GAEBELEIN'S CONCISE COMMENTARY ON THE WHOLE BIBLE

Other books by

ARNO C. GAEBELEIN

The Book of Psalms
The Prophet Ezekiel
The Gospel of Matthew
The Gospel of John
The Acts of the Apostles
The Revelation

The Conflict of the Ages: The Mystery of Lawlessness

GAEBELEIN'S CONCISE COMMENTARY ON THE WHOLE BIBLE

ARNO C. GAEBELEIN

LOIZEAUX BROTHERS
Neptune, New Jersey

REVISED EDITION, JULY 1985
SECOND PRINTING, JULY 1989
Originally published as *The Annotated Bible*

*A Nonprofit Corporation Devoted to the Lord's Work
and to the Spread of His Truth*

Library of Congress Cataloging in Publication Data

Gaebelein, Arno Clemens, 1861-1945.
Gaebelein's concise commentary on the whole Bible.

Rev. ed. of: The annotated Bible. 1970.
1. Bible—Commentaries. I. Gaebelein, Arno Clemens, 1861-1945. Annotated Bible. II. Title. III. Title: Concise commentary on the whole Bible.
BS491.G32 1985 220.7 85-10089
ISBN 0-87213-209-9

PRINTED IN THE UNITED STATES OF AMERICA

CONTENTS

THE NEW TESTAMENT

PUBLISHER'S FOREWORD

A publisher is constantly faced with the need to make hard decisions. When the stock of any publication is exhausted, the decision must be made whether or not to reprint. Naturally there are various aspects to consider; sales, of course; but also cost; and certainly demand. But there is another facet also important in our thinking, and that is the value of the ministry of the title under consideration.

Thus when we realized our supply would soon be exhausted of Dr. A. C. Gaebelein's four-volume set of *The Annotated Bible,* these various aspects were considered in detail.

A reprint of the four big volumes would mean a steep increase in price. Would such a high cost be good stewardship for those who would purchase it? Was its ministry worth it?

We went through our files, finding letters like these:

> *From a missionary:* It would be a pity to let it go out of print. It has contributed to my ministry of the Word through many years of missionary work in Africa. It is clear and concise, and comprehensive enough to meet the need of the researcher time and time again. I have found it of tremendous value as a Bible study aid. Often when seeking an answer to a perplexing problem, or assembling material for an article on a particular subject, I have gone to this comprehensive work and obtained needed help. Issues side-stepped in some commentaries are fairly examined and an opinion expressed which often launches one on further investigation. One is seldom disappointed, and often happily satisfied.

> *Another wrote:* Dr. Gaebelein gave us a very splendid running commentary on the Bible. You often find insights and emphases in Dr. Gaebelein's work that are missing elsewhere. He was a grand and glorious warrior for the truth.

Yes, the ministry is worth reprinting.

But what about the cost? Surely we must do *something* with the purchaser in mind?

We are proud to present the result of our planning: this convenient, single-volume edition of The Annotated Bible, complete in every respect, and just about half the cost of what the four-volume reprint would have been!

This edition has been planned with the modern student in mind. It has been retitled GAEBELEIN'S CONCISE COMMENTARY ON THE WHOLE BIBLE. It has been edited to change the roman numerals to arabic for easier use by today's readers. A few obsolete footnotes have been deleted. *The Annotated Bible* is here complete, only new in name and format, the result of ten years of labor by a giant among Bible teachers of the first half of the twentieth century, author of scores of expositions and other Biblical works that gave him an international reputation. His influence still lives through the lives of many who heard him during his ministry of over fifty years in many parts of the United States and Canada. And also through the added lives of those to whom his written ministry is still thus available.

LOIZEAUX BROTHERS

THE BOOK OF
GENESIS

Introduction

The first book of the Bible is called in the Septuagint (the Greek translation of the Old Testament) "Genesis." Genesis means "origin." The Hebrews call it by the first Hebrew word "Bereshith"—in the beginning. It is the book of all beginnings. We can trace here the beginnings of creation and everything else, except God, who has no beginning. The book of Genesis is the great foundation upon which the entire revelation of God rests. The marvellous structure of the Bible, composed of the different books, written by different instruments of the Spirit of God at different times, is built upon this great, majestic book. It is the root out of which the tree of God's revelation has grown. Internal evidences prove the most complete unity, that is the work of one chosen instrument, Moses, and that it is not of a composite authorship. But more than that, the book of Genesis establishes the divine unity of the Bible. The last book of the Bible, the Revelation, confirms this. Genesis tells of the origin of all things; Revelation reveals the destiny of all things.

It is an interesting study, profitable and suggestive, to trace the great doctrines of the Bible in this first book. They are all found somewhere in Genesis, either in typical foreshadowings or in direct words. Here, too, we may discover the dispensational and prophetic truths of the Bible in germ. Genesis 3:15 is the prediction out of which the rest of prophecy has been developed. The entire New Testament in its doctrinal statements rests upon this book. It is quoted there as the Word of God scores of times. If the revelations of Genesis, especially the opening chapters, the supreme foundation, if these chapters were myths, the entire New Testament would have to be given up as unauthoritative. Indeed, the great doctrines in Romans, starting from the fact that man is a fallen being and lost, would be just as much myths, if the fall of man were a myth. The Lord Jesus Christ has put His seal to this great book.

The Criticism of Genesis

The book of Genesis, being the foundation of the whole Bible, and of such vast importance, it does not surprise us that the enemy of the truth of God has directed first of all his attacks against this book to break down its authority. A hundred years ago and less the cunning inventions of the father of lies, directed against the inspiration of Genesis and its unity, occupied mostly, if not altogether, the minds of theologians and scholars. It is different now. The stock of trade of the destructive critics, differing but little from that of accredited infidels, has become the common property of evangelical Christendom. The rationalistic theories concerning the date and authorship of Genesis are now liberally and almost universally displayed. In theological seminaries they are openly taught and hundreds of men, who claim to be teachers of the oracles of God, deny the inspiration of the book of Genesis.

The Paternity of Higher Criticism

That such a denial is not of God is self-evident. But it is interesting to examine the source from which the destructive criticism of Genesis and the Pentateuch has come. The man who has been called the "Sir Isaac Newton of criticism" is Jean Astruc. He was a French physician, a freethinker, who led a wicked, immoral life. In 1753 this man gave to the world his doubts in a work which he called, "Conjectures Regarding the Original Memoirs in the Book of Genesis." In this work he taught that the use of the two names of God in Genesis, Elohim (translated by God) and Jehovah (translated by Lord) showed that two different documents were used in the composition of the book. The hypothesis of a Jehovist and Elohist writer, so called, was invented by this unsaved man. It was, however, reserved for a German scholar and rationalist to formulate the denial of the unity and inspiration of Genesis into a system. This man was Professor Eichhorn. He coined the phrase, "higher criticism," and is therefore called the "father" of it. He introduced successfully into the theological institutions of Germany the theory of Astruc. On account of his great learning his invented higher criticism took hold upon the minds of thousands of people. But who was

Professor Eichhorn? Let another higher critic give the answer. Ewald, himself such a powerful factor of this most dangerous infidelity, wrote: "We cannot fail to recognize that, from the religious point of view the Bible was to him a closed book."

Such is the paternity of the now widely accepted higher criticism: an immoral, infidel Frenchman and an unconverted, blind leader of the blind, a German Professor.

Their Disciples

After Eichhorn came other men, such as Vater and Hartman, who tried to undermine the Mosaic authorship of Genesis by still another theory. Professor DeWette, of Heidelberg, followed closely in the steps of infidel Eichhorn. Bleeck taught still another theory. Then we mention Ewald, Hupfeld, Prof. Kuenen, Dr. Davidson, Robertson Smith, Canon Driver, George Adams Smith, Professor Briggs, W. Harper, Marcus Dods and many others, who may all be fitly called the disciples of the immoral Frenchman and the infidel German. For instance, George Adams Smith saith: "The framework of the first eleven chapters of Genesis is woven from the *raw material of myth and legend."* And the works of this man and others are now sold at popular prices by so called Christian publishers.

A Complicated Science

They call this kind of criticism scientific. It surely has all the marks of so-called science. Speculation, uncertainty and complicated statements are the leading characteristics of this criticism. They claim now that the Pentateuch (the five books written by Moses) were never written by him, but that these books consist of four diverse documents. These they designate as follows: 1. The Jehovist. 2. The Elohist. 3. The Deuteronomist. 4. The Priestly Code. The authorship of Moses has been completely given up and it is claimed that the earliest part of the Pentateuch was written perhaps six hundred years after Moses' death. They put the date of the greater part of these five books after the Babylonian captivity.

A writer has recently given a fine description of this higher critical "scientific" nonsense, part of which we quote:

> They conjecture that these four suppositive documents were not compiled and written by Moses, but were probably constructed somewhat after this fashion: For some reason, and at some time, and in some way, someone no one knows who, or why, or when, or where, wrote Jehovist. Then someone else, no one knows who, or why, or when, or where, wrote another document, which is now called Elohist. And then at a later time, the critics only know who, or why, or when, or where, an anonymous personage, whom we may call Redactor I, took in hand the reconstruction of these documents, introduced new material, harmonized the real and apparent discrepancies, and divided the inconsistent accounts of one event into two separate transactions. Then some time after this, perhaps one hundred years or more, no one knows who, or why, or when, or where, some anonymous personage wrote another document, which they styled Deuteronomist. And after awhile another anonymous author, no one knows who, or why, or when, or where, whom we will call Redactor II, took this in hand, compared it with Jehovist and Elohist, revised them with considerable freedom and, in addition, introduced quite a body of new material. Then someone else, no one knows who, or why, or when, or where, probably, however, about 525, or perhaps 425, wrote the Priestly Code; and then another anonymous Hebrew, whom we may call Redactor III, undertook to incorporate this with the triplicated composite Jehovist, Elohist, and Deuteronomist, with what they call redactional additions and insertions (Canon Hague).

This describes the infidel mudpuddle into which these "great" scholars have plunged and into which they would like to lead the sheep and even the little lambs.

The Mosaic Authorship

"All tradition, from whatever source it is derived, whether inspired or uninspired, unanimously affirms that the first five books of the Bible were written by one man, and that man was Moses. There is no counter-testimony in any quarter." With these words, Prof. William Henry Green begins his learned work on the unity of Genesis. Other learned men in past generation up to the present time stand firm for the Mosaic authorship of Genesis, and thereby affirm the fact of revelation. The cry of the higher critics—"ripe scholarship," "access to better sources," etc.—is a bluff. The best scholarship stands by the truth. Some of the arguments advanced against Moses as writer of Genesis are exactly the argument for it and the evidences of inspiration. For instance, the use of the name of God as Elohim and Jehovah. Elohim is the name of God as Creator—Jehovah is His name as entering into covenant relation with man. The use of these names is a precious evidence of the work of the Spirit of God and not an evidence of different writers and documents.

The highest authority that Moses wrote Genesis and the other four books, and that Genesis is the revelation of God, is the Lord Jesus Christ. He spoke repeatedly of Moses and reminded His hearers of the historic facts as given in Genesis. This fact is met by the critics with the statement that our Lord was not a critical scholar and limited in His knowledge. Such statements are akin to blasphemy.

Needed Information

The information concerning the criticism upon this great Bible book we are about to study is much needed. Many Christians hear of higher criticism without knowing what it is and how it originated. The information given shows that it originated with wicked men and that it is an attempt to destroy the very foundations upon which the whole Scriptures rest. Sometimes higher critics have a way of telling uninformed Christians that the views they hold are the consensus of the best scholarship. This is untrue. Others, again, who have imbibed these views hide the worst features of them. For this reason we deem it expedient to give this information.

The study of Genesis will deepen the faith in the inspiration and revelation of the first book of the Bible. There is nothing which convinces of the divinity of the Bible like the prayerful and spiritual study of the Bible itself. And the Bible has nothing to fear. It needs neither apology nor concessions.

Revelation or Myth?

A Few Objections Considered

From the sides of infidelity, higher criticism and a certain class of scientists objections are made against the opening chapters of Genesis. Not only is the Mosaic authorship denied but the revelation contained in these chapters is branded as unscientific and at variance with the facts revealed by science. Others class these sublime truths concerning creation, the fall of man, the deluge, etc., with the legends of primitive nations and thus the fact of revelation is altogether denied. Inasmuch as these wicked statements are heard on all sides from pulpits and chairs of educational institutions, it becomes necessary that we consider briefly some of these objections and uncover their absolute worthlessness. The purpose of our work forbids a more extended treatment of these objections. Many helpful and interesting books have been written by scholars against these attacks. Elsewhere in this booklet the reader will find a number of works mentioned which deal with these attacks in a masterly way.

Is the Creation Account Contradicted by Science?

That the creation account is unscientific and in clash with the discoveries of modern science is one of the common statements. It has, however, no foundation whatever. The proofs that there is no error in the account of creation as revealed in the first chapter of Genesis, have been furnished by the investigation of science. The order of creation as given in the first chapter is the order, which, after years of searching—the most laborious searching—science has discovered. Over and over again has science with its guesses and speculations been forced to bow in submission before the simple and brief description of the creation in God's Word. There is no clash between the Bible and the results of true scientific research. Geology, astronomy, and other sciences have had to retrace their steps more than once and acknowledge their mistake; the first chapter of Genesis will never have to do that.

Years ago scientists ridiculed the divine statement that the first thing called into existence was light: "let there be light," and that the sun was made on the fourth day. That sneer is forever silenced, for science has found out that light existed first. Again for a long time it was denied that vegetation came first before animal life was on this globe. This denial has likewise been stopped by scientific discoveries. Other evidences that the Bible is right and science had to accept the truthfulness of the creation account we must pass by. What scientists should explain is, how in a simple record of a few verses, which antedates all scientific research and discovery, such accurate information is given without any error whatever. Where did Moses get his marvellous knowledge which the scientific research of the nineteenth century confirms correct in every way? There is only one answer. It is the revelation of God.

This becomes still more evident when the creation chapter in Genesis is compared with the conceptions of the origin of the earth as found in the records of the oldest nations. What ridiculous things were believed concerning creation and the universe! Why did Moses not write the same childish things but instead gives a majestic account of the creation of the earth and the heavens? The answer is and ever will be, his account is the revelation of God how the earth and the heavens came into existence.

Is There a Contradiction Between the First and Second Chapters of Genesis?

Another favorite argument against the infallible record of creation is that the first and second chapters are contradictory. A certain New York preacher stated some years ago in *Appleton's Magazine* this supposed difficulty. He said, "How can we trouble about reconciling Genesis and science" while the two accounts of the first two chapters "are so hopelessly at variance?" Criticism has used this alleged discrepancy as an argument for its infidel theories. There is, however, no contradiction between these two chapters. The second chapter in Genesis is not another history of creation nor does it contradict the account in the first chapter. The historical account of creation as a whole is found in Genesis 1—2:3. The division of chapters in the authorized version is unfortunate. From chapter 2:4 to the close of the chapter we have not a historical account of creation at all, but a divine statement of the relationships of creation, that is, man's place in it as its head. There are no contradictions in anything. Genesis 1:27 is said to clash with 2:21-22. Such a clash does not exist. Gen 1:27 does not say that man and woman were created together, nor does it say that the woman was created directly and not formed as revealed in the second chapter.

The Myths of Ancient Nations

It is a well known fact that ancient nations such as the Chaldeans, Egyptians, Phoenicians, Hindus, possessed myths in which one can hear now and then a faint echo of a primeval revelation and knowledge, which must have been in possession of all mankind at one time. That such was the case Romans 1:21-23 fully confirms. All mankind knew God and was acquainted with the great facts of history, the events recorded in the first eleven chapters of Genesis. As they became vain, their foolish heart was darkened, they rushed into idolatry. Their traditions, however, here and there give glimpses of the truth they once knew. It is impossible to give here evidences of it as discovered in the Assyrian tablets, which have something to say of the creation and the deluge, known now as "the Chaldean Genesis." Other traces are found in ancient Phoenican sources as well as in India, among the Romans and the Greeks, Babylonians, Chinese and other nations. However, all these, including "the Chaldean Genesis" are miserable contortions.

There are a few resemblances and many more differences between the Biblical and especially the Babylonian accounts. It is claimed that Moses, or since Moses did not write according to this infidel theory, somebody else, made use of these myths in writing the opening chapters of Genesis. This farfetched invention has no foundation at all. The book of Genesis is not the offspring of Babylonian tradition. God gave to Moses the account of creation and the beginnings of history by direct revelation as the blessed foundation of all subsequent revelation in His holy Word. The man, who boasts of scholarship, and brands the first eleven chapters of Genesis as myths, putting them alongside of the traditions of ignorant ancient nations, but reveals his ignorance and blindness.

The Deluge

This great catastrophe has also been denied and ridiculed. It is painful to mention all these denials, but it is needful to call attention to these attacks on the foundation of the Bible. Hundreds of men, who claim to be exponents of Christianity speak of Noah as a myth and the deluge reported in Genesis as an unconfirmed event. Traditions of the flood are found among all nations and exhibit in many cases a very striking agreement with the divinely given record. These traditions are found in India, China, Egypt, and Greece as well as among the Chaldeans and Babylonians. Peruvians, Mexicans, Greenlanders, and the Teutonic races possess these traditions. Geology also gives the most decisive evidence of such a judgment by water through which the earth passed. The surface of the earth exhibits a deposit, which originated after a universal flood and which is called *diluvial* (flood) land. Vast quantities of bones and teeth of antediluvian animals, masses of rock and boulder, carried by the flood, are found in this diluvial deposit. Many pages could be filled with such evidences.

Nothing Left Unattacked

Nothing has been left unattacked in the opening chapters of Genesis. The existence of paradise, the fall of man, the curse, the story of Cain and Abel, Enoch's translation, the tower of Babel and every other recorded event has been denied and is increasingly denied. That our Lord referred repeatedly to these first chapters of the Bible and thereby confirmed their historicity and revelation, is not at all taken in consideration by these enemies of the Word of God.

But the foundation rock of the Bible, the book of Genesis stands as firm as it ever stood. It can never be moved. Let them dig away! Let them dash against it with their heads. They will perish, but God's Word abideth forever. In a day when apostasy sweeps through Christendom like a mighty avalanche, let us cling closer to the living Word of the living God and hold fast the testimony of its inerrancy. And now with thankful hearts and a prayer for the Holy Spirit's guidance we come to the book itself.

The Division of Genesis

Every book of the Bible has a key and also hints on the division of the book. The correct way in unlocking the book is to use the key and the Division as given by the Holy Spirit in the book itself. The book of Genesis has been divided in perhaps more different ways than any other book. In looking through Genesis for a characteristic word we have no difficulty in finding it in the word "generations" (Hebrew: *toledoth*). It is used eleven times in this book. The first time the word generations occurs is in chapter 2:4. The creation account stands therefore by itself. This gives us twelve sections.

I. **THE CREATION ACCOUNT** (1—2:3)

II. **THE GENERATIONS OF THE HEAVENS AND THE EARTH** (2:4—4)

III. **THE GENERATIONS OF ADAM** (5—6:8)

IV. **THE GENERATIONS OF NOAH** (6:9—9:29)

V. **THE GENERATIONS OF THE SONS OF NOAH** (10—11:9)

VI. **THE GENERATIONS OF SHEM** (11:10-26)

VII. **THE GENERATIONS OF TERAH** (11:27—25:11)

VIII. **THE GENERATIONS OF ISHMAEL** (25:12-18)

IX. **THE GENERATIONS OF ISAAC** (25:19-35)

X. **THE GENERATIONS OF ESAU** (36:1-8)

XI. **THE GENERATIONS OF ESAU'S SONS** (36:9-43)

XII. **THE GENERATIONS OF JACOB** (37:2—50:26)

We fully agree with the scholarly remarks of Prof. Green about the importance of this division. "These titles are designed to emphasize and render more prominent and palpable an important feature of the book, the genealogical character of its history. This results from its main design, which is to trace the line of descent of the chosen race from the beginning to the point where it was ready to expand to a great nation, whose future organization was already foreshadowed, its tribes being represented in the twelve sons of Jacob, and its tribal divisions in their children. The genealogies contained in the book are not merely incidental or subordinate, but essential, and the real basis of the whole. They are not to be regarded as addenda to the narrative, scraps of information introduced into it; they constitute the skeleton or framework of the history itself."

"There is, accordingly, a regular series of genealogies of like structure, or rather one continuous genealogy extending from Adam to the family of Jacob. This is interrupted and suspended from time to time, as occasion requires, for the sake of introducing or incorporating facts of the history at particular points where they belong; after which it is resumed again precisely at the same point, and proceeds regularly as before until it reaches its utmost limit, thus embracing the entire history within itself."

It is interesting to note the beginning and the end of these sections. We leave this as a suggestion with the reader. The reign of death after the entrance of sin is in full evidence in these sections. "Death reigned from Adam to Moses" (Romans 5:14). The last section ends with Joseph's death "and he was put in a coffin in Egypt."

In our annotations, following the above division, we shall trace the historical account and point out some spiritual and dispensational truths giving many hints, which may be followed in a more extended study of this great book.

Analysis and Annotations

I. The Creation Account

The manner in which the book of Genesis begins leaves no doubt that it is the revelation of God. The creation account is historical truth. The question is how was it given? An answer to this question claims that the Jews obtained the account from the records of other nations concerning the origin of the universe and that they altered it according to their own religious ideas. This is an impossibility. The ancient heathen nations considered God and the universe one and had absolutely no knowledge of the existence of God independent of the universe, nor did they know anything of a creation of the world. Here is something wholly different from all the theories, mythologies and other inventions of the human race. How then was it given? By revelation of God is the only answer.

No human being knew anything about the origin of the heavens and the earth. Man cannot by searching find out God, nor can man discover how the earth was created and all things came into existence. How ridiculous the statements and opinions on the creation of men called great thinkers, not to speak of the equally foolish beliefs of the nations of the past. But here is what God makes known, how He called all things into existence. He makes known that the universe is not eternal but that He created it. The whole account is of wonderful grandeur and yet of the greatest simplicity; so simple that a child can read it and understand the truth, but so profound that the greatest men have bowed before it.

It is not the purpose of this Bible study course to enter into details or we would write at length on the evolution theory with its invented "protoplasm." There are many questions which the evolutionists cannot answer and many difficulties which they cannot explain. Their scientific assertions and speculations require one to believe what is against reason, while God never expects us to believe what is contrary to reason. It is far more simple to accept God's revelation. "By faith we understand that the worlds have been framed by the Word of God, so that what is seen hath not been made out of things which appear" (Heb. 11:3). This disposes of evolution and the other theories of unbelieving men, who reject God's Word.

The statement which one hears so often from sneering lips that the creation account is unscientific has no foundation. That it is nonscientific is an entirely different matter. Galileo, the astronomer, truthfully said, "The Scriptures were given, not to tell us how the heavens go, but to teach us how to go to heaven." Yet, as already mentioned in our introduction, science had to acknowledge over and over again the correctness of the creation account and withdraw the objections and assaults which had been made.

THE ORIGINAL CREATION OF GOD (1:1)

A ruined creation and the brooding spirit (1:2)

The Restoration of the Earth

1. The first day—Light (1:3-5)
2. The second day—The dividing of the waters (1:6-8)
3. The third day—The earth out of the waters and vegetable life appears (1:9-13)
4. The fourth day—The lights in the heavens (1:14-19)
5. The fifth day—Living creatures in the waters and in the air (1:20-23)
6. The sixth day—Living creatures made and man created in God's image (1:24-31)
7. The seventh day—God's rest (2:1-3)

The first verse of the book of Genesis and of the whole Bible stands alone in majestic greatness. Like some mountain peak rising from the valley in solitary grandeur with its snow-capped summit, it inspires awe. In the Hebrew the verse is composed of seven words. When that beginning was in which God created the heavens and the earth is not revealed. It must have been many millions of years ago; God only knows it and science can never discover it. It is incorrect to say that it was 6,000 years ago. God does not speak of Himself; no statement concerning His existence or His eternity is given. How different from the myths and speculations of pagan nations. God's Name mentioned for the first time in the Bible is *"Elohim."* It is in the plural indicating God's great dignity and power as well as the fact that God is triune. (See the "Let us make man," in verse 26.) Elohim is God's name as Creator. This verse answers all the different "isms" about God and His creation, while its depths cannot be sounded. Here atheism is answered; polytheism (the many gods of the heathen) is exposed to be false. The verse disproves materialism as well as pantheism, that God and the universe are one.

It is of the greatest importance to understand that the condition in which the earth (not the heavens) is described in the second verse is not how God created it in the beginning. Scripture itself tells us this. Read Isaiah 45:18. The Hebrew word for "without form" is *tohu,* which means waste. "The earth was waste and void." But in the passage of Isaiah we read, "He created it not a waste." The original earth passed through a great upheaval.A judgment swept over it, which in all probability must have occurred on account of the fall of that mighty creature, Lucifer, who fell by pride and became the devil. The original earth, no doubt, was his habitation and he had authority over it which he still claims as the prince of this world. Luke 4:5-6 shows us this. The earth had become waste and void; chaos and darkness reigned. What that original earth was we do not know, but we know that animal and vegetable life was in existence long before God began to restore the earth. The immense fossil beds prove this. But they likewise prove that man was not then on the earth. Between the first and second verses of the Bible there is that unknown period of millions of years of which geology gets a glimpse in studying the crust of the earth. God waited His own time in majestic calmness when He would begin to carry out His plans He had made before the foundation of the world.

When that time arrived God began to bring order into the chaos and restored His creation so that the earth which is now and the heavens above came forth. The Spirit moving (brooding) upon the waters and His Word were the agents through which it was accomplished. Read John 1:1-3; Col. 1:15-16; Heb. 1:2-3. We do not follow the historical account and the six days' work, but call attention to the correspondency between the first three days and the last three. The seventh day stands by itself.

First day: Light
Second day: Dividing of waters
Third day: The earth out of the waters and vegetable life
Fourth day: Solar system and lights
Fifth day: Life in the waters
Sixth day: Life on the earth and man created
Seventh day: God rests

The word "create" is used only three times. In the first verse it applies to the original creation, when God called everything into existence out of nothing. Then we find it in verse 21 in connection with the calling forth of living creatures (*nephesh*—soul) and in verse 27 in connection with man. The other word used is the word "made." This necessitates the existence of material which is shaped into something; the word "create" does not require existence of matter. The light which came forth on the first day was light before the sun, a fact well known to science.

The creation of man is the crowning act of the Creator and precedes His rest. "Let us make man" is the counsel of the Godhead. God then created man in His own image. In the second chapter we read that He formed him out of the dust of the earth and breathed into his nostrils and man became a living soul.

The deeper Lessons of the Creation. The Creation account has a most interesting typical and dispensational meaning. In dealing with the individual in redemption and dealing with ruined creation by the fall of man, God follows the order of the six days' work. (F.W. Grant's *Genesis in the Light of the New Testament* develops this fully.) We give a few hints. The ruined creation wasted and void, covered with the dark waters and in darkness is the picture of fallen man. The two agents God used in the restoration of the ruined creation, the Spirit and the Word are the agents of the new birth. "Born of the Spirit" and of the "incorruptible seed of the Word of God." In redemption God uses the word "create" not the word "made," because what we receive by faith in His Son is not a mending of an old nature, but we are a new creation; created in Christ Jesus. David prayed, *"Create* in me a clean heart." The work of the first day is touched upon in 2 Cor. 4:6. "For God, who commanded the light to shine out of darkness hath shined in our hearts." When that light shines upon us it reveals the ruin of ourselves. The second day brings before us the separation, which follows the manifestation of the light. The third day stands for resurrection, for the earth came out of the waters and brings forth grass, herbs and trees, yielding fruit. Throughout the entire Bible this meaning of the third day may be traced.[1] The spiritual truth

[1]It is the day of resurrection and restoration. Gen. 22:4; 40:20-22; 42:18; Ex. 15:22; 19:11; Numb. 7:24; Josh. 2:16; 2 Kings 20:5; Esther 5:1; 9:18; Hos. 6:2, John 2:1; Luke 13:33.

here is that if the Light has shone in and we believe we are "risen with Christ" and the fruit bearing, which is the result of this. The fourth day directs our attention heavenward; there we are seated together in heavenly places in Christ Jesus. The fifth day brings before us again the restless waters and the life manifested there. Out of the midst of these waters life comes. Even so in Christian experience down here. The sixth day points to the time of the completion of the new creation, while the seventh day reveals the eternal rest.

Dispensationally the lessons from the first chapter in Genesis are still more interesting.

The first day: The age before the flood: The light shines in.
The second day: The age of Noah.
The third day: The age of Abraham and his seed.
The fourth day: The present age: Christ the Sun; the moon typical of the church. Individual believers represented by stars.
The fifth day: The restless waters: The times of the Gentiles ending; "the sea and the waves roaring." The great tribulation.
The sixth day: The kingdom rule established over the earth in the second coming of Christ.
The seventh day: The eternal ages: God is all in all.

It is equally interesting to see that the same dispensational truths gather around the names of seven of the prominent actors of the book of Genesis. These are: Adam, Seth, Noah, Abraham, Isaac, Jacob, and Joseph. We quote from another:

Adam gives us the beginning, when, with the entrance of God's Word, light comes into the soul of a sinner, and God meets him *as* such with the provision of His grace (chapter 3).

Then (4—5), we have the history of the two "seeds," and their antagonism—a story which has its counterpart in the history of the world at large, but also in every individual soul where God has wrought, and where the "flesh lusteth against the Spirit, and the Spirit against the flesh, and these are contrary the one to the other."

Next, Noah's passage through the judgment of the old world into a new scene, accepted of God in the sweet savor of sacrifice, is the type of where salvation puts us—"in Christ, a new creation: old things passed away, and all things become new" (6—11:9).

Abraham's Canaan-life—pilgrim and stranger, but a worshiper, gives us the fruit and consequence of this—a "walk in Him" whom we have received (11:10—21).

Then, Isaac, our type as "sons" (4:28), speaks to us of a self-surrender into a Father's hands, the door into a life of quiet and enjoyment, as it surely is (22—24:33).

Jacob speaks of the *discipline* of sons, by which the crooked and deceitful man becomes Israel, a prince with God—a chastening of love, dealing with the fruits of the *old* nature in us (26:34; 37:1).

While Joseph, the fullest image of Christ, suffers, not for *sin*. but for *righteousness'* sake, and obtains supremacy over the world and fulness of blessing from the Almighty One, his strength (*Genesis in the Light of the New Testament*).

How marvellous all this is! And yet we touch only upon the surface. The highest evidence for the Word of God is the Word itself. No man or human genius could have ever produced such a document as the first chapter of Genesis, which contains in embryo all the subsequent revelations of God. It is God's revelation.

II. The Generations of the Heavens and the Earth

Man in Innocency before the Fall (2:4-25)

1. The earth his abode (2:4-6)
2. The creation of man (2:7)
3. The garden of Eden (2:8-14)
4. Man in the garden. His commission (2:15-17)
    a. To keep the garden
    b. The commandment
5. No helpmeet for Adam found (2:18-20)
6. The formation of the woman (2:21-22)
7. The union (2:23-25)

This is not a new version of the creation or a repetition of the account in the preceding chapter. The relationships of the created man to nature and to His Creator are now more specifically introduced. The name of God appears now no longer as "Elohim" but another name precedes the word Elohim; it is the name "Jehovah." This name is used because it is the name of God in relationship with man. Jehovah is the Son of God.

In verse 7 we have the creation of man revealed. Jehovah God formed him out of the dust of the earth; He breathed into his nostrils the breath of life. Here is that which distinguishes man from the beast. The animals also are living souls, but not immortal. Man alone became a living soul by the inbreathing of Jehovah Elohim and that constitutes man immortal.

The garden of Eden was situated in a fertile, pleasant plain, somewhere near the two streams still known by their names, the Euphrates and the Tigris (Hiddekel). The tree of life represents Christ, while the rivers of water are clearly the types of the Holy Spirit. What the tree of knowledge of good and evil was no one knows. The command was given to test man in his innocency. Adam unfallen had not the knowledge of good and evil. That knowledge was acquired by the fall. The test, therefore, involved not some great moral evil but simply the authority and right of God to prohibit something. The tree of knowledge then represented responsibility.

"Thou shalt surely die" means literally "dying thou shalt die." This does not mean "eternal death," but "physical death."

The formation of the woman is highly typical. Adam is the figure of Him who was to come (Rom. 5:14), the last Adam. Here Christ and the Church are foreshadowed. The deep sleep into which Adam was put by Jehovah Elohim is typical of the death of the cross. The woman, built out of his side, is the type of the Church. As the helpmeet of Adam was bone of his bone, and flesh of his flesh and also the bride of Adam, so is the church the body and the bride of Christ. The woman was brought to Adam and presented to him. But Christ will present the Church to Himself (Eph. 5:27). Marriage is indicated in verse 24 and quoted in Matt. 19:5, 1 Cor. 6:16, and Eph. 5:31. Both were naked, the suitable condition for innocence.

CHAPTER 3

The Fall of Man

1. The serpent and the woman (3:1-5)
2. The fall and the immediate results (3:6-7)
3. Jehovah Elohim questions Adam (3:8-12)
4. His question to the woman (3:13)
5. The curse upon the serpent (3:14-21)
6. The first prophecy (3:15)
7. The sentence upon the woman (3:16)
8. The sentence upon the man (3:17-19)
9. The faith of Adam and God's answer (3:20-21)
10. The expulsion and the guarding cherubim (3:22-24)

Another actor is now introduced, the adversary of God. His person and his history are not revealed here. The last book of the Bible speaks of him as "the great dragon, that old serpent, called the Devil and Satan" (Rev. 12:9). Our Lord called him "the murderer from the beginning" and "the father of lies." He used a creature of the field to deceive the woman and to ruin the restored creation by the introduction of sin. The word "serpent" is in the Hebrew *"nachash,"* which means "a shining one." It is evident that this creature was not then a reptile like the serpent of to-day. The curse put the serpent into the dust. This creature Satan possessed and perhaps made still more beautiful so as to be of great attraction to the woman. He transformed himself in this subtle way, "The serpent beguiled Eve through his subtlety" (2 Cor. 11:3), "And no marvel; for Satan himself transforms himself into an angel of light" (2 Cor. 11:14). Of this marvellous being having access to the garden of Eden we read in Ezekiel 28:13.

Some brand the opening verses of Genesis 3 as myth. If it were, all else in God's Word concerning man and his redemption would collapse. Others look upon it as an allegory, but it is a historical fact and this revelation gives the only explanation of the origin of evil and its existence.

Speaking to the woman Satan awakened doubt in God's Word. In speaking of God he avoided the word "Jehovah," but only spoke of God. Then he acts as the accuser of God and uttered his lie, which, as the father of lies he still continues, "ye shall not surely die." The crime of the devil by which he fell, that is, pride, is also shown in the words "ye shall be as gods." The woman listened to the tempter's voice. She saw it was good and that it was pleasant; she desired, she took, she ate and gave unto her husband. It is the beginning of the lust of the flesh, the lust of the eyes and the pride of life. (Compare with the temptations of the last Adam, the Lord Jesus, in the wilderness.)

Their eyes were opened at once. They discovered their nakedness and made themselves coverings from fig leaves. When they heard the voice of Jehovah Elohim they hid themselves. Shame and fear were the immediate results of the fall. What the first parents did to hide their nakedness by sewing fig leaves together is still the natural man's occupation. Man attempts by the labor of his hands, by his religious profession and morality to cover his nakedness.

Jehovah Elohim came to seek that which was lost. Adam did not seek the Lord, but the Lord sought him and Eve.

The curse was then pronounced upon the serpent and the earth was cursed on account of man and sentence pronounced upon the man and the woman. The evidences of all this are about us. The sentence "dying thou shalt die," that is physical death, the wages of sin, was not executed at once.

The first prophecy in verse 15 announces the

seed of the woman, Christ, and His triumphant work over the serpent and his work as well as the death of the seed. Out of this first prediction all prophecy is developed. Space forbids to enlarge upon this great verse.

Adam believed God's Word for he called now his wife "Eve." The word Eve is *Chavah* in Hebrew, and means "life." God answered his faith by making unto Adam and Eve clothes of skin. Jehovah Elohim must have slain an animal, perhaps a lamb, to provide the skin. The first blood must then have been shed and the Lord provided the covering for Adam and Eve. Its meaning as a type needs no further comments.

They were driven out of Eden so as to avoid the possibility of taking of the tree of life and live forever. This is used as an argument that man through the fall lost his immortal soul. It only refers to the body. If they had eaten of the tree of life they would have lived forever in the body and physical death would then not have been possible.

The cherubim are not symbols but actual beings. We find them elsewhere revealed, Ps. 18:10; Ezek. 1:5; 10-1; Rev. 4—5. The flaming burning sword is symbolic of the holiness of God.

With the third chapter of Genesis the waiting of the heavens and of the earth began: Heaven waiting to send Him forth to deal with the question of sin and the earth waiting for redemption and deliverance. What marvellous chapters these first three chapters of the Bible are! The entire Word of God rests upon them and is linked with them.

CHAPTER 4

After the Fall and the Two Seeds

1. Cain and Abel (4:1-2)
2. Their offerings (4:3-5)
3. The divine remonstrance (4:6-7)
4. Abel slain by his brother (4:8)
5. Cain's judgment (4:9-16)
6. Cain and his offspring and the progress of the world (4:17-24)
7. Seth in place of Abel (4:25-26)

This chapter is filled with many lessons. Here are types of the Seed of the Woman, Christ. Christ as the Good Shepherd, the death of Christ, the shedding of blood, the atonement, righteousness by faith, the self-righteousness of the sinner and his rejection are here indicated. We find in this chapter types of the Jewish nation and their blood-guiltiness as well as the record of the progressing civilization of that age.

Eve's first son was Cain (acquired of Jehovah). This tells of her faith; she believed her first born was the promised seed. Cain, however, is the type of the natural man, the flesh, the offspring of the serpent. The second son born was Abel (vapor).

Cain's offering and worship was that of the natural, self-righteous man, who needs no blood, but trusts in his character and good works. Cain did not believe in what Jehovah Elohim had declared concerning sin, the penalty of sin; and he did not believe in the prediction of Gen. 3:15. God had cursed the ground, but Cain brought of the fruit of the ground. To-day the masses of professing Christians "go in the way of Cain" (Jude 10-11).

Abel's offering consisted of the firstlings of the flock. He believed himself a sinner who had deserved death. He believed in substitutionary sacrifice (Heb. 11:4).

Abel is a type of Christ. Abel was a shepherd. There is no report of evil about him. He was hated by his brother without a cause. Abel died on account of his brother's sin.

Cain, who hated his brother Abel, foreshadows the Jew, who rejected Christ and delivered Him into the hands of the Gentiles and shed innocent blood. As Cain had blood-guiltiness upon himself, the blood of his brother Abel, so there is blood-guiltiness upon the Jewish race. "His blood be upon us and our children," was their demand. Cain's judgment is typical of the punishment which came upon the Jewish people. Like Cain, they were driven from Him; became wanderers over the face of the earth; bearing a mark, everybody is against them. Cain went with his wife (one of his sisters) to the land of Nod. He built a city. His hope was in earthly things. The progress of the Cainites is given. Polygamy began with Lamech. Jubal became inventor of harp and pipe. Tubal-Cain was the worker in brass and iron. Then there is a song of defiance celebrating murder. The age advanced in civilization, inventions, making the earth under the curse attractive; on the other hand, lust, violence, vice, and crime increased. But Cain's seed was also religious following Cain's worship. The name of El (God) appears in some of Cain's offspring.

The third son of Adam was Seth. From him springs the Seed. Seth is the type of Christ risen from the dead. Abel, the first, died; Seth, the second, lives. "Then people began to call at the name of Jehovah." True worship is only possible in the Second Man, Christ risen from the dead.

III. The Book of the Generations of Adam

CHAPTER 5

Adam and His Seed Through Seth

1. Adam (5:1-5)
2. Seth (5:6-8)
3. Enos (5:9-11)
4. Cainan (5:12-14)
5. Mahalaleel (5:15-17)
6. Jared (5:18-20)
7. Enoch (5:21-24)
8. Methuselah (5:25-27)
9. Lamech (5:28-31)
10. Noah (5:32)

Here we find the record of the seed of Seth. There is a striking contrast with the record of the Cainites in the previous chapter. The Cainites were progressive, built cities and made inventions. Nothing is said of the God-fearing generations in this chapter accomplishing great earthly things. They were pilgrims and strangers, waiting for better things. In the fourth chapter the word "die" is not mentioned. Nothing is said of the duration of the life of Cain and his seed. Eight times in the fifth chapter we read, "and he died." One did not die. We learn from this that the Lord keeps a record of the lives, the work and the years of His people. His saints are in His hands.

The names of ten generations translated give a startling revelation. In them we read the faith of the pious generations before the flood and for what they waited.

Adam	Man
Seth	Set
Enos	Frailty
Cainan	Deplorable
Mahalaleel	The Blessed God
Jared	Descends
Enoch	Teaching
Methuselah	Death sent away
Lamech	Powerful
Noah	Rest, Comfort

The record of Enoch must be compared with Jude 14-16 and Hebrews 11:5. He was translated before the great judgment swept over the earth. Enoch is a type of the living saints at the close of the present age, who will be changed in a moment, in the twinkling of an eye. Study Enoch's walk, Enoch's faith, Enoch's testimony, Enoch's suffering and Enoch's translation with the help of the New Testament passages.

CHAPTER 6:1-8

The Increasing Corruption

1. The sons of God and the daughters of men (6:1-2)
2. The warning of Jehovah (6:3)
3. Increased wickedness (6:4-6)
4. Judgment announced (6:7)
5. Noah found grace (6:8)

The question is who are the sons of God who took the daughters of men. The general view is that the sons of God were the pious descendants of Seth and the daughters of men, the Cainitish offspring. However, there are strong arguments against it.

1. There is no proof in the text that the daughters of men were only the descendants of the Cainites. The text supports the view that in "daughters of men" the natural increase of the whole human family is meant, and not a special class.

2. The theory that "sons of God" must mean pious people can likewise not be sustained. The term sons of God is never applied in the Old Testament to believers. Isaiah 43:6 refers to the future gathering of the godly remnant of Israel. That the believer is a son of God, predestined to the son—place, with the spirit of sonship in him, crying, "Abba, Father," is exclusively a New Testament revelation.

3. The result of the marriage of the sons of God with the daughters of men were children, who were heroes, men of the Name. If the sons of God were simply the pious Sethites, who mixed with the Cainites, it is hard to understand why the offspring should be a special race, heroes, men of the Name. The giants were Nephilim, which means "the fallen ones."

"Sons of God" is the term applied in the Old Testament to supernatural beings, both good and evil. Angels good and fallen are termed sons of God in the Old Testament. Satan himself is reckoned among the sons of God in Job 1:6, and 2:1. The term sons of God must mean here supernatural evil beings. These evil beings came down out of the air and began to take possession of such of the daughters of men as they chose.

"For if God spared not the angels which sinned, but cast them down to hell, and delivered them unto chains of darkness, to be reversed unto judgment; and spared not the old world, but saved Noah the eighth, a preacher of righteousness, bringing in the flood upon the world of the ungodly" (2 Pet. 2:4, 5).

Here we have a New Testament hint on Genesis 6:1-5. The Scripture declares that the fallen angels are still loose; here, however, are angels, which sinned and God did not spare them. Another passage in Jude's Epistle is still more significant: "And the angels which kept not their first estate, but left their own habitation, He hath reserved in everlasting chains under darkness unto the judgment of the great day." This statement in Jude is linked with the sin of Sodom and Gomorrah.

We stand not alone in this exposition. "The sons of God, in my judgment, mean the same beings in Genesis as they do in Job. This point will suffice to indicate their chief guilt in thus traversing the boundaries which God appointed for His creatures. No wonder that total ruin speedily ensues. It is really the basis of fact for not a few tales of mythology which men have made up."[2] God has veiled the awful corruption and we dare not intrude into the secret things.

May we remember that our Lord has told us, "As it was in the days of Noah, so shall it be when the Son of Man cometh."

The Spirit of God was then pleading with men. His work as the hindering one is indicated in verse 3.

Read, 1 Peter 3:20, "For Christ indeed once suffered for sins, the just for the unjust, that He might bring us to God; being put to death in flesh but made alive in the Spirit, in which also going He preached to the spirits, which are in prison, heretofore disobedient, when the long-suffering of God waited in the days of Noe, while the ark was preparing." This passage does not teach that Christ after His death, went into Hades to preach, but the meaning is that His Spirit through Noah preached to the spirits of men living at that time, and who were then disobedient and are now in prison.

God in His long-suffering waited yet 120 years, during which His Spirit preached through the preacher of righteousness, calling to repentance.

The withdrawing of the Spirit of God is clearly taught in 2 Thess. 2:7. This age will end in the same manner as the age before the flood, "the Spirit not always pleading with man."

[2]W. Kelly, *Lectures on the Pentateuch.*

Jehovah, beholding the earth, saw that the wickedness of man was great, and every imagination of the thoughts of his heart only evil continually. Before we read Jehovah's verdict, "for he indeed is flesh." And again, "The end of all flesh is come before me, for the earth is full of violence through them, and behold, I will destroy them with the earth."

IV. The Generations of Noah

CHAPTER 6:9-22

Before the Flood

1. Noah walked with God (6:9-10)
2. The earth filled with violence (6:11-13)
3. The building of the ark commanded (6:14-21)
4. Noah's obedience (6:22)

It was grace which constituted Noah just and enabled him to walk with God. Hebrews 11:7 gives a full definition of Noah's faith. Seven things are shown concerning Noah:

Warned of God	The ground of faith
Things not seen	The realm of faith
He feared	The exercise of faith
Prepared an ark	The work of faith
Saved His house	The results of faith
Condemned the world	The testimony of faith
Heir of righteousness	The reward of faith

The ark is a type of Christ. The word "gopher" means atonement, and the word "pitch," meaning the same, is translated more than seventy times in the Bible by "to make atonement."

The ark had a window above—looking towards Heaven and not upon the earth and its judgment beneath. It had one door and only one in the side. All blessedly applicable to Christ and salvation. The deluge which came, flood of waters, covering all, so that the end of all flesh came, is a type of the death of Christ. In His death judgment was passed and executed upon all flesh. The waves and billows rolled over His innocent head. He passed through death and judgment for us and has made Himself our perfect ark, our hiding place. In Him we are lifted above the judgment waters.

CHAPTER 7

Noah in the Ark and the Judgment by Water

1. Commanded to enter the ark (7:1-4)

2. Noah's obedience (7:5-9)
3. The judgment by water (7:10-24)

Noah is a type of the Lord Jesus. In the one, Noah, his house was saved. He carried them above and through the judgment waters. Noah is also a type of the Jewish remnant which will pass through the great tribulation and the judgments to come.

The ark of gopher wood, pitched inside and outside with pitch, is a type of the Lord Jesus Christ; Noah preparing the ark, the type of Christ, accomplishing salvation, having finished it.

The deluge is a type of the death of Christ. "All Thy billows and Thy waves have gone over Me" (Ps. 42:7). This was done when on the cross. He who knew no sin was made sin for us. As the earth was covered in the deluge, so the judgment passed over Him, in whom the end of all flesh has come.

"And Jehovah said unto Noah, 'Come thou and all thy house into the ark.' " After the ark was finished came the invitation to enter in. The invitation "come" still goes forth. "Come unto Me"—will it last forever?

The beasts, clean and unclean, taken into the ark, as well as the fowls of the air, give us the hint that creation will share the blessed effects of salvation. The subsequent prophetic word and Romans 8:19-23, tell us of a coming deliverance of groaning creation.

"And they that went in unto Noah, went in male and female of all flesh, as God (Elohim) had commanded him, and the Lord (Jehovah) shut him in" (verse 16). In this verse we have Elohim and Jehovah used. God, as Creator, had commanded Noah; Jehovah had announced the judgment, and the ark which had been preparing represented the patient and merciful Jehovah. And now as the hour of mercy was past, Jehovah shut the door. He who had given an open door shut it at last.

Noah and his house in the ark were saved and safe. And so are we in Christ Jesus our Lord.

"The rain was forty days and forty nights upon the earth" (verse 12). Here for the first time in the Word do we find the number forty. It is not the last time. Forty means endurance and testing. Moses was forty days on the mountain, his life was divided into three forties. Forty years Israel was in the wilderness. Elijah knew the forty days, and Ezekiel lay forty days on his right side, a typical action (Ezekiel 4). Jonah preached, "yet forty days and Nineveh shall be destroyed"; and Christ was forty days in the wilderness to be tested.

CHAPTER 8

Noah Remembered

1. Noah remembered (8:1-3)
2. The ark resting (8:4-5)
3. The raven sent forth (8:6-7)
4. The sending forth of the dove (8:8-12)
5. The waters dried up (8:13-14)
6. The command to leave the ark (8:15-17)
7. Noah's obedience (8:18-19)
8. The altar and the covenant (8:20-22)

Especially instructive are verses 6 to 12 in our chapter. Noah opened the window at the end of forty days, and he sent forth a raven. This bird flew to and fro until the waters were dried up from off the earth.

Then he sent forth a dove three times. The first time she found no resting place, and Noah took her back into the ark. The second time she returned with an olive leaf in her mouth, and the third time she did not return at all, and finds her abiding place in the earth.

That the dove is the type of the Holy Spirit needs hardly to be stated. In this outward symbolic form He came upon our Lord. But what does the black raven represent? The raven is the type of evil, a representative of the god of this age and the flesh as well. We may see in the raven flying to and fro until the waters were dried up, a type of the prince of the power in the air, the devil. His work and activity the devil describes himself as "going to and fro in the earth, and walking up and down in it" (Job 1:7; and 2:2). He is doing this still, but there is a time coming when the black raven will stop his restless flight. When this present age ends with divine wrath revealed once more, and the waves of divine judgment have rolled over the earth, then Satan, the devil, that old serpent, will be bound a thousand years.

The dove and her threefold departure is a type of the coming and presence of the Holy Spirit in the earth sent forth from the Lord.

First, she comes forth and finds no resting place. This represents the Holy Spirit in the Old Testament, where he was not present in the earth to find a rest, to abide. The second departure of the dove may be taken as a type of the Holy Spirit's presence in this age. The dove found a resting place and still she did not stay, but came back to the ark with an olive leaf. This olive leaf was the witness that the judgment waters had passed and that new life had developed. It also signifies peace. So the Holy Spirit is present in this age as the result of the finished work of Christ. The third time the dove did not return. So there is an age in the future when the Holy Spirit will be poured upon all flesh. During the first and second sending forth of the dove, the raven was also present. Both flew over the earth. When the dove went forth the third time the waters were gone and there was no more raven.

The word "altar" is mentioned here for the first time in the Bible. The altar is for worship. Here then worship is for the first time revealed. We worship, having passed from the old into the new, standing on the ground of resurrection. We know that death and judgment is passed, and therefore we worship in spirit and in truth. Christ is our altar; and in the sacrifices Noah brought, Christ is also typically represented. Only he is a true worshiper who knows Christ and the perfect work He has done. "Jehovah smelled the sweet savor." This reminds us of John 4: "But the hour cometh, and now is, when the true worshipers shall worship the Father in Spirit and in truth, for the Father seeketh such to worship Him." Not service is a sweet savor to God, but worship.

CHAPTER 9

The Earth Replenished

1. The divine commission (9:1-7)
2. The covenant with Noah (9:8-11)
3. The token of the covenant (9:12-17)
4. The family of Noah (9:18-19)
5. Noah's drunkenness (9:20-24)
6. Noah's prophecy (9:25-27)
7. Noah's death (9:28-29)

A new start is made after the judgment by water and Noah is blessed by God. Like Adam and Eve they are commissioned to fill the earth, but nothing is said of having dominion over the earth.

In Genesis 1:29 we read that man was to eat the green herb and the fruit of the trees, but now there is permission given to eat every moving thing that liveth. It seems clear that before the deluge meat was not eaten. There are not a few advocates of total abstinence from meat in our day. The adherents of delusions like thesophy and others tell us that a vegetable diet will ennoble man, deliver him from the lust of the flesh, make him pure and good and fit to approach God. With all the abstinence from meat before the deluge the people were not better, but ended in the flesh and perished in it. In 1 Tim. 4 we read of those who live in the latter times and depart from the faith, and among the characteristics given is the following: "Forbidding to marry, and commanding to abstain from meats which God has created to be received with thanksgiving of them which believe and know the truth. For every creature of God is good, and nothing to be refused, if it be received with thanksgiving."

And why is the blood made so prominent? Four times we read the word "blood" in verses 4-6. The book of Leviticus gives the answer, "For the life of the flesh is in the blood, and I have given it to you upon the altar, to make an atonement for your souls; for it is the blood that maketh an atonement for the soul" (Lev. 17:11). The sanctity of the blood is here shown forth. Even the hunter in Israel had to keep it in view. "And whatsoever man there be of the children of Israel, or of the strangers that sojourn among you which hunteth, or catcheth any beast or fowl that may be eaten; he shall even pour out the blood thereof, and cover it with dust. For it is the life of all flesh; the blood of it is for the life thereof; therefore I said to the children of Israel, Ye shall eat the blood of no manner of flesh; for the life of all flesh is the blood thereof; whosoever eateth it shall be cut off" (Lev. 17:13, 14). So the hunter had to stop, and pour out the blood. All points to the blood of the Lamb.

God established His covenant with Noah and his seed and put the token of the covenant in the clouds. The rainbow speaks of a passed judgment of His salvation and remembrance.

Another universal judgment by water will never come again (verse 15). Another judgment is in store for this planet. "The world that was then, being overflowed with water, perished; but the heavens and the earth, which are now, by the same word are kept in store, reserved unto fire against the day of judgment and perdition of ungodly men" (2 Pet. 3:6-7).

Interesting is Noah's prophecy after his drunkenness.

Ham (black) is not mentioned in the curse, but the son of Ham, Canaan (the merchantman). Ham's deed revealed the unbelieving condition of his heart, while Shem's and Japheth's action manifest divine grace in covering up the nakedness. God's eye beheld Canaan and his subsequent career in his descendants. He inherits the curse. How literally it was carried out! Shem, meaning "name," becomes the family in which Jehovah, the Name, is to be revealed. Jehovah is the God of Shem. Soon we shall see a son of Shem, Abram, and his seed becoming the depository of Jehovah's revelation. Later Jehovah speaks and reveals His name by which He wishes to be known forever to another son of Shem, Moses. "Thus shalt thou say unto the children of Israel, Jehovah, the God of your fathers, the God of Abraham, the God of Isaac and the God of Jacob hath sent me unto you; this is my name forever, and this is my memorial unto all generations" (Ex. 3:15). He does not call Himself "the God of Japheth" but "the God of Shem." Shem's supremacy is here indicated. It is a far-reaching prophecy.

Japheth means "expansion." His sons are Gomer, Magog, Madai, Javan, Tubal, Meshech, Tiras, and the sons of Gomer and Javan are mentioned in the next chapter. They expanded and Japheth dwells in the tents of Shem, partakes of Shem's blessing and responsibility. Some take "He shall dwell in the tents of Shem," the "he" as referring to God, but this is incorrect. It means Japheth and reminds us of the parable of the olive tree in Romans 11.

Shem's blessing consisted (1) In being the carrier of the Name, Jehovah. (2) In controlling Canaan and being the master over him. (3) The giving shelter to Japheth and let him be sharer of the blessing. It is the germ of all following prophecy and we wait still for its end fulfillment.

V. The Generations of the Sons of Noah

CHAPTER 10

Shem, Ham, and Japheth and Their Seed

1. The sons of Japheth (10:2-5)
2. The sons of Ham (10:6-20)
3. The sons of Shem (10:21-32)

Here we have the beginning of the nations. God knows them and keeps track of the nations of the earth. The order of the sons of Noah is here changed. Japheth comes first. Ham's place is unchanged. Shem comes last. This order is given in view of Noah's prophecy. Among the descendants of Ham we find Nimrod, a mighty hunter. His name means "Let us rebel." Here also we find Babel mentioned for the first time. Babylon has for its founder "a mighty one in the earth—a mighty hunter." Mentioned here for the first time Babylon is seen springing from the race which is under a curse, and having for its founder a mighty one in the earth, a second Cain. We have here the birth of Babylon, while the entire Bible, from now on to the eighteenth chapter of the "book of the Revelation of Jesus Christ," gives us its development, its Satanic opposition to all that is from above, and its final great fall and destruction. Babylon! what a sinister word! Both city and system, such as is seen in its finality in Rev. 17 and 18, are Satan's stronghold.

It would be interesting to follow all these names and trace them in the Scriptures and in history. But this we cannot do.

CHAPTER 11:1-9

The Tower of Babel and the Scattering of the Nations

1. The unity of the nations in Shinar (11:1-2)
2. Their attempt: "Let us make" (11:3-4)
3. The divine answer: "Let us go down" (11:5-7)
4. The Result (11:8-9)

All the earth had one language. This is also proven by philological research. The whole human family journeyed together. They left the mountainous regions and went down to the plain. This expresses their descent morally; they turned away from God, though they had the knowledge of God (Rom. 1:18-19).

Notice the absence of the name of God in the beginning of the chapter. They had excluded Him. "They said . . . let us make . . . and they had . . . let us build ourselves . . . let us make ourselves a name." It is self-exaltation and defiance of God. It was full rebellion against God.

The tower they attempted to build was to reach into heaven. It is the first concentrated effort of man against God his maker and against Jehovah. It represents a God-defying and man-deifying confederacy. We cannot follow Babylon in its different aspects. There was the ancient city, the enemy of Jerusalem. There is the present day Babylon, a lifeless, professing Christendom, both Romanism and Protestantism. There is the future Babylon (Rev. 17—18). Concentration and confusion marks Babylon. Compare the "Let us" here with the prophetic second

Psalm, when in the future, nations will confederate against God and His anointed. God came down in divine irony to look at their city and tower and to scatter them by the confusion of languages. And when the rebellion of the second Psalm is reached, He will laugh and hold them in derision.

VI. The Generations of Shem

CHAPTER 11:10-26

From Shem to Terah

Here again we find ten names prominent. The same number we have in Genesis 5. Both genealogies in chapters 5 and 11 end with a man to whom God reveals Himself and with each a new dispensation begins, Noah and Abram. Notice the decreasing years of life. Shem was 600 years old, the grandfather of Abram only 148. The line of Shem was degenerating; some of the names indicate this. Terah (delay), the father of Abram, was an idolator. The descendants of Shem worshipped idols (Joshua 24:2). When the line of Shem had failed God called Abram.

VII. The Generations of Terah

CHAPTER 11:27-32

Terah's Family and His Death

Terah with the persons mentioned in verse 31 went forth from Ur to go into the land of Canaan. Terah died in Haran. Chapter 12:1 and Acts 7:1-4 makes it clear that this going forth was by divine revelation.

CHAPTER 12

The First Events in Abram's Life

1. The call and the promise (12:1-3)
2. Abram's obedience (12:4-6)
3. The second communication of Jehovah (12:7-9)
4. Abram in Egypt and first denial of Sarai (12:10-20)

We come now to a new beginning, the Abrahamic covenant. It marks the beginning of that wonderful race, the seed of Abraham, the people of Israel. Abraham's name is mentioned 74 times in the New Testament. How closely his history is interwoven into New Testament doctrine. This may be learned by consulting the following passages: John 8:56; Acts 7-2; Rom. 4:1-16; Gal. 3:6-18; Heb. 11:8-19; James 2:21-23. What a satanic lie it is to brand the existence of this great man of God as a myth! Such is often done in "Christian" (?) schools and pulpits. We give a few hints on this chapter:

The sovereign grace of God in the call of Abram. Shem had the promise of the Name. Jehovah was to reveal Himself in Shem. We learned from the eleventh chapter that the line of Shem had run into decay and was departing from God. In the midst of this ruin in which Abram was involved, he became the object of divine election and Jehovah in His grace manifested Himself to Abram and called him.

The delay at Haran. "The God of Glory appeared unto our father Abraham, when he was in Mesopotamia, before he dwelt in Charran." "Then came he out of the land of the Chaldeans, and dwelt at Charran; and from thence, when his father was dead, he removed him into this land, wherein ye now dwell" (Acts 7:2-4). The call came to Abram in Mesopotamia. They left their country and dwelt in Haran. Here Abram tarried till his father Terah died. The delay in going to the land to which God had called him was on account of Terah. Typically, Terah stands for the flesh, the ties of nature. This is always in the way to carry out fully the call of God and enter into full and blessed realization of God's calling. While delaying in Haran (Haran means "parched"), God did not reveal Himself anew to Abram.

Death set Abram free, and by death freed from the ties of nature he journeyed on to the land of Canaan. The death of Terah, the liberating factor in Abram's experience, is typical of the death of the Lord Jesus Christ. We have died in Him. The cross of Christ has set us free.

Abram was "sanctified unto obedience." Sanctified means "separated." The call of God meant separation for Abram. "Get thee out of thy country and from thy kindred, and from thy father's house." Now there was no further delay. "Abram departed, as the Lord had spoken to him." The calling involved obedience which was readily yielded. All this is typical of the individual believer.

It was by faith. What faith is stands here fully manifested. "By faith Abraham, when he was called out into a place which he should after receive for an inheritance, obeyed; and he went out, not knowing whither he went" (Heb. 11:8). He took God's infallible Word and left all; walked by faith and not by sight; he hoped for things he saw not. Faith ever finds its most precious resting place upon the naked Word of God.

The promises. "And I will make of thee a great nation, and I will also bless thee and make thy name great; and thou shalt be a blessing. And I will bless them that bless thee, and curse him that curseth thee; and in thee shall all families of the earth be blessed" (verses 2 and 3). And all God promised to Abram He hath kept. Every word has been literally fulfilled. Nations upon nations who hated Abraham's seed, his natural descendants, have found to their great sorrow how true Abraham's God is. These promises still hold good. To the seed of Abraham belong still the promises (Rom 9:4). The nations of the earth, all the families are unconsciously waiting to be blessed by Abraham's seed. Salvation is still of the Jews.

Abram worships. He built an altar unto Jehovah, who appeared unto him. Again he built an altar, with Bethel on the west and Ai on the east, and there he called upon the name of Jehovah. The revelation of Jehovah produces worship. The basis of worship is a conscious and precious relation with Jehovah. Abram knew Jehovah's grace toward him, therefore he worshipped Him and called upon His name.

Abram's failure was the result of leaving Bethel and going down to Egypt (typical of the world).

CHAPTER 13

The Return from Egypt and Separation from Lot

1. Back to Bethel (13:1-4)
2. The strife (13:5-7)
3. The separation. Lot in Sodom (13:8-13)
4. The third communication of Jehovah (13:14-18)

Abram is graciously brought back. Abram could not have remained in Egypt forever. So the believer who has wandered away from the Lord will be restored. How precious the altar at Bethel must have been to him. Dispensationally Abram's going down to Egypt foreshadows the going down of his posterity.

Lot's character is brought out in his selfish choice. He had not so much followed the Lord as he followed Abram. He is self-centered, and unlike Abram looking to the things unseen, he is occupied with the things which are seen, with the earth and earthly possession. Lot is a type of the world-bordering, carnally minded, professing Christian. He lifts up his eyes and beholds a well-watered plain, beautiful as the garden of the Lord. He chooses all the plain of Jordan and pitched his tent toward Sodom. That Sodom and Gomorrah were fast ripening for the day of burning and destruction, that the men in Sodom were wicked and sinners well known in the day when Lot made his choice, is not taken into consideration by him. There was no prayer, no consultation with the Lord from the side of Lot. His eyes behold only the beautiful and well-watered plain; there must have been a feverish haste to make his decision. Nor did Lot go at once into Sodom. He nears Sodom gradually. Perhaps at first he had no thought of having fellowship with the wicked men of Sodom, but he got there all the same. All is written for our learning. Decline begins gradually, but always leads into the world.

And Abram gazed too over the fertile plains. Some time after he looked again. "And he looked toward Sodom and Gomorrah, and toward all the land of the plain, and beheld, and lo, the smoke of the country went up as the smoke of a furnace" (19:28). Was Abram sorry then for his choice? Do not look upon the fairness of the world; remember a little while longer and wrath and judgment will be poured upon the world now under condemnation.

Another communication and promise is received by Abram from Jehovah.

CHAPTER 14

The First Recorded War and Lot's Deliverance

1. The battle of the confederacy (14:1-10)
2. Sodom and Gomorrah spoiled (14:11-13)
3. Abram's rescue (14:14-16)
4. Sodom's king to meet Abram (14:17)
5. Melchizedek (14:18-20)
6. The king's offer and Abram's answer (14:21-24)

The record of the first war is here foreshadowing the last great warfare still to come. Amraphel, King of Shinar, has been historically located by excavated tablets in 1901. The code of Amraphel (Khammurabi) was discovered in Susa. It dates back to 2139 B. C. Some 800 years the laws of Amraphel governed the people of Central Asia. The discovery of this code was a severe blow to higher criticism which claimed that writing before Moses was unknown. What interests us most is Melchizedek. He is mentioned as a type of Christ in Psalm 110 and Hebrews 7. This chapter in Hebrews must be read with Genesis 14.

Melchizedek was a human being. We do not believe that he was a supernatural being manifested in the form of man. He was king of peace and king of righteousness and priest as well, uniting the office of priest and king and prophet in himself. The way he is introduced in this first book, where genealogies abound, without descent, having in this sense neither beginning of days nor end of life (Heb. 7:3), makes him a very strong type of Christ, the Son of God.

Like Melchizedek, Christ unites in His person kingship and priesthood. However, though Christ is a priest after the order of Melchizedek, He does not yet fully exercise His Melchizedek priesthood. As priest after the order of Melchizedek He must have His own throne, for which he is still waiting on the throne of His Father.

Therefore when He comes again He will be the Priest upon His throne and crowned with many crowns (Zech. 6:12-14)

The sinister temptation of Sodom's king was rejected by Abram because Melchizedek had made known the name of God in a new way, "The most high God." Abram uses this new title and adds "Jehovah" to "the most high God."

Dispensationally it shows the future events after the conflict, the time of wars by confederacies of nations, in which the seed of Abraham will be so much concerned, when the enemies of God and of Israel will be overcome, and the King of Peace, the King of Righteousness, the great Priest, the Lord Jesus Christ, will appear to bless His earthly people. Then Israel will acknowledge Him as Abram did Melchizedek. "The Most High God," is one of God's millennial names.

CHAPTER 15

The Fourth Communication and the Covenant and the Vision

1. The fourth communication (15:1)
2. Abram's answer (15:2-3)
3. The promised seed (15:4-5)
4. Abram counted righteous (15:6)
5. Continued communication (15:7-8)
6. The divided animals (15:9-11)
7. The vision (15:12-17)
8. The covenant made (15:18-21)

The connection with the previous chapter is extremely precious. Abram had honored the Lord and now the Lord honored him. Then the seed is promised. That seed promised is Isaac; Christ is typified by him. "Abram believed in the Lord and He counted it to him for righteousness." The fourth chapter of Romans must be closely studied at this point for it is the commentary to the promise given and Abram's faith. He is commanded to take the different animals and to divide them.

All these animals are mentioned later in the book of Leviticus and as sacrifices are typical of Christ, while the fowls which came down upon the carcasses and which Abraham drove away (Gen. 15:11) are types of evil. (See Matthew 13, the birds which pick up the seed; the fowls which make nests in the tree.) But the divided pieces and the turtledove and pigeon, exposed to the fowls, are also typical of Israel, divided and cut through, while the fowls may be taken as types of nations who feast upon Israel. The deep sleep which fell upon Abraham, signifying death, and the horror of a great darkness, are likewise types of what was to come upon the seed of Abraham. After God had spoken of the coming affliction of the children of Abraham and announcing the judgment of their troubles, a smoking furnace and a burning lamp passed between the pieces. The smoking furnace, the spectacle of a fire and the dark smoke from it, showed to the eye, what God had spoken to the heart of His servant. The smoking furnace is the type of Egypt and the tribulation through which the sons of Jacob and their seed had to pass. The burning lamp is the type of God's presence with them. Thus we read: "But the Lord hath taken you and brought you forth out of the iron furnace, out of Egypt to be unto Him a people of inheritance, as ye are this day" (Deut. 4:20; 1 Kings 8:51). In Egypt the fire burned, as in the furnace, and the great darkness settled upon Abraham's seed.

CHAPTER 16

Abraham and Hagar

1. Sarai's suggestion (16:1-3)
2. Abram's action (16:4)
3. Sarai and Hagar (16:5-6)
4. Hagar in the wilderness (16:7-9)
5. The birth of Ishmael announced (16:10-14)
6. Ishmael born (16:15-16)

The fifteenth chapter may be called Abram's faith chapter. The sixteenth is the chapter of unbelief. It was impatience which forced Sarai and Abram to act for themselves. Unbelief is impatience and impatience is unbelief. Faith waits patiently for the Lord, and on the Lord, to act. "He that believeth shall not make haste." Abram and Sarai attempted to help the Lord to fulfill His promise. What a failure they made of it! On account of it there was great trouble in his house.

But the incident has a deeper meaning. Read Gal. 4:21-31. This gives us the typical meaning and how the Lord overruled even this failure. Sarai represents the covenant of grace; Hagar the law covenant. Hagar was an Egyptian; Sarai a princess. The law brings into bondage, grace makes free.

Abram was eighty-six years old when Ishmael was born. The next chapter tells us that Abram was ninety and nine years old when the Lord spoke to him again. Thus for thirteen years Abram's life seems to have been barren of communications from the Lord. What a harvest of the flesh.

CHAPTER 17

The Fifth Communication and the Covenant Repeated

1. The communication and Abram worships (17:1-3)
2. The enlarged promise (17:4-8)
3. The covenant sign (17:9-14)
4. Sarah's seed promised (17:15-16)
5. The laughter of Abraham (17:17)
6. Abraham's plea for Ishmael (17:18-22)
7. Abraham's obedience (17:23-27)

The promises which the Lord now gives to Abram are most complete. His name is changed; he is now to be called Abraham, which means "the Father of many," because he is to be the Father of many nations.

Upon this follows the institution of circumcision. This is a portion which is extremely rich in its teachings. Let us notice that in Romans the Holy Spirit explains the meaning of this ceremony. "For we say that faith was reckoned to Abraham for righteousness. How was it then reckoned? When he was in circumcision, or in uncircumcision? Not in circumcision, but in uncircumcision. And he received the sign of circumcision, a seal of the righteousness of the faith which he had yet being uncircumcised. . . ." (Rom. 4:10, 11). Circumcision was, therefore, the seal of righteousness of faith. Some fourteen years previous Abram had been constituted righteous, because he believed God, and it was counted unto him for righteousness. First righteousness by faith and then the seal. Of believers it is said in the New Testament that they are circumcised. "In whom also ye are circumcised with the circumcision made without hands in putting off the body of the flesh by the circumcision of Christ" (Col. 2:11). The circumcision of Christ is the death of Christ; in Him the body of the flesh is put off. We have died with Him, are dead and buried and risen with Him. "For we are the circumcision, which worship God in the spirit and rejoice in Christ Jesus and have no confidence in the flesh" (Phil. 3:3).

Sarai's name is also changed. The promised seed is to be from her. "His name is to be Isaac" which means laughter. The end of the chapter shows Abraham's obedience.

CHAPTER 18

The Sixth Communication and Jehovah Visits Abraham

1. The manifestation (18:1-2)
2. Abraham's welcome (18:3-8)
3. The promise repeated (18:9-10)
4. Sarah's laughter (18:11-15)
5. The departure towards Sodom (18:16)
6. Abraham's intercession (18:17-33)

This most remarkable visitation was the answer of Jehovah to Abraham's obedience of faith. The one in the middle was none other than Jehovah in human form; the other two were angels. "Before Abraham was I am," He said when on earth. Here Abraham is face to face with Him.

Sarah's laughter when the son is promised to her is the laughter of unbelief. She looked to her womb, which was a grave. Her laughter was made the occasion of that blessed word Jehovah spoke. "Is anything too hard for the Lord?" From the place of sweet communion they now proceed towards the scene where a great judgment was to be enacted.

"Shall I hide from Abraham that thing which I do?" is another gracious word. Abraham was the friend of God. The Lord said to His disciples, "The servant knoweth not what his Lord doeth, but I have called you friends; for all things that I have heard of My Father I have made known unto you" (John 15). Yes, He has told us all about the things to come, the doom of the world and the secrets of His coming. And then follows that wonderful intercession before the Lord. How He pleads! What humility and yet boldness! Blessed privilege of all saints the prayer of intercession, which the great Intercessor, the Lord Jesus Christ, loves to hear from the lips of His children, for it is the echo of His own heavenly occupation.

CHAPTER 19

The Destruction of Sodom and Gomorrah

1. The angels visit (19:1-5)
2. Lot and the Sodomites (19:6-11)
3. The destruction of Sodom announced (19:12-13)
4. Lot and his sons-in-law (19:14)
5. Lot brought forth (19:15-17)
6. Lot's request (19:18-20)
7. The escape (19:21-25)
8. Lot's wife (19:26)
9. Abraham looks on (19:27-29)
10. Lot's shame (19:30-38)

This is a chapter of judgment. How great the contrast with the preceding one! There Abraham sat under the tent door and the Lord appeared unto him; here two angels come to Sodom at even and Lot sits in the gate of Sodom. Joyfully Abraham had run to meet the heavenly visitors and willing the Lord and His companion had entered in to be comforted by Abraham. Lot invites the angels likewise but they say "Nay; but we will abide in the street all night." Only after Lot pressed upon them greatly "did they enter his house." The feast was not like Abraham's feast of fine meal and a calf, but only unleavened bread. Poor, selfish Lot! He had gone down to Sodom; from the tent pitched toward Sodom he had landed in Sodom and there he had no longer a tent, but he had a house. He had settled down and given up his character as pilgrim. His daughters had become perfectly at home in Sodom and married unbelieving Sodomites. More than that Lot had taken a position in Sodom. "He sat in the gate of Sodom" and the mob said "This fellow came in to sojourn and he will be judge" (verse 9). He held an influential position there and most likely attempted the reformation of Sodom. That he was greatly troubled is learned from the New Testament . . . "he was vexed with the filthy conversation of the wicked" (2 Peter 2:7). Lot is the picture of thousands of Christian believers, who are carnally minded and worldly. There are many who have settled down in the world, from which they have been separated and delivered by the death of Christ and like Lot they will be saved "so as by fire."

From the fourth verse to the eleventh in this chapter we find a short description of the awful wickedness of Sodom. Its gross immoralities, the fearful fruits of the lust of the flesh have since then become proverbial. In this connection we may well remember the words of our Lord Jesus Christ, "Likewise also as it was in the days of Lot . . . even thus shall it be in the day when the Son of Man cometh" (Luke 17:28-30). This Christian age will not end in universal righteousness; it will end in apostasy from God and His Word, in iniquity and lawlessness, and these will be followed by a fiery judgment. Indications of such an ending of this age of boasted progress are numerous and becoming more pronounced. Among these immoralities, the looseness of the marriage ties, and adulteries are prominently in the lead. The great cities of Christendom are modern Sodoms and the immorality in them is perhaps worse than in the ancient, lewd cities of the valley of Jordan. This will be getting worse and worse and the end will be judgment. And now the angels give the message of the impending judgment. Sodom was to be destroyed by fire. Lot believed the message, but when he had spoken the word to his two sons-in-law, "Up get you out of this place; for the Lord will destroy this city," they took it as a joke and believed not. They might have been saved if they had believed. They perished in Sodom. Even so it is now at the end of this age. "Knowing this first, that there shall come in the last days scoffers, walking after their own lusts, and saying, Where is the promise of His coming?" (2 Pet. 3:3, 4). If one preaches and teaches the soon coming of the Lord Jesus Christ, to be revealed from heaven with His mighty angels in flaming fire taking vengeance on them that know not God, and that obey not the Gospel of our Lord (2 Thess. 1:7, 8), he is laughed at and scorned, called a pessimist. Perhaps the two sons-in-law called Lot a pessimist.

Notice verse 24. "Then Jehovah rained upon Sodom and Gomorrah brimstone and fire from Jehovah out of heaven." Here was a Jehovah on earth and He called to Jehovah in heaven.

Lot's history ends in shame. Moab and Ammon begotten in wickedness have a history of shame. No record is given of the death of Lot.

CHAPTER 20

Abraham in Gerar

1. Abraham in Gerar (20:1)
2. Second denial of Sarah (20:2)
3. God's dealing with Abimelech (20:3-7)
4. Abimelech and Abraham (20:8-18)

Note Abraham's going down to Egypt in chapter 12 and now going to Gerar and denying again Sarah. In chapter 26 Isaac goes also to Gerar and denies Rebekah. It shows what the flesh is.

But Abraham is greatly honored by the Lord. The Lord called him a prophet. Abraham prayed and God healed Abimelech.

CHAPTER 21

Isaac and Ishmael and the Covenant with Abimelech

1. Isaac's birth (21:1)
2. His circumcision (21:4-8)
3. Ishmael mocking (21:9)
4. Sarah's demand (21:10-11)
5. God speaks to Abraham (21:12-13)
6. Hagar and Ishmael cast out (21:14-16)
7. The intervention of God (21:17-21)
8. The covenant with Abimelech (21:22-34)

Isaac, the promised seed, was born at the set time as God had spoken.

As there was a set time when the promised son was born to Abraham, so there was an appointed time when God gave His Son "when the fulness of time was come, God sent forth His Son." There is also a set time, when the First-Begotten will be brought into the world again, His second coming. Then it will be the set time for Israel, too, when God remembers His promises and when He visits and does all, what He has spoken concerning them. "Thou shalt arise and have mercy on Zion; for the time to favor her, yea, the set time is come" (Psalm 102:13).

Isaac's name means laughter, the laughter of God in view of man's helplessness. Isaac the promised one, the only one, in his wonderful birth and in his name is a type of the promised seed, the Lord Jesus Christ. He is God's laughter over Satan, sin and death.

Sarah laughed again, but it is the laughter of joy. The word the Lord spoke to her: "Is anything too hard for the Lord?" wrought faith in her heart. "Through faith also Sarah herself received strength to conceive seed, and was delivered of a child when she was past age, because she judged Him faithful who had promised" (Heb. 11:11). We have called attention before to the allegory in Gal. 4:21-31. This passage gives meaning to the historical account. Sarah stands for the grace covenant; Hagar for the law covenant. As soon as the Seed came (Christ) the law was cast out. The law was only the schoolmaster till Christ came. Hagar's son also typifies the flesh. Isaac is typical of the nature which grace bestows.

No sooner was Isaac weaned and a great feast made than the son of Hagar, the Egyptian, mocked. Ishmael manifests his true character. As long as there was no Isaac, nothing is heard of Ishmael; the presence of Isaac makes known what was in the son of the bond-woman. The presence of the new nature makes known what the flesh really is and it is fulfilled what is written "The flesh lusteth against the Spirit and the Spirit against the flesh."

Here we have also a dispensational picture. According to the passage in Galatians Hagar corresponds to Jerusalem which is now, the one who is in bondage with her children. As Hagar wandered in the wilderness so the natural descendants of Abraham have become wanderers. It is on account of that "covenant of grace" that rich grace in the Lord Jesus Christ, which they rejected that they are cast out. But they are like Hagar in the wilderness of "Beersheba," which means translated, "well of the oath," reminding us of the oath of God and His gifts and calling, which are without repentance. Like Hagar's eyes their eyes are blinded and they see not the "well of water" which is for them. A time, however, will come when their eyes will be opened and when they shall draw water out of the wells of salvation (Isaiah 12:3). The rest of the chapter is taken up with the record of the covenant, which Abimelech made with Abraham. He, who had been healed in answer to the prayer of Abraham, now acknowledges openly that God is with his servant. This shows the faithfulness of God to His promises. Abraham is blest and is a blessing. In the grove of Beersheba he called on the name of Jehovah, the everlasting God.

CHAPTER 22

The Testing of Abraham

1. God's command (22:1-2)
2. Abraham's obedience (22:3-6)
3. Isaac's question and Abraham's answer (22:7-8)
4. Isaac upon the altar (22:9-10)
5. The interference from above (22:11-12)
6. Jehovah-Jireh (22:13-14)
7. The second message and Abraham's return (22:15-19)
8. Nahor's offspring (22:20-24)

God now tested Abraham. True faith has to be tested; it is an evidence that there is faith when tests come upon the believer. God knew Abraham, and when the proper moment had come in his life, God spake the words to him by which he was to be tested. What a test it was!

That promised son, that beloved one to take him and to slay him upon an altar! Reason might have said, God promised this son, he was given by God's own power, all my hope and expectation center in him; how can God demand him to be slain? But faith does not question God's Word, and has no "why?" to ask of God. Such faith was manifested by Abraham when in the beginning God told him to go out of his land, to a land that He would show him. He went out in faith and knew not whither he went. But God brought him to the land. He knew God's faithfulness. And now once more he is asked to go out, to the land of Moriah to an unknown mountain, and to take his beloved son along to give him up. Was his heart really all for God? Does he love Him and depend on Him supremely? Would he be willing to part with the only one and give him up? This is the test. The record shows there was not a moment's hesitation on Abraham's side. No word escaped from his lips. The only answer which he gave to God was that he rose up early in the morning and began at once the journey with Isaac. What an obedience it was!

What a word of faith it was when he said, "Abide ye here with the ass, and I and the lad will go yonder and worship and come again to you." Hebrews 11:17-19 gives us the secret of it.

We behold them going together, Isaac now carrying the wood. Abraham laid the wood upon him. An old Hebrew exposition of Genesis paraphrases this by saying "he laid the wood upon him in the form of a cross." And only once does Isaac speak asking for the lamb. To which Abraham replied, "My son, God Himself will provide a lamb for a burnt offering." Then they go together, and Isaac opened not his mouth again "like a lamb led to slaughter." He allows himself to be bound upon the altar. He had absolute confidence in his father and is willing to be slain by him; there was no struggle to be free. He is obedient to his father Abraham, even obedient unto death. The typical meaning of the event is as simple as it is precious. Isaac is the type of that "Only Begotten." In Abraham we behold "the Father," who spared not His only begotten Son, but delivered Him up for us all. But how great the contrast! God gave Him, the Son of His love for a sinful, rebellious world. And when the hour came and the Son was nailed upon the wood there was no hand to stay. He was led to slaughter like a lamb and opened not His mouth; and then we hear Him cry, "My God, my God, why hast Thou forsaken me?" God's hand was upon Him and He, the Holy One, was smitten by God. This is the Lamb God Himself has provided; "the ransom" He has found, typified also by the ram caught in the thicket. And in the angel of Jehovah, He Himself was present upon the scene, knowing all that which He would do and suffer, when the appointed time had come. How wonderful is His written Word! And we touch in these brief notes but a little of the foreshadowings and truths revealed in this chapter. The binding of Isaac upon the altar and the taking from the altar foreshadow the death and resurrection of Christ.

"Jehovah-Jireh," the Lord has seen, is the great foundation. From that provision, the gift of His Son and His obedience unto death, even the death of the cross, flows forth the great redemption: Jehovah-Rophecah (Exodus 15:26), the Lord thy healer, is next. Then follow Jehovah Nissi, the Lord my banner, (victory Ex. 17); Jehovah Shalom, Jehovah is peace (Judges 6:24); Jehovah Roi, Jehovah, my shepherd (Psa. 23:1); Jehovah Zidkenu, Jehovah our righteousness (Jer. 23:5, 6); Jehovah Shamma, Jehovah is there (Ez. 48:35).

CHAPTER 23

The Death of Sarah

1. Sarah dies (23:1-2)
2. The grave obtained (23:3-18)
3. The burial of Sarah (23:19-20)

We call the attention to the typical meaning of the death of Sarah.

She is the type of the nation Israel and her death in this chapter signifies the death of Israel, nationally. This must be brought in connection with the previous chapter. There we learned that Isaac was upon the altar and taken from it. This is typical of the death and resurrection of the true Isaac, the Promised One, the Lord Jesus Christ. Immediately after, Sarah dies, the one from whom Isaac came. And so after the Lord Jesus Christ had died and was raised from the dead, the nation from whom He came, according to the flesh, passes off the scene. Israel, like Sarah, is buried in the midst of the children of Heth, that is the Gentiles. But Israel has the promise of restoration typified by resurrection. God has promised to open the national grave of Israel and bring them back to the land, which He has given to the seed of Abraham forever. This typical application becomes still more striking and irrefutable by what follows in the twenty-fourth chapter. Here we find the call of the bride who is to comfort Isaac, after his mother's death.

It is interesting that Sarah is the only woman, whose age is mentioned in the Bible.

CHAPTER 24

The Bride Sought for Isaac

1. The commission to the servant (24:1-9)
2. The obedience and prayer of the servant (24:10-14)
3. The prayer answered (24:15-21)
4. The gifts of the servant (24:22-26)
5. The servant received (24:27-33)
6. The servant's message (24:34-36)
7. The commission and answered prayer stated (24:37-49)
8. The bride chosen (24:50-60)
9. The journey to meet Isaac. (24:61)
10. The meeting and the marriage (24:62-67)

This is one of the longest chapters in the Bible. The connection with the previous chapters is obvious. All has a typical meaning. The promised son is the type of the Lord Jesus Christ. When he was upon the altar and taken from the altar we saw a prophetic picture of the death and resurrection of our Lord. In the preceding chapter the death of Sarah stands for the national death of Israel from whom Christ came according to the flesh; this national setting aside of Israel occurred after Christ was risen from the dead and had returned to the Father. And here in chapter 24 we behold Isaac, the son and heir, with the father and the father sending forth his servant to seek a bride for Isaac. Typically we see in this chapter the call and homebringing of her, who is the comfort of the Son, after Israel's failure and national death, the church.

Abraham is now old (140 years). He was very rich in possessions, but his greatest treasure was the son of his love who was with him in Canaan. And Isaac is the father's delight and the object of his love and thoughts. He is to have a wife to share his riches. In sending forth the servant (probably Eleazar) Abraham tells him twice, "Beware thou that thou bring not my son thither again." The son is not to leave the father's side; the bride is to be brought to him. And Abraham is assured of the success of the mission of the servant.

The application is easily made. Canaan, where the three dwell, Abraham, the father; Isaac, the son, and the servant, is the type of the heavens. Abraham typifies the Father and Isaac the Son. The Son who died, raised from the dead, seated as the Heir of all things at the right hand of God, is to have one destined from before the foundation of the world to share His riches and His glory. For her, the Church, He died and purchased her with His blood. For the pearl of great price He sold all He had.

And whom does the servant foreshadow? He is the oldest servant; he ruled over all Abraham had; he was with him from the beginning. Who is represented by the servant who went forth in obedience and whose sublime mission was crowned with such results? The servant is the type of the Holy Spirit. He was sent forth after Christ was glorified and with the day of Pentecost He began His blessed mission on earth. The testimony of the Holy Spirit and His work in calling out the church is blessedly foreshadowed in this chapter. He testified of the Father and the Son; how rich the father is and that Isaac is the heir of all the riches. And so the Holy Spirit does not speak of Himself but of the Father and of the Son and makes known the eternal purposes of the Father, and as the Servant's mission did not fail, so the mission of the Holy Spirit in the present age cannot fail.

And richer still, in typical meaning, is the story of the chosen one, Rebekah. We give a very few hints. She heard the message the servant brought. She believed all he said. She had never seen Isaac and she was attracted to him. The jewels of silver and of gold and the raiment the servant gave to Rebekah were the evidences of the riches of the unseen bridegroom and the tokens of his love. And when they asked her, "Wilt thou go with this man?" she answered, "I will go." There was no delay.

All is very simple in its application. The sinner hears the testimony and is to believe the report. If the Word is received in faith and accepted then we receive "the earnest of our inheritance," the Holy Spirit. The heart through grace becomes detached from the world and attached to Him, who loveth us and whom we love, though we have never seen Him.

"The servant took Rebekah and went his way." He took charge of her. How long the journey lasted we do not know. Most likely she was ignorant of the journey and how soon she was to meet Isaac. But the bridegroom Isaac must have ever been in her heart and before her eyes. And so are God's called out ones, who constitute the church, while on the journey, in charge and keeping of the Holy Spirit. We do not know how long the journey towards the meeting place may last.

From the well of Lahai-roi (the living and the seeing one) Isaac came. Isaac and Rebekah met. The servant presented her to Isaac and gave his report. As Isaac came forth from Lahai-roi, so our Lord will come forth from the place where He is now. He will come into the air to meet His own (1 Thess. 4:15-18). No doubt Isaac waited for Rebekah and as Rebekah expected to meet him so are we to wait for His Son from heaven. We shall see Him as He is. Before the night came Isaac took her into his tent, and then the marriage (Rev. 19).

CHAPTER 25:1-11

Abraham's Posterity From Keturah and His Death

1. Abraham's offspring from Keturah (25:1-4)
2. Isaac the heir (25:5-6)
3. Abraham's death and burial (25:7-11)

Abraham's marriage to Keturah and the offspring from her concludes the history of this remarkable character. That this took place after Isaac's marriage (typifying the marriage of the Lamb) makes it very interesting. After the church is completed and the present age ends the seed of Abraham will be blessed for the nations of the earth and nations will be born and walk in the light. This will be the result after Israel's restoration. Then all the families of the earth will be blessed in Abraham's seed. Abraham's posterity from Keturah stands for the millennial nations.

And Isaac is seen above all these. He still dwelt at Lahai-roi. He alone is the heir and the others received only gifts. So Christ is the Heir of God and His church will be with him far above all the earthly blessings of the age to come. Abraham died 175 years old, which means, he lived till Jacob and Esau were 15 years old. The phrase "gathered to his people" is used only of six persons. Of Abraham (25:8); Ishmael (verse 17); Isaac (35:29); Jacob (49:29-33); Aaron (Num. 20:24); and Moses (Deut. 32:50). Here we add a few words translated from the German and written by Dr. Kurtz, late professor of the University of Dorpat:

> The human race has had four ancestral heads, to each of whom the divine blessing is granted: "Be fruitful and multiply." Of these, Abraham is the third; for he, too, is the head and founder of a new race, or of a new development. The direct reference of that blessing, in the case of the first and second, is to descendants after the flesh; in the case of the fourth, Christ (see Psalm 22:30—110:3; Isa. 53:10), to a spiritual seed, but in the case of Abraham, to both; for his spiritual seed was appointed to be manifested through the medium of his seed according to the flesh, agreeably to the promise: "In thee and in thy seed shall all the nations of the earth be blessed." The children of Abraham, according to the flesh, are countless in number. Nations have arisen and disappeared, but his descendants proceed onward, through all ages, unmixed and unchanged. Their history is not yet closed; the blessing given to his seed, still preserves them unharmed, under every pressure of the nations around them, and amid all the ravages of time. But the peculiar feature which distinguishes Abraham does not, properly, belong to him naturally, as a member of the human family, or as an individual of a particular nation, but is found in his spiritual character. Where this character, which is faith, is manifested, we find the true children of Abraham (Gal. 3:7, 29; Rom. 9:6-8). Faith was the polar star, the very soul, of his life. The ancient record, anticipating a development of two thousand years, remarked of him, first of all: "He believed in the Lord; and he counted it to him for righteousness" (Gen. 15:6); and after these two thousand years had elapsed, Christ said of him: "Abraham rejoiced to see my day: and he saw it, and was glad" (John 8:56). Abraham's true position and importance cannot, therefore, be fully appreciated, until we recognize in him the father of them that believe (Rom. 4:11); and innumerable as the stars of heaven, and glorious as they are, are his spiritual children, the children of his faith.

VIII. The Generations of Ishmael

1. Ishmael and his sons (25:12-16)
2. The death of Ishmael (25:17-18)

In chapter 16:12 we find the prediction that Ishmael should dwell in the presence of his brethren. In verse 18 we find the fulfilment. The names we find here may be traced in other Scriptures. For instance in Isaiah 60, the great chapter of the millennial kingdom, we have Nebajoth and Kedar mentioned (verse 7). The number twelve, twelve princes, links Ishmael closely with Israel. When Israel is blest in the future and receives the promised Land for his glorious possession, the posterity of Ishmael will not be forgotten.

IX. The Generations of Isaac

CHAPTER 25:19-34

Esau and Jacob

1. Rebekah barren and the answered prayer (25:19-22)

2. The birth of Esau and Jacob (25:23-26)
3. The growth of the boys (25:27-28)
4. Esau sells his birthright (25:29-34)

It was 25 years after Abraham entered Canaan before Isaac was born. It was 20 years after Isaac's marriage before the birth of Esau and Jacob. The barren condition of Rebekah led Isaac to exercise faith and to cast himself upon the Lord for help. And He answered him. God delights to take up what is weak and barren and manifest His power in answer to prayer. Before the children were born the Lord had declared, "the elder shall serve the younger." The struggle in Rebekah's womb reminds us of the struggle between the two seeds (Ishmael and Isaac) in Abraham's household. God's sovereignty is here solemnly made known. He knew them before they were born and He made His choice according to His own sovereign will and purpose. "And not only this; but when Rebekah also had conceived by one, even by our father Isaac (for the children being not yet born, neither having done good or evil, that the purpose of God according to election might stand, not of works but of Him that calleth), it was said unto her, The elder shall serve the younger, as it is written, Jacob have I loved but Esau have I hated" (Rom. 9:11-13). That this does not refer to any unconditional and eternal condemnation is clear. It must be noticed that the statement "Esau have I hated" does not appear in Genesis, but in the last book of the Old Testament. Then the character and defiance of Edom had become fully established. In Genesis the Lord speaks only of having chosen Jacob and what creature of the dust can challenge His right to do so.

Then Esau sold his birthright. It fully brought out the defiance of his wicked heart (Hebrews 12:16-17). The blessings of the birthright he sold consisted in three things: 1. The father's blessing and the place of head of the family; 2. The honor of being in the direct line of the promised One—Shem-Abraham-Isaac; 3. The exercise of the domestic priesthood. All this Esau despised for a carnal gratification. How numerous are his followers in our days who might have greater blessings, but they are lovers of pleasure more than lovers of God.

CHAPTER 26

Isaac in Gerar

1. The famine (26:1)
2. Jehovah appears unto Isaac (26:2-5)
3. Isaac in Gerar where he denies Rebekah (26:6-11)
4. Isaac's prosperity and the digging of wells (26:12-22)
5. Jehovah appears at Beer-sheba (26:23-25)
6. Isaac and Abimelech (26:26-33)
7. The wives of Esau (26:34-35)

When the famine came Jehovah commanded Isaac not to go to Egypt. As Isaac is the type of Christ risen from the dead and Egypt is the type of the world, this command has a significance. Isaac is separated from Egypt as Christ and His people are, who share in Him a heavenly place. We also notice, while the Lord spoke to Abraham that his seed should be like the sand of the sea (the natural descendants) and the stars of heaven (the spiritual seed) to Isaac the Lord promises the seed as the stars of heaven; this confirms the typical character of Isaac.

In Gerar he failed as his father failed. And while Sarah was seized by Abimelech, Rebekah is not touched nor separated from Isaac. Christ and His church are inseparable.

The digging of the wells and Isaac's patience fully manifests his character; a little picture of the patient suffering of the Son of God "who when He was reviled, reviled not again; when He suffered, He threatened not." Then Jehovah appeared unto him again and he receives still greater blessings as the reward of his obedience.

When Esau was 40 years old he manifested his defiance still more by taking wives of the Hittites to the grief of his parents.

CHAPTER 27

The Story of Jacob and the Deception of Rebekah and Jacob

1. Esau sent for (27:1-4)
2. Rebekah's deception (27:5-17)
3. Jacob's deception (27:18-25)
4. Jacob blessed (27:26-29)
5. The discovery (27:30-40)
6. Esau hates Jacob (27:41)
7. Rebekah advises Jacob to flee (27:42-46)

With this chapter the story of Jacob begins. Three periods of his life are especially to be noticed: 1. His life in Canaan; 2. His departure from the land and his servitude in Padan-aram;

3. His return to the Land. The history of his descendants, the people Israel, may be traced in this. They were in the land; now they are away from the land scattered among the nations; like Jacob they will return to the land. Isaac knew the Word of God, "the elder shall serve the younger," yet he wanted to bless Esau. This was failure on his side. Yet he blessed Jacob by faith (Heb. 11:20). Rebekah wants to comply with the divine declaration but uses unholy means trying to aid God by her own devices to fulfill His Word. Jacob obeys his mother and makes use of the deception. Esau deceives, too, for he claimed a blessing to which he had no right before God and man. The flesh and its sinful ways is fully manifested in this chapter, nevertheless the will of God was accomplished.

Isaac lives after this event 43 years longer, but with this he passes from the page of history. Of his death and burial by Esau and Jacob we hear later. His life was characterized by patient endurance and suffering and his faith consisted in quietness and waiting.

CHAPTER 28

Jacob's Departure to Padan-Aram and His Vision

1. Isaac sends Jacob away and gives his blessing (28:1-5)
2. Esau's action (28:6-9)
3. Jacob's vision and vow (28:10-22)

We enter with this upon the interesting wanderings of the third patriarch, Jacob. God was pleased to reveal Himself to the three illustrious men, Abraham, Isaac and Jacob, as He did not before. In Exodus 3:4-15 Jehovah reveals Himself to Moses and Jehovah calls Himself "the God of Abraham, the God of Isaac and the God of Jacob. This is My name forever." In Abraham, as we have seen, we have the type of the Father; in Isaac the type of the Son and now in Jacob we shall find the type of the work of the Holy Spirit. Jacob in his history foreshadows the history of Jacob's sons.

Jacob's departure stands for Israel's expulsion from their own land to begin their wanderings and suffering, till they are brought back again to the land sworn to the heads of the nation. In the chastening which passed over him we see God's governmental dealings with Israel.

The vision at Bethel is mentioned by our Lord in John 1:51. The Jehovah who stood above the ladder Jacob saw is the same who spoke to Nathaniel, "Hereafter ye shall see heaven open and the angels of God ascending and descending upon the Son of Man." It is the vision of the future. Jehovah in that vision gave the promise of the land to Jacob and told him that his seed shall be as the dust of the earth. Notice while to Isaac the promise is of a heavenly seed to Jacob a seed as the stars of heaven is not mentioned. Still more was promised to Jacob. Read verse 15. "I will not leave thee until I have done that which I have spoken to thee about." Here again is Sovereign Mercy. What did Jacob do to merit all this? Why should God meet him thus? Did he think of the Lord and call on Him for mercy before he slept on the stone? Nothing whatever. And Jehovah kept His promise and did all He had promised. "I will not leave thee" is a repeated promise. See Deut. 31:6; Josh. 1:5; 1 Chronicles 28:20; Hebrews 13:5-6. "Happy is he that hath the God of Jacob for his help, whose hope is in Jehovah his God" (Ps. 146:5). And He is our God and our Lord and in His grace keeps and leads us and does all He has promised. Thus God met Jacob at Bethel (the house of God), assured him of His watching care over him and of a return home in peace. Though Israel is now nationally set aside and they are dispersed, yet God watches over them, keeps them and will lead them back in his own time.

The ridiculous claim that "the coronation stone" in London is the stone upon which Jacob slept needs no refutation. Leading geologists declare unanimously that this stone did not come from Palestine.

CHAPTER 29

Jacob with Laban

1. Jacob's arrival at Padan-aram (29:1-4)
2. His service for Rachel (29:15-20)
3. Laban's deception (29:21-25)
4. Jacob receives Rachel 29:26-31)
5. Leah's sons (29:32-35)

The Lord brought him to Padan-aram, where he was to dwell as an exile for twenty years. During these twenty years Jehovah did not manifest Himself to him, even as Israel dispersed among the nations has no communications from the Lord. His sojourn in Padan-aram produced suffering, the disciplinary dealings of God with him. He reaps in a measure what he had sown. He deceived his father Isaac and now Laban deceives him in different ways, especially by substituting Leah for the beloved Rachel. A week after he received Leah, Rachel was given to him. But though he possessed her, he had to serve seven years for her.

Interesting are the names of the sons of Leah. Reuben (behold a Son!); Simeon (hearing); Levi (joined); Judah (praise). It is the order of the gospel.

CHAPTER 30

Jacob with Laban

1. The sons of Bilhah: Dan and Naphtali (30:1-8)
2. The sons of Zilpah: Gad and Asher (30:9-13)
3. The children of Leah: Issachar, Zebulon and Dinah (30:14-20)
4. The birth of Joseph (30:22-24)
5. Jacob's request to return (30:25-26)
6. Laban's confession and Jacob's prosperity (30:27-43)

Little comment is needed on this. The avarice and deceit of Laban is matched by the dexterity and cunning of Jacob. Joseph's birth marks an important event. It is then that Jacob said unto Laban, "Send me away that I may go unto mine own place and to my country." All this is likewise typical. Rachel the first loved represents Israel; Leah, the Gentiles. The names Reuben, Simeon, Levi and Juda (see translations) tell out the story of His grace towards the Gentiles. Rachel, the barren, was remembered and gave birth to Joseph (adding), the one who was made great among the Gentiles and the deliverer of his brethren, and therefore the type of Christ. How interesting that Jacob thought at once of returning when Joseph had been born. But he had to wait six years more.

CHAPTER 31

Jacob's Servitude Ended and Flight from Laban

1. Laban's behavior and God's commandment (31:1-10)
2. The dream vision to return to the land (31:11-16)
3. Jacob's flight (31:17-21)
4. Laban warned (31:22-24)
5. Laban's accusation (31:25-30)
6. Jacob's answer (31:31-42)
7. The covenant between Jacob and Laban (31:43-55)

The twenty years had expired. Laban's hatred and the hatred of his sons had increased. When the crisis had been reached the voice of Jehovah was heard. "Return unto the land of thy fathers and to thy kindred; and I will be with thee." This is the first time Jehovah spoke since the vision at Bethel. Jacob then laid the matter before his wives and relates a dream in which the angel of the Lord had spoken to him. What comfort it must have been for him to hear "I have seen all that Laban doeth unto thee." The Lord watched over Jacob and though Laban hated him Jacob prospered. So Israel in the dispersion, hated by the Gentiles, increases and prospers.

Rachel and Leah consented to flee and Jacob departs with his great wealth, his cattle and his goods. Soon Laban pursued and overtook Jacob. God warned the Syrian to beware how he treated Jacob. It seems that the main reason of the pursuit was the teraphim (household gods) which Rachel had stolen and which Laban wanted to recover. Idolatry was practised in the household of Laban, though he used the name of Jehovah (verse 49). The dialogue between Jacob and Laban is intensely interesting.

CHAPTER 32

Jacob's Fear of Esau and Prayer at Peniel

1. The vision at Mahanaim (32:1-2)
2. The message to Esau (32:3-5)
3. Esau's coming and Jacob's fear (32:6-8)
4. Jacob's prayer (32:9-12)
5. Preparing to meet Esau (32:13-23)
6. Jacob's prayer at Peniel (32:24-32)

What a welcome it was when he came near to his land, that the angels of God met him. They were like divine ambassadors sent to welcome him back to assure him of God's presence and protection. When the remnant of Israel returns in the future to the promised land, the angelic hosts will not be absent. They have a share in the regathering and restoration of the people Israel (Matt. 24:31). But he faced the greatest trouble, his brother Esau. Fear drives him to prayer. It is a remarkable prayer: 1. He acknowledges his utter unworthiness; 2. He gives God the glory for all he has received; 3. He cries for deliverance; 4. He reminds God of the promises given at Bethel. And the Lord heard and answered his prayer. The returning remnant of Israel during the great tribulation will confess and pray in the same manner.

The night experience at Jabbok was not a dream, nor a vision, but an actual occurrence. The same person who appeared to Abraham at

Mamre (chapter 18) appeared to Jacob that night. It is often stated that Jacob wrestled with the Lord who came to him that night; it is the other way, the Lord wrestled with Jacob. And He appeared in that memorable night as Jacob's enemy and opponent. Jacob uses the same carnal weapons with which he had in the past contended against God; he meets Him in his own natural strength. That stubborness is overcome by the Lord touching the hip-joint of Jacob, dislocating it. In this way He completely crippled his strength and now Jacob could wrestle no more. In utter weakness and helplessness he could but cling to Him and ask a blessing. "By his strenth he had power with God, yea he had power over the angel and prevailed; he wept and made supplication unto Him" (Hos. 12:3-4). The weeping and supplication was his strength. His name is changed. From now on his name is "Israel"—a Prince with God. And the descendants of Jacob, at the time of Jacob's trouble (Jer. 30:7), will make a similar experience and have their Peniel.

CHAPTER 33

The Reconciliation of Esau

1. Jacob meets Esau (33:1-17)
2. In the city of Shechem and the altar erected (33:18-20)

The reconciliation is effected, but Jacob is the same man of deceit. He tells his brother he will follow him to Seir. But he goes instead to Succoth. He built an altar there, but it is not the worship God expected. He should have gone to Bethel and fulfilled his vow.

CHAPTER 34

Defilement of Dinah

1. The defilement (34:1-3)
2. Hamor's proposal (34:4-12)
3. The deceitful answer of Jacob's sons (34:13-24)
4. The males of Shechem slain (34:25-29)
5. Jacob's shame and grief (34:30-31)

If Jacob after the Peniel experience had gone to Bethel instead of building a house at Succoth and buying a parcel of a field, perhaps this sad event might never have occurred. God permitted it for the humiliation of His servant Jacob. Again he reaps what he had sown and the deceit of the father is reflected in the deceit of some of his sons.

CHAPTER 35

Jacob at Bethel and Three Deaths

1. The divine commandment (35:1)
2. The defilement put away (35:2-4)
3. The journey to Bethel and the altar (35:3-7)
4. Deborah, Rebekah's nurse, dies (35:8)
5. God appears to Jacob (35:9-15)
6. Benoni-Benjamin and Rachel's death (35:16-20)
7. The twelve sons of Jacob (35:21-16)
8. Isaac's death (35:27-29)

The Lord did not leave Jacob in Shechem amidst the evil and corrupting influences. The Lord now reminded him of what had happened long ago and of the unfulfilled vow he had made when he had his dream-vision. And he responded. His house, however, was first cleansed from the defilement; the strange gods among them, most likely teraphim or household gods, had to be put away. After that was done he gave the order to go to Bethel to make an altar there unto God. They gave up their gods and earrings; the latter must have been in the shape of figures representing idols. And after this cleansing they became a mighty host, the terror of God fell upon the cities through which they journeyed. The altar is built and the place called El Bethel (God of the House of God). Rebekah's nurse died. After chapter 49:31 Rebekah is no longer mentioned; not even her death. This corresponds with that which she typifies, the church. Jacob as we learned foreshadows the history of the earthly people of God and as that is related no more mention of Rebekah is made. Then God met him again and Jacob becomes Israel in reality.

Rachel gives birth to another son at Ephrath and dies there. The one born has a double name. "Benoni," which means "son of sorrow"; "Benjamin," which is "the son of the right hand." Here we have another type of the Lord Jesus Christ, His humiliation and exaltation. Bethlehem is here mentioned for the first time in the Bible.

After the names of the twelve sons of Jacob are given and Reuben's evil deed is recorded we hear of the death of Isaac. He died 180 years old and his sons Esau and Jacob buried him. We now add a little diagram, which gives the family tree of the patriarchs down to the end of this book.

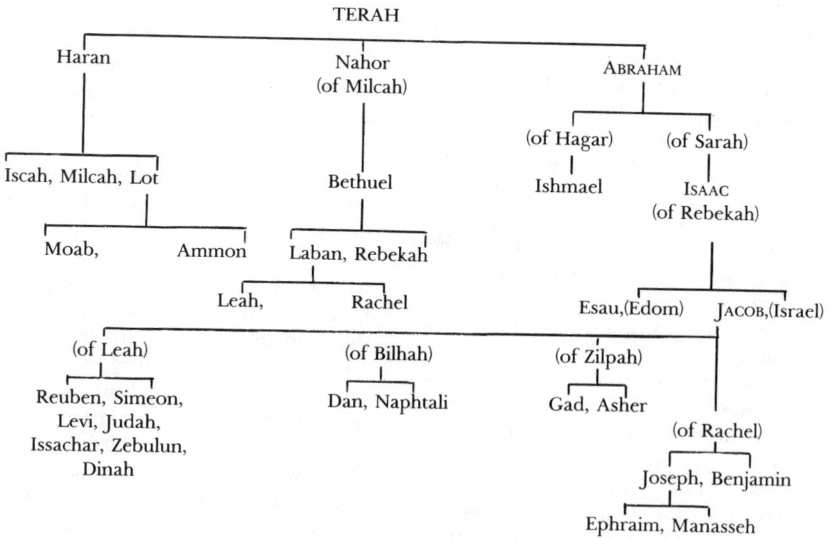

X. The Generations of Esau

1. Esau in Canaan, his wives and sons (36:1-5)
2. Esau leaving Canaan and in Edom (36:6-8)

XI. The Generations of Esau in Mount Seir

1. Sons of Esau (36:9-10)
2. Sons of Eliphaz (36:11-12)
3. Sons of Reuel (36:13)
4. Sons of Aholibamah (36:14)
5. Dukes of Eliphaz (36:15-16)
6. Dukes of Reuel (36:17)
7. Dukes of Jeush (36:18)
8. Dukes of Horite and kings of Edom (36:20-43)

We point out a few interesting facts in these two generations of Esau and Esau's sons. In verse 6 we read that Esau went into the country from the face of his brother Jacob. It came at last to a pronounced and complete separation between Esau and Jacob. Jacob dwelt in the land in which his father was a stranger. And Edom became the treacherous foe to the people of Israel. Read Obadiah, verses 8-16. From the concubine of Eliphaz was born Amalek, one of the terrible enemies of Israel with whom there was to be a continual warfare (Exodus 17:8,14).

And what a prolific progency of the wicked Esau! The Hebrew names tell the story of their expansion, their wickedness and power. What was not of God developed rapidly, as it does now, in the earth.

XII. The Generations of Jacob

CHAPTER 37

The Story of Joseph

1. Jacob dwelling in Canaan (37:1)
2. Joseph's character and feeding the flock (37:2)
3. Beloved of his father (37:3)
4. Hated by his brethren (37:4)
5. The dream of the sheaves (37:5-8)
6. The dream of the sun, moon and stars (37:9-11)
7. Joseph seeks his brethren (37:12-17)
8. The plot against Joseph (37:18-22)
9. Joseph in the pit and sold (37:23-28)
10. Reuben's grief (37:29-30)
11. The deception of Jacob's sons (37:31-32)
12. The grief of Jacob (37:33-35)
13. Joseph in Egypt (37:36)

The story of Joseph is one of the most interesting in the whole Bible. The Holy Spirit has devoted more space to the life of Joseph than He devoted to Abraham. The reason for this must be sought in the fact that the story of Joseph foreshadows the story of Christ. Some critics have made out that the story of Joseph is an invention and that the record was written hundreds of years after Moses. However, archeological evidence has fully and completely established the historical character of Joseph. Two of the El Amarna tablets show that a Semite held such a high position as attributed to Joseph. Others, while they believe in the historicity of Joseph, deny that his life is typical of our Lord. Such a denial is akin to spiritual blindness. It is true nowhere is a statement made that Joseph typifies Christ, but throughout this age all teachers of the Word have treated the life of Joseph as foreshadowing Christ. Stephen in his great address before the Jewish council mentions Joseph (Acts 7:9-14); the Messianic application must have been in his mind.

The life of Joseph falls into two periods; his humiliation and his exaltation. In these two parts the sufferings of Christ and the glory that should follow are blessedly foreshadowed. There is no other type so perfect as that of Joseph. In our annotations we shall not be able to point out all the comparisons; only the leading ones we give as a hint.

Israel loved Joseph more than all his sons and that reminds us of Him who is the Father's delight. Joseph was separated from evil, even as Christ was. Joseph had a coat of many colors, the expression of the Father's love; thus God honored His Son. And as Joseph was hated by his brethren without a cause, so Christ was hated (John 15:25). The dreams foretold Joseph's future exaltation; he saw things in heaven and things on earth bowing before him, even as before Christ things in heaven and on earth must bow the knee.

Then the father sent forth his beloved Joseph to seek his brethren who were lost. Israel put Joseph into their hands. All this foreshadows God's unspeakable gift in sending His only begotten Son into this world to seek what is lost.

Then note the following typical suggestions. When he came to his brethren, they conspired against him to slay him. "Come now therefore let us slay him, and cast him in some pit." And in John 5:16 it is written that the Jews sought to slay Christ. The brethren stripped Joseph of his coat, as our Lord was stripped of His garment. He was cast into the pit and they sat down to eat bread. And the Pharisees who had delivered up the Lord Jesus sat down to eat the passover, while the soldiers, who had parted the garments sat down to watch them. They sold him as the Lord was sold and Judah was the one who said "let us sell him." This brings the betrayal by Judas to our mind.

And Jacob is deceived by his sons as he deceived his father. The coat stained by the blood of a kid reminds us of the skin of the kid with which he had deceived Isaac.

CHAPTER 38

Judah and Tamar

1. Judah's marriage to the Canaanitish woman (38:1-2)
2. His sons: Er, Onan and Shelah (38:3-5)
3. Tamar married to Er and Onan (38:6-10)
4. Tamar waiting for Shelah (38:11)
5. Her deception and Judah's sin (38:12-16)
6. The birth of Pharez and Zarah (38:27-30)

Historically this chapter comes before the thirty-seventh. The higher critics are one against the other in their unbelieving speculations over the composition of this chapter. It is inserted here for a most interesting purpose. Judah's history foreshadows the history of the Jews after they had rejected the Lord Jesus. His connection with a Canaanite (trafficker) and his marriage to the daughter of Shuah (riches) shows what the Jews have been ever since they rejected Christ. His offspring is Er (enmity) and Onan (wickedness) till the significant third one comes, Shelah (the sprout) pointing to the godly remnant of that nation in the future. (On that remnant see chapter on Isaiah.)

And Tamar's sin, so dark and vile, shows forth the grace of God. We find her name and the names of her two sons in the genealogy of Christ (Matthew 1).

CHAPTER 39

Joseph In Egypt

1. In Potiphar's house (39:1-6)
2. Tempted by Potiphar's wife (39:7-18)
3. Joseph in prison (39:19-23)

Potiphar, the master of Joseph, was an officer of Pharaoh. His name means "devoted to Ra," a god of Egypt. Why is it stated a number of times that Potiphar was an Egyptian? Discoveries have shown that Egypt had come at that time under a new dynasty; therefore it is repeatedly stated that Potiphar, the Egyptian, was retained in his official position. Joseph in Egypt is the type of Christ among the Gentiles. Jehovah blessed the Egyptian's house for Joseph's sake.

The temptation of Potiphar's wife brings out the marvelous character of Joseph. The critics in rejecting this story have dug their own pit into which they have fallen. A number of critics (Von Bohlen, Tuch, and others) claim "that Joseph could never have seen his master's wife, for the women were secluded and had separate apartments." Monuments and Egyptian paintings have shown that the women were not secluded, but mingled freely with the men. Woman in the hieroglyphics is called neb-t-en pa, which means "mistress of the house." An ancient papyrus was discovered containing "the romance of the two brothers." It contains an episode similar to that of our chapter. It fully bears out the fact that the temptation of Joseph is not a myth and it is thought that this event in Joseph's life formed the basis for the romance of the two brothers.

Joseph suffered innocently, but the prison in which he was confined becomes the high road to power and glory. How much greater were the sufferings of Him, who was not only innocent, but holy.

CHAPTER 40

Joseph the Interpreter of Dreams

1. The fellow prisoners (40:1-8)
2. The dream of the chief butler (40:9-11)
3. The interpretation (40:12-13)
4. Joseph's request (40:14-15)
5. The dream of the chief baker (40:16-17)
6. The interpretation (40:18-19)
7. The fulfilment (40:20-22)
8. Joseph forgotten (40:23)

He was reckoned among the trangressors. To the one he spoke the word concerning life, while the other heard the message of death. Thus Christ was reckoned among the evildoers. To the one crucified with Him He said, "Today thou shalt be with Me in paradise," while the other malefactor railed and died in his sins.

Critics do not believe even this simple story and deny the culture of vines in Egypt. But the Egyptian paintings have given them the lie. They picture the pressing of the grapes in a cup, which was a religious ceremony. Joseph was forgotten; two years longer he had to remain in prison. What exercise of patience and faith he must have had!

CHAPTER 41

Joseph's Exaltation

1. Pharaoh's dreams (41:1-7)
2. Joseph brought from the prison (41:8-15)
3. Joseph's humility (41:16)
4. The revealer of secrets (41:17-32)
5. Joseph's wise counsel (41:33-36)
6. Pharaoh's answer (41:37-40)
7. Joseph's exaltation and marriage (41:41-46)

All is so simple that little comment is needed. The dreams impressed Pharaoh, because the cow was a sacred animal, the emblem of Isis. At last Joseph is remembered and brought out of the prison and his raiment is changed. All this finds an application in the life of our Lord. He was taken out of the grave. Compare verse 16, Joseph's humility, with the humility of another Hebrew prisoner, Daniel in Babylon. (See Dan. 2:27-30.)

The seven years of plenty and the seven years of famine are typical. This age will close with the seven years of tribulation.

And this dream of Pharaoh and Joseph's interpretation has been remarkably confirmed by the hieroglyphic inscriptions. One was discovered in 1908 which tells of the seven years of famine, because the Nile did not overflow. It has been ascertained that this was the very time when Joseph was in Egypt.

Then follows Joseph's exaltation. The name of this Pharaoh was Apepi. His father and grandfather were for a time co-regents with him. He recognized the presence of the Spirit of God in Joseph. Note the beautiful comparisons with our Lord. Pharaoh said, "I have set thee over all the land of Egypt." Of Christ we read, "Thou didst set Him over the works of Thy hands." Joseph said, "God hath made me lord of all Egypt" and Christ is "Lord over all." Joseph is arrayed in royal vesture, and Christ is crowned with glory and honor. The word "Abrech" was cried before him. This word means "bow the knee." According to Prof. Sayce of Oxford "Abrech" is the Sumerian "Abrok," which means the seer. This would call for prostration. Thus every knee must bow before our exalted Lord. The name by which he was called is in the Septuagint "Psomtomphanech." This is an Egyptian name, meaning "saviour of the world." The word Zaphnethpaaneach means "revealer of secrets." Even so Christ after He was rejected by His own brethren became the Revealer of secrets and the Saviour of the world.

Before the seven years of famine came Joseph received his bride, Asenath, the Gentile, and Christ will have His beloved with Him before the years of tribulation and judgment come. All had to come to Joseph for corn, as all must come to Christ for the bread of life.

CHAPTER 42

The First Visit of Joseph's Brethren

1. Joseph's brethren sent to Egypt (42:1-5)

2. Joseph meets his brethren (42:6-16)
3. Put in prison for three days (42:17)
4. Joseph's demand (42:18-20)
5. The accusing conscience (42:21-23)
6. Joseph weeps and Simeon bound (42:24)
7. The return of the nine (42:25-38)

The famine years bring Joseph's brethren to repentance and after the deepest exercise Joseph makes himself known to them and they find forgiveness and deliverance. Thus it will be during the tribulation of the last days of the present age. The remnant of Israel will pass through that time called "Jacob's trouble" and be saved out of it. Then the Lord Jesus Christ will make Himself known to His brethren, according to the flesh.

Joseph's treatment of his brethren, whom he recognized, was harsh, so that they might be led to acknowledge their sin. And they readily confess their guilt on account of having sold their brother and take the harsh treatment and imprisonment they received as a just retribution. And Joseph understood all their words so that he wept. And He who was rejected by His own has a loving sympathy for this nation. Simeon remains behind; while Joseph demands Benjamin. The grief of Jacob is pathetic.

CHAPTER 43

The Second Visit to Joseph

1. The journey to Egypt with Benjamin (43:1-15)
2. The kindness of Joseph (43:16-34)

CHAPTER 44

The Feigned Dismay and the Bringing Back

1. The cup concealed and the dismay (44:1-13)
2. The return to Joseph's house (44:14-34)

CHAPTER 45

Joseph Reveals Himself

1. He reveals himself (45:1-3)
2. His address (45:4-13)
3. He kissed his brethren (45:14-15)
4. Pharaoh's command (45:16-20)
5. His brethren sent away and their return to Jacob (45:21-28)

These three chapters belong together because they lead up to the great climax in the story of Joseph. The nobility of the character of Joseph is here fully brought out. Besides being a wise man, the great statesman of Egypt, he had a heart of tender love. Seven times we read of Joseph that he wept. The trial with the cup, which had been hidden in Benjamin's sack, was the needful and decisive test. Benjamin had become the object of Jacob's love. The trial with the cup was to bring out whether they cherished the same bitter feelings against Benjamin which had governed their conduct towards Joseph. Their behaviour now reveals the great change which had taken place. They confess that their iniquity has been found out and Judah, the spokesman, manifests the most affectionate reverence for his old father and the ardent love for his younger brother.

But who is able to describe the scene when Joseph made himself known to his brethren, when they had come the second time? It is a chapter of great tenderness. Some day He who was rejected and disowned by His brethren, the Lord Jesus Christ, will come the second time. Then when the deep anguish, the soul exercise of the Israel of the end time has reached the climax, He will come and they that pierced Him shall look upon Him. He will forgive them their sins and remember them no more (Romans 11:26-27).

CHAPTER 46

Jacob Goes Down to Egypt

1. Israel's departure and the vision (46:1-4)
2. The journey and the arrival in Egypt (46:5-7)
3. The offspring of the sons of Jacob (46:8-27)
4. Israel meets Joseph (46:28-30)
5. Joseph's directions concerning Pharaoh (46:31-34)

The whole family of Jacob, consisting of seventy souls, exclusive of the wives and the servants, came to Egypt. Once more God appears to Israel, but addresses him as Jacob. He gives him permission to go down to Egypt and assures him of His presence. They were directed to the land of Goshen, which was east of Memphis. And what a meeting it was, when Joseph fell around his father's neck and kissed him!

This emigration to Egypt was, without doubt, directed by the Lord for the purpose of guarding against the dispersion of the family, as well as against its admixture with strangers, during the important period which had arrived, in which it was appointed to be developed as a nation; neither of these unfavorable results, which would have been inevitable in Canaan, could follow in Egypt: for Goshen afforded ample room for their increasing numbers, on the one hand, while, on the other, the aversion of the Egyptians to shepherds (46:34) effectually prevented the formation of ties between them by intermarriage. Besides, the opportunity which was furnished for becoming acquainted with the wisdom of Egypt, and also the pressure of the future bondage, may have been both designed to serve, in the hands of God, as means for training and cultivating the chosen nation. And the transition from a nomadic to an agricultural life, which was designed to constitute the foundation of the polity of Israel on acquiring independence and a home in the promised land, may also be assigned, in its incipient stages, to this period.[3]

CHAPTER 47

The Settlement in Goshen

1. Before Pharaoh (47:1-10)
2. The settlement (47:11-12)
3. Joseph's wise administration (47:13-26)
4. Jacob's request (47:27-31)

Jacob and some of his sons were presented to Pharaoh, who received them graciously, and Jacob blessed Pharaoh. The great and powerful monarch of the great land of Egypt was blessed by the poor old Jacob. He is more than blessed, but a blesser, a type of what Israel is yet to be for the nations of the earth.

There is no discrepancy in verse 11, for Goshen is also called Rameses. We likewise get a glimpse in this chapter of the wonderful administration of Joseph during the years of famine. Verse 27 speaks of Israel's prosperity in the land. Notice how the names of Jacob and Israel are used. He requested to be buried in Canaan and Joseph promised to carry out his wish.

CHAPTER 48

Jacob adopts Ephraim and Manasseh

1. The sons of Joseph brought to Jacob (48-1-2)
2. The words of Jacob (48:3-7)
3. Ephraim and Manasseh presented (48:8-14)
4. Jacob's blessing (48:15-16)
5. Joseph's interference (48:17-20)
6. Jacob's last words to Joseph (48:21-22)

The adoption of Joseph's sons is interesting and instructive. As the offspring of the Gentile wife Asenath they were in danger of becoming gentilized and thus forget their father's house. Jacob frustrated this by adopting the sons. It was an action of faith. "By faith, Jacob, when he was dying, blessed both the sons of Joseph; and worshipped leaning on the top of his staff" (Hebrews 11:21). Again the younger is preferred. When Jacob speaks of "the Angel, the Redeemer" (literal translation) he speaks of Jehovah who appeared unto him, whom he met face to face at Peniel. Full of hope, dying Jacob predicted the return of his offpsring to the land of Canaan.

[3]J. H. Kurtz, *Sacred History.*

CHAPTER 49

Jacob's Prophecy

1. The call of Jacob: "Gather yourselves together" (49:1-2)
2. The prophecy concerning his sons (49:3-27)
    - Reuben (49:3-4)
    - Simeon and Levi (49:5-7)
    - Judah (49:8-12)
    - Zebulun (49:13)
    - Issachar (49:14-15)
    - Dan (49:16-18)
    - Gad (49:19)
    - Asher (49:20)
    - Naphtali (49:21)
    - Joseph and Benjamin (49:22-27)

The last words of Jacob to his sons are often called "the blessings." What he said is rather a prophecy. Concerning Judah he saith the most because from Judah there was to come the Shiloh, that is, the Messiah. Jacob's prophecy covers in a remarkable way the entire history of Israel, past, present and future. We give a few brief hints, which will be helpful in a closer study of this important chapter. Seven periods of Israel's history are given here.

I. Reuben, Simeon and Levi show the character of the nation up to the time of Christ. II. Judah points clearly to the period of this nation when our Lord was on the earth. III. Zebulun and Issachar, where the sea and commerce, indolence and service are prominent, describes Israel scattered among the nations during this age. IV. Dan shows Israel apostate during anti-Christ (Dan is left out in Revelation 7). V. Gad, Asher and Naphatali describe the godly remnant during the great tribulation. VI. Joseph speaks of the second coming of Christ; and VII. Benjamin, the son of the right hand, of the righteous rule of the King.

CHAPTER 50

The Burial of Jacob and Joseph's Return and Death

1. The grief of Joseph (50:1-3)
2. The burial (50:4-13)
3. The return to Egypt (50:14-23)
4. The death of Joseph (50:24-26)

This great book which begins with the perfect and good creation of God ends with a burial and the last words are "a coffin in Egypt." What havoc sin has wrought. Jacob died 147 years old and after his body was embalmed was carried to Canaan. Read in connection with Joseph's death Ex. 13:19, Josh. 24:32 and Hebrews 11:22.

Genesis and Geology

Genesis is a relevation from God; geology is a discovery of man. A revelation from God can be augmented by God only; a discovery by man may be improved, matured, advanced, ripened progressively, till the end of the world. We therefore assume that Genesis is perfect and beyond the possibility of contradiction or improvement by us; and we equally assume that geology, because the discovery of man, and the subject of the investigation of man, may be improved by greater experience and more profound acquaintance with those phenomena which lie concealed in the bosom of the earth, waiting for man to evoke, explain, and arrange them. I am sure, therefore, that Genesis, as God's Word, is beyond the reach of the blow of the geologist's hammer; or the detection of a single flaw by microscope or telescope; it will stand the crucible of the chemist; and the severer the ordeal to which it is subjected, the more pure, resplendent, and beautiful it will emerge, indicating its origin to be from above, and its issue to be the glory of God, and the supreme happiness of mankind. Geology has before now retraced its steps; Genesis never. Before now it has been discovered, that what were thought to be facts incontrovertible were fallacies. It is found that phenomena described and discussed as true, were mistakes and misapprehensions, which maturer investigations have disposed of; and therefore I am not speaking dogmatically and without reason, when I say, that while Genesis must be true, geology—having already erred, may err again, and some of its very loudest assertions, made rashly by those who have least acquaintance with its data—may yet be proved to be wrong. But certain facts in it are now beyond all dispute. Let geology and Genesis be alleged to clash, and the discovery from the depths of the earth contradict the text from the page of the Bible; in such a case, I would submit first these questions: Are you sure that there is a real contradiction between the fact of geology and the text of the Bible, or is it only a contradiction between the fact discovered by science, and the *interpretation* that you put upon the text of the Bible? In the next place, if there be in any instance contradiction between a clear text of the Bible and a supposed fact or discovery made by the geologist, my inference, and without hesitation, is, that the geologist must have made a mistake, that Moses has made none; and therefore the advice we give to the geologist is, not to say, God's work beneath contradicts God's Word without, but just to go back again, read more carefully the stony page, excavate more laboriously in the subterranean chambers of the earth, and a maturer acquaintance with the facts of science may yet elicit the desirable result, that there is harmony where we thought discord, and perfect agreement where to us there seemed only discrepancy and conflict. We have instances of the possibility of some deductions of science being wrong in other departments of it. Astronomy was once quoted as contradicting the express declarations of the Word of God; maturer acquaintance with it has proved its perfect coincidence. Again, the hieroglyphics on the banks of the Nile, as deciphered by Young and Champollion, were instanced to prove a far greater age of the human race than that declared in the Bible; but subsequent investigation showed that the hieroglyphics were wrongly interpreted, not that God's Word was untrue. The traditions of the Chinese were viewed as upsetting the records of the Mosaic history, but subsequent investigation has proved that those were wrong, and that God's Word is true.

The Bible, whether we take it in Genesis or in the Gospels, contains no error; it has not a single scientific error in it. Yet it was not designed to teach science; but wherever it touches the province of science, it touches so delicately that we can see the main object is to teach men how to be saved, while its slight intimations of scientific principles or natural phenomena have in every instance been demonstrated to be exactly and strictly true. If the Bible said in any part of it, as the ancient philosopher alleged, that there were two suns, one for the upper hemisphere, and the other for the lower, then science would prove that Scripture was wrong; or if the Scripture said, as the Hindus believe, that the earth is a vast plain, with concentric seas of milk, honey, and sugar, supported by an elephant, and that the earthquakes and convulsions of the globe are the movements of that elephant as he bears it on his back, then science would have proved that to be absurd; and if Scripture has asserted it, such assertion would be demonstrably untrue. But the striking fact is that you find no such assertion, nor anything approaching such assertions in the Bible. How comes it to pass, then, that Moses has spoken so purely and truly on science where he does speak, and has been silent where there was such a provocative to speak—his very silence being as significant as his utterance? How happens it that Moses, with no greater education than the Hindu, or the ancient philosopher, has written his book, touching science at a thousand points so accurately, that scientific research has discovered no flaws in it; and has spoken on subjects the most delicate, the most difficult, the most involved; and yet in those investigations which have taken place in more recent centuries, it has not been shown that he has committed one single error, or made one solitary assertion which can be proved by maturest science or the most eagle-eyed philosopher to be incorrect scientifically or historically? The answer is, that Moses wrote by the inspiration of God, and therefore what he writes are the words of faithfulness and of truth. *(Cumings.)*

Dictionary of the Proper Names of Genesis with Their Meaning

A

Abel—Vanity, vapor.
Abel-mizraim—Mourning of Egypt.
Abidah—Father of knowledge.
Abimael—My father from God.
Abimelech—My father is king.
Abraham—Father of many.
Abram—Father exalted.
Accad—Band; city of Nisibis.
Achbar—Mouse; Swift.
Adah—Adorned.
Adam—Man (red).
Adheel—Sorrow from God.
Admah—Red earth.
Adullamite—From Adullam; Restingplace.
Aholibamah—Tent of the high place.
Ahuzzath—Possession.
Ajah—A young hawk.
Akan—Wresting.
Allon-bachuth—Oak of weeping.
Almodad—Beyond measure.
Alvah—Wickedness.
Alvan—Unrighteous.
Amalek—A nation that licks up.
Amorite—Mountain dweller.
Amraphel—Uttering dark sentences.
Anah—An answer.
Anamin—Gushing of the waters.
Aner—Exile; Sprout.
Aram—Exalted.
Aran—Wild goat.
Ararat—High or holy ground.
Arbah—Four.
Ard—Fugitive (uncertain).
Areli—Lion of God.
Arioch—Strong lion.
Arkite—One who gnaws.
Arodi—Roaming, untamed.
Arphaxad—Laying on or at the side.
Arvadite—Break loose; Wanderer.
Asenath—Devoted to the goddess Neith.
Ashbel—Fire of Bel; or, Correction of God.
Asher—Happy.
Ashkenay—Scattered fire.
Ashteroth-Karnaim—Dougle-horned Astarte (Phoenician); Venus.
Asshur—Step.
Asshurim—Steps.
Atad—Bramble.
Avith—Ruins.

B

Baal-hanan—Baal is merciful.
Babel—Confusion.
Bashemath—Pleasant smell.
Becher—First born.
Bedad—Solitary, separate.
Beeri—My well.
Beer-lahai-roi—Well of the living and seeing.
Beersheba—Well of the oath.
Bela—Devouring.
Benammi—Son of my people.
Benjamin—Son of the right hand.
Ben-oni—Son of my sorrow.
Beor—Torch; Burning.
Bera—Excelling in evil.
Beriah—Unfortunate.
Bethel—House of God.

Bethlehem—House of bread.
Bethuel—Separated of God.
Bilhah—Timid.
Bilhan—Their fear.
Birsha—Son of wickedness.
Bozrah—Sheep fold.
Buz—Contempt.

C

Cain—Acquisition; Acquired of Jehovah.
Cainan—Deplorable.
Calah—Completion, old age.
Calneh—Complete wailing (Cal-neh.)
Canaan—Merchant; Trafficker.
Caphtorim—Crowns.
Carmi—My vineyard.
Casluhim—Barren mountains.
Chedorlaomer—Handful of sheaves.
Cheran—Their lamb; Joyous shouts.
Chesed—Meaning is unknown.
Chezib—Lying.
Cush—Black.

D

Damascus—City of activities.
Dan—Judging.
Deborah—Bee, or her words.
Dedan—Their leading forward.
Diklah—Palm tree.
Dinah—Vindicated; Judgment.
Dinhabah—She gives judgment.
Dishan—Their threshing; Gazelle.
Dishon—A thresher.
Dodanim—Leader, or loves.
Dothan—Decrees.
Dumah—Silence.

E

Ebal—Heaps of barrenness.
Eber—He that passes over, a passenger.
Edar—A flock.
Eden—Delight, according to others, a plain.
Edom—Red.
Ehi—My brother.
Elah—Strength, an oak.
Elam—Forever, eternal.
El-bethel—God, God's house.
Eldaah—God's knowledge.
El-elohe-Israel—God, the God of Israel.
Eliezer—My God is help.
Eliphaz—My God is fine gold.
Elishah—My God is salvation.
Ellasar—Of uncertain meaning.
Elon—Mighty; Oak.
El-Paran—The might of their adorning.
Emims—Terrors.
En-mishpat—Fountain of judgment.
Enoch—Dedicated; Teaching.
Enos—Frail, mortal man.
Ephah—Darkness.
Epher—A young hart.
Ephraim—Great fruitfulness, doubly fruitful.
Ephron—A fawn; Of dust.
Ephrath—Fruitful.
Er—Watcher; Stirring up; Enmity.
Eri—My watching; My enmity.
Erech—Length.
Esau—Hairy.
Eschol—A cluster.
Eshban—Very red.
Ethiopia—Black.
Euphrates—Fruitfulness; Sweet water.
Eve— Life, life giver.
Ezbon—Uncertain meaning; perhaps, Hastening of the son.
Ezer—Help.

G

Gad—Good fortune is come; Invading.
Gaham—Flame, burning.
Galeed—Heap of witness.
Gatam—Coming in touch.
Gaza—Fortified.
Gera—Rumination.
Gerar—Sojourning.
Gershon—Outcast, stranger.
Gether—Turning aside; A spy.
Gihon—Breaking forth.
Gilead—Rocky; Heap of witness.
Girgasites—Dwellers in swamps.
Gomer—Completion.
Gomorrah—Heap or bundled together.
Goshen—Meaning obscure.
Guni—Protected.

H

Hadar—Honor, ornament.
Hadad—Sharp, noisy.
Hadoram—Exalted people.
Hagar—Flight, sojourner.
Haggi—My feast.
Hai—Ruins.
Ham—Hot; Black; Sunburnt.
Hamathite—Defender; Fortress.
Hamor—An ass.
Hamul—One who has been pitied.
Hanoch—Dedicated.
Haran—Their Mountain; Parched.
Havilah—Trembling in pain (childbirth).

Hazarmaveth—Court of death.
Hazezon-Tamar—Pruning of the palm.
Hazo—Vision.
Heber—A company; also, Passing through.
Hebron—Fellowship.
Hemam—Destruction; Crushed.
Hemdan—Delight.
Heth—Dread; Fear.
Hezron—Walled in; Division of song.
Hiddekel—The swift; Tigris.
Hirah—Nobility.
Hittite—Same as Heth.
Hivite—Together; Villagers; Winding.
Hobah—Hiding place.
Hori } Dwellers in caves.
Horites
Hul—Writhing in pain.
Huppim—Coverings.
Husham—Haste.
Hushim—Hasters.
Huz—Counsellor.

I

Irad—City of witness.
Iram—Belonging to their city.
Isaac—Laughter.
Iscah—Gaze upon, or She will see.
Ishbak—He will remain.
Ishuah—He will be equal.
Ishmael } God will hear.
Ishmaelites
Israel—Prince with God.
Issachar—Bringing wages; He will be hired.
Isui—He will level.

J

Jaalam—He will hide.
Jabal—A river.
Jabbok—He will pour out.
Jachin—He will establish.
Jacob—The supplanter.
Jahleel—Hope of God.
Jahzeel—Allotted of God.
Jamin—Right hand.
Japheth—Expansion.
Jared—Descent.
Javan—Clay (Greece).
Jebusite—Treader down.
Jegarsahadutha—Heap of witness.
Jehovah-jireh—The Lord will see.
Jemuel—Day of God.
Jerah—Moon.
Jetheth—Strengthener; A nail.
Jetur—Encircle; Defence.
Jeush—Gathering together.
Jezer—Form; Purpose.
Jidlaph—He will weep.
Jimnah—Right-handed; Prosperity.
Job—One who returns.
Jobab—Crying aloud.
Jokshan—Ensnaring.
Joktan—He will be small.
Jordan—Descending.
Joseph—Let him add.
Jubal—Musician.
Judah—Praise.
Judith—Jewish; Praising (in Phoenician form).

K

Kadesh—Set apart; Devoted to licentious idolatry.
Kadmonites—Ancients.
Kedar—Dark-skinned.
Kedemah—Eastward.
Kemuel—Congregation of God.
Kenaz—Hunter.
Kenites—Acquiring.
Kenizzites—Hunter.
Keturah—Incense; Fragrance.
Kirjath-arba—City of four.
Kittim—Subduers.
Kohath—Congregation; Waiting.
Korah—Ice.

L

Laban—White.
Lahai-roi—The living and seeing one.
Lamech—Powerful.
Leah—Weary.
Lehabim—Flames.
Letushim—Hammered ones.
Leummim—Nations.
Levi—Joined.
Lot—Covering.
Lotan—Covering up.
Lud } —of uncertain meaning;
Ludim— perhaps, to shine.
Luz—Perverting.

M

Maachah—Oppression.
Machir—Seller.
Machpelah—Double; Folded together.
Madai—My extension.
Magdiel—Preciousness of God; others: Mighty tower.
Magog—Expansion, overtowering.
Mahalaleel—Praise of God; The Blessed God.

Mahalath—Stringed instrument; Harp; also, To be weak.
Mahanaim—Two hosts or camps.
Malchiel—My King is God.
Mamre—Fatness; Strength.
Manahath—Gift; Resting place.
Manasseh—Forgetfulness.
Marah—Bitterness.
Masrekah—Vineyard.
Massa—Bearing patiently; A burden; An utterance.
Matred—Thrusting forward.
Medan—Strife.
Mehetahel—Benefited of God.
Mehujael—Destroyed of God; or, Blot out that Jah is God.
Merari—My bitterness.
Mesha—Deliverance brought.
Meshech—Drawing out.
Mesopotamia—Exalted.
Methusael—Dying who are of God.
Methuselah—Death sent away.
Mezahab—Waters of gold.
Mibsam—Sweet smell.
Mibzar—Defence.
Midian / *Midianites* } Contention; Strife.
Milcah—Queen.
Mishma—Hearing.
Mizpah—Watch-tower.
Mizraim—Egypt; Double distresses.
Mizzah—From sprinkling.
Moab—From father; Water of father.
Muppirm—Anxieties; Shakings.

N

Naamah—Pleasantness.
Naaman—The same as Naamah.
Nahath—Rest.
Nahor—Snorter.
Naphish—Refreshment.
Naphtali—My wrestling.
Naphtuhim—Openings.
Nebajoth—Exalted places.
Nimrod—Rebel.
Nineveh—House of Ninus.
Noah—Comfort.

O

Obal—Stripped of leaves.
Ohad—To be wild; Joined together.
Omar—Eloquent.
On—Light; Sun (Egyptian).
Onam—Vanity; Iniquity.
Onan—Iniquity.
Ophir—Abundance.

P

Padan-aram—Plain of Aram (Mesopotamia).
Paran—Abundance of foliage.
Pathrusim—Southern countries.
Pau—Crying out.
Peleg—Division.
Peniel—Face of God.
Perrizites—Country folks.
Phallu—Distinguished.
Pharaoh—The King; a title.
Pharez—Breach.
Phichol—Mouth of all.
Philistines—Land of wanderers.
Phut—Extension.
Phuvah—Mouth.
Pildash—Flame of fire.
Pinon—Distraction.
Pison—Great increase.
Potiphar—Devoted to Ra (Egyptian).
Poti-phera—The same meaning.

R

Raamah—Roaring; Thunder.
Rachel—An ewe.
Rameses—Son of the sun.
Rebekah—Typing; rope.
Rehoboth—Streets.
Rephaims—Giants.
Resen—Bridle.
Reu—Friend, associate.
Reuben—Behold a son.
Reuel—Friend of God.
Reumah—Exalted.
Riphath—Crushing.
Rosh—Chief; Head.

S

Sabtah—Breaking through.
Salah—Sent forth.
Salem—Peace.
Samlah—Covering; Enwrapping.
Sarah—A princess.
Sarai—My princess.
Saul—Asked for.
Seba—Drink thou; Drunkard.
Seir—Rough, hairy.
Sephar—Numbering; Census.
Serah—A princess; same as Sarah.
Sered—Fear; Trembling.
Serug—A branch.
Seth—Set; Appointed.
Shalem—Peace.

Shamah—Hearing.
Shaul—Asked for (Saul).
Shaveh-Kiriathain—Plain of cities.
Sheba—To the oath.
Shebah—The same.
Shechem—Shoulder.
Shelah—Sent forth; Sprout.
Sheleph—Drawn out.
Shem—Name.
Shemeher—Name of wing.
Shepo—Prominent.
Shillem—Retribution.
Shimron—A keeper.
Shinab—Tooth of father.
Shinar—Dispersing.
Shobab—Backsliding.
Shuah—Sink down; Depression; also: Riches.
Shuni—Quiet; My rest.
Shur—A wall.
Sichem—Shoulder.
Siddim—Plains; Name of a valley.
Sidon—Fishing.
Simeon—Hearing in obedience.
Sinite—Clay.
Sitnah—Accusation; Enmity.
Sodom—Scorching; Burning; Locked up (Arabic).
Succoth—Booths.
Syria—Lifted up; Sublime.

T

Tamar—A palm tree.
Tarshish—Subjection; Scattering.
Tebah—Slaughtering.
Tema—Desert; Southern region.
Teman—The same.
Terah—Delay.
Thahash—Badger; Seal.
Tidal—Fear; Reverence.
Timna—Restraint.
Timnah—The same.
Timnath—A portion.
Tiras—Desire.
Togarmah—Breaking bones.
Tola—Little worm; (Cocus-cacti: from which comes the scarlet color).
Tubal—Flowing forth.
Tubal-cain—Coming forth of Cain.

U

Ur—Light.
Uz—Counsel.
Uzal—Flooded; Going to and fro.

Z

Zaavan—Great unrest.
Zaphnath-paaneah—Revealer of secrets.
Zarah—Sun rising.
Zeboim—Troops.
Zeboiim—The same.
Zebulun—Habitation.
Zemarites—Double cuttings off.
Zepho—Watchfulness.
Zerah—Rising of light.
Zibeon—Of many colors.
Zilpah—Dropping.
Zillah—Shadow.
Zimran—Their song.
Ziphim—Smelters.
Zohar—Whiteness; Light.
Zuzims—Murmuring; Commotions.

Chronological Arrangement of Some Leading Persons and Events in Genesis

	B. C.
The creation of Adam	4004
The birth of Seth	3874
Enos born	3769
Cainan born	3679
Mahaleel born	3609
Jared born	3544
Enoch born	3382
Methuselah born	3317
Lamech born	3130
Adam's death	3074
Enoch's translation	3017
Noah's birth	2948
The Flood	2348
Peleg born	2247
Naber born	2155
Terah's birth	2126
Noah's death	1998
Abraham's birth	1996
Abraham's call in Ur	1945
Terah's death	1921
Second call to Abraham	1921
Abraham in Egypt	1920
His return	1912
Abraham takes Hagar	1911
The birth of Ishmael	1910
The Covenant sign given	1897
Birth of Isaac	1896
Sarah's death	1859
Isaac's marriage	1856

Jacob born	1836
Abraham's death	1821
Marriage of Esau	1796
Death of Ishmael	1773
Jacob's flight	1759
His marriages	1752
Jacob's flight	1739
Meets his brother	1738
Jacob at Bethel	1731
Death of Rachel	1728
Joseph sold	1727
Joseph in Egypt	1717
Death of Isaac	1716
Joseph interprets dreams	1715
Egyptian famine	1707–01
Jacob's death	1689
Joseph's death	1635

THE BOOK OF
EXODUS

Introduction

The word "exodus" means "way out" or "going forth." The book has been given this Greek name because it relates to the history of the deliverance of the children of Israel from the house of bondage and how they were led forth by the power of God. It needs hardly to be stated that this second book of the Pentateuch is closely linked with Genesis. Without the events recorded in the final chapters of Genesis, the book of Exodus would have no meaning; without the continuation of the story of Israel in Egypt, the book of Genesis would be in an unfinished state. The promises given by God to the patriarchs which we find recorded in Genesis, make this book a necessity. For instance, we read in Genesis 15:13-14: "And He said unto Abram, Know of a surety that thy seed shall be stranger in a land that is not theirs and shall serve them; and they shall afflict them four hundred years; and also that nation, whom they shall serve, will I judge; and afterward they shall come out with great substance. To Jacob the Lord said, I am God, the God of thy Father; fear not to go down to Egypt; for I will there make a great nation of thee" (Genesis 46:3). The fulfillment of these predictions and promises, as well as others, are seen in the book of Exodus.

"And"

The close connection with the book of Genesis is also learned by the first little word with which Exodus begins. It is the Hebrew conjunction "ve." The Authorized Version has translated it with "now," but it really means "and." Each of the four books, which, besides Genesis constitute the Pentateuch, begins with this little word. It fully establishes the fact that these books form one great record and must have been written by one instrument. Originally the present division of the writings of Moses into five books did not exist. He wrote in a continuous way, which formed one record. The division into five parts, we doubt not, was made under the guidance of the Holy Spirit.

The Higher Criticism

The book of Exodus has been treated by the higher critics in the same manner as the first book of the Bible. Its inspiration and the Mosaic authorship have been denied as well as the great judgments and miracles of which we read in Exodus. What ridiculous inventions have been made to explain some of the miracles wrought by the power of God we care not to follow.

The school of the destructive Bible criticism claims that Exodus is of a composite origin. The same confusing nonsense of a "Jehovist-Elohist-Priestly" narrative with a number of redactors, with which they dissect Genesis, has been applied to Exodus. Canon Driver, an ardent disciple of the fathers of higher criticism, makes the following statement: "The two main sources used in Exodus are those now generally known as 'Jehovist—Elohist,' the chief component parts of which date probably from the seventh or eighth century before Christ, and the 'Priestly' which is generally considered to have been written during or shortly after the Babylonian captivity." According to these statements Moses had nothing whatever to do with the composition of this book. We do not care to invite our readers to a closer inspection of this higher critical dissecting room, nor do we wish to burden our pages with the infidel assertions of these so-called "learned men." It is a hopeless labyrinth of theories and contradictions, which lead gradually but surely into the outer darkness. Yet these pernicious inventions are taught in many colleges and seminaries of the different evangelical denominations.

A Jewish rabbi of considerable learning, after a close examination of the arguments produced by the critics, has of late shown their absolute worthlessness from a literary point of view. He declares, "All these and similar analyses of the sources of Exodus and the conclusions based thereon are entirely wrong . . . . The theory that the book of Exodus was compiled from previous works is not sufficiently supported; and the attempt to analyze it into its component parts is a hopeless one, for all the elements of the book are closely welded together into one harmonious whole (Rabbi Dr. Benno Jacob of Goettingen, Germany).

But it does not take scholarship to discover the truth of the last sentence, that "all the elements of the book are closely welded together into one harmonious whole." Every intelligent reader of Exodus makes this discovery. The impression is at once created that only one person wrote this book, and that this person was intimately acquainted with the history of the period which Exodus treats. That the author was Moses is indisputable.

In Exodus 24:4 we read, "And Moses wrote all the words of the Lord." In Chapter 34:27 another command to write is given, "Write thou these words." The Hebrews speak of the Pentateuch as "the law," and "the law of Moses." The book of the law, the law of Moses, now divided into five parts, was in existence at the time of Joshua (Joshua 1:8).

The Witness of the New Testament

Our Lord Jesus Christ, the infallible Son of God, perfect in knowledge, said to the Sadducees: "And as touching the dead, that they rise, have ye not read in the book of Moses, how in the bush God spake to him, saying, I am the God of Abraham, and the God of Isaac and the God of Jacob" (Mark 12:26). Our Lord thus gives positive evidence that Exodus is the book of Moses. See also Luke 20:37. Exodus is quoted twenty-five times by Christ and His apostles, and there are almost as many allusions to it scattered throughout the New Testament books. The rejection of the inspiration of Exodus means the rejection of the inspiration of the entire New Testament, and worse than that, it means the rejection of the testimony of the Son of God.

Israel's Birthday Book

The book of Exodus may well be called "Israel's birthday book." Israel entered Egypt as a family and left Egypt as a nation, brought forth by the grace and power of God. Jehovah calls Israel "my Son, my Firstborn" (Exodus 4:22).

The national birthday of Israel is recorded in this book. First we find the travail pains in the house of bondage, preceding the birth. The birth itself takes place in the twelfth chapter, when sheltered by blood they went out, to leave Egypt behind. The memorable month in which they were redeemed by blood was now to be "the beginning of months," the beginning of a new year, the starting point of their national existence. Then followed their deliverance and redemption by the power of God at the Red Sea, the giving of the law and the statutes and their divine calling as a nation to be "a kingdom of priests and an holy nation."

Typical Teachings

Perhaps no other Old Testament book is so rich in typical teachings as Exodus. The power of Satan and God's salvation by blood are most clearly revealed in the first part of the book. The Lord Jesus Christ and His work in redemption are foreshadowed throughout the book. The two great phases of the gospel of God, so fully and blessedly revealed in the Epistle to the Romans, are found in type in Exodus. These two phrases are, redemption from the guilt of sins and redemption from the power of sin. The former is seen in type in Israel's Passover experience, and the latter is typified by the overthrow and destruction of the Egyptians in the Red Sea. These two great events give us two aspects of the death of Christ.

And how rich and full in typical meaning is the tabernacle with its different appointments and its priesthood. Here we find Christ everywhere. Various experiences of God's people may be traced in the conflicts and victories of Israel, their failure and unbelief. The annotations of the different chapters take notice of all this.

Dispensational Foreshadowings

Equally important are the dispensational foreshadowings. Israel's suffering in Egypt is typical of their history of sorrow and tears until their final restoration and fulfillment of God's promises to them as a nation takes place. God's dealing in judgment with Egypt foreshadows future judgments in store for the world. The deliverance out of Egypt is a pattern of their future deliverance, when they will be brought back. To this Jeremiah 16:14 refers: "Therefore, behold, the days come, saith the Lord, that it shall no more be said, As the Lord liveth that brought up the children of Israel out of the land of Egypt, but, As the Lord liveth, that brought up the children of Israel from the land of the north, and from all the countries, whither He had driven them." The life of Moses, as a type of Christ, gives other dispensational hints of great interest. It is a most blessed book. May He guide us by His Spirit and unfold its precious truths to our hearts.

The Division of Exodus

We do not find in the book of Exodus a characteristic word like the word "generation" in Genesis, which points out the division in that book. Exodus contains a continuous story. We believe the key text for this book is found in the third chapter, in the words which the Lord spoke out of the burning bush to Moses, whom He called to be the leader of His people. We find them in chapter 3:7–8.

> And the Lord said, I have surely seen the affliction of My people which are in Egypt, and have heard their cry by reason of their taskmasters; for I know their sorrows; and I am come down to deliver them out of the hand of the Egyptians; and to bring them up out of the land unto a good land flowing with milk and honey, unto the place of the Canaanites, and the Hittites, and the Amorites, and the Perizzites, and the Hivites, and Jebusites.

These are beautiful words. They tell us that the Lord took notice of the affliction of His people and heard their cry. He was now ready to act in their behalf and to deliver them out of the house of bondage. In the eighth verse we have the two parts of Exodus indicated. The Lord announced two things He would do for His people. 1. I am come down to deliver them out of the hands of the Egyptians. 2. And to bring them up out of the land unto a good land flowing with milk and honey. Exodus has two great parts which correspond to these two statements.

I. ISRAEL'S DELIVERANCE OUT OF THE HANDS OF THE EGYPTIANS

1. **The House of Bondage** (1:1-22)
2. **Moses the Chosen Deliverer** (2—4:28)
3. **Moses and Aaron in Egypt** (4:29—7:13)
4. **The Nine Plagues; the Tenth Judgment Announced** (7:14—11:10)
5. **Redemption by Blood: The Passover and the Law of the Firstborn** (12—13:16)
6. **Redemption by Power** (13:7—14:31)
7. **The Song of Redemption** (15:1-21)

II. THE JOURNEY TOWARDS THE PROMISED LAND. ISRAEL AT SINAI

1. **The Experiences in the Wilderness** (15:22—18:27)
2. **At Sinai: The Covenant and the Law** (19—24:18)
3. **The Tabernacle and the Priesthood** (25—31:18)
4. **Israel's Sin and Rebellion** (32:1-35)
5. **Moses' Intercession and its Results** (33—34:35)
6. **The Building of the Tabernacle** (35—39:43)
7. **The Tabernacle Set Up: The Finished Work and the Glory** (40:1-38)

We learn from this division and analysis that the first section begins with the groans of the enslaved people in the house of bondage and ends with the song of redemption, sung by the redeemed and delivered nation. The beginning of the second section shows the redeemed people in the wilderness of Shur and describes their experiences; it ends with the finished work and the glory of the Lord filling the tabernacle. Both sections are prophetic. Israel's groans and captivity will end in deliverance. Their wilderness wanderings will yet terminate in a future of glory, with Jehovah in their midst.

Analysis and Annotations

I. Israel's Deliverance Out of the Hands of the Egyptians

1. The House of Bondage

CHAPTER 1

1. The names of the children of Israel; their increase (1:1-7)
2. The new king and his policy (1:8-11)
3. The continued increase (1:12)
4. Their hard bondage (1:13-14)
5. The midwives commanded (1:15-16)
6. Their disobedience and God's reward (1:17-21)
7. Pharaoh's charge to all his people (1:22)

The opening verses take us back once more to the end of Genesis; as already stated the word "now" (literally, "and") makes Exodus a continuation of the previous book. They had come into Egypt while Joseph was already there. Joseph and all his brethren had passed away, but their descendants multiplied rapidly. The Hebrew word "increased" means "swarmed." The seventh verse emphasizes their wonderful increase both in numbers and in power. Inasmuch as a comparatively short time had elapsed after Joseph's death, some 64 years only, infidelity has sneered at the description of this increase. It is generally overlooked that besides the 70 souls which came into Egypt a very large number of servants must have accompanied them. Abraham had 318 servants born in his house. Jacob had a still larger number. And they had been received into the covenant, though they were not natural descendants. The command of circumcision extended to "every man child in your generations, he that is born in the house, or bought with money of any stranger, which is not thy seed" (Gen. 17:12). There may have been thousands of such servants besides immense herds of cattle. Yet even this does not fully explain the great increase. It was miraculous, the fulfillment of the promises given to the patriarchs. God witnessed thereby that they were His people.

The Egyptian account given by their historian Manetho, speaking of the Hyksos, the shepherd kings of the East, is in all probability a distorted account of the increase and influence of the Israelites. A new king, or dynasty, then arose. Josephus, the Jewish historian, states: "The government was transferred to another family." The debt which Egypt owed to Joseph was forgotten.

The increasing Israelites filled the Egyptians with terror, hence the attempt to crush them by hard labor and the cruel taskmasters. They were used in the construction of some of the great monumental buildings and became the slaves of the Gentiles. The ruins of cities bear witness to it, for they were composed of crude brick and in many of them straw was not used (chapter 5:10-12). The oppression was in degrees. But the more they were afflicted, the more they multiplied and grew. Here we may read the history of Israel among the Gentiles. Their increase and expansion has produced what is known as "anti-Semitism." The Gentiles fear the Jews. Their miraculous increase always takes place when oppression and persecution is upon them. When they are oppressed then God's time for deliverance draws nigh.

Their oppression and sorrow in Egypt was also permitted for their own good. The idolatry of Egypt began to corrupt the chosen people. See Joshua 24:14; Ezek. 20:5–8; 23:8.

The attempt to destroy all the male children follows next. Satan, who is a murderer from the beginning, manifested his cunning and power in this way. He desired to destroy the seed of Abraham so as to make the coming of the Promised One impossible. The murder of Abel was his first attempt. Here is an attempt on a larger scale, which was followed by many others. See Exodus 14, 2 Chron. 21:4, 17; 22:10; Esther 3:6, 12, 13; Matt. 2, etc. Throughout the history of Israel during this age Satan has made repeated attempts to exterminate this wonderful people, because he knows God's purpose concerning their future. His final attempt is recorded in Rev. 12.

Pharaoh was the instrument of Satan, and is a type of him. Blessed is the record of the faithful Hebrew midwives. They were pious women. Satan tried to use woman again for his sinister purposes, but he failed. Later we find that the wicked Pharaoh was defeated by the faith of a Hebrew mother and by the loving kindness of his own daughter (chapter 2). And God rewarded the actions of these women. They received honors; their families increased and were blest. When Pharaoh saw his attempt frustrated he appealed to his own people to commit wholesale murder. They began to sow an awful seed; the harvest came when years later there was no house in Egypt without one dead, when the firstborn were slain. Galatians 6:7 applies also to nations, "Whatsoever a man soweth, that he shall also reap." God honored the Hebrew midwives because they honored Him. The retribution came upon cruel Egypt in God's own time.

And yet there are other lessons. Egypt is the type of the world; Pharaoh the type of the prince of this world. The bondage of sin and the wretchedness of God's people, still undelivered, are here depicted. God permitted all so that they might groan for deliverance. The house of bondage opens the way for redemption by blood and by power.

2. Moses the Chosen Deliverer

CHAPTER 2

Moses: His Birth, Education, Choice, and Exile

1. His birth and concealment (2:1-4)
2. His rescue and education (2:5-10)
3. His choice and failure (2:11-14)
4. His exile (2:15-20)
5. His marriage (2:21-22)
6. The answered cry (2:23-24)

The history of the chosen deliverer, recorded by himself under the guidance of the Spirit, follows the dark picture of Israel's suffering. He was the offspring of a son and daughter of Levi. His name was *Amram* (chapter 6:20 and Num. 26:59). His wife's name *Jochebed.* As we saw in Genesis, Levi means "joined," and Levi was the third son of Jacob (Gen. 29:32-35). Here we have a typical hint of the true Mediator, joined to God and man. Levi was Jacob's third son, and Moses the third child of a son of Levi. The number "three" is the number of resurrection. It all foreshadows Christ. Pharaoh's command had been to cast the male children into the river. The river is the type of death (Jordan, for instance). By death Satan tried to oppose God's purposes. The babe was in danger of death; Satan's hatred through Pharaoh was directed against this child as Herod through Satan's instigation tried to kill the newborn King in Bethlehem.

The child was beautiful. Acts 7:20 states he was (literally) "beautiful to God." For three months he was hid and then his own mother prepared the ark of bulrushes and laid him in the reeds at the river's brink, in the place of death. The word "ark" is the same as in Gen. 6:14 and the pitch with which it was daubed reminds us likewise of Noah's ark. The dark waters were kept out. It was not alone the natural love of the mother which acted, but faith. "By faith Moses, when he was born, was hid three months by his parents, because they saw that the child was beautiful; and they were not afraid of the King's commandment" (Heb. 11:23). What faith this was! First they saved the child by faith for three months and then the mother's faith prepared the little casket, the place of safety, and in faith committed the ark of bulrushes to the river's brink. But while faith depends on God's power and trust in God's Word, it also fears nothing. They were not afraid of the king's commandment. And God acted as He always will in answer to faith. He guided Pharaoh's daughter to the very spot where the child rested with his sister standing afar off. Her faith did not fully measure up to the faith of the mother; but even this was God's leading. According to Jewish tradition the name of Pharaoh's daughter was Thermoutis. The weeping babe stirred her compassion. And what these tears accomplished! Not the smiling face, but the tear-stained countenance of sorrow, lead to the far-reaching results of deliverance. How it reminds us of Him who was the Man of Sorrows, who wept and went into the dark waters of death and judgment.

The mother receives her child again, whom she gave up in faith, and then the child becomes the son of Pharaoh's daughter, who gave him the Egyptian name "Moses," which means "saved from the water." The beautiful faith of Moses' mother here meets its full rewards; Satan is confounded; and the marvelous wisdom of God is displayed. Who would have thought that the one who had said, "If it be a son, then ye shall kill him," and, again, "Every son that is born ye shall cast into the river," should have in his court one of those very sons, and *such* a son." The devil was foiled by his own weapon, inasmuch as Pharaoh, whom he was using to frustrate the purpose of God, is used of God to nourish and bring up Moses, who was to be His instrument in confounding the power of Satan. Remarkable providence! Admirable wisdom! Truly, Jehovah is "wonderful in counsel and excellent in working." May we learn to trust Him with more artless simplicity, and thus our path shall be more brilliant, and our testimony more effective.[1]

In Egypt Moses received his instruction and education. What followed is more freely revealed by Stephen in his Spirit-given message.

> And Moses was learned in all the wisdom of the Egyptians, and was mighty in words and in deeds. And when he was full forty years old, it came into his heart to visit his brethren the children of Israel. And seeing one of them suffer wrong, he defended him, and avenged him that was oppressed, and smote the Egyptian: For he supposed his brethren would have understood how that God by his hand would deliver them; but they understood not. And the next day he shewed himself unto them as they strove, and would have set them at one again, saying, Sirs, ye are brethren; why do ye wrong one to another? But he that did his neighbor wrong thrust him away, saying, Who made thee a ruler and a judge over us? Wilt thou kill me, as thou didst the Egyptian yesterday? (Acts 7:22-28).

He had learned the wisdom of Egypt, but not yet the wisdom of God. He manifested zeal for his brethren, but it was not according to knowledge. He attempted a deliverance before the time. Yet it was an action of faith.

> By faith Moses, when he was come to years, refused to be called the son of Pharaoh's daughter. Choosing rather to suffer affliction with the people of God, than to enjoy the pleasures of sin for a season; Esteeming the reproach of Christ greater riches than the treasures in Egypt: for he had respect unto the recompense of the reward. By faith he forsook Egypt, not fearing the wrath of the king: for he endured, as seeing Him who is invisible (Hebrews 11:24-26).

He acted in self will, assuming the office of a judge and leader, without having received the divine call. It was faith, nevertheless, which led

[1]C. H. Mackintosh, *Exodus.*

Moses into this path and to make this remarkable choice. His heart was filled with deep sympathy for his suffering kinsmen and he yearned for their salvation. He was, however, not received by them; they rejected him. He left the palace and, perhaps, the throne, and came to his own to take up their cause. It all points to Him, who left the glory and came to His own and they received Him not. When Moses came the first time to his brethren to deliver them, "they understood not" (Acts 7:25). But they understood when he came the second time, as Israel will understand, when He, who is greater than Moses, comes the second time.

He became an exile in Midian and met Reuel. His name also is Jethro (3:1). Reuel means "friend of God." He also was a priest, no doubt a true worshipper of God. Moses received a daughter of the Midianite, Zipporah, for his wife. Rejected by his own people, he entered into union with a Gentile. All this is typical. Christ after His first coming, rejected by His own, receives her, who shares His rejection and who will come with Him, when He comes the second time. The church is here indicated.

The forty years spent by Moses in Midian were, as we express it, the best years of his life. He had forty years' training in Egypt, and then the Lord took him aside into His school to train him for the great work for which he had been chosen. In the obscurity of the desert he was prepared to be "a vessel fit for the Master's use." How blessed must have been his experience, away from man, away from Egypt's pleasures, alone with God. Thus the Lord has dealt with all His servants. Elijah came forth out of the wilderness and went back to Cherith, Ezekiel was alone at the river Chebar. Paul spent his schooling days in Arabia. Blessed are His servants who follow His leading into the desert place, to find their never-failing source of strength in communion with their Lord, who receive their service from Himself, and then go forth to serve.

We give a little diagram of the genealogy of Moses and his brother Aaron.

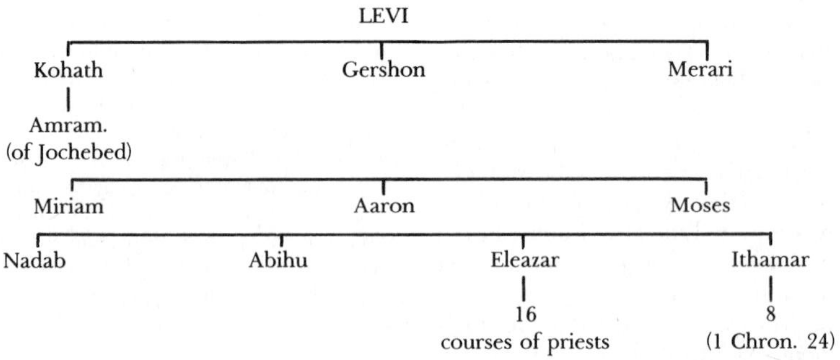

CHAPTER 3

The Burning Bush and the Call and Commission of Moses

1. The vision of the burning bush (3:1-3)
2. Jehovah speaks and calls Moses (3:4-10)
3. Moses' answer (3:11-12)
4. The name revealed (3:13-14)
5. The commission of Moses (3:15-18)
6. The promise (3:19-22)

The two last verses of the preceding chapter form the introduction to the great manifestation of Jehovah in the burning bush and the call of Moses. God's time had come. He heard their groaning, He remembered the covenant, and looked upon His suffering people. The scene is at Horeb, called here the mountain of God by anticipation. Moses had become a shepherd, that occupation which the Egyptians despised (Gen. 46:34). It was part of God's training by which he became "very meek above all the men which were upon the face of the earth" (Num. 12:3). In his shepherd character he is the type of Christ.

The burning bush is the picture of the suffering people, the wretched slaves in Egypt. It was a thornbush. Thorns being the results of sin, it typifies the sinfulness and worthlessness of the people. The fire is the symbol of their suffering and tribulation. It has the same meaning as the "smoking furnace" Abraham saw in his vision. Later God called Egypt the "iron furnace" (Deut. 4:20). The thornbush, however, is not consumed. All the fires of persecution and tribulation could not consume Israel. In the flame of the fire in the midst of the burning bush the angel of the Lord appeared. This was the secret of the preservation of the bush; God was there and kept them. "When thou walkest through the fire, thou shalt not be burned; neither shall the flame kindle upon thee" (Is. 43:2). He is with all His people in their affliction; He preserves them and carries them through the fire. But the fire is also the figure of God's consuming and purifying holiness. All that is unholy must be consumed by the fire. "Our God is a consuming fire."

The angel of Jehovah, who addressed Moses out of the burning bush reveals His name. It shows that the Angel of Jehovah (God the Son) is God. He calls Himself the God of Abraham, the God of Isaac and the God of Jacob. The triune God is thus revealed as Father, Son and Holy Spirit. In Abraham, as the Father, in Isaac as the Son and in the experience of Jacob as the Holy Spirit. Our Lord quotes these words and silenced with them the unbelieving Sadducees, who rejected the doctrine of resurrection (Matt. 22:31, 32). The words Jehovah spoke to Moses are the expressions of His sovereign grace. What had they merited? What could they do to secure His intervention? Nothing whatever. They were in Egypt, a lot of miserable slaves, given more or less to idolatry, a sinful people. It was grace which looked upon them and heard their cry. It was grace which came down to deliver them. The work of salvation He came to do was all His own work. It foreshadows His coming down in incarnation for the work of salvation. Note the five words: 1. I have surely seen the affliction of my people; 2. I have heard their cry; 3. I have known their sorrow; 4. I have come down to deliver them; 5. And to bring them up out of the land into a good land. He is ever the same, Jehovah, who changeth not. He ever sees, hears and knows and acts in behalf of His people. He never leaves nor forsakes.

And when the Lord called Moses to send him to Pharaoh to lead His people forth, he answered, What am I that I should go to Pharaoh and that I should bring forth the children of Israel out of Egypt? Forty years before in self-confidence he had undertaken the work and had run before he was sent, and now he had learned humility and his weakness. God answered his confessed distrust with the all-sufficient assurance, "I will be with thee." When He sends forth He goes along to accomplish His own purposes. What encouragement for all who wait on the Lord and conscious of their own weakness, go forth in service.

In response to another question, God reveals His name. "And God said unto Moses, I AM THAT I AM, and He said, Thus shalt thou say unto the children of Israel, I AM hath sent me unto you." God had made Himself known to Abraham as Jehovah (Genesis 15:7). But here He gives the explanation of His name Jehovah. The patriarchs knew the name Jehovah, but the blessed significance of that name was not known to them. He reveals Himself as the Self-Existing One, THE I AM THAT I AM. He is the One, which is, which was, which is to come (Rev. 1:4). And this wonderful Name of the Unchanging, Living One, the Eternal, the Name unsearchable in its depths is the Name of our Lord who has redeemed us. When about to act in the deliverance of His enslaved people to lead them out and to bring them in, He makes Himself known as the I AM. "Before Abraham was I AM" (John 8:58). Our ever-blessed Lord is the I AM, who spoke to Moses. And what is Jehovah, the I am for His people? Well has it been said, "Jehovah, in taking this title, calling Himself 'I AM,' was furnishing His people with a blank check, to be filled up to any amount. He calls Himself I AM, and faith has but to write over against that ineffably precious name whatever we want."

In verse 15 we have the hint of Jehovah's eternal relationship with His people Israel. He is still and ever will be the God of Abraham, of Isaac and of Jacob. "This is my name *forever* and this is my memorial unto *all generations.*" Here is the hope for Israel. He hath not cast them away; He is their God still and His gifts and calling are without repentance.

The commission to Moses follows, and Jehovah telling beforehand that the king of Egypt would not let them go also promises Moses that He would smite Egypt and that when the exodus takes place, they were not to go empty-handed. This is in fulfillment of a previous promise (Gen. 15:14).

CHAPTER 4:1-28

Moses' Objections, Jehovah's Answer and the Return to Egypt

1. The first objection (4:1)
2. The two signs and Jehovah's assurance (4:2-9)
3. The second objection (4:10)
4. Jehovah's answer (4:11-12)
5. Moses' request (4:13)
6. Jehovah's anger and answer (4:14-17)
7. The command to return to Egypt (4:18-23)
8. The event by the way in the inn (4:24-26)
9. The meeting of Moses and Aaron (4:27-28)

The division of chapters at this point is unwarranted. Moses' objections reveal his unbelief and self-distrust. Jehovah's patience and condescending grace are blessedly manifested. Moses first expressed his doubt that the people would not believe him and his mission. Though he saw the vision of the burning bush and heard Jehovah's voice, which assured him of His presence and power, yet did he not believe. His former experience with his people, and the fact that generations had passed since Jehovah had appeared to an Israelite must have led him to express this doubt.

The Lord gave him three signs: the rod cast down, which became a serpent; the leprous hand; and the water turned into blood. The first two signs were carried out in Jehovah's presence. Moses cast his rod on the ground and it became a serpent, and he fled from it. In obedience to Jehovah's command, Moses took the serpent by the tail and it became a rod. The rod Moses held was his shepherd's rod. It is the emblem of government and power. Moses cast it on the ground and out of his hand the rod became a serpent. The serpent stands for the power of Satan. Egypt (the type of the world) is under the control of Satan. The serpent was worshipped in Egypt. It was used as the emblem of the goddess Ranno and also used as a sign of royalty. The serpent, Satan, had usurped the place of government and power. But Jehovah can deal with the serpent and this is seen by Moses' taking the serpent by its tail so that it became a rod. The sign was to inspire and teach confidence. The sign of the leprous hand teaches another lesson. Sin, typified by leprosy, and cleansing from sin are indicated in this sign. Israel was in a leprous condition, but the power of Jehovah could cleanse his people. When Moses came the first time to deliver his people, they treated him as an outcast; but when he put his hand in his bosom the second time to act the reproach was removed.

The third sign teaches how the blessing, the water of the Nile, is to be changed into a curse. It is the sign of judgment to come upon Egypt. Moses, in receiving these signs and the power to enact them, is a type of Christ. He will take the rod, the government, into His blessed hand, and then Satan's dominion ends. He will cleanse and restore His people and smite Egypt, the world, with judgment.

Moses' second objection was his slow speech and slow tongue. The same unbelief is here in evidence. Had he but believed "I will be with thee," and that the "I AM" would be His tongue and his speech, this objection would never have come from his lips.

How gracious Jehovah's answer: "Now, therefore, go, I will be with thy mouth and teach thee what thou shalt say." Every servant of the Lord, who serves under Him, can appropriate this great promise. And still Moses hesitates. What patience from the side of the Lord! He now makes another gracious provision. Aaron is to be his spokesman. This was for Moses' humiliation. Then Moses' objections were silenced. Grace is fully illustrated in the call of Moses and how the Lord dealt with him.

Jethro sanctions his return to Egypt. The Lord prepared his way as He always does, when He sends forth His servant. He took his wife and sons, who were still young, for he set them on an ass. This shows that his marriage to Zipporah did not take place immediately after his arrival in Midian. Then he took his rod, which is now called "the rod of God," and the Lord gave him the solemn message to Pharaoh. Israel is to be nationally God's firstborn son. Jehovah's demand is, Let my son go, that he may serve Me. God's firstborn is to be brought out of Egypt, where service for God was impossible. Then follows the message of death and judgment for Egypt.

What comes next is closely connected with the message to Pharaoh. There was a stumbling block in Moses' family. Circumcision, which stands for the sentence of death, had not been executed in the case of one of Moses' sons. No doubt Zipporah made objections to this rite and kept her husband back from doing what he knew was imperative. This failure of Moses stood in his way to carry out the divine commission. The hand of the Lord was upon Moses, and he was in danger of being cut off for his sin, for he had been disobedient and yielded to his wife. Then Zipporah is forced to do herself what she hated and the reproach was removed. The words "surely a bloody husband art thou to me," were addressed to Moses. She had been forced, as it were, to purchase him again by the shedding of the blood of her beloved son. She received him back as one who had been in the realm of death and was joined to him anew. It must have been there that Moses brought the sacrifice of separation by sending Zipporah and the sons back to Jethro (chapter 18:2). What a meeting it must have been which took place between Aaron and Moses. They met in the Mount of God and kissed each other. Compare with Num. 20:27,28.

3. Moses and Aaron in Egypt

CHAPTERS 4:29—5:23

Before the Elders and Before Pharaoh

1. Before the elders of Israel (4:29-31)
2. Before Pharaoh, and his answer (5:1-4)
3. The increased oppression (5:5-19)
4. Israel's complaint and Moses' prayer (5:20-23)

The people were willing and believed. Notice they believed *after* the signs were done. Faith was followed by worship. It is almost a constitutional thing with the Jew to see first and then believe. Compare with John 20:26-29.

Then the messengers of God appeared before Pharaoh. This must have been in his capital Zoan (Psalm 78:43). Jehovah made of Pharaoh seven demands. They are found in chapters 5:1; 7:16; 8:1; 8:20; 9:1; 9:13; 10:3. Satan's power now becomes more fully manifested. Israel is Jehovah's people and He must have His chosen ones out of Egypt and fully delivered. The objects of his love and grace must be completely freed from the miserable slavery of sin and Satan. The typical application as to man's condition as a sinner is so well known that we need not to follow it in detail.

Pharaoh's attitude is that of defiance, though he spoke the truth when he said, "I know not Jehovah." The threat of coming judgments is disbelieved. His answer was increased burdens marked by the most awful cruelty. It was Satan's rage through Pharaoh in anticipation of Jehovah's intervention in the redemption of His people. As far as Israel is concerned this will yet be repeated during the great tribulation. Then Satan's wrath will be great, for he knows his time is short and the Lord will deliver the remnant of Israel (Rev. 12:12-17). It is the same in the individual experience. Satan will not let his victims go. When sin and the power of the flesh is felt, then comes the conflict and Satan's rage.

What discouragement for the poor slaves in Egypt! They had rejoiced in faith and worshipped because Jehovah's servants had announced deliverance, and now a darker night had settled upon them; but it was only the harbinger of the glad dawn of the redemption. They murmured while Moses, deeply perplexed, turned to the Lord in prayer. Moses was a great man of prayer. He cast his burden upon the Lord.

CHAPTER 6:1-27

Jehovah's Answers and the Genealogy

1. Jehovah answers Moses (6:1-13)
2. The Genealogy (6:14-27)

Moses' "wherefore" and "why," his outburst of impatience, is graciously met by Jehovah. In His answer He speaks more fully of Himself as Jehovah, and what He will do in behalf of His afflicted and oppressed people. I am Jehovah, is His solemn declaration. Note the continued utterances of what He is and what He will do. I appeared unto Abraham; I have heard; I have remembered; I will bring you out; I will rid you out of their bondage; I will redeem you; I will take you to be for Me a people; I will be to you a God; I will bring you into the land; I will give it to you for a heritage; I am Jehovah. In Ezekiel, chapter 36, the reader will find Jehovah's "I will" concerning the future restoration of His people Israel.

No condition is mentioned; for their salvation as well as ours, is "not of works" but of grace alone. The source of all is His love (Deut. 7:7, 8). Salvation is Jehovah's work and not ours. Thus while the patriarchs knew the name of God as Jehovah, the full revelation of Jehovah, working in the gracious performance of His promises, they knew not. Verse 3 means that they did not understand the name Jehovah, though they knew that name. Then follows the record of "the heads of their fathers' houses." He knows them by name. He comes down where the slaves are, and calls them by name, thus identifying Himself with them. And then He knew, as He does now, every groan, every burden, every spot upon which the whip of the cruel taskmaster had fallen. This is the precious lesson of this register of names. No other genealogy is found in Exodus. What a great redeemer is Jehovah, our Lord Jesus Christ! All praise and glory be to His holy Name.

CHAPTERS 6:28—7:13

The Renewed Commission and Before Pharaoh Again

1. Renewed commission and renewed hesitation (6:28-30)
2. Jehovah's instructions (7:1-9)
3. Before Pharaoh and the sign of the rod (7:10-13)

Once more Moses received his commission, and again he hesitated on account of his poor speech. After all the gracious words Jehovah had spoken he pleads again his weakness. It shows what the unbelieving heart is. Twice Jehovah said that Moses should be a god. A god to Aaron (4:16) and a god to Pharaoh (7:1). He received divine authority and power over Pharaoh, while he was to his spokesman Aaron a god, because the word he uttered to him to communicate to Pharaoh was the word of the Lord. "And I will harden Pharaoh's heart." This was stated before in chapter 4:21. Eighteen times we read of the hardening of Pharaoh's heart. However, different words are used in the Hebrew to show an important distinction. One means to "make firm" or "strong." The other, "to make stubborn." These two words show Pharaoh's hardening of his own heart and God's hardening after he continued in his wicked way. After it is five times declared that Pharaoh hardened his heart, then God began His hardening and made Pharaoh's heart stubborn. Pharaoh hardened himself, then God hardened him. Pharaoh had his opportunities and as he refused and continued in unbelief, God made him stubborn. God hardens as a judicial act because man refuses His Word. God never hardens first nor compels a man to be an unbeliever. A solemn warning is contained in this. Thousands harden their hearts now, and ere long apostate Christendom will be hardened by God without remedy (2 Thessalonians 2).

Moses' age was 80 years and Aaron's 83 when they spoke to Pharaoh. They are before the monarch to show a miracle. Moses did not use his rod as before the elders of Israel, but it was Aaron's rod which was cast down and became a serpent. There is likewise another word used for serpent. In chapter 4:3, it is *nachash*, the same word as in Genesis 3. But the word used in chapter 7 is *thanin*, which the Septuagint translates *dragon*. This does not show that there were two different records, but that the two events have a different significance. Aaron's rod, which later blossomed, is the type of the resurrection of the Lord Jesus, the mighty victor over Satan, sin and death. Aaron's rod swallowing the rods of the magicians of Egypt seems to indicate the complete triumph of Jehovah over him who has the power of death.

The question is, was the action of the magicians a real miracle or produced by juggling? Snake charming was carried on in ancient Egypt. However, these magicians were the instruments of Satan, who manifested his power through them. What they did were "lying wonders." The names of two of these endued with demoniacal powers are given in 2 Timothy 3:8, Jannes and Jambres. Such manifestation of demon power is found to-day in spiritualism and will be fully revealed during the days of Antichrist at the end of this age (2 Thess. 2:9-12). Pharaoh's heart was hardened (literal translation) because he wilfully rejected the sign given.

4. The Nine Plagues and the Tenth Judgment Announced

CHAPTER 7:14-25

The First Plague

1. The plague announced (7:14-19)
2. The judgment executed (7:20-25)

Nine judgment plagues follow, and after they had passed, the tenth, the great judgment, fell upon Egypt. There are striking and different characteristics of these plagues. Aaron uses his rod in the beginning of the plagues, while Moses stretches out his rod and hand in the last three, not counting the slaying of the firstborn. Some of them were announced beforehand, others were not announced and came without warning. We give them now in their order: 1. Water turned into blood; 2. Frogs; 3. Lice; 4. Flies; 5. Murrain; 6. Boils; 7. Hail; 8. Locusts; 9. Darkness (see Psalm 105:26-36). The process of the hardening of Pharaoh's heart progresses with these judgments till God hardened him completely. After the first plague his heart was hardened (or firm) and deliberately he set himself to do this. Note this process in chapters 8:15; 8:19; 8:31; and 9:7. When this present age closes with the great tribulation and the vials of God's wrath are poured out upon an unbelieving world, the hearts of the earthdwellers and Christ rejectors will be hardened and thus ripe for the day of wrath. The book of Revelation acquaints us with this solemn fact.

"The plagues of Egypt are founded on the natural features which Egypt presents, so that they are unprecedented and extraordinary, not so much in themselves, as on account of their power and extent, and their rapid succession when Moses simply gives the command. As they are, consequently, both natural and supernatural, they afford both to faith and to unbelief the freedom to choose (in Pharaoh, unbelief prevailed); they are, besides, adapted to convince the Egyptians that Jehovah is not merely the national God of the Israelites, but a God above all gods, who holds in his hand all the powers of nature likewise, which Egypt was accustomed to deify" (J. H. Kurtz).

The water of the river Nile was turned into blood. The Nile was worshipped by the Egyptians and now this great river was polluted. Strange that even orthodox commentators can state that the change in the water was a change in color produced by red earth or by a certain water plant. But we know a real change took place, for the water stank and the fish died. Thus the Nile, known as Osiris, became an object of abomination and death. The messengers of Satan imitated this miracle also. This plague lasted seven days.

CHAPTER 8

The Second, Third, and Fourth Plagues

1. The demand and the plague of frogs announced (8:1-4)
2. The plague executed (8:5-7)
3. The request of Pharaoh and the frogs removed (8:8-15)
4. The divine command for the third plague (8:16)
5. The plague executed (8:17)
6. The confession of the magicians (8:18-19)
7. The renewed demand and the plague of the flies announced (8:20-23)
8. The plague executed (8:24)
9. Pharaoh's promise and his refusal (8:25-32)

The different demands made of Pharaoh to let God's people go and Pharaoh's objections are of much interest. In Jehovah's demands to let His people go we have God's purpose that His people must be completely brought out of Egypt (the world) and be separated unto Him. Before they could worship and serve Him they had to be delivered from Egypt. It is so with us. Pharaoh is the type of Satan, the god of this age. He made his objections, as Satan makes his opposition to a full and complete deliverance of God's people. Study Pharaoh's objections: In chapter 8:25, he says, "Go ye, sacrifice to your God in the land." Then in verse 28 he makes a compromise, but they must not go far away. In chapter 10:9-11 he desired the men to go, but the rest and their belongings were to stay behind. The final compromise is in chapter 10:24. In these objections and compromises we read Satan's attempt to keep God's people ensnared with the world and thus hold them under his control and power. How well he has succeeded in Christendom.

If we connect the last verse of the previous chapter it seems it was on the seventh day, the day of rest, the Sabbath, which Israel must have completely forgotten, when the Lord again spoke to Moses and announced the second plague. This consisted of frogs, which proceeded from the worshipped, sacred Nile. The rationalistic higher critics have tried to explain this plague also as a natural occurrence. But they do not explain how it is that they came as soon as Aaron stretched his hand over the waters of Egypt and that they died by the millions after Moses' prayer. Surely Pharaoh was better than the modern day critics, for he acknowledged at least that it was a miracle of Jehovah (verse 8). Frogs were also connected with Egyptian idolatry. One Egyptian goddess called *Hekt* appears with the head of a frog. Frogs stand for unclean things. See Revelation 16:13. The magicians enabled by Satan's power also imitated this miracle. But with this their power in counterfeiting ceased.

The third plague consisted in lice, or rather "gnats." It came like the sixth and ninth plague, without any previous warning. They smote the dust and divine power for judgment brought out of the dust these tormenting insects. The very soil of Egypt now was turned into a curse. God now restrained the demoniacal powers of imitation and the wicked magicians had to confess, not for the glory of Jehovah, but for their own protection, "this is the finger of God."

The fourth plague was still more disastrous and significant. The appeal was made in the morning (Jeremiah 25:4; 26:5; 29:19). Swarms of flies covered all Egypt. These were not the common house flies, but a more powerful insect, the bite of which was exceedingly painful. There were different kinds of them. He sent divers sorts of flies among them, which devoured them (Psalm 78:45). They fastened themselves upon men and tormented them. It was another blow against the idols of Egypt. The beetle was reverenced as the symbol of creative power and the Egyptian Sun-god had a beetle's head. This plague did not touch Israel. Jehovah showed that Israel is His people. All the terrible punitive judgments did not touch His people. And this was a sign. The word "division" in verse 23 means "redemption." Jehovah is here clearly revealed as the author of the plague judgments. His supreme authority stands out prominently. After the removal of this plague, Pharaoh hardened his heart anew.

CHAPTER 9

The Fifth, Sixth, and Seventh Plagues

1. The fifth plague: the grievous murrain (9:1-7)
2. The sixth plague: boils (9:8-12)
3. The warning given (9:13-21)
4. The seventh plague: hail (9:22-35)

In the demand God calls Himself "the Lord God of the Hebrews" (see also verse 13 and 10:3). The fifth plague strikes animal creation. Cattle, such as mentioned in the opening of this chapter, formed the most important part of the wealth of Egypt. Egypt's wealth is therefore stricken. But God waited and warned before He executed this judgment. Jehovah's power sheltered Israel in Goshen and not a beast suffered there. Notice Pharaoh's curiosity. He *sent* to see if Israel had escaped and found that not one had died. What an evidence that the Lord God of the Hebrews is *the* Lord. Yet his heart was hardened.

The next plague came without warning, unannounced. Moses and Aaron sprinkled the ashes of the furnace, and it became a boil upon man and beast. The magicians may have attempted then another counterfeit move, but the boils broke out on them. If they were of the priestly class they had become defiled by the nasty sores. The priests were obliged to be scrupulously clean in everything. The ashes of the furnace have a double meaning. Egypt in its fiery persecution of Israel is called a furnace. Divine retribution now came upon them in the boils, which must have burned as fire. But the furnace may have been the altar in Egypt upon which sacrifices were offered to their god Typhon. Most likely the Egyptians brought such sacrifices to stay the plagues, and now the very thing in which they trusted is turned into a plague. This plague was the first which endangered human life, and therefore the forerunner of the death which Pharaoh would bring upon himself and his people by his wicked opposition.

The seventh plague is ushered in by a solemn warning and more lengthy address to Pharaoh. A very grevious hail is threatened to fall upon man and beast; the hail was to kill all found in the open field. Note verse 16 and compare with Romans 9:17. God dealt with Pharaoh in this way that he might know Jehovah and His power and that through what Jehovah did His name might be made known throughout the earth. Jehovah's holiness, omnipotence, justice, as well as His patience and longsuffering are revealed in these judgments, foreshadowing all future judgments to come for this earth. The report of what Jehovah had done in Egypt spread soon to other nations, and inspired a holy awe (Exodus 15:14-16). It was a loving and gracious advice God gave through Moses (verse 19). No doubt there were many Egyptians who believed and escaped. The unbelieving suffered. Divine mercy still lingered. Those of the Egyptians who believed the divine warning must have belonged to the mixed multitudes which went out with Israel (chapter 12:38).

The fearful hail was accompanied by fire (lightning) which ran along the ground, and thunderings. These are called in the Hebrew "the voices of God." The tempest is the type of God's wrath in judgment. Hail is mentioned repeatedly in Revelation and there it is called "the plague of hail" (Rev. 8:7, 11:19, 16:21). The plagues of Egypt will be repeated on this earth during the great tribulation. Note Pharaoh's confession, which shows that this plague had made a deep impression on him (verse 27). Pharaoh used the name of "Jehovah" and the name of God (Elohim). "Intreat Jehovah that there be no more voices of God" (literal rendering). What a desperately wicked thing the human heart is. He sinned more after this than before.

CHAPTER 10

The Eighth and Ninth Plagues

1. The eighth plague: locusts (10:1-17)
2. Pharaoh's renewed confession and refusal (10:16-20)
3. The ninth plague: darkness (10:21-16)
4. Pharaoh's anger (10:27-29)

The eighth plague is introduced by another warning; the ninth came without it. As a result of the eighth plague, Pharaoh confessed his sin against God and against Moses and Aaron; but after the ninth plague drove Moses from his presence and threatened the divine messenger with death.

Locusts covered the face of the whole earth and every green thing was destroyed. On the ravages of the locusts we find a vivid description in the book of Joel. Locusts are typical of God's punitive judgments. The locusts plague was aimed to show the impotence of the Egyptian god Serapis, in whom the Egyptians trusted as the protector against the locusts. Locusts are likewise mentioned in a symbolical way in Revelation 9:1-12.

In the ninth plague, darkness covered Egypt for three days. Beautiful must have been the vision of the land of Goshen. Out of the dense darkness the light shone brightly in the miserable abodes of the children of Israel. "All the children of Israel had light in their dwellings." Note again the book of Revelation, chapter 16:10, 11.

The sun as the source of light was worshipped in Egypt. If Menephtah was the Pharaoh of the exodus, as some hold, this plague has a special significance. A sculptural image of this Pharaoh is preserved. His hand is outstretched in worship, and underneath stand in hieroglyphics these words: "He adores the sun; he worships Hor of the solar horizons." Suddenly darkness, which could be felt, came upon Egypt. Pharaoh and all Egypt learned now that their idols were helpless. Darkness is the withdrawal of light. It stands for the solemn truth of the forsaking of God. (We may well think here of the darkness which enshrouded the cross and the unfathomable cry of our Lord, "My God, My God, why hast thou forsaken Me?") God was about to abandon Egypt, the darkness was the herald of it. All Egypt was to be plunged into the severest of all judgments, the death of the firstborn. This darkness was God's final appeal to repentance. For three days they were shut in and all business was suspended. Rich and poor, king and beggar, the learned and the ignorant, all classes were shrouded in that awful darkness. The suspense must have been frightful. What was to come next? God waited, and in that silence and darkness appealed to their conscience. How slow God is to judge; it is His strange work. In infinite patience He waited before He dealt the final blow to Egypt. Thus He waits now and warns till at last His patience ends and His threatened judgments sweep the earth. The last objection and compromise by Pharaoh is found in verse 24, but Moses answered "not an hoof shall be left behind." Jehovah's demands and purposes concerning the completest separation from Egypt stand and must be literally executed.

CHAPTER 11

The Tenth Plague Announced

1. God's Word to Moses and to the people (11:1-3)
2. The tenth plague announced to Pharaoh (11:4-8)
3. Pharaoh's unbelief and his heart hardened (11:9-10)

In chapter 10:29 we hear Moses say to Pharaoh, "I will see thy face again no more." In this chapter, however, we hear him address Pharaoh once more concerning the tenth plague judgment. The announcement made to Moses and recorded in the first verse of this chapter occurred before the interview of the previous chapter and verses 4-8 in chapter 11 is the continuation of Moses' address to Pharaoh after he had spoken the words in chapter 10:29. The eleventh chapter is therefore a supplement to the tenth. The command to ask (this is the correct word; 'borrow' is incorrect) of the neighbors jewels of silver and gold had already been given in chapter 3:22. The death of all the firstborn in Egypt is announced to Pharaoh. A great cry shall be throughout all Egypt, but Israel should also be exempt of this last plague as the previous plagues were not shared by them. "Not a dog shall point his tongue (literal translation) against Israel," promising perfect rest and peace in the coming night of death and sorrow.

Verses 9 and 10 mark the close of Moses' interviews and negotiations with Pharaoh, which began in chapter 7:8. The right rendering of verse 9 is "And the Lord had said unto Moses." Moses left Pharaoh in a great anger. Judgment was now ready to fall.

5. Redemption by Blood, the Passover and the Law of the Firstborn

CHAPTER 12

The Passover Instituted and Kept, the Death of the Firstborn and the Exodus

1. The Passover instituted and the feast of unleavened bread (12:1-20)
2. The command given to the people and obeyed (12:21-28)
3. The death of the firstborn in Egypt (12:29-30)
4. The departure of the children of Israel (12:31-36)
5. From Rameses to Succoth (12:37-39)
6. The fulfillment of the 430 years (12:40-42)
7. The ordinance of the Passover (12:43-51)

This is the birth chapter of Israel as a nation. The birthpangs are about over and the deliverance is at hand. The first thing announced is the change of the year (verses 1, 2). A new beginning is made with the deliverance out of the house of bondage; the past is left behind and blotted out. This is typical of the new birth of the individual. The month which marks this new beginning is *Abib,* the "green ear" month, because the corn was then in the ear. After the captivity it was called *Nissan* (Nehemiah 2:1; Esther 3:7). It is our April.

Verses 1-14 give the instructions concerning the Passover, and verses 15-20 those concernnig the feast of unleavened bread. The Passover Lamb is a most blessed type of the Lord Jesus Christ in His work. He is the Lamb of God and our Passover (John 1:29; 1 Cor. 5:6, 7; 1 Peter 1:18, 19). The chapter is extremely rich in typical foreshadowing and spiritual truth. The spotless character of our Lord is indicated in that the lamb had to be without blemish. Taken out, separated, and a male; all has a meaning. For four days the lamb had to be set aside before it was to be killed. This was done to discover if there would be a flaw, some defect in it, which would unfit the lamb for the sacrifice. Here we are reminded of the four Gospel records in which the holy, spotless life of Him is told out who gave His life for a ransom. The lamb was to be killed by the whole congregation, even as it was with Christ. It was to be killed "between the evenings." That is between noon and the night, the afternoon; that is when Christ died. And what more could we say of the roasting with fire and other instructions, which all foreshadow the death and suffering of the Lamb of God? We call attention to the fact that Satan did not want to have the Lord Jesus put to death on the Passover feast. Satan knew He was the true Lamb, and he tried to prevent His death at the predicted time (Matt. 26:5; Mark 14:2). But the Lamb of God, the true Passover, died at the very time appointed, thus fulfilling the Scriptures. The shedding of the blood and its application is the prominent thing in the Passover. The word "pesach" means to "pass through," and "to pass over." God passed through Egypt in judgment; it was also liable to fall upon the people Israel. They were guilty before God and had deserved the same judgment which was about to fall upon Egypt. But Jehovah provided a sacrifice and in the shed blood a shelter and complete deliverance. The blood secured all they needed as a sinful people and as it was sprinkled in obedience to Jehovah's command perfect peace and rest was obtained. "When I see the blood, I will pass over you." The blood was the token for Jehovah. They were not to see the blood, but He in passing through saw the blood. *Faith* in what Jehovah had said and what had been done gave peace to all in the dwellings. The blood of Christ is thus blessedly foreshadowed. Peace has been made in the blood of the cross. Upon the Lamb of God, the holy Substitute, the sentence of death was executed and now whenever God sees the blood there He passes by, no more condemnation, but perfect justification. Wherever there is faith in the blood, there is the enjoyment of perfect peace. The blood of the Lamb and the assuring word of Jehovah, "When I see the blood I will pass over you," were the solid foundations of Israel's shelter and peace in that awful night of death and judgment. And they are our solid foundations too. We quote helpful words from another.[2]

"While outside the house the blood of atonement spoke to God, to whom it was addressed; inside He provided that which was to satisfy *them,* and enable them for that path with Him upon which they were now so shortly to go forth. The lamb is theirs to feed upon, and God is bent upon their enjoying this provision of His love. The lamb, too, must all of it be eaten. If the household were too little for the lamb (we read nothing of the lamb being too little for the house), then, says the Lord, let him and his neighbor next unto his house take it. God would have Christ apprehended by us. He would have our souls sustained, and He would have Christ honored. We are to *eat*—to appropriate to ourselves what Christ is; and what we appropriate becomes, in fact, part and parcel of ourselves. This laying hold of Christ by faith makes Christ to be sustenance indeed to us, and Himself to be reproduced in us.

"Death God ordains as the food of life; and it is as sheltered and saved from death that we can feed upon death. It is not merely vanquished and set aside; it is in the cross the sweet and wonderful display of divine power and love in our behalf, accomplished in the mystery of human weakness. Death is become the food of life, and the life is life eternal."

The eating of the Passover lamb (verses 9-11) is full of meaning. It is the type of feeding upon Christ, occupation with His blessed Person. And that is what we need to keep our feet in the way of peace.

The feast of unleavened bread is mentioned next. Leaven means corruption; it is the type of sin. The lesson of holiness, which God looks for in His redeemed people, is here before us. The old leaven must be purged out. The leaven of malice and wickedness must be put away (1 Cor. 5:6-8). We are delivered from the power of indwelling sin. Saved by grace our calling is to holiness. Spiritually to keep the feast of unleav-

---

[2]*Numerical Bible,* Vol. I, p. 172.

ened bread means to live in the energy of the new nature and that is the walk in the Spirit. The bitter herbs mentioned in verse 8 with the unleavened bread speak of self-denial and self-judgment. The terrible judgment fell that fourteenth day, or between the fourteenth and fifteenth day of Abib. All Jehovah had announced in judgment was literally carried out. There was not a house where there was not one dead. So God will yet put all His predicted judgments for this age into execution and a hardened world will find out the truth of His word.

Then the Exodus took place, and they left with the riches of the Egyptians. The whole experience of Israel in Egypt and their deliverance is typical of their coming final and glorious deliverance.

From Rameses (city of the sun) the city of earthly splendor, they went to Succoth, which means "booths." There pilgrim character is now brought out. The wilderness begins. Redemption by blood makes us pilgrims and strangers, for we are no longer of the world, though we are in it. The mixed multitude came along. They were Egyptians stirred up by the mighty judgment events, which had taken place (Numbers 11:4; Nehemiah 13:3). They became a snare to the Israelites.

A word on verses 40 and 41 will terminate these brief annotations of this remarkable chapter. The 430 years' sojourning does not mean that it was 430 years since Jacob and his sons had come to Egypt. "The self-same day" means the fifteenth day of the seventh month; it was the day on which Abraham left Ur to go forth in obedience to the divine command.

CHAPTER 13:1-16

The Sanctification of the Firstborn

1. The separation commanded (13:1-2)
2. Remember this day: the memorial (13:3-10)
3. The separation of the firstborn (13:11-16)

The firstborn had been delivered in a special manner in Egypt and because Jehovah had delivered them they were to be sanctified unto Him. There is an inseparable connection between redemption and holiness. What the Lord has redeemed He claims for Himself. Here we have a definition of sanctification; it is separation unto God. But let us notice that salvation out of the house of bondage is the foundation of all. The same order is more fully revealed in the New Testament. In Romans 3—5:11 we read of our salvation corresponding to the type in Exodus 12 and that is followed by the exhortation to holiness, separation unto God (chapter 6). We are saved unto holiness. The blood of atonement has sanctified us unto God. The more we realize this great redemption by blood, the more we shall yield ourselves and our members unto God.

Upon verse 9 and 16 as well as Deut. 6:4-9 and 11:13-21 the Hebrews have built their ordinance of the phylacteries. They use leather strips with Scripture verses contained in a small box. These they put at certain times when they pray upon their hand and forehead. Thus they try to fulfill these words literally. It is only an outward ceremony and corresponds to certain usages in ritualistic Christendom. They were to retain those commandments in their hearts and practise them as well. The ass is especially mentioned. Why? It is an unclean animal and used here to show that unredeemed man is on the same level with the ass and must either be redeemed or die.

6. Redemption by Power

CHAPTER 13:17-22

From Succoth to Etham

1. God's leading (13:17-18)
2. Joseph's bones carried away (13:19)
3. The pillar of cloud and the pillar of fire (13:20-22)

Jehovah now begins to lead His redeemed people forward. God chose their way for them, as He chooses the way for us. He was with His people, therefore He led them in His way. If His people are in His way He is with them and all is well. If we are not in His way He cannot be with us in the fullness of His power. What grace and tenderness is revealed in the fact that the Lord did not permit them to go through the land of the Philistines! They had to learn lessons in God's way, which they could never have learned in the shorter way through the land of the Philistines (Deut. 8:2-4). He wanted them to escape trials and other experiences which might discourage them. Nor were they fitted for the warfare which would have resulted from the journey through the country of the Philistines. He would not suffer to have them tried above that they were able to bear. He deals thus with all His people. "But God is faithful, who will not suffer you to be tempted above that ye are able;

but will with the temptation also make a way to escape that ye may be able to bear it" (1 Corinthians 10:13).

It was Moses who took the bones of Joseph with him. They must have rested in a magnificent sarcophagus known to Moses. Joseph's request was not forgotten. It may have been the word, which Israel remembered in the house of bondage; they did not lose sight of the fact that redemption had been promised and that Joseph had looked forward to it (Genesis 1:25). "And as the people bore his honored ashes through the desert, these being dead spoke of by-gone times, they linked the past and the present together, they deepened the national consciousness that Israel was a favored people, called to no common destiny, sustained by no common promises, pressing toward no common goal" (Bishop G. A. Chadwick).

The pillar of cloud and of fire was the outward sign of Jehovah's presence with His people. By day and by night He guarded and led His people. The Keeper of Israel does not sleep nor slumber. He journeys along with them. It was but one pillar and Jehovah was present in it (chapter 14:24). The glory of the Lord appeared in that cloud (16:10; 40:34; Numbers 9:15). That glory cloud filled Solomon's temple and was seen retreating and returning to heaven (Ezek. 11:22-25). It will be seen again when the King comes back from heaven's glory and His glory will be established over Jerusalem (Isaiah 4). The sign of the Son of Man may be the Shekinah cloud.

CHAPTER 14

The Pursuit of the Enemy and Redemption by Power

1. The coming of Pharaoh announced (14:1-4)
2. The pursuit and Israel troubled (14:5-12)
3. Moses speaks to the people (14:13-14)
4. The Lord speaks to Moses (14:15-18)
5. The passages through the Red Sea (14:19-22)
6. The Egyptians overthrown (14:23-29)
7. The great work accomplished (14:30-31)

While the marching host of Israel was ignorant of Pharaoh's device and the threatening danger, Jehovah's eye was watching every move the enemy made. He knew what Pharaoh would do and Jehovah had planned how to deliver Israel completely by His power from the Egyptians. That Jehovah might be honored upon Pharaoh and all his host, He told His people to encamp in a place which made their position, from a human standpoint, almost hopeless. They were hemmed in by mountains and the sea was in front of them and behind them the Egyptian host was soon to appear. Only the outlook upward to heaven was unobstructed. From there help had to come. Pharaoh appeared to bring them back into bondage. Then the unbelief of the redeemed people, whom Jehovah had so marvelously led forth, is manifested. Though their lot had been so severe in Egypt and Jehovah's power upon Egypt had been seen in the terrible judgments, yet they regretted that they had left Egypt. It was unbelief. They feared that the God who had taken such pains to deliver them out of Egypt, who had led them out and was visibly present with them, would now abandon them, so that they would die in the wilderness. How many Christians give way again and again to such an unreasonable doubt. "Unbelief leads to interpret God in the presence of the difficulty, instead of interpreting the difficulty in the presence of God. Faith gets behind the difficulty and there finds God in all His faithfulness, love and power."

Verses 13 and 14 are the words to faith. The Lord was now taking up their case and fighting their battles. It was no longer the question of Pharaoh and Israel, but Pharaoh and Jehovah. But notice the words are Moses' words, as given to him by the Spirit of God. After he had spoken them and assured the people that all their enemies were to be wiped out, he began to pray, for the Lord said to him, "Wherefore criest thou unto Me?" This is followed by the command to go forward, to stretch out the rod over the sea and the assurance that the sea would be divided so that they should pass through to the other side.

In verse 19 we learn that the Angel of God—that is Jehovah—who went before the camp of Israel, removed and went behind them. Thus the pillar of cloud descended between them and their enemies; they were involved in the deepest darkness, while Israel had light throughout the night. Moses did according to the word of the Lord. The east wind from the Lord caused the sea to go back; a strong wind, which blew all night, divided the sea. Higher criticism has tried to explain this miracle as a natural occurrence, but they overlooked the fact that on the right and on their left the waters were a wall. It was a grave, so to speak, into which Israel passed, when God's power had made the way through it. It was faith which led them through. "By faith they passed through the Red Sea as by dry land; which the Egyptians assaying to do, were drowned" (Hebrews 11:29).

When Pharaoh and his army followed to pursue them, Jehovah acted in judgment. "In the morning watch Jehovah looked unto the host of the Egyptians through the pillar of fire." It was not a thunderstorm which confused them, but they saw the Lord in His majesty and the fearful judgment overtook them after Moses had stretched out his hand over the sea. The overthrow of the Egyptians came "when the morning appeared." Not one of them remained, but Israel saw the Egyptians dead upon the seashore.

This great deliverance by the power of God has many lessons. It foreshadows the future judgment which is in store for the enemies of Israel, when the Lord "in the morning watch" looks upon them. Greater still are the typical lessons in connection with our redemption in Christ. The Red Sea is a type of the death of Christ. Deliverance from sin by being dead with Christ is the aspect which the Red Sea passage illustrates. It is the truth so fully brought out in Romans 6, 7 and 8. When Israel had passed through the Red Sea and reached the other side, we have a type of resurrection. Dead with Christ and risen with Him; our old enemy is gone, and we can look upon our enemies as dead. Many pages of annotations could be given in following this story. We must leave the fuller application to our readers. Victory is on our side. Redeemed by blood, God's power is with us, the power of His Spirit, who is given to us of God. We are not asked to fight our enemy, the old man, or to subdue him. God has done this for us in the death of Christ.

7. The Song of Redemption

CHAPTER 15:1-21

1. Jehovah acknowledged and praised (15:1-2)
2. The victory celebrated as His victory (15:3-10)
3. His holiness praised (15:11-13)
4. His enemies tremble (15:14-16)
5. Thou shalt bring them in (15:17-18)
6. The judgment and salvation (15:19)
7. The women's chorus (15:20-21)

This is a great chapter. It is the first song in the Bible. In Egypt was no singing for Israel but only weeping and groaning. Nor did they sing in Babylon (Psalm 137:2-4). There is to be a future song for Israel in connection with their coming great deliverance (Isaiah 12). Moses sang this song. It is his first song; his last song is that great prophetic outburst recorded by him in Deut. 32. The song of Moses, the servant of God, is mentioned in Rev. 15:3.

This whole song breathes the spirit of praise and worship. The destructive criticism has not left this song unchallenged. They object to it on account of the prophetic utterance in verses 17 and 18, as if this were impossible to say at that time, thus ruling out the inspiration by the Holy Spirit. A closer study of this song will be very profitable. Note the expression "Jehovah is a *man* of war." This foreshadows His incarnation and His coming as the mighty King, who conquers his enemies (Psalm 45:3; 46:8-9; Isaiah 63:1-7, Revelation 19:11). The whole song is prophetic. What Jehovah has done in the judgment of His enemies and the complete deliverance of His people that He will do again. It is interesting to compare this outburst of praise in which Miriam[3] (Mary) and the women joined with the song of praise of Hannah (1Sam 2:1-10), the praise of the mother of our Lord, Mary, in Luke 1:46-55, and Zechariah's words in Luke 1:68-79. The whole atmosphere of Exodus 15:1-21 is that of praise and adoration, joy and victory; such is yet in store for the earth and for Israel, when that goal is reached, of which verse 18 speaks, "Jehovah shall reign forever and ever."

Exodus 12 foreshadows our deliverance from the guilt of sins (Romans 1—5:11). Chapter 13 teaches God's claim on those He has delivered, which is separation unto Himself. Chapter 14 tells in type of our deliverance from the power of sin. The song of redemption contained in chapter 15 points us to the beautiful ending of Romans 8, the song which every delivered believer can sing (Romans 8:31-39).

II. The Journey Towards the Promised Land and Israel at Sinai

1. The Experiences in the Wilderness

CHAPTER 15:22-27

In the Wilderness of Shur

1. Marah (15:22-26)
2. Elim (15:27)

---

[3]Miriam is significantly called "Aaron's sister," not Moses'. She could not rank with Moses. Leadership did not belong to her. She was subordinate to Moses, as Aaron was.

They went out into the wilderness of Shur. Shur was a great wall of protection which Egypt had erected. The surrounding country was called by that name. The trials of the wilderness journey at once begin; typical of our passage as redeemed ones through this world. Redemption has for a consequence the wilderness. We are in Christ crucified unto the world and the world unto us. The bitter waters are the first wilderness experience of the nation. It is a hint of what their subsequent history would be. Naomi in the book of Ruth called herself "Mara." "Marah," the bitterness, is the perfect picture of the world under sin and death. Then came the first wilderness murmuring. Six more are reported in Exodus and Numbers: Exodus 16:2; 17:2,3; Numbers 11:33, 34; 14:2; 16:41; 21:5. God had a remedy. The tree is typical of the cross. The tree was not discovered by Moses, but by Jehovah. Christ went into the deep, dark waters of death; by Him the waters were made sweet for those who believe on Him. Now the bitterness of death is passed, and if we find the bitterness in the world through which we pass as pilgrims and strangers and we follow the path which He went while in the world, then murmuring will be forever excluded if the heart sees Christ and following in His steps, looks upon every bitter experience as the fellowship of His sufferings. Compare the tree for healing with Rev. 22:2.

In verse 26 Jehovah speaks of Himself as *"Jehovah Ropheka,"* the Lord thy Healer. The bitter waters showed them that they needed Jehovah in the wilderness as much as they needed Him in their deliverance from Egypt and Pharaoh's power. And now He offers Himself as their healer. He takes gracious care of His people while they follow Him in the path of obedience. Some have pressed this promise to such an extent that they say sickness in a Christian is the result of direct disobedience; a Christian has no need of being sick, etc. This is wrong, and has led into theories which are far from sane and scriptural.

Marah is followed by Elim with its twelve wells of water and seventy palm trees. A beautiful oasis in the desert, giving them a foretaste of Canaan. What a place of refreshing and peace it must have been. So in our experience many a Marah is followed by an Elim, as the cross is followed by the crown. Elim means "trees," and they must have been of luxuriant growth, planted by the wells of waters. So Israel after their Marah experience, when Jehovah has forgiven their sins and healed all their diseases, in the day of their future blessing and glory, will be like trees planted at the water brooks and will draw water out of the wells of salvation (Isaiah 12:3).

CHAPTER 16

In the Wilderness of Sin

1. The renewed murmuring (16:1-3)
2. The bread from heaven promised (16:4-10)
3. The promise fulfilled and the quails and bread given (16:11-14)
4. Instructions concerning the gathering (16:16-18)
5. The manna corrupted (16:19-21)
6. The manna and the Sabbath (16:22-31)
7. The manna kept for a memorial (16:32-36)

After they removed from Elim, they encamped by the Red Sea (Numbers 33:10). They came into the wilderness of sin. The Hebrew word means "thorn," the bush in which Jehovah had appeared to Moses in the Hebrew is "Sineh," a thornbush. The second murmuring takes place. This gives a deep glimpse into the desperately wicked condition of the human heart. God had brought them out of the house of bondage; they wished themselves back. God had sheltered them beneath the blood; they wished the judgment might have carried them away. They were ready to leave the ground of redemption, guided by Jehovah, and turn back to Pharaoh to become slaves once more. What infinite patience and grace the Lord manifested toward them. All this is repeated in the lives of many believers. It need not to be so and it will not, if Christ and the redemption we have in Him as well as our glorious inheritance which is before us, is a reality in our lives.

Heaven offers now to minister to the daily need of such a people. The glory of the Lord was seen again out of the cloud (verse 7, 10). The bread from Heaven was given. It is described as small in size, round, white like coriander seed, like wafers made with honey and hard. Rationalists have tried to explain the giving of this bread in a natural way. In a certain part of the desert is found a tree from which exudes at certain times an eatable gum and falls to the ground in the form of small cakes; this, it is claimed, explains the manna. But they do not explain how it is that the Israelites received the manna in every part of the desert, that they received it in such immense quantities that the hundred thousands were fed by it and it lasted for forty years. It ceased as miraculously as it was given (Josh. 5:12). The word "manna" is from the Hebrew "Man-hu," the question, "What is that?" It is designated as the bread from heaven (Psalm 78:24; 105:40). Our Lord speaks of it as the bread from heaven in John 6, a chapter which is of importance in connection with the typical meaning of the manna. But quails were given first and in the morning dew, and after it arose, the manna. The quails and the manna are both the types of Christ, the food for God's people. The dew after which the manna is seen, speaks of the Holy Spirit, who ministers Christ. Each gathered the bread which had come down according to his eating. Each got what he wanted, and not more. So Christ meets the need we have of Him if only our need of Him were greater and felt more.

It could not be hoarded up, but had to be gathered every morning. We must feed on Christ daily in living faith. Yesterday's experience and enjoyment cannot feed us to-day. We must gather afresh, and let the dew, the Holy Spirit, minister to our hearts. Many live on past experiences, and become puffed up. Stagnation and corruption follow. The Sabbath is mentioned in connection with the manna and it is the *first time* that the Sabbath for Israel as a nation is spoken of. To feed on Christ, the bread from heaven, means rest for the soul. The keeping of the manna in the golden pot (Hebrews 9:4) tells us of what our Lord said concerning the bread from heaven, "He that eateth of this bread shall live forever." The true manna endureth to eternal life and we shall eat in His own presence in glory "the hidden manna" (Revelation 2:17).

CHAPTER 17

At Rephidim

1. The water from the rock (17:1-7)
2. The conflict with Amalek (17:8-16)

From Sin they went to Dophkah and Alush before they came to Rephidim (Numbers 33:12, 13). Again there was no water and Moses feared they might stone him. Without following the historical record we point out some of the most interesting lessons of the two events at Rephidim. The Rock is a type of Christ. Jehovah stood upon the rock to be smitten, even as "God was in Christ" (2 Cor. 5:19). The smiting by the rod, used in judgment upon the river of Egypt, is the type of the death of Christ. There could be no water till the rock was smitten. There could be no water till Christ had died. The water from the cleft rock is the type of the Holy Spirit, who was given as the result of the finished work of Christ. Exodus 16 and 17 go together and John 6 and 7 go together likewise. In Exodus 16 we find the manna and in John 6 the bread of life. In Exodus 17 the water out of the rock, the type of the Holy Spirit; in John 7 the Lord Jesus announces the coming gift of the Holy Spirit. "If any man thirst, let him come unto Me and drink. He that believeth on Me, as the Scripture hath said, out of his belly shall flow rivers of living water. But this He spake of the Spirit, which they that believe on Him should receive; for the Holy Spirit was not yet given, because that Jesus was not yet glorified" (John 7:37-39). "They drank of that spiritual Rock that followed them, and that Rock was Christ" (1 Corinthians 10:4).

The first conflict followed. There was no conflict at the Red Sea, but immediately after the water had been given in such wonderful abundance, Amalek appeared. Amalek is the type of the flesh. The conflict illustrates Galations 5:17. "The flesh lusteth against the Spirit, and the Spirit against the flesh, and these are contrary, the one to the other, so that ye should not do the things ye would." The flesh and its lusts, which war against the soul (1 Peter 2:11), are represented by Amalek. And Amalek attacked Israel, and Israel, Amalek. The attack was made when Israel in unbelief had asked, "Is the Lord among us or not?" Even so, when God's people do not reckon in faith with the presence and the power of the Lord the flesh rises up; but if we walk in the Spirit we shall not fulfill the lusts of the flesh.

Joshua is here mentioned for the first time. He was twenty-seven years younger than Moses, that is fifty-three years. He is the type of the Lord Jesus Christ, the captain of our salvation. Moses, on top of the hill, represents Christ risen from the dead and at God's right hand, to appear in the presence of God for us as our advocate. Aaron and Hur at Moses' side typify His priesthood of loving sympathy and His righteousness. ("Hur" means "white," the color used for righteousness.) But the hands of Christ never hang down. He ever liveth and intercedes for us.

Amalek is not destroyed and the flesh is not. Amalek's end comes when Christ comes (see Numbers 24:17-20). The conflict with Amalek, the flesh, continues as long as we are in the body.

In verse 14 we have the first command to

Moses to write. Not so long ago critics claimed that writing at Moses' time was unknown. The tablets of Lachish and Tel-el-Amarna have silenced this foolish assertion. The memorial altar, "Jehovah Nissi," the Lord is my banner, tells us of victory. "The assurance of victory should be as complete as the sense of forgiveness, seeing both alike are founded upon the great fact that Jesus died and rose again. It is in the power of this that the believer enjoys a purged conscience and subdues indwelling sin. The death of Christ having answered all the claims of God in reference to our sins, His resurrection becomes the spring of power in all the details of conflict afterwards. He died *for* us, and now He lives *in* us. The former gives us peace, the latter gives us power."

CHAPTER 18

Moses and Jethro

1. The coming of Jethro (18:1-5)
2. Moses' and Jethro's communion (18:6-12)
3. Jethro's advice (18:13-23)
4. Moses' action (18:24-27)

This chapter concludes the first section of the second part of Exodus. We have in it a beautiful dispensational foreshadowing of things to come. God had redeemed Israel, delivered them from Pharaoh's host, manifested His power and had given them victory. The priest of Midian, a Gentile, now comes, having heard all that Jehovah had done for Moses and for Israel, his people. Zipporah, Moses' wife, and his two sons are with him. What a happy reunion. And there was praise unto Jehovah from the lips of the Gentile as well as burnt offering and sacrifices for God. It foreshadows what will take place when Israel is finally restored and delivered. Then the Gentiles will come and "many nations shall be joined unto the Lord in that day" (Zech. 2:11). Read Jeremiah 16:14-21. First Jehovah's power in the restoration of His scattered people is mentioned; then the coming of the Gentiles is announced. "The Gentiles shall come unto thee from the ends of the earth."

Moses judging, and the faithful men, fearing God, judging with him, may well remind us of that day, when He who is greater than Moses will judge the earth in righteousness. Then we shall have share with Him. "Do ye not know that the saints shall judge the world?" (1 Cor. 6:2).

What grace is and grace has done and will do is the most beautiful and precious revelation of Exodus up to the end of the eighteenth chapter. Jehovah took notice of the poor slaves. He heard their cry. He sent them a deliverer. He smote Egypt with great tribulation and judgment. He sheltered His people under the blood. He led them forth as His redeemed people. Their enemies perished through His power and He brought them through the Red Sea. He gave them bread from heaven and water out of the rock. Victory was on their side and the glory of His name extended to the Gentiles. But over our brief and imperfect annotations we have to write, "Not the half has been told."

2. At Sinai: The Covenant and the Law

CHAPTER 19

Israel at Sinai and the Covenant

1. Israel before Mount Sinai (19:1-2)
2. The covenant and calling of Israel stated (19:3-6)
3. The covenant accepted (19:7-15)
4. The glory of the Lord at Sinai (19:16-25)

Sinai is mentioned 31 times in the Pentateuch and only three times more in the rest of the Old Testament. In the New Testament the word occurs only in Acts 7:30, 38 and Gal. 4:24, 25. The place where the law was given is a barren wilderness of high towering rocks. Moses went up to God and Jehovah reminded the people first of all of His gracious dealing with them. Then He revealed His purposes concerning them as a nation. They were to be His peculiar treasure above all people and to be unto Him a kingdom of priests and an holy nation. This purpose is founded upon a theocracy, that is, He Himself would reign over them as King. For this He must ask obedience from them. How else could they be a kingdom of priests and a separated people, unless they harkened to His voice, and kept His covenant? But it is still the purpose of grace. Jehovah in His grace would make all this possible if they had received it. The law which followed, with its principle, obedience, as the place of blessing, never led to the realization of Israel's calling, nor ever will. When at least Israel becomes the kingdom of priests, it will be through grace and not of works.

It was a fatal thing, which all the people did when they answered together, "all that the Lord hath spoken we will do." It was a presumptuous declaration, which sprang from self-confidence and showed clearly that they had no appreciation for that grace which had visited them in Egypt and brought them hitherto. They had received grace, they needed grace. With the vow they had made, they had put themselves under the law. The legal covenant had its beginning with the rejection of the covenant of grace, and the legal covenant ends with the acceptance of grace. God permitted all this for a wise purpose. For what the law serves, why it was given, is fully answered in the New Testament (See Romans 7 and Galatians 3). In this we cannot enter here.

At once the scene changes. The character of the law they had chosen and its ministration unto death is manifested in the outward phenomena of clouds and darkness and in the first mention of death since they had left Egypt. "Whosoever toucheth the mount shall surely be put to death." On the third day the glory of the Lord appeared. The thunderings, lightnings, the trumpet, the trembling of the mountain, the voice of God, which accompany the manifestation of Jehovah, may be traced throughout the Bible. All this will be repeated in His glorious second coming. (Deut. 33:1-3; 1 Sam. 2:10; Psalm 18:7-16; Heb. 3; Rev. 10:4, etc.)

CHAPTER 20

The Covenant Revealed

1. The Ten Commandments (20:1-17)
2. Jehovah's gracious provision (20:18-26)

This law covenant is now stated. It was given three times. First orally here, when God spake all these words. Then in Exodus 31 Moses received the tables of stone, "written with the finger of God," the same finger which later wrote on earth in the sand (John 8). The first tables were broken and Moses was commanded to hew two tables of stone upon which Jehovah again wrote the Ten Commandments (Ex. 34:1). This law was given to Israel exclusively, which is seen in the opening word. The voice of God spoke these words so that the people heard Him speak. In what sense the law was given by the ministration of angels (Acts 7:53; Gal, 3:19, Heb. 2:2) is not revealed here. Our Lord has divided the Ten Commandments into two sections. The first three go together and speak of duties towards God and the seven which follow of duties towards our fellowmen. And He who gave this law expounded the law and filled it full when He appeared on earth in humiliation. And after He lived that holy life on earth He went to the cross and the curse of the law rested upon Him (Gal. 3:13). The law given in these commandments shows man's condition. Most of the commandments are negative, "thou shalt *not.*" It is a prohibition of the will and natural tendency of man. Man is a sinner, and the law was given to make a full demonstration of it. Read Rom. 5:12-14, 20; 7:6-13; Gal. 3:19-29. May we fully understand that this law cannot give righteousness nor life and that it is not in force as the rule for the Christian in order to receive blessing from God. We are not under that law but under grace. But grace teaches us to live righteously, soberly and godly in this present evil age. The righteous requirements of the law are fulfilled in us, who walk according to the Spirit.

The altar is mentioned and in the sacrifice we behold Christ. "But further, God will meet the sinner at an altar without a hewn stone or a step—a place of worship which requires no human workmanship to erect, or human effort to approach. The former could only pollute, and the latter could only display human 'nakedness.' Admirable type of the meeting place where God meets the sinner now, even the Person and work of His Son, Jesus Christ, where all the claims of law, of justice, and of conscience are perfectly answered! Man has, in every age and in every clime, been prone, in one way or another, to 'lift up his tool' in the erection of his altar, or to approach thereto by steps of his own making; but the issue of all such attempts has been 'pollution' and 'nakedness.' "[4]

CHAPTER 21

Different Judgments

1. Master and servant (21:1-11)
2. Concerning injury to the person (21:12-32)
3. Concerning property (21:33-36)

The Three Chapters which follow the giving of the Ten Commandments give the practical application of the decalogue in the daily life. The duties towards the fellowmen are demonstrated in part. There are seven sections to these three chapters; each section contains ten precepts.

The servant occupies the first place. He was to obtain his freedom for nothing after serving six years. In Deuteronomy we read that the

[4]C. H. Mackintosh, *Notes on Exodus.*

master is commanded not to let him go empty-handed, but give him of his flock, his threshing floor and his winepress. In this Israel was to remember their own deliverance from the house of bondage (Deut. 15:12-18). If the servant chose to remain with his master forever, his ear was to be bored through as the sign of perpetual servitude. This was a custom in other nations as well and signified that the servant was, as it were, fastened by the awl to the house (Deut. 15:17).

The Hebrew servant is put so prominently in the foreground because the Son of God became a servant and has chosen the perpetual service. Psalm 40:6 and Hebrews 10:5 show that it is typical of the Lord Jesus Christ. Notice what it says in our chapter: "And if the servant shall plainly say, I love my master, my wife and my children, I will not go out free." It was love which decided the Hebrew servant to be a servant forever. And it was love which brought Him to this earth to do the Father's will, and love for the church. "He loved the church and gave Himself for it." And He loves us as individuals. This corresponds to the love of the servant to his wife and his children. Christ was a servant on earth; He is serving in glory now as the priest and advocate of His people, and in glory "He will gird Himself . . . and will come forth and serve them" (Luke 12:37).

This is followed by judgments concerning the injury of a person. Injury of a person had to be punished in a manner corresponding to the injury. The principle of retribution is marked throughout these laws. Smiting father or mother, man-stealing, and cursing the parents was punishable with death. Many pages might be written to follow these laws in detail. Read verses 23-27, and compare with Matthews 5:38-48.

Notice again the mention of the servant in verse 32. The price of a servant was thirty shekels of silver. The redemption price of a free Israelite was fifty shekels (Lev. 27:3); that of a slave, thirty shekels. How it reminds us again of Him who was sold for thirty pieces of silver (Deut. 11:12).

CHAPTER 22

Further Judgments

1. Concerning theft (22:1-5)
2. Concerning neglect in case of fire (22:6)
3. Concerning dishonesty (22:7-15)
4. Concerning immoralities and forbidden things (22:16-20)
5. Concerning oppression (22:21-28)
6. Concerning offerings to God (22:29-31)

These laws need no further comment; they are good and just. The wisdom of them is the wisdom from above. We call attention to verse 18: "Thou shalt not suffer a witch to live." The nations with which Israel came in contact were given to the most satanic cults and the powers of Satan were manifested among them. Demoniacal possessions abounded, and witchcraft, sorceries, asking the dead, and other abominations were practised. Witchcraft and sorceries, communicating with the wicked spirits is therefore more than a possibility. It can be traced throughout the history of the human race and whenever nations ripened for judgment this form of evil became prominent. The female sex was then, as it is still the case, principally addicted to this sin. In our day it flourishes in spiritualism, Christian Science, theosophy, and other cults.

CHAPTER 23

Further Judgments and Directions

1. Concerning unrighteous dealings of various kinds (23:1-9)
2. Concerning the seventh year (23:10-13)
3. Concerning the three feasts (23:14-19)
4. Promises concerning the possession of the land (23:20-33)

We call attention to the words concerning the seventh year. The seventh day was the day of rest. The seventh year was to give the land rest; it was to rest and lie still. Besides this there was the jubilee year, which occurred every seven times seven years, that is, the fiftieth year was the year of jubilee, in which liberty was proclaimed. We hope to examine this more closely and learn its typical and prophetic significance when we read the book of Leviticus (chapter 25). The seventh year was especially meant for the poor. Whatever grew by itself belonged to them, and what they left the beasts of the field were to eat. What gracious provision this was! How merciful and gracious our God is!

The three feasts are next mentioned. The connection with verse 13 is obvious. It is a warning concerning other gods. The feasts were designed to keep Jehovah, His power and His grace, as a living reality before the nation. The three feasts are: The feast of unleavened bread in memory of the exodus; the feast of the first fruits, also called the feast of weeks, because it came seven weeks after the feast of unleavened bread (Lev. 23:15-16; Deut. 16:9), and still another name is "the feast of the first fruits of the wheat harvest." It was now known by the name of *Shavuoth.* The third feast came on the fifteenth day of the seventh month (Lev 23:34), and is the feast of ingathering, known as *Succoth,* the feast of tabernacles. Of all this we shall learn more in Leviticus. The last clause of verse 19 has led to ridiculous speculations among the rabbis. It is looked upon by the Jews as a prohibition against eating flesh prepared with milk (see Deuteronomy 14:21).

We must not overlook in our study verses 20-23. Who is this angel? He is called in chapter 33:15, "the face of Jehovah" (literal translation). The name of God is in Him; God revealed Himself in Him. His voice must be obeyed. He has power to pardon transgressions or not to pardon them. This angel is not a created being, but the same who appeared in the burning bush; the same of whom Jacob said, "The angel, the Redeemer." It is Jehovah Himself, the Son of God. The ancient synagogue paraphrased this person by using the expression "Memra," which means "the Word." They have believed and taught that "the Word" brought Israel out of Egypt; "the Word" led them in the pillar of a cloud; "the Word" confounded the Egyptian host. And they paraphrased "the angel" by "the Word."

CHAPTER 24

The Ratification of the Covenant and the Glory of Jehovah

1. Moses called into Jehovah's presence (24:1-2)
2. The covenant ratified and the sprinkling with blood (24:3-8)
3. In the presence of God and Jehovah's glory (24:9-18)

This chapter is a fitting conclusion of this second section of the second part. It begins with the giving of the law and ends with the glory of the Lord. Moses alone was to come near to Jehovah; Aaron, Nadab and Abihu with the seventy elders of Israel, had to worship afar. Moses is a type of Christ in his exclusive privilege and attitude. Twice the people make the promise to keep the covenant, not realizing what they were doing. Then the blood was sprinkled upon the altar, upon the book of the covenant (Heb. 9:19), and on the people. In this way the covenant was ratified. This sprinkling of the blood here has not the meaning of atonement. It rather stands for the penalty of the broken covenant. The blood standing for life given, was a solemn warning that the penalty of disobedience would be death. At the same time the offerings and the blood point to Christ. He came and took the curse of the law upon Himself. When He came to give His life a ransom for many, the people, so occupied with the ordinances, the law and the traditions of men, cried, "This blood be upon us and upon our children." Ever since blood-guiltiness rests upon them and the curse of their own law is their portion till they shall look upon Him whom they have pierced.

The people were afar off; the leaders were not to come nigh, and had to worship afar off. The blood of the Lord Jesus Christ, however, makes nigh and we can draw nigh. The legal covenant ever puts man into a solemn and guilty distance from God; the covenant of Grace brings man nigh to God. The presence and glory of God appeared. Moses was on the mount forty days and forty nights.

3. The Tabernacle and the Priesthood

CHAPTER 25

The Tabernacle

1. The freewill offering and the materials (25:1-9)
2. The ark (25:10-22)
3. The table of showbread (25:23-30)
4. The golden candlestick (25:31-40)

This is another intensely interesting portion of this great book. To give a few annotations and hints on the tabernacle is an extremely difficult task, for there is such a wonderful mine of wealth here that a book of hundreds of pages could not contain all.

The tabernacle concerning which the Lord instructed Moses was the earthly place of worship of Israel; it was the means of a continued relationship of a holy God with a sinful people. But besides this the tabernacle and its worship foreshadow in the completest way the person and work of our Lord Jesus Christ. The epistle to the Hebrews bears witness to this. The types in the tabernacle are simply inexhaustible. The word "tabernacle" in the Hebrew is *mishkan,* which means dwelling-place. The construction and arrangement were not left to man. God gave Moses the instructions and showed to him a pattern.

The materials are mentioned first, and they are to be supplied by His willing people. The Hebrew expression is literally, "every one whom his heart drove." Only His people, not strangers, could furnish the material. And they had to give with the heart. The same principle holds good in the New Testament. The support of the Lord's work by unsaved people and the methods of the world are wrong; they have not the blessing of God. We do not touch upon the materials now, but shall do so later.

The ark of shittim wood is the first thing mentioned. Man builds differently. Man lays first a foundation, builds the walls, works from the outside to the inside. God begins within. The ark with the mercy seat is where Jehovah dwelt, "between the Cherubim." It is, therefore, a type of Christ. The shittim wood, that is, acacia, grows in the desert, out of a dry ground (Is. 53:2). It is of all the wood the most durable, almost imperishable. We have in it the type of the humanity of Christ. The gold which covered it is typical of His deity. The mercy seat fitted the ark. It was of the same dimensions as the ark. The Hebrew word is *kapporeth,* which means covering, and has reference to atonement. The two cherubim faced each other and looked down upon the mercy seat, where the blood was sprinkled. They are always seen in the Word in connection with the throne (Ezek. 1; Rev. 4). Beautiful is verse 22.

The table of showbread still tells us of Christ, for it is of the same material as the ark. What was on the table, the showbread and all its blessed lessons we shall consider in Leviticus. The table and the bread are typical of Christ, who sustains us in fellowship with God.

The golden candlestick is the next article of furniture described. It was of pure gold. Three times almonds are mentioned. From the book of Numbers we learn that the almond, on the blossoming rod of Aaron, is the type of Christ in resurrection. The candlestick typifies Christ in heaven's glory, outshining the glory of God. It also is the type of Him, risen from the dead, giving the Holy Spirit, who is seen as the sevenfold Spirit in the candlestick. See and compare with Rev. 1:4, 13, 20; 3:1 and 4:5.

CHAPTER 26

The Tabernacle and its Construction

1. The curtains (26:1-6)
2. The coverings (26:7-14)
3. The boards (26:15-30)
4. The vail (26:31-35)
5. The hangings for the door (26:36-37)

While the tabernacle is a type of the heavenly places (Heb. 9:23) it is also a type of Christ, who tabernacled among men. The wonderful foreshadowings we find here down to the minutest details is an evidence of inspiration. We must confine ourselves to a very few things.

The colors used were blue, purple, scarlet and white. Blue is the color of heaven, purple that of royalty, scarlet the color of blood, and the white tells of righteousness. The ten curtains of fine twined linen which surrounded the tabernacle typify the holy, spotless humanity of our Lord. How the colors tell out the blessed story of the gospel, that heaven's King came down to shed His blood, we need not to follow in detail. The loops of blue and taches of gold which unite the curtains tell of Him likewise.

"We have here displayed to us, in the 'loops of *blue*,' and 'taches of *gold*,' that *heavenly* grace and *divine* energy in Christ which enabled Him to combine and perfectly adjust the claims of God and man; so that in responding to both the one and the other, He never for a moment marred the unity of His character."

The curtains of goats' hair were to be a tent over the tabernacle and the tent had other coverings of rams' skins, dyed red, and covering of badgers' skin. These coverings hid the ten curtains of the fine twined linen, and their beauty. Thus He was not beheld in His lovely character when on earth. The goats' hair covering reminds us of the divine statement, "He hath no form nor comeliness; and when we shall see Him, there is no beauty that we should desire Him" (Is 53:2). The rams' skins, dyed red, are the symbol of His devotion and obedience to God, even unto the death of the cross. The badgers' skins are taken to mean His holy determination and steadfastness.

Christ and his people are typified in the board of shittim wood (the same as in the ark and the table) resting in the sockets of silver. The silver was the ransom money (chapter 30:11-13); out of it the sockets were made (chapter 38:25-28). The whole frame work of the tabernacle rested in that which tells of atonement. Thus we stand in Christ and we are one with Him, separated from the world as the boards were separated from the earthly sockets of silver. And as we look upon this frame work, with the bars of shittim wood uniting the boards (typical of Christ) we may well think of Eph. 2:21: "In whom all the building fitly framed together groweth unto an holy temple in the Lord."

The vail as described in verses 31-35 is interpreted in Heb. 10:2. It marked the division of the holy and the most holy, or Holy of Holies. Like the inner curtains this vail typifies the holy humanity of our Lord. That vail barred the entrance into the presence of God. But it was rent by the hand of God, when our Lord had laid down His life on the cross. Christ is the way into the presence of God, "by a new and living way, which He hath consecrated for us, through the vail, that is to say, His flesh." Therefore we have boldness to enter into the holiest by the blood of Jesus. The hanging for the door of the tent has the same meaning, Christ the way.

CHAPTER 27

The Tabernacle Concluded

1. The altar of brass (27:1-8)
2. The court of the tabernacle (27:9-19)
3. The oil for the lamp (27:20-21)

The brazen altar stood at the door of the tabernacle. Later we find in this book the golden altar of incense mentioned. It stood between the golden candlestick and the brazen altar. This altar was likewise of shittim wood. Instead of gold, here was brass, because the altar is the type of the cross where Christ met the burning heat of divine justice. Upon this altar the burnt offering was brought and wholly consumed, speaking of Him who knew no sin and was made sin for us. The altar was hollow, the sacrificial fires burned mostly within. This tells of His work on the cross and the sufferings "within," when He was forsaken of God; they are for us unfathomable. The horns on the four corners of the altar indicated that His great work on the cross should go forth in worldwide proclamation.

The court of the tabernacle had for a wall fine twined linen. This was symbolical of the righteousness of God. This excludes the sinner from His presence. But there was a gate (verse 16) in which the colors reappeared. Blue, purple and scarlet were seen there. The gate typifies Christ. If an Israelite entered through that gate in the linen wall, which shut him out, he found, after entering in, that the same fine twined linen shut him in. Even so, if we enter in through the one door, Christ, the righteousness of God which condemned us, covers us. There were also hooks and fillets of silver and sockets of brass, telling once more the story of atonement and divine righteousness executed in judgment.

CHAPTER 28

The Priesthood

1. Aaron and his sons (28:1)
2. The garments mentioned (28:2-4)
3. The ephod (28:5-14)
4. The breastplate (28:15-30)
5. The robe of the ephod (28:31-35)
6. The mitre (28:35-38)
7. The ordinary garments (28:39-43)

This chapter is still richer in typical lessons, a very few of them we can notice. Two chapters are devoted to the priesthood. Aaron is the type of Christ. The sons of Aaron are types of Christians representing false worshippers (Nadab and Abihu) and true worshippers (Eleazar and Ithamar.) The holy garments are mentioned first, but not in the order as they were put on. The correct order is found in Leviticus 8:7-9. The garments were for glory and beauty, typifying Him who is altogether lovely. The ephod stands first. Ephod in Hebrew means "to bind on"; it held the breastplate in position. It was of gold, blue, purple, of scarlet, fine twined linen, with cunning work. How beautifully it was wrought we read in Exodus 39:3. The same material as in the curtains was used in the ephod; gold is added and the figures of the cherubim are absent. It all tells us of Himself and His priestly service in behalf of His people. The two onyx stones Aaron wore on his shoulders with the names of the twelve tribes engraven, are the type of Christ, carrying His people upon His shoulders. The shoulder is the symbol of power. From the moment He puts His sheep He has found upon His shoulder (Luke 15:5) to the blessed day, when He gathers His own, He carries them in His power.

Read verse 11 how these names were put into the stones. They were ineffaceable and could not be blotted out. It speaks of our security in Christ. The breastplate consisted of twelve stones. Every one of these stones has a meaning, which we cannot follow here, and the names of the twelve tribes were engraved upon these precious stones. The breastplate was "upon his heart when he goeth in unto the holy place." The words "upon his heart" are twice repeated in verse 30. Here we have the blessed type that Christ carries all His people upon His heart of love. That the breastplate be not loosed from the ephod (verses 26-28) blue lace was attached. There was no possibility that the breastplate could shift; there is no possibility that His love for His own can ever grow less. His power and

His love go together. In the breastplate there were also placed "Urim and Thummim," which means "lights and perfections." Seven times they are mentioned: Ex. 28:30; Lev 8:8; Num. 27:21; Deut. 33:8; 1 Sam. 28:6; Ezra 2:63; Neh. 7:65. In two of these passages only Urim is mentioned and in Deut. 33:8 Thummim stands first. It is not certain in what the Urim and Thummim consisted. Some think they were two costly stones drawn as a lot in difficult questions. Others think it was one stone which by various scintillations gave an answer from the Lord. Israel did not need to be in darkness about any matter. We possess as believers a gift in us to guide and direct our steps; it is the Holy Spirit. He is our Urim and Thummim. The robe of the ephod was entirely blue. Christ is our *heavenly* highpriest. Bells and pomegranates, the types of testimony and fruit, were around the robe. "His sound shall be heard when he goeth in." That happened when He as a priest went in to God and Holy Spirit came and the gospel bells began to ring. And fruit in the conversion of souls ever followed. The bells also rang when Aaron came out from the presence of God. Even so when our Lord comes again a fresh testimony in power will be heard yielding wonderful fruit.

The "holy crown" Aaron wore is equally suggestive. "Holiness unto the Lord" was on the golden plate. So He is our holy Priest and we are holy priests with Him. Read Zech. 14:20, 21.

CHAPTER 29

The Consecration of the Priests

1. Aaron and his sons wash with water (29:1-4)
2. Aaron clothed (29:5-7)
3. The consecration (29:8-25)
4. The food of the priests (29:26-35)
5. God's meeting place (29:36-46)

In Leviticus we find the record of their consecration, which is linked there with the offerings. Here it is only the instruction, while in Leviticus we find the act of the consecration. We touch upon it briefly; in Leviticus, we shall follow it a little closer. First they were washed with water. This is the type of the washing of regeneration. It stands for the new birth, which is by the water (the Word) and the Spirit (John 3:5). It is the one washing of which our Lord spoke to Peter (John 13:10). This puts all believers into the position of priests before God; we are a holy priesthood. But Aaron towers above his sons; we see him separated from them (verses 5-7). This is on account of typifying Christ. Aaron was washed with water like his sons because he was a sinner. It made him typically what Christ is essentially, that is, holy. The sons of Aaron represent Christians; all true believers are one with Christ as Aaron's sons were. But Aaron was anointed alone before the blood was shed, besides wearing already his priestly garments. In this he is a very striking type of our Lord. He was anointed with the oil, the Holy Spirit, in virtue of what He is in Himself.

Notice the sacrifices brought. First, Aaron and his sons put their hands upon the head of the bullock, which was then slain. The blood was put upon the horns of the altar, and then all the blood was poured at the base of the altar. It was a sin offering. Then there were two rams. The first one was for a burnt offering. The significance of these different offerings we shall examine in the book of Leviticus. The blood of the second ram was put upon the tip of the right ear, the thumb of the right hand, and the great toe of the right foot of Aaron and his sons. The ram was killed after they had laid their hands upon his head. Then the blood and the anointing oil was sprinkled upon them and their garments. This was the consecration proper. It tells us how they were set apart completely. Thus in redemption we are set apart to be a holy priesthood, to have our ears open to hear His voice and receive from Him, the hand set apart to act for Him, and the foot to walk with Him. In all this we see Christ and ourselves linked by grace with Him, as Aaron's sons were so fully identified with Aaron.

Then there was the wave offering put into the hands of Aaron and his sons, and what this wave offering was is learned from verses 22, 23. It all expresses Christ, and is a sweet savor. The breast and the left shoulder of the ram of consecration (verse 22), as well as all else which had not been offered to God, belonged to the priests. This tells of practical enjoyment of the love of Christ (the breast) and the enjoyment of His strength (the shoulder) who bears us up. It was eaten in the holy place, and the unleavened bread had to be used.

In verse 33 we find the English word "atonement" for the first time. The Hebrew word is *kaphar*, to cover. Of this likewise we shall have more to say when we read the book of Leviticus.

In the concluding section of this chapter we read God's promises, "where I will meet you and speak there unto thee;" "I will meet with the children of Israel;" "I will dwell among the children of Israel." The meeting place is the burnt offering altar. The daily offerings make known what the work of Christ is to God. And that is the place of the blessing.

CHAPTER 30

The Altar of Incense and the Worshippers

1. The altar (30:1-10)
2. The atonement money (30:11-16)
3. The brazen laver and the unction of the Spirit (30:22-33)
4. The incense (30:34-38)

This is a beautiful chapter, filled with blessed lessons. We have before us instructions concerning true, priestly worship. The brazen altar was of shittim wood, but this altar is of shittim wood covered with pure gold. The altar of brass tells of the work of Christ on the cross when judgment fell upon Him. There we learn in faith that our sins and guilt were fully met. The golden altar typifies Christ as entered into heaven. He is an altar there likewise, a place of sacrifice, but not a bleeding sacrifice. As believers we are a holy priesthood to offer up spiritual sacrifices, acceptable to God by Jesus Christ (1 Pet. 2:5). "By Him, therefore, let us offer the sacrifice of praise to God continually, that is, the fruit of our lips confessing His name." The altar of incense stands for this true, heavenly worship. There is a warning not to offer strange incense. In Leviticus (10:1-3) the additional warning is against strange fire. Strange incense is that kind of worship which is called ritualistic; a mere outward form, which puts a man in the place of leader in worship. Strange fire is a soulical, emotional worship, which is destitute of the Holy Spirit, who alone gives power to worship.

And those who come as true worshippers must be redeemed. This is seen in verses 11-16. Here is a confession of the fact that all are lost, all on equal footing, and all need redemption.

The brazen laver is mentioned next. This was for the washing of the hands and feet, symbolical of the washing of water by the Word, the cleansing from daily defilement. This is so blessedly illustrated in the washing of the feet of the disciples by our Lord. We must be cleansed, self-judged and self-denied, separated from evil, if we are to be true worshippers before the altar of incense. No real communion with God is possible save on the ground of personal holiness. Later we shall find that the laver was made of the looking-glasses of the assembling women (38:8). The Word of God is the true looking-glass where we see ourselves as we are, and then go to Him who is our laver for cleansing.

The holy anointing oil is the type of the Holy Spirit. He is needed for worship in the Spirit. A closer examination of the principal spices and their possible meaning, we must pass over. Notice that this oil was not to be poured upon man's flesh, "neither shall ye make any other like it" (verses 32-33). "The natural man cannot receive the things of the Spirit of God for they are foolishness unto him; neither can he know them, because they are spiritually discerned." The flesh is so corrupt that the Holy Spirit can have nothing to do with it. And how much the Spirit and His real work is counterfeited in these days.

The ingredients of the incense are also given. It is typical of the wonderful fragrance Christ is to God. His life on earth, His obedience, His death on the cross, His presence in Glory, all He is and all He does are of unspeakable fragrance and value to God.

CHAPTER 31

The Workmen and the Sabbath

1. The workmen called (31:1-11)
2. The Sabbath law emphasized (31:12-17)
3. Moses receives the tables of stone (31:18)

The call of the builders of the tabernacle follows the instructions. The plan and worship of the tabernacle was by divine appointment, only God could give such a plan foreshadowing the redemption work of His Son. To carry out this plan, the Lord called His own workmen by name and filled them with His Spirit, so that they could do the work in a manner which would please Him. "I have called; I have given; I have filled" are the words of Jehovah showing that He selected and qualified the two men to undertake the work. The New Testament ministry rests equally in the hands of the Lord. He has the exclusive right to select His servants for the ministry. As the risen Lord in Glory He gave some apostles; and some, prophets; and some, evangelists; and some, pastors and teachers; for the perfecting of the saints, for the work of the ministry, for the edifying of the body of Christ (Eph. 4:11-12). And whom He calls into the work of the ministry He also qualifies. His

Spirit gives the wisdom and power to carry out the work into which the Lord calls. It is therefore all of Him; no room for boasting or jealousy.

What confusion would have resulted if certain Israelites had decided to do part of the work and others, calling themselves "superintendents," had directed the construction of the tabernacle, or a committee selected the design of the breastplate and another committee examined drawings of the cherubim. Great is the confusion in the professing church with its man-made, self-appointed ministry, with its organizations, committees and worldly methods. The truth so clearly revealed in the New Testament epistles concerning the ministry in the body of Christ and the Holy Spirit who fits for this ministry, is almost entirely forgotten. But wherever there is the divine call and divine qualification through the Spirit of God, there the work is done and is accompanied by the power and blessing of God.

The principal workman called was Bezaleel, the grandson of Hur of the tribe of Judah. He had an assistant in Aholiab, as well as others who were wisehearted and to whom God gave wisdom (verse 6). Bezaleel means, "in the shadow of God"; this tells of his trust, filled with the Spirit of God in wisdom and understanding. He may well be taken as a type of the Lord Jesus Christ. Uri means "Light of Jehovah"; and Hur means "white." All these words point clearly to the great workman selected by God to fashion a dwelling place for Him and to make a kingdom of priests unto God, the Lord Jesus Christ. And as Bezaleel did all as God commanded so that He was pleased, so our Lord has done the work in perfect widsom to the eternal glory of God His Father.

Aholiab, Bezaleel's assistant, means "tent of my father." Ahisamach has the meaning "brother of support." This, likewise, reminds us of our Lord. Bezaleel belonged to the tribe of Judah, the leader in the camp of Israel, and Aholiab to Dan, the last in the camp. Thus the first and the last were selected to do the work. What a glorious time is yet to come when all Israel, saved by grace in that day of His appearing, filled with the Spirit and divine wisdom, erects the great millennial temple (Ezek. 40—48).

The Sabbath law is re-stated and emphasized. This was also done when the manna was given. Here the Sabbath is especially mentioned as "a sign between Me and you in your generations." The Sabbath is altogether a Jewish institution; it is always mentioned when Israel is seen in their responsibility in the special position given to them. Here the penalty for breaking the Sabbath is stated for the first time; it is death. Notice the peculiar expression in verse 17, that the Lord rested on the seventh day *and was refreshed.* He must have looked forward to His own work on the cross and the marvellous results of this work.

We quote from another some well-put distinctions between the Sabbath Israel had and could not keep, and the Lord's day. This distinction is of importance in the days when some consciences are disturbed by teachers who would force the seventh day upon those who are under Grace.

1. The Sabbath was the *seventh* day; the Lord's day is the *first.*

2. The Sabbath was a *test* of Israel's condition; the Lord's day is the *proof* of the Church's acceptance, on wholly unconditional grounds.

3. The Sabbath belonged to the *old* creation; the Lord's day belongs to the *new.*

4. The Sabbath was a day of *bodily* rest for the Jew; the Lord's day is a day of *spiritual* rest for the Christian.

5. If the Jew worked on the Sabbath, he was to be put to *death;* if the Christian does not work on the Lord's day, he gives little proof of *life;* —that is to say, if he does not work for the benefit of the souls of men, the extension of Christ's glory and the spread of His truth. In point of fact, the devoted Christian who possesses any gift is generally more fatigued on the evening of the Lord's day than on any other in the week, for how can he *rest* while souls are perishing around him?

6. The Jew was *commanded* by the *law* to abide in his tent; the Christian is *led* by the spirit of the *gospel* to go forth, whether it be to attend the public assembly or to minister to the souls of perishing sinners.[5]

How higher criticism, the whole rationalistic school, and their brethren, the infidels, have amused themselves with verse 18. Why should this be thought to be impossible with God? Their sneers but reveal their darkened and wicked hearts. God had made the tables and wrote on them (chapter 32:16).

---

[5]C. H. Mackintosh, *Notes on Exodus.*

4. Israel's Sin and Rebellion

CHAPTER 32

1. The people in rebellion (32:1-6)
2. Jehovah threatens his wrath (32:7-10)
3. Moses beseeches Jehovah (32:11-14)
4. Moses descends and in the camp (32:15-29)
5. Moses' offer and failure (32:30-35)

This chapter records the breaking of the covenant by Israel's sin, rebellion against Jehovah, and idolatry. Here we find man's heart fully uncovered, that wicked heart of unbelief. What manifestations of God's power they had seen! Their eyes beheld the dreadful judgments which fell upon the land of Egypt and wiped out the Egyptian hosts. They were guided by the visible sign of Jehovah's presence. He had given them manna, yea, they were eating that bread the very day on which they rebelled. The smitten rock had yielded water. God had entered into covenant with them. And now when Moses delayed, they requested of Aaron, "Up, make us gods." God was not mentioned at all by the rebellious mass. It seemed Moses and not God was the object of their faith. The heathen had gone that way and "changed the glory of the uncorruptible God into an image made like to corruptible man, and to birds, and four-footed beasts and creeping things" (Rom. 1:23). The favored nation shows that their heart is as corrupt as the heart of the Gentiles, who know not God. They plunged into the degradation of idolatry. The unseen One, the One who had honored Abraham's faith, who spake to the fathers, was rejected by them, and they preferred a golden calf fashioned with a graving tool. And Aaron plays the leading part in this awful scene of degradation and wickedness. He announces a feast unto the Lord, after he had made the golden calf from the golden ear-rings (copied, no doubt, after the Egyptian idol Apis; see Ps. 106:19-20). Then the people "rose up to play"; wild dances, licentious and filled with the abominations of the heathen, the flesh let loose, is what followed. The people were naked (verse 25).

Alas! the same has been repeated on "Christian" ground. The ritualistic, religious worship, appealing to the senses, filled with God, Christ and the Holy Spirit dishonoring counterfeits, the inventions of the "religious nature" of man under satanic control, is nothing but idolatry. It rejects the invisible One, who demands our faith and trust, and puts something else in His place. That is idolatry. All God's true people are in danger of that sin in the most subtle forms. Whenever we lean on the arm of flesh and not exclusively upon the "I Am," our gracious Lord, then we are guilty of the same sin. "Little children, keep yourselves from idols" (1 John 5:21).

As Moses went up, so our great High Priest has gone to the Father. We see Him not, but we know He is there and will come back again. May we live by faith during His absence and be kept from idols.

Then Jehovah told Moses what was going on in the camp. Note that He said to Moses, "thy people which thou broughtest out of the land of Egypt." The Lord puts them, so to speak, upon Moses and commits them into his hands. Moses only needed to say the word and the rebellious nation would have been consumed and Moses and his offspring would become a new beginning. It was a test of Moses, but Jehovah knew beforehand what His servant would do. Beautiful is Moses' intercession. He uses the same words the Lord had used. "Thy people which Thou hast brought forth out of the land of Egypt." The Lord had put them into Moses' hands; Moses puts them back upon the Lord. How wonderful was Moses' intercession in their behalf. He reminds Him of His promises and the covenant made with Abraham, Isaac and *Israel* (avoiding the word Jacob). His intercession is typical of our great intercessor before the throne.

The covenant was broken and the first tables of stone were broken. The golden calf was burnt and ground to powder. This was cast into the water (the brook, Deut. 9:21), and the children of Israel had to drink it. They had to drink their own shame; a humiliating experience. Aaron is questioned first, and he adds a new sin to the one already committed. (Compare verse 24 with verse 4). The sons of Levi gathered themselves to Moses. They, too, had shared in the rebellion, but were now the first to confess and take their stand with the Lord. Judgment follows and three thousand fell by the sword. They did not spare their nearest relations (Deut. 33:9). Besides this, the people were plagued (32:35). Moses returned to the Lord. But he failed in his proposition. "None of them can by any means redeem his brother, nor give unto God a ransom for him" (Ps. 49:7). Yet Moses' willingness to be blotted out of the Book foreshadows Him who alone could do the atoning work. He offered himself without spot unto God, (Heb. 9:14) and gave His life a ransom for many. He died for that nation (John 11:51, 52).

5. Moses' Intercession and its Results

CHAPTER 33

Repentance and Intercession

1. The word of the Lord and the people's repentance (33:1-6)
2. The tabernacle without the camp (33:7)
3. Moses enters the tabernacle (33:8-11)
4. Moses' prayer and Jehovah's answers (33:12-17)
5. Moses' request (33:18-23)

The words of the Lord, with which this chapter begins, reveal Him as the covenant-keeping Jehovah. He remembers His covenant, though they are a stiff-necked people. Yet He is a holy God and if He were to be in their midst they would be consumed. They had to take the place in self-judgment and acknowledge their guilt and separation from the Holy One. They were obedient to this demand and stripped themselves of their ornaments. In this place they had taken the Lord could show them mercy.

The word "tabernacle" here in this chapter means "tent" and of course is not the real tabernacle, for that had not yet been erected. It was a tent which had been used as a place of worship, It now had to occupy a place outside of the camp. All who wanted to seek the Lord had to go to the "tent of meeting," outside of the camp. See Hebrews 13:13. Christ and His gospel is now rejected; the professing people of God are in rebellion and apostasy; the call, therefore, is to go outside of the camp, bearing His reproach. Christ occupies this place in Laodicea, the phase of Christian profession in these last days. He is outside, standing at the door and knocking. And there, "outside of the camp," the Lord spake unto Moses, as a man speaketh unto his friend. Again he represents Christ as mediator, only our mediator is higher than Moses. And through Christ we have access into His presence. "Outside of the camp" leads to the closest communion with Himself. The Lord talked to Moses out of the cloud and then Moses turned again into the camp. Joshua remained in the tabernacle and did not enter the camp. All is written for our learning. Though we go "outside of the camp" yet we have a solemn duty and responsibility towards those in the camp. May we discharge these.

Moses' prayer pleads now grace, and upon that the Holy One answers graciously. But His face Moses could not see. Read and compare with John 1:18 and 14:9.

CHAPTER 34

The Result: The Second Covenant and the Glory

1. The command to hew two tables of stone (34:1-4)
2. The proclamation of Jehovah (34:5-7)
3. Moses' worship and prayer (34:8-9)
4. The covenant restated (34:10-26)
5. The second tables written (34:27-28)
6. The glory upon the face of Moses (34:29-25)

The command is given to Moses to hew two tables of stone like the first, which Jehovah Himself had hewn and which were broken by Moses. The first were hewn of one stone; the second of two stones. Moses was permitted to furnish the material for the second tables, while the Lord had furnished it for the first. The second tables were given as the result of the intercession of Moses. But God wrote the words on the second tables of stones as He had done on the first.

The manifestation of Jehovah recorded in this chapter is deeply interesting. In chapter 33:21-23 the Lord promised Moses a vision. This is now fulfilled. Jehovah came down from heaven in a cloud and stood with him there; He proclaimed the name of Jehovah. This reminds us of Exodus 19:24. What Moses saw is not stated. The Lord had come down to him and the descended Lord made known the name of the Lord. It is a most blessed hint on the incarnation of Jehovah and the manifestation of the name of Jehovah through Him, who is Jehovah. "For the law was given by Moses, but grace and truth came by Jesus Christ" (John 1:17). The descended Lord makes known grace, but also divine righteousness. The full manifestation of grace could not be then made known; only in the cross of Christ, where God's righteousness is revealed, grace shines forth in all its marvelous glory. In the gospel of Jesus Christ the justification of the ungodly is announced as well as the glorious inheritance of eternity for justified believers. Of this the law had nothing to say, for it could not give righteousness and God never meant to give to man eternal glory by keeping the commandments.

Moses worshipped and bowed his head toward the earth. His prayer to Jehovah is that He might come among them. He confessed the sinful condition of the people and asks for pardon. He includes himself. In chapter 33:5 Jehovah called the people stiff-necked. Moses then did not use this word; but here when Jehovah speaks of grace he pleads this charge of Jehovah for forgiveness and mercy. This is a blessed foreshadowing of the gospel of grace. But there is another lesson here. Moses realizes that the presence of Jehovah who had uttered such gracious words, if He were among them, would result in their forgiveness. The Holy One of Israel will some day be in the midst of His earthly people, then He will forgive their sins and remember them no more, and they will be His inheritance.

In the statements of the renewed covenant the separation of the people from the inhabitants of Canaan is made prominent. They were to have nothing to do with the impure and abominable idolatries of these nations. He called His people unto holiness. Moreover, they were to destroy their altars, their images and their groves. The word groves is "asherah." It was an image used for the most lascivious practices, commonly known as the phallic worship. It flourished among all the ancient nations, but was especially used by the Canaanites. When Israel later fell in with these abominations, the judgment fell upon them. The commandments concerning the feasts, the Sabbath, and the firstfruits are repeated.

The conclusion of this chapter is used in 2 Cor. 3.

When Moses was on the mountain the first time to receive the first tables of stone no glory was seen on his face, because the covenant was altogether legal and not a ray of glory can come from that. The second time, because grace and mercy were mingled with it, glory shines from the mediator's face. But they could not look upon that glory. He had to cover his face with a vail. Thus grace and glory are covered in the law. This vail is done away in Christ. In Him grace and glory in the most perfect splendor shine forth. And it is a glory which does not wane, but increases. "But we all with open face beholding as in a glass the glory of the Lord, are changed into the same image from glory to glory, even as by the Spirit of the Lord" (2 Cor. 3:18)

Of Israel it is written, "But their minds were blinded, for until this day remaineth the same veil untaken away in the reading of the Old Testament, which veil is done away in Christ. But even unto this day, when Moses is read, the vail is upon their hearts. Nevertheless, when it shall turn until the Lord, the veil shall be taken away" (2 Cor. 3:14-16). And that glorious day is coming, when they will believe.

6. The Building of the Tabernacle

CHAPTER 35

The Commandments Concerning the Tabernacle Remembered and the Offerings

1. The Sabbath law emphasized (35:1-3)
2. The offerings restated (35:4-10)
3. The tabernacle and its furniture restated (35:11-19)
4. The offerings given (35:20-29)
5. The workmen and the teachers (35:30-35)

It is interesting to review the events and steps which lead to this consummation in Exodus, the setting up of the tabernacle. After Jehovah had redeemed His people and led them through the wilderness to Mount Sinai, dealing with them in grace, the law covenant was made. It was broken by them in their rebellion and idolatry. Intercession and another covenant followed, mingled with grace. And now there is obedience and the tabernacle is put up. And when it was finished the glory filled the place, showing that God was well pleased. Jehovah dwelt there with His people. In New Testament times, the true church is His dwelling place, "an habitation of God through the Spirit." When the age to come, the millennium is reached, He will again dwell in the midst of Israel and manifest His visible glory in Jerusalem and above the city. Then comes eternity when God is all in all. "And I heard a great voice out of heaven saying, Behold, the tabernacle of God is with men, and He will dwell with them" (Rev. 21:3).

The Sabbath rest is once more mentioned. This is not a vain repetition, nor is it the mark of imperfection, or the work of different writers, as the critical school has claimed. Rest precedes the work, not work precedes the rest. This is the blessed spiritual principle. This cannot be under the law, but it is blessedly so under grace. We rest in Him, and He gives us rest so that we can labor and give back to Him.

All the details commanded by Jehovah concerning the tabernacle are repeated and also the material to be furnished by the people in free will offerings. How needful was the repetition! He had made the specifications show what they were to bring, as He has shown in His Word the service and work He expects of His people. And then we behold their willing service. Men and women came and brought their gifts. How it must have refreshed His heart. The women are prominently mentioned. The willing heart and the cheerful giver are also seen in the New Testament. When in the future the day of Christ's power dawns (His second coming) His earthly people, Israel, will be willing to bring their all to His feet: "Thy people shall be willing in the day of Thy power" (Ps. 110:3). Then they will build that great and glorious millennial temple, the house of prayer for all nations.

Once more the two leading workmen are mentioned by name and the fact is made known that the Spirit of God fitted them for the work. But something is added here which we do not find in chapter 31, "And He hath put in his heart that he may teach, both he and Aholiab, the son of Ahisamach, of the tribe of Dan." Besides having the spirit of wisdom they also had the gift of teaching, to pass on to others what they had learned.

CHAPTER 36

The Work Carried Out

1. The work begun (36:1-4)
2. The over-supply in the offerings (36:5-7)
3. The curtains (36:8-13)
4. The covering of the tent (36:14-19)
5. The boards and the sockets of silver (36:20-30)
6. The bars (36:31-34)
7. The vail and the hanging for the door (36:35-38)

In the abundant offerings, more than was needed, we see the results of the grace of God. Every morning the offerings were presented. So large was the supply that they had to be restrained. What a contrast with the professing people of God in our days! How little self-sacrifice and self-denial; how little willingness to spend and be spent. The methods used to help along the work of the Lord, such as collections from unbelievers, are condemned by the word of God. The willingness of the people was the fruit of the spirit of God. The different curtains and coverings, boards and bars and the vail and hanging were prepared. In chapter 30 we saw God began with that which is within; the building began with the outside things.

CHAPTER 37

The Ark, The Table, the Candlestick, and the Incense Altar, the Oil and Incense

1. The ark made by Bezaleel (37:1-9)
2. The table of shittim wood (37:10-16)
3. The candlestick (37:17-24)
4. The incense altar (37:25-28)
5. The oil and incense (37:29)

The word of Jehovah is literally carried out, because the Holy Spirit was in the workmen. Compare verses 1-9 with 25:10-22; verses 10-16 with 25:23-30; verses 17-24 with 25:31-40; verses 25-28 with 30:1-10; verse 29 with 30:22-38. Notice that the ark is mentioned especially as the work of Bezaleel.

CHAPTER 38

The Burnt Offering Altar, the Laver, the Court and the Metals Used

1. The altar of burnt offering (38:1-7)
2. The laver (38:8)
3. The court (39:9-20)
4. The amount of metal used (38:21-31)

The pattern as previously given is closely followed and everything done according to the divine command. Nothing was left in the work to the choice of the workmen. They had the pattern and the spirit of God gave the power to carry it out. Thus God expects us to work and serve after His own pattern in the power of the indwelling Spirit. He will eventually carry out all His revealed plans and purposes concerning this earth. Women furnished the material for the laver. They gave their looking glasses, which were of shining metal. (See Job 37:18.) They were pious women of Israel who gave willingly what must have been a costly possession. They assembled at the door of the tabernacle. The Chaldean paraphrase is "of the mirrors of the women, which came to pray at the door of the tabernacle."

Interesting is the estimate of the amount of metal used. *Gold* occupies the first place: 29 talents and 730 shekels. Silver was given by every male a half of a shekel (the atonement money). The number of men from 20 years and upward was 603,550; so they gave 301,775 shekels of silver. Then there was the brass (copper). Precious metals, like gold and silver, were plentiful in Egypt, which had immense gold mines.

CHAPTER 39

The Priestly Garments and the Work Finished

1. The material used (39:1)
2. The ephod (39:2-7)
3. The breastplate (39:8-21)
4. The robe, the bells and pomegranate (39:22-26)
5. The coats (39:27-29)
6. The holy crown (39:30-31)

7. The work finished (39:32-43)

All is done "as the Lord commanded." This expression is used seven times in chapter 39 (verses 1, 5, 7, 21, 26, 29, 31). It is again repeated exactly seven times in chapter 40, the last chapter of Exodus (verses 19, 21, 23, 25, 27, 29, 32). Seven is the number of perfection and completion. All had been well done and Jehovah was pleased and could own the work, of which He was the originator. Blue, purple, and scarlet, the colors of heaven, royalty and blood, are given in the preparation of the holy garments. It tells once more of Him who is the priest. The order is significant. The heavenly color comes first, for He came from heaven's glory. The kingly color next; He manifested Himself in His kingly power, and the blood color last, He died and shed His blood. Urim and Thummim are not mentioned in the list, for they could not be made.

The work was finished and all presented to Moses for inspection. The principal parts are mentioned once more. With what joy Moses must have looked upon the ark, the curtains, the boards, the altars, the laver and the garments of beauty and glory. There was no flaw in anything. With what liberality and zeal the great work had been accomplished. Then Moses blessed the children of Israel.

7. The Tabernacle Set Up, the Finished Work and the Glory

CHAPTER 40

1. Jehovah gives the directions (40:1-15)
2. Moses' obedience (40:16)
3. The tabernacle set up (40:17-19)
4. The ark brought in (40:20-21)
5. The furniture placed and the offerings brought (40:22-29)
6. The laver and the court (40:30-33)
7. The glory of the Lord filled the tabernacle (40:34-38)

While the people had offered and the chosen workmen labored in the production of the tabernacle, the Lord had not spoken. He looked upon His people as they carried out His commands. But after Moses had blessed them, then the Lord spoke and commanded the setting up of the tabernacle on the first day of the first month. He directs the placing of the different pieces of furniture. The table with the shewbread was to be arranged, water to be put into the later, the anointing of all was to follow, the priests to be washed, clothed and anointed. All was carried out again. Moses did according to all the Lord commanded him. The building of the tabernacle and all the work connected with it occupied not quite six months. The tabernacle was reared in the first month in the second year on the first day of the month. The setting up began with the sockets, in which the boards were placed. The testimony was put into the ark (the tables of stone). Then after the ark had been brought in, Moses hung the curtain. The holy part of the tabernacle was next arranged. The table was placed on the right side towards the north, and the shewbread was laid upon it. Of all this we shall read in Leviticus, where the typical meaning will be pointed out. The altar of burnt offerings was placed before the door of the dwelling of the tabernacle and the laver between the tabernacle and the altar. Moses burned sweet incense and offered the burnt offering and meat offering.

When Moses had looked upon all that had been done, he was well pleased and blessed the people (39:43). When Jehovah looked upon the finished work and saw that all was according to His heart, He was well pleased. His approval was witnessed to by the cloud, which covered the tabernacle, and His glory filled the place. He entered in to take possession of it. Moses had to stand back; He could no longer go into the place where Jehovah dwelt.

While here the cloud covered all and the glory filled the whole place, later the cloud drew back into the most holy place to dwell above the outspread wings of the cherubim. Moses and the priests could then enter the holy place without coming in touch with the sign of Jehovah's presence, which was hidden from human gaze by the curtain of the holy of holies.

As long as the cloud rested upon the tabernacle the children of Israel remained in camp; when it moved, they continued their journey. This had a blessed meaning for the people of God and has its lessons for us. The cloud in its movements made known Jehovah's will. We have no such external sign to declare the will of God to us. We have the internal presence of the Holy Spirit. And He guides us through His Word, which we must consult for direction and guidance. All this we shall find fully stated in Num. 9:15-23; when we reach that "wilderness book" we hope to point out some of its lessons.

We state once more the fact that Exodus begins with a groan and the first part ends with the song of redemption. The second part begins with Israel's wilderness wandering and ends after the work was finished with the glory of the Lord filling the tabernacle. The Lord Jesus Christ and His Word is foreshadowed in the entire book. Glory is the great goal of all He has done. He has reached down and set the miserable slaves of sin and Satan free; He changes our groans into songs of victory, because He, the Lamb of God, shed His blood. He guides His people home. Glory will yet cover Zion, the place of His rest. In the day of His glorious manifestation, when He appears in glory and majesty as the King of Kings, the glory cloud will be seen again in the midst of the redeemed Israel (Isa. 4:4-6). And in all eternity, the ages to come, His glory will be with the redeemed and the redeemed will share His glory.

"And I heard a great voice out of heaven saying, Behold, the tabernacle of God is with men, and He will dwell with them, and they shall be His people, and God Himself shall be with them, and be their God. And God shall wipe away all tears from their eyes; and there shall be no more death, neither sorrow nor crying, neither shall there be any more pain, for the former things are passed away" (Rev. 21:3-4).

Appendix A

The Atonement Money[6]

EXODUS 30:11-16

The word silver in Hebrew is frequently translated *money.* It was indeed, the precious metal ordinarily in use, in all transactions of buying and selling; and even at this day, in many countries, it is the current money of the merchant. Francs, dollars, thalers, scudi, are all coins of silver; and mercantile transactions are generally calculated in one or other of these coins, in most of the countries of Europe, and indeed of the world.

We have two memorable instances in Scripture, where life was bartered for silver. Joseph for twenty, and the Son of God for thirty pieces. The idea therefore, of price or value, especially attaches to this metal. It ranks also with us, as one of the precious metals; and though not displaying the brilliant glory of the gold, it is especially beautiful, by reason of its soft purity and unsullied whiteness; and like gold, it corrodes not, and wastes not in the fining pot, though subject to the intense heat of the furnace.

The silver, used in the construction of the tabernacle, was all derived from the atonement money.

The whole range of God's truth rests upon two great verities: the Lord Jesus, the Son of God, the Son of Man—and His work of atonement on the cross. Throughout the history of God's ancient people, type after type, and shadow upon shadow, reiterated the absolute necessity of atonement. And while the law prescribed commandments, to obey which Israel fatally pledged themselves, it at the same time contained abundant ritual observances, which testified to man's incapability and need, and prophesied of One, who while they were yet without strength, should, in due time, die for the ungodly. As a covenant of works, it was a ministration of death. But to one who was really a child of Abraham, it must have shone out, like the face of Moses, with a prophetic glory; and have pointed onwards to the Lamb of God; in whom all the shadows of good things to come passed into substance.

This type before us, of the atonement-money, preached a very clear and blessed gospel. It told out the great truth, that birth in the flesh availed nothing. An Israelite might trace up, in unbroken succession, his descent from Abraham, or from one of Jacob's sons. Still, that sufficed him not, if he desired to be entered on the roll as one of God's soldiers and servants. The Jews, in the time of the Lord, could say, "We be Abraham's seed"; and the Samaritan sinner claimed Jacob as her father. But they were captives of the devil, and of fleshly lusts; and their human pedigree had not raised them out of the dominion of sin. God had therefore enjoined that, whenever Israel were numbered as His people, every man must give a ransom for his soul. The price was fixed by God himself. Each man, whether poor or rich, must bring the same. One could not pay for another; but every one must tender his own ransom-money, of pure silver, and of perfect weight. "Half a shekel, after the shekel of the sanctuary, (a shekel is twenty gerahs) a half-shekel shall be the offering of the Lord" (Exod. 30:13). Other gospel truths here shine out. When the question came to be one of ransom, the poor and the rich, the foolish and the wise, the ignorant and the learned, the immoral and the

---

[6]Henry W. Soltau, *The Tabernacle, Priesthood and the Offerings.*

moral, stood on the same level. Each person was estimated by God at the same price. He proved Himself no respecter of persons. And so it is still. The third chapter of the Epistle to the Romans defines the state of every one in the whole world, and levels the way for the gospel. John the Baptist prepared the way of the Lord by his voice, calling all to repentance, declaring all to be in one condition, needing change of heart. And the Lord Jesus began to speak of the great salvation to hearts thus prepared. The chapter above referred to makes the path straight for the proclamation of justification through faith in Christ, by pronouncing that all are under sin; that every mouth must be silent; that all the world is guilty before God; and that there is no difference between the religious Jew, and the irreligious Gentile; for, "all have sinned, and come short of the glory of God."

Another truth enunciated in this type is, that salvation must be an individual, personal matter; between the soul and God. Every man has to bring his own half-shekel. One of the devices of Satan at the present day—and it is spread far and wide—is the way in which he obscures this truth, by inducing whole communities to believe they are Christians; made such, either by baptism, or by some formal profession of religiousness; and placing, in the lips of thousands, "Our Saviour," and "Our Father"; and thus beguiling them into the thought that they are included in a general redemption of mankind, which affects the whole human race. Constantly, therefore, in speaking to persons, we find the reply: O yes, we are all sinners: and Christ has died for us all.

Each individual Israelite had to present himself to the priest, bringing with him his own piece of money as a ransom; and his name would then be entered in God's book. The Lord Jesus, in the 6th chapter of John, says: "Except ye eat the flesh of the Son of Man, and drink His blood, ye have no life in you." Eating and drinking are actions which one cannot perform for another. The food, taken into the mouth, becomes one's own, and ministers strength and nourishment to the body. So, the death of Christ must be appropriated by each to himself. The soul has to say, *My* Saviour; *My* Lord; *My* God. *I* have been crucified with Christ. Christ loved *me,* and gave Himself for *me.* Just as assuredly as the Israelite of old had to eat the manna he had collected for his own sustenance; or according to his eating, to make his count for the lamb.

The half-shekel was to be of silver; the unalloyed, unadulterated metal. Three things are probably here presented to us in type: the Lord Jesus as God—as the pure and spotless One—and as giving His life a ransom for many. The silver, being a solid, imperishable precious metal, may have this first aspect: its chaste whiteness representing the second; and its being ordinarily employed as money or price, may point out its fitness as a type of the third.

The *weight* was also defined by God: "the shekel of the sanctuary"; kept as a standard in the tabernacle; and perhaps bearing some stamp or inscription to authenticate it. Its weight was twenty gerahs. The half-shekel, brought by each man who desired to be numbered, was to be compared with this. God kept the just weight and the just balance; and His priest would neither take dross instead of silver, nor receive less weight of the precious metal than was required by the Lord. With confidence the true-hearted Israelite would ring out the silver sound, from his half-shekel before the priest: with confidence would he see it put into the balance. And, in the blessed antitype, with confidence does the believer sound out, in the ears of God, and of the great High Priest of His sanctuary, his full dependence on Christ and His precious blood. He knows that this price is up to the full estimate demanded by God. He has one standard of perfection and purity, against which He weighs the hearts, spirits, and actions of men. Everything short of this standard, every one who fails to reach this sterling value, will be comdemned; like the Babylonian prince, who was weighed in the balances and found wanting. To come short of the glory of God, is to be in the distance and darkness of corruption and death. How wondrous the grace, which has provided One, in whom we are raised from the depth of human misery, degradation and ruin, to the height of the throne and glory of the Most High! How passing knowledge, that love of God, which has not hesitated to plunge into judgment and wrath, His only-begotton Son, and to shed the blood of Christ like water, in order to redeem, from filthiness and sin, the worthless and the vile; and to number them among the hosts of light and glory, in the courts above!

There is a manifest allusion to the atonement-money in 1 Peter 1:18; "Forasmuch as ye know that ye were not redeemed with corruptible things, as silver and gold, from your vain conversation, received by tradition from your fathers; but with the precious blood of Christ, as of a Lamb without blemish and without spot."

An allusion, by way of contrast. What men consider precious metals, and free from impurity and corrosion, God calls "perishable" and "corruptible." He says that gold and silver "canker" and "rust."

The man who amasses wealth is an object of praise and envy. "Men will praise thee when thou doest well to thyself" (Ps. 49:18). But in this epistle, gain is denominated filthy lucre. The redemption, which God has paid for us, is no amount of corruptible things, as silver and gold. Lebanon is not sufficient to burn, nor the beasts thereof sufficient for a burnt-offering. Nothing less than the precious blood of Christ would avail. God has valued our salvation at no less cost, than the pouring out of His soul unto death.

The Hebrew word, from which the words *ransom* and *atonement* are derived, has a variety of senses all bearing on the same truth. Thus, we find the word includes the thought of covering over our sin; as a covering of pitch covers over the wood on which it is spread (Gen. 6:14).

The blood of the atonement blots out the page of sin, and hides it from the eye of God. The secret sins, which have stood out in their glaring evil, in the light of His countenance, are hidden by the blood sprinkled on the mercy-seat. It also means, to *appease* or *pacify.* Thus Jacob sent a present to (*atone* or) appease his brother Esau (Gen. 32:20). "The wrath of a king is as messengers of death: but a wise man will (*atone* or) pacify it" (Prov. 16:14). "That thou mayest remember, and be confounded, and never open thy mouth any more, because of thy shame, when I am (*atoned* or) pacified towards thee" (Ezek. 16:63).

This is the sense of the word in the New Testament—*propitiation;* God's wrath being appeased in Christ through the shedding of His blood (1 John 2:2; and 4:10).

Pardon and *forgiveness* are included in the word. "The blood shall be [atoned, or] forgiven them" (Deut. 21:8).

Hezekiah prayed, "The good Lord (atone, or) pardon every one" (2 Chron. 30:18); also, to *reconcile.*

"A sin-offering brought in (to atone, or) to reconcile withal, in the holy place" (Lev. 6:30).

"And when He hath made an end of (atoning, or) reconciling the holy place" (Lev. 26:20).

"Poured the blood at the bottom of the altar, and sanctified it, to make (atonement, or) reconciliation upon it" (Lev. 8:15).

"So shall ye [atone, or] reconcile the house" (Ezek. 45:20; also 15 and 17).

In the New Testament also, the word *atonement* is synonymous with *reconciliation.*

"To make reconciliation for the sins of the people" (Heb. 2:17).

"We have now received the atonement" (Rom. 5:11; margin—reconciliation).

"Reconciling of the world" (Rom. 11:15).

"That He might reconcile both unto God in one body by the cross" (Eph. 2:16).

"By Him, to reconcile all things to Himself" (Col. 1:20).

To put off, or *expiate.*—"Mischief shall fall upon thee; thou shalt not be able to put it off" (margin—expiate; Isa. 47:11).

To disannul.—"Your covenant with death shall be disannulled" (Isa. 28:18).

Ransom, or, *satisfaction*—Deliver him from going down into the pit: I have found a ransom" (Job 33:24).

"A great ransom cannot deliver thee" (Job 36:18).

"Nor give to God a ransom for him" (Psa. 49:7).

Satisfaction.—"Yet shall take no satisfaction for the life of a murderer" (Num. 35:31).

In the New Testament.—"To give His life as a ransom for many" (Matt. 20:28; Mark 10:45).

Lastly: *To purge or cleanse.*—"Purge away our sins, for Thy name's sake" (Psa. 79:9).

"By mercy and truth, iniquity is purged" (Prov. 16:6).

"This iniquity shall not be purged" (Isa. 22:14).

"By this, therefore, shall the iniquity of Jacob be purged" (Isa. 27:9).

"The land cannot be cleansed of the blood" (Num. 35:33).

We shall perceive from these various quotations, that the same Hebrew word translated *atonement,* signifies also, covering over; appeasing; forgiveness; reconciliation; expiation; disannulling; ransom or redemption; satisfaction; and cleansing.

One sense of *our* word atonement is, at-one-ment; two opposing parties being brought together in agreement as one. And the means whereby this is effected, the payment of a price, ransom or satisfaction. So, this beautiful type of the half-shekel or silver, shadows forth the precious blood of Christ, as the redemption price provided by God. And, when the sinner estimates its all-sufficient value in the presence of God, he answers the action of the Israelite in paying down the silver half-shekel; as it is beautifully expressed in 1 Pet. 2:7: "Unto you which believe, He is precious"; or, as it might be rendered, "He is the preciousness" your full satisfaction, and value also before God.

We have also another important aspect of truth portrayed in this type—*viz.:* that redemption *brings* us to, and *fits* us for God. The Israelite, who paid his ransom-money, was numbered as a soldier and a servant for God. A place was assigned him in the battlefield; and he had his position in the camp, appointed with reference to the tabernacle, the dwelling-place of God in the midst of the hosts. From henceforth Jehovah was his Leader, his Lord, his King. In like manner, the believer is redeemed to God, by the blood of Christ, from the world, and from slavery to sin and Satan; that he may be a soldier and a servant of the Most High; to be led, guided, and sustained by Him, who has called him out of darkness, into His marvellous light.

Two other words deserve our notice in this passage (Exod. 30:13-14). "Every one that *passeth* among them that are numbered." And the word *"offering"* (30:13-15). The allusion, in verses 13 and 14 is to the sheep passing under the rod of the shepherd, as he numbers them (Ezek. 20:37). "I will cause you to pass under the rod: and I will bring you into the bond of the covenant." The priest took the place of a shepherd, counting the sheep of God's hand. And as the true mark of the sheep came under his eye, in the ransom-money offered by each, he entered each in the book of the covenant. So the good Shepherd has laid down His life for the sheep; and they are entered in the Lamb's book of life, because the atonement-price has been paid for each.

The word *offering* is a peculiar word in the Hebrew, signifying something that is lifted off the ground and presented on high; and is the word translated *heave-offering.* All the various offerings brought by the Israelites, as contributions for forming the tabernacle, the enumerated (Exod. 25:2-7) are called heave-offerings. This atonement-money was a peculiar piece of silver, separated off to God, and lifted, as it were, from the earth, with the special object of being paid into His treasury, as a ransom for the soul. So has the Lord Jesus been lifted up, first on the cross, to pour out His blood a ransom for many; and secondly, He has been exalted, and made very high, "to be a Prince and a Saviour, for to give repentance to Israel, and forgiveness of sins" (Acts 5:31).

This ordinance was transgressed by David, as related in 2 Sam. 24, 1 Chron. 21. Israel had settled down in self-contentedness and pride; David their king and shepherd, himself drinking into the same spirit. Satan, by God's permission, was allowed to tempt the king, and provoke him, by whisperings of vanity and self-exaltation, to number Israel. The desire in David's heart was, not that God might be glorified and His promise made manifest, in the vast increase of His people; but that he, the king, might congratulate himself on the number of his subjects. "Number ye the people, *that I may know.*" "Bring the number of them to me, *that I may know it.*" Joab, to whom the command was given, though himself an ambitious worldly-minded man, yet was keen-sighted enough to perceive that this desire of his master was not of God. He even had some insight into David's sin. He looked upon Israel as a people belonging to Jehovah; and on David, as committing a trespass in having them numbered for himself. But, like all unbelievers, though he could point out the fault, he was not able to direct David to the remedy. He did not allude to the atonement-money.

One result of this numbering was that even cities of the Hivites, and the stronghold of Tyre, were included in the tale; which could never have been the case had the silver half-shekel been required. At the present day, unconverted inhabitants of earth are too often classed as of the church of God, by reason of the same neglect, *viz.:* that they are not required to confess openly their confidence in the precious blood of Christ, before being reckoned among the hosts of God.

David's heart soon smote him after the numbering was completed; he fully confessed his own sin and folly; he at once cast himself on the mercies of God for pardon, and preferred being dealt with in chastisement immediately from the Lord rather than fall into the hands of men. Accordingly, the plague (which had already been threatened, in Exod. 30:12) broke out amongst the people; and the destroyer stayed not his hand until the Lord, listening to the humiliation of David, and appeased by the burnt-offering, presented at the threshing-floor of Ornan the Jebusite, said "It is enough." David in his intercession, manifests a soul restored to the Lord; and proves that he has discovered his former error; for he speaks of Israel as sheep, and as the people of the Lord; whereas he had numbered them as fighting-men, and for his own glory.

Also the price of the spot for the altar is paid in shekels of silver. There may be some reference to this in the atonement-money. The apparent discrepancy between the fifty shekels, mentioned as the purchase-money in 2 Sam.

24:24, and the six hundred shekels of gold in 1 Chron. 21:25, may be reconciled on the supposition that the former money was paid for the mere spot on which the altar itself was erected; whereas the latter was the purchase-money for the whole place of the threshing-floor.

The blessed words "it is enough" were again, in principle, uttered by Jehovah from heaven, when He raised the Lord Jesus from the dead. Satisfaction had been completedly made: the sword of vengeance had been buried in the heart of God's own Son; the precious blood had been poured out; the full redemption-price had been rendered; and Jesus was raised from the dead; at once the proof of the perfect value of His own death, and to receive the due reward of His loving faithful obedience. "It is enough" may be a fitting superscription for the half-shekel ransom-money.

It appears that the question asked of Peter, (Matt. 17:24) "Does not your master pay tribute?" (or, according to the margin, the didrachma) had reference to this ransom-money. Probably the payment, which had been instituted in Exod. 30, of a half-shekel, when the Israelties were numbered, had in the course of time been converted by the Jewish rulers into a kind of poll-tax, payable for the uses of the temple. Peter, with his usual readiness, or rather rashness, answered the question in the affirmative, without referring, as he should have done, to the Lord Himself for a reply. And when he was come into the house, Jesus anticipated his request for the ransom-money, (to the payment of which he had just committed the Lord) by putting the question, "What thinkest thou, Simon, of whom do the kings of the earth take custom or tribute? of their own children, or of strangers?" The Lord thus addresses him as Simon, instead of Peter. The Apostle had relapsed into the natural man; and Jesus uses the name, which Peter had received from his earthly parents, instead of the new name, given him on his confession of faith.

Peter had forgotten the late glorious scene of the transfiguration, when the Voice had sounded from the excellent glory, "This is my beloved Son: hear ye Him;" and he had committed two errors. Instead of harkening to Jesus, and learning of Him, he had acted on his own self-confident judgment; and instead of owning the Lord as the Son of God, he had lowered Him down to the position of a stranger, or captive, from whom a ransom was demanded by God.

This serves to explain the Lord's question quoted above. Peter replies to it—to his own condemnation—"of strangers." Jesus saith unto him, "Then are the children free." Jesus came to declare *the Father.* "He that hath seen Me, hath seen the Father." He had come to redeem them that were under the law; that those who believed on Him might receive the adoption of sons. Liberty of sonship, and not the bondage of servantship, not the slavery of bondmen confined under rigid commandments, was the liberty that Christ came to proclaim. The law, even in its type of the atonement-money, did not intimate the blessing of sonship. Grace and truth, which came by Jesus Christ, placed the believer in the freedom of new birth; as many as received Christ, were born of God. But Peter had not yet received the spirit of sonship. The Holy Ghost had not yet been sent from the risen Christ; and thus the apostle mingled up and confounded adoption and bondage, and lowered the Son down to the position of a stranger.

This is an instructive lesson to our souls; for the spirit of bondage is constantly working within us. It is of the flesh, of nature. It springs from Simon, the son of Jonas, instead of from Peter, a child of God. If we have known God, or rather, are known of God, we are no longer aliens or strangers, but children and heirs; and the spirit of slavery cannot dwell with the spirit of the Son. Law and grace can never be united.

The Lord Jesus, having claimed for Himself and Peter the liberty of children, adds: "Notwithstanding, lest we should offend them, go thou to the sea, and cast a hook, and take up the fish that first cometh up; and when thou hast opened his mouth, thou shalt find a piece of money (a stater), that take and give unto them for Me, and thee." Thus, one piece of silver, brought up from the depth of the sea, was paid into God's treasury, in which piece Jesus and Peter were both included. There seems to be a wonderful significance in this. The sea yielded up the precious ransom-money. The depths, with their billows and waves of wrath and death, were, so to speak, the birthplace of atonement. Jesus rose not alone, but inseparably linked on with His Church—one with Him in all His own preciousness—presented in Him to God in glory—laid up and hidden in God's treasury above.

Whatever God's demand against Peter, the blessed Lord was involved in the same demand: Peter's responsibility became Christ's—"for Me and thee"—and thus is Jesus now in the presence of God for us, to answer every liability, to render payment in the full for all our infirmities and sins, to save, to the very end, all that come unto God by Him. He has bound us up with Himself, in one bundle of life; and we can never look upon Him now, without also beholding in union with Him, the whole ransomed church of God, one precious piece of silver in God's temple above.

Appendix B

The Jewish Year

Abib or *Nivan*—First month (April)
Fourteenth day—Passover Feast
Sixteenth day—Firstfruits of the Barley Harvest
Zif—Second month (May)
Sivan—Third month (June)
Sixth day—Feast of Weeks or Pentecost
Firstfruits of the Wheat, etc.
Thammuz—Fourth month (July)
Ab—Fifth month (August)
Elul—Sixth month (September)
Tisri—Seventh month (October)
First day—Feast of Trumpets
Tenth day—Day of Atonement
Fifteenth day—Feast of Tabernacles. Succoth
Bul—Eighth month (November)
Chislev—Ninth month (December)
Twenty-fifth day—Feast of Dedication
Tebeth—Tenth month (January)
Shebat—Eleventh month (February)
Adar—Twelfth Month (March)
Fourteenth and Fifteenth days—Purim

The Jewish year beings with a feast commemorating the great deliverance out of Egypt. It ends with a feast commemorating another deliverance. Heman is a type of the Antichrist. Read the book of Esther.

THE BOOK OF
LEVITICUS

Introduction

The third book of the Pentateuch is Leviticus. It has been called by this name because it gives fully the functions of the Levites. The Hebrews have given the book the name *"Va-yikra,"* the first word in the Hebrew text, meaning, "And He called."

The little word "and" connects the book closely with the preceding one. Its beautiful relation to the book of Exodus we hope to show later. The opening verses of Leviticus solemnly declare that the words contained in this book are the very words of Jehovah. "And the Lord called unto Moses and spake unto him out of the tabernacle of the congregation, saying, Speak unto the children of Israel," etc. In no other book of the Bible is such stress laid upon the fact that Jehovah speaks, and nowhere do we find so many repetitions of this fact. Twenty-four times we find the divine command, "speak unto the children of Israel"—"speak unto Aaron." Thirty-six times occurs the phrase "the Lord spake." Twenty-one times the speaking One says, "I am the Lord (Jehovah)," and as often, "I am the Lord your God." No other proof is needed that the Lord is speaking on every page of this book. Moses received the very Word of God. He wrote the words as he had received them from the Lord. Any other belief is untenable.

And here we must add the testimony of the New Testament Scriptures. Those contain at least forty references to the book and its ordinances. When our Lord Jesus Christ, the infallible Son of God, was on earth, the book of Leviticus, as well as the entire Pentateuch, was known and believed to be the Word of God, and written by Moses. Our Lord set His seal to this, and repeatedly bore witness to the Mosaic authorship and inspiration of the Pentateuch, called "the Law of Moses." How He confirms the book of Leviticus may be seen by turning to the following passages: Matthew 8:4 and Lev. 14:3-10; Matthew 12:4 and Lev. 24:9; Matthew 15:3-6 and Lev. 20:9; John 7:22 and Lev. 12:3. Without giving other New Testament references we briefly mention the Epistle to the Hebrews, which contains so many allusions to the levitical institutions, the priesthood and sacrifices, their typical meaning and realization in the person and work of Christ. This remarkable Epistle alone, in its God-breathed unfoldings, bears an incontrovertible testimony to the divine, as well as Mosaic, origin of Leviticus. And to this must be added another fact. The closer study of this book will disclose the fact that the different rites and divinely appointed institutions are indeed the "shadow of good things to come." The gospel of the grace of God is inseparably connected with the entire book of Leviticus. Nowhere else do we find the redemption-work of Christ so fully and so blessedly told out as in this book. The beauty and wisdom of all is from above.

An Astonishing Assertion

Leviticus, then, is by its own testimony the Word of God. The Son of God and the Holy Spirit in the New Testament confirm this testimony. The work of Christ and the gospel are foreshadowed in it and closely linked with the levitical institutions. In view of these great facts, believed and cherished by the people of God, including the most scholarly and devout, how astonishing is the assertion now so generally made by the boasting rationalistic school of higher criticism, that Leviticus is "a priestly forgery of the days after Ezra"! One is loath to refer again to this most dangerous infidelity which has become so widespread throughout all Christendom. Our times, however, demand a positive and outspoken condemnation of this modern day infidelity, which comes in the garb of an angel of light, with the claim of being reverent and devout, but behind which stands the dark and sneering shadow of the enemy of God. Higher criticism has consigned Leviticus to a date after the Babylonian captivity. According to these "scholars" the priestly laws were collected in Babylonia and were brought back to Palestine. Some even go so far as to claim that the levitical institutions were influenced by the institutions of Babylon. But enough of this! We do not want to fill our pages with the inventions of those blind leaders of the blind. If the book of Leviticus was not written by Moses, given to him directly by Jehovah Himself, then this book is a colossal fraud and forgery. Inasmuch as so many "theological" professors deny the inspiration and Mosaic authorship of Leviticus, this book has been branded as a concoction of falsehoods. Such is the logical consequence. We let another scholar speak on this matter: "While the Lord Jesus taught in various ways that Leviticus contains a law given by revelation from God to Moses, these teach that it is a priestly forgery of the days after Ezra. Both cannot be right; and if the latter are in the right, then—we speak with all possible deliberation and reverence—Jesus Christ was mistaken, and was therefore unable even to tell us with inerrant certainty whether this or that is the Word of God or not. But if this is so, then how can we escape the final inference that His claim to have a perfect knowledge of the Father must have been an error; His claim to be the incarnate Son of God, therefore, a false pretension, and Christianity, a delusion, so that mankind has in Him no Saviour?

"But against so fatal a conclusion stands the great established fact of the resurrection of Jesus Christ from the dead; whereby He was with power declared to be the Son of God, so that we may know that His word on this, as on all subjects where He has spoken, settles controversy, and is a sufficient ground of faith; while it imposes upon all speculations of men, literary or philosophical, eternal and irremovable limitations.

"Let no one think that the case, as regards the issue at state, has been above stated too strongly. One could not well go beyond the often cited words of Kuenen on this subject: 'We must either cast aside as worthless our dearly bought scientific method, or we must forever cease to acknowledge the authority of the New Testament in the domain of the exegesis of the Old.' With good reason does another scholar exclaim at these words, 'The Master must not be heard as a witness! We treat our criminals with more respect.' So then stands the question this day which the first verse of Leviticus brings before us: In which have we more confidence? in literary critics, like a Kuenen or Wellhausen, or in Jesus Christ? Which is the more likely to know with certainty whether the law of Leviticus is a revelation from God or not?

"The devout Christian, who through the grace of the crucified and risen Lord 'of whom Moses, in the law, and the prophets did write,' and who has 'tasted the good word of God,' will not long hesitate for an answer."[1]

To this we say, heartily, "Amen," If these critics, whose real difficulty is the "puffed up head" and "the empty heart" were to turn in humility of mind and in dependence upon the Spirit of God to the Word itself, casting their "little learning" to the winds, they would soon learn the wisdom of God and repent of their foolishness.

The Message of Leviticus

We have pointed out the fact that Leviticus has in itself the unmistakable imprint of divine revelation. What then is its message? One word gives the answer. The word "holy." Ninety times this word is found in the twenty-seven chapters. And here we call the attention to its relation to the book of Exodus. We found in our study of Exodus that redemption is there blessedly foreshadowed. The message of Leviticus is that which is the outcome of redemption, "holiness unto the Lord," "sanctification." In the New Testament the sanctification of a redeemed people is revealed in a twofold aspect: Sanctification by the precious blood of atonement, and sanctification by the Spirit of God. The first is the foundation of all, and the second is the result of it. We see, therefore, that the book of Leviticus begins with the divine instructions concerning the offerings, in which the perfect work of the Lord Jesus Christ and His perfect life are typically foreshadowed. It is perhaps the most complete as well as wonderful description of His work and sacrifice which we possess. In their typical meaning the first seven chapters can never be exhausted. Then follows the divine account of the consecration of the priesthood, telling us typically that a redeemed and sanctified people, a holy priesthood (1 Pet. 2:5), can draw nigh and enter into His presence. Access and worship are thus most blessedly illustrated. Practical sanctification in a separated walk and holy living is demanded by the different statutes and laws. And these typify the work of the Holy Spirit in the believer. All this, and much else, makes the study of Leviticus of great interest and value. It is needed in our days. The fundamental truths of the gospel, typically foreshadowed in Leviticus, are the truths mostly denied or belittled. And all that know the gospel, and rest upon the finished work of the Lord Jesus Christ, will surely find

[1]S. H. Kellogg, *Leviticus.*

in this book new beauties of Him, who is altogether lovely, and learn more what His great work as our substitute meant to Him and what it means for us.

Prophetic Foreshadowings

By far the greater number of the types of Leviticus have found their fulfillment in the life and death, the resurrection and priesthood of our Lord. Others, however, are still unfulfilled. This is especially true in connection with some of the feasts of Jehovah. The feast of trumpets, the ingathering at the full harvest, the Sabbatic year, the year of jubilee await their glorious fulfillment in a future day, when Israel shall be restored as a nation. These prophetic foreshadowings will be pointed out in the annotations.

The Time When Leviticus Was Given

Different views are held concerning the period of time consumed in the giving of these words of Jehovah. It is evident that Leviticus and Numbers 1—10:10 were given between the first day of the month and the twentieth day of the second month, that is of the second year after their departure from Egypt.

The Scope and Division of Leviticus

Leviticus containing the divine instructions for a redeemed people reveals a progressive order. A rapid glance at the contents will demonstrate this at once. First the Lord gives to the people, whom He brought out of Egypt, His communications concerning the different sacrifices. After these offerings are described, and the law concerning them is given, the account of the consecration of Aaron and his sons, his fellow-priests, follows, and how they began their priestly functions. The judgment of Nadab and Abihu for presenting strange fire is closely connected with this. God demanding holiness in His redeemed people comes next in this book. The account of the great day of atonement, when Aaron entered the Holiest for a brief season, precedes the precepts for the people of God in which their walk in separation from evil is so fully entered upon. The great day of atonement is the center of the book of Leviticus; everything in the book is related to that day. The next which follows, after the giving of instructions of a holy walk, is the divine appointment of the different feasts, and the laws connected with these feasts, especially the great year of jubilee. This, with a chapter on things vowed and devoted, closes the book. It is most interesting to note this last chapter, for it contains the consummation of the book, and foreshadows the time when God will receive what belongs to Him, and when He will be all in all. The words "unto Jehovah"—"holy to Jehovah"—"it is Jehovah's"—occur fourteen times in this last chapter. (The word "Lord" in Leviticus, as throughout the Old Testament, is in the Hebrew "Jehovah.") "Holy unto Jehovah" is mentioned thrice in the closing verses of Leviticus. And this is in keeping with the message of the book. Jehovah is holy; His people must also be holy. "Ye shall be holy: for I the Lord your God am holy" (chapter 19:2). The last verse of Leviticus states once more the solemn fact of the beginning of the book, that Jehovah spake all these words unto Moses.

This brief sketch shows the unity of the book of Leviticus and its progressive revelation. That it could be the patchwork of different writers or the product of after exilic days, as claimed by the rationalists, is impossible. A closer study of this book, so directly communicated by Jehovah to Moses, shows the marvellous wisdom of God. Only the omniscient Lord could give such instructions and institutions, which foreshadow His gracious ways in redemption. We shall aim, as much as this is possible, in our annotations, to point out the wonderful types and prophecies of Leviticus. Here the atoning work of Christ, the results for His people, their privileges and responsibilities are most blessedly outlined. Israel's future restoration connected with the coming day when they shall see Him, who is typified by Aaron, when they shall look upon the pierced One, and their great national day of atonement dawns, the millennial times of blessing and glory and the great Jubilee: all is more than indicated by the Divine communications.

The Division of Leviticus

The brief outline of the scope of the book shows that the division is not difficult to make. As this book is so little known, we suggest first of all a careful reading of the book, noting the three general parts.

These are the following: 1. The offerings and the priesthood (1—10). 2. Laws and precepts (11—22). 3. The feasts of Jehovah (23—27). In our study we shall divide the book in a way which, we trust, will make the study not alone helpful, but interesting. We divide the book in seven parts, which we give first of all, so that the reader can have the contents of the entire book for a careful survey at his command. It will help much in the study of Leviticus to go over this division a number of times and if possible to memorize the parts and contents of the chapters before following the analysis and studying the annotations.

I. THE OFFERINGS AND THE FOUNDATION OF HOLINESS

1. **The Burnt Offering** (1:1-17)
2. **The Meal Offering** (2:1-16)
3. **The Peace Offering** (3:1-17)
4. **The Sin Offering** (4:1—5:13)
5. **The Trespass Offering** (5:14—6:7)
6. **The Laws of the Offerings** (6:8—7:38)

II. THE PRIESTHOOD AND THE RESULTS OF HOLINESS

1. **Aaron and His Sons and Their Consecration** (8:1-36)
2. **The Functions of the Priesthood Exercised** (9:1-24)
3. **Nadab and Abihu: The False Worship and its Results** (10:1-20)

III. HOLINESS DEMANDED

1. **The Clean and the Unclean** (11:1-47)
2. **Childbirth Law. Inherited Sin** (12:1-8)
3. **Leprosy. Type of Indwelling Sin** (13:1-59)
4. **The Cleansing of the Leper** (14:1-57)
5. **Concerning Issues: Man's Weakness and Defilement** (15:1-33)

IV. THE DAY OF ATONEMENT: IN THE HOLIEST

1. **The Day of Atonement** (16:1-34)
2. **The Testimony Concerning the Blood** (17:1-16)

V. PRACTICAL HOLINESS IN DAILY LIFE

1. **Different Relationships** (18:1-30)
2. **Different Duties** (19:1-37)
3. **Warnings Against Special Sins and their Penalty** (20:1-27)
4. **Laws for the Priests** (21:1—22:33)

VI. THE HOLY FEASTS AND SET TIMES

1. **The Feasts** (23:1-44)
2. **Priestly Duties; the Light and the Shewbread** (24:1-9)
3. **Blasphemy: Israel's Sin Foreshadowed** (24:10-23)
4. **The Sabbatic Year and the Year of Jubilee (25:1-55)**
5. **The Blessings and the Curse: Israel's History (26:1-46)**

VII. VOWS AND DEVOTION

1. **The Claims of Jehovah Realized** (27:1-34)

Analysis and Annotations

I. The Offerings
the Foundation of Holiness

1. The Burnt Offering

CHAPTER 1

1. The bullock (1:1-9)
2. The sheep or the goat (1:10-13)
3. The doves or pigeons (1:14-17)

Jehovah spoke out of the tabernacle which had been set up and upon which the cloud descended, filling the Holy of Holies with the glory of the Lord. Thus Leviticus is closely linked with the ending of the book of Exodus. Out of that glory, from between the cherubim, the same Person spoke to Moses, who had spoken to him out of the burning bush and on Mount Sinai. The first three chapters with which Leviticus opens form one utterance of Jehovah. The second utterance begins with chapter 4:1. This first utterance of Jehovah is concerning three offerings: the burnt offering, the meat offering, and the peace offering. They are distinguished from the other two offerings by being called "a sweet savour (or odour) to Him." This tells of the value and acceptability of these offerings. No direct reference to sin is made in connection with the "sweet savour" offerings. For Israel these three offerings were the divinely appointed means to approach Him, who dwelt in the Sanctuary. The sin and trespass offerings had more specially to do with their sins and were the means of restoring communion with God. The burnt offering stands first among the offerings because it foreshadows in a most precious and simple way the perfect work of Christ, who through the eternal Spirit offered Himself to God. This offering was wholly consumed, and was therefore also called "whole burnt offering" (Deut. 33:10; Psalm 51:19). It was a holocaust. It went up entirely to God; the priests could not eat of it. The altar upon which it was brought was called the altar of burnt offering, while the fire upon that altar was never permitted to go out. Every part of it typifies Christ offering Himself completely to God; the sweet odour is unto God and it is for the believer's acceptance in Him. A few hints on this offering and the other offerings will be sufficient to show their typical meaning.

First the bullock is mentioned. The ox gives us the highest type of Christ offering Himself. Like the sheep and goats used in the burnt offering, the ox was easily gotten. He needed not to be hunted or be gotten by man's efforts; the ox and the other domestic animals used were, so to speak, ready and willing. Led from the green pastures to be killed before the Lord, the ox is the type of Christ, who left the Father's glory and presence to do His will and give Himself as the willing sacrifice (Psalm 40:6-8; Hebrews 10:1-6). But the ox is also the type of the servant, and reminds us of Christ, the obedient servant, who came not to be ministered to, but to minister and give His life as a ransom for many. There was to be no blemish whatever in the animal. Even so Christ was without blemish, holy and undefiled. The type was to be without blemish, Christ is without blemish, and the Church which He loved and for which He gave Himself will be through His gracious work without blemish, having no spot or wrinkle or any such thing (Eph. 5:27).

The offerer had to offer it of his own voluntary will. The correct rendering is (verse 3) "for his acceptance." This reveals the great purpose of the burnt offering. Through Christ as the sin offering, as we shall see later, the believer knows that all sins are paid for and put away. The burnt offering leads us higher. The spotless One offered Himself unto God and we are accepted in Him. The believer is therefore completely identified with the perfect obedience and devotion of the Lord Jesus Christ and accepted as His willing sacrifice was accepted by God and a sweet odour unto Him.

The offerer had to put his hand on the head of the sacrifice. This simple act identified the offerer with the offering. It also stands for faith, for the hand is for taking hold. Thus faith must lay hold in faith on Christ and become identified with Him. God and the believing soul meet in the One, who offered Himself. In connection with the command to put the hand on the head of the sacrifice we find the statement: "it shall be accepted for him to make atonement for him." While we saw before the believer's acceptance in Christ, here the fact is made known that the sacrifice is accepted in the offerer's place and that the burnt offering makes atonement. And because "without shedding of blood is no remission of sins" the ox had to be killed. The Hebrew word "killing" has a sacrificial meaning. The offerer had to slay the victim himself to indicate that he deserved the death which the animal suffered in his place. The next thing done was the sprinkling of the blood by the priests round upon the altar by the door of the tabernacle. Thus He who knew no sin was made sin for us; and His blood has made atonement. And how blessed it is to see it was done "before the Lord" (verse 5). How exceedingly precious and of inestimable value the devotedness of Christ, His obedience unto the death of the cross, and the shedding of His blood must be in God's holy sight! Thus everything in the burnt offering foreshadows the blessed truth—"Christ hath given Himself for us an offering and a sacrifice to God for a sweet smelling savour" (Eph. 5:2).

The victim was flayed, cut into pieces. His inwards and his legs were washed with water. The head and the fat, as well as the other parts including the inwards and the legs, were put in order on the wood upon the altar. It was then completely consumed by fire and rose up a sweet savour unto the Lord. All has its typical meaning. All is exposed to the Divine gaze and all witnesses to the perfection and excellencies of Him who gave Himself. The fat is typical of His internal excellencies. The inwards and the legs washed in water apply to Christ's holy character in His affections and in His walk in perfect accord with the Word (the water). The wood tells of His humanity which He took on for the suffering of death. The fire was the fire from heaven. It is not, as often taken here, the symbol of Divine wrath consuming the sacrifice, but it has another meaning. It is the figure of God's perfect delight in the devotion of His ever blessed Son. God rested in Christ and found His fullest satisfaction in Him. The Hebrew has different words for burning. The one that is used here is the same as used for the burning of incense. This in itself shows that it has no connection with wrath. The continual fire upon the altar in connection with this greatest of all the offerings, tells us of God's perpetual delight in the work of Christ, what He is and what He has done.

What became of the skin of the ox? Chapter 7:8 gives the answer. It belonged to the priest. And thus the burnt offering aspect of the death of Christ covers and hides all, who trust in Him.

Next we find that sheep and goats could also be brought as a burnt offering. The highest grade was the ox and the grades which followed, the sheep and the goat. This was in case the offerer was poor and could not bring the more costly ox. It also represents the faith of the offerer. A lower faith and estimate of Christ which does not reach up to the highest conception, however, does not affect the acceptance of the offerer. The inferior offerings typified Christ and were therefore a sweet savour unto God, who beheld in all the same perfect sacrifice. Our faith should rest completely upon God's estimate of Christ and His work. The sheep is the type of Christ in His devoted self-surrender, unresisting and silent (Isaiah 53:7). The goat offering clearly typifies the substitutionary character of the work of the Lamb of God on the cross. The goat is more linked with the sin offering aspect of the death of Christ. Here also the fact is made known that the lamb and goat offering is to be brought on the side of the altar *northward* before the Lord (verse 11). It stands typically for distance and not the same nearness is recognized as in the first grade offering.

Turtle-doves and pigeons are the lowest grade of burnt offerings. These were for the poorest of the people and they express typically the weakest faith in Christ and the lowest estimate of His work. But here also we read that it was accepted as an offering made by fire, of a sweet savour unto the Lord. These birds speak of Christ as do the ox and the lamb. The dove is the bird of peace, love and sorrow. The dove pictures Him as holy and undefiled, filled with tenderness and love. The bird was put to death by "wringing off its head," the type of the violence done to Him, who was so tender and loving. The crop and the feathers (correct meaning, "filth") were cast away. As those were unclean they had to be thrown away so as to make the type correspond to Him, who is undefiled and holy.

2. The Meal Offering

CHAPTER 2

1. The general instruction (2:1-3)
2. Baked in the oven (2:4)
3. Baked in a pan (2:5-6)
4. Baked in a frying pan (2:7)
5. Presented unto the priest (2:8-11)
6. The oblation of the firstfruits (2:12-16)

The word "meat" should be changed throughout this chapter to "meal." This offering or oblation is closely connected with the burnt offering. No doubt it could not be brought apart from the sacrificial animal. The meal offering is the type of Christ in His perfect humanity and holy, devoted character. It was not for atonement even as the holy humanity of Christ and devotedness of His life could not atone for sins. It is called "most holy" for in His humanity He was "that holy thing." The fine flour, sifted and pure, coming from the corn of wheat, is the apt and beautiful type of His perfect humanity. The oil, so prominent in this offering, is the type of the Holy Spirit. The oil was connected in a two-fold way with this offering. The fine flour was mingled with oil. This is typical of the incarnation, His conception by the Holy Spirit, His whole being Spirit-filled. It is a blessed illustration of Luke 1:35. Leaven was *entirely* absent. "Unleavened fine flour" and "no leaven" is repeatedly stated by Jehovah. It had to be excluded, for leaven is a type of evil, and no evil was in Him.

Nor was any honey permitted in the fine flour. Honey is the type of the sweetness of human nature apart from grace; the picture of fallen nature in an amiable character, yet sin connected with it. Leaven is fermentation; and the sweet honey is the cause of it. It was not allowed in the fine flour, for nothing of an unholy sweetness was in Christ. Only the oil was mingled with the flour. But the oil was also poured upon the flour. This is the type of the Holy Spirit, as He came upon Christ, the anointed One. He was on earth the One whom the Father had sealed (John 6:27); in the meal offering "salt" had likewise a place. It is the type of the separating power of holiness. Believers, born again, have the Holy Spirit in the new nature, and by the Spirit are sealed. Thus we are enabled to walk even as He walked, and show forth His excellencies. We add here a beautiful tribute to the perfect humanity and the moral glory of Christ:

This meal offering of God, taken from the fruit of the earth, was of the finest wheat; that which was pure, separate and lovely in human nature was in Jesus under all its sorrows, but in all its excellence, and excellent in its sorrows. There was no unevenness in Jesus, no predominant quality to produce the effect of giving Him a distinctive character. He was, though despised and rejected of men, the perfection of human nature. The sensibilities, firmness, decision (though this attached itself also to the principle of obedience), elevation and calm meekness, which belong to human nature, all found their perfect place in Him. In a Paul I find energy and zeal; in a Peter, ardent affection; in a John, tender sensibilities and abstraction of thought, united to a desire to vindicate what he loved which scarce knew limit. But the quality we have observed in Peter predominates and characterizes him. In a Paul, blessed servant though he was, he did not repent, though he had repented. . . . In him in whom God was mighty toward the circumcision, we find the fear of man break through the faithfulness of his zeal. John, who would have vindicated Jesus in his zeal, knew not what manner of spirit He was of, and would have forbidden the glory of God, if a man walked not with them.

But in Jesus, even as man, there was none of this unevenness. There was nothing salient in His character, because all was in perfect subjection to God in His humanity, and had its place, and did exactly its service, and then disappeared. God was glorified in it, and all was in harmony. When meekness became Him He was meek; when indignation, who could stand before His overwhelming and withering rebuke? Tender to the chief of sinners in the time of grace; unmoved by the heartless superiority of a cold Pharisee (curious to judge who He was); when the time of judgment is come, no tears of those who wept for Him moved Him to other words than 'Weep for yourselves and for your children,'—words of deep compassion, but of deep subjection to the due judgment of God. The dry tree prepared itself to be burned. On the cross, when His service was finished, tender to His mother, and intrusting her in human care, to one who (so to speak) had been His friend, and leaned on His bosom; no ear to recognize her word or claim when His service occupied Him for God; putting both blessedly in their place, when He would show that, before His public mission, He was still the Son of the Father, and though such, in human blessedness, subject to the mother that bare Him, and Joseph His father as under the law, a calmness which disconcerted His adversaries; and in the moral power which dismayed them at times, a meekness which drew out the hearts of all not steeled by opposition. Such was Christ in human nature.[2]

And frankincense was thereon. This is the fragrance, unspeakable in its value, as it went up from His blessed life to God.

But the meal offering was baked in an oven, in a pan and in a frying pan or cauldron. These are the types of the testings and trials in His holy humanity. He was made perfect through suffering as the captain of our salvation (Heb. 2:10). The oven typifies the temptations from the side of Satan—known only to the Lord Himself. The pan tells of the more evident testings and trials through which He passed, enduring the contradiction of sinners and all the opposition and hatred heaped upon Him. The frying pan or cauldron speaks of the combining trials and sorrows of an outward and inward nature. But all, whether the oven, the pan or the cauldron, brought out His perfection.

The meal offering was then burnt upon the altar, a sweet odour to Jehovah. The priests could eat the remainder of the meal offering. As priests of God, constituted thus through the grace of God, it is our holy and blessed privilege to feed on Himself, and the feeding on Christ will ever keep us in conscious nearness to God, and wean us away from earthly things.

The oblation mentioned in verse 12 refers to the "new meal offering" in which leaven was permitted, and which was not to be burnt. This we shall find more fully mentioned in chapter 23:15-20. When we reach that chapter we shall speak of its significance as the wave offering. The oblation of the firstfruits (verses 14-16) consisted in green ears of corn dried by fire, even corn beaten out of full ears. He again is typified here as the green corn, which was dried (roasted) in the fire. It points to His holy life, His death and His resurrection. However, all this is more fully revealed in the wave sheaf after Passover in connection with Pentecost. This we shall find in the contents of the twenty-third chapter of the book.

3. The Peace Offering

CHAPTER 3

1. The ox (3:1-5)
2. The sheep or goat (3:6-17)

This is the third "sweet savour offering," and is closely linked with the burnt offering, but it differs from it, especially, in that part of it was to be eaten. The peace offering also had the character of a thank offering (7:11-13). As it was offered on the altar *upon* the burnt sacrifice, it cannot therefore be separated from Christ offering Himself as the burnt offering. Leviticus 7:11-34 contains the law of the peace offering

---

[2] J. N. Darby, *Synopsis of the Bible.*

and tells of the eating of the peace offering, which is not mentioned in the third chapter. It typifies the gracious results accomplished for the sinner by the death of Christ. The blood is sprinkled upon the altar, which is for propitiation. Fellowship therefore results with praise and thanksgiving. As we shall learn more fully from the seventh chapter about the feeding upon the breast and the shoulder of the peace offering, we pass all this by. However, we call attention to the prominence given to the fat of the sacrifice. It is the type of the inward energy of Christ, expressed in doing the Father's will, even unto death; and this is called "the food of Jehovah." He delights in this. The happy scene of how the priests, the offerer and his friends partook of that of which God partakes Himself, we shall see later.

4. The Sin Offering

CHAPTER 4—5:13

1. The second utterance of Jehovah (4:1-2)
2. The sin offering for the high priest (4:3-12)
3. The sin offering for the congregation (4:13-21)
4. The sin offering for the ruler (4:22-26)
5. The sin offering for one of the people (4:27-35)
6. The sin offering for special inadvertent offences (5:1-13)

The burnt offering, meal offering, and peace offering typified the absolute and blessed perfection and devotion of Christ, and are therefore the sweet savour offerings. The remaining offerings, the sin and trespass offerings, are not called a sweet savour. In these offerings we see Christ typified as the bearer of the sins of His people. And as such He had to take upon Himself the judgment of God. This, no doubt, is the reason why these two offerings are not called a "sweet savour"; for God does not delight in judgment. Judgment is His strange work (Isaiah 28:21). Note also that the preceding three offerings were voluntary, the two remaining were compulsory. Forgiveness had to be sought and secured by them. In the actual approach of man to God, the sin offering always occupied the first place; the burnt offering followed. As we have seen the burnt offering is mentioned first, because it tells out the perfection and infinite worth of Him in whom, according to the eternal purpose of God, we are accepted. And now as accepted in the Beloved One, made nigh and brought into fellowship with God, the need which we have on account of our sins is fully met in the work of Christ, who bore our sins in His own body on the tree.

It is impossible to follow all the manifold types in connection with the sin offering for the priest, the ruler, and the congregation. The details of it demand a very careful and minute study which we cannot attempt here. We can treat the sin offering only in a general way. The bullock is the sin offering for the anointed priest and for the whole congregation (verses 4 and 13). Like in the burnt offering, the offerers had to identify themselves with the offering by laying their hands on the head of the bullock. But this difference must be noticed: in the burnt offering the believer is seen identified with Christ and accepted in Christ; in the sin offering Christ became identified with us in our sin. Sin was transferred to Him as our substitute. "The Lord hath laid on Him the iniquity of us all." The blood then was sprinkled seven times before the Lord. Some of it was put upon the horns of the altar of incense; while the blood of the bullock, the greater portion of it, was poured at the bottom of the altar of burnt offering.

The skin of the bullock with the whole bullock was burned without the camp. The Hebrew word for "burned" is different from that used in the burnt offering. The word used in connection with the sin offering is "saraph"; it speaks of the burning of judgment. The commentary to this is Hebrews 13:11-12. "The bodies of those beasts whose blood is brought into the sanctuary by the high priest for sin, are burned without the camp. Wherefore Jesus also, that He might sanctify the people with His own blood suffered without the gate." With the case of a ruler having sinned the offering was a kid of the goats, a male; and in the case of any one of the common people having sinned through ignorance still other instructions are given.

It is evident, therefore, that there is a graduated scale in these different instances. Why so? Because of a most solemn principle. The gravity of sin depends on the position of him that sins. It is not so, that man is prone to adjust matters, though his conscience feels its rectitude. How often man would screen the offense of him that is great, if he could! The same might be hard on the poor, friendless, and despised. The life of such at any rate seems of no great account. It is not so with God, nor ought it to be in the minds and estimate of His saints. And another witness of this in the last instance is not without interest for our souls. Only to one of the common people is allowed the alternative of a female lamb instead of a kid (verses 32-35), the offering of which for his sin is reiterated with the same minute care.

When the anointed priest sinned, the result was

precisely such as if the whole congregation sinned. When a prince sinned, it was a different matter, though a stronger case for sacrifice than where it was a private man. In short, therefore, the relationship of the person that was guilty determines the relative extent of the sin, though none was obscure enough for his sin to be passed by. Our blessed Lord on the other hand meets each and all, Himself the true anointed priest, the only One who needs no offering—who could therefore be the offering for all, for any. This is the general truth, at least on the surfrace of the sin offering. The offence that was brought foward, confessed, and judged becomes the substitute in this case for him that was guilty; and the blood was put in the care of individuals on the brazen altar, as it only needed to be dealt with in the place of sinful man's access to God.[3]

In studying the interesting details of the sin offerings it must be remembered that all is the "shadow of good things to come," and that the good things which have come, and which we now enjoy, as believers in Christ, are far higher and more blessed than the types could reveal.

5. The Trespass Offering

CHAPTERS 5:14—6:7

1. The trespass against Jehovah (5:14-19)
2. The trespass against man (6:1-7)

The brief section which gives instruction concerning the trespass offering contains twice the statement, "Jehovah spake unto Moses" (5:14 and 6:1). Sin is here looked upon as an injury done. The trespass offering was always a ram without a blemish out of the flock (verses 15, 18; 6:6). First the wrong is mentioned done in holy things of Jehovah or something done against His commands, and secondly, wrongs done against his neighbor, which Jehovah also reckons as done against Himself. There is no need to define the wrong done in the holy things of Jehovah. The word trespass in the Hebrew means "to act covertly." It was no doubt an attempt to defraud Jehovah in the holy things, as defrauding is prominent in connection with the wrong done to the neighbor. The offering of the ram, which, of course, typifies Christ, is not described here, but in chapter 7:1-10. But another feature is made prominent which contains a most interesting truth. Restitution had to be made in each trespass against Jehovah and against man, and in each case the fifth part of the whole had to be added. In the wrong done against Jehovah the fifth part was given to the priest; and in the wrong done against the neighbor the one who had been defrauded received it. This shows forth the blessed effect of the redemption work of Christ. He has not only restored what He took not away, but added more to it. God manifested thus His gracious power by giving greater blessing to His people and bringing greater glory to Himself.

6. The Laws of the Offerings

CHAPTER 6:8—7:38

1. The law of the burnt offering (6:8-13)
2. The law of the meal offering (6:14-18)
3. The offering of the high priest (6:19-23)
4. The law of the sin offering (6:24-30)
5. The law of the trespass offering (7:1-10)
6. The law of the sacrifice of the peace offerings (7:11-38)

After Jehovah had given to Moses by direct communication the different offerings, in what they were to consist, and how they were to be brought, different laws concerning these offerings were added by Jehovah. They are mostly addressed to Aaron and his sons (6:8,14,19,24). They acquaint us therefore with the relation of the priest to the offerings. In the law of the trespass and peace offerings we do not find an address to Aaron and his sons. The proper way to study the offerings is to consider first what is said in the beginning of Leviticus and then to read the laws of the offerings in connection with each to learn their relation to the priest and the people.

The law of burnt offering—It was the duty of the priest to keep the burnt offering upon the altar and the fire of the altar had to be kept burning in it. It is especially stated that the burnt offering shall be upon the hearth upon the altar all night unto the morning. This continual burnt offering with the fire, which never went out, is the type of Christ, who continually offers Himself to God and in whom all believers have the assurance of their full acceptance. It was different with the sin offering; there could not be a continuous sin offering, for Christ giving Himself as an expiatory sacrifice cannot be a continuous act. But it is different with the burnt offering. While on earth He ever presented Himself before God and the fire of His devotion never went out. And thus He continues in

[3]W. Kelly, *Introduction to the Pentateuch.*

the heavenly sanctuary, appearing in the presence of God for us. This never ceases. It is morning by morning, evening by evening. And how blessed that the night is mentioned! The night is the present age; and it will be followed by the morning, when the day dawns. What comfort is here provided for us! While we are down here in the wilderness, tested, tried, failing and stumbling our perfect burnt offering is ever present with God and the sweet savour arises from it. By it we are kept, though we are a sinning people. It has also a blessed meaning for Israel. This is Israel's night. By the burnt offering sacrifice even Israel is kept during the dark night of their unbelief for the blessing which shall surely come in the morning, when He is revealed again. Then they will behold Him as their burnt offering, whom they had despised and rejected during the night of wandering and tribulation; then they will confess their sin and acknowledge He was bruised on account of their iniquities.

But while this is the blessed meaning of the burnt offering for the believer and for repenting and believing Israel, for the unbeliever there is another fire which will never go out. And we must see the practical application as well. This blessed continual burnt offering must lead His believing people to give themselves continually and manifest their devotion in practical holiness. "God delights to have us remind Him (though He can never forget it) of the work of His dear Son, and that we have here our occupation and live in the fragrance of His acceptance. This is really the foundation of all practical holiness, as it is of rest and satisfaction to the soul. Christ is our righteousness before God; we are accepted in the Beloved; in Christ we are as Christ, even in this world. Here the perpetual sunshine settles down on us; it is the true Beulah land for the saint, where the birds sing ever and the heart goes forth in perpetual melody" (*Numerical Bible*). Our answer to the continuous burnt offering in our behalf must be a life of devotion to God. Space forbids to follow the equally precious application of the other priestly actions.

The law of the meal offering—As we learned in connection with the second chapter, the meal offering foreshadows Christ on earth, that blessed and holy life which was lived here in entire devotion. The principal thing here is that Aaron and his sons, the priests, were to eat of it. God had His portion in it, but the priests were to share it. All believers are priests in Christ, and as such have this precious food to enjoy. That food is Christ, and that means communion with God. To enjoy Christ, feed on Him, the bread come down from heaven; to meditate upon all His loveliness and grace, is our blessed privilege, who are brought into His fellowship. Note that it says "it shall be eaten unleavened in a holy place." This means that only in the place of separation, where grace has put us, can we enjoy this feast. The feeding on the meal offering will keep us in the sanctuary in His presence.

The offering of the high priest—Distinct from the general meal offering is that meal offering which the high priest had to bring on the day of his anointing. This had to be wholly burned unto Jehovah. No priest was permitted to taste this and partake of it. It had to be offered half of it in the morning and half of it at night. There is another distinction. Oil was mixed with it, but oil was not poured upon it. We saw what the oil mixed with the fine flour meant, and that the pouring of the oil upon the fine flour typified the Holy Spirit as He came upon Christ at His baptism. Now inasmuch as this pouring of the oil is omitted here, this meal offering seems to typify the blessed life of our Lord before His public ministry began. The hidden years, as we term them, were yielded completely to God, and as the Holy Spirit has not given us a record of those years we cannot feed on them. This, no doubt, is the typical meaning of this special meal offering of the high priest "on the day of his anointing."

The law of the sin offering—This law contains interesting details concerning the sin offering. It had to be killed in the place where the burnt offering was killed. The priest that offered it for sin had to eat it, and he typifies Christ. This means His identification with sinners, when in our stead He bore our sins in His own body on the tree. But the priests also could eat of it. The work of atonement, the sin-bearing, no fellow priest could share with Him. He alone could do this great work. Nevertheless we eat of the sin offering if we identify ourselves in humiliation and confession with the sins and failures of the saints of God. The holiness of the sin offering is especially emphasized. It is called "most holy." The earthen vessel in which it was boiled had to be broken and the brazen pot had to be scoured and rinsed. This typifies the unique and most precious, as well as holy character, of the great work accomplished by the sin bearer on the cross.

The law of the trespass offering—This also is called "most holy." Here the killing of the sacrifice, the sprinkling of the blood, the presentation of the fat, etc., and the burning upon the altar, omitted in chapters 5:14—6:7, are now commanded. Restitution is the prominent thing at the first mention of the trespass offering. It reveals the joy of God in what has been accomplished by Christ in His redemption work. But restitution must rest for a foundation upon atonement. This is now therefore brought out in the law of the trespass offering.

The law of the peace offering—But one more remains. We discover that the peace offering is removed out of its connection. The order in the beginning of Leviticus is: burnt offering, meal offering, peace offering, sin offering, and trespass offering. The first three were the "sweet savour offerings." The third sweet savour offering, the peace offering, is put last in the laws of the offering. The peace offering represents the blessed results of the work of Him, who has made peace in the blood of His cross, in whom all who believe are justified and have peace with God. And the first thing mentioned is most blessed and intimate communion and enjoyment with thanksgiving. The pierced cakes, unleavened mingled with oil, etc., typify Christ. In this blessed feast Christ, as everywhere, has the pre-eminent place. The enjoyment of peace and its resulting communion is impossible apart from Christ. We must ever let the Holy Spirit remind us of what He is and what He has done for us. But what does it mean that the Israelite had to bring an offering of *leavened* bread with the sacrifice of his peace offerings for "thanksgiving"? Leaven was forbidden at Passover, in the meal offering, because it is the type of evil. Here and in the two loaves of the Feast of Weeks it was not only permitted, but commanded. In Christ there was no leaven; but in His saints, though made nigh by blood, there is still leaven, the corruption of the old nature. How harmonious with the teaching of the New Testament! We leave this to our readers to follow with prayer, searching, and, we trust, exercise of soul.

Rich and full is indeed this portion, the concluding section; one feels like touching upon every detail and meditate on these precious pictures, foreshadowing our blessings and privileges in Christ.

We must pass all these riches by, but pray that His Spirit may open up the mines of divine wisdom and comfort to every child of God. But one more phrase we mention. The priests had their portion in the peace offering. The priest, who burns the fat upon the altar represents Christ. Aaron and his sons received the breast of the sacrifice. The shoulder of the peace offering belonged to *the* priest for an heave offering. Like Aaron and his sons, priests of God, we can feast upon the breast, the type of His love, and thus enjoy His affections. The shoulder is the seat of power. And power belongs to Him alone, who loveth us and hath washed us from our sins in His own blood and hath made us priests and kings. May this first part of Leviticus (so often ignored) become a source of much joy and blessing to His people. The few hints we could give will, under God, show the way how these types should be studied.

II. The Priesthood and the Results of Holiness

1. Aaron and His Sons and Their Consecration

CHAPTER 8

1. Aaron (8:1-12)
2. Aaron and his sons (8:13-21)
3. The consecration (8:22-30)
4. The sacrificial feast (8:31-36)

The second part of Leviticus is historical and gives the account of how Aaron and his sons were consecrated as priests and how they exercised their priesthood. The judgment, which fell upon the two sons of Aaron ends this interesting section.

The voice of Jehovah spoke again, commanding that Aaron and his sons should now be taken and be consecrated. The ceremony took place "at the door of the tabernacle of the congregation." The entire congregation of Israel was gathered together to witness the event. This statement has been severely attacked by the critics, who reject this report as untrustworthy inasmuch as a congregation of several millions could hardly have gathered at the door of the tabernacle. For this reason the critics have branded the account as legendary. "But, surely, if the words are to be taken in the ultraliteral sense required in order to make out this difficulty, the impossibility must have been equally evident to the supposed fabricator of the fiction; and it is yet more absurd to suppose that he should ever have intended his words to be pressed to such a rigid literality."[4] But the words do not necessarily mean that every individual was present at the door of the tabernacle and all remained there for the entire seven days of ceremonial observance. Perhaps only the representatives of the tribes were called to witness all that was done; these appointed leaders represented the whole assembly of Israel. All was carried out according to the divine command. Not less than twelve times is reference made to this fact in the eighth chapter. It was all according to divine appointment. Aaron was called of God to this office, and in this he was a type of Christ in His office-work as priest. "And no man taketh this honour unto himself, but he that is called of God as was Aaron. So also Christ glorified not Himself to be made an high priest, but He that said unto Him, Thou art my Son, today have I begotten thee" (Heb. 5:4-5). As Aaron and his work was appointed by God, so the work of our Lord in connection with sin. Aaron did "all the things which the Lord commanded by the hand of Moses," and Christ completely did the will of Him that sent Him. That blessed will is foreshadowed in the priestly office and the priestly work.

Without following the historical account in every detail we point out some of the leading types in this great chapter. The principal actors are Aaron and his sons. Aaron occupies the leading and prominent place; his sons are associated with him. He is, as stated above, a type of Christ. His sons typify those who are called into the priesthood in their Christian profession. The priesthood of the sons of Aaron depended upon their relationship to him. Without Aaron they could not be priests at all. Our relationship to Christ constitutes us priests. The Priesthood of Christ rests upon His Sonship, and believing on Him we become children of God and also priests with Him. The sons of Aaron typify the Christian profession; two of his sons were taken in a judgment. They foreshadow the true and the false in Christendom. But there is still another application. Israel's national priesthood is also foreshadowed. "Ye shall be unto Me a kingdom of priests" (Exod. 19:6) is God's calling for the nation. They will yet possess that priesthood. "But ye shall be named the priests of the Lord, men shall call you the ministers of our God" (Is. 61:6). This will be accomplished with the second coming of Christ. A part of the nation will then be swept away in judgment, while the believing remnant will exercise the functions of the priesthood in the ngdom. These two classes are typified by the sons of Aaron.

The first thing mentioned is the "washing with water." This washing of water is the type of the new birth. This is beautifully illustrated by the symbolical action of our Lord in the washing of the disciples' feet (John 13:2-12). The feet washing corresponds to the wahing the priests had to do when they went into the tabernacle, and typifies the daily cleansing by the Word the believer needs to continue in fellowship with God. When Peter demanded to have his hands and head washed the Lord told him "He that is washed needeth not save to wash his feet, but is clean every whit; and ye are clean, but not all." By these words the Lord told Peter that inasmuch as they all had believed on Him, with the exception of Judas Iscariot, they were washed and clean every whit. And in other Scriptures the same symbol is used: "Born of the water and the Spirit" (John 3:5); "the washing of regeneration" (Titus 3:5); "our bodies washed with pure water" (Heb. 10:22). But this could never apply to the Lord Jesus Christ. He needed no washing, no regeneration, for He is holy and undefiled.

Aaron was then clothed with the holy garments, invested with his official robes. These are described in detail in Exodus 28. (The annotations on Exodus give the typical meaning of the garments. This description of the official dress and what is typified by it should be carefully studied.) The investiture of the sons of Aaron took place *after* the anointing of the tabernacle and Aaron as high priest. Christ and His work is put into the foreground. He is anointed with the oil of gladness above His fellows (Ps. 45:7; Heb. 1:9). But linked with Him are His fellows, His seed, the many sons He brings to glory. Their garments, including the breeches (Exodus 28:42) (not mentioned here), were of pure white linen, the type of the holiness and righteousness into which the grace of God has brought us in Christ. We are a holy priesthood. See also Rev. 4:4. "And round about the throne were four and twenty thrones, and upon the thrones I saw four and twenty elders sitting clothed in *white raiment;* and they had on their heads crowns of gold." "And to her was granted that she should be arrayed in fine *linen, clean* and *white;* for the fine linen is the righteousness of the saints" (Rev. 19:8).

The tabernacle, the altar, the laver and finally Aaron were anointed with the holy oil. The oil was sprinkled upon the altar seven times. No

[4] S. H. Kellogg, *Leviticus.*

blood was shed for atonement. All this has its blessed significance. While by this ceremony the tabernacle with all that was in it was sanctified and consecrated, it also typifies the consecration of all through Christ. The anointing of Aaron is the type of the anointing of our Lord. "God anointed Jesus with the Holy Spirit and with power" (Acts 10:38).

After the investiture of the sons of Aaron came the sacrifice of the bullock for a sin offering. This was followed by the ram of the burnt offering. Then the sacrifice of a second ram, the ram of consecration. Aaron and his sons laid their hands upon the head of the bullock and also upon the heads of the rams before they were killed. The sin offering had to come first for Aaron's sin and those of his sons. Aaron was a sinful man, Christ was not. But His gracious identification with us is here foreshadowed. The burnt offering, speaking of the perfection of Christ, was alone a sweet savour unto the Lord. For Aaron and his sons it had the meaning of their full consecration to the service of God. The second ram was for consecration; the literal rendering from the Hebrew is "the ram of fillings," because of verse 27, where we read that their hands were filled to wave it all as a wave offering before the Lord. The blood of this second ram was put upon the tip of the right ear of Aaron, upon the thumb of the right hand and upon the great toe of his right foot. The same was done to Aaron's sons. Their whole bodies were thus set apart for the service of God in virtue of the blood which had been shed. It is the most blessed type of sanctification by that "better blood," the blood of Christ. The ear is for hearing; we are set apart to hear the Word of God and yield obedience to it. The hand is set apart to serve and to do His will, and the feet to walk in His ways. No such sanctification was possible till the blood had been shed. All this foreshadows our sanctification by blood, and the results of this sanctification. The anointing oil was also sprinkled with the blood (of the peace offering) upon Aaron and his sons and their garments. The sacrificial feast, which followed is interesting and full of meaning. They fed upon the ram and the unleavened bread.

"This sacrificial feast most fitly marked the conclusion of the rites of consecration. Hereby it was signified, first, that by this solemn service they were now brought into a relation of peculiarly intimate fellowship with Jehovah, as the ministers of His house, to offer His offerings, and to be fed at His table. It was further signified, that strength for the duties of this office should be supplied to them by Him whom they were to serve, in that they were to be fed of His altar. And, finally, in that the ritual took the specific form of a thank offering, was thereby expressed, as was fitting, their gratitude to God for the grace which had chosen them and set them apart to so holy and exalted service.

"These consecration services were to be repeated for seven consecutive days, during which time they were not to leave the tent of meeting; obviously, that by no chance they might contract any ceremonial defilement, so jealously must the sanctity of everything pertaining to the service be guarded" (S. H. Kellogg).

How necessary for us who are constituted "a holy priesthood to offer up spiritual sacrifices" to feed thus on Himself, who is ever before us in these ceremonies. It is at the Lord's table, when we eat and drink in remembrance of Him, we feed on Him and then exercise our holy priesthood of praise and worship. The seven days mean typically our life down here during which our consecration continues. The seven days stand for this age when a "heavenly priesthood" is feasting (the Church), and when the seven days end something new begins. The eighth day which follows marks this new beginning.

2. The Functions of the Priesthood Exercised

CHAPTER 9

1. The new offerings of the priests (9:1-14)
2. The people's offerings (9:15-21)
3. The fulness of blessing and glory (9:22-24)

A service follows the consecration of the priests, in which they officiated; hitherto Moses had acted by divine command. The service ordered is of great significance. For seven days, during the days of their consecration, a bullock had been offered for Aaron and his sons, and yet at the beginning of the eighth day a young calf for a sin offering and a ram for a burnt offering are needed. This reminds us of Hebrews 10:4, "For it is not possible that the blood of bulls and of goats should take away sins." But there is a deeper meaning here. In connection with these new offerings on the eighth day the promise is given "today the Lord will appear unto you," and "the glory of the Lord shall appear unto you." We must look for a prophetic, dispensational foreshadowing. And such we have here.

We have seen that Aaron and his sons typify a heavenly priesthood, Christ, and those who are priests with Him. But Aaron and his sons also typify the nation Israel. While the seven days of the consecration feast foreshadow the present age in which believers in Christ feast and exercise the functions of their spiritual priesthood, the eighth day stands for the beginning of the coming age in which the Lord will appear unto His people Israel and when His glory is manifested. Then Israel will become the kingdom of priests. The sin offering and burnt offering brought again shows that it is in virtue of the blessed work of Christ. Then "all Israel," the remnant of that day, will be saved and "there shall be a fountain opened to the house of David and to the inhabitants of Jerusalem for sin and for uncleanness" (Zech. 13:1). The offerings for the people in our chapter suggest this prophetic application. When the seven days, the present age, is ended, then Israel will look upon Him, whom they have pierced and mourn for Him (Zech. 12:10).

A still more interesting event is given in the close of our chapter. Aaron came down from the altar where he had brought the offerings to bless the people. Immediately upon that he withdrew and entered with Moses into the holy place. Moses and Aaron were then invisible to the people. But they came forth, and a second blessing was pronounced upon the people. Nothing is said of how long both were in the holy place. We have here the beautiful types of the work of Christ and the blessing, which results from it for His people. As Aaron came forth the *second* time, so Christ will come the second time to bless His people Israel with peace. Moses, the leader of the people, typifies kingship, and Aaron the priesthood. Both coming out of the holy place foreshadow the second coming of Christ, the King—Priest. Melchisedek was king of righteousness and king of peace and priest as well, the type of Christ. When Christ comes again He will receive His throne and be a priest upon that throne. All this will mean glory for Him, glory for the church, glory and blessing for Israel, and glory for the earth. Then the glory of the Lord will appear, as it appeared when Moses and Aaron blessed the people. The fire came out from before the Lord. The Shekinah-Glory appeared and the flashing fire falling upon the altar consumed the offerings and the fat. The Lord thereby showed His approval of all that had been done. Jewish tradition claims that the fire which was never to cease burning was started in this divine act.

3. Nadab and Abihu: The False Worship and Its Results

CHAPTER 10

1. The false worship and the judgment (10:1-7)
2. New instructions (10:8-15)
3. The neglect of Eleazar and Ithamar (10:16-20)

The ceremonies were ended and the people, beholding the glory of the Lord, had worshipped. A terrible occurrence follows the beautiful ending to the previous chapter. Nadab and Abihu, two sons of Aaron, offered strange fire before Jehovah. The fire before Jehovah devoured them and they died before the Lord. The sin consisted in taking strange fire, which Jehovah had not commanded; most likely it was fire they produced themselves, instead of taking the fire from off the altar (Lev. 16:12). The whole action was in utter disregard of the commandment given and an act of disobedience. This sin in the form as committed by Nadab and Abihu was never repeated. However, the principle of this sin is to be seen on all sides and in many forms in Christendom. It was "will worship." It was doing that in their own will, what God had not commanded. And in Christian worship, so called, how much there is which is will worship! How numerous the carnal things, the inventions and traditions of men, used in worship which have not alone no sanction whatever in the Word, but are altogether contrary to a true worship in the Spirit. Well has one said: 'When one goes into many a church and chapel and sees the multitude of devices by which, as it is imagined, the worship and adoration of God is furthered, it must be confessed that it certainly seems as if the generation of Nadab and Abihu was not yet extinct; even although a patient God, in the mystery of His long suffering, flashes not instantly forth His vengeance." The fire of judgment, however, will some day fall upon all the false worship and make an end of it.

What induced them to act in this way so that the judgment of God fell upon them? The warning which follows this incident gives a strong hint on the possible cause of their presumptuous deed. Read verses 8 and 9. The warning against strong drink hints, no doubt, that they had been under the influence of strong drink. It must have been intoxication. May we remember that there is also another intoxication, which is a strange fire and which God hates. How much of Christian service and activity is there which is not done under the leading of the Holy Spirit. Then there are the so-called "revivals," with their purely soulical emotion and carnal means which are used. The unscriptural, and alas! sometimes even vulgar language used by a certain class of evangelists, aiming at excitement and popularity, the forced and often spurious results, heralded to increase the fame of the leader, the aim to receive large financial remuneration, etc., belongs all to the strange fire. In one word, all which is not done in worship and in service in dependence on the Holy Spirit and under His guidance in obedience to the Word, is strange fire.

The judgment of the two sons of Aaron makes known the holiness of Jehovah, who dwelled in the midst of His people. In some respects it is analogous to the judgment of Ananias and Sapphira in the New Testament (Acts 5).

Aaron held his peace. Grace sustained him, so that he could submit to the divine judgment without a murmur, though his heart was greatly burdened (verse 19). He and his sons were not to mourn the dead according to priestly custom. Then follows the command to abstain from the use of wine and strong drink when they were exercising their priesthood. The reason first is stated in verses 10-12. "That ye may put a difference between holy and unholy, and between unclean and clean; and that ye may teach the children of Israel all the statutes, which the Lord hath spoken unto them by the hand of Moses."

"The prohibition of wine and strong drink when going into the tent of meeting connects itself, of course, with the sin of Aaron's sons: and for us plainly covers all fleshly stimulus, which prevents clear discernment of what is or is not according to the mind and nature of God. For us also who are called to walk in the light of God's presence continually, this is not a casual, but a constant rule. The impulse of nature needs the restraining of Christ's yoke; even where, as the apostle says, things are lawful to us, we must still not be brought under the power of any (1 Cor. 6:12). And how easily do they acquire power!" (*Numerical Bible*).

Commandments previously given to them are then restated. The judgment demanded this. All what follows in this chapter may be looked upon as the effect of the judgment which had fallen upon Nadab and Abihu. Eleazar and Ithamar failed in not eating the sin offering, and only the intercession of Aaron kept them from judgment. The earthly priesthood has failure stamped upon it.

III. Holiness Demanded

1. The Clean and the Unclean

CHAPTER 11

1. Concerning the beasts on the earth (11:1-8)
2. Concerning things in the water (11:9-12)
3. Concerning flying and creeping things (11:13-23)
4. Concerning defilement with dead bodies (11:24-40)

The chapters which form the third section of Leviticus are by some taken to give evidence that not Moses, but another person arranged the material of the book. Even men who do not deny the inspiration of the book claim that the hand of a redactor is here discovered. In their opinion chapter 16 should follow immediately after the tenth chapter, because the first verse of the sixteenth chapter connects with the death of Nadab and Abihu. We do not agree with this view, but believe that the arrangement as we have it, is as Moses made it. Immediately after the solemn judgment Jehovah spoke again unto Moses and Aaron. Each chapter begins with the statement "And Jehovah spake." The holy One now demands that His people whom He has redeemed and made nigh, must be a holy people. The fact of man's sin and defilement is fully demonstrated in this section.

The eleventh chapter consists in commandments concerning clean and unclean animals. In chapter 20:24-26, the reason for this distinction is given. "But I have said unto you: Ye shall inherit the land and I will give it unto you to possess it, a land that floweth with milk and honey; I am the Lord your God, which have separated you from other people. Ye shall therefore put a difference between clean beasts and unclean, and between unclean fowls and clean; and you shall not make your souls abominable by beast, or by fowl, or by any manner of living thing that creepeth on the ground, which I have separated from you as unclean. And ye shall be holy unto me: for I the Lord am holy, and have severed you from other people, that ye should be mine."

All those beasts were unclean which do not both chew the cud and divide the hoof (see also Deut. 14)—those fishes were unclean which have not both fins and scales—and those birds were unclean which are known as birds of prey, as well as insects (with the exception of certain locusts) and flying mammalia. The subject before us deserves a far deeper and more extended study than we can give it here. We are obliged to confine ourselves to but a few hints. We need not to devote much space to the wisdom revealed in these laws. As God is the author of them they must necessarily reveal His wisdom. It is interesting that all civilized races abstain from the use of the greater part of the animals, which this code prohibits. With the exception of a number of forbidden animals, civilized nations partake of only such which these laws permit. And those which are commonly eaten, such as the oysters, the hog and others, prohibited in this code, science has shown to be more or less responsible for certain diseases and therefore dangerous as a food. The discoveries made by science fully demonstrate the wisdom of these distinctions between the different animals. These laws in their literal meaning are, of course, no longer binding; the religious observance of them was not a permanent thing, and is done away with in the New Testament. The church has no such laws distinguishing between the clean and unclean animals. The clean typify the Jew and the unclean the Gentile. Peter's vision on the housetop of Joppa warrants this interpretation (Acts 10). The clean, the Jews, and the unclean, Gentiles, are, in believing, gathered into the one body. Read Colossians 2: 16-17, where the fact is stated that Leviticus 11 is no longer in force. (While these laws have no longer a *religious* significance, it is wise to follow them as much as possible. Orthodox Jews who hold strictly to these dietary laws and keep them are far more free from certain diseases than Gentile races, which ignore these laws. It has also been shown by statistics that the mean duration of Jewish life averages much higher than that of others.)

But there is also a deeper meaning to all this. Yet in looking for deeper and spiritual lessons, one must be guarded against a fanciful and far-fetched application. This has often been done. It is obvious that these laws concerning the clean and unclean, teach the path of separation, which Jehovah has marked out for His redeemed people. Only that which is clean according to the divine estimate was to be their food. And we, as His redeemed people, must feed spiritually upon the food God has provided for us, that is Christ. The clean and the unclean, all show certain characteristics, which may well be studied. In the New Testament unclean animals are used to represent unbelievers and unsaved persons. The dog and the swine are thus used (2 Peter 2:22). The sheep, as everybody knows, typifies a believer. The characteristics of the clean animals may therefore give some typical lessons on the characteristics of those who believe, and the unclean, characteristics of those who believe not. However, we repeat, these things must not be pressed too far. It is interesting to see the prominence given to the chewing of the cud and the dividing of the hoof. These two things found together in an animal constituted them clean. Those which only chewed the cud, but did not divide the hoof, and others dividing the hoof and not chewing the cud, were unclean. The feeding and the walking are thus made prominent. A Christian, born again, and therefore clean, must feed upon the Word, meditate upon it constantly, like "chewing the cud." The feet stand for the walk, and that must correspond with the feeding upon the Word. The clean fish had to have fins and scales. The fins are for swift movement through the waters and the scales for defense. This too is not without meaning.

2. Childbirth Laws and Inherited Sin

CHAPTER 12

1. The man-child (12:1-4)
2. The maid-child (12:5)
3. The offerings (12:6-8)

The childbirth laws as contained in this chapter are full of meaning. The woman is constituted unclean by the birth of a child. When a man-child was born, she was to be unclean for seven days, and her purification was to end thirty-three days after that; forty days after childbirth. (A. Bonar, in his work on Leviticus, makes the following conjecture: "May it have been the case that Adam and Eve remained only forty days unfallen! These forty days would thus be a reminiscence of that holy time on earth. The last Adam was forty days on earth after His resurrection, recalling to mind earth's time of paradise.") In case of the birth of a maid-child the days of uncleanness were just double, fourteen and sixty-six. But why was this? The key to the spiritual meaning of this chapter is found in this very fact. "Adam was not deceived, but the woman being deceived was in the transgression" (1 Tim. 2:14). It was by the woman that the fall was brought about through the Serpent. The facts that sin is in the world, how it came into the world and that sin is inherited, transmitted from generation to generation, are made known in this brief chapter. The woman is constituted unclean because she is a sinful creature. Her sorrow and pain in childbirth, which no science nor discovery can remove, is a definite witness to the truth as contained in the third chapter of Genesis. And because she is a sinful creature and unclean, her offspring too is sinful and unclean, for "who can bring a clean thing out of an unclean?" What later David expressed, when he stood in the light, confessing his sin, is here seen in the childbirth laws. "Behold I was shapen in iniquity; and in sin did my mother conceive me" (Psalm 51:5) And one well may think here of her who was a sinful woman like every other woman, but who conceived by the Holy Spirit, Mary, the virgin. The One born of her had no sin, but is "that holy thing" called the Son of God (Luke 1:35).

On the eighth day the male child was to be circumcised. Both "circumcision" and "the eighth day" are of spiritual significance. The eighth day is the type of resurrection, the new creation. Circumcision is given in the New Testament in its true meaning. See Romans 6:6; Col. 2:11; Phil. 3:3. This indicates the manner in which God hath dealt with inherited sin in the cross of His blessed Son, our Saviour and Lord. Then follows the commandment concerning the offerings, when the days of purification were ended. It was for both the male and the female, the same offering, a lamb and a young pigeon or turtle dove. "And if she be not able to bring a lamb, then she shall bring two turtles or two young pigeons." Read and compare with Luke 2:22.

3. Leprosy: Type of Indwelling Sin

CHAPTER 13

1 Leprosy in a person (13:1-46)
2. The infected garment. (13:47-57)
3. The cleansing of the garment (13:58-59)

The entire chapter treats of leprosy. It has been argued from the side of critics that the disease described here is not the one we know as leprosy, but only a similar disease of the skin. The arguments advanced to support this objection are silenced by Matthew 8:1-4. The man who came to our Lord had leprosy. The Lord told him "show thyself to the priest, and offer the gift that Moses commanded, for a testimony unto them." From this we learn that Leviticus 13 and 14 speak of the real disease, so loathsome and, from human side, incurable. The twelfth and thirteenth chapters of Leviticus are closely linked together. Inherited sin is the theme of the preceding chapter. Its cure is also indicated in circumcision and the offering. Leprosy is the type of indwelling sin and its awful corruption. This horrible disease was chosen by the Lord to typify sin on account of its vileness. Like sin it is progressive and eventually affects the whole being; it is hereditary and incurable. As the disease progresses the victim becomes more and more insensible to his dreadful condition and is even content with it.

"In view of all these correspondences, one need not wonder that in the symbolism of the law leprosy holds the place which it does. For what other disease can be named which combines in itself, as a physical malady, so many of the most characteristic marks of the malady of the soul? In its intrinsic loathsomeness, its insignificant beginnings, its slow but inevitable progress, in the extent of its effects, in the insensibility which accompanies it, in its hereditary character, in its incurability, and, finally, in the fact that according to the law it involved the banishment of the leper from the camp of Israel—in all these respects, it stands alone as a perfect type of sin; it is sin, as it were, made visible in the flesh."[5]

The Lord had much to say about the examination of persons suspected of having leprosy, and how the disease was to be detected. First the case of leprosy is stated when it rises spontaneously, showing itself in the skin and the hair. Then follows the case where leprosy rises out of a boil and out of a burn (verses 18-28), and finally leprosy on the head or beard and its diagnosis (verses 27-44).

But these general applications of leprosy as a type of sin do not fully explain the lessons of this chapter. We must remember that Israel is viewed as Jehovah's redeemed people. As such they must keep out of their midst that which defiles. The same principle we find in the New Testament in connection with the church, the assembly of God. Leprosy, indwelling sin, showing itself in any member of the people of God, works havoc. It dishonors God and defiles others. Discipline must be exercised. "Therefore put away from among yourselves that wicked person" (1 Cor. 5:13). The priest was the person to examine closely the suspected person and pronounce the disease as leprosy, according to the signs given by the Word of God. On the one hand the priest had to watch that no real leper be kept in the congregation of Israel, and on the other hand, he had to be equally careful that none was put out of the congregation who

[5] S. H. Kellogg, *Leviticus.*

was not a leper. "Holiness could not permit any one to remain in who ought to be out; and on the other hand, grace would not have any one out who ought to be in." In the New Testament this solemn duty falls upon those who are spiritual (Gal. 6:1). Note how God commanded that the suspected one should not be treated in a hasty manner. After the priest had looked upon him, the diseased one was to be shut up for seven days. On the seventh day the priest was again to look on him. Then he was again shut up for seven more days. And after all the seeing and looking upon, the priest was to consider. It showed the necessity of great care. How easy it is to condemn a brother as living in sin, showing leprosy in his conduct; a hasty action in excluding a real child of God from Christian fellowship is as sinful as permitting a wicked person in that fellowship. We cannot enter into the different signs of leprosy. Much which has been written on it by some good men is strained.

When an Israelite was found to have the true leprosy, he had to be without the camp. "And the leper in whom the plague is, his clothes shall be rent, and his head bare, and he shall put a covering upon his upper lip, and shall cry, Unclean, unclean. All the days wherein the plague shall be in him he shall be defiled; he is unclean, he shall dwell alone, without the camp shall his habitation be" (verses 45-46). Thus the poor leper was excluded from the congregation of Israel and from the tabernacle of Jehovah. The rent clothes, the bare head, the covering upon the lip, all showed his sad and deplorable condition. So the unsaved sinner is shut out from Jehovah's presence on account of his defilement and has no place among the people of God. Without the camp! Read the solemn words in Rev. 21:27 and 22:11, 15. The sinner unforgiven and not cleansed will be forever shut out of the presence of a holy God. And one, who is a child of God and belongs to the family and people of God, and permits indwelling sin to work out, is unfit for both fellowship with God and fellowship with His people. But notice it says, "all the days wherein the plague shall be in him he shall be defiled." Here is the ray of hope. Only as long as it was in him was he excluded. Recovery from the evil thing which defiles and disturbs our fellowship is blessedly revealed in the New Testament. It has to be brought into the light, must be confessed and put away (1 John 1). And above all, we have an Advocate with the Father, Jesus Christ the Righteous.

Leprosy in the garment is also reckoned with, and its cleansing by washing is commanded. A garment is that which belongs to a person and is used by him. It is typical of contamination by sin in our earthly occupation. The cleansing by the water is the type of the Word of God, which uncovers the leprosy in our ways and can cleanse us.

4. The Cleansing of the Leper

CHAPTER 14

1. The cleansing of the leper (14:1-32)
2. Leprosy in the house and its purification (14:33-54)

The cleansing and restoration of the leper is full of significance, foreshadowing once more the blessed work of our Saviour. Two parts in this ceremonial are to be noticed first of all. The first thing done was to restore the leper among the people from whom he had been put away. The second part of the ceremony restored him fully to communion with God. The first part was accomplished on the first day; the second part on the eighth day. A careful distinction must be made between the healing and the cleansing. All the ceremonies could not heal the leper. Jehovah alone could heal that loathsome disease. But after the healing, the cleansing and restoration had to be accomplished. However, what was done for the leper is a most blessed illustration of the work of Christ and of the gospel in which the believing sinner is saved, and the sinning saint cleansed and restored. The leper outside the camp could not do anything for himself. He was helpless and could not cleanse himself; it had to be done for him. The priest had to make the start for his cleansing and restoration. He had to go forth out of the camp to seek the leper; the leper could not come to the priest, the priest had to come to him. Well may we think here of Him, who left the Father's glory and came to this earth, the place of sin and shame, where the lepers are, shut out from God's holy presence. He came to seek and to save what is lost.

Two birds which the priest commanded to be taken for the leper are a beautiful type of Christ in His death, and Christ risen from the dead. The birds are typically belonging to heaven. The first bird was killed in an earthen vessel over running water. This likewise typifies Christ. The earthen vessel stands for the humanity of Christ. The running water is the Holy Spirit, who filled Him and then He gave Himself and shed His precious blood. And that blessed blood of atonement is what cleanses from all sin, and on account of that blood the leper can be restored. The second bird did not die, but was set at liberty to take up a heavenward journey. The second bird was dipped into the blood of the bird that was killed over the running water. This bird typifies Christ in resurrection. The bird in its upward flight, singing perchance a melodious song, bearing upon its white wings the precious token, the blood, typifies Christ in His accomplished work, risen from the grave and going back from where He came. He died for our offences and was raised for our justification. But with the living bird there was also used the cedar wood, the scarlet and the hyssop; these, with the living bird, were dipped into the blood. What do these things signify? Scarlet is the bright and flashing color, which typifies the glory of the world (Dan. 5:7; Nahum 2:3; Rev. 17:3-4; 18:12,16). Cedar wood and hyssop are things of nature.The cedar stands in God's Word always for that which is high and lofty. The insignificant small hyssop typifies that which is low.

"From the lofty cedar which crowns the sides of Lebanon, down to the lowly hyssop—the wide extremes and all that lies between—nature in all its departments is brought under the power of the cross; so that the believer sees in the death of Christ the end of all his guilt, the end of all earth's glory, and the end of the whole system of nature—the entire old creation. And with what is he to be occupied? With Him who is the antitype of that living bird, with blood-stained feathers, ascending into the open heavens. Precious, glorious, soul-satisfying object! A risen, ascended, triumphant, glorified Christ, who has passed into the heavens, bearing in His sacred person the marks of an accomplished atonement. It is with Him we have to do: we are shut up to Him. He is God's exclusive object; He is the centre of heaven's joy, the theme of angels' song. We want none of earth's glory, none of nature's attractions. We can behold them all, together with our sin and guilt, forever set aside by the death of Christ" (C. H. Mackintosh).

It is a beautiful illustration of the great truth stated in Galatians 6:14. "God forbid that I should glory, save in the cross of our Lord Jesus Christ, whereby the world is crucified unto me, and I unto the world." The leper was sprinkled seven times with the dipped bird, scarlet, cedar wood and hyssop. It was put upon him. And thus it is upon us, redeemed by blood, to live as dead unto the world. Throughout the entire ceremony the leper did nothing. Only after the blood was sprinkled and the bird set loose began he to wash his clothes, shave off his hair, and wash himself in water. After we are saved and cleansed we must go to the Word and cleanse by it our habits and our ways.

The second part of the ceremony on the eighth day restored the leper completely to his privileges. All is done again "before the Lord," a phrase missing in the first part of the ceremony, but repeatedly mentioned in the second part. The trespass offering occupies the prominent place. And the blood of the lamb was put upon the right ear, the thumb of the right hand and upon the great toe of the right foot. The symbolical meaning is clear; the ear is cleansed and restored to hear the Word; the hand to serve and the foot to walk. The blood of atonement in its cleansing power is therefore blessedly foreshadowed in this ceremony. It has the same meaning as it had in the consecration of the priests. The leper was like one who came out of the realms of death and corruption to become again a member of the priestly nation. The oil was put then upon the blood. Where the blood was, the oil was also applied. The work of the Holy Spirit in the sanctification of the redeemed sinner is typified by this anointing. The oil was then poured upon him, the type of the unction of the Holy One, which is upon all who are redeemed by blood.

But there is still another lesson connected with all this. The delay in the full acceptance of the healed and cleansed leper and his full reinstitution and presentation before the Lord on the eighth day is of deeper meaning. The eighth day in the Word of God represents the resurrection and the new creation. We are now as His redeemed people healed and cleansed but not yet in the immediate presence of the Lord. The seven days the cleansed leper had to wait for his full restoration and to enter in, typify our life here on earth, waiting for the eighth day, the blessed morning, when the Lord comes and we shall possess complete redemption and appear in the presence of Himself and behold His glory. The eighth day came and it was impossible for the leper, upon whom the blood of the sacrificial bird had been sprinkled, to be kept out from appearing in His presence and receive the blessings of full redemption. Even so there comes for us, His redeemed people, the eighth day. May we also remember that the leper, waiting for the eighth day, had to cleanse himself by the washing of water (verse 9). "Having therefore these promises, dearly beloved, let us cleanse ourselves from all filthiness of the flesh and spirit, perfecting holiness in the fear of God" (2 Cor. 7:1). "And every man that hath this hope in Him purified himself, even as He is pure" (1 John 3:3).

Nor must we forget Israel typified in this entire ceremony. Israel blinded is morally like a leper. They are outside and separated from Jehovah on account of their condition. In the future the remnant of Israel will be cleansed and then wait for that full restoration which God in His gracious purposes has promised unto them.

Then follows a description of the plague of leprosy in a house. Leprosy, like other diseases, is caused by germs. These germs existing in the blood of the victim also may exist outside of the body, and under favorable conditions, especially in darkness, multiplying rapidly, spread the infection over a house and its contents. Bacteriology after years of laborious research has discovered these facts. Moses did not know about these bacteria in a house, but Jehovah knew.

The house with leprosy in it has often been applied to Israel. What was done to the house to arrest the plague is applied to what God did to His people. But the plague re-appeared and culminated in the rejection of Christ; then the house was completely broken down. Others apply it to the church and see that the leprosy has entered into the professing church and will some day terminate in the complete judgment of Christendom. We do not believe this to be the entire meaning of leprosy in the house. It likewise typifies the presence and working of sin in the place where man has his abode, that is, the material creation of God. All has been dragged down by the fall of man. All creation is under a bondage of corruption, made subject to vanity and therefore travaileth in pain and groaneth. But there is hope, for groaning creation is to be delivered. Then for the cleansing of the house the same ceremony with the two birds was enacted and the house was cleansed by the sprinkling of the blood. This is typical of the work of Christ as it will eventually bring blessing to all creation and all things will be reconciled (Col. 1:20). But here is also indicated the judgment by fire which is in store for the earth (2 Peter 3:10). Then there will be a new heaven and a new earth.

Concerning Issues: Man's Weakness and Defilement

CHAPTER 15

1. The uncleanness of a man (15:1-18)
2. The uncleanness of a woman (15:19-33)

The whole chapter shows the deplorable physical condition into which man has been plunged by sin. The issues mentioned were therefore an evidence of the presence of sin in man's nature with the curse upon it, and constitutes man and woman unclean in the sight of God. "Not only actions, from which we can abstain, but operations of nature which we cannot help, alike defile; defile in such a manner and degree as to require, even as voluntary acts of sin, the cleansing of water and the expiatory blood of a sin offering. One could not avoid many of the defilements mentioned in this chapter, but that made no difference; he was unclean." Fallen human nature in its weakness and defilement is taught, and that this human nature is impure and polluting even in its secret workings. The blood and the water cover all this. It must be noticed that the water and the different application of water is constantly mentioned throughout this chapter. The water always typifies the Word by which our way is to be cleansed.

"Again, we learn that human nature is the ever-flowing fountain of uncleanness. It is hopelessly defiled; and not only defiled, but defiling. Awake or asleep, sitting, standing, or lying, nature is defiled and defiling: its very touch conveys pollution. This is a deeply humbling lesson for proud humanity; but thus it is. The book of Leviticus holds up a faithful mirror to nature: it leaves 'flesh' nothing to glory in. Men may boast of their refinement, their moral sense, their dignity: let them study the third book of Moses, and there they will see what it is all really worth in God's estimation" (C. H. Mackintosh).

The case of the woman with an issue of blood (Matthew 9:18-26) is stated in verses 25-27. How great must have been her trial and her sorrow during the twelve years of her uncleanness. Still greater was her faith and the testimony she bore to the holy Person of our Lord. All what came in touch with such an unclean person became unclean. She believed both that her touch could not make Christ unclean, for He is holy, and that His power could heal her.

IV. The Day of Atonement: In the Holiest

1. The Day of Atonement

CHAPTER 16

1. The command how Aaron was to enter (16:1-5)
2. The presentation of the offerings (16:6-10)
3. The blood carried into the Holiest (16:11-19)
4. The scapegoat (16:20-22)
5. Aaron's burnt offering and that for the people (16:23-25)
6. The ceremony outside of the camp (16:26-28)
7. Cleansed and resting (16:29-34)

A brief rehearsal of the ceremonies of this great day of atonement, with a few explanatory remarks, will help in a better understanding of this chapter. The day of atonement was for the full atonement of all the sins, transgressions and failures of Israel, so that Jehovah in His holiness might tabernacle in their midst. On that day alone the Holiest was opened for the high priest to enter in. That all connected with this day is the shadow of the real things to come, and that in the New Testament we have the blessed substance, is well known. The Epistle to the Hebrews is in part the commentary to Israel's great day of atonement. The way into the Holiest by the rent vail which is revealed in the Epistle to the Hebrews, was not made known on the day of atonement. The day itself was celebrated on the tenth day of the seventh month, and it was a Sabbath of rest in which they were to afflict their souls (chapter 23:27-29). What is called "afflict" was fasting, the outward sign of inward sorrow over sin. When this was omitted the atonement did not profit anything "for whatsoever soul it be that shall not be afflicted in that same day, he shall be cut off from among his people." Only true faith mainfested by repentance gives the sinner a share in the great work of atonement.

Aaron is the central figure in the day of atonement. All is his work with the exception of the leading away of the scapegoat. Aaron is the type of Christ. Aaron had to enter the Holiest with the blood of sacrifice, but Christ entered by His own blood. "Neither by the blood of goats and calves, but by His own blood He entered in once into the holy place, having obtained eternal redemption for us" (Heb. 9:12). Aaron had to come into the holy place with a sin offering and a burnt offering. Nothing is said about a meal or a peace offering. These would be out of keeping with the purpose of the day. As we have seen, the sin and the burnt offerings foreshadow the perfect work of Christ in which God's righteous claims are met and in which atonement is made for the creature's sins. Aaron had to lay aside his robes of beauty and glory and put on white linen garments after he had washed his flesh in water. Christ did not need fine linen garments, nor was there any need in Him for washing. Aaron wearing these garments and washed in water typifies what Christ is in Himself. Aaron had to take next two kids of the goats for a sin offering and a ram for a burnt offering. He had to offer the bullock of the sin offering (chapter 4:3). Such an offering for Himself Christ did not need (Heb. 7:27). But Aaron's offering was an atonement for his house. And Christ is Son over His house, whose house we are (Heb. 3:6). The bullock offering made by Aaron typifies therefore the aspect of Christ's work for the Church. The two goats were for the people Israel. Lots were cast by Aaron, and one goat was taken by lot for Jehovah and the other for the scapegoat. After the choice by lot had been made Aaron killed the sin offering for himself and his house. Then having taken a censer full of burning coals of fire from off the altar, with his hands full of sweet incense, he entered within the vail, into the Holiest. The cloud of incense covered the mercy seat. He then sprinkled the blood with his finger upon the mercy seat eastward and seven times before the mercy seat. How blessedly all this foreshadows Christ and His work! The incense typifies the fragrance of His own person, and the sprinkled blood is the type of His own precious blood, in which God accomplishes all His eternal and sovereign counsels of grace.

"The blood which is sprinkled upon the believer's conscience has been sprinkled 'seven times' before the throne of God. The nearer we get to God, the more importance and value we find attached to the blood of Jesus. If we look at the brazen altar, we find the blood there; if we look at the brazen laver, we find the blood there; if we look at the golden altar, we find the blood there; if we look at the vail of the tabernacle, we find the blood there; but in no place do we find so much about the blood as within the vail, before Jehovah's throne, in the immediate presence of the divine glory."

In Heaven His blood forever speaks,
In God the Father's ears.

Then the first goat was killed and the blood was also sprinkled in the same manner. "And he shall make an atonement for the holy place, because of the uncleanness of the children of Israel, and because of their transgressions in all their sins; and so shall he do for the tabernacle of the congreation that remaineth among them in the midst of their uncleanness" (verse 16). "And almost all things are by the law purged with blood; and without shedding of blood is no remission. It was therefore necessary that the patterns of the things in the heavens should be purified with these; but the heavenly things themselves with better sacrifices than these" (Heb. 9:22-23). Christ brought the one great sacrifice on the cross and then entered into heaven itself. Having made by Himself purification of sins He sat down on the right hand of the Majesty on high. Christ Himself, in the Holiest, is the blood-sprinkled mercy seat. Aaron and his presence in the Holiest behind the vail is described in verse 17: "And there shall be no man in the tabernacle of the congregation when he goeth in to make an atonement in the holy place, until he come out, and have made an atonement for himself, one for his household, and for all the congregation of Israel." We see again the difference which is made in the atonement for Aaron and his household and the atonement for all the congregation of Israel. It foreshadows the atonement made by the one sacrifice of Christ for the church and for Israel. Israel, however, does not yet possess the blessings and fruits of this atonement on account of their unbelief. We shall soon see how this great day of atonement foreshadows the forgiveness of their sins in the future. The true priest having gone into heaven with His own blood and being there alone, the day of atonement is now. And we who believe and constitute His church have boldness to enter into the Holiest by the blood of Jesus, by a new and living way which He hath consecrated for us through the vail, that is to say, His flesh. This entire age is the day of atonement, and it will end when He comes forth again.

When the work was finished by Aaron and he had come forth again the live goat was brought. Aaron then put his hands upon it and confessed over him all the iniquities of the children of Israel, all their transgression, and all their sins. All these were put symbolically upon the head of the goat and a fit man sent the goat away into the wilderness. "And the goat shall bear upon him all their iniquities unto a land not inhabited; and he shall let go the goat in the wilderness." We cannot follow the different views expressed on the meaning of the second goat. However, we mention a few. The word for scapegoat is in the Hebrew *azazel*. Some take it that Azazel is an evil being. Inasmuch as it saith that one goat is to be for Azazel, Azazel must also be a person. Some critics claim that all this is a kind of relic of demon worship; such a statement is not only wrong, but pernicious. Others claim that the goat sent to Azazel in the wilderness shows Israel's sin in rejecting Christ, and that they were on account of it delivered to Satan. There are still other views which we do not mention. Jewish and Christian expositors declare that Azazel is Satan, and try to explain why the goat was sent to him.

The best exposition we have seen on this view is by Kurtz: "The blood of the first goat was carried by him into the holiest of all, on this day (on which alone he was permitted to enter) and sprinkled on the mercy-seat. The sins for which atonement was thus made, were put upon the head of the second goat, which was sent away alive into the wilderness of Azazel (the evil demon, represented as dwelling in the wilderness), in order that the latter might ascertain all that had been done, and know that he no longer retained power over Israel. This whole transaction expressed the thought that the atonement made on this day was so complete, and so plain and undeniable, that even Satan the Accuser (Job 1 and 2; Zech. 3; Rev 12:10,11) was compelled to acknowledge it. In the sacrifice of this day, consequently, the sacrifice of Christ is shadowed and typified more clearly than in any other, even as we read in Heb. 9:12: "By His own blood He entered in *once* into the holy place, having obtained *eternal* redemption for us.

There is no need for all these speculations. "Azazel" is not at all an evil being or Satan. The Hebrew word signifies "dismissal"—"to depart." It is translated in the Septuagint (Greek version of the Old Testament) with *eis teen apopompee,* which means "to let him go for the dismissal." Both goats are for sin offering. The first goat represents Christ dying for the sins of His people. The second goat laden with those sins which were atoned for by the blood of the first goat, represents the blessed effect of the work of Christ, that the sins of His people are forever out of sight. It is a blessed harmony with the two birds used in connection with the cleansing of the leper.

And here the dispensational aspects come in. Before the transgressions of Israel could be confessed over the scapegoat and before the goat could be sent forever away with its burden, never to return, the high priest had to come out of the Holiest. As long as he remained alone in the tabernacle the scapegoat could not carry off the sins of the people. When the Lord appears the second time, when He comes forth out of Heaven's glory as the King-Priest, then the blessed effect of His death for that nation (John 11:51) will be realized and their sins and transgressions will forever be put away. Then their sins will be cast into the depths of the sea (Micah 7:19) and they shall no more be remembered (Is. 43:25). That this is the true meaning of the scapegoat taking the sins of the people into the wilderness and therefore forever out of sight, we shall learn also in the twenty-third chapter. The feasts and holy seasons mentioned there are: Passover (redemption by blood); firstfruits (resurrection); feast of weeks (Pentecost); feast of trumpets (the re-gathering of Israel); the day of atonement (when Israel repents and is forgiven); the feast of tabernacles (millennial times). Israel therefore is unconsciously waiting for Christ's return as their forefathers waited outside, till Aaron came back to put their sins on the scapegoat.

Of the many other interesting things for brief annotation we but mention the rest connected with this great day (verse 31). In the Hebrew "Sabbath of rest" is "Sabbath sabbatizing." No work had to be done on that great day. The work was completely on God's side, man must not attempt to supplement that work. But let us also remember the dispensational application. When Israel's great national day of atonement and repentance comes, when they shall look upon the One, whom they pierced and the great mourning and affliction of soul takes place (Zech. 12:9-12), the glorious Sabbath will follow. Rest and glory will come at last to them as His redeemed people, while the glory of the Lord will cover the earth and all the earth will have rest.

2. The Testimony Concerning the Blood

CHAPTER 17

1. Concerning slain animals (17:1-9)
2. Concerning the eating of blood (17:10-16)

This chapter needs little comment. Everything in this chapter speaks of the sanctity of the blood, what great value God, to whom life belongs, places upon the blood and with what jealous care He watches over it. The center of all is verse 11: "For the life of the flesh is in the blood: and I have given it to you upon the altar to make an atonement for your souls, for it is the blood that maketh an atonement for the soul." Every slain animal had to bear witness to this fact. Even the hunter had to pour out the blood and cover it with dust. No blood was to be eaten. But in the New Testament we are commanded to eat spiritually of the flesh of the Son of God and to drink spiritually His blood.

V. Practical Holiness in Daily Life

1. Different Unholy Relationships

CHAPTER 18

1. Separation and obedience (18:1-5)
2. Unholy relationships (18:6-18)
3. Vile and abominable practices (18:19-23)
4. Judgment threatened (18:24-30)

This section of Leviticus contains the words of Jehovah addressed to His people, whom He had redeemed and in whose midst He dwelt. They are to be a holy people. About thirty times in this section we find the solemn word "I am Jehovah. Ye shall be holy: for I, Jehovah your God, am holy." This is Jehovah's calling for His people. Four times in the beginning of this chapter the Lord tells His people "I am Jehovah" (verses 2, 4, 5 and 6). His name was upon them and therefore they are to manifest holiness in their life and walk. This demand and principle is unchanged in the New Testament, in the covenant of grace. His people are exhorted to walk "as obedient children, not fashioning yourselves according to the former lusts in your ignorance, but as He, who hath called you is holy, so be ye holy in all manner of conversation, because it is written, Be ye holy for I am holy" (1 Peter 1:14-16). Brought nigh by blood, knowing the blessed relationship into which Grace of God has brought us, our solemn duty is to present our bodies a living sacrifice, holy and acceptable unto God. The Spirit of God, the Spirit of holiness and power, is bestowed upon us that we can walk in the Spirit and fulfill not the lusts of the flesh. Israel was not to walk after the doings of the land of Egypt which they had left, nor after the doings of the land of Canaan whither they were going. And the church is told the same thing in the New Testament. "This I say therefore, and testify in the Lord, that ye henceforth walk not as other Gentiles walk, in the vanity of their mind, having the understanding darkened, being alienated from the life of God through the ignorance that is in them, because of the blindness of their heart; who being past feeling have given themselves over unto lasciviousness, to work all uncleanness through greediness" (Eph 4:17-19).

And Jehovah's words reveal all the degradations and vile abominations human nature, the nature of sin and death, is capable of. He is the searcher of hearts and Jehovah only can sound the depths of the desperately wicked heart of man. The incestuous relationships against which the Lord warns were commonly practised among the Gentiles. These unholy impure things are still common in the world, not alone among the heathen, but also in the so-called civilized world. The laxity of the marriage laws, divorces and other evils in the same line are the curse of our age. Polygamy is forbidden in verse 18. All that would destroy the sanctity of the family and bring in abuse is solemnly warned against and forbidden. In the New Testament the Spirit of God emphasizes the absolute purity of the family relation and how the Christian family is to be a witness of the holiness and love of Jehovah to make known the mystery of Christ and the church (Eph. 5:22-32).

Molech worship is forbidden. Read 1 Kings 5:7; 2 Kings 23:10; Jer. 32:35; 7:31 and 19:5). The awful worship of Molech is described in these passages. The most unnatural crimes and vile things mentioned in verses 22-23 were connected with the idolatries of the nations which surrounded Israel. These things were practised in Egypt and in Canaan. Romans 1:18-32 gives the inspired history of the degradation of the Gentile world. Idolatry and moral degradation always go together. The fearful road of the apostasy in Christendom is no exception. Rejection of God's revelation leads into idolatry (not necessarily idols of wood and stone) and moral declension. The days of Lot, the grossest licentiousness of Sodom, are predicted to precede the coming of the Son of man (Luke 17:26-32).

A solemn warning concludes this chapter. The inhabitants of Canaan were to be cast out on account of their vileness. Jehovah would not spare His people if they practised these things. They did commit all this wickedness. Israel cast out of the land, the homeless wanderer, bears witness to the fulfillment of this solemn warning.

2. Different Duties

CHAPTER 19

1. Honoring parents and fearing God (19:1-8)
2. The care of the poor (19:9-10)
3. Against stealing and lying (19:11-12)
4. Against oppression (19:13-14)
5. Against unrighteousness in judgment (19:15-16)
6. Thou shalt love thy neighbor (19:17-18)
7. Different commands and prohibitions (19:19-37)

Many of these duties enjoined upon a people called to holiness, the different commands and prohibitions, are of much interest. It is true, believers are not under the law. This, however, does not mean that we should refrain from reading and studying these commands. Jehovah changes not. May we remember that our call, like Israel's, is unto practical holiness in life. Our responsibilities are even greater. Many lessons are here for us which will greatly help us in our walk as His people. The provision made for the poor (verses 9-10 compare with Ruth 2:14-16) manifests the loving care of Jehovah. God has special regard for the poor and strangers. His blessed Son became poor and was indeed a stranger in the world He created. His people had no heart for Him and He was hungry, while His disciples had to take ears of corn from the field to satisfy their hunger. The Lord Himself was the owner of Israel's land (Lev. 25:23), and as owner He charged His servants to be unselfish in the use of the bountiful provision He was making for their temporal need.

Note the precept concerning the laborer. "The wages of him that is hired shall not abide with thee all night until the morning" (verse 13). This again reveals the gracious care of the Lord. How little such care and consideration for the poor and the servant is found in our day! If these simple instructions were followed the discontent of the poor and the unrest of the laborers would not be as prominent as they are now. Israel failed in this. They cheated the poor and hired servants (Amos 8:5-6). What is to be in the last days of the present age we find in James 5:4: "Behold the hire of the laborers, who have reaped down your fields, which is of you kept back by fraud, crieth; and the cries of them that have reaped have entered into the ears of the lord of Sabaoth." The divine plea for the poor and the laborer is utterly disregarded in the last days, and Jehovah has to take up their case.

The deaf and the blind are also mentioned. The defenceless and helpless with the poor and the hired servant are the objects of His special care.

In verse 19 the raising of hybrid animals is forbidden. Anything "mingled" God despises.

His people are to avoid this, even in the smallest things.

Heathen superstitions, such as using enchantments and observing times are forbidden by Jehovah. These are unworthy of a redeemed people linked with Jehovah. All superstitions, such as dreading certain days and numbers ("Friday" or "13"), and other foolish observances, alas! found so much amidst professing Christians are heathenish and dishonor God, who alone knows and controls the welfare and future of His people. All "cuttings in your flesh for the dead" were also prohibited. Thus the pagans did who have no hope. Such sorrow, expressed in fearful lamentations and frenzied outbreaks, were unworthy of Israel, as they are more so for Christian believers (1 Thess. 4:13). Those who have familiar spirits (mediums) and wizards were not to be consulted.

> But it is truly most extraordinary that in Christian lands, as especially in the United States of America, and that in the full light, religious and intellectual, of the twentieth century, such a prohibition should be fully as pertinent as in Israel! For no words could more precisely describe the pretensions of the so-called modern spiritualism, which within the last half century has led away hundreds of thousands of deluded souls, and those, in many cases, not from the ignorant and degraded, but from circles which boast of more than average culture and intellectual enlightenment. And inasmuch as experience sadly shows that even those who profess to be disciples of Christ are in danger of being led away by our modern wizards and traffickers with familiar spirits, it is by no means unnecessary to observe that there is not the slightest reason to believe that this which was rigidly, forbidden by God in the fifteenth century B.C., can now be well-pleasing to Him in the nineteenth century A.D. And those who have most carefully watched the moral developments of this latter-day delusion, will most appreciate the added phrase which speaks of this as "defiling" a man. *(S. H. Kellogg)*

It will be wise to meditate carefully on all these commands and prohibitions. They reveal the tenderness, the wisdom and the holiness of God.

3. Warnings Against Special Sins and their Penalties

CHAPTER 20

1. Warning against Molech-worship and familiar spirits (20:1-8)
2. Warning against cursing parents (20:9)
3. Criminal and vile connections (20:10-21)
4. Exhortations to obedience and separation (20:22-27)

This chapter reveals the justice of God in dealing with criminals. The death penalty is most prominent. It is pronounced upon the following crimes: Molech worship; dealing with familiar spirits (spiritualism); different forms of incest and sodomy. Men advocate now the abolishment of death penalty without considering the outraged justice of a holy God. The object of these severe penalties imposed by Jehovah were the satisfaction of justice and the vindication of a broken law. A closer examination of these warnings and the penalties attached will reveal the seriousness of the offences against the theocratic government set up in the midst of Israel, and the perfect justice of every penalty. It is a serious matter if critics find fault with these solemn statements, denying their authority and judging the holy and infallible Judge.

The chapter gives a testimony against the awful drift of our times in the lax laws concerning marriage, divorces and its attending evils so very much in evidence among the so-called Christian nations.

4. Laws for the Priests

CHAPTER 21

1. Laws concerning the person of the priests (21:1-6)
2. Laws concerning their family (21:7-9)
3. Laws concerning the high priest (21:10-15)
4. Concerning blemishes (21:16-24)

We come now to the special laws and precepts for the priestly class among the people. The preceding laws concerned the nation as such. The requirements of the priests are the highest in the entire book of Leviticus. Responsibility is always according to relationship. The priests, as we have seen before, typify the church. The grace of God has given to us the place of nearness in Christ, access into the Holiest and constituted us priests. The holiness required of the New Testament believers corresponds to this blessed relationship.

Many are the lessons given here. 2 Tim. 3:16-17 applies to this part of Leviticus. These divine requirements and laws are given even for us "for reproof, for correction, for instruction in righteousness." May we read with prayer and ponder over these words of Jehovah. We point again to the marriage relation. This was especially guarded. Only a virgin of his own people was he permitted to take for wife. A woman upon whose character there was a spot, who was immoral or divorced, could not be the wife of a priest. And should not God's people in the New Testament, as holy priests, be equally cautious? We have an answer in 1 Cor. 7:39. No child of God, a holy priest, should unite in marriage with an unbeliever. The harvest from the acts of disobedience in unholy alliances is often disastrous.

Interesting is this section concerning blemishes in the priestly generations. These blemishes were: blindness, lameness, deformity of the nose, any outgrowths in the skin, broken footed, broken handed, crookbacked or of small stature, etc. Such a one was not permitted to come nigh to offer the bread of his God. He could not go in unto the vail nor come nigh unto the altar. Nevertheless, he could eat the bread of his God, both of the most holy and of the holy. His deformity or blemish deprived him not of his priestly position, nor was he anything less than a son of Aaron. He was excluded from the functions of the holy priesthood. Our spiritual defects, the blemishes which often are upon us as a holy priesthood, typified by lameness (defective walk), blindness (defective sight), arrested growth (dwarf), etc., all these blemishes do not affect our sonship nor our priestly position. But they do interfere with the enjoyment of the communion into which grace has brought us. On account of spiritual defects we cannot enter into the fullest exercise of our priestly privileges and functions. Yet grace permits us to eat of the bread of God.

And Christ as our Priest is without any defect or blemish. "For such an high priest became us, who is holy, harmless, undefiled, separate from sinners, and made higher than the heavens" (Heb. 7:26).

CHAPTER 22

1. Care to be exercised in holy things (22:1-16)
2. Care in the enforcement of the law of offerings (22:17-33)

Uncleanness such as mentioned in the first part of the chapter prohibited the partaking of holy things. Strangers who did not belong to the priestly house and even the married daughter of the priest, not living in the priestly household, were not permitted to eat of the offering of the holy things. Holy things have to be used in a reverent and holy way. The same principle holds good in the New Testament. We may well think here of the Lord's table. Read 1 Cor. 11:23-31. Coming to the Lord's table to remember Him requires self-judgment.

The instruction concerning sacrifices, their unblemished character and what constitutes an acceptable offering are all of great interest with many spiritual lessons. But space forbids our enlarging upon them.

VI. The Holy Feasts and Set Times

1. The Holy Feasts and Set Times

CHAPTER 23

1. The Sabbath (23:1-3)
2. The feast of Passover and feast of unleavened bread (23:4-8)
3. The firstfruits (23:9-14)
4. The feast of weeks (23:15-22)
5. The blowing of trumpets (23:23-25)
6. The day of atonement (23:26-32)
7. The feast of tabernacles (23:33-44)

This is one of the grandest chapters in Leviticus, filled with the choicest truths and prophetic from beginning to end. The holy feasts and set times, appointed by Jehovah, to be kept yearly by Israel, cover indeed the entire realm of redemption facts. The dispensational dealings of God with Jews and Gentiles are clearly revealed in these feasts. We have to look at each of these divisions separately to point out the way to a deeper study, which no child of God should neglect.

1. The Sabbath—This is in itself no feast, but a set time, a holy convocation after the six work days. What it signifies we have already seen in the study of Genesis and Exodus. The reason why the Sabbath is put here first is on account of its prophetic meaning. "There remaineth a rest for the people of God." The Sabbath is the type of that rest yet to come, when redemption is consummated. When all the work is accomplished, foreshadowed in the feasts and set times of Israel, the great rest-keeping will begin. Faith can enjoy it even now. In the Sabbath the blessed outcome of all is revealed.

2. The Passover and feast of unleavened bread—The Passover, with the lamb slain and its body eaten, occupies the first place. It typifies the blessed work of the Lamb of God, His redemption work on the cross. And this is the foundation of every thing, as we have seen in the levitical offerings and ceremonial. In this finished work, and the shed blood, God rests, and here the believing sinner has found his rest. The feast of unleavened bread is closely connected with the Passover, so that it cannot be separated from it. Leaven stands for sin and unleavened bread for holiness. The feast of unleavened bread therefore typifies the result of the work of Christ on the cross, which is holiness. Again we meet the great truth that Jehovah has redeemed His people to be separated unto Himself. They were not to do a servile work, but to bring an offering by fire unto Jehovah. On the first and on the seventh day no servile work was to be done. It typifies the fact that in redemption there is no servile work, but a joyous manifestation of Christ, the sweet savour in the power of the Holy Spirit.

3. The firstfruits—While the Passover-feast foreshadows the death of Christ, the waving of the sheaf of the firstfruits is the blessed type of the resurrection of our Lord Jesus Christ. It was just one sheaf waved before Jehovah, the earnest of the harvest which was to follow. "But now is Christ risen from the dead, and become the firstfruits of them that slept" (1 Cor. 15:20). "But every man in his own order: Christ the firstfruits; afterward they that are Christ's at His coming" (1 Cor. 15:23). The grain of wheat had fallen into the ground and died. But He liveth; the full ear of the sheaf waved before Jehovah typifies the abundant fruit which He brings unto God. And it was waved before Jehovah "on the morrow after the Sabbath." The morrow after the Sabbath is the first day of the week, the glorious resurrection morning. In connection with the waving of the sheaf of firstfruits there were offerings. But of what kind? "An he-lamb without blemish for a burnt offering unto the Lord," a meal offering and a drink offering. No sin offering was demanded, for that was accomplished when He died. The offerings were a sweet savour, telling forth once more the blessedness and value of His own person and work. And in Him we are accepted; with Him the firstfruits we shall be forever.

4. The feast of weeks—After seven Sabbaths had passed by, fifty days counted, a new meal offering was brought and two wave loaves baken with leaven. This is the feast of Pentecost (named on account of the fifty days). It is also called the feast of weeks, as seven weeks had passed by. Exactly fifty days after the waving of the firstfruits, on the morrow of the Sabbath, when Christ arose, the Holy Spirit came down out of heaven to form the church on earth. The meal offering as we saw in the first part of the book is the type of Christ in His perfect humanity. Pure flour, oil mingled with it, and oil poured upon it. Here is a *new* meal offering. It does not typify Christ, but those who are one with Him, His believing people. The oil, the Holy Spirit came on the day of Pentecost upon them, as the oil was poured upon the meal offering.

The two loaves, baken with leaven, typify also the church. Sin is still there. Pure flour was in the loaves (the new nature), but baken with leaven (the old nature). The two loaves, no doubt, refer us to the Jews and Gentiles, which compose the new meal offering. And here is the sin offering, which was absent at the waving of the sheaf of firstfruits on the morrow after the Sabbath. The leaven and the sin offering indicate the presence of sin, as it is the case. Yet the loaves are waved in the presence of Jehovah and fully accepted.

The two loaves were a wave offering before Jehovah. Thus the church is presented unto Him "a kind of first-fruits" (James 1:18); the two loaves, the product of the wheat, the firstfruits of Christ's death and resurrection.

We must not overlook verse 22. The harvest here, we doubt not, is the same as in Matthew 13:39. When that end of the age comes, the church will be taken into the garner; the firstfruits will be with Christ. The poor and strangers, Gentiles, will even then be remembered in mercy.

5. The blowing of trumpets—With this holy convocation we are led upon new ground. The feasts we have followed typify that which is past; the death of Christ, the resurrection of Christ, and the formation of the church by the Holy Spirit on the day of Pentecost. The three set times which follow, the memorial of blowing of trumpets, the day of atonement and the feast of tabernacles await their great fulfillment in the near future. The first thing after the two wave loaves are completely presented unto Jehovah, when this age is about to close, will be the blowing of the trumpets. It is the call of God to the remnant of His people, their re-gathering. A long period of time is between Pentecost and the blowing of the trumpets. This interval is the present age. The Lord does not re-gather His earthly remnant till His heavenly people, the church, is complete. Read and carefully consider Isaiah 27:13; 58; Joel 2:1. Matthew 24:31 is the re-gathering of His elect earthly people after He has come. But the blowing of the trumpets on the first day of the seventh month precedes the great day of atonement and is the heralding of that approaching day. All this, studied with the light God has given to us in the entire word of prophecy, is intensely interesting.

6. The day of atonement—We have already pointed out the dispensational meaning for the people of Israel in our annotations on the sixteenth chapter. When the great high priest, our Saviour and Israel's King, comes forth out of the Holiest, when He comes the second time in power and glory, Israel will look upon Him whom they have pierced and mourn for Him. And He will take away their sins, typified by the scapegoat. "In that day there shall be a fountain opened to the house of David and to the inhabitants of Jerusalem for sin and uncleanness" (Zech. 13:1). Their great day of atonement will be a Sabbath of rest unto them and glory will cover their long desolate land once more.

7. The feast of tabernacles—The final feast began on the fifteenth day of the seventh month. It is the feast, which comes after the sin of Israel has been removed. It was the feast of ingathering of the products of the year and a memorial of Israel's dwelling in booths in the wilderness. The feast of tabernacles foreshadows the coming glory of the millennium, Israel's glorious inheritance and the Gentiles gathered with redeemed Israel in the kingdom. It will be the time of the complete harvest, the time of rejoicing, when sorrow and sighing will flee away. It comes after the harvest (the end of the age) and the vintage (the winepress of the wrath of God). How beautiful is the order in these three last holy convocations! The blowing of the trumpets; the remnant of Israel called and gathered; the day of atonement; Israel in national repentance looking upon Him, whom they pierced, when He comes the second time; the feast of tabernacles; the millennium. "And it shall come to pass that every one that is left of all the nations which came against Jerusalem, shall even go up from year to year to worship the King, the Lord of hosts, and to keep the feast of tabernacles" (Zech. 14:16). It is the great memorial feast of millennial times. Perhaps it will be during that feast that the King of Israel, the King of kings, the Lord of lords, will appear in visible glory in Jerusalem to receive the homage of the representatives of the nations of the earth. What a day that will be! The eighth day which we meet here again points us to that which is beyond the millennium. The story of the twenty-third chapter is marvellous! Only God in His infinite wisdom could give us such an unfolding and foreshadowing of His eternal counsels and purposes. We rehearse it briefly. The Sabbath is the type of the end, which will come after the accomplishment of all His purposes; the eternal rest. Passover, the type of the death of Christ; the waving of the firstfruits, the type of the resurrection of Christ; Pentecost, the type of the coming of the Holy Spirit for the formation of the Church. Then Israel's restoration and fullest blessing comes in. How blind men must be who can call all these beautiful things fable and legends! In these poor critics there is once more fulfilled the Word of God, "professing themselves to be wise, they become fools" (Rom 1:22).

2. Priestly Duties: The Light and the Shewbread

CHAPTER 24:1-9

1. The light (24:1-4)
2. The shewbread (24:5-9)

This chapter is not disconnected from the preceding one as some claim; nor is it the work of a redactor as the critics teach. It is most beautifully linked with the dispensational foreshadowings we found in the feasts of Jehovah. Between Pentecost and the blowing of the trumpets there is, as stated before, a long period of time. When the church was formed, after the sheaf of the firstfruits had been waved, Israel was nationally set aside and night settled upon them. Maintained by the high priest, a light was to be kept shining continually from evening till morning; it was the light of the golden lampstand with its lamps. The lampstand typifies Christ and the high priest also is a type of Christ. Here is a hint of the testimony which shines forth in Christ and through the heavenly priesthood (the church) during the night, the present age. But Israel also will some day shine forth and be a light-bearer (Zech. 4:1-14).

Then there was the shewbread. They were set in two rows, six on a row, upon the pure table before the Lord. Shewbread means literally "bread of the face," that is, the bread before God. Pure frankincense was also put upon them. No doubt, dispensationally, we have in the shewbread another picture of those who are now

His people (the church), while the twelve loaves also typify Israel as a nation.

3. Blasphemy and Israel's Sin Foreshadowed

CHAPTER 24:10-23

1. The blasphemy (24:10-22)
2. The penalty executed (24:23)

The blasphemer who blasphemed the Name and cursed, foreshadows the sin of Israel. They sinned and blasphemed that holy Name: and on account of the rejection of the Lord Jesus Christ, the curse has come upon them. But it will not be permanent. The remnant of Israel will be saved in the future day, when He comes back and they shall welcome Him: "Blessed is He that cometh in the Name of the Lord." The Jews have based upon this incident of the blasphemer the traditional belief that it is sinful to pronounce the Name of Jehovah. For this reason they substitute the word "Adonai."

The twenty-fourth chapter shows in its first part the twofold testimony maintained in the sanctuary, the light and the shewbread; it ends with an incident which foreshadows the sin of Israel when they blasphemed and rejected the Lord of Glory.

4. The Sabbatic Year and the Year of Jubilee

CHAPTER 25

1. The Sabbatic year (25:1-7)
2. The jubilee (25:8-12)
3. The jubilee and the land (25:13-28)
4. The jubilee and the dwelling houses (25:29-34)
5. The jubilee, the poor and the bondmen (25:35-55)

This is the great restoration chapter in Leviticus. All is connected pre-eminently with Israel's land. The application, which has been made, that this chapter foreshadows a universal restitution of all things, including the wicked dead and Satan as well, is unscriptural. If such a restitution were true the Bible would contradict itself. The Sabbatic year could only be kept after Israel came into the land. "When ye come into the land which I give you, then shall the land keep a Sabbath unto the Lord." And Jehovah uttered these words from Mount Sinai and not from the tabernacle (Lev. 1:1). Every seventh year, the land which belongs to Jehovah, and which was not to be sold, had to enjoy complete rest. See what gracious promises Jehovah had given in connection with the Sabbatic year (25:20-22). Jehovah was the Lord of the land, the owner of the land, and Israel received the land as a gift; they were the tenants. Beautifully the Lord said: "Ye are strangers and sojourners *with Me.*" When Israel sinned and broke the laws of Jehovah, when they did not give the land its rest, the Lord drove the people out of the land. Read here 26:32-35. "And I will bring the land into desolation; and your enemies which dwelt therein shall be astonished at it. And I will scatter you among the nations, and will draw out a sword after you, and your land shall be desolate, and your cities waste. Then shall the land enjoy her Sabbaths, as long as it lieth desolate, and ye be in your enemies' land; even then shall the land rest, and enjoy her Sabbaths. As long as it lieth desolate it shall rest; because it did not rest in your Sabbaths, when ye dwelt upon it." This prediction has been fulfilled. Israel is scattered among the nations of the earth and the land is desolate, a witness for the Word of God. Jehovah in giving the law concerning the Sabbatic year, gave to His people a picture of that coming rest, and the assurance of joy and blessing. But they failed.

The year of jubilee shows clearly the restoration which is in store for Israel and Israel's land. It points once more to the millennial times of blessing and glory. How blessedly is that coming age of restoration and of glory seen in the year of jubilee! Without entering into details we give a few of the divine statements. What did the jubilee year mean to Israel? Liberty was proclaimed; every man returned to his possession; every man to his family; all wrongs were righted and the redemption of the bondmen took place. Seven times the word "return" is used; and oftener the word "redeem." It was the time of returning, the blessed time of restoration and redemption.

And how was this year of jubilee ushered in? By the sound of the trumpet of the jubilee on the tenth day of the seventh month, in the day of atonement. This great year of returning and redemption began with the day of atonement. Most likely after the high priest had returned from his holy office work and sprinkling of blood; after he had put the sins of the people upon the scapegoat and that sacrificial animal bearing upon its head Israel's sin had vanished in the wilderness, the trumpet sounded. What all this means we have seen in the annotations of the "day of atonement" chapter. The year of jubilee begins, when our Lord comes back from the Holiest and appears in the midst of His people. And this time of restoration, blessing and glory is not confined to Israel's land. It means more than the promised blessings for that land. We have the year of jubilee in Romans 8:19-23.

We must not forget the significance of the time, the fiftieth year. The day of Pentecost came fifty days after the resurrection of Christ from among the dead. And the fiftieth day brought, as the result of the death and resurrection of Christ, the gift of the Holy Spirit, and the formation of the church began. It came on the eighth day, the first day of the week. The year of jubilee may well be termed another Pentecost. On that day a great outpouring of the Spirit of God will take place (Joel 2:28). The kingdom with all its glories and blessings will be established upon the earth. And how much more might be added to these blessed foreshadowings of the good things to come!

5. The Blessing, the Curse and Israel's History

CHAPTER 26

1. Obedience and the blessings (26:1-13)
2. Disobedience and the curse (26:14-39)
3. The restoration (26:40-46)

This great chapter is very fitting for the close of this book. We have no types here, but direct utterances of Jehovah. Israel's history and their future restoration is here predicted. He reminds them that He brought them out of the land of Egypt; they are His people. Therefore He wants obedience. If this is yielded blessings would be the results. These promised blessings consisted in abundance of rain, great fruitfulness of their land, peace in the land, deliverance from wild beasts and the sword, victory over their enemies. They would multiply and His covenant would be established with them; more than that: "I will walk among you, and will be your God and ye shall be My people." What blessings Jehovah held out to them! They never possessed them in fulness. Some day Israel and Israel's land will enter into these blessings. Then Moses' last word will be true: "Happy art thou, O Israel; who is like unto thee, O people saved by the Lord, the shield of thy help, and who is the sword of thy excellency! and thine enemies shall be found liars unto thee; and thou shalt tread upon their high places" (Deut. 33:29).

But how dreadful the threatened judgments on account of a broken covenant! Judgment after judgment is announced, one greater than the other, every blessing is changed into a curse and the culminating threat is expulsion from the God-given land and dispersion, world-wide, among the nations. The nation called to blessing is threatened with the most awful judgments and disasters. And all these have become historical facts. Jewish history of many weary centuries records the constant fulfillment of these solemn declarations. We have therefore in this chapter, in the predicted curses and the literal fulfillment, a most valuable and powerful evidence of inspiration. The Jew and his history, the land and its desolation, is God's standing witness for the Gentiles that the Bible is the Word of God.

"The fundamental importance and instructiveness of this prophecy is evident from the fact that all later predictions concerning the fortunes of Israel are but its more detailed exposition and application to successive historical conditions. Still more evident is its profound significance when we recall to mind the fact, disputed by none, that not only is it an epitome of all later prophecy of Holy Scripture concerning Israel, but, no less truly, an epitome of Israel's history. So strictly true is this that we may accurately describe the history of that nation, from the days of Moses until now, as but the translation of this chapter from the language of prediction into that of history."[6]

To this another fact must be added. It is predicted in this chapter that the people passing through judgment devastated by the sword, famine and pestilence, would continue to exist in their enemies' land. Israel's preservation throughout the long period of these executed judgments is a miracle. It cannot be explained in any other way. And the land itself bears witness to all this. It used to be one of the richest of all lands. But ever since the people Israel are driven out of the land and no longer possess it, desolation has come upon it. How remarkable this is!

"We point to the people of Israel as a perennial historical miracle. The continued existence of this nation up to the present day, the preservation of its national peculiarities throughout thousands of years, in spite of all dispersion and oppression, remains so unparalleled a phenomenon, that without the special providential preparation of God, and His constant interfer-

[6]S. H. Kellogg, *Leviticus.*

ence and protection, it would be impossible for us to explain it. For where else is there a people over which such judgments have passed and yet not ended in destruction?" (Professor Christlieb)

Some have speculated on the statement that, they should have the judgments upon them seven times. However, these "seven times" cannot mean the exact duration of Israel's dispersion. The "seven times," however, foreshadow the time of Jacob's trouble, the last seven years of the times of the Gentiles, during which their judgments will be the severest.

This important chapter closes with a promise of restoration. Confession of sin, acknowledgment of their guilt, humiliation and deep sorrow for their iniquity opens the way to this restoration. It will at once be seen that this connects again with the day of atonement. It is the year of jubilee. Then Jehovah remembers His covenant and remembers the land (verse 42). To this future repentance of the remnant of Israel and their re-gathering, the restoration of the land to the people and the people to the land, the entire prophetic Word bears witness.

VII. Concerning Vows

The Claims of Jehovah Realized

CHAPTER 27

1. The singular vow (27:1-8)
2. The sacrifice (27:9-13)
3. Concerning the house (27:14-15)
4. Concerning the land (27:16-25)
5. Concerning the firstling (27:26-27)
6. Devoted things (27:28-29)
7. All holy to Jehovah (27:30-34)

This last chapter in Leviticus concerns vows and devoted things. Israel is still in view here. At Horeb they had made their vow of being obedient and devoted to the Lord, but they could not meet the claims of what that vow meant. The sanctification as demanded in this book they could not fulfill. But grace is seen connected with it. The grace which is yet to flow out to Israel, the chosen nation. Sanctification by law is impossible; grace alone can sanctify. All mentioned is connected with the people. The house to be holy to Jehovah (verse 14) is Israel. The land too is mentioned, as well as the year of jubilee. The house, Israel, becomes Jehovah's; and the land also belongeth then to Him. The thought which runs through this final chapter of Leviticus is that Jehovah will have His own and God finally will be all in all.

May God's Spirit lead us into these blessed types and may we, as His bloodbought people, sanctified in Christ, walk in sanctification in the power of His Spirit.

Appendix

Sprinkling the Blood upon the Mercy Seat (Chapter 16)

In the order of the sacrifices Aaron first killed the bullock, the sin offering which was for himself to make atonement for himself and for his house. This bullock is three times recorded as the sin offering for *himself* (16:6,11); and wherever the atonement made by it is mentioned it is said to be for himself and his house (16:6,11,17). So closely are the high priest and his house linked on together; doubtless to draw our attention to the oneness between Christ and His house—only with a striking contrast also—Aaron's bullock for sin suffered for himself and his house—he being *himself* a sinner, and his house composed of sinners *like himself.*[7] Our High Priest knew no sin, and offered up Himself solely therefore on behalf of others.

Aaron next took the censer full of coals of fire from off the altar before the Lord, and his hands full of sweet incense beaten small, and brought all within the vail, and put the incense upon the fire before the Lord, that the cloud of the incense might cover the mercy-seat upon the testimony, that he might not die.

The censer was apparently a golden censer. If we refer to the Epistle to the Hebrews, chapter 11, a description of the tabernacle is given us on this day of atonement. No incense altar is mentioned standing in the holy place; but the golden censer in the holiest. The cherubim also, shadowing the mercy-seat are called "cherubim of *glory.*" On this day of atonement the coals of fire were moved from off the incense altar, and the golden censer being filled with them was carried within the vail. For the time therefore, the incense altar was inactive, and is not alluded to probably on that account in the ninth

---

[7]Throughout the Epistle to the Hebrews, the high priest and the people are alone alluded to; there is no mention made "of *his house*" Heb. 5:3; 7:27; 9:7. *The house* when spoken of is God's house, and Moses, not Aaron, the head over it; the whole assembly of Israel being included in "the house" (Heb. 3:2).

chapter of Hebrews. Jehovah appeared in the cloud upon the mercy-seat—the cloud of *glory*—and this may be the reason why the cherubim are called "cherubim of *glory.*" Aaron notwithstanding the washing of his flesh, and the linen garments with which he was clothed, could not enter the holiest with the blood of atonement unless he could personally shelter himself under a cloud of incense. A perfume, not his own, but provided according to minute directions given by God.

Two epithets are especially attached to the incense, "*pure,*" and "*holy*"—and it was to be holy for the Lord (Exod. 30:35,37). The frankincense, which was one ingredient of the incense, betokened purity. The word "pure" is connected with it (Exod. 30:34; Lev. 24:7), and the Hebrew word *levohnah* has the appropriate signification of whiteness. One of the Hebrew words for the moon is almost the same as that for frankincense—"fair as the moon" (Cant. 6:10). There is one of whom it is truly said, "Thou art fairer than the children of men"; whose unsullied purity formed a wondrous contrast with every other human being. A purity, a righteousness so made manifest upon the cross that even a Roman centurion exclaimed, "Certainly this was a righteous man" (Luke 23:47). The cloud of incense beaten small, as it wafted itself up to God, attracted with its singular perfume that Gentile soldier. Purity and holiness are not to be found here except in one whose graces were fully displayed before God.

The incense was compounded of three sweet spices besides the frankincense, "stacte, onycha, and galbanum." The two last are not known; but the stacte is manifestly derived from a word signifying "*to drop,*" both in the Hebrew, and in the Greek translation. A sweet spice that spontaneously dropped from the tree which produced it. Another emblem of the grace of the Lord Jesus, the Son of Man. Grace and truth came by Jesus Christ. His paths dropped fatness; wherever He went, true love, sympathy, and pity flowed from His heart towards the weak, the weary, and the afflicted. He was the true Man in the midst of falsehood and deceit in human beings all around Him. True in His affection; true in His words; true in His sympathies; true in His rebukes of evil as well as in His forgiveness of sin. It is blessed to turn from the hypocrisies of our own hearts, and of men around us, and contemplate Him "who did no violence," "neither was guile found in His mouth" (Isa. 53:9; 1 Pet. 2:22). There was no *effort* in Him; He simply lived, manifesting life in all He did and said. There was no affectation of spirituality; He *was* what He *appeared to be.* Thus His words and ways were not forced. His sanctity was not assumed. He had nothing to lay aside when He came into the presence of others. He put on nothing to gain their admiration. He was always Himself, living in the presence of God, ever pleasing God. Blessed contrast with men who have to assume religiousness to hide their own evil, who think that roughness is sincerity, and who are unnatural oft-times even in the very presence of God.

The incense "tempered together pure and holy" may have reference to the sweet fragrance which the Man Christ Jesus ever presented to God. The Israelites were forbidden to make a perfume like it, "to smell thereto." Christ is not to be imitated by a false humility to gratify one's own self-conceit. There may be a shew of wisdom and humility by which men satisfy their own flesh, but this is like an imitation of the holy perfume to smell thereto. If we are imitators indeed of Him we must first have been washed in His precious blood, and be born of God. To follow Him would involve self-crucifixion instead of self-admiration.

The golden censer was *filled* with burning coals, and Aaron's hands were *filled* with incense. The vessel that held the fire—type of the holiness of God—was full. The altar from which that fire had originally been taken was a place where holiness of God was exhibited in no scanty measure; and the censer was also filled, that in the very holiest itself that consuming fire might again be presented according to the divine estimate.

The high priest's hands were also full of sweet incense. He had to grasp that holy compound to the full extent of his ability, that his filled hands might answer to the filled censer. He then put the incense on the fire before the Lord, and the cloud of the incense covered the mercy-seat, and mingled with the cloud of glory upon the mercy-seat, in which Jehovah appeared.

We must here draw a contrast betwixt Aaron and Christ. The Lord Jesus presented Himself to God on the morning of His resurrection—called of God an High Priest, after the order of Melchizedek. His entrance into heaven itself was like the bringing in of fresh incense before God; for He entered on the ground of His perfect obedience unto death, even the death of the cross. God had been glorified in Him, on that very earth where God had been so dishonoured by man; and when for the first time a

Man stood in the presence of the glory of God before "the throne of the Majesty in the heavens," a cloud of human fragrance (may we not say?) mingled itself with the cloud of divine glory. What a wondrous addition to the heaven of heavens! What an added glory was the entrance of the risen man there for the first time as the risen man—a man able to stand before God on the ground of His own righteousness, His own obedience, His own purity, His own holiness; and also able to say to God, "I have glorified Thee on the earth, I have finished the work which Thou gavest Me to do."

May we not with reverence contemplate this resurrection of Jesus, and His thus presenting Himself before God in heaven itself, as a marvellous change in the economy of the heavens? One who bore the likeness of the creature, standing in the midst of the throne of the Most High in such nearness to God? What indeed has God wrought! What marvels has He accomplished through His blessed Son!

Aaron next took of the blood of the bullock and sprinkled it with his finger upon the mercy-seat and before the mercy-seat, seven times. So also he did with the blood of the goat, the sin offering for the people. Having sheltered himself under the cloud of incense, he was able to bring this record of death, the blood, and sprinkle it under the glory of God upon the mercy-seat, and upon the ground before the mercy-seat; first by way of atonement for himself and his house; and next on behalf of the people.

What a singular ritual this. The emblem of death placed where God in His glory manifested Himself. What a wondrous coming together of things in themselves opposed to one another. A record of life *poured out on account of sin,* brought into the holy of holies. And yet how this shadowy ritual portrays to us the truth in which our souls rejoice. The great engima of truth solved to faith in the death of God's Son.

It was said of the Aaronic high priest that "he entereth into the holy place every year with blood of *others,*" (Heb. 9:25) or, as it might be rendered, *strange* or *foreign* blood (*alotrio,*) seeing there was no affinity between the blood of a bullock, and a goat, and himself, a human being. It is written of Christ that "He by his *own (idiou)* blood entered in once into the holy places," (Heb. 9:12) and the word "*His own*" is again repeated (Heb. 13:12).

Aaron had to make atonement for himself as well as for his house. His own blood would have been of no avail for others, or for himself, for he was a sinner. Our High Priest is "holy, harmless, undefiled, separate from sinners, and made higher than the heavens"; and what He is now in the glory that He was when on earth, as far as regards holiness and harmlessness. Free from all human infirmity—the Son—who offered up Himself.

Aaron had to sprinkle the mercy-seat *eastward,* because his approach into the holiest was from the east, and he had to sprinkle before the mercy-seat, to establish a footing for himself before God; for his own feet would have defiled the ground before the mercy-seat. The Lord Jesus has His own rightful place—the Lamb as it had been slain in the midst of the throne—and He enables us *sinners* by nature to enter into the holiest by His blood, "by a new and living way, which He hath new made for us, through the veil, that is to say, His flesh."

We have no threat of "*lest he die*" held out to us in our approaches to God; but our very way is a *living* way, made *new* in contrast to all other ways of old, and ever new with the fresh sprinkled blood, in contrast with the blood only sprinkled once a year. The sacrifice of Christ is as fresh in all its life-giving value, and in all its cleansing power to-day, as it was on the very day it was first offered. The blood of Christ has ever its full, and fresh, and living value, in contrast with the blood of victims which had to be renewed daily and yearly.

(The word translated "*consecrated,*" is as the margin of the Bible has it, "*new made.*" The word "*new*" is a remarkable one, literally meaning "fresh slain," *(prosphaton),* and is used by the Spirit of God apparently to mark the contrast between the way on the day of atonement of old, when the blood must have at once ceased to keep its value, because it became stale, and had to be renewed every year; and the constant fresh value of the precious blood of Christ, as of a lamb just slain.)

Aaron had to make atonement for the holy place, and for himself, his household, and the congregation of Israel. "*The holy place,*" throughout this chapter where the word "*place*" is in italics, signifies the "*most holy,*" verses 2, 16, 17, 20, 23, 27. Called "the holy sanctuary" in verse 33. No one was to be with him, or enter the tabernacle until he had completed that important work of atonement. Atonement properly speaking is all Godward; and is accomplished by one alone. The sinner who is atoned for has no part in the work. It is accomplished entirely by another. He is passive, and ignorant of the fact, until God reveals it to him by His Spirit through the Word. It is most important for the peace of the soul that this should be fully understood. And this type makes it very plain. Not one of the congregation, nor one of Aaron's house was with him whilst he thus acted for them before God. They could not be aware whether even he was alive in the sanctuary, or what he had accomplished there. They were not in any attitude of prayer or supplication outside; but they silently waited in suspense till he came out; then they knew he had fulfilled all God's requirements; this being proved by the fact that he was alive.

The whole work of atonement, from beginning to end, has been accomplished by Christ alone; whether we look at the commencement of the work in the shedding of His blood on the cross, or at its completion in His resurrection as the great High Priest, and entering in, "once for all, by His own blood into the holy places, having obtained eternal redemption" (Heb. 9:12). This is emphatically stated in the Epistle to the Hebrews: "when He had by *Himself* purged our sins," 1:3; "this He did once when He offered up *Himself,*" 7:27; "He hath appeared to put away sin by the sacrifice of *Himself,*" 9:26. Alone upon the cross, the Lamb of God slain on account of sin. Alone in resurrection, the firstfruits of them that slept. Alone in the holiest with God, the great High Priest. He has offered one sacrifice for sins for ever, and has by Himself perfected the whole work of reconciliation which God committed to Him.

The sinner troubled in conscience on account of his sins, is not called upon by efforts of his own to reconcile God to himself. Every attempt of his own of this kind is the expression of an unbelieving heart, calling in question the full eternal redemption which Christ has obtained for us. He has to believe in a reconciliation accomplished. An atonement completed. A salvation finished. And that by the Lord Jesus Himself alone.

The "atonement for the holy place was because of the uncleanness of the children of Israel, and because of all their transgressions in all their sins"; or it might perhaps be rendered, "he shall make atonement upon the holy place, *from* the uncleanness of the children of Israel, and *from* their transgressions *in respect to,* or *on account* of all their sins."

Throughout this chapter uncleanness is in the plural (Heb. *tumoth*). *Uncleannesses* twice in ver. 16, and once in ver 19. It seems especially to refer to personal defilements originating from man's very nature, the constitution of his body, or from disease. Transgressions are also mentioned. Sin is that evil thing in which we are conceived, which renders us utterly unclean from our very birth; children of wrath by nature. The corrupt body is an outward evidence of the evil taint which pervades us. Our mortal flesh, mortal as to every part; without a spot of it free from death and corruption, is a proof of what we are by nature as regards our whole being, unclean perishing sinners.

Transgressions are sins made manifest in direct acts contrary to the revealed mind of God. Atonement had to be made with reference to the uncleanness of Israel, and their transgressions. These two manifestations of evil indicating their sins.

The law had no full type of the entire corruption of man. One of the objects for which it was given, was to develop that corruption in overt acts: "wherefore then the law? It was added because of transgressions" (Gal. 3:19).

"Moreover the law entered that the offence might abound" (Rom. 5:20). It was "the strength of sin" (1 Cor. 15:56). In the types therefore which form part of the law, we do not discover that great truth, that a man is so irremediably a sinner by nature as to need new birth, a new existence.

Perhaps *leprosy* affords the nearest type of the entire uncleanness of the human being. But even here the priest could only deal with the *manifestations* of the disease. In interpreting these shadows therefore we have to go deeper than the types themselves. The atonement made by Christ does not only answer to God for *us* as regards *our* uncleanness, but also in respect to the unclean nature itself, in which we entered this world as children of the first Adam. Our unclean selves; and here we must be careful to distinguish between *ourselves* and our corrupt *nature.* The atonement made by Christ has not in any way cleansed, improved, or reconciled our flesh, our evil nature; for that is so irremediably bad that all that God could do with it was utterly to condemn it. In the death of Christ for sin, God has "condemned (damned) sin in the flesh" (Rom. 8:3). "Our old man is crucified with Him that the body of sin might be destroyed," (Rom. 6:6). The body of the sins of the flesh have been put off from us as regards all judgment and wrath of God. *We* (not our evil nature) have been reconciled to God (2 Cor. 5:18; Col. 1:21).

This is the great aspect of atonement. For what troubles us most is the constant presence of an evil heart, an evil nature; an inclination for sin, which will make itself to be felt notwithstanding all our efforts towards practical holiness, and notwithstanding we are new creatures in Christ, and notwithstanding the presence of the Holy Spirit dwelling in us. As believers we have a right to look at this, the old man, and say, it has been crucified; it has been condemned once for all; it has been judged under the full wrath of God, poured out upon His own Son for us. And there is "now no condemnation" of any kind to us—no condemnation on account of this evil nature which we still know to exist—no condemnation on account of weakness, failures, ignorances, sins. The uncleannesses and transgressions of the people entered the sanctuary of God, and had to be met by the blood of atonement; or otherwise wrath must have burst forth from before the Lord upon the people, or God must remove His dwelling-place from the midst of them.

"The patterns of things in the heavens were purified with these (sacrifices), but the heavenly things themselves with better sacrifices than these. For Christ is not entered into the holy places made with hands, the figures of the true; but into heaven itself, now to appear in the presence of God for us" (Heb. 9:23, 24). (This is the only place where the word *sacrifices* occurs in the plural, when the death of the Lord Jesus is spoken of. In all probability it is used to express the fact of His one sacrifice embracing every varied aspect of the *many sacrifices* offered under the law.)

Notwithstanding our manifest sins and uncleannesses, of which to a great extent we are unconscious, Christ has opened the way for us into the very glory of God—He has preceded us there with His own most precious blood—and now we can draw near with confidence, without defiling with our presence the holiest of all. We can confess our sins before the mercy-seat itself. We can bring our deep necessities, and find mercy and grace to help us. We can offer thanksgiving, praise and worship which God can accept because of the sweet savour of that precious blood. We can say, without fear, "thou hast set our iniquities before thee, our secret (sins) in the light of thy countenance" (Psa. 90:8), because we know Christ is in the presence of God for us; His precious blood is in the very light of the glory of God on our behalf. The sins which have reached to heaven have been covered; blotted out by that sprinkled blood. "We have come to God, the judge of all." We have heard His sentence pronounced upon us as guilty and defiled sinners. We have seen that sentence executed in the death of His own Son. We have been justified from sin through that death, "justified by his blood" (Rom. 5:9; 6:7).

We have come "to Jesus the mediator of the new covenant"; the High Priest in the presence of God for us, ministering to us all the blessings of that new covenant. We have come "to the blood of sprinkling that speaketh better things than that of Abel"; the blood of sprinkling *upon* the mercy-seat, and *before* the mercy-seat. God said to Cain respecting the blood of Abel, "the voice of thy brother's blood crieth unto me from the ground, which hath opened her mouth to receive thy brother's blood from thy hand" (Gen. 4:10, 11). The blood cried for vengeance. The blood of sprinkling to which we have come, speaketh incessantly mercy and grace; answers every accusation; calls down ceaseless blessings; cleanseth from all sin; utters a voice which delights the ear of God; and which enables Him to open His hand and fill us with good. The word "*speaketh*" is a blessed word, in contrast not only with the blood of Abel which cried for vengeance, but with the blood of bulls and of goats, which spoke but for a moment, and effected nothing in reality. Whereas this blood speaketh on and on with a ceaseless still small voice of power, until the day of full redemption, when the resurrection of the Church in glory will manifest for ever its mighty efficacy: and the voice of the precious blood will continue to sound until Israel, God's *chosen nation,* and others redeemed out of the world during the 1000 years reign of Christ, are clothed with immortality (Henry Soltau).

THE BOOK OF

NUMBERS

Introduction

The fourth book of the Pentateuch bears in the Greek translation of the Old Testament (Septuagint) the title *Arithmoi,* of which the Latin *Numeri* and our English "Numbers" are translations. It is called by this name because the people Israel are twice numbered in this book. The first time when they started on their journey, and the second time at the close of their thirty-eight years wandering (chapters 1, and 26). The Hebrews have given to this book the name *Be-Midbar,* which means "in the wilderness."

It is the wilderness book and covers the entire period of Israel's history from the second month of the second year after the Exodus from Egypt to the tenth month of the fortieth year. However, the years of wanderings are passed over in silence, only the different camps are mentioned. Our annotations point out the significance of this.

The Author of Numbers

Numbers is closely linked with Leviticus, though it differs greatly from it. Moses wrote the record of the events in the wilderness as he wrote the instructions Jehovah gave concerning the worship of His people. Only a person who was contemporaneous with the events recorded in Numbers could have been the author of this book. In chapter 33:2 we find a statement to the effect that Moses wrote their goings out according to their journeys. If Moses did not write the book, who then was the author? If the Mosaic authorship is denied the genuineness and trustworthiness of the entire book must be given up. Higher criticism, so called, claims that Moses did not write Numbers and that the book itself was not contemporary with the events it describes. They call attention that throughout the book Moses is referred to in the third person. They make much of chapter 12:3, as bearing definite testimony against Moses as the author. (For the explanation see our annotations on that chapter.) The same documents, compilers and redactors, etc., which, as it is claimed, composed the other books of the Pentateuch, and put them into shape in which we have them, centuries after Moses lived, are also brought into play in connection with Numbers. It would be more than unprofitable to follow these foolish theories which have laid the foundation to the most serious denials of the revelation of God.

Interesting History

The story of Numbers is of deep interest. We do not need to follow here the events in detail as recorded in the different chapters; this will be our happy task as we study this book. The Lord had the people numbered first. They had to show their pedigree that they really belonged to the people of God. Then the camp was set in order. The service of the Levites in connection with the tabernacle was appointed. Everything was in readiness for the journey towards the land and the possession of the land. Jehovah Himself went before the camp. Then comes the sad history of Israel's failure, their murmuring and unbelief. They became wanderers and their carcasses fell in the wilderness.

In the Light of the New Testament

Every careful reader of the New Testament Scriptures knows that Numbers is there repeatedly quoted. The Lord spoke to Nicodemus about the serpent which Moses lifted up in the wilderness (chapter 21:9) and spoke of it as a type of His death on the cross. Balaam is mentioned by Peter, Jude and in the book of Revelation. Korah and the awful rebellion under him is used by Jude in his brief testimony concerning the apostasy of the last days.

But above all must we remember in the closer study of the book of Numbers that the Holy Spirit has called special attention to the experiences of Israel in this book in its typical character and as a solemn warning for us as pilgrims in this present evil age. The failure of Israel on account of unbelief to enter into the promised land and possess it foreshadows the failure of Christendom to possess the heavenly things in Christ. We follow this more fully in the annotations. All this is fully authorized by the divine statement in 1 Cor. 10:1-12.

Moreover, brethren, I would not that ye should be ignorant, how that all our fathers were under the cloud, and all passed through the sea; And were all baptized unto Moses in the cloud and in the sea; And did all eat the same spiritual meat; And did all drink the same spiritual drink: for they drank of that spiritual Rock that followed them: and that Rock was Christ. But with many of them God was not well pleased: for they were overthrown in the wilderness. Now these things were our examples, to the intent we should not lust after evil things, as they also lusted. Neither be ye idolaters, as *were* some of them; as it is written, The people sat down to eat and drink, and rose up to play. Neither let us commit fornication, as some of them committed, and fell in one day three and twenty thousand. Neither let us tempt Christ, as some of them also tempted, and were destroyed of serpents. Neither murmur ye, as some of them also murmured, and were destroyed of the destroyer. Now all these things happened unto them for ensamples: and they are written for our admonition, upon whom the ends of the world are come. Wherefore let him that thinketh he standeth take heed lest he fall.

And again it is written, "For whatsoever things were written aforetime, were written for our learning, that we through patience and comfort of the Scriptures might have hope" (Rom. 15:4). Read also Hebrews 3:7-19; 4:1-6. The entire wilderness experience of Israel as recorded in this book will yield to us deeper lessons if we seek them with prayer and a heart which is willing to know and to do His will. These typical and spiritual applications have been made as far as our limited space permits. Much more may be discovered in this great book; our annotations, we hope, will be used, under God, to point out the way.

The faithfulness of Jehovah in the midst of the most awful failures of His people and how He kept them and manifested His grace towards them is one of the beautiful things of this book.

The Levites and their Service

In the wilderness book only the service of the Levites is mentioned. Their responsibility in a service divinely given in taking charge of the things of the tabernacle (all typical of Christ and His work) is typical of our service into which the Lord calls each member of His body.

In this book we find likewise the first of the greater prophetic utterances of the Bible. The parables of Balaam form a great prophecy. The Appendix gives a full exposition. May it please God to use the analysis and annotations which now follow.

The Division of Numbers

The division of this book is very simple if we follow the historical account it contains. There are three parts to it. We give them and the leading contents of the different chapters.

I. THE PREPARATION FOR THE JOURNEY

1. **The People Numbered** (1:1-54)
2. **The Camp Put in Order** (2:1-34)
3. **The Levites and their Ministrations** (3—4)
4. **The Sanctification of the Camp and the Nazarite** (5—6)
5. **The Offerings of the Princes** (7:1-89)
6. **The Consecration of the Levites** (8:1-26)
7. **Passover and Jehovah with His People** (9:1-23)
8. **The Trumpets of Silver** (10:1-10)

II. THE JOURNEY STARTED AND THE PEOPLE'S UNBELIEF, FAILURE AND PUNISHMENT

1. **The Departure and the First Failure** (10:11-36)
2. **At Taberah and Kibroth-Hattavaah** (11:1-35)
3. **The Rebellion of Miriam and Aaron** (12:1-16)
4. **At Kadesh Barnea and Israel's Unbelief** (13—14)
5. **Various Laws, the Sabbath Breaker, and the Tassels upon the Garment** (15:1-41)
6. **The Rebellion of Korah and the Murmuring of the Whole Assembly** (16:1-50)
7. **The Priesthood of Aaron Confirmed** (17:1-13)
8. **The Priesthood and Iniquity and the Recompense of the Priests** (18:1-32)
9. **The Red Heifer and the Law of Purification** (19:1-22)
10. **At Kadesh in the Fortieth Year, Murmuring and Conquests** (20—21)

III. EVENTS IN THE PLAINS OF MOAB AND FACING THE LAND

1. **Balaam and His Parables** (22—24)
2. **Israel's Sin with the Daughters of Moab and the Zeal of Phinehas** (25:1-18)
3. **The Second Numbering of the People** (26:1-65)
4. **The Daughters of Zelophehad, the Death of Moses and his Successor Announced** (27:1-23)

5. **Order of the Offerings and the Set Times** (28—29)
6. **Concerning Vows** (30:1-16)
7. **The War against the Midianites** (31:1-54)
8. **The Tribes of Reuben, Gad, Half-Manasseh and their portion** (32:1-42)
9. **The Encampments in the Wilderness** (33:1-49)
10. **Instructions Concerning the Conquest and the Boundaries of the Land** (33:50—34:29)
11. **The Cities of Refuge** (35:1-34)
12. **The Security of the Inheritance** (36:1-13)

Analysis and Annotations

1. The Preparation for the Journey

1. The People Numbered

CHAPTER 1

1. The command to number (1:1-4)
2. The appointed helpers for the work (1:5-16)
3. The congregation assembled (1:17-19)
4. The twelve tribes numbered (1:20-46)
5. The Levites separated unto the tabernacle service (1:47-54)

It was exactly one month after the erection of the tabernacle that the Lord gave the commandment to Moses to number the people. This is seen by comparing the first verse of Numbers with Exodus 40:17. It must not be overlooked that there was a previous numbering of the people in connection with the atonement money. Then all who were twenty years and above, the same as in this census, were numbered. This took place nine months before, and the number of men twenty years and over was 603,550. The same number is given in this first chapter. See Exodus 38:25-26 and Numb. 1:46.

The numbering was "after their families by the house of their fathers." And those to be numbered were "all from twenty years old and upward, all that are able to go forth to war in Israel." They had to declare their pedigrees after their families, and only those who could do that had a place in this mustering and could be warriors. This showing of their pedigree was necessary on account of the mixed multitude which had joined themselves to the people of God. "And a mixed multitude went up also with them" (Exod. 12:38). This mixed multitude that was among them fell a lusting (Numb. 11:4). Therefore only those who could show by their pedigree their rightful place among the people of God were mustered and could go to war. Our pedigree, which gives us a place among the people of God, is the new birth, by which we become children of God. And our calling is to a spiritual warfare, not with flesh and blood, but against the devil and his wiles and the wicked spirits (Eph. 6:11-12).

The significance of the statement "all that are able to go forth to war in Israel" must not be overlooked. God wanted His people to go forward and reach in a few days the land of promise, enter in and conquer that land. How this plan was frustrated by their unbelief, and the men of twenty years and over died in the wilderness, without seeing the land is the sad history of this book.

Moses and Aaron were called to be the leaders in numbering the people by their armies. As we saw in Exodus, both Moses and Aaron are typical of Christ. He knoweth His people and His watchful eye rests upon each. With Moses and Aaron were associated the princes of the tribes mentioned in verses 5-16. The names of these princes are of deep interest when we translate them into English. The prince of Reuben is Elizur, "My God is a rock." The Prince of Simeon, Shelumiel, "At peace with God." The Prince of Judah, Nahshon, "A diviner." Then comes Nathaniel, "The gift of God." The Prince of Issachar, Zebulun, is represented by Eliab, "My God is father." Joseph has his double portion and Ephraim has Elishama, "My God hath heart." Manasseh's Prince is Gamaliel, "My God is a rewarder." Benjamin has Abidan, "My father is judge." The Prince of Dan is Ahiezer, "Brother of help." Asher has Pagiel, "Event of God." Gad's Prince is Eliasaph, "God addeth," and Naphtali is represented by Ahira, "Brother is evil." Nearly all these names are an encouragement to faith. These helpers in forming the mighty army speak by their names of the victory and blessing in store for His people if they go forward in faith. (The deeper lessons connected with it are pointed out in an excellent manner in the *Numerical Bible.*)

The different tribes, except Levi, were then numbered. We give a table which gives the result of this numbering and also the second numbering thirty-eight years later. The comparison in interesting:

	First Numbering Ch. 1	Second Numbering Ch. 26	
Reuben	46,500	43,730	2,700 *decr.*
Simeon	59,300	22,200	37,100 *decr.*
Gad	45,650	40,500	5,150 *decr.*
Judah	74,600	76,500	1,900 incr.
Issachar	54,400	64,300	9,900 incr.
Zebulun	57,400	60,500	3,100 incr.
Manasseh	32,200	52,700	20,500 incr.
Ephraim	40,500	32,500	8,000 *decr.*
Benjamin	35,400	45,600	10,200 incr.
Dan	62,700	64,400	1,700 incr.
Asher	41,500	53,400	11,900 incr.
Naphtali	53,400	45,400	8,000 *decr.*
Total	603,550	601,730	1,820 *decr.*

The tribe of Levi is not included. The end of this chapter gives the reason. They were not to be among the warriors, but appointed over the tabernacle of testimony, over all the vessels, and what belonged to it. They were to bear it and their place was round about the tabernacle. Their service, divinely appointed and the beautiful lessons connected with it, we shall follow more fully in our annotations of the third and fourth chapters.

2. The Camp Put in Order

CHAPTER 2

1. The command (2:1-2)
2. The east-side: Judah, Isaachar and Zebulun (2:3-9)
3. The south-side: Reuben, Simeon and Gad (2:10-16)
4. The position of the Levites (2:17)
5. The west-side: Ephraim, Manasseh and Benjamin (2:18-24)
6. The north-side: Dan, Asher and Naphtali (2:25-34)

The camp is now divinely arranged and put in order. Nothing was left to themselves. Jehovah spoke and gave the instructions, how every man of the children of Israel was to pitch by his own standard, with the ensign of their father's house over against, round about the tabernacle. The tabernacle where Jehovah dwelt was in the midst. Around this center the tribes were grouped in four camps, an east side, a south side, west side and north side, three tribes on each side. Rabbinical tradition adds many interesting details which may be true. According to this tradition each had its own standard with the crests of its ancestors. On the east, above the tent of Nahshon, there shone a standard of green, because it was on an emerald (the green stone) that the name of Judah was engraved upon the breastplate of the high priest. Upon this standard was a lion, according to the words of Jacob, "Judah is a lion's whelp." Towards the south, above the tent of Elizur, the son of Reuben, there floated a red standard, the color of the Sardius, the stone upon which Reuben's name was written. Upon his standard was a human head, because Reuben was the head of the family. And Reuben means, as we saw in Exodus, "Behold a son," typical of Him who became the Son of man. On the west, above the tent of Elishama, the son of Ephraim, there was a golden flag on which was the head of a calf, because it was through the vision of the calves or oxen that Joseph had predicted and provided for the famine in Egypt; and hence Moses, when blessing the tribe of Joseph (Deut. 33:17) said, "his glory is that of the first-born of a bull." Towards the north, above the tent of Ahiezer, the son of Dan, there floated a motley standard of red and white, like the Jasper, in which the name of Dan was engraven upon the breastplate. In his standard was an eagle, the great foe of serpents, because Jacob had compared Dan to a serpent; but Ahiezer had substituted the eagle, the destroyer of serpents, as he shrank from carrying an adder upon his flag. This, we remind our readers, is Jewish tradition, and very interesting.

A little diagram will bring the camp more vividly before us.

The Lord, we repeat, arranged the camp, with Judah facing towards the sunrise; this indicates the promised goal and also reminds us of the rising of the Sun of Righteousness, the coming of the Lord, when the wanderings of His people will end. And Jehovah was in the midst of His people to guide and protect them, to supply their needs. He is still the same. His New Testament people are also put in order by Him, and He is in the midst. However, there are not different standards around which His people gather, but there is only One, which is Christ. We do not think it profitable to enter into some of the rationalistic objections made in connection with this camp and its enormous number of occupants. They say, among other things, that such a mass of people could not possibly have lived for any length of time in the peninsula of Sinai, inasmuch as the natural produce of the desert could not have sustained them. But they forget that the book of Numbers does not say they lived upon what the desert yielded, but that they were miraculously sustained. These objections, whether they come from a vile French

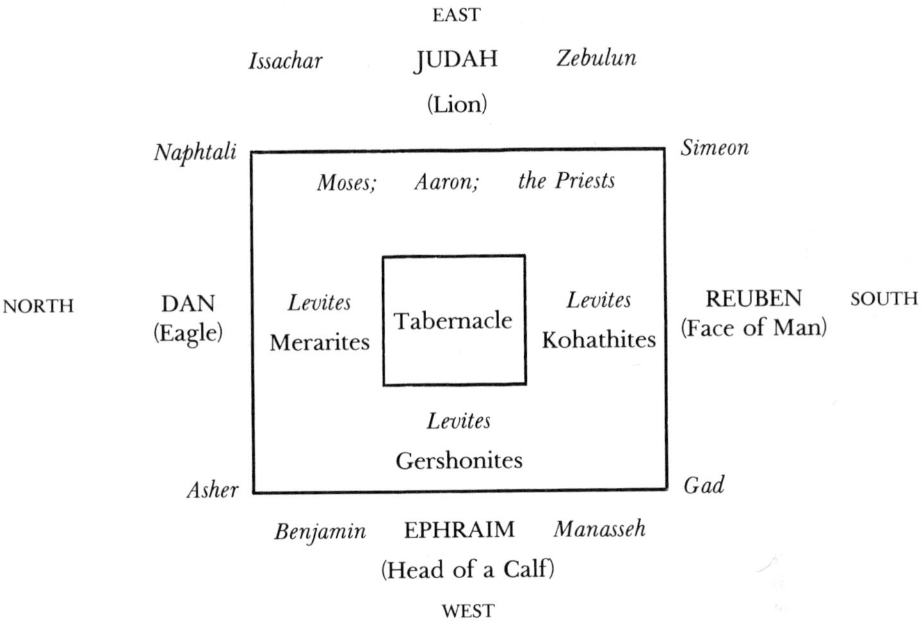

infidel or a cultured, higher critic, are the offspring of an unbelieving heart.

3. The Levites and their Ministrations

CHAPTER 3

1. The generations of the priests (3:1-4)
2. The tribe of Levi and their ministry (3:5-10)
3. The Levites substituted for all the first-born (3:11-13)
4. The numbering of the Levites ordered (3:14-20)
5. Gershon (3:21-26)
6. Kohath (3:27-32)
7. Merari (3:33-37)
8. Moses, Aaron and Aaron's sons (3:38)
9. The numbering completed (3:39)
10. The separation of the Levites in place of the first-born (3:40-51)

The supremacy of the tribe of Levi shows the sovereignty of God. Divine grace is fully revealed in the selection of this tribe. This tribe could not be chosen on account of a meritorious character. We read in Jacob's prophecy words concerning Simeon and Levi which reveal their sin. "O my soul, come thou not in their secret; unto their assembly, mine honor, be not thou united, for in their anger they slew a man, and in their self-will they digged down a wall. Cursed be their anger, for it was fierce; and their wrath, for it was cruel: I will divide them in Jacob, and scatter them in Israel" (Genesis 49:6-7). Yet out of this tribe Jehovah took Moses for the leader of His people, Aaron and his sons for priests, and the whole tribe instead of all the first-born for the special ministry. This is a most blessed illustration of sovereign grace. They were brought into this wonderful place of blessing and privilege by grace. In the eighth chapter we read of the cleansing of the Levites (8:5-7).

The difference between the ministry of the priests and the Levites must be noted. The book of Leviticus acquainted us with the work of Aaron and his sons, but it had nothing to say about the ministry entrusted to the Levites. The priests had given to them the ministry of the sanctuary, where they acted as worshippers and intercessors. The work of the Levites as given in this chapter, and that which follows, was of a more outward nature. They had to guard the tabernacle, to attend to its erection and taking down, to bear the different parts, all of which was ordered in all its details by Jehovah.

Levi means "joined." The grace of God had joined them to the Lord and His ministry. Christian believers are joined to the Lord and are both priests and Levites, possessing priesthood and ministry. Our priesthood consists in the ministry of the sanctuary, in worship and intercession. Our Levite ministry is many sided. It is given to us from the Lord to be exercised towards men. We bring spiritual sacrifices, the fruit of our lips, the sacrifice of praise unto God. The whole life of a Christian is to have the Levite character of ministry. "For me to live is Christ" is our service as the Levite lived for the tabernacle and its service. All Christian believers are priests and all have a ministry.

The generations of Aaron and Moses are mentioned first in this chapter. While elsewhere we read of Moses and Aaron, Aaron's name here stands first. His name is put first because he typifies Christ as Priest, upon whose intercession all depends. The Levites were then brought to Aaron to minister unto him and keep his charge. Jehovah claims them for His own instead of all the first-born. "Therefore the Levites shall be mine." "Mine shall they be, I am Jehovah." The first-born were sanctified unto the Lord because of deliverance. They knew therefore that they were sanctified unto Jehovah and owned by Him. And this is our blessed knowledge in Christ. We are delivered, sanctified, belong to Him and to keep His charge, rendering the service into which He has called us. May our hearts be led into the enjoyment of all this.

The difference between the numbering of the tribe of Levi and the other tribes must be noted. In the previous chapter those were numbered who were twenty years and over, but the Levites were numbered "every male from a month old and upward." This difference was because they were in place of the first-born, which were at the tender age of weakness and helplessness either redeemed or given up (18:16).

The sons of Levi made prominent as the heads of eight families, are, Gershon, Kohath and Merari.

Gershon (exile) with his sons, Libni and Shimei, were 7,500 souls. Their place was on the west-side of the tabernacle, over against Ephraim. (See diagram in the previous chapter.) They had charge of the tabernacle, the tent, the coverings and the hangings of the door of the tabernacle.

Kohath (assembly) with the Amramites, Izeharites, Hebronites and Uzzielites, were 8,600 souls. Their place was on the south side and they had charge of the ark, the table, the candlestick, the altars, the hanging and all the service thereof.

Merari (bitter) with the family of Mahlites and Mushites were 6,200 souls and their place was on the north-side, over against Dan. Their service consisted in handling the boards of the tabernacle, pillars, sockets, pins and cords. Each had his specific work given. There could be no misunderstanding about it. How strange it would have been if these 22,000 Levites had formed committees and sub-committees to divide the work and direct in it! All this would have brought in disorder. All they needed to do was to do the work into which the Lord had called them. All the instructions were given; obedience to these instructions, and faithfulness in the discharge of it were the essential things. The same is true in connection with the church. Every member in the body of Christ has a service to render. Each member is put into place by the Lord Himself and He gives to each the service, as He gave to these sons of Levi and their families their specific work in and around the tabernacle. "Now there are diversities of gifts, but the same Spirit. And there are differences of ministries, but the same Lord. And there are diversities of operations, but it is the same God, that worketh all things in all" (1 Cor. 12:4-6). How little this truth is recognized! Much of what is called Christian service is service in self-will and therefore lacks power and blessing. As these Levites knew their work, because the Lord had spoken and called them into it, so every member of the body of Christ is to know his calling and his service.

"We, as Christians, are very apt to jostle one another; indeed, we are sure to do so if we do not each one pursue his own divinely appointed line of work. We say *"divinely* appointed," and would press the word; we have no right to choose our own work. If the Lord has made one man an evangelist, another a teacher, another a pastor, and another an exhorter, how is the work to go on? Surely, it is not by the evangelist trying to teach, and the teacher to exhort, or one who is not fitted for either trying to do both. No; it is by each one exercising his own divinely imparted gift. No doubt, it may please the Lord to endow one individual with a variety of gifts; but this does not, in the smallest degree, touch the principle on which we are dwelling, which is simply this, every one of us is responsible to know his own special line and pursue it. If this be lost sight of, we shall get into hopeless confusion. God has His quarry-men, His stone-squarers, and His masons. The work progresses by each man attending diligently to his own work. If all were quarry-men, where were the stone-squarers? if all were stone-squarers, where were the masons? The greatest possible damage is done to the cause of Christ, and to God's work in the world, by one man aiming at another's line of things, or seeking to imitate another's gift. It is a grievous mistake, against which we would solemnly warn the reader. Nothing can be more senseless. God never repeats Himself. There are not two faces alike, not two leaves in the forest alike, not two blades of grass alike. Why, then, should any one aim at another's line of work, or affect to possess another's gift? Let each one be satisfied to be just what his Master has made him. This is the secret of real peace and progress."[1]

Worship holds the first and highest place. This is for us His people most clearly stated in the New Testament. Devotion to the Lord Jesus Christ in our life is the highest form of service and all other service must flow, and will flow, from faithfulness to the Person of our Lord.

Gershon and his sons had charge of the coverings and the fine linen. Gershon means exile, a stranger. The fine linen is typical of righteousness. The coverings, hangings, which divided off and separated the different parts of the tabernacle, must have the meaning of separation. His service points us to the fact that we are separated ones and strangers in the world. This separation must be witnessed to by practical righteousness.

Merari had charge with his sons of the boards, the sockets, pins and cords. These held the building together. We stated in the annotations on Exodus (chapter 26) that Christ and His people are typified in the boards of shittim wood, resting in the sockets of silver. The framework of the tabernacle, with the bars of shittim wood uniting the boards, is a type of that building of which we read in Ephesians, "a building fitly framed together," the church. The work of Merari suggests the thought of union.

It is interesting to compare this wilderness service as outlined above with the exhortation in Eph. 4:1-3. Knowing God's calling, in possession of God's highest and best, as revealed in that Epistle, passing through the wilderness, we are to walk worthy of that calling.

1. In all lowliness and meekness; manifesting Christ: Kohath-service.

2. With longsuffering, etc.; practical righteousness: Gershon-service.

3. Keeping the unity of the Spirit; united in the one body: Merari-service.

And if we walk thus we shall make known the excellencies of Him, who hath called us from darkness to His marvellous light and exercise in obedience the special gift He has given to us as members of His body.

The numbering then proceeded. The number of those fit for service was 8,580.

Kohathites	Able men	2,750	
	Unable	5,850	
Total			8,600
Gershonites	Able men	2630	
	Unable	4,870	
Total			7,500
Merarites	Able men	3,200	
	Unable	3,000	
Total			6,200
Total			22,300

But how many among God's people are unfit for service, being out of conscious fellowship with God and conformed to this present evil age! May it please the Spirit of God to awaken such to see anew their calling and their blessed privileges as priests and Levites unto God.

But while it is impossible to restore the house, that is the professing church, so sadly divided and broken in pieces, it is not impossible for the individual believer to live and serve according to the divine ideal.

In verse 38 we find the place given where Moses, Aaron and the priests were to encamp. It was before the tabernacle, that is, on the east side. The number of the Levites is given as 22,000. If we add the number of the Gershonites, Kohathites and Merarites, 7,500, 8,600 and 6,200, we get 22,300. Here is a difficulty which seems to remain unsolved. The total number in verse 39 must be correct, for in verse 46 we read that the number of the first-born exceeded the total number of the Levites by 273.

CHAPTER 4

The Service of the Levites and their Numbering

1. The children of Kohath; their service (4:1-20)
2. The sons of Gershon; their service (4:21-28)
3. The sons of Merari; their service (4:29-33)
4. Their numbering for service (4:34-49)

[1]C. H. Mackintosh, *Notes on Numbers.*

This chapter enters more fully into the service of the Levites. They are mustered for service "from thirty years old and upwards even unto fifty years old." As we saw in the previous chapter, their service was to carry the holy things of Jehovah through the wilderness. The wilderness is for us the type of the world through which we pass, and our business as Christians is to manifest Christ. We must guard the holy things of our faith as jealously as the Levites guarded the tabernacle and its sacred contents, and this must be done by us with the testimony of our lips and the testimony of our lives. The service of the Kohathites, Gershonites and Merarites is full of blessed instructions for us, at which we can but briefly hint. In the previous chapter Gershon stands first, as he is the first-born. Here the first-born has to take a secondary place and Kohath is put first. The lesson is that the divine appointment for service is not the matter of natural relation and endowment, but of grace. The sons of Kohath had to carry the most holy things. All of them typify Christ in His humanity as our Redeemer and Lord. This stands first. It is occupation with Christ, and therefore fellowship with God.

4. The Sanctification of the Camp and the Nazarite

CHAPTER 5

1. Concerning the leper, the issue and defilement of the dead (5:1-4)
2. Concerning restitution (5:5-10)
3. Concerning the wife suspected of adultery (5:11-31)

So far we had the outward arrangement of the camp. This chapter tells us that the camp had to be holy and therefore must be cleansed from that which defiles. Divine directions are given concerning the unclean person, the restitution of anything unjustly taken and what is to be done with a wife suspected of adultery. Leprosy could not be tolerated in the camp in the midst whereof Jehovah dwelt. The persons who had an issue and had come in touch with the dead, as well as the leper, both male and female, were to be put without the camp. This command was at once obeyed. "And the children of Israel did so, and put them out without the camp." The typical meaning of leprosy we learned from Leviticus as well as the meaning of the issue. Sin is typified thereby as manifested in and through one who belongs to the people of God. While here we have the divine command to put the unclean person out of the camp, we have the equally divinely given command in the New Testament: "Put away from among yourselves that wicked person" (1 Cor. 5:13). The principle is the same whether in the camp of Israel or in the church of the Lord Jesus Christ. To touch the dead also defiled. If it was a dead person, the one who touched the same was considered unclean for seven days (Numb. 19:11); if a man touched a dead animal it rendered him unclean till the evening (Levit. 11:27, 39, 40). To purify such who had become defiled in this manner, the ordinance of the red heifer was given. In no other portion of the Law is made so much of this form of defilement as in Numbers. This is in keeping with the character of the book. Israel passing through the wilderness came face to face with death on all sides. Spiritually the application is not hard to make. The world through which God's children pass is the enemy of God, alienated from Him and lying in the wicked one. Death is stamped upon it and the world is under condemnation. By the cross of Christ we are crucified to the world and the world is crucified unto us. The Word of God therefore exhorts us not to be conformed to this world (Rom. 12:2). We are not to love the world nor the things in the world (1 John 2:15-17). James tell us that whosoever will be a friend of the world is the enemy of God (James 4:4). Against defilement with the world in its different phases the child of God must constantly be on his guard. The camp must be holy, because Jehovah is in the midst. All what defiles belongs outside.

The wrong committed in the camp (verses 5-10) must be confessed, restitution be made, and, according to the law of the trespass-offering, the fifth part must be added to it. Unconfessed sin could not be tolerated in the camp where Jehovah dwells. And the same principle we find in the New Testament. "The grace of God, which has brought in unlimited forgiveness, would be rather a calamity if it did not enforce confession. Can one conceive a thing more dreadful morally than a real weakening of the sense of sin in those brought nigh to God? It may seem so where there is only a superficial acquaintance with God. Where the truth hath been hastily gathered and learned on the surface it is quite possible to pervert the gospel to an enfeebling of the immutable principles of God, ignoring His detestation of sin, and our own necessary abhorrence of it as born of God. Whatever produces such an effect is the deepest wrong to Him and the greatest loss to us. This is guarded against here. [2]

In the next paragraph concerning the wife suspected of adultery, no positive defilement or sin is in view, only the suspicion of it. A careful reading of the passage is suggested. The offering of jealousy is described in detail, but the brief character of our annotations forbids a closer examination. We can only point out that the offering consisted not of fine flour as in the meal-offering, but of barley meal, which was coarser. No leaven was mixed with it, for that would have implied before the test, the guilt of the accused woman. Nor was oil and frankincense put on the offering, no joy and worship could be connected with this offering of jealousy. Then the priest took holy water in an earthen vessel and the dust of the tabernacle floor and put it into the water. This also has a symbolical meaning. The water stands for the Word, and the dust typifies death and the curse. It was a most solemn ceremony of a searching nature. The innocent one had nothing to fear; the drinking of the bitter water that causeth the curse but resulted for her in vindication. The guilty one was found out by Jehovah and the curse rested upon her. This ordinance is also applicable to Israel as the unfaithful wife of Jehovah.

CHAPTER 6

The Nazarite

1. The vow of a Nazarite (6:1-8)
2. The defilement of the Nazarite (6:9-12)
3. The law of the Nazarite (6:15-21)
4. The blessing of Aaron and his sons (6:22-27)

The word Nazarite means, one who is separated. The vow of the Nazarite meant separation *unto* Jehovah and separation in three things: 1. Separation from wine and strong drink, vinegar of wine, vinegar of strong drink, liquor of grapes, moist or dried grapes, from all that is made of the wine-tree, from the kernels even unto the husks. 2. His hair was to grow long and no razor was to come upon his head. 3. He was to be separated from the dead. This Nazarite vow was only for a certain period of time and not permanent. When it ended he shaved his head and drank wine.

This entire chapter concerning the Nazarite is of intense interest for it contains many helpful and most blessed lessons for us. It is needless to say that no more vows like the vow of the Nazarite can be made in the literal sense of the word, just as there is no longer a special class of priests among God's people. A Nazarite was a separate one, a saint, and such are we in Christ Jesus. But while the grace of God has constituted us saints, the practical living out of our Nazariteship remains with us. It must be the matter of the willing heart, the heart, which, in devotion to the Lord, yields itself to Him. The wine, strong drink, and all which comes from the vine stands for earthly joys, for pleasures, for that which is pleasing to the old nature. The wine and strong drink stand typically for the intoxicating pleasures which this poor, lost world indulges in and which the god of this age so often uses to dull the heart and the spirituality of the saints. But there are other things mentioned, which in themselves are harmless, like the moist grapes and dried grapes. These represent also earthly joys of a harmless character, but which cannot give to the believer the joy in the Lord which His heart craves. Christ is to be our all in all, the saint does not need anything whatever of earthly joys to sustain him. Christ is sufficient. Asaph reveals the true Nazarite spirit, when He said, 'Whom have I in heaven but Thee? and there is none on earth that I desire beside Thee" (Ps. 73:25). Paul in writing to the Philippians gives the expression of a Nazarite: "For me to live is Christ." "And furthermore, I consider all things but loss for the sake of the surpassing knowledge of Christ Jesus, my Lord; for whom I suffered the loss of all things, and count them but dung, that I may win Christ" (Phil. 3:8).

"Legality this is not. Legality is the spirit of self-righteousness, or of slavish dread, never of love, or desire after Christ, or of expectation from Him, such as that of which we have been speaking. Carry these ever so far, they can never land you in that in the direction of which they do not even point, but away from it. He who speaks of himself as doing but one thing was neither a legalist nor an extremist. He was simply a man into whose heart, forever filling it, the glory of Christ had shined.

"Let us not confound this, however, with the spirit of asceticism that has peopled monasteries with men fleeing vainly from this world, or scattered through the desert the abodes of the recluse. Nor let us imagine as involved in it any 'death to nature,' in which what God has made or instituted is branded as if it were unclean. It is striking that just in these two epistles in which Christian position is most emphasized (Ephe-

[2]W. Kelly, *Lectures on the Pentateuch.*

sians and Colossians) the duties of earthly relationships are most largely dwelt upon. The lilies of the field could be seen by Him who as Son of Man was here on earth for us arrayed in glory beyond all Solomon's. His hands indeed had made them, and if not a sparrow fell to the ground without His Father, He could say, 'I and My Father are one.' Still as ever is it true that the Lord's works are manifold, and in wisdom has He made them all: the earth is full of His riches; yea, and His works are sought out of all them that have pleasure therein.

"But the Christian Nazarite is *Christ's:* therefore in his pleasures, in his business, in his duties, Christ is before him, with him, over him. He has fellowship with the Father and the Son, and there is nothing for him outside this. Here is the principle which makes him of necessity a stranger to what *they* find pleasure in, who find none in Him. The world's 'vine of wine,' as a whole, he is separate from" (F. W. Grant, *Numerical Bible*).

The long hair of the Nazarite is not difficult to interpret. 1 Cor. 11:1-15 gives the key. "If a man have long hair, it is a shame unto him. But if a woman have long hair, it is a glory to her; for her hair is given her for a covering." The long hair of the woman testifies of the authority under which she is put. The long hair of the Nazarite therefore showed that he had humbled himself, made of himself no reputation. He took the place of dependence and loneliness. He gave up his rights and became nothing. And this is the place of blessing and power. The Christian Nazarite in his practical separation to the Lord, loves the low place and delights to follow after Him who emptied Himself and stooped so low. The separation from the dead has the same meaning as in the previous chapter. May it please God to give the writer and every reader of these lines a deeper longing to live as a true Nazarite, separated unto the Lord.

The Nazarite vow ended. Our separation is only as long as we are in the wilderness. The time came when the Nazarite, having fulfilled his vow, drank wine. A time of joy is coming for the saints of God, when His words shall be fulfilled. "I will not drink henceforth of this fruit of the wine until that day when I drink it new with you in my Father's kingdom" (Matt. 26:29). Then in His presence, delivered completely from sin and an evil world, we shall have joy unending, and instead of the place of lowliness we shall be exalted and share His throne with Him. Oh! for a thousand lives to devote to the Lord Jesus Christ!

The blessing with which this chapter ends gives a precious revelation of the triune God. Three times the Name of Jehovah was put upon the children of Israel; the Father-God, who keeps; Jehovah the Son, who is gracious; Jehovah the Holy Spirit, who gives peace. And there are certain people who deny the triune God and claim that no such doctrine is found in the Bible! How great will be the blessing, when He comes the second time to bless His people and all creation!

5. The Offerings of the Princes

CHAPTER 7

1. The princes present their offerings (7:1-3)
2. The command concerning these offerings and the Levites (7:4-11)
3. The twelve princes and what they offered (7:12-88)
4. Moses hears the voice from the mercy-seat (7:89)

This is the longest chapter in Numbers. The princes of Israel appear to bring their free-will offerings in six covered wagons drawn each by two oxen. No command had been given. With a willing heart they devoted of their possessions to the service of the sanctuary. The Lord accepting the offerings gave directions that the Gershonites and Merarites were to receive the wagons and the oxen for their service. The sons of Gershon received two wagons and four oxen and the sons of Merari four wagons and eight oxen. The gift was according to the service into which Jehovah had called them. The Merarites had to take care of the heavy boards and the Lord provided the means to carry the burden and render the service. For all service into which He calls His people, He also provides the strength and the means for the service. The sons of Kohath received nothing. They needed no wagons and oxen; their service was to carry the precious things upon their shoulders.

The critics of the Word of God have found fault with the lengthy statements and repetitions concerning the twelve princes and their offerings. If these critics had penned this chapter, they would have given these offerings in a verse or two. But what unbelief belittles and rejects, is precious to faith. The details of the offerings and repetitions are written by the Holy Spirit, that we may know that Jehovah takes notice of the devotion and sacrifice of His people. He keeps a record of it all. The same eye, which followed the princes as they approached the tabernacle with their wagons, saw the two mites, which the poor widow deposited into the treasury; the same eye sees us. He will not forget the least service rendered unto Him.

All the twelve are called princes, except Nahshon of Judah. He, as the leader, the representative of Judah, must be the type of the Lord Jesus Christ, and He is more than a prince. We give a bird's eye view of the persons named and their gifts.

1. Judah: *Nahshon* (7:12)
2. Issachar: *Nethaniel* (7:18)
3. Zebulun: *Eliab* (7:24)
4. Reuben: *Elizur* (7:30)
5. Simeon: *Shelumiel* (7:36)
6. Gad: *Eliasaph* (7:42)
7. Ephraim: *Elishama* (7:48)
8. Manasseh: *Gamaliel* (7:54)
9. Benjamin: *Abidan* (7:60)
10. Dan: *Ahiezer* (7:66)
11. Asher: *Pagiel* (7:72)
12. Naphtali: *Ahira* (7:78)

12 Silver Chargers, each 130 shekels.
12 Silver Bowls, each 70 shekels.
12 Gold Spoons, each 10 shekels.
Total Shekels of Silver, 2400
Total Shekels of Gold, 120
Of beasts for sacrifice:

Bullocks	12
Rams	12
Lambs	12
Goats	24
Rams	60
He-Goats	60
Lambs	60
Total	240

Jehovah expressed His approval and His joy, after the offerings had been presented, by speaking to Moses in an audible voice, from between the Cherubim. The promise given in Exodus 25:21, 22 was fulfilled.

6. The Consecration of the Levites

CHAPTER 8

1. The lighting of the candlestick (8:1-4)
2. The consecration of the Levites (8:5-22)
3. The charge to the Levites repeated (8:23-26)

The candlestick is the type of Christ as in the sanctuary, that is, Christ in glory. The lighting of the seven lamps introduced in the beginning of the wilderness book is of blessed meaning. The seven lamps were to illuminate the candlestick of beaten gold, throw their light upon the candlestick so that the gold and beautiful workmanship might be seen. The oil in the seven lamps represents the Holy Spirit. Spiritually applied we have the picture here of the Spirit of God shedding light upon Christ. For this He is given to His people, to glorify Christ. And this is the great need of the people of God in their journey through the wilderness. The eyes of the pilgrim and stranger, the passenger passing through the wilderness, must be fixed upon Christ in glory.

The consecration of the Levites consisted in sprinkling with water, shaving the whole body, washing of their clothes. They had to stand before the tabernacle of the congregation and the whole assembly of the children of Israel was gathered together. The children of Israel had to put their hands upon the Levites. The whole congregation became thus identified with the service of the Levites. The Levites represented the entire congregation of Israel and served in their behalf. The sprinkling with water in their consecration stands typically for the purification from sins. This they could not do for themselves, another had to do it. But the sharp razor they were able to take to remove from their bodies all the hair, which stands for that which belongs to the flesh, the old nature. They had also to wash their clothes, which typically signifies the water (the Word) applied to our habits and to our ways. The lessons are many. He who would be a true Levite in service must constantly use the sharp knife of self-judgment to remove all what is of self.

Their period of service was fixed. It was uniform, from 25 to 50 years. It was a gracious provision that at 50 the Levite was permitted to retire from the harder work. There is no clash here with the statement of chapter 4. From 25 to 30 they could do the lighter work of the tabernacle, even as the Levites over 50 years were exempt from the harder tasks. The Lord still fixes the period in which His servants are to serve Him, as He also looks out for their comfort (John 21:12, 18-19).

7. Passover and Jehovah with his People

CHAPTER 9

1. The command to keep the Passover (9:1-3)
2. The Passover kept (9:4-5)
3. Provision in case of defilement (9:6-14)
4. Jehovah with His people (9:15-23)

Jehovah next commands His people to keep the feast of redemption, Passover. And they obeyed at once. The first Passover was held in Egypt, the second in the wilderness at Sinai, with their faces turned towards the land of promise, and it was next celebrated in the land of Canaan. This shows how essential the blood is for everything. The blood delivers out of Egypt, it keeps in the wilderness and brings into the land of promise. Here in the wilderness they looked back to redemption as it had been accomplished in Egypt, the sprinkled blood of the paschal lamb had delivered them, and they looked forward to the land towards which they journeyed. Jehovah, who had delivered them out of Egypt by blood, carried His people through the wilderness, supplying all their wants, and brought them in virtue of that redemption blood, the ever blessed type of the precious blood of the Lamb, into the land of Canaan. We have the Lord's table where we enjoy the feast of redemption, feeding on Himself and His great love. There we look back to the Cross where He died, and praise Him for our deliverance. There we look forward to the blessed goal "till He comes." And we know that while on the way all our need shall be supplied, according to His riches in glory in Christ Jesus.

A gracious provision was made for the men who were defiled by the dead or were on a journey afar. They could keep the Passover a month later, in the second month on the fourteenth day. The men who were defiled made a confession of it. And Moses not knowing what to do about their case turned to the Lord for instruction, which was immediately given. The grace of God met this need in a blessed way. There was time given for cleansing and for return from the journey and then a month later they could keep the Passover. None was to be shut out from the feast of redemption which God in His grace had provided for His people. Confession and self-judgment are needed in keeping the Lord's Supper. If the wanderer but returns he finds a welcome at the table He has spread for His people. What grace the Lord manifests towards His people! But how little grace those who are the objects of His love and grace manifest towards each other! If one, however, did neglect the Passover wilfully, he was to be cut off from among his people. Such neglect showed that he had no heart for Jehovah and His redemption.

And the cloud was with His people. In that cloud Jehovah was present, He was with His people. They tarried and journeyed according to the command of the Lord. The cloud by day and the pillar of fire by night. "So it was alway." He did not leave His dwelling place in the midst of the people. All their movements were ordered by the cloud, that is, by the Lord Himself.

That mighty camp of over 600,000 men of twenty years and over, the 22,000 Levites and the hundreds of thousands of women and children, were dependent on the cloud. They could make no plans of their own. They did not know where they would go the next day. When they camped they did not know for how long it would be; when they marched they were ignorant how long it would last. Their eyes had to be fixed every morning, every night and throughout the day upon the cloud. They had to look up. Daily they were dependent upon Jehovah and upon the cloud for guidance.

And does He do anything less for His people living in the present age? Is the promise of guidance confined to Israel? Is it still His promise to His trusting child, "I will guide thee with mine eye"? Every Christian knows that he is under His care and under His guidance. If He guided Israel thus, how much more He will guide us who are, through grace, members of His body, one spirit with the Lord! How often we frustrate the manifestations of His power and His love by choosing our own path.

"Thus is was with Israel, and thus it should be with us. We are passing through a trackless desert—a moral wilderness. There is absolutely no way. We should not know how to walk, or where to go, were it not for that one most precious, most deep, most comprehensive sentence which fell from the lips of our blessed Lord, *'I am the way.'* Here is divine, infallible guidance. We are to follow Him. 'I am the light of the world: he that followeth Me shall not walk in darkness, but shall have the light of life' (John 8). This is living guidance. It is not acting according to the letter of certain rules and regulations; it is following a living Christ—walking as He walked, doing as He did, imitating His example in all things. This is Christian movement—Christian action. It is keeping the eye fixed upon Jesus, and having the features, traits and lineaments of His character imprinted on our new nature, and reflected back or reproduced in our daily life and ways.

"Now this will assuredly involve the surrender of our own will, our own plans, our own management, altogether. We must follow the cloud: we must wait *ever,* wait *only* upon God. We cannot say, We shall go here or there, do this or that, to-morrow, or next week. All our movements must be placed under the regulating power of that one commanding sentence (often, alas! lightly penned and uttered by us), *'If the Lord will'* " (C. H. Mackintosh).

8. The Trumpets of Silver

CHAPTER 10:1-10

1. The silver trumpets (10:1-2)
2. How they were to be used (10:3-10)

The silver trumpets were also given for guidance. They made known the mind of the Lord in an audible way. The cloud was seen. It stands for guidance by the eye. The silver trumpets were heard. When Israel was gathered together the trumpets were blown. "When ye blow an alarm, then the camps that lie on the east side shall go forward; when ye blow an alarm the second time then the camps that lie on the south side shall take their journey." They were used in time of war and the promise of victory and deliverance is connected with it. And in the days of gladness, in solemn days, in the beginning of the months, at the burnt offerings and peace offerings these trumpets were to be blown. And in the future there will be a use for the trumpet in connection with the gathering of Israel (feast of trumpets). Read Isaiah 27:12-13; Joel 2:1. Thus all was ordered for them by the Lord. The sound of the trumpets was to them the voice of God giving direction and a comforting assurance at the same time. They typify the Word of God. It must not be overlooked that the sons of Aaron, the priests, had to blow the trumpet. They were in holy communion with the Lord and made known His will to the people. As Israel was dependent on the sound of the trumpets, so are we dependent as His people on the testimony of His Word. His will is ascertained in priestly intimacy with Himself.

This ends the first part of this interesting book. It shows how Jehovah made all preparations and provisions for the wilderness journey of His people. He had them numbered, the camp was arranged and put in order, the service of the Levites appointed. The offerings were brought, the Levites consecrated, the Passover celebrated and the guidance by the cloud and silver trumpets given. All was ready for the journey.

II. The Journey Started. Israel's Unbelief, Failure and Punishment

1. The Departure and the First Failure

CHAPTER 10:11-36

1. The cloud moves (10:11-13)
2. The standard of the camp of Judah (10:14-17)
3. The standard of the camp of Reuben (10:18-21)
4. The standard of the camp of Ephraim (10:22-24)
5. The standard of the camp of Dan (10:25-28)
6. The first failure (10:29-32)
7. The cloud leading (10:33-36)

It was on the twentieth day of the second month, in the second year, that the cloud was taken up from off the tabernacle and the signal was given for the camp to break up. The wilderness journey begins and we shall soon be face to face with the sad story of Israel's failure, a failure which is repeated in the history of Christendom. What a magnificent spectacle it must have been when the camp of Israel moved for the first time in its divinely arranged order! No pen can describe the scene. The cloud moved and advanced towards the wilderness of Paran. Judah with his flowing standard led by Nahshon comes first. Then the tabernacle was taken down and the sons of Gershon and Merari set forward carrying the different parts of the tabernacle. In the second chapter instruction was given that the tabernacle was to set forward with the camp of the Levites in the midst of the camp. Here the order is changed. We shall find later the reason for this. Then the other camps followed, all in perfect order with Dan the rear guard of all the camps. Was it possible that one not an eye-witness could have given such a remarkable and minute description of all this? Only the person who was actually there and saw it with his own eyes could have written this account. No compiler living a few hundred years later could have produced such a work.

How beautiful the order in the camp! What a contrast with the disorder and confusion which followed so soon! And this has all been repeated in Christendom.

The incident between Moses and Hobab is significant. The first failure is recorded and it is on the side of Moses. He turned to his father-in-law, a man who knew the wilderness well, and said, "Leave us not, I pray thee; forasmuch as thou knowest how we are to encamp in the wilderness, and thou mayest be to us instead of eyes." Criticism has pointed this out as one of the marks of imperfection in this book and calls it a contradiction. It is a contradiction, but not in the sense as infidelity takes it. It gives a perfect picture of what the human heart is, and therefore is a mark of the perfection of this record. Jehovah had offered Himself as the leader of His people. He was to be eyes for them. And Moses as the human leader of the host of Israel, knowing Jehovah and His promise, turns to a poor Midianite and expects guidance and directions of him! How true it is what one has said, "We find it hard to lean upon an unseen arm. A Hobab that we can see inspires us with more confidence than the living God whom we cannot see. We move on with comfort and satisfaction when we possess the countenance and help of some poor fellow-mortal, but we hesitate, falter and quail when called to move on in naked faith in God." Every Christian believer knows this tendency of the heart. Every failure begins with leaning on the arm of flesh and leaving out the Lord. And now we understand why the tabernacle was taken to the front and out of the place in the middle of the camps. Jehovah anticipated this failure and graciously, not in judgment, He acts towards His people. "The ark of the covenant of the Lord went before them in the three days journey to search out a resting place for them." They wanted to find a resting place through Hobab's guiding eye for the tabernacle and the camp, and now Jehovah in unspeakable condescension and marvellous patience proceeds to search out a resting place for His people. Thus while we fail, He never fails His people. "Oh! for faith to trust Him more."

2. At Taberah and Kibroth-Hattaavah

CHAPTER 11

1. The first complaint and the punishment (11:1)
2. The first prayer and the answer (11:2-3)
3. The manna rejected (11:4-9)
4. Moses' complaint and request (11:10-15)
5. The institution of the seventy elders (11:16-30)
6. The quails given and the wrath of Jehovah (11:31-35)

They were now facing the land which was only a short distance away. The ark had sought out a resting place for them. Jehovah had graciously made all provision for their need and comfort. If enemies came victory was on their side, for with the setting forward of the ark Moses said, "Arise Jehovah and let Thine enemies be scattered; and let them that hate Thee flee before Thee." No hardships whatever they had encountered. What else was necessary but to trust Jehovah, praise His Name and possess the land which He had promised to them. Instead of acting thus they complained. It is the first complaint after the camp had been set in order. Their murmuring must have been on account of the journey, which after the long repose at Sinai seemed hard to them. It shows what man is with an evil, stubborn heart. Failure is stamped on man's history everywhere. It can be traced throughout the Word of God. Every age has this mark. Judgment fell as the result of this murmuring upon those in the uttermost parts of the camp. Most likely those who complained fell behind and expressed a desire not to go forward. Among these the fire burned; no record, however, is given of the first judgment. It must have been tempered with mercy. And the people did not turn to Jehovah in this hour of punishment, but cried to Moses. When he prayed the fire was quenched and the name of the place was called Taberah, which means "burning."

Alas! they did not profit by the chastening. The second murmuring is more pronounced and more definite. The mixed multitude were a large number who had joined the exodus. They did not know the reality of redemption as Israel did, because they were Egyptians, most likely the so-called "Fellahs." This multitude fell a lusting and infected the children of Israel. They wept and spoke lightly of the bread from heaven. Such a mixed multitude without the knowledge of redemption is found in the professing church. They have crept in unawares and have been and still are a fearful detriment to the people of God. No unregenerated person has a place in the church of God. They cannot eat and enjoy the manna God has given, but constantly lust after the food of Egypt. (Compare Numb. 11:4-5 with Deut. 8:8. Egypt's food consisted in six things. Seven things are mentioned as food in the land.) In connection with the despised manna we find a description of that God-given food. It is, as we learned from Exodus, the type of Christ, the food God has given to His people. And how often that food is neglected and Egypt's food preferred to the Word of God!

Moses' complaint follows. He seems discouraged and downcast as he looks over the vast camp and sees everybody weeping. It was failure in Moses also, who did not fully trust Jehovah that He could take care of His people and endow him, the leader of His people, with His own strength. The Lord met his weak and discouraged servant and told him to call the elders, seventy of them, and the Spirit, who was upon Moses, was to be put upon them. They were to share the burden with him. But while this delivered him from some of the care it also lost him dignity. Again Moses addressed Jehovah and expressed doubt about the feeding of the six hundred thousand footmen. "Shall the flocks and the herds be slain for them to suffice them? or shall all the fish in the sea be gathered together for them to suffice them?" And the Lord rebuked him. The elders who received the Spirit prophesied and did not cease. What they prophesied is not revealed in the record. They uttered the words of God, exhorting the people in their increasing departure from Jehovah. Prophecy is always put into the foreground in the days of failure and apostasy. Here we also learn that prophecy is a gift. While Moses failed, Joshua also made a failure in being envious because Eldad and Medad prophesied in the camp. He was jealous not for Jehovah, but for Moses. "And Moses said until him, enviest thou for my sake? would God that all the Lord's people were prophets, and that the Lord would put His Spirit upon them." This wish of Moses' is realized in the church, for all His believing people now have the gift of the Spirit. And the remnant of God's earthly people will yet be prophets upon whom the Spirit of God is poured out. This will be accomplished in the future when the Lord has come.

The end of the chapter shows Jehovah's bountiful provision in sending the flesh they had desired. But the wrath of the Lord was kindled against them, and while they were eating a great plague broke out. There was no repentance. Greedily they fell upon what God had provided. It was only to satisfy their lust; the giver they did not see behind the gift. The rebellious, stubborn heart, unrepenting, was there, making use for their own destruction what the Lord had given. Hence the severe judgment. The quails typify Christ. Professing Christendom speaks of Christ, but there is no repentance, no self-judgment, only the form of godliness, but the power is denied. The judgment of God must rest upon such. Kibroth-Hattaavah means "graves of lust."

3. The Rebellion of Miriam and Aaron

CHAPTER 12

1. Miriam and Aaron speak against Moses (12:1-3)
2. The interference of the Lord (12:4-9)
3. Miriam leprous (12:10)
4. Aaron's confession and intercession (12:11-12)
5. Moses' prayer and Miriam's restoration (12:13-16)

Open rebellion against Moses by his own brother and sister is the next step in the story of failure. Envy was at the bottom of it. The words Miriam and Aaron spoke reveal that they aimed at Moses' position. Miriam was a prophetess (Exod. 15:20). Aaron had the dignity of the priesthood. Pride, the crime of the devil (1 Tim. 3:6), lead them to speak against their own brother. Miriam was the leader in this rebellion, for her name stands first and the judgment falls upon her. She may have been moved to jealousy by the elders having received the Spirit and exercising the gift of prophecy among the people. And Aaron reveals the weakness of the flesh. It is the second time he failed in this manner. He could not resist the clamoring of the people when they demanded the golden calf and here he cannot resist his sister, who became the willing instrument of Satan, like the first woman (1 Tim. 2:14). Moses had a Cushite woman for wife. This typifies the great truth of the union of Christ and the church, that Gentiles were to be joint-heirs and joint-members of the same body. But it seems that the Cushite wife of Moses was only a subterfuge and an attempt to reflect upon the moral character of the man of God, whose position they envied.

(If this thought is followed out in its dispensational meaning, it becomes very interesting. The natural relations objected to this union, as the Jews were moved with jealousy when the gospel was preached to the Gentiles and the Gentiles believed. The book of Acts bears abundant testimony to this fact.)

"And the Lord heard it." Magnificent words these! and the Lord also said, "Wherefore then were ye not afraid to speak against my servant Moses?" It is a serious thing to speak against any servant of God. The Lord will always guard those who serve Him and vindicate their character. Moses did not take the case in his own hands. He did not answer back. His gracious character stands out in majestic greatness. How hard it is for a man who holds a high and honored position to bear any attack in silence and not to open his mouth! Moses kept silent, for he was very meek above all the men which were upon the face of the earth. In this he is a blessed type of Him who was meek and lowly; who reviled not when He was reviled, who opened not His mouth.

But did Moses really write the third verse? And if he did, does this not prove that he spoke well of himself? Some claim that this is an addition to the text. "The self-praise on the part of Moses which many have discovered in this description of his character, and on account of which some even of the earlier expositors regarded this verse as a later gloss, whilst more recent critics have used it as an argument against the Mosaic authorship of the Pentateuch, is not an expression of vain self-display, or a glorification of his own gifts and excellences which he prided himself upon possessing above all others. It is simply a statement which was indispensable to a full and correct interpretation of all the circumstances and which was made quite objectively with reference to the character which Moses had not given to himself, but had acquired through the grace of God.[3] This fully meets the difficulty.

And Jehovah speaks well of His servant Moses. He is declared faithful. With him He speaks and the similitude of Jehovah he is to behold. Compare with Hebrews 3:5-6. A greater than Moses is here! Christ is faithful as Son over God's house. Aaron confesses his sin and Miriam's sin. She is leprous and excluded from the congregation of Israel, where she tried to be the leader, but graciously restored at the appointed time as the result of the prayer of Moses. And may we not read here Israel's story, leprous now, but some day healed and restored?

4. At Kadesh-Barnea and Israel's Unbelief

CHAPTER 13

1. The command to search out the land (13:1-3)
2. The names of the spies (13:4-16)
3. Directions given (13:17-20)
4. Their explorations (13:21-25)
5. The report they brought (13:26-33)

The crisis is reached with this chapter. The events of the preceeding chapters are the prelude to the complete failure and disaster. To understand the situation we must consult Deut. 1:21-24. Moses spoke in faith when he said, "Behold, the Lord thy God hath set the land before thee; go up and possess it, as the Lord God of thy fathers hath said unto thee; fear not, neither be discouraged." And the people's answer was that men be sent to search out the land. It was unbelief once more. They wanted to see first before they acted upon the Word of God. The saying also pleased Moses. No doubt he asked the Lord and received an answer from Him, which is recorded in the opening verses of this chapter.

Leading men are selected to act as spies. Reuben here stands first, Simeon follows, Levi is left out, for the Levites were not to have an inheritance in the land, Judah (praise) is the third. Caleb, the son of Jephunneh, who represents the tribe of Judah is here mentioned for the first time. Caleb means "brave," "whole hearted." Joshua's name is given also as "Oshea."Oshea means "saviour" and Joshua is "Jehovah is Saviour." The name of Joshua is found some 250 times in the Bible. He is the type of the Lord Jesus Christ. The name "Jesus" is the Greek equivalent. Caleb and Joshua were the only two in the whole company who trusted in Jehovah. And Jehovah rewarded them for their faith. Another interesting name is "Sethur" (verse 13). His name means "mysterious." The four letters of the name of Sethur give the number 666. He may have been the leader of the opposition, as Anti-christ has this number (Rev. 13).

They found the land exactly as it had been described. "We came unto the land whither thou sentest us, and surely it floweth with milk and honey; and this is the fruit of it." They brought a great cluster of grapes, pomegranates and figs. These tell us of spiritual food and service, which is for those who possess the land, our heavenly portion in Christ. They could not deny that Jehovah's promise was true. They carried the evidences of it upon their shoulders while they carried unbelief in their hearts. They looked at the children of Anak, the giants, which dwelled in the land and not to Jehovah, who had delivered them from the Egyptians. If they had reckoned with the Lord and trusted Him, not they, but the giants would have appeared to them as grasshoppers. Caleb said in faith, "Let us go up at once and possess it." Their unbelieving hearts refused and declared, "We are not able to go up." They brought an evil report of the land. The Hebrew for "bringing up an evil report" is in Prov. 10:18 translated "uttering a slander." Unbelief slanders God; it is an insult to the Lord.

And all this has many lessons for us. The church is called to possess a heavenly portion. This is typified by Canaan. Christendom has made a worse failure than Israel by not entering into the inheritance and by turning back to the world. And besides this, there are the lessons connected with our individual experience.

[3]Keil and Delitzsch, *The Pentateuch.*

CHAPTER 14

The Rebellion of the People, Moses' Intercession and the Divine Sentence

1. The rebellion (14:1-10)
2. The intercession of Moses (14:11-25)
3. The divine sentence (14:26-39)
4. The presumption of the people and the defeat (14:40-45)

The words of unbelief of the ten spies yielded an awful harvest among the people. The camp was transformed into a camp of despair, weeping and crying during the night. Outpsoken rebellion against Moses and Aaron was heard on all sides. Worse than that took place; they accused Jehovah of deception. Such is unbelief! They are ready to select a captain and march back to Egypt. Moses, Aaron, Joshua and Caleb stand alone among the hundreds of thousands of murmuring, rebellious Israelites and the mixed multitude. They fell on their faces, no doubt in the attitude of prayer and worship, to tell the Lord. They tried to stem the swelling tide of rebellion. Read the supplementary words in Deut. 1:29-31. "Jehovah is with us!" This was the word of cheer and comfort. Their answer was the stones with which they were ready to stone the servants of the Lord. Unbelief had robbed them of all reason, blinded their eyes and rushed them into despair and prompted them to become murderers.

Beautiful is the scene of Moses' intercession. He stands out as a striking type of our great Mediator, the Lord Jesus Christ. Jehovah's offer to Moses to make a new start after destroying the rebels and to make Moses a greater nation, even than Israel, is rejected. He does not want glory for himself, but he is jealous for Jehovah's name and glory. And in the intercession he reminds Jehovah of His own words He had spoken to him when on the mountain (Exod. 34:5-9). And upon this magnificent intercession Jehovah said, "I have pardoned according to thy word." Another, our ever blessed Lord, has secured forgiveness for His sinning people. Grace now reigns through righteousness. Connected with this forgiveness is the divine declaration that the earth shall be filled with the glory of the Lord. The grace which has secured pardon will yet establish glory on this earth. In spite of Israel's failure and the failure of man in this dispensation of grace, glory must ultimately cover this earth. This will be in the day when our Lord is revealed in all His glory. The measure of Israel's sin is full. They had tempted the Lord ten times (Exod. 14:11-12; 15:23-24; 16:2; 16:20; 16:27; 17:1-3; 22; Numb. 11:1; 11:4; 14:2). The divine sentence is pronounced. "Your carcasses shall fall in this wilderness, and all that were numbered among you, according to your whole number, from twenty years old and upward, who have murmured against me." Only Caleb and Joshua are an exception. Up to now they had been pilgrims, but now they became wanderers (verse 33). The ten spies were carried away by the plague. Their unbelief resulted in the disaster which came upon all the people as they were the first witnesses of the divine displeasure. "They could not enter in because of unbelief" (Heb. 3:19). And Christendom in its failure to lay hold in faith of the heavenly calling and heavenly possession, has lost its pilgrim character and has become the wanderer, minding earthly things.

Another failure follows. The divine sentence pronounced upon them resulted in mourning and a lip-confession, "we have sinned." True repentance and self-judgment there was not. They tried to make their error good in their own strength and they attempted to go up without the ark and without Moses. "Whereas at first they had refused to enter upon the conflict with the Canaanites through their unbelief in the might of the promise of God, now, through unbelief in the severity of the judgment of God, they resolved to engage in the conflict by their own power, and without the help of God, and to cancel the old sin of unbelieving despair through the new sin of presumptuous confidence" (Dr. F. Delitzsch). And Christendom, stripped of its power, tries to meet the giants of sin and wickedness in the same way, only to suffer defeat in all their attempts.

5. Various Laws, the Sabbath-Breaker, and the Tassels on the Garments

CHAPTER 15

1. Concerning offerings in the land (15:1-16)
2. The second communication concerning offerings (15:17-31)
3. The Sabbath-breaker (15:32-36)
4. The tassels on the garments (15:37-41)

The historical account is here interrupted. What the critics have to say about this chapter speaking of it as an evidence of the patchwork of different persons, we care not to follow. Our space is too valuable for that. The chapter is beautifully in order at this point. God gave two communications to Moses (verses 1 and 17). In the foreground of these communications stand the comforting assurance, "When ye come into the land." Jehovah assured them that in spite of all their failure He would give them the land and that He would bring them there. While the great mass died in the wilderness they received nevertheless the assurance that the rest would reach that land. And then they would bring the sacrifices and offerings. God's faithfulness stands here in contrast with man's failure. We cannot enter into the details of this chapter. The offerings speak of Christ as they always do. The stranger is also mentioned (verses 14-16). There was to be one law and one custom for Israel and for the stranger among them. The stranger is placed upon the same level with the Jew. While in Exod. 12:48 the circumcision of the stranger who would keep Passover is commanded, nothing is said here of this rite as touching the stranger. And this is not without meaning.

"Israel had forfeited everything. The rebellious generation was to be set aside and cut off; but God's eternal purpose of grace must stand, and all His promises be fulfilled. All Israel shall be saved; they shall possess the land; they shall offer pure offerings, pay their vows, and taste the joy of the kingdom. On what ground? On the ground of sovereign mercy. Well, it is on the self-same ground that "the stranger" shall be brought in; and not only brought in, but "*as* ye are, *so* shall the stranger be before the Lord" (C. H. Mackintosh).

All will find its final great fulfillment in the day when wandering Israel is restored to the land. And that day seems no longer far off. God will keep His promises, for His gifts and calling are without repentance. The annotations in Leviticus will help in understanding verses 22-31. The burnt offering and the sin offering typify the atoning death of our Lord. The presumptuous sin mentioned in verses 30-31 is illustrated by the case of the Sabbath-breaker. And there is a deeper lesson connected with it. Rest is procured through the finished work of Christ. The sinner who refuses this offered rest and passes it by, substituting for it his own works, acts presumptuously and will be cut off. He has despised the word and the work of Jehovah. It is the "anathema" of the Epistle to the Galatians.

The tassels of blue, the heavenly color, (in Hebrew 'Tsitsith'; still worn by orthodox Jews in literal fulfillment of the command) were to remind them of the commandments so that they would do them and not go after strange things. It was a help to a separated, a holy life. May we be constantly reminded by the Word of God of an holy and heavenly calling and be delivered from worldliness.

6. The Rebellion of Korah

CHAPTER 16

1. The rebellion of Korah (16:1-19)
2. The punishment (16:20-35)
3. Eleazar and his work (16:36-40)
4. The murmuring of the whole congregation (16:41-43)
5. The staying of the plague (16:44-50)

The history is now resumed and we have the worst episode of Israel's history in the wilderness before us. We have seen and followed the steps downward and toward this fearful rebellion and the terrible punishment which followed. It started with unbelief. This tragedy is mentioned in the New Testament. In the Epistle of Jude we read, "Woe unto them! for they have gone in the way of Cain, and ran greedily after the error of Balaam for reward, and perished in the gainsayings of Korah." This little Epistle gives a prophetic picture of the apostasy of the professing people of God during our age. This apostasy began in the days of Jude and is now fully developed in the end of the age. Unbelief is given in Jude's Epistle as the starting point of the departure from God (verse 5), and Israel's unbelief is used as the picture of the unbelief of Christendom. Besides Cain (the one who rejects the sacrifice) Balaam and Korah are mentioned as types of the apostasy. The consummation of the apostasy is opposition to Christ, His blessed office-work and glory. And this seems to have been reached in our day. The opposition will continue and become more outspoken, more widespread, till the judgment by fire in the day of the Lord falls upon the apostates.

The leader of the rebellion was Korah, a Kohathite. It will be remembered that the Kohathites had the choicest service among the Levites; they carried the very best upon their shoulders, the sacred things of worship. The departure from God and rebellion against His Word often begins with those who claim the office of teachers and preachers. Such is the case in our times. Korah's name means "hail; ice." May not this indicate the coldness of his heart? Even so the apostate teachers of the last days, mere hirelings like Balaam, are only natural men, not having the Spirit (Jude 19). Their mouths may speak great swelling words, their hearts have never tasted the love of Christ; they know Him not, or they would not betray Him.

The sons of Reuben, Dathan and Abiram, and On, besides two hundred and fifty, joined the revolt. Their attempt was a complete overthrow of the constitution which had been given to Israel and the establishment of another order and other leaders. They themselves sought recognition and Korah aimed at the priesthood of Aaron and would have it himself. Verses 8-10 indicate this. Korah and his associates aimed at God's appointed highpriest. And Moses put this serious matter in the hands of the Lord.

Moses and Aaron could not deal with this rebellion. The glory of the Lord appeared. Divine judgment falls upon them. Dathan and Abiram, their wives, their sons and their little ones, besides the ringleader Korah, are swallowed up by the earth and went down alive into the pit. (It is also foreshadowing the judgment to come upon the apostates when the Lord appears the second time. See Rev. 19:20.) The two hundred and fifty who had taken presumptuously censers with incense, thereby defying the priesthood, are consumed by fire. It must be noted that the sons of Korah did not perish. A careful reading of verses 27-33 will bring out this fact and chapter 26:11 settles it beyond a doubt, "notwithstanding the children of Korah died not." Sovereign grace saved the sons of Korah from the awful fate of the father. They were saved from the pit. Mercy was remembered in wrath. What grace bestowed upon them may be learned by consulting the following passages: 1 Chronicles 6:54-67; 9:19-32;26:1-20; 2 Chron. 23:3, 4, 19; 31:14-18. They had the cities of refuge, were keepers of the gates of the tabernacle; were over the chambers and treasuries of the house of the Lord; the instruments of the sanctuary, the wine, oil, etc., were in their charge; they were mighty men of valor; strong men; they were the royal guards. And more than that, the Holy Spirit inspired them to write some of the beautiful Psalms. Read Psalm 84, "How amiable are thy tabernacles, O Lord of hosts." What meaning this Psalm has when studied in the light of the story of Korah! They were faithful, devoted in their service because they knew that they had been saved from the pit. And we have the same deliverance and knowledge of it. Should we be less faithful and devoted?

Interesting is Eleazar's priesthood and ministry. As the third son of Aaron and in his ministry here he typifies the priesthood of Christ. The censers are kept as a memorial and as a warning. This ministry of Eleazar and Aaron staying the plague with the censer of incense, when the whole congregation revolted, is a confirmation of the divinely appointed priesthood and its efficacy. The preservation of the sinning, murmuring people depended upon the exercise of the priesthood. Blessed be God for Him who has made atonement, and whose priesthood in the presence of God keeps His people.

What higher criticism has made of this may be learned by the following statement:

> "From the plain account of the text it appears that Aaron separated the men and women suffering with the plague from those not yet attacked, and then he piled the censer with incense and swung it between the hosts, so that not a germ in the air could pass over from the plague-stricken to those not yet attacked by the disease.
>
> The disinfecting of the air and separating of the sick from the well was dictated by Moses, who had learned in Egypt all the science of his day, and the Egyptian priests were master of many secrets which we have to learn over again." How absurd!

7. The Priesthood of Aaron Confirmed

CHAPTER 17

1. The divine command (17:1-5)
2. The rods before Jehovah (17:6-7)
3. The blossoming rod of Aaron (17:8-13)

Little comment is needed on this chapter. The blossoming and fruit bearing rod of Aaron is another confirmation of the priesthood. Standing among the dying, "making an atonement," he is a type of Christ in His atoning work. The blossoming rod is the beautiful figure of resurrection. The rods were absolutely dead, not a sign of life was there. And Aaron's rod received life during that night and life was there in its abundance, buds, blossoms and almonds. Christ risen from the dead, the firstfruits of them that slept, is here blessedly foreshadowed. It was life from the dead and finds its application too in connection with the sinner who is dead in trespasses and sins, while it also foreshadows the spiritual resurrection of Israel. The murmurings of the children of Israel were taken away by the rod of Aaron preserved before the testimony or else they would have died. The blossoming rod preserved was a provision for the wilderness journey. In Hebrews we read,

"Wherein was the golden pot of manna, and Aaron's rod that budded, and the tables of the covenant" (Heb. 9:4). The manna God's people need constantly in the wilderness as well as the ministry of Him who ever liveth and intercedeth for us. In 1 Kings 8:9 we read, "There was nothing in the ark save the two tables of stone." They were then in the land. When we reach our eternal home the manna and the intercession of a merciful high priest are no longer needed.

The rebellion of Korah yielded after all something. It added two things to the tabernacle, the plates from the censers for the covering of the altar and Aaron's blossoming rod.

8. Priesthood and Iniquity and the Recompense of the Priesthood

CHAPTER 18

1. The iniquity borne by the priesthood (18:1-7)
2. The recompense of the priests (18:8-19)
3. The inheritance of the priests (18:20-32)

"Aaron, thou and thy sons and thy father's house with thee shall bear the iniquity of the sanctuary, and thou and thy sons with thee shall bear the iniquity of your priesthood." This is evidently in answer to the question, "Shall we be consumed with dying?" (17:13) The ministry of the priests and the Levites keeping the charge of the tabernacle and the charge of the altar "that there be no wrath any more upon the children of Israel" (verse 5). The priesthood which had been the object of rebellion was to be their security. If it had not been for the priestly service they would have all been consumed by the wrath of God. Christ is again here in view, He who ever liveth and intercedeth for His own people; Jesus Christ the righteous, who is the propitiation for our sins. He bore the iniquity and the wrath Himself.

The recompense of the priests is fully described in the second section of this chapter. In conclusion of it we read, "It is a covenant of salt forever before the Lord unto thee and to thy seed with thee." It is an indissoluble and inviolable covenant. The recompense of the priest and his house must be applied to the reward which Christ has, the joy which is His and His people, His house, sharing it with Him. The two sections harmonize beautifully. Aaron had no inheritance in the land. His inheritance is the Lord. "I am thy part and thine inheritance among the children of Israel." The Levites had no inheritance in the land, but received tithes. Aaron's was the better portion, and such is ours in Christ.

9. The Red Heifer and the Water of Purification

CHAPTER 19

1. The provision appointed: The red heifer and the ashes (19:1-10)
2. The use of the water of purification (19:11-22)

This is a most interesting chapter. The ordinance of the red heifer and the water of purification is nowhere mentioned in Leviticus. The day of atonement, so prominent in Leviticus, is not referred to in Numbers at all. The provision of the water of purification is characteristic of the wilderness book. The people were dying by the thousands, and means had to be provided for the cleansing of those who became defiled by contact with the dead. The ashes of the red heifer used in the way as described in this chapter were for the cleansing of the defiled. Without following the details of this new ordinance in the wilderness we point out briefly its typical meaning. That the red heifer is a type of Christ no one can fail to see. "For if the blood of bulls and goats and the ashes of an heifer sprinkling the unclean sanctifieth to the purifying of the flesh, how much more shall the blood of Christ, who through the eternal Spirit offered Himself without spot to God, purge your conscience from dead works to serve the living God?" (Heb. 9:13-14) This fully warrants the typical application. The red heifer was to be without spot, wherein is no blemish is the type of Christ, without spot and blemish. It had to be an heifer upon which never came a yoke. A yoke is put on an animal to restrain the wild nature, to bring it to subjection. Our blessed Lord needed no yoke, for He came willingly. "Lo, I come to do Thy will." Nowhere is the color of a sacrificial animal mentioned but here. Red is the color of blood. It is the type of His obedience unto death. The heifer was slain without the camp. So Christ suffered without the camp (Heb. 13:12). The sprinkling of the blood seven times toward the tabernacle is the type of the blood of atonement. Everything of the red heifer was consumed by fire and into the fire was cast cedar wood, hyssop and scarlet. These things typify the world. (See cleansing of the leper in Lev. 14). The world and all its glory is judged in the judgment of the cross.

Here is the essential difference between this and all other offerings: it is an offering once offered which (ideally, at least) never needs to be renewed. In all other cases, if any man sinned, fresh blood had to be shed, a fresh sacrifice to be made; but in this, the *virtue* remained of what had already been offered: the ashes were the memorial of an already accepted work. (*F. W. Grant*)

The ashes of the red heifer were gathered up by a clean man and put outside of the camp in a clean place. Water was used with the ashes and was sprinkled upon the defiled persons, upon the tent and all the vessels. This was the mode of their purification. It is all so full and rich that it would take many pages to explain all the blessed lessons connected with it. We need constant cleansing because we pass through the wilderness, the world, and death is stamped upon everything. The death of Christ has made provision for our cleansing, as it has provided for the removal of our guilt. The living water is the type of the Holy Spirit. Defilement with the world interrupts communion with God. The death of Christ and the work of the Holy Spirit through the Word cleanse us from that defilement. See 1 John 1.

"If we walk in the light, as He is in the light, we have fellowship one with another, and the blood of Jesus Christ His Son cleanseth us from all sin" (1 John 1). But if we fail to walk in the light—if we forget, and, in our forgetfulness, touch the unclean thing, how is our communion to be restored? Only by the removal of the defilement. And how is this to be effected? By the application to our hearts and consciences of the precious truth of the death of Christ. The Holy Ghost produces self-judgment, and brings to our remembrance the truth that Christ suffered death for that defilement which we so lightly and indifferently contract. It is not a fresh sprinkling of the blood of Christ—a thing unknown in Scripture—but the remembrance of His death brought home, in fresh power, to the contrite heart, by the ministry of the Holy Ghost.

10. At Kadesh in the Fortieth Year: Murmuring and Conquest

CHAPTER 20

1. The death of Miriam (20:1)
2. The murmuring of the people (20:2-5)
3. The divine instruction (20:6-8)
4. Moses' and Aaron's failure (20:9-13)
5. Edom's refusal (20:14-22)
6. The death of Aaron (20:23-29)

Between the nineteenth and twentieth chapter lies the unrecorded period of almost 38 years, the wandering of the children of Israel in the wilderness. In chapter 33 we find their different camps mentioned. In verse 38 of that chapter we read, "And Aaron the priest went up into the mount Hor at the commandment of the Lord, and died there, in the fortieth year after the children of Israel were come out of the land of Egypt, in the first day of the fifth month." The death of Aaron is recorded in the twentieth chapter. It was therefore about 37 years and six months when the spies had been sent out and their arrival in the desert of Zin. The critics have made this unrecorded period the occasion of attack upon the Mosaic authorship of this book. They suppose that the last historian who wrote on the Pentateuch left out a great deal of the history of the forty years wanderings. There was nothing to record but the scenes of death and sorrow; the entire theocratic covenant was suspended, and therefore theocratic history has no occurrence to record. It is even so now during the present age, during which Israel is set aside and wanders among the nations of the world.

During all these years of wandering in the wilderness circumcision was not carried out (Joshua 5:2-5). What else happened during this unrecorded period in the wilderness may be learned from a number of passages. "But the house of Israel rebelled against Me in the wilderness; they walked not in My statutes, and they despised My judgments, which if a man do, he shall live in them; and My sabbaths they greatly polluted. Then I said, I would pour out My fury upon them in the wilderness to consume them" (Ezek. 20:13, etc.). "Have ye not offered unto Me sacrifices and offerings in the wilderness forty years, O house of Israel? But ye have borne the tabernacle of your Moloch and Chiun your images, the star of your god, which ye made to yourselves" (Amos 5:25, 26). "Then God turned, and gave them up to worship the host of heaven, as it is written in the book of the prophets, O ye house of Israel, have ye offered to me slain beasts and sacrifices by the space of forty years in the wilderness? Yea, ye took up the tabernacle of Moloch, and the star of your god Remphan (worship of Saturn) figures which you made to worship them" (Acts 7:42, 43). They continued in stubbornness and rebellion and became idolators. But oh! the mercy of God! He continued to feed them and gave them water. "These forty years the Lord thy God hath been with thee, thou hast lacked nothing" (Deut. 2:7). "And I have led you forty years in the wilderness; your clothes are not waxen old upon you, and thy shoe is not waxen old upon thy foot" (Deut. 19:5). What marvellous compassion! And thus He still deals in mercy with His wayward wandering people. (Psalm 90, standing at the beginning of the fourth section of the book of Psalms (Numbers) was written by Moses, no doubt, when he saw them dying.)

This chapter, which brings us to the last year of their journey, begins with death and ends with death. In the middle we find the record of the failure of Moses and Aaron.

Miriam is the first to die, and her brother Aaron followed her four months later. Hundreds of thousands had passed away; their carcasses fell in the wilderness. And the new generation which has come up also murmured like their fathers and brethren. Such is the heart of man! "Would God that we had died when our brethren died before the Lord!" The Lord commanded Moses to take the rod and speak to the rock, and He promised that the rock should give water. No word of displeasure came from the lips of the gracious Lord, who had compassion with His people. Moses took the rod from before the Lord as He had commanded him. But he also took the rod in his hand with which he had smitten the rock, according to the Lord's command in Exodus 17:5-6. But the words Moses spoke were far from being gracious. "Hear now ye rebels; must we fetch you water out of this rock?" God had not called His people rebels. And Moses' words are far from meek. He makes it appear as if he could supply the water. "They angered Him also at the waters of strife, so that it went ill with Moses for their sakes. Because they provoked his spirit so that he spake unadvisedly with his lips" (Ps. 106:32-33). And greater still was his failure when he took *his* rod and not the blossoming rod of Aaron and smote the rock twice. The first smiting of the rock in Exodus 17 with Moses' rod, the rod of judgment is the type of the death of Christ. This should not be repeated; one smiting was enough just as the death of Christ once for all has opened the floodgates of divine grace. Aaron's rod, the type of Christ in resurrection, was sufficient, and but the word spoken would bring forth the water. But the anger of Moses marred this scene. He completely lost sight of the gracious Lord and misrepresented Him by his action. "Moses failed, departed from the rich grace of God, fell back on judgment, and judgment accordingly dealt with him." It was a grievous sin, and on account of it he was not fit to lead Israel into the land. And Aaron, equally weak in faith, shared Moses' fate. Edom then bars the way for the hosts of Israel and would not let them pass through their land. And Aaron dies on Mount Hor, after Moses had, in obedience to the Lord, removed his priestly garments and put them upon Eleazar.

CHAPTER 21

Murmuring and Conquest

1. Opposition of King Arad (21:1-3)
2. Murmuring and the fiery serpents (21:4-7)
3. The serpent of brass (21:8-9)
4. Journeying and singing again (21:10-20)
5. Sihon and Og (21:21-35)

The first victory is here recorded. The Lord delivered Canaanites into the hands of Israel, and according to their vow they utterly destroyed them and their cities.

But in spite of this victory the people became again discouraged because of the way, and they spoke against God and against Moses. "Our soul loatheth this light bread." Here we may trace our own individual experience. As one has said, "A time of victory has to be watched, lest it be a precursor of danger. A time of defeat on the other hand constantly prepares one for a fresh and greater blessing from God, so rich is His grace."

The punishment by the fiery serpents follows. Jehovah provided a remedy in the serpent of brass,[4] which was put on a pole. "And

---

[4]"It is less easy to arrive at the interpretation of the serpent that was lifted up, in its purely symbolical character, that is, to ascertain the aspect which it presents, when regarded from an Old Testament point of view. The serpent appears to have been almost universally received by antiquity as a *symbol of healing,* or the healing art; this symbolization probably originated when it was ascertained that some of the most efficacious remedies of nature are precisely the most dangerous poisons. When we, accordingly, regard the serpent, in the present instance, as a symbol of healing, we obtain from such a view a bond of union between the symbol and the type; we are, also, enabled by this view to explain the fact that idolatrous worship was rendered to the brazen serpent till the reign of Hezekiah, who destroyed it" (2 Kings 18:4) J.H. Kurtz.

it came to pass that if a serpent had bitten any man when he beheld the serpent of brass, he lived." Our Lord has given us the meaning of this remedy. "As Moses lifted up the serpent in the wilderness, so must the Son of man be lifted up, that whosoever believeth in Him should not perish, but have everlasting life" (John 3:14, 15). The type is so simple and clear that we refrain from enlarging on it. Dr. Martin Luther in one of his sermons on John 3 made the following statements: "In the first place, the serpent which Moses was to make was to be of brass or copper, that is to say, of a reddish color (although without poison) like the persons who were red and burning with heat because of the bite of the fiery serpents. In the second place, the brazen serpent was to be set up on a pole for a sign. And in the third place, those who desired to recover from the fiery serpent's bite and live, were to look at the brazen serpent upon the pole, otherwise they could not recover or live." In these three points we find the typical character of the brazen serpent. "God sending His own Son in the likeness of sinful flesh, and for sin, condemned sin the flesh" (Rom. 8:3). "He hath made Him to be sin for us who knew no sin" (2 Cor. 5:21). This took place when Christ was lifted up, when He hung on the cross. And now "there is life in a look at the Crucified One." By His sacrificial death, life, even eternal life is the present and eternal possession of the sinner who believes on the Son of God.

And now we see them journeying on, healed and victorious. Nine places are mentioned. The last is Pisgah, from which they get a vision of the land and can look back over the desert lands which are now forever behind them. Two songs are recorded. Israel begins now to sing again. There were no songs in the wilderness, nothing but murmurings. The first time they sang was at the Red Sea, and now as they are nearing the land they break out once more in song. The first is a battle-song, which speaks of victory; the second song is on account of the water from the digged wells. Spiritually considered, the victory and the abundant water may well be brought in connection with Him who is typified in the brazen serpent. There is not alone life by faith in Him, but God gives us freely with Him all things. There is victory, there is the abundance of water, the gift of the Holy Spirit. The princes digged the well. But how? It was not a laborious task. They did it with their staves. It is the sweet picture of grace supplying the need. It seems as if the brazen serpent incident is a marked turning point. And in a future day the remnant of Israel shall look upon Him whom they have pierced (Zech. 12:10). "Behold He cometh with clouds; and every eye shall see Him, and they also which pierced Him." Then Israel will be healed, have victory and sing a new song. Read the song prophetically given in Isaiah 12. "Therefore with joy shall ye draw water out of the wells of salvation." And then a still greater victory is won. Israel conquers Sihon, king of the Amorites, and Og the giant-king of Bashan. Both typify the powers of darkness in the world in their resistance to God's people. But victory is on our side because God is for us and with us.

Numerous critical points in the text we have to pass by. We mention but one in connection with the book of the wars of Jehovah. This book has been declared to be of different origin. The critics have made much of it by the fragmentary character of verses 14-16. Some state "that it is a work dating from the time of Jehoshaphat, containing the early history of Israel." All these statements are mere theories and invention. The book of the wars of Jehovah was undoubtedly a collection of odes of the time of Moses himself in celebration of the wonderful and glorious acts of the Lord. These critical points and questions raised are of no importance whatever.

III. Events in the Plain of Moab Facing the Land

1. Balak and Balaam and Balaam's Parables

CHAPTER 22

1. Balak's message to Balaam (22:1-20)
2. The journey of Balaam (22:21-35)
3. Balaam with Balak (22:36-41)

The last section of the wilderness book begins with the story of Balak and Balaam. An enemy, the Gentile Balaam, has to speak the words of prophecy, predicting wonderful blessing and glory for the hosts of Israel. The advancing Israelites inspired terror and Balak (waster), the king of Moab, not willing to meet Israel in open battle, sent for Balaam (devourer of the people) to put his powerful magic spell upon Israel and curse them.

Balaam, originally a heathen magician of an ordinary class, was, very probably (like Jethro, Exodus 18) and Rahab (Joshua 2) conducted to the acknowledgement of Jehovah by the overpowering influence of the wonderful deeds of God in Egypt and in the wilderness, which made a deep impression on all of the surrounding nations (Exodus 15:14; Joshua 5:1). He resolved to serve Jehovah and to perform his enchantments henceforth in the name of Jehovah. Analogous instances in the New Testament occur in Matt. 12:27; Acts 19:13; and, particularly, in Acts, ch. 8, which relates the case of Simon the sorcerer, the Balaam of the New Testament. Such a combination of heathenish magic with the service of Jehovah, could not be permanent, and the experience of Balaam would necessarily soon compel him to abandon the one or the other. When the message of Balak reached him, the period of decision arrived—the test was applied, and Balaam was found wanting.

Balak send gifts to Balaam, but he declined the invitation as the result of divine instructions. He could not resist the second deputation, which was more imposing than the first. God gave him permission on the condition that he was to say nothing but what God would tell him. How God's anger (not Jehovah, the covenant name) was kindled against him and the ass saw the angel of Jehovah, how the Lord opened the mouth of the ass and all the other details the reader will find in the text, so that a repetition here is not needed. Infidelity and higher criticism scoff at the incident of the speaking ass. One of their arguments is that the story of the speaking ass is disproven by the fact that Balaam carried on a conversation with the beast without expressing any astonishment at all at the occurrence. This is admirably answered by Augustinus: "Balaam was so carried away by his cupidity that he was not terrified by this miracle, and replied just as if he had been speaking to a man, when God, although He did not change the nature of the ass into that of a rational being, made it give utterance to whatever He pleased for the purpose of restraining his madness." That the ass saw the angel of the Lord first, before Balaam saw him, does not present any difficulty at all.

Naturalists tell us that irrational animals have a much keener instinctive presentiment of many natural phenomena, such as earthquakes and storms, than man. The horses, for instance, sometimes will see dangers when the rider is entirely ignorant of what is ahead.

"Jehovah opened the mouth of the ass." An omnipotent God can do this; why then should it be thought impossible? It is unbelief which makes objection to a miracle of this kind. If the occurrence did not happen, and must be classed as they claim, with legends, what becomes of the inspiration of the New Testament? The Holy Spirit through Peter confirms the miracle (2 Peter 2:15-16).

Balaam is used in the Epistle of Jude and in the corresponding testimony in the second Epistle of Peter (chapter 2) as well as in the message to Pergamos, as a type of the apostates in Christendom. "They ran greedily after the error of Balaam for reward" (Jude 2). "Following the way of Balaam, the son of Beor, who loved the wages of unrighteousness" (2 Peter 2:15). They make merchandise of the things of God. They deny the Master, who bought them, and exercise a religious office for "filthy lucre's sake." We shall find additional information on this matter in the twenty-fifth chapter.

The Parables of Balaam

CHAPTERS 23—24

1. The first parable (23:1-10)
2. Balak's surprise and Balaam's answer (23:11-12)
3. At Zophim (23:13-17)
4. The second parable (23:18-24)
5. Balak's request and Balaam's reply (23:25-30)
6. Balaam's third parable (24:1-9)
7. Balak's anger and Balaam's firmness (24:10-14)
8. Balaam's fourth parable (24:15-24)
9. Balaam and Balak separate (24:25)

The parables of Balaam compose the first great prophetic utterance of the Bible. They are remarkable in every way. The language is sublime. The unwilling prophet is forced to say what Jehovah put into his mouth. Here is a hint on inspiration. The thoughts and revelations of Jehovah are put into Balaam's lips by the Spirit of God, so that he had to utter them. How did Moses find out what was said by Balaam? Balak would surely not report the sayings to Moses; Balaam did not tell Moses. What transpired at the different stations where Balak and Balaam were, was not known to Israel. The Holy Spirit gave the correct report of all that took place and all what was said to Moses.

These parables are of such importance and interest that we give a complete exposition and point out the prophetic meaning. *The reader will find this exposition and a metrical version of these parables at the close of these annotations on Numbers.*

But what was said of Israel is also true, spiritually, of the church. We wish all our readers would follow this thought. Israel was a separated people; so is the church. God keeps His covenant with Israel and does not go back on

His Word; the same is true of His spiritual people. He does not behold iniquity or perverseness in His redeemed people; this speaks of justification. God is with His people to bless them and give them complete victory over all their enemies. These are but brief hints.

2. Israel's Sin with the Daughters of Moab. Phinehas

CHAPTER 25

1. The transgression and the anger of Jehovah (25:1-5)
2. Phinehas' action (25:6-9)
3. Phinehas and his reward (25:10-15)
4. The Midianites to be smitten (26:16-18)

The sin of Israel was the result of Balaam's work. He could not turn Jehovah from Israel (no enemy can), but he could turn Israel from God. While we do not read here that the fornication and idolatry into which Israel fell was Balaam's work, elsewhere this information is given. See Numbers 31:16 and Rev. 2:14. The stumbling block, which this instrument of Satan put into the way of Israel, by which they committed fornication and idolatry, were the daughters of Moab. Pergamos in the second chapter of Revelation is prophetically that period of the church which began with Constantine the Great. Then the church left the ground of separation and was wedded to the world. Spiritual fornication was committed and idolatry followed in its train. This was Satan's work as much as Balaam's act was. And to-day we see Christendom in the sad condition of Israel at Shittim. Separation is given up completely. Judgment will be visited ere long upon apostate, adulterous Christendom as it fell upon Israel. In the plague 24,000 died. In 1 Cor. 10:8, we read, "Neither let us commit fornication as some of them committed, and fell in one day three and twenty thousand." The record in Numbers speaks of a previous punishment when the heads of the transgressors were hung up before the Lord against the sun. Traditions among the Jews states that the number of those who were thus punished was a thousand, so that only 23,000 perished in the plague. In verse 9 this thousand is reckoned in, while in Corinthians they are left out.

Then followed an outrageous act of defiance (verse 6). The name of the Midianitish woman was Cozbi (my lie). By the zeal of Phinehas the people were saved from further judgment and Jehovah was glorified. He was zealous for His God and made an atonement for the children of Israel. He received for reward an everlasting priesthood. It is another type of Christ in His righteousness and holy zeal for God.

3. The Second Numbering

CHAPTER 26

1. The command to number (26:1-4)
2. The census taken (26:5-50)
3. The total number (26:51)
4. The inheritance (26:52-56)
5. The Levites (26:57-62)
6. The new generation (26:63-65)

The reader will find the comparison of these two numberings in the annotations of the first chapter. The increase and decrease of the different tribes may be learned by consulting that table. The many names in their meaning teach many lessons of interest. At the close of the chapter we have the fact stated that the penal sentence which God had pronounced upon the people who came out of Egypt (Numb. 14:29, 38) had been executed. God kept His Word, as He always will.

"Of the vast total of upwards of 600,000 then enumerated, Caleb and Joshua alone had their names registered in the present census. This, however, is to be understood with a qualification. It is evident from Josh. 14:1; 22:13, that both Eleazar and Phinehas did actually enter into the promised land. How is this consistent with the statement here made? We reply that the sentence of exclusion applied to the other tribes which were enumerated on two former occasions, and in which the Levites were not embraced. We do not read that they had any share in the transaction which brought the divine denunciation upon the mass of the people. This tribe did not, like the others, send a spy into Canaan, nor does it appear that it concurred in the general murmuring which the report of the spies occasioned."

4. The Daughters of Zelophehad, the Death of Moses and His Successor Announced

CHAPTER 27

1. The daughters of Zelophehad (27:1-11)
2. Moses' death announced and his request (27:12-17)
3. Joshua appointed (27:18-23)

The question of the daughters of Zelophehad was concerning their inheritance. Their father had died in the wilderness and there were no sons. They expected and claimed a possession among the brethren of their father. They fully counted on the Lord and His goodness, though their case was not met by the previous instructions. "It is impossible for God to be like a poor man, who says, 'You expect more good than I am prepared to bestow.' God could not make such an answer. He always gives more. Whatever may be the petition of faith, the answer of grace never fails to go beyond it." The answer given to Moses was that they were surely to receive their inheritance.

Moses' departure is announced by Jehovah. He cannot go over Jordan on account of his sin. But the Lord graciously permits him to go upon the mountain and view the land of promise in all its glory. Beautiful is Moses' answer to Jehovah. He does not speak of himself, nor does he think of his own interest. The people of God and their need are upon his heart. If they are taken care of he is satisfied and content with his own lot. What a blessed spirit of unselfishness he manifested! Joshua is the appointed successor, who is to lead the people into the land as Moses had led them out of Egypt. Moses and Joshua are both the types of Christ. Verse 21 is the key to understand the typical significance. "And he (Joshua) shall stand before Eleazar, the priest, who shall ask counsel for him." Aaron's priesthood, as we learned in Exodus and Leviticus, is the type of Christ in His sacrificial work on the cross. Eleazar, his successor, typifies the resurrection-heavenly priesthood of Christ. Moses is in different ways the type of Christ, as we have seen in his official and personal character; Joshua is the type of Christ in Spirit, who acts in His people by the Holy Spirit. Therefore Joshua has to stand before Eleazar the priest. He had, so to speak, to depend upon Eleazar, as the work of the Holy Spirit in the believer is dependent on the priesthood of Christ in glory.

5. The Offerings and the Set Times

CHAPTER 28

1. The daily offerings (28:1-8)
2. The Sabbatic offerings (28:9-10)
3. The monthly offerings (28:11-15)
4. The Passover (28:16-25)
5. The firstfruits (28:26-31)

CHAPTER 29

1. The blowing of trumpets (29:1-6)
2. The day of atonement (29:7-11)
3. The feast of tabernacles (29:12-16)
4. The second day offering (29:17-19)
5. The third day offering (29:20-22)
6. The fourth day offering (29:23-25)
7. The fifth day offering (29:26-28)
8. The sixth day offering (29:29-31)
9. The seventh day offering (29:32-34)
10. The eighth day offering (29:35-40)

These two chapters go together. They tell of Jehovah's portion which he is to receive in the worship of His people. The second verse reveals this. "Command the children of Israel to say unto them, My offering and My bread for My sacrifices, made by fire, for a sweet savour unto Me, shall ye observe to offer unto Me in their due seasons." Needless to say that all speaks of Christ. He is seen in all the offerings, in the lambs, the young bullocks, the ram, the meal offerings and all the others. In Christ God has found His delight. In Leviticus we saw that aspect of the different offerings by which God has met our need in Christ and His blessed work; but here Jehovah speaks of these offerings as being "My bread." The heart of God feeds, humanly speaking, upon Christ. The sweet savour-offerings are the prominent feature of these two chapters. The sin-offerings take a secondary place. As we learned in Leviticus, the offerings which are a sweet odor in the presence of God are those which typify the matchless worth and blessed devotion of the Lord Jesus Christ.

Leviticus 23 must be studied with these two chapters. The reader should turn to that chapter and see the meaning of the different feasts as given in the annotations. We call attention to the enlarged command concerning the feast of tabernacles. Ten verses are given in Leviticus 23 to the feast of tabernacles, but in Numbers 29 not less than twenty-seven are devoted to this feast. The seven days of the entire feast are mentioned with the different sacrifices, which were to be brought. They were to be brought in the following order and numbers:

First day	13 Bullocks	2 Rams	14 Lambs	1 Goat
Second day	12 Bullocks	2 Rams	14 Lambs	1 Goat
Third day	11 Bullocks	2 Rams	14 Lambs	1 Goat
Fourth day	10 Bullocks	2 Rams	14 Lambs	1 Goat
Fifth day	9 Bullocks	2 Rams	14 Lambs	1 Goat
Sixth day	8 Bullocks	2 Rams	14 Lambs	1 Goat
Seventh day	7 Bullocks	2 Rams	14 Lambs	1 Goat

In all there are 70 bullocks, 14 rams, 98 lambs, and 7 goats. And besides these there were the daily burnt offerings and meal offerings. Why this detail in Numbers? And why should the feast of tabernacles begin on the first day with 13 bullocks and there be a gradual decline? As we learned in Leviticus, the feast of tabernacles the last of the feasts, foreshadows the millennium. The character of the millennium will therefore help us to understand some, at least, of the typical meaning of these offerings. The large number of offerings, especially the double seven in the lambs, which are offered, stand for the praise which Jehovah will receive during the age to come. But it is not perfect praise. The number thirteen on the first day is an incomplete number. It lacks one to make it perfect. And then we see that the number decreases from thirteen down to seven on the seventh day of the feast. The millennium, as we know from Revelation (chapter 20), ends in failure. There will be most likely a decline in devotion to God and full obedience to His will. A look at the above table shows that there is something which mars. The goats, only one each day, are for sin offering, for sin will be possible during the millennium, however, it will be very exceptional. The twice fourteen lambs means fulness of redemption which will be enjoyed unhindered in the coming age. The eighth day has the same offerings as the day of atonement. The eighth day in Scripture marks a new beginning; it is the day of the new creation. Following the feast, the eighth day stands for eternity. The precious work of Christ will never be forgotten in the ages to come.

6. Concerning Vows

CHAPTER 30

1. The vow of a man (30:1-2)
2. The vows of women (30:3-16)

The entire chapter treats of vows. It also has a deeper meaning. There is a sharp contrast between the vow of a man and the vows of virgins, widows or wives. The vows of women could be set aside under certain conditions. The husband or the father could disallow the vow. But if they kept their peace or if she was a widow or divorced, she had to keep the vow. It was different with the man; he was not to break his word, but to do according to all that proceeds out of his mouth.

The man who keeps his word, who does all that he vowed, typifies the Lord Jesus Christ. He has completely done the work He voluntarily bound Himself to do. The woman represents the nation Israel. They made a vow at Sinai which they could never keep. "Alas, when the gracious proffer of redemption came, though they had been even then long under the penalty of it, they refused redemption, held stubbornly to their broken contract, and remain under it to-day, the enduring lesson, published in every land, of what the law is for those who seek righteousness by it" (*Numerical Bible*).

Some day the vow under which Israel has put herself will be disallowed, then Israel is received back into favor. "And the Lord shall forgive her" (verse 8).

7. The War Against the Midianites

CHAPTER 31

1. The command to fight Midian (31:1-6)
2. The war (31:7-12)
3. The cleansing (31:13-24)
4. The spoil taken (31:25-47)
5. The oblation of the officers (31:48-54)

War is commanded next by the Lord. The Lord said to Moses, "Avenge the children of Israel of the Midianites; afterward shalt thou be gathered to thy people." This is, therefore, the last thing in the official life of Moses. This war against Midian had been commanded before (25:16-18), the execution had been delayed. It was now to be carried out and the Midianites were to suffer for the wicked thing they had done to Israel by seducing them to the idolatrous worship of Baal Peon. Phinehas, the high priest, accompanied the army of 12,000 men. They were victorious and slew the kings of Midian; Balaam also was slain (verse 8). His wish, "let me die the death of the righteous," was not granted unto him, for he remained in his wickedness.

This war of revenge has a significant meaning. The key is found in the third verse, which, literally translated, reads: "Arm some of yourselves unto the war, and let them go against Midian, *to execute the vengeance of Jehovah upon Midian.*" There is another day of vengeance coming which will fall heavily upon the Gentile world. The Lord will avenge His people Israel and judge the nations for the sin they committed against them. Of this the prophetic Word speaks often. That day is closely linked with Israel's restoration to the land. Then the true

Sheep,	675,000.	The soldiers,	337,500;	therefrom to the Lord.......	675.
		The people,	337,500;	therefrom to the Levites....	6,750.
Beeves,	72,000.	The soldiers,	36,000;	therefrom to the Lord.......	72.
		The people,	36,000;	therefrom to the Levites....	720.
Asses,	61,000.	The soldiers,	30,500;	therefrom to the Lord.......	61.
		The people,	30,500;	therefrom to the Levites....	610.
Persons,	32,000.	The soldiers,	16,000;	therefrom to the Lord.......	32.
		The people,	16,000;	therefrom to the Levites....	320.

King-Priest will appear, like Phinehas, who was with the army of Israel (Isaiah 63:1-6; 2 Thess. 1:7-9).

Purification took place and the spoil was divided. This table may be studied in connection with verses 25-47.

When the officers returned they discovered to their great joy that they had not lost a single man. God's power had been with them and kept them in a miraculous way. They brought a magnificent oblation. The gold they offered was brought into the tabernacle for a memorial.

8. The Tribes of Reuben, Gad, Half-Manasseh and their Portion

CHAPTER 32

1. The petition of Reuben and Gad (32:1-5)
2. The rebuke by Moses (32:6-15)
3. Their answer (32:16-19)
4. Moses' reply (32:20-24)
5. The final agreement (32:25-41)

Failure is now again manifested. Reuben and Gad looked upon the beautiful territory which had been taken from the two Amorite kings, Sihon and Og. As Reuben and Gad were especially rich in cattle and the territory was one of great fertility, they were anxious to possess the land. The half-tribe Manasseh evidently made the same request and joined Reuben and Gad (verse 33). A lengthy controversy followed between Moses and these tribes. Moses saw at once the evil which was connected with such a request. They despised the land of promise. God had commanded them to possess that land. By their request they showed readiness to disobey God. Furthermore by desiring the land of Jazer and Gilead they would become separated from their brethren; they would let them go to fight alone in the land. The whole request manifested selfishness.

Compare them with Lot and his selfish choice (Gen. 13). He lifted up his eyes and beheld all the plain of Jordan, that it was well watered, even as the garden of the Lord, He then chose the plain of Jordan. How he suffered for it we know well from the divine record. Reuben and Gad also looked upon the good land and with the same selfishness as Lot requested the land. Consult 1 Chron. 5:25, 26 and 2 Kings 15:29, to find out how their descendants had to pay for the selfishness of their ancestors. They went a whoring after the gods of the people of the land and were the first carried away into captivity.

We see in their behaviour the picture of the Christian who is worldly-minded, who walks according to the flesh. He does not enter into the promised land and prefers earthly things to spiritual things. The story of Christendom is also written here.

9. The Encampments in the Wilderness

CHAPTER 33:1-49

1. The first stage: From Egypt to Sinai (33:1-15)
2. The second stage: From Sinai to Kadesh (33:16-17)
3. The third stage: From Rithmah to Kadesh—The 38 years wandering (33:18-36)
4. The fourth stage: From Kadesh to the plain of Moab—The fortieth year (33:37-49)

The chapter shows most blessedly how the eye of God follows the journeys and wanderings of His people and how He keeps record of them. Nothing escapes His watchful eye. And He leads His people in spite of their failures to the promised goal. Notice the long list of encampments of their wanderings with no history. Many lessons must be written here which God's people have not been able to understand. The Hebrew names given in this long list of stations shed much light on what may have taken place.

10. Instructions Concerning the Conquest and the Boundaries of the Land

CHAPTERS 33:50—34

1. Command to drive out the inhabitants of the land (33:50-56)

2. The division of the land (34:1-15)
3. The names of the men who shall divide the land (34:16-29)

The extermination of the Canaanites is first of all demanded. Everything of idolatry was to be destroyed. The land was to belong to a holy people who belong to Jehovah, therefore the Canaanite with his abominations had to be driven out of the land. "If ye will not drive out the inhabitants of the land from before you, those that ye let remain of them shall be pricks in your eyes and thorns in your sides and shall vex you in the land wherein ye dwell. Moreover, it shall come to pass, that I shall do unto you as I thought to do unto them" (33:55-56). The same warning was repeated by Joshua in his last address (Josh. 33:13). They did not drive them out as they were commanded, and they had to suffer in consequence of their disobedience.

The land of Canaan does not typify heaven, but our heavenly portion in Christ. In the annotations of the book of Joshua we hope to follow this more fully. The enemies in the land typify the wicked spirits, Satan and his powers. With these is our warfare, and we are commanded, like Israel, to conquer them. The boundaries of the land are given, and we find at the close of the chapter the names of the men who were to divide the inheritance unto the children of Israel. Notice the difference which is in the boundaries here as compared with Genesis 15:18. The promise given to Abraham and to his seed was under the covenant of grace, but Israel entered into the land under the law-covenant. If they had kept the law-covenant and had been obedient to Jehovah, they would have received the whole land. This they could not do. The original promise made to Abraham and his seed will be fulfilled in the future when the Lord will bring Israel back to possess the land. This will be in the millennium. The land will then be divided in a new way, revealed in the closing two chapters of Ezekiel.

11. The Cities of Refuge

CHAPTER 35

1. The provision of the Levites: Forty-eight cities (35:1-8)
2. The cities of refuge (35:9-34)

The cities of the Levites were scattered through the land. Genesis 49:7 is therefore fulfilled. The provision of cities for refuge is full of interest. The careful study of the purpose of these cities is recommended. Note especially that they were provided to give shelter for those who had killed a person unawares. The avenger of blood (Hebrew: *goël*, which means to redeem) pursued the person and the city of refuge gave shelter. The death of the high priest resulted in liberty for all who were in the cities of reuge. It was the signal that they could return to their possessions (verse 28).

Israel's history may be easily read in this chapter in connection with the cities of refuge. The innocent blood shed is the blood of Christ. Blood guiltiness is upon the nation. They did it ignorantly, even as He prayed on Calvary's cross, "Father, forgive them for they know not what they do." They are on account of this blood-guiltiness kept out of their inheritance, and yet they have had their city of refuge and have been preserved till the time comes when they are set free and return to the possession in the land. And that will be when the Priesthood of Christ as now exercised by Him in glory ends, when He comes forth as the King-Priest to exercise the Melchisedek priesthood. The names of the cities are not given in the book of Numbers. They were: Bezer, Ramoth, Golan, Kedesh, Shechem and Hebron (Deut. 4:41-43; Josh. 20:7). The cities are also types of Christ because they gave shelter. He is our refuge and our hiding place.

12. The Security of the Inheritance

CHAPTER 36

1. The applicants and their statement (36:1-4)
2. The response of Moses (36:5-12)
3. The epilogue (36:13)

The chapter explains itself. But what is the lesson? It is evident that the inheritance given by the Lord must remain with those to whom it is given. And this brought security and comfort to the daughters of Zelophehad. It brings security and comfort to our hearts when we consider that our inheritance in Christ can never be taken from us. It belongs to us and we belong to the inheritance. The same is true of Israel with its earthly inheritance, the promised land.

Thus ends the wilderness book, a marvellous book, like every other portion of God's holy Word. May we remember in the study of this book, as stated in the introduction, that "all these things happened unto them for ensamples; and they are written for our admonition upon whom the ends of the world are come" (1 Cor. 10:11). May we pass the time of our sojourning here with fear, realizing our separation unto God, the priestly and Levite service which belongs to us till we reach our eternal inheritance.

Appendix

The Prophecies of Balaam

Numbers 23—24

The healing of Israel by the believing look on the brazen serpent stands at the end of their murmurings in the wilderness. Israel was victorious once more, and songs of praise and victory are heard in the camp. And now, after the sad history of their disobedience is almost ended, a prophet pronounces remarkable blessings over the wonderful nation, the nation so miraculously saved from Egypt, guided and kept and healed. This voice of prophecy comes from the lips of a Gentile, and a Gentile king hears the message first, in which, besides Israel, the king of Moab and all his Gentile successors are so eminently concerned.

Balak (waster) saw all that Israel had done to the Amorites. He knew that the people had come out of Egypt. He was sore afraid; the fate of the Egyptians and Amorites seemed to foretell his own; his heart, therefore is filled with fear and hatred, and he desired to oppose and curse Israel. He allied himself with the elders of Midian. It is nothing less than the history of anti-Semitism in a nutshell. Gentile nations, Christian in name, still hate and fear the people whom no Pharaoh and no soothsayer could overcome, a people disobedient, judged and suffering, still always conquering. Like Balak, opposing Gentile nations and kingdoms will yet rise in fear and hatred against Israel before Israel's coming King will sweep them aside, and what Balak heard from the prophet's lips in his day—the complete destruction of the world-powers by the appearing of the glorious king of Jeshurum—will be the fate of these nations. Balak sends for Balaam, a prophet and a soothsayer. Who was Balaam? His name is a terrible one, the devourer of people; his father, Beor, the consumer; his native place, Pethor, meaning "interpretation." He must have known Jehovah to some extent, for he asked of Him and God answered his request. At the same time he was known for his skill in cursing nations and for his readiness for gold and silver to destroy them by his powerful spells. He may have practiced his soothsaying for many years, becoming rich by it, when, probably, one day he heard of Jehovah, who had done such great things for and among the wandering nation. Most likely for selfish reasons he sought God, like Simon, the sorcerer, who offered the apostles money for the power to heal the sick; thus Balaam may have desired the acquaintance of God, seeking revelations from Him for the sake of gain, and Jehovah revealed Himself to him. It is very significant that Balaam is mentioned in that important prophetic Epistle of Jude, where he stands as a type of the great apostasy at the end of this age. Balak, the representative of the anti-Semitic world-powers, and Balaam, the half-hearted prophet, a type of apostate Christendom, forming an alliance against Israel.

The parables which Balaam is obliged to give by the power of God, are divided into four parts. He utters them from three points, all mountain-tops. The first from the high places of Baal, the second from the summit of Pisgah, and the last from Peor. From these mountain-tops Balak and Balaam had a good view of the camp of Israel. Each one of the three points is nearer to the camp and a more complete view obtained from them. It seems Balak tried to diminish the number of Israel and their strength in the eyes of Balaam, for he took him first to a place from which he saw only a part, the utmost part, the fourth part of the people. Seeing that his scheme failed, Balak took Balaam to Pisgah; from there the view was more complete, and then at least to Peor, from which point he saw the twelve tribes of Israel with their flags in camp. Upon each mountain Balaam had seven altars erected, and two sacrifices, a bullock and a ram, are brought upon each altar. The whole proceedings were evidently calculated to make all as impressive and solemn as possible. On the heights of Baal, Balaam says to Balak: "I will go, may be Jehovah will come to meet me, and whatever He may say to me I will declare to thee." He went to a bare height and God met him there and put a word in his mouth. Next is Pisgah; here Balaam tells Balak to stand by the burnt offering, "while," he says,

"I go to meet," in the authorized version it says "the Lord," but that does not appear in the original. In Hebrew it reads, "I will go to meet—yonder." He tried to impress Balak once more with his mysterious power, and in proceeding to Mount Peor, Balak, utterly disheartened by the continued blessing of Israel from Balaam's lips, demands that he is neither to curse nor to bless. Balaam, however, knows that it pleased the Lord to bless Israel; he no longer goes out to meet with enchantments; he drops the mask, and now the Spirit of God comes upon him. Balak's anger is kindled after this third parable, and while he smites his hands together the prophet opens his mouth once more and utters the sublimest of all his prophecies, after which he went to his place soon after to meet with his terrible fate.

I.

And now we will read the parables themselves and study their wonderful meaning. The first from the heights of Baal:

> From Aram Balak hath fetched me,
> The King of Moab—from the mountains
> of the East.
> Come, curse me Jacob,
> Come and denounce Israel!
> How shall I curse? God hath not cursed,
> How shall I denounce? The Lord hath
> not denounced,
> For from the top of the rocks I see Him
> And from the hills I behold Him.
> Behold a nation that dwelleth alone,
> Not to be reckoned among the nations.
> Who counted the dust of Jacob?
> By number the fourth part of Israel.
> Let me die the death of Jeshurum,
> And let my last end be like his.

This first inspired utterance of Balaam speaks of the general character of Israel as the chosen people of God. It is, so to speak, the foundation, the key-note for all he is about to say by divine inspiration to Balak. We may divide this first parable into four parts.

1. After stating the fact of Balak's call and his wish that he should curse Jacob and denounce Israel, he states the impossibility to curse and to denounce—for God hath not cursed him, He hath not denounced him. In the original the name El, God, stands in connection with Jacob, and Jehovah, the covenant-keeping God, with Israel. When Balak's deputation came to Balaam, God had said to him, "Thou shalt not curse the people, for they are blessed." And now what God told him there in the secret place he is to speak here in public. It is the truth which we find all through the Word of God, Israel's blessed calling, the seed of Abraham blest and to be a blessing. How many have tried to curse Jacob and to denounce Israel? They have never succeeded, for Isaiah's vision has been fulfilled in all generations, "No weapon that is found against thee shall prosper, and every tongue that shall rise against thee in judgment thou shalt condemn." No magic, no voice, no power, no tongue can counteract the decree of God. Jacob and his seed is blest of God. Oh that men would understand it, but alas, they are wise in their own conceits, and boasting against the broken off branches they think of Jacob as accursed and denounce Israel, and thus dishonor God and make Him a liar.

2. With his hands before his eyes, Balak gazes upon the fourth part of the Israelitish camp from the tops of the rocks and from the hill and sees a second general characteristic of the people, namely, that Israel is to be a separated people. Israel is Ho-Am, the nation, and as such different from the nations and not to be reckoned among them.

Here then we have the destiny of Israel, a destiny the same for all times—a peculiar people, separated from all other nations. As far as Old Testament times are concerned, this decree of God can hardly be denied; but many Christians have stated and believe that in these New Testament times Israel has ceased to be a peculiar people, and that there is no difference between them and the other nations. Experience, however, teaches differently. Truly the seed of Abraham is to-day mingling with the nations, scattered in fact among all the nations, and there the sons of Jacob have not lost their peculiar characteristics. Assimilation has been attempted, and quite often by themselves, but rarely if ever has it been successful. God has kept Israel as His own separated people as truly as He has separated and keeps unto Himself by His Holy Spirit a spiritual, heavenly people, the church. All movements endeavoring to rob Israel of its peculiarity and separation have failed, and thus Israel remains a stranger in a strange land. What a tremendous testimony the Zionistic movement is in this direction! It is a movement to establish a Jewish state for the Jewish people in the Jewish land, and in itself a confession that assimilation with other nations is impossible. In speaking the Word of our God to the scattered Jews, God's future purpose in Israel as a nation must not be overlooked.

3. In the third place, we have the wonderful increase. "Who has counted the dust of Jacob?" The promise to Jacob when he went out from Beer-Sheba was, "Thy seed shall be as the dust of the earth." It stands for the earthly promises and earthly blessings which are Jacob's. What a sight it must have been for Balaam and Balak, standing beside their smoking altars, and down, way down in the desert, tent after tent is to be seen; but still it is only the fourth part, and appears like the dust of the earth—a people having passed through so much affliction and punishment, yet in spite of it all, strong and numerous as ever. In looking over the past, a still grander picture presents itself to us. Israel has wandered through a greater desert and through greater afflictions and punishments than ever before; they have been a people scattered and peeled, yet how wonderfully God has kept them, and more than ever they are like dust, down-trodden yet ever increasing, and multiplying, to the astonishment of their enemies. Who counted the dust of Jacob? The question is often asked, How many Jews are living to-day in the world? We tried to give a conservative estimate, still some tell us it is too low and others too high. The fact is no one seems to be able to get a correct number of the Jews living. Surely they are increasing rapidly all over the earth, and it is more true than ever before, "Who counted the dust of Jacob?"

4. Balaam's exclamation forms a fitting conclusion to his first parable. "Let me die the death of Jeshurum and let my end be like his." We do not think that Balaam had so much the physical death of Israel in view, as their hope and glorious end, the glorious end of ages when the God of Jeshurum will reveal Himself once more for the salvation of His people and brings vengeance upon their enemies. Of that glorious end which is Israel's, that glorious morning after a night of storm and disaster, he has here the first glimpse, and in his next parable the Holy Spirit puts it before him and before Balak in detail. It remains only to be said that the contents of this first parable are in part a repetition of God's promises to Abraham, but now the promise is not given to a member of Abraham's family, but put into the mouth of a Gentile to transmit it to the Gentile king.

II.

Next they are on top of Mount Pisgah, on the fields of Zophim. Balaam, after having been away from Balak hastens back, and filled with a greater degree of inspiration, it seems, he bursts forth:

Rise up Balak and hear!
Listen to me, son of Zippor!
God is not a man to lie;
Nor son of Adam to repent.
Hath He said and will He not do it?
Or spoken and shall not make it stand?
Behold I have commanded to bless:
Yea, he hath blessed and I cannot change it.
He hath not beheld iniquity in Jacob:
Nor has he seen travail in Israel:
Jehovah, his God is with him,
The shout of a king is in his midst.
God bringeth them out of Egypt:
He hath strength like that of the wild ox:
No enchantment there is against Jacob,
There is no divination against Israel.
In its time shall it be said of Jacob and of Israel.
What hath God wrought?
Behold the people rise up as a lioness!
And as a lion does he raise himself up!
He shall not lie down till he eat of the prey,
And drink the blood of the slain.

What an awful rebuke this was to unbelieving Balak. He surely had expected a change in the mind of that God whose aid and help Balaam was to invoke. Maybe, he thought that God would once more, after a second request, allow Balaam, as at the time when Balak's princes came to him, to speak a more favorable word; instead of that with an awful commanding voice—for thus it must have been—Balaam shouts to Balak to rise and listen. He hears now that God's promises to Israel are unchangeable, they can never be reversed. The same truth we have not alone from Balaam's lips, but likewise from the lips of Paul, the servant of the Lord, who after giving his wonderful prophetic testimony concerning his own beloved Jewish nation, cries out in exaltation, "The gifts and calling of God are without repentance." God is ever the covenant-keeping God, and every word which has come from His loving heart through the prophets to His people Israel He will yet fulfill. Balak, in his unbelief and his ignorance, as well as his hatred against Israel, is, alas, a sad type of Christendom, apostate, disbelieving the promises of the God of Abraham, ignorant of His purposes concerning Israel, and, therefore, despising and cursing those whom they should honor and love. Again, in this parable, we notice four principal thoughts, which now bring us a step nearer to Israel, Israel's calling and Israel's future, just as Balaam and Balak were on Pisgah's mountain-top nearer to the camp than on the heights of Baal.

1. He hath not beheld iniquity in Jacob nor seen travail (or perverseness) in Israel. It seems to us a very significant fact that in all of Balaam's parables sin and guilt are never mentioned. However, it does not say here that Israel is without iniquity or evil travail, but the statement is that God hath not beheld iniquity and not seen perverseness in Israel. Truly Israel had sinned against God during their travels in the wilderness. Israel was likewise punished for it, but their apostasy was never hopeless. In all their iniquity and perverseness they are still His beloved children, and the promise is theirs very definitely, that the seed of Israel can only be cast away for all that they have done if the heavens above can be measured and the foundations of the earth searched out beneath (Jeremiah 31:36, 37). That, of course, means that it will never come to pass. But more than that, to Israel belongs the promise of forgiveness, when, indeed, the eyes of God will not behold iniquity in Jacob nor will He see perverseness in Israel. In Micah, the last chapter and last three verses, is one of these sweet national promises to Israel, "Who is a God like unto thee, that pardoneth iniquity, and passeth by the transgression of the remnant of His heritage? He retaineth not His anger forever, because He delighteth in mercy. He will turn again and have compassion upon us; He will tread our iniquities under foot, and Thou wilt cast all their sins into the depths of the sea. Thou wilt perform the truth to Jacob, and the mercy to Abraham, which Thou hast sworn unto our fathers from the days of old." God looking upon Israel and no iniquity, God beholds His people and no perverseness; their sins forgiven and remembered no more.

2. In the second place notice the statement of Balaam, "Jehovah his God is with him, and the shout of a king in his midst." This was true in part when Balaam looked upon the camp of Israel. I wonder if Balaam's prophetic eye did pierce that cloud of glory, which in all its splendor was resting in the midst of Israel? Maybe he saw in that cloud, what the prophet Ezekiel saw in his vision, a throne, and upon the throne one like the Son of Man surrounded by the sign of the first covenant, a rainbow. There was no king in the midst of Israel at that time; Jehovah was King. Prophetically all points to the time when Israel's travail and iniquity will have an end, and He whose name is ever Emanuel will be the King in the midst of His redeemed people.

3. In the next place we notice that Balaam speaks of that deed of salvation, the redemption of Israel from the house of Egypt, which stands in the Old Testament as a type not only of our redemption in the blood of the Son of God, but likewise as the type of that future deed of God when He will gather His outcast children from the four corners of the earth. (See Jeremiah 16:14-15.) It is important that in the next parable Balaam repeats the same words only in another connection. Connected with the fact in this parable that God brought Israel out of Egypt stands the statement that there is no enchantment against Jacob and no divination against Israel. Egypt could hold Israel for centuries, but Egypt's wickedness ripened, and when the hour had come there was no power in the air nor upon the earth which could prevent the carrying out of the judgments of God upon Egypt, and the mercies upon Israel. No enchantment and no divination will ever frustrate God's plan in the future.

4. And then in the fourth place: In its time shall it be said of Jacob and of Israel, "What hath God wrought?" Just a glimpse is given here of that time of conquest in Israel and through Israel, when the people shall rise up as a lioness, when she shall not lie down till she has eaten the prey and drunk the blood of the slain; which not only Balaam in his next parables has to make plainer because the vision now hastens towards the end, but likewise which all the prophets from beginning to end have revealed. We shall see more of this in the third parable of Balaam.

From the top of Peor, Balaam now beholds Israel abiding in their tents according to their tribes. The Spirit of the Lord comes upon him. It is no longer meeting with the Lord and receiving it from Him, but the Spirit is upon him and through the Spirit he receives a higher revelation. He is now fully persuaded that Israel is to be blessed and he yields himself without resistance to God.

> The oracle of Balaam, son of Beor,
> Even the oracle of the man with eyes that
>   had been shut:
> His oracle who heard the words of God,
> Who seeth with the vision of the Almighty;
> Falling, but his eyes uncovered:
> How goodly are thy tents, O Jacob!
> Thy tabernacles, O Israel!
> As valleys are they spread forth
> As gardens by the river's side;
> As aloe trees that Jehovah planted;
> As cedars beside the waters!
> Water poureth from his buckets,
> And his seed is in many waters:

And his king shall be higher than Agag,
And his kingdom shall be exalted.
God bringeth him out of Egypt;
He hath strength like that of the wild ox
He shall eat upon the nations, his adversaries,
Yea, he shall break their bones,
And smite them through with his arrows,
He couched, he lay down as a lion;
And as a lioness, who will rouse him?
Blessed is he that blessed thee,
And cursed is he that curseth thee!

Balaam, forced to speak, is now made to proclaim the victory of the nation of destiny and what God will do among them.

1. We notice first a description of Israel: "Goodly tents, beautiful tabernacles spread forth as valleys, gardens by the river side, aloe trees and cedars beside the waters, waters poured from his buckets, seed in many waters." Every Sabbath day and at every feast commanded by God, in entering the synagogue, this beautiful description of Israel's happiness is chanted by the orthodox Jews. Still it has not yet been realized, and whatever spiritual lessons for the church we may derive from it, we do not care to follow them at this time. Israel still living in miserable huts, no tabernacles among them, far from being like gardens by the riverside, and aloe trees and cedars beside the waters. Truly his seed in many waters, but not in honor and peace, but dishonor and unrest. The prophetic eye, however, sees it all accomplished, and Balaam's vision leaps over centuries and centuries to the time of the end when Israel's unbelief has ended and once more the tribes are gathering to take possession of the land, their glorious inheritance. When that great Sabbath day commences, that day of the Lord, Israel's hope will be realized, and what the pious orthodox Jew to-day sees in faith and often repeats with tears in his eyes, will then be a blessed reality. How goodly are thy tents O Jacob, thy tabernacles O Israel. In the highly poetical strain we realize the type of the living Spirit, the water poured from His buckets.

2. In two lines Balaam speaks of the king and kingdom which is to be exalted. Agag was the title of the king of the Amalekites, the national enemy of Israel. Haman was an Agagite; he came from Amalek, a fitting type of Antichrist, and here Balaam sees a king coming, who is higher than Agag, than all the powers which are anti-Semitic, and that king will have a kingdom which will be exalted. It is hardly necessary to enlarge upon this.

3. We notice now for the second time the repetition, "God bringeth him out of Egypt," but after the phrase, he hath strength like that of a wild ox, he changes his words. In the second parable we saw that he continues saying, "there is no enchantment against Jacob and no divination against Israel," while in this he says after stating, "God bringeth him out of Egypt, he shall eat up the nations, his adversaries, yea, he shall break their bones and smite them through with his arrows." It seems in the second parable Egypt of the past is meant, and in this parable, it is Egypt of the future, as already quoted from Jeremiah, the regathering of the people through the high and wonderful hand of the Lord. Connected with that second Egypt, that great and wonderful deed of Jehovah's, when the whole nation will be redeemed and spirit-filled in that day; connected with that is the judgment of the nations, which are the adversaries of Israel. There is a wonderful similarity between the story in Exodus and the future history of Israel, and the nations still unwritten on the pages of history and only visible by eyes of faith in the word of our God, who will speak again and not keep silence. The words, "he couched, he lay down as a lion and as a lioness will rouse him," is a quotation from Jacob's prophecy of Judah, but here applied to the entire nation, which will become through the lion of the tribe of Judah the lioness who will lie down and spring upon its prey and drink the blood of the slain. The last stanza of the first part of the third parable is again a repetition of God's promise to Abraham now seen in its fulfillment; both declare from an enemy's mouth how surely, how fully every utterance of God shall come to pass.

However, the prophecy in these parables is still incomplete, something is lacking which must be said. Step by step the Lord and the Spirit led Balaam up to the consummation, and while Balak's anger is kindled and like a raving maniac he stamps with his feet and smites his hands together, crying to Balaam, "I called thee to curse mine enemies and lo, thou hast altogether blessed them these three times, flee to thy place," and while Balak denied him the honor he had promised, Balaam in a divine defiance, the fire of God burning forth from his eyes, turns once more to Balak and says, "Behold I am going to my people; come, I will admonish thee what this people shall do unto thy people in the last days." Then—

The oracle of Balaam, son of Beor,
Even the oracle of the man with eyes that had been shut!
The oracle of one that heareth the sayings of God
And who knoweth the knowledge of the Most High;
Seeing with the vision of the Almighty;
Falling, but his eyes uncovered:
I see him, but not now;
I behold him, but not nigh:
There hath come a star out of Jacob,
And a sceptre hath risen out of Israel,
And hath smitten through the sides of Moab,
And dashed against each other all the sons of tumult.
And Edom is a possession—
Seir also a possession—his enemies;
And Israel doeth valiantly.
Yea, out of Jacob one hath dominion,
And destroyeth what is left from the city.

And he looked upon Amalek and took up his parable, saying—

Amalek first of the nations!
And his latter end, destruction!

And he looked at Kenites and took up his parable, saying—

Firm is thy dwelling place,
And thy nest fixed in the rock!
But the Kenite shall be ruined,
Until Asshur carry thee captive away.

And he took up his parable, saying—

Who shall live when God appointeth this?
And ships shall come from the coasts of Kittim,
And shall afflict Asshur, and afflict Eber,
And he also . . . to destruction.

And Balaam rose up and went and returned to his place and Balak also went his way.

This is the most remarkable parable of Balaam, and surely it is the very breath of God. He boasts himself of knowing the knowledge of the Most High, seeing with the vision of the Almighty. After this introduction he speaks again that he sees Him and beholds Him. However, not now and not nigh. We recollect that in the first parable he said likewise from the top of the rocks, "I see him and from the hills I behold him." There it was the nation, here it is a person; namely, the King of Israel whose shout he had heard before among the wonderful people. The description of this coming King is glorious. First he sees Him as a star coming out of Jacob, and then he calls Him a sceptre risen out of Israel, smiting through the sides of Moab and turning against each other all the sons of tumult. In consequence of this Edom becomes His possession, likewise Seir; all His enemies are conquered and Israel stands with the King and does valiantly. It is a very pronounced Messianic prophecy relating to the time when the kingdom is to be restored to Israel. Many teachers of God's Word have made a mistake in applying this prophecy to the time of the first coming of the Lord Jesus Christ. The Jews recognize the prophecy as relating to the King Messiah. One of their false messiahs was known by the name Bar-Chochva, the son of a star. We also notice that after he has taken Edom and Seir for his possession, Balaam says, "Yea, out of Jacob one hath dominion and destroyeth what is left from the city." In these words reference is made to His reign and rule in the coming age. The vital point of this last parable of Balaam is the prophecy concerning the fate of the Gentile powers. We have first Moab, who is smitten through the sides; the sons of tumult are connected with Moab and who are dashed against each other; Edom and Seir, Amalek, Asshur, Eber, and the ships coming from the coast of Kittim. All these nations having passed away stand nevertheless in a very pronounced relation to the great day of the wrath of the Lord, when He whose right it is will appear once more. In fact they seem to come again to the front in the latter day. We will quote here a remarkable passage from the prophet Jeremiah, which relates to Moab. Jeremiah 48:47, "Yet will I bring again the captivity of Moab in the latter days, saith the Lord." In chapter 49:6, we read, "And afterward I will bring again the captivity of the children of Ammon, saith the Lord." And in the 39th verse, "But it shall come to pass in the latter days that I will bring again the captivity of Elam, saith the Lord." All these nations have been judged in the past, and their descendants are hard to find, yet God knows and in His own way and in His own time He will have every one of His words fulfilled.

What else do we see in this last parable of Balaam than the judgment of the world powers? Later Nebuchadnezzar, another Gentile ruler like Balak, had a dream, and he saw the great image, the wonderful picture of the four kingdoms of the world; and Daniel, a true prophet of Jehovah, not like Balaam, interpreted the dream for Nebuchadnezzar, but what Nebuchadnezzar dreamed and Daniel saw in his vision

Balaam here sees in his last vision from the top of Peor. Wonderful description of the time when the stone cut out without hands smashes the proud image and reduces it to dust! Wonderful vision later seen by Zechariah, the four carpenters who are being raised up to conquer the four horns who have scattered Israel, Judah and Jerusalem (Zechariah 1). There is no doubt that Asshur stands for the first of the Gentile empires, that is Babylon, and Eber probably for the other, the Medo-Persian, while Kittim, the isles of the west, stand for the Greek and Roman rule.

THE BOOK OF
DEUTERONOMY

Introduction

The fifth book written by Moses is called Deuteronomy on account of an erroneous Greek translation of Chapter 17:18. The words "a copy of this law" were translated by mistake "a second law." Deuteronomy means "second law." The Hebrews call it *haddeborim,* which means "the words."

This book does not contain a second law, as suggested by the word Deuteronomy; nor is the book a mere repetition of the law previously given in Exodus, Leviticus and Numbers. The analysis and annotations as given in this work show that such is not the case. Dr. Martin Luther remarks on this book: "Deuteronomy is a compendium and summary of the whole law and wisdom of the people of Israel, wherein those things which relate to the priests and Levites are omitted, and only such things included as the people generally are required to know." This is a correct view. It is "a hortatory description, explanation, and enforcement of the most essential contents of the covenant revelation and covenant laws, with emphatic prominence given to the spiritual principle of the law and its fulfilment; and with a further development of the ecclesiastical, judicial, political and civil organization which was intended as a permanent foundation for the life and well-being of the people in the land of Canaan. There is not the slightest trace, throughout the whole book, of any intention whatever to give a new or second law."

The book of Deuteronomy is the book which demands *obedience*. Obedience is the keynote of almost every chapter. It is the great lesson of the book. Obedience in the spirit of love, flowing from a blessed and enjoyed relationship with Jehovah, is the demand made of His people. Over and over again in this final portion of the Pentateuch the people Israel are reminded of the great goodness and faithfulness of Jehovah. How He redeemed them out of the house of bondage, carried them through the wilderness, guided them, gave them food, sustained them is repeatedly stated. And He, who chose Israel and dealt thus with them has a perfect claim on their love; that love is to be expressed by obedience. There are some misguided believers who pass by this magnificent book as if there were no lessons to be learned here. To do this is a very serious mistake. No book in the Bible must be ignored. Each bears its own peculiar character and message. We do well to look under the guidance of the Holy Spirit for the spiritual lessons which are written for us here. Is the principle of the book of Deuteronomy, obedience to Jehovah and His Word in the spirit of love and godly fear, abandoned in the New Testament? We answer, it is as prominent there as it is in this fifth book of Moses. New Testament believers, forming the body of Christ, are brought into the highest possible relationship with the Lord. They possess a position which Israel never possessed and of which even their greatest prophets were ignorant. Christian believers are one with the Lord Jesus Christ. Everywhere in the Gospels and in the Epistles this relationship into which the grace of God has brought believers forms the basis of exhortation to love the Lord and to obey His Word; to live unto Him. "He that hath My commandments, and keepeth them, he it is that loveth Me; and he that loveth Me shall be loved of My Father, and I will love him, and will manifest Myself to him. . . . If a man love Me he will keep My words, and My Father will love him, and We will come unto him and make Our abode with him. He that loveth Me not, keepeth not My sayings, and the Word which ye hear is not Mine, but the Father's, who sent Me" (John 14:21, 23, 24). "If ye keep My commandments, ye shall abide in My love; even as I have kept My Father's commandments and abide in His love" (John 15:10). May God's people everywhere be reminded, in the days of laxity and worldiness, that the Lord who has redeemed us and has washed us from our sins in His own blood, claims our love and obedience. This fact makes the book of Deuteronomy, if carefully studied in a spiritual way, of great importance to every child of God. If read it is bound to produce a response from every heart indwelt by His Spirit and a closer walk with God and more childlike obedience will be the result. It is deeply interesting at the same time to study this old book. This book, three thousand years old, having power to touch the heart and the life of all who receive its message, is an evidence in itself of its divine origin. Well has it been said: "Take any human writing of the same date as the book of Deuteronomy; if you should lay your hand on some volume written three thousand years ago, what would you find? A curious relic of antiquity—something to be placed in the British Museum, side by side with an Egyptian mummy, having no application whatever to us or to our time—a musty document—a piece of obsolete writing, practically useless to us, referring only to a state of society and to a condition of things long since passed away and buried in oblivion."

Higher Criticism and Deuteronomy

On account of the sublime character of this book, Deuteronomy has been the object of the special attacks by the critics. These boasting "scholars" have left nothing unattacked, but have defiled with their foolish theories and inventions the perfect Word of God. Throughout our studies in the preceding books, we have touched repeatedly upon their arguments and repudiated their claims. It is quite impossible to follow here the history and development of the criticism of Deuteronomy. There is a reason, which we hope to state later, why this book has been the special object of these satanic attacks, to rob it of its authority. And we wish to add, that nowhere else in their criticism are the critics so at sea and often contradicting each other, as in their attacks upon Deuteronomy. All deny, of course, the Mosiac authorship. The dates are placed many centuries after Moses. To show how these "learned" gentlemen agree, we give a few names of professors and others and what they say about the date of the book. Oettli and others assume that is was composed during the earlier, but post-Solomonic, time of the kings. Vatinger and Koenig claim it was written under Hezekiah. Ewald, Riehm, Smith, Kautsch, etc., teach it was composed under Manasseh's reign. De Wette, Bleck, Welshausen, Reuss, Dillman, etc., believe it was written when Josiah was king. Gesenius and a host of modern critics put the composition of Deuteronomy during or even after the Babylonian captivity. Here is harmony!

If Deuteronomy was not written by Moses immediately before his death, then the book has no claim whatever upon our confidence. It must be rejected as a colossal fraud. And if this book was not written by Moses and therefore must be classed as a forgery, then the testimony of the Lord Jesus Christ concerning this book would have to be dismissed as untrustworthy; that would rob Him of His infallibility. Furthermore the entire New Testament teaching would be affected by it, for the New Testament writers in their inspired testimony make constant use of the book of Deuteronomy.

Higher Criticism is Infidelity

Higher criticism is infidelity and that of the most dangerous kind, because it comes in the garb of an angel of light and often claims to be a friend and a helper, to lead people into the truth. All the prominent infidels (and most of them, if not all, immoral men) ridiculed the idea that Moses wrote Deuteronomy.

We quote from that well-known infidel, who lived more than a hundred years ago, Thomas Paine:

"In Deuteronomy the style and manner of writing marks more evidently than the former books that Moses is not the writer." "Though it is impossible for us to know identically who the writer of Deuteronomy was, it is not difficult to discover him professionally, that he was some Jewish priest who lived, as I shall show in the course of this work, at least 850 years after Moses."

Recently an official of high standing in the Methodist Episcopal Church wrote a book in which he followed closely in the tracks of German infidel critics. He made the following assertions:

"It is clear, say our modern authorities, that he (Moses) could not have been the author of this book (Deuteronomy). For reasons equally convincing, it is evident that the book must be the product of a period or periods far later than that of Moses." "The date of its origin is probably not far from the middle of the sixth century B.C."

Is there any difference between the statements of the infidel Thomas Paine and the Methodist preacher of prominent standing? Both speak the same language. Doubly sad it is, when the men, who adopt this destructive criticism, are destitute of any scholarship whatever. They are but weak echo-men of others.

Our Lord and Deuteronomy

Our Lord Jesus Christ put special honor upon this book. It is this book which He quoted exclusively when Satan came to Him with his vile temptations. Three times He took His answers from that one book, quoting chapter 6:13, 16;8:3; 10:20. This certainly is highly significant. He, who knew the Word so well, might have gone to any other portion and used it with equal effect. But He chose to take refuge behind this book and draw the weapon from it to defeat Satan, who now tries, by his instruments, to destroy the trustworthiness of the book in which the Lord Jesus Christ so firmly believed as the very Word of God. And our Lord no doubt foresaw all this modern day infidel criticism. Did He know anything of the authorship of Deuteronomy? Would He have quoted from this book if it had been a forgery? If these words are not truly the Word of God, though claiming to be that, then they are falsehoods. How could Satan have been defeated by falsehoods? Alas! these critics go so far in their blasphemy, that they charge Christ with ignorance, or that He acquiesced in a popular error of His times! The testimony our Lord has given to this book is sufficient to establish its divinity as well as the Mosaic authorship.

But there is another reason why He selected Deuteronomy in answering the Devil. As we have seen Deuteronomy tells of obedience. Hence the One who had come to be obedient, yea obedient unto death, the death of the cross, went to that book, which speaks of obedience, to show how He submitted to the will of His Father and to defeat Satan thereby. Our Lord therefore bore witness also to the very character of the book itself.

In the New Testament

Equally striking it is that the Lord in many other instances made use of Deuteronomy. And the Holy Spirit in almost every portion of the New Testament connects His testimony with this great book. We earnestly request our readers to study the following passages and turn to these references. This not only shows how Deuteronomy is made use of in the New Testament, but it will help in understanding the book. Deut. 1:16, 17; 16:19 and John 7:24; James 2:1. Deut. 4:2; 12:32 and Matt. 5:18; Rev. 22:18-19. Deut 4:7 and James 4:8. Deut. 4:29-31; 31:6 and Hebrews 11:6; 8:8. Deut. 5:5 and Gal. 3:19. Deut. 7:8 and 1 John 4:10. Deut. 9:7, 24; 10:16 and Acts 7:51. Deut. 9:15, 19 and Hebr. 12:18. Deut. 10:17 and Acts 10:34 and 1 Tim. 6:15. Deut. 13:14 and 2 Cor. 6:15. Deut. 4:2; 26:19; 28:9 and 1 Peter 2:9. Deut. 15:11 and Matt. 26:11; John 12:8. Deut. 16:20 and 1 Tim. 6:11. Deut. 17:6; 19:15 and Matt. 18:16; John 8:17; 2 Cor. 13:1; Hebr. 10:28. Deut. 18:15 and Acts 3:22; 7:37; John 1:21; 6:14; Matt. 17:5. Deut. 18:16 and Heb. 12:19. Deut. 18:19 and Luke 10:16; John 10:48; Acts 3:23. Deut. 18:18 and John 12:49. Deut. 19:19; 17:7 and 1 Cor. 5:13. Deut. 19:21 and Matt. 5:38. Deut. 21:6 and Matt. 27:24. Deut. 21:23 and Gal. 3:13. Deut. 22:22 and John 8:4. Deut. 23:25 and Matt. 12:1. Deut. 14:1 and Matt. 5:31; 19:3. Deut. 24:14 and James 5:4. Deut. 25:3 and 2 Cor. 11:24. Deut. 25:4 and 1 Cor. 9:9; 1 Tim. 5:18. Deut. 25:5 and Matt. 22:24. Deut. 27:26 and Gal. 3:10. Deut. 29:3 and Rom 11:8. Deut. 29:18 and Heb. 12:15. Deut. 30:6 and Rom. 2:29. Deut. 30:11 and Romans 10:6-8. Deut. 31:26 and Rom. 3:19. Deut. 32:21 and Rom. 10:19. Deut. 32:35 and Rom. 12:19; Heb. 10:30. Deut. 32:43 and Rom. 15:10.

And if Deuteronomy were not true, not the Word of God, what then? Every part of the New Testament would collapse.

Interesting Prophecy

But Deuteronomy is also a book of prophecy. Moses is called in it a prophet. He exercises His office in this final book he wrote. From Pisgah he beheld the land in all its beauty. But before he had that vision, he had seen the future of the people, who had been his charge during the weary years through the desert sands. How wonderful it is that he, their appointed leader, who knew the people so well, uttered prophecies, which cover the past, present and future history of Israel. How minutely curses, which were to come upon the people, are predicted in this book! How minutely they were fulfilled and are still in course of fulfillment.

His great song (chapter 32) is wholly prophetic. It is, if rightly understood, a key to the entire prophetic Word. What is yet to come upon the nation, both in judgment and in blessing, was beheld by Moses.

His last message was the blessing. The man, the faithful servant of Jehovah, to whom was given the ministry of the law (which can do nothing but curse), ends his earthly testimony by uttering a blessing. That blessing will yet come upon the sons of Jacob and all nations will rejoice in coming days, when His people is brought back and all His promises are fulfilled. May it please God to make the study of this book a great blessing to all His people.

The Division of Deuteronomy

I. THE FIRST DISCOURSE OF MOSES AND RETROSPECT

1. **Introduction** (1:1-5)
2. **From Horeb to Kadesh** (1:6-46)
3. **After the Forty Years: Conflict and Conquest** (2—3)
4. **Hearken, O Israel!** (4:1-40)
5. **The Three Cities of Refuge** (4:41-43)

II. THE EXPOSITION OF THE LAW AND THE STATUTES, EXHORTATIONS AND WARNINGS, BLESSING AND CURSE

1. **The Proclamation of the Decalogue** (4:44—5:33)
2. **The First Commandment and What It Involves** (6:1-25)
3. **The Possession of the Land and Their Separation** (7:1-26)
4. **Thou Shalt Remember! Provision and Warning** (8:20)
5. **Warning Against Self-Righteousness and Their Previous Failures** (9—10:11)
6. **Jehovah's Love and His Requirements of His People** (10:12-22)
7. **Israel's Responsibility: The Blessing and the Curse** (11:1-32)
8. **The Place of Worship** (12:1-32)
9. **Warning Against False Prophets and Their Punishment** (13:1-18)
10. **The Children of God and Their Separation** (14:1-29)
11. **The Year of Release and Liberation of Hebrew Slaves** (15:1-18)
12. **The Firstlings and the Three Feasts** (15:19—16:17)
13. **Justice and the Choice of a King** (16:18—17:20)
14. **The Rights of the Priests and Levites, the True and the False Prophet** (18:1-22)
15. **Laws for Israel in the Land** (19:1-21)
16. **Concerning Future Wars** (20:1-20)
17. **The Expiation of an Uncertain Murder and Various Instructions** (21:1-23)
18. **Against Inhumanity and Different Violations, False Testimony and Sins of Adultery** (22:1-30)
19. **The Congregation of Jehovah: Its Constitution and Holiness** (23:1-25)
20. **Concerning Divorce and Laws of Mercy** (24:1-22)
21. **Various Laws and Responsibilities** (25:1-19)
22. **First Fruits and Prayer** (26:1-19)
23. **The Memorial of the Law at Mount Ebal, Gerizim and Ebal** (27:1-26)
24. **The Blessing and the Curse** (28:1-68)
25. **The Repetition of the Covenant and the Restated Curse** (29:1-29)
26. **The Dispersion and the Return: The Final Appeal** (30:1-20)

III. THE FINAL WORDS OF MOSES AND THE VISION OF THE FUTURE

1. **Moses' Final Charge, the Written Law Delivered, and Jehovah's Word to Moses** (31:1-30)
2. **The Song of Moses** (32:1-43)
3. **The Blessing of Moses** (32:43—33:29)
4. **The Death of Moses** (34:1-12)

Analysis and Annotations

I. The First Discourse of Moses and Retrospect

I. The Introduction

CHAPTER 1:1-5

The people were still on this side of Jordan in the wilderness. The second verse, containing a parenthetical statement, gives the story of their unbelief, as recorded in the Book of Numbers. "There are eleven days' journey from Horeb by the way of Mount Seir unto Kadeshbarnea." They might have reached the place they occupied now, facing Jordan and the land, in eleven days. It took them almost forty years. Unbelief had kept them back. It was towards the end of the fortieth year, in the eleventh month, that Moses began his wonderful addresses. In the first month of that memorable year Miriam had died (Numb. 20:1). His brother Aaron had died in the fifth month (Numb. 33:38). Moses was soon to follow him at the close of the fortieth year, at the ripe age of one hundred and twenty. Forty years were spent by Moses in the palaces of Egypt; forty years he was a shepherd in the land of Midian and forty years he was the leader of God's people through the wilderness. Before he went to the top of Pisgah to behold the land and to die, he pours out his heart in the presence of all Israel. His words were "according unto all that the Lord had given him." All he had received from the Lord, he passed on faithfully to the Lord's people. "Moses verily was faithful in all God's house, as a servant, for a testimony of those things, which were to be spoken afterward" (Heb. 3:5). Once more, therefore, he placed the words of the Lord before their hearts. This is the blessed object of ministry, to make known what God has revealed. True ministry is to deliver the message received. "For I delivered unto you first of all that which I also received" (1 Cor. 15:3). Moses declared the Law unto them (verse 5). The Hebrew word "declare" means "to make plain." It is used in Habakkuk 2:2.

2. From Horeb to Kadesh

CHAPTER 1:6-46

1. The command to go in and to possess the land (1:6-8)
2. The appointment of judges reviewed (1:9-18)
3. The failure to possess the land (1:19-33)
4. The judgment of God (1:34-46)

In the beginning of our annotations we must guard once more against the misleading conception, that the book of Deuteronomy is nothing but a rehearsal of previous history. On account of this wrong estimate, the book has not received the close study it deserves and God's people have missed the blessing, which results from such a study. It is true, Deuteronomy contains much that is retrospective, but it is far from being mere repetition. Spiritual lessons are found here, which are very much needed at the present time.

God had spoken at Horeb, "Ye have dwelt long enough in this mount." This communication is not found in the book of Numbers, though the opening chapters of that book presuppose such a command. Not a word is said here of the cloud and the trumpets, the twofold means by which Jehovah guided and directed His people. We therefore learn, that the Lord also spoke in direct words to them. He had watched their dwelling at Horeb; the purpose He had with them at that mountain was accomplished and now they had been instructed to move. It reveals the loving interest the Lord took in His people and in their movements. And He is still the same, who controls the tarrying and the journeying of His people. Every word in verses 7 and 8 reveals the divine purpose to lead His people at once into the land, which He had sworn unto Abraham, Isaac and Jacob (Genesis 22:16). The land was set before them; all they needed was to go forward in faith and possess it. They failed miserably.

The nation had greatly multiplied and Moses was not able to bear them alone (Exodus 18:17-18; Num. 11:14). To guard against any misunderstanding of his word: "I am not able to bear you myself;" Moses added the gracious wish "the Lord God of your fathers make you a thousand times so many more as ye are and bless you, as He hath promised you!" These beautiful words still breathe the warmth of the loving heart of Moses and they are also expressing his faith in the promise of Jehovah. Provision was made for the relief of Moses. There is no discrepancy here with the statements in Exodus and Numbers on this matter. Moses in his address does not give a repetition of the historical-chronological facts, and circumstances, but simply mentions them incidentally as leading up to the main object of his address. It was failure on his part, when he complained of his burden. We learned this in our annotations of Numbers 11. May we think here of the great burden-bearer, our Lord, who never fails His people and who never complains. We can cast our burdens and cares upon Him and shall ever find that He careth for us.

The sending out of the spies is next mentioned. Here we find the hidden things uncovered and the motives are given, which prompted the people to ask for the spies. They asked for the spies themselves. So we learn that the wish did not come from the Lord, nor from Moses. When Jehovah saw the desire of their hearts and heard their request, He commanded the sending out of the spies. He knew in what it would result. Moses was ignorant of that, therefore, the saying pleased him well. If the people had faith in God they would have been obedient at once and gone up to possess the land. The story of their unbelief and rebellion follows. Fearful was the accusation, which came from their lips. "Because the Lord hated us, He hath brought us forth out of the land of Egypt to deliver us into the hands of the Amorites, to destroy us." What ingratitude and blindness! The Lord, who had so graciously delivered them out of Egypt, who had overthrown the hosts of Egypt, who had given them the bread from heaven and water out of the rock, Him they accused of hatred.

The words of Moses to inspire the murmuring people with new courage (verses 29-31) do not appear in the book of Numbers. Deuteronomy is clearly not a mere rehearsal of what took place. Moses honored the Lord by the words he spoke. He did not share the unbelief of the people. The concluding paragraph of the first chapter shows the judgment, which fell upon that unbelieving generation. The opening words of Moses in this book are of a solemn character. Unbelief and disobedience had brought judgment upon the people. God's demands here and throughout this book are faith and obedience as the expression of faith. Confidence in Him and obedience, unswerving obedience He asks of us; He can never dispense with these. We find these demands of Jehovah everywhere. Obedience is the way to blessing and the enjoyment of what Jehovah is, while disobedience plunges into darkness and despair. And how significant are the burning exhortations to obedience from the lips of the servant of God, whose failure by being disobedient and self-willed had deprived him from entering into the land!

3. After the Forty Years and From Conflict to Conquest

CHAPTER 2

1. From Kadesh to the land of the Amorites (2:1-23)
2. The command to possess (2:24-25)
3. The conquest of Sihon (2:26-37)

The many days in the first verse are the thirty-eight years. We must notice the little word "we." "We turned and took our journey into the wilderness." Moses, Aaron, his sons, Joshua, Caleb and the faithful Levites turned back with the unfaithful, murmuring Israelites. Moses and all who had not shared in the unbelief of the people submitted to the sovereign will of the Lord. How strange it would have been if they had complained in sharing in the judgment of the mass of the people. This is true obedience and humility. "God resisteth the proud, but giveth grace to the humble; submit yourselves, therefore, to God" (James 4:6-7). The faithful ones shared the trials, the sorrows, the hardships of the murmuring multitudes. And Jehovah was with them and in gracious tenderness. Can there be anything more beautiful than the testimony of Moses he gives in verse 7! "For the Lord thy God hath blessed thee in all the works of thy hand; He knoweth thy walking through this great wilderness: these forty years the Lord thy God has been with thee; thou hast lacked nothing." Well may we ponder over it. The people, who had accused Him, insulted Him, disbelieved His word, this people He carried through the great wilderness so that they lacked nothing. May we take courage. Our failures, our short-comings, our unbelief do not arrest the gracious tenderness of His loving heart.

Intensely interesting is the divine injunction not to molest Edom, Moab and Ammon. The great principle which goes through Deuteronomy is very outstanding in this command of Jehovah. He guided them, gave His instructions and they were to depend on Him and be obedient to His will. They might have coveted to possess the plains of Moab or Mount Seir and the lands of Ammon. The Lord forbade them to do so. Disobedience would have been disastrous. Though Edom had harrassed Israel greatly and displayed an arrogant pride, yet Jehovah would not give Edom's possession to Israel. He remembered His word "I have given Mount Seir unto Esau for a possession" (Gen. 32:3; 36:6-8; Josh. 24:4). They were, therefore, not to seek what the Lord had not given to them. And this is obedience and a lesson of faith. What happy contentment there would be among God's people, if this rule were followed.

The same command not to discuss the Moabites and Ammonites (blood relations to Israel) is given. The races of giants are mentioned, which occupied the territories of Moab, Ammon and Edom. They had different names as stated in the text. Emim means "the terrible ones;" Zamzumim has the meaning "to murmur and meditate." This may have some reference to demon possession as seen in some of the present day mediums of spiritism. They were powerful and extremely vicious beings, given up to the control and service of Satan.

Then Jehovah called to action. "Rise up,[1] take your journey, and pass over the river Arnon, behold I have given into thine hand Sihon the Amorite, King of Heshbon, and his land, begin to possess it and contend with him in battle." Obedience is again the demand. While the statement in verse 25 "I begin to put the dread of thee and the fear of thee upon the nations that are under the whole heaven" has been taken as hyperbolical, it also has a prophetic meaning. The Gentiles fear the Jews and the nations stand in dread of them. Some day the Jewish race will be the head of the nations of the world. Sihon's measure of wickedness and cruelty was full. His

[1]In verse 13, "Now rise up, *said I*"—the words in italics "*said I*" must be omitted. Not Moses, but Jehovah gave the command.

spirit was hardened like Pharoah's and Israel completely overthrew him and his kingdom. "The Lord our God delivered all unto us" (verse 36). Read Psalm 136:19-26. It was His mercy. And His mercy endureth forever and is blessedly on our side. May we walk in obedience and find His mercy acting in our behalf.

CHAPTER 3

1. The conquest of Og (3:1-11)
2. The land possessed (3:12-20)
3. Joshua in the place of Moses (3:21-29)

In obedience to the word of the Lord, they went to battle against Og, the king of Bashan. Obedience to the Lord and its results and blessing are the marks of the second and third chapters of Deuteronomy, while the first chapter shows disobedience and its fruit.

The kingdom of Og in Bashan was a powerful kingdom. The cities had high walls with gates and bars. Their number was sixty. Archaeological research has proven the existence of strong and fortified cities in that territory, the ruins of which may still be seen. The oldest dwellings and ruined towers of Hauran (Bashan) are described by C. Von Raumer in the following words: "Simple, built of heavy blocks of basalt, roughly hewn, and as hard as iron, with very thick walls, very strong stone gates and doors, many of which were about eighteen inches thick, and were formerly fastened with immense bolts, of which traces still remain; such houses as these may have been the work of the old giant tribe of Rephaim, whose king, Og, was defeated by the Israelites 3,000 years ago." King Og was a giant, belonging to the remnant of the giant tribe of Rephaim. His iron bedstead is mentioned by Moses. There is nothing exaggerated about it. The bed was about twelve feet long and six feet broad, which does not mean that Og was as tall as that. Moses must have mentioned the bedstead of the slain giant, to remind the people of the great victory which the Lord had given them and to inspire them with confidence in the possession of the land. The Lord, who overthrew Og would certainly not fail them when they entered the land and met the enemies there.

They utterly destroyed men, women and children of every city. Many an infidel has sneered at this statement and blasphemed God, charging Him with cruelty and injustice for allowing such an extermination of human beings. God is righteous. These people were steeped in all kinds of vices and wickedness, similar to the depravity and vilest corruption of the Canaanites. God had to deal in judgment with them. He could not permit them to exist, and as the sovereign God He dealt with them in His righteous government.

"Now, the question is, Are we competent to understand these ways of God in government? Is it any part of our business to sit in judgment upon them? Are we capable of unraveling the profound and awful mysteries of divine providences? Can we—are we called upon to—account for the tremendous fact of helpless babes involved in the judgment of their guilty parents? Impious infidelity may sneer at these things; morbid sentimentality may stumble over them; but the true believer, the pious Christian, the reverent student of holy Scripture, will meet them all with this one simple but safe and solid question, 'Shall not the Judge of all the earth do right?'

"This, we may rest assured, is the only true way in which to meet such questions. If man is to sit in judgment upon the actings of God in government—if he can take upon himself to decide as to what is and what is not worthy of God to do, then, verily, we have lost the true sense of God altogether. And this is just what the devil is aiming at. He wants to lead the heart away from God; and to this end, he leads men to reason and question and speculate in a region which lies as far beyond their ken as heaven is above the earth. Can we comprehend God? If we could, we should ourselves be God" (C. H. Mackintosh).

This is a good answer to the infidel scoffer and should satisfy every Christian as well. The time is coming when the Lord will deal again in righteousness with this earth and then the slain of the Lord will be many.

The goodness and faithfulness of the Lord is thus unfolded by Moses in his address; it was meant for an encouragement to their faith and obedience. Next he speaks to them of the land, which the tribe of Reuben, Gad and half Manasseh received. We learned in our study of the book of Numbers that it was in self-will that they made the request. They were disobedient. Their failure is here completely overlooked by Moses. How beautifully this illustrates the grace of God!

He also reminded them of Joshua's call to be his successor; it took place at that time, after the conquest of the land on the east of the Jordan. He had seen what the Lord had done and that was an assurance of what the Lord would do in the future. All is worded so as to encourage confidence in the Lord and obedience to His command. And is it not even so throughout His entire Word? Everything in His Word urges us on to trust in Him with fullest confidence. Happy are we if we do so and manifest that confidence by a loving obedience.

Then we find a prayer of Moses, which is unmentioned in Numbers. It is a beautiful prayer. He pleaded with the Lord to let him go over to see the good land. It could not be, on account of his sin at the waters of Meribah. Meekly he tells out the story of failure in the presence of the people and gives the Lord's answer to him. Divine government had to shut him out from the land, but grace took him to the top of Pisgah to see, in company with the Lord, the land of promise.

3. Hearken, O Israel!

CHAPTER 4

1. Obedience demanded (4:1-8)
2. The covenant to be observed (4:9-14)
3. Take heed unto yourselves lest ye forget (4:15-24)
4. The warning (4:25-31)
5. Israel, the chosen nation (4:32-40)

"Now therefore hearken, O Israel" marks the beginning of the exhortation to keep the law of the Lord. First he had shown the goodness and faithfulness of the Lord and upon that Moses admonishes them to be true to Jehovah and to the covenant. The same order is followed in our great New Testament Epistles. What the Lord has done for us, His grace and faithfulness, always occupies the first place; this is followed by our responsibilities to walk worthy of the Lord. The first great discourse of Moses in its two main features, the retrospect of what Jehovah had done and Israel's obligation to keep the law to enjoy the blessings of the covenant, is the key to the entire book.

They were to hearken and to do. Hearing and doing stand in the foreground of this section. The result of obedience is life and possession of the land. "That ye may live" does not mean the possession of eternal life, but a long earthly life in the promised land. See chapters 5:33; 6:2; 8:1; 11:21; 16:20; 25:15; 30:6, 16;32:47. Nothing was to be added to the law and nothing to be taken from it. Alas! this warning has not been heeded. The elders with their traditions and commandments of men, added to the law and put the word of man above the Word of God, while later the Sadducees took away from the law and reduced the Word of God to the level of the word of man. The same is done to-day in ritualistic and rationalistic Christendom.

His voice had spoken to them; they had heard His words. They were privileged above all other nations. "For what nation is there so great, who hath God so nigh unto them, as the Lord our God is in all things that we call upon Him for? And what nation is there so great, that hath statutes, and judgments so righteous as all this law, which I set before you this day?" Therefore, they had great responsibility. Three times Moses told them to take heed (verses 9, 15 and 23). He warned them to beware of idolatry. They were to serve only Jehovah for He had brought them forth out of the iron furnace, to be unto Him a people of inheritance. He had delivered them and made them His own people, therefore, they were to obey Him. Solemnly Moses said, "I call heaven and earth to witness against you this day,[2] that ye shall soon utterly perish from off the land whereunto you go over Jordan to possess it; ye shall not prolong your days upon it, but shall utterly be destroyed." Moses in speaking these words had the first prophetic glimpse of their coming history of idolatry, followed by national ruin. This vision widens and he beheld them scattered among the nations. Verses 30 and 31 refer not only to past history, but they are yet to find a fulfilment in the latter days. It is the first prophetic note we hear in Deuteronomy from the lips of Moses. More fully he speaks of it towards the end of his farewell message to the people he loved so well.

Especially beautiful are the closing verses of this section (verses 33-40). What a display of what Jehovah had done for them, how He had revealed Himself and His power in their behalf! Therefore, He was entitled to a wholehearted obedience from His people. "Know therefore this day, and consider it in thine heart, that the Lord He is God in heaven above, and upon the

[2]It has been stated Luke 23:43 is this Old Testament idiom in the New Testament, as if our Lord meant to say: "Verily I say unto thee to-day, thou shalt be with Me in Paradise." However, this is positively wrong. It is the argument advanced by the teachers of the soul-sleep. The same hint is made in the *Companion Bible*. The comma does not belong after "to-day" but after "thee" as we have it in the English Bible.

earth beneath; there is none else." And what greater works He has made unto us His people, that great salvation in His blessed Son, our Lord! He has the right to claim our full obedience. May we consider constantly, who He is and what He has done for us and we shall yield to Him the obedience He looks for in His people.

4. The Three Cities of Refuge

CHAPTER 4:41-43

1. The cities set apart (4:41-42)
2. The cities named (4:43)

The first address being ended, an action of Moses takes place. To detect here the hand of an editor, who added these verses, as critics claim, cannot be sustained. The cities of refuge were mentioned in Numbers. Here the three on this side of Jordan are given. Then there were three more on the other side of which we read in chapter 19 and in the book of Joshua. As stated in our annotations in Numbers, the cities of refuge are typical of Christ, who is our shelter from the avenger. Scattered through the land for the gracious purpose of sheltering the slayer, they also bear a prophetic testimony. They speak of Israel's hope.

"These cities of refuge, set at intervals through the land of Israel, are a garrison for it from God, which even still, in ruin, as the land is, watch over it, as ministers of unchanging grace, and prophets of now near-coming glory. This people of God, separated to Him in the wonderful way attested by their annals,—what, after all, has been their condition for many and long centuries of subjection to hostile races? They have been strangers and wanderers, Cain-like, and indestructible as Cain,—a nation surviving even in death, but as if to perpetuate only the memory of the doom under which they lie,—the doom of an awful fratricide. Such is, in fact, their condition,—a condition hopeless to most yet, though it may be now with a streak of gray dawn widening upon it. But these cities of refuge have all the time been watch-towers set to face eastward, ramparts round prostrate Zion, upon which the watchmen hold not their peace, and give Him no rest, till He establish it again,—yea, till He make it a praise upon earth (Isa. 62:6, 7).

"They are His pledge, in view of what has in fact come to pass, that what He has foreseen cannot thwart His purposes, nor their sin His long-foreshown grace. Preach they may in sackcloth, but it is good tidings that they preach, of a place of security even for homicides,—for those for whom His plea shall yet avail, 'They know not what they do.' "[3]

The meaning of the three names are of equal interest. "Bezer" means "defence," a fortified place. Such Christ is for all who trust in Him. In Him we have our shelter and blessing as well. "Ramoth" means "heights." Our Lord occupies the exalted, the pre-eminent place and shelter in Him, we share His place as we read in the second chapter of Ephesians. "Golan" means "joy" or "their rejoicing." Even so we have in Him, who is our refuge, our joy and He has His joy in us.

II. The Exposition of the Law, Exhortations and Warnings, Blessing and Curse

1. The Proclamation of the Decalogue

CHAPTERS 4:44—5:33

1. The introductory words (4:44-49)
2. The law proclaimed (5:1-21)
3. Moses, the mediator (5:22-33)

First a general announcement is given of the discourse on the law. The fact is emphasized, that it was set before them after they came forth out of Egypt. Then the victories over Sihon and Og are mentioned once more and that they now possessed their land. Why this repetition? It was to remind them of the goodness and faithfulness of Jehovah, whose law they were about to hear expounded. It was to be a helpful encouragement to them and stimulate their obedience, while it also was the pledge of greater victories and blessings to come. Jehovah would keep His promise.

All Israel is gathered about Moses. The aged servant, so soon to leave their midst, now solemnly begins to utter the main discourse, which composes this book. The first verse of the fifth chapter contains the four words, which are found so often in this book of moral responsibility and practical obedience. These words are "hear" (over thirty times); "learn" (seven times); "keep" (thirty-nine times); "do" (almost one hundred times). These are therefore characteristic words of this great book. They were to hear, and hearing to learn, and learning to keep, and keeping to do. And this is still Jehovah's de-

[3]F. W. Grant, *Notes on Deuteronomy.*

mand of us His people. All who have a spiritual nature love to have it so. What is more delightful and blessed, than to hear Him speak, to learn of Him, to keep His Word and to do what He tells us!

Jehovah had made a covenant with them, not with their fathers, the patriarchs. The law covenant was made 430 years after Abraham. Moses then speaks in their hearing the words of the decalogue. The words differ somewhat from the twentieth chapter in Exodus, showing again that Deuteronomy is not a mechanical repetition of previous history. Higher criticism with its confused and confusing theories has made the best of this difference. Upon this difference critics claim that Moses could not have been the author of both. Says a critic: "Indeed he could not have written either in its present form, because that in Exodus is Jehovistic, and older than the record in Deuteronomy" (Dr. Davidson). Such an assertion simply shows the blindness of these men of supposed learning and scholarship. Anyone can see that the records in Exodus and Deuteronomy differ. We do not need scholarship for that. The mysterious person, whom the critics call "Deuteronomist" certainly possessed the record in Exodus and could have easily copied the exact words. But why is there a difference? Exodus gives the history; Deuteronomy does not repeat that history, but in restating the decalogue, Moses makes such comments which are in perfect keeping with the object of Deuteronomy. If Deuteronomy claimed to be a literal repetition of the history recorded in Exodus and Numbers, then one might speak of discrepancy.

> "Deuteronomy proves that we have here a grave and instructive reference to the commandments formally given in the second book of Moses. Such moral motives as are added are therefore as appropriate in Deuteronomy as they could not, ought not to, be in Exodus. The remembrance of their own estate as slaves in Egypt till delivered by Jehovah is most suitable in verse 15; but it is certain that this is an appeal to their hearts, not the ground stated by God in promulgating the fourth commandment. All is perfect in its own place, and the imputation of self-contradiction as baseless as it is malicious and irreverent. But one must only expect this from men whose aim is to reduce the inspired writers to their own level, and who think that piety can co-exist with fraud, yea, with fraudulent falsehood about God."

Moses left out purposely certain statements he uttered when the law was given through him in Exodus; and he added by way of comment other words in fullest keeping with the moral purpose of his message to the people. This is most evident in connection with the commandment to keep the Sabbath-day holy. in Exodus 20 we find the words "for in six days the Lord made heaven and earth, the sea, and all that in them is, and rested the seventh day; wherefore the Lord blessed the Sabbath-day and hallowed it." This reference to creation is omitted now by Moses, but he adds another spiritual motive to keep that day. "And remember that thou wast a servant in the land of Egypt, and that the Lord thy God brought thee out thence through a mighty hand and by a stretched out arm; therefore, the Lord thy God commanded thee to keep the Sabbath-day" (verse 15). We see at once that the characteristic of Deuteronomy is maintained. The people are reminded of the faithfulness and goodness of Jehovah, His gracious dealing with them, and that is made the ground of their responsibility to obey His Word. See in connection with the Sabbath Exodus 31:12-17. It was a sign between Jehovah and Israel. We refer the reader to our remarks on the Sabbath in the analysis of Exodus.

Moses then confirms the record in Exodus. "And He wrote them in two tables of stone, and delivered them unto me." They possessed them. Moses was also appointed as mediator, the type of Him, who is mediator between God and man, our Lord Jesus Christ. And He has done more than Moses did; He made atonement. The people had recognized their sinful distance from God as well as their merited condemnation (that which is the purpose of the law), and therefore had asked for the mediator. Note verse 29: Jehovah speaks, the One who searches the heart and knows what is in man. Absolute obedience is again demanded in the closing verses of this chapter.

2. The First Commandment and What It Involves

CHAPTER 6

1. Hear, therefore, O Israel! (6:1-3)
2. The first commandment (6:4-5)
3. The remembrance of these words and practical obedience (6:6-25)

"Hear, O Israel! The Lord our God is one Lord." Much has been made of this verse by orthodox Jews, who reverence it greatly. They call it the "Shema" after the first word "Hear." It is often used by Jews and Unitarians to deny the three persons of the Godhead. The Hebrew word "echod" (one), however, excludes forever such a denial, for it means a *compound unity*. The Hebrew has another word which expresses exactly what Jews and Unitarians, who reject the three persons in the Godhead, believe. It is the word "yochid"; this has the meaning of *a single one*.

"Jehovah, our Elohim is one Jehovah," thus the name of God is used in this verse. The verse states that to Him alone the name of Jehovah (the Self-existing One) rightfully belongs, He is the one who is absolutely God. It is the testimony against the polytheism (many and different gods) of the Gentiles, which surrounded Israel on all sides. And therefore, because He is the one God, and none beside Him, He must be loved with all the heart, with all the soul, with all the might. The heart with all its affections and energies must belong to Him. To believe on Him and to know Him must ever result in giving Him the heart. Spirit, soul and body must be devoted to Him. This is the first and the great commandment (Matthew 22:38; Mark 12:29-30). And we know this Jehovah as our Redeemer, who came and died in our stead. The New Testament fully reveals the claims He has on those, for whose redemption He paid the price with His own blood. "We love Him, beause He first loved us" (1 John 4:19). "And this commandment have we from Him, that he who loveth God loveth his brother also" (verse 21). "This is the love of God, that we keep His commandments" (1 John 5:3). "For ye are bought with a price; therefore, glorify God in your body, and in your spirit, which are God's" (1 Cor. 6:20).

Verses 6-9 are literally carried out by orthodox Jews. They write these words on parchment and put them in little boxes, which they bind with strips of leather to their foreheads and upon the hand. These are the phylacteries. They also put them in tin-boxes and nail them on the doors of their houses. All His words are worthy to be constantly remembered. The Word must be hid in the heart. It is to be in the family. It is never to be forgotten, whether we sit in the house, or walk, or rest, or rise up. Such a true spiritual remembrance of His words will increase and constantly produce devotion and obedience to the Lord. How solemn the warning not to forget Jehovah in the days of blessing and prosperity! (verses 10-15) How often they did forget Jehovah in the days of peace and earthly blessing.

Verse 16 is of deep interest. "Ye shall not tempt the Lord your God, as ye tempted Him in Massah." The tempting of the Lord at Massah was questioning His presence among them (Exodus 17:7). Our Lord made use of this word when the devil demanded that He should cast Himself from the pinnacle of the temple. Satan then quoted Scripture in His presence. The enemy knows how to do that; but he either leaves something out from the Word or he adds something to it. In quoting from Psalm 91, he omitted seven words, "to keep thee in all thy ways." Satan knew the obedience of Christ and he tried to make our Lord act in obedience to the Word by testing God's Word. But such was not God's way; it was not according to His command to cast Himself from the pinnacle of the temple. If He had done it, it would have been an act of self-will and therefore disobedience. And that is why Satan left out those seven words. But what did our Lord do? He did not call Satan to task for mutilating the Scriptures, but quoted another Scripture to show His unswerving obedience. "Again it is written, Thou shalt not tempt the Lord thy God." He would not tempt God. He quoted the book of Deuteronomy, because it is the book of obedience, and He had come not to do His own will, but the will of Him who sent Him. He also quoted the words in 8:3 and 10:20. How this fact confirms the inspiration and genuineness of Deuteronomy, we have already mentioned in our introduction.

3. The Possession of the Land and Their Separation

CHAPTER 7

1. The command to destroy the Canaanites (7:14)
2. The command to destroy their idolatry (7:5-11)
3. The promise of blessing and help (7:12-26)

Seven nations are mentioned as occupying the land, which God gave to Israel. These nations were steeped in the most awful licentiousness and practised the vilest abominations. There are different reasons to believe that Satan possessed them in a peculiar manner. God had tolerated these nations for many centuries. He waited in His mercy before the sword of justice was unsheathed. The measure of their wickedness was now full, the time for judgment had come. The Lord called Israel to be the executioner of that awful judgment. And whenever they carried out the divine judgment, not sparing any one, they had an object lesson of the holiness and righteousness of God. Their sons and daughters were not to marry any members of these doomed nations. That would result in apostasy from Him and in idolatry. All their altars, their images and their groves they were to destroy. They were a holy people. But the Lord did not choose them because they were more in number than other nations. Jehovah loved them. Solemnly they are once more told that the Jehovah who hath set His love on them is a faithful, a covenant keeping God. He keeps His covenant and mercy with them that love Him and keep His commandments. But He also repays them that hate Him. Promises of blessings follow. If they are obedient, if they hear, keep and do (verse 12) the Lord would bless them. It is refreshing to read all these gracious promises. May they encourage us to trust in Him and walk in obedience. In Christ even greater blessings than these are put on our side. We know from subsequent history, how completely Israel failed to carry out all these instructions. They practised the vile abominations of the nations they were commanded to destroy. God had to deal with them in judgment. Instead of the blessings enumerated in verses 12-24, the curse was visited upon them. God's gifts and calling are without repentance; in a future day the remnant of Israel will inherit these things through the grace of God.

4. Thou Shalt Remember! Provision and Warning

CHAPTER 8

1. Remember the forty years and Jehovah's care (8:1-6)
2. The gracious provision in the land (8:7-10)
3. Warning against forgetting Jehovah (8:11-20)

Admonition to obedience begins this chapter. Disobedience and what will result from it closes it. Between the first and last verses we find extremely precious words. They are called upon to remember the experiences of the wilderness. It was Jehovah, who led them and watched over them. The wilderness experience was made a blessing to them. It taught them the blessed lessons of humility and brought out all that was in their hearts. And this corresponds to our own experiences. Jehovah's care over them had been manifested. They had to learn in the wilderness the lessons of dependence upon God. He supplied their need. They were fed with manna. Their raiment waxed not old. Their feet did not even swell (Chapter 29:5; Neh. 9:20-21). "As a man chasteneth a son, so the Lord thy God chasteneth thee." And thus He still deals with His people, whom He loves and whom He has redeemed in His Son, the people He is leading home to Himself through the wilderness. Oh, that we may trust Him fully and yield ourselves to Him in obedience!

"How wonderful to think of God's patient grace and painstaking love with His people in the wilderness! What precious instruction for us! With what intense interest and spiritual delight we can hang over the record of the divine dealings with Israel in all their desert-wanderings! How much we can learn from the marvelous history! We, too, have to be humbled and proved, and made to know what is in our hearts. It is very profitable and morally wholesome."

Verse 3 was quoted by our Lord, when Satan asked Him to turn stones into bread. His perfect obedience to God was again revealed, when our Lord defeated Satan by quoting this verse.

He also gives them a glimpse of the good land. There would be abundance of water, no scarcity of food, wheat, barley, vines, fig trees, pomegranates, oil and honey. Then there were the hidden treasures in the mountains. These things speak typically of our blessings, the spiritual blessings, with which we are blessed in Christ Jesus, to which we are fully entitled, but which we can only enjoy if we walk in faith and obedience to His Word. Another solemn warning is given to them by their loving leader. The warning is against highmindedness and forgetting the Lord, who has done all these things. The warning was not heeded and what Moses testified against them overtook them in their national history. May we also remember here the warning God has given to Gentile Christendom, not to be highminded, but to fear (Romans 11:17-24).

5. Warning Against Self-Righteousness and Their Previous Failures

CHAPTERS 9:1—10:11

1. The warning (9:1-6)
2. The failures of the past (9:7-24)
3. The intercession of Moses (9:25-29)
4. The results of the intercession (10:1-11)

This chapter and the first eleven verses of the tenth are aimed against the spirit of self-righteousness. First there is the warning. This is followed by their shameful history of the past, which showed that a boast of being righteous, or having any righteousness had to be positively excluded in their case. They had been rebels and they owed their existence wholly to the mercy of God and that was secured by the intercession of Moses. They were, therefore, to understand that the good land was not given to them for their righteousness; they were a stiffnecked people. How humbling the recital of their failures, their rebellion and murmuring against Jehovah, must have been! And Moses added to it, which must have cut them to the very heart. "Ye have been rebellious against the Lord from the day that I knew you" (verse 24). Mercy alone had saved them and had effected their restoration. How easy it is for our poor hearts, not different from theirs, to forget all we were and that we owe all we are to the grace of God. Self-righteousness is an abomination in God's sight. True faith and obedience means a true humility.

The chronological order is not followed by Mses in the first part of the tenth chapter. That is known by the historical account. Verses 6 and 7 are a parenthesis. The beginning of verse 8, "At that time," does therefore not stand in connection with the death of Aaron, but it refers to the time when the broken covenant was restored. Higher critics have made much of this as a glaring contradiction. There is no such contradiction here and the apparent difficulty is easily solved by understanding the parenthetical character of verses 6 and 7. But why should such an historical statement be here introduced by Moses by way of a parenthesis? The answer is not difficult to find. Moses describes the gracious results of the intercession. Not only was the covenant restored, but also the institution and maintenance of the priesthood. Moses reminds the people of this gracious gift on the part of their God, by recalling to their memory the time when Aaron died and his son Eleazar was invested with the high priesthood in his stead.

6. Jehovah's Love and His Requirements of His People

CHAPTER 10:12-22

1. Jehovah's delight and love (10:12-15)
2. Admonition to fear and serve Jehovah (10:16-22)

This section is especially precious. Jehovah speaks through Moses and reminds His people of Himself and His Love and what He requires of them. "Behold the heaven and the heaven of heavens is Jehovah's thy God, the earth also, with all that therein is." What a marvellous call to fear and serve such a Lord! What He required of them was a loving obedience, to fear Him, to walk in all His ways, to love Him and to serve Him. They were to be followers of Jehovah their God. He is God of gods, Lord of lords, great, mighty, terrible. His goodness again is revealed by Moses as an incentive to love and to obey Him. He cares for the fatherless and loveth the stranger; for this reason they were to love the stranger. Yet far greater is our knowledge of our Lord Jesus Christ, who loveth us and hath washed us from our sins in His own blood and made us priests and kings unto God His Father. And this carries with it a higher obligation to serve Him, to love Him and to walk in obedience, than Israel's obligation.

"Well then, let us ever bear in mind—yea, let us have it deep, deep down in our hearts, that according to our privileges are our obligations. Let us not refuse the wholesome word 'obligation,' as though it had a legal ring about it. Far from it! It would be utterly impossible to conceive any thing further removed from all thought of legality than the obligations which flow out of the Christian's position. It is a very serious mistake to be continually raising the cry of 'Legal! legal!' whenever the holy responsibilities of our position are pressed upon us" (C. H. Mackintosh).

7. Israel's Responsibility, the Blessing and the Curse

CHAPTER 11

1. Therefore thou shalt love the Lord thy God (11:1-9)
2. If ye hearken unto my commandments (11:10-21)
3. The blessing and the curse (11:22-32)

The great characteristic teaching of this book, obedience springing from love to Jehovah, is still further developed in this chapter. It begins with a "therefore." The last verse of the previous chapter shows that Jehovah had kept the promise made to the fathers of the nation. Then once more the mighty acts of Jehovah are reviewed. His miracles and acts done in Egypt; what He did at the Red Sea and what He did unto them in the wilderness—therefore thou shalt love the Lord thy God. They were also to love Him and keep His words in view of the land they were about to possess. What He had done and what He was going to do for them, called for the love and obedience of His people. May we heed the same call. The result of obedience in loving and serving the Lord would be the first and the latter rain, fruitful fields and abundant harvests. Jehovah would also drive out the enemies and give them the land. Blessing and curse are solemnly set before the people by their leader. Of the mount of blessing, Gerizim, and the mount of curse, Ebal, we shall hear more fully later (chapter 17).

(The foolish theory that "latter rain" means a spiritual revival and is a special "outpouring of the Holy Spirit" has no foundation at all in the Word of God. Such "spiritualizing" leads and has led into confusion.)

8. The Place of Worship

CHAPTER 12

1. The overthrow of false worship (12:1-4)
2. The true place of worship (12:5-14)
3. Concerning eating and the blood (12:15-28)
4. Warning against the abominations of idolatry (12:29-32)

The law, and love as the fulfilment of that law, was the main subject of the words of Moses up to the close of the eleventh chapter. The chapters which follow also contain expositions of the different statutes, as well as exhortations to obedience and warnings against departure from Jehovah. How significant that worship occupies the prominent place! A false worship must be completely extirpated, for it would lead their hearts away from the one Jehovah. All images and pillars were to be destroyed. True worship is ever linked with obedience to and love for Jehovah. False worship is apostasy.

The one place is mentioned repeatedly, the place, which Jehovah has appointed for worship (verses 5, 11, 14, 18, 21 and 26). What disobedience if they left that one place and turned somewhere else to worship! The subsequent history of God's ancient people teaches the awful results of such a course. We have in the New Testament also commandments to worship. Our worship is in spirit and in truth. It is not connected with an earthly place, an earthly altar; but we worship in the power of the Spirit in heaven itself, where our forerunner is. But Christendom has a false worship which apes after the ritualistic Jewish worship. In that worship we find also images, holy places, etc., and that is in the sight of God as great an abomination as the Canaanite worship, which Israel found in the promised land.

We do not touch here again upon the eating of flesh, the sanctity of the blood, etc. All this we have had in Leviticus to which we refer the reader. Nor do we enter into the alleged contradictions, which the modern day infidels, in the camp of Christendom, claim exist here. It is but blindness (we fear often wilful blindness), which can bring such criticism and accusations against the Word of God.

9. Warnings Against False Prophets and Their Punishment

CHAPTER 13

1. The first case: The false prophet and dreamer (13:1-5)
2. The second case: Temptation to idolatry from blood-relations (13:6-11)
3. The third case: The apostasy of a city (13:12-18)

Three cases are mentioned. The false prophet or a dreamer of dreams, who confirms his claims by a sign or a miracle, yet whose aim is to seduce to idolatry, is to be put to death. False teaching, which leads from God, is an abomination. It results finally in the most awful moral corruption. A false prophet may do signs and wonders to prove thereby that what he teaches is truth. Signs and miracles are therefore no evidence of the truth. Spiritualism and Christian Science claim to be the truth and they often refer to the evidences of supernatural manifestation and miraculous healings which take place in their cults. Satan can work signs and miracles. He does so in these delusive systems of the last days and God permits it to prove thereby His people. In the light of Matthew 24:23-25, 2 Thess. 2:8-12 and Rev.13:12-14 the first five verses of the chapter we study are of great interest. The false prophet to come, the personal and final Antichrist will do lying wonders and the many who received not the love of the truth will be permitted to believe the lie. One does well to be on the guard whenever teachers claim some special power or signs. The second warning is against a more subtle snare, when the deception worketh secretly, emanating from a blood relation. If it is the dearest one, no pity is to be shown to him. The third case is that, when a whole city has departed from the Lord and serves other gods and practices the abominations of idolatry. It was to be completely destroyed and the city burned with fire. Such will be some day the awful fate of apostate Christendom, having rejected God's Son and the gospel.

10. The Children of God and Their Separation

CHAPTER 14

1. The declaration of relationship: A holy people (14:1-2)
2. Their food as a separated people (14:3-21)
3. Concerning tithes (14:22-29)

Ye are the children of the Lord your God. Because God had chosen them to be a peculiar people unto Himself, above all the other nations, they were to be an holy people. To them belongeth still "the adoption" (Rom. 9:4). God called Israel His firstborn son and that nation holds that place, in the divine purpose, among the nations. Sonship in the New Testament, bestowed upon the individual believer, who is possessed by the Spirit of Sonship (the Holy Spirit) and who is an heir of God and joint-heir with Christ, is infinitely higher, than Israel's national and earthly calling. Therefore our responsibility is so much greater. The children of the Lord were not to participate in the sinful customs of the heathen, who have no hope. No disfigurement as mentioned in the first verse was permitted. The Lord whom they served is a Lord of life; they belonged wholly to Him; they were not their own. To sorrow like those who have no hope is also forbidden in the New Testament (1 Thess. 4:13). Then follows once more the reminder concerning the clean and the unclean. See Leviticus 11 and the annotations. The laws concerning the food Israel was to eat and to abstain from were given in Leviticus to Moses and Aaron; in Deuteronomy the whole congregation hears these instructions. A number of animals are also mentioned in Deuteronomy, which we do not find in Leviticus. Thus their separation is once more emphasized. They belonged to a holy Lord and were to be an holy people. We have for our food the living Bread, which came down from heaven. And as we feed on Christ, abiding in Him, we become also like Him. It has been well said "for a Christian to participate in the vanities and follies of a sinful world would be to use a typical phrase, like an Israelite eating that which had died by itself." How sad the condition of the great majority of those who profess Christianity, who run after this present evil age and are conformed to it!

The tithe mentioned in verses 22-29 is peculiar to Deuteronomy and forms one of the supplementary laws. Israel and the land, they were to possess, belong to Jehovah. The tithe gave expression to the fact of the proprietorship of the Lord. And when they came before Jehovah to eat before Him in the spot where He had placed His Name, they owned in His presence all His goodness and mercies and rejoiced in the Lord. Verses 28 and 29 are more fully developed in chapter 26:12-19. Annotations are given there on the happy scene when, at the end of every third year, the Levite, the stranger, the fatherless and the widow were to eat and be satisfied.

There is a gathering place for His people in the New Testament. "Where two or three are gathered together in My Name there am I in the midst of them." And when we remember His love at His table, we rejoice in Him and He rejoices in us. But the gathering of Israel in connection with the tithe also looks forward to the coming days when there will be a gathering for Israel and the nations. See Isaiah 2:1-4; 11:10; Zech. 14:16-17.

11. The Year of Release and Liberation of Hebrew Slaves

CHAPTER 15:1-18

1. The year of release (15:1-11)
2. The liberation of the Hebrew slaves (15:12-18)

The poor and those who have no possession were to be remembered in kindness and have a share in the blessings. Linked with this law are the laws not to force and oppress the poor, the year of release and the liberation of the slaves. The great Sabbatic year, the seventh, brought the release. See Exodus 23:10 and Leviticus 25:2-7. Here we have an enlarged exposition of the previously given law. The debtor was not to be pressed then for what he owed and nothing was to be exacted from him. While the land rested all debts and obligations had also to rest. It does therefore not mean a complete remission of all debts forever. And linked with this merciful institution is the promise of blessing. Obedience to these gracious laws would bring to them great blessing. Especially interesting is verse 6. "For the Lord thy God blesseth thee, as He promised thee; and thou shalt lend unto many nations, but thou shalt not borrow; and thou shalt reign over many nations, but they shall not reign over thee." Even to-day in their blindness and dispersion this promise is being fulfilled. Who does not know that the Jews are the money lenders of the nations? Kings and princes have borrowed from this wonderful people. Some day when the time of our fulness and blessing comes, this promise will be fully accomplished and Israel will reign over the nations, be the head and no longer the tail.

The poor were also to be treated in great kindness. What grace and love breathes in verses 7-11! Twice we read "thou shalt open thine hand wide." "Thou shalt open thine hand wide unto him, and shalt surely lend him sufficient." "For the poor shall never cease out of the land, therefore, I command thee, saying, Thou shalt open thine hand wide unto thy brother, to thy poor, and to thy needy, in thy land." Throughout the Word of God the poor are mentioned to be remembered in kindness and some most blessed promises are given to those who obey these gracious words. See Proverbs 14:21; 19:17; 22:9; 28:8, 27; Ps. 41:1. Oppression of the poor is a sin, which God specially marks. See Isaiah 3:14, 15; 10:2; Ezek. 18:11-13; Amos 2:6; 4:1; 5:11; James 2:6. When the Lord comes He will remember the poor and deliver them. See Ps. 72:2, 4, 12, 13; 113:7; 132:15; Isaiah 11:4.

The teaching of some, who say that we are not under the law but under grace, and therefore do not need to pay any attention whatever to these gracious words, which Jehovah bound upon the hearts of Israel, is fatally wrong. "Under grace" is often used to cover a selfish life. The grace, which has saved us, which pledges our eternal security in Christ, demands of us that we be followers of God. This is learned from the exhortations of the New Testament. "As we have therefore opportunity, let us do good unto all men, especially unto them who are of the household of faith" (Gal. 6:10). "But to do good and communicate forget not; for which sacrifices God is well pleased" (Heb. 13:16). "The Lord loveth a cheerful giver" because "He giveth to all and upbraideth not." "It is more blessed to give than to receive."

The liberation of the slave is also stated in Exodus 21, to which we refer the reader. The Hebrew woman is mentioned here. In Exodus 21 only the male slave is spoken of. But why is it given here again? Is it a mere repetition? It is not. The Lord gives through Moses the mode in which this law is to be kept. His loving kindness shines out once more in the gracious addition made here. "And when thou sendest him out free, thou shalt not let him go away empty." This verse and verses 14-15 are not found in Exodus 21. How blessedly He cared for the poor slaves. They were set free, laden down with the riches of the flock, the floor and the winepress. Other lessons connected with this we must leave untouched.

12. The Firstlings and the Three Feasts

CHAPTERS 15:19—16:17

1. Concerning the firstlings (15:19-23)
2. Passover (16:1-8)
3. Feast of weeks (16:9-12)
4. Feast of tabernacles (16:13-17)

What is said in the closing verses of chapter 15 is supplementary to the law given concerning the first-born in Exodus 13:2, 12 and Numbers 18. They were not to be worked or sheared. "Before the Lord thy God shalt thou eat it, year after year, in the place which the Lord shall choose, thou and thy household." Nothing which had a blemish, was lame or blind could be sacrificed. The spotless Lamb of God is here in view once more and the type is given how we are to feed on Him in the presence of God, in the sanctuary.

The feasts were mentioned in Exodus 12; Levit. 23; Numb. 28—29. Here only the Passover, the feast of weeks and the feast of tabernacles are given. The critics claim that there is contradiction between this chapter and the laws concerning the feasts in the previous books of the Pentateuch. Such contradiction, however, does not exist. That only these three feasts are mentioned here is in full harmony with the character and message of Deuteronomy.

Obedience, as we have repeatedly learned from the study of past chapters, is the demand of Jehovah from His people. The three prominent feasts were absolutely obligatory. Three times in a year all the males were commanded to appear before the Lord to keep these three feasts. No such demand was made in keeping the feast of trumpets and the day of atonement. Because these three feasts were to be obeyed, they are mentioned in Deuteronomy. The objections of the critics spring (as all other objections and criticisms) from the lack of spiritual discernment. The contradiction they see is only another evidence of the perfection of His Word. "The place, which Jehovah thy God will choose" occurs six times in this chapter. This was not mentioned in Exodus, Leviticus or Numbers. This again is characteristic of the book. Over twenty-five times mention is made of the place which Jehovah will choose, the gathering place of His people in His presence, and this demands obedience. What these feasts mean typically and dispensationally may be learned by consulting the annotations of Leviticus 23. The fact is also to be remembered that they came out of Egypt (verses 3 and 12). They are commanded to rejoice on the feast of weeks (Pentecost) and on the feast of tabernacles (typical of the time of joy and blessing in the coming age); but the statement "thou shalt rejoice" is omitted in connection with Passover. Redemption is typified in that feast. This calls forth gratitude and praise to God. The solemnity of the death of the Lamb of God and the judgment our Lord had to pass through, must be the reason why the command to rejoice is absent.

13. Justice and the Choice of a King

CHAPTERS 16:18—17:20

1. Appointment of judges and their instruction (16:18—17:1)
2. The higher court at the place He chooses (17:8-13)
3. The choice and right of the king (17:14-20)

This chapter leads us upon new ground. The obligations of the religious life of Israel were stated in the first part of chapter 16 and now the government of the people in the land is commanded. "Just as in its religious worship the Israelitish nation was to show itself to be the holy nation of Jehovah, so was it in its political relations also. This thought forms the link between the laws already given and those which follow. Civil order, that indispensable condition of the stability and prosperity of nations and states, rests upon a conscientious maintenance of right, by means of a well-ordered judicial constitution and an impartial administration of justice (F. Delitzsch). Judges and officials were to be appointed and a higher judicial court for more difficult cases to be established, the latter at the place of the sanctuary. Idolatry is prominently mentioned again because it is the most serious matter, both individually and nationally, to forsake the one Jehovah. Apostasy from Jehovah and His covenant is wickedness. Chapter 16:21-22 also has reference to idolatry. The idolatrous altars and images were set up under, or, beside green trees. See 1 Kings 14:23; 2 Kings 17:10; Jerem. 17:2. Then there is provision made for the choice of a king. The Lord foresaw Samuel's time, when the people would reject Him as their King and desire to be like other nations; and foreseeing their failures He made provision for this emergency.

"And yet the wisdom and grace of God are only the more, not the less, conspicuous in this provision. True, of Saul it was said, 'I gave thee a king in Mine anger, and took him away in My wrath' (Hos. 13:11). But this only brings out God's real choice—David, 'the beloved,' type of One who is indeed that, and in whom a King is found who reigns forever. He is the One of whom the king that Deuteronomy announces is the shadow. Brought forth when priesthood has failed in Eli, and prophet in Samuel, the true king is God's resource for Israel and the earth. For neither priesthood nor prophecy alone will set right the earth, or bring in the time when it shall be filled with the glory of the Lord. He must come to whom the throne belongs, and who shall bring back judgment to righteousness; He in whom Prophet, Priest, and King are one,—a threefold cord that never shall be broken" (*Numerical Bible*).

A comparison of verse 16 and 17 with 1 Kings 9-11 is most interesting. What failure man is in himself! And Solomon was the wisest and most influential of all the kings. This fact that Solomon did the very opposite from what the king should do has led the critics to say that this passage was written after Solomon. As if God did not know all this beforehand! But there is not allusion to Solomon's kingdom at all in the words Moses spoke.

14. The Rights of the Priests and the Levites, the True and the False Prophet

CHAPTER 18

1. The rights of the priests and Levites (18:1-8)
2. Forbidden things (18:9-14)
3. The true and the false prophet (18:15-22)

The priests, the Levites, were the servants of Jehovah and had no inheritance with Israel, but Jehovah Himself was their inheritance. How the people were to minister unto them is now commanded by Moses. They were both dependent on the Lord and closely identified with Him. And this is true of us, who are in Christ constituted priests and called to the Levite service.

Of great interest are verses 9-14. The nations who possessed the land practised evil things, through which Satan manifested his awful power to lead astray and to corrupt. His people were to beware of these things. We, too, are warned not to intrude into those things which we have not seen (Col. 2:18). Moses puts together the words which the language contained for the different modes of finding out the future and discovering the will of God. Passing a son or daughter through the fire, the awful Moloch service, is forbidden once more (Levit. 18:21).

Then follow all the abominable things. There are seven of them mentioned, which come under the term "divination": 1. Observer of times, predicting good or bad things by observation of the heavens and circumstances; 2. Enchanter. The Hebrew word is *menachesh* connected with *nachash* the Hebrew word for serpent. It means one who murmurs enchantments; 3. Witch; 4. Charmer; 5. A consulter with familiar spirits; 6. A wizard, who has access to an unlawful wisdom; 7. The necromancer, who asks the dead. These abominations existed then and they exist to-day. Clairvoyancy, palmistry, astrology, soothsaying, fortune-telling, spiritualistic seances, theosophy, the formulas and treatments of "Christian Science" are a few of the modern names of this ancient demonism. It is awful to see their growth as the end draws near. What is claimed to be "psychical research," studying "occult phenomena," is nothing less than stepping upon the same territory of evil. And Satan uses these wicked things, his familiar spirits, and asking the dead to prepare the way for the great delusion of the end, with its signs and lying wonders. Spiritualism with its demon-possessed mediums, psychical research, theosophy, Christian Science, are Satan-cults. They are an abomination to Jehovah and His righteous judgment will soon fall upon them. We add here the solemn warning of another.

I take this opportunity of solemnly warning every soul—more particularly the young—from levity in hankering after that which they do not understand, and very especially in the way of giving up their will to any but the Lord Jesus. This is the essential point of danger. I do not raise the smallest doubt that there are powers in the natural world which lie quite beyond the explanation of men. It is not my wish therefore to excite a kind of hue and cry against that which may not be yet explained. Let us avoid the presumption of supposing that we can account for everything. But in our ignorance (which the wisest most feel and own) this wisdom at least ought to belong to the least of God's children, that they know in whom they believe, and they have His word and His Spirit, and can count on infinite love and power as well as wisdom on their behalf. They can well afford therefore to leave what is beyond themselves or any others in the hands of God their Father. They with sorrow see others rush in who have nothing higher, who have no God to count on or look to. But above all beware. Whenever any one asks you to give up your mind or will to another—were it but for a moment—there is the evident hand of the devil in it. *This* is no question of physical powers, or of what is naturally inexplicable. What is behind giving up yourself, your will, to any one but God, is plain enough in its character and consequences; it is too easy to understand it. The divine axiom is that the Lord and He alone has a right to you. Consequently such a demand proves that Satan is taking advantage, it may be of what is natural, but certainly of you (W. Kelly).

The Prophet promised in verse 15 is the Lord Jesus Christ. Acts 3:22-23 refers us to this prophecy. Acts 7:37 also confirms the fulfilment of Moses' prediction in the person of Christ.

15. Laws for Israel in the Land

CHAPTER 19

1. Concerning the cities of refuge (19:1-13)
2. Removing a landmark (19:14)
3. The punishment of a false witness (19:15-21)

Here again we have not a repetition of the previous law concerning the cities of refuge (Numb. 35:9-34), but an earnest admonition to be obedient to those laws. The three cities on the east of Jordan were named in chapter 4. Here the other three in the midst of the land are in view. They were to be in a place of easy access with a prepared way leading to them. Grace and judgment are illustrated in the case of the slayer, who killed his neighbor ignorantly and he who killed his neighbor purposely. When the slayer reached the city he found a shelter there and lived, for he had done it ignorantly. Grace gave him shelter and he knew he was safe. For the wilful murderer there was no mercy, but judgment. "Thine eyes shall not pity him." Obedience was demanded in all these utterances of Moses.

16. Concerning Future Wars

CHAPTER 20

1. Words of encouragement (20:1-4)
2. The fearful and faint-hearted (20:5-9)
3. Concerning seiges (20:10-20)

In the appointed warfare there was no need to fear the enemies. The priest was commissioned to speak words of encouragement not to fear, nor to tremble, nor to be terrified by the horses and chariots. The divine assurance was threefold: Jehovah goeth with you, to fight for you, to *save* you. This presupposes their obedience. If they were obedient, they had nothing to fear. Victory was on their side. And we too need to fear nothing in our warfare with the wicked spirits (Eph. 6). The Lord is on our side and if we resist the devil he will flee from us.

But if Israel was disobedient and departed from the Lord, He fought against them and their enemies overcame them. See also Zech. 14:3 about the time when Jehovah will overcome the nations who gather against Jerusalem at the close of the age. The faint-hearted and the fearful as well as those who might hanker after their possessions and become homesick were not to go into the battlefield. They were unfit for warfare, because they did not wholly trust in Jehovah. There was a most merciful arrangement, which consisted in an offer of peace to a besieged city. (The cities of the Canaanitish nations are not included.) Peace was the first thing proclaimed. If the offer was accepted the lives of the inhabitants were saved. If not and the people resisted the proclamation of peace and therefore showed the wickedness of their hearts, resisting God, the city was besieged. All the males were to be smitten with the sword, but the women and little ones were saved. It was different with the wicked inhabitants of the land. Their utter destruction was demanded. The reason for this is again stated in verse 18. The fruit trees during a siege were not to be cut down, for they sustained life.

17. The Expiation of an Uncertain Murder and Various Instructions

CHAPTER 21

1. The expiation of an unknown murder (21:1-9)
2. Concerning a wife, who had been a prisoner of war (21:10-14)
3. The right of the firstborn (21:15-17)
4. The punishment of a rebellious son (21:18-21)
5. The burial of one who hanged on a tree (21:22-23)

The expiation of an unknown murder seems to find an interesting application in the case of the nation itself. Bloodguiltiness is upon them for they cried "His blood be upon us and upon our children." And the nation has suffered as the result of it. But there is a full expiation coming through Him who prayed for them on the cross, "Father, forgive them for they know not what they do." He died for them as the heifer (the type of Christ) died in the rough valley (the type of His deep humiliation) for the unknown murder. Then the prayer in verse 8 will be graciously answered, when Israel turns to the Lord in the day of His manifestation. "Be merciful, O Lord, unto Thy people Israel, whom Thou hast redeemed, and lay not innocent blood unto Thy people of Israel's charge. And the blood shall be forgiven them."

The woman captive desired by an Israelite for wife could not be one of the Canaanitish races for they were to be all slain; but other Gentiles are meant. She was to be mercifully protected. Polygamy is taken in consideration in verses 15-17 and a law is given in view of it to guard against an abuse in favor of a beloved wife. The son of the hated wife, if he is the firstborn, cannot be defrauded of his birthright; he must receive the double portion. If we look deeper we shall find here too the dispensational lesson concerning Israel's relation to Jehovah. Israel has been the unfaithful wife, but she will be reinstated in due time and receive the blessing promised unto her.

The stubborn and rebellious son, who is to be stoned to death, is but another type of the finally disobedient in Israel. While in the future the penitent and believing remnant of Israel will be reinstated in Jehovah's favor and inherit the glorious things promised to them, the apostate part of that nation, going on in self-will and rebellion, will be cut off in judgment. The prophetic Word predicts such a stubborn and rebellious condition among the great mass of that people before the Lord comes. But the same judgment also falls upon the rebellious, disobedient among the Gentiles, those who profess to be children of God, but their disobedience shows that they are not.

The close of this remarkable chapter plainly refers to our blessed Lord and His work on the cross. Galatians 3:13 quotes verse 23 and applies it to the Lord Jesus.

18. Against Inhumanity and Different Violations, False Testimony and Sins of Adultery

CHAPTER 22

1. Laws against inhumanity (22:1-12)
2. Concerning false testimony (22:13-21)
3. Sins of adultery (22:22-30)

Laws on the second table are now more fully expounded by Moses. The love to the neighbor is to be expressed by guarding and preserving that which is his property. The strayed and fallen animal belonging to another had to be helped. To leave them in that condition would have been a violation of the law "love thy neighbor as thyself" as well as an act of inhumanity.

Another interesting law is the one which forbids woman to wear man's garments (verse 5). "The immediate design of this prohibition was not to prevent licentiousness, or to oppose idolatrous practices; but to maintain the sanctity of that distinction of the sexes, which was established by the creation of man and woman, and in relation to which Israel was not to sin. Every violation or wiping out of this distinction —such as even the emancipation of women— was unnatural, and therefore "an abomination in the sight of God." Yet to-day we find a universal movement in the world for the complete emancipation of women, which ignores and even defies the place which the Creator and the Redeemer has given to woman.

The law concerning the bird's nest manifests the Creator's care and His people are to recognize it. The keeping of this law has the same promise as the commandment relating to obedience to parents. Diverse seeds were forbidden. Spiritually we find a lesson here. There are two seeds, the good and the bad. The good seed stands for the truth. It must not be mixed with error. The truth must be kept unmixed. The opposite is done to-day as never before in the history of Christendom. They were not to plow with an ass and an ox together. They were not to wear a mixed garment. And we are exhorted not to be unequally yoked with unbelievers, but be separated in our habits, in life and walk, unto the Lord. The concluding part of the chapter reveals the heart of man in its deceitfulness and corruption.

19. The Congregation of Jehovah and Its Constitution and Holiness

CHAPTER 23

1. The constitution of the congregation of Jehovah (23:1-8)
2. The cleanness of the camp in time of war (23:9-14)
3. Concerning the escaped slave and the harlot (23:15-18)
4. Usury forbidden (23:19-20)
5. Concerning vows (23:21-23)
6. The neighbor's vineyard and field (23:24-25)

The congregation of Israel is called in this chapter "the congregation of Jehovah." And because it was the congregation of Jehovah, all that is unclean and which defiles had to be kept out of it. The same principle applies to the New Testament assembly, which is called the Church of God. Only those who are born again and therefore clean have a right to belong to the church.

(The following interesting typical meaning of verses 1-8 is taken from the *Numerical Bible*:

> First, then, we have the assembly in its refusal of all discordant elements; and here the exclusion of the unsexed male is based on the need of maintaining the integrity of the creature. Mutilation was a reproach to God; and thus the whole spirit of asceticism is condemned and excluded both for Israel and for us to-day. The word of "bastard," "one born of corruption," only occurs once beside in Zech. 9:6, is explained by the Rabbins, and received by commentators in general as meaning "one born of incest or adultery." Typically, one corruptly born is not the mere child of nature; but rather one corruptly introduced among the people of God. "Baptismal regeneration," as the ritualist holds it, is such a birth; and the Moabite and the Ammonite following here emphasizes this thought, though it be true that they are not distinctly reprobated for their birth, but for their enmity to the true people of God, and their employment of Balaam to curse. But even thus does the false professor, like an Ammonite or a Moabite, show his birth to-day. The Edomite is the simple natural man, and for him there is more hope, and the Egyptian is classed with him, though only in the third generation (dead and risen with Christ) could they enter the congregation of the Lord.

Cleanness and purity had to be preserved in Israel's camp. They were constantly to remember "Jehovah thy God walketh in the midst of thy camp . . . therefore shall thy camp be holy; that He see no unclean thing in thee, andurn not away from thee." All uncleanness and uncleanliness of the body was considered for this reason an evil thing. The Lord gave even such instructions as these, because He wanted His people to be clean and separated unto Himself. And how it behooves us to take heed to all these things. Jehovah is not alone with us, in the midst of His people, but God the Holy Spirit has made our bodies His temples. "What! Know ye not that your body is a temple of the Holy Spirit, who is in you, whom ye have from God, and ye are not your own? For ye were bought with a price, *therefore glorify God in your body*" (1 Cor. 6:19-20).

And how beautiful it is that the poor, escaped slave found in the congregation of Jehovah a refuge! He was not to be oppressed. But the Israelites, who practised the abominable things of the flesh under a religious garb (verse 17) were an abomination unto the Lord.

Verses 24 and 25 prove that Jehovah is the owner of the land and He invited the hungry one to satisfy his hunger, to be His guest, so to speak. But the right of the tenant of the land was also respected. See on plucking the ears of corn (Matthew 12:1; Luke 6:1).

20. Concerning Divorce and Laws of Mercy

CHAPTER 24

1. Concerning divorce (24:1-5)
2. Concerning pledge and slavery (24:6-7)
3. Concerning leprosy (24:8-9)
4. Concerning the oppression of the poor (24:10-15)
5. Concerning injustice (24:16-18)
6. The stranger, the fatherless and the widow remembered (24:19-22)

Matthew 19:1-9 must be studied with the words of Moses on divorce. The Pharisees asked the Lord "why then did Moses then command to give a writing of divorcement, and to put her away?" But they erred when they called Moses' word a commandment. It was only something which Moses allowed. Adultery according to the law was punishable with death. "He saith unto them, Moses, because of the hardness of your hearts, suffered you to put away your wives; but from the beginning it was not so. And I say unto you, Whosoever shall put away his wife except it be for fornication, and shall marry another, committeth adultery; and whosoever marrieth her that is put away doth commit adultery."

No part of the handmill, the millstone, was to be taken as a pledge, for that would have deprived the person of the necessary instrument in the preparation of food. Manstealing was forbidden under penalty of death (Ex. 21:16).

Merciful are the laws found in verses 10-15. If these laws were obeyed how many questions would be solved and how much injustice would be abolished. See also James 5:4. Mercy was to be shown to the poor in remembrance of their former condition in Egypt.

21. Various Laws and Responsibilities

CHAPTER 25

1. Corporal punishment (25:1-3)
2. Thou shalt not muzzle the ox (25:4)
3. The brother-in-law's marriage (25:5-10)
4. Concerning a sinful freedom (25:11-12)
5. Concerning divers weights and measures (25:13-16)
6. Concerning the conquest of Amalek (25:17-19)

Corporal punishment is mentioned in the first paragraph of this chapter. But this also was tempered with mercy. Not more than forty stripes were to be administered in the presence of the judge. The rabbinical instructions put the limit at thirty-nine—"forty save one." Five times our blessed apostle Paul was punished in this manner, for we read, "Of the Jews five times received I forty stripes, save one" (2 Cor. 11:24).

In comparison with the cruel beatings and tortures so universally found among the Gentile races the law concerning corporal punishment appears very merciful. The chastisement was not to be severer than it could be endured. It speaks typically also of the chastisement His people have to undergo.

The ox was not to be muzzled when he treaded out the corn.

"Who goeth a warfare any time at his own charges? who planteth a vineyard, and eateth not of the fruit thereof? or who feedeth a flock, and eateth not of the milk of the flock? Say I these things as a man? or saith not the law the same also? For it is written in the law of Moses, Thou shalt not muzzle the mouth of the ox that treadeth out the corn. Doth God take care for oxen? Or saith He *it* altogether for our sakes? For our sakes, no doubt, *this* is written: that he that ploweth should plow in hope; and that he that thresheth in hope should be partaker of his hope" (1 Cor. 9:7-10).

"For the Scripture saith, Thou shalt not muzzle the ox that treadeth out the corn. And, the laborer is worthy of his reward" (1 Tim. 5:18). These are most blessed comments on this verse, which otherwise would be rather obscure. The toiling ox is the type of the servant and his ministry. And this has its rewards.

The commandment given by Moses, that a surviving brother is to marry his brother's widow is seen in its working in the story of Ruth and the kinsman—redeemer. The law itself was founded upon an old traditional custom, which we find already in Genesis 38:8-11. Moses here recognized this custom was not to be considered compulsory.[4]

[4]"The taking off of the shoe was an ancient custom also, adopted, according to Ruth 4:7, in cases of redemption and exchange, for the purpose of confirming commercial transactions. The usage arose from the fact, that when any one took possession of landed property, he did so by treading upon the soil, and asserting his right of possession by standing upon it in his shoes. In this way the taking off of the shoe and handing it to another became a symbol of the renunciation of a man's position and property."

And Amalek was to be remembered, Amalek, who feared not God. When Israel had rest in the land and all the other enemies were conquered, then the remembrance of Amalek was to be completely blotted out. As we saw from our annotations in Exodus Amalek typifies the flesh, while Egypt is the type of the world. The complete perishing of Amalek is seen in Balaam's parables. When the sceptre rises out of Israel (the second coming of Christ), when He comes that shall have dominion, then Amalek shall perish forever (Numb. 24:20). When we are indeed in the land and possess our inheritance, when all our enemies are gone, then the remembrance of Amalek, the old flesh, will be blotted out forever.

22. Firstfruits and Prayer

CHAPTER 26

1. The basket of first-fruits, confession and rejoicing (26:1-11)
2. Obedience yielded and prayer (26:12-15)
3. Jehovah acknowledges His people (26:16-19)

The possession of the land is anticipated and a most beautiful ceremony is appointed for confession and worship in the place the Lord chose to place His Name there. The first of all the fruit of the land was to be gathered and put in a basket. This basket was presented unto the priest with the following words: "I profess this day unto the Lord thy God, that I am come unto the country which the Lord sware unto our fathers for to give us." The priest then set it down before the altar. It was an acknowledgment of His Grace and His faithfulness in keeping His promise and bringing them into the land. The Lord had brought them in and the basket of fruits witnessed to the fact that they possessed the good things promised unto them. They could truly say, the Lord kept His Word, He promised us this land and now we are in it; it is ours. And we know, as saved by grace and in Christ, that we are blessed with every spiritual blessing in the heavenlies. We too are brought in and have the right of access into His presence. And this blessed consciousness that we are redeemed and belong to Christ is essential to true worship in spirit and in truth.

Most beautiful is the confession Moses gave to Israel, to be used when the basket of firstfruits was set before Jehovah. "A Syrian ready to perish was my father." Lovely words! They brought to remembrance what they were and the grace which Jehovah manifested, when that Syrian ready to perish was called out. And this is but a picture of what we are by nature, "ready to perish." Then comes the story of Egypt and their deliverance out of the house of bondage. Even so we are delivered. They were to rejoice in every good thing the Lord had given unto them; and we rejoice in the Lord and all His goodness to us. And this joy was practically expressed in giving to the Levite, the stranger, the fatherless, the widow; they ate and were filled. Thus they could tell Jehovah, "I have not transgressed Thy commandments, neither have I forgotten them." While we rejoice in the Lord, know that we are saved and worship in the spirit, may we also remember that it is written, "But to do good and to communicate forget not; for with such sacrifices God is well pleased." How often we forget this! Yet it must ever be an outflow from true worship.

23. The Memorial of the Law at Mount Ebal; Gerizim and Ebal

CHAPTER 27

1. The memorial to be set up in the land (27:1-8)
2. Gerizim and Ebal (27:9-26)

Little comment is needed on this chapter. The memorial stones were to be set up on Mount Ebal. Upon that mountain the curses of the law were to be uttered. The blessings were to be pronounced upon Mount Gerizim. However, on Gerizim were no stones with the law written upon it. How strikingly this illustrates the true ministration of the law! It cannot give blessing, but it must curse man. "For as many as are of the works of the law are under the curse; for it is written, Cursed is every one that continueth not in all things which are written in the book of the law to do them" (Gal. 3:10). Then the tribes are divided to stand upon Gerizim to bless and upon Ebal to curse. But where are there words of blessing in connection with Gerizim? Not one. The law cannot give blessing. But the word "cursed" we find twelve times in this chapter. What a confirmation that the law holds out no blessing for man, but can do nothing but curse. But, blessed be God! upon Mount Ebal there stood not alone the great stones with plaster, with the words of the law upon them, but there was also an altar unto Jehovah, for burnt offerings and for peace offerings, for rejoicing before the Lord. And this speaks of Christ, who has redeemed us from the curse of the law.

24. The Blessing and the Curse

1. The blessing promised (28:1-14)
2. The curse announced (28:15-68)

This is one of the most solemn chapters in the Pentateuch. Orthodox Hebrews read in their synagogues each year through the entire five books of Moses. When they read this chapter, the Rabbi reads in a subdued voice. And well may they read it softly and ponder over it, for here is prewritten the sad and sorrowful history of that wonderful nation. Here thousands of years ago the Spirit of God through Moses outlined the history of the scattered nation, all their suffering and tribulations, as it has been for well nigh two millenniums and as it is still. Here are arguments for the divine, the supernatural origin of this book which no infidel has ever been able to answer; nor will there ever be found an answer.

It would take a great many pages to follow the different predictions and show their literal fulfilment in the nation, which turned away from Jehovah and disobeyed His Word. What a warning this chapter is to Gentile Christendom! "If God spared not the natural branches, take heed lest He also spare not thee" (Rom. 11:21).

Apart from such general predictions as found in verses 64-66 and fulfilled, as everybody knows, in the dispersion of Israel, there are others, which are more minute. The Roman power, which was used to break the Jews, is clearly predicted by Moses, and that in a time when no such power existed. Read verses 49-50. "The Lord shall bring a nation against thee from far, from the end of the earth, as swift as the *eagle* flieth, a nation, whose language thou shalt not understand." The eagle was the standard of the Roman armies; the Jews understood many oriental languages, but were ignorant of Latin. "Which shall not regard the person of the old, nor show favor to the young." Rome killed the old people and the children. "And he shall beseige thee in all thy gates, until thy high and fenced walls come down, wherein thou trustedst, throughout all thy land" (verse 52). Fulfilled in the siege and overthrow of Jerusalem by the Roman legions. "The tender and delicate woman among you, which would not adventure to set the sole of her foot upon the ground for delicateness and tenderness, shall eat their children, for want of all things in the siege and straitness wherewith thine enemy shall distress thee in thy gates" (54-57). Fulfilled in the dreadful sieges of Jerusalem, perhaps the most terrible events in the history of blood and tears of this poor earth. Every verse beginning with the fifteenth to the end of this chapter has found its oft repeated fulfilment. It does not surprise us that the enemy hates this book, which bears such a testimony, and would have it classed with legends.

25. The Repetition of the Covenant and the Repetition of the Curse

CHAPTER 29

1. The repetition of the covenant (29:1-15)
2. The repetition of the curse (29:16-29)

The words of the covenant are once more brought to their remembrance. Once more all the goodness of the Lord towards them is unfolded by Moses, how the Lord had dealt with Egypt and how their eyes had seen the signs and great miracles. (Verses 5 and 6 are the direct words of Jehovah, ending with the declaration, "I am the Lord, your God.") Again the forty years are mentioned, during which their clothes and their shoes did not get old. God took care of them and provided for their needs in the wilderness. Bread from heaven was their portion and therefore they had no need of stimulants, such as wine and strong drink (verse 6). But in the midst of these words, calling to remembrance the goodness and faithfulness of the Lord, we find a solemn statement: "Yet the Lord hath not given you an heart to perceive, and eyes to see, and ears to hear, unto this day" (verse 4). In all the manifestations they had remained without understanding and their heart was not touched and broken down. Therefore these gracious dealings are here repeated, that they might receive understanding and love and obey the Lord with all their heart. But they were a stiffnecked people, their heart of stone. How fully Israel's history illustrates the words of our Lord, "that which is born of the flesh is flesh!" Later, when Israel went deeper and deeper into apostasy, Isaiah received the message, "Hear ye indeed, but understand not; and see ye indeed and perceive not. Make the heart of this people fat and make their ears heavy, and shut their eyes, lest they see with their eyes and hear with their ears and understand with their heart, and convert and be healed" (Is. 6:9-10). Judicial blindness came upon them when they rejected the Lord of Glory (Matt. 13:14-15; John 7:40; Acts 28:26-27). See also Stephen's testimony given in the power of the Holy Spirit (Acts 7:51-52). But a day is coming when there will be for that nation a New Testament (Jer. 31:31-34; Heb. 8:7-11). Then Ezekiel 36:24-31 will be fulfilled. A careful reading of these passages will be helpful.

Here the Lord reminded them of what He had done for them to show them the claim He has on their obedience. "Keep therefore the words of this covenant, and do them, that ye may prosper in all ye do."

After an earnest appeal to enter into the covenant, including the little ones, the stranger, the hewer of the wood and the water-carrier (Josh. 9:21, 27), we find the curse mentioned once more as the result of departure from the Lord. Especially interesting are verses 22-24. Such evil is to come upon them and upon the land, that "the stranger that shall come from a far land, shall say, when they see the plagues of that land, and the sickness which the Lord has laid upon it . . . even all nations shall say, Wherefore hath the Lord done thus unto this land? What meaneth the heat of this great anger?" Strangers from far lands, tourists and pilgrims, have visited Palestine in fulfilment of this prediction and in view of the deplorable condition of that land have often asked these questions and known their answer. "Then men shall say, Because they have forsaken the covenant of the Lord God of their fathers, which He made with them, when He brought them forth out of the land of Egypt."

26. The Dispersion, the Return and the Final Appeal

CHAPTER 30

1. The message of hope (30:1-10)
2. The final appeal (30:11-20)

These things, which Moses spoke into the ears of the people were to come to pass. And they have been fulfilled. The people Israel are scattered among all the nations, and yet they have not been assimilated by the nations. They are kept as a separate people. Connected with the prediction of their dispersion is the message of hope, the prophecy relating to their return. The Lord promises, that if they return unto Him and obey His voice, that He will return unto them. "Then the Lord thy God will turn thy captivity, and have compassion upon thee, and will return and gather thee from all the nations, whither the Lord thy God hath scattered thee" (verse 3). That will come to pass when this present age closes. Then when the greatest trouble, the time of Jacob's trouble is upon them (Matt. 24) they will return. The Lord Himself will return, as announced in the above verse, and gather them from all the nations. He will bring them back into their land; they will possess it once more. Spiritual blessings will also come upon them and upon their children. Earthly blessings will be multiplied unto them and the Lord will rejoice over them, because they are a converted, an obedient people. God's gifts and calling, which are without repentance, will then be fully accomplished in that nation. "Behold I will gather them out of all countries, whither I have driven them in mine anger, and in my fury, and in great wrath; and I will bring them again unto this place, and I will cause them to dwell safely. And they shall be my people and I will be their God" (Jer. 32:37-38). "For I will take you from among the nations, and gather you out of all countries, and will bring you into your own land" (Ezek. 36:24). Many more passages might be added from other portions of the prophetic Word. Moses, the prophet, speaks of that which all the other prophets after him have restated, confirmed, and enlarged. Israel's present condition, dispersed among the nations of the earth, is not permanent. God will bring them back and keep all the promises of blessing. How wonderful are some of the visions of glory relating to the time, when this will be accomplished. Read Isaiah 24; 60; 61; 62, etc.; these magnificent promises of blessing are not for a spiritual Israel, as people sometimes term the church, but for the literal Israel. Some say, the return predicted by Moses and the other prophets was fulfilled when a remnant of Jews came back from Babylon. This is incorrect for neither were the people scattered among all the nations, nor did the small remnant, which came back from the Babylonian captivity, enjoy the glories and blessings predicted in the prophetic Word. Another return will take place, when their once rejected King comes back. The Old Testament is practically a sealed book to every person who does not believe in a literal restoration of Israel to their land.

The final appeal of Moses as given in the

second part of this chapter, has for its leading note "obedience," the characteristic word of this entire book. Notice in the last verse the significant statement, that the Lord, who is to be loved and whose voice is to be obeyed, is their life. "For He is thy life."

III. The Final Words of Moses and the Vision of the Future

1. Moses' Final Charge, The Written Law Delivered, and Jehovah's Word to Moses

CHAPTER 31

1. The final charge of Moses (31:1-8)
2. The written law delivered (31:9-13)
3. Jehovah's word to Moses—Moses to Joshua (31:14-23)
4. A prophecy (31:24-30)

The final words of Moses to the people are full of tenderness and affection. There he stood, an hundred and twenty years old, a witness to the grace of His God. His eye was still the eye of youth, for it knew no dimness. And his frame was not bowed down by old age; there was no sign of feebleness about him (34:7). The words "I can no more go out and come in" are not in clash with the statement about his physical condition. He knew that he had to die because the Lord had told him so. He encouraged the people to trust in the Lord and assured them that the Lord would give them victory. "He it is who doth go with thee; He will not fail thee nor forsake thee." Precious words these! And the same Jehovah is on our side, never to leave nor forsake His people. May we walk in the obedience of faith and find that His promise is true. Then followed an impressive scene. Joshua is called and in the sight of all Israel Moses addressed him. Joshua would bring them into the land. The same words given to Moses by the Lord to address to Joshua were spoken again to Joshua by the Lord Himself (Josh. 1).

The law, which Moses had written was next delivered unto the Levites. "Moses wrote this law." Could there be a more emphatic statement than this! And this declaration that Moses wrote this law is confirmed by our Lord, the same Lord who spoke to Moses and whose words and laws Moses committed to writing. The denial of the Mosiac authorship includes the denial of the infallibility of the Son of God. It is infidelity. The infidels of the past ridiculed the teaching that Moses wrote the five books of the law. The infidels of Christendom do now the same. And this law was to be read before all Israel at the feast of tabernacles. They were to be dependent upon the Word of God and learn, fear, and obey by reading and hearing it. Our dependence is the same. Apart from believing and obeying the Word, spiritual life, walking in the Spirit, in fellowship with God, is impossible.

Then the Lord appeared in the tabernacle in a pillar of cloud, when Moses and Joshua presented themselves in the tabernacle of the congregation. The omniscient One, who knows everything from the beginning, announced the failure and apostasy of the nation, with whom He had dealt in such marvellous kindness, and who had been the witnesses of His power and glory. They would break the covenant and apostatize. He would forsake them also, because they turned away from Him to go a whoring after other gods. He would hide His face. All the predicted and threatened evils and troubles would come upon them. And their past, as well as present history, proves the solemn truth of these divine words. And there is one more chapter of their shameful history to be written. "The great tribulation" is still future. It will sweep over them in the days when the apostate nation will accept the false messiah, the Anti-christ, he who comes in his own name.

And Jehovah was to give Moses a song, which he was to teach Israel. The song is found in the chapter which follows. It has for its foundation the words of the Lord in verses 16-21. And Moses was obedient and wrote the same day and taught it to the children of Israel. It was a witness against them. It is so to-day. How striking that they should read this great final book of the law, read their own curses, their own history, past, present and future, and still abide in unbelief!

The parallel with the church is easy to recognize. Apostasy and failure were predicted for the latter days of the church on earth; that prediction was made in the very beginning of the church. How abundantly it has found its fulfillment! Compare Moses' words in verse 29 with the words of Paul, the apostle to the Gentiles, in Acts 20:29-30.

2. The Song of Moses

CHAPTER 32:1-43

1. The introduction and the theme (32:1-4)
2. The foolish people (32:5-6)
3. How Jehovah loved them (32:7-14)

4. Their apostasy (32:15-18)
5. The results of the apostasy (32:19-33)
6. Jehovah's final dealing with Israel (32:34-42)
7. The glorious consummation (32:43)

The song of Moses is a great prophecy. The first great prophetic utterance is found in the parables of Balaam. The second prophetic discourse is this song. The song of Moses embraces the entire history of Israel, past, present and future. It bears in a most remarkable way every mark of being a prophetic testimony from the inspired leader of God's people. The men, who deny this and who boast of literary ability, must be wilfully blind. The critics have denied to a man, that Moses wrote a single word of this song. But they have not informed us who wrote this wonderful ode. "The assertion that the entire ode moves within the epoch of the kings, who lived many centuries after the time of Moses, rests upon a total misapprehension of the nature of prophecy" (Keil).

Moses began his song by calling heaven and earth to hear the words of his mouth. What he was about to say concerned indeed heaven and earth. Isaiah too began his book with the same call (Isa. 1:2). The name of Jehovah is exalted. He is the Rock and His work is perfect. He is a God of truth, just and right. But His people, what are they? Their character is described in verses 5 and 6. How He uncovers the true nature of the people, who had acknowledged Him as Jehovah! Corrupt, perverse, crooked, foolish, unwise, are the terms used to describe their character. The failure they would be, their apostasy and the necessity of disciplinary dealings of Jehovah with them, are thus mentioned in the first stanza of this song.

The third section, verses 7-14, reveals the goodness and the love of the Lord for them. The eighth verse has a deep meaning. "When the Most High divided to the nations their inheritance, when He separated the sons of Adam, He set the bounds of the people according to the number of the children of Israel." This verse carries us backward. The boundaries of the nations were made by God with a direct reference to the children of Israel. The name of God used here, "the Most High," is the millennial title, which He will have when His blessed Son our Lord receives His Kingdom. (See Genesis 14:19.) When that time of blessing comes and Israel converted is no longer the tail but the head of the nations, this divine division will then be fully made known. And how they are reminded again what Jehovah did for them! "He found him, He led him, instructed and kept him." Verses 9-14 are wonderful words. And they apply to us spiritually as they described Jehovah's goodness to Israel.

But how great is the contrast when we reach the fourth section of this prophetic song? (See verses 15-18.) The first step in their apostasy is the forsaking of God and the worshipping of false gods. The next step is, they "lightly esteemed the rock of His salvation." No doubt this latter statement refers to the rejection of the son of God, when He appeared in the midst of His people.

The awful consequences of this rejection are seen prophetically. Here again we have history prewritten. But these predictions were so minutely fulfilled, the unbelieving heart of man refuses to accept these words as being the words of Moses. Here again we have a striking evidence of inspiration. God foretells through Moses the future of an apostate people. Compare verse 21 with Romans 10:19 and 11:10-11. The call of the Gentiles is anticipated in Moses' song; salvation came to us Gentiles by their fall. It seems almost as if they are going to perish completely as a nation. But the song changes suddenly. Jehovah will yet arise in their behalf. It will be in a time when their power is gone, when they are helpless and their enemies press down upon them as never before in their long, dark night of suffering and tears. That will happen in the end of this present age, during the predicted time of great trouble, which is to come upon them. Compare verse 39 with Hosea 5:15—6:3. The judgment, which is announced by Moses in verses 40-42 is the judgment which will fall upon Gentile nations in the day when the Lord appears in His glory. To follow this throughout the entire prophetic Word is as helpful as it is interesting.

The last verse of this song (verse 43) shows the glorious consummation. After the storm of judgment and indignation, peace will come to this earth. The nations will learn war no more; they will learn righteousness. Then the world will be converted. The Lord will be merciful unto His land and to His people. The blessings and glories promised to Israel have come. Therefore the nations will rejoice with His people. The song of Moses is the key to all prophecy.

3. The Blessing of Moses

CHAPTERS 32:44—33:29

1. Introduction (32:44-52)

2. Jehovah's manifestation (33:1-5)
3. The blessing of Reuben, Judah and Levi (33:12-17)
4. The blessing of Benjamin and Joseph (33:12-17)
5. The blessing of Zebulon and Issachar (33:18-19)
6. The blessing of Gad, Dan, Nephtali and Asher (33:20-25)
7. Happy art thou, O Israel! (33:26-29)

Moses and Joshua (same as Hoshea) spoke the song in the ears of the people. They had to learn it. He exhorts them once more to set their hearts to do all these words. "It is not a vain thing for you; because it is your life." But they could not keep the law and therefore could not obtain life and the blessing promised to them. The law cannot bestow life and blessing. It can only curse. But grace gives life. To illustrate this very fact, that the law is for condemnation, the death of Moses is once more announced by Jehovah, as well as his sin at Meribah-Kadesh. He could see the land from afar, but could not enter in. The great man through whom the law was given, the humble Moses, the self-sacrificing, faithful servant of Jehovah, on account of the one transgression, was excluded from the possession of the land.

In the foreground of Moses' prophetic blessing of the tribes stands a description of the manifestation of Jehovah in His glory. This theophany is more than a description of how Jehovah came from Sinai. It is a prophetic picture of how He will come again. Compare this with Habakkuk 3. The blessing of the tribes is different from the blessing which Jacob put upon his sons when they gathered about him (Genesis 49). Jacob foresaw the entire history of his offspring. (The reader is referred to the section on Genesis, where the different periods of the nation are given as indicated in Jacob's prophecy.) The blessing of Moses describes the blessing, which the people Israel will enjoy, when the Lord has been manifested. For this reason it is correct to say (a fact seldom mentioned by exposition), the blessing of Moses is an inspired expansion of the last verse of his song. That verse (32:43) speaks of the Lord's people rejoicing and the Gentiles rejoicing with them.

What Israel will possess and enjoy during the millennium are the contents of these last utterances of Moses. As a closer exposition of these blessings is beyond the scope of these annotations, we confine ourselves to a few hints which will show the way to a deeper study of this remarkable closing section of Deuteronomy. Reuben's, Judah's and Levi's blessings reveal the salvation of the Lord that Israel will enjoy in that coming age of blessing. Benjamin's and Joseph's blessings picture most beautifully the things which the sacred nation will enjoy during the millennium. This section is a most precious one. Zebulun's and Issachar's blessings make known the fact, that the nation will enjoy the abundance of the seas (the Gentiles). The correct translation of verse 19 is "they shall call the peoples (Gentiles) to the mountain." The mountain is Mount Zion and the Lord's house, which will be a house of prayer for all nations. The nations will go there to worship (Isa. 2:1-4). We have therefore a prophetic description of the blessings which Gentiles receive through a saved Israel. The blessings of Gad, Dan, Naphtali and Asher, speak of the full blessing and supremacy the converted and restored nation will enjoy.

Simeon is left out. We shall not give the different explanations which are offered, nor burden our pages with the unworthy theories of higher criticism.

(Reuben (behold a son!); Simeon (hearing); Levi (joined); Judah (praise). This is the order of the sons of Jacob according to their birth. It tells out the gospel. In the blessing of Moses the order is: Reuben (behold a son!); Judah (praise); Levi (joined). Simeon (hearing) is left out. When the Lord comes Israel will behold Him as the Son and will break out in praise and worship and become joined to Him. No "hearing" is needed then. We pass this on to our readers for consideration. We have nowhere seen this application.)

We quote the beautiful ending of this chapter in a revised metrical version:

There is none like the God of Jeshurum (upright),
Who rideth on the heavens for thy help,
And in His majesty, upon clouds.
The eternal God is thy home
And underneath, the everlasting arms.
And He shall drive out the enemy from
before thee,
And shall say: Destroy!
Then Israel shall dwell in safety alone,
The fountain of Jacob,
In a land of corn and new wine,
His heavens also shall drop down dew.
Happy thou, O Israel!
Who is like thee, people saved by Jehovah,
The shield of thy help,
And the sword of thy excellency!
Surely thine enemies shall crouch before thee,
And thou shalt tread upon their high places.

And the same Jehovah is our Lord. May we know Him more fully as our home, with the everlasting arms underneath and taste the happiness of our salvation, till we shall see Him face to face.

4. The Death of Moses

CHAPTER 34

1. The death and burial of Moses (34:1-7)
2. The mourning of the people (34:8)
3. The conclusion of the book (34:9-12)

This chapter was not written by Moses, but is an addition by another chosen instrument.

The home-going of this great man of God is beyond description. What a scene it must have been when he ascended Nebo to the top of Pisgah! And the Lord met him there and showed him the land and said: "This is the land, which I sware unto Abraham, unto Isaac, and unto Jacob, saying, I will give it unto thy seed. I have caused thee to see it with thine eyes, but thou shalt not go over thither." What vision it must have been! What peace and joy must have filled the heart of the servant of God! Then he died. Jewish tradition has woven many stories around this event. One, however, is so beautiful that we must mention it. "At God's command Moses crossed his hands over his breast and closed his eyes; and God took away his soul with a kiss. Then heaven and earth and the starry world began to weep for Moses."

And the Lord buried Moses. How and where is unrevealed. Jude informs us that Michael, the archangel, contended with the devil about the body of Moses. No doubt Satan tried to bring the buried body to light and to seduce Israel to worship the body of their departed leader. What honor Jehovah put after all upon His servant! He is the only one who was buried by the Lord, and he appeared on the Mount of Transfiguration with the Lord. And the beautiful testimony concerning him by the Spirit of God at the end of this book! "And there arose not a prophet since in Israel whom the Lord knew face to face."

May it please God to bless this book and its many lessons to our hearts. May He grant unto us to live and walk dependent upon and obedient to His Word.

THE BOOK OF
JOSHUA

Introduction

The book of Joshua heads in the Hebrew arrangement of the Old Testament Scriptures, that division which is called "the former Prophets." It is the first book in the Bible which bears in its title the name of a person.

Joshua means "Jehovah is Saviour"; the Greek name for Joshua is Jesus. In our study of the previous books, beginning with Exodus, we have met his name at different times and have learned much of this great man of God. He was the Son of Nun, an Ephraimite (Num. 13:8), grandson of Elishama (1 Chron. 7:26-27). In Exodus we saw him as the leader of Israel against Amalek. He is mentioned as Moses' servant and attendant (Ex. 24:13; 32:17-18); as the servant of Moses, he did not depart out of the tabernacle (Ex. 33:11). He went with Moses, up into the mount of God.

We meet him again in Num. 11:27-29. In Num. 13:8, 16 we find him as one of the spies sent to Canaan. With Caleb he had confidence in God and His promises, and bravely exhorted the people to trust the Lord and go forward. His name, however, is not given at all during the thirty-eight years' wandering in the wilderness. In Deuteronomy he is divinely pointed out as Moses' successor. Moses and Joshua presented themselves in the tabernacle of the congregation, and after the Lord had announced the approaching death of Moses, Joshua hears the charge from the lips of the passing leader of God's people. "Be strong and of a good courage; for thou shalt bring the children of Israel into the land, which I sware unto them; and I will be with thee" (Deut. 31:23). In the analysis and annotations of the book itself we shall have abundant occasion to study the character of Joshua more fully.

The Authorship of the Book

Jewish tradition makes Joshua the author of the book which bears his name. There is no reason why this should be denied. No other person was more fitted to write down the great events, connected with the entrance of Israel into the land, than Joshua. As Moses by inspiration wrote the account of how the Lord brought out His people from Egypt, so Joshua is the instrument, divinely chosen and equipped, to give the story of how the Lord brought them in. That another person should be the author of the book of Joshua appears unreasonable.

The modern critics, however, deny that Joshua had anything whatever to do with the book as we possess it. These wise men have discovered what equally learned and pious men of passed generations, seemingly did not know. They tell us that the date of the composition of Joshua is very late and that it is not the work of one man at all, but a compilation from the same sources that have been utilized in the Pentateuch. These are termed Jehovist (J.)[1]; Elohist (E.); Priestly Code (P.); Deuteronomist (D.) and still another Deuteronomist, termed D^2. This so-called "science," higher criticism, tries to show which is which. And to these must be added a number of redactors, revisors and editors, who all had a hand in putting the book of Joshua into the shape in which we have it now. Well has it been said:

"One is tempted to say of this complicated but confidently maintained scheme, that it is just too complete, too wonderfully finished, too clever by half. Allowing most cordially the remarkable ability and ingenuity of its authors, we can hardly be expected to concede to them the power of taking to pieces a book of such vast antiquity, putting it in a modern mincing machine, dividing it among so many supposed writers, and settling the exact parts of it written by each!"

And now we must mention in connection with the authorship of the book of Joshua, the Hexateuch theory.

The Hexateuch Theory

The word "Hexateuch" means "six-fold book." The five books written by Moses, Genesis to Deuteronomy, are called "Pentateuch," that is, "five-fold book." The critics claim that

[1]The letters behind the names are used by the critic to indicate these different sources. W. H. Bennett in 1895 published Joshua in a number of colors, indicating the various documents.

the book of Joshua belongs properly to the five books of the law, thereby adding a sixth book. This combination they call the Hexateuch. In itself this appears harmless. However, a closer examination reveals that this invention is the offspring of unbelief. They call attention to the fact that throughout the Pentateuch the land of Canaan and its final conquest and inheritance by Israel is mentioned and presupposed. The following passages are generally pointed out: Gen. 13:14-17; 15:13-16; 26:3; 28:13-15; Ex. 3:8, 17; 32:13; 33:1-3; Num. 13:17, 27:18-23; Deut. 1:38; 3:21; 31:3-6. Upon those passages predicting the future occupation and possession of Canaan, the critics base the claim that the same person or persons who wrote the Pentateuch must have also written the book of Joshua. We quote the exact words of one of the leading critics. "It is self-evident that a writer who has commenced his narrative by the brilliant promises made to the patriarchs, is bound to conclude it by showing us their accomplishment; to say the least, it would be impossible for him to pass that accomplishment in silence."

Such a claim involves the denial of the possibility of prediction of future events. This denial is in very fact the whole foundation of the destructive criticism of the Bible; and such a denial is unbelief. To explain, in a scientific way, as it is termed, the predictions found in the Bible, all kinds of theories have been invented. These theories attempt to explain away the supernatural in the Word of God. Thus different Isaiahs have been invented, because the one Isaiah, who wrote the book which bears his name, must be denied an account of such a marvellous prediction as the mention of Cyrus, the king unborn, when Isaiah lived. Daniel is rejected as the author of the book of Daniel and a "pious Jew" (without a definite name) living hundreds of years after Daniel, has to pose as the author of that prophetic book, because, according to the critics, Daniel could not have foretold the events recorded in his prophecies. And the book of Joshua, for the same reason, must have been composed by the same author or authors, compiler or compilers of the Pentateuch. Of course the critics deny that Moses had anything to do with the writing of the first five books of the Bible. If they were to assign the composition of the book of Joshua to Joshua, and the Pentateuch to Moses, the denial, that there can be no genuine prediction, could not be sustained. And this supposed "Hexateuch," the six-fold book, is relegated to a very late period.

But all this Hexateuchal invention is easily disproven. The Hebrews always reverenced the five books, universally ascribed to Moses. They look upon them, and rightly so, as standing by themselves in solitary grandeur. The Hebrew Old Testament has three parts, *Thora* (Pentateuch), *Neviim* (Joshua, Judges, Samuel, Kings, Isaiah to Malachi, except Daniel), and *Kethubim* (Psalms, Proverbs, Job, Song of Solomon, Ruth, Lamentations, Ecclesiastes, Esther, Daniel, Ezra, Nehemiah and Chronicles). To link Joshua with the five books of Moses is a thing unknown among the Hebrews. The book of Joshua was never bound together with the law. No manuscript has ever been found which links Joshua with the Pentateuch. The Pentateuch always stood alone by itself and was jealously guarded by the Hebrews. The critics are unable to furnish any proof that originally the Pentateuch and Joshua were combined.

We state another fact, which overthrows the Hexateuch theory. The Pentateuch is the model of the entire Bible. The five-fold division can be traced in both Testaments. The Book of Psalms, for instance, in the Hebrew Bible has five divisions. The ancient Hebrews called therefore the Psalms "the Pentateuch of David."Each division corresponds in a remarkable degree with the character of the different books written by Moses. The New Testament also has five parts which correspond to the Pentateuch: Gospels (Genesis); Acts (Exodus); Pauline Epistles (Leviticus); General Epistles (Numbers); Revelation (Deuteronomy). All this shows that the Hexateuch is a man-made theory pure and simple. It is invented by such, who refuse to accept the supernatural in the Bible.

We cannot follow the different other objections made against the book of Joshua, as being written by Joshua. These objections are easily answered and we need not to burden our readers with these controversial matters which are of no value at all. We shall, however, in our annotations, call attention to some questions raised by the critics. The study of the book itself will furnish continued evidence, that it is written by inspiration.

The Historical Events and their Typical Meaning

The book of Joshua records the entrance of the people Israel into the promised land, how this entrance was effected by the power of God, the conflicts which arose when they came into the land, the partial conquest and the division of the land among the tribes. All this is fully given in our analysis and followed in the annotations of the different chapters.

There is no other historical book in the Bible so rich in typical foreshadowings as the book of Joshua. It is inexhaustible and full of blessed meaning and encouragement to every child of God, because these historical events typify Christian position, Christian experience and Christian conflict. We shall find that a part of Joshua illustrates for us in a typical way the Epistle to the Ephesians. We point out a few of the leading types; the annotations will give the details and touch upon others as well.

Joshua is, of course, a type of Him whose earthly Name he bears. He is the first one in the Word of God who bears that ever blessed Name. As already stated Joshua is the same as "Jesus," the Greek form for Joshua. Joshua therefore typifies Christ. The earthly people Israel typifies the heavenly peoples and the earthly possession promised and given to Israel is the type of the heavenly possession given to His heavenly people. However, Canaan is not the type of heaven, the place into which the believer enters in the future. Canaan could not be the type of heaven for two reasons. The first is, Israel's conflict when they came into the land. They had to fight their way through the land. Their battles, so to speak, began after they had crossed Jordan. They got into the land without even lifting a single sword or spear. But no sooner were they in the land, their fighting began. This can never be said of heaven. When we reach the Father's house all conflicts will be forever ended and Satan will be completely bruised under our feet.

The second reason why Canaan cannot mean heaven is, that Israel could be driven out of the land. This is not possible with heaven. It is impossible that the place into which God's grace brings us could ever be lost to a child of God. Canaan is the type of the heavenly position and possession which the believer has in Christ Jesus. It corresponds to that which in Ephesians is called "in heavenly places," or as better rendered "in the heavenly." It is the heavenly sphere, the heavenly, spiritual blessings given to us in Christ Jesus.

Jordan is not the type of the death of the believer, but Jordan typifies in Joshua the death of Christ, by which we are separated into this blessed heavenly possession. We are brought into it by the death of Christ, as Israel was brought into Canaan through the passage of Jordan.

The passage of Jordan, the erection of the memorial stones, the events at Gilgal, all find a most blessed typical application, illustrating our redemption in Christ as well as our privileges and responsibilities.

The enemies of Israel, the Canaanites, were usurpers of a land which did not belong to them. They were steeped in wickedness. Immoralities of the most abominable nature were connected with their idolatries. They practised sorcery, divinations; they asked the dead and had familiar spirits. Satan and his demons had complete control over them. They are the types of the "wicked spirits" with which a heavenly people wage their warfare. See Ephesians 6:10-13. All these typical applications we shall make in the annotations.

The division of the land among the tribes has its many typical lessons for us, who are called to possess and enjoy our heavenly possession.

The Dispensational Aspect

The book of Joshua has also a marked dispensational aspect. Israel is yet to possess the promised land in the dimensions in which they never possessed it. God brought them in under Joshua, the second one. The first one, Moses, could not bring them in. When our Lord Jesus Christ appears the second time, He will gather His people from the wilderness of the nations and will give them the land and they shall occupy their full inheritance.

The fall of Jericho, the overthrow of Israel's enemies, the battle at Gibeon, the division of the land, the rest, which followed, all have their striking and most interesting dispensational meaning.

May it please God to make the study of the book of Joshua a blessing to the hearts of His people.

The Division of the Book of Joshua

The division of the book of Joshua is not difficult to make. The opening chapters are taken up with a description of the entrance of the people into the promised land and the conflicts with the enemies. This is followed by the record of the division of the land among the tribes. The book closes with the last words of Joshua, as Deuteronomy closed with the final words of Moses. The death and burial of Joshua and a few other historical statements are added to the book. These, of course, were not written by Joshua.

I. THE ENTRANCE OF THE PEOPLE INTO CANAAN AND THE CONFLICTS

1. **The Entrance Commanded and Success Promised** (1:1-18)
2. **The Spies and Rahab's Faith** (2:1-24)
3. **The Passage of Jordan** (3:1-17)
4. **The Memorial Stones** (4:1-24)
5. **At Gilgal** (5:1-15)
6. **The Fall of Jericho** (6:1-27)
7. **Achan's Sin and Israel's Defeat** (7:1-26)
8. **The Overthrow of Ai** (8:1-35)
9. **The Gibeonites and their Victory** (9:1-27)
10. **The Victorious Conquest** (10—12)

II. THE DIVISION OF THE LAND

1. **Instructions Given: The Two and a Half Tribes** (13:1-33)
2. **Caleb's Request and Inheritance** (14:1-15)
3. **The Portion of Judah** (15:1-63)
4. **The Portion of Ephraim** (16:1-10)
5. **The Portion of Manasseh** (17:1-18)
6. **The Portion of the Rest of the Tribes** (18—19)
7. **The Cities of Refuge** (20:1-9)
8. **The Portion of the Levites** (21:1-45)

III. THE FINAL WORDS OF JOSHUA AND THE EPILOGUE

1. **The Two and a Half Tribes** (22:1-34)
2. **Joshua's Two Addresses** (23:1—24:28)
3. **The Epilogue** (24:29-33)

Analysis and Annotations

I. The Entrance of the People into Canaan and the Conflicts

1. The Entrance Commanded and Success Promised

CHAPTER 1

1. The Lord speaks to Joshua (1:1-9)
2. Joshua speaks to the people (1:10-15)
3. The answer of the people (1:16-18)

The little word "now" with which this book begins is in the Hebrew "and." It links the book with Deuteronomy and the other books of the Pentateuch. It also shows that the previous books were in existence, for the mention of Moses, his death, and Joshua, the minister of Moses, presupposes that the reader knows all about them. But there is a stronger evidence in the eighth verse of the chapter, that the Pentateuch was then completely written. The term "This book of the law" applies to the five books written by Moses.

Joshua begins with the statement of Moses' death and ends with the record of Joshua's death. The book which follows, the book of Judges, begins with the statement of Joshua's death. Moses and Joshua are closely linked together. Both are beautiful types of the Lord Jesus Christ. Moses, the servant, is the type of Christ, the perfect servant of God. Joshua typifies Christ in and among His people in the power of His Spirit.

He leads His people victoriously into the promised possession. Moses' death also typifies Christ. The people could not enter the land as long as this servant of God was living. After his death the land could be possessed. So after the death of Christ the heavenly inheritance is thrown open.

The Lord mentions once more the death of His servant. "Precious in the sight of the Lord is the death of His Saints" (Ps. 116:15). After that the command to enter the land is given. The land promised to the seed of Abraham is God's gift. "The land which I do give unto them." They beheld that land across the river with its beautiful hills and mountains and its fertile valleys. The third verse contains a condition. "Every place that the sole of your feet shall tread upon, that have I given unto you, as I said unto Moses." They had to appropriate what God had given and as they appropriated it, they would possess and enjoy the land. If they made it their own by putting their feet upon the land, whether mountain or valley, it became theirs in reality. This required energy. As stated in our introduction, Canaan typifies the heavenly places mentioned in the Epistle to the Ephesians. We are blessed in Christ with every spiritual blessing in the heavenly places (Ephes. 1:3). All is the gift of the grace of God. Unsearchable riches, far greater than that land, even in its widest dimensions, belong to us. The unsearchable riches of Christ are by the death of Christ put on our side. We must take possession in the energy of faith, as Israel had to plant their feet upon the territory and conquer it. If we are apprehended of Jesus Christ, we also must apprehend. "I follow after, if that I may apprehend that for which I am also apprehended of Jesus Christ" (Phil. 3:12). Israel failed in the wilderness and Israel failed in the possession of the land. And greater still is our failure in not claiming in faith our possessions in Christ.

The words the Lord addressed to Joshua are extremely precious. "I will be with thee," stands first. He was with Joshua and gave him the promise "There shall not any man be able to stand before thee all the days of thy life." And this is true of us. He is with us, indwelling us; His Spirit is with us and His power on our side. God is for us; who can be against us? "I will not fail thee, nor forsake thee." He never fails His people. Divine strength and power are on our side. In the midst of the conflict He will never forsake His people.

After these assuring and encouraging words come the exhortations to obedience. "Be strong and very courageous." Notice the courage is linked with the law (the Word of God) and obedience to it, as well as meditation in it day and night. Joshua was put in dependence on the written Word. So are we. Spiritual growth and enjoyment are impossible apart from meditation in the Word and obedience to it. The Word and obedience to it, separates us, and keeps us separated. And we need courage to obey. It requires courage in an ungodly age, a blinded world with its eyeblinding god (Satan) "to observe to do according to all that is written." It becomes more difficult as the present age draws to its close, to fight the good fight of faith, to appropriate in faith the spiritual blessings, to stand and withstand the wiles of the devil. But if we are obedient His strength will sustain us and give us victory. We constantly need the courage of faith, which looks to God and which is expressed by obedience to His Word. "God's strength is employed in helping us in the paths of God's will, not out of it. Then no matter where we go, what the difficulties are, how long the journey seems, He makes our way prosperous."

Joshua addressed the officers of the people and especially the Reubenites, Gadites, and half the tribe of Manasseh. They had made their choice and had found rest on this side of Jordan. But they were not to be exempt from the approaching warfare; they are commanded to help their brethren by passing with them over Jordan. Then after their brethren had found rest, they were to return to their rest. They could not escape the conflict, though they had no reward in the land itself.

2. The Spies and Rahab's Faith

CHAPTER 2

1. The spies sent forth (2:1)
2. Rahab's faith and works (2:2-14)
3. The escape of the spies and assurance given (2:15-21)
4. The return of the spies (2:22-24)

The historical account needs not to be restated. Joshua, who was one of the spies sent out by Moses, now sends two spies to view the land, even Jericho. Jericho was the great stronghold of the enemy, surrounded by high walls. Jericho means "fragrance" and is a type of the world. (It is interesting to note that in the Hebrew Jericho differs in its spelling in Joshua from that in Numbers. This proves certainly a different authorship.) It is situated near Jordan, the river which typifies death and judgment. The King of Jericho is the type of Satan, the god of this age. The city was grossly immoral, so that it is not strange that the spies came to the house of an harlot. Some have tried to change her character by making her to be an innkeeper. But it cannot be done on account of the word used in the record here and also in the New Testament. Why should even such an attempt be made? Rahab, the harlot, is a beautiful type of the power of the gospel of grace. "By faith the harlot Rahab perished not with them that believed not, when she had received the spies with peace" (Hebews 11:31). Her faith she witnessed to by works. "Likewise also was not Rahab the harlot justified by works, when she had received the messengers, and had sent them out another way?" (James 2:25) Rahab belonged to the doomed race, the race against which the curse had been pronounced. In the doomed city she practised her vile occupation. But she heard the report and she believed. She confessed her faith in Jehovah, the God of the heaven above and of the earth beneath. She had a reason for this faith, for she said, "We have heard how the Lord dried up the water of the Red Sea for you, when ye came out of Egypt" (verse 10). She prayed for mercy for herself and her father's house. She knew judgment would overtake Jericho, that she was a sinner and needed salvation. She believed in Jehovah and believed, that while He is a holy God, who had dealt in judgment with Egypt, that He is also merciful. She trusted in that mercy and appealed to it in her prayer. She claims assurance of salvation and that of her house and she received it in positive terms.

The scarlet-line by which the spies escaped is bound by herself in the window. It was a token to her and a sign to the coming executioners of judgment, when Jericho fell. They saw that scarlet-line; but she was not told to look upon it. How scarlet speaks of the blood needs hardly to be mentioned. It is the type of being sheltered by the blood. "When I shall see the blood, I will pass over you," was spoken to Israel, behind the blood-sprinkled door posts. The scarlet-line has the same meaning. And we must not forget that two living witnesses gave her the assurance of Salvation. Thus we have our assurance in Him, who died for our sins and who was raised on account of our justification.

By hiding the spies and lying to the King of Jericho, she shows her faith and the weakness of it. To her was also given a place of honor in the first chapter of the New Testament as one of the ancestors of Him who, according to the flesh, is the Son of David.

Dispensationally the application is equally interesting. When Israel is about to be restored to their land, a witness is sounded forth once more, the preaching of the gospel of the kingdom (Matt. 24:14). Before the judgments of the Lord are executed in the world, those will be saved during the end of the age who, like Rahab, hear and believe this last kingdom message. They will do good to the Jewish messengers of this final testimony, before the coming of the Lord in power and in glory, as Rahab did good to the spies, the messengers of Joshua. They are those to whom the Lord will say, "What ye have done to the least of these, My brethren, that have ye done unto Me." Rahab was saved and remained in the land to enjoy the earthly blessings with Israel. So the Gentiles, who hear and believe the last message, who have done good to the messengers of the King, the Lord's brethren, will be saved from the wrath to come. For a more complete unfolding of this interesting theme, we refer the reader to the exposition of the Olivet discourse in the Gospel of Matthew.

3. The Passage of Jordan

CHAPTER 3

1. The Ark of Jehovah going before (3:1-6)
2. Jehovah's words to Joshua (3:7-8)
3. Joshua's words to the people (3:9-13)
4. The passage accomplished (3:14-17)

The River Jordan divided the people from the promised land. To be in the land Jordan had to be crossed. Jordan, overflowing all its banks at that time (verse 15), rolled its dark waters between them and their God-given possession. Only the power of God could bring them through those dark waters. It was a miracle which took place, when a way was opened and "the waters which came down from above stood and rose up upon an heap . . . and those that came down toward the sea of the plain, even the salt-sea, failed and were cut off" (verse 16). Unbelief has always branded this miracle as a legend. The destructive criticism has done the same. This is the second time the Lord made a way for His people through the waters. He made first a way for them through the Red Sea, by which Israel was separated from Egypt and from their enemies. The passage of Jordan separated them from the wilderness and brought them into the land.

Both, the Red Sea and Jordan, are types of the death of Christ in its blessed results for His people. The Red Sea experience typifies the fact that the believer, through the death and resurrection of the Lord Jesus Christ, is dead to sin and dead to the law. The passage through Jordan is the type of the fact, that the death and resurrection of Christ brings us into the heavenly places; we are seated together in Christ in heavenly places.

And how was the passage accomplished? We read now nothing more of the movement of the pillar of cloud and of fire, so prominent at the Red Sea and during the wilderness journey. The ark of the covenant of the Lord appears in the foreground to lead the way and made a way through the overflowing waters. Taken up by the priests, carried towards the river, as soon as the priests touched the brim of it, the waters were stemmed back, till all the people had passed over on dry ground. The ark with the blood-sprinkled mercy seat is the type of our Lord Jesus Christ. It is the type of our Lord going into the deep waters of death to make a way through them for His people. The distance between the ark and the people was to be two thousand cubits. It illustrates the fact that our Lord had to do this work alone. Peter declared that he would go with Him into death, but the Lord told him, "Thou canst not follow Me now, but thou shalt follow Me hereafter." There was none with Him, when He made the way, but He takes all His people through death into resurrection life and glory.

In the midst of Jordan, the mighty waters standing as a heap above, the priests that bare the ark of the covenant of the Lord stood firm on dry ground, until all the people were passed clean over Jordan. It was a dry way, not a drop of the dark, muddy waters were left. It shows the truth, that the power of death (typified by the waters of Jordan) is completely gone; nothing is left of it. The work is accomplished for all His people. Not one is left behind; the weakest and the smallest pass over. What effect it must have had upon the enemies, and especially upon Jericho! Jericho was but five miles away. No doubt they watched the hosts of Israel before the passage. They felt secure on account of the mighty waters of Jordan, which seemed to bar the Israelitish invasion. How panic-stricken they must have become when they saw or heard of the great miracle and that God's people had reached the other shore! But one person was calm in Jericho. One enjoyed peace and rest and did not fear. The one from whose window there streamed the scarlet line.

4. The Memorial Stones

CHAPTER 4

1. The first memorial (4:1-8)
2. The second memorial (4:9)
3. The return of the priests with the ark (4:10-18)
4. The encampment at Gilgal (4:19-24)

Jehovah commanded that the great event should be remembered by a memorial. From the river-bed, where the priest's feet stood firm, twelve men, one from each tribe, were to carry twelve stones and leave them at the first lodging place in the land, that is, at Gilgal. These memorial stones were to tell subsequent generations the story of God's faithfulness and power in bringing His people through Jordan into the land. Another memorial of twelve stones was set up by Joshua in the midst of the river, where the priests stood with the ark. This whole record has been much questioned by the critics; it has been charged that there are two different accounts. Professor George Adam Smith states: "For instance, in the story of the crossing of Jordan, as told in Joshua 3 and 4, there are two accounts of the monument set up to commemorate the passage. One of them builds it at Gilgal on the west bank with stones taken from the river-bed by the people; the other builds it in the bed of the river with twelve stones set there by Joshua. (The same view is held by Friedrich Bleek; no doubt Prof. G. A. Smith has it from him.) Such criticism reveals the astonishing weakness of that entire school. Why should the ninth verse of the fourth chapter be looked upon as an interpolation, or as another account of one transaction? There is nothing in the text to warrant such a statement. The fact is there are two transactions. The one by the twelve men, who take the twelve stones and set them up at Gilgal. The other by Joshua, who puts twelve stones in the river-bed.

But if these critics but knew a little more of the spiritual and typical significance of all these events and transactions, they would soon learn better. What do these two memorials mean? They tell out the story what God has done for His people. In the midst of Jordan the children of Israel could see the pile of twelve stones Joshua had put there as a memorial. As they looked upon them and the waters rushing about them, they remembered that where these stones are, there the ark halted and the waters were cut off and His people passed over.

The typical application is not hard to make. The twelve stones in the river-bed tell out the story of the death of Christ and our death with Him. We *are* dead to sin and to the law as well as crucified unto the world. We must, therefore, reckon ourselves dead unto sin.

The other memorial was erected at Gilgal. As they looked upon these stones and their children asked them, "What mean these stones?" they could point to them and say, as these stones were taken out of Jordan on the dry land, so had they been brought out of Jordan into this land of promise. This memorial is the type of the fact "that we are alive unto God in our Lord Jesus Christ." We are a new creation in Christ Jesus, the old things are passed away, behold all things are become new. It is the memorial which tells us, that we are raised up and seated in Christ in the heavenly places. These two great truths seen in this double memorial must ever be remembered by God's people, as Israel was charged to remember the passing over Jordan and the bringing into the land.

5. At Gilgal

CHAPTER 5

1. The terrified enemies (5:1)

2. Circumcision commanded and executed (5:2-9)
3. The Passover kept (5:10)
4. The old corn of the land (5:11-12)
5. The captain of Jehovah's host (5:13-15)

The events at Gilgal are of much interest. Jehovah had brought His people over Jordan. All His promises were kept. He had promised to deliver them out of Egypt and to bring them into the land of Canaan. All is now accomplished. The wilderness is behind them and they face the marvellous land with its riches and resources, the land flowing with milk and honey. The advance and the conquest is next in order. At the Red Sea their enemies were slain by the power of God, but now, after the power of God had brought them into the land, the real conflict begins.

Gilgal, the new ground gained and occupied by the people brought over Jordan, is the type of the resurrection-ground upon which our feet have been planted. That we are risen with Christ and seated in Him in the heavenly places must be constantly remembered, as Israel could never forget at Gilgal that they had been brought over Jordan into the land. The memorial stones served as a constant reminder.

But before they could advance a number of things took place. First we read of the fear which took hold on the kings of the Canaanites. Their hearts melted. They were the instruments of Satan under whose control they were; their fear denotes Satan's fear. He knew the power of Jehovah, which had brought them into the land. The enemy is defeated by the death and resurrection of our Lord. Through death He has annulled him, who has the power of death, that is the devil. Being in Christ, risen with Christ and seated in Him in the heavenly places, we can look upon the enemy as conquered. Yet it is only in the Lord and in the power of His might that we are strong. Apart from Him we become the easy prey of our enemy. What an encouragement to Israel it must have been, when they learned, as no doubt they did, that the mighty enemies, who had inspired such terror to their fathers over thirty-eight years ago, were now trembling. Israel's fear was gone, because God's power was on their side. What confidence we should have when we remember that "we are translated from the power of darkness into the kingdom of the Son of His love"! Victory is on our side. All we need to do is to put on the whole armour of God, to resist the devil and he will flee from us.

Circumcision is next commanded by Jehovah. "At that time the Lord said unto Joshua, Make thee sharp knives and circumcise again the children of Israel the second time." This command was carried out at once and the reproach of Egypt was rolled away. Therefore the place was called Gilgal, which means "rolling." The circumcision was carried out on all the males, who were born in the wilderness (verses 5 and 7). The rite of such deep meaning had been neglected. No doubt they had plenty of excuses for that during the wilderness journey. No command was given to circumcise during the thirty-eight years' wandering. It was suspended; it may have been a punishment for their unbelief. But now all is changed. They are in the land. The Passover, the great memorial feast, was about to be kept. The uncircumcised could not eat the Passover. The reproach of Egypt, for as uncircumcised they were the same as in bondage in Egypt, in no covenant with Jehovah, is rolled away. The visible token of belonging to Jehovah was now borne by every male in the camp.

Joshua exhibited the courage of faith in circumcising the thousands of Israelites at that time. His action has been called "most unmilitary." He put the vast majority of his fighting men into an unfit condition. What if these Canaanites should have fallen upon the settlers in their territory? May Joshua not have remembered the dastardly crime of the sons of Jacob? See Genesis 34:24-26. He knew no fear; his first concern was to yield obedience to God. They tarried for several weeks at Gilgal.

What are the typical lessons of all this? Circumcision stands for the carrying out of the sentence of death to the flesh. The death of Christ is for His people a circumcision. "In whom also ye are circumcised with the circumcision made without hands, in putting off the body of the flesh by the circumcision of Christ" (Col. 2:11). But this fact that we are dead to sin by the circumcision, the death of Christ must be carried out practically. The sharp knife has to be applied to the flesh and the things of the flesh. The members, which are on earth, must be mortified, which means, put into the place of death, where the death of Christ has put them. If it is not done the reproach of Egypt will rest upon His people and they are unfit to enjoy their heavenly possession, and unable to advance in the things of Christ.

Gilgal, therefore, stands for the judgment of self. This is the place of our strength and power. Israel had always to return to Gilgal; when they did not they were defeated. Defeat, failure in our walk, always drives us back to self-judgment and humiliation. Victory and blessing may keep us from it; and that is our real spiritual danger.

Passover is kept next. See Numbers 9 and our annotations there. What blessed memories must have come to them? They remembered that fearful night in Egypt and how Jehovah had passed over them, when He saw the blood of the lamb. Notice the difference between these two Passovers. The first they kept as guilty; they needed protection. But now they keep it as delivered and brought into the land. And we have a feast of remembrance likewise, the Lord's table. "Do this in remembrance of Me." It must be kept by us on resurrection-ground, realizing that we are dead with Christ and risen with Him; self-judgment is needed as well.

"The remembrance of the past is often an excellent preparation for the trials of the future, and as often it proves a remarkable support under them. It was the very nature of the Passover to look back to the past, and to recall God's first great interposition on behalf of His people. It was a precious encouragement both to faith and hope. So also is our Christian Passover. It is a connecting link between the first and second comings of our Lord. The first coming lends support to faith, the second to hope. No exercise of soul can be more profitable than to go back to that memorable day when Christ our Passover was sacrificed for us. For then the price of redemption was paid in full, and the door of salvation flung wide open. Then the Son sealed His love by giving Himself for us. What blessing, whether for this life or the life to come, was not purchased by that transaction? Life may be dark and stormy, but hope foresees a bright to-morrow. "When Christ, who is our life, shall appear, then shall ye also appear with Him in glory" (Professor W. G. Blaikie).

Then the manna ceased and they ate the old corn of the land. Both foods are typical of Christ, the food God has given to His people. The manna is the type of Christ, on earth, in humiliation. The old corn is Christ in Glory. May we constantly feed on both.

Then Joshua meets before Jericho the man with the drawn sword. What a courageous man Joshua was! He meets the stranger alone. Most likely he had no sword, while the man had his sword drawn. He soon hears who the stranger is. It is the same One who appeared to Moses in the burning bush, to Abraham at Mamre, to Jacob at Peniel and to others afterward. It is Jehovah in visible form. These theophanies were surely not incarnations, yet they foreshadowed the incarnation of the Son of God. Here Jehovah who in the fulness of time became Man, appears as a man of war, as Captain of the host of the Lord. The host are Israel. And He is the Captain of our salvation.

The book of Joshua is the book of conflicts and conquests. The sword is freely used in carrying out the divine judgments upon the ungodly tenants of the land. Yet the *first* drawn sword, mentioned in the book, is in the hand of the Lord as He appeared unto Joshua. He fights for His people. He will yet execute the righteous judgments in the earth. It will be when He appears the second time.

6. The Fall of Jericho

CHAPTER 6

1. The divine instruction (6:1-5)
2. The instructions followed (6:6-19)
3. The fall of Jericho (6:20-21)
4. Rahab remembered (6:22-25)
5. The curse upon Jericho (6:26-27)

We do not enlarge upon the history of the chapter, which needs no comment. The fall of Jericho by the power of God, as described in this chapter, has also been ridiculed by infidels. Others have tried to explain the occurrence in a natural way. It has been said that the marching Israelites, by tramping around the city for seven days, weakened the walls, and the trumpet blasts and shouting of the people brought about their collapse. How utterly ridiculous! But what are the typical and dispensational lessons of this interesting chapter?

Jericho is the type of the world, as already stated in the annotations of the second chapter. As Jericho falls and is laid in ruins as soon as Israel is in the land, so the world is laid in ruins for the believer who apprehends his position in Christ. Our faith is the victory which overcometh the world. It was faith which obtained the victory over Jericho. A faith which trusted in the Lord; a faith which acted in obedience to the divinely given instructions. "By faith the walls of Jericho fell down, after they were compassed about seven days" (Hebrews 11:30). And we must walk in faith and in the power of His Spirit, as crucified unto the world and the world crucified unto us. The world must remain in ruins for the believer who walks in the Spirit, as Jericho was not to be rebuilt.

It is a remarkable circumstance, in various aspects, that Jericho, the first and the strongest city of the land, is taken in this peculiar manner, without a single stroke of the sword. This result was intended, on the one hand, to furnish the faith of the Israelites with unquestionable evidence of the success of their future warlike movements, which now commenced, and, on the other hand, to secure them in advance, from a carnal reliance on their own strength, and from all vainglorious tendencies to ascribe their success to their own courage, their own intelligence, and their own power.

We must also think here of the walls, the hindrances, the obstacles in our lives as believers, as we pass through the world. The enemy often tries to terrify us by these, as he discouraged Israel at Kadesh by the walled cities. Alas! we often do what Joshua did not do before Jericho. We measure the walls, we study the difficulties, we are occupied with our perplexities and trials. We reckon with the walls, instead of reckoning with the Lord and His power. By faith walls still fall down.

Richer is the meaning of the fall of Jericho viewed in the light of prophecy. Jericho is the type of the world *ripe* for judgment. The high walls are types of the walls of unbelief, apostasy, wickedness and self-security. *Seven* days Israel had to march around the walls. *Seven* priests with *seven* trumpets were there. On the *seventh* day they had to march around *seven* times and blow the *seven* trumpets. Note the number "seven." It stands for divine completion. How it all reminds us of the last book of the Bible with its *seven* seals, *seven* trumpets and *seven* vials. The trumpets, however, in Joshua are the trumpets of jubilee. The great jubilee, the time of blessing for this earth comes, when judgment is executed. As the walls of Jericho fell, so comes the day, when all the high and exalted things will be laid low (Isaiah 2:10-22) The stone will fall out of heaven (Christ in His second coming) smiting the image, representing the world-power. Complete ruins will be the result, never to be built again; but the smiting stone becomes a mountain, filling the earth. It is the prophetic picture of the coming kingdom.

"The details of the fall of Jericho seem *not*, however, to be facts of present experience, but prophetic of actual judgment when it comes; and this is quite as we might expect. We see by them, however, that the people of God have to maintain the testimony as to these things: compassing the city and blowing the trumpets until the city falls; although it be only in the meantime to awaken the scorn of the men of the world, as they hear the frequent alarm of that which seems never to come. But it comes, comes steadily nearer, is surely even now at the door, and how urgent should be our testimony, which, if of no effect upon the mass, yet helps to fill Rahab's house, where the true scarlet-line, as despicable in men's eyes as that of old, shields with the power of the Almighty the prisoners of hope.[2]

How blessedly the promise was kept to Rahab and her house! No doubt that scarlet line was the object of ridicule in Jericho. She alone and her house escaped the dreadful judgment. The entire walls fell; but one small portion was kept standing, the portion upon which her house stood.

Jericho was built three times and three times razed to the ground. It was first destroyed under Joshua. Then Hiel, the Beth-elite rebuilt it in Ahab's reign (822-790). He experienced the curse of Joshua. Compare Joshua 6:26 with 1 Kings 16:34. Hiel's city was destroyed by the Herodians in 3 B.C. The next year Archelaus built Jericho again, the Jericho standing in the days of our Lord. This was destroyed by Vespassian 68 A.D.

7. Achan's Sin and Israel's Defeat

CHAPTER 7

1. The defeat of Israel (7:1-5)
2. The source of the defeat revealed (7:6-15)
3. The transgressor found out (7:16-23)
4. The judgment of Achan (7:24-26)

The insignificant place Ai brings defeat. Joshua sent men to view Ai. What authority was given to him to do so? There was no need to send spies once more, for the Lord had said, that the whole land was given to them. They report Ai a place without walls and recommend that only two or three thousand men be sent up. Defeat follows.

Ai means "ruins." It is mentioned for the first time in Genesis 12. Abraham built his altar between Bethel (House of God) and Ai. Ai is another type of the world. But the source of the defeat was Achan's sin. The shekels of silver and gold, the Babylonian garment, had blinded his eyes. These things were to be "accursed," which literally means devoted; devoted to the treasury of the Lord (6:19). Joshua had given the command that such should be the case, and

---

[2]F. W. Grant, *Joshua.*

also announced, that disobedience would bring trouble upon Israel. Achan's sin was responsible for the defeat of the people. He confesses, "I saw—I coveted—I took." The same old story, first enacted in the garden of Eden. The evil in the midst of the people of God, unjudged, becomes the most powerful agent against Israel and withholds God's power and blessing. It is so still. As soon as we cling to the things of the world, the enemy gets an advantage over us, and we have little power and cannot advance in the things of Christ. Ah! the Achans in our lives! Judge self; bring the evil thing into the light and victory and blessing will follow. Joshua's prayer and Jehovah's answer; Achan's sin discovered and forced confession; the judgment which falls upon him and his house; the heap of stones raised over him—all is of interest and instruction, which our limited space forbids to follow in detail.

The valley of Achor is mentioned in Hosea 2:15 as a door of hope. The place and door of hope is in Him, who died not for his sins, but who took the sin and guilt of the nation upon Himself.

The valley of Achor was not only the place of national repentance, and of a national repudiation of sin, but it was also the place of a great and tragic national expiation. Israel had sinned, and so Israel had suffered, but it was the sin of one man that had brought judgment on the camp. Now, observe, the sin of a single man was imputed to Israel, and became Israel's sin, and because of that imputation of sin, the wrath of God fell on the whole nation. But when the sin of that one man was discovered, and when it was confessed before God, then the sin imputed to the congregation reverted on to the head of the one criminal. Thus the penalty due to a national sin was actually carried out upon him whose guilt had involved the nation in judgment; and as the deadly stones were hurled upon him, that man in his death was not only reaping the reward of his disobedience, but the sin of the nation was being expiated in the death of the individual; and thus was opened 'a door of hope' through 'the valley of trouble,' whereby Israel might enter the land of promise, and find her vineyards from thence.—Aitken.

8. The Overthrow of Ai

CHAPTER 8

1. The advance commanded (8:1-2)
2. The strategy of Joshua (8:3-13)
3. Ai's defeat (8:14-29)
4. Joshua's obedience (8:30-35)

Sin confessed, judged and put away restored communion with the Lord. If any burden remained upon the mind of Joshua, it was removed by the repeated words of comfort and cheer. "Fear not, neither be thou dismayed." The failure is no longer mentioned, but instead, comfort and assurance is given and victory promised. He deals in the same gracious way with us, whenever we have failed and humbled ourselves before Him in self-judgment. However, their former presumption is not overlooked by Jehovah. The capture of Ai is hard work for them. They had to learn the lesson. Their pride and self-reliance was dealt with by Jehovah, who ever wants His people in the place of lowliness and weakness. Instead of 3,000 men, ten times as many had to go up and engage in the warfare.

The Lord commanded Joshua to stretch out the spear toward Ai. This corresponds to the uplifted hands of Moses in the warfare against Amalek in Exodus 17. It was a token of the presence of divine power in securing the complete victory. We read nothing of Joshua's arm with the spear becoming weak, as it was with the uplifted hands of Moses. "For Joshua drew not his hand back wherewith he stretched out the spear, until he had utterly destroyed all the inhabitants of Ai" (verse 26). It was an act of faith, and divine power supported the outstretched arm.

Then, after the victory, Joshua built an altar unto the Lord God of Israel, in Mount Ebal. He is doing this in obedience to the previously given command. See Deuteronomy 27:2-8. What an impressive scene it must have been when "he read all the words of the law, the blessings and the cursings, according to all that is written in the book of the law."

"Both mounts belong to the range of Mount Ephraim; the elevated valley of Shechem lies between them. The transaction probably took place in the following manner. Six tribes occupied each mount; the priests, standing below in the valley with the ark of the covenant in their midst, turned toward Mount Gerizim as they solemnly pronounced the words of blessing, and then, looking towards Mount Ebal, repeated the words of cursing; all the people responded to each of the words, and said: 'Amen!' Ebal, the Mount of cursing, is naked and bald; Gerizim, the mount of blessing, is green and fertile. The circumstance that the mount of cursing was assigned for the writing of the law, the erection of the altar, and the offering of sacrifice, is highly significant; the cause lies in the intimate relations existing between the curse, on the one hand, and the Law and Sacrifice, on the other— the former brings a curse, or gives a sharp point to it, the latter abolishes it" (J. H. Kurtz).

9. The Gibeonites

CHAPTER 9

1. The confederacy of the enemies (9:1-2)
2. The deception of the Gibeonites (9:3-13)
3. The failure (9:14-15)
4. The deception discovered (9:16-27)

Israel now comes face to face with the other inhabitants of the land. These enemies, which Israel encountered, are the types of our enemies, and the conflict of God's earthly people is typical of our conflict. There is, however, a difference. Israel's enemies were flesh and blood; ours are not. Israel's conflict was in the land; ours is with the wicked spirits in the heavenly places. Israel was asked to drive them out; we are not asked to do this, but to resist the devil. Israel's land rested from the conflict; we shall not rest till we are with Him, when Satan will be bruised under our feet. Read Ephesians 6:10-17.

The Canaanites are the types of the evil powers, with whom we have to wage our warfare. As the Canaanites opposed the possession and enjoyment of the land, so the aim of the wicked spirits is to keep us back, to hinder us in possessing and enjoying our spiritual blessings in Christ Jesus.

The Gibeonites were Hivites. They came with deceptions, knowing well what was their lot. The deceptions were inspired by the father of lies.

In Ephesians 6, we are especially warned against the wiles of the devil. We are to stand against the wiles of the devil. Elsewhere we read that he transforms himself into an angel of light. The Gibeonites illustrate these wiles of the devil. Not alone had they their mouldy bread and old wineskins, as a kind of credential to back up their lies, but they talked very piously. What are these wiles of the devil? We have to turn to the so-called "religious world" to find them. The "religious world," which speaks piously of God and Christ, is at best hypocrisy, phariseeism. Ritualism, Galatianism, man-made ordinances, belong to the wiles of the devil. Philosophies, traditions of men, delusive doctrines, cunningly devised fables, all these belong to the wiles of the devil (Colossians 2). Such systems as Christian Science, spiritism, Russellism, Bahaism, higher criticism, theosophy and others belong to the wiles of the devil. So does "social-reform." These world reformers, "Christian" socialists, talk piously like the Gibeonites, but the devil's wiles are underneath.

And these wiles of the devil are multiplying. Satan, knowing that his time is short, does all he can to keep God's people from enjoying their blessings and from advancing in spiritual things.

The Gibeonites, with their pious talk, were received into the congregation of Israel, just as the professing church is receiving the world into the church. The failure was with Israel. They asked not counsel of the Lord. Had Joshua gone in the presence of the Lord, He would soon have exposed the deceptions of the Gibeonites. Here is where our failure comes in likewise. Never can Satan, with his superior knowledge and his wiles, get an advantage over us, if we hold closely to the Word of God, the Sword of the Spirit, and if we ask counsel of the Lord through His Word and in prayer. The covenant made had to stand. It would have been unrighteousness, if Israel had acted differently. How many unequal yokes there are among God's people, entered into without having asked counsel of the Lord!

And there is generally no escape, but suffering in consequence. Israel had to stand much on account of the unholy alliance with the Gibeonites. What a man sows that he will reap. Read 2 Samuel 21:1-6.

10. The Victorious Conquest

CHAPTER 10

1. Adoni-zedec and his confederacy (10:1-6)
2. The war (10:7-11)
3. The miracle (10:12-15)
4. The victory won (10:16-21)
5. The five kings slain (10:22-27)
6. Further conquests (10:28-43)

The name Jerusalem is mentioned here for the first time in the Bible. (Salem in Genesis 14:18, is generally taken to be Jerusalem. See Psalm 76:2. The ancient tablets give the name as *Ur-Salim*. But the name "Jerusalem" is found the first time in Joshua 10:1.) It is in connection with war, and the next time we find Jerusalem on fire (Judges 1:8). This may be taken as a prophecy of the history of that city. Yet something better is in store for Jerusalem. Adoni-zedec is here the King of Jerusalem. His name means "lord of righteousness." He represents the counterfeit king in opposition to Him who is Jerusalem's true King, the true Melchizedec, King of righteousness and King of peace. He is a type of Anti-christ. On account of Gibeon having gone over to Israel, Adoni-zedec forms an alliance, which he heads as leader. His confederates are given by name. We give the meaning of their names in parenthesis, which will be helpful in a deeper study of these types. Hoham (the noise of a multitude), King of Hebron; Piram (the wild ass), King of Jarmuth; Japhia (causing brightness); King of Lachish; Debir (an oracle), King of Eglon. This satanic alliance was aimed at Gibeon and at Israel as well. And Gibeon appealed to Joshua for help.

Notice that they sent to Gilgal, the first camp of Israel. Joshua and the people were at Gilgal, and from Gilgal they ascended. At Gilgal they saw the memorials of God's power, and encouraged by a direct message from Jehovah they went forth to war. Blessed are we, if in our spiritual warfare we go forth from Gilgal (the place of self-judgment and of power).

The great miracle of the standing still of the sun and the moon occurred then. The way this miracle has been held up to ridicule is known to everybody. Infidels of all generations have sneered at it. Critics have followed, as they always do, close in their footsteps. But even good men have found difficulties here and tried to explain it with their human wisdom. One explanation given is that the Hebrew word *dum,* to stand, means rather that the sun was to cease to give its light. Upon this the statement is made, that Joshua's command was that the sun and moon should cease giving their light, and not that they should cease continuing their apparent motion. Herder in his "*Hebraische Poesie*" says:

"It is astonishing that this fine passage has been so long misunderstood. Joshua attacked the Amorites in the early morning, and the battle continued till night; that is, for a long day, which seemed to protract itself into night, to complete the victory. The sun and moon were witnesses of Joshua's great deeds, and held their course in the midst of heaven till the triumph was perfect. Who does not recognize this as poetry, even if it had not been quoted from the Book of Poems on Heroes. In the usual language of the Hebrews such expressions were neither bold nor unusual."

These are the attempts of man, by which he tries to explain the supernatural by the natural. The occurrence is a miracle. It says the sun stood still. But how is that when science tells us the sun does not move? We give the answer from Kurtz in his *Sacred History,* because it is the most concise statement we have ever seen:

"A voucher from the Old Testament for the promise in Mark 11:23, 24, 'Whosoever shall say unto this mountain, Be thou removed, &c..' is furnished by Joshua's bold word of faith with its fulfilment. It was his prayer that the light of day might be prolonged, and the darkness of night be retarded, until he had secured the object for which he pursued the enemy: he obtained the answer which he sought by the miraculous power of his faith. No investigation respecting the natural means which produced this supernatural effect can furnish valuable results. The command of faith is pronounced in the sense which *Joshua* assigns to the words; the divine answer is given in the sense in which *God* understands them. No arguments that are either favorable or unfavorable to any particular system of astronomy are furnished by the occurrence."

The miracle must have stricken with terror the fighting nations, for they worshipped the sun and the moon.

Signs in heaven are frequently mentioned in the Word.

Read and study carefully the following passages: 2 Kings 20:11; Is. 38:8; Amos 8:9; Isaiah 13:10, 60:20; Ezek. 32:7; Joel 2:10, 31; 3:15; Matt. 24:29; Rev. 6:12; 8:12; 9:2; 16:8. When the age ends with the battle of Armageddon and the Lord Jesus Christ appears the second time in great power and glory, these signs as predicted in some of these passages will be fulfilled. The sun and moon will be darkened. What terror will take hold upon the great masses of Christendom, who reject the miracle and Christ! Read Revelation 6:12-17.

What is the book of Jasher, mentioned in verse 13?

The Book of Jasher (or, *of the Upright,* that is, Israel) was a collection of sacred war-songs, and may have, possibly, formed a continuation, in a certain sense, of the "Book of the Wars of the Lord" (Numbers 21:14; 2 Samuel 1:18). The collection was probably commenced in the wilderness, and, at different periods, received additions.

The fact that it is no longer in existence proves its noninspiration.

Great are the victories described in this chapter. See verse 41 as to the territory which was covered. From Kadesh-barnea unto Gaza, all the country of Goshen unto Gibeon. And why? Because the Lord God of Israel fought for Israel (verse 42). If God is for us, who can be against us! "And Joshua returned, and all Israel with him, unto the camp of Gilgal." How wonderful it is to return after our victories to Gilgal, the place of self-judgment and confessed weakness. How often our victories and blessings are more dangerous than our failures and defeats!

Further Conquests

CHAPTER 11

1. Jabin and his confederacy (11:1-5)
2. The divine encouragement (11:6)
3. The victory (11:7-14)
4. The obedience of Joshua (11:15)
5. The continued conflict with the kings (11:16-23)

The Kings of the north formed the second confederacy, headed by Jabin, King of Hazor. Jabin means "understanding" and Hazor, "an enclosure." He with other kings, and with them "much people even as the sand that is upon the seashore in multitude, with horses and chariots very many," came to fight against Israel. These different confederacies opposing the rightful owners of the land may be taken as types of the opposition from confederate nations which Israel will have to face during the great tribulation.

Did Joshua fear in the presence of such a powerful enemy? If he feared, his fear must have vanished completely when Jehovah said, "Be not afraid of them, for to-morrow about this time will I deliver them up all slain before Israel; thou shalt hough their horses, and burn their chariots with fire." The Lord assured Joshua, and with such an assurance he rushed at once against the enemy by the waters of Merom. It does not matter how strong the enemy is, how cunningly his plans are laid, how he may come upon us with an host to terrify; if we are right with the Lord and on the Lord's side, we shall be more than conquerors. The victory is complete; their chariots are burned and the horses were disabled by cutting the sinews of their legs. The latter no doubt had for its purpose to make it impossible for His people to trust in human resources. If they had used these horses, they might have put their confidence in them. "Some trust in chariots and some in horses; but we will remember the Lord our God" (Psalm 20:7).

At Hazor, as in other cities and places, the divine command of utter extermination of all human beings was literally carried out. "There was not any left to breathe." An awful picture indeed it is! Infidels have made the best of it by denouncing these records and blaspheming the righteous and holy God. Others again have tried to excuse the Israelites by saying that it was the customary thing 1,500 years before Christ to treat conquered nations in this way. But it was God Himself who commanded their extermination. Joshua and Israel had no choice whatever in the matter. They acted in obedience to the divine will. God's time for the execution of His righteous judgments had come and He used Israel as His instrument. To Abraham the word was spoken concerning his seed, "In the fourth generation they will come hither again; for the iniquity of the Amorites is not yet full." The iniquity of these nations had reached such a degree, that God's wrath and holy vengeance had to fall upon them. They were given to the most awful abominations and practised unspeakable immoralities. The hour of judgment had come. The whole race was to be swept away. And who dares to question God's sovereign right to do so. Should not the Judge of all the earth do right?

Nor must we forget that the judgment of Canaan, as well as the judgment of Egypt, is prophetic. Judgment and wrath are in store for this earth. The divine sword will some day be unsheathed again. The conditions of the earth are such that God must judge. Thousands are hardening their hearts; ere long, as it was with the Canaanites (verse 20), the Lord will harden their hearts. These judgments are written in language which cannot be misunderstood.

Notice Joshua's obedience. He left nothing undone. He obeyed the Word; he followed closely the divine instructions. That led to success and blessing.

The Conquered Kings

CHAPTER 12

1. The kings on the other side of Jordan (12:1-6)
2. The kings on this side of Jordan (12:7-24)

"The land rested from war" is the concluding statement of the previous chapter. It was after Joshua had made war a long time with all those kings (11:18). Deut. 6:10-11 was also fulfilled. "And it shall be, when the Lord Thy God shall have brought thee into the land, which

He sware unto thy Fathers, to Abraham, to Isaac and to Jacob, to give thee great and goodly cities, which thou buildest not, and houses full of all good things, which thou filledst not, and wells digged, which thou diggedst not, vineyards and olive trees, which thou plantedst not." The list of kings which is given in this chapter needs no comment. Thirty-one are mentioned as conquered by Joshua. The land was only 150 miles from north to south, and 50 miles from east to west. Criticism has also objected to this, as if so many kings could not exist in so small a territory. Professor Maspero, one of the foremost archaeologists, fully confirms the Bible-record. We quote from him:

"The Canaanites were the most numerous of all these groups, and had they been able to amalgamate under a single king, or even to organize a lasting confederacy, it would have been impossible for the Egyptian armies to have broken through the barrier thus raised between them and the rest of Asia; but, unfortunately, so far from showing the slightest tendency towards unity or concentration, the Canaanites were more hopelessly divided than any of the surrounding nations. Their mountains contained nearly as many states as there were valleys, while in the plains each town represented a separate government, and was built on a spot carefully selected for purposes of defence. The land, indeed, was chequered by these petty states, *and so closely were they crowded together, that a horseman travelling at leisure could easily pass through two or three of them in a day's journey.*" Of the richer country towards the north he writes: "Towns grew and multiplied upon this rich and loamy soil."

II. The Division of the Land

The divine record concerning the division of the land, as it is before us in these chapters, is often looked upon merely as history barren of any spiritual meaning. Many expositors pass over the greater part of it or give only geographical information. However, a deeper meaning must be sought here; there are many and blessed lessons in spiritual and dispensational truths hidden in these chapters. Why should the Holy Spirit have recorded all these things if they have no meaning whatever? It is written, "*All* Scripture is given by inspiration of God, and is profitable for doctrine, for reproof, for correction, for instruction in righteousness" (2 Timothy 3:16). This surely applies to all Scripture, including the chapters which contain nothing but names. Again it is written, "Now all these things happened unto them (Israel) as types, and they are written for our admonition, upon whom the ends of the ages have come" (1 Corinthians 10:11). "For whatsoever things were written aforetime were written for our learning, that we through patience and comfort of the Scriptures might have hope" (Romans 15:4). We dare not deny these chapters in Joshua a spiritual application in the light of these plain words of the Spirit in the New Testament.

In the study of the previous books we have discovered (especially in Genesis) the fact that the meaning of the Hebrew names are of deep significance and often helpful in the types as well as the spiritual and dispensational lessons. Here is a wide field, which has been but little covered. Hundreds of names are found in this second part of Joshua. They all have a meaning and through these names we can learn the lessons the Spirit of God has written there for our learning. Yet caution is needed. While some ignore this study entirely, others swing into the opposite direction and are fanciful in their application. This must be avoided.

We are sorry that the scope of our work does not permit a more detailed exposition and research. If we were to give way to the desire to do this we would have to write a volume. But we hope, with His gracious help, to give such hints which will help in a more extended, private study. (F. W. Grant in the *Numerical Bible* gives excellent help, both in the meaning of the names and in application. We know of no other attempt in this direction and acknowledge our own indebtedness to him. This, of course, does not mean that we endorse all the translations or applications he gives.)

1. Instruction Given: The Two and One-half Tribes

CHAPTER 13

1. Jehovah speaks to Joshua (13:1-7)
2. Inheritance of the two and one-half tribes (13:8-33)

About seven years had gone by since the passage over Jordan and Joshua, being old and advanced in years, is addressed by the Lord. He takes care of His servants in their old age and provides for their comfort. Much land was yet to be possessed. Israel never responded to the fulness of God's gift to them. How great their failure, as well as our failure as His spiritual people, to possess our possessions, which God's grace has put on our side!

The unpossessed land is described in verses 2-7. It was never possessed in full by Israel, nor did they ever have the land, as promised to them from the Red Sea to the River Euphrates. God's gifts and calling being without repentance (Romans 11:29) the time must yet come when they receive that land in the dimensions as promised in Exodus 23:31. When their restoration comes with the coming of their once rejected King, our Lord, this promised land will be possessed by the nation.

These undisposed enemies may well be taken as the types of our spiritual enemies. The Philistines, who were not Canaanites, stand in the foreground. Their origin may be traced in Genesis. They were sons of Ham and sprang from Egypt. The name "Palestine" is derived from "Philistine." They typify the power of corruption to the people of God. The Philistines today, which keep God's people back from the enjoyment of their inheritance, are the corrupt forms of Christianity, Rome and her daughters. Note the five princes of the Philistines and their residence. Gaza (strong); Ashdod (I will spoil); Ashkelon (the fire of infamy); Gath (wine-press, a type of wrath); Ekron (uprooting). These names describe the character of these powerful enemies of Israel. We leave it with the reader to apply them to that powerful ecclesiastical world-system, Rome. The Avites belonged to the gigantic races, which dwelt in the land. The name means "perverters." Satan with his powerful agencies perverts the truth and keeps God's people in bondage.

And the Lord promises to drive them out (verse 6). With His own power He was ready to dispossess these wicked usurpers, if Israel was but willing to advance in faith and act upon His promise. Here is where they failed. Oh! that we might see that God is on our side in the conflict and in the possession of our inheritance.

The inheritance of the two tribes and a half, Reuben, Gad and half Manasseh is then restated and confirmed.

2. Caleb's Request and Inheritance

CHAPTER 14

1. The inheritance by lot (14:1-5)
2. Caleb's request (14:6-15)

Judah's portion comes first, and as they draw near to Joshua to receive their inheritance by lot (See Proverbs 16:33 and Acts 1:26) at Gilgal (note the recurrence of this place and its significance), Caleb, the son of Jephunneh, steps to the front. It was not forwardness or love of the pre-eminence which led him to do this, but the burning zeal in that old, yet youthful soul. He comes to claim the inheritance, which forty-five years ago Moses had promised unto him. Caleb was eighty-five years old. "As yet I am as strong this day as I was in the day that Moses sent me; as my strength was then even so is my strength now, for war, both to go out and to come in." One can almost see him standing before Eleazar, Joshua and the heads of the tribes. What a beautiful testimony he gives to the faithfulness of the Lord! He could say, "I wholly followed the Lord my God." He stands for the man who trusts his God, who reckons not with earthly circumstances and conditions, but with the Lord and His promised power. They that honor Me, I will honor. Forty years old was Caleb when he was put among the spies and when, with Joshua, he honored God and His Word. The reward of faith became evident in his life. Mental vigor and physical strength remained unimpaired. And now he claims his inheritance. Patiently he had waited for forty-five years. The hour has come. He claims the mountain with its Anakim, the giants, the fenced cities, the great cities. That beautiful mountain with its strenuous task is the claimed inheritance. Old age is often characterized by "the pride of life." The lust of the flesh is peculiar to youth; the lust of the eyes, the desire of increase in earthly things to enjoy them, comes with middle life, and in old age temptation is "the pride of life." But not so with the man of faith. Listen to his humble language. He does not pride himself on his faith and trust in God; he knows nothing of self-confidence. "If so be the Lord will be with me, then I shall be able to drive them out, as the Lord said."

In our day of departure from God and unbelief, may we be like Caleb, "wholly following the Lord." We, too, wait in faith and in patience for the promised inheritance, which some day will be ours, when He comes to reward His Saints. Then as Israel's land had rest from war (verse 15) we shall enter into our rest from strife and conflict.

3. The Portion of Judah

CHAPTER 15

1. The south-border of Judah's portion (15:1-4)
2. The eastern and northern border (15:5-11)
3. The western border (15:12)

4. Caleb's conquest (15:13-19)
5. Inheritance according to families (15:20-63)

This is a chapter which contains many names; nearly one hundred and fifty are recorded. With the help of a good concordance, or dictionary of Hebrew names, the English meaning may be ascertained. However, many of these names may be derived from different roots and have therefore a different meaning, while the meaning of others is rather obscure. For the reason already stated we cannot follow the possible meaning and application of these names. The lesson, however, is that the Lord distributed the inheritance to His people and placed them as it pleased Him. He knew their faithfulness and their ability, and accordingly they received their portion. And we, too, as members of His body, receive our portion and inheritance from Himself, "dividing to every man severally as He will" (1 Corinthians 12:11).

Caleb's conquest is of additional interest. In the previous chapter we learned of his faith and how he honored the Lord. He acknowledged that the Lord had kept him alive; by His mercy he had been spared (14:10). He claimed His portion, and in humility of faith he expected success and victory. He gets Hebron, which means "communion." The application in spiritual lines is interesting. Faith longs for Hebron, for communion. But the giants, the Anakim, are there, to keep away from real communion with God. They must be dispossessed. Caleb drove out the three sons of Anak. Their names are Sheshai, which means "my fine linen," reminding us of our own righteousness (*Shesh* is the Hebrew word used for the fine linen in the tabernacle. In this way we get "Sheshai," *my* fine linen); Ahiman, the meaning of this word is "who is my brother?" which may be applied to pride of desent; Talmai, the third son of Anak, means "abounding in furrows," the pride of achievement. Pride in different forms is the hindrance to real communion with God. Pride has to be dethroned in the heart and in the life of His people. Only as we follow the Lord wholly, as Caleb did, shall we conquer and enjoy our Hebron in the Lord Jesus Christ. And he also had Debir (Oracle—the voice speaking); Kirjath-sepher means "city of the book." Thus Hebron, communion, is closely linked with the written Word and the voice which speaks there. And in Achsah, Caleb's daughter, we have another side of faith represented. When Caleb said unto her, "What wouldest thou?" she answered, "Give me a blessing; for thou hast given me a south land; give me also springs of water. And he gave her the upper springs and the nether springs." It is faith which asks much and receives much.

4. The Portion of Ephraim

CHAPTER 16

1. The lot for the children of Joseph (16:1-4)
2. Ephraim's portion (16:5-9)
3. Ephraim's failure (16:10)

A wonderful lot was that of Joseph, beginning at Jordan, the river of death, up to Bethel, which means "the house of God." Then the portion of Ephraim comes first. Ephraim with the blessed inheritance to be "doubly fruitful" (the meaning of Ephraim) fails. "They drove not out the Canaanites that dwelt in Gezer." Josephus, the Jewish historian, remarks on this: "They grew effeminate as to fighting any more against their enemies, but applied themselves to the cultivation of the land, which producing them great plenty and riches, they indulged in luxury and pleasure." No doubt this tradition is correct. How this has been repeated in Christendom! What Ephraim became, joined to idols, we read in the prophet Hosea.

5. The Portion of Manasseh

CHAPTER 17

1. Their names (17:1-6)
2. Their border (17:7-13)
3. The complaint and the answer (17:14-18)

Half of the tribe of Manasseh had their inheritance on the other side of Jordan, having joined themselves to Reuben and Gad. The rest of Manasseh are now named according to their families. These are: Abiezer, Helek, Asriel, Shechem, Hepher and Shemida. The son of Hepher, Zelophehad, had no sons (see Numbers 27:1-11); the names of the five daughters are given here again. They claim now the inheritance which the Lord had given to them. They, too, exhibit the courage of faith. May we also claim in faith that inheritance which belongs to us through the grace of God.

The complaint of the children of Joseph shows dissatisfaction with their lot; it was selfishness. Joshua takes them by their word. His answer reminds us of the divine command given in chapter 13. "Every place that the sole of your foot shall tread upon, that have I given unto you, as I said unto Moses." Yonder were the stately forests, the wooded hills and mountains, inhabited still by the Perizzites and the giants. All they needed to do was to go there and drive them out and they would possess a larger portion. But this answer but brings out their unbelief and failure. They plead weakness; it was nothing less than unbelief, for they looked to the iron chariots the Canaanites possessed, instead of looking to the Lord and trusting His power. They refused to meet the enemy and have their borders enlarged under these conditions. What a contrast with bold and humble Caleb! And yet Joshua encourages them. He urges them to go forward and possess the forest and cut it down. It was his challenge to their faith. Faith does not reckon with chariots, with difficulties.

6. The Portion of the Rest of the Tribes

CHAPTER 18

1. The tabernacle at Shiloh (18:1)
2. The remaining seven tribes (18:2-10)
3. The lot of Benjamin (18:11-28)

The tabernacle of the congregation is now set up at Shiloh. Shiloh means "peace," "security." The land was then subdued before them. Shiloh is now the center. From there the operations proceed. Seven times after this Shiloh is mentioned in the book of Joshua: Chapter 18:8, 9, 10; 19:51; 21:2; 22:9, 12. Read these carefully and see what happened in connection with Shiloh, the place of rest. The tabernacle remained at Shiloh till the Philistines came and took the ark, as recorded in 1 Samuel 4:11. Then it was at Nob in the days of Saul, then at Jerusalem, at Gibeon in the beginning of Solomon's reign (2 Chronicles 1:3). It never got back to this first resting-place.

At that time seven tribes still remained without an inheritance. They seemed to be content without any inheritance whatever. Most likely they had also become tired of war. Theirs had been a strenuous experience. It was difficult work to go forth and conquer, to occupy new territory and meet the enemies. They must likewise have come into possession of many things for their comfort, which were unknown to them in the wilderness; and with the natural and plentiful resources of the land they became self-indulgent and were at ease. Joshua's earnest appeal suggests such a state of the people. "How long are ye slack to go to possess the land which the Lord God of your fathers hath given you?" And their negligence in not possessing the land avenged itself, for the unpossessed land with its enemies became "scourges in their sides and thorns in their eyes." What ingratitude it was, after God's wonderful power had brought them in, that they should neglect to avail themselves of so great a gift! Such is man, always a failure in himself. It needs hardly to be said, that all this finds an application with ourselves, whom the Lord has brought into a better land and richer inheritance. How slack we are to go to possess the land! How many neglect so great salvation! Joshua then gave instructions and the men selected walked through the land and made a survey of it.

The inheritance of Benjamin is described in the remaining portion of this chapter. Their lot fell into a steep, mountainous country; many of the cities they received were in high places, indicated by such names as Gideon (hilly); Gibeath (a hill); Gaba (elevation); Ramah (the height); Mizpeh (watch-tower), etc. May we ascend the heights of glory we have in Christ, and walk in our high-places, with feet as swift as the hinds' feet (Habakkuk 3:19). And we too have our "Mizpeh," the place of watching and waiting for Him, who will lead us into our wonderful inheritance in the day of His coming glory.

"Benjamin was counted the least of the tribes (1 Samuel 9:21), and when, with other tribes, it was represented by its chief magistrate, it was rather disparagingly distinguished as 'little Benjamin with their ruler' (Psalm 68:27). Yet it was strong enough, on one occasion, to set at defiance for a time the combined forces of the other tribes (Judges 20:12, etc.) It was distinguished for the singular skill of its slingers; seven hundred, who were left-handed, 'could every one sling stones at an hair-breadth and not miss' (Judges 20:16). The character of its territory, abounding in rocky mountains, and probably in game, for the capture of which the sling was adapted, might, in some degree, account for this peculiarity.

"Many famous battles were fought on the soil of Benjamin. The battle of Ai; that of Gibeon, followed by the pursuit through Bethhoron, both under Joshua; Jonathan's battle with the Philistines at Michmash (1 Samuel 14), and the duel at Gibeon between twelve men of Saul and twelve of David (2 Samuel 2:15, 16); were all fought within the territory of Benjamin. And when Sennacherib approached Jerusalem from the north, the places which were thrown into panic as he came near were in this tribe. 'He is come to Aiath, he is passed through Migron; at Michmash he layeth up his baggage; they are gone over the pass; they have taken up their lodging at Geba; Ramah trembleth; Gibeah of Saul is fled. Cry aloud with thy voice, O daughter of Gallim! Hearken, O Laishah! O thou poor Anathoth! Madmenah is a fugitive, the inhabitants of Gebim gather themselves to flee. This very day shall he halt at Nob; he shaketh his hand at the mount of the daughter of Zion, the hill of Jerusalem (Isaiah 10:28-32, R. V.). In later times Judas Maccabeus gained a victory over the Syrian forces at Bethhoron; and, again, Cestius and his Roman troops were defeated by the Jews" (*Expositor's Bible*).

The tribe counted the least, "little Benjamin," came into possession of the richest inheritance, which is abundantly witnessed to by the names of the different cities, if we diligently search out their meaning. God delights to take up what is little and make it great. (Saul of Tarsus, our great Apostle Paul (Paul means "little"), was of the tribe of Benjamin. He possessed and enjoyed his inheritance in the heavenlies.)

CHAPTER 19

1. The inheritance of Simeon (19:1-19)
2. The inheritance of Zebulun (19:10-16)
3. The inheritance of Issachar (19:17-23)
4. The inheritance of Asher (19:24-31)
5. The inheritance of Naphtali (19:32-39)
6. The inheritance of Dan (19:40-48)
7. The inheritance of Joshua (19:49-51)

The many names of cities and villages, the inheritance of the remaining six tribes, we must leave untouched. Blessed and deep spiritual lessons are written in all these names. Simeon's inheritance is closely connected with that of Judah. "Their inheritance was in the midst of the inheritance of the children of Judah." Simeon means "hearing" and Judah means "praise." Thus the two are linked together. If our hearts are open to hear and our faith appropriates we praise and worship and enjoy our God-given inheritance in the Lord Jesus Christ. And the different cities have a blessed meaning. Diligent and prayerful searching will discover the hidden treasures which faith prizes more than gold, and which are "sweeter than honey." Let us glance briefly at Asher to give a little illustration of this. Asher means "happy," commonly translated by "blessed" (Psalm 1:1; 32:1; 119:1). The Lord's people must be a happy people. Moses had pronounced them so (Deuteronomy 33:29). A few of the cities and boundaries of Asher and their meaning will show in what the happiness of God's people consists. Helkath means "portion"; the Lord Himself is the portion of His people. He is our joy and happiness. Hali means "an ornament worked out with pain." We possess that which Christ has worked out for us in His death. Ahamelech means "God is King." This is a sweet morsel to faith. Amad, "an eternal people," speaks of our security, that we belong to God and nothing can separate us from Him. Misheal, "feeling after God," tells of the longing of the new nature, which finds happiness in God. Hammon, "sunny"; Kanah, 'He has purchased"; Zidon, "taking the prey"; Hosah, "trust"; Ummah, "union"; Aphek, "strength"—these and others are easily seen as giving spiritual lessons on the happiness of the people of God who enjoy in faith the inheritance.

After all had received their portions Joshua received his. It was Timnath-serah, which means "an abundant portion." The portion of Joshua is the blessed type of the inheritance, which the Lord Jesus Christ has received. We must not overlook the fact that the children of Israel gave Joshua the inheritance. Christ is our inheritance and we are His inheritance. He has an inheritance in the saints (Ephesians 1:18). May we give Him that inheritance.

7. The Cities of Refuge

CHAPTER 20

1. The ordinance repeated (20:1-6)
2. The cities named (20:7-9)

The reader will find the meaning of the ordinance of the cities of refuge in Numbers and Deuteronomy, so that we do not need to repeat it here. But only three cities are mentioned in the Pentateuch. Here the three cities in the land are added. Kedesh was in Naphtali. Kedesh means "sanctuary," and Naphtali means "wrestler—struggler." Christ is the refuge for the struggling sinner. Shechem means "shoulder," and is the type of service. He who is the perfect servant, who ministered and gave His life, is the place of refuge. Kirjath-arba, which is Hebron, is the third, and Hebron means "communion." This we find in Him. Bezer (defense), Ramoth (heights) and Golan (rejoicing) were the other three beyond Jordan, named already in the Pentateuch.

8. The Portion of the Levites

CHAPTER 21

1. The Levites, the children of Aaron, and their portions (21:1-8)
2. Kohath (21:9-26)
3. Gershon (21:27-33)
4. Merari (21:34-40)
5. The Lord's faithfulness (21:41-45)

In chapters 13:14, 33 and 14:3, 4 the statement is made that Moses gave no inheritance to the Levites. The Lord was their inheritance. After the tribes had received their allotments the heads of the fathers of the Levites came to Joshua and Eleazar with a petition. They based their petition upon the Word of God spoken to Moses. "Command the children of Israel, that they give unto the Levites of the inheritance of their possession cities to dwell in; and ye shall give also unto the Levites suburbs for the cities round about them" (Numbers 35:2). The people were obedient and gave them cities out of their several inheritances. But the cities were also assigned by lot, so that the Lord assigned them their habitations. How it must have pleased Him to see His Word remembered, obeyed and acted upon! They were scattered throughout the entire domain of Israel. The Kohathites and the children of Aaron had thirteen cities in the tribes of Judah, Benjamin and Simeon, and two more in Ephraim, Dan and Manasseh. The Gershonites were placed in cities in eastern Manasseh, Issachar, Asher and Naphtali. The Merarites were in Zebulun and among Gad and Reuben. The divine purpose in scattering them over the land was, no doubt, that they might exercise a beneficent influence in divine things to exhort the tribes to worship Jehovah, to remind them of His goodness and to restrain them from idolatry. At the close of this chapter we read of the faithfulness of the Lord. He gave them the land; He gave them rest; He gave them victory. "There failed not ought of any good thing which the Lord had spoken." All God's promises will be in due time accomplished.

III. The Final Words of Joshua and the Epilogue

1. The Two and One-half Tribes and the Altar Ed

CHAPTER 22

1. Joshua's address (22:1-6)
2. The tribes dismissed and their return (22:7-9)
3. The great altar erected (22:10)
4. War proposed (22:11-12)
5. The mission of Phinehas and the explanation (22:13-29)
6. The explanation accepted (22:30-31)
7. The altar Ed (22:32-34)

A beautiful scene is before us. Joshua, the aged servant of God, called the Reubenites, the Gadites and half of Manasseh. Their selfish choice is selecting their portion on this side of Jordan is found in Numbers. They had, however, to pass over Jordan with the other tribes and help them in the conflict (chapter 1:12-18). The promise they had made was conscientiously kept and the time for their return to their habitations had come. Joshua commends them for their faithfulness, and exhorts them to love the Lord, to walk in all His ways, to keep His commandments, to cleave unto Him and to serve Him. May we also heed these words. Only as we walk in all His ways and are obedient to His Word can we enjoy the fellowship and the spiritual blessings which belong to us. They returned with great riches, with silver, gold, brass, iron and raiment.

They erected, after their homegoing, a great altar (Hebrew: An altar great to the sight). It was of immense size, so that it might be seen far and wide as a silent witness. When the rest of Israel heard of this altar, and thinking that it meant a separate worship, instituted by these two and a half tribes, they were ready to go to war. They exhibited great zeal for the Lord and were ready to carry out His Word. See Exodus 20:24; Leviticus 17:8-9; Deuteronomy 7:5-13; 8:7-13. But while they were zealous, they also exhibited wisdom and sent Phinehas with ten princes to investigate the supposed apostasy. The explanation follows and is accepted. The altar was then called Ed, which means "witness." It was to bear witness between them, that the Lord is God, and that the tribes, though separated by Jordan, are one people. But where is to-day the witness in Christendom that there is one body? That witness seems to have been lost.

2. Joshua's Two Addresses

The First Address

CHAPTER 23

1. The people gathered (23:1-2)
2. God's faithfulness remembered (23:3-5)
3. Exhortations to obedience (23:6-11)
4. Warning (23:12-13)
5. Conclusion of first address (23:14-16)

It was about eight years after the Lord had given rest unto Israel, that the aged Joshua called for all Israel and their elders to assemble in his presence. He was very old and the time of his departure at hand. The purpose of his first address is to remind the people and their elders of the Lord's faithfulness in keeping all His promises, and to exhort them to be faithful to Him and to warn them of the results of apostasy. He exhorts them with the same message, which the Lord had given to him in the beginning of the book. Compare verse 6 with chapter 1:7. He had been obedient to this command and the Lord had done all for him He had promised. Joshua was a man of faith and courage, an excellent character.

"He is characterized by conscientious fidelity to the Law, and unclouded theocratical sentiments. He is deliberate and prudent when he acts himself, for he conducts the wars of the Lord; but he becomes prompt, bold and decided, when the Lord sends him. His courage is humility, his strength is faith, his wisdom is obedience and the fear of the Lord. He has a gentle spirit, but does not betray weakness; the evidence of the latter is furnished by his strict judgment in the case of Achan, and the scrupulous exactness with which he executes the Lord's sentence respecting the Canaanites. Such a union of gentleness and rigor, of simplicity and prudence, of humility and grandeur of sentiment, presents evangelical features. This peculiarity of his character, combined with the peculiarity of that age of the kingdom of God in which he lived, and also of the position which he occupied, adapts both himself and the work which he performed to be highly significant types of the future. He conducts the people into the land of promise and of rest; but there remains a better rest into which his archetype, who bears the same name, conducts the people of God (Hebrews 4:8,9); he carries on the wars, and executes the judgments of the Lord, in which are shadowed the victories and judgments of Christ.

"The sentiments which govern Joshua, pervade the people in general in his day. The whole history of the chosen people presents no other period in which they were generally animated by such zeal in the cause of the theocracy, by such conscientious fidelity to the Law, by such vigorous faith and sincere fear of God as that generation manifested. It was the period of first love, and, in this aspect, may be compared with the first centuries of the Christian Church."[3]

And we need, as His people, the courage of faith to stand for the Lord and for His Word in the days of departure from God. And Joshua's warning was sadly fulfilled in the subsequent history of Israel.

The Second Address

CHAPTER 24:1-28

1. The gathering at Shechem (24:1)
2. Historic retrospect and exhortations (24:2-15)
3. The answer given by Israel (24:16-18)
4. Joshua's answer (24:19-20)
5. The promise made (24:21)
6. Joshua's appeal and the repeated promise (24:22-24)
7. The covenant made and Joshua's final word (24:25-28)

In Joshua's second and last address to the people at Shechem we have first a historic retrospect. It must not be overlooked, that the words of Joshua are not his own, but the words given to him by the Lord. "Thus saith the Lord, God of Israel," is the manner in which he begins. The retrospect is a marvel in terse statements and rehearsal of the entire history of Israel, beginning with the call of Abraham. Its object is to remind the assembled congregation once more of the mercies and faithfulness of Jehovah. How soon they may be forgotten! Yet upon remembering what we are by nature and what the Lord in His infinite grace has done for us, depends a true walk with God. The Spirit of God, through Joshua, shows that Abraham was called away from idolatry and traces all Jehovah did for him and his seed. Notice the different acts of the Lord. I took your father Abraham—I led him—I multiplied his seed—I gave him Isaac—I gave—I sent Moses—I plagued Egypt—I brought you out—I brought you into the land. All the promises made in Exodus and Deuteronomy concerning the possession and conquest of the land had been fulfilled. Read Exodus 23:28 and Deuteronomy 7:20 and compare with verse 12. He gave them a land for which they did not labor.

The covenant is then renewed. Beautiful are Joshua's words, "As for me and my house, we will serve the Lord." He had served Him all his life and on the eve of his departure, he renews his vow. With such an enthusiastic, consecrated and successful leader, the people could only answer in the affirmative. They renewed their

---

[3]J. H. Kurtz, *Sacred History.*

previous promise to serve the Lord. The answer they gave is an echo of Joshua's words. They repeat what Jehovah had so graciously done unto them. Joshua's answer to the enthusiastic reply of the people was "Ye cannot serve the Lord." He well knew by the light of the Spirit of God that this people, so stiffnecked in the past, would soon depart from this resolution and follow other gods. Besides this, Joshua knew the final words of Moses, the great prophecies concerning the apostasy of the nation, their deep fall into idolatries and their coming dispersion among the Gentiles. With the Word of God before him, he could not believe that the future of the people, whom Jehovah had brought out and brought in, would be a future of obedience and blessing. He is not deceived by the enthusiasm which had taken hold of the assembled congregation. We also have in the New Testament the predictions and the warnings concerning the course of the professing church on earth during the present age. We do well to heed these. If not we shall be deceived in expecting that which is nowhere promised for this age.

"The predictions of the Church's course have so little ambiguity that it is marvelous that the smooth preaching of peace, and the comforting assurance of progressive blessing, could ever gain credence with those who boast in an 'open Bible,' But the Bible can be but little 'open' as long as man's pride and self-seeking hang their imaginative veil before it; and the Church, believing herself heir to Israel's promises, has largely refused to accept the lessons of Israel's career, which she has so closely followed. Thank God, we are near the end of the strange history of almost two millennia; and for us the end is the coming of the Lord" (F. W. Grant).

The covenant was thus renewed and a great stone set up as a witness. How long did it last? Our next book gives the answer: "And the children of Israel did evil in the sight of the Lord, and served the Baalim" (Judges 2:11). "And they forsook the Lord and served Baal and Ashtaroth" (verse 13).

3. The Epilogue

CHAPTER 24:29-33

1. Joshua's death and burial (24:29-31)
2. The bones of Joseph buried (24:32)
3. Eleazar's death (24:33)

Moses, the instrument through whom the law was given, was buried by the Lord, no doubt a hint that some day the Lord would put away the law, with its curse, as we learn in the New Testament. Joshua was buried by the people in his own inheritance; he died ten years younger than Moses, that is 110 years old. Joseph had reached the same age, having died some 200 years before. Genesis 1:25, Exodus 13:19 and Hebrews 11:22 must be consulted to understand the burial of his bones recorded here. They had carried those bones all through the wilderness and never attempted to bury them till they were settled in the land. The book closes with the account of Eleazar's death.

Appendix

The Dispensational Aspect of the Book of Joshua

The book of Joshua foreshadows the great coming events in which Israel, Israel's land and the nations are concerned. Everything in Israel's history is prophetic. The events connected with the lives of the patriarchs, Abraham, Isaac and Jacob, as well as the story of Joseph, have a prophetic dispensational meaning. Israel in the furnace of Egypt foreshadows Babylon, and also the great dispersion in which they are now. Their persecutors then were Gentiles, who hated them and would not let them go; Gentiles are still troubling them and will persecute them during the time of the end. Their remarkable experiences and preservation in Egypt are the types of their miraculous keeping, and no less miraculous increase among all the nations of the world, among whom they have been scattered. The plagues which fell upon Egypt are typical of the judgments of God, which will fall upon the world at the close of the present age. Their Exodus from Egypt teaches similar lessons. The passage through the Red Sea, their slain enemies and the song of praise, as given in Exodus 15, have likewise a dispensational aspect. So has the visible presence of Jehovah. As He was there with His people, so will He be with them again.

As we have seen in the study of Numbers, the parables of Balaam are great prophecies touching the future of Israel. When the dying people were looking upon the brazen serpent, and the healing which resulted, may also be taken as a type of their future looking upon Him, whom they have pierced. There is therefore also a dispensational foreshadowing in the book of Joshua. We shall mention seven things.

I. The Possession of the Land

That goodly land in its great dimensions is still Israel's land, the land of promise. They have yet to possess it from the Euphrates to the River Nile. To say that Israel will never receive the land and possess it in the future as a redeemed people, would mean the same as accusing God of breaking His promise and oath-bound covenants.

As surely as we are in Christ the heirs of God and joint-heirs with the Lord Jesus Christ, so surely will Israel inherit and possess the land. As there was a definite time for Israel to cross Jordan and possess the land, so is there a definite time when God will bring them in again. It will be when the measure of wickedness of the nations, who are the present possessors of the land, is filled up, as the wickedness of the Canaanites was filled up in Joshua's days. When that time comes God will once more remember the covenant, and He will give the land back to His people and bring them in through Joshua.

The land is God's gift. We have often talked with Jews and Zionists. Some years ago a Zionistic leader mentioned in our presence their plans of getting the land back gradually, and eventually buy the whole land. We asked him: "What would you think, if your horse had been stolen by a thief, and you knew the thief, went to him and offered him a hundred dollars to buy your horse back? Would it not be the most nonsenical as well as unjust dealing? You Zionists are trying to buy back the land from the power which has no right to have the land." That power holds stolen property. And, besides, this land, according to the law, is not to be bought nor to be sold. To-day the power which holds Palestine, Turkey, is crumbling to pieces. It is only the question of time when the fate of Palestine has to be decided.

II. Joshua Their Leader

As we have mentioned before in the annotations, Joshua means "Jehovah is Saviour." Moses, the first one, could not bring them in, but Joshua, the second divinely appointed leader, brought them in. Moses is the type of Christ's first coming, and Joshua the type of the second coming of Christ. It is at the second coming of our Lord that Israel will receive the land. He will restore to them the God-given inheritance.

Under Joshua the people were no longer stiff-necked, but obedient and submissive, willing followers of Him who led them forth. This will be the case when the Lord Jesus Christ returns. Then they will be His willing people (Psalm 110:3). Joshua was magnified before the eyes of all Israel, even as Christ will be magnified when He comes again. At the close of the fourth chapter of Joshua we read that all the people may know and fear the Lord. This surely will be the result of the second Coming of our Lord.

III. The Spies and Rahab

God's abounding grace is illustrated in the salvation of Rahab and her house. In the New Testament we find her with three other Gentile women in the genaelogy of our Lord in Matthew's Gospel. We read of her in Hebrews 11 and in the Epistle of James. The meaning of these passages has already been pointed out. The scarlet line, and her security and salvation from judgment, we have also seen in the annotations. But the story has still another application.

The two spies entered the land in advance of the whole nation. They were faithful and courageous men, and took their lives into their own hands. They may well be taken as a type of the faithful remnant, which will be a kind of an advance guard entering into the land, before the rest of Israel is taking possession. The King of Jericho, who seeks their lives, is the type of that wicked one, the counterfeit king and messiah. Their flight to the mountains reminds us of the word of warning given by our Lord in His Olivet discourse, "Let them that be in Judea flee unto the mountains." Rahab, who believed and hid the spies and was saved on account of it, foreshadows those of the nations, who believe the last message concerning the coming of the King and the judgment in store for this earth. They will do good to the Jewish remnant, as Rahab did hide the spies. When the Lord comes and takes the seat upon the throne of His Glory, He will say to them: "What ye have done to the least of these, My brethren, ye have done unto Me." Rahab remained in the land and enjoyed blessings with Israel. So the nations, who believe during the great tribulation, will remain on the earth, and not be swept away by the divine judgments.

IV. The Events at Gilgal have a Prophetic Significance

The circumcision of Israel, as carried out by Joshua, is the type of the spiritual circumcision which the Lord will effect for the whole nation. Of this the Word of prophecy speaks: "And the Lord thy God will circumcise thine heart and the heart of thy seed, to love the Lord thy God with all thine heart and with all thy soul, that thou mayest live" (Deuteronomy 30). "Behold I will gather them out of all countries, whither I have driven them in My anger, and in My fury and great wrath; and I will bring them again unto this place, and I will cause them to dwell safely. And they shall be My people, and I will be their God. And I will give them one heart, and one way, that they may fear Me forever, for the good of them, and of their children after them" (Jeremiah 32:37-39). "Then I will sprinkle clean water upon you, and ye shall be clean; from all your filthiness and all your idols will I cleanse you. And a new heart will I give you, and a new spirit will I put within you. And I will take away the stony heart out of your flesh, and I will give you an heart of flesh" (Ezekiel 36:25-28). Then the reproach, which has rested upon them for so long, will be rolled away. They will become the head of all the nations of the world.

V. The Fall of Jericho and the Overthrow of Israel's Enemies

As stated in the annotations, Jericho is the type of the world ripe for judgment. The number seven, in its frequency in the fall of Jericho, the reader will find more fully described in the annotations of chapter 6. The walls of Jericho fell without the single sword being lifted up. The breath of Jehovah laid them flat. So shall the day come when the power of God will throw down the high and lofty things.

The warfare which Israel carried on is likewise prophetic. Israel was used to execute God's vengeance upon the wicked nations of Canaan. It will be repeated in the future. "Thou art My battle-ax and weapons of war; for with thee will I break in pieces the nations, and with thee will I destroy kingdoms" (Jeremiah 51:20). Read also Micah 5:8-9; Ezekiel 39:10; Zechariah 2:6; Zechariah 14:14.

VI. Battle at Gibeon

It was the most remarkable battle in Israel's history. There was no day like it, nor ever after, because the Lord hearkened unto the voice of Joshua. The Lord fought for Israel. The sun stood still, and the moon stayed until the people had avenged themselves upon their enemies. This is a prophetic type of the coming day of the Lord. What will happen in that day? Habakkuk, seeing that day and describing its detail, tells us, "The sun and the moon stood still in their habitation, at the light of thine arrows, as they went, at the shining of thy glittering spear. Thou didst march through the land in indignation; thou didst thresh the nations in anger. Thou wentest forth for the salvation of thy people, for salvation with thine anointed; thou woundest the head of the house of the wicked by laying bare the foundations to the neck" (Habakkuk 3).

VII. The Division of the Land and Israel's Rest

They came into the land, and the land was divided unto them by lot. Though it was not a permanent rest, yet the land had rested from wars for a time, and the tabernacle was set up at Shiloh. The prophetic Word tells us, that when Israel is brought in, they shall no more be plucked out of the land. There is in store for them a great Sabbath, a great jubilee, when His people and His land will have rest. It will be after the Lord has come. Then the land will be re-divided. See Ezekiel 47—48. Israel's land will then become, with its magnificent temple, the gloryland of this earth, the center of the Kingdom.

THE BOOK OF THE
JUDGES

Introduction

The previous book began with the statement: "Now after the death of Moses, the servant of the Lord, it came to pass"; the book of Joshua is, therefore, closely linked with Deuteronomy. The book of Judges has for its opening word a similar announcement: "Now after the death of Joshua it came to pass." Judges is, therefore, the book which contains Israel's history after the occupation of the promised land and the death of Joshua. It covers about 320 years, extending to the judgeship of Samuel. In Acts 13:20 we read: "And after that He gave them judges about the space of four hundred and fifty years, until Samuel the prophet." This is a general statement and does not claim a chronological character. It is founded on the addition of the numbers mentioned in Judges. Some of these synchronize with others and must be deducted from the total.

"We find one express and clearly fixed chronological point in 1 Kings 6:1, according to which 480 years intervene between the departure out of Egypt, and the building of the temple, in the fourth year of Solomon's reign; after the necessary deductions have been made, about 320 years remain for the age of the Judges. The chronological data in the book of Judges agree with this result, if the Ammonite oppression of the east-Jordanic territory (Jephthah, Ibzan, Elon, Abdon) are assumed as contemporaneous with the Philistine oppression of the west-Jordanic territory (Eli, Samson, Samuel). In this case, Eli's priesthood preceded the term of Samson's labors; the first operations of Samuel (merely prophetic in their character), belong to Samson's term, and it was only after the death of the latter that he assumed the office of a Judge. It may, indeed, appear a singular circumstance, that the book of Judges should not refer to Eli and Samuel, and that the two books of Samuel should not mention Samson, but both circumstances are readily and satisfactorily explained by the difference in the objects for which these books respectively were written. The books of Samuel design to relate the history of David, the necessary introduction of which is an account of Saul, Samuel, and Eli, the events of whose lives are interwoven with those which belong to the earlier years of David's career; and here no reference whatever to Samson was required. The book of Judges, on the other hand, relates nothing concerning Eli, because he was not a judge, in the peculiar sense of that word, but presided over public affairs merely in the capacity of a high-priest; and it related nothing concerning Samuel, since his later acts, when he officiated as a judge, no longer belong to the period of Israel's repeated apostasy from Jehovah, which it is the design of this book to describe."[1]

The main part of the book of Judges is given to the sad history of Israel's departure from God, their chastisement and deliverance through the mercy and faithfulness of the Lord. The divinely given predictions through Moses, recorded in Deuteronomy, are now seen passing into history. Joshua's warning is being fulfilled. "Know for a certainty that the Lord your God will no more drive out any of those nations from before you; but they shall be snares and traps unto you, and scourges in your side, and thorns in your eyes, until you perish from off this good land which the Lord our God hath given you" (Josh. 23:13). The whole nation disintegrates. All goes to pieces. The whole sad story of decline is written in two statements, one at the beginning and the other at the end of the book. In the beginning of this book they asked the question of who is first to go up to fight the Canaanites (chapter 1:1). At the end they ask who is to battle against their own, to fight the children of Benjamin (20:18). They began in the Spirit and ended in the flesh. First, they fought the common foe, then they fought each other.

The book of Judges, therefore, records the complete failure of the people of God and the graciousness of the Lord. Perhaps nowhere else in the Word of God do we find the patience and faithfulness of Jehovah towards an unfaithful and backsliding people so fully made known as in Judges.

The instruments Jehovah used were the

---

[1]J. H. Kurtz, *Sacred History.*

judges. They were raised up by God in the days of declension to bring about deliverances from the enemies, who had been permitted to bring Israel into servitude. They were, therefore, more than what the word judge in our language denotes. They were prophets in action. Their persons show how God has chosen the weak things to accomplish His purposes. One was left-handed. Another used an ox-goad; still another pitcher and trumpets and one had for a weapon the jawbone of an ass. One was a woman. There were thirteen judges. Six declensions are clearly marked by the phrase that the children of Israel did evil in the sight of the Lord (3:7, 12; 4:1; 10:6; 8:1). And these six main declensions resulted in corresponding punishments followed by gracious deliverances through the Judges.

What is the value and meaning of this historical book? If it has no other object beyond acquainting us with Israel's history, a deeper study would indeed be useless.

Again we refer to that familiar New Testament word, which fully authorizes us to read these histories in their typical bearings. "Now all these things happened unto them as types; and they are written for our admonition, upon whom the ends of the ages have come" (1 Cor. 10:11). "For as many things as have been written before have been written for our instruction, that through endurance and through encouragement of the Scriptures we might have hope" (Rom. 15:4).

We have learned from the study of the Pentateuch, especially from the history of Israel in Egypt, her experiences in the wilderness and entrance into the promised land, how indeed all these things are types and what blessed lessons are written everywhere for our instruction. The history of the book of Judges finds also a most interesting and important typical application. The book of Joshua typifies the heavenly blessings of the people of God and the heavenly inheritance (corresponding to Ephesians). The book of Judges unfolds in a typical way the sad story of the decline, apostasy, dissension and corruption of the professing church on earth. The different errors and evils of Christendom may be traced here as well as the different revivals and restorations. The flesh and the world and what allegiance these lead to, slavery and misery with distance from Jehovah, and how the Lord can deliver and bring back His people, are the prominent lessons of this book. Like Joshua and the Pentateuch, Judges is so full and rich in these spiritual types and instructions that they cannot be exhausted. We touch upon these things in the analysis and annotations. May they prove to be helpful hints to a deeper study of this neglected book. And blessed are we if we discover our individual experience, our failures, our need and the faithfulness of our gracious Lord in this book and thus learn more of Him.

The Division of the Book of the Judges

The history of the different declensions in Israel, their oppression by the enemies, and the work wrought by the judges the Lord raised up, begins with chapter 3:5 and is continuously related to the end of chapter 16. The opening chapters of the book are a general introduction, part of which touches upon the contents of the book itself. Chapters 17—21 are an appendix to the main part. The events recorded in these closing chapters must have occurred a little while after the death of Joshua, during the life-time of Phinehas, the high-priest (20:28). They give a glimpse of the sad internal conditions of the people, how every man did that which was right in his own eyes. Their complete failure towards God and towards themselves as the people of God is clearly seen in these records.

This gives us a threefold division of the book of Judges.

I. THE INTRODUCTION—ISRAEL'S FAILURES AND THE RESULTS

1. **Israel's Failure in mingling with Canaanites** (1:1-36)
2. **The Angel at Bochim and the history of the entire Book** (2:4—3:4)

II. THE DECLENSIONS, PUNISHMENTS AND DELIVERANCES

1. **The Sin of Idolatry and Othniel** (3:5-11)
2. **Second Declension: Under Moab—Ehud and Shamgar** (3:12-31)
3. **Third Declension: Under Jabin and Deborah and Barak** (4:1—5:16)
4. **Fourth Declension: Under Midian and Gideon, Tola and Jair** (6:1—10:5)
5. **Fifth Declension: Under the Philistines and Ammon. Jephthah, Ibzan, Elon and Abdon** (10:6—12:15)
6. **Sixth Declension: Under the Philistines and Samson** (13—16)

III. THE APPENDIX: ISRAEL'S INTERNAL CORRUPTION

1. **Micah's idolatry and its punishment** (27—28)
2. **Israel's moral condition and the War on Benjamin** (19—21)

Analysis and Annotations

I. The Introduction: Israel's Failure and the Results

1. Israel's Failure in mingling with the Canaanites

CHAPTER 1

1. The question and the answer (1:1-4)
2. Adoni-Bezek (1:5-7)
3. Jerusalem (1:8)
4. Judah's victory and failure (1:9-20)
5. The children of Benjamin and their failure (1:21)
6. The failures of others (1:22-36)

The book begins with an inquiry of the Lord. This was immediately after the death of Joshua. From chapter 2:7-10 we learn that the people served the Lord during the days of Joshua and the elders who had seen the great works of the Lord and who outlived their leader. Israel looked to the Lord for guidance. They feel their dependence upon Him. How different the history of His people would have been if they had maintained this dependence on the Lord, and acted always in subjection to Him! And the Lord answered the inquiry as He always delights to answer those who put their trust in Him. Judah is to go up to fight against the Canaanite, and the Lord promises victory. The first sign of weakness follows at once. Judah invites Simeon his brother to go with him to fight against the Canaanites, and he promises in return to help Simeon in conquering his lot. It showed that Judah had not full confidence in Jehovah. He put some dependence in his brother, as if he needed his help to gain the promised victory. How often His people have dishonored the Lord by trusting in something besides Himself. Judah going forward by divine command, yet asking the help of Simeon, gained victories, yet he could not drive out the inhabitants of the valley, for they had chariots of iron (verse 19). What is iron to omnipotence! Had Judah gone forth in utter dependence on Jehovah and in His promise, "I have delivered the land into his hand," the chariots of iron would have not stopped him.

But there were great victories, the blessed assurance that Jehovah is with His people, if they go but forward. Adoni-Bezek is punished in the same manner as he in his wickedness had done to others. Infidels have often found fault with the extermination of the Canaanites. The confession of Adoni-Bezek answers these objections. "As I have done, so God hath requited me." Their punishment was just and well deserved.

The eighth verse is of interest. In Joshua 10:1 Jerusalem is mentioned for the first time in the Bible and that in connection with war. Here the city is smitten by the sword and burned with fire. This has been her history over and over again, and will be again in the future, till the times of the Gentiles are fulfilled.

Then there is mentioned once more the most refreshing picture of Caleb, Othniel and Achsah. (See Joshua 15:16-19.) Othniel, which means "lion of God," is the center of it. God delights in whole-heartedness and the victories of His people.

The rest of this first chapter has failure stamped upon it. Benjamin, the warrior tribe permitted the Jebusites to dwell with them and did not drive them out. There is not even a reported attempt. The command of the Lord was wholly ignored by them. They were in the worst condition (chapters 20—21). Manasseh failed. Ephraim did not drive out the Canaanites that dwelt in Gezer. Zebulun, Asher and Naphtali all failed to dislodge the enemies God had commanded them to destroy entirely. And Dan instead of conquering was conquered. The Amorites forced them into the hill country. Unbelief, lack of confidence in Jehovah, was the cause of it all. These enemies here are typical of the flesh and the fleshly lusts in the believer And these lusts, the carnal nature, must be put and kept in the place of death. We are enabled to do this by faith in our Lord Jesus Christ and through the power of the Holy Spirit, who is given to us of God. If we walk not in the Spirit, that is, in faith, we shall be overcome by these things; instead of conquering we will be conquered. The old nature not triumphed over will bring us into bondage as it is with so many of God's children.

2. The Angel at Bochim and the History of the Entire Book

CHAPTERS 2:1—3:4

1. The angel at Bochim (2:1-5)
2. Israel's obedience remembered (2:6-16)
3. Israel's strange gods (2:11-15)
4. Israel's history under the judges outlined (2:16-18)
5. The nations left to prove Israel (2:19—3:4)

The opening event of this chapter is significant. The Angel of the Lord came up from Gilgal to Bochim. This Angel is Jehovah Himself. His own words reveal this fact. In Joshua's time after the land had been possessed the Angel of the Lord, Jehovah in visible form, was with them and as leader of the Lord's host led them on in the conquest (Joshua 5:13-15). Israel had left Gilgal, the place where the reproach had been rolled away, the place of the "sharp knives," typical of self-judgment. It was for Israel the place of strength and power for victory, as it gave the flesh nothing to glory in. They had left Gilgal. How often we, who are crucified with Christ, leave our Gilgal and instead of glorying in the Lord and having no confidence in the flesh, we too act in self-confidence. The place to which the Angel went was "Bochim." It means "weepers." It was the best place for Israel to be after all their failures to do what the Lord had commanded them. It is the place today for us in the midst of the worldliness in which so many of the Lord's people have drifted, as well as the divisions which exist among those, who are members of the one body, and other evils besides. But Bochim, the place for weeping, must be the place of self-judgment and confession. It was not so for Israel. They wept when the plain words of Jehovah told them their disobedience and when they heard what should follow. "I will not drive them out before you; but they shall be as thorns in your sides, and their gods shall be a snare unto you." But we do not read anything of a true repentance and return unto Jehovah.

From chapter 2:6—3:4 we have the history of the whole period of judges outlined. There is first mention made of their obedience and service, how they began in the Spirit. The second generation, as it is always the case, leads to failure. For the first time we read the words which, as already stated, appear in six other places in this book. "And the children of Israel did evil in the sight of the Lord." They forsook Him, the loving, gracious Jehovah, whose kindness and tender mercies are so fully revealed in their past history and instead of serving such a God, they served Baal and Ashtaroth. Connected with this Canaanite "religion" were the vilest immoralities by which they were dragged down to the level of these doomed nations. All moral corruption, social and political confusion is the result of turning away from God. Romans 1:19-32 reveals the awful steps down. Christendom in apostasy, turning away from God and from the light, leads to moral corruption as well. Turning away from the truth means being turned into fables.

The Lord then acted in behalf of His backslidden people and raised up judges (verses 16-18). The result was recovery, and once more the people under these revivals rejoiced in victory over their enemies and the promised covenant blessings. Self-judgment, which is true repentance, had to precede each revival. They cried unto the Lord; they sought His face, and then deliverance came. Even so it is in the individual experience of the children of God.

Yet in spite of these revivals in Israel the tendency is downward. "When the judge died they returned and corrupted themselves beyond their fathers . . . they ceased not from their own doings, nor from their stubborn way." So it has been in the professing Church. Revivals have come and gone, but it is has not remedied the wayward conditions, and the departure from God and His Word becomes more and more pronounced till the final great apostasy is reached. The only complete deliverance can be the coming of the Lord which we do not find fully revealed in the types of the book of Judges.

II. The Declensions, Punishments and Deliverances

1. The Sin of Idolatry and Othniel

CHAPTER 3:5-11

1. The first declension (3:5-7)
2. Sold to the king of Mesopotamia (3:8)
3. The deliverance through Othniel (3:9-11)

The first declension, bondage and deliverance is briefly related. We see how Israel went from bad to worse. First, the wicked nations they were to exterminate dwelt amongst them. Then the children of Israel established some relationship with them and dwelt amongst these nations. First, the children of Israel permitted them to exist in their midst; then the doomed nations gained the power over Israel and the people of God became dependent on them. The third step down is inter-marriage. They did exactly what Jehovah had forbidden (Deut. 7:2). Then they began to serve their idol-gods. It began by "forgetting the Lord." The application to the individual believer and to the professing church can easily be made. If He is forgotten, who has redeemed us and made us His own, an alliance with the world is soon formed and rapid decline follows. The same story is written in the message to Ephesus, which stands prophetically for the Apostolic age. "I have against thee that thou hast left thy first love" (Rev. 2:4). Leaving the first love means to have no longer the Lord Jesus Christ as the all-absorbing object before the heart. Thus the decline began in the Church, and it always begins in this way in the individual believer.

Chushan-Rishathaim, king of Mesopotamia, becomes their lord and they served him eight years. This king is the first punitive instrument in Jehovah's hands. His name very significantly reveals the very condition into which Israel had plunged. Chushan-Rishathaim means "the blackness of double wickedness." They had become doubly wicked, leaving Jehovah and serving strange gods.

When they cried unto the Lord out of the depths of their misery and sin, casting themselves once more upon Jehovah and turning their backs upon the strange gods, the Lord answered and sent a saviour[2] who saved them. It is the same Othniel of whom we read in chapter 1:13 and Joshua 15:17. Othniel means "lion of God," and as he was of Judah, he is the type of Him, who is the Lion of the tribe of Judah. Upon him rested the Spirit of the Lord. The king of Mesopotamia was given into his hands, and a rest of fifty years followed for Israel. Thus we too must return to the Lord and expect our deliverance from Him. What grace towards His people is manifested in this first deliverance!

2. Second Declension Under Moab—Ehud and Shamgar

CHAPTER 3:12-31

1. The second declension: serving Eglon, king of Moab (3:12-14)
2. Ehud raised up (3:15)
3. Eglon, king of Moab, slain by Ehud (3:16-25)
4. The deliverance by Shamgar (3:31)

When they continued to do evil Jehovah used Eglon, king of Moab to punish their disobedience and evil-doings. With him there is Ammon and Amalek, a trinity of evil. The city of Palms is Jericho (Deut. 34:3) a type of the world, as we saw from Joshua. Moab pictures typically an outward, empty, Christian profession. Amalek is the type of the lusts of the flesh which flourish with those, who have the form of godliness but deny the power thereof. How many to-day have become captives of Moab! The greater part of Protestantism, with a name to live, yet dead, is in that deplorable condition.

They served Eglon eighteen years. For the second time they cried unto the Lord and again He answered graciously by raising up Ehud, the son of Gera, the left-handed Benjamite. The story of the deliverance wrought by him is interesting. Without repeating the history of the chapter we give briefly its typical meaning. Ehud's father was Gera, which means "meditation." This is needed first of all to get deliverance from a mere profession or world prosperity with its attending evils to bring the soul to a blessed realization of its possessions and blessings in Christ. Ehud means "I will give praise." Here is the deliverance for God's people out of a dead formalism. Meditation on the Word leads to a believing possession of the realities of redemption in our Lord Jesus Christ. This is followed by praise, the confession of His Name. Then Moab's bondage is ended.

Ehud was left-handed, showing the weakness of the instrument. The two-edged dagger is the type of the Word of God, while the hand which grasps it illustrates how faith is to use the sword of the Spirit. Then Ehud, the Son of Gera, the left-handed, thrust the two-edged dagger into the fat belly of Eglon. Fat is the emblem of prosperity, the prosperity of the world by which so many of God's people become captivated. The sword of the Spirit must be plunged into that which is of the world, the lust of the flesh, the lust of the eyes and the pride of life.

"Face to face in this solemn place, in solemn silence and alone they stand; the fat, prosperous world; and poor, left-handed faith. The scene is quickly over. Into the very belly of Eglon sinks the sharp sword of Ehud; the very belly, the centre of all that is of the world and not of the Father; of 'the lust of the flesh, the lust of the eye, the pride of life'; that which flesh serves (Phil. 3) and which is never satisfied, is pierced through and through. With what result? *Its true*

---

[2]The authorized version has 'deliverer.' The correct translation is 'saviour.'

nature is fully exposed. Let us not be so falsely delicate as not to profit by this strong-worded truth. The prosperity of the world, fat and flourishing as it appears externally, is seen under the stroke of God's word—in the light of Jesus, whom it crucified, being the Son of the living God—as nothing but '*dirt.*' Yea, so says another Benjamite, who well knew how to wield that sword: 'I count all things but loss, for the excellency of the knowledge of Christ Jesus my Lord; for whom I have suffered the loss of all things, and do count them *but dung* that I may win Christ and be found in Him.' How much does this leave of fat Eglon alive?"[3]

Then the trumpet of victory was blown. Even so is our faith the victory which overcometh the world.

Shamgar's work seems to have been closely connected with that of Ehud. He smote the Philistines with an ox-goad. The ox-goad is like the sword, an emblem of the Word of God. Then the land had rest for eighty years.

3. Third Declension: Under Jabin, Deborah, and Barak

CHAPTER 4

1. Sold into the hand of Jabin (4:1-2)
2. The cry of the children of Israel (4:3)
3. Deborah and Barak (4:4-11)
4. The conflict and Jael's deed (4:12-24)

Ehud the mighty instrument of Jehovah had died, and again the children of Israel lapsed into evil. Then the Lord sold them into the hand of Jabin, King of Canaan, that reigned in Hazor. His captain was Sisera, which dwelt in Harosheth of the Gentiles. A powerful oppressor he was, for this King had nine hundred chariots of iron and oppressed Israel twenty years. About one hundred and thirty years before Joshua had overcome Jabin, King of Hazor. "He took Hazor and smote the King thereof with the sword, for Hazor before him was the head of all these kingdoms." All were slain and Hazor was burnt with fire. And now the Lord sold them into his hand. This Jabin is a successor of the one whom Joshua had killed. Hazor had been built again out of its ruins. We see, so to speak, a resurrection of an old enemy. It is significant too that this declension and captivity under Jabin is the third one. As mentioned in annotations on Genesis the number three stands everywhere in the Word for revival and resurrection. The former enemy enslaves Israel once more. How often has this been the case in the history of the church, and how true it is to-day. Satan knows how to revive old errors and evils and use them to bring God's people into captivity. And is it not so in our individual experience? Some sin which overpowered us was through the grace and strength of Christ and of His Spirit mastered, and its power broken. But can that same sin not be revived? Is it forever gone? If there is neglect of prayer, no child-like dependence in true humility, no watchfulness, it will, like Jabin, return and domineer over us in even greater power than before. Jabin means "discerning"—"understanding." This city Hazor, where he dwelt, means "enclosure." This Jabin represents human intellect, the understanding of the natural man, which is corrupt and opposed to God and to His revelation. It is the wisdom of the world. Jabin is in his own "enclosure," which rejects and excludes what God has given. The Christian believer is called upon to bring every thought into captivity to the obedience of Christ. "Casting down imaginations (reasonings), and every high thing that exalteth itself against the knowledge of God, and bringing every thought to the obedience of Christ" (2 Cor. 10:5). Man's own thoughts, his natural understanding, must be completely subjected to God's Word. How much of this spirit of exaltation against the knowledge of God is about us and in the professing church! Higher criticism belongs here. All the errors in doctrine, affecting always the Person of our Lord, are the results of putting the thoughts of man above the Word of God. Then in connection with this we must think of the sects and parties, the works of the flesh, that is the natural man and his reasonings, which have divided the body of Christ. These divisions are "the enclosures" of Jabin. "As the enemy of the people of God, it is the wisdom of the world with which we have here to do—a wisdom which reigns in its own 'enclosure,' shut up, as is the constant fashion, in cliques and parties and philosophies, by which it elevates itself over what is outside its boundary. The spirit of it is easily manifest as that of self: self-interest, self-assertion, self-satisfaction, the true 'trader' or Canaanite spirit, that of gain. The inroad of this into the Church was early indeed. 'All seek their own, not the things of Jesus Christ,' was said, in the apostle's days, of those at Rome (Phil. 2:21). Of the Ephesian elders it was prophesied, 'Also of your own selves shall men arise,

[3] F. C. Jennings, *Notes on Judges.*

speaking perverse things, to draw away disciples after them' (Acts 20:30). But already at Corinth the sects and parties produced by such attempts were being formed, as we know, and the true people of God were becoming subject to Jabin's rule; and this has developed much more widely since, even until the Church of God has been broken up into various denominations, to the dishonor of the *One* Name which is upon us all" (F. W. Grant).

Then once more the children of Israel cried unto the Lord. Jabin's mighty oppression and the humiliation connected with it had become so great that they turned to the Lord. How beautiful it is to see throughout these declensions, that the Lord seemed just to wait for this one thing, His people to cry to Him. As soon as they cried He answered. He is the same to-day. How willing and ready He is to break all the chains of His people and save them from the hands of all their enemies! True revivals always started in deep humiliation, in self-judgment, in prayer. But alas! the state of such, who have departed from the faith, who are the willing captives of Satan, who love this present evil age and who do not cry to the Lord! The Lord brought deliverance through a woman, Deborah, the prophetess. The weaker vessel is now summoned to judge. The name Deborah means "the Word." It is the Word and the Word of God alone which can deliver from the wisdom of this world and from error and sin. But Deborah is married. She is the wife of Lapidoth. Lapidoth means "firebrands." He is typical of the Holy Spirit. The Word, and the Spirit in the Word give the victory and deliver. And Deborah did not dwell in an "enclosure." She dwelt under the palm tree between Ramah and Bethel. The palm tree typifies the spiritual prosperity of the believer. This we enjoy if we let the Word in the power of the Spirit judge us. Then we have our Ramah (heights) the blessed knowledge of our standing in Christ and Bethel (House of God) our fellowship with Him. That is where our palm tree, our spiritual blessing lies.

Deborah sent for Barak. Barak means "lightning." Here we have judgment indicated. The Word calls for judgment and judgment will surely come, as it was executed through Barak upon Jabin and his host.

And so this age ends with the lightning flash of judgment, when the bundled up tares will be burned with fire. All the wisdom of this world, higher criticism, Christian Science, falsely socalled, and every other form of evil will then pass away. All error will end forever with the coming of our Lord. But there is a second woman mentioned in this chapter, Jarel the wife of Heber. She slew Sisera, the wicked captain of Jabin, with the tent pin. Her deed is specially celebrated in song.

CHAPTER 5

The Song of Deborah and Barak

1. The praise of Jehovah (5:1-5)
2. The condition of the people and their deliverance (5:6-11)
3. The celebration of the victory and the victors (5:12-22)
4. The fate of the enemy (5:23-31)

This is one of the prophetic songs of the Bible. It is full of the fire of passion and enthusiasm, reflecting the character of the woman through whom the deliverance had been wrought. It has been classed with the barbaric outbursts of the battle-hymns and odes of triumph of heathen nations, likened to some wild chant of a victor, whose blood-thirst has been quenched in the cruel overthrow of his enemies. Such estimates of this song, so often made by the critics of the Bible, are incorrect. Deborah speaks as a prophetess. She begins with ascribing praise to Jehovah; she ends with Jehovah. This prophetic outburst is marked by limitations. She has no glimpse of the final victory which is mentioned in other songs of triumph, and especially in the Psalms. There are phrases which the Holy Spirit utters through Deborah, which He used in other prophetic songs. The following passages of Scripture may be compared with Deborah's words and will be helpful in the closer study of this chapter. Exodus 15:1-9; Deut. 32:1-3, 16-17; Psalm 67:1-4, 8, 11, 34-35; Psalm 83:9-10; Habak. 3:1-4; Psalm 18:7; Psalm 77:11-12; Luke 1:28, 71-74.

While all this is true and we do not forget that Deborah was the chosen instrument, raised up to effect the great deliverance, we also must recognize the strong human element which is so prominent. One must beware of giving to the deeds done, especially to the deed of Jael in its detail, divine sanction and endorsement. It was an act of courage and of faith; she was moved by faith and that faith led her to kill Sisera, the enemy of Israel.

"The act of Jael, who smote a nail into the temples of the sleeping Sisera, does not claim our approbation; still, when we estimate the character of the act, the extenuating circumstances are entitled to attention—the times in which she lived, her ardent and enthusiastic devotion to the cause of Israel, the general and glowing hatred of the tyrannical oppressor of the people, etc. If such considerations are allowed to plead in favor of a Charlotte Corday, much more appropriately do they vindicate the act of a Jael. The same remark applies to the act of Ehud, which, according to our moral principles, was an assassination worthy of reprobation alone."[4]

Meroz is especially mentioned (verse 23). Deborah speaks with authority then, and has her message from the Angel of the Lord. He said: "Curse ye, Meroz, curse ye bitterly the inhabitants thereof; because they came not to the help of the Lord, to the help of the Lord against the mighty." Meroz might have helped, but they lived there in luxuries. Meroz means "built of cedars"; they dwelt in palaces of cedars and lived in ease, unconcerned about the condition of their brethren. And the angel of the Lord said that they did not call up to the help of the Lord. The indifference they manifested in not helping their brethren is thus charged as not helping the Lord against the mighty. As in the New Testament so here the Lord identifies Himself with His suffering people. God deliver His people to-day from the indifference of Meroz, which is high treason against the Lord and His cause! Verses 24-31 are a vivid description of what took place. The mother of Sisera is seen awaiting the return of her victorious son. She expects nothing but good and her wise ladies are with her. It is a remarkable irony. Thus all the enemies of Jehovah will perish, while for those who love Him there is glory and rest in store. Deborah could only express a longing that the enemies might perish, and those that love Him be as the sun in might and splendour. It was her prayer. We know more through the full light of prophecy how the enemies of God will perish and the glory shall be for those who love Him.

4. Fourth Declension: Under Midian and Gideon, Tola and Jair

CHAPTER 6

1. Israel's suffering from Midian (6:1-6)
2. Their repentance and the divine answer (6:7-10)
3. Gideon, the deliverer, chosen (6:11-24)
4. The restored worship (6:25-32)
5. The gathering for the conflict (6:33-35)
6. The sign of the fleece (6:36-40)

After Deborah and Barak the land had fifty years' rest, and when again they did evil they were delivered into the hand of Midian for seven years. It was a most cruel oppression which they suffered and on account of their repeated unfaithfulness. They sank now lower than during the previous declensions and captivities. They were stripped of everything and greatly impoverished. The Amalekites came also and made common cause with Midian against Israel.

The word Midian means "strife." Midian is typical of the world in its opposition to and separation from God. Midian and Moab are often seen together. Both typify the world as the enemy of God. The Midianites with Moab tried to get Balaam to curse Israel (Num. 22:6). Moab and Midian were the means of bringing God's judgment upon Israel through the woman Balaam brought into the midst of God's people. Then Israel was joined to Baal-Peor, and the Lord told Moses: "Vex the Midianites and smite them" (Numbers 25:17). Amalek represents the flesh with its lusts. The world and the flesh ever combine to enslave God's people and rob them of their blessings; "greatly impoverish them" as Midian did to Israel. How the Church has been spoiled by Midian and is to-day in the sad condition typified by Midian's power of Israel, we cannot follow at great length. The world is in the Church—separation is given up and the methods of the world have become the methods of the Church. In the Church message to Pergamos, Balaam and the stumbling-block he cast before the children of Israel, are mentioned. It represents that period of the Church when the Church gave up her separation and settled down in the world. (The seven Church messages in Rev. 2 and 3 are prophetic of the history of the Church on earth. Pergamos is that period which began with Constantine.)

And the same application of Midian must be made of the individual believer. How God's Word warns against the world and the corruption which is through lust. "Love not the world, neither the things that are in the world. If any man love the world, the love of the Father is not in him" (1 John 2:15). "Ye adulterers and adulteresses, know ye not that the friendship of the world is enmity with God? Whosoever therefore will be a friend of the world is the enemy of God" (James 4:4).

When they cried to the Lord a prophet was sent to them. The deliverer they looked for is

[4]J. H. Kurtz, *Sacred History.*

withheld for a time to deepen their need and burden their souls with a greater sense of the evil they had done. The unnamed prophet brings therefore a twofold message: The message of God's faithfulness and the message of their disobedience.

Next we see an angel of the Lord under an oak in Ophrah. Gideon, the son of Joash, threshed wheat by the winepress to hide it from the Midianites. The angel greeted him. "The Lord is with thee, thou mighty man of valour." And Gideon addressed him telling out the burden of his soul. If the Lord be with us why then is all this befallen us? But now the Lord hath forsaken us. It was the language of despair. "Then the Lord looked upon him and said, Go in this thy might, and thou shalt save Israel from the land of the Midianites; have not I sent thee?" And still Gideon is reluctant to believe the message and the Lord tells him "Surely I will be with thee, and thou shalt smite the Midianites as one man." The Lord had called him, and when He calls He also fits for the service and is with the servant. Oh! the blessed word "I will be with thee." And the One who spoke to Gideon is the same, who has left to us the precious word, "Lo, I am with you always even to the end of the world." Then Gideon brought his offering upon the rock, and the Angel of the Lord with his staff brought the fire which consumed it all, while He departed from Gideon's sight. Then it dawned upon Gideon that he had been face to face with Jehovah, and he feared death. A blessed message came to him then. "Peace be unto thee; fear not; thou shalt not die."

Then he built an altar and called it "Jehovah-shalom"—the Lord is peace. All is full of meaning. The offering he brought typifies Christ; so does the rock upon which it was brought. The fire consumed it all, carried it upward to God. And upon that the assurance of peace is given. Even so He is our peace. Blessed be God for such a precious, beautiful name—"Jehovah-shalom"—the Lord is peace. So we need not to fear, for He has made peace through the blood of His cross, and He is our peace. And therefore like Gideon we need an altar to worship. True peace with God, and the enjoyment of Himself as our peace, leads to worship, yea, it demands worship. Such the Father seeketh. As holy priests we come, made nigh by His precious blood, and bring our spiritual sacrifices. If Christ were constantly enjoyed, the facts of our redemption of blood never forgotten, Midian, this poor world, could never impoverish us. And deliverance out of worldliness and a new separation unto Him must needs have for its starting point a heart—return to Himself, who is our peace.

Then Gideon does what his name (cutter down) means. Baal's altar must fall down. He began his great work at home. It was a bold deed by which he put himself completely on the Lord's side and stirred up the wrath of the enemy. And then the enemies gather for the battle. The Spirit of the Lord then came upon Gideon. He was endued with the Spirit for the approaching deliverance. The enemies were coming in like a flood, but the Spirit of God lifted up a standard against them.

Finally Gideon asked his signs. He still hesitated. And the wonderful patience and condescension of Jehovah in meeting poor, wavering Gideon! The fleece in the midst of the ground is the type of Israel in the midst of the nations. The dew is the symbol of divine grace and mercy. It is the Lord who forsakes and who refreshes Israel. Israel to-day is like the fleece without the dew, while the ground, the Gentiles, possess of the grace of God. But ere long the dew will fall upon Israel again and the time of their blessing and fulness will come.

CHAPTER 7

The Victory of Gideon

1. The sifting of Gideon's army (7:1-8)
2. The dream of the Midianite (7:9-15)
3. Victory through weakness (7:16-25)

Gideon "the cutter down," now also called Jerubbaal "the contender with Baal," after his faith had been strengthened, pitched his camp at the well of Harod (trembling). The Lord did not need the large army he had gathered, lest Israel would say: "Mine own hand hath saved me." First 22,000 were let go. They were afraid. What an evidence of the sad conditions among the people. Jehovah had commanded through Moses this test. "And the officers shall speak further unto the people, and they shall say, What man is there that is fearful and faint hearted? Let him go and return unto his house, lest his brethren's heart faint as well as his heart" (Deut. 20:8). Faint heartedness and fear are but unbelief. Faith is courage and does not reckon with iron-chariots, with the powers of Midian, but with an omnipotent Lord. After the 22,000 had left, 10,000 remained and the Lord said again, "The people are too many."

Only 300 were selected who took up water out of the brook in their hands as they drank. Kneeling down, drinking in leisure, is the natural way for man to do. They showed thereby that they were inclined to take matters easy and to satisfy their need to the full. Taking the water into the hand and lapping it like a dog is not the natural way for man to drink. They were less absorbed with satisfying their natural wants. They showed thereby their eagerness to press on. Thus the army was narrowed down to the 300 whom the Lord would use in His service. How many of the Lord's people to-day like Gideon's army are unfit for service? Unbelief and too much occupation with earthly things, the creature wants, stand in the way.

To encourage Gideon still more the Lord permitted him to overhear how a soldier related his dream. That dream was like Nebuchadnezzar's great dream given by the Lord. The loaf of barley bread which smote the tent is another figure of the Word of God. Midian and Amalek, the world and the lusts of the flesh, can only be dealt with and overthrown by the Bread of Life, the living and abiding Word of God.

Read in connection with Gideon's victory 2 Cor. 4:4-12. Here we find a blessed application. The light hath shined into our hearts, so that it might shine out. The pitchers, the earthen vessels, represent our old self. If the light is to shine out, the victory to be won, the old self must be broken to pieces.

CHAPTER 8

Internal Strife, Gideon's Failure and End

1. The strife (8:1-9)
2. The complete deliverance (8:10-21)
3. Gideon's failure and end (8:22-32)
4. Israel's failure after Gideon (8:33-35)

Internal strife follows. The two princes of Mideon, Oreb and Zeeb, were slain (7:25). Oreb means "raven" and Zeeb means "wolf." Oreb, the raven, is slain on the rock and Zeeb, the wolf, at the winepress. The raven, the bird which represents darkness and evil, is the type of corruption; the wolf is the destroyer of the sheep. The rock and the winepress typify the Lord Jesus Christ and His Cross. There the victory over both was won. The internal strife was born in selfishness. Ephraim chided him sharply, because he had not called them to the fight. Gideon's wise and gracious answer averted the threatening dissension. How beautifully it illustrates Phil. 2:1-5. All church strifes begin with self-seeking vain-glory. The remedy is "in lowliness of mind let each esteem the other better than themselves."

A greater victory follows after the internal strive had been overcome. The men of Succoth and of Peniel, Israelites, mocked Gideon and refused him help. They were really secret allies of Midian. After the victory these mocking, half-hearted Israelites were whipped by Gideon with the briers and thorns of the wilderness to teach them the needed lesson. How often we also in half-heartedness, world-bordering and being occupied too much with earthly things, need the thorns and briers, anxieties, disappointments and sufferings to bring us into line.

When they wanted to make Gideon king he refused. But while he refused that honor he tries to grasp another, the priesthood. He gathers the gold to make a priestly ephod and put it in Ophrah. It became a snare for all Israel as well as for Gideon, for they went "a whoring after it." The gold was taken from the enemy. It was a self-glorification of the victor Gideon. He and all Israel forgot that the glory belonged to Jehovah. Gideon claimed an honor which did not belong to him. Even so it has been done on Christian ground. A false priesthood with man in place of the Lord and His work, the instruments used in the power of the Spirit of God exalted instead of Him who furnished the instrument, these are the lessons which may be traced here in Gideon's sad failure. How many a servant of Christ, forgetting 1 Cor. 4:7: "And what hast thou that thou didst not receive? Now if thou didst receive it, why dost thou glory, as if thou hadst not received it?" has fallen into the same snare, and as a result lost his power and blessing! The many wives of Gideon and the concubine of Shechem tell the other side. Amalek (the flesh) spoiled him. Like priest, like people. Israel went whoring after Baal and forgot once more Jehovah.

CHAPTER 9

Abimelech the King, and His Wickedness

1. The murder of Gideon's sons (9:1-6)
2. Jotham's parable (9:7-21)
3. Scenes of strife and destruction of Shechem (9:22-49)
4. Abimelech's end (9:50-57)

The story of Abimelech is intensely interesting in its typical meaning. Abimelech was the offspring of an unlawful union: the son of Gideon and the concubine in Shechem. He was half Israelite and half Canaanite. Abimelech means "my father was king"; he claims therefore supremacy, lordship over the people Israel on the basis of succession. His father had refused that honor; the bastard offspring claims it. He gains his object by a conspiracy and by murdering the sons of his father, with the exception of Jotham, who hid himself. And this domineerer over the people bears the name of the Philistine kings.

This illustrates perfectly that corrupt system of Christendom which is half Christian and half heathenish—Rome. It is like Abimelech—a bastard system. She is called in Revelation "Jezebel," the heathen woman who was married to an Israelitish king. Rome claims apostolic succession through Peter, who disclaimed any preeminence, but rather warned against "lording over God's heritage." Ecclesiastical assumption to control and govern the people of God, so prominent in corrupt Christendom, is clearly indicated in Abimelech's act of putting himself forward as king. And the murderous spirit of Abimelech is there likewise.

Jotham (Jehovah is perfect), the youngest son of Gideon, is the witness against it. He uttered a parable from Gerizim. The olive, the fig-tree and the vine refused to reign over the trees. The bramble becomes king to devour with fire the cedars of Lebanon. He applied the parable to Abimelech, who had been made king.

"The tendency of man's heart is to make another king than God, to put leaders in His place, and thus to destroy the use and blessing for which the olive, the fig, the vine, the various gifts of God, are given. But just those who are really worthiest will most surely refuse to leave their spheres of happy service, their sweetness, and their fruit, to go to 'wave over,'—flutter idly in the wind over the trees. Thus royalty comes naturally to the thorn-bush,hich need give up nothing, but which has thus nothing in its gift but thorns,—such as, indeed, the men of Succoth (chapter 8:16) were taught with. But worse would come than this—the fire of God's wrath, which, from this side and from that, would destroy both king and people" (*Numerical Bible*).

Three years later the prediction in Jotham's parable comes true; fire came out from Abimelech and devoured the men of Shechem; and fire came out from Shechem and devoured Abimelech. It was God who sent an evil spirit between Abimelech and the men of Shechem. Then there is the revolt of Gaal, (loathing), the son of Ebed (servitude), and he opposed Abimelech. Something similar came to pass in Christendom. On account of the domineering rule of Rome there was the revolt against her. The overthrow of the ecclesiastical oppressor was attempted. But Gaal's attempt fails. He is overcome. Abimelech and his officer Zebul are victorious. The revolt has failed. Even so to-day Rome is gaining, and those who "protested" once against her wickedness, now are following her pernicious ways once more. Abimelech's end was brought about by a piece of a *millstone* which a woman cast on him, and a young man thrust him through with a sword and he died. It was a fearful end in judgment. Even so it is written of Babylon, the mother of harlots, Rome. "And a mighty angel took up a stone like a great *millstone*, and cast it into the sea, saying, Thus with violence shall that great city Babylon be thrown down, and shall be found no more." . . . "And in her was found the blood of prophets, and of saints, and of all that were slain upon the earth" (Rev. 28:21, 24).

CHAPTER 10:1-5

Tola and Jair

1. Tola judging twenty-three years (10:1-2)
2. Jair judging twenty-two years (10:3-5)

These are but brief records but not without meaning. Tola means, translated, "a worm." What a contrast with the proud, wicked, domineering Abimelech! Here is one, who takes the place in self-abasement. It reminds us of Him, whose voice we hear in the great Atonement Psalm "I am a worm and no man." Tola, no doubt, typifies our Lord in His humiliation. When Abimelech's awful rule is ended, He who was obedient unto death, the death of the cross, will come to reign in righteousness.

And this seems to be more fully brought to our attention in Jair, the judge, who followed Tola. His name means, "enlightener." He is a type of our Lord in His coming as "the Sun of Righteousness." The thirty sons, who rode on thirty ass-colts and had thirty cities, must mean the rule of that kingdom to come in which His sons, His co-heirs, will have a part, as Jair's sons had authority over these cities.

5. Fifth Declension: Under the Philistines and Ammon. Jephthah, Ibzan, Elon, and Abdon

CHAPTER 10:6-18

1. The great declension (10:6-9)
2. Their cry and the Lord's answer (10:10-14)
3. Confession and self-judgment (10:15-18)

This is the greatest declension yet. They did evil again, served Baalim, Ashtaroth, the gods of Syria, Zidon, Moab, Ammon and the Philistines. They were then sold by the Lord into the hands of the Philistines and into the hands of the children of Ammon. Ammon has rightly been taken to typify rationalism in every form and the wicked doctrines, the denials of the faith, which follow in its train. Christian Science, Russellism, higher criticism, Seventh Day Adventism, Unitarianism and a host of other "isms" are of the Ammonite tribe. The Philistines typify ritualism. Like Ammon and the Philistines, these two enemies distress sorely the people of God from all sides. Then they cried unto Him and confessed their sins, and Jehovah reminded them of all His goodness in past deliverances and threatened them that He would not deliver them. "Go and cry unto the gods which ye have chosen; let them deliver you in the time of your tribulation." But when they continued to plead and to confess, when they put away the strange gods, when they began to serve Him again, though He had denied their first cry—His soul was grieved for the misery of Israel. What a compassionate Lord He is! Then they gathered together and encamped at Mizpah—the watchtower.

CHAPTER 11

Jephthah and the Ammonites

1. Jephthah's covenant (11:1-11)
2. The messages to Ammon (11:12-28)
3. Jephthah's vow and victory (11:29-33)
4. Jephthah keeps his vow (11:34-40)

Jephthah the judge who delivered Israel from the servitude of Ammon was the offspring of an unholy union "the son of an harlot." Then he became an outcast and had to flee from his brethren. He dwelt in the land of Tob (goodness) and vain, or worthless, men gathered unto him. Yet he was a mighty man of valor. He was therefore an humble instrument, despised and rejected by his own. But finally those who rejected him had to send for Jephthah to be their saviour from the hands of the children of Ammon. They had to own him as their leader, whom they had hated and cast out on account of his lowly birth. He reminds us of our Lord, who was hated by His own and who is yet to be their deliverer.

Jephthah means "he opens." Gilead, to which he belonged, means "witness." The enemy, Ammon, as we stated in the annotations of the previous chapter, typifies for us rationalism and the wicked errors connected with it, which distress the people of God. Here then we have in a simple yet blessed way the deliverance from those evils indicated. It needs "a true witness," one who "opens." The witness of an opened Word, the testimony of the Word of God and with it the Spirit of God, will make an end of error. It is the only true way to combat the wicked departures from the faith so prominent in the last days. How God in this book bears witness in types to the one remedy for all the declensions and backslidings of His people! Othniel has Debir "the Word"; Ehud with his sword, the sword of the Spirit; Shamgar and his oxgoad; Deborah and Lapidoth, the Word and the Spirit; the barley loaf which smote down Midian's tent and Jephthah, the one who opens, the true witness.

Jephthah made a hasty vow. It was bargaining with Jehovah, as Jacob did. And when his daughter met him first the awful vow was carried out. In reading the story one can hardly escape the literal offering up of the child.

"It is true that a mode of interpreting this vow and its fulfilment has been proposed, according to which Jephthah's daughter was not offered as a sacrifice, but devoted to a life of celibacy, and consecrated to the service of the tabernacle; and the confirmation of this view has been sought in the institution of an order of females who served before the tabernacle (Exod. 38:8; 1 Sam. 2:22; Luke 2:37). Luther already remarked: 'Some maintain that she was not sacrificed, but the text is too clear to admit of this interpretation.' But stronger evidence of her sacrifice than even the unambiguous words of the vow afford, is found in the distress of the father, in the magnanimous resignation of the daughter, in the annual commemoration and lamentation of the daughters of Israel, and, particularly, in the narrative of the historian himself, who is not able to describe clearly and distinctly the terrible scene on which he gazes both with admiration and with abhorrence. The Law undoubtedly prohibited human sacrifices as the extreme of all heathen abominations (Lev. 18:21, Deut. 12:31, etc.). But the age of the Judges had descended to a point far below the lofty position occupied by the Law."[5] And yet there are difficulties in connection with literal interpretation. The word burnt-offering is in the Hebrew "an offering that ascends."

"The great Jewish commentators of the Middle Ages have, in opposition to the Talmud, pointed out that these two last clauses ('shall surely be the Lord's and I will offer it up for a burnt-offering') are *not* identical. It is never said of an *animal* burnt offering that it 'should be to Jehovah,' for the simple reason that as a burnt offering it *is* such. But where human beings are offered to Jehovah, there the expression is used, as in the case of the firstborn among Israel and of Levi (Num. 3:12, 13). But in these cases it has never been suggested that there was actual human sacrifice. If the loving daughter had devoted herself to *death*, it is next to incredible that she should have wished to have spent the two months of her life conceded to her, not with her broken-hearted father, but in the mountains with her companions" (A. Edersheim).

Whatever it was, one thing stands out very prominently, the loyalty of Jephthah to Jehovah and the obedience and surrender of the daughter.

CHAPTER 12

The strife—Jephthah's Death—The Other Judges

1. The strife and the slaying of the Ephraimites (12:1-6)
2. Jephthah's death (12:7)
3. Ibzan, Elon and Abdon (12:8-15)

The strife of Ephraim and their question reminds us of what hapens under the judgeship of Gideon. There the soft answer turned away wrath. How different it is here. Jephthah in self-exaltation shows a far different spirit. Notice the "I" in his answer. "I was at great strife"—'I and my people"—"I called you"—"I saw"—"I put my life in my hand." A great strife follows. The Gileadites take the fords of Jordan and those who said "Sibboleth" were slain. Horrible record! Forty-two thouand Ephraimites were murdered. And this sad extermination of brethren has its sequel in Christendom. Shibboleth means "flood," that which divides. Sectarianism is undoubtedly in view here. How God's people have suffered under it and still suffer! It is true "every test that divides the people of God from one another, and not from their enemies, is another false 'shibboleth.' " May God graciously deliver His people from all sectarian strife, which is but the work and the fruit of the flesh (Gal. 5:19-21).

Three judges follow after Jephthah's death. These correspond to their typical meaning to Tola and Jair after Abimelech's lordship had been broken. Ibzan of Bethlehem. Ibzan means "shining"—"splendour." Then there is Elon, which means "strength"; and Abdon, the meaning of which is "service," the son of Hillel, "praising." These three give us a little glimpse of "Him who will come in splendor and in strength"—that is "in power and great glory," to set things right. Then all strife and disorder will end and happy service and praise will follow.

6. Sixth Declension: Under the Philistines and Samson

CHAPTER 13

1. Israel delivered to the Philistines (13:1)
2. Manoah and his wife (13:2-23)
3. Samson born (13:24-25)

The sixth and last declension of Israel in this book is now before us. This section has deep and interesting lessons. The darkest period is reached. The Philistines lorded over Israel. We miss in connection with this declension the statement which occurs in every preceding departure from Jehovah: "And the children of Israel cried unto the Lord." Here is no cry recorded nor a return unto the Lord. It seems the greatest indifference controlled the people so that there was no desire to cry to the Lord. And when we come to the deliverance we find that it was an imperfect one. "He shall begin to deliver Israel out of the hand of the Philistines" (verse 5), is the divine announcement of Samson's work. And how did he end? He died as a captive of the Philistines. But what does the Philistine typify? He represents the religious man, one who has the form of godliness but knows not the power, the ritualistic Pharisee. We quote from *Notes on Judges* by F. C. Jennings:

> Turning to the tenth chapter of Genesis, we find the genealogy of the Philistines. They are the children of Ham, and Ham is, as his name denotes, the 'black one' or sunburnt. Dark indeed, but darkened by the sun. God wanted a man who should show us, as in

[5] J. H. Kurtz, *Sacred History.*

a figure, or picture, what He sees man who is turned away from Himself (light), so He brings on to the stage of this world a "black man," a man made black by the sun, and crystalizes the sorrowful truth in his name, Ham. A very clear picture of the "old man." The sun has shone upon him indeed, but he has not received the light. He has rejected the light—has not come to the light, has hated the light, and, of course, it has not enlightened him; but it must have had some effect. What is it? It has been only to *darken* him. We may truthfully say that if he had never had light he would not have been dark as he is, and the brighter the light, the darker he has become. Now this is surely the picture of the Pharisee rather than the Publican. It was the Pharisee, the religious man, who was warned "if the light which is in thee be darkness, how great is that darkness." It was the Pharisee, the religious man, not the Publican, of whom the Lord testified that his deeds were evil. It was the Pharisee, the religious man of that day, who with the very Light of the World—the true, bright light shining clearly right before his eyes—*asked for a sign!* As if one should ask for a light at noonday—what would it prove but his blindness? Oh, blind Pharisee, Oh, dark Pharisee, Oh, thou child of Ham, thou unregenerate religionist, thou unconverted church-member, how great was, and is even up to this day, thy darkness— a "black man" indeed!

The marks of the Philistine are given as follows:

First. Wherever there is an introduction of carnal principles—that is, principles that the flesh can understand and approve—into the things of God, there is the Philistine.

Second. Wherever there is the teaching of some other way into the land of blessing than by the Red Sea and Jordan (the Cross of Christ) there is the Philistine.

Third. Wherever there are claims to sole authority over the refreshing fountain of God's Word, which is then tightly shut up, there is the Philistine, for that is how his ancestors treated Abraham's wells.

Fourth. Wherever you get uncertainty as to sins forgiven—a dread, cold fear that all is not well, for there is no knowledge of a sacrifice that takes away sin—there is the work of the Philistine.

Fifth. Wherever you get principles that would bind the energy of faith, there is the Philistine. And one may still further question whether there are not other phases of Philistinism, far more subtle and dangerous in these last days, than these open expressions of it. The Philistine women of whom we shall read were not warriors, but they were always the ensnarers of the Nazarite.

And who is the deliverer out of the hands of the Philistine? A Nazarite. (See our annotations on Numbers 6 of what the Nazarite is and represents. A careful perusal of that chapter is needed to understand the typical meaning of Samson.) Even so the heart knowledge of Christ, our blessed place in Him, as well as the *practical life of separation unto which we are called,* is the power which delivers from the evil of Philistinism. The Angel of the Lord appeared to the wife of Manoah and later also to Manoah. Her name is not givn. He announces to her, who was barren, the birth of a son, who was to be a Nazarite unto God from the womb. The mother herself was to abstain from wine and strong drink and defilement with any unclean thing. The messenger, the Angel of the Lord, is the same who had come from Gilgal to Bochim, the Captain of the Lord's host, He who appeared to Moses in the burning bush, Jehovah Himself. When asked what is thy Name? He answers: "It is Wonderful" (Isaiah 9:6). Then He ascended in the flame of the altar. Samson was born and Jehovah blessed him. The Spirit of the Lord even in his young days began to move him in Mahaneh-dan, the camp of Dan. (Dan means "judging.")

CHAPTER 14

The First Deeds of Samson

1. The woman in Timnath (14:1-4)
2. The killing of the young lion and the honey in the carcass (14:5-9)
3. The marriage feast and the riddle (14:10-14)
4. The riddle answered (14:15-18)
5. Thirty Philistines slain by Samson (14:19-20)

Samson was called of God to be a true Nazarite, but in his life which was to manifest the Nazarite character he failed. "He went down to Timnath" is a foreboding beginning. It was a step in the wrong direction. He stepped upon the territory of the enemy to enter into an alliance with the Philistines. He meets one of the daughters of the Philistines, a woman in Timnath. Two other women we find in Samson's life, an harlot of Gaza and Delilah. They are alike, representing the "wiles of the devil." They lead him down and ultimately accomplish his downfall and death. Timnath means "portion assigned." He left his occupation to seek a portion with the Philistines. Yet it was of the Lord in the sense that He permitted it for a wise purpose. And in that wrong course he came to the vineyards of Timnath and met the roaring lion. The lion is the type of Satan (Amos 3:8; 1 Pet. 5:8). He roared at the Nazarite, as Satan still roars against any one who bears the marks of separation unto God. Then in the power of the Spirit who came upon Samson he rent the lion as a kid. Then he saw the woman and she pleased him well. Strange contrast! In the power of the Spirit he tore the lion and then falls victim to the enemy in another form. How often this is the case in the experiences of God's people. Afterwards he found in the carcass of the lion the swarm of bees and the honey, which he ate and also gave to his parents. "Out of the eater came forth meat, and out of the strong came forth sweetness." Our blessed Lord has conquered Satan and as the result of that mighty overthrow and victory, accomplished on the Cross, we have our meat, our sweetness, our salvation and blessing.

Another application besides the above and also of the believer's personal experience in conquering by faith the enemy and receiving sweetness through it, has been suggested: "The occurrences which took place when Samson visited Timnath, the residence of the woman (the lion, and the honey afterwards found in the carcass), were highly significant, and adapted to instruct both him and his people. He seems himself to be aware, in some degree, of their importance, as he introduces them in his riddle. The lion, namely, is an image of the kingdoms of the world which are hostile to the kingdom of God; the attack, the struggle, and the victory thus acquire a symbolical meaning. The riddle also includes a truth of great importance, the evidence of which is furnished in manifold ways by the history of the world, and which admits of an appropriate application even to our times. The attack of the lion was an image of the Philistine invasion; the eater furnished Israel with meat and sweetness, the destroyer brought salvation and blessings with him; for the yoke of the Philistines was a chastisement, designed to lead the people to repentance, and terminate in their renewed acceptableness before God."

Then he is in very bad company. He went down to Timnath alone. He met the woman, then he made a feast and was surrounded by thirty Philistines as companions. He had allied himself with the enemy. And this compromise, this mingling with the enemies of the cross of Christ, is the common thing to-day and has led to the grieving of the Spirit and the loss of power. "For example, the modern system of revival—to which our Samson, in his failure, so closely answers—in which, whilst there doubtless often is more or less of true faithful service, yet to effect the end *an alliance even with the enemy is sought*; the aid of the world is sought in obtaining deliverance *from* the world! Fleshly attractions, eloquent speakers, exquisite music, cunning schemes for gathering crowds to attract crowds; all the churches closed except one, thus awakening a natural excitement; all these are daughters of the Philistine, very fair, all serving religion and pleasing us well; but very, very dangerous. For whilst at first they may not appear serious, they point to the possibility of their becoming so in the future; nor do they ever radically aid, but always hinder, the Nazarite."

He gives the riddle to the Philistines and makes a wager. The woman, now Samson's wife, wept and continued till he told her the secret, "and she told the riddle to the children of her people." Here was his weak point, which eventually resulted in his shameful downfall and humiliating experience. He could not keep a secret. But it was all the results of his going down, forming an alliance with the enemy he was called to overcome. He did not see that he had stepped in the wrong direction. He blamed the Philistines and not himself. "If ye had not plowed with my heifer, ye had not found out my riddle." Then he slew thirty Philistines to make good his promise and thus openly declared his hatred and antagonism to the enemy for the first time.

CHAPTER 15

The Conflict with the Philistines: Bound Yet Free

1. The damage done to the Philistines (15:1-8)
2. Bound by his own brethren (15:9-13)
3. The deed with the jawbone (15:14-17)
4. His prayer and the answer (15:120)

He discovered next the true character of the Philistines. His wife has been given to another. Nothing came of his alliance with the Philistines but trouble and unpleasantness for himself. Was it of the Lord when he took the 300 foxes (literally, jackals; it would have been hard work to catch 300 foxes, for they go alone, but jackals go in packs) and the firebrands to destroy the corn, the vineyards and olive-groves? We find that there is no record that the Spirit of the Lord came upon him for this work. He acted out of revenge, because they had given his wife to another, whom as an Israelite with the Nazarite vow upon himself, he should never have taken. It was anger and not a judgment commanded by the Lord. And touching the jackal, an unclean beast, he had defiled himself. How often God's people act in the same way in an undignified manner, biting and devouring each other and like Samson destroying corn, vineyards and olives, the types of spiritual blessings. Whenever an unchristlike spirit manifests itself among the children of God, the spirit of malice, envy and vain-glory, the people of God are robbed of their joy and peace. The Philistines paid him in the same coin. They burnt his wife and her father. Then he slew the Philistines with a great slaughter and dwelt in the rock Etam (literally, the cleft of the rock). It was a safe place for him against "their ravening," the meaning of Etam. And we too have our safe place in the cleft of the rock. His own brethren bind him out of fear for the Philistines, but in the Spirit of the Lord he bursts now the new cords and with the jawbone of an ass he slew a thousand men. It is now faith which acts. It was a feeble thing he used; boasting was excluded. Nor was it his own physical strength which accomplished the deed, but the Spirit of the Lord, who had come upon him. The jawbone having done its work is cast away.

> He will not keep it. It might become a snare to him: Israel might go a-whoring after it as after Gideon's ephod. It has served his purpose, now let it go—after all it is nothing more than the poor jawbone of a dead ass! Oh, that we could learn something from this! It is such a day to exalt the poor, foolish instruments that God, in His goodness, may use. Do not we everywhere hear what a wonderful man is such a man! What marvellous power in the gospel! What beauty of exposition! What magnetism! What a smart man is he! Yes, indeed, just as well might Samson say, 'What a powerful jawbone! What a wonderful jawbone! What a magnetic jawbone! No, no, put the poor jawbone where it belongs, lest it detract from the glory of Him to whom all glory alone is due."[6]

Then after the victory he thirsts and God cleaves a place in *Lehi.* "God clave the hollow that was in Lehi" and water flows forth to refresh him. A beautiful picture of Him who was smitten that the refreshing waters of life may flow forth.

CHAPTER 16

Delilah, and Samson

1. In Gaza (16:1-3)
2. Delilah and her victory over him (16:4-20)
3. The captive of the Philistines (16:21)
4. The feast of Dagon and Samson's death (16:22-31)

Down he goes again, and this time to Gaza, the Philistine stronghold. There he unites himself with a harlot. We are here reminded of the history of the Church. The harlot typifies that system which in Revelation is called by the same name, she who seduces to commit fornication, Babylon the great, Rome. Rome is the capital of Philistinism, ritualistic Christendom, as Gaza was the capital of the Philistines. But the attempt of the Philistines to kill him fails. He carries the gates, posts and bars of the city and took them to the top of the hill before Hebron. We may see in it a little picture of the recovery from the power of the harlot in the Reformation movement. But it was not Samson's last visit and farewell to Gaza. We shall see him there again, stripped of his power, his eyes put out, a ridiculed captive. We find him first at Sorek. He is entangled with Delilah, which means "exhausted." He loves her and she becomes the fearful instrument of his downfall. She is the type of the world, the fair, pleasure-loving, religious world, which aims, like Delilah, to rob the true Nazarite of his separation, the real power of the Christian life. It would take pages to describe the subtleties, the cunning ways, the wiles of the fair Delilah of the last days. And even then we would have to say "not the half has been told." And how she presses upon the Nazarite! Again and again he deceives her and keeps his secret. He knows well she is after his destruction. Like a moth attracted to the light though burning awaits it, he goes back to the dangerous sport, till at last, vexed unto death, he tells her his secret. Again he sleeps upon her knees. The locks of hair fall under the razor. Then she, the fair Delilah, afflicts him. Her caresses become blows and his strength went from him. "And he awoke out of his sleep, and said, I will go out as at other times before, and shake myself. And he wist not that the Lord was departed from him." Alas! the sad story, how it has been repeated in the individual experiences of many believers. Flirting with the unholy principles of this present evil age is a dangerous thing. Loving the world will end, if unchecked, in disaster for the child of God. And the remedy is the close walk in heart dependence and heart devotion to the Lord Jesus Christ. And thus it has happened and still more happens in our days with the Church. Stripped of her strength, her confessed weakness, lowliness, separation and utter dependence on the Lord, the Philistines have come upon her, lulled to sleep by Delilah's wiles. There is a shaking too, like Samson's shaking. Efforts are made by a pow-

---

[6] F. C. Jennings, *Notes on Judges.*

erless Church and they do not know that the power is no longer there, for the Spirit is grieved and quenched. That is the sad state of the professing Church as seen in those of Laodicea (Rev. 3:14-17).

Oh, the sad picture of the Nazarite shorn of his locks, naked in this sense; eyes put out, blind, bound in fetters, grinding in the mill! What sport the Philistines had with him! And is a Church robbed of power, naked and blind, not a sadder spectacle? The end of Samson was a great victory. He had learned his lessons. Thoroughly humbled and chastised he must have repented of all his sin and folly. His hair grew again. He cries to Jehovah between the pillars, where he made sport. Then follows his prayer. "O Lord God, remember me, I pray thee, and strengthen me; I pray thee, only this once, O God, that I may be at once avenged of the Philistines for my two eyes." Then he bowed himself, and an awful catastrophe follows when the house collapsed and he and the vast multitude of Philistines were slain and buried in the ruins.

III. The Appendix: Israel's Internal Corruption

Micah's and Dan's Idolatry and Its Punishment

CHAPTER 17

The Images Made and the Hired Priest

1. The stolen money restored and the images (17:1-6)
2. The Levite hired for a priest (17:7-13)

The last five chapters of the book form an appendix. The events given did not occur after Samson's death, but they happened many years before. These chapters are not in chronological order but arranged in this way to teach the root of the evil and its results. This answers much, if not all, of the objections of the critics. These chapters reveal the internal corruption which existed in Israel during the different declensions. Idolatry and lawlessness are the two characteristic features. True worship and dependence on God is given up and then follows the dreadful fruit of this, which is hatred, strife culminating in lawlessness. The predictions in the New Testament reveal the same two phases. Departure from the faith is followed by moral corruption (1 Tim. 4:1; 2 Tim. 3:1-4). Then we find in these chapters a statement which does not appear elsewhere in the book. "There was no king in Israel" is the statement made four times (17:6; 18:1, 19:1; 21:25). A king was needed to remedy these sad internal conditions, this departure from God and strife of one against the other. This is an evident link with and preparation for the history which follows. Even so in this age of evil, darkness and cunning lawlessness; what the world needs is a king, the King of Righteousness and Peace. Wen He comes, order will be brought out of chaos, all strife and war, all bloodshed and lawlessness will cease.

Into what a scene this chapter introduces us! The thieving son, the cursing mother. He, for the fear of the curse (true faith was not there, but superstition), restores the money and that ungodly woman can say, "Blessed be thou of the Lord, my son." Then she used two hundred shekels of silver and has two images made. Micah, whose wicked life belies his name (Micah means "who is like Jehovah"), had a house full of gods, made an ephod, teraphim and then "ordained" one of his sons for a priest. Then a wandering Levite passed by and to make his idolatrous worship a little more "religious" he hires the Levite to be a "father" and "a priest." He also promises him a yearly salary, his board and clothing. Then he settled down and said, "Now know I that the Lord will do me good, seeing I have a Levite to my priest."

There is no need of much comment. The typical application is seen at a glance. Here is a man-made god, a man-made worship and a man-made priest. Such is the state of ritualistic Christendom. Much of that which is called worship is simply man-made and dishonors God as much, or even more, than the idolatry of heathendom. And how the false priesthood is here typified! We have but one Priest as the people of God and that is our gracious Lord. Through His infinite grace all true believers are constituted priests with Him. We are a holy and a royal priesthood. Any other priesthood is man-made and a wicked assumption which has corrupted and is corrupting Christianity. The hirelings too are represented in this scene. Religious service is so much reduced to a commercial basis. And there is the delusion of thinking that the Lord must surely bless and give prosperity.

The Levite himself is another sign of the times. He is of the Levites of Judah, has been for a while in Bethlehem-judah and wandered away again to find, where he may, another temporary resting place. His is the restless foot of a stranger where he might have claimed inheritance, and he is ready to find a home where he should have been a stranger. Little solicitation prevails with him: his sustenance, a suit of clothes, a salary, has prevailed with many in all ages of the world, and the Levite exchanges his ministry for priesthood in the house of Micah, where the idolatry of the place is sanctified with Jehovah's name. All this is simple enough to read by those that care, and Christendom has exhibited every detail of this transformation—not, alas, as it would seem, a long process: a manufactured priesthood for manufactured gods, all covered with a fair name of orthodoxy, and men doing with great satisfaction what is right in their own eyes!

CHAPTER 18

The Danite Idolatry

1. The Danites seek an inheritance (18:1-12)
2. Their robbery (18:13-26)
3. Laish taken and idolatry consummated (18:27-31)

The history of this chapter is closely linked with the preceding. The tribe of Dan had failed to take the God-given inheritance (Josh. 19:40-46). "The Amorites forced the children of Dan into the mountain: for they would not suffer them to come down to the valley" (Judges 1:34). Then in self-will, entirely disregarding the will of God, they sent out spies to seek another inheritance. They meet Micah's priest, the hireling. Micah's idolatrous outfit including the hired priest are taken by the invaders. The hireling sees an advantage for himself, his "usefulness" is enlarged for filthy lucre's sake. Then they killed the people of Laish and set their city on fire. The whole tribe of Dan becomes idolatrous. We have in all a picture of complete apostasy.

2. Israel's Moral Condition and the War on Benjamin

CHAPTER 19

The Levite and His Concubine

1. The Levite and the unfaithful woman (19:1-21)
2. The fate of the concubine (19:22-30)

The results of departure from God are now revealed in the awful corruption and violence so faithfully recorded in this chapter. The moral condition of Israel has gone down to the same level of the Canaanites; they sank even lower than the nations whom God had doomed to destruction. We do not repeat the horrible details of this deed of lust and violence. Apostasy from God, rejection of the truth is followed by moral corruption. Romans 1:26-32 shows the vileness of the Gentiles, who turned their backs to the light and did not glorify God. 2 Timothy 3:1-5 contains the description of the moral corruption of the last days of the present age, the conditions of those who claim to be "religious" and yet are apostates. The days of Lot, with their vileness, are to precede the coming of the Son of Man (Luke 17:28-30). Evidences that such moral corruption and violence exist to-day throughout professing Christendom are only too numerous.

CHAPTER 20

The Horrible War

1. The Levite's story (20:1-7)
2. The uprising (20:8-11)
3. The slaying of the Israelites (20:12-25)
4. Benjamin exterminated except six hundred men (20:26-48)

This and the concluding chapter bring before us the awful harvest of what had been sown. "For whatsoever a man soweth, that shall he also reap" (Gal. 6:7). They had sown the wind and now reaped the whirlwind. Violence and lawlessness result in the slaying of 40,000 Israelites and 25,000 of the tribe of Benjamin. Nearly the entire tribe was wiped out. From Dan to Beersheba into the land of Gilead they gathered at Mizpeh to hear the story of the Levite. Benjamin refused to give up the wicked men and instead of humbling themselves, acknowledging the dreadful guilt and bringing the guilty ones to judgment, they gathered themselves together to fight their own brethren. Their company was small in comparison with the mighty host of Israel. The divine counsel was that Judah should go up first to battle with Benjamin. What a contrast with the beginning of the book! There they were to fight against the common foe; here against their own brethren.

"But to be fit to be used of God to deal with evil involves much more than readiness to be His instrument. They are *too ready*, as we see in the result. Their wrath is too prompt, too implacable, too unsparing. Theirs is the reckless haste of vengeance, and not the solemn discrimination of divine judgment. They remember not their own sins, bring no sin offering to God, no tears of penitence. They build on their numbers; no doubt on the justice of their cause, also, but in self-righteousness and without self-suspicion. Thus they go up to smite, and they are smitten heavily, disastrously. Benjamin, the wrong-doer, is wholly victorious."

Here too are the lessons for God's people in judging what is evil amongst them. Then the children of Israel went to Bethel (House of God) and with prayer and fasting waited on the Lord and brought the offerings. Then the Lord gave them the assurance of victory. Benjamin is smitten, their women and children are wiped out. Only six hundred men escaped to the rock of Rimmon. All their cities were burned.

To even greater scenes of violence, bloodshed and desolution this poor world, which has rejected God and His beloved Son, is hastening on.

CHAPTER 21

The Repentance About Benjamin

1. Sorrow of the people and Jabesh-Gilead smitten (21:1-15)
2. The restoration of Benjamin (21:16-25)

A tribe of the nation was almost entirely exterminated. Then the oath they had made not to give their daughters to wife to the Benjamites left assured the complete extinction of the tribe. The dreadful work they had done dawned suddenly upon them and weeping before Jehovah they said, "Why is this come to pass in Israel that there should be to-day one tribe lacking in Israel?" The answer surely was, it came to pass on account of their departure from God and their sins. Thus people ask when they behold the scenes of bloodshed and war, as we see in our times, why is this? and are even ready to blame God, instead of thinking of sin and its curse. Then once more they acted themselves and committed another deed of violence. Jabesh-Gilead is destroyed; only four hundred virgins are saved. These were given to the Benjamites. But what hypocrisy they showed in having a feast of Jehovah and commanding the Benjamites to steal the daughters of Shiloh! Failure and decline is written in this book. God's faithfulness towards His people whom He loves is not less prominent.

"This is Israel, the people of God: infirm and wavering where good is to be accomplished; quick and decisive where patience and forbearance would become them; tolerant of what is only of themselves; scrupulously keeping an insane oath, yet managing to evade it by a jesuitry that deceives no one. Such is the people of God, and such is Christendom to-day; and such it has been. Let us search our hearts as we read the record,—not given as a record without purpose in it. How solemn is the repetition at the end of what has been the text of these closing chapters: "In those days there was no king in Israel: *every man did what was right in his own eyes"* (*Numerical Bible*).

THE BOOK OF
RUTH

Introduction

This book, containing the beautiful story of Ruth, is closely linked with Judges. The beginning of the book makes this clear: "Now it came to pass in the days when the Judges ruled." The events happened during the period of the judges. It therefore belongs next to that book. In the Hebrew Bible it occupies another place. We find it there next to the Song of Solomon, followed by Lamentations. Five books are called by the Jews "Megilloth" and are read by them at different feasts commemorating past events. The Song of Solomon is read during Passover; Ruth at Pentecost; Lamentations on the ninth day of the month Ab in memory of the destruction of Jerusalem; Ecclesiastes is read during the feast of Tabernacles and Esther they read when they celebrate Purim.

The author of the book of Ruth is unknown. The conclusion of the book shows that it must have been written after David had been made king. However the late date assigned to it by the critics, after the exile, is incorrect. We do not enter into their arguments. Any intelligent reader must see at once that its place between Judges and Samuel is the right place, for it is as sequel to the former and an introduction to the latter. If we read the books of Samuel we discover that they do not contain any reference whatever to the ancestors of the house of David. To supply this deficiency is one of the reasons why this book was written. It is more than probable that Samuel is the author.

The story is so familiar that we do not need to repeat it in this brief introduction. Ruth the Moabitess is the chief character in the story. She who was cursed by the law becomes married to Boaz and as we learn from the ending, Ruth is the great-grandmother of David. Her name appears therefore in the first chapter of the New Testament in the list of ancestors of Him, who is David's son and David's Lord. She is the third Gentile woman in the genealogy of our Lord. The two Canaanitish women, Tamar and Rahab, precede her. The promises made to Abraham that the Gentiles were to receive blessing through his seed are confirmed through the history of these Gentile women among the ancestors of David and our Lord.

The typical dispensational meaning of the story of Ruth is interesting and has many blessed lessons. (The best application we have seen is in the *Numerical Bible* to which we acknowledge our indebtedness.) Ruth is often given as a type of the Church, as the bride of Christ. This application is difficult to make and leaves much of the beautiful story unexplained. Naomi represents Israel in unbelief, widowed and in bitterness. Ruth is the type of the remnant, who is called and received back by grace (like the sinners of the Gentiles) identifying itself with Israel's ruin, as Ruth identified herself with Naomi. The Kinsman-Redeemer, who espouses their cause and through whom Naomi's bitterness is changed to joy, who marries Ruth, is the type of the Redeemer, Christ. We shall follow briefly this correct dispensational foreshadowing in the annotations. A special division of this little book is not needed. The story has been divided into four chapters which makes another division unnecessary.

Analysis and Annotations

CHAPTER 1

The Story of Naomi: Orpah and Ruth

1. Naomi and her sorrows (1:1-5)
2. The return (1:6-13)
3. Orpah turning back. Ruth cleaving (1:14-18)
4. Naomi and Ruth in Bethlehem (1:19-22)

The story begins with a famine. Elimelech, "my God is king," and Naomi, "pleasant," leave Bethlehem, "the house of bread," to go to the land of Moab, the heathen country. The story ends in Bethlehem with a marriage. Naomi far from the land, in unbelief and bitterness, bereft of Elimelech, her two sons also dead, Mahlon, which means "sick," and Chilion "pining," pictures Israel's condition, away from the land, no longer married unto Jehovah, but forsaken. Like Naomi, Israel has had trouble upon trouble and sorrow upon sorrow. There is no hope for Naomi amidst the Gentiles in Moab, as there is no hope for Israel among the nations. Hearing that Jehovah had visited His people with bread, she arose that she might return from Moab. Then Orpah said farewell to remain in Moab, while Ruth, the Moabitess, clave unto Naomi. She had faith and the beautiful words she addressed to Naomi were the expression of that faith. Not alone did the poor Moabitish woman say "thy people shall be my people," but also "thy God my God." It was grace which had drawn her. She thus clung closely to Naomi, became one with her in all her misery, yet with a faith, a confidence in Naomi's God, which Naomi did not possess. When Israel sets her face homeward once more, there will be in the midst of the unbelieving nation a remnant, searching for the promised blessing, longing for God, a remnant[1] which ultimately will come in touch with the mighty Kinsman-Redeemer and inherit through Him the promised blessings. This remnant is represented in Ruth, cleaving to Naomi. But the objection may be raised that Ruth was a Gentile. How can she represent the remnant of Israel? Israel through her unbelief has become practically the same which the Gentiles are. They are "Lo-Ammi," not my people (Hosea 1:9). The grace which called and saved Gentiles will call and draw them. Therefore this remnant is called "according to the election of grace" (Romans 11:5-6).

Naomi is back in Bethlehem, empty and with a bitter spirit. She calls herself "Mara" which means bitter. This pictures Israel's return in unbelief. And it was at the time of the barley harvest. The harvest, as our Lord tells us, is the end of the age. When that end comes, after the true church has been gathered home, Israel, like Naomi, with a believing, trusting remnant cleaving to her, represented in Ruth, will return.

CHAPTER 2

Gleaning in the Field

1. Ruth gleaning in the field of Boaz (2:1-3)
2. Grace shown to Ruth by Boaz (2:4-17)
3. Ruth hears concerning Boaz (2:18-23)

Boaz comes now upon the scene. His name means "in Him is strength." He is called "a mighty man of wealth." As the kinsman-redeemer he is a beautiful type of the Lord Jesus Christ. He is the one in whom there is strength, the rich one. Ruth knows at first little of him and the coming relationship with the wealthy one. Boaz is related to Elimelech, whose name "my God is king" is typical of Israel's faith. Through Elimelech only Naomi (the nation Israel) has a claim on Boaz. And she can only lay claim through Ruth. Even so Israel has a claim on the blessings promised to her through the remnant which returns to Him in the beginning of the harvest, the end of the age; that remnant, as stated before, is represented in Ruth.

How simple and beautiful is the story which follows. The mighty man of valor knows evidently all about her, though he does not act at once in her behalf. He appears on the harvest field. Beautiful greeting he brings! "The Lord be with you"; and they answer him, "The Lord bless thee." Gracious are his words to her, who had cast herself upon his grace, for Ruth had said to Naomi, "Let me now go to the field and glean ears of corn after him in whose sight I shall find grace." She anticipated in faith, though she did not fully know what grace was awaiting her. Even so the remnant of Israel in the last days. How he permits her to continue in the humble work. He provides for her. She is only to glean in his field. She is not to be molested; his gracious power shields her. She can also drink of the water he provides. Then she falls on her face. Beautiful are her words of humility, "Why have I found grace in thine eyes, that thou shouldst take knowledge of me, seeing I am a stranger?" Then she hears from his lips that he knows all about her. More than that. He assures her of coming blessings, blessings Ruth will get because she trusted; blessings not of works, the law covenant, but of grace, because she believed. "The Lord recompense thy work, and a full reward be given thee of the Lord God of Israel, under whose wings thou art come to trust."

All foreshadows dispensationally the soul-exercise of the believing remnant of Israel, when the harvest begins, and the gracious dealing of the Lord with that remnant. Another application may also be made on spiritual lines of a soul which seeks blessing and how the Lord deals in His grace with those that seek Him. This we cannot follow in these brief annotations. Then he comes closer to her. She receives

[1]Of this remnant called through the grace of God, after the true Church has left this earthly scene, the prophetic Word has much to say. Read: Is. 6:13; 10:21-22; 11:11; Micah 4:7; Zeph. 2:7; Ezek. 9; Rom. 11:5 and many other passages. In the Psalms we read the future prayers of this remnant, the sorrows and sufferings they will have and the glorious deliverance when the King comes.

from his own hands. He also, unknown to her, gives instructions that "handfuls on purpose" are to be dropped, just for her. What evidences that the mighty, wealthy Boaz loves the poor stranger, Ruth! So the remnant will gradually learn of His love. And we also find our comfort here. We glean in His Word. It is typified by the wheat, the barley and the corn. Then when we feel our need and dependence on Him, and plead, as we always should, our ignorance, He drops the handfuls on purpose, so that we find just what we need for our spiritual sustenance and comfort.

And Naomi tells her something about Boaz. But she only calls him "one of our redeemers." She should have said he is the redeemer. The secret who he is and what he will do for her, the trusting Ruth, she will learn only from himself. So unbelieving Israel does not know the full story of Him, who is the Redeemer. Boaz, Christ Himself, will make it known when He reveals Himself in His grace and power to the remnant of His people.

CHAPTER 3

At the Feet of Boaz

1. Naomi instructs Ruth (3:1-5)
2. At his feet (3:6-7)
3. The discovery (3:8-13)
4. The six measures of barley (3:14-17)
5. He will not rest until he have finished the thing (3:18)

What follows in the realization of redemption must be connected with Leviticus 25, the law concerning the redemption of an inheritance and the other law about the marriage of a brother-in-law as given in Deut. 25:5-12. See the annotations on that passage. Naomi gives instructions to Ruth which are based upon that law. But notice it is the question of the rest. "My daughter, shall not I seek rest for thee, that it may be well with thee?" She then is seen resting at his feet. Blessed truth indeed which even Naomi realizes, rest can only be found at the feet of the redeemer. This truth is known to all His beloved people. He promises rest and He giveth rest. Like Mary it is the good part for us to be at His feet.

But what is Boaz's occupation when Ruth seeks him to claim her full blessing? "Behold he winnoweth barley tonight in the threshing floor." The winnowing is a sifting process by which the wheat is separated from the chaff. Read Matthew 3:12. The threshing floor is Israel. The dark night of tribulation is coming for them, when the mighty One will do the work of separating among His people. "His fan is in His hand." In that coming night the believing remnant will seek, like Ruth, the place at His feet and claim Him as their own redeemer. Critics and unbelievers have often sneered at this scene and suggested evil motives. They do the same with other portions of the Word of God. Only an evil mind can read evil into this beautiful scene. It was at midnight when Boaz became conscious of her presence and asked, "Who art thou?" She answered, "I am Ruth." She owns all she is and prays that he may cover her, "for thou art a redeemer." Notice the steps. His question—her answer and prayer because she believed in him as the kinsman redeemer.

She tarried there during the night. "And she lay at his feet till the morning." Then she left not empty handed!

CHAPTER 4

The Redemption and Marriage

1. The other kinsman (4:1-5)
2. His refusal (4:6-8)
3. Boaz's redemption (4:9-10)
4. The marriage (4:11-13)
5. Naomi's happiness (4:14-17)
6. The ancestry of David (4:18-22)

And now the other redeemer, who cannot redeem, appears. Boaz sits in the gate and hails the one whom he knew as he passeth by. He calls him not by name but said, "Ho, such a one! turn aside, and sit down here." If Boaz had not called him he would surely have passed by. Then ten men also sit down. The case is stated and the other redeemer is willing to redeem the land. But when he hears that he also must take Ruth the Moabitess, he declares his powerlessness to do it. "I cannot redeem it for myself, lest I mar mine own inheritance. Redeem thou my right to thyself; for I cannot redeem it." Whom does this unnamedor stranger, the Moabitess? This powerless redeemer is the law. Ten witnesses are there confirming his inability to do it. These represent the Ten Commandments. The curse of the law rested upon the Moabitess for it is written, "An Ammonite or Moabite shall not enter into the congregation of the Lord, even to the tenth generation forever" (Deut. 23:3). Therefore the law could not bring in Ruth, but only keep her out. Her case is indeed hopeless from the point of the law. Grace alone can help her. And this grace is beautifully seen in Boaz. He acquires both the land and Ruth, the Moabitess. "And Boaz took Ruth and she became his wife." It is a blessed type of Him who has paid the redemption price for the land and the people. The great day is coming after He had the fan in His hand, at the time of the harvest, when He will redeem both by His gracious power. Then all the blessings will follow—which are but faintly seen in Ruth's union with Boaz. "For thou shalt break forth on the right hand and on the left; and thy seed shall inherit the Gentiles, and make the desolate cities to be inhabited. Fear not, thou shalt not be ashamed; neither be thou confounded: for thou shalt not be put to shame. For thou shalt forget the shame of thy youth, and shalt not remember the reproach of thy widowhood any more. For thy Maker is thine husband; the Lord of hosts is His name; and thy Redeemer is the Holy One of Israel; the God of the whole earth shall He be called" (Is. 54:3-5). "Thou shalt no more be termed Forsaken; neither shall thy land be any more termed Desolate. But thou shalt be called Hephzi-bah, and thy land Beulah; for the Lord delighteth in thee, and thy land shall be married" (Is. 62:4).

The conclusion of this precious little book is the generations of Pharez ending with David. Ruth became the great-grandmother of David.

THE FIRST BOOK OF
SAMUEL

Introduction

The two books of Samuel and the two books of Kings bear in the Greek Version of the Old Testament (the Septuagint) the name First, Second, Third, and Fourth Books of Kingdoms. In the Latin Version, known as the Vulgate, they are called the Books of Kings. In Hebrew manuscripts and the earlier printed editions of the Hebrew text, both the books of Samuel appear as one; the same is true of the book of Kings. It must also be remembered that in the Hebrew Bible, the books of Samuel belong to that section which Jewish authorities have named "The Former Prophets." The books of Samuel are, therefore, classed by the Jews with the writings of the Prophets.

The Authorship

The books bear the name of Samuel. This, however, does not mean that Samuel is the author of these books. That would be impossible, inasmuch as the greater part of them contains events which transpired after the death of Samuel. The only hint in Scripture about the authorship of these two books is found in 1 Chronicles 29:29: "Now the acts of David the King, first and last, behold, they are written in the book of Samuel the Seer, and in the book of Nathan the Prophet, and in the book of Gad the Seer." Ancient tradition among the Jews assigns to Samuel the authorship of the first twenty-four chapters of the first book of Samuel. These chapters contain what may be termed the life of Samuel up to the time of his death. The twenty-fifth chapter begins with the record of his death. It is reasonable that Samuel wrote these opening chapters of the first book which bears his name. That Samuel did write is fully established by chapter 10:25: "Then Samuel told the people the manner of the Kingdom, and wrote it in a book and laid it up before the Lord." The same Jewish tradition credits Nathan the Prophet and Gad the Seer with having written the remainder of the two books. The passage in the first book of Chronicles seems to support this view. Evidently Samuel began to write these books, which, for this reason, were called by his name. Modern criticism rejects this view and claims that the books of Samuel could not be the work of men who lived during the reign of Saul and David. We do not give their speculative theories and conflicting opinions, which are of no value whatever in the spiritual study of the text. The best scholars believe that these books belong to a very early period, and that the critical view of a compilation of certain documents and fragments, immediately before the exile, cannot be sustained. "The minute sketches and vivid touches with which these books abound prove that their author speaks what he knows and testifies what he has seen" (John Eadie). Some of the more important objections higher criticism has raised against the early date of the books of Samuel and the alleged discrepancies we shall point out and answer in our annotations.

The Continuation of Israel's History

These books contain the continuation of the history of the people Israel. The opening chapters cover the period of the Philistine oppression, during which Samson began to deliver Israel out of the hands of the Philistine (Judges 13:5). As stated in our introduction to the book of Judges, Samuel's first operations fall into the same time when Samson was acting as judge. Samuel assumed the office of judge after the death of Samson. In the beginning of the Philistine oppression these two boys were born, both devoted to the Nazariteship and both to a definite work. There is, however, a difference between the two, as Edersheim puts it: "Samuel was God-granted, Samson God-sent; Samuel was God-dedicated, Samson was God-demanded. The work of Samson ended in self-indulgence, failure and death; that of Samuel opened up into the royalty of David."

The final statement with which the book of Judges closes is the following: "In those days there was no king in Israel; every man did that which was right in his own eyes." This shows that Israel was looking forward towards having a king; the need of a king was recognized, for the government by judges had wrought no deliverance for the people. The ruin into which Israel had fallen, besides being described in the closing chapters of Judges, is also seen in the opening chapters of Samuel. The priesthood is corrupted. Eli is old and weak; his sons, Hophni and Phinehas, were wicked men. The Philistines smite them again. Then they used the ark of the covenant to overcome the foe; but instead there is more defeat. The ark of God is captured by the Philistines and taken to Ashdod. After the return of the ark Samuel called the people to repentance. "Then the children of Israel put away Baalim and Ashtaroth, and served the Lord" (1 Sam. 7:4). The result was victory over the Philistines. Samuel then judged Israel; he also made his sons judges. Like Eli's sons, they were ungodly. "They turned aside after lucre, and took bribes, and perverted judgment" (1 Sam. 8:3). It was at that time that the elders of Israel made their demand. "Behold thou art old, and thy sons walk not in thy ways, now make us a king to judge us like all nations" (1 Sam. 8:5). With this the crisis is reached. A king is demanded and the Lord grants their request. They had rejected Him as king over them.

The two institutions which we find now definitely introduced among Israel are the prophetic order and the monarchy. Samuel heads the order of the prophets and is also chosen to crown the first two kings. That the kingly office in the midst of Israel had been anticipated is learned from Deut. 17:14-15. "When thou art come into the land which the Lord thy God giveth thee, and shalt possess it, and shall dwell therein, and shalt say, I will set a king over me, like as all the nations that are about me. Thou shalt in any wise set him a king over thee, whom the Lord thy God shall choose; one from among thy brethren shalt thou set king over thee; thou mayest not set a stranger over thee, who is not thy brother." Thus the demand was anticipated and provision made for it in the law.

Foreshadowing the True King and His Kingdom

Israel had to have a monarchy established in her midst to foreshadow the true King and His Kingdom. That true King of Israel, the promised One, and His dominion had already been mentioned by Balaam. "A sceptre shall rise out of Israel"—"Out of Jacob shall come He that shall have dominion" (Numbers 24:17-19). Hannah in her inspired outburst of praise and her prophetic vision beheld that true king. "He shall give strength unto his King and exalt the horn of his Anointed" (1 Sam. 2:10). It is Israel's true King, the Anointed, the Christ, she beheld.

Saul, the first king, is the people's choice and ends in complete failure. Then David comes upon the scene; he is God's choice; the king after His own heart. But he also fails. However, he is a type of Him who is both David's Lord and David's son, the root and offspring of David, our Lord Jesus Christ, the true King of Israel. David and Solomon are faint shadows of the true King and His work both in judgment and in the Kingdom of peace. The historical records in the books of Samuel are especially rich in typical and dispensational lessons and teach many spiritual truths. We hope to point out many of them as we follow the text in the annotations.

The Division of First Samuel

Inasmuch as the first book of Samuel contains the record of Samuel's labors and the anointing of the two first Kings of Israel, Saul and David, Saul's reign and David's exile, we divide the book into three sections. In the first section we find the birth, childhood and judgeship of Samuel; in the second, the anointing and coronation of Israel's first King, Saul, his reign and rejection. In the third section David, his anointing, and exile are before us. We give these sections and subdivisions as we shall follow them in our analysis and annotations.

I. SAMUEL THE PROPHET AND JUDGE

1. **The birth and Childhood of Samuel** (1:1-28)
2. **Hannah's Prophetic Song** (2:1-10)
3. **The Failure of Eli and His Sons** (2:12-36)
4. **Samuel's Call and Prophetic Ministry** (3:1-21)
5. **The Judgment of Eli and his Sons—Ichabod** (4:1-22)
6. **The Ark in the hands of Philistines and Its Return** (5:1—7:2)
7. **The Return unto Jehovah and the Deliverance** (7:3-14)
8. **Samuel Exercising His Office and His Failure** (7:15—8:3)

II. KING SAUL—HIS REIGN AND REJECTION

1. **The King Demanded** (8:4-22)
2. **The Story of Saul and His Anointing** (9:1—10:16)
3. **The Open Acclamation of Saul as King** (10:17-27)
4. **The King's First Victory: the Kingdom Renewed at Gilgal (11:1-15)**
5. **Samuel's Witness and Warning** (12:1-25)
6. **The First Failure of Saul and Its Results** (13:1-23)
7. **Jonathan's Heroic Deed of Faith** (14:1-52)
8. **War with Amalek: Saul's Disobedience and Rejection** (15:1-35)

III. DAVID, THE KING AFTER GOD'S HEART—HIS EXILE AND SUFFERING

1. **David Anointed King and the Departure of the Spirit from Saul** (16:1-23)
2. **David and Goliath** (17:1-58)
3. **Jonathan and David and Saul's Jealousy** (18:1-30)
4. **Saul's Renewed Attempt and David's Escape** (19:1-24)
5. **Jonathan Protects David and Their Separation** (20:1-42)
6. **David's Varied Experiences** (21—27)
7. **Saul and the Witch at Endor** (28:1-25)
8. **David and Achish and Ziklag Destroyed and Avenged** (29—30)
9. **The Death of Saul** (31:1-13)

Analysis and Annotations

I. Samuel the Prophet and Judge

1. The Birth and Childhood of Samuel

CHAPTER 1

1. Elkanah and his wives (1:1-8)
2. Hannah's prayer and vow (1:9-18)
3. The prayer answered and Samuel born (1:19-20)
4. The child weaned and presented unto the Lord (1:21-28)

The descent of Samuel opens the book. The names are of striking significance. Elkanah means "acquired of God." He was the son of Jeroham (tenderly loved), the son of Elihu (my God is He), the son of Tohu (prostration), the son of Zuph (honeycomb). They were pious generations from which the great man came. Elkanah had two wives. Hannah (grace) the much beloved was barren; Peninnah (pearl) had children. The fact that Hannah's name stands first makes it probable that her barren condition led Elkanah to marry a second wife. (See Deut. 21:15.) Elkanah was an Ephraimite. But from 1 Chronicles 6:20-28 we learn that Samuel and his father were of levitical descent. This has been pointed out as a discrepancy. It is however not at all inconsistent with the statement that Samuel's father was of Ephraim. He was one of those Levites to whom cities were assigned in the portion given to the tribe of Ephraim (Josh. 21:20).

Each year Elkanah went to Shiloh to sacrifice unto the Lord of Hosts. It is noteworthy that the name of God as "Lord of Hosts" (Jehovah Zebaoth) appears here for the first time in the Bible. (It is found 281 times in the Bible. It is not found in the Pentateuch; it occurs some 80 times in Jeremiah and 50 times in Zechariah.) It is the name of God as the Lord of power, the Lord of all the hosts of heaven and earth. That it is used the first time in the book which reveals the Kingdom is especially appropriate.

Hannah in her visits to Shiloh presents a sorrowful picture. She is beloved and receives a double portion from Elkanah, while Peninnah, her adversary, provoked her on account of her childless condition, so that she wept and did not eat at the feast. Then she arose from the sacrificial feast which she had not tasted and sought the presence of the Lord. There she wept and vowed a vow that if the Lord of hosts would grant her a man-child she would give him back to the Lord and he should be a Nazarite. She cast herself upon the Lord and laid hold on Him. Samuel therefore was the child of prayer, asked of the Lord; his whole life afterwards manifests the spirit of prayer and dependence.

Then Eli the priest is mentioned for the first time. He was astonished seeing her thus engaged in silent prayer and accused her of drunkenness. His astonishment and accusation are a witness to the sad state of Israel. Evidently few ever sought the presence of the Lord, and his reproof makes it evident that it was not an uncommon thing that drunkenness prevailed during the feasts at Shiloh.

Hannah's prayer was answered. The son is born and was called Samuel, which means "heard of God." Little did she know of the mighty work her son was called to do; her prayer was answered far beyond her thought. She did not go up again to Shiloh till the child was weaned. Then she went up to fulfill her vow and presented him unto the Lord. Before Samuel could begin to serve the Lord he had to be weaned. "As a weaned child no longer cries, frets, and longs for the breast, but lies still and is content, because it is with its mother, so the soul must be weaned from all discontented thoughts, from all fretful desires of earthly good, waiting in stillness upon God, finding its satisfaction in His presence, resting peacefully in His arms."[1] He began to minister at once unto the Lord before Eli the priest (2:11). He was brought up in the sanctuary and became that solid, earnest, prayerful man of God. It is the weaning and the sanctuary every servant of Christ still needs. And Hannah had given back to the Lord what He so graciously had bestowed upon her. This should be the case with all our prayer-answers.

2. Hannah's Prophetic Song

CHAPTER 2:1-10

1. The praise of Jehovah—God (2:1-3)
2. Jehovah's power and grace in deliverance (2:4-8)
3. The prophetic outlook (2:9-10)

Hannah's heart filled with the Holy Spirit overflows with a marvellous utterance. Higher criticism claims "that this beautiful sacred lyric could not have been sung by Hannah in the circumstances as described. The words of verse 5 alone approach her situation, and doubtless led to the insertion of the psalm in its present context." They also say "that the Virgin's song (Luke 1:46-55) is largely modelled on the song of Hannah" (Prof. A.R.S. Kennedy). Such statements deny inspiration. Hannah's and Mary's songs are so much alike because the same Spirit spoke through both. Why should it be thought impossible for pious Hannah to give forth such sublime and far reaching words which stand so closely related to all subsequent prophecy, if we believe that the Holy Spirit inspired her as He did Isaiah and other prophets?

As every other song given by the Spirit of God, so her song begins with extolling the Lord, glorifying His name. The first four stanzas give her own experience. She knows Jehovah and rejoices in His salvation. Especially beautiful are the utterances the Spirit of God makes through her in describing Jehovah's power and grace in deliverance. We must think here first of all of our Lord Jesus Christ. He went down into the dust of death and was raised from the dead. He was brought down to the grave and brought up; He became poor and is made rich; He was made low and is lifted up (verses 6-7). And therefore He reaches down to our misery and raiseth the poor out of the dust, and lifteth the beggar from the dunghill to set them among princes to inherit the throne of glory. What a glimpse she, whose name means "grace," had of grace which stoops so low and lifts so high! Her words came nearest in the Old Testament to the gospel of grace as revealed in the New. With the middle of the eighth verse she speaks of the future. The day of the Lord with its judgment bursts into view. The feet of His Saints will be kept; the wicked will be in darkness; the adversaries broken to pieces. Then heaven is no longer silent. The Lord judges. The King, Israel's true and once rejected King, our Lord Jesus Christ, will be exalted. In the beginning of the books of Kingdoms heaven's true King is seen in prophetic vision.

The ministering child Samuel before the Lord is a most beautiful and sweet picture. Faithfully his little hands did whatever they could do, and Jehovah was well pleased with it.

3. The Failure of Eli and His Sons

CHAPTER 2:12-36

1. The wicked sons of Eli (2:12-17)
2. Samuel before Jehovah and Hannah blessed (2:18-21)
3. The empty warning of Eli (2:22-26)
4. Judgment announced (2:27-36)

The corruption of the sons of aged Eli is next exposed. They were sons of Belial; they knew not Jehovah, and yet they ministered in the outward things of the sanctuary. It could result only in the worst corruption. They handled holy things and were wicked in heart and life. It has been well said "a holiness that is but external is the worst unholiness." It is so to-day in Christendom. Men who know not Jehovah, who are not serving the Lord but themselves and are thus under the control of Satan, the god of this age, minister in the things of God. It results in all kinds of departures and corruption. It is the curse of Christendom. "The sin of the young men was very great before the Lord, for the men despised the offering of Jehovah." Beholding such wicked conduct in the priests men became disgusted with all religious performances and the truth they forshadowed.

[1]Perowne, *The Psalms.*

They turned away from the offering of Jehovah. It is so still. An unholy, unselfish ministry is the greatest stumbling block to the great mass of the people.

And then the contrast! The child Samuel in his little ministry is mentioned once more. What a charming picture he must have been in his little ephod and the little robe furnished by his loving mother! Upon him a mere child, so innocent and simple, the white linen robe had been bestowed. Everything else in Shiloh was corrupted.

Eli makes an attempt to warn his sons of their immoral and wicked conduct. His weak effort but reveals the state of his own soul. The law demanded as a penalty the death of the offenders. The lack of zeal in Eli's remonstrance made no impression upon his wicked sons. Then an unnamed man of God came to Eli and carried to him the message of judgment. Hophni and Phinehas are to die both in one day. Then there is the promise of the raising up of a faithful priest. Such a priest was Zadok, but the promise finds its ultimate fulfillment in Him who is the King-Priest, our Lord Jesus Christ.

4. Samuel's Call and Prophetic Ministry

CHAPTER 3

1. Samuel's call (3:1-9)
2. The message from Jehovah (3:10-18)
3. Samuel the prophet (3:19-21)

After the priesthood had so completely failed and divine judgment had been pronounced, Samuel receives his call to the prophetic office. He continued his ministrations as a Levite during the time that the word of the Lord was precious (literally, rare); there was no vision. Up to this time Samuel had not known the Lord nor had the word of the Lord been revealed to him (verse 7). It must have been near the hour of dawn, for the tabernacle lamp was not yet gone out, when the voice of Jehovah called Samuel by name. He knew him, as He knows all His own by name. Three times the voice called and three times he ran unto Eli. Then Eli understood that Jehovah called the child and he instructed him to answer at the next call—"Speak, Jehovah, for thy servant heareth." Jehovah then appeared and stood and called again. Samuel in answering omits the word "Jehovah" Eli had told him to use. He may have omitted the name Jehovah out of reverential fear. He hears thus from Jehovah's lips the message of doom for Eli and his house, which he faithfully transmitted to Eli in the morning. He kept nothing back and Eli bowed to it in resignation; however, he did not repent. "By the faithful discharge of a commission so painful, and involving such self-denial and courage, Samuel had stood the first test of his fitness for the prophetic office. Henceforth "the word of the Lord" was permanently with him. Not merely by isolated commissions, but in the discharge of a regular office, Samuel acted as prophet in Israel. A new period in the history of the kingdom of God had commenced, and all Israel, from Dan to Beer-sheba, knew that there was now a new link between them and their God, a living centre of guidance and fellowship, and a bond of union for all who were truly the Israel of God."[2]

5. The Judgment of Eli and His Sons—Ichabod

CHAPTER 4

1. The fulfilled prediction: The death of Eli's sons (4:1-11)
2. The death of Eli (4:12-18)
3. Ichabod (4:19-22)

Israel then renewed the conflict with the Philistines and suffered defeat. It seems that they acted in self-confidence, and when the battle was lost they readily acknowledged the hand of the Lord in the disaster: "Wherefore has the Lord smitten us to-day before the Philistines?" But there was no self-judgment, no repentance, no crying unto the Lord. The ark of the covenant of the Lord is brought out of Shiloh. They trust in the ark instead of Jehovah; they expect salvation from the ark of gold and wood: "it may save us out of the hand of our enemies." Alas! "the two sons of Eli, Hophni and Phinehas, were there with the ark of the covenant of God" (verse 4). They forgot Jehovah whom they had offended and insulted. How could He bless and deliver His people when such sons of Belial were associated with the sanctuary? A worse defeat followed. Thirty thousand Israelites fell, among them the sons of Eli. The Philistines, first terrified by the presence of the ark, gain a great victory and capture the ark.

On the words "these are the gods that smote the Egyptians with every plague in the wilderness" Wellhausen, the well known critic, remarks: "Either an

[2]A. Edersheim, *Bible History*.

excusable inaccuracy, or a copyist's slip." He meant that the Egyptians were not smitten in the wilderness, but in their own land. However, Wellhausen did not see that the Philistines said this. They expressed their inaccurate knowledge of what had happened and Samuel reports it as if it was spoken by the Philistines.

The tidings of the awful disaster reach Eli, ninety-eight years old and totally blind. When he heard that the ark of God was taken, he fell backward, broke his neck and died. Significant is the final paragraph of this chapter. The wife of Phinehas in child-birth also hears of the capture of the ark and the death of Eli, her father-in-law, the death of her husband and his brother. Dying, she named her baby son "Ichabod," which means "no glory." The glory had departed from Israel. Israel had indeed brought forth, by her departure from God, the condition of "Ichabod." The ark as the glory of God's manifest presence among His people was gone. "He forsook the tabernacle of Shiloh, the tent which he placed among men; and delivered his strength into captivity, and His glory into the enemy's hand" (Ps. 78:60-61). In a higher sense the word "Ichabod" is written over that which professes to be the church, but which has departed from the truth. The power and the manifest presence of Jehovah are lost. And many individual Christians have drifted into the same conditions by their sinful and worldly ways.

6. The Ark in the Hands of the Philistines and Its Return

CHAPTER 5

1. The ark in the house of Dagon (5:1-5)
2. The Philistines smitten by Jehovah (5:6-12)

The ark was brought to Ashdod, the leading city of the Philistines, and set up in the temple dedicated to Dagon, the chief god of the people. It was half fish and half man, the symbol of fertility. Before this idol the ark was set up. In their blindness they imagined that Dagon had conquered the God of Israel. The next morning they found Dagon fallen with his face to the earth before the ark. It was the Lord who did it and not an accident. The next morning the whole idol-image, except the fish-part, is fallen upon the ground. "The head of Dagon and both the palms of his hands lay cut off upon the threshold." The God of Israel demonstrated His power over the gods of the Philistines, yet they continued to reverence even the threshold where the fragments of their idol had lain. Such is the darkness of fallen man.

A severer visitation came upon the Philistines; they were smitten with malignant boils. At the same time a plague of field mice destroyed the fields and the harvest (4:4, 11, 18). It reminds us of the plagues of Egypt. Yet the Philistines did not repent of their sins, but carried the ark of God about, but wherever it was carried the same punishment came upon the people. Yet there was no repentance from the side of the Philistines. All this becomes still more interesting if we consider what the Philistines as the enemies of the people of God represent. (See annotations on Judges.) The world is to experience the judgments and plagues of God in a future day foreshadowed in these plagues which came upon the land of the Philistines; and there will be no turning to God. In the book of Revelation, where these final judgments upon a wicked world and an apostate world-church are described, we hear not a word of repentance. The answer God receives will be blasphemy of His name. "And they blasphemed the God of heaven because of their pains and sores, and repented not of their evil deeds" (Rev. 16:11).

CHAPTERS 6:1—7:2

1. The counsel of the Philistines (6:1-9)
2. The ark at Beth-shemesh (6:10-20)
3. The ark at Kirjath-jearim (6:21—7:2)

The ark had remained among the Philistines seven months. For them they were months of suffering and deadly destruction. Now they plot to get rid of the ark and of Him whose hand rested so heavily in judgment upon them. The advice of the heathen priests and diviners is that the ark should be sent away with votive offerings of gold, representing that which had plagued them. This was a heathen custom, which has also been adopted and is practiced by Roman Catholicism, the great Philistine system of Christendom. In Romish churches, especially at shrines, one can find hundreds of votive offerings to God by those who are suffering affliction to appease the wrath of God. It is heathenish and denies Him who shed His blood for our redemption. And as these Philistine priests had some knowledge of God's judgment upon Egypt they added to their counsel a warning reminding them of Pharoah and Egypt. Their unbelief and superstition are manifested by the way they returned the ark. But the power of the Creator is seen in the incident.

"In result it is proved conclusively that Jehovah is the God of Creation, supreme above all the natural instincts: the kine, though unaccustomed to a yoke, take the cart with its sacred burden directly away from where their calves are shut up, even while lowing after them, and take the straight road to Bethshemesh, a priestly city near the Israelite border. There, at the border, they stop, still under the eyes of the Philistine lords, at a great stone upon which the Levites place the ark, and where the kine are offered up a burnt offering to Jehovah.

> Thus the Philistines have Jehovah's sovereignty demonstrated to them in the precise terms which they have themselves chosen,—the goodness of God thus meeting them with what should have turned them from idolatry forever and brought them to His feet. But they go back, after all, to worship instead the humbled Dagon (*Numerical Bible*).

The ark reaches Beth-shemesh (house of the sun) the nearest point across the border. It is welcomed with much rejoicing, but they forgot the holiness of God and looked into the ark, and the people of Beth-shemesh were smitten. As Beth-shemesh was only a small town it is generally taken that the number of the slain as given in verse 19 was changed by the mistake of a copyist. Various readings give smaller numbers; but that is immaterial.

The ark is removed from Beth-shemesh to Kirjath-jearim, "the city of the woods." It was an humble place where the ark abode for twenty years. It was brought into the house of Abinadab; his son Eleazar (my God is help) was set aside to keep it. David found it there (Psalm 132:6). The ark never returned to Shiloh again.

7. The Return Unto Jehovah and the Deliverance

CHAPTER 7:3-14

1. Samuel's message and the response of the people (7:3-4)
2. Gathered at Mizpah (7:5-6)
3. The deliverance (7:7-14)

Samuel now is seen beginning his great national ministry. The message he brings is the message of repentance and the assurance of faith. In simple words he addressed the people, who no doubt were prepared for it by their long period of humiliation. He demands that their true return to the Lord must be practical; the strange gods and Ashtaroth must be put away. If they serve the Lord only, deliverance out of the hands of the Philistines would come. The message was at once obeyed. Every true return to the Lord must manifest itself in the same way. True repentance without self-judgment and self-surrender is impossible. The earnest appeal and whole-hearted response by the people led to the great gathering at Mizpah (the watchtower). It was a day of humiliation and prayer. Samuel said "I will pray unto the Lord for you." He was the child of prayer and the man of prayer (8:6; 12:19, 23). "Samuel among them that call upon His name; they called upon the Lord and He answered them" (Ps. 99:6). There was confession of sin and they drew water, and poured it out before Jehovah. It was a symbolical act showing the undone and helpless condition of Israel. "We must needs die, and are as water spilt on the ground" (2 Sam. 14:14). When the Philistines came up against them they were afraid and acknowledged prayer as their only refuge and help. "Cease not" they appealed to Samuel, "to cry for us unto the Lord our God." And afterwards he offered a whole burnt offering unto the Lord. This offering represents Christ. Then Samuel cried unto the Lord and the Lord answered him. The elements of a true return unto the Lord and a true revival among God's people are found in this great national movement. While Samuel offered the burnt offering and interceded for Israel the Philistines drew near. Then came the interference from the Lord. It was a supernatural thundering which discomfited the Philistines, and they were smitten. Israel gains a great victory. They pursue the enemy to Beth-car (house of the lamb). Between Mizpeh and Shen the stone called by Samuel "Ebenezer" is put up as a memorial. Ebenezer means "stone of help." "Helped—but only 'hitherto'! For all Jehovah's help is only 'hitherto'—from day to day, and from place to place—not unconditionally, nor wholly, nor once for all, irrespective of our bearing."[3]

8. Samuel Exercising His Office and His Failure

CHAPTERS 7:15—8:3

1. Samuel the Prophet-Judge (7:15-17)
2. His failure (8:1-3)

---

[3]A. Edersheim, *Bible History*.

Samuel's activity as the great prophet-judge is now seen. He had a blessed circuit of ministry, which has its spiritual lessons for us. He first visited Bethel (the house of God). Judgment must begin there. When Jacob was obedient to the divine call "Arise and go up unto Bethel," he buried the strange gods, the household gods under the oak of Shechem. So the evil things must be put away. Then came Gilgal (rolling). There the reproach of Egypt was rolled away (Joshua 5). This is what we need, to be freed from the world, dead to it and the world dead to us. Mizpeh (watch tower) was his third station. This is our constant need to be on our guard and watch against the foe, as well as look upward and forward from Mizpeh to that blessed home where He is and which we shall surely share with Him. This is represented in Ramah (heights) where Samuel had his home. But there is failure. Samuel makes the mistake in making his sons judges. Because he was a judge and a prophet and had success in it, his sons are to follow him in the same capacity. God does not work by succession, nor does He transmit gift and power from father to son. The so-called "apostolic succession" and traditional authority is an invention and one of the greatest factors in the corruption of Christianity. The Lord alone can call to service and give gifts for the ministry. Joel and Abiah were judges in Beersheba, but walked not in his ways, but turned aside after lucre, and took bribes, and perverted judgment. And this opened the way for the introduction of the monarchy in Israel.

II. King Saul: His Reign and Rejection

1. The King Demanded

CHAPTER 8:4-22

1. The king demanded (8:4-9)
2. The rights of the king (8:10-22)

The kingly government is now to be established through the deliberate and untheocratic self-determination of the people. Jehovah was their invisible King, and Him they rejected by requesting a king like all the nations. The motives for the demand of a king are three: 1. The old age of Samuel and the unfitness of his sons; 2. The desire to be upon the same footing with other nations; 3. To have a leader and fight their battles (verse 20).[4] Samuel was displeased by the request, but the man of prayer turned to the Lord and received from Him the needed direction. The Lord comforts the heart of His servant "for they have not rejected thee, but they have rejected Me, that I should not reign over them." As they did to Jehovah, so the Lord told His servant, do they also unto thee. The servant is identified with His Master. It reminds us of the words of our Lord: "If they have persecuted Me, they will persecute you also." We are called to share His reproach. And they were to have a King according to their own choice. Later the Lord reminded Israel through Hosea of this event. "I will be thy King; where is any other that may serve thee in all thy cities? and thy judges of whom thou saidst, give me a king and princes? I gave thee a king in mine anger, and took him away in my wrath" (Hos.13:10-11). Then Samuel describes the manner, literally the rights, of the king. Military service, harsh and compulsory, forced labour and other evils are spread before them. Yet they refused to hearken and the Lord said again: "Hearken unto their voice, and make them a king."

2. The Story of Saul and His Anointing

CHAPTERS 9:1—10:16

1. Saul the son of Kish and the lost asses (9:1-10)
2. Samuel and Saul (9:11-24)
3. Saul anointed King (9:25—10:16)

And now the Lord gives them a king according to their choice. "He should possess all the natural attractions and martial qualities which the people could desire in their king; he should reflect their religious standpoint at their best; but he should also represent their national failings and the inmost defects of their religious life; that of combining zeal for the religion of Jehovah, and outward conformity to it, with

[4] "The state or political organization reaches its highest development when royalty is introduced. The King of Israel is not, however, intended to be an autocratic but a theocractic king; the prophet and the priest, in their official capacity, did not occupy a subordinate, but a co-ordinate rank. As men and as citizens, they were under an obligation, like all other subjects, to obey the king; but with respect to their prophetic and priestly offices, they were dependent on God alone, and by no means on the king" J. H. Kurtz, *Sacred History*.

utter want of real heart submission to the Lord, and of true devotedness to Him" (A. Edersheim). They obtained exactly what they wanted. God's choice for them would have been a different character, one who seeks Him and is in subjection to Him, as we shall find in the king after God's heart, King David. But now He gives to the people what they had asked for.

Saul means "asked." The genealogy of Saul is given; the five names in their original meaning suggest the pride and self-glorification of the natural man. Saul is described as an ideal man, "a young man" (literally, "in the prime of manhood") and goodly; and there was not among the children of Israel a goodlier person than he; from his shoulders and upward he was higher than any of the people. Saul, ignorant of the divine purpose, sets out to seek the lost she-asses of his father. Little did he know how the search would end and that he would soon become the head of the nation, which had gone more astray than the lost asses (Is. 1:3). A small matter it was going forth to look for animals which had strayed away; but the guiding hand of Jehovah was there. The search is futile. The servant then suggests a visit to the man of God, none other than Samuel. Saul seems to have no knowledge of Samuel. He is willing enough to seek the man for counsel but he is troubled about the present for the man of God. It shows the tendency of the natural man to give in order to get from God. The servant has the fourth part of a shekel of silver which he offers to give to the man of God. Verse 9, containing a parenthetical statement, is not a gloss by a later hand, as the critical school maintains. The difference between seer and prophet is an interesting one. A prophet is one who speaks for God being moved by God; he is the mouthpiece of the Lord. The term seer suggests the knowledge the prophet had. The people were more concerned about the seer than the prophet. Thus Saul shows the state of his heart. He does not seek God, nor the prophet as the man and mouthpiece of God; only the seer.

Then Samuel and Saul meet for the first time. First Saul and the servant meet maidens going out to draw water, and they directed them to the heights where a sacrificial feast was to be held. And the Lord had spoken into Samuel's ear the day before that the man of Benjamin would come. All had been ordered by the Lord and Samuel, knowing the expected one would come had reserved the shoulder of the peace offering for him (9:23-24).(See annotations on Leviticus.) What the Lord had said to Samuel concerning Saul reveals His gracious purpose of love towards Saul. Though he was the people's choice yet the Lord was willing to make him much more, even the saviour of this people Israel (9:16). Samuel tells Saul that the asses were found, so that he was relieved of the anxiety. And when Samuel acquaints him that all Israel desires him, he speaks of his own littleness (9:21). It reminds us of that other Saul of the tribe of Benjamin, the Apostle Paul, whose name means "little." However Saul, the son of Kish, knew nothing of real self-judgment. It was rather the language of surprise than the expression of a deep, heartfelt humility. Then we see them in communion, and afterwards Samuel anoints him with the holy anointing oil and kissed him. The anointing is the symbol of power conferred upon him and also implies dependence upon the Holy Spirit, typified by the oil. The kiss was given in token of homage. Thus Saul became the first king in Israel. Samuel also gave him three significant signs, which all came to pass. They were given to Saul to assure him of all which had taken place and to teach him certain spiritual lessons. He was assured that God is with Him (10:7). The Spirit of God also came upon him and he prophesied.

"By this, as in the case of judges, we are, however, not to understand the abiding and sanctifying presence of the Holy Ghost dwelling in the heart as His temple. The Holy Ghost was peculiarly "the gift of the Father" and "of the Son,"and only granted to the Church in connection with and after the resurrection of our blessed Lord. Under the Old Testament, only the manifold influences of the Spirit were experienced, not His indwelling as the Paraclete. This appears not only from the history of those so influenced, and from the character of that influence, but even from the language in which it is described. Thus we read that the Spirit of Elohim "seized upon" Saul, suddenly and mightily laid hold on him,—the same expression being used in Judg. 14:6,19; 15:14; 1 Sam.16:13; 18:10."

3. The Open Acclamation of Saul as King

CHAPTER 10:17-27

1. The lot at Mizpeh (10:17-21)
2. The acclamation of the King (10:22-27)

Samuel called once more a national gathering at Mizpeh. The lot is now to be cast. But before this is done the Lord through Samuel reminds them once more of their serious mistake: "And ye have this day rejected your God, who Himself saved you out of all your adversities and your tribulations; and ye have said unto Him, Nay but set a king over us." They had not heeded this warning before and now they are to receive what they had asked in their self-will. The lot was therefore but an outward, empty ceremony. It fell on Saul, the son of Kish. He could not be found. Why did he hide? Some say it was humility and modesty. It was not that, but rather fear of the responsibility he was now to assume. And that revealed lack of confidence in God of whose power he had received such evidences. All foreshadows the coming failure of the people's king. When he is presented before the people it was seen that he towered above them all. When Samuel introduced him, "See ye him whom the Lord hath chosen," there was a wave of fleshly enthusiasm. And all the people shouted and said, God save the King. (literally, Live the King!) Now they had a king like the other nations, a king who reflected their own carnal, unspiritual condition. How his heart must have been lifted up with pride even then! Once more Samuel tells them the manner of the kingdom; it was undoubtedly a restatement of Deut. 17:14-20. And Saul did not assume leadership at once. He went home to Gibeah. A faithful company whom God had touched accompanied the king, while the sons of Belial despised him and brought no present. There was opposition to him. He showed the wisdom of the natural man by holding his peace. He was as a deaf man.

4. The King's First Victory and the Renewal of the Kingdom at Gilgal

CHAPTER 11

1. The victory over Ammon (11:1-11)
2. The kingdom renewed (11:12-15)

Nahash the Ammonite encamped against Jabesh-gilead. Nahash means "the serpent." This invasion took place before Saul had been made king. From chapter 12:12 we learn that it really was the occasion why Israel demanded a king. In despair the inhabitants of Jabesh-gilead offered to make a covenant with this old foe of Israel, whom Jephthah had so successfully fought. Ammon represents typically the enemy of God's people characterized by evil doctrines and perversions of the truth of God. How often compromise is made with the most subtle errors which emanate from Nahash, the serpent! But he makes his condition, their right eyes are to be plucked out. We speak of the eye of faith, and typically we may apply it in this way. All errors and false doctrines blind the eyes of faith and rob God's people of their true vision.

Then Saul acts for the first time. However his actions are characteristic of his spiritual condition. We read nothing of prayer; he did not seek the presence of the Lord. It is true, the Spirit of God came upon him, but that does not mean that he was right with God. The Spirit of God came also upon Balaam to prophesy. Even so the Spirit came upon King Saul with external power in the same sense as He came upon the judges. The anger which he manifested, the methods he employed to stir up the people, the threat he makes and his leaning on Samuel for authority (verse 7) all show again the lack of true faith. He is but the man in the flesh who knows not the Lord.

At Gilgal the kingdom is renewed. The people are united and suggest the killing of the sons of Belial mentioned in the previous chapter. Saul forbids it and acknowledges that the Lord had wrought salvation that day. But there is no real outburst of praise. They were at Gilgal, the place which typifies death to the flesh. Here Saul is made king before the Lord. But while Saul and the people rejoiced nothing is said of Samuel's joy. The man of God looked deeper, for he knew that all was only skin deep and that the Lord, whom they had rejected from being king over them, could not be pleased with their outward joy.

5. Samuel's Witness and Warning

CHAPTER 12

1. His witness to his own integrity (12:1-5)
2. His warning (12:6-15)
3. Heaven's answer (12:16-19)
4. His words of comfort (12:20-25)

What a scene! The man of God, the man of prayer, now advanced in years, stands before them. "I have walked before you from my childhood unto this day." Here was not a Nazarite who had failed like Samson, but one who had lived out his Nazariteship in the fullest sense of the word. What unselfish service he had rendered and how he loved his own people! In all this he is a type of that greatest servant who came in the fulness of time not to be ministered unto, but to minister and to give his life a ransom for many. His witness to his own integrity reminds us also of Paul's words in the Epistle to the Corinthians (2 Cor.11:6-9; 12:14-17). The whole nation acknowledged Samuel's integrity. A brief historical retrospect follows in which Samuel points out their sin of forgetting Jehovah. ("Bedan" in verse 11 should be "Barak.") Their present condition was like that of their fathers, unbelief and disobedience.

It was the time of the wheat harvest. Samuel prayed for a witness from heaven upon his words. Then it thundered and rained. It never thunders and rains in Palestine at that time of the year (May and June). A guilty fear seized upon them and they requested intercession. This reminds us of that coming harvest, the end of the age (Matth. 13:39). Then Jehovah will thunder in judgment and the repentance of the people of Israel will follow. However true repentance did not take place here when Samuel prayed. Beautiful are his words of comfort. How he manifests the work and character of a true prophet! Here is also the assurance for Israel. "For Jehovah for His great name's sake will not forsake His people, because it hath pleased Jehovah to make you His people." His gifts and calling are without repentance.

6. The First Failure of Saul and Its Results

CHAPTER 13

1. The failure of Saul (13:1-9)
2. Samuel's sentence (13:10-14)
3. Israel's deplorable condition (13:15-23)

Omit the first verse of this chapter as it does not belong into the text. In self-confidence Saul has dismissed the greater part of the people; only 2000 remained with him and 1000 with his son Jonathan. Saul is now passing through a test. Hath he true faith which counts and depends on God? Is he obedient to His word as given by the prophet? Jonathan appears here for the first time. His name means "the Lord hath given." He is the opposite from his poor father; the son is a man of real faith and zeal for God. In smiting the garrison of the Philistines he manifested that faith. He counted on God and in dependence on Him he acted. And what did Saul do? "And Saul blew the trumpet throughout all the land, saying, let the Hebrews hear." It was not the action of faith but the result of his own proud heart. Significant it is that he avoids the word Israel. The Lord never speaks of "My people the Hebrews," their original, national name; it is always "My people Israel." He leaves out the God of Israel. It all reveals the character of Saul. Then Saul gets the credit of having smitten the garrison of the Philistines, and when they gathered in all their strength the people are paralysed by fear, and instead of advancing in the name of Jehovah they seek the caves, the thickets, the rocks, the high places and the pits. And some of the Hebrews even crossed the Jordan. Saul remains in these demoralized conditions at Gilgal, followed by some of the people trembling. It is all unbelief; like king, like people. They fear the Philistines and distrust Jehovah. And Saul at Gilgal! He might have remembered the captain of the Lord's hosts and sought His presence and help. All shows the chosen king knew not the Lord. Samuel's word to him (chapter 10:8) was not forgotten by Saul. He wails, but not long enough. The test is on. The people stay a few days and then begin to scatter. They have no faith; neither has the king. True faith waits on God and trusts in Him. Faith knows that man's extremity is God's opportunity. Saul makes an outward effort to be obedient, while in his soul he knows no subjection to the Lord and to His way. At last the breaking point is reached. He intrudes into the priestly office. The burnt offering, without any meaning under these circumstances, is brought by Saul and immediately after, perhaps before the seven days had fully expired, Samuel appears.

The king's own words reveal once more his character and they are his condemnation. He was tested and the test revealed a heart which did not fear the Lord, had no confidence in Him and is disobedient to His word. And Samuel delivers his message. Sentence is pronounced. Another, a man after the Lord's own heart, is to take his place. And the deplorable condition of Israel! The Philistines speak also of them as Hebrews. Instead of being dependent upon the Lord for everything, they were the slaves of their oppressors, dependent upon them. This is the place into which unbelief can put the people of God.

7. Jonathan's Heroic Deed of Faith

CHAPTER 14

1. Jonathan's victory (14:1-23)
2. Saul's adjuration and Jonathan's deed (14:24-32)
3. Saul's first altar and unanswered inquiry (14:33-37)
4. Jonathan condemned and saved (14:38-45)

5. Saul's battle and success (14:46-48)
6. Saul's family (14:49-52)

Jonathan, one of the most beautiful characters of the Bible, with a kindred spirit, his armour bearer, goes forward to attack once more the outpost of the Philistines. Saul knew nothing of it. The King is surrounded by a small company, among them the relations of Eli. They had an ephod, needed for inquiry from Jehovah, but we do not read of its use. Jonathan and his armour bearer and their conversation are blessed illustrations of true faith. What simplicity it reveals! Jonathan knew the Lord and knew that He loves His people and therefore would overthrow their enemies. He tells the armour bearer "it may be that the Lord will work for us, for there is no restraint to the Lord to save by many or by few." And the armour bearer, whose name we do not know, but known to God, answered him: "Do all that is in thine heart; turn thee; behold I am with thee according to thy heart." They were in blessed unity. They cast themselves upon the Lord and let Him decide what they were to do. And the Lord, as He always does, answers to their faith. In spite of the difficulties, the sharp rocks, which they had to ascend, difficulties which are always connected with true faith, they overcome the foe. The Lord was there, for it was His battle and the earth quaked. But twenty men were slain by the two. A great confusion followed. The multitude melted away as they beat each other, and the Hebrews which had been with the Philistines turned against them. It was the Lord who saved Israel that day (verse 23).

Then Jonathan and his armour bearer were missed. Saul made an attempt in consulting the Lord, which did not succeed. Saul's adjuration was unnecessary and made in self-will. His oath is but the working of the natural man. In his blindness he thinks he can help along the complete defeat of the enemy by his legal injunction. On account of this foolish oath the people were in distress; legalism always puts burdens and distress upon the people of God. His own son Jonathan, ignorant of his father's commandment, takes a little honey on the end of the rod and receives refreshment by it. Honey is the type of natural things and their sweetness. Their use in the right way is not forbidden. Like Jonathan we must touch them only with the end of the rod and take a little. If Jonathan had gone down on his knees and filled himself with all the honey he could eat, it would not have refreshed but incapacitated him for the conflict. Jonathan was revived by the little honey he had taken, while the people fainted. But a worse result of Saul's commandment happened. The famished people ate meat with the blood. Thus Saul's restriction of a lawful thing led to the breaking of a divine commandment.

Saul erects his first altar, for he feels the need; perhaps less than that, he only fears the judgment of God. There is no answer from God when he inquired "Shall I go down after the Philistines?" What follows shows us again the impetuous and stubborn heart of Saul. Self-righteous and self-willed he is ready to slay his own son; the people rescued him from his own hands. What humiliation for King Saul!

8. War with Amalek: Saul's Disobedience and Rejection

CHAPTER 15

1. The commission to destroy Amalek (15:1-9)
2. Saul's disobedience and rejection (15:10-23)
3. Saul's confession (15:24-31)
4. The doom of Agag (15:32-35)

From verse 48 in the previous chapter we learn that Saul smote the Amalekites. Samuel is sent by Jehovah with a new message to Saul telling him to smite Amalek again and to destroy utterly all that they have. It involves another task for Saul. He had been fully established as king and is therefore called upon to discharge his responsibilities and prove that he is fit for the position which he held. Amalek is the great foe of God's people and typifies, as we have seen in our annotation on Exodus (chapter 17), the flesh and its lusts. Israel should have war with Amalek from generation to generation, and the remembrance of Amalek was to be completely blotted out. Even so the flesh is always the enemy of the children of God. "The flesh lusteth against the Spirit and the Spirit against the flesh." It is enmity against God. With this enemy Saul was to war and to destroy them utterly. But Saul at heart was nothing but an Amalekite. He gathers his army to do what Jehovah had demanded. The Lord gives Amalek into his hands. Then comes the significant "but."—"But Saul and his people spared Agag, and the best of the sheep, and of the oxen, and of the fatlings, and the lambs, and all that was good and would not utterly destroy them, but everything that was vile and refuse, that they destroyed utterly."

"The lesson is a deeply solemn one, and wider in application than perhaps we would easily allow. If Amalek stands here as elsewhere for the lusts of the flesh, alas, is it not true that we measure our judgment of these often more by our own tastes than by the simple letter of the Word of God? How easy it is to judge the multitude of things, and spare the worst of all, the Agag! And things which *minister* to the lusts of the flesh are unhesitatingly allowed, if only they are not what to common estimate would be considered vile. Our judgments, how apt are they to be those of the world at large rather than of God,—in the light of nature rather than of the sanctuary!" (*Numerical Bible)*

Then the Lord, who had been the silent witness of all this, told Samuel about it. A night of sorrow and of prayer followed for the man of God. How he must have pleaded with the Lord for unhappy Saul! Samuel and Saul meet. Strange words which came from the lips of disobedient Saul: "Blessed be thou of the Lord! I have performed the commandment of the Lord." It was a falsehood. He then hears the sentence. "When thou wast little in thine own sight thou becamest the head of the tribes of Israel, and the Lord anointed thee King over Israel!" And now he had become great in his own sight and little in the sight of the Lord. Solemn are the prophet's words to him. "Behold to obey is better than sacrifice, and to hearken than the fat of rams. For rebellion is as the sin of witchcraft, and stubbornness is as iniquity and idolatry. Because thou hast rejected the word of the Lord, He hath also rejected thee from being king." This was the irrevocable sentence of Jehovah. Alas! Saul's confession but reveals his true character once more. He sinned and transgressed against the voice of the Lord, because he feared the people and hearkened to their voice. Such a one was unworthy to be king over the Lord's people. It is a sad spectacle, the unrelenting Samuel and the deposed king. And Samuel deals with Agag in judgment as he deserved it.

The statement "and Samuel saw Saul no more until the days of his death" is taken by critics in connection with chapter 19:24 as an indication of the diversity of the sources from which the books of Samuel have been derived. But it is incorrect. Samuel did not come to see Saul again, though Saul prophesied before Samuel. However chapter 28:11-19 must be connected with Samuel's final word to Saul in this chapter.

III. David, the King After God's Heart—His Exile and Suffering

1. David Anointed King and the Departure of the Spirit from Saul

CHAPTER 16

1. David anointed king (16:1-13)
2. The Spirit departs from Saul and David with Saul (16:14-23)

The king after the people's heart has failed and is set aside, and now Jehovah brings forth His king after His own heart. That king like Jonathan, a man of faith, is devoted to Jehovah and in perfect subjection unto Him. Furthermore, from the tribe of Judah (Judah means "praise") he is a worshipper through whom the Spirit of God pours forth the sweetest strains of praise and worship. He prospers into a great kingdom and Jehovah makes an oathbound covenant with him (2 Sam. 7). That covenant points us to the true King, who according to the flesh is of the seed of David. Saul could not foreshadow that King. There is absolutely nothing in Saul which could remind us of the King who is yet to rule over this earth in righteousness. It is different with the life and reign of David. Everywhere we may discover most blessed types of our Lord Jesus Christ, the son of David. Because this king after God's own heart is to give a typical vision of the coming true King, David had to pass through suffering first before he could receive the kingdom and its glory. From now on in this book we shall follow the sufferings of the king after God's heart.

Samuel is interrupted in his mourning for Saul by a new command to fill his horn with oil for the anointing of another king. That king is to be chosen from the sons of Jesse the Bethlehemite. A sacrificial feast is appointed in connection with the approaching anointing of the son of Jesse, and Samuel is obedient and went to Bethlehem. Then he called Jesse and his sons to the feast. Then the seven sons of Jesse pass by, but the chosen one is not among them. Only one was left, the youngest who kept the sheep. He is brought in. Now he was ruddy (literally, "reddish," perhaps referring to auburn hair) and withal of a beautiful countenance and goodly to look upon; and the Lord said, Arise, anoint him, for this is he. David the son of Jesse was anointed and the Spirit of the Lord came upon him. And so David became the Lord's anointed. David means "beloved";

he is a shepherd, typifying the Beloved One, the good, the great and the chief Shepherd. What a contrast with Saul!

An evil spirit from the Lord began then to trouble Saul after the Spirit of the Lord had departed from him. What a sad spectacle he now presents! When he had been anointed, the Spirit also came upon him and he became another man. His pride, self-will, disobedience and stubbornness we have followed, and now the Spirit departs and in judgment upon the deposed King an evil spirit was permitted to come upon Saul. "Evil as well as good has its commission from God,—not its existence, but its liberty to act, and the limits of its action." It was no doubt a case of demon possession. He had rejected the Word of God and was given over into the hands of a demon. Such is also the case in the days of apostasy which are now upon Christendom. They depart from the faith and follow seducing spirits and doctrines of demons. Doctrinal apostasy and the moral evils following such an apostasy is the work of demons. God still permits as an act of judgment that demons possess those who are disobedient and rebel against Him. Then David is called in to sing to the afflicted King and to soothe him. And he loved him greatly and David became his armour bearer. "And it came to pass, when the evil spirit from God was upon Saul, that David took an harp, and played with his hand; so Saul was refreshed, and was well, and the evil spirit departed from him." Here we have a beautiful type of the Lord Jesus Christ. His sweet words, the ministrations of His Spirit refresh the soul and drive out the evil spirit. When the unhappy king had been quieted and the ministry of the young shepherd-king was no longer needed, he returned to his home and to his shepherd life; to feed his father's sheep (17:15).

No discrepancy exists between 1 Sam. 16:19-23 and the question which Saul subsequently asks: "Whose son is this youth?" (17:55-58) The king had not been previously anxious to become intimately acquainted with the origin and family-connections of one who merely bore his arms and served as his harper; but when the latter is on the point of becoming his son-in-law, it is naturally a matter of interest to him to acquire a more accurate knowledge of the personal history of David.

2. David and Goliath

CHAPTER 17

1. Goliath of Gath, the Philistine (17:1-11)
2. David's errand and inquiry (17:12-30)
3. David's offer to fight Goliath (17:31-40)
4. David's victory (17:41-54)
5. Saul's inquiry (17:55-58)

Modern critics are practically unanimous in regarding the story of this chapter as unhistorical. One of the leading arguments they advance is the statement found in 2 Sam. 21:19 that the slayer of Goliath was Elhanan the son of Jair-oregim, a Bethlehemite. But if we consult still another passage we find that Elhanan slew the brother of Goliath. "And Elhanan the son of Jair smote Lahmi the brother of Goliath the Gittite" (1 Chron. 20:5). It is therefore no discrepancy at all. A closer examination into this matter we cannot undertake here. If the account in 1 Sam. 17 were unhistorical the jealousy of Saul against David would be inexplicable.

David, the Lord's anointed, in his great deed, is constituted the deliverer of Israel. The deed of the young shepherd is one of the greatest recorded in the Bible. It was simple trust in the Lord of hosts, the God of the armies of Israel, which won the overthrow of the boasting Philistine. In typical application the story of David and Goliath is especially rich; we can pass on but a little of it. A prayerful and diligent search will reveal much more. Goliath, the giant, is the type of Satan, the prince of this world, who has the power of death. He also typifies that which is connected with the enemy of God, which is under the leadership of Satan. This is suggested by the number "six." Six is in Bible numerics the number of man in opposition to God. His height was six cubits. He had also six pieces of armour (verses 5-7). The number six is also prominent in another giant, who was slain by Jonathan, the son of Shimeah. He had six fingers on each hand and six toes on each foot (2 Sam. 21:20). Nebuchadnezzar's image of gold also has the number six connected with it (Dan. 3:1). In Revelation we find the number of the beast, that coming man of sin, and his number is 666; it represents the utmost defiance of God, the fullest manifestation of sin. The bold and defiant language Goliath used, the terror he inspired among the people of God, find easy application to Satan and his power.

And David is the type of our Lord Jesus Christ. His father sent David on a mission to his brethren. It reminds us of Joseph who was sent to seek for his lost brethren. Both are types of Him whom the Father sent into the world. (Jesse means "Jehovah is living.") He came to the camp in lowliness and then was misunderstood and wrongly accused by his own brethren. And thus our Lord was treated by His own. We must not overlook the prominence given to the reward which he is to receive who slays Goliath. "The King will enrich him with great riches, and will give him his daughter, and make his father's house free in Israel." Well may we see here a type of the reward of Him who became poor for our sake. And David took the stones from the brook, out of the water, the type of death. Then after he struck the giant with the stone, he took Goliath's sword and slew him and cut off his head. Even so our Lord Jesus Christ by death destroyed him that had the power of death, that is, the devil (Hebr. 2:14). And now Israel and Judah, the types of the true people of God, can arise and shout for joy and gain a complete victory over the conquered foe (verse 52). And this took place at Ephes-dammin (the boundary of blood) and the valley of Elah (the mighty one). It speaks of the blood and the power, death and resurrection. What evidences we have in these historical events and their typical application of the inspiration of the Bible! And David had said to Goliath that the victory Jehovah would give him should bring about "that all the earth may know there is a God in Israel." All the earth will yet see and know His salvation.

The alleged difficulty of verses 55-58 we have already explained at the close of the previous chapter.

Note objections made by critics to verse 54. They say it is "curious anachronism, since David's future capital was still in the hands of the Jebusites." However, Jerusalem, west of Moriah, had been taken by Judah. The Jebusites only held Jebus, or Zion, south of Moriah. See Judges 1:7-8. Higher criticism abounds in misstatements of the Scriptures.

3. Jonathan and David— Saul's Jealousy

CHAPTER 18

1. Jonathan's love for David (18:1-4)
2. The beginning of Saul's jealousy (18:5-16)
3. David's marriage (18:17-30)

A beautiful scene opens this chapter. Jonathan, the man of faith, loves David. He was about 40 years old and David about 17. Jonathan made a covenant with David and loved him as his own soul. He showed also his great devotion by giving to David, his robe, his garments, his sword, his bow and his girdle. Thus he stripped himself of all for David's sake. Such devotion and love should we manifest towards Him, who is greater than David. No doubt Jonathan's devotion was kindled by the deed young David had done in slaying Goliath. And when we think of what our Lord has done for us the devotion to Him increases.

And David the anointed is the obedient servant and conducts himself wisely. The days of suffering and exile are now rapidly approaching. The song of the women, "Saul hath slain his thousands, and David his ten thousands," angers the rejected King. Again the demon possesses him because he gave way to his temper. He nourished the feeling of hatred against David. "He eyed David from that day forward." When the evil spirit came upon him he prophesied. This has been hard to understand to some. Several translators have translated "raved"; but that cannot be done, for the word prophesy is the same as in chapter 5:5. Prophesying means to speak by inspiration; it does not always mean the prediction of future events. Now there is besides a divine inspiration, also a satanic inspiration. Certain cults which claim restoration of certain gifts claim inspiration, which has often been traced to the influence of demons. Saul uttered words which were the result of the indwelling evil spirit. Then he attempted twice to kill David with the javelin. This was no doubt an attempt from the side of Satan to do away with him from whose loins the promised seed, the Redeemer, was to come. The Lord shielded David and Saul was afraid of him, because the Lord was with him.

And now David has also gained the love of all Israel and Judah. Saul then offers to make David his son-in-law. Underneath it all was the mad King's plotting to get rid of David and have the Philistines kill him. How blinded Saul had become! The Lord's anointed was in the Lord's own hands and his life was precious in His sight. It has its precious lessons for us likewise.

Merab is promised to him to become his wife, but Achiel receives her instead. (See 2 Sam. 21:8 and read 'Merab" instead of "Michal.") Then he received Michal, who loved David. We shall meet her again later when she was restored to the King by Abner and later mocked the King of Israel. And Saul, after his scheme failed, became David's enemy continually.

4. Saul's Renewed Attempt and David's Escape

CHAPTER 19

1. Saul and Jonathan (19:1-7)
2. Saul's new attempt to kill David (19:8-10)
3. David's escape (19:11-18)
4. Saul's pursuit and his helplessness (19:19-24)

The lost King goes from bad to worse. First he tried to spear David; then he attempted to take his life through having him killed by the Philistines, and now he speaks openly to his own son and to all his servants that David must be killed. Therefore loving Jonathan warned David and he hid himself. Then Jonathan persuades his father to desist and Saul uttered a meaningless oath "As the Lord liveth, he shall not be slain." And Jonathan brought David to Saul.

Thus Jonathan is seen as a peacemaker.

But David's great victory (verse 8) starts the king's hatred again and the javelin flies once more, but only strikes the wall from where he had slipped away. Then David fled and when he comes to his house his faithful wife tells him of the great danger and let him down through a window. They watched the house to kill him. The fifty-ninth Psalm throws interesting light upon this part of David's history and has of course prophetically a wider application.

And Michal practised a deception. Like Rachel she possessed teraphim, the idol-images in so much use among the Chaldeans and other nations. These were forbidden by Jehovah and yet they were secretly used (Judges 17:5; 18:14). Michal's image must have been of considerable size; she arranged it in the bed and then said to messengers "he is sick." When the deception is discovered she lies again and said that David threatened her life. That the Scriptures record these misdeeds is but an evidence of their genuineness, however the Holy Scriptures never sanction these things. In all these attempts on David we see a foreshadowing also of the attempts which were made on the life of our Lord.

And David fled to Samuel, who had a kind of a school for prophets at Naioth in Ramah. Saul's pursuit is in vain and he is helpless to touch the Lord's anointed. Divine power was engaged in behalf of David, and Saul himself, stripped and naked, lying down all night and all day has to bear witness to it.

"The 'schools of the prophets,' which were placed under the direction of experienced and approved prophets, afforded to younger men an opportunity of becoming qualified to perform the duties of the prophetic calling. The selection and the admission of individuals who were suited for the prophetic office by their personal character, and who had a divine call, undoubtedly depended on the prophetic judgment of those who presided over these institutions. As prophecy was a gift and not an art, the instructions which were imparted probably referred merely to the study of the law, and were intended to awaken and cultivate theocratical sentiments, as well as promote a growth in spiritual life, for herein a suitable preparation for the prophetic office necessarily consisted. There are also indications found which authorize us to conclude that the revival of sacred poetry, as an art, and that theocratico-historical composition also, are to be ascribed to these religious communities as their source. Such schools existed in Ramah, Jericho, Beth-el, and Gilgal (1 Sam. 19:18; 2 Kings 2:3, 5; 4:38)" J. H. Kurtz.

5. Jonathan Protects David and Their Separation

CHAPTER 20

1. David with Jonathan (20:1-10)
2. The strengthened bonds and the token (20:11-23)
3. Saul's attempt to kill Jonathan (20:24-34)
4. David separated from Jonathan (20:35-42)

We do not need to enlarge upon this beautiful story of the further devotion of Jonathan to David. What friendship and affection is here! Indeed the chapter contains one of the most charming incidents in this book. When David told Jonathan of his great danger, Jonathan refused to believe it. But David knew there was but a step between him and death. The conversation which took place in the field is most pathetic. Both were men of faith putting their trust in Jehovah and hence this great affection. Jonathan also was deeply conscious of David's destiny as the Lord's anointed. Verses 14 and 15 bear witness to this. "And thou shalt not only while I live show me the kindness of the Lord, that I die not. But also thou shalt not cut off thy kindness from my house for ever, no, not when the Lord hath cut off the enemies of David every one from the face of the earth." Then Jonathan caused David to make a covenant with him, for he loved him as he loved his own soul. And Jonathan had to taste his father's anger. Vicious are Saul's words to his own son, and in wrath he threw a javelin at him to smite him. How this illustrates Satan's hatred, both against Christ and those who are one with Him, as David and Jonathan were one.

Then comes the parting. They kissed one

another, and wept one with another till David's weeping exceeded (literally, "till David wept loudly"). Jonathan went into the city and David into the suffering of the exile. They met but once more (23:16-18).

6. David's Varied Experiences

CHAPTER 21

1. David at Nob with Ahimelech (21:1-9)
2. David's flight to Achish, King of Gath (21:10-15)

With this chapter begins the record of David's wanderings as an exile. A number of Psalms were written by him during this period of the rejection of the Lord's anointed. We shall point out some of them. These Psalms are prophetic also foreshadowing the rejection and the sufferings of Christ as well as the tribulations of the pious remnant of Israel during the closing years of the age, preceding the coming and enthronement of the King of Israel, our Lord. He reached Nob after his separation from Jonathan. At Nob the tabernacle of the Lord had been established and Ahimelech (my brother is King) the son of Ahitub (22:9) and great-grandson of Eli, was now exercising the priesthood. Nob was not far from Jerusalem, north of the city (Isaiah 10:32).

He appeared before Ahimelech in a deplorable condition. It was on a Sabbath when the King's son-in-law appeared unarmed and hungry. Ahimelech became afraid and suspicious, but David invented a falsehood to allay the suspicions of the high priest. The truthfulness of the Word of God is demonstrated in this faithful report of David's failure. He was not fully trusting in his God and the result was the exercise of an endeavour to protect himself which led to the deception. How different the actions of Him who according to the flesh was the son of David! "Who did no sin, neither was guile found in His mouth; who when He was reviled, reviled not again" (1 Pet. 2:22-23). Then he and his companions ate the hallowed bread. Our Lord called the attention of the Pharisees to this when they murmured because His disciples had plucked the ears of corn on the Sabbath (Matth. 12:1-8; Mark 2:23-28; Luke 6:1-5). There are no discrepancies between the account in Samuel and the words of our Lord. Our Lord speaks of David and they that were with him, while in the record here we read that Ahimelech asked David "Why art thou alone, and no man with thee?" The young men who are mentioned later (verses 4 and 5) may have at first kept out of sight. In Mark 2:26 our Lord mentions Abiathar as high priest. This is not a discrepancy, for Abiathar was the son of Ahimelech and exercised priestly function and also was high priest (1 Sam. 30:7). The story of eating the shewbread which was not lawful for him to eat is full of interest if compared with the words of our Lord. There was an inquiry of the Lord and then Ahimelech gave him the hallowed bread. (See 22:10.) On account of the ruin in Israel everything had become common and David and his companions did not sin in eating the shewbread; the "bread of presence" as it is called. And so our Lord was rejected, as David was, and justifies the conduct of His disciples by referring the Pharisees to David's action. (For a complete exposition see the annotations on Matthew, chapter 12.) "We can see in David rejected the type of a greater, who as such has abrogated Jewish and legal ordinances in order to give to His people the true communion with Himself of which the shewbread speaks." Thus the shewbread typifies the true bread, which we use for our sustenance, as David needed it for his physical keeping.

Then Doeg (the fearful) is mentioned. He was an Edomite and a prominent servant of Saul. David knew with the presence of Doeg that his secret was now discovered and Doeg later told Saul about it (22:9). He also received the sword of Goliath. With it he had slain the giant and, as we showed before, it is the type of Him who by death has destroyed him who has the power of death. The victory our Lord has won through death is the weapon against all our enemies.

Then we find David in Gath among the Philistines. Strange place he had selected for his protection! Why should he have gone to the strongest enemies of God and of His people? He had acted in unbelief and unbelief was dragging him down lower and lower. Instead of fleeing to God, he turned to Gath. And then for self-preservation, because he had been discovered, he feigned madness. The King of Gath drove him away. The Lord was far better than his fears. The gracious deliverance set his heartstrings vibrating with praise. Here we would ask the reader to turn to Psalm 34, which David wrote, according to the inscription, when Ahimelech drove him away and when he departed. (There is no discrepancy here. The Philistine kings were called "Abimelech" as the rulers of Russia are called "Czar," the rulers of Turkey, "Sultan." Achish was Abimelech of the Philistines.)

CHAPTER 22

1. In the cave of Adullam (22:1-2)
2. In Moab and Gad's message (22:3-5)
3. Saul's discovery of David's visit to Nob (22:6-10)
4. The murder of the priests (22:11-19)
5. David and Abiathar (22:20-23)

Next we find him in the cave of Adullam (a witness). Here a strange company gathers around the rejected king. It consisted of 400 men. He became their captain. Some of them were in distress, others in debt, and discontented. Such were attracted to the rejected David. It was a blessed scene foreshadowing Him to whom all can gather who are in distress, who feel their debt, their sinfulness, their sorrow and their need. And a greater One than David is here. Our Lord rejected, but owned by those who acknowledge their need, has power to meet it all in the riches of His grace. They with their captain, the Lord's anointed were "outside of the camp." Such a place there is to-day for all who know Him, who is rejected of men and so much dishonored in that which claims and bears His name. "Let us go forth therefore unto Him without the camp, bearing His reproach" (Heb. 13:13). And later those who had gathered around David in the cave, and suffered with him, were specially remembered (2 Sam. 23:8-39). "If we suffer we shall reign with Him" (2 Tim. 2:12). Psalm 57 was written by David when he fled to the cave. And when he was in the cave he prayed. This prayer is embodied in Psalm 142. It was answered too when the Lord sent to him the 400 men. What food for meditation and reflection is here!

Then he came to Moab. His father and mother were there with him. He thought of making his nest there, yea, more than a nest, "a hold"; it was not according to the mind of the Lord. His ancestress of blessed memory, Ruth, the Moabitess, had left the land of Moab to dwell in Israel; her great-grandson David leaves the land to dwell in Moab. Again it was unbelief. He tried to escape the troubles which were in store for him. He had to learn patience and endurance. Therefore the Lord sent the prophet Gad with the message to depart. In all his unbelief and failures the Lord did not forsake him, but His watchful, loving eye followed His rejected servant. He cared and provided for him. No harm could reach him. He was not in Saul's hands but in the hands of the Lord. And this is our happy lot. In a psalm he saith "Thou tellest all my wanderings."

A frightful scene follows. Doeg the Edomite tells Saul of what happened at Nob. Saul, demonized Saul, orders the slaughter of the priests and while the servants of Saul refused the bloody work, the Edomite executed the command. Abiathar the son of murdered Ahimelech told David. He knew of Doeg's words to Saul about the shelter Ahimelech had given him. At that time David wrote Psalm 52. Prophetically Doeg, the Edomite, is the type of that cunning man of sin.

Beautiful are David's words to Abiathar (verse 23). They suggest the blessed assurance of salvation and preservation all receive who in faith turn to the Lord Jesus Christ.

CHAPTER 23

1. The victory over the Philistines at Keilah (23:1-13)
2. In the wilderness of Ziph (23:14-26)
3. Saul's return (23:27-29)

Keilah was about six miles southeast of Adullam. David heard of the invasion of the Philistines that they were fighting against this walled city. And he inquired of the Lord, through Abiathar, who had an ephod (verse 6). David's inquiry of the Lord shows the man of faith in his submission to the Lord. He had his lapses, but at heart he owned the Lord and wanted to glorify Him. Twice he asked the Lord; the second time evidently to quiet the fears of the six hundred men who were now with him. The Lord gave him the victory. Then poor, blinded Saul thought David was now shut up in Keilah and could not escape. He knew not the Lord and His power to protect His own. While Saul plotted, David prayed and depended on the Lord, who told him that Saul would come to Keilah and that the men of Keilah would deal treacherously with him and his men. In the wilderness of Ziph Saul sought him every day, but God did not deliver him into his hands. And David learned by experience what the name of Ziph means; it means "refining." In the refining process of suffering and endurance the shepherd-king was fitted for his coming exaltation. In this he is not a type of our Lord, but we can read our own experience here. For the last time Jonathan and David met. He came to strengthen David's hand in God. This is the true purpose of the fellowship of the Saints. What a noble character was Jonathan!

"It is difficult to form an adequate conception of the courage, the spiritual faith, and the moral grandeur of this act. Never did man more completely clear himself from all complicity in guilt than Jonathan from that of his father. And yet not an undutiful word escaped the lips of this brave man. And how truly human is his fond hope that in the days to come, when David would be king, he should stand next to his throne, his trusted adviser, as in the days of sorrow he had been the true and steadfast friend of the outlaw! As we think of what it must have cost Jonathan to speak thus, or again of the sad fate which was so soon to overtake him, there is a deep pathos about this brief interview, almost unequalled in Holy Scripture, to which the ambitious hopes of the sons of Zebedee form not a parallel but a contrast" (A. Edersheim).

The Ziphites after Jonathan's visit discovered David's hiding place to Saul but Saul could not reach him nor touch the Lord's anointed. But David at that time cried mightily to God, "Save me, O God"—"Hear my prayer, O God; give ear to the words of my mouth"; these were some of his utterances recorded in Psalm 54, which was written at that time.

CHAPTER 24

1. In the wilderness of En-gedi (24:1-8)
2. David's words to Saul (24:9-15)
3. Saul's answer to David (24:16-22)

Saul continues in the pursuit of David and with 3000 chosen men he sought David at the rocks of the wild goats. It was in En-gedi, which means "the fountain of the young goat." There were wild rocks and the fountains of water and here David had found his refuge and strongholds. God trained him also amidst the hardships and difficulties suggested by the rocks, while the fountain suggests the refreshing which was also his blessed portion. Perhaps in that trying wilderness he poured out his heart in the way as recorded in Psalm 63. It is certain that he developed constantly in his faith and trust in God. And a test is now permitted to come upon him. Saul had entered a cave. David and his men were in the sides of the cave. But a few steps between him and the unsuspecting Saul! An uplifted sword, one stroke and Saul's career would have been ended. Is he going to do it? Will he take his case out of the hands of the Lord and become his own avenger? And his men remind him of an unrecorded word, which the Lord had spoken to David (verse 4) which David might have used to justify the slaying of Saul. Faith conquers. He looks upon Saul as being still the Lord's anointed and only cut off a part of the skirt of Saul's garment. What magnanimity it was! And even for this his tender conscience smote him. A marvellous, eloquent address to King Saul was delivered by David. He tells him all what he had done and what is in his heart and thus shows the purpose of his soul to leave it all with the Lord. This is faith's language. The Man of God who walks by faith can await the Lord's own time. And thus the case was not Saul against David, but Saul fighting David's Lord. The outcome is obvious. And Saul? His reply, given in the voice of weeping, acknowledged the wrong he had done and the righteous cause of David as well as the future of David, that he would receive the Kingdom of Israel. He also made David swear not to cut off his seed. He is broken down and deeply moved. Yet his heart is unchanged.

CHAPTER 25

1. The death of Samuel (25:1)
2. Nabal and his refusal (25:2-13)
3. Abigail's deed and her prayer (25:14-31)
4. David's answer to Abigail (25:32-35)
5. Nabal's death (25:36-38)
6. Abigail becomes David's wife (25:39-44)

After the death of Samuel, briefly mentioned in the beginning of this chapter, David went still further south into the wilderness of Paran. An interesting story, the story of Nabal and Abigail, is told in this chapter. David had won a great victory over himself and over Saul. The next event records a great failure. He loses his self-control completely, and instead of manifesting the magnanimity he showed towards Saul, he breaks out in a rage and in the violence of his temper he was ready to kill Nabal and his entire household. God alone in His gracious intervention saved him from committing a crime as heinous as the one Saul committed when he slew Ahimelech, his fellow-priests and the inhabitants of Nob. How he failed! How different He was, whose rejection and suffering David foreshadowed, our Lord! What a contrast with His meekness! David was out of touch with the Lord and we read nothing here of David asking the Lord about sending the ten young men to Carmel, nor did he enquire of the Lord, when in the heat of his spirit he ordered the four hundred men to proceed on their dreadful errand.

It is true the provocation was great. He had sent the young men with a message of peace to Nabal, requesting the rich man for a little help. David had regarded the property of Nabal and his shepherds were not molested. The exiled king had a right to expect the little help he asked. And Nabal was an unbeliever. He did not believe in David as the Lord's anointed King, but looked upon him as a slave who had left his master. He refused and insulted the King's messengers. Nabal means "fool." He is a type of natural man and especially those who reject the Lord and His message of peace. His words "my bread"—"my water"—"my flesh"—"my shearers" and the whole story reminds us of that other fool of whom our Lord spoke. He also spoke of "my barns"—"my fruits"—"my goods" (Luke 12:16-21).

David was restrained from his evil purpose by the intervention of beautiful Abigail, the wife of Nabal. When she heard what her husband had done she at once prepared a magnificent present for David and his men. It was a princely gift, including two skins filled with wine. All this she did without consulting her husband. And the place she takes before David, her supplications, her confession, her humble prayer for forgiveness, her delicate reference to the king's sinful haste to shed blood, her faith in David's coming exaltation and her concluding request, "then remember thine handmaid"—all is so rich and beautiful. Abigail the woman with understanding and of a beautiful countenance typifies the true believer and may also be taken as a type of the church. Nabal to whom she is bound as wife is typical of the old nature, the flesh. But Nabal died and Abigail was married to David; even as the believer is dead to sin, dead to the law and is now married to another, even to Christ (Rom. 7:4). We leave it to the reader to follow these hints in their application.

CHAPTER 26

1. The Ziphites and Saul's pursuit (26:1-4)
2. David again spares Saul (26:5-12)
3. David's words to Abner (26:13-16)
4. David's words to Saul (26:17-20)
5. Saul's confession and David's reply (26:21-25)

Hachilah, where we find David now, was six miles east of Ziph and about half-way to Engedi. The Ziphites once more reveal his hiding place to Saul. And Saul was rushing forward to his doom when with his three thousand chosen men he took up the hunt again. The two, the rejected king and God's true king, are close together and David finds Saul in the trench and the people round about. With David were Ahimelech, the Hittite and Abishai, the son of Zeruiah, the sister of David. They creep up to sleeping Saul. Once more his enemy is given into his hands and once more David does not want to take his case out of the Lord's hands. He is true to his own words (24:15). Abishai, David's own nephew, counsels the smiting of Saul. But David does not want to touch the Lord's anointed. He declares "the Lord shall smite him" or "his day shall come to die." He leaves him in the Lord's hands to deal with him as it pleases Him. He acts in faith. Would to God that all the Lord's people would act at all times in the same manner, when they suffer persecution. The sleep which had fallen upon the company was of the Lord. He can keep awake (Esther 6:1) and He can put to sleep, to suit His own will and purpose. Then David took Saul's spear, perhaps the same he had cast at him and his water-cruse. Alas! poor, apostate Saul had been deprived before of what these two things mean spiritually; he had lost his weapon to fight in faith and righteousness, he knew no longer the water, which refreshes the soul. How the spear and the water-cruse are lost to-day to nominal, disobedient, apostate Christendom!

The sleeping company is aroused. He ridicules and chides Abner for his unwatchfulness. Saul recognized David's voice and the last discourse between the two kings follows. We call attention to two statements. David witnesses to his faith and trust in the Lord. He trusts Him that He will deliver him out of all tribulation. Saul's last words to David are prophetic. "Thou shalt both do great things, and also shall prevail." David did not hear Saul's voice again after this, nor did Saul see David again. The sad history of poor, lost Saul will soon be consummated in his visit to the witch at Endor and his miserable end.

CHAPTER 27

1. David's unbelief (27:1-2)
2. With Achish, King of Gath (27:3-7)
3. His slaughter and deception 27:8-12)

David became despondent. After all the gracious evidences that the Lord was with him, shielded him and guarded his very footsteps, he relapses in unbelief. Such is the heart of man! He fears for his life and then takes once more his case out of the Lord's hands and flees to Achish the king of Gath. He had been there before and at that former visit he feigned insanity and the Philistinian Ahimelech Achish of Gath had driven him away. Now he is welcomed by Achish, for he brings a small army of 600 young men with him and receives Ziklag to dwell in with his two wives and his household. And Saul after this sought him no more.

David abode there one year and four months; a long time to be away from the Lord. And at the same time he made raids upon the enemies of God and His people. He invaded the Geshurites, the Girzites and the Amalekites. It was not a real work for God, but the result of a self-centered heart and its aim was selfishness. It shows how a person whose heart is out of touch with God may outwardly be engaged in fighting evil for selfish reasons. David shared in the spoils, yet he deceived the King of the Philistines. And the road leads down. Unbelief drags down, lower and lower. David, as we learn from the beginning of the next chapter, beame the body guard of Achish and with his men is to fight Israel. A sad record it is. How often God's people followed the same road.

7. Saul and the Witch at Endor

CHAPTER 28

1. David fully joined to Achish (28:1-2)
2. Forsaken Saul (28:3-6)
3. The command to seek a witch (28:7)
4. Saul's visit to Endor (28:8-14)
5. Samuel's solemn message (28:15-20)
6. Saul's despair and departure (28:21-25)

Saul's final plunge towards his awful end is the main topic of this chapter. Israel had adopted necromancy, asking the dead, and other occult and wicked practices of the Canaanitish nations. They had those who were possessed by demons; the so-called mediums of spiritism and the modern day psychical research endeavors follow the same paths. Saul had cleared the land of these necromancers. Saul became frightened by the advancing Philistines. But when he asked the Lord there was no answer. Then in despair he sought the woman with the familiar spirit at Endor. Disguised he sneaked away to the woman. And he swears unto her in the Lord's name to exempt her from all punishment in breaking the law. What presumption! He demands to see Samuel. The woman no doubt had the power to communicate with wicked spirits, who represented themselves as those who had died. It is the same in spiritualism. The messages which are transmitted through the women mediums in that cult do not emanate from the dead at all, but from lying spirits, who impersonate the dead. More than once has this been practically demonstrated. When this woman at Endor saw Samuel, she cried out in fear and at the same time she recognized the king, who told her not to be afraid.[5] She had not expected the return of Samuel from the realms of death. Was it really Samuel or only an apparition? There can be no doubt whatever that it was Samuel who came up. It was by God's own power and permission that he appeared to pronounce the final doom upon Saul. And what a message it was! "The Lord is departed from thee and become thine enemy;"—"the Lord hath rent the kingdom out of thine hand;"—"the Lord will deliver Israel with thee into the hands of the Philistines." Then came the announcement of his death and the death of his sons. "Tomorrow shalt thou and thy sons be with me." This means that they were to die. Perhaps the more correct rendering is given in the Septuagint version, which reads: "Tomorrow shalt thou and thy sons with thee be fallen."

Solemn is the record of Saul as given in 1 Chronicles 10:13. "So Saul died for his transgressions which he committed against the Lord, even against the Word of the Lord, which he kept not, and also for asking counsel of one that had a familiar spirit, to enquire of it." Such was the condition and doom of the people's king, before God's king came into power. Here is a striking and significant type of the conditions on the earth before God's King, our Lord Jesus Christ, the son of David and Israel's King is enthroned. The kings of the earth and nominal Christendom are disobedient to the Word of God. They like Saul commit transgressions against the Lord and follow seducing spirits and doctrines of demons (1 Tim. 4:1). It is said that a number of European rulers have their own mediums and necromancers. But the kings of the earth defying God and His laws will be dragged lower still. The spirits of demons, work-

[5]It has been suggested that the word "Samuel" should be Saul in verse 12. The woman, it is said, recognized Saul, which would explain the second half of that verse. However, there is no reason why such a change should be made.

ing miracles, will yet go forth, during the closing years of this present age, and possess the kings of the earth and the whole world and gather them together to the battle of that great day of God Almighty, the battle of Armageddon (Rev. 16:13-16). This is foreshadowed in Saul's apostasy and in Saul's end.

8. David and Achish and Ziklag Destroyed and Avenged

CHAPTER 29

1. The objections of the Philistine lord (29:1-5)
2. Achish dismisses David (29:6-11)

While David's enemy, Saul, heard his coming doom, David was still with the enemies of God's people. The Philistines were gathered against Israel and David was with Achish ready to fight against the Lord's people. The lords of the Philistines however object to his presence. They still remember the song of bygone days and fear treachery. Then follows the description of how Achish and David parted. David's words expressing his great willingness to stay with the enemies of God show how deep a believer may fall when he has wandered away from God. He calls wicked Achish "my lord the King" and his own people Israel, whose anointed king he was, "the enemies." God's mercy kept him from plunging deeper than that.

CHAPTER 30

1. The Amalekites destroy Ziklag (30:1-5)
2. David's distress and return unto the Lord (30:6-8)
3. David pursues the Amalekites (30:9-10)
4. The young Egyptian and the defeat of the enemy (30:11-20)
5. The threatening dissension and David's decision (30:21-25)
6. The spoil sent to Judah (30:26-31)

The chastening hand of the Lord now rests heavily upon wayward, backsliding David. The Amalekites had destroyed Ziklag. The entire city was burned to the ground and the women and children were taken away captive by the Amalekites. The people rose up against David and were ready to stone him. He reaps the fruit of his sowing. He had gone into an alliance with the enemies of God and His people, and now he finds that the Lord permitted the enemy to touch his possessions. The Lord through affliction, loss and sorrow spoke to the heart of David. How humiliating that his followers were ready to stone him! They understood that his behaviour had brought upon them the disaster, that he was another Achan (Joshua 7). It was then that he turned to the Lord. "David encouraged himself in the Lord his God." Here we see the difference between him and Saul. Affliction and sorrow, the chastenings of the Lord, recall the true believer and bring him back to the Lord. He sought the presence of the Lord and once more through Abiathar, who had the ephod, enquired of the Lord. And here graciously the Lord met His servant who had failed Him! There is no word of rebuke on account of the 16 months David had wandered from the Lord, but instead the Lord assures His servant that he would recover all.

The incident of the young Egyptian is very interesting. David appears now once more as a type of our Lord. He did not foreshadow the Lord Jesus during the months he was with the Philistines. The Egyptian is a type of the unsaved. He is an Egyptian (the type of the world); he was found in the field ("the field is the world" Matth.13). He was the slave of an Amalekite. Amalek as we have seen in the annotations of Exodus (chapter 17) and in Judges, is a type of the flesh. Behind it stands Satan. Thus the unsaved, the one who is not born again, is of the world and a slave of Amalek, serving the flesh under Satan's dominion. The physical condition of this young Egyptian also typifies the spiritual condition of the unsaved. And David in showing him mercy is a type of Christ. The young man's confession, the bread and water given to him, can easily be applied in the gospel. The story of the Egyptian reminds us of the parable of the good Samaritan in the Gospel of Luke. The young Egyptian is assured of his safety; the slave of the Amalekite becomes the servant of the king. The company to which he belonged is eating and drinking and dancing. They rest secure dreaming of no danger, when all at once the battle cry of the king is upon them. It is the picture of the world. Thus sudden destruction will come upon them. And David recovered all.

How differently the dissension, which threatened among David's men, would have turned out had he still been away from the Lord. But now he acts in the sweetness of grace. The great spoil is distributed among the different cities of Judah. Well may we think here of the victory of our coming King in which His people will share through His infinite grace.

9. The Death of Saul

CHAPTER 31

1. Saul wounded in battle (31:1-3)
2. Saul a suicide (31:4-6)
3. The victorious Philistines (31:7-10)
4. The bodies recovered and burnt (31:11-13)

A sad ending to one of the saddest stories of the Bible. Jonathan, Abinadab and Melchishua, Saul's sons, fall first. Then Saul is wounded. He asks his armour bearer to make an end of his sufferings. There is no evidence whatever of his repentance and turning unto the Lord. He died as he had lived in rebellion against Jehovah. The armour-bearer refused to kill Saul; then he fell upon his own sword and committed suicide. He is the first suicide mentioned in the Bible. Ahithopel (2 Sam. 17:23); Zimri (1 Kings 16:18) and Judas Iscariot (Matth. 27:5) are other suicides recorded in the Word. The first chapter of the second book of Samuel tells us of an Amalekite who slew Saul. This is not a contradiction at all as some have declared. First Saul asked his armour-bearer to slay him; he refused. Then he fell upon his sword but was not wholly successful. In anguish he leaned upon his spear and when the Amalekite came along, he told him that his life was still in him (2 Sam. 1:9) and he slew him. His end is sad and has its solemn lessons. His sin was the sparing of Amalek, we say again, the type of the flesh. Of this sin Samuel had reminded him in his message of doom (28:18). His disobedience ended in self-destruction. Such is sin. And an Amalekite made the end of him. Sin allowed and followed will do its dreadful work in the end, as this Amalekite, spared by Saul, ends his life.

The triumph of the Philistines is complete. Saul's body is held up to scorn in the idol-house of the Philistines and afterward his body and the bodies of his sons are recovered and buried by Jabesh. The people's choice, King Saul, has gone down in ruin and shame. All looks hopeless now. Israel's hope centers now in the coming king after God's own heart, David the son of Jesse. How he foreshadows the true King and his coming kingdom, He who is the hope of Israel, the hope of the world, as well as the hope of the church, we shall find in the second book of Samuel.

THE SECOND BOOK OF

SAMUEL

The Division of Second Samuel

The second book of Samuel contains the history of David after Saul's death, his reign over Judah and over all Israel, as well as the great events which transpired during his reign. The center of the book is the record of his fall, the chastisements which he had to pass through as a result of his sin and his subsequent restoration after the rebellion of his son Absalom. The last four chapters form an appendix in which various episodes in David's life are recorded; it tells us of the victories of the King. Much in this book, even more so than in the previous history, has a typical meaning, which we shall follow as far as the purpose of our annotations permits. We make the following division:

I. DAVID KING OF JUDAH AND THE EVENTS OF HIS REIGN

1. **David's Lamentation for Saul and Jonathan** (1:1-2)
2. **David Anointed King over Judah** (2:1-7)
3. **Abner's Revolt and the War which Followed** (2:8-32)
4. **Abner's Deeds and End** (3:1-39)
5. **The Death of Ishbosheth** (4:1-12)

II. DAVID KING OVER ALL ISRAEL AND THE EVENTS OF HIS REIGN

1. **David Anointed King Over All Israel** (5:1-5)
2. **David's Conquest of Zion and Victory Over the Philistines** (5:6-25)
3. **The Ark Brought to Zion** (6:1-23)
4. **The Lord's Promise to David and the Covenant** (7:1-29)
5. **The Extension of His Kingdom** (8:1-18)
6. **David and Mephibosheth** (9:1-13)
7. **The War with Ammon and Syria** (10:1-19)

III. DAVID'S SIN, CHASTISEMENTS AND RESTORATION

1. **David's Great Sin** (11:1-27)
2. **The Message of God and David's Confession. The Beginning of the Chastisements** (12:1-31)
3. **Further Chastisement: Amnon, Tamar and Absalom** (13:1-39)
4. **David and Absalom** (14:1-33)
5. **Absalom's Conspiracy and David's Flight** (15:1-37)
6. **The Sorrows and Testings of the King** (16:1-23)
7. **Absalom, Ahithophel and Hushai** (17:1-29)
8. **The Civil War and Absalom's Death** (18:1-33)
9. **The Return of the King** (19:1-43)
10. **The Revolt of Sheba** (20:1-26)

IV. THE APPENDIX TO THE HISTORY OF DAVID

1. **The Famine and the Wars with the Philistines** (21:1-22)
2. **David's Song of Deliverance** (22:1-51)
3. **The Last Words of David and the Record of the Mighty Men** (23:1-39)
4. **David's Failure: the Altar on the Threshing Floor of Araunah** (24:1-25)

Analysis and Annotations

1. DAVID KING OF JUDAH AND THE EVENTS OF HIS REIGN

1. David's Lamentation for Saul and Jonathan

CHAPTER 1

1. The Death of Saul and Jonathan announced to David (1:1-10)
2. David's great Grief (1:11-12)
3. The Amalekite slain (1:13-16)
4. David's Lamentation (1:17-27)

David heard of the death of Saul and Jonathan from the lips of the Amalekite, who also brought him the crown and the bracelet of the dead king. The story of this young man has been branded by some as a falsehood, invented to gain favor from David. It is not necessary to reconcile the supposed contradiction of the

Amalekite's story with the account of Saul's death in the last chapter of the preceding book, by saying the Amalekite lied to David. We have explained this in the annotations of chapter 31. When the Amalekite said to David, "So I stood upon him, and slew him, because I was sure that he could not live after that he was fallen," he referred to the fact that Saul had fallen upon his own sword, in committing suicide and was in great suffering. And great was David's grief when he hears the sad news. He and his companions wept and fasted in mourning over Saul, Jonathan and the people of the Lord. Then he commanded the Amalekite to be slain because he had smitten the Lord's anointed; thus he honored Saul in his death, while the Amalekite received the punishment for his deed. Then David broke out in his great lamentation over Saul and Jonathan. The eighteenth verse as given in the authorized version is unintelligible. The Hebrew reads "and he bade them teach the children of Judah the bow;" the words "the use of" are supplied. Others read instead "the song of the bow" and claim it has reference to this lamentation, which David taught Judah. (See verse 22.) The book of Jasher (the upright) is never mentioned again (Joshua 10:12-14). The lamentation of David is a wonderful outpouring of soul. First he speaks of the calamity which has come to Israel in the death of Saul and Jonathan (verses 19-22); then he extols the virtues of both. What grace this manifests if we consider that Saul had hunted David and put upon him so many afflictions! He does not refer to it in a single word. Beautiful beyond description are his loving words on Jonathan.

I am distressed for thee, my brother Jonathan:
Very pleasant hast thou been unto me.
Thy love to me was wonderful,
Passing the love of women.

But there is one whose love is greater than David's love for Jonathan, even our Lord Jesus Christ.

2. David Anointed King over Judah

CHAPTER 2:1-7

1. David's inquiry of the Lord (2:1-3)
2. Anointed king over Judah (2:4)
3. His message to the men of Jabesh-gilead (2:5-7)

The first thing mentioned of David after his lamentation over Saul and Jonathan is that he inquired of the Lord. He would not do a single step towards claiming the rights which belonged to him without consulting the Lord. It shows how David, with all his faults, was in submission to the Lord. He waits on the Lord ready to follow His guidance and in this David acknowledged his complete dependence on Him who had chosen him as His King over His people. In this he is a type also of our Lord Jesus. The answer came to him at once that he was to go up into the cities of Judah. Then the men of Judah came and anointed him king over the house of Judah. There is nothing ostentatious about it nor does he take any steps whatever to extend his God-given rights beyond the tribe of Judah. His first act as king was to thank the men of Jabesh-gilead for the kindness they had done in the burial of Saul. He also exhorted them to be strong and announced his kingship over Judah.

3. Abner's Revolt and the War which Followed

CHAPTER 2:8-32

1. Abner makes Ish-bosheth king over Israel (2:8-11)
2. The defeat of Abner (2:12-17)
3. Abner and Joab and Joab's victory (2:18-32)

God's king began his reign in quietness, and opposition and open revolt followed at once. Abner, who had been the captain of Saul's host, took a son of Saul by the name of Ish-bosheth and made him king in Gilead. The original name of this son was "Esh-baal," which means "the fire of Baal" (1 Chronicles 8:33). "Ish-bosheth" was his other name; it means "man of shame." He seems to have been a weakling and a tool in Abner's hand. Ish-bosheth's influence was soon extended over all Israel and the false King ruled, while David was only acknowledged by the faithful men of Judah. David's reign over Judah was seven years and six months. Here are faint hints of what will be repeated in the future history of Israel. Another Ish-bosheth, a pretender to the throne of Israel, the false king, will be in the earth. He comes in his own name, with no claim whatever to the throne. And the true King, like David, will only be acknowledged by a faithful remnant of his people. The seven years and a half remind us of the last period of Israel's history when these things come to pass. However, Ish-bosheth's weakness and especially his end makes a fuller application on these lines impossible.

The other prominent person is Joab, the son of Zeruiah, who went out with the servants of David. (Joab was David's nephew. See 1 Sam.

26:6; 1 Chronicles 2:16.) They met Abner's force about six miles northwest of Jerusalem by the pool of Gibeon. Then followed at Abner's suggestion a conflict between twelve young men of Benjamin, the subjects of Ish-bosheth, and twelve of David's servants. A wicked scene followed. They slaughtered each other at Helkath-hazzurim, "the field of sharp swords," after which there was a severe battle which ended with the defeat of Abner. All this shows the sorrowful conditions which existed among Israel, foreshadowing again the worse conditions throughout this age and especially at the close of it. Then follows the record of the three sons of Zeruiah, Joab, Abishai and Asahel. Asahel followed hard after Abner and though repeatedly warned by Abner, continued in his pursuit till Abner in self defense slew him. The battle ended with the loss of nineteen servants of David and Asahel, while Abner lost 360 men. "Shall the sword devour forever?" was Abner's question. As long as God's true King does not occupy the throne, ruling in righteousness and in peace, wars and bloodshed will continue. The sword cannot be stopped till He reigns. In His coming kingdom nations will learn war no more and beat their swords into plowshares.

4. Abner's Deeds and End

CHAPTER 3

1. The long war and its results (3:1)
2. David's family (3:2-5)
3. Abner's defiant deed (3:6-7)
4. Abner and Ish-bosheth (3:8-11)
5. Abner's defection to David (3:12)
6. David's request (3:13-16)
7. Abner with David (3:17-22)
8. Abner's end (3:23-30)
9. David's lamentation over Abner (3:31-39)

The first verse speaks of the long war between the house of Saul and the house of David. And David waxed stronger and stronger. The weakness of the king in giving way to the flesh is next faithfully recorded; his self-indulgence in his different marriages. Alas! he began his sowing in the flesh from which later he was to reap such a sad harvest. Six sons are mentioned, born to David by his six wives. Three of these sons became a source of sorrow and grief to him. Ammon's vile deed is found in chapter 13. Absalom was a still greater trial to him. Adonijah became the rival of Solomon (1 Kings 1:5). In this record of taking these different women as wives, in this gross indulgence of the flesh, he prepared himself for the great sin of his life. Disorder and much confusion followed. Abner's deed in taking Rizpah insulted Saul's house and Ish-bosheth protested and Abner's fury came upon the weakling whom he had made king. Then suddenly Abner professed belief in David's God-given kingdom. His arrogant pride is seen in verse 10; as if it was in his power to set up the throne of David over all Israel, from Dan to Beer-sheba. The poor counterfeit king was silenced. Then we see Abner entering negotiations with David. Had David again relapsed that he fell in with Abner? We do not hear a word that he inquired of the Lord. He makes a condition under which Abner is to see his face. Michal, Saul's daughter, the first wife he had, who was now the wife of Phaltiel, is to be brought to him. He then received her after his request to Ish-bosheth, while her husband accompanied her as far as the border of Judah. The subsequent history, Michal's mockery, shows that it was a mistake for David to take her back. How different all would have been if David had inquired of the Lord.

Abner, the shrewd schemer, was then entertained by David in a great banquet at which occasion he offered to make David ruler over all Israel. And David listened and sent him away in peace. But was it God's way and God's plan to have His anointed made king through such an instrument? Abner's death frustrating his plans gives the answer. Joab, moved by envy, jealousy and bitter hatred, slew Abner in the same way as he had slain his brother Asahel. He died for the blood of Asahel he had shed. An insinuation is made as if Joab's deed was justified as the avenger. This however could not be sustained by the law for Abner's death in slaying Asahel was in self-defence. But David cleared himself from so abominable a deed. "I and my kingdom are guiltless before the Lord forever from the blood of Abner." A public mourning is instituted in which Joab is forced to partake and the king lamented over Abner. "And all the people took notice of it, and it pleased them, as whatsoever the king did pleased all the people." The king's wise behaviour had its effect upon the people and thus his kingdom was strengthened.

5. The Death of Ish-bosheth

CHAPTER 4

1. Ish-bosheth in despair (4:1-3)
2. Mephibosheth, the lame son (4:4)

3. The end of Ish-bosheth (4:5-8)
4. The punishment of the murderers (4:9-12)

Abner's death meant the speedy end of Ish-bosheth's pretentious reign. Baanah and Rechab were his captains and became his murderers. While Ish-bosheth was resting in the heat of the day they sneaked in and murdered the sleeping son of Saul, then brought the head to David. They claimed to be instruments of God in the execution of the wicked deed, expecting approval and a reward from David. But the king received them in a different way. Here David's trust in Jehovah breaks through the dark clouds and the King's heart is revealed. "As the Lord liveth, who hath redeemed my soul out of all adversity." He acknowledges the Lord's gracious help in the past and his present confidence in Him. His case had rested in Jehovah's hands and in the ghastly deed of the two captains the King did not see Jehovah's intervention in his behalf, but he looked upon them as murderers. Swift judgment was executed upon them. David is now through these circumstances the sole and undisputed claimant of the throne of Israel and his anointing as king over all Israel must speedily follow. Through all the sad occurrences since Abner had made Ish-bosheth king, David had maintained his integrity. In all the evil deeds, the bloodshed and cold-blooded murders he had no part. He acted in justice. In this at least he is a type of Him who will reign over the earth in righteousness.

We must not overlook verse 4 in which Jonathan's son Mephibosheth is mentioned for the first time. He was the only representative of Saul's line, a helpless cripple. His story and David's kindness to him we shall soon follow.

II. David King Over All Israel and the Events of His Reign

1. David Anointed King over all Israel

CHAPTER 5:1-5

1. David anointed king over all Israel (5:1-3)
2. Duration of his reign (5:4-5)

The events of the reign of David over Judah had a beneficial effect upon all Israel. After Ish-bosheth's death all the tribes of Israel came to David at Hebron. It is a blessed scene when they appear to anoint him King over all Israel. 1 Chronicles 12 should here be consulted. In that chapter the names of those are given who stood by David. In verse 38 we read: "All these men of war, that could keep rank, came with a perfect heart to Hebron, to make David king over all Israel; and all the rest also of Israel were of one heart to make David king." The coming of all Israel to Hebron was one of the most magnificent spectacles in the history of the nation. One only needs to take a pencil and add the numbers mentioned in 1 Chron. 12:24-37 to find what a great army had gathered to make David king. There were 1222 chiefs and 339,600 men. Here we see a united Israel swept by a tremendous enthusiasm. Now they own him as their own bone and flesh; the victories of the past are remembered as well as the divine promise that he, David the Bethlehemite, should be the shepherd of Israel as well as their captain.

But there is coming for Israel a greater day than the day in Hebron, when they anointed David king. It foreshadows but faintly the glorious day when their long rejected King-Messiah, the Son of David, comes again. Then they will own Him and He will own them. They will also know and remember all God has done through Him. He will then indeed be the Shepherd and King of Israel. All this and much more is foreshadowed in David's coronation and his reign. David is the type of the coming reign of our Lord as "King of Righteousness" while Solomon and his reign typify Him as "King of Peace." And David made a covenant with them in Hebron as the Lord Jesus will enter into covenant with the nation in the day of His return.

Then the duration of David's reign is given. Seven years and six months he reigned over Judah and over all Israel and Judah 33 years. The record here does not speak of the great feast which was made at Hebron. We find this also mentioned in 1 Chronicles 12:39-40. It is typical of the time of joy and rejoicing in Israel and throughout the world, when the true King has come. Then the great feast of which Isaiah speaks will take place (Is. 25:6-10).

2. David's Conquest of Zion and Victory over the Philistines

CHAPTER 5:6-25

1. David's conquest of Zion (5:6-10)
2. Hiram King of Tyre (5:11-12)
3. David's additonal concubines and wives (5:13-15)
4. The victory over the Philistines (5:17-25)

Zion is closely linked with David's anointing as king over all Israel. Here 1 Chronicles 11 must be read for a more complete account of what took place. Jerusalem is now to become the capital of the great kingdom. The oldest name was Salem; the name of Jebus was given to it by the Jebusites (Judges 19:10). After David's conquest the ancient name was restored and it became known as Jerusalem ("habitation of peace"). The town had previously been taken (Judges 1:8) but the stronghold of the upper city, Mount Zion, remained in the hands of the Jebusites. David took the stronghold. Jebusite means "the one who treads down." It reminds us of the words of our Lord, "Jerusalem shall be trodden down by the Gentiles until the times of the Gentiles are fulfilled" (Luke 21:24). Jerusalem and Zion are still trodden down by the Gentiles. The day is coming when the King will end all this. Jerusalem is yet to be "the city of the great King." (Ps. 48). Here we have once more a prophetic foreshadowing of what will take place, only on a larger scale, when He, who is greater than David, begins His long promised reign in the midst of His people. After this we shall find much more about Zion, especially in the prophets and in the psalms. It is the place Jehovah has chosen (Ps. 132:13-14). To this place, where his throne was, David also brought the ark. When our Lord establishes His kingdom, Zion will be the glorious and the beautiful place. "This is my rest forever; here will I dwell; for I have desired it" (Ps. 132:14). Then He will bless out of Zion (Ps. 128:5); and out of Zion shall go forth the law (Is. 2:3). He will be enthroned upon the holy hill of Zion (Ps. 2:6); the rod of His strength cometh out of Zion (Ps. 110:2); Zion will be the joy of the whole earth (Ps 48:2).

Then Hiram, the King of Tyre, is mentioned. He sent messengers to David, as well as cedar trees, carpenters and masons, and they built David a house. It must be understood that we have in this and the events which follow not a strict chronology. The children mentioned here were born at a later period. All is put in here to show how David grew great and that the Lord was with him. Hiram, the Gentile king, and the messengers he sent, are typical of that day, when our Lord reigns in Zion and "the Kings of Tarshish and the isles shall bring presents"—when all nations shall serve Him (Ps. 72:10-11).

The Hebrew names of the eleven sons of David are of deep significance. It seems the story of the redemption which is in Him, whom David foreshadows, is made known in these names. Shammuah (heard); Shobab (returning); Nathan (he is given); Solomon (peace); Ibhar (the Lord chooses); Elishua (my God is salvation); Nepheg (budding); Japhia (glorious); Elishama (God heareth); Eliada (whom God knoweth); Eliphalet (my God is escape). This is a most blessed revelation contained in those names; and some Christians can say there is no meaning in names! Read them in their meaning and ponder over each as telling forth the very gospel story from start to finish.

Twice David enquired of the Lord concerning the Philistines. Once he is told to go up and the Lord gave him the victory and he burned the images of the Philistines. It is another picture of how the coming King will make an end of idolatry. Again he asked the Lord and was told not to go up. Then the Lord smote the Philistines Himself. In all David was obedient.

3. The Ark Brought to Zion

CHAPTER 6

1. The ark fetched by David (6:1-5)
2. Uzzah: his error and death (6:6-9)
3. The ark in the house of Obed-edom (6:10-11)
4. The ark brought into David's city (6:12-19)
5. Michal's mockery of David (6:20-23)

It is of importance to read 1 Chronicles 13 for a better understanding of how the ark was brought from Kirjath-jearim to David's city. The book of Chronicles contains these larger records because in that book these events are described in their theocratic character, while in Samuel the outward aspect of David's kingdom is followed. David issued the call that the people with the priests and the Levites should gather to bring again the ark of God (1 Chron. 12:2-3). However we do not read anything more about the Levites, who alone were commissioned to carry the ark. It is evident that David neglected to follow the divine instructions given in the law concerning the handling of the ark. (See Numbers 4.) This neglect may be traced to the fact that David did not inquire of the Lord. The way they transported the ark was the way of the Philistines (1 Sam. 6:7). When Uzzah put forth his hand to steady the ark, he was smitten for his error and died. God had spoken to His people and taught them the lesson that the ways of the Philistines and disobedience to His Word in holy things demands His judgment. How many in the past and more so to-day act like Uzzah when in service for God they employ the methods of the world and disregard entirely His Word. Godly fear and faithful submission to the Word of God are essentials in true service for God. Service without these is often a snare and results in dishonour.

Then the progress of the ark was arrested, because David filled with fear would not remove it to his city. The ark found a resting place for three months in the house of Obed-edom (servant of Edom); he was a Levite and therefore authorized to care for the ark (1 Chron. 26:1-5). Blessing rested upon his house. The judgment of Uzzah and the blessing of Obed-edom had a great effect upon David. "So David went and brought up the ark of God from the house of Obed-edom into the city of David with gladness." This is all we find in our chapter. But how did he bring the ark up? 1 Chronicles 15 gives the answer. "Then David said, none ought to carry the ark of God but the Levites; for them hath the Lord chosen to carry the ark of God, and to minister unto Him for ever." The sons of Kohath, Merari, Gershom, etc., are given there. All is now done in accordance with the Word of God and blessing follows. And David filled with divine joy danced, girded with a linen ephod, before the Lord. After the ark had been set in its proper place in the tabernacle which David had pitched and the burnt offerings and peace offerings had been brought, he blessed the people in the name of the Lord. In his dancing the king had taken a place amidst the people. And Michal, who is called here not the wife of the king, but "the daughter of Saul," despised David. She looked upon David's holy joy as an indecent humiliation, while the king declared he would even be more vile than thus and base in his own sight. What a contast with the pride of Saul which is now manifested in his daughter Michal. And what happened when the ark had been put into the tabernacle? 1 Chronicles 16:4-36 tells us how David appointed Levites to minister and then he delivered into the hands of Asaph and his brethren a great Psalm of praise. And that sublime utterance looks forward to a far more glorious day, when the Lord dwells in Zion in the midst of an obedient people. Then the heavens will be glad and the earth rejoice and among all the nations it will be said "Jehovah reigneth"; and even nature will sing in the presence of the Lord (I Chron. 16:31-36).

4. The Lord's Promise to David and the Covenant

CHAPTER 7

1. David's desire (7:1-3)
2. Nathan receives the message for David (7:4-17)
3. David in the presence of Jehovah (7:18-29)

We reach now a climax. The Lord speaks and reveals His great purposes He had in His eternal councils for David, the king after His own heart. We behold the king in peace sitting in his own house; he had rest from all his enemies. In pious meditation the heart of the king had but one great thought, one great ambition. The prophet Nathan is in his presence and to him he speaks. "See now, I dwell in an house of cedar, but the ark of God dwelleth within curtains." And Nathan told him to do all that was in his heart. But he had spoken without divine authority. God knew all David planned and what was in his heart. While His prophet encouraged David to carry out his wishes, God meant otherwise.

That night Nathan received an important message. The Lord told Nathan that David thought of building Him a house, but that the Lord would build David a house. Then He promises him a son. "He shall build an house for my name, and I will establish the throne of his kingdom for ever." Solomon is first in view, but he is only a type of Him, who said while on earth "a greater than Solomon is here." In Christ alone this great covenant-promise is to be fulfilled. Chastening for his offspring is announced, but a disannulment of the covenant is impossible, for God's gifts and calling are without repentance. "But my mercy shall not depart away from him, as I took it from Saul, whom I put away before thee. And thine house and thy kingdom shall be established forever before thee, thy throne shall be established forever." More than that, this great covenant was confirmed by the oath of Jehovah. "Once I have sworn by My holiness that I will not lie unto David. His seed shall endure forever, and his throne as the sun before Me" (Ps. 89:35-36). And when He was about to come, the Son of David according to the flesh, but also David's Lord, He who spoke these words to Nathan, it was divinely announced "the Lord God shall give unto Him the throne of His father David. And He shall reign forever and of His kingdom there shall be no end" (Luke 1:32-33). That throne and that kingdom He has not yet received. He fills the Father's throne in the highest heaven, but all heaven and earth wait for the appointed time when He will come again to claim His crown-rights and receive the world-wide kingdom, which David in inspired songs of praise so often beheld (Ps. 72). "And this prophecy refers neither only to Solomon nor only to Christ; nor has it a twofold application, but it is a covenant-promise which, extending along the whole line, culminates in the Son of David, and in all its fulness applies only to Him. These three things did God join in it, of which one necessarily implies the other, alike in the promise and in the fulfilment: a unique relationship, a unique kingdom, and a unique fellowship and service resulting from both. The unique relationship was that of Father and Son, which in all its fulness only came true in Christ (Heb. 1:5). The unique kingdom was that of Christ, which would have no end (Luke 1:32, 33; John 3:35). And the unique sequence of it was that brought about through the temple of His body (John 2:19), which will appear in its full proportions when the New Jerusalem comes down out of heaven (Rev. 21:1-3).

"Such was the glorious hope opening up wider and wider, till at its termination David could see 'afar off' the dawn of the bright morning of eternal glory; such was the destiny and the mission which, in His infinite goodness, God assigned to His chosen servant. Much there was still in him that was weak, faltering, and even sinful; nor was he, whose was the inheritance of such promises, even to build an earthly temple. Many were his failings and sins, and those of his successors; and heavy rods and sore stripes were to fall upon them. But that promise never failed."[1] And to this we add, nor will the promise ever fail in the future. Even now all is preparing for Him who alone is the Hope of the world. "Thy Kingdom come" is still the prayer, nor will it ever come till the King's coronation day arrives. And Nathan delivered faithfully the great covenant message. David's response is beautiful, yea it measures up to the fullness of grace the gracious Lord had bestowed upon him. He does not seek the fellowship of Nathan to talk over this unspeakably wonderful promise. He sat before the Lord. All the thoughts in him, planning to work and to build the Lord a house, were forever hushed. He is in His presence as a worshipper, pouring out his grateful heart. Jehovah's grace has touched the innermost cords of his soul; they give forth their sweet vibrations, which ascend in a holy melody to the courts above. He is humbled, bowed in the dust. Who am I, Lord God? and what is my house that thou hast brought me hitherto?—He believes all he has heard; he trusts in every word. His prayer is "do as thou hast said." What an hour it was when the king with the message of grace and mercy was in the presence of the Lord! May we who are the recipients of even greater grace in our Lord Jesus Christ respond to that grace as David did.

[1]A. Edersheim, *Bible History.*

5. The Extension of His Kingdom

CHAPTER 8

1. The Philistines and Moab smitten (8:1-2)
2. Hadadezer overthrown (8:3-8)
3. Further conquests and triumphs (8:9-14)
4. David's reign and his associates (8:15-18)

Great conquests and victories follow. David arose from the presence of the Lord to go forth to conquer. With such a message he had heard, assuring him of the Lord's presence and power, of the success of his kingdom, he began to extend his kingdom over the different nations which surrounded the land. The Lord was with him and preserved him withersoever he went. The history of these wars for the enlargement of the kingdom of David we shall have occasion to follow a little closer in our annotations of the first book of Chronicles. The extension of the kingdom of our Lord when He comes and begins His kingly work among the nations, to rule them with a rod of iron, is foreshadowed in these events.

When we read in verse 15 of David's reign executing judgment and justice we have another faint picture of the rule of the coming King. The leading officers of the kingdom are mentioned. Joab was the general over his army; Jehosaphat the recorder. Zadok and Ahimelech were the priests; Seraiah the scribe. Benaiah had charge of the Cherethites and Pelethites; these two names mean "executioners and runners," while David's sons were also ruling with him. Order prevailed in all things. When that true kingdom will be established on earth there will also be those who rule under the King, who have charge over five or ten cities (Luke 19:17-18). David's sons who ruled with him may represent typically believers who are sons of God in Christ and fellowheirs with Him.

6. David and Mephibosheth

CHAPTER 9

1. Mephibosheth brought to David (9:1-6)
2. Grace and mercy shown to him (9:7-13)

The story of Mephibosheth is the first thing mentioned after the government of David had been fully established. Typically it reveals the gospel in a beautiful way, and dispensationally the kindness of God which will be manifested in the coming kingdom. Mephibosheth is a type of the sinner and the condition which he is in. He was helpless, being lame of both feet. How he became lame is found in chapter 4:4. He fell and became lame, a helpless cripple. It reminds us of the fall of man and the helpless condition into which sin has put man. Therefore he could not come to David. He had to be carried into the king's presence. The sinner cannot come of himself to the Saviour; He has to seek him out. And David wanted to show him "the kindness of God" for Jonathan's sake. Thus the kindness and love of God our Saviour toward man hath appeared (Titus 3:4). God for Christ's sake shows His great kindness to sinful man. Mephibosheth means "shame out of the mouth"; when he hears from David's lips what kindness was prepared for him he confessed with his mouth his own shame and nothingness. "What is thy servant that thou shouldst look upon such a dead dog as I am?" And what words of grace came from David's lips! Surely the kindness of God is here fully made known. He is lifted from his low place of shame to take a place at the King's table "as one of the King's sons." It is the kindness of God as made known in the gospel of His Son our Lord Jesus Christ. He takes us out of our shame and makes us one of His sons. "So Mephibosheth dwelt in Jerusalem; for he did eat continually at the king's table; and was lame on both feet." When the kingdom has come the King will show such grace and kindness to the poor and needy (Isaiah 11:1-5; Ps. 72:1-4).

7. The War with Ammon and the Syrians

CHAPTER 10

1. David and Hanun (10:1-5)
2. Ammon and the Syrians smitten (10:6-19)

The chapter with the war against Ammon and the Syrians is the prelude to the great sin of David. While Joab is carrying on the siege of Rabbah, the last city of the Ammonites, David, no doubt flushed with the great victory and prosperity, remained in his house and committed his awful sin. The war with Ammon originated through the insults which Hanun the King of Ammon had heaped upon David's ambassadors. David wanted to show kindness also to Hanun as his father Nahash had shown kindness to David. We have no record of this kindness. In this endeavour David did certainly not follow the right course, for Ammon was an enemy, and while Nahash showed some kindness to David during his exile, he also had reproached Israel and was ready to thrust out the right eyes of the men of Jabesh-gilead (1 Sam. 11:1-3). Hanun's deed in treating David's peaceful messengers in so shameful a way showed that he was a wicked man like his father and not worthy of David's kindness. Had he inquired of the Lord the messengers would have been spared these indignities. Ammon then formed an alliance with the Syrians, but Joab smote them. The greatest victory is recorded in verses 15-19. The king appeared himself to lead his hosts against the mighty foe and their overthrow followed. It foreshadows the day of final victory over the rebellious nations, led by the beast (Rev. 19:19-20) when the true King comes to fight against those nations.

III. David's Sin, Chastisement and Restoration

1. David's Great Sin

CHAPTER 11

1. David's great sin (11:1-5)
2. David sends for Uriah (11:6-13)
3. The murder of Uriah (11:14-25)
4. David makes Bath-sheba his wife (11:26-27)

We see the king once more in his house. He sent Joab, his servants and all Israel to battle again against Ammon. Was it not his business as king to go forth with Israel as he had done before? Instead he remains in ease and comfort at home. Evidently he rested all day on his couch, during the heat of the day, and when the cool evening came he walked upon the roof of his house. He had been in self-indulgence and was self-satisfied with his great achievements. The spirit which characterized later Nebuchadnezzar when he walked in his palace (Dan 4:4) puffed up with pride, which preceded his great humiliation, was no doubt David's spirit also. Had he remained in the presence of the Lord, humble and depending on Him, as we saw him after the Lord had spoken through Nathan (7:18) this awful sin would not have happened. How often it has been repeated in the experiences of God's people! Nor did this great sin like a mighty giant ensnare him suddenly. The way for it had been prepared. He had given way to the flesh before in taking wives and concubines. We read nothing of self-restraint or self-judgment in his life up to his fall. And had he not disobeyed the law in multiplying wives unto himself? It is written: "Neither shall he multiply wives to himself, that his heart turn not away" (Deut. 17:17). Had he really walked constantly in the presence of the Lord he would have heeded the warning of His law. What warning there is for all believers! The flesh is the same to-day as it ever was; it does not change. We are told "to make no provision for the flesh" (Rom. 13:14). Paraphrased this means, do not nourish the flesh by the indulgence of it; flee fleshly, youthful lusts. And now the culmination is reached. "I made a covenant with mine eyes; How then should I look upon a maid;" thus spake Job (Job :1). David knew no such covenant. He looks where he should not have looked and sin soon follows. It is a solemn illustration of James 1:14-15. "But every man is tempted, when he is drawn away of his own lust and enticed. Then when lust hath conceived, it bringeth forth sin, and sin when it is finished, bringeth forth death." The king of all Israel had become another Achan. "I saw—I coveted—I took" (Josh. 7:21).[2] And sin follows sin. The offspring of sin is sin. What cunningness and deception followed. But honest Uriah frustrates his wicked plan. Did not David's conscience smart under it? No doubt it was deadened. Then he becomes actually the murderer of Uriah the Hittite. When the news of the death of Uriah is announced to David, hypocrisy is crowned in the words of the King, "Let not this thing displease thee, for the sword devoureth one as another." And here we read still the dreadful record, the sin of David and how God dealt with it.

"David, too, has faced that ever since, and faces it still: he will face it ever. It is put away, that sin, yet it remains, and will remain, type of all sins of his people, and of God's dealing with them: out of the holy light of eternity they will never pass,—out of our memories never! Here is man, here is his condemnation,—redeemed, saved, justified man! Thyself, reader; myself. Cease ye from man forever!—from ourselves, sinner or saint! Turn we to God forever, and let us ascribe greatness and salvation to Him alone.

"This is what an unexercised conscience can bring a David to. This is what lack of self-judgment, with temptation and opportunity, may make a saint! Shall we not cry afresh, with David himself, 'Search me, O God, and know my heart; try me, and know my thoughts; and see if there be any wicked way in me, and lead me in the way everlasting'?" *(Numerical Bible)*

And seven days later the equally guilty woman becomes David's wife. And she became the mother of Solomon. We find her mentioned in the genealogy of Matthew 1. Surely grace and mercy covered their sin. Yet what a trail of sorrow, misery and unrest follows! We shall find in chapters which follow the awful results. Incest, fratricide, rebellion, civil war and the king a fugitive! What a man soweth that he will also reap.

2. The Message of God and David's Confession and the Beginning of the Chastisement

CHAPTER 12

1. The Lord's message through Nathan (12:1-4)
2. David's anger (12:5-6)
3. Thou art the man! (12:7-9)
4. The chastisement (12:10-12)
5. David's confession (12:13)
6. The death of the child announced (12:14)
7. The death of the child and David's grief (12:15-23)
8. Solomon born (12:24-25)
9. Rabbah taken (12:26-31)

The Lord was displeased with what David had done. Nathan comes with his message in the form of a parable. His outburst of anger and condemnation of the injustice done to the poor man shows that he did not think of his own case. Yet sorrow and unrest were his portion; he tried to cover up his sin and as a result was in the deepest agony. Psalms like the sixth,

---

[2]"It need scarcely be pointed out, how this truthful account of the sins of Biblical heroes evinces the authenticity and credibility of the Scriptural narratives. Far different are the legendary accounts which seek to palliate the sins of Biblical personages, or even to deny their guilt. Thus the *Talmud* denies the adultery of David on the ground that every warrior had, before going to the field, to give his wife a divorce, so that Bathsheba was free. We should, however, add, that this view was controverted" A. Edersheim.

the thirty-eighth, the thirty-second and others tell us of the deep soul exercise through which he passed. Then Nathan pointed at him with his soul piercing, "Thou art the man!" First the prophet tells him all the Lord had done for him; he reminds him of all God's kindness. What had David done? He had despised the Lord's commandment; had killed Uriah the Hittite with the sword and taken his wife. Then the chastisement is announced. He had slain Uriah with the sword of the children of Ammon—the sword should now never depart from his house. He had taken Uriah's wife—others should take his wives. He had done it secretly—but, said Jehovah, I will do this thing before all Israel, and before the sun. We shall find the sentence executed in chapters 13:28-39; 16:21-22; 18:14.

Then the King's heart broke. "I have sinned against the Lord." It was at that time that, his soul filled with deepest sorrow, and yet illumined with the light from above, he uttered that wonderful penitential Psalm, the fifty-first. "Against Thee, Thee only, have I sinned, and done this evil in Thy sight, that Thou mightest be justified when Thou speakest, and be clear when Thou judgest." All the inward corruption now is revealed to him, as many a saint after him has found out by bitter experience that in our flesh there dwelleth no good thing. "Behold I was shapen in iniquity and in sin did my mother conceive me" (Ps. 51:5). And when he prayed "take not Thy Holy Spirit from me"—he must have had a vision of Saul, the mad King, when the Spirit had left him and an evil one possessed his heart. But David knew God and God knew David. He is in the light and uncovers all in His presence. Then David announced the divine mercy, "the Lord hath also taken away thy sin." And Nathan added "because by this deed thou hast given great occasion to the enemies of the Lord to blaspheme, the child also that is born unto thee shall surely die." That was the bitterness of it. Up to the present time infidels and rejectors of the Word of God point to David's sin and blaspheme, though the very things they sneer at are the things which they practice. The child died and David's grief was great. All his fasting and night long prayer did not change the divine sentence. But he also knew the comfort of hope and expresses it beautifully. "I shall go to him, but he shall not return unto me."

And has it no meaning that Solomon's birth is recorded immediately after these sad and solemn incidents? Solomon means "peaceful." Peace had come to his heart; the divine favour was restored unto him, yet the chastisement grievous and sore would follow him in the future. And then the Lord named also Solomon. He called him "Jedediah." This means "beloved of Jehovah." He is the blessed type of God's on Son. For us He is "peace"—He who hath made peace and our sin is covered by His precious blood. To God He is "the Beloved." The record of the fall of Rabbah closes this chapter. What is recorded in verse 31 was cruel and barbarous. (However, there is a doubt about the translation. It has been rendered in the following way: "And he set them to saws and iron picks and iron axes and made them labor at the brick kiln.") Ammon did horrible things to the women of Israel. (See Amos 1:13.) A fearful retribution came upon them. How often it has been repeated in history, even down to the 20th century with all its boasted civilization, now collapsed in the greatest and most awful war the world has ever witnessed. And thus it will continue to the end, till the true King comes.

3. Further Chastisement: Amnon, Tamar, and Absalom

CHAPTER 13

1. Amnon's wicked desire (13:1-5)
2. The incest (13:6-14)
3. His hatred (13:15-18)
4. Amnon murdered (13:19-36)
5. Absalom's flight (13:37-39)

"Behold I will raise up evil against thee out of thine own house." This was Jehovah's sentence and it is now carried out. The evil which he had nourished in his heart, the passion which he had fed now breaks out in his own family. His oldest sons and Tamar, a daughter of David, half sister to Amnon, are the chief actors in the first tragedy. Amnon means "faithful." Thus he should have been, but he is the very opposite. Brought up in the midst of scenes of license, as it must have been in David's harem, the lust of the flesh gets the upper hand and the awful deed, a positive transgression of the law (Lev. 20:17) is committed. The deed had been precipitated by a satanic adviser, Jonadab, a subtle man, and when it was done violent hate gave way to the violent passion of Amnon. Unhappy Tamar, outraged, insulted and hated, appears with her virgin-princess gown torn, ashes on her head, her hand on top of her head (the oriental way of expressing a heavy burden) and crying, and her brother Absalom discovers the reason of her sorrow. He then hated his brother Amnon. David heard of it also and was very wroth, but he made no attempt to deal with his son. We do not read a word that he even rebuked him. "The gloss of the Septuagint is likely to be correct, that David left unpunished the incest of Amnon with Tamar, although committed under peculiarly aggravating circumstances, on account of his partiality to him as being his first born son. This indulgence on the part of his father may also account for the daring recklessness which marked Amnon's crime. But a doting father, smitten with moral weakness, might find in the remembrance of his own past sin an excuse for delay, if not a barrier to action; for it is difficult to wield a heavy sword with a maimed arm" *(History of Judah and Israel).*

After two years the reckoning day comes. Absalom (the father of peace) becomes the murderer of his brother. It was an awful deed. In the midst of merrymaking, Amnon filled with wine, with no chance to repent, is cruelly slain. The sword is unsheathed and fell upon David's house. The harvest is on. What a man soweth that he will reap—murder for murder. It was an awful blow to David, for Amnon, his beloved first-born, the son of Ahinoam, was dead. Exaggerated tidings reach the court of David. "Absalom hath slain all the King's sons and there is not one of them left." And wicked Jonadab, the instigator of Amnon's crime, appears again and acts as comforter of the king. Jonadab is one of the most abominable characters in Bible history. We do not read of him again. Absalom, the fratricide, fled to Talmai, his maternal grandfather. He remained there three years; so this chapter covers a period of five years. Alas! who was responsible for it all? The scenes of lust and murder, outrage and bloodshed, revolt and rebellion, sorrow upon sorrow, grief upon grief, start with David's great sin. Pardoned he was, restored in every sense of the word, yet God maintains His holiness and chastised His servant.

4. David and Absalom

CHAPTER 14

1. Joab's scheme (14:1-3)
2. The woman of Tekoah before the king (14:4-20)
3. Joab brings Absalom to Jerusalem (14:21-24)
4. Absalom's beauty (14:25-27)
5. Absalom sees his father (14:28-33)

In all these records of those sad events we hear not a word that David inquired of the Lord. Joab now appears upon the scene again and that for evil, though he did not mean to do evil to the king. He concocts a scheme by which Absalom is to be brought back into the favor of the king. This he must have tried many times before, for verses 19 and 22 indicate this. It seems almost as if Joab imitated Nathan, when he came with his message to David. But God had not sent him and David's conscience was not touched. The wisdom he used was not the wisdom from above, but the wisdom of a cunning man. The whole story was deception and "the wise woman" of Tekoah lent herself as a willing instrument. And David finds out that it is all a plot and, blinded by a mere love for Absalom, without thinking of the claims of God in this case, he becomes a willing victim to the scheme of Joab. And so Absalom was brought back. The King commands, "Let him turn to his own house, and let him not see my face." It was an evil hour when it happened. Absalom's rebellion and the king's exile were the fruit of the unscrupulous plot of Joab.

Absalom's physical beauty was great with magnificent hair. (The statement that his hair weighed 200 shekels is undoubtedly the error of a scribe who copied the manuscript. The Hebrew letters which stand for 20 and for 200 are similar. It should no doubt be 20 shekels.) He was thus fitted to do the work of winning the people to himself and became the leader of a rebellion. The deed he had done in avenging the crime against his sister was most likely looked upon by the mass of the people as a noble and heroic deed. That behind the beautiful exterior there was a proud, violent and evil spirit may be seen in his deed, when after Joab's refusal to come to him, he set the barley field of Joab on fire. Then a reconciliation between David and Absalom followed: "Once more we notice here the consequences of David's fatal weakness, as manifested in his irresolution and half-measures. Morally paralysed, so to speak, in consequence of his own guilt, his position sensibly and increasingly weakened in popular estimation, that series of disasters, which had formed the burden of God's predicted judgments, now followed in the natural sequence of events. If ever before his return from Geshur Absalom had been a kind of popular hero, his presence in Jerusalem for two years in semi-banishment must have increased the general sympathy."

5. Absalom's Conspiracy and David's Flight

CHAPTER 15

1. Absalom steals the hearts of the men of Israel (15:1-6)
2. His conspiracy (15:7-12)
3. The flight of the king (15:13-37)

The beautiful prince gradually prepared for the great conspiracy of which we read now and which made of his own father the Lord's anointed, an exile. Chariots and horses with fifty men to run before him won no doubt the admiration of the people. His evident interest in their welfare, kissing those who sought his presence and advice, endeared him still more to the men of Israel. To this must be added his open words, which must have quickly circulated among the people, "Oh, that I were made judge in the land, that every man which hath any suit or cause might come unto me, and I would do him justice."

This continued for about four years. ("Forty" is incorrect. Ancient versions have "four years" which we take is the correct number. Others have suggested that the 40 years should be reckoned from David's anointing (1 Sam. 16:13). This, however, is unlikely.) During this time he stole the hearts of the men of Israel. All is now ripe for the great rebellion. He lies to his father about an alleged vow he had made at Geshur. The unsuspecting King said, "Go in peace." So he arose and went to Hebron. The signal is given at which all the tribes of Israel were to say, "Absalom reigneth in Hebron." Then he sent for David's counsellor, Ahitophel. He was away from Jerusalem at Giloh, a short distance from Hebron, which would seem that he also was in league with Absalom. Ahitophel (the brother of folly) was the grandfather of Bath-sheba. As his name so was his deed in joining the revolution, through which he may have thought of avenging the shame which had been put upon his family by David's sin.

When David hears the news he said to his servants who were with him in Jerusalem, "Arise and let us flee." Fear now takes hold on him. He feared for himself and for his city. Yet he passed through the deepest soul-exercise and clung to the Lord in all the chastisement which followed, stroke after stroke, upon him. The third Psalm gives the culmination of this. It bears the inscription, "A Psalm of David when he fled from Absalom his son." In spite of his fears he trusted the Lord. "But Thou, oh Lord, art a shield for me; my glory and the lifter up of mine head" (Ps. 3:3). It is claimed that Psalm 49 also refers to this period of his life. If that is correct then David was sick at the time of Absalom's rebellion. Verse 9 in that Psalm would have a meaning in connection with Ahitophel, the traitor. John 13:18 makes it clear that Judas Iscariot is predicted; but Ahitophel is a type of Judas, like him he was a suicide. Another Psalm which was probably written during the rebellion of Absalom and which speaks of Ahitophel's treachery is Psalm 55. The king and his household left the city and all the people after him. All the Cherethites and Pelethites (executioners and runners) and six hundred which came after him from Gath accompanied the King. And not all was bitterness. Ittai (with Jehovah) the Gittite, and his devotion to the King, must have greatly comforted David's heart. He was a stranger and an exile, who had come but yesterday to David. He told him to return to abide with the king (that is, Absalom). Beautiful is his answer, which strongly reminds us of the blessed words of Ruth, the Moabitess (Ruth1:16). What noble purpose he expresses! He wants to be with the king in life or in death. Grace has linked us even closer with our Lord. Ittai in his devotion and attachment to the king is a blessed type of those who are true to the Lord in the days of His rejection.

And there was much weeping as David passed over Kidron. Our Lord passed over that brook also to enter the garden (John 18:1) where He offered up prayers and supplications with strong crying and tears. The ark had been carried along, but now the king directed Zadok to carry it back to the city. "If I shall find favour in the eyes of the Lord, He will bring me again, and show me both it and his habitation." Beautiful it is to see that in all his great sorrow, conscious that it was the hand of the Lord which chastised him, in all his affliction he does not forget the Lord. He trusts in His mercy. Deep submission breathes in these words.

What a sight the weeping king, barefooted, his head covered, ascending Olivet! A type of Him who also ascended Olivet and wept (Luke 19:41). Then Hushai (hasty) met David. Alas! for the evidence of unbelief in the king, in planning to have Hushai return to the city and feign friendship for Absalom so as to defeat the counsel of Ahitophel.

6. The Sorrows and Testings of the King

CHAPTER 16

1. Lying Ziba (16:1-4)
2. Shimei curses and stones David (16:5-14)
3. Absalom enters Jerusalem (16:15-19)
4. Ahitophel's wicked counsel (16:20-23)

Ziba in great craftiness meets the exiled king with provisions and acts as the false accuser of Mephibosheth. And David hastily puts all that belongs to Mephibosheth into his hands. Strange that David could believe in the falsehood of Ziba. How could one who was a helpless cripple aspire to possess a kingdom? Mephibosheth had been deceived (19:26) by Ziba and David readily believed the lying story.

Shimei (my fame) appeared, cursing David, stoning him and his servants. His accusation that he was responsible for "all the blood of the house of Saul" was unfounded and unjust. He was not responsible for the death of Saul and Jonathan, and equally guiltless of the death of Abner and Ishbosheth. And yet David saw something else in the curses of Shimei and in calling him a bloody man. The blood of Uriah which he had shed must have suddenly come to his mind. And when Abishai offers to kill Shimei, David rebuked him. (See Luke 9:52-56.) "Let him curse, because the Lord hath said to him, Curse David"—"Let him alone, and let him curse; for the Lord hath bidden him." He realizes Shimei is but an instrument in the Lord's hands; He had permitted it and David acknowledges thus that he had deserved the curses. "It may be that the Lord will look on mine affliction, and that the Lord will requite me good for his cursing this day." His eyes now look to the Lord whose chastening hand rested so heavily upon him.

Absalom is now in Jerusalem and Hushai succeeds in his commission given to him by David. He deceives Absalom. Whom did Hushai mean, when he said, "Whom the Lord and this people, and all the men of Israel choose, his will I be, and with him will I be"? They can only be applied to David; most likely in his heart he meant David. But it was flattery which wicked Absalom gladly accepted. Absalom followed the vile counsel of Ahitophel and committed the unnatural crime to show to all Israel that the breach between him and his father David was beyond remedy. God's predicted judgment upon David had come literally true. (See chapter 12:11-12.) The world will yet find out that God's judgments, though long delayed, will find ultimately their literal fulfilment.

7. Absalom, Ahitophel, and Hushai

CHAPTER 17

1. The counsel of Ahitophel and Hushai (17:1-14)
2. The counsel made known to David (17:15-22)
3. Ahitophel commits suicide (17:23)
4. Absalom pitched in Gilead (17:24-26)
5. The kindness of Shobi, Machir and Barzillai (17:27-29)

Ahitophel's counsel was aimed at the person of David only. He wanted to have him killed and thus by the death of the one man bring all Israel back. But Ahitophel had not reckoned with David's Lord, who loved him and in all the chastisement through which he had to pass, was still his Lord and his Keeper. It was not Hushai who defeated the counsel of Ahitophel, but the Lord. "For the Lord had appointed to defeat the good counsel of Ahitophel, to the intent that the Lord might bring evil upon Absalom." Hushai was evidently not present when Ahitophel spoke. When he came to Absalom and asked his opinion he gave a different advice which Absalom and all the men of Israel adopted. The Lord gave the counsel through Hushai and then made Absalom and his men to follow the advice of Hushai. Hushai then communicated with Zadok and Abiathar as David had advised him. We do not follow the interesting story in its details. David heard of the counsel and the uncertainty of Absalom's movement and passed over Jordan into safety. Thus through Hushai's conspiracy, acting as a spy for David, the king had been saved. But would he have been lost if Hushai had not been acting the spy? The Lord would not have forsaken the king and though He used Hushai's counsel yet David was the loser after all. He lost the opportunity of seeing the Lord's power and and intervention in his behalf. And how much we also lose by want of faith in Him, with whom nothing is too hard.

Ahitophel seeing his counsel defeated and unable to slay the king set his house in order and committed suicide. As stated before he is a type of Judas Iscariot, the betrayer of our Lord, as Ahitophel was the betrayer of David. Like Ahitophel Judas hanged himself (Matth. 27:5).

8. The Civil War and Absalom's Death

CHAPTER 18

1. The battle in the forest of Ephraim (18:1-8)

2. The death of Absalom (18:9-18)
3. The tidings of his death and David's grief (18:19-33)

And now everything is ready for the battle and the victory. The army of David consisted of three divisions, Joab, Abishai and the faithful Ittai had the command. David was ready to go forth with his warriors, but the people refused to let him go. What a testimony they gave concerning him! "Thou art worth ten thousand of us." But of Him, who according to the flesh is the Son of David, we say, "He alone is worthy." The king then stood by the gate of Mahanaim to see the departure of his troops. As his generals Joab, Abishai and Ittai left him he gave them the message, "Deal gently with the young man, even with Absalom." The battle took place in a wild jungle forest, most likely with many steep rocks and gulches. Absalom lost 20,000 men "and the forest (on account of rocks and gulches) devoured more people that day than the sword devoured."

Absalom fled, but his flight was arrested when his head caught in the bough of an oak, as Josephus states, entangled by his hair. "And he was taken up between the heaven and the earth and the mule that was under him went away." The first one who saw him would not smite him, not for a thousand shekels of silver, for he had heard the king's request. Then Joab, unscrupulous Joab, whose scheme had brought Absalom back into the presence of the king, took three darts (literally "staves") and thrust them through the heart of Absalom while he was yet alive. Most likely the unfortunate rebel son was unconscious through the impact with the tree. The armour bearers made a complete end of him. Joab's deed was unjustifiable in veiw of the king's command to deal gently with Absalom. Absalom's body was cast into a pit and covered with a very great heap of stones, a criminal's monument. He had looked for a more honorable death, for he had reared a pillar in his lifetime, which he called after his own name, "for he said, I have no son to keep my name in remembrance." Those who claim that the books of Samuel are a patchwork of a number of writers who made use of different sources, refer us to chapter 14:27 and point out the discrepancy. But why should there be? Absalom may have put up this monument before he had any sons, or he may have lost his two sons.

And then comes the record of how the tidings were carried to David. The watchman announces that he recognizeth in the swift runner Ahimaaz the son of Zadok. "And the King said, He is a good man, and cometh with good tidings." All is well—is his message, while the anxious father-heart but paying little attention to the victory won, inquired for the young man Absalom. Cushi the second runner makes his appearance and he carries the tidings of Absalom's death, which he transmits to David in a tender and cautious manner. And then that grief! How pathetic! The weeping King, crying out over and over again: O my son Absalom, my son, my son Absalom! Would God I had died for thee, O Absalom, my son, my son!

"The conduct of David in reference to his profligate son, is certainly extraordinary, but is not occasioned by weakness of character, which would be inconsistent with the judicial severity with which he banished him from his presence during five years. The shameful and sinful conduct of Absalom may be viewed in two aspects: it exhibits, on the one hand, the operation of the curse which David's sin brought upon his house (2 Sam. 12:10), and the influence of the iniquity of the fathers, which is visited upon the children (Exod. 20:5); it exhibits, on the other hand, Absalom's own degeneracy and profligacy, which fit him to be the bearer of the family-curse. It was not in the latter, but in the former aspect, that David regarded the conduct of Absalom, for his own guilt is so grievous in his eyes, that, in comparison with it, he deems Absalom's wickedness to be inconsiderable. Hence arises the deep and boundless compassion with which he surveys his reprobate son. David's treatment of Shimei may be regarded in the same light; his consciousness of his own great guilt causes him to overlook the guilt of that criminal."[3]

9. The Return of the King

CHAPTER 19

1. The continued grief of the king (19:1-8)
2. The return of the king (19:9-16)
3. Mercy shown to Shimei (19:17-23)
4. Mephibosheth's joy (19:24-30)
5. Barzillai and Chimham (19:31-40)
6. Strife between Judah and Israel (19:41-43)

What grief must have been David's that "the victory of that day was turned into mourning"? And the people went about on tip-toe, like peo-

[3]J. H. Kurtz, *Sacred History.*

ple ashamed after defeat. A great stillness pervaded everything, only broken by the loud and wailing voice of David: "O, my son Absalom, O, Absalom my son, my son!" All mourned with him. But what a man must this David have been to endear himself to his men, that his personal grief became so completely theirs?

Then Joab acted. He speaks as a wise statesman. It was a bold rebuke, but well deserved, for David's continued mourning was more than weakness; it was selfishness. That he greatly resented the words of condemnation of Joab may be learned from the fact that immediately after he appointed Amasa as commander in chief of his army instead of Joab. The word was also spoken to bring the king back to Jerusalem from exile and he returned.

Once more Shimei appears upon the scene; he brings with him a thousand men of Benjamin and Ziba also. Shimei fell down before the King and implored his forgiveness. Though Abishai suggested his death, the mercy Shimei craved was readily granted and the King sware unto him. But the mercy shown was at the expense of righteousness. The ultimate fate of Shimei we shall find recorded in 1 Kings 2.

Mephibosheth appears next with undressed feet, untrimmed hair and unwashed clothes; he had been thus since the flight of the King. Ziba's deception practised on the King is now discovered. But David's conduct towards lame Mephibosheth cannot be justified. The impatience David showed when Mephibosheth speaks is proof that he felt guilty at the rash word he spoke to Ziba. Then he tells Mephibosheth that he and Ziba should divide the land. This was injustice. The deception of Ziba had deserved punishment. Beautiful is Mephibosheth's answer. It shows a love and devotion which is almost unsurpassed in the Bible. "Yea, let him take all, forasmuch as my lord the King is come again in peace to his own house." It was a sweet echo of Jonathan's love for David. It hardly needs to be pointed out that in all this David still acts as a natural man and not as guided by Jehovah and His Spirit. His object was to make himself still more attractive with the people and conciliate the different factions. If he had acted in faith, remembering that the Lord had called him into the kingdom and that He was able to keep him, he would not have tried to gain his end by such means. The bright picture in this chapter is aged and unselfish Barzillai. And the strife between Judah and Israel on account of the King is the first indication of the great division and the internal strifes, which many years later broke out among the people. Thus failure is seen on all sides.

10. The Revolt of Sheba

CHAPTER 20

1. Sheba's revolt (20:1-2)
2. The ten concubines shut up (20:3)
3. Amasa's failure (20:4-6)
4. Joab and the death of Amasa (20:7-13)
5. Joab, the wise woman and the death of Sheba (20:14-22)
6. David's officials (20:23-26)

The final revolt in David's reign was headed by a wicked man, whose name was Sheba. Israel sided with him, probably as the result of the dissension recorded at the close of the previous chapter. Judah remained loyal to David. The act of David in shutting up unto the day of their death the ten concubines to live in widowhood was necessitated on account of what had taken place (16:21). Amasa being now the leader of the hosts of David (19:13) is called to subdue the revolt; but he proves a failure and could not mobilize the army. Abishai is commissioned then and with him is also Joab. All the mighty men, including the executioners and runners (Cherethites and Pelethites) pursued after Sheba. Then Amasa appeared on the scene. Joab was girded around his loins with a sword which was in the scabbard and the sword fell out. Joab picked up the sword but Amasa did not see the sword in his hand. Then Joab took Amasa by the beard with his right hand, while he held the sword in his left. Then he smote Amasa deliberately so that he died. He might have lied himself out of the accusation that he murdered Amasa by saying he fell into the sword and that it was an accident. But 1 Kings 2:32 gives the reckoning with unscrupulous Joab for the innocent blood he had shed. Jealousy had led Joab to murder Amasa. And Sheba was killed in Abel, the city in which he sought shelter. On the advice of the woman mentioned in the story, he was beheaded. The revolt ended.

IV. The Appendix to the History of David

1. The Famines and the Wars with the Philistines

CHAPTER 21

1. The Famine and the Gibeonites (21:1-14)
2. The Wars with the Philistines (21:15-22)

The fourth section of the second book of Samuel is an appendix to the history of David. When the great famine happened in the days of David we do not know. After the famine had returned year after year, for three years, David inquired of the Lord. Why did he not inquire in the first year? It is an evidence of the low spiritual state which prevailed at that time. The answer which David received revealed the cause of the judgment which rested upon the land. It was Saul and the blood-guilt in having slain the Gibeonites. The story of the Gibeonites is recorded in Joshua 9. They got in among Israel through deception and Joshua had made peace and a league with them. Though they belonged to the nations doomed to death they were permitted to live and became the hewers of wood and the drawers of water (Josh. 9:26-27). Jehovah's name and an oath assured them of their safety. Saul had violated this covenant and slain some of them. This wrong is now to be righted. David did not inquire again of the Lord what he should do but consulted the Gibeonites instead. And the Gibeonites demand not silver nor gold of Saul and of his house, "neither for us shalt thou kill any man in Israel." After that they asked that seven men of his sons be delivered unto them and they would hang them up unto the Lord in Gibeah. And again in haste the king promised to do so. Their demand, though piously worded, was not according to the law of God. Children were not to be put to death for the sins of their fathers (Deut. 24:16). Saul was the guilty one and he had died. How atonement for the broken covenant and the blood guilt was to be made remained for the Lord to say. David, not asking direction from Him, but turning to the Gibeonites, had failed again. And the Gibeonites in their awful demand shared the bloodthirsty cruel character of the Canaanites. David carried out the awful request. He spared Mephibosheth. Two sons of Rizpah, a concubine of Saul, and five sons of Merab (Michal in the Authorized Version is incorrect), Saul's eldest daughter, are the victims. They were hanged by the Gibeonites and then left hanging. Sad it is to think that the horrible deed might have been averted if but David had again turned to the Lord and inquired of Him. And another law is broken, when these bodies were kept hanging for months. "And if a man have committed a sin worth of death, and he be put to death, and thou hang him on a tree, his body shall not remain all night upon the tree, but thou shalt in any wise bury him that day." Surely the Lord could not sanction the deed so opposite to His own law. One of the most terrible scenes recorded in the Bible follows. Rizpah, the concubine of Saul, watched by her dead from April till fall, when it began to rain again. Six months she abode there, the only resting place the coarse sackcloth, above her the putrifying corpses of the seven men, including her two sons. While the hot oriental summer lasted she kept her awful watch and chased away by day the screeching birds of prey, while her nights were disturbed by the hungry howls of wolves and jackals. Could there be a more pathetic picture! And she gained something by it. When David hears of it he is stirred to action. The bones of Saul and Jonathan and the seven men who had been hanged were buried. And after that God was entreated for the land. It seems then that David turned to God and He was favorable to the land.

In the record of the battles with the Philistines four giants are mentioned. They represent the power of darkness, which the people of God must overcome.(For a full typical application we refer the reader to the *Numerical Bible.*)

2. David's Song of Deliverance

CHAPTER 22

1. The praise of Jehovah (22:1-4)
2. The sorrows of the past (22:5-7)
3. God's presence and intervention (22:8-20)
4. Reward and approval (22:21-28)
5. The judgment of the enemies (22:29-43)
6. The exaltation above the adversaries (22:44-49)
7. The praise of Jehovah (22:50-51)

It would take many pages to give an exposition of this great song which in the Book of Psalms, with a few changes, is known as Psalm 18. He uttered these words through the Spirit of the Lord. "The Spirit of the Lord spake by me and His word was in my tongue" (22:2). It is therefore a great prophetic utterance. The song takes us beyond David and his experience. His sufferings and deliverances are indicated, but they are but prophetic of Him, whose sufferings and whose victory are foreshadowed in David's life and experience. The great deliverance psalm includes therefore prophetically the story of David's greater Son, our Lord Jesus Christ. In verses 5-7 we have David's suffering when an exile, persecuted by Saul; prophetically the suffering of Christ, who was compassed by the waves of death and who was plunged beneath these dark waves and saved out of death. Verses 8-20 describe the intervention. Nothing in the life of David could be made to fit this; but being a prophetic utterance there is no difficulty to trace here the resurrection of Christ, who was brought forth into a large place (verse 20). "He delivered me, for He delighted in Me" can only be truthfully applied to Christ. And all looks forward to a still greater intervention and manifestation of God. Verses 21-28 equally can only be true of our Lord. "For I have kept the ways of the Lord, and have not wickedly departed from my God." It is impossible to say that David spoke of himself. The history we have traced gives a far different story. But every word is true if we think of David's Son, our Lord. And the judgment and exaltation described in the closing stanzas of this song will be realized in Him into whose hands the Father has committed all judgment. He will be "the head of the nations" and a people will serve Him (verses 44-45). That David had before his heart the great covenant-promise (chapter 7) and that his vision was enlarged so that he beheld "His Anointed" and His coming manifestation and kingdom becomes sufficiently clear in the last two verses of the song.

3. The Last Words of David and the Record of the Mighty Men

CHAPTER 23

1. His last words (23:1-7)
2. The names and records of David's mighty men (23:8-39)

In his last words an even greater and clearer vision is given to King David. "If Psalm 18 was a grand Hallelujah, with which David quitted the scene of life, these 'his last words' are the divine attestation of all that he had sung and prophesied in the Psalms concerning the spiritual import of the kingdom which he was to found in accordance with the divine message that Nathan had been commissioned to bring to him. Hence these 'last words' must be regarded as an inspired prophetic utterance by David, before his death, about the King and kingdom of God in their full and real meaning" *(History of Judah and Israel).* And this King is Christ and the kingdom that which will be set up with the second coming of Christ. As the translation in the authorized version is weak we give here a corrected translation:

David the son of Jesse saith,
And the man who was raised on high saith,
The anointed of the God of Jacob,
And the sweet Psalmist in Israel:
The Spirit of the Lord spake by me,
And His word was on my tongue.
The God of Israel said,
The Rock of Israel spake to me:
A righteous ruler over men.
A Ruler in the fear of God,
Like the light of the morning when the sun riseth,
A morning without clouds;
When the tender grass cometh forth out of the earth,
Through the clear shining after the rain.
But my house is not so with God.
Yet He has made me an everlasting covenant
Ordered in all and sure;
For this is all my salvation—all my delight,
Although He maketh it not to grow.
But the wicked shall be all of them as thorns thrust away,
For they cannot be taken with the hand;
And the man that toucheth them,
Must have iron and the staff of a spear
And they shall be utterly burned with fire in their dwelling.

Little comment is needed; just a little help to open up the words of the dying King. The righteous ruler over men, a ruler in the fear of God is our Lord. Thus He will yet rule over the earth in righteousness. And when He comes to rule, there cometh the morning without clouds when the earth will be refreshed, through the clear shining, the brightness of His glory, after the rain; after judgment is passed. Then David confesseth that his house is not so with God. His hope, his salvation, all his delight is in the covenant made with him; it centers in the fulfilment of the Davidic covenant. And the wicked will suffer the fire of His wrath.

In blessed keeping with this last great prophetic utterance of the King are the records and the names of the mighty men of David. They were the men who loved David, stood by him, showed their loyalty and devotion to the King. And others are given, of whom we read no definite deeds. The last name is Uriah the Hittite. The spiritual meaning is not hard to find. Before the judgment seat of Christ all will be made manifest. When He comes to be the righteous Ruler, to usher in the morning without clouds, those will be remembered who were loyal and devoted to Him in His rejection. No name and no deed, even the smallest, will then be forgotten. What an incentive this should be, especially in the solemn days in which we live, when we see the day approaching, to serve Him and be as devoted to our absent, but coming Lord, as David's mighty men were to him. In our annotation on 1 Chronicles where we find these records also we hope to point out some of the details of the deeds of David's mighty men (1 Chronicles 11).

4. David's Failure: the Altar on the Threshing Floor of Araunah

CHAPTER 24

1. The numbering of the people (24:1-9)
2. The sin acknowledged and Gad's message (24:10-14)
3. The pestilence (24:15-17)
4. The altar on the threshing-floor of Araunah (24:18-25)

The final chapter of the books of Samuel is of much interest and importance. "And again the anger of the Lord was kindled against Israel, and He moved David against them to say, Go, number Israel and Judah." In 1 Chronicles 21:1 we read "And Satan stood up against Israel, and provoked David to number Israel." This has often been pointed out as a discrepancy and contradiction. Criticism has explained it in the following way: "Of surpassing interest for the study of the progressiveness of revelation in the Old Testament period is the form which the chronicler has given to this verse. To his more developed religious sense the idea was abhorrent that God could be subject to moods, and incite men to a course of action for which He afterwards calls them to account. Accordingly he writes: And Satan stood up against Israel and moved David to number Israel." There is no contradiction here nor do the two accounts need an explanation as the above. Israel had committed some sin which brought upon them the displeasure of Jehovah. Satan the accuser was then permitted to influence David. The statement, "He (God) moved David," also means in Hebrew, "He suffered him to be moved." He permitted Satan to do his work. In 1 Tim. 3:6 we read that pride is the condemnation (or as it is literally "the crime") of the devil. And Satan the accuser moves David with national pride to number the people. It is significant that preceding this record are the names and achievements of the mighty men of David. No doubt his heart swelled with much elation over his victories and great achievements. While David's eyes were blinded by Satan, Joab saw the danger. In 1 Chron. 21:3 we read that he said to David: "The Lord make His people an hundred times so many more as they be; but, my Lord the King, are they not all my Lord's servants? Why doth my Lord require this thing? Why will he be a cause of guilt to Israel?" The King's word prevailed and reluctantly Joab and the captains went forth to carry out the King's command. It was altogether a military census. But the census was not completed (1 Chronicles 27:24).

David's heart then smote him and we see him coming to the Lord and confessing his sin. "I have sinned greatly in that I have done; and now I beseech thee, Lord, take away the iniquity of Thy servant; for I have done very foolishly." It was a true confession he made that night. Then the Lord sent the answer through the prophet Gad. The Lord leaves the choice to David. Either three years of famine, three months of flight or three days of pestilence. (This is according to 1 Chron. 21:12; 2 Sam. 24:13 records seven years, which must be the error of some copyist.) And here the man of faith asserts himself. "Let us now fall into the hand of the Lord; for His mercies are great, and let me not fall into the hand of man." And the Lord did not disappoint His servant's faith in His mercy. When the angel stretched out his hand upon Jerusalem to destroy it the Lord said, It is enough; stay now thine hand. And the angel of the Lord, the same who appeared to the patriarchs, to Moses, Joshua and others, was by the threshing floor of Araunah the Jebusite. Once more David's voice is heard in confession. "I have sinned, and I have done wickedly; but these sheep, what have they done? Let Thy hand, I pray thee, be against me, and against my father's house." He was willing to be the one sufferer for his people; in this he is a type again of our Lord, the sinbearer. He is commanded to rear an altar upon the threshing-floor of Araunah. "It was a fitting spot for mercy upon Israel, this place where of old faithful Abraham had been ready to offer his only son unto God; fitting also as still outside the city; but chiefly in order that the pardoning and sparing mercy now shown, might indicate the site where, on the great altar of burnt-offering, abundant mercy in pardon and acceptance would in the future be dispensed to Israel" (A. Edersheim). It was the place upon which the temple was built (1 Chron. 21:28—22:1). And Araunah the Jebusite offered willingly the threshing floor and the sacrificial animals. But David would not consent. "Neither will I offer burnt offerings unto the Lord my God of that which doth cost me nothing." For fifty shekels of silver he bought the oxen and the threshing floor. Then the burnt offerings and peace offerings ascended unto Jehovah as a sweet savour. And Jehovah answered by fire (1 Chron. 21:26). And David before that altar, who buys and offers, thus meeting the claim of God, is a type of our Lord who bought us with the great price and offered Himself. And even so as this book closes with the Lord being merciful to His land and people, the plague stayed, so will Israel in the future receive and enjoy His mercy. It will be the result of the one sacrifice.

THE FIRST BOOK OF THE
KINGS

Introduction

In the introduction to the books of Samuel we stated that the first and second books of the Kings are called in the Greek version of the Old Testament the third and fourth books of Kingdoms and in the Latin version the third and fourth books of the Kings. The two books, which were originally undivided and formed one book, contain the history of Israel under the government of the kings. The same period of history is also covered in the two books of the Chronicles. However there is a great difference between the books of the Kings and the books of the Chronicles. The books of the Kings were written before the captivity; the books of the Chronicles after that event (1 Chron. 6:15). The books of the Kings trace the history of the kings from the prophetic viewpoint; the books of the Chronicles from the priestly. Kings gives the history from a human point of view, Chronicles from the divine standpoint. After Solomon's wonderful reign and the division of the kingdom the history of the kings of Israel is mostly given while much less is said of the kings of Judah. The books of the Chronicles are characterized by an almost entire absence of the history of the kings of Israel; they are mentioned only in case of absolute necessity. After the genealogical tracings the history of the kingdom of David is followed in detail down to the Babylonian captivity. The blessing and grace of God as manifested towards the house of David is beautifully given in Chronicles. The story centers around the temple. In the introduction to Chronicles and more so in the annotations we shall point out more fully these interesting and striking differences, the blessed marks of inspiration.

The Authorship of Kings

Much has been written on the possible instrument who was used in putting these records together as we have them now. Critics have much to say on the different compilers, redactors, editors, etc., who all had a hand in putting these histories together. They speak of proximate sources and primary sources and later additions and redactions. To say the least it is bewildering and unprofitable to follow, what they term, their scientific method. That the author of these two books had certain sources or documents, besides traditional accounts at his disposal, cannot be denied. But we maintain that he was chosen by the Lord to write these records of the kings and was guided by the Holy Spirit as he wrote. The books of the Kings have the mark in every way of being the work of one person and not a number of persons, followed by others who edited their writings. Unity of style can be clearly followed throughout the books; there is uniform mode of expression which would be quite impossible with a number of authors or compilers. See and compare 1 Kings 22:43 with 2 Kings 14:3-4; 1 Kings 12:31 with 2 Kings 17:32; 1 Kings 11:43 with 2 Kings 13:13. Jewish tradition declares that the prophet Jeremiah was the instrument chosen to write the two books of the Kings. While no one can say with certainty that this is true, much is in favor of this view. There is a striking similarity of style and idiom between the language of Kings and the language employed by Jeremiah. Perhaps no one was better fitted to write the wonderful history of Solomon's failure, the division of the Kingdom, the apostasy of Israel, the chastisements of the Lord, than the prophet of tears, the man of God whose loving messages were to a backslidden Israel.

Spiritual And Prophetic Truths

There is much spiritual and prophetic truth to be found in these records. Solomon's wonderful reign, and the building of the house of the Lord contains great foreshadowings of the coming kingdom of our Lord Jesus Christ. Solomon's reign of peace marks the climax of the history of Israel. In him the promise made unto David (2 Sam. 7) found its first fulfillment. As head over the people, as king of righteousness ruling in righteousness, as king of peace, exercising also priestly functions, furthermore, in taking Pharaoh's daughter and the Gentiles seeking after him and much else he is a type of the coming King in whom the covenant promises made to David will be fully realized. There are many spiritual lessons to be found in the decline among Israel. Elijah's and Elisha's ministries, their messages and miracles, have a deeper prophetic and spiritual meaning. To write a large volume on these two great historical books and trace in them God's way in government as well as the prophetic foreshadowings would be a far easier work than to condense them in brief annotations. However we hope and pray that even these few hints we could give will be used by our Lord to help His people into a better knowledge of His Word. The chronological table of the kings of Judah and Israel, and of contemporary events, which follows this introduction should be freely consulted in the study of the text.

The Division of the First Book of the Kings

The first book of the Kings contains the record of the reign of Solomon and the glory of his great kingdom of peace. But that glory soon passed away through the failure of Solomon and the great united kingdom becomes a divided kingdom. In the last six chapters we read of Elijah, the Tishbite, the great prophet of God and his activity during the reign of wicked Ahab. We make the following division:

I. DAVID'S LAST DAYS AND THE CROWNING OF SOLOMON

1. **Adonijah's Exaltation to be King** (1:1-27)
2. **The Anointing of Solomon and Adonijah's Submission** (1:28-53)
3. **David's Charge to Solomon and David's End** (2:1-11)

II. SOLOMON'S GLORIOUS REIGN, HIS FAILURE AND END

1. **The Righteous Judgment of Solomon** (2:12-46)
2. **Jehovah Appears to Solomon—His Prayer and the Answer** (3:1-28)
3. **Solomon's Princes and Officers: The Prosperous Kingdom and the King's Great Wisdom** (4:1-34)
4. **The Building of the Temple and Its Dedication** (5—8)
5. **Jehovah Appears unto Solomon and the Greatness of the King** (9:1-28)
6. **Solomon and the Queen of Sheba: His great Riches and Splendour** (10:1-29)
7. **Solomon's Failure: Judgment Announced and the Beginning of the Disruption** (11:1-43)

III. THE DIVIDED KINGDOM

1. **Rehoboam and the Revolt of the Ten Tribes** (12:1-33)
2. **Jeroboam and Rehoboam and their Reign** (13—14)
3. **Abijam and Asa: Kings of Judah** (15:1-24)
4. **Kings of Israel** (15:25—16)

IV. THE PROPHET ELIJAH AND KING AHAB

1. **Elijah's Prediction and His Miracles** (17:1-24)
2. **Elijah on Mount Carmel: The Answered Prayer** (18:1-46)
3. **Elijah in the Wilderness and on Mount Horeb** (19:1-21)
4. **King Ahab, His Wicked Reign and Downfall** (20—22)

Analysis and Annotations

I. David's Last Days and the Crowning of Solomon

1. Adonijah's Exaltation to be King

CHAPTER 1:1-27

1. David's decrepitude (1:1-4)
2. Adonijah's self-exaltation (1:5-9)
3. The plot of Nathan and Bath-sheba (1:10-14)
4. Bath-sheba and Nathan before the king (1:15-27)

David was about 70 years old and extremely feeble. The strenuous life he had led, the exposures and hardships of his youth, the cares and anxieties of his reign, and the chastenings through which he passed on account of his great sin, and much else were responsible for this enfeebled condition. It is but another illustration of that rigid law, What a man soweth that shall he reap. It was a premature decay with the complete loss of natural heat. While the king was in this helpless condition Adonijah (My Lord is Jehovah) exalted himself to be king and like his unhappy brother Absalom he prepared chariots and horsemen and fifty men to run before him. Like Absalom he also was of great

CHRONOLOGICAL TABLE

OF THE KINGS OF JUDAH AND ISRAEL, AND OF CONTEMPORARY EVENTS

According to Keil, Winer, Clinton, and Usher

Year from the Separation of the Two Kingdoms	KINGS OF JUDAH Reigned:	Year from the Accession of the Kings of Judah	KINGS OF ISRAEL Reigned:	Year from the Accession of the Kings of Israel	CONTEMPORARY EVENTS	DATE BEFORE CHRIST			
						Keil	Winer	Clinton	Usher
1	REHOBOAM, 17 years	1st	JEROBOAM, 22 years	1st	Shishak King of Egypt	975	975	976	975
					Shishak enters Jerusalem	971	970		
18	ABIJAM, 3 years			18th		957	957	959	958
20	ASA, 41 years			20th		955	955	956	955
22		2nd	NADAB, 2 years			953	954	955	954
23		3rd	BAASHA, 24 years			952	953	954	953
					Zerah the Ethiopian	940			
					Bed-Hadad. I of Syria	939			
45		26th	ELAH, 2 years			930	930	930	930
46		27th	ZIMRI, 7 days			929	928	930	929
46		27th	OMRI, and TIBNI,			929	928	930	929
			4 years			925	924		
50		31st	OMRI, sole king						
			8 years						
					Building of Samaria	924	923		
57		38th	AHAB, 22 years		Ethbaal, King of Tyre and Sidon				
61	JEHOSHAPHAT, 25			4th		918	918	919	918
	years					914	914	915	914
					Ben-Hadad II of Syria				
					Battle of Ramoth-gilead	897	897		
78		17th	AHAZIAH, 2 years			897	897	896	898
79		18th	JEHORAM, 12 years			896	896	895	896
					War of Israel and Judah against				
	JEHORAM, co-regent				Moab (Moabite Stone)				
	for 2 years?			5th		891			
86	JEHORAM, sole ruler					889	889	891	892
	6 years			12th		884	885	884	885
91	AHAZIAH, 1 year								
					Hazael, King of Syria				
					Second Battle of				
					Ramoth-gilead				
92	ATHALIAH, 6 years		JEHU, 28 years		Murder of Ahaziah and Jehoram	883	884	883	884
					by Jehu. Lycurgus in Sparta, 884				
98	JOASH, 40 years			7th	Athaliah slain	877	878	877	878
					Pygmalion, King of Tyre. His				
					sister Dido founds Carthage,				
					143 years after the				
					building of the Temple				
						856	856	855	856
119		22nd?	JEHOAHAZ, 17 years		Judah invaded and Jerusalem	840	840	839	841
135		37th	JOASH, 16 years		threatened by the Syrians				
					Ben-Hadad III, King of Syria				
137	AMAZIAH, 29 years			2nd	Joash, King of Judah, murdered	838	838	837	839
					War of Amaziah against Edom				
					Attack of Moab upon Israel				
					War between Judah and Israel				
					Jerusalem occupied by the Israelites				
151		15th	JEROBOAM II, 41			824	825	823	825
			years		Successful War of Israel				
					against Syria				
165	UZZIAM, 52 years			15th?		810	809	808	810
					Ammon becomes tributary to				
					Judah. The Philistines humbled				
192			Death of JEROBOAM II,			783	784		
			Interregnum						
			for 11 years						
203		38th	ZECHARIAH, 6		First year of the Olympiads, 776				
			months			772	772	771	773
204		39th	SHALLUM, 1 month			771	771	770	772
204		39th	MENAHEM, 10 years			771	771	770	772
					Pul, King of Assyria				
					Israel becomes tributary				
					to Assyria				
215		50th	PEKAHIAH, 2 years			760	760	759	761
216		52nd	PEKAH, 20 years		Murder of Pekahiah	759	758	757	759
217	JOTHAM, 16 years			2nd		758	758	756	758
					Building of Rome, 753				
					Nabonassar, King of				
					Babylon, 747				
					Rezin, King of Syria				
233	AHAZ, 16 years			17th		742	741	741	742
					Ahaz invokes the help of				
					Assyria against Syria				
					and Israel				
					Tiglath-pileser, King of Assyria				
					The Assyrians occupy the land				
					east of the Jordan, and the				

Year from the Separation of the Two Kingdoms	KINGS OF JUDAH Reigned:	Year from the Accession of the Kings of Judah	KINGS OF ISRAEL Reigned:	Year from the Accession of the Kings of Israel	CONTEMPORARY EVENTS	DATE BEFORE CHRIST			
						Keil	Winer	Clinton	Usher
					north of Palestine, and lead the people captive				
					The Philistines conquer the western part of Judah				
236		4th	PEKAH murdered, Interregnum 8½ years?			739	738		
					So, King of Egypt	730	729	730	730
245		12th	HOSHEA, 9 years, tributary to Assyria		Shalmaneser, King of Assyria (Media and Babylonia.) Growth of the Assyrian Empire in Asia				
248	HEZEKIAH, 29 years			3rd	Attempt of Hoshea to rebel against Assyria. Invasion of the Assyrians. Siege of Samaria	727	725	726	726
253		6th	DESTRUCTION OF THE COMMON-WEALTH OF ISRAEL		Deportation of the Ten Tribes	722	721	721	721
					Sargon, King of Assyria. Siege of Ashdod (Isa. 20:1)				
					Alliance between Judah and Egypt				
261					Siege of Jerusalem by Sennacherib	714	712		
					War between Sennacherib and Tirhakah				
					Destruction of the Assyrians by "the Angel of the Lord"				
					Embassy from Merodach-baladan				
277	MANASSEH, 55 years					698	696	697	698
					Esarhaddon, King of Assyria, sends fresh Colonists to Samaria				
332	AMON, 2 years				Scythian hordes pass through Palestine (Herod I, 104, etc.)	643	641	642	643
334	JOSIAH, 31 years				Murder of Amon	641	639	640	641
					Nabopolassar, founder of the Babylonian Temple, father of Nebuchadnezzar	626	625		
					Draco in Athens				
					Invasion of Assyria by Egypt. Alliance of Assyria and Judah. Victory of Megiddo by Pharaoh-nechoh, Josiah slain	610	609		
365	JEHOAHAZ, 3 months					610	609	609	610
365	JEHOIAKIM, 11 years				Jehoiakim put on the throne by the King of Egypt. Judah subject to Egypt	610	609	609	610
369	Commencement of the Exile				The Egyptians beaten by the Chaldees in the Battle of Carchemish. Taking of Jerusalem by Nebuchadnezzar	606	606		607
376	JEHOIACHIN, 3 months				Second Conquest of Jerusalem and Deportation	599	598	598	599
					Jerusalem and the Temple plundered by the Chaldees				
376	ZEDEKIAH, 11 years				Zedekiah made king by the Chaldees	599	598	598	599
					Zedekiah rebels against Nebuchadnezzar, and turns towards Pharaoh-hophra, King of Egypt (Jer. 44:30; Ezek. 17:15). Jerusalem besieged. Attempted relief of Jerusalem by the Egyptians (Jer. 37:5, etc.; Ezek. 17:17, etc.)		590		
387	DESTRUCTION OF JERUSALEM								
387	Gedaliah Babylonian Governor in Judea, 2 months				Death of Zedekiah. Majority of the Jews carried to Babylon (3rd deportation)	588	588	587	588
391	Last Deportation of the Jews to Babylon (Jos. *Ant.* 10:97; comp. Jer. 52:30?)				Gedaliah murdered. Many of the Jews retire into Egypt	588	588		
						584	584		

Judah lies desolate (2 Chron. 36:21; Zech. 7:14). Occupation of part of the country by the Philistines and Edomites. The latter take the southern territory (Ezek. 35:10). Hebron part of Idumea (Jos. *Jew. Wars,* 4:9, 7).

physical beauty. There is a significant sentence which reveals the weakness of David towards his favorite children, a weakness which has borne its sad fruits in many families. "And his father had not displeased him at any time in saying, Why hast thou done so?" There had been no discipline in David's family; he had spared the rod. By right of primogeniture he thought of claiming the throne. However, he must have known that his younger brother Solomon had been selected by David to fill the throne after him. But Adonijah knew not the Lord nor was he subject to His will. In his selfish ambition he was upheld by Joab and Abiathar, the priest. No doubt but both of these men sought their own interests; Joab to continue in his position he held with David; Abiathar to get supremacy over Zadok his rival in the priesthood. But Zadok the priest, who ministered at Gibeon (1 Chron. 16:39), Benaiah, who had charge of the Cherethites and Pelethites (2 Sam. 8:18), Nathan, the faithful prophet, Shimei (not the one who cursed David), Rei and David's mighty men kept aloof from the revolt. They remained true to Jehovah and to His anointed. Then Adonijah made a sacrificial feast to give his self-exaltation a religious air. He invited all the king's sons, his brethren, and the men of Judah; but Nathan, Benaiah, David's mighty men and his brother Solomon were not called. It was meant to be his coronation. In this revolt, preceding the enthronement of God's king, Solomon, the king of peace, we have another foreshadowing of what will precede the reign of the Prince of Peace, our Lord. It seemed as if Adonijah might succeed. But Nathan, the prophet, begins to act. In agreement with the mother of Solomon the plan is made to discover what Adonijah had done to the aged King. Bath-sheba goes in first and after a while Nathan appeared to tell the King the same story he had heard from the lips of his wife. She reminded David of his oath, that Solomon her son was to be the successor to the throne, and after telling him of Adonijah's act, she appealed to him to proclaim now who was to sit upon the throne. She speaks to him repeatedly as "My lord the King." And when Nathan appeared before David he also said, "My lord O King." Some have gathered from this that aged David had become filled with the pride of life. However, the honour done to him may have been true reverence for the Lord's anointed King.

2. The Anointing of Solomon and Adonijah's Submission

CHAPTER 1:28-53

1. The renewed promise to Bath-sheba (1:28-31)
2. The anointing of Solomon commanded (1:32-37)
3. Solomon made king (1:38-40)
4. The consternation of Adonijah (1:41-49)
5. Adonijah's fear and submission (1:50-53)

Bath-sheba had withdrawn while Nathan was before the king. She is called back and David once more assures her that Solomon her son should reign after him. Then David commands that Solomon be anointed king without further delay. His instructions are at once carried out. Zadok the priest, Nathan the prophet, and Benaiah caused Solomon to ride upon King David's mule and brought him to Gihon. The priest anointed him king and the people rejoiced with great joy. But what joy will come to this earth when He who is greater than Solomon will be enthroned and receive His great kingdom, which is only faintly foreshadowed in Solomon's glorious reign! All David did was according to Jehovah's will and purpose. Solomon was a mere youth when he was anointed. In 1 Chronicles 28 and 29 where the most impressive scene is fully described which followed Solomon's anointing, we find David's own words concerning him, "Solomon my son, whom alone God hath chosen is yet young and tender, and the work is great" (1 Chr. 29:1). We shall follow the remarkable utterances of King David at that occasion when we reach the Chronicles. Like Saul and David, King Solomon was likewise anointed a second time. "And they made Solomon the son of David king the second time, and anointed him unto the Lord to be the chief governor, and Zadok to be priest" (1 Chronicles 29:22). And while the people were rejoicing in Gihon over God's true King, Adonijah's feast was about ended. Abiathar's son Jonathan appeared on the scene. Adonijah said, "Come in; for thou art a valiant man, and bringest good tidings." And the tidings he brought were good tidings for God's people: "Solomon sitteth on the throne of the Kingdom." Fear and consternation took hold on Adonijah and his guests and while the people gathered around Solomon, Adonijah and his company scattered. When another One, the greater Son of David, is enthroned and the glad tidings flash forth, He has taken His throne, all His enemies will be scattered and be made the footstool of His feet.

Adonijah took hold of the horns of the altar

(Exodus 21:12-14). Solomon promises him that his life would be spared, "but if wickedness shall be found in him, he shall die." Mercy shown and righteousness demanded were the first acts of King Solomon. In this he is a type of Him who will reign in peace and execute mercy and righteousness on the earth. Righteousness will reign in the millennial Kingdom and evil doers will be cut off.

3. David's Charge to Solomon and David's End

CHAPTER 2:1-11

1. David's charge (2:1-9)
2. David's end (2:10-11)

We call attention again to 1 Chronicles 28 and 29 where we find the record of the great assembly of all the princes of Israel and David's great address to them. He then made known to all Israel that the Lord had chosen Solomon to occupy the throne. He speaks there of the covenant promise,that his son should build the house of the Lord and His courts. He exhorted the people to keep the commandments and then spoke in tenderest words to young Solomon. "And thou, Solomon my son, know thou the God of thy father, and serve him with a perfect heart and with a willing mind . . . take heed now; for the Lord hath chosen thee to build an house for the sanctuary; be strong and do it" (1 Chron. 28:1-10). Then he gave to his son Solomon the patterns for the temple. These had been made under the guidance of the Spirit of God. The immense treasures are mentioned which David had dedicated for the temple worship. Of all this we find nothing in the record of the first book of the Kings. Here only the general history of God's government in Israel is given from the prophetic point of view. What Chronicles represents we shall state in our annotations on those books.

The charge of David to Solomon recorded in the opening verses of this chapter was given privately. Its main purpose was to exhort his son to punish Joab and Shimei and to show kindness unto the sons of Barzillai. Critics have attacked David's character on account of this charge. Renan in his history of the people Israel goes so far as to say that the incident is "a revelation of the black perfidy of his hypocritical soul." However, the charge to Solomon to execute vengeance upon these two men is not a stain upon King David. The punishment was well deserved. Joab had killed Abner and Amasa. Shimei had in great vileness cursed God's King. Both were wicked men. David's own guilt had no doubt compelled him to neglect the solemn duty demanded by justice. He therefore asked Solomon to vindicate divine justice and raise it up from the defeat it had sustained by punishing Joab and Shimei with death, while kindness is to bestowed upon the righteous. From the prophetic view-point we get a glimpse of the coming righteous judgment of the King, our Lord Jesus Christ, who will execute the vengeance of God and punish the evil doers, and reward the righteous in His kingdom. Then David passed away and was buried after his forty-year reign in the city of David. He died in good old age, full of days, riches and honour (1 Chron. 29:28). His memory was always cherished by the nation. Peter on the day of Pentecost spoke of his burial place: "His sepulchre is with us unto this day" (Acts 2:29). In the coming day of the glorious manifestation of the Son of Man, who also bears the title Son of David, when He shall receive the throne of His father David, King David in resurrection glory will have a great share in that Kingdom.

II. Solomon's Glorious Reign. His Failure and End

1. The Righteous Judgment of Solomon

CHAPTER 2:12-46)

1. Solomon upon the throne (2:12)
2. Adonijah's request (2:13-18)
3. Bath-sheba before Solomon (2:19-21)
4. Solomon's answer and sentence upon Adonijah (2:22-24)
5. Adonijah executed (2:25)
6. Abiathar thrust out (2:26-27)
7. Joab and Shimei executed (2:28-46)

"Then sat Solomon upon the throne of David his father; and his kingdom was established greatly." Solomon and his glorious reign foreshadows the reign of that greater Son of David, our Lord, in whom the covenant promise made to David will be fully accomplished. The section which begins with the statement of Solomon's enthronement is deeply interesting and full of the richest typical and prophetic meaning. Solomon's righteous judgments, his wisdom, his reign in peace, but especially the building of the temple foreshadow Him who will ere long receive the throne and build the temple of the Lord (Zech 6:13). Inasmuch as the critics reject the literal fulfilment of the oath-bound Davidic covenant and the prophetic foreshadowing of the recorded events, they also condemn Solomon's righteous judgment which occupies the foreground of his reign. We quote from one of these critics: "The reign of Solomon began with a threefold deed of blood. An eastern King surrounded by the many princes of a polygamous family, and liable to endless jealousies and plots, is always in a condition of unstable equilibrium; the death of a rival is regarded as his only safe imprisonment" (Canon Farrar). In such statements God's governmental ways in righteousness and retribution are entirely ignored.

Adonijah the wicked rebel on probation visits Bath-sheba. He acknowledges freely that the Lord had given the Kingdom to his brother. Then he desired that Bath-sheba should ask her son Solomon to give Abishag the Shunammite to him as wife (1:3). Bath-sheba was completely won by the pathetic plea of Adonijah and did not discover the wicked plot which was hidden beneath his request. Beautiful is the reverence which Solomon showed to his mother. He arose from his throne, he bowed himself unto her, (the Septuagint version reads "he kissed her") and he made her sit on his right hand. How he honored and loved her! It may foreshadow the love of Him for the believing remnant of Israel, His beloved people, who will have a share in His coming Kingdom. When Bath-sheba states Adonijah's request the keen discernment and wisdom of Solomon are at once apparent. "And why dost thou ask Abishag the Shunammite for Adonijah? ask for him the kingdom also; for he is mine elder brother; even for him, and for Abiathar the priest, and for Joab the son of Zeruiah." Adonijah's request was a scheme to obtain the kingdom. Most likely it was concocted by Abiathar and Joab. To marry a deceased king's wife or concubine was, according to Oriental customs, paramount with claiming the rights of the king (2 Sam. 12:8; 16:21-22). Now Abishag was not the wife of David in the sense of the word, yet she must have been considered as belonging to the departed king. Had Solomon granted the request he would have hopelessly degraded himself in the eyes of the people (2 Sam. 2:7). Adonijah aimed by this cunning scheme at the throne of Solomon and attempted to obtain the kingdom. Then Solomon pronounced judgment, which Adonijah fully deserved. He was put to death that day. It has been suggested by certain critics that Solomon had a more selfish, carnal reason for putting his elder brother to death. "If, as seems almost certain," declares a higher critic, "Abishag is the fair Shulamite of the Song of Songs, there can be little doubt that Solomon himself loved her, and that she was the jewel of his seraglio." But there is absolutely no evidence that Abishag is identical with Shulamite; nor does Jewish tradition sustain such a theory. It is a mere supposition.

Abiathar is next dealt with. His life is spared but Solomon thrusts him out of the priesthood, thus fulfilling the word of the Lord concerning the house of Eli (1 Sam. 2:31-36). Zadok becomes exclusively priest (verse 35). Joab and Shimei are both executed. Though Joab caught hold of the horns of the altar it did not save him; he paid now by a just retribution for the wicked deeds he had done. Shimei was commanded to remain in Jerusalem; disobedience would mean certain death. When he disobeyed, the sentence of death was executed upon him. And here we have another glimpse of the government of the kingdom in the coming age. In the present age grace reigns through righteousness; in the kingdom age, when the Lord rules over all, righteousness reigns. Disobedience will be swiftly met by judgment as it was with Shimei.

2. Jehovah Appears to Solomon His Prayer and the Answer

CHAPTER 3

1. Affinity with Pharaoh and Pharaoh's daughter (3:1)
2. Solomon loved the Lord (3:2-4)
3. Jehovah appears to Solomon (3:5-15)
4. The wisdom granted and exemplified (3:16-28)

We shall now see how the Lord kept His promise He made unto David in the establishment of his kingdom. After the execution of the demanded judgment Solomon entered into affinity with Pharaoh King of Egypt (probably the last King of the 21 Tanitic dynasty) and married his daughter. She was with him in David's city until he made an end of building his own house, the house of the Lord and the wall of Jerusalem round about. She was a Gentile and Jewish tradition states that she became a Jewish proselyte. This union was prophetic of the blessing Gentiles were to receive in union with Him whom Solomon typifies. It was grace which took up Pharaoh's daughter and made her share the riches and honors of Solomon. And Solomon loved the Lord. At Gibeon he offered a thousand burnt offerings. Gibeon was one of the high places where the priests performed their functions (1 Chron. 16:36-40). The tabernacle and the brazen altar were there, but not the ark of the covenant. However, he also approached the ark and stood before it to render thanks unto Jehovah. (Another application may be made to the Jewish remnant of the end of the age the same way as Ruth typified that remnant. See Annotations on Ruth. That remnant is called through grace; the Jews through unbelief are in the same place as the Gentiles. The grace which saved and called the Gentiles will draw and call them and bring them into union with the King.)

A most blessed incident followed. As stated before Solomon was a youth when he was anointed king. Eusebius states that he was only 12 years old; Josephus gives his age as 15 years. He was probably not yet 20 years old when he became King. He felt deeply two things, his own littleness and his great responsibility in governing the multitude of people. It was while still at Gibeon that Jehovah appeared unto him in a dream and said: "Ask what I shall give you." What grace this was, but it also searched his innermost soul. And this offer was not made exclusively to Solomon. He who appeared unto Solomon and put this gracious question to him, when He was on earth clothed in the garb of a servant, yet greater than Solomon in all his glory, said: "Ask, and it shall be given you" (Matt. 7:7). And again He said: "Whatsoever ye shall ask in my name, that will I do" (John 14:13). It is faith's prerogative to hear Him speak thus to our hearts and to make use of His great offer. Solomon's answer is beautiful. He acknowledged God's great mercy and kindness. Then he confessed his own weakness and helplessness. "I am but a little child; I know not how to go out or come in." He speaks of his responsibility and duty towards God's people and then utters his request: "Give therefore Thy servant an understanding heart to judge Thy people, that I may discern between good and bad, for who is able to judge this Thy so great a people?" It pleased the Lord as it always pleases Him when His people confess their littleness and expect help from Him. The request is granted. "So there was none like thee before thee, neither shall any arise like unto thee." Wisdom from above filled his soul. The book of Proverbs bears witness to this great understanding the Lord gave to him. But He added much more; He gave him riches and honour. "Seek ye first the Kingdom of God, and His righteousness and all things shall be added unto you" (Matthew 6:33). And the same Lord does still, to all who put their trust in Him, exceeding abundantly above all they ask or think. "He giveth us richly all things to enjoy" (1 Tim. 6:17). Then there was a conditional promise. "And if thou wilt walk in My ways, to keep My statutes, and My commandments, as thy father David did walk, then I will lengthen thy days" (verse 14). Alas! Solomon did not fulfill the condition. He forsook the Lord and died when he was not quite 60 years of age. He awoke and behold it was a dream. But it was more than a dream. That the prayer had been answered and that the wisdom of God was in him to do judgment is evidenced in the incident which follows and which needs no further comment. In his wisdom he is a type of our Lord Jesus who is the wisdom of God. And the justice he administered in his kingdom is typical of the righteous judgment of our Lord when He rules as king over the earth. "He shall not judge after the sight of His eyes, neither reprove after the hearing of His ears, but with righteousness shall He judge the poor" (Is. 11:1-4).

3. Solomon's Princes and Officers The Prosperous Kingdom and the King's Great Wisdom

CHAPTER 4

1. The Princes (4:1-6)
2. The Officers (4:7-19)
3. The prosperous kingdom (4:20-28)
4. Solomon's great wisdom (4:29-34)

"So King Solomon was king over all Israel." A list of the princes and the twelve officers is given first. Their names fit in perfectly with the character of the kingdom, foreshadowing the coming and better kingdom of our Lord. We give the names of the princes with their meaning. Azariah, "Jehovah is help"; Elihoreph, "my God is reward"; Ahiah, "Brother of Jehovah"; Jehoshaphat, "Jehovah judges"; Benaiah, "Built up by Jehovah"; Zabud, "Gift bestowed"; Ahishar, "Brother of ability"; Adoniram, "Lord of Heights."

Then we have here the record of a remarkable increase of Judah and Israel "as the sand which is by the sea in multitude." It reminds us of the promise made to Abraham, "in multiplying I will multiply thy seed as the stars of the heaven and as the sand which is upon the sea shore" (Gen. 22:17). Such an increase will come during the reign of God's appointed King, the Prince of Peace. His kingdom reached from the river (Euphrates) to the border of Egypt. Even so had Jehovah spoken to Abraham that his seed should possess the territory from Egypt unto Euphrates. This was realized in Solomon's kingdom. Now the Jews hold not even the little land called Palestine. When the true King comes the promised territory will be given once more to the seed of Abraham. It was a time of great prosperity. Another prophetic hint we find in the fact that the great multitude were in peace, "eating and drinking and making merry." Such will be the universal state of the people in the coming Kingdom when "every man shall call his neighbor under the vine and the fig tree" (Zech 3:10), as under Solomon's reign Judah and Israel dwelt safely every man under his vine and fig tree (verse 25). Solomon had also great stables full of horses and many chariots. He had 4000 horses; the number 40,000 in verse 26 is evidently the error of a copyist. (See 2 Chron. 9:25.) There was much to be supplied for the provision of the court of the King. See the daily need; but they lacked nothing. How great the need there is in the world during the absence of the true King! But when He comes to reign "He will satisfy the poor with bread" (Ps. 132:15).

And how marvellously the Lord answered the King's petition! The greatness of Solomon's wisdom, the manysidedness of its character as well as the world-wide impression this wisdom made is recorded in verses 29-34. "Happy is the man who findeth wisdom, and the man who causeth understanding to go forth; for merchandise with it is better than merchandise of silver, and the gain from it than the most fine gold" (Prov. 3:13-14). The King expressed in these words his own experience. His wisdom was greater than the wisdom of the wise men of the East and greater than Egypt. (Compare 1 Chron. 2:6. Ethan, 1 Chron. 6:44; 15:17, 19. Ps. 89 [Inscription]; Heman see 1 Chron. 6:33; 25:5. Psalm 88 [Inscription].) He spake 3000 proverbs and made 1005 songs. The book of Proverbs contains hundreds of his sayings. But not all these proverbs were preserved and only a few of his songs (Song of Solomon and a few Psalms). Creation itself was known by the great King. (See verse 33.) According to an apocryphical book (Wisdom of Solomon) he had knowledge of kosmogony, astronomy, the alteration of solstices, the cycles of years, the natures of wild beasts, the forces of spirits, the thoughts of men, the qualities of plants and roots. Jewish tradition even declares that he could converse with the wild beasts. This knowledge of creation was not a perfect knowledge. However, it also reminds us of the glorious time when the secrets of nature, lost through the fall of man, will be restored through Him, who will deliver groaning creation (Rom. 8:21).

4. The Building of the Temple and its Dedication

CHAPTER 5

Hiram King of Tyre

1. Hiram sends servants to Solomon (5:1)
2. The message of Solomon (5:2-6)
3. Hiram's answer and league with Solomon (5:7-12)
4. Solomon's workmen (5:13-18)

In connection with 1 Kings 5—8 the chapters in 2 Chronicles should be read which give a more extensive account (2 Chronicles 2—5:11). Solomon now begins the great work, which may be called his life work, the building of the house of the Lord. Hiram heard of Solomon's enthronement, and sent messengers to Solomon. This Gentile king was a lover of David. David had made before his death abundant material for the building of the house and Hiram had supplied much of it (1 Chron. 22:4). Solomon requested that Hiram furnish cedar trees from Lebanon for the building of the house and Hiram agrees to float them down the coast. According to the request of Hiram, Solomon supplied Hiram's household with 20,000 measures of wheat and twenty measures of oil. Hiram also sent a master-workman by name of Huram whose mother was a Jewess (2 Chron. 2:13-14; 1 Kings 7:14). This cooperation of the Gentiles in building the temple is also prophetic, for the riches of the Gentiles are promised to Israel (Is. 40:6; 54:3). Jews and Gentiles will unite to manifest His glory. A large number of workmen were needed. Two classes were employed. First there were 30,000 men out of Israel raised by a levy; 10,000 worked by relays of 10,000 a month. The second class was composed of strangers (1 Kings 5:15; 2 Chron. 2:17-18), 150,000 in number; 70,000 were burden bearers and 80,000 hewers in stone. Over all were 3300 officers (verse 16) with 550 chiefs (1 Kings 9:23), of whom 250 were native Israelites (2 Chron. 8:10). The great stones and the costly (splendid) stones and hewed stones are especially mentioned. They were for the foundation of the house. These stones may illustrate all those who as "living stones" are built up a spiritual house (1 Pet. 2:5). Through Grace all those are taken out of nature's place and prepared to fit into that marvellous temple of the Lord "fitly framed together—an holy temple in the Lord" (Eph. 2:21).

CHAPTER 6

The Description of the Temple

1. The date of the beginning of the building (6:1)
2. The house, the porches and side chambers (6:2-10)
3. The divine charge (6:11-14)
4. The internal arrangements (6:15-22)
5. The cherubim (6:23-30)
6. The doors (6:31-35)
7. The inner court and the temple finished (6:36-38)

Three chapters are taken up with the description of the temple, its contents, Solomon's house of the forest of Lebanon and with the dedication of the house of the Lord. Rich foreshadowings are here which we must pass over in greater part. Books could be written on these three chapters. However, we hope to point out the way for a closer study of the temple. The building of the temple commenced in the month of Zif (splendour), the second month when nature bursts forth in all her splendour. There comes a morning without clouds (2 Sam. 23:4) with glorious splendour, when He, for whose coming all is waiting, will build the temple (Zech. 6:12). It took seven years to finish the house. The temple was erected on Mount Moriah. There was an immense foundation of great hewn and splendid stones, a platform upon which the temple was built. This great foundation remains to the present day, known by the name "Haram-esh-Sheref," and upon it there stands now the Mosque of Omar. One stone alone is thirty-eight feet and nine inches long. "This great stone is one of the most interesting stones of the world, for it is the chief corner stone of the temple's massive wall. Among the ancient Jews, the foundation corner stone of their great sanctuary on Moriah was regarded as the emblem of moral and spiritual truths. It had two functions to perform; first, like the other foundation stones, it was a support for the masonry above, but it had also to face both ways, and was thus a bond of union between the two walls .... The engineers, in order to ascertain the dimensions of this foundation stone, worked round it, and report that it is three feet eight inches high, and fourteen feet in length. At the angle it is let down into the rock to a depth of fourteen inches, but, as the rock rises towards the north, the depth at four feet north of the angle is increased to thirty-two inches, while the northern end seems entirely embedded in the rock. The block is further described as squared and polished, with a finely dressed face .... Fixed in its abiding position three thousand years ago, it still stands sure and steadfast" (from report, "Recent Discoveries in the Temple Hill").

Still more interesting is the fact that the men who made an exploration of this temple wall, some 3000 years old, discovered certain marks. We quote from the Palestine Exploration report: "I must now speak somewhat fully on a subject which has engaged public attention for some time, and has already given rise to many conjectures, namely, the 'writings,' either painted on or cut into the stones, discovered lately on the bottom rows of the wall, at the south-east corner of the Haram, at a depth of about eighty feet there, where the foundations lie on the live rock itself. I have examined them carefully in their places—by no means an easy task. The ventilation at that depth is unfavourable to free breathing; nor is the pale glimmer of the taper, or the sudden glare of he magnesium wire, calculated materially to assist epigraphical studies.... I have come to the following conclusions:—First: The signs cut, or painted, were on the stones when they were first laid in their present places. Secondly: They do not represent any inscription. Thirdly: They are Phoenician. I consider them to be partly letters, partly numerals, and partly special mason's, or quarry, signs. Some of them were recognisable at once as well-known Phoenician characters; others, hitherto unknown in Phoenician epigraphy, I had the rare satisfaction of being able to identify on absolutely undoubted antique Phoenician structures in Syria, such as the primitive substructures of the harbour at Sidon. No less did I observe them on the bevelled stones taken from ancient edifices and built into later work throughout Phoenicia. For a striking and obvious instance of this, the stones of which (old Phoenician stones to wit) immured in their present place at subsequent periods, teem with peculiar marks identical with those at Jerusalem." Thus the stones testify to the fact that strangers, Phoenicians and others were employed. This rock foundation, which has remained unshaken, is an illustration of Him, the rock of ages, upon whom everything rests.

The dimensions of the house were twice the size of those adopted in the tabernacle; the whole length was 60 cubits, the breadth 20 cubits, and the height also 20 cubits. The interior was lined with boards of cedar, the house was overlaid with gold, and a wall surrounded the whole. The upper chambers were 10 cubits high, on which account the height of the whole building is stated to have been 30 cubits. The porch before the entrance of the temple was 10 cubits in length and as many in breadth, and here were placed two massive pillars of brass, named Jachin (he shall establish, or, steadfastness) and Boaz (in Him is strength). On the other three sides a building was erected three stories in height, which rose to two-thirds of the height of the house of the temple. The sancturay, 40 cubits in length, contained the golden altar of incense, ten candlesticks of gold, and ten tables of gold. The holiest of all was a cube of 20 cubits; it contained two cherubim made of the wood of the olive-tree, overlaid with gold, and 10 cubits in height, whose expanded wings touched in the middle, and, on the opposite sides, touched the walls.

In verse 7 we find a remarkable statement: "And the house when it was building, was built of stone made ready before it was brought thither, so that there was neither hammer nor axe nor any tool of iron heard in the house, while it was in building." Thus orderly and quietly proceeds the erection of that spiritual house, the Church, destined to be the holy temple in eternity. However, the temple itself does not exactly prefigure the Church. It is a type of the Father's house above where God dwells. The chambers or dwellings round about remind us of the words of our Lord: "In my Father's house are many mansions" (literally: abodes, dwellings). It is a blessed hint that God will have His people dwelling with Him. But the temple is also prophetic of another temple which will yet stand on the earth when our Lord reigns. His glory will cover and fill that house, which will be a house of prayer and worship for all nations.

After the description of the dimensions of the house, and after he had built it and built the chambers, the word of the Lord came to Solomon telling him that His dwelling among the children of Israel depended upon Solomon's faithfulness. Soon the failure came in and Ezekiel saw later the departure of the glory of the Lord from the temple and from Jerusalem.

And in the house gold was the prominent feature. The word "gold" occurs eleven times in this chapter. All was overlaid with gold. Besides this there were "glistening stones, and of divers colours" (1 Chron. 29:2). Everything was of pure gold; the sanctuary might have been called the golden house. The floor was overlaid with gold, the walls, the doors and ceiling were covered with pure gold, and the walls had inlaid precious stones (2 Chron. 3:6). Gold is the emblem of divine righteousness and divine glory. Therefore the whole sanctuary witnessed to the glory of righteousness which is in keeping with the prophetic foreshadowing of this house. How much greater will be the glory and the manifestation of divine righteousness when the true King builds the house and manifests His glory!

Another interesting feature present was the cherubim. While the cherubim which belonged to the ark of the covenant remained unchanged, for it was the same ark which was in the tabernacle, Solomon put on either side of it the big figure of a cherub carved of olive wood and overlaid with gold. Each was ten cubits high. The two with their wings met over the mercy seat, while the wing of the one touched the wall on the south and the wing of the other touched the wall on the north. Then instead of these cherubim, like those on the ark, looking downwards towards the mercy seat, they looked outwards (2 Chron. 3:13). "Inwards" really means "towards the house" or "outwards." And this is in harmony with the reign of righteousness which is foreshadowed in Solomon and the temple. "At that time, righteousness reigning and being established, these symbols of God's power can look outwards in blessing, instead of having their eyes fixed on the covenant alone. During the time there was nothing but the covenant, they gazed upon it; but when God has established His throne in righteousness, He can turn towards the world to bless it according to that righteousness."

CHAPTER 7

The House of Solomon and Pharaoh's Daughter
The Furnishings of the Temple

1. The house of the forest of Lebanon (7:1-7)
2. The royal palace and the house of Pharaoh's daughter (7:8-12)
3. The master workman (7:13-14)
4. The great pillars and chapiters (7:15-22)
5. The brazen sea (7:23-26)
6. The ten lavers with their carriages (7:27-40)
7. Hiram's work (7:41-47)
8. The golden utensils for the interior (7:48-51)

The description of the palace buildings come next. These buildings are called "Solomon's own house" (verse 1). The buildings consisted of the following: The house of the forest of Lebanon (verses 2-5). The porch of pillars (verse 6). The porch of judgment, where the king judged (verse 7). The house where the king dwelt (verse 8). The house where Pharaoh's daughter dwelt "like unto his house" (verse 8). The wall which surrounded the great court. Seven things are mentioned in connection with the palace buildings. While the temple was God's dwelling place the palace buildings were the dwelling place of the king and his wife, Pharaoh's daughter. From there the king executed judgment. Here we have prefigured the glorious administration of the kingdom, when our Lord judges in righteousness. The house of the forest of Lebanon is the type of His glory among the Gentiles. And inasmuch as the house of Pharaoh's daughter was closely connected with Solomon's house it is written "we are his house" (Hebrews 3:6), we have here foreshadowed the association of the Church with Christ in His coming reign of glory. Everything in the temple and in the palace buildings was glorious and revealed the immense riches of the great king. What a day it will be when the riches and glory of Christ will be manifested and when the saints of God will share it all!

Then Solomon sent and fetched Hiram out of Tyre. This was not the king, but a master workman. His father was a Tyrian and his mother by birth of the tribe of Dan was a widow and had married a man of Naphtali. This reconciles an alleged discrepancy. (See 1 Kings 7:14 and 2 Chron. 2:13.) In Chronicles he is called Huram. (Probably Huram-abi (Abi—meaning "my father") was his correct name.) His mother belonged to the same tribe to which Aholiab the coworker of Bezaleel belonged. (See Exodus 31:1-6.) The two pillars of solid brass Jachin (he will establish) and Boaz (in him is Strength) are first described. They were a new thing for the house of the Lord. The outward support these pillars afforded speak of Him who is the support of everything and whose power upholdeth all things. Read Jeremiah's words concerning these pillars (Jer. 27:19, etc.) and the fulfilment (2 Kings 25:13-17; Jerem. 52:17). All the vessels mentioned were made on a much larger scale, and greater in number, than those of the tabernacle. The great molten sea supported by twelve oxen which looked towards the North, South, East and West, the river wrought like a cup, like lilies, contained two thousand baths (about 16,250 gallons of water). (2 Chron. 4:5 has 3000 baths: this must mean the actual capacity of this colossal vessel, while the 2000 measures in 1 Kings gives the usual contents of the laver.) Here the priests and Levites performed their ablutions. The water was drawn from the big reservoir. There was a large supply. Living waters in abundance will flow forth from Jerusalem in the coming kingdom ages. The oxen (the burden bearing beast) are typical of service. Of all this we shall find more in Chronicles. Then all the things which David had dedicated, the silver, the gold and the vessels were put by Solomon among the treasures of the house of the Lord.

CHAPTER 8

The Dedication of the Temple

1. The great assembly (8:1-2)
2. The transportation of the ark (8:3-9)
3. The glory of the Lord filling the house (8:10-11)
4. Solomon's opening words (8:12-21)
5. Solomon's great prayer (8:22-53)
6. Solomon's benediction (8:54-61)
7. The sacrifices and the feast (8:62-66)

The ark of the covenant is now to be transported out of David's city to be put into the most holy place, under the wings of the great cherubim. The ark was carried, according to the instructions in the law, by the priests. A great sacrificial ceremony also took place; so many sheep and oxen were sacrificed that "they could not be numbered for multitude." The ark now had found a resting place (Ps. 132:8). The staves by which the ark had been carried were now drawn out. They were not to be removed (Ex. 25:15); but now they were pulled out, but remained there as a memorial of their journeys and the Lord's faithfulness in bringing them into the promised rest. But in the ark nothing was found but the two tables of stone; Aaron's rod and the pot of manna were missing. (Hebrews 9:4 has reference to the ark in the Tabernacle). The rod of Aaron was the emblem of the priestly grace which had accompanied them on their journey and the manna was their food in the wilderness. Both Aaron's rod and the pot of manna were provisions for the wilderness; they would not have been in keeping with the reign of glory and peace, as well as the rest they now enjoyed. Thus when we are brought into glory we have no more need of priestly intercession and help, nor do we need the manna any longer. But the law was not missing, for as regards that earthly kingdom over which our Lord will yet reign, its foundation and administration will be the law of righteousness.

When the ark had been placed the glory-cloud filled the house. Jehovah had appeared in His glory to dwell in the house. And when that future temple will be on the earth as seen by Ezekiel in his great temple-vision, the glory will return and fill the house, and more than that, the whole earth will be filled with His glory (Ezek. 43:1-5; Num. 14:21).

Then Solomon spoke. A great and marvellous dedicatory and intercessory prayer follows. It must be noticed that in all, especially in the bringing of the sacrifices, Solomon assumes the full character of priest. He acts as the king-priest, another Melchizedek, King of Salem. And this he was, king of righteousness in his judgments and king of peace. In all this he foreshadows Him, who is a priest forever after the order of Melchizedek. "He shall be a priest upon His throne" (Zech. 6:13) is the still unfulfilled prediction. Now He is upon the Father's throne as the priest and advocate of His people. When He comes again He will have His own throne and be also a priest. We have therefore in Solomon's functions in dedicating the temple and in the bringing of the sacrifices a prophetic type of our Lord in His future royal priesthood. First, Solomon turned towards the Most Holy filled with the glory of the Lord and said: "I have surely built Thee an house to dwell in, a settled place for Thee to abide in forever." Then he blessed the congregation. He mentions once more David, his illustrious father, and the covenant-promise. "And the Lord hath performed His word that He spake, and I am risen up in the room of David my father, and sit upon the throne of Israel as the Lord promised, and have built an house for the name of the Lord God of Israel" (verse 20). And yet the covenant-promise had not seen its accomplishment; the failure of Solomon and the passing of the glory witnesses to that. Yet Solomon, his reign of peace and prosperity and especially his great work in the building of the temple foreshadows the great coming fulfillment of the Davidic covenant in the enthroned Christ upon the throne of his father David. A closer study of the great prayer we must leave with the reader. The different petitions are of deep interest and the kingdom characteristics are prominent. "The prayer sets the people under the form of a righteous government, abounding indeed in kindness and forgiveness, yet one which will not hold the guilty innocent; and it presents God as the people's resource, when the consequences of their sin fall upon them according to the principles laid down by Moses in Deuteronomy and elsewhere" *(Synopsis of the Bible).* And in the prayer mention is made "that all people of the earth may know Thy name, to fear Thee, as do Thy people Israel; and that they may know that this house, which I have builded, is called by Thy name" (verse 43). This looks forward to the ingathering of the nations into the kingdom, when nations will be joined to a God-fearing Israel. (See Zech. 2:11; 8:23.) The feast mentioned which followed the dedication feast is the feast of tabernacles. And this is again highly typical for the feast of tabernacles is as a type unfulfilled. While it pointed back to the time when they were in the wilderness, living in tents and journeying towards the land of promise, it also pointed to the future, when the name of Jehovah was to be known among all the nations of the earth, when the nations would come to worship the Lord of Hosts (Zech. 14). The conjunction of the dedication of the temple with the feast of tabernacles was more than significant, it was prophetic. It is only when the Lord Jesus Christ occupies the throne and He builds the Temple of glory, that the nations will seek after Him and be converted. (See our annotations on Leviticus 23.) And while the king prayed and blessed the people, the people full of happiness and joy blessed the king. Heaven and earth rejoiced. It is the climax of Israel's history in the land.

5. Jehovah Appears unto Solomon and the Greatness of the King

CHAPTER 9

1. The second appearance of the Lord to Solomon (9:1-9)
2. Transactions with Hiram (9:10-14)
3. The levy of the king (9:15-23)
4. Pharaoh's daughter occupies the house (9:24)
5. The king's offerings (9:25)
6. Solomon's navy (9:26-28)

Jehovah's righteous government in the midst of His people Israel had now been established. This government was given and entrusted to Solomon the son of David, so that, in a sense, Solomon occupied the throne of the Lord. All depended upon the faithfulness of Solomon. Therefore the Lord appeared unto him the second time, not to say once more: "Ask what I shall give thee," but to assure him that He would keep His promise made to David and if he would be faithful his throne would be established. Then He warns against disobedience. If he serves other gods, Israel was to be cut off from the land and the house would be forsaken. How all this came to pass, Solomon's idolatry, disobedience, the subsequent shameful history of Israel's apostasy, we shall soon have to follow. Then God used Nebuchadnezzar to carry out the judgment upon Jerusalem and the temple. Another son of David will receive some day the throne and the government will rest in His hands. In Him all will be accomplished which the prophets have spoken and which was foreshadowed in Solomon.

The transaction with Hiram is interesting. Besides furnishing Solomon with timber he also gave him gold; this amounted to 120 talents of gold. Solomon gave to Hiram twenty cities in Galilee. When he came to look at them, he was displeased with them and called them Cabul, which probably means "as nothing." These cities may have been given to King Hiram for the gold Solomon had received from him. The cities were later restored to Solomon by Hiram, most likely after Solomon had paid back the gold Hiram had furnished.

The activity of the great King in building fortresses and cities is described in this chapter. Hazor became under him a stronghold in defence of Syria. The plain of Jezreel had for a protection Megiddo. Gezer and Baalath were other strongholds. Tadmor is Palmyra, called so by the Greeks and Romans, while it is called still to-day Tadmor. In this chapter (verse 18) the name is given in Hebrew as "Tamar"; in 2 Chron. 8:4 it is "Tadmor." Tamor means "palm tree," the same as Palmyra. Chronicles uses Tadmor because it was known by that name after the exile.

And Solomon had a fleet of ships, manned mostly by the experienced shipmen of King Hiram. Another fleet is mentioned in 10:22, a navy of Tharshish, which, with Hiram's navy, sailed every three years to fetch gold, silver, ivory and apes and peacocks. Ophir has been variously located. Peru, the Molucca Islands, Armenia, Arabia and parts of Africa have been suggested. All these statements show the great prosperity of the kingdom.

6. Solomon and the Queen of Sheba: His great Riches and Splendour

CHAPTER 10

1. The visit of the Queen (10:1-13)
2. Solomon's enormous wealth (10:14-15)
3. The targets and shields (10:16-17)
4. The ivory throne (10:18-20)
5. The abundance of gold and the depreciation of silver (10:21-22)
6. The greatest living monarch (10:23-26)
7. His chariots and horsemen (10:27-29)

The visit of the Queen of Sheba, who had heard of Soloman's wisdom, is the next recorded event of much interest and significance. It illustrates what was previously stated in chapter 4:34. Sheba was known to such ancient writers as Strabo and Pliny. It was the center of a vast commercial empire in the southwestern part of the Arabian peninsula. The ruins which are still to be seen testify of a great civilization. (See Isaiah 60:6; Psalm 72:15; Jerem. 6:20; Ezek. 27: 22; 38:13.) She heard and came; she communed with Solomon and brought presents; she was filled with wonder at all she heard and saw and declared: "Behold the half was not told me." Then she uttered her praise: "Happy are thy men, happy are these thy servants, which stand continually before thee, and that hear thy wisdom. Blessed be the Lord thy God, who delighteth in thee, to set thee on the throne of Israel, because the Lord loved Israel forever, therefore made He thee King, to do judgment and justice." Then she gave gold, spices and precious stones of an enormous value. In all this glory which came to Solomon we have a prophetic type of the glory which will come to Him, who is greater than Solomon. When He occupies the throne, the Gentiles will seek Him and praise the King as the Queen of Sheba praised Solomon. "The kings of Tarshish and of the isles shall bring presents; the kings of Sheba and Seba shall offer gifts. Yea, all the kings shall fall down before Him; all nations shall serve Him. . . . And He shall live, and to Him shall be given of the gold of Sheba; prayer also shall be made for Him continually, and daily shall He be praised" (Ps. 72:10-15). This great Kingdom Psalm will be fulfilled when our Lord comes again. "The abundance of the sea shall be converted unto Thee, the forces of the Gentiles shall come unto Thee. The multitude of camels shall cover Thee, the dromedaries of Midian and Ephah; all they from Sheba shall come, they shall bring gold and incense; and they shall shew forth the praises of the Lord" (Is. 60:5-6). All these and many other prophecies will be fulfilled in the future kingdom of our Lord. The visit of the Queen of Sheba foreshadows all this. See also the warning of our Lord in Matth. 12:42.

And what riches and glory the king possessed! Everything was of gold. His throne was of solid ivory overlaid with gold. Twelve wonderful lions stood on the one side and on the other. All the drinking vessels were of gold. Silver depreciated in his days; it was worth next to nothing. "The King made silver to be in Jerusalem as stones, and cedars made he to be as sycomore trees" (verse 27). Compare this with what will take place in the coming kingdom of our Lord. "Instead of the thorn shall come up the fir tree, and instead of the brier shall come up the myrtle tree" (Is. 55:13). "For brass I will bring gold, and for iron I will bring silver, and for wood, brass, and for stone, iron" (Is. 60:17).

7. Solomon's Failure: Judgment Announced and the beginning of Disruption

CHAPTER 11

1. Solomon's polygamy and departure from God (11:1-13)
2. Hadad the Edomite (11:14-22)
3. Rezon the second adversary (11:23-25)
4. Jeroboam (11:26-40)
5. Solomon's reign and death (11:41-43)

"But—." An ominous word with which this chapter begins. It introduces us to the sad picture of Solomon's great apostasy. "He shall not multiply horses to himself, nor cause the people to return to Egypt, to the end that he should multiply horses, for as much as the Lord hath said unto you, ye shall henceforth return no more that way. Neither shall he multiply wives to himself, that his heart turn not away, neither shall he greatly multiply to himself silver and gold" (Deut. 17:16-17). The Lord anticipated a royal form of government for Israel and gave these instructions concerning the King. The first failure is seen in the previous chapter. He multiplied horses and brought them out of Egypt. Egypt is the type of the world. God had answered his prayer and then added riches and everything else. But his heart was captivated by riches and luxuries. No doubt he loved these things and multiplied silver and gold. The Devil's crime, pride, was found in him. His heart was lifted up (Deut. 17:20). But worse than all he multiplied wives. The sad record is found in the opening verses of this chapter. Then his heart was turned away by his wives and concubines after other gods. David, though his trouble also originated in polygamy, had always, in all his sin and failure, clung to Jehovah. In this sense David's heart was perfect with the Lord his God. He did not turn away from the Lord, nor did David go after strange gods. Solomon's guilt was great. The Lord had appeared twice to him; He never appeared to David. And with all the Lord had done for Solomon, the evidences of His grace towards him, the house he could build, the superior wisdom he had, the great king departed from the Lord. Such is the heart of man, desperately wicked. It becomes now evident that the oathbound covenant concerning a man to sit upon the throne of David with a glorious kingdom established, must be fulfilled in another son of David. Solomon fails. The kingdom is rent from him. The glory departs. Never again were the scenes of glory repeated in the kingdom of Israel. But when David's Lord and David's Son appears, the King of Righteousness, the Prince of Peace, the kingdom and the glory will be restored to Israel.

It has been stated that Solomon himself was not actually guilty of idolatry. If he built the places of idolatrous worship for his many wives only, he was guilty of the sin of idolatry. The abominations were then introduced. Luxuries, wealth, self-indulgence, the lust of the eyes, the lust of the flesh and the pride of life led into idolatry. It is the same in the closing days of the present age. Ashtoreth, a Phoenician goddess, was worshipped with impure rites. Milcom (Molech) was the idol-god of the Ammonites. Chemosh was the sun-god and war-god of the Moabites.

And the Lord who had appeared twice unto Solomon, the Lord who had commanded him not to go after other gods, was now angry with Solomon. Judgment is announced. Two adversaries were stirred up at once against Solomon, Hadad the Edomite and Rezon of Syria, who abhorred Israel.

Jeroboam, a servant of King Solomon (verse 11) lifted up his hand against the king. Ahijah the prophet, attired in a new garment, meets the future king of the ten tribe division and tore his garment into twelve pieces. "And he said to Jeroboam, Take thee ten pieces, for thus saith the Lord, the God of Israel, Behold I will rend the kingdom out of the hand of Solomon, and will give ten tribes to thee." But the message of the Lord through Ahijah also declared His faithfulness to David. Jehovah still speaks of "David my servant"; he is "to have a light always before Me in Jerusalem, the city which I have chosen to put My name there." The house of David in the midst of all the evil is not forgotten. There will be affliction, "but not forever" (verse 39). And Jeroboam also has the opportunity of having a house "as I built for David" on the condition of obedience. But ambitious Jeroboam did not keep the statutes and commandments of the Lord.

And Solomon? Not a word of repentance! No tears like those his father wept. No confession as it came from David's lips. Only one thing is stated. Only one act is mentioned of apostatized Solomon. He sought to kill Jeroboam. After a reign of 40 years, Solomon passed away not quite 60 years old.

III. The Divided Kingdom

1. Rehoboam and the Revolt of the Ten Tribes

CHAPTER 12

1. The revolt of the northern tribes (12:1-20)
2. The threatening war averted (12:21-24)
3. Jeroboam's wicked schemes (12:25-33)

Rehoboam (enlarger of the people) is the only son of Solomon mentioned in the Bible (1 Chron. 3:10). Ecclesiastes 2:18-19 and 4:13-16 seem to give a hint that his father was fearful about his reign in his stead. In 2 Chronicles 10:13 we find the history of Rehoboam more fully, which we follow in the annotations of that book. He was the son of the Ammonitess Naamah. During the first three years he was outwardly faithful, but after that he drifted like his father into idolatry and its moral evils (1 Kings 14:23-24; 2 Chron. 11:13-17). He forsook the law of the Lord and the people followed him (2 Chron. 12:1). The polygamous tendency of his father and grandfather were also indulged by him (2 Chr. 11:21). Jeroboam who had fled into Egypt (11:40) was recalled and the history of the revolt follows. Jeroboam was made king over the ten tribes, while Rehoboam reigned over Judah. What took place was from the Lord "that He might perform His saying, which the Lord spake by Ahijah the Shilonite unto Jeroboam the son of Nebat" (12:15). The disruption of the kingdom had taken place. Up to the deportation of the ten tribes under Shalmaneser (722 B.C.) covers 253 years. During that time thirteen kings reigned over Judah and twenty over the ten tribes; there were also two periods of lawlessness. The apostasy of the ten-tribe kingdom was complete; none of their kings served the Lord. Under Ahab and his two sons Ahaziah and Joram the Baal worship became universal. It was different with the kings of Judah. A number of them were God-fearing (Asa, Jehoshaphat, Uzziah, Jotham, Hezekiah and Josiah). Others were wicked blasphemers as we shall see from their history. It is also noteworthy that the reign of the wicked kings was shorter than the reign of those who feared the Lord.

After the stoning of Adoram, Rehoboam's collector, Rehoboam fled to Jerusalem and gathered an army from Judah and Benjamin to fight against Israel to bring back the kingdom to the son of Solomon. Shemaiah (heard of Jehovah), a man of God, brought the message from the Lord not to fight against Israel. They were obedient and the war was averted. Many Israelites, who were true to Jehovah, as well as all the priests and Levites remained in the Kingdom of Judah. (As failure had come in, prophecy at once reappears. Shemaiah must have been a very courageous man to stand in face of a gathered army of 180,000 men, an angry king and an angry people and declare a message which must have been decidedly unwelcome. And one cannot but admire the gracious submission of king and people.)

Jeroboam made Shechem his capital. He also built the ancient Penuel (the face of God, Gen. 32:30; Judges 8:8), but he did not meet the Lord there like Jacob. Then the step was done which precipitated idolatry. To protect his kingdom and keep the people back from the true worship of Jehovah, he placed, with the consent of the people, in Dan and Beth-el on the northern and southern boundaries of his kingdom, two calves of gold. Thus with an unspeakable blasphemy he said: "It is too much for you to go up to Jerusalem; behold thy gods, O Israel, which brought thee up out of the land of Egypt." The lowest class of the people were chosen as priests. Then he also offered sacrifices unto the calves that he had made. All was devised of his own heart and God's Word was completely set aside. It corresponds to the great apostasy of Romanism with its wicked, blasphemous rites.

2. Jeroboam and Rehoboam and their Reign

CHAPTER 13

The Man of God from Judah

1. The man of God and Jeroboam (13:1-10)
2. The temptation and lying message (13:11-19)
3. Judgment announced (13:20-22)
4. The fate of the man of Judah (13:23-32)
5. Jeroboam's impenitence (13:33-34)

A dramatic scene opens this chapter. The idolatrous King is engaged in his religious ceremony when an unnamed man of God interrupted him. He did not rebuke Jeroboam, but addressed himself to the altar, uttering a remarkable prophecy: "Behold, a child shall be born unto the house of David, Josiah by name; and upon thee shall he offer the priests of the high places that burn incense upon thee, and men's bones shall be burned upon thee." More than 300 years later, and nearly a century after the ten tribes had been carried away captive, this prophecy was fulfilled (2 Kings 23:15-18). The man of God announced the unborn king by name and also what he would do, just as Isaiah announced the unborn King Cyrus and his work. Higher criticism has labored in vain to destroy this great evidence of prophecy. Then the man of God added a sign which happened literally in the presence of the king. The angry king commanded the seizure of the prophet, but the outstretched arm withered. The withered arm was restored in answer to the prophet's prayer. Jehovah was seeking in mercy even Jeroboam in all his wickedness. It was unsuccessful, for it is written: "After this King Jeroboam returned not from his evil way." The man of God and what happened to him occupies the greater part of the chapter. The King invited him to a feast, probably an idol feast, and wanted to give him a reward. He refused both because the Lord had charged him not to eat bread nor drink water, nor return the same way he came. The man of God was to have no fellowship with the works of darkness. The same principle is laid down for God's people in the New Testament (2 Cor. 6:14-18; Eph. 5:11; 2 John 9-11). Then comes his great failure, showing that while he was a messenger of God, his heart was not altogether right with God. It was through the old prophet that a lying spirit induced him to disobey the Word of the Lord. And when the old prophet announced his coming judgment we read not a word that he turned to the Lord with confession and prayer. Then the predicted fate overtook him. It is a solemn lesson which teaches us obedience to the Word of God. "It teaches us that, whenever God has made His will known to us, we are not to allow any after thought whatever to call it in question, even although the latter may take the form of the Word of God. If we were nearer to the Lord, we would feel that the only true and right position is to follow that which He told us at first. In every case our part is to obey what He has said." The lion who had killed the disobedient prophet remained for a time with the body without touching it. It was to show the divine character of the judgment. If we look upon Jeroboam's departure from God and idolatrous worship as typical of the corruption of Romanism, we may see in the Man of God from Judah, who rebuked the false altar, a type of Protestantism. Like the prophet who delivered the message faithfully but became disobedient, Protestantism is disobedient to the Word of God and the judgment of God will overtake it in the end.

CHAPTER 14

The Passing of Jeroboam and Rehoboam

1. Sickness and death of Jeroboam's son (14:1-18)
2. Jeroboam's reign and death (14:19-20)
3. Rehoboam's apostasy, punishment and death (14:21-31)

We come now to the passing of both kings, Jeroboam of Israel and Rehoboam of Judah. Abijah (Jehovah is my father), the son of wicked Jeroboam, was sick. "That child was the one green spot in Jeroboam's life and home; the one germ of hope. And as his father loved him truly, so all Israel had set their hopes on him. Upon the inner life of this child, its struggles and its victories, lies the veil of Scripture silence; and best that it should be so. But now his pulses were beating quick and weak, and that life of love and hope seemed fast ebbing. None with the father in those hours of darkness, neither counsellor, courtier, prophet nor priest, save the child's mother."[1] Then the unhappy king remembered Ahijah, who had first announced his exaltation to be king (11:31). Disguised the wife of Jeroboam proceeds to Shiloh not to ask prayer for the sick son but to find out (as if consulting a fortune teller) what should become of the child. Ahijah was blind. What

---

[1]A. Edersheim, *Bible History.*

need was there for Jeroboam's wife to feign to be another? And the Lord saw her coming and announced her approch to blind Ahijah. She hears from his lips not good tidings, but a message of judgment. Judgment upon the house of Jeroboam is announced and when the feet of the mother entered Tirzah once more the child would die. Concerning the child, Ahijah, the prophet, said: "In him there is found some good thing toward the Lord God of Israel in the house of Jeroboam." Thus the little one was saved and removed from the evil to come upon the house of Jeroboam. Then Jeroboam died. In 2 Chronicles 20 we read "the Lord struck him and he died." Nadab reigned after him for only two years.

Then follows the passing of Rehoboam. (In 2 Chronicles 11 we find the fuller record. He had 18 wives and 60 concubines. His family consisted of 28 sons and 60 daughters.) His reign was begun well, but he also turned against the Lord, and Judah did evil in the sight of the Lord. Idolatry and immorality flourished. A corrupted worship led to a corrupted life. Departure from God and His Word leads always to moral decline. Our times bear witness to this. Then the punishment came in the fifth year of his reign. Shishak, King of Egypt, took Jerusalem and carried away the treasures of the house of the Lord and of the King. He took away the golden shields of Solomon so that Rehoboam had to substitute shields of brass. Shishak was the founder of the twenty-second dynasty. Jeroboam had been with him (11:40), and it is not improbable that at his instigation Shishak made his expedition to Jerusalem. In the temple ruins of Amon at Karnak, near Thebes, are recorded more than sixty Ephraimitic cities that paid tribute to Shishak, also the names of many more Judean cities; there also is a picture of Rehoboam. The detailed description of Shishak and his invasion, the work of Shemaiah the prophet in averting a greater disaster, we find in 2 Chronicles 12.

3. Abijam and Asa, Kings of Judah

CHAPTER 15

1. Abijam of Judah (15:1-8; 2 Chronicles 13)
2. Asa of Judah (15:9-24; 2 Chronicles 14—16)

Abijam is called in Chronicles Abijah; in 2 Chron. 13:21 he is called Abijahu. Abijam was undoubtedly the older form. It is possible that on account of his great address of rebuke to Jeroboam (2 Chron. 13:4-12) they may have called him Abijah (Jehovah is my father). He ascended the throne in the eighteenth year of Jeroboam's reign and was king for three years. Here we find the statement that he walked in all the sins of his father and that his heart was not perfect with the Lord as the heart of David his father. The statement in chapter 11:36 is repeated, that for David's sake did the Lord his God give him a lamp in Jerusalem. It was a custom (and is still so among the Fellaheen in Palestine) to keep a lamp constantly burning in the tent. The extinction of the lamp signified the removal of the family. The Lord remembered the house of David and his covenant and on account of that covenant the deserved judgment was held back. The war he fought with Jeroboam is not given in Kings but in Chronicles. We shall follow his history with the text in Chronicles.

Then his son Asa (who will heal), a mere boy, began to reign. During the first ten years of his reign the land had rest (2 Chron. 14:1). He is the first King of Judah of whom it is said, he did right in the eyes of the Lord, as did David his father. A great reformation took place. The Sodomites with their abominations, the result of idolatry, he ended; the idols were removed. His grandmother, Maachah, was removed by him from being a queen because she had made an idol, which Asa destroyed and burnt. (Most likely on account of his youth Maachah was regent during Asa's minority.) And in Chronicles we read more of his good work. He was faithful to Jehovah, though he also failed in the end. The war with Zerah the Ethiopian is recorded in 2 Chronicles 14, as well as other deeply interesting events during his reign. We do not touch those at this time. Our book here only records the war with Baasha, King of Israel, and Asa's strange alliance with Ben-hadad, King of Syria, to whom he presented the silver and gold which Shishak had left in the house of the Lord, and also the treasures of the King's house. Baasha had fortified Ramah, which meant the complete isolation and domination of Jerusalem. Asa, forgetful of his experience with Zerah and the manner of getting the victory (see his beautiful prayer, 2 Chron. 14:11), and that the Lord who had smitten Zerah could also smite Baasha, feared the rival king and renewed the God-dishonoring league with Syria which his father Abijah had made. What followed after this league, the divine exhortation and judgment delivered through Hanani the prophet and Asa's end, we shall follow in Chronicles.

Asa's sin and failure consisted in not trusting the Lord wholly, but using other means for deliverance. Hanani told him "thou hast relied on the King of Syria, and not on the Lord thy God." "For the eyes of the Lord run to and fro throughout the whole earth, to show Himself strong in the behalf of them whose heart is perfect toward Him. Herein thou hast done foolishly; therefore from henceforth thou shalt have wars" (2 Chr. 16:7-9). Then Asa imprisoned the faithful messenger. Alas! how often the failure of Asa has been repeated among God's people! Many begin well but lose the freshness of their faith. In our own days we behold on all sides Asa-movements, no perfect confidence in the Lord, but reliance upon all kinds of world schemes and alliances which make it impossible for the Lord to manifest the fullness of His power.

4. Kings of Israel

CHAPTERS 15:25—16

1. Nadab, King of Israel (15:25-32)
2. Baasha, King of Israel (15:34—16:7)
3. Elah, King of Israel (16:8-14)
4. Zimri, King of Israel (16:15-20)
5. Divisions (16:21-22)
6. Omri, King of Israel (16:23-28)
7. Ahab (16:29-34)

Six kings of Israel are now mentioned. Asa saw them all ascending the throne of Israel. The first mentioned is Nadab, the son of Jeroboam, who followed in his father's footsteps. His reign was cut short by an uprising of one of the house of Issachar, Baasha. He smote Nadab at Gibethon (Josh. 19:44; 21:23). Baasha then smote all the house of Jeroboam. Thus was the prediction of Ahijah, the prophet of Shiloh, fulfilled. "Because of the sins of Jeroboam which he sinned, and which he made Israel sin, by his provocation wherewith he provoked the Lord God of Israel to anger." God's predicted judgments never fail in the end. The judgments written over against our own age, this evil age, will some day be executed by the Lord as all other judgments which were threatened against Israel.

The new dynasty headed by Baasha began in the third year of Asa's reign. Baasha reigned twenty-four years. He sinned as Jeroboam did, though he had been the executer of God's judgment upon the descendants of the wicked king. He had not heard Jehovah's voice speaking in the events of the past. Then came the message of the Lord to Baasha through Jehu, the son of Hanani (2 Chronicles 19:2; 20:34). He reminds him that the Lord had raised him out of the dust (his family was unknown) and He had made him prince over Israel. He followed Jeroboam and Jeroboam's fate, and the fate of his house would now also be the fate of Baasha, who had executed the divine sentence. "I will make thy house like the house of Jeroboam, the son of Nebat." Such is divine justice.

Elah his son followed. His rule lasted not quite two years. He was in Tirzah. While the army was away fighting the Philistines, Elah in the house of his steward Arza ("earthliness") became drunk and was killed by his captain, Zimri, who at once began to reign in his place. He only reigned seven days and the only deed mentioned, besides his awful death, is the slaying of all the house of Baasha "according to the Word of the Lord, which He spake against Baasha by Jehu the prophet." Omri was made king by all Israel and with him began another dynasty. His first act was to besiege Tirzah where Zimri was, who set the king's palace on fire and perished in the flames. A division followed, but Omri prevailed. In all these sad records the fruits of the departure from God and from His Word are seen. They can easily be traced in the history of other nations down to our own times, the days which have brought the most awful bloodshed in the world's blood drenched history. It is all the result of sin. And Omri was worse than all that were before him, and his son Ahab was the climax of all wickedness in the Kingdom of Israel. There was no improvement, but a steady decline till God's hand smote them in judgment. Ahab introduced Baal-worship in Israel. This was the result of his marriage to Jezebel (dunghill), the daughter of Ethbaal (with Baal), King of Zidonians. "Ahab did more to provoke the Lord God of Israel to anger than all the Kings of Israel that were before him." The last verse of this chapter records a presumptuous action. Hiel (God liveth) built Jericho. He found out that the word of God spoken 500 years before (Josh. 6:26) was true.

IV. The Prophet Elijah and King Ahab

1. Elijah's Prediction and Miracles

CHAPTER 17

1. Elijah's message to Ahab (17:1)
2. At the brook Cherith (17:2-7)

3. With the widow of Zarephath (17:8-16)
4. The widow's son restored to life (17:17-24)

Upon this scene of complete departure of God, when Ahab and his heathen wife worshipped Baal and all the vileness connected with that cult flourished in Israel, there appeared suddenly one of the greatest of God's prophets, Elijah (my God is Jehovah) the Tishbite. "A grander figure never stood out even against the Old Testament sky than that of Elijah. As Israel's apostasy had reached its highest point in the time of Ahab, so the Old Testament antagonism to it in the person and mission of Elijah."—"He was the impersonation of the Old Testament in one of its aspects: that of grandeur and judgment" (A. Edersheim). His miracles, like those of Moses, have a judicial character. Heaven is shut in answer to his prayer and fire falls from heaven at his word. The last promise in the Old Testament is concerning Elijah the prophet who is to appear before the coming of the great and dreadful day of the Lord, to turn the heart of the fathers to the children and the heart of the children to their fathers (Mal. 4:5-6). See also the Lord's words concerning the coming of Elijah (Matth. 17:10-13). He appeared with Moses on the transfiguration mountain. In the book of Revelation two witnesses are mentioned who witness among Israel before the great day of the Lord comes. Though their names are not given, the miracles they perform clearly show that these witnesses will be like Moses and Elijah. "These have power to shut heaven, that it rain not in the days of their prophecy (Elijah), and have power over waters to turn them to blood and to smite the earth with all plagues, as often as they will (Moses)." "And if any man will hurt them fire proceedeth out of their mouth and devoureth their enemies (Elijah)" Rev. 11:5-6. James speaks of Elijah also and tells us he was a great man of prayer.

He appeared suddenly upon the scene and said to wicked Ahab, "As the Lord God of Israel liveth, before whom I stand, there shall not be dew nor rain these years, but according to my word." He had, no doubt, like other great servants of God, his training in secret.

The passage in James gives us the key: "Elias was a man subject to like passions as we are, and he prayed earnestly that it might not rain" (James 5:17). It was in secret that he sought God's presence and wrestled in prayer till the Lord sent him forth with the message of judgment. Prayer, persevering prayer, is the one great need in the days of declension and departure from God, and it is the one resource of God's faithful ones. And how little true and continued waiting upon God there is in the days of apostasy! When Elijah delivered the message to Ahab and said "according to my word" he did not speak presumptuously, but as standing in the Lord's own presence as his mouthpiece he had a perfect right to speak thus with divine authority.

As soon as he had delivered the message the Lord told him to hide himself by the brook Cherith. There he was miraculously fed by the ravens. He was in the appointed place and the Lord took care of him in His own way. Rationalistic critics have made the absurd statement that the word "orebim"—ravens—should be "arabim," which means Arabs.[2] But the Lord had commanded the birds, so shy in their nature, to supply His servant with the needed food. Twice every day they ministered to his wants. How this shows the omnipotence of the Lord. There is nothing too hard for Him. If we are in the right place, the place He assigns to us, we shall find that He still provides for those who trust and obey. The brook dried up. Surely his faith was being tested. Then he was sent to a destitute Gentile widow, who faced starvation. And concerning her the Lord said: "I have commanded a widow woman there to sustain thee." The Lord who commanded the ravens, commanded the widow. The Lord delights to take the weak things and use them for His glory. And how did Elijah find her? Preparing the last meal for herself and her child. Her faith was tested. She was to make first a little cake for Elijah and bring it unto him and afterwards to do the same for herself and her son. She obeyed and "the barrel of meal wasted not neither did the cruse of oil fail, according to the Word of the Lord." Here was greater faith than in Israel. See also Luke 4:26. The story foreshadows the bringing in of the Gentiles to know the Lord. And when the widow's son fell ill and died and was restored by Elijah and he delivered him to the mother saying: See, thy son liveth—she made the blessed confession: "Now by this I know that thou art a man of God and that the Word of the Lord in thy mouth is truth." The truth of resurrection both physical and spiritual is here foreshadowed.

---

[2]Thus Canon Farrar in the *Expositor's Bible:* "The word (orebim) may equally well mean people of the city Oreb, or of the rock Oreb; or merchants as in Ezek. 27:27; or Arabians.

2. Elijah on Carmel: The Answered Prayer

CHAPTER 18

1. The command to see Ahab (18:1)
2. Elijah's response (18:2)
3. Ahab and Obadiah (18:3-6)
4. Elijah and Obadiah (18:7-15)
5. Elijah meets Ahab (18:16-18)
6. Elijah's demand (18:19-20)
7. The events on Carmel (18:20-40)
8. The answered prayer (18:41-46)

The judgment of God as announded by Elijah continued its allotted time. A Greek historian, Menander of Ephesus, in his account of the acts of Ethbaal (the father of Jezebel, Ahab's wife), says: "Under him there was a want of rain from a certain month till the same month the following year." And Josephus, the Jewish historian who quotes this, adds, "by these words he designed the want of rain that was in the days of Ahab." It was in the third year of the drought that Elijah is commanded to show himself to Ahab. Elijah obeys. Great distress and famine were everywhere. Then we see Ahab and Obadiah, the governor or steward of his house, looking for a little pasture so that they might save the horses and mules alive. Obadiah (servant of Jehovah), holding a high position with Ahab, feared the Lord greatly. He belonged to the faithful remnant who did not bow the knee to Baal (1 Kings 19:18). He must have had severe tests of faith and much courage. It showed faith and devotion in hiding the Lord's prophets. Jezebel, the wicked idolatrous woman, used the civil power to kill off the true prophets. Her aim was to exterminate completely the men of God who stood for the truth. We find her mentioned in Revelation 2:20. There she is used to represent Rome, the harlot, and her spiritual fornication and idolatry. Rome, like Jezebel, has persecuted the Lord's servants and killed them (Rev. 18:24). Jezebel had evidently left the palace of Samaria and was at Jezreel, but Ahab and Obadiah were still in Samaria making a survey of the land. Then Obadiah met Elijah. The prophet requests Obadiah to announce his presence to Ahab. But Obadiah feared that such a message might cost him his life. Had not the whole country been searched for Elijah? And what if the Spirit should carry Elijah away? Then he pleads his kindness to the hundred prophets whom he saved when murderous Jezebel slew the prophets. From all this we learn that Obadiah, pious and faithful, was full of fear and trembling. He and the other faithful ones in Israel during the dark days of Ahab and Jezebel typify that faithful remnant of Israel during the end of the present age, suffering and persecuted during the great tribulation. Ahab and Elijah met, and the prophet, clothed with power, rebuked the apostate King: "I have not troubled Israel; but thou and thy father's house, in that ye have forsaken the commandments of the Lord, and thou hast followed Baalim." What would have happened if the daughter of Ethbaal, demon-possessed Jezebel, had been present? The great gathering suggested by Elijah would hardly have taken place. But she was in Jezreel and was ignorant of what was taking place. Ahab gathers all Israel and the 450 prophets of Baal upon Mount Carmel as demanded by Elijah. It is said that upon that mountain there stood two altars, one dedicated to Jehovah and another altar of Baal. This place Elijah chose for the vindication of Jehovah. To describe the scene, one of the grandest in the history of Israel, would take many pages. To his solid statement demanding decision—"How long halt ye between two opinions? If Jehovah is God, follow Him; but if Baal, then follow him"—the people had no answer. Then follows his great declaration as the only prophet of Jehovah, while 450 prophets of Baal stood over against him. Then the sacrifices are suggested "and the God that answereth by fire, let him be God." And all the people answered, it is well spoken. Then follows the wild crying of the prophets of Baal from early morning till noon; Elijah's sarcasm and the greater frenzy of the Baal worshippers. A wild scene followed. Crying louder and louder, they cut themselves with knives and lancets till the blood flowed. But there was no answer and no voice. Then Elijah repaired the altar of Jehovah, that was broken down. What a reminder the twelve stones were with which he built the altar! The sacrifice had been put upon the altar with the wood. Three times the altar had been drenched with water, so that the trench was filled with water. And now the time for the evening sacrifice, that significant time had come. A simple prayer follows. Jehovah's vindication is demanded and that he is Jehovah's servant. "Hear me, O Lord, hear me, that this people may know that Thou art the Lord God, and that Thou hast turned their heart back again." Then Jehovah answered by fire and everything was consumed. The people who witnessed the indescribable scene fell on their faces and cried: "The Lord He is God—the Lord He is God." Thus Jehovah manifested His power in the vindication of His name and in answer to His servant's prayer; and the people were brought back to the confession of the name of the Lord. His great mission to which the Lord had called him had been accomplished and the prophets of Baal, wicked and guilty as they were, received their deserved judgment. And here we have a foreshadowing of events to come. Apostasy from the Lord and from His Word is increasing. Before the age closes it will be universal, though the Lord will have a faithful remnant even in the dark days of the age. His name is dishonored and rejected. But that blessed name will be vindicated by a manifestation of His power in judgment. "For behold, the Lord will come with fire, and with His chariots like a whirlwind, to render His anger with fury, and His rebuke with flames of fires. For by fire and by His sword will the Lord plead with all flesh; and the slain of the Lord shall be many" (Is. 66:15-16).

Higher criticism has not left these records unattacked. They speak of "the legendary narratives in which Elijah's history is enshrined." All is done to discredit these records and to make them appear doubtful. But the verdict given by these men who sit in judgment upon the Word of God, that the scene on Carmel is unhistorical, is a false verdict which shows lack of real research. Nothing whatever can be brought forward to question the historicity of this great scene, while much confirms it.

Then follows Elijah's word to Ahab: "Get thee up, eat and drink, for there is a sound of abundance of rain." It was spoken in faith. The Lord had said to him: "I will send rain upon the earth" (18:1). And then came his prayer. He knew the Lord's will and the Lord's promise, and then persevered in prayer, and when the answer was in sight then he exercised faith once more by sending a message to Ahab. Then the heaven was black with clouds and wind and there was a great rain. The hand of the Lord was also upon Elijah and he ran before Ahab's chariot to the entrance of Jezreel. It was supernatural power which sustained him (Is. 60:31).

3. Elijah in the Wilderness and upon Mount Horeb

CHAPTER 19

1. Elijah's flight and despondency (19:1-8)
2. Upon Mount Horeb (19:9-18)
3. Elisha called (19:10-21)

Elijah perhaps stopped at the very door of the palace where wicked Jezebel dwelt. He would remain with Ahab to the very last before he went in to face the queen. Should not Elijah have remained and gone even before Jezebel to bear his testimony? Instead he becomes terrified of wicked Jezebel. Had he hoped that what had taken place on Carmel would result in bringing not alone Ahab back to Jehovah, but also influence Jezebel? If such was his expectation he must have been bitterly disappointed. Jezebel seeks to kill him and he flees for his life. All what follows is the result of unbelief. This verifies James' statement in his Epistle: "Elias was a man subject to like passions as we are." Then in despair and unbelief he requested to die. He is altogether occupied with himself and did not look to God. Instead of seeking the wilderness, his training school, to pour out his heart before God, to get new strength in communion with the Lord, "he requested for himself that he might die."

"The heart of Elijah and the hand of God led the prophet into the wilderness, where, overwhelmed perhaps, yet precious in Jehovah's sight, he will be alone with God. Elijah's forty days' journey in the wilderness has only a partial resemblance to the forty days which Moses spent with God, in the same Horeb to which the prophet was going, or to those which Jesus spent in the wilderness for conflict with the enemy of God and man. In the two latter cases nature was set aside. Neither Moses nor the Lord ate or drank. As for Elijah, the goodness of God sustains the weakness of tried nature, makes manifest that He considers it with all tenderness and thoughtfulness, and gives the strength needed for such a journey. This should have touched him, and made him feel what he ought to be in the midst of the people, since he had to do with such a God. His heart was far from such a state. Impossible, when we think of ourselves, to be witnesses to others of what God is! Our poor hearts are too far from such a position" *(Synopsis of the Bible).*

In Mount Horeb the Lord spoke to him: "What doest thou here, Elijah?" It was the gentle rebuke of a loving God. He was not in the place where the Lord wanted him as His servant. It is a great contrast—Elijah on Mount Carmel and Elijah on Mount Horeb in a cave. On Carmel he stands the man of faith, filled with a holy zeal for Jehovah. On Horeb hidden in the cave because he fled from Jezebel. And how many children of God may learn something from this question: "What doest thou here?" They are drifting into the world while others have left the sphere of service into which the Lord called them. And Elijah's answer shows his self-occupation. It is what he had done; what he was and the threatening danger to lose his life. But that danger was far greater when they searched country-wide for him and when the Lord preserved his life by the ministry of the ravens and by the widow-woman.

His answer has in it the spirit of bitterness and accusation. Then the Lord passed by. The storm, the earthquake and the fire preceded His coming; these are always connected with Jehovah's presence and manifestation. Then came "a still small voice" Elijah knew so well. He wrapped his face in his mantle and then he answered the question once more, but in an humbled spirit. He receives the commission to anoint Hazael, King of Syria; Jehu (Jehovah is he), the son of Nimshi (Jehovah reveals), he is to anoint King of Israel and Elisha is to be his successor. All three are called as instruments of judgment upon Israel's idolatry and the house of Ahab. Then the Lord announced that He had a faithful remnant of 7000 in Israel who had not bowed the knee unto Baal. (See its prophetic meaning in Romans 11:3-6.)

4. King Ahab: His Wicked Reign and End

CHAPTER 20

Ahab's War with the Syrians and His Victory

1. The siege and relief of Samaria (20:1-21)
2. The victory at Aphek (20:22-34)
3. A prophet's symbolical action and his message (20:35-43)

Two expeditions of Ben-hadad (son of the Sun) against Israel are recorded in this chapter. When Ben-hadad forced the war and insulted the King of Israel, Ahab prepared for the battle. Then a prophet came to Ahab, most likely one of those who had been hidden by Obadiah. He brought a message from the Lord. "Thus saith Jehovah, Hast thou seen all this great multitude? behold I will deliver it into thine hand this day; and thou shalt know that I am Jehovah." From this we may gather that a spiritual revival must have taken place in Israel after the manifestation of Jehovah on Carmel. Jezebel, after her rage on account of Elijah's deed, is not mentioned again till after Ahab's failure. The Lord in graciousness gave to Ahab another evidence that He is the Lord and can smite the enemies of Israel. The Syrians were defeated. Another message came to Ahab through the prophet. A year later Ben-hadad made another expedition against Israel. "And there came a man of God, and spake unto the King of Israel, and said, Thus saith Jehovah, because the Syrians have said, The Lord is the God of the hills but not the God of the valleys, therefore will I deliver all this great multitude into their hand, and ye shall know that I am the Lord." A great victory followed at Aphek. But Ahab let Ben-hadad, who had defied Jehovah, live. More than that, he treated him like a friend and brother, had him come into his chariot, and made a covenant with him. In showing such clemency to the enemy of God, Ahab revealed the state of his soul. He had no heart for the Lord and was bound to follow his wicked ways.

Then one of the sons of the prophets (Josephus saith it was Micaiah; 22:8) was commanded by the Lord to ask another prophet to smite him. The prophet refused the unquestioning obedience demanded from a prophet and therefore the judgment of God overtook him. The purpose of God in bringing the judgment message home to Ahab is carried out nevertheless. Then Ahab pronounced his own doom for showing leniency to Ben-hadad.

CHAPTER 21

Naboth's Vineyard

1. Naboth's refusal (21:1-4)
2. Jezebel's wicked deed (21:5-16)
3. Elijah pronounces divine judgment (21:17-24)
4. Ahab's wickedness and confession (21:25-27)
5. The Lord's mercy (21:28-29)

No comment is needed on the story of Naboth's vineyard. Jezebel, the wicked, and Ahab's submission to her was his ruination. On her Satanic suggestion one of the most wicked deeds recorded in Bible history is done. Naboth is murdered to obtain his vineyard. The measure of Ahab's apostasy and wickedness is now filled to overflowing. For the wicked king the tidings of Naboth's death were welcome tidings. No inquiry follows, but in self-satisfaction he goes to take possession of the beautiful vineyard of Naboth. But his enjoyment, as it is always with the enjoyment of sin, did not last very long. No sooner had the innocent blood been spilt, than Jehovah, who saw and knew the foul deed, sent Elijah with the final message of doom and judgment for the guilty pair. Ahab was still in the vineyard. His eyes still feasted on the beautiful scene before him. His thoughts were occupied with the pleasures of sin when suddenly Elijah appeared. "I have found thee," were the prophet's first utterances. "Be sure your sin will find you out." Then follows the sentence already indicated in the words of the disguised prophet in the previous chapter. "I will make thine house like the house of Jeroboam the son of Nebat, and like the house of Baasha the son of Abijah, for the provocation wherewith thou hast provoked Me to anger, and made Israel to sin. And of Jezebel also spake the Lord, saying, The dogs shall eat Jezebel by the wall of Jezreel. Him that dieth of Ahab in the city the dogs shall eat; and him that dieth in the field shall the fowls of the air eat." How literally this sentence was carried out we shall find in the subsequent history. But Ahab having humbled himself hears a merciful message from Elijah's lips. "Because he humbled himself before Me, I will not bring evil in his days, but in his son's days will I bring evil upon his house." How merciful the Lord is to all who humble themselves!

CHAPTER 22

The Death of Ahab

1. Jehoshaphat and Ahab (22:1-12)
2. The prophet Micaiah (22:13-28)
3. The battle and Ahab's death (22:29-40)
4. Jehoshaphat of Judah (22:41-50; 2 Chron. 19—20)
5. Ahaziah, King of Israel (22:51-53)

Three years passed without war between Syria and Israel. In the third year Jehoshaphat of Judah came down to Ahab. Jehoshaphat's son and heir-apparent had married Athaliah the daughter of Ahab. An unholy alliance had therefore been formed between the royal families. Jehoshaphat, who knew better, was in this very unfaithful, and though the Lord did not forsake him chastisements came upon him and his house. The prophet Jehu, son of Hanani, met him after he came back from the battle of Ramoth-Gilead and said to him: "Shouldst thou help the ungodly, and love them that hate the Lord? Therefore is wrath upon thee from before the Lord" (2 Chron. 19:2). Ahab, under the predicted judgment of God, asked Jehoshaphat: "Wilt thou go with me to battle to Ramoth-Gilead?" And gladly the good King of Judah answers: "I am as thou art, my people as thy people, my horses as thy horses." And Ahab in all his wicked apostasy had prophets, four hundred of them. Jehoshaphat was, no doubt, troubled in his conscience, and demanded that Ahab inquire of the Lord. The prophets he had, used no longer the name of Baal, but the name of Jehovah. And they all prophesied success. Jehoshaphat, however, was suspicious and asked for a prophet of the Lord. From this we may gather that there was something about them by which the King of Judah knew that they were not Jehovah's prophets. Ahab then sent for Micaiah the son of Imlah. Both kings occupied thrones and were clad in their robes in the entrance of the gate of Samaria. All the false prophets prophesied and one Zedekiah made horns of iron to produce a vivid impression of the coming victory. Then Micaiah appeared. The faithful prophet tells the kings what he had seen. It is a revelation he had. Jehovah permitted a lying spirit to possess Ahab's false prophets and they were prophesying lies. And Micaiah predicted the defeat of Israel. The words of Micaiah are of much importance. What happened in Ahab's day, when the Lord permitted a lying spirit to deceive and lead the wicked into ruin, will happen again at the close of this present age. God will send a strong delusion that they should believe a lie (2 Thess. 2). Unclean spirits will then be on the earth, even as they begin already and by lying words, lying miracles and signs, lead the Christ-rejecting masses into judgment.

Then the battle. Ahab disguised himself and Jehoshaphat wore his robes. It was more than cowardice in Ahab; he feared the judgment which was hovering over him and tried to avert the coming fatal stroke. Jehoshaphat was almost miraculously saved, but Ahab was miraculously killed. A soldier drew a bow at venture. That arrow was guided by a higher hand. It found the disguised King of Israel. It found the small opening in the King's harness. A little while later the dogs were licking his blood as they washed his blood stained chariot. Thus the word of the Lord was fulfilled. Jehoshaphat's full record we shall consider in Chronicles and Azariah's in the beginning of the second book of the Kings.

THE SECOND BOOK OF THE

KINGS

The Division of the Second Book of the Kings

The second book of the Kings is a continuation of the history of the kingdoms of Israel and Judah up to the time of the captivities. As stated in the introduction to the book of Kings, both books were originally undivided. In the opening chapters Elijah the prophet is seen once more in his final ministrations, followed by his translation. Then Elisha comes upon the scene. In and through his ministry and miracles Jehovah manifested His power in behalf of His people. It was Jehovah's gracious appeal to Israel to return unto Him. The history of decline and apostasy in Israel and Judah follows after that. The house of Israel was first carried into captivity through Assyria. In the Kingdom of Judah a revival took place under Hezekiah, which was followed by a reaction under Manasseh and Amon. After Josiah's reform and death Judah's doom was sealed. The book ends with the record of the seige of Jerusalem and the captivity. Hosea and Amos exercised their prophetic offices in the northern Kingdom, while Isaiah, Jeremiah, Joel, Obadiah, Micah, Nahum, Habakkuk and Zephaniah were the prophets of Judah. Ezekiel prophesied among the captives, while Daniel was in Babylon. The division of this second part of the book of the Kings is therefore easily made.

I. ELIJAH'S FINAL MINISTRY AND TRANSLATION

1. **Elijah and Ahaziah** (1:1-18)
2. **Elijah's Translation** (2:1-11)

II. THE PROPHET ELISHA

1. **The Beginning of His Ministry** (2:12-25)
2. **Jehoram, Moab and Elisha** (3:1-27)
3. **The Miracles** (4:1-44)
4. **Naaman and His Healing** (5:1-27)
5. **Elisha and the Syrians** (6:1-33)
6. **Elisha's Prediction and its Fulfilment** (7:1-20)
7. **The Famine Predicted and Further Events** (8:1-29)
8. **The Anointing of Jehu** (9:1-10)

III. THE PERIOD OF DECLENSION AND APOSTASY

1. **Jehu, King of Israel and His deeds** (9:11-37)
2. **Jehu's Judgments, the Baal-worship Destroyed, and Jehu's Death** (10:1-36)
3. **Athaliah and Jehoida's Revival** (11:1-21)
4. **Jehoash, the Temple Repairs, and the Death of Jehoash** (12:1-21)
5. **Jehoahaz and Jehoash, the Death of Elisha** (13:1-25)
6. **Kings of Israel and Judah** (14—15)
7. **King Ahaz and Assyria** (16:1-20)
8. **Assyria Conquers Israel and the Captivity** (17:1-41)

IV. THE REIGN OF HEZEKIAH, MANASSEH AND AMON

1. **Hezekiah and Sennacherib's Invasion** (18:1-37)
2. **Hezekiah and Isaiah and the Deliverance** (19:1-37)
3. **Hezekiah's Illness, Recovery, Failure and Death** (20:1-21)
4. **Manasseh and Amon** (21:1-26)

V. THE REIGN OF JOSIAH

1. **The Revival** (22:1-20)
2. **The Results of the Revival and the Death of Josiah** (23:1-30)

VI. THE FINAL APOSTASY OF JUDAH AND THE CAPTIVITY

1. **Jehoahaz and Jehoiakim** (23:31-37)
2. **Jehoiachin and Zedekiah: The Beginning of Judah's Captivity** (24:1-20)
3. **The Seige of Jerusalem and Judah's Complete Overthrow** (25:1-30)

Analysis and Annotations

I. Elijah's Final Ministry and Translation

1. Elijah and Ahaziah

CHAPTER 1

1. Moab's rebellion (1:1)
2. The illness of Ahaziah (1:2)
3. Elijah's message (1:3-8)
4. Ahaziah's messengers and their fate (1:9-15)
5. Elijah before the king and Ahaziah's Death (1:16-17)
6. Jehoram becomes king (1:18)

The rebellion of Moab is here briefly mentioned. Both Omri and Ahab had oppressed Moab, and after Ahab's death this rebellion took place. The complete report is found in the third chapter. That ancient monument known by the name of the Moabite stone contains a most interesting record of this revolt and the oppression by Omri and his son Ahab. This record is as follows: "Omri (was) King of Israel, and he oppressed Moab many days, for Chemosh (Moab's idol-god) was angry with his land. His son (Ahab) followed him, and he also said, I will oppress Moab." (See Appendix for a complete translation of the record on this monument.) However, if it were not for the Bible no one would know that the inscription on the Moabite stone is truthful. The Bible proves the record genuine, and not the record the genuineness of the Biblical account. The Bible does not need such confirmation.

Ahaziah, the wicked son of a wicked father, had an accident and sent his messenger to inquire of Baal-zebub, the god of Ekron. Baal-zebub means "lord of flies." According to rabbinical tradition, he was worshipped in the form of a fly; and so addicted were the Jews to this cult that they carried a small image in their pockets, kissing it from time to time. Vile practices were also connected with its worship. What awful blasphemy the Pharisees uttered when they accused our Lord of using Beelzebub, the prince of demons! (Matt. 12:24. Beelzebub is given in the Greek as Beelzebul, which means "lord of idolatrous sacrificing.")

The messengers of Ahaziah never reached Ekron. The Lord had heard the charge to the king's messengers and He sent a messenger (angel means in Hebrew "a messenger") to Elijah the Tishbite. The angel of the Lord commanded the prophet to meet the men the king had sent forth to inquire of Baal-zebub and to announce the coming death of Ahaziah. The message is faithfully delivered; the messengers return to Ahaziah and he heard the words of Elijah from their lips. He knew at once who the mysterious person was who had turned back his messengers. The king sent therefore a captain with his fifty men to arrest the prophet. The captain addressed Elijah as a "Man of God" and commanded him in the name of the king to come down from the hill. But Elijah, fearless as he was, took up the word of the captain and appealed to his God to let fire come down from heaven. It was at once carried out and the captain with his fifty men were consumed by fire. The same fate overtook the second expedition, whose captain urged the prophet's obedience more than the first, for he said, "Come down quickly." The judicial character of Elijah's ministry is here once more in evidence. Critics have more than once condemned his action and called him "arrogant and merciless," while others deny the historicity of the event altogether. "Terrible as this answer was, we can perceive its suitableness, nay, its necessity, since it was to decide, and that publicly and by the way of judgment (and no other decision would have been suitable in a contest between man and God), whose was the power and the kingdom—and this at the great critical epoch of Israel's history" (*History of Israel*). Compare this fire judgment with Luke 9:54-56. When this present dipensation of grace is ended, judgment by fire will be meted out to the enemies of God (Rev. 11:5). During the great tribulation (Matt. 24:22) the fiery judgments will be on the earth (Rev. 8:5), preceding the visible manifestation of the Lord, who shall be revealed from heaven with His mighty angels in flaming fire taking vengeance on them that know not God, and that obey not the gospel of our Lord Jesus Christ (2 Thess. 1:7-8).

Elijah could consistently command fire to come down from heaven and consume those who dishonored and despised in him the prophet and servant of God. But when the disciples of Jesus, in a similar case (Luke 9:54-56) desired to imitate that example, the Lord restrained them, and said: "Ye know not what manner of spirit ye are of." Elijah here acted as the representative of the law, which showed no indulgence, but the disciples of Christ were the representatives of the gospel which proclaims the remission of sins. The old covenant necessarily alarmed and subdued the enemies of the kingdom of God by minatory language and punitive measures, while the new covenant designed to disarm and, if possible, to win them by forgiving love (J. H. Kurts).

A third company was sent out by Ahaziah. Mercy was shown to this captain and his fifty men, for the captain feared God and honored Elijah as His representative. His words breathe humility and his prayer showed that he owned the power of God. such mercy is also in store for those who humble themselves when the coming judgments are in the earth. Then Elijah appeared before Ahaziah in person and delivered the God-given message and the wicked King died according to the Word of the Lord.

2. Elijah's Translation

CHAPTER 2:1-11

1. From Gilgal to Jordan (2:1-6)
2. The divided Jordan (2:7-8)
3. Elisha's request (2:9-10)
4. Elijah goes up to heaven in a whirlwind (2:11)

The time for Elijah's departure had now come, and the Lord, whom he had served so faithfully, "would take up Elijah into heaven by a whirlwind." As Lord He graciously orders the time and the manner of the departure of His servants (John 21:18-22). His coming translation was known to him, to Elisha and to the sons of the prophets. The latter belonged to the schools of the prophets.

The "schools of the prophets," which were placed under the direction of experienced and approved prophets, afforded to younger men an opportunity of becoming qualified to perform the duties of the prophetic calling. The selection and the admission of individuals who were suited for the prophetic office by their personal character, and who had a divine call, undoubtedly depended on the prophetic judgment of those who presided over these institutions. As prophecy was a gift and not an art, the instructions which were imparted, probably referred merely to the study of the law, and were intended to awaken and cultivate theocratical sentiments, as well as promote a growth in spiritual life, for herein a suitable preparation for the prophetic office necessarily consisted. There are also indications found which authorize us to conclude that the revival of sacred poetry, as an art, and that theocratic-historical composition also, are to be ascribed to these religious communities as their source. Such schools existed in Ramah, Jericho, Beth-el, and Gilgal (1 Sam. 19:18; 2 Kings 2:3, 5; 4:38). Those who frequented them, had, usually, reached the age of manhood already, and in some cases, were married men. They lived together in a society or community, which often embraced a large number of members, and were occasionally employed as prophetic messengers by their teachers (2 Kings 9:1). However, the prophets were not invariably trained in these schools; several are named who were taken at once from civil life and invested with the prophetic office (*Sacred History*).

The goodness and power of God was now to be manifested in taking him into heaven without passing through death. The Jewish synagogue and the church have always believed the record of his departure, but it has been reserved to the destructive criticism to deny the translation of Elijah. The following statements are taken from Canon F. W. Farrar's exposition of the second book of Kings. "Knowing that he was on his way to death, Elijah felt the imperious instinct which leads the soul to seek solitude at the supreme crisis of life." "His death, like that of Moses, was surrounded by mystery and miracles, and we can say nothing further about it." How strange that a scholar and expositor can speak twice of the death of Elijah, when the record so clearly establishes the fact that he was taken up into heaven in a whirlwind and that he did not die at all!

He appeared with Moses when our Lord was transfigured. According to Peter's inspired comment the transfiguration scene foreshadows the power and coming of our Lord Jesus Christ (2 Peter 1:16-21). As He stood in glorious majesty upon that mountain so will He come to this earth once more and bring His saints with Him. Moses is the representative of those saints, who died and are raised from the dead; Elijah represents that company, who will be caught in clouds to meet the Lord in the air, departing from the earth without dying (1 Cor. 15:51-53; 1 Thess. 4:13-18).

Elisha clings close to Elijah. He had previously cast his mantle (the symbol of the prophetic office) upon Elisha, and he was then not quite ready to follow him fully. (See 1 Kings 19:19-20. Compare with Luke 9:62.) But now we see Elisha following Elijah from Gilgal to Bethel, from Bethel to Jericho, and from Jericho to Jordan. He proves himself worthy of the mantle, to exercise the holy office as the prophet of the Lord. He covets in answer to Elijah's request a double portion of the spirit which was upon Elijah to rest upon him. (According to the marginal reading, "the portion of the first born son," which was twice as much as that of the other sons. See Deut. 21:17.) Elijah's answer is conditional. If Elisha saw Elijah taken up into heaven, it should be so, and if not, then his request was not to be granted. And while they yet talked the chariot of fire, and horses of fire appeared and Elijah went up by a whirlwind into heaven. The chariot of fire with its horses of fire were the symbol of the presence of the Lord of Hosts (Psalm 104:3-4; Isa. 66:15; Hab. 3:8), but Elijah went up by the whirlwind. We know he was translated; he passed on without dying, but the details of it are not made known.

Elisha following Elijah, his request and the vision of glory, are suggestive about true service for God. Only as we follow the Lord wholly, as Elisha followed Elijah, and look to the coming glory, are we fit and fitted for service.

II. The Prophet Elisha

1. The Beginning of His Ministry

CHAPTER 2:12-25

1. The mantle used (2:12-14)
2. The sons of the prophets (2:15-18)
3. The healing of Jericho's waters (2:19-22)
4. Judgment upon the scoffers (2:23-25)

Both Elijah and Elisha are types of our Lord Jesus Christ. Their names indicate this. Elijah means "my God is Jehovah," and Elisha, "my God is salvation." Suffering, affliction and rejection are prominent in the life of Elijah, but it ended for him by being taken into heaven. It foreshadows the path of Him who was rejected by His own, cast out by the world and who has gone to heaven. In Elisha and his ministry, sovereign grace towards Israel in apostasy and ripening for judgment, is the predominant feature, foreshadowing Him who appeared in the midst of His people, ministering grace and truth (John 1:14, 18). (Another typical application is to look upon Elisha's ministry as typifying what will be bestowed upon Israel and upon the Gentiles with the return of our Lord Jesus Christ.)

Elisha had seen Elijah's departure into heaven, and when he saw him no more "he took hold of his own clothes, and rent them in two pieces." He thus expressed his grief, but at the same time he took Elijah's mantle (symbolical of the prophetic ministry, which had fallen upon him) and used it at once. He smites with it the waters of Jordan and the Lord God of Elijah answers faith by parting the river. It was the first miracle of his administration. "So shall the waters of difficulty, nay, the cold flood of death itself, part, if we smite in faith with the heaven given garment; so shall the promise of God ever stand sure, and God be true to His Word; and so may we go forward undauntedly, though humbly and prayerfully, to whatever work He gives us to do" (A. Edersheim).

The sons of the prophets then acknowledged Elisha. They are seen ever after in close fellowship with the prophet; they belonged to the faithful remnant in Israel. However, not having witnessed Elijah's translation they were unbelieving and thought that the Spirit might have transported the prophet (1 Kings 18:12; Ezek. 3:14; 8:3). They were not obedient to Elisha's command and urged him to send, till he was ashamed and yielded to their request. After a three days' unsuccessful search they returned and now they had to be ashamed, when their master told them, "Did I not say unto you, Go not?" They were like the disciples of our Lord "slow to believe."

The second miracle is one of mercy, followed by a miracle of judgment. The healing of Jericho's waters is a miracle of much significance. Jericho is a type of the world under the curse (Joshua 6). The water was naught and the ground barren. A new cruse with salt is brought. The salt is put into the waters and the prophet said: "Thus saith the Lord, I have healed these waters; there shall not be from thence any more death or barren land." When He, who is greater than Elisha, comes back to this earth again, now under the curse and death reigning upon it, the curse will be removed; there will be healing as it was for Jericho. The other miracles of grace and mercy teach the same lesson.

The third miracle is one of judgment. Judgment well deserved fell upon those who despised the chosen messenger of God. The mockers were not "little children," but young men. They were of Bethel, and no doubt associated with the wicked worship established there (1 Kings 7:25-33). They were infidels and scoffers. They mocked the translation of Elijah and taunted Elisha. The curse of the Lord fell upon them. Forty-two of their number were torn by she-bears. The punishment has been declared by critics "disproportionate to the offence." It certainly is not when the offence is considered as an insult to the man of God, who had gone to heaven and to the prophet who had taken his place; besides, these young men had scoffed at the power of God. And we must not overlook the fact that present day mockers and rejecters of the ministry of the gospel and grace of God will also receive their punishment in due time (2 Peter 3:3-7).

2. Jehoram, Moab, and Elisha

CHAPTER 3

1. Jehoram, King of Israel (3:1-3)
2. Moab's rebellion (3:4-9)
3. Elisha's message and prediction (3:10-20)
4. The defeat of Moab (3:21-27)

In chapter 1:17 we read, "And Jehoram reigned in his stead (Ahaziah) in the second year of Jehoram, the son of Jehoshaphat, King of Judah." (He was associated with his father in the government of the kingdom. See 2 Kings 8:27; 2 Chronicles 21:6.) There was, therefore, a Jehoram, king over Judah, as well as a king of Israel by the same name. They are also known by the name Joram. Joram and Jehoram are used interchangeably. In 2 Kings 1:17 and 2 Chron. 22:6 both kings are called Jehoram; in 2 Kings 9:15, 17, the King of Israel is called Joram; in 2 Kings 8:21, etc., the King of Judah is called Joram; comparing 2 Kings 8:16 and verse 29 we find these two names inverted. We mention this to clear up a possible difficulty some may find here. Jehoram was another son of Ahab, the brother of Ahaziah. A partial reformation was attempted by him, but he continued in the sins of Jeroboam, the son of Nebat (1 Kings 12:25-33).

The full record of Moab's rebellion is now given. Jehoram formed an alliance with Jehoshaphat, the King of Judah and the King of Edom. Jehoshaphat had been in league with Ahab (1 Kings 22) and now we see him in a similar alliance with Ahab's second son. It was an alliance displeasing to the Lord and Jehoshaphat was troubled in his conscience about it. The same question he had put to Ahab, he now puts to Ahab's son, "Is there not here a prophet of the Lord, that we may inquire of the Lord by him?" (1 Kings 22:7). Jehoshaphat knew the Lord, but was in evil company. When the three kings met in Elisha's tent, the prophet manifests the boldness of Elijah in rebuking the wicked King of Israel. But he honors the King of Judah. "As the Lord of hosts liveth, before whom I stand,surely, were it not that I regard the presence of Jehoshaphat the King of Judah, I would not look toward thee, nor see thee." But there was also a rebuke for the good King of Judah. The Spirit of God was grieved and Elisha had not the power of prophecy. He needed a minstrel first to calm his own agitated spirit and get into the condition of soul to utter the needed message. How it should have humbled the king, who served Jehovah, that after calling for a prophet of the Lord, the divine mouthpiece was unable to prophesy at once! Unholy alliances hindered the manifestation of the Spirit of God. Such is the case almost everywhere in our days of departure from the truth of God.

Then the ditches which had been made in obedience to the command given through Elijah were miraculously filled with water. On the next morning the Moabites saw the water and imagined that it was blood, on account of the reflection from the rising sun. "And they said, This is blood; the kings are surely slain, and they have smitten one another, now therefore Moab to the spoil." The onrushing Moabites were met by the Israelites and Elisha's prediction was fulfilled in the defeat of the Moabites and the devastation of their own land. It was the supernatural gift of water "when the meal-offering was offered" which led to the defeat of the enemy and the victory for Israel. And God has supplied the water of life through Him who is the true meal offering.

Kir-hareseth alone was left intact, all other cities were razed, all wells stopped up and every good tree cut down. (Kir-hareseth is repeatedly mentioned as the stronghold of Moab. See Isaiah 16:7.) On the devastation of Moab remarks a commentator, that the spirit of the times must be considered and that the half barbaric nations of that time all did this. But could the devastation of Moab hundreds of years before Christ have been any worse than the devastation of Belgium, Poland and Galicia in the twentieth century after Christ?

Then in despair the King of Moab did the horrible thing of sacrificing his eldest son, the one to reign after him. He offered him upon the wall, in plain sight of Israel, as a burnt offering, to conciliate his god Chemosh, who is mentioned on the Moabite stone. (See Appendix.)

3. The Miracles

CHAPTER 4

1. The widow's oil multiplied (4:1-7)
2. The Shunammite and her reward (4:8-17)
3. The son of the Shunammite raised from the dead (4:18-37)
4. The deadly pottage healed (4:38-41)
5. The multitude fed (4:42-44)

In the previous chapter Elisha appeared as the saviour of Israel, and now he acts in behalf of the widow of one of the sons of the prophets. His name is not given. Elisha had known him as one who feared the Lord. And now the widow deeply in dept, about to lose her two sons, appealed to the prophet. In answer to Elisha's question what she had in her house she told him that her whole possession consisted in a pot of oil (in Hebrew, anointing oil). She then was told to borrow empty vessels, not a few. Behind closed doors she was to pour out. All the borrowed vessels were soon filled and when the empty vessels were all filled and no other to be filled, the oil stayed. The oil was to be sold to satisfy the creditor and the rest to be used to sustain the widow and her sons. The Lord is the father of the widows and heareth their cry; this is beautifully illustrated in this miracle. Then there is the lesson for faith. The vessels had to be produced to be filled; if there had been more vessels the oil would have filled them all. The limitation was not in the supply of oil, but in the empty vessels to receive the oil. There is an abundance of grace and in faith we can always come with our empty vessels to receive out of His fulness grace upon grace.

Then the great woman of Shunem is introduced for the first time. She belonged to the godly in Israel and did not know the prophet, but it did not take her long to discover that he was a holy man of God. It is a blessed picture to see this man of God walking through the land, possessing nothing and acting in grace in the midst of Israel's ruin. In the words of another, "Poor indeed, while making many rich; seeming to possess all things, yet really having nothing. Receiving bounty and care in the ordinary need of life from those in whose behalf he, at the same time, is opening resources which were altogether beyond man. And, besides, he walks alone in the world, and yet all wait on him.

"All this gives us a strong expression of the ways of One who could call Himself Master and Lord, receiving the homage of faith, even while He had not where to lay His head. In all this our prophet is marking out for us, as in a reflection, the path of the Lord Jesus in one of its most striking, remarkable characters" (J. Bellett).

The pious Shunammite prepared for the lonely pilgrim a little chamber with its simple furnishings in her own house. And the man of God appreciated the kindness shown to him, and, learning that she had no son, Elisha told her "about this season, according to the time of life, thou shalt embrace a son." Like Sarah she believed and received her son. And when the child died, what faith the Shunammite exhibited! The son of promise was dead, yet in the midst of her great sorrow she could say, "It is well." Like Abraham, when he put the son of promise upon the altar, the Shunammite counted on resurrection and believed on Him who can raise the dead. She had lost her son for a while, but not her faith.

And how her faith clings to Elisha! Not Gehazi with the staff can help, but Elisha is needed. And her faith is rewarded. Her child is raised from the dead. The Holy Spirit mentions her in the New Testament. "Women received their dead raised to life again" (Heb. 11:35).

We see in her a true and faithful Israelitish woman, who, in a time of general apostasy, owned Jehovah alike in her life and her home. Receiving a prophet, because of Him who had sent him, because he was a holy man of God—and with humility and entire self-forgetfulness—she received a prophet's reward in the gift most precious to a Jewish mother, which she had not dared to hope for, even when announced to her. Then, when severely tried, she still held fast to her trust in the promise—strong even when weakest—once more self-forgetful, and following deepest spiritual impulse. And, in the end, her faith appears victorious—crowned by Divine mercy, and shining out the more brightly from its contrast to the felt weakness of the prophet. As we think of this, it seems as if a fuller light were shed on the history of the trials of an Abraham, an Isaac, or a Jacob; on the inner life of those heroes of faith to whom the Epistle of the Hebrews points us for example and learning (Heb. 11), and on such Scripture sayings as these: "Jehovah killeth, and maketh alive: He bringeth down to the grave, and bringeth up" (1 Sam. 2:6); "Know that Jehovah hath set apart him that is godly for Himself: Jehovah will hear when I call unto Him" (Psalm 4:3); or this: "All the paths of Jehovah are mercy and truth unto such as keep His covenant and His testimonies" (Psalm 25:10). (*Bible History*).

And here we must also think of Him, whom Elisha but faintly foreshadows. He raises the spiritually dead now, all who hear His voice, as He will raise the physically dead in the future.

In Gilgal the eighth miracle of Elisha took place. The humble pottage which was being prepared for the sons of the prophets had been spoiled by the addition of a wild and poisonous gourd. Then Elisha cast meal into the pot and the pottage became eatable—"there was no harm in the pot." The meal is typical of our Lord, who was cast into the scene of death and through His death hath brought healing.

The miraculous feeding of the multitude was Elisha's ninth miracle; prefigures the miracles of our Lord (Matt. 14:19-21, etc.).

4. Naaman and His Healing

CHAPTER 5

1. Naaman, the leper (5:1)
2. The testimony of the maid of Israel (5:2-4)
3. The message to the king of Israel (5:5-8)
4. Naaman and Elisha (5:9-19)
5. Gehazi; His sin and punishment (5:20-27)

The story of this chapter is peculiarly rich in its spiritual and dispensational meaning. Naaman, captain of Ben-hadad, the King of Syria, was a Gentile. He was no common man. In all his greatness and might, with all the honors heaped upon him and wealth at his command, he was an unhappy and doomed man, for he was a leper. Leprosy is a type of sin. Here, then, is a picture of the natural man, enjoying the highest and the best—but withal a leper. And then the little captive, taken from Israel's land, away from her home and family—what a contrast with the great Naaman! In her captivity she was happy, for she knew the Lord and knew that the prophet in Samaria, the great representative of Jehovah, could heal leprosy. She knew and she believed. The grace which filled the heart gave her also a desire to see the mighty Naaman healed; the same grace gave her power to bear witness.

And how the Lord used the simple testimony! The King of Syria heard of it and addressed a letter to the King of Israel demanding that he should recover Naaman from his leprosy. And Naaman departed with "ten talents of silver and six thousand pieces of gold besides ten changes of raiment." And the King of Israel, Jehoram, no doubt, was filled with fear, for he thought the King of Syria was seeking a pretext to quarrel with him. While he readily acknowledged that God alone has the power to heal, he did not look to the Lord nor did he think of the mighty prophet, whose very name declared that God is salvation. In helpless and hopeless terror, in the despair of unbelief he rent his clothes.

It was then that the man of God spoke reproving the King, asking that Naaman come to him. Then Naaman, with his horses and chariot, laden with the treasures, stood at the door of the house of Elisha. The prophet through a messenger told the leper, "Go and wash in Jordan seven times, and thy flesh shall come again to thee, and thou shalt be clean." Well may we think here of our Lord Jesus, who cleansed the leper, and in doing so manifested Himself as Jehovah. But how He shines above all!

> When the leper comes to Him, it is not as with the king, "Am I God, that I should heal a man of his leprosy?" nor is it as with the prophet, "Go wash in Jordan, and be clean." No; but He reveals Himself at once in the place and power of God. 'I will, be thou clean.' Elisha was but a preacher of Jesus to Naaman; the Lord Jesus was the lepers' cleansing, the healing God. Elisha did not venture to touch the leper. This would have defiled him. But our Lord 'put forth His hand and touched him;' for He, with the rights of the God of Israel, was above the leper, and could consume and not contract the defilement (J. G. Bellett).

And Naaman's wrath and indignation were stirred by Elisha's command. The great and mighty captain with his treasures expected a different reception from the prophet. He expected him at least to do what heathen priests with their enchantments did, to call on the name of the Lord his God and strike his hand over the place of leprosy. He rejects the remedy which grace had provided because it humbled him into dust and stripped him of all his pride. It is just this the sinner needs. Naaman had to learn that he was nothing but a poor, lost leper. All his silver and gold could not purchase cleansing for him. He needed humiliation and the obedience of faith. And so he learned as his servants reasoned with him, and instead of returning in a rage to Damascus as the helpless leper, he obeyed the given command and dipped himself seven times in Jordan—"and his flesh came again like unto the flesh of a little child, and he was clean." Jordan is the type of death, as we saw in the study of Joshua. Our Lord was baptized by John in that river, for He had come to take the sinners' place in death. Naaman bathing in Jordan typifies death and resurrection in which there is cleansing and healing for the spiritual leper, but it is the death and resurrection of our blessed Lord. As we believe on Him who died for our sins according to Scripture, and was raised for our justification, we are born again and made clean. It is the one way of salvation, the only way, revealed in every portion of God's holy Word. "Saved by grace through faith (in Him who died for our sins), it is the gift of God, not of works, lest any man should boast."

And the blessed results of true salvation are seen at once in Naaman the Syrian. He is fully restored and healed. He stands now before the man of God, no longer the proud, self-trusting Naaman, but an humble believer. He confesses the Lord with his lips. He offers also a gift to Elisha. ("A blessing" means a gift.) He could not give anything to effect his cleansing, but after the healing he offered willingly. But Elisha refused the reward offered to him. He had freely received and freely he gave (Matt. 10:8). Then he requested "two mules' burden of earth." This was to be used to build an altar unto Jehovah in Syria. It was an outward expression of his faith and would be a testimony among the heathen that there is but one Lord to be worshipped. And there was the tender conscience (verse 18). Finally he departed in peace. "Go in peace"; the same words our blessed Lord used repeatedly. And Gehazi's covetousness earned him the leprosy from which grace had delivered the Syrian Gentile. The story is full of solemn lessons.

Dispensationally Naaman stands for the Gentiles. Through Him who is greater than Elisha salvation has been extended to the Gentiles, while Gehazi, who was closely connected with Elisha, but who had hardened his heart, is a type of Israel.

5. Elisha and the Syrians

CHAPTER 6

1. The lost axe-head recovered (6:1-7)
2. Elisha makes known Ben-hadad's plans (6:8-12)
3. Elisha's arrest planned (6:13-17)
4. The blinded Syrians led to Samaria (6:18-23)
5. Samaria beseiged (6:24-30)
6. The king's wrath against Elisha (96:31-33)

It has been truly said that the miracle of the swimming axe-head reveals the condescension of divine power and the grace of benevolence. We see the great man of God in fellowship with the sons of the prophets. He goes with them and when they are in distress the power of God is manifested through him. Rationalistic critics have always ridiculed the miracle of the swimming iron. "The story is perhaps an imaginative reproduction of some unwonted incident," saith Farrar, the higher critic. Then he adds, "all the eternal laws of nature are here superseded at a word, as though it were an every day matter, without even any recorded invocation of Jehovah, to restore an axe-head, which could obviously have been recovered or resupplied in some less stupendous way than by making iron swim on the surface of a swift-flowing river" *(Expositor's Bible)*. And Ewald, the German critic, explains, "he threw on to the spot where it had sunk a piece of wood cut to fit it, which caught it up"! These men all aim at the denial of miracles of any kind. They delight in making an omnipotent God, in whom they profess to believe, a helpless slave to the laws of nature, a God who has neither power nor inclination to set aside these laws in behalf of His trusting people. We say it again, the rationalistic critic is an unbeliever of the worst type.

There is much comfort for God's trusting children in the miracle of the swimming iron. The mighty power of God condescends to help those who trust even in the smallest things of life. Our Lord fills the throne in glory and is the upholder of all things, yet as the sympathizing priest, He enters into the lives of His people. His power answers faith, if we but learn to bring our little troubles to Him as the man came in distress to Elisha.

When war broke out between Ben-hadad and the King of Israel, Elisha made known the secret counsels of the King of Syria. The man of God, walking in constant fellowship with Jehovah, received this supernatural information, and thereby an additional evidence was given to apostate Israel that the Lord is for His people and a very present help in time of trouble. Then one of Ben-hadad's servants suggested that it was Elisha's work, and the king in his blindness sent a great host to capture Elisha. (Certainly not Naaman as some have surmised. Yet the knowledge that Elisha had been the instrument of healing the Syrian captain moved some unknown servant of Ben-hadad to suggest that Elisha was responsible for the revelation of the king's plans.) What Ahaziah attempted with Elijah (chapter 1), Ben-hadad now undertakes with Elisha. But Elisha, who acts in grace, does not call down fire from heaven to devour the men who compassed Dothan. Elisha's servant (not Gehazi) is terror stricken when he beheld the beseiging host. Elisha knows no fear, for he knows "they that are with us are more than they that be with them." He had seen the chariots of Israel and the horsemen thereof before (2:12). He knew that the Lord's hosts compassed him about. He did not need to pray for himself, that he might see, for he saw, because he believed. He prayed for his servant that his eyes might be opened. Then the servant saw, "and behold, the mountain was full of horses and chariots round about Elisha." Angelic ministry and protection may be termed one of the lost comforts which God's people have. They are still "ministering spirits to minister unto the heirs of salvation."

"I doubt not, a host or constellation of angels, those heavenly creatures, which, excelling in strength, stand in the presence of God, or go forth to minister on account of those who are heirs of salvation. For of them we read that 'God maketh His angels spirits (winds) and His ministers a flame of fire'; and again, 'The chariots of God are twenty thousand, even thousands of angels.' At the divine behest, they get ready to serve in whatever the exigency of the saint, or the occasion under the throne of God, may require. They formed a travelling chariot to convey Elijah to heaven, and to carry Lazarus to Abraham's bosom. They now form chariots of war, when Elisha is beleaguered by the hostile bands of Syria. Either singly or in company they visit the elect on earth, and either alone or in concert celebrate the joy of heaven in the audience of the earth. They have drawn the sword to smite a guilty city, or with the strong hand of love dragged the too reluctant one forth from the doomed city. They are either as winds or as fire. They are messengers of mercy, and executors of judgment, as 'the Lord' who 'is among them' may command. They attended on Mount Sinai when the law was published, and they hovered over the fields of Bethlehem when Jesus was born. And here, in their order and strength, they are as a wall of fire, a wall of salvation, round about the prophet.

> Very blessed all this is. And still more blessed to know, that ere long, the hidden glories, which are now only known to such faith as Elisha's, will become the manifested things; and the threatenings of the enemy, the noise and the din and clang of arms, which are the present apparent things, full of fears and sorrows for the heart, shall have rolled by, like the past thunder-storm, but to leave the sunshine the brighter (*Meditations on Elisha*).

Elisha then prayed that the beseiging host should be smitten with blindness. The prayer was at once answered. He led on the Syrian forces into Samaria. But was it not deception when the man of God said to the blinded enemies, "I will bring you to the man whom ye seek," leading them into Samaria? It was not. Samaria was the home of the prophet and he was then on his way there. His object was to demonstrate to the Syrians, as well as to the King of Israel, that Jehovah is the God and all-sufficient helper of His people. What mercy he then showed to his captives. Jehoram would have smitten them, but Elisha fed them and had them sent away in peace. In this he is a type of Him who taught, "Ye have heard that it hath been said, Thou shalt love thy neighbor, and hate thine enemy. But I say unto you, Love your enemies, bless them that curse you, do good to them that hate you, and pray for them which despitefully use you and persecute you" (Matt. 5:43-44).

Some time after Ben-hadad besieged Samaria and a great famine followed, and there was such a distress that women ate their own offspring. It was but a fulfilment of the threatened judgments upon an apostate people (Levit. 26:29; Deut. 28:53). The same horror occured during the siege of Jerusalem by Nebuchadnezzar (Lam. 4:10) and also, according to Josephus, during the seige by Titus 70 A.D. The wicked nature of the king asserted itself in blaming Elisha for the misfortune which had fallen upon his kingdom. He seeks to slay the man of God. After all the mighty miracles God had wrought by the hands of Elisha, the representative of Israel, wants to kill the prophet. This also foreshadows our Lord, when they sought to kill Him after His gracious ministry. But Elisha knew the murderous purpose of the king ere the messengers came. He called the king by the right name "this son of a murderer," for such Ahab was. And when the king appeared in person he said, "Behold this evil is of the Lord, what should I wait for the Lord any longer?" He realizes the impending judgment on account of Israel's sin.

6. Elisha's Prediction and Its Fulfilment

CHAPTER 7

1. Elisha's prediction (7:1)
2. The unbelieving lord (7:2)
3. The four lepers and their discovery (7:3-8)
4. The day of good tidings (7:9-15)
5. The prediction fulfilled (7:16-18)
6. The death of the unbelieving lord (7:19-20)

When the worst had come, Samaria starving to death, the king in despondency, Elisha's life threatened, then the mercy and kindness of God is revealed once more. The prophet announces the good news of salvation and deliverance. All is typical of the gospel of grace. The unbelieving lord who rejected the good news and refused to believe it represents those who reject the gospel. All in this chapter is intensely interesting and suggestive.

The great victory was accomplished by the Lord alone. His chariots had frightened the Syrian camp and put them to flight. The bread and the water, the silver and gold and raiment, all was His provision for a starving, dying people, and the four lepers in despair, facing certain death, were the first to discover God's victory for them and the people. Their great need led them to find the needed salvation. Well may all this be applied to our Lord's work for us and to the provision of the gospel. He alone worked out the great salvation and provided all, that sinners dying and lost (represented by the lepers) may come to eat and drink, without money and without price. It was a day of good tidings. Such is the still lasting day of salvation, the day of grace. The lepers who had their fill first and had tasted God's great salvation, could not hold their peace. Through them the whole city hears of the provision made. And the people went out to see how wonderfully the prediction of Elisha had been accomplished. All enjoyed it. But the unbelieving lord perished, a warning that he that believeth not must die in his sins. The repetition at the close of this chapter of the words of the unbeliever recorded in the beginning of this story, is of solemn meaning. God is true to His Word, the Word which promises life to all who believe and which threatens eternal punishment to all who believe not. "He that believeth on the Son hath everlasting life, and he that believeth not the Son shall not see life, but the wrath of God abideth on him."

7. The Famine Predicted and Further Events

CHAPTER 8

1. The famine predicted (8:1-2)
2. The Shunammite's land restored (8:3-6)
3. Elisha with Ben-hadad and Hazael (8:7-15)
4. Jehoram King of Judah (8:16-19; 2 Chronicles 21:5)
5. The Revolt of Edom (8:20-21; 2 Chronicles 21:8-10)
6. The Revolt of Libnah (8:22-23; 2 Chronicles 21:10)
7. Death of Jehoram (8:24; 2 Chronicles 21:19-20)
8. Ahaziah and Jehoram (8:25-29; 2 Chronicles 22)

The threatened judgment upon the house of Ahab is now rapidly approaching. Elisha, knowing the secrets of the Lord, predicts the seven years famine. "Surely the Lord God will do nothing, but He revealeth His secrets unto His servants the prophets" (Amos 3:7). The Shunammite, that godly woman, is here introduced once more. As her husband is not mentioned she may have been a widow. Elisha warns her of the coming famine, and she heeded the warning and sojourned for seven years in the land of the Philistines. After her return all was restored unto her by the King. The introduction here of Gehazi, the servant of Elisha, has drawn the fire of the critics. "As it is unlikely that the king would converse long with a leper, and as Gehazi is still called 'the servant of the man of God,' the incident may here be narrated out of order" (*Expositor's Bible*). But not so. It is fully in order. Gehazi was known as the servant of Elisha and is mentioned by his former position so that all doubt about his personality might be removed. That the deposed servant was with the apostate king is of much interest and has its lessons.

"It seems to me that Gehazi stands here in a grievous position. Smitten by the hand of God, because his heart clung to earth, even in the presence of Jehovah's mighty and long-suffering testimony, he is now a parasite in the king's court, relating the wonderful things in which he no longer took part. This poor world grows weary enough of itself to lead it to take some pleasure in hearing anything spoken of that has reality and power. Provided that it does not reach the conscience, they will listen to it for their amusement, taking credit to themselves perhaps for an enlarged and a liberal mind, which is not enslaved by that which can yet recognize philosophically in its place. But that is a sad position, which makes it evident that formerly we were connected with a testimony, whilst now we only relate its marvels at court. Nevertheless God makes use of it; and it does not follow that there was no truth in Gehazi. But to rise in the world, and entertain the world with the mighty works of God, is to fall very deep" (*Synopsis of the Bible*).

Elisha after this went outside of Israel's land to Damascus. Guided by the Lord, whom he served so faithfully, he paid a visit to the sick King of Syria. By referring to 1 Kings 19:15 we find that the commission to anoint Hazael, King over Syria, had been given to Elijah. There is no record from which we learn that Elijah had done so. And now Elisha meets Hazael, who came to him as the messenger of the sick King Ben-hadad, bringing costly presents. And the king asked the question, "Shall I recover of this disease?" The prophet's answer was brief. The sickness itself was not fatal, he would certainly recover and yet the Lord had shown to him that the king should surely die. This meant while the sickness in itself would not result in Ben-hadad's death, he should nevertheless die by other means.

Then Elisha's countenance fell and the man of God wept. Then Elisha told Hazael he wept on account of the horrible atrocities which he would commit against the children of Israel.

The fulfillment of Elisha's prediction is found in chapters 10:32, 12:17, 13:3. Weeping Elisha foreshadows our Lord weeping over Jerusalem when He saw what was to come upon the city He loved so well. And Hazael, with a mock humility, expressed surprise. But the prophet revealed the innermost thoughts of his wicked heart by telling him he would be king over Syria; this was his aim. And so he returned to Ben-hadad, bringing a mutilated message and murdered the king immediately after.

The record of the kings of Judah and Israel is now briefly given. All is fast ripening for the long threatened judgment. After the death of Jehoshaphat, his son Jehoram became sole ruler over Judah. He walked in the evil ways of the kings of Israel and the record tells the reason, "for the daughter of Ahab was his wife." After him came his son Ahaziah. Again wicked Athaliah, his mother, is mentioned. (The marginal reading "grand-daughter" is correct. She was Ahab's daughter and Omri's grand-daughter.) His connection with Ahab is made prominent. He did evil also in the sight of the Lord and made an alliance with the son of Ahab, Joram (or Jehoram), who was still king in Israel. Joram was wounded by the Syrians and Ahaziah, King of Judah, visited him in Jezreel. Alas! the unholy alliance of Jehoshaphat, King of Judah, with the wicked murderer, Ahab, King of Israel (1 Kings 22) had resulted in the marriage of his son with Athaliah, the wicked daughter of a wicked father. And Jehoram, Jehoshaphat's son, was dragged down by her and she became the ruination of her son Ahaziah. A dreadful harvest!

8. The Anointing of Jehu

CHAPTER 9:1-10

1. The commission (9:1-3)
2. Jehu anointed (9:4-10)

The hour of judgment for the house of Ahab has come. The instrument for it, mentioned long ago to Elijah (1 Kings 19:16-17), appears now upon the scene. The army of Joram, King of Israel, beseiged Ramoth-gilead and Jehu was the captain of the forces. Joram was recovering from his wounds in Jezreel. Then Elisha called one of the sons of the prophets. Handing him a box of oil he sent him to Ramoth-gilead. He was to look out for Jehu, the son of Jehoshaphat, the son of Nimshi, and anoint him King over Israel. Then he was not to tarry, but to flee. (Jehu means "Jehovah is He"; Jehoshaphat, "Jehovah judges"; Nimshi, "Jehovah reveals." Significant names!)

The messenger carried out the commission and at the same time states the judgment work into which God had called him. He was to execute judgment on the house of Ahab, to avenge the blood of the prophets and the Lord's servants at the hand of Jezebel. The whole house of Ahab was to perish like Jeroboam (1 Kings 14:10) and that of Baasha (1 Kings 16:3). "And the dogs shall eat Jezebel in the portion of Jezreel, and there shall be none to bury her." More than fifteen years had passed since Jehovah through Elijah had announced the doom of the house of Ahab and the doom of Jezebel. And now the hour of execution had come. God will judge in the end, though He is never in haste to execute His threatened judgments. The day is surely coming when the Lord will judge this world, when especially Jezebel (Rev. 2:20), Babylon the Great, the mother of harlots and abominations of the earth, drunken with the blood of the saints, the Romish apostate "church," will receive her judgment. "And in her was found the blood of the prophets, and of saints, and of all that were slain on the earth" (Rev. 17:5-6, 18:24).

III. The Period of Declension and Apostasy

1. Jehu, King of Israel and His Deeds

CHAPTER 9

1. Jehu is king (9:11-13)
2. Jehoram, King of Israel slain (9:14-26)
3. Ahaziah slain (2 Chronicles 22:9)
4. Jezebel and her end (9:30-37)

Jehu revealed the secret anointing as King over Israel, and under the blare of the trumpets the army hails him as King. "Jehu is King!" Oh! for that day when our Lord Jesus will be hailed as King to begin His righteous judgment over the earth.

The Assyrian monuments bear interesting testimony to a good deal of the history contained in 2 Kings. Our space forbids a fuller mention of this. The name of Jehu has a place in the obelisk of black marble which Layard discovered at Nimrood. The Assyrian form of his name is "Yahua." Shalmaneser II (860-825 B.C.) erected this obelisk and inscribed on it the annals of his reign in 190 lines in cuneiform characters. Five rows of bas-relief illustrate the annals. The second row pictures the bearers of the tribute of Jehu to the Assyrian King. The obelisk is in the British Museum.

He begins at once his awful judgment-work. He is just an instrument used by a holy and righteous God to execute His vengeance. Of real communion with the Lord he knew nothing. Nothing of the fear of the Lord or exercise of soul towards Him is recorded, nor do we read that he ever worshipped or called upon the name of the Lord. There was zeal and obedience in the execution of the judgments of the Lord.

"But how awful in its character! On what a fearful journey does it send this sword of the Lord! From Ramoth to the vineyard of Naboth, from thence to the going up to Gur, from thence to Jezreel, from thence to the shearinghouse, and from thence to Samaria, and all the road marked by blood!—blood, too, appointed in righteousness to be shed! For though the sword that shed it cared not for righteousness, yet in its action the Lord was pleading with the flesh of Ahab and his house—as, by and by, He will have a greater pleading, even with all flesh, and the slain of the Lord shall be many. And what shall be the rapidity and the stretch of the divine judgment then! What will be the journey of the sword of the Lord, or the 'grounded staff' in that day, when 'as the lightning cometh out of the east and shineth even unto the west, so shall also the coming of the Son of Man be!"

The record itself of how Joram and Ahaziah fell under the judgment executed by Jehu needs but little comment. Jehoram sent messengers from Jezreel, which Jehu detained, while he drove on furiously. Then Joram, with his nephew Ahaziah, King of Judah, went to meet Jehu. When they met, the arrow of Jehu pierced Joram's heart and his body was cast into the field of Naboth, the Jezreelite, "according to the word of the Lord." Ahaziah fled, but was smitten "at the going up of Gur." He tried to reach Megiddo and there he died.

Then comes Jezebeel, the wicked. She died as she had lived, in wickedness and pride. She knew she had to die. The evil tidings had reached Jezreel, where once in younger days she was queen and mistress. She painted her face to make herself look beautiful. Did she attempt to attract Jehu? Hardly that, for she was an old woman, having a grandson twenty-two years old (2 Kings 8:26). It was a proud defiance—she would meet death like a queen. The miserable, doomed woman, the dunghill of all vileness (Jezebel means "dunghill"), the instigator of crimes, looked out of the window, while Jehu's chariot came thundering on. Then she spoke, "Is it peace—Zimri! murderer of his master?" It was a bold taunt. Zimri had murdered his master, but reigned only seven days (1 Kings 16:9-19). She reminds him of Zimri's deed and Zimri's fate. Eunuchs threw her out of the window. The blood bespattered the wall and the prancing horses. The chariot of Jehu rushed on over her body. He did not pay any attention to her mangled body. Jehu entered the royal palace to feast and afterwards gave command to bury the cursed woman. But little was left of her. And Jehu said, "This is the word of the Lord, which He spake by His servant Elijah the Tishbite, saying, In the portion of Jezreel shall dogs eat the flesh of Jezebel." God's judgments are often slow, but they are sure.

2. Jehu's Judgments, Baal-worship Destroyed, and His Death

CHAPTER 10

1. The judgment upon the house of Ahab (10:1-11)
2. The relations of Ahaziah slain (10:12-14; 2 Chron. 22:8)
3. Jehonadab spared (10:15-17)
4. The Baal worship destroyed (10:18-28)
5. Jehu's record (10:29-31)
6. Israel cut short (10:32-33)
7. Jehu's death (10:34-36)

And now Jehu, the instrument, chosen for judgment, continued his judgment work without showing mercy. The long threatened national judgment upon Israel had begun.

The hint which Jezebel had given him concerning Zimri and the possibility of a rebellion may have influenced Jehu to put away the descendants of Ahab. There were seventy sons, which, according to Hebrew phraseology, means his grandsons and their offspring. He concocts a clever scheme by which the elders of Samaria and the guardians of the grandsons of Ahab were forced to kill the seventy. This was done probably to head off a rebellion against him. Then, according to the custom of those days, the ghastly evidence of the deed was piled in two heaps at the entering in of the gate. Then he addressed the people, showing that while he had slain his master, they were also guilty in slaying these seventy persons, and finally he added the justification of the deeds. "Know now that there shall fall unto the earth nothing of the Word of the Lord, which the Lord spake concerning the house of Ahab, for the Lord hath done that which He spake by His servant Elijah." So Jehu slew all that remained of the house of Ahab in Jezreel, and all his great men, and his kinsfolks, and his priests, until he left him none remaining.

Then forty-two princes and the sons of the brethren of Ahaziah (2 Chron. 22:8) were slain. They were on the way to Jezreel, which showed their guilty affiliation with the wickedness of Jezebel. They were taken alive and then were slain at the pit of the shearing house, probably a cistern called Beth Eged.

Next he met Johonadab, the son of Rechab. The Rechabites belonged to the Kenites (1 Chron. 2:55). They are first mentioned in Gen. 15:19. A part of this tribe had followed Israel (Num. 10:29-32) and settled in the south of Judah (Judges 1:16), where they became attached to the Amalekites (1 Sam. 15:6). Jethro, Moses' father-in-law, was a Kenite (Judges 1:16) and so was Jael, who slew Sisera (Judges 4:17). See the record of Jonadab and his work for the tribe in Jeremiah 35:1-16. Jehu recognized him as a friend and took him into his chariot. He may have been acquainted with Elijah; and the great work he did, as made known by Jeremiah, in separating them unto the Lord may have been brought about by the threatened judgment by Elijah and its execution through Jehu, of which Jonadab knew and part of which he witnessed.

Then in great subtility Jehu destroyed the worshippers of Baal who appeared at his summons in their festive vestments. Thus Jehu destroyed Baal out of Israel. But the summary of Jehu's reign gives a mournful picture. Like Jeroboam, the son of Nebat, Jehu did not depart from the golden calves at Beth-el and at Dan. Nor did he take heed to walk in the law of the Lord God of Israel with all his heart. He is a sad illustration of a man who may be used of God and yet is disobedient in his own life; executing God's plans, yet knowing nothing of real communion. But the Lord did not forget even this imperfect service (verse 30).

3. Athaliah and Jehoiada's Revival

CHAPTER 11

1. Athaliah's wicked reign (11:1-3; 2 Chron.22:10-12)
2. Joash (Jehoash) proclaimed king (11:4-12; 2 Chron. 23:1-11)
3. The death of Athaliah (11:13-16; 2 Chron. 23:12-15)
4. Jehoiada's revival (11:17-21; 2 Chron. 23:16-21)

Athaliah, the wicked daughter of a wicked pair (Ahab and Jezebel), the widow of Joram, King of Judah, Jehoshaphat's son and the mother of Ahaziah, who had been slain by Jehu, destroyed the seed royal. She did so because she wanted the authority herself. It was an awful deed, inspired by him who is the murderer from the beginning. And Satan aimed through her at something of which his instrument was ignorant. It was one of the many attempts Satan made to exterminate the male offspring to make the coming One, the promised Saviour, the seed of the woman, impossible. Had he succeeded through Athaliah in the destruction of the royal seed of David, the promise made to David would have become impossible. Notice the first little word in the second verse, "But." Satan's attempt failed. The watchful eye of Jehovah and His power frustrated it all. A wicked woman killed her own children and a godly woman was used to keep one of the royal seed alive.

Jehosheba ("the Lord's oath" is the meaning of her name), through whom the covenant-oath was sustained, was the wife of Jehoiada (meaning "the Lord knows"), the high-priest (2 Chron. 22:11); he was brother-in-law to Ahaziah (2 Chron. 22:11) and Jehosheba was probably a half sister of Ahaziah. She took the young child from among the King's sons and hid him first in the bed-chamber and then in the house of the Lord till the seventh year. Well may we see here a most beautiful type of our Lord Jesus Christ. Like Joash He was doomed to death, yea, He died. But He was raised from the dead and is now hidden in the house of God above, the heavens having received Him. Joash, the heir of the throne of David, was hidden till the seventh year even as the true heir to the throne of David is now hidden in the presence of God till the six years (six the number of man's day, the present age) are passed. And when the seventh year comes—the beginning of the coming age, He will be brought forth as Joash was brought from his hiding place and be crowned king.

A remnant selected by Jehoiada saw the king first. It is a great scene this chapter describes. The company brought together, armed with King David's shields and spears, the king's son brought into the midst, Jehoiada putting the crown upon his head, anointing him with oil, they clapped with their hands and shouted "God save the King." Greater will be the scene when He will be crowned King of Kings, whose right it is to reign. Athaliah, the usurper, appears on the scene, attracted by the noise. She is face to face with the crowned king and receives now her well-deserved punishment outside of the house of the Lord. A great revival followed. A covenant was made by Jehoiada between the Lord and the king and people "that they should be the Lord's people." Baal's altars and images are broken. The king sits upon his throne. All the people of the land rejoiced and there was peace. All these blessed results are faint foreshadowings of what is yet to be when the usurper is cast out, when the true King is crowned. Then Israel will be in truth the Lord's people, idolatry will cease, the land and the people will rejoice and the city be quiet.

4. Jehoash, the Temple Repaired, and the Death of Jehoash

CHAPTER 12

1. Jehoash's (Joash) Reign (12:1-3; 2 Chron. 24:2)
2. The Failure of the Priests (12:4-8; 2 Chron. 24:4-5)
3. The Temple Repaired (12:9-16; 2 Chron. 24:8-14)
4. Hazael and Jehoash (12:17-18)
5. The Death of Joash (12:19-21; 2 Chron. 24:25-27)

Great things had the Lord done both in Israel and in Judah. As we have seen there were numerous divine interpositions in the downward course, but all led to the final judgments upon both. Revivals took place, but they were not lasting and the reactions which followed produced a greater apostasy. This also is the course of the present age, which will end in a greater departure from God and in a corresponding greater judgment than Israel's. "The people had fallen away from the divine purpose of their national calling, and become untrue to the meaning of their national history. From this point of view the temporary success of these reform movements may be regarded as a divine protest against the past. But they ultimately failed because all deeper spiritual elements had passed away from rulers and people." "And still deeper lessons come to us. There is not a more common, nor can there be a more fatal mistake in religion or in religious movements than to put confidence in mere negations, or to expect from them lasting results for good. A negation without a corresponding affirmation is of no avail for spiritual purposes. We must speak because we believe; we deny that which is false only because we affirm and cherish the opposite truth. Otherwise we may resist; and enlist unspiritual men, but we shall not work any deliverance in the land" (A. Edersheim).

The reign of Jehoash had begun well. The record tells us that he did which was right in the sight of the Lord as long as Jehoiada was priest. But what happened after the departure of Jehoiada? The answer is indicated in verse 3 and fully given in 2 Chron. 24:17-22. The king, who had received such kindness from Jehoiada, ordered the stoning of Zechariah, the son of Jehoiada, because he delivered a faithful message to the king against his idolatry.

The leading work of Jehoash's reign was the repairing of the temple. This had become necessary because the family of Athaliah had broken it up and used the dedicated things in the worship of Baal (2 Chron. 24:7). The king took the initiative, but the neglect of the priests made the work practically impossible. Then the work was taken up in earnest by Jehoiada, and voluntary contributions received. A large sum was collected which was exclusively used for the repairing of the temple. When this was completed the balance was used for the purchase of the sacred vessels (2 Chron. 24:14).

Then Hazael began his wicked work and threatened Jerusalem. Joash bought him off by turning over to him all the hallowed things of the temple and the treasures of the palace. Not a word is said that Jehoash sought the Lord or prayed. It shows only too clearly that Jehovah, the present help in time of trouble, had been forgotten. The death of the king, murdered in the house of Millo followed soon. In our annotations of Chronicles we shall hear more of his history. Then Amaziah reigned in his stead.

5. Jehoahaz and Jehoash of Israel, Elisha's Death

CHAPTER 13

1. The reign of Jehoahaz and his death (13:1-9)
2. Jehoash King of Israel (13:10-13)
3. Elisha and Joash (13:14-19)
4. The death of Elisha (13:20-21)
5. Hazael and his death (13:22-25)

Jehoahaz, the son of Jehu, reigned after the death of his father (10:35) and here we learn that he also followed in the abominable worship which Jeroboam had instituted in Bethel and in Dan. The Lord delivered therefore Israel into the hands of Hazael of Syria and into his son's hand. Jehoahaz prayed to the Lord and the Lord, so abundant in mercy, hearkened, for He saw the oppression of Israel, because the King of Syria oppressed them. Verses 5 and 6 form a parenthesis. The seventh verse tells of the havoc which the King of Syria had wrought among Israel. The prayer of Jehoahaz, though heard, was not fully answered at once. The parenthetic verses (5 and 6) must be looked upon as giving a summary of the entire history; God sent a saviour and yet they continued in their sins. Joash, the son of Jehoahaz, was the first one through whom a partial deliverance was wrought (verse 25) and the full deliverance came under the grandson Jeroboam II (14:25-27). We have here a good illustration of how the Lord hears prayer and how in His sovereignty and all-wise purposes He may delay the answer for many years. It should be enough for God's people to know that prayer is heard and to leave the answer with Him, who does all things well. And so Jehoahaz saw nothing but oppression (verse 22) though he had turned unto the Lord and had prayed. It was a trial of faith.

After his death his son Jehoash (also called Joash, distinguished from the King of Judah of the same name) reigned. There was no change for the better. Verses 10-13 are another brief summary giving briefly the character of his reign, his death and his successor.

The deathbed scene of Elisha and Joash's visit follows. Over sixty years Elisha had been the prophet of God. The last we heard of this great man of God was when he sent his messenger to anoint Jehu. Forty-five years had passed and no ministry of Elisha is recorded. He was quite forgotten and neglected. The same was the case with Daniel in Babylon. When apostasy advances, the Lord's true prophets are not wanted; they share the rejection of the Lord and His Truth. Joash then visited the dying prophet. From this we may gather that his abode was known and that Joash realized that Elisha's death would be a great loss. He utters the same words which Elisha spoke when Elijah went to heaven. He wept and still his words were the words of unbelief, as if with Elisha's death "the chariot of Israel and the horsemen thereof," the protection and blessing for Israel would have an end. Then follows the symbolical shooting of the arrows and the smiting of the ground. Half-heartedly the unbelieving king enters into that which Elisha had made so plain. It was Joash's lack of faith, indicated by smiting the ground but thrice, which made the complete victory over the Syrians impossible. Only "three times did Joash beat him (Hazael's son Ben-hadad) and recovered the cities of Israel" (verse 25). If he had faith it would have been five and six times.

Elisha had died. A corpse about to be buried was hastily cast into the sepulchre of Elisha, where his bones rested. "And when the man was let down, and touched the bones of Elisha, he revived and stood up on his feet." This final miracle bears a great and blessed testimony. Here an application must be made concerning Him who is foreshadowed in Elisha's ministry of grace. It is by faith in Him who died that sinners receive life and are raised up from the dead. To touch Him in faith means to live. And Israel, moreover, is typically represented by the dead man and through Him who died for that nation, Israel is yet to live.

6. Kings of Israel and Judah

CHAPTER 14

1. Amaziah's reign over Judah (14:1-7; 2 Chron. 25)
2. The conflict between Israel and Judah (14:8-11; 2 Chron. 25:17-24)
3. Judah's defeat and Jerusalem taken (14:12-14)
4. Jehoash and his successor (14:15-16)
5. Death of Amaziah (14:17-20; 2 Chron. 25:26-28)
6. Azariah, King of Judah (14:21-22)
7. Jeroboam II (14:23-29)

Amaziah, a son of Joash, began his reign over Judah. His mother was Jehoaddan (Lord is pleased) of Jerusalem. He did right in the sight of the Lord and yet he followed the errors of his father. His first deed was to deal in judgment with the two servants who had murdered his father in Millo, both of whom were sons of Gentile women (2 Kings 12:19-21; 2 Chron. 24:26). He feared, however, the Word of God. The additional record which is found in Chronicles we shall not follow here, but do so in the annotations of that book. He raised a large army and hired besides 100,000 Israelitish mercenaries at a tremendous cost. He gained a victory over Edom. All the cruelties practised then we shall find recorded in Chronicles. He became lifted up by his victories and then challenged Jehoash, the King of Israel. That King answered by a parable. The thistle in Lebanon is Amaziah; the cedar is Jehoash, King of Israel. The wild beast that was in Lebanon overcoming the thistle (Amaziah) is Jehoash's army. And the King of Israel gave him a solemn warning to desist. But proud Amaziah paid no attention to Jehoash's words. God was behind it all. "It came of God, that He might deliver them into the hand of their enemies, because they sought after the gods of Edom" (2 Chron. 25:20). A complete defeat of Amaziah followed and Jerusalem was taken. And Jehoash "took all the gold and silver, and all the vessels that were found in the house of God with Obed-Edom, and the treasures of the King's house, the hostages also and returned unto Samaria." After this humiliating defeat there followed a revolution in Jerusalem and the unhappy King fled to Lachish, where he was slain. His body was brought back to Jerusalem for burial.

The brief record of the reign of Jeroboam II concludes this chapter. The Prophet Jonah, the son of Amittai is here mentioned. This same Jonah made later the experience which the book of Jonah relates and to which our Lord refers as a historic fact. Hosea and Amos also prophesied at that time in Israel.

(The books of Hosea and Amos, especially the latter, shed much light upon the history of the Kingdom of Israel under Jeroboam and his son. This will be pointed out in annotations of both books.)

CHAPTER 15

1. Reign and death of Azariah (Uziah) (15:1-2; 2 Chron. 26).
2. Reign and death of Zachariah (15:8-12)
3. Reign and death of Shallum (15:13-15)
4. Menahem, King of Israel (15:16-18)
5. Pul of Assyria and Menahem (15:19-20; 1 Chron. 5:26)
6. Death of Menahem (15:21-22)
7. Pekahiah and his death (15:23-26)
8. Pekah and his death. Hoshea (15:27-31)
9. Jotham, King of Judah (15:32-38; 2 Chron. 27)

Eight kings are mentioned in this chapter. Of five it is said they did evil in the sight of the Lord. One was a leper; four were murdered; one committed unspeakable cruelties.

Azariah is first mentioned. In 2 Chronicles his name is Uzziah; but he is also called by this name in the present chapter (verses 13, 30, 32 and 34). Different explanations of the use of this double name have been given. We insert here the one advanced by Edersheim as the most satisfactory.

"The usual explanation either of a clerical error through the confusion of similar letters, or that he bore two names seem equally unsatisfactory. Nor is the meaning of the two names precisely the same—Azariah being 'Jehovah helps'; Uzziah, 'My strength is Jehovah.' May it not be that Azariah was his real name, and that when after his daring intrusion into the sanctuary (2 Chron. 26:16-20), he was smitten with lifelong leprosy, his name was significantly altered into the cognate Uzziah—'My strength is Jehovah'—in order to mark that the 'help' which he had received had been dependent on his relation to the Lord. This would accord with the persistent use of the latter name in 2 Chronicles—considering the view-point of the writer—and with its occurrence in the prophetic writings (Hosea 1:1; Amos 1:1; Isa. 1:1, 6:1, 7:11). And the explanation just suggested seems confirmed by the circumstance that although this king is always called Uzziah in 2 Chronicles, yet the Hebrew word for 'help,' which forms the first part of the name Azariah, recurs with marked emphasis in the account of the divine help accorded in his expeditions (2 Chron. 26:7, 13, 15)."

As his intrusion into the priestly office and his punishment for it is found in full in the second book of Chronicles, we shall follow it there.

Then follows the brief record of Zachariah (The Lord remembers), King of Israel. He became king of Israel in the thirty-eighth year of Uzziah, King of Judah. He was the son of Jeroboam II and the fourth and last ruler of the dynasty of Jehu. Thus was literally fulfilled the Word of The Lord (2 Kings 10:30). His reign lasted only six months. Shallum assassinated him in public. The murderer occupied the throne only one month. Shallum means "requital." As he did to Zachariah so Menahem did to him. All was now lawlessness in apostate Israel. Departure from God and the true worship came first and that opened the way for moral corruption and lawlessness. The same is true of this present Christian age. It also ends in apostasy, moral corruption and lawlessness. Hosea testified faithfully to these conditions. "And the revolters are profound to make slaughter, though I have been a rebuker of them all"—"They will not frame their doings to turn unto their God, for the spirit of whoredoms is in the midst of them and they have not known the Lord. And the pride of Israel doth testify to his face; therefore shall Israel and Ephraim fall in their iniquity, Judah also shall fall with them" (Hosea 5:2-5).

Josephus here informs us that Menahem was the military leader of Zachariah, the murdered King. When Tiphash refused his authority he executed a terrible, barbaric punishment. "All the women therein that were with child be ripped up." And God in His eternal justice permitted the same punishment to fall upon Samaria (Hosea 13:16; Amos 1:13).

And now for the first time the Assyrian is mentioned, the power used by God to execute judgment upon the Kingdom of Israel. The meaning of the Assyrian in prophecy we shall point out later. Pul, King of Assyria, came against the land. In verse 29 Tiglath-pileser is mentioned as king of Assyria. Are these two different kings or are they the same person under different names? The identity of Pul with Tiglath-pileser II has been proved, after the most painstaking research, beyond the possibility of a doubt. The Assyrian monuments bear witness to this fact. (*Assyrian Echoes of the Word* by Laurie and *Fresh Light from the Ancient Monuments* by Prof. Sayce, are helpful books on these and other questions.) In the annals of Tiglath-pileser the record is found that he received tribute from *"Minikhimmi Samirina"*—this is Menahem the Samaritan. Pul was evidently one name of the Assyrian ruler and later he assumed the title of Tiglath-pileser II. This does not clash at all with the statement in 1 Chron. 5:26. Through paying an immense amount of tribute (almost two million dollars) the Assyrian was kept back. Menahem's son, Pekahiah, after his father's death, ruled two years in Israel. He also was assassinated. Pekah headed the conspiracy and killed him. Under his reign, doing evil in the sight of the Lord, Tiglath-pileser came again and devastated a part of the land "and carried them captive to Assyria." This marks the beginning of the end. This invasion took place after his wicked attack upon Jerusalem with Rezin of Damascus during the reign of Ahaz, King of Judah. He tried to overthrow the house of David (2 Kings 16:1-8; 2 Chron. 28; Isa. 7:4-8). Wicked Pekah, who had killed so many Jews (2 Chron. 28:6) was murdered by Hoshea, who reigned in his stead. His death had been predicted by Isaiah (Isaiah 7:16).

The full record of Jotham, King of Israel, is given in the book of Chronicles. It was in those days that the Lord began to send against Judah Rezin, the King of Syria, and Pekah, the son of Remaliah. Judah, like Israel, was degenerating fast and the Lord chastised them by judgments.

7. King Ahaz and Assyria

CHAPTER 16

1. King Ahaz and his reign (16:1-4; 2 Chron. 28)
2. The invasion by the two kings (16:5-6)
3. Ahaz appeals to Assyria (16:7-8)
4. Ahaz in Damascus and the idolatrous altar (16:9-18)
5. Death of Ahaz (16:19-20; 2 Chron. 28:26-27)

Righteous Jotham had for his successor a wicked son. Ahaz "walked in the way of the Kings of Israel, yea, and made his son pass through the fire according to the abominations of the heathen, whom the Lord cast out from before the children of Israel." (This refers to the horrible rite of child-sacrifice. Ahaz was the first among the kings who did this. As the apostasy increased this awful ceremony became more frequent. 2 Kings 17:17; 21:6; 23:10; See Mic. 6:7; Jerem. 7:31; 19:5.) For additional wickedness he committed see 2 Chron. 28:2, 21-25. He burnt incense in the valley of the son of Hinnom and burnt his children in the fire.

"But this was to revive the old Canaanitish and Phoenician worship, with all its abominations and all its defilements. The valley of Gihon, which bounds Jerusalem on the west, descends at its southern extremity into that of Hinnom, which in turn joins at the ancient royal gardens the valley of Kidron, that runs along the eastern declivity of the Holy City. There, at the junction of the valleys of Hinnom and Kidron, in these gardens, was Topheth—'the spitting out,' or place of abomination—where an Ahaz, a Manasseh, and an Amon, sacrificed their sons and daughters to Baal-Moloch, and burnt incense to foul idols. Truly was Hinnom 'moaning,' and rightly was its name Gehinnom (valley of Hinnom—Geheena), adopted as that for the place of final suffering. And it is one of those strange coincidences that the hill which rises on the south side of this spot was that 'potter's field,' the 'field of blood,' which Judas bought with the wages of his betrayal, and where with his own hands he executed judgment on himself. History is full of such coincidences, as men call them; nor can we forget in this connection that it was on the boundary-line between the reigns of Jotham and Ahaz that Rome was founded (in 752 B.C.), which was destined to execute final judgment on apostate Israel" (A. Edersheim).

Isaiah, Micah, Hosea and Oded then exercised their prophetic offices. When Rezin, King of Syria, and Pekah, the son of Remaliah, King of Israel, came against Jerusalem and besieged Ahaz, he appealed to Tiglath-pileser to save him out of their hands, instead of crying to Jehovah for the deliverance He had promised to His people. The king also took the silver and gold from the Lord's house and presented it to Tiglath-pileser. Then after Ahaz had declared himself the vassal of Assyria ("I am thy servant"), Tiglath-pileser conquered Damascus. The inscriptions of Tiglath-pileser mention this fact. We refer again to Isaiah 7. The alliance with the Assyrian was opposed by Isaiah. He told Ahaz "at the end of the conduit of the upper pool" to ask a sign of any kind of the Lord God, to allay the fears of the king and give an evidence that the Lord would preserve the house of David. And furthermore Isaiah had taken with him his son Shear-jashub, which means "the remnant shall return," prophetic also of the preservation of a remnant. When wicked Ahaz refused, the prophet uttered that great sign which was to take place over seven hundred years after, that the virgin should conceive and bring forth a son, even Immanuel. The house of David might be punished and chastised, but there could be no full end of the royal family, for the promised One had to come from David and receive in due time the promised kingdom. And Isaiah also predicted that the Assyrian, in whom Ahaz had put his trust, should come upon them (Isa. 7:17). What Pekah did to Judah and Oded's testimony against Pekah we shall learn from the Chronicles.

The erection of a new altar in the Temple by Ahaz according to the pattern of the idol-altar, opened the door wide for the unlawful worship in the Temple of God. He found a willing helper in Urijah (the Lord is light), who conducted the worship "according to all that King Ahaz commanded." And greater profanation followed. He even shut up the doors of the house of the Lord (2 Chron. 28:24), which probably meant a complete cessation of the services in the Holy Place. The gods of Damascus were worshipped by him in connection with this altar (2 Chron. 28:23). And in Christendom an even greater profanation of worship has come to pass. True Christian worship is in spirit and in truth. Roman Catholicism has erected altars patterned more or less after the ancient Babylonish worship.

7. Assyria Conquers Israel and the Captivity

CHAPTER 17

1. Hoshea, Israel's last king (17:1-2)
2. Shalmaneser imprisons Hoshea (17:3-4)
3. Israel carried into captivity (17:5-6)
4. Retrospect and Israel's sins (17:7-23)
5. The colonization of Samaria (17:24-41)

Israel's last king was Hoshea. His name means "deliverance." It indicates what might have been had he and the people repented of their sins. The record of his character is brief. "And he did that which was evil in the sight of the Lord, but not as the kings of Israel before him." This does not mean that he improved. The golden calves had been taken away by the Assyrian from Bethel and Dan, so that he could no longer sin like Jeroboam, the son of Nebat, and the other kings of Israel. Hosea had predicted this (Hosea 10:5-8).

Shalmaneser, King of Assyria, then came against him, and Hoshea became his servant. The Biblical account is meagre, but the Assyrian inscriptions have a great deal to say about this period. Shalmaneser's name is given in these inscriptions as *"Salmanu-ussir"* and Hoshea's as *"A-usi."* From these inscriptions we learn that after the siege of Samaria had lasted two years Shalmaneser was succeeded by Sargon, who took Samaria in the first year of his reign. While Sargon is not mentioned in the record here it is significant that the capture of Samaria is not attributed to Shalmaneser. Both passages, 2 Kings 17:6 and 18:10-11, speak only of the king of Assyria. These inscriptions declare that Sargon captured Samaria, led away 27,290 of its inhabitants and appointed a governor over Samaria. There is also a record of the deportation of Israel and the colonization of the land. What would these interesting ancient inscriptions mean if it were not for the Bible? Again we say they are proven true because the Word of God confirms them.

Hoshea had, after he had become the vassal of the king of Assyria, made a conspiracy against the king by sending messengers to So, king of Egypt, and then he refused to pay the tribute. (The proper reading of "So" is given as "Seve" or "Sava." By the Greeks he is called "Saba Kon" on the monuments "Shabaka," in cuneiform inscriptions "Shabi-i.") He was imprisoned and we hear nothing whatever of his fate. (Hosea 10:7 tells of his death.) Samaria completely in the hands of the king of Assyria the people were carried away captives into Assyria. The places are given, but beyond this little is known. Nor do we know anything about their subsequent history. They did not return from the captivity. Various attempts have been made to locate them. The American Indians, the Afghans, Armenians, Nestorians and others have been mentioned as the descendants of the ten tribes, but no substantial evidence can be given to verify this supposition. The so-called "Anglo-Israel theory" is so full of unreasonable speculations and inventions that it does not deserve any consideration. God knows where they are located, and in His own time He will surely gather them and together with the remnant of the house of Judah bring them back to their land. At that time the many unfulfilled promises made to Israel and to Judah will all be literally fulfilled.

There is next given a solemn retrospect of the history of the house of Israel. Judah is also mentioned. The record shows the awful apostasy and the great patience of Jehovah in delaying the threatened judgment.

The account of the colonization of Samaria by the King of Assyria is interesting. It gives the history of the Samaritans, which emanated from this mixture of races and religions and which were responsible for much trouble after the return of the Jewish remnant from the exile. The priest who was returned from Assyria to teach religious rites to the colonists settled in Bethel, where Jeroboam had instituted the idolatrous worship, which had dragged Israel down, produced a new religion, partly Israelitish and partly heathenish, like the mixed multitude which dwelt in the land.

Thus ended the Kingdom of Israel. Out of the nineteen kings which reigned seven were murdered, one died from wounds received on the battlefield, one died from a fall out of the window, one was struck down by the judgment of God and one committed suicide.

IV. The Reign of Hezekiah, Manasseh and Amon

1. Hezekiah and Sennacherib's Invasion

CHAPTER 18

1. Hezekiah, King of Judah (18:1-3; 2 Chron. 29-32)
2. The Revival (18:4-7)
3. Victory over the Philistines (18:8)
4. Israel's captivity (18:9-12)
5. Sennacherib's invasion (18:13-16)
6. Sennacherib's messengers and message (18:17-25; 2 Chron. 32:9-19)
7. The request of Hilkiah, Shebna and Joah (18:26)
8. Rabshakeh's insulting answer (18:27-37)

Hezekiah (strength of Jehovah) was the pious son of a very wicked father. It is refreshing to read now after the long list of kings who did evil in God's sight that Hezekiah "did that which was right in the sight of the Lord, according to all that his father David did." According to the book of Chronicles, the first thing he did was to open the doors of the house of the Lord (which Ahaz his father had closed) and repair them (2 Chron. 29:3). This was a true beginning. We shall find in Chronicles the details of the great revival and the restoration of the temple-worship, the keeping of the Passover, as well as the other reforms which took place under his reign. All these will be considered in the annotations on Second Chronicles. He destroyed also all forms of idolatry. Especially mentioned is the brazen serpent which Moses had made. This interesting object had been preserved since the days when Moses had lifted it up in the wilderness, the wonderful type of Him who knew no sin and who was made sin for us on the cross. The children of Israel in their apostasy had made the brazen serpent an object of worship. He broke it in pieces and called it Nehushtan, which means "brazen." Thus negatively and positively a great reformation was accomplished. The secret of it all we find tersely stated in one sentence. "He trusted in the Lord God of Israel." Because he trusted Jehovah, Jehovah was with him. "And the Lord was with him, and he prospered whithersoever he went forth." This is the way of all true recovery and the way to blessing.

The evil alliance with the king of Assyria, which his father had made, the God-fearing king refused to own. "He rebelled against the king of Assyria and served him not." Immediately after he smote the ancient enemy of God's people, the Philistine. (The fate of Samaria, the Kingdom of Israel, is once more mentioned in verses 9-12 obviously because chronologically it followed Hezekiah's victory over the Philistines.) In annotations of Judges we learned the typical significance of the Philistines. They represent ritualistic Christendom. After Hezekiah's restoration of the true worship of Jehovah and after the breaking down of all false altars and idol worship, a complete victory over the Philistines has a special meaning. Ritualism, the deadly foe of true worship, can only be overcome by a return to that true worship and trust in the Lord. Protestantism attempted this, but it has failed.

The rebellion of Hezekiah against Assyria may have been under the reign of Shalmaneser. Then followed Sargon, who was succeeded by his son Sennacherib. In all probability Sennacherib was co-regent with his father Sargon. The Assyrian inscriptions concerning Sennacherib covering this period are very interesting though not always correct and often mixed and confusing. In the fourteenth year of Hezekiah, Sennacherib came against all the fenced cities of Judah and they fell before him. Isaiah 10 gives us additional information on this invasion. True, Hezekiah's faith was severely tested. Sennancherib had not yet come near to Jerusalem and Hezekiah sent him to Lachish, saying "I have offended; return from me; that which thou puttest on me will I bear." It was not according to faith, but the godly king had acted in fear and unbelief. No mention is made by Isaiah of this occurrence, nor do we find a record of it in the Chronicles. The tribute was very heavy, amounting to over one million and a half dollars. Hezekiah had to use the silver and the gold of the Temple and the palace to meet this obligation.

Then Sennacherib decided to attack Jerusalem. Here we have three accounts of what took place: 2 Kings 18—19; 2 Chron. 32 and Isaiah 36—37. These Scriptures should be carefully read and compared. From 2 Chron. 32:1-8 we learn the wise preparations Hezekiah made in anticipation of the coming attack. The water supply for the invading army was cut off; he made strong fortifications; he reorganized the army. But the best of all are the words he addressed to the people. "Be strong and courageous, be not afraid nor discouraged for the king of Assyria, nor for all the multitude that is with him; for there be more with us than with him. With him is an arm of flesh, but with us is the Lord our God to help us, and to fight our battles." These were noble words. No wonder the people leaned upon them in that hour of trial. We hear in them an echo of Isaiah's faithful ministry. The head of the expedition and negotiations for the surrender of Jerusalem were entrusted to the "Tartan," the commander-in-chief of the army: "Rabsaris," which has been explained to mean "chief of the eunuchs" and Rabshakeh, the Assyrian title of "chief captain." The message which Rabshakeh brought was delivered from the same spot where Isaiah stood when he gave his message to Ahaz (Isa. 7:3). The words of the emissary of Sennancherib were coarse; they reveal the blindness of a heathen, who thought of Jehovah having been offered by Hezekiah's great reformation (verse 22). Politically and religiously it was misrepresentation. He ended up with a lie, "The Lord said to me, Go up against this land and destroy it."

When the representatives of Hezekiah requested for the sake of the populace not to speak in Hebrew, but in Aramean, which the common people did not understand, Rabshakeh became very abusive and shouted a vulgar appeal to the people. It needs no further commentations. The people were obedient to the king. They answered not a word. And the king's representatives return to the king with clothes rent.

2. Hezekiah and Isaiah and the Deliverance

CHAPTER 19

1. Hezekiah's message to Isaiah (19:1-5)
2. Isaiah's answer. (19:6-7)
3. Sennacherib's message to Hezekiah (19:8-13; 2 Chron. 32:17)
4. Hezekiah's Prayer (19:14-19; 2 Chron. 32:20)
5. Jehovah's answer through Isaiah (19:20-34)
6. The deliverance (19:35; 2 Chron. 32:21-22)
7. Sennacherib's death (19:30-37)

And Hezekiah also rent his clothes. In deep humiliation and sorrow the pious man went to the house of the Lord and sent messengers to Isaiah. This is most blessed. He did not call a counsel of his advisers, a meeting of the captains to talk the matter over; nor did he send first to the prophet. Faith knows a better way than that. He went straight into the presence of the Lord and the sending to Isaiah was secondary. Many of our failures as His people are due to the fact that we do not go to the Lord first.

And equally beautiful is his message to God's prophet. He mentions not himself in the danger of Jerusalem. It is the honor of Jehovah which is at stake; the honor of the living God is at stake. The Assyrian had defied the God of Israel. Yea, Hezekiah's comfort was that Jehovah had heard it all and knew it all. What lessons and what comforts are here for us also! Then he requests prayer.

The divine answer through Isaiah was brief. Be not afraid! The blessed assurance for faith first—Fear not! The promise of deliverance is the second thing in Isaiah's answer.

Another message in the form of a letter is sent by Sennacherib to the king. Again Hezekiah goes with it straight to the Lord. He read it and went up into the house of the Lord and spread it before the Lord. What blessing there would be in the lives of all God's people; what wonderful evidences of His power and His love we might have if all things which happened unto us were at once taken into the presence of God and spread before Him!

And the beautiful answer to Hezekiah's prayer sent through the prophet! The Lord had heard, He had seen. All what had taken place He knew and any word which had been spoken. The message ends with the assuring word, "I will defend this city, to save it, for Mine own sake, and for my servant David's sake."

That night the judgment stroke fell. The whole Assyrian army of 185,000 men was smitten by the angel of the Lord. Prophetically it stands for the end of the Assyrian who will enter Israel's land during the great tribulation and who will perish like Sennacherib's army.

Sennacherib dwelt after that in Nineveh. There he was murdered by his own sons. An Assyrian cylinder in the British Museum contains a record of this deed.

3. Hezekiah's Illness, Recovery, Failure, and Death

CHAPTER 20

1. Hezekiah's illness and recovery (20:1-11; 2 Chron. 32:24)
2. Hezekiah's failure (20:12-19; 2 Chron. 32:25-31)
3. The death of Hezekiah (20:20-21; 2 Chron. 32:32-33)

Hezekiah's sickness must have occurred about the second invasion of the Assyrian. Then the prophet Isaiah delivered to him the message of approaching death. "Thus saith the Lord, Set thine house in order, for thou shalt die, and not live." The message made a deep impression on the sick king. He turned his face to the wall; he prayed and wept sore. Though he was a pious man he was greatly agitated and deeply moved when he heard the announcement of his coming departure. The meagre knowledge God's saints had in Old Testament times on the things beyond the grave, as well as the conception that an untimely death denoted divine disfavor produced no doubt much of this grief. How differently saints in New Testament times can face death! Life and immortality is now brought to life by the gospel, and we know that absent from the body means to be present with the Lord, and to depart and be with Christ is "far better."

Hezekiah's prayer was at once heard and answered. It is one of the most striking answers to prayer. Isaiah had not gone very far, he had just reached the middle of the court, when he was commanded to turn back and bring to Hezekiah the answer. Seven things are contained in this new message to the weeping king. "I have heard thy prayer"; "I have seen thy tears"; "I will heal thee"; "Thou shalt go up to the house of the Lord"; "I will add unto thy days fifteen years"; "I will deliver thee"; "I will defend the city." And Isaiah was also commanded to use means. "Take a lump of figs. And they took and laid it on the boil and he recovered." If this simple remedy had been neglected, if there had been disobedience, the recovery would not have taken place. The third day is mentioned on which he should go up to the house of the Lord. For Israel there is also in store the third day, when they will be raised up nationally and worship the Lord (Hosea 6:2). Then there was the sign of the shadow turning backward ten degrees on the dial of Ahaz. Hezekiah's experience is a great encouragement for God's people to pray.

> It is interesting to learn that Ahaz had—probably on his visit to Damascus (2 Kings 16:10)—seen and brought to Jerusalem some of the scientific appliances of the great empire of the East. It is impossible to determine whether this mode of measuring the progress of time (not strictly hours) was by a sun-dial, the invention of which Herodotus ascribed to the Babylonians. According to Ideler it was a *gnomon,* or index, surrounded by concentric circles, by which the time of the day was marked by the lengthening shadow. But the term "steps" seems rather to indicate an obelisk surrounded by steps, the shadow on which marked the hours, so that the shadow falling in the morning westwards first on the lowest step, gradually ascended to the plane on the top, and after midday again descended the steps eastwards. As the text seems to imply that there were twenty such "steps," they must have marked the quarters of an hour, and in that case the event has happened about half-past two o'clock p.m. (*Bible History*)

And the promise the Lord had given, "I will deliver thee and this city out of the hand of the king of Assyria; and I will defend this city for Mine own sake, and for my servant David's sake," was wonderfully fulfilled in the complete destruction of Sennacherib's army. The last we hear of this great king is the failure when he was lifted up with pride and did not give the glory to God. Merodach-baladan,[1] King of Babylon, sent letters and a present to Hezekiah when he heard of his sickness and his miraculous recovery. This is the first time we hear of a king of Babylon. The ambassadors came possibly to form with Hezekiah a league against Assyria. Hezekiah was favorably impressed, "he hearkened unto them," and then he made a display of all his possession. He had hearkened unto them and pleased with the attention shown

[1]Berodach is the error of some scribe. See Isaiah 39:1.

to him and the presents the king of Babylon had sent to him, he became lifted up in his heart, he boasted of his wealth and his possessions. Then Isaiah had another message for him. The Babylonian captivity is announced; remarkable in itself. How verses 17 and 18 were fulfilled is well known.

4. Manasseh and Amon

CHAPTER 21

1. Manasseh's reign of wickedness (21:1-9; 2 Chron. 33:1-9)
2. The word of the Lord against it (21:10-15)
3. Manasseh's end. (21:16-18; 2 Chron. 33:18-20)
4. Reign and death of Amon (21:19-26; 2 Chron. 33:20-25)

Hezekiah had a wicked father and his son Manasseh did not follow the example of his father, but became even more wicked than Ahaz, his grandfather. Manasseh means "forgetting." No doubt Hezekiah named him thus because the Lord had delivered him and thus made him forget his troubles and trials. He was born three years after Hezekiah's recovery from sickness. And now Manasseh forgot all the goodness and mercy of the Lord and plunged headlong into the worst apostasy. All the vile practices of the Canaanites and the Sodomites were revived by him. The Moloch-worship flourished, sorcery and the practice of demonism as well. The corruption was more vile than the corruption of Samaria. It was even worse than the corruption of the Canaanites. "Manasseh seduced them to do more evil than did the nations whom the Lord destroyed before the children of Israel." And still more evil is recorded of this king. "Moreover Manasseh shed innocent blood very much, till he had filled Jerusalem from one end to the another" (verse 16). Josephus declares that he killed all the righteous in Jerusalem and it is not unlikely that the tradition of aged Isaiah's violent death under Manasseh's reign is correct. Then the Lord sent to him His judgment message, announcing the coming doom of Jerusalem. Of his conversion and subsequent reign nothing is said in Kings. We find the record of these interesting events in Chronicles. His conversion was indeed a miracle of grace.

After his death Amon ruled as king and followed all the wickedness of his father Manasseh. Terrible is the record of this lost soul. "And he humbled not himself before the Lord as Manasseh his father had humbled himself; but Amon trespassed more and more" (2 Chron. 33:23). He was murdered by his servants.

V. The Reign of Josiah

1. The Revival

CHAPTER 22

1. Josiah begins to reign (22:1-2; 2 Chron. 34:1-2)
2. The temple repaired (22:3-7; 2 Chron. 34:8-13)
3. The law discovered (22:8-9; 2 Chron. 34:14-21)
4. The reading of the law and its results (22:10-14)
5. The words of Huldah, the prophetess (22:15-20)

After the violent death of Amon his eight-year-old son Josiah (sustained by Jehovah) began to reign. Under him the greatest reformation and revival took place. While he was yet young he began to seek after the God of David, his father. Afterward he began to purge Judah and Jerusalem. The carved images and molten images as well as the altars of Baal were destroyed by him. "And he burnt the bones of the priests upon the altars, and cleansed Judah and Jerusalem" (2 Chron. 34:5). Thus was fulfilled the prophecy uttered more than three hundred years before by the man of God from Judah (1 Kings 13:2). Perhaps the prophecy had been forgotten, the unbelievers may have ridiculed its fulfillment. But when God's time came He saw to the literal fulfillment of His own Word. It is so today. Rationalists scoff at the Word of God. Others spiritualize the predictions of the Bible and do not believe that they will ever be fulfilled. This is one of the characteristics of the last days of the age (2 Peter 3:3-7).

We must leave it to the reader to study the details of the great reformation-revival which took place under Josiah. In the annotations on Second Chronicles we point out some of its lessons. After the breaking down of the idols and idol-altars the temple was repaired. The law was also found by Hilkiah the high-priest. The Word of the Lord written by Moses in the Pentateuch had most likely been hidden away by Manasseh. It was the accusing voice of God against the wickedness of the king. Strange it is that it is not mentioned in connection with the repentance and conversion of Manasseh. And when the law was read to the king by Shaphan, the king rent his clothes.

"Here we have a tender conscience bowing under the action of the Word of God. This was one special charm in the character of Josiah. He was, in truth, a man of an humble and contrite spirit, who trembled at the Word of God. Would that we all knew more of this! It is a most valuable feature of the Christian character. We certainly do need to feel, much more deeply, the weight, authority, and seriousness of Scripture. Josiah had no question whatever in his mind as to the genuineness and authenticity of the words which Shaphan had read in his hearing. We do not read of his asking, 'How am I to know that this is the Word of God?' No; he trembled at it. He bowed before it. He was smitten down under it. He rent his garments. He did not presume to sit in judgment upon the Word of God, but, as was meet and right, he allowed that word to judge him.

"Thus it should ever be. If man is to judge Scripture, then Scripture is not the Word of God at all. But if Scripture is, in very truth, the Word of God, then it must judge man. And so it is, and so it does. Scripture is the Word of God and it judges man thoroughly. It lays bare the very roots of his nature—it opens up the foundations of his moral being. It holds up before him the only faithful mirror in which he can see himself perfectly reflected. This is the reason why man does not like Scripture—cannot bear it—seeks to set it aside—delights to pick holes in it—dares to sit in judgment upon it. It is not so in reference to other books. Men do not trouble themselves so much to discover and point out flaws and discrepancies in Homer or Herodotus, Aristotle or Shakespeare. No; but Scripture judges them—judges their ways—their lusts. Hence the enmity of the natural mind to that most precious and marvellous book which carries its own credentials to every divinely prepared heart" (*Things New and Old*).

The direct result of reading the Word of God was more than outward grief and repentance. The king gave the command, "Go ye, inquire of the Lord for me, and for the people and for all Judah." Jeremiah and Zephaniah were then upon the scene, but we do not read anything of them in the record. It is Huldah the prophetess, the wife of Shallum (retribution), the son of Tikvah (meaning "hope") the son of Harhas (meaning "extremely poor"). That he had to inquire of a woman, the weaker vessel, must have been humiliating to the king. And Huldah's message is one of judgment. To Josiah personally good is promised. He was not to see the evil. In spite of the great reformation-revival, judgment would fall upon Judah and upon Jerusalem (verses 15-17).

And here is an important lesson for our own times. Reformations and revivals cannot keep back the decreed judgments of God. Often it is thought that great waves of reformation and revival movements are evidences that the world is getting better and that only good is in store for this age. It is forgotten that this age is an age marked by departure from God, by the rejection of His own blessed Son and by the perversion of the truth of God. It will culminate in the great apostasy and the manifestation of the man of sin—the son of perdition. Christendom has been even more unfaithful than Israel in Old Testament times. Judgment is in store for this age and for that which claims to be the church. The Lord has announced this long ago and it will surely come as judgment came upon Judah for all the abominable things they did. Reformation-revival movements are evidences, too, that the threatened judgment is not far away. As the end approaches God warns us and His Spirit presses home the truth once more to awaken the consciences of men. In 2 Chron. 36:15 we read the following words: "And the Lord God of their fathers sent to them by His messengers, rising up betimes, and sending; because He had compassion on His people, and on His dwelling place." But the next verse declares the failure of what the Lord had done in His compassion. "But they mocked the messengers of God, and despised His words, and misused His prophets, until the wrath of the Lord arose against His people, till there was no remedy." No remedy! an awful word it is. Judah in spite of the gracious revival under Josiah hastened on to the predicted doom, and so does this present age.

2. The Results of the Revival and the Death of Josiah

CHAPTER 23:1-30

1. The People hear the law (23:1-2; 2 Chron. 34)
2. Josiah makes a covenant (23:3)
3. The great reformations (23:4-20)
4. The Passover celebrated (23:21-23; 2 Chron. 35)
5. Further statements concerning Josiah (23:24-27)
6. The death of Josiah (23:29-30)

It is a great scene with which this chapter opens. The king feels now his responsibility towards the people. All the elders of Judah and Jerusalem were called together by him. Then there was a great procession of people headed by the king, followed by the elders, the priests and the prophets and all the people both small and great. The king read before this vast assembly all the words of the book of the covenant. The king standing on a pillar, or platform, made a solemn covenant to walk after the Lord and to keep His commandments. All the people stood by it. But it did not last very long. As far as the king was concerned there can be no question that it was real with him. However, if we read the opening chapters of Jeremiah we find that the people's consecration was but skin-deep. They did not turn unto the Lord with the whole heart, but in falsehood (Jer. 3:10).

The description of the cleansing of Judah and Jerusalem of all the abominable things (verses 4-20) shows the awful depths of vileness and wickedness into which the professing people of God had sunk. All the abominations of the flesh connected with the worship of Baal and Ashera and a host of other things flourished in the land. "And he slew all the priests of the high places that were there upon the altars, and burned men's bones upon them and returned to Jerusalem" (verse 20).

The keeping of the Passover, the blessed feast of remembrance of what Jehovah had done, follows immediately after the cleansing of the land. The full account we find in Chronicles where we give further comment (2 Chron. 35:1-19). But the record declares that "there was not holden such a passover from the days of the judges that judged Israel, nor in all the days of the kings of Israel, nor of the kings of Judah." The same was said of Hezekiah's passover (2 Chron. 30:26). Hezekiah's passover was greater than any previous one and Josiah's feast was even greater than that of his great-grandfather.

And all the workers with familiar spirits (the demon possessed mediums) and other wickedness he cut off. In all this Josiah pleased Jehovah and the Spirit of God testifies to it. "And like unto him was there no king before him, that turned to the Lord with all his heart and with all his soul, and with all his might, according to all the law of Moses; neither after him arose there any like him." Yet after these words there stands written once more the judgment message so soon to be accomplished upon Judah and Jerusalem.

Josiah died, having been shot on the battlefield at Megiddo. The Chronicles contains the details of his death (2 Chron. 35:20-27).

VI. Final Apostasy of Judah and the Captivity

1. Jehoahaz and Jehoiakim

CHAPTER 23:31-37

1. The three months' reign of Jehoahaz (23:31-33; 2 Chron. 36:1-2)
2. Jehoakim made king (23:34-37; 2 Chron. 36:4-5)

Chronicles tells us that immediately after the death of Josiah, the people of the land took Jehoahaz (which means "Jehovah holds up") and made him king. He was not the Lord's choice, but the people's choice. He was not the eldest son and therefore the action of the people was an unlawful and a lawless one. He was an evil-doer; Josephus speaks of him as having been vile. In the brief period he reigned he may have attempted to restore the immoral rites which his father had so completely crushed. He may have opposed Pharaoh-necho, King of Egypt.

As Josephus explains it, "Necho had, after the battle of Megiddo, continued his march towards Syria. Thither, at Riblah, 'in the land of Hamath,' the victor summoned the new Jewish King. On his arrival, Jehoahaz, who had been crowned without the leave of Necho, was put in bonds. Necho does not seem, on this occasion, to have pursued his expedition against Assyria. The great battle at Carchemish, to which the chronicler refers by anticipation (2 Chron. 35:20), was fought on a second expedition, three years later, when the Egyptian army under Necho was defeated with great slaughter by Nebuchadnezzar, the son of Nabopalassar. This was after the fall of Nineveh, and when the Babylonian or Chaldean empire had taken the place of the Assyrian. But on the present occasion Necho seems to have returned, before encountering the Assyrians, into Egypt, whither 'he brought' with him Jehoahaz, who died in captivity." (See Jeremiah 22:11-12.)

Then the king of Egypt took the oldest son of Josiah, Eliakim, changed his name to Jehoiakim and made him King over Judah. Jehoiakim means "Jehovah raiseth up"; this name was probably selected to impress the people. He reigned eleven years. It was a most disastrous time and the beginning of the end. God's mighty prophets Jeremiah, Ezekiel, Habakkuk, Zephaniah and also Urijah were then warning and delivering their great messages.

"The reformatory work of Josiah gave place to a restoration of the former idolatry (compare

2 Chron. 36:8). As in previous reigns, it was connected with complete demoralization of the people (compare Jer. 7:9-15; 17:2, 19:4-9; Ezek. 8:9-18). And this not only among the laity, high and low, but equally among the priests and prophets (compare Jer. 23:9-14). All the louder rose the voices of the prophets Jeremiah, Urijah and Habakkuk. But their warnings were either unheeded and scorned, or brought on them persecution and martyrdom (2 Kings 24:4; Jer. 26:10, 11, and especially verses 20-23). Otherwise, also, it was a wretched government, characterized by public wrong, violence, oppression and covetousness. While the land was impoverished, the king indulged in luxury and built magnificent palaces, or adorned towns, by means of forced labor, which remained unpaid, and at the cost of the lives of a miserable enslaved people (Jer. 22:13-18; Hab. 2:9-17)" (A. Edersheim).

The book of Jeremiah will give us much more of the history of this wicked king and our annotations will lead us back to the ending days of Judah and Jerusalem. He tried to put Urijah to death because he prophesied against Jerusalem. The prophet fled to Egypt. Jehoiakim sent for him and slew him with the sword and threw his body into the graves of the common people (Jer. 26). He himself was buried with the burial of an ass (Jer. 22:18-19). Another infamous deed he committed was the cutting with the penknife of the scroll upon which Jeremiah had written the Word of God, casting it into the fire (Jer. 36).

2. Jehoiachin and Zedekiah: The Beginning of Judah's Captivity

CHAPTER 24

1. Jehoiakim, Servant of Nebuchadnezzar, and His Death (24:1-5; 2 Chron. 36:6-7)
2. Jehoiachin (24:6-10; 2 Chron. 36:8-9)
3. The first deportation to Babylon (24:11-16)
4. Zedekiah, the last king, and his rebellion (24:17-20)

The foe of Judah, the chosen instrument of the Lord to execute His wrath upon the people and the city, now comes to the front. Jeremiah had predicted the coming judgment; Isaiah and the other prophets did the same. Then Jehoiakim proclaimed a fast (Jer. 36:9). It was nothing but hypocrisy. Immediately after, he cut the scroll to pieces and cast it into the fire. Jeremiah and his secretary Baruch hardly escaped with their lives. Nebuchadnezzar, King of Babylon, bound Jehoiakim in fetters to carry him to Babylon (2 Chron. 36:6). This was not done because Nebuchadnezzar was suddenly called to Babylon. The book of Daniel introduces us more fully to this great monarch, the head of the times of the Gentiles; we give in the annotations on that book more information about his character and history.

Nabopalassar, founded the new Babylonian empire, which began the period of the Chaldees—as they are chiefly known to us in Scripture. Here we may at once indicate that he was succeeded by his son, Nebuchadrezzar (or Nebuchadnezzar), and he in turn by his son, Evil-merodach, who, after two years' reign, was dethroned by his brother-in-law, Neriglissar. After four years (559-556 B.C.) Neriglissar was succeeded by his youthful son, Laborosoarchod. After his murder, Nabonidos (Nabunit, Nabûnâ'id) acceded to the government, but after seventeen years' reign (555-539 B.C.) was dethroned by Cyrus. The eldest son of Nabonidos, and heir to the throne, was Belshazzar, whom we know from the book of Daniel, where, in a not unusual manner, he is designated as the son, that is, the descendant of Nebuchadrezzar (Dan. 5:2, 11, 18). We infer that, while his father, Nabonidos, went to meet Cyrus, to whom he surrendered, thereby preserving his life, Belshazzar had been left as "king" in Babylon at the taking of which he perished in the night of his feast, described in Holy Scripture. (See *The Prophet Daniel,* by A.C. Gaebelein.)

Jehoiakim became a vassal of Nebuchadnezzar. Three years later he rebelled. Punishment followed swiftly. It was "at the commandment of the Lord."

After the death of Jehoiakim, buried with the burial of an ass (Jer. 22:18-19), his son Jehoiachin reigned in his stead. He was eighteen years old when he ascended the throne and reigned only three months and ten days (2 Chron. 36:9). (2 Chronicles 36:9 gives his age as eight years, evidently the error of a scribe.) He is also known by the names of Joiachin (Ezek. 1:2) and Coniah (Jer. 22:24, 28, 37:1). Then Nebuchadnezzar besieged Jerusalem. The city surrendered and the long predicted punishment was executed. At the first invasion under the reign of Jehoiakim, when Nebuchadnezzar besieged Jerusalem, a part of the vessels of the house of God were transported to Babylon, as well as the noble children, among whom were Daniel and his companions (Dan. 1:1-6). With the second siege and conquest of Jerusalem all was taken and the people were taken away captives, among them was the prophet Ezekiel (Jer. 52:28; Ezek. 1:1-2; Jer. 29:1).

A remnant, however, was left behind; Jehoiachin was carried into captivity. The last chapter of this book gives his fate. He never returned. Important is to note the curse which was pronounced upon him. Jeremiah pronounced it upon Coniah (Jehoiachin). "Write ye this man childless, a man that shall not prosper in his days; for no man of his seed shall prosper sitting upon the throne of David and ruling any more in Judah" (Jer. 22:28-30). He had children; no offspring of the line of Solomon was ever to occupy the throne of David. But there were the descendants of David through another line, that is, Nathan's; no curse rested upon that line. The virgin Mary, the mother of our Lord, was of David through Nathan (Luke 3:31). Joseph, to whom Mary the virgin was espoused, was a son of David through Solomon's line.

Nebuchadnezzar made Mattaniah, the youngest son of Josiah, King over Judah (compare verse 18 with chapter 23:31). His name means "the gift of Jehovah" and he changed it into Zedekiah, "the righteousness of Jehovah." Here is no doubt a prophetic hint. When Judah and Jerusalem went down in judgment, in unspeakable ruin and shame, God indicated in the very names of the last king that there would yet come from David's line He, who is His own precious gift and in whom righteousness will be given and established. Zedekiah filled full the measure of wickedness and finally rebelled against the king of Babylon.

3. The Siege of Jerusalem and Judah's Complete Overthrow

CHAPTER 25

1. The last siege and complete overthrow (25:1-21; 2 Chron. 36:17-20)
2. Gedaliah (25:22-26)
3. Jehoiachin's captivity and release (25:27-30)

Zedekiah's rebellion was a great offence. He had sworn in Jehovah's name to be loyal to Nebuchadnezzar (2 Chron. 36:13; Ezek. 17:13). We find more light thrown upon this king and his rebellion in the book of Jeremiah. Ambassadors from Edom, Moab, Ammon, Tyre and Sidon came to Jerusalem to see Zedekiah (Jer. 27). A combined revolution was probably contemplated. Zedekiah sent at the same time a message to Nebuchadnezzar in Babylon (Jer. 29:3); the prophet Jeremiah used this opportunity to send a God-given communication to the exiles in Babylon (Jer. 29:1, etc.). The news of Zedekiah's schemes must have reached the captives, for they expected an early return. (The prophet Ezekiel was especially used to warn against these false hopes. See annotations on Ezekiel.) False prophets, Satan's instruments, gave them their lying messages. Prominent among them was Hananiah who received his deserved punishment for his lying words (Jer. 28). Once more the city was besieged. A great famine prevailed. What happened in the doomed city and Jeremiah's great ministry as well as suffering may be learned from his prophecies. Consult especially the following passages: Jer. 21:1-2; 37:3; 34:2-6; 38. Jeremiah charged with treacherous designs had been cast into a dungeon, but was later delivered out of the miry pit and brought before the king, who declared himself willing to follow Jeremiah's advice. What followed we give from Edersheim's *Bible History:*

> Meantime the siege was continuing, without hope of relief. Tyre suffered straits similar to those of Jerusalem, while Ammon, Moab, Edom and the Philistines had not only withdrawn from the alliance, but were waiting to share in the spoil of Judah (Ezek. 25). At length a gleam of hope appeared. An Egyptian army, under their King Hophra, the grandson of Necho, advanced through Phoenicia, and obliged the Chaldeans to raise the siege of Jerusalem (Jer. 37:5-7). The exultation and reaction in Jerusalem may be imagined—and it was probably in consequence of it that Jeremiah, who still predicted calamity, was cast into prison (Jer. 37:4). But the relief of Jerusalem was brief. The Egyptian army had to retire, and the siege of Jerusalem by the Chaldeans was resumed, and that under even more disadvantageous circumstances to the besieged.
>
> To the other calamities that of famine was now added (2 Kings 25:3). Of the horrors of that time Jeremiah has left a record in the Book of Lamentations (comp. 1:19, 2:11, 12, 20; 4:3-10). The last resistance was soon overcome. On the ninth day of the fourth month (Tammuz), in the eleventh year of Zedekiah, the enemy gained possession of the northern suburb (2 Kings 25:4; Jer. 39:2, 3; 52:6, 7). Before the middle gate the Babylonian captains held a council of war (Jer. 39:2, 3). Then the king and all the regular army sought safety in flight during the darkness of the night (Jer. 39:4). As the Chaldeans held the northern part of the city, they fled southwards. Between the two walls, through the Tyropoeon, then out of the "fountain-gate," and through the king's garden, they made haste to gain the Jordan.
>
> But their flight could not remain unobserved. They were pursued and overtaken in the plains of Jericho. The soldiers dispersed in various directions. But the king himself and his household were taken captives, and carried to the headquarters at Riblah, where Nebuchadnezzar himself was at the time. Here Zedekiah was formally arraigned and sentence given against him. His daughters were set free, but his sons were slain before him. It was the last sight the king saw.

His eyes were put out; he was bound hand and feet with double fetters of brass, and so carried to Babylon. There he died in ward (Jer. 52:11).

The remainder of this mournful tale is soon told. After the flight and capture of the king, the city could not long hold out. A month later, and on the seventh day of the fifth month (Ab) Nebuzar-adan ('Nebo gave posterity') penetrated into the city. The temple was set on fire, as well as the king's palace. The whole city was reduced to ruins and ashes, and the walls which had defended it were broken down (2 Kings 25:9, 10). After three days the work of destruction was completed; and ever afterwards was the 10th (9th) of Ab mourned as the fatal day of Jerusalem's fall (Jer. 52:12; Zech. 7:3, 5, 8:19). "The rest of the people left in the city,' and those who had previously passed to the enemy, together with the remnant of the multitude,' were carried away (2 Kings 25:11). We can scarcely be mistaken in regarding these captives as the chief part of the non-combatant population of Jerusalem and Judah.

Jeremiah's history and how he was found in prison when Jerusalem fell we shall learn from his book.

The administration of the conquered country was then entrusted by Nebuchadnezzar to Gedaliah, the son of Ahikam (2 Kings 22:12; Jer. 26:24). Gedaliah dwelt on Mizpah. He held his office only two months and was murdered by Ishmael, the son of Nethaniah (Jer. 40:8-16 and 41:1-9).

Jehoiachin's release needs no further comment. In the second book of Chronicles we shall follow again this mournful history. The seventy year captivity was on. The Word of the Lord through Jeremiah that "the land should enjoy her Sabbaths, for as long as she lay desolate she kept Sabbath, to fulfill three score and ten years" (2 Chron. 36:21).

We add the words of another:

> Again is the land keeping Sabbath. And again is it "stillness unto God," till His voice shall waken land and people, Whose are land and people, dominion and peace: till He shall come who is alike the goal and the fulfillment of all past history and prophecy—"a light to lighten the Gentiles, and the glory of Thy people Israel."

Appendix

THE MOABITE STONE

This ancient monument was discovered by R. F. Klein in 1868 at Dîbân in Moab.

The inscription consists of thirty-four lines (the last two being undecipherable), and was written by Mesha, King of Moab to commemorate his successful revolt from the yoke of Israel, recorded in 2 Kings 1:1 and chapter 3; and to honor his god Chemosh, to whom he ascribed his successes.

The writing is in the ancient Hebrew characters, which continued in use down to 139 B.C., but was gradually replaced by the modern square Hebrew characters which are in use today.

1. "I, Mesha son of Chemosh-Melech King of Moab, the Di-
2. bonite. My father reigned over Moab thirty years and I reign-
3. ed after my father. I made this monument to Chemosh at Korkhah. A monument of sal-
4. vation, for he saved me from all invaders, and let me see my desire upon all my enemies. Om-
5. ri [was] king of Israel, and he oppressed Moab many days, for Chemosh was angry with his
6. land. His son followed him, and he also said: I will oppress Moab. In my days Che[mosh] said;
7. I will see my desire on him and his house. And Israel surely perished for ever. Omri took the land of
8. Medeba and [Israel] dwelt in it during his days and half the days of his son, altogether forty years. But there dwelt in it
9. Chemosh in my days. I built Baal-Meon and made therein the ditches; I built
10. Kirjathaim. The men of Gad dwelt in the land of Ataroth from of old, and built there the king of
11. Israel Ataroth; and I made war against the town and seized it. And I slew all the [people of]
12. the town, for the pleasure of Chemosh and Moab: I captured from thence the Arel of Dodah and tore
13. him before Chemosh in Kerioth: And I placed therein the men of Sh(a)r(o)n, and the men
14. of M(e)kh(e)rth. And Chemosh said to me: Go, seize Nebo upon Israel; and
15. I went in the night and fought against it from the break of dawn till noon: and I took
16. it, and slew all, 7,000 men, [boys?], women, [girls?]
17. and female slaves, for to Ashtar-Chemosh I devoted them. And I took from it the Arels of Yahveh, and tore them before Chemosh. And the king of Israel built
18. Jahaz, and dwelt in it, while he waged war against me; Chemosh drove him out before me. And
19. I took from Moab 200 men, all chiefs, and transported them to Jahaz, which I took,
20. to add it to Dibon. I built Korkhah, the wall of the forests and the wall
21. of the citadel: I built its gates, and I built its towers. And
22. I built the house of Moloch, and I made sluices of the water-ditches in the middle
23. of the town. And there was no cistern in the middle of the town of Korkhah, and I said to all the people, Make for

24. yourselves every man a cistern in his house. And I dug the canals for Korkhah by means of the prisoners
25. of Israel. I built Aroer, and I made the road in [the province of] the Arnon. [And]
26. I built Beth-Bamoth, for it was destroyed. I built Bezer, for in ruins
27. [it was. And all the chiefs] of Dibon were 50, for all Dibon is subject; and I placed
28. one hundred [chiefs] in the towns which I added to the land: I built
29. Beth-Medeba and Beth-diblathaim and Beth-Baal-Meon, and transported thereto the [shepherds]? . . .
30. and the pastors] of the flocks of the land. And at Horonaim dwelt there
31. . . .And Chemosh said to me, Go down, make war upon Horonaim. I went down [and made war]
32. . . .And Chemosh dwelt in it during my days. I went up from thence. . ."

Translation by Dr. Neubauer

THE FIRST BOOK OF THE
CHRONICLES

Introduction

The books of the Chronicles are called in the Hebrew *"Dbri-Hayyomim"* which means "words of the days," that is the events of the times. In the Greek translation they are known by the name *"Paraleipomena,"* that is "things omitted." Our English title "Chronicles" is adopted from the Latin translation, the Vulgate, because the title there is *"Liber Chronicorum."*

In the English Bible the Chronicles occupy a different place from that in the original Hebrew Bible. As stated before, the Hebrew Scriptures are divided into three main divisions; the law, the prophets and the writings. This last section of the Hebrew Scriptures contains the following books: Psalms, Proverbs, Job; the five books known as *Megilloth,* Canticles, Ruth, Lamentations, Ecclesiastes and Esther. These are followed by Daniel, Ezra, Nehemiah and Chronicles. The Chronicles therefore stand at the close of the Hebrew Scriptures. That this arrangement is not without meaning in connection with the New Testament, has been pointed out by others. "The genealogies with which Chronicles begins lead up to the genealogy of Matthew 1 and the commencement of the New Testament. They end with the ending of the kingdom, and the question of Cyrus, "who is there?" (2 Chron. 36:23) is followed by another "Where is He?" (Matthew 2:2) and the proclamation of the kingdom by the true King and His forerunner. Chronicles begins with the first Adam and leads on to the last Adam."

Authorship and Date

Ezra has been mentioned as the possible author of Chronicles, which, however, cannot be proven. Nothing whatever is known of the instrument who was used to write these historical books. From the prominence which is given to the history and organization of the Levitic priesthood and the deep interest shown in the minor officials of the temple, especially the singers, it has been surmised that the author may have been a Levite. Beyond this nothing definite can be said. The author used by the Spirit of God must remain unknown to man, but he is known to God. In the books are mentioned repeatedly other books and histories to which the author of Chronicles refers. These include the following: a book of the kings of Israel and Judah, (2 Chron. 27:7; 35:27; 36:8); a book of the kings of Judah and Israel (2 Chron. 16:11; 25:26; 28:26; 32:32); a book of the kings of Israel (2 Chron. 24:27); a commentary of the books of Kings (2 Chron. 24:27); a history of the prophets Samuel, Nathan and Gad (1 Chron. 29:29); a history of the prophets Nathan, Abijah, the Shilonite, and Iddo (2 Chron. 9:29); a history of the prophets, Shemaiah and Iddo (2 Chron. 12:15); a history of the prophet Jehu (2 Chron. 20:34); a commentary of the prophet Iddo (2 Chron. 13:22); Isaiah's history of Uzziah (2 Chron. 26:22); a history of the prophet Isaiah (2 Chron. 32:32) and a history of the prophet of Manasseh's day (2 Chron. 33:19). It will be seen that there are just twelve sources mentioned. It will be seen that the first four are historical and the remaining eight are prophetic. While some of these references must have been books and histories now unknown to us, the main references are to the preceding books of the kings and to the first part of the prophet Isaiah.

The date of Chronicles is fixed by the first book. 1 Chron. 6:15 shows that the book was written after the captivity. We find also the names of the descendants of Zerubbabel given in 1 Chron. 3:19-24. Inasmuch as Zerubbabel was one of the leaders of the exile, who returned from the captivity, and his descendants are given, Chronicles must have been written some time after the return from Babylon. The diction of the books of Chronicles also bears witness to this. The Hebrew is substantially the same which is employed in the books of Ezra, Nehemiah and Esther, which were written immediately after the captivity. It is mixed with Aramaeisms, which marks the corruption of the pure Hebrew by the Chaldaean language which the captives learned in Babylon. The pure Hebrew had been lost in Babylon. Even the orthography bears witness to it as every Hebrew scholar knows.

Rationalistic Objections

Rationalists, the so-called higher critics, speak

much of the discrepancies and contradictions contained in Chronicles. That there are variations from previous records cannot be denied, but variations are not contradictions. That there are certain corruptions in the text must be acknowledged, and some of them will be pointed out in the annotations. But the charge that the writer of Chronicles contradicts himself, is wholly unfounded. The following passages have been used to demonstrate this supposed contradiction: 2 Chron. 14:1 and 2 Chron. 15:19; 2 Chron. 14:2 and 2 Chron. 15:17; 2 Chron. 17:6 and 2 Chron. 20:33; 2 Chron. 30:26 and 35:18. A careful perusal will show that there is nothing contradictory between these passages. Higher criticism is often superficial and we fear just as often wilfully blind and even ready to cast doubt upon the inspired records.

The Marks of Inspiration

The omissions and additions we find in the Chronicles in comparison with the books of Samuel and Kings are not the marks of an imperfect human hand. They are the marks of inspiration. We found that the books of Kings contained the history of God's government in Israel. Kings omits much of the history of the house of Judah and only touches upon that which relates to the connection of Judah with the house of Israel during that period.

"The books of the Chronicles give us the history of the same period under another aspect, that is, that of blessing and of the grace of God: and, more particularly, they give us the history of the house of David with respect to which this grace was manifested. We shall see this verified in a multitude of instances.

"These books preserve God's history of His people, recorded by the Holy Ghost, as He loved to remember it, exhibiting only such faults as require to be known in order to understand the instructions of His grace" *(Synopsis of the Bible).*

It is in these distinctions we discover the supernatural guidance of the penman.

Parallel Passages

A comparison with the books of Samuel, Kings and certain chapters in Isaiah is necessary in the study of Chronicles. To assist in this, we give a complete list of the parallel passages with which Chronicles should be studied.

1 Sam. 27	1 Chron. 12:1–7
1 Sam. 29:1–3	1 Chron. 12:19–22
31	1 Chron. 10
2 Sam. 5:1–5	1 Chron. 11:1–3
5:6–10	1 Chron. 11:4–9
5:11–16	1 Chron. 14:1–7
5:17–25	1 Chron. 14:8–17
6:1–11	1 Chron. 13
6:12–23	1 Chron. 15 and 16
7	1 Chron. 17
8	1 Chron. 18
10	1 Chron. 19
11:1–27	1 Chron. 20:1
12:29–31	1 Chron. 20:1–3
23:8–39	1 Chron. 11:10–47
24:1–9	1 Chron 21:1–6
24:1–9	1 Chron. 27:23, 24
24:10–17	1 Chron. 21:7–17
24:18–24	1 Chron. 21:18—22:1
1 Kings 2:1	1 Chron. 23:1
2:1–4	1 Chron. 28:20, 21
2:10–12	1 Chron. 29:23–30
2:46	2 Chron. 1:1
3:4–15	2 Chron. 1:2–13
5	2 Chron. 2
6	2 Chron. 3:1–14; 4:9
7:15–21	2 Chron. 3:15–17
7:23–26	2 Chron. 4:2–5
7:38–46	2 Chron. 4:6, 10, 17
7:47–50	2 Chron. 4:18–22
7:51	2 Chron. 5:1
8	2 Chron. 5:2; 7:10
9:1–9	2 Chron. 7:11–22
9:10–28	2 Chron. 8
10:1–13	2 Chron. 9:1–12
10:14–25	2 Chron. 9:13–24
10:26–29	2 Chron. 9:25–28; 1:14–17
11:41–43	2 Chron. 9:29–31
12:1–19	2 Chron. 10
12:21–24	2 Chron. 11:1–4
12:25	2 Chron. 11:5–12
12:26–31	2 Chron. 11:13–17
14:22–24	2 Chron. 12:1
14:25–28	2 Chron. 12:2–12
14:21, 29–31	2 Chron. 12:13–16
15:1	2 Chron. 13:1, 2
15:6	2 Chron. 13:2–31
15:7, 8	2 Chron. 13:22; 14:1
15:11, 12	2 Chron. 14:1–5
15:13–15	2 Chron. 15:16–18
15:16–22	2 Chron. 16:1–6
15:23, 24	2 Chron. 16:11–14
22:1–40, 44	2 Chron. 18
22:41–43	2 Chron. 17:1; 20:31–33
22:45	2 Chron. 20:34
22:47–49	2 Chron. 20:35–37
22:50	2 Chron. 21:1

2 Kings 1:1; 3:4, 5	2 Chron. 20:1–3
8:16–19	2 Chron. 21:2–7
8:20–22	2 Chron. 21:8–15
8:23, 24	2 Chron. 21:18–20
8:25–27	2 Chron. 22:1–4
8:28, 29; 9:1–28	2 Chron. 22:5–7, 9
10:11–14	2 Chron. 22:8
11:1–3	2 Chron. 22:10–12
11:4–20	2 Chron. 23
11:21; 12:1–3	2 Chron. 24:1–3
12:6–16	2 Chron. 24:4–14
12:17, 18	2 Chron. 24:23, 24
12:19–21	2 Chron. 24:25–27
14:1–6	2 Chron. 25:1–4
14:7	2 Chron. 25:11–16
14:8–14	2 Chron. 25:17–24
14:17–20	2 Chron. 25:25–28
14:21, 22; 15:1–4	2 Chron. 26:1–15
15:6, 7, 27, 28	2 Chron. 26:22, 23
15:32–35	2 Chron. 27:1–8
15:38	2 Chron. 27:9
16:1, 2	2 Chron. 28:1, 2
16:3, 4, 6	2 Chron. 28:3–8
16:7	2 Chron. 28:16–19
15:29	2 Chron. 28:20
16:8–18	2 Chron. 28:21–25
16:19, 20	2 Chron. 28:26, 27
18:1–3	2 Chron. 29:1, 2
18:13	Isa. 36:1
18:14–16	2 Chron. 32:2–8
20:1–11	2 Chron. 32:24: Isa. 38
20:12–19	Isa. 39:1–8
18:17–37	2 Chron. 32:9–19; Isa. 36:2–22
19:1–5	2 Chron. 32:20; Isa. 37:1–4
19:6, 7	Isa. 37:6, 7
19:8–19	2 Chron. 32:17; Isa. 37:8–20
19:20–37	2 Chron. 32:21; Isa. 37:21–38
20:20, 21	2 Chron. 32:32, 33
21:1–16	2 Chron. 33:1–9
21:17, 18	2 Chron. 33:18–20
21:19–26	2 Chron. 33:21–25
22:1, 2	2 Chron. 34:1–7
22:3–20	2 Chron. 34:8–28
23:1–3	2 Chron. 34:29–32
23:21–23	2 Chron. 35:1–19
23:24–26	2 Chron. 34:33
23:28–30	2 Chron. 35:20–27
23:30–33	2 Chron. 36:1–3
23:34–37	2 Chron. 36:4, 5
24:8, 9	2 Chron. 36:9
24:15–17	2 Chron. 36:10
24:18, 19	2 Chron. 36:11, 12
24:20	2 Chron. 36:13–16
25:8–21	2 Chron. 36:18–21

The reader should look up these parallel passages. Especially should the previous annotations in Samuel and Kings be read in connection with Chronicles.

The Division of the First Book of the Chronicles

The first book of the Chronicles begins with genealogies which start with Adam and lead up to the time of the restoration from the captivity and sometime after. The tables do not mention all the names; many are omitted. This makes clear at once the object of these long lists of names. Only those are recorded who were related to the accomplishment of the purpose of God and who were the divinely chosen channels through whom the Lord carried out His purpose. Many lessons may be gathered from these genealogies, so often considered unprofitable. Even to those opening chapters of Chronicles, applies the statement in 2 Timothy 3:16, "All Scripture is given by inspiration of God, and is profitable for doctrine, for reproof, for correction, for instruction in righteousness." The main part of the book begins with the miserable end of Saul, the crowning of David at Hebron and the establishment of his kingdom. Especially is that made prominent which is passed over in the books of the Kings, David's relation to the public worship of God and to the building of the temple, which his son Solomon built after him.

We divide the first book of the Chronicles into four parts:

I. THE GENEALOGIES

1. **From Adam to the Edomites** (1:1-54)
2. **The Sons of Israel and the Tribe of Judah** (2:1—4:23)
3. **Simeon, Reuben, Gad and Manasseh** (4:24—5:26)
4. **Levi** (6:1-81)
5. **Issachar, Naphtali, half Manasseh, Ephraim and Asher** (7:1-40)
6. **Benjamin** (8:1-40)
7. **The Record of the Inhabitants of Jerusalem after the Return** (9:1-44)

II. THE OVERTHROW AND END OF SAUL (10:1-14)

III. THE CROWNING OF DAVID AND ESTABLISHMENT OF HIS KINGDOM

1. **David in Hebron** (11:1-47)
2. **David's Warriors and Friends** (12:1-40)
3. **The Ark removed from Kirjath-jearim** (13:1-14)
4. **David's Increase and Blessing** (14:1-17)
5. **The Ark Brought to Jerusalem** (15:1—16:3)
6. **The Great Celebration** (16:4-43)
7. **The Covenant and the Promise** (17:1-27)
8. **David's Wars and Successful Reign** (18:1-17)
9. **The Wars with Ammon, Syria and the Philistines** (19—20)
10. **The Numbering of the People and the Punishment** (21:1-30)

IV. PREPARATIONS FOR THE BUILDING OF THE TEMPLE AND DAVID'S DEATH

1. **The Preparations and Charge to Solomon** (22:1-19)
2. **The Numbering and Arrangement of the Levites** (23:1-32)
3. **The Twenty-four Courses of the Priests** (24:1-31)
4. **The Singers and Musicians of the Temple** (25:1-31)
5. **The Porters and other Temple Officers** (26:1-32)
6. **The Captains, Princes, and Various Officers and Counsellors** (27:1-34)
7. **The Last Acts of David and His Death** (28—29)

Analysis and Annotations

I. The Genealogies

1. From Adam to the Edomites

CHAPTER 1

1. Adam to Noah (1:1-4)
2. The sons of Japheth (1:5-7)
3. The sons of Ham (1:8-16)
4. The sons of Shem (1:17-23)
5. From Shem to Abraham (1:24-27)
6. Ishmael and his sons (1:28-31)
7. Abraham's sons from Keturah (1:32-33)
8. The sons of Isaac (1:34)
9. The sons of Esau (1:35-42)
10. The kings and dukes of Edom (1:43-54)

The nine chapters of genealogical tables is the largest collection of Hebrew names in the Bible. These names are full of the deepest interest, as they often bear in their meaning a message. We have pointed out this fact many times in the annotations of the preceding books. Here is unquestionably a mine of great wealth for the diligent searcher: many lessons connected with these names have been but little understood. (A good concordance or dictionary of these names and their meaning is needed for such research.) The names given in this chapter are all found in the book of Genesis (chapters 5, 10, 11, 25 and 36.) The ten generations before the flood, ending with Noah begin the list. The descendants of Cain are not mentioned. Then follow the names of the offspring of Noah's sons, Japheth, Ham and Shem. Fourteen nations descended from Japheth; thirty-one from Ham and twenty-six from Shem. No person is able to trace all these races in history, but He who has recorded their names knows also their history and their wanderings. And so He knows all His creatures. But above all does He know His own people by name.

Shem's line is followed to Abraham, the father of the nation. The sons of Abraham are mentioned first as Isaac and Ishmael, not in their right order, Ishmael preceding Isaac. The sons of Ishmael are therefore given first, as well as the sons which Abraham had from Keturah. Then follows the statement, "And Abraham begat Isaac. The sons of Isaac: Esau and Israel" (verse 34). Esau's sons and descendants are given before the sons of Israel; those we find in the second chapter. Then follows the list of the kings and dukes (or chiefs) of Edom. King Joab (verse 44) is considered by some to be Job and that he ruled in Dinhabah (Genesis 36:32).

2. The Sons of Israel and the Descendants of Judah (2:1—4:23)

CHAPTER 2

From Israel to Caleb

1. The sons of Israel (2:1-2)
2. The sons of Judah (2:3-12)
3. The offspring of Jesse (2:13-17)
4. The descendants of Caleb (2:18-24)
5. The descendants of Jerahmeel (2:25-41)
6. Other descendants of Caleb (2:42-55)

After the twelve sons of Israel (Jacob) are named, Judah and his sons are mentioned. The entire chapter is devoted to the descendants of Judah. Judah is given the prominent place, because from this tribe the promised Messiah was to come (Gen. 49:8-12). The sons of Jesse (verses 13-17) are given, seven in number. In 1 Sam. 16:5-11 and 17:12-14 eight are mentioned. This is not a discrepancy. One of these sons probably died childless and his name would therefore have no place in this genealogy. Prominent in this chapter are the sons of Hezron, Jerahmeel, Ram (the Aram of Matt. 1:3) and Chelubai. The latter is Caleb. Caleb is here given as a son of Hezron. Is this the same Caleb who was one of the spies, the son of Jephunneh (Num. 13:6, 30; 14; 6, 24, etc)? Critics claim that he is the son of Jephunneh and pointed this out as one of the inaccuracies. However, it is impossible that Caleb the son of Hezron, could be identical with Caleb, the son of Jephunneh. Caleb the son of Hezron was the great-grandfather of Bezaleel (verses 19-20), who was selected with Aholiab to do the work in connection with the tabernacle (Exod. 31:2). He must therefore have been the ancestor of Caleb the son of Jephunneh. And furthermore, Caleb the son of Jephunneh is mentioned in Chapter 4:15. That in verse 49 a daughter of Caleb (Achash) is mentioned is not sufficient proof that the son of Jephunneh is meant.

CHAPTER 3

From David to Zedekiah

1. The sons of David (3:1-9)
2. David's line to Zedekiah (3:10-15)
3. The sons of Jeconiah (3:16-24)

Six sons were born to David during his reign in Hebron. Four are mentioned as the offspring from Bath-shua, another name for Bath-sheba (2 Sam. 11:3). Then follow the names of other nine sons. As the name Elishama appears twice, it has been suggested that one is Elishua (2 Sam. 5:15). Eglah is called David's wife. Some claim that it is Michal, who became childless after her mockery when David danced before the ark. Then the line of Solomon is traced up to Zedekiah. The usurping Queen Athaliah (2 Kings 11:3) is omitted, for she was not of the house of David. Then follows the list of the sons of Jeconiah. The name "Assir" which follows Jeconiah in verse 17 means "the captive." "Jeconiah, the captive," is the proper rendering. His son Salathiel was therefore born in the captivity (Matt. 1:12). Jeconiah was written "childless," which does not mean that he was to have no sons, but that no son of his should sit upon the throne of David (Jer. 22:30). The son of Salathiel was Zerubbabel (Matt. 1:12; Ezra 3:2, 5: 2; Hag. 1:1, 12). It seems that, in some way, the different names as they appear in the Hebrew text were dislocated. The following arrangement has been suggested to remove the difficulty.

"And the sons of Jeconiah, the captive, Salathiel, his son. And the sons of Salathiel; Zerubbabel and Shimei; and the sons of Zerubbabel; Meshullam, Hananiah and Shelomith their sister. And Hashubah, and Ohel, and Berechiah, and Hasadiah, Jushab-hezed. And Malchiram, and Rephaiah, and Shenazar, Jecamiah, Hoshama, and Nedabiah. The sons of Hananiah; Pelatiah and Jesiah; the sons of Rephaiah; his son Arnan, his son Obadiah, his son Shecaniah."

CHAPTER 4:1-23

Additional Genealogies of Judah

1. The sons of Judah (4:1-8)
2. Jabez more honorable (4:9-10)
3. Further descendants of Judah (4:11-20)
4. Descendants of Shelah (4:21-23)

Hur and Shobal, mentioned in the first verse, were the sons of Caleb the son of Hezron. The families of the Zorathites sprang from Reaiah, the son of Shobal. Jabez is especially mentioned. Jabez means "He causes pain." "And Jabez called on the God of Israel, saying, Oh that Thou wouldest bless me indeed, and enlarge my coast, and that Thine hand might be with me, and that Thou wouldest keep me from evil, that it may not grieve me! And God granted him that which he requested." The occasion when this prayer-vow was uttered is not given; probably it was made in connection with the expulsion of the Canaanites from the land and the acquisition of their territory. It was a simple prayer of child-like faith. For blessing, for increase, for companionship and for preservation Jabez cast himself upon the God of Israel, and He granted him his request. Blessing came to Jabez's soul; his coast was enlarged; the hand of the Lord was with him and kept him from evil. God never disappoints faith.

Then we have mentioned in this chapter the craftsmen; Geharashim (verse 14) means "valley of the craftsmen"; the workers in fine linen (verse 21); and those who were potters (verse 23).

3. Simeon, Reuben, Gad, and Manasseh

CHAPTERS 4:24—5:26

1. The sons of Simeon (4:24-43)
2. The sons of Reuben (5:1-10)
3. The children of God and half Manasseh (5:11-26)

The account of the Simeonites is interesting. Some of their families had increased so much that they had no pasture for their flocks. Some went then to Gedor and found fat pasture and quietness. Others went to Mount Seir, and five hundred of them smote the Amalekites.

Reuben was the firstborn, and the Chronicles state briefly why Reuben was not mentioned first in these genealogies. His birthright was given to the sons of Joseph. Judah, however, had the pre-eminence "of him came the prince." This refers to David and to Him who came from him after the flesh, Messiah the Prince. The Syriac version makes this paraphrase, "of Judah is the King, the Messiah." In verse 6 Tiglath-pileser is mentioned. (Not Tiglath-pilneser; it is an erroneous spelling.) He carried away Beerah, the Prince of the Reubenites.

The Hagarites, mentioned in verse 10, were no doubt the descendants of Hagar through Ishmael. They were nomads, who wandered over the desert lands of the trans-Jordan territory. The tribe of Gad occupied the lands north of Reuben and eastward from the Jordan to the desert.The genealogies of the chiefs mentioned here were compiled during the reign of Jotham of Judah and Jeroboam of Israel (verse 17). Another war with the Hagarites is recorded in verses 18-22. (Some take that this is the same war mentioned in verse 10.) Here prayer is mentioned again. "They cried to God in the battle, and He was entreated of them; because they put their trust in Him." The Lord delights to record those who trust in Him.

4. Levi

CHAPTER 6

1. The high-priestly line (6:1-15)
2. Levitical genealogies (6:16-30)
3. David's chief musicians (6:31-48)

The high-priestly line is first given, starting with Levi, and followed down to the exile. From Eleazar the son of Aaron, twenty-two generations are named. Moses is not mentioned in this list. With Aaron his brother he is called a priest (Psalm 99:6), yet he was chosen as the great leader of the people before the consecration of the levitical priesthood. This is the reason why his name is not found here. The last priest named before the captivity is Jehozadak (also called Jozadak). He was carried into captivity and was the father of Joshua, the high-priest, who returned from Babylon (Ezra 3:2; 5:2; Neh. 12:26; Hag. 1:1, 12; Zech. 6).

After the genealogies of the sons of Levi, who were not priests, the list of the names of David's singers and musicians is given. "These are they whom David set over the service of song in the house of the Lord, after that the ark had rest. And they ministered before the dwelling place of the tabernacle of the congregation with singing, until Solomon had built the house of the Lord in Jerusalem, and then they waited on their office according to their order." Heman stands first. He was Samuel's grandson. Psalm 88 is by Heman, the Ezralite. Asaph, the son of Berachiah (verse 39), was the poet-prophet. Psalms 50 and 73—88 bear his name. The sons of Asaph are later mentioned as choristers of the temple (1 Chron. 25:1-2; 2 Chron. 5:12; Ezra 2:41, etc.). Two other prominent persons bore the name of Asaph; Asaph, the recorder to King Hezekiah (2 Kings 18:18; Isaiah 36:3), and Asaph, the forester under Artaxerxes (Neh. 2:8). Ethan or Jeduthun (1 Chron. 9:16, 16:41, 25:1; 2 Chron. 35:15) is the author of Psalm 89.

5. Issachar, Naphtali, half Manasseh, Ephraim, and Asher

CHAPTER 7

1. Issachar (7:1-5)
2. Of Benjamin (7:6-12)
3. Naphtali (7:13)
4. Half Manasseh (7:14-19)
5. Ephraim (7:20-29)
6. Asher (7:30-40)

The other tribes are given except Dan and Zebulun, which are missing. Issachar's had the territory between the highlands and the Jordan valley. Their warriors numbered 87,000 taken most likely from David's census. Only three sons of Benjamin are mentioned in verse 6; five are given in chapter 8:1. What became of the other five? In Genesis 46:21 we find ten names. The others had most likely become extinct in the awful slaughter recorded in Judges (Judges 20). All these tables are more or less imperfect. This does not in any way affect the question of inspiration. No doubt there are deeper lessons connected with many of these names and arrangement of them, which we do not know.

"These genealogies were imperfect. The condition of Israel bore the impress of the ruin which had befallen them; but also that of the goodness of God who had brought back a remnant, and who had preserved all that was needful to place those who formed it in the record of His people. If the needful proof to give them a title to this were wanting, such as were of the people ceased to enjoy their proper privileges, and the priests their sacerdotal position, until a priest stood up with Urim and with Thummim. For these genealogies served as a means to recognize the people. Happy he who had preserved his own, and who had so appreciated the heritage of Jehovah as to attach value to it! It was a proof of faith; for it might have been said, Of what use are these genealogies in Babylon?" (*Synopsis of the Bible*)

6. Benjamin

CHAPTER 8

1. The genealogies of Benjamin (8:1-28)
2. The house of Saul (8:29-40)

In comparing this list with Gen. 46:21 we find some differences. The names of Benjamites include many who were born in the captivity and who returned to the land and dwelt in Jerusalem. Twice we read "those dwelt in Jerusalem" (verses 28, 32). Some of the names are found in the list of restored exiles in Ezra (chapter 2). Benjamin being brought back from the exile, their loyalty to Judah and the temple was rewarded by God. The following passages will give further light on Benjamin's connection with Judah and sharing the blessing of the return from Babylon (Ezra 1:5; chapter 2; 4:1; Neh. 7; 11:4, 7, 31; 12:34).

The genealogy of Saul stands last in this chapter. The overthrow of Saul in chapter 10 forms the beginning of the historical records in Chronicles. The son of Jonathan mentioned in verse 34 as Merib-baal is Mephibosheth (2 Sam. 4:4).

7. The Record of the Inhabitants of Jerusalem after the Return

CHAPTER 9

1. The restoration (9:1-2)
2. Different residents in Jerusalem (9:3-9)
3. The priests (9:10-13)
4. The Levites (9:14-16)
5. Porters and Levites; their duties (9:17-34)
6. The house of Saul (9:35-44)

All Israel was reckoned by genealogies, which means that from the beginning of the nation, public records were kept. The name of every individual and the family and tribe to which they belonged were carefully registered. This complete registry was contained in the book of the kings of Israel and Judah, which does not mean the two books of Kings. The genealogies contained in the preceding chapters were condensed from the larger registry in the archives of Israel and Judah. Such genealogical registers were likewise kept during the captivity. The names registered in the rest of this chapter are the names of the inhabitants of Jerusalem after the exile. Almost all the names are also found in Nehemiah 11 with some marked differences. The genealogy of the house of Saul is repeated once more (see 8:29-38), evidently, as the connecting link with the next chapter.

It is beyond the scope of our work to follow these genealogical registries at greater length, or to attempt the solution of many supposed difficulties.

II. The Overthrow and End of Saul

CHAPTER 10

1. The overthrow and death of Saul (10:1-7)
2. The burial of Saul and his sons (10:8-12)
3. The cause of Saul's failure (10:13-14)

1 Samuel 31 contains the same record of Saul's miserable end and trial. The writer of Chronicles uses the departure of Saul to introduce the history of the king after God's own heart, why God had dealt with Saul in judgment, and that the kingdom was turned unto David, the son of Jesse. The fatal battle between the Philistines and Israel took place in Mount Gilboa. Gilboa is south-east of the plain of Esdraelon which runs from Carmel to the Jordan valley. The cause of this war is unknown. Saul suffered a great defeat and many were the slain of Israel which fell in Gilboa. Among them were Saul's three sons, Jonathan, Abinadab, also called Ishui (1 Sam. 14:49), and Melchi-shua. Then Saul himself was hit by an archer and wounded. Fearing abuse and insults from the Philistines, he requested his armor bearer to draw his sword and to kill him, but he was afraid, because Saul was the Lord's

anointed. Then the unhappy king took his own sword and fell upon it. The armor bearer also committed suicide. The reader will find in annotations on 2 Samuel 1 the story of the Amalekite explained.

The victory of the Philistines was complete. The people forsook their cities and these were occupied by the Philistines. When the plunderers came searching for the slain, in order to strip them of their belongings, the bodies of Saul and his sons were found. Then the body of Saul was stripped and beheaded and the armor was brought into the house of their gods, (Ashtaroth, the Phoenician Venus) and the gory head fastened as a trophy in the house of Dagon. 1 Sam. 31:10 tells us that the body was fastened to the wall of Beth-shan, but here we read that only the head was fastened in the house of Dagon. Beth-shan was a mountain fortress, and here the bodies of Saul and his unfortunate sons were fastened.

"And now night with her dark mantle once more covered these horrible trophies. Shall the eagles and vultures complete the work which, no doubt, they had already begun? The tidings had been carried across the Jordan, and wakened echoes in one of Israel's cities. It was to Jabesh-gilead that Saul, when only named but not yet acknowledged king, had by a forced night-march brought help, delivering it from utter destruction (1 Sam. 11). That had been the morning of Saul's life, bright, and promising as none other; his first glorious victory, which had made him king by acclamation, and drawn Israel's thousands to that gathering in Gilgal, when, amidst the jubilee of an exultant people, the new kingdom was inaugurated. And now it was night; and the headless bodies of Saul and his sons, deserted by all, swung in the wind on the walls of Beth-shan, amid the hoarse music of vultures and jackals.

"But it must not be so; it cannot be so. There was still truth, gratitude, and courage in Israel. And the brave men of Jabesh-gilead marched all the weary night; they crossed Jordan; they climbed that steep brow, and silently detached the dead bodies from the walls. Reverently they bore them across the river, and ere the morning light were far out of reach of the Philistines. Though it had always been the custom in Israel to bury the dead, they would not do so to these mangled remains, that they might not, as it were, perpetuate their disgrace. They burned them just sufficiently to destroy all traces of insult, and the bones they reverently laid under their great tamarisk tree, themselves fasting for seven days in token of public mourning. All honor to the brave men of Jabesh-gilead, whose deed Holy Scripture has preserved to all generations!" (*Bible History*).

Sad and solemn is the final record of King Saul in these historical books. "So Saul died for his transgression which he committed against the Lord, even against the Word of the Lord, which he kept not, and also for asking counsel of one that had a familiar spirit, to inquire of it" (1 Sam. 28:6-7). He had disobeyed God, rejected His Word and then turned to the agency of Satan, to a demon instrument for help and advice. This is the road of apostasy. The road of the apostasy in Christendom so prominent in the closing days of our age is the same. It is departure from the faith and giving heed to seducing spirits and doctrines of demons (1 Tim. 4:1). It is a turning away from the truth, the Word of God, and turning to fables (2 Tim. 4:4).

III. The Crowning of David and the Establishment of His Kingdom

1. David at Hebron

CHAPTER 11

1. David crowned king (11:1-3)
2. Jerusalem becomes David's capital (11:4-9)
3. The record of David's mighty men (11:10-47)

From the second book of Samuel we learned that the crowning of David in Hebron occurred after the death of Ishbosheth (2 Sam. 5). The previous reign of David for seven and a half years and his failures are here omitted. We shall find that Chronicles does not record all the failures and sins of David and Solomon. The blessing and the grace of God toward the house of David are made prominent throughout. Acknowledged by all Israel as belonging to them, a great leader, Jehovah's choice to feed His people Israel and to be their prince, all the elders came to Hebron before the Lord and anointed David king.

The conquest of Jerusalem (Jebus) followed. It was still in the hands of the Jebusites, but David took the stronghold of Zion. Joab distinguished himself and became chief. This is unmentioned in 2 Sam. 5. He built the city from Millo. Millo means "filling up" so that it may have been a big embankment which connected the city of David with the Temple mount. See 1 Kings 9:15 and 2 Chron. 32:5.

The record of David's mighty men are mentioned here in the beginning of his reign. In Second Samuel we read of them at the end (2 Sam. 23:8-39), preceding Solomon's reign. When the true King begins His reign, typified by both David and Solomon, those who were loyal to the Lord and faithful to Him will be remembered. The first name mentioned is Jashobeam, a Hachmonite. In Samuel his name is given as Josheb-basshebeth, the Tachmonite. They were probably alternative names for the same person. Jashobeam means "the people shall return" and his other name in Samuel means "one who sits in a seat." Hachmonite means translated "the wise." According to Samuel he slew 800 and here in Chronicles he slew 300 at one time. Probably these are both correct; he slew 800 at one occasion and 300 at another. The second name is Eleazar (help of God) the son of Dodo (his beloved). His deed is more fully given in 2 Sam. 23:9. Shammah, the third one of the three mighties is omitted here (2 Sam. 23:11).

Bethlehem shows the deepest devotion to David from the three who broke through the line in response to David's wish. It was not a command but only a desire expressed, yet they were ready to give their lives, for they were ambitious to please David. May we think here of Him who is greater than David. He, who sat on Sychar's well said to the woman "give me to drink." He longs for the refreshment from His own and we must be ambitious to please Him. It means to break through the hostile ranks of our enemies, as the three men did.

Abishai (father of gift) the younger brother of Joab and nephew of David slew 300 men. Benaiah's deeds include the slaying of an Egyptian giant almost eight feet tall. In the list of the mighty men Uriah, the Hittite (verse 41) is included. He was a brave and devoted warrior which makes David's deed so much more abhorrent (2 Sam. 11).

2. David's Warriors and Friends

CHAPTER 12

1. The Benjamite warriors with David at Ziklag (12:1-7)
2. The other warriors (12:8-22)
3. Those who came to make him king (12:23-40)

And now those are given by name who stood by David, when he was an outcast, rejected and persecuted by Saul. They were mighty men, his helpers in war. The leading company were of Benjamin, the tribe to which Saul belonged. These joined him when he was at Ziklag. In the wilderness of Judah certain of the Gadites separated themselves unto him, "whose faces were like the faces of lions and they were as swift as the roes upon the mountains." May we remember again that all this is written for our learning. Our Lord is rejected and we can stand by Him, as these mighty men stood by David. Men with faces like lions, bold and courageous, are needed, as well as those as swift as the roes upon the mountains, in doing His bidding in true service. They braved the floods of Jordan and swept all hindrances out of the way to reach David, and when David spoke to them to ascertain why they had come, the Spirit of God sent through Amasai a message which must have greatly cheered his heart. "Thine are we, David, and on thy side, thou son of Jesse." May we say to Him whose we are and whom we serve, "Thine we are, O Lord, and on Thy side, Thou Son of God." Other valiant men of Manasseh also joined him and helped him greatly.

Then a wonderful gathering took place. From everywhere they gathered to make David king. Even from the most northern parts of the land, from Issachar, Zebulun and Naphtali they came for one of the greatest events which happened in Israel's history. If we tabulate the figures given in verses 23-37 we have the following results:

	Men	
Of Judah	6,800	
Of Simeon	7,100	
Of Levi	4,600	
With Jehoiada, the "prince" (not high-priest of Aaron)	3,700	
Zadok and his father's house	———	22 chiefs.
Of Benjamin	3,000	
Of Ephraim	20,800	
Of half Manasseh	18,000	
Of Issachar	———	200 leaders.
Of Zebulun	50,000	
Of Naphtali	37,000	1,000 chiefs.
Of Dan	28,600	
Of Asher	40,000	
Of the 2½ tribes east of Jordan	120,000	
Total	339,600	1,222 chiefs, etc.

This immense company of people came and they had all one desire and one thought, "to make David king." They were not of a double heart. There was no dissenting voice; they were of one heart, they came with a perfect heart to make David king.

A great feast was kept. They brought bread on asses and on camels and on mules and on oxen, and meat, meal, cakes of figs, and bunches of raisins, and wine and oil and oxen and sheep abundantly. There was joy in Israel. But how much greater will be the joy, and what a feast will be made, when He is made King, not alone over Israel, but when He will be enthroned as King of kings and Lord of lords!

3. The Ark Removed from Kirjath-jearim

CHAPTER 13

1. The consultation about the ark (13:1-5)
2. The attempt and the failure (13:6-14)

The first thing after the coronation which concerned David was the ark. This reveals the fact that the king had the things of the Lord upon his heart. He at once consulted with the captains about bringing the ark from Kirjath-jearim. The ark is mentioned forty-six times in the two books of Chronicles.[1] In Chronicles David's gracious words are recorded, which he addressed to the assembly of Israel, "If it seem good unto you and that it be of the Lord our God . . . let us bring again the ark of our Lord to us; for we inquired not at it in the days of Saul." The whole scene manifests a true religious enthusiasm and deep concern to follow the ways of Jehovah. David and all Israel went up to Kirjath-jearim and carried the ark upon a new cart. David and all Israel played before God with all their might, even with songs and with harps and with psalteries, with cymbals and trumpets. But in all this great and human rejoicing, David did not conform to Jehovah's ways. According to God's laws covering the handling of the ark, only the Levites were to touch it. They were to carry it on their shoulders and not to place it in a cart (Num. 4:5, 15). All this had been violated. The divine displeasure was fully manifested when Uzza put forth his hands to hold the ark, because the oxen had stumbled. Uzza was stricken with sudden death. He forgot that the ark was the emblem of Jehovah's presence in the midst of His people. See annotations on 2 Samuel 6.

[1]The titles are the following: ark, 15 times; the ark of God, 12 times; the ark of the Covenant of the Lord, 11 times; the ark of the Lord, 4 times; the ark of the Covenant of God, of Thy Strength, of our God and Thy holy ark, each once.

4. David's Increase and Blessing

CHAPTER 14

1. Hiram (14:1-2)
2. David's family (14:3-7)
3. The Philistines defeated (14:8-17)

The reader is referred to 2 Sam. 5:11-16 for the comment on verses 1-7. Beeliada is called in 2 Sam. 5:16 Eliada. Beeliada was probably changed to Eliada. David's great victory over the Philistines is also recorded in 2 Sam. 5:17-25. He inquired of God and being permitted to go, he smote them at Baal-perazim, where also the idol images were burned with fire (in obedience to Deut. 7:5, 25). It was a great victory. Baal-perazim means "possessor of breaches." In Isaiah the victory over the Philistines is used as a prophecy of the coming future judgment of the earth. "For the Lord shall rise up as in mount Perazim, He shall be wroth as in the valley of Gibeon, that He may do His work, His strange work, and bring to pass His act, His strange act" (Isaiah 28:21). A second time the Philistines came, and David, obedient to the divine instructions, gained another great victory. His fame went into all lands and the fear of him was brought by the Lord upon all nations.

5. The Ark Brought to Jerusalem

CHAPTER 15:1—16:3

1. The true preparation to fetch the ark (15:1-15)
2. The great procession (15:16-24)
3. The ark brought back (15:25—16:3)

The ark rested in the house of Obed-edom for three months. During that time David prepared a place for the ark of God and pitched a tent. Warned by what had happened, his conscience aroused, David said, "None ought to carry the ark of God but the Levites, for them hath the Lord chosen to carry the ark of God, and to minister unto Him forever."

It is to be observed, that, although the death of Uzza had its origin in the guilty forgetfulness of David, it nevertheless gave occasion through grace to his being set in his true position for the regulation and appointment of all that concerned the Levites' service. It is always thus with regard to faith, for the purposes of God are fulfilled in favor of it. Man in his zeal may depart from the will of God, and God will chasten him, but only to bring him into more honor, by setting him more completely in the position which God has purposed, and in the understanding of His ways, according to which He will magnify His servant (*Synopsis of the Bible*).

All Israel and especially the Levites were gathered together. All is now done according to the divine directions. The former failure was owned and the priests and Levites sanctified themselves to bring up the ark. They carried the ark of God upon their shoulders with the staves as God had commanded.

A great procession was also requested by David and arranged by the Levites. David loved singing and music as the expression of praise unto the Lord. The instruments mentioned are the psaltery, which was like a long box with a convex sounding board, over which wire strings were stretched; the harp and the cymbal. The latter was a brass instrument with a ball attached. The great procession was headed by a choir of singers and musicians under the leadership of Heman, Asaph and Ethan. In the middle of the procession was the ark, preceded by Chenaniah (established by the Lord), the chief of the Levites. Then there were the two door-keepers of the ark, Berechiah (blessed of the Lord) and Elkanah (God has purchased) and seven priests, who sounded the trumpets before the ark, and two more door-keepers. "Alamoth" in verse 20 must have been a choir of virgins (Alamoth means virgins). Such is the meaning of the word in the inscription of Psalm 46. In Psalm 58, where a great procession is mentioned in connection with the removing of the ark (no doubt commemorating the return of the ark to Jerusalem) we read of women publishing the tidings (verse 11 marginal reading) and there we hear also of the damsels in the procession. (Read also Psalm 132 and notice its connection with the event of this chapter.) "The singers went before; the players of the instruments followed after, among them were the damsels playing with timbrels" (Psalm 68:25). But the sixty-eighth Psalm describes prophetically another great procession and celebration, when He comes in great power and glory. "Sing unto God, ye kingdoms of the earth; O sing praises unto the Lord—to Him that rideth upon the heaven of heavens" (Psalm 68:32-33).

And so the ark was brought to Jerusalem and set in the midst of the tent. It was a time of great rejoicing and feasting. But what will it be when not an ark, the symbol only of the divine presence, is in the midst of the people, but when the once rejected King appears in the midst and receives the homage and praise of Israel!

(Comment on Michal and her mockery is made in the parallel passage in 2 Samuel. We omit in annotation in Chronicles all which has been previously mentioned in Samuel and Kings.)

6. The Great Thanksgiving Psalm

CHAPTER 16:4-43

1. David's appointment (16:4-6)
2. The Psalm of praise and thanksgiving (16:7-36)
3. The Levites and the public worship (16:37-43)

A great thanksgiving Psalm was then delivered by David into the hand of Asaph and his brethren. The view of modern critics, that this Psalm is post-exilic, does not call for any refutation, for the text declares that David himself delivered the hymn to Asaph. The Psalm is made up of portions of different Psalms. See Psalm 105:1-15; 96:1-13; 106:47-48; 107:1; 136. A careful study will show the far reaching meaning of this composite Psalm. It is a great prophecy. It begins with the celebration and praise of what Jehovah has done. Israel is called to remember His covenant. It is not the covenant at Sinai, with its conditional promises, but the unconditional, the grace-covenant, made with Abraham, an everlasting covenant that his seed is to have the land. But prophetically the Psalm points to the time when "His judgments are in all the earth"; it is at that time when the covenant made with Abraham will be remembered. Such a time will come according to the prophetic Word. Verse 22, "Touch not Mine anointed, and do My prophets no harm," speaks of Israel's preservation; for Israel is His anointed, a kingdom of kings and priests. The day must come when the covenant made with Abraham will be realized and when Israel shall possess the land, after their wanderings from nation to nation (verse 20). Then there will be a throne in Zion and a King shall reign in righteousness, even Christ (Psalm 2).

Then Psalm 96 is quoted. It is a Psalm which looks forward to the kingdom on earth, when the nations acknowledge Jehovah and bow in Hi presence. The blessed age of glory, of which the prophets have so much to say, the unreached goal of the glorious future of the earth, the millennium, is pictured in this Psalm.

Fear before Him, all the earth
The World is established, it cannot be moved,
Let the heavens be glad,
And let the earth rejoice.
And let them say among the nations,
The Lord reigneth.
Let the sea roar, and the fulness thereof,
Let the fields rejoice and all there is therein;
Then shall the trees of the wood sing out,
At the Presence of the Lord,
Because He cometh to judge the earth.

The praise of Israel concludes the thanksgiving Psalm. We repeat, it is prophetic. It looks onward to the time when the Lord will deliver His people, when the promises made to the fathers will all be fulfilled, when the nations of the earth will know the Lord and when He will reign over all. Such is Israel's future. When He has been merciful to His land and to His people, the nations will rejoice (Deut. 32:43).

At the close of this chapter we notice how King David regulates everything that was to be done before the ark.

"The placing of the ark in the capital of Israel, thus making it 'the city of God,' was an event not only of deep national, but of such typical importance, that it is frequently referred to in the sacred songs of the sanctuary. No one will have any difficulty in recognizing Psalm 24 as the hymn composed for this occasion. But other Psalms also refer to it, amongst which, without entering on details that may be profitably studied by each reader, we may mention Psalms 15, 68, 78, and especially Psalm 101, as indicating, so to speak, the moral bearing of the nearness of God's ark upon the king and his kingdom.

> Faith, apprehending the counsels and the work of God, could see in the establishment of the ark in Zion, the progress of God's power and intervention towards the peaceful and glorious reign of the Son of David. The sure mercies of David were as bright to the eye of faith as the dawn of day, in that the ark of the covenant had been set up by David the king in the mountain which God had chosen for His everlasting rest *(Synopsis of the Bible).*

7. The Covenant and the Promise

CHAPTER 17

1. David's plan to build a house (17:1-6)
2. The covenant and the promise (17:7-15)
3. David's praise and prayer (17:16-27)

After the ark had found its resting place in a tent the king became deeply concerned about the building of a house. He contrasted his own house of cedars with the humble dwelling place of the ark of the covenant. The desire to build a house for the Lord was expressed to Nathan, who told David, without having consulted the Lord, "Do all that is in thine heart, for God is with thee." That night the message came to Nathan, "Go and tell David my servant, Thus saith the Lord, Thou shalt not build Me a house to dwell in, for I have not dwelt in a house since the day that I brought up Israel unto this day, but have gone from tent to tent, and from one tabernacle unto another. Wheresoever I have walked with all Israel, spake I a word to any of the judges of Israel, whom I commanded to feed My people, saying, Why have ye not built Me a house of cedars?" What condescension and what identification with His people these words reveal!

> When Israel was a slave, God became his Redeemer; when he dwelt in tents, God abode in one also; when in conflict, God presented Himself as captain of Jehovah's host; when settled in peace, God establishes Himself in the house of His glory. The interval was the probation of His people on earth. God abode in the tent, and even His ark is taken. He interposes in grace for deliverance.
>
> "Christ also, since we were born of woman, is born of a woman; since His people were under the law, He is born under the law; now that He will have a heavenly people, He is on high for us; when He comes in glory, we shall come with Him, and reign when He reigns, but in these last we are with Him," *(Synopsis of the Bible).*

As we have already considered the great Davidic covenant and its meaning (2 Sam. 7) as well as David's worship and prayer, we refer the reader to the annotations of that chapter. Solomon, David's son, is first in view, but he is only a type of Christ, David's greater Son and David's Lord as well. In Christ alone, this great covenant-promise is to be fulfilled. It is still all future, for the Son of David, rejected of His own, does not sit and rule upon the throne of His father David. He has gone to heaven, occupying the throne of God, sitting at His right hand up to the time when His enemies will be made His footstool. Then, when He appears the second time, the angelic announcement will come true, "and the Lord God shall give unto Him the throne of His father David."

And what words David spoke to Him, whose grace had made such promises! Humility, faith and confidence answered grace.

8. David's Wars and Successful Reign

CHAPTER 18

1. War with the Philistines (18:1)
2. War with Moab (18:2)
3. War with Zobah (18:3-4)
4. War with Damascus (18:5-11)
5. Wars with Edom (18:12-13)
6. David's administration (18:14-17)

After such glorious experiences David went forth as the victorious warrior-king to conquer the enemies of Israel. He first smote the Philistines, subdued them and took Gath and her towns. Gath, the chief city of the Philistines, is called in 2 Sam. 8:1 "Metheg-ammah," which means "the bridle of the mother city." Then he smote Moab and they became his servants and brought presents. Great are the conquests and victories of David recorded in this chapter. From Hadarezer, King of Zobah, he took 1,000 chariots, 7,000 horsemen and 20,000 footmen. (2 Sam. 8:4 has 700, which is a copyist's error.) Then the Syrians came to help the King of Zobah and lost 22,000 men. Then the Syrians also became his servants and brought presents. "And the Lord gave victory to David whithersoever he went." In all this we see foreshadowed the triumphs of our Lord Jesus Christ, when He comes as the victorious King and His enemies shall all be subdued.

All the spoil taken, the shields of gold, were brought to Jerusalem. From Tibhath and from Chun, cities which belonged to Hadarezer, David took very much brass. The brazen sea, the pillars and the vessels of brass for the temple were made by Solomon out of this material. Silver and gold which he carried away from all the conquered nations were all dedicated unto the Lord. And in a future day shall the silver and the gold of the Gentiles be brought to Jerusalem (Isa. 60:6, 17; Psalm 72:10). So David reigned over all Israel, and executed judgment and justice among all his people.

9. The Wars with Ammon, Syria and the Philistines (19—20)

CHAPTER 19

1. Hanun's insult to David's servants (19:1-5)
2. Joab's victory (19:6-16)
3. David's victorious campaign (19:17-19)

See annotations on 2 Samuel chapter 10. The occasion of the war with the Ammonites was the insult to the messengers of David whom he had sent to the son of King Nahash. Nahash had died and David sent the messengers to comfort Hanun concerning his father. It gives a little glimpse of the tenderness of David. "But the princes of the children of Ammon said to Hanun, Thinkest thou that David doth honor thy father, that he hath sent comforters unto thee? Are not his servants come unto thee for to search and to overthrow and to spy out the land?" When the Ammonites realized the insult to David's messengers, they spent 1,000 talents of silver (about $375,000) to hire chariots and horsemen. Joab was victorious. Then the king himself took charge and gathered all Israel. A great victory was the result.

In 2 Samuel the great sin of David follows the victory over the Syrians. In our comment on the fall of David, we have pointed out the connection between the victory of David and his sin. David's fall is omitted in Chronicles because the grace of God is the prominent feature and grace had completely covered David's great sin.

CHAPTER 20

Joab and David take Rabbah

1. Rabbah destroyed (20:1-3)
2. The Philistine giants slain (20:4-8)

Rabbah was the capital of Ammon (Deut. 3:11; Josh. 13:25) and was taken by Joab. David tarried in Jerusalem (so fatal to him, 2 Sam. 11:1) and Joab smote Rabbah and destroyed it. Then David appeared also upon the scene. Joab had summoned David to help in the overthrow of the city (2 Sam. 12:27, etc). The crown mentioned was probably the crown of Milcom, their idol-king. It was of solid gold set with precious stones. David received the crown and precious stones, even as our Lord Jesus receives the glory and will appear crowned with many crowns (Rev. 19:12). On verse 3 see annotations 2 Sam. 2:31. The overthrow of the giants followed. First Sibbechai slew Sippai of the children of the giants; in 2 Sam. 21 his name is given as Saph. Elhanan slew Lahmi of Goliath. (The words "the brother of" are in italics and must be omitted. It was another giant who had the same name as the giant of 1 Sam. 17.) Then David's nephew Jonathan, the son of Shimea, David's brother, slew the last of the giants. He had six fingers on each hand and six toes on each foot and was of great stature. These giants were the special instruments of the power of darkness. They have a typical significance.

The notion of a giant in Scripture is always connected with evil, the lifting up of man against God, the symbol of pride and self-sufficiency, as well as of oppressive power. He is the opposite of the little and the lowly, the humble in heart, with whom God delights to dwell; but thus may stand for the tyranny of a lust, as in the case of Og, or of a Satanic delusion, as with Goliath himself. In those before us we must see, what we have seen in their kinsman, the monstrous delusions which abide in a system of error such as Philistinism depicts, the ecclesiastical "mystery of lawlessness" of Christian times *(Numerical Bible).*

And in the last one overcome by Jonathan (gift of the Lord), we see a type of the final ecclesiastical leader of the apostasy, the man of sin. The number "six" points to this (Rev. 13:11-18).

10. The Numbering of the People and the Punishment

CHAPTER 21

1. David's failure in numbering the people (21:1-7)
2. David's confession and the message of God (21:8-12)
3. David's answer and the punishment (21:13-17)
4. The altar in the threshing floor of Ornan (21:18-30)

On the alleged discrepancy between the statement in 2 Sam. 24:1 "And again the anger of the Lord was kindled against Israel, and He moved (literal: He suffered him to be moved) David against them to say, Go, number Israel and Judah," and 1 Chron. 21:1 "And Satan stood up against Israel and provoked David to number Israel"; see annotations on 2 Sam. 24. Israel had committed some sin and deserved punishment. This is clear from the statement in 2 Sam. 24:1. The direct cause of the visitation, however, was David's pride, and may have been connected with the desire of constituting his kingdom as a great military power. He wanted to know the strength of the nation and glory in it, and the king forgot that the Lord had increased Israel and all he was and had was of God. What a difference between David here and David sitting in the presence of the Lord after hearing Nathan's message! (17:16). Nothing humbles so as being in the presence of the Lord. The lust of the flesh in self-indulgence had led to his awful sin with Bathsheba, and now the lust of the eyes and the pride of life had entangled him. Satan stood behind it all and the sin committed, pride and self-exaltation, was according to Satan's character. Then David confessed (verse 8) and the Lord sent the prophet Gad to him announcing the modes of punishment from which he was to make his choice. The recovery of David, his real knowledge of God and the working of His grace in his heart are manifested by the fact that he committed himself to God, choosing rather to fall into the hands of God than into the hands of his enemies. The Lord sent the pestilence. David saw the angel of the Lord. Then David and the elders clothed in sack cloth were on their faces. At the sight of the angel with his drawn sword stretched over Jerusalem, David confessed again, but his prayer becomes an intercession; he takes the sin upon himself and prays "let Thine hand, be on me, and on my father's house; but not on Thy people that they should be plagued." This prayer was speedily followed by mercy. The site of the future house of the Lord was then acquired. (See comment on 2 Sam. 24.) Ornan and his four sons had also seen the angel and they were afraid (verse 20). And the Jebusite was willing to give the threshing-floor and all within it. And when the site had been acquired by purchase and the altar was built, burnt-offerings and peace-offerings were brought. Heaven answered by fire. "And the Lord commanded the angel; and he put up his sword again into the sheath thereof." All is blessedly typical of Him who is the true burnt-offering, as well as the peace-offering.

It is interesting to see the order unfolded here in the establishment of the sovereign grace: first of all, the heart of God and His sovereign grace in election, suspending the execution of the deserved and pronounced judgment (verse 15); next, the revelation of this judgment, a revelation which produces humiliation before God and a full confession of sin before His face. David, and the elders of Israel, clothed in sackcloth, fall upon their faces, and David presents himself as the guilty one. Then, instruction comes from God, as to that which must be done to cause the pestilence judicially and definitively to cease, namely, the sacrifice in Ornan's threshing-floor. God accepts the sacrifice, sending fire to consume it, and then He commands the angel to sheathe his sword. And sovereign grace, thus carried out in righteousness through sacrifice, becomes the means of Israel's approach to their God, and establishes the place of their access to Him.

IV. Preparations for the Building of the Temple

1. The Preparations and Charge to Solomon

1. The material (22:1-5)
2. The charge to Solomon (22:6-16)
3. The charge to the princes (22:17-19)

God had accepted the sacrifice. The judgment had passed. Prayer had been answered and David, therefore, could truthfully say "this is the house of the Lord God, and this is the altar of the burnt-offering for Israel." The place had therefore been pointed out on which the temple was to be reared. And from now on up to the twenty-eighth verse of chapter 26 all concerns the house which is to be built. The temple is from now on prominently in the foreground and that which the book of Kings does not mention, David's great interest in making preparations for it, is recorded in these chapters. And so we see David with great energy making vast preparations. It shows again how grace had worked in his heart. All else seems to have been forgotten by him. Only one desire controls the king, to make provision of everything necessary for the construction of the Temple. And the house, according to David's conception "must be exceeding magnificent, of fame and of glory throughout all countries." His heart burned with zeal to glorify Jehovah, whose mercy and grace he knew so well and who had kept and prospered him in all his ways. "I will therefore now make preparation for it," David said. Then he prepared abundantly before his death. David, making preparation for the temple his son was to put up, is not without a very striking typical meaning. Both David and Solomon are types of our Lord Jesus Christ. David typifies Him in His humiliation and suffering, Solomon in His exaltation and glory. What Christ has done in His grace results in the coming glory. This is foreshadowed in the preparations David made for the house and the glorious reign of his son. If this is kept in mind these historical statements will take on a blessed meaning.

He gathered the strangers (the descendants of the Canaanites) and he set them at work. Stones, iron and timber all were prepared before hand on a large scale. Then he called for Solomon, young and tender in years, and addressed him. First he restated the reason why he had been barred from building the house. Then he recited the promise made to him that his son should have rest and build a house for His name. "For his name shall be Solomon, and I will give peace and quietness unto Israel in his days. He shall build a house for my name." David believed all the Lord had spoken through Nathan, and, believing the promise, he had made all preparations and was telling his son about it.

Then he exhorted him to build the house, to keep the law of the Lord and to take heed. "Be strong, and of good courage and dread not nor be dismayed." Once more he speaks of all he had done in preparation of the house of the Lord. Even in the days of trouble and adversity he had prepared for the house and remembered the claims of Jehovah. Immense amounts of gold and silver, the spoils of wars, had been stored up by him. Many millions of dollars in gold and silver were in his possession and devoted for the one object. And Solomon was to add unto it. Then he told him to arise and to be doing. In the same way he commanded the princes of Israel to help his son Solomon.

May this teach us who know the riches of the grace of God in Christ Jesus our Lord, to be as devoted to Him, as zealous to glorify Him, as David was in making these preparations for the building of the temple.

2. The Numbering and Arrangement of the Levites

CHAPTER 23

1. Solomon made king (23:1)
2. The number of the Levites (23:2-6)
3. The Gershonites (23:7-11)
4. The sons of Kohath (23:12-20)
5. The sons of Merari (23:21-23)
6. The service of the Levites (23:24-32)

David, in his seventieth year, made Solomon king. It is the first time, and afterwards (29:22) he was made king the second time.

"The first time Solomon was made king, when grace was fully established in the altar built on the threshing-floor of Ornan, where the son of David, as the prince of peace, was to build the temple. Solomon is introduced as the head of all that was being established, and as holding the first and supreme place in the mind of God—the one on whom all the rest depended, which could not even exist now without him. The house, the whole order of the house, and its government, all referred to Solomon; and thus his identification with David, in that both were on the throne at the same time, makes it much easier to understand the type of Christ in this. It is *one* person, whom His sufferings and victories place on the throne of glory and of peace. For at this moment, although the result of the glory was not yet manifested, God had given rest unto His people, that they might dwell at Jerusalem" *(Synopsis of the Bible)*.

After he had made Solomon king, David devoted himself still more to the house of the Lord. He ordered and arranged everything. So when the temple was built, Solomon had only to carry out the plans his father in divine wisdom had made. All is typical of Him who has ordered all things in His infinite grace.

The census of the Levites gave their number from thirty years and upwards, at 38,000. Of these 24,000 were appointed to attend, set forward the work of the house of the Lord; 6,000 were officers and judges; 4,000 were porters and 4,000 praised the Lord with the instruments David had made to praise therewith (Amos 6:5).

3. The Twenty-four Courses of the Priests

CHAPTER 24

1. The twenty-four courses (24:1-19)
2. The organization of other Levites (24:20-31)

In the previous chapter we read of 24,000 Levites set apart for the service. In the next chapter we find twenty-four leaders of song and music appointed, and here David instituted twenty-four courses of priests. Each of these ministered a full week, from one sabbath to the next. These courses were not only continued by Solomon, but also by Hezekiah and Josiah. From Luke 1:5, we learn the same order was still followed in the days our Lord was born. Zecharias belonged to the eighth course, that of Abijah.

In the book of Revelation (chapter 4, etc.) we read of twenty-four elders clothed in white raiment, crowned and seated upon twenty-four thrones. They represent symbolically all the redeemed brought into glory. This number is obviously an allusion to the arrangement of the priesthood made by David for the service of the temple under the glorious reign of Solomon, the blessed type of the reign of Christ in glory. As these twenty-four courses of Priests were to minister during Solomon's glorious reign, they are typical of the redeemed, the holy and royal priesthood, associated with the Lord Jesus Christ when He occupies His throne of glory.

4. The Singers and Musicians of the Temple

CHAPTER 25

1. Sons of Asaph, Jeduthun and Heman (25:1-7)
2. Their division by Lot into twenty-four (25:8-31)

As we have seen before, Asaph, Jeduthun (Ethan) and Heman were the master leaders in song and music; their service was eminently spiritual, for we read "they should prophesy." Heman especially is called the king's seer in the words of God. This is a significant expression. How much there is in what is termed "worship", which has nothing whatever of the words of God in it. In most of the songs used in our times there is little of the words of God and many contain unscriptural and sentimental phrases. Israel's worship in song and music was to be spiritual, prophesying and in the words of God. Christian worship is not less. It is to be in spirit and in truth. "Let the Word of Christ dwell in you richly in all wisdom; teaching and admonishing one another in psalms and hymns and spiritual songs, singing with grace in your hearts to the Lord" (Col. 3:16). Asaph had four sons, Jeduthun six, and Heman fourteen, equal to twenty-four. They were divided into twenty-four courses of twelve men each, equal to 288, who served a week in turn. The names of six of the sons of Heman form, in the Hebrew, a complete sentence. Giddalti, Romamti-ezer, Joshbekashah, Mallothi, Hothir and Mahazioth (verse 4) may be rendered in English:

> I have magnified and I have
> raised up help;
> Sitting in trouble, I have spoken
> oracles plentiful.

This fact has aroused the suspicion of the critics regarding the genuineness of this entire list of names. "Now this sentence," saith a critic, "is either an obscure and ancient prayer which hath been mistaken for a list of names by the compiler, or else the compiler has purposely strung together those significant names in such order as to form a sentence" (W. R. Harvey-Jellie). But it is not the mistake of the compiler or an invention. We read that God gave to Heman these sons and the pious Israelite named his sons so as to produce this meaning. There are many such messages in names throughout the Bible. (See annotations on Genesis 5.)

5. The Porters and other Temple Officers

CHAPTER 26

1. The porters (26:1-12)
2. The keepers of the gates (26:13-19)
3. The Levites over the treasures (26:20-28)
4. Officers and judges (26:29-32)

Ninety-three porters are mentioned, which held the position of chiefs. The whole number of porters was 4,000 (23:5). Asaph in verse 1 must be changed to Ebiasaph (9:19), for Asaph was not a Korahite, but a Gershonite. Obed-edom is especially mentioned. God blessed him (verse 5). He had sheltered the ark (8:14), "and the Lord blessed the house of Obed-edom, and all that he had." And here the blessing is seen in a remarkable increase. "All these of the sons of Obed-edom; they and their sons and their brethren, able men for strength for the service, were three score and two of Obed-edom" (Psalm 127:3). How faithful the Lord is. He did not forget Obed-edom's service and rewarded him richly.

Then there were the gate keepers. The temple was still unbuilt, no plans had been drawn by man, but the Lord had revealed the plan to David (28:11-13), and he ordered the keepers of the gates according to the divine plan. Then follows the appointment of the Levites who had charge over the treasures and the appointment of officers and judges. Their number was 6,000 (Chap. 23:4). They were divided into three classes: 1. For the outward business of Israel (verse 29). 2. Those who had the oversight of Israel beyond Jordan westward, 1,700 persons, for all the business of the Lord, and for service of the King (verse 30). 3. The third class consisted of 2,700 who were rulers for every matter pertaining to God, and affairs of the king (verses 31-32). All was divinely planned and arranged through David in anticipation of the glorious reign of his son. And even so all is planned and appointed for the coming reign of the King of Righteousness and the King of Peace.

6. The Captains, Princes, and Various Officials

CHAPTER 27

1. The twelve captains (27:1-15)
2. The princes of the twelve tribes (27:16-22)
3. The unfinished numbering (27:23-24)
4. Various officers (27:25-34)

We have here the military organization of David's kingdom. The army comprised all males over twenty years of age. The host had twelve divisions each of 24,000. It is remarkable how the number twenty-four occurs again and again. Twelve is the governmental number and twice twelve, that is, twenty-four, would indicate a perfect and complete government such as will be established when Heaven's King of Glory is enthroned. In the list of the Princes of Israel the tribe of Dan is numbered last. There is something significant about this. Dan, as we have seen, is not mentioned in the chronological register, nor is this tribe mentioned in Rev. 7. Dan is called a serpent (Genesis 49:17); it may be that the coming false Messiah will come out of Dan. Gad and Asher are not mentioned in the list.

7. The Last Acts of David and His Death

CHAPTER 28

The Great Assembly

1. The Address of David to the assembly (28:1-10)
2. The patterns, the gold and the silver delivered to Solomon (28:11-19)
3. His encouraging words to Solomon (28:20-21)

The events in this chapter connect with Chapter 23:1. There we find the brief statement that David was old and full of years and that Solomon his son was made king over Israel. Then follow the chapters which acquaint us with the preparations David had made for the building of the temple and the arrangements of the Levites, etc., for the temple service. And now the threads of the narrative which were dropped are taken up again. A great and representative audience was called by David when he made Solomon king. All the princes of Israel and the captains and mighty men in Jerusalem came together. As we know from the book of Kings the aged monarch was weak in his body. But when the hour came to address the great assembly he arose and stood upon his feet. The three attitudes of David are suggestive. He was, on his face, a penitent, (2 Sam. 1:12; 1 Chron. 21:16); he sat in His presence as a worshipper (1 Chron. 17:16), and now he stood on his feet as a servant. The words he spoke before the assembly are similar to those he addressed to his son Solomon in private (1 Chron. 22). After he had spoken all these words, in which he once more traced the gracious dealings of the Lord with him, he admonished his son to know the God of his father, to serve Him with a perfect heart and a willing mind. "If thou seek Him, He will be found of thee; but if thou forsake Him, He will cast thee off forever." Then he exhorted him again to build the house. "Be strong and do it."

After this David handed over the patterns of the porch, the temple houses, the treasuries, the upper chambers and the inner rooms and of the place of the mercy seat. How did the king obtain these patterns? He had them by the

Spirit. The authorized version prints Spirit with a small "s." It was not his own spirit who planned it. A certain commentator says it means that these patterns had been "floating in his mind." The sentence "the pattern of all that he had by the Spirit" means that the Holy Spirit had revealed it all to him. It was given to him by inspiration as the pattern of the tabernacle and all belonging to it had been given to Moses also by revelation. Then he turned over to Solomon the immense quantities of gold and silver and other materials he had so faithfully collected for the construction of the Temple.

CHAPTER 29

The Final Words and Actions of David and His Death

1. The exhortation (29:1-5)
2. The response (29:6-9)
3. David's praise and prayer (29:10-20)
4. The sacrifices and enthronement of Solomon (29:21-25)
5. The reign of David and his death (29:26-30)

Then David spoke once more to the assembled princes and captains. What tenderness and concern as well as devotion his words reveal! "Solomon my son, whom alone God hath chosen, is yet young, and tender, and the work is great, for the palace is not for man, but for the Lord God." Once more the aged king speaks of the vast preparations he had made for the house of God. He would also contribute largely from his own treasures. The gold and silver, precious and glistening stones amounted in value to many million dollars. The gold of Ophir mentioned was the purest and finest known in that day (Job 22:24; 28:16; Isaiah 13:12). And all he had done was because he had set his affection to the house of my God. He loved it so much and therefore he gave and consecrated such vast treasures. And here we may remember Him who was richer than David, who gave more than David ever could give. "For ye know the grace of our Lord Jesus Christ, that though He was rich, yet for your sakes He became poor that ye through His poverty might be rich" (2 Cor. 8:9). After he had told of this own devotion he said, "And who then is willing to consecrate his service this day unto the Lord?" The Hebrew is "to fill his hand to-day to Jehovah." It means that whosoever gave willingly, as he himself had done, would fill his hand with a free will offering unto the Lord. Christian giving should always be looked upon in this light. It is giving unto the Lord. And David's great liberality and example brought a great response. An immense offering was given.

"Drams" is in Hebrew "daric," a Persian gold coin weighing about 130 grains. The word is found also in Ezra 8:27. It was probably called "daric" after Darius and therefore shows that Chronicles was written after the captivity.

"Then the people rejoiced, for that they offered willingly, because with perfect heart they offered willingly to the Lord, and David, the King, also rejoiced with great joy." The joy of giving took hold of all. "It is more blessed to give than to receive" (Acts 20:35). How great must have been the joy of the king as he beheld the fruits of his own devotion in the willingness of his people! And here again we must think once more of our Lord. It is His gracious example in giving Himself for us, His people, which will lead us on to sacrifice, to give, to spend and be spent. And how great His joy if His people follow thus after Him.

It is a great inspired outburst of David which follows. How He praises! Verses 10-13 are one of the greatest outbursts of praise and worship found in the Old Testament. Then what humility! "But who am I, and what is my people that we should be able to offer so willingly after this sort? for all things come of thee, and of thine own have we given thee . . . all this store that we have prepared to build thee a house for thine holy name cometh of thine hand, and is all thine own." A most beautiful sight is an aged saint whom God hath used and honored and who is humble. Alas! how many become lifted up and walk in pride. Then David prayed for the people and for his son Solomon. "And all the congregation blessed the Lord God of their fathers, and bowed down their heads, and worshipped the Lord, and the King" (verse 20). All foreshadows that day of which we read in Psalm 110:3, "Thy people shall be willing in the day of thy power." That will be when the King, the Prince of Peace, will take His glorious throne, when He begins to rule.

After the large number of sacrifices had been brought and they had eaten before the Lord on that day with great gladness, Solomon was made king the second time, even as his father David passed through the same experience. This double event has no doubt a definite typical meaning in connection with our Lord in as much as both, David and Solomon, are types of the Lord Jesus Christ. When Solomon was made king the first time he was but anointed with oil (1 Kings 1:39) and acclaimed as king, but he did not occupy the kingly throne. But when he was made king the second time he sat upon the throne "and all Israel obeyed him." "The Lord magnified Solomon exceedingly in the sight of all Israel and bestowed upon him such royal majesty as had not been on any king before him in Israel." We see therefore (though no commentaries mention it) that these two occasions are typical of the first and the second coming of our Lord. Our Lord was anointed king when He came the first time, but He received not the throne. When He comes the second time He receives the throne and God will bestow upon Him "royal majesty" and "all Israel" will obey Him.

Then follows the record of the reign and death of David. There is no clash between the account of David's last days in the closing chapters of the second book of Samuel and the opening chapters of First Kings. The record in Chronicles is in fullest keeping with the purpose and object of this book. Blessing and grace is manifested to the end, and David's failings are passed over.

Appendix

Chronological Table

According to Professor Keil, from the Exodus to the Building of the Temple by Solomon

(Compare Judges 11:26 and 1 Kings 6:1)

Principal Events		*Years of their duration*	*Date before Christ*
The Exodus		..	.. 1492
Giving of the Law on Mount Sinai		..	from 1492 to 1491
Death of Moses and Aaron		in the 40th year	.. 1453
Conquest of Canaan by Joshua		7	1452 to 1445
Division of Canaan to the invasion of Chushan Rishathaim		10	1445 to 1435
Death of Joshua		..	about 1442
Wars of Israel against the Canaanites		..	from 1442
Expedition against Benjamin (Judges)		..	about 1436
Oppression by Chushan Rishathaim		8	1435 to 1427
Othniel, and rest of Israel		40	1427 to 1387
Oppression by the Moabites		18	1387 to 1369
Ehud, and rest of Israel		80	1369 to 1289
Victory of Shamgar over the Philistines		..	.. ..
Oppression by Jabin		20	1289 to 1269
Deborah and Barak, and rest of Israel		40	1269 to 1229
Oppression by the Midianites		7	1229 to 1222
Gideon, and rest		40	1222 to 1182
Abimelech		3	1182 to 1179
Tola		23	1179 to 1156
Jair		22	1156 to 1134
Eli for forty years		..	1154 to 1114
Then: *In the East*	*In the West*	40	1134 to 1094
Oppression by the Ammonites, 18 years: 1134-1116	By the Philistines Loss of the Ark	..	about 1114
Jephthah, 6 years: 1116-1110	Samson's deeds	..	1116 to 1096
	Samuel as a prophet		from 1114
Ibzan, 7 years: 1110-1103	Samuel judge	19	1094 to 1975
Elon 10 years: 1103-1093	Saul king	20	1075 to 1055
Abdon, 8 years: 1093-1085	David at Hebron	7	1055 to 1048
	David at Jerusalem	33	1048 to 1015
	Solomon to the building of Temple	3	1015 to 1012
Total		480	years.

THE SECOND BOOK OF THE

CHRONICLES

The Division of the Second Book of the Chronicles

Originally the two books of the Chronicles formed one book and were undivided. The period of the history of the people, Israel, covered in this book is the same as in the books of the Kings. It begins with the Solomonic reign, the building and dedication of the temple, and ends with the captivity of Judah. The closing of Chronicles proves the post-exilic time of its composition, for it mentions Cyrus the King of Persia and his restoration proclamation. The history, however, is almost exclusively the history of the house of Judah. Israel's history is very briefly touched upon. Inasmuch as Chronicles is written from the priestly and the divine viewpoint, everything centers around the temple of Jehovah. There are most interesting descriptions of Solomon's reign, the temple and the worship, which we do not find in the parallel chapters in the first book of Kings. The reader should make use of the parallel passages given in connection with the introduction to the Chronicles and then read the annotations in Kings, as we shall not repeat, in the annotations of this second book of the Chronicles, what has already been given. We shall point out what is peculiar to Chronicles. We divide the book into four sections.

I. THE REIGN OF SOLOMON (1—9)

1. **The Beginning of His Reign and the First Vision** (1:1-17)
2. **The Building of the Temple** (2—4)
3. **The Dedication of the Temple** (5:1—7:10)
4. **The Second Vision** (7:11-22)
5. **Solomon's Prosperity and Activities** (8:1-18)
6. **The Queen of Sheba and Solomon's Death.** (9:1-31)

II. THE REBELLION OF THE TEN TRIBES (10:1-19)

III. THE HISTORY OF THE KINGS OF JUDAH AND EVENTS LEADING UP TO THE CAPTIVITY (11—36:14)

1. **Decline and Apostasy under Rehoboam and Abijah; Asa and his Reformation and Failure.** (11—16)
2. **Reformation under Jehoshaphat** (17—20)
3. **Decline and Apostasy under Jehoram, Ahaziah and Athaliah** (21—22)
4. **Reformation under Joash, and Joash's Apostasy** (23—24)
5. **Decline and Apostasy under Amaziah, Uzziah, Jotham and Ahaz** (25—28)
6. **Reformation under Hezekiah** (29—32)
7. **Decline and Apostasy under Manasseh and Amon** (33:1-25)
8. **Reformation under Josiah** (34—35)
9. **The Final Decline and Apostasy** (36:1-14)

IV. THE CAPTIVITY AND THE EPILOGUE (36:15-23)

Analysis and Annotations

I. The Reign of Solomon

1. The Beginning of Solomon's Reign and the First Vision

CHAPTER 1

1. The Lord was with him (1:1)
2. At Gibeon (1:2-6)
3. The first vision (1:7-12)
4. His riches and prosperity (1:13-17)

The events connected with the beginning of Solomon's reign and recorded in 1 Kings 1—3:3 are omitted in Chronicles. Second Chronicles begins with the statement that Solomon was strengthened in his kingdom, and the Lord his God was with him, and magnified him exceedingly. This shows the keynote of Chronicles. It is Jehovah's gracious dealing with the house of David and the bestowal of the promised blessing. In 1 Kings 3:3 we read that Solomon loved the Lord.

Here more of Gibeon is mentioned than in Kings. "Gibeon was a great city, as one of the royal cities" (Joshua 10:2). Later Gibeon became the possession of the tribe of Benjamin and was made a priest-city. It was about two hours from Jerusalem. When Saul had destroyed Nob, the tabernacle was removed to Gibeon, where it remained till Solomon built the house of the Lord (1 Chron. 16:39, 21:29; 1 Kings 3:4; 2 Chron. 1:3). The ark had been brought from Kirjath-jearim, not far from Gibeon, to the tent which David had pitched for it in Jerusalem (2 Sam. 6:2; 1 Chron. 13:5-6), with the tabernacle and the brazen altar, that Bezalel, the son of Uri, the son of Hur, had made remained at Gibeon. The high place at Gibeon means the elevation upon which the tabernacle and the altar stood. Originally there was at the same spot a Canaanitish place for the worship of idols. As long as the temple, that central place for worship chosen by God (Deut. 12:11), was not standing, the worship of Jehovah in the Gibeon high place was not sinful. After the temple was built the high places became centers of idolatrous practices. Solomon and all the congregation with him gathered at Gibeon and sought the brazen altar and offered a thousand burnt offerings upon it. He began with this act of worship and it was the same night that God appeared unto Solomon. The Lord drew graciously near to him as the result of the sacrifices upon the brazen altar. The burnt-offering is the type of the perfect devotion and sacrifice of our Lord Jesus Christ, and it is this which makes us nigh. On the meaning of the great vision, God's offer to Solomon, the King's answer, see 1 Kings 3.

After the vision and the Lord's promise, "I will give thee riches and wealth and honor," we hear of Solomon's horses, horsemen and chariots. In 1 Kings, we find the same paragraph in another setting, that is, in chapter 10:26-29. He had 1,400 chariots and 12,000 horsemen and 4,000 stalls for horses. A great commerce seems to have been fostered by Solomon. While this showed the promise fulfilled, in that the Lord gave him riches and wealth, it also showed an unlawful desire for increase which was forbidden (Deut. 17:16). Read comment on 1 Kings 10:26-29.

2. The Building of the Temple

The Beginning and Appeal to Huram

CHAPTER 2

1. Solomon's purpose (2:1)
2. The workmen (2:2)
3. The message to Huram, King of Tyre (2:3-10)
4. Huram's answer (2:11-16)
5. Solomon numbers the strangers (2:17-18)

In 1 Kings 5, Solomon purposed to begin the great work to which he had been called, to build an house for the name of the Lord and an house for his kingdom (1 Kings 7:1; 2 Chron. 8:1). Then he levied a very large body of men from among the people to labor in cutting the timber and hewing stone for the temple and the palace of Solomon. Of these 70,000 were carriers; 80,000 were quarry men and 3,600 overseers. In 1 Kings 5:13, we read of a levy of 30,000 men. These must be considered additional workmen, for they were sent to Lebanon.

Solomon then sent a message to Huram (the same as Hiram), the King of Tyre. Hiram had sent before messages to Solomon, when he heard of his enthronement. They of Tyre had already brought cedar trees in abundance to David for the building of the Temple (1 Chron. 22:4). He loved Solomon as much as he loved his father David, for when Hiram heard the words of Solomon he rejoiced greatly and said, "Blessed be the Lord this day, who hath given unto David a wise son over this great people." To him Solomon sent a message. He reminded him of the dealings his father David had with him, and requested "even so deal with me." He acquainted him with his work, "Behold I build an house for the name of the Lord my God," and that it would be a great house, "for great is our God above all gods." Then he requested that Hiram would send him a master-workman and more material, cedar trees, fir trees and algum trees or almug trees (1 Kings 10:11), the red sandalwood, highly valued among the ancient nations, out of Lebanon. In return he offered to Hiram's servant wheat, barley, wine and oil, twenty thousand measures of each. 1 Kings 5:11 tells us that besides this gift to the workers in timber, twenty thousand measures of wheat and oil were yearly given by Solomon to the household of Hiram.

And Huram's answer reveals that he was a believer in Jehovah, for he acknowledged Him as the Creator and as the lover of His people (verses 11-12). The King sent Huram, a skilful worker whose mother was a Jewess (1 Kings 7:14). This Gentile co-operation in the construction of the temple is interesting, and also prophetic. Jews and Gentiles, Israel and the nations will yet unite to glorify the Lord. And the strangers who were in Israel, also Gentiles, were the servants of the King.

CHAPTER 3

The Building of the Temple

1. The place (3:1-2)
2. The dimensions (3:3)
3. The porch and holy place (3:4-7)
4. The most holy (3:4-18)
5. The brazen pillars (3:15-17)

First, the place is mentioned where the house of the Lord was built, "in Mount Moriah (Gen. 2), where the Lord appeared unto David his father, in the place that David had prepared in the threshing floor of Ornan the Jebusite." The building began in the second day of the second month in the fourth year of Solomon's reign. From 1 Kings 6:1 we learn that this was the 480th year from the Exodus. Counting forty years to one generation we have exactly twelve generations. This figure can be chronologically verified. The internal measurement given in verse 3 is sixty cubits long (about ninety feet), twenty cubits wide (about thirty feet), and thirty cubits high (about forty-five feet). Then there was the porch. The height of the porch is given as 120 cubits, which is evidently the error of a copyist; it should be twenty cubits, or perhaps thirty . For the full description see annotations on 1 Kings 6. Notice again the description of the cherubim overlaid with gold. These are not the cherubim upon the ark, but they were great figures made by Solomon. Each was ten cubits high. Their great wings met over the mercy seat upon which were the cherubim, which look down upon the mercy-seat. The Solomonic cherubim looked outwards. The word "inward" in verse 13 is a wrong translation. On the meaning of this attitude of these gigantic cherubim, see comment on 1 Kings 6:23-30. In verse 14, the veil is mentioned, of which we read nothing in 1 Kings 6. This veil was woven of the same material and in the same manner as the one in the tabernacle (Exod. 26:31).

The two pillars called Jachim (He will establish) and Boaz (In Him is strength) are the symbols of the stability of the government of this earth in the glorious reign of Christ, which is typified by the reign of Solomon and the house he built.

CHAPTER 4

The Vessels that were for the House

1. The altar of brass (4:1)
2. The molten sea (4:2-5)
3. The ten loaves (4:6)
4. The ten candlesticks (4:7)
5. The ten tables (4:8)
6. The court (4:9-10)
7. The work of Huram (4:11-17)
8. The work of Solomon (4:18-22)

The altar of brass, twenty cubits long, twenty cubits broad and ten cubits high, is not mentioned in the book of Kings. In the south-east of the court of the temple, stood the molten sea, which rested upon twelve oxen, three looking northward, three looking westward, three southward and three eastward. It received and held 3,000 measures of water. (3,000 measures was the full amount it could contain; the usual contents, however, were 2,000 measures [1 Kings 7:26].) The molten sea was for the priests and the Levites to perform their ablutions. It is typical of that cleansing which His people need and which is so graciously provided by the Lord Himself. The immense quantity of water contained in the molten sea suggests the unlimited provision grace has made. In Revelation 4:6, we read that before the throne was a sea of glass like crystal. This sea of glass is an allusion to the molten sea in Solomon's temple. But it is not a sea of water, but of glass like crystal, because the redeemed (symbolically seen in the twenty-four elders) in glory do no longer need cleansing. They have entered upon a perfect and fixed state of holiness. The ten lavers with their bases were for the washing of the sacrifices. We see that instead of one laver there were ten; and there were also ten candlesticks and ten tables. Everything was an increase and on a large scale, while the whole house and its contents represented an untold wealth. It all foreshadows that coming glorious Kingdom of Christ. Then there will be the increase and the blessing typified by the ten lavers, the ten candlesticks and the ten tables. The brazen scaffold, five cubits long, five cubits broad and three cubits high which Solomon had made upon which he stood and kneeled in prayer (2 Chron. 6:13) is not mentioned in this chapter.

The Priest's court was enclosed by a wall of hewn stones and a row of cedar beams (1 Kings 6:36). It had massive gates covered with brass. What Huram had worked for Solomon and Solomon's own work concludes this chapter and the account of the building the temple.

3. The Dedication of the Temple

CHAPTER 5

The Ark Brought in the Temple

1. The completion of the temple (5:1)
2. The assembly called by Solomon (5:2-3)
3. The ark carried to its place (5:4-9)
4. The contents of the ark (5:10)
5. The praise and the glory (5:11-14)

The reader will find the comments on the dedication of the temple in the book of Kings (1 Kings 8). Verses 11-13 are not given in the record of the first book of Kings. The Levites exercised their holy office. What a sight it must have been when Asaph, Heman and Jeduthun in the lead with their sons and brethren, all clothed in white linen, with cymbals, psalteries and harps, stood at the east end of the altar, and with them an hundred and twenty priests sounding the trumpets! And they were as one, to make one sound. It expresses the unity of God's people. The one supreme thought and aim was to praise and thank the Lord. This was the one mind in which they all were as one. Then the mighty volume of many voices, the sound of the trumpets, cymbals and instruments of music broke forth. The one note in praise was "He is good; for His mercy endureth forever." When the foundation of the second house was laid this praise was again uttered (Ezra 3:11). It must be remembered that David in his great prophetic psalm of praise ended with this note of praise "O give thanks unto the Lord; for He is good; for His mercy endureth forever. . . . Blessed be the Lord God of Israel for ever and ever. And all the people said 'Amen' and praised the Lord" (1 Chron. 16:34-36). In Psalm 136 we find twenty-six times "His mercy endureth." How rich was that mercy towards Israel! He had graciously guided and kept them. He brought them into the land and all their enemies had been subdued. The house had been built and all had been accomplished. And greater mercy is for Israel in the future. He will re-gather them. All their enemies will be silenced. Another house will once more stand in Jerusalem and the covenant-promise made to David will be completely realized in the enthronement of the coming King upon the hill of Zion (Psalm 2). What praises His redeemed and restored people will then utter, when the Lord has been gracious to His people and to His land! (Psalm 65:1, 147:12) The scene here at the dedication of the temple foreshadows the future praise of Israel in the Kingdom which our Lord will bring and establish when He comes again.

And when this mighty praise ascended to Jehovah, when they made but one sound, heaven answered. The house was filled with the cloud. The visible symbol presence of Jehovah had come, as it came at the consecration of the tabernacle (Exod. 40:34-35). "Whoso offereth praise glorifieth me" (Psalm 50:23). "As an holy priesthood we are to offer spiritual sacrifices acceptable to God by Jesus Christ" (1 Peter 2:5). "By him therefore let us offer praise to God continually, that is, the fruit of our lips giving thanks to His name" (Heb. 8:15). And if Israel had but one thought and made but one sound, how much more should we, His heavenly people, enjoying greater riches and a greater nearness than Israel ever had, be of one mind in praising His name!

CHAPTER 6

Solomon's Address and Dedicatory Prayer

1. Solomon's address to the congregation (6:1-11)
2. Solomon's dedicatory prayer (6:12-42)

The report of Solomon's address is the same as recorded in 1 Kings 8:12-21. The opening statement of this chapter has been well characterized as a pregnant expression of the king's realization of the mystery of the Being of Jehovah, the all-creative God, as well as the condescension displayed in His self-limitation to dwell amongst men. (See Exodus 19:9; 20:21; Lev. 16:2; Deut. 4:10; 5:22.) The prayer is nearly the same as in Kings (1 Kings 8:22-50). However, 1 Kings 8:51-61 is omitted and a few additional verses are added. The opening words of his great prayer are in acknowledgment of the greatness of Jehovah and the fulfillment of what God had promised to David, that is, the promise as it relates to him as David's son and the building of the house. He asks next that his prayers and the prayers of God's people may be heard as they ascend from the place where His Name is honored. Sin is acknowledged in connection with this request. "And when Thou hearest, forgive." In what follows, the different troubles are mentioned and Jehovah is implored to hear and to forgive. It is the model prayer for Israel. Confession of sin and prayer for forgiveness is linked with all petitions. Sin is acknowledged as the one cause of all troubles and disaster. Israel was thus taught in the prayer of Solomon to cast itself with supplication and repentance for sin upon Jehovah, and to find that the Lord heareth and delivereth His people. The subsequent history of Judah gives numerous instances of answered prayer. Note the omissions from the prayer report in 1 Kings 8 and the different closing of the prayer in the account in Chronicles. It is explained by the prophetic character of Kings and the priestly character of Chronicles. Psalm 132:8-10 is touched upon in verses 41-42.

CHAPTER 7:1-10

The Answer by Fire—the Sacrifices and the Feast

1. The answer by fire (7:1-3)
2. The sacrifices (7:4-7)
3. The feast of tabernacles (7:8-10)

A fuller manifestation of Jehovah's favor and presence followed the great prayer of the king. First the cloud had appeared and now the fire came down from heaven and consumed the burnt offering and the sacrifices; and the glory of the Lord filled the house. This is complementary to 1 Kings 8:63-64. Nothing is mentioned of this answer by fire upon the sacrifices in the book of Kings. And now all the children of Israel saw the fire and the glory of the Lord; and they bowed themselves and worshipped, praising the Lord and saying, as the Levites had said before, "He is good, for His mercy endureth forever." So all Israel will see in a future day the glory of the Lord and the coming Lord in glory and worship Him (Zech. 12:10). The house was dedicated by the King and all the people. (The Hebrew word used for dedicate is the word "*channuka.*" The Jews keep a feast called by that name.) The feast which followed was the feast of tabernacles. Its prophetic significance is mentioned in previous annotations.

4. The Second Vision

CHAPTER 7:11-22

1. All finished by Solomon (7:11)
2. The divine answer and the warning (7:12-22)

A second time the Lord appeared unto Solomon. At this time He did not say again "Ask what shall I give thee," but He assured him that Solomon's prayer had been heard and He had chosen the dedicated place for Himself. He graciously assures the king that if He has chastised His people by sending drought, locusts or pestilence and they humble themselves, and seek His face, turning away from their wicked ways, that He will forgive and heal their land. There can be no recovery apart from the conditions mentioned in these verses. His people who have failed must first humble themselves, pray, seek His face, and turn away from their evil ways. The warning given in verses 19-22 had passed into history and found its literal fulfillment.

5. Solomon's Prosperity and Activities

CHAPTER 8

1. The fortifications of cities (8:1-6)
2. The subjection of the strangers (8:7-10)
3. The removal of the daughter of Pharaoh (8:11)
4. The perfected service (8:12-16)
5. The expedition to Ophir (8:17-18)

The activities of the King included the fortification of certain cities. (See 1 Kings 9.) First the cities are mentioned which Huram restored to Solomon. These are the cities which Solomon had previously given to him for security. 1 Kings 9:10-14 explains this statement which otherwise would be obscure. All the strangers, the Canaanites, dwelling in the land were put into subjection and had to pay tribute to Solomon. They were the servants. "But of the children of Israel did Solomon make no servants for his work; but they were men of war, and chief of his captains and captains of his horsemen and chariots." It foreshadows the age in which all will be put in subjection under Him who will be King to rule in righteousness (Isaiah 32:1; Heb. 2:8). Then His own people will serve Him, for they "shall be willing in the day of His power" (Psalm 110:3). The only mention made of the daughter of Pharoah in Chronicles is in this chapter (verse 11). He married her in the beginning of the reign. Her removal to the house Solomon had built for her now took place. On the typical meaning of Pharaoh's daughter see 1 Kings 3:1. The worship in the house was then carried on in a perfect way. At the appointed times all was done and all David, the man of God, had commanded was carried out (verse 14). There was no departure from the commandment of the king, so the house of the Lord was perfected. It foreshadows a perfect obedience and worship which the earth will see when the true King has come. Then, as it was in Solomon's day, the King's commandment will be the absolute rule for everything (verse 15).

6. The Queen of Sheba, Solomon's Riches and Honors, and Solomon's Death

CHAPTER 9

1. The visit of the Queen (9:1-12)
2. The riches of Solomon (9:13-16)
3. The ivory throne (9:17-19)
4. Further riches and honors of Solomon (9:20-29)
5. The death of Solomon (9:30-31)

The account of the visit of the Queen of Sheba is the same as it appears in 1 Kings 10. The fame of Solomon had spread far and wide, and the Queen of Sheba comes to bring her tribute to admire and praise his wisdom and to give him presents of glorious things and of great value. And more than that. "King Solomon passed all the kings of the earth in riches and wisdom." A type of the coming King who will be head of all. "And all the kings of the earth sought the presence of Solomon, to hear his wisdom that God had put in his heart. And they brought every man his present, vessels of silver, and vessels of gold, and raiment, harness and spices, horses and mules, a rate year by year" (verses 23-24). In annotations on 1 Kings 10, we have pointed out how all this glory and the wealth of Solomon and Jerusalem foreshadows the fulfillment of many prophecies concerning the glorious reign of our Lord Jesus Christ. Greater splendor and glory will rest upon Him and come to Jerusalem than in Solomon's reign. Many beautiful descriptions of that coming glory, foreshadowed in this chapter, we find in different parts of the prophetic Word (Isa. 60:3-14, 66:10-13; Psalm 72).

As nothing is said in the first part of Chronicles on David's sin, so the sin and failure of Solomon is passed over in this part of Chronicles. His reign is described as unmarred by failure, a reign of undimmed glory. Such will be the reign of Him who is greater than Solomon. Solomon's failure, however, is indicated in this chapter. The horses out of Egypt mentioned in verse 28, and the fact that he multiplied horses and sought the gold of Ophir, shows that he became lifted up.

> Solomon enjoyed the sure promises of God. He sins in the means by which he seeks to satisfy his own lusts; and although the result was the accomplishment of the promise, yet he bears the consequences of so doing. Outwardly only the fulfillment of the promise was seen. In fact there was something else. Without sending for horses from Egypt, and gold from Ophir, Solomon would have been rich and glorious, for God had promised it. By doing this he enriched himself, but he departs from God and from His word. Having given himself up to his desires after riches and glory, he had multiplied the number of his wives, and in his old age they turned away his heart. This neglect of the word, which at first appeared to have no bad effect (for he grew rich, as though it had been but the fulfillment of God's promise), soon led to a departure more serious in its nature and in its consequences, to influence more powerful, and more immediately opposed to the commands of God's word, and at last to flagrant disobedience of its most positive and essential requirements. The slippery path of sin is always trodden with accelerated steps, because the first sin tends to weaken in the soul the authority and power of that which alone can prevent our committing still greater sins—that is, the word of God, as well as the consciousness of His presence, which imparts to the word all its practical power over us *(Synopsis of the Bible).*

II. The Rebellion of the Ten Tribes

CHAPTER 10

1. Rehoboam made king (10:1)
2. Jeroboam's return from Egypt and his request (10:2-5)
3. Rehoboam's answer (10:6-15)
4. The revolt and Rehoboam's flight (10:16-19)

What followed Solomon's fall when he turned away from the Lord, who so graciously had appeared unto him twice, is unrecorded in the Chronicles. 1 Kings 11:9-43 contains these events. Jeroboam, the son of Nebat, had lifted up his hand against Solomon (1 Kings 11:27). He planned secretly a revolt against the king, and when he went out of Jerusalem, most likely to carry out his plans, the prophet Ahijah met him, and in renting his own garment into ten pieces announced that God would take the kingdom out of the hand of Solomon and give to Jeroboam the ten tribes. Then Solomon sought to kill Jeroboam and he fled into Egypt, and was in Egypt until Solomon died. It is here where the account in Chronicles comes in. Rehoboam (enlarger of the people), the only son of Solomon mentioned in the Bible, went to Schechem, where all Israel had come together to make him king. Jeroboam had returned from Egypt and appeared on the scene, sent by the people to conduct negotiations in their behalf. Jeroboam demanded a lightening of the heavy burden of forced labor and taxation which Solomon had put upon them. If this request would be granted they were ready to serve Jeroboam. The King asked for three days to consider the demand. He first turned to the aged men and consulted those who had been closely associated with his father. They advised him to use kindness to avert the threatening rebellion. "A soft answer turneth away wrath, but grievous words stir up anger" (Prov. 15:1). If Rehoboam had heeded this inspired saying of his father, he would have followed the advice which had been given. But instead he turned to the young men, "the young men (Hebrew: children) that had grown up with him." They readily gave advice how the peoples' demand, "Ease somewhat the yoke that thy father did put upon us," should be answered. It was foolish advice. The threat to increase their burdens, and that while his father had used whips he would use scorpions (a cruel whip to which pieces of sharp metal were attached) was to overawe the people and bring them into submission. It seems almost impossible that Rehoboam should follow such advice. If Eccles. 2:18-19 applies to this son of Solomon, the father's fears were well founded. He certainly showed that he was not a wise man, but a fool. Yet there was another reason why Rehoboam listened to the foolish counsel. "So the king hearkened not unto the people, for the cause was of God, that the Lord might perform His Word, which He spake by Ahijah, the Shilonite, to Jeroboam, the son of Nebat." And the offended people answered the king with the same spirit and declared their independence. In contempt they said, "And now David see to thine own house." Then foolishly Rehoboam sent one of the officials who were hated on account of their office, Hadoram, who was over the tribute. The people became infuriated and stoned him to death. King Rehoboam had to make haste to escape a similar fate. The revolt had come. "And Israel rebelled against the house of David." The words spoken to Solomon (1 Kings 11:11-13) were now fulfilled.

III. The History of the Kings of Judah. Events Leading up to the Captivity

1. Decline and Apostasy under Rehoboam, Abijah and Asa

CHAPTER 11

Rehoboam's Reign

1. The forbidden war (11:1-4)
2. The national defence (11:5-12)
3. Jeroboam's wickedness and Rehoboam's strength (11:13-17)
4. Rehoboam's family (11:18-23)

The provocation to go to war with the tribes which had revolted was great. Rehoboam was ready to start the civil war. He gathered 180,000 men of Judah and Benjamin to fight against Israel and to restore the tribes to his kingdom. Shemaiah, the man of God, the prophet in Judah, received a message from the Lord, which he faithfully delivered. "Ye shall not go up, nor fight against your brethren; return every man to his house, for this thing is done of me." It required courage to deliver such a message in the midst of the great preparations for war. Rehoboam and the people obeyed and did not go to war. They must have realized that if they disobeyed they would have fought against God. And the Lord also blessed the king and his people for believing the Word and being obedient. He always blesses when there is obedience. He built and fortified fifteen cities. "He fortified the strongholds, and put captains in them and store of victuals and of oil and wine." In several places he put shields and spears. Thus he made ready for a possible invasion from the side of Egypt, for Jeroboam, his rival, had been there. Rehoboam's fears were well founded, as we shall find in the next chapter.

Then there was a great exodus of priests and Levites from the domain of Jeroboam. As we learned from 1 Kings 12:25-33, Jeroboam established a wicked worship, setting up two golden calves at Beth-el and Dan. The priests he made were taken, not from the sons of Levi, but from the lowest of the people (1 Kings 12:31). The true priest and Levites who had remained with him were cast off from executing their holy and God-given office. He also had priests "for the devils." The Hebrew word translated "devils" means "hairy ones" and "goats." In Egypt the sacred goat was worshipped and Jeroboam's worship was patterned. The priests and Levites who were driven away by Jeroboam strengthened the Kingdom of Judah. They had a wholesome influence upon the otherwise weak son of Solomon. "They made Rehoboam, the son of Solomon, strong." They all walked in the way of David and Solomon for three years. Most likely fear had much to do with it. We read nothing of turning to the Lord and seeking His face.

His family record is given. Mahalath is mentioned as his wife, a daughter of Jerimoth, probably the son of one of David's concubines (1 Chron. 3:9). Then he took Maacah, a granddaughter of Absalom. According to Josephus, Maacha's mother was Tamar, the daughter of Absalom (2 Sam. 14:27). He had many wives and concubines. The polygamous tendencies of his father and grandfather were thus indulged by him, and in all probability his apostasy started from this sin. But he acted wisely and dispersed all his children throughout the whole country. Having twenty-eight sons and many more daughters, there were great possibilities of conspiracies, which he avoided by scattering them in different directions.

CHAPTER 12

Rehoboam's Apostasy, Punishment, and Death

1. Rehoboam's apostasy (12:1)
2. Punishment through Shishak (12:2-12)
3. Death of Rehoboam (12:13-16)

The kingdom had been established; Rehoboam had strengthened himself and lived in the indulgence of the flesh. Then followed the awful plunge into apostasy. "He forsook the law of the Lord and all Israel with him." Idolatry in the high places and under every green tree was established and fostered by him. "And there were also Sodomites in the land, and they did according to all the abominations of the nations which the Lord cast out before the children of Israel" (1 Kings 14:22-24).

Then Shishak came from Egypt against Jerusalem with an immense army. He was the first king of the twenty-second, or Bubastic dynasty. In his army were the Lubims (Libyans), Sukkims (desert tribes) and the Ethiopians. The cities which Rehoboam had built and fortified could not keep him out, for the Lord had brought him to punish Jerusalem. When Jerusalem was threatened and the Egyptian hordes were about to proceed against Jerusalem, Shemaiah, the man of God, appeared once more. He brought the solemn message from the Lord, "Ye have forsaken me, and therefore have I left you in the hand of Shishak." That for which the Lord always looks first of all, when His people have sinned and departed from Him, was done by the princes and the king. "They humbled themselves." And when the Lord saw that they humbled themselves and were returning to Him, He had compassion on them. Some deliverance was granted and the wrath was not poured out upon the city. And He is still the same gracious Lord, always ready to forgive His people, when they return unto Him. However, the pride of Rehoboam had to be dealt with and, therefore, Shishak was permitted to take away the immense riches which Solomon had stored up in the treasures of the house of the Lord and in the king's house. The shields of gold were also carried away. Sad is the record of this son of Solomon: "And he did evil, because he prepared not his heart to seek the Lord." Had he prepared his heart to seek the Lord, he would not have done the evil which he did. The only thing which can keep from evil is to seek the Lord and walk in obedience to His Word. Rehoboam's reign, with the exception of three years in which he walked in the way of David and Solomon, was a reign of trouble. Besides Shishak's invasion "there were wars between Rehoboam and Jeroboam continually" (verse 15).

CHAPTER 13

The Reign of Abijah

1. The beginning of his reign (13:1-2)
2. War with Jeroboam (13:3-19)
3. Death of Jeroboam (13:20)
4. Abijah's family (13:21-22)

Abijah is called in Kings, Abijam, and in 2 Chron. 12:21, Abijahu. His reign was not of a long duration; he outlived his father Rehoboam only three years. His mother was Maachah (2 Chron. 11:20). She is called here Michaiah, probably because she was the queen-mother. There is no discrepancy between chapter 11:20 and the second verse of this chapter, in which she is called the daughter of Uriel of Gibeath. Josephus is probably correct when he states that Uriel was the husband of Tamar, the daughter of Absalom. In chapter 11:20, she is called a daughter of Absalom or rather grand-daughter, for one word is used in Hebrew for daughter and grand-daughter. (Abishalom in 1 Kings 15:2 is the same as Absalom.)

Of Abijah's evil walk, and that his heart was not perfect with the Lord, the Chronicles has nothing to say. That is found in Kings. That things went from bad to worse under Abijah's brief reign may be learned from the fact that his son Asa had to institute a reformation, and Maachah, the mother of Abijah and grandmother of Asa, had to be put away, because she had put up an Asherah, a vile idol-image in a grove (1 Kings 15:13; 2 Chron. 15:16). Chronicles gives an account of Abijah's war with Jeroboam. The two armies of Judah and Israel faced each other; Abijah had 400,000 men and Jeroboam 800,000. There is no reason to doubt the accuracy of these figures, as some critics have done. Both sides were confident of victory. Jeroboam had twice as many men as Abijah, and they were "mighty men of valor." He trusted in his superior number. It was different with Abijah, King of Judah. Before the battle began the king delivered a remarkable address in which he expressed his confidence in Jehovah. The Lord had given the kingdom to David and to his sons by a covenant of salt, said Abijah. The covenant of salt refers to a very ancient custom. When a guest had been entertained in a tent and partaken of salt with his host, the obligation of the latter towards his guest was one of inviolable sanctity. The covenant of Jehovah with David was like a covenant of salt, that is, inviolable. Abijah believed in that covenant. Then he mentioned Jeroboam, whom sarcastically he calls "the servant of Solomon," his revolt, his idolatry, his opposition to the priesthood. He closed his address with a confident statement. "Behold, God Himself is with us for our captain, and His priests with sounding trumpets to cry alarm against you." Then the warning: "O children of Israel, fight ye not against the Lord God of your fathers, for ye shall not prosper." Abijah won the battle. When they were encircled by the enemy they cried to Jehovah in their hour of need, and He was faithful to His own word (Numb. 10:9). When the priests sounded with the trumpets, when they shouted, no doubt in faith and anticipation of Jehovah's interference, then God smote Jeroboam and all Israel and delivered them into their hands. They had prevailed because they relied upon the Lord God, and so shall we prevail if we trust in the Lord. With that battle Jeroboam's strength was broken. The wicked king, whose awful idolatry was the ruin of Israel, never recovered his strength. The Lord struck him and he died.

CHAPTER 14

The Reign of Asa

1. The death of Abijah and Asa becomes king (14:1)
2. The good beginning (14:2-8)
3. His victory over Zerah (14:9-15)

Asa, (which means "healing" or "who will heal?"), the son of Abijah, began his reign well. He did what was right in the sight of the Lord. The strange altars, the high places and the images were taken away and the groves cut down. He was not satisfied with this work, but he also commanded Judah to seek the Lord. The land was quiet. The Lord blessed him and the land for the faithful work which had been done. "The land had rest, and he had no war in those years, because the Lord had given him rest." It was a remarkable work for one so young; probably Asa was not yet twelve years old when he became King. Maachah, his grandmother, most likely had some oversight as "queen-mother." (In 1 Kings 15:13 she is called the mother of Asa; the same is the case in our book 15:16. Mother in these passages has the meaning of grandmother.) Notice the great prosperity which followed the work he had done. "The Kingdom was quiet before him." Cities were built and fortified. They readily acknowledged that it was all of God. "Because we have sought the Lord our God, we have sought Him, and He hath given us rest on all sides." So they built and prospered.

But faith had to be tested. A powerful army under the leadership of Zerah, an Ethiopian, came against Judah. The battle was to take place in the open field, in the valley of Zephathah. Before the forces ever clashed Asa cried to the Lord. His prayer is most beautiful and simple. It still breatheth freshness and has been a help to all God's trusting people in all ages. "Lord it is nothing with thee to help, whether with many, or with them that have no power; help us, O Lord our God; for we rest on thee, and in thy name we go against this multitude. O Lord, thou art our God, let not man prevail against thee." What confidence and trust! He put the whole matter upon the Lord. Their enemies were His enemies. In His name, resting on Him, they went forth. May we know and practice the same confidence. Such a prayer could not remain unanswered. The Lord smote the Ethiopians and gave to His people a great victory.

CHAPTER 15

The Reign of Asa, Warning and Reformation

1. The warning message of Azariah (15:1-7)
2. Asa's response and reformation (15:8-19)

But the Lord knew the danger which threatened Asa. He had begun well. He was faithful to Jehovah, and he and the people had a wonderful demonstration that the Lord hears and answers prayer. Would he continue and end as well as he had begun? The Spirit of God came at this important time upon Azariah (whom the Lord helps). When victorious Asa returned the prophet met him and delivered his message. It was a needed and timely message, for the danger for God's people is always the greatest after a victory is won and outward success and prosperity is enjoyed. "The Lord is with you, while ye be with Him; and if ye seek Him, He will be found of you; but if ye forsake Him, He will forsake you." This has, of course, nothing to do with the question of salvation and the possession of eternal life, which the believer hath in Christ. To bear a real testimony, fruit unto God and have the victory at all times, a close walk with the Lord is needed. Apart from this, God's people are helpless and must needs dishonor their Lord. Verses 3-6 picture the results of departure from the Lord, such as were among Israel during the period of the Judges. "Be ye strong therefore, and let not your hands be weak; for your work shall be rewarded."

And Asa hearing these words, believed what the prophet had said and then acted upon them. It is the true path to blessing, learning, believing and obeying. The abominable idols were removed and the altar before the porch of the Lord, which had fallen into disuse, was renewed by him. (2 Chron. 8:12). A great sacrificial scene followed. In connection with it they entered into a covenant to seek the Lord. The religious enthusiasm ran so high that they determined to put to death every person who did not seek the Lord. And when they sought Him with their whole desire He was found of them and gave them rest. These are precious and encouraging words. He is the Lord, who changeth not. It is still true to-day and ever will be true. He will be found by those who seek Him with their whole desire.

CHAPTER 16

Asa's Relapse and Death

1. War between Asa and Baasha (16:1-6)
2. Hanani's rebuke (16:7-9)
3. Hanani imprisoned (16:10-11)
4. Asa's illness and death (16:12-14)

Much has been made by critics of the supposed wrong date, the thirty-sixth year of the reign of Asa. Compare 1 Kings 15:33 with the first verse of this chapter to see the apparent discrepancy. If the invasion of Judah by Baasha occurred shortly after the events recorded in the previous chapter, it was in the thirty-sixth year after the revolt of the ten tribes. This presents a possible solution. Others think it is the error of a scribe.

As the dates in 2 Chron. 15:19; 16:1 are incompatible with that of Baasha's death (1 Kings 16:8), and consequently, of course, with that of Baasha's war against Asa, commentators have tried to obviate the difficulty, either by supposing that the numeral 35 refers, not to the date of Asa's accession, but to that of the separation of the kingdoms of Judah and Israel, or else by emendating the numeral in the book of the Chronicles. The latter is, evidently, the only satisfactory solution. There is manifestly here a copyist's mistake, and the numeral which we would substitute for 35 is not 15 but 25—and this for reasons too long to explain *(Bible History).*

Asa relapsed and failed when Baasha, King of Israel, came against Judah and built Ramah. (See annotations, 1 Kings 15 and 16.) In unbelief Asa made an alliance with the King of Syria. He feared Baasha very much. In Jeremiah 41:9, we read of a pit which he made for fear of Baasha; probably to hide there. "The fear of man bringeth a snare." How this reveals the weakness of man! After all the evidences of the Lord's mercy and power Asa could forsake thus the Lord and enter into an unholy alliance with a heathen king. He gained the object he sought and Baasha was forced to abandon his plan. But God had been a witness of it all. He sent through Hanani (graciously given by the Lord the meaning of his name) and rebuked the king for what he had done. The Lord reminds him of the far greater host which threatened him (14:9-15) and the deliverance He had wrought. Beautiful are the final words of Hanani. "For the eyes of the Lord run to and fro throughout the whole earth, to show Himself strong in behalf of them whose heart is perfect toward Him." The Lord looks for faith, for confidence. Our hearts are perfect toward Him when we trust Him and are obedient to His Word. Then all His power is with us and for us.

Wars to the end was the punishment announced upon Asa. And Asa showed his true state of soul, when, instead of saying, "I have sinned," he began to rage; when instead of beseeching Hanani to pray for him, he put him in prison. He was away from the Lord and his behavior made it known. Stricken by disease, no doubt to humble him and bring him back to the Lord, he sought not the Lord, but the physicians. These were in all probability magicians; who used enchantments. There was no return unto the Lord; no repentance.

2. Reformation under Jehoshaphat

CHAPTER 17

Jehoshaphat's Reformation and Increase

1. The Lord was with Jehoshaphat (17:1-5)
2. The revival under his reign (17:6-9)
3. His increase (17:10-19)

Jehoshaphat, the son of Asa, began his reign by strengthening himself against Israel. The Lord was with him, because he walked in the first ways of his father David, which means David's faithful walk before his great sin. The Lord greatly blessed him by establishing his kingdom and in giving him riches and honor in abundance. The Lord kept all His promises. When Jehoshaphat saw the evidences of divine blessing, his heart was lifted up in the ways of the Lord. This does not mean that he was puffed up, but that he became encouraged to go on in the good way he was following. The high places and groves were removed by him. In 1 Kings 22:43, we read that he did not take away the high places and that the people offered incense there. The work was not completely done. While he personally wanted to see it accomplished and commanded that it be done, the people failed in fully carrying out his wishes. "For as yet the people had not prepared their hearts unto the God of their fathers" (20:33). Another work he did, was the sending out of teachers to instruct in the knowledge of the Lord. Their names are interesting. Ben-hail, "son of strength"; Abadiah, "servant of the Lord"; Zechariah, "the Lord remembers"; Nethaneel, "gift of God"; Michariah, "Who is like the Lord?" He also sent priests and Levites. "And they taught in Judah and had the book of the law of the Lord with them and went about throughout all the cities of Judah and taught the people." It was a revival in teaching and in the study of the Word. No true revival can take place unless it is connected with the Word.

And the results soon came. The fear of the Lord fell upon the surrounding kingdoms. They feared to touch the people who were thus blessed. The Philistines brought presents and tribute silver; the Arabians immense herds of cattle. It was all a fulfillment of Deut. 11:22-25. Judah had a phenomenal increase. Without doubt this chapter presents one of the best scenes in the kingdom of Judah.

CHAPTER 18

Jehoshaphat's Sinful Alliance with Ahab

1. The alliance with Ahab (18:1-3)
2. Ahab's false prophets (18:4-11)
3. Micaiah's prophecy (18:12-27)
4. The fatal battle at Ramoth-Gilead (18:28-34)

The same record also appears in 1 Kings 22, to which the reader may turn for further annotations. Jehoshaphat's prosperity became a snare to him. Riches and honor he had in abundance. No doubt lifted up in his heart and self-secure, saying perhaps, "I am increased in goods and have need of nothing," on a certain day he joined affinity with Ahab. Jehoshaphat's son Jehoram married Ahab's wicked daughter Athaliah (21:6). This was a fatal step for Jehoshaphat and the house of Judah. It brought him into alliance with Ahab, the wicked; he almost lost his life on account of it; only his prayer saved him (18:31); and Athaliah introduced the vile idolatries of Ahab into Judah (22:3) and became the murderess of the royal seed (22:10-12).

The historical account of Jehoshaphat's alliance with Ahab, the false prophets, the prophecy of Micaiah, the battle of Ramoth-Gilead, is commented upon in the record of the first book of the Kings.

That Jehoshaphat knew the Lord and was His is blessedly illustrated in verses 31-32. In the hour of need, the king in such bad company turned to the Lord and cried to Him. There was an immediate answer and the King of Judah was saved. What a power prayer is! May all God's people make use of it. As we have said previously, "Jehoshaphat was miraculously saved, but Ahab was miraculously killed."

CHAPTER 19

Rebuke and Restoration

1. The rebuke by the prophet (19:1-3)
2. Further revival and restoration (19:4-11)

At sun-down Ahab, the King of Israel died, while his ally Jehoshaphat, saved through the mercy of God, returned to his home in peace in Jerusalem. Then Jehu, the son of Hanani, met him. Asa, the father of Jehoshaphat, had been rebuked by Hanani, and had put him in prison for it. The son of Hanani rebukes Jehoshaphat. We read no answer from the king, but his actions show that the rebuke went home to his conscience. He must have repented of the unholy alliance with the enemy of the Lord. Jehu said to him, "Shouldest thou help the ungodly, and love them that hate the Lord? Therefore is wrath upon thee from before the Lord." This principle is the same in the New Testament. God's people are a separated people. "Be ye not unequally yoked together with unbelievers, for what fellowship hath righteousness with unrighteousness? and what communion hath light with darkness?" (2 Cor. 6:14). And the Lord acknowledged the good Jehoshaphat had done and his attitude, a heart prepared to seek God.

Graciously had Jehovah restored the king who had failed and dishonored Him. He had returned in peace, bowed before the divine rebuke and dwelt in Jerusalem. Then he went out again to do service for the Lord. He became at once active in bearing testimony and helping God's people, bringing them back to the fear of the Lord. He caused judgment and righteousness to be executed in the land. Notice how in this revival the Lord is before Jehoshaphat; eight times in verses 4-11 the Lord is mentioned.

CHAPTER 20

Judah Invaded, Jehoshaphat's Prayer and Deliverance

1. The invasion (20:1-2)
2. Jehoshaphat's great prayer (20:3-13)
3. Jehovah's answer through Jahaziel (20:14-17)
4. Prostrated before the Lord (20:18-19)
5. The great deliverance (20:20-25)
6. In the valley of Berachah (20:26-30)
7. The record of Jehoshaphat (20:31-34)
8. Alliance with Ahaziah (20:35-37)

An invasion of Judah by Moab, Ammon and others followed. Then Jehoshaphat feared and set himself to seek the Lord and proclaimed a fast throughout Judah. Though the enemy was nearing Jerusalem and the danger was great, there was no disorder or confusion. They all looked to Jehovah and that gave them calmness. In troubles and trials God's people must always look first to the Lord and seek His face. A great company gathered together, even from the cities in Judah, to seek the Lord. It was one of the most remarkable prayer meetings reported in the Bible. The king stood in the midst of the large congregation. And what a prayer it was he uttered! What earnestness and faith breatheth in every word! He addressed God as in heaven and as the ruler over all the kingdoms of the nations. In His hand there is power and might; none is able to withstand Him. It is a good way in approaching God to remember what a wonderful and almighty God and Lord He is. Then Jehoshaphat speaks of His dealing with His people Israel and speaks of Abraham—"thy friend forever." The prayer of Solomon in dedicating the house is mentioned (verse 9). Then he tells the Lord of the invasion, and the object of Ammon and Moab "to cast us out of thy possession which thou hast given us to inherit." Most beautiful is the ending of his prayer. "O, our God, wilt Thou not judge them?" They were His enemies, for they came against His land and His people. "For we have no might against this great company that cometh against us; neither know we what to do; but our eyes are upon Thee." Here is the spirit and soul-attitude which pleases God. Whenever and wherever it is manifested God's answer and gracious help is not far away. But it is just this spirit of dependence and expectation from the Lord which is so little known among God's people.

In the midst of the congrgation was a Levite by name of Jahaziel (he will be seen of God), of the sons of Asaph. Upon him came the Spirit of the Lord and through him there came the answer, "Ye shall not need to fight in this battle; set yourselves, stand ye still, and see the salvation of the Lord with you, O Judah and Jerusalem; fear not, nor be dismayed; to-morrow go out against them, for the Lord will be with you." And the heavenly answer was believed. The king took the lead in bowing his head with his face to the ground. The people did likewise. In anticipation of the coming victory the Levites praised the Lord with a loud voice.

The next morning the divine direction was obeyed. The king addressed the people to have faith in God. Then he appointed singers arrayed in their official garments to go before the army and sing as if it were a triumphal procession: "Praise the Lord; for His mercy endureth forever." (The expression, "beauty of holiness" is literally, "holy array.") We read nothing of swords or spears. They needed no weapons. Probably they left them at home, for the Lord had said, "Ye shall not need to fight in this battle." And when they began to sing and praise, trusting in the promise, the Lord began His work in overthrowing and destroying their enemies. The invading armies were annihilated and none escaped.

A great praise-service in the valley of Berachah (blessing) followed. Jehoshaphat in the forefront of them, with the people returned to Jerusalem with joy. They came to Jerusalem with psalteries and harps and trumpets unto the house of the Lord. And the kingdoms feared God when they heard what the Lord had done.

The prophetic application of all this is not difficult to make. Jehoshaphat and the people with him are typical of the remnant of God's earthly people, that God-fearing remnant which dwells in the land and in Jerusalem during the great tribulation. The prayer of Jehoshaphat, the divine answer and the great deliverance, foreshadows the cry for help and deliverance of that remnant, while the overthrow of their enemies, with the coming of the Lord, is foreshadowed in the deliverance of Jehoshaphat and the people. The praise will be great in Jerusalem, when the Lord acts in behalf of His believing remnant, at the close of the times of the Gentiles. Then the kingdoms of the earth will fear God.

It would be well if Jehoshaphat's life had ended with this beautiful scene. But it does not. He entered another unholy alliance, for commercial reasons, with wicked Ahaziah, King of Israel. The ships to go to Tarshish never reached their destination; they were broken. "Again had Jehoshaphat to learn in the destruction of his fleet at Ezion-Gaber that undertakings, however well planned and apparently unattended by outward danger, can only end in disappointment and failure, when they who are the children of God combine with those who walk in the ways of sin."

And how many Christians have made the same experience! God cannot bless the believer when he is in fellowship with an unbeliever.

3. Decline and Apostasy under Jehoram, Ahaziah and Athaliah

CHAPTER 21

The Reign of Jehoram

1. Jehoram's wicked reign (21:1-7)
2. Revolt of Edom (21:8-9)
3. Revolt of Libnah (21:10-11)
4. The message of Elijah (21:12-15)
5. Judah invaded (21:16-17)
6. Jehoram's sickness and death (21:18-20)

Jehoram was Jehoshaphat's firstborn. Jehoshaphat had six other sons to whom he gave great riches, but the kingdom was given to Jehoram. He walked in wickedness. "For he had the daughter of Ahab to wife and he wrought that which was evil in the sight of the Lord." When Jehoram was in power, he slew all his brethren with the sword and also princes in Israel. The daughter of the murderer Ahab may have instigated the horrible crime. Jehoshaphat had joined affinity with Ahab (18:1), and married his son Jehoram to Athaliah. "What a man sows that will he reap." His unholy alliance began to bear fruit. And how often have Christian parents seen their children depart from God and follow altogether the wicked ways of the world, because they themselves had set the example. Then the enemies of Judah came and different revolts took place.

The writing which came to Jehoram from the prophet Elijah is interesting and presents some difficulties. Elijah had been translated a number of years before. To solve the difficulty some say that the name Elijah should be Elisha, who was then living and ministering in connection with Samaria. There is no need of doing this. It does not say that Elijah sent that writing, but it says: "There came a writing from Elijah the prophet." Elijah knew Jehoshaphat and he knew his son Jehoram, who was for several years the co-regent of his father. The Lord showed him beforehand the evil course Jehoram would take, and how he would follow the wicked ways of Ahab, Elijah knew so well. Then he received the message exposing the wickedness of Jehoram, "like to the whoredoms of Ahab," and announcing the judgment to come upon Jehoram. This message was probably intrusted by Elijah to Elisha, and when the proper moment had come this man of God delivered the writing to Jehoram, telling him at the same time that it was from Elijah.

Fearful was the end of this murderous and idolatrous king. He died of sore diseases, unrepenting, and thus as a lost soul passed into the blackness of darkness forever (Jude 13). And his people made no burning for him (burning incense) like the burning of his fathers; neither was he buried in the sepulchres of the kings.

CHAPTER 22

Ahaziah and Athaliah

1. Ahaziah and his evil reign (22:1-4)
2. His alliance with Ahab's son (22:5)
3. At Jezreel (22:6-7)
4. Jehu's judgment and Ahaziah's end (22:8-9)
5. Athaliah (22:10-12)

When the Philistines and Arabians invaded Judah they carried away the treasures of Jehoram, and slew his sons. Only Jehoahaz the youngest son was left (21:17). He is also known as Ahaziah and Azariah. These names in Hebrew have the same meaning "upheld by Jehovah." Poor, young Ahaziah still reaps the harvest of the unfortunate alliance of his grandfather Jehoshaphat. The leaven is doing its dreadful work. His mother Athaliah, granddaughter of the wicked Omri and daughter of Ahab, was his counsellor to do wickedly. He therefore did evil in the sight of the Lord, like the house of Ahab, for they were his counsellors, after the death of his father, to his destruction. What might have been if his grandfather Jehoshaphat had not made affinity with Ahab and his house and marrying his son Jehoram to Athaliah! Ahaziah's end, after he went with his uncle Jehoram, the son of Ahab, and the circumstances connected with it we have already annotated in Second Kings. Athaliah's awful crime in slaying the seed royal and the miraculous preservation of Joash, the reader will also find explained in 2 Kings 11:1-3.

4. Reformation Under Joash

CHAPTER 23

Joash King and Athaliah's Execution

1. Joash made king (23:1-11)
2. Athaliah slain (23:12-15)
3. Jehoiada and the revival (23:16-21)

The annotations to this interesting page in the history of Judah have already been made in connection with 2 Kings 11. We therefore pass over the preservation of the young child Joash and his hiding away in the Lord's house, on this account. However we call attention to the differences in the two accounts in 2 Kings 11 and 2 Chron. 23. As stated before the book of Chronicles is written from the priestly and Levitical view point; this explains the greater detail about Jehoiada, the priest, given in Chronicles. A careful study and comparison of the two chapters will show that there are no discrepancies.

"The differences, and even more the similarity, in the narratives of the event in the books of Kings and Chronicles have suggested what to some appear discrepancies of detail. It is well to know that, even if these were established, they would not in any way invalidate the narrative itself, since in any case they only concern some of its minor details, not its substance. The most notable difference is that in the book of Kings the plot and its execution seem entirely in the hands of the military; in Chronicles, exclusively in those of the priests and Levites. But in Chronicles also—and indeed, there alone—the five military leaders are named; while, on the other hand, the narrative in the book of Kings throughout admits the leadership of the priest Jehoiada. And even a superficial consideration must convince that both the priests and the military must have been engaged in the undertaking, and that neither party could have dispensed with the other. A revolution inaugurated by the high-priest in favor of his nephew, who for six years had been concealed in the Temple, and which was to be carried out within the precincts of the Sanctuary itself, could no more have taken place without the co-operation of the priesthood than a change in the occupancy of the throne could have been brought about without the support of the military power. And this leaves untouched the substance of the narrative in the two accounts (A. Edersheim).

Athaliah received her just recompense. The youthful Joash occupied the throne of David, and the faithful priest Jehoiada was the instrument who brought about the needed revival. The beginning was in a solemn covenant. It was a covenant which bound the young ruler and the people together to be true to Jehovah, as it is demanded of the Lord's people; there was also a covenant between the King and the people (2 Kings 11:17). And the revival under the priestly direction began by the destruction of the idols and false worship and a return to Jehovah and the true worship of His Name. Every true revival must needs begin the same way. Tested by this standard most of the present day revivals are found wanting. "And he set the porters at the gates of the house of the Lord, that none which was unclean in anything should enter in." The house of the Lord was guarded against all that is unclean. How different from the corruption which is tolerated in Christendom, in that which is "the house," the professing Church.

CHAPTER 24

The Temple Repaired, Apostasy and its Results

1. Joash's reign (24:1-3)
2. The failure of the priests (24:4-7)

3. The temple repaired (24:8-14)
4. Death of Jehoiada (24:15-16)
5. The apostasy (24:17-22)
6. The Syrian invasion (24:23-24)
7. The death of Joash (242:25-27)

Joash was seven years old when he began his reign and reigned forty years. As long as Jehoiada the priest lived, he did what was right in the sight of the Lord. The account of the repairing of the temple needs no further comment here. (See annotations on 2 Kings 12.) Jehoiada, the faithful priest, who had so much to do with these important events during this crisis, died 130 years old. Being connected by marriage with the royal house and in appreciation of the great work he had accomplished "because he had done good in Israel, both toward God, and toward His house," they buried him among the kings. After his death it became manifest that the revival which had taken place had its mainstay in the good priest; Joash's convictions and faithfulness to Jehovah were but skin-deep. A reaction set in, as it has been so often in the history of the Church. He listened to the evil counsel of the princes of Judah, and then they left the house of the Lord God and became idolators. The result was wrath from God upon Judah and Jerusalem for this trespass. Such is man in his corrupt nature! But the gracious Lord did not give them up. His righteousness demanded judgment, yet in infinite mercy he sent prophets to bring them back. These unnamed prophets testified against them, but they would not give ear. They hardened their hearts against the Lord and His prophets.

A worse deed followed. Jehoiada had a son by name of Zechariah; he was the cousin of the king. Upon him came the Spirit of God and he announced the fact that because they had forsaken the Lord, He had also forsaken them (2 Chron. 15:2). Like Stephen, the first martyr of the church, Zechariah had touched the sore spot; when they heard these things, they were cut to the heart. Then they stoned Zechariah as their offspring later stoned Stephen. It was worse than base ingratitude from the side of Joash that he gave the commandment to murder the son of Jehoiada. The king remembered not the kindness which Jehoiada his father "had done him, but slew his son."

But there is a difference between the last words of this martyr-prophet and the last words of the first martyr of the Church. Stephen prayed: "Lord lay not this sin to their charge" (Acts 7:60). Zechariah said: "The Lord look upon it and require it." Typically he represents the tribulation martyrs of the Jewish remnant, who will give the testimony concerning righteousness and the coming King at the end of the present age, and whose blood will cry for vengeance to heaven (Rev. 6:9-11). There can be no doubt our Lord meant this Zechariah when He uttered the words in Matthew 23:35. It is true He speaks of him as the son of Barachias (blessed of Jehovah); but this is not a difficulty. Barachias was another name Jehoiada bore and well suited to his character. Our Lord informs us of the place where he was slain, "between the temple and the altar." Joash, completely forsaken by the Lord, was defeated by the Syrians. Great diseases came upon him and he was murdered by his own servants. Like Jehoram he was not buried in the sepulchres of the kings.

5. Decline and Apostasy under Amaziah, Uzziah, Jotham and Ahaz

CHAPTER 25

The Reign of Amaziah

1. The record of Amaziah's reign (25:1-4)
2. The war against Edom (25:5-13)
3. His idolatry and the divine rebuke (25:14-16)
4. The war between Judah and Israel (25:17-25)
5. The death of Amaziah (25:26-28)

Joash's son Amaziah (strength of the Lord) took up the government in Judah when he was twenty-five years old. His mother's name, Jehoaddan, means "Jehovah is pleased." Perhaps it was through her influence, as her name indicates godliness, that her son began the reign well. He did that which was right in the sight of the Lord. But the Lord, who looks deeper and knows the heart of man, knew that it was "not with a perfect heart." He dealt out justice to the murderers of his father, and also adhered closely to the law of God. In the account in 2 Kings 14 but a passing statement is given on the war with Edom. The details are recorded in the present chapter. He gathered a large army and hired 100,000 mighty men of the kingdom of Israel. It was a hasty deed and showed that Amaziah was not acting in faith. A man of God appeared next and warned him to have nothing to do with the 100,000 hirelings, "for the Lord is not with Israel." This is a good test still in all undertakings. Every believer should ask before he enters upon anything: Can the Lord approve of it? Is the Lord with it? But Amaziah had already paid the hundred talents to the soldiers. So he asked about the money. And the man of God gave a beautiful answer. "The Lord is able to give thee much more than this." Whenever believers face pecuniary losses on account of being true to the Lord and to His Word, they should remember that the Lord, who is thus honored, is able to make up for it and give much more. How many have found out that this is true! He dismissed the hirelings and Israel was angry. Cruel was Amaziah's deed done to the Edomites. After smiting 10,000 of them he took another 10,000 captive and brought them unto the top of the rock and cast them down so that they were broken in pieces. It was a horrible crime. The deed was committed in the wild regions of Selah or Petra (2 Kings 14:7). Evidently Amaziah had become greatly impressed with the magnificent rock temples which he saw in Mount Seir. In their weird and grand temples the Edomites practised their abominable idol-worship with human sacrifices. Some of these "gods" of the children of Seir, Amaziah brought back from his expedition and set them up to be his gods. A prophet rebuked him with a statement of much force. And the king answered with a sneer and a threat, showing how hopeless was his case. Then the prophet became silent after he made the solemn declaration: "I know that God hath determined to destroy thee, because thou hast done this, and hast not hearkened to my counsel" (verses 15-16).

The comment on the war between Amaziah and the king of Israel is given in 2 Kings 14. Amaziah was slain in Lachish.

CHAPTER 26

The Reign of Uzziah

1. The beginning of his reign (26:1-5)
2. Uzziah's success and fortifications (26:6-15)
3. Uzziah's sin and leprosy (26:16-21)
4. The death of Uzziah (26:22-23)

The Son of Amaziah, Uzziah, in his sixteenth year, was made king by the people. In Second Kings 15 he is called Azariah. (In the annotations on 2 Kings 15:1-2 an explanation is given on this double name of Uzziah.) Isaiah was then prophet in Judah (Isaiah 1:1). Isaiah's name is mentioned in verse 22. Hosea (Hosea 1:1), Amos (Amos 1:1) and Zechariah (2 Chronicles 26:5) were also prophets during his reign. The latter is not, of course, the Zechariah whose wonderful visions are written in the book which bears his name. Uzziah built Eloth and restored that important harbor to Judah (2 Kings 14:22). From Eloth and Ezion-Geber Solomon's ships had gone to Ophir (1 Kings 9:26-28; 2 Chron. 8:17-18). Probably during the days of Joram (also called Jehoram) of Judah, when Edom revolted, Eloth also must have become independent. Uzziah did that which was right in the sight of the Lord. He sought God in the days of Zechariah, of whom we know nothing else but what is mentioned in verse 5. The Zechariah of Isaiah 8:2 cannot be identified with the Zechariah here, for the one mentioned by Isaiah lived much later. The better rendering of "who had understanding in the visions of God," is, "who was his (Uzziah's) instructor in the fear of God." Then follows the statement "as long as he sought the Lord, God made him prosper." And this is still true with all of God's people.

He waged a most successful warfare against the ancient foe of Israel, the Philistines. Previously, under the reign of Jehoram (2 Chron. 21:16-17), as so often before, God had used the Philistines to chastise His people, but now He used Uzziah to punish them for their wickedness. Then the Ammonites brought gifts and Uzziah's fame spread as far as Egypt. A great restoration work was, after that, carried on by him; he restored and fortified the northern wall of Jerusalem, which had been broken down under Amaziah (2 Chron 25:23). Then there was a marked re-organization of the army of Judah and the defense of Jerusalem was greatly strengthened. "And his name spread far abroad; for he was marvellously helped, till he was strong." Alas! for the next little word! How often we find it in Scripture. "But—!" "But when he was strong, his heart was lifted up to his destruction, for he transgressed against the Lord his God, and went into the temple of the Lord to burn incense upon the altar of incense." How solemn these words are! What a warning they contain to all God's people! When the heart of man is lifted up, when pride is followed, transgression is not far behind. "Pride goeth before destruction, and a haughty spirit before a fall" (Prov. 16:18). How well it is for God's children to be much on their faces and humble themselves before the Lord. To be little in one's own eyes and make nothing of self is true greatness and the place of safety, where Satan stands defeated. And the danger of success and prosperity!

Uzziah invaded the priestly office which did not belong to him. It was a small matter to put some incense upon the altar. It was done in self-will and in defiance of the Lord's order and ordinance. It was a rejection of that office which foreshadowed the work of the true priest, our Lord Jesus Christ. And to-day in Christendom we see much of the same spirit, and that which is far worse, the total rejection of the Lord Jesus as sin-bearer and the great high priest. Uzziah became a leper and died a leper. He was buried as an outcast in the field and not in the sepulchres of the kings. In the year he died Isaiah had his great vision (Is. 6:1). Isaiah's opening chapters give a good description of the religious and moral condition of Judah at the close of Uzziah's reign.

CHAPTER 27

The Reign of Jotham

1. The reign of Jotham (27:1-6)
2. The death of Jotham (27:7-9)

The record of the reign of Jotham is brief in both 2 Kings and in Chronicles. He did also what was right in the sight of the Lord. The statement "howbeit he entered not into the temple of the Lord" means that he did not act as Uzziah, his father did, when he intruded into the functions of the priesthood. However, in spite of the good example of the king, the people continued in their departure from Jehovah. "And the people did yet corruptly." All the evils of a false worship continued and were not stopped. The state of the people is pictured by Isaiah in chapters 1—5 and also in the book of the prophet Micah. These portions of the Word of God are needed to get a better understanding of the conditions which prevailed during the reign of Jotham. Jotham was a godly man and in his reign of sixteen years did much good. All his wars were successful. "He became mighty, because he prepared his ways before the Lord his God." And this statement is the key of all his success and prosperity. He lived and walked in the presence of the Lord. He was guided, strengthened and kept by Him. And this is what all God's people need. It is still the way, the only way to blessing and success, to prepare our ways before the Lord. Jotham is one of the few Bible-characters of whom nothing evil is recorded. Yet the people over which he ruled continued in corruption and apostasy from God.

CHAPTER 28

The Reign of Ahaz

1. The record of his reign (28:1-4)
2. The punishment of Ahaz (28:5-8)
3. The message of Oded and its results (28:9-15)
4. Further punishments of Ahaz (28:16-25)
5. Death of Ahaz (28:26-27)

On Ahaz his wicked reign and apostasy, as well as the war with Syria and the invasion of Judah by Israel, see our annotations on 2 Kings 16. It was at that time that Isaiah ministered in Judah (Isa. 7). Pekah, the son of Remaliah, slew in one day 120,000 men "because they had forsaken the Lord their God ." It was a terrible punishment which fell upon Ahaz. Zichri, a mighty man of Ephraim, slew the son of Ahaz, Maaseiah, also the governor and Elkanah, who was next to the king. A still larger number of Jews were taken captive. The interesting record of the prophet Oded is only given here in Chronicles. Who Oded was we do not know. He was a true and courageous prophet of Jehovah in the midst of idolatrous Samaria nearing so rapidly its predicted doom. Only a true prophet clothed with the Spirit of power could utter such a daring message, which in a time of victory and enthusiasm was calculated to humble the people. And he made the demand, "deliver the captives again, which ye have taken captive of your brethren, for the fierce wrath of the Lord is upon you." It was the Word of the Lord, and they knew only too well that every word spoken was true, and the heads of Ephraim (the northern kingdom) were deeply impressed and convicted. They said, "Ye shall not bring the captives hither." They acknowledged that Israel had transgressed. "For our trespass is great, and there is fierce wrath against Israel." Then follows one of the beautiful scenes in Chronicles. This dark chapter is relieved by the mercy which was shown. "And the men which were expressed by name rose up, and took the captives, and with the spoil clothed all that were naked among them, and arrayed them, and gave them to eat and to drink, and anointed them, and carried all the feeble of them upon asses and brought them to Jericho, the city of palm trees, to their brethren." It reminds us of two passages in the New Testament: Luke 10:30-37, the parable of the good Samaritan, and Matthew 25:31-40. We leave the application which can be made with the reader. Ahaz and his alliance with Assyria as well as Ahaz's further idolatry are commented upon in Second Kings.

6. Reformation under Hezekiah

CHAPTER 29

Hezekiah and the Beginning of the Revival

1. The record of his reign (29:1-2)
2. The purification of the temple (29:3-19)
3. The restored worship (29:20-30)
4. The great offerings (29:31-36)

Compare chapters 29—32 with 2 Kings 18—20 and the annotations given there. The reformation which took place under the reign of the godly son of ungodly Ahaz was a thorough and remarkable one. He did right in the sight of the Lord, according to all his father David had done. In the records of most of the former kings this phrase if missing. It shows that Hezekiah followed the ways of the man after God's own heart. His father had shut up the doors of the house of the Lord (28:24). The first thing Hezekiah did was to open the doors and to repair them. And this was in the first year of his reign, in the first month. There was no delay; he began at once. He fully realized that, in order to have the Lord's presence and blessing, the work must begin at the sanctuary. It has been well said, that piety and the work of righteousness were manifested in Jehoshaphat; great energy and faith was displayed in Hezekiah; and we shall find in Josiah profound reverence for the Scriptures, for the book of the law. And such is the need of the professing Church in the days of decline and apostasy. A revival of profound reverence for the Scriptures, and a whole hearted turning to the law and the testimony, the Word of God, is specially needed. Hezekiah gathered the priests and the Levites. In his great address he acknowledged the sins of the nation. Confession, as it always must, stands in the foreground. "For our fathers have trespassed, and done that which was evil in the eyes of the Lord our God, and have forsaken Him, and have taken away their faces from the habitation of the Lord, and turned their backs." For this reason the wrath of the Lord rested upon them. He called upon them to sanctify themselves and to carry forth the filth out of the holy place. As for himself, it was in his heart to make a covenant with the Lord. No doubt this had been made in secret in the presence of the Lord. Every true revival begins in this way.

The address and appeal found willing hearts among the servants of God. The Levites arose. The three leading families of Gershon, Kohath and Merari, were represented. Then there were two from the family of Elizaphan; two of the descendants of Asaph; two of Heman and two of Jeduthun. They gathered their brethren and went into the inner part to cleanse it. They did not begin on the outside to work towards the inner part. All true work must begin in the inner part.

The true worship was restored and great offerings were brought. The praises they sung were the Psalms, "the words of David and Asaph the singer." Consult 2 Kings 18 on the abolishment of the idols and the destruction of the brazen serpent. Chronicles emphasizes the great restoration work of the temple, in harmony with its priestly character.

CHAPTER 30

The Passover

1. Preparations for the great Passover (30:1-14)
2. The celebration of the Passover (30:15-22)
3. The concluding festive days (30:23-27)

The Passover is next celebrated. It was, so to speak, the birthday of the nation, and typified the great redemption by the blood of the true Passover-Lamb. It had not been kept for a long time and as the proper yearly time for its celebration had passed, the first month, they concluded to keep it in the second month. The law had made provision for that and therefore what they did was according to the Word. (See Num. 9:6-13 and the annotations given there.) And the king recognized the unity of the people of God and their need. Therefore he sent letters to all Israel and Judah, also to Ephraim and Manasseh, that they should come to the house of the Lord, to keep the passover unto the Lord God of Israel. The posts went with the letters throughout the entire land. The letter in itself is beautiful and was addressed to the children of Israel, not mentioning the sad division which had taken place. A considerable part of the house of Israel, the ten tribes, had already been carried into captivity. The letter reached, therefore, only the remnant which escaped out of the hand of the Kings of Assyria (30:6; 2 Kings 15:19; 1 Chron. 5:26). It was the Spirit of God who would bring all the people of God together around the table of the great feast. He always unites God's people. And the posts passing along even unto Zebulun with the God-given message of the king, were treated by some of the remnant with mockery. But others humbled themselves and came to Jerusalem. Without such humbling a coming together of the people of God is not possible.

The great feast then was kept by the great multitude after they had taken away the false altars. They killed the passover. The priests sprinkled the blood, which they had received from the Levites. Many of them who had come were not cleansed; Hezekiah prayed for them. "The good Lord pardon every one." And the Lord hearkened and healed the people, so that the divine threat was not carried out (Lev. 15:31). The feast of unleavened bread was also kept for the appointed seven days with great gladness; yet throughout the days of gladness and remembering Jehovah confession was made to the Lord (verse 22). Everything shows that the Spirit of God was in the great revival. Other festive days followed with more gladness. The king gave great gifts and the princes did likewise, while a great number of priests gave their continued service. Not since the days of Solomon, when he had dedicated the house and reigned over Israel, had Jerusalem seen anything like it. The whole scene ended by the priests blessing the people (Num. 6:23-27). Heaven heard and rejoiced with His people.

Dispensationally the great revival foreshadows what will take place when the King of Israel will occupy the throne and reign, when all Israel is united and back in the land (Ezek. 37), when His people will worship and praise the Holy One of Israel.

CHAPTER 31

The Results of the Revival

1. The destruction of the false worship (31:1)
2. The king's appointments (31:2-21)

All was done by Hezekiah for the orderly continuance of the service in the house of the Lord. The order of the courses of the priests, after David's arrangement, which had been abandoned during the preceding apostasy, was once more settled. What was needed for the public sacrifices of the congregation was willingly given, as well as other things, by the king and the people.

"For the personal support of the ministering priests and Levites nothing more was required than the re-enactment of the ancient provision of firstfruits, tithes, and firstlings (Ex. 23:19; Num. 18:12, 21, etc.; Lev. 27:30-33). These together with 'the tithe of dedicated things' (Lev. 27:30; Deut. 14:28), were now offered in such quantity as not only to suffice for the wants of the priesthood, but to leave a large surplusage, to the thankful joy and surprise of Hezekiah and the princes. In answer to the king's inquiry the high-priest Azariah explained that the large store accumulated was due to the special blessing bestowed by the Lord on a willing and obedient people (2 Chron. 31:5-10). The collection of this store began in the third month—that of Pentecost—when the wheat harvest was completed, and it ended in the seventh month—that of Tabernacles, which marked the close of the fruit harvest and of the vintage. And these contributions, or dues, came not only from Judah, but also from 'the children of Israel' (verse 6); that is, from those in the northern kingdom who had joined their brethren in returning to the service and the law of their Lord.

"For the storage of these provisions, Hezekiah ordered that certain chambers in the temple should be prepared, and he appointed officials, who are named in the sacred text, alike for the supervision and the administration of these stores (verses 11-19). Again and again it is noted with what 'faithfulness' one and the other duty were discharged by each in the special department assigned to him (verses 12, 15, 18)."

Such were the results of the revival produced by the Spirit of God. A united people, the destruction of all false worship, the restoration of Jehovah's worship, great willingness in giving and much sacrifice, obedience to the Lord and to His Word. Such must be the results of every true revival among God's people. Great is the record of the good King Hezekiah: "He sought his God, he did it with all his heart, he prospered."

CHAPTER 32

Sennacherib's Invasion, the Deliverance, and the Passing of Hezekiah

1. Sennacherib's invasion (32:1-2)
2. The king's counsel and trust in God (32:3-8)
3. Sennacherib's threatening and arrogance (32:9-16)
4. Sennacherib's defiance of God (32:17-19)
5. Hezekiah's and Isaiah's prayer (32:20)
6. The deliverance (32:21-23)
7. Hezekiah's illness, pride and departure (32:24-33)

As this part of Hezekiah's history is also found in 2 Kings 20 and we have given already the necessary annotations in connection with these chapters, we do not repeat them here. His prayer and Isaiah's ministry are reported in Second Kings and omitted in Chronicles. So are the details of his illness, his prayer, Isaiah's comforting words, and the details of his failure when he exposed his wealth to the ambassadors. The account of the defiance of Sennacherib's servants is also very much condensed in Chronicles. Both 2 Kings 19—20 and 2 Chronicles 32 must be read together. But we find also additions here. Notably among these are the beautiful words of Hezekiah. After he had done all in his power in defence of the city, cutting off the water, building walls, raising up towers, making darts and shields, appointing captains, he uttered his comforting message. "Be strong and courageous, be not afraid or dismayed for the King of Assyria, nor for all the multitude that is with him, for there be more with us than with him. With him is an arm of flesh; but with us is the Lord our God to help us, and to fight our battles." (See 2 Kings 6:16. No doubt the king had a record of the events of Elisha's ministry and words.) No wonder the people rested themselves upon the words of Hezekiah. They are good and helpful words to rest upon in faith in all our warfare down here.

7. Decline and Apostasy under Manasseh and Amon

CHAPTER 33

1. Manasseh's wicked reign (33:1-10)
2. Manasseh's imprisonment and restoration (33:11-13)
3. His reign after restoration and his death (33:14-20)
4. The reign of Amon (33:21-25)

Manasseh, the twelve year old son of Hezekiah, did not follow the ways of his father, but did evil in the sight of the Lord. He had no godly Jehoiada, like Joash, to stand by him and guide him. He was surrounded, no doubt, by counsellors, but they were evil counsellors. Instead of following the example of his father, he followed that of his wicked grandfather Ahaz. In reading the record of his evil doings we get the impression that he hasted in undoing all his father had done. The corrupt worship on the heights was restored by him, and he added at the same time the Phoenician rites of Baal and Asherah, the Chaldean worship of the host of heaven (the sun and the stars). The altars for this wicked worship were placed in the outer and inner courts of the house of the Lord. More than that, he set a carved image in the house of God. This was an image of an idol; the vilest, unnameable practices were introduced into the place which was to be holy. "And he caused his children to pass through the fire in the valley of Hinnom." As we saw in Second Kings, his grandfather Ahaz was the first one to introduce this horrible Canaanitish custom in Judah. The sins of the Sodomites were openly practiced.

"Alike the extent and the shameless immorality of the idolatry now prevalent, may be inferred from the account of the later reformation by Josiah (2 King 23:4-8). For, whatever practices may have been introduced by previous kings, the location, probably in the outer court of the temple, of a classs of priests, who, in their unnaturalness of vice, combined a species of madness with deepest moral degradation, and by their side, and in fellowship with them, that of priestesses of Astarte, must have been the work of Manasseh" (A. Edersheim).

Then there were enchantments, witchcraft and wizards, and he dealt also with a familiar spirit. This was demon-power manifested as it is to-day in spiritualism and similar cults. So wicked was his work that he made Jerusalem to err, and to do worse than the heathen whom the Lord had destroyed before the children of Israel (verse 9). "Moreover Manasseh shed innocent blood very much till he filled Jerusalem from one end to another" (2 Kings 21:16). "And the Lord spake to Manasseh, and to his people, but they hearkened not" (verse 10). God's prophets bore faithful witness against these awful deeds. Isaiah, Jewish tradition claims, suffered martyrdom under Manasseh's reign. But though the Lord sent His messages, they did not hear. In 2 Kings 21:10-15, we have preserved the message which the Lord sent by His servants the prophets. But Second Kings has nothing to say of the conversion and restoration of this wicked man, one of the greatest miracles of grace on record. The king of Assyria came and bound Manasseh in fetters and carried him to Babylon. A certain class of higher critics, a number of years ago, used to sneer at this record, and denied its historicity because it is entirely missing in the book of Kings.

"It was called in question for this reason, that there was not ground for believing that the Assyrians exercised supremacy in Judah—far less that there had been a hostile expedition against Manasseh; and because, since the residence of the Assyrian kings was in Nineveh, the reported transportation of Manasseh to Babylon (verse 11) must be unhistorical. To these were added, as secondary objections, that the unlikely account of a king transported in iron bonds and fetters was proved to be untrustworthy by the still more incredible notice that such a captive had been again restored to his kingdom."

But these objections have been completely refuted by an Assyrian monument. On this monument the Assyrian king is pictured leading two captives with hooks and rings. The inscription runs as follows: "I transported to Assyria men and women . . . innumerable." Among other names given is the name *"Minasi sar matir Jaudi"* which means "Manasseh, King of Judah." Then carried away, no doubt much disgrace and suffering put upon him, his conscience awakened. He humbled himself and prayed and found mercy. What a manifestation of divine mercy! Jewish tradition often refers to Manasseh's conversion as the greatest encouragement to repentant sinners. Such mercy will yet be shown to the remnant of Israel, when they turn unto the Lord "whose mercy endureth forever." And the evidences of the genuineness of the conversion of Manasseh are not lacking. He acted faithfully after his return and repaired the altar and commanded Judah to serve the Lord God.

The utter corruption of human nature is seen in the case of his son Amon. With the awful experience of his father before him, and no doubt exhorted by Manasseh to serve the Lord and be true to Him, he followed deliberately the bad example of his father's idolatry. He trespassed more and more and did not repent like his father Manasseh, but died in his sins. Under his reign the wickedness reached a higher mark than under any previous king.

8. Reformation under Josiah

CHAPTER 34

The Reign of Josiah and the Reformation

1. The record of his reign (34:1-2)
2. The beginning of the reformation (34:3-7)
3. The house of the Lord repaired (34:8-13)
4. The law of Moses found and read (34:14-21)
5. Hulda, the prophetess (34:22-28)
6. The law read and the covenant (34:29-33)

The contents of this chapter are found also in Second Kings, chapters 22:1—23:30. Inasmuch as this has been covered by our annotation, we do not need to repeat it here. However, we add a paragraph from the *Synopsis of the Bible.*

"We find in Josiah a tender heart, subject to the word, and a conscience that respected the mind and will of God: only at last he had too much confidence in the effect of this to secure blessing from God, without the possession of that faith which gives intelligence in His ways to understand the position of God's people. God, however, makes use of this confidence to take Josiah away from the evil He was preparing in the judgments which were to fall upon Judah, the knowledge of which should have made Josiah walk more humbly. At the age of sixteen he began by the grace of God to seek Jehovah; and at twenty he had acquired the moral strength necessary for acting with energy against idolatry, which he destroyed even unto Naphtali. We see here how sovereign grace came in; for both Hezekiah and Josiah were the sons of extremely wicked fathers.

"Having cleansed the land from idolatry, Josiah begins to repair the temple; and there the book of the law was found. The king's conscience, and his heart also, are bowed under the authority of the word of his God. He seeks for the prophetic testimony of God with respect to the state in which he sees Israel to be, and God makes known to him by Huldah the judgment about to fall upon Israel; but tells him at the same time that his eyes shall not see the evil."

CHAPTER 35

The Keeping of the Passover and Josiah's Death

1. The Passover kept (35:1-19)
2. The death of Josiah (35:20-27)

In the eighteenth year of his reign, Josiah, like his great-grandfather Hezekiah, kept the Passover. No doubt the reading of the law had made this feast once more an urgent necessity. Moreover they had made a solemn covenant "to walk after the Lord, to keep His commandments, His testimonies and His statutes, and to perform the words of the covenant written in the book." Therefore in the appointed time, on the fourteenth day of the first month, they kept the memorial feast, the last before the house of Judah was carried into captivity. (Hezekiah's Passover was kept in the second month. See 2 Chronicles 30:2-3.) And all was done by the godly king "according to the word of the Lord"—"as it is written in the book of Moses." It was obedience to the Word. And such an obedience is needed in the days of decline in the professing Church. It is this which pleases

God. The Passover kept was even greater than that of Hezekiah (verse 18). All Judah and Israel (those who were still left) kept the great feast.

The death of this excellent man and king of Judah has its lessons. The king of Egypt, who was Necho, also called Pharaoh-Necho, came up to fight against Charchemish by Euphrates. Josiah went out against him. But did Josiah ask counsel of the Lord? Was the good man guided by the Lord when he went out against Necho, who did not intend to attack Judah? The evidence is conclusive that Josiah acted of himself and was not directed by the Lord. The Egyptian king rebuked him. Necho had not come against Judah. God had commanded him to make haste and fight against Assyria. Josiah should have known what the prophets had announced about Assyria and its overthrow. Thus Necho sent his ambassadors to give a warning. Necho was on a mission which he knew was of God. Josiah opposed him. "Forbear thee from meddling with God, who is with me, that He destroy thee not." But he gave no heed. The king who had cleansed Jerusalem and Judah, who had repaired the temple, obeyed the word and kept the Passover, neglected to ask the Lord in this matter and then continued in the wrong course. Perhaps pride played here also an important part. It would have greatly humbled him if he had desisted from his uncalled for warfare. How all this has been repeated and is being repeated in the individual experience of Christians needs hardly to be pointed out. Many who were much used like Josiah, stumbled and fell, when they ceased to depend on the Lord and acted in self-will. Like Ahab (2 Chron. 18:29) he disguised himself. The arrow found him as it was with Ahab. He was pierced in the valley of Megiddo; he died in Jerusalem. There was great lamentation. The lamentations of Jeremiah are not the lamentations as we possess them in the book which bears that name. Jeremiah, however, refers to him (Jer. 22:10-13; Lam. 4:20). In Zechariah 12:10-14 the lamentation in the valley of Meggido is mentioned. It is connected there prophetically with another lamentation for another son of David, who was pierced. And He, our Lord, was pierced and wounded for our transgression. When He comes again to fill the throne of His father David, the people shall mourn for Him, but in a different way as they mourned for Josiah. Josiah was the last good king of the house of David who reigned. But there is another one coming who shall rule in righteousness (Is. 32:1).

9. The Final Decline and Apostasy

CHAPTER 36:1-14

1. Jehoahaz's reign (36:1-7)
2. Jehoiachin's brief reign (36:8-10)
3. Zedekiah (36:11-14)

As the complete record of these three final rulers is given in the second book of Kings, the annotations are made there. Nothing needs to be added. It was the final plunge before the awful judgment overtook Jerusalem and Judah. And there will be a final plunge into apostasy in connection with the professing Church, before the predicted judgment with the coming of our blessed Lord will end this present evil age and usher in His glorious kingdom.

IV. The Captivity and the Epilogue

CHAPTER 36:15-23

1. The captivity (36:15-21)
2. The epilogue (36:22-23)

In infinite patience the Lord still waited for the return of His people. Judgment is His strange work, but He delighteth in mercy. He sent them messengers who exhorted them and brought the messages of God, because He had compassion. But they mocked the messengers, despised God's gracious offers and misused His prophets, till there was no remedy. An awful statement! Apostasy and defiance of God increased to such an extent, till there was no remedy. The threatening clouds of judgment broke at last and the people were carried away into the captivity. "To fulfill the word of the Lord by the mouth of Jeremiah, until the land had enjoyed her sabbaths, for as long as she lay desolate she kept sabbath to fulfill three-score and ten years." And this age too is, with its rejection of God's best, approaching a day when there will be no remedy and the judgment will fall.

The epilogue takes us after the seventy year captivity. Cyrus had been named by Isaiah almost two hundred years before he was born (Is. 44:28). God accomplished His purpose through this Persian king. We shall follow his history in Ezra and his work and what it foreshadows in Isaiah.

THE BOOK OF
EZRA

Introduction

In the Hebrew Bible the books of Ezra and Nehemiah are placed at the close of the third division of the Jewish canon, which is called "Ketubim." In the Talmud, the Massorah, the Septuagint, and in the writings of Josephus, Ezra and Nehemiah are treated as one book. It is claimed that originally Chronicles with Ezra and Nehemiah formed one book. The last two verses with which Second Chronicles closes are repeated in the opening chapter of Ezra.

(The order of the books in the Hebrew Bible is as follows: I Tora (the law) Genesis—2 Kings, except Ruth; II Nevijin (the prophets) Isaiah—Malachi, except Lamentations and Daniel; III Ketubim (the Writings) Psalms, Proverbs, Job, Song of Solomon, Ruth, Lamentations, Ecclesiastes, Esther, Daniel, Ezra, Nehemiah and Chronicles.)

Ezra, the Author of the Book

No valid proof can be given that the Jewish and early Christian view, that Ezra is the author of the book which bears his name, is incorrect. He was a pious, deeply spiritual man. His genealogy is found in chapter 7:1-6. We learn that he was a lineal descendant of Phineas, the son of Eleazar, the son of Aaron; and therefore Ezra was a priest. (See chapter 7:11; 10:10, 16.) He was also a scribe—"a ready scribe in the law of Moses, which the Lord God of Israel had given" (7:6); "a scribe of the words of the commandments and of the statutes of Israel" (7:11). We find him first mentioned in the seventh chapter. The record is given that he went up to Babylon . . . "and the king granted him all his request, according to the hand of the Lord God upon him." He received permission from King Artaxerxes I (Longimanus) in the seventh year of his reign (458 B. C.) to lead a number of the people back to Jerusalem. His beautiful, godly character may be seen in the three last chapters of the book, in which he is the principal actor. He was a great man of prayer and worship, with a childlike trust in the Lord, with great zeal for God and an intense interest in His people and their welfare. Much is said of Ezra in talmudical literature, where his greatness and worthiness is celebrated. According to these traditions he was in meekness and godliness like Moses. It is said that he first introduced the Hebrew alphabet in square characters, and that he made the massorah and punctuation of the Scriptures. He is also considered to be the author of the Jewish canon, and to have rewritten the whole of the Old Testament from memory. Most likely he wrote Chronicles besides the record contained in this book. It is more than likely that he collected the Psalms in a book and arranged them under the guidance of the Spirit of God in the order in which we possess them now. His great reformation work we shall point out in the annotations.

The Story of the Book

The book of Ezra records chronologically the return of the remnant to Jerusalem and the events which took place after their return. The rebuilding of the temple and its dedication are fully described, while Nehemiah records the rebuilding of the wall and the city. The edict of Cyrus permitting the Jews to return and urging the rebuilding of the temple is followed by the list of names of those who returned under Zerubbabel, a son of David, to Jerusalem. The given number is 42,360. After their re-establishment they proceeded with the building and dedication of the altar, after which the foundation of the temple was laid. Then the mongrel race, the Samaritans, came offering their fellowship in the building of the temple; their co-operation was positively rejected. Then the adversaries troubled them, hired counsellors against them, and for a number of years the work stopped. A letter addressed to the king of Persia is inserted in chapter 4 and is written in Aramaic (Chaldean). (The Aramaic portions of Ezra are chapters 4:8—6:18 and 7:12-26.) Then appeared in the midst of the discouraged remnant, when the work had ceased, the two great post-exilic prophets, Haggai and Zechariah. As a result of the fiery exhortations of Haggai and the glorious visions of Zechariah, a revival took place and under Zerubbabel with Joshua the highpriest, the prophets helping, the building of the house began. Next the governor Tatnai appeared, attempting to stop their work; but he did not succeed. He appealed to the king in a letter which is also given in full in Aramaic; he was confident that he would succeed in ending the work of the remnant. Ezra had access to these documents and reports them in the Chaldean language in which they were written. But when Darius the king instituted a search there was found in Achmetha, in the palace of Media, a roll with the record of Cyrus, which Tatnai the governor had insinuated was a falsehood, used by the remnant to continue the work. Then Darius made a decree by which Tatnai and his companions were commanded not to interfere any more with the work of the house of God, but that the Jews should build the house. The decree also appointed a generous contribution day by day from the king's goods for the Jews. The hostile governor was forced to carry out the decree of the king. After that the temple was completed and dedicated. They kept the feast of Passover and unleavened bread. This concludes the first section of the book.

Many years after these events had taken place, Ezra comes upon the scene. Ezra's work is described, and how, authorized by the decree of Artaxerxes, he headed an expedition of exiles, who returned to Jerusalem. Artaxerxes' letter is given in full in the language used by the Chaldeans (Aramaic). Ezra's outburst of praise follows the decree of the king. A list of all who joined Ezra in the return is found in the beginning of the eighth chapter. They gathered at the river Ahava, encamping there for three days. Ezra discovered that none of the sons of Levi were in the company. A number of these were soon added to the returning exiles. Before the journey was started there was a fast and humiliation before God; they looked to Him for a straight way and for protection. They departed from Ahava on the twelfth day of the first month and reached Jerusalem on the first day of the fifth month, the Lord graciously protecting them from robbers. After that follows the great reformation work in which Ezra dealt with the deplorable moral conditions into which the people had fallen.

The Spiritual and Dispensational Application

This interesting historical account of a return of a remnant from Babylon contains a message for us. Divine principles are revealed in this book, which find their application to God's people at all times. These spiritual and dispensational lessons will be pointed out in the annotations.

The Division of the Book of Ezra

This book is divided into two sections. After the edict of Cyrus there is a return to Jerusalem under Zerubbabel, the rebuilding of the temple and its dedication. Then after sixty years the return under Ezra took place.

I. THE RETURN UNDER ZERUBBABEL AND THE REBUILDING OF THE TEMPLE (1—6)

II. THE RETURN UNDER EZRA AND HIS REFORMATION (7—10)

Analysis and Annotations

I. The Return Under Zerubbabel and the Rebuilding of the Temple

CHAPTER 1

1. The proclamation of Cyrus (1:1-4)
2. The response of the chiefs of Judah and Benjamin (1:5-6)
3. The vessels of the house of the Lord restored (1:7-11)

Verses 1-4. Cyrus (meaning "the Sun") the King of Persia was, according to ancient historians, the son of Cambyses, Prince of Persia, and Mandam, daughter of Astyages, King of the Median Empire. The theory that he was the offspring of Ahasuerus and Esther, and was trained by Mordecai and Nehemiah, lacks all historical foundation. The heart of Cyrus in the beginning of his reign was stirred by the Lord, because the time had come that the Word of the Lord spoken by the mouth of the prophet Jeremiah might be fulfilled. And this was the Word of the Lord spoken by Jeremiah: "For thus saith the Lord, that after seventy years be accomplished at Babylon I will visit you, and perform my good word toward you, in causing you to return to this place" (Jere. 29:10). The seventy years were ended and God was about to act in behalf of His people Israel. Daniel was praying in Babylon after also having read the words of Jeremiah (Dan. 9:1-2). Cyrus was the chosen instrument of the Lord to bring about the return of the Jews and the rebuilding of the temple. Almost two hundred years before his birth the Lord had revealed his name and his work to the prophet Isaiah. Twice Isaiah mentions the name of this Persian King: "That saith of Cyrus, He is my shepherd, and shall perform all my pleasures, even saying to Jerusalem, Thou shalt be built, and the temple, Thy foundation shall be laid. Thus saith the Lord to His anointed, to Cyrus, whose right hand I have holden, to subdue nations before him; and I will loose the loins of kings, to open before him the two leaved gates; and the gates shall not be shut" (Isa. 44:28, 45:1). "I have raised him up in righteousness, and I will direct all his ways; he shall build my city and he shall let go my captives, not for price nor reward, saith the Lord of Hosts" (Isa. 45:13). This was written by this prophet of God over a century before the temple was destroyed by Nebuchadnezzar. Previously in Isaiah Jehovah had spoken his challenge to the idol-gods to show their power: "Let them bring forth, and show us what shall happen, let them show the former things, what they be . . . or declare us things for to come; show the things that are to come afterward" (Isa. 41:22-23). In naming Cyrus the king, and the great work he would do for the exiles and for Jerusalem, the Lord demonstrates His power to declare things to come and to make the future known. And who would doubt that an omniscient God, who knows all things, the end from the beginning, could do this? Only infidels and destructive critics. The latter have invented a Deutero-Isaiah who, it is claimed, wrote the above prophecies concerning Cyrus after he had come into existence and done the work.

It will be seen that the Spirit of God through Isaiah spoke of Cyrus as the shepherd, the anointed, the man of my counsel (Isa. 46:11); whom the Lord loveth (48:14); whose right hand the Lord upholdeth (45:1); who will perform the Lord's pleasure (44:28); and yet he is also called "a ravenous bird from the East" (46:11). Cyrus is, as the chosen instrument, a type of the Messiah, Christ. A comparison of Cyrus with Christ, the work Cyrus did for Israel and the work Christ will do in His second coming, is interesting.

The proclamation which Cyrus issued and sent in writing throughout his kingdom speaks of God as "the Lord God of heaven," and in his edict Cyrus declares, "He hath charged me to build Him a house at Jerusalem, which is in Judah." How did Cyrus receive this knowledge? Beyond question he knew Daniel, and may have heard from his lips the history of Nebuchadnezzar as well as the great prophecies. This prophet may also have acquainted Cyrus with the prophecies of Isaiah. According to Josephus, the great Jewish historian, Cyrus read the book of Isaiah himself. When he came to the place in which Isaiah mentioned him by name, an earnest desire and ambition seized upon him to fulfill what was written in these prophecies. From the record here we learn that it was the Lord who stirred him up to issue the proclamation. In it permission was granted to those Jewish exiles throughout his kingdom to return to Jerusalem to build the house of the Lord; and those who remained were to help with silver and gold, with goods and beasts, besides free-will offering for the house of God. Thus God's Word spoken over two hundred years before was fulfilled in this proclamation of Cyrus: "He shall let my captives go;" "Saying to Jerusalem, Thou shalt be built; and to the temple, Thy foundation shall be laid"; these were the two great prophetic statements of the work he was to do. And so it came literally to pass. All predictions of a future restoration of Israel to their land, not through a Gentile king, but through the coming of Heaven's King, the Shepherd of His sheep, will soon find all their literal fulfillment likewise.

Verses 5-6. There was at once a response from the heads of the fathers of Judah and Benjamin, and the priests and Levites. What joy must have filled their hearts when they read the proclamation of Cyrus. What they had longed and prayed for had come at last. God was acting in their behalf and His promises were about to come to pass. It was the Lord who stirred them to action and to turn their faces towards Jerusalem. But not all were ready to go back; only a small remnant was willing. The great majority preferred to remain in Babylon. There was nothing to attract them to Jerusalem—the city of ruins, with the once magnificent temple in ruins. Those who returned, loved Jerusalem, the place the Lord had chosen, where alone the appointed offerings and sacrifices could be brought. They belonged to those who sat by the rivers of Babylon and wept when they remembered Zion and said, "If I forget thee, O Jerusalem, let my right hand forget her cunning; if I do not remember thee, let my tongue cleave to the roof of my mouth, if I prefer not Jerusalem above my chief joy" (Ps. 137). And the Jews who remained helped them generously in every way.

Verses 7-11. Then Cyrus restored the vessels of the house of the Lord, which Nebuchadnezzar had brought from Jerusalem and put into the house of his gods (Daniel 1:2). His grandson, Belshazzar, defiled them at his licentious feast (Dan. 5:2). In that night Belshazzar was slain and Babylon fell. No doubt Cyrus had these vessels collected and carefully guarded. Mithredath the treasurer handed them to Sheshbazzar the prince of Judah. This prince was Zerubbabel: Sheshbazzar was the name the Babylonians had given him. He was born in Babylon; his name means "stranger in Babylon." He became the princely leader of the returning exiles. Besides being mentioned in Ezra we find his name also in the book of Zechariah. In all there were 5,400 vessels of gold and silver which were handed over to Zerubbabel to take back to Jerusalem. How it all shows that God had not forgotten His people, and when His appointed time came He manifested His power in their behalf. Nor has He forgotten His promise to bring a remnant back from the great dispersion among all the nations of the world. When that return comes, a greater than Zerubbabel the prince of Judah will be the leader. The Lord Jesus, the Son of David, will be their Deliverer.

CHAPTER 2

1. The leaders (2:1-2)
2. The names of the returning exiles (2:3-35)
3. The priests (2:36-39)
4. The Levites and singers (2:40)
5. The porters and Nethinim (2:42-54)
6. Solomon's servants (2:55-58)
7. Those of doubtful descent (2:59-63)
8. The number of the whole company (2:64-67)
9. The offering of the house of God (2:68-70)

Verses 1-2. This chapter contains the names of the returning remnant. It is a specimen page of the records which God keeps, and from which we may learn that He remembers His people, whom He knows by name and whose works are not forgotten by Him. In the book of Nehemiah this list is repeated (chapter 7) with an additional record of those who helped in building the wall. He has a book of remembrance (Mal. 3:16); and the apostle reminded the Hebrew believers of this fact when he wrote: "For God is not unrighteous to forget your work and labor of love, which ye have showed toward his name, in that ye have ministered to the saints and do minister" (Heb. 6:10). There were twelve leaders. Only eleven are given by Ezra; in Nehemiah's record we find an additional name (Nahamani), making twelve in all. Zerubbabel was the leader of the returning captives. His name means "seed of Babylon." He is called the son of Shealtiel, the son or grandson of Jeconiah, and was therefore a descendant of David. His name appears in the two genealogies of Matthew (1:12) and Luke (3:27). In 1 Chronicles 3:19 he is called the son of Pedaiah, who was Shealtiel's brother. This double ascription of parentage may probably be accounted for by Pedaiah having contracted a levirate marriage with Shealtiel's widow. The second leader was Jeshua, also called Joshua. He was a son of Jehozadak and grandson of the high priest Seraiah. Zerubbabel, the princely leader, son of David, and Joshua, the highpriest, are types of Christ. (See Zech. 4 and 6.) Nehemiah is not the Nehemiah who led the other expedition years later; nor is Mordecai the uncle of Queen Esther, who was an old man and evidently remained in Shushan (Esther 10:3). The names Nehemiah and Mordecai were quite common among the Jews. The names of some of the others appear in a slightly changed form in Nehemiah; it was a Jewish custom to call a person by different names.

Verses 3-35. The descendants of the different persons are now given. In all we find 24,144 descendants. Their individual names are not recorded but the Lord knows them all, and cared for each member and sustained them in the journey homeward. Even so He knows all His sheep and keeps every member of His body, leading them home to glory. If some of the numbers do not agree with Nehemiah's record, there is no doubt a good reason for it. For instance, the descendants of Arah are here 775 and in Nehemiah we find only 652 recorded. Probably 775 had enrolled their names but only 652 went. All the names recorded may be traced in other portions of the Scriptures.

Verses 36-39. The different temple officials are recorded next. These are priests, Levites, singers, porters and Nethinim. The priests are first mentioned. In 1 Chronicles 24 there are mentioned twenty-four courses. Jedaiah, Immer and Harim are found in the record of the Chronicles. In all there were 4,289 priests who went back. And these constituted four courses only.

Verses 40-41. Only seventy-four Levites returned. This was a very small number. (Hodaviah should be read Judah; chapter 3:9.) There were more singers than Levites. The children of

Asaph, that sweet and blessed singer in Israel, were one hundred and twenty-eight. No doubt they encouraged the returning exiles in song, by the spirit of praise and worship. The Babylon experience, so beautifully expressed in Psalm 137, was passed. "By the rivers of Babylon, there we sat down, yea, we wept, when we remembered Zion. We hanged our harps upon the willows in the midst thereof. For there they that carried us away required of us a song; and they that wasted us required of us mirth, saying, Sing us one of the songs of Zion. How shall we sing the Lord's song in a strange land?" All was changed now. God was working. Deliverance had come and singing no doubt was heard again among the returning hosts. But why were so few Levites ready to go back? According to the divine instruction in the Law they were to have no inheritance save in the Lord. It was a test of faith to return under these circumstances, and for this reason many Levites must have tarried in Babylon, where things were abundant. Those who returned were tested (Neh. 13:10).

Verses 42-54. The names of the porters and Nethinim. There were in the company one hundred and thirty-nine porters. The Nethinim were temple servants. The word means "given" or "devoted," i.e., to God. We find this name in only one other passage (1 Chron. 9:2). According to Ezra 8:20 this order originated with King David. Jewish tradition identifies them with the Gibeonites, whom Joshua appointed as helpers to the Levites (Josh. 9:3-27). Whatever their origin, they were devoted servants of God assigned to certain duties in the temple.

Verses 55-58. Then comes the record of the children of Solomon's servants. These with the Nethinim were three hundred and ninety-two. Nothing certain is known of these additional servants, whose duty seems to have been similar to that of the Nethinim. Some regard them as the descendants of the strangers whom Solomon had enlisted in the building of the temple (1 Kings 5:13).

Verses 59-63. These verses tell us of the great caution exercised by the people not to tolerate one in their midst whose origin was in any way doubtful. They were determined that Israel should be an unmingled Israel. Therefore they were most careful in examining the genealogies to exclude all who could not be clearly established as true Israelites, for none but such should engage in the work. The true family of God was now marked out and all who could not clearly prove their connection were set aside. There were six hundred and fifty-two who had joined the company from the Babylonish places Tel-melah, Tel-harsa, Cherub, Addan and Immer. They were the children of Delaiah, of Tobiah and Nekoda. These could not show their descent. They were allowed to return with the rest, but their names are not found in Ezra 10:25-43 or in Nehemiah 10:15-28. And also children of priests sought their register among those that were reckoned by genealogy, but they were not found; they were therefore counted as polluted and put from the priesthood. Tirshatha is the governor (a Persian title meaning "your severity"); his name was Sheshbazzar, the official title of Zerubbabel, the prince (chapter 1:8). Nehemiah also had that title (Neh. 8:9). Zerubbabel, the governor, ruled that those uncertified priests should not eat of the most holy things, till there stood up a priest with Urim and Thummim. And how many are there today in the professing Church who are in the same uncertainty. While making an outward profession, they have no assurance, they have no clear title and do not know that they belong to the holy priesthood into which grace brings all who have been born again. The Church has become a great house (2 Tim. 2:20-21) in which we find the true children of God and those who are such only in profession. If there is to be a return from the Babylon which Christendom is today, the same principle of separation must be maintained. Only those who are born again, who can "show their father's house," constitute the members of the body of Christ.

Verses 64-67. The number of the whole congregation was 42,360. There were also 7,337 servants and maids, among them two hundred singers; the latter must be distinguished from those mentioned in verses 41 and 70. Singing was evidently a very prominent occupation on the journey towards the homeland! Their groans were ended. The captivity was behind and freedom before. How beautiful the chanting of their great psalms must have been as they journeyed on. But greater still will be the time when the wandering remnant, so long scattered among the nations, turns homeward; when through the coming of their King their groans will end forever, and when they sing the Hallelujah chorus in the kingdom of righteousness and peace.

There were likewise 736 horses, 245 mules, 435 camels and 6,720 asses.

Verses 68-70. These last verses tell us of what happened when they came to Jerusalem. They must have sought at once the ruins of the former temple, for that is the spot they loved. Significant it is that though it was razed to the ground, it still existed in the mind of God, and also in the thoughts of the people. It does not say "when they came to the ruins," but "when they came to the house of the Lord." And then the hearts of the fathers were touched, and they gave after their ability unto the treasurer of the work 61,000 drams and 5,000 pounds of silver and one hundred priests' garments. They were faithful in their giving, not according to the Law, the tenth part, but after their ability. And in the New Testament the rule for the Church as to giving is stated in 1 Cor. 16:2, "Upon the first day of the week, let each one of you lay by him in store as God hath prospered him."

CHAPTER 3

1. The altar set up (3:1-3)
2. The feast of tabernacles celebrated (3:4)
3. The sacrifices brought (3:5-7)
4. The foundation of the temple laid (3:8-13)

Verses 1-3. How long the journey lasted is not stated. The previous chapter in its close states that all dwelt in their cities—"and all Israel in their cities." The significant seventh month (Tishri) with its holy convocation (feast of trumpets, day of atonement and feast of tabernacles) having come, the remnant gathered "as one man to Jerusalem." It was the time for such a general gathering, for the feast of trumpets is typical of the restoration of Israel, a restoration which was not fulfilled in the return of this remnant; only foreshadowing it. This gathering "as one man to Jerusalem" reminds us of that other gathering in Jerusalem centuries later "when they were all with one accord in one place" (Acts 2:1) and the Holy Spirit came down from heaven and all were baptized into one body, the Church. There is only one body, and all true believers are put into that body by the same Spirit. This oneness was manifested in the beginning of the church on earth (Acts 2:41-47; 4:23, 32). While its outward expression is lost, yet still the unity of the Spirit in the bond of peace can be kept. (Sectarianism is a denial of that unity.) Whenever the Spirit of God is permitted to manifest His power unhindered among God's people, the result is always in bringing them together. The Spirit of God never divides, but unites.

Then Jeshua the highpriest with his brethren priests, also Zerubbabel and his brethren, built the altar of the God of Israel, to be enabled to bring the burnt offerings as commanded in the law. Obedience to the Word of God was their first concern. Fear was also upon them because of the people of those countries, therefore they felt the need of protection. They knew Jehovah is the Shield and the Refuge of His trusting people. First they were obedient to His Word by setting up the altar for worship and approach to God in the appointed way, and then they trusted Him that He would keep them in the midst of their enemies. The altar and the burnt offerings morning and evening are typical of Christ, who is the altar and the burnt offering. Whenever the Spirit of God sends a true recovery and revival He will make the Lord Jesus Christ and His blessed finished work the first thing. He leads His people together, and then in true worship around the Person of the Lord. This worship centers for the true Church in the Lord's Supper, that precious feast of remembrance.

Verse 4. Next they kept the feast of tabernacles—as it is written (Lev. 23:33-36). They manifested a holy zeal in rendering a complete obedience to the law of their fathers. The feast of tabernacles typifies the consummation when the kingdom has come and the full harvest. Another remnant of Israel will return in the future, under different circumstances, and then when Messiah, the King, is in the midst of His people, the feast will find its fulfillment. We learn from this how exact the returned exiles were to be in obedience to the Word of God. Without having the house to worship in, destitute of almost everything, they earnestly tried to please God by leaving the ways of Babylon and submitting to the Word of God. This is another mark of the power and energy of the Spirit of God in His gracious work or recovery; He leads back to the Word of God and gives power to walk in obedience.

Verses 5-7. It was a complete return to the law of God. Continual burnt offerings were offered, new moons and the set feasts of Jehovah were kept. Then the spirit of sacrifice was also manifested—they offered a free-will offering unto the Lord. And though the foundation of the temple was not yet laid, they gave money to the masons and to the carpenters in anticipation of the laying of the foundation and building of the temple. Meat, drink and oil were given to them of Zidon and Tyre, to bring cedar trees from Lebanon to the sea of Joppa. Permission had been given to do this by King Cyrus.

Verses 8-13. We doubt not that their faith also was tested in the beginning, for nine months passed by before the work began. It was in the second month of the second year after their arrival in Jerusalem, when the Levites from twenty years and upward were appointed by Zerubbabel and Jeshua "to set forward the work of the house of the Lord." The leaders were foremost in the work, and associated the people with themselves in the blessed enterprise. They were "laborers together" (1 Cor. 3:9). They took hold of the work in earnest. The order in this chapter is the building of the altar-worship; obedience to the Word of God, and then whole-souled and united service for the Lord. This is the order still for God's people. And in that work God's order was not ignored but conscientiously followed, for the Levites are mentioned first (Numbers 4; 1 Chron. 23:24). In all things they adhered strictly to the Word of God. And when the work was actually begun a holy enthusiasm took hold of them, and all the people praised the Lord with a great shout. It was a great celebration, led by the priests in their apparel, with trumpets. Next came the sons of Asaph with cymbals. Their praise was after the ordinance of David, King of Israel. They sang together by courses in praising and giving thanks unto the Lord "because He is good, for His mercy endureth forever toward Israel." Then all the people shouted with a great shout. The Spirit of praise took hold upon their hearts. They celebrated the goodness and mercy of Jehovah towards His people, which are endless. But there were also tears. The old men, priests and Levites, and others who still remembered the Solomonic temple in its great beauty, wept with a loud voice; while others shouted aloud for joy. The voice of the shouting and of the weeping was so mingled together that it could not be discerned. The tears were occasioned by remembering the glories of the former days, which had passed away.

Joy was in His presence and acceptable. Tears confessed the truth and testified a just sense of what God had been for His people, and of the blessing they had once enjoyed under His hand. Tears recognized, alas! that which the people of God had been for God; and these tears were acceptable to Him. The weeping could not be discerned from the shout of joy; this was a truthful result, natural and sad, yet becoming in the presence of God. For He rejoices in the joy of His people, and He understands their tears. It was, indeed, a true expression of the state of things *(Synopsis of the Bible)*.

And when we too remember the former things and present conditions in the ruin and confusion all around us in that which professes His Name, we also weep. And yet we shout and praise Him when we remember His mercy, which endureth forever.

CHAPTER 4

1. The offer of the Samaritans refused (4:1-6)
2. The letter to King Artaxerxes (4:7-16)
3. The king's reply (4:17-22)
4. The work is stopped (4:23-24)

Verses 1-6. The adversaries were the Samaritans. (There is an interesting correspondence with the book of Acts. After the Spirit of God had begun His blessed work, the enemy from without and then within started his hindering work.) They had watched silently the work of restoration and then appeared before Zerubbabel and the chief of the fathers and said unto them, "Let us build with you, for we seek your God, as ye do, and we do sacrifice unto Him since the days of Esar-haddon, King of Assur, who brought us "up hither." These words revealed their true origin. They were a mongrel race settled by heathen kings in the conquered territory of the house of Israel, the ten tribes. We find the history relating to them in 2 Kings 17:24. The king of Assyria brought men from Babylon, Cuthah, Ara, Hamath, and Sepharvaim and colonized them in Samaria. They were a wicked lot, and the Lord punished them by sending lions in their midst. Then they appealed to the Assyrian king and expressed a desire to get acquainted with the "manner of the God in the land." Priests of Jeroboam, who were captives, were then sent to them. One of these priests taught them in Beth-el the corrupt worship which had been the downfall of the ten tribes. The result was "they feared the Lord, and made unto themselves of the lowest of them priests of the high places." They served their own idols at the same time. The record saith, "Unto this day they do after the former manners, they fear not the Lord, neither do they after their statutes, or after their ordinances, or after the law and commandment which the Lord commanded the children of Jacob, whom He named Israel." These Assyrians married Israelitish women who had been left in the land. (In the British Museum is a cylinder containing the annals of Esar-haddon, giving the deportation of the Israelites and the settlement of colonists in their place.) These corrupt people with their well sounding words remind us of the Gibeonites in Joshua's day. They illustrate the wiles of the devil. The leaders of the remnant refused them participation in the building of the house of the Lord. They realized that they were a separated people and to permit these Samaritans to come in would have been disobedience to the Word of God, bringing His displeasure upon them. If they had been permitted to link themselves with the people of God, corruption and disaster would have been the result. But Zerubbabel and Jeshua endowed with divine wisdom knew that they were adversaries and had no call and no right to engage in the work of the Lord. It was a decisive reply they received. "Ye have nothing to do with us to build an house unto our God; but we ourselves together will build unto the Lord God of Israel, as King Cyrus, the King of Persia, hath commanded us." At once they were unmasked. They turned against them, molested them, and hired counsellors against them to frustrate their purpose. They also wrote an accusation against the inhabitants of Judah and Jerusalem. The Hebrew word (used only in this passage) is "sitnah," cognate with the noun "Satan." Satan was the power behind these Samaritans and their efforts to hinder the work. Their method was Satan's method. These Samaritans may well be compared with the large masses in Christendom who have a form of godliness and deny the power thereof. Like the Samaritans the unsaved multitudes in professing Christendom pretend to serve the Lord, but they are the enemies of the Cross, and their belly is their god, they mind earthly things. The New Testament demands separation from such (2 Cor.6:14-18; 2 Tim. 3:5; 2 John 11). Fellowship with them is disastrous, for they are only natural men, not having the Spirit and are therefore unfit for Christian fellowship, for they are serving the world and its god.

Verses 7-16. Bishlam, Mithredath and Tabeel, Persians, and officials of the government, probably closely identified with the Samaritans and residents of Jerusalem, wrote a letter to King Artaxerxes. (Ahasuerus is a regal title, meaning "the venerable king"; Artaxerxes also is such a title, meaning "the great king.") With the eighth verse begins an Aramaic section of the book, which extends to chapter 6:18. The Syrian tongue was Aramaic. The letter is a very cunningly devised document, full of misrepresentation and falsehood, inspired by him who is "the liar, and the father of it." They accused the Jews of building Jerusalem and setting up the wall. This was a falsehood, for only the house was being built and not the wall or the city. What they said about the city, its former character of rebellion, was true, and the accuser made use of the past sins of the nation. But God had again been gracious to His people and turned their captivity. Reminding the king of the possible danger if the city were built again and fortified by a wall; and the loss of revenue, they inspired fear in the king's heart. The same accuser of the brethren, liar and falsifier, who stood behind these letter writers, is still at work and will continue till he is cast out (Rev. 12).

Verses 17-22. The king received the letter and instituted a search into the former history of Jerusalem, which verified what the letter claimed, and he commanded at once that the city should not be built. The falsehood that they were building the city and the wall was not discovered. The enemy was successful. Yet a faithful God watched over it all.

Verses 23-24. We can well imagine that when the letter was read before Rehum and Shimshai and their companions, with what a feverish haste they must have rushed up to Jerusalem, and made them cease from the work by force and power. "Then ceased the work of the house of God which is at Jerusalem. So it ceased unto the second year of the reign of Darius, King of Persia." The remnant was severely tested, and at that time there set in a decline. The former energy seems to have left them, as we find when we consider Haggai's message. Nor do we read anything at the close of this chapter about turning to the Lord in prayer.

CHAPTER 5

1. The prophetic ministry of Haggai and Zechariah (5:1)
2. The result of their ministy (5:2)
3. Tatnai's interference (5:3-5)
4. The letter to Darius (5:6-17)

Verse 1. At that critical time when the enemy seemed to have triumphed, and they were losing their interest, God graciously intervened by sending them His two messengers the prophets Haggai and Zechariah. Their great prophetic messages will be more fully taken up in our annotations on the books which contain their prophecies. The voice of prophecy is always heard when the people of God are in decline. The greatest prophets appeared at the darkest period of Israel—Elijah, Elisha, Isaiah, Jeremiah, Ezekiel, Daniel. Two months before Zechariah began his prophetic ministry Haggai lifted up his voice and addressed Zerubbabel and Joshua (Jeshua). It was the Word of the Lord which he communicated to the princely and priestly leaders of the people. This first message gives an interesting light upon the situation of the remnant. (Read Haggai 1.) The people were saying "The time is not come, the time that the Lord's house should be built." This they must have said on account of their enemies; they were waiting for a more providential time, when they could pursue the building of the house. The next words of Haggai reveal the moral condition of the people: "Is it time for you, O ye, to dwell in ceiled houses, and this house lie waste?" Then the exhortation, "Consider your ways." From these words we learn that they had settled down in comfort and were more occupied with building themselves houses than with finishing the house of the Lord. And God had dealt with them for this neglect; they had suffered on account of it (Hag. 1:6-11).

Verse 2. When the burning message of Haggai was delivered the Lord revived them again. They arose from their state of apathy and began to build the house of the Lord, the prophets of God helping them. The book of Haggai tells us that they all obeyed the voice of the Lord their God . . . and the people did fear before the Lord. No sooner had they obeyed and feared the Lord than another message came through the prophet: "I am with you, saith the Lord." They no longer feared their enemies, nor the King's command, but they feared the Lord, and at once the work was vigorously resumed and the house finished (6:15). The Word of the Lord was used in their revival. Every true and genuine revival always started and always will start with the Word of God, hearing and believing what God has spoken.

Verses 3-5. This new start attracted at once the attention of their enemies. Tatnai, governor on this side of the river and Shethar-boznai with their companions appeared on the scene. (In cuneiform tablets of the first and third years of Darius Hystaspis, a governor Ustnai is mentioned. He is described in Assyrian as the governor of the province.) They asked the questions, "Who hath commanded you to build this house, and to make up the wall? What are the names of the men that make this building?" ("We" in verse 4 is "they," Tatnai and his companions. See verse 10.) Thus the enemy made another effort to hinder the work. He never fails to attack that which is done to the glory of God. But these enemies did not reckon with the Keeper of Israel who neither sleeps nor slumbers. Little did they know that what they were doing would lead to victory for God's people and would result in finishing the house of God. The eye of God was upon the elders of the Jews. He gave them strength, courage and assurance, so that they could persevere in the work. God was with them, and who then could be against them? God restrained Tatnai from giving order to suspend the work, so that they worked right on. Blessed are all the servants of the Lord who toil in the fear of the Lord, knowing that His eye is upon them and that He sustains all who put their trust in Him.

Verses 6-17. Then Tatnai and his associates sent a letter to King Darius, which gives the unreported details of their visit to Jerusalem. The letter tells us that the house was built with great stones and timber in the walls, and that all prospered in their hands. Zerubbabel and his companions had answered the inquiries to Tatnai as follows: "We are the servants of the God of heaven and earth." Thus they gave a witness of themselves and then related what had taken place, and how Cyrus had made the decree to build the house of God. The letter stated that Sheshbazzar (Zerubbabel) had laid the foundation and that the house was still unfinished. Then follows the request: "Now, therefore, if it seem good to the king, let there be search made in the king's treasure house, which is there at Babylon, whether it be so, that a decree was made of Cyrus the King to build this house of God at Jerusalem, and let the king send his pleasure to us concerning the matter." The builders must have had perfect peace about this letter, knowing that the Lord was with them.

CHAPTER 6

1. The search of the king and the result (6:1-5)
2. The command of Darius (6:6-12)
3. The king's command obeyed (6:13)
4. The house finished (6:14-15)
5. The dedication of the house (6:16-18)
6. The feast of Passover and unleavened bread (6:19-22)

Verses 1-5. King Darius had a search made in the place where the records of the empire were kept, "in the house of the rolls." The word "rolls" is "books" and these consisted of clay tablets on which the cuneiform inscriptions were preserved. Neither the Aramaic nor the Hebrew language has a word for clay tablets. Whole libraries of such clay tablets were found at Nineveh and elsewhere, and can now be seen in different museums. The searchers found the desired record at Achmetha (the Ecbatana of

Greek writers, the capital city of Media, which is the modern Hamadan). Divine providence had preserved this interesting command of Cyrus, and the same providence guided the searchers to the place where it was kept. From it we learn interesting details. Cyrus gave instructions concerning the foundations, the height and the breadth of the building; the expenses were to be met from the King's house, i.e., the royal treasure house. Persian Kings controlled the religious affairs of the nation; but Cyrus acted under divine guidance of the Lord (1:1).

Verses 6-12. Darius answered the communication of Tatnai and Shethar-boznai at once. He commands, "Be ye far from hence," do not hinder the work; let the work of this house of God alone. And furthermore he directed that the Jews were to be assisted in the building of the house by the paying of the expenses. Darius was anxious that the house should be built and speedily completed. The material mentioned was for the sacrifices and offerings. Young bullocks, rams and lambs for the burnt offerings. Wheat, oil and salt for the meal offering, and wine for the drink offering. All these things were to be given to the priests without fail day by day. "That they may offer sacrifices of sweet savour unto the God of heaven, and pray for the life of the King and of his sons." God was working again, and used Darius as His instrument for the accomplishment of His own purposes. All the enemy was doing to hinder the work turned out to its furtherance. How often this has been in the history of Israel and the Church. The decree of Darius demanded the death penalty for all who altered the command he had given. "And the God that hath caused his name to dwell there destroy all kings and peoples that shall put their hand to alter and to destroy this house of God which is at Jerusalem. I Darius have made a decree; let it be done with speed." These words warrant a belief that Darius had knowledge of the God of heaven. The events which transpired during the reign of Nebuchadnezzar in the Babylonian Empire, when Daniel was there, as well as the things which happened under the reign of the other Darius (Daniel 6) may have been fully known to Darius Hystaspis who gave this decree. And solemn were his words that God would destroy all kings and people who alter or destroy this house of God. How this came repeatedly to pass history tells us. (Antiochus Epiphanes, Herod and the Romans defiled and destroyed the house, and God's wrath came upon them for it.)

Verse 13. What Darius commanded was speedily done. All opposition ended and the enemies were completely defeated. God had undertaken in behalf of His trusting people, whose faith had been revived through the messages of Haggai and Zechariah.

Verses 14-15. With revived zeal the elders builded, and they prospered, through the prophesying of Haggai the prophet, and Zechariah the son of Iddo. Haggai's ministry stirred up the conscience of the people, exhorting them to consider their ways, which must have led them to seek His face. Zechariah is the prophet of glory. The vision of glory, the ultimate victory of God's people, the coming of the King and setting up of His kingdom, the future overthrow of all their enemies—this vision of the coming glory became an inspiration for them. God's people need this two-fold ministry which is so abundantly supplied in the Word of God. They builded and finished the house according to the commandment of the God of Israel, and according to the decree of the great Kings Cyrus and Darius. ("And Artaxerxes, King of Persia," some claim should be omitted from the text.) The house was finished on the third day of the month of Adar, which was in the sixth year of the reign of Darius the King.

Verses 16-18. Then the dedication of the house took place. It was a feast of great joy. "The feast of dedication" which the Jews keep (Chanukah) does not commemorate the dedication of this house, but the cleansing of the temple from the defilement of Antiochus Epiphanes. Tradition claims that Psalms 138, 146, and 148 were composed by Haggai and Zechariah, and used in the dedication ceremony. But what a contrast with the magnificent dedication of the Solomonic temple! Here they offered a hundred bullocks, two hundred rams, four hundred lambs, and for a sin offering twelve he-goats. At the dedication of the first temple Solomon offered 22,000 oxen and 120,000 sheep (2 Chron. 7:7). And the greatest contrast with Solomon's temple, the glory cloud; the visible sign of Jehovah's presence which filled the house; was absent. No glory came to manifest the fact that Jehovah dwelt in the midst of His people. In the future another temple will stand again in Jerusalem, and into that temple the glory of the Lord will enter once more (Ezek. 43:1-3). It is the millennial temple which will be erected by converted Israel after the King has come back. Of this glorious event Zechariah bore witness: "Sing and rejoice, O daughter of Zion, for, lo, I come, and I will dwell in the midst of thee, saith the Lord. And many nations shall be joined unto the Lord in that day, and shall be my people; and I will dwell in the midst of thee, and thou shalt know that the Lord of hosts hath sent me unto thee" (Zech. 2:10-11). These prophetic words were certainly not fulfilled in the dedication of the second temple, nor have they been fulfilled since. Perhaps this prophecy was the prophecy of hope and comfort for the godly then, as well as Haggai's prediction (Hag. 2:7-9). But note well the obedience to God's Word manifested in the dedication service—"as it is written in the book of Moses."

Verses 19-22. The feast of Passover and unleavened bread was kept also by the children of the captivity. Those who had separated themselves from the filthiness of the heathen were not proselytes, Gentiles who turned to Israel; they were Jews who had married heathen women (10:11). They were true to the written Word. As to the meaning of this feast see our annotations on Exodus 12, Leviticus 23 and 1 Corinthians 5.

The connection is exceedingly beautiful. The house of their God finished, His people celebrated the memorial of their redemption from the land of Egypt, and thus remind themselves, to the praise of Jehovah, of the ground on which they stood, and of the fact that the foundation of all their blessing, of all God's actings in grace towards them was the blood of the slain Lamb. This, according to the word of Moses, was "a night to be much observed unto the Lord for bringing them out from the land of Egypt: this is that night of the Lord to be observed of all the children of Israel in their generations" (Exodus 12:42). Nothing could show more distinctly that these children of the captivity were at this moment in possession of the mind of the Lord than their observance of the Passover. Passing by the glories of the kingdom, they travelled upward until they reached the charter of all they possessed, whether in title or in prospect, and there confessed God as the God of their salvation. They thus built on what God was for them on the ground of the blood of the Passover lamb, and they found in that, as individual souls ever find, a rock which is both immutable and immovable. Their hearts were in this feast; "for," as we read, "the priests and the Levites were purified together, all of them were pure." (See Numbers 9:10-14.) They discerned what was due to Him whose feast they kept (E. Dennett).

II. The Return Under Ezra and His Reformation

CHAPTER 7

1. The journey of Ezra to Jerusalem (7:1-10)
2. The decree of Artaxerxes (7:11-26)
3. Ezra's thanksgiving (7:27-28)

Verses 1-10. The record of the return under Zerubbabel and the rebuilding of the temple ends with the previous chapter. Many years passed after the temple had been built before the godly Ezra and his companions returned to Jerusalem. No record whatever is in existence covering the years which intervened between Zerubabbel's expedition and work, and Ezra's expedition. The critics claim that "it was in these apparently barren years that the priestly code was elaborated by the priests who had not left Babylon, and that part at least of the second half of Isaiah (chapter 40, etc.) was composed and put together in Babylon." But what historical foundation for their theory can they offer? There is nothing in existence which in any way warrants such claims. The evidence that Moses wrote the Pentateuch and that Isaiah is the author of the entire book which bears his name is overwhelming. The theory of a priestly code, that the priestly laws of Leviticus were collected in Babylon and brought back by Ezra, is an invention.

What became of Zerubbabel is not known. But we know that a sad decline among the returned remnant set in. Their moral and religious condition had suffered a severe relapse. Perhaps these very conditions moved Ezra to leave Babylon and go to Jerusalem.

It was in the seventh year of Artaxerxes, King of Persia, that Ezra went up. The genealogy of Ezra is given, showing that he was a direct descendant of Aaron, the chief priest. Ezra was "a ready scribe in the law of Moses, which the Lord God of Israel had given." A blessed testimony that the Law of Moses was given by God, and not put together piece-meal, corrected, revised and added to by different hands. Ezra, occupied with the Law and the Word of God, desired to go up to Jerusalem. God put it into his heart, and the Gentile King granted him all his request. In all this the hand of the Lord is acknowledged. "According to the hand of the Lord his God upon him." This phrase we meet a number of times (7:6, 9, 28; 8:18, 22, 31); and it shows how this man of God trusted in the Lord for guidance. He saw His hand in having all his request granted by Artaxerxes. It was the good hand of God who brought him to Jerusalem (7:9). His hand strengthened him (7:28). The good hand of the Lord is again acknowledged in bringing them ministers (8:18) and in deliverance (8:31). The same hand which was for good upon Ezra, which guided, kept and shielded him, is still upon all His people who trust Him and are obedient to His Word. (The character of our work forbids an attempt to enlarge upon the identity of the different rulers mentioned in Ezra and Nehemiah—which is a difficult matter, involving a careful examination of chronology. We suggest a good book on chronology *The Romance of Bible Chronology,* by M. Anstey.)

With Ezra a company of people went up to Jerusalem, 1,496 in all. They left on the first day of the first month, and arrived on the first day of the fifth month, corresponding to the end of July or beginning of August. The distance they travelled by way of Carchemish was over 800 miles.

In verse 10 we have the secret of Ezra's piety: "For Ezra had prepared his heart to seek the Law of the Lord, and to do it, and to teach in Israel statutes and judgments." Diligently and prayerfully he sought the truth and the will of God in the Word of God. The law of the Lord was his joy and delight. How he must have searched the Scriptures with deep exercise of soul. This is the foundation of godliness. The heart must enter into the things of God as revealed in His Word. And his aim was "to do it;" to live according to the truth God had given him. Finally, the third desire of Ezra was "to teach in Israel statutes and judgments." Heart preparation in the Word, obedience to the Word, must be the marks of the true servant of the Lord.

Verses 11-26. The copy of the letter that Artaxerxes gave to Ezra is now recorded. This section is again in Aramaic. In the salutation of the letter Artaxerxes calls himself "king of kings" and addresses Ezra as the scribe of the law of the God of heaven. There can be no question that Artaxerxes was divinely moved in all he did. The decree states that all Israelites, priests and Levites in his realm who are minded of their own free will to up to Jerusalem, may go with Ezra. The name of God, the law of God, the house of God are constantly used in this document. Then the King and his seven counsellors freely gave silver and gold "unto the God of Israel, whose habitation is in Jerusalem." In a future day, when all Israel is saved, when Christ comes again, the Gentiles and their kings will offer their silver and gold (Isaiah 60; Ps. 62:10-11). Besides the silver and gold Artaxerxes and his counsellors gave, there were other offerings of non-Jews and of the Jewish residents of Babylon. The king had perfect confidence in Ezra. After buying bullocks, rams, lambs, etc., the king wrote, "And whatsoever shall seem good to thee, and to thy brethren, to do with the rest of the silver and the gold, that do after the will of your God."

Verses 27-28. Then Ezra broke out in a beautiful doxology. He blessed the Lord God of his fathers. He had put all this in the King's heart. And Ezra was strengthened as the hand of the Lord His God was upon him.

CHAPTER 8

1. Those who returned with Ezra (8:1-14)
2. The gathering at Ahava (8:15-20)
3. The fast proclaimed (8:21-23)
4. The appointment of guardians (8:24-30)
5. The departure and arrival in Jerusalem (8:31-36)

Verses 1-14. The names of those who gathered around Ezra and went up with him are here recorded. In view of the magnificent decree and liberality of Artaxerxes, the company was very small. The majority preferred Babylon, and remained there. The faithful ones are known to God, and their names are here forever written in His Word. Though the Gentile monarch had given the decree, and the people were abundantly supplied with all necessary means, the undertaking was one of faith. They came out of Babylon trusting the Lord; they marched on in faith. It must be especially noticed that only males are mentioned. The mixed marriages of which we read in the next chapter most likely were the result of the fact that no women had joined Ezra's expedition.

Verses 15-20. Ezra gathered them together at the river that runneth to Ahava, which probably was a branch of the Euphrates, near Babylon. There they dwelt in their tents for three days. They were pilgrims and strangers, and had gone forth like Abraham, the father of the nation. Ezra viewed the people and discovered the absence of the Levites. While a small number of Levites had gone up with Zerubbabel, none had joined Ezra. Only two priests were present, Gershon, son of Phinehas, and Daniel, son of Ithamar. What indifference this reveals! They had settled down in the enemy's land and were satisfied to remain there. They were minding earthly things, and the things of God were forgotten by them. Still they were Levites in their holy calling. It is so today with many who are no doubt saved, but they are worldly-minded, and have but little desire to live in the separation demanded by Him from His people. Ezra was not willing to leave the Levites behind, knowing how absolutely necessary they were for the house of God. How Ezra must have looked to God! Then he acted, and through the good hand of God, which he once more acknowledged, a number of Levites and Nethinim joined the party.

Verses 21-23. He proclaimed a fast. The man of God felt the need of seeking God's face and His gracious protection. The fasting was the outward sign of deep humiliation and an expression of their dependence, "to seek of Him a straight way, for us and for our little ones, and for all our substance." The need of guidance as well as protection was fully recognized by the gathered company, and they trusted the Lord for both. This is still the blessed way of faith for God's servant, and for the children of God. How great would be the success and the blessing if at all times and in all service God's people would first seek His face, humble themselves in His presence and trust Him fully. Ezra had told the king that he trusted the Lord, that His hand is upon all them for good that seek Him, and so he was ashamed to ask a military escort to protect them against robbers, who might waylay them and rob them of their possessions. He knew His God was the best shield, and His angels, the ministers used in guarding His people and keeping evil away from them, would be the unseen companions of the caravan. "So we fasted and besought our God for this, and He was intreated of us." Their prayers were answered. And He still answers faith.

Verses 24-30. Faith in God did not make Ezra careless. He felt his great responsibility and made the most careful preparations. He set apart twelve of the chief priests, Sherebiah, Hashabiah, and ten of their brethren with them. Levites were also selected by him (8:30). To their custody he committed the holy vessels, as well as the silver and the gold which had been so freely given. Then he gave them the charge, "Ye are holy unto the Lord; the vessels are holy also and the silver and gold are a freewill offering unto the Lord God of your fathers. Watch ye and keep them, until ye weigh them before the chief of the priests and Levites, and chief of the fathers of Israel, at Jerusalem, in the chambers of the house of the Lord." He had weighed into their hand 650 talents of silver (about $1,250,000) and of gold 100 talents (about $3,000,000) besides the costly vessels of silver and gold. This careful weighing of everything when they received the costly treasures, and the weighing when they delivered the same in Jerusalem, does not mean that Ezra entertained any doubt as to the honesty of the priests and Levites. It was done to avoid all suspicion. The same principle is laid down in the New Testament for the Church: "Provide for honest things, not only in the sight of the Lord, but also in the sight of men" (2 Cor. 8:21).

Verses 31-36. Then the departure was made on the twelfth day of the first month. In faith and complete dependence on God they set out towards the land of their fathers. And the Lord honored their faith. "And the hand of our God was upon us, and He delivered us from the hand of the enemy, and of such as lay in wait by the way. And we came to Jerusalem, and abode there three days." They must have had many narrow escapes, but as they constantly trusted in the Lord, in His good hand of mercy and power, He delivered them from all dangers. The Lord who answered their faith and kept them is the same today, and never disappoints faith. His hand is the same as then, and we too can experience His gracious deliverance. The journey occupied not quite four months. The three days at the end of the journey correspond to the three days before the journey began at the river Ahava (8:15). What praise they must have rendered to God during these three days in Jerusalem, when their eyes beheld once more the beloved city and the house of the Lord!

On the fourth day the treasures were turned over and were weighed in the house of God. This was done by Meremoth, the son of Uriah, the priest. He is mentioned by Nehemiah as one of the builders of the wall (Neh. 3:4, 21). With him was Eleazar, the son of Phinehas. Associated with them were Jozabad, the son of Jeshua (mentioned also in 10:23 and Neh. 7:7) and Noadiah, the son of Binnui. Thus in the house of God account was rendered, as all His people will have to give an account before the judgment seat of Christ.

Burnt offerings were then offered, twelve bullocks for all Israel, ninety-six rams, seventy-seven lambs and twelve he-goats for a sin offering. It is especially to be noticed that the small remnant which had returned embraced in their faith all Israel. "All Israel" will some day be saved and be brought back to the land, through Him who is the true burnt and sin offering. And as their faith included all their brethren, the whole house of Israel, though they were not with them, so our faith must include all the saints of God.

After having discharged their solemn obligation, giving God the first place, they "delivered the king's commissions unto the king's lieutenants, and to the governors on this side of the river; and they furthered the people and the house of God."

CHAPTER 9

1. Ezra's astonishment and grief (9:1-4)
2. Ezra's confession and prayer (9:5-15)

Verses 1-4. When all these things had been done (that are related in chapter 8:33-36) Ezra was confronted by a very sad condition of the people, and even the priests and the Levites. The princes (civil leaders) came to Ezra and told him that the demanded separation according to the law, between God's people and the Canaanitish inhabitants of the land, had not been obeyed. The people had taken of their daughters for themselves and of their sons "so that the holy seed have mingled themselves with the people of the lands; yea the hand of the princes and rulers hath been first in this trespass." Not alone had they intermarried, but they were also doing according to their abominations. Not alone had they fallen into the evil things of the former inhabitants of the land, the Canaanites, but they were also contaminated with the wicked things of the Ammonites, the Moabites, the Egyptians and the Amorites. In doing this they had wilfully broken the command of the Lord as given in Exodus 34:12-16. God's people were to be holy, a separated people. Israel was married unto Jehovah; their marriage to the heathen was disobedience to the law and unfaithfulness to Jehovah. It was an alliance with the world. God demanded separation of Israel; He demands the same of His people in the New Testament. "But as He who hath called you is holy, so be ye holy in all manner of conversation; because it is written, Be ye holy, for I am holy" (1 Peter 1:15-16). Like Israel, believers in the New Testament are said to be married unto Christ (Romans 7:4; 2 Cor. 11:2). And therefore God's Spirit warns against alliance with the world. "Be ye not unequally yoked together with unbelievers" (2 Cor. 6:14). "Love not the world, neither the things that are in the world" (1 John 2:15). "Ye adulterers and adulteresses, know ye not that the friendship of the world is enmity with God? Whosoever therefore would be a friend of the world, maketh himself an enemy of God" (James 4:4). That the returned remnant, after a few years of the completion of the temple and after the gracious and remarkable deliverance from Babylon, could plunge into such depths of degradation, shows what the heart of man is. As it has been said, when saints fall into sin, it is sometimes into worse and grosser forms of sin than those committed by the people of the world. It equally manifests the infinite patience and long-suffering of God, in bearing with His people and not dealing with them at once in judgment.

Let us listen to the words of pious Ezra, what he said and did after receiving this sad report. "And when I heard this thing, I rent my garment and my mantle, and plucked off the hair of my head and of my beard, and sat down astonished. Then were assembled unto me every one that trembled at the words of the God of Israel, because of the transgression of those that had been carried away; and I sat astonished until the evening sacrifice." He was seized with horror. The rending of his garments was the outward expression of his indignation and grief (Gen. 37:29; Lev. 10:6; Judges 11:35; Esther 4:1). The plucking of the hair is also a sign of sorrow (Job 1:20; Ezek. 7:18). But how his heart must have felt the dishonor done to Jehovah's holy Name! How he was deeply affected by the sins of the people. Would to God such a spirit of deep grief and humiliation were more manifested today over the sad and worldly conditions of those who profess that worthy Name! His grief and sorrow brought others, who were also trembling at the words of God, to his side, and he sat in their presence astonished till the evening sacrifice.

Verses 5-15. When the evening sacrifice came he arose from his deep affliction and sorrow, with his garments rent. It is the sacrifice, the burnt offering, which leads him to approach God; he trusted in the efficacy of the sacrifice as the ground on which he could appear before God. He knew by sacrifice he could come near to God and receive the answer. All this blessedly foreshadows the sacrifice of Christ and our approach to God through His finished work on the cross. The prayer which follows is like Daniel's great prayer (Daniel 9:4-19). Daniel also received his answer at the time of the evening sacrifice. Ezra fell upon his knees and spread out his hands unto the Lord. What a confession of sins and deepest humiliation breathe in the opening sentences of this remarkable prayer! He is ashamed and blushes to lift his face up to God. Iniquities are owned as covering the head of the people and "the guiltiness is grown unto the heavens." Not alone is the present guilt acknowledged, but he owns the guilt of the nation from its very start. Furthermore he declares God's righteousness and justice in dealing with them in judgment. "For our iniquities have we, our kings, and our priests, been delivered into the hands of the kings of the lands, to the sword, to captivity, and to spoiling, and to confusion of face, as it is today." He confessed the sins of the people and owned it all in His presence. Such humiliation and confession is always pleasing to God, for "God resisteth the proud, but giveth grace unto the humble" (James 4:6).

Then, after having confessed and owned the sins of his brethren and justified God in His judgment upon them, he mentions the grace which had been manifested towards the people in bringing back the remnant from the captivity. The remnant through His mercy had escaped, and God had given them "a nail in His holy place" (Isaiah 22:23). Like a nail in the wall fixed and immovable, so God had established them in Jerusalem. And after the recital of all these mercies, he brings into the light of God's presence their sin, their disobedience and ingratitude once more (9:10-12).

It should also be observed that Ezra does not once pray for forgiveness. Nay, with any intelligence of the mind of God, it was impossible that he should do so. When there is known evil in our hearts or in the assembly, our first responsibility is to judge it, not to pray for forgiveness. Thus, when Joshua lay on his face before the Lord, after the defeat of Israel by the men of Ai, the Lord said, "Get thee up; wherefore liest thou thus upon thy face? Israel hath sinned," etc. And yet how often does Satan beguile the Lord's people, in a time of manifested evil, by suggesting through one or another, Let us pray about it. Confess our sins we surely should, but even then only as seeking grace and strength to deal with the evil, and to separate ourselves from it; for if Ezra lay before the Lord in this chapter owning his people's guilt, we shall see him in the next energetic in dealing with the sin he had confessed, and resting not until it had been put away.[1]

CHAPTER 10

1. The effect of Ezra's prayer on the people (10:1-4)
2. Ezra summons an assembly (10:5-8)
3. The gathering, confession and the evil judged (10:9-17)
4. The register of those who had married strange women (10:18-44)

[1]E. Dennett, *Exposition of Ezra.*

Verses 1-4. Ezra's prayer, confession and humiliation were before the house of the Lord." The people saw his great sorrow and his tears, they heard his words confessing the nation's sins. It produced a wonderful effect among the people. "There assembled unto him out of Israel a great congregation of men and women and children, for the people wept very sore." Was this great weeping real contrition over their disobedience? or did they weep in anticipation of the separation from the wives they had taken? No doubt they thought of what the demanded separation would mean for them; yet it was an aroused conscience which produced the tears of repentance.

Schechaniah's voice is heard in behalf of the people. He was a son of Jehiel. His own father is mentioned among those who had taken strange wives (10:26). His words then must have condemned his own father. He said, "We have trespassed against our God, and have taken strange wives of the people of the land." He acknowledged the sin of the people violating the direct commandment of the Lord. But he also had confidence in the mercy of God, that not all was lost on account of their disobedience, "yet now there is hope in Israel concerning this thing." Yet this hope and mercy could only be realized by self-judgment and by putting away all the wives and such as were born of them. He therefore said, "Let us make a covenant with our God to put away all the wives, and such as are born of them, according to the counsel of my Lord, and of those who tremble at the commandment of our God; and let it be done according to the law." The law demanded the dismissal of these wives and children, for they were unclean, and admission into the congregation of Israel had to be denied to them. How different it is under grace! In 1 Cor. 7:10, etc., we read what grace has done even for an unbelieving husband who is sanctified by the believing wife, and the unbelieving wife who is sanctified by the believing husband, and that their children are not unclean, but holy.

Then Schechaniah addressed weeping Ezra: "Arise! for this matter belongeth unto thee; we also will be with thee; be of good courage and do it." These words must have dried Ezra's tears, for they evidence the answer to his humiliation and prayer. Confession, humiliation, self-judgment and putting away the evil are always the condition of the restoration of God's people.

Verses 5-8. Ezra took hold at once. The priests,

Levites and all Israel had to swear that they would act upon this word. But Ezra's grief was not ended. He arose and went into the chambers of Johanan, the son of Eliashib. He did not eat bread, nor did he drink water. He still mourned because of the transgression of the people. God's presence was sought by this deeply spiritual man of God, and in His holy presence he felt anew the sin of the people. What deep soul exercise Ezra passed through! This is what is so sadly lacking in our own days. So many make light of the sin and worldiness of those who profess the Name of Christ, there is but little heart searching, true humiliation and self-judgment to be seen. Such is the spirit of Laodicea.

A proclamation was then made. The time to act had come. All the returned captives were to gather themselves together in Jerusalem. It had to be within three days. Neglect of this commandment meant the confiscation of their substance and separation from the congregation of Israel.

Verses 9-17. The great gathering takes place. They all obeyed the Word. We see them sitting in the wide space before the house of the Lord. They were a trembling, frightened company, on account of this matter and also the great rain, for the cold and rainy season had started in. Ezra addresses the multitude in simple but firm words. Once more he mentions their sin and the guilt which rests upon them on account of it. He demands confession, and separation from the peoples of the land and from the strange women. There was an immediate response: "As thou hast said concerning us, so must we do." Then a plan is inaugurated to bring the separation about in as speedy a manner as possible. What self-denial and heartaches this must have meant! In verse 15 we read of those "who were employed about this matter." But the translation of this sentence is more than doubtful. It has been rendered "they stood up against this." If there was opposition it was not opposition to the separation decree. They probably opposed the method which had been suggested; they may have demanded an immediate action.

Verses 18-44. The examination of the whole matter as agreed upon began on the first day of the first month (Nisan—March-April), the time of the New Year, the new beginning according to Exodus 12:1. Then follows the list of the men who had married the strange women. God's record is again before us in these names. The names of the priests come first. Theirs was the greater responsibility and guilt. The sons of Joshua head the list. What an illustration of what man is, that the sons of the high-priest, who, with Zerubbabel, had been such great instruments of the Lord to lead the first captives back, should corrupt themselves with these women! They gave their hand that they would put away their wives, and confessing themselves guilty, they brought a ram for an offering. In all, seventeen priests were guilty, and six Levites. The guilty singers and porters are given by name in verse 24. Then follow eighty-six more names who had all defiled themselves by strange women.

Ezra's great work was finished. In Nehemiah we read how he was still active, ministering to the people in spiritual things, in reading and expounding the Word of God (Neh. 8:8).

THE BOOK OF
NEHEMIAH

Introduction

The book of Nehemiah is the latest of the historical books of the Old Testament. It is the continuation of the history of the company of people which had returned under Zerubbabel and Ezra to the land. In Ezra we saw the remnant getting back and rebuilding the temple, the place of worship. In Nehemiah we have the record of the rebuilding of the walls of Jerusalem, and the restoration of the civil condition of the people, the partial and outward re-establishment of the Jews in the land. The book bears the name of Nehemiah, because he is the leading person in the recorded events, and likewise the inspired author of the main portion of this record. Two other persons by the name of Nehemiah are mentioned in the books of Ezra and Nehemiah. One was the son of Azbuk (Neh. 3:15) and the other belonged to the returning remnant under Zerubbabel (Ezra 2:2 and Neh. 7:7). From these, Nehemiah the son of Hachaliah must be distinguished. His genealogy is obscure. Besides being the son of Hachaliah, the only other mention of his family is found in chapter 7:2; there he speaks of his brother Hanani. Some class him as a priest for the reason that he heads the list of priests. But his name is given there as the princely leader of the people. As to his office, he carried two titles. He is called "Tirshatha" in chapter 8:9, which means ruler or governor. In chapter 12:26 his title is also governor; the word used is "pechah," the Turkish word "pasha."

There can be no doubt that this man of God wrote chapters 1 to 7:5; it is an autobiography. Chapter 7:6-73 is a quotation of a register of names, which differs in numerous places from the register in Ezra 2:1-70. Both were probably copied from public documents, perhaps from the book of Chronicles mentioned in chapter 7:23. The discrepancies between Ezra 2 and Nehemiah 7 show that Nehemiah did not copy from Ezra's record. Chapters 8 to 10, it is claimed by some, were not written by the hand of Nehemiah. It has been suggested that Ezra is the author. The remaining section, chapters 11 to 13, bears the clear mark of Nehemiah's pen.

The History it Contains

Nehemiah was the cupbearer in the palace of Shushan, serving Artaxerxes the King. When he learned the deplorable condition of the people in the land of his fathers, he sat down, wept and prayed. The king discovered the source of Nehemiah's sorrow, and permitted him to go, giving him full authority to rebuild the wall of Jerusalem and to help his people. This was in the year 445 B.C. Nehemiah reached the city the same year, and was for twelve years actively engaged in the welfare work of Jerusalem. The city wall was finished and the work done in spite of the many hindrances and obstacles the enemy put in the way. Sanballat, the Moabite, and Tobiah, the Ammonite, were Nehemiah's chief enemies. With them were allied the Arabians, Ammonites and Ashdodites. They tried to hinder the work by mocking the workmen, then by threatening them with violence. When their attempts failed to arrest the restoration of the wall, then they tried craft. Nehemiah came out victorious. And there were also internal troubles among the people, threatening disruption. Thus as Daniel the prophet had announced, the wall was rebuilt and the work finished in troublous times (Dan. 9:25).

After the city had been fortified, the wall built, religious reforms were inaugurated. At the watergate the law was read and expounded by Ezra the priest. The feast of tabernacles was also celebrated, followed by a solemn fast, repentance and a prayer of humiliation and confession of sins. A covenant then was made. In all this Nehemiah was assisted by the pious Ezra. About 432 B.C. Nehemiah returned to Babylon. His stay there does not seem to have been very long, and he went back to Jerusalem. After his return he demanded the separation of all the mixed multitude from among the people. He also expelled the Ammonite Tobiah from the chamber which the high priest Eliashib had prepared for him in the temple. Then he chased away the son-in-law of Sanballat, a son of Joiada the high priest. According to the Jewish historian Josephus, Nehemiah died at an advanced age.

Interesting light has been thrown on this book

and the conditions of the Jews of that period by the recent discovery of Aramaic papyri near Assouan. These papers were written twenty-four years after Nehemiah's second visit to Jerusalem, and sixteen years after the death of King Artaxerxes; they were therefore probably written during the lifetime of Nehemiah. These papyri speak of the Jewish colony in the land, and the house of the Lord with its worship, as well as what the enemy did to the people.

The Spiritual Lessons

Nehemiah is a beautiful character well worth a close study. He was a man of prayer, who habitually turned to God, seeking His wisdom and His strength. The rebuilding of the wall, the different gates, and the men who toiled there, the attempts of the enemies and their defeat, all contain truths of much spiritual value and help. The reader will find the spiritual and dispensational lessons pointed out in the annotations of each chapter.

The Division of Nehemiah

The contents of the book are best divided into three sections.

I. **HOW NEHEMIAH RETURNED TO JERUSALEM AND THE BUILDING OF THE WALL** (1—7)

II. **THE SPIRITUAL REVIVAL** (8—10)

III. **THE PEOPLE ESTABLISHED, THE DEDICATION OF THE WALL, AND NEHEMIAH'S FINAL ACTS** (11—13)

Analysis and Annotations

I. How Nehemiah Returned to Jerusalem and the Building of the Wall

CHAPTER 1

1. Nehemiah hears of the condition of Jerusalem (1:1-3)
2. His great sorrow, and prayer (1:4-11)

Verses 1-3. "The words of Nehemiah (the Lord is comfort) the son of Hachaliah." It is therefore the personal narrative of his experience which is before us in the first six chapters of this book, in which he describes his soul exercise, and how the Lord made it possible for him to return to Jerusalem, and how the wall was rebuilt. Nehemiah was a young man, born in captivity holding a position of nearness to the great Persian king and living in the beautiful palace of Shushan. He lived in luxuries, and was an honored servant of the king. It was in the month of Chisleu, in the twentieth year (445 B.C.) when Hanani his brother (7:2) visited him with certain men out of Judah. The question he asked them at once shows the deep interest he had in God's people. "I asked them concerning the Jews that had escaped, which were left of the captivity, and concerning Jerusalem." Though he had never seen Jerusalem, the city of his fathers, he loved Jerusalem and felt like all pious captives, so beautifully expressed in one of the Psalms—"If I forget thee, O Jerusalem, let my right hand forget her cunning. If I do not remember thee, let my tongue cleave to the roof of my mouth, if I prefer not Jerusalem above my chief joy" (Ps. 137:5-6). Though he lived in prosperity his heart was with his people. It was bad news which they brought him. The remnant was in great affliction and reproach, the wall of Jerusalem in a broken-down condition, and the gates burned with fire.

Verses 4-11. This sad news overwhelmed him with great sorrow. He sat down and wept; his mourning continued certain days. If Nehemiah was so affected by the temporal condition of Jerusalem and the affliction of the remnant, how much more should believers mourn and weep over the spiritual conditions among God's people. Yet how little of this sorrowing spirit over these conditions is known in our day! It is needed for humiliation and effectual prayer. Nehemiah did not rush at once into the presence of the king to utter his petitions. He waited and fasted certain days and then addressed the God of heaven (Ezra 6:9). He reveals in the opening words of his prayer familiarity with the Word of God. "I beseech thee, O Lord, the God of heaven, the great and terrible God (Deut. 7:21; 10:17; Dan. 9:4) that keepeth covenant and mercy with them that love Him and keep His commandments (Deut. 7:9; 1 Kings 8:23) let thine ear now be attentive (2 Chron. 6:40; Ps. 130:2) and thine eyes open (2 Chron. 6:40) that thou mayest hearken unto the prayer of thy servant." After these scriptural expressions, expressing confidence in the power and faithfulness of God, Nehemiah confessed his sin and the sins of his people. "Yea, I and my father's house have sinned. We have dealt very corruptly against thee, and have not kept thy commandments, nor thy statutes, nor the judgments, which thou commandest thy servant Moses." Ezra had prayed a similar prayer, and before him Daniel in Babylon (Dan. 9). There is no flaw revealed in Nehemiah's character, as there is none in Daniel's life, yet both of these men of God went on their faces and confessed their sins and the sins of the people. They realized that they had a share in the common failure of His people. And so are we all blameworthy of the spiritual decline and failure among God's people, and should humble ourselves on account of it. It is this which is pleasing to the Lord and which assures His mercy.

But Nehemiah was also trusting in the promise of God. He was a man of faith, and cast himself upon the word of God, knowing what the Lord had promised He is able to do. "Remember, I beseech thee, the word that Thou commandest thy servant Moses." The promise in Deut. 30:1-5 is especially upon his heart and mentioned by him in the presence of the Lord. In the near future this great national promise of the regathering of Israel from the ends of the earth will be fulfilled, in that day when the Lord returns. The exercise and prayer of Nehemiah will be repeated in the Jewish believing remnant during the time of Jacob's trouble, the great tribulation. Furthermore Nehemiah claims the blessing for the people on account of their covenant relation with Jehovah. They are His servants, His people, "whom thou hast redeemed by thy great power and by thy strong hand." And how he pleads for an answer. "O Lord, I beseech thee, let now thine ear be attentive to the prayer of thy servant, and to the prayer of thy servants, who delight to fear thy name"—others were also praying—"and prosper, I pray thee, thy servant this day and grant him mercy in the sight of this man." He meant the powerful monarch Artaxerxes. Yet in God's presence he looked upon him only as a man, and he knew God could use this man in behalf of His people, as He had used Cyrus.

CHAPTER 2

1. The King's question (2:1-2)
2. The King's permission (2:3-8)
3. The arrival in Jerusalem and the night-ride (2:9-16)
4. The resolution to build the wall (2:17-18)
5. The ridicule of the enemy, and Nehemiah's answer (2:19-20)

Verses 1-2. The last sentence of the previous chapter, "For I was the king's cupbearer," belongs to this chapter. Nehemiah is seen exercising the functions of the King's cupbearer to minister to the joy and pleasure of the monarch. Notice that it was four months after his prayer. Hanani had visited his brother Nehemiah in the month Chisleu, the ninth month, and Nisan is the first month of the Jewish year. How many prayers he must have offered up during these three months! How patiently he waited for the Lord's time! He carried a heavy burden upon his heart, expressed in a sad countenance, which was at last noticed by Artaxerxes. "Why is thy countenance sad, seeing that thou art not sick? this is nothing else but sorrow of heart," said the king. Then was Nehemiah sore afraid fearing the king's displeasure.

Verses 3-8. Nehemiah answered the king and acquainted him with the reason of his sadness, "why should not my countenance be sad, when the city, the place of my father's sepulchres, lieth waste, and the gates thereof are consumed with fire?" From the meek answer Nehemiah gave we learn that his forefathers were inhabitants of Jerusalem, and he belonged therefore to the tribe of Judah. Instead of the angry outburst Nehemiah feared, the king asked graciously, "For what dost thou make request?" How his heart must have been stirred when the king uttered these words! He had prayed four months before that the God of heaven grant him "mercy in the sight of this man." And now the answer to his prayer was at hand. When the king had asked for his request, Nehemiah prayed again to the God of heaven. He found time to pray between the words of the king and the answer he gave him. His lips did not speak, his knees were not bowed, nor did the king see any other sign that Nehemiah prayed. Yet there was earnest believing and prevailing prayer. It was an ejaculatory prayer, the soul's cry to God, carried swiftly by the Holy Spirit to the throne of God. This man of God every step of the way cast himself upon God; prayer was his constant resource. Such is our privilege. As we walk in His fellowship we too shall pray and look to the Lord as Nehemiah did. It is a blessed occupation to cultivate a prayerful mind; indeed it is the breathing of the new life. Whatever our experiences, the heart which is in touch with God will always turn to Him even in the smallest matters. After Nehemiah had stated his request the king granted what he had asked. His prayers were answered; God had touched the heart of the monarch. "So it pleased the king to send me; and I set him a time." The requested letters to the governors beyond the river to convey him till he came to Judah, and to Asaph the forester to furnish him with timber needed for the work, were granted to him. In this, like pious Ezra (Ezra 7:6; 8:18, 22) Nehemiah saw the power of God displayed—"according to the good hand of God upon me." Faith not only depends on God, but also sees His gracious hand and gives the glory to Him. In faith Nehemiah could say "my God," like Paul in writing to the Philippians (Phil. 4:19).

Verses 9-16. He crossed the river Euphrates and traversed Transpotamia till he reached Samaria. He delivered the letters. Sanballat, the Horonite, and Tobiah, the servant, the Ammonite, Samaritans, are here mentioned for the first time. Sanballat may have been the governor of the Samaritan mongrel race. They were grieving exceedingly at Nehemiah's appearing, when they heard he had come "to seek the welfare of the children of Israel."

Sanballat (hate in disguise) is called the Horonite, an inhabitant of Horonaim, which was a southern Moabite city (Isa. 15:5; Jerem. 48:3, 5, 34) and Tobiah, the servant, an Ammonite. They came from Moab and Ammon, blood-relations of Israel, being bastard offspring of Lot. The Moabite and Ammonite were not to come into the congregation of God forever; the curse rested upon them. They did not meet Israel with bread and water when they came forth from Egypt. They hated the people of God, and had hired Balaam the son of Beor to curse Israel (Deut. 23:3-6). They were the bitter enemies of Israel, which explains the displeasure of Sanballat and Tobiah when Nehemiah came with the king's credentials. They represented typically those who profess to be children of God, but are not born again; their profession is spurious and carnal, and as mere religionists, with a form of godliness but destitute of its power, they are the enemies of the cross of Christ and of the real people of God.

Nehemiah continues his narrative. "So I came to Jerusalem and was there three days." We can well imagine, though he does not inform us of it, that these three days were more than days of rest from the strenuous journey. They were days of waiting on God, renewed prayer for guidance and wisdom. He was alone with his God. When the three days of waiting were over he began a night ride to inspect the condition of the different gates and the wall. When all was quiet and people asleep, this servant of God went on this memorable night inspection, accompanied by a few men. No one knows what God had put in his heart; he kept it a secret. There was no boast that he had come to do a big work, and no heralding of his plans. The man of faith, who trusts God, can go and act without making known what the Lord has commissioned him to do. He alone rode on an animal; the others walked. It must have been a sad journey as he passed from gate to gate in the walls. Desolation and debris everywhere. The gates were burned to ashes, and finally the rubbish in the way was so great that the animal he rode could no longer pass through. And how he must have sighed when his eyes beheld the ruin and havoc, the results of the judgment of God on account of Israel's sin!

And how many other true servants of God have spent nights like this in considering the failure and ruin among God's people, burdened with sorrow and deep concern, sighing and groaning, with hearts touched like Nehemiah's, ready to do the Lord's will.

Verses 17-18. The rulers, the Jews, the priests and nobles were ignorant of all he had done. On the morning after that night journey, he called the people together to tell them what the Lord had put in his heart. But with what meekness and tenderness he speaks to them! He does not reproach them or charge them with unfaithfulness and neglect. He does not assume the role of a leader, but identifies himself with the people. "Ye see the distress that *we* are in"—he might have said, "You see the distress you are in." Then he told them of what God had done. But we find not a word of credit to himself, nor of the lonely hours spent during that sleepless night. Then the people resolved to rise up and build.

Verses 19-20. Sanballat, Tobiah and a third one, Geshem the Arabian (an Ishmaelite) were at hand with their sneers. "They laughed us to scorn, and despised us, and said, What is this thing that ye do? Will ye rebel against the king?" They realized that Nehemiah had come to build the wall of exclusion, and bring the people back to their God-given separation; therefore these outsiders began at once to antagonize the messenger of God. Magnificent is Nehemiah's answer. "The God of heaven, He will prosper us." He puts God first. Knowing that they were doing His will in rebuilding the wall, he had the confidence and assurance that God was on their side and none could hinder. "Therefore we His servants will arise and build." This was their determination to do the work. "But ye have no portion, nor right, nor memorial in Jerusalem." It is the refusal of their fellow help. Though they might have claimed a relationship with the people of God, yet did they not belong to Israel. Their help was not wanted. What a contrast with the unseparated condition which prevails in the professing church in what is termed "work for the Lord," in which the unsaved and ungodly are asked to participate!

CHAPTER 3

1. The builders of the sheep gate (3:1-2)
2. The builders of the fish gate (3:3-5)
3. The repairers of the old gate (3:6-12)
4. The repairers of the valley gate (3:13)
5. The repairers of the dung gate (3:14)
6. The repairers of the gate of the fountain (3:15-25)
7. The repairers of the water gate (3:26-27)
8. The repairers of the horse gate (3:28)
9. The builders of the east gate and the Gate Miphkad (3:29-32)

Verses 1-2. The work is begun at once. We shall not point out the location of these different gates, nor study the topography of Jerusalem in the days of Nehemiah, as others have done. There are most helpful, spiritual lessons to be learned from the building of the wall and the repairing of the gates. A wall is for protection and to keep out what does not belong in the city. In Ezra's work we saw the restoration of the true place of worship. The wall surrounding the place where the people gathered once more in the true worship of Jehovah typifies the guarding of that place of privilege and blessing. A wall of separation is needed to keep out that which is undesirable and which would hinder and mar the true worship. (Even in connection with the millennial temple a wall is mentioned, "to make a separation between the sanctuary and the profane place" Ezek. 42:20.) Even so a church, an assembly, composed of true believers who gather together in that worthy Name, and unto that Name, must be protected from the world and all which dishonors Christ, or that which is contrary to sound doctrine, must be excluded. This is the true New Testament principle in connection with the true Church, foreshadowed in the building of the wall surrounding the place where the Lord had set His Name.

The third chapter is a remarkable one. We see the people of God at work building and repairing, every one doing the work in a certain place. Here is the record of the names, where and how they labored. God keeps such a record of all His servants and their labors. When all His people appear before the judgment seat of Christ this book will be opened "and every man shall receive his own reward according to his own labor" (1 Cor. 3:8).

Ten gates are mentioned in this chapter. In chapter 8:16 we read of "the gate of Ephraim" and in chapter 12:39 of "the prison gate." If we add these two to the ten mentioned in this chapter we have twelve gates (Rev. 21:12). The first gate at which the work started is the sheep gate. Through this gate the sacrificial animals were led to the altar, the constant witness to the fact that "without the shedding of blood there is no remission" and the types of Him who was "led as a lamb to the slaughter." The sheep gate at which the work started is typical of the blessed work of the Lamb of God, He who bore our sins in His body on the tree, the offering of His spotless, holy body by which we are sanctified. The lesson here is that the person and work of Christ is the starting point of a true restoration, and that the cross of Christ, the work of God's Son has accomplished, must be guarded above everything else. At the close of this chapter this sheep-gate is mentioned once more. After making the circuit of all the gates, we are led back to this first gate. It is with this great truth, the gospel of Christ, that all repairing of the inroads of the world and the flesh, must start and terminate. This gate suggests Him who said, "I am the door; by me if any man enter in he shall be saved, and shall go in and out, and find pasture" (John 10:9). There is no other gate which leads to life and into God's presence.

Eliashib (God will restore) the highpriest, with his brethren, builded the sheep gate, sanctified it and set it up. It was priestly work. The tower of Meah and the tower of Hananeel are mentioned. Meah means "a hundred" and it reminds us of the parable in which our Lord mentions the man who had a hundred sheep. Hananeel means "to whom God is gracious." Significant names. There is no doubt that this sheep gate is the same one mentioned in John 5:2, which affords still another application. The men of Jericho, once under the curse, but now in the place of nearness and blessing, toiled next to the highpriest. What grace this reveals! Zaccur (well remembered) the son of Imri (the towering one) also was there.

Verses 3-5. Next was the fish gate. This was separated from the sheep gate by the portion of the wall which the men of Jericho and Zaccur repaired. Outside of that gate may have been a fish market, or it may have been the gate through which the fishermen passed to catch fish. It reminds us of the words of our Lord, "Come ye after me, and I will make you to become fishers of men" (Mark 1:17). After we have passed through the sheep gate we must go through the fish gate, to catch fish, to be soul-winners. In this way, leading others to Christ, bringing sinners to a knowledge of the Saviour, the Church is built up. Hassenaah (lifted up) was the builder there. Then Meremoth (strong), Meshullam (repaying a friend) and Zadok (just) repaired next to the fish gate. "And next unto them the Tekoites repaired; but their nobles did not put their necks to the work of their Lord." The prophet Amos was a Tekoite who had prophesied many years before, a simple herdman and gatherer of sycamore figs. He was chosen of the Lord, and here other humble instruments of Tekoa, used in doing the work, are immortalized in this record. Their nobles were slackers. They had no interest in the work of their Lord. And so there are such who do not work for the Lord, and in that coming day will suffer loss, though they are saved.

Verses 6-12. The next gate is the old gate. This gate was probably the same which elsewhere is called "the corner gate" (2 Kings 14:13; Jer. 31:38). Jehoiada ("the Lord knows") and Meshullam repaired this gate. This gate may also remind us of Him "whose goings forth have been from of old, from everlasting," who is the cornerstone, upon whom all rests. Next repaired Melatiah, the Gibeonite, and Jadon, the Meronothite, the men of Gibeon and Mizpah. The Gibeonites, on account of their deception by which they had obtained a covenant of peace with Israel in Joshua's day, had been made "hewers of wood and drawers of water." Here we behold some of them participating in the great work. Of the others we mention Rephaiah, who was a wealthy man, who did not hire a substitute, but labored with his own hands, toiling with the rest. Shallum, the son of Halohesh, was another man of power and wealth; he and his daughters repaired like the rest. What a sight it must have been when these zealous men cleared away the debris and repaired the gates, and among them the daughters of Shallum!

Verse 13. The valley gate was repaired by Hanun (gracious) and the inhabitants of Zanoah (broken). The valley typifies the low place, humility. How needed this is in service for God, for "God resisteth the proud, and giveth grace to the humble."

Verse 14. The dung gate was repaired by Malchiah, and he was the ruler of Beth-haccerem (the place of the vineyard). This gate was used to carry out the refuse and filth from the city. This gate reminds of the exhortations that God's people must cleanse themselves from all filthiness of the flesh and the spirit "for God hath not called us unto uncleanness, but unto holiness" (1 Thess. 4:7).

Verses 15-25. The gate of the fountain was next to the dung gate. The fountain, ever flowing, is a blessed type of the Holy Spirit, who indwells the believer and is in him, the well of living water springing up, like a fountain, into everlasting life (John 4:14). It is suggestive that the fountain gate came after the dung gate. If a believer cleanses himself from that which defiles, the Spirit of God will be unhindered, filling the believer and using him as a vessel meet for the Master's use. Shallun (recompense) the son of Colhozeh (wholly seer) the ruler of Mizpah (watchtower) repaired and built that gate. And these names fit in beautifully with the Spirit of God as the fountain of life and power. We cannot mention all the names which follow. (A good concordance like Strong's or Young's gives most of the Hebrew proper names in a reliable translation. We suggest the study of the names of those who repaired as interesting and helpful.) Nor do we know anything whatever of the individual history of those zealous Israelites, who reconstructed and restored the wall and gates of Jerusalem. God knows each one and has preserved their names, though unknown by the world, in His Word. Surely "the memory of the just is blessed" (Prov. 10:7) and some day they, with us and all His servants, will receive the reward.

Verses 26-27. The water gate is mentioned and the Nethinim, who were servants and dwelt in Ophel (the high place) are connected with this gate. This gate suggests the Word of God so frequently spoken of under the symbol of water (John 3:5, 13:1-16; Eph. 5:26; Ps. 119:136). It is very interesting to notice that while the servants are mentioned in connection with the water gate, it does not say that they repaired the gate. The Word of God needs no building up or improving; it builds up those who bow to its blessed authority.

Verse 28. The horse gate (2 Kings 11:6; Jer.

31:40) suggests warfare and victory. In a world of evil the people of God wage a warfare. We wrestle not with flesh and blood, but with the wicked spirits. Paul speaks of the believer as a soldier of Christ. Victory is on our side, though the forces of evil may threaten on all sides.

Verses 29-32. The east gate was repaired and kept by Shemaiah, the son of Shechaniah. From Ezekiel's prophecy we learn that the Shekina glory left from the east gate, and that when the glory returns to dwell once more in the temple, the great millennial temple of Ezekiel's vision, the glory of the Lord will enter through the east gate. The east gate faces the rising sun. It suggests the coming of the Lord for His people. And here the two names fit in beautifully. Shemaiah means "heard of the Lord"; even so He will hear His people and some day will answer their prayer for His coming. Shechaniah means "habitation of the Lord." We shall be with Him.

The Miphkad gate was repaired by Malchiah (the Lord is King) the goldsmith's son. Miphkad means "the appointed place" or "a place of visitation." It was probably the gate in which the judges sat to settle disputes and controversies. It suggests the judgment seat of Christ.

Thus we learn that the wall surrounding and protecting the gathered people suggests the cross as the starting point; service; Christ as Lord; humility; cleansing from defilement; filling with the Spirit; the Word of God and its power; warfare and victory; the coming of the Lord and the judgment seat of Christ.

CHAPTER 4

1. The indignation and sneers of the enemies (4:1-3)
2. Nehemiah's ejaculatory prayer (4:4-6)
3. Conspiracy, and more prayer (4:7-9)
4. Nehemiah's precautions and confidence (4:10-23)

Verses 1-3. Sanballat (hate in disguise) having heard of the successful building of the wall, became very angry and mocked the Jews. And Tobiah the Ammonite used sarcasm. He said that which they build will be so weak that one of the foxes, which infested the broken-down walls (Ps. 63:10) could break these newly built walls again.

Verses 4-6. The answer to these sneers was prayer. The language these two enemies used was provoking, but Nehemiah's refuge is prayer. Hezekiah did the same when the Assyrian taunted him and defiled the God of Israel. It is another of the brief ejaculatory prayers of Nehemiah. There are seven of them in this book: chapters 2:4; 4:4-6; 5:19; 6:14; 13:14, 22, 29. He prayed, "Hear, our God, for we are despised, and turn their reproach upon their own head, and give them for a prey in the land of captivity; and cover not their iniquity, and let not their sin be blotted out from before thee; because they have provoked thee to anger before the builders." He cast himself wholly upon God and with this prayer Nehemiah and the people put the matter in the hands of the Lord. They were an object of contempt, as His people who were doing the work of the Lord wanted to have done. Sanballat and Tobiah were the enemies of God. This prayer reminds us of the many imprecatory prayers in the psalms. When in the future another remnant of the Jews returns to the land, they will face in the great tribulation more powerful enemies than this remnant had to contend with. The man of sin, the Antichrist, will be in control, and it is then that they will pray these prayers, some of them almost like Nehemiah's prayer (Ps. 109:14).

The work was not hindered by the taunts of the enemy. "So built we the wall; and all the wall was joined together unto the half thereof, for the people had a mind to work." If only God's people are in touch with God and cast themselves wholly upon Him, all the efforts of the enemy are unavailing.

Verses 7-9. As the work progressed and the Samaritan enemies saw that their taunts were unsuccessful, they became very wroth and conspired to use force and fight against Jerusalem. Sanballat and Tobiah had gathered others, the Arabians, Ammonites and Ashdodites, to hinder the work. Behind them stood the same enemy of God, Satan, who always hinders the work of God. His work of opposition is the same in every age. A very serious time had come to the builders of the wall. The enemy was threatening to fall upon them, and perhaps destroy what they had built. "Nevertheless we made our prayer unto our God." It was prayer, dependence on God, first. The next thing they did was to take precaution against the enemy—"and set a watch against them day and night, because of them." But was not prayer enough? Why the setting of a watch if they trusted the Lord? If they had not done this it would have been presumption on their part. Their action did not clash with their trust in God.

Verses 10-23. There was also discouragement in their midst. As the apostle wrote of himself, "without were fightings, within were fears" (2

Cor. 7:5), this was true of them. They became timid and fainthearted. It was Judah, the princely tribe, whose emblem was the lion, which showed discouragement and was ready to give up in despair. But Nehemiah made no answer to the complaint "we are not able to build the wall." The best remedy was to keep right on praying, working and watching. The adversaries intended to make a surprise attack and slay the workmen and cause the work to cease. That was their plan; but they did not reckon with God, who watched over His people. Ten times the Jews which were scattered among these adversaries warned them of the great danger of the coming attack. This was another discouragement. Then Nehemiah acted in the energy of faith. He knew God was on their side and that He would fight for them. He prepared the people for the threatening conflict and armed them with swords, spears and bows. Then he addressed them with inspiring words. "Be not afraid of them: Remember the Lord, great and terrible, and fight for your brethren, your sons and your daughters, your wives and your houses." All was at stake. No mercy could be expected from the wicked adversaries. It was a blessed battle-cry he gave to them: "Remember the Lord." If He is remembered and kept before the heart defeat is impossible. The great preparation was soon reported to the enemies, by which they knew that their attack had become known. Nehemiah saw in it all God's gracious and providential dealings, "God had brought their counsel to nought." Then he continued to work at their task of building the wall. But they did not become careless. They continued to be on their guard. "Every one with one of his hands wrought in the work and with the other hand held a weapon." A trumpeter stood at Nehemiah's side. If he sounded the alarm they were to gather together; then, said Nehemiah, "our God shall fight for us." "So we laboured in the work, and half of them held the spears from the rising of the morning till the stars appeared." We leave it with the reader to apply all this to our spiritual warfare against our enemies. The Sword of the Spirit is the Word of God, and constant watching is needed for that.

CHAPTER 5

1. The complaint of oppression (5:1-5)
2. Nehemiah's rebuke and demands (5:6-13)
3. Nehemiah's generosity (5:14-19)

Verses 1-5. The internal conditions among the toiling people were serious. The work which was done in rebuilding the walls was a labour of love; no wages were paid. As the people were thus engaged their other occupations, including agriculture, had to be neglected. As a result the poor had been driven to mortgage their lands, vineyards and houses in order to buy corn, because of the dearth. The rich had taken advantage of this and had enslaved their sons and daughters, and there seemed to be no prospect of redeeming them. The rich Jews by usury oppressed the poor, who had lost their lands and houses. There was therefore a great cry of the people and of their wives against their brethren the Jews. It was a sad condition; the enemy was doing his work in the camp (Acts 6:1). Oppression of the poor is especially displeasing to God and His Spirit condemns and warns against it (Amos 2:6; 5:12, 8:4-8; Prov. 14:31; 22:16; 28:3; and James 5:1-6).

Verses 6-13. Righteous Nehemiah, when he heard all this, was moved with indignation and righteous anger took hold on him. Nehemiah, the Governor, writes, "I consulted with myself." No doubt much prayer was connected with this self-consultation. He then rebuked the nobles and rulers for having done what the law of God forbids and condemns (Exod. 22:25; Lev. 25:36-37; Deut. 23:19; Ps. 15:5) to exact usury. A great assembly was called in which their conduct was denounced unsparingly. "We after our ability have redeemed our brethren the Jews, which were sold unto the heathen; and will ye even sell your brethren? or shall they be sold unto us?" When Nehemiah came to Jerusalem he had freed those Jews who were in bondage to the heathen on account of some debt, and these rich usurers were selling their own brethren. They had no answer to give but were convicted of their evil deeds. He then demanded full restitution, "Restore, I pray you, to them even this day, their lands, their vineyards, their olive yards, and their houses, also the hundredth part of the money, and of the corn, the wine and the oil, that ye exact of them." The appeal was effectual. They were at once ready to restore, to require nothing more of them, and to do all Nehemiah had demanded. It was a great victory. Had the oppression continued and the internal strife, it would have resulted in disaster. How often these internal strifes and acts of injustice have brought reproach upon the people of God, and dishonor to that worthy Name! (Gal. 5:15; James 3:16.) They had to give an oath to do this, and solemnly Nehemiah shook his lap and said, "So God shake out every man from his house, and from his labour, who performeth not this promise, even thus be he shaken out and emptied." An "Amen" from the great congregation followed, and they acted upon the promise.

Verses 14-19. The closing verses show the generosity and self-denying character of this man of God. It reminds us somewhat of the apostle Paul and his testimony concerning himself (1 Cor. 4:12; 2 Cor. 12:15-16; 1 Thess. 2:9-10). In all he had done as a servant of God he had the comfort that God knew and would be his Rewarder. "Think upon me, my God, for good, according to all that I have done for this people." He will have his reward, and so will all His people, who serve in behalf of God's people as Nehemiah did.

CHAPTER 6

1. The attempt to entice Nehemiah (6:1-4)
2. The attempt to intimidate him (6:5-9)
3. The attempt through a false prophet (6:10-14)
4. The wall finished (6:15-16)
5. The conspiracy between Jewish nobles and Tobiah (6:17-19)

Verses 1-4. Defeated in all previous efforts to hinder the work and to do harm to the builders of the wall, the enemies made new attempts to make them cease from the work. Sanballat, Tobiah, Geshem the Arabian, with the other enemies, had heard that the wall was about finished. Sanballat and Geshem sent the message to Nehemiah, "Come, let us meet together in one of the villages in the plain of Ono." Nehemiah knew their scheme, "they thought to do me mischief," probably to assassinate him, or make him a prisoner. He therefore answered, "I am doing a great work, so that I cannot come down; why should the work cease, whilst I leave it, and come down to you?" Four times they tried to entice him, and four times he gave the same answer. Apparently Sanballat and Geshem offered a friendly meeting on neutral ground, suggesting some kind of an alliance. But Nehemiah, whole-hearted as he was, refused to come down and stop the important God-given work. He would not turn aside from the place given to him by the Lord and the work which he had been called to do. Maintaining this separation was his safeguard. In our own days of worldly alliance and compromise, when deceitful workers abound on all sides, who are like the Samaritans, who feared the Lord outwardly and served their own gods (2 Kings 17:33) the only way of escape is to act like Nehemiah did and have no fellowship with such.

Verses 5-9. After this failure they attempted to intimidate Nehemiah. Sanballat sent his servant the fifth time, and while the previous communications were sealed this one was in the form of an open letter. In this letter Nehemiah was slandered and a threat made to accuse him of treason to the king of Persia. Maliciousness breathed in every word of this open letter. With a clear conscience, knowing that all was a wicked invention, Nehemiah answered this new attack. "There are no such things done as thou sayest, but thou feignest them out of thine own heart." He recognized what they tried to do and afresh Nehemiah looked to his God. "Now therefore, O God, strengthen my hands." As it was in Nehemiah's day so it is still. Wherever the work of the Lord is done and God's servants labor to glorify Him, the enemy will rise up and hinder the work. When the Lord opens a door, then many adversaries will appear. The sneers, the hatred, the wiles and the lies of the world are the same today, because behind them stands the same person who acted through Sanballat, Tobiah and Geshem—Satan, the god of this age.

Verses 10-14. Shemaiah's message was the message of a false prophet. He told Nehemiah that they would come to slay him. He supposed that Nehemiah would flee after receiving this information in the form of a message from the Lord. But Nehemiah said, "Should such a man as I flee? and who is there, that, being such as I am, would go into the temple to save his life? I will not go in." He was a man of faith, in fellowship with God and he at once knew that the message was not from Him. He perceived God had not sent him. Shemaiah was the hireling of the adversaries. It was a cleverly laid plan, not only to frighten Nehemiah, but to make him sin, so that they might have something against him. It seems that Shemaiah was ceremonially unclean; that is probably the meaning of "shut up." He was not fit in that condition to be in the house of God, within the temple. And Nehemiah too, not being a priest, would have transgressed had he followed Shemaiah's suggestion. This was the cunning scheme. With this hireling prophet there were also other prophets and a prophetess, by the name of Noadiah.

Verses 15-16. "So the wall was finished in the twenty-fifth day of the month Elul, in fifty and two days." How grateful they must have been when their task was finished! Critics have remarked that fifty-two days is too short a time to accomplish that much work. But a large number of people as well as the servants of Nehemiah (5:16) worked incessantly. The material, too, was ready, for they probably had to dig out the old stones to put them back into the right place; no new stones needed to be hewed and transported. God had worked and given His blessing. The success of it, next to God, was due to persevering prayer, personal and united effort, constant watchfulness and unfailing courage. And their enemies were more cast down, "for they perceived that this work was wrought of our God."

Verses 17-19. The final paragraph of this chapter reveals another sad condition which resulted from disobedience to the law. Mixed marriages were responsible for it. Nehemiah only reports this serious fellowship of the nobles of the Jews and his enemy Tobiah. We shall read later how Nehemiah dealt with those who had allied themselves with this Ammonite (chapter 13).

CHAPTER 7

1. Provisions made for the defense of the city (7:1-4)
2. The genealogy (7:5-65)
3. Their whole number (7:65-69)
4. The gifts for the work (7:70-73)

Verses 1-4. The wall had been finished and the doors set up. Porters, singers and the Levites were appointed, and Nehemiah gave to his brother Hanani and Hananiah, the ruler of the castle, charge over Jerusalem. The porters were gate keepers. These gate keepers are named in Ezra 2:42, and here in this chapter in verse 45. Their duty was to open the gates and bar them at night. Nehemiah's instructions are given in the text, "Let not the gates of Jerusalem be opened until the sun be hot; and while they stand by, let them shut the doors, and bar them: and appoint watches of the inhabitants of Jerusalem, every one in his watch, and every one to be over against his house." The city was carefully guarded. Every one who entered the city had to do so in broad daylight, and a system of watches was established for the purpose of watching the gates of the city day and night. It seems the Hebrews before the exile, and some time after, had three night watches of four hours each. Later, at the time our Lord was on earth, they had four night watches (Mark 13:35). It was wisdom to guard the entrances to the city so as to keep out those who had no right to enter. As there were many enemies who might sneak in and do harm, this scrutiny and these watches were of great importance and necessity.

This caution exercised by Nehemiah in regard to watching those who entered the gates gives a lesson concerning the Church. The New Testament teaches the same caution as to those who are to be admitted to Christian fellowship, and those who are to be refused. Unregenerated persons have no right in a true church or assembly, nor any one whose life is not right, nor who holds doctrines contrary to the faith delivered unto the saints. "If there come any unto you, and bring not this doctrine, receive him not into your house, neither bid him God speed: for he that biddeth him God speed is partaker of his evil deeds" (2 John 10-11). But if even in the Apostolic days "certain men crept in unawares," as Jude writes (Jude 4) how much greater is this evil in these Laodicean days.

Verses 5-65. This chapter corresponds to the second chapter in Ezra; the annotations given there need not be repeated here. But we notice Nehemiah's statement, "My God put it into my heart." As a godly man, he acknowledges the hand of the Lord and His guidance.

Verses 66-69. The number of the whole congregation is given as 42,360. If we turn to Ezra 2:64 we find the same statement. There are differences between these two lists which prove that they are not identical.

Verses 70-73. The gifts for the work are mentioned more fully by Nehemiah. See Ezra's record, chapter 2:68-70. The amounts in both records do not agree, and it is generally charged that it is due to different traditions, or copyists' errors. But there is no real discrepancy. Ezra mentions what *some* of the chiefs of the fathers offered. Nehemiah records what he himself gave (Tirshatha is Nehemiah's Persian title as governor) besides the chiefs and the rest of the people.

II. The Spiritual Revival

CHAPTER 8

1. The reading of the law before the water gate (8:1-8)
2. A day of joy and not of mourning (8:9-12)
3. The keeping of the feast of tabernacles (8:13-18)

Verses 1-8. This interesting chapter gives the record of a gracious revival through the reading of the law. All the people gathered themselves together as one man in the street that was before the water gate, the place which suggests the cleansing and refreshing power of the Word. And as a united people they had but one desire, to hear the law of Moses, which the Lord had commanded, to Israel. They gave orders to Ezra that he should bring the book of the law. This the people knew was the Word of the Lord, and for this they hungered. Every true revival must begin with the Word, and in believing submission to what the Lord has said. So, it has been in all the great revivals of the past, and so it will be in the future. The great need today is "back to the Bible"; and to listen to its message as the message of God. How willingly and joyfully Ezra must have responded, and how it must have cheered the aged servant of the Lord! He brought the law before the congregation both of men and women, and those that understood in hearing (children of a certain age). Critics say that Ezra's law of Moses must not be understood as meaning the Pentateuch; they claim that it was a collection of different laws, and part of the so-called "priestly codex," which even then, according to the critical school, was not completely finished. Inasmuch as the destructive criticism denies that Moses is the author of the Pentateuch, they are obliged to resort to these arguments in order to sustain their theory. There is no valid reason to doubt when the book of the law of Moses was demanded and Ezra brought it before the people, that it was the Pentateuch, which the Jews call *Torah,* the law.

Then followed under great attention the reading, from the morning until the midday. Ezra stood upon a pulpit of wood, which was a raised platform which had been made for this purpose. Alongside of Ezra were thirteen men; in all, counting in Ezra, fourteen men faced the people. They probably took turns in reading from the law. Their names are interesting if we look at their meaning—Mattithiah (gift of the Lord); Shema (hearing); Anaiah (answer of the Lord); Uriah (the Lord is Light); Hilkiah (portion of the Lord); Maaseiah (work of the Lord); Mishael (who is as God is); Malchijah (King is the Lord); Hashum (wealthy); Hashbaddanah (esteemed by judging); Zechariah (the Lord remembers); Meshullam (reward). These names are suggestive of the Word itself. Then Ezra unrolled the parchment seen by all the people. Great reverence was manifested to the Word by all the people standing up. Then Ezra blessed the Lord, the great God. Amen, Amen was the people's answer, with the lifting up of their hands. Then they bowed their heads and worshipped the Lord with their faces to the ground. Ezra and the people believed that what they read is the Word of God. Hence this reverence, this praise and the attitude of submission. How little reverence for the Word of God our generation manifests! This too is a fruit of the destructive criticism, which has put the Bible on the same level with common literature. Thirteen others are mentioned who, with the Levites, caused the people to understand the law. Some think it means that the people did not understand Hebrew, and that the Hebrew text had to be translated into Aramaic. This is probably incorrect. Hebrew was not unknown after the captivity, for Haggai, Zechariah and Malachi spoke and wrote in that language. It rather means the interpretation of what had been read, that is, an exposition of it. The names of these thirteen expositors are also of interest. The first is Jeshua, which means "Jehovah is salvation"; this is the great truth which all Bible exposition must emphasize.

Verses 9-12. When the people heard the words of the Law they wept. They were conscience stricken on account of their individual and national sins; they judged themselves. The Word had been believed; their godly sorrow had been expressed by tears, and so they were ready for the words of comfort and cheer the Lord gave through Nehemiah, Ezra and the Levites. "This day is holy unto the Lord your God; mourn not nor weep . . . go your way, eat the fat, and drink the sweet, and send portions to them for whom nothing is prepared; for this day is holy unto our Lord; neither be ye sorry; for the joy of the Lord is your strength." And this was done. They were the Lord's people, separated unto Himself, and as they remembered all His goodness, they rejoiced in Him. Refreshed themselves, they were to remember those "for whom nothing was prepared."

Verses 13-18. The feast of tabernacles was kept by them. They came in reading the law to the command of Moses that the children of Israel should "dwell in booths in the feast of the seventh month." Olive, pine, myrtle and palm tree branches were to be used to construct booths in commemoration of the wilderness journey. This was done at once by them in obedience to the Word. Thus we have three facts concerning the Word in this chapter; reading the Word, believing the Word, and obeying the Word. Hence there was great gladness in keeping the feast of tabernacles. The words, "for since the days of Joshua the son of Nun unto that day had not the children of Israel done so," present a difficulty. We read in Ezra 3:4 that the feast of tabernacles was celebrated immediately after the arrival of Zerubbabel; nor does it seem possible that God-fearing kings in the past overlooked this feast. 1 Kings 8:2 and 65 shows that Solomon kept this feast of the Lord. It therefore cannot mean that the people of Israel had neglected the keeping of the feast of tabernacles for a thousand years. The emphasis must be placed upon the word "so"—it means that never before had the feast of tabernacles been kept in such a manner. The reading of the Word and the revival which followed produced such a joyful and whole-hearted keeping of the feast, as had not been the case since the days of Joshua.

CHAPTER 9

1. The public humiliation and confession (9:1-5)
2. The great confession and prayer (9:6-38)

Verses 1-5. Two days after the feast of tabernacles had been concluded this humiliation and confession of sin took place. The assembled congregation fasted, with sackcloth and earth upon them. Separation was next. Evil confessed must mean evil put away. They separated themselves from all strangers, and after their confession they worshipped the Lord. Here again is the right order of a spiritual revival. Reading, hearing and believing the Word always comes first; humiliation, self-judgment, confession and true worship follow.

Verses 6-38. The Levites who occupied the platform (called here stairs) called upon the people to stand up and to bless the Lord and His glorious Name. Then follows the prayer. It is the longest recorded prayer in the Bible and is much like Daniel's prayer (Dan. 9) and Ezra's prayer (Ezra 9). These three prayers deserve a careful comparison and study.

First there is a beautiful invocation and outburst of worship. "Thou art the Lord, even thou alone; thou hast made heaven, the heaven of heavens, with all their host, the earth and all things that are thereon, the seas and all that is therein, and thou preservest them all; and the host of heaven worshippeth thee." Here is the praise of the Creator, whose power is acknowledged, as well as the Preserver of His creation. The covenant of God with Abraham and the seed of Abraham is next mentioned (9:7-8) and then follows the account of the deliverance of their fathers from Egypt. He was their Redeemer (9:9-11). The experience of the wilderness is stated in verses 12-21. The Creator-Redeemer led them in a pillar of cloud by day and in a pillar of fire by night; He spoke with them, gave them His commandments. He supplied them with bread from heaven and water from the rock. Then follows the story of their disobedience, and with what graciousness the Lord had dealt with their fathers. "Thou gavest also thy good Spirit to instruct them, and withheldest not thy manna from their mouth, and gavest them water for their thirst. Yea, forty years didst thou sustain them in the wilderness, and they lacked nothing; their clothes waxed not old, and their feet swelled not." The possession of the land of Canaan is given in verses 22-25, revealing God's faithfulness and His power in behalf of His redeemed people. Verses 26-30 cover the period of the judges and the prophets. In all the mercy of God is exalted. Then comes the prayer for mercy, with the acknowledgment of their sins as a nation.

CHAPTER 10

1. Those who sealed the covenant (10:1-27)
2. The obligations of the covenant (10:28-39)

Verses 1-27. The last verse of the preceding chapter mentions a covenant. "And yet for all this we make a sure covenant, and write it; and our princes, our Levites, and our priests, seal unto it." In this chapter we find the names of the heads of the different houses who sealed the covenant, which means they put their signature to it. According to talmudical tradition these signers constituted "the Great Synagogue." Originally it consisted of 120 members, but later only 70 belonged to it. Its covenants were as follows: (1) Not to marry heathen women; (2) to keep Sabbath; (3) to keep the Sabbatical year; (4) to pay every year a certain sum to the Temple; (5) to supply wood for the altar; (6) to pay the priestly dues; (7) to collect and to preserve the Holy Scriptures.

The list is headed by Nehemiah with his official title as Governor (Tirshatha). In verses 2-8 the priestly houses are given. The Levitical houses are recorded in verses 9-13. From the book of Ezra we learn that only four priestly houses and only two Levites had returned under Zerubbabel. Here we have twenty-one priestly and seventeen Levitical houses. This shows a marked increase. The chiefs of the people were forty-one houses; their names are given in verses 14-27.

Verses 28-29. Besides the heads of the houses recorded in this chapter there were the rest of the people, priests, Levites (the individuals), porters, singers and the Nethinim (Ezra 2:43); they all had separated themselves and entered into a curse, and into an oath. The word "curse" has the meaning of an imprecatory expression in the form of an oath. There must have been some formula in connection with singing the covenant, in which the signers declared that if they broke the covenant God would do something to them (the curse) and then by a direct oath swore to keep the covenant. The obligations of the covenant are given in the rest of this chapter. These obligations may be summed up in one word, "obedience." They covenanted to obey the law of the Lord and to do all the commandments.

III. THE PEOPLE ESTABLISHED, THE DEDICATION OF THE WALL, AND NEHEMIAH'S FINAL ACTS

CHAPTER 11

1. The willing offerers (11:1-2)
2. The heads of the residents of Jerusalem (11:3-24)
3. The inhabitants outside of Jerusalem (11:25-36)

Verses 1-2. A splendid example of self-sacrifice is given in these two verses. Certain men willingly offered themselves to dwell in Jerusalem, and the people blest them for the willing sacrifice. It must be explained that Jerusalem was not then a very desirable place for residence. The enemies of the city seeking to destroy the fortifications and harm the inhabitants were constantly active. There was much danger for those who dwelt in the city itself. For this reason the great majority of the returned captives preferred to live outside of the walls of Jerusalem. It was decided to make every tenth man to dwell in Jerusalem. The decision was made by lot. But then these volunteers came to the front and displayed self-denial and courage.

Verses 3-24. Here is another register of names recorded in God's book, and not forgotten by Him. The children of Judah, the children of Benjamin, the priests who acted as temple officials, the Levites, the Nethinim, and those with special callings are all named. Some day the Lord will be their Rewarder for their faithful service, as He will be the Rewarder of all His people.

Verses 25-36. Those who lived outside of Jerusalem, in villages, are tabulated in the closing verses of this chapter.

CHAPTER 12

1. Priests and Levites at the time of the return under Zerubbabel and Joshua (12:1-9)
2. The descendants of Joshua, the high-priest (12:10-11)
3. The heads of the priestly houses in the time of Joiakim (12:12-21)
4. Heads of Levitical houses (12:22-26)
5. The dedication of the walls (12:27-43)
6. Provisions for the priests and Levites, and other temple officials (12:44-47)

Verses 1-9. The names of the priests and Levites, who went up under Zerubbabel, the son of Shealtiel, and Jeshua (or Joshua), the High-priest, are recorded first. Ezra, mentioned in the first verse, is not the Ezra of the book of Ezra. According to the seventh verse these persons "were the chiefs of the priests and of their brethren in the days of Jeshua." They constituted the heads of the twenty-four courses into which the priesthood was divided (1 Chron. 24:1-20). Only four heads of these courses had returned from the captivity; Jedaiah, Immer, Pasher and Harim. These were divided by Zerubbabel and Jeshua into the original twenty-four; but only twenty-two are mentioned in this record. The Abijah of verse 4 is one of the ancestors of John the Baptist (Luke 1:5)

Verses 10-11. This is the important register of the high-priests, the descendants of Jeshua, or Joshua. From now on in the history of the Jewish people chronological reckonings were no longer made by means of the reign of kings, but by the successions of the high-priests. Jaddua is unquestionably the same who is mentioned by Josephus, the Jewish historian. In his high-priestly robes he met Alexander the Great as he besieged Jerusalem, and was the means of saving Jerusalem. Alexander fell on his face when he saw Jaddua, for the great king claimed to have seen this very scene in a dream vision. Inasmuch as Jaddua was not in office till a considerable time after the death of Nehemiah, the name Jaddua must have been added later, under the sanction of the Spirit of God, so that Jaddua's descent might be preserved.

Verse 12-26. The heads of the priestly houses in the time of Joiakim (the son of Jeshua, verse

10) are here recorded, as well as the heads of the Levitical houses. The sentence, "also the priests, in the reign of Darius the Persian" (Darius Codomannus 336-331), was probably added later, under the direction of the Holy Spirit. Further comment on the recorded names is not needed.

Verses 27-43. A full and interesting account of the dedication of the walls follows the register of the names. The singers are mentioned first (verse 27-30) for it was the occasion of praise and great rejoicing. They gathered from everywhere to celebrate the dedication with singing, with cymbals, psalteries and with harps. No doubt the Psalms were used by this multitude of singers, as they gave thanks in holy song. What singing and rejoicing there will be some day when "the ransomed of the Lord shall return and come to Zion with songs and everlasting joy upon their heads" (Isa. 35:10)! A great procession was made around the walls. This was the main ceremony of the dedication. The procession was in two great companies, one going to the right, and the other to the left. The one company was headed by Nehemiah and the other probably by Ezra, the scribe. Hoshaiah (set free of the Lord) and half of the princes of Judah are mentioned first in the one company. The two companies gave thanks, no doubt responding one to the other. Perhaps they used Psalms 145—147. Thus singing and praising the Lord they came to the house of the Lord. Here the greatest praise was heard, by the whole company. Seven priests blew the trumpets and eight others with them. The singers' chorus swelled louder and louder, so that the joyous sound was heard even afar off. Great sacrifices were offered and everybody rejoiced. It was God by His Spirit who produced this joy, "for God had made them rejoice with great joy."

Verses 44-47. The servants of the Lord, the priests and the Levites, were not forgotten. They brought their tithes and there was an abundant provision for all. Such were the blessed results under the spiritual revival of Nehemiah and Ezra. But when we turn to the last book of the Old Testament, to Malachi, we learn that declension must soon have set in, for we hear there the very opposite from what is recorded here. "Will a man rob God? Yet ye have robbed me. But ye say, Wherein have we robbed thee? In tithes and offerings" (Mal. 3:8). Therefore a curse rested upon the nation (Mal. 3:9-12).

CHAPTER 13

1. The separation of the mixed multitude (13:1-3)
2. The unholy alliance repudiated (13:4-9)
3. Nehemiah's action in behalf of the Levites and singers (13:10-14)
4. Provision for Sabbath observance (13:15-22)
5. Nehemiah's protest (13:23-29)
6. His own testimony as to his work (13:30-31)

Verses 1-3. "On that day" does not mean the same day when the wall had been dedicated. It was a considerable time later, for we read in verse 10 that the Levites had not received their portion. It was different when the wall was dedicated. On a certain day when the law was read again, they came to the passage in Deuteronomy 23:3-5, where it is written that an Ammonite and a Moabite should not enter into the assembly of God forever. Obedience followed at once, "they separated from Israel all the mixed multitude."

Verses 4-9. Here we have the first indication of declension, which in Malachi's days reached a climax. Tobiah was an Ammonite, and with Sanballat and Geshem had strenuously opposed the building of the wall (chapter 6). Eliashib, the priest, who had the oversight of the chambers of the house of the Lord, had allied himself with the enemy of Jerusalem and prepared for this man a great chamber in the temple. There he had stored his household goods (verse 8). Nehemiah had been absent from the city, paying a visit to the Persian court, and during his absence all this hapened. It was probably right after his return from King Artaxerxes in Babylon that the law was read that led to the separation from the mixed multitude, and this in time led to the discovery of the priest's alliance with Tobiah. Nehemiah acted quickly, being deeply grieved. He could not tolerate such an alliance and profanation of the house of the Lord. How much greater and more obnoxious are the unholy alliances in Christendom, and the profanation of God's best.

Verses 10-14. During Nehemiah's absence the tithes had not been given, and the Levites and singers had received nothing. In consequence they left the city and the house of God was forsaken. It is possible that the people had been outraged by Eliashib's alliance with Tobiah, and had refused the tithes. Nehemiah set all things in order, and he appointed also treasurers. On his prayer in verse 14 see chapter 5:19.

Verses 15-22. Another evidence of the declension which had set in after the spiritual revival was the laxity in observing the Sabbath. Nehemiah saw some on the Sabbath day treading winepresses; others brought all kinds of burdens on the Sabbath to Jerusalem; while still others sold victuals. And men of Tyre sold fish and other wares to the people on the Sabbath. We are sure that during Nehemiah's absence the law of God was no longer read, or they could not have fallen into this evil. All declension begins with the neglect of the Word of God. Then Nehemiah contended with the nobles. "What evil thing is this that ye do, and profane the Sabbath day? Did not your fathers thus, and did not our God bring all this evil upon us, and upon this city? Yet ye bring more wrath upon Israel by profaning the Sabbath."

Again, he not only rebuked the evil, but acted energetically, and the Sabbath day was sanctified.

Verses 23-29. Alas! the flesh is flesh, and will ever be the same. Some Jews turned back and deliberately married again women of Ashdod, Ammon and Moab. Their offspring talked a mongrel language. Nehemiah acted in holy zeal. He cursed them, smote them and plucked off their hair. And Joiada, the son of Eliashib the High-priest, who had made an alliance with Tobiah, had married a daughter of Sanballat, the Horonite. Nehemiah refused to have anything to do with him—"I chased him from me."

Verses 30-31. The final thing we hear of Nehemiah is his testimony concerning himself and his prayer, "Remember me." In the day of Christ in glory, this great man of God will surely be rewarded for his earnest and faithful service.

THE BOOK OF
ESTHER

Introduction

The book of Esther is one of the five books which the Jews call Megilloth (Rolls). They appear in the Hebrew Bible in the following order: 1. Canticles, that is, Solomon's Song, read in connection with Passover; 2. Ruth, read on the feast of weeks (Pentecost); 3. Lamentations, used on the ninth day of the month Ab, commemorating the destruction of the temple, which happened twice on the same day, first by Nebuchadnezzar and then afterwards by the Romans; 4. Ecclesiastes, which is read during the celebration of the feast of tabernacles; 5. The book of Esther, read on the feast of Purim. The Jews hold this little book in the highest esteem; they call it "The Megillah" and thereby give it the place of pre-eminence among the other Megilloth. The ancient Rabbis give it a place next to the Torah, the law. Maimonides taught that when the Messiah comes every other book of the Jewish Scriptures will pass away, but the law and the book of Esther will remain forever. . . . Yet many objections have been made against this book. Its rightful place in the canon of the Old Testament has been hotly contested by Jews and Christians.

We mention the two leading objections. The first objection is that the name of God does not appear in this book. Some ancient teachers have tried to overcome this objection by the theory that the name of Jehovah is found a number of times in the initial letters of certain sentences, which letters spell the sacred name. Jehring, Bullinger and others have adopted this attempt to vindicate the book. But this is at best only a fanciful endeavour to do away with this objection. We believe the Holy Spirit is the author of the book of Esther and has given in it a correct report of this remarkable episode in Jewish history. He does not conceal things and to use initial letters of certain words to produce another word is an extremely unsafe method of Bible study. The Spirit of God had a valid reason why He omitted the name of God, which we state later.

Some have suggested that inasmuch as Esther was to be used in connection with the feast of Purim (a feast of merry-making) the name of the Lord was omitted on purpose to avoid its irreverent use amid the scenes of feasting and drinking. Professor Cassel in his lengthy commentary on Esther states that the omission of the name of God was an act of prudence and caution from the side of the person who wrote this account. Others claim that the report was taken mostly from Persian records, which would explain the absence of the name.

It is true the name of God is absent, but God is nevertheless present in this little book. We find Him revealed on every page, in His providence, in His overruling power, in the preservation and deliverance of His covenant people. God cared for His people and watched over them, though they were unfaithful to Him. He frustrated the plan of the enemy. It is true they did not call on Him, but nevertheless His sovereignty in grace is displayed towards them. God's government is therefore revealed in this book though His name is unmentioned.

The second objection is that the canonicity of the book should be rejected because it is not quoted in the New Testament. But this objection also breaks down when we remember that seven other Old Testament books are unquoted in the New Testament Scriptures. Destructive criticism has made other objections of a minor character; we do not need to mention these. Amongst those who had no use for this book is found Martin Luther, who went so far as to say that he wished the book might not exist at all. The evidence that the book is true, with its remarkable story of the great deliverance of a part of God's people, is found by the celebration of the feast of Purim by the Jews. If such a thing as the book of Esther records had not occurred then the Purim feast could not be explained.

The author of the book of Esther is unknown. Some think of Mordecai, others mention Ezra and Nehemiah as possible authors; but this is only guesswork. It is certain that one person wrote the entire account with the exception of chapter 9:20-32, which probably was added by another hand. The style is extremely simple; the Hebrew used is much like that of Ezra and Nehemiah. It contains some Persian words.

The purpose of the book of Esther has admirably been stated by Professor Cassel: "It is a memoir written by a Jew to all his people who are scattered in the extensive countries of Persia, in which are recorded the wonderful interpositions of Providence in their deliverence from destruction, which appeared to be certain. It has no other purpose but to narrate this; it is not called upon to give information about other matters; albeit it gives a picture of Persian court life, the like of which is found nowhere else."

It brings out the great fact that the Jewish people out of their own land, and no longer in any outward relation to God, are nevertheless the objects of His gracious care. This broken relationship seems to be reason why the name of God is avoided in the book. In spite of their unfaithfulness they are still His people, for God's gifts and calling are without repentance. He covers them with His protecting hand and watches over them and in His own way and His own time acts in their behalf, delivering them from their enemies.

Significant it is that the history in the book of Esther concludes the historical books of the Old Testament. The conditions described therein continue during the times of the Gentiles till finally the great deliverance comes for the people Israel. Jewish expositors have compared Esther to the dawn of the morning, that it is like the dawn which announces the end of the night.

It is a prophetic forecast of their history and is especially typical of the coming days of Jacob's trouble when they shall be delivered.

The typical-dispensational application is of much interest, for it illustrates some of the prophecies in a practial way. Vashti, the Gentile wife, may be looked upon as Christendom, to be set aside for her disobedience, and Esther, the Jewess, takes her place. This reminds us of the parable of the two olive trees in Romans 11 and the final execution of the divine threat that the grafted in branches, Gentile Christendom, are to be cut off and the broken off branches, Israel, put back upon their own olive tree.

Haman, the wicked enemy of the Jews, a descendant of Agag, the first enemy Israel met in the wilderness, is an illustration of the future enemy Israel will face. He is called "Haman the wicked" (chapter 7:6). The numerical value of the Hebrew letters composing the words "Haman the wicked" is exactly 666.

Mordecai is a type of the Lord Jesus Christ in His coming glorious exaltation. The complete triumph of the Jews over their enemies, the joy and peace, recorded at the close of this book, are typical of the time when Christ reigns on earth. We give at the close of each chapter hints on the typical and dispensational application which can be made of this history.

Analysis and Annotations

The Banquets and Queen Vashti Disowned

CHAPTER 1

1. The first feast of the king (1:1-4)
2. The king's feast unto all the people (1:5-8)
3. The queen's feast for the women (1:9)
4. The queen's refusal to appear at the king's feast (1:10-12)
5. The queen put away (1:13-22)

Verses 1-4. King Ahasuerus, one of the leading characters of this book, is known in history as Xerxes I. The name Ahasuerus is an appellative, which means the chief king, or the king of all kings. Xerxes, the son of Darius Hystaspes, bore this title, king of kings. This title is also given to him in the cuneiform inscriptions. One of these reads as follows: "I, the mighty king, king of kings, king of populous countries, king of this great and mighty earth, far and near." His dominion extended from East to West, even from India unto Ethiopia. He had a universal kingdom. The capital of his empire was Shushan, which had a beautiful situation surrounded by high mountains, traversed by streams and abounding in a luxurious vegetation. Since the time of King Darius it became the residence of the Persian kings. The word "palace" is better translated by fortress or castle. And in the third year of his reign he made the great feast unto all his princes, and his servants, and all the nobles of Persia and Media were before him. He then showed the riches of his glorious kingdom and entertained the nobles and princes for six months.

Verses 5-8. This sumptuous feast was followed by a second banquet to which all the inhabitants of the capital were invited. It was held in the garden of the palace and lasted for seven days. The decorations were in white, green, blue, fastened with cords of fine linen and purple to rings of silver and pillars of marble. Upon a pavement of red, white, blue, and black marble (a mosaic floor) stood the couches of gold and silver. The royal wine was served out of vessels of gold not two of which were alike. The king displayed his enormous wealth and his abundant possessions. "And the wine of the kingdom was in abundance, according to the bounty of the king." And there was perfect freedom; each could drink to his heart's content. The king had instructed the officers "that they should do according to every man's pleasure."

Verse 9. Queen Vashti (Vashti means "beautiful woman") is now introduced. She made a separate feast for the women in the royal house which belonged to her husband, the king. Such feasts were frequently given by royal women of the East. Nothing is said how long her feast lasted.

Verses 10-12. The king's heart being merry with wine, he commanded his seven chamberlains to bring Vashti in her royal apparel to the feast, so that the peoples and the princes could admire her great beauty. The seven chamberlains were eunuchs who held important offices. Mehuman was the chief officer; Biztha, according to the meaning of his name, the treasurer; Harbona, the chief of the bodyguard; Bigath, who had charge over the female apartments; Abagtha, the chief baker; Zethar, the chief butler, and Carcas, the chief commander of the castle. These dignitaries were sent to accompany the queen to the feast of Ahasuerus. She refused to obey the king's command. Her refusal has been differently interpreted. According to Persian custom the Persian king held all for slaves except the legitimate wife. Was it in defiance of the king's order or out of self respect? She may have refused to show that she could not be dictated to by a drunken husband and that she was unwilling to show herself in the midst of revelry. Perhaps she did not care to come because she had a feast of her own. Then the king became extremely angry.

Verses 13-22. At once the wise men were called, the astrologers, the magi and sorcerers (Dan 2:2). His privy council consisted of seven princes, the princes of Persia and Media, who were next to the king, sat with him and the wise men to take up this serious matter. The question is, "What shall we do unto the Queen Vashti according to law, because she had not done the bidding of the king Ahasuerus by the chamberlains?" The case is thus turned over by the king into the hands of the wise men and the seven princes. These decide that Vashti has wronged the king and furthermore by her refusal had set a dangerous example to all the subjects of the king. Much contempt and wrath would follow throughout the empire. They advise that Vashti is to lose her royal estate, that she be put away. The king sanctions it and issued at the same time a decree to be published throughout his great kingdom that all wives should honor their husbands. The Persian kings were great autocrats and ruled with an iron hand. Their laws were irrevocable. "It is certainly no fable which is told of Xerxes, viz., that when the inundation of the Hellespont had destroyed all bridges, he gave order that it should be beaten with rods for disobedience (Herodotus 7:35). But it was more easy for him to beat the sea than to obtain that which his edict demanded."

The letters were dispatched by the excellent postal service, which according to the historian Herodotus, Persia possessed. Memucan had brought about the downfall of the queen; she disappears completely. Jewish tradition gives several reasons why Memucan was so hostile to Vashti. One is that his own wife had not been invited to Vashti's feast and another, because he wanted his own daughter promoted and become the queen.

Typical Application

The Persian king claimed the title King of Kings, which belongs only to the Lord Himself. The great feast which he made reminds us of another feast which the Lord has spread. Ahasuerus' feast was on the third year of his reign and appointed to show the riches of his kingdom and the honor of his excellent majesty. The gospel feast to which God invites, is prepared in His Son, who died and was raised on the *third day,* and this feast shows forth exceeding riches of His grace in kindness towards us. And those who accept become partakers of the heavenly calling, nobles and princes, who shall reign with Him in His coming kingdom. The invitation is, "Come for all things are now ready." There is enough for all; enough to fill to overflowing. The wine is the symbol of joy; it cheereth God and man (Judges 9:13). As the king had his joy with his subjects in this earthly feast, so God rejoices in those who come to the table of His love, and those who accept His invitation rejoice in Him. The couches of gold and silver at the King's feast were for rest. Gold and silver are symbolical of righteousness and redemption, and these are the couches, the resting places for the believer. And as Ahasuerus invited all to come to his feast, with no other conditions, but to come, so God wants all men to be saved and offers the riches of His grace without money and without price. While the Persian king displayed the glories of his great kingdom, God displays the glory of His grace.

In Vashti we see a type of the refusal of the invitation. She had been invited to come and grace the feast with her presence; she would not come. It reminds us of the parable of our Lord, in which He speaks of the great supper, a symbol of the gospel, and the bidden guests who made excuses for not coming. She had her own feast, which she probably would not leave. How many there are who refuse the gospel invitation because they love their own things best. And Vashti is banished. She is put away. And this is the siner's fate who refuses to obey the gospel of Jesus Christ.

Vashti too may be taken as a type of professing Christendom, those who have the form of godliness and deny the power thereof, whose god is their belly and who are the enemies of the cross, disobedient to God. Some day Christendom will be disowned by the Lord; He will spew Laodicea out of His mouth. Then the King of Kings will call another to take the place of apostate Christendom.

Esther Chosen Queen and Mordecai's Discovery

CHAPTER 2

1. The suggestion (2:1-4)
2. Mordecai and Esther introduced (2:5-7)
3. Esther brought to the king's house (2:8-11)
4. Esther chosen as queen (2:12-18)
5. Mordecai's discovery and exposure of the plot (2:19-23)

Verses 1-4. This probably did not happen immediately after the feast. We learn this from verse 16 in this chapter. He took Esther in the place of Vashti in the seventh year of his reign, but the feast described in the opening chapter happened in the third year. About four years elapsed. During these years, profane history tells us, Ahasuerus (Xerxes I), undertook a campaign against Greece with which many misfortunes were connected. He must have returned exhausted and unhappy. Then his conscience spoke. He probably missed the companionship of Vashti and he remembered her and what was decreed against her. But why did the monarch not take Vashti back into favor and forgive her, if remorse troubled him? As nothing more is said of Vashti it is more than probable that she was put to death. Perhaps the unfortunate war, the great losses he had sustained, were looked upon by the king as being the punishment for his drunken wrath against the queen. Then the courtiers made their suggestions which is in fullest keeping with the customs of Persia and still practised by oriental sultans and shahs. Fair young virgins are to be brought to the harem, the house of the women, under the custody of Hegai, the king's chamberlain and keeper of the women. The king was well pleased with this suggestion.

"One cannot but admire the simple, quiet historical style of our narrative. Laying aside all the reports which only would prolong our way of coming to the essential part of the contents of the book, there is nothing omitted which would contribute to the historical and psychological introduction and illustration. How much is necessary to happen before Israel could have ready help in time of need! What great things, according to the external appearance, must precede, in order to make it possible that a Jewish girl by the influence of her charms ascend the throne of the Persian Empire! The great conference of all the officers of the state, the dreadful war with Greece, and the unfortunate issue of the same, were they not in the hands of Providence so many stepping stones in the path of Esther's ascendancy? In order to replace the loss of Vashti, a woman of equal endowments must be sought for the king, wherever and however it might be! How many things must subserve to the frustration of Haman's wicked plan! The wrath of Xerxes against Greece, and his wrath against his wife. Court intrigues against the powerful influences of a wife, and the vain conceit of offended sovereignty? First drunkenness, then homicidal passion, then new excited sensuality, were the sad instruments which preceded Israel's redemption.

"When the people were delivered, they could well be penitent when they considered the way in which Vashti—though not herself guiltless—was one of the main causes of their deliverance. And if deep penitence must have resulted from the reflection that a woman like Vashti had to die a violent death in order that the people of God should live,—what kind of penitence must the thought call forth when we remember that Christ gave His Life in order that Israel and the Gentiles might live" (Professor P. Cassel).

Verses 5-7. These verses introduce us now to the leading actors in this book. Mordecai, the Jew, was the son of Jair, the son of Shimei, the son of Kish, a Benjamite; who had been carried away from Jerusalem with the captives which had been carried away with Jechoniah king of Judah, whom Nebuchadnezzar the king of Babylon had carried away.

Here we face one of the inconsistencies charged by higher criticism. But their mistake is quite apparent. Then claim that Mordecai belonged to the captives carried away by Nebuchadnezzar. Then they say, that being the case Mordecai must have been over 130 years old and Esther at least 70 years. But does it say that Mordecai was carried away at the time of King Jechoniah? It was not Mordecai who was carried away but his great-grandfather Kish. "The clear and instructive intentions of the historian in this genealogical passage are evident. He points out, through the enumeration of the four generations from Kish to Mordecai, the time which elapsed since the banishment of Jechoniah, which took place before the destruction of the temple. The period of about 120 or more years which since then elapsed to the sixth year of Xerxes are exactly expressed by the four generations. We have also some intimation concerning the period of the narrative, which is assigned to the reign of Xerxes I. That Kish was a Benjamite, is only told for the purpose of distinguishing him from other men with the same name who belonged to the tribe of Levi. One might have thought it impossible that Biblical expositors should commit the mistake of making the information concerning the exile of Jechoniah refer to Mordecai himself—an idea for which there is neither textual nor historical foundation, but rather both against it" (Professor Cassel). Mordecai had brought up Hadassah. She was an orphan, fair of form and good of countenance, his uncle's daughter. Mordecai had adopted her. Hadassah means "myrtle" and Esther "star." Critics have identified the name Esther with Babylonian goddess Isthar (similar to Ashtoreth), and they also claim that Hadassah was the Babylonian title for the same goddess. But such statements are mere inventions.

Verses 8-11. Esther on account of her great beauty was taken with the many other virgins in obedience to the King's command. Jewish tradition informs us that Mordecai, her guardian and second father, had kept her concealed, in order not to be obliged to deliver her to the royal agents, but people who knew her, and who had not seen her for some time drew the attention of the agents to the concealment. She with the others is placed in charge of Hegai the keeper of women. In all we see the hand of the Lord preparing step by step the help needed for the preservation and deliverance of His people during the approaching crisis. And Esther pleased Hegai; he showed her kindness. This kindness was expressed in furnishing her the means of improving her appearance, such as cosmetics and perfumes, according to Oriental customs. Then she received no doubt beautiful garments and jewelry to enhance her person still more. Then the best place in the house of the women was given to her and the seven maids who waited on her. (Very interesting and curious is the Jewish tradition concerning these seven servants. This tradition as preserved in the Targumim makes their names to correspond with the work of the six days of creation. Thus the fourth maid-servant's name was "Starlight" because on the fourth day the heavenly bodies came into view. Remarkable is the name of the maid who attended her on the sixth day—Friday; her name was "Lamb." On the seventh day, the Sabbath, the servant's name, who waited on her was "Rest": she reminded Esther of the Sabbath. And the Servant who attended her after the day after the Sabbath (Our Lord's day) bore the name of the mystical bird Phoenix, the symbol of light, rising out of the fire and out of death. It is certainly interesting, to say the least, to find such traditional statements.)

And Esther had not showed her people and her kindred. This was done on the advice of Mordecai. This has been characterized as deception, extraordinary adroitness, and cowardice. It was neither. Divine Providence ordered it thus. Inasmuch as Esther's parents were dead such concealment of nationality was not difficult; had her parents lived it would have been next to impossible. Had it been known that she belonged to the alien race, intrigues for her destruction would have soon been set afoot. Haman's wicked endeavour may even then have been in process of planning. Mordecai walking daily before the court of the women's house, proves his great concern for his adopted daughter.

Verses 12-18. The description of verses 12-14 is a perfect picture of Persian customs and the licentiousness of Persian and other Oriental rulers. In due time Esther's turn came to be presented to the king. "She required nothing." Professor Cassel in his exposition gives the best exposition of this statement. The other women could not find enough artificial means with which to make an impression upon the king. But Esther cared nothing about these things. She had no such ambitious desires. Her heart did not burn to become something illustrious, yet unbecoming to a Jewess. Reluctantly she must have left her home, and reluctantly she must have put on the ornaments. She was wanted, and was ordered to appear, and therefore she obeyed Hegai and allowed herself to be prepared for the occasion. She was compelled to be there, while no doubt in heart she detested the whole affair.

She was brought in to the king. Attracted by her beauty he set the royal crown upon her head and the Jewish maiden became queen in the place of Vashti. This took place in the month Tebeth in the seventy year of the reign of Ahasuerus.

Then a great feast was made, even Esther's feast, a release was made, probably a release of prisoners and taxes and gifts were bestowed. God in His providence.

Verses 19-23. This paragraph contains another important providential event which in the subsequent history plays a very leading part. The opening words of verse 19 have been pronounced obscure by critics. "And when the virgins were gathered together the second time." Jewish expositors have explained this as meaning a conspiracy, that the enemies of the new queen had collected more virgins so that in some way Esther might be eclipsed and placed into the background. It is claimed by others that the words "the second time" should be omitted from the text as there is some doubt about them. If this is done the statement would then refer to the gathering of the virgins mentioned in the eighth verse of the chapter. But the suggestion that the second gathering was an act of conspiracy might be the true meaning; it would show the purpose of the unseen enemy and it also explains the watchfulness of Mordecai. He sat at the king's gate. It was according to oriental cutom a place of public resort, where news was heard and conversation with friends and others were carried on. The suggestion by some that Mordecai sat in the king's gate because he was an official of the government must be dismissed as incorrect.

Verse 20 informs us of two interesting facts. Esther did not disclose her nationality and she continued in humble obedience to her foster father as if she were still under his roof and not the great queen. The royal glory and dignity which surrounded her on all sides had not affected her in the least. She had not forgotten that the whole royalty was not a matter of pleasure to her, but only an act of obedience, the providential purpose of which she did not know, but which she found out afterward. Her interest was with Mordecai outside and not with the royal splendour inside.

Let us note the providential leading in all this. If Esther had revealed her connection, if it had become known that Mordecai at the gate was her uncle and she his adopted daughter, he would not have remained in the obscure position before the gate. Then the conspirators would have been cautious and not spoken within the hearing of such a person so closely related to the queen. The knowledge of the planned attempt upon the life of the King Mordecai owed to the fact that nobody knew who he was and therefore paid no attention to him.

The conspirators were Bigthan and Teresh. They sought to lay hands on the king. According to Jewish tradition they intended to put a venomous reptile in the king's cup when he was about to drink. The plot was overheard by Mordecai who at once communicated the fact to Esther and she told the king of it in the name of Mordecai. She did so guided by the divine hand, which is so evident in this remarkable history. The plot is at once investigated and the report is found true. The conspirators were hanged and the event is historically recorded in the book of the Chronicles. (King Ahasuerus, Xerxes, lost his life by assassination in 465 B.C. Artaban, the commander of his cavalry, conspired with Mithridates, his confidential chamberlain, who admitted him into the king's bedroom, and Artaban stabbed him to death while he slept.)

Esther had saved the king's life by giving him the report of Mordecai. And Mordecai received no reward. His faithfulness was evidently forgotten; but God had ordered it all.

Typical Applications

Dispensationally Esther typifies the Jewish remnant, which will be called by the King of Israel, our Lord, when Gentile-Christendom has been disowned and set aside for its unfaithfulness, as Vashti was set aside. The parable of the good and the wild olive tree in Romans 11 is thus illustrated by Vashti and Esther. The branches of the wild olive tree—professing Christendom (but not the true Church) which were grafted in upon the root of the good olive tree (Israel and the Abrahamic covenant) on account of their failure will be cut out and cast aside. The broken off branches (the remnant of Israel) will be put back upon the root of the good olive tree. (See annotations on Romans 11 or for a fuller exposition read "The Jewish Question," an exposition of Romans 11 by A. C. Gaebelein.) This remnant will then be brought into definite relationship with the Lord, pass through the period of the great tribulation, foreshadowed in Haman's wicked plot, and then receive the kingdom, be delivered and have part in the kingdom, as it was the case with Esther, Mordecai and the Jews at Shushan.

The gospel application is also of interest. The humble Jewish girl is raised to the place of a queen, to the place beside the King. She did not seek that place. It never entered into her mind to receive such a place. She was sought for. All this illustrates the gospel by which the beggar upon the dunghill is raised to sit amongst princes and to inherit the throne of glory (1 Samuel 2). She, who was a foreigner, becomes married to the king, to share his glory, his riches and his honors. And so the believing sinner becomes one spirit with the Lord, a member of His body "flesh of His flesh and bone of His bones," to share His eternal glory and His eternal riches.

HAMAN AND HIS WICKED PLOT

CHAPTER 3

1. The promotion of Haman and Mordecai's faithfulness (3:1-6)
2. Haman's proposal and the King's assent (3:7-11)
3. The proclamation of death (3:12-15)

Verses 1-6. How long after these things the history of this chapter came to pass is not definitely stated. It probably happened after a short interval. We are now introduced to Haman, the Son of Hammedatha the Agagite. Him the king promoted and set his seat above all the princes. The tracing of this man's name is of interest. Its meaning is "A magnificent one." Philologists derive it from the Persian god Haoma or Hom, who was thought to be a spirit, possessing life-giving power. There can be no doubt that his name has a religious sentiment connected with and his activity shows zeal in religious things. What interests us the most is that he was a descendant of Agag, the king of Amalek (1 Sam. 15:8) who descended from Esau, Jacob's brother and enemy. Amalek is always the bitter enemy of Israel. His final overthrow will come with the second coming of Christ. Thus Balaam announced in his prophetic utterance. When the sceptre at last rises out of Israel to smite the nations, then Amalek will find his end. "And when he looked on Amalek, he took up his parable and said, Amalek was the first of the nations, but his latter end shall be that he perish forever" (Numbers 24:17-20). This Haman, the Amalekite, is later called "the Jew's enemy" (verse 10). He foreshadows that final enemy, who arises to trouble Israel and attempts their extermination before the King of Israel appears. The dispensational and typical applications at the close of this chapter deal more fully with this interesting character.

And all the king's servants bowed down and did him reverence. They paid to him the honor of a god. Nearly all these Oriental rulers claimed divinity. Artaban is saying to Themistocles, according to Plutarch "The important thing with us Persians is that a king is worshipped and looked upon as the very image of God." As the king's representative this worship was extended to Haman. But Mordecai did not bow down because such reverence involved the recognition of a false god and was against the commandment of God. Mordecai may have remembered Isaiah's great prediction, "To Me every knee shall bow and every tongue shall swear." According to Jewish tradition Haman wore on his coat the image of an idol and that this was the reason why Mordecai refused. The king's servants warned Mordecai and when this was not heeded they told Haman. What a noble figure! In the midst of the worshipping servants bowing deep before Haman stands erect Mordecai, the Jew. He manifested faith in God. He trusted in Him who had delivered Daniel's companion out of the fiery furnace, when they refused to worship the image set up by Nebuchadnezzar. He trusted the same God who had stopped the lion's mouths when Daniel would not pay divine honors to Darius, the Persian king.

And when Haman discovers that Mordecai was a Jew and that his refusal was not wilful disobedience but inspired by faith in God, in obedience to His law, the Amalekite hate is stirred up in his wicked heart, and he became full of wrath. An unseen being, he who is the murderer from the beginning, told him to make this occasion for destroying all the Jews in the Persian Empire.

Verses 7-11. And now Haman waits on his unseen master, the devil. They cast the lot before Haman, from day to day, and from month to month, to the twelfth month, which is the month Adar. He wanted to find out the month which would be best suited for the execution of his wicked plot. Soothsaying, familiar spirits, asking the dead, divining by the flight of birds or by the liver of a slain animal, prognostigators and astrologers, flourished among the Egyptians, the Babylonians, the Persians and all other pagan nations. Behind it all is the Devil and his fallen angels. And these things are still practised, not alone in China and India, but in the very midst of professing Christendom. Spiritism, the worst form of demonism, is ever on the increase. Astrology, asking the dead, consulting the demons, casting the lot, getting messages through the so-called "ouija board" (in use in China, the land of demon possessions, for over 2000 years) is made use of today by countless thousands among the supposedly "Christian nations." We see what kind of progress the world has made. The same superstitions, the same evils morally and in religious matters, the same demon powers whose fellowship the greater part of the race invites, as 3000 and more years ago.

Through the lot he imagines that the twelfth month, the Jewish month Adar, is the month to execute the plot. Jewish tradition explains this in the following way: "When he came to make observations in the month Adar, which comes under the zodiacal sign of the fish, Haman exclaimed, "Now they will be caught by me like the fish of the sea." But he did not notice that the children of Joseph are compared in the Scripture to the fish of the sea, as it is written: And let them multiply as the fish in the midst of the earth" (Genesis 48:16; marginal reading).

And now he approacheth the king who was ignorant of Haman's dark counsel. He tells the king of a certain people which inhabit his kingdom. He avoids mentioning their names. If he had the plot would not have succeeded for Xerxes must have been well acquainted with the illustrious history of the Jews and he knew that ever since Cyrus the policy of the Persian Empire had been the protection of the Jews. Haman's accusation is twofold. First: Their laws are diverse from those of every people. Second: Neither keep they the king's laws. And then the verdict: It is not for the king's profit to suffer them. They were a separate people, following their God-given law. It was this religious side which stirred up the hatred of Satan and through Haman he urges now the wholesale murder of the race. And Haman like his dark master, Satan, was cunning enough to anticipate an objection from the side of the king. Would not his kingdom suffer financially if a whole people is wiped out? To remove this financial consideration he offers to pay 10,000 talents of silver for the desired slaughter of the Jews (about 20 million dollars). With it he tempted the avarice of the king and at the same time tickled his pride by implying that it must be a trifle to him to lose a whole people who were only worth the price of 10,000 talents. And Haman probably speculated that this great sum he offered, the greater the sum was the more flattering it would appear to the fancy of the king to waive it. Oriental monarchs were known for doing such things in a boastful spirit. This Haman knew well.

Then the king gave him his ring. It was a ring to seal a document. Every ring had a seal. The transfer of the royal ring with the royal seal denoted the transfer of kingly authority and power to the recipient. Haman was therefore invested with royal authority. The haughtiness of the king appears now. Not alone does he turn over his signet-ring but he also makes Haman a present of the enormous sum he had offered to the king. In cold blood Xerxes gives over the to him unknown people into the hands of this wicked enemy.

Verses 12-15. A great activity is here described. An Empire-wide proclamation, a veritable proclamation of death was issued. The king's scribes were called on the 13th day of the month. Research has established the fact that the 13th day of the month was called by the Persians Tir (the meaning of which is "lot"). All the king's satraps, the governors of every province, the princes of every people who had become identified with the Persian empire were notified in different languages of what should take place on the 13th day of the month Adar. The proclamation was written in the name of the king and sealed with his ring in Haman's possession. "And letters were sent by posts into all the king's provinces, to destroy, to slay, and to cause to perish, all Jews, both young and old, little children and women, in one day, even on the thirteenth day of the twelfth month, which is the month Adar, and to take the spoil of them for a prey." And this horrible decree was sent in haste throughout the land. The king and Haman sat down to a banquet, while the capital, Shushan, was perplexed and deeply stirred.

Typical Application

Haman illustrates the coming man of sin, the beast of Revealtion 13. As remarked in the introduction, his title "Haman the wicked" (7:6) represents in the numerical value of the Hebrew letters which compose this title the number 666. (See Revelation 13:18.) This future coming one will be like Haman the enemy of the Jews and one of Satan's masterpieces. Haman was to be worshipped and revered. And the man of sin will demand divine worship and with the help of the first beast, the little horn of Daniel 7, he seeks to exterminate the Jews. He will manifest greater cunning than Haman and use the political power to accomplish his purpose. Mordecai in his refusal is a type of the godly Jewish remnant to worship the man of sin.

The proclamation of death pronounced upon a whole race of people, everyone doomed to death, none exempted, typifies the condition in which the whole race is spiritually. The law on account of sin is such a proclamation. The soul that sinneth shall die. The wages of sin is death. The helpless condition in which the death doomed Jews found themselves is a picture of the helpless condition of man as a sinner. Nothing the Jews did could save them; no weeping nor pleading could change things. All this may be enlarged upon and helpfully applied to man's condition as a sinner.

The Consternation of the Jews—Mordecai and Esther

CHAPTER 4

1. The great lamentations of the Jews (4:1-3)
2. Esther's discovery (4:4-9)
3. Esther's helplessness (4:10-12)
4. Mordecai's answer (4:13-14)
5. Esther's decision (4:15-17)

Verses 1-3. When Mordecai heard of what had been done and the plan to exterminate his people became known to him he rent his clothes. This and the putting on of sackcloth and ashes were the outward expressions of the most intense grief. The sackcloth was a coarse haircloth of a black color. Then his bitter cry and wailing was heard in the midst of the city. Because of the sackcloth, which was also used as a sign of mourning over the dead among the Persians, it was regarded as unclean, and inasmuch as the palace of the king was looked upon as a clean and holy place, Mordecai could not enter the king's gate. He had to stand outside the wall. And throughout the provinces as the proclamation became known and was read by the condemned race, there was the same weeping and wailing with fasting. Prayer unquestionably was also connected with this grief.

Verses 4-9. Esther in the secluded portion of the palace knew nothing of the great edict which had gone forth. Her maids and chamberlains, whom she may have used to keep in touch with her uncle, then informed her that Mordecai was missing inside of the gate and that he was sitting outside in a most pitiable condition, weeping and wailing. How this report must have shocked Esther! She was exceedingly grieved and then sent raiment to Mordecai. This was according to Persian custom in connection with mourning over the dead that the nearest relations should send the mourner new garments, to put these on instead of the sackcloth. The Jews must have conformed to some of these customs. Esther thought that some one of the family of Mordecai had died. But Mordecai refused the garments for he was not mourning over death. This must have mystified Esther still more. She therefore sent Hathach, one of the king's chamberlains, her personal attendant, to Mordecai to find out the cause of his mourning.

And Hathach went forth. Mordecai told him of Haman's plot. As he possessed a copy of the decree he gave it to Hathach to deliver to Esther and then Mordecai's message to Esther. "To charge her that she should go in unto the king, to make supplication unto him, and to make request before him, for her people." He did not say "for this people" but "for her people." This made known to Hathach Esther's Jewish origin. Mordecai knew the great favor Esther had found before the king and he hoped that her supplication would avert the doom of the race. There is nothing said of Mordecai calling upon God, no record of his supplications to the God of Abraham. Undoubtedly he did call on Him. This is in accord with the character of the people; they are seen as out of the land and out of touch with the Lord. Yet Jehovah in unchanging mercy watcheth over them. And Hathach delivered the message.

Verses 10-12. Esther sent the answer. Mordecai heard the alarming news that the king was unapproachable. Esther herself had not seen his face for a whole month. To enter the king's presence unbidden would mean sure death. Death to all "except such to whom the king shall hold out the golden sceptre, that he may live." Esther thus informed Mordecai that she is subject to the same law, and if she transgresseth it, no exception would be made, though she be the queen.

Verses 13-14. Mordecai's answer to Esther is a sublime one. It would have been quite natural for Mordecai to say "If thou canst not save all the people, at least save me, and the house of thy father, for thou belongest to the unassailable house of the king." He does not think of his personal interest and safety; it is the salvation of his people which is upon his heart. He knows that Esther is in a position not only to be saved herself, but also to save her people. He gives her to understand if she does not act now and if she holds her peace deliverance for the Jews would be granted through another source. She would lose a great opportunity and she and her father's house would perish. In these words Mordecai expressed his deep conviction that the Jewish people cannot perish. He knew the history of the past and trusted God that He would find a way out at this time also. And he believed more than this, that Providence had put her on the throne just to effect the deliverance: "Who knoweth whether thou art not come to the kingdom for such a time as this?"

"The answer of Mordecai is a masterpiece of eloquence. He who loved and cherished Esther as a daughter, seeks now that she should risk her life for the deliverance of Israel. He wills it, because he believes in the deliverance; because he draws from the history of Israel the assurance that as a race they cannot become extinct, and because he sees in the exaltation of Esther the divine purpose to use her in the deliverance. He encourages her to act and to risk her life and this he did by stimulating her faith in an overruling providence and that therefore she had nothing to fear."

Verses 15-17. She responded to this eloquent appeal; her believing heart had laid hold on the suggestion of her uncle. The Jews are to be gathered together in Shushan, she requests, for three days and three nights, neither to eat nor to drink. She would do the same with her maidens. "And so will I go in unto the king, which is not according to the law, and if I perish, I perish."

Fasting in the Old Testament is always the symbolic form of prayer; it cannot be disassociated from prayer. In giving this command she expressed her dependence on God and put Him first before attempting to go in to the king. And then her noble word—If I perish, I perish. Her faith measured up to Mordecai's expectation. She is ready to sacrifice herself in order to save her people. How it reminds us of Him who did more than say, "If I perish, I perish," who gave Himself and took upon Himself the curse of the law. And Mordecai did according to all that Esther had commanded him.

Typical Application

In the weeping, and wailing of Mordecai and the Jews, the rent clothes, the sackcloth and the ashes, we have a prophetic foreshadowing of the earnest turning to God of the Jewish remnant during the end of this age. How vividly Joel speaks of this man in the name of Jehovah. "Therefore also now saith the Lord, turn ye even to me with all your heart, and with fasting and with weeping, and with mourning (Joel 2:12). And then comes for them the final deliverance as revealed by Joel and foreshadowed in the deliverance of the book of Esther. Mordecai's faith and Esther's noble decision are equally typical of the trust and confidence of that godly portion of the Jewish people who will pass through the time of Jacob's trouble (Jeremiah 30:4) and who will be delivered out of it.

As we pointed out in the previous chapter, the great proclamation typifies what God has said as to the race of sinners, that the wages of sin is death. "Cursed is every one that continueth not in all things that are written in the book of the law to do them." The whole race is therefore under condemnation. And the Jews read this awful proclamation and reading they believed, and believing what was written they gave expression to their grief in fasting and turning to God. Alas! that God's proclamation telling the sinner of his dreadful condition, of the death and wrath which hangs over him is less believed than the proclamation of the Persian enemy of the Jews. Yet to know and to enjoy real salvation and deliverance, the realization of our real condition as lost sinners is eminently necessary.

As already stated, Esther is a faint type of our Lord in that she was willing to sacrifice herself in behalf of her people; while He gave that blessed life and died for that nation (John 12:27).

ESTHER AND THE KING AND HAMAN'S DELUSION

CHAPTER 5

1. Esther before the king and her request (5:1-8)
2. Haman's delusion (5:9-14)

Verses 1-8. On the third day Esther put on her royal apparel, a significant day in Scripture as we point out in the typical application of this chapter. The days of fasting and agony were passed and she is seen no longer attired in sackcloth but in royal garments. It is of great interest that Rabbinical exposition (Midrash) gives a tradition that in her great anxiety and anguish of soul she uttered the opening sentence of Psalm 22, "My God, my God, why hast Thou forsaken me?" She made use of the very words which the most ancient Jewish exponents understood as referring to the Messiah and which came from the lips of our Lord when He bore our sins in His body on the tree.

Clothed in her majestic robes, probably wearing the crown the king had placed upon her head, she entered in and stood in the inner court, which was the entrance gate to the pillared hall at the opposite end of which the king sat on his throne. The king saw her and she obtained favour—grace—in his sight.

And the king held out the golden sceptre which was in his hand. So Esther drew near, and touched the top of the sceptre. The beautiful typical meaning of this the reader will find at the close of this chapter. The royal sceptre, the emblem of royal power is extended towards her, the sign of the king's favour, and she touched the sceptre. (The Latin translation—the Vulgate—translates "she kissed the sceptre.") In touching the sceptre she expressed her need of it. She touched the royal sceptre of power and authority—because from this she seeks and expects deliverance. And it was the touch of faith. And so at once the king recognizing her action and what was behind it said, "What wilt thou, Queen Esther? And what is thy request? It will be given thee even to the half of the kingdom." Instead of asking for a big gift she requests that the king and Haman be present at a banquet she had prepared. The initials in the Hebrew of the sentence "Let the king and Haman come" spell the word Yahweh, which is Jehovah. This the rabbis used to prove that the name of God is mentioned in this book. While this is merely fanciful, we know that Jehovah is revealed in the manifestation of His power in behalf of His people. It must have mystified the king that such a request came from Esther. But she made the petition for she wanted Haman to be present when she uncovered the plot to the king. And the king urged haste upon Haman. He was hurrying to his doom. At the banquet he repeated his question to find out what her petition was. It was customary among oriental kings that petitions were offered and then easily granted at banquets. He repeats his offer also that even if it is the half of the kingdom, it is to be performed. This benevolence of the king proved to the queen his affection for her and hence the success of her great mission. She still holds back her petition. She invites to another banquet on the next day when she promises to make known her petition. In this she exhibited great wisdom. She made the king curious and expectant.

Verses 9-14. Haman's pride produces delusion. He congratulates himself over the honour the Queen has done him. It was a day of joy and gladness of heart. And how he was moved with indignation when he beholds again Mordecai standing up and not doing him the honour which in his delusion he thinks is now more due him than before. Why did he not kill him at once? According to Persian law one who sat at the king's gate put himself under the protection of the king. As long as he was there he was safe. Now this being the case, if Haman had killed Mordecai, his enemies would have reported the matter to the king that he had murdered one who had placed himself under the protecting wings of the king, who had appealed for protection. Haman knew the possible consequences. Therefore he fetched his friends and his wife Zeresh. He gives a review of his riches and his honors including the latest of being invited by the queen. Then he tells of his vexation. "Yet all this availeth me nothing, so long as I see Mordecai the Jew sitting at the king's gate." Then comes from his friends and his wife the advice. The suggested gallows are made to hang Mordecai and Haman waits, perhaps impatiently, for the morrow when he would go in merrily to the king and request the execution of the Jew. In his delusion and pride he did not know that he built the gallows for himself.

Typical Application

This chapter is especially rich in its symbolical, typical and dispensational meaning. It was on the third day that Esther came forth to enter into the presence of the king. The third day throughout Scripture is the day of resurrection and life, the day of blessing and glory. On the third day in the first chapter of Genesis the submerged earth came out of the waters and brought forth its beautiful vegetation. This speaks of resurrection and it is the first time this type is found in the Word of God. Many times after that the third day in the history of Israel is mentioned, as well as the third time, and each time it carries with it the same lesson. (See 2 Kings 20:5; Jonah and his experiences, etc.) All these passages are blessed types of Him who was raised on the third day after He finished the work the Father gave Him to do. And so is Esther a type. She passed typically through a death experience in her fasting, with deep anguish of soul. If I perish, I perish, she had said; ready to sacrifice herself. When she stands in her royal garments before the king on the third day with her death experience behind she reminds us of Him who left the grave behind and is now garbed in resurrection glory. The golden sceptre tells of divine righteousness, power and grace. That sceptre is extended to all who come to God in that blessed and worthy Name. We can come with boldness to the throne of grace, obtaining mercy and finding grace to help in time of need. And there are other gospel applications which we can make. Esther's entering in to the king was not according to law. Law excluded her from the presence of the king. So we are excluded from being in God's presence, because we are sinners. But love has made a way through the Beloved One in whom we are accepted. And the banquet which Esther made for the king was for more than giving refreshment to him who loved her, as we can refresh Him also. It was a banquet to expose the enemy, to stop his accusation and take his power away from him. And all this is graciously accomplished in a spiritual way through the cross and the resurrection of Christ.

If we look upon Esther as a type of the Jewish remnant we see in her fasting and agony the tribulation through which this remnant passeth. But there comes a third day. This prophecy declares. "After two days will He revive us; on the third day He will raise us up, and we shall live before Him" (Hosea 6:1). The third day will surely come when Israel will rise out of the dust and when the golden sceptre will be extended to His earthly people.

In Haman we see the arrogant pride of the enemy of God and the final enemy of the Jewish people. "Pride goeth before destruction, and a haughty spirit before a fall" (Prov. 16:18), was true of Haman, it is true of all who walk in pride and will finally be exemplified in the total defeat of him, who exalteth himself above all that is called God.

THE SLEEPLESS NIGHT AND MORDECAI'S EXALTATION

CHAPTER 6

1. The sleepless night (6:1-3)
2. The exaltation of Mordecai (6:4-11)
3. Haman anticipates his doom (6:12-14)

Verses 1-3. A sleepless night is the next event. The king wanted to sleep but sleep refused to come. What was the cause of his insomnia? Some say too much excitement and anxiety in connection with his kingdom; others that he was speculating on the petition the queen would make on the morrow. The ancient Jewish expositors say that God took his sleep away from him. And this is the correct answer. His wakefulness was ordered by God. Next God puts it into his heart to order the book of record of the chronicles to be brought so that they might be read to him, not to produce sleep but to spend the sleepless night in a profitable way. Once more we see the hand of God in directing the reading of the record of Mordecai's discovery of the plot against the king's life and how he had saved the king. The deed of Mordecai had been unrewarded through the wise purpose of the Lord; and now it is brought to light by the same providence. In that memorable, sleepless night the machinations of revenge, so finely spun in the dark, are suddenly arrested and their exposure becomes assured. And let us remember that the same providence still works, mysteriously and openly in the lives of God's people.

The king hears that Mordecai had not been rewarded. His pride and dignity were suddenly stirrred up. He felt it was not just that such a deed should go unrewarded. It must also have come to his mind that this Mordecai had not reminded the king of his deed, by sending a petition for a reward or by requesting a favour, so common in oriental life. He had kept silent.

Verses 4-11. The king must have been indignant that such a matter had been overlooked and he wants to have the matter rectified at once. He asks "Who is in the court?" Whosoever would be there would have to carry out the king's commission. He did not expect that Haman was waiting outside. Perhaps he also had a sleepless night, nervously excited as he thought that soon Mordecai would dangle from the gallows; and how he would enjoy the banquet of Esther on the same day. He was in a great hurry and desired that the execution of the despised Jew should take place in the early morning. All is working together and God's majestic hand is seen every step of the way! "Never was there exhibited a more frivolous and thoughtless judgment than that shown by many higher critics in their light estimation of the book of Esther. For surely there can be no more beautiful description of the impending dramatic catastrophe than that with which the whole of this book is full. At the moment when the mind of the king has but one thought, to compensate Mordecai with the long-merited honour and dignity, and so much the more because it ought to have been done long ago, at the very moment when he looks for a person to carry out his plans, just then, Haman appears on the scene" (Professor Cassel).

And the king asks Haman, "What shall be done unto the man whom the king delighteth to honour?" In his blind self-love, his deluded pride, Haman thought he was the man to whom the king would do still more honour. Well says a writer in the Talmud—"inasmuch as the writer of the book of Esther knew what was in Haman's heart, he must have been inspired in writing this account."

And pride fills his lips with an extraordinary demand. When his wicked lips spoke the words, he must have imagined himself clad in royal apparel riding the king's charger, wearing his crown, and thus led forth through the city, announced by the town-crier that he is the man whom the king delighteth to honour.

The king speaks: "Make haste and take the apparel and the horse, as thou hast said and do even so to Mordecai the Jew, that sitteth at the king's gate, let nothing fail of all thou hast spoken."What a thunderbolt this must have been for Haman! While he dreamt of his own honour and greatness he is suddenly awakened by the unalterable command of the king, whose word is law, to do all he had spoken to the man whom he hated and despised, whose death warrant he expected to have signed by the king. He could not tarry in the king's presence for the king demanded haste. He could not parley with the king; that would have been an insult. All that was left to Haman was to make haste and take the apparel and the horse to Mordecai. He arrayed him and then led him through the city and proclaimed before him the king's message. And Mordecai? His mouth must have been filled with laughter and with praises to his God, when his deadly enemy came to do him honour. How great was his triumph in the marvellous exaltation brought about by the keeper of Israel, who neither sleeps nor slumbers! The Jews read the entire book of Esther on the Purim feast. When the reader reaches this passage he reads the record with a raised and triumphant voice.

Verses 12-14. Mordecai is back at the gate; Haman in bitter disappointment, with evil forebodings, his head covered, the sign of grief, returns to his wife and friends. When they hear what happened they told him that his case would be hopeless. In the conflict between the Jew and the offspring of Amalek, victory is on the side of the Jew. (Exod. 17:16; Numb. 24:20; Deut. 25:17-19) And then the king's chamberlains knocked at the door to hurry Haman to Esther's banquet.

Typical Application

The great lesson of this chapter is the wonderful working of divine providence. Surely "God works in a mysterious way, His wonders to perform." And how He cares for His people and watcheth over them! He is still the same, for He is the Lord who changeth not.

And Mordecai stands out in this chapter as another type of our Lord. All the men of God in Old Testament history, in their humiliation and exaltation, like Joseph, Moses, David, etc., are types of the humiliation and exaltation of our Lord.

What was done to Mordecai will also be some future day the happy lot of Israel when they will be delivered out of the hand of their enemies.

THE SECOND BANQUET AND HAMAN'S MISERABLE END

CHAPTER 7

1. The second banquet and Esther's petition (7:1-4)
2. Haman's exposure (7:5-6)
3. Haman's miserable end (7:7-10)

Verses 1-4. Esther at this second feast knew that the God of her fathers was at work and that all the hatred against her race came not from the heart of the king, but centered in Haman. In the events of the sleepless night and what followed she must have seen the display of the hand of God. And now she utters her delayed petition. Her peititon is that her life may be spared as well as her people. How astonished the king must have looked as he gazed upon his beautiful wife and learned from her lips that her life was in danger. And still greater must have been his surprise when he hears, "For we are sold, I and my people, to be destroyed, to be slain, and to perish." What a scene! The handsome queen, her marvelous earnestness and eloquence in pleading for her life and for her people; the darkening, astonished countenance of the king, the blanching face of Haman and the others in the banquet hall in great excitement.

And her heart-rendering plea, perhaps mingled with tears wich coursed down her cheek, did not fail to produce the desired effect.

Verses 5-6. The king must have been more than astonished; he must have been angry. Who dared to plot against the life of the beautiful qeeen and deprive him of her? Who dared to sell her and her people for slaughter? Even then before he hears from Esther the name of the man, he must have realized, that the crouching Haman is the man. "Who is he, and where is he that durst presume in his heart to do so?" Her answer is brief but eloquent. With flashing eyes and pointing her finger to the guest at her side she said, "An adversary and an enemy, even this wicked Haman!" The scene is beyond comparison. Then Haman was afraid before the king and the queen. He anticipated the fearful storm which would break over his head.

Verses 7-10. The king arose in his wrath. Close to the banquet hall was the garden. There the king went in the heat of his wrath and the great excitement which had seized upon him and made him speechless. When an oriental king or sultan arises angry from his own table, then there is no mercy for him that causeth it. (See Rosenmueller *Oriental Studies on Esther.*) In the meantime Haman begs cowardly for his life. He must have fallen at her feet with weeping and wailing. And Esther did not open her lips. Then Haman in his agonizing plea falls upon the couch where Esther was. At that moment the king re-entered the banquet hall. He has regained his speech and when he beholds Haman on the couch he utters a word of bitter sarcasm, as if he had designs upon the honour of the queen. No sooner had the king spoken the word, the attending servants covered Haman's face. This was a Persian custom. The face of a criminal was covered to indicate that he was no longer worthy to behold the light and that darkness of death would be his lot.

The gallows which Haman had prepared for Mordecai is used for his own execution. Critics point out the statement that the gallows 50 cubits high (80 feet) stood in Haman's house and they raise the question "How could an 80 foot long pole be gotten into any one's house?" But the word gallows means in the Hebrew "tree." Probably a tree standing in the garden of Haman was made ready with a rope to hang the hated Jew. It is characteristic of the critics to take such minor things to discredit the accuracy of Scripture.

Typical Application

Haman illustrates the work and the ignominious end of the final Anti-christ who troubles Israel. Haman had almost succeeded. But when the proper moment came God acted in behalf of His people and Haman falls forever. So that coming man of sin will almost succeed, but in the end of the great tribulation, the final 1260 days or three years and a half, with which this age closes, the power of God will be displayed in the complete victory over this enemy of God and man. Haman's end came by the decree of the king and the Anti-christ will be destroyed by the coming of the King of kings and Lord of Lords.

Mordecai's Exaltation and the Second Proclamation

CHAPTER 8

1. Mordecai's exaltation (8:1-2)
2. Esther's second petition (8:3-8)
3. The second proclamation (8:9-14)
4. The joy of the Jews (8:15-17)

Verses 1-2. Esther the Queen receives from the king the possessions of Haman, the enemy of the Jews. Then she revealed what Mordecai was to her, her uncle and foster-father. The king had taken the signet-ring of authority from the hand of Haman. The same ring Mordecai received. Esther honoured her uncle by placing him over the house of Haman.

Verses 3-6. But while Mordecai had become the prime-minister of Persia, Haman the Agagite had been executed, and all his property given to the queen, the horrible decree still stood; the first proclamation was still in force. Something had to be done to complete the deliverance of her people. Her life and Mordecai's life had been spared, but what about her beloved people? It is true the fateful day was still in the future, but the evil decreed and not yet recalled had to be met in some way. Once more she enters into the presence of the king. Once more the king holds out the golden sceptre, from which we learn that his decree was still in force and that, therefore, Esther once more risked her life. But she knew he loved her. Knowing this she cast herself at his feet and besought him with tears to put away the mischief of Haman, and his devices he had devised against the Jews. Her pleading and her tears were not in vain. Her petition is that the letters of Haman, demanding the destruction of her people, should be reversed. "For how can I endure to see the evil that will come upon my people? or how can I endure the destruction of my kindred?" The king answers her. But the former decree cannot be revoked; it must stand. Laws made by Persian kings could not be altered or changed. (See Daniel 6:15.) A revocation of the edict is impossible and the former proclamation therefore stands. This Persian custom had for its foundation the idea that a "decree" must be looked upon in the light of an emanation from the king as a person with divine authority. But inasmuch as Mordecai had now the signet-ring, which authorized him to issue decrees in the name of the king, he could do anything he pleased and write to the Jews in the name of the king and this second proclamation would also be irrevocable.

Verses 7-14. Then followed a great activity. The scribes were called and Mordecai dictated the message. It was addressed to the governors and princes of the whole empire from India to Ethiopia and written in many languages. He wrote in the name of the king and sealed it with his ring. The letters were dispatched by posts on horseback, riding on swift steeds that were used in the king's service. The proclamation contained the following good news: "The king grants the Jews in every city to gather themselves together, and to stand for their life, to destroy, to slay, and to cause to perish, all the power of the people and province that would assault them, their little ones and women, and to take the spoil of them for a prey, upon one day in all the provinces of King Ahasuerus, that is upon the thirteenth day of the twelfth month, which is the month Adar." The proclamation of death stood, but alongside of it there was given a proclamation of life. They needed not to die. Their enemies were given into their hands. Acting upon this second proclamation, believing its contents, they learned that while the first decree stood and could not be revoked, the second decree set them free from death and gave them liberty.

Verses 15-17. How things had changed under God's merciful dealings with His people! When that first decree was issued Mordecai sat in sackcloth and ashes and all the Jews wept and wailed. But now when the second decree was announced Mordecai went forth from the presence of the king in royal apparel of blue, white and purple, the Persian colours. (They illustrate the ancient Persian view about the world. White the colour of light, blue, the sky, and purple was brought in connection with the sun.) On his head he had a great crown of gold. There was great joy in the city of Shushan. The Jews had light, and gladness, and joy, and glory. Throughout the vast kingdom there was nothing but joy. Furthermore many people became Jews.

Typical Application

In Mordecai's exaltation as given in this chapter, in Haman's possession handed over to the queen and her uncle, in the authority which both received, we have a fine foreshadowing of what will take place when the final Haman is overthrown. That will be when the times of the Gentiles are passed and the King, our Lord, has come back. Then Israel will get her great blessings, promised long ago by a covenant-keeping God.

Like it was in Mordecai's and Esther's day, the riches of the Gentiles will be given unto them. "Then thou shalt see, and flow together, and thine heart shall fear, and be enlarged; because the abundance of the sea shall be converted unto thee, the wealth of the Gentiles shall come unto thee" (Isaiah 60:5). Israel restored will then be the head of the nations and no longer the tail. As many people became Jews as recorded in the last verse of this chapter, so in that coming day, ten men out of all languages of the nations shall take hold of the skirt of a Jew and say, "we will go with you, for we have heard that God is with you" (Zech. 8:23). "And many nations shall be joined unto the Lord in that day" (Zech. 2:11). All this blessing for the Jews in Persia was brought about by the heroic deed of Esther, who passed through a great struggle, who risked her life that her people might be saved. And the promised blessings and glory can only come to the people Israel through Him who gave His life, the true King and Shepherd of Israel, the Lord Jesus Christ.

In gospel application the second decree or proclamation is of much interest. It typifies and illustrates the good news. As we saw, the first decree illustrates the sentence of death passed upon the whole race on account of sin. The second decree does not cancel the first, but declares that which liberates from death, sets free and gives power. And that is the good news as it is given in the cross of Christ. Death is met by death; the death of the Son of God in the sinner's place, bearing the curse, sets free from the law of sin and death. Thus the sinner's doom is fully met in the death of Christ. "This second decree has been nailed to the cross of

Christ, it has been revealed in His sacrificial death, written with His blood, sealed by His bowed head, uttered by His expiring cry. It has a twofold effect. First, the sinner who avails himself of it, who believes, is saved. It arrays all the forces of righteousness on his side and enables him to find his surest protection in that which but for the work of Christ must have condemned him. Then it puts him in a position to rise up against his enemies by whom as a captive he was enslaved and to lead his captivity captive. From the condemnation of the law and from the cruel dominion of sin believing sinners are equally delivered by the proclamation of the gospel in the cross of Christ, as the Jews had righteous power given to them over their enemies.

But faith was necessary for the Jews. They had to believe the second proclamation as they believed the first. Woe unto the Jews when that thirteenth day of the month Adar came and they acted not upon the second decree. Then the first decree would have been carried out upon their heads and they would have suffered death. So must the sinner believe the first decree—that death is sentence as a sinner; then he must believe the second decree "Christ died for the ungodly"—there is life in a look to the crucified One. And as the Jews had light, gladness, joy, and glory because they believed, even so he who believes the good news has salvation peace, joy and glory.

The Thirteenth Day of Adar and the Feast of Purim

CHAPTER 9

1. The resistance and victory of the Jews (9:1-11)
2. Esther's petition (9:12-16)
3. The institution of Purim (9:17-19)
4. The messages of Mordecai and Esther (9:20-32)

Verses 1-11. The fateful day, the thirteenth day of Adar, came and with it the retribution for the enemies of the Jews. On that day they gathered together to withstand all who would assault them. The princes and governors and all other officials of the king helped the Jews, because they knew the influential position which Mordecai held and that he waxed greater and greater. Theirs was a great victory. In Shushan itself 500 were slain and 300 more in another part of the city; there were 75,000 slain in the provinces. The ten sons of Haman were slain; their Persian names are given.

Verses 12-16. The king heard the report of the number of his subjects slain in Shushan the fortress and then asks the queen to make a petition. She requests that an additional day be given to continue the work in Shushan and that the ten sons of Haman be hanged on gallows. But had they not slain already 500 in Shushan? The 500 were killed in the palace, or, as that word should be rendered, citadel, fortress; the extra day was requested to continue the retributive work in the city itself. The request was granted and the ten sons of Haman were hanged. On the spoil, the goods and possessions of those slain, they did not touch, probably to avoid false accusations, though the decree gave them permission to spoil their enemies. When Jews read in orthodox synagogues the book of Esther they read the names of Haman's ten sons in one breath, as quickly as possible, intimating thereby that they all were exterminated at one and the same time.

Verses 17-19. With the fourteenth day of Adar they rested and made it a feast of rejoicing. The Jews in Shushan celebrated the thirteenth and fourteenth day and rested on the fifteenth day. This was the origin of the traditional feast of Purim still kept by the orthodox Jews in commemoration of the great deliverance and the wonderful history of Mordecai and Esther. It is mostly celebrated by public reading of this book and by the distribution of gifts.

Verses 20-32. The final section of this chapter gives the account of a message which Mordecai sent to the Jews in the provinces of the Persian kingdom enjoining them to observe these days, the feast of Purim. Queen Esther also wrote with all authority confirming this second letter of Purim.

Typical Application

What happened to the enemies of the Jews in Shushan and the Persian provinces will be the lot of all whose who hate them. This is often made known in the prophetic Word. Thus spake Balaam: "His king (Israel's King) shall be higher than Agag, and His kingdom shall be exalted. God brought him forth out of Egypt; he hath as it were the strength of an unicorn; he shall eat of the nations his enemies and shall break their bones, and pierce them through with arrows" (Numbers 24:7-8). The Lord Himself will arise in behalf of His people and judge their enemies, for it is written, "I will render vengeance to mine enemies and will reward them that hate me" (Deut. 32:41). In this respect this little book with its history is a prophecy of the ultimate victory of God's chosen people over their enemies. In all their history it has been true, and will be finally true in the fullest sense of the word what Isaiah wrote: "No weapon that is formed against thee shall prosper; and every tongue that shall rise against thee in judgment thou shalt condemn (Isaiah 54:17).

The ten sons of Haman, so fully identified with the wicked father, are also not without meaning. The final form of the Gentile government in the close of the age was revealed to Daniel. It consists of ten kingdoms, seen in Nebuchadnezzar's dream image and in Daniel's ten-horned beast, forming once more the Roman empire. It will be domineered over by the little horn, who works together with the man of sin. The ten sons of Haman and their miserable end are another illustration of prophetic truth.

Ahasuerus and Mordecai: the Conclusion

CHAPTER 10

The three verses with which this book closes tell us of the greatness of King Ahasuerus. Here also is the record of the increasing greatness of Mordecai. He was next unto King Ahasuerus, great among the Jews, accepted of the multitude of his brethren, seeking the wealth of his people and speaking peace to all his seed. A blessed type of Him who is greater than Mordecai and who will some day bring peace to His earthly people and who will speak peace to the nations. The precious little book ends with peace.

THE BOOK OF
JOB

Introduction

The book of Job belongs to the poetical books of the Old Testament. The other poetical books are: The Psalms, Proverbs, Ecclesiastes, The Song of Solomon and Lamentations. In the Hebrew Bible they are found in the third section, called Kethubim (the Writings, Hagiographa). The arrangement in the Hebrew Bible differs from that in our English version. It is as follows—Psalms, Proverbs, Job, Song of Solomon, Lamentations and Ecclesiastes.

It needs to be explained that Hebrew poetry is different from the poetry of occidental languages. It knows nothing of rhymed verses, though a rhythmical arrangement is quite often noticeable. The fundamental law of Hebrew poetry is parallelism, which is also very frequently found in the other books which are not classed as poetical. This parallelism has been divided in a threefold form. The *synonymous,* in which the same sentiment is repeated in different but equivalent words, as in Ps. 25:4, "Show me Thy ways O Lord, Teach me Thy paths"; the *antithetical,* in which the parallel members express the opposite sides of the same thought as in Psalm 20:8.

> They are brought down and fallen,
> But we are risen and stand upright.

The synthetical or constructive, in which the two members contain two disparate ideas, which, however, are connected by a certain affinity between them, as in Prov. 1:7:

> The fear of the Lord is the beginning of wisdom
> But fools despise wisdom and instruction.

The book of Job is in the form of a great dramatic peom, in which we have the following actors: Job of the land of Uz and his wife; his three friends Eliphaz, Bildad and Zophar; Elihu the son of Barachel, and Jehovah and the accuser, Satan. The question arises at once, since this book is cast in the form of a drama, is it romantic fiction or history? The critical school declares that it must not be regarded as history at all, though it is claimed that the author may have had some traditional material of a righteous man who was a great sufferer and then the poet worked out the drama, adding fictitious matter. To show the mode of the reasoning of the critical school we quote from Dr. A. S. Peake, who says in his expository work on Job: "That this book must not be regarded as historical is shown by the account of the heavenly councils, by the symbolic numbers of Job's family and flocks, by the escape of one messenger and one only from each catastrophe, by the exact doubling of his possessions at the end of the trial. And even more obvious is that the speeches of Job and his friends cannot be literal reports of actual speeches, since they mark the highest point attained by Hebrew poetical genius, and since no such debate could be imagined in the patriarchal age." But if we believe that this book, like all the other books of the Bible, is given by inspiration, all these objections fall to the ground. Man knew not what was going on in heaven, but the Lord can reveal these unseen things and make known what happens in His own presence. If the record of the scenes in heaven in chapters 1 and 2 are not historical, not revelation, then they are mere human inventions, unworthy of our confidence. And why is it impossible that a controversy such as this book records could not have taken place in the patriarchal age? Evidently the author believes that the patriarchal age was too unenlightened to produce such brilliant speeches. Such reasoning is the natural offspring of evolution.

The book of Job is real history. Job is not the creation of a great, unknown poetic genius, some ancient playwright, he was a real person, who lived; the book gives the great and remarkable experience of his life. The first statement with which the book opens is sufficient to show the historicity of Job. "There was a man in the land of Uz, whose name was Job." Two other books in the Bible speak of him also as a historic person. Twice in the fourteenth chapter of Ezekiel we find him mentioned alongside of Noah and Daniel (Ezek. 14:14, 20). He is therefore not any more fictitious than Noah and the prophet Daniel. In the New Testament the apostle James mentions his name and calls attention to his patience.

Who Was Job?

Who was Job, when and where did he live? These questions cannot be definitely answered. According to rabbinical tradition he lived in Abraham's times, or, according to another tradition, he lived when Jacob's sons were grown up. If the latter view is true then he might be the Job who is mentioned as Issachar's son in Genesis 46:13. But there are also many other traditions which are very fanciful and mostly legendary. The land of Uz has been located somewhat east of Palestine, in the great fertile lands of North-eastern Idumea. That he must have lived in patriarchal days is proven by the contents of the book itself. We have no mention in this book of the law, nor of the levitical institutions, priesthood and sacrifices. (Sacrifices are mentioned in the beginning and the end of the book. But no priest is indicated. It is the primitive way of approaching God by a sacrifice.) Nothing is said of the history of Israel, nor is there a quotation from the writings of the prophets. We move evidently in this book in a time before the law was given and before Abraham's seed constituted a nation.

The Author and Date of the Book

Who wrote the book of Job cannot be determined. Some think is was Job himself to whom God by His Spirit dictated the book after he had passed through the suffering. Some suggest Elihu as the chosen instrument to preserve this experience of Job. Not a few believe that Moses wrote the book. It matters but little who the penman was; we know that behind that pen stood the Spirit of God, who after all is the real author of this and every other Bible book.

The critics have made havoc with the probable date when the book was written. We quote again Dr. Peake, who in discussing the date of Job weaves in a piece of pernicious Bible exegesis which strikes deeper than a late date for Job. "The problem (of the date when Job was written) is no longer in its elementary stage. It has been long pondered and discussed, and this agrees best with a date considerably later than that of Jeremiah. Several scholars have placed it towards the close of the Exile, contemporary with Isa. 40—55. A comparison of the two writers discloses correspondence which cannot be accidental. There are especially close points of contact between the figure of Job and that of the suffering servant of Jehovah. The servant is to be identified with the historical Israel, which had died in the Exile and was to be restored to life by a return from captivity and re-establishment in its old home. The meaning of its suffering and death is closely connected with its mission to the world. That mission was to bring to the Gentiles the knowledge of the true God. . . . The sufferings of Israel are accordingly interpreted as vicarious; by its stripes the nations are healed." Isaiah 53, that sublime prophecy of Christ the sin-bearer, is thus interpreted as meaning the nation and then by an involved argument the authorship of Job is put into the time when the imagined "Deutero-Isaiah" wrote his part, which the ancient Jews and the Church of the past always believed to have been the work of the one Isaiah, and being the divine prediction of the suffering Christ. In their antagonism to the Bible as the infallible Word of God, the critics declare also that Job must have been written in post-exilic times, on account of Satan being mentioned and "Satan (they say) occurs in no early literature, but only in Zechariah and Chronicles."

And this is called scholarship! The fact, however, is that the Hebrew of the book of Job is in style not the Hebrew of a later, but of very early times. Traces of the Chaldee language are found in the Hebrew of Job. Yet these peculiarities which are antagonistic to a pure Hebrew style are really an evidence to the very oldest date in which this book must have been written. They are not in reality Chaldeisms, but rather Arabicisms, and are proof of a very great antiquity of the book, and show that its composition was made when Hebrew and Arabic had not diverged. That is why one of the greatest oriental scholars, Gensenius, wrote: "There is in this book much that is analogous to the Arabic language, or that may be explained by it." Inasmuch then as the book exhibits a fine picture of patriarchal times and its language also bears witness to a very early date all the objections of the critics are void.

The Story of the Book

The book begins with a prologue in which we are introduced to the central figure, Job. We hear of him as an excellent, God-fearing man, surrounded with great prosperity. Then the scene changes and the veil is drawn aside from the unseen world. We see what is going on in heaven and how Satan, the accuser of the brethren, when the Lord mentions His servant Job, sneers in Jehovah's face "Doth Job serve God for nought?" and then challenges God to put forth His hand and to touch all that he hath.

Satan is confident that Job would curse Him to His face. How Satan is permitted to carry out his own suggestion, we read in the first chapter. Yet after Job is stripped of all, he did not sin nor did he charge God foolishly.

Again we are in heaven and the same scene is before us. Satan, defeated in his first attempt, demands that the Lord touch the body of Job, his bone and his flesh, and he is confident Job would curse God. The Lord again permits Satan to do what he demanded with one restriction, Satan cannot touch Job's life. And soon we see Job covered from head to foot with sore boils scraping himself with a potsherd, sitting among the ashes. Only once does his wife appear upon the scene. She said to him, what Satan put into her heart: "Dost thou still retain thine integrity? Curse God and die." Job answered her and in all this did not Job sin with his lips. After that the dark shadow disappears. He has lost the battle. God is victor.

Then begins the main portion of the book when the three friends of Job, having heard of his affliction, come to comfort him. Three times each delivers himself of an address, except Zophar who speaks only twice. And eight times Job answers. The subject of the controversy is the mystery of suffering. The result of this lengthy controversy is tersely stated in chapter 32:2-3. Job through it all justified himself rather than God; the three friends with all their fine orations had not found an answer and yet had condemned Job. Then comes the great testimony of Elihu; this is followed by the words which Jehovah speaks. Then after Job is in the dust and cries out "Behold I am vile, I abhor myself!" comes an epilogue. The storm is gone; the sun breaks through the receding storm clouds and the book ends with the Lord blessing the latter end of Job more than his beginning.

The Message of the Book

The message of the book of Job is concerning the suffering of the righteous. Why do the godly suffer? How can their suffering be harmonized with the righteousness of God? If God is love and He loveth His saints why have they afflictions? In one word the theme of the book is the mystery of suffering. The answer to these questions concerning the suffering of the godly is twofold. God permits their suffering for His own glory. This we learn in the first two chapters. God received glory to Himself when Job, enabled by His grace and by His power, sinned not in the midst of the fiery trials through which he passed. Then God permits the righteous to suffer for their own good. It was a wholesome experience for Job; the sufferings chastened him and he received great blessing. This is the double answer in the book of Job as to the suffering of God's people. And yet there is a mystery of suffering which will only be fully bared when God's saints are in His presence and "know as we are known." Till then we walk in faith, trusting Him who has told us "that all things must work together for good to them that love God."

The Division of the Book of Job

The division of the book of Job is not difficult to make. There is first a prologue, that is followed by the main portion of the book, and in conclusion we have an epilogue. We divide the book into seven parts which we shall follow in a closer analysis with the annotations on the most important truths.

I. THE INTRODUCTION (1:1-5)

II. THE CONTROVERSY BETWEEN JEHOVAH AND SATAN AND THE RESULTS (1:6—2:10)

III. THE CONTROVERSY BETWEEN JOB AND HIS FRIENDS

1. First Series of Controversies
- **The Friend's Arrival (2:11-13)**
- **Job's Lament (3:1-26)**
- **Eliphaz's Address (4—5)**
- **Job's Answer (6—7)**
- **Bildad's Address (8:1-22)**
- **Job's Answer (9—10)**
- **Zophar's Address (11:1-20)**
- **Job's Answer (12—14)**

2. Second Series of Controversies
- **Eliphaz's Address (15:1-35)**
- **Job's Answer (16—17)**
- **Bildad's Address (18:1-21)**
- **Job's Answer (19:1-29)**
- **Zophar's Address (20:1-29)**
- **Job's Answer (21:1-34)**

3. Third Series of Controversies
- **Eliphaz's Address (22:1-30)**
- **Job's Answer (23—24)**
- **Bildad's Address (25:1-6)**
- **Job's Answer (26—31)**

IV. THE TESTIMONY OF ELIHU (32—37)

V. JEHOVAH'S TESTIMONY AND CONTROVERSY WITH JOB (38—41)

VI. THE CONFESSION OF JOB (42:1-6)

VII. THE EPILOGUE AND JOB'S RESTORATION AND BLESSING (42:7-17)

Analysis and Annotations

I. The Introduction

We are at once introduced to the leading person of this book. "There was a man in the land of Uz, whose name was Job and that man was perfect and upright, and one that feared God and eschewed evil." As already stated in the introduction, the land of Uz was east of Palestine and probably a part of Idumea, or in close proximity to the land of Edom. This seems to be confirmed by Lamentations 4:21: "Rejoice and be glad, O daughter of Edom, that dwellest in the land of Uz." Uz is also mentioned in Jeremiah 25:20. It must have been on the borderland of Edom, if it was not a part of it. In Genesis 22:20-21, we read of the sons of Abraham's brother Nahor; among them are two named Uz and Buz. (Elihu was of Buz, Job 32:2.)

The meaning of the name Job is "persecuted" or "afflicted." His character is described as most excellent. He was perfect, which of course does not mean that he was sinless, without any flaw in his character. He was a wholehearted man with a well-balanced solid character. In his dealings with others he was righteous, always upright and doing the right thing. He feared God, walking in the fear of God, which proves that he was a child of God, born again; and therefore he shunned evil in every form. This brief description of Job shows that he was an unusual man. The Lord Himself bore witness to this fact, for He said to Satan, "there is none like him in the earth."

Great blessing rested upon him and upon his house. His family consisted of seven sons and three daughters. Of cattle he had seven thousnd sheep, three thousand camels, five hundred yoke of oxen and five hundred she-asses and a very great household. He was in every way, in his character, in his enormous wealth, the greatest man of the children of the east. His was the position of a prince among men with a princely household. Then follows a pleasing scene, a sample of how he conducted himself. His sons and daughters lacked nothing; they feasted and enjoyed life together in the midst of the great prosperity with which God had blessed them. There is nothing to indicate that it was sinful pleasure in which they indulged. But Job had a tender conscience. He wanted to make provision in case his children had sinned and "cursed God in their hearts." The Hebrew for "curse" is "bless" and the meaning is to renounce God, to forget and turn away from Him. Notice that Job feared some such thought of turning away from God might have entered their young hearts; and that is where all turning away from God starts. And therefore pious Job rose up early in the morning and besides sanctifying them he also offered burnt offerings according to the number of them all. He knew God's holiness and the true mode of approach, by a sacrifice, the shedding of blood "without which there is no remission of sins." How far he himself entered into the joys of his family we do not know; nor does he mention himself as needing a sacrifice.

II. The Controversy Between Jehovah and Satan and the Results

CHAPTER 1:6-22

1. A scene in heaven, Jehovah's challenge and Satan's accusation (1:6-12)
2. Satan's power manifested (1:13-19)
3. Job's great grief and great victory (1:20-22)

Verses 6-12. Suddenly the scene changeth. We are no longer on earth but heaven is opened and we read what is going on before the throne of God. While Job on earth with his loved ones is enjoying himself something takes place in heaven in which he is prominently concerned and yet he is ignorant of all.

The whole scene is intensely interesting. It is not fiction but revelation, and what is here recorded actually took place, and something like it still goes on in heaven. A parallel passage is found in 1 Kings 22:19. The prophet Micaiah saw the Lord sitting on His throne and all the host of heaven standing by Him on His right hand and on His left. And then the Lord permitted as a judgment upon Ahab, that a lying spirit should enter Ahab's prophets to deceive Ahab.

Heaven as a place is not fiction. There is an uncreated heaven where God's throne and dwelling place have always been. From the passage here we may gather that there are certain times when all heavenly tenants, good and evil, have to assemble before the Lord. The sons of God came to present themselves before the Lord. The expression "sons of God" does not mean believers on earth (the sonship of a believer is a New Testament truth), but supernatural beings, the angels. According to this book these sons of God shouted for joy in the hour of creation (38:7). Other Scriptures speak of such heavenly gatherings. (See Psalm 89:5-7; Zech. 4, etc.) And Satan came also among them. He likewise must appear before the Lord. Satan means "adversary." In this character, as the accuser of the brethren he is seen in the last book of the Bible and according to Revelation 12 he is still active in the same capacity as in the days of Job, and has still access to the throne of God, till the hour comes when his doom begins with being cast out of heaven. Destructive criticism pronounceth Satan a Babylonian or Persian myth, a reproduction in Hebrew literature of the Persian fable of Ahriman. But even the French infidel Renan said of the Satan of the Scriptures, "This is quite a different person from the Ahriman of the Zend-Avesta. It is not the spirit of evil existing and acting for himelf." He is not independent of God; as one has correctly stated it, "Satan can go only to the end of his chain." The critical assertion that the belief in a Satan originated after the exile is historically incorrect. The serpent in Genesis 3 is Satan. Originally he was Lucifer, the son of the morning (Isaiah 14), the cherub that covereth (Ezekiel 28) and this great creature of God fell by pride. (See "The History of Satan" in *Studies in Prophecy* Our Hope Press, and the larger work on *Satan, His Person, Work Place and Destiny,* by F.C. Jennings.)

He is forced to give an account to Jehovah. He walked to and fro in the earth and walked up and down in it. He therefore is not in hell. The New Testament tells us that he is "the god of this age" and that his throne is here on earth. He still walks up and down and to and fro. Then God calls his attention to Job and approves his character that there is none like Job. Satan knew Job and hated Job, as he still knows and hates every child of God and is moved with malice towards God's people. And so at once he sneers into the face of the Lord the challenge, "Doth Job fear God for nought?"—"Hast not Thou made an hedge about him, and about his house, and about all that he hath on every side? Thou hast blessed the work of his hands, and his substance is increased in the land. But put forth thine hand now, and touch all that he hath and he will renounce thee to thy face." Then the Lord delivers Job to Satan; gives him the permission to take all that he hath, only upon the person of Job he was not permitted to lay his vile hands. But let us notice that the accusation of Satan is the result of Jehovah's challenge. We quote another.

"It is carefully to be remarked here, that the spring and source of all these dealings is not Satan's accusations, but God Himself. God knew what His servant Job needed, and Himself brings forward his case and sets all in movement. If He demands of Satan if he had considered His servant Job, it is because He Himself had. Satan is but an instrument, and an ignorant though subtle instrument, to bring about God's purposes of grace. His accusations result really in nothing as against Job, save to disprove their truth by what he is allowed to do; but, for Job's good, he is left to his will up to a certain point, for the purpose of bringing Job to a knowledge of his own heart, and thus to a deeper ground of practical relationship with God. How blessed and perfect are God's ways! How vain in result the efforts of Satan's against those that are His!" (*Synopsis of the Bible*)

The controversy then is not between Satan and Job, but between Jehovah and Satan. Job is not so much on trial as the Lord Himself. Is God able to keep His servants loyal when the greatest afflictions pass over them? Has the Lord the power to sustain them? To manifest this power, to show forth His own glory, He permits the suffering of the saint. There are many blessed and comforting truths connected with all this. The best is that we learn that the Lord lovingly watches His people, as He watched Job and spoke well of him and that it is an honor not chastisement when He permits afflictions and sorrow to come.

Satan could not attack the righteousness of Job, but he impeacheth his motives in serving God. In this he only revealed his own character. He attributes the godliness of Job to the selfishness in Job. Then comes his challenge. The conflict is on and it is to be seen if one who is the Lord's, who trusts in Him, can be made by adversities to turn his back upon God and forsake Him; or is God able to keep?

Verses 13-19. "So Satan went forth from the

presence of the Lord." The accuser now acts the roaring lion. And now his work against Job begins. But caution is needed here lest powers be ascribed to Satan which he in reality does not possess. Satan is only a creature and does not share the attributes of God. He is not omnipotent; nor is he omniscient, nor omnipresent. If he displays powers it is with divine permission only. Of course here are secrets which we cannot fathom nor fully understand. Questions upon questions might be asked on this subject which the finite mind cannot answer; problems are here which no human can solve. But we know that all God's ways are perfect, yet past finding out.

And so here he is permitted to use powers to carry out his purposes. If God had not said, "Behold all that he hath is in thy power," he would have had no power.

Four calamities overtake Job's possessions and household. Satan stirred up the Sabeans (Hebrew: Sheba), a nomadic people, probably robber tribes and under his direction they plunder Job of his most valuable cattle and murdered the servants. No sooner had this happened than another messenger announced that the fire of God, probably not lightning, had fallen from heaven and the sheep and servants who were there had been completely destroyed. Then came the third calamity. The Chaldeans robbed Job of his camels and killed his servants who had charge of them. And then the last affliction which is the greatest of them all. A hurricane tore down the house and his loved ones were killed. His wife is not mentioned. Satan did not touch her for he intended to use her as a tool and as his mouthpiece. Thus suddenly, without any warning whatever, in the midst of earthly happiness, yea, real piety, Job, the great and prosperous Job had been stripped of all he had. Satan had done his work well. He knew how to be cruel and reserve the worst blow to the last. And all this happened not only under the all-seeing eye of God, but with His own permission.

Verses 20-22. And Job? Not a murmur escapes his lips. He arose; he expressed his great grief by renting his robe, shaving his head. But then he fell as a worshipper upon the ground and uttered the never to be forgotten words, "Naked came I out of my mother's womb, and naked shall I return thither; the Lord gave, and the Lord hath taken away; blessed be the name of the Lord." It was a great victory. Satan had failed completely. The Lord remained the refuge of Job and underneath the everlasting arms.

CHAPTER 2:1-10

1. Jehovah's second challenge and Satan's answer (2:1-6)
2. Job stricken (2:7-8)
3. Job's wife, Job's answer and victory (2:9-10)

Verses 1-6. Once more the sons of God, and Satan among them, present themselves before the Lord. It must have been immediately after Job's afflictions had come upon him. Probably the Lord called the assembly. The victory is on the Lord's side. Satan is defeated and his defeat is known to the heavenly hosts, who undoubtedly watched the tragedies which had been enacted on earth and who, with joy, had listened to Job's marvellous words. Triumphantly the Lord said to Satan, "And still he holdeth fast his integrity, although thou movedst me against him, to destroy him without cause." Then comes Satan's sneer. He has not given up hope. "Skin for skin, yea, all that a man hath will he give for his life. But put forth Thine hand now and touch his bone and his flesh, and he will renounce thee to thy face." This is bold and horrible language; it shows Satan's knowledge of human nature. And God tells Satan, 'Behold, he is in thine hands." What an evidence that Satan can do nothing against the saints of God without His permission. What a comfort this is! Satan is absolutely under the control of God. And if God permits him to do his evil work, he judiciously designs, God's own love and power are on the side of His afflicted people; His own gracious faithfulness will be demonstrated in the trial. The suffering saints still learn the lesson which Job had to learn, his own nothingness, and that God is all in all. But there is a gracious restriction. The Lord said, "Only spare his life." Satan might sift Job; his life he could not touch, for the lives of God's people are in the hand of the Lord.

Verses 6-8. Satan does not delay long. He carries out his commission and useth his power to the utmost. "He smote him with sore boils from the sole of his foot unto his crown." What was the disease? It may have been the disease known as Elephantiasis, a disease of a horrible nature. Other diseases are mentioned also which correspond with the symptoms given in the brief description. "The symptoms given agree better with those of the Biskra sores, an oriental disease, endemic along the southern shores of the Mediterranean and in Mesopotamia. It begins in the form of papular spots, which ulcerate and become covered with crusts, which are itchy and burning sores" (Professor Macalister). It must have been the most loathsome disease Satan could think of.

"And he took him a potsherd to scrape himself; and he sat among the ashes." What a sad transformation! The great eastern emir, who erstwhile was so rich and influential, stripped of all his possessions, reduced to the most abject poverty, afflicted with a vile and extremely painful disease, takes his place upon the dunghill, amidst the ashes of the burnt refuse. He considers himself an outcast, unfit for a human dwelling.

Verses 9-10. Then his wife makes her only appearing in this drama. She is seen but once and only once she speaks. She must have followed him with weeping and wailing outside to the ash-heap. And now she speaks, but not of herself. Satan uses her as his instrument. He speaks through her. "Dost thou still retain thine integrity? Renounce God and die." That is exactly what Satan had spoken in God's presence, that Job would do this very thing. And now he uses the woman to suggest suicide to Job.

But noble is the answer of the afflicted saint of God. He detects in her language impiety—"thou speaketh as one of the impious (this is the meaning of foolish) women speaketh." Only those who do not know God can speak as you have spoken, is the meaning of his rebuke. What? shall we receive good at the hand of God, and shall we not receive evil? The power of God it was which produced such wonderful submission. His grace enabled him to pass through it all without sinning. What a record! "In all this did not Job sin with his lips!" Satan's defeat is complete. His mouth is stopped. If he appears again before Jehovah he must stand in silence; the last word does not belong to him, but to God. And so is coming the day when Satan's defeat is complete, when he will be completely bruised under the feet of God's people.

III. The Controversy Between Job and His Friends

1. First Series of Controversies

CHAPTER 2:11-13

The Friends' Arrival

We now enter upon the main section of the book. The dark shadow of the accuser of the brethren has disappeared and in his place Job's three friends appear upon the scene. The news of the awful misfortunes had reached them; they made an appointment together to mourn with him and to comfort him. As they are now taking a prominent part in this drama we must examine their names and get some knowledge as to their personality. The first friend is Eliphaz the Temanite. Teman is in Idumea. He may have been the son of Esau (Genesis 36:10-11). His name means "my God is fine gold." Teman was noted for its wisdom. "Is wisdom no more in Teman?" (Jeremiah 49:7). The second is Bildad the Shuhite. His name means "son of contention," which expresses the character he reveals in his speeches. His name can also be identified with the patriarchal age. Shuah was the sixth son of Abraham by Keturah (Genesis 25). He is also mentioned in connection with Esau, Edom and Teman. Shuah means "depression or prostration." The third friend is Zophar the Naamathite. Of his origin we know nothing. His name means "to twitter" like a bird chirps and twitters. And his addresses, consisting in violent utterances, reveal the senseless and harmless twittering of a bird.

There can be no question that all three were, like Job, God-fearing men. They formed with Job in the patriarchal age a kind of intellectual and religious aristocracy, in the midst of the surrounding idolators. How long their journey took after the news of Job's condition had reached them we do not know. It must have been months later after Job was first stricken, that they came to visit him. During that time the disease of Job developed fully; his misery did not become less. At last the friends arrived. And as they saw the ash-heap and the miserable figure upon it, they knew him not. He was so disfigured and distorted by the suffering and the disease that they failed to recognize him. They had known him in the days of his great prosperity, when young men were held by his personality in awe, when old men arose to do him honor, when princes refrained from talking and nobles held their peace (29:7-10). What a sad spectacle to see him in this deplorable condition. Their sympathy is expressed by weeping, the rending of their garments and the sprinkling of dust upon their heads toward heaven. What pain it must have given them when they saw that his grief and and suffering were so great! The follows an impressive silence of seven days and seven nights. They are stricken dumb and find no words to utter. But while their lips did not speak their minds were deeply engaged with the problem which ere long they would take up in controversy with the afflicted one. And the question uppermost must have been, "How can God, a righteous God, permit this good man to be in this condition?"—"Why is he stripped of all and in this horrible condition?"

CHAPTER 3

Job's Lament

1. Job curses the day of his birth (3:1-9)
2. He longs for death (3:10-23)
3. The reason why (3:24-260

Verses 1-9. The silence is broken by Job. Alas! his lips do not utter praises now, but he cursed the day of his birth. It was a sore trial for Job to look into the faces of these pious friends, in perfect health and strength, and he, even more pious than they, stricken and smitten of God. It was an aggravation of Job's grief and sorrow.

But let us notice though Job gives way to his feelings in this passionate outburst, he did not renounce God, nor is there a word of rebellion against Him. All through his address in answer to the arguments of his friends he does not lose sight of God, and over and over again expresses confidence in the unseen One, as in that matchless utterance, "Though He slay me, yet will I trust" (13:15).

Unmanned by the presence of his friends he curses the day of his birth. The chapter, and in fact all the chapters which follow, should be read in a good metrical version.

Perish the day when I was born to be,
And the night which said a man-child
is conceived.
That day! may it be darkness;
Let not God regard it from above,
Neither let the light shine upon it.
Let darkness stain it and the
shade of death.
Let densest clouds upon it settle down.
Let gathering darkness fill it with alarm.
That night—let gloom seize upon it.
Let it not rejoice among the days of the year.
Let it not come into the number of the months.

We give this as a sample of a metrical version. As the full quotation of the text is beyond the compass of our work, we recommend to our readers the translation of the Old Testament made by John Nelson Darby. It is the best we know and all poetical sections are given in this metrical arrangement.

Jeremiah, the great weeping prophet, also broke out in the midst of sorrow and treachery, in a similar lament, which reminds us of Job's words.

Cursed be the day wherein I was born.
Let not the day in which my mother
bare me be blessed.
Cursed be the man who brought tidings
to my father,
Saying, A man-child is born unto thee,
making him glad.
Wherefore came I forth out of the womb
To see labour and sorrow
That my days should be consumed with shame?

Such expressions are the failures of poor, frail man. And He who knoweth our frame and remembereth that we are but dust, is like a father who pitieth His children (Psalm 103:13-14). Since critics associate the sufferings of Job with the suffering Servant of the Lord in Isaiah's great prediction (Isaiah 53), we also can make this application, but not as meaning the nation, but our Lord Jesus Christ. What are Job's sufferings in comparison with the sufferings of our Lord! Job sat upon an ash-heap, but the Son of God was nailed to the cross and then He was forsaken of God. Never did a murmur escape those blessed lips.

(The correct translation of verse 8 is as follows:

Let those engaged in cursing days, curse this day;
Who are ready to rouse Leviathan.

It voices heathen superstitions and myths.)

Verses 10-23. He next wishes that he had died at the time of his birth and he looks upon death as a great relief and rest, saying:—

There the wicked cease from troubling
And there the wearied are at rest.

We see from these expressions that his mind turned to death as the great emancipator. Moses and Elijah exhibit the same trend of thought and weakness; so did disappointed Jonah when he said, "It is better for me to die."

Weighed in the light of the New Testament all these expressions are found wanting. Death is not a friend whose visit is to be desired, but an enemy. The hope of God's people in affliction and sorrow in the light of the gospel is not relief by death, but the coming of the Lord. The promise of the New Testament, "We shall not all sleep but be changed in a moment, in the twinkling of an eye" (1 Cor. 15:52) is unknown in the Old Testament, for it is one of the mysteries hidden in former ages. Job's language is that of a man in despair; he seems to have quite forgotten the bright and blessed days of the past and fears a hopeless future.

Verses 24-26. In this final paragraph Job states the reasons for his lament and longing for death to release him. We quote the last two verses.

For the thing which I greatly
  feared is come upon me,
And that which I was afraid
  of is come unto me.
I was not careless, neither had I quietness
Neither was I at rest; yet trouble came.

He evidently in the days of his prosperity feared that just such calamities might overtake him. He knew the testing times would come and had no quietness. But now as they have come and the three anticipated evils overwhelmed him he would be glad to find the grave.

CHAPTERS 4—5

The First Address of Eliphaz

1. He rebukes Job (4:1-5)
2. The righteous are not cast off (4:6-11)
3. An awe-inspiring vision (4:12-21)
4. Experience and exhortation (5:1-16)
5. Happy is the man whom God correcteth (5:17-27)

With this chapter the long and tedious controversy between Job and his three visitors begins. His pitiful lamentation brings forth the addresses of his friends. Eliphaz and Bildad speak thrice, each answered by Job, and Zophar twice with corresponding rebuttals by Job. Job delivers his last word, the lengthy speech of chapters 27—31 in which he gives a summary of what he contended for, namely, his own integrity, but the problem of his suffering remains unexplained.

The controversy is progressive. The thought which the three friends follow is that all suffering is the result of the justice of God and therefore punitive. For this principle they contend in a dogmatic way. As the controversy continues they become more harsh, suspicious and finally almost abusive. Job's answers are first marked by despair; then hope enters in. In a measure he rises above his sufferings in answering his friends in a sharp way. He has the last word, but, as already stated, the mystery and problem of his suffering is not cleared up.

Eliphaz's address is first in the series of controversies in which each maintains the punitive character of suffering and each answer given by Job (chapters 6—7; 9—10; 12—14) is filled with despair reflecting the state of his mind. After these preliminary remarks we briefly examine each address and Job's answers.

Chapter 4:1-5.. Eliphaz is the most dogmatic of the three friends and in his first address makes much of the greatness and justice of God. He had come to comfort; but little comfort could he bring to the afflicted one. He begins very politely. "If one replied to thee (to Job's lament) wouldst thou be grieved? But who can refrain from speaking?" But at once he stabs Job to the heart.

Behold thou hast instructed many
And thou hast strengthened the weak hands
Thy words have upholden him that was stumbling;
And thou hast strengthened oft the feeble knees.
But now it is come upon thee and what grief!
Because it toucheth thee, thou art troubled.
Hath not thy piety been thy confidence,
And the perfection of thy ways thy hope?

All this was of course perfectly true. But he did not understand what Job needed in his suffering. The words of Eliphaz, the wise man from Teman, must have acted upon Job like an application of an irritant to a bleeding wound. What Job needed was tender sympathy, a good Samaritan, to pour oil and to give him wine. But Eliphaz reveals in this at once the harshness of his nature, the lack of discernment between the suffering of the righteous and the wicked, and finally he develops into a false accuser.

Verses 7-11. Eliphaz had told Job he was a pious and righteous man (verse 6). And now he tells him: "Remember I pray thee, who ever perished, being innocent? Or when were any righteous ones cut off?" Only those that plow iniquity and sow wickedness reap what they have sown. God makes such to perish in His wrath. They are cut off even if they were like strong lions. What dogmatic logic! Job, if thou art righteous and suffering thus, then God is destitute of all justice; but if God is justice, then thou hast plowed iniquity and sown wickedness and all thy suffering is thine own harvest.

Verses 12-21. The words which follow, describing a vision which Eliphaz had, are so sublime that we must quote them.

Now a thing was brought secretly to me,
Mine ear did catch a whispering thereof.
In thoughts from visions of the night
When deep sleep falleth upon men:
Great fear came upon me, and trembling too,
It made my very bones to shake.
Then a spirit passed before my face;
The hair of my flesh stood up—
I stopped—but nothing could I then discern—
I looked, and lo, I saw a form
Silence: and then I heard a voice—

"Shall mortal man be more just than God?
Shall a man be purer than his Maker?
In His own servants He trusteth not,
His angels He chargeth with folly.
How much more than they that dwell
in houses of clay
Whose foundation is the dust,
Who are crushed as the moth!
From morning to evening are they smitten
They perish utterly, without any regarding it.
Is not their tent-cord plucked up within them?
They die and without wisdom."

This vision describes the greatness and majesty of God and of course is again true. That it was a real vision cannot be doubted. Man's punity, his utter nothingness, is thus made known in this vision. But did this meet the need of afflicted Job? It could not explain the reason of Job's suffering. And something like this is suggested by these words—Job, you are just like other men before God; your present experience of affliction testifies to this. You thought you were right with God and that He blessed and protected you, but as He is holy and just, your suffering shows, you are reaping the consequences of your sin, as others do.

Chapter 5:1-16. He gives Job next a bit of experience, which is very true indeed. But the insinuation is wrong. He reasons from experience that suffering is the lot of the wicked, and therefore Job must belong to that class. The advice he gives to Job is in full keeping with his dogmatic assertion.

For man is born to trouble, as
the sparks fly upwards.
But as for me I will seek unto God,
And unto God commit my cause;
Who doeth great things and unsearchable,
Marvellous things without number.

But the advice, while good, is most subtle, for it is built upon wrong premises. He maintains his previous assertion that Job was an ungodly sinner, reaping what he had sown; with this in view he spoke these words.

Verses 17-27. The first address of Eliphaz closes with a marvellous climax upon the same wrong premises, that Job had sinned, that he must seek God, but Job had not renounced God; he had not left Him. Otherwise this final utterance of Eliphaz tells out the gracious power of the Almighty in a most blessed way. Read these verses and get the help and comfort which they breathe.

CHAPTER 6—7

Job's Answer

1. His Despair justified by the greatness of his suffering (6:1-7)
2. He requests to be cut off (6:8-13)
3. He reproacheth his friends (6:14-30)
4. The misery of life (7:1-7)
5. Two questions: Why does God deal with me thus? Why does He not pardon? (7:8-21)

Chapter 6:1-7. He meets first of all the reproach and accusation of Eliphaz (4:1-5). Because his sufferings are so great his utterances are so desperately wild. If Eliphaz only would consider this he would find how enormous the pressure is "heavier than the sand of the seas" which weighs him down and he would have shown the sympathy and tenderness for which Job longed. And then the description of what his agony is:

For the arrows of the Almighty are within me
The heat whereof my spirit drinketh up.
God's terrors now against me are arrayed.

This inward suffering of his soul was even greater than the loathsome disease which covered his body. He felt that God's hand in holy anger was upon him and he knew not what he learned afterward, that all was love and compassion from God's side. Satan must have had a share and part in these increasing soul-agonies of Job. But has he not a perfect right to complain? The animals in God's creation do not complain without reason. If the wild ass has grass and the ox fodder, they utter no sound. Nor would he complain if all was well with him. But his afflictions are like loathsome meat, and should he not murmur and complain. It is all the language of despairing grief.

Verses 8-13. And now he returns to his great lamentation:

Oh that I might have my request;
And that God would grant me the thing
I long for!
Even that it would please God to crush me;
That He would let loose His hand, and
cut me off!

This is still greater despair. And that he looks upon as comfort; yea, he would exult in pain that spareth not. It would end his sufferings and then after death he need fear nothing. He was conscious that he was right with God. "For I have not denied the words of the Holy One." Here is the first note of self-righteousness, of justifying himself, which later on becomes more pronounced in his answers.

Verses 14-30. The sympathetic kindness he expected from his friends had not come. Eliphaz's address gave the evidence of it.

E'en to th' afflicted, love is due from friends;
E'en though the fear of God he might forsake.
But my brethren have dealt deceitfully, like a brook
Like streams whose flowing waters disappear,
And are hidden by reason of the ice
And of the snow, which, falling, covers them.[1]

He had been bitterly disappointed in his friends. Their silence first, their wailing, and the outward signs of deepest grief, had led him to hope for comfort from their lips. They were like water brooks promising an abundant supply of refreshing water in winter time when not needed. But—

What time it waxeth warm, they disappear
When it is hot they vanish from their place.
The travelling caravans by the way turn aside
They go up into the waste, and perish.

Such were his friends. They were like dried up brooks in the summer's heat. He had not asked them to give.

Did I say, Give unto me?
Or, Offer a present for me of your substance?
Or, Deliver me from the Adversary's power?
Or, Redeem me from the Oppressor's hand?

Nothing like this he had asked of their hands; all he craved was kind and tender sympathy. He urges them to teach him, to show him in what he has sinned, if he suffers for his sins. He urges them to look straight into his face and see if he is lying. He solemnly assures his friends of his innocence.

If only Job had not looked to his friends but to Him whose goodness and mercy he knew so well, he would not have suffered such disappointment. And what a contrast with David's faith: "Yea, though I walk through the valley of the shadow of death, I will fear no evil, for Thou art with me; Thy rod and Thy staff they comfort me."

Chapter 7:1-7. This section is one of great beauty, describing human existence and the misery connected with it, as it was so markedly in his own case.

[1]*Companion Bible.*

As soon as I lie down to sleep, I say:
How long till I arise, and night be gone?
And I am full of tossings till the dawn.
My flesh is clothed with worms, and clods of earth;
My broken skin heals up, then runs afresh.
Swifter than weaver's shuttle are my days,
And they are spent without a gleam of hope.

It is the picture of despair. The dark shadow of the enemy who had so wrongfully accused him must have told him "without a gleam of hope" as if God had now forsaken him.

Verses 8-21. Why did God deal with him in this way? He thinks God must be his enemy and asks:

Am I a sea? or a monster of the deep;
That Thou settest a watch over me?

He had dreams too, not like the dreams of Eliphaz which reveal the greatness of God, but dreams of terrifying visions, so that he loatheth his life.

. . . I would not live always:
Let me alone; for my days are vanity.

Poor, suffering, despairing Job! To think of Him whose love had been so fully demonstrated in the past, as his enemy and to pray to Him, "Let me alone," was indeed horrible despondency. And if he has sinned, why does not God pardon and take away his iniquity? But this is not confession of sin. A different thing it is when finally he cries out, "Behold I am vile, I abhor myself."

CHAPTER 8

Bildad's Address

1. How long, Job? (8:1-7)
2. Enquire of the former age (8:8-10)
3. God's dealing with the wicked and the righteous (8:11-22)

Verses 1-7. Bildad the Shuhite now speaks to Job. He is less dogmatic than Eliphaz, and less courteous, but more outspoken. He must have lost his patience listening to Job's reply. Especially does he resent what Job had said about God, the insinuations which had fallen from his lips. But we shall see he too follows the logic of Eliphaz, that God punishes Job for his sins. He starts in at once to rebuke Job for what he had said. How long, Job, wilt thou speak these things? How long shall the words of thy mouth be like a mighty wind? By the latter expression he insinuates that Job's speech was tempestuous like the wind, and as empty as the wind. He declares, what certainly is the truth, that God cannot be unrighteous. In this way Bildad called a decisive halt to the dangerous utterances Job had made, forced to it by Eliphaz's cold and dogmatic assertions. Job, inasmuch as he repudiated the accusation of being a sinner, and being punished for his sins, was rapidly approaching the verge of charging God with being unjust. Then Bildad deals a cruel blow to the man upon the ash-heap. He tries to illustrate the principle he defends, that God only punishes sinners, by the children of Job, that they sinned and were wicked and therefore God dealt with them in His righteousness. It has been freely rendered in this wise:

> It may be thy sons 'gainst Him have sinned
> And He, through their rebellion, cut them off.

How that must have pained Job! Then he exhorts Job to seek God diligently and it would not be in vain. He has his "ifs." "If thou wouldest seek unto God"—and —"If thou wert pure and upright."

Verses 8-10. But he is a traditionalist. He appeals to the past. "For inquire, I pray thee, of the former age, and apply thyself to that which their fathers have searched out." We, in our generation, are but of yesterday, and know nothing. Zophar also appealed to the fathers.

Verses 11-22. And here we have the wisdom of Bildad as he learned it from the past. It is all true and sublimely stated; the wicked cannot prosper; their doom is certain. On the other hand God will not cast off the perfect man. But Job is in the place of one who is cast off; therefore he must belong to the wicked who do not prosper. This is hidden beneath Bildad's rhetoric. Yet beautiful are the closing sentences of his first address, the truth of which was fully acknowledged by Job in his reply.

> But perfect men God never casts away
> Nor takes He evil-doers by the hand.
> Wait! Then one day He fills thy mouth
> With laughter and thy lips with joyous shouts.
> And they who hate thee shall be clothed
> with shame,
> And tents of wicked men exist no more.

CHAPTERS 9—10

Job Answers Bildad

1. The supremacy and power of God (9:1-10)
2. How then can Job meet Him? (9:11-21)
3. He destroyeth the perfect and the wicked (9:22-24)
4. Confession of weakness and the need of a daysman (9:25-35)
5. Murmuring against God (10:1-17)
6. Welcoming death (10:18-22)

Chapter 9:1-10. The final words of Bildad seemed to have had a momentary soothing effect upon Job. Of a truth it is so. But here is the question, How can a man be just with God? And what a God He is! If a man contend in argument with Him, of a thousand things he could not answer one. Even if it is the wisest among men, and strongest, who stood up against Him, he did not prosper. He moveth and overturneth mountains; He makes the earth to tremble, bids the sun and it does not shine. He made the mighty constellations in the sky, Arcturus, Orion and Pleiades—

> Who doeth mighty things works, past finding out,
> And wondrous things, in number infinite.

How then can a man be just with such a God of power and greatness?

Verses 11-21. And such a Being Job declares is for him inaccessible.

> Behold, He passeth, but I see Him not,
> He sweepeth by, but is invisible.
> Lo, He doth seize; who then can hold Him back?
> Or who shall say to Him, What doest Thou?
> Should God at length His anger not avert,
> Helpers of pride must stoop beneath His hand
> How then can I address and answer Him?
> Or choose my words in argument with Him?

How can Job confront such a one? Should he attempt to justify himself, his own mouth and lips would instantly condemn him; and if he were to say, I am perfect and blameless, He would only prove his perverseness.

Verses 22-24. But the words which follow sound almost like the ravenings of a madman. He speaks out, but not in the fear of God. He assumes indifference and says that it is all the same to him, whether he is right or wrong, for God destroyeth the perfect and the wicked alike; in other words He is an unjust God. When the pestilential scourge marcheth through the land and slays suddenly, He but mocks at the innocent who are taken away. The earth is given by Him into the hands of the wicked; injustice reigns everywhere. If God has not done all this, who then is it? Horrible words these which must have been whispered in his despairing soul by that being who is as much the accuser of God to the brethren, as the accuser of the brethren before God.

Verses 25-35. Then he confesseth his impotence. His days are swiftly passing. He cannot clear himself. He expresses his fear that God will not hold him innocent; He will account him guilty. If then he is wicked all his labours are in vain. Whatever he does cannot change matters. Even if he bathed himself in water pure as snow, and washed his hands with soap, so as to be as clean as he never was before, yet God would surely plunge him into the ditch. All self-help, and self-improvement is in vain. But then a ray of light. He needs another to help him, to bring him in touch with God, to make him just with God. He calls for a daysman, an umpire, one that might lay His hand on God and on him, the sinner, so that the rod be taken from him and he be freed from fear. The daysman we find later in this book foreshadowed. But He has come; Christ Jesus our Lord.

Chapter 10:1-17. And now the darkest of all. Not so much is it the physical agony, the boils and running sores, torturing him, as it is the bitter consciousness that he is loosing hold on God, that he begins to look upon Him no longer as a loving friend, but as a harsh, unmovable tyrant. It is a death struggle through which he passeth. His soul is weary of his life and so he tells out the bitterness of his heart. What accusations are here! Bold language indeed for the creature of the dust, and such an afflicted creature as he was—"I will say unto God—Show me wherefore Thou contend with me." He charges God that He planned his calamity and destruction (verses 6-13). It is as if Job confesseth in his blindness by his words that he is in the hands of an all-powerful, merciless being, not a God of love and justice, but an enemy.

Verses 18-22. What then is the use of living? Oh, if he only had been carried from the womb to the grave!

CHAPTER 11

Zophar's First Address

1. Job's multitude of words rebuked (11:1-6)
2. The greatness and omniscience of God (11:7-12)
3. That Job repent and receive the Blessings (11:13-20)

Verses 1-6. The third friend of Job is in every way the weakest. Speaking last he must have been the youngest of the three. He lacks the dignity of Eliphaz and the gentleness of Bildad, nor does he possess the depths of either. Evidently Job's speech has taxed his patience and irritated him.

> Should not thy mass of words be answered?
> And a man so full of talk, should he
> be justified?
> Can thy boastings make men hold their peace?
> And when thou mockest, shall no man
> make thee ashamed?
> For thou sayest 'My doctrine is pure
> And I am clean in His eyes.'
> But Oh that God might speak
> And open His lips against thee.
> That He would show thee the secrets
> of wisdom,
> That is manifold in effectual working!
> Know therefore that God exacts not more
> than thine iniquity deserveth.

One can almost feel the boisterous spirit in which this rebuke must have been delivered.

Verses 7-12. He now reminds Job of the greatness and omniscience of the God whom he accused. Could he by searching find out God or find out the Almighty unto perfection? "It is high as heaven; what canst thou do? Deeper than Sheol; what canst thou know? The measure thereof is longer than the earth, and broader than the sea." But more than that He is an omniscient God, the searcher of hearts. He knoweth vain men and seeth iniquity also. So far it all seems well.

Verses 13-20. So far all sounds well, but now he follows the same argument as his friends. He too believes that Job is a wicked man who has hidden iniquity, and that this must explain his affliction. So he turns exhorter and calls on him to repent. Set thine heart aright, he tells Job; stretch out thy hands towards Him. Put iniquity away, do not permit iniquity to be in thy tents! He talks as if he is very sure, more so than Eliphaz and Bildad, that Job is guilty of much sin. Then he draws a charming picture of the blessed results if Job confesses and repents. He would forget his misery "as waters that are passed away."

Everything is painted by him in the rosiest colors as if he knew what God would do for Job. The time did come when Job got richer blessings than those outlined by Zophar. And what Zophar said, "Yea, many shall make suit unto thee" (marginal reading: entreat thee), came actually true when Eliphaz, Bildad and Zophar had to humble themselves before this Servant of God. Zophar's final word is a warning of the fate of the wicked. It was meant for Job. The blunt, rough way of Zophar, who does not contribute anything new and fresh to the controversy, makes Job more confident that he is right and he gives a remarkable answer.

CHAPTERS 12—14

Job's Answer to Zophar

1. His sarcasm (12:1-6)
2. He describes God's power (12:7-25)
3. He denounces his friends (13:1-13)
4. He appeals to God (13:14-28)
5. The brevity and trouble of life (14:1-6)
6. The ray of light through hope of immortality (14:7-22)

Chapter 12:1-6. He answers not only Zophar but the others as well. Before this Job had expressed his disappointment in them, rebuked them for their unkindness, and assailed as worthless their arguments, but now he treats them in a very sarcastic manner.

> No doubt but ye are the people
> And wisdom shall die with you.

Was he then without any understanding or inferior to them? Do you think I am ignorant of the things you have spoken to me about? You mock me; I am nothing but a laughingstock. You as my neighbors come to me and say, "He calls on God, that He should answer him." Yet I am the just, the perfect man; you make sport of me. You are at ease and treat the one who is down, overwhelmed by misfortune, with contempt. But remember:

> The tents of robbers prosper,
> And they that provoke God are secure;
> Abundance does He give unto them.

This is what Zophar had claimed in his address, that the wicked do not prosper. (See Job 11:2, 14, 19, 20.) Robbers often prosper and those who are secure are often those who provoke God. Perhaps his friends with their prosperity might belong to that class.

Verses 7-25. This is also in answer to Zophar's argument. Zophar had spoken of the greatness of God. The wisdom which Zophar had tried to impress upon him is so elementary that the beasts themselves know something about it.

> But ask now the beasts, and they
> shall teach thee;
> And the fowls of the air, and they
> shall tell thee;
> Or speak to the earth, and it
> shall teach thee;
> And the fishes of the sea shall
> declare unto thee.
> Who knoweth not in all these,
> That the hand of the Lord hath
> wrought this?
> In whose hand is the soul of
> every living thing,
> And the breath of all mankind.

Job outstrips Zophar's speech in every way. He is ahead in the controversy. In verses 12-13 Job seems to have Bildad's statement in mind (8:8-9), and he declares now that with God is wisdom and might; He hath counsel and understanding. But what follows, while true in itself, is but the one side of God's doings, and the darkest pessimism, such as suited his mind. God spoils counsellors, maketh judges fools, looseth the bonds of kings, leadeth priests away spoiled, overthroweth the mighty, pours contempt on princes; He increaseth the nations and destroyeth them.

> He taketh away the heart of the chiefs
> of the people in the earth,
> And causeth them to wander in a
> wilderness where there is no way.
> They grope in dark without light,
> And He maketh them stagger like
> a drunken man.

It is a dreadful picture Job has drawn of God by the one-sided description of His greatness. Not a word of His love and mercy. It is in full keeping with his despairing heart.

Chapter 13:1-5. He had told in the previous words that he was not an ignorant man. What his wise friends had told him he understood perfectly; both nature and history had taught him the greatness of God which they had emphasized. What ye know, I know; I am not inferior to you. I am just as good as you are. What he desires is not to speak with them but to the Almighty; he wants to reason with God. The parallelism of verses 4 and 5 is interesting and has been rendered as follows:

> But as for ye, plastered with lies are ye,
> Physicians of no value are ye all
> Would ye but altogether hold your peace;
> That, of itself, would show that ye are wise.

Still stronger is his rebuke as found in verses 7-13. He warns them that their whole course is wrong. They are presumptuous in talking deceitfully for God. All this he speaks in self-defense, that he is innocent, and with it the subtle accusation against God once more, that He is unjust. He also warns them that "He will surely reprove you" and this came true.

Verses 14-28. Then his words addressed to God Himself. He dares to approach Him. Knowing the greatness and awfulness of God, and perhaps conscious too of not having Him honoured as he should have done, he says, this would be the meaning of the rather difficult verse (14), "Come what may I take my life in my hand and risk it." The paraphrase of the *Companion Bible* expresses it correctly.

> Aye, come what may, I willingly the risk
> will take; and put my life into my hand.

But at that moment when he makes this resolve His faith breaks through and he utters one of the sublimest words which ever came from human lips. "Yea, though He slay me, yet will I trust in Him." And thousands upon thousands have spoken it after him, thus honouring God with faith's sweetest song in the night.

He wants God to hear his speech diligently and have declaration come into His ear. He expresses his hope that God would yet declare him just, that is justify him, then who will dare to contend with him? And then that pleading of his with so much pathos! Relieve me from the sufferings, withdraw thine hand far from me, which rests upon me; and let not thy terror make me afraid. Then call Thou, and I will answer (verses 20-22). Or let me speak, he says, and answer Thou me. Then once more the right note, that note which finally must be sounded to the full in his wretched misery—"How many are mine iniquities and sins? Make me to know my transgression and my sins." But it was only momentarily. He breaks out in fresh charges against God. His self-righteousness has blinded him so that he asks, "Wherefore hidest Thou Thy face, and holdest me for Thine enemy?" Horrible charges he brings against His Maker, the charges of injustice (verses 26-28). He wanted to listen to God, but He gives Him no chance to speak. When finally God speaks, Job is in the dust.

Chapter 14:1-6. A true picture he has drawn in these words of man's frailty. Besides this unclean, for, who can bring a clean thing out of an unclean? Not one. He requests that he might be let alone "till he shall accomplish as an hireling his day."

Verses 7-22. There is hope for a tree, he declares, though cut down, but it may sprout again. "But man that dieth, and wasteth away; yea, man giveth up the ghost, and where is he?" He speaks of man "who lieth down and riseth not." That is the language of man apart from revelation. It is the expression of one who is in darkness and uncertainty. Frequently teachers of errors, like soul-sleep, the annihilation of the wicked, etc., in defense of their false teachings quote Job and the utterances of these friends as if these were true revelations from God, when their words are only the expressions of the human mind, and often false and misleading. What Job spoke and his friends is given in an unfailing inspired account, but revelation is a different matter altogether.

Then Job's desire is to be hidden in Sheol, until His wrath be past. "That Thou wouldest appoint me a set time, and remember me!" In this he expresseth the wish to believe that there is hope and that some one might give him the assurance about it—"If a man die, shall he live again?" But this ray of hope is only for a moment and once more he gives way to despair and continues his awful suspicions that God is his enemy. The first series of controversies are a complete failure. Job by justifying himself has dishonored God, and his friends by condemning him and not giving him the comfort he needed have sinned as well.

2. The Second Series of Controversies

CHAPTER 15

Eliphaz's Second Address

1. Tells Job that he is self-condemned (15:1-6)
2. Charges him with pride (15:7-16)
3. The wicked and their lot (15:17-35)

Verses 1-6. His second address is not as lofty as his first. Job's language has evidently annoyed him very much. He characterizes his words as vain, unprofitable, which can do no good. He charges him with having cast off fear and having become one who restrained devotion before God. He tells Job that what he has spoken only confirms their views of him, that he is a wicked man and suffers justly for his sins.

> Thine own mouth condemneth thee and not I;
> Yea, thine own lips testify against thee.

Verses 7-16. Wrong as Eliphaz's rebuke is, he adds still another charge. He tells him he is filled with pride. What Job knows they know also. "What knowest thou, that we do not know? What understandeth thou, which is not in us?"

And why does Thine heart carry thee away?
And why do thine eyes wink? (in pride)
That thou shouldest turn thine
anger against God
And cause such words to issue from
thy mouth.

Then, as he did in his first address, Eliphaz speaks once more of the holiness of God. "Behold He putteth no trust in His holy Ones. Yea, the heavens are not clean in His sight."

Verses 17-35. Here we have another description of the wicked, their miserable lot and what is in store for them. What he said was meant to terrify Job. Every word must have cut deep into Job's miserable soul, for he knew with Eliphaz he was a wicked, impious man. We see that Eliphaz said nothing new. He re-stated the former argument.

CHAPTERS 16—17

Job's Reply to Eliphaz

1. Miserable comforters are ye all (16:1-5)
2. Oh God! Thou hast done it! (16:6-14)
3. Yet I look to Thee (16:15-22)
4. Trouble upon trouble; self-pity (17:1-12)
5. Where is now my hope? (17:13-16)

Chapter 16:1-5. How masterfully he meets their wrong accusations and how he brings forth his suffering afresh, yet always with that horrible nightmare, God is not for me, but against me! Such things Eliphaz spoke he had heard before. What are you anyway? Nothing but miserable comforters. If they were in the condition in which he is, he would also speak. "But I would strengthen you with my mouth, and the solace of my lips should assuage your grief." I would never treat you as you treat me.

Verses 6-14. And now he charges God with being responsible for all. What does he say? "Thou hast made me desolate. . . . Thou hast laid fast hold on me. . . . He hath torn me in His wrath and persecuted me. . . . He has gnashed upon me with His teeth. . . . He hath delivered me to the ungodly." Remarkable is verse 10. "They have gaped upon me with their mouth; they have smitten me upon the cheek reproachfully; they gather themselves against me." This was done to another Sufferer, the Lord Jesus Christ. But He murmured not; He did not dishonour God as Job did, but glorified Him. It is interesting to make a contrast between these two sufferers. It brings out the perfection and loveliness of our Saviour.

Verses 15-22. But in all these ravings, faith, which slumbers in his breast, asserts itself, and tries to awake. He says "my witness is in heaven, and He that voucheth for me is on high." Thus he clings to God. How beautiful this word suits us, who know Him who has gone on high and who voucheth for us there, needs hardly to be pointed out. But Job knew Him not as we know Him. Once more he desires that daysman. "O that one might plead for man with God, as a man pleadeth for His neighbour!"

Chapter 17:1-12. What a pathetic description of his troubles! And he cannot deliver himself from the obsession that God is the author of it all.

Verses 13-16. And what is his hope now? How dark and evil his thoughts! The grave is to be his house, the darkness his bed. Corruption, his father, the worm his mother and his sister. He and his hope will go down to the bars of the pit, and rest together in the dust. But we shall soon hear another confession from his lips.

CHAPTER 18

Bildad's Second Address

1. New reproaches (18:1-4)
2. Once again, the wicked and what they deserve (18:5-21)

Verses 1-4. Bildad has the good sense in this second oration to be very brief. He, like Eliphaz, pays his compliments to Job and reproaches him. How long are you going to speak yet any way! You, you tell us that we are like the beasts, stupid and ignorant! Keep on with your nonsense you but tear yourself in your anger; it is all unavailing and not changes things for thee. This is the meaning of his rebuke.

Verses 5-21. Then the favored theme, the wicked and what is in store for them. Apart from the falsity of the application of all Bildad says to Job, his words are certainly true and very poetic. Thus he speaks of the wicked and his fate:

Terrors make him afraid on every side,
And chase him at his footsteps.
Through pangs of hunger his strength declines,
Calamity ever stands ready at his side,
The members of his body to consume,
Yea, death's firstborn his members shall destroy.
His confidence be rooted out of his tent,
It shall lead him away to the king of terrors.
They that are none of his shall dwell in his tent,
And upon it brimstone shall descend.

All his words, though true, were consummated cruelty. It must have been torture and agony unspeakable for suffering Job to hear himself thus portrayed as the wicked man, whose lot is well deserved.

CHAPTER 19

Job's Reply to Bildad

1. How long will ye vex my soul? (19:1-6)
2. And I am not heard! (19:7-12)
3. Forsaken of men he pleads to be pitied (19:13-24)
4. Faith supreme (19:25-27)
5. The warning to his friends (19:28-29)

Verses 1-6. Bildad's scathing speech did not bring Job into the dust. He acknowledges the words vexed his soul and broke him in pieces, but he does not change his view-point. He repudiates the guilt with which they charged him and continues to blame God.

Verses 7-12. Afresh he breaks forth in accusing God. He charges Him with not answering his prayers. "He hath stripped me of my glory, and taken the crown from my head. He hath broken me down on every side, and I am gone." He imagines that His wrath is kindled against him. But what a display of divine mercy and patience! God looked upon the worm in the dust and pities him, as He still pities His children.

Verses 13-24. Then the description of his forsaken condition. Read it in these verses. His brethren, his kinsfolk, his wife, all have turned against him. His servants look upon him as an outcast. Young children even despise him. Then the wail for pity: "Have pity upon me, have pity upon me, O, ye my friends."

Verses 25-27. But what a change! Suddenly light breaks in. He does not speak by himself, but the Spirit of God enlightens his soul and utters words which stand in striking contrast with all his previous wailings. The witness he bears is not without difficulties in point of translation. Darby's translation is as follows:

And as for me, I know that my Redeemer liveth
And at the Last, He shall stand upon the earth;
And if after my skin this shall be destroyed
Yet from out of my flesh I shall see God.
Whom I shall see for myself
And mine eyes shall behold and not another:-
Though mine eyes be consumed within me.

The Companion Bible paraphrases the text in an excellent way:

I know that my Redeemer ever liveth,
And in the latter day on earth shall stand;
And after worms this body have consumed,
Yet in my flesh I shall Eloah (God) see,
Whom I, e'en I, shall see upon my side,
Mine eyes shall see Him—stranger now no more:
For this my inmost soul with longing waits.

And the Redeemer of whom he speaks, enabled to utter these words of faith by the power of another, is the Lord Jesus Christ, the risen, living, coming Redeemer, the victor over death and the grave. Here is the testimony of the book of Job to the hope of the coming of the Lord, the resurrection of the body and the glorification of the saints.

Verses 28-29. How astonished his friends must have been at this wonderful outburst from his lips, which but a few moments ago almost blasphemed God. He asks them why they persecute him, inasmuch as the root of true faith is in him. He warns them that there is judgment.

CHAPTER 20

The Second Address of Zophar

1. Zophar's swift reply (20:1-3)
2. Another description of the life and fate of the wicked (20:4-29)

Verses 1-3. Zophar, the twitterer, begins his reply to Job with impatient haste. Job's words, probably those found in chapter 19:2-3, and the last two verses, have made him angry. He boils over with indignation. He is ready now to confirm the testimony already given and wound the suffering servant of God still more.

Verses 4-29. He follows the same path and there is again nothing new in his argument. The description of the wicked is great; no fault can be found with what he says about those who are ungodly. The triumphing of the wicked, and the joy of the ungodly is for a moment only. He is bound to perish swiftly; like a dream, like a vision he vanisheth away. His children remain poverty stricken. He may swallow down riches, but he vomits them up again. And so he continues in his portrayal of the ungodly. Wrath is finally coming upon him. Such is the portion of the wicked man from God. But the serious mistake Zophar made is twofold. Job had pleaded for pity. Not a word of pity comes from Zophar's lips. The whole address is meant to tell Job "Thou art that man!" And the second mistake, he does not consider for a moment Job's utterance which could not come from the lips of an ungodly person, but from one who knows God.

CHAPTER 21

Job's Reply

1. Hear my solemn words—then mock on (21:1-6)
2. His testimony concerning the experiences of the wicked (21:7-26)
3. Your answers are nothing but falsehoods (21:27-34)

Verses 1-6. This answer shows that Job gets the upper hand over his accusing friends in this controversy. In a masterly way he meets their arguments. He wants them to hear diligently, and if they choose, after he has spoken, they may mock on. He is not complaining to man, or making his appeal to these human friends. He begins to look for another helper, even to God.

Verses 7-26. Zophar's eloquent words concerning the wicked are taken up by Job and he proves that experience shows another side besides the one Zophar had made so prominent. The wicked often live to a ripe old age and possess great power. They have large families and their houses are safe from fear; nor is the chastening hand of God upon them. They prosper and all goes well with them; their cattle increase. They sing to the timbrel and to the harp and rejoice at the sound of the pipe. They love pleasure and have a good time. Then suddenly Job changeth the description. They spend their days in prosperity—but in a moment they go down to Sheol. It reminds us of Asaph's great Psalm (73) in which he describes the prosperity of the wicked: "When I thought to know this it was too painful for me; until I went into the sanctuary of God; then understood I their end. Surely Thou didst set them in slippery places; Thou castedst them down to destruction."

Job declares they reject and defy God; they laugh at the thought of praying to Him. Then he gives his own, personal testimony "the counsel of the wicked is far from me." In this he shows his friends that they are wrong in classing him with the wicked. Then he continues in unfolding the problem of the wicked and how God deals with them.

Verses 27-34. Without enlarging upon the final statements of his answer, we only remark that Job shows that his friends have not only failed to convince him, but their answers are insincere and nothing but falsehoods. The victory is on his side; yet the problem, "why do the righteous suffer and how can their suffering be harmonized with a righteous God," remains as unsolved as before.

3. The Third Series of Controversies

CHAPTER 22

The Third Address of Eliphaz

1. Is not thy wickedness great? (22:1-6)
2. In what Job had sinned (22:6-11)
3. The omniscience of God and the ways of the wicked (22:12-20)
4. Eliphaz's exhortation and promise (22:21-30)

Verses 1-5. The third cycle of addresses begins again with Eliphaz, the wise man from Teman. He tries to maintain his dignity and lofty conception, but he proves too well that Job's accusation of insincerity is well-founded. He starts out with reminding Job of the majesty of God. Can then a man be profitable to God? Is it any pleasure to the Almighty when thou art righteous? Or does He gain anything by it if thou art perfect in thy ways? Since then God has no interest in man's righteousness, and He cannot punish Job for his righteousness, he draws the conclusion that Job is a great sinner. Is not thy wickedness great? Neither is there an end to thine iniquities.

Verses 6-11. And now having made the assertion, according to his logical conclusions, he attempts to show that Job not alone must have sinned, but in what his sin consists. He charges him with avarice, with cruelty, with dealing in a heartless way with widows and with the fatherless. Then he tells Job that is "why these snares are around thee and thou art covered with darkness and with the waters of affliction." The astonishing thing is that every word of what Eliphaz says is a lying invention. Job later gives the most positive proof that all was a concoction of falsehoods. The Word of the Lord concerning Job shows up Eliphaz as a miserable liar, for the Lord had said concerning Job, "there is none like him in the earth, a perfect and an upright man." Would the Lord have spoken this if Job had outraged the laws of humanitarianism and withheld water and bread from the destitute or stripped the naked of their clothing? But how could Eliphaz ever stoop so low? It was but the result of his iniquitous logic. Job must be a sinner; he is a wicked man and without any real facts he draws his conclusions that Job must have done these things and charges him positively with it. The same fatal logic is still with us. Evil, for instance, comes upon a servant of the Lord Jesus Christ; he passeth through affliction, sorrow upon sorrow comes upon him, then someone suggests that his life must be wrong and the slanderous tongue soon charges some specific evil.

Verses 12-20. Eliphaz speaks next of God's omniscience and then again brings in the favoured theme of himself and his friends, the wicked and their defiance of God. Then in self-righteousness he declares—"But the counsel of the wicked is far from me." Strange it is this word which came from Job's lips first (21:16). Evidently Eliphaz repeats this phrase to mock and to insult Job.

Verses 21-30. Once more as before he turns exhorter. Acquaint now thyself with Him and be at peace, thereby good shall come unto thee. He gives him instruction what he is to do, and what God will do for him if he acts upon his advice. But while the exhortations are all proper, they are altogether out of place with Job. For if Job acted upon this advice and would repent according to Eliphaz's demand he would by doing so assent to the false and lying accusations of his three friends. He would acknowledge himself the wicked man they had made him out to be. What he says as to restoration is almost prophetic of what should come to Job in blessing at the close of his trial.

CHAPTERS 23—24

Job's Reply

1. O that I knew where I may find Him (23:1-8)
2. Trusting yet doubting (23:10-17)
3. Hath God failed? (24:1-12)
4. Job's further testimony as to the wicked (24:13-25)

Chapter 23:1-9. Job here does not disprove at once the false charges of Eliphaz. He can afford to wait till later, till their mouths are completely silenced. Then he speaks the final word. He acknowledgeth that he is still rebellious. His hand which is upon him is heavier than all his groanings. Then that outburst which reveals the longing of his tried and tempest-tossed soul—"Oh, that I knew where I might find Him, that I might even come to His seat! I would order my cause before Him, and fill my mouth with arguments." Then in blinded self-righteousness he speaks a bold word: "I would know the words He would answer to me, and understand what He would say to me." He is so sure of it all that he declares "He would give heed to me." How different it was when the Lord did speak and Job's lips are sealed, only to open in expression of deepest self-abhorrence. Yet even in the words he speaks here, still in the dark as to the reason of his suffering, he demonstrates that he is not the defiant wicked man, but one who longs for God.

Verses 10-17. Trusting yet doubting expresseth the sentiment of what he says next. Trust is expressed in the beautiful utterance, "But He knoweth the way that I take; when He hath tried me I shall come forth as gold." Yet it is self-vindication which speaks next, not in God's presence, but to clear himself before his friends. "My foot held fast to His steps." Doubt follows for he still considers God, not his friend, but his enemy.

Chapter 24:1-12. The rendering of the opening verse is difficult to make. It has been paraphrased in this wise: "Since, then, events from the Almighty are not hid, why do not they who love Him know His ways?" This perhaps expresseth the true meaning of his thought. He shows what so often happens on the earth and which seemingly indicates a failure of God in His righteous government. Why is it all? And never before in the history of the race has Job's charge of the failure of God been so prominent as in our evil days.

> From city and from houses groans ascend;
> With shrieks those being murdered cry for help
> Yet God regards not this enormity.

Verses 13-25. He describes the paths of the wicked again and yet they seem to escape the retribution in this life which they so well deserve. They even have security. And Job still is haunted by the thought that in these facts there is found an evidence that God is favorable to them. Death surely comes to them "yet a little while and they are gone" but what comes after death he does not mention. Then boldly he raiseth himself up and says, "And if it be not so now, who will prove me a liar, and make my speech of no account?" What an assertion that all he declared is infallibly true!

CHAPTER 25

The Third Address of Bildad

1. What God is (25:1-3)
2. What man is (25:4-6)

Verses 1-3. Bildad's arguments are exhausted. He has reached the end of his resources and Zophar does not open his lips again. Nevertheless Bildad's final word is of great force and beauty, with deep meaning. He gives a picture of what God is.

> With Him dominion is reverence;
> He maketh peace in His high places.
> The number of His hosts who can count?
> And upon whom doth not His light arise?

How pregnant with meaning these four sentences!

Verses 4-6. And what is man, man the creature of the dust, the earthworm.

> How then can man be just with God?
> Or he be pure who is of woman born?
> Behold for Him the moon hath no brightness,
> And even the stars are not pure in His sight.
> How much less man, that is but a worm!
> Or any mortal man—nothing but a worm!

CHAPTER 26

Job's Reply

1. A sarcastic beginning (26:1-4)
2. Job also knows and can speak of the greatness of God (26:5-14)

Verses 1-4. You have helped me greatly, Bildad, me, who am without power. Whom does thou instruct anyway? And what kind of a spirit is it which speaks through thee? In other words he means to say, I have no more use for your argument at all.

Verses 5-14. But let me, Bildad, tell you something about the greatness of God before which your words pale into nothing. And so he utters a description of God's greatness which is indeed greater than Bildad's. And after this sublime unfolding of God's greatness and power, he truthfully says:

> Lo these are but the outlines of His ways
> A whisper only do we hear of Him
> But who can comprehend the thunder
> of His power?

Job's Closing Words in Self-Vindication

CHAPTER 27

1. My righteousness I hold fast (27:1-6)
2. The contrast between himself and the wicked (27:7-23)

Verses 1-6. Zophar, the third friend, no longer speaks. Perhaps Job paused after his remarks in answer to Bildad and waited for Zophar's criticism. Perhaps that young hot-head hid his inability of advancing another argument under an assumed disgust. Critics have assigned verses 7-10 and 13-23 to Zophar and claim that Job did not speak them at all. But other critics, like Wellhausen, Kuenen and Dillman say that these verses are a later insertion. We do not need to waste our time by examining these claims of the inventive genius of these scholars. There is nothing to them. Job now becomes bolder, knowing that his friends had spent their last arrow against him. He still accuseth God that He has taken away his right and wronged him. And he is determined, more so than ever before, not to give in to the abominable logic of his friends. "My righteousness I hold fast, and will not let it go; my heart does not condemn me as long as I live." It is the vindication of himself.

Verses 7-23. And this self-vindication he pursues when he pictures the godless and contrasts them with himself, showing that he cannot be identified with these. How could this description of the godless ever be applied to himself? True, he had suffered like the wicked suffer, but will his end be like theirs? Thus he tries to show them that they had done him an injustice, for he was an upright man, who in spite of his misery held on to God.

CHAPTER 28

1. The treasures of the earth (28:1-6)
2. The better treasures (28:7-22)
3. God knoweth the way and the true wisdom (28:23-28)

Verses 1-6. This part of the monologue of Job does not seem to have much relation, if any, to the controversial matter of the previous chapters. He speaks first of the treasures of the earth, the riches which man seeks after, but which do not last, and are so often man's undoing. Job shows that he had a good knowledge of mining operations. He knows of veins of silver and how gold is refined. Iron is taken out of the earth and copper molten out of stone. Then he describes how the miner with his mining lamp makes an end to the darkness when he digs into the mountains and then he sinks a shaft. They are so far down that the foot which passeth above knows nothing where they are. The dangers of mining he also mentions—"they hang (suspended by ropes) afar from men, they swing to and fro." All this man does, risking life and comfort, to get gold and the treasures of the earth.

Verses 7-22. But there are better treasures, truer riches than these. Job evidently aims at a contrast with what man seeks in earthly things and the better things which are for him. There is a better way than digging into the earth for gold and precious stones.

> There is a path no bird of prey has ever known,
> Nor has the eagle's eye discovered it.
> A path which no proud beast hath ever trod;
> Not e'en the lion ever passed that way.

But these paths are not for finding treasures of the earth; and so there is another way to get other riches, far better than silver and gold. Then he speaks again of what man does to bring hidden things to light, how he lays his hand on the flinty rock and overturns the mountains in his mining operations, stemming the subterranean waters, and all to bring the hidden treasures to light. Then he asks: "But where can wisdom be found? And where is the place of understanding?" Alas! man does not know the price of wisdom; it is not found in the deep, nor in the sea. Gold cannot buy it, nor silver. The price of wisdom is above rubies, the gold of Ophir, the precious onyx (beryl) or the sapphire. "Whence then cometh wisdom?"

Verses 23-28. Here is the answer: "God understandeth the way thereof. Yea, in all His creation, He knows the way and much more so in redemption He is in the person of His blessed son, the way to Himself, and in Him all the treasures of wisdom and of knowledge are hid." Then comes the revelation of true wisdom: "Behold, the fear of the Lord, that is wisdom; and to depart from evil is understanding." God has spoken to his heart and answered the question concerning wisdom and understanding. And ere long Job himself will demonstrate in his experience the meaning of this verse. In reverence and fear he then turns to Him, bowing in the dust; from evil, yea, from himself he turns, departs and finds the true wisdom and understanding.

CHAPTER 29

1. His past prosperity and honors (29:1-10)
2. The good works he did (29:11-25)

Verses 1-10. The words spoken by Job were wholesome words, showing that his mind was moving in another channel, but now he reverts to the old complaint in self-occupation, self-pity and self-vindication. What a horrible thing this old self! And before the sun can scatter his dark night, that self must be laid into the dust of self-abhorrence. And so we hear him review the past. Some 20 times he says "I" in this chapter. It reminds one of the man in Romans 7 with his "I." Retrospect is good if it is done with praise and in humility. Not once does Job utter a word of praise. It is all spoken to remind his friends, as well as himself, what a great man he was. How often it is with the Lord's servants, that they live in the past and then nourish a most subtle pride.

Verses 11-25. What a prominent place he used to occupy and the good works he did! The words need no further comment; what he means is on the surface. He glories in his good character and in his good works. Self is triumphant. His friends well knew that every word he spoke of his past greatness was true and not a lie.

CHAPTER 30

1. His present humiliation and shame (30:1-19)
2. No answer from God: completely forsaken (30:20-31)

Verses 1-19. He had spoken of his past greatness and now he describes his present misery. Ah! the bitterness if it—those younger than I have me in derision! Alas! through it all we hear nothing but pride. He scorns those who were so much beneath him. And those who were scourged out of the land, these children of fools and base men, mock him, the former prince among men. "I am become their song; I am a byword to them; they abhor me; they spit in my face." Then he describes his affliction. "Days of affliction have taken hold upon me—the pains that gnaw me take no rest." He is in the mire and has become like dust and ashes.

Verses 20-31. He brings in God again. Thou dost not answer me! Heaven had been silent to all his pleas. What a dreadful charge: "Thou art turned to be cruel to me; with the might of Thy hand Thou persecutest me"! He thinks himself completely forsaken, not knowing that God's thoughts towards him were thoughts of love and peace. His skin is black, he says, his bones are burned with heat. No joy for him, nothing but weeping.

CHAPTER 31

1. My chastity and righteousness (31:1-12)
2. My philanthropy (31:13-23)
3. My integrity and hospitality (31:24-34)
4. Let God and man disprove me (31:35-40)

Verses 1-12. His final word is the final word in his self-righteous vindication. He gives Eliphaz the lie. He gives a review of his life to prove that he is clean in the sight of God and of man. Even if after this outburst his friends would have an inclination to answer him they could not have done so. He silenced them for good. But what are his declarations after all? Nothing else but the filthy rags of his own righteousness, the vain boastings of a good, moral man, such as we hear on all sides. He shows that in his character he was morally pure. The gross sins of the flesh he had avoided. He had even abstained from a look which might stir his passion. He knew that God watched him and therefore the sin of adultery was shunned by him; he did not sin against a neighbour's wife. If he had ever done that, then let the sanctity of his home and his own wife be violated. Then he enumerates his great philanthropy. He had respect of the widow; he shared his bread with orphans; those who were naked he had clothed.

Verses 24-34. He was not a worshipper of gold, a covetous man, nor had he worshipped like others about him, the sun and the moon, or what sun-worshippers did, kissing the hand and wafting it towards the sun. He was a hospitable, a kind hearted man; nor did he cover his transgressions as Adam did, nor did he hide his iniquity in his bosom. His was a walk in integrity.

Verses 35-40. 'Lo, here is my signature, let the Almighty answer." I sign my name to all I have said; I swear to it. Let mine enemies also bring forth his accusations and sign them also. He challengeth God and man. And even to the land he appeals that all his transactions were just. Job's words are ended. One feels like saying, "Thank God!"

His final word may be condensed in one sentence: "I am clean." The next time he speaks and opens his lips, he says, "Behold I am vile." How he came to this the rest of the book will teach us.

IV. The Testimony of Elihu

If the book of Job were now ended the last word would be Job's. Furthermore the enigma of suffering would remain unexplained and God's character would stand impeached. Eliphaz, Bildad and Zophar ceased answering Job because he was righteous in his own eyes. But suddenly another appears on the scene. Nothing is said how he came to be there; yet he must have listened to the controversy, for he sizeth up the whole situation and boils down the whole matter in a few terse statements. Critics and most expositors have spoken rather slightingly of Elihu. We heard some years ago a prominent Bible teacher speak of him as "a young theologian who has just been ordained and who thinks he has a lot of knowledge." Others call him "a conceited young philosopher" and that his babbling should be treated with silent contempt. Such statements only prove that the men who make them have not gone deep into the meaning of this book and that they lack in spiritual discernment. Just such a one, sent by God, is needed to exercise a mediatorial function and to prepare the way for the Lord Himself to come upon the scene. It is generally pointed out that God rebukes him in the words of chapter 38:2. But God speaks to Job who applies it to himself. The vindication of Elihu from such criticism of man is found in the last chapter.

CHAPTERS 32—33:7

1. Elihu introduced (32:1-5)
2. I waited, but now must speak (32:6-22)
3. His address to Job (33:1-7)

Verses 1-5. As Elihu had listened to the different addresses his wrath was stirred up. His name is very suggestive. Elihu means "my God is He"; Barachel—"the Blessed God"; the Buzite, "the rejected One" of Ram, and Ram means "exhalted." These are names which find their fullest application in the person of our Lord, whom Elihu in his mediatorial work represents. But why was his wrath kindled? Because Job justified himself rather than God and because Job's friends had found no solution of the problem, yet they condemned Job. This is indeed the result of the whole controversy in a nutshell. From the fourth verse we learn that he was a younger man; he maintained silence because they all were elder than he.

Verses 6-22. He tells them why he waited and did not speak before. He thought "days should speak, and multitude of years should teach wisdom," so he was not a froward, conceited young man. But he acknowledges the spirit and that the inspiration of the Almighty gives understanding. Depending on that he must speak. He tells the three friends in plain words that they did not convince Job, nor did one of them answer his words. With Job, Elihu says he has no controversy and he does not intend to use the speeches of the three men. Verse 15 is a soliloquy in the third person, spoken by Elihu as he looked on the three men. Then he says that he must speak. He is filled with words and the mighty constraint of the spirit within him, makes him like wine which has no vent and is ready to burst like new bottles.

Chapter 33:1-7. The chapter division here is unfortunate. The opening verses belong properly to the preceding chapter. What a difference between Elihu's words in addressing Job and the way the three other men had acted. He is calm, gentle and kind. He assures him that what he is going to say comes from the Almighty. Now, Job, if thou canst answer me, arrange thy words and stand up. "Behold, I am according to thy wish in God's stead." We believe with this Elihu refers to Job's desire for a daysman. Now in the person of Elihu he has come. He encourages Job not to be afraid, for "I am also formed of clay." How beautifully all this may be applied to the true Daysman, our Lord, we leave to the meditation of the reader.

CHAPTER 33

1. Elihu rebukes Job (33:8-13)
2. How God deals with man (33:14-22)
3. How God in grace recovers (33:23-30)
4. Mark well, Job, hearken unto me (33:31-33)

Verses 8-13. Elihu treats Job in a dignified, yet firm manner. He speaks as one who is sure of the whole matter. He has heard Job's speeches; he knows the mistake Eliphaz, Bildad and Zophar made, in treating Job as a suspicious character, a hypocrite and a godless man. No such wrong accusations are made by Elihu. He knows where Job's trouble lies and already spoke of it (32:2); it is his self-justification and pride stands behind it. But Elihu's zeal is for the honor of the name and character of God. What Job had said in charging God he must rebuke. He therefore quotes Job's utterances in his previous addresses. Without entering into a lengthy argument to disprove the charge of Job, or to explain the mystery of the sufferings Job underwent, he utters one masterly sentence. "Behold in this (his wrong charges against God) thou art not just. I will answer thee, *that God is greater than man.*" Well spoken! God is greater than man, therefore His ways are past finding out, yet all must be perfect and righteous. And because God is God—"Why dost thou strive against Him? for He giveth not account of any matter of His."

Verses 14-22. But God, though He is greater than man, does not pass by man or ignore him. Elihu speaks of two different ways in which God deals with man. The first is in a vision of the night, in a dream. When there was no Bible, the revelation of God, God spoke to man individually by dreams and visions. He does not do so any longer for we have His completed Word in which His will is made known unto us. The purpose of this way of dealing with man is to withdraw him from an evil way and to warn him so that he may leave the pride which man nourisheth in his bosom; to keep his soul from the pit and his life from perishing by the sword.

But there is another way in which God deals with man, the way of affliction and suffering. The description Elihu gives of a sufferer fits Job's case exactly. To understand this method of God in dealing with man there is need of a messenger from God, a mediator, one who comes in, a daysman to interpret the meaning of the affliction and God's object in it. It is not a common interpreter who can do this, but one of a thousand—yea, He is needed who is "the chiefest among ten thousand." This interpreter is to show unto man his uprightness. But whose uprightness, or righteousness, is meant? It has been translated by "to show unto man what is right for him"; and so most expositors explain that it means the interpreter tells the sufferer how to do right before God; and critics even suggest that the word "uprightness" should be changed to "fault ." There is a deeper meaning here. The word "his" should be spelled with a capital "H"—not man's, but God's righteousness, the interpreting messenger is to show to the afflicted one. The following paraphrasic translation puts it in the right way:

> Then, then, He speaks to him by messenger
> Who can interpret; One 'mong thousands chief,
> Who will reveal to man HIS righteousness.
> Then He doth show him grace (divine and saith:)
> "Deliver him from going down to death;
> A ransom I have found—redemption's price."

In these words we have Him declared who is the revealer of God's love and righteousness, the Son of God, though His Name is not mentioned, yet He is the only One who reveals to sinful man His righteousness. He has paid redemption's price, He has made atonement and therefore He can deliver the sinner from going down to the pit. Here we have the gospel in the book of Job. Then the blessed results. His flesh becomes as fresh as a young child; this is the new birth He prays to God as His redeemed child and He shows Him grace and beholds His face with joy, even the face of a loving Father. This is the way God bestows upon man His righteousness through Him, His well-beloved Son, who has found the ransom. He sings a new song. "I have sinned, and perverted that which was right, and it profited me not. He hath redeemed my soul from going into the pit, and my life shall behold the light."

Verse 31-33. After this glowing utterance in which Elihu brings in God in His grace, he turns to Job. "Hast thou anything to say, then answer me." But Elihu waits in vain. Job's lips are sealed.

CHAPTER 34

1. Hear my words ye wise men (34:1-4)
2. The refutation of Job's accusation of God (34:5-30)
3. Job needs testing to the end (34:31-37)

Verses 1-4. In beginning this part of the address, in which Elihu vindicates God's character against Job's insinuations, he addresses the friends of Job, and perhaps others who were gathered there. He wants them to pay the closest attention to what he will say.

Verses 5-20. This is the main burden of his address; it is taken up with refuting Job's charge against God. He treats Job with all fairness and quotes what he said before. The wrong Job had done in his words is found in verses 5-9. Then Elihu brings forth the refutation that God is unjust. He shows that God is righteous. He is God and the Almighty and He cannot do that which is evil and unrighteous. If sin or wickedness were in Him He would not be God. His creation bears witness to this. He sustains all in His goodness. Note verse 14 in its true rendering, "Should He set His heart upon Himself," what then would become of man? All flesh would then expire and man would turn to dust again. But He does not set His heart upon Himself. Finally Elihu demonstrates the righteousness of God from His greatness and his omniscience. His judgments also declare that He is righteous (verses 26-30) .

Verses 31-37. And Job has not yet learned the lesson; he needs more testings. Did ever a word like the following come from his sinful lips? "I have borne chastisement, I will not offend any more." Has he asked in humility to be taught? Or has he said, "If I have done iniquity I will do it no more"? Alas! his spirit in spite of all affliction, was still unbroken. "Would that Job were tried unto the end, because he answered like wicked men, for he addeth rebellion unto his sin, He clappeth his hands among us, and multiplieth his words against God."

CHAPTER 35

1. Remember the greatness of God (35:1-8)
2. Why God is silent and does not answer (35:9-16)

Verses 1-8. Job having kept silence Elihu continues and asks him if this is sound judgment, what he had said, "My righteousness is greater than God's righteousness." This was the logical conclusion which Elihu drew from some of his words. Because God did not care for him the sufferer what profit was it to him if he had not sinned? Then Elihu answers and his friends as well by following Job's unjustly charge. He points out the greatness of God and that cannot in any way be affected by what man does. That was Job's contention. Look at the heavens which are higher than the creature of the dust. If thou hast sinned by thy many sins, what canst thou do to Him? If thou are just, what givest thou to Him? Thy sin may hurt thee, and thy righteousness may profit thee; how canst thou claim that He has afflicted you in an unrighteous way? In all this Elihu had accommodated himself to Job's wrong reasoning.

Verses 9-16. Furthermore, Elihu shows that this reasoning of Job is utterly false. Job had contradicted himself. God takes notice of man. Then he gives the reasons why God does not answer the cry of the afflicted. It is not His indifference but man's sin and forgetfulness of Him. None saith, "Where is God my Maker, who giveth songs in the night?" The true reason is the evil-doer's pride. God will in nowise hear vanity. Pride, vanity, self-will and all that goes with it makes it impossible for a righteous God to hear. And therefore Job's contention that it does not matter with God whether a man sins or is righteous is disproven.

CHAPTER 36:1-21

1. God's care over the godly (36:1-7)
2. The purposes of affliction (36:8-18)
3. Job to consider this (36:19-21)

Verses 1-7. Elihu had told Job in the last verse of the preceding chapter that he had opened his mouth in vanity and had multiplied words without knowledge. That should have explained to Job the reason why God did not answer. There could be no reply from Job and so Elihu continues. He is not through yet with speaking in behalf of God. Sublimely he stands up for God. "I will ascribe righteousness to my Maker." He tells Job, "One that is perfect in knowledge is with thee." How could he say this? Because Elihu knew in speaking for God His Spirit would speak through him to Job. All Job had said was wrong. Though God is mighty, yet does He not despise any. He does not preserve the life of the wicked, nor does He withdraw His eyes from the righteous. But the day is coming when God will reward the righteous.

He seateth them with kings upon the throne
He makes them sit in glory; raised on high.

Beautiful truth! It is a glimpse of the gospel again, as expressed also in Hannah's song of praise (1 Samuel 2).

Verses 8-18. But what about the afflictions of the righteous? Here Elihu speaking in God's behalf lifts the veil. He permits them to be bound in fetters and in sorrow's bonds, so that He, the righteous God, may show to them their deeds, to uncover their transgressions which have for its source that which God hates, pride (the crime of the Devil; 1 Tim. 3:6). It is love and kindness, not his wrath and displeasure, which are revealed in the afflictions of the righteous. He wants to instruct them by suffering. And if they hearken and learn the lesson, they shall spend their days in prosperity, and end their earthly existence in peace and pleasantness. It was a call to Job to acknowledge this, it is a prophecy that ere long he would find it out, when God has accomplished His purpose with him, and his end would be peace and prosperity. The wicked do not heed this and therefore perish. Let any man refuse to hear Him and harden his heart against Him, they shall perish among the unclean. He would have led out Job in a broad place, but if Job continues in the argument of the wicked, reasoning and pleading as they do, charging God falsely, then let him beware. "Because there is wrath, beware lest He take thee away with His stroke, then a great ransom cannot deliver thee." We dare not meddle with this verse as others have done. Let it stand as it is, this solemn truth! There is wrath and if man does not hearken to God His wrath in judgment will be displayed and the great ransom, not even the great ransom, can deliver.

Verses 19-21. These verses contain wholesome words of exhortation addressed to Job to take heed and not to regard iniquity.

CHAPTER 36:22—37

1. God's power and presence in nature (36:22-33)
2. The thunderstorm (37:1-5)
3. The snow and the rain (37:6-16)
4. Elihu's concluding remarks (37:17-24)

Chapter 36:22-33. The chapter division in the Authorized Version is at fault. These concluding verses of the thirty-sixth chapter begin the final section of Elihu's testimony. Unspeakably great in every way, in diction and reverence, is this man's witness to the ways of God in creation's work. They show that he speaks not of himself, but the One who is perfect in knowledge speaks through him. God's power is displayed in nature and man should extol His work and gaze in wonder upon it.

Lo! God is Great—greater than we can know;
The number of His years past finding out.
Tis He who draweth up the vapour clouds,
And they distil from heaven in rain and mist,
E'en that which from the low'ring skies does fall,
And poureth down on man continually.
Can any man explain the rain-clouds balancings,
The rumbling thunders of His canopy?
Behold He spreadeth out His light thereon
While making dark the bottom of the sea.
Yet He His judgment executes by these;
By these He giveth food abundantly.
He graspeth in His hand the lightning flash
And giveth it commandment where to strike.
Of this the noise thereof quick notice gives
The frightened cattle warn of coming storm.
(*Companion Bible*)

How beautiful! It also proves the antiquity of the book. In early days man knew the Creator by His works and was fully occupied with them (Romans 1:20-21).

Chapter 37:1-5. And now the thunderstorm. His voice is heard in the thunder, His power displayed in the lightning and Elihu, in vivid description, trembles.

He thundereth with His voice of Majesty
One cannot trace Him, though His voice be heard.
God's voice is wondrous when He thundereth.
Great things He doth; we comprehend them not.

And if He is so wonderful in nature, His ways there past finding out, how much more in His providential dealings. Yet whether in nature or in providence, His ways are perfect.

Verses 6-16. The description of God's perfect ways in nature are continued by Elihu. The snow and the rain, the hot blast of the summer, the biting frost of winter, the formation of ice by His breath and the storms, all is in His hands and controlled by Him. O Job! hearken, hearken! Stand still and consider the wondrous works of God.

Verses 17-24. And now the concluding words of his great, God-given testimony. They are to impress Job and all of us with the frailty, the nothingness of man. "Touching the Almighty, we cannot find Him out; He is excellent in power; and in judgment and plenteous justice He will not afflict. Men do therefore fear Him; for none can know Him, be they ere so wise." This must be man's true attitude. This should have been Job's place before the Almighty. Surely the beautiful and powerful testimony of Elihu must have been a spiritual anaesthetic to Job. But more than that, it clears the way for the Almighty to speak.

V. The Lord's Testimony to Job and Controversy with Him

CHAPTER 38:1-38

1. The Lord speaks to Job (38:1-3)
2. The questions of the Lord (38:4-38)

Verses 1-3. The voice of man is hushed; the voice of the Lord begins to speak. The Almighty, the Creator, the Lord of All comes now upon the scene. He too, like Elihu, had been the silent listener; He heard Job's complaint and wailing and the babblings of his friends. Elihu's wonderful utterance, inspired by the Lord, was ended. The thunderstorm is on, no doubt a literal storm, the dark clouds gather—

Then from the North there comes a golden light.
God appears in wondrous Majesty (chapter 37:22).

The golden light of God's own presence and glory overshadows the scene. Out of the whirlwind His own voice is heard. It is that voice which David in the "thunderstorm-Psalm" (Psalm 29) so wonderfully describes. The voice which is upon the waters—full of majesty, the voice which breaketh the cedars; the voice which divideth the flames of fire. When David thus extolled the voice of the Lord, he shows the demands of that voice. "Give unto the Lord, O ye mighty, give unto the Lord glory and strength. Give unto the Lord the Glory due unto His Name; worship the Lord in the beauty of holiness." And that voice, though terrible in majesty, will bring peace. "The Lord will bless His people with peace." What a scene it must have been there in the land of Uz, when the voice of the Lord spoke out of the whirlwind! We can imagine how good Elihu stepped aside and covered his face. And Eliphaz, Bildad and Zophar, terror-stricken, fell on their faces in the dust, while silent Job, awe-struck, dares not to look up. And what He speaks is for the one great purpose to humble Job, to bring him in the dust.

Job's last utterance was this: Oh, that the Almighty would answer me (31:35). He answers Him now. "Who is this that darkeneth counsel by words without knowledge?" What a blunder expositors have made of speaking of Elihu's gentle words, and true words, as "a harsh judgment" and that God rebukes him in this verse. No; God does not rebuke Elihu who had exalted His Name and His works. He rebukes Job. He had darkened counsel by the multitude of his senseless words. God answers Job. He is going to ask him questions.

Verses 4-38. If we were to examine these questions minutely, which the compass of our work does not allow, we would have to write many pages. There are 40 questions which the Lord asks of Job, His creature, concerning His own works in creation. They relate to the earth and its foundations upon which all rests, the bounds of the sea—

When I decreed for it My boundary
And set its bars and doors and to it said,
Thus far—no farther, ocean, thou shalt come:
And here shall thy proud waves be stayed.

He asks about the morning light and the unknown depths, the unexplored depths of the sea, with their hidden secrets, and the gates of death. He questions as to the elements, the treasuries of the snow, the storehouse of hail, the rain, the winds and the ice—

Whose is the womb whence cometh forth the ice?
And heaven's hoar-frost, who gave it its birth?

As turned to stone, the waters hide themselves;
The surface of the deep, congeal'd, coheres.

And what about the things above, the stars and their wonderful constellations?

Canst thou bind fast the cluster Pleiades?
Or canst thou loosen great Orion's bands?
Canst thou lead forth the Zodiac's monthly signs?
Or canst thou guide Arcturus and his sons?

And then the rain clouds, the lightnings and their control. What questions these are. They cover every department of what man terms "natural sciences"—geology, meteorology, geography, oceanography, astronomy, etc. Job had not a single answer to these questions and if he had spoken his words would have been folly. And we, 3000 years or more after, with all our boasted progress, scientific discoveries of the great laws of nature, are still unable to answer these questions in a satisfactory way. All the boastings of science of getting at the secrets of creation are nothing but foam. One breath of the Almighty and man's speculations, apart from Him and His Word, are scattered to the winds. But what is the aim of the Lord in putting these questions? To show that God is greater than man and to humble man, to bring Job to the needed true knowledge of himself and to deliver him from the pride of his heart.

CHAPTERS 38:39—39

1. The beasts of prey (38:39-41)
2. The wild goats, the ass, the unicorn and the ostrich (39:1-18)
3. The horse, the hawk and the eagle (39:19-30)

Chapter 38:39-41. God's own wisdom and power in nature, as witnessed to by Himself, is followed by His witness as to the sustenance of His creatures, how mercifully He provides for their need. This section begins with the query, "Knowest thou?" Could he hunt the prey of the lion, or fill the ravenous appetite of their young? God considers the young, even so unclean a bird as the raven has its food provided by God. Wonderful it is to read that the young ravens in their helplessness cry to God. The beasts acknowledge the Creator by their instincts and look to Him for food, though it be not the sweet song of a lark, but only the croak of a raven. How it reminds us of the witness of the same Creator who speaks here, when He was clothed in creature's form. "Consider the ravens; for they neither sow nor reap; which neither have storehouse nor barn; and God feedeth them. How much more are ye better than the fowls" (Luke 12:24). And striking it is that He begins by calling Job's attention to the wild beasts first, though they are now man's enemy through man's sin. God in His infinite wisdom and benevolence cares for them.

Chapter 39:1-18. Then what about the goats of the rock and their young? His omniscient eye beheld them out in the desert rocks and He watched over their young. Could He then not watch the footsteps of His higher creature, even His offspring, man? Then the wild ass, also a desert animal. He cannot be tamed. God made him so. The unicorn (the aurochs) with his strength is known to God also. He has the power to make him the willing slave; man cannot do it. And the peacock with its goodly wings and the ostrich, which leaveth her eggs in the earth, and warmeth them in dust. Who takes care of these hidden eggs, which the foot might crush and wild beasts break? It would be amusing, if it were not so sad, when critics declare that the author of "the poem" made a mistake when he speaks of the eggs of the ostrich. But it is not an "author" who speaks, but the Creator Himself and He knows more about His creatures than all the "scientists" in the world.

Verses 19-30. Next the description of the noble horse. Did Job give the war horse his strength or clothe the neck with the rustling mane, or make him leap like the locust? The picture of the war horse in battle is sublime also. God shows to Job a glimpse of His works, and the wisdom which has created them, as well as His care in keeping them. Such a God is He whom Job has maligned.

The hawk too may teach him a lesson. Is it by Job's instructions that the hawk soars high into the air, and is it by his command that the eagle mounts and builds his nest in the dizzy heights, from where he spys his prey? No answer could Job give. His silence is assent. God is great and unsearchable and Job but the rebellious worm of the dust.

CHAPTER 40

1. The answer demanded (40:1-2)
2. Job's answer (40:3-5)
3. Jehovah's appeal to Job (40:6-14)
4. Behold behemoth! (40:15-24)

Verse 1-3. Now comes the direct word of Jehovah out of the storm-cloud to Job. He addresses him as "he that reproveth God." He had contended with the Almighty and now the Almighty Job had judged faces him and demands an answer. Let him answer.

Verses 3-5. And Job answers; and what an answer it is! It is the answer for which God was waiting. "Lo! I am vile; what shall I answer Thee? I will lay my hand upon my mouth." He acknowledges that he had spoken too much and that now he cannot answer and proceeds no further. He is completely silenced, acknowledges his own nothingness and vileness, that his words were wrong and that he has nothing else to say. He was convinced that such a God who had spoken to him of creation and His creatures, making known His power, wisdom and care, could never be unjust in His dealings with man.

Verses 6-14. But Jehovah, the searcher of hearts, has not yet finished. Job's abominable pride must be laid bare. Jehovah asks him the serious question, 'Wilt thou disannul My judgment? Wilt thou condemn Me, that thou mayest be righteous? Hast thou an almighty arm like God, or canst thou thunder with a voice like His?" Then he tells him: "Deck thyself now with majesty and glory." Array thyself with majesty and power. Come and take My place and then thus arrayed let Job be in God's place, rule and deal with proud man and the evil-doers.

Send far and wide thy overflowing wrath;
And on each proud one look, and bring him low;
Each proud one single out, and humble him;
Yea, crush the evildoers where they stand;
Hide them away together in the dust;
And in the deepest dungeon have them bound.

It is Divine irony, but needed in order to humble Job still more. He who was so proud and had so stubbornly defended his righteousness in self-jutification and God-accusation, how could he do what Jehovah asked him to do?

But if he were to do it, then Jehovah would be ready to own to him "that thy right hand to save thee will suffice." It all strikes home to the proud, self-righteous heart of Job.

Verses 15-24. The Lord asks Job to consider the behemoth; it is undoubtedly the hippopotamus (the Greek for river-horse). A description of this powerful beast follows. He calls the behemoth the "chief of the ways of God," one of His greatest works in animal creation. The behemoth is one of Job's fellow-creatures "which I made as thee." He eateth grass like an ox. He has tremendous strength in his loins and legs. He takes its rest under the shady trees and fears nothing:

Suppose the stream should swell,
  he will not blench
For he believes that Jordan he can drink.
Shall any take him while he lies on watch?
Or with a ring shall any pierce his nose?

Behemoth then is a powerful, uncontrollable beast which lives for itself. How weak then is man as contrasted with this beast in possession of such marvellous strength. Yet it is only a beast and Job is a man. How abominable then must Job's pride and boasting appear in the sight of the Lord.

CHAPTER 41

1. Leviathan, the untamable beast of power (41:1-11)
2. Its description (41:12-24)
3. His remarkable strength (41:25:34)

Verses 1-11. The leviathan has generally been identified with the crocodile. Like the behemoth, the leviathan is a strong and untamable beast. Jehovah asks, Canst thou draw up leviathan with a hook? Canst thou pierce his jaw with a reed? Will he make a covenant with thee? Wilt thou take him for a servant forever? Then He declares that he is fierce, and even at the sight of him one is cast down. And if a creature is so mighty and strong what must the One be who called this creature into existence? Verses 10 and 11 should be rendered as follows: "Who then is able to stand before Me (the Creator) who did give to me first that I should repay him? since all beneath the heavens is mine."

Verses 12-24. A more detailed description of the leviathan follows. His frame is strong; his outer garment, so invulnerable, who can strip it off? His teeth are terrible, who can open the doors of his face (his mouth)? His scales, his armour, are his pride. Here is a good description of the crocodile's hide. The scales are so near each other that no air can come between them; they are joined one to another, they stick together, that they cannot be sundered. His sneezings flash forth light and his eyes are like the eyelids of the morning. The eyes of the crocodile are visible quite a distance under water. The Egyptians therefore used the crocodile's eyes in the hieroglyphics for the dawn of the morning. The entire description shows what a terrible beast it is.

Verses 25-34. Then his great strength is unfolded. If one lay at him with the sword, it cannot avail. The dart, the spear and the pointed shaft make no impression upon him. He counteth iron as straw and brass as rotten wood. The arrow cannot make him flee; clubs are counted as stubble. The final statement concerning leviathan is "He is king over all the sons of pride."

This last word is significant—"He is King over all the sons of pride." It has a deeper meaning. In Isaiah 27:1 we read: "In that day the Lord with His sore and strong sword shall punish leviathan the piercing serpent, even leviathan the crooked serpent; and He shall slay the dragon that is in the sea." Here leviathan typifies the power of darkness. Both the behemoth and the leviathan typify Satan, his character and his rule. He is king over all the sons of pride. These two beasts are likewise a good description of the beasts spoken of in Revelation, which at the end of this age will manifest their power and pride as Satan's masterpieces. And now the deduction which Job could easily make. If he is proud then he belongs to leviathan the king who rules over the sons of pride. Jehovah has touched the secret in Job's bosom. He has searched out the depths of his heart. Pride, the Devil's crime, has been cherished by him. And now with the heart laid bare by Jehovah's dealing we shall hear Job's voice once more.

VI. The Confession of Job

CHAPTER 42:1-6

Critics claim that Job's answer is misplaced and that it really ought to be put in connection with chapter 41:3-5. This is another evidence of the lack of spiritual discernment of these "great" scholars. They treat the Word of God as literature only and criticise it as such. We have seen that the additional words of Jehovah were needed to bring Job completely into the dust and bring from his lips the confession which alone could satisfy Jehovah and be the great blessing for himself. This confession we have now before us.

Then Job answered the Lord and said:
I know that Thou canst do all things,
And that no purpose of Thine can be withstood.
Who is this that hideth counsel
without knowledge?
Therefore have I uttered that
which I understood not.
Hear I beseech Thee and I will speak;
I will demand of Thee, and I will
speak and declare Thou unto Me.
I heard of Thee by the hearing of the ear;
But now mine eyes seeth Thee,
Wherefore I abhor myself, and repent
In dust and ashes.

Here we have his full answer, his complete prostration before Jehovah. He acknowledgeth first Jehovah's supreme power. He is omnipotent and can do all things. Then he quotes Jehovah's own words (38:2; 40:2). Thou hast asked me, "Who is this that hideth counsel without knowledge?" It is strange that some expositors can misapply these words as if the Lord again rebuked Elihu. No, as we have shown before, He rebukes Job for his wild and audacious charges he had made against the Lord. And now Job acknowledgeth that Jehovah's rebuke is right. It is all true, he saith, I uttered things I did not understand, things too wonderful for me, beyond my ken. Hear me now, Jehovah, I will speak. Once more he quotes Jehovah's word. Thou hast said (40:2), "I ask of thee, answer ME." Here then is my answer, he replies—I heard of Thee by hearing of the ear; but now mine eyes hath seen Thee—this is my answer now—I abhor myself. In dust and ashes I repent.

Face to face with Jehovah, His power and His holiness prostrate Job in the dust. No creature can stand and boast in His presence. His plea of innocence, of righteousness, of philanthropy and all the boastings of his former greatness is gone. He seeth himself stripped of all; he stands in Jehovah's presence in nakedness and shame. Nor does he say that he abhors now what his mouth hath spoken, but it is himself, his wicked, proud self, which he abhors. He has taken the place of greatness. Now Jehovah can come forth and lift him up and raise him to blessing and glory. This great scene corresponds with the vision of Isaiah when he beheld the Lord and cried out "Woe is me! for I am undone; because I am of unclean lips" (Isaiah 6:5). And Daniel also! (Daniel 10) Peter on the Lake of Galilee was face to face with Him, who hath spoken to Job, the same and not another, and when he seeth His power and realizeth this is Jehovah, Peter falls at His feet and like Isaiah, Daniel and Job, acknowledges his nothingness. "Depart from me, for I am a sinful man, O Lord."

The enigma of the book of Job is solved. God permitted the afflictions to come upon His servant Job, not only to manifest His power, but for Job's good, to draw him into the place of nearness and of blessing. And that place is the dust, 'in dust and in ashes."

This is the place which all God's saints must own. And blessed are we, beloved reader, if we follow the wooings of grace, if we let His Spirit put us daily into that place, so that the Lord's hand may be prevented from putting us there by suffering and affliction.

VII. The Epilogue: Job's Restoration and Blessing

CHAPTER 42:7-17

1. Jehovah's message to Job's friends (42:7-9)
2. Job's restoration (42:10-15)
3. The conclusion: Peace (42:16-17)

Verses 7-9. Like the beginning of the book, the prologue, the epilogue is not in a poetic measure, but in prose. The Lord addresseth Eliphaz as the most prominent one of the three friends of Job. His wrath is kindled against the three. Though they had apparently stood up for Him and defended His character, yet under the searchlight of the Omniscient One, who searcheth the hearts of men, they are found wanting. The charges they had brought against his servant Job, were false. They had wickedly accused Job, whom He had declared to be "a perfect and an upright man." In all their charges they had slandered God. Then the Lord said, "for ye have not spoken of Me the thing that is right, as My servant Job hath." Here is a beautiful lesson. Job hath confessed and Jehovah hath forgiven. He forgets all Job's sinful utterances; He remembers them no more. But in infinite grace He takes the few sentences scattered throughout Job's speeches in which he honoured the Lord and expressed trust in Him and with these He is well pleased. It must have been a sweet music in Jehovah's ear when Job said, "Though He slay me yet will I trust." And so He acknowledgeth Job as His servant. They must bring sacrifices—a burnt offering; and that blessedly shows us the cross.

"And my Servant Job shall pray for you; for Him I will accept. . . ." Sweet scene now as Job prays for his humbled friends. How it again reminds us of Him, who ever liveth and maketh intercession for His people. Him God hath accepted in His great sacrificial work on the cross, and we are accepted in Him.

So Eliphaz the Temanite, Bildad the Shuhite, and Zophar the Naamathite went, and did according as the Lord commanded them; and the Lord accepted Job. This is the last as to Job's friends.

Verses 10-15. And now Job's restoration and double blessing. All his kinfolks return with all his acquaintances and sit down to a meal in sweet communion. What about his bodily disease? Nothing is said of that. But assuredly the Lord touched his suffering body, and He who spoke to the leper, must have spoken to Job, "Be thou clean," and the loathsome disease vanished, and as Elihu had said, his flesh became like that of a young child. They also brought him money and rings of gold. They were not presents to enrich him, the Lord did that for Job, but simply to show how happy they were over Job's healing and restoration.

All his wealth becomes twice as large as before. The Lord blessed the latter end of Job more than his beginning. While his possessions are doubled, his sons and daughters are not. He gives him also seven sons and three daughters. This does not mean, as some suppose, that they were not new sons and daughters, but that the restoration is that in resurrection. Such view is untenable. The sons and daughters were born to him. The names of the three daughters are given. Jemimah (a dove); Keziah (cassia); Keren-happuch (flashes of Glory). Such were the blessed results of Job's experience, expressed by these names. Purified and humble like the dove; cassia, which is fragrance, worship and adoration; and the flashes and splendour of glory.

Verses 16-17. We have reached the end. It is an end of peace, a perfect day. Four generations he beholds and at the ripe old age of 140 years he is gathered to his fathers. In consulting the Septuagint version we find a long addition to the last verse which begins with this statement: "and it is written that he will rise again with those whom the Lord raises up." Then follows Job's genealogy. It is taken from some apocryphal writing but it shows that the hope of the resurrection of the body was believed in ancient days. Surely Job will be there, "in that day" and his great utterance, "I know that my Redeemer liveth," and the hope of seeing Him will be realized.

"Ye have heard of the patience of Job, and have seen the end of the Lord; that the Lord is very pitiful, and of tender mercy" (James 5:11). And all His people know this matchless truth, that the Lord in all His dealings with His people "is very pitiful and of tender mercy." In our annotations we have pointed out repeatedly the comparison of Job in his sufferings with the

Lord, our Saviour, and His holy sufferings in the sinner's place. It brings out the perfection of Him who is altogether lovely.

An application to Israel can also be made. If this is followed out it will prove of much interest. Israel, like Job, is suffering, self-righteous, but some day the nation will come face to face with Jehovah and be humbled in the dust. Then their restoration when they will receive double of the Lord's hand for all their sins (Isaiah 11:2).

THE BOOK OF
PSALMS

Introduction

"Although all Scripture breatheth the grace of God, yet sweet beyond all others is the book of Psalms." This is the ancient witness of Ambrose. And Luther said "You might rightly call the Psalter a Bible in miniature." Hundreds of similar testimonies could be added. The Psalms have always been one of the choicest portions of the Word of God for all saints, Jewish and Christian. The ancient Jews used the Psalms in the temple worship. The so-called "Great Hallel," consisting of Psalms 113—118 was sung during the celebration of Passover, Pentecost and the feast of tabernacles. Daily in the temple Psalms were sung in a prescribed order. The Jews still use them in all their feast days and in the synagogue.

The Psalms are mentioned in connection with praise in the New Testament (Col. 3:16; James 5:13). The Church from the very start has used them in public and private devotion. All branches of Christendom use them today; Protestantism, Romish and Greek Catholicism make use of them in responsive reading or chanting. And even more so are they used and have always been used by individuals, because the heart finds in these songs and prayers, the different experiences of human life, and the different emotions. The sufferer steeped in sorrow finds in this book the experiences of suffering and sorrow; he finds more than that, encouragement to trust God and the assurance of deliverance. The penitent soul finds that which suits a broken and contrite heart. The lonely one, helpless and forsaken, reads of others who passed through the same experience. Then there is comfort, joy and peace, as well as hope. They stimulate faith and confidence in the Lord and are breathing a spirit of worship and praise which produce reverence and praise in the heart of the believer.

The Lord Jesus and the Psalms

But there is another reason why believers love the Psalms. The Lord Jesus is not only revealed in this book as nowhere else (as we shall show later) but He used the Psalms throughout His blessed life on earth and even in glory. Here are His own prayers prewritten by the Spirit of God. The expression of sorrow, loneliness, rejection and suffering describe what He passed through in His life of humiliation. The praise and worship, the trust and confidence in God, express likewise prophetically that life of obedience and trust. We believe when He spent nights in prayer to pour out His heart before His Father, on the mountain or in the desert, He must have done so by using the Psalms. He used the Psalms speaking to His disciples; with Psalm 110 He silenced His enemies. Gethsemane is mentioned in the Psalms; and in the suffering of the cross He fulfilled all that the Psalms predict. In resurrection He used the twenty-second Psalm: "Go and tell My brethren." He opened to His disciples the Scriptures "that all things must be fulfilled, which were written in the law of Moses, in the prophets, and in the Psalms, concerning Me" (Luke 24:44) as He had before told the two on the way to Emmaus "Ought not Christ to have suffered these things and to enter into His glory?" And beginning at Moses and all the prophets, He expounded unto them in all the Scriptures concerning Himself. When He ascended on high and took the seat at God's right hand, and God welcomed Him to sit down and to be the priest after the order of Melchisedec it was according to the Psalms. And in His messages from the throne in speaking to the churches He uses the Psalms (Rev. 2:27). And when He comes again the Hallelujah chorus of the ending of this book will be sung by heaven and earth and all the predicted glory, as given in the Psalms, will come to pass. This book then ought to be precious to us, because it was precious to Him and makes Him known to our hearts. The Spirit of God also quotes the Psalms more frequently in the Epistles than any other Old Testament book.

The Title of the Book

Our English word "psalms" is taken from the Greek word employed in the Septuagint translation—*"psalmoi";* this means "songs." It is also frequently called Psalter. This word is also Greek, from "Psalterion," a harp or any other stringed instrument.

The Hebrews call this book *"Tehillim,"* which means to make a joyful sound, or praises. It is in the Hebrew Bible in the third division, the *"Kethubim"* section. It is the great poetical book of the Old Testament. We refer the reader to our remarks on Hebrew poetry in the introduction to the book of Job. The poetry of the Psalms is of a lyric character. The real great beginning of lyric poetry is with King David. He was remarkably gifted and yet it was not natural gift which produced these wonderful utterances but it was the Spirit of God who tuned his harp. Our space is too valuable to pay much attention to the critical school with their denials of the Davidic authorship of different Psalms, and that which is worse, the denial of the Messianic predictions of the Psalms. If these critics were but seekers after the fine gold, the precious gems of truth and divine knowledge, so richly stored in this mine, they would cease criticising and become worshippers.

The Authorship of the Different Psalms

Nearly one-half of the Psalms, seventy-three in all, were given by the Holy Spirit through the Shepherd King of Israel, David, who is rightly called the sweet singer of Israel.

The following are the *Davidic* Psalms: 3—9; 11—41 (except Psalm 33); 51—70; 86; 101; 103; 108; 109; 110; 122; 124; 131; 133; 138—145.

Asaph has twelve Psalms: Psalm 1 and Psalms 73—83.

The children of *Korah* composed eleven Psalms: Psalms 43, 44—49, 84, 85, 87 and 88.

One by *Heman the Ezrahite* Psalm 88 and one by *Ethan the Ezrahite* Psalm 89; one by *Moses,* Psalm 90.

That makes 99 Psalms whose authors are known; the remaining 51 have no inscription.

The Collection and Arrangement of the Psalms in the Present Form

From the foregoing paragraph we learn that the known authors of the Psalms are: David, Asaph, the Children of Korah, Moses, Heman, and Ethan. If we take into consideration that other Psalms were written during the exile we see that the authors are centuries apart. The people Israel possessed these Psalms in an uncollected form; they laid about loose, so to speak. Someone at some time collected them in a book, in the form we have them now.

Who did this valuable collecting and arranging of these Psalms we do not know for it is not revealed. But this we can say of certainty that the Hebrew saint who did it was called to do it by the Spirit of God and the very arrangement of these Psalms in the book as we have it now is the perfect work of the Holy Spirit.

Here we clash with the critics who speak of "different editors arranging and re-arranging at different occasions." They claim, for instance, that the statement at the close of Psalm 72 "The prayers of David the son of Jesse are ended," shows that it is misplaced because other Davidic Psalms come later, and that probably this is the work of some editor, etc. But the phrase at the close of Psalm 72 rather means something different, as we take it. The Seventy-second Psalm reveals the glories of the coming kingdom of Him who is greater than Solomon, and David, getting a glimpse of it, declares. "The prayers of David, my prayers are ended; I have nothing greater to ask, than what this Psalm reveals."

The work the unknown collector has done shows that it is the work of one person guided by the Spirit of God.

Let us suppose that we had in our possession a basket containing 150 precious stones, diamonds, rubies, sapphires, emeralds and pearls and we went with this basket to some jeweler with the request to arange these gems in a necklace. How would he go about? Would he take out a stone at random and put it on a string and then take another, and another till he had strung them all? Certainly not. He would examine each stone. He would study the value of every emerald and sapphire, the brilliancy of each diamond and the lustre of every pearl. Then he would continue to study where each belongs on that chain so as to tell out its own value in relation to the other.

And here were 150 gems of greater value than earthly gems, gems of divine inspiration. They are to be arranged in perfect order so that each gem has the right place, to tell out its own story, in this book. Who else could do this but He who knows the value and meaning of these Psalms! The Spirit of God through His chosen instrument put these Psalms together and therefore we have in the arrangement a most wonderful, consecutive revelation. It is this knowledge which so many readers of the Psalms have missed. Generally one Psalm is read without considering that this Psalm stands in some relationship to the preceding one and to those which follow, that it is only a link in a chain. Just as Romans 6 leads to Romans 7 and Romans 7 to Romans 8, so it is with the Psalms. And here we shall discover the divine wisdom. These Psalms come in clusters and must be treated as belonging together to get the real spiritual and especially prophetic message. We give the most simple illustration of this fact found in the book known to many readers of the Psalms: Psalm 22 is a prophecy of Christ in His suffering, or the good Shepherd who gives His life for the sheep. Psalm 23 shows Him as the great Shepherd of the sheep and Psalm 24 reveals Him as the coming, chief Shepherd in glory. The many other most interesting interrelation of Psalms the annotations will point out. Before we give the great message of the book of Psalms we call attention to other matters of importance in the study of this remarkable book.

The Hebrew Terms in Connection with the Psalms

In many of the Psalms we find the beginning a Hebrew word. For instance in Psalm 8 "To the Chief Musician upon the Gittith," or in Psalm 16 "Michtam of David." It is now a question whether these terms belong to the Psalm with which they are connected in our English Bibles, or to the preceding Psalm. When we read the last chapter of Habakkuk we find a psalmodic phrase at the close, "To the chief singer upon Neginoth." Upon this the interesting theory has been advanced that the different titles in the Psalms should be the subscription of the preceding one. In other words, to give an illustration, the words standing at the beginning of Psalm 8 "To the chief musician upon the Gittith," belongs to Psalm 7. Our work does not permit a minute examination of this. Such a misplacement could of course easily happen when we remember that the Hebrew manuscripts were written without a break. (Dr. J. W. Thirtle of England, to whom we are indebted for this suggestion, has written a volume on it, *The Titles of the Psalms.* We recommend it to those who desire to follow it more closely.)

We give in alphabetical arrangement the Hebrew titles and their English meaning.

Aijeleth-Shahar. Psalm 22. "The hind of the dawn." The early light preceding the dawn of the morning, whose first rays are likened to the shining horns of a hind. (Delitzsch)

Alamoth. It means "concerning maidens." It is found in the beginning of Psalm 46.

Al-Tashcheth. "Destroy not," in Psalms 57—59 and in Psalm 75.

Gittith. "Winepresses," in Psalms 7, 80 and 83.

Jeduthun. "Praise giver," in Psalms 39, 62, and 77.

Mahalath. "Sickness." Delitzsch says on the meaning the following "Upon Mahalath signifies after a sad tone or manner, whether it be that Mahalath itself is a name for such an elegiac kind of melody, or that it was thereby designed to indicate the initial word of some popular song. So that we may regard 'Mahalath' as equivalent to piano or andante." This would correspond to Psalm 53 where this word is found.

Mahalath Leannoth. It means "sickness unto humiliation." It stands connected with Psalm 88.

Maschil. "Instruction," found in Psalms 32, 42, 44, 52—55, 74, 78, 88, 89, 142.

Michtam. "Engraven," in Psalms 16, 56—60.

Muth-Labben. "Death for the son." It is found as the superscription of Psalm 9.

Neginoth. "Smitings," in Psalms 4, 6, 54, 55, 61, 67 and 76.

Nehiloth. "Possessions," in Psalm 5.

Sheminith. "The Eighth Division" or "upon the Octave," in Psalms 6 and 7.

Shiggaion. "Loud Crying," Psalm 7.

Shoshannim. "Lilies," in Psalms 45 and 69.

Shoshannim-Eduth. "Lilies of testimony," Psalm 53. Eduth (testimony) is found in Psalm 60.

The word *Selah* occurs 71 times in the Psalms. It means "To pause," with a secondary meaning to "lift up." We can take it as an indication that in reading we should pause, meditate and then lift up our hearts in praise and prayer.

The Alphabetical Psalms

A number of the Psalms in the Hebrew are in an alphabetical arrangement; that is, certain verses begin with a letter of the Hebrew alphabet. This arrangement is not always perfect. Psalms 9 and 10 contain (the two together) the letters of the alphabet with several missing. Psalms 25 and 26 are also incomplete in the alphabetical scope. Psalm 37 has a perfect alphabetical character. Other alphabetical Psalms are Psalms 111 and 112. The most perfect Psalm in this respect is the longest in the book, Psalm 119.

The Psalms and the New Testament Scriptures

As already stated the Psalms are quoted by the Spirit of God more than any other Old Testament book. This is significant and a divine indication of the great importance of these inspired gems. We give now a list of quotations as found in the New Testament and also those passages where the Psalms are alluded to.

Matthew 4:6 (Psalm 91:11). This first quotation is by the Devil. By this he showed his great knowledge of the Word and its meaning. Matthew 13:35 (Psalm 78:2). Matthew 21:42 (Psalm 118:22). Matthew 27:43 (Psalm 110). John 2:17 (Psalm 69:9). John 6:31 (Psalm 78:24, 25). John 7:42 (Psalm 132:11). John 10:34 (Psalm 82:6). John 13:18 (Psalm 41:9). John 15:25 (Psalm 35:19; 49:4). John 19:24 (Psalm 22:18). John 19:28 (Psalm 69:21). John 19:36 (Psalm 34:20). John 20:17 (Psalm 22:17). Acts 1:20 (Psalm 69:25). Acts 1:16 (Psalm 41:9). Acts 2:25 (Psalm 16:8). Acts 2:34 (Psalm 110:1). Acts 4:25 (Psalm 2:1, 2). Acts 13:33 (Psalm 2:7). Acts 13:35 (Psalm 16:10). Romans 3:4 (Psalm 51:4). Romans 3:12 (Psalm 14:2). Romans 3:13 (Psalm 140:3). Romans 4:6 (Psalm 32:1, 2). Romans 11:9,10 (Psalm 69:22, 23). Romans 15:10 (Psalm 117:1). Ephes. 4:8 (Psalm 68:18). 2 Cor. 4:13 (Psalm 116:10). Hebrews 1:10-12 (Psalm 102:25-27). Hebrews 1:8-9 (Psalm 45:6-7). Hebrews 1:13 (Psalm 110:1). Hebrews 2:6 (Psalm 8:4). Hebrews 4:3 (Psalm 95:11). Hebrews 4:7 (Psalm 95:7). Hebrews 5:6 (Psalm 110:4). Hebrews 7:17 (Psalm 110:4). Revel. 2:27 (Psalm 2:9).

This is not by any means a complete list of quotations, for there are many more passages. We have quoted only the most prominent. See also Psalm 2:7-9 in Hebrews 1:5 and Revel. 2:27. Psalm 4:4 in Ephesians 4:26. In Psalm 6:8. Matthew 11:16 in Psalm 8:2. Psalm 7:6 in 1 Corinth. 15:25-27. Psalm 9:8 in Acts 17:31. Psalm 19:4 in Romans 10:18. Psalm 22:1 in Matthew 27:46. Psalm 22:21 in 2 Tim. 4:17. Psalm 24:1 in 1 Cor. 10:26. Psalm 27:1 in Hebrew 13:6. Psalm 34:8 in 1 Peter 2:3. Psalm 40:6-8 in Hebrews 10:5-7. Psalm 41:9 in Mark 14:18 and John 13:18. Psalm 48:2 in Matthew 5:35. Psalm 50:14 in Hebrews 13:15. Psalm 55:22 in 1 Peter 5:7. Psalm 56:4 in Hebrews 13:6. Psalm 69:21 in Mark 15:36. Psalm 79:6 in 2 Thess. 1:8. Psalm 89:27, 37 in Revel. 1:5 and 3:14. Psalm 97:6 in Hebrews 1:6. Psalm 104:4 in Hebrews 1:7, etc.

In all about 50 Psalms are directly and indirectly quoted and alluded to in the books of the New Testament.

The Message of the Psalms

It would be imposible to give a complete review of the great message contained in the Psalms. A close study of each Psalm only can bring this out fully and even then we probably touch but the surface of this marvellous mine of wisdom and knowledge. That a part of the message is the experience of the saint in the world, his trials, sorrows, the persecutions he suffers, his dependence on God, his deliverance and much else, is known to all readers of this book. Yet it must be remembered that the experiences are those of Jewish saints; true Christian experience is higher. In the midst of persecutions from the enemies, these Jewish saints call to God to destroy their enemies, to burn them up like stubble. The New Testament demands that saints should love their enemies. What these imprecatory Psalms mean and how perfectly in order they are in the message of this book we shall show in the annotations. Nor do we find in these experiences salvation made known as it is in the gospel dispensation. While the writers of the Psalms call on the Lord and use different names by which they call Him, as rock, fortress, shepherd, shield, etc., nowhere do we find that one ever utters the word "Father," nor is there a declaration of the sonship of the saint nor do we find anything of the blessed hope of glory to be with Him in the Father's house. The message of praise, giving thanks, adoration and worship is another prominent feature. But true Christian worship and praise is of a higher note and order. No such doxology like the doxology of Ephes. 1:3 is found anywhere in the Psalms. Yet the Christian believer, with the light of the full gospel revelation, indwelt by the same Spirit who gave the Psalms, can get the sweetest comfort and encouragement from the experiences recorded in these songs.

While this is part of the message of this book, the great message is the message of prophecy. The book of Psalms is pre-eminently a prophetic book. The New Testament warrants us to say this for the quotations from the Psalms are overwhelmingly on prophetic lines. It is not said too much when we say that all the great prophetic messages of the prophets of God, and their visions concerning the future are wonderfully given by the Psalms and many of them are enlarged. The prophetic scope of the Psalms is truly marvellous. Yet this feature of it is the most neglected in the study of the book. It is rarely ever studied as a prophetic book; the devotional study has always been in the lead.

What then is the prophetic message of the Psalms? The prophecies of the Psalms comprise the following three themes:

1. The prophetic message concerning the Messiah, His humiliation and His exaltation. There are more prophetic statements on this theme of all themes in the Psalms, than in the book of Isaiah or in any of the other prophetic

books. As already stated in the paragraph of this introduction relating to the Lord Jesus and the Psalms, we have in many of them the pre-written prayers of our Lord, as well as the expressions of His sorrow and grief. The story of His life of loneliness down here, the hatred which He met, the rejection from the side of the nation; the betrayal and other features of His humiliation are found over and over again in the Psalms. While the chosen instruments passed through experiences of sorrow and trial, the Spirit of God pictures in them Him who could say "Behold and see if there be any sorrow like unto my sorrow which is done unto me" (Lament. 1:12). But the application of these Psalms to the person of our Lord needs great caution. Some teachers have erred grievously in this matter. We heard several years ago of a Bible teacher applying Psalm 38:7 to our Lord: "For my lions are filled with a loathsome disease, and there is no soundness in my flesh." And this teacher declared that the Lord suffered thus because He took upon Himself our sickness and diseases. Such teaching must be severely condemned for it is positively false. Nor must other similar expressions be put into the mouth of our Lord. He had no need to complain of sins for He had no sin. He had no need to use the Fifty-first Psalm.

The sufferings of the cross are prophetically revealed in the twenty-second Psalm and in others as well. Then the glory which is to follow, the kingship of Christ, His kingdom is wonderfully predicted in many Psalms. His first coming in humiliation, to be rejected and to die; His second coming to be accepted and to reign over the earth, these are the two great prophetic messages of the Psalms. It is of much interest to note the order of the four great Messianic Psalms which we find in the first section of the book. The Spirit of God calls our attention to them in the New Testament. The Second Psalm is the first; here the divine sonship of our Lord is made known. The Eighth Psalm is next quoted; there He is the Son of Man. In Psalm 16 we see Him as the Obedient One and in Psalm 22 obedient unto death, the death of the cross. Son of God—Son of Man, obedient, obedient unto death, the death of the cross. And with each of these Psalms His glory is connected.

2. The second prophetic theme of the Psalms we mention are the sorrows, trials and suffering of Israel and their coming deliverance, restoration, blessing and glory. We do not mean by this the prediction of their present wanderings and the affictions which are upon the nation as a result of having rejected the Christ, but the experiences through which a godly Jewish remnant will have to pass when this present age closes in its predicted darkness and apostasy. Of this time Jeremiah speaks as the time of Jacob's trouble. "Alas! for that day is great, so that none is like it; it is even the time of Jacob's trouble; but he shall be saved out of it." That remnant will appear when the purpose of this present dispensation, the out calling of the people for His Name (the Church) is accomplished. A remnant of His earthly people, energized by the Spirit of God, will turn to the Lord and pass through that time of trouble, of which our Lord speaks as the great tribulation. It will be the travail time for them. They suffer from the side of ungodly nations and pray for deliverance. (See Isaiah 63:15-64.) The Psalms give us the completest picture of their harrowing experiences. Here we read their sorrows, their afflictions. We hear their prayers, their cry "How long, O Lord, how long!" We hear them plead that the Lord might intervene and come down to save them. The nations about them persecute them. The land, which is partially restored, is invaded again. Then we read in the Psalms of a wicked man who domineers over them; one who breaks the covenant. This is the man of sin, the final Anti-christ. And as they pray for deliverance, they cry to God for vengeance, to deal with their enemies and with His enemies according to His righteousness. This will explain perfectly the imprecatory prayers we find here and there in this book.

Suddenly the scene changeth. Their prayers are answered. Heaven opens and the long expected King returns. Their tears are wiped away; their moans are changed to songs, their agonizing cries are turned to laughter. They are delivered and receive the blessing as His people, their land is blest and they become the channel of blessing and mercy to the nations of the earth. It is all intensely interesting and fascinating.

3. The third prophetic theme shows the future glories in store for His redeemed people, for the nations of the earth and for creation itself. In other words we have prophecies relating to the coming kingdom. The prophetic teaching of the Psalms annihilates postmillennialism. These prophecies show conclusively that there can be no blessing for Israel, for the nations, for the earth, no peace and prosperity, no world conversion, till the King comes back. The book ends with the mighty hallelujahs, the glorious consummation when heaven and earth will sing

His praises. How well Handel caught this message when in his Oratorio, "The Messiah," he concludes all with a mighty hallelujah chorus. Our annotations will adhere to this threefold prophetic message. The task is difficult to condense these great truths. Far easier it would be to write a book of a thousand pages than one of a hundred. It is all so rich and glorious.

The Division of the Psalms

The unknown collector of these Psalms has divided the book into five sections, which we must maintain and follow. These five sections correspond in a remarkable manner with the five books with which the Bible opens, the Pentateuch. This was known to the ancient Jews, for they call the Psalter "the Pentateuch of David." The Aramaic comment (Midrash) on Psalm 1:1 declares that "Moses gave to the Israelites the five books of the law and corresponding with these David gave them the five books of the Psalms."

I. THE GENESIS SECTION—Psalms 1—41. This section has the same character as the book of Genesis in that it has much to say about man. We have first a contrast between the righteous and the ungodly. After that a contrast between the first man, Adam, and the second Man who was made a little lower than the angels (Psalm 8). Here also is a description of the wicked one, in whom in some future day the defiance of the ungodly will culminate. This man of sin, the Anti-christ, is revealed in Psalms 9 and 10; the tribulation which is yet to come for man is revealed in the Psalms which follow. The Christ, the last Adam, in His obedience, even the obedience unto the death of the cross, His salvation and His glory are unfolded (Psalms 16—41). The first book ends with a blessing and a double Amen.

II. THE EXODUS SECTION—Psalms 42—72. Like in the book of Exodus, where the story is written how God redeems by blood and by power, we see a people groaning and moaning. The opening Psalms show a people oppressed and longing for God. This is the godly Jewish remnant. Then we find their prayers answered by the coming of the King (Psalm 45). Redemption by power then takes place and the blessings of the kingdom, when Christ has returned, are revealed in a number of Psalms. The Seventy-second Psalm, the conclusion of this second book gives the reign and the kingly glory of Christ. This book also ends with a double Amen and the statement, so very appropriate to this book, "And let the whole earth be filled with His glory." The book of Exodus ends with the glory of the Lord filling the tabernacle, the Exodus portion of the Psalms ends with His glory filling the whole earth.

III. THE LEVITICUS SECTION—Psalms 73—89. This is the briefest section. The theme of Leviticus is "holiness unto the Lord." In this section we are brought into the sanctuary and we behold the holiness of the Lord in dealing with His people. The Asaph Psalms are put into this section and nearly every Psalm has something about the sanctuary, the congregation, Zion and approaching the Lord. It also closeth with a benediction and a double amen.

IV. THE NUMBERS SECTION—Psalms 90—106. The first Psalm of this section is the Psalm Moses wrote, in all probability when he saw the people dying in the wilderness. The second Man is seen in Psalm 91. Here we have the prophetic Psalms which show that the times of unrest and wanderings will cease, when the Lord reigneth and when the nations will worship Him. No rest and no peace till then. This section ends with an amen and a hallelujah.

V. THE DEUTERONOMY SECTION—Psalms 107—150. In this section, as it is in Deuteronomy, the Word is magnified. The Lord Jesus Christ quoted this book of Deuteronomy exclusively in His conflict with the devil. Christ is seen as the Living Word in the beginning of this section. His rejection, His exaltation, His return and the hallelujah times which follow are once more revealed in a cluster of Psalms (109—113). Then follows the consummation, deliverances, the end-ways of God, His praise and His glory. This section ends with five hallelujah Psalms. It is the hallelujah chorus of completed redemption.

Analysis and Annotations

I. THE GENESIS SECTION: BOOK ONE: PSALMS 1—41

Psalms 1—8

PSALM 1

The Godly and the Ungodly

1. The godly, his character and his fruit (1:1-3)
2. The ungodly in comparison with the godly (1:4-6)

The first eight Psalms are the Psalms in embryo, just as the opening chapters of the book of Genesis are the Bible in a nutshell. Throughout the Psalms we can trace the subjects of these eight Psalms, the godly and the ungodly; but especially the great theme of the Psalms, Christ, the Perfect Man, the King rejected, the suffering of the righteous during the time of His rejection, the King enthroned and all things put under His feet. These are the leading themes of Psalms 1—8.

Psalms 1 and 2 are introductory to the entire collection, put there by the Holy Spirit. In some ancient manuscripts the first Psalm is not numbered, in others the First and Second Psalms are put into one. The First Psalm begins with a beatitude and the second ends with a beatitude. The righteous man, negative and positive, nothing evil in him, no fellowship with sinners, and positive, obedience and entire devotedness to God, does not mean the natural man. The godly One is the perfect One who walked down here separated from sinners, and devoted to God. He walked in obedience, in dependence on God and in communion with Him, and therefore the blessing, honor and glory are His. But the godly man is also the believer, born of God, separated, a saint, who delights in the things of God, meditates in His Word day and night. It is still more, a description of what the true believing remnant of Israel will be some day, "like a tree planted by the rivers of water, that bringeth forth his fruit in his season." Such is converted, redeemed Israel's future as revealed here and also by Isaiah: "Thy people shall all be righteous, they shall inherit the land forever, the branch of My planting, the work of My hands, that I may be glorified" (Isaiah 60:21). We behold then in these opening verses of the Psalms the Lord Jesus Christ as the perfect Man, the individual believer in his separation and devotion, and what Israel, saved and converted, will be in the future.

(The Romish church has a volume called "The Psalter of the Virgin Mary compiled by Doctor St. Bonaventura." It is in Latin and contains the 150 Psalms, greatly abridged, and each addressed to Mary. Psalm 1 begins as follows: "Happy is the man that loves thy Name, O Virgin Mary, thy grace will comfort his soul. Ave Maria." Psalm 19: "The Heavens declare thy glory, O Virgin Mary." Horrible blasphemy!)

Then the ungodly: "Like the chaff which the wind driveth away" is a prophecy of the time when the ungodly are dealt with in judgment, when "He will thoroughly purge His floor, and gather His wheat into the garner, but He will burn up the chaff with unquenchable fire" (Matt. 3:12). Then the ungodly will forever disappear and cease troubling the righteous. They will have no place in the assembly of the righteous in millennial times.

PSALM 2

The Rejected King

1. The rejection and the coming confederacy (2:1-3)
2. Jehovah's attitude and interference (2:4-6)
3. The coming of the King and his inheritance (2:7-9)
4. Warning and exhortation (2:10-12)

Verses 1-3. The rejection of the perfect Man, the Son of God, by man, is here revealed. It is the first psalm quoted in the New Testament. See Acts 4:25-28. In this quotation it is applied to the Jews and Gentiles gathered together against the Lord, and against His Christ. This rejection continues throughout this present age; it becomes more marked as the age draws to its close. Finally the nations with their kings and also apostate Israel will form a great confederacy, they will form a tumultuous throng, taking counsel together for one great purpose, Satanically conceived and executed, to defy God and His Christ. The generallisimo will be Satan through the beast. It is the gathered confederacy as seen in Revelation. "And he gathered them together in a place called in the Hebrew tongue Armageddon" (Rev. 16:16). "And I saw the beast, and the kings of the earth, and their armies, gathered together to make war against Him that sat on the horse (Christ) and His army" (Rev. 19:19).

Verses 4-6. Heaven is silent till the appointed time comes. Here we have, as in Psalm 110, the exalted position of the rejected Christ: He sitteth in the heavens; His place is at the right hand of God. He shares the Father's throne. In infinite patience He is waiting, silent to all what wicked men do in dishonouring His Name. But when on earth the final rebellion takes place, then He will laugh at them and hold them in derision. (The Jewish comment contained in the ancient "Yalkut Shimoni" is interesting. "Like a robber who was standing and expressing his contempt behind the palace of the king, and saying, If I find the son of the king, I will seize him, kill him, and crucify him, and put him to a terrible death; but the lord mocks at it.") Then He who has so long spoken in love, will speak in wrath and begin the execution of God's judgments which are committed into His hand. Then will He be established as God's King upon the holy hill of Zion.

Verses 7-9. And now we hear Him speak; He proclaims God's counsel concerning Himself. He declares who He is, "the Son of God"—"Thou art My Son, this day have I begotten thee." (See the New Testament comment, Acts 13:33,34.) It is not a declaration of His eternal Sonship (though that is implied), but speaks of Him as the Incarnate One and the Risen One. And His second coming will be the completest vindication of His Sonship. It will demonstrate that He whom the nations rejected is the Son of God, who walked on the earth, who died, rose from the dead, ascended upon high and is manifested in power and glory. Then every mouth will be stopped and every knee must bow. He asks the Father and He gives Him the nations for His inheritance and the uttermost parts of the earth for His possession. In His prayer in John 17 (the model of His priestly intercession throughout this age of grace), He said, "I pray not for the world." When His present priestly ministrations cease, that is, when His own have been received by Him in glory, then will He ask for the world and receive the kingdoms of this world, to shepherd the nations with a rod of iron and execute judgment among them.

Verses 10-12. The exhortation and warning closes this perfect and beautiful Psalm. It is meant especially for that time when the final revolt takes place. The appeal goes forth then to turn to the Lord, to kiss the Son—"for in a little will His anger kindle." So even at that time mercy still is waiting. Critics object to the use of the Aramaic word "bar"—son—and give as the correct translation "receive instruction" or "do homage." The word "bar" is used in place of the Hebrew "ben" for the sake of euphony. "Blessed are they that put their trust in Him." That is true of all at all times. It is our blessedness.

Sorrows and Trials of the Godly Remnant (3—7)

PSALM 3

1. Persecution and comfort (3:1-4)
2. Arise Jehovah! Save me, O my God (3:5-8)

The five Psalms which follow bring before us the godly remnant of Israel, their sorrows and trials during the end of the age, while the expected Redeemer and King has not yet come. While this is the dispensational aspect, the application is wider. The trials and sorrows are common to all saints, who live in accordance with their calling apart from the world which rejects Christ; and the comfort belongs to them likewise.

Verses 1-4. The Psalm was written by David when he fled from the face of Absalom. Persecution is mentioned first. The remnant is suffering persecution and that from their own unbelieving brethren, who sneer at them and mock. "There is no salvation (deliverance) for him from God." But the godly trust in Jehovah as a shield about them, giving protection; He is my glory and the lifter up of mine head. Thus David encouraged himself in the Lord and so do all saints in persecution and the remnant when they are persecuted in the time of Jacob's trouble.

Verses 5-8. The simple faith produces peace and quietness. He has slept in peace even if myriads of people should set themselves around him. He cries to Jehovah to arise and to save. Then faith looks back and remembers that God hath smitten the enemies in the past, and broken the teeth of the ungodly. He acknowledgeth that salvation belongeth to the Lord, it is of Him and that His blessing rests upon His people who trust in Him. Viewed in connection with the remnant of Israel in the coming tribulation all this takes on an interesting meaning. It is called a morning hymn.

PSALM 4

1. The cry to Jehovah (4:1-3)
2. The warning to the enemies (4:4-5)
3. The assurance of faith (4:6-8)

Verses 1-3. The fourth Psalm is closely connected with the third; the third is "a Morning Psalm" and the fourth "an Evening Hymn." He calls God "God of my righteousness" and He knows that He will act in righteousness toward him, be gracious and hear prayer. Then the appeal to the sons of men, who love emptiness and seek after a lie. They should know that the Lord hath set apart the godly for Himself and therefore He will hear.

Verses 4-5. This expresseth the concern of the godly for those who reject the Lord, it is a warning appeal to turn from their evil ways, to offer the sacrifices of righteousness and to trust Jehovah.

Verses 6-8. The mocking words "who will show us any good?" the challenge of unbelief, is met by prayer and the assurance of faith. "Lift upon us the light of Thy countenance, Jehovah." This we shall find later is a choice prayer of the Jewish saints in the tribulation. (See Psalm 80.) His heart is filled with joy; he knows he is safe. "For Thou, Lord, only makest me dwell in safety." Such is the experience of the godly, who trust the Lord. Their hearts are filled with gladness; their safety is the Lord.

PSALM 5

1. The cry to God the King (5:1-3)
2. Hating iniquity and trusting in mercy (5:4-7)
3. Prayer for guidance and judgment (5:8-12)

Verses 1-3. In the third Psalm trust is expressed in God as shield; in the fourth the prayer is to the God of righteousness. "Hearken unto the voice of my cry, my King and my God." It is a fresh and more intense prayer, because evil increaseth and abounds. The cry is to God as King. David calls Him King, as the Jewish remnant will pray to the King and look for the coming of the King. The Church looks for the Lord, for the Bridegroom. Nowhere is the Lord Jesus Christ spoken of as the King of the Church.

Verses 4-7. The holiness of God is recognized and shared by the godly in hating iniquity. His confidence is in a sin- and iniquity-hating God, a holy God. He has no pleasure in wickedness or in folly. Falsehood He hates and liars He will destroy. Such are the enemies of God and his enemies also. The bloody and deceitful man mentioned in verse 6 is the first mention of the man of sin, the false Christ, who will persecute Jewish saints in the future. And how beautiful it is to see faith breaking through the gathering storm clouds again—"But as for me I will come into Thy house in the multitude of Thy mercy, in Thy fear I will worship toward Thy holy temple." The final victory is seen by faith.

Verses 8-12. Prayer for guidance stands first. "Lead me, Jehovah, in Thy righteousness because of mine enemies." What these enemies, especially the future enemies of Israel will be, their character, is described and this is followed by prayer for judgment. Here is the first imprecatory prayer (verse 10). This and the other imprecatory prayers will be prayed during the final days of this age, when the wicked are ripe for judgment. It will be answered and then the righteous will be delivered and have joy (verses 11, 12). All this we shall find very much more prominent in the Exodus section of the Psalms.

PSALM 6

1. The cry of repentance (6:1-3)
2. In deep distress (6:4-7)
3. Jehovah has heard (6:8-10)

Verses 1-3. Here we have the deep soul exercise of the godly expressed. In the midst of the trials and sorrows they search their hearts. The persecution of the enemies is used under God to bring His people in the dust. And so they feel the trial and sorrow which passeth over them as divine displeasure against sin. They feel it is the chastening hand of God which rests heavily upon them. Perhaps bodily sickness is also indicated. They cry, Jehovah how long? It is a night experience, of deepest woe and agony. We know that all things must work together for good to them that love God and that our loving Father does not chasten in the heat of wrath.

Verses 4-7. But there is deeper distress. There is groaning, the couch is covered with tears, the eyes are sunken in because of grief. The remnant is put into the place of dust, and that is the place of blessing and deliverance.

Verses 8-10. Faith again is victorious. The Lord hath heard the voice of my weeping; heard the voice of my supplication; He will receive my prayer. The last verse is prophetic. All the enemies will be ashamed, they shall be suddenly ashamed. That will be when the Lord returns to save His people.

PSALM 7

1. Confidence and prayer (7:1-2)
2. Unjust persecution (7:3-5)
3. Arise Jehovah! (7:6-10)
4. God's dealings in government (7:11-16)
5. Thanksgiving (7:17)

Verses 1-2. It has been suggested that over this Psalm should be written the sentence, "Shall not the Judge of all the earth do right?" David appeared to God to judge His cause, that a righteous God cannot but save the righteous and judge the wicked. David sang this unto the Lord concerning the words of Cush, the Benjamite. Who Cush was we do not know. He must be a type of the man of sin. David appeals to God who is his refuge, to save and rescue him. The lion stands ready to tear him to pieces.

Verses 3-5. He knows it is unjust persecution he is suffering. If he had done evil to others he might well be treated in this way.

Verses 6-10. Then follows the appeal to Jehovah to arise in His anger, and to awake for him the judgment He has commanded, when the peoples are assembled for judgment. This appeal from the lips of the remnant will be answered by the manifestation of the Lord.

Verses 11-16. God's judgments in righteousness will overtake the wicked. It is a prophetic description of that day when the wickedness of the wicked comes to an end and the righteous are established. Verses 14-16 are another description of the man of sin, the wicked one.

Verse 17. A word of praise closes this series of Psalms in which the millennial name of Jehovah is given: "The Most High." We see that the overthrow of the wicked brings the praise of Jehovah, as it will be heard on earth when He has come back. In reviewing these Psalms, beginning with the Third, we have a morning hymn (3), followed by an evening hymn (4); then a night experience (5), followed by the deepest night (6) and the breaking of the morning, when the Judge ariseth and the wickedness of the wicked comes to an end (7).

PSALM 8

The Son of Man: All Things Put Under His Feet

1. A little lower than the angels; crowned with glory (8:1-5)
2. All things put under Him (8:6-8)
3. How excellent is Thy Name over all the earth (8:9)

Verses 1-5. In this Psalm we behold Christ again, and here as Son of Man. Three times this Psalm is quoted in the New Testament; in Matthew 21:16, 1 Corinth. 15:27 and Hebrews 2:6-9. The latter passage shows clearly who the Son of Man is who was made a little lower than the angels, for the suffering of death, to taste death for everything and who is now crowned with glory and honor.

(The inscription of this Psalm is "upon Gittith"—the winepress. If the theory is correct that the titles of the Psalms were misplaced, then "Gittith" should belong to the preceding Psalm, where it would find a good application. But it is equally in place in the beginning of this Psalm, for the Son of Man went into the winepress, the suffering of death when He shed His precious blood.)

The Psalm begins with praise; it will be His praise in that coming day when all things are put under His feet as the second Man, the last Adam, then His Name will be excellent in all the earth and His glory will be set in the heavens (the New Jerusalem). The little children in the temple who sang their Hosannahs when the Lord Jesus was there foreshadow this coming praise. Many expositors have made of "the son of Man" Adam, the first man; but he is the type of the last Adam; the Lord Jesus is meant as Hebrews 2:6-9 tells us so clearly.

Verses 6-8. The first man lost his dominion through sin, the second Man has bought it back by His death. When He comes again then all things will be put under His feet. During His absence "we see not yet all things put under Him." He must reign till all enemies are put under His feet.

Verse 9. The Psalm closes with the same praise with which it begins. It is the future praise of Him, who was made a little lower than the angels and whose Name in that day will be excellent in all the earth. We beheld Him as the perfect Man, as the King, rejected by men, enthroned by God, with the nations for His inheritance, in the opening Psalms. Then followed (Psalms 3—7) the experiences of the godly during His absence, especially the Jewish remnant and the Eighth Psalm shows Him as Son of Man, who comes for the deliverance of His people and receives the dominion over all the earth.

The Godly Remnant. The Wicked One and His Followers (9—15)

PSALM 9

1. The praise of the Most High (9:1-2)
2. Millennial deliverances and glories (9:3-12)
3. Prayer for divine intervention: Faith's Vision (9:12-18)

Verses 1-2. Psalms 9—15 continue the great prophetic story. Once more the godly remnant is before us and in this section the wicked one, the man of sin, is also revealed. The first part of this Psalm is a prophetic vision of what will be on earth, when the Son of Man has come and when all things are put under Him. His triumph is celebrated. We doubt not what is written here will be the comfort of that company of believing Jews at the end of the age as they anticipate in faith what will be when the King comes. But how much more we His heavenly people should praise Him, and declare His wondrous works in grace.

Verses 3-12. What it will mean when the Lord reigns is told out in these verses. His enemies will be defeated; He rebukes the nations and destroys the wicked; He judgeth the world in righteousness, and He is a refuge for His people. The Lord will dwell in Zion, Israel will sing praises and become the witness amongst the nations.

Verses 13-20. Up to the previous verse we saw the glorious results for Israel when the Son of Man comes. But that has not yet come. Faith realizeth it. In verse 13 we hear the voice of supplication of those who in faith look forward to the promises, but who suffer in the midst of the trials of the ending days of the age. They are hated and suffer and long to shew forth praises in Zion. Then once more the vision of faith what must happen ere long to the nations and to the wicked (15-18). The plea "Arise, O Lord," is the prayer for His glorious manifestation.

This Psalm and the next are linked together by the letters of the Alphabet (in Hebrew). Ten letters are used in this Psalm and five in the next. Six letters are dropped out in this alphabetical composition. The irregularity may be explained as in harmony with the time of tribulation when everything on earth is broken and out of joint.

PSALM 10

1. The cry of Jehovah and what causeth it (10:1-2)
2. That wicked one (10:3-11)
3. Prayer for divine Intervention: Faith's Vision (10:12-18)

Verses 1-2. Here is a renewed cry to Jehovah and why? Because the wicked in his pride persecutes the poor. The wicked is that coming man of sin.

Verses 3-11. That persecutor of the saints of God is now prophetically revealed in his arrogant pride, defiance of God and oppression of the poor and needy. Such will be the character of the beast out of the earth, the man of sin and son of perdition (2 Thessal. 2). We shall get other photographs of the same person in other Psalms.

Verses 12-18. Significant prayers these. And they will be prayed by that future remnant. Arise—lift up Thy hand—forget not—Thou hast seen it—break Thou the arm of the wicked! And then faith seeth the answer. "The Lord is King forever and ever." The prayer of the humble has been heard. The man of the earth no more oppresseth.

PSALM 11

1. Faith's resources in the day of trouble (11:1-4)
2. The recompense for the righteous and the wicked (11:5-7)

Verses 1-4. Their refuge is the Lord, in Him they trust as we, His heavenly people, know Him as our hiding place in the time of trouble. That coming day of trouble is the time "when the foundations are destroyed." It is the time of apostasy and confusion. But their comfort is "Jehovah is in His holy temple, the Throne of Jehovah is in heaven."

Verses 5-7. But faith also reckons with the day of retribution and judgment, when the days of tribulation are ended. Then the wicked receive their punishment. But the righteous shall behold His face.

PSALM 12

1. The arrogancy of the wicked in the last days (12:1-4)
2. Then Jehovah will act and deliver His people (12:5-8)

Verses 1-4. It is the time of departure from the Lord; the godly and faithful have ceased. It is a mass of corruption, lying lips, flattering lips, proud lips. They reject the Lord. "Who is lord over us?"

Verses 5-8. Then faith sees the coming intervention. The Lord will speak. "Now will I arise, saith Jehovah, I will set him in safety whom they would puff." Jehovah will keep His people in these coming dark days, "when the wicked walk on all sides and the vilest men are exalted."

PSALM 13

1. How long? Answer me, Jehovah (13:1-4)
2. The victory of faith (13:5-6)

Verses 1-4. Four times "How long?" The trial of faith becomes more severe. Sorrow is in the heart and an enemy is outside. Has then Jehovah forgotten? The hearts begin to despair; an answer is demanded, it must come "lest I sleep the sleep of death."

Verses 5-6. But here comes the change. Faith triumphs and is victorious. "I have trusted in Thy mercy; my heart shall rejoice in Thy salvation. I will sing unto Jehovah, for He hath dealt bountifully with me."

PSALM 14

1. The days of Noah repeated (14:1-6)
2. Salvation and glory (14:7)

Verses 1-6. As it was in the days of Noah so shall it be when the Son of Man cometh. Here we have a prophetic forecast of these coming days of corruption and violence. Iniquity abounds, wickedness is on all sides. None doeth good, none seeketh after God. While all this is used by the Spirit of God in the Epistle to the Romans to describe the condition of the race at large, here dispensationally it describes the moral conditions in the end of the age.

Verse 7. Will this end? Is there to be a better day than violence and wickedness? When will that day come? It comes when the salvation comes out of Zion (Romans 11:26), when the Lord bringeth back the captivity of His people, when Israel is restored. That will be when the Lord returns.

PSALM 15

1. The question (15:1)
2. The answer (15:2-5)

Verse 1. The connection with the previous Psalm is obvious. When He comes and that promised salvation becomes reality, who then shall sojourn in His tabernacle? Who shall dwell in His holy hill? Who will become a partaker of that kingdom, when the King is set upon the holy hill of Zion?

Verses 2-5. The answer is given. The character here described is impossible for the natural man. To walk uprightly, to work righteousness, to speak the truth in the heart and practise righteousness in life is only possible if man is born again. So Israel will be born again, receive the new heart and the Spirit and thus enter the kingdom.

A Revelation of the Christ of God
(16—24)

PSALM 16

1. The obedient One (16:1-3)
2. The path He went (16:4-8)
3. Death and resurrection (16:9-11)

In the nine Psalms which compose this section Christ is marvellously revealed. We notice an interesting progress in the messianic message of this section, culminating in the manifestation of the King, the Lord of Glory in Psalm 24. In the Sixteenth Psalm we behold Christ in His obedience on earth. See also Paul's testimony in Acts 13:35.

Verses 1-3. Here we hear Him speak; it is not David who speaks of himself. This we learn from Acts 2:25, when Peter quoted this Psalm and states that David spoke concerning Him (Christ). As the all obedient One, in humiliation He lived the life of faith and dependence on God. He took the place of lowliness in which He said to Jehovah, "Thou art my Lord." And this humiliation was for the saints and the excellent, His own people in whom is all His delight.

Verses 4-8. In that path the Lord was His portion and His cup, He was His All, nor did He want anything beside Him. "Thou maintainest my lot." Thus He could say "the lines are fallen to me in pleasant places, yea, I have a goodly inheritance." And so He walked in obedience, learning obedience though He was the Son, with the Lord always set before Him.

Verses 9-11. These last three verses show that He went into death, the death of the cross as seen in Psalm 22, with the assurance that His soul should not be left in sheol and that His body should not see corruption. It is the promise of resurrection and after that glory, the way of life through death into the presence of God, to the right hand of God, where there is fullness of joy and pleasures for evermore. It is a beautiful prophecy of Him who walked on earth in obedience, devoted to God, dying the sinner's death, His resurrection and His presence in glory. We shall find these precious prophecies concerning Himself more fully revealed in this section.

PSALM 17

The Prayer of Christ Against the Enemy

1. The Righteous Intercessor (17:1-5)

2. Prayer for deliverance (17:6-12)
3. The deliverance (17:13-15)

Verses 1-5. This Psalm is blessedly linked with the foregoing one. We hear Christ interceding for the saints in whom is His delight (16:3). He pleads His own perfection. He is righteous; His prayer does not come from feigned lips. Not David, but Christ alone could truly say, "Thou hast proved my heart; Thou hast visited me in the night; Thou hast tried me. Thou findest nothing." By the Word of God He had walked and was kept from the paths of the destroyer. What a grand testimony to inspiration we have in verse 4 when the Spirit of Christ declares beforehand that Christ would walk in obedience to the Word and that Word is called here "the Word of Thy lips," which came from the mouth and heart of God.

Verses 6-12. It is a marvellous prayer for His own with whom He so perfectly identifies Himself. The seventh verse is the key, for He prays, "Show Thy marvellous loving-kindness, delivering those who put their trust in Thee by Thy right hand from those rising up against them." He pleads for His beloved saints that they may be kept as the apple of the eye, and hidden under the shadow of His wings. He speaks as for Himself, but it is for the saints, those that trust God, and God hears Him and answers. The enemy threatens His people on earth and therefore we find the plural in verse 11, "they have now compassed us in our steps."

Verses 13-15. The final prayer is to the Lord to arise and to rescue His suffering people from the wicked one, who is the sword in the hand of the Lord. Then when the Lord ariseth His people will behold His face in righteousness and in awakening shall be satisfied with His likeness. Oh, blessed Hope! which is ours too, when shall it be!

PSALM 18

The Story of God's Power in Behalf of Christ

1. In the jaws of death (18:1-6)
2. God appearing and delivering (18:7-18)
3. God gave Him glory (18:19-27)
4. His enemies subdued (18:28-42)
5. The head of the nations (18:43-45)

Verses 1-6. This is another remarkable Psalm. Though David wrote it not everything could be his experience. He was a prophet (Acts 2:30) and prophesied; much in this Psalm is prophecy describing the deliverance of Christ from the jaws of death and the glory God has given Him, and this deliverance and glory also concerns the remnant of His earthly people in "that day." The Psalm begins with an outburst of praise and it ends with His praise among the nations. Hebrew authorities tell us that the proper translation of "The Lord is my Rock" is "Jehovah, my cleft of the rock." It is Christ the rock, cleft for us, in whom the believer has found His refuge. And He Himself was saved from His enemies and in Him His people are saved and will be saved from their enemies (verse 3). It is His own death experience which is described in verses 4-6. "The sorrows of death compassed me, and the floods of Belial (marginal reading) made me afraid." Then in His distress He called and cried unto God and was heard.

Verses 7-18. In these verses we have the answer in behalf of Christ. It is a wonderful description of God's power and His appearing. It is the manifestation and glory of Jehovah in deliverance. "He sent from above, He took Me, He drew me from great waters. He delivered me from my strong enemy, and from them which hate me for they were too strong for me." This describes His resurrection.

At the same time while all this shows His experience as the author and finisher of the faith, it is also the experience of His trusting people, and the deliverance of that remnant living during the tribulation period.

Verses 19-27. The Lord has recompensed Him for His righteousness. He not only raised Him from the dead "but gave Him glory." He was brought forth into a large place. He was delivered because God delighted in Him and He has rewarded Him. Verse 23 as it stands in the authorized version can not apply to Christ. It is in fact a poor translation. The translation in the *Numerical Bible* is very satisfactory. "I was also perfect with Him and kept myself from perverseness being mine."

Verses 28-42. He will save an humble people and all His enemies will be conquered by Him. While much in this section was David's experience, who overcame all his enemies, in its prophetic meaning it must apply to the Lord Jesus. Verses 37-42 speak prophetically of this coming great victory when all His enemies will be made the footstool of His feet.

Verses 43-45. He becomes the head of the

nations. "Thou hast made me the head of the nations" cannot apply to David and his experience, but it is David's Son and David's Lord who will head the nations of the earth. It is the coming kingdom which is described in verse 44. "As soon as they hear of me they shall obey me, the strangers (Gentiles) shall submit themselves unto me." The marginal reading is suggestive, "they shall yield feigned obedience unto Me," which tells us that the obedience of many during the kingdom reign of our Lord will not be whole-hearted and therefore the revolt at the end of the thousand years (Revel. 20). His praise will then be heard among the nations (Verses 49-50).

PSALM 19

Christ in Creation and in Revelation

1. In creation (19:1-6)
2. In revelation (19:7-11)

Verses 1-6. This Psalm also bears witness to Christ as Creator and as revealing Himself through the Word. The two great books, Creation and Revelation, bear witness to Him. The Heavens which declare the glory of God were created by Him (Col. 1:16; John 1:3). And there is a testimony to Him in creation which is continuous. "Day unto day uttereth speech and night unto night showeth knowledge." (See Romans 1:20) The sun is especially mentioned, for the sun is the type of Christ. "As a bridegroom coming out of His chamber he rejoiceth as a strong man to run his course. His going forth is from the end of the heavens, and his circuits unto the end of it and nothing is hid from the heat thereof." He is the Sun of Righteousness, who will arise some day with healing beneath his wings.

Verses 7-11. The second witness to Him is the Law of Jehovah, the testimony and the precepts of the Lord. It is His written Word. This Word comes from Himself and speaks of Himself. What this Word is and what it produces and the practical use of the testimony of the Lord as well as prayer are mentioned in these verses.

The nineteenth Psalm is an introduction to the next five Psalms, which tells us more fully of the person of Christ, the Creator and Revealer, in His great work as Redeemer.

PSALM 20

Christ and His Salvation as Contemplated by His People

1. What God has done for Christ (20:1-4)
2. The salvation His people enjoy (20:5-9)

Verses 1-4. "My Redeemer" was the last word of the previous Psalm. Christ the Redeemer of His people is revealed in this Psalm. His death and sacrificial work, revealed in Psalm 22, are here anticipated. He who humbled Himself has been heard by Jehovah, He has set Him upon high (marginal reading), He has sent Him help, He has accepted His great offering, the whole burnt offering which typifies the death of the cross. All the desires of His heart are given to Him and all His counsels will be fulfilled. The believing remnant is contemplating the Redeemer and His salvation. Because He has been heard, because His offering is accepted, because He is set on high, they possess salvation *Verses 5-9.* This salvation is now celebrated in inspired song. It is anticipatiopatory of that coming salvation. They will rejoice in His salvation, His heavenly people, now rejoice in it. Banners, the symbol of victory won, will be set up. The intercessions of His Anointed (Christ) will be answered, all enemies are bowed down and fallen. "But we are risen and stand upright" refers to the day of Israel's national and spiritual resurrection. In anticipation of the trouble of the last days we read the prayer of this godly remnant. "Save Lord! Let the King hear us when we call."

PSALM 21

The King's Glory Anticipated and Contemplated

1. The King's power, glory and salvation (21:1-6)
2. His victory over the enemies (21:7-13)

Verses 1-6. This is another Messianic Psalm in anticipation of the glory of the King. The prayers He offered up are all answered. (See Ps. 20:4) He shares the strength of Jehovah as the Risen and Exalted One. The desire of His heart is fulfilled, as it will be when the kingly crown of pure gold is set upon His head, the head which was once crowned with thorns. He had gone down into the jaws of death and then received life, yea, eternal life, as the head of the new creation, which shares this life He has received. And His glory is great in Jehovah's salvation, the salvation which the Lord has planned and which He has accomplished, wh)ch is His glory.

Verses 7-13. Here once more the downfall and complete overthrow of the enemies, when the King reigns, is prophetically anticipated. Then we hear in the last verse a prophetic prayer, that all this might be accomplished. "Be Thou exalted, Lord, in Thine own strength." And when He is exalted, then Israel redeemed will sing—"So will we sing and praise Thy power."

(How the critics have made havoc with all these Psalms, trying to find a solution, when the Lord Jesus is the only solution as He is the key to all the Scriptures! The Targum reads in verses 1 and 7 "King Messiah" and Jewish interpretation has mostly been on Messianic lines. Perowne writes on this kingly Psalm "Each Jewish monarch was but a feeble type of Israel's true King; and all the hopes of pious hearts still looked beyond David or David's children to Him who should be David's Lord as well as David's Son.")

PSALM 22

The Sufferings of Christ and the Glory That Follows

1. The suffering (22:1-21)
2. The glory (22:22-31)

Verses 1-21. In many respects this Psalm is the most remarkable in the entire book and one of the sublimest prophecies in the whole Bible. The sufferings of Christ and the glory that should follow are here wonderfully foretold. The inscription mentions *Aijeleth Shahar,* which means "the hind of the morning." Jewish tradition identifies this hind with the early morning light, when the day dawns and the rays of the rising sun appear like the horns of the hind. The eminent Hebraist Professor Delitzsch, makes the following remark: "Even the Jewish synagogue, so far as it recognizes a suffering Messiah, hears His voice here, and takes the hind of the morning as a name of the Shechinah, and makes it a symbol of coming redemption. And the Targum recalls the lamb of the morning sacrifice, which was offered as soon as the watchman on the pinnacle of the temple cried out, "The first rays of the morning burst forth." All this is very suggestive. The inscription also tells us that the Psalm was written by David. "We know, however, of no circumstances in his life to which it can possibly be referred. In none of the persecutions by Saul was he ever reduced to such straits as those here described" (Perowne). David's personal experience is all out of question. He speaks as a prophet, such as he was (Acts 2:30) and the Spirit of God useth him to give one of the completest pictures of Christ, His suffering and glory, which to David must have been a mystery, so that with other prophets, he searched and enquired as to its meaning. (See 1 Peter 1:10-12). Our Lord in uttering the solemn word with which this Psalm begins in the darkness which enshrouded the cross gives us the conclusive evidence that it is He of whom the Psalm speaks. The Spirit of God equally so in Hebrews 2:11-12 shows that it is Christ. And the glory-side of this gem of prophecy proves fully that none other than the Christ of God is meant.

The precious, blessed, unfathomable work of the sinbearer on the Cross and its far reaching results in blessing and glory is here unfolded to our faith, as well as for our joy and comfort. The heart of the atonement occupies the foreground, not the physical sufferings, but the suffering He endured from the side of God, when He made Him who knew no sin, sin for us. "My God, My God, why hast Thou forsaken me?"—But Thou art holy! That is the answer to the "Why?" And when the blessed One was thus forsaken, and faced as the substitute of sinners the holy, sin-hating God, He finished the work, the work which enables God to be just and the justifier of all who believe in Jesus. "It is finished!" was His triumphant shout, expressed in the Greek by one work—"tetelestai." And our Psalm ends with a similar word—"He hath done"—the Hebrew word "ohsa" expresseth the same thought—it is finished.

Still more astonishing are the details of His physical sufferings, which were all so minutely fulfilled on Calvary. Here we find foretold the piercing of hands and feet, the excessive thirst He suffered, the terrible agony by hanging suspended, every bone out of joint; the laughter and hooting of his enemies, the very expressions they used surrounding the cross are given here, and the dividing of the garments and casting lots over them and other details are prophetically revealed. And to this must be added another fact. Crucifixion was an unknown method of death in Jewish law. Among ancient nations the Roman penal code alone seems to contain exclusively this cruel penalty; Rome evidently invented it. Yet here this unknown death penalty is described in a perfect manner. What an evidence of divine inspiration!

And the critics, how they have tried to explain away this great prophecy! And they are still trying to explain it away. Some apply it to

Hezekiah; others say it may describe the sufferings of Jeremiah; still others say it is the Jewish nation. And some try to make it out as being only coincident that the Hebrews had such a piece of literature and that one of their own, Jesus of Nazareth, made such an experience. Surely these infidels are fools, for only a fool can adopt and believe such a method of reasoning against these conclusive evidences of revelation.

Verses 22-31. The deliverance of the sufferer comes in with the twenty-first verse. Thrice He calls for help. "Haste Thee to help Me"—"Deliver my soul from the Sword"—"Save me from the Lion's Mouth." Then we hear of the answer: "Thou hast answered Me from the horns of the wild-oxen." He was surrounded by the dogs (Gentiles) and the assembly of the wicked (Jews) as memtioned in verse 16, but now God has answered Him. The sufferings are ended and the glory begins. The horns of the wild-oxen denote power; the power of God answered Him and raised Him from the dead and gave Him glory. We therefore behold Him at once as the risen One with a great declaration. "I will declare Thy name unto my brethren." And thus He spake after His passion and resurrection, "Go and tell my brethren that I ascend unto my Father and your Father, and to my God and your God." This brings out the first great result of His finished work. It is the Church, His body, brought into this definite and blessed relationship with Himself. In the midst of the congregation (the Church) He sings praises. He is in the midst. "For both, He that sanctifieth, and they who are sanctified are all of one; for which cause He is not ashamed to call them brethren, saying, I will declare Thy name unto my brethren, in the midst of the church will I sing praise unto Thee" (Hebrews 2:11-12). And then the circle widens. Israel too will praise Him, all the seed of Jacob will glorify Him. The ends of the earth shall remember and turn unto the Lord. All the kindreds of the nations will worship Him. He will receive the kingdom and the glory. Thus this Psalm, which begins with suffering, ends with glory, a glory yet to come for Israel and the nations of the earth.

PSALM 23

Christ, the Great Shepherd

1. Assurance (23:1-3)
2. Comfort (23:4-6)

Verses 1-3. Well has it been said "without Psalm 22, there could be no Twenty-third Psalm." While the former Psalm reveals Christ as the good Shepherd, who gives His life for the sheep, this Psalm makes Him known as the great Shepherd of the sheep, whom the God of peace hath brought again from the dead, through the blood of the everlasting covenant (Hebrews 13:20). And all who deny the atoning work of Christ have no claim whatever upon the assurance and comfort of this Psalm.

But we must not overlook the fact that the first application of the Twenty-third Psalm must be made in connection with that godly remnant of Israel of a future day. While He is individually the Shepherd of all who trust in Him, He is also nationally the Shepherd of Israel. The Patriarch Jacob spoke of this when he said, "the God which fed me," or, literally, "my Shepherd." In Psalm 53:1 the Lord is spoken of as being the Shepherd of Israel nationally, while in another Psalm the pious in Israel declare "we are the people of His pasture, and the sheep of His hands." In Isaiah 40:11 we have record of another national promise made to His people Israel—"He shall feed His flock like a Shepherd" and Micah calls Israel "the flock of Thine inheritance" (Micah 7:14). The entire thirty-fourth chapter of Ezekiel reveals Him as the Shepherd and His future work when He will gather graciously the scattered sheep of Israel and lead them back to their own land. This Psalm has therefore a wider national application, especially in connection with the already mentioned godly remnant who look forward during the time of Jacob's trouble, the great tribulation, to His visible manifestation. It will be their comfort, when they walk through the valley of the shadow of death, when their enemies arise threateningly on all sides. Then they will say, "I will fear no evil, for Thou art with me" and again "Thou preparest a table before me in the presence of mine enemies." Their hope is expressed in holy anticipation as dwelling finally in the house of the Lord forever, that is the hope of sharing the blessings and glories of the millennial reign.

Much has been written devotionally on this Psalm. Hundreds of books have been published, but it has never been exhausted nor ever will be. The assurance of the first three verses belong to every believer on the Lord Jesus. He is individually the Shepherd and each child of God can say, "Jehovah is my Shepherd," the Shepherd who never fails, who never changeth, the Jehovah Jireh—the Lord who provides. He gives pasture, peace and rest, with the never failing waters, the supply of His Spirit. Then He restoreth after failure and leads in paths of righteousness for His Name's sake.

Verses 4-6. And here is the comfort for all earthly circumstances, no matter where the path may be. Goodness and mercy are in store for all His sheep and the blessed goal to be with Him, not in an earthly house, where yet His glory is to dwell visibly, but in the Father's house with its many mansions.

A good way to read this Psalm is by asking the question, "What shall I not want?"

I shall not want—

Rest—for He makes me to lie down in green pastures.

Drink—for He leadeth me beside the still waters.

Forgiveness—for He restoreth my soul.

Guidance—for He leadeth me in the paths of righteousness.

Companionship—for Thou art with me.

Comfort—for Thy rod and Thy staff comfort me.

Food—for Thou preparest a table before me.

Victory—in the presence of mine enemies.

Joy—Thou anointest my head with oil.

Overrunning Joy—for my cup runneth over.

Everything in time—for goodness and mercy shall follow me.

Everything in eternity—for I shall dwell in the house of the Lord forever.

PSALM 24

The Chief Shepherd, the King of Glory

1. Who shall dwell with Him when He comes? (24:1-6)
2. The glorious manifestation of the King (24:7-10)

Verses 1-6. This Psalm may have been composed and used on the occasion of the removal of the ark from the house of Obed-Edom, to the city of David on Mount Zion (2 Sam. 6). It is a millennial Psalm and describes how the Lord will enter His glorious dwelling place on Mount Zion when He appears in power and in glory. When the King comes back He will choose Zion for His glorious rest, as so many prophecies tell us, and reign from there, while another house of the Lord, the great millennial temple filled with His glory, will then be built. Who then shall ascend into the hill of the Lord? Or who shall stand in His holy place? That these questions have nothing to do with the church, which at that time is as the glorified body with the Lord, is obvious. The character of those who will enter into His presence when He comes back to earth to dwell in Zion, and who will share the blessings of the kingdom, is that of practical righteousness, which is the fruit of faith. This company includes those Israelites who believed during the tribulation, who turned to the Lord, and also the company of Gentiles who learn righteousness when the judgments of the Lord are in the earth (Isaiah 26:9).

Verses 7-10. Here we have the glorious manifestation and entry of the King into His House and dwelling place. It is a most sublime description. It has nothing to do with the ascension of our Lord; it is His glorious return and entry into the earthly Zion to fill it once more with His visible glory. And the King of Glory is the Lord of Hosts. Jehovah of Hosts, He is the King of Glory. He who was forsaken on the cross is now crowned with many crowns.

This Psalm concludes this series which so wonderfully tells out the person and work of Christ.

Psalms 25—39

The fifteen Psalms which follow give the deep soul exercise of the godly. All fifteen, except the thirty-third, are marked as Psalms of David. Much of it expresses undoubtedly his own individual experience during the days of his suffering and at other occasions. Prophetically these Psalms give again the experience of the godly remnant of Israel in the time of trouble, preceding the coming of the King. We also can trace in these experiences much which concerns our Lord in His earthly life, when as the Holy One He lived that perfect life of obedience and trust, suffering too among the ungodly. But great caution is needed in the application of these Psalms to our Lord. Here we find expressions which could never be true of Him, who knew no sin. For instance some have applied Psalm 38:7: "for my loins are filled with a loathsome disease and there is no soundness in my flesh" to the Lord Jesus, simply to sustain the theory that He carried literally our diseases in His body. This is positively wrong. His body was a holy body. Death had no claim on it nor could disease lay hold on that body. But many of these experiences are unquestionably the experiences of the Perfect and Righteous Man, the second Man, walking in the midst of sinners.

These fifteen Psalms are rich in spiritual food, yet it must always be remembered that strictly speaking it is not Christian experience, but the experience of Jews under the Law dispensation, and it needs spiritual discernment in using these utterances for ourselves with our heavenly calling and spiritual blessings in Christ Jesus. We give but one illustration of what we mean.

The much beloved thirty-seventh Psalm with its blessed promises which we as Christian believers have a right to enjoy and to claim contains the promise, "But the meek shall inherit the earth; and shall de,ight themselves in the abundance of peace" (verse 2). This is promised to the godly Jews who wi,l inherit the earth. The Church does not inherit the earth, but hers is a heavenly possession. When our Lord in the kingly proclamation, the sermon on the mount, said, "Blessed are the meek, for they shall inherit the earth," He quoted from the thirty-seventh Psalm. This promise has therefore nothing whatever to do with the Church, but is a kingdom promise for the godly in Israel.

(It is deplorable that of late not a few of God's people have been confused by "new light" concerning the kingdom. This theory claims that John the Baptist and the Lord Jesus never offered the promised kingdom to Israel, but that the kingdom of heaven is equivalent with the present dispensation.)

The scope of our work does not permit a detailed exposition of these fifteen beautiful Psalms. We must leave it to the reader to ponder over them prayerfully and to enjoy their blessed comfort, yet always "dividing the Word of Truth rightly."

PSALM 25

Prayer for Mercy and Deliverance

1. Dependence on the Lord (25:1-7)
2. Confidence and assurance (25:8-14)
3. The Lord the refuge in trial and distress (25:15-22)

Verses 1-7. This is another alphabetical Psalm, though not perfect in structure as two letters of the Hebrew alphabet (v and k) are missing. This great prayer-psalm begins with the expressions of trust in Jehovah. The soul is uplifted and calm in His presence. Depending on the Eternal One, the soul knows that none that wait on Him shall be ashamed. David found this true in his own experience; so have generations upon generations of His people, and the godly of Israel in the future will make the same experience. They will turn to Him and inquire for His ways, His paths and His truth. Here are their prayers: "Show me—lead me—teach me—remember Thy mercies—remember not my sins—remember me." And He will answer, yea, He will remember their sins and iniquities no more and remember them in mercy. Our prayer as Christian believers is also for guidance, but we know that our sins are put away, that He hath saved us.

Verses 8-14. Here we find expressions of confidence and assurance. He guides the humble in judgment, He teaches the humble His way, a truth which all His people may well remember. The godly in Israel, fearing the Lord, express their confidence that their seed shall inherit the earth and that "all the paths of the Lord are mercy and truth unto such as keep His covenant and His testimonies." Yea, they know His secrets through His Word; this godly remnant will see and enjoy His covenant, the new covenant. (See Jeremiah 31:31-34.)

Verses 15-20. They are in distress, a net has entangled their feet; they are desolate and afflicted, in affliction and pain, the burden of sin is upon them, enemies hate them with cruel hatred. They look away from self and from man and are turning their eyes only to the Lord. From Him their deliverance must come. "Redeem Israel, O God, out of all his troubles." And that prayer will be answered.

PSALM 26

An Appeal on Account of Righteousness

1. Pleading integrity (36:1-5)
2. Separated unto the Lord (36:6-8)
3. Be gracious unto Me (36:9-12)

Verses 1-5. The opening verses remind us of the First Psalm and well may we put these words into the lips of the perfect man, who walked in integrity and was separate from sinners. Here we find no confessions of sin, no pleadings for forgiveness, but instead an avowal of conscious uprightness and separation from wicked men as well as love for His house and for the place where His honour dwells. It is the godly remnant pleading not exactly moral perfection, but uprightness of heart, which has led them apart from the apostate part of the nation. They hate the congregation of evil doers, and on account of this they look for divine vindication. No Christian believer pleads on such grounds with God. We plead that worthy Name, the grace of our Lord Jesus Christ.

Verses 6-8. The washing of the hands in innocency is a Jewish figure. See Deut. 21:6. They cleanse themselves from defilement to approach His altar as the priests had to wash their hands and feet (Exodus 30:17-21).

Verses 9-12. Then their prayer—redeem me and be merciful unto me—gather not my soul with sinners—all the pleading of integrity of heart and separation from evil-doers has not produced assurance of acceptance, though in hope they look forward to the day when in the congregations they will bless the Lord. How different the assurance which grace gives to us, that we are redeemed and the fullest mercy is on our side.

PSALM 27

Holy Longings and Anticipations

1. Confidence in the Lord (27:1-3)
2. Longings and anticipations (27:4-6)
3. Earnest prayer in trial and trust in the Lord (27:7-14)

Verses 1-3. This Psalm leads us deeper. We repeat that primarily it is a rehearsal of David's experience, perhaps at the time of Absalom's rebellion. Here faith breaks through in triumph, with deep longings for the house of the Lord and for His presence, which is followed by a description of the trials through which the godly Israelites will pass in the future. He is light, salvation and the strength of life; thus faith lays hold on the Lord and in view all fear and terror must vanish. "The Lord is my light and my salvation; whom shall I fear? the Lord is the strength of my life; of whom shall I be afraid?" It belongs to us all. Yet greater is the shout of faith uttered on the pinnacle of our great Salvation Epistle, Romans 8—"If God be for us, who can be against us?"

Verses 4-6. Heart longings and blessed anticipations follow. They long for the earthly sanctuary, we for our heavenly abode. Their desire is to dwell in the house of the Lord—to behold the beauty of the Lord—to inquire in His temple. And we too desire to be with Him, to behold Him face to face, and what it will mean then to inquire in His holy temple! What it will be when up yonder we shall no longer look into a glass darkly! Then follows praise. Their heads will be lifted up—"therefore will I offer in His tabernacle sacrifices of joy; I will sing, yea, I will sing praises unto Jehovah." And while Israel will sing on earth when their earthly hope and deliverance has come, the praises of His church will fill the heavens above.

Verses 7-14. Once more we hear the cry in distress. The present trouble which is upon them comes into view. They plead, "leave me not, neither forsake me, O God of my salvation"—a prayer which no true Christian believer needs to pray.

PSALM 28

Prayer For Judgment and Praise For the Answer

1. Prayer for judgment (28:1-5)
2. Praise for the answer (28:6-9)

Verses 1-5. Their cry now increaseth because of their enemies, the enemies of Israel in the last days. They breathe out cruelty to them (27:12). They pass through the valley of the shadow of death and if He does not answer and remains silent they be like those that go down to the pit. Hence the imprecatory prayer, "Give them according to their deeds, etc." (verse 4)

Verses 6-9. In faith the answer is anticipated and praise is given for it. The Psalm ends with a prayer. "Save Thy people (Israel), and bless Thine inheritance, and lift them up forever." The next Psalms bring the answer.

PSALM 29

The Judgment Storm

1. Give unto the Lord the glory of His Name (29:1-2)
2. The day of the Lord described as a thunderstorm (29:3-9)
3. The calm after the storm—the Lord is King (29:10-11)

Verses 1-2. The voice of His trusting people is hushed; His voice is now heard. From Psalm 25 to 28 we have seen the soul exercise of the remnant of Israel, we heard their prayers, we learned of their hopes and anticipations and of their trials and sorrows. Their last prayer in the preceding Psalm was "Save Thy people," and now He is seen arising to save them. His glory and strength, the glory of His Name, is now to be manifested.

Verses 3-9. This is one of the most wonderful poetic descriptions we have in the Bible. The day of the Lord, when He will be manifested in wrath and in mercy, is described under an onrushing thunderstorm. The mighty tempest passes from north to south. Jehovah thundereth, great waters sweep along, His voice is heard with power. The mighty cedars of Lebanon are broken by the fury of the storm. The cedars of Lebanon are symbolical of the high and exalted things which will be broken to pieces in that day. (Read Isaiah 2:11-14.) Lebanon and Sirion, the lofty mountains, skip like a young unicorn. The mountains will be shaken by mighty earthquakes and all the governments, typified by mountains, will also be shaken. He is manifested with flames of fire, the lightning of His righteousness, which ushers in His glorious reign. Then the hind is made to calve—it means Israel's new birth, while the forests (the nations) are stripped and laid low. And in His temple, that greater house, whose maker He is, earth and heaven, "all that is therein uttereth glory" (literal translation).

Verses10-11. The storm is past. The Lord has come. The judgment flood is gone. Jehovah now has taken His throne. He is King and blesseth His people with peace. The name of Jehovah is found 18 times in this Psalm and this Jehovah is our ever blessed Lord and Saviour Jesus Christ.

PSALM 30

A Psalm of Praise

1. Praise for deliverance (30:1-5)
2. The Past experience (30:6-12)

Verses 1-5. The inscription says that the Psalm was written by David as a song of dedication of the house. It probably means the house of the Lord mentioned in 1 Chron. 22:1. The Psalm must be looked upon as expressing prophetically the praise of the nation for the deliverance and when that greater house of the Lord will be on the earth (Ezekiel 40, etc.) David's experience, of course, stands in the foreground. It is generally assumed that David was sick unto death and that the Lord raised him up. But this foreshadows the experience of the remnant of Israel. They approached the pit, while their foes were ready to rejoice over them, but the Lord intervened, and they were saved and healed. Then the singing begins (verse 4). Weeping had endured for a night, the dark night of tribulation, but joy came with the morning, that blessed morning for which all is waiting, when the day breaks and the shadows flee away.

Verses 6-12. This is a rehearsal of the experiences through which they passed. Mourning for them is turned into dancing; the sackcloth is taken off and the garments of joy and gladness are put on. Then His glory will be manifested and will sing His praise throughout Israel's land and the whole earth will be filled with His glory.

PSALM 31

The Enemies of Israel and the Victory

1. The prayer for deliverance (31:1-18)
2. The victory (31:19-24)

Verses 1-18. Many saints have turned to this Psalm for encouragement in time of trouble and sorrow. And there is much in it which helps the trusting soul. Notice the different names of Jehovah—my rock—my house of defense—my strong rock—my fortress—my strength—God of truth. But like the previous Psalms this one also unfolds prophetically the sufferings of the remnant of Israel during the last days of this age.

Yet likewise we may think of Him who endured the contradiction of sinners. The words "into Thine hand I commit My spirit" were used by our Lord when He laid down His life on the cross (Luke 23:46).

Verses 19-24. The outcome of all the suffering and trials will be victory for the godly. His goodness will be displayed in their behalf; He will answer the voice of their supplications in the coming great deliverance. The faithful ones will be preserved, the proud rewarded for their evil deeds.

PSALM 32

Fullest Blessing

1. The blessedness of righteousness imputed (32:1-5)
2. The blessedness of hiding-place (32:6-7)
3. The blessedness of guidance and preservation (32:8-11)

Verses 1-5. This is the first of the 13 Maschil Psalms, the Psalms of special instruction. They tell us of the understanding which the godly in Israel will have in spiritual things (Daniel 12:10). All these Maschil Psalms have reference to the last days. The foundation of this Psalm is David's own experience. See the application of it in Romans 4. This blessedness of being justified by faith, and all that is included, will be the portion also of the godly in Israel during the end of the age, after the true Church has been caught up. They will pass through David's experience and enjoy the "sure mercies of David."

Verses 6-7. And the Justifier is the hiding-place, the refuge. As He is now the hiding-place for His trusting people, so will He be their hiding-place. The floods of great waters point clearly to the great tribulation. They will be preserved as it is written concerning this godly remnant by Isaiah: "Come, my people, enter thou into thy chambers, and shut thy doors about thee; hide thyself as if it were for a little moment, until the indignation be overpast" (Isaiah 26:20).

Verses 8-11. Then the blessedness of guidance and preservation. His eye will rest upon them and with His eye He will guide them, as He watches over and guides all His people. And finally the righteous kept and delivered will shout for joy.

ALM 33

The Future Praise of Jehovah

1. The call to praise Jehovah (33:1-3)
2. His praise as the Creator (33:4-9)
3. His praise of His governmental dealings (33:10-17)
4. His praise as the Keeper and Deliverer of the Righteous (33:18-22)

What the last verse of the preceding Psalm exhorts to shout for joy, is in this Psalm more fully unfolded. Such praise the Lord has not yet received, it looks forward to millennial times when all earth fears the Lord and all the inhabitants stand in awe of Him (verse 8). Now they oppose and defy Him and His Word. Then the counsel of the nations will be brought to nought and His people Israel, His own nation, will be blessed. The last verse is a prayer that His mercy may be bestowed upon His people Israel, who hope in Him.

PSALM 34

The Perfect Praise of His Redeemed People

1. His praise for salvation (34:1-10)
2. The instructions of the righteous (34:11-16)
3. His redemption remembered (34:17-22)

This is another alphabetical Psalm, only one letter is omitted. It is primarily the praise of David after his escape from Gath, as the inscription tells us. Prophetically it is the praise of His redeemed and delivered people, delivered from all their fears (verse 4) and saved out of all their troubles (verse 6). Such will be their worship and praise in the coming day, while they themselves will be teachers and instructors in righteousness (verses 12-16; see 1 Peter 3:10-12).

Verse 20 is a literal prophecy concerning our Lord and was literally fulfilled (John 19:36). But the believer also can claim this promise, for we are His bones. "It intimates to the believer the limitation within which the power of the oppressor is confined, with whom he is in ceaseless conflict. As the same Scripture which contains the record of Messiah's sufferings provided also that no bone of Him should be broken, so it is with the saint." They will be kept by His own power. The last two verses of this Psalm shows the judgment of the wicked and the deliverance of the righteous in that day. We have seen once more how Psalm is linked with Psalm.

PSALM 35

The Cry for Justice and Divine Help

1. The cry of distress (35:1-10)
2. The contrast? (35:11-18)
3. Prayer for vindication and victory (35:19-28)

This Psalm introduces us again to the suffering of the righteous, giving another prophetic picture of the distress of the remnant. When David composed this Psalm we do not know. But He casts himself completely on the Lord and calls to Him for help and vindication. Thus the godly have always done when surrounded by the enemies who persecuted them. The condition of the godly when violence is in the earth during the time of Jacob's trouble is here fully pictured, and their prayers prewritten by the Spirit of God. They look to Him to fight against their enemies, so that they may be confounded and put to shame, that they might be like the chaff before the wind, driven away. These are imprecatory petitions, such as a Christian is not authorized to pray, but these petitions will be perfectly justified in those final days, when judgment is decreed upon the enemies of God. The godly act in righteousness towards the wicked, but they reward evil for good, showing that they are ripe for judgment. And therefore their plea, "How long, O Lord, wilt Thou look on?" (verse 17) "Rescue my soul from their destructions, my darling from the lions." This reminds us of the Twenty-second Psalm where this expression applies to our Lord. The remnant suffers with Him. And then their faith looks forward to the time of vindication and victory.

PSALM 36

Contrasts

1. What the wicked is and does (36:1-4)
2. What Jehovah is and does (36:5-9)
3. Prayer and trust in His loving kindness (36:10-12)

The wicked are described in their wickedness, with sin in the heart, no fear of God; filled with pride and flattery, speaking evil and doing evil. "But evil men and seducers shall wax worse and worse, deceiving, and being deceived" (2 Tim. 3:13). This is the divine forecast for the last days and these opening verses of this psalm show the wicked of the last days. But what a Lord He is whom they do not fear! What a contrast! And the righteous know His mercy, His faithfulness, His righteousness and His judgment. Only good is in store from His side for those who trust in Him. His lovingkindness is excellent, He covers them with the shadow of His wings, He satisfies them abundantly with the fatness of His house. Such will be the hope and comfort of the godly when the wicked wax worse and worse, till the day comes when the workers of iniquity shall fall, unable to rise again.

PSALM 37

The Blessed Lot of the Righteous Contrasted with the Wicked

1. Waiting for Jehovah and His promise (37:1-11)
2. The doom of the wicked and the portion of the righteous (37:12-20)
3. The ways of the righteous and the wicked (37:21-29)
4. God's gracious ways with the righteous (37:30-40)

This Psalm is also alphabetical in structure and somewhat proverbial in character. It is full of sweet comfort and encouragement to faith. All the saints of God have fed on its beautiful statements, and the coming saints of Israel will find help and strength in it for their souls. He who trusts in the Lord and waits for Him needs not to fret on account of evil-doers; they will soon be cut off. But what is the righteous man to do? Trust in the Lord—delight thyself in Him—commit thy way unto the Lord—rest in the Lord. If God's people will but do this all is well, for He who never faileth adds His promises. He promises safety, the fulfilment of the heart's desire; He will bring it to pass and bring forth righteousness as the light. Waiting for the Lord will end for the godly of that coming day, when the evil-doers will be cut off in judgment and when those who waited on the Lord shall inherit the earth. This is Israel's promise which will be realized for the godly remnant when the Lord appears in glory in their midst. These brief hints will help in the study of the entire Psalm. It must be looked upon as prophetic, pointing to the day when the wicked troubles no more, when his end is come and when the Lord exalts the righteous to inherit the land.

PSALM 38

The Suffering Saint and Confession of Sin

1. Suffering and Humiliation (38:1-8)
2. Looking to the Lord (38:9-15)
3. Confession and prayer (38:16-20)

This Psalm is read by the Jews on the day of atonement. It pictures great suffering in body and soul; it reminds us in different ways of the book of Job. (See and compare verse 2 with Job 6:4; verse 4 with Job 23:2; verse 11 with Job 19:13; the loathsome disease, with no soundness in the flesh, also reminds of Job's experience.) And the suffering one looks to Jehovah, He is his hope. He confesses his sins, pleads, "Make haste to help me, O Lord of my salvation." And that cry will always be answered.

PSALM 39

Deep Soul Exercise in View of Man's Frailty and Nothingness

1. The vanity of life (39:1-6)
2. Self-judgment and prayer (39:7-13)

This Psalm is connected closely with the preceding one and shows deep soul exercises. In the midst of trial, with God's hand resting upon the sufferer, he had been silent before his enemies. Before the Lord he did not maintain silence but pours out his heart, confessing the vanity of his fleeting life which appears to him as a hand-breadth and altogether vanity. Beautiful is verse 7. "And now, Lord, what wait I for? My hope is in Thee." All else the saint waits for in this little life down here is vanity except the Lord. These two Psalms have also their special application to the suffering remnant, who learn the vanity of all things and wait for the Lord only.

PSALM 40

Christ the Obedient One and the Fruit of His Work

1. The path of the Obedient One (40:1-12)
2. His prayer and His comfort (40:13-17)

Verses 1-12. The Fortieth and Forty-first Psalms are Messianic. Our Redeemer and Israel's Redeemer is blessedly revealed in them both and with the testimony to Him the first book of the Psalms closes. Psalm 40 begins with what may be termed "Christ's resurrection song." He came and went as the sin-bearer into the horrible pit (Hebrew: the pit of destruction) and the miry clay, and the power of God brought Him out, raised Him from the dead, set His feet upon a rock and established His goings (His ascension). A new song is put into His mouth, "even praise unto our God." It is the song of redemption which He sings first and all who believe on Him joinin that song. That is why we read "our God." The many who shall see it are those who trust in Him who was delivered for our offenses and raised again for our justification. And who can tell out the wonderful works He has done in redemption; "they are more than can be numbered." Verses 6-8 are quoted in Hebrews 10. The ears opened, literally "digged ears," refers us to Exodus 21. The New Testament quotes the Septuagint translation, made undoubtedly with the sanction of the Holy Spirit, "a body hast Thou prepared Me." In verses 13-17 we hear Him pray as the sin-bearer of His people, as we hear Him say in verse 12 that the sins He bore are more than the hairs upon His head. The doom of those who reject and despise Him, and the blessing of all who love His salvation are likewise mentioned.

PSALM 41

Faith and Unbelief in View of the Cross

1. Faith in Him and the Results (41:1-3)
2. Unbelief and its hatred (41:4-9)
3. The vindication of the Christ of the cross (41:10-13)

The poor one (literally: the miserable, exhausted one) is the Lord Jesus suffering on the cross. Blessed are they who understand as to Him, who consider Him, for it means deliverance, salvation, preservation, victory and happiness. But unbelief mocks and sneers at Him. They speak against Him, make evil devices against Him, the sin-bearer, that an evil disease (literally: a thing of Belial) is upon Him and that He shall rise no more. All this points back to the cross and is still true of the unbeliever who rejects the cross. Verse 9 refers to Judas who betrayed Him. See John 13:18 and notice when our Lord quotes from this Psalm He omits the words "whom I trusted," for the Omniscient One knew Judas, and did not trust him. And He, the Poor and Needy One, the Miserable One, the Forsaken One, had His prayer answered; He is the Risen One (verse 10); in God's own presence, before His face (verse 12). The first book of the Psalms ends with praise, prophetic of the praise which is yet to fill all the earth. Amen and Amen.

II. The Exodus Section: Book Two: Psalms 42—72

The second division of the book of Psalms corresponds to the book of Exodus, the second book of the Pentateuch. That book begins with the groans and moans of a suffering people in Egypt and after redemption by blood and by power, ends with the glory of the Lord filling the tabernacle when the work was finished. Ruin, oppression, suffering and sorrow, ending in deliverance and redemption, is the order in which the Psalms in this section are arranged. It is a most interesting study and we regret that we cannot enter into all the details, to explore these mines of prophecy. The oppressed, persecuted people, who suffer surrounded by the ungodly, is that same godly remnant of Israelites. Their deliverance comes by the visible manifestation of the Lord, the second coming of our Lord. The Psalm which concludes this Exodus of the Psalms is the 72, the great Kingdom Psalm, when His Kingdom has come and the King reigns in righteousness.

Psalms 42—49

The first eight Psalms form the first section. Here the remnant is seen in great distress, having fled from Jerusalem on account of wickedness during the time of the great tribulation (Daniel 12:1), longing for deliverance. Then we learn how that deliverance comes by the manifestation of the King and the results which follow that deliverance.

PSALM 42

Longing after God in the Midst of Distress

1. Longing after God and His sanctuary (42:1-6)
2. Distress and the comfort of hope (42:7-11)

This is the second Maschil Psalm, for instruction of the godly of that day. The remnant looks towards the sanctuary, the house of God, from which they are separated and driven away. They are panting after God, as the hart panteth after the water brooks. Their cry comes from "the land of Jordan"—Jordan, the type of death,and from the Hermons (which means "ban"), from the hill Mizar (littleness). The enemy taunts, "Where is thy God?" For them deep calleth unto deep and they cry out "all Thy waves and billows are gone over me." They suffer with Him, bearing His reproach, over whose blessed head the waves and billows also passed. "Why hast Thou forgotten me?" they cry to God and remind Him of the oppression of the enemy. Yet hope and trust fills their soul.

PSALM 43

The Cry Against the Ungodly Nation and Antichrist

1. The cry to God (43:1-2)
2. Send out Thy light and truth (43:3-5)

Here their enemies are mentioned, the ungodly nation, serving the beast (Revel. 13:11-18). The deceitful and unjust man, is that coming man of sin, the son of perdition, who then has taken his seat in the temple of God in Jerusalem (2 Thess. 2). They realize their help must come from the Lord to lead them to the holy hill and the sanctuary. They call for the coming of Him who is "the Light and the Truth."

PSALM 44

The Increased Cry for Deliverance

1. My King, O God! Command deliverances (44:1-8)
2. Trouble upon trouble and confusion (44:9-21)
3. Awake! Arise for our help! (44:22-26)

The third Maschil Psalm. They remember the days of old, what God did for His covenant people in the past, how He gave them the land with an outstretched arm and delivered them from their enemies. They own Him as King and call on Him to command deliverances for Jacob. Then they utter their complaint and describe the great troubles and calamities they are facing; they are spoiled, like sheep appointed for meat, scattered, scorned and derided. Yet they have not forgotten Him. Then follows the cry for the Deliverer and for deliverance. "Arise for our help, and redeem us for Thy mercies' sake."

PSALM 45

The Answer: The King Messiah and His Glory

1. The King in His majesty and power (45:1-5)
2. His throne and His glory (45:6-8)
3. With the King, sharing His glory and kingdom (45:9-17)

This beautiful Psalm, a perfect gem, gives the answer to the prayer of distress, "Arise for our help," with which the preceding Psalm closed. It is also a Maschil Psalm and a traditional view claims Solomon as the author. And how the critics have laboured, without success, to explain away its Messianic meaning! The Jews have borne witness to this fact. The Chaldean Targum paraphrases verse 2 by saying, "Thy beauty, O King Messiah, is greater than that of the sons of men." And the eminent Jewish expositor Aben-Ezra says, "This Psalm treats of David, or rather of his son the Messiah." But the first chapter in the Hebrew Epistle establishes forever that the Lord Jesus Christ is here prophetically revealed. It has the inscription "upon Shoshannim" (lilies). Here the theory that the inscriptions belong to preceding Psalms breaks down, for He is the Lily of the Valley, revealed now as the King, the Beloved One.

What sublime descriptions of the Person of our Lord! Here is His perfect Humanity, fairer than the children of men, with grace poured into His lips. His kingly glory, His manifestation in glory, executing the vengeance of God upon His enemies and delivering His waiting people. Here is His deity, for the King is God, "Thy Throne, O God, is forever"; His cross, He loved righteousness and hated iniquity, and the oil of gladness which is upon Him in resurrection glory, and His fellows share His glory. He receives the kingdom. With Him is the queen at His right hand in gold of Ophir, the Lamb's wife, to share His rule and reign with Him. The King's daughter is Israel, now all glorious within, born again, with garments of wrought gold, the symbol of glory. Her companions are nations now brought to the King. From henceforth the Name, which is above every other name, will be remembered and His people will praise Him forever and ever.

PSALM 46

The Deliverance and What Follows

1. God is our Refuge and Strength (46:1-3)
2. His coming in power and glory (46:4-7)
3. What follows His manifestation (46:8-11).

This is "a song upon Alamoth," which means "maidens' voices" and calls to remembrance the song which Miriam and the women sang when the Lord redeemed His people by power at the Red Sea. The remnant delivered relates prophetically the experience of deliverance. They trusted in God as their refuge and strength, though the earth was moved and the mountains carried into the sea. Then He appeared and helped His people "at the dawn of the morning." The nations raged, the kingdoms were moved—then His voice was heard, while His people shouted "Jehovah of hosts is with us." They call next to behold the desolations which judgment has wrought. Then, and only then follows peace and all wars are ended. "He maketh wars to cease unto the ends of the earth, He breaketh the bow and cutteth the spear asunder."

PSALM 47

He is King Over All the Earth

1. In the midst of His people (47:1-5)
2. The praise of His delivered people (47:6-9)

And now we see prophetically how the redeemed people clap their hands and shout unto God with the vo)ce of triumph, for Messiah is King and then they sing praises unto the King, for He is King over all the earth and highly exalted. Every knee must bow and every tongue confess.

PSALM 48

The Judgment of the Nations and the Millennium

1. Jerusalem the city of the King (48:1-3)
2. The confederated nations scattered (48:4-7)
3. The millennium (48:8-14)

Jerusalem is now seen as the city of the great King. His glorious throne will there be established, and Mount Zion becomes the joy of the whole earth. Verses 4-7 show what preceded the coming of the King. The nations had come against Jerusalem (Zech. 14), a mighty confederacy was assembled. He came and scattered them by His judgments. Then Jerusalem is established forever; His millennial reign begins.

PSALM 49

Retrospects and Meditations

1. Hear this, all ye peoples! (49:1-4)
2. His message of retrospect and encouragement (49:5-20)

If such is the outcome and the goal of the purposes of God concerning His people, why should they fear in the days of evil, which precede the coming glory? The ungodly will pass away no matter how great their riches are, nor can they redeem themselves; their way is folly; like sheep they are laid in the grave and death feeds on them. But different is the lot of the righteous. They shall have dominion over them in the morning, when the night of suffering and trouble is ended. They will be redeemed from the power of the grave and He shall receive them, "for He will swallow up death in victory."

Psalms 50 and 51

PSALM 50

The Demands of a Righteous God

1. His coming and His call (50:1-6)
2. The God of Israel speaks (50:7-13)
3. The demands of righteousness (50:16-21)

Psalms 50 and 51 belong together. In the first God is described coming to Israel, proclaiming His righteousness and demanding righteousness from His people and in the second Israel makes confession of sin. Psalm 50 is by Asaph. He describes the Lord shining out of Zion, coming in glory as the righteous Judge to judge His people. When the Lord appears His people will be gathered in His presence, for He has a controversy with them; He declares unto them the righteousness which He as their God requires. He does not want their ritual services, sacrifices and offerings, but He requires that which is the fruit of true faith, the sacrifice of thanksgiving and practical righteousness of life. He uncovers their moral condition and warns, "Now consider this, ye that forget God, lest I tear you in pieces, and there be none to deliver."

PSALM 51

The Confession

1. Conviction and prayer for forgiveness (51:1-8)
2. Prayer for cleansing and restoration (51:9-13)
3. Bloodguiltiness acknowledged (51:14-17)
4. Prayer for Zion (51:18-19)

This great penitential Psalm, according to the inscription, was the outburst of confession and repentance of David when Nathan had uncovered his sin. Well has it been said, "So profound a conviction of sin, so deep and unfeigned a penitence, so true a confession, a heart so tender, so contrite, a desire so fervent for renewal, a trust so humble, so filial in the forgiving love of God, are such as we might surely expect from 'the man after God's own heart.' " We cannot enter into all the petitions and expressions of sorrow over sin which are found in this remarkable Psalm. It goes deep in confession and brokenness of spirit. All the saints of God know something of such deep soul exercises on account of sin.

We point out the prophetic meaning of the Psalm. It is the future confession of Israel of their sin and especially their bloodguiltiness which is upon that nation. It is therefore the answer of penitent Israel to the words of the righteous judge in the preceding Psalm. David had bloodguiltiness upon him. And when the Jews delivered the Holy One into the hands of the Gentiles they cried, "His blood be upon us and upon our children." This bloodguiltiness will then be confessed when the Lord comes, when they look upon Him whom they pierced and shall mourn for Him (Zech. 12:10). Isaiah 53 is a similar confession which Israel will yet make. It will be the time of their deep contrition, national repentance and weeping. Then they will become the teachers of the Gentiles, to teach transgressors His ways, that sinners be converted unto Him. They will sing aloud of His righteousness, when the Lord has taken away their sins. Then they will bring sacrifices of righteousness and the Lord will do good to Zion and build Jerusalem.

PSALM 52

The Proud and Boasting Man

1. The character of the man of sin (52:1-7)
2. The character of the righteous (52:8-9)

The four Psalms which follow (all Maschil Psalms) give mostly a prophetic picture of the man of sin, the final Antichrist, the false messiah-king, under whom the godly in Israel will especially suffer. He is first described as the mighty man, the super-man, who boasts in evil. He is also a lying, deceitful man, "working deceitfully" and having a "deceitful tongue." But God is going to deal with him, destroy him forever, take him away, pluck him out of his dwelling place, and out of the land of the living. He will be destroyed with the brightness of the Lord's coming (2 Thes. 2:8).

PSALM 53

The Apostasy Under the Man of Sin

This Psalm is in greater part the same as the fourteenth. It is the description of the apostasy, the complete turning away from God and opposition to God, which will hold sway when Satan's mighty man is on the earth. Then the godly remnant will sigh for the coming of salvation out of Zion.

PSALM 54

The Prayer of the Godly

1. The prayer for salvation (54:1-3)
2. The assurance of faith (54:4-7)

During that final apostasy when the man of sin is revealed, the saints among the Jews will suffer persecution as the prophetic Word elsewhere reveals. Here is another prophetic record of their prayers, with a believing anticipation of deliverance.

PSALM 55

In the Throes of the Great Tribulation

1. Prayer for help (55:1-3)
2. Longings to escape (55:4-8)
3. The great tribulation (55:9-21)
4. The comfort of hope (55:22-23)

The man of sin, the Antichrist, stands out prominently in this Psalm. Because of him and his oppression, the godly remnant calls for help. They are overwhelmed with horror and beholding the abomination, they wish for wings like a dove and escape from the storm and the tempest of the great tribulation. This is in accordance with Matthew 24:15-16, which refers to the same time. They will actually flee to the mountain and will be away from Jerusalem as we learned in Psalm 42. The great tribulation has begun and of Jerusalem it will be true "wickedness is in the midst thereof, deceit and guile depart not from her streets." And this wicked one, the Antichrist, is one of the nation, not a stranger, the man with a flattering tongue, who even walked in the house of God. And now his character and the character of his followers is exposed as they turn against the godly. Hence the imprecatory prayer (verse 15). Here is the 70th week of Daniel's prophecy, the last seven years, divided into half. In the first half the Antichrist is the man who claims friendship, with words smooth as butter, but in the middle of the week he breaks the covenant and puts his hands against such as are at peace with him (verse 20).

Psalms 56—60

PSALM 56

The Faithfulness of God, the Comfort of His People

1. Trust and Comfort (56:1-9)
2. Praise for anticipated deliverance (56:10-13)

These five Psalms which are grouped together are Michtam Psalms. This one was written by David when the Philistines took him at Gath. The inscription Jonathelem-rechokim has been rendered by the Septuagint translators as "upon the people driven afar from the holy place," the literal rendering is, "The dove of silence in far off places." On account of the great tribulation, the abomination in Jerusalem, seen in the previous Psalm, the godly have left the city and here we have the expressions of their trust in the faithfulness of their God. Whatever the enemy may do they can say in all their wanderings and with all their tears, "Thou tellest my wanderings, put Thou my tears into Thy bottle, are they not in Thy book?" Blessed comfort is ours too.

PSALM 57

Perfect Trust in God

1. Sheltered until the trouble is past (57:1-5)
2. Deliverance and praise (57:6-11)

The inscription is Al-taschith, which means "destroy not"; it is the Michtam of David when he fled from Saul. It shows us once more the exercise of faith in the godly of Israel. In the shadow of His wings they take refuge till these calamities are overpast. They look for intervention from above, from where it will surely come at the close of the days of tribulation. "He shall send from heaven, and save me." Then they know they will be delivered in anticipation of which the voice of praise is heard. "Be Thou exalted, O God, above the heavens, let Thy glory cover all the earth."

PSALM 58

A Judgment Psalm

1. Why God must judge (58:1-5)
2. The judgment executed (58:6-11)

"Do ye of a truth in silence speak righteousness?" (literal rendering of the first verse). Righteousness is not heard on earth. Wickedness and violence are on the earth, therefore God must arise and deal with these conditions in judgment. It will overtake the wicked and the imprecatory prayers will be answered. Then the righteous will be glad when he seeth the vengeance and it will be said, "Verily there is a reward for the righteous; verily He is a God who judgeth the earth."

PSALM 59

Gentile Enmity Against Israel

1. Surrounded by nations (59:1-8)
2. Their judgment anticipated (59:9-17)

Another Michtam of David when he was persecuted by Saul. While in previous Psalms we saw prophetically the remnant of the last suffering from their own ungodly brethren and the Antichrist, here the nations are their enemies. The word "heathen" should always be translated "nations." They will surround Jerusalem. This is mentioned in verse 6. They are like the dogs, the term used for Gentiles in the Word. The godly pray for deliverence and in faith sing of His power—"I will sing aloud of Thy mercy in the morning"—that coming morning when the shadows flee away.

PSALM 60

The Lord with His People

1. Confessions and prayer (60:1-5)
2. The inheritance anticipated (60:6-8)
3. Faith's certainty (60:9-12)

This Psalm, "Shushan-Eduth" (the lily of testimony), also a Michtam of David, has for its beginning a confession of the godly in Israel. The Lord they acknowledge had scattered them and is angry with them. They pray for restoration. "That thy beloved may be delivered, save with Thy right hand and hear me." Then He hears and answers in His holiness and His people rejoice as once more they possess their earthly inheritance. The casting of the shoe upon Edom means the subjugation of Edom, taking possession and making Edom a servant.

Psalms 61—68

PSALM 61

The Identification of the King with His People

1. His cry and their cry (61:1-4)
2. His answer and exaltation (61:5-8)

The following eight Psalms are grouped together leading up again to the final deliverance of Israel and the glory of the Lord. The question in connection with this Psalm is, who is the king whose years shall be from generations to generations, that is forever, who shall abide in God's presence forever? The ancient Jewish Targum says it is King Messiah, which is the true answer. This is the key to this Psalm. The King, Christ, is seen as identified with the remnant. He walked on earth trusting, having as the dependent Man His shelter in God. And so does the godly remnant trust and fleeing to the rock which is higher than they, find their shelter there also. And when the King comes back they will have their full deliverance.

PSALM 62

Waiting and Trusting

1. He only (62:1-2)
2. Persecuted (62:3-4)
3. My expectation from him (62:5-12)

This Psalm is not difficult to interpret. It has always been food for the saints of God. Faith in God in the midst of adversity and persecution, waiting on Him, expecting salvation, deliverance and defense only from Him is beautifully expressed. Like all these Psalms this one also gives us a prophetic glimpse into the experience of the remnant of Israel. But it has its practical value for us likewise. The first verse literally rendered is, "Only unto God my soul is silence"; that is, hushed in His presence, in confident submission. To expect all from Him, nothing from man, to look away from self and magnify the Lord, is the secret of a life of rest and victory.

PSALM 63

Heart Longings

1. To see Thy power and glory (63:1-4)
2. Satisfied longings (63:5-11)

A Psalm of David when he was an outcast in the wilderness of Judah. Thus it fits in well with the outcast remnant, thirsting after God, longing to see His power and His glory displayed. And these longings are created in their hearts by the Holy Spirit, as in our hearts also. These longings will be satisfied in the coming day of His manifestation, when His people shall praise and worship Him.

PSALM 64

The Wicked and their End

1. The power of the wicked displaced (64:1-6)
2. Their sudden end (64:7-10)

This Psalm stands in contrast with the preceding ones. The outward circumstances, the deeds and power of the wicked, are seen again. But suddenly the Lord will act and strike down the wicked. He will avenge His own elect, who cry day and night unto Him. (See Luke 18:1-7. The widow in this parable is the godly Israelitish remnant.)

PSALM 65

The Times of Restitution and Refreshing

1. Spiritual blessings (65:1-5)
2. Earthly glories and blessing (65:6-13)

The four next Psalms unfold prophetically the times of restitution of all things as spoken by the mouth of His holy prophets since the world began. Here we get the visions of Israel's restoration, her spiritual blessings and her praise unto the Lord. and what will be the result for the nations and for all creation. We recommend a careful study in details by comparing Scripture with Scripture. In this Psalm Zion is mentioned first. It will be the joy of the whole earth and His praises will sound forth from the glorious place of His rest. Then He who answereth prayer unto Him, who is the desire of all nations, all flesh will come. The nations will be gathered into the kingdom. Israel's transgression will be purged away and they will be fitted to draw near and be satisfied with the blessings of His house, that future holy temple which will be filled with His glory (Ezekiel 43). The terrible things in righteousness with which the Lord has answered the pleadings of His suffering people, are His judgments, the vengeance of God. The results will be "peace on earth, Who stilleth the roaring of the seas, the roaring of their waves, and the tumult of nations." Verses 9-13 show that the curse which rests now upon creation will then be removed and even creation itself will shout for joy and sing.

PSALM 66

The Praise and Worship of the Millennium

1. What God hath wrought! (66:1-7)
2. Israel's praise and worship (66:8-20)

"Shout aloud unto God, all the earth! Sing the glory of His Name, ascribe to Him glory, in His praise." This will be done in the coming kingdom age. And Israel will be the leader of that praise, calling upon the nations to join into the glory song. "All the earth shall worship Thee, and shall sing unto Thee, they shall sing Thy Name, Israel will worship in the beauty of holiness, and this people, now a holy nation and kingdom of priests, become His witnesses." "Come and hear all ye that fear God, and I will declare what He has done for my soul."

PSALM 67

The Fullest Blessing

This brief Psalm does not permit any division. It is closely linked with the preceding one, telling us of the fullest blessings in store for Israel and the whole earth, when the new day has dawned and the King reigns. If this little Psalm in its prophetic message were understood it would end forever all postmillennial misconceptions as to the conversion of the world. Israel prays that the Lord may be gracious to them as He will in that coming day. As a result of Israel's conversion by the coming of the Lord, His way will be known upon the earth and His salvation among the nations. Then the peoples will praise, and the nations will be glad and rejoice. The Lord will be King of nations (verse 4) and the earth yield her increase. Here is God's way for the full blessing the earth and the race needs. Israel prays "God shall bless us" and as the result "all the ends of the earth shall fear Him." But Israel's blessing is inseparably connected with the return of our Lord. No blessing and restoration till He comes again.

PSALM 68

The Great Redemption Accomplished

1. The introduction (68:1-3)
2. The proclamation of His Name and of His acts (68:4-6)
3. A historic review (68:7-12)
4. Israel's place of blessing and the Redeemer (68:13-19)
5. His victory over the enemies (68:20-23)
6. The great procession (68:24-29)
7. The conversion of the nations and the kingdom (68:30-35)

This is one of the greatest Psalms. The Name of God is found in it in seven different forms: Jehovah, Adonai, El, Shaddai, Jah, Jehovah-Adonai and Jah-Elohim. The opening verses mention three great facts of the accomplished redemption. God arises—the enemies are scattered—the righteous rejoice. See Numb. 10:35. Praise then begins. Verse 4 correctly rendered is "Sing unto God, sing forth His Name, Cast up a way for Him that rideth in the deserts" (not heavens). See also Isaiah 62:10. The word used for deserts (araboth) refers to the regions south of Jerusalem, Jordan and the Dead Sea. The One who comes as the glorious King is He who hath passed through the scenes of death and has the power to lead from death to life. He delivers His earthly people who waited for Him, while the rebellious dwell in a parched land. The manifestation of the God of Israel at Sinai (verse 7, etc.) is the type of His future manifestation. Verse 13, "Though ye have lain among the sheepfolds (Israel)—wings of a dove covered with silver and greenish gold." The dove, as the sacrificial bird, is a type of Christ, but it is also applied to godly Israel in the Song of Solomon, when they are addressed as "O my dove." It applies therefore to both. The wings are covered with silver and gold. Silver stands for redemption and the greenish gold, the finest, for glory. Christ has brought redemption and glory, and under His blessed wings, Israel enjoys and possesseth both. Then the mount of God where His glory will be seen where He dwells forever. Verse 18 is quoted in Ephesians 4:8. He, the Redeemer of Israel, had descended first into the lower parts of the earth, even into the depths of death and the grave. Then He ascended into glory. But notice, it saith here that this ascended One received gifts for men, but in Ephesians we read that He communicates that which He hath received as the risen and glorified One. The Holy Spirit adds to it in Ephesians. But He also omits something. He leaves out "even for the rebellious." This refers to rebellious Israel and has no place in the Epistle which concerns the church alone. Then His victory over enemies and the lawless leader, the Antichrist (verses 20-23). The wonderful procession, He the triumphant leader, the head of the new creation (verses 24-29). And finally the world and the nations bowing before Him. There will be a temple in Jerusalem once more, as we saw before. The kings of the earth will go there to worship and to bring presents. And then peace on earth, true peace, lasting peace, universal peace, which the world tries to have now while we write this, without the Prince of Peace. "He scattereth the peoples that delight in war" (verse 30). Peace on earth in the Psalms always follows the visible and glorious manifestation of the King.

Psalms 69—72

PSALM 69

The Suffering and Rejected Christ

1. Hated without a cause (69:1-6)
2. Bearing reproach (69:7-12)
3. His own prayer (69:13-21)
4. The retribution (69:22-28)
5. His exaltation and the glory (69:29-36)

Psalms 69—72 go together and lead us prophetically from the suffering and rejected Christ to the glory of His kingdom in the Seventy-second Psalm. The Sixty-ninth Psalm, like the Forty-fifth, bears the inscription, "upon Shoshanim" (lilies). It concerns Christ and indirectly also the people who suffer for His sake. The Spirit of God in the New Testament quotes this Psalm repeatedly. See verse 4 and John 15:25; verse 9 and John 2:17 and Romans 15:3; verses 22-23 and Romans 11:9-10; verse 25 and Acts 1:20. Verse 21 was literally fulfilled as we find from the Gospels, Matthew 27:34, 48; Mark 15:23, 36; Luke 23:36 and John 19:28-30. No further evidence is needed that the Lord Jesus Christ in His suffering and rejection is here described. Yet the critical school attempts to deny the prophetic aspect. Referring to verse 21 and what the Gospels say about our Lord's words, "I thirst" that the Scriptures might be fulfilled, Prof. Davidson saith in the Century Bible "the fulfilment of Scripture referred to must not be understood as the accomplishment of a direct prophecy." And again in commenting on verses 22-23, quoted by the Spirit of God in Romans 11, the same professor declares, "These imprecations are among the darkest and fiercest in the Psalter. The gulf which separates these verses from 'Father forgive them,' marks the impassable limits of typology." But it does not in the least. The words apply to the nation as righteous retribution from the side of God after they rejected His Son. In His heart there is still the same love, for they are still beloved for the Father's sake. But these imprecations also belong rightly into the lips of the remnant against the antichristian oppressors of the last days. Well may we read the Psalm and think of all His suffering and sorrow in our behalf. The Psalm ends with His praise, the exaltation and victory of the Christ who died for the ungodly.

PSALM 70

This Psalm is "to bring to remembrance." It is the repetition of the last five verses of the Fortieth Psalm. The cross is again made known and the attitude of men towards that cross, those who reject Him and those that love His salvation.

PSALM 71

Israel's Song of Hope

1. Declaration of trust (71:1-11)
2. Anticipations of faith (71:12-18)
3. Revival and victory (71:19-24)

This Psalm, which bears no inscription whatever, gives another prophetic picture of the faith and the anticipations of faith as found in the godly of Israel, when the salvation is about to come out of Zion. They look to Him who is all sufficient to deliver and to save them. The Psalm may well be called Israel's song of hope. It abounds in many beautiful, refreshing statements, equally precious to us.

PSALM 72

The Kingdom Psalm

1. The King, who reigns in righteousness (72:1-4)
2. His kingdom from sea to sea (72:5-11)
3. The blessings and the kingdom (72:12-20)

The last Psalm of this Exodus section describes the establishment of the promised kingdom, the kingdom of heaven on earth. Surely the Spirit of God directed the arrangement of the Psalms, and put each into the right place. Here we have a beautiful prophecy of what is yet to be and for which all is waiting now, in a time when every form of government has failed and law and order seems to go to pieces. The King and the King's Son is the Lord Jesus Christ, He who came as the Only-Begotten from the bosom of the Father to this earth, to seek the lost sheep of the house of Israel, offering them first the promised kingdom. His own received Him not. In previous Psalms we heard the voice of His complaints, His sorrows and saw the sufferings of the cross. But here we behold Him enthroned as the King of Righteousness and the King of Peace. Righteousness and peace He alone can bring to man and He will surely bring both for the whole earth when the cloud brings Him back. Then He will be feared and worshipped as long as the sun and moon endure, for all times. Showers of blessing will fall and the righteous will flourish, while the wicked can trouble the righteous no more. Abundance of peace will be the lot of mankind then and His kingdom will include all the kingdoms of the earth. His enemies will lick the dust and kings will bring Him presents. And the blessings of His Kingdom! All the subjects in His kingdom will share them and all creation as well. The doxology of this section is the greatest of all. "And let the whole earth be filled with His glory. Amen and Amen."—The prayers of David the Son of Jesse are ended. Let us quote once more Prof. Davidson what he makes of this. "A note, probably added by the editor of the Elohistic collection, to mark the end of a group of Davidic Psalms." What blindness! David had seen the glories of the kingdom of Him who is His Lord and His Son and then declared "his prayers are ended." He has nothing more to pray for.

III. The Leviticus Section: Book Three: Psalms 73—89

The third division of the book of Psalms corresponds in character to the third book of the Pentateuch, th% book of Leviticus. That is the book of the Sanctuary, of Holiness. And this section, which is the shortest, also has the same character. Each Psalm brings the sanctuary of Israel in view, with the same prophetic-dispensational character as in the first two books. *The Companion Bible* gives the following division of the 17 Psalms: Psalms 73—83, The Sanctuary in Relation to Man. Psalms 84—89, The Sanctuary in Relation to Jehovah.

Psalms of Asaph Concerning the Sanctuary (73—77)

PSALM 73

The Problem of the Suffering of the Righteous

1. The perplexity (73:1-9)
2. Departure from God (73:10-14)
3. The sanctuary and the solution (73:15-28)

Eleven Psalms by Asaph open this Leviticus section. The clean heart is mentioned at once, and the assurance that truly God is good unto Israel and to those of clean heart. But here is the old question, the wicked prosper in spite of all their pride, their violence and corruption, while the righteous suffer. The prosperity of the wicked had an evil effect too upon the people, who departed from God. And Asaph's steps had well nigh slipped, as some said, "Verily I cleaned my heart in vain and washed my hands in innocency." Then he turns to the sanctuary and finds the solution In the light of God and His holiness he sees their end. Desolation is coming upon them in a moment, they are utterly consumed with terrors. Then having had the vision of the sanctuary he grieves over his foolishness, like a beast which does not know God. But could there be more beautiful words than those in verses 23-26! Read and enjoy them. But the experience of Asaph will be the experience of the godly remnant.

PSALM 74

The Enemy in the Sanctuary

1. The Prayer on account of the enemy (74:1-3)
2. The work of the enemy (74:4-9)
3. Intercession for intervention (74:10-23)

This is a Psalm for instruction, a Maschil Psalm. The enemy is seen in the sanctuary. This has been applied to the defilement of the temple by Antiochus Epiphanes, but prophetically it rather refers to that end-time, when the enemy will defile the temple with the abomination of desolation (Matthew 24:15). Then the remnant loving the sanctuary tells the Lord about it as we read in this Psalm, and in a mighty intercession pleads for intervention. "O deliver not the soul of thy turtledove (Israel) unto the multitude of the wicked—Have respect unto the covenant, for the dark places of the earth are full of the habitations of cruelty." How true that will be during the great time of trouble. And then the cry to God to arise.

PSALM 75

The Divine Answer

1. Christ the righteous Judge (75:1-5)
2. His judgment (75:6-10)

It is Christ as King who is pictured in this Psalm coming to answer the pleas of His people in behalf of His sanctuary. The translation in our version of the opening verses is faulty. "We give thanks to Thee, O God, we give thanks—Thy Name is near! When I have taken the set time, I, even I, will judge uprightly. Though the earth and all the inhabitants thereof are melting, I myself set up its pillars." Then He executes His judgments. He deals with the wicked, the horn lifted up, the man of sin. He putteth down and lifteth up. The wicked will be cut off and the righteous exalted.

PSALM 76

Divine Government Established and Maintained

1. The Prince of Peace reigns (76:1-6)
2. The day of wrath and what it brought (76:7-12)

We behold the Lord now in Judah, the Lion of the tribe of Judah, His Name great in Israel! In Salem He has His tabernacle and in Zion His dwelling place. There, as the Prince of Peace, He broke the arrows, the shield, and sword and battle. The stouthearted were spoiled. Judgments were heard from heaven; the earth feared and was still, then the meek of the earth were saved. The Lord is terrible to the kings of the earth, the final confederacy of nations. How wonderful the order of these Psalms!

PSALM 77

The Distressed Saint and His Comfort

1. The distress (77:1-10)
2. The comfort (77:11-20)

This Psalm shows the distress of the saint in deepest exercise of soul. He earnestly seeks the Lord and never leaves off; "my hand was stretched out in the night, and failed not" (literal translation of verse 2). He moaned and complained and his spirit was overwhelmed. Then in still greater distress he asks, "Will the Lord cast off forever?—Is His mercy come to an end forever?"—"Hath God forgotten to be gracious?" The comfort comes to him as he thinks of God's past dealings, as he remembers His work of old. He realizeth "Thy way, O God, is in the sanctuary, who is so great a God as our God?" He remembers how God redeemed His people Israel in the past, and this being His way as a holy God, the God of the Sanctuary, He will redeem again and manifest His power. One can easily see how this Psalm also is Israelitish and finds its application in the last days.

Psalms 78—83

PSALM 78

A Historical Retrospect

1. The call to hear (78:1-8)
2. Ephraim's failure (78:9-11)
3. His dealings in power and mercy (78:12-55)
4. The continued provocation (78:56-64)
5. His sovereign grace in chosing David (78:56-64)

This historical retrospect needs no further comment. It is God speaking to the hearts of His people through their own history from Egypt to David. How graciously He dealt with them all the way! The crowning fact is His sovereign grace in choosing Judah, Mount Zion which he loved, building there His sanctuary, and choosing David His servant to feed Jacob His people and Israel His inheritance. Here we may well think of the Son of David, God's Anointed in whom God's sovereign grace is made known and who will yet feed Jacob and Israel His inheritance.

PSALM 79

Lamentation and Prayer on Account of the Enemy

1. The Enemy in Jerusalem (79:1-4)
2. How Long, Lord? (79:5-13)

Zion, the place He loves, mentioned in the preceding Psalm, is here prophetically seen in desolation. The nations have come into the inheritance, Jerusalem is become a heap of ruins, the temple is defiled. The dead bodies of His servants and His saints lie unburied, and the people are a reproach, a scorn and a derision. A similar prophecy we found in the Seventy-fourth Psalm, which should be compared with this Psalm. While Jerusalem and the temple has seen more than once such desolations, we must view these predicted calamities as being the final disaster which is yet to overtake the city. Read Daniel 9:27; Matthew 24:15, Rev. 11, and Rev. 13:11-18. And in that day of calamity where shall the faithful turn? They cry to Him whose faithfulness is proven by the dealings of the past and assured by the Davidic covenant. How long, Lord? Pour out Thy wrath upon the nations and the kingdoms, the ten kingdoms and the little horn of Daniel 7. They pray, "Remember not our former iniquities—Help us, God of our Salvation." Then when the answer comes they will give Him never ceasing praise.

PSALM 80

Looking to Heaven for Help Through the Man at His Right Hand

1. Calling to the Shepherd (80:1-4)
2. The ruin of His inheritance (80:5-16)
3. The Man of the right hand (80:17-19)

This Psalm continues the same theme. They call now definitely to the Shepherd, He who is enthroned in glory between the Cherubim. They ask Him to "shine forth," to manifest Himself in glory and power for their salvation, to answer their cries for help. Three times they plead, "Turn us again, O God, and cause Thy face to shine, and we shall be saved." Ancient Jewish comments on this verse say that the face which shines upon Israel is the Messiah. Even so when His face shines, when He is manifested in glory His earthly people will be saved. And they know Him. They speak of Him as "the Man of Thy right hand," as "the Son of Man whom Thou madest strong for Thyself." It is our Lord who sits at the right hand of God, waiting till His enemies are made the footstool of His feet (Psalm 110). Criticism refuses to accept this. They say, "Of course Israel is meant" (*Century Bible* on the Psalms, p. 88).

PSALM 81

Hope Revived: His Gracious Return to Israel

1. The blowing of the trumpet (81:1-5)
2. His loving call to His people (81:6-12)
3. Gracious results promised (81:13-16)

Hope has revived and singing is commanded. What interests us most is the call to blow the trumpet in the new moon. The blowing of the trumpet, in the feast of trumpets (Leviticus 23), marks the beginning of Israel's New Year. Dispensationally it stands for the regathering of Israel and is followed by the day of atonement, that future day, when they shall look upon Him whom they pierced (Zech. 12:10) and after that the final feast, the harvest feast of tabernacles, a type of the millennium. Thus with the blowing of trumpets begins the revival of Israel's hope in answer to the prayers of the preceding Psalm. And He Himself addresses His people and promises as a result of hearkening to His voice deliverance from their enemies and other blessings.

PSALM 82

Concerning Judgment

1. The Judge with His righteous judgment (82:1-5)
2. Arise O God! Judge the earth (82:6-80)

His own presence in the congregation of God (Israel) means a righteous judgment. Israel is then owned as His congregation (Numb. 27:17). The judges among them were called gods; the Hebrew word for judges in Exodus 21:6 is "elohim"—gods, mighty ones. Our Lord refers to this verse 6 in John 10:34. But they were unrighteous in their judgments and so He comes Himself to execute judgment and to do justice to the afflicted and needy. And more than that, He will judge the earth and the nations.

PSALM 83

The Final Enemies Overthrown

1. The enemies in confederacy (83:1-8)
2. Their complete defeat and fate (83:9-18)

Elsewhere in prophecy we read of the confederacies of nations, Israel's enemies, coming against the land of Israel in a final great onslaught. There will be an invasion from the north mentioned in Isaiah 29; Joel 2; Daniel 8:9-12, and in Zech. 12:2. Then there will also be Gog and Magog invading the land (Ezek. 38, etc.). It seems the former is in view here. The godly remnant prays and speaks of these invading hosts as "His enemies" calling upon the Lord to deal with them. Their satanic object is to cut them off from being a nation. They remind the Lord of what He did with Israel's former enemies and treat them likewise, so that Jehovah may become the Most High (God's millennial Name) over all the earth.

Psalms 84-89

PSALM 84

In View of the Sanctuary

1. Heart longings (84:1-7)
2. In the sanctuary (84:8-12)

The two next Psalms are of the sons of Korah, who themselves are monuments of saving grace. (They were saved from the fate of Korah; see Numb. 26:10-11.) In these precious outpourings of the heart for the sanctuary of the Lord, we read prophetically the heart longings of the remnant of Israel. They are not yet in possession of the fullest blessings but look forward now to an early realization of all their hopes of being at His altars again. And all they long for will be their happy and lasting portion. They will go from strength to strength; He will be their Sun and Shield; He will give grace and glory. Verse 9 shows us our Lord. "Behold, O God our Shield, look upon the face of Thine Anointed (Christ)." It is through Him that all this will be accomplished.

PSALM 85

All Promised Blessings Realized

1. What grace has done (85:1-3)
2. Prayer for the fulfilment (85:4-9)
3. Righteousness and peace (85:10-13)

What will come to Israel when Christ returns to be their King is blessedly made known in the opening verses of this other Korah Psalm. Favour will rest upon the land; the captivity of Jacob is brought back; their iniquity is forgiven and their sin covered; His wrath is turned away. Hence they pray that all this may speedily be accomplished as it surely will in the days when heaven will send Him back. Then He will speak peace to His people and His saints and glory will dwell in the land, even their land (verses 8-9). Then righteousness and peace will kiss each other and truth shall spring out of the earth.

PSALM 86

A Prayer

1. The prayer of the poor and needy one (86:1-9)
2. The praise of His Name (86:10-17)

This Psalm has for an inscription "A prayer of David." We can hear in it the voice of the Son of David, our Lord, pleading in the place of humiliation, and also the pleadings of the remnant saints. The prophetic element enters in with verse 9. "All nations whom Thou hast made shall come and worship before thee O Lord." This will be the glorious result of His humiliation. Into the many and precious details of this Psalm we cannot enter. The name of the Lord (Adonai) is found seven times in this Psalm.

PSALM 87

Zion and Its Coming Glories

Another Korah Psalm. Zion is the object of Jehovah's love where He will manifest His glory. Glorious things are spoken of the city of God. This we learn from many visions of the prophets. When these prophecies are fulfilled and the glory has come, then Rahab (pride—Egypt) and Babylon shall know, as well as Philistia, Tyre and Cush. Nations will be born again and turn to the Lord and share the blessings of the kingdom. Then the singers will sing "All my springs are in Thee," in Him who dwelleth in Zion. The Christian believer gives now this testimony and knows its blessed truth, that Christ is all and in Him we have all our resources. But what will it be when nations with Zion shall know this!

PSALM 88

The Deepest Soul Misery Poured Out

1. In deepest misery and distress (88:1-7)
2. Crying and no answer (88:8-18)

This is a Maschil Psalm by Heman the Ezrahite. See 1 Kings 4:31; 1 Chronicles 6:33, 44; 25:4. It is a Psalm of deepest distress, picturing the darkest experience with no ray of light or word of comfort. That it describes the real experience of a saint no one would doubt. But in it we can hear again the voice of sorrow of Him who was the Man of Sorrows and acquainted with grief. It is His testimony concerning that He passed through as the Great Sufferer. "Thou hast laid me into the lowest pit, in darkness, in the deeps. Thy wrath lieth hard upon me, and Thou hast afflicted me with all Thy waves."—"Thy fierce wrath goeth over me, Thy terrors cut me off." Such was His experience when on the cross. The Christ in humiliation and suffering is mentioned so frequently to remind His people of the costprice of deliverance and glory, and that His must be the glory and the praise.

PSALM 89

God's Faithfulness: His Oath-bound Covenant with David

1. Jehovah's faithfulness (89:1-18)
2. His covenant with David (89:19-37)
3. The ruin and desolation (89:38-45)
4. How long, Lord? Remember! (89:46-52)

A Maschil of Ethan, a Merarite (1 Chron. 6:44; 15:17). The greater part of this Psalm extols Jehovah's lovingkindness and faithfulness and makes prominent the covenant with David. We must of course look beyond David and behold Him, the Son of David in whom this covenant will be ratified. Viewed prophetically this Psalm becomes intensely interesting. Verses 4-37 tell us of all the blessings which will be on earth when our Lord, the Son of David, is King. He is the Firstborn, higher than the kings of the earth (verse 27). All His enemies will be beaten down, they are scattered (verses 10, 22). Justice and judgment will be the foundations of His throne, mercy and truth will go before His face (verse 14). His people will be blessed and walk in the light of His countenance; He will be the glory of their strength, their defense and their King (15-18). His seed (including the heavenly people, the Church, and the earthly people) shall endure forever, and His throne as the days of heaven (29, 36). The past ruin of the house of David and the people Israel, the result of unbelief and disobedience, covered with shame instead of glory, is described in verses 38-45 and the prayer follows that the Lord may remember what He has sworn to David.

THE NUMBERS SECTION: BOOK FOUR: PSALMS 90—106

The Ninetieth Psalm begins the fourth book of Psalms, corresponding in different ways with the book of Numbers. It opens with the only Psalm written by Moses in the wilderness when the people were dying on account of unbelief, and is followed by a Psalm which shows the second Man, the Lord as the head of a new creation. In this book are found numerous millennial Psalms, showing us prophetically when under Christ, in the day when all things are put under His feet, the wilderness experiences of His people end, glory comes to Israel, the nations and all the earth.

Psalms 90—93

PSALM 90

Man's Condition of Sin and Death

1. The Eternal One (90:1-2)
2. Frailty and Death because of Sin (90:3-10)
3. The Prayer: Return Jehovah! How long? (90:11-17)

This Psalm of Moses shows what man is as a sinner, picturing his nothingness, the misery and frailty of his life, and death. The race dies, but does not become extinct, for He says, "Return ye children of men. They are carried away as with a flood, they are as a sleep-like grass which groweth up. In the morning it flourisheth, and groweth up; in the evening it is cut down and withereth." And time to the Eternal One is as nothing, for a thousand years are to Him as nothing. (See 2 Peter 3:8.) It is true, every statement as to frailty, uncertainty and death, of the entire race. But even in this Psalm of the first man with sin and death, we must see the prophetic aspect. If Verses 7-8 are true of those who died in the wilderness, they are also true of God's earthly people in the time of their trouble. "For we are consumed by Thine anger and by Thy wrath are we troubled. Thou hast set our iniquities before Thee, our secret sins in the light of Thy countenance." Hence their plea to return. The prayer with which this Psalm of death closes becomes illuminated when we look at it dispensationally. "Return, O Lord, how long? And let it repent Thee concerning Thy servants. O satisfy us early with Thy mercy; that we may rejoice and be glad all our days.—Let Thy work appear unto Thy servants and Thy glory unto their children." It is the expression of hope uttered by His earthly saints.

PSALM 91

Christ, the Second Man

1. In dependence (91:1-2)
2. In security (91:3-8)
3. His triumph and exaltation (91:9-16)

This Psalm has no inscription. Its author is unknown, but we know it is the testimony of the Spirit of God concerning the second Man, our Lord. Satan knew this also for he quoted this Psalm to our Lord in Matthew 4, omitting the words "in all thy ways" (verses 11-12 and Matthew 4:6). It is the Psalm God's people love to read on account of its precious assurances given to those who put their trust in Him. In a larger and prophetic sense we have here the blessings of God's power in the kingdom age when under the rule of the King His people will be kept from all evil. But let us not forget that we have in it a prophetic picture of our Lord as He walked as the dependent Man on the earth. He dwelled in the secret place of the Most High and trusted in Him, walking in perfect obedience. Death had no claim on His life, for He knew no sin. No evil could come near Him. Angels ministered unto Him. The lion and the adder—Satan in his two-fold character, as the powerful enemy and as the sneaking, hidden serpent—He tramples under His feet. And some day the enemy will also be completely bruised under the feet of His people. Then His exaltation, "I will set Him on high."

PSALM 92

A Psalm of Praise

1. Praise for His works (92:1-5)
2. The enemies who perish (92:6-9)
3. The happy lot of the righteous (92:10-15)

The inscription tells us it is a Psalm for the Sabbath day. The rest for His people comes when the Lord arises, delivers them, and the enemies perish. This Psalm looks forward to that rest, the coming great Lord's day. The praise is on account of the work Jehovah has done, His redemption work in behalf of His people. "Thou hast made me glad through Thy work—I will triumph in the work of Thy hands." Then the wicked shall perish, and all the workers of iniquity shall be scattered, while the saints of God shall flourish like the palm tree.

PSALM 93

Jehovah Reigneth

This is a kingdom Psalm by an unknown author. The Lord reigneth in majesty. And under His reign the world is established; He is above all the floods of many waters, none can withstand Him. Revelation 11:15-18 may be read in connection with this brief kingdom Psalm. The angry nations mentioned in this passage correspond with the floods of waters mentioned in the Psalm.

PSALMS 94—100

PSALM 94

Prayer for the Execution of the Vengeance of God

1. The Prayer on account of the enemy (94:1-7)
2. Expostulation with the wicked (94:8-13)
3. The comfort of the righteous (94:14-23)

The seven Psalms which follow lead on to the full establishment of the kingdom on earth and most of these Psalms celebrate His judgment reign, and the blessings of the age to come. We start once more with a Psalm which pictures vividly the trials of the days which precede the coming of the Lord and the coming of His kingdom. The Spirit of God has arranged these Psalms, as we have by this time learned, in such a manner as to lead from suffering to glory, the path which He went and which His people are appointed to follow also. Hence we see in this Psalm the wicked persecuting and breaking in pieces the people of God, and the righteous remnant is calling to the God to whom vengeance belongeth to show Himself, that is, to manifest His glory in their behalf. The voice of faith we hear also, the assurance that the Lord will not forsake His people nor His inheritance, that the Lord will intervene in behalf of His own and cut off the wicked.

PSALM 95

In Anticipation of His Coming

1. Singing unto Him? (95:1-5)
2. Let us worship and bow down (95:6-11)

It is a call to Israel in anticipation of the soon appearing of the expected Saviour-King. The next Psalm will show that He has come. How are they, His people, to welcome Him? With singing, with confession (this is the literal translation of thanksgiving in verse 2), with worship and prostration. And there is the warning now not to harden their hearts, not be like their fathers who could not enter into His rest. His people must welcome Him as a willing, as an obedient people and such will be the humble remnant, having passed through the gracious discipline of the tribulation days. The end verses are quoted in Hebrews 3 and 4.

PSALM 96

The Lord Has Come

1. The new song (96:1-3)
2. The Lord supreme (96:4-6)
3. Glory unto His Name (96:7-10)
4. Creation celebrating (96:11-13)

And now He has come and is manifested in the earth. The singing times begin and will last for a thousand years, when they will merge into the never ceasing songs of eternity. It is a call now to make the glad and glorious news known in all the earth and to make His glory known among the nations. That will be the work of converted Israel. Not much comment is needed; it is all so plain if we just see it refers to His visible return. And while Israel rejoices, the nations hear that He reigneth, all creation will rejoice as well, for He takes the curse away and delivers creation from its groans.

PSALM 97

His Glorious Reign

1. Jehovah reigneth (97:1-5)
2. In righteousness and with glory (97:6-12)

He reigneth! Earth and the multitude of isles will now rejoice, for He whose right it is occupies the throne and all unrighteousness, wickedness and idolatry will be banished. Zion and the daughters of Judah rejoice and all the righteous rejoice. It is the time of singing and of joy. And the heavens will reveal His righteousness, while angels worship Him (verse 7 and Hebrews 1:6). What glory scenes will then take place upon this earth!

PSALM 98

The New Song

1. The call to sing (98:1-3)
2. The response (98:4-6)
3. The praise of all (98:7-9)

The Lord by His coming has done wonderful things. He has brought salvation and victory; He has made known His salvation, His righteousness in judgment was seen by the nations. He has also remembered the house of Israel in His mercy and all the ends of the earth have seen the salvation of God. And therefore the call to sing the new song. And all the world and creation will join in.

PSALM 99

The Reign of Righteousness

1. His throne (99:1-3)
2. Judgment and righteousness executed (99:4-6)
3. His gracious dealings (99:7-9)

It is a Psalm of the righteous government. The Lord who reigns is holy, demands obedience. He is holy and must be worshipped. Moses and Aaron were His priests in the past and Samuel among them that called upon His Name. He dealt graciously with His people in the past and forgave them, and the same Lord now reigneth and will deal in righteousness and mercy with His people.

PSALM 100

Nothing but Praise

It is Israel's voice in praise which we hear in this brief Psalm, which so fittingly concludes this series of great millennial Psalms. They exhort that all the earth should make a joyful noise unto the Lord, to serve Him and come before Him with singing. The third verse tells us that they are the speakers. All are to enter His gates with thanksgiving and come into His courts with praise. How often is this Psalm used in a spiritualised way, making the gates and the courts some church building. But we worship in spirit and in truth and not in an earthly house. The gates and courts have reference to that future temple, which will be a house of prayer for all nations.

Psalms 101—106

PSALM 101

The Righteous King Speaketh

1. The character of the King (101:1-3)
2. His righteous demands of His subjects (101:4-8)

A Psalm of David. He speaks as king concerning himself and those in his kingdom. But it is evident that once more he speaks as a prophet concerning the true King, the Son, whom God had promised through him, our Lord Jesus Christ. He is a King of perfect righteousness, which David was not. This true King is in complete fellowship with Jehovah, for He is one with Him. He will not tolerate evil in His kingdom of righteousness. The proud and wicked are not suffered by Him. He will destroy early (morning by morning) the wicked out of the land and all evil doers will be cut off from the city of the Lord. Those who walk in a perfect way shall serve Him.

PSALM 102

Christ the King in His Humiliation

1. In the place of humiliation and dependence (102:1-7)
2. His enemies (102:8-11)
3. The set time for Zion (102:12-16)
4. The blessings which follow (102:17-22)
5. The God-man in His work (102:23-28)

That this Psalm is a prophecy concerning the sufferings of Christ, His humiliation and death, and the gracious results which flow from it, is confirmed by the quotation in the first chapter of the Epistle to the Hebrews. In that chapter His work and His glory are unfolded. Here we have both. First we have a prophetic picture of the lonely One, like a pelican, an owl in the desert and as a sparrow alone upon the house top. What a deep humiliation for Him who created all things (verses 23-28) to take the lowest place, even like a sparrow. Then we read how His enemies reproach Him. He eats His bread like ashes and mingles His drink with weeping. He suffers more than that, in making atonement—God's indignation and wrath is upon Him.

Next we read something of the joy which was set before Him on account of which He endured the cross, despising the shame. Here is part of the travail of His soul. God will through Him, have mercy upon Zion when the set time to favour her has come. All nations will then fear His Name, and all the kings behold His glory. And Zion shall assuredly be built when the Lord appears in glory, His second coming. Then the glorious results when "the people are gathered together (in the kingdom) and the kingdoms serve the Lord." The closing verses tell us of His glory as the God-Man. The Man who suffered thus is the Lord of all, Jehovah the Creator. The Spirit of God alone could teach the true application of these words and He has done so in Hebrews 1:10-12.

PSALM 103

The Praise of Israel

1. The benefits of full salvation (103:1-7)
2. Merciful and gracious (103:8-18)
3. His throne and His kingdom (103:19-22)

This is the well-beloved Psalm, because God's people love it for its precious and beautiful expressions, telling out the full salvation of our Saviour Lord and the gracious compassion which He manifests towards His own. But we must not overlook the prophetic aspect, which but few believers have recognized. It is really the hymn of Praise which will be sung by redeemed and restored Israel. Theirs will be a whole-souled praise. Their iniquities are forgiven, their diseases are healed, their life is redeemed from the pit, they are crowned with lovingkindness and tender mercies. Their youth is renewed like the eagle's (Isaiah 40:28-31), which will be fulfilled then). And then the riches of mercy towards His beloved people! His Throne and His kingdom are seen in the closing verses and everything blesses Him.

PSALM 104

Creation's Praise

1. The Creator (104:1-4)
2. The foundations of the earth (104:5-9)
3. His works manifesting His kindness (104:10-23)
4. How manifold are Thy works (104:24-30)
5. Rejoicing in His works: Hallelujah! (104:31-35)

He is now praised as the Creator by creation. He is seen in His creator-glory. When the kingdom is established that glory will then be manifested. Verse 4 is quoted in Hebrews 1 showing that the glory of the risen Christ is here likewise revealed. The angels of God will ascend and descend upon the Son of Man. Then creation will be in its rightful place and man will see His glory there. The earth will be filled with His Riches (verse 24). Then too sinners will be consumed out of the earth and the wicked be no more for He is King. The Psalm ends with hallelujah. His people and all creation will praise Him.

PSALMS 105 and 106

The Memories of the Past

The last two Psalms of this fourth section review the entire history of Israel up to the time of the judges. It is the story of God's faithfulness and mercy, and the story of their shameful failure and apostasy. He is ever mindful of His covenant, and that covenant is mentioned first, as the foundation of all. Then how He watched over them. The story of Joseph is mentioned, followed by the rehearsal of the deliverance out of Egypt. Psalm 106 is couched in words of confession, showing their failure all the way, sinning, forgetting, lusting, unbelieving and disobedient. Only infinite mercy and grace could save such a people. Prophetically these Psalms express the repentance and national confession of Israel, when the Lord has saved them. Then with a new heart, the nation born again, with a new spirit within them, they read their history aright and learn to know the God of Jacob as never before. It is the fulfillment of Ezekiel 36:31. "Then shall ye remember your own evil ways, and your doings that were not good, and shall loathe yourself in your own sight for your iniquities and for your abominations."

THE DEUTERONOMY SECTION: BOOK FIVE: PSALMS 107—150

The final section of the book of Psalms, the fifth, is just like Deuteronomy. It shows God's ways with Israel, the end of these ways in deliverance not only for His people, but for their land, for the nations of the earth, for all creation. The book ends with the Hallelujah Chorus of redemption.

Psalms 107—108

PSALM 107

Israel's Deliverances

1. The wanderers regathered (107:1-9)
2. The prisoners released (107:10-16)
3. The fools healed (107:17-22)
4. Brought to the haven of rest (107:23-32)
5. The praise of His ways (107:33-43)

In the book of Deuteronomy, in Moses' great prophecies, we read of the scattering of the nation, the lot which should befall them as a disobedient people, becoming wanderers among the nations. But we read also of the promised regathering and the promises of restoration (Deut. 30). How harmonious it is to find the first Psalm of the Deuteronomy section celebrating this promised regathering and restoration! Again we see the divine power which guided the hand of the instrument who arranged these Psalms. And they thank and praise Him for this accomplished salvation. As wanderers amongst the nations they suffered and yet perished not as the peculiar nation; but now they are brought back to the city of habitation, to their own land. They had rebelled against the words of God and sat as prisoners in darkness and shadow of death; but now they are released and He brought them out of the darkness, out of judicial blindness, out of national and spiritual death, into life and light. They were fools on account of their transgressions; but now His Word has healed them. They were the storm tossed nation upon the restless waves of the sea, the emblems of the nations of the world; but now the storm is passed, the sea of nations is calm and He has brought them into the desired haven. For all this they praise Him. They are now "Israel His glory" through whom and in whom He has glorified Himself.

PSALM 108

Israel's Praise for Salvation

1. Israel's praise (108:1-4)
2. The inheritance (108:5-9)
3. Through God alone (108:10-13)

This Psalm is not a patchwork of two other Psalms as the critics declare (Ps. 72:8-12 and 60:7-14), but it comes in as a Psalm of David to give another hint on Israel's praise in the day of deliverance. Their heart is fixed to sing His praise. It is a praise not only amongst themselves, but a praise among the nations. Where they were once a byword they are now a blessing. And their deliverance and possession they will enjoy is not of themselves; it is through God and His power. The second part of the Psalm looks back to the time when deliverance had not yet come.

Psalms 109—113

PSALM 109

Christ in Humiliation

1. Despised and rejected (109:1-5)
2. The rejectors and their fate (109:6-20)
3. The Christ in His sorrow (109:21-25)

The five Psalms which are next grouped together belong to the most interesting in the whole collection. They give a marvellous prophecy concerning Christ, His rejection, exaltation and coming glory. In Psalm 109 we see Him rejected. In Psalm 110 He is at the Right hand of God, waiting till His enemies are made His footstool, returns as the victorious King and becomes the Priest after the order of Melchisedec. The three Psalms which follow, all Hallelujah Psalms, show forth His glory and His kingdom.

Psalm 109 gives us once more the story of His rejection. We hear the complaints from Himself, indited by His Spirit. He is the hated One. They fight against Him without a cause. They reward Him with evil for good, and His love, the love which sought them, they answer with hatred. Verses 6-15 have reference to Judas who betrayed Him and applies to all those who reject Him. Verse 8 is quoted by Peter in Acts 1:20. Of the betrayer it is said, "He loved cursing, so let it come unto him; as he delighted not in blessing, so let it be far from him." But this is true of all who reject Christ. All the cursing and punishment which come upon the rejectors of Christ are self-chosen. In the closing verses we hear the weeping, sorrowful voice of the Rejected One.

PSALM 110

The Psalm of the King-Priest

1. His person, exaltation and waiting (110:1)
2. His manifestation and His glory (110:2-4)
3. His judgment and His glory (110:5-7)

Seven verses only, but what revelations and depths we find here! The Psalm is frequently quoted in the New Testament. Who is the person of whom the first verse testifies? Here is the critics' answer. "Is the Psalm Messianic? Looking at it by itself, and without prepossession, one would not say that it is, for the writer has in mind some actual ruler of his own day, and his references are to events of his own times" (Prof. Davidson). But what about the words of our Lord in Matthew 22:41-46? In the light of these words every critic who denies the Messianic meaning of this Psalm is branded as a liar. And such they are. Our Lord shows that David wrote the Psalm, that he wrote by the Spirit, that the Psalm speaks of Him, as David's Lord and David's Son. To deny these facts is infidelity. And the Holy Spirit useth the Psalm to show the exaltation of Christ. See Acts 2:34-35; Hebrews 1:13 and Hebrews 10:12-13.

How well it fits in with the preceding Psalm. The Rejected One is the Risen One. His work on earth as the sin-bearer is finished. God raised Him from the dead and exalted Him to His own right hand. There He waits for the hour when God will make His enemies His footstool. This is not accomplished by the preaching of the gospel, nor by the work of the Church, but by God when He sends Him back to earth again and He will bind Satan and all His enemies will be overthrown. The rod of His power will proceed out of Zion and He will rule in the midst of His enemies. Then in that coming day of power, His people (Israel) will be a willing people, who will shine in the beauty of holiness in the dawning of the morning. He will be the true Melchisedec, a Priest upon His own throne. Then His judgment work and His Victory, judging nations and the wicked head of nations. "He shall drink of the brook in the way, therefore shall He lift up the head." He was the humbled One, who drank of death, and now is the exalted One. (For a complete exposition see the author's pamphlet "The Royal Psalms.")

PSALM 111

Hallelujah! He Has Done It

This is the first Hallelujah Psalm, following Psalm 110, in which He is praised for what He is and for what He has done. It is a perfect alphabetical Psalm: not a letter of the Hebrew alphabet is missing. It shows the perfect One and the perfect praise He will receive when He is on the throne as the King-Priest. The next Psalm is also perfect in its alphabetical character. Both Psalms have 22 lines, each prefixed by a letter of the Hebrew alphabet in their right order. All then will be order and all human speech can say will be said in praise of Him who has done it. Read the Psalm and see how His work in redemption is praised. He has now sent redemption to His people. Verse 9 is quoted in Zacharias' song, Luke 1:68, showing that in faith he too looked forward to the time of the kingdom.

PSALM 112

Hallelujah! The Righteous are Blessed

The second Hallelujah Psalm tells of blessedness of the righteous in the day the Lord is enthroned. It is preeminently Israel. His seed will be mighty upon the earth—wealth and riches will be in their house. And the righteous character, their righteous acts are given. "He hath dispersed, He hath given to the poor." While this is done by the Jews even today in their unbelief, what will it be in the day they know Him and worship the King? See Paul's answer in Romans 11:12-15. The desire of the wicked is then perished. Righteousness reigns.

PSALM 113

Hallelujah! Praise His Name!

This third Hallelujah Psalm begins with a Hallelujah and ends with Hallelujah. It is given in the authorized version as "Praise ye the Lord" (as in all these Psalms). It would be more sublime to maintain this grand old Hebrew word "Hallelujah." His Name is praised. "Praise the name of the Lord—Blessed be the Name of the Lord." Yea from the rising of the sun unto the going down, from one end of the earth unto the other, the Lord's Name is praised. He is above all nations. What Hannah so beautifully uttered in her song of Praise has come. "He raiseth up the poor out of the dust, and lifteth the needy out of the dunghill; that He may set him with princes, even with the Princes of His people." That is Israel redeemed by Him. And so is "the barren woman, a joyful mother of children."

Psalms 114—117

PSALM 114

Retrospect

As in the book of Deuteronomy God's ways with His people are reviewed so we find in some of these Psalms the reminders of God's dealing with Israel in the past. Here it is first of all the deliverance out of Egypt and what happened then, the type of the greater deliverance effected by the power of God. (See Jeremiah 16:14-15.)

PSALM 115

Who Their God Is?

1. Israel's God (115:1-3)
2. In Contrast with Idols (115:4-8)
3. O Israel Trust in the Lord (115:9-18)

Here Israel acknowledges her Saviour-Lord, unto Him alone is glory due. The nations had asked, Where is now their God? (Ps. 43:3, 10; 79:10) The Contrast between the God of Israel and the dumb idols of the nations follows. But Israel's God, the Lord, who has delivered them, is the living God and therefore the exhortation to trust Him who blesseth His people. Israel's resolve closes this Psalm: "But we will praise the Lord, from this time forth forevermore. Hallelujah."

PSALM 116

The Praise of Israel for Deliverance from Death

1. The Deliverance—Experience (116:1-9)
2. Thanksgiving (116:10-19)

Redeemed Israel expresseth in this Psalm her love to Jehovah for His gracious deliverances, for answered prayer and for His salvation. They were, during the great tribulation, as a faithful remnant; surrounded by the sorrows of death, the pains of Sheol were upon them. Death stared them in the face. Then they cried to the Lord, and, as of old, He heard them and sent deliverance. He dealt bountifully with them, delivered them from death, the eyes from tears, the feet from falling. And now they serve Him, taking the cup of salvation and performing their vows unto the Lord. The death of those who died in the tribulation period as martyrs is mentioned in verse 15. "Precious in the sight of the Lord is the death of His saints." Compare with Revel. 14:13, which also refers to the Jewish martyrs during the tribulation. The Psalm ends with another hallelujah.

PSALM 117

This is the shortest Psalm. All the earth, all the nations, are now called upon to praise, because His merciful kindness has been great towards His people Israel. And their blessing means the blessing of the world. See the significant and interesting verse in Deut. 32:43, the last note of Moses' prophetic song. Hallelujah.

Psalms 118—119

PSALM 118

Christ the Head of the Corner

1. His mercy endureth forever (118:1-7)
2. The past experience (118:8-12)
3. Jehovah My Salvation (118:13-19)
4. The rejected stone the head of the corner (118:20-29)

This Psalm is the last one which is used from ancient times by the Jews in celebrating the Passover in the home. The Psalms sung begin with Psalm 113 and end with this Psalm, the One hundred-eighteenth. It is called the "Hallel," the Praise. Our Lord sang together with His disciples this Hallel (Matthew 26:30; Mark 14:26). The One hundred-eighteenth Psalm was therefore the last which they sang, before the Lord with His disciples that memorable night when He was betrayed, went to the Mount of Olives. And speaking to the chief priests and elders our Lord applied this Psalm to Himself. See verse 22 and compare with Matthew 21:42. Furthermore verse 26 is also used by our Lord in Matthew 23:39. So there is no question that the Spirit of God speaks of Him in this Psalm. It has been suggested that this Psalm was written and used in connection with the completion and consecration of the second temple. That it was used in other feast days, apart from Passover, seems evident; perhaps in connection with the feast of tabernacles. The Psalm begins with thanksgiving for His mercy manifested towards Israel in their deliverance. Nations had compassed them about, but in the Name of the Lord they were cut off. Therefore Israel sings "The Lord is my strength and song, and is become my salvation." The voice of rejoicing and salvation is therefore in the tabernacles of the righteous (verses 14, 15). They are delivered from death. Note the "gates of righteousness" in verse 19, through which they wish to enter in to praise the Lord. But immediately after we read, "This gate is the Lord's, the righteous shall enter it." It is Christ the Door, through which Israel also must enter, as every other sinner must use Him as the gate, the door of salvation. We read therefore at once "I will praise Thee for Thou hast heard me and art become my salvation."

And then the verse concerning the stone which the builders rejected and which has become the head of the corner. His people rejected Him and He became for them the stone of stumbling and a rock of offence. They were nationally broken to pieces (Matthew 21:44). Then He became the cornerstone of another house, the church, of which He is the chief cornerstone. In the day of His second coming He will be the smiting stone, striking down Gentile dominion (Daniel 2) and grinding opposing nations to powder (Matthew 21:44). And after that He will be the cornerstone for His people Israel, upon whom all rests. This is indeed marvellous in their eyes as it is also to us. The cry "Hosanna," or "Save now" (verse 25) and "Blessed is He that cometh in the Name of the Lord" is the welcome of Israel to her returning King.

PSALM 119

The Law Written on Their Hearts and the Praise of the Word

This is the longest and most perfect Psalm in the whole collection. It is an alphabetical acrostic. It is composed of 22 sections, each having eight verses, 176 verses in all. Each section begins with a different letter of the alphabet and each verse of the different sections begins also with the corresponding letter of the section. Eight times each letter of the alphabet is mentioned in the 22 sections. The number eight in the Word has the meaning of resurrection, death is gone and life has come. Israel has passed from death to life and now extols the Word and the Law of God. The time has come when it is fulfilled what the Lord spoke through Jeremiah concerning the new covenant, "I will put my law in their inward parts and write it in their hearts." We behold then in this Psalm the joy of Israel in knowing the Word, in praising the Word and being obedient to the Word. In each verse except verses 90 and 122 the Word is mentioned and the following terms are employed: Law, commandment, word, saying, path, way, testimonies, judgments, precepts and statutes.

We give the twenty-two sections under the different Hebrew letters with a brief succession as to their contents:

Aleph: 1-8. The blessedness of those who obey His Word. *Beth:* 9-16. Cleansing by the Word. *Gimmel:* 17-24. The quickening by the Word. *Daleth:* 25-32. The uplift of the Word. *He:* 33-40. The power of the Word. *Vau:* 41-48. Victory through the Word. *Zayin:* 49-56. Comfort through the Word. *Cheth:* 57-64. Preservation through the Word. *Teth:* 65-72. The pricelessness of the Word. *Jod:* 73-80. Testimony through the Word. *Caph:* 81-88. Affliction and the Word. *Lamed:* 89-96. The Word eternal. *Mem:* 97-104. Wisdom through the Word. *Nun:* 105-112. The Word the lamp and the light for all occasions. *Samech:* 113-120. The wicked and the Word. *Ain:* 121-128. Separation and deliverance through the Word. *Pe:* 129-136. Communion through the Word. *Tsaddi:* 137-144. Zeal for the Word. *Koph:* 145-152. Experience through the Word. *Resh:* 153-160. Salvation through the Word. *Schin:* 161-168. The perfection of the Word. *Tau:* 169-176. Prayer and praise through the Word.

The whole Psalm is a marvellous evidence of verbal inspiration. But what will it be when the Word will thus be exalted and lifted to its proper place of supremacy through righteous Israel!

PSALMS 120—134

The Psalms of Degrees

Fifteen brief Psalms follow, called songs of degrees, or, ascents. They were in all probability used by Israel going up to Jerusalem three times a year to celebrate the feasts of the Lord—"Whither the tribes go up, the tribes of the Lord, a testimony for Israel, to give thanks unto the name of the Lord." They are indeed Psalms of "the goings-up" for we rise higher and higher as we read through them. Prophetically they give us again the steps from trial and suffering to the glorious consummation.

As they are so simple in language and construction no lengthy annotations are needed. Psalm 120 begins with distress, picturing again the suffering of the righteous godly remnant. In Psalm 121 the Keeper of Israel, the Covenant Keeping God, is revealed, who has made heaven and earth and neither sleeps nor slumbers. He has kept Israel in all their troubles and saved them. Psalm 122 brings us to Jerusalem and the house of the Lord. The redeemed ones go up to worship there. Thrones are there also for judgment, the thrones of which our Lord speaks in Matthew 19:28. Peace and prosperity have come.

In Psalm 123 there is another cry to Jehovah to be gracious and the next one, Psalm 124 celebrates the deliverance of Israel. "Blessed be the Lord." Men arose against them, but the Lord delivered His people. Mount Zion comes in view in Psalm 125. It cannot be moved, it abideth forever. Then when the word and the law go forth from Zion and Jerusalem there will be peace upon Israel. Psalm 126 celebrates the returning of the captives and this is the song they sing: "The Lord has done great things for us, whereof we are glad." Psalm 127 acknowledges the Lord as the One from whom all blessing and help must come. Psalm 128, which follows, shows the blessing which will be enjoyed when the Lord reigneth and blesseth His people out of Zion. Then we have a description of Israel's affliction in the past and how the hand of the Lord delivered them out of all their afflictions—Psalm 129. And in Psalm 130 we have a Psalm calling for forgiveness and waiting for the plenteous mercy and redemption which is promised to His people. Psalm 131 shows Israel prostrate, hoping in the Lord. Then follows the beautiful One hundred thirty-second Psalm in which Zion and its King is prophetically unfolded. It begins with the promise made by David to build a house, but the Lord made a covenant instead with him. "The Lord hath sworn in truth unto David; He will not turn from it; of the fruit of thy body will I set upon Thy throne" (Acts 2:30). And that is Christ, as the Son of David. He will choose Zion; it is His resting-place. His enthroned in Zion and what is connected with it is found in verses 13-18.

The One hundred thirty-third Psalm gives a blessed picture, not of the church, as it is so often taught, but of the great brotherhood of Israel, when once more they are a nation before the Lord. Then the Spirit will flow upon them and through them. In the last songs of the ascents, Psalm 134, we behold them in the house of the Lord, in the temple, lifting up their hands in worship in the sanctuary, praising the Lord and calling for blessing out of Zion.

Psalms 135—136

PSALM 135

Israel's Knowledge and Praise of the Lord

1. Knowing and praising His Name (135:1-7)
2. Deliverances of the past remembered (135:8-12)
3. His Name endureth forever (135:13-21)

The last song of ascents (134) showed Israel's praise in the sanctuary. The two Psalms which come next show this worship and praise more fully. This Psalm begins with a hallelujah and ends with a hallelujah. It will be an endless praise. The servants who stand in the house of the Lord and in the courts are called to praise Him. Israel cleansed and redeemed is now His servant (Zech. 3:7). They are His peculiar treasure (verse 4—Exod. 19:5). Then once more the remembrance of the deliverances of the past, the contrast with the idols of the nations (like Psalm 115) and the call to the house of Aaron, the house of Israel, the house of Levi and all that fear Him, to bless the Lord.

PSALM 136

His Mercy Endureth Forever

This is a historical Psalm of praise, as His grateful people Israel think of all He has done. Twenty-six times we read "His mercy endureth forever." The Psalm begins with a threefold call to give thanks unto the Lord, the God of gods, and the Lord of lords; the triune God is thus adored. And after this the brief sentences which rehearse His mighty deeds of the past as Creator and as the God of Israel, ea followed by the praise of His mercy. This Psalm was undoubtedly used in the Temple worship. The Jews in their ritual call it "the great Hallel." It will probably be used in the future, when in the new temple Israel will sing the praises of His Name.

PSALM 137

Remembering the Exile

This Psalm is in remembrance of the Babylonian captivity written by an unknown person. Some have named Jeremiah, but he was not in Babylon. The Psalm expresseth the never dying love for Zion in the heart of Israel. The same love is alive today after an exile of almost two thousand years. "If I forget thee, O Jerusalem, let my right hand forget its cunning. Let my tongue cleave to the roof of my mouth, if I remember thee not; if I prefer not Jerusalem above my chiefest joy." But this Psalm also looks forward to the day when divine retribution will be measured out to the daughter of Babylon, when Israel's enemies will be punished for their sins committed against His people. The fate of the final Babylon as given in Isaiah 13:16 corresponds with the last verse of this Psalm. See also Isaiah 47:6.

PSALM 138

A Psalm of Deliverance

This is a Psalm of David giving praise to the Lord for deliverance. The harp is now no more hanging idle on the willows, but is tuned afresh to praise His Name. It is not alone David's praise who cried and the Lord answered him, it is the praise of Israel for accomplished deliverance from the exile and therefore the kings of the earth are also mentioned. "All the kings of the earth shall praise Thee O Lord, when they hear the words of Thy mouth."

PSALM 139

In the Divine Presence

1. His omniscience (139:1-6)
2. His omnipresence (139:7-12)
3. Praising Him (139:13-18)
4. Delighting in His holiness (139:19-24)

Here we see the people of God in the light of God, standing in His presence. He is an omniscient and an omnipresent God. How marvellously this is given in this Psalm! And what a comfort to know that He knoweth, that He seeth, that He is about us, around us, with us everywhere, that His hand leads, that His hand upholds the saint, and that darkness and light are both alike to Him. And this God has fashioned us, He is our Creator. And the thoughts of God mentioned in verses 17 and 18 may be applied to the thoughts of His love in redemption. How precious are these thoughts in which He has remembered the sinner's need. They are indeed more than the sand. And with the knowledge of God's omniscience, His omnipresence, His thoughts of love and grace, the saint loves God's holiness, separating himself from the wicked, counting God's enemies his enemies, hating those who rise up against God. And then that prayer—"Search me, O God, and know my heart; try me and know my thoughts. And see if there be any wicked way in me, and lead me in the way everlasting." Can you pray thus daily in the presence of an omniscient and omnipresent Lord?

PSALMS 140—142

These three Psalms are Psalms of David. The third one in this series, 142 is another Maschil, the last Maschil Psalm, being a prayer when David was in the cave. In these Psalms the distress of Israel, the godly remnant of Israel, is again remembered. In Psalm 140 we see prophetically the evil and violent man, that man of sin of the last days. And therefore have we one more imprecatory prayer for the destruction of the wicked (verse 10). The last verses look forward to the overthrow of the wicked and the exaltation of the righteous.

In Psalm 141 the righteous are seen in separation from the wicked, and the prayer for preservation. Psalm 142 contains continued prayer for deliverance. The psalmist's voice is lifted up to the Lord. Before Him he poured out his complaint and before Him he showed his trouble; not before man, but before the Lord. He knew when his spirit was overwhelmed that the Lord knew his path. All these experiences of trial and trouble will be repeated among the godly remnant, as all God's people have passed and are still passing through similar soul-exercises.

PSALMS 143—145

In Psalm 143 the enemy is mentioned again, the enemy who pursued David. "For the enemy has persecuted my soul; he has smitten my life down to the ground; he has made me to dwell in darkness, as those that have long been dead." How this again reminds us of the death experience of the pious remnant when the man of sin, the Antichrist will rule in Israel's land. Prayer for deliverance follows. Hear me speedily—Hide not Thy face from me—Cause me to hear Thy lovingkindness—Deliver me, O Lord, from mine enemies, I flee unto Thee to hide me!

The next Psalm riseth higher. Faith lays hold on God. Israel, as David did, will look in faith to Him who has the power to deliver His trusting ones. "My Goodness, and my Fortress; my high tower and my deliverer; my shield and He in whom I trust; who subdueth the peoples under me" (literal translation). They acknowledge before Him their nothingness, days like shadows passing away. We see how this prayer too brings the final days of the age and the coming deliverance by the intervention from above before us. "Bow Thy heavens, O Lord, and come down; touch the mountains and they shall smoke. Cast forth lightning, and scatter them. Shoot out Thine arrows, and destroy them. Send Thine hand from above; rid me and deliver me out of the great waters (the great tribulation) from the hands of the strangers (the Gentiles). Whose mouth speaketh vanity, and their right hand is a right hand of falsehood" (144:5-8). Then bursts forth the new song which anticipates the answer for this great prayer, the answer which the coming Lord brings to His suffering people, by His manifestation in power and in glory. Verses 12-15 anticipate the days of earthly blessings when the King has returned and rules in righteousness.

Psalm 145 is a magnificent outburst of praise. While it is David's praise, it is also the praise of Him who is the leader of all the praises of His people, the Son of David, our Lord. He is singing praises in the great congregation (Psalm 22:25) composed of His redeemed people Israel and the nations of the earth. It is an alphabetical Psalm, all letters of the Hebrew alphabet are given except one, the letter "nun." The *Numerical Bible* gives the following helpful suggestion: "I cannot but conclude that the gap is meant to remind us that in fact the fullness of praise is not complete without other voices which are not found here; and that those missing voices are those of the Church and the heavenly saints." In the book of Revelation we have the record of this full praise. See Chapter 5 and the fourfold Hallelujah in the beginning of Chapter 19. In this Psalm we find the celebration of the power of God displayed in judgments and in the deliverance of His people. Here we read likewise of His great lovingkindness in "The Lord is gracious and full of compassion; slow to anger and of great mercy." See Exodus 34:6-7. He has come to dwell in the midst of His people. The kingdom has come and His saints speak now of the glory of that kingdom. They will talk of His Power. "Thy kingdom is an everlasting kingdom, and Thy dominion endureth throughout all generations." The mercies of the Lord displayed in that coming kingdom are the subject of the praise in verses 14-21. We learn now why this great praise Psalm was preceded by Psalms of distress and prayer. It is in remembrance of the sufferings of His trusting people in the last days, and to magnify the Lord, who alone will save them and that unto the praise of His Name.

PSALMS 146—150

The Hallelujah Chorus

The five Psalms with which this marvellous book closeth are all Psalms of praise. The word "praise" is found in the Hebrew thirty-seven times. Each one of these Psalms begins and ends with a hallelujah; there are ten hallelujahs.

First is a hallelujah which celebrates Himself, He who is the God of Jacob. Precious vision of Him who delights to call Himself "the God of Jacob," the God who loves the sinner and has redeemed His people. Who is He? The Creator of all, by whom and for whom all things were made (verse 6). The Lord of judgment and redemption; the Lord who looseth the prisoners, openeth the eyes of the blind, raiseth them that are bowed down—and He will reign for ever. *Hallelujah.*

Psalm 147 is the hallelujah for what He has done for His people Israel. They praise Him now in the beauty of holiness. He hath built Jerusalem; He hath gathered the outcasts of Israel; He hath healed the broken hearted and bound up their wounds. He manifests His glory too by the heavens above. And nature is now in full harmony, restored and blessed. But Jerusalem is the center of praise and glory. He hath blessed Zion and her children (verses 12-14). *Hallelujah.*

The notes of praise swell higher and higher. In Psalm 148 it is heaven and earth which sing His praises. The heights above, the angels, the heavenly hosts, the sun, the moon, the stars, the heaven of heavens, His eternal dwelling place, praiseth Him. And so does all the earth. The creatures of the deep praise Him, so do the hills and the mountains, the trees of the field, beasts, cattle, birds and creeping things. The kings of the earth, all races of men praise Him, who is worthy of all praise. *Hallelujah.*

Psalm 149 is the hallelujah of the new song. Israel redeemed is leading the glory-hallelujah song. The children of Zion are joyful in their King. They sing praises unto Him. They praise Him for victory and blessing. He has executed vengeance upon the ungodly. All His saints have honour and Glory now. *Hallelujah.*

And the finale, the last Psalm! It is the praise to the full. We have seen the "crescendo" of praise in these Psalms and now we reach the "fortissimo," the loudest and the strongest praise. With this the great redemption is consummated. Look at this Psalm. It begins with hallelujah and after this first hallelujah we find nothing but praise—praise Him—praise Him—praise Him! Let all that hath breath praise the Lord. *Hallelujah!*

Do you praise Him now? Oh let us give Him as our Lord, Him who hath redeemed us by His own Blood, who will soon gather us home to be like Him and forever with Him, let us give Him praise. Let us sing our hallelujahs now, songs of praise in the night, while we wait for the break of day, the morningstar. And the end of all for earth and heaven will be the hallelujah chorus, a praise which will never die in all eternity. *Hallelujah!*

THE BOOK OF
PROVERBS

Introduction

The title of this book in the Hebrew Bible is "Mishle," which is derived from the verb "Mashal," to rule, hence short sayings which are given to govern life and conduct. It also has the meaning of "resemblance," that is a parable. Many proverbs are concentrated parables. Our English word "proverbs" comes from the word "proverbia"used in the Latin translation. Traditionally the authorship of the whole book is attributed to Solomon, but the book itself does not claim this, nor does it sustain the Solomonic authorship of the entire collection. The major portion of the book is attributed to Solomon and there can be no question that he is the author of it. In First Kings 4:32 we read that the great king uttered 3,000 proverbs in which the wisdom given to him is illustrated. But the book does not contain this number of proverbs.

Chapter 25 begins with the statement: "These are also proverbs which the men of Hezekiah, King of Judah, copied out." This pious king must have had a great interest in compiling and preserving certain portions of the Word of God. According to this statement in Proverbs he must have commissioned certain scribes to add to the previous collection of proverbs by Solomon, other proverbs, which up to that time had re-ained uncollected. Then in chapter 30 we find the words of Agur the son of Jakeh, and in chapter 31 the words of King Lemuel.

From these facts which appear in the book it is clear that the composition of the entire book of Proverbs cannot be attributed to Solomon. The book begins with "The Proverbs of Solomon the Son of David, King of Israel". In the beginning of chapter 10 we read again: "The Proverbs of Solomon". It seems clear then that in chapters 1—24 we have the proverbs of Solomon; chapter 25 to the end contains also proverbs by the king, except the last two chapters. In all probability the scribes of Hezekiah who copied out the proverbs of chapters 25—29 added the last two chapters. What criticism states, that "the later chapters of this book point to the second or third century before Christ," is only an assertion.

Another feature of this book is, that numerous times a person is addressed as "My son," and the personal pronoun is often used "thou, thee, thy," etc. The sections where we find this are chapters 1—9; 19:20—24:34; and 27—29:27. Who then is the person addressed? Does Solomon address some one or is it Solomon himself who is addressed? Dr. J. W. Thirtle in his *Old Testament Problems* distinguishes between proverbs written *by* Solomon and those which were written *for* him. All those which are addressed to "My son," and in which the personal pronoun is used, it is claimed, are given to Solomon by "wise men or teachers" and that all these sententious sayings were given to young Solomon by these men to fit him for rulership. But this produceth other difficulties. The proverbs of Solomon would in this case be very few in comparison with the size of the book, and furthermore we do not know who these wise men or teachers were who instructed the king and wrote such words of wisdom.

It seems to us that there is another way in which these sections containing the personal address, "My son," may be explained. When the Lord appeared unto Solomon in Gibeon, He said unto him, "Ask what I shall give thee." Then Solomon asked for an understanding heart, to discern between good and bad. Then the Lord said, "Lo I have given thee a wise and understanding heart" (1 Kings 3:5, etc.). His prayer was answered. Then the Lord must have spoken to him by His Spirit and given him the instructions he needed as the king over His people Israel. It is more than probable that the sections in which the address "My son" and the personal pronoun is used contain the heavenly instructions given to the young king in the beginning of his reign by the Lord Himself. One cannot be dogmatic about this, but if such was the case the difficulties disappear. There is no need to put these proverbs for Solomon into the mouths of unknown wise men. It was th% Lord who spoke to Solomon, addressing him thus and Solomon guided by the Spirit of God penned all these words. But it seems that the beginning of chapter 4 contains a brief autobiography of Solomon relating to his training. If wise men or teachers had spoken these words their names would have been mentioned and their sayings would have appeared in a different setting, without being found in different sections of the book.

As Dr. Thirtle has pointed out, these sayings, instructions given to Solomon, as we take it by the Lord in answer to his prayer for an understanding heart, cover certain commands relating to Israel's kings, as given in the law of Moses. These commands we find in Deut. 17:14-20.

"When thou art come unto the land which the Lord thy God giveth thee, and shalt possess it, and shalt dwell therein, and shalt say, I will set a king over me, like as all the nations that are about me; thou shalt in any wise set him king over thee, whom the Lord thy God shall choose: one from among thy brethren shalt thou set king over thee: thou mayest not set a stranger over thee, which is not thy brother. But he shall not multiply horses to himself, nor cause the people to return to Egypt, to the end that he should multiply horses: forasmuch as the Lord hath said unto you, Ye shall henceforth return no more that way. Neither shall he multiply wives to himself, that his heart turn not away: neither shall he greatly multiply to himself silver and gold. And it shall be when he sitteth upon the throne of his kingdom, that he shall write him a copy of this law in a book out of that which is before the priests the Levites: And it shall be with him, and he shall read therein all the days of his life; that he may learn to fear the Lord his God, to keep all the words of this law and these statutes, to do them: That his heart be not lifted up above his brethren, and that he turn not aside from the commandment, to the right hand, or to the left: to the end that he may prolong his days in his kingdom, he, and his children, in the midst of Israel."

Now in the sections of Proverbs, pointed out above, in which the personal address is used, some instructions are given which correspond to the commandments relating to the king, as found in the passage from Deuteronomy which we have quoted. Of special interest are the repeated warnings against the "strange woman." The strange women against which the Spirit of God warned him in his youth, are the women of other nations, Gentiles. The passage in Deuteronomy says, "Neither shall he multiply wives to himself, that his heart turn not away." The Spirit of the Lord anticipated the sad end of the great and wise king and therefore warned him against the strange woman, under the picture of the harlot, who ensnares and whose ways end in death. But the heavenly wisdom which had instructed him and warned was not heeded. It is written, "King Solomon loved many strange women, together with the daughter of Pharaoh, women of the Moabites, the Ammonites, Edomites, Zidonians, and Hittites; of the nations concerning which the Lord said unto the children of Israel, Ye shall not go in to them, neither shall they come in to you, for surely they will turn away your heart after their gods. Solomon clave unto these in love" (1 Kings 11). Then followed his downfall. "It came to pass, when Solomon was old, that his wives turned away his heart after other gods." Then he worshipped Ashtoreth, Milcom and Chemosh and other idol gods. The words of wisdom the Lord gave him, thus giving him understanding, were not heeded and the allurements of the strange woman, of which his inspired pen had warned, became a mournful fact in his own history.

The literary form of these proverbs is mostly in the form of couplets or distichs. The two clauses of the couplet are generally related to each other by what has been termed parallelism, according to Hebrew poetry. Three kinds of parallelism have been pointed out.

1. Synonymous Parallelism. Here the second clause restates what is given in the first clause.

Judgments are prepared for scorners
And stripes for the back of fools. Proverbs 19:29

2. Antithetic Parallelism. Here a truth which is stated in the first clause is made stronger in the second clause by contrast with an opposite truth.

The light of the righteous rejoiceth,
But the lamp of the wicked shall be put out.
Proverbs 13:9

3. Synthetic Parallelism. The second clause develops the thought of the first.

The terror of a king is as the roaring of a lion—
He that provoketh him to anger sinneth
against his own life. Proverbs 20:2.

The Teachings of Proverbs

The Proverbs, speaking generally, give moral teachings as to human conduct, often giving the contrast between the righteous and the wicked. But besides this there is much which goes deeper. Many of these short sayings can be applied to the Lord Jesus Christ and to the gospel. There is one portion which speaks definitely of the Son of God, our Lord, who is Wisdom. This is found in chapter 8:22-31. When we read in chapter 13:7, "There is that maketh himself poor, yet hath great wealth," we can well think of Him who was rich and became poor for our sake that we by His poverty might be rich. Then there are verses which speak of a friend, "There is a friend that sticketh closer than a brother" (18:24). "A friend loveth at all times, and is born as a brother for adversity" (17:17). Well do we think, in reading such and similar verses in this book, of our Lord, who is the friend of sinners. Proverbs in spiritual instruction and application has an inexhaustible wealth.

The Spirit of God makes use of this book in quoting from it in the New Testament: Chapter 1:16 is quoted in Romans 3:15; 3:11-12 in Hebrews 12:5-6, also in Rev. 3:19; 3:34; in James 4:6 and 1 Peter 5:5; 4:26 in Hebrews 12:13; 10:12 in 1 Peter 4:8; 11:31 in 1 Peter 4:18; 25:21-22, in Romans 12:20; and 26:11 in 2 Peter 2:22.

Proverbs ought to be studied by believers as diligently as any other portion of God's Holy Word. The prayerful searcher will soon be rewarded by many nuggets of divine truth.

We make another suggestion on the study of this book. Many of the lessons given in these proverbs are illustrated by the lives of the godly and ungodly recorded in the Bible. It will prove a most helpful occupation to fit the experiences of these two classes as found in the Word of God to many of these proverbs.

The Division of Proverbs

As already stated in our introduction the book of Proverbs, as a book, was not in existence in the days of Solomon; it was completed through the interest, no doubt inspired interest, of King Hezekiah. That Solomon wrote the proverbs as attributed to him is beyond question.

The scope of this book is quite simple for it is clearly marked in its contents.

We find seven sections.

I. **INSTRUCTIONS OF WISDOM GIVEN TO SOLOMON:** Chapters 1—9

II. **THE PROVERBS OF SOLOMON:** Chapters 10:1—19:19

III. **INSTRUCTIONS GIVEN TO SOLOMON:** Chapters 19:20—24:34

IV. **THE PROVERBS OF SOLOMON COLLECTED BY HEZEKIAH:** Chapters 25—26

V. **INSTRUCTIONS GIVEN TO SOLOMON:** Chapters 27—29

VI. **THE WORDS OF AGUR THE SON OF JAKETH:** Chapter 30

VII. **THE WORDS OF KING LEMUEL TAUGHT HIM BY HIS MOTHER:** Chapter 31

It will be seen at a glance that instructions given to Solomon alternate with the proverbs of Solomon, teaching others as he first had been taught. The description of the virtuous woman in the last chapter is in the Hebrew in the form of an acrostic. The twenty-two letters of the Hebrew alphabet are found in these verses, just like in the alphabetic Psalms and in Lamentations.

Analysis and Annotations

A detailed analysis, as we have made it in other books, cannot be fully made in this collection of proverbs. Most of them are detached and each has a message by itself. To interpret each separately, to point out the many spiritual lessons, as well as prophetic application, to show their relation to other portions of the Word of God and to explain them by incidents taken from the Bible, would require volumes; and even then the spiritual meaning would not be exhausted. All we can do is to hint at their meaning and give some annotations which, under God, may be helpful in the closer study of this book.

I. Instructions of Wisdom Given to Solomon

CHAPTER 1

1. The Introduction (1:1-7)
2. Warning against evil companions and covetousness (1:8-19)
3. The appeal of wisdom (1:20-33)

Verses 1-7. The introductory words of these verses present the object of the book. These proverbs were given to Solomon, and contain instructions he received from the Lord. They are given to him that he might know wisdom. The word 'wisdom' is the characteristic word of this book for it occurs in the original language 42 times, which is 6 times 7. Six in Scripture is the human number, while 7 is the divine number. Wisdom is the first thing to be acquired, and that is followed by instruction, or admonition, to receive the instruction, the discipline of wisdom. The instructions are in justice, judgment and equity and they give subtilty to the simple. The word "subtilty" means prudence; the word "simple" has the meaning of "guileless." Solomon was a young man when the Lord answered his prayer for a wise and understanding heart, and in these proverbs given to him he received "knowledge and discretion" (thoughtfulness). Thus by the Word of God comes wisdom and that produceth understanding and a moral character in the man who trusteth in the Lord and is obedient to Him. To hear marks the wise man, and hearing will increase learning, learning will give understanding so that proverbs can be understood and also the interpretation. The latter word is only used once more in the Old Testament. It has the meaning of "satire." The words of the wise and their dark sayings (riddles) are the words of the wise men of this world, the philosophers. The meaning is not that these wise men were the instructors of the young monarch, but that the divinely given proverbs rightly understood would protect him from accepting the foolish things of human wisdom, of philosophy. "This verse (6) intimates that the aim of the book is to confer an initiation which will make the possessor free of all the mysteries of the wise" (T. T. Perowne).

Verse 7 contains the keynote to the entire book. (See 9:10; Eccles. 12:13; Job 28:28; Psalm 111:10.) The word "fear" means a godly fear, reverence. This fear of the Lord is mentioned fourteen times in Proverbs. This childlike reverence, so sadly lacking among the young of our day, is the beginning of knowledge; there is no true knowledge apart from the fear of the Lord. It means to acknowledge the Lord, adore and worship Him, bow in faith to His revelation and put it above everything else. The foolish despise wisdom and instruction, they follow the philosophies of this world. To acknowledge the Lord to reverence and fear Him is thus written over the portal of the house of wisdom.

Verses 8-19. The practical instructions begin with an exhortation of obedience to the father and mother. "My son" is the address of the Lord to Solomon, who thus acknowledges him as His child. Obedience to parents is not only commanded in the law dispensation; it is as prominent in the dispensation of grace, as we learn from Ephesians 6:1 and Colossians 3:20. One of the marks of the last days among those who profess Christianity who have the form of godliness but have not the power of it, is "disobedience to parents" (2 Timothy 3). Such disobedience, so prominent to-day among professing Christians, is coupled with disobedience to God and rejection of His Word. Much of the ungodliness to-day has its source in this disobedience. This is followed by warning against wicked associates, those who are lawless and desperate men, thieves and murderers, who pass through the country greedy for gain. Solomon is exhorted not to walk in the way with them. The one who fears the Lord walks in separation and keeps away from the paths of the wicked. Verse 16 is quoted by Paul in the third chapter of Romans. There is a striking resemblance of this passage to Psalm 10 in which we have a description of the wicked, prophetically indicating the man of sin. (See annotations on that Psalm.)

Verses 20-23. Wisdom now speaks and wisdom in this first section of Proverbs is a person, a divine person. The eighth chapter gives us a wonderful vision of that Person, the Son of God, who is the Wisdom. First stands the call of Wisdom. The call may be answered or rejected. Wisdom promises if the call is obeyed, "Behold, I will pour my Spirit unto you, I will make known my words unto you." But if the call is refused the consequences will be disastrous. The appeal of wisdom closes with a precious promise.

> But whoso hearkeneth unto me shall dwell safely
> And shall be quiet from fear of evil.

This appeal of wisdom, the call, the promise, the refusal and the calamity of the refusal to listen to Him who speaks furnishes an excellent theme for preaching the Gospel to the unsaved.

CHAPTER 2

1. The pursuit of wisdom and its results (2:1-9)
2. Preservation from the evil man and the strange woman (2:10-19)
3. The path of the righteous (2:20-22)

Verses 1-9 This second chapter of divine instructions begins with an exhortation to pursue after Wisdom. The sayings of Wisdom, that is the Word of the Lord, must be received, laid up, the ear must incline to hear them, the heart must be applied to understanding. In verse 3 mention is made of prayer. There must be crying after knowledge and for understanding and that must be followed by seeking and searching. If these conditions are fulfilled then the fear of the Lord is one's portion as well as the knowledge of God. These are excellent instructions for the study of the Word of God. If followed then the Lord will give wisdom (James 1:5). He layeth up sound wisdom for the righteous. He Himself is the Wisdom and in Him are laid up all the treasures of wisdom and knowledge (Colossians 2:3). He also is a shield (the better word for buckler) to them that walk uprightly, and the way of His saints is preserved by Him.

Verses 10-19. When Wisdom entereth the heart and the soul rejoiceth in true knowledge, what blessed consequences will follow! There is preservation and deliverance. The way of the evil man, the proud, the ungodly and their crooked ways hold out no attraction to those who love and seek wisdom. Then for the first time the strange woman, the foreign woman is mentioned. While a prostitute is meant, the warning to Solomon was to beware of the allurement of those who were outside of the commonwealth of Israel, the heathen Canaanitish cults in which prostitution played such a prominent part. If we look on these instructions as given to a young man, we see the temptations outlined which are peculiar to the young—disobedience to parents, evil companions and the lust of the flesh.

Verses 20-22. He who ordereth his conduct according to divine instruction will walk in the way of the good and keep the paths of the righteous, dwelling in the land of promise while the wicked have no such hope.

CHAPTER 3

1. The call and promise of wisdom (3:1-10)
2. Happy is the man that findeth wisdom (3:11-20)
3. Promise and instruction (3:21-25)

Verses 1-10. The call to obedience is followed by promise. The promise is like all the promises to an earthly people "for length of days and long life". Here are some blessed exhortations loved and cherished by all His people (verses 5-7). How happier, and more fruitful the children of God would be if they obeyed constantly this instruction: "In all thy ways acknowledge Him and He shall direct thy paths."

Verses 11-20. Verses 11-12 are quoted in Hebrews 12. The man who findeth wisdom, that is, who knows the Lord, is happy. If we look upon wisdom as personified in the Lord Jesus Christ we can read "His ways are pleasantness, and all His paths are peace. He is a tree of life to them that lay hold on Him, and happy is every one that retaineth Him" (17-18).

Verses 21-34. The words of the Lord kept are life to the soul, grace to the neck; they insure safety; they protect and keep by day and by night. Each verse has a blessed meaning. This chapter ends with the promise that the wise shall inherit glory while the promotion of fools will be shame.

CHAPTER 4

1. Solomon's training (4:1-9)
2. Hear, O my son: Receive my sayings (4:10-19)
3. My son, attend to my words. (4:20-27)

Verses 1-9. This passage shows the early training which Solomon received and he passeth on the instructions. It is said that these verses formed a model for many Puritan homes in England and the Scotland of the covenant. He was the beloved one, his father's true son. Note the different exhortation, about wisdom: Forget it not; forsake her not; love her; exalt her. Then the promises: She shall preserve thee; she shall keep thee; she shall promote thee; she gives honor; an ornament of grace for the head and a crown of glory. If we take wisdom and make it the Lord Jesus Christ and His Word, what blessed food for the soul we will enjoy!

Verses 10-19. Here we find instructions for Solomon and all the godly with the corresponding promises. Then there is the warning concerning the path of the wicked and a contrast between the way of the righteous and the way of the wicked.

> But the way of the righteous is as the
> dawn of light
> That shineth more and more unto the
> perfect day.

This is a blessed statement. As soon as we accept the true wisdom, the Lord Jesus Christ, we enter upon a way which faceth the east, the sunrise. The light of the coming dawn illumines that path, and at some time the perfect day will break when all shadows flee away.

Verses 20-27. Instructions to receive and to obey the words of wisdom are the contents of this address. The eye is never to be taken off from the words of the Lord; they are to be kept in the midst of the heart. How important to listen to such counsel, even for us His children:

> Keep thy heart with all diligence;
> For out of it are the issues of life.

CHAPTER 5

1. Shun the strange woman and sinful passion (5:1-14)
2. The life of chastity (5:15-23)

Verses 1-14. It is a warning against literal fornication and the accompanying spiritual fornication, turning away from the worship of Jehovah and worshipping idols. The dreadful results of sinful lust are vividly described. How many a young man has found out the truth as given in these words in his licentious life.

> And thou mourn at thy latter end
> When thy flesh and thy body are consumed.

Solomon received these repeated warnings, yet after great prosperity and honor came to him, and his glory spread in every direction, like many a rich and successful man of to-day, these warnings were not heeded and he had to experience in his own life the truths of these words he had penned by the Spirit of God.

Verses 15-23. Here we have a sweet exhortation and picture of marital fidelity and a picture of true love in family life. How the Christian family should manifest something greater than this is revealed in Ephesians 5.

CHAPTER 6

1. The surety (6:1-5)
2. The sluggard (6:6-11)
3. The naughty, good-for-nothing person (6:12-19)
4. The strange woman (6:20-35)

Verses 1-5. These are instructions concerning contracts, in being surety for a neighbor and the danger connected with it.

Verses 6-11. The sluggard is commanded to go to the ant for a lesson. (See also 30:25.) The ant is a marvellous little creature. That which modern science has found out by close observation of the life of this little insect is here tersely stated by the words of the Lord, the Creator. They swarm in the woods and in the fields; they work day and night; they capture, train and nourish aphides, which they use as a kind of slave. They build vast and symmetrical mounds, which they use as homes and barns, and which are, relatively to the size of the tiny builders, three times larger than the Egyptian pyramids. They march and labor in unison, have their own wars, nourish their sick, and all is done without a chief, an overseer or a ruler. Yet man with a higher intelligence and a higher work to do can be a sluggard.

Verses 12-19. The description of the sluggard is followed by that of a worthless person. It is a son of Belial (the term used in the Hebrew) whose picture is drawn. He is a naughty person, a good-for-nothing, a man of iniquity; he has a lying mouth. A minute description of his way and work is given; everywhere he makes mischief and causeth division. But suddenly there comes the calamity upon him. He shall be broken and that without remedy. Such is the way of the man who despiseth wisdom, follows his old nature and plunges ultimately into the outer darkness. Finally there will yet appear "the man of sin," that wicked one, in whom all these evils will culminate and he shall suddenly be broken without remedy. (See Daniel 11:45.) We do well to read carefully the six things which the Lord hateth (6:16-19).

Verses 20-35. The words of the Lord, the commandment and the law as stated here, are of unspeakably great importance. They are to be in the heart and about the neck.

> When thou walkest, it shall lead thee;
> When thou sleepest, it shall watch over thee;
> And when thou wakest, it shall talk with thee.

They are a lamp and a light; they are the way of life. Then follows another description of the evil woman, a warning not to lust after her beauty nor to be taken by her eyelids. These oriental women painted their faces; by plucking their eyebrows they made them almond-shaped. Alas! that in the society of the twentieth century the women and girls of a so-called Christian civilization should do the same thing, and we fear, for the same purpose as the whorish woman described in this chapter.

CHAPTER 7

The entire chapter is a continuation of the strange woman and the warning against her. The Word and the law of the Lord will keep the obedient son from her. If Solomon had obeyed the Word of God, not to multiply wives (Deut. 17:17) his end would not have been spent in the degrading fellowship with the harlots of other nations. The description is very graphic. What the word pictures is as prominent in the great centers of Christendom as it was thousands of years ago in Babylon and Egypt. And so it is still true:

> She hath cast down many wounded;
> Yea, many strong men have been slain by her.
> Her house is the way to hell,
> Going down to the chambers of death.

But think of Solomon after having received these inspired descriptions and warnings, that he should have been forgetful of them all.

CHAPTER 8

1. The call and appeal of wisdom (8:1-11)
2. What wisdom is and what wisdom gives (8:12-21)
3. Wisdom; the Person, who He is (8:22-31)
4. The renewed appeal (8:32-36)

Verses 1-11. This is one of the most interesting chapters in the entire book. It begins with a call and appeal of wisdom, much like the call and appeal of the first chapter. If wisdom calls, has a voice, then wisdom must also be a person. Who personified wisdom is we learn most blessedly in this chapter. Wisdom calls to the sons of men; wisdom speaks of plain and excellent things; she speaks the truth; her words are the words of righteousness; wisdom is better than rubies.

Verses 12-21. This section may well be looked upon as an introduction to the sublime revelation in verses 22-31. Wisdom is a person and what wisdom gives, the power wisdom has, makes it clear that wisdom is a divine person. Kings and princes rule by that person, as well as the nobles and judges of the earth. The powers that be are ordained by this wisdom. And that person says:

> I love them that love Me
> And those that seek Me early shall find Me.

This wisdom has riches and honor to bestow; has durable riches and righteousness; the fruit of it is better than fine gold; those that love the wisdom will receive an inheritance. In the next place we hear who that person is.

Verses 22-31. The Wisdom is the Son of God. The personification of wisdom is found in the person of the Lord Jesus Christ. This wonderful passage is a great prelude to the incarnation and the subsequent redemption work of the Son of God. Here Solomon beheld the highest of all; he had a vision of the Messiah of Israel, the Son of David, whose wisdom, peace and kingdom of peace and glory he but faintly foreshadowed. The critical school must of course deny this application to our Lord. "The passage played a great role in subsequent thought, for it lies at the back of much of the speculation of Philo, and at a subsequent period was greatly employed by Christian theologians in support of their doctrine of the person of Christ through their identification of wisdom in this passage with Logos (the Word) of the fourth Gospel" *(New Century Bible).*

Wisdom was possessed by the Lord in the beginning of His ways, before His works of old. But that is the beginning without a beginning. In the beginning was the Word; and because the Word, the Son of God, is God, He like God has no beginning. The word "possessed" has also the meaning of "formed". "This word has been a battleground of controversy since the days of the Arian heresy. But it is well to remember that, all theological questions apart, it is impossible to understand the word, whatever rendering of it we adopt, as indicating that wisdom ever had a beginning, or was ever properly speaking created. Wisdom is inseparable from any worthy conception of Him who is "the only wise God" (1 Tim. 1:17), and therefore is like Him "from everlasting to everlasting" (Perowne). Wisdom, the Son of God, was always with God from everlasting. Before there ever was anything created, before the mountains were settled, or even the earth had been made, He was. And when creation began He was there. He, the Son, was by Him, as one brought up with Him. From the greater revelation in the New Testament we learn that all things were created not only for Him, but also by Him (Colossians 1:16). Wisdom speaks: "And I was continually His delight, rejoicing always before Him." This can only be true of God the Son. And furthermore He says: "Rejoicing in the habitable part of His earth; and My delight was with the sons of men." His delight was so great, that He laid by His glory, and left His eternal dwelling place to become man and redeem man by the death of the cross.

It is interesting to observe that this glimpse, this adumbration of a great truth, which was only to become fully clear in Christ Jesus our Lord, was advanced a little in clearness and completeness by a book which is not considered to be inspired, the so-called Book of Wisdom, in a passage which must be quoted: "For she (i.e., Wisdom) is a breath of the power of God, and a pure influence flowing from the glory of the Almighty; therefore can no defiled thing fall into her. For she is the brightness of the everlasting light, the unspotted mirror of the power of God and the image of His goodness. And being but one, she can do all things; and remaining in herself, she maketh all things new; and in all ages entering into holy souls, she maketh them friends of God and prophets. For God loveth none but him that dwelleth with Wisdom. For she is more beautiful than the sun, and above all the order of stars; being compared with the light, she is found before it."

Verses 32-36. Then follows the renewed appeal. Wisdom says, "Whosoever findeth me findeth life." How true of our Lord; in Him we find and have life. note the two occurrences of "blessed" in this paragraph.

CHAPTER 9

1. The invitation of Wisdom (9:1-12)
2. The contrast with Folly. (9:13-18)

Verses 1-12. The first section of Proverbs closeth with a contrast of Wisdom and Folly, both personified. The one, our Lord, the other under the symbol of a foolish woman. Wisdom sends forth her invitation after her house is built and the feast is spread. It reminds us of the parable of the great supper (Luke 14). Here too is the gracious invitation, "Come, eat of my bread and drink of the wine which I have mingled."

Verses 13-18. Folly too has her house and sitteth in the door on a seat in the high places of the city to call to her victims. She invites to the stolen waters, so sweet to the natural man, to eat bread in secret places, equally pleasant. But what is the end? "The dead are there; . . . her guests are in the depths of hell." The foolish woman is the world with its lusts.

II. The Proverbs of Solomon: Chapters 10—19:19

Beginning with the tenth chapter we have the collection of proverbs given by inspiration through Solomon. In this section the personal address, "My son," and the personal exhortations are missing. It will be noticed that each verse in this section contains a proverb, consisting each of two lines, mostly of an antithetic character, except 19:7, which has three lines instead of two (a tristich).

It is impossible to give a detailed analysis of these chapters, nor can we take up each proverb separately for meditation. This must be left to each reader. By comparing Scripture with Scripture, and a prayerful study of these terse sayings, the heavenly wisdom given in these chapters can readily be found. There is no end to practical application. Yet even in these chapters a certain order is maintained. The contrast in each chapter is between the righteous and the wicked, between right and wrong.

CHAPTER 10

The Godly and the Ungodly in Life and Conduct

The opening proverbs are concerning treasures, earthly substance. What an important sentence, "Treasures of wickedness profit nothing!" Throughout these proverbs there are the warnings concerning getting riches, or as it is expressed in a modern phrase "getting rich quick" (28:20), and the dangers connected with it.

These grave warnings of Wisdom are especially needed at the present time in England and America, when the undisguised and the unrestrained pursuit of riches has become more and more recognized as the legitimate end of life, so that few people feel any shame in admitting that this is their aim; and the clear unimpassioned statements of the result, which always follows on the unhallowed passion receive daily confirmation from the occasional revelations of our domestic, our commercial and our criminal life. He that is greedy of gain, we are told, troubleth his own house. An inheritance may be gotten hastily at the beginning, but the end thereof shall not be blessed. A faithful man shall abound with blessings, but he that maketh haste to be rich (and consequently cannot by any possibility be faithful) shall not be unpunished. He that hath an evil eye hasteth after riches, and knoweth not that want shall come upon him. 'Weary not thyself,' therefore, it is said, 'to be rich;' which, though it may be the dictate of thine own wisdom, is really unmixed folly, burdened with a load of calamity for the unfortunate seeker, for his house, and for all those who are in any way dependent upon him *(Expositor's Bible).*

There are also warnings against being slack, which maketh poor, while the hand of the diligent, he that is up and doing, maketh rich. We find promises and assurance for the godly like these: "Righteousness delivereth from death . . . the Lord will not suffer the righteous, the soul of the righteous to famish . . . blessings are upon the head of the just . . . the memory of the just is blessed."

The walk and conduct of the two classes are contrasted, especially in relation to the mouth and lips. The walk of the righteous is the sure walk (10:9); the mouth of the righteous is a well of life, it is a fountain for good (10:11). In this proverb we are reminded of John 4:10 and 7:38, the believer indwelt by the Holy Spirit welling forth waters of life. While violence covers the mouth of the wicked and hatred does nothing but stir up strife, love, the true love in the heart of the just covereth all transgressions. (See 1 Peter 4:8 and James 5:20.) Whoever has understanding his lips speak wisdom. In all these proverbs there is something to be learned in a practical way and many blessed lessons are written here for all who desire to walk righteously, godly and soberly in this evil age. Here is a test, for instance, "He is in the way of life that heedeth correction" (10:17, corrected translation). But as soon as one forsaketh reproof he errs. How well it would be if children of God would daily consider verse 19. "In the multitude of words there wanteth not sin, but he that refraineth his lips is wise." The fear of the wicked, the fear of the Lord, the hope of the righteous and the expectations of the wicked are furthermore contrasted in this chapter.

CHAPTER 11

The Contrast Continued

The continued contrast in this chapter between the righteous and the wicked contains many precious gems, sweet to faith and wholesome for instruction. In the second verse there is a warning as to pride. Pride and shame are vitally linked together, as is lowliness and wisdom. Lowliness therefore is true wisdom. A Rabbinical comment on this passage says, "Lowly souls are filled with wisdom as the lowly places are filled with water." Again riches are mentioned. They profit nothing in the day of wrath. (See Zephaniah 1.) But righteousness delivereth from death (11:4). What wisdom there is in verse 8, "The righteous is delivered out of trouble, but the wicked cometh in his stead." Even so will it be when the Lord comes and gives rest and deliverance to His own and trouble and wrath to the wicked (2 Thess. 1). Verse 19 has been rendered:

> He that is steadfast in righteousness
> is so unto life,
> And he that pursueth evil doeth so
> unto his own death.

The delight of the Lord, declares the next proverb, is in the way of the upright, who remain steadfast in righteousness.

In verse 30 we read that the fruit of the righteous is a tree of life, not the righteous is a tree of life, but the fruit of the righteous, which means that he gives forth blessing and life to others, and that is here expressed in one sentence, "and he that winneth souls is wise." (See Daniel 13:3.)

CHAPTER 12

The Contrast in Relation to Various Conditions

In these proverbs we have the righteous mentioned, his thoughts, his words, his domestic relationship, his attitude toward animal creation (12:10); his diligence; all is contrasted with the wicked in these beautiful antithetic expressions of wisdom. The thoughts of the righteous are right (12:5), because his heart is right; his words bring deliverance (12:6); in speaking truth he showeth forth righteousness (12:17); his tongue is health (12:18); the lip which uttereth truth shall be established for ever (12:19); he knows nothing of lying lips, but dealing truly he is the Lord's delight (12:22). All is summed up in one statement, with which the chapter closeth: "In the way of righteousness there is life; in the pathway thereof there is no death." Happy are we if we know this way, which is Christ Himself, and if we follow Him. Verse 21 speaks of the blessing of the righteous, "There shall no evil happen to the just," that is, all things must work together for good.

CHAPTER 13

The Contrast: Advantage and Disadvantage

The contrast in Proverbs concerning the righteous and the wicked is continued in this chapter, showing mostly the advantage of the righteous, illustrating a statement found in the prophet Isaiah: "Say ye to the righteous, that it shall be well with him, for they shall eat the fruit of their doings" (Isaiah 3:10). Then the contrast: "Woe unto the wicked! It shall be ill with him, for the reward of his hands shall be given him" (verse 11). The righteous eats good by the fruit of his mouth; the trangressor receives violence. There is fatness for the soul of the diligent and nothing for the soul of the sluggard. Righteousness keepeth; wickedness overthrows. While the light of the righteous rejoiceth, the lamp of the wicked shall be put out. These are some of the contrasts.

In verse 7 is a statement which may be applied to our Lord: "There is that maketh himself poor, yet hath great riches." He who has all the riches made Himself poor for our sake.

Then there is warning against pride. In fact the proverbs abound in these warnings. "By pride cometh contention" (verse 10). To the proud who refuseth correction cometh poverty and shame (verse 18).

CHAPTER 14

The Wise and The Foolish: The Rich and The Poor

The contrast now concerns the wise and the foolish, the rich and the poor. Let us see some of these contrasts. "In the mouth of the foolish is a rod of pride, but the lips of the wise shall preserve them" (14:3). The foolish shoots forth his foolishness like a branch. Separation from the foolish man is commanded in the seventh verse. The wise cannot have fellowship with the foolish, as the believer is not to be yoked to the unbeliever. Fools make a mock at sin (14:9). The word "sin" in the original means "trespass offering." That is exactly what the foolish man does, including the religious fool; he denies both sin and the blessed provision God has made to deliver from the guilt and power of sin. But among the righteous, says the next line, there is favor (acceptance). Because the righteous owns himself a sinner, judgeth himself and accepts God's redemption through the one sacrifice.

How true it is "the heart knoweth his own bitterness, and a stranger does not intermeddle with its joy" (14:10). We can tell our troubles and sorrows to others, but the bitterness of the heart cannot be revealed, but it is known to One who is touched with our sorrows and the bitterness of life through which we pass, for He Himself passed through it also.

Here is another deep saying, which shows that behind this wisdom uttered by the wise king, there is another who knows all what is going on in human life and in the heart. "Even in laughter the heart is sorrowful, and the end of that mirth is heaviness" (10:13). How often the sorrowful, the downcast covers all with forced laughter and no one suspects that underneath the mirth there is heaviness. This is true of children of the world, the foolish who reject true wisdom and know not the Lord Jesus Christ.

Of the poor and the rich we read that the poor is hated; the rich has many friends (10:20). He that oppresseth the poor reproacheth his Maker; but he that honoreth Him hath mercy on the poor" (10:31). To deal kindly with the poor and the lowly is God-like. The righteous will manifest his righteousness in a practical way by considering the poor.

Precious are two other proverbs in this chapter.

> In the fear of the Lord is strong confidence;
> And His children shall have a place of refuge.
> The fear of the Lord is a fountain of life,
> To depart from the snares of death. (14:26-27)

CHAPTER 15

The Better Things

One can read through the proverbs recorded in this chapter and ask the question, What are the better things?

A soft answer which turneth away wrath is better than grievous words (verse 1). The tongue of the righteous which useth knowledge aright is better than the mouth of fools (verse 2). Better is the prayer of the upright than the sacrifice of the wicked (verse 8). Better is he that followeth after righteousness than the way of the wicked, for the one the Lord delights in, the other is an abomination (verse 9). Better is the heart that seeketh knowledge than to feed on foolishness (verse 14). Better is a little with the fear of the Lord than great treasure and trouble therewith (verse 16). This fits many in our own days. Better is a dinner of herbs where love is, than a stalled ox and hatred therewith (verse 17). Better it is to be slow to anger than wrathful (verse 18). Better is the plain way of the righteous than the thorny way of the slothful (verse 19). Better is to hear reproof than to refuse it (verse 32).

Some other deep sayings are found in this chapter. For instance in verse 11.

Sheol and destruction are
before the Lord,
How much more then the hearts
of the children of men.

(Destruction, or Abaddon, is used in Revelation 9:11.)

All is known to the Lord. The unseen world as well as the future; all eternity is known to Him. All is naked and open before Him. He knoweth the hearts of men, yea even our thoughts afar off, before they ever pass through our finite minds.

Twice prayer is mentioned in this chapter, in verses 8 and 29. Not alone does the Lord delight in the prayer of the upright, but He also heareth them. "The Lord is far from the wicked, but He heareth the prayer of the righteous."

CHAPTER 16

In the Light of the Lord

The name Jehovah (Lord) appears eleven times in this chapter of Proverbs. The Lord has the final word, for to man belong the preparations (or plans) of the heart; but from the Lord is the answer of the tongue. It is the same thought as in our English proverb—"Man proposes—God disposes." Man loves to justify himself, his ways are clean in his own eyes; but the Lord weigheth the spirits; He is the judge of ways and motives. Our works are to be committed (literal: rolled upon) unto the Lord, then establishment and blessing will follow. It is strange that these three verses were omitted in the Septuagint version of the Old Testament.

The Lord hath made all things for Himself, yea, even the wicked for the day of evil (verse 4). Much error has been taught in connection with this verse. Some have taught that God made some wicked. It is not said that God makes a man wicked, for "He made man upright" (Eccles. 7:29), but being wicked by his own choice he comes under the irrevocable law which dooms him to "the day of evil," of calamity and punishment. By this, the Apostle teaches us, even in its final and most awful form, is revealed not the arbitrary predestination, but "the righteous judgment of God" (Romans 2:5-11, T. T. Perowne).

The abomination to the Lord is to be proud in heart. Pride, not only pride as it works out in deeds, but pride as nourished in the heart, seen by the eyes of the Lord alone, is equally an abomination to Him. How much there is in these days! The second stanza of this proverb speaks of joining hand in hand, or hand to hand. It is the much praised "team-work," confederation, alliance, etc., to do a big work and make a big name. Much of this attempt of doing "big things" in the day of "small things" has its source in the pride of the natural man.

In the sixth proverb of this chapter we have a Gospel text. The word mercy is literally "grace." The word "purged" is the word translated elsewhere by "covered" or "atoned." In the Lord Jesus Christ and His work is revealed "grace and truth" and by His work so blessedly finished on the cross our iniquity is covered. Then comes the fear of the Lord which results in departing from evil.

If a man walks in righteousness, in true humility, if he pleaseth the Lord, then his enemies will be silenced and not talk against him. Only too often the charges brought against the children of God by the enemies of truth, are the result of not walking in the truth.

Comforting to faith is the ninth verse. We may devise, plan, and often worry as we make our plans but behind it stands the Lord and in spite of our failures and mistakes "He directeth" the steps of the righteous.

Twice more the name of the Lord is given in this chapter. "And whoso trusteth in the Lord, happy is he" (verse 20). The only true happiness is to know the Lord, to trust Him and to follow Him. Inasmuch as we may increase in knowledge of Him, in confidence and in practical obedience our happiness is an increasing happiness. In the last verse we read that the disposing of the lot is of the Lord. The lot was used in the Old Testament. It is mentioned rarely in the New Testament, once preceding the day of Pentecost (Acts 1:26).

After the Holy Spirit came to guide and direct no lot is needed any longer. We pass over the many other blessed instructions recorded in this chapter. Private meditation and prayer unlock the many riches deposited in them.

CHAPTER 17

Diverse Proverbs

Of the twenty-eight proverbs found in this chapter we point out but a few. "The fining pot is for silver and the furnace for gold; but the Lord trieth the hearts" (verse 3). Man may try silver and gold, but God only the hearts. And

He tries the hearts by the refining process, trials and afflictions, the process which rests in His own hands. (See Psalm 66:10-12; Mal. 3:3-4; 1 Peter 1:7.)

"He that covereth a transgression seeketh love, but he that repeateth a matter separateth very friends" (verse 9). To cover a transgression does not mean to ignore sin. How he who has sinned and is in transgression is to be dealt with is given to us in Galatians 6:1-5. To act in the spirit of love towards one who has sinned is Christ-like. To repeat the matter, gossip about it, harp on the shortcomings and failure, is Satan-like, for he is the accuser of the brethren.

"A friend loveth at all times, and a brother is born for adversity" (verse 17). This is beautifully illustrated in the case of David and Jonathan (1 Sam. 18—20). And the great Friend, the brother born for adversity, is the Lord Jesus Christ. He loveth at all times; His love is limitless and timeless. It is the love which passeth knowledge.

CHAPTER 18

Proverbs of Personal Instruction

There is first a warning against separation produced by desire, that is for gratification and pleasure, and not for a righteous purpose. Such a one becomes an enemy of true wisdom and one who intermeddleth with all wisdom. This proverb finds a New Testament illustration in Alexander the coppersmith, as well as Hymenaeus and Philetus, and Diotrephes of whom John writes in his epistle. A fool foams out his own folly. This proverb in verse 2 is illustrated by many of the critics of the Bible. They have no delight in true understanding but their own hearts are laid bare by their mad oppositions to God's Holy Word.

The fool's mouth, his lips, the talebearer (whisperer), and the slothful are the themes of the proverbs in verses 6-9. Then we read "The Name of the Lord is a strong tower; the righteous runneth into it and is safe" (verse 10). The Name (Ha-Shem, in Hebrew) stands for Jehovah Himself. He is the place of refuge, of shelter, protection and safety for all who in faith turn to Him. In Him is our peace and safety. The Hebrew meaning of "is safe" is "set on high." Even so if we flee to Him and become His, we are exalted in Him, seated in Christ in heavenly places.

Another proverb of solemn meaning is found in verse 12. "Before destruction the heart of man is haughty, and before honor is humility." Scripture abounds in illustrations of these two lines. The truth stated here is still being manifested in the lives of men and women. The only place of safety for God's people is the place in the dust, the place of humility.

"Death and life are in the power of the tongue; and they that love it shall eat the fruit thereof" (verse 21). The Epistle of James (chapter 3) speaks in the same manner of the power of the tongue and its misuse. Evil words will bring evil results. But the tongue speaking the words of life and love, as given in the gospel of our Lord Jesus Christ, is a power for good, the power of life—and oh! what shall the harvest be in that day!

CHAPTER 19:1-19

Further Proverbs on Personal Instruction

One may be poor, but walking in integrity, he is far ahead of him who is perverse in his lips and is a fool. Then we find proverbs about fretting against the Lord; warning against false witness and speaking lies and other matters. We call special attention to verse 12.

> The King's wrath is as the roaring of a lion,
> But his favour is as dew upon the grass.

It may be applied to Him who is The Lamb of God and also the Lion of the tribe of Judah. Some day He will roar in His displeasure and manifest the wrath, so well deserved by the world. But even then His grace will be revealed, for in wrath He will remember mercy, the mercy promised to Israel. "I will be as the dew unto Israel; he shall grow as the lily, and cast forth its roots as Lebanon" (Hosea 14:5).

We then read of a foolish son, a contentious wife, concerning houses and riches, a prudent wife. There is a warning against slothfulness, and exhortation to keep the commandments and to pity the poor, for giving to the poor means lending to the Lord. The son is to be chastened as long as there is hope and a warning against sinful wrath. This verse marks the end of this section of proverbs.

III. Instructions Given To Solomon

CHAPTER 19:20-29

Beginning with the twentieth verse of chapter 19 the personal address begins again and we read repeatedly the phrase "My son" up to the twenty-fifth chapter. This section corresponds therefore with the first nine chapters, containing the instructions which Solomon received from the Lord and which he records in these chapters.

Once more there is the call, like in the opening chapters, to hear, to give attention. "Hear counsel, and receive instruction, that thou mayest be wise in thy latter end." The Lord knew beforehand what "the latter end" of Solomon would be. The wise man who warned against the fool, the backslider, the unjust and the man who forsakes counsel and the Lord, himself illustrates the truths given in these proverbs by turning away from the Lord. Alas! he did not hear counsel, and therefore instead of being wise in his latter days he became a fool. The truth expressed in verse 22 was Solomon's portion as long as the fear of the Lord governed his conduct. He was satisfied, had peace and prosperity; but when he no longer feared the Lord, evil came upon his kingdom and it was divided. "Wherefore the Lord said unto Solomon, Forasmuch as this is done of thee, and thou has not kept My covenant and My statutes which I have commanded thee, I will surely rend the kingdom from thee, and will give it to thy servant" (1 Kings 11:11).

CHAPTER 20

Proverbs as to Personal Conduct

Proverbs of warning and instructions as to personal conduct are found mostly in this chapter; a number of them are of special interest if applied to Solomon. The first one is concerning wine and strong drink. As the use of wine among the people of Israel was legitimate the warning is against intemperance (Deut. 14:26). The Bible gives many illustrations of the truth of this proverb-warning. We may think of Noah, Lot, Nabal, Ben-hadad, Belshazzar and others.

From all the good things we select the following. In verse 3 is instruction which makes for peace. It is the fool who meddles and thus produceth strife, but it is an honor for man to cease from strife. In verse 13 we find a warning against self indulgence. In verse 19 the talebearer and flatterer is mentioned. The sin of flattery should be avoided by all the godly for it nourisheth pride and works nothing but evil.

Many great and noble men have been ruined by admiration and popularity, who might have thriven, growing greater and nobler, in the fiercest and most relentless criticism. Donatello, the great Florentine sculptor, went at one time of his life to Padua, where he was received with the utmost enthusiasm, and loaded with approbation and honors. But soon he declared his intention of returning to Florence, on the ground that the sharp assaults and the cutting criticisms which always assailed him in his native city were much more favorable to his art than the atmosphere of admiration and eulogy. In this way he thought that he would be stimulated to greater efforts, and ultimately attain to a surer reputation.

Verse 22 gives another beautiful instruction. "Say not, I will recompense evil; but wait on the Lord, and He shall save thee." To put everything in the hands of the Lord, to trust Him and wait for His own time, that is true wisdom. But it is a lesson hard to learn. The twelfth chapter of Romans gives the same instruction. "Dearly beloved, avenge not yourselves, but rather give place unto wrath; for it is written, vengeance is mine; I will repay, saith the Lord." Also 1 Thess. 5:15: "See that none render evil for evil;" and 1 Peter 3:9; "Not rendering evil for evil, or railing for railing." How blessed it is to wait on the Lord, to bide His own time, and in waiting to know that He does all things well. Thrice in this chapter the king is mentioned: in verses 2, 26 and 28. These verses may be applied to Him, who is greater than Solomon, the King of kings and the Lord of lords. When He comes again He will deal with the lawless and with His enemies, but His throne is not only a judgment throne, but it is also upheld by mercy.

CHAPTER 21

Personal Instructions as to Life and Conduct

In the proverbs of this chapter the Lord is mentioned five times. "The king's heart is in the hand of the Lord, as the rivers of water: He turneth it whithersoever He will" (verse 1). The rivers of water are "water-courses," the irrigation system known to the ancients, opening and shutting sluices directed the flow of the waters. Thus the Lord governs the king's heart as He directs the affairs of men. The Lord pondereth the hearts (verse 2). The same truth is stated in chapter 16:2; self-justification suits the natural man but the Lord testeth all hearts. How well it is to remember in all our conduct, that truth, so comforting to the believer, expressed by Peter, "Thou knoweth all things." More acceptable than sacrifice to the Lord, is to do righteousness and judgment (verse 3). This may be compared with 1 Sam. 15:22, Hosea 6:6; Micah 6:6-8. The words of our Lord in the Gospel of Matthew give the same truth. "But go ye and learn what that meaneth, I will have mercy, and not sacrifice" (Matt. 9:13). At the close of the chapter two additional statements are made concerning the Lord; "There is no wisdom nor understanding, nor counsel against the Lord" (verse 30). No matter how man may plan, how cunning the enemy may be, it will all come to naught, for the Lord is above all. How well Eliphaz the Temanite expressed this truth when he said: "He disappointeth the devices of the crafty, so that their hands cannot perform their enterprise. He taketh the wise in their craftiness; and the counsel of the froward is carried headlong" (Job 5:12-13). Safety is not by the horse prepared against the day of battle, nor by might or by power, but safety is of the Lord (verse 31). How well then to look away from man and look to the Lord and to know in Him is our safety. The other proverbs in this chapter giving direction as to life and conduct, warning against the high look and the proud heart, getting of treasures by a lying tongue, against heartlessness in refusing to hear the cry of the poor, against loving pleasure and luxurious living, against coveteousness and other matters do not need further annotations.

CHAPTER 22

Instructions Continued

Better than great riches, better than silver and gold is a name and loving favor. If a person has riches and a bad name and is not well thought of, he is less honorable than the poor man who has a name and good reputation. In Ecclesiastes, Solomon says: "A good name is better than precious ointment" (Eccles. 7:1). The third verse has a wise message: "The prudent man foreseeth the evil and hideth himself; but the simple pass on, and suffer for it." The Lord has revealed in His Word the evil which is in store for the sinner and the impenitent. He also has prepared a hiding place, an ark of safety, in His Son, our Lord. The prudent believeth the Word and flees to the refuge; the simple, the unbelieving, pass on and suffer for it when the evil comes. Humility and the fear of the Lord has a reward, while thorns and snares are in the way of the froward. sowing and reaping is found in verses 8 and 9. He that soweth iniquity reaps vanity, or calamity; he that has a bountiful eye, who looks upon the poor and needy with kindness and supplies their wants reaps blessing.

In verse 11 we read, "He that loveth pureness of heart, for the grace of his lips the king shall be his friend." In such, whose hearts are pure and whose words are gracious, the Lord, the King, delights.

Beginning with verse 18 we find another call to hear, and to apply the heart to His knowledge: "For it is a pleasant thing if thou keep them within thee, they shall withal be fitted in thy lips. That thy trust may be in the Lord, I have made known to thee this day, even to thee." This is the personal message to Solomon by the Lord, heeded by him for many years and finally disobeyed.

The proverb of verse 28: "Remove not the ancient landmarks, which thy father has set," is a restatement of Deut. 19:14. It is repeated in chapter 23:10. In Job 24:2 we read "Some remove the landmarks." These landmarks were for Israel sacred things, for their possessions were staked off according to the Lord's will; to meddle with them was a transgression. While Israel, God's earthly people had landmarks, God's heavenly people also has landmarks of the heavenly realm, the blessed doctrines of the Word of God, which constitute the faith once and for all delivered unto the saints. And how man removes these landmarks in our day! How true it is, "Some remove the landmarks," that which our fathers cherished, believed and trusted in. The rationalist, the ritualist and the delusionist do it constantly and thus destroy the foundation upon which everything rests.

CHAPTER 23

Instructions Continued

The opening proverbs of this chapter treat of self-restraint in curbing the appetite and give manners to be observed in the presence of a superior. Warnings against riches and their uncertainty are contained in verses 4 and 5. How well it would be if the great mass of professing Christians, and some true believers also, would consider this instruction: "Labor not to be rich." But this exhortation as well as the exhortation in 1 Timothy 6:1-10 is overlooked, and many who profess to have their riches in Christ, in the heavenly places and never ending glory, weary themselves with earthly gain, and aim to become wealthy. But riches have wings; they can fly away swiftly as does the eagle when he mounts heavenward. This too is mentioned in the epistle to Timothy, in which those who are rich are charged not to be highminded, nor trust in uncertain riches, but to be rich in good works. The evil eye mentioned in verse 6 has nothing to do with the superstitious belief that some person with an evil eye can cast a spell to harm others. It means a dishonest, insincere person, one who is pharisaical. While he urges to eat and drink, puts on a friendly front, in his heart he entertains other thoughts.

Not to envy sinners is commanded in verse 17; one who walks in fear of the Lord all the day long looks to their end, though they may prosper now, their prosperity will end, but the expectation of him who fears the Lord will not be cut off.

Beginning with verse 22 is another call to hearken. Parents are to be obeyed. The truth is to be bought and never to be sold, as well as wisdom, instruction and understanding. There is a price often to be paid for the possession of the truth. Some have suffered even unto death to possess the truth, and in its defense. Then in verse 26 is the familiar exhortation, "My Son, give me thy heart, and let thine eyes delight in my ways." This word is often misued when applied to sinners, the unsaved. It is addressed to a son. The gospel does not come to the sinner with the exhortation "give"; the sinner has nothing to give. The gospel comes with an offer and if the offer of free grace is accepted, the believing sinner becomes a child of God, a son of God and an heir. Such a one is to yield his whole heart to the Lord, and his eyes are to delight in His ways. Thus Jehovah spoke to Solomon. The chapter ends with proverbs relating to self-indulgence, the sin of intemperance and all that goes with it.

CHAPTER 24

Instructions Continued

In the final instructions of this chapter we find first a description of the evil men. Their heart studieth destruction; their lips talk mischief. This theme is repeatedly referred to in this chapter. In verse 15 the evil man is addressed not to lay wait for the righteous and not to spoil his resting place. The Lord takes care of the righteous; he may be overcome by misfortunes seven times, yet will he rise again. Different it is with the wicked when he falls into mischief. Yet there must be no rejoicing over the fall of the enemy, nor gladness when he stumbleth. This displeaseth the Lord. Still higher is the command of the New Testament, "Love your enemies; . . . recompense no man evil for evil; . . . overcome evil with good." There is to be no fretting because of evil men nor envy (verses 1 and 19). Why should the righteous be envious at the wicked in their prosperity? The Thirty-seventh Psalm enters more fully into this; but here the same answer is given in a terse way. The wicked have no reward; their candle will be put out. Their calamity riseth suddenly, and who knoweth the ruin of them both? which means that the Lord and the king, will deal with the wicked. Another proverb of this chapter we mention: "If thou faint in the day of adversity thy strength is small" (verse 10). The hour of trial is the hour which brings the test. When adversity brings despondency, and even worse, murmuring, it is an evidence that the heart does not fully trust the Lord.

The last section of this chapter is introduced by the statement, "These things also belong to the wise," or as it may be rendered, "These also are sayings of the wise." The chapter ends with a vivid description of the slothful. His field and vineyard bear witness to his character. They are grown over with thorns and covered with nettles and the stone wall is broken down. And why all this? "Yet a little sleep, a little slumber, a little folding of the hands in sleep." An illustration of this sluggard can be found a thousand times over again in our own land.

IV. The Proverbs of Solomon Collected by the Men of Hezekiah

CHAPTER 25

Here begin the proverbs which the good king Hezekiah, under the guidance of the Spirit of God, added to this book. "This title is interesting as affording a proof that a revival of literary activity accompanied the revival of religion and of national prosperity which marked the reign of Hezekiah. The men of Hezekiah were doubtless a body of scribes engaged under the direction of the king in literary labors."

Very fittingly the opening verses of this collected portion of proverbs relate to the king. While it is the glory of God to conceal a thing, the glory of kings is to search out a matter. God has many things concealed as to Himself, the great universe, creation and His ways in providence; but kings should inquire diligently into the matters brought before them and search them out in their administration of justice. Some day the great King who is coming, the King of Kings, who knows all the secrets of God as well as the hearts of men, will search out all things and bring the hidden things to light. When that day comes the fifth verse will see its accomplishment.

> Take away the wicked from before the king—
> And His throne shall be established
> in righteousness.

When He comes to establish His throne of righteousness, to rule as the true Melchizedek, the King of Righteousness and of Peace, the wicked and evildoers will be taken away in judgment. Only then can there be a righteous government. Verses 6 and 7 remind us of the parable of the great supper spoken by our Lord in Luke 14.

Verses 21 and 22 are quoted by the Holy Spirit in the Epistle to the Romans (12:20). And that is followed by another saying as to the conduct of the righteous man. "The north wind driveth away rain; so does an angry countenance, a backbiting tongue." The backbiter does the work of Satan and the Lord hates the slandering tongue as He hates the flattering tongue. The believer can show an angry countenance, without sinning, and cut short the pernicious work of the backbiter (Ephesians 4:26). Verse 28 gives a good definition of true self-control, the rule over one's own spirit.

CHAPTER 26

Concerning the Fool and the Sluggard

Eleven times we meet the word fool in this chapter. Three different words are used in the Hebrew for fool. The first is "avil" which signifies weakness. The second word "kesil" occurs nearly fifty times, means fat or dense. The third word is the Hebrew "nabal," which is derived from the verb to fade, or to wither; it means a vulgar, bad man who has given himself over to wickedness. The natural man in his condition, his darkened mind, his sinfulness answers to much that is said about the fool in this book. As snow in summer and rain at harvest time are quite impossible in Palestine, so is honor for a fool. A fool may utter a curse, as they often do, and wish something evil, but being causeless, it will not be fulfilled. The fool needs correction, the stripes for his back; he deserves no answer, and if he is answered it must be according to his folly. The foolish questions mentioned in the New Testament may well be considered here (Titus 3:9). The tenth verse is doubtful in its translation. A better suggested rendering is the following:

> A master workman formeth all
> himself aright,
> But he that hireth a fool hireth
> a transgressor.

That is, a master does everything right; a fool spoils everything. The eleventh verse is quoted in 2 Peter 2:22. The Apostle applies it to the outward professor of Christianity who turns back to the world after a period of profession and reformation. The true child of God is never described as a dog, nor could the other sentence in Peter's Epistle mean a true believer. "The sow that was washed turned to her own wallowing in the mire." A hog may be washed, yet in spite of the washing he is still a hog. So a sinner may profess salvation yet may never have been born again, and after a brief period of profession turn again to his old sins and habits.

The slothful man, the man that deceiveth his neighbor, the talebearer, the contentious man, the lying tongue and the flattering mouth, furnish other proverbs. How true it is "A flattering mouth worketh ruin." Every godly man and woman should hate and avoid flattery.

V. Instructions Given to Solomon

In the three chapters which follow 27—29 we find the change we have noticed before. These proverbs are addressed to a person and the phrases "My son" and the personal address, "thou," "thy" and "thyself," are again used in these chapters. Like the previous sections, so here we find instructions which were given to Solomon.

CHAPTER 27

Instructions and Warnings

The opening proverb warns against procrastination. No one can be sure of what the next day may bring forth. True wisdom is not to trust the future day, for it may never come, nor are we to dwell in the past. While it is today we must live and act and leave nothing undone which can be done today. How true this is of salvation which is offered for today—now is the day of salvation. How many have been lost forever by procrastination, by thinking a more convenient time would come. Well has one said, "The thief which cheats us of our days and beggars us of our wealth is the specious thought that tomorrow belongs to us." The illusion is as old as the world, but is today as fresh and powerful as ever. James 4:13-14 gives the same lesson. In the second verse we find a warning as to self-praise. Self-praise is one of the worst forms of pride, that pride which another proverb states (16:18-19) "goeth before destruction, and a haughty spirit before a fall."

"Open rebuke is better than secret love" and "faithful are the wounds of a friend; but the kisses of an enemy are deceitful" (verses 5-6). A wise man welcomes open criticism and rebuke, though such rebuke may wound, yet being given by the faithfulness of a friend, it is far better than the deceitful kisses of a flattering enemy. The 14th verse may be linked with these statements. "He that blesseth his friend with a loud voice rising early in the morning, it shall be counted a curse unto him." Insincerity lurks behind such loud, pharisaical protestations of friendship.

A great truth is given in verse 19: "As in water face answereth face, so the heart of man to man." The still pool of water was man's first mirror. Gazing in it the face is relected. As truly as the face seen in the pool is like the face which the water reflects, so truly does one man's heart reflect the other's. Though there may be culture, education and a certain refinement, underneath each human being there is the same corrupt, fallen human nature.

CHAPTER 28

Warnings and Instructions Continued

The wicked is a coward; the righteous man, because he trusteth in the Lord and knows the Lord is on his side, is as bold as a lion. It is the conscience which makes a coward of the wicked man.

This chapter has many sharp contrasts and important warnings and exhortations. We point out a few. Those who forsake the law, turn their backs upon the revelation of God, refuse obedience to Him, praise the wicked, they make common cause with them. Those who keep the law, obey God's Word, are contenders for the faith (verse 4). Evil men are blind, but with seeking the Lord comes understanding, the blind eyes are opened (verse 5). A wise son is he who keepeth the law; such was Solomon till he plunged into apostasy and darkness (verse 7). Then in the ninth verse is another pithy saying. He "that turneth away his ear from hearing the law, even his prayer shall be abomination." It is the same truth as stated in Psalm 66:18, "If I regard iniquity in my heart, the Lord will not hear me."

An important message is contained in verse 13. "He that covereth his sins shall not prosper; but whoso confesseth and forsaketh them shall have mercy." Every attempt to cover up sin is a failure. How much of this is done today, not merely the covering of individual sins, but the denial of sin itself. The modern theology useth much ingenious argumentation which tries to make out of sin something else; speaks of it as a mere defect, as if it were some kind of a taint in the blood, a hereditary and therefore unavoidable weakness, something for which man is not responsible. All these inventions, which sweep aside the declarations of the infallible Word of God, are "covering up." No mercy can there be for those who deny sin and sins. The fig leaves must be torn away with which man still tries to cover his nakedness. There must be confession, repentance, self-judgment and then of course trust in Him who died for the ungodly. The next proverb (verse 14) contains a beatitude. "Happy"—or "blessed"—"is the man that feareth always." He who has found forgiveness is sheltered by the precious blood, walks in newness of life and in godly fear all the day long.

We mention verses 25 and 26: "Trust in the Lord brings blessing; and he that trusteth in his own heart is a fool."

CHAPTER 29

The Final Instructions

These final instructions given in proverbs cover the similar ground as those in the previous chapters. Wisdom shines out in each, and the contents of every proverb shows that the author is not Solomon but He who is perfect in knowledge. "He that being often reproved hardeneth his neck shall suddenly be destroyed, and that without remedy." Scripture abounds with examples of cases of hardening the neck and the heart, like Pharaoh, Ahab and others. This proverb will be finally proven to be the truth when an ungodly age will end with judgment for those who were often reproved and continue in sin.

Once more the sin of flattery is mentioned. "A man that flattereth his neighbor spreadeth a net for his feet" (verse 5). Flattery is akin to lying and can never be right, but is always a mistake, which results in the gravest consequences. More servants of the Lord have been spoiled by flattery than in any other manner. It is literally, as this proverb says, "spreading a net for his feet."

In verse 23 we read, "A man's pride shall bring him low, but honor shall uphold the humble in spirit." It should be connected with the proverb in chapter 26:12, "Seest thou a man wise in his own conceits? There is more hope of a fool than of him." Pride always brings low; humility always brings up. The highest place is the lowest place. "The fear of man bringeth a snare; but whoso putteth his trust in the Lord shall be safe" (verse 25). The fear of man is born of unbelief. The Christian who fears man shows clearly that he is not looking to the Lord, but to man. The fear of man surely bringeth a snare, it leads to men-pleasing and men-praising. And because one seeks the honor which comes from man and not the honor which cometh from God only, man, his approval or disapproval, is feared. The fear of man is as dangerous, as subtle and as un-christianlike as flattery, talebearing, backbiting, whispering and the other evil things mentioned in these proverbs.

This chapter concludes the proverbs of Solomon. As we have se, the instructions which he received, first from the Lord, and the instructions which were given such which were for his conduct and life, for guidance and direction, and the proverbs which were revealed to him to give to others. We express once more the belief that every true Christian should devote more attention to these God-given instructions. How much there is in all of them for all classes of believers!

VI. The Words of Agur the Son of Jakeh

CHAPTER 30

Some hold that Agur is another name for Solomon. This opinion is also upheld by the Talmud, which speaks of six names which belonged to the King: Solomon, Jedidiah, Koheleth, Son of Jakeh, Agur and Lemuel. But this opinion cannot be verified, nor do we know who Agur the son of Jakeh was. The Septuagint and the Vulgate have translated the Hebrew words and formed a sentence out of them. "Agur" means "assembler" and Jakeh has the meaning of "pious," so that some think that Agur means an unknown godly man who gathered these sayings and they were embodied in this book. We leave the name as it is, and believe that Agur, the son of Jakeh, is the name of the author of this chapter. "Whoever Agur was, he had a certain marked individuality; he combines meditation on lofty questions of theology with a sound theory of practical life. He was able to give valuable admonitions about conduct. But his characteristic delight was "to group together in quatrains visible illustrations of selected qualities or ideas" (R. F. Horton). The opening verse also tells us that he spoke to Ithiel (God with me) and Ucal (I shall be able). The *Revised Version* has a marginal reading instead of the two names Ithiel and Ucal: "I have wearied myself, O God. I have wearied myself O God, and am consumed." We do not adopt this.

The structure of the chapter itself is different from the other chapters in this book. It begins with a prologue, containing his confession, in which he shows a spirit of deep abasement and acknowledgment of his own ignorance (verses 2-3).

This is followed by five questions concerning creation and the Creator and His Son (verse 4).

The questions are answered by God's revelation. This is indicated in the next two verses (5 and 6).

Next comes a prayer by Agur the son of Jakeh (verses 7-9).

One proverb follows next in the tenth verse. After that come the so-called "quatrains," six groups of proverbs each consisting of four things. Between the second and third group a single proverb is inserted (verse 17) and at the close of the chapter stands another proverb.

In the prologue he takes the low place, and in his confession manifests the deepest humility, with no taint of pride, thus illustrating the true humility enjoined in the proverbs of Solomon. Because he confessed that he had no understanding nor knowledge of the holy, the Lord gave him all what he lacked.

The questions he asks are concerning the

Creator. "Who is He that hath ascended up into heaven and descended? Who hath gathered the wind in His fists? Who hath bound the waters in a garment? Who hath established all the ends of the earth? What is His Name, and what is His Son's Name, if thou canst tell?" He knows there is a Creator. He cannot question the eternal power and Godhead, which alone can account for this ordered universe. He has not, like many thinkers, ancient and modern, dropped a plummet down the broad deep universe, and cried, No God. He knows there is a God; there must be an intelligence abled to conceive, coupled with power able to release this mighty mechanism. But Who is it? What is His Name or His Son's Name? Here are the footsteps of the Creator; but where is the Creator Himself? (*Expositor's Bible*) By searching God cannot be found out; the fullest answer is given in the New Testament. We are reminded of John 3:13. We know Him who has ascended, because He descended from heaven; Who is the Lord and Creator of all, now in God's presence as the glorified man, and some day He who ascended into heaven will descend again.

That in the next place the Word of God is mentioned, that is the written revelation of God, is not without meaning. Man needs this revelation to know the Lord, and have the question answered which human speculation and scientific research can never answer. On account of the statement "add thou not unto His words" critics have surmised that the canon of the Old Testament must have been completed when this chapter was written. They have put the date long after the exile. But such a conclusion is unwarranted. God had commanded long before that nothing should be added to His words (Deut. 4:2). The prayer of Agur in verses 7-9 is closely linked with the foregoing verses. He prays for deliverance from vanity and lies, that he may have a true and honest heart, so necessary for the reception of the truth of God; then he prays to have neither poverty nor riches. Poverty might induce to steal and take the name of God in vain, then His Word would be rejected by him; and riches would mean the same, as it might lead him to say, Who is the Lord?

The proverb in the form of a command in verse 10 is isolated from the trend of thought in this chapter. The first quatrain comes next in verses 11-14. Four times the word generation is used, describing the classes of people frequently mentioned in the preceding chapters of proverbs. Then follow four things which are insatiable. The climax is reached gradually. The horseleach (or vampire) has two daughters by name of "Give." Even so is the poor heart of man; and there are three and four things of the same character; the unseen regions into which disembodied spirits are going day after day, year after year; the barren womb; the earth upon which rain descends yet is never filled with water, and the fourth thing, the fire, which never saith, it is enough, which consumes till nothing is left. These unsatiable things mentioned are symbolical of the condition of the natural man, always taking in yet always, restless and never satisfied.

Then there are four things inscrutable: The way of the eagle in the air; the way of the serpent on a rock; the way of a ship in the midst of the ocean; and the way of a man with a maid (verses 18-20).

Four disquieting things are given in verses 21-23. In verses 24-28 the four little things, yet wise, are pictured. They are the ants, the conies, the locusts and the lizard (not spider as in the A. V.). Here are lessons for man: the sluggard, the fool, the evil man, and other characters touched upon in proverbs are put to shame by the sagacity of these little things. Four graceful things conclude these sayings: A lion, a greyhound, an he-goat and a king, against whom there is no rising up. So may the righteous man act. Bold as a lion, swift as the greyhound to carry out the Lord's will in the Lord's service, climbing the steeps like the he-goat, and always victorious like a king undefeated. We see that these statements of Agur have a definite bearing upon the entire book of Proverbs inasmuch as they restate and illustrate the different characters, such as the ungodly, the unwise, the fool, the sluggard, the proud, the righteous, the godly, the humble, etc., mentioned in the book. Agur's message ends with a word of counsel to exercise self-restraint.

VII. The Words of King Lemuel Taught Him By His Mother

CHAPTER 31

The Virtuous Woman

"The words of King Lemuel, the prophecy that his mother taught him"; this is the superscription of this chapter. Who is King Lemuel? No king by that name is known. We do not hesitate in saying that it is Solomon. It means "unto God" one who is devoted to the Lord. In all probability Solomon's mother called her boy by this name, and here is the record therefore of the instruction given by Solomon's mother. The warning is once more, and that very earnestly (shown by the thrice asked "what?" What shall I say unto you?) against licentiousness, against wine and strong drink. The brief words of the mother's exhortation end with a request to act righteously as king, to stand up for those who are appointed to destruction, to plead the cause of the poor and needy.

The final portion of the book of Proverbs is a description of the virtuous woman. This section is quite different from the rest of the book, like many Psalms and the Lamentations it is alphabetically arranged. The virtuous woman, who is far more valuable than rubies, is described in her home as a faithful wife, a painstaking mother and the competent mistress of her household. There is no need to allegorize this description and apply it to the Church, as some have done. But this virtuous woman stands out in prominent and bright relief—a relief against the descriptions of "the strange woman," the adulteress so repeatedly mentioned in Proverbs (2:16-20; 5:1-23; 22:14; 23:27, etc.). One of the proverbs is expanded in this beautiful picture drawn by the Spirit of God: "Whoso findeth a wife findeth a good thing, and obtained favor from the Lord." But how few of the modern women reach this ideal! How few among Christian women measure up to it!

Thus ends the book of Proverbs, the book filled with practical instructions, warnings; food for thought and meditation; filled with wholesome counsel, with direction and guidance, the wisdom which is from above.

THE BOOK OF
ECCLESIASTES

Introduction

The book of Ecclesiastes has difficulties which have puzzled both the expositor and the reader. We do not mean the question of authorship so much as the contents. It has been branded as pessimism, and not a few have declared that it is unworthy of the Holy Spirit and should never have been added to the other books of the Bible. In spite of all these perplexities connected with the book and hasty judgments, it has a definite place in the organism of the Holy Scriptures, and without this book the revelation of God would be incomplete.

The title the book bears in our English translation comes from the Septuagint, and is an attempted translation of the Hebrew word "Koheleth", which Luther in the German version translated with "Preacher" (Prediger); it is thus translated in the King James version in the opening verse of the book—"The words of the preacher." But the Hebrew word Koheleth can hardly mean preacher. It is dervied from the verb "kahal" which means "to gather" or "assemble." The word "Kahal" has been translated "congregation," or as the Greek of the Septuagint translates it "ecclesia." Koheleth is feminine, evidently a word specially provided, and it has been suggested that this was done to correspond to "wisdom" in Proverbs, which is also the feminine gender (Prov. 1:20). Perhaps the word "debater" comes nearest to the meaning of the original. The word Koheleth is found nowhere else in the Bible; but in Ecclesiastes it occurs seven times, three times in the beginning, once in the middle and three times at the end of the book.

The Authorship and Date

Both Jewish and Christian tradition ascribe this book to King Solomon. The book itself does not leave us in doubt about it. Chapter 1:12-16 is conclusive. If this is disputed, as it is almost universally among rationalistic critics, and also by some who are not rationalists, we may well ask the question who wrote Ecclesiastes? The higher critic is unable to give a satisfactory answer. They give the date of the book and its composition about 250-235 B. C. The book itself shows that this is impossible, for the author of it lived at a time when Israel had reached the zenith of prosperity and glory. That time was during Solomon's reign. If Solomon was not the author, then another person living during the reign of Solomon must have written the book. But everything shows that only Solomon could have been the author fit and fitted to write this book.

As already stated Jewish teachers and Christian teachers give decisive testimony for the Solomonic authorship. In a Jewish commentary of Ecclesiastes (Midrash Koheleth) which was written almost 1,200 years ago, a large number of learned and ancient rabbis bear witness to the fact that Solomon is the author. The Targum, or paraphrase, on this book, composed in the sixth century A. D., with many other Jewish commentators, speaks of Solomon as the writer of Ecclesiastes. Equally uniform is the testimony of the teachers of the early church. The critics fully acknowledge this consensus of Jewish and Christian opinion and they have an explanation for it. They say these scholars and commentators "wanted the faculty of historical criticism, one might almost say, of intellectual discernment of the meaning and drift of a book or individual passages, . . . and that they had no material for forming that opinion other than those which are in our hands at the present time" (Dr. E. H. Plumbtree in *The Cambridge Bible*). We shall see what the "intellectual discernment" is, of which critics constantly boast, and we shall find that it is but another term for "infidelity."

It was Luther, the great German reformer who, as far as we know, began first to cast doubt upon this book. In his "Table Talks" he said; "Solomon did not write the book himself, but it was composed by Sirach in the time of the Maccabees. It is, as it were, a Talmud put together out of many books, probably from the library of Ptolemy Euergetes, King of Egypt." He was followed by Grotius in 1644 who also denied that Solomon is the author. "From that time onward," says a critic, "the stream of objections to the Solomonic authorship has flowed with an ever increasing volume." No doubt it is still flowing, and that stream carries those who trust themselves to it farther and farther away from childlike trust in God's Holy Word.

Some of the Objections of Critics

The main objection is on linguistic lines. Hebraeists have pointed out that there are several scores of words and forms in Ecclesiastes which are found only in the post-exilian books and literature; some they claim originated even later. Professor Delitzsch makes the bold statement, "If Ecclesiastes is of Solomonic origin, then there is no history of the Hebrew language." And another scholar states, "We could as easily believe that Chaucer is the author of Rasselas as that Solomon wrote Ecclesiastes." But not so hasty, gentlemen! There is another side to this question of the foreign words in this book, which, after all your objections, still is believed to be Solomon's. Your objection on these linguistic peculiarities is really an evidence for the Solomonic authorship of this book. The words which are Aramaic (and Aramaic belongs to the same branch of language as the Hebrew Semitic) have been proven by other scholars to be in common use among the nearby nations who used the Chaldean language. Solomon was a scholar himself. No doubt all the available literature of that age and of the surrounding nations was at his disposal, and he was familiar with it. It is said of him, "His wisdom excelled the children of the East country and all the wisdom of Egypt, for he was wiser than all men." That Solomon used Aramaic words is perfectly logical; but it would have been strange if such words had been absent from this book, with its peculiar character and message. That Solomon's foreign diplomacy, as well as marriages with foreigners also made him familiar with Aramaic words and sayings is quite possible. Then we might add that no unimpeachable proof has ever been given that the Aramaic words and forms used by Solomon were of later date at all. At any rate objections to the date and authorship of a Bible book on purely philological evidence suits those perfectly who approach the Word of God as they approach any other literary production.

Another objection is made on account of the statement in chapter 1:12, "I, the preacher, was king over Israel." It seems almost childish that these scholars raise such a point; it shows the weakness of their case. They declare that the writer of the book says, "I, the preacher, was king over Israel," and that this could not have been written by Solomon, who never ceased to be king. This objection is foolish. It is not at all the question of the fact that the writer of the book reigned as king, but rather what was his position at the time when he wrote the book?

Another objection is the absence of the name of Jehovah in this book. It has been said, "A book coming from the Son of David was hardly likely to be characterized, as this is, by the omission of the name Jehovah." This objection springs from the deplorable ignorance of the critics concerning the message and purpose of this book. The omission of the name of Jehovah and the use of the name of God as Elohim exclusively is a mark of the genuineness of the book. We shall refer to this later when we touch on the character and message of Ecclesiastes.

We mention but one more of the objections. They say "That the book presents many striking parallelisms with that of Malachi, which is confessedly later than the exile and written under the Persian monarchy, probably 390 B.C."

This studied objection can readily be answered by anybody. In fact we have seen no valid objection whatever. Every one can be satisfactorily answered. A mature scholar, Dean Milman, wrote many years ago: "I am well aware that the general voice of German criticism assigns a later date than that of Solomon to this book. But I am not convinced by any arguments from internal evidence which I have read."

The Message of Ecclesiastes

No other book in the whole Bible is so perplexing, if not confusing to the average reader as is Ecclesiastes. It is a book filled with hopelessness and despair, depicting the difficulties and disappointments of life, and the hollowness of temporal things; at the same time it seemingly sanctions a conduct which clashes with the standards of holy living as revealed in other portions of the Scriptures. The utter absence of any praise, or expression of joy and peace, as it is in the group of other books to which Ecclesiastes belongs (Job, Psalms, Proverbs and Solomon's Song) is another striking characteristic.

The problem is solved in the very beginning of the book itself. In the first verse we are introduced to the illustrious author of the book, who calls himself "Koheleth," and "the son of David, King in Jerusalem." This ought to settle the question for ever. If another man wrote as the critics maintain centuries later and assumed that he is "the son of David and King of Jerusalem," he was a fraud. But why does Solomon write? What is the theme he follows? What is the object of his debate or discourse? The next two verses give the answer to these questions and the solution of the problem. Vanity of vanities, saith Koheleth; vanity of vanities—all is vanity. "What profit hath a man of all his labor which he taketh under the sun?" Here are two words which arrest our attention. The first one is "vanity," used five times in the second verse. It occurs many times throughout the book and is frequently connected with "vexation of spirit" (literally, pursuit of the wind). The word "vanity" means that which soon vanishes, nothingness. It is used for the first time by Eve when she had her second son, whom she called "Abel." So the great king, the wisest of men in his discourse in which he seeks and searches out by wisdom concerning all things that are done under heaven (verse 13), and in all his searching independent of Jehovah's revelation, he discovers that all is vanity and vexation of spirit.

The second word which we notice is "under the sun." This expression is found twenty-nine times in this book. Now that which is "under the sun" is on the earth. There is, of course, something which is above the sun, that is heaven, the heavenly things. Ecclesiastes then is occupied with earthly things, with what man does apart from God, that is the natural man. The book describes the things under the sun, shows that all what man does, his pursuits, his labors, whatever undertaken and all that is connected with it, is nothing but vanity and vexation of spirit, ever unsatisfying and filled with sorrow and perplexity. The writer makes it clear that in all his searching and description of the things under the sun he does not depend on divine revelation, on that which is above the sun, but he reacheth his results through the light which nature gives; his resources are within himself. This is confirmed by the phrase, "I communed with my own heart," which occurs seven times in the book. The book of Ecclesiastes is therefore the book of the natural man apart from divine revelation. This is the reason why the name Jehovah (God's name as He enters in covenant relation with man) is omitted and the name of God is only expressed by Elohim, that is His Name as Creator. It shows what the natural man is, the life he lives, and the world in which he lives with its fleeting vanities. Ecclesiastes is embodied in the Holy Scriptures for one purpose, to show to the natural man the hollowness and vanity of all that is under the sun, and to convince him thereby to seek and find that which is better, that which is above the sun.

"It is the experience of a man who—retaining his wisdom, that he may judge of all—makes trial of everything under the sun that should be supposed capable of rendering men happy, through the enjoyment of everything that human capacity can entertain as a means of joy. The effect of this trial was the discovery that all is vanity and vexation of spirit; that every effort to be happy in possessing the earth, in whatever way it may be, ends in nothing. There is a canker worn at the root. The greater the capacity of enjoyment, the deeper and wider is the experience of disappointment and vexation of spirit. Pleasure does not satisfy, and even the idea of securing happiness in this world by an unusual degree of righteousness cannot be realised. Evil is there, and the government of God in such a world as this is not in exercise to secure happiness to man here below—a happiness drawn from things below and resting on their stability" (*Synopsis of the Bible*).

Natural men, and even infidels, have put a kind of a seal upon the character of the book. The French infidel Renan praised it as being the only charming book that a Jew had ever written, a book, he added, that touched our grief at every point, while he saw in the writer one who ever posed but was always natural and simple. Frederick the Great, equally infidel, regarded it as the most valuable book in the whole Bible.

Revelation and Inspiration

In the study of this book the important distinction between what is "revelation" and what is "inspiration" must not be overlooked. What Solomon sought out, the conclusions he reached, the things he found as he communed with his own heart, all is recorded in this book by divine inspiration. But this inspired record is not revelation in the sense, for instance, as the Epistle to the Ephesians. It is not divine revelation for man to be guided by. It is not revelation concerning that which is above the sun, nor the future. We mention this because those who hold the evil doctrines of soul-sleep and also annihilation turn to Ecclesiastes and quote (9:5, 10) as being "the word and revelation of God" when it is not.

The book too directs to Christ. There is that which is above the sun, that which is not vanishing, but abiding. The old creation demands a new creation and that has been made possible in Christ.

The Division of Ecclesiastes

It has been charged "that the book is very far removed from the character of a systematic treatise and therefore does not readily admit of a formal analysis." This verdict is far from being right. The analysis and division of the book depends on the right viewpoint concerning the contents of it. As we have stated in our introduction Ecclesiastes is the book of the natural man searching out the things under the sun and the conclusions he reached. The division of the book should be made with this theme in mind.

After reading the book carefully a number of times one finds that there are two main parts. The first six chapters form the first part and the remaining six chapters constitute the second part. In the first part the search of the wise man brings out the fact what the chief good is not, how all things under the sun are vanity and vexation of spirit. In the second part the search leads to certain conclusions. The chief good is sought for in wise conduct but in all we are still on the ground of the natural man.

PART I. CHAPTERS 1—6

1. **THE PROLOGUE AND THE SEARCH BEGUN:** (1—2)
2. **THE RESULTS OF THE SEARCH:** (3—4)
3. **EXHORTATIONS ON DIFFERENT VANITIES AND CONCLUSIONS:** (5—6)

PART II. CHAPTERS 7—12

1. **THE GOOD ADVICE OF THE NATURAL MAN, DISCOURAGEMENT AND FAILURE:** (7—9:12)
2. **THE PRAISE OF WISDOM AND PHILOSOPHY, THE FINAL WORD AND THE GREAT CONCLUSION:** (9:13—12)

Analysis and Annotations

PART 1. CHAPTERS 1—6

1. The Prologue and the Search Begun

CHAPTER 1

1. The introduction and prologue (1:1-11)
2. The seeker; his method and the results (1:12-18)

Verses 1-11. In the general introduction we have already referred to the opening verses as giving the information who the author is and what is the object of his treatise. So sure is the critical school that Solomon is not the king mentioned that one says "the fact that Solomon is not the author, but is introduced in a literary figure, has become such an axiom of the present day interpretation of the book, that no extended argument to prove it is necessary." Still another makes the following remarks as to the date of the book: "I shall presume that we have in this book, a late, perhaps the very latest, portion of the Old Testament canon; and that the book was written, not in the palmy days of the empire of Solomon, but at a time when the Jewish people, once so full of aspirations to universal empire, always so intolerant of foreign supremacy, was lying beneath the yoke of Persian or Syrian or Egyptian kings; when the Holy Land had become a province, ruled by some Eastern satrap, and suffering from the rapacity and corruption inherent at all times in such government" (Dean Bradley). Such presumptions spring from ignorance about the message of the book. We shall find in the text the above assertions refuted and a confirmation likewise of the Solomonic authorship.

"Before following the Preacher in his great quest it should be noted that he is to be viewed as a man who himself belongs under the sun. Whether the word Koheleth is rendered "preacher," "debater," or "assembler," or "one of an Assembly," the whole tenor of the teaching proves it is wisdom from under the sun, natural wisdom, that is speaking. The wisest of men undertakes to observe and experiment with life under the sun, in order to find out for all men the outcome of all his searchings, and then rehearses all to an assembly of his fellows. He is not supposed to know any divinely-revealed wisdom, or to have heard of a righteousness of faith, or of divine mercy, or of forgiveness of sins. He is to make answer as a natural man to whom is given the resources and helps common to natural men, only he is wiser and richer than they, and so must bring the final answer for all. And also he is a Hebrew and knows of one living and true God. When he says "thou," in advice or warning, it is not so much to some disciple or "son" he is speaking as to himself, or he is then assuming a high ground, far above " the maddening crowd," but it is soon apparent how, in these most exalted frames of the pious and philosophic mind, he is still only a natural man, for he is found, soon after, in the depth of despair uttering his disgust and hate of life and exclaiming: "The whole is vapor and a chasing of the wind." That "thou" is, after all, a sign that he is talking to himself, telling what he and all men under the sun ought to do, but utterly fail to do.

Not only does he pronounce the verdict of "vanity" for all, but he resorts to the same passing mirthful enjoyment he commends to all; but he would do it all before God. He is indeed wiser and more serious than other men, only to become more perplexed and sorrowful than they.

On him hangs more heavily than on other men

> . . . the burden of the mystery
> . . . the heavy and the weary weight
> Of all this unintelligible world.

He, if any, can say, "I know there is nothing better for them." He is king and can lay the whole world under contribution to furnish the means for answer. "What can the man do who cometh after the king?"

He repeatedly says, "I have seen all the works that are done," all the "oppressions," and "all the labor that I have labored at." And so he is to speak for the world, for the race, for man, for high, for low, wise and foolish, rich and poor, in hut and hall, living and dying. And he speaks as before God. He, of all men, feels a strange fear, seeing that somehow man's imperfect vain life under the sun is mysteriously related to and controlled by the unalterable purpose and work of God.[1]

The first note as to vanity is found in verses 4-11. There is a law of repetition, or circle-movement. It works in the sphere of nature as well as in human life. Generation follows generation; the sun has his circle; the winds too have their currents in which they blow from north to south and south to north; the waters also are subject to the same law. History repeats itself, for the thing that has been, is that which shall be and that which is done is that which shall be done. There is then, no new thing under the sun; nothing is new, all is repetition, a monotonous unchangeableness. Man is in the midst of it; he too is subject to this law. Everything then under the sun is restless, unstable (except the earth itself, which abideth forever: verse 4) hollow and empty, therefore all is vanity. Here is a picture of unrest, weariness, if not melancholy and despair.

[1]W. J. Erdman, *Ecclesiastes.*

Verses 12-18. On the critical objection that Solomon is meant in verse 12 see the general introduction. The great king, filled with wisdom and learning, rich and prosperous as none ever was before him in Jerusalem, nor after him, gives his heart to search out everything that is done under heaven. When he says: "I communed with mine own heart," he states the method of his search. He does it by meditation and not through revelation. He searches not in the light which comes from above, but that which comes from nature and by observation. He tells us a little more of himself. "Lo, I am come to great estate, and have gotten more wisdom than all they that have been before me in Jerusalem; yea, my heart had great experience of wisdom and knowledge." Is this language not sufficient to establish beyond the shadow of the doubt that Solomon speaks? And if not Solomon, who was it who dared to write these words? And what are the given results by the great and wise king of Jerusalem? The result is twofold. "I have seen all the works that are done under the sun; and behold all is vanity and vexation of spirit"—the pursuit of the wind, that is chasing air-bubbles. And another conclusion: "For in much wisdom is much grief; and he that increaseth knowledge increaseth sorrow" (verse 18). What a verdict from such a man as Solomon was. He had all things man can enjoy; all pleasures and honors; great possessions, chariots, horses, palaces and a large estate and he exclaims "nothing but travail!" "Nothing but vanity and vexation of spirit!" It all leaves me empty; it does not satisfy.

But he had given himself to wisdom. He possessed unusual wisdom. The king was what we would term today a great scientist. He excelled in wisdom all the children of the East country. Proverbial in his days was "the wisdom of Egypt"; yet his wisdom was greater. His fame was in all nations round about. Philosophy and poetry were his great achievements. "And he spake of trees, from the cedar tree that is in Lebanon even unto the hyssop that springeth out of the wall; he spake also of beasts, and of fowl, and of creeping things and of fishes" (1 Kings 4:29, etc.). He was a great botanist, an ornithologist and zoologist. He traced God's wonders in nature, that which the natural man can so easily do. But what about all this wisdom? Did it satisfy his soul? We listen to his answer: "I perceived that this also is vexation of spirit." The more knowledge the more sorrow. Alas! how true it all is!

But is there something else which satisfies?

Is there a higher wisdom and knowledge? There is, but in the book of the natural man it is unrevealed. That which satisfies, which is not vanity and vexation of spirit, is that which is above the sun, and not under it. From above the sun He came, who is the wisdom of God, the son of God. He has come and gone, but brought to the poor thirsting and hungry heart of man the true knowledge. He who died for our sins and is now back above the sun, is He "in whom are hid all the treasures of wisdom and knowledge" (Col. 2). That which alone can satisfy is Christ.

CHAPTER 2

The Results of the Search and Different Vanities

1. His personal experience (2:1-11)
2. Various vanities and a conclusion (2:12-16)

Verses 1-11. Here we find first of all the king's personal experience. He experimented, so to speak, with that which is the possession of the natural man, a fallen nature. In that nature are found three things: the lust of the flesh, the lust of the eyes and the pride of life. We can trace these three things in the opening verses. The lust of the flesh in verses 1-3; the lust of the eyes in verses 4-6, and the pride of life in verses 7-8. He said in his heart, Go to now, I will prove thee: that is, I will try now to satisfy thee, that is myself, my heart. He said to himself, "enjoy pleasure." He laughed and had mirth; he tried wine, laid hold on folly. Then he made great works, built houses, planted vineyards, laid out beautiful oriental gardens with fruit trees, all kinds of shrubbery, with pools of water, springs and waterfalls—all so pleasing to the eye—the lust of the eyes. To all this he added servants and maidens, with great possessions. He gathered silver and gold and treasures such which only kings could obtain, gifts, probably from other monarchs, perhaps those which the Queen of Sheba brought. He also paid attention to music, had men singers, women singers, and an orchestra. Then, self-satisfied, he leans back and says, "So I was great and increased more than all that were before me in Jerusalem; also my wisdom remained with me" (verse 9). Who can doubt even for a moment that all this could mean any other person but Solomon; none but he could speak thus. But to make sure, he did not leave a single desire unsatisfied, for "whatsoever mine eyes desired I kept not from them, I withheld not my heart from any joy." Well, he had tried everything, every pleasure, everything that is beautiful to the eye; he was surrounded with every comfort, had all honor and glory, was wealthy and esteemed. Does he then sing and in a blessed peace of mind is he content and satisfied? Far from it. "Then—then"—when he had done all these things and had every desire fulfilled—"then I looked on all the works that my hands had wrought, and on the labor that I had labored to do; and, behold, all was vanity and vexation of spirit; and there was no profit under the sun." It is a groan instead of a song. But that sounds pessimistic. It is the pessimism into which sin has put man. Whatever man does and seeks in satisfying that old nature, whatever his pursuits, his labors and his achievements in life, if it is that and nothing else, in the end it is nothing but vanity and a chasing of the wind.

Thank God! there is One who can still the hunger and thirst of the soul, who graciously invites, "If any man thirst, let him come unto Me and drink."

Verses 12-26. He now turns in search for happiness in another direction. The old, old question, "Is life worth living?" after all he had stated must be answered negatively—if all is vanity and vexation of spirit and there is no profit under the sun, in anything that man enjoys, labors for and obtains, then life is not worth living. He had been disappointed in his search, but now he turns to something more ideal and not materialistic as the former things. "Then I saw that wisdom excelleth folly, as far as light excelleth darkness." He turns philosopher, but it is of no avail, for it leads in the same road and ends with the same groan—vanity and vexation of spirit. While wisdom is superior to folly as far as light is superior to darkness, yet wisdom cannot help man, cannot give him peace nor give him happiness. There is one event which happens to the wise men and to the fool: that event is death. As it happeneth to the fool, so it happeneth unto me. What then was the good that I was more wise? He at once concludes "this also is vanity." Death, according to the conception of the natural man, apart from revelation, plunges the wise man and the fool into oblivion, "there is no remembrance of the wise more than of the fool for ever; seeing that which now is in the days to come shall all be forgotten and how dieth the wise man as the fool?" (verse 16) Such is the reasoning of the natural man. By revelation we know that there is remembrance. But it leads Koheleth, the King, almost to despair. He hates life. If the pursuit of pleasures, the lust of eyes and the pride of life left me empty, and were found out to be nothing but vexation of spirit, so that life is not worth living, equally so, he finds out, that wisdom in itself and its possession brings the same results—vanity of spirit—I hated life! Then he speaks of labor done. He has labored to leave it all to the one who comes after him, and he may be a fool and not a wise man. Or he may have labored wisely and it is left all to one who never did anything, a sluggard. All he brands as vanity and ends by saying, "For what hath a man of all his labors, and of the vexation of his heart wherein he hath labored under the sun? For all his days are sorrows, and his travail grief; yea his heart taketh no rest in the night. This is also vanity."

The conclusion reached is that, apart from God, man has no capacity to enjoy his labor. Verse 25 has been metrically rendered as follows:

> The good is not in man that he should
> eat and drink
> And find his soul's enjoyment in his toil;
> This, too, I saw is only from the hands of God.

2. Further Results of the Search

CHAPTER 3

1. The times of man under the sun (3:1-11)
2. When then is the good? (3:12-15)
3. Concerning judgment and the future (3:16-22)

Verses 1-11. There is a time for everything. Twenty-eight "times" are mentioned, beginning with the time of birth and ending with the time for peace. Everything has a fixed time: Life-death; seeding-harvesting; killing-healing; breaking-down building-up; weeping-laughing; mourning-dancing, etc. These are the times of the entire race; that is what human life is. All moves and changes; all appears unto him profitless. "What profit hath he that worketh in that wherein he laboreth? What is the gain of it, to be born and to die, to plant and to pull up, to weep and to laugh, to mourn and to dance, to get and to lose, to love and to hate? But he advanced a step. He recognizeth that all this travail must be of God, who has produced these never ceasing changes, so that men's hearts might be exercised thereby." "I have seen the travail which God has given to the sons of men to be exercised in it." Yeah, there is something which is in man. "God hath set the world in their heart," the correct rendering is, "God hath set eternity in their heart" (verse 11). Man has the sense of the infinite in his heart.

All that time offers, all these changes cannot satisfy, nor can man with eternity in his heart find out the truth about it by himself. He may feel but cannot understand.

Verses 12-15. What then is the good? To what can man in such condition, with such constant changes, and with an unsatisfied feeling of the infinite in his heart resort to? The searcher gives his results. Let man rejoice and do good in his life. Let him eat and drink and enjoy the food of all his labor. But let him also do so fearing God in view of God's judgment, for "God requireth that which is past." This is about as far as the natural man can see.

Verses 16-22. The thought of judgment expressed in verse 15 is now more fully taken up. It seems as if a ray of light now breaks in. There must be from the side of God's judgment. Under the sun he saw in the place of judgment wickedness, and in the place of righteousness, wickedness was there also. Then he said in his heart, "God shall judge the righteous and the wicked." He draws the conclusion that the present injustice must be dealt with by God. But here he stops short. He may surmise, but certainly he has not. Instead of advancing in his searchings as a natural man he comes back to his old wail of vanity. "I said in mine heart, it is because of the sons of men that God may prove them, and that they may see they themselves are but as beasts. For that which befalleth the sons of men befalleth beasts; even one thing befalleth them: as the one dieth so dieth the other; yea, they have all one breath; and man hath no preeminence above the beasts: for all is vanity." It shows that as far as life beyond the present is concerned all is darkness for man. He may have "eternity set in his heart", but he has no light. Death comes alike to man and beast; they die and are gone, hence the conclusion, "man hath no pre-eminence above the beast." But man has, as the revelation of God teacheth. But here we do not listen to God's revelation but to the searchings and observations of man only. The natural man knows, "all" men and beasts "go to one place, all are of the dust, and all turn to dust again," Then there is just a faint suggestion of something which might be beyond the grave. The correct rendering of verse 21 is, "Who knoweth whether the spirit of man goeth upward, and the spirit of the beast goeth downward to the earth?" Man and beast share the same being, draw breath in the same way, spring from the dust, return to the dust, but who can give assurance that the spirit of man really goeth upward? Who knoweth if this is really true. Who has come back and told us the truth about it? Who knoweth? Such is still the cry of the natural man with all his boasted discoveries and research. Finally he reacheth the same goal as Koheleth—all is vanity. Oh! blessed truth as given by revelation and above all in the person of our Lord and His precious gospel! Man indeed has the pre-eminence and is not like the beast that perisheth. Redeemed by Him who became man, to die for our sins, not only the spirit of the redeemed goeth upward but in its time the body will leave the dust and be changed like unto the glorious body of Him, who as glorified man sits at the right hand of God.

Returning to the wise king with his search, in view of all this, which he has brought forth in this chapter he gives his counsel as to what man is to do under these harassing circumstances. "Wherefore I perceive that there is nothing better than that a man (the natural man) should rejoice in his own works, for that is his portion; for who shall bring him to see what shall be after him?" (See also 6:12).

CHAPTER 4

Observations of Different Wrongs

1. Concerning oppressions (4:1-3)
2. Concerning envy of fools and the rich (4:4-7)
3. Concerning the miser (4:8-12)
4. Concerning popularity (4:13-16)

Verses 1-3. He observes that the world is filled with oppressions. This connects with the statement made in the previous chapter, (verse 16). Criticism declares in connection with this passage that it could not have been written by Solomon, nor does it, they claim, describe the conditions of the people Israel during the reign of the king. One commentator asks, "Can this bitter experience be drawn, I asked in passing, from the golden day of Solomon, from the high noon of Hebrew prosperity, as sketched in the book of Kings?" They apply it to the days of the Ptolemies. But Solomon does not say that the oppressions were in Jerusalem at all. He says that he saw "all the oppressions that are done under the sun." As the great king was in touch with other nations he knew what oppression, poverty, tears and sorrow are in the world, and that the oppressed, the grief stricken, the downtrodden, have no comforter. It is so still, "under the sun." Oppression and all that goes with it is still the history of part of the race and will be as long as sin reigns. Injustice and unredressed wrongs have been the order for almost six thousand years. So deep is his sorrow over these conditions that he declares it would have been better for both the living and the dead if they had never existed at all.

Verses 4-7. In continuing his observations he mentions the successful man, the man who has made life worth living. But success breeds envy. It makes his life bitter. Instead of being loved the successful man is hated; what else then is it but vanity and vexation of spirit! But now another extreme. It is the sluggard, the lazy man, the fool who eats his own flesh. But here is the best human wisdom can suggest. Avoiding both extremes, he declares, "Better is an handful with quietness, than two handsful with labor and vexation of spirit."

Verses 7-12. Another vanity is observed. Some are misers, heaping up riches and treasures untold. He has no relations, no children, no brother; even companionship and friendship are unknown to him. He lives his solitary life. His ambition is to labor and gather riches, but his eyes are never satisfied with riches; he wants more and more all the time. This also is vanity and is a sore travail.

Verses 13-16. Popularity is another vanity and vexation of spirit. No lot is abiding. Upon the throne sits an old and foolish king. He is dethroned and is replaced by a youth out of prison.

3. Exhortations on Different Vanities

CHAPTER 5

1. Concerning worship and vows (5:1-7)
2. Concerning extortions (5:8-9)
3. The vanities of wealth (5:10-17)
4. The conclusion (5:18-20)

Verses 1-7. The writer, King Solomon, seems to have been exhausted in his descriptions as to the things under the sun. He pauseth and turns to something different. He meditates on worship, that man aims to get in touch with the unseen God. "He seems to turn to himself again and communes with his heart on the loftier heights of what proves to be, after all, but natural religiousness, and what cannot save him from the depths of unbelief, ignorance and despair, in which he is soon hopelessly floundering. Mindful of man's jaunty liberalism and enslaving superstitions, rash vows and wordy prayers, shallow reverence and dreamy worship—dreamy and unreal because full of entreating vanities and worldly business, the speaker earnestly exhorts the multitude going to the house of God to have few words and slow and solemn steps in their worship and vows; but even then he does so like a natural man himself, knowing only of a God far away, who is looking upon the sinful on earth with cold judicial eye, ready to destroy the work of man in wrath."[2] The natural man may fear God, fear Him with a slavish fear, make an attempt to worship Him and do something, yet he does not know God nor can he know Him by himself. Christendom, even to-day, bears witness to the worship of the natural man. Yet this natural religion, which recognizeth the existence of a Creator, speaks of Him as the All-wise, the Omnipotent and the Eternal, makes an attempt to worship in a house by ceremonies and ritual, or that which takes on a more liberal form, does not meet the needs of man. God is still in heaven and man on earth (verse 2), and a vast distance between—an unbridged gulf. To bring man to God, to give him peace and assurance, to deliver him from fear, revelation is needed that which is "above the sun." The gospel of Jesus Christ is the only provision.

Verses 8-9. Once more he calls attention to oppression, the extortions so common "under the sun," and he shows that One higher than they will some day judge them, for He has regard for the poor and the oppressed.

Verses 10-17. He speaks now of wealth and of earthly prosperity. Silver does not satisfy, nor is he that loveth abundance satisfied with the increase. It is vanity. Earthly happiness in the things under the sun is a vain hope. The reasons why riches, and what goes along with them, cannot give true enjoyment have been searched out by the wise king and the results of his observations are given in these verses. "As he came forth from his mother's womb naked so shall he go again as he came, and shall take nothing for his labor, which he may carry away in his hand . . . and what profit hath he that laboreth for the wind?" (See 1 Timothy 6:7).

Verses 18-20. What then has he seen and learned in observing all these vanities? He draws the conclusion that it is good and comely for one to eat and to drink, and then to enjoy to fullest extent the good which he has obtained all the days of his life, the life and length of days given him by the Creator. And if God has given him riches and wealth and the capacity to enjoy it, then he ought to take his portion and rejoice in his labor. Such a spirit of enjoyment will make him forget the evil in his day; it will carry him over the disagreeable things of life. "For he shall not much remember the days of his life, because God answereth him in the joy of his heart." The latter phrase means that God Himself corresponds to his joy, for real enjoyment is a God-acknowledging spirit.

CHAPTER 6

Disheartening Contradictions

1. Riches—Inability to enjoy them (6:1-2)
2. Having All—Yet no fill of the soul (6:3-9)
3. The sad ending wail (6:10-12)

Verses 1-2. The first evil the wise searcher sees as a discouraging contradiction is, that God giveth a man riches, wealth, and honor so that he does not lack in anything whatever. But God does not give him the power to enjoy it, a stranger instead eats thereof. This makes impossible what he stated in the closing verses of the preceding chapter. The cherished desires of man have found no fulfilment. And if he has seen this evil, so do we still see it also. Where then is "the good and comely" of chapter 5:18? This is vanity and it is an evil disease, he confesseth.

Verses 3-9. But here is more of life's bitterness. If one should beget a hundred children and live to a very ripe old age, so old he becomes that it seems as if there is to be no burial for him at all, yet his soul is not filled with good—what then? "I say that an untimely birth is better than he, for it cometh in vanity and departeth in darkness, and the name thereof is covered with darkness; moreover it has not seen the sun nor known it; this hath rest rather than the other: yea, though he live a thousand years twice told, and yet enjoy no good; do not all go to one place?" It is a sad, sorrowful picture, yet every word of it is true as to man's existence. With all his long life and all it brings, riches and power, his soul has not the fill it needs, that which satisfies. His life ends at last and then there is the one place—the region of the unknown, the Sheol, where they all go. And about that one place there is no light; it is felt existence after death but of what nature? All is darkness! Better, far better off, is the untimely birth.

In verse 7 he comes back again to the labor

[2]W. J. Erdman, *Ecclesiastes.*

that man does. It is for the mouth, yet it does not satisfy—the appetite is not filled. The hunger returns, and man must labor to satisfy it and yet it is never filled. The fool and the wise make the same experience. The wise has no advantage over the fool; and the poor man who has something to eat in sight is far better off than the rich, whose desires wander, seeking that which gratifies. Vanity and vexation of spirit! We may all sum it up in a brief sentence: Man under the sun, whatever he does, all his labors, all his riches, all his seeking for good, all his achievements cannot satisfy him, it cannot give that which the soul of man craves and needs. Nor can it ever be discovered by the searcher, the wise man, the philosopher, the scientist. What man needs is not anything "under the sun" but that which is "from above the sun."

Verses 10-13. Who knoweth what is good for man in this life that is—what is it that can satisfy the heart and soul of man? He spendeth all the days of his vain life as a shadow. For who can tell a man who shall be after him under the sun? It is the wail of darkness and despair. Who knoweth? Not the natural man. But the question which man cannot answer, God has graciously, blessedly and eternally answered in His Son, the Lord Jesus Christ. With Peter we too cry out, "Lord to whom shall we go? Thou hast the words of eternal life" (John 6:68).

Part II. Chapters 7—12

1. The Good Advice of the Natural Man, Discouragement and Failure

CHAPTER 7

1. The better things (7:1-14)
2. The anomalies (7:15-18)
3. The strength of wisdom, yet none perfect (7:19-22)
4. The worst thing he found (7:23-29)

Verses 1-14. All had been tested by the royal searcher; all was found out to be vanity and vexation of spirit. Darkness, discouragement, uncertainty and despair were the results. The good, that which is right and comely for men, supposedly, found had also turned unto vapor, empty and hollow like the rest. He starts now in a new direction; he turns moralist and philosophizeth on the better things. He climbs high with his reason and deductions. He had come to the conclusion that life is not worth living. Having riches, possession of everything, were found out nothing but vanity. Perhaps being good, having the better things morally, and doing good, will satisfy the heart in "which is set eternity," the soul of man. And so he makes his observations in seven comparisons.

A good name better than precious ointment; the day of death better than the day of birth; the house of mourning is better than the house of feasting; sorrow is better than laughter; the rebuke of the wise better than the songs of fools; the end of a thing better than the beginning; the patient in spirit better than the proud in spirit. He has used his highest power to reasoning in reaching these conclusions, similar to the conclusion of other wise men, moralists and philosophers among the pagans. The different "sacred writings" of other nations, the Greek, Roman, Persian, Hindu, Chinese, etc., poetry and ethics as well as philosophies of all these nations give a definite proof that Ecclesiastes is the book of the natural man, that reason speaks and not revelation. For these "sacred writings" and philosophies are on the same line as our book. But does this satisfy? Can man thereby attain perfection? His heart has passions which man cannot control. Oppression makes a wise man mad (verse 7); anger is in his bosom (verse 9). Again he mentions wisdom. It is a good thing, just as good as an inheritance; it profits to see the sun, but not above the sun. Wisdom and wealth are both good as a defense; both give life, animate the person who possesses them, give a certain amount of enjoyment. But can both wisdom and wealth give a solution of man's problem? Who can make that straight which God hath made crooked? His ways are mysterious, unsolvable as far as man is concerned; man cannot solve the providential dealings of God. Prosperity is followed by adversity and adversity by prosperity; He sets one over against the other. But who by his reason, by his wisdom, can find out what God will do in the future, what His dealings will be? In the very reading of all these statements one feels like walking in a dense fog. Some statements are beclouded so that it is difficult to ascertain the correct meaning that the searcher is really aiming at. Perhaps this is the case to teach the lesson how man, with his finite reason searching for light, apart from revelation, wanders in darkness and ends in confusion.

Verses 15-18. Prosperity and adversity, controlled by a higher power; how are they meted out? No one knows when they come; they come to the righteous and to the wicked. He has seen the righteous perish in his righteousness and the wicked prolongs his days in his wickedness. How does the natural man, the philosopher, meet this difficulty? He answereth it by what is called "common sense." "Be not righteous overmuch, neither make thyself overwise; why should thou destroy thyself?" Do not overdo it, strike a happy medium; avoid any kind of excess; be not too self-righteous for you might become puffed up and then you destroy yourself. Here is more "common sense" of the natural man. Be not overmuch wicked, neither be thou foolish; why shouldst thou die before thy time? Enjoy yourself, but avoid too much wickedness; have a good time but avoid excesses. Not too much righteousness and not too much wickedness; just a happy middle way; such a way, thinks the natural man, is not compatible with the fear of God.

Verses 18-22. Wisdom is strength. He had tried wisdom; he tells us what he proved by wisdom. But the wise man makes a wise confession: "I said I will be wise; but it was far from me." He owns his ignorance. Everything has left him unsatisfied. He cannot find out by wisdom that which is far off and exceeding deep. All is imperfection. "There is not a just man on the earth, that doeth good, and sinneth not" (verse 20).

Verses 25-29. Again he applies his heart to know, to search and to go to the root of the matter—to know the wickedness of folly, even of foolishness and madness. And what does he find? "I find more bitter than death the woman whose heart is snares and nets, and her hands as bands." He speaks here as a Hebrew with the knowledge at least of what happened to man. God hath made man upright, but they have sought out many inventions. And woman was deceived by the serpent and her heart is often a snare and a net and her hands drag down into the vile things of the flesh. Here, at least, is an acknowledgement that sin is in the world and has corrupted the old creation, but what about the remedy? He knows nothing of that, for the new creation which lifts man out of the condition where sin has put him is the subject of the revelation of God.

CHAPTER 8

1. Prudence before kings (8:1-10)
2. Of the righteous and the wicked (8:11-13)
3. The conclusion (8:14-17)

Verses 1-10. What else had he seen? What were his further discoveries? He is still ardent in praising wisdom, though he had confessed "that it was far from him." Wisdom makes the face to shine and the boldness of the face becomes changed. He cautions as to the governmental powers in the world, urges prudence and submission. He is a keen observer. But nothing can deliver from the power of the grave. The tyrannic ruler ruleth over another to his own hurt, but the power of the tyrant does not deliver him from the power of the grave and he is soon forgotten.

Verses 11-13. But here is a true statement, which the natural man discovers by observation, for instance, in reading the pages of history. "Because sentence against an evil work is not speedily executed, therefore the heart of the sons of men is fully set in them to do evil." Evil will be punished; man knows that by experience. And he knows "that it shall be well with them that fear God, which fear before Him. But it shall not be well with the wicked, neither shall he prolong his days which are as a shadow, because he feareth not God." But what about his former saying, "Be not righteous overmuch—be not overmuch wicked?" He is in perplexity. But his reason, which has approved of "fearing God," by which he knows that it shall be well on earth with the righteous, is now staggered, when he sees just men unto whom it happeneth according to the work of the wicked, and wicked men to whom it happeneth according to the work of the righteous. Nothing but contradictions! Like a shipwrecked man who strikes out amidst the raging waves to reach the land, and is constantly thrown back by the waves he tries to master, with all his wisdom, his searching, his conclusions and nice sayings, he is thrown back, and once more he cries his "vanity."

Verses 15-17. He is at the end of his wit. He moralized, spoke of things better; made his observations and gave exhortations; a measure of light he has to judge certain things, but the darkness is too overwhelming. His boasted wisdom has left him stranded completely. What then shall he say? In spite of the higher tone he assumed, he is back at his old conclusion, only more emphatic than before: "Then I commended mirth, because a man hath no better thing under the sun than to eat, and to drink, and to be merry; for that shall abide with him of his labor the days of his life, which God giveth him under the sun." Enjoy life! There is no better thing! Thank God through revelation we know "the better part," that which satisfies and which abides. Then comes the confession of utter helplessness in verse 17. A man, the natural man, cannot find out, he is not able to find out anything.

CHAPTER 9

1. The common fate (9:1-6)
2. Make the best of life (9:7-10)
3. The great uncertainty (9:11-12)

Verses 1-6. Here is another conclusion. The righteous and the wise with their works are in the hands of God. One event is in store for all, for the righteous, the wicked, the good, the clean, the unclean, the one who sacrificeth and the one who sacrificeth not—the grave is the one common goal. In that goal there is the end of all human toil and ambition. But even with this knowledge that all go one way, and the certainty of it, man does not reckon with it at all; "the heart of the sons of men is full of evil, and madness is in their hearts while they live." They live on with madness in the heart; then comes death. Surely reason, dark reason, says "a living dog is better than a dead lion"; the dead lion has nothing left of all his majestic awe, but if man is alive, though he be as a dog, it is the better thing. Surely everything here is pessimism gone to seed. And what in this darkening perplexity does the searcher have to say about the dead? "The dead know not anything, neither have they any more reward; for the memory of them is forgotten" (verse 5). And again, "There is no work, nor device, nor knowledge, nor wisdom in the grave (Sheol) whither thou goest." But is this the truth? Is this a doctrine of the faith delivered unto the saints? Is this the revelation of God? A thousand times, No! It is the verdict which the natural man, pagan or infidel philosopher, pronounceth. But revelation, the life and immortality brought to light by the gospel, tells us something entirely different. Yet these sentences penned when the searcher finds himself in the most despairing condition, are used by men and women, who claim to be Christians, to prove the abominable doctrines of "soul-sleep," that after death the soul plunges into a state of unconsciousness, and that the wicked are annihilated. Christian doctrine? NO! but paganism, and a denial of the revelation from above the sun.

Verses 7-10. Therefore, because "death ends it all," that unbelievable conclusion of the natural man, make the best of life. Feast well and enjoy your wine, be sure and let the wine of earthly joys make your heart merry. Dress spotlessly in the heights of fashion; be well groomed; put ointment on your head. Have a good time with your wife; enter into everything energetically—for a little while longer and you reach the common fate. Is this also "revelation" for faith to follow, or is there something better from above the sun? The New Testament answers blessedly this question.

Verses 11-12. He returns—to speak another word. Even this is not satisfying. A man knoweth not his time, "As the fishes that are taken in an evil net, and as the birds that are caught in the snare, so are the sons of men snared in an evil time, when it falleth suddenly upon them."

2. Praise of Wisdom and Philosophy, the Final Word and the Great Conclusion

CHAPTER 9:13-18

Before he had declared that wisdom is strength. He comes back to this statement and gives an illustration of it. He is in a calmer mood, but what does his meditation amount to? Only to show that this also is vanity.

CHAPTER 10

This chapter contains a series of proverbs, expressing the wisdom and prudence of the natural man. Here are a number of observations and all show that there is a practical value in wisdom and that it has certain advantages. These maxims are of a differen kind than the proverbs in the preceding book. There we are face to face with the wisdom which is from above, here it is the wisdom of man. The name of the Lord is not mentioned once. Similar philosophic utterances can be traced in the literature of other ancient nations. They need no detailed annotations.

CHAPTER 11

1. Proverbs concerning man's work (11:1-6)
2. The vanity of life (11:7-10)

Verses 1-6. These continued proverbs concern the work of man and begin with exhortations to charity and are followed by the wise acknowledgement that no one knows the works of God, who is the maker of all. All this knowledge is within the compass of the natural man.

Verses 7-10. After these philosophic proverbs he comes back to his former finding—vanity. So to speak he sums up life in one verse, "Truly the light is sweet and a pleasant thing it is for the eyes to behold the sun." It is a great thing to have life. A different strain from his despondency, when life seemed not worth living. Alas! there is another "but." "But if a man live many years, and rejoice in them all; yet let him remember the days of darkness; for they shall be many. All that cometh is vanity." Yes, let him enjoy himself in the present, but there is "a dead fly in the ointment" (10:1). There is looming up the dark future; days of darkness are coming for him—it is the grave, and human reason, philosophy, science nor anything else can bring light into this baffling darkness. "All that cometh is vanity!" Thank God, through revelation we know that those who believe His revelation, and believe on Him, whom God has sent, who is the propitiation for our sins, who conquered death and the grave—for such, "all that cometh is glory!"

Is it sarcasm that follows? He calls upon the young man to rejoice in his youth. Have a good time! Walk in the ways of thine heart, that heart out of which nothing but evil can come, and in the sight, not of the all-seeing eye of God, but of thine eyes. Do as you like! Follow my previous advice—be not righteous overmuch; be not too wicked; follow the middle road and enjoy yourself. Then comes a weighty sentence, "but know thou that for all these things God shall bring thee to judgment." But is not this revelation? Can the reason of man discover that such will be the case? Reason does know the law in nature "that whatsoever a man sows that he shall also reap." Reason beholds this law working not only in nature, which teaches man many things, but also in history, so that the philosopher can say, "the history of the world is the judgment of the world."

CHAPTER 12

1. Youth and old age (12:1-8)
2. The concluding epilogue (12:9-14)

Verses 1-8. Childhood and youth are vanity! That is the concluding sentence of the previous chapter. The vanities of life, the doom and darkness of the grave are uppermost in his mind, and the final word he speaks, ere he closeth with his epilogue, is the same with which he began his search, the search which brought out so many things, yet nothing in reality—as in the beginning of the book, so now he cries out, "Vanity of vanities, saith the preacher, all is vanity" (verse 8). He has come back in all his reasoning to the place from which he started.

Once more he speaks of youth and exhorts, "Remember now thy Creator in the days of thy youth." This advice is given in connection with the thought expressed in chapter 11:9, "God will bring thee into judgment." Yet the natural man cannot obey this command. He then points to that which is inevitable. The balmy days of youth and energy will be followed by years in which man says, "I have no pleasure in them," the days of old age. Then death stalks in and the dust returns to the earth as it was and the spirit to God who gave it (verse 7). The description of the approach of old age is extremely beautiful. Clouds begin to cast a shadow over the spirit; sorrows multiply, one comes after the other as "clouds return after rain." The keepers of the house (the hands) tremble with weakness, and the strong men (the knees) become feeble. But a few of the grinders (the teeth) are left and those that look out of the windows (the eyes) are darkened. Then the doors are shut in the streets, the ears become dull and can no longer hear the familiar sound of the grinding at the mill; he is troubled with sleeplessness and no longer enjoys pleasure. He is troubled with fears. His hair becomes snow-white like the almond tree in bloom and the least thing becomes a heavy burden; the appetite is gone. Age has come and man is ready to go to his "age-long home." The silver cord is snapped (the spinal column), the gold bowl is broken (the brain), the pitcher is broken at the fountain (the heart), and the wheel broken at the cistern (the blood and its circulation). But if he speaks of an age-long home, what is that home? And he speaks now of the spirit returning to God, but what does it mean? There is no answer, no light on these questions, for the natural man, even at his best, and in highest wisdom, cannot find the truth for himself about that "home" nor what it means—the spirit return to God. And thus he ends, "All is vanity."

But if we turn to the gospel, the gospel of God, the gospel of His Son, the Lord Jesus Christ, the gospel which is from above the sun, which reaches down to lost man under the sun, that blessed gospel lifts man higher and higher, till redeemed, saved by grace, washed in the blood of the Lamb, he reaches the place above the sun, the Father's house with its many mansions, the eternal home of the saints of God.

Verses 9-14. The final great conclusion remains. He reaches the high-water mark of his reasoning wisdom. Let us hear the conclusion of the whole matter: "Fear God and keep His commandments, for this is the whole duty of man. For God shall bring every work unto judgment with every hidden thing, whether it be good or whether it be evil." This is great wisdom, but does it help man? Does it bring comfort to his soul? Does it carry with it that which satisfies his heart? God is in heaven and man on the earth, he said before. There is an immeasurable distance between. And this masterly conclusion of the royal searcher still leaves God and man apart, with not even the faintest glimmer of light. Man is a sinner; how can his sins be forgiven? How can man, with a sinful heart, "obey commandments"? What about that judgment of every hidden thing? Alas! no answer; and man, struggling man, lost, sinful man, face to face with that which the highest natural wisdom can produce, must quake and tremble.

Hence Ecclesiastes is the way-preparer for the gospel of Jesus Christ. Like every other Old Testament book it points and leads to Christ, in whom all problems are solved, all questions answered, in whom the old creation ends and the new begins.

THE SONG OF
SONGS

Introduction

The Song of Solomon, as this book is called in the St. James Version, is the third book of which Solomon is the author, preceded by Proverbs and Ecclesiastes. In the Hebrew Bible it occupies a different place. It is found there in the section called "Kethubim," the Hagiographic division. It belongs to the so-called "Megilloth" or rolls and is placed first among them—Song of Solomon, Ruth, Lamentations, Ecclesiastes and Esther. In the synagogual service it has been appointed to be read on the eighth day of Passover, the feast of redemption. This is suggestive, for, as we shall see, this Song is a love-song, expressing the love of Messiah for His people.

A better title for this book is "the Song of Songs." It corresponds to the Hebrew beginning of the book in Hebrew—*Shir Ha-shirim.* It is called "Song of Songs" in the Septuagint (*Asma Asmaton*) and also in the Vulgate (*Canticum Canticorum*). This title expresses most fully the spiritual meaning of this little book.

Needless to say that this beautiful song has suffered much from the hands of the men who claim to be critics of the Word of God. We do not care to repeat the charges which have been made against this Song as being sensuous, if not immoral, in its suggestions. Such is the verdict of the natural man, who, by such criticism, reveals the state of his own heart.

The Solomonic authorship has likewise been attacked, and it is claimed that the book was written long after Solomon's day. Wellhausen, the German critic, declares that "the most original of the Hagiographic writings is the song of Solomon; the names and things which occur in it assign it clearly to the second half of the Persian period. We see from it that the law had not yet forbidden love-poetry to the Jews, and had not made the enjoyment of life impossible." Nearly all the other critics have placed the date after the exile. The objections against the composition of the book in Solomon's period are mostly on account of a few words, which critics think were unknown to the people during Solomon's reign. What we have stated on these philological objections in the introduction to Ecclesiastes holds good in the case of this book also. While Wellhausen and others have denied the Solomonic authorship and date, other scholars have declared that the song itself has all the marks of Solomon. Among these marks Professor Delitzsch mentions "the familiarity with nature, the fulness and extent of the book's geography and artistic references, the mention of so many exotic plants and foreign things, particularly of such objects of luxury as the Egyptian horses."

Neither the Jews nor the early church doubted the authenticity of Solomon's Song. It formed part of the Hebrew Canonical Scriptures from very ancient times, and there is no valid reason why it should be rejected or the Solomonic authorship be denied.

Another question which has been raised is as to the unity of the contents. Inasmuch as different voices are heard speaking in this little book, and it being composed of dialogues as well as monologues, some critics claim that the book is not a unity, but rather a collection of love poems, similar to those written by Burns and Heine. One critic (Budde) endeavors to prove that the book is a collection of folk-songs sung at weddings, which some unknown hand collected. But the unity of the book in tone and its language disposes of this theory, nor is there any ground to call it, as some have done, a Hebrew drama.

The Story of the Song

It is the story of the love of King Solomon for Shulamith, the bride, who by turns is a vinedresser, shepherdess, midnight inquirer, etc., while the king is described in all his beauty, as the beloved one. In this way the Jewish interpreters as well as the vast majority of Christian commentators have understood the story of the song.

But there is also a different explanation of the story, the so-called "literalist." It was first proposed by an expositor by name of Jacobi in 1771, and was later adopted by Herder, Umbreit, the critic Ewald, and the French infidel Renan and others. In England it found an able defender in Dr. Ginsburg. Briefly stated this literalist explanation is as follows:

There lived somewhere at Shulem a widowed mother, several sons and a beautiful daughter. They were farmers. One day while the damsel tended the flocks, while resting under an apple tree, she met a beautiful young shepherd to whom she was later espoused. One morning this youth invited her to accompany him into the field, but as her brothers were anxious for her reputation they sent her away to take care of the vineyards. She then requested him to meet her in the evening, and, as he did not keep his appointment, and fearing that he might have had an accident, she searched for him and found him. One day she met accidentally King Solomon, who happened to be on a summer visit to that neighborhood. Enraptured by the beauty of the damsel, the king took her to his royal tent, and there, assisted by court ladies, endeavored with alluring flatteries and promises, to gain her affections, but without effect. Released from the presence of the king, the girl sought her beloved shepherd. But the king took her with him to Jerusalem in great pomp, in the hope of dazzling her with his splendor; but neither did this prevail; for even while there she told her beloved shepherd, who had followed her to the city that she was anxious to be with him.

The shepherd, on hearing this, praised her constancy, and such a mutual demonstration of their love took place, that several of the court ladies were greatly affected by it. The king was still determined to win her affections and watched for a favorable opportunity, and with flatteries and allurements, surpassing all former ones, tried to obtain his purpose. He promised to give her the highest rank, if she would comply with his wishes, but she refused, declaring that her affections were pledged to another. The king then was obliged to dismiss her, and the shepherdess with her beloved returned to her native place.

There are at least three reasons why this view must be rejected. In the first place, it makes havoc with the order of the book. The text must be cut up, and a veritable "grasshopper-method," jumping from one place and chapter to another, must be employed in order to put such a story together. In the second place, it is contrary to all the Jewish and Christian interpretation of the past; they all must be branded as erroneous if this literalist explanation is the true one. And finally it makes King Solomon, who as King of Peace, and in the glory of his kingdom, is a type of Christ, the Messiah, a vile tempter, who tries his utmost to seduce the shepherdess.

We therefore believe that it is the story of Solomon's love for his bride, the Shulamith, as believed by the vast majority of Jewish and Christian expositors.

The Allegorical Meaning

That this song has a deep, mystical and spiritual meaning has always been recognized. The Jews have looked upon it in this light and some orthodox Jews forbade it to be read till a person had reached the thirtieth year. It has been called by them "the Holy of Holies." Jewish interpretation has rightly explained this love-song as typifying the love of Jehovah for his people Israel and His union with His people. We believe this is the correct interpretation, only it is not Israel, the whole nation, but rather the godly remnant. The Song of Songs shows forth the affections which the King-Messiah creates in the heart of this remnant at the time of the re-establishment of their relationship with Himself, when once more they enter into that blessed relationship, which has been severed for such a long time. Here, then, is a blessed revelation in a mystical form of Christ's devoted love for the remnant of His people and Jerusalem, and the heart response which comes from that remnant.

The Larger Application

This interpretation does not exclude another and larger application to Christ and the Church. Such an application is fully warranted by the teaching of the New Testament. While the Messiah loves the remnant of His people Israel, whose love and heart devotion He will animate in the future, when they are taken back into His favor, He also loved the Church and gave Himself for it. Both Israel's union with the Messiah, the Lord God, and the greater union of the Church and Christ, are typified in both Testaments by the marriage relation. The following passages will demonstrate this fully: Isa. 54:5, 52:5; Jer. 3:1; Ezek. 16:23 and many others; in the New Testament: Matt. 9:15, 22:2, 25:1; John 3:29; 2 Cor. 11:2; Eph. 5:23, 32; Rev. 19:7, 22:17.

The teaching of some that only Israel is the bride of Christ must be rejected. It is true that the Church, as the body and bride of Christ, is unrevealed in the Old Testament, but it is anticipated, and we have a perfect right therefore to apply the precious statements in this song of love to ourselves.

This has been done in the past. The history of the application to the Church is of much interest. We touch upon it briefly.

Hippolytus (225 A. D.) was the first commentator of Solomon's Song and he states that the primary application is to Israel and next to the Church. Origen developed this application to the Church and her union with Christ more fully. After him the identification of the bridegroom and the bride with Christ and the Church became the predominant one. Athanasius, Gregory of Nyssa and Jerome followed more or less the interpretation and application made by Origen. Jerome's view was that the bride and the bridegroom were Christ and the Church, or Christ and the soul. Augustine agreed with him also, but restricted the meaning to the union of Christ and the Church.

Theodore of Mopsuestia, a great expositor of the Word of God, gave the Song a more literal explanation. Chrysostom, Theodoret and nearly all the great exegetes of the early Church teach that the Song typifies the love of Christ for His Church.

In the Middle Ages the mystical school made great use of this portion of the Word of God. Thus Bernard of Clairvaux preached not less than eighty sermons on the first two chapters. To mention all the expositors of the Middle Ages and more recent ones would fill pages.

The critical school has broken away completely from the spiritual application to Christ and the Church. "The admixture of this carnal imagery," says Dr. Harper in the *Cambridge Bible,* "With the more spiritual passion of the bride and her lover has grown repulsive to us as it could not be formerly."

The Division of the Song

Different divisions of this song have been made; none appears to be satisfactory. We believe the best way to study the Song of Songs is to take it up verse by verse without attempting a detailed division and analysis.

Annotations

Song of Songs

In studying this Love Song the primary application to the remnant of Israel must not be lost sight of. It is to be kept in mind that we are on Jewish ground and that the perfect assurance of that perfect love, which we know as members of His body, is lacking. The deeper spiritual applications which the individual believer may make in heart communion with the Lord, must be left to each person. In a certain sense we are here in the "Holiest" of all, for love-communion with our Saviour-Lord is the most precious thing. It produces that worship and adoration which is so acceptable in His sight, the worship in the Spirit. Our annotations will therefore be more of a general nature, but, we trust, under God, helpful to a deeper study of the book.

CHAPTER 1

The bride speaks first. She is occupied with the Beloved One. What He is, and all His kindness and loveliness have produced in her heart the love and admiration she expresses. The first rapturous outburst is, "Let Him kiss me with the kisses of His mouth; for Thy love is better than wine." She does not mention the Beloved by name; for her there is but One, beautifully illustrated by Mary when she came to the sepulchre and seeking Him said to the one she supposed to be the gardener, "If thou has borne Him hence." The kiss expresseth reconciliation (Luke 15:20), it is the token of peace, and above all, of affection. Thus the remnant of Israel will long for Him, for reconciliation, peace, and His affections. But true believers, the members of Himself, know in fullest assurance their reconciliation in Him; that He is peace and enjoy His affection. His love is better than wine. Wine is the symbol of earthly joys and pleasures; far better than anything under the sun is His love.

In verse 3 His worthy Name is described as "ointment poured forth." It is because of all He is and all He gives. Well do we sing, "How sweet the Name of Jesus sounds in a believer's ear." The passage reminds us of Mark 14:3. For all who know Him His Name is the Name above every other name. But while we know His Name in all its preciousness, His own people Israel, the godly among them, will know Him likewise in the future. The virgins mentioned here, loving Him, are those separated ones in Israel who refuse to fall in line with the antichristian delusion of the great tribulation. We find them mentioned in Rev. 14:1-5.

The bride desires to be drawn by Him and knows that if He draws all will run after Him. Then the King appears and brings her into His chambers, typifying full communion of love. Joy and rejoicing are the results. Verses 5-6 are the bride's confession. She confesseth she is black, which does not denote at all, as some have taken it, that she was an Ethiopian. It means sunburnt, as she declares, "Look not upon me because I am black, because the sun has looked upon me." She passed through the scorching heat of affliction and sorrow, yet she is comely (Ezek. 16:10); through His mercy and kindness not forsaken. The daughters of Jerusalem the bride addresses are those of the nation, who do not yet share her knowledge of the Beloved, the Messiah. Israel had been called to be "the keeper of the vineyards," that is, the keeper of nations and to be a blessing to them; but she had failed; not even her own vineyard did she keep. It is her confession to Him whom she now knows and longs for.

And she wants to belong to Him only, and be with Him where He is. She seeks shelter in the place where He makes His flock to rest at noon; for her soul loves Him. For her He is become the shepherd of Israel, who has found His sheep (Isa. 49:10; Ezek. 34:13-15.) And if the remnant of Israel thus longs for Him and His precious fellowship, how much more should we, His heavenly people, love Him and be attached to Him only! Then He speaks in verse 8. Because of her confession He calls her the fairest among women. She is to go forth "by the footsteps of the flock." What He says of her, what she is, He Himself has produced in her and for her. The horses imply energy and swiftness (same as in the New Testament); the ornaments the gifts of His love (Ezek. 16:11). Interesting is verse 11, "We will make beadrows of gold with studs of silver." The Jews believe that both God and the Messiah are Kings. "We" denotes the Father and the Son; the beadrows of gold and studs of silver denote the joy and the nuptial crown for the bride (Esther 2:17; Ezek. 16:12). Thus Messiah will crown His faithful ones in Israel, while His church will be crowned in glory.

Then the bride speaks again of her affections in the rest of the chapter. While the bridegroom calls her fair, she in return cries out, "Behold, Thou art fair, my Beloved, yea, pleasant."

CHAPTER 2

The voice of the bride is heard again in the opening verses of this chapter; some understand it as meaning the Messiah speaking of Himself as the Rose and the Lily of the valley, but it is rather the bride. She is in her purity and separation like the lily among thorns, among the apostates of the nation during the end of the Jewish age. Of the Messiah she speaks as the apple-tree. She has no fruit of herself, but rests under Him as the blessed fruit-bearer. Under Him she finds her shelter, while He protects her and she can enjoy His fruit under His shadow. There she, and all true believers have rapture and rest and enjoy His fruit, which is sweet to the taste. The Bridegroom has brought her to His own place. She is in the house of wine (the better translation, instead of banqueting house). Unlimited joy and gladness are now her portion; the banner of love is over her; while she revels in His love, and He, too, rests in His love, for all His gracious purposes towards the godly remnant of Israel are accomplished. The spiritual application to the church is easily made. In verse 7 she charges the daughters of Jerusalem not to disturb in any way the love-relations she enjoys, till He please, till the rest of the daughters of Jerusalem, too, shall know Him, according to His own purpose. It is interesting to note that several times the phrase, "I charge you daughters of Jerusalem" is found in this song. Each time it is followed by His coming. Here we read, "The voice of my Beloved! Behold He cometh!" It is His coming as Messiah revealing Himself to the bride. In chapter 3:6 He comes as King Messiah; His Name is revealed as Solomon, the Prince of Peace. Then once more the same phrase, "I charge you, O daughters of Jerusalem," is found in chapter 8:4-5, and here the bride is coming out of the wilderness with Him, leaning on her Beloved, not the supposed shepherd lover, but King Messiah.

The rest of this chapter bears witness to the correctness of the Jewish interpretation. All shows that it refers to the time when the remnant of Israel knows Him and is enjoying the blessings and the glories promised unto them. The winter is past, the time of death and coldness; the rain is over, spring-time is at hand. The morning without clouds is breaking! Flowers appear; the birds begin their song; the cooing of the bird of love, the turtle dove, is heard. Furthemore, the fig tree putteth forth her green figs (the national fruit-bearing of the once cursed fig tree); the vines, too, begin to give the tender grapes. Who cannot see in the imagery of all these statements that millennial times are about to begin! Then there is His call to her, "Arise, my love, my fair one, and come away." Be wholly for Me! He calls her "My dove." She is in the clefts of the rock, and He Himself is that rock, where His people are hidden away and find shelter. He longs for her and she longs for Him. His eyes are upon her, His beloved bride, and her eyes upon Him. Joyfully the bride cries out, as the assurance of His great love stirs her soul, "My Beloved is mine and I am His." Yet the fullness has not yet come. It is all still in blessed anticipation of the time of fullest manifestation—"until the day dawn and the shadows flee away." "Turn my Beloved," she calls to Him, "Be Thou like a gazelle or a young hart," swift in Thy coming, upon the mountains of Bether, the mountains of spices and frankincense, when the time of worship begins.

CHAPTER 3

The scene changes. The bride is now alone and in the darkness of the night. She is seeking her Beloved and is unable to find Him. Her heart is filled with the same love she exhibits in the previous chapter, but the joy and comfort she lacks. We see her walking through the streets and in the broadways, looking for Him whom her soul loveth; she sought Him but found Him not; Then the watchmen of the night which pass through the street came across the seeking one and she eagerly inquires, "Have ye see Him whom my soul loveth?" They have no answer for her, probably they knew not what she meant. No sooner had she passed them by, when she found Him. All this is prophetic, as it reveals the soul exercise of that godly remnant of Israel during the night of tribulation. There is no need of giving a meaning to every detail.

As already stated, His coming described in verses 6-11 is His coming as King Messiah. In the last verse we have the key. "Go forth, daughters of Zion, and behold King Solomon, with the crown wherewith His mother crowned Him, in the day of His espousals, and in the day of the gladness of His heart," His mother is Israel. Israel gave birth to Him according to the flesh, as it is also seen in the great vision of the Apocalypse (Rev. 12). In that day when He comes up from the wilderness, like pillars of smoke, in the Shekinah cloud, when He comes the mighty victor, yet the true Solomon, the Prince of Peace, who speaks peace to the nations, His mother Israel will crown Him Lord of all.

CHAPTER 4

The King, the Bridegroom speaks of her, who is "perfect through His comeliness put upon thee" (Ezek. 16:14). He tells out all she is in His sight and loving estimation. He has called her from the lions' den, from the mountains of the leopards (verse 8); she has passed through the fires of persecution and tribulation and now His heart expresses His delight in her. There are eight descriptions of her beauty. He tells her, "Behold thou art fair, my love, behold thou art fair." And after the description of the beauty He beholds in her, whom He has brought out of the wilderness and out of the lions' den, He says, "Thou art all fair, my love; and there is no spot in thee." He assures her of His delight in her. It is all His own workmanship; she has not made herself fair without a spot. His grace and power have accomplished it for her. And what is true of the bride-remnant of Israel is also true of the Church. In Him we have our completeness and perfection; His own comeliness and glory is bestowed upon us. The happy day is coming for Him and for us when He will present the church to Himself, "a glorious Church, not having spot, or wrinkle, or any such thing, but that it should be holy and without blemish" (Eph. 5:27).

In verses 12-15 we have a beautiful description of the garden, the land of Israel in which His beloved is now planted once more. Here are found the precious fruits, as well as the spikenard and all the trees of frankincense. There is the fountain, the well of living waters; this as well as the north wind and the south wind, typifies the Holy Spirit. And she invites Him to come to His garden. "Let my Beloved come into His garden and eat its precious fruit."

CHAPTER 5

The Bridegroom answers the invitation extended to Him when the bride had said, " Let my Beloved come into His (not her) garden." He says, "I am come into My garden, My sister, My spouse." She is both sister and spouse." When He speaks of her as sister, He owns the national relationship. In Matthew 12:46-50 He disowned that relationship because they rejected the offer of the kingdom, but now it is re-established and the godly portion of Israel becomes the spouse. In His garden, the product of His love and His death, He finds now His enjoyment, His joy and His satisfaction. He invites others to come and partake. "Eat, O friends; drink, yea, drink abundantly, beloved ones."

But there is no response here from the side

of the bride. She exhibits slothfulness. He is seen now standing outside; His head is filled with the night dew and standing at the door He knocks (See Rev. 3:20). The comment on this difficult portion of the Song, as given in the *Synopsis of the Bible,* is especially helpful.

"Alas, what hearts are ours! We turn again to ourselves as soon as we are comforted by the testimony of the Lord's love. The Bridegroom's sensitive and righteous heart acts upon her word, and He retires from one who does not listen to His voice. She arises to learn of her own folly, and the just delicacy, with respect to herself, of His ways whom she had slighted. How often, alas! do we act in the same manner with regard to the voice of His Spirit and the manifestations of His love! What a dreadful loss, but, through grace, what a lesson! She is chastised by those who watch for the peace of Jerusalem. What had she to do in the streets at night, she whom the Bridegroom had sought at home? And now her very affection exposes her to reproof, the expression of its energy placing her in a position that proved she had slighted her Beloved. If we are not in the peaceful enjoyment of the love of Christ, where He meets with us in grace, the very strength of our affection and our self-condemnation causes us to exhibit this affection out of its place, in a certain sense, and brings us into connection with those who judge our position. It was right discipline for a watchman to use towards a woman who was wandering without, whatever might be the cause. Testimonies of her affection to her Beloved at home, the love of her own heart, do not concern the watchman. Affection may exist; but *He* has to do with order and a becoming walk. Nevertheless her affection was real and led to an ardent expression of all that her Beloved was to her—an expression addressed to others, who ought to understand her; not to the watchman, but to her own companions. But if sloth had prevented her receiving Him in the visitations of His love, her heart, now disciplined by the watchman and turned again to her Beloved, overflowing with His praises, being taught of God, knows where to find Him."

The words recorded in verse 9 are no doubt addressed to the bride by the rest of the nation. How beautiful is her answer! She speaks of Him as "the chiefest among ten thousand." Here is symbolical language. White tells us of His holiness; ruddy reminds us of His love, so fully expressed in the shedding of His blood. His cheeks were once smitten; Grace is in His lips; the belly speaks of His bowels of mercy; His eyes are the eyes of love; the gold is the symbol of His Deity; the hair is the symbol of His perfect humanity. After giving ten features of His beauty, she has exhausted herself and in ecstacy cries out, as thousands upon thousands in every generation have done, "Yea, He is altogether lovely . . . this is my friend." Blessed are all who can repeat these words and who can say, "This is my friend."

CHAPTER 6

The description of Her Beloved was addressed to the daughters of Jerusalem. Their answer is recorded in the beginning of this chapter. Her outburst of praise, her glowing testimony of Him, created the desire in the hearts of others to become His. "Whither is thy Beloved gone? . . . We will seek Him with thee." The bride answers and then in words of precious assurance she declares, "I am my Beloved's and my Beloved is mine."

Then the Bridegroom speaks in loving praise of her. He speaks of that which she is for Him. He owns that remnant as "the only one" of her mother (the nation Israel). Nor is she alone His dove, but she is fair as the moon and clear as the sun; glory covers her and she is like an army with banners displayed.

He went down into the garden, to look at the verdure of the valley, to see if His vine budded, and suddenly, before He is aware, His love makes Him like Ammi-nadib, which means 'the chariots of my willing people' (Psalm 110:3). He leads them forth in triumph and in glory.

CHAPTER 7

The rapturous outburst in praise of the bride, the saved and glorified remnant of Israel, with which this chapter begins, must not be put into the lips of the bridegroom, the Messiah-King. It is the praise of the daughters of Jerusalem, who now recognize her as the beloved of the King. Her highest confession is found in this chapter. He begins to speak of her with verse 6, "How fair and pleasant art thou, my love, in delights." She answers His expressions of love. "I am my Beloved's, and His desire is toward me." This is the highest—to know she posseseth Him and that His heart's delight is in her. This, too, is our happy knowledge. We know He belongs to us; we are Christ's and in us He has, and finds, His delight. Blessed is the scene with which this chapter closes. He calls on her to go forth with Him into the fields, to go to the vineyards, to see the budding and blossoming, the blooming pomegranates, the choice fruits new and old, all laid up for the Beloved.

This takes us into millennial times. It will be the time of fruit bearing and glory for Him in the fields, in the vineyards, among all the nations of the world. "For as the earth bringeth forth her bud, and as the garden causeth things that are sown in it to spring forth; so the Lord God will cause righteousness and praise to spring forth before all nations" (Isa. 61:11). "Truth shall spring out of the earth, and righteousness shall look down from heaven. Yea, the Lord shall give that which is good and our land shall yield her increase" (Psa. 85:11, 12).

Israel restored in fellowship with the King will share in the fullest sense these coming blessings and glory.

CHAPTER 8

The last chapter of the song is a review of the whole. There is unquestionably a recapitulation of the entire book. The bride's desires are once more given to be loved and caressed by Him. For the last time we have the charge to the daughters of Jerusalem and once more the coming is announced. "Who is this that cometh up from the wilderness leaning upon her Beloved?" She returns with Him. The Beloved is mentioned seven times in the book. There is the voice of the Beloved (2:8); the call of the Beloved (2:10); claiming the Beloved (2:16); opening the Beloved (5:5); praising the Beloved (5:9-16); leaning on the Beloved (8:5) and longing for the Beloved (8:14).

Here again the apple tree is found (2:3). It is Christ. There the Lord awoke her and manifested Himself to her. From Christ alone she derives her life. Thus only can Israel give birth to this remnant, which, at Jerusalem, shall become the earthly bride of the great King, which desires to be, and shall be, as a seal upon His heart, according to the power of a love that is strong as death, that spares nothing and yields nothing. The little sister of verse 8 has been interpreted as meaning Ephraim, the ten tribes, who will then also come into remembrance and blessing. Solomon's vineyards at Baal-hamon (master of multitudes) points clearly to the converted nations in the millennium and then His own vineyard. Israel is mentioned in verse 12.

The Song of Songs ends with a prayer, "Haste my Beloved, and be Thou like a gazelle or a young hart upon the mountain of spices." Thus the remnant of Israel will plead in the future, that He may come and be manifested in His glory; but the bride of Christ, the Church, prays "Even so, Come Lord Jesus."

In conclusion, we mention the attempt made by some, to trace in this Song of Songs the entire history of the Church. We give the divisions made for those who desire to examine this interpretation. John the Baptist's Ministry is claimed to be covered by chapters 2:8—3:5. The Ministry of the Lord Jesus on earth is traced in chapters 3:6—5:1. From the agony in Gethsemane to the conversion of Samaria is thought to be in chapters 5:2—8:5. Then chapter 8:5-14 is said to be a picture of the times when the Gentiles were first called to the revelation and the coming of the Lord.

We think the safest interpretation is that which holds closely to the Jewish meaning, as we have done in these brief annotations.

THE PROPHET
ISAIAH

Introduction

The opening verse of this great book gives us information concerning the prophet Isaiah and the period covered by his official ministry. "The vision of Isaiah the son of Amoz, which he saw concerning Judah and Jerusalem, in the days of Uzziah, Jotham, Ahaz and Hezekiah, kings of Judah." Of his personal history we know but little. Jewish tradition claims that he was related to King Uzziah. That he must have come from a prominent family may be gathered from the fact that he had ready access into the presence of the kings of Judah, Ahaz and Hezekiah, and probably also the others. That he was married we learn from the book. He had two sons which bore prophetic names. The one was Shear-Jashub (a remnant shall return), prophetically indicating that God would leave a remnant of His people. The second son was Maher-shalal-hash-baz, which means "hasting to the spoil, hurrying to the prey," prophetic of the coming and threatening invasion of Assyria.

Nothing else is said of his personal history in the book which bears his name nor do we find anything about his death. There is a trustworthy tradition that he lived during the reign of Manasseh, also that he suffered martyrdom, because he reproved the vices and idolatries rampant during the reign of that wicked king. This tradition says that the mode of his death was by being sawn asunder. (See Hebrews 11:37 which, in case this tradition is true, would apply to Isaiah.) Josephus, the great Jewish historian, speaks of the cruel persecutions under the reign of Manasseh in the following words: "He barbarously slew all the righteous men that were among the Hebrews; nor would he spare the prophets, for he every day slew some of them, till Jerusalem was overflowed with blood."

The Times of Isaiah

Isaiah lived during the eighth century before Christ. This is fully confirmed by the chronology of the kings of Judah mentioned in the first verse of the book. To understand fully the prophecies which he made in the name of Jehovah, a good knowledge of the times in which he lived and acted as Jehovah's mouthpiece is eminently necessary. We shall enter into it a little more fully to help the student of this book.

Isaiah must have lived to a very old age, for it is quite certain that for fully seventy years he exercised his God-given office. Two hundred and forty years before Isaiah the kingdom of Israel had been divided, after Solomon's apostasy. The glory had departed from both the kingdom of Israel or Samaria (also called Ephraim), and the kingdom of Judah. Both had been greatly affected by civil wars and conflicts with other nations. The kingdom of Israel sunk deeper and deeper, ruled over by a number of depraved kings, who plunged the people into the grossest idolatries with the accompanying immoralities, so that God's righteous judgment fell upon it first. During the prophetic ministry of our prophet the judgment fell on the ten tribe kingdom of Israel. About the year 736 B. C., Tiglath-Pileser, the Assyrian king, had killed Rezin, the king of Damascus, with whom Pekah the king of Samaria had made an alliance. Tiglath-Pileser then invaded the northern kingdom of Israel, took many cities in Gilead and Galilee and carried the inhabitants into his own country. (See 2 Kings 16:5-9; Amos 1:5, etc.) This was the first captivity of Israel. The rest of the inhabitants of Samaria, the kingdom of the ten tribes, were carried away by the successor of Tiglath-Pileser, that is Shalamaneser. (Read about this in 2 Kings 17:3-18, 1 Chronicles 5:26, and Hosea 8:16). Now, Isaiah's home was in Jerusalem, the capital of the kingdom of Judah, and he witnessed from there the calamity which had come upon the ten tribes.

Isaiah began his ministry under the reign of Uzziah. He was a good king, a worshipper of the Lord, yet he did not remove the places of idolatrous worship. He had a sad end (2 Kings 15:1-5). He is also called Azariah. Chapter 6 in Isaiah tells us that he had his great vision in the year when this king died of leprosy.

The son of Uzziah, Jotham, reigned in his stead. He did not trouble himself about the high places and the idolatrous groves, and the condition of the nation was that of corruption (2 Kings 15:32-26). He built cities, castles and towns; he prepared for war in time of peace. The ancient Assyria had seen its end with Sardanapulus and in its place arose the two kingdoms of Assyria and Babylonia. Babylonia soon took the lead and Assyria was joined to the Chaldean monarchy. The dissolution of the great Assyrian monarchy took place during the reign of Jotham, yet we have not evidence that Isaiah uttered a definite prophecy during the reign of Jotham. He probably did, but we cannot locate it in the book.

Then came Ahaz, the twelfth king of Judah. He was an ungodly ruler and his reign was marked by disaster. (See 2 Chronicles 28; 2 Kings 16.) In idolatry such as burning incense in the valley of Hinnom, and burning his children in the fire of idol worship, he was as wicked, or almost so, as his grandson Manasseh. As a punishment the Lord sent the kings of Syria and Samaria against him. In one day Pekah the king of Syria killed a large number of Jews and took 200,000 captive. They were only saved from deportation by the intercession of the prophet Obed. The full record of this is found in 2 Chronicles 28. Then Ahaz trembled before this strong alliance and resolved in calling in the aid of the Assyrian.

It was at that time that prophet and king met at the waterworks as recorded in chapter 7. The prophet assured the wicked monarch that Jerusalem had nothing to fear from Syria and Samaria, that Jehovah would protect Jerusalem. He urged Ahaz to ask a sign, which he refused to do. Then the Lord gave him a sign, that of the virgin who should conceive and bring forth a son and call his name Emmanuel. It is a prediction concerning the virgin birth of Israel's Redeemer-King, the Son of God. The thought is this; How can Jerusalem and Judah perish as long as He, the Messiah, David's Son and David's Lord, has not come? Isaiah also told the king that the menace then threatening would be speedily removed, but that his alliance with the Assyrian would bring disaster. But Ahaz, though he saw a fulfillment of the prophecy concerning the kings of Syria and Samaria, did not heed the warning. When an invasion of the Edomites and Philistines threatened (2 Chronicles 28:17, etc.), he turned again to his old ally, the king of Assyria. He made him costly presents. Tiglath-Pileser, as already stated above, conquered the kings of Syria and Samaria. Ahaz visited his heathen friend and ally in Damascus, and when he saw there a beautiful altar, he sent a model of it to Urijah, the priest, in Jerusalem, who constructed one like it, and afterward Ahaz used it to commit idolatry and all the abominations which go with it. (See 2 Kings 16.) But the prophecy about disaster through the Assyrian king was not fulfilled during the lifetime of this wicked king. It came with Sennacherib's invasion during the reign of the next king Hezekiah. He invaded the land but could not touch Jerusalem.

Hezekiah, the son of Ahaz, was the very opposite to his wicked father. He was one of the most godly kings which occupied the throne of David. He started in with overturning the altars of idolatry and cutting down the groves where his predecessors had permitted the wicked religious ceremonies of heathendom. Then the temple was renovated. He also destroyed the brazen serpent which Moses long ago had made, and which had been preserved as an object of idolatry, much as ritualistic Christendom worships the literal cross of wood or metal. He restored furthermore the observance of Passover. After his successful war with the Philistines, he decided to cast off the yoke of the Assyrian by not paying the tribute which his father Ahaz had promised to pay. Then Sennacherib advanced with a large army and spread ruin in every direction. Hezekiah fortified Jerusalem and prepared for a siege (2 Chronicles 22:1-8). Then he sent ambassadors to the Assyrian and sued for peace. Sennacherib demanded a large sum of money and gave him assurance that the army would be withdrawn (2 Kings 18:13-15). Hezekiah agreed and stripped even the temple of its treasures to pay the vast sum. Then Sennacherib went down to Egypt but was defeated by Tirhaka, king of Ethiopia. Maddened by the defeat he approached Jersualem again, and sent messengers from Lachish and demanded its surrender. Hezekiah then spread the whole matter before the Lord, in the house of the Lord, and received the answer that the city was safe. Isaiah's ministry in all this is found in the historical portion of his book. When Sennacherib dared to advance towards the city, the angel of the Lord slew 185,000 of his men in one night. It must be remembered that a large portion of the prophecies of Isaiah up to chapter 39 are occupied with these events, and can only be rightly understood in the light of the history of Judah of that period.

Concerning the Authorship of Isaiah

We have stated before that according to Jewish tradition Isaiah perished by the hands of wicked men by being sawn asunder. Equally wicked men have "sawn him asunder" in a different way. We mean the so-called "higher or destructive critics." Did Isaiah really write this book? Could it be the work of one man? Are there not evidences of a composite authorship? These and other questions have been raised, and their answers given by men whose boast is of superior scholarship, of greater knowledge than the knowledge of the past generations; men who blasphemously assert that their finite brains have absorbed more knowledge in these matters than the infinite Lord of Glory, the Lord Jesus Christ, possessed in the days of His dwelling on earth.

For some 2,500 years no one ever thought of even suggesting that Isaiah did not write the book which bears his name. The criticism of this book and the denial of this great prophet being the sole author of it is a very modern thing. It started with a man by the name of Koppe, who attacked, in 1780, the genuineness of chapter 1. He was followed by another theologian who expressed doubt as the Isaiah being the author of chapters 40—66, generally called the second part of Isaiah. Rosenmueller, the notorious Eichorn, the Hebraist Gesenius, Ewald and others took a hand in it in sawing Isaiah asunder, each questioning certain portions of the book. The great Leipzig professor, Franz Delitzsch, also joined the band of "scientific butchers," and declared that the second part of Isaiah is of post-exilic authorship. This was done by him in 1889, and after this with the year 1890 a veritable flood of criticism set in, led, by Canon Driver, George Adam Smith, Duhm, Stade, Hackman, Cornill, Cheyne and many others. Their infidel discoveries have been readily accepted in this country and are now being taught in Methodist colleges, in the Union Theological Seminary of New York, the Chicago University, in Baptist, Presbyterian and other denominational institutions. But let it be said that there are also scholars just as mature as these critics who stand up for the Isaiahan authorship of the whole book. We mention Stier, Weber, Strachey, Naegelsbach, Barnes, Bodenkamp, Cobb, Benjamin Douglass, Green, Thirtle, and many others.

The critics have invented a Deutero-Isaiah, that is a second Isaiah, who should have written the second part. Then another set of "scholars" with their scientific microscope discovered that this Deutero-Isaiah could not have written everything of this second part; that there was a third, or Trito-Isaiah, who wrote chapters 55—66. They also found out with their scholarship that parts were written in Babylon, and other parts in Palestine. They are still at it, "sawing Isaiah asunder." To mention their methods, their hair-splittings, their philological objections and their claims would fill pages, and we would, if we were to follow it, oblige our readers to examine the inventions of the natural, darkened heart of man, which does not believe in God. There are 1,292 verses in the book of Isaiah. Out of these the ultra critics allow 262 verses to be genuine and the rest, 1,030 verses, are rejected by them.

We repeat here what we say in the studies of Isaiah at the close of our analysis and annotations.

But what does all this mean? It is a denial of what is written in the first verse of this book, "The vision of Isaiah, the son of Amoz, which he saw concerning Judah and Jerusalem, in the days of Uzziah, Jotham, Ahaz and Hezekiah." And if several men wrote this book, if part was written during the Babylonian captivity and other parts added after the captivity, then this statement with which the book begins is untrue. This first verse assures us that the book is a whole, that all we find in it is the vision of one man. To deny this breaks down the truthfulness of the book and reduces it to the level of common literature. This is what the critics have done. But the book of Isaiah is quoted in the New Testament. The Jews always believed this book to have been written by Isaiah. They held this belief when our Lord was on the earth. He Himself read in the synagogue of Nazareth from chapter 61 which critics deny to be the writing of Isaiah. Quotations from Isaiah are frequently found in different parts of the New Testament. Twenty-one times we read of Isaiah and his words in the New Testament. The phrases used are the following: "Spoken by the prophet Esaias;" "Fulfilled which was spoken by Esaias;" "Well did Esaias prophesy;" "In the book of the words of Esaias;" "As said the prophet;" "These things said Esaias;" "Well spake the Holy Spirit by Esaias," "Esaias also saith;" "Esaias saith." This is evidence enough that the Lord and the Holy Spirit through the evangelists and the Apostle Paul set their seal to this uncontradicted and unanimous belief that Isaiah wrote this book. The critics by their methods impeach the testimony of the Lord Himself or charge the infallible Lord of Glory to have been limited in His knowledge and that He acquiesced in the current traditional belief of the Jewish people, knowing better Himself.

All the arguments of the critics are disproven by the book itself. One only needs to study this book and the careful study will bring out the unanswerable fact of the unity of the book of Isaiah. Only one person could have written such a book and that person did not write it by himself, but was the mouthpiece of Jehovah. This is the conclusion of an intelligent and spiritual study of the book itself. The silly and arbitrary restrictions the critics make, that Isaiah could not have written certain passages, because it was beyond his horizon, or that he could not have mentioned Cyrus, the Persian king, by name, over 150 years before he was born, springs from the subtle infidelity which is at the bottom of the destructive criticism, which denies the supernatural altogether.

The Message of Isaiah

The name Isaiah means "Jehovah saves" or "Jehovah is salvation." He has well been called the evangelical prophet. There are more direct quotations as well as indirect allusions to this great book in the New Testament than from any other prophetic book. Josephus relates that Cyrus, the Persian king, was greatly moved by the reading of the book of Isaiah, one of the evidences, that Isaiah was not compiled after the exile. In the passage where Josephus speaks of the edict issued by Cyrus permitting the Jews to return, he says: "This was known to Cyrus by his reading the book which Isaiah left behind him of his prophecies; for this prophet has said that God had spoken thus to him in a secret vision, 'My will is that Cyrus, whom I have appointed to be king over many and great nations, send back My people to their own land, and build My temple.' This was foretold by Isaiah 140 years before the temple was demolished. Accordingly, when Cyrus read this and admired the divine power, an earnest desire and ambition came upon him to fulfill what was so written." The early church held Isaiah in great esteem and recognized its great message. When Augustine had been converted he asked Ambrose which book he would advise him to study first. Ambrose told him, "The prophecies of Isaiah." All the great men of God, the instruments of the Spirit of God like Luther, Calvin, Knox and others acknowledged the greatness of this book and its message.

What Peter says as to the contents of the writings of the prophets of God is more true of Isaiah than of any of the other prophetic books except the Psalms. "The Suffering of Christ and the glory that should follow." Isaiah's message reveals the Redeemer and King of Israel. He is the "Holy One of Israel" mentioned by this title twenty-five times. The Redeemer of Israel is Jehovah the Creator. He announced His virgin birth, the child to be born of the virgin, the Son given, and reveals the titles of that Son (9:6). He describes Him in His lowliness, His tenderness, His miracles, as the servant of Jehovah, and above all as the sin-bearer in that wonderful fifty-third chapter. But how much more Isaiah was permitted to reveal of His glory! He pictures in prophetic vision that kingdom which is yet to come, and which will come with the return of our Saviour-Lord. The details of His coming, His glory and His kingdom are unfolded in the special lecture on this subject which the reader finds with the other lectures at the close of the annotations.

Another great message is the predictions of future glories for and blessings for Israel, Jerusalem and the nations. These have been grouped by us in the third lecture on Isaiah under the following heads: (1) Israel's Restoration to their Land, (2) Israel's Spiritual Blessings, (3) The Blessings for the Land, (4) The Future of Jerusalem, (5) The Future Blessings of the Nations, (6) The Blessings for all Creation.

The Division and Scope of Isaiah

The book is an organic whole which proves that it can never be the piecemeal work of a number of men who assumed the name of Isaiah. That the language of the second part differs so much from the style of the first is no argument against the unity of the book at all. The style changes according to the character of the prophecy. "His style is suited to the subject and changeth with it. In his denunciations and threatenings, he is earnest and vehement; in his consolations, he is mild and insinuating. He so lives in the events he describes that the future becomes to him as the past and present" (Hengstenberg). If we believe that Isaiah was but the mouthpiece of Jehovah, that he wrote under the guidance and direction of the Holy Spirit, as He moved him and put the words into his pen, all difficulties disappear. But as we have already stated the scope of the book is conclusive evidence of both, the inspiration of the book and its Isaiahic authorship.

There are two great sections first of all. The one, chapters 1—35, contains the earlier prophecies. Chapters 40—66 the later prophecies. Between these two portions is a historical parenthesis contained in chapters 36—39.

In the earlier prophecies judgments are announced upon Jerusalem, Judah and upon nations, while blessings of the future are also given, but they take a secondary place. In the later prophecies we likewise read of judgments but the major portion reveals the glories and blessings of the future.

In the earlier prophecies the Assyrian invasion as it took place is announced, giving at the same time a prophetic forecast of a future invasion from the north in the time of the end. In the later prophecies the Assyrian is no longer mentioned. The Babylonian captivity announced in the thirty-ninth chapter is seen by the prophet as past and he predicts the return and beyond that the return of the remnant from the greater dispersion and the final glory of the kingdom with the coming of the King.

We shall now give the scope and division of these books.

I. The Earlier Prophecies (1—35)

1. **Prophecies under the Reign of Uzziah, Jotham and Ahaz** (1—12)
2. **The Judgment of the Nations and the Future Day of Jehovah** (13—27)
3. **The Six Woes. Judgment Ruins and Restoration Glories** (28—35)

Each section of the earlier prophecies foretells great judgments but each section ends with the vision of a regathered and restored people.

The Historical Parenthesis (36—39)

II. The Later Prophecies (40—66)

1. **In Babylon: Deliverance Promised through Cyrus** (40—48)
2. **The Servant of Jehovah: His Suffering and His Glory** (49—57)
3. **Jewish History in the Endtime: The Glory of Israel and of the Coming Age** (58—66)

Each section begins with a chapter which is the key to the whole section. Each concludes with a description of the two classes which compose the nation especially in the last days, and that there is no peace for the wicked but punishment.

Analysis and Annotations

The reader will find that every chapter has been analyzed as to its contents. We have not made copious annotations, because the three lectures on the book of Isaiah as found at the close of the analysis cover the contents of this book in such a manner that detailed annotations for a study of the book can be omitted. We suggest that all who desire to study this great prophecy in a closer way read carefully the introduction, and after that the three lectures on "The Scope of Isaiah," "The Messianic Predictions" and "Future Glories and Blessings." These lectures should be carefully studied and every passage should be looked up. After this has been done, take up the book section by section and follow the analysis we give and consult the lectures whenever needed.

I. The Earlier Prophecies (1—35)

1. Prophecies under the Reign of Uzziah, Jotham, and Ahaz (1—12)

CHAPTER 1

Jehovah's Case Against Judah and the Promise of Restoration

The title of the book and contents (1:1)
The moral and religious decline of the nations (1:2-15)
Jehovah's exhortation and appeal (1:16-20)
The result of obstinate refusal (1:21-24)
The promise of restoration (1:25-31)

The promised restoration of Jerusalem is still future. The "afterward" when the earthly Jerusalem is to be called "The City of Righteousness" refers to the second coming of Christ. Compare with Jeremiah 33:14-26.

CHAPTER 2

Zion's Future Glory and the Day of Jehovah

The glories in the latter days (2:1-4)
Exhortation to walk in the light (2:5)
The corruption of the people (2:6-9)
The day of Jehovah (2:10-22)

The vision of verses 1-4 is altogether future. When Israel is converted and in possession of the land, when once more a house of Jehovah will stand in Israel's land, then this great prediction will be fulfilled. Compare with Micah 4:1-5. The Day of the Lord (Jehovah) is the day of His visible manifestation to deal with the earth in judgment. Compare with Isaiah 24, etc., Zephaniah 1.

CHAPTER 3

Judgments upon the Rulers and the Daughters of Zion

The Judgment against the rulers (3:1-7)
Jerusalem's sad condition (3:8-9)
Jehovah's message (3:10-15)
The worldliness of the daughters of Zion (3:16-23)
Their humiliation in judgment (3:24—4:1)

This chapter describes the corrupt conditions among the professing people of God in Isaiah's day. A similar corruption and worldliness prevailing in our age demands divine judgment.

CHAPTER 4

Zion's Future Cleansing and Glory

Israel regathered and cleansed (4:2-4)
Jehovah's visible glory revealed (4:5-6)

The Branch of the Lord (Jehovah) is the Lord Jesus Christ. After judgment has been executed cleansing is promised and glory is established on Mount Zion.

CHAPTER 5

The Song of the Vineyard and the Six Woes

The song of the vineyard and Jehovah's lament (5:1-4)
The judgment upon the vineyard (5:5-7)
The wild grapes (5:8-23)
First woe against covetousness (5:8-10)
Second woe against fleshly lusts (5:11-17)
Third woe against mockers (5:18-19)
Fourth woe against moral insensibility (5:20)
Fifth woe against conceit (5:21)
Sixth woe against lawlessness (5:22-23)
Jehovah's anger and the invader announced (5:24-30)

Compare the song of the vineyard with Matthew 21:33-44. The wild grapes of Israel fully correspond to the wild grapes of nominal Christendom. "If God spared not the natural branches, take heed lest He also spare not thee" (Rom. 11:21).

CHAPTER 6

The Prophet's Vision and New Commission

The time of the vision (6:1)
Jehovah of hosts (6:2-4)
The prophet's woe (6:5)
The cleansing (6:6-7)
"Here am I. Send me." (6:8)
The new commission (6:9-10)
The limitation of the judgment (6:11-13)

Note the eight steps: vision, conversion, self-judgment, cleansing, self-surrender, communion, commission, intercession. This vision is the glory of Christ (John 12:41). The fulfillment of the hardening judgment of the nation, the blinding of their eyes did not set in completely in Isaiah's day. Study carefully Matt. 13:14-15; John 12:39-41; Acts 28:25-27.

However, Israel's blindness is not permanent.

CHAPTER 7

The Prophet before King Ahaz

The king in trouble (8:1-2)
Isaiah sent and his message (8:3-9)
A sign offered and refused (8:10-12)
The sign: The virgin birth (8:13-16)
The advent of the Assyrian (8:17-25)

Study carefully the historic setting of this chapter and 2 Chronicles 28:1-27. See lecture on "Messianic Predictions." In verse 14 the virgin birth of Christ is announced. Much of the controversy is around the word "virgin" (almah), which the critics declare does not mean a virgin, but a young married woman. However, they err. In Genesis 24:43, Exod. 2:8, Psalm 68:25, Song of Sol. 1:3, etc., the same word is used, and it means "virgin" in these and other passages. The Septuagint, a Greek translation of the Old Testament made some 300 years B. C., translates the Hebrew "almah" with "pardenos," the Greek for virgin. Matthew 1:23 confirms this Messianic prediction.

CHAPTER 8

Jehovah's Word Through Isaiah and the Assyrian Announced

The divine instruction and Maher-shalal-hash-baz (8:1-4)
The Assyrian to come (8:5-8)
The answer of faith (8:9-10)
A word to the faithful remnant (8:11-20)
The coming great distress (8:21-22)

The names are significant. Isaiah heard the word "Maher-shalal-hash-baz," and then is told to call his newborn son by this name. The name means "swift for spoil, hasty for prey." Isaiah's other son was named "Shear Jashub," which means "a remnant shall return." The names of the sure witnesses are equally full of meaning. Urijah (Jehovah is light), Zechariah (Jehovah remembers), and Jeberechiah (Blessed of Jehovah).

Verses 14 and 15 are deeply interesting. It is the rejection of Immanuel, Christ. Compare with chapter 28:16 and read the following passages: Luke 2:34, 20:18; Matthew 21:44; Rom. 9:32, 33; 1 Pet. 2:8.

Also note the quotation of verse 18 in Hebrews 2:13. The great distress is a description of what awaits apostate Israel.

CHAPTER 9

The Message of Hope Concerning Israel's Future and the Impending Judgments

The Messiah, His Name, His rule, His kingdom (9:1-7)
Judgment upon Israel (9:8-12)
The impenitent nation (9:13-17)
The wrath of Jehovah (9:18-21)
Unrighteous judges and three questions (10:1-4)

Matthew 4:12-16 quotes the opening verses of this chapter. This applies to His double advent. The first and second coming of the Lord are wonderfully blended together in verses 6-7. The nation in impenitence and God's wrath against them has had its past and present fulfillment. It is not yet exhausted. It looks forward to the coming day of wrath.

CHAPTER 10

The Assyrian, His invasion of Immanuel's land, and His end

The first four verses belong to the preceding chapter.
A description of the Assyrian enemy (10:5-11)
The overthrow of his army announced (10:12-15)
The punishment (10:16-19)
The return of the remnant (10:20-23)
The faithful remnant comforted (10:24-27)
The Assyrians march against Jerusalem (10:28-32)
Jehovah's intervention (10:33-34)

This is an interesting and important chapter. The Assyrian enemy was used by God to punish his people. In chapters 7 and 8 his coming was announced. In this chapter we read a fuller description of this great troubler and how he invaded the land of Israel. God addresses him as the rod He uses in anger against His people. While all this had a past fulfillment a similar invasion of the land of Palestine will be enacted before the times of the Gentiles close and the King of Kings appears. The Assyrian of the end time comes from the North; therefore he is called in Daniel's prophecy "the King of the North." Antiochus Epiphanes is a type of this final outward foe of Israel. Study carefully with this chapter Is. 14:24-25; Is. 30:31-33; Micah 5:1-7; Daniel 8:23-26; 11:40-45; Psalm 74:1-10; Psalm 89. Jehovah shall suddenly make an end of him. Verses 33-34 compare with Daniel 11:45.

CHAPTER 11

The Coming King and His Kingdom

The King: Who He is and what He will do (11:1-5)
The peace and blessing He brings (11:6-10)
The gathering of scattered Israel (11:11-16)

It is a great vision of the future which this chapter unfolds. The critics deny that the blessed Person mentioned in the opening verses is our Lord Jesus. They think Hezekiah or Josiah is meant. 2 Thess. 2:8 shows that it is our Lord. Link verses 1-5 with chapter 9:6-7. Again His coming in humiliation and His coming in exaltation are here interwoven. We behold His reign in righteousness. Verses 6-10 need not to be spiritualized, as it is so often done. Romans tells us (8:18-23) that a literal groaning creation, travailing together in pain until now, will be delivered of its groans and curses. The hour of deliverance strikes with the "manifestation of the Sons of God." However, this manifestation does not take place till the Lord is manifested the second time. In the coming kingdom to be established on earth and ruled over by the King from above, creation will be put back into its original condition.

Israel's regathering will be from a worldwide dispersion. It will be "the second time." It does not and cannot mean the return from Babylon, but the return from their present exile of almost 2,000 years.

CHAPTER 12

Israel's Salvation Hymn

When Israel will sing (12:1)
What Israel will sing (12:2-3)
To whom Israel will sing (12:4-5)
The Holy One in the midst (12:6)

It is Israel's future song of praise for salvation. Read in this light what a wonderful meaning this little chapter has. The song will be sung by the delivered and blessed remnant "in that day." In what day? When the Lord arises to judge; when He is manifested in His glory; when He brings back the captivity of His people.

2. The Judgment of the Nations and the Future Day of Jehovah (13—27)

CHAPTER 13

The Burden of Babylon

Jehovah's call to the judgment of Babylon (13:1-5)
The day of Jehovah: When Babylon falls (13:6-16)
Babylon overthrown (13:17-22)

The great judgments announced in this part of Isaiah were only partially fulfilled in the past. The great Babylon which came into existence as the mistress of the world after this prophecy had been given, fell by the Medes (verse 17 and Daniel 5). The judgment of this Babylon is meant here first. But the Babylon of the past is the type of a Babylon of the future, another mistress of the ecclesiastical and commercial world. It is yet to appear in its final form (Rev. 17—18). Its fall comes in the day of the Lord. This great day is described in verses 6-16 in this chapter.

CHAPTER 14

Israel's Restoration and Blessing After Babylon is Fallen and the Burden of Philistia

Israel's restoration and exaltation (14:1-2)
The proverb against the king of Babylon (14:3-11)
The triumph over Lucifer (Satan) (14:12-20)
Babylon's destruction (14:21-23)
The Assyrian broken (14:24-27)
The burden of Philistia (14:28-32)

When the last great Babylon is overthrown the Lord will remember His people and Jerusalem in mercy. He will then set His people in rest in their own land. The king of Babylon here in this chapter is not Nebuchadnezzar, nor his grandson Belshazzar, but the final great king of Babylon. It is the little horn of Daniel 7, the great political head of the restored Roman empire. Behind this final king of the times of the Gentiles looms up Satan, who energized that wicked and false king. The description of him who was "Lucifer," the light-bearer, and his fall is of deep interest.

CHAPTER 15

The Burden of Moab

The Destruction Announced (15:1-9)

CHAPTER 16

The Burden of Moab Continued

God's call to Moab to repent (16:1-5)
Moab's pride and judgment (16:6-14)

The fifteenth and sixteenth chapters form one prophecy. Moab's land bordered on the land of Israel. The historical facts concerning Moab may be studied and followed through the following passages: 1 Sam. 14:47; 2 Sam. 8:2; 2 Kings 1:1; 3:4; 2 Chronicles 20; 2 Kings 8:20; 24:2. Moab's sin and judgment are frequently mentioned by the prophet. See Amos 2:1-3. A great past judgment of Moab's is described in 15:1-9. The call in chapter 16:1 to send a lamb has nothing to do with Him who is "the lamb of God." The exhortation becomes clear by reading 2 Sam. 8:2 and 2 Kings 3:4, 5. Christ, however, is in view in verse 5, chapter 16. A remnant of Moab is to be left and in the time of the end we find Moab mentioned again. Read Isaiah 11:14 and Daniel 11:41. The final ruin of Moab is described in Isaiah 25:10-12.

CHAPTER 17

The Burden of Damascus and Judgment upon Ephraim

Damascus to be a ruinous heap (17:1-3)
Judgment upon Ephraim (17:4-11)
Woe to the enemies of Israel (17:12-14)

Damascus was the ancient city of Syria, mentioned for the first time in Gen. 15. Syria and Ephraim had made common cause against the house of David. Tiglath-pileser, King of Assyria, executed the judgment upon Damascus and made of it a ruinous heap. But the judgment is also future. And the enemies of Israel, which trouble His people, will be troubled "in that day." It is a solemn word with which this chapter closes, "This is the portion of them that spoil us, and the lot of them that rob us."

CHAPTER 18

When Israel Will be Brought Back

The land beyond the rivers of Ethiopia (18:1)
The ambassadors sent (18:2)
The trumpet blown and Jehovah's Message (18:3-6)
Israel restored to Mount Zion (18:7)

An interesting prophecy concerning a nation of great power, which will be used in the bringing back of God's ancient people.

CHAPTER 19

The Burden of Egypt

The Judgment announced (19:1-15)
Egypt blest with Israel in the last days (19:16-25)

Egypt has passed through many judgments. Hundreds of years after the divine predictions had been given the Word of the Lord was accomplished. The final judgment upon Egypt comes in that day when the Lord appears in visible glory. Egypt will come, like other nations, to the front once more at the close of the times of the Gentiles. But mercy is also in store for Egypt. Egypt will be called "His people." When the Lord smites Egypt that land will return to Him. It will then be lifted out of the dust and receive a place of blessing only second to that which Israel will enjoy.

CHAPTER 20

The Near-Punishment of Egypt by Assyria

Isaiah walks naked and barefooted (20:1-2)
The meaning of his action (20:3)
Egypt punished by Assyria (20:4-6)

A strong party in Jerusalem looked to Egypt for help from the threatening Assyrian invasion. This prophecy shows the utter hopelessness of expecting help from Egypt. The victory of Assyria over Egypt is predicted.

CHAPTER 21

The Burdens of the Desert of the Sea, of Dumah, and Arabia

The burden of the desert of the sea (Babylon) (21:1-10)
The burden of Dumah (21:11-12)
The burden upon Arabia (21:13-17)

The fall of Babylon is predicted, for Media is mentioned. This event was over two centuries in the future. Isaiah beholds the Persian hosts advancing. Such is prophecy, "history written in advance."

CHAPTER 22

The Burden of the Valley of Vision (Jerusalem)

Jerusalem's deplorable state (22:1-4)
The invading armies (22:5-7)
The siege and the calamity (22:8-14)
Shebna (22:15-19)
Eliakim (22:20-25)

This is another intensely interesting prophecy. Jerusalem has passed through many sieges and at last in part the prophecy has been fulfilled. But there is another siege of Jerusalem impending. It will come after the message of the fall of the final Babylon. See Zechariah 14. Still more interesting are Shebna and Eliakim, mentioned in this chapter. Shebna, the proud one, is the usurper, the type of the Antichrist. Eliakim is the type of Christ, He whose right it is to reign. It is Christ displacing Antichrist, which is seen in verses 15-25. Compare 22:22 with Rev. 3:7.

CHAPTER 23

The Burden of Tyre

Tyre's great disaster (23:1-5)
The complete overthrow (23:6-14)
Tyre's future restoration and degradation (23:15-18)

Tyre typifies the commercial expansion and glory of the world. Behind this commercial glory stands Satan, the god of this age. Read Ezekiel 28:11-19. Nebuchadnezzar carried out judgment upon Tyre (Ezek. 29:17-18). A revival of Tyre is also predicted. We call attention to a statement in the beautiful Forty-fifth Psalm, a millennial Psalm. When the King appears, surrounded by His own, "The daughter of Tyre shall be there with a gift" (Ps. 45:12). It is what is indicated in Isaiah's vision, "And her merchandise and her hire shall be holiness to the Lord."

CHAPTER 24

The Day of Jehovah

Jehovah dealing with the earth (24:1)

All classes affected (24:2)
The Desolations described (24:3-12)
The Jewish Remnant during the trouble (24:13-20)
The punishment of the high ones and kings (24:21-22)
Jehovah's reign in Mount Zion and Jerusalem (24:23)

A marvellous chapter. Not a word of it has ever been fulfilled. The great day of Jehovah is that day of which Isaiah speaks in chapter 2, Zephaniah in chapter 1, Zechariah in chapters 12—14 and every other prophet. It is the day of 2 Thess. 1:7-10.

Notice that chapters 24—27 are a continuous prophecy. To break them into chapters has been a mistake. Study the phrase "in that day." Find what Jehovah will do in the day of His manifestation. He will judge and He will bless. Singing begins in that day.

The high ones in verse 21 are the wicked spirits in the heavenly places (Ephesians 6). The Kings on earth are the Kings mentioned in Psalm 2 and Rev. 19:19. Their visitation after many days will be a visitation of judgment and not of blessing.

CHAPTER 25

Israel's Praise and the Blessings of the Kingdom

The praise of the delivered nation (25:1-5)
The blessing for all nations during the Kingdom (25:6-8)
Israel rejoicing after waiting (25:9)
Moab and Israel's enemies judged (25:10-12)

In the foreground of this chapter stands another hymn of praise, which redeemed Israel will sing in "that day." Jehovah has done wonderful things for His people. Compare with chapter 12:5; Psalm 46:8-9, etc.

The blessings for all nations are described in verses 6-8. The mountain is Zion (Isaiah 4:5-6, Psalm 132:13-14). From there the streams of blessing will gush forth. Then "all the ends of the earth shall remember, and turn unto the Lord, and all the kindreds of the nations shall worship before thee" (Ps. 22:27). Darkness will be removed and all tears wiped away. All this does not relate to the eternal state, but to conditions on the earth.

CHAPTER 26

Judah's Glory Song

Praise for Jehovah's faithfulness and mercies (26:1-6)
The experiences of waiting during the night (26:7-11)
The assurance of peace and deliverance (26:12-18)
Assurance of restoration and preservation (26:19-21)

We call attention to verses 12-21. Annihilationists base upon these words the evil doctrine that the wicked are not raised, but destroyed. The fact, however, is that verses 13 and 14 do not teach a physical resurrection. The teaching is that the lordship of other nations over Israel is forever gone. No other lords will ever rise again to domineer over Israel.

Death and resurrection are often used in the Old Testament as symbols of Israel's national death and national resurrection. See Hosea 6:2; Ezek. 37; Dan. 12:2 and verse 19 of the present chapter.

CHAPTER 27

Israel's Enemies Overthrown and the Great Restoration

Assyria, Babylon and Egypt punished (27:1)
What Jehovah has done and will do (27:2-11)
The vineyard established and the glorious consummation (27:12-13)

This is a fitting finale to the second section of this book. Israel's chief enemies are indicated by the leviathan, the serpent and the dragon. Behind them stands the serpent and the dragon, Satan. When these enemies are overthrown and Satan is bound then "Israel shall blossom and bud, and fill the face of the world with fruit."

The last word tells of Israel's literal regathering under the blowing of the trumpet (Matt. 24:31) and their future worship in Jerusalem. The ending of the first and second sections are alike. They reveal Israel's future glory and blessing.

3. The Six Woes of the Prophet, Judgment Ruins and Restoration Glories to Come (28—35)

CHAPTER 28

The First Woe and the Message of Assurance

Ephraim addressed (28:1-6)
Jerusalem equally corrupt and guilty (28:7-8)
The prophet mocked (28:9-10)
The prophet's answer (28:11-13)
Their covenant with death (28:14-15)

The message of assurance (28:16-22)
How Jehovah judges (28:23-29)

The first woe is directed against the ten tribes, Ephraim. The judgment is that which fell upon them through the invasion of Sennacherib. Yet glory is also in store for the scattered, so-called, lost tribes. A remnant will return. Verse 5 describes this glory.

The prophecy here and in the subsequent chapters was not by any means fulfilled when the Assyrian came into Israel's land. Its greater fulfillment is in the future, when the Assyrian once more invades Israel's land. See chapter 10. The covenant with death and agreement with hell (verse 15) must be compared with Daniel 9:27. It is the time when the apostate Jewish nation enters into a covenant with the coming prince and worships Antichrist. This verse and the message from the Lord in verses 16-22 are deeply interesting.

CHAPTER 29

The Second Woe Against Ariel and the Third Woe

The fall of Ariel (Jerusalem) predicted (29:1-4)
Their enemies dealt with by Jehovah (29:5-8)
The people's condition: Blinded and religious formalists (29:9-14)
The third woe (29:15-16)
In that Day: Joy and blessing for the meek and iniquity punished (29:17-24)

Ariel means "the lion of God." It is one of the names of Jerusalem. A great siege of Jerusalem is predicted. Neither Sennacherib's invasion nor the siege of Jerusalem by the Romans accomplished this prophecy. At the end of this age the King of the North (Assyrian) and confederate nations with him will besiege Jerusalem. Of this the chapter gives us the history. Sennacherib's army is a type of the King of the North. Read again chapter 10 and study with this chapter before us Zech. 12—14; Micah 4:11; 5:4-15, and especially the last part of Daniel 11. After that last siege of Jerusalem "that day" will bring blessing for the faithful and punishment for the wicked.

CHAPTER 30

The Fourth Woe Against Alliance With Egypt

The alliance and its failure (30:1-7)
The written table against the rebellious people (30:8-14)
Jehovah's word of encouragement (30:15-17)
The nation blest and restored (30:18-21)
Idolatry ceases and the land restored (30:22-26)
The accomplishment by the coming of the Lord (30:27-33)

While this chapter had a significance, like all these prophetic utterances, for the people in Isaiah's day, its complete revelation can only be grasped in the light of what is yet to come. The Jewish people have never yet possessed the blessings of verses 18-20. These will come as a result of the second coming of Christ. See verse 30.

CHAPTER 31

The Fifth Woe Against Them that Go Down to Egypt

The Egyptian Alliance condemned again (31:1-3)
Jehovah promises to deliver Jerusalem (31:4-9)

All looks forward towards the future. It is Jerusalem's glorious future. The Lord will deliver it; He will preserve it (verse 5).

CHAPTER 32

The Coming King and His Kingdom

The King and His rule (32:1-8)
The careless women addressed (32:9-12)
The judgment of the land and the city (32:13-14)
The hope of the future (32:15-20)

The connection with the previous chapter is obvious. In chapter 31:4-9 the coming of the Lord for the deliverance of His people and the punishment of their enemies is predicted. "So shall the Lord of Hosts come down to fight Mount Zion and the hill thereof." And now in the beginning of chapter 32 the coming King and His righteous reign is revealed. The King is the Man Christ Jesus, "a hiding place from the wind and a cover from the tempest."

Verses 13-14 describe once more the judgment which rested upon the land and the city. But it is not permanent. "Until the Spirit be poured upon us from on high." This great outpouring of the Spirit connected with the restoration of Israel's land has not yet taken place. It comes in that day. Read Joel 2.

CHAPTER 33

Sixth Woe Against the Assyrian and What Is to Follow

The judgment announced (33:1)
The prayer of the faithful remnant (33:2-6)
The judgment executed (33:7-13)
The judge in the midst of Zion (33:14-16)
The King beheld in His beauty (33:17-23)
Healing and forgiveness the result of the coming of the King (33:24)

This is the last mention which is made of the Assyrian apart from the historical chapters. Here again the judgment of the final Assyrian is in view. When the Lord arises and is exalted the judgment of the last great enemy of Israel will be executed. This judgment scene is described in verses 9-13. The prayer of the faithful remnant is recorded in verses 2-6. The remnant is that portion of the nation which holds to Jehovah and His word in the last days. Their prayer will be answered by the King, whom they shall see in His beauty. What Zion will be then and what the Lord will be to His earthly people is seen in the rest of the chapter.

CHAPTER 34

The Day of Jehovah

Addressed to the world: Jews and Gentiles involved (34:1)
The shaking of the earth and the heavens (34:2-8)
The day of vengeance (34:9-17)

This is one of the darkest chapters in the Bible. A worldwide judgment is described such as has never taken place in the history of the world. The indignation of the Lord is then upon all nations and upon their armies. Like chapter 33, it tells of the great judgments to come.

CHAPTER 35

Restoration Glory and the Kingdom

Creation blest and the glory of the Lord revealed (35:1-2)
The spiritual and material blessings of the kingdom (35:3-9)
The return of the ransomed of the Lord (35:10)

What follows the great judgments of the day of Jehovah, when our Lord Jesus Christ is revealed from heaven in flaming fire, is now brought forward in this final chapter of the first great part of Isaiah's vision. The unscriptural view, that the coming of the Lord in judgment means the complete end of the world, is once more answered. After judgment ruin comes restoration glory. What that glory is we find in this chapter. Read it carefully and also the "Studies in Isaiah" which follow this analysis. The last verse shows the ransomed of the Lord returning to Zion, delivered from sorrow and sighing, filled with joy and singing salvation songs. It is the bringing back to their own land of a delivered people.

A brief word of review. Each section of Part I—chapters 1—35—foretells great judgments. Judgments upon Jerusalem, the land of Judah, the nations, the whole world. These visions were not at all fulfilled in the past judgments. The day of the Lord ("in that day" ba yom hahu, a phrase so often used by Isaiah) will bring these threatened judgments. But there are the predictions of restoration and blessing, which always follow that day. Each of the three sections end with the vision of a regathered and restored people, brought back to their land. The scope is perfect because it is divine.

THE HISTORICAL PARENTHESIS (36—39)

The center of the book of Isaiah is a brief but deeply interesting historical account of events during the reign of King Hezekiah. His name is mentioned not less than thirty-one times in these chapters. His great works in reformation and otherwise are recorded in 2 Kings 18:4-7, 2 Chron. 29—30:5-22, 2 Kings 20:20. From Proverbs 25:1 we learn that he was a great lover of the Word of God, for he had it copied, perhaps by many scribes. He was 25 years old when he ascended the throne and reigned 29 years, 727-699 B. C. No doubt he was one of the greatest kings of Judah.

The events recorded in these chapters are not put together chronologically. The king's sickness, prayer and recovery occurred before the attempts of Sennacherib to take Jerusalem and the subsequent complete overthrow of the Assyrian hosts. This arrangement has its meaning. These historical chapters are designed for an appendix to the earlier prophecies (1—35) and for an introduction to the later prophecies (40—66). The Assyrian enemy is repeatedly predicted in the earlier prophecies. Indeed he is seen as the enemy of God's people, the rod of God's anger to punish His disobedient people. How the Assyrian came and the angel of the Lord smote the camp is therefore put first, because it is related to the first prophecies of Isaiah. In connection with Hezekiah's pride in chapter 39 the future Babylonian captivity is announced. The later prophecies look upon the people as in Babylon, assuring the remnant of restoration, not alone from the dispersion in Babylon but the future great restoration, the regathering from all countries.

We give a brief analysis of these four chapters and leave it to the reader to gather up the blessed lessons of confidence in God, dependence upon Him, of prayer, as well as others, in which these chapters abound.

CHAPTER 36

The Threatening Enemy

The Assyrian invasion (36:1-3)
Rabshakeh's mockery (36:4-10)
Eliakim, Shebna, and Joah's Request (36:11)
Rabshakeh's address in Hebrew defying God (36:12-20)
The silence of the people (36:21)
The terror of Eliakim, Shebna, and Joah (36:22)

CHAPTER 37

Hezekiah in the House of the Lord and Sennacherib's Second Attempt

Hezekiah's humiliation and Isaiah sent for (37:1-5)
The message from the prophet (37:6-7)
Rabshakeh's letter (37:8-13)
Hezekiah's prayer (37:14-20)
The prayer answered (37:21-35)
The army of Sennacherib judged (37:36)
The judgment upon Sennacherib (37:38)

CHAPTER 38

Hezekiah's Sickness and Healing

Isaiah's startling message (38:1)
Hezekiah's prayer (38:2-3)
The prayer heard and the sign (38:4-8)
The king's sorrow and joy, a psalm of praise (38:9-20)
The remedy for the recovery (38:21-22)

The message of approaching death startled the king because at that time he had no son. If he had died what then would have become of the Messianic hope through the house of David? Beautiful it is to hear the Lord say through Isaiah, "Thus saith the Lord, the God of David, thy father." Before that Isaiah gave him the message "For I will defend this city to save it for Mine own sake and for My servant David's sake."

CHAPTER 39

Hezekiah's Self-Exaltation

The ambassadors of Merodach-baladan (39:1)
Hezekiah's boasting (39:2)
Isaiah's inquiry (39:3-4)
The Babylonian captivity announced (39:5-7)
Hezekiah's submission and comfort (39:8)

The prediction of Isaiah of the Babylonian captivity, fulfilled through King Nebuchadnezzar about 100 years after these words were spoken, is startling. The reader will bear in mind that the Assyrian was not yet overcome, for the sickness and self-exaltation of Hezekiah preceded the judgment of Sennacherib's army. The Assyrian and not Babylon was the threatening enemy. God's Spirit alone could enable him to make such a prediction.

II. The Later Prophecies of Comfort and Glory (40—66)

Like the first part this second part of Isaiah has three sections. The three sections of the first part revealed the judgments to come upon the Jewish people, Jerusalem, the nations and the earth. The three sections of the second part reveal the great blessings in store for the people of Israel, Jerusalem, the nations and the earth, after the judgments are passed. These sections give the past, present, and the future history of the Jewish people.

In the first section (40—48) they are seen prophetically in Babylon, but about to be delivered and brought back to the land. Cyrus is predicted as the chosen instrument. However, this section looks also beyond the return of the remnant from Babylon. Their present dispersion and coming restoration is predicted as well. In the second section (49—57) we find this period of their history more fully brought forward. In this section the servant of Jehovah is more fully revealed. He came to His own and they received Him not. They hid their faces from Him and esteemed Him not. In consequence of this rejection Israel is not gathered (49:5), while those who are afar off, the Gentiles and the isles of the sea, hear of the salvation of God. It is the present age which can be traced in this section. Israel not gathered and the rejected One is given for a light to the nations. The great central figure in this section is the suffering servant of Jehovah (chapter 53).

In the third section we discover their future history. Here we see Him, who suffered, as the victorious King. A remnant is seen back in the land and the glories and blessings of the future burst forth in marvelous splendor.

1. In Babylon: Deliverance Promised Through Cyrus (40—48)

CHAPTER 40

The Opening Message: Key and Introduction to this Section

Comfort for His people (40:1)
The voice in the wilderness (40:3-5)
The prophet's message (40:6-8)
The message to Zion (40:9-11)
The supremacy of Jehovah (40:12-26)
Comfort for Jacob and Israel (40:27-31)

The first verses of this chapter are the key and introduction to the entire section. The Lord now speaks in comfort to Jerusalem and announces the pardoning of her iniquity and that in blessing she will receive double for her sins. In verses 3-11 the first and second coming of Christ are again blended together. John the Baptist was that voice crying in the wilderness (John 1:23). Not in Matthew, but in Luke, Isaiah 40:3-5 is quoted with the exception of verse 5. In its place the Holy Spirit saith, "And all flesh shall see the salvation of God." The glory of the Lord will be revealed with the second Advent. When that glory appears Israel is saved, in the meantime the salvation of God is offered to the Gentiles. Jehovah speaks in this chapter of Himself and the evidences that He is God. This is the peculiar feature of the entire section. All is spoken to encourage the faith of His people. Blessed lessons we find here. Verses 27-31, however, will only be fully realized in the future kingdom.

CHAPTER 41

Jehovah's Challenge

The address to the islands and the peoples (41:1)
Jehovah's question, Cyrus and his ways predicted (41:2-4)
Nations troubled on account of Cyrus (41:5-7)
Israel as Jehovah's servant (41:8)
The message of comfort and assurance of restoration (41:9-20)
Jehovah's second challenge: He alone can declare things to come (41:21-24)
The future things revealed (41:25-29)

Cyrus is here mentioned for the first time, though not yet by name. He is in view in verses 2-3 and 25. His work as a mighty conqueror is outlined and the consternation of the surrounding nations on account of it is described. Verses 18-20 go beyond the times of Cyrus. They can only be fulfilled when He who is greater than Cyrus will appear.

CHAPTER 42

The True Servant of Jehovah

The Servant of Jehovah and His mission (42:1-4)
His future work among the nations (42:5-9)
The future song of redemption glory (42:10-13)
Jehovah's manifestation in power (42:14-17)
The address of exhortation to the deaf and blind nation (42:18-25)

Matthew's Gospel (12:20) tells us that this servant is the Lord Jesus Christ. Mark the different phases of His character and work while on earth and His future work when He appears again. The song of redemption glory will be sung only when He is manifested. Israel is seen as a people robbed and spoiled. None saith "Restore." This is their present condition.

CHAPTER 43

Jehovah Speaks in Comfort to His People

What Jehovah is and will be to Israel (43:1-7)
Second address to the blind and deaf people (43:8-13)
Jehovah deals with their enemies (43:14-17)
Blessed things to come: They shall show forth My praise (43:18-21)
Jehovah's loving appeal and promise to remember their sins no more (43:22-28)

Chapters 43—45 must be studied together. Jehovah speaks in these chapters as nowhere else in the prophetic Word. Note the many declarations Jehovah makes. "I have redeemed thee," "I will be with thee," "I have loved thee," "I have made him," "I am the Lord, " "I will make a way in the wilderness." All God's people can lay claim to these blessed words of promise and assurance. Ultimately Israel will possess and enjoy these great blessings.

CHAPTER 44

Jehovah Continues to Speak

Spiritual blessings promised by the gift of the Spirit (44:1-5)
Jehovah the First and the Last (44:6-8)
Idolatry rebuked (44:9-20)
Remember! Return! Sing! (44:21-23)
The faithful Jehovah, the Redeemer (44:24-27)
Cyrus named (44:28)

The outpouring of the Spirit upon Israel's seed promised in the beginning of the chapter has not yet taken place. Compare with chapter 32:15 and 59:21. Verses 21-23 look forward to the coming age of blessing. Then Israel will be "Jehovah's servant" on the earth; then their transgressions will be blotted out. Then the heavens, the earth, the mountains and the trees will break forth in singing. In verse 28 Cyrus is mentioned by name. This great Persian King was then in the distant future an unborn being. Jehovah knew him and named him through Isaiah. He calls him "my shepherd" and predicts his work. Josephus declares that when Cyrus found his name in the book of Isaiah, written 220 years before, an earnest desire laid hold upon him to fulfil what was written.

CHAPTER 45

The Word of Jehovah to Cyrus, to Israel and to the Ends of the Earth

Thus saith Jehovah to Cyrus (45:1-13)
Thus saith Jehovah: Israel shall be saved (45:14-17)
Thus saith Jehovah to the ends of the earth: Every knee to bow (45:18-25)

Cyrus is called in this chapter God's anointed (Messiah). Jehovah called him by name, but it was for the sake of Israel. But it is well to bear in mind that Cyrus, God's instrument, called and prepared to make the restoration of a remnant possible, is likewise a type of Christ, through whom alone the promises of God to the nation can be accomplished.

Note the statements "Israel shall be saved in Jehovah with an everlasting salvation" (verse 17). "All the ends of the earth will be saved" (verse 22). Then idolatry will be rebuked (49:9-20). But notice the order. First Israel must know salvation and as a result the ends of the earth will look and be saved. The most precious gospel truths found here are well known.

CHAPTER 46

Babylon Is to Fall

The Babylonian idols carried by the beasts (46:1-2)
How Jehovah carries His people (46:3-4)
The divine reproach (46:5-7)
A ravenous bird (Cyrus) to come from the east (46:8-11)
Salvation in Zion (46:12-13)

The opening verses are comforting. The helplessness of the Babylonian idols is described. They have to be carried. They cannot deliver out of captivity, for they themselves have gone into captivity. But Jehovah carries His people from birth to old age. The last verse takes us beyond the fall of the Babylon of the past. When the final Babylon described in Revelation is accomplished then it will be true "I will place salvation in Zion for Israel my glory."

CHAPTER 47

A Description of the Fall of Babylon

Babylon's degradation announced (47:1-3)
Israel acknowledges the redeemer (47:4)
Retribution for Babylon (47:5-7)
The destruction swift and sure (47:8-15)

In chapter 14 a similar description of Babylon and the fall of the king of Babylon is recorded. All has its meaning for the future.

CHAPTER 48

The Divine Restatement Concerning His People, Their Condition and Future

Their condition and Jehovah's predictions (48:1-8)
Jehovah acts for His Name's sake (48:9-11)
"I am He" (48:12-16)
Israel's future blessing (48:17-21)
No peace for the wicked (48:22)

This chapter touches once more upon the different phases of Jehovah's messages from chapters 40—47. Israel's apostate condition, Jehovah's sovereign grace and mercy towards them, Cyrus (verses 14-15), the blessings of the future for a converted remnant of His people, are all mentioned again. Solemn is the declaration that whatever Jehovah does, whatever comfort and peace He bestows, however grand and glorious the blessings of the future are, the wicked are forever excluded. There is no peace unto the wicked.

This chapter closes the first section of the second part of Isaiah. Babylon, Cyrus and Jehovah's majesty and glory, revealed in predicting future things, the helplessness of idols and Jehovah's mercy and power manifested in the restoration and blessing of His people are the leading features of this section.

2. The Servant of Jehovah, His Suffering and His Glory (49—57)

CHAPTER 49

The Servant of Jehovah and His Mission

The servant speaks of himself (49:1-3)
He complains of failure (49:4)
Jehovah's answer to him (49:5-13)
Zion speaks (49:14)
Jehovah's answer (49:15-26)

This entire chapter is the key to the whole section. The Servant of Jehovah, the Lord Jesus Christ, stands in the foreground. He is seen as the Rejected One, who complains that He has labored in vain. The ultimate result of His Work is prophetically described. In the opening verses He speaks of His call. To bring Jacob to God is why He appeared in the midst of His own. But Israel is not gathered, for they rejected Him (verse 5). The nation abhorreth Him. Israel's gathering was not accomplished at the first advent. The nation was set aside. By their fall salvation came to the Gentiles. This is fully revealed in verses 6-7. In verses 8-13 we find the future work of Christ as King. When it is accomplished the heavens will sing and the earth will be joyful. Zion's present complaint (verse 14) is answered by promises of restoration.

CHAPTER 50

Ther Servant Speaks of His Determination and Suffering

(Verses 1-3 belong to the preceding chapter.)
The cause of Zion's present desolation (50:1-3)
The Servant's self-witness (50:4)
His obedience and His suffering (50:5-6)
His victorious triumph (50:7-9)
The two classes: Those who fear Him and those who reject Him (50:10-11)

The Suffering One is speaking. Little comment is needed on this chapter if the reader will use the above outline.

CHAPTER 51

Jehovah Encourages His Faithful People, the Remnant of Israel

The call to remember Abraham (51:1-2)
Zion to be comforted (51:3)
His righteousness near and His arm to judge the people (51:4-6)
Fear ye not (51:7-8)
The prayer of faith (51:9-11)
Jehovah answers (51:12-16)
The suffering of the nation to end (51:17-23)

The Lord speaks to His faithful people. He reminds them of Abraham and the covenant. He assures them that the wilderness of Zion shall become like Eden, like the garden of the Lord. Judgment shall overtake the earth. It is beautiful to see how the faithful pray in faith after this message from Jehovah (verses 9-11), and how Jehovah answers them (verses 12-16).

CHAPTER 52

Zion Awakening and the Coming of the Lord

(It is unfortunate that chapter 52:1-12 is detached from chapter 51 and that the last 3 verses of chapter 52 are detached from the chapter which follows. The correct division is chapter 51—52:12, chapter 52:13—53:12.)
Zion called to awake (52:1-5)
"In that day" Behold it is I (52:6)
The results of the return of Jehovah (52:7-12)
The Servant's suffering and glory (52:13-15)

The last paragraph of chapter 52 gives the divine declaration that the suffering and affliction of Israel is to end. "Behold I have taken out of thine hand the cup of trembling, even the dregs of the cup of my fury; thou shalt no more drink it again" (51:22). Now Zion assured of the end of suffering is called upon to awaken and put on beautiful garments. She is to arise from the dust. Such is the glorious future of Jerusalem. Verses 7-12 reveal the blessed results of the Coming of the Lord. Then it shall be said, "Thy God reigneth." Then and not before "all the ends of the earth shall see the salvation of our God" (5:10).

Verses 13-15 connect with chapter 1. Chapters 51—52:12 are parenthetical.

CHAPTER 53

The Sinbearer and His Victory

The marred visage and His exaltation (52:13-15)

His life and His rejection by the nation (53:1-3)
The work of the Sinbearer: smitten, afflicted and bruised (53:4-6)
His submission and His deliverance (53:7-9)
His glorious reward (53:10-12)

In "Messianic predictions," at the close the reader will find hints on this great chapter. We do not repeat them here. The New Testament fully bears witness to this great vision of the cross of Christ, the vicarious suffering of the Son of God and its blessed results. To reject them as meaning Christ and His work of atonement is equivalent to the rejection of the revelation of the New Testament and especially the rejection of the Person of our Lord. The chapter is one of the greatest in this book. After chapter 52 the Servant of Jehovah is no longer mentioned. He is seen in the next section as the King coming with power and executing the judgments of God.

CHAPTER 54

Israel Called to Sing

The blessings of restoration (54:1-6)
Mercy bestowed (54:7-10)
The earthly glory of Jerusalem (54:11-14)
Jehovah keeps and defends His people (54:15-17)

After the cross the singing. What singing there will be in the earth when at last "they will look upon Him, whom they have pierced." Israel will some day know the full meaning of Isaiah 53, and when He is owned at last the glories and blessings of restoration will, through infinite grace, be bestowed upon them. Enlargement and faithfulness will be the results. The shame of Israel's youth and long widowhood is ended. The forsaking is ended. Everlasting kindness will be their happy portion. The fear and sorrow of Israel are ended because "He hath poured out His soul unto death."

CHAPTER 55

Salvation's Offer and Provision

The invitation to everyone and the promise (55:1-2)
The sure mercies of David (55:3-5)
The exhortation to seek and to forsake (55:6-7)
God's thoughts and God's ways (55:8-11)
The joy, peace and glory of the future (55:12-13)

The scope and application of this chapter must not be limited. While Israel eventually will break forth in singing as the result of believing on Him, whom they once despised, the invitation to a free and full salvation goes forth to every one. It is the great gospel invitation in this book. But the national promises to Israel are in evidence in verses 3-5. And when Israel is redeemed the invitation to salvation will go forth as never before. Now individuals are saved. Then nations will be brought into the kingdom. "Nations that knew not thee shall come unto thee because of the Lord thy God, and for the Holy One of Israel; for He hath glorified thee."

CHAPTER 56

Salvation Enjoyed by the Strangers and Eunuchs

Strangers and servants joined unto the Lord to serve Him and to love the Name of the Lord (56:1-8)

The first eight verses of this chapter stand by themselves. Strangers to the commonwealth of Israel and eunuchs are gathered in. It is the result of the gracious invitation of the preceding chapter and that again is the result of the work of the Servant of Jehovah and His vicarious suffering. While these verses look forward to the kingdom we have in them a hint of what God does now in gathering strangers. The gathering of the others in verse eight can only take place when the outcasts of Israel are brought in.

Chapters 56:9—57:14 must be read continuously.

CHAPTERS 56:9—57:21

The Condition of the Apostate Nation and the two Classes

The condition of the shepherds of Israel (56:9-12)
Apostate Israel (57:1-14)
The two classes (57:15-21)

The final chapter of this second section corresponds to the last chapter of the first section (chapter 48). The sad condition of the people Israel is pictured. This is their national apostasy throughout this age, while strangers are joined to the Lord and the church is gathered. The worst is yet to come. Chapter 57:9 looks forward to the great apostasy during the great tribulation. The king is the Antichrist, who takes his seat in the temple and claims worship (2 Thess. 2). They worship him, the masterpiece of Satan, and thus they debase themselves unto hell.

Gracious is the promise to the feeble remnant, those who are contrite and humble. "I have seen his ways and will heal him. I will lead him also and restore comforts unto him and to his mourners." Peace is promised to him that is afar off (Gentiles) and to him that is near (Israel). It will be fully realized in the kingdom. "But the wicked are like the troubled sea, when it cannot rest, whose waters cast up mire and dirt. There is no peace, saith my God, to the wicked." It is the same solemn declaration which stands last in chapter 58. Comfort and peace for all, except for the wicked. It is a complete answer to the heresy of the present day, which claims that all Israel, including the wicked dead, will be saved and have a share in the Kingdom of Peace.

3. Jewish History in the Endtime: their Future Glory and the Glory of the Coming Age (58—59)

This third and last section of the vision of Isaiah can only be understood and appreciated if it is studied in the light of other prophecies which predict the final events with which the times of the Gentiles close. That period consists of 7 years, the last 3 1/2 being the great tribulation. According to these predictions a part of the Jewish nation will be back in their land. These returned Jews will consist of two classes, a faithful remnant who own their condition, trust in Jehovah and in the national promises, and an unbelieving mass. The latter will be the large majority and hate their own brethren. In their unbelief they will build another temple and eventually will accept the false Messiah, the Antichrist. The struggles and troubles of the endtime can easily be traced in this last section. The faithful remnant, their fears and hopes, their sufferings and prayers are written here, as well as their deliverance through the coming of the King, the Lord Jesus Christ. The prophetic descriptions of the future of Jerusalem, the land of Israel, the restored nation, the spiritual blessings and the glories in store for this earth are the most magnificent in the entire book.

CHAPTER 58

The Condition of the People, Repentance, and the Blessings to Follow

The Prophet's commission (58:1)
The transgression and sins of Jacob uncovered (58:2-5)
The divine requirements (58:6-7)
What Jehovah promises (58:8-14)

Once more the Prophet is commissioned to cry and this time to call the people to repentance. Such will be the case during the time of the end. The first advent of the Lord was heralded by John the Baptist, who called the nation to repentance. The second advent will be preceded by another call to repentance. It is before us in this chapter. See also Malachi 4:5-6.

In verses 9-14 we have all the great future blessings of the converted remnant of Israel described. It is the entire section in embryo.

CHAPTER 59

Apostasy and Confession, Jehovah's Intervention and the Coming of the Redeemer

The deplorable condition of the people (59:1-8)
The confession (59:9-15)
Jehovah's intervention (59:16-19)
The coming of the Redeemer (59:20-21)

The corruption of the people during the endtime is first described. But grace is at work and a part of the people confess their sins. They confess that they are in darkness, that they are blind, that they stumble and are like dead men. They confess that salvation is far from them. They confess their lying, their departure from God and their revolt. It is their future repentance. Then Jehovah sees and intervenes. He answers the confession in person. He comes to repay the adversaries. He comes in mighty judgment power. As a result they will fear His name. The Redeemer then comes to Zion and appears for the salvation of them that turn from transgression. Compare this with Romans 11:25-32.

CHAPTER 60

The Glory Chapter: The Morning of a New Age and Its Blessing

The light and glory has come (60:1)
The darkness before the morning (60:2)
The conversion of the Gentiles (60:3)
The dispersed brought home (60:4)
The conversion of the world (60:5-9)
Jerusalem restored and glorified (60:10-16)
The theocratic kingdom established: Its material and spiritual glories (60:17-22)

A small volume might be written on this glory chapter. The reader will note how all stands connected with chapters 58—59. First the call to repentance, then the uncovering of Jacob's transgression, their confession, the answer of Jehovah by His personal manifestation. He deals with His adversaries and appears as Redeemer in Zion. Then the glory light breaks forth. It is the dawn of the morning. That morning was preceded by gross darkness—universal apostasy and corruption. After the glory has broken forth the kingdom age begins. The conversion of the Gentiles will take place and Jerusalem will be indeed the city of a great King. Then at last all the people will be righteous. How strange that Christendom should ignore these majestic predictions and their divine order.

CHAPTER 61

The King, Jehovah's Messenger: His People and their Salvation Song

Jehovah's Messenger and His work (61:1-5)
His people a kingdom of priests and their work (61:6-9)
The salvation song (61:10)
The blessings of the whole earth (61:11)

Luke 4 tells us that the Lord Jesus Christ applied the opening verses to Himself. The destructive criticism denies both the Isaiah authorship of this chapter and its messianic application. The satanic origin of this kind of criticism is here fully exposed. But our Lord did not quote the whole of verse 2. He only read up to "the acceptable year of the Lord." This sentence marks the work He did in His first advent. The day of vengeance is introduced by His second advent. The results of His second coming are described in the verses which follow. Then Israel will be the kingdom of priests and a holy nation (Exod. 19). They will sing the song of salvation (verse 10). Righteousness and praise will follow.

CHAPTER 62

Zion's Glory

He will not rest (62:1)
The new names (62:2-5)
The intercession and the answer (62:6-9)
The accomplishment at hand (62:10-12)

The intercession in the beginning of the chapter is that of Christ. He will not rest till He has accomplished His purpose in His earthly people and in Zion. When it is accomplished Gentiles and kings will witness it. Zion then shall be called by a new name. The forsaken one will no longer be forsaken; the desolation of the land will cease. She shall be called Hephzibah (my delight in her); the land will be Beulah (married). All points to the glorious consummation of the kingdom, and other watchmen intercede and give Him no rest till He establish and make Jerusalem a praise in the earth. Faithful Jews, men of prayer will during the great tribulation call on God to make good His Word and fulfil His promises. May God's people even now plead and intercede for the hastening of all His purposes. "Behold, thy salvation cometh, behold His reward is with Him and His work before Him." Note the results of His coming in verse 12.

CHAPTER 63

The Executor of the Day of Vengeance

The glorious appearing (63:1)
The day of vengeance (63:2-6)

Rev. 19:11-21 corresponds to this marvelous description of the coming King. Before in this section we read of the day of vengeance, the Lord's intervention in behalf of His people and the overthrow of their enemies. The day of vengeance is now beheld by the prophet. The acceptable year is closed and judgment sweeps the earth. Often this chapter is quoted as meaning the salvation work of Christ. It has nothing to do with that. It is His judgment work. It is unfortunate that the sixty-third chapter is not ended in our Bibles with the sixth verse. Verses 7-19 belong to chapter 64.

CHAPTER 63:7-19—64:12

The Great Intercessory Prayer

Jehovah's loving kindness and power in the past remembered (63:7-14)
Their deepest need (63:15)
The cry of faith, Thou art our Father (63:16)
The increasing plea (63:17-19)
The prayer for Jehovah's manifestation (64:1-4)
Confession and humiliation (64:5-7)
The cry for mercy and help (64:8-12)

This is one of the greatest prayers in the Bible. The prophet no doubt prayed it first of all, and the Spirit of Christ through him. But its full meaning will be reached when the faithful remnant of Israel in the endtime cries for help and deliverance during the great tribulation. When Daniel discovered that the end of the Babylonian captivity was at hand, he uttered a great prayer (Daniel 9). The same beautiful spirit of a contrite heart, confession of sin, trust in Jehovah, pleading for Jerusalem and expectation of deliverance, which characterizes Daniel's prayer is seen in this great prayer. Many of the prayers in the book of Psalms are the prayers of the remnant suffering in the land before the second advent.

The remaining two chapters contain the answer to this prayer.

CHAPTER 65

Jehovah's Answer: The Rebellious and Their Judgment, the Faithful and Their Blessings

The divine rebuke to the apostates (65:1-8)
The elect seed (65:9-10)
The judgment of the apostates (65:11-12)
The blessings of Jehovah's servants and the contrast (65:13-16)
The glories and blessings of the future (65:17-25)

The first eight verses give a description of the iniquities practised by apostate Israel. Judgment will overtake them in the day of vengeance. Then the blessings of Jehovah's true servant (the remnant) are declared. They shall eat, drink, rejoice and be blessed. All is contrasted with the wicked who have forsaken the Lord. A marvelous revelation concerning the future is given in verses 17-25. When will all this be accomplished? It begins with the day of Jehovah; that day of the Lord is one thousand years. At the close of it the new heavens and a new earth will be created. Then, when eternal ages begin the complete fulfilment is reached. But the blessings of the Millennium are also before us. Jerusalem is created a place of rejoicing and His people, the people of the kingdom, Jews and Gentiles, obedient to the laws of the kingdom, will enjoy the material blessings here predicted. And groaning creation is seen once more delivered.

CHAPTER 66

The Finale: The Two Classes and the Prophecy of Isaiah in a Retrospect

The apostates and their wicked worship (66:1-4)
The remnant suffering and encouraged (66:5)
The sudden manifestation of the Lord (66:6)
The nation's rebirth (66:7-9)
Jerusalem's supremacy and glory (66:10-14)
The warning of judgment (66:15-18)
The regathering after judgment (66:19-21)
The blessings for the righteous (66:22-23)
The destiny of the wicked (66:24)

This great chapter is the fitting conclusion of the prophecy of Isaiah. The leading predictions contained in Isaiah concerning the future are once more restated. The opening verses have mystified many readers of this book. The apostate part of the Jewish nation, restored in unbelief (a restoration now going on), erect a temple once more and resume their ancient worship. This worship without faith in Jehovah is an abomination before Him. It were as if they offered swine's blood. Their coming judgment is announced in verse 4. The pious remnant, the praying remnant is seen once more. They tremble at the Word of the Lord. The unbelievers in their own nation hate them. They are mocked because they expect Jehovah's intervention from above. "Let the Lord be glorified"—they say in ridicule (verse 5). Then the coming of the Lord takes place. This is described in the sixth verse. The nation's rebirth, the supremacy and glory of Jerusalem, additional warnings, the gathering of the people into the kingdom, the blessedness of the righteous and the destiny of Jehovah's enemies conclude the chapter and the book.

The reader will have noticed that each section of the second part begins with a chapter which is the key and introduction to the section. Each concludes with a description of the two classes which compose the nation in the last days and emphasizes the fact that for the wicked there is no peace, but punishment. Each section reveals a person. The first section reveals Cyrus, under whom the remnant returned from Babylon; the second, the suffering Servant of Jehovah; the third, the King of Glory to execute vengeance and deliver His people. May He give us to see these wonderful things to come. May the vision of the future be the inspiration of our lives.

THE SCOPE OF ISAIAH

It is a great book which bears the name of Isaiah. The scope of the book and the contents are of indescribable grandeur. The more it is read, the more its majestic greatness takes hold of the heart and mind of the reader. The revelations and predictions it contains are the foundations of our faith. They unfold the future of Israel, describe the glories of the kingdom to come and the blessings in store for this earth. Isaiah is the prophet of the future. The supernatural origin of the writings of this noble prophet is in evidence throughout the entire book.

The Work of the Critics. Perhaps no other book has been of late years so much attacked by the destructive critics as the book of Isaiah. This in itself is an evidence of its genuineness and inspiration. Satan through his instruments attacks especially those parts of God's Word where the Holy Spirit has revealed the Person of our Lord, His work and His coming kingdom. It is the first move towards the rejection of the Person of Christ. In reading some of the critical works on Isaiah one is reminded of a dissecting room. These critics follow the tactics of the Jewish King Jehoiakim. He took the penknife and cut the scroll upon which God's message through Jeremiah was written. I wonder if archaeologists will some day find that penknife. If so it ought to be presented as a precious relic to the school of the destructive critics who might build a shrine for it in one of their institutions.

It would be interesting to follow the history of this criticism. We fear, however, it would not be very edifying to us who are believers in the inspiration of this book. What the critics have especially attacked is the authorship. They tell us that the book of Isaiah is of a composite origin. Isaiah did not write the entire book which bears his name. For about 2500 years no one ever thought of even suggesting that Isaiah did not write the book. Then they invented an unknown person who is called the Deutero-Isaiah, i.e., a second Isaiah, who is said to have written the sublime chapters 40—66. With this they did not stop. They found out that this Deutero-Isaiah only wrote chapters 40—55 and a Trito-Isaiah wrote the greater part of chapters 55—66. With their supposed learning they discovered that some of these chapters were written in Babylon and others in Palestine. Some of the most radical critics have even gone beyond this.

To give the result of the work of the critics, men like George Adams Smith, Canon Driver and A. B. Davidson, declare that out of the 66 chapters, which compose the book of Isaiah forty-four were not written by Isaiah. Others cut out more than that so that actually they claim out of the 1292 verses found in the book of Isaiah only 260 were penned by the prophet.

But what does all this mean? It is a denial of what is written in the first verse of this book. "The vision of Isaiah, the son of Amoz, which he saw concerning Judah and Jerusalem, in the days of Uzziah, Jotham, Ahaz and Hezekiah." And if several men wrote this book, if part was written during the Babylonian captivity and other parts added after the captivity, then this statement with which the book begins is untrue. This first verse assures us that the book is a whole, that all we find in it is the vision of one man. To deny this breaks down the truthfulness of the book and reduces it to the level of common literature. This is what the critics have done. But the book of Isaiah is quoted in the New Testament. The Jews always believed this book to have been written by Isaiah. They held this belief when our Lord was on the earth. He Himself read in the synagogue of Nazareth from chapter 61, which the critics deny to be the writing of Isaiah. Quotations from Isaiah are frequently found in different parts of the New Testament. Twenty-one times we read of Isaiah and his words in the New Testament. The phrases used are the following: "Spoken by the prophet Esaias"; "Fulfilled which was spoken by Esaias"; "Well did Esaias prophesy"; "In the book of the words of Esaias"; "As said the prophet Esaias"; "The saying of Esaias the prophet"; "These things said Esaias"; "Well spake the Holy Spirit by Esias"; "Esias also saith"; "Esias saith." This is evidence enough that the Lord and the Holy Spirit through the evangelists and the Apostle Paul set their seal to this uncontradicted and unanimous belief that Isaiah wrote this book. The critics by their methods impeach the testimony of the Lord Himself or charge the infallible Lord of Glory to have been limited in His knowledge and that He acquiesced in the current traditional belief of the Jewish people, knowing better Himself.

All the arguments of the critics are disproved by the book itself. One only needs to study this book and the careful study will bring out the unanswerable fact of the unity of the book of Isaiah. Only one person could have written such a book and that person did not write it by himself, but was the mouthpiece of Jehovah. This is the conclusion of an intelligent and spiritual study of the book itself. The silly and arbitrary restrictions the critics make, that Isaiah could not have written certain passages, because it was beyond his horizon, or that he could not have mentioned Cyrus, the Persian king, by name, over 150 years before he was born, springs from the subtle infidelity which is at the bottom of the destructive criticism, which denies the supernatural altogether.

Turning to the book we find that there are two great parts:

1. The earlier prophecies (1—35)
   Historical parenthesis (36—39)
2. The later prophecies (40—66)

In the first part we find that Isaiah witnessed against the moral and religious conditions of the people. Judgments are announced upon Jerusalem, Judah and upon the nations. Judgments to come are the leading features in the first 35 chapters. The blessings of the future after the execution of these judgments are also revealed, but they take a secondary place. We see in the first part the gathering of the storm-clouds, we hear the rolling thunders of divine judgment, and in the distance the calm and sunshine after the storm. The second part is introduced with the words of comfort, "Comfort ye, comfort ye, my people." While we read also of judgments in this part the great revelation of the later prophecies of Isaiah is the restoration which is in store for Jerusalem and the great blessings which the nations and the earth will receive when Jerusalem has been restored and her people redeemed.

In the first part the Assyrian is announced to come against Jerusalem. The Assyrian invasion stands in the foreground. This Assyrian enemy however is the prophetic type of another external foe, who appears in the endtime. Then the deliverance of Jerusalem is announced and the Assyrian completely overthrown. In the second part the Assyrian enemy is no longer mentioned. From this we conclude that these chapters were written after the Assyrian period. Israel's restoration from Babylon and from the greater dispersion which has lasted so long is predicted in the second part. The wonderful results of this restoration are here revealed. These two parts are therefore inseparable. The Isaiah who wrote of judgments is the Isaiah who makes known the blessings. The entire book gives the history of Israel, past, present and future. Both parts reveal Him who is the Holy One of Israel, the Redeemer. His incarnation, His obedience as God's servant, His rejection, His suffering and death, His second coming and kingdom rule are progressively revealed from chapters 1—66.

The division of the first part. If we omit chapters 36—39, which are historical, we find that the main divisions of the first part are three.

First division (1—12). In this division we find first Israel's sin and apostasy; their hardening; God's judgment upon them. This is followed by a vision concerning the future, 2:1-5. Six woes are pronounced in chapter 5 upon the apostate nation. We find the birth of the Redeemer announced. His Person, His work and His future glory are indicated. The Assyrian is mentioned for the first time; his pride and overthrow are pictured. The section closes with a vision of the future. The second coming of Christ, the restoration of the people Israel and what will come in blessing to the Gentiles and to creation is predicted. It closes with a beautiful song of praise, which redeemed Israel will sing in that day. Attention has often been called to the fact that the opening verses and chapters of a book give the key for the whole book. The first twelve chapters of Isaiah contain the whole book of Isaiah in embryo.

Second division (13—27). Here we find first the judgments upon different nations announced. Babylon's judgment stands in the foreground. When that final judgment falls upon Babylon and its king, Israel will find mercy and in a triumphant utterance celebrate the fall of the king of Babylon. All this has a meaning for the future. Then judgments are announced against other nations. Palestina, Moab, Damascus, Ethiopia, Egypt, Elam, Arabia and Tyre are mentioned. Eleven chapters, 13—23, are taken up with those judgments, which were only partially fulfilled in the past.

With the twenty-fourth chapter the subject of judgment is continued. Chapters 24—27 contain a great prophecy. The judgment announced is the coming judgment for this world when the Lord Jesus Christ appears the second time. All classes are affected by it and the high ones that are on high (Satan and his angels) and the kings on earth are involved in it. This portion ends with several songs of praise. The remnant of Israel praises Jehovah for deliverance and for His mercy to Jerusalem. Then there is a prophecy concerning the blessings of the future, when the Lord in connection with the blessing bestowed upon Israel will make a feast of fat things for all people. The last verse of this section announces once more the regathering of His scattered people to bring them back to Jerusalem. The great trumpet mentioned in 27:13 is the same of which the Lord speaks in Matthew 24:31, only our Lord tells us in addition that the angels will be used in this service.

Third division (28—35). In this section we find first six woes. The first section also contained six woes. The first woe is against Ephraim. Then follows the woe against Ariel (Jerusalem) that distress is to come upon this city. Blessing is promised after this visitation. Then there is a third woe against those who seek to hide their counsel from the Lord and their works are in the dark. The fourth woe is upon those who enter into an unholy alliance with Egypt, seek help there instead of the Lord. The fifth woe is directed against those who trust in the arm of flesh, in horses and chariots. The sixth woe is against the Assyrian destroyer. But alongside of these woes we find the promises of blessing to Israel in the future. A king is to reign in righteousness. The work of righteousness is to be peace. Jerusalem and Israel's land is to be desolate till the Spirit be poured out from on high, then the wilderness shall be a fruitful field (32:13-20). The 34th chapter is a great prophecy of the future day of the Lord when His indignation will be upon all nations and when His fury will be poured out upon all nations and when His fury will be poured out upon all their armies. It is the day of the Lord's vengeance and the year of recompenses for the controversy of Zion (verse 8). The last chapter in this section, chapter 35, shows again the future blessings for Israel and for the earth and the return of His people to Zion. And they come with singing. "And the ransomed of the Lord shall return, and come to Zion with songs and everlasting joy upon their heads; they shall obtain joy and gladness, and sorrow and sighing shall flee away."

We call attention to the fact that these three great sections follow the same course and end in the same way. The ending of each section reveals the restoration of Israel, the singing of the redeemed people and the blessing which will result from restored and blest Israel for the nations and for the earth.

In dividing the earlier prophecies of Isaiah into three sections we have not considered chapters 36—39. These chapters are of a historical character. Hezekiah's experience with the Assyrian invasion, Hezekiah's prayer, the prophet's message to the king, the destruction of the Assyrian army, the king's sickness and recovery and his fall into pride, are the contents of these four chapters. They may be looked upon as an appendix to the first part of Isaiah's vision and the preface to the second part. The Assyrian and his destruction is the culmination of the first part; the prediction of Isaiah concerning the Babylonian captivity (chapter 39:6-7) opens the way for the later prophecies.

The division of the second part. In these later prophecies we find likewise three great sections. However the character of the predictions found in the second part differs much from the earlier prophecies. The historical settings so prominent in the first part are entirely absent in the second. We briefly hint at the structure and contents of these three divisions.

The first division (40—48). This section begins with the message of comfort to Jerusalem. The first two verses of the fortieth chapter are the keynotes of the great symphony of Israel's future blessing and glory, which gradually breaks forth in this part, swelling higher and higher. "Comfort ye, comfort ye my people, saith your God. Speak ye comfortably to Jerusalem (literally: to the heart of Jerusalem) and cry unto her, that her warfare is accomplished, that her iniquity is pardoned; for she hath received of the Lord's hand double for all her sins." Throughout these later prophecies we find the comfort in store for His people, that their wanderings will end in restoration, their enemies will be conquered and their sins pardoned. Should it surprise anyone that the language employed in these great messages differs very much from the language of the first and earlier prophecies?

We find in this opening section a great deal of the majesty and glory of the God of Israel. A contrast is made between Israel's God and the idols of the nations. The one great proof brought forward is that the God of Israel has the power to predict future events. Read chapter 41:21-25. All this is spoken to encourage the faithful remnant of Israel to trust in Jehovah. In view of the Babylonian captivity, which Isaiah had announced this is of special meaning. Again and again Jehovah speaks in these chapters of Himself and His power to forgive, to save and to deliver. "I am He—the first and the last—I even I am the Lord; and beside me there is no saviour—I am the Lord your Holy One, the creator of Israel, your King—there is no God beside me—a just God and a Saviour"; these are a few of the direct utterances of Jehovah through Isaiah in this section. Jehovah has the power to save and to deliver His people.

Here we read of "the servant of Jehovah." It has a twofold meaning. The redeemed remnant of Israel is spoken of as the servant of the Lord. This is what Israel will be in the future. But this title as used in the opening verses of chapter 42 refers to Christ.

The people of Israel are prophetically seen in this section in Babylon but about to be delivered from Babylon. The great deliverer Cyrus, whom God called, is named in this portion of the book. The Lord who speaks of His power to tell the future things manifests this power in naming an unborn being and telling beforehand what his work was to be. Cyrus and his mission are recorded over 150 years before this Persian king was born and the record is found in chapter 44:24—45:25. Cyrus is called "the anointed"—"my shepherd"—"whose right hand Jehovah upholdeth"—"who performs all Jehovah's pleasure." He is likewise called "a ravenous bird from the east" (46:11). The return from Babylon is predicted to take place through the instrumentality of this king. But a greater restoration through a greater Anointed One, the Redeemer of Israel, is promised in these chapters. The end of the section looks forward to that great coming restoration. The last verse declares "there is no peace, saith the Lord, unto the wicked."

The second division (49—57). This section brings the servant of Jehovah prominently before us. It is no longer the redeemed Israel, nor Cyrus, but the Lord Jesus Christ comes fully into view. The opening verses of chapter 49 with which this division begins are again the keynote to the entire section. The Servant of the Lord is here called Israel, for He is the true Israel. In Him God is glorified. He Himself breaks out in the mournful complaint. "I have labored in vain, I have spent my strength for naught." He is called to bring Jacob to God, yet Israel is not gathered. But the Gentiles hear of Him, whom Israel refuses. "I will also give thee for a light to the Gentiles, that thou mayest be my salvation unto the end of the earth." All is indicated in these verses what the Servant of the Lord would do. His people, the nation, would despise Him and Israel would not be regathered at once but the Gentiles were to hear of Him. In chapter 50:4-11 we read again of Him. Here His suffering is mentioned more fully. "I gave My back to the smiters and My cheeks to them that plucked off the hair; I hid not My face from shame and spitting" (50:6). The last time this Servant, the Christ, is mentioned by Isaiah is in chapter 53. Here we find the marvellous portrait of Him who suffered, died as the sinbearer and of His exaltation. After the sublime fifty-third chapter the Servant of the Lord is not mentioned again.

This section also speaks of what is in store for Israel when at last they believe in Him whom they once despised. The most glorious promises follow the fifty-third chapter. The fifty-fourth chapter has never yet seen its fulfillment and can only be fulfilled when the remnant of Israel bows before the One whom they once despised. These chapters of this section look forward to their future blessing. The last verse of the second division is the same as the last verse of the first division, "There is no peace, saith my God, to the wicked."

The third division (58—66). This is the great finale of Isaiah's symphony of Israel's coming restoration and redemption. It is the most majestic and sublime portion of the book. Here the remnant of Israel takes a more leading part. While in the previous chapters of these prophecies we hear promises of restoration in this concluding division we see a small and feeble remnant actually back in the land. It has nothing to do with the small remnant which returned from Babylon. It is a remnant of believing Jews brought back to the land and suffering in the midst of the great tribulation which precedes the glorious manifestation of the Lord and the literal fulfillment of the promises of the blessing for Jerusalem. We have a record of their soul exercise, their troubles and their prayers in chapter 63:7—64:12. In chapter 64:1 they pray for the coming of the Lord. And that coming in great power and glory is described in this division. The Redeemer comes to Zion and He comes bringing the day of vengeance for all His enemies (chapter 59:20; 63:1-6). But who is able to expound the glorious things which are spoken of Jerusalem and the future of His redeemed people? Beginning with the sixtieth chapter we find an almost unbroken prediction of what is to be in the day when the Redeemer comes to Zion, what it will mean for His earthly people, for Jerusalem, for the nations and for all creation. This section is closely linked with certain predictions in the earlier prophecies; in fact, these closing chapters are expansions of the former vision of Isaiah as found in chapters 2:1-5; 11—12, and others. The last chapter is a resume of the great events predicted before. Here once more we read of the sudden manifestation of the Lord from heaven, the deliverance of the remnant of His people, the peace like a river for Jerusalem, the bringing back of the scattered sheep of Israel, the fiery judgments of the Lord and the conversion of the Gentiles. The last verse reveals the judgment upon the wicked. Their worm shall not die; their fire shall not be quenched. This fully corresponds with the ending of the two previous divisions, when the Lord saith, "there is no peace for the wicked."

The same order of revelation prevails in the second part of Isaiah as in the first. We have seen how every division in the first part closed with predictions of blessing for Israel, their restoration and the glory of Jerusalem as well as the blessings which the whole earth will receive when that has come to pass. The same revelation is contained on a larger scale in the second part. The same order of events is maintained. And how solemn it is that the each division of the later prophecies of Isaiah in the second part of his book closes with the declaration of the punishment, yea, the eternal punishment of the wicked. There is no peace for the wicked. Their worm dies not; their fire is not quenched. Evil teachers claim there is a restitution of all things including the wicked dead. Isaiah in his vision makes known what that promised restitution of all things is. The restoration of Israel; the restoration of Israel's land; the restoration of Jerusalem; peace for this earth; deliverance for groaning creation—all these he reveals. But solemnly God has said, "There is no peace for the wicked."

The great unity of the book of Isaiah proves that he wrote the entire book. The arrangement and contents tell us that it is not the work of man, but of the Spirit of God.

Messianic Predictions in Isaiah

It would be of much interest and profit if we could take up each division of this great prophetic book and study some of its revelations. This we cannot do. But we shall point out two great topics which are progressively revealed in the vision of Isaiah. We shall study first the messianic unfoldings in this book, and then the great coming events, such as Israel's future blessings in the earth and the blessings of the kingdom to come.

Of all the prophets Isaiah saw the most about Christ. Only the book of Psalms contains a larger number of messianic predictions. Every glory of our Lord and every phrase of His life on earth were beheld by this great man of God. His incarnation, His growing up in Nazareth, His public ministry, His message to the people, His rejection by the nation, His sufferings, the shame and the cross, His death with its meaning, His resurrection, His ascension, His glorious exaltation and future manifestation as well as His work as Prophet, Priest and King, are all found in this book. We shall point out some of these great predictions and the connection in which we find them.

The Redeemer promised is Jehovah Himself. That the Messiah is Jehovah Himself, who appears on earth in the midst of His people, God manifested in the flesh, is seen in this entire book. The call of Isaiah to the prophetic office was in a great vision in which he saw Jehovah and His glory (Chapter 6). Whom he beheld is explained in the Gospel of John, the Gospel which tells us so fully of the essential deity of the Lord Jesus. "These things said Esaias when he saw His glory and spake of Him" (John 12:41). He who was on the earth and whom His own received not is the One whose glory Isaiah saw in the temple vision.

He is called throughout Isaiah "the Holy One of Israel." Twenty-five times this title of the Lord, who deals in judgment and in mercy with His people, is found in Isaiah. Read 1:4; 5:19, 24; 10:20; 12:6; 17:7; 29:19; 30:11, 12, 15; 31:1; 37:23; 41:14, 16, 20; 43:3, 14; 45:11; 47:4; 48:17; 49:7; 54:5; 55:5; 60:9, 14. This phrase is found in only six other passages in the Old Testament. The Holy One of Israel is Jehovah; He is the Redeemer of His people. "Our Redeemer Jehovah of hosts is his name, the Holy One of Israel" (47:4). "Thus saith Jehovah, thy Redeemer, the Holy One of Israel" (48:17). This Holy One is the Creator. "The Holy One hath created it" (41:20). He hath stretched the heavens and laid the foundations of the earth (41:13). He appeared as the Holy One in their midst and they knew Him not but despised Him. In chapter 50:2-9 He is beheld as the One who clothes the heavens and who gives His back to the smiters. In chapter 49:7 the Redeemer, Jehovah, the Holy One, is seen as despised and abhorred by the nation. At His second coming Isaiah predicts Israel shall discover that the rejected and despised One is Jehovah. "Therefore My people shall know My Name, therefore they shall know that I am He" (52:6). The words "I am He" (Ani Hu) is a divine Name and our Lord used it when He said to the woman at the well "I am " and to the company in the garden Gethsemane.

In chapters 7 and 8 His name is revealed as "Immanuel," God with us. Throughout Isaiah's vision the Redeemer, the Anointed One who is rejected by the nation, who suffers and dies, who comes again to dwell in the midst of His people, is Jehovah.

His incarnation. The first messianic prediction in Isaiah relates to the incarnation of the Son of God. We find it in chapter 7:14. As it is well known its messianic character is denied by Jews and by the higher critics. The virgin birth is clearly predicted in these familiar words by Isaiah and the Holy Spirit in the first chapter of the New Testament tells us of the fulfillment of the words spoken by the Lord through Isaiah. In the first chapter of Luke the full announcement of the birth of Immanuel by the virgin is made by Gabriel to Mary. The rejection of this first great prophecy of the incarnation means the rejection of the incarnation itself.

Such alas! has been the case. We do not attempt to enter into the objections which are made against Isaiah 7:14. Not one of them has any foundation. The authority of the New Testament is sufficient to any believer.

The historic setting, however, is interesting and solves the problem why Isaiah received just this message at that time. Ahaz was threatened by King Pekah of Israel and by Rezin of Damascus, because he refused to make common cause with them against Assyria. He preferred the friendship of Assyria. When it became known that these two kings were planning an attack upon Jerusalem, Ahaz and the whole city were terror stricken. He decided at once to send to Assyria for help. How he sent messengers with valuable gifts to Tiglath-Pileser and called himself his servant and his son, is written in 2 Kings 16:7-8.

Isaiah was then told by God to meet Ahaz at the waterworks of Jerusalem and to take his son Shear-Jashub along. The meaning of this name is "the remnant shall return." In his interview with the king the prophet exhorts him to be true to Jehovah and that the house of David has nothing to fear. If he accepted the divinely given message he would be quiet and delivered of his fear and faint-heartedness. Then God offers Ahaz a sign, either in the depth or in the heights above. But the unbelieving king refused the offer. His wicked heart dreaded the consequences of such a sign. He did not want to be near to God and get a sign that God was near to him. He felt that in such a case he would have to abandon what God condemns and give up the alliance with the Assyrian. Then God gives the sign. It is the sign of the birth of the Messiah. The Deliverer is first announced in the Bible as being the seed of the woman; then as coming of the seed of Abraham from Isaac and Jacob; then of Judah and finally that He should be of the house of David. Here the prediction is narrowed down to the fact that He should be born of a virgin, necessarily of the house of David. Ahaz the King of Judah feared for Jerusalem and the royal line. He had no cause to fear for God promised David a son to come from his loins, He whom King David addressed as his Lord, the root and offspring of David. The house of David was perfectly secure. Thus the unbelief of Ahaz was made the occasion for this great prediction. Christ to be born of the virgin and yet "God manifested in the flesh."

In chapter 9:6 the incarnation is announced once more and in a prophetic vision it i seen as already accomplished, "For unto us a child is born, unto us a son is given." The child is the Son of the virgin and He is God's unspeakable gift, the Son. As Man born of the woman He will have the overnment upon His shoulder and possess the throne of David. This looks forward to His second coming. The Son given is the Wonderful, Counsellor, the Mighty God, the Everlasting Father, the Prince of Peace. His humanity and deity are here blended together.

His life and ministry on earth. The leading features of this blessed life and service on earth are revealed in Isaiah. We call attention to a few of the more prominent predictions.

His lowliness. He who was rich became poor for our sake. This poverty seems to be indicated in Isaiah 7:15, "butter and honey shall He eat." His lowliness is more fully predicted in 53:2, "For He shall grow up before Him as a tender plant, and as a root out of the dry ground; He hath no form and comeliness; and when we shall see Him, there is no beauty that we should desire Him."

The Servant of the Lord. As such He is filled with the Spirit. "And the Spirit of the Lord is upon Him, the Spirit of wisdom and understanding, the Spirit of counsel and might, the Spirit of knowledge and of the fear of the Lord" (11:2). "Behold My servant whom I uphold, Mine elect in whom my soul delighteth; I have put My Spirit upon Him" (42:1). His method is seen; He is unostentatious in His service. "He shall not cry, nor lift up, nor cause His voice to be heard in the street" (42:2-3). His loving tenderness. "A bruised seed shall He not break and the smoking flax shall He not quench; He shall bring forth judgment unto truth" (42:3). These words are applied to Him in the New Testament (Matthew 12:18-20). His obedience we find predicted in chapter 50:5: "The Lord hath opened mine ear, and I was not rebellious, neither turned away back." His message is given likewise. "The Spirit of the Lord God is upon me; because the Lord hath anointed me to preach good tidings unto the meek; He hath sent me to bind up the broken-hearted, to proclaim liberty to the captives, and the opening of the prison to them that are bound, to proclaim the acceptable year of the Lord" (61:1-2). It is a well known fact that our Lord read these words in the synagogue of Nazareth and pronounced them fulfilled. He also gives us a very important hint in reading this prediction. He stopped short in reading this passage. The rest belongs to His second coming. The first and second coming of Christ are repeatedly blended together.

As servant of the Lord He brings light. "The people that walked in darkness have seen a great light; they that dwell in the land of the shadow of death upon them hath the light shined" (Matthew 4:15-16).

His miracles are also touched upon. In chapter 35 we read: "Then the eyes of the blind shall be opened and the ears of the deaf shall be unstopped. Then shall the lame man leap as an hart, and the tongue of the dumb sing." When He appeared in the midst of His people He did these miracles to prove to the nation that He had the power of the kingdom in His hands; however Isaiah 35 looks forward to the kingdom, which is yet to come.

His rejection by the people Israel. This rejection was predicted by Isaiah. As already quoted in chapter 49:4, He is seen as despised and abhorred by the nation, so that He mournfully complains, "I have labored in vain, I have spent my strength for nought." On account of this rejection "Israel is not gathered" (verse 5). More fully is this rejection of the Servant of the Lord seen in the great fifty-third chapter. "He is despised and rejected of men; a man of sorrows and acquainted with grief; and we hid as it were our faces from Him; He was despised and we esteemed Him not."

His mission to the Gentiles. While Israel is predicted to reject this servant, the Gentiles are to see His light and rejoice in His salvation. It is true most of these predictions await His future work, when He comes again and the Gentiles will be given to Him for an inheritance, but they also imply what is now in force. "I the Lord have called thee in righteousness, and will hold thine hand and keep thee, and give thee for a covenant of the people, for a light of the Gentiles" (42:6-7). "It is a light thing that Thou shouldest be My servant to raise up the tribes of Jacob and to restore the desolations of Israel that Thou mayest be my salvation to the end of the earth" (49:6). Through Him Gentiles are saved now and when He comes again even the ends of the earth will know Him and He will reign over the Gentiles. Unto Him every knee must bow and every tongue shall swear (45:23).

The sufferings of Christ. It was given to Isaiah to behold 700 years before the Son of God appeared on earth an almost complete picture of the sufferings of Christ and their vicarious character. How the obedient servant was to be treated by men is for the first time mentioned in chapter 50:6: "I gave My back to the smiters and My cheeks to them that plucked off the hair, I hid not My face from shame and spitting." But the great revelation of the sufferings of Christ is found in the famous fifty-third chapter. It is the culmination of the second part of Isaiah. The center of the chapter is "brought as a Lamb to the slaughter." The most ancient as well as reliable Jewish expositors apply the chapter to Messiah. The great expositors of the Church in the past have all read the story of the cross of Christ in this chapter. The New Testament repeatedly quotes Isaiah 53 and knows no other fulfillment than in Him, who was the man of sorrows.

The Spirit-filled evangelist Philip heard the eunuch reading from this chapter and then opened his mouth and preached Jesus unto him. The infidel Jews have invented a theory which teaches that the nation's sufferings are described and not the Messiah's. This wicked denial the destructive critics have fully indorsed.

The last three verses of chapter 52 belong to the fifty-third chapter. If we count them to the great chapter we find five progressive parts: 1. The Servant—His suffering and His exaltation, so that the nations are astonished at Him and kings shut their mouths. It is the keynote of the prediction that follows (52:13-15). 2. His life and His rejection by the nation (53:1-3). 3. His sufferings; smitten, afflicted, wounded and bruised (53:4-6). 4. His submission and His deliverance (53:7-9). 5. His glorious reward (53:10-12).

But what is all contained in this matchless chapter! We have in it a description of the Servant, the vicarious sufferer, the triumphant victor as nowhere else. Twelve great statements are made concerning His work on the cross: 1. He hath borne our griefs. 2. Carried our sorrows. 3. He was wounded for our transgressions. 4. Bruised for our iniquities. 5. The chastisement of our peace was upon Him. 6. With His stripes we are healed. 7. The Lord has laid on Him the iniquity of us all. 8. For the transgression of my people was He smitten.

9. Made His soul an offering for sin. 10. He shall bear their iniquities. 11. He bears the sin of many. 12. Made intercession for the transgressors.

His holy, spotless character is revealed. As a lamb He suffered in patience. He had done no violence nor was deceit in His mouth. He suffered and died for others. He suffered for His people (John 11:50-51). It was God who smote Him, the Lord who bruised Him, who put Him to grief. There is in the whole Bible no grander unfolding of John 3:16 than this great chapter. Whoever rejects Isaiah's vision of the Sinbearer, rejects the gospel and denies the atoning work of the cross.

We also behold His grave, we see Him risen in this chapter, exalted, interceding, justifying many, having a seed, an offspring as the last Adam, securing the travail of His soul and dividing the spoil with the great. Ah! who can tell out the majestic grandeur of this great peak in God's revelation! After this great vision, the Servant of the Lord is not mentioned again, nor His sufferings. The glory side comes more fully in view in chapters 54—66. And it will be fully realized when Israel has confessed Him, whom they once rejected.

The predictions of glory and the second coming of Christ. More numerous and richer are the messianic predictions, which reveal His exaltation and the fact of His glorious second coming.

Isaiah beheld His personal, visible and glorious coming, not as the sufferer but as the King. He saw Him coming in majesty and glory. His glory is seen in these visions as covering Jerusalem and the land and eventually the whole earth. He comes to Zion to redeem His people and deliver them out of the hands of their enemies. He comes to overthrow the wicked one and to execute the judgments of God on the earth. He comes to establish peace and dwell in the midst of His people and rule as King over the nations. We can call attention to a very few of the many predictions from different chapters; our remaining study will bring this great theme more fully to our view.

"He shall judge among the nations and shall rebuke many people; and they shall beat their swords into plowshares and their spears into pruninghooks; nation shall not lift up sword against nation, neither shall they learn war any more" (2:4). This is the program of God. Peace on earth will thus be accomplished. It follows His visible manifestation. He appears in the glory of His majesty and will alone be exalted in that day (2:10, 11). His glory will cover Jerusalem (4:5). "With righteousness shall He judge the poor and reprove with equity for the meek in the earth; and He shall smite the earth with the rod of His mouth and with the breath of His lips shall He slay the wicked" (11:4). "The earth shall be full of the knowledge of the Lord, as the waters cover the sea" (11:9). "Cry out and shout, thou inhabitant of Zion; for great is the Holy One of Israel in the midst of thee" (12:6). "I will punish the world for their evil and the wicked for their iniquity" (13:11). "Therefore I will shake the heavens, and the earth shall remove out of her place in the wrath of the Lord of Hosts, and in the day of His fierce anger" (13:13). "The Lord of hosts shall reign in Mount Zion and in Jerusalem and before his ancients gloriously" (24:23). "And it shall be said in that day, Lo this is our God, we have waited for Him and He will save us; this is the Lord we have waited for Him, we will be glad and rejoice in His salvation" (25:9). "The Lord cometh out of His place to punish the inhabitants of earth for their iniquity" (26:21). "Behold a King shall reign in righteousness" (32:1). "And the Glory of the Lord shall be revealed and all flesh shall see it together (40:5). "And the Redeemer shall come to Zion, and unto them that turn from transgression in Jacob, saith the Lord" (59:20). "Arise, shine for thy light is come and the glory of the Lord is risen upon thee" (60:1).

"Who is this that cometh from Edom, with dyed garments from Bozrah? this that is glorious in His apparel, traveling in the greatness of his strength? I that speak in righteousness, mighty to save. Wherefore art Thou red in thine apparel, and Thy garments like him that treadeth in the winefat? I have trodden the wine-press alone; and of the people there was none with Me: for I will tread them in Mine anger, and trample them in My fury; and their blood shall be sprinkled upon My garments, and I will stain all My raiment. For the day of vengeance is in Mine heart, and the year of My redeemed is come. And I looked, and there was none to help; and I wondered that there was none to uphold: therefore Mine own arm brought salvation unto Me; and My fury, it upheld Me. And I will tread down the people in Mine anger, and make them drunk in My fury, and I will bring down their strength to the earth" (63:1-6).

"For behold, the Lord will come with fire, and with His chariots like a whirlwind, to render His anger with fury, and His rebuke with flames of fire. For by fire, and by His sword, will the Lord plead with all flesh: and the slain of the Lord shall be many. For I know their works and their thoughts; it shall come, that I will gather all nations and tongues; and they shall come, and see My glory. And I will set a sign among them, and I will send those that escape of them unto the nations, to Tarshish, Pul, and Lud, that draw the bow, to Tubal and Javan, to the isles afar off, that have not heard My fame, neither have seen My glory; and they shall declare My glory among the Gentiles" (66:15-16; 18-19).

These are a few of Isaiah's predictions concerning the future glory of our Lord and the work of judgment and mercy He will execute. May it be our delight to meditate on these great prophetic unfoldings of the Person and the glorious work of our Lord, till some day we shall be face to face with Himself and through grace become partakers of His glory.

Future Glories and Blessings

The book of Isaiah abounds in great predictions of glories and blessings in store for this earth and its inhabitants. Not one of these have been fulfilled in the past, nor are they now in process of fulfillment. They must therefore be fulfilled in the future. To this we might add that not one of these great predictions can be fulfilled till the predicted judgments have taken place.

Isaiah uses some 45 times the phrase "in that day." He uses these words almost exclusively in the earlier prophecies contained in chapters 1—35. This day is the day when Jehovah is manifested and when He deals in judgment with the earth. We give a few of the more prominent passages in which that day is mentioned (chapter 2:10-22). Here the day is described as bringing the exaltation of the Lord and the utter casting down of all that is lofty and high (chapter 13:9-13). These words tell us that it is the day in which the world will be punished for its wickedness and that heaven and earth will be shaken (chapter 24). In this great judgment chapter we read that all classes will be affected by it, the earth will reel to and fro like a drunkard and be removed like a cottage. Then the kings on earth will be punished. The high ones on high, the wicked spirits in the heavenlies, will be shut up in prison. This great day Isaiah beheld is the day "when the Lord Jesus shall be revealed from heaven with His mighty angels in flaming fire taking vengeance on them that know not God, and that obey not the gospel of our Lord Jesus Christ." Such a day has not yet been. It will surely come. Never before have things been so ripe for that day as they are now.

Whatever we find in future glories and blessings in Isaiah is always in connection with that day. The glories and blessings do not precede that day, but the day precedes the glories and blessings promised. Therefore we say the fulfillment of these great predictions has not been in the past, they are not now being fulfilled and they cannot be fulfilled till the storm clouds of divine judgment have swept over this earth and the Lord has been manifested.

The great majority of Christians hold the unscriptural view that in the Church and through the Church the visions of Isaiah are fulfilled in a spiritual way. But they forget the great day in Isaiah and the fact stated that the glories and blessings predicted follow that day.

What then are these predicted glories and blessings? We find that the larger number of them belong to the people Israel. We look at these first.

The future blessings of Israel. This wonderful people has a wonderful future. God has not cast them away and to them still belong the promises and the glory. Israel is set aside throughout this present age and judicially blinded. Isaiah had to announce this fact. We find that in the vision which called him into the prophetic office the message was given to him that the nation should not hear and that their eyes should be blinded. The consummation of this predicted blindness came after they had rejected Christ. We find these words of Isaiah (6:10) quoted three times in the New Testament. In Matthew 23:13-15. Israel had then rejected Him and He began to teach the mysteries of the kingdom of heaven in parables. In John 12:40 when the Lord was about to suffer and to die. In Acts 28:27 at the close of the book of Acts after the gospel had been preached to them by the Holy Spirit come down from heaven. They rejected it and the last statement of the Apostle of the Gentiles, who loved his people so well, is a significant one, "the salvation of God is sent unto the Gentiles and they will hear it." Since then the message Isaiah received has been fully carried out. They are judicially blinded and scattered among the nations. Their land is desolate. Their city is trodden down by the Gentiles. Their sufferings and woes have been indescribable. God has hidden His face from them and in His wrath He has forsaken them.

But Isaiah's vision tells us likewise that this condition is not to be permanent. The curse will be changed into blessing and they will receive double for all their sin.

Their restoration to the land. They will be brought back to the land. In chapter 11:10-12 we find one of these unfulfilled predictions of Israel's restoration. It has been taught that these words were fulfilled in the return of the remnant from Babylon. Notice, however, that it saith "and gather together the dispersed of Judah from the four corners of the earth." It speaks of a gathering from a world-wide dispersion, not from the Babylonian captivity. It includes the islands of the sea and it is distinctly stated that the Lord shall set His hand again the *second* time to recover the remnant of His people. The entire chapter shows that it is a future thing.

In chapter 14:1-2 is another unfulfilled prediction. "For the Lord will have mercy on Jacob and will yet choose Israel, and set them in their own land." The nations are mentioned as helping them to return. This fact is indicated elsewhere in Isaiah (chapters 18:7, 66:20). This regathering is stated in 27:13. "And it shall come to pass in that day, that the great trumpet shall be blown and they shall come which were ready to perish in the land of Assyria, and the outcasts in the land of Egypt and shall worship the Lord in the holy mount of Jerusalem." Also read 35:10; 43:5-6; 49:10-12. All the great predictions in the later prophecies concerning Israel's glorious state in the land make such a regathering necessary.

The spiritual blessings. The calling of Israel as a nation is stated in Exodus 19:5-6. "Now therefore if ye will obey my voice, indeed, and keep my covenant, then ye shall be a peculiar treasure unto me, above all people, for all the earth is mine. And ye shall be unto me a kingdom of priests and a holy nation." Up to now this has never been; yet God's gifts and calling are without repentance. The day is coming when the Lord in His infinite grace will bestow upon the remnant of His people such spiritual blessings, that they will be healed of all their backslidings and become a holy nation and a kingdom of priests in the earth.

This is beautifully revealed in the first song of redemption in chapter 12. Closely connected with their regathering predicted in the preceding chapter is their grateful expression for the spiritual blessings they received. His anger is turned away, comfort has come at last. They sing and praise for Jehovah has done excellent things. Then the Lord gives them rest from their sorrows, fear and hard bondage (14:3). The songs of redemption in chapters 25—26 celebrate the same blessings. The forgiveness of their sins is promised in chapter 33:24, "the people that dwell therein shall be forgiven their iniquity." "I, even I, am He that blotteth out thy transgressions for mine own sake, and will not remember thy sins" (43:25). "I have blotted out, as a thick cloud, thy transgressions, and, as a cloud, thy sins return unto me, for I have redeemed thee" (44:22). This is followed by a song. "I will bring near My righteousness; it shall not be far off, and My salvation shall not tarry and I will place salvation for Israel My glory" (46:13). Read also 54:6-10. Then the Spirit of God will be poured out upon them. This is promised in chapter 32:15. The promise is connected with their restoration to the land. The same promise is found in chapter 59:20-21. First the Redeemer comes to Zion and the Spirit is promised unto Israel and Israel's seed. These great future blessings are especially revealed in chapters 61 and 62. "But ye shall be named the priests of the Lord, men shall call you the ministers of our God." Thus their priestly calling among the nations will be realized. But when? After the day of vengeance, the second coming of the Lord (verse 2). The same blessings are stated in verses 7 and 10. Then they shall be called "the holy people," "the redeemed of the Lord" (62:12). In one day the new birth of the nation will take place (66:8).

But let us understand that these blessings are not for the apostate portion of the nation. Millennial Dawnism, as well as others, claims that all Israel will receive these blessings, not alone the wicked element which sides with the man of sin and worships him, but also all the past generations who died in their sins will be raised up and brought back to the land and possess these things. No such teaching is found in the Word. Ezekiel 37, the vision of the raising up of the dry bones, has nothing to do with a physical resurrection; it is a type of their national restoration. Ezekiel 20:38 makes it clear that the rebels, the apostates, will have no share in these blessings. These will not enter into the land saith the Lord. Two parts of the people will be cut off and die and the third part only shall be brought through the fire.

The blessings for Israel's land. The land of Israel, Palestine, is called by Isaiah "Immanuel's land" (8:8). Desolation has come upon it on account of the transgressions of the people. It is now an unfruitful land, a land of wastes and ruins. But there is a glorious future for Immanuel's land and He who lived His blessed life in that land, where He shed His blood and died, will also make it a glorious land. We can only link a few passages together where this is promised. Read 30:23-26; 60:17-22; 61:4; 62:4-5; 65:21-24.

The future of Jerusalem. Jerusalem, still trodden down by the Gentiles, has a glorious future. It will become the great capital of the kingdom, which will cover the whole earth. In chapter 1 Isaiah speaks of Jeusalem as a harlot and that murderers dwell in it. This is true now and blood-guiltiness rests upon it. But *afterward,* Isaiah announces, "thou shalt be called the city of righteousness, the faithful city." That will be after the Lord has come. Then "out of Zion shall go forth the law and the Word of the Lord from Jerusalem" (2:3). The Holy One of Israel will make His dwelling place there and cover it with His glory (4:2-6; 11:9-10; 12:6; 24:23). Then they will rejoice on account of it. "In that day shall this song be sung in the land of Judah; we have a strong city; salvation will God appoint for walls and bulwarks" (26:1). 33:20-21 shows another picture of Zion and Jerusalem. Also 54:11-14; Jerusalem will be a praise in the earth (62:7). "But be glad and rejoice forever in that which I create; for behold I create Jerusalem a rejoicing, and her people a joy. And I will rejoice in Jerusalem and joy in My people, and the voice of weeping shall no more be heard in her, nor the voice of crying" (65:18-19). What a beautiful word this is! His people rejoice in Him and He rejoices in them. Jerusalem has become at last the place of joy and peace and Jerusalem is His joy. Then He will fully have the travail of His soul and be satisfied. Once more Jerusalem is mentioned in the last chapter. "Rejoice ye with Jerusalem, and be glad with her, all ye that love her, rejoice for joy with her, all ye that mourn for her" (66:10). The nations redeemed will rejoice. But we may well think of the joy of the glorified saints, including all the saints, both the Old Testament and New Testament saints. They all loved Jerusalem. We love Jerusalem, and when He rejoices in the accomplishment of His purposes we shall rejoice with Him. His joy will be our joy in glory.

The future blessings of the nations. Closely linked with these great future blessings and glories for Israel His people are the blessings of the Gentiles. The many predictions which concern the Gentiles cannot be fulfilled till Israel and Jerusalem have entered into their blessing. The conversion of the world is nowhere taught to take place in this present age through the church, but it is always found in connection with converted Israel. This is an important principle. The day of the Lord will bring great judgments for the Gentile world. When these judgments are in the earth the inhabitants of the world will learn righteousness (chapter 26:9). The Lord will deal in great and world-wide judgments with the Gentiles, especially with those which had the light and turned from the light. But there will be Gentiles who turn to God during these great judgments and believe the testimony, the gospel of the kingdom, preached at that time (Matthew 24:14). What are the blessings promised to these nations? We touch upon a few. In chapter 2:2-4 we find one of the most comprehensive. The nations will go up to that house of the Lord, which is yet to be built and which will be, according to another prophecy, a house of prayer for all nations. This great prediction is sadly spiritualized. It is applied to the church; and the fulfillment was, it is claimed, when the Lord selected the twelve apostles on a mountain. It has nothing whatever to do with the church nor with the church age. When Jerusalem has been restored, the nations which are left will go there to worship. Then war will end and not before. This is God's peace program. In 11:9-10 we read that the earth will be filled with the knowledge of the Lord and the Gentiles will seek Him. The great things, which He hath done, will be known in all the earth (12:5). Greater still is the vision of chapter 15:6-8. A feast of fat things will be made. Now God has spread the gospel feast and invites all to come. "Come, for all things are now ready." But the invitation to this feast will soon end. Then comes "the supper of the great God," a fearful judgment to which the fowls of heaven are invited (Rev:19:16-18). This is followed by the feast of all peoples. The veil which is now over the heathen nations will be destroyed and all tears will be wiped away; the tears of sickness, the tears of want, the tears of affliction, the tears of sorrow. The gathering of the nations will be to Israel; they will be joined to them and thus the kingdom will extend over the whole earth. "Lift up thine eyes round about and behold, all these gather themselves together and come to thee" (49:18). World conversion, the multitude of nations brought to the knowledge of God (not into the Church) is beautifully predicted in chapter 60. First we see the glory of the Lord shining forth; this is His second coming. But in what state does He find the earth? "Behold, darkness shall cover the earth and gross darkness the people." This is the apostasy, the moral and spiritual darkness the Lord will find on the earth. It will soon be changed by His glorious appearing. The Gentiles will then be brought to that light.

"And the Gentiles shall come to thy light, and kings to the brightness of thy rising. Lift up thine eyes round about, and see; all they gather themselves together, they come to thee: thy sons shall come from far, and thy daughters shall be nursed at thy side. Then thou shalt see, and flow together, and thine heart shall fear, and be enlarged; because the abundance of the sea shall be converted unto thee, the forces of the Gentiles shall come unto thee. The multitude of camels shall cover thee, the dromedaries of Midian and Ephah; all they from Sheba shall come: they shall bring gold and incense; and they shall show forth the praises of the Lord. All the flocks of Kedar shall be gathered together unto thee, the rams of Nebaioth shall minister unto thee: they shall come up with acceptance on Mine altar, and will glorify the house of My glory. Who are these that fly as a cloud, and as the doves to their windows? Surely the isles shall wait for me, and the ships of Tarshish first, to bring thy sons from far, their silver and their gold with them, unto the name of the Lord thy God, and to the Holy One of Israel, because He hath glorified thee. And the sons of strangers shall build up thy walls, and their kings shall minister unto thee; for in My wrath I smote thee, but in My favor have I had mercy on thee. Therefore thy gates shall be open continually; they shall not be shut day nor night; that men may bring unto thee the forces of the Gentiles, and that their kings may be brought. For the nation and kingdom that will not serve thee shall perish; yea, those nations shall be utterly wasted" (60:3-12).

This is the vision of the kingdom to come. That coming age, introduced by the visible and glorious coming of Christ, will mean the end of idolatry and the worshipping of the Lord. "All flesh shall come to worship before Me, saith Jehovah" (66:23).

The blessings for all creation. In Romans 8 we read of the future and complete deliverance of groaning creation. It will come with the manifestation of the sons of God. That manifestation takes place when the Lord Jesus Christ comes again. He who created all things and whose creation was marred by sin; He who came into His creation and died for the creature's sin, will in that coming day deliver creation from its curse. The blessings of a delivered creation were beheld by Isaiah.

"The wolf also shall dwell with the lamb, and the leopard shall lie down with the kid; and the calf and the young lion and the fatling together; and a little child shall lead them. And the cow and the bear shall feed; their young ones shall lie down together: and the lion shall eat straw like the ox. And the sucking child shall play on the hole of the asp, and the weaned child shall put his hand on the cockatrice' den" (11:6-8).

Also read chapter 65:25. Only the serpent will continue to crawl in the dust as an abiding witness of Satan and sin; also as a warning, for after the kingdom age Satan will be loosed for a little season (Rev. 20:7).

All waits for the coming of these great blessings and glories. We insist again that they cannot come till "that day" of Isaiah's vision has appeared. It will surely come, though it has tarried long. Judgment ends the present age and blessings for Israel, the nations and all creation are the characteristics of the age to come. The church and her heavenly destiny was not seen by Isaiah. In the New Testament we read exclusively of the church, how it began and how it will suddenly end. When the predicted judgments smite the earth the true Church is gathered home and is in His presence. Her destiny is not an earthly kingdom, an earthly Jerusalem, but with the King, the Lord of Glory in the heavenly Jerusalem. The destiny of the church is not to be ruled over in the kingdom, but to rule over the kingdom. May God's Spirit give unto us the power to enjoy these great revelations and rejoice in them even before they are accomplished.

THE ACTORS OF THE PERIOD OF ISAIAH

Chronologically Arranged

Before Christ	
765	Isaiah born
789-740	Uzziah
784-745	Jeroboam II
745-727	Tiglath-pileser III
740	The call of Isaiah's vision, chapter 6
740-736	Jotham
738	Arpad, Calno, Carchemish and Damascus taken by Tiglath-pileser III
745-737	Menahem
737-736	Pekahiah
736-730	Pekah
736-727	Ahaz
734	Syro-Ephraimitic war; Gaza captured by Tiglath-pileser III; Galilee carried captive to Assyria
732	Damascus taken by Tiglath-pileser III
730-722	Hoshea
727-699	Hezekiah
727-722	Shalmaneser IV
722	Fall of Samaria; end of the kingdom of Israel
722-705	Sargon II
721-709	Babylonia under Merodach-Baladan
720	Battle of Karkar; Sargon II conquers Arpad, Hammath and Damascus. Battle of Raphia
717	Sargon II conquers the Hittites, takes Carchemish, their capital
714	Hezekiah's sickness
712	Merodach-Baladan sent messengers to Hezekiah
711	Siege of Ashdod by Sargon II
709	Merodach-Baladan driven from Babylonia by Sargon II
705-681	Sennacherib
703	Merodach-Baladan again king over Babylonia
701	Siege of Jerusalem by Sennacherib; Judah, Moab, Edom, Ammon and Philistia made to pay tribute. Tirhakah (afterwards "king of Ethiopia") head of the Egyptian army under Shabaka
699-643	Manasseh, king of Judah. Tradition claims that under Manasseh, Isaiah suffered martyrdom

THE PROPHET
JEREMIAH

Introduction

This book starts with information concerning the person of Jeremiah, the time when he was called to the office of a prophet, and the period of time during which he exercised his ministry.

Jeremiah means "exalted of the Lord," or, "established by the Lord." He was the son of Hilkiah. Some have identified the father of Jeremiah with the high-priest Hilkiah, who was such a power in Josiah's great reformation work. This is incorrect. The high-priest Hilkiah was of the line of Eleazar, as recorded in 1 Chronicles 6:4,13. The father of the prophet Jeremiah was, we read in the first verse of this book, of the priests that were in Anathoth; the priests who lived there were of the line of Ithamar. (See 1 Kings 2:26; 1 Chronicles 24:3, 6.) Anathoth, the home of Jeremiah, was in Benjamin, about three miles northeast of Jerusalem.

The first time the Word of the Lord came to young Jeremiah, for he was but a child, was in the thirteenth year of King Josiah, or just a year after the eventful reformation accomplished by that good man. We know but little of the activity of the prophet during the subsequent reign of Josiah. Only one message is timed "in the day of Josiah the King" (3:6). In the history of that illustrious king of Judah, we read nothing of Jeremiah, with the exception of the brief statement "and Jeremiah lamented for Josiah" (2 Chron. 35:25). It seems that the third verse gives the period covering the larger part of the ministry of this prophet. The Word of the Lord came unto him "also in the days of Jehoiakim, the son of Josiah, king of Judah, unto the end of the eleventh year of Zedekiah, the son of Josiah, the king of Judah, unto the carrying away of Jerusalem captive in the fifth month."

The book which bears this prophet's name abounds in personal allusions. In fact no other prophet in his character, in the exercise of his soul, and in his experience is so fully portrayed as Jeremiah; not even Ezekiel and Daniel whom, with Habakkuk and Zephaniah, were his contemporaries. The study of this great man of God is deeply interesting.

He has been called "the weeping prophet" and is generally known by that name. No other prophet wept like Jeremiah. That outburst in his lamentations, "For these things I weep; mine eye, mine eye, runneth down with water" (Lam. 1:16) shows how tender hearted he was, and how his tears flowed freely. But he was something else beside the weeping prophet. He was a man of great courage, with the boldness of a lion. In the presence of His Lord he was prostrate and broken, one who trembled at His Word, filled with godly fear. He was a man of prayer and faith in the Lord and faithful in the discharge of his great commission.

His Life of Service and Suffering

His lot was one of great solitude; he was divinely commanded to remain unmarried (16:2). He was forbidden to enter the house of joy and feasting (16:8). Reproach and derision were his daily portion (20:8). He was betrayed by his own kindred (12:6), and his fellow citizens at Anathoth wanted to kill him (11:21). Then, in the first part of his book, we read of the inner struggles he had, the spiritual conflict, when everybody was against him. In the bitterness of his spirit he spoke of himself as "a man of contention to the whole earth" (15:10). He even doubted whether his whole work was not a delusion and a lie (20:7), and like Job he cursed the day of his birth (20:14). When the Chaldeans came to the front and Jeremiah heard from the Lord that Nebuchadnezzar was called as His servant to receive the dominion from His hands (27:6), Jeremiah urged submission. This stamped him as a traitor. False prophets appeared who contradicted him with their false messages; he committed his cause to the Lord. On one occasion when the temple courts were filled with thousands of worshippers, he appeared and uttered the message that Jerusalem would be a curse, that the temple should share the fate of the tabernacle at Shiloh (26:6). Then the great conflict began. The priests, the false prophets and the people demanded his death (26:8). The Lord graciously protected him through chosen instruments. Still greater were his sufferings under Zedekiah. His struggles with the false prophets continued; they called him a madman

(29:26), and urged his imprisonment. He then appeared in the streets of Jerusalem with bonds and yokes upon his neck (27:2), showing the coming fate of Judah. A false prophet broke the offensive symbol and gave a lying message that the Chaldeans should be destroyed within two years. Then the Egyptian army approached, and the Chaldeans hastened away; it created a dangerous condition for Jeremiah. He sought to escape to his home town Anathoth; it was discovered, and he was charged with falling to the Chaldeans as others did (37:14). In spite of his denial, he was thrown into a dungeon. Later he was thrown into the prison pit by the princes to die there. From that horrible fate he was again mercifully delivered. When the city fell, Nebuchadnezzar protected his person (39:11), and after being carried away with other captives as far as Ramah, he set him free. It was left to him whether he would go to Babylon to live under the special protection of the king, or remain in the land with the governor Gedaliah. He chose the latter. But Gedaliah was murdered by Ishmael and his associates. Then the people forced him to emigrate with them to Egypt. The last glimpse of the prophet's life we have of him is in Tahpanhes, uttering there a final protest and a great message. Nothing is known of the details of his death.

"He is preeminently the man that hath seen afflictions (Lam. 3:1). He witnessed the departure one by one, of all his hopes of national reformation and deliverance. He is forced to appear as a prophet of evil, dashing to the ground the false hopes with which the people were deluded. Other prophets, Samuel, Elisha, Isaiah, had been sent to arouse the people to resistance. He has been brought to the conclusion, bitter as it is, that the only safety for his people lies in their acceptance of that which they think is the worst evil, that brings on him the charge of treachery. If it were not for his trust in the God of Israel, for his hope of a better future to be brought out of all this chaos and darkness, his heart would fail within him. But that vision is clear and bright, and it gives to him, almost as fully as to Isaiah, the character of a prophet of glory. He is not merely an Israelite looking forward to a national restoration. In the midst of all the woes he utters against the nearby nations, he has hopes and promises for them also. In that stormy sunset of prophecy, he beholds, in spirit, the dawn of a brighter day. He sees that, if there is any hope of salvation for his people, it cannot be by a return to the old system and the old ordinances, divine though they had once been. There must be a new covenant. That word, destined to be so full of power for after ages, appears first in his prophecies. The relations between the people and the Lord of Israel, between mankind and God, must rest, not on an outward law, with its requirements of obedience, but on an inward fellowship with Him and the consciousness of entire dependence. For all this the prophet saw clearly there must be a personal center. The kingdom of God could not be manifested but through a perfect righteous man, ruling over men on earth. They gather round the person of Christ, the Jehovah Zdidkenu—the Lord our Righteousness, the Son of David, Israel's coming king."

The Authorship of Jeremiah

The book begins with "The words of Jeremiah," and it closes with chapter 51:64 with the statement, "thus far are the words of Jeremiah." The final chapter is an addition of a historical character. That Jeremiah must be the author of the greater part of the book is proven by the many personal references which only the prophet himself could have written. No other prophet was so frequently commanded to write as Jeremiah was. "Write thee all the words that I have spoken unto thee in a book" (30:2). "Take thee the roll of a book and write therein all the words that I have spoken" (36:2). Then Baruch witnessed that he wrote all these words which came from Jeremiah's lips in a book (36:18); and when the roll was burned the Lord said, "Take thee again another roll, and write in it all the former words that were in the first roll" (36:28). "So Jeremiah wrote in a book" (51:60). Who are the men who try to make us believe that Jeremiah did not write these words? Baruch, his secretary, who took the dictations from the lips of the prophet (36:27) may have arranged, under the direction of Jeremiah, the different prophecies. The language used is the language of his time and is tinged with Aramaic. The style does not compare with that of Isaiah.

There are, of course, many difficulties in connection with the text. For instance, the Greek version (the Septuagint) differs more widely from the Hebrew than that of any other portion of the Old Testament. Numerous passages like 7:1-2, 17:1-4, 23:14-26, etc., are omitted in the Greek version. Inasmuch as the Hebrew is the oldest and the Septuagint was made from the Hebrew, the latter is the correct text. The critical school has made much out of these apparent difficulties and the disorder and unchronological character of the book. Therefore Jeremiah has suffered just as much in the dissecting room of the destructive critics as Isaiah and Moses. Thus Peake in his commentary on Jeremiah uses nine symbolic letters to show which is which.

J. Which stands for the prophecies of which Jeremiah is most likely the author. *S.* This stands for certain supplementers. *JS.* This stands for the words of Jeremiah worked over by a supplementer; nobody knows who he was. *B.* This means Baruch and his production. *BS.* This means that Baruch's words were supplemented by some more unknown supplementers. *R.* This stands for Redactor, whoever he was. *I.* Here we have an unknown author who, according to the critics, wrote chapter 10:1-6. *K.* Here is another unknown gentleman, the author of 17:19, etc. *E.* This letter denotes extracts from 2 Kings.

It is of little interest to quote the ramblings of Duhm, Ryssell, Hitizig, Renan and others about the authorship and compilation of Jeremiah. Not one of these scholars agrees. They have theories but no certainties. How simple it is to believe the beginning and the end of this book, that here are "the words of Jeremiah." And though King Jehoiakim tried to destroy these words, they still live and they will live on in our days, in spite of the successors of the wicked king, the professors of apostasy, who are trying to give Christendom an abridged Bible.

That the book appears disjointed and is unchronological is no argument against its authenticity. The *Companion Bible* gives the following: "The prophecies of Jeremiah do not profess to be given in chronological order; nor is there any reason why they should be so given. Why, we ask, should modern critics first assume that they ought to be, and then condemn them because they are not? It is the historical portions, which concern Jehoiakim and Zedekiah that are chiefly so affected; and who was Jehoiakim that his history should be of any importance? Was it not he who cut up the Word of the Lord with a penknife and cast it into the fire? Why should not his history be cut up? Zedekiah rejected the same Word of Jehovah. Why should his history be respected?"

The Message of Jeremiah

His message is first a message which charges the people with having forsaken Jehovah. The sins of the people are uncovered, especially the sins of false worship and idolatry. Connected with this are the appeals to return unto the Lord with the promises of the mercy of Jehovah. The impenitent condition of the people is foreseen and judgment is announced. Then follow the messages which make known Jehovah's determination to punish Jerusalem, and further announcement of the impending judgment. But while Jeremiah gave the messages of warning of the coming disaster of Nebuchadnezzar's conquest, he also received prophecies concerning the future. Thus in chapter 23 we find a great prophecy of restoration. He speaks of the days when the righteous Branch, the King, is to reign, when Judah will be saved and Israel dwell safely. Who that King is, every believer knows. His name is "Jehovah our Righteousness." It is the Lord Jesus Christ. Greater still is the great prophecy contained in chapters 30—31. Here we find the prophecy of the new covenant to be made with the house of Judah and the house of Israel. Chapter 33 contains another prophetic restoration message. Chapters 46—51 contain prophecies against Gentile nations.

The personal experience and the sufferings of this prophet are of a typical character, like the experiences and sufferings of other men of God in the Old Testament. The following passages make Jeremiah a type of Christ: Chapter 11:19, 13:17, 20:7 (last sentence), 20:10, 26:11, 15; Lamentations 1:12, 3:14.

The Divisions of Jeremiah

We have already referred in the introduction to the charge made by the critics that the book of Jeremiah is unchronological and lacks proper arrangement. Says one critic, "as the book now stands, there is nothing but the wildest confusion, a preposterous jumbling together of prophecies of different dates." Attempts have therefore been made to reconstruct the book on a chronological basis, but none of these are satisfactory. On the other hand, some able scholars have come to the conclusion that we possess the book substantially in the same state as that in which it left the hands of the prophet and his secretary Baruch. We believe this is correct. If Jeremiah was guided by the Spirit of God in writing and dictating his great messages, he wrote them down just as the Spirit wanted to have them written down. If some things appear disjointed, or out of the chronological order, there must be some wise purpose in it. We shall discover this as we proceed with the analysis and in our annotations.

To enjoy fully the book of Jeremiah a good knowledge of the historical setting is eminently necessary. We have given many references in the annotations which will help in this direction.

We call attention first to the two main divisions of the book. The first constitutes the greater part of the book, from chapters 1—45. This portion has the full ministry of the prophet during the reign of Josiah, the brief reign of Jehoahaz (Shallum; see chapter 22:10-12); the reign of Jehoiakim, Jehoiakin (Coniah) and the reign of Zedekiah. The second division contains the prophecies against Gentile nations, that is chapters 46—51. The last chapter is an appendix corresponding in its history to 2 Kings. Some have looked upon this appendix as the introduction to the Lamentations.

The prophecies historically according to the reign of Josiah, Jehoahaz, Jehoiakim, Jehoiakin, and Zedekiah may be arranged as follows:

Under the Reign of Josiah. The call of Jeremiah and probably the greater part of chapters 1—6.

Under the Reign of Jehoahaz. The prophecy contained in chapter 22:10-12.

Under the Reign of Jehoiakim. Chapters 7—20, 25—26, 35—36, 46:1-12, 47, 49.

Under the Reign of Jehoiakin (Coniah; Jeconiah). Chapters 22 and 23.

Under the Reign of Zedekiah. Chapters 21, 24, 27, 28, 29, 30—34, 37—44, 46:13-28, 50 and 51.

We make the following divisions for the study of this book:

I. THE PROPHET'S CALL TO REPENTANCE, THE NATION'S IMPENITENCE, AND THE JUDGMENT ANNOUNCED (1—13)

II. THE PROPHET'S MINISTRY BEFORE THE FALL OF JERUSALEM, THE PROPHECIES OF JUDGMENT AND RESTORATION, THE PERSONAL HISTORY OF JEREMIAH, HIS FAITHFULNESS AND HIS SUFFERING (14—39)

III. AFTER THE FALL OF JERUSALEM (40—45)

IV. THE PROPHECIES CONCERNING THE GENTILE NATIONS (46—51)

V. THE HISTORICAL APPENDIX (52:1-34)

The different subdivisions will appear in the analysis.

Analysis and Annotations

I. The Call to Repentance, the Impenitence of the People, and the Judgment Announced

CHAPTER 1

The Call of the Prophet

1. The introduction (1:1-3)
2. The divine call (1:4-10)
3. The renewed call and the first visions (1:11-19)

Verses 1-3. The first three verses introduce us to the person of the prophet, to the time the Word of the Lord came unto him, and to the sphere of his ministry. Jeremiah's father, Hilkiah, was a priest of the line of Ithamar; his home was Anathoth of Benjamin. (See general introduction.)

Verses 4-10. "Then the Word of the Lord came unto me" (verse 4). The prophet is the writer who tells us how he was called into the office of a prophet. A sovereign, omniscient and omnipotent Lord speaks to and informs the young Jeremiah that He knew him, that his call was prenatal. He had been chosen and set apart for the specific work which he now was to undertake. (See Isa. 49:1; Gal. 1:15, 16). What comfort this assuring knowledge must have been to the prophet in his trying ministry, in the persecutions which were his portion and the suffering he passed through! The Lord had called him, the Lord knew all that would take place, and He had the power to sustain him. And he is the same Lord today, and Jeremiah's comfort is still the comfort of His trusting people.

Jeremiah expresses at once his fear. Like Moses (Exod. 4:10), he manifests self-distrust. He was but a child, not in the sense of a mere child, but a youth. The Septuagint translates it, "I am too young." After that the Lord encouraged him by the promise of His presence, "I am with thee to deliver thee." Then He touched his mouth and said, "Behold, I have put my words in thy mouth." He was the mouthpiece of Jehovah, Who commissioned him to fulfill a ministry over nations and kingdoms, to announce the overthrow of them by the judgments of the Lord.

Verses 11-19. Some think that this renewed call came in the beginning of the reign of Jehoiakim. There is nothing in the text to indicate this. The first vision is that of the rod of the almond tree. The Hebrew word for almond is *"Shakad,"* which means to watch, to wake early. It is the first tree which shows the return of spring. It denotes the early fulfillment of the judgment purposes of the Lord. The vision of the seething pot toward the north denotes the coming invasion by the kingdom of the north, that is, the Babylonians under Nebuchadnezzar. Then follows the renewed commission with a threat in case of disobedience; if his fearfulness would lead him to abandon the commission. More than that, the Lord, knowing the fears of the servant He had called and separated, encouraged him and once more promised him, "I am with thee saith the Lord, to deliver thee."

CHAPTERS 2:1—3:5

Expostulation and Impeachment

1. His love and kindness to Jerusalem (2:1-3)
2. The unfaithful people (2:4-11)
3. The two evils and the results (2:12-18)
4. Impeachment (2:19-30)
5. Expostulation (2:31-37)
6. Jehovah waiting to show mercy (3:1-5)

Verses 1-3. The first message Jeremiah received begins with reminding Jerusalem of the kindness Jehovah bestowed upon the nation in her youth, and how she went after Him in the wilderness. He had separated Israel to belong to Him, to be a holy nation, the first fruits of His increase, which probably means that other nations should through Israel be called to know Him. He was their protector and those who tried to devour them would be held guilty.

Verses 4-11. After Jehovah had called to the remembrance of the people the days of her youth, He reproves them for their unfaithfulness. This is the opening chapter of the roll which Jehudi read in the presence of Jehoiakim, which he threw into the fire after he had mutilated it with his penknife (chapter 36:23). The remonstrance starts with a pathetic question: "What iniquity have your fathers found in Me, that they are gone far from Me, and have walked after vanity, and are become vain?" Was there anything unrighteous in Him: had He dealt in a treacherous way? Was the fault in Jehovah that they had left Him? They had not thought on His faithfulness as He had led them out of Egypt, through the desert and the shadows of death. It was forgotten by them, and when Jehovah brought them to the land of promise they had defiled the land. Priests, pastors and prophets had apostatized. Thus Jehovah states His case to plead with them and their children. Their folly and ingratitude were worse than that of heathen nations. Such was the failure of the favored nation. The failure of Christendom is even greater when we think of the greater manifestation of God's love in the gift of His Son, and the greater blessing and deliverance.

Verses 12-18. The two evils are, forsaking Jehovah, the fountain of living waters, and the hewing for themselves cisterns, broken cisterns that can hold no water. Jehovah was the storehouse of the living waters, put at the disposal of His people without money and without price. But instead of confessing, "All my springs are in Thee," they had left Him, the source of life and comfort; and turned to broken cisterns of their own invention, as well as to the idols and worshipped them. It is so among the professing people of God in this dispensation; the two evils are present with us also. The result for Israel was enslavement. The young lions came (the Assyrian invasion) and made the land waste. Noph (Memphis) and Tahpanhes (Daphnae), that is, Egypt, did the same. It came as the fruit of having forsaken the fountain of living water.

Verses 19-30. The impeachment begins with the solemn statement: "Know therefore and see that it is an evil thing and bitter, that thou hast forsaken Jehovah Thy God, and that my fear is not in Thee, saith the Lord God of hosts." They had broken the covenant and played the harlot. The noble vine He had planted had degenerated. Their iniquity was marked before the Lord, and nothing that they did could remove the stain (verse 22). Yet they denied their guilt of going after idols. And when the Lord tells them, "withhold thy foot from being unshod," that is, running so much after strange gods, so that the feet become unshod, by wearing out the sandals, they boldly declared, "There is no hope; no, for I have loved strangers, and after them will I go." Their backs and their faces were turned from Jehovah. But when the time of trouble comes, they will say, "Arise, save us." But could or would the false gods they had made respond and save them? Some day a remnant of that nation will turn to the Lord and cry, "Arise, save us," and He will answer.

Verses 31-37. Israel's conduct was incomprehensible. Once more it is the "Why" of Jehovah. What had He done that they should turn away from Him? Can a maid forget her ornaments, or a bride her attire? Yet His people had forgotten Him, who had loved and adorned them, days without number. He will plead with them because they said, I have not sinned.

Chapter 3:1-5. Here is the first time the gracious invitation is given, "Return again to Me, saith the Lord." And how many times after, the Lord pleads in the riches of His mercy for His people to return unto Him and offers them forgiveness.

The Call to Repentance and Judgment Announced (3:6—6:30)

CHAPTER 3

1. The contrast between backslidden Israel and treacherous Judah (3:6-11)
2. The call to return and the promised glory (3:12-18)
3. The future true repentance predicted and anticipated (3:19-25)

Verses 6-11. The message which begins with the sixth verse was given to Jeremiah during the reign of Josiah. There is then, first of all, a contrast between Israel (the ten tribes) and her sister Judah. (Compare with Ezekiel 23.) The house of Israel, the northern kingdom was judged first by the Lord. She played the harlot; after she had done so, the Lord said, "Turn thou to Me." She refused, and her treacherous sister the house of Judah saw it. And when the Lord dealt with the house of Israel in judgment and they were carried away, Judah did not fear but played the harlot. The tenth verse proves conclusively that the reformation under Josiah was not a true spiritual revival: "And yet for all this her treacherous sister Judah hath not returned unto Me with her whole heart, but feignedly, saith the Lord."

Verses 12-18. Here is a message to be proclaimed toward the north, calling on backsliding Israel to return. He promises mercy to them. One hundred years before, the house of Israel had gone northward as captives. The Lord knew where they dwelt and sent them this message of mercy. He knows today where the house of Israel is, the ten tribes, and at some future time the gracious offer given here will be consummated in their return. These verses are prophetic. They speak of the time when the chosen people will return. Then Jerusalem will be called "the throne of the Lord." Israel will be converted. All the nations will be gathered unto the Name of Jehovah; the house of Judah with the house of Israel will be reunited. That will be when the King our ever blessed Lord comes back.

Verses 19-25. What the future true repentance of the people will be is here predicted and anticipated. There will be weeping and supplications. They will acknowledge that true salvation is in the Lord. They will confess their sins and their disobedience.

CHAPTER 4

1. True repentance and what it means (4:1-4)
2. The alarm sounded: Judgment comes (4:5-13)
3. The doom of the rebellious people (4:14-22)
4. The desolation of Israel's land through judgment (4:23-31)

Verses 1-4. A return must be a return unto Him, Jehovah; anything less is insufficient. Their abominations must be judged and put away. Every return of backsliders must be in the same way—a true return to the Lord with confession of sin, self-judgment, and abandonment of evil. The circumcision of the heart means regeneration. (See chapter 31:31-34, and Ezek. 36:26.)

Verses 5-13. This is the first definite announcement of the coming judgment from the north, which Jeremiah had seen in the vision of the boiling pot toward the north (chapter 1). The lion who comes, the destroyer of the Gentiles, who makes the land desolate, is Nebuchadnezzar, the king of Babylon. It is a very vivid description of the approaching judgment. Verse 10 means not that Jeremiah is reproaching the Lord for having deceived the people. Jeremiah did not preach peace, but the false prophets did. They came and spoke in the name of Jehovah, that there should be peace; and Jehovah permitted as a judgment these prophets, and the message of these prophets. And thus they were deceived.

Verses 14-22. The doom of Jerusalem and Judah is sealed; there can be no escape. Their ways and their doings brought all upon them. And when Jeremiah hears it from the lips of the Lord, he breaks out in a lament: "My bowels, My bowels! I am pained at my very heart. My heart maketh a noise in me; I cannot hold my peace, because thou hast heard, O my soul, the sound of the trumpet, the alarm of war."

Verses 23-31. Then the prophet has a vision of what will happen to the land of Israel, when the judgment threatened above has passed over it. The unscriptural invention and wicked teachings of Seventh Day Adventism applies this passage to the whole earth and teaches that when the Lord comes the whole earth will be laid waste. Like Isaiah 24, only Israel's land is in view. It must be not overlooked that the Lord said: "The whole land shall be desolate; yet will I not make a full end." This is Israel's hope.

CHAPTER 5

1. The apostate conditions of Jerusalem (5:1-9)
2. The impending judgment (5:10-18)
3. Sowing and reaping (5:19-29)
4. The horrible thing (5:30-31)

Verses 1-9. So degenerate had the inhabitants of Jerusalem become that the Lord promised if but one man could be found in the city who executed judgment and sought the truth, He would pardon Jerusalem. It was a general apostasy. A similar apostasy is predicted for the end of our age. "Nevertheless when the Son of Man cometh shall He find the faith on the earth? They were foolish, saith the Lord; they broke the yoke and burst the bonds; they have refused to return. They were as fed horses in the morning; every one neighed after his neighbor's wife. Shall I not visit these things, saith the Lord; and shall not my soul be avenged on such a nation as this?"

Verses 10-18. The judgment messages had not been believed by the people (verse 12). What the invader from the north will do to Israel is described in verses 15-18. Again the promise is given, "I will not make a full end with you." The Lord keeps in the midst of His people a remnant.

Verses 19-29. Their sowing was bringing a harvest. They asked, "Wherefore doeth the Lord our God all these things unto us?" He answers them that they had sown their evil seed in forsaking the Lord and serving strange gods; the harvest would be serving strangers in a strange land. The good things promised had been turned away by their sins and iniquities. The question of verse 9 is repeated in verse 29. And what was true of that generation, is true of this present age also. The seed which is being sown is Bible rejection; the rejection of the gospel of Christ, the seed of apostasy, will bring a harvest of judgment as it did with Israel.

Verses 30-31. False prophets, false priests and the people were satisfied with it. How is it going to be in the end? Both prophets and priests were in league against the prophet of God. They misled the people; they were a curse instead of a blessing. It is not unlike the religious conditions in Christendom today.

CHAPTER 6

1. The call to the children of Benjamin (6:1-8)
2. Corruption and the deserved judgment (6:9-26)
3. The prophet addressed (6:27-30)

Verses 1-8. The children of Benjamin are exhorted to flee for safety on account of the evil from the north. There were probably among the Benjamites God-fearing men. Those who heeded the call fled and escaped. It is a warning message which follows: "Be thou instructed, O Jerusalem, let my soul depart from thee; lest I make thee desolate, a land not inhabited." But they heeded it not.

Verses 9-26. They did not hear because they had uncircumcised ears, neither had they delight in the Word of the Lord. How true this is today of the great mass of professing Christians! The Lord will now no longer restrain His fury; He will pour it out upon them. Covetousness, the love of money, as it is in our day, was the controlling passion. Prophet and priest dealt falsely; their one message, like the one message of the prophet and priest today, was peace, peace, when there was no peace. Then once more the judgment from the north is announced (verses 18-26).

Verses 27-30. In the final paragraph of this chapter the Lord speaks intimately to the prophet. He is encouraged and strengthened. He is set as a tower and as a fortress. What a position of honor! May we consider it as we are as His believing people surrounded by the flood of apostasy; that we, too, are called to be a tower and fortress.

The Prophet's Temple Address (7—9)

CHAPTER 7

1. Amend your ways and your doings (7:1-15)
2. No prayer-answer to be expected (7:16-20)
3. Sacrifices rejected; Obedience demanded (7:21-28)
4. Jerusalem's rejection (7:29-34)

Verses 1-15. We call this next address of the prophet "the temple address," because he was commanded to stand in the gate of the Lord's house. There he stood, a solitary figure, and said: "Hear the Word of the Lord, all ye of Judah, that enter in at these gates to worship Jehovah." Their worship was but external. They trusted in the temple of the Lord, as if with the house itself some kind of a blessing was connected and the house would shield them from disaster. Micah gives the same delusion of the apostate people: "Yet will they lean upon the Lord, and say, Is not the Lord among us? no evil can come upon us" (Micah 3:11). Such a false trust in ordinances and outward worship is only too evident in Christendom also. The masses of unsaved people with their religious observances think it is a protection and insures the Lord's help and blessing. They trusted in lying words. They were thieves, murderers, adulterers, perjurers and idolators, and they thought if they go to the house of the Lord they would be delivered from these abominations. The Lord calls upon them to amend their ways and their doings, to work a better righteousness. They had made His house a den of robbers. This verse (verse 11) was quoted by our Lord in Matt. 21:13. He tells them of the fate of Shiloh when it was overthrown on account of the wickedness of Israel; such would be the fate of the temple (Psa. 78:60). They would be cast out as the whole seed of Ephraim had been cast out.

Verses 16-20. The Lord told the prophet that no prayer of intercession would be answered. "I will not hear thee." What a word this is, coming from Him, who had told Israel to cry unto Him and He would answer. They had provoked Him by making cakes to the queen of heaven. They had fallen in with the worship of a female idol, so prevalent among the idolatrous nations which surrounded them, like the Phoenicians, the Assyrians, the Egyptians and the Babylonians. The Babylonian Venus, Ishtar, was called by them the queen of heaven. The Assyrian called her Beltis, the female form of Baal; they placed in the sculpture a star over her head and called her "the mistress of the heavens." The Phoenicians worshipped this "queen of heaven" under the name of Ashtoreth or Astarte. This wicked worship, with which all kinds of immoral ceremonies were connected, had been adopted by the Jews. The women made cakes to present to this goddess. Jewish tradition tells us that the image of the idol was stamped on each cake. This worship of "the queen of heaven" is perpetuated in the mystical Babylon, Rome, the great whore and mother of harlots (Rev. 17). Mary is called by Romanists "the queen of heaven" and "mistress of the heavens." It can be proven that Mariolatry is but the continuation of the Babylonish worship of the goddess they called "queen of heaven." If the Lord was provoked to anger because the women of Israel brought cakes to this queen of heaven, how much more is He provoked to anger with the idolatries of papal Rome?

Verses 21-28. He brands their sacrifices as worthless. He gave no command concerning burnt offerings and sacrifices in the day He brought them out of Egypt. Destructive critics have built upon this verse (22) a puerile argument to prove that the law of sacrifices was not given by Moses, but introduced many centuries later. When the Lord first led them out of Egypt, He gave them no laws as to sacrifices, but asked obedience. They harkened not; nor did they in Jeremiah's day. It is a nation that obeyeth not the voice of the Lord, nor receiveth correction.

Verses 29-34. The hair was cut off as a sign of mourning (Job 1:20). Jerusalem is to lament in the high places. They have defiled His house. On the heights of Tophet, in the valley of the son of Hinnom, they had burned their children as a sacrifice to Molech (2 Kings 23:10). The days were now to come when the same place should become the place of slaughter. The carcasses of the people should then be meat for the beasts of the earth; they should lie there unburied. Such was to be Jerusalem's rejection and judgment.

CHAPTER 8

1. The horrors of the invasion (8:1-3)
2. Hardened hearts and retribution (8:4-12)
3. Utter destruction threatened (8:13-17)
4. The prophet's lamentation (8:18-22)

Verses 1-3. These verses must not be detached from the preceding chapter. The division of chapters is often unfortunate in this book. The invaders from the north would even have digged out the bones of the dead. Kings, priests, prophets and people who had worshipped the sun, the moon and the stars should be exposed and spread out before the sun and moon, remain unburied and become dung. We doubt not that all this was literally done during the Chaldean invasion.

Verses 4-12. They did not repent of their wickedness. Theirs was a perpetual backsliding.

The stork knows his appointed time; the turtle, the crane and the swallow observe the time of their coming, but they had hardened their hearts in such a manner that they knew not the judgment of the Lord. Hence the retribution (9-12).

Verses 13-17. The thirteenth verse shows the desolation which will fall upon the land when the Lord arises. The words of verses 14-16 were spoken by the prophet and not by the impenitent people as some take it. The 16th verse is extremely vivid.

Verses 18-22. His heart was faint in him. He is overwhelmed with sorrow. The harvest was passed, the summer gone and they were not saved. It is a mournful outburst.

Verses 23-26. The days were coming when judgment would strike Jews and Gentiles, for the uncircumcised Gentiles and for Israel, uncircumcised in heart. In view of these days of judgment the prophet exhorts to stop their boasts in wisdom, in might and in riches, for all availeth nothing. "But let him that glorieth glory in Me, that he understandeth and knoweth Me, that I am the Lord which exercise loving kindness, judgment and righteousness, in the earth, for in these things I delight, saith the Lord." May we also glory in Him and not in the things of the dust, the temporal, the passing things, which are but for a moment! Let us remember "the coming of the Lord draweth nigh."

CHAPTER 9

1. The prophet's complaint and Jehovah's answer (9:1-9)
2. The cause of desolation and destruction (9:10-16)
3. The call for the mourning and wailing women (9:17-22)
4. Glorying in the Lord in view of judgment (9:23-26)

Verses 1-9. Here again is a deplorable break. The opening verses of this chapter belong to the preceding one. The prophet still speaks. He is overwhelmed with sorrow; his eyes are fountains of tears. He weeps day and night over the slain. He wishes himself away in some wilderness, to be alone and separated from the adulterous generation. Then follows a description of the moral corruption of the people. The Lord answered him and once more asks the question: "Shall not I visit them for these things? saith the Lord; shall not my soul be avenged on such a nation as this?" (See chapter 5:9, 29.)

Verses 10-16. Jerusalem will be heaps, ruins and a den of dragons. The cities of Judah will be desolate. But why is it like this? Because they forsook His law, obeyed not His voice, and practiced idolatries. Therefore their portion would be wormwood and gall. They would be scattered among the nations.

Verses 17-22. The time of wailing and mourning is at hand. "For death is come up into our windows, and is entered into our palaces, to cut off the children from without and the young men from the street." Pestilence was to sweep over them and enter into their habitations. Hence the call to the professional wailers to sing the mournful dirges of death. These wailing women are also called "wise women," for they dabbled in magical, occult things, in familiar spirits and in soothsaying.

CHAPTER 10

The Vanity of Idols

1. Be not dismayed at the signs of heaven (10:1-5)
2. The contrast: The vanity of idols and the Lord, the King of Nations (10:6-18)
3. The affliction of the prophet and his prayer (10:19-25)

Verses 1-5. The heathen paid attention to the signs of heaven, such as eclipses, comets, meteoric showers, etc. They were dismayed at these things. All they did, their customs and observances in connection with idol worship, was nothing but vanity.

Verses 6-18. Idols are nothing, but the Lord God of Israel is all. He is the King of Nations, who rules over all. He is the true God, the living God, the everlasting King. At His wrath the earth trembles and the nations shall not be able to abide His indignation. He made the earth by His power; He established the world by wisdom; He stretched out the heavens by His discretion. But what is man? Brutish in his knowledge.

Verses 19-25. Here we see how Jeremiah identified himself with the afflictions and sorrows of Jerusalem. In his prayer he pleads that the judgment might be only for correction and not for a complete and perpetual consummation. "O Lord correct me, but with judgment; not in thine anger, lest thou bring me to nothing." He calls for judgment upon the nations. Well may we see in pleading Jeremiah, the weeping prophet, who is afflicted in Jerusalem's affliction, who identified himself with his people, a type and picture of Him who is greater than Jeremiah.

CHAPTER 11

The Broken Covenant and the Plot Against Jeremiah

1. The broken covenant (11:1-17)
2. The plot revealed and Jehovah's answer (11:18-23)

Verses 1-17. Jehovah had made a covenant with His people. He tells the prophet about it and the responsibility which was connected with that covenant. They were to obey His voice. Then should they be His people and He their God. And of this covenant it was written, "Cursed be the man that obeyeth not the words of this covenant." The prophet answered the Lord: "So be it Lord" (Amen). Then he is commanded to proclaim this covenant and tell the people that they had broken the covenant. They had followed the evil example of their fathers. They had burned incense to the idol gods. Therefore the prophet again is told not to pray for this adulterous generation, "for I will not hear them in the time they cry unto Me in their trouble." Yet the Lord in spite of it all still calls them "My Beloved," though they had broken the covenant and worked lewdness. Verse 16 is used by the Spirit of God in Romans 11, the chapter which begins with the assurance that God has not cast away His people. The branches of the green olive tree are broken. Yet there is hope; they are still beloved for the Father's sake.

Verses 18-23. The Lord revealed unto him their doings. He was ignorant of it, like a lamb or an ox brought to the slaughter. They wanted to cut him off from the land of the living. He calls for vengeance upon them, which is in full keeping with the law dispensation and God's righteous government.

> Righteousness characterizes the saint as well as love, and has its place where there are adversaries to that love and to the blessing of the loved people. It is the Spirit of prophecy, not the gospel, no doubt because prophecy is connected with the government of God, not with His present dealings in sovereign grace. Hence in the Revelation vengeance is called for by the saint. *Synopsis of the Bible.*

The men of Anathoth had intimidated him by saying, "Prophesy not in the name of the Lord, that thou die not by our hand." The Lord answers him that their young men should die by the sword, and their sons and daughters by famine. No remnant of them should be left.

CHAPTER 12

The Prophet's Prayer and the House Forsaken, Yet Compassion

1. The prophet's prayer (12:1-6)
2. The house forsaken, yet compassion (12:7-17)

Verses 1-6. In his outburst of grief and in great mental perplexity Jeremiah states the old question, why does the righteous man suffer, why does the wicked prosper? And then the prayer for His intervention. Such will be again the case with the godly remnant in the end of this present age. They will suffer and be persecuted as godly Jeremiah was and pray as Jeremiah prayed: "Pull them out like sheep for the slaughter, and prepare them for the day of slaughter." The imprecatory psalms are of the same prophetic meaning. Jehovah's answer tells him that greater trials were in store for him (verses 5, 6).

Verses 7-17. The house is to be forsaken. The dearly beloved is to be given into the hands of the enemies. The sword of the Lord would now devour them. But there is the warning to the nations who touch His inheritance. He will deal with them in judgment as He dealt with Judah. Then we find the promise, "I will return and have compassion on them." This is still future. The compassion for Israel comes in the day of His return.

CHAPTER 13

Signs, Warnings, and Exhortations

1. The linen girdle and the filled bottles (13:1-14)
2. Hear and give glory (13:15-21)
3. The justice of the judgment (13:22-27)

Verses 1-14. The prophet enacts a sign, that of the linen girdle. After he had put on the girdle, he was told to hide it in a hole of the rock of the Euphrates. After many days, he was commanded to dig for the girdle. It was found marred and profitable for nothing. Was this only a vision, or did the prophet actually make the long journey to the Euphrates and then repeat it after many days? The latter is quite improbable, nor can the command be called a vision. The question is what river is meant, the river Euphrates or another river by a similar name? The Hebrew word for Euphrates is *"Perath,"* and the word river is generally added to this word. In the text here it is missing. Now, three miles north of Anathoth there was a small river by the name of *"Parah"* (Josh. 18:23). It probably means this place to which the prophet was commanded to go. Both words in the Hebrew spring from the same root.

The meaning of this symbolical action is explained. A girdle belonged to the priest. Israel was called to be the priestly nation. As a girdle cleaveth to the loins of a man, so the Lord had chosen Israel to cleave unto Him, "that they might be unto Me for a people," and for a name and for a glory. And as the girdle had become marred and profitable for nothing, so even would their pride, that in which they gloried as the chosen people, be marred.

The bottles filled with wine, dashed one against the other, are the symbol of their sin-intoxication and their destruction.

Verses 15-21. How patient and merciful is Jehovah! He interrupts His judgment message by calling on the people, whom He still loves, to give ear and to give glory to Jehovah. It is the utterance of the prophet, the outpouring of His love towards His people. The prophet addresses the king and the queen: "Humble yourselves." And then his heart seems to break in anticipation of their obstinacy. "But if ye will not hear; my soul shall weep in secret places on account of your pride, and mine eye shall weep sore, and run down with tears, because the Lord's flock is carried away captive."

Verses 22-27. Wherefore? they asked. And He answers, "For the greatness of thine iniquity . . . because thou hast forgotten Me and trusted in falsehood." Woe unto thee, Jerusalem! wilt thou not be made clean? When shall it be? But could they do it themselves? "Can the Ethiopian change his skin, or the leopard his spots? Then may ye also do good, that are accustomed to evil." The new heart is needed (Ezek. 36); the new birth of which the Lord spoke to the teacher in Israel.

II. The Prophet's Ministry Before the Fall of Jerusalem, the Prophecies of Judgment and Restoration, the Personal History of Jeremiah, His Faithfulnesss and His Suffering

CHAPTER 14

The Great Drought, the Sword, the Famine, and the Pestilence

1. The description of the drought (14:1-6)
2. The prophet's priestly intercession (14:7-9)
3. The answer (14:10-18)
4. The renewed prayer (14:19-22)

Verses 1-6. The vivid description of the great drought is given in these verses. The little ones sent forth for water returned empty handed. It is the picture of distress.

Verses 7-9. And now the prophet's voice as intercessor is heard. Like Daniel (chapter 9), in his great prayer Jeremiah acknowledges the nation's sin as his own. But he trusts in the Lord and knows that He is "the hope of Israel," the Saviour. Blessed statements of faith which came from His lips: "Thou, O Lord, art in the midst of us—we are called by Thy Name—leave us not" (verse 9)! The Saviour and hope of Israel has surely not given up His people, though judgment had to do its work.

Verses 10-18. They wandered away from Him, saith the Lord in answering Jeremiah. Their iniquities will be remembered and their sins visited. This is the demand of a righteous God. He is not going to hear their cry; the sword of the famine and the pestilence will consume them. Jeremiah tells the Lord about the message of the false prophets. They had promised peace, just as the false teachers in Christendom do today. But they prophesied lies in His name; He had not sent them, nor commanded them nor had He spoken to them.

Verses 19-22. What soul stirring petitions these are! It is not the impenitent nation which speaks, but the prophet is pleading in the place of the people and for them.

CHAPTER 15

The Prophet's Deep Soul-Exercise

1. The answer (15:1-9)
2. The prophet's grief and sorrow and Jehovah's answer (15:10-21)

Verses 1-9. The preceding prayer is now answered and the Lord tells Jeremiah that if Moses and Samuel, these two great men of intercessory prayer, were pleading, judgment would not be averted. What is in store for those who are appointed to death, for the sword, for the famine, for captivity, will be accomplished. There is no escape. They will be removed among all kingdoms on account of Manasseh's great sin (2 Kings 21:11-15). The terrors of judgment are described in verses 7-9. Their children will be taken; widows increase; the mother of seven children faints, because they are all taken from her.

Verses 10-21. Jeremiah is overwhelmed. He pronounces a "woe" upon himself and declares that his mother has given birth to one who is a man of strife, of contention to the whole land. He has faithfully discharged his duty; he loved his people and they hated him beyond measure. Every one cursed him, as if he were a wicked man. What anguish of soul this implies! But then the Lord was near to cheer and comfort him, as He is near to us when we are in sorrow and all is dark and we are in despair. It would be well with him and with those, who, like Jeremiah, trust the Lord. But the remnant, too, would suffer with the nation's portion (13-14). This brings out another prayer from Jeremiah's heart. He pleads for revenge upon his adversaries, and then prays, "Take me not away in Thy longsuffering, know that for Thy sake I have suffered rebuke." But while he prayed he also used the Word of God. "Thy words were found, and I did eat them." He fed on the bread of life. The word was unto him the joy and rejoicing of his heart. He knew from the Word that he was called by His Name. And we also can turn to the Word and feed on it. But how few can say, "Thy Word is the joy and rejoicing of my heart." That Word on which Jeremiah fed, which filled his sorrowful heart, led him to separation. It will lead us also to separation in the evil day of departure from God and the threatening judgment. He sat alone; He refused to have anything to do with the assembly of mockers, those who denied His Word and His Name, who listened to the false prophets with their false message. Verse 18 must be interpreted in the sense that Jeremiah speaks as representing the godly remnant of Israel. There was such a remnant then in the midst of the wicked mass, there will be such a remnant again in the future, during the great tribulation, or, as Jeremiah calls that time, "The time of Jacob's trouble." They suffer in the trials and judgments; they are fearful, yet trusting. Jeremiah is representative of this remnant. The answer the Lord gives in verses 19-21 must be explained in the same light. Verse 21 will find its final fulfillment of the future remnant when the Lord returns and redeems them from the hand of the wicked and the hand of the terrible, the two beasts of Revelation 13.

The Coming Calamities: Restoration Promised, Ruin Imminent on Account of Judah's Sin and Concerning the Sabbath (16—17)

CHAPTER 16

1. The coming calamities (16:1-13)
2. The coming days of restoration and blessing (16:14-21)

Verses 1-13. In view of the coming calamities Jeremiah is bidden to remain unmarried and not to raise a family. The verses which describe the coming calamities need no further annotations.

Verses 14-21. The great dispersion was announced by the Lord in the preceding verse: "Therefore will I cast you out of this land, into a land that ye know not, neither ye nor your fathers; and there ye shall serve other gods day and night; where I will not show you favor." But is this to last forever? Is this dispersion permanent? Will they always be homeless wanderers? The next verse gives the answer: "I will bring them again into their land that I gave unto their fathers." They will be brought back from the land of the north and from all lands where they had been driven. It will be a greater deliverance than the deliverance out of Egypt. Critics have found fault with these verses: "They are out of place here, but whether inserted by accident, or whether to modify the painful impression of the prophecy of judgment in which they are inserted, we cannot say" (Prof. A. S. Peake). They are not out of place, nor inserted by some unknown hand. The Lord declares His gracious purposes which will yet be accomplished. That these verses were not fulfilled in the return of the small remnant from Babylon is obvious. They will be fulfilled in the future, when the house of Israel and the house of Judah will be re-established in the land. Then the so-called "lost tribes" will be found again by Him for whom they were never lost, "For Mine eyes are upon all their ways, they are not hid from My face neither is their iniquity hid from Mine eyes." He will send fishers and hunters to bring them forth. It is the same of which our Lord speaks in Matt. 24:31. The elect of whom the Lord speaks are not a spiritual Israel, but the elect nation Israel. Then the voice of the prophet is heard in verse 19 with a blessed prophetic declaration: "The Gentiles shall come unto Thee from the ends of the earth, and shall say, Surely our fathers have inherited lies, vanity and things wherein there is no profit." It denotes the conversion of the world, which in prophecy never precedes the restoration of Israel, but always follows that great coming event. (See Rom. 11:12, 15; Acts 15:14-17).

CHAPTER 17

1. Judah's sin (17:1-4)
2. The curse and the blessing (17:5-11)
3. The worship of Jeremiah (17:12-18)
4. Concerning the Sabbath (17:19-27)

Verses 1-4. The sin of Judah was idolatry, engraven with a pen of iron, the point of a diamond, upon their heart (from whence it proceeded) and he horns of their altars. They had destroyed but a few years before the asherim (translated groves, a kind of sacred post), and now their children turned back to the abominable heath cults. His anger and judgment must now be their portion.

Verses 5-11. A curse is pronounced upon him who trusteth in man, who departeth from the Lord. For such a one there is no hope; he shall not see good; he must be an outcast, like the heath in the desert. And such is the natural condition of man, his heart is departed from the Lord, he trusteth in himself, making flesh his arm to defend and to uphold. But blessing is for the man who trusteth in the Lord, whose hope the Lord is. Verse 8 contains the same truth as Psalm 1:3. It is a description of the God-fearing in Israel, who knew the Lord, trusted and hoped in Him. He had called them to this place of blessing; He had encouraged them to trust in Him; He had manifested His glory and His power in their midst. But they turned away from Him, they leaned not on Him, but on the arm of flesh, on Egypt. The heart is the source of it, deceitful above all things and desperately wicked. The question, "Who can know it?" is answered, "I the Lord search the heart." He has sounded the depths of it and in His omniscience knew the shameful history of Israel, and all their backsliding. So He knew and knows what we are, yet in sovereign love and grace He has loved us and bears with His own.

Verses 12-18. The worship of the prophet stands here also for the worship and soul exercise of the godly remnant of the Lord's people. The sanctuary of the godly is the glorious high throne, that throne which we know as the throne of grace. In verse 14 there is expressed by the prophet in behalf of the God-fearing the need of His salvation. They mocked the prophet, "Where is the Word of the Lord? Let it come." So they will hate the remnant of the future (Isa. 66:5). And we know the prediction in Peter's second Epistle (2 Peter 3). Verse 18 corresponds to the imprecatory psalms. What Jeremiah prays, was fulfilled upon that evil generation; and some day the imprecatory psalms will be fulfilled when the Lord deals again in judgment with the nation.

Verses 19-27. Kuenen and other critics deny the Jeremianic authorship of this passage. It is not out of keeping with the message of the prophet. The Sabbath of which he is commanded to speak is the standard of Israel's spiritual condition, for it is the weekly reminder of Israel's covenant relation with Jehovah. If they neglected the divine command, as they always did in their departure from the Lord, it was the outward evidence that they had broken the covenant. If they really returned to the Lord they would show it by keeping the solemn Sabbaths and the Lord would bless them. But they obeyed not. This passage as well as others is used by the pernicious Seventh Day Adventistic cult, which denies grace and turns back to the law. But the Sabbath has nothing to do with the Church, nor has the Church anything to do with the Sabbath. The Sabbath is an institution of the law in connection with Israel. The great documents addressed to the church, the Epistles, never mention the Sabbath once, nor is there anywhere in the Epistles an exhortation to keep the Sabbath.

CHAPTER 18

The Potter and the Clay

1. In the potter's house and the message (18:1-17)
2. The plot against the prophet and his prayer (18:18-23)

Verses 1-17. He was commanded to go to the house of a potter and watch his work. The vessel Jeremiah sees fashioned out of clay is marred; it did not turn out well. Then the clay was taken up again and made in another vessel as it seemed good to the potter to make it.

Then came the message: "O house of Israel, cannot I do with you as this potter? saith the Lord. Behold as the clay is in the potter's hand, so are ye in my hand, O house of Israel." If the creature of the dust can do as he pleases with the clay, how much more the Sovereign God. The Holy Spirit evidently uses this in Romans 9:20-32.

If a nation is threatened with destruction and that nation turns to the Lord, He will repent of the evil pronounced upon them. This is fully illustrated in the case of Jonah's prediction, God-given as it was, of Nineveh's overthrow. Nineveh repented and the judgment was not executed upon that generation. But if the Lord has promised a nation good and that nation does evil in His sight, He will repent of the good He had promised unto them. Thus the potter's action is used to convey a great lesson, the lesson of God's sovereignty, to do as He pleaseth, yet always in perfect righteousness. If Israel had owned then the sin and guilt and turned to the Lord, He would have acted in sovereign grace towards them. Their answer was: "There is no hope; but we will walk after our own devices, and we will every one do the imaginations of his evil heart." What depravity and wicked boldness these words reveal! They refused to believe the message of the Lord. They pushed aside the hand which would snatch them out of the fire. They acknowledged the evil heart and deliberately declared to continue in wicked defiance of Jehovah. And is it any better in professing Christendom today? The answer of the Lord, an answer of kindness and long suffering follows.

Verses 18-23. They arose in rebellion against the messenger of Jehovah. They hated him. They would smite him with the tongue, malign him, bring false accusations against him. But the man of God does not take up their contentions. Like Hezekiah when the enemy reviled him, Jeremiah turned to the Lord. He tells the Lord all about it. Then he prays for judgment to fall upon them. Here once more we must look upon these words prophetically. Such expressions as used by the prophet here will, during the great tribulation, come from the lips of the remnant of Israel, who suffer from their enemies and who righteously call for heaven's vengeance, which will fall upon these enemies when Jehovah, our Lord, is manifested in glory.

CHAPTER 19

The Broken Bottle

1. The broken bottle and the message (19:1-13)
2. The fate announced in the court of the Lord's house (19:14-15)

Verses 1-13. He was to get a potter's earthen bottle accompanied by elders and priests, and go to the valley of the son of Hinnom. There he should proclaim the words Jehovah would breathe into him. The message is another judgment message and needs no further comment. In Tophet, the valley of Hinnom, they had worked their abominations, burnt their sons with fire. Now it should become the valley of slaughter, so that their carcasses should be eaten by the fowls and wild beasts. He would cause them to eat the flesh of their loved ones. It was fulfilled during the siege of Jerusalem (Lam. 4:10). Then he broke the bottle as a sign that thus the people and the city should be broken.

Verses 14-15. When the prophet returned from the valley of Hinnom he took his place in the court of the Lord's house and declared the fate of the city.

CHAPTER 20

Pashur: Jeremiah's Perplexity and Complaint

1. Pashur and Jeremiah (20:1-6)
2. Jeremiah's great perplexity and complaint (20:7-18)

Verses 1-6. A great scene now follows the message in connection with the broken bottle. The great Pashur, the chief governor in the house of the Lord had heard of the message. He smites Jeremiah and puts him in the stocks, which must have been some form of cruel torture by which the victim was rendered helpless, besides being exposed to the vulgarity of the people who passed by and would taunt him. In this position Jeremiah remained all night before the high gate of Benjamin. In the morning he was released. He then speaks as only an inspired prophet can speak. His name Pashur (which means "most noble") should now be "Magor-missabib," which means "terror on every side." The awful fate of Pashur and his own is predicted. He is dumb, perhaps even then terror-stricken, as he looks into the flashing eyes of the man of God and listens to the fiery words.

Verses 7-18. What follows now is a most passionate outburst, revealing an unspeakable emotion of the soul, as perhaps nowhere else in the prophetic Scriptures. Even critics acknowledge this as "one of the most powerful and impressive passages in the whole of the prophetic literature, a passage which takes us, as no other, not only into the depths of the prophet's soul, but into the secrets of his prophetic consciousness." "Lord," he cries, "Thou has deceived me, and I was deceived." The *Revised Version* has translated it, "Thou has persuaded me," but that is not correct. He acknowledges himself deceived, or enticed. He is troubled with doubt. He speaks of his great trials. He is a laughing stock—he is a reproach and a derision all the day. He tried to stop mentioning Him and not to speak any more in His name; but he tried to turn back upon his commission. But then the fire burned within him; his conscience became as a burning fire. He had heard defaming; his best friends had said "We will denounce him." They thought of taking revenge on him.

But suddenly faith is victorious. He must have remembered the words of the Lord in connection with his commission, "For I am with thee saith the Lord, to deliver thee" (chapter 1). And so he cries out, "The Lord is with me." He prays to see His vengeance on his enemies, for unto Him he had revealed His cause. And then the singing! "Sing unto the Lord, praise ye the Lord; for He has delivered the soul of the needy from the hand of the evil-doers." Such is the experience of the godly remnant in fears and doubts, troubled on all sides, fleeing to Jehovah, till the singing times come, when He appears for their deliverance and the hallelujahs will sweep the earth and the heavens.

But his grief overwhelms him. Perhaps he thought again of all the sneers and mockeries, of all the harsh words, the unfaithful friends and the physical pain he endured. He is occupied with himself and the soul struggle begins anew and culminates in a near collapse. He curses, as Job did, the day in which he was born.

CHAPTER 21

The Prophetic Warning

1. Zedekiah's inquiry (21:1-2)
2. Jehovah's answer through Jeremiah (21:8-14)

Verses 1-2. It has been said that this chapter is historically misplaced and therefore must be considered an evidence of the composite authorship of this book. The Spirit of God for some reason unknown to us has put it in this place. Zedekiah sent unto Jeremiah Pashur (a different one from the Pashur in the preceding chapter) to inquire as to Nebuchadrezzar, the King of Babylon. This is of course Nebuchadnezzar. The form of his name found in Jeremiah is derived more correctly from the Babylonian, which is "Nabukudurri-usur." Here the great king is mentioned for the first time in Jeremiah. The wicked Zedekiah may have remembered God's dealing with Hezekiah when the Lord annihilated the army of Sennacherib, the Assyrian. Then Zedekiah said: "Peradventure the Lord will deal with us according to all His wondrous works, that he may go up from us."

Verses 3-14. Zedekiah (whose name was Mattaniah), the ungodly king, who had been made king by Nebuchadrezzar after he had carried away captives from Jerusalem, heard a message of judgment from Jeremiah. The Babylonian king's army was again before the city, because Zedekiah had revolted and broken his agreement with the king. How could Zedekiah even imagine that a righteous Lord had a message of peace for him? The Lord Himself will now fight against Jerusalem and its wicked king. The enemy will do the appointed judgment work; "he shall smite them with the edge of the sword; he shall not spare them, neither have pity, nor have mercy." The king is to be taken captive. Then he addresses the people and the house of David in no uncertain words, which need no further comment.

Concerning the Kings of Judah (22:1—23:8)

CHAPTER 22

1. The message in the house of the king of Judah (22:1-9)
2. Touching Shallum, the King of Judah (22:11-12)
3. Concerning Jehoiakim and his fate (22:13-19)
4. Concerning Coniah and his fate (22:20-30)

Verses 1-10. What a figure Jeremiah was as he stood, obedient to the divine command, before the royal palace to deliver his God-given message! The door of mercy still is open. Let them execute judgment, let them stop oppressing the stranger, the widows and orphans, let them shed no longer innocent blood, then the house of David shall prosper. If not, the house shall become a desolation. The nations astonished at the destruction and overthrow of the city will hear the answer that it is "because they have forsaken the covenant of the Lord their God and worshipped other gods and served them."

Verses 11-12. He is also called Jehoahaz (1 Chron. 3:15; 2 Kings 23:30, 31). He was carried away by Pharaoh-Necho into Egypt; he will return.

Verses 13-19. This wicked king and his evil doings are described in these verses. He was a cruel despot, who built his palaces by forced labor; covetousness, shedding of innocent blood, oppression and violence characterized his reign. Then his ignominious burial, the burial of an ass, is predicted. It means that an ass has no burial and so Jehoiakim would have no burial; he is the only kind of Judah whose burial is not recorded. It may be possible that Jeremiah added these words by divine command, after this king had cut the roll to pieces and burned it in the fire (Jer. 36). The prophet wrote the same words contained in the roll (all these chapters beginning with chapter 2 constitute the roll the king burned), and many others were added. Most likely because he had done that wicked work in cutting the Word of God to pieces and casting it into the fire, this special shameful end was announced. Beware you cutters of the Bible, you mutilators of the Word of God, your end, too, will be an ignominious end!

Verses 20-30. Coniah, also called Jehoiachin, Joiakim and Joachim, after a brief reign of a few months had been carried away to Babylon to die there. Then the prophet's voice breaks in with a mighty appeal, "O earth, earth, earth, hear the word of the Lord." Every true believer feels like shouting these words in the present days of departure from God and rejection of His Word. Then there is a prediction as to Jeconiah, "Write ye this man childless, a man that shall not prosper in his days; for no man of his seed shall prosper, sitting upon the throne of David and ruling any more in Judah." A curse was thus pronounced upon the house of David in the line of Solomon. But there was still the line of Nathan the son of David. Messiah, the Son of David, could therefore not spring from the line of Solomon; he must come from the line of Nathan. Joseph, the husband of the virgin Mary of Nazareth was a son of David through the line of Solomon, the disinherited line; but Mary of Nazareth was a daughter of David through the line of Nathan.

CHAPTER 23:1-8

1. The false shepherds (23:1-4)
2. The True Shepherd (23:5-8)

Verses 1-4. The word "pastors" means "shepherds." Ezekiel received a larger message about these false shepherds, the hirelings who did not feed the flock. (See annotations of Ezekiel 34.) The scattered remnant of the Lord's flock (not the Church, but the remnant of Israel) will yet be gathered out of all countries, be fruitful and increase, no longer fearful, dismayed or in want. It is a prophecy concerning the time when the Shepherd of Israel, their King as well, is manifested.

Verses 5-8. A great Messianic prophecy follows. "The Righteous Branch," the Son of David, whose name is "The Lord our Righteousness" (Jehovah Zidkenu) is the Lord Jesus Christ. He is the King who will reign and prosper, executing judgment and justice in the earth. The prophecy is unfulfilled. He came as the Son of David, the promised King. He offered that kingdom to Israel; they rejected Him. But He is coming again, and in that day of glory this great prediction will be accomplished. His people Israel will be saved (Rom. 11:25-27). Their wonderful restoration from the north and from all the countries will then take place.

CHAPTER 23:9-40

Condemnation of the False Prophets

1. Jeremiah's lament on account of the false prophets (23:9-14)
2. The condemnation of these prophets (23:15-32)
3. Forgotten and forsaken (23:33-40)

Verses 9-14. The prophet is overwhelmed because of the wicked prophets, because in the Lord's house wickedness was found. The false prophets of Samaria had led the people into idolatry and the prophets of Judah were guilty of all kinds of immoralities. Like priests, like people; they all became unto the Lord as Sodom, and the inhabitants of Jerusalem like Gomorrah.

Verses 15-32. They will be fed with wormwood and will have to drink gall. On account of their false message of peace (verses 17, 18), the whirlwind of divine judgment will fall upon them and upon the head of the wicked. They prophesied lies in the name of Jehovah; they were prophets of the deceit of their own heart. They tried to make the people forget the Name of Jehovah. Such is today still the work of apostate teachers, who speak out of the deceit of their hearts, who prophesy lies and who aim at the Name which is above every Name. How different is the word of the Lord, from the idle dreams of these false prophets. "Is not My word like as a fire? saith the Lord; and like a hammer that breaketh the rock in pieces?" (verse 29). Three times the Lord declares He is against these prophets (verses 30-32).

Verses 33-40. If they ask the question, "What

is the burden of the Lord?" the answer is to be, "I will cast you off." The burden, or word of the Lord is not to be mentioned again to them. They will be utterly forgotten and forsaken, with everlasting reproach and perpetual shame upon them.

CHAPTER 24

The Two Baskets of Figs

1. The vision of the two baskets of figs (24:1-3)
2. The vision interpreted (24:4-10)

Verses 1-3. Jeconiah, with the choicest of the nation, had been carried away into captivity. A large portion remained, and were not taken away, and these attributed their escape from exile to some goodness in them. At that time the prophet had a vision. He saw set before the temple two baskets of figs. The one basket was filled with good figs, the second basket with bad figs.

Verses 4-10. The good figs are symbolical of those who were carried away into captivity. They were sent away for their good. He promises them good things. They are going to return; He is going to build them; He will plant them. More than that, He will give them a heart to know that He is the Lord. For they shall return unto Me with their whole heart. They are never to be plucked up. This prophecy evidently goes beyond the return of the small remnant from Babylon, yet partially at least it was fulfilled. The bad figs are those who remained with Zedekiah in Jerusalem, but they also should be removed into all the kingdoms of the earth, "to be a reproach, a proverb, a taunt and a curse."

CHAPTER 25

The Seventy Years' Captivity and the Judgment of the Nations

1. The retrospect (25:1-7)
2. The seventy years' captivity announced (25:8-11)
3. The punishment of Babylon and its king (25:12-14)
4. The wine-cup of fury for the nations (25:15-29)
5. The day of the Lord and wrath of God (25:30-38)

Verses 1-7. The prophet in the fourth year of Jehoiakim addresses the people of Judah and the inhabitants of Jerusalem. The fourth year of Jehoiakim was also the first year of Nebuchadrezzar. In this eventful year the battle of Carchemish was fought and Nebuchadrezzar defeated Egypt. The supremacy of Babylon had been insured. At this critical time the prophet gives a retrospect of his ministry among them. From the thirteenth year of Josiah he had spoken to them, but they had not heard. The Lord sent other servants, too, but they did not hear. He puts before them their stubbornness and how they provoked the Lord to anger.

Verses 8-11. And now the solemn verdict is announced. The northern power is coming against this land, headed by King Nebuchadrezzar, who is here called for the first time by the Lord, "My servant." All mirth and joy will be taken from them; the whole land shall be a desolation, and they shall serve the king of Babylon for seventy years.

Verses 12-14. When the seventy years are ended the Babylonian nation and its king (Belshazar) would be punished for their iniquity. All that is written in this book of Jeremiah, concerning Babylon is to be accomplished (including the final desolation). Daniel in Babylon, when he read the book of Jeremiah, dwelt perhaps on this passage, and turned to the Lord in that remarkable prayer recorded in the ninth chapter of the book which bears his name.

Verses 15-29. While the Lord thus judged Jerusalem, should the other nations go unpunished? And He answers, "Ye shall not be unpunished, for I will call for a sword upon all the inhabitants of the earth, saith the Lord of hosts" (verse 29). This prophecy is most remarkable. It predicts a world war. All nations shall drink and be moved and be mad because of the sword. It includes all the kingdoms of the world which are upon the face of the earth (verse 26). Have we not seen something like this during the past, most horrible war of history? And may this not be the prelude to the day of the Lord, when these nations will have to face the Judge and judgment?

Verses 30-38. The *Yom Jehovah,* the day of the Lord, is now announced by the prophet. It is that great future day ushered in by the visible and glorious manifestation of the Lord. All the prophets speak of that day as the day of consummation and glory. It is equally prominent in the New Testament (Matt. 24:30; 2 Thess. 1:7-10; 2 Peter 3:7-10; Rev. 19:11-21, etc.). Jeremiah beholds Him coming from above, with a shout, not the shout with which He calls His own together (1 Thess. 4:17), but the shout of judging wrath. He will plead with all flesh. The slain of the Lord shall be many. The howling of the shepherds, the false leaders, because their end is come, concludes this great vision.

CHAPTER 26

Threatened with Death and His Deliverance

1. The temple like Shiloh, and Jerusalem to be a curse (26:1-7)
2. Threatened with death (26:8-11)
3. Jeremiah's defense (26:12-15)
4. History remembered and the prophet's deliverance (26:16-24)

Verses 1-7. We are now taken back to the beginning of the reign of Jehoiakim. (Compare with chapter 7.) The Lord still waits in patience for their repentance. With holy boldness the prophet stands in a place where the worshippers pass to enter the temple and announces the message. The temple is to be like Shiloh, that is forsaken (Psa. 78:60). Jerusalem is to be a curse.

Verses 8-11. Then he was arrested for his faithfulness and threatened with death, "Thou shalt surely die." The priests and the prophets were his accusers before the princes. How often this has been repeated in the history of God's true witnesses! During pagan Rome as well as papal Rome, the false priests and false prophets hated and despised God's witnesses and persecuted them. It is so in our times.

Verses 12-15. He makes his defense in a few dignified words. He tells them he is Jehovah's messenger. He tells them that he is in their hands, but warns them if they kill him they shed innocent blood. This courage was born of faith. He knows that he is in His hands.

Verses 16-24. The princes and people were deeply impressed and declared that he was not worthy of death. This encouraged certain elders to speak, in whose heart some fear seems to have been left. They remembered the prophet Micah, the contemporary of Isaiah, who spoke similar words in the days of Hezekiah (Micah 3:12). Hezekiah did not have Micah killed. They warned against so rash a deed. They also mentioned the case of the prophet Urijah, who had also prophesied, as Jeremiah did. He had fled to Egypt, but was brought back; then Jehoiakim killed him. We do not know why his case is mentioned in this connection, unless it is to show the difference between good Hezekiah and wicked Jehoiakim. Then Ahikam, the father of Gedaliah, who was governor under Nebuchadnezzar, stood by him, and he was delivered.

CHAPTER 27

The Optimism of the False Prophets Contradicted

1. The call of Nebuchadnezzar to be the servant of God (27:1-11)
2. The call to submit and to serve the king of Babylon (27:12-22)

Verses 1-11. It was in the earlier part of the reign of Zedekiah (Jehoiakim in verse 1 is a clerical error, see verses 3 and 12) that Jeremiah is commanded to make bonds and yokes to put them on his neck; then he was to send them to the surrounding nations by the ambassadors at the court of Zedekiah. The verses which follow are of much importance and interest. God speaks as Creator, and in His sovereignty He appoints Nebuchadnezzar as head over the nations and over the beasts of the field also over the fowls of heaven (Dan. 2:38), not permanently, but for a time. God appointed a new form of government, because Jerusalem had failed, and the theocratic government as vested in the house of David was to pass away. An imperial head is chosen by the Lord from among the Gentiles. He constitutes Nebuchadnezzar His servant; with him and his rule begin the times of the Gentiles. He is the golden head in the dream-image he saw, which young Daniel interpreted by Divine revelation. The times of the Gentiles are fully revealed in Daniel's great prophecies. The predicted end of these times are not passed into history; we are still living in the times of the Gentiles. They end with the second, visible coming of Christ, when Gentile world-dominion, as it started with Nebuchadnezzar, will end, and the kingdom of heaven begins.

> This fact—that God has committed power in this world to a man—is very remarkable. In the case of Israel, man had been tried on the ground of obedience to God, and had not been able to possess the blessing that should have resulted from it. Now God abandons this direct government of the world (while still the sovereign Lord above); and, casting off Israel whom He had chosen out from the nations, grouping the latter around the elect people and His own throne in Israel, He subjects the world to one head, and committing power unto man, He places him under a new trial, to prove whether he will own the God who gave him power, and make those happy who are subjected to him, when he can do whatever he will in this world.

Whoever refuses now the new governmental order will be punished by the Lord; the nations that put their neck under the yoke of Nebuchadnezzar, to serve him, will remain in their land.

Verses 12-22. He speaks to the king and to the priests and calls them to submit to the new government established with Nebuchadnezzar. He urges them not to believe the lying prophets with their false, optimistic message, who promised smooth things. Every message they uttered, contradicted the Word of God. It is the same in Christendom today. The rationalistic critics have a message of unscriptural optimism concerning the conditions of this age, which contradicts everything made known in the prophetic Word. Part of the vessels from the temple had been carried away. The false prophets said that these vessels would shortly be returned. The Lord dispels this lying message, for He reveals through His prophet that the remaining vessels shall also be taken to Babylon.

CHAPTER 28

1. Hananiah, the false prophet (28:1-11)
2. The judgment of Hananiah (28:12-17)

Verses 1-11. One of these lying prophets became very bold, and declared that he had a message from the Lord that the yoke of the Babylonian king was to be broken, and that within two years the temple vessels would be brought back. Jeremiah said "Amen"—let it be so! But he knew it could not be so, for the Lord had spoken to him; he gives a test. Then Hananiah became still more arrogant. Jeremiah had about his neck the yoke (chapter 27:2). Hananiah took it off and broke it and declared again that within two years the yoke of Nebuchadnezzar should be broken. What applause he must have earned from the unbelieving masses about him!

Verses 12-17. Instead of yokes of wood there should be yokes of iron, the prophet tells Hananiah. He exposes him as a deceiver whom the Lord had not sent, and announces his fate, that he should die this same year. He died in the seventh month of the same year.

CHAPTER 29

Jeremiah's Letter to the Exiles

1. Jeremiah's letter (29:1-23)
2. Concerning Shemaiah and his false prophecies (29:24-32)

Verses 1-23. King Zedekiah sent Elasah and Gemariah on a diplomatic mission to King Nebuchadnezzar. Jeremiah used the occasion to send a letter by them to the exiles. The letter first of all makes it clear that their stay in Babylon will not be transitory. They are to settle down, build homes, marry, rear families, take wives for their sons and husbands for their daughters. They were to seek the peace of Babylon, for Babylon's peace would mean their own peace. The latter injunction has often been forgotten by the Jews during the past 1900 years, since their great dispersion; often have they fomented strife among the nations where they are strangers.

The false prophets had predicted a speedy return. Some of these false prophets had gone with them to Babylon and were present in the prison camp on the banks of the river Chebar. We read in Ezekiel 11:3 that they ridiculed the Divine command and gave wicked counsel. They felt themselves secure. Ezekiel continued the message of Jeremiah. (See annotations of Ezekiel.) Once more the seventy years are mentioned and what is to take place after they have expired. "For I know the thoughts that I think toward you, saith the Lord, thoughts of peace and not evil, to give you an expected end." He promises an answer to their cry, and if they seek Him, He will be found. How gracious and merciful He is towards His own! In His own time all His gracious purposes will be fully accomplished in that nation, as they were partially accomplished in the return of a remnant after the exile. Verse 14 speaks of the larger return "gathered out from all the nations." But those who persistently continued in disobedience, who listened to the false prophets will suffer the predicted fate; for such there will be no deliverance. Two of the false prophets are mentioned by name, Ahab and Zedekiah (not the king). Besides being false prophets, they were adulterers and whoremongers. King Nebuchadnezzar roasted them in the fire (22-23).

Verses 24-32. Shemaiah, a Nehelamite, which means "the dreamer," was also in Babylon, and when the captives received the letter from Jeremiah, he answered the letter The letter was received by a certain Zephaniah, of whom he inquired, "Why hast thou not reproved Jeremiah of Anathoth, which maketh himself a prophet to you?" When Zephaniah received this letter he read it to Jeremiah. The Lord exposes the Nehelamite as a deceiver, and his judgment is announced.

The Glorious Future of the Nation
(30—31)

CHAPTER 30

1. The time of Jacob's trouble (30:1-11)
2. Zion's desperate condition and the promise of deliverance (30:12-17)
3. Restoration and glory (30:18-24)

Verses 1-11. The critics have made havoc with this great prophecy. De Wette, Hitzig, and other rationalists, claim to have discovered that this chapter, and those which follow, are the work of the spurious "second Isaiah." The critics, with their present day echoes in different colleges, reject these chapters as not being Jeremianic. They are totally wrong. This great prophecy, which begins with the thirtieth chapter, is quite in order after all these judgment messages, announcing the doom of Jerusalem and of the nation. What then about the future, that future which all their fathers had cherished, the promises which rested upon the covenant Jehovah made with David? Was now everything to be plotted out and no national hope left? The last siege of Jerusalem was in progress; soon all the threatened judgments would pass fully into history. How perfectly in order is it that now should be given a message of the glorious future of the nation.

Jeremiah is commanded to write in a book all the words Jehovah had spoken; quite sufficient evidence that Jeremiah is the author and that this book is not a patchwork of different supplementers, redactors and compilers.

The first promise in verse three is concerning the coming days in which the people Israel and Judah will return to their God-given land to possess it. Has this promise been fulfilled? Expositors generally say that it was fulfilled in the return from the captivity. But this is not so. Here is a promised return not only of the house of Judah, but a return of the ten tribes also. This has never taken place. In spite of the "British-Israel" hallucination, every sane Bible reader realizes that the house of Israel is still scattered among the nations. This restoration promise will be accomplished in the future. Then we hear what will precede that restoration. It will be a time of great trouble, even the time of Jacob's trouble (Matt. 24; Mark 13), the great tribulation revealed in other portions of the prophetic Word, notably in Daniel and Revelation. When that time comes "Jacob will be saved out of it." The yoke of the last Gentile world-power (the revived Roman Empire, the ten-horned Beast of Dan. 7 and Rev. 13) will then be broken (verse 8) and they will serve the true David, David's Lord and David's Son, our Lord (verse 9). Then follows the message of comfort. How well history has confirmed this one sentence of verse 11: "Though I make a full end of all nations whither I have scattered thee, yet will I not make a full end of thee."

Verses 12-17. Here is a reminder of Zion's desperate condition and shameful history and how He had to chastise His people and wound them with the wound of an enemy. Such is still their lot and will be down to the end of this age, a people scattered and afflicted, devoured and spoiled by the nations. But when the time comes, the time of mercy for Zion, her enemies will be dealt with. In arrogant unbelief, these nations, so called "Christian nations," said "Zion is an Outcast"—"whom no man seeketh after" (verse 17); but the Lord says, "I will restore health unto thee, and I will heal thee of thy wounds."

Verses 18-24. The city then will be built again. The voices of praise and joy will be heard once more. He will glorify and increase them. He will be their God and they shall be His people. The whirlwind will strike "the head of the wicked," the wicked false king, the false Messiah, Antichrist. The next chapter is the continuation of this great prophecy.

CHAPTER 31

1. The home-going of the nation (31:1-9)
2. The joy of salvation (31:10-14)
3. The preceding tribulation, sorrow and repentance (31:15-21)
4. Assurance (31:22-26)
5. The new covenant (31:27-34)
6. The everlasting nation (31:35-40)

Verses 1-9. Sovereign grace will bring them back and give them the songs of salvation. It is true of Israel "I have loved thee with an everlasting love, therefore with loving kindness have I drawn thee"; it is equally true of us. What day of joy it will be when they go back home once more, never to leave the old homeland again! Then the watchmen on mount Ephraim cry, "Arise ye, and let us go up to Zion unto the Lord our God." Can there be anything more touching and beautiful than verses 8-9?

Verses 10-14. The nations are addressed. Oh! that the great nations of today might have an ear to hear this message, "He that scattered Israel will gather him, and keep him as a shepherd does his flock." His promises made to

Israel will not fail. The nations should understand, as they do not, that Israel will yet become the head of all the nations of the earth. What singing that will be in that day of which the prophet speaks (verse 12). What rejoicing after their sorrow! What fullness will be theirs!

Verses 15-21. Rachel weeping for her children (verse 15) is quoted in Matthew 2 in connection with the killing of the boys in Bethlehem. It has also a future fulfillment, when once more Satan will manifest his power as the murderer during the tribulation. But the promise, "They shall come again from the land of the enemy" and "Thy children shall come again to their own border," clearly shows that captivity is likewise meant from which Rachel's children (Joseph and Benjamin, i.e., Ephraim) shall return after the final tribulation and weeping. Physical resurrection is not in view here. Therefore, the next verse speaks of Ephraim moaning and in repentance. Then God's gracious answer "Is Ephraim my dear son?—I will surely have mercy upon him."

Verses 22-26. Backsliding Israel is exhorted and the assurance is given, "A woman shall compass a man." It refers to Israel as the woman, the timid, weak, forsaken one, who now will compass a man: that is have power given unto her to become the ruler. (Some have translated this difficult passage, "The woman shall be turned into a man.") Then follows the promise of assurance.

Verses 27-34. In the preceding verse we read that Jeremiah awoke, so that this message must have come to him in a vision by night, and sweet was his sleep. How refreshing must have been to his troubled soul this wonderful prophecy! The great prediction in these verses is the one concerning the new covenant. This covenant is not made with Gentiles, nor even with the church as so often erroneously stated. It is the new covenant to be made with the house of Israel and the house of Judah. This is fully confirmed in the Epistle to Hebrews (Hebrews 8:8-13). The old covenant is the law-covenant, which the Lord did not make with Gentiles, but with Israel exclusively. The new covenant is of grace. The ground of this new covenant is the sacrificial death of the Lord Jesus Christ, His blood, as we learn from His own words when He instituted the supper. He died for that nation, and therefore all Israel will yet receive the promised blessing of this new covenant. This prophecy is therefore still unfulfilled, for Israel does not enjoy this new covenant now. In the meantime, while Israel has not yet the blessings of this new covenant, Gentiles, who by nature are aliens from the commonwealth of Israel and strangers from the covenants of promise, believing in Christ, possess the blessings of this new covenant to the full. In that coming day of Israel's return, the nation, Israel and Judah, will be born again, know the Lord, and their sins will be remembered no more.

Verses 35-40. This word of Jehovah is a complete answer to those in Christendom who think that God has cast away Israel, that they are no longer the chosen people. The Lord makes a condition, "If heaven above can be measured, and the foundations of the earth searched out beneath, I will also cast off all the seed of Israel for all they have done saith the Lord." Neither has heaven been measured, neither has the depth of the earth been searched out, nor will this ever be accomplished. What a faithful covenant-keeping God He is! Verses 38-40 have never been fulfilled in the past.

CHAPTER 32

Jeremiah in Prison

1. Shut up in the court of the prison (32:1-5)
2. The revelation of the Lord concerning Hanameel (32:6-15)
3. The prophet's prayer (32:16-25)
4. Jehovah's answer (32:26-44)

Verses 1-5. The siege of Jerusalem began in the ninth year of Zedekiah's reign. It was in the tenth year, a year later (39:1) that we find Jeremiah in prison. In order to understand this imprisonment Jeremiah 37:11-21 must be consulted. He was first thrown as a prisoner into the house of Jonathan the scribe. It was a dungeon, perhaps some underground place. He was consigned there. It was a horrible place, for Jeremiah was afraid he might die there (37:20). Zedekiah seems to have been somewhat favorably inclined towards him. He asked him secretly to his palace and after Jeremiah told the king, in answer to his question about a word from the Lord, that the king should be delivered into the hands of the king of Babylon, Zedekiah on his request released him from the dungeon and put him into the court of the prison, and was kept by the king's order from starvation (37:21). Here, in our chapter, is the full text of his faithful message; had it been less faithful he might have been released.

Verses 6-15. The coming of his cousin with the request to buy his field in Anathoth is divinely announced. The right of redemption was Jeremiah's. (See Leviticus 25:25.) Hanameel came, and Jeremiah, realizing that it was of the Lord, bought the field, paying for it seventeen shekels of silver. The sale was legally transacted and executed; there being two rolls, one sealed, the other open. It was all delivered to Baruch, the faithful secretary of the prophet, mentioned here for the first time. He was instructed to put all in an earthen vessel. By his action the prophet proved his simple faith in the promised return.

Verses 16-25. What a beautiful prayer it is which came from the lips of the prisoner! He acknowledges first of all, as we all do in believing prayer the power of God, that there is nothing too hard for the Lord. Then he speaks of the loving kindness and righteousness of the God of Israel, and mentions the past history of the nation. What the Lord had predicted against the city and the nation had been done; the city was given to the Chaldeans. "What Thou hast spoken is come to pass; and behold Thou seest it." He then mentions the fact that the Lord had told him to buy that field. Then the prayer is interrupted, like Daniel's prayer.

Verses 26-44. The answer the Lord gave to praying Jeremiah is twofold. Jeremiah had said in faith, "There is nothing too hard for the Lord." The Lord answered him, "Behold, I am the Lord, the God of all flesh; is there anything too hard for Me?" Then He announces first of all the fate of the doomed city (verses 28-35). After this comes once more the message of comfort and peace looking forward to that blessed future when Israel is gathered out of all countries, brought back to the land—when they shall be His people (verses 36-44.)

CHAPTER 33

New Message of Restoration and Blessing

1. The call to pray and Jerusalem's overthrow (33:1-5)
2. Future blessing and glory (33:6-14)
3. The Branch of Righteousness; Jerusalem's new name (33:15-18)
4. Jehovah's faithfulness (33:19-26)

Verses 1-5. Jeremiah is still in prison, as we learn from the first verse. The siege of Jerusalem is on. Then the Lord said, "Call unto Me, and I will answer thee, and show thee great and mighty things, which thou knowest not." What an offer and what an assurance! Then the Lord speaks of the great and mighty things, announcing first the overthrow of Jerusalem. The demolished houses of Jerusalem are coming to be used in the defense to serve against the mounds and the sword. There will be great slaughter. (The Hebrew text of verses 4 and 5 has many difficulties.)

Verses 6-14. The next great and mighty things revealed are the future blessings and glory. Health and cure, abundance of peace and truth, a complete return from the captivity of both Judah and Israel, cleansing from all their iniquity, complete forgiveness, all are promised; and let it be remembered none of these promises has been realized. Verses 9-13 also concern the future restoration of the land and the city. What a day is yet to come when "the voice of joy, and the voice of gladness, the voice of the bridegroom, and the voice of the bride, the voice of them that shall say, Praise the Lord of Hosts" is heard, when Zion sings her beautiful redemption songs. "Behold the days come, saith the Lord, that I will perform that good thing which I have promised unto the house of Israel and the house of Judah." The delay may be long and still deferred according to His eternal purposes; but at the appointed time these days will surely come.

Verses 15-18. "In those days" in the coming days, the days of blessing and glory, when Christ comes the second time, He, the Branch of Righteousness will occupy the throne of His father David. (See Luke 1:32.) Then salvation for His people will have come, and the city will receive a new name, the name of Him whose glory covers it, "the Lord our Righteousness." Likewise will the temple worship be restored. (See annotations on Ezekiel's millennial temple.)

Verses 19-26. This is similar to 31:35, etc. His gifts and calling are without repentance. The Davidic covenant stands. He does not cast away His people.

CHAPTER 34:1-7

Jeremiah Warns Zedekiah

The besieging army was before the walls of Jerusalem when the prophet is commanded to go to the king and tell him that the city will soon be burned. He announced also Zedekiah's fate. He could not escape, but would be delivered into the hands of the king of Babylon. He would see Nebuchadnezzar eye to eye, speak with him mouth to mouth, and then be taken to Babylon. Ezekiel said he should not see Babylon (Ezek. 12:13). Both statements are true. He saw the king as a prisoner at Riblah and there his eyes were put out (2 Kings 25:6, 7), and then he was taken away to Babylon. Yet he was not to die by the sword, but in peace. And Jeremiah discharged faithfully his message.

CHAPTER 34:8-22

The Message of Condemnation

The king had made a covenant that all Hebrew slaves should be released (Exod. 21:1-6; Deut. 15:12-18). The princes and people agreed, but afterwards broke the covenant. The message of condemnation tells them, since they had done this, that the Lord will set them free to fall a prey to the sword, the pestilence and famine. The text explains itself.

CHAPTER 35

The Faithful Rechabites and the Unfaithful Jews

1. The command concerning the Rechabites (35:1-11)
2. The lesson for the Jews (35:12-19)

The Rechabites were Kenites and were numbered with the children of Israel (1 Chron. 2:55). During the reign of Jehoiakim the incident of this chapter happened. The critics may rave against the "unchronological" construction of Jeremiah jumping from one period into another, but there we see the guiding hand of the Spirit in the arrangement of these events. It is perfectly in order that this should come next to the chapter which relates the broken covenant. A careful reading and study of this chapter will bring out the lesson of their faithfulness to their father's command, and the unfaithfulness of the Jews to God's command.

CHAPTER 36

The Indestructibility of the Word of God

1. The writing of the roll (36:1-4)
2. The reading of the roll (36:4-20)
3. The king cuts and burns the roll (36:21-26)
4. The indestructibility of the Word of God (36:27-32)

Verses 1-4. Once more we are taken back to the fourth year of Jehoiakim. Jeremiah is now commanded to commit all the words Jehovah had spoken to him to writing. It was for the purpose that the people might hear of all the evil and that they might yet consider it and turn to the Lord to be forgiven. How gracious and merciful He is! He then dictated all the words to Baruch, who wrote them down. But, asks a critic, how could he remember all he had spoken? The same Spirit who communicated the messages to him, re-communicated them to the prophet.

Verses 4-20. Jeremiah was "shut in," which, however, does not mean that he was a prisoner (see verse 19); it probably means that he was not permitted to enter the Lord's house on account of some ceremonial impurity. So he sent Baruch, his amanuensis, to read the scroll to the people on the fasting day, and when all the people had come together, Baruch read the roll at the entry of the new gate. Michaiah, one of the sons of Gemariah, was deeply moved by what he had heard, went to the place where the princes sat in counsel and told them what he had heard from Baruch's lips. Baruch was then commanded to appear before the princes to read the roll to them. What they heard frightened them. They declared they would tell the king.

Verses 21-16. The king sent for the roll. The king listened to but a few of the leaves. Then, energized by the devil, he pulled out his penknife, cut the roll, and, to make sure that the roll would be destroyed, he cast it into the open fire, and with keen satisfaction he watched till the roll was consumed. Elnathan, Delaiah, and Gemariah tried to keep him from doing this evil deed, but he refused to listen to them. These three had at least some reverence for the Word of God, and therefore the Holy Spirit records their names. The king was not satisfied with this. His satanic anger was so aroused that he wanted to have Baruch and Jeremiah apprehended. Like the mad king Saul, he probably thought of killing them both. But the Lord hid them.

What Jehoiakim did, has been done over and over again. It is being done today as never before in the history of Christendom. It is being done by the destructive critics, in colleges and universities; it is done by the men who have produced the *Shorter New Testament* and the *Shorter Old Testament,* by those who advocate an abridged Bible, by others who, like the English writer Wells, want a new Bible. The same power of darkness is behind all these wicked attempts to mutilate the Word of God. Jehoiakim's work is nothing in comparison with these twentieth century infidels, because these aim at the most precious, the most blessed revelation of God, the doctrine of Christ. Their condemnation will be far greater than that of the Jewish king.

Verses 27-32. But did the king destroy the Word of God? One might just as well speak of destroying God Himself. Neither God nor His Word can ever be affected by the efforts of men inspired by the emeny of the truth of God. The Word of God endureth forever. It is, like God, eternal. How the Bibles have been burned a thousand times over again! In pagan Rome and papal Rome Satan has raged against the Bible. His Word lives on. And now the devil, camouflaged as an angel of light, in the guise of "devout scholarship" and "reverent criticism" tries it again. His Word lives on! Emperors and popes, philosophers and infidels who attacked the Bible are gone; the Bible is still with us. Jeremiah is told to take another roll. Once more the Lord dictates the same words to him, and Jeremiah again dictates them to Baruch, "with many like words," including a judgment message of the miserable end of the wicked king.

Jeremiah and Zedekiah and the Fall of Jerusalem (37—39)

CHAPTER 37

1. Jeremiah's warning (37:1-10)
2. Jeremiah's arrest (37:11-21)

Verses 1-10. To understand more fully these chapters it must be remembered that the besieging army before the gates of Jerusalem was temporarily withdrawn, because an Egyptian army had appeared against it. This was no doubt an occasion for the false prophets to preach their false hope, so that the people were deceived. Once more Zedekiah sent to the prophet a deputation (21:1) after Nebuchadnezzar had made him king. The occasion was on account of the withdrawal of the Chaldean army (verse 5). They thought that it was surely a good sign and expected a favorable message. The false hope with which they were deceiving themselves was swept away by the word of Jehovah as it came to the prophet (verses 7-10). There was no hope and after Zedekiah had rebelled (see our annotations on 2 Kings), the king of Babylon came and burnt the city with fire.

Verses 11-21. When the Chaldean army had left, Jeremiah went forth to go to his hometown Anathoth, for what is not revealed. He may have gone to claim his portion which belonged to him as priest. When, in the gate of Benjamin a captain arrested him, charging the prophet with desertion, he denied the charge. Such a charge could easily be made on account of Jeremiah's former exhortation to submit to the Chaldeans. He is put in prison in the house of Jonathan the scribe; but later the dungeon is changed to the court of the prison. (See the annotations to 32:2.)

We give a diagram which illustrates the chronology of the siege of Jerusalem and the fall of the city.

	I. The Siege begun in the ninth year	
39:1		Siege begun
	34:10	Manumission of slaves
	I. The Siege raised temporarily in the ninth or tenth year	
37:3-10=	=21:1-7	Jeremiah consulted by deputies from the king.
	34:8-22	Re-enthralment of slaves.
37:11-16		Jeremiah seized, and imprisoned in Jonathan's house.
	III. The Siege renewed in the ninth or tenth year	
37:17-21	=32:1-5 =34:1-7	Jeremiah brought in tenth year to be secretly consulted by the king: put afterwards in court of guard.
	32:6-44	Field bought by Jeremiah.
	33:1-26	Further prophecy in court of guard.
38:1-3=	=21:8-10	Jeremiah advises people to desert to Chaldeans.
38:4-6		Jeremiah put in miry dungeon.
38:7-13		Jeremiah restored by Ebed-melech to court of guard.
38:14-28		Jeremiah consulted by king in third entry of Temple: remanded to court of guard.
	IV. The Siege ended in the eleventh year	
39:1-14		City taken and destroyed.

CHAPTER 38

1. Jeremiah in the dungeon and his rescue (38:1-13)
2. Jeremiah with Zedekiah: His last appeal (38:14-28)

Verses 1-13. Jeremiah is next accused of high treason. The charge is based on his message, given to him by the Lord: "He that goeth forth to the Chaldeans shall live." Like the conscientious objectors during the past war, they accused him of being unpatriotic. "This man seeketh not the welfare of this people, but the hurt." They demand his life. In the sixth verse we see him in a deep dungeon, into which he was put by means of ropes. And Jeremiah sank into the vile mire. This reminds us of Him, our blessed Lord, who was also accused by false witnesses, and who went Himself into the horrible pit and the miry clay, into the deepest suffering and the jaws of death, to take us out of the dungeon, where sin has put us. The wicked princes evidently meant to leave Jeremiah in that dungeon to suffer a horrible death.

But the servant of the Lord was not in the hands of the princes, but in the hands of his Master. God chooses for the deliverer a slave, an Ethiopian, Ebed-melech (servant of the king). The heart of this Ethiopian eunuch was touched with pity. He goes to the king, who seems to have been ignorant about what had been done to Jeremiah and tells him that Jeremiah is likely to starve to death in the filthy hole where they had put him. The king commands the eunuch to act at once with thirty men to deliver Jeremiah. With what tenderness, to spare the man of God all needless pain, Ebed-melech carried out the king's wish (verse 12)!

Verses 14-28. This is a great dramatic scene. Zedekiah sends once more for Jeremiah. We suppose the filth of the dungeon was still clinging to the prophet's garments. The king wants to know something. "Hide nothing from me," he demands. He may rest assured that the prophet of holy courage hides nothing. But Jeremiah asks two questions: "Wilt thou not surely put me to death? And if I give thee counsel, wilt thou not hearken unto me?" The first question the king answers: "I will not put thee to death." The second question he leaves unanswered. His heart was hardened like Pharaoh's heart.

He gives him once more the message of Jehovah: Go forth to the king of Babylon, acknowledge his authority, believe in My Word and thou shalt live and thine house; then Jerusalem will not be burned. But if not, then you cannot escape and the doom of the city is sealed. The king shrinks from such a surrender. Terrors of an imaginary kind seize hold on him. He fears the Babylonian king will deliver him into the hands of the Jews who had deserted already, and that they would mock him and ill-treat him. Jeremiah pleads once more. It is his final appeal: "Obey, I beseech thee, the voice of the Lord." But the king refuses. The final request he made of Jeremiah but reveals his miserable character. The last interview has ended. Jeremiah remains in the prison and was there when Jerusalem was taken.

CHAPTER 39

1. The fall of Jerusalem and the fate of Zedekiah (39:1-9)
2. Nebuchadnezzar's kindness to Jeremiah (39:10-14)
3. Ebed-melech's reward (39:15-18)

Verses 1-9. The Word of God comes true; the prophecy of Jeremiah is vindicated! The mighty army of Nebuchadnezzar returned to the city; for many months the siege goes on under indescribable suffering. How horrible it must have been! Then the city fell and the victors rushed in; the work of slaughter and burning began. According to Jewish tradition it was on the ninth day of the month Ab. On the same date in the year 70 of our era, the city was destroyed again and the temple burned, announced some forty years before by one greater than Jeremiah, the Lord Jesus Christ. Ever since, Jerusalem has been trodden down by the Gentiles and is so still. The prophetic Word tells us of a final great tribulation which will sweep over the land, and the restored, unbelieving nation, and once more armies will gather before the city.

Zedekiah tried to escape with his men of war, but is captured. Cruelly his boys are slaughtered in his sight—the last thing his eyes beheld, for immediately after his eyes were put out. Bound with chains he is led to Babylon. All the houses of Jerusalem go up in flames; the walls are demolished and the remnant of the people are carried away prisoners (52:4-16). The poorest are permitted to remain and were treated mercifully. God remembers the poor and they are spared. For all we know, these poor people, who had nothing, were the godly, those who wept over the conditions and who cried to God for help. Their prayer, the prayer of the needy, was answered.

Verses 10-14. And if the poor were remembered, the prophet was likewise treated with great kindness. The Babylonian king commanded: "Take him, and look well to him, and do him no harm; but do unto him even as he shall say unto thee." Nebuzar-adan found the great man of God in the prison. The princes had to come and take him from the prison house of humiliation. What an exaltation! He dwelt among the people. He cast his lot with the poor, who had nothing. We doubt not Nebuchadnezzar knew much of the history we have followed, that which transpired in Jerusalem during the siege. Perhaps he even knew the great messages concerning himself. But it was the Lord who made him act as he did. His loving eye was open above His servant, who had served so faithfully.

Verses 15-18. And now the deliverer of Jeremiah, the Ethiopian eunuch, receives his reward. This message was previously given before the city fell into the hands of Nebuchadnezzar, when Jeremiah was still in prison. It is put here into this place for a very definite purpose, which once more answers the puerile charges of the critics.

It is when judgment comes that the faithful are rewarded. This is the lesson. While the ungodly fell and were carried away, the poor remained and were spared; Jeremiah is well treated, and Ebed-melech receives his reward. So will it be when the Lord comes.

III. After the Fall of Jerusalem (40—45)

CHAPTERS 40—41

The Treachery in the Land and the Flight to Egypt

1. Jeremiah's choice (40:1-6)
2. Gedaliah and Ishmael's deed (40:7—41:3)
3. Ishmael's further atrocities and retreat (41:4-18)

Verses 1-6. The opening paragraph of this chapter tells us of the choice which was given to Jeremiah. He was loosed from the prisoner's chains and told by the captain of the guard "If it seems good unto thee to come with me into Babylon, come and I will look well unto thee, but if it seem ill unto thee to come with me to Babylon, forbear; behold all the land is before thee, whither it seemeth good and convenient for thee to go, thither go." Jeremiah decided to stay with his people in the land.

Verses 40:7—41:3. The history of this section is as follows: Gedaliah had been made governor by the victorious king. When the captains heard it they came to him at Mizpah and Gedaliah exhorted them to loyalty to the Chaldeans. Then Gedaliah is warned that Baalis, the King of Ammon, has sent Ishmael to assassinate him, but Gedaliah refuses to believe the report. Then Johanan declares himself ready to kill Ishmael, so that the dreadful results of the murder of the governor Gedaliah might be averted. Gedaliah thinks it is all slander and forbids it. In the seventh month Ishmael, with ten men, who are being entertained by Gedaliah, murders him and all the Jews and Chaldeans, who are present. It is a horrible story.

Verses 41:4-18. The next day Ishmael met eighty men who came from the north; he invited them to come to Gedaliah, who was dead in his house. When they came to the place he slew them, except ten men, who offered to reveal to him hidden treasures of food. Then he carried off all the rest of the people who were left in Mizpah, to go to the land of Ammon. When Johanan and the captains heard of what Ishmael had done, they pursued him unto Gibeon, but Ishmael with eight men escaped to the Ammonites. Johanan took those whom they had rescued out of the clutches of the monster Ishmael, and, fearing the Chaldeans, purposed to go to Egypt.

CHAPTER 42

1. Jeremiah the intercessor (42:1-6)
2. The answer from Jehovah (42:7-22)

Verses 1-6. The remnant, the few who were left after the terrible happenings recorded in the preceding chapter were now cast upon the Lord and besought the prophet to pray for them: "That the Lord thy God may show us the way wherein we may walk, and the thing that we may do." They believed in Jeremiah as a man of God. He promises to do so, and when the answer comes he will not keep back anything.

Verses 7-22. The answer came ten days later. Then the word of the Lord came unto Jeremiah. If he had spoken of himself, sat down and thought out by himself what they were to do now he would have waited ten days. But it was not his counsel, not his opinion or advice; the Lord's answer to the divine counsel is that they should abide in the land and that the king of Babylon would not hinder them in any way. Then the Lord would plant them and build them up. The Lord promises them mercies and salvation. But if they went down to Egypt, the Lord's anger would be upon them and judgment would overtake them.

In their hearts they had a desire to go to Egypt. He who is the searcher of hearts knew all about it. They used deceit, and now the Lord, knowing that they would not obey, announced through the prophet that they should die by the sword, the famine and the pestilence.

CHAPTER 43

1. The rebellion against Jeremiah (43:1-7)
2. Jeremiah's prediction about the conquest of Egypt (43:8-13)

Verses 1-7. No sooner had Jeremiah finished communicating the divine answer, but the captains and the proud men denounced him. They charged him that he spoke falsely, that all he had said was at the instigation of Baruch, that both were traitors. Then the leaders did not obey the voice of the Lord to dwell in the land; they took the remnant of Judah (verse 5 is explained by 40:11-12) all the people, including Jeremiah and Baruch, to lead them down to Egypt, and finally they settled in Tahpanhes (Daphne), which was in the northeastern part, on the road out of Egypt to Palestine.

Verses 8-13. Then Jeremiah was commanded by the Lord to take great stones and bury them at the entry of Pharaoh's house in Tahpanhes, so that all the men of Judah could be witnesses of it. In 1886 the Egyptologist, Professor Petrie, excavated at Tahpanhes a brick pavement before a kind of a palace, which probably was the place where Jeremiah hid the stones. The ruin was *Kasr el Bint Jehudi,* which means, "the palace of the daughter of Judah," the place evidently assigned to the daughters of Zedekiah. (See verse 6.) The word brick-kiln means a pavement of bricks. Then, after having buried the stones, he announced that Nebuchadnezzar would come and set his throne there also, that he would conquer Egypt, smite it and burn the idol temples there. Such an invasion took place about 568 B.C., when the Egyptian King Amasis was defeated. The pillars mentioned in verse 13 are obelisks, and Beth-Shemesh means "the house of the Sun" (Heliopolis or On).

CHAPTER 44

1. The message to the Jews (44:1-10)
2. Their punishment (44:11-14)
3. Worshipping the queen of heaven (44:15-19)
4. Jehovah's answer (44:20-28)
5. The sign: Pharaoh-Hophra's Defeat (44:29-30)

Verses 1-10. The message is concerningall the Jews who were now dwelling in Egypt. Besides being in Tahpanhes, they were also in Noph (Memphis) and in Pathros, which was in the upper Egypt. Not long ago ancient papyri in Aramaic were discovered which show that there was a Jewish colony in that part of Egypt. Jeremiah reminds them in his message how God had dealt with Jerusalem and Judah on account of their idolatries, though He had sent prophets to warn them. And now they were doing the same thing in Egypt. "You too bring now utter ruin upon yourselves and all your own."

Verses 11-14. This announces their coming punishment. "Behold I will set my face against you for evil, and to cut off all Israel." They are to be punished as Jerusalem was.

Verses 15-19. What heart-hardness to say to the man of God, "We will not hearken." They intended to perform their vows to worship "the queen of Heaven." All they said was, it was well with us when we worshipped the queen of Heaven in the homeland. The women seem to have been concerned mostly in this, but they did so with the knowledge and the consent of their husbands. See about the queen of Heaven and the worship, chapter 7 and the annotations there. They claimed that all the disaster which had come on them was the result of abandoning their evil practices. What defiance and wickedness, the fruit of their unbelieving hearts! Still greater is the defiance and wickedness of today, when the cross and the gospel of Christ are deliberately rejected.

Verses 20-28. The answer is plain enough, and they heard what their fate would be for their deliberate unbelief and disobedience. These are solemn words, and the Lord said, "They shall know whose Word shall stand, Mine or theirs." God's Word will always stand, and so will those who stand by the Word of God and put their trust in it.

Verses 29-30. He gives them a sign that such will be the case. Hophra is to be given into the hands of his enemies. This happened a few years before Nebuchadrezzar defeated Amasis, who had succeeded Hophra.

CHAPTER 45

This is the shortest chapter and contains a special message to Baruch, the companion and secretary of the prophet Jeremiah. It must be noticed that this did not take place in Egypt, where now the prophet and his friend sojourned, but it was in the fourth year of Jehoiakim. Baruch had just finished writing the words which Jeremiah dictated. It was no doubt a strenuous task, and when Baruch laid down his pen, the work having been finished, the Lord sent him a special message, showing that He had not forgotten the faithful scribe. He, too, was deeply exercised over the existing conditions; he shared the grief and sorrow of the prophet. But there must have been a measure of disappointment in Baruch's heart. Had he expected some special recognition? Was he seeking something for himself, expecting great things? Had he planned and was he lifted up with some high ambition? It would seem that such was the case, for He who knows the thoughts of His creatures from afar said to him: "And seeketh thou great things for thyself? Seek them not." It is the very heart of the old nature to seek great things, to be ambitious for earthly possessions and honors, to please oneself. God's people need to watch against this more than against anything else. It is the very crime of the devil, pride (1 Tim. 3:6). Every high ambition must be dethroned; the only ambition worthy of a child of God is to please Him, who lived on earth, never pleasing Himself, who made of Himself no reputation. How it ought to ring in our hearts daily: "Seeketh thou great things? Seek them not." Seek not recognition in this poor age; wait for His day. And Baruch is assured of God's protection and care.

IV. The Prophecies Concerning the Gentile Nations

CHAPTER 46

Concerning Egypt

1. Prophecy about Pharaoh-Necho (46:1-12)
2. Nebuchadnezzar's invasion of Egypt (46:13-26)
3. A message of comfort (46:27-28)

Verses 1-12. This Pharaoh made an attempt to invade the territory of the king of Babylon, but was defeated by Nebuchadrezzar in a battle on the river Euphrates at Carchemish. This prophecy was given about eighteen years before the fall of Jerusalem. All was literally fulfilled.

Verses 13-26. This was given after the fall of Jerusalem, when the remnant had gone to Egypt. (See chapters 43 and 44.) This also was fulfilled. Verse 26 promises a future restoration of Egypt. Compare this with Isaiah's prophecy (19:19-25).

Verses 27-28. This blessed message of comfort also awaits its final great fulfillment in the coming days of promised blessing for Jacob's seed.

CHAPTER 47

Concerning the Philistines

This brief chapter is concerning the inhabitants of the borderland of Canaan, called Philistia. This announced judgment was fulfilled a short time after it was spoken by the prophet.

CHAPTER 48

Concerning Moab

1. The overthrow of Moab (48:1-10)
2. The humiliation of Moab (48:11-19)
3. Reaping what they sowed (48:20-28)
4. Destroyed on account of its pride (48:29-47)

With these divisions the chapter may be studied in detail. Moab was of incestuous offspring (Gen. 19:37). Israel is now exhorted to flee and save itself because Moab is to be destroyed. Moab's national deity was Chemosh, who was also worshipped by the sister nation, the Ammonites. Chemosh was probably the same as Molech. He is now to go forth into captivity with his priests and princes. On verse 10 critics say: "This bloodthirsty verse is surely not Jeremiah's." But they forget that the whole prophecy is introduced with, "Thus saith the Lord," and the critic's knife, which cuts out certain verses from this chapter, mutilates the Word of God. There is no valid reason to brand this and other verses as the work of some supplementer.

The chief places of Moab are mentioned. "The horn of Moab (horn the emblem of power) is cut off and his arm is broken, saith the Lord." And why this judgment? "For he has magnified himself against the Lord." They were filled with pride, yea, they were exceedingly proud. The Lord speaks of it thus: "His loftiness and his arrogancy and his pride and his haughtiness of heart." How God detests pride! In both Testaments it is marked out as the great abomination in the sight of God. Filled with pride and haughtiness, they derided Israel, God's people; whenever Israel was mentioned "they skipped for joy" (verse 27). Of verses 28 and 29, critics declare that they are mostly derived from Isaiah 15 and 16. These two chapters contain a similar prophecy about Moab, but these utterances by Jeremiah are not copied from Isaiah, but are a divine repetition of the coming judgment of that people. "Woe be unto thee Moab! the people of Chemosh perisheth! for thy sons are taken captives, and thy daughters captive." This is the final word in this predicted judgment of Moab. And thus Moab was broken.

The last verse speaks of a territorial restoration of Moab, not of a restitution of that wicked generation, as some teach. We do not know where a remnant of Moab is today, to possess in millennial times their former land; nor do we know how the Lord is going to accomplish it. But we know He will fulfill His own Word and we do not need to invent some scheme of how it will be done.

CHAPTER 49

Concerning Ammon, Edom, Damascus, Kedar, and Elam

1. Concerning the Ammonites (49:1-6)
2. Concerning Edom (49:7-22)
3. Concerning Damascus (49:23-27)
4. Concerning Kedar and Hazor (49:28-33)
5. Against Elam (49:34-39)

Ammon was the younger brother of Moab, and, like the Moabites, the Ammonites were a wicked people, though they had no cities like Moab, but were restless wanderers; they were also the enemies of Israel. The predicted judgment has come. Where is Ammon today? In what tribe or nation is a remnant preserved? Only the Omniscient One knows. But their captivity, like that of Moab, will be brought back again in the days when Israel becomes the head of the nations.

Edom, springing from Esau, was the most outspoken enemy of Israel. In our annotations on the prophecy of Obadiah we return to this chapter. Their complete judgment is here announced. "For, lo, I will make thee small among the nations and despised among men. Thy terribleness has deceived thee and the pride of thine heart, O thou that dwellest in the clefts of the rock, that holdest the height of the hill. Though thou shouldest make thy nest as high as the eagle, I will bring thee down from thence, saith the Lord" (49:15-16). Here at least the critics concede that this is a true description of the dwelling places of Edom of old. "Its capital, Petra, lay in an amphitheater of mountains, accessible only through a narrow gorge, called the *Sik,* winding in with precipitous sides from the west; and the mountain sides round Petra, and the ravines about it, contain innumerable rock-hewn cavities, some being tombs, but others dwellings in which the ancient inhabitants lived" (Canon Driver). No restoration for Edom is promised. Damascus's anguish and sorrow is predicted next, followed by a prophecy concerning various Arabian tribes; Kedar and Hazor are to be smitten. The final prediction is as to Elam. Elam was east of South Babylonia and the lower Tigris, later known as Susians. This prophecy was given at the beginning of Zedekiah's reign. Elam became an ally of the Persian kingdom. Here her overthrow is foretold as well as her restoration "in the latter days."

CHAPTERS 50—51

Babylon

These two final chapters contain a great prophecy concerning Babylon, her overthrow and doom. The fifty-first chapter closes with the statement "thus far are the words of Jeremiah." There is a direct statement that Jeremiah wrote all these words. We find it at the close of chapter 51:59-64. "Jeremiah wrote in a book all the evil that should come upon Babylon, even all these words that are written against Babylon." It would be a brazen infidelity which says Jeremiah did not write all these words. Yet the almost universally accepted view of the critics is that these chapters cannot be the work of Jeremiah. The German infidel, Professor Eichhorn, the man who coined the phrase "higher criticism," started this denial; Kuenen, Budde and others have followed in his steps. Others have modified this radical view and concede the possibility that Jeremiah may have been the author of these two chapters. No believer in the Word of God can have a moment's doubt as to this question.

An analysis of these two chapters would be difficult to make. We therefore point out some of the leading parts of this great utterance. The prophecy covers both the doom of Babylon as it has been and the doom of another, the mystical Babylon, so prominent in the last book of the Bible, in which also two chapters are devoted to Babylon. Some hold that the literal Babylon is meant in Revelation; that the city in Mesopotamia must be rebuilt; that it will finally become the one great world center domineering the religious, commercial and political affairs of all the world, and that when this has taken place Jeremiah's prophecy will be fulfilled. A careful examination of this theory will show that it is untenable. It would mean that all the great world-centers of today must be wiped out first, and London, New York, and others would have to yield their supremacy to the restored Babylon. The chapters in Revelation show us clearly that a Babylon of a mystical nature is meant, which in spirit, in worldly glory and corruption corresponds to the ancient Babylon. This mystical Babylon is Rome. This has been the interpretation of the chapters of Revelation from the earliest times and is still maintained, with a few exceptions, by all sound and spiritual expositors of the Word of God.

The message begins with the command to publish among the nations the conquest of Babylon, that Bel (lord) is put to shame and that Merodach (the chief god of Babylon, known as Marduk in Babylonian inscriptions) is dismayed. The gods of Babylon are put to confusion on account of the fall of the city. The disaster comes from the north (Medo Persia, the conqueror of Babylon; Daniel 7). Verses 4-7 predict the return of the nation thoroughly penitent. That the return of a small remnant after the defeat of Babylon does not exhaust this prophecy is obvious. The return promised here comes in the day when the times of the Gentiles are over, when Babylon and the Babylon spirit will pass away, when all false gods fall and the Lord is exalted in that day. Then the lost sheep of Israel will be found and gathered again. The invasion under Cyrus is described in verses 9-10. The fall of the Babylon in Revelation is not brought about by an invasion such as is described here, but by the ten horns of the beast, the revived Roman empire (Rev. 17:16; Dan. 7). Verse 13 announces the complete overthrow of the city, to become the hindermost of the nations, a wilderness, a dry land and a desert. This ruin was not at once carried out, but gradually ancient Babylon became all that. The ruins of this once powerful city have been located north of Hilla, a town of about 25,000 inhabitants. Koldewey, of the German Orient Society, laid bare by excavation many of the ruins, showing that the city covered twelve square miles; great streets and canals, and the ruins of the Marduk temple have been found. These ruins can never be rebuilt (Isa. 47). There is nothing which indicates that this once glorious city is to have a revival and then be destroyed once more and remain a wilderness after its destruction at some future time.

In her fall Babylon only reaped what she had sown. "For it is the vengeance of the Lord; take vengeance upon her; as she hath, do unto her" (verse 15). The same verdict is pronounced upon the Babylon of the end time, when Rome will once more have supremacy, when the present day Babylon-spirit will concentrate in a great world federation. "Reward her even as she rewarded you, and double unto her double according to her works; in the cup which she hath filled fill to her double" (Rev. 18:6). The nations will then drink of the cup of God's wrath and judgment as the literal Babylon did. Coupled with these judgment predictions are the future blessings of Israel. When the Lord overthrows the final Babylon, as seen in the book of Revelation, when the great whore is judged and her seat, Rome, in Italy, goes up in smoke, then Israel's day of glory and blessing breaks. "In those days, and in that time, saith Jehovah, the iniquity of Israel shall be sought for, and there shall be none; and the sins of Judah, and they shall not be found; for I will pardon them whom I leave as a remnant" (50:20; see chapter 31:34; Micah 7:18, and Rom. 11:25-28). After still more predictions concerning the fall and doom of Babylon (verses 21-32), we find another prophecy of comfort. When the times of the Gentiles end with the complete dethronement of Babylon in its mystical meaning as pictured in Revelation, the Redeemer of Israel will arise to plead the cause of His people Israel. The fiftieth chapter ends with an additional description of the desolation of Babylon.

The fifty-first chapter is a continued prophecy of the doom and utter desolation of the proud mistress of the nations. Much here connects with Rev. 18. The remnant of Israel is addressed in verses 5 and 6. Compare with Rev. 18:4. It is the same command to flee Babylon, a principle which is in force today as regards the true church and her separation from ecclesiastical evil. The golden cup mentioned in verse 7 is also mentioned in Revelation in chapter 17:4, in the description of papal Rome and her evil abominations. In the rest of the chapter God's dealing in judgment is wonderfully told out, prophetic of that coming day when the Lord will deal with the world in judgment. This must be the reason why such an extended prophecy is given. It all goes beyond the judgment of the literal Babylon. We call attention to the last verses of this long chapter. We read there that the prophet, after he wrote down all these words against Babylon, gave the book to Seraiah, chief chamberlain of Zedekiah. This was before the fall of Jerusalem. Seraiah was evidently the brother of Baruch (32:12). While Jeremiah knew the significant position that Babylonia, and especially King Nebuchadnezzar, had been given by the sovereign Lord, on account of which he urged submission to the Chaldeans; he also knew even then, before Jerusalem fell, of Babylon's fall and doom. Seraiah went to Babylon and he was to read the roll there, probably not in public, but in private. After reading, he was to speak certain words (verse 62), then bind a stone to the roll and cast it into the Euphrates. When the roll was sinking he was to say, "Thus shall Babylon sink and shall not rise again." In our New Testament book of prophecy we read: "And a mighty angel took up a stone like a great millstone, and cast it into the sea, saying, Thus with violence that great city Babylon be thrown down, and shall be found no more" (Rev. 18:21). That great predicted end of all God-defiance and opposition, typified by Babylon and its past glory, will surely come. Jeremiah uttered his last word.

The last chapter of Jeremiah is not from his pen; some other inspired writer was moved by the Holy Spirit to add the history of the capture of Jerusalem and the fate of the people.

The substance of this appendix is found in 2 Kings 24:18-20 and 25:1-21, 27-30. The reader will find in the second book of Kings our annotations on this history. But why is it added here once more? Evidently to show how literally the judgment predictions and divine warnings given through Jeremiah were fulfilled. For a time the false prophets had their way; their lying messages, their words of delusion and false hope were listened to and believed. The lot of the prophet of God was a lonely lot; he was rejected and he suffered. Yea, often the weeping prophet was discouraged and filled with gloom. But the time came when he was vindicated and God's Word was vindicated, while the false prophets were found out to be liars and deceivers.

In our own day we have the false prophets still with us, men and women, who deny the truth and teach error. They speak of world improvement, world betterment, and world conquest. What God has spoken concerning "wrath and judgment to come" is set aside. Those who preach and teach according to the infallible Word of God, who see no better world, no universal righteousness and peace, are branded as pessimists. The "day of the Lord" and the "coming of the Lord" are sneered at. But as the Word of God spoken by Jeremiah was vindicated, so the Word of God will be vindicated again, till all the enemies of the written Word, the Bible, and the living Word, Christ, are silenced forever.

THE BOOK OF
LAMENTATIONS

Introduction

In the Hebrew Bible, the small book which follows in our English Bible the book of Jeremiah, is placed in the portion which is called "Kethubim" (the writings). It is one of the five, so called "Megilloth." The Septuagint translation begins with a brief paragraph which is not found in our version: "It came to pass that, after Israel was taken captive and Jerusalem was made desolate, Jeremiah sat weeping and lamented with this lamentation over Jerusalem, and said . . .;" then the first chapter begins. The Vulgate (Latin) translation has adopted this statement and also the Arabic version.

There can be no question that Jeremiah is the inspired author of these outbursts of grief, as well as confession of sin and dependence on Jehovah. Yet this has not only been seriously questioned, but positively denied. Critics claim that probably chapters 2 and 4 must have been written by an eye-witness of Judah's conquest; they deny that it was Jeremiah and think it must have been one of the exiles. The claim is made because it appears to them that these two chapters lean strongly on Ezekiel and parts, they say, must have been copied after Ezekiel's writings. The other chapters, they say, are much later. Critics like Budde and Cheyne put the third chapter in the pre-Maccabean period towards the end of the third century. All is nothing but guesswork, which is proved by the different theories of these scholars, which clash with each other. To show the superficial method of these men we shall give a few of the star arguments against the Jeremianic authorship of Lamentations. They say that 4:17 could hardly have been written by Jeremiah because the writer includes himself with those who had expected help from Egypt. But the critic does not see that the prophet identifies himself with the nation, as Daniel did. The, again, they object to 4:20, because it speaks of Zedekiah in such a way as Jeremiah would never have spoken of him. But how do they know? Zedekiah was still the Lord's anointed, even as David recognized down to the sad end of Saul, the king as the Lord's anointed. Instead of being an argument against the authorship of Jeremiah, it is one for it.

Then these "literary" critics claim that the smooth and beautiful style cannot be Jeremiah's. "The whole style of these poems, though exquisitely beautiful and touching, and studded with the thoughts of the great prophet, is absolutely different to anything we find in the long roll of Jeremiah's great work. It is too artificial, too much studied, too elaborately worked out" (A. B. Davidson). If A. B. Davidson and other critics had just a little faith in divine inspiration they would not write such puerile criticism. As if the Spirit of God could not change the style and manner of the writings of one of His chosen instruments!

The Lamentations are correctly divided into five chapters in a very remarkable way. Chapters 1 and 2 consist each of twenty-two verses of three lines each. All is written in a certain meter. Each verse begins in both chapters with the successive letters of the Hebrew alphabet. They are acrostics. The third chapter has instead of 22 verses, 66 verses, that is 3 x 22. The first three verses of this chapter begin each with the first letter of the Hebrew alphabet; the next three with the second letter, so that in these 66 verses the Hebrew alphabet is again followed. The fourth chapter is also arranged in the same manner, acrostically, each of the 22 verses begin with the letters of the Hebrew alphabet. The last chapter shows no such arrangement. We doubt not that in all this there may be a hidden, a deeper meaning, which no saint of God has yet discovered.

The message of this book is extremely precious. It is a pity that so few of God's people have ever paid a closer attention to this book. Here is indeed a great mine of comfort and spiritual instruction which will prove very wholesome to all those who walk with God.

When Israel suffered in Egypt the Lord said: "I have surely seen the affliction of My people" (Exod. 3:7). Lamentations shows the same blessed fact, that Jehovah has a loving and deep interest in the afflictions of His people through which they pass on account of their sins. He who had to chastise His people is nevertheless moved with compassion in their behalf. Yea, in their affliction He Himself is afflicted and He yearns over them. The feelings, deep emotions of sorrow and humiliation, expressed by the mouthpiece of Jehovah, Jeremiah, were produced by the Spirit of Christ, in the heart of the prophet.

"There is nothing more affecting than the sentiments produced in the heart by the conviction that the subject of affliction is beloved of God, that He loves that which He is obliged to smite, and is obliged to smite that which He loves. The prophet, while laying open the affliction of Jerusalem, acknowledges that the sin of the people had caused it. Could that diminish the sorrow of his heart? If on the one hand it was a consolation, on the other it humbled and made him hide his face. The pride of the enemy, and their joy in seeing the affliction of the beloved of God, give occasion to sue for compassion on behalf of the afflicted, and judgment on the malice of the enemy" *(Synopsis of the Bible).*

Prophetically we may look upon these lamentations as embodying the soul-exercise of the godly remnant of God's earthly people passing in a future day through the great tribulation. That beautiful prayer found in the last chapter will then be answered, "renew our days of old" and all the glorious promises given to Israel will then be fulfilled.

No further division of this book is needed; the division into five chapters is perfect.

CHAPTER 1

Jerusalem's Great Desolation and the Sorrow of His People

The chapter begins with an outburst of grief over Jerusalem's desolation. Once she was a populous city; now she is solitary. Once she was great among the nations, like a princess among provinces, and now she is widowed. Then in the next verse we hear her weeping; she weeps all night long; none is there to comfort her; her friends have turned against her, they have become her enemies. She was disobedient to her Lord, she rejected His Word, she gave up her holy place as His separated people and now "she findeth no rest." The Lord's hand is upon her for the multitude of her transgressions. The hopeful note we find in verses 8-11. Here is confession of her guilt and shame; here is humiliation and appeal to the Lord on account of the enemy. "See, O Lord, and behold; for I am become vile." Such humiliation and self-judgment is pleasing in the Lord's sight.

In verse 12 Jerusalem speaks: "Is it nothing to you, all ye that pass by? Behold, and see if there be any sorrow like unto my sorrow, which is done unto me, wherewith the Lord hath afflicted me in the day of His fierce anger." The passer-by who beholds the ruins of Zion is asked to look upon the desolations and then to consider that the Lord in His righteous anger smote her, who is still His beloved. Well may we think of Him, who had to say, "See if there be any sorrow like unto My sorrow," who was smitten and afflicted, upon whom Jehovah's rod rested, over whose blessed head all the waves and billows of Divine judgment-wrath rolled, He who is the Beloved, the Son of God, our Lord. Again the prophet breaks out in weeping, "His eye runneth down with water." He is deeply affected over the desolation and judgment which has taken place. But a greater One, greater than Jeremiah, stood centuries after before the same city, brought back from the ruin of Jeremiah's time. And as He beheld that city He wept, because His omniscient eye beheld a still more appalling judgment for city and nation.

Forsaken, uncomforted, distressed, humiliated, sighing and crying, owning her rebellion, vindicating Jehovah and His righteousness, Jerusalem sits in the dust, "abroad the sword bereaveth, at home there is death."

CHAPTER 2

What the Lord Has Done

The great catastrophe continues in vivid description throughout this chapter also. Not an enemy has done it, not Nebuchadrezzar and his Chaldean hordes, but the Lord is the executor of all. The beauty of Israel He cast down; He swallowed up the habitations of Jacob; He burned against Jacob like a flame; He bent His bow like an enemy; He poured out His fury like fire; He was as an enemy. These are a few of the many expressions with which the righteousness of the Lord in judging His people is acknowledged.

And what a great description of Jerusalem and her inhabitants we read in verses 8-16. Gates broken down; king and princes among the Gentiles; law abandoned; no more visions! Elders on the ground in sackcloth and ashes; virgins hanging their heads; children and sucklings swooning in the streets—and all that pass by clap their hands, hiss, and wag their head at the daughter of Jerusalem.

"The Lord hath done what He had devised; He hath fulfilled the Word that He had commanded in the days of old." Oh! that the people today would hear and believe that God will yet fulfill other judgment messages and deal with the world on account of its sin. The chapter ends with a prayer.

CHAPTER 3

The Prophet's Suffering and Distress

This chapter is intensely personal. None but Jeremiah could have written these wonderful expressions of sorrow, the sorrows of the people of God into which he entered so fully, in such a way that they become his own. He shared all their afflictions, bore them himself and then was hated by them. It was the Spirit of Christ who created these feelings in the heart of the prophet. In reading these words of deep distress and the words of faith and waiting for Him, we must look beyond Jeremiah and see a picture of our Lord, "the Man of sorrows and acquainted with grief," His sorrow and His afflictions, the emotions of His holy soul, as well as the experiences and soul exercise of the believing remnant of Israel in days to come.

The prophet speaks of himself as one who is smitten by the rod of God's wrath, the man that hath seen affliction. He had not deserved that wrath; the wrath and affliction have come upon a sinful people, but he identifies himself with them. What must have been the suffering and the affliction of our Lord when He, at the close of His blessed life, suffered and died the death of the cross! The rod of righteousness fell on Him. More than Jeremiah did, He tasted that wrath, when He who knew no sin was made sin for us. "He (God) hath bent His bow, and set me as a mark for the arrow. He hath caused the arrows of His quiver to enter into my reins. I was a derision to all my people and their song all the day" (verses 12-14). He speaks of "the wormwood and the gall" (verse 19); of the "smitten cheek filled with reproach" (verse 30).

Through such suffering Jeremiah passed as well as the godly of all ages, as well as those in the future. Jeremiah's affliction but faintly foreshadows the afflictions of the Afflicted One. But while Jeremiah suffered with Jerusalem and for Jerusalem, he was not destitute of comfort. He knew the Lord and He sustained him in his affliction. How beautifully he speaks of the mercies of the Lord, of His compassions which never fail, of the greatness of His faithfulness (verses 22,23). Such is the comfort still of all those who know the Lord; it is the song in the night: "The Lord is my portion, saith my soul; therefore will I hope in Him. The Lord is good unto them that wait for Him, to the soul that seeketh Him." All His saints speak thus when they feel the chastening hand of the Lord. He has full confidence in the Lord and knows "He doth not afflict willingly," and that "the Lord will not cast off for ever." And again, "though He cause grief, yet will He have compassion according to the multitude of His mercies."

Beginning with verse 40, a real return is described. There is self-examination: "Let us search and try our ways and turn again to the Lord." This is followed by prayer: "Let us lift up our hearts with our hands unto God in the heavens." Then comes confession: "We have transgressed and have rebelled; Thou hast not pardoned." It describes prophetically the repentance of a Jewish remnant when this present age ends and the Lord is about to be manifested in visible glory. Jeremiah's lament over Jerusalem's condition and the nation's state is once more recorded in verses 45-47. "Thou hast made us an offscouring and refuse in the midst of the people. All our enemies have opened their mouths against us. Fear and snare is come upon us, desolation and destruction." Such will also be the complaint of the suffering remnant. This chapter ends with an imprecatory prayer. "Render unto them a recompense, O Lord, according to the works of their hands. Give them sorrow of heart, thy curse unto them. Persecute and destroy them in anger from under the heavens of the Lord." It is like the imprecatory prayers in the Psalms, prayers which will be prayed when the godly in Israel suffer under their enemies in the great tribulation.

CHAPTER 4

The Departed Glory and the Cup of Shame

This new lament begins with a description of the former glory of Zion and its present wretchedness; the glory is departed:

How is the gold become dim! The most pure gold changed!
The stones of the sanctuary are poured forth at the top of every street.
The precious sons of Zion, just like fine gold—
How are they now esteemed like earthen pitchers, the work of the potters' hands!
Even the jackals draw out the breast, giving suck to their young—

The daughter of my people is become cruel, like the ostriches in the wilderness.
The tongue of the sucking child cleaveth to the roof of his mouth for thirst.
The young children ask bread, no man breaketh it unto them.
They that did feel delicately are desolate in the streets.
They that were brought up in scarlet embrace dunghills.

What degradation and shame! The Lord had called Zion to be like the pure gold, precious and glorious. In his beautiful parable, Ezekiel speaks thus of Jerusalem's glory: "Thus wast thou decked with gold and silver; and thy raiment was of fine linen and silk and broidered work; thou didst eat fine flour, and honey, and oil; and thou wast exceeding beautiful, and thou didst prosper in a kingdom" (Ezekiel 16:13). The gold is become dim, the pure gold changed. Instead of the linen and silk there is sackcloth and ashes; instead of the flour, the honey, and the oil, there is want and famine. When the golden-glory departed from Zion, then the Lord revealed that Nebuchadnezzar is "the head of gold," the starting point of the times of the Gentiles. The glory had departed and Zion had to drink of shame and want to the full on account of her sins (verse 6). And what a contrast now between what the Nazarites and nobles of the nation were once and what they are now. They were purer than snow, whiter than milk; and now they are blacker than coal. They were ruddy in body; and now their skin cleaveth to their bones. What a horrible transformation sin had wrought! Sin is a robber; sin brings its wages. It robs of glory and gives nothing but suffering, shame and death. All that God had spoken long ago, the very curses generation after generation had read in the book of the law (Deut. 28:56, 57; Lev. 26:29), had come upon them. The kings of the earth, the inhabitants of the world, knew that Jerusalem was unconquerable, for the Lord of all the earth was Zion's King and Lord. What no earthly power could have done, to enter Jerusalem and spoil the city, the Lord had done, "on account of the sins of her prophets, the iniquities of her priests, that have shed the blood of the just in the midst of her." Jerusalem was built again. Once more after the seventy years the city was restored, the temple rebuilt. Then the Just One came, the Messiah of David, the Lord of Glory. They shed the blood of the Just One, and now, as verse 14 says, "They wander about blind."

And Edom! She had rejoiced at Zion's overthrow, even as Gentiles have despised Israel. But there is judgment in store for the nations, mercy for Israel, when the punishment is accomplished. "He will no more carry thee away into captivity."

CHAPTER 5

The Prayer of Hope

The lamentations end with a prayer: "Remember, O Lord, what is come upon us; consider and behold our reproach." It is the prayer of confession and of hope, which reaches the heart of the God of Israel. The prophet, in behalf of the nation, pours out his confession: "The crown is fallen from our head; woe unto us that we have sinned." And there is hope in the Lord who remaineth, whose throne is from generation to generation. The prayer, "Turn Thou us unto Thee, O Lord, and we shall be turned; renew our days as of old" (verse 21) will some day be blessedly answered. The Eightieth Psalm contains the same prayer a number of times, and there He is mentioned who will yet save His people Israel from their sins. "Let Thy hand be upon the Man of Thy right hand, upon the Son of Man whom Thou madest strong for Thyself. So will not we go back from Thee; quicken us and we will call on Thy Name. Turn us again O Lord God of hosts, cause Thy face to shine, and we shall be saved."

"The prophet now presents in this chapter the whole affliction of the people *to God,* as an object of compassion and mercy. This is an onward step in the path of these deep exercises of heart. He is at peace with God; he is in His presence; it is no longer a heart struggling with inward misery. All is confessed before Jehovah, who is faithful to His people, so that he can call on God to consider the affliction in order that He may remember His suffering people according to the greatness of His compassions. For Jehovah changes not (5:19-21). The sense of the affliction remains in full, but God is brought in, and everything having been recalled and judged before Him, all that had happened being cleared up to the heart, Jeremiah can rest in the proper and eternal relations between God and His beloved people; and, shutting himself into his direct relations with his God, he avails himself of His goodness, as being in those relations, to find in the affliction of the beloved people an opportunity for calling His attention to them. This is the true position of faith—that which it attains as the result of its exercises before God at the sight of the affliction of His people (an affliction so much the deeper from its being caused by sin).

"This book of Lamentations is remarkable because we see in it the expression of the thoughts of the Spirit of God, that is, those produced in persons under His influence, the vessels of His testimony, when God was forced to set aside that which He had established in the world as His own. There is nothing similar in the whole circle of the revelations and of the affections of God. He says himself, How could He treat them as Admah and Zeboim? Christ went through it in its fullest extent. But He went through it in His own perfection with God. He acted thus with regard to Jerusalem, and wept over it. But here man is found to have lost the hope of God interposing on His people's behalf. God would not abandon a man who was one of this people, who loved them, who understood that God loved them, that they were the object of His affection. He was one of them. How could he bear the idea that God had cast them off? No doubt God would re-establish them. But in the place where God had set them, all hope was lost forever. In the Lord's own presence it is never lost. It is in view of this that all these exercises of heart are gone through, until the heart can fully enter into the mind and affections of God Himself. Indeed, this is always true.

"The Spirit gives us here a picture of all these exercises. How gracious! To see the Spirit of God enter into all these details, not only of the ways of God, but of that also which passes through a heart in which the judgment of God is felt by grace, until all is set right in the presence of God Himself. Inspiration gives us not only the perfect thoughts of God, and Christ the perfection of man before God, but also all the exercises produced in our poor hearts, when the perfect Spirit acts in them, so far as these thoughts, all mingled as they are, refer in the main to God, or are produced by Him. So truly cares He for us! He hearkens to our sighs, although much of imperfection and of that which belongs to our own heart is mixed with them. It is this that we see in the book of Lamentations, in the Psalms, and elsewhere, and abundantly, though in another manner, in the New Testament" *(Synopsis of the Bible).*

THE PROPHET
EZEKIEL

Introduction

From the opening verses of the book we learn that Ezekiel was the son of Buzi, the priest, and belonged consequently to the much honored Zadok family. That he knew the nobility of Jerusalem well and was intimate with them may be indirectly learned from the eleventh chapter. Rabbinical tradition makes Buzi (which means "contempt") a son of Jeremiah. There is no evidence for this. Eleven years before the complete ruin of the city and the temple by the King of Babylon, Ezekiel was carried away into the captivity. This deportation is recorded in 2 Kings 24:14. Before Ezekiel with the princes and the mighty men were taken into captivity, others had been removed to Babylon, notably Daniel and his three companions. Ezekiel must have known Daniel personally. His name is found three times in this book (14:14, 20; 38:3).

Ezekiel was not a youth, as generally supposed, when he was deported to Babylon, for the matured character of a priest which appears in his writings and his full and intimate acquaintance with the temple service render such a supposition highly improbable. Jewish tradition declares that he exercised already the prophetic office before he was carried away.

The name Ezekiel means "strengthened by God." It has been stated by some that this is not the original name of the prophet, but his official title, which he adopted on account of his ministry among the people. Very interesting on this controverted point is the statement in a rabbinical comment. The declaration is made that the prophets of God received their significant names, so closely linked with and expressive of the character of their messages, from above, and not according to the will of their earthly parents. God called them to their work and had them named accordingly before they ever entered upon their offices as prophets. We believe this may be correct, especially in view of Jeremiah 1:5.

Where He Ministered

The place where we find Ezekiel is the river Chebar. This river is now known by the name *Kabour.* It emptied into the Euphrates north of Babylon and was also called *Nar-Kabari,* the great canal. Here Nebuchadnezzar had started a colony of captives. In chapter 3:15, the name of the place is given; it was at Tel-abib. In this settlement the prophet seems to have lived. Two passages in the book tell us that he had his own house (3:24, 8:1). We also know that he was married (24:16-18). The death of his wife is the only event he mentions of his personal history, and that would probably have not been recorded if it were not connected with his prophetic office. The prophecies he uttered among the captives are carefully dated. The first date is found in chapter 1:1-2.

Ezekiel and Jeremiah

Ezekiel's great prophetic ministry is closely connected with that of Jeremiah. When Ezekiel had his first great vision on the banks of the river Chebar, Jeremiah had already been a prophet for thirty-five years. Only a few years more remained for this great man of God. That Ezekiel must have been acquainted with Jeremiah and his messages of warning and exhortation is more than likely. Yet it is strange there is not a single reference to Jeremiah in the entire book of Ezekiel. It is strange in view of the fact that the messages of these two men have so much in common. Critics make the assertion that Ezekiel as a prophet was molded by the teaching of Jeremiah. Kuenen claims that Ezekiel must have been for many years the close student of Jeremiah's writings. Before Ezekiel proceeded to write his own prophecies, his mind, it is claimed, had become so saturated with the ideas and language of Jeremiah that every part of his book betrays the influence of his predecessor. This view would make Ezekiel an enthusiastic admirer and copyist of Jeremiah. But in the book of Ezekiel the phrases "Thus saith the Lord God"—"The Word of the Lord came unto me"—occur over and over again. The words he spoke, the mighty messages he delivered, were not produced by the influence of Jeremiah nor by his example, but by the Spirit of God. Other critics have even done greater dishonor to this chosen instrument of the Lord and to the Word he preached. We quote from *The New Century Bible:* "It would appear that there runs through all the prophet's activities, at least in the earlier period, a strain of mental abnormality—perhaps of actual malady. By some writers this has been supposed to be a form of catalepsy. Probably Ezekiel was no more a cataleptic than Paul; with equal probability he was what would now be called a 'psychical subject,' and as such liable to trances—and perhaps a clairvoyant." Such are the ridiculous things invented by men, who claim scholarship, and whose aim is to deny the supernatural origin of the words and the visions of the prophets of God.

The fact is that Jeremiah and Ezekiel were called by Jehovah to specific ministries. In their characters and natural temperaments they differed greatly. Jeremiah, assuming, as a very young man, his prophetic office during the reign of Josiah, was called to deliver the messages of the awful judgments which were to come upon Jerusalem and had to witness these in their execution. He was an extremely kind, gentle, and tender-hearted man. Jeremiah is the prophet of a dying nation; the agony of Judah's prolonged death struggle is reproduced with tenfold intensity in the inward conflict which rends the heart of the prophet. Ezekiel was of a different temperament. The deep soul exercise we find so often in Jeremiah, his tender, loving sympathies, are almost entirely absent in Ezekiel. He lacked the emotional character of Jeremiah. He was a man of great energy and vigor; he was stern and had a deep sense of his human responsibility. Both prophets uncover the corrupt conditions of Judah and condemn them. The condemnations in Ezekiel are far more severe than those in Jeremiah. The style of Ezekiel is also different from that employed by his contemporary.

In all this he differs from Jeremiah; and more so in the greater and more complete visions concerning the future.

His Ministry

There is an evident connection between the communication which Jeremiah sent from Jerusalem unto the captives in Babylon and the beginning of Ezekiel's ministry. The letter of Jeremiah is found in chapter 29 of the book of Jeremiah. It is an interesting document. It seems to have been occasioned by a number of false prophets who had appeared among the captives, and who encouraged the rebellious and disobedient spirit which prevailed among the exiles. They prophesied falsely, led the people away, and awakened the delusive hope of an early return from the captivity. While Jeremiah continued to minister to the feeble few and the poor, who were left behind, Ezekiel was engaged among the captives and contended against these false prophets and against the false hopes of the people who gave no evidences of repentance. Inasmuch as Jerusalem had not yet been completely destroyed by Nebuchadnezzar, the captives, who had listened to the false prophets, expected a speedy return to their own land. To dispel this false hope Jeremiah had sent them the message, "For thus saith the Lord, that after seventy years be accomplished at Babylon I will visit you, and perform My good word toward you, in causing you to return to this place" (Jer. 29:10). Ezekiel then labored also to dispel this false hope preached by the prophets, whom the Lord had not sent. By his stern and solemn words, by divinely commanded actions and symbols, he had to deliver the message that there was no hope for Jerusalem. When the catastrophe came at last, his ministry changed. He comforts the disappointed and heartbroken people and delivers his great restoration messages.

This great prophet had to do certain divinely commanded things in the presence of the people who were living in deception after having listened to the false prophets. In chapter 3:24-26 he had to shut himself up, bind himself, and then he was made dumb. Then he was commanded to lie upon his right side and upon his left for 430 days (4:4-8). In chapter 4:9 he had to eat unclean bread. Then he had to shave his head and beard (5:1); to carry a captive's baggage (12:3-7); when his wife died, he was not to mourn (24:15-20); and again he lost his speech (24:27). The key to all this is found in chapter 24:24.

The visions of glory Ezekiel had belong to some of the greatest recorded in the Word of God. Much in the beginning of the book reminds of the last book of the Bible, the Revelation. We mention a few passages to be compared: Ezekiel 1 with Rev. 4 and 5. Ezekiel 3:3 with Rev. 10:10. Ezekiel 8:3 with Rev. 13:14, 15. Ezekiel 9 with Rev. 7. Ezekiel 10 with Rev. 8:1-5. The critics declare upon this striking correspondency that "much of the imagery of Revelation is borrowed from Ezekiel."

The Division of the Book

A careful reading of the book of Ezekiel shows, in the first place, that the prophet received messages and saw visions before the final destruction of Jerusalem, and after that catastrophe had taken place in fulfillment of his inspired predictions, he received other prophecies. The predictions preceding the fall of Jerusalem are the predictions of the judgment to fall upon the city and upon Gentile nations, the enemies of Israel. The predictions Ezekiel received after the city had been destroyed are the predictions of blessing and glory for Israel and Jerusalem in the future. The first part of the book has found a fulfillment in the destruction of the city by Nebuchadnezzar. The second part is awaiting its fulfillment at the close of the times of the Gentiles, when Israel will be regathered, restored and the glory of the Lord returns to another temple, which Ezekiel beheld in a magnificent vision. All will be accomplished when the Lord returns to dwell in the midst of His people, so that the name of the city will be "Jehovah-Shammah"—"the Lord is there" (48:35). These two main divisions are clearly marked in the book itself. In chapter 33:21, after the prophet had received a renewed call as watchman, we read: "And it came to pass in the twelfth year of our captivity, in the tenth month, in the fifth day of the month, that one that had escaped out of Jerusalem came unto me, saying, The city is smitten." This detemines the two parts.

To show the perfect and orderly arrangement of the whole book of Ezekiel we shall give a complete analysis.

I. PREDICTIONS BEFORE THE DESTRUCTION OF JERUSALEM

Section A. Judgment Predictions Concerning Jerusalem (1—24)

1. The Vision of the Glory of the Lord and the Call of the Prophet (1—3:14)
2. The Judgment Announced, Four Signs and Their Meaning, and the Two Messages. (3:15—7:27)
3. Visions in Relation to Jerusalem (8—11)
4. Signs, Messages, and Parables (12—19)
5. Further and Final Predictions Concerning the Judgment of Jerusalem (20—24)

Section B. Predictions of Judgments against the Nations (25—32)

1. Against Ammon, Moab, Edom, and the Philistines (25:1-17)
2. Against Tyrus and Zidon (26—28)
3. Against Egypt (29—32)

II. PREDICTIONS AFTER THE DESTRUCTION OF JERUSALEM

Section A. The Watchman and the Shepherds (33—34)

1. The Renewed Call of Ezekiel as watchman (33:1-20)
2. Ezekiel's Mouth Opened After Jerusalem's Fall (33:21-33)
3. Message Against the shepherds of Israel (34:1-19)
4. The True Shepherd and restoration Promised (34:20-26)

Section B. Judgment Announced Against Mount Seir and Israel's Final Restoration Promised (35—36)

1. The Message Against Seir and Idumea (35:1-15)
2. The Message of Comfort for Israel (36:1-38)

Section C. The Future Blessings of Israel, the Nation Regathered, Their Enemies Overthrown and the Millennial Temple (37—48)

1. The Vision of the Dry Bones and Judah and Israel Reunited (37:1-28)
2. The Last Enemies, Gog and Magog, and Their Destruction (38—39)
3. The Millennial Temple, and Its Worship, the Division of the Land (40—48)

Analysis and Annotations

I. Predictions Before the Fall of Jerusalem

A. Judgment Predictions Concerning Jerusalem (1—24)

CHAPTERS 1:1—3:14

The Vision of Glory and the Call of the Prophet

1. The introduction (1:1-3)
2. The vision of glory (1:4-28)

3. Ezekiel's call and commission (2:1-8)
4. The roll eaten and the repeated commission (2:9—3:14)

Verses 1:1-3. The introductory words give us the time when Ezekiel was among the captives by the river Chebar. Four things are mentioned by Ezekiel, who is evidently the author of this book, for he uses the personal pronoun—the heavens were opened—he saw visions of God—the word of the Lord came unto him—the hand of the Lord was upon him. Ezekiel is the only prophet in the Old Testament of whom it is said that he saw the heavens opened. Four times the New Testament mentions opened heavens (Matt. 3:16; John 1:51; Rev. 4:1; 19:11). He then saw the visions of God concerning His governmental dealings with His people Israel. Then the hand of the Lord was also upon him when the word of the Lord had come unto him. Notice the order: An opened heaven, a vision, the call, and enablement by the power of God. Such is still the order for the servants of the Lord. The phrase, "The hand of the Lord was upon him," or came upon me, is found seven times in Ezekiel, in chapters 1:3, 3:14 and 22, 8:1, 23:22, 37:1, 40:1.

Verses 4-28. Then he had his great and wonderful vision, which is repeatedly mentioned in his book. We find it mentioned again in chapters 10 and 11, where it is seen departing from Jerusalem. Its return is promised in connection with the great millennial temple after the Lord's return (chapter 43). The vision is the vision of the glory of the Lord (1:28). The vision comes from the north, for a storm cloud of divine indignation from the north (Babylon) was to burst over the house of Judah. The whirlwind, the cloud, and the fire Ezekiel beheld are symbols of glory, the divine presence and judgment. (See Psa. 18:8-13; Hab. 3; Jer. 4:12-13). The vision then indicated the presence of the God of Israel and His glory, ready to deal in judgment with His apostate people. The living creatures are the same as mentioned and seen in Rev. 4:6-9. They are the cherubim, not fictitious creatures or symbols, but real beings. Their position is in connection with the throne. But upon the throne there was one who had the likeness as the appearance of a man. And this man was enshrouded in glory, with the rainbow about him. All this shows forth the glory of Him who is God' vision, glory and presence, the Son of God. It anticipates the Lord Jesus Christ, His exaltation upon the throne, government and judgment resting in His hands, who is now the Man in the glory. While the cherubim with their fourfold faces also symbolize the Lord Jesus, here in this vision they are seen in connection with judgment. It is the same in Revelation (Rev. 6; 15:7). And then the wheels and their work. In them was the spirit of these great creatures; the rims of the wheels (not rings) were full of eyes. There was an orderly movement of these wheels. The wheels are on the chariot upon which rested the throne of God. They show forth and symbolize the purposes of God in the execution of His inerrant governmental dealings on earth. God controls it all, and His Spirit directs every movement. Much that is ridiculous has been written on this, and some would-be expositors claim that Ezekiel beheld an aeroplane.

"Intelligence, strength, stability and swiftness in judgment, and, withal, the movement of the whole course of earthly events, depended on the throne. This living energy animated the whole. The cherubic supporters of the throne, full of eyes themselves, moved by it; the wheels of God's government moved by the same spirit, and went straight forward. All was subservient to the will and purpose of Him who sat on the throne judging right. Majesty, government and providence united to form the throne of His glory. But all the instruments of His glory were below the firmament; He whom they glorified was above" (*Synopsis of the Bible).*

Verses 2:1-8. We see Ezekiel prostrate upon his face. Then a voice spoke, not the voice of a cherubim; while in Revelation the cherubim speak, in Ezekiel they are silent. Jehovah addressed Ezekiel as son of man; the title which is found exactly one hundred times in this book. Daniel only besides Ezekiel is called by this name. Our Lord called Himself by that name and used it in connection with His suffering, exaltation, glory, and coming again. Ezekiel, too, passed through much suffering, passing symbolically through sufferings which the nation at large was to undergo. He is, therefore, in a measure a type of the Messiah, who took Israel's sin and shame upon Himself.

The Word which spoke was followed by the Spirit—"and the Spirit entered into me when He spoke unto me." Thus the Word and the Spirit are always connected. Then Ezekiel received his commission. He is sent to an impudent and hard-hearted people. His message is to begin with: "Thus saith Jehovah-God." The sender is the Lord; the message is from Him. Then the sender gives also assurance and encouragement.

Verses 2:9—3:14. Compare the roll here with Zech. 5:1-4; with the one of Rev. 5, which the Lamb receives and opens, and the little roll in Rev. 10:9, 10. These rolls have the same meaning, namely, the Word itself, the message of tribulation and judgment, which is written therein.

The Word must be received and eaten, that is the spiritual lesson. Ezekiel obeyed. It was self-surrender and though the message was a hard message, yet it was sweet unto him. Compare with Jer. 15:16. Ezekiel was to speak the words of the Lord unto them; and the sender predicts failure. "The house of Israel will not hearken unto thee, for they will not hearken unto Me." It was to make no difference to the prophet. His commission was to speak Jehovah's words. Then cherubim and wheels are in motion. He is lifted up and Jehovah's hand is strong upon him.

CHAPTERS 3:15—7:27

The Judgment Announced, the Four Signs and Their Meaning, and the Two Messages

This section extends from chapter 3:15 to the close of the seventh chapter. The prophet is told of his great responsibility as watchman, and has to enact four signs. Two solemn messages close this section. The first message predicts that the sword is to come upon the land and disperse them; the second message predicts the end.

1. The new charge and Ezekiel's new experience (3:15-27)
2. The sign of the tile (4:1-3)
3. The sign of the prophet's physical position (4:4-8)
4. The sign of the famine and the defiled bread (4:9-17)
5. The sign of the shaving of head and face (5:1-4)
6. The message of denunciation (5:5-17)
7. The first judgment message: I will bring a sword upon you (6:1-14)
8. The second judgment message: The end is at hand (7:1-27)

Verses 3:15-27. He had been transported by the power of God from the river Chebar to Tel-abib, where a number of captives dwelt. He sat for seven days in their presence without opening his lips. (See Job 2:13.) The silence of Ezekiel was broken by the Lord, who spoke to him and gave him a new charge, that of a watchman unto the house of Israel. His duty was to be twofold: First, to hear the word of the Lord from His own lips, and then to give the warning. It is a solemn message and charge, making known to the prophet his great responsibility.

The passage, as well as the corresponding one in chapter 33:1-20, has been often used in the defence of what is termed "falling from grace,"—that a true believer, who is saved by grace, may by sinning become unsaved again and then perish in his sins like the wicked. The words "fallen from grace" are found only once in the Bible, that is in Gal. 5:4. The context shows what they mean. If a believer goes to the law to be justified before God, if he tries by his own works, and by ordinances, to be righteous before God, he abandons the ground of grace. The dispensation in which we live is the dispensation of grace; grace reigns through righteousness unto eternal life through Jesus Christ our Lord (Rom. 5:21).The message delivered by God to Ezekiel is in fullest keeping with the character of the law-covenant, though grace is also manifested in it. Righteousness has not the same meaning here as in the New Testament. We are constituted righteous by faith in Jesus Christ. It is now not the question of doing righteous deeds in order to be saved and live. We are saved by grace through faith. "Now to him that worketh is the reward not reckoned as of grace but as of debt. But to him that worketh not, but believeth on Him, who justifieth the ungodly, his faith is reckoned for righteousness" (Rom. 4:4). And he who is justified by faith has peace with God. The true believer may sin, but he does not deliberately practice and live in sin, for "he that is born of God doth not commit (practice) sin" (1 John 3:9). If he falls in sin, a gracious provision is made. We have an Advocate with the Father, Jesus Christ the righteous, and therefore we can confess our sins; forgiveness and cleansing follow according to the divine promise (1 John 1:9, 2:1-2).

Then he was commanded to go into the plain, where he again beheld the glory of the Lord and fell on his face. After that, he was shut up in his house; they were to put bands upon him and bind him. He was not to go among the captives, and God made him dumb (verses 25-26). Yet this dumbness was not complete or constant. Finally it ceased altogether. That was after Jerusalem had fallen (33:21-22). The dumbness was a sign to the nation—the sign of God's displeasure and the coming judgment upon Jerusalem (24:27).

Verses 4:1-3. The word tile means "brick." They were used by the Babylonians to preserve their records, and many have been found marked with building plans, etc. The sign of the tile foretells the siege of Jerusalem and Jehovah's opposition against the city.

Verses 4-8. While in the preceding sign Jehovah's action against Jerusalem was pictured, in this new sign a portrayal is given of the punishment which should come upon the inhabitants of the city. In his own person Ezekiel had to experience the great degradation and judgment which was to fall upon all the people. The critical school has invented all kinds of theories to explain, or rather to explain away, the divine command given to the prophet. They say that probably Ezekiel suffered from some form of epilepsy or catalepsy; they also point out the physical impossibility for a man to lie continuously for 390 days on his left side. But it says nowhere that the Prophet should be in that position day and night during these allotted days. The 390 and 40 days are symbolical. They mean years, giving us a total of 430 years. This reminds us of Exod. 12:40-41, where the sojourning of the children of Israel in Egypt is given as 430 years.

But the 390 years apply more specifically to Israel, the period of unfaithfulness of the ten tribes, beginning with Jeroboam (1 Kings 11:31). The 40 years describe the unfaithfulness of the house of Judah. The captives were reminded by the prophet's position of the shameful history of their long apostasy. But more than that. The Lord said to Ezekiel: "I have laid upon thee the years of their iniquity . . . so shalt thou bear the iniquity of the house of Israel." The sign, therefore, pictured the actual punishment which was now to fall upon the nation.

Verses 9-17. Both the sign of the famine and the bread baked in an unclean manner predict the horrors of famine in connection with the siege of Jerusalem, and how the people in the subsequent captivity among the Gentiles should live in defilement.

Verses 5:1-4. The sharp knife is the symbol of the king of Babylon. (See Isa. 7:20.) He was God's instrument in the execution of His wrath; the people are represented by the hair. The third part of the hair burned with fire pictures the fate of a part of the people during the siege. The pestilence and the famine were also to consume them. Only a few in number, a small remnant, were to be preserved, as indicated when Ezekiel took a few hairs and bound them in his skirt.

Verses 5:5-17. These solemn words should be carefully read. In connection with them there ought to be read Jeremiah's lamentations, for Jeremiah's outburst of sorrow shows the literal fulfillment of this message. (See Verse 10 and compare with Lamentations 4:10.)

Verses 6:1-14. The mountains of Israel are mentioned first, because they were the places where the people practiced idolatry; they were the high places so often mentioned in the historical books. (Read Lev. 26:30-33.) Hundreds of years before, Moses wrote these words; and now they were all to be fulfilled. But the Lord also promised that a remnant should be left. That remnant would acknowledge the evil they had done. "They shall loathe themselves for the evils which they have committed in all their abominations." The words "because I am broken with their whorish heart" mean, literally translated, "When I shall have broken their whorish heart which has departed from Me." No judgment which has ever come upon Israel made a complete end of the nation. A remnant always remained and returned to the Lord. (See Rom. 11:5.) During the greatest and longest judgment which has come upon that nation, their world-wide dispersion during this present age, there is also a remnant still among them. When the Lord resumes His dealings with them during the last seven years of the times of the Gentiles, with which our age closes, a remnant from among them will turn to Him and be saved. That remnant will be carried through the judgments of the great tribulation and receive the promised kingdom.

Verses 7:1-27. This chapter closes the first great message of Ezekiel. This great judgment message is written in beautiful language, which, in the authorized version, is marred by numerous incorrect renderings. The reader will find a reliable metrical translation in our larger commentary on Ezekiel.

First, the end is announced to come upon the entire land; it could no longer be averted.

There is another day coming in which the Lord will deal in fearful judgments with this earth. Now is the day of salvation in which God speaks in love through His Son. When wickedness and apostasy has reached its climax, the day of salvation will end and "the day of vengeance of our God" will begin. Then He will speak in His wrath and vex them in His sore displeasure (Psa. 2:5). Then will they say to the mountains and rocks, "Fall on us and hide us from the face of Him that sitteth on the throne, and from the wrath of the Lamb; for the great day of His wrath is come; and who shall be able to stand?" (Rev. 6:16-17). God's judgments for the future are as sure as were His judgments in the past. There is a set time, the day of the Lord, when He, to whom the Father has given all judgments, will tread "the winepress of the fierceness of the wrath of God, the Almighty" (Rev. 19:15).

Then follows a solemn description of the doom of Jerusalem and the reasons why such a judgment is executed.

CHAPTERS 8—11

Visions in Relation to Jerusalem

1. The vision of abomination in the temple (8).
2. The vision of the linen-clothed man with the ink-horn (9).
3. The vision of the coals of fire (10).
4. The vision concerning the leaders: The glory departs (11).

Chapter 8. This vision shows the abomination which prevailed in the temple of Jehovah.

In the visions of God, Ezekiel is brought to the door of the inner gate that looks to the north. Here was the image of jealousy, which provoketh to jealousy. Some have taken this and the following visions to be retrospective. It has been said, "It was as if he were translated back to Jerusalem, and to the time when these things were occurring." Such is the view of some critics; however, it is untenable. These visions would lose their meaning if the prophet seemed to be translated back to Jerusalem and to the time when these abominations had happened in Israel's past history. Later we find the names of persons given, whom he saw. They certainly were living persons known to the prophet Ezekiel and his contemporaries. One of them died while Ezekiel prophesied (11:13).

What was the image of jealousy which provoketh to jealousy? It was an idol. The word is used in Deut. 4:16, where it is translated "graven image." It is also found in 2 Chron. 33:7, 15, where it refers to the idol, which Manasseh had made and put up in the temple.

After Manasseh's idolatry came Josiah's great reformation. After his death, Judah plunged into greater wickedness under the reign of wicked kings, and a revival of idolatry followed once more. Such a wrath-provoking idol was beheld by the prophet. This image they worshipped. "Son of man, seest thou what they do?" They must have lain prostrate before that idol. And yet the glory of the God of Israel was still there.

That there will be a similar scene enacted in a future temple, during the great tribulation, is well known to all students of prophecy. (See 2 Thess. 2 and Rev. 13.)

The prophet saw creeping things and beasts worshipped; the elders and the people were practising Egyptian idolatry of the most degrading kind. Jaazaniah, the son of Shaphan, is especially mentioned. Shaphan was the scribe, who received from the high priest, Hilkiah, the book of the law, and read it before King Josiah (2 Kings 22:8-11; Jer. 39:14). The son of this God-fearing scribe was the leader of the idolators. And these idol worshippers, each in his chamber of imagery (probably individual cells), said: "This Lord seeth us not; the Lord has forsaken the earth." They denied His omniscience and omnipresence. The apostasy in Christendom is going the same road.

The women wept for Tammuz, the Babylonian "Dumuzi," the god of spring, who dies, and revives each year. It was a vile, obscene cult, for with the worship of Tammuz were connected immoral, licentious ceremonies. Sun-worship was the crown of all these abominations. (See verses 16-18).

Chapter 9. The six men mentioned are angels, into whose hands the city is given. Angels are used in judgments past and future. (See Matt. 13:41; 16:27; 2 Thess. 1:7-8.) Angels are likewise prominently mentioned in the book of Revelation. There is a striking correspondency between this chapter and Revelation 7:1-3. Those who sigh and weep constitute the remnant which have no sympathy with the abominations. They are marked for preservation. Thus a remnant was then kept. Well may we remember that now, in the professing church, in the midst of the apostasy, there is also a faithful remnant who sigh and cry and who have the special promise of the Lord (Rev. 3:10).

The word "mark" in the Hebrew is "Tav," the last letter in the Hebrew alphabet. Its literal meaning is "cross." This letter "T" was a cross in the older Hebrew script as well as in the Phoenician and Samaritan. The Egyptians also used a cross in their language, with them it was a sign of life. Ancient Jewish tradition gives the information that the blood sprinkled in Egypt on the doorpost (Exod. 12:23) was in the form of a cross. All this is interesting. To this we may add that in Gen. 4:15, the mark set upon Cain, an entirely different word is used.

Then the command was literally executed.

Chapter 10. Once more the glory vision appears. The linen clothed man who had done the marking in the previous chapter is now executing judgment. Who is He? Evidently more than an angel. That he is a supernatural being is clear. He held the place of pre-eminence among the other angels (chapter 9:2-4). This angel is the Angel of the Lord, the same who appeared to the patriarchs, to Moses, Joshua, Gideon, Manoah, and to others. It is the Son of God in the garb of an angel. In the same form he also appeared to Daniel on the banks of the river Hiddekel. "Then I lifted up mine eyes, and looked, and behold a certain man clothed in linen, whose loins were girded with fine gold of Uphaz. His body also was like the beryl, and his face as the appearance of lightning, and his eyes as lamps of fire, and his arms and his feet like in color to polished brass, and the voice of his words like the voice of a multitude" (Dan. 10:5-6). Here we have a complete description of the same person whom Ezekiel saw taking the coals of fire and scattering them over Jerusalem. Judgment upon the guilty city came from His hands.

When we turn to the book of Revelation, we find a similar scene which has not yet been enacted. A careful comparison of this scene here with Rev. 8:3-5 is suggested. This angel who presents the prayers before the throne and who casts the judgment fires on the earth is the same who received the seven-sealed book (Rev. 5:1). It is the Son of God, the Lord Jesus Christ.

Then the glory of the Lord departed from the threshold of the temple; over its portals "Ichabod" (the glory is departed) was now to be written.

Chapter 11. The priests and the leaders of the nation were steeped in wickedness, defied God and the judgments His prophets had announced. They devised mischief (or iniquity) and gave wicked counsel. Their wicked counsel consisted in disobedience against Jehovah and His Word. In regard to the judgment they said, "It is not the time to build houses; this is the cauldron and we are the flesh." They knew of Jeremiah's letter which he had sent to the elders who were carried away captives. In that letter, Jeremiah, believing God's Word concerning the long duration of the captivity, gave the advice, "Build ye houses and dwell in them" (Jer. 29). They ridiculed that divinely given advice. They still thought themselves safe in Jerusalem. The phrase "this is the cauldron" means the city of Jerusalem; and we are the "flesh" themselves. As the flesh in the cauldron is preserved from the fire by the cauldron itself, so they felt themselves secure in the doomed city. That these wicked leaders were still in the city shows that the judgment in chapter 9 was not a complete judgment. It began at the sanctuary, and the wicked worshippers Ezekiel saw in his vision were smitten first of all, while the man with the inkhorn marked the entire remnant for preservation. Then the Spirit fell upon Ezekiel and he uttered Jehovah's message.

The message of judgment is followed by a message of mercy. Verses 14-21 are yet to be fulfilled in that nation. The final departure of the visible glory of the Lord concludes this chapter. It held its ascension from the Mount of Olives. From the same place, He who is the Lord of Glory and reveals the glory of the Lord, went back to the Father. And when He returns "His feet shall stand upon the Mount of Olives" (Zech. 14). It will be at that blessed time when Israel and Jerusalem will behold the return of the glory, which Ezekiel beheld departing from city and temple.

CHAPTERS 12—19

Signs, Messages, and Parables

1. Signs given through the prophet (12:1-20).
2. The message of speedy judgment (12:21-28).
3. The message against false prophets and prophetesses. (13).
4. The message against the elders (14).
5. The parable of the vine given to the fire (15).
6. The parable of the abandoned child and Israel's whoredom (16).
7. The parable of the riddle of the two eagles and the vine (17).
8. The message of the righteous judgments of God (18).
9. The Lamentations for the Princes of Israel (19).

With the twelfth chapter a new section of this book begins, ending with chapter 19.

Verses 12:1-20. They were a rebellious house and the prophet is told to do something, that they might consider. He was to attire himself like one who goes on a journey with sandals on his feet, a staff in his hand, a burden on his shoulder. He was told to move from place to place. The meaning of all this is explained in verses 8-16. The prince in Jerusalem is Zedekiah. His attempt to flee from Jerusalem, and his fate of having his eyes put out by the king of Babylon, his captivity and death are here clearly predicted. The following passages must be read and studied in connection with this chapter (Jer. 39:4, 52:10-11; 2 Kings 25:1-7).

Verses 12:21-28. The false prophets had

preached a false hope, "The days are prolonged and every vision faileth." God had announced another message. Had they believed what God had spoken, that judgment was imminent, they would have surely repented and turned unto the Lord. Unbelief was responsible for their condition; in this they were sustained by lying prophets. And the Lord answered these false prophets. He changed the lying message and told them "the days are at hand"—the effect of every vision. All false visions, divinations and hopes were to cease. His Word is now to be done.

Chapter 13. And now the Lord speaks through Ezekiel about the false prophets in the midst of His people. They prophesied out of their own hearts; or as it might be rendered, "Who prophesy from their own mind without having seen." Such they were and such are the false teachers of this present age (2 Peter 2:1-2). Of such our Lord warned: "Beware of false prophets, which come to you in sheep's clothing, but inwardly they are ravening wolves" (Matt. 7:15). Every man who prophesies out of his own heart, who utters his own mind, whose preaching and teaching is not according to the oracles of God, is a false prophet, a blind leader of the blind. Like false prophets in Israel the false teachers in Christendom are the cause of the spiritual condition of the professing people of God. Of all such it is true what the Lord said through Ezekiel: "They have seen vanity and lying divination, saying, "The Lord saith, and the Lord has not sent them." They are self-called and self-sent. Behind them stands the father of lies (1 Kings 22:19-23; 1 Tim. 4:1). Next we find in verses 8-16 their condemnation and punishment. But there were also false women prophets; they practised occultism.

All this is also done in the very midst of Christendom in the twentieth century. Women prophets, the most subtle instruments of Satan, are plentiful in these days. The fact has often been pointed out that the prominent leaders in the evil cults of the last days are women. There has been a strange modern-day revival of occult practices upon Christian ground. Spiritualism, Theosophy, and Christian Science belong to this class. All three started with women. Spiritualism with its mediums, fortune-tellers and necromancers is almost entirely in the hands of women, who claim to be religious leaders. The same is true of theosophy, with its Hindu philosophy, and occultism, surrounded with an air of unholy mysticism. Christian Science is closely related to these two cults. Its founder practiced for a time the calling of a medium.

Significant is the description of their evil testimony as given in verse 22.

Chapter 14. These inquiring elders, with wickedness in their hearts, give another illustration of the depth of degradation in which the people had sunk. He who searches the hearts knew what was in them. They came with pious, religious pretensions. It sounded well to inquire of the Lord and seek the prophet-priest for that purpose. Their hearts were full of evil. While their lips spoke of asking the Lord, their hearts were full of idolatry. They liked idolatry. Their hearts were in it and this stumbling-block of their iniquity they had put before their faces, which means they openly defied the Lord God of Israel by their doings. "Should I be inquired of at all by them?" To seek the Lord and inquire of Him in such a condition reveals a brazen spirit and the deepest depravity. Yet this also belongs to the conditions in which the professing people of God are when judgment overtakes them.

Verses 12-23 contain an additional judgment message. The threatened judgment cannot be averted; it is unavoidable. Famine is to come and the noisome beasts, symbolical of Gentile world powers, as Daniel beheld them in his vision (Dan. 7). The judgment message closes again with a message of mercy and comfort for the remnant.

Chapter 15. This is the first of three parables to demonstrate still further the delusion of their false hope that deliverance would come. The vine is a type of Israel (Psa. 80:8-12; Isa. 5:1-6, and Hosea 10:1). The vine is only good for one thing, which is the bearing of fruit; apart from this it is worthless. The wood cannot be used for anything whatever. It is good for nothing but burning. Nebuchadnezzar carried out this sentence (2 Kings 25:9). It reminds us also of the parable of the vine our Lord spoke, in which, speaking of the unfruitful branch, He said, "Men gather them and cast them into the fire, and they are burned" (John 15:6). Some apply this also to Israel; it means the professing believer, who professes to be a branch in the true vine.

Chapter 16. This chapter consists of four sections: 1. The parable of the abandoned child. 2. Jerusalem's idolatries and moral degradation (verses 15-34). 3. The doom of Jerusalem and the promise of restoration (verses 35-59). 4. The covenant remembered (verses 60-63).

The parable of the abandoned child, and what the gracious Lord did for the little one is a most beautiful demonstration of what He had done in His sovereign love and grace for Jerusalem.

It must be read first with this in mind. But this sweet parable illustrates also, as few other portions in the Old Testament do, the grace which the Lord bestows upon the believer in the gospel. Thy father an Amorite and thy mother a Hittite reminds us of what is true of all men, so tersely expressed in David's confession, "Behold I was shapen in iniquity and in sin did my mother conceive me" (Psa. 51:5). Like the child pictured in the parable, we are lost, perishing in the field (the world). What could that perishing child do to save itself? Even so we cannot do anything to save ourselves. The Lord passing by had compassion and spoke His Word of power—Live. He came from heaven to this earth, into the field to seek and save what is lost. He found man in the vile and helpless condition so aptly pictured by the miserable child. And more than that, He died to save man. He gave His life so that we might live. The first thing He does for the believing sinner is to give him life. When the spiritual dead hear His voice they live. The washing with water, the anointing with oil (type of the Holy Spirit), the announcement "thou becamest Mine," as well as the clothing, the beautifying and the crowning, all illustrate what His marvelous grace does for the trusting, believing sinner. It is all grace from start to finish, from the impartation of life in the new birth to the crowning in glory.

Upon this beautiful background of Jehovah's love and mercy, there is written next the dark picture of Jerusalem's whoredoms, symbolical of her wicked idolatries. It started all with pride (verse 15). Jerusalem did not acknowledge the giver. Instead of worshipping Him, they established the high places and conformed to all the wicked Canaanitish practices. Verses 15-34 give the depth of Jerusalem's apostasy.

Then the Lord addresseth her whom He loved, and who had turned away from Him as a harlot. Her doom and judgment is announced which once more is followed by the promise of mercy and restoration. The restoration of Sodom and her daughters has puzzled many. It has been used by Universalists, Russellites, Restorationists, teachers of Reconciliationism and other errorists to back up their inventions of a second chance of the wicked dead, or the ultimate salvation of the entire race. The restoration promises have nothing to do with the restoration of the wicked dead. They are promises of national restoration. It is a mistake to look in the Old Testament for any doctrines concerning the future state. Three facts will show this error of making the Old Testament teach the restoration of the wicked.

1. The Old Testament is not that part of the divine revelation where teachings and doctrines about the future state are given.

This is a most important fact. The Old Testament shows man as upon the earth, on this side of death, and not beyond death. The future of Israel on the earth, their supremacy and destiny of glory amidst the nations of the earth, the judgments of God in the earth, as well as the future blessings for the nations inhabiting the earth during the coming age, are all clearly revealed in the Old Testament. The state after death, that which is beyond this life, is shrouded in mystery in the Old Testament Scriptures. That great judgment, the great white throne judgment, is nowhere mentioned in the Old Testament, nor do we read a word there of "the second death." Resurrection of the dead, no doubt, was known to individual saints of Old Testament times; the Spirit of God revealed it to their hearts, but as a doctrine, resurrection is not found in the Old Testament. In Psalm 16 is revealed the hope of resurrection of the body, and there is a prophecy of the resurrection of our Lord.

2. Should we find anything in the Old Testament concerning the future state, the state of the righteous and the unrighteous after death, such a hint or statement can only be rightly understood and interpreted by the great doctrine concerning the future state as revealed in the New Testament.

By this, of course, we do not say that the Old Testament needs correction by the revelation of the New, nor do we say that the Old is inferior to the New; all *is* the Word of God. However, as the Old Testament does not show man's condition after death, any passage which appears to relate to such a condition must be interpreted by the full light as given in the New Testament.

3. If such passages as Ezekiel 16:53 and Ezekiel 37:1-14, etc., teach the restitution of the wicked by resurrection for another chance, we must then find such a doctrine of the restoration most clearly and fully revealed as one of the great doctrines of the New Testament.

In vain, however, do we look in the New Testament for such a restoration—second probation doctrine. Such a doctrine is not even hinted at in the New. However, the New Testament gives the fullest revelation concerning resurrection and the future state. It tells us that there is indeed a resurrection of the body for every human being. This revelation of resurrection as contained in the New Testament leaves no room whatever for the Sodomites and all the wicked idolatrous Israelites to be raised up for another chance. Our Lord, in John 5:29, reveals a twofold resurrection, a resurrection unto life and a resurrection unto damnation. The human race, those who have died, are therefore in resurrection divided into two classes; they must come forth either unto life or unto damnation: there is no middle class. Later the New Testament teaches a first resurrection, an out-resurrection from the dead. Only those who have believed and died in Christ will have a share in this resurrection. Both Old and New Testament saints belong to it, but none have a part in it who died in their sins. The rest of the dead, meaning of course, the wicked dead, are not raised up till after the thousand years. This is a second resurrection, and this takes place not when the Lord comes the second time, but after His millennial reign (Rev. 20). The subjects of this second resurrection appear before the great white throne and are cast into the lake of fire. Now, these teachers claim that the return of Sodom and Samaria to their former estate means their resurrection for another chance when the Lord comes. But, as these departed, wicked people are wicked still, how can they have part in the first resurrection when the Lord comes, which is the resurrection of the righteous?

They surely cannot belong to this resurrection. And there is nowhere in the New Testament a word about another special resurrection in which all the wicked are raised from the dead for another chance. After the resurrection of the righteous dead there is but one more resurrection, the resurrection of the wicked unto damnation. In the light of these facts the flimsy theory built upon misapplied texts of the Old Testament, texts which relate to national restoration and blessing, breaks down completely. And now, having seen what the statements in this chapter of Ezekiel do not mean, let us see what is their meaning. While these statements annot mean the resurrection of individuals, they mean a *national* restoration. There is promised in many passages of the Old Testament a national restoration of Israel. The ten tribes are to be brought back to their former possessions. Historically they have been lost. But they are not lost to God. He knows where they are. He has kept track of them, and in His own time He will make good the promises of their restoration and will bring back the remnants of the house of Israel, now scattered still among the nations. The Jews will also be restored to their territory. Repeatedly this national restoration of the ancient people is promised under the picture of a resurrection. But to other nations there is also promised such a national restoration in the days to come, when the Lord comes and begins His Kingdom reign over the earth. Such a national revival is beyond a doubt promised for a future day to Moab, Ammon, Assyria, and Egypt. Edom and Babylon, however, are doomed as nations and no revival whatever is promised to them

We do not know, of course, how God will accomplish these promises of restoration and national revivals, and how He will gather the remnants of these former nations from the great sea of nations. We can leave this and other difficulties with Him who will see to the fulfillment of all these things.

Chapter 17. The great eagle mentioned first is Nebuchadnezzar. (See Jer. 48:40 and 49:22). He came to Lebanon and took the highest branch of the cedar, the symbol of the house of David, which was conquered by this eagle. Nebuchadnezzar made the youngest son of Josiah king over Judah and called him Zedekiah. This action is described in verse 5. The other great eagle is Hophra, the king of Egypt. To him Zedekiah turned for help. The interpretation and application of this parable is given in verses 11-21. The following passages should be read as helpful to the understanding of these verses: 2 Chron. 36:13; Jer. 27:1-2, 37:5-7, 52:11.

Israel's hope and Israel's future come once more into view in verses 22-24. The cedar is the royal house of David. God in His sovereignty promises to take "of its young shoots a tender one and I will plant it upon a high and eminent mountain." This tender one is the Messiah, the Son of David. It is the same promise as given in the book of Isaiah. "And there shall come forth a rod out of the stem of Jesse, and a Branch shall grow out of his roots" (Isa. 11:1). "For He shall grow up before Him as a tender plant and as a root out of a dry ground" (Isa. 53:2). The high and eminent mountain typifies Mount Zion, and the kingdom of Messiah is pictured in the closing verses of the chapter. The high tree which is brought low, the green tree which is dried up, is the symbol of Gentile world-power. The low tree which is exalted and the dry tree which is made to flourish stands for the restoration of the kingdom to Israel when the Son of David, our Lord, comes again. Then the high tree will be cut down and the now flourishing Gentile dominion will dry up; Israel the low tree will be exalted, and the long, dry and barren nation will bring its blessed fruit.

Chapter 18. In verses 1-4, we find the false accusation against God and the divine answer, and this is followed in verses 5-9 by the conditions of life, "The soul that sinneth, it shall die" (verse 4). But the conditions to have life and to be just cannot be fulfilled by sinful man; nor is in these verses "eternal life" in view; these are not conditions to secure "eternal life," but to escape physical death in the announced judgment. The conditions which bring death are given in verses 10-13. The son does not die for his father's sins, as they thought in their wrong reasonings (verses 14-20). All their accusations that the Lord is unjust are completely answered in the final paragraph of this message (verses 21-32).

Chapter 19. This lamentation has two sections. The lamentations for the princes come first (1-9), and that is followed by the lamentation for the land of Judah (10-14).

The princes are Jehoahaz and Jehoiachin. King Jehoahaz was carried away captive into Egypt (2 Kings 23:33); his fate is lamented in verses 1-4. King Jehoiachin was taken to Babylon and he is lamented in verses 5-9. In the lamentation for the land of Judah the vine is once more mentioned. The vine is burned, the fruit devoured and there is no scepter in Judah.

CHAPTERS 20—24

Further and Final Predictions Concerning the Judgment of Jerusalem

1. Jehovah rehearses His mercies bestowed upon Israel (20)
2. The impending judgment announced (21)
3. Jerusalem's sins and whoredom (22—23)
4. The parable of the boiling pot and the last word. (24).

Chapter 20. The chapter contains a divine retrospect and an arraignment of the people for their national sins. The following division will greatly assist in an analytical study of this chapter. Verses 1-9 describe the nation's sins in Egypt. Verses 10-17 give the history of the first generation which came out of Egypt. It is a wonderful condensed rehearsal of all they were and what the Lord had done for them. The record of the second generation is contained in verses 18-26. This is followed by a description of their unfaithfulness and sins in the land (verses 27-32). Judgment then is announced and a future restoration promised. Verses 40-44 are yet to be fulfilled. The fire of judgment to sweep over the south field (Judah) is announced in the final paragraph (verses 45-49).

Chapter 21. A solemn message is given to the prophet: "Behold I am against thee, and will draw forth my sword out of its sheath, and will cut off from thee the righteous and the wicked." It was to be a widespread judgment, against all flesh. Ezekiel was commanded to sigh with bitterness before their eyes and was to tell them the cause of his grief (verses 1-7). The sharpening of the sword of judgment is given in verses 8-17. It was hanging over their heads, ready to strike at any moment. The question is asked, "Should we then make mirth?" Is this the time of mirth, worldly pleasures and enjoyment? Not for the faithful in Israel. Nor is the present solemn time a time of mirth for those who know the signs of the times and what God has revealed concerning things to come.

The king of Babylon and his divination is vividly pictured in verses 18-24. The Babylonians used different kinds of enchantments, etc., to ascertain what they should do. The king stands at the cross-roads. Shall he go to Rabbath or against Jerusalem? He used arrows and put on one the name of "Rabbath" of the Ammonites; on the other "Jerusalem." Then he shook them to and fro (correct rendering—"he made his arrows bright"). In verse 22, we see the result of this divination. He has in his hands the arrow with "Jerusalem" on it.

The wicked prince and the Coming One are seen in verses 25-27. Here Christ and Antichrist are contrasted. There can be no question that Zedekiah is first of all in view as the profane wicked prince of Israel. But the prophecy looks far beyond Zedekiah. It is the coming wicked prince, the one who comes in his own name, the final Antichrist, the false Messiah, or, as he is also called in Revelation, the false prophet. That verse 25 refers to the time of the end, is seen by the words, "in the time of the iniquity of the end" (correct translation). The same phrase appears in Dan. 11:35-39, "the time of the end," and the person described in that passage is the Antichrist, the wicked prince. It is the time of the future great tribulation "when the transgressors are come to the full" (Dan. 8:23). This false Christ will claim priestly and kingly honors. He is the beast out of the earth, (Rev. 13) having two horns like a lamb, but speaking as a dragon. The two horns represent the priesthood and the kingship he assumes. And this, we learn from verse 26, is the character of the wicked prince of Israel of whom Ezekiel speaks. Again, we must correct the faulty translation of the authorized version: "Remove the mitre and take off the crown"; the word "diadem" is mitre, the head-dress of the high-priest (Exod. 28:4). He wears the mitre of the priest and the crown of the king. He is Satan's final counterfeit (like the pope) of the Priest-King. In verse 27, the overturning times are mentioned. Thrice it is stated, "I will overturn." Even so will it be at the time of the end until He comes whose right it is.

Verses 28-32 give the announcement of judgment upon the Ammonites.

Chapters 22—23. Before the sharpened sword of justice and retribution does its dreadful work, the Lord uncovers the guilt and vileness of the city and lays bare the corruption of her prophets, priests, and princes, as well as of the people. The violence and abomination of Jerusalem are revealed in verses 1-16; the smelting furnace in verses 17-23 is the symbol of Jehovah's fiery indignation against Jerusalem and its inhabitants. The corruption of the prophets, priests, and princes is fully uncovered in the closing section of chapter 22 (verses 23-31).

In chapter 23 Samaria and Jerusalem are called two sisters, Aholah and Aholibah, in their ungodly relation with Assyria and Chaldea. Aholah means "her tent." Aholibah, "my tent is in her." The latter denotes the fact that the true sanctuary was in Judah. The sins and vileness of both are portrayed throughout this long chapter, as well as the deserved punishment.

Chapter 24. The exact date is given by the prophet. It was the tenth day of the tenth month in the ninth year. What happened also on that date we find recorded in 2 Kings 25:1: "And it came to pass in the ninth year of his reign in the tenth month, in the tenth day of the month, that Nebuchadnezzar, King of Babylon, came, he and all his host, against Jerusalem, and pitched against it; and they built forts against it round about." How did Ezekiel know about all this? It was the Lord who gave him this information and led him to record the date. This is the statement of the second verse: "Son of man, write thee the name of the day, even of this selfsame day, the king of Babylon set himself against Jerusalem this same day." What does higher criticism have to say to this? We quote a recent commentator: "These verses (2) force on us in the clearest fashion the dilemma—either Ezekiel was a deliberate deceiver or he was possessed of some kind of a second sight!" What about divine revelation? This the "learned" men refuse to think even possible. The boiling pot announced is the symbol of Jerusalem.

Verses 15-18 announce the death of Ezekiel's wife, and he is commanded not to mourn or weep; all the customary signs of grief are forbidden him. While he faithfully delivered the message in the morning, even his wife was taken from his side. Death had dissolved the marriage union and taken from the prophet the beloved wife. Even so the relationship between Jehovah and Jerusalem was now completely to be severed. The question of the people and the answer is found in verses 19-27. Read verses 26-27 and compare with chapter 33:21,22.

CHAPTERS 25—32

Predictions of Judgments Against the Nations

1. Prophecies concerning Ammon, Moab, Edom, and the Philistines (25)
2. Concerning Tyrus (26)
3. The glory of Tyrus and Her Fall (27)
4. The prince of Tyrus (28)
5. Concerning Egypt (29—30)
6. Pharaoh's greatness and his overthrow (31)
7. Lamentations and the great funeral dirge (32)

Chapter 25. The eight chapters as analyzed above are on prophecies concerning nations which were in touch with Israel. These predictions concern seven nations, and these are divided into four d three. The first four were the immediate neighbors of Israel. The first message concerns the Ammonites (verses 1-7). Both Ammon and Moab had a racial connection with Israel and were the incestuous offspring of Lot (Gen. 19:37-38). They were in constant conflict with Israel. Their evil character is revealed in this message. Moab is mentioned next (verses 8-11). We give several passages which may be consulted about Moab and the character of the people (Jer. 48:29; Isa. 16:6). There is promised for both Ammon and Moab a national restoration in the latter days, that is, when the Lord comes (Jer. 48:47, 49:6). Let us remember that these nations were proud in the extreme. And these judgments upon proud, self-exalting, God-forgetting nations, are not confined to the past. They will be repeated in the future when He will judge the nations.

Verses 12-14 concern Edom. The descendants of Esau, Edom, were closer to Israel than Ammon and Moab. Edom's deeds were more prominently against the people of God, more wicked and defiant, than the others. Israel was especially commanded not to abhor an Edomite (Deut. 23:7). Amos shows the sin of Edom

(Amos 1:11). So does Obadiah (verses 3-4). The cruel Herods, the types of the man of sin, were Edomites. The judgment upon Edom is to be executed by Israel. This is to take place in a future day. (See Obadiah, verses 17-21 and Amos 9:11-12.) The final paragraph is concerning the Philistines (verses 15-17). The Philistines dwelt on a narrow strip on the seashore and were the long continued enemies of the people Israel. Jeremiah speaks of them (chapter 47). See also Amos 1:6-9, Joel 3:4; Isa. 14:29-32. The vengeance of the Lord fell upon the coast of Palestina, the Philistines, and they experienced the fury of the Lord. He dealt with them who had corrupted His people. And so God will deal in due time with all His enemies.

Chapter 26: A lengthy prophecy concerning Tyrus is found in this and in the chapters which follow. These great predictions have found a startling fulfilment. History confirms all that Ezekiel spoke should come to pass. In verses 1-14 we have the overthrow of the powerful city predicted.

The city of Tyrus (which means rock) was partly built upon an island off the mainland in the Mediterranean Sea. It was an ancient Phoenician city and is mentioned in Scripture for the first time in Joshua 19:29, where it is called "the strong city." It had a wonderful commerce, a description of which in its variety, we find in the twenty-seventh chapter. It was inhabited by seafaring men, and the prophet Isaiah describes this wealthy and influential city as "the crowning city, whose merchants are princes, whose traffickers are the honorable of the earth" (Isa. 23:8). We read in the next chapter how Syria, Persia, Egypt, Spain, Greece and every quarter of the ancient world laid their choicest and most precious things at the feet of Tyre, who sat enthroned on ivory, covered with blue and purple, from the isles of Elishah. Her beauty was perfect (Ezek. 27:11). During the reign of David and Solomon, Tyre came into great prominence, playing an important role in the commercial, political and religious history of Israel. Hiram, King of Tyrus, sent cedar trees to Jerusalem, as well as workmen, who built David a house (2 Sam. 5:11). How Tyrus aided in the construction of the temple and the palace under Solomon's reign, may be learned by consulting the following passages: 1 Kings 5:1-12; 7:13-14; 1 Chron. 14:1, 2 Chron. 2:3, 11. When the ships of Solomon sailed away to Ophir, "Hiram sent in the navy his servants, ship-men that had knowledge of the sea, with the servants of Solomon, and they came to Ophir, and fetched from thence gold, four hundred and twenty talents, and brought it to King Solomon" (1 Kings 9:27-28). She sinned against Jerusalem and the people of God. Joel and Amos, Isaiah, and Jeremiah mention her and her well-deserved judgment (Joel 3:4-6; Amos 1:9-10; Isa. 23; Jer. 47:4).

In the third verse of our chapter, we read the divine announcement of Tyre's fate: "Behold I am against thee, O Tyrus, and will cause many nations to come up against thee, as the sea causes its waves to come up. And they shall destroy the walls of Tyrus, and break down her towers; I will also scrape her dust from her, and make her like the top of a rock." It was to become a place for the spreading of nets and a spoil to the nations. This great judgment was not all at once carried out. Nebuchadnezzar came first against her as predicted in verses 7-11. He besieged Tyre on the mainland and after thirteen years took the city; while that part of Tyrus which was built upon the island in the sea, protected by the fleet of Tyrus, escaped. Then came for her seventy years when she was forgotten, as predicted by Isaiah (23:15). After these years had passed Tyrus saw a startling revival. The island city became more powerful and wicked than before; "she committed fornication with all the kingdoms of the world upon the face of the earth" (Isa. 23:17). The continental Tyrus, however, remained in ruins.

Centuries passed and it seemed as if Ezekiel's prophecy concerning Tyre's complete overthrow would remain unfulfilled. It was about 240 years after when the literal fulfillment of this prophecy was accomplished. Alexander the Great came against the city built on the island. After seven months the city was taken by means of a mole, by which the forces of Alexander could enter the city. In constructing this mole, Alexander made use of the ruins of the old city. The stones, timber and the very dust of the destroyed city was laid into the sea to erect the causeway which accomplished the utter ruin of the wealthy city. And thus Ezekiel's prophecy was fulfilled. "And they shall lay thy stones and thy timbernd thy dust in the midst of the water." The complete end of Tyrus had come. "And thou shalt be no more, though thou be sought for, yet shalt thou never be found again" (verse 21). So completely was the work done by Alexander, depositing the debris of the ruins of Tyrus on the mainland into the sea, that its exact site will remain undeterminable. And Alexander the Great fulfilled still another prophecy. Before he came on his mission, directed by God, to make an end of the proud and wicked city, Zechariah, the great post-exilic prophet, had once more announced the fate of Tyrus. "And Tyrus," said the Lord through Zechariah, "did build herself a stronghold, and heaped up silver as the dust, and fine gold as the ruin of the sheets." This was after Nebuchadnezzar had destroyed the Tyrus on the mainland and she became the great island city. "Thus," said Zechariah, "behold, the Lord will cast her out, and He will smite her power in the sea, and she shall be devoured with fire" (Zech. 9:3-4). Alexander did this: he laid proud Tyrus in ashes. What an evidence that all these words are divine!

The effect of the fall of Tyrus and a lamentation over that fall are revealed in verses 15-21. There is a description of the descent of Tyrus into the pit (verses 19-20). The last sentence of verse 20, "And I shall set glory in the land of the living," means the coming glory of the earthly Zion, the glory in store for Israel.

Chapter 27. Verses 1-25 give an interesting description of the world-wide commerce and glory of this proud world city. "Sic transit gloria mundi," thus passeth the glory of the world! Of the proud and wicked mistress of the sea nothing but ruins remain and her very site is no longer known. What her past glory was is made known by the prophet, yet Ezekiel never had been to that city, nor did he have any knowledge of her grandeur, her great wealth and far reaching commerce. God revealed all unto him.

The description of her great commerce reminds us of that coming world-system as described in the last book of the Bible, the Revelation. Babylon the Great will be both an ecclesiastical and commercial world center. Her commerce is just like the commerce of Tyrus (Rev. 18:12-13). The fall of Tyrus is fully given in verses 26-30.

The description of Tyrus as a ship as given in the first part of this chapter is here maintained. Tyrus is to be shipwrecked. The east wind is Nebuchadnezzar, who came against the proud city to accomplish part of her ruin; and Alexander the Great, as we saw in our previous study, completed the work. A comparison with Revelation 18 will bring out the striking correspondency. When finally Babylon the Great falls, that coming religious-commercial world-system, with Rome as a center, her fall and desolation, will surely be greater than the fall of Tyrus. For this all is rapidly preparing.

Chapter 28. The prince of Tyrus, or, as he is also called, the king, was, according to the Jewish historian Josephus, Ithobalus, known in the Phoenician annals as Ithobaal II. He was the consummation of the pride and wealth of Tyrus; the terrible pride of the city headed up in him. His heart was so lifted up that he claimed to be a god and that he occupied the very seat of God. He boasted of greater wisdom than the wisdom of Daniel. He is a type of the final Antichrist, the man of sin. Behind the wicked prince and king, there is seen another power, Satan. Satan was the power behind the throne of the Tyrian king, as Satan is still the god of this age, who controls the kingdoms of the world. Inasmuch, then, as Tyrus is a type of the commercial glory of the world, its wealth and pride, foreshadowing the final great world-city or world-system, Babylon, the ruler of Tyrus, spoken of as prince, foreshadows the Antichrist; while as king, Satan himself stands behind him as the domineering power. The descriptions given of Satan as an unfallen being show that he was originally a marvelous being, full of wisdom and perfect in beauty. From Jude's Epistle, we learn that even Michael still recognized in him the grandeur of his unfallen past, and did not bring a railing accusation against him (Jude verses 8-10). He was in Eden, the garden of God, and every precious stone was his covering. It is a description of Satan's original place and of his great beauty. Furthermore, he was the anointed cherub that covereth; the Lord had set him to be this. As the anointed, divinely chosen cherub he held an exalted position in connection with the government of the throne of God. Everything shows that this majestic creature possessed a place of great dignity, being "upon the holy mountain of God," walking up and down in the midst of the stones of fire, he was ever present and moving about in the fiery glory of a holy and righteous God. "Thou wast perfect in thy ways from the day that thou wast created till unrighteousness was found in thee."

In verses 20-26 the judgment upon Zidon, some twenty miles north of Tyrus, is predicted. For some years Zidon was even more prominent than Tyrus. She was burnt after a revolt against Artaxerxes Ochus in 351 B.C., but later rebuilt.

Chapters 29—30. First Egypt's desolation is announced (verses 1-12). The king of Egypt addressed in this prophecy was Pharaoh-Hophra, called in Greek, Apries. He was the grandson of Pharaoh-Necho, who defeated King Josiah at Meggido (2 Chron. 35:20-27). King Zedekiah of Judah expected help and relief from Pharaoh-Hophra, when Jerusalem was besieged. The

Egyptian army under Hophra advanced through Phoenicia and forced the Chaldeans to raise the siege of Jerusalem (Jer. 37:5-7). But the relief was only temporary, for the Egyptian army had to retire. The prophet Jeremiah announced also the doom of Hophra, associating it with Zedekiah's doom: "Thus saith the Lord, Behold I will give Pharaoh-Hophra, King of Egypt, into the hands of his enemies, and into the hand of them that seek his life; as I gave Zedekiah, King of Judah, into into the hand of Nebuchadnezzar, King of Babylon, his enemy, and that sought his life" (Jer. 44:30).

But have these predictions been fulfilled? Did Egypt pass through a period of forty years' desolation and did a restoration take place after the forty years? Critics claim that these predictions were never literally fulfilled and that Nebuchadnezzar did not invade Egypt during the reign of Hophra. They point to the historical evidence that Amasis followed Hophra as King of Egypt, and under his reign Egypt was in a very flourishing condition. The historian, Herodotus, gives this information, and it is fully confirmed by Egyptian records on monuments. But did the prophet Ezekiel predict that Egypt should be invaded by Nebuchadnezzar during the reign of Pharaoh-Hophra? His predictions of disaster for Israel by trusting in Egypt had been used by the Assyrian officer in addressing Hezekiah: "Now, behold, thou trustest upon the staff of this bruised reed, upon Egypt, on which, if a man lean, it will go into his hand, and pierce it; so is Pharaoh, King of Egypt, unto all that trust on him" (2 Kings 18:21). And so it was. Egypt gave no help to Israel and only wounded them grievously, as a staff which breaks under the weight of him who leaneth upon it breaks and pierces the hand. Whenever God's people turn to Egypt (the type of the world) for help, and form ungodly alliances, they do so to their own hurt and shame.

Verses 13-16 predict a future restoration of Egypt. Isaiah also shows its future history, both in judgment and in blessing (chapter 19). Yet the prediction of Ezekiel that Egypt after the forty years should be restored and be the basest of all kingdoms and shall have no more rule, but be in a diminished condition, excludes the application of this prophecy to the coming millennium. Egypt had such a period of forty years' devastation, though the exact history of it may not be known to us. Prophecy is not learned by historical events, but history is revealed in prophecy. We believe prophecies, not because history has measured up to them, but we believe them because they are the inerrant Word of God. After Egypt's sorrowful forty years' experience and dispersion, this proud country went into a steady decline, and the Word of God was literally fulfilled when it became the basest of kingdoms, so that Israel put confidence no longer in Egypt. After Nebuchadnezzar's raid, Egypt declined and sank lower still under the Persians and the Ptolemies, until she became the granary of Rome. And this degradation has continued throughout the centuries of this age, so that Egypt is literally the basest of the kingdoms. That she will play her part in the future at the close of our age we learn from Daniel's prophecy (Dan. 11:36-45). Egypt will rise into prominence ere long in connection with the present-day world conflict.

Then follows another prediction, the conquest of Egypt by Nebuchadnezzar, the King of Babylon (verses 12-21). This also was literally fulfilled. In chapter 30 we find first a prophecy as to the desolation of Egypt and her allies (verses 1-13).

The prophet's first utterance is concerning the day, "Howl ye! Alas for the day! For the day is near, even the day of the Lord is near, a cloudy day; it shall be the time of the Gentiles." What day is this? Other prophets mention the day of Jehovah as a day of judgment and wrath when the Lord will deal in His righteousness with the nations of the earth (Isa. 2, 13:6, 9; Joel 1:15, 2:1, 11, 3:14; Amos 5:18, 20; Obad. 15; Zeph. 1:7, 14; Zech. 14:1, etc). This day in its final meaning is the day on which the Lord Jesus Christ will be visibly revealed from heaven. It is mentioned in the New Testament in 1 Thess. 5:2; 2 Thess. 2:2 (where "day of Christ" should be rendered "day of the Lord") and 2 Peter 3:10. This day will bring "man's day" to a close and usher in a new age, when righteousness shall reign as grace reigns now. This day of coming judgment of all nations is seen also here in a prophetic perspective. All previous judgments of nations as announced by God's prophet's, nations which sinned against Israel the chosen people, foreshadow *the* one great day, when the times of the Gentiles end in the revealed manner (Dan. 2:34, 7:10-14). What came upon Egypt in the past through divine judgment will happen to the Gentile nations in the future at the close of our age, "when the Lord Jesus shall be revealed from heaven with His mighty angels, in flaming fire, taking vengeance on them that know not God, and that obey not the Gospel of our Lord Jesus Christ" (2 Thess. 1:7-8). Ever since the times of the Gentiles began with Nebuchadnezzar the divinely appointed head (Jer. 27:4-8), this day of the Lord has been drawing near, till now, with the stupendous present-day events, we can see this day rapidly approaching.

Two weeks after the lamentations over Pharaoh, the prophet uttered this solemn and most impressive elegy over the multitude of Egypt and the heathen nations who have gone into sheol. It has been called a weird Dantesque funeral march over the whole heathen world; but it is more than that. We look here into sheol and see the nations gathered there, stripped of their glory, in deepest abasement and shame. Their bodies are in the pit, the grave, and their souls in sheol, the unseen regions. God's patience was exhausted with them, the measure of their wickedness became full; then judgments swept them off the earth and they passed away and descended into sheol. And what irony there is connected with it! "Whom does thou surpass in beauty? Go down and be thou laid with the uncircumcised." And as the king came there with his multitudes, whom did they find there? Asshur, that is Assyria, is mentioned first: "Asshur is there and all her company." She was a cruel, pitiless, destructive power, and now she, who once caused "terror in the land of the living," is helpless, with all her power gone in the unseen world. Elam, Meshech, Tubal, Edom, the princes of the North, and the Zidonians are named as being in existence there. Once great powers, but now cut off, they lie with the uncircumcised in weakness and disgrace. While in chapter 31:16 the dead and gone nations were comforted over Pharaoh who descended into sheol; in this passage Pharaoh, who sees these nations, now is himself comforted as he discovers his former enemies there.

A similar statement about sheol as a place of departed nations, who are nevertheless conscious, is found in the book of Isaiah. There the king of Babylon is seen in his descent into sheol. "Sheol from beneath is moved for thee to meet thee at thy coming; it stirreth up the dead for thee, all the chieftains of the earth; it hath raised up from their thrones all the kings of the nations. All they shall speak and say unto thee, Art thou also become weak as we? Art thou become like unto us? Thy pomps are brought down to the grave, and the noise of thy viols, the worm is spread under thee, and the worms over thee?" (Is. 14:9-11). Solemn words these are behind which stands the undeniable truth of a conscious and eternal existence of the human race. But only the New Testament Scriptures give the full light upon the future state.

The destruction of the principal cities of Egypt is announced in verses 13-19. All has been literally fulfilled. Noph is Memphis, the seat of the worship of Ptah and Apis. The city "No" is Thebes, the ancient capital of Egypt, called by the Greeks "Diospolis," the city of Jupiter. Her ruins bear witness of the past, indescribable splendor. The great temple of Carnac stood there. The other places mentioned are Sin, which is Pelusium, now completely buried in sand. Aven is Heliopolis, the center once of sun-worship; Pi-beseth is Bubastis, where the sacred cats were mummied, likewise a desolation now. Theaphnehes or Daphnis also passed through judgment. What a remarkable fulfillment of what the Lord had announced through His prophet! May we here be reminded in our solemn times that the same omniscient Lord, who knows the end from the beginning, has spoken concerning this age, now closing in its predicted apostasy. Nations today steeped in bloodshed; nations filled with covetousness and hatred; an apostate professing Christendom and the indifferent masses have written over against them the judgment-wrath of the coming king. And He who fulfilled the words spoken through Ezekiel will also fulfill every other prediction uttered by His holy prophets and apostles.

The chapter closes with a prophetic description of the work of King Nebuchadnezzar, whom God used to execute His righteous judgments.

Chapter 31. Pharaoh's greatness is described in the first part of the chapter (verses 1-9). He is compared to the Assyrian, once so powerful and proud. The fall and desolation of the proud monarch under the picture of a tree follows in verses 10-14. The overthrow of Egypt and the resulting consternation among the nations is predicted in the last section of this chapter (verses 15-18).

Chapter 32. The lamentation over Pharaoh is contained in verses 1-10, followed by the final announcement of the sword of the King of Babylon, Nebuchadnezzar, in verses 11-16. The most interesting part in this last chapter of these great predictions of national judgments is the funeral dirge and the unveiling of the unseen world (verses 17-32).

II. Predictions After the Destruction of Jerusalem (33—48)

CHAPTERS 33—34

A. The Watchman, the False Shepherds, and the True Shepherd

1. The renewed call of Ezekiel as watchman (33:1-20)

2. Ezekiel's mouth opened after Jerusalem's fall is announced (33:21-33)
3. Message against the shepherds of Israel (34:1-19)
4. The True Shepherd and restoration promised (34:20-26)

Chapter 33: 1-20. The commission of Ezekiel as watchman corresponds to the same call in chapter 3:16-21. In verses 10-20 the prophet announces certain principles of divine justice.

The exiles knew that the just wrath of God rested upon them as a nation and that their sins were unforgiven. Therefore they asked, "If our transgressions and sins be upon us, and we pine away in them, how should we then live?" They also accused the Lord of inconsistency by saying, "the way of the Lord is not equal" (verse 20; see also 18:25, 29). The answer Jehovah sends them makes known the principles on which He will deal with them individually as a just God. "O ye house of Israel, I will judge you every one after his ways." Judgment rested upon them as a nation, but the individual still could turn to the Lord in repentance. What a wonderful declaration it is which is recorded in verse 11! "Say unto them, as I live, saith the Lord God, I have no pleasure in the death of the wicked; but that the wicked turn from his way and live; turn ye, turn ye from your evil ways; for why will ye die, O house of Israel?" What compassion and mercy! As it was a day of judgment which had come upon them, true repentance was the needed thing. A past righteousness could not shield them from the judgment if sin had been committed. "As for the wickedness of the wicked, he shall not fall thereby in the day that he turneth from his wickedness." The wicked confessing and forsaking his sin would find mercy and forgiveness, while those who were impenitent would surely die and not live. "None of his sins that he hath committed shall be mentioned unto him; he hath done that which is lawful and right; he shall surely live." And this gracious promise was given in anticipation of the work of the cross, the redemption by the blood of Christ, by which God's righteousness is declared in passing thus over sins of Old Testament believers who turned to God (Rom. 3:25). The principles of divine justice are summed up in verses 18 and 19: "When the righteous turneth from his righteousness, and committeth iniquity, he shall even die thereby. But if the wicked turn from his wickedness, and do that which is lawful and right, he shall live thereby." Needless to say, all this must be viewed as under the law-covenant. But their complaint that the way of the Lord is not equal was wrong; it was their way which was not equal. They were to be judged each according to what he had done.

Verses 33:21-33. In chapter 24:27, the promise had been given to Ezekiel that when the one who escaped from Jerusalem when it fell, arrived, the prophet should no longer be dumb. This dumbness evidently does not mean that he was continually silent, without uttering a word, for he prophesied what is written in chapters 25—32. He was to be dumb concerning Israel; the intervening chapters, before the messenger came, concern other nations. And now that promised messenger arrived and his mouth was opened again to prophesy about Israel. The first message is one of rebuke, describing their condition.

Verses 34:1-19. The shepherds of Israel were the kings and princes and all who had authority over them. The prophet Jeremiah had received a similar message (Jer. 23:1-2). These shepherds of Israel were responsible for the deplorable condition of the flock. Utterly selfish, they cared not for the sheep of His pasture; they feared not God nor did they have a heart for God's people. The flock was scattered and spoiled.

Such was the sad condition of the people Israel. And when the Lord Jesus appeared in their midst to seek the lost sheep of the house of Israel, He found them as sheep without a shepherd, and He had compassion upon them (Mark 6:34). But they rejected Him and the Shepherd was smitten. Zechariah's prophecy was fulfilled: "Awake, O sword, against My Shepherd, and against the man that is My fellow, saith the Lord of hosts. Smite the shepherd and the sheep shall be scattered, and I will turn Mine hand upon the little ones" (Zech. 13:7). The false shepherds, the Pharisees and the Sadducees, were a curse to the people, and the leaders were against the Shepherd. They delivered Him into the hands of the Gentiles. And now for nearly 2,000 years the sheep have been scattered and peeled, wandering among the nations of the earth (Luke 21:24). What is their hope and coming blessing we learn from this great prophecy.

(What is said in this chapter of the false shepherds who ill-treated the flock of God, His ancient people, may also be applied to the false shepherds, the hirelings in the professing church. See Acts 20:28-35 and 1 Peter 5:2-3.)

In verses 7-10, judgment is pronounced upon these false shepherds, and after that the Lord announces the deliverance of His flock (verses 11-19).

"Behold, I myself, even I, will search for My sheep and will seek them out." Jehovah arises in behalf of His scattered sheep. He will Himself exercise the office of a true shepherd, seeking out His flock. The cloudy and dark day (the times of the Gentiles) is gone and another morning breaks, the morning for which His people have waited so long. What He will do at this time for His scattered sheep is now fully proclaimed. "I will bring them out from the people, and gather them from the countries, and will bring them to their own land, and feed them upon the mountains of Israel by the rivers, and in all the inhabited places of the country. I will feed them in a good pasture, and upon the high mountains of Israel shall their fold be; there shall they lie down in a good fold, and in a fat pasture shall they feed upon the mountains of Israel. I will feed My flock, and I will cause them to lie down, saith the Lord." And all this has not yet come to pass. Some apply these words to the restoration of a remnant from the Babylonian captivity and see no future fulfillment of these promises. It is evident that the returning remnant did not possess these blessings. Others make a spiritual application and claim that it means the Church and the blessing which Gentiles will receive as the sheep of Christ. This is the common path which most commentators follow. It needs no lengthy refutation, for neither Ezekiel, nor the other prophets know anything of the Church and the "other sheep," Gentiles saved by grace and with believing Jews constituting the one flock (John 10:16; Ephes. 3:1-6). This is unrevealed in the Old Testament. These gracious words of promise have not yet been fulfilled, nor will they be fulfilled as long as the Church, the body of Christ, is being gathered out from all nations. All must wait till God's purpose in this age is accomplished. When the Church is complete as to its elect number, when the Lord has come for His saints and the true Church has passed from earth into glory, then will the Lord turn in mercy to His people Israel and these promises given by Ezekiel will be fulfilled.

Verses 20-26. Some have applied this to Zerubbabel, the head of Judah at the return from the Babylonish captivity; this is done by those who deny a future restoration of Israel. Others take these words in a strictly literal sense and teach that David the King will become the head of the nation once more, and raised, from the dead, will be the one shepherd over His people. It is not David, but He who is according to the flesh the Son of David and David's Lord as well. The one Shepherd can only be the Messiah. Numerous passages show that David's name is used in a typical sense. Jeremiah announced, "They shall serve the Lord their God, and David their King, whom I will raise up unto them" (Jer. 30:9). Here David stands typically for Christ, the Messiah of Israel, for He is raised up unto them when Jacob's trouble is ended (verses 1-7). Of Him Jeremiah speaks more fully in chapter 23:5-6: "Behold, the days come, saith the Lord, that I will raise unto David a righteous Branch, and a King shall reign and prosper, and shall execute judgment and justice in the earth. In His days Judah shall be saved, and Israel shall dwell safely; and this is the name whereby He shall be called, the Lord our Righteousness." The two, Judah and Israel, will be reunited by the one Shepherd. The Messiah of Israel is also mentioned by Hosea as David: "Afterward shall the children of Israel return, and seek the Lord their God and David their King, and shall fear the Lord and His goodness in the latter days" (Hosea 3:5). Isaiah speaks of the sure mercies of David, and adds, "Behold I have given Him for a witness to the people, a leader (prince) and commander to the people." It is therefore not David, raised from the dead, but the Prince of Peace, who was here once to seek the lost sheep of the house of Israel and who comes again to save the remnant of His people Israel and to receive the Throne of David (Isa. 9:6-7).

When the Lord is doing all that is promised here and the remnant has accepted the long rejected Messiah-King, a covenant of peace and blessing will follow. "And I will make with them a covenant of peace, and will cause the evil beasts to cease out of the land, and they shall dwell safely in the wilderness and sleep in the woods. Peace will come to the land and to the whole earth with His coming. The evil beasts, the Gentile world powers (Dan. 7) will no longer devastate the land. All will be peace and safety, so that they can sleep peacefully in the woods. "There shall be showers of blessing" (verse 26). How often a hymn is sung based upon this promise:

> There shall be showers of blessing,
> This is the promise of love.

But how few who sing it know that the promise belongs first of all to Israel. When the Lord comes, the showers of blessing will be poured forth upon His people and upon all nations. It will be "the times of refreshing" (Acts 3:19). Verses 27 and 28 give a brief description of the millennial kingdom. Groaning creation will then be delivered and the wild beasts will have their natures changed (compare verse 28 with Isa. 11:6-9 and Rom. 8:19-22). There is no need to speculate on the meaning of "the plant of renown," which will be raised up. It is none other than He, who, as to His humiliation, is described as "a tender plant" and "as a root out of a dry ground" (Isa. 53:2). But now He appears in all His glory, and becomes the plant of renown. Their shame and suffering will then be over. He will be their God and they will be His people.

CHAPTERS 35—36

Judgment Announced and Israel's Final Restoration Promised

1. The message against Mount Seir and Idumea (35)
2. The message of comfort to Israel (36)

Chapter 35. This is another judgment message, which is closely related to the coming restoration of Israel. When the Lord is merciful to His people and bestows upon them the promised blessings, He will also deal with their enemies in judgment. Edom was the most bitter enemy of Israel, their blood-relation. The judgment threatened here was executed upon Edom; but it has a prophetic meaning of the judgment which is in store for the enemies of God's people when the times of the Gentiles end and God arises in behalf of His suffering and persecuted people.

Then, in verses 14-15, we hear of the time of rejoicing which will come for His people when their enemies are judged (Deut. 32:43).

Chapter 36. With this chapter the great prophetic utterances of Ezekiel begin concerning the future restoration and blessing of Israel. From here on to the end of the book, all is still unfulfilled, nor can it be fulfilled until the Lord Jesus Christ comes again and is enthroned as King. The first seven verses announce once more the future judgment of Israel's enemies. Then comes the promised return to the land (verses 8-15). The mountains of Israel, barren so long, shall be inhabited again. Israel's past sins and chastisement are reviewed in verses 16-20, and then comes that great message of restoration and blessing through grace in that day when their once rejected King returns and they bow before Him. The characteristic words in verses 23-28 are the words "I will do." It is the word of sovereign grace. Eighteen times Jehovah says what He will do. They are the "I wills" of Israel's hope and coming glory.

He will gather them from among the nations and all countries and bring them back to their own land. Only a superficial expositor can speak of a fulfillment when they returned from Babylon. But even if this were so, though it is not, the verses which follow have never been fulfilled in the past. The cleansing of the nation is next promised: "I will sprinkle clean water upon you and ye shall be clean." It refers us to the water mixed with the ashes of the red-heifer, which was sprinkled with a hyssop on the unclean, typifying the precious blood of Christ in its cleansing power (Heb. 9: 13-14, 10:22). Thus, when the people of Israel believe on Him and look upon Him whom they pierced (Zech. 12:10), they will be cleansed. "In that day there shall be a fountain opened to the house of David and to the inhabitants of Jerusalem for sin and for uncleanness" (Zech. 13:1). Then follows the promise of the new birth of Israel. "A new heart will I also give you, and a new spirit will I put within you." The stony heart is to be taken away and they will receive a heart of flesh. Our Lord had this passage in mind when He talked with Nicodemus about the new birth. Nicodemus, the teacher in Israel, was ignorant of the fact that this new birth for Israel is necessary in order to be in that coming kingdom and to receive its blessings. Therefore the Lord said to him, "If I have told you earthly things (about Israel and the new birth as the way into the kingdom) and ye believe not, how shall ye believe if I tell you of heavenly things?" (the heavenly blessings which follow His sacrificial death).

CHAPTERS 37—48

The Future Blessings of Israel, the Nation Regathered, Their Enemies Overthrown, the Millennial Temple, and the Division of the Land

1. The vision of the dry bones and Judah and Israel re-united (37)
2. Gog and Magog and their destruction (38—39)
3. The millennial temple, its worship, and the division of the land (40—48)

Chapter 37. The future restoration of Israel, both nationally and spiritually, is now shown to the prophet in a vision. What these dry bones represent and what their revival mean, is explained by the Lord Himself. It may be used in application in different ways, to illustrate certain truths, but the true and only interpretation is the one which is given by the Lord in verses 11-14. But there is an erroneous interpretation of a serious nature which is widely taught and believed among many Christians. Because "graves" are mentioned, beside the dry bones and their resurrection, it is being taught that the vision means physical resurrection. Systems, like Millennial Dawnism, *alias* International Bible Student Association and others, which teach the so-called larger hope, a second chance for the impenitent dead, the restitution of the lost, teach that all the Israelites who have died in their sins will be brought out of their graves and then be saved. They use this vision to confirm this invention. An advocate of this theory declared that all the Christ-hating Pharisees and Sadducees who lived when our Lord was on earth would be raised up when He comes and then believe on Him. Matthew 23:39 was used by him as an argument. These restitution teachers also teach that inasmuch as Israel will have a second chance when they are raised from the dead, the Gentile dead will share also in the same. It needs no argument to refute this. The Word of God teaches a twofold resurrection: A first resurrection and a second resurrection, a resurrection of the just and a resurrection of the unjust (John 5:28-29). According to the above theory, there would have to be a third resurrection, a resurrection for a second chance and ultimate salvation of those who died in their sins. Of such a resurrection the Bible knows nothing.

In this vision of the dry bones, physical resurrection is used as a type of the national restoration of Israel. It is used in the same way in Daniel 12:2. In that passage the sleep in the dust of the earth is symbolical of their national condition. And when their national sleep ends there will be an awakening. When we read here in Ezekiel of graves, it must not be taken to mean literal graves; the graves are symbolical of the nation as being buried among the Gentiles. If these dry bones meant the physical dead of the nation, how could it be explained that they speak and say, "Our bones are dried up, and our hope is lost?" The same figure of speech is used in the New Testament. Of the prodigal it is said, "For this my son was dead, and is alive again" (Luke 15:24). Yet he was not physically dead, nor was he made alive physically. Therefore, this vision has nothing whatever to do with a physical resurrection. The late Dr. Bullinger, whose erroneous suggestions have led astray some, also taught that the vision of the dry bones includes resurrection as well as restoration.

Equally bad is that spiritualizing method which takes a vision like this, as well as the hundreds of promises of a coming restoration, and applies it all to the Church, ignoring totally the claims of Israel and their promised future of glory. This is the general trend of commentators.

Verses 15-28 predict the reunion of Judah and Israel with one king over them. That King is our Lord. Then the angelic message given to the Virgin when the coming incarnation was announced will be fulfilled: "The Lord God shall give unto Him the throne of His Father David, and He shall reign over the house of Jacob forever and of His Kingdom there shall be no end" (Luke 1:32-33).

Chapters 38—39. There will be at that time of restoration a great and final invasion of the land of Israel. Gog and Magog will invade the land "that is brought back from the sword, and is gathered out of many people." The invaders come "against the mountains of Israel which have always been waste; but it is brought forth out of the nations, and they shall dwell safely, all of them." In verse 11, the evil purpose of the invader is made known. From all this we learn that the invasion takes place at the time when the Lord has brought back His people and resumed His relationship with the remnant of Israel.

The invasion will happen some time after the beastly empire with its beasthead, the revived Roman empire, in its final ten kingdom form and the clay, with the little horn as leader (Dan. 7; Rev. 13:1-10) and the false prophet, the personal Antichrist (Rev. 13:11, etc.) have been dealt with in judgment (Rev. 19:19-20). The stone out of heaven has then fallen upon the feet of the great dream image of Nebuchadnezzar; and as far as the western confederated world power is concerned, it is now ended. But other nations gather now for an assault. It is a northern confederacy which sweeps southward to invade the land, as Antiochus Epiphanes did in the past, as well as the Assyrian in the days of Isaiah. These final invading hosts, under the leadership of a powerful king, come like a storm, and like a cloud to cover the land.

But who are they?

The leader is the prince of Rosh (not as the authorized version has it "the chief prince") of Meshech and Tubal. This prince is the head of the confederacy and with him allied are Persia,

Cush, Phut, Gomer and Togormah. They come out of the north, or, as it is in Hebrews, "out of the uttermost north" (verse 15). Inasmuch as the Prince of Rosh is addressed in verse 3 as Gog, we take it that Gog is the name given to this prince and leader of these nations. His dwelling place is in the land of Magog. We know from Genesis 10:2, that Magog was the second son of Japheth. Gomer, Tubal and Meshech were also sons of Japheth; Togormah was a grandson of Japheth, being the third son of Gomer. Magog's land was located in what is called today the Caucasus and the adjoining steppes. And the three, Rosh, Meshech, and Tubal were called by the ancients Scythians. They roamed as nomads in the country around and north of the Black and the Caspian Seas, and were known as the wildest barbarians. We learn from this that the invading forces, which fall into Israel's land in the future, when Israel has been regathered, come from a territory north of Palestine which today is in the hands of Russia. And here we call attention to the prince, this northern leader, or king, who is the head of all these nations. He is the prince of Rosh. Careful research has established the fact that the progenitor of Rosh was Tiraz (Gen. 10:2), and that Rosh is Russia. All students of prophecy are agreed that this is the correct meaning of Rosh. The prince of Rosh, means, therefore, the prince or king of the Russian empire. But he also is in control of Meshech and Tubal, which are reproduced in the modern Moscow and Tobolsk. Russia, we may well conclude from this, will furnish the man who will lead this confederacy of nations. We write this at a time when Russia is passing through horrors upon horrors. A revolution changed the autocratic government into a democracy, and that gave way to anarchy, produced by satanic powers. From what is written in this chapter, we learn that Russia will ultimately return to the old regime, and will once more become a monarchy to fulfill her final destiny as made known in this sublime prophecy. Well known it is that Russia has been in the past the most pronounced and bitterest enemy of the Jewish people. What she passes through today is but a fulfillment of what the Lord has spoken: "I will curse them that curse thee." Today, the Jews in Russia may have bright hopes of getting their rights and complete emancipation at last. For a time this may come to pass, but ultimately Russia will turn against them; and, as Pharaoh did, when Israel had left his domain, so this coming king of the north, the prince of Rosh, when Israel is back in the land, will turn against them.

With him come the other nations. Persia, which is even now in part occupied by Russia, will finally be a vassal to this prince of Rosh. Ethiopia and Phut are also in this confederacy. There also is Gomer and all its bands. Gomer, says Delitzsch, "is most probably the tribe of the Cimmerians, who dwell, according to Herodotus, on the Maeotis, in the Taurian Chersonesus, and from whom are descended the Cumri or Cymry in Wales and Britain, whose relation to the Germanic Cimbri is still in obscurity." Valuable information is given in the Talmud; Gomer is there stated to be the Germani, the Germans. That the descendants of the Gomer moved northward and established themselves in parts of Germany seems to be an established fact. All this is of much interest. Germany did not belong to the Roman empire, at least the greater part of Germany was never conquered by Rome. She will therefore not participate in the Western confederacy. Will she then become united to Russia and march under the prince of Rosh into the land of Israel? We cannot be sure about all these things. This, however, we know, that a powerful confederacy of nations, under the leadership of the prince of Rosh, Meshech and Tubal, will come up against Immanuel's land, when Israel has been restored and dwells safely.

The judgment and destruction of the invading hosts are vividly pictured in the thirty-fourth to thirty-ninth chapters as well as their burial. Compare verses 17-20 with Rev. 19:17-18; though the great supper in Revelation and Jehovah's sacrifice here in Ezekiel are not identical, yet both are judgments. The final paragraphs of this chapter (verses 21-29) give the promise of glory.

The last verse contains an important statement. The Lord says that He hides His face no more from them. This in itself shows that all this is not yet here; for still He hides His face from them. The hiding of His face from them will be no more when His Spirit is poured upon them. "I have poured out My Spirit upon the house of Israel, saith the Lord God." There comes then a time when the house of Israel, the literal descendants of Abraham, will receive an outpouring of the Spirit of God. Such is also the message of Joel, in which restoration and spiritual blessing, through the outpouring of the Spirit are blended together (Joel 2). We call attention to another passage which should be linked with the statement in this chapter. Isaiah

32:13-18 is a very striking prophecy. There is an announcement made first of all concerning the judgment which is to fall upon Israel's land. "Upon the land of My people shall come up thorns and briers; yea, upon all the houses of joy in the joyous city," etc. But this is not to last forever. An "until" follows. "Until the Spirit be poured upon us from on high." This is the same future outpouring of the Spirit of God. Up to now it has not been. The Holy Spirit on the day of Pentecost came to form the body of Christ; but this outpouring in connection with Israel has another significance.

Chapters 40—48. The final nine chapters of this book form the climax of the great prophecies of Ezekiel; they belong to the most difficult in the entire prophetic Word. Once more the hand of the Lord rests upon the seer and in the visions of God he is brought into the land of Israel. In the very beginning of this grand finale we learn therefore that the visions concern the land of Israel. Let us remember, that after the fall of Jerusalem had been announced to Ezekiel (chapter 33:21), his prophetic utterances and visions concern the future when Israel is to be regathered and restored to the land. The previous two chapters dealt with the last invasion of the land of Israel and the complete overthrow of Gog and its hordes. The vision contained in this last section follows after Israel's final deliverance. So much is clear as to the time when the prophecies of these eight chapters will be accomplished. They have not been fulfilled in the past, certainly not in the remnant which returned under Zerubbabel and Ezra. Nor have these prophecies been fulfilled since then. All is future. Only when the Lord has gathered Judah and Israel, when He has established His glorious Kingdom in their midst and delivered His people and the land from the last invader, will this last vision of Ezekiel become history.

This disposes then at once of the different modes of interpretation employed by so many expositors of this book. These are the following:

1. The theory of interpretation which looks upon the vision of these chapters as fulfilled in the return of the remnant from Babylon. One of the expositors who follows this line stated that these visions are "an ideal representation of the Jewish state about to be restored after the captivity." It does not need much argument to show that this mode of interpretation is erroneous. The temple which the remnant built does in no way whatever correspond with the magnificent structure which Ezekiel beheld in his vision. The fact is, if this temple is a literal building (as it assuredly is) it has never yet been erected. Furthermore, it is distinctly stated that the glory of the Lord returned to the temple and made His dwelling place there, the same glory which Ezekiel had seen departing from the temple and from Jerusalem. But the glory did not return to the second temple. No glory cloud filled that house. And furthermore no high priest is mentioned in the worship of the temple Ezekiel describes, but the Jews after their return from Babylon had high priests again. Nor can the stream of healing waters flowing from the temple as seen by Ezekiel be in any way applied to the restoration from the Babylonian captivity. Expositors who follow this mode of interpretation claim that all has been fulfilled and that there is nothing in store for Israel in the future. It is the most superficial method and totally wrong.

2. Another interpretation claims that the whole vision sprang from the imagination of the prophet. That it is all an ideal description of something which the expositor himself is unable to define. This mode of interpretation needs no further mention and answer.

3. The third interpretation of these chapters is the allegorical, which spiritualizes everything, and claims that the Christian Church, its earthly glory and blessing, is symbolically described by the prophet. This is the weakest of all and yet the most accepted. But this theory gives no exposition of the text, is vague and abounds in fanciful applications, while the greater part of this vision is left unexplained even in its allegorical meaning, for it evidently has no such meaning at all.

(What strange applications have been made of this vision! We quote from *The New Century Bible,* which says concerning this temple:

> Its details shed a light nowhere else vouchsafed to us upon the ideals of *Hebrew art,* influenced perhaps, by Babylonian masterpieces, yet entirely national and Puritan; and they embody in material form Ezekiel's sober but intense conception of religion, as completely as the Gothic cathedrals translate into concrete and abiding stone and marble the soaring visions of mediaeval Christianity.

The true interpretation is the literal one which looks upon these chapters as a prophecy yet unfulfilled and to be fulfilled when Israel has been restored by the Shepherd and when His glory is once more manifested in the midst of His people. The great building seen in his prophetic vision will then come into existence and all will be accomplished.

But while we are sure of the strictly future fulfillment of this final vision, the many details which abound in these chapters can hardly be fully interpreted as to their meaning. Much is obscure. That all has a deeper meaning we do not doubt; and here and there we shall offer suggestions, but many things we shall have to pass over. Before we turn to the text and open up the contents of these chapters, a telescopic view of the whole section is in order and will be helpful in our further studies.

As it will be impossible to give a detailed explanation of this future temple we give an analysis of these chapters. Our larger work on Ezekiel will be found helpful in a better understanding of this portion of this book.

I. THE DESCRIPTION OF THE TEMPLE (40—47)

CHAPTER 40

1. The introduction (40:1-4)
2. The gate toward the east (40:5-16)
3. The outer court (40:17-27)
4. The inner court (40:28-37)
5. The tables for the offerings and the chambers for the inner court (40:38-47)
6. The porch of the house (40:48-49)

CHAPTER 41

1. The holy place (41:1-2)
2. The most holy (41:3-4)
3. The side chambers (41:5-11)
4. The hinder buildings and the measurement (41:12-14)
5. Description of the interior of the temple (41:15-26)

CHAPTER 42

1. The priest's chambers in the inner court (42:1-14)
2. The final measurements (42:15-20)

II. THE TEMPLE WORSHIP (43—44)

CHAPTER 43

1. The return of the glory of the Lord and filling the house (43:1-9)
2. The address to the nation (43:10-12)
3. The dimensions of the altar (43:13-17)
4. The offerings to be bought (43:18-27)

CHAPTER 44

1. The outward eastern gate for the prince (44:1-3)
2. The charge concerning the stangers and the rebellious tribes (44:4-14)
3. The charge concerning the priests, the sons of Zadok (44:15-27)
4. The inheritance of the priests (44:28-31)

CHAPTER 45

1. The portions of the priests, the Levites, of the whole house of Israel, and the prince (45:1-8)
2. Concerning the prince (45:9-17)
3. The feast of Passover and the feast of tabernacles (45:18-25)

CHAPTER 46

1. The worship of the prince (46:1-8)
2. Further instruction as to worship (46:9-15)
3. Concerning the prince, his sons and his servants (46:16-18)
4. A final description of places in the temple (46:19-24)

III. THE VISION CONCERNING THE LAND (47—48)

CHAPTER 47

1. The waters of healing from the temple (47:1-12)
2. Borders of the land (47:13-21)
3. Concerning the stranger in the land (47:22-23)

CHAPTER 48

1. The portion of the seven tribes (48:1-7)
2. The oblation for the sanctuary, for the city, and for the prince (48:8-20)
3. The gates of the city and its new name (48:30-35)

Without entering into the measurements, the architecture, and other features of this great temple, we point out a few things which are important. First, as to the contents of the interior of this temple. The words "silver and gold" are not mentioned once in Ezekiel 40—48. Silver typifies grace in redemption, being the ransom money. Gold typifies divine righteousness. Both are absent in the millennial temple, for what the silver and gold foreshadows is now realized in His redeemed earthly people. The heavenly Jerusalem has gold in it, but silver is not mentioned in the description of the city in Revelation 21.

The chief ornaments in this temple are cherubim and palm trees; they were along the wall of the temple. So it was in the temple of Solomon. "And he carved all the walls of the house round about with carved figures of cherubim and palm trees and open flowers within and without" (1 Kings 6:29).

A palm tree was between cherub and cherub. As stated in the previous chapter, palms are the emblems of victory and remind us of the feast of tabernacles. They were seen high above on the posts. Cherubim speak of the presence of the Lord, who enters this house and is worshipped here. But the cherubim here have only two faces and not four as in the opening vision of this book (1:10-12). As often stated, these celestial beings tell out the Lord Jesus Christ in His personal glory. The lion, His kingly glory; the face of a man, His true humanity; the face of an ox, His servant character; and the face of an eagle, His heavenly origin and destiny, Son of God. It is not without meaning that the face of a man and the face of a young lion are seen on these cherubim and each face looks upon a palm tree. Its symbolical meaning is obvious. The Lord Jesus Christ has come again and visited the earth and the temple and appeared as the Glorified Man and the Lion of the tribe of Judah. His is the victory and the glory. When at last this temple stands in Israel's land, and its meaning and measurements, as well as other details, are fully known and understood, it will be known then that His blessed work, victory and person are symbolically seen throughout this house.

In the forty-third chapter we read of the returning glory. The glory will fill this house.

We must notice here especially, that the vision the prophet beheld was "according to the appearance of the vision" he saw before the destruction of the city; "the visions were like the visions," which he saw "by the river Chebar." This points back to the first chapter, when first by the river Chebar the heavens were opened to Ezekiel the priest, and he saw visions of God. At the close of that chapter, we read after the recorded vision, "This was the appearance of the likeness of the glory of the Lord." The same vision of glory appeared again to him when Ezekiel had left the river Chebar and gone into the plain (3:22-23). Then he had witnessed the gradual and solemn departure of the glory of the Lord. "Then the glory of the Lord departed from off the threshold of the house, and stood over the cherubim. And the cherubim lifted up their wings, and mounted up from the earth in my sight . . . They stood at the door of the east gate of the house of the Lord, and the glory of the God of Israel was over them above" (10:18-19). Then finally the Shekinah went up and disappeared. "And the glory of the Lord went up from the midst of the city and stood upon the mountain which is on the east side of the city" (11:23).

The similarity of the departure of the glory of the Lord from the temple before its destruction by Nebuchadnezzar and its future return to the temple of Ezekiel's vision is most interesting. It is the same glory which departed, which returns; it is the same Lord, who resumes relationship with His earthly people. The withdrawal of the visible glory of the Lord meant the departure of His gracious presence from among His people, which was followed by judgment. The return of the visible glory means the return of His gracious presence among them, and that the judgment, which has lasted so long, is forever gone. The departure of glory was through the east gate and was finally seen upon the mountain at the east side of the city; the return is from the way of the east, and the glory of the Lord enters through the east gate. But it is not only a visible glory, but the Lord Himself is in the Shekinah, Ezekiel beheld above the firmament and the cherubim, when he saw the glory of the Lord at the river Chebar, he heard His voice. And here also His voice is mentioned "like the sound of many waters." From verses 6 and 7, we learn, that after the glory had entered the house, the Lord addressed the prophet out of the house.

The Lord Himself in all His glory is manifested and enters the temple, the place of His rest and glory. The cherubim will be seen in person, and from the New Testament we learn that angels will be with Him also. His glory will then cover Israel's land and the earth. "His glory covered the heavens, and the earth was full of His praise. And His brightness was as the light; He had bright beams out of His side[1] and there was the hiding of His power." This is how Habakkuk describes the same manifestation of the glory of the Lord and the coming of the Lord of glory. (See Isa. 40:5, 58:8, 60:1-2, 66:18). Isaiah's great vision may be viewed as foreshadowing this manifestation of His glory. He saw the Lord sitting upon a throne and His train filled the temple. The seraphim cried one unto

[1]Marginal reading.

another, and said, Holy, holy, holy is the Lord of hosts, the whole earth is full of His glory. And as the prophet was cleansed and his iniquity taken away, and as he became the messenger of the Lord (Isa. 6), so the nation Israel will be cleansed and forgiven and become the messenger of Jehovah. (Such an application seems warranted in view of the message Ezekiel received from the Lord to the people, verses 6-12.)

When the Spirit had transported the prophet into the inner court of the temple, he discovered that the glory of the Lord filled the house. We repeat it, no such thing happened when the returned Jewish remnant had entered the temple. When the old men, who had seen the Solomonic temple and knew of its glory, beheld the foundation of the second temple, they wept (Ezra 3:12). When the house was dedicated, no glory returned, no cloud was seen, no Shekinah filled the house. Nor is it a spiritual glory, the glory of the church, as so many seem to believe.

But Haggai, who with Zechariah prophesied during the rebuilding of the temple, uttered a significant prophecy while that second house was building—a prophecy which must be linked with Ezekiel's vision of the returning glory: "For thus saith the Lord of Hosts: yet once it is a little while, and I will shake the heavens, and the earth, and the sea, and the dry land. And I will shake all nations, and the desire of all nations shall come, and I will fill this house with glory" (Haggai 2:6-7). This was not the house they were building. It is a future house, a future temple. That house will be built when the heavens and the earth are being shaken, when all nations shake, and when the desire of all nations, the King of Glory, the Prince of Peace, our Lord comes. Then this house will be filled with glory.

It will be a visible glory. It will be a permanent glory. He will now dwell gloriously in the midst of the children of Israel (verse7). This visible glory will be seen over Jerusalem, like as it was of old, a cloud by day and a shining, flaming fire by night. "And Jehovah will create over every dwelling place of Mount Zion, and over its convocations a cloud by day and a smoke and the brightness of a flame of fire by night, for over all the glory shall be a covering" (Isa. 4:5).

Another acknowledged difficulty is the one concerning the restored sacrifices and ordinances.

But what do these ordinances mean? Here are priests again standing before an altar, bringing bloody sacrifices, burnt offerings, sin offerings and peace offerings. Is this to be taken literally also? Some expositors have stated that all this had a meaning in the past and could only be true in connection with the second temple. Others attempt to read into it a spiritual meaning. All, or nearly all commentators, think it inconceivable that such sacrifices could ever be brought again in a future temple. Those expositors who combat the premillennial coming of the Lord and the literal restoration of Israel, consider the supposed impossibility of a satisfactory explanation of this part of Ezekiel's visions, the collapse of the premillennial argument.

Sacrifices of bulls and goats were brought by Israel in their past history; the Lord commanded His people to do this. Every Christian knows that these sacrifices foreshadowed the work of Christ, His great sacrifice on the cross. In themselves these sacrifices Israel brought could not take away sins, nor give rest to the conscience, nor could they make the worshipper perfect. The Epistle to the Hebrews demonstrates this fully.

All these sacrifices had a prospective character, looking forward to the work of the cross. And when the Lamb of God died, when His blessed lips uttered the never-to-be-forgotten words, "It is finished," and God's hand rent the veil from top to bottom, the prospective character of these sacrifices was forever ended. The new and living way into God's presence, into the holiest, had been made by His blood. During this age Israel has no temple, and all their Levitical ordinances can no longer be practised by them. As Hosea declared, they are without a sacrifice (Hos. 3:4).

God, during this age, our present age, which began with the rejection of Christ by Israel and ends with His return, is gathering a heavenly people, the Church. The Church has for its worship no earthly place, no temple, but worships in spirit and in truth, in a heavenly sanctuary. There are no sacrifices, priests, altars, in connection with the true Church, the body of Christ. Christ is all. He is the sacrifice, the priest and the altar. That the enemy has produced upon Christian ground a ritualism which is aped after the Jewish system and which denies as such the gospel and Christianity, is well known. They have invented altars, and sacrifices, and priests. This is the Judaizing of the Church, "the other gospel which is not another," upon which the Spirit of God has pronounced the curse of God (Gal.1). The day is coming when the Lord will deal in judgment with the apostate church which denies His Son and His work, while His true church will be taken to the place which He has prepared.

After the prophecy of the division of the land, comes the majestic ending, the last message this man of God uttered: "And the name of that city from that day shall be 'Jehovah Shammah,' the Lord is there." It is a fitting finale to this great book. In its beginning, we see the glory of the Lord departing. Throughout the pages of the book we read of Israel's rebellion, Jerusalem's judgments, the nation's disobedience and rejection. Then follow the messages of hope—Israel's conversion, the regathering of the twelve tribes, the final conflict, the returning glory of the Lord; and from that day the name of the city will be Jehovah Shammah. Because He has manifested His gracious presence in the midst of His people and established His throne, blessed His people with all the spiritual and national blessings promised by His holy prophets, destroyed all their enemies, and covered all with His visible glory once more, therefore the city will have the name "Jehovah is there." What a glory it will be for Him. The city through which He once walked with weary feet, the Son of God garbed in servant's form, the city through which He was dragged, when the cross was laid upon His shoulders, the city which cast Him out, the city outside of which He endured the cross and despised the shame—that same city will be made in that day of glory spot of the earth.

THE PROPHET
DANIEL

At the close of the history of Hezekiah, the noble king of Judah, as reported by the prophet Isaiah, is found a significant prophecy. Hezekiah, like so many other good men before and after him, had fallen into the crime of the devil, pride (1 Timothy 3:6), and the Lord through the prophet Isaiah announced therefore the future judgment upon the royal house of David: "Behold the days come, that all that is in thine house, and that which thy fathers have laid up in store until this day shall be carried to Babylon, nothing shall be left, saith the Lord. And of thy sons that shall issue from thee, which thou shalt beget, shall they take away, and they shall be eunuchs in the palace of the king of Babylon. Then said Hezekiah to Isaiah, Good is the word of the Lord which thou hast spoken. He said, moreover, For there shall be peace and truth in my days" (Isaiah 39:6-8).

About one hundred years after this startling prophecy was literally fulfilled. The opening verses of the book of Daniel introduce us to this. The Babylonian king came and besieged the city of Jerusalem and conquered it. Among those carried away was Daniel and his companions. Daniel, as we learn from the third verse of the first chapter, was of princely descent.

This young man, the captive in Babylon, became, through the marvellous providence of God, one of the leading figures and prominent actors in the great Babylonian empire, under the reign of Nebuchadnezzar. He was made, in spite of his youth, a great man—the prime minister of Babylon.

Of his personal history, his character and remarkable experiences we know more than of any of the other prophets of God. As a mere lad he was brought to the strange land as a captive. We behold him and his companion, true to Jehovah, maintaining their God-given place of separation. He honored Jehovah and Jehovah honored him. Soon the Lord used the young captive by revealing unto him the forgotten dream of Nebuchadnezzar and the interpretation of the dream. Then followed the exaltation of the obscure captive; and afterwards he seemed to have been the close companion of the great Gentile monarch, who acknowledged finally the Lord-God of Israel as his God. Then God honored him by giving him the great visions of the future, so remarkable in their scope. The Lord appeared unto him; he talked with angels, and the messenger Gabriel addressed him as "the man greatly beloved."

As an old man he had been quite forgotten during the reign of the grandson of Nebuchadnezzar, Belshazzar; only the queen mother, the aged wife of Nebuchadnezzar, remembered him. In that memorable night when Babylon fell the old prophet interpreted the handwriting on the wall, though old in years, still young in his faith. Under the reign of Darius he was cast among the lions, on account of his devotion to Jehovah, and wonderfully delivered.

What a man of prayer he was we learn from the ninth chapter. He reached a very old age, continuing even into the reign of Cyrus, and when his great work was done, ere the Lord called him home, he received the promise: "But go thy way till the end be; for thou shalt rest, and stand in thy lot at the end of days" (12:13). In the great faith chapter of the Hebrew Epistle his name is not mentioned, but his deeds are there. "Who through faith subdued kingdoms, wrought righteousness, obtained promises, stopped the mouths of lions" (Hebrews 11:33).

The Authenticity of Daniel

Perhaps no other book of the Bible has been so much attacked as the book of Daniel. It is a veritable battlefield between faith and unbelief. For about 2,000 years, wicked men, heathen philosophers and infidels have hammered away against it; but the book has proved to be the anvil upon which the critics' hammers have been broken into pieces. The book has survived all attacks, and we need not fear that the weak and puerile critics, the most subtle infidels of Christendom in our day, can harm the book. It has been denied that Daniel wrote the book during the Babylonian captivity. Kuenen and Wellhausen and their imitating disciples like Canon Farrar, Driver and others of inferior calibre, claim that the work was not written in the Exile, but centuries later. Daniel had nothing to do with the book at all; a holy and gifted Jew wrote it instead, and it is avowed fiction.

Such are a few of the infidel statements made against this sublime book. These critics follow the wicked assailant of Christianity of the third century, Porphyr, who contended that the book of Daniel is a forgery, that it was written during the time of the Maccabees, after Antiochus Epiphanes, so clearly foretold in this book, had appeared. The whole reasoning method of the destructive Bible-criticism may be reduced to the following: Prophecy is an impossibility, there is no such thing as foretelling events to come. Therefore a book which contains predictions must have been written after the events which are predicted. But how could the man who committed such a forgery be a pious Jew? No, the book of Daniel is either divine or it is the most colossal forgery and fraud. No middle ground is possible.

We give a few of the evidences which answer the infidel attacks upon this great fundamental prophetic book.

It should be enough for every Christian that our Lord, the infallible Son of God, mentions Daniel by name in His great prophetic discourse delivered on Olivet (Matthew 24:15). There can be no question that our Lord at least twice more referred to the book of Daniel. When He speaks of Himself and His coming again in the clouds of heaven as the Son of Man, He confirms Daniel's vision in chapter 7:13, and when He speaks of the stone to fall in Matthew 21:44, He confirms Daniel 2:44-45. How does the critic meet this argument? He tells us that our Lord accommodated Himself to the Jewish views current in His day. They say, perhaps He knew better, and some say that He did not know. In other words, they deny the infallibility of our Lord, and with this invention that He accommodated Himself against His better knowledge, they accuse our Lord of something worse. When the Lord uttered the words, "Daniel the prophet" He put at once His unimpeachable seal on both the person and the book of Daniel.

But there are other evidences. The heathen Porphyr declared that the book was written during the days of the Maccabees; as stated above the modern critics have echoed the opinion of that lost heathen soul. But the Septuagint version of the Old Testament, which was made before the time of the Maccabees, contains the book of Daniel. It was in the hands of the learned Hebrews, who translated in the third century before Christ the Hebrew Scriptures into the Greek. The book therefore antedates the time of Antiochus Epiphanes.

Furthermore during the days of the Maccabees a book was written, the first book of the Maccabees, a historical account of those eventful days. This Maccabean work not only presupposes the existence of the book of Daniel, but shows actual acquaintance with it, and therefore gives proof that the book must have been written long before that period (1 Macc. 1:54, compare with Daniel 9:27; 2:49 and Daniel 3).

The reliable Jewish historian Josephus also furnisheth historically an evidence for Daniel. He tells us that when Alexander the Great, who is mentioned in Daniel's prophecy (chapter 8), came to Jerusalem in the year 332 B.C., Jaddua the high priest, showed him the prophecies of Daniel, and Alexander was greatly impressed with them.

Then we have the testimony of another prophet of the exile, the prophet Ezekiel. He speaks twice in the highest terms of Daniel, whose contemporary he was. (See Ezekiel 14:14-20 and 28:3.)

Daniel also betrays such an intimate acquaintance with Chaldean customs and history, as well as their religion, such as none but one who lived there and was an eye-witness could have possessed. For instance, the description of the Chaldean magicians perfectly agrees with the accounts found in other sources. The account of the insanity of Nebuchadnezzar is confirmed by the ancient historian Berosus.

Then there has been a most striking vindication of this book through the Babylonian excavations, tablets, cylinders and monuments. Into this we cannot fully enter, but we cite but one of the most striking.

The name of Belshazzar furnished for a long time material to the infidels to reject the historical accuracy of the book. The father of Belshazzar was Nabonnaid, who was not a son of Nebuchadnezzar at all. How then could Belshazzar be a grandson of Nebuchadnezzar?This objection is seemingly strengthened by the fact that no ancient historians include in the list of Babylonian kings the name of Belshazzar.

Berosus, who lived about 250 years after the Persian invasion, gives the following list of Babylonian monarchs:

Nabuchodonosar (Nebuchadnezzar). Evil Marudak, who is the Evil Merodach of the Bible. Neriglissor. Laborosoarchod. Nabonnaid. Cyrus, the Persian conqueror.

Different attempts were made to clear up this difficulty, but they failed. Now, if Daniel wrote his book he must be correct. But the critics are ever ready to put the doubt not on the side of history, but on the side of the Bible.

So they said Berosus was not mistaken and that if Daniel really had written the book which bears his name he would have been historically correct. This is how matters stood up to 1854. In that year Sir Rawlinson translated a number of tablets brought to light by the spade from the ruins of the Babylonian civilization. These contained the memorials of Nabonnaid, and in these the name of Bil-shar-uzzar appeared frequently, and is mentioned as the son of Nabonnaid and sharing the government with him. The existence of Belshazzar and the accuracy of Daniel were at once established beyond the shadow of a doubt.

Daniel was promised by Belshazzar to become the third ruler in the kingdom (Dan. 5:16).

Why the third and not the second? Because Nabonnaid was the first, Belshazzar his son was the second and vice-regent. Nabonnaid had a daughter of Nebuchadnezzar for wife and therefore Belshazzar from his mother's side was the grandson of Nebuchadnezzar.

But have the critics learned by this complete defeat? Have they profited by this experience and will they leave the Bible alone? Not by any means. They will continue to look for flaws in the infallible Book. Some day they will discover the seriousness of their work.

The Important Prophetic Message of Daniel

It is impossible to overestimate the importance of the book of Daniel. It is the key to all prophecy; without a knowledge of the great prophecies contained in this book the entire prophetic portion of the word of God must remain a sealed book. One of the reasons why so few Christians have a correct knowledge of the prophetic forecast in the Bible is the neglect of the book of Daniel. The great prophetic portions of the New Testament, the Olivet discourse of our Lord (Matthew 24 and 25), and above all the great New Testament book of prophecy, the book of Revelation, can only be understood through the prophecies of Daniel.

To both, the Babylonian king and God's prophet, were revealed the political history of the "times of the Gentiles" (Luke 21:24). The rise and fall of the great monarchies, Babylonia, Medo-Persian, Graeco-Macedonia and the Roman, are successively revealed in this book. The appointed end of these times and what will follow the times of the Gentiles is made known. Our generation lives in the very shadow of that end. Then there are prophecies relating more specifically to Jerusalem and the Jewish people, showing what will yet come for that city and the nation.

It will be impossible in our brief annotations to do justice to all the details of this prophetic book. The larger work on the prophet Daniel by the author of *The Annotated Bible* should be carefully studied with the accompanying pages.

The Division of Daniel

The book of Daniel is written in two languages, in the Hebrew and in the Aramaic, the language of Chaldea. The first chapter is written in Hebrew, in style closely allied to the Hebrew used in the book of Ezekiel. Chapters 8—12 are likewise written in the Hebrew language. But chapters 2:4—7:28 are written in the Aramaic language. This gives an additional argument for the authenticity of the book. The author was conversant with both languages, an attainment exactly suited to a Hebrew living in exile, but not in the least so to an author in the Maccabean age, when the Hebrew had long since ceased to be a living language, and had been supplanted by the Aramaic vernacular dialect. Daniel was led to employ both languages for a specific reason. What concerned these great monarchies, Babylonia and Medo-Persia, was written in the language with which they were familiar. What concerned the Jewish people was written for them in Hebrew. We shall not follow the linguistic division of the book.

We find in the book two main sections:

I. DANIEL IN BABYLON, NEBUCHADNEZZAR'S DREAM, AND HISTORICAL EVENTS

Chapter 1. Daniel and His Companions in Babylon

Chapter 2. The Great Prophetic Dream of Nebuchadnezzar.

Chapter 3—6. Historical Events

II. THE GREAT PROPHECIES OF DANIEL

Chapter 7. The Night Visions of Daniel

Chapter 8. The Vision of the Ram and the He-Goat

Chapter 9. The Prophecy of the Seventy Weeks

Chapter 10. Preparation for the Final Prophecy

Chapter 11. The Wars of the Ptolemies and Seleucidae Predicted and the Coming Events of the End
Chapter 12. The Great Tribulation and Israel's Deliverance

Analysis and Annotations

I. Daniel in Babylon, Nebuchadnezzar's Dream, and Historical Events

CHAPTER 1

Daniel and His Companions in Babylon

1. The introduction (1:1-2)
2. The king's command (1:3-5)
3. Daniel and his companions (1:6-21)

Verses 1-2. Divine judgment, which had threatened so long, had finally fallen upon Jerusalem. It was executed by the divinely chosen instrument, Nebuchadnezzar. Three times he came against Jerusalem. In 606 B.C. he appeared the first time. This is the visitation mentioned here. In 598 he came again and carried away more captives, including Ezekiel. In 587 he burned the city and the temple.

Verses 3—5. As already stated in the introduction the young captives of the king's seed and of the princes (both of Judah) was in fulfillment of prophecy. They were to be added to the king's court and to receive special royal favors, instructions in the wisdom and language of the Chaldeans and have the privileges of the king's table.

Verses 6—21. Daniel means, "God is my Judge"; Hananiah, "Beloved of the Lord"; Michael, "Who is as God"; Azariah, "The Lord is my help." These beautiful names were soon changed into names of heathen meaning, to blot out the very memory of Jehovah. Daniel becomes Belteshazzar (Bel's prince); Hananiah is named Shadrach (illumined by the sun-god); Mishael is called Meshach (who is like Shach-Venus); and Azariah is changed to Abednego (the servant of Nego).

The purpose of the four expressed their loyalty to the God of their fathers and their obedience to His law. The Lord rewarded them for their loyalty and faithfulness, as He is still the rewarder of all who trust in Him and walk in separation.

CHAPTER 2

Nebuchadnezzar's Dream and Its Interpretation

1. The forgotten dream (2:1-13)
2. The prayer meeting in Babylon and the answer (2:14-23)
3. Daniel before the king (2:24-28)
4. The revelation and interpretation of the dream (2:29-45)
5. The promotion of Daniel and his companions (2:46-49)

Verses 1—13. The king had a dream which was occasioned by thinking concerning the future (verse 29). God answered his desire by this dream, which made a great impression on him. But he had forgotten the dream. The soothsayers, wise men and magicians, who were kept by him to interpret dreams, were unable to reveal the forgotten dream: they confessed their utter helplessness. The king condemned them to death. Inasmuch as Daniel and his companions were counted among the wise men, "they sought Daniel and his companions to be slain."

Verses 14—23. And now Daniel steps to the front. But there is no haste and no hurry connected with it, for "He that believeth shall not make haste." He is brought before the king and promises to the king the meaning of that dream. It was the language of faith; he had confidence in God. He knew that the same Jehovah who had given another captive wisdom, Joseph in Egypt, was his God also. Then there was a prayer meeting in Babylon. While the condemned wise men, the astrologers and magicians trembled for fear of death, Daniel and his companions asked "mercies of the God of heaven concerning this secret." The prayer was speedily answered.

Verses 24—28. After Daniel had praised the God of heaven he requested an audience with the king. How beautiful he is in the presence of the mighty monarch! What an opportunity to glorify himself! But he hides himself completely and gives God all the glory. Then he tells the king that in the dream he is about to relate God has made known unto him "what shall be in the latter days."

Verses 29—45. Daniel then told to the king the forgotten dream:

> Thou, O King, sawest, and behold a great image. This great image, whose brightness was excellent, stood before thee; and the form thereof was terrible. This image's head was of fine gold, his breast and his arms of silver, his belly and his thighs of brass, his legs of iron, his feet part of iron and part of clay. Thou sawest till that a stone was cut out without

hands, which smote the image upon his feet that were of iron and clay, and brake them to pieces. Then was the iron, the clay, the brass, the silver and the gold broken to pieces together, and became like the chaff of the summer threshing-floors; and the wind carried them away, that no place was found for them; and the stone that smote the image became a great mountain, and filled the whole earth (verses 31-35).

The great man image is the prophetic symbol of the "times of the Gentiles." This expression "The times of the Gentiles" is not found in the book of Daniel, but it is a New Testament phrase. Our Lord used it exclusively. In that part of His prophetic discourse which is reported in the Gospel of Luke and which relates to the fall of Jerusalem and the dispersion of the nation, our Lord said: "And they shall fall by the edge of the sword, and shall be led away captive into all nations; and Jerusalem shall be trodden down of the Gentiles until the times of the Gentiles shall be fulfilled" (Luke 21:24). Now, the times of the Gentiles did not begin when Jerusalem rejected the Lord from heaven. Our Lord does not say that the times of the Gentiles were then ushered in. The times of the Gentiles started with the Babylonian captivity by Nebuchadnezzar. The glory of the Lord departed from Jerusalem. The other great prophet of the captivity, Ezekiel, beheld the departure of the Shekinah. "Then did the Cherubim lift up their wings, and the wheels beside them; and the glory of the God of Israel was over them above. And the glory of the Lord went up from the midst of the city, and stood upon the mountain which is on the east side of the city" (Ezek. 11:22-23). But before that Jeremiah recorded a remarkable word. These are the words of Jehovah concerning Nebuchadnezzar:

I have made the earth, the man and the beast that are upon the ground, by My great power and by My outstretched arm, and have given it unto whom it seemed meet unto Me. And now have I given all these lands into the hands of Nebuchadnezzar the king of Babylon, My servant; and the beasts of the field have I given him also to serve him. And all nations shall serve him, and his son, and his son's son, until the very time of his land come: and then many nations and great kings shall serve themselves of him. And it shall come to pass, that the nation and kingdom which will not serve the same Nebuchadnezzar the king of Babylon, and that will not put their neck under the yoke of the king of Babylon, that nation will I punish, saith the Lord, with the sword, and with the famine, and with the pestilence, until I have consumed them by his hand (Jeremiah 27:5-8).

Jerusalem had been supreme because the throne and the glory of Jehovah was there. Though Assyria, Egypt and Babylon had tried repeatedly to overthrow Jerusalem, they were held in check by the power of God and divine intervention, but when the measure of the wickedness of Jerusalem was full, Nebuchadnezzar was chosen to become the first great monarch of the times of the Gentiles. The dominion was then taken away from Jerusalem and transferred to the Gentiles.

Therefore the golden head in this prophetic man-image represents Nebuchadnezzar and the Babylonian empire. The chest of silver, according to divine interpretation, stands for an inferior monarchy which was to follow the Babylonian empire. This second world empire is the Medo-Persian. The belly and thighs of brass represent the third great monarchy, the Graeco-Macedonian. The fourth great monarchy which was to rise during the times of the Gentiles, represented by the two legs of iron, is the iron empire, Rome. Here, then, is history pre-written. God, who knows the end from the beginning, revealed in this dream the course of the times of the Gentiles, beginning with the Babylonian monarchy and followed by three more: The Medo-Persian, the Graeco-Macedonian and the Roman. Notice the process of deterioration as indicated in the composition of this image: Gold, silver, brass, iron, and finally the iron getting less and clay taking a prominent place. It shows that politically the times of the Gentiles are not improving.

Everything which this image represents has been fulfilled, except the last portion, when a stone falls out of heaven and strikes the ten toes and the clay, so that the whole colossal figure goes to pieces, the different constituent metals become like the chaff on the summer threshingfloor and the striking stone becomes a mountain and fills the whole earth.

The fourth Empire, the Roman, has not yet fulfilled its history. The final form, and with it the final form of the times of the Gentiles is yet to pass into history. This final form is symbolically seen in the ten toes and the clay, in the feet of the image. The territory which constituted the now extinct Roman empire will in the near future undergo a political revival. It will reappear in a confederated Europe, except certain countries which never belonged to the Roman empire. In that confederacy will be kingdoms to the number of ten; the clay represents democracies, the rule by the people and for the people. The late great war has brought such a political combination into our times. Such is the future and end of the times of the Gentiles, as foretold in the feet of the image.

But what does the smiting stone represent, the stone which abolisheth the image and becomes itself a great mountain filling the whole earth?

The Stone is Christ. That the stone represents Christ is seen from the Scriptures. "Behold, I lay in Zion for a foundation a stone, a tried stone, a precious cornerstone, a sure foundation" (Isa. 28:16). Zechariah speaks of this stone with seven eyes upon it and engraven. We read of Him in the New Testament as the foundation stone of the church, the cornerstone, the stone rejected by the builders. Most interesting is His own word in the Gospel of Matthew: "And whosoever shall fall on this stone shall be broken: but on whomsoever it shall fall, it will grind him to powder" (Matt. 21:44). Here we have Israel's sin and judgment and the fate of the Gentiles. Israel stumbled against this stone; for them He was a stumblingstone and rock of offence. In consequence they were broken as a nation. But the Gentile world, rejecting Him, will be broken when the stone falls. They will be ground to powder by the falling stone. Our Lord must have had the dream of Nebuchadnezzar in mind when he spake these words. The falling stone of which He speaks and the striking stone in the dream mean the same Person, Himself.

The stone doing its work in smiting the image is a prophecy of the second coming of our Lord. The mountain filling after that the earth foreshadows that kingdom which will be established with the return of Christ and His enthronement as King of kings.

Verses 46-49. The heathen monarch then acknowledged Daniel's God in a threefold way: The God of Gods (the Father); the Lord of Kings (God the Son); the Revealer of Secrets (God the Holy Spirit). Daniel is lifted from the place of humiliation to a place of exaltation. He did not forget his companions; they share honor and glory with him. It is a beautiful picture of that day when our Lord will receive the throne and when His own will not be left behind in sharing with Him His glory.

Historical Events (3—6)

The four chapters which follow the great dream of Nebuchadnezzar are of a historical character. They do not contain direct prophecies, but record certain events which transpired during the reign of Nebuchadnezzar, his successor and grandson Belshazzar, and Darius, the Mede. On the personal history of these three persons and where they are found in profane history we have little to say, as a deeper examination of this subject would lead us too far and would be tedious. But this much must be said that the criticism which charged Daniel with being incorrect has been completely silenced by the Babylonian cylinders of Cyrus and Nabonnaid and the so-called annalistic tablets, the very records of those days. It is true the personality of Darius the Mede has not yet been definitely located historically. However, we do not believe the Bible because its historical statements can be verified from profane history. We believe the Bible because its records are divinely inspired and therefore correct. What would we know of the genuineness of these ancient tablets and cylinders covered with cuneiform inscriptions if it were not for the Bible? These witnesses from the stones, which indeed cry out, do not verify the Bible, they are rather declared genuine and correct by the Word of God.

These four chapters then give us historical events. Each has a prophetic meaning, though direct prophecy is not found in them.

These chapters describe the moral conditions which held sway during the two first world empires; they indicate prophetically the moral conditions which continue to the end of the times of the Gentiles. Five things may be traced in these four chapters: The moral characteristics of the times of the Gentiles; what will happen at the close of these times; the faithful remnant in suffering; their deliverance and the Gentiles acknowledging God, as King and the God of heaven.

CHAPTER 3

The Image of Gold

1. The image of gold (3:1-7)
2. The faithful three (3:8-18)
3. The miraculous deliverance (3:19-25)
4. The worshipping king (3:26-30)

Verses 1-7. He had an immense statue of gold made, the image of a man, no doubt, and he set it up in the plain of Dura in the province of Babylon. It was idolatry and the deification of man. Idolatry and the deification of man are then the first moral characteristics mentioned which are to prevail during the times of the

Gentiles. The times of the Gentiles produce a religion which is opposed to the God of heaven. The image was sixty cubits high and six broad. Seven is the divine number and six is the number of man. Sixty cubits and six reminds us of that familiar passage in the book of Revelation, where we have the number of a man given, that mysterious number "six hundred three-score and six," that is 666. The image then represents man, but the climax of man was not yet reached. However, the beginning foreshadows the end of the times of the Gentiles. That end is described in chapter 13 of Revelation.

The civil power tried to force this universal religion upon the people. The great governors, judges, captains and rulers had to appear for the dedication of the image. But then the whole thing had a religious aspect. Listen, after looking at this great awe-inspiring image of gold—the sweetest music—the cornet, the flute, the harp, the sackbut, psaltery, dulcimer and all kinds of music sounds forth. No doubt the Chaldean priests approached chanting some sweet Babylonian song. Why all this? To stir up the religious emotions and aid in this way the worship of an idol. It is intensely interesting that the ancient Babylonian worship, with its ceremonials and chanting is reproduced in Rome, which is called in Revelation, Babylon. (The book by Alexander Hyslop, *The Two Babylons,* gives reliable and important information on this fact.)

Verses 8-18. The companions of Daniel refused to worship the image and were cast into the fiery furnace. Notice their wonderful trust in God.

Verses 19-25. The very men who cast them down were consumed by the flames. But when the king looked towards the furnace he beheld to his great astonishment not three men bound and burning up, but four men loose and actually walking in the fire. "They have no hurt and the form of the fourth is like the Son of God." And when they brought up from the fiery furnace, no smell of fire was about them, not even a hair was singed, only the bands which had bound them were burned off. The fire had set them free but it could not touch them. But did the king speak true when he beheld the fourth like the Son of God? Little did he know what he said or what it meant, but assuredly he saw in that fire the Son of God, Jehovah, for He had promised His people, "When thou walkest through the fire thou shalt not be burned; neither shall the flame kindle on thee." The faithful Lord kept His promise to His trusting servants.

And has not all this been repeated throughout the times of the Gentiles especially during the Roman Empire? Pagan Rome persecuted the true worshippers of God and in great persecutions multitudes suffered martyrdom. But think of what is worse, Papal Rome, that Babylon the Great, the mother of harlots. There we find the images and the sweet music, the prostrations and political power enforcing unity of worship. The fiery furnaces were there, the stake, the most awful tortures for those who were faithful to God and to their Lord. Think of the story of the Waldensians and Huguenots. And while for these noble martyrs, for whom there is a martyr's crown in the coming day of Christ, there came no deliverance and their bodies were consumed by the fire, yet the Son of God was with them and with praising hearts and a song upon their lips, He carried them through the fire.

And during the great tribulation will a faithful remnant of Jews suffer under the man of sin, as these three Hebrews suffered; but they will likewise be delivered.

Verses 26-30. Once more Nebuchadnezzar acknowledged God and made a decree that severe punishment should be the lot of all who say anything amiss against the God of Daniel's companions.

CHAPTER 4

The Tree Vision of Nebuchadnezzar

1. The king's proclamation (4:1-3)
2. The king relates the tree vision (4:4-18)
3. Daniel interprets the vision (4:19-27)
4. The tree vision fulfilled, the king's abasement and his restoration, (4:28-37)

Verses 1-3. This chapter is in form, at least in part, of a proclamation. This proclamation must have been written after the king had passed through the experience recorded in this chapter.

Verses 4-18. Read carefully the vision the king had and compare with Ezekiel 31:3 and Matthew 13, the parable of the mustard seed. In each case the great big tree is the symbol of pride and self-exaltation.

Verses 19-27. The prophet's interpretation of this dream needs no further comment. A careful reading will make it clear in its meaning.

Verses 28-37. Twelve months later he walked in the palace of the kingdom of Babylon. Then with a haughty mien he utters the fatal words:

"Is not this great Babylon, that I have built for the house of the kingdom by the might of my power and for the honor of my majesty." Notice the personal pronoun. But while he yet uttered these words a heavenly voice was heard which announced that the kingdom is departed from him. What Daniel had said in his interpretation is repeated from heaven. The same hour was the thing fulfilled upon Nebuchadnezzar and he was driven from men and did eat grass as the oxen, and his body was wet with the dew of heaven, till his hairs were grown like eagles' feathers, and his nails like birds' claws. And after the seven times had passed over him his understanding returned unto him and he blessed the Most High.

The great characteristic here is pride and self-exaltation. As judgment came upon the great monarch in the beginning of the times of the Gentiles, so judgment will yet fall upon this proud and self-exalting age of the Gentiles. That great big, political and religious tree will some day be hewn down and be destroyed.

And Nebuchadnezzar's great humiliation in becoming a beast for seven times (seven years), points us to the end of this Gentile age once more. (The attempt to ascertain from this "seven times" the length of the times of the Gentiles as some do lacks the support of Scripture. The seven times mean seven years.) Apostasy from God will be the great characteristic of that end. There will be no more looking up to God, but the attitude of the beast will be the attitude of the nations. We see much of this already. They mind earthly things and become the "earth-dwellers" so frequently mentioned in the book of Revelation. Madness and bestiality will seize upon the Gentiles, after the One who hinders, the Holy Spirit is removed. Then proud and apostate Christendom will believe the lie and follow the beast with its lying wonders. This will last seven times, that is, seven years.

The stump of the great tree which remains in the field suggests the fact that the judgments which fall upon the nations in the time of the end will not completely destroy all nations. Many of them will be swept away. For those who wilfully rejected the gospel and turned away from the truth, there is no hope. But there are others which will be left and when these judgments are in the earth, the nations learn righteousness.

The millennium is also seen in this chapter in the restoration of Nebuchadnezzar and in the praise He gives to the Most High. In the previous chapter the three friends of Daniel speak of "our God," but in this chapter we hear of "the Most High." It is the millennial name of God. We see then in the fourth chapter the pride and self-exaltation of the Gentiles, and how the Gentiles will be humiliated and judged. First there is self-exaltation, that is followed by judgment, and then follows restoration and the acknowledgement of the Most High.

That nothing more is now reported of Nebuchadnezzar, that the last which we hear of him in Scripture is his acknowledgment of the Most High, is also not without meaning. It foreshadows the universal acknowledgment of God in the kingdom which the God of heaven will set up, when the stone fills as the mountain the whole earth.

CHAPTER 5

Belshazzar's Feast

1. Belshazzar's licentious feast (5:1-4)
2. The writing on the wall (5:5-9)
3. Forgotten Daniel (5:10-16)
4. The message of Daniel (5:17-31)

Verses 1-4. This feast of wickedness and blasphemy needs no further annotations. But it shows the great decline morally in the great Babylonian empire. Nebuchadnezzar, no doubt, had handled the golden vessels of the house of the Lord most carefully. He had stored them away, fearing to misuse them. The grandson sent for these vessels to drink out of them wine with his harlots and to praise his idols.

Verses 5-9. A mysterious finger then wrote over against the candlestick on the wall. The king saw plainly the part of the hand that wrote. The feast of licentiousness became suddenly a feast of gloom and consternation. Nor could the astrologers and wise men read the writing which had appeared on the wall.

Verses 10-16. At this point the queen, the aged widow of Nebuchadnezzar, appeared on the scene and called attention to an old man, who played such an important part during the reign of her husband. Daniel is sent for.

Verses 17-31. Daniel refused the honors of the king. He knew that ere long the blaspheming king would be no more. And Daniel was more than an interpreter of the handwriting on the wall. He is God's prophet and messenger, as a reading of this portion of the chapter shows.

This chapter reveals the blasphemous character of the end of the Babylonian monarchy. Blasphemy, rejection of God's truth are about us on all sides. There is a "Mene, Mene, Tekel" for apostate Christendom and for that final phase of Babylon as revealed in Rev. 17 and 18.

CHAPTER 6

Under Darius the Mede and Daniel in the Lion's Den

1. The decree of Darius (6:1-9)
2. Daniel's faith and steadfastness (6:10-15)
3. Daniel cast into the lion's den and the deliverance (6:16-24)
4. The Decree of Darius (6:25-28)

Verses 1-9. From the opening of this chapter we learn that Daniel also held a very high position in the beginning of the second monarchy, which had conquered Babylonia. He was preferred above all the other presidents and princes. This created jealousy. They devised a very cunning plan and made the king sign a decree, which they were sure Daniel would break. Inasmuch as the law of the Persians and Medes was irrevocable they were sure that the hated old man would be cast into the lion's den.

Verses 10-15. It is a beautiful scene. When Daniel knew the decree had been signed, he went calmly back into his house and with his windows open towards Jerusalem he prayed and gave thanks to the Lord. He looked away from earthly circumstances and looked to the Omnipotent One. The accusation followed. The king now discovers that he is in a desperate condition. His law demands that Daniel be cast to the lions, but his heart filled with love for Daniel would have liked to save him, but he found no way of delivering him.

Well may we think here of another law and another love. God, a holy and righteous God and a God of love, found a way to save man. God's holy law condemns man, who is a sinner and the curse of the law rests upon him. God's love is set upon the world, and He "so loved the world that He gave His only Begotten Son, that whosoever believeth on Him should not perish, but have everlasting life." The curse of the law came upon Him who knew no sin and who was made sin for us, and therein is love manifested. Daniel is cast into the lions' den as our blessed Lord was given to the lion (Psalm 22:21), and a stone is laid upon the mouth of the den and it is sealed with the king's signet. He is so to speak in a grave, as good as dead in the eyes of the world, for who has ever heard of hungry lions not devouring a man. And all this brings before us that other place, the tomb in the garden, where He was laid and the stone before it, which bore the seal of the Roman world power. But as Daniel could not be hurt by the lions, so He who went into the jaws of death could not be holden by death. The tomb is empty and He is victor over death and the grave. All this is blessedly foreshadowed in this experience of God's prophet.

The Lord in whom Daniel trusted and whom he served delivered him from the lions. His accusers and their families were given to the ferocious beasts, which devoured them at once.

Verses 25-28. King Darius also acknowledged the God of Daniel.

The final characteristic of the times of the Gentiles is man worship. The heads of these empires including the Roman Caesars claimed divine honors. Papal Rome also puts up man as the viceregent of the Lord. And all about us we find the deification of man. Finally there comes the head of all this apostasy, the son of perdition, the man of sin, who demands worship for himself (2 Thessalonians 2).

II. The Great Prophecies of Daniel

CHAPTER 7

1. The night vision of the three beasts (7:1-6)
2. The night vision of the fourth beast (7:7-8)
3. The judgment vision (7:9-12)
4. The son of man and His kingdom (7:13-14)
5. The interpretation of the visions given (7:15-28)

Verses 1-6. The sea in the vision is the type of nations (Rev. 17:15). The three first beasts he saw represented the same great monarchies which were shown to Nebuchadnezzar in his dream by the gold, silver and brass. The lion Daniel saw first rising out of the sea stands for the Babylonian empire symbolized by the lion (Jere. 4:7). The plucking of the wings and the man's heart must refer to Nebuchadnezzar's insanity and restoration (chapter 4). The bear is the emblem of the Medo-Persian monarchy (corresponding to the chest of silver in the image). One side of the bear was raised up, higher than the other, because the Persian element was the strongest. The three ribs denote the conquest of three provinces by this power. The leopard with four heads and wings is the picture of the great Alexandrine empire, the Graeco-Macedonian (corresponding to the belly and thighs of brass in the image).

The four wings denote its swiftness, the four

heads the partition of this empire into the kingdoms of Syria, Egypt, Macedonia and Asia Minor. It is seen in the next chapter as the rough he-goat with a notable horn (Alexander the Great) and the little horn (Antiochus Epiphanes). The fourth beast was not seen in the first vision. Before we turn to the second night vision of the prophet we call attention to the fact that in the selection of beasts to represent these world powers who domineer the times of the Gentiles, God tells us that their moral character is beastly. The lion devours, the bear crushes, the leopard springs upon its prey.

Verses 7-8. This represents Rome, corresponding to the two legs of iron and the ten horns with the little horn between has the same meaning as the ten toes on the feet of the image. The little horn we find more fully mentioned in another portion of this chapter. Thus the prophet beheld the same monarchies revealed in the second chapter under the emblem of ferocious beasts. Such the nations are and in their standards and national emblems they have borne witness to their beastly characters. Notice also here the same process of deterioration as in the image. The monarchies degenerate from lion to bear, from bear to leopard and then into a great nondescript.

Verses 9-12. This vision bring us to the close of the times of the Gentiles. When the fourth beast with the ten horns and the little horn, the last thing spoken of this world empire, is in full swing, then the end comes. It is a great judgment scene which is here before us. How different the end of this age as revealed in the Word and as it is believed in Christendom. The great mass knows nothing whatever about this age coming to an end. It will go on indefinitely, so they believe, and its future is world progress, better times and the triumph of the Christian civilization. But others concede that a judgment must come and they think of the judgment here as the universal judgment, the great white throne judgment. This judgment is not the last judgment at all. It is a judgment which precedes the final judgment by 1,000 years. This judgment here must be read in connection with passages like Matthew 25:31-46 and Rev. 19:19-21. In reading the last passage no one can doubt that we have the same judgment here revealed to Daniel. But who is the one who occupies the central place in this vision of judgment? There can be but one answer. It is our ever blessed Lord and Saviour Jesus Christ. John 5:22 gives the conclusive answer: "For the Father judgeth no man, but hath committed all judgment unto the Son." The Ancient of Days is the Lord Jesus Christ. It is still more demonstrated if we turn to John's great Patmos vision.

Verses 13-14. These words are so plain that every Christian knows what they mean. They describe the second coming of Christ and the kingdom He then receives from the Father's hands. If this passage were more considered, Christians would stop speaking about the kingdom now. No kingdom till Christ comes again. Both the judgment vision and the vision of His coming to receive the kingdom correspond to the stone which smites the image and as a mountain fills the whole earth.

Verses 15-28. First, Daniel hears about the four beasts. But there is a significant statement in verse 18, the saints of the Most High receiving the kingdom.

Who are the Saints of the Most High? The fact that the term "Most High" is in the plural and may also be translated with "the most high or heavenly places" has led some expositors to say that the saints are the same who are seen in the Epistle to the Ephesians in which "the heavenly places" are repeatedly mentioned: in other words, the saints which compose the Church. It is true the Church will be with the Lord in Glory and "we shall reign over the earth," but this does not necessarily mean that the saints here represent the Church. There are other saints besides "Church saints." The saints of whom Daniel was thinking were his own beloved people. To that people is promised a kingdom in the days of the Messiah. With Him, the Lord in glory, there is a heavenly people, so as Messiah and the Son of Man in connection with the earth He has an earthly people, saints which will receive and possess with Him that kingdom which will fill the whole earth. These saints are the Godfearing Jews, who pass through the great tribulation and inherit the blessings and promises which God gave through their own prophets.

Another important matter is the little horn of whom now Daniel hears more fully. The ten horns are kings and the little horn in their midst will be the final imperial head of the revived Roman empire, that world domineering person of whom we read repeatedly in the Word of God. He must be distinguished from another one, the personal anti-Christ, the man of sin and son of perdition. In Revelation the revived Roman Empire is seen in chapter 13: 1-10, and the second beast which John saw rising from the sea is the false Christ having two horns like a lamb but speaking like a dragon (Rev. 13:11, etc.) A closer study of these coming leaders of the end time is needed to understand the details; here we but point the way. Our larger work on Daniel will give help on all these chapters.

CHAPTER 8

The Ram and the He-Goat

1. The vision (8:1-14)
2. The interpretation of the vision (8:15-27)

Verses 1-14. Beginning with this chapter to the end of the book prophecy will lead us mostly upon Jewish ground. While some of these prophecies were fulfilled in the past, most of them are related to the future when the great end fulfillment takes place before the coming of the Son of Man in the clouds of heaven to receive the kingdom. The phrases "the latter times," "the time of the end," "in the last end of the indignation," appear several times in these chapters. These phrases describe the same period of time mentioned in the seventh chapter, "a time, times and dividing of times;" the 1,260 days or 43 months in the book of Revelation. It is the great tribulation which is recorded in the last chapter of this book.

The time and place of the vision in this chapter are given in the beginning. The ram, according to divine interpretation (verses 15, etc.), is the Medo-Persian monarchy—the silver kingdom, the kingdom also typified by the bear. The he-goat with a notable horn is the Graeco-Macedonian monarchy and the notable horn is Alexander the Great. In 334 B. C., Alexander leaped like a swift he-goat across the Hellespont and fought his successful battles, then pushed on to the banks of the Indus and the Nile and then onward to Shushan. The great battles of the Granicus, Issus and Arbella were fought, and he stamped the power of Persia and its King, Darius Codomannus, to the ground. He conquered rapidly Syria, Phoenicia, Cyprus, Tyre, Gaza, Egypt, Babylonia, Persia. In 329 he conquered Bactria, crossed the Oxus and Jaxaitis and defeated the Scythians. And thus he stamped upon the ram after having broken its horns. But when the he-goat had waxed very great, the great horn was broken. This predicted the early and sudden death of Alexander the Great. He died after a reign of 12 years and eight months, after a career of drunkenness and debauchery in 323 B. C. He died when he was but 32 years old. Then four notable ones sprang up in the place of the broken horn. This too has been fulfilled, for the empire of Alexander was divided into four parts. Four of the great generals of Alexander made the division namely, Cassander, Lysimachus, Seleucus and Ptolemy. The four great divisions were, Syria, Egypt, Macedonia and Asia Minor.

Then a little horn appeared out of one of these divisions; it sprung up out of Syria. This little horn is of course not the little horn mentioned in the previous chapter, for the little horn in Daniel 7 has its place in connection with the fourth beast (Rome), while this one comes from a division of the third beast, the Graeco-Macedonian monarchy.

History does not leave us in doubt of how and when this great prophetic vision was fulfilled. This little horn is the eighth king of the Seleucid dynasty. He is known by the name of Antiochus Epiphanes; after his wild and wicked deeds he was called Epimanes, the madman. Long before he invaded the pleasant land (Israel's land), Daniel saw what he would do. He conquered Jerusalem. He took away the daily sacrifice in the temple and offered a swine and swine's blood upon the altar. He introduced idol worship, devastated the whole land and killed some 100,000 Jews.

In verses 13-14 is an angelic conversation. The 2,300 days (literal days) cover just about the period of time during which Antiochus did his wicked deeds. When they were ended Judas Maccabaeus cleansed the sanctuary about December 25, 165 B. C.

We believe these 2,300 days are therefore literal days and have found their literal fulfillment in the dreadful days of this wicked king from the north. There is no other meaning attached to these days and the foolish speculations that these days are years, etc., lacks scriptural foundation altogether. Such views and fanciful interpretations bring the study of prophecy into disrepute. We have special reference to the Seventh Day Adventist delusion. They teach the abominable falsehood that the Lord Jesus Christ did not enter into the Holiest till the year 1844 had been reached, because this is according to their reckoning 2,300 years after Cyrus had issued the command to build the temple. That this is a denial of the gospel itself and satanic is self-evident.

Verses 15-27. Gabriel is the interpreter of the whole vision. It should be carefully studied. It points to a future fulfillment.

Gabriel told Daniel that the vision has a special meaning for the time of the end. Four different expressions are used to denote the time of the final fulfillment of the vision: (1) "The time of the end" (8:17); (2) "The last end of the indignation" (8:19); (3) "The latter time of their kingdom" (8:23); (4) "When the transgressors are come to the full" (8:23).

Once more, at the close of the age, before the Lord comes in visible glory, in the days of the great tribulation, the time of Jacob's trouble, an invasion from the north takes place. Israel's land will once more undergo the horrors of a devastation, foreshadowed by Antiochus Epiphanes. The king of the north, as he is also called in Isaiah's prophecy, "the Assyrian," will do this work. For details and other prophecies relating to this coming event see our exposition of Daniel, pages 102-118.

CHAPTER 9

The Prophecy of the Seventy Weeks

1. The time and occasion of Daniel's prayer (9:1-2)
2. The prayer (9:3-19)
3. The answer and the prophecy of the seventy weeks (9:20-27)

Verses 1-2. It was in the first year of Darius, of the seed of the Medes, that Daniel understood by the sacred writings of his people, especially by the prophecy of Jeremiah, that the end of the years of the captivity was at hand. The promises in the Word of God led him at once to seek the face of the Lord and he poured out a wonderful prayer in His presence.

Verses 3-19. It has three parts: Verses 4-10: Confession of the failure of his people and acknowledgment of God's covenant mercies. Verses 11-14: The deserved curse as written in the law of Moses. Verses 15-19: Pleadings for mercy to turn away His anger and to remember His city, Jerusalem and His people. Throughout this prayer we read how completely he identified himself with the sins, the failure, the shame and the judgment of the people of God. This is remarkable. As we have seen from the first chapter, he was brought to Babylon when quite young and belonged even then to the believing, God fearing element of the nation. Yet he speaks of the nation's sins, their rebellion, their transgressions of the law and their wicked deeds as if they belonged to him. Of all the Bible characters Daniel appears as the purest. The failures of Abraham, Moses, Aaron, David and others are recorded, but Daniel appears with no flaw whatever in his character. As far as the record goes he was a perfect man. Of course he too was "a man of like passions" as we are, and as such a sinner. Yet this devoted and aged servant with such a record of loyalty to God and to His laws confesses all the people's sins and the curse and shame, which came upon them, as His own.

Verses 20-27. The prayer was not ended. How near heaven is may be learned from verses 20-32. Heaven is not far away, for there is no space and no distance with God. When Daniel began his confession and humiliation the Lord called Gabriel and instructed him what he should tell the praying prophet, and then Gabriel was caused to fly swiftly through the immeasurable space, and before Daniel ever reached the "Amen" the messenger stood before him and stopped his prayer. What blessed assurance! The moment we pray in the Spirit and in His Name our voices are heard in the highest heaven.

We give a corrected text of the great prophecy, perhaps the greatest in the entire prophetic Word.

> Seventy weeks are apportioned out upon thy people and upon thy holy city to finish the transgression and to make an end of sins, and to cover iniquity, and to bring in the righteousness of the ages, and to seal the vision and prophet, and to anoint the holy of holies. Know therefore and understand: From the going forth of the word to restore and to rebuild Jerusalem unto Messiah, the Prince, shall be seven weeks and sixty-two weeks. The street and the wall shall be built again, even in troublous times. And after the sixty-two weeks shall Messiah be cut off, and shall have nothing; and the people of the prince that shall come shall destroy the city and the sanctuary; and the end thereof shall be with overflow, and unto the end war, the desolations determined. And he shall confirm a covenant with the many for one week; and in the midst of the week he shall cause the sacrifice and the oblation to cease and because of the protection of abominations there shall be a desolator, even until the consummation and what is determined shall be poured out upon the desolator (verses 24-27).

The literal translation of the term "seventy weeks" is "seventy-sevens." Now, this word "sevens" translated "weeks" may mean "days" and it may mean "years." What then is meant here, seventy times seven days or seventy times seven years? It is evident that the "sevens" mean year weeks, seven years to each prophetic week. Daniel was occupied in reading the books and in prayer with the seventy years of Babylonian captivity. And now Gabriel is going to reveal to him something which will take place in "seventy-sevens," which means seventy times seven

THE SEVENTY PROPHETIC YEAR WEEKS OF DANIEL'S PROPHECY

Seven Weeks	Sixty-two Weeks—434 Years		The Great Unreckoned Period	The Last Week—7 Years	
49 years later the street and wall built Artaxerxes in the month Nisan gives edict to rebuild Jerusalem 445 B.C.	From the word to restore and build Jerusalem seven weeks and sixty-two weeks (483 years) till Messiah the Prince The 69 weeks, or 483 years, expired A.D. 32 In the week they expired Christ died on the cross as predicted. Messiah shall be cut off and shall have nothing	End of 69th week, April 10, 32 A.D.	The Romans under Titus destroy the city and sanctuary, 70 A.D. Jews are scattered among all nations Jerusalem trodden down Desolations till the end The mystery hid in former ages made known (the Church) World-wide preaching of the gospel Apostasy of Christendom Part of the Jewish nation returns to the land in unbelief (Zionism) The coming of the Lord for His saints. Dead saints raised and living saints changed (1 Thess. 4:13-18)	First half, 3½ years, 1260 days	Roman prince (little horn, Dan. 7) makes a covenant with the Jews Jewish people fully restored and temple worship resumed Many other predicted events in prophets and Revel. fulfilled The covenant broken
				The Middle of the Week	
				Second half, 3½ years, 1260 days The Great Tribulation	Sacrifices and oblations cease Antichrist in Jerusalem Image set up and its worship demanded Great tribulation Jerusalem in distress The little horn (Dan. 8), the king with fierce countenance The Lord appears to deliver His people

The end of the seventieth week brings in the Righteousness of Ages through the second coming of the Lord. The kingdom established. All vision and prophecy fulfilled. Jerusalem a praise in the earth. Universal peace. Nations learn war no more.

years. The proof that such is the case is furnished by the fulfillment of the prophecy itself. Now seventy-seven years makes 490 years.

What is to be accomplished. Verse 24 gives the great things which are to be accomplished during these seventy-year weeks or 490 years. They are the following: (1) To finish the transgression; (2) To make an end of sins. (3) To cover iniquity; (4) To bring in the righteousness of ages; (5) To seal the vision and prophet; (6) To anoint the Holy of Holies.

It must be borne in mind that these things concern exclusively Daniel's people and not Gentiles but the holy city Jerusalem. It is clear that the finishing of transgression, the end of sins and the covering of iniquity has a special meaning for Israel as a nation.

Now, these seventy year-weeks are divided into three parts. The first part consists in seven weeks, that is seven times seven, 49 years. During these 49 years the street and the wall of Jerusalem was to be rebuilt and the complete restoration accomplished. The reckoning of this time begins in the month Nisan, 445 B. C., when the command was given (Nehemiah 2). Then follows the second division consisting of 62 weeks of years, that is sixty-two times seven, 434 years. At the close of these 434 years, or 483 years reckoned from the month Nisan in 445 B. C., Messiah the Prince should be cut off and have nothing. Messiah the Prince is none other than the Lord Jesus Christ. Here then is a startling prediction of the death of Christ, the Messiah rejected by His people and not receiving the kingdom which belongs to Him as the Son of David. The sixty-two weeks, or 434 years, expired on the day our Lord rode into Jerusalem for the last time; during that week He was crucified. (For full proof see *The Coming Prince,* by Anderson, and our book on the Prophet Daniel.)

Then we have a remarkable prediction concerning the fate of Jerusalem after the nation rejected the Lord Jesus Christ: "And the people of the prince that shall come shall destroy the city and the sanctuary; and the end thereof shall be with an overflow, and unto the end war, the desolations determined." Who is "the prince that shall come?" Expositors have erred seriously in making of this prince the Lord Jesus Christ. This prince is not our Lord. It is the little horn predicted in Daniel 7 to rise out of the Roman Empire in the time of the end, when the Roman Empire is revived politically and has its ten horns. Therefore "*the people* of the prince that shall come" are the Roman people. Here then is a prediction that the Romans were to take the city and burn the sanctuary. How literally this has been fulfilled! And all this was revealed when the Roman Empire was not yet in existence. Such are the marvels of divine prophecy. After that there are to be wars and desolations for Jerusalem and the Jewish people. It is the same that our Lord predicted when He said: "They shall fall by the edge of the sword, and shall be led away captive into all nations" (Luke 21:24).

But all this leaves seven years, that is one week, unaccounted for. We have up to now 483 weeks, and there are to be 490 years. The last week of seven years is still future. The course of the Jewish age was interrupted. It is an unfinished age. Between the 483 years which ended when the nation rejected the Lord of Glory and the beginning of the last seven years of the Jewish age, this last year-week is this present age, the unreckoned period of time during which God does His great work in sending forth the gospel of His grace to the Gentile nations, to gather out of them a people for His Name. This age of grace is still on but it will end some day when God's purpose is accomplished. Then the true Church will be gathered home to glory and the Lord will turn again to His people Israel and the last week of Daniel will pass into history. During these seven years the Prince that shall come, the little horn of Daniel 7, will enter into a covenant with the Jewish people. Not with all of them, for there is a remnant of godly Jews who will not accept this one (indicated by the expression "the many"—see correct translation). In the middle of the week he breaks that covenant and the result will be the great tribulation, the time, times and half of a time, 1,260 days, 42 months of Daniel 7 and Rev. 13. When this great tribulation ends the Lord Jesus Christ comes back and the great things mentioned in verse 24 will be accomplished.

CHAPTER 10

The Preparation for the Final Prophecy

This chapter contains the preface to the final great prophecies as found in the last two chapters of this book. The certain man who appeared unto Daniel at the banks of the river Hiddekel (Tigris) was the Lord. Compare with Revelation 1, where John, the beloved disciple, beheld Him in a vision of glory. Daniel's vision is a pre-incarnation vision of the same One whom John beheld after His resurrection and in His glorified humanity.

The delayed answer by the angelic messenger is explained by the power of darkness. A powerful demon-prince, a satanic agency, having control over Persia, so that he claimed the title the prince of Persia, kept back the answer. Then the prophet was strengthened.

CHAPTER 11

The Wars of the Ptolemies and Seleucidae Predicted
The Coming Events of the End

1. The wars of the Ptolemies and Seleucidae (11:1-35)
2. The time of the end and the man of sin (11:36-45)

Verses 1-35. Here we have history prewritten and the greater part of this chapter (verses 2-35) is fulfilled historically. So accurate are these predictions and their subsequent fulfillment that the enemies of "the Scripture of truth" have declared that it could never have been written by Daniel several hundred years before these persons came into existence and fought their battles. The pagan Porphyry in the third century in his "Treatise against Christians" bitterly attacked the belief that Daniel wrote these predictions. He argued that all was written after the events had taken place. The same arguments are used by the critics. Such is this most subtle infidelity that it can make use of the statements of a poor heathen in opposition to the divine revelation.

The prophecies given here were minutely fulfilled during the years 301 B. C., to 168 B. C. History verifies everything. The history covers a good part of the Persian and Graeco-Macedonian Empires, but mostly the wars of the Ptolemies and Seleucidae. Artaxerxes, Darius, Alexander the Great, Ptolemy Lagris, the King of the South, Ptolemy Euergetes, Seleucus Calinicus, Ptolemy Philopater, Antiochus Epiphanes, even the Roman fleet (the ships of Chittim), all enter into this prophecy. A detailed exposition of the prophecy and its fulfillment would fill many pages.

Before we pass on we desire to say again that all in these verses we have briefly followed has been historically fulfilled. We point out a mistake in which some have fallen. In verse 31 we read of "the abomination that maketh desolate." Our Lord in His Olivet discourse (Matthew 24:15) said: "When ye therefore shall see the abomination of desolation, spoken by Daniel the prophet, stand in the holy place (whoso readeth let him understand)." Some believe that when our Lord spoke these words he referred to Daniel 11: 31, and that this is the abomination of desolation. This is not quite correct. The abomination that maketh desolate of verse 31 is past and happened in the days of the atrocities committed by Antiochus Epiphanes. The abomination of desolation to which our Lord refers is mentioned in chapter 12:11, and it points, as we shall find later, to the abomination set up by the Antichrist, the second beast, in the middle of the week. The typical meaning of Antiochus Epiphanes and his crimes in the land of Judea and against Jerusalem we have already learned in connection with chapter 8.

Verses 36-45. The time of the end is mentioned in verse 35. What is to befall Daniel's people in the latter days as Daniel was told in chapter 10:14 is now revealed. Between verses 35 and 36 we must put a long and unreckoned period of time. Antiochus Epiphanes and the victorious Maccabees end the historical fulfillment of the predictions of the great prophecies in the first part of this chapter, and since then over 2,000 years have come and gone and the fulfillment of verses 36-45 have not yet been. First we read of a wilful king. Who is this king so fully pictured in verses 36-45?

Many expositors of Daniel apply this passage to Antiochus Epiphanes because they see not the important interval which exists between verses 35 and 36. However, a closer examination of the description of this king shows that he cannot be Antiochus. He is another person altogether, and as we shall see later, will be a Jew and assume kingly honors in the midst of the Jewish people. Antiochus was a Gentile. Others again identify this King with the first beast in Revelation 13, and say that the head of the revived Roman Empire, one like Napoleon I is meant, while others see here a reference to the pope in Rome. And whether the head of the Roman power, or the pope, or perhaps Mohammed, the term "Antichrist" is freely applied to each. Those who see the papacy here and the Romish corruption make some startling applications which are extremely fanciful.

The wilful king is the Antichrist. The Jewish people rejected their King, the Messiah, who came to His own, the Lord Jesus Christ. Our Lord told the Jews: "I am come in My Father's name, and ye receive Me not; if another shall come in his own name, him ye will receive"

(John 5:43). This other one has not yet come. We have his photograph here. He appears in Israel's land in the time of the end as a counterfeit Messiah and takes also the place of king in their midst. This wilful king, the personal Antichrist who deceives the apostate mass of the Jewish people, is repeatedly mentioned in the Old Testament prophetic Word. Isaiah speaks of him and his end (Isa. 30:33, 57:9). Zechariah calls him "the idol shepherd" (Zech. 11:15-17). He is repeatedly mentioned in the Psalms as "the wicked man"—"the man of the earth"—the bloody and deceitful man." In the book of Revelation he appears as the second beast out of the land (Palestine) (Rev. 13:11-17). The two horns like a lamb as he is described there show clearly that he imitates Christ. He has the spirit of the dragon and appears as a religious leader, for this reason he is also called "the false prophet" in the book of Revelation (chapters 16:13, 19:20, 20:10).

In the New Testament he is called in the writings of John "the Antichrist". (See 1 John 2:18-22, 4:3; 2 John 7). Another great prophecy of the same person is found in 2 Thess. 2, where he is called "the man of sin, the son of perdition." The early Church believed that this evil person will be a real man, a Jew, and be energized by Satan. That he is the papal system or something else was invented later.

In verses 40-45 we have a prophecy of the wars and conflicts during the time of the end. The false king, Israel's false Messiah, the Antichrist, plays an important part in these conflicts. Then there are the kings of the south and of the north. The king of the south comes out of Egypt. His antagonist is the king of the north. The king of the south will be overthrown by the powerful king of the North, the same who is typified by the Antiochus Epiphanes. (Read about this invasion in Joel 2 and Zechariah 14.)

While the king of the north and his proud hosts are thus overthrown by the army of the Lord, what becomes of the wilful king, the Antichrist in the city? The king of the north cannot touch him. But the Lord Himself will deal with that wicked one. "Whom the Lord shall consume with the spirit of His mouth, and shall destroy with the brightness of His coming" (2 Thess. 2:8). Thus ends the great conflict of the time of the end. The eternal abode of the satanic instruments of the time of the end, the beast, that coming prince, the Antichrist and the king of the north will be the lake of fire.

CHAPTER 12

The Great Tribulation and Israel's Deliverance

"And at that time." What time? The time of the end, the time of trouble such as never was before; the same time to which our Lord refers in Matthew 24:21.

Michael, the great prince which standeth for the Jewish people, is now also mentioned again. He will stand up and take a leading part in the events of that time. From the book of Revelation we learn (chapter 12) that there will be war in heaven, that is where Satan has his dominion now as the prince of the power of the air. Michael, assisted by his angels, will cast out the great dragon, the devil and his angels. They will be forced down to the earth. Then when Satan and his angels are cast out the great tribulation will be instituted (Rev. 12:12). Michael will stand up in another sense and take a definite part in the deliverance of Daniel's people. It is not fully revealed what that will be.

The deliverance of which we read in these verses and the awakening of those "who sleep in the dust of the earth" has likewise been grossly misinterpreted. Because expositors have not seen the application of all this to the Jews in their future history in the land, they have read the church in here, and even what they term a general resurrection on a general judgment day. But we shall see now what is meant by the deliverance of Daniel's people.

Physical resurrection (as so often stated: a general resurrection) is not taught in the second verse. Physical resurrection is used as a figure of the national revival of Israel in that day. They have been sleeping nationally in the dust of the earth, buried among the Gentiles. But at that time there will take place a national restoration, a bringing together of the house of Judah and of Israel. It is the same figure as used in the vision of the dry bones in Ezekiel 37. This vision is employed by the men, who have invented the theory of a second chance and larger hope for the wicked dead to back up their evil teaching, but anyone can see that it concerns not the Gentiles but the Jewish people and that it is not a bodily resurrection, but a national revival and restoration of that people. Their national graves, not literal burying places, will be opened and the Lord will bring them forth out of all the countries into which they have been scattered.

There will be two classes, the godly and the ungodly. The ungodly accept the false Messiah, and in their national revival, shame and everlasting contempt awaits them, while the others, the godly, will enjoy life in the kingdom. The wise in verse 3 are the Jewish teachers and witnesses in the endtime, those which compose the godly remnant. A special reward will be theirs during the kingdom, they shall shine as the stars forever. The same holds good, only in a higher sense for all those who are witnesses for Him during this age, who are faithful to Christ.

Then Daniel is addressed and beholds angels once more, as well Him who appeared clothed in linen, none other than the Lord. Then Daniel asked his final question.

Verses 11-12 have puzzled many readers of the book. Different theories are given.

But what is the meaning of these 1,290 and 1,335 days? Can there be anything plainer than the fact that these 1,290 and 1,335 days are literal days? Who authorizes us to make of these days years? By what process of exposition are we to arrive at the conclusion that "days" mean "years?" It is worse than folly to do that.

Now, the great tribulation lasts for 1,260 days. But here we have 30 days or a whole month added. The Lord will be manifested at the close of the great tribulation of 1,260 days, 3½ years. Matthew 24:29-31 teaches us this. The extra month will in all probability be needed to make possible certain judgment events especially with the overthrow of the nations which came against Jerusalem and the judgment of nations as given in Matthew 25:31. We cannot speak dogmatically on all this. But certain it is that 1,335 days after the Antichristian abomination had been set up in Jerusalem, that is, 75 days, or 1½ months beyond the time of the great tribulation, the full blessing for Israel and the establishment of the glorious rule of Israel's King, the once rejected Lord Jesus Christ, will have come, for it is written, "Blessed is he that waiteth and cometh to the thousand, three hundred and five and thirty days." This is as far as any teacher can safely go, and here we would rest.

THE PROPHET

HOSEA

Introduction

The Minor Prophets begin with the book of Hosea. There are twelve of these books which are called by the name "minor prophets" not because their contents are of less authority than the preceding prophetic books, but on account of their size. The Jews considered them one book and the Talmud says of them, "our fathers made them one book, that they might not perish on account of their littleness." The term "minor prophets" was used by the church in early days. Augustinus states: "The prophet Isaiah is not in the books of the twelve prophets who are therefore called minor, because their discourses are brief in comparison with those who are called 'greater' because they composed considerable volumes." Jewish tradition claims that the present arrangement was made by the great synagogue formed by Ezra. This arrangement is not chronological. Joel precedes Hosea, while Hosea, Amos and Jonah were nearly contemporary; Obadiah is difficult to place. The introduction to the book enters into the question of date. Micah, the Morasthite, ministered between the years 757 and 699 B. C. Nahum, the complement and counterpart of the book of Jonah, also prophesied during the period of Isaiah. Habakkuk is later than the preceding prophets. He speaks of the invasion of the land by Chaldeans as imminent; his prophetic office was probably exercised during the second half of Manasseh's reign. Zephaniah prophesied under the reign of Josiah, between 642 and 611 B. C. Haggai, Zechariah and Malachi are post-exilic.

Hosea and His Times

The first verse of the book determines the period of Hosea. He prophesied while Uzziah was reigning in Judah and Jeroboam II in Israel, as well as during the time when Jotham, Ahaz and Hezekiah were kings over Judah. His whole prophetic ministry covers probably over seventy years, so that he must have reached a very old age. His prophecy is directed almost exclusively to the house of Israel, which had degenerated in a short time and Hosea lived during these awful years. Jeroboam II was almost the last king who ruled by the appointment of the Lord. After him kings made their way to the tottering throne of Israel by murdering their predecessors. Shallum slew Zechariah; Menahem slew Shallum; Pekah killed the son of Menahem; Hosea killed Pekak. All was anarchy in Israel.

The religious conditions were still worse. Nearly all these usurpers had made alliances with foreign powers which resulted in the introduction of the immoral, corrupt Phoenician and Syrian idolatry. The first Jeroboam had set up a rival worship so that the people would not go to Jerusalem to worship in the divinely appointed way. Jeroboam had been in Egypt (1 Kings 11:40; 12:2) where he had seen nature worshipped in the form of a calf. This worship he introduced in the identical words which their fathers had used when they worshiped the golden calf in the wilderness. (See Exodus 32:4 and 1 Kings 12:28). Outwardly the different ceremonies of the law, the feasts of Jehovah, the new moons and Sabbath days, the sacrifices and offerings were maintained, but all was a corrupt worship. The calf was the immediate object of that idolatrous worship. They sacrificed to the calf (1 Kings 12:32); they kissed the calf (Hosea 13:2) and swore by these idol-calves (Amos 8:14). As Dr. Pusey states: "Calf-worship paved the way for the coarser and more cruel worship of nature, under the names of Baal and Ashtaroth, with all their abominations of consecrated child sacrifices, and horrible sensuality." It led to the most awful sins and degradation. Here is a description of the moral conditions prevailing in the days of Hosea, a condition brought about by the false worship and departure from God. Hosea and Amos acquaint us with it. All was falsehood (Hosea 4:1; 7:1, 3); adultery (Hosea 4:11, 7:4, 9:10); bloodshed (Hosea 5:2; 6:8); excess and luxury were supplied by secret or open robbery (Hosea 4:2; 10:13; 11:12; 4:11; 7:5; 6:4-6; Amos 4:1); oppression (Hosea 12:7; Amos 3:9-10); false dealing (Hosea 12:7; Amos 8:5); perversion of justice (Hosea 10:4; Amos 2:6, 7); grinding of the poor (Amos 2:7, 8:6). Adultery was consecrated as an act of worship and religion (Hosea 4:14). The people, the king and the priests were all steeped in debauchery. Corruption had spread everywhere; even the places once sacred through Jehovah's revelation, Bethel, Gilgal, Gilead, Mizpah, Shechem, were special scenes of vileness and wickedness. Remonstrance was useless for the knowledge of Jehovah was wilfully rejected; they hated rebuke. To understand the message of Hosea and Amos these conditions, both religious and moral, must be fully understood.

The Message of Hosea

Like the message of other prophets Hosea's message is one of judgment and future mercy. He announced the coming judgment as certain and irreversible. They were to be led away into captivity. His sons and daughters born to him by Gomer, the daughter of Diblaim, expressed this coming judgment in their names which were given to them by divine direction. "Lo-Ruhamah"—I will have no mercy; and "Lo-Ammi"—not my people. Then he announced in the name of the Lord, "I will cause the kingdom of the house of Israel to cease;" "I will have no mercy upon the house of Israel:" "They shall be wanderers among the nations;"—"They shall not dwell in the Lord's land;"—"Israel is swallowed up; she shall be among the nations like a vessel in which is no pleasure." In the greater portion of his message there is an exposure of the people's moral condition and their impenitent state.

But there is also the message of mercy, which is found in the very beginning of the book. Here are a few of these comforting words, which still await their fulfillment in the day when they shall "seek the Lord their God, and David their King (the Messiah); and shall fear the Lord and His goodness in the latter days" (3:5):—"I will betroth her to me forever;"—"They shall fear the Lord and His goodness;"—"He will raise us up, and we shall live in His sight;"—"Till He come and rain righteousness upon you;"—"I will ransom them from the power of the grave, I will redeem them from death;"—"I will heal their backsliding;"—"I will be as the dew unto Israel, He shall grow as the lily, and cast forth its roots as Lebanon."

"It belongs to the mournful solemnity of Hosea's prophecy that he scarcely speaks to the people in his own person. The ten chapters, which form the center of the prophecy, are almost wholly one long dirge of woe, in which the prophet rehearses the guilt and the punishment of his people. If the people are addressed, it is, with very few exceptions, God Himself, not the prophet, who speaks to them; and God speaks to them as their judge. Once only does the prophet use the form so common in other prophets 'saith the Lord.' As in the three first chapters, the prophet, in relation to his wife, represented the relation of God to His people, so in these ten chapters, after the first words of the fourth and fifth chapters;—'Hear the word of the Lord, for the Lord has a controversy with the inhabitants of the land;'—'Hear ye this, O priests;'—whenever the prophet uses the first person, he uses it not of himself, but of God. 'I,'—'My,'—are not Hosea, and the things of Hosea, but God and what belongs to God. God addresses the prophet in the second person. In four verses only of these chapters does the prophet himself apparently address his own people Israel, in two expostulating with them (9:1, 5); in two calling them to repentance (10:12 and 12:6). In two other verses he addresses Judah, and foretells their judgment mingled with mercy (4:13). The last chapter alone is one of almost unmingled brightness; the prophet calls to repentance, and God in His own person accepts it, and promises large supply of grace" (Dr. Pusey).

We learn then from the message of this book, what is so largely written in all the prophets, that there is a glorious future in store for all Israel. Judah and Israel both will receive the promised blessing and glory in that day when the King comes back, when Ephraim joyfully cries out "I have seen Him" (14:8).

The conditions in Israel also find their counterpart in our own times. Christendom has turned its back in greater part upon the true worship, rejects the truth, yea the highest and the best God has given, the Gospel of Christ, hence the moral decline and apostasy and ere long a greater judgment than that which fell upon Israel.

The Division of Hosea

Hosea (meaning "salvation") in his style is abrupt and sententious. As already stated in the introduction he is the prophet of the ten tribes, though Judah is also mentioned by him. The book begins with two symbolical actions commanded by Jehovah, to illustrate Israel's adulterous condition and Jehovah's enduring love for His people in spite of their faithlessness. This is followed by a terse prophecy as to the condition of the people for many days and their return in the latter days (chapters 1-3).

The main portion of the book begins with the fourth chapter. This part begins with "Hear the Word of the Lord." In this section their religious and moral degradation through the priests and their coming ruin is announced. Then follows a description of the judgment which was to come upon Ephraim (the house of Israel) and also upon Judah. This is beheld by the prophet in a solemn vision (5:8-15), followed by a brief prophecy as to what will take place when the remnant of Israel returns unto the Lord (6:1-3). Then the Lord reproves them for their inconstancy, their immorality, their lewd priests. From chapter 7 to 13 we have similar remonstrances, with renewed announcements of the judgments on account of their wickedness, idolatries, leagues with heathen nations; the judgment is to be exile. What is to be their lot is predicted. This punishment is not to be delayed; it will, however, not destroy them, but purge them, leaving a remnant. The last chapter is one of gracious promise of what will take place in the day of their return. The division of this book is therefore twofold.

I. THE REJECTION OF ISRAEL AS AN ADULTEROUS WIFE AND HER FUTURE RECEPTION AND RESTORATION: (1—3)

II. THE MESSAGES OF EXPOSTULATION, JUDGMENT, AND MERCY: (4—12)

There are different subdivisions which will be pointed out and followed in the analysis and annotations.

The book of Hosea is quoted a number of times in the New Testament. See Matt 2:15, 9:13, 12:7; Rom. 9:25, 26; 1 Cor. 15:55; 1 Peter 2:5, 10.

Analysis and Annotations

I. The Rejection of Israel as the Adulterous Wife and Her Future Reception and Restoration

CHAPTER I

Israel's Sin and Promise of Restoration

1. The introduction (1:1)
2. The prophet's marriage and birth of Jezreel (1:2-5)
3. The birth of Lo-Ruhamah (1:6-7)
4. The birth of Lo-Ammi (1:8-9)
5. The future restoration (1:10-11)

Verse 1. This superscription gives the period of Hosea's ministry. First stands the statement that the word of the Lord came to him. Hosea means salvation; his father's name, Beeri, means "my well." Both are typical names. Critics have pointed out that Hosea was undoubtedly a resident of the northern kingdom of Israel, yet he mentions but one of the kings of Israel, Jeroboam, while four kings of Judah are given in this introduction. Inasmuch as Hosea long survived Jeroboam, the king of Israel, and the Judaic kings extend far beyond the time of the one Israelitish king, it has been alleged that the second part of the superscription does not harmonize with the first. Such is not the case. The superscription is made in this manner for some purpose. Hosea marks his prophecy by the names of the kings of Judah, because in Judah the theocracy remained. He mentions Jeroboam (the Second), whose reign ended in the fourteenth year of Uzziah, because he was the last king of Israel through whom God acted and vouchsafed help to the rival kingdom. All the other kings of Israel who came after Jeroboam, by whom the Lord sent deliverance to the ten tribes (2 Kings 14:27) were therefore recognized by the prophets of God; the kings which followed were robbers and murderers, whose names the Spirit of God finds unfit to mention in the prophetic ministry of Hosea.

Verses 2-5. In the beginning of his ministry, when Hosea was a young man, the Lord commanded him to take unto him a wife of whoredoms and children of whoredoms, and that for the reason, because the land hath committed great whoredoms, departing from the Lord. This command was at once executed by the prophet; he took to wife Gomer, the daughter of Diblaim.

We are confronted with an interesting question. What is the nature of these transactions? Were they real events, that Hosea literally took this woman and had children by her, or were they nothing but pictorial, visionary illustrations of the spiritual adultery and unfaithfulness of Israel? Did the prophet actually and literally enter into such an impure relationship, or, is it wholly an allegory? Luther supposed that the prophet called his lawful wife and children by these names at a certain time to perform a kind of drama before the people and thus remind them of their apostasy. The objectors to the literalness of this incident, and defenders of the allegorical explanation, have pointed out that it would be unworthy of God to command and sanction such an unchaste union. The allegorical meaning is entirely excluded by the text, which speaks of a literal transaction. All is related as real history, the marriage and the birth of the children. We quote first Dr. Pusey's words in support of the literal meaning of this command by the Lord.

"We must not imagine things to be unworthy of God, because they do not commend themselves to us. God does not dispense with the moral law, because the moral law has its source in the mind of God Himself. To dispense with it would mean to contradict Himself. But God, who is absolute Lord of all things which He made, may, at His sovereign will, dispose of the lives or things which He created. Thus, as sovereign Judge, He commanded the lives of the Canaanites to be taken by Israel, as, in His ordinary providence, He has ordained that the magistrate should not bear the sword in vain, but has made him His minister, a revenger to execute wrath upon him that doeth evil. So, again, He, whose are all things, willed to repay to the Israelites their hard and unjust servitude by commanding them to spoil the Egyptians. He, who created marriage, commanded to Hosea whom he should marry. The prophet was not defiled by taking as his lawful wife, at God's bidding, one defiled, however hard a thing this was."

This is the strongest defense of the literal interpretation of this incident. But there is another interpretation possible, which we believe is the correct one. As the context shows the symbolical meaning of Hosea's marriage is to illustrate Israel's unfaithfulness. But Israel was not always unfaithful; she played not always the harlot. Of necessity this had to be symbolized in the case of the prophet's marriage. The question then arises, was Gomer, the daughter of Diblaim an impure woman when Hosea married her, or did she become unchaste after her marriage to the prophet? We believe the latter was the case. The Hebrew does not require the meaning that she was impure at the time of the marriage; in fact, as already indicated, the supposition that Gomer lived the life of a harlot before her marriage to the godly prophet, destroys the parallelism, which the prophet's message embodies, with the relation of God to Israel. The expression "a wife of whoredoms and children of whoredoms" simply intimated to Hosea what the woman he married was going to be. If not taken in this sense it would mean that Gomer had already children when Hosea married her.

Gomer was called "a wife of whoredoms" by the omniscient Lord, in anticipation of her future conduct. She fell and became immoral after her union with Hosea, and not before. In this way she became a symbol of Israel, married unto the Lord, but afterwards became the unfaithful wife. With this view, the entire prophetic message of Hosea in the beginning of this book harmonizes. The name of the woman is likewise suggestive. Gomer, the daughter of Diblaim, means "Completion—a double cake of figs." Israel's wickedness is symbolized as complete and the double cake of figs is symbolical of sensual pleasures. And the prophet in spite of her unfaithfulness still loved her and did not abandon her. This illustrates Jehovah's love for Israel.

Then she bore him a son. Expositors have stated, "The children were not the prophet's own, but born of adultery and presented to him as his." But that can not be the meaning in view of the plain statement "she conceived and bare *him* a son."

The Lord commands him to call this son "Jezreel." Jezreel has likewise a symbolical meaning. It means "God shall scatter" (Jer. 31:10); but it also means "God shall sow" (Zech. 10:9). Thus Israel was to be scattered and sown among the nations. Jezreel was the valley in which Jehu executed his bloody deeds. On account of his hypocritical zeal, the blood of Jezreel is now to be avenged, and the kingdom of the house of Israel would cease. Thus the name Jezreel (resembling in sound and form "Israel") indicates the speedy end of Israel, scattered and sown among the nations, on account of their whoredoms (see Ezek. 23).

Verses 6-7. Next a daughter is born. Here "bare him" as found in verse 3 is omitted. The prophet receives a name for her—Lo-ruhamah, which means "not having obtained mercy." Interesting are the two renderings of the Holy Spirit of this passage in the New Testament. In Romans 9:25 it is rendered "not beloved" and in 1 Peter 2:10, "hath not obtained mercy." Love and mercy were now to be withdrawn from Israel and they were to be taken away utterly.

Then the house of Judah is mentioned. They shall be saved by the Lord their God, because He has mercy on them. Their salvation was not by bow, by sword, or by battle, horses and horsemen. It was only a little while later when the Assyrian, who was God's instrument in the execution of judgment upon Israel, came before the gates of Jerusalem, but Jerusalem was saved in the manner as predicted here, not by bow or sword, but the angel of the Lord smote the army of 185,000 in one night. And later Judah was saved and a remnant brought back from Babylon. Then there is a future salvation for Judah in the end of the age.

Verses 8-9. Another son is born and "God said, Call his name Lo-Ammi, for ye are not my people and I am not your God." Lo-Ammi means "not my people." Lo-Ruhamah and Lo-Ammi are symbolical of Israel's rejection and the withdrawal of God's mercy. That this is not to be permanent the next two verses make this clear.

Verses 10-11. Abruptly we are transported from the present into the distant future, and a prophetic utterance of great depth follows. The tenth verse is quoted by the Holy Spirit in Romans 9 and gives full light on the meaning of the passage here. God's sovereignty is the theme of the ninth chapter of Romans: "And that He might make known the riches of His glory on the vessels of mercy, which He has afore prepared unto glory, even us, whom He hath called, not of the Jews only, but also of the Gentiles. As He saith also in Osee (Greek form of Hosea), I will call them My people, which were not My people; and her beloved, which was not beloved. And it shall come to pass, that in the place where it was said unto them, Ye are not My people, there shall they be called the children of the living God" (Rom. 9:23-26). Here is the commentary of Hosea 1:10. It means first that Israel shall be reinstated; but it also means the call and salvation of the Gentiles, and Gentiles called in sovereign grace are to be constituted "the sons of the living God." It is a prophetic hint on the blessing to come to the Gentiles, and that blessing is greater than Israel's.

The eleventh verse is a great prophecy and remains still unfulfilled. Some expositors claim that it was fulfilled in the return of the remnant of Jews under Zerubbabel. But the Babylonian captivity is not in view here at all. The great day of Jezreel will come, when King Messiah, our Lord returns. Then shall Judah and Israel be gathered together under one head, and gather once more to their national feasts in the land.

CHAPTER 2

Appeal and Punishment for Unfaithfulness
The Resumed Relationship

1. The appeal and complaint (2:1-5)
2. The punishment for unfaithfulness (2:6-13)
3. The resumed relationship and its great blessing (2:14-23)

Verses 1-5. Who is addressed in the first verse of this chapter? Some think the children of the prophet are meant. The godly in Israel, those who obtained mercy, are addressed, for the Lord acknowledges such still as "Ammi"—my people. The godly are to plead with the rest of Israel their mother, but who is disowned by Jehovah as the wife, on account of her adulterous conduct. Then the Lord threatens her with severe punishment because of her unfaithfulness. She is to be stripped naked and be as in the day she was born (see Ezek. 16:4). Nor would there be mercy for her children because the mother, Israel, continued to go after her lovers.

Verses 6-13. Her way is to be hedged up with thorns; a wall of separation is to be raised and to keep her from her lovers. And if she follow after them and make a sinful alliance with them (symbolical of the idol worship of heathens which Israel practised) she would not find them. Thus she might return to her first husband, to Jehovah. Israel had received from the Lord corn, wine, oil, silver and gold. Then they attributed it all to Baal and used it in idol worship. In verses 9-13 the punishment is fully made known. She is to be left alone; the gifts and blessings will be withdrawn; her lewdness is to be uncovered, all mirth will cease and the days of Baalim, spent in licentious worship, would be visited upon her in judgment.

Verses 14-23. Immediately after the announcement of her punishment follows the assurance of future mercy. Israel's conversion is promised (verses 14-17) and the great mercies of Jehovah's covenant are to be renewed (verses 18-23). The Lord of love will not forever abandon His people and though Israel has played the harlot so long, with no willingness to return unto Him, He Himself in infinite love is going to woo her back. He will allure her, as He brings her into the wilderness, and there speak "to her heart" (the Hebrew meaning). That will be in the coming day when the Lord will remember the remnant of His people during the time of Jacob's trouble and save them in that day. Then she will get her vineyards, her place of blessing, promised to Israel as His earthly people. The valley of Achor shall be the door of hope. In that valley Achan died, on account of whom all Israel had fallen under the ban (Josh. 7). There judgment had been enacted and after that blessing was restored to Israel and the ban was removed. Achor means "troubling." When Israel is in that great trouble, the great tribulation, the valley of trouble will become the door of hope, for then the Lord will forgive them their sins, cover them with His grace and redeem them by His power. Then the singing times begin again for Israel. "She shall sing there as in the days of her youth, and as in the day when she came up out of the land of Egypt." Songs of praise on account of accomplished redemption by Jehovah's power will then burst forth (Exod. 15; Isa. 12). She will be fully restored to her former relationship, typified by marriage. "It shall be in that day, saith the Lord, that Thou shalt call Me Ishi (my husband), and shalt call Me no more Baali (my master)." She will be re-married to the Lord, symbolically speaking, and become the earthly wife of Jehovah, while the church, the espoused virgin, becomes in glory the Lamb's wife (Rev. 19:6-8).

But greater blessing will be connected with that coming day of blessing, when Israel is received back (Rom. 11:15). Verse 18 tells us that creation will then be blest; the time of its deliverance has come. Here the same is indicated as in Isaiah 11:6-7 and Romans 8:21. The end of wars comes then and universal peace blesses the whole earth. This is always the order in the divine forecasts. First, Israel has to be brought back, and after that the blessings for the earth and the nations, including that peace, which the blinded world-church tries to secure without the Lord Jesus Christ. All these promises as to the future of Israel, her restoration and spiritual blessings, are unrealized. "It is infatuation to think that all this was fully accomplished in the return of a remnant from the captivity. The result is that even Christians, misled by this miserable error, are drawn away into the rationalistic impiety of counting God's Word here mere hyperbole to heighten the effect, as if the Holy Spirit deigned to be a verbal trickster, or a prophet were as vain as a litterateur. No; it is a brighter day, when the power of God will make a complete clearance from the world of disorder, misrule, man's violence and corruption, as well as reduce to harmless and happy resubjection the entire animal kingdom."

In that day all the great covenant blessings will return to redeemed Israel. Betrothed again to Jehovah in righteousness, in judgment, in faithfulness and mercies, Israel will know Jehovah. There will be an uninterrupted line of blessing from the heavens down to every earthly blessing. Heavens and earth will be gloriously united, and in answer to the call of His people the heavens will hear and cover all with blessing, for Satan's power is now gone. Israel is no more Lo-Ammi, but they will be "His people" and He will be "their God," while the redeemed nation itself will be a blessing in the earth.

CHAPTER 3

Israel's Past, Present, and Future

1. The past (3:1-3)
2. The present (3:4)
3. The future (3:5)

Verses 1-3. The command here is not that the Prophet should enter into relation with another woman, but it concerns the same Gomer, the unfaithful wife. It seems she left the prophet and lived in adultery with another man. "And Jehovah said unto me, Go again, love a wife, who is beloved of her friend and who is an adulteress; just as Jehovah loves the children of Israel, who have turned towards other gods, and love raisin cakes" (correct translation; used in the idolatrous worship). She is not called "thy wife," simply "a wife"; yet the prophet is told to love the adulterous wife. This woman, whom the Lord commands Hosea to love, he had loved before her fall; he was now to love her after her fall, and while in that condition, in order to save her from abiding in it. It was for her sake that she might be won back to him. Such is the love of Jehovah for Israel.

He bought the adulteress for half of the price of a common slave (Exod. 21:32); it denotes her worthlessness. The measure of barley mentioned reminds of the offering of one accused of adultery, and, being the food of animals, shows her degradation likewise. He thus was to buy her back, not to live with him as his wife, but that she might sit as a widow, not running after others, but wait for him during an undefined, but long season, until he would come and take her to himself. While she was not to belong to another man, he, her legitimate husband, would be her guardian. Israel's spiritual adultery is in view in all this.

Verse 4. Here we have direct prophecy, a very remarkable one, as to Israel's present condition. It is to be their state for "many days."

These "many days," unreckoned, are the days of this present age, in which Israel is in the predicted condition, while God visits the Gentiles, to gather through the preaching of the gospel a people for His Name, that is, the church. Their condition is to be threefold: Without a civil polity, without king or prince; without the appointed Levitical worship, no sacrifice; without the practice of idolatry, to which they had been given, without image, ephod and teraphim—the distinctly priestly garment, the ephod; the teraphim, the tutelary divinities, which they used before the captivity. Before the captivity they had kings; now they have none, would have none; after the captivity Judah had princes; no princes during the "many days." The real approach to God according to the Levitical service was to cease, for during the "many days" there would be no sacrifice. This has been Israel's condition for nineteen hundred years. What a wonderful forecast of the present we have here! Clearly then, this describes the present condition of Israel—the most anomalous spectacle the world has ever seen—a people who go on generation after generation without any of those things which are supposed to be essential for keeping a people in existence. They have lost their king, their prince; they have neither the true worship nor the worship of idols. They are unable to present a sacrifice, because they have no temple and no more priesthood. Here is an evidence of the supernaturalness of the Bible, one which no Jew nor destructive critic can deny.

Verse 5. Afterward—in the latter days. These two statements open and end the prophecy concerning their future. The "afterward" is not yet; the latter days are still to come. Their future is returning and seeking the Lord, their God and David their king. This is Christ. Nearly all the rabbinical writers and expositors explain it in this way. David himself this could not be. It is He who is David's Son and David's Lord, our Lord (Ezek. 37:23, 24). Here we have the prediction of the future conversion of Israel to the Lord, in the latter days, the days of His coming again.

(The Targum of Jonathan says on Hosea 3:5: "This is the King Messiah; whether he be from among the living or from the dead. His name is Messiah. The same explanation is given by the mystical books Zohar, Midrash Shemuel and Tanchuma. The greatest authorities among the Jews are one in declaring that 'the last days' mean the days of the Messiah; we have reference to Kimchi, Abarbanel, Moses Ben Nacham and many others.)

II. The Message of Expostulation, Judgment, and Mercy

CHAPTER 4

The Lord's Controversy with His People

1. The condition of the people (4:1-5)
2. The loss of their priestly relation (4:6-11)
3. Israel's idolatry (4:12-19)

Verses 1-5. This chapter begins with a terse description of the condition of the professing people of God. First, we have the negative side—no truth, no mercy, no knowledge of God. And there was no truth, because they had rejected the Word of the Lord, hence the result no mercy and no knowledge of God. It is so still whenever and wherever the Word of God is set aside. Then follows the positive evil which was so prominent in their midst: Swearing, lying, killing, stealing, committing adultery, and abundant shedding of blood. Such was the continued moral condition of the house of Israel, the ten tribes. It was all the result of having rejected the Word of the Lord and having turned away from Him. The result of unbelief, destructive criticism and denial of the truth is today, as it was then, swearing, lying, stealing, killing and the immoralities of our times. Therefore judgment would overtake all, even the land itself.

Verses 6-11. The people were destroyed for lack of knowledge, the knowledge of God and His truth. They had lost their place of nearness to the Lord, their priestly character into which the Lord had called the nation (Exod. 19). Therefore they would be rejected to be no longer in priestly relationship to Jehovah. And the priestly class was as corrupt as the people—"like people like priests." They were to be punished for their ways and their doings.

Verses 12-19. Having left Jehovah they had turned to idols, asked counsel of a piece of wood and practised divination. This abominable idol worship was practised upon the tops of mountains. There, under trees, they gave themselves over to the vile rites of Baalpeor and Ashtaroth, both men and women abandoned themselves to the grossest sins of the flesh. And the Lord threatens that He would leave them alone in their vileness and not correct them, that they might be brought back. The first chapter of Romans is illustrated by verse 14; they glorified not God, became idolators and then God gave them up to their vile affections.

Then there is a warning to the house of Judah

in verse 15. The most sacred places, like Gilgal, had become the scene of the idolatry of the ten tribes. Bethel, the house of God, became a Beth-aven, the house of vanity. If Judah offended and committed the same whoredoms, she would not escape judgment. The warning was unheeded.

"Ephraim (the ten tribes) is joined to idols; let him alone." Ephraim was too far gone; further remonstrances would not help, and so the evil is permitted to go unchecked, to run its full course.

CHAPTER 5:1—6:3

The Message to the Priests, the People, and the Royal House; Judgment, Affliction and the Future Return

1. The message of rebuke (5:1-7)
2. The judgment announced (5:8-15)
3. The future return and the blessing (6:1-3)

Verses 1-7. The first verse shows who is addressed: the priests, the house of Israel and the house of the King. Judgment was in store for them, for Mizpah and Tabor, the places of hallowed memory, had been turned by their idolatrous worship into a snare. An old and interesting tradition among the Jews states that at Mizpah the apostates waited for those Israelites who went up to Jerusalem to worship there, to murder them. The next verse seems to indicate something like this tradition.

"And the apostates make slaughter deep; but I am a chastisement to them all." (See also chapter 6:9.) And the Lord saw it all. "I know Ephraim, and Israel is not hid from Me." He knew the whoredoms of Ephraim and the defilement of Israel. Their evil deeds kept them from returning to their God, for the demon of whoredoms had taken complete possession of them and it kept them in sin and rebellion. Pride was the leading sin of Ephraim, it was to testify against them and both Israel and Ephraim would stumble on account of their guilt and Judah would share the same fate. And though they go with their flocks of sheep and their herds, willing and ready to sacrifice, they shall not be able to find Him, for He hath withdrawn Himself.

Verses 8-15. Then follows a vision of judgment. The judgment is seen as having already fallen upon the guilty nation. The horn (Shophar) is blown in Gibeah and the trumpet in Ramah; the alarm is sounded. Gibeah and Ramah were situated on the northern boundary of Benjamin. The enemy was behind Benjamin pursuing. There will be no remedy and no escape (verse 9). "The princes of Judah have become, like the removers of landmarks: I will pour out upon them my wrath like water" (verse 10). A curse is pronounced in the law upon those who remove the landmarks (Deut. 27:17). Judah instead of taking warning from the disaster coming upon the northern kingdom, the ten tribes, sought gain by an enlargement of their own border. The princes of Judah, instead of weeping over the calamity, rejoiced at the removal of Israel as the means of removing the boundary line and increase their estate. Wrath was in store for Judah. To Ephraim the Lord would be as a moth. To the house of Judah He would be as rottenness. The moth destroys. Both terms, moth and rottenness, are symbols of destroying influences working against the house of Israel and the house of Judah (Isa. 50:9, 51:8; Psalm 39:11; Job 13:28). Then they turned to the Assyrian for help and to King Jareb. But there was no help. Jareb is not a proper name, it is an epithet applied to the king of Assyria and means "He will contend" or "He will plead the cause." Like a lion would be the Lord to Israel, and like a young lion to Judah. The same symbolical language is used in Isaiah in connection with the Assyrian, the rod of God's anger (Isa. 10). "Their roaring shall be like a lion, they shall roar like young lions; yea, they shall roar, and lay hold of the prey, and shall carry it away safe, and none shall deliver it" (Isa. 5:29). Thus judgment came upon them and they were carried away as a prey. And like the lion after his attack withdraws to his den, so the Lord would withdraw from them, leave them and return to His place, waiting till their repentance comes and they seek Him early in their affliction.

The last verse of this chapter has a wider meaning than the past judgment which came upon the house of Israel. The Lord of glory came to earth and visited His people. He came with the message and offer of the kingdom to the lost sheep of the house of Israel. He came unto His own, but His own received Him not. After they had rejected Him, delivered Him into the hands of the Gentiles to be crucified, He returned to His place. There He is now at the right hand of God, waiting for that day, when the remnant of Israel will repent and seek His face (Acts 3:19-20). That will be in their coming great affliction, in the time of Jacob's trouble.

Chapter 6:1-3. The division of the chapter at

this point is unfortunate. The three verses of chapter 6 must not be detached from the previous chapter. Here we have the future repentance of the remnant of Israel, that is during the great tribulation. Believingly they will acknowledge His righteous judgment and express their faith and hope in His mercy and the promised blessings and restoration. They express what their great prophet Moses so beautifully stated in His prophetic song, that great vision given to him, ere he went to the mountain to die. "See now that I, even I, am He and there is no god with Me; I kill, and I make alive; I wound, and I heal; neither is there any that can deliver out of My hand" (Deut. 32:39). "After two days will He revive us; on the third day He will raise us up, and we shall live in His sight (literally, before His face)." They have been dead spiritually and nationally, but when the two days of their blindness and dispersion are over, there is coming for them the third day of life and resurrection. Jewish expositors have pointed out the fact that a day is with the Lord as a thousand years. They state that they will be in dispersion for two days, that is, two thousand years, after which comes the third day of Israel's glorious restoration. One Rabbinical commentator says: "The first day we were without life in the Babylonian captivity, and the second day, which will also end, is the great captivity in which we are now, and the third day is the great day of our restoration." Like Jonah was given up by the fish on the third day, so comes for Israel a third day of life and glory. Then the latter and the former rain will fall upon their land again, and, blest by Him, their Saviour-King, they will live in His sight. But the passage, no doubt, also points to the resurrection of our Lord, the true Israel in a hidden way.

CHAPTER 6:4-11

Divine Mourning over Ephraim and Judah

1. What shall I do to thee? (6:4-6)
2. Their transgression (6:7-11)

Verses 4-6. The Lord grieves and mourns over the condition of the people whom He loves. After the brief glimpse given of their great future of glory we are brought back into the days of Moses. The Lord grieves and mourns over His people whom He loves, who today are still beloved for the Father's sake (Rom. 9). But while He loved them, their love was like the morning cloud, like the dew, vanishing soon away. The morning cloud looks beautiful, gilded by the rays of the rising sun, but it quickly disappears through the heat of the sun; the dew glitters in the early morning, but soon it is gone. Thus was their love, fluctuating and changing. How often is the love of His heavenly people like the morning cloud and the dew! Thank God that His love never changes! The Prophets He had sent to them came, therefore, with words of condemnation, instead of words of comfort and cheer. They came to hew, as stone or wood is hewn, and the message of judgment they proclaimed condemned them; this is the meaning of the sentence, "I have slain them by the words of My mouth."

Verses 7-11. "Yet they like Adam have transgressed the covenant; they have dealt treacherously against Me." As God had made known His covenant to Adam, given him a commandment, so He had made a covenant with them and made known unto them His will. Like Adam they had transgressed the covenant. Adam had been called into relationship with His Creator and a place of blessing and favor in Eden had been given to him. He transgressed, and after his fall he was driven out. This happened to Israel. Called of God, who entered with them into a covenant and gave them the land of promise, but when they transgressed, like Adam, they were also driven out.[1] Iniquity and blood was everywhere. Even the priests lurked as a band of robbers and murdered the travelers on the way to Shechem, one of the cities of refuge. (Note correct translation: "Upon the way they murder (those who go) to Shechem" verse 9.) The horrible thing was that Israel was steeped in whoredoms; they were not only spiritually adulterers, but following the idol worship they lived in literal harlotry and lewdness. Judah, too, would get a harvest. But the final sentence of this chapter, "When I return the captivity of My people," is a prophecy, not concerning the return from Babylon, but that other great restoration which is yet to come. Looked upon in

[1]Attention has been called to an important distinction. Man is called a sinner. The Gentiles as such are never called transgressors. We read in the New Testament of sinners of the Gentiles, but never "transgressors" of the Gentiles. Adam was under a law, which he broke and by it he became a transgressor. Israel was under the law, which they broke and became transgressors. But no covenant existed with the Gentiles, nor had they the law given to them; hence while they are lost sinners, they are not called transgressors in the sense in which the covenant people are called transgressors.

this light the entire verse is prophetic. "For thee, also, Judah a harvest waits, when I shall turn the captivity of My people." When God restores His people in His promised covenant mercies then Judah will be visited by judgment as it will be in the end of this age.

CHAPTER 7

The Moral Depravity of Israel

1. Their moral depravity (7:1-7)
2. Mingling with heathen nations (7:8-16)

Verses 1-7. All the gracious efforts of the Lord to heal Israel resulted in a greater manifestation of the iniquity of Ephraim. Instead of turning to Him in true repentance and self-judgment their evil heart turned away from Jehovah, and they continued in their downward course. They did not consider that the Lord would remember all their evil deeds and punish them for it. The king and the princes, the political heads were as corrupt as the priests, they were pleased with the impenitence and wickedness of their subjects. Then follows a graphic description of their moral depravity. They were adulterers, burning with lust, "like an oven heated by the baker, who rests, stirring up (the fire), after he has kneaded the dough until it be leavened." They indulged in all the vile, obscene practices connected with the idol worship of the heathen about them. They were also drunkards and were heated with wine as they were with lust. They made their heart like an oven; their baker (meaning their own evil will and imagination) slept all night, but, awakening in the morning, their lust is stirred up again. Nor did anyone call upon the name of the Lord.

Such was the moral depravity of a people with whom the Lord had entered into covenant, the favored nation. The source of it was unbelief and the rejection of His Word. The sad history of Israel is repeated in professing Christendom today.

Verses 8-16. The Lord called Israel to be a separated nation, but Ephraim mingled with the heathen (not, people) and is compared to a cake not turned. They adopted heathen ways, heathen manners and heathen vices. Like an unturned cake, which is black and burnt on the one side, while above it is unbaked, such was Ephraim's condition. Such a cake was fit for nothing; it had to be thrown away. The strangers with whom they mingled devoured their strength, nor did they not notice the signs of their speedy national decay. This is the meaning of the statement, "Gray hairs are here and there upon him, and he does not know it." Furthermore, Ephraim is likened to a silly dove without understanding. Instead of flying back to Jehovah their help and rest, they fluttered, like a moth around the flame, around Egypt and Assyria, trying to find deliverance there. But while fluttering from Egypt to Assyria and from Assyria to Egypt, they did not see the net which was spread for their destruction—that net was Assyria itself. In this net the Lord caught them; their freedom would be ended and captivity begin. Then follows the divine Woe. "Woe unto them! for they have wandered from Me. Destruction upon them, that they have transgressed against Me!" The divine lament cried after them, "I would have redeemed them, but they spoke lies against Me." While they may have cried with their mouth, their heart did not. They were like a deceitful bow on which the archer cannot depend, so the Lord could not depend upon Israel. God had, to apply the symbol, bent Israel as His own bow against evil and idolatry, but they turned themselves against Him.

CHAPTER 8:1—9:9

The Apostasy is Followed by Judgment

1. The judgment announced (8:1-7)
2. The apostasy which resulted in judgment (8:8-14)
3. Warning against self-security (9:1-9)

Verses 1-7. The prophet is commanded to sound the alarm of the impending judgment. The message is that the enemy will come swift as an eagle upon house of the Lord, which here does not mean the temple (which was in connection with Judah), but Israel as the chosen people was the house, the dwelling-place of the Lord. All their spurious profession, their false claim, "My God, we know Thee, we, Israel," will go for nothing, because they transgressed the covenant and the law. The obnoxious thing they did is stated in verse 4. They had separated themselves from Judah and chosen their own kings and princes in self-will, thus putting themselves outside of the theocracy; idolatry speedily followed. In Bethel they had erected the worship of the calf, the great abomination in the sight of the Lord. He rejects their corrupt worship, and ere long the calf of Samaria will be broken to pieces, like the golden calf their fathers made in the wilderness. They sowed the wind and the whirlwind would be the harvest (chapter 10:13, 12:2; Job 4:8; Prov. 22:8). They sowed vanity and evil; the tempest of destruction would be their reaping. What they sowed would not yield fruit at all. The Hebrew contains a play of words, *"Tsemach* brings no *Quemach,"* which may be rendered, "shoot brings no fruit."

Verses 8-14. Israel had been swallowed up by the nations, that is, by mingling with them. By their doings they have become like a despised vessel. Their sin was going up to Assyria, like a wild ass, suing there for love and favor. They were like a stubborn brute going here by itself. Ephraim was even worse than the stubborn ass. They formed unnatural alliances with the Gentiles. There they gave presents, hiring lovers, literally rendered, "Ephraim gave presents of love" to practice her whoredoms. They forgot their Creator, God; their sacrifices Jehovah despised. Therefore the judgment.

Chapter 9:1-9. Under the reign of Jeroboam II Israel enjoyed great prosperity. It seems they had a bountiful harvest, corn and wine was in abundance. They gave themselves over to feasting and rejoicing. It was at such an occasion when the Lord sent this warning against their own security. Their captivity is announced where they would eat things unclean and feast days will no longer be possible. Then the prophet beholds them as already in the Assyrian captivity. They went away and turned towards the south to escape the sure destruction. But "Egypt will gather them, Memphis will bury them." Their precious things of silver will give way to thistles and thorns. The day of visitation was at hand; their iniquities are remembered and their sins will be visited.

CHAPTERS 9:10—11:11

Retrospect, Israel's Failure and Ruin

1. Israel once beloved, now fugitive wanderers (9:10-17)
2. Their guilt and punishment (10:1-11)
3. Exhortation and rebuke (10:12-15)
4. The mercy of a merciful God (11:1-11)

Verses 10-17. Like a wayfaring man who finds grapes and figs in the desert and delights in them, so the Lord found Israel in the desert and they were His pleasure when He led them out of Egypt. But they requited His love by going after Baal-Peor, one of the filthiest gods of heathendom. To this they consecrated themselves and practiced their vile abominations. Therefore the glory which He had given to His people will fly away like a bird and their licentious worship of unnatural vices would avenge itself so that there would be no pregnancy and no birth; the promised increase would stop. It seems verses 14-17 are an outburst of the prophet. How literally the sentence has been fulfilled. "They will be wanderers."

Chapter 10:1-11. Here is another retrospect, Israel once called to be a thriving vine (not empty), called to be fruitful; but Israel did not bring forth the expected fruit. As the nation abounded and prospered they increased their idol altars; as the land yielded its increase in the same measure they made their images. Their heart was smooth, or deceitful, for this they will now have to suffer. "Their heart is smooth; now will they make expiation." They will have no more king. The smooth or deceitful heart is described in verse 4, while in the verse which follows the judgment upon their calves they worshipped is announced. It, the calf, will be carried to Assyria to be made a present of to the king. The high places will be destroyed and thorns and thistles will overgrow its altars. Then they will say to the mountains, "Cover us!" and to the hills, "Fall upon us!" Well, it is to read in connection with this prophetic statement what our Lord said about the judgment of Jerusalem in Luke 23:30 and what is written in connection with the breaking of the sixth seal in Revelation 6:16.

Gibeah is mentioned (verse 9). The corruption of Gibeah is also noted in chapter 9:9. The horrible abomination of Gibeah is recorded in Judges 19 in consequence of which the tribe of Benjamin was almost wiped out. And the people had become as wicked and guilty as Benjamin at Gibeah. The nations are now to be used to punish Israel. "And the nations will gather themselves against them, when I bind them for their offences" (verse 10, literal translation).

Verses 12-15. Here is a break in the judgment message. If they would return to the Lord and would sow righteousness, they would reap mercy. But such sowing is impossible unless the fallow ground is broken up, that is, true repentance and a heart return unto the Lord. "For it is time to seek the Lord, until He come and rain righteousness upon you." In what infinite patience He waited for the repentance of His people! But while He would save them, they would not! Still God's gifts and calling are without repentance and the day will come when a remnant of Israel will seek the Lord; then He will come and rain righteousness upon them.

How different was their condition! The Lord rebukes them, for they had ploughed wickedness, and reaped iniquity. The noise of war is now heard; Shalman (a contracted form of Shalmanezer, the King of Assyria) is advancing and shall destroy all their fortresses as he destroyed Beth-arbel. (There is no further record of Beth-arbel and its destruction.) And who was responsible for all this havoc and the impending calamity? "Thus has Bethel done to you, for the evil of your great evil. In the early morning the king of Israel shall be utterly cut off." Bethel was the seat of Israel's idolatry, it drew God's wrath and finally ended the monarchy in Israel and their national existence.

Chapter 11:1-11. This chapter starts with a beautiful allusion to Israel's youth, when in sovereign love He called Israel, His firstborn son, out of Egypt, redeeming them by blood and power (Exod. 4:22-23). But this passage is quoted in the second chapter of the Gospel of Matthew: "That it might be fulfilled which was spoken of the Lord by the prophet, saying, Out of Egypt have I called My Son" (Matt. 2:15). The blending together of Israel and Christ is very interesting. Christ is the true Israel and goes through the entire history of the nation, without failure and in divine perfection. He was carried as an infant into the land where Israel suffered in the fiery furnace; and finally He died for that nation and in some future day through Him, the true Israel (called such in Isa. 49), Israel's great future and glory will come to pass.

But while the Son of God, the true Israel, was perfect and holy in all His ways, Israel was unfaithful. This record of Jehovah's faithfulness and mercy is here unfolded. He sent them prophets who called them, but they turned away from Him and gave themselves over to the Baalim and the idol-gods. How loving He had been to them! He led them, took them into His arms and healed them. He drew them with cords of love and was towards them "as those that would raise the yoke-strap over their jaws, and I reached out to them to eat" (verse 4). It is a beautiful picture of His great gentleness with them. Perhaps some of them were anxious to turn to Egypt and find a home there and thus escape the cruel Assyrian. But the Lord declares that they shall not return to Egypt, but Assyria is to be their king, because they refused to return. The sword of judgment would do its work completely (verses 6-7). Then follows a most wonderful outburst of deepest sorrow over the stubborn nation:

> How should I give you up, Ephraim?
> How shall I surrender thee, Israel?
> How should I make thee like Admah?
> Or set thee like Zeboim?
> My heart is turned within me;
> My repentings are kindled together.

It is the same Lord who speaks here, who centuries later stood before the city and broke out in loud weeping when He beheld the city: "If thou hadst known, even thou, at least in this thy day the things which belong unto thy peace! but now they are hid from thine eyes" (Luke 19:42). "O Jerusalem, Jerusalem, thou that killest the prophets and stonest them which are sent unto thee, how often would I have gathered thy children together, even as a hen gathereth her chickens under her wings, and ye would not! Behold your house is left unto you desolate. For I say unto you, ye shall not see Me henceforth, till ye shall say, Blessed is He that cometh in the name of the Lord" (Matt. 23:37). How He loves His people! And though He has punished them, He does not forsake them; He will not be angry forever; He is a covenant keeping God, "For I am God and not man" (verse 9). "For I am the Lord, I change not; therefore ye sons of Jacob are not consumed" (Mal. 3:6). And so here, this chapter of Jehovah's mercy ends with the assurance of their future restoration and blessing. "They will follow the Lord." That will be "when like a lion He roars." That is the day when He appears again as "The lion of the tribe of Judah." Then, in that day, like a bird from Egypt they will hasten back and like a dove from Assyria. "Then will I make them dwell in their houses, saith the Lord." Here is another prophecy of their restoration to their own, God-given home land.

CHAPTERS 11:12—12:14

The Indictment

1. Ephraim's indictment (11:12—12:2)
2. Remembrance of the past (11:3-6)
3. What Israel had become (11:7-14)

Chapter 11:12—12:2. Lying and deceit had been Ephraim's course towards Jehovah; instead of trusting Him and following Him faithfully they had attached themselves to idols, while Judah still outwardly cleaved to Jehovah, though it was in a rambling way. The word translated "ruleth" means rambling. The better rendering of the sentence is "and Judah is also rambling towards God (or unbridled against Him) and towards the faithful Holy One." But while outwardly Judah seemed to be all right, Ephraim fed on wind, was occupied with the vain, the empty things, increased in lies and desolation and turned to Assyria and Egypt for help, sending as a present olive oil to the latter and making a covenant with the former (see 2 Kings 17:4). Then the mask is torn from Judah's face. The Lord had a controversy with them also and would repay them according to their evil deeds.

Verses 3-6. Jacob's sons are now reminded of Jacob's experience. Though he was so weak and sinful yet the Lord in marvellous grace met him. The experience at Peniel is recalled. "Yea, he had power over the angel, and prevailed; he wept and made supplication unto Him." There he learned the sufficiency of grace and his strength was made perfect in weakness. The angel who appeared unto him that night was none other than the Son of God. What a reminder it was to them. "He found him (Jacob) in Bethel!" In the very place where the Lord found Jacob and Jacob found the Lord, they had set up their awful, God-defying idol worship. Where God had shown such mercy there they practised now their abominations. Jehovah, the God of hosts, was still the same. He is the Lord who changes not. He was waiting still for their return. To such a God, who keeps His covenant promises they were urged to return and prove their true return by keeping mercy and justice and by waiting on Jehovah continually. But the call of grace and mercy was unheeded.

Verses 7-14. The Lord calls apostate Israel a merchant, that is in Hebrew "Canaan." (Canaan means traffic; see Ezek. 17:4.) They had become Canaanites with the balances of deceit, loving to oppress. They had become fraudulent merchants, by cheating and oppression. Their wrong attitude towards Jehovah, having forsaken Him, led to a wrong attitude towards their fellowmen. Instead of repenting they boasted, "I am become rich, I have found me out substance." They were breaking the law continually (Lev. 19:36 and Deut. 25:13-16). Yet in all their lawbreaking they prided themselves of being a righteous nation. "In all my labors they shall find no iniquity in me that were sin." How all this fits a good part of the Jews today is too well known to need further comment.

Some day it will be different through the grace and mercy of the never-changing Lord. He is the Jehovah who delivered them out of Egypt; all their blessing and prosperity they owed to Him; He had guided and preserved them, and all their sinning would not diminish His faithfulness to them. They are going to dwell again some day in tents, a reference to the feast of tabernacles, that great feast which typifies the coming millennial blessings for restored Israel. Such had been the continued testimony of the prophets He had sent, who announced the coming judgments and the final blessings in a future day. But now everything was ruin on account of their idolatry. Gilgal was the seat of a part of their idolatry (chapter 4:15, 9:15). Then once more they are reminded of their progenitor Jacob. He fled before Esau his brother, yet though he was weak he served faithfully for a wife and for a wife he kept guard and Jehovah guarded and blest him. So He would concern Himself with them again. The twenty-sixth chapter of Deuteronomy throws light on this passage. But what was Ephraim's condition? Instead of acknowledging all Jehovah had done for Jacob and his offspring they provoked Him to bitter anger, therefore the Lord would punish them.

CHAPTER 13

Ephraim's Ruin and Judgment

1. Ruin and judgment (13:1-8)
2. It is thy destruction, O Israel! (13:9-11)
3. Mercy to follow wrath (13:12-14)
4. The desolation of the nearing judgment (13:15-16)

Verses 1-8. In the beginning Ephraim was humble, and knowing his dependence, he spoke with trembling. Then he became puffed up, exalted himself in Israel, loving the pre-eminence, it led on to the schism from Judah and the house of David. The next step after this separation from Judah was idolatry, then the dying of the nation began. This sad history of Ephraim, revealing the steps of decline, beginning with self-exaltation and ending in ruin and death, has often been repeated in the individual history of countless multitudes among the professing people of God.

Then they went from sinning to sinning, from bad to worse, just as in our own days, the apostates in Christendom go from bad to worse in fulfillment of 2 Timothy 3:13. "But evil men and seducers shall wax worse and worse, deceiving and being deceived." Idolatry flourished on all sides. They added idol images in Gilgal and

Beersheba to the golden calves (Amos 8:14). Then the judgment is announced. Just as the rising sun quickly disperses the morning clouds and the dew, so they should pass away (chapter 6:4). They would be like the chaff driven with a whirlwind out of the threshing floor (Psa. 1:4, 35:5; Isa. 17:13, 41:15-16); they would be like the quickly evaporating smoke, which comes out of the windows of a house without a chimney.

Then the Lord reminds them of their former relationship and that He is the true God, "and there is no Saviour beside Me." In the land of the wilderness He knew them and there He cared for them and provided all their needs. But instead of acknowledging Him, they became full; self-exaltation followed, and then they forgot Him. Throughout the Word of God self-exaltation, pride is always given as the starting point of departure from God and the consequent ruin.

Verses 7-8 are interesting. They are to be rent by wild beasts, which, symbolically, represent the Gentiles. The ten tribes were carried away by the Assyrian, while later, when Judah met its judgment, the whole land was devastated by the lion-empire (Babylonia); by the bear (Medo-Persia); by the leopard (the Graeco-Macedonia); and finally by the dreadful beast, "the beast of the field shall tear them," the Roman power.

Verses 9-11. "It is thy destruction, O Israel, that thou art against Me, against thy help." What they had done in lifting themselves up, in forsaking Jehovah was spiritual and national suicide. They were alone responsible for their destruction. Where was their king to save them out of such ruin and destruction? The house of David with which the covenant had been made they had forsaken. He reminds them again of an episode in their past history, when they, their fathers, were rebellious and asked for a king. Such kings like Saul had been their kings which reigned over the ten tribes.

Verses 12-14. Ephraim deliberately held on to his sin. Their iniquity was bound up; it was laid by in store. The reference is to the oriental custom of tying up money and other valuables into a bundle and hiding it somewhere. It was done for security. So the Lord would see to it that their sins and iniquity would not be forgotten; all their sins were preserved for punishment (see Deut. 32:34). Sorrow and great trouble should come upon them. It has been thus in the past, it will be so in the future, in the time of "Jacob's trouble" (Jer. 30:7). When that time comes, when all their hope and strength is gone (Deut. 32:36-43) then He will deliver. Then all the enemies will be put down. Redemption from death and the plagues will come; they will be ransomed from the power of Sheol (not hell). Israel will be raised from its national death—sleep. Long she has been buried among the nations, without spiritual and national life, like those who are in the power of Sheol. But Jehovah will deliver the faithful portion of Israel and Judah, and they will rise from the dust of the earth, the symbol of their national resoration. To use this passage, as it has been done, to teach the restitution of the wicked, is wrong. It has nothing to do with the wicked dead and their future, but all applies to the restoration of Israel. (See the annotations of chapters 16 and 37 of the Prophet Ezekiel.)

Verses 15-16. These verses describe the horrors of the coming judgment by the Assyrians (2 Kings 8:12, 15:16, and Amos 1:13).

CHAPTER 14

The Return and the Glorious Redemption

1. The exhortation to return (14:1-3)
2. The glorious redemption (14:4-9)

Verses 1-3. This chapter is a wonderful finale to the messages of Hosea. What tender entreaties! What gracious assurance! What glorious promises of a future redemption! It is Jehovah beseeching His people, those who had forsaken Him, outraged His character of holiness and who had despised Him. First is the call to return. God's hands are tied as long as His people stay away from Him and do not return to Him in true repentance. No true salvation and deliverance for His people is possible without a true heart return unto Him. It is this for which He looks and waits.

Then the Lord Himself puts His word and a prayer into their mouth. He loves to provide all. "Take with you words and turn to Jehovah and say unto Him, Forgive all iniquity, and receive us graciously, so will we render the calves of our lips." Could their poor, darkened and mistrusting hearts ever even have imagined to ask thus of Him? Their consciences were defiled; the burden of guilt was upon them. But Jehovah does not mention their sins and their guilt, but tells them just to pray for forgiveness and for a gracious reception. And He who tells His wayward people to pray, to turn to Him, to pray for forgiveness, He who assures them that

He hears, assures them of a gracious receiving, will never fail. How full of comfort these sentences are to all His people at all times! We can imagine that in Hosea's day there were individual Israelites who took these words to heart. After them generations of Jews read them and turned individually to the Lord, found forgiveness and became the objects of His grace. And we too, as His people, when we have gone back in our spiritual life, can find our comfort here, and appropriate all this in faith as we act upon His Word. In the future the remnant of Israel will take these gracious exhortations to heart, and before the glorious redemption is given to them return to the Lord with this prayer.

"So will we render the calves of our lips." Literally rendered it is "we will pay as young oxen our lips," i.e., present the prayers of our lips as a thankoffering; we will be worshippers. Such is the result of a real return unto the Lord with sins forgiven and restored to His fellowship. The days of singing are coming for Israel in that day when they return unto Him and He appears in His glory to be enthroned as King. It will usher in the singing times for all the world, including groaning creation, then delivered. Then follows the evidence of their genuine repentance. It is expressed in words suited to the condition of Ephraim in Hosea's day. They repudiate Assyria; they acknowledge that no salvation is there, but only in Jehovah. No longer will they trust in their own strength and in the strength of their horses; no longer will they turn to idols and call them "Our God," but they will acknowledge Him in whom the fatherless findeth mercy. Israel, God's firstborn son, had been the prodigal, was fatherless, though the Father's love never gave them up. But now the prodigal returns and knows there is One in whom the fatherless findeth abundant mercy. All this true repentance will be manifested at the close of this age, when the remnant of Israel turns to the Lord.

Verses 5-9. His gracious answer to such repentance follows. Three times Jehovah speaks "I will." This is the word of sovereign grace. (See annotations on Ezekiel.) The three "I wills" are: (1) I will heal their backslidings; (2) I will love them freely; (3) I will be a dew unto Israel. They are arranged in a most blessed order. Mercy, love and gracious refreshment resulting in fruitfulness and beauty, such is the order. The past is wiped out, the present is love and the future is glory. Like the lily, like Lebanon and like the olive-tree, Israel is to be. The lily denotes beauty; they will be clad in the beauty of holiness. Lebanon stands for strength and stability; they will become the nation of power which can never be moved. Then they shall be once more the olive-tree; the broken off branches will be put back (Rom. 11: 16, etc.). The blessings of the restored Israel in the millennium are given in the seventh verse.

Beautiful is verse 8. "Ephraim (shall say), "What have I to do any more with idols? I hear and I look upon Him; I am like a green fir tree. From Me is thy fruit found." Ephraim, the cake half turned, Ephraim, of whom it was said, he is joined to idols, leave him alone, now repudiates the idols. And why? I hear and I look upon Him! The vision of the Lord turned the stubborn heart. It is so still; the great power is to hear Him, to look upon Him. In that day Israel will look on Him whom they pierced, the great turning point in their future history. Then the nation will yield the fruit through their fellowship with Him. Blessed ending of this prophecy. "For the ways of Jehovah are right, and the just shall walk in them; but the transgressors shall fall therein."

THE PROPHET
JOEL

Introduction

Joel means "Jehovah is God." This name occurs frequently in the Old Testament (1 Sam. 8:2; 1 Chronicles 4:35, 5:4, 8, 12, etc.). The prophet Joel was the son of Pethuel. Numerous guesses have been made about his personality. A tradition states that he was from Bethom in the tribe of Reuben. In 1 Chronicles 24:16 a man by name of Pethaliah is mentioned. Some have connected him with the father of Joel, Pethuel, claiming upon this that Joel belonged to a priestly family; but this, as well as other claims cannot be confirmed. Jewish expositors make the statement that Pethuel was Samuel, because Samuel had a son by name of Joel; but, inasmuch as the sons of Samuel were evildoers this is incorrect. The book itself does not give even a single hint as to his personal history.

When and Where Joel Lived

As to the time and place, when and where he exercised his prophetic office, we are not left in doubt. He prophesied not like Hosea among the ten tribes, but he was a prophet of Judah. The entire prophecy bears witness to it; this fact has never been disputed. It is different with the date of Joel. Destructive criticism has assigned to Joel a post-exilic date, with some very puerile arguments. For instance they claim that the mention of the walls of Jerusalem (chapter 2:7, 9), point to a date after Ezra and Nehemiah. Such an argument is not an argument of a scholar but of school-boy. Critics also object to an early date because the Greeks are mentioned in chapter 3:6. But the Greeks are also mentioned in an inscription of Sargon (about 710 B. C.), and long before that in the Armana letters a Greek is also mentioned, as stated in "Higher Criticism and the Monuments" by Professor Sayce.

The best Jewish and Christian scholarship has maintained a very early date of Joel. When the editor published his larger work on Joel, in which he puts the date between 860 and 850 B. C., Professor H. A. Sayce of Oxford, one of the greatest scholars of our times, wrote in a personal letter to the writer: "Let me thank you heartily for your very interesting exposition of Joel. I am glad to see a work of the kind on conservative lines; the attempts to find a late date for the prophet rests on arguments which to the inductive scientist are no arguments at all." This strong statement and endorsement of a very early date for Joel certainly outweighs the arguments of certain critics who possess nothing like the scholarship of the Oxford professor.

There is nothing mentioned in Joel of the Assyrian period 800-650, nor is there anything said of the Babylonian period 650-538, hence Joel must have prophesied before the Assyrian period, that is in the ninth century B. C., or he must have lived after the exile. The latter is excluded, therefore Joel exercised his office as prophet in Judah during the middle of the ninth century, as stated above, about 860-850 B. C. This view is abundantly verified by different facts found in the book itself.

Now, the date of Amos is generally accepted as being in the middle of the 8th century before Christ. In the first chapter of the book of Amos there is an undoubted quotation from the book of Joel. (See Joel 3:16 and Amos 1:2). Dr. Pusey makes the following argument out of this fact:

"Amos quoting Joel attests two things. (1) That Joel's prophecy must, at the time when Amos wrote, have become a part of Holy Scriptures, and its authority must have been acknowledged; (2) That its authority must have been acknowledged by, and it must have been in circulation among, those to whom Amos prophesied; otherwise he would not have prefixed to his book those words of Joel. For the whole force of the words, as employed by Amos, depends on being recognized by his hearers, as a renewal of the prophecy of Joel. Certainly bad men jeered at Amos, as though this threatening would not be fulfilled."

The seven strongest reasons for the early date of Joel are the following:

1. Joel charges the Philistines with having invaded Judah, captured the inhabitants, and sold them as slaves. Now, according to 2 Chron. 21:16, this happened under Joram, B. C. 889-883. And they suffered the punishment predicted for their crime, under Uzziah, 2 Chron. 26:6. Hence Joel could not

have written this book before B. C. 889, nor later than 732.

2. The Phoenicians, i. e., those of Tyre and Sidon, who in the days of David and Solomon were the allies, had in later times become the enemies of Judah. They too had been guilty of selling Jewish prisoners to the Grecians. Joel predicts that they also shall be punished for this crime—a prediction fulfilled in the time of Uzziah, B. C. 811-759. This proves that Joel must have prophesied before the days of Uzziah.

3. The Edomites (3:19), are ranked among the enemies of Judah. They came from the same stock as the Jews, and on account of their sin against their brethern, their country was to become a perpetual desolation. From 2 Kings 8:20, comp. with 2 Chron. 21:8, we learn that they became independent of Judah in the time of Joram, B. C. 889-883. They were again subdued, and their capital city Petra captured, B. C. 838-811, though the southern and eastern parts of their territory were not conquered until the reign of Uzziah, about B. C. 830. The prophet must have exercised his ministry, therefore, prior to the latter date.

4. The fact that no mention is made of the invasion by the Syrians of Damascus proves that Joel was one of the early prophets. This occurred in the latter part of the reign of Josiah, B. C. 850-840.

5. The high antiquity of Joel is proved by the fact that he makes no reference to the Assyrian invasion of the two Jewish kingdoms in B. C. 790. On the other hand, Amos clearly alludes to it (6:14).

6. Another proof is derived from the relation between Joel and Amos. The latter was certainly well acquainted with the writings of the former.

7. The mention of the Valley of Jehoshaphat is a circumstance leading to the same conclusion. It took this name from the memorable victory there gained over Moab and Ammon. The way in which Joel refers to it shows that this event must have been a comparatively recent one, and that the memory of it was still fresh.

On these grounds we conclude that in fixing the time of this prophet, we cannot take for our *terminus a quo* an earlier date than B. C. 890, nor for our *terminus ad quem* a later one than 840. It most probably falls between B. C. 860-850. Joel therefore is probably the oldest of the Minor Prophets.

The Prophecy of Joel

The prophecy of Joel is one which extends from his own time to the time of Israel's restoration and blessing in the day of the Lord. The style of the brief prophecy is sublime. To show its beauty we give a corrected metric version. It must be read through several times to grasp its vivid descriptions, the terse and solemn utterances, the full, smooth phrases, and above all the revelation it contains. His utterances are distinguished by the soaring flight of imagination, the originality, beauty and variety of the similes. The conceptions are simple enough, but they are at the same time bold and grand. The perfect order in which they are arranged, the even flow, the well compacted structure of the prophecy are all remarkable.

He may well be called "The Prophet of the Lord's Day." Five times he mentions this day. Chapters 1:15, 2:1-12, 10-11, 30-31, and 3:14-16. The great theme then is "The Day of the Lord," that coming day, when the Lord is manifested, when the enemies of Israel are judged, when the Lord restores and redeems Israel.

The occasion of the book and prophecy of Joel was a dreadful scourge which swept over the land of Israel. Locusts swarms had fallen upon the land and stripped it of everything green. There was also a great drought. All was a chastisement from the Lord. Hence we see in the first chapter the penitential lamentations of old and young, priests and people. Then the vision widens in the second chapter. The locusts appear no longer as a scourge of literal insects; they become typical of an invading army. This hostile army invades the land from the North and makes the land a wilderness. The alarm is sounded in Zion; the repentance of the people follows. Then comes the great change in this picture of desolation and despair. The day of the Lord is announced. He acts in behalf of His people. He delivers them from the northern Army; He restores what the locusts had devoured; the land is restored and the latter rain is given. At the close of the second chapter stands the prophecy which predicts spiritual blessings through the outpouring of the Spirit of God upon all flesh, a prophecy which has not yet been completely fulfilled, which is not now in process of of fulfillment, but which will be accomplished in the day of the Lord. The last chapter is the great finale of this symphony of prophecy. Here the judgment of the nations is vividly portrayed; what the day of the Lord will bring, and what will follow in blessing is the final theme.

But few Christians have ever given much heed to this prophetic book. There are many important truths in this book. A great deal of confusion might have been avoided if more attention had been given to the setting in which the prediction of the outpouring of the Holy Spirit upon all flesh is found. The Pentecostal delusion is built up mostly upon the wrong interpretations of this prophecy.

The Division of Joel

The divisions of the prophecy of Joel, as found in our English version, cannot be improved upon. We follow it in our analysis and annotations.

The Book of Joel

A Metric Version

CHAPTER 1

1. The Word of Jehovah which came to Joel, the Son of Pethuel.
2. Hear this, ye aged men
And open the ear ye inhabitants of the land!
Hath this happened in your days,
Or even in the days of your fathers?
3. Relate it to your children
And your children to their children,
And their children to another generation.
4. What the *Gazam*[1] left, the *Arbeh* hath devoured
And what the *Arbeh* left, the *Jelek* hath devoured
And what the *Jelek* left, the *Chasel* hath devoured.
5. Awake, ye drunkards and weep!
And howl all ye drinkers of wine
Because of the sweet wine,
For it is taken away from your mouth.
6. For a nation has come up upon my land
Mighty and without number—
His teeth—lion's teeth—
The jaw teeth, that of a lioness.
7. He hath made my vine for a desolation
And my fig tree broken off;
Peeled off completely and cast it away;
Its branches are made white.
8. Lament like a virgin!
Girded with sackcloth for the husband of her youth.
9. Cut off is the meat and drink offering
from the house of Jehovah.
10. "Wasted is the field
Mourning is the land—
For wasted is the corn
The new wine is dried up
The oil faileth."
11. Be ashamed, husbandmen!
Howl—vine dressers!
For the wheat and the barley.
Because the harvest of the field is lost.
12. The vine is dried up
And the fig tree faileth
The pomegranate, also the palm and the apple tree.
All the trees of the field are withered.
Gone is joy from the children of men.
13. Gird yourselves and lament, O ye priests,
Howl, ministers of the altar;
Come lie down in sackcloth all night
Ye ministers of my God.
For withholden from the house of your God
Are the meat offering and the drink offering.
14. Sanctify a fast.
Call a solemn gathering.
Bring together the Elders
All the inhabitants of the land
In the house of Jehovah your God
And cry unto Jehovah
15. Woe! For the Day!
Because near is the day of Jehovah
Even like destruction from Shaddai[2] it comes.
16. Is not the food cut off before our eyes?
From the house of our God joy and gladness.
17. The seeds have perished under their clods.
The garners become desolate
The storehouses are broken down
For withered is the corn.
18. Hear the cattle groan!
The herds of cattle are bewildered,
For there is no feeding place for them.
Also the flocks of sheep are made to suffer[3]

[1]We leave these four words untranslated for reasons which will be given in the exposition.

[2]The only time Shaddai (Almighty) is used in Joel. In the Hebrew there is a resemblance of sound between "destruction" and "Shaddai."

[3]The Hebrew word, which we translate "made to suffer" means in its root "to be guilty."

19. To Thee, Jehovah, I cry,
For the fire has consumed the goodly places of the desert
And a flame hath burned all the trees of the field.
20. Also the cattle of the field look up[4] unto Thee
For the streams of water are dried up,
And a fire hath consumed the goodly places of the desert.

CHAPTER 2

1. Blow the trumpet in Zion,
Sound an alarm in the mount of my holiness.
Let all the dwellers of the land tremble,
For the day of Jehovah cometh,
For it is near at hand.
2. A day of darkness and gloom
A day of clouds and thick darkness,
Like the dawn spread upon the mountains;—
A people numerous and strong!
Never hath there been the like before,
Neither shall the like come again,
In the years of many generations.
3. A fire devoureth before them,
And behind them a flame burneth;
Before them the land is as the garden of Eden,
And behind them a desolate wilderness,
Yea, and nothing can escape them.
4. Their appearance is like the appearance of horses,
And like the horsemen shall they run.
5. Like the noise of chariots,
On the mountain tops, they shall leap,
Like the crackling of a flame of fire devouring the stubble,
Like a strong people set in battle array.
6. Before them the peoples are in distress
All faces turn to paleness.
7. They run like mighty men
They climb the wall like men of war;
And they march each one in his ways,
And they turn not aside from their ranks.
8. Nor doth one press upon another.
A mighty one[5] marches in the high road.
They fall upon the dart, but are not wounded.
9. They spread themselves in the city.
They run along upon the wall,
They climb up into the houses,
They enter in by the windows like a thief.
10. The earth trembleth before them,
The heavens shake,
The sun and the moon are darkened,
And the stars withdraw their shining.
11. And Jehovah uttereth His voice before his army
For very great is His host,
For He that executeth His Word is mighty;
For great is the day of Jehovah and very terrible,
And who can stand it?
12. Yet even now, saith Jehovah,
Return unto Me with all your heart,
With fasting and with weeping and with mourning.
13. And rend your heart and not your garments,
And return unto Jehovah your God,
For He is gracious and merciful,
Slow to anger and of great loving kindness
And repenteth Him of the evil.
14. Who knoweth He may return and repent
And leave a blessing behind,
An oblation and a drink offering
For Jehovah your God.
15. Blow the trumpet in Zion,
Sanctify a fast.
16. Call out a solemn assembly,
Gather the people.
Sanctify a congregation.
Assemble the old men.
Gather the children,
And those that suck the breasts;
Let the bridegroom leave his chamber
And the bride her closet;
17. Let the priests, the ministers of Jehovah,
Weep between the porch and the altar,
And let them say:—
"Spare Thy people, O Jehovah,
And give not Thine heritage to reproach

[4]Another word different from the 19th verse is used, though nearly all translators use "cry." It is more a groaning, desirous looking up.

[5]This is the literal meaning.

That the nations should rule over them.[6]
Wherefore should they say among the peoples
Where is their God?"
18. Then Jehovah will be jealous for His people:
And will have pity on His people.
19. And Jehovah will answer and say to His people:
Behold I am sending to you the corn,
The new wine and the oil;
And ye shall be satisfied therewith,
And I will no longer make you
For a reproach among the nations
20. And I will remove afar from you the One from the North
And will drive him into a dry and desolate land,
His face toward the Eastern sea
His rear toward the Western sea
And his stench shall arise
And his ill odour shall ascend,
For he hath lifted himself up to do great things.
21. Fear not, O Land
Be glad and rejoice,
For Jehovah doeth great things.
22. Fear not, ye beasts of the field!
For the pastures of the desert spring forth,
The tree beareth her fruit
The fig tree and the vine give their strength.
23. Ye children of Zion, be glad and rejoice
In Jehovah your God;
For He giveth you the early rain in righteousness,
He causeth to descend for you the showers,
The early and the latter rain as before.
24. And the floors shall be full of corn,
And the vats shall overflow with new wine and oil.
25. And I will restore to you the years,
Which the *Arbeth* hath eaten.
The *Jeel,* the *Chasel* and the *Gazam,*
My great army, which I sent among you.
26. Then ye shall be in abundance, and be satisfied
And praise the name of Jehovah your God,
Who has dealt wondrously with you,
You My people shall never be ashamed.

[6]Or, "they that should be a byword of the nations."

27. And ye shall know that I am in the midst of Israel,
And that I Jehovah am your God, and none else.
And My people shall never be ashamed.
28. And it shall come to pass afterwards,
I will pour out My Spirit upon all flesh,
And your sons and your daughters shall prophesy;
Your old men shall dream dreams,
Your young men shall see visions.
29. Yea, even upon the men servants and the maid servants,
In those days will I pour out My Spirit.
30. And I will give wonders in the heaven and on earth,
Blood, and fire and pillars of smoke.
31. The sun shall be turned to darkness,
And the moon into blood,
Before the great and terrible day of Jehovah come.
32. And it shall come to pass
Whosoever shall call on the name of Jehovah shall be saved.
For in Mount Zion and in Jerusalem shall be deliverance,
As Jehovah hath said,
Even for the remnant whom Jehovah shall call.

CHAPTER 3

1. For behold in those days and in that time,
When I shall bring back the captivity of Judah and Jerusalem;
2. I will also bring together all nations,
And will bring down into the valley of Jehoshaphat;
And there will I judge them on account of My people,
And My heritage Israel, whom they have scattered among the nations,
And they divided My land.
3. And they cast lots for My people,
They gave a boy for a harlot,
And sold a girl for wine, and drank it.
4. Yea also, what have ye to do with Me, O Tyre and Sidon,
And all the borders of Philistia?
Would you requite Me with retaliation?
If you retaliate
Swiftly and speedily will I bring your recompense
Upon your own head.

5. Because ye have taken My silver and gold,
And have brought into your temples My very best things
6. And the children of Judah and of Jerusalem,
Ye sold to the children of the Greeks,
That ye might remove them far from their border.
7. Behold I will raise them up out of the place whither ye sold them,
And I will return the retaliation upon your own head.
8. And I will sell your sons and your daughters
Into the hands of the sons of Judah.
And they shall sell them to the Sabeans to a far off nation.
For Jehovah hath spoken it.
9. Proclaim this among the nations:
Declare a war!
Arouse the mighty ones!
Let all the men of war draw near, let them come up!
10. Beat your ploughshares into swords,
And your pruning hooks into spears.
Let the weak say, I am strong.
11. Come together,
All ye nations round about
Gather yourselves together.
Thither cause thy mighty ones to come down,
O, Jehovah!
12. Let the nations arise and come up
To the valley of Jehoshaphat,
For there will I sit to judge all the nations round about
13. Put in the sickle,
For the harvest is ripe;
Come—Tread!
For the wine-press is full,
The vats overflow;
For their wickedness is great.
14. Multitudes, multitudes in the valley of decision!
For the day of Jehovah is at hand in the valley of decision.
15. The sun and the moon are darkened
And the stars withdraw their shining.
16. And Jehovah shall roar from Zion,
And send forth His voice from Jerusalem;
And the heavens and the earth shall shake;
But Jehovah will be a refuge for His people
And a fortress for the sons of Israel.
17. And ye shall know that I, Jehovah, your God,
Dwell in Zion, My holy mountain;
And Jerusalem shall be holy,
And strangers shall no more pass through her.
18. And it shall come to pass in that day
That the mountains shall drop down new wine,
And the hills shall flow with milk,
And all the river beds of Judah shall be full with waters,
And a fountain shall come forth from the house of Jehovah,
And shall water the valley of Shittim.
19. Egypt shall be a desolation
And Edom shall be a desolate wilderness.
For their violence against the children of Judah,
Because they shed innocent blood in their land.
20. But Judah shall abide forever.
And Jerusalem from generation to generation.
21. And I will purge them from the blood
From which I had not purged them
And Jehovah will dwell in Zion.

Analysis and Annotations

I. THE PLAGUE OF LOCUSTS

II. THE COMING DAY OF THE LORD: THE RUIN, THE REPENTANCE AND THE RESTORATION

III. THE EVENTS OF THE DAY OF THE LORD: ISRAEL'S ENEMIES JUDGED AND THE KINGDOM ESTABLISHED

I. The Plague of Locusts

CHAPTER I

1. The prophet's appeal (1:1-4)
2. The call to the drunkards (1:5-7)
3. The call to the people and the priests (1:8-14)
4. The day of the Lord and the suffering land (1:15-18)
5. The prayer of the prophet (1:19-20)

Verses 1-4. The prophet announces that it is the Word of Jehovah he utters, which came to him. Verses 2 and 3 are an introduction to the description which follows the great calamity which had befallen the land. It is in the form of an appeal. What had happened to the land is of such a fearful character that it is unprecedented. The visitation of the land by the locust plague is to be related to future generations, because there is a great prophetic meaning as to the future attached to the locusts, which will be pointed out later. The fourth verse we render in a way our own, leaving the words of the destroying insects untranslated.

> What the *Gazam* left, the *Arbeh* hath devoured;
> And what the *Arbeh* left, the *Jelek* hath devoured;
> And what the *Jelek* left, the *Chasel* hath devoured.

We left the Hebrew words untranslated because they do not express insects of different species; they are one insect, the locust, in a fourfold stage. Gazam means "to gnaw off;" Arbeh is "to be many"; this is the common name of the locusts on account of their migratory habits. Jelek is "to lick off," and Chasel means "to devour or consume." The locust passes through a fourfold stage in its development to full growth. First, it is the gnawing locust, when first hatched; then it gets its wings and flies about; after that it starts in its destructive work by licking off whatever it finds, and, finally, it reaches its full growth and devours everything in its path. (Many foolish applications have been made of these locusts. One of the most ridiculous is the one made by a certain woman-healer in her book *Lost and Restored.*)

The locust plague which laid Israel's land bare was a judgment from the Lord. It was one of the judgments the Lord sent upon Egypt, and Moses had prophetically announced that the Lord would use them to punish his people (see Deut. 28:38, 42).

But these literal locusts, which fell literally upon the land and destroyed in a short time all vegetation, are symbolic of other agencies which were to be used later in Israel's history to bring judgment upon the land and the people. They are typical of Gentile armies, as stated in the second chapter, where the Lord calls them "My great army." Here is unquestionably a prophetic forecast as to the future of the land. From Daniel's prophecy we learn twice that four world-powers should subjugate Israel and prey upon the land: Babylonia, Medo-Persia, Graeco-Macedonia and Rome. Zechariah, also, in one of his night visions, beheld four horns, and these four horns scattered Judah and Jerusalem. We see, therefore, in the locusts, first, the literal locusts which destroyed everything in vegetation at the time Joel lived, and these locusts are symbolical of future judgments executed upon the land and the nations by the prophetically announced world-powers. At the close of the "times of the Gentiles," during which Jerusalem is trodden down, the final invasion of the land takes place; it is this which is described in the second chapter.

Verses 5-7. The first swarm had probably appeared in the fall; only the vineyards had not yet been harvested. They attacked the vineyards and speedily the vines and the grapes disappeared under the onslaught. The drinkers of wine were therefore to suffer first. That there was much drunkenness among the people Israel, especially in the days of their prosperity, may be learned from Amos 6:1-6; Isa. 5:11, 24:7-9, 28:7, etc. In verse 6 the locusts are described as a nation, mighty without number, with lion's teeth. This confirms the typical application to Gentile nations of the future who would devastate the land. See, furthermore, Numbers 13:33, Isaiah 40:22 and Jeremiah 51:14, where the same comparison is made.

Verses 8-14. On account of the great disaster the people are called to mourn and put on sackcloth. "Lament like a virgin, girded with sackcloth, for the husband of her youth." This is a significant expression. Israel in her relationship to Jehovah is here indicated. We are reminded of Isaiah 3:26 concerning Jerusalem, "And her gates shall lament and mourn, and she, being desolate, shall sit on the ground;" and Isaiah 54:6, "For the Lord hath called thee as a woman forsaken and grieved in spirit, and a wife of youth, when thou wast refused, saith thy God." So great was the havoc wrought that the meal and drink offering was cut off from the house of the Lord so that the priests mourned, the servants of Jehovah. This is their mournful chant:

> Wasted is the field,
> Mourning is the land,
> For wasted is the corn,
> The new vine is dried up,
> The oil faileth.

This is followed by the call to lament for the husbandmen and vinedressers. The whole harvest was gone, and besides the failure of the vine, the fig tree the other trees are also mentioned, yea, "all the trees of the field are withered." On account of the severity of this visitation joy had left the children of men.

Then comes the definite call to the priests to lament and cry unto Jehovah and to sanctify a fast (verses 13-14). But there is no record of a response. At the close of this chapter the Prophet alone raises his voice to Jehovah. We shall learn in the second chapter of the time of the national repentance of Israel.

Verses 15-18. For the first time we meet the day of the Lord (Yom Jehovah), that phrase used so frequently in all the prophetic books. The 15th verse is an exclamatin of the Prophet as before his vision that day appears. In the midst of the weird description of the calamity, present in Joel's day, he beholds a greater judgment approaching. It is the same day he beholds which the other prophets mention; each time Joel uses this expression it means the coming day of the Lord, still approaching. It may be noticed that the five passages in Joel in which "the day of the Lord" is mentioned are progressive.

For a comparative study of this important phrase we quote the leading passage of the different prophets.

Isaiah. The phrase "in that day" is found many times in his book. We mention 2:2-5, 10-22; 4; 13:6-13. The great glory predictions of Isaiah 54, 60, 61 and 62 are all related to this day.

Jeremiah. He also speaks of that day (chapters 25:30-33; 30:18-24).

Ezekiel. Chapters 7 and 8. From chapters 37—38 we have the record of great events both of judgment and blessing which will come to pass in connection with that day. While *Daniel* does not use in his book the phrase "day of the Lord" nearly all his great prophecies are connected with that day. It is the day in which the stone smites the great image, representing the times of the Gentiles, and demolishes it; the day on which "the Son of Man" comes in the clouds of heaven to receive the kingdom. *Hosea* points to that day in chapters 2 and 3, as well as in the closing chapter. *Amos* witnesses to it in chapters 1:2, 6:3, 9:2, 15. *Obadiah,* who lived about the same time as Joel, speaks of the day in verse 15 of his brief prophecy. *Micah* in his prophecy refers to it in chapter 5:15. In *Nahum* the day is described in which the Lord will deal in judgment with the wicked world cities (see chapter 1:1-9). The third chapter of *Habakkuk* reveals that day. *Zephaniah* has a great deal more to say about that day than the preceding prophetic books (chapters 1:14-18; 2 and 3). *Haggai* bears witness to it in chapter 2:6-7. (Compare with Heb. 12:26-29.) *Zechariah* uses the phrase "in that day" many times, especially in the last three chapters. *Malachi* reveals the day in chapters 3:1-3 and 4:1-3).

We learn from all this what a prominent place the day of the Lord occupies in the prophecies. It must be so, for it is the day of manifestation and consummation. Joel beheld here for the first time this day.

Then follows an additional description of the great calamity which had come upon the land in Joel's day (verses 16-18).

Verses 19-20. Joel was, like all the other prophets, a man of prayer. No other mention is made by the prophet concerning himself, but this brief word is sufficient to give us a glimpse of his inner life and his trust in the Lord. He cried to Jehovah in the great distress.

II. The Coming Day of the Lord: The Repentance and Restoration of Israel

CHAPTER 2

1. The alarm sounded and the day at hand (2:1-2)
2. The invading army from the north (2:3-11)
3. The repentance of the people and cry for help (2:12-17)
4. "Then." The great change (2:18)
5. Promises of restoration, and the early and latter rain (2:19-27)
6. The outpouring of the Spirit upon all flesh (2:28-31)
7. Deliverance in Mount Zion and Jerusalem (2:32)

Verses 1-2. With this chapter we reach the heart of the prophecy of Joel. The description of the literal locust plague is now no longer continued. As we have shown the literal locusts in their different stages were symbolical of nations laying waste the land as the locusts had done. Dispensationally the first chapter stands for the entire times of the Gentiles, which began with Nebuchadnezzar (Dan. 2:36-38), and they continue till the time comes when the God of heaven sets up a kingdom that cannot be destroyed. The second chapter takes us at once to the end of the times of the Gentiles, when the day of the Lord is to be enacted. Before the Lord appears in that day, the greatest distress will be upon the land and the people; there will be a great time of trouble such as never was before (Matt. 24:21). The remnant of His people will cry to the Lord for intervention and for deliverance, and the Lord will answer their cry and deliver them. Then their land becomes once more like the garden of Eden, there will be a great outpouring of the Spirit upon all flesh and from Jerusalem the great kingdom-center blessings will extend to all the nations.

This whole chapter as well as the next one is therefore unfulfilled. Nothing of it has been fulfilled. Before it can be fulfilled a part of the people Israel must be restored to the land of promise and the ancient ceremonies and institutions be at least partially restored.

The chapter begins with the sounding of the alarm for "the Day of Jehovah cometh, for it is near at hand." The last prophetic week of Daniel is now in process of fulfillment and near its end. (See annotations on Dan. 9.) A part of the people are back in the land, having returned there in unbelief, just as we see it today in the Zionistic movement. But in their midst will also be found a God-fearing remnant. The blowing of the trumpet shows that they have revived their ancient custom (Num. 10:1, 2, 9). We also mention that trumpets are often connected with the appearing of the Lord and the restoration of Israel. In the second verse the day is described and may be compared with Zephaniah 1:15-16 and Isaiah 60:2. Then there is an invading army announced which is fully described in the verses which follow. The words, "As the dawn spread upon the mountains," are a description of the day and not of the army, as some have taken it. On the one hand the day of the Lord is a day of darkness and gloom, on the other hand it is "like the dawn spread upon mountains." After the darkness, the morning light will break "the morning without clouds" (2 Sam. 23:4).

Verses 3-11. Many armies in past history have occupied the land of Israel and wasted it, but here is the coming great invasion from the north. This invasion is mentioned in the prophet Isaiah also. The Assyrian who came in Isaiah's day to take Jerusalem is the type of the final Assyrian who threatens the land and the people with destruction. He is also prefigured by Antiochus Epiphanes, who came into the land of Israel as the predicted little horn, rising from one of the divisions of the Graeco-Macedonian Empire (Dan. 8).

This army of Israel's enemies finds the land like the garden of Eden; it has been restored through political Zionism, irrigated and cultivated. The Jews are at it now, determined to make Palestine the garden-spot of the world, their Eden, as it has been said. Then comes the rude awakening. They thought themselves safe; they dreamed that their plans they had made without trusting in the Lord and without true repentance, had fully succeeded. But now the greatest trouble of their long history of blood and tears is at hand. The land is once more stripped of its beauty.

> Before them the land is as the garden of Eden,
> And behind them a desolate wilderness,
> Yea, and nothing can escape them.

The Lord uses these destructive hosts to humble His people, to show them that He is their help, when this great calamity is upon them. The symbolical language here is characteristic of other prophecies.

> The earth trembleth before them;
> The heavens shake,
> The sun and the moon are darkened,
> And the stars withdraw their shining
> * * *
> For the Day of the Lord is great and very terrible.

Compare this with the following passages: Isa. 13:13; Hab. 1:6, 12; Zech. 14:3, 4.

Verses 12-17. Here is the Lord calling to His people to return unto Him with true repentance (compare with Hosea 5:15—6:1). And during that great tribulation there will be a truly penitent portion of the people who turn to Him in the manner described in this chapter. It is this remnant which will be saved in that day, while the impenitent part will be cut off in judgment. Ezekiel 20:38 and Zech. 13:8-9 speak of this. What Moses spoke long ago now takes place (Deut. 30:1-4). The many prophetic prayers recorded in the Psalms, as pointed out in the annotations of that book, will then be offered up by this godly waiting remnant (Psa. 44:13-14, 115:2-3, 79:9-10, etc.). This mourning and prayer for deliverance precedes the visible manifestation of the Lord in the day of His coming. When at last deliverance has come there will be another lamentation. This is found in Zech. 12:9-14 and in Rev. 1:7.

Verse 18. "Then Jehovah will be jealous for His land and will have pity on His people." Here is the great change. Up to this point we have seen nothing but calamity and judgments. Literal locusts had devoured the land—the types of nations which would prey upon the land. They came, and Jerusalem was trodden down by the Gentiles. The times of the Gentiles terminated in Jacob's trouble, out of which they are to be saved (Jer. 30:7). We saw their great repentance. Here is the answer from above. When their power is completely gone (Deut. 32:36), *then* will the Lord be jealous for His land and pity His people. Often this little word "then" is found in the prophetic Word marking the great change, from Israel's past judgments and rejection to deliverance and glory. The following passages should be carefully examined and compared with the 18th verse here: Isa. 14:25, 24:23, 32:16, 35:5-6, 58:8, 14, 60:5, 66:12; Ezek. 28:25-26, etc.

The Lord's personal manifestation is not mentioned here. The deliverance does not come apart from the second coming of our Lord. The entire prophetic Word bears witness to this. "Then shall the Lord go forth and fight against those nations as He fought in the day of battle. And His feet shall stand in that day upon the mount of Olives, which is before Jerusalem" (Zech. 14:3-4). "When the Lord shall build up Zion, He shall appear in glory" (Psa. 102:16). "The Lord shall go forth as a mighty man, He shall stir up jealousy like a man of war; He shall cry, yea, roar; He shall prevail against His enemies" (Isa. 42:13).

Verses 19-27. Here is His gracious answer. He will bless their land and make it fruitful once more, as it used to be, the land flowing with milk and honey. It is foolish to spiritualize the terms corn, new wine and oil. Yet it has been done. One of the older commentators of this book says on this verse about corn, wine and oil, that it has been fulfilled in the church. The corn he applies to the body of Christ, the wine to the blood of Christ, and the oil to the Spirit. Earthly blessings, such as belong to His earthly people are exclusively in view. Then they shall be no longer a reproach among the nations. Inasmuch as they are still a reproach we know that this promise is still future in its fulfillment. The one from the north will be overthrown and pass away forever. That all this cannot mean the Babylonian captivity and the small remnant which returned to the land may be learned from the statement "no longer" a reproach.

Because the Lord does all this they are commanded to rejoice, the children of Zion, which does not mean a spirtual Zion, but God's only true Zion. The early and the latter rain is restored to the land. Of late this term, too, has been strangely misapplied. It has been claimed that the early and latter rain mean spiritual blessing. The early rain, it is said, means the day of Pentecost, when the Holy Spirit was poured out, and the latter rain, these deluded people tell us, is another Pentecost, a greater manifestation of the Spirit. This latter rain, they teach, consists, according to their conception, in a restoration of "pentecostal gifts" and is especially evidenced in making strange sounds, which, it is claimed, is the original gift of tongues. This unscriptural teaching has led to all kinds of fanaticism and worse things than that.

Nowhere in the Bible is there warrant for us to believe that "the early and latter rain" has a spiritual significance. To say that the early rain and the latter rain typify blessings and manifestations of the spirit of God, peculiar to the opening of this present age and to its close is extremely fanciful and cannot be verified by the Scriptures. It is strange that even men who seem to possess considerable light have endorsed this kind of exposition, which has worked such harm among so many Christian people. There is absolutely no prediction anywhere in the New Testament that the present age is to close with "a latter rain" experience, a time when the Holy Spirit is poured out and that in greater measure. This age, according to divine revelation, ends in apostasy and complete departure from God and His truth (2 Thess. 2:3-12). After the Holy Spirit came on the day of Pentecost, for the formation of the Church, the body of Christ, there is nowhere to be found a promise in the Church Epistles that another outpouring is to take place, by which a part of the Church is to get into possession again of the different sign gifts. The enemy of souls has made good use of these distorted teachings to bring in his most subtle delusions.

The rain has altogether a literal meaning. Read carefully the following passages for a confirmation: Lev. 26:4; Deut. 11:14-17; 1 Kings 8:33-35 and Jer. 3:3.

Then all the harm done by the locusts, the army the Lord used in judging His people, will be restored. "And My people shall never be ashamed" (verse 27). This again is sufficient proof that all this remains unfulfilled.

Verses 28-32. This interesting passage invites our closest attention. The almost general interpretation of this prophecy has been that it found its fulfilment on the day of Pentecost, when the Holy Spirit was poured forth. Most expositors confine the fulfilment to that event while others claim that Pentecost was only the beginning of the fulfilment and that the event which occurred once continues to occur throughout this Christian age. We quote from one of the best commentaries. "But however certain it may be that the fulfilment took place at the first Christian feast of Pentecost, we must not stop at this one Pentecostal miracle. The address of the Apostle Peter by no means requires this limitation, but rather contains distinct indications that Peter himself saw nothing more therein than the commencement of the fulfilment, but a commencement indeed, which embraced the ultimate fulfilment, as the germ enfolds the tree; for if not only the children of the apostles' contemporaries but also those that were afar off—i.e., not foreign Jews, but the far off heathen, were to participate in the gift of the Holy Spirit, the outpouring of the Holy Spirit which commenced on Pentecost must continue as long as the Lord shall receive into His kingdom those that are still standing afar, i.e., until the fulness of the Gentiles shall have entered the kingdom of God."

There is, however, no Scriptural foundation for the statement that the outpouring of the Holy Spirit commenced on Pentecost must continue throughout this present age. The Holy Spirit came on the day of Pentecost. He was poured out once, and nowhere in the New Testament is there a continued or repeated outpouring of the Holy Spirit promised. The difficulty with interpreting this great prophecy of Joel of having been fulfilled on Pentecost and being fulfilled throughout this age is that which follows in the next two verses. Wonders in heaven and on earth, fire, pillars of smoke, a darkened sun and a blood-red moon are mentioned, and that in connection with the day of Jehovah, which, as we have seen is the great theme of Joel's vision. These words have been generally applied to the destruction of Jerusalem, which followed the day of Pentecost. The spirtualizing method has been fully brought into play to overcome the difficulties the 30th and 31st verses raise. The terrible day of Jehovah, it is claimed, is the destruction of Jerusalem. Thus we read in the commentary of Patrick and Lowth: "This (verse 30) and the following verse principally point out the destruction of the city and the temple of Jerusalem by the Romans, a judgment justly inflicted upon the Jewish nation for their resisting the Holy Spirit and contempt of the means of grace." We quote another leading commentator on Joel 2:30, Dr. Clarke. He states: "This refers to the fearful sights, dreadful portents and destructive commotions by which the Jewish polity was finally overthrown and the Christian religion finally established in the Roman empire. See how our Lord applies this prophecy in Matthew 24:29 and the parallel texts." And in verse 31 ("the sun shall be turned into darkness") Clarke says "it means the Jewish polity, civil and ecclesiastical, shall be entirely destroyed." Others give these words the same spiritualized meaning. These learned doctors tell us that Joel 2:30 and 31 relate to the destruction of the nation, and the civil and ecclesiastical polity of the Jews! This is a fair example of the havoc which a Bible interpretation makes, which ignores the great dispensational facts revealed in the Word of God. But inasmuch as the 32d verse, the last verse in this second chapter of Joel, reveals that there shall be deliverance in Mount Zion and in Jerusalem after these signs and wonders, and the continuation of the prophecy in the third chapter shows the judgment of the enemies of the people Israel, God's ancient people, such interpretations appear at once as fundamentally wrong.

It is strange that all these expositors use the word "fulfilment" in connection with this prophecy, saying, that Peter said that the day of Pentecost was the fulfilment of what is written by Joel. But the Holy Spirit did not use the word "fulfilment" at all. He purposely avoided such a statement. In so many passages in the New Testament we find the phrase "that it might be fulfilled," but in making use of the prophecy in Acts, chapter 2, this phrase is not used and instead of it we read that Peter said, "But this is that which was spoken by the Prophet Joel" (Acts 2:16). There is a great difference between this word and an out and out declaration of the fulfilment of that passage. Peter's words call the attention to the fact that something like that which took place on the day of Pentecost had been predicted by Joel, but his words do not claim that Joel's prophecy was there and then fulfilled. Nor does he hint at a continued fulfilment or coming fulfilment during this present age. The chief purpose of the quotation of that prophecy on the day of Pentecost was to point out to the Jews, many of whom were scoffing, that the miraculous thing which had happened so suddenly in their midst was fully confirmed by what Joel had foretold would be the effect of the outpouring of the Spirit. The outpouring of the Holy Spirit had taken place, but not in the full sense as given in the prophecy of Joel. He came for a special purpose, which was the formation of the Church and for this purpose He is still on earth.

Without following the events on Pentecost and their meaning it is evident from the entire prophecy, which precedes this prediction of the outpouring of the Spirit, that these words have never been fulfilled. We might briefly ask, What is necessary according to the contents of this second chapter in Joel, before this prophecy can be accomplished? We just mention what we have already learned before in our exposition. The people Israel must be partly restored to their land, that great invasion from the north, bringing such trouble to the land must have taken place, then there must also have come the intervention of the Lord and He must be jealous for His land and pity His people, then at that time this great outpouring of the Spirit of God will take place. It stands in the closest connection with the restoration of Israel. The promises which are Israel's (Rom. 9:4) may be grouped into two classes, those which pertain to the land, earthly blessings and supremacy over the nations, and spiritual blessings, such as knowing the Lord, walking in His ways, being a kingdom of priests and prophets. The earthly blessings are accomplished by the power of Jehovah when He is manifested as their deliverer and the spiritual blessings will be conferred upon them by the outpouring of the Spirit.

The word "afterwards" with which this prophecy is introduced refers to the same period of time as the phrase "in the latter days," that is, the days when the Lord will redeem His earthly people and be merciful to His land.

Therefore when the Holy Spirit came on the day of Pentecost it was not in fulfilment of Joel's prophecy. This prophecy has never been fulfilled nor will it be fulfilled during this present age, in which the Church is being formed, which is the body of the Lord Jesus Christ. After this is accomplished the Lord will begin His relationship with His earthly people, when He appears in His day then they will experience the fulfilment of this great prediction.

There are numerous passages in the Old Testament which shed interesting light upon this future outpouring of the Spirit (see Isa. 32:15, 44: 3-4, 59:19-21; Ezek. 36:27-28, 37:14, 39:29).

Verse 32. The great coming outpouring of the Spirit upon all flesh will result in salvation. It is blessedly true now that "whosoever shall call on the name of the Lord shall be saved," but it will be also true in that day. The word our Lord spoke, "salvation is of the Jews" will find its largest fulfillment. The nations will then be joined to the Lord in the kingdom (Zech. 2:11).

III. The Events of the Day of the Lord: Israel's Enemies Judged and the Kingdom Established

CHAPTER 3

1. The judgment of the nations (3:1-8)
2. The preceding warfare of the nations and how it ends (3:9-16)
3. Jehovah in the midst of His People (3:17-21)

Verses 1-8. The first verse specifies the time when Jehovah will do what He announces in the two verses which follow. It will be in those days, in that time, when the captivity of Judah and Jerusalem is brought back. Clearly then up to this time this cannot yet have been, for the captivity of His people is not yet ended. They are still scattered in the great dispersion among the nations of the earth. The time is future when the captivity of Judah and Jerusalem is brought back. Israel, the ten tribes are not mentioned here, but they are included in the prophecy; they will likewise be brought back. Joel only mentions Judah, because His prophecy was addressed to Judah and Jerusalem. The captivity , or dispersion, which is the same thing, of the people Israel will not end till divine power accomplishes it according to the many promises in the Word of God. And when at last the heavens are silent no longer and Jehovah in His power begins to fulfil His promises and their captivity ends, it will mean judgment for the nations.

It is Jehovah Himself who speaks, what He is going to do in that day, when He arises and has mercy on Zion. "I will also bring together all nations and will bring them down into the valley of Jehoshaphat." How the Lord will bring these nations together and then accomplish His purpose is revealed in verses 9-12. We therefore pass it by for the present till we reach the second part of this chapter. But here is also the place mentioned where this great judgment of nations will be executed. It will be in the valley of Jehoshaphat. The word means translated "Jehovah judges." This name occurs elsewhere in the Word of God. King Jehu was the son of Jehoshaphat and he was the son of Nimshi (2 Kings 9:2). Significant names of the king who had to judge, for Jehu means "He is Jehovah;" Jehoshaphat, "Jehovah judges;" Nimshi, "Jehovah reveals."

In 2 Chronicles 20 we read the account of King Jehoshaphat's victory over hostile nations.

But the place where this took place is not the valley of Jehoshaphat, but it was called "Berachah," that is blessing. We mention this for some expositors have claimed that the place where King Jehoshaphat brought judgment upon these nations is the valley of which Joel speaks.

The valley of Jehoshaphat must be looked for in the immediate vicinity of Jerusalem. It is generally placed in the valley of the Kidron on the East of Jerusalem. It may not yet be in existence. In Zechariah 14 we read of the same events which are here predicted. When the Lord appears His feet will stand on the Mount of Olives in that day. The Mount of Olives will then cleave in the midst and there will be formed a very *great valley* (Zech. 14:4). This great valley may be the valley where the Lord judges the nations.

In the valley of Jehoshaphat the Lord will deal with the nations and His judgment will be on account of His people and heritage Israel. The nations scattered them and divided His land. They treated His people like slaves, casting lots for His people, sold a girl for wine and drank it.

The great sin of the nations, the Gentile world-powers, is the sin against Israel. This is repeatedly mentioned by God's prophets. The foundation of the judgment of the nations of which our Lord speaks in Matthew 25 is likewise the treatment of the Jew. Read also Psalms 79:1-3, 83:1-6; Isaiah, 29:1-8; 34:1-3; Jeremiah 25:13-17; Zechariah 1:14-15, 12:2, 3.

In Joel's day such wickedness as described here of casting lots for His people and selling boys and girls was partially known. The Philistines had done this, as well as Tyre and Sidon. But these words were fulfilled during the Babylonian captivity and in that great dispersion which was brought about by the Roman Empire. After the destruction of Jerusalem in the year 70 the very thing happened spoken by the prophet. Nearly a million and a half of human beings perished in Jerusalem and the land in that awful warfare. Over 100,000 were taken prisoners. These hundred thousand Jews were disposed by Titus according to Josephus in the following manner: "Those under seventeen years of age were publicly sold; of the remainder, some were executed immediately, some sent away to work in the Egyptian mines (which was worse than death), some kept for public shows to fight with wild beasts in all the chief cities; only the tallest and most handsome were kept for the triumphal procession in Rome." Jews were sold for so small a price as a measure of barley; thousands were thus disposed of. And what else could we add from the history of centuries, the cruel and terrible persecutions God's heritage suffered, the thousands and tens of thousands massacred, tortured, outraged and sold as slaves. Have we not beheld but recently similar horrors in Germany? And that history is not yet finished. Outbreaks of hatred against the heritage Israel are still to come and the time of Jacob's trouble soon to come will eclipse all their former suffering. It will be a time of trouble such as has not been from the beginning of the world until now nor ever shall be (Matt. 24:21). The day will come when the Lord will judge the nations for the evil they have done.

Verses 9-16. This is a prophecy showing what precedes the judgment of these nations. The judgment hosts of the Lord, the angels, are seen coming down, then He appears in all His majesty, while sun and moon are darkened. It is a great dramatic scene which the Spirit of God unfolds. We arrange it, adding the different speakers, to bring out its full value:

The Lord speaking:
Proclaim this among the nations;
Declare a war,
Arouse the mighty ones,
Let all the men of war draw near,
let them come up!

Beat your ploughshares into swords,
And your pruning hooks into spears.
Let the weak say, I am strong.

Come together
All ye nations round about
Gather yourselves together.

The Prayer of the Prophet:
Thither cause Thy mighty ones to come down,
O Jehovah!

The Lord speaking:
Let the nations arise and come up
To the valley of Jehoshaphat,
For there will I sit to judge all
the nations round about.

The Lord to His judgment hosts:
Put in the sickle,
For the harvest is ripe;
Come—Tread!
For the wine-press is full,
The vats overflow;
For their wickedness is great.

The Prophet beholding the gathering:
Multitudes, multitudes in the

valley of decision!
For the day of Jehovah is at hand
in the valley of decision.

The sun and the moon are darkened
And the stars withdraw their shining.

And Jehovah shall roar from Zion
And send forth His voice from Jerusalem;
And the heavens and the earth shall shake;
But Jehovah will be a refuge for His people
And a fortress for the sons of Israel.

Throughout the prophetic Word we read that great nations confederated will oppose God and His purposes when this age closes. There will be a great western confederacy, the restored Roman Empire. (See annotations on Dan. 2 and 7.) There will also be a great northeastern alliance of nations. This is in view here. Consult Psalm 2, 68:1-6; Isaiah 29:1-8, 34:1-3; Jeremiah 25:29-33; Ezekiel 38, Zechariah 12, 14, and Revelation 19:19. Judgment then falls upon these opposing nations. The judgment is mentioned as reaping and treading the winepress, the same as in Revelation 14:14-20.

Verses 17-21. Like nearly all the other prophetic books Joel ends with the vision of the kingdom and the Lord dwelling in the midst of His people. He will appear in all His glory. Jehovah will be a refuge for His people. Then they will come to that knowledge which they so long refused, that the delivering Jehovah is their God. But the Jehovah who appears there is none other than the Lord Jesus Christ, the one who was in their midst and who was delivered by the people to be crucified. What a day it will be when "They will look upon Him whom they have pierced and mourn for Him" (Zech. 12:10). He will dwell in Zion, the mountain of glory. The glory from above will find a resting place on that holy hill. There He will be enthroned as King (Psa. 2:6). From there the glory will be spread over all (Isa. 4:5-6; Psa. 68:16). "For the Lord hath chosen Zion; He hath desired it for His habitation. This is my rest forever; here will I dwell for I have desired it" (Psa. 132:13-14). It is the literal Zion and not something spiritual. Even good expositors of the Bible have missed the mark. One good commentator says: "For Zion or Jerusalem is of course not the Jerusalem of the earthly Palestine, but the sanctified and glorified city of the living God, in which the Lord will be eternally united with His redeemed, sanctified and glorified Church." Such exposition emanates from ignorance of God's purposes with His earthly people and in not dividing the Word of Truth rightly.

Joel speaks also of the judgment which will fall upon Egypt in that day. Isaiah also tells of judgment, but through him we learn that Egypt will turn to the Lord and the Lord will graciously heal Egypt (Isa. 19). Judah will abide forever. His people will be cleansed. Jehovah, our ever blessed Lord, will dwell in Zion. The happy and glorious state of the land and the whole earth during the millennium is thus tersely stated. For when He reigns there will be righteousness and peace; glory will cover the earth as the waters cover the deep. Thus ends the great vision of Joel, the son of Pethuel. May the eye of faith behold these blessed revelations and may we live in anticipation of what is soon to be.

THE PROPHET
AMOS

Introduction

A few years before the prophet Hosea began to witness against the apostasy of the house of Israel, the ten tribes, and announced the coming judgment, there appeared in Bethel, the seat of idolatry a peasant by the name of Amos. He was not a citizen of the ten-tribe kingdom, but belonged to Tekoa, a small town in the south country of Judah. We learn from the book that he was a herdman and a gatherer of the fruit of the sycamore trees. Some have thought he was a man of wealth, in possession of large flocks of sheep and herds of cattle, but this cannot be confirmed. He was just an humble peasant and while engaged in his calling, not being a prophet or the son of a prophet, the Lord suddenly called him to leave his work and said unto him "Go, prophesy unto My people Israel" (chapter 7:14-15). Amos means "bearer" or "burden." In obedience to this command he appeared in Bethel to discharge his prophetic duty and deliver the messages of Jehovah to the people. It was a strange occurrence that a prophet should come out of Judah to prophesy to Israel, it probably attracted wide attention, for such a thing had never happened before nor after. It greatly aroused Amaziah, the priest of Bethel, who reported the case to Jeroboam, the king of Israel. The message the priest sent to the king was the following: "Amos has conspired against thee in the midst of the house of Israel, the land is not able to bear all his words. For thus saith Amos, Jeroboam shall die by the sword, and Israel shall surely be led away captive out of their land" (7:10). Evidently the priest did not await the king's answer for he tried to intimidate the prophet and drive him away, but Amos was a man of courage, he boldly resisted the priest and announced the fate of the priest and his family.

The Time of His Prophecy

There is no difficulty with the age in which he prophesied. This is stated in the opening verse of the book. "In the days of Uzziah, King of Judah, and in the days of Jeroboam, the son of Joash, King of Israel, two years before the earthquake." Jeroboam II became king in the fifteenth year of the reign of Amaziah, King of Judah. Jeroboam reigned forty-one years. As Amaziah reigned over Judah twenty-nine years and was followed by Uzziah, Jeroboam's reign was during fourteen years of Amaziah's reign and covered twenty-seven years of Uzziah's reign. Amos' activity was during the period when Uzziah was king in Judah, in the second half of Jeroboam's reign. The earthquake which is mentioned, two years before which Amos began his work, cannot be placed chronologically. It is also mentioned by Zechariah (14:5). The time then is around 810-782 B.C. As we have shown in the introduction to Joel, Amos knew Joel's prophecy, because Joel preceded him by at least a half a century. Amos was therefore somewhat earlier than Hosea and part of his ministry was contemporary with Hosea.

The Characteristics of His Times

Under the reign of Jeroboam II the northern kingdom of Israel flourished as never before nor after. There was a great external prosperity. Therefore, we find that the prophet mentions the rich, their great wealth and luxury, their arrogant pride and self-security and the oppression of the poor. Underneath it all was an awful moral corruption, the fruit of the false worship. In this state of prosperity, immorality and false worship they did not dream of any coming calamity whatever. Such were the days in which the herdman of Tekoa appeared upon the scene to give an inspired testimony against the nation.

The Style of Amos

Attention has been called to the fact that the prophet's style and composition show the former herdman in the use of certain words and in many figures and similes drawn from nature and rural life. But he also shows a very close acquaintance with the Mosiac law and the history of the people to whom he belonged. The style also shows great rhetorical power, great depths of thought, and truly poetic expressions.

"Amos expressed his thoughts in words taken from the great picture book of nature, which, being also written by the hand of God, so wonderfully expresses the things of God. Scarcely any prophet is more glowing in style, or combines more wonderfully the natural and the moral world, the Omnipotence and Omniscience of God" (Dr. Pusey). Augustinus selected Amos as an illustration of unadorned eloquence. And another learned scholar speaks of him thus, "Let any fair judge read his writings, thinking not who wrote them, but what he wrote, and he will come to the conclusion that this herdman is in no wise behind the very chiefest prophets; in the loftiness of his thoughts and the magnificence of his spirit, nearly equal to the highest; and in the splendor of his diction and the elegance of the composition scarcely inferior to any" (Bishop Lowth, *De Poesi Sacra*).

He gives us a splendid example of inspiration. The Lord called him, gave him the message, filled the simple herdman with the wisdom from above so that he burst out in these eloquent utterances. At the same time the Lord in using him as His mouthpiece did not set aside his personality, he uses his shepherd idiom, and the truth of God is expressed through him in the terms of nature, with which he, as a child of nature, was so familiar.

The Message of Amos

The message concerns chiefly Israel, the ten-tribe kingdom, their spiritual and moral condition, yet Judah is also noticed by him, as well as the different nations, surrounding Israel, their Gentile enemies. The book consists of the prophecies he uttered in Bethel, which follow the two introductory chapters. The people are reproved and their sins uncovered; judgment for them and for the nation is announced. The end of the book brings in the promise of deliverance and restoration. The great prophecy in the ninth chapter (9:11-12) was quoted by James in the first great church-council in Jerusalem (Acts 15).

The Division of the Book of Amos

The book of Amos consists of three parts. The first part comprises the two opening chapters which form the introduction to the book. In them we find the judgments announced in store for the nations surrounding Israel, but Judah and Israel are also included.

From the third chapter to the end of the sixth is the second part. Here are recorded four prophecies given by the Lord through Amos. Three of them begin with "Hear this Word" and the last in chapter six begins with "Woe." The third part, chapters seven to nine, give the five visions which Amos had. The first two judgment visions were not carried out on account of the intercession of the prophet. The third vision is that of the plumb-line; the fourth, the vision of the basket with ripe fruit. In the last vision he beheld the Lord standing alongside of the altar, ready to smite. The conclusion of the ninth chapter is a prophecy concerning the restoration of Israel, the rebuilding of the tabernacle of David and the blessings of the kingdom. We follow this division.

I. JUDGMENT OF THE NATIONS, JUDAH, AND ISRAEL (1—2)

II. THE PROPHETIC MESSAGES UNCOVERING THE CONDITION OF THE PEOPLE (3—6)

III. THE FIVE VISIONS OF THE PROPHET (7—9)

Analysis and Annotations

I. Judgment Announced Against the Nations, Judah, and Israel

CHAPTER 1

1. The introduction (1:1-2)
2. Damascus (1:3-5)
3. Philistia (1:6-8)
4. Tyre (1:9-10)
5. Edom (1:11-12)
6. Ammon (1:13-15)

Verses 1-2. It has been pointed out that Amos does not say like so many of the other prophets, "the Word of the Lord which came unto me," but he begins his prophecy with the statement "the words of Amos." The fact of divine inspiration, however, is expressed in the next words "which he saw." His messages, like the messages of all the prophets, were given to him in vision. As stated in the general introduction to this book, this first verse determines the exact time when the herdman of Tekoa appeared with his message. The earthquake mentioned must have been a disastrous one, for there was a great flight of people (Zech. 14:5).

Then follows his first utterance which Joel recorded in his prophecy, "the Lord roars out of Zion." Inasmuch as Joel prophesied in Judah and Amos appeared from Judah in Bethel of the ten-tribe kingdom, this sentence of coming judgment was probably unknown to his hearers. He sounded the alarm at once as to the coming judgment on account of which the shepherds would mourn and the beautiful, luxurious Carmel would wither; it would bring disaster upon all.

Verses 3-5. Six nations are mentioned against which judgment is announced, five in this chapter and Moab in the beginning of the second. Eight times we read "saith the Lord." Then in each judgment prediction we find the phrase, "for three transgressions or four . . . I will not reverse it." The meaning of it is that the measure is full and that the judgment cannot be averted. Fire is prominently mentioned as the mode of judgment. These nations were the enemies of Israel. The Syrians were the great enemies of Israel and treated them with awful cruelties. The threshing of Gilead with iron instruments took place when Hazael of Damascus conquered the land east of Jordan (2 Kings 10:32-33; 13:7). Hazael murdered Ben-hadad and Elisha predicted all the horrible things he would do to Israel. When the man of God wept and Hazael asked him the reason, Elisha answered, "Because I know the evil that thou wilt do unto the children of Israel; their strongholds wilt thou set on fire, and their young men wilt thou slay with the sword, and wilt dash their children, and rip up their women with child" (2 Kings 8:12). Damascus was broken and the predicted judgment came. It was executed through the King of Assyria, Tiglath-Pileser, who drove the Syrians back to Kir, from which they had come (2 Kings 16:9).

Verses 6-8. Philistia is represented by Gaza. They also mistreated Israel and sold them into the hands of Edom (2 Chron. 21:16). The cities of Philistia, Gaza and its palaces would be consumed by fire. There would be an end to the Philistines, "the remnant of the Philistines shall perish saith the Lord."

Verses 9-10. Tyrus, the capital of Phoenicia, had also sinned against Israel by delivering them into the hands of their great enemy Edom. Their sin was especially heinous because David and Solomon had made a covenant with the King of Tyre, hence no King of Judah or Israel had ever warred against Tyre (2 Sam. 5:11; 1 Kings 5:1-5).

Verses 11-12. Edom was closely related to Israel, yet they hated more than the heathen nations hated Israel. At every opportunity Edom expressed this hatred by deeds of cruelty. What an awful record! "He did pursue his brother with the sword, and did cast off all pity, and his anger did tear perpetually, and he kept his wrath forever." In Obadiah we find more concerning Edom.

Verses 13-15. Wicked Ammon had tried to exterminate the people for selfish reasons "to enlarge their border." What horrible deeds to rip open women with child! Nor is this confined to the barbarous warfare of 3,000 years ago; the same was done in other wars down to our own days. Judgment would overtake them also.

In meditating on these terse judgment messages we must remember while these nations of the past have ceased existing as nations, and the predicted judgment came long ago, that these nations are typical of the other nations, who also sin against Israel and whose judgment will come "in that day."

CHAPTER 2

1. Moab (2:1-3)
2. Judah (2:4-5)
3. Israel (2:6-16)

Verses 1-3. So fierce was the hatred of Moab that they dishonored the bones of the king of Edom. "Moab burned the bones of the king of Edom into lime" (see 2 Kings 3:26-27). The fire of judgment came upon Moab and her glory, too, departed like the glory of the other nations.

Verses 4-5. While the measure was full of these nations, who had heaped transgressions upon transgressions, Judah and Israel were as guilty, yea, even more guilty, than these nations. The same significant phrase "for three transgressions and four" is used in connection with both. If the punishment of the nations could not be held back, but had to come, so Judah and Israel could not escape. Judah's sin was the rejection of the law of the Lord; instead of listening to the voice of the Lord and to His prophets, they harkened to the false prophets, who, with their lies, caused them to err, and the children walked in the evil footsteps of their fathers. The sin of Judah was apostasy. That is the great sin today among the professing people of God, Christendom. Fire was to devour the cities and palaces of the nations and fire was to come upon Judah and the palaces of Jerusalem. Nebuchadnezzar fulfilled this prophecy.

Verses 6-16. Inasmuch as Amos was sent to Israel the indictment and judgment of them occupies more space than the rest. Verses 6-8 give a description of their sins. The poor suffered through their coveteousness, they lived in unspeakable vileness, they were idolatrous. Those who were condemned by judges and paid their fines furnished the money to the judges to buy wine for their heathenish orgies.

Then the Lord reminds them of all His mercies and loving kindness in the past. He destroyed the Amorite; He led them through the wilderness to possess the land. He instituted the Nazarite. In spite of all these manifold mercies they continued in their evil ways, grinding the poor, defying God and His law and in their moral depravity.

> Behold, I will press you down
> As the full cart presses the sheaves.
> Then shall flight be lost to the swift,
> And the strong shall not confirm his strength,
> And the hero shall not save his life.
> He that beareth the bow shall not stand,
> And the swift-footed shall not save,
> And the rider of the horse shall
> not save his life.

II. The Prophetic Messages Uncovering the Condition of the People

CHAPTER 3

The First Discourse

1. There is cause for judgment (3:1-8)
2. The coming judgment visitation (3:9-15)

Verses 1-8. "Hear this word that the Lord hath spoken against you, O children of Israel, against the whole family which I brought up from the land of Egypt, saying, You have I only known of all the families of the earth, therefore will I punish you for all your iniquities." This is the solemn beginning of the special messages addressed to the nation by the humble herdman of Tekoa. The Lord had singled them out from the other nations. He had separated them unto Himself. With His mighty power and outstretched arm He had delivered them from the house of bondage and brought them to the land promised unto their fathers. He had revealed Himself and made known His will to them exclusively. He had entered with them into covenant and called them to be a kingdom of priests and a holy nation (Exod. 19:6). Hence their responsibility was very great, for the degree of relationship is always the degree of responsibility. The divine election of the twelve tribes does not insure against punishment, but that intimate relationship into which the Lord had entered with Israel broken and violated by sin, demanded a correspondingly great punishment. To whomsoever much is given of him shall much be required. Our Lord expressed the same truth in Matthew 11 when he denounced the cities in which great miracles had been done and they believed not and declared that it shall be more tolerable for Tyre and Sidon in the day of judgment than for them.

To demonstrate the rightful cause of judgment Amos speaks now in a number of brief similes. There are six of them in the form of questions. "Can two walk together, except they be agreed?" Fellowship is only possible on the ground of separation; a holy God demands a holy people. In their state of licentious idolatry and gross injustice the Lord could not own them. Then follow brief questions indicating that which would happen to them. Like a roaring lion, or a young lion, the Lord would come upon them. They will be caught in a snare and a trap. The blowing of the trumpet denotes that evil was to come upon them. "Shall there be evil in a city, and the Lord has not done it?" It is hard to believe that certain men have taken this statement and teach on account of it that God is the author of moral evil—of sin. The context shows that this is not in view here at all. A holy God who cannot be tempted with evil, who is light and in whom there is no darkness at all, does not put moral evil in the world. The evil is of a punitive character such as invasion by hostile forces, the sword, the famine and the pestilence.

And the Lord Jehovah will do nothing, but He revealeth His secrets unto His servants, the prophets. These secrets are made known to us in the prophetic Word and not, as some claim, in special visions. The Spirit of God, the author of the Word, shows to God's people in His Word things to come (John 15:15; 1 Cor. 2:10-16). The result of such knowledge of the secrets of the Lord concerning the future is stated in 2 Peter 3:17, "Ye therefore, beloved, seeing ye know these things before, beware lest ye also, being led away with the error of the wicked, fall from your own steadfastness." (See also 2 Peter 3:14).

Verses 9-15. This paragraph begins with a striking call. The speaker is the Lord and He addresses the prophets and commands them to cry in the palaces of Ashdod (Philistia) and in Egypt so that they may see and know the wicked acts of Samaria, and thus bear witness against Israel. Thus the Lord exposed them to their enemies. Then the coming adversary is announced who would encircle the land and humiliate the proud nation, so that her palaces would be spoiled. Then the herdman speaks in a parable familiar to him from his life as a shepherd. When the beast of prey devours a sheep the shepherd must bring proof of it, so he is anxious to recover a part of the slain animal and tries to snatch away from the devouring lion either the legs of the sheep, or even a small piece of the ear, so as to show the rest was eaten by the lion. Such would be the case with the people in their luxurious living, and only a small remnant is to escape the coming slaughter by the lion, the Gentile world power. The transgressions of Israel will be visited; the idol altars of Bethel will be overthrown in that visitation and all their prosperity and luxury would then end and instead of living in winter and summer houses, they would become homeless.

CHAPTER 4

The Second Discourse

1. Divine threatening and irony (4:1-5)
2. Yet have ye not returned unto Me (4:6-11)
3. Prepare to meet thy God (4:12-13)

Verses 1-5. The prophet addresses them as "kine of Bashan, that are in the mountain of Samaria." The cows of Bashan were noted for their sleek and well-fed condition, feeding on the choicest of pasture. The term is descriptive of Israel's prosperous condition as well as their beastly character. They were selfish and cruel, for they oppressed the poor and crushed the needy. It seems that women are mostly here in view, which explains the fact that the comparison is with kine and not with bulls. They asked their masters to supply them means for debauchery. But what happens to dumb cattle would happen to them in their luxurious and selfish life. They would be taken with hooks and their posterity with fishhooks, and they would be taken away. The last sentence of verse 3 is correctly translated "Ye shall be cast away to Har (mountain) Monah." It has been surmised that this means Armenia.

Then follows a statement of bitter irony. "Go to Bethel and sin; at Gilgal multiply transgression." Go on in your idolatry in these sacred places of your past history! In Bethel the Lord had revealed Himself to the progenitor Jacob; in Gilgal on the banks of the Jordan, the reproach of Egypt had been rolled away (Joshua 5), and these favored places were now the scenes of their wicked idolatries. It is also mockery when the prophet says, "Offer a sacrifice of thanksgiving with leaven," for leaven always typifies sin.

Verses 6-11. The Lord had sent different chastisements upon them at different times. There had been famines, drought; yea, it had rained here and there, while lots of ground received rain others remained parched, so that they might recognize in it the hand of God. He smote them with mildew and blasting; the locusts came and devoured vegetation; there were frightful pestilences and other judgments, but they did not return unto Him. Five times in this paragraph we find the same statement, "Yet have ye not returned unto Me." They were an impenitent nation and hardened their hearts as Pharaoh did. They were incorrigible, though they knew that through His mercy they were "as a firebrand plucked out of the burning."

In the book of Revelation we read of a similar condition in the coming days when the Lord deals with the earth in the decreed and revealed judgments. It is written that the inhabitants of the earth, in spite of these judgments falling upon the earth, do not repent of their sins.

Verses 12-13. And now they were to come face to face with Himself as the Judge.

CHAPTER 5

The Third Discourse

1. The lamentation (5:1-3)
2. Seek the Lord and ye shall live (5:4-15)
3. The wailing (5:16-20)
4. The captivity announced (5:21-27)

Verses 1-3. This chapter begins with a lamentation over the fallen daughter of Israel. "She shall no more rise" has been used as an argument against the future and literal restoration of Israel. The prophet has only the present government of God over that generation in view and does not deny at all a future rising as so abundantly predicted in the prophetic Word.

"There is none to raise her up," nor could she raise herself up. But the day will come when the Lord in grace will raise her.

Verses 4-15. Here the Lord entreats Israel once more to desist from her idolatrous way and to seek Him instead of the worship at Bethel and Gilgal, for judgment would surely be executed there. "Seek ye Me and ye shall live." Then again, "Seek the Lord and ye shall live," and in case of disobedience, He, whom they refused, would fall like fire upon the house of Joseph. The house of Joseph is mentioned because the tribe of Ephraim was the most powerful tribe in the kingdom of Israel, and Joseph was the father of Ephraim. Again they are told to seek Him "Who maketh the seven stars (the Pleiades) and Orion." These two great constellations were well known to the ancients (Job 9:9; and 38:31). And He also turneth the shadow of death into morning and darkeneth day to night. This is an illustration of the judicial actions of the Lord. As in nature He turns night into day, and the day into dark night, so He turns the deepest misery and sorrow into joy and happiness, and changes the bright day of prosperity into the night of woe and disaster. He is the Lord of judgment, who controls the waters of tribulation and wrath, the floods of judgment, and makes them pass over the earth.

Verses 10-13 give a description of the moral condition of Israel. They were unrighteous and loved the ways of unrighteousness; if the judge in the gate judged righteously they hated him for it, those who spoke uprightly they abhorred. The poor they trampled into the dust and extorted the distribution of corn from them. They had built fine houses of hewn stone, but they were not to enjoy them nor the wine from their pleasant vineyards (Deut. 28:30, 39). The Lord knew their transgressions and the greatness of their sins.

Still there was hope, for the Lord is merciful and slow to anger. Judgment is His strange work. Therefore once more we hear His pleadings, "Seek good and not evil that ye may live, and so the Lord God of hosts shall be with you, as ye have spoken." "Hate evil and love good!"

Verses 16-20. As judgment comes there shall be wailing in the streets, wailing with the husbandman, and there will be wailing in all vineyards as the Lord passes through in His judgment. "For I will pass through thee" reminds us of Egypt in the passover night when the Lord passed through Egypt to smite. And now the death wail was soon to be heard in the midst of His people.

And still another evil was in their midst. Some of them brazenly desired the announced "day of the Lord," the day of His manifestation to come. It originated in their false boast that they are the covenant people. They knew from the former prophets that the day of the Lord would rid them of their enemies, then Israel would be fully redeemed and blest and the Lord's glory would be manifested in the sight of the nations. Such was Joel's vision concerning "that day." Such was their false hope while they lived on in sin. But the herdman, Amos, pronounced a woe upon them for desiring that day. What good will that day be to the impenitent nation? It is a day of darkness and not light. Then follows a parable such as a child of nature, as Amos was, would make. He describes a man who flees from a lion and fortunately escapes; but then he meets a bear; him he escapes likewise. Exhausted he reaches his house, and like one about to faint, he leans his hand on the wall; a small serpent out of the crevice bites him and he perishes miserably. So would the day of the Lord overtake them. How different it is with the true believer. He desires, not the Day of the Lord, but the coming of Him, who has promised His own, "I will come again and receive you unto Myself, that where I am ye may be also."

Verses 21-27. The Lord despised their outward worship; their feast days and different offerings were not well pleasing in His sight. It was all a hollow pretense of honoring Him, and all their songs were hateful to Him.

But this departure from Him was not a new thing in their history. They were always a stiffnecked people. Even in the wilderness did they not bring Him sacrifices and offerings, but instead they bore the tabernacle of Moloch and Chiun (or the booth of your king and the pedestal of your images, the star of your gods). Then follows the verdict, "Therefore will I cause you to go into captivity beyond Damascus, saith the Lord, whose name is the God of Hosts."

CHAPTER 6

The Fourth Discourse

1. Woe to them that are at ease in Zion (6:1-6)
2. The punishment announced (6:7-14)

Verses 1-6. This woe concerns the great men, the chiefs of the nation, who were sunk into a godless self-security, and dreamt on in their darkness, while the clouds of judgment were gathering above them. They were to go from Calneh to Hamath and then down to Gath of the Philistines. Calneh was built by Nimrod in the land of Shinar (Genesis 10:10); Hamath was the capital of a Syrian kingdom, and Gath the center of Philistia. These places were the places of vileness and corruption. But were the kingdoms of both Judah and Israel any better than these?

While some desired the day of the Lord others put it far off, they refused to believe that judgment was impending. It was so in Ezekiel's time when the people said "The days are prolonged and every vision faileth " (Ezekiel 12:22). So it is in Christendom. The evil servant (Matthew 24) says "My Lord delayeth His coming," and as a result he acts outrageously. What were the results in Israel when the evil day was put far off? They committed violence; violence increased in the land. They lived luxuriously on beds of ivory and ate the best of the flock. They danced and made merry; they drank wine but none was exercised over the hurt of Joseph, the spiritual condition of the people.

Verses 7-14. They were now to go away as captives. There should be utter desolation. There would be a multitude of dead, so that they could not follow their ancient custom in burying them; they would have to burn them. Then the one who burns the corpses asks the last person in the house whether there is any one still with him, and the answer is No, but keep silence! For the name of the Lord is not to be invoked. It means that the speaker fears that the other one might mention the name of the Lord and in doing so bring down upon himself an additional judgment. Everything is to be smitten. What they had done could no more secure blessing and salvation than horses could run upon a rock and one plowing upon a rock with oxen. The nation which is announced in the last verse is the Assyrian.

III. The Five Visions of the Prophet

CHAPTER 7

Three Visions and the Opposition Against Amos

1. The vision of locusts (7:1-3)
2. The vision concerning the fire (7:4-6)
3. The vision of the plumbline (7:7-9)
4. Opposition against Amos (7:10-17)

Verses 1-3. In the first vision Amos saw how the Lord prepared locusts (not grasshoppers as in the A.V.). They started in with their destructive work, just as they did in the day of Joel. Then Amos interceded in behalf of the sinful nation, "O Lord, God, forgive, I beseech Thee, by whom shall Jacob rise for he is small?" He confessed and pleaded forgiveness, acknowledging their helplessness. With such a spirit the Lord is well pleased and the praying prophet received the answer from the Lord, "It shall not be."

Verses 4-6. He beheld a furious fire sweeping everything before itself so that it even devoured the great deep, the floods of water. This represents a more severe judgment than the previous one. This judgment also was kept back by the intercession of the prophet. But when the time came for judgment by the Assyrian, symbolized by the locusts and the fire, no intercession could change it. Tiglath-Pileser and Shalamaneser finally made an end of the sinful ten tribe kingdom.

Verses 7-9. He saw the Lord standing upon a wall with the plumbline to see if the wall was straight. The test by God's Word and God's holy law shows that all is crooked and must be condemned. Therefore, the announcement, "I shall pass by it no more. And the high places of Isaac shall be desolate, and the sanctuaries of Israel shall be laid waste; and I will rise against the house of Jeroboam with the sword." The false worship and the monarchy in Israel will be completely swept away by the judgment.

Verses 10-17. This is an interesting and instructive occurrence. Amaziah, the apostate priest at Bethel, who had charge of the idol worship, accused the prophet falsely before King Jeroboam. It was a religious political accusation. Thus the enemy accused Jeremiah also (Jeremiah 37:14-15); he did the same with our Lord and His apostles. At the same time Amaziah, the priest, sent an insulting message to Amos, saying, 'Seer, go and flee into the land of Judah, and eat there thy bread; there thou mayest prophesy." He tried to intimidate him, urging him to return to Tekoa in Judah where he came from. He received a courageous answer from the herdman-prophet. "I am no prophet, nor a prophet's son, but I was a herdman and a gatherer of sycamore fruit. The Lord took me from following the flock; He said unto me, Go and prophecy to My people Israel."

The insinuation was that Amos prophesied for the sake of a living. Amos refutes the false charge and then announced the doom of the false priest and the doom of his family.

CHAPTER 8

The Fourth Vision: The Basket With Summer Fruit

1. The vision (8:1-3)
2. Israel ripe for judgment (8:4-10)
3. The coming days of famine (8:11-14)

Verses 1-3. In his fourth vision the prophet beholds a basket of summer fruit. The Hebrew shows that it was a basket filled with ripe fruit. The ripe fruit is a symbol that Israel was ripe for the harvest of judgment. The message of the Lord to the prophet is, "The end is come upon My people Israel; I will not again pass by them any more." The songs would be changed into howling lamentations and many should be slain.

Verses 4-10. Once more the wealthy and prosperous portion of the nation is addressed, their sinful practices are exposed and it is shown that they were ripe for judgment. The rich oppressed the poor; they took away from the poor what belonged rightfully to them. They cheated by making the measure small and increased the price. They were the profiteers of that time. They also used false balances. Then they sold the refuse of the wheat. All may be compared with James 5:1-6 where the same conditions are pictured, prevailing in Christendom, before the Lord comes. For all this they did the land would have to tremble and every one mourn.

"And it shall come to pass in that day, saith the Lord God, that I will cause the sun to go down at noon, and I will darken the earth in the clear day." Much nonsense has been written on this verse especially from the side of the Adventists, as if there has been a certain time "a dark day" in fulfillment of this prophecy. Some expositors have made of it a mere eclipse of the sun. The verse, while it has a certain application to that generation, whose glory should end like the sun going down at noon, has its final meaning in the coming day of the Lord, which all the prophets announced. It is the same our Lord predicts in Matthew 24:29-30. For Israel the bitter day of mourning, lamentation and woe would come.

Verses 11-14. A great famine is announced. It is not to be a famine for bread, or thirst for water, but a famine of hearing the words of the Lord. His Word and the light of His revelation is to be completely withdrawn from them. The Word of the Lord which they despised they would then desire to seek in vain. They will wander hither and thither from sea to sea, from the north to the east; they shall run to and fro to seek the Word of the Lord and shall not find it. Such was the case with them when the cruel Assyrian power took hold on them and carried them away. Such a judgment too is fast approaching for Christendom which in its apostasy rejects the Word of the Lord, turns to fables, till the day comes when the Spirit will leave and as a result there will be a famine of the Word, no comfort and no help for those who are ripe for judgment.

CHAPTER 9

The Passing of a Kingdom and the Coming of the Kingdom

1. The fifth vision: The passing of a kingdom (9:1-10)
2. The coming of the kingdom (9:11-15)

Verses 1-10. In his fifth vision the prophet saw the Lord standing by the altar. He utters His word. The description of what is to take place is very vivid. He stands by the altar and the people are assembled before Him. He smites the lintel of the door, so that everything trembles and the building falls upon them, cutting all of them in the head and none can escape. Even if they break into sheol (not hell, but the world of spirits in the unknown regions), from thence His hand will take them; if they climb into heaven, He would bring them down. If they hide themselves on the top of Carmel He would search for them and take them out. If they conceal themselves from His sight in the bottom of the sea, He would command the serpent to bite them. It is to be an all consuming judgment with no possibility of escape.

Even as they went into captivity the sword of judgment would follow them. "Thence will I command the sword, and it shall slay them; and I will set Mine eyes upon them for evil, and not for good." He is the Lord who has all power to do this (verses 5-6). They had degraded themselves down to the level of the heathen nations, hence they were unto Him like the Ethiopians. Then He calls them "the sinful kingdom." This kingdom is to pass away from the face of the earth; there is no hope for its restoration. But the Lord in mercy promises that the house of Jacob is not utterly to be destroyed. In His own time He will assemble the outcasts of Israel with dispersed Judah and lead them back to their land. In the meantime they will be sifted among all nations, as wheat is sifted in a sieve, but not the least grain shall fall on the ground. The sinners of His people will die by the sword.

Verses 11-15. While the sinful kingdom, the ten-tribe kingdom of Israel, is passed away and will never come into existence again, there is another kingdom which will come, into which Judah and Israel will be gathered with the nations of the earth. This kingdom of heaven, promised to David, is now announced by the prophet. "In that day will I raise up the tabernacle of David that is fallen, and close up the breaches thereof; and I will raise up its ruins, and I will build it as in the days of old." This prophesy is quoted by James in Acts 15:15-16 at the first great church council held in Jerusalem. On that occasion the Holy Spirit used the prophecy of Amos to unfold the program of God concerning the future. Yet there is no church council, no general conference, general assembly or general association which reckons in any way with that which the Spirit of God has laid down as the program of the future. We learn from the passage in Acts that during this age the Gentiles are visited to gather out from among them a people for His Name (the Church). When this is accomplished the Lord returns, and, as a result of His return, the restoration of the tabernacle of David takes place: that is, the kingdom will be restored to His people, the kingdom of heaven comes and the Lord Jesus Christ will be enthroned as its king upon the throne of David. Then the conversion of the world will take place.

This is seen here in the passage before us. Verse 12 tells us that when the tabernacle of David is raised up, when "that day" has come, His people restored and saved will possess the remnant of Edom and all the nations. The last three verses of the prophecy of Amos describe the millennium in its earthly blessings. It also shows the permanent blessing and glory into which redeemed and restored Israel has entered, "They shall no more be pulled up out of their land which I have given them, saith the Lord thy God."

THE PROPHET
OBADIAH

Introduction

Of Obadiah we know nothing but his name, which means "servant of Jehovah." There are numerous men mentioned in the Old Testament by that name, but it is impossible to identify any one of these with Obadiah, or to trace him. "The silence of Holy Scriptures as to the prophet Obadiah stands in remarkable contrast with the anxiety of men to know something of him. They hoped that Obadiah might prove to have been the faithful protector of the prophets under Ahab; or the son of the Shunamite, whom Elijah called to life, or the Obadiah whom Jehoshaphat sent to teach in the cities of Judah, or the Levite who was selected, with one other, to be the overseer set over the repair of the temple in the reign of Josiah. Fruitless guesses at what God has hidden! God has willed that his name alone and this brief prophecy should be known in this world" (Dr. Pusey).

Inasmuch as nothing is known of this man of God, nor anything stated under whose reign he uttered his prophecy, the guesses about the time he lived are numerous and very contradictory. The critics have assigned to Obadiah dates removed from each other by above 600 years. We quote again from Pusey's commentary: "The punishment of Edom the prophet clearly foretells, as yet to come; the destruction of Jerusalem, which, according to our version is spoken of as past, is in reality foretold also. Unbelief denies all prophecy. Strange, that unbelief, denying the existence of a jewel—God's authentic and authenticated voice to man—should trouble itself about the age of the casket in which the jewel rests. Yet so it was. The prophets of Israel used a fascinating power over those who denied their inspiration. They denied prophecy, but employed themselves about the prophets. Unbelief denying prophecy had to find out two events in history, which should correspond with these two events in this prophet—a capture of Jerusalem and a subsequent judgment of Edom. And since Jerusalem was first taken under Shishak, king of Egypt, in the fifth year of Rehoboam 970 B.C., and Josephus tells us that in 301 B.C. Ptolemy Lagus treacherously got possession of Jerusalem, unbelieving criticism has a wide range in which to vacillate. And so it reeled to and fro between these two periods, 970 B.C. and 301 B.C."

Obadiah does certainly not belong to the prophets of the captivity, nor to the post-Exilic prophets. The position given to him in the Hebrew arrangement of the prophetic books bears witness to that. The internal evidence shows that he is one of the earliest prophets, if not the earliest. If we turn to Jeremiah 49:7-22 we find a very striking similarity between the words of Jeremiah and the words of Obadiah concerning Edom. The question is whether Jeremiah used Obadiah's words or Obadiah made use of Jeremiah's message. It has been pointed out that it is a peculiar characteristic of Jeremiah that he often leans upon the utterances of the earlier prophets, and in his writing their thoughts, words and symbols are often reproduced. Compare Jeremiah 47 with Isaiah 14:28-32; Jeremiah 47 with Isaiah 15 and 16; Jeremiah 49:1-6 with Amos 1:13-15, etc. When we point out this characteristic of the book of Jeremiah we do not mean to say that this man of God was a copyist, who slavishly copied the utterances of the earlier prophets. He had the books, or scrolls, of the earlier prophets before himself and the Spirit of God led him to use them; thus the Spirit of God repeated through Jeremiah the testimony of his predecessors and confirmed their God-given utterances. Jeremiah knew and possessed the prophecy of Obadiah, so that we can say with certainty that Obadiah is earlier than Jeremiah.

Now, Obadiah in his utterance lays bare the wicked behavior of Edom in a time when Judah and Jerusalem were plundered by hostile forces. The statement of some of the critics that the eleventh verse means only the taking of Jerusalem by Nebuchadnezzar is an assumption. The fact is the prophet does not speak of the destruction of the city, but that Jerusalem was plundered.

Can this historically be located? There can be no question but it must have reference to the time when the Philistines and the Arabs invaded the city in the reign of King Jehoram. Then the Edomites threw off the Judean supremacy (2 Kings 8:20-22; 2 Chronicles 21:8-10). They also planned a great massacre of the Jews who were in the land of Edom at that time (Joel 3:19; Amos 1:11). It was then that the treacherousness of Edom and its evil spirit became fully manifested. But there can be no question, as we show in the annotations, that the description of their evil spirit against their kin includes the after history, the fall of Jerusalem under Nebuchadnezzar, the opposition of Edom during the times of the Maccabees and the future revival and doom of Edom. It is, therefore, quite well established that Obadiah lived and uttered his prophecy during the reign of Jehoram.

Obadiah

In a corrected version

1. The vision of Obadiah,
Thus saith the Lord Jehovah concerning Edom:
We have heard tidings from Jehovah,
And an ambassador is sent among the nations.
Arise ye! Let us arise against her to battle!
2. Behold, I have made thee small among the nations;
Greatly art thou despised!
3. The pride of thy heart has deceived thee,
Thou dweller in the clefts of the rock, in the lofty habitation;
Who saith in his heart:
Who will bring me down to the ground?
4. Though as high like the eagle,
And though thou hast made thy nest among the stars,
Thence will I bring thee down,
Whispers Jehovah.
5. If thieves came to thee.
If robbers by night—
How art thou destroyed!
Would they not steal until they had enough?
If grape gatherers had come unto thee,
Would they not leave some?
6. How is Edom searched out
His hidden things laid bare!
7. Even to the border
Have all the men of the covenant sent thee;
They have deceived thee, prevailed against thee,
Those that were at peace with thee;
Thy bread have they placed as a snare under thee.
There is no understanding in him.
8. Will not I in that day,
Whispers Jehovah,
Destroy the wise out of Edom,
And understanding out of mount Esau?
9. And thy valiant ones, O Teman, shall be dismayed,
When every man is cut off from mount Esau
By slaughter.
10. For the violence of thy brother Jacob,
Shame shall cover thee,
And thou shalt be cut off forever.
11. In the day that thou stoodest on the other side,
In the day when strangers took captive his army
And foreigners entered his gates,
And o'er Jerusalem cast lots,
Thou also wast one of them.
12. And thou shouldest not have looked on the day of thy brother,
On the day of his calamity;
Thou shouldest not have rejoiced over the sons of Judah
In the day of their destruction;
Nor spoken proudly in the day of distress.
13. Thou shouldest not have entered into the gate of My people
In the day of their ruin
Thou shouldest not have looked on his misfortune
In the day of his calamity.
And stretched not out thy hand for his possession
In the day of his destruction.
14. And thou shouldest not have stood at the cross-roads
To cut off his fugitives;
Neither shouldest thou have delivered up his remnant
In the day of distress.
15. For near is the day of Jehovah upon all nations.
As thou hast done will they do to thee;
Thy reward will be upon thy head.
16. For as ye have drunken on the mountain of my holiness,
All the nations shall drink continually,
And drink and swallow down,
And be as though they had never been.
17. But upon mount Zion shall be deliverance; there shall be holiness;
And the house of Jacob shall possess their possessions.

18. And the house of Jacob shall be a fire.
And the house of Joseph a flame.
And the house of Esau for stubble;
And they will kindle upon them and devour them,
And there shall be none remaining of the house of Esau;
For Jehovah has spoken it.
19. And the south country shall possess the mountain of Esau,
And the plain the Philistines;
And they shall possess the fields of Ephraim,
And the field of Samaria;
And Benjamin shall possess Gilead.
20. And the captives of this army of the children of Israel
Will possess of the Canaanites as far as Zarepath,
And the captives of Jerusalem who are in Sepharad
Shall possess the cities of the south.
21. And Saviours shall go up on mount Zion,
To judge the mountain of Esau.
And the kingdom shall be Jehovah's.

Analysis and Annotations

The brief prophecy of Obadiah is composed of two parts: Verses 1-16 concern Edom and its destruction and verses 17-21 reveal the establishment of the kingdom in Israel and Israel's restoration and victory. We shall give brief annotations to assist in the understanding of this prophecy by making a threefold division:

1. Edom's humiliation and ruin (verses 1-9). 2. Edom's sin against Israel and the day of the Lord (verses 10-16). 3. The kingdom of the restoration of Israel (verses 17-21).

Verses 1-9. In order to understand Obadiah's prophecy, Edom's origin and history must be taken into consideration. The Edomites were the offspring of Esau. Of him it was said that Esau the Elder should serve Jacob the younger. The character of Esau was soon manifested and his offspring soon became powerful. In Genesis 36 we read of the generations of Esau, who is Edom; there the dukes, the national chiefs, are prominently mentioned. Long before Israel had kings, Edom had such rulers, "And these are the kings that reigned in the land of Edom before there reigned any king over the children of Israel" (Gen. 36:31). In Exodus 15 we read of the dukes in Edom being amazed and in Numbers 20 of the King of Edom. His outrageous behavior towards the kin of Edom is recorded in Numbers 20:14-21. Though the children of Israel promised not to drink the waters in the territory of Edom, or take their fruit without paying for it, Edom refused to give Israel passage; while Israel turned meekly away from Edom. Thus Edom branded itself as the enemy of the people of God. They had an undying hatred against the children of Israel, the sons of Jacob. They had an envious dislike of the people of God. Later it was attacked by Saul and conquered for David by Joab (2 Sam. 8). During the reign of Jehoram (or Joram) they revolted and gained independence.

When Judah and Israel began to decline Edom became more and more arrogant and rejoiced in the evil which came upon the people of God. Their dwelling place was the former possession of the Horim, a race which lived in caves in the mountainous region, much like the prehistoric cave dwellers on the North American continent. Edom possessed then the so-called troglodyte dwelling places cut into the cliffs of sandstone; these rocky habitations were suited to their warlike character and gave them the shelter they needed. Hence they are mentioned in verse 3 as "dwelling in the clefts of the rock." The ruins of Petra still bear witness to its former grandeur. The wickedness of Edom continued and when the Chaldeans came to destroy Jerusalem they also seemed to have shown their hatred. We read in Psalm 137:7, "Remember, O Lord, the children of Edom in the day of Jerusalem, who said raze it, raze it, even to the foundation thereof." They were also in evidence during the Maccabean period and later in the person of Herod the Great, an Edomite, reigned in Jerusalem. The judgment pronounced upon Idumea, their dwelling place, has found a startling fulfillment.

But this does not end the story of Edom; there will be a future revival of Edom and an ultimate history. This will be at the close of the age, when the Lord regathers all Israel and Judah and ten tribes will be reunited, then and before Edom will appear once more in prominence. No one knows where and what Edom is today. One might almost surmise that the Turk must have some connection with Edom in his horrible hatred and outrages against the Armenians, who, as it is claimed by some, may contain remnants of the ten tribes. But all this is mere speculation. When God's time comes the Edomite will manifest their national, undying hatred against the sons of Jacob, but Israel victorious will lay their hand on Edom (Isa. 11:14).

We read of this future judgment upon the country of Edom, Idumea, in Isaiah 34:6:

"And all the host of heaven shall be dissolved, and the heavens shall be rolled together as a scroll, and all their hosts shall fall down, as the leaf falleth off from the vine, and as a falling fig from the fig tree. For My sword shall be bathed in heaven; behold it shall come down upon Idumea, and upon the people of My curse, to judgment." It is unfulfilled to the present time, but it will be fulfilled when "the Lord hath a sacrifice in Bozrah, and a great slaughter in the land of Idumea" (verse 6), that is, in the future day of the Lord. As the context shows in Isaiah 34:8, it will be that day, "For it is the day of the Lord's vengeance, and the year of recompense for the controversy of Zion." Then comes the utter desolation of Edom (Isa. 34:9-17; see also Ezek. 25:12-14; 35; Isa. 63:3 and Lam. 4:21-22). While Obadiah's prophecy has been partially fulfilled, it awaits its final accomplishment in the day of the Lord.

The prophecy begins with the announcement that tidings had come from the Lord which was heard by the prophet and by the people; an ambassador is sent forth among the nations to summon them to go up in battle against Edom. The hour for Edom's overthrow has come. The Lord has made them small among the nations. It was pride which brought them low so that they would be greatly despised. As the dwellers in the rocks they thought themselves secure and boasted of it by saying, "Who will bring me down to the ground?" But the humiliation of Edom had been decreed by the Lord and no power could arrest its execution. Their nests were high as the eagles, yea, even so high that their habitations seemed to be among the stars, yet the Lord would bring them down. His destruction would be complete; the spoilers would not be like the thieves, who steal till they have enough; or like the grape-gatherers who leave something behind. There would be a clean sweep, everything searched out, even the hidden things. Even those in whom they trusted, with whom Edom made a covenant would deceive them and prevail against Edom. Those with whom they made an alliance and gave hospitality would turn against Edom and prove treacherous, though they had eaten bread with them. Their friends of the heathen nations, whom they stirred up against Israel, would forsake them completely and the Lord would destroy the wise out of Edom and understanding out of Mount Esau. Even the wise men will not be able to help them; their wisdom and understanding will not avail. Teman is mentioned because it was known for its wise men; Eliphaz, who spoke so well to Job was a Temanite (Job 4:1). And the prophet Jeremiah in his testimony against Edom wrote, "Is wisdom no more in Teman? Is counsel perished from the prudent? Is their wisdom vanished?" (Jer. 49:7). But now their wise and valiant ones would be cut off by slaughter.

Verses 10-16. Her sin of violence against her brother Jacob comes now in special remembrance. On account of it shame would cover them and they would be cut off forever. When Jerusalem was in trouble and the Philistines and Arabs plundered the city (2 Chron. 21:16-17), they stood on the other side and revolted (2 Chron. 21:8-10). And more than that, they joined in plundering the city. Thus it was afterwards when the Babylonians came against Jerusalem, Edom rejoiced; they spoke proudly. Perhaps what is recorded in verses 12-14 happened repeatedly. They stretched out their hands for the possession of God's people. They placed themselves at the crossroads to cut off the fugitives and delighted to deliver up into the hands of their enemies the remnant which was left.

All this will be repeated once more, when another great prophecy will be fulfilled and Jerusalem is once more surrounded by hostile nations (Zech. 14:1-5). Not a few superficial Bible students thought when Jerusalem was captured during the war, and all looked bright for political Zionism, that the promises were now being fulfilled. There is coming another siege of Jerusalem, preceding the glorious appearing of the King of Israel, our Lord. That siege is prophetically described by Zechariah. Among those nations will be found Edom once more. Once more they will manifest their malice and hatred against Jerusalem.

Then, to show the link of connection between the future and the past, the prophet announces the day of the Lord. "For near is the day of Jehovah upon *all nations.*" This day has not yet been. There have been judgments upon nations like Egypt, Babylon and others, nations which were nations of power and culture, which have fallen under the dealings of a righteous God; these judgments of the past did not bring that day which Obadiah announced, of which Joel after him so fully speaks. The day of the Lord upon all nations is future. When it comes it will mean judgment for all nations, including Edom, Moab and others named in the Scriptures of Truth; and that day will be immediately followed by an age of blessing and glory such as the earth and race had never known before. It will bring divine retribution. "As thou hast done will they do unto thee." The nations of the earth will have to drink of the cup of His fury and wrath.

Verses 17-21. The final section of Obadiah's brief prophecy concerns the kingdom, the victory over the enemies and the restoration of His people. Mount Zion will come into its own; there will be deliverance and there shall be holiness. What God had promised to be the remnant of His people will be accomplished, and they will be a holy people and then hold their possessions, all that the Lord in His infinite grace had promised unto them. The house of Esau will be consumed, so that none shall be remaining of Esau, while Israel will occupy Edom's territory.

The saviours mentioned in the last verse of this prophecy (or deliverers) must mean the chosen instruments which go forth to teach all nations and make known the glory of the King in their midst. For "the kingdom shall be the Lord's."

THE PROPHET JONAH

Introduction

The question as to the reality of the person of Jonah is answered by 2 Kings 14:25. In this passage we find him mentioned as the prophet who prophesied during the reign of Jeroboam II. His name means "dove," and his father's name Amittai means "the truth of the Lord." He was from "Gath-Hepher"—the winepress of the well is the meaning of these two words. Thus Jonah also belongs to the earlier prophets and the book bearing his name, written by himself, occupies the right place in the Old Testament. A Jewish tradition states that Jonah was the son of the widow at Zarephath, whom Elijah raised to life; but this is only an invention with no evidence whatever.

The Book and Experience of Jonah

The book of Jonah is of a different nature from the books of the other Minor Prophets and their personal experiences and activities as reported in the historical books. The book of Jonah has no direct prophecies in it, yet the experience it records is a great prophecy.

We do not give the contents of the book in this introduction, but shall follow all in the annotations. As is well known, the miraculous history of the book of Jonah has been widely attacked by infidelity. When the Old Testament was translated into the Greek (the Septuagint) heathen philosophers and other writers ridiculed it and made sport with the book. Their objections and ridicule are reproduced in the school of the destructive criticism. We hear that men who boast of great scholarship declare that Jonah never lived, that the story of the book of Jonah is an imagination of some great literary genius. Says that archcritic, Canon F. W. Farrar, in *The Expositor's Bible:* "Of Jonah we know nothing more. For it is impossible to see in the book of Jonah much more than a beautiful and edifying story, which may or may not rest on some surviving legends." But as some one has said, it requires less faith to credit this simple excerpt from Jonah's history than to believe the numerous hypotheses that have been invented to deprive it of its supernatural character. The great majority of these hypotheses are clumsy and far-fetched, doing violence to the language, and doing despite to the spirit of revelation. These infidel inventions are distinguished by tedious adjustment, laborious combinations, historical conjecture and critical jugglery.

Some critics who do not want to reject altogether the story of Jonah, suppose that it may have had some historical basis, though in the form we have it today is fanciful and mythical. Another critic regards it as a dream Jonah had in the ship. Still another critic views the book as an historical allegory, descriptive of the fate of Manasseh, and Josiah his grandson. What wild fancy this critic indulged in may be seen from the fact that he compared the ship to the Jewish monarchy, while the casting away of Jonah symbolized the temporary captivity of Manasseh!

Many critics treat it as an allegory based upon the Phoenician myth of Hercules and the sea-monster. To quote a few more, simply to show what foolish thgs the darkened mind of man, who thinks he has attained scholarship, can invent in order to disprove the truth of God, we mention the theory that when Jonah was thrown into the sea he was picked up by a ship having for a figurehead the head of a great fish. Another one says that probably Jonah took refuge in the interior of a dead whale which was floating about near the spot he was cast overboard.

The great majority of the critics today deny the historicity of the book of Jonah and claim that its material has been derived from popular legends, that it is fiction with a moral design. The moral lessons and its religious meaning have even a wider range than these hypotheses. The theories do not merit a special refutation.

Is it History or Myth?

There is nothing in the account which would justify any critic to charge it with being allegory. It is cast in the form of a narrative and has all the literary characteristics of a personal experience. The sole reason why the critics have classed it with myths and deny its authenticity is the miraculous element in the book. Any one who believes in an omnipotent God, a God who does wondrous things, will have no difficulty whatever in accepting this book as a true history. We might also add that all the earlier Jewish sources confirm the historicity and literalness of the book of Jonah. Furthermore, the book is very simple and pure Hebrew.

The Highest Evidence

The highest authority that Jonah lived, and had the experience recorded in this account is the Lord Jesus Christ. The words which He spoke, who is the Truth, are plain and unimpeachable. There can be no secondary meaning; "For as Jonah was three days and three nights in the whale's belly, so shall the Son of Man be three days and three nights in the heart of the earth. The men of Nineveh shall rise in judgment with this generation, and shall condemn it, because they repented at the preaching of Jonah, and behold, a greater than Jonah is here" (Matthew 12:40-41). Our Lord tells us that there was a prophet by the name of Jonah and that he had the experience related in the book which bears his name. To deny this is tantamount to denying the knowledge and the truthfulness of God. This is exactly what sneering critics do. They have even gone so far as to say that if our ever blessed Lord knew better than He spoke, He acted thus for expediency's sake, so as not to clash with the current opinions among His contempories. Others boldly say that He did not know, for He had not access to the sources which are at our command today. In other words the destructive critic claims to have more knowledge than the Lord Jesus Christ possessed in His days on earth.

Professor A. C. Zenos (in the *Standard Bible Dictionary)* says: "The New Testament does not commit Jesus Christ or its own authors to one or the other of the contending theories." This is a poor statement. The Lord Jesus did commit Himself fully to the historicity of Jonah. *The New Century Bible,* a destructive work, makes the following declaration: "We are not to conclude that the literal validity of the history of Jonah is established by this reference"—that is, the words of our Lord in Matthew 12:40. But the man who wrote this overlooked the fact that the Lord in all His allusions to the Old Testament events always speaks of them as actual, literal events, and, therefore, establishes their literal validity. For instance, "As Moses lifted up the serpent in the wilderness" . . . "As it was in the days of Noah" . . . "As it was in the days of Lot." Then in the next verse in Matthew's Gospel, the Lord speaks of the queen of the south's visit to Solomon as a real, literal fact. Why then should He not have spoken of the history of Jonah as a literal fact?

The truth is that the Lord Jesus Christ placed such emphasis upon the book of Jonah because it foreshadowed His own experience as the Redeemer, and because He knew of what apostate Christendom would do with this book and its record. There is no middle ground possible; either this book of Jonah is true, relates the true and miraculous history of this prophet, or the Lord Jesus Christs is not the infallible Son of God. His person and His work stand and fall together with the authenticity of Jonah.

"Our Lord singled out this particular miracle about Jonah, which has been thought of great difficulty, and affixes to it His own almighty stamp of truth. Can you not receive the words of the Lord Jesus Christ against all men that ever were? The Lord Jesus has referred to the fact that Jonah was swallowed by a great fish, call it what you will—I am not going to enter into a contest with naturalists, whether it was a shark, or a sperm-whale or another. This is a matter of very small account. We will leave these men of science to settle the kind (if they can); but the fact itself, the only one of importance to us to affirm, is that it was a great fish that swallowed and afterwards yielded up the prophet alive. This is all one need to affirm—the literal truth of the fact alleged. There is no need to imagine that a fish was created for that purpose. There are many fishes quite capable of swallowing a man whole. But the fact is not only affirmed in the Old Testament, but reaffirmed by our Lord Himself and applied to Himself. Any man who disputes this must give an account before the judgment seat of Christ" (W. Kelly).

The Typical-Prophetic Meaning of Jonah

The typical-prophetic meaning of the story of Jonah is authorized by the words of the Son of God. His experience typifies the death, the burial and the resurrection of our Lord, as well as the gospel message which goes forth to the Gentiles. Furthermore, Jonah's experience is prophetic also of the entire nation. The annotations will enter more fully into these interesting and important foreshadowings.

The Division of the Book

The division of the book is very simple. We maintain the chapter division as made in the authorized version.

Chapter 1 gives the record of Jonah's commission, his disobedience and the consequences. Chapter 2 contains his prayer and his deliverance. Chapter 3 has the account of his obedience in preaching to Nineveh. Chapter 4 contains the account of Jonah's discontent and correction.

Analysis and Annotations

CHAPTER 1

The Commission of the Prophet, His Disobedience, and the Consequences

1. The commission (1:1-2)
2. The disobedience (1:5)
3. The consequences (1:4-17)

Verses 1-2. The record begins with the same word with which all historical books in the Bible begin, like Joshua, Judges, Ruth, Samuel, etc. The commissin given to Jonah was to go to Nineveh, that great city, and to cry against it on account of its wickedness.

Nineveh was the great capital of the Assyrian nation; it is mentioned for the first time in Genesis 10:11. Its great size is mentioned in chapter 3:3, where we read it was "three day's journey." Ancient Greek and Roman writers state that it was the largest city in the world in that day. All these statements of its enormous size have been verified by modern excavations. The word of the Lord came to Jonah to visit this city and deliver the message. Seven times the phase "the word of the Lord came to Jonah" is used in this book.

Verse 3. Jonah rose up at once, but instead of going to the east towards Nineveh he fled in the other direction. Tarshish in Spain was his goal. It is also stated that he fled from the presence of the Lord. This cannot possibly mean that he fled from the presence of Him whom he knew as the omnipresent One. The Psalm of David which speaks of this expressly was then in the possession of Israel, and Jonah must have known it: 'Whither shall I go from Thy Spirit? Or whither shall I flee from Thy presence? If I ascend up into heaven, Thou art there: if I make my bed in sheol, behold, Thou art there. If I take the wings of the morning and dwell in the uttermost parts of the sea; even there shall Thy hand lead me, and Thy right hand shall hold me" (Psalm 139:7-10). He did not flee from the presence of the Lord in the sense of escaping His knowledge and authority. It means that he left the land of Israel where Jehovah dwelt; he fled from the service-commission he had received.

If we look for a motive of this disobedient prophet we find it given in the book itself. In chapter 4:2 we read, "Therefore I fled before unto Tarshish, for I knew that Thou art a gracious God, and merciful, and slow to anger, and of great kindness, and repentest Thee of evil." But why should he fear that God might be merciful to Nineveh and save the city? It was undoubtedly a national spirit which possessed the prophet. It has been suggested that the prophet knew that the Assyrian would be used by the Lord as the instrument to punish Israel and that he thought if Nineveh would perish the people Israel might be saved. Inasmuch as God might show mercy to Assyria, Assyria would then be used as the rod upon Israel, and for this reason he was disedient to the commission. But the direct prophecy that the Assyrian would be the staff in the hand of the Lord to bring judgment upon Israel was made through Isaiah (chapter 10), and that relevation had not yet been given, for Jonah lived before the prophet Isaiah. It was rather the fear Jonah had as a Jew that the conversion of the Gentiles might rob his nation of the distinction of being the nation of election, to whom Jehovah had revealed Himself exclusively. He therefore went to ppa where he engaged passage on a ship which was to bring him to Tarshish, which he never reached. It was at Joppa where centuries later another Jew, who was also jealous for his nation, had a vision which made it clear that the gospel should be preached to the Gentiles. That Jew was Peter (Acts 10).

Verses 4-17. No sooner had the ship set sail but a terrible tempest arose, sent by the Lord. The danger of shipwreck was imminent. The heathen mariners became terrified and besides crying each one to their gods, they threw the wares overboard to lighten the ship, so that it might weather the storm. But we do not read anything about Jonah calling on his God. Was it an evil conscience which led him to seek sleep in the sides of the ship? Or did he seek sleep because he was in despair? Or was his action produced by the calmness of faith, that he knew himself in the hands of the Lord? Perhaps his action shows more than anything indifference and an astonishing self-security.

The shipmaster aroused him from his sleep, asking him why he slept and demanded that he call upon his God. The lot is cast and it fell upon Jonah. He might have confessed before but he waited as long as he could. The questions they asked him he answers readily. He confesses that he is a Hebrew, that he fears the Lord, the God of heaven, the creator of sea and land. His confession filled them with fear; they also knew that he had been disobedient for he told them about it. It was a noble confession and shows that though he had fled from the presence of the Lord his heart still clung to Him. He answered the question, what shall we do unto thee, that the sea may be calm unto us? by pronouncing his own sentence. "Take me up, and cast me forth into the sea; so shall the sea be calm unto you; for I know that for my sake this great tempest is upon you." Again we must say these are noble words. He is ready to sacrifice himself and trusts the Lord and His mercy. After the mariners made an unsuccessful attempt to row the ship to land, and calling upon the Lord not to lay upon them innocent blood, they cast Jonah into the raging sea, and the sea became calm. As a result the heathen sailors feared Jehovah exceedingly, offering a sacrifice unto Him and making vows, while the Lord prepared a great fish to swallow up Jonah, in whose belly Jonah remained three days and three nights. Some have stated that the Lord created a special sea-monster for this purpose, but the Hebrew word does not mean "create" it means "appoint." It certainly was not a whale, for whales rarely ever are seen in the Mediterranean sea, nor can a whale swallow a human being on account of the narrowness of its throat. It was probably a species of sea-monster frequently found in that sea and known by the scientific name *squalus carcharias,* which can easily swallow a human being whole. But the miracle was not that such a fish came up from the depths of the sea and swallowed the prophet, but that Jonah was miraculously preserved in the fish.

The Typical Application

1. Jonah is a type of the Lord Jesus Christ. As already pointed out in the introduction the words of our Lord sanction this application. But as He said when He spoke of Solomon "a greater than Solomon is here," so He also said "a greater than Jonah is here."

We point out a few of the applications and contrasts. Jonah was sent with a message of judgment; the Son of God came with the message of love and salvation. "For God sent not His Son into the world to condemn the world, but that the world through Him might be saved" (John 3:17).

Jonah was disobedient, acting in self-will, fleeing from the presence of the Lord. The Son of God was obedient; He never did His own will but the will of Him that sent Him. The words He spoke were not His own. "The word which ye hear is not mine, but the Father's who sent me." He always had the Father set before Himself and was uninterruptedly in His presence.

Jonah, indifferent and self-secure, was fast asleep in the ship while the storm raged and the ship was in danger of going down. The Lord Jesus was asleep in the ship on Galilee, and though the ship was filling with water He was undisturbed, knowing that He was safe. He did what Jonah did not and could not do. He rebuked his fearful disciples and rebuked the wind and the waves; the storm was suddently hushed.

Jonah bore a faithful witness; but how much greater is His witness. He is called "the faithful Witness" (Rev. 1).

Jonah sacrificed himself in order to save those who were about to perish. But how much greater His sacrifice! Jonah's fate came upon him on account of his sin and disobedience. The Lord Jesus Christ did not suffer for His sins, for He had none, being the Holy, the Sinless One. He died exclusively for others and died for the ungodly. But did Jonah actually die? Did death fasten upon him? Was his body miraculously preserved so that it did not see corruption? Was it a literal resurrection when the fish vomited him out? Jonah did not die physically. But his experience typifies the death and the burial of Christ, and also His physical resurrection. How could Jonah have prayed and cried to the Lord out of the belly of the fish if his physical life had ceased? It was a miracle, however, that Jonah was kept alive.

The three days and three nights have troubled a good many expositors. Not a few teach that in order to bring together the three days and three nights during which our Lord was in the grave, He must have died either on Wednesday or Thursday. The three days and three nights must be interpreted according to Hebrew usage. In Luke 24:21 we read that the two who met the risen Lord said, "And beside all this, today is the third day since these things were done." That was on the first day of the week. Reckoning back, Saturday would be the second day and Friday the first day, the day on which Christ died.

2. Jonah is a type of the Jewish Nation. In the

Jewish synagogical ritual the book of Jonah is read on the Day of Atonement. The writer is indebted to an old orthodox Jew for the information why this story is read on their great day of fasting and prayer. He said, 'We are the Jonah." Like Jonah the nation was called to bear witness to the Gentiles. And as Jonah did not want the knowledge of Jehovah to go to the Gentiles, so the Jews filled with national pride of being the elect nation opposed God's purposes. (See Acts 13:6-12, 44-52; 14:19-20; 17:5-9; 18:12, etc.)

Disobedient as Jonah, the nation left the presence of the Lord. Jonah engaged passage on a merchant-ship, and the Jew became a trafficker. Like as it was with Jonah, storm and disaster came upon the nation after their great act of disobedience, when they rejected Christ, and opposed His purposes. Like Jonah, in the midst of all their troubles they did not deny, nor deny now, their nationality, their faith in God; they also confess in some of their prayers, at least the orthodox Jews, why it is that they are in trouble, that they have sinned and turned away from the Lord.

Jonah was cast overboard into the sea. The sea represents the nations; that is where the Jews were cast. As a result of the casting away of Jonah the heathen sailors turned to the Lord and sacrificed unto Him. In Romans 11:11 we read, "through their fall (the Jews) salvation came to the Gentiles to provoke them to jealousy." The belly of the fish represents the grave of the Jews among the nations. They became nationally and spiritually dead. But as the fish did not digest Jonah, so the nations have not digested the Jew. They remain unassimilated, just as Balaam predicted, "This nation shall dwell alone and not be reckoned among the nations." The national preservation of Israel is one of the great miracles in history, just as the preservation of Jonah in the belly of the fish was a miracle.

CHAPTER 2

Jonah's Prayer and Deliverance

1. The prayer (2:1-9)
2. The deliverance (2:10)

Verses 1-9. Some expositors have called attention to the fact that the prayer is not one offered up for deliverance, but it is a thanksgiving for the accomplished deliverance. But this is answered by the opening verse of this chapter, in which we are told that he prayed unto the Lord his God out of the fish's belly. When he found that he had escaped the death he anticipated and that the power of God kept him alive, he realized that the Lord his God would also deliver him; in faith he praised Jehovah for the coming deliverance. His prayer is composed almost entirely of sentences found in Psalms. We give the references. Verse 2 reminds of Psalms 18:6, 7 and 120:1. The word "hell" is the Hebrew "sheol," the unknown region. See also Psalm 30:3. Verse 3 contains a quotation from Psalm 42:7, "All thy waves and billows passed over me." In connection with verse 4 consider Psalm 31:22. Verse 5 is found in Psalm 18:4, except the seaweed which crowned his head as he went into the deep; also Psalm 69:2. The thanksgiving in verse 6, "Yet hast Thou brought up my life from the pit, O Lord, my God" is closely allied to Psalm 30:3. The first part of verse 7 is from Psalm 142:3 (marginal reading) and 143:4. The second part is found in Psalm 5:7 and 18:6. The eighth verse reminds of Psalm 31:6 and the ninth verse is to be connected with Psalm 42:4.

The last utterance before the Lord commanded the fish is a triumphant shout, "Salvation is of the Lord," a truth which many preachers in Christendom do not know.

Verse 10. The God of creation manifested His power over His creation by impelling the fish to release its prisoner. The place at which the fish vomited out Jonah is not mentioned; it was probably not very far from the seaport Joppa where he embarked.

The Typical Application

1. As to the Lord Jesus Christ. Our Lord went into the jaws of death and died the sinner's death, the substitute of sinners. Most of the passages from the Psalms which Jonah embodied in his prayer are prophetic predictions of the sufferings of Christ. He cried to God for deliverance and was heard. (See Hebrew 5:7) The answer was His resurrection. Over His blessed head passed the waves and billows of a Holy God, when as the substitute He hung on the cross. He knew more than Jonah could ever know what it meant, "The sorrows of death compassed me, and the floods of ungodly men made me afraid." The Sixty-ninth Psalm is Messianic and the words Jonah used, "I sink in deep mire where there is no standing; I am come into deep waters, where floods overthrow me," tell us of the deep sufferings through which He passed. While Jonah's head was wound about with the seaweeds of the deep, our Lord bore the crown of thorns, the emblem of the curse, upon His blessed head.

It was on the third day that the fish vomited out Jonah. The third day is marked in the Word of God as the day of resurrection. (See Genesis 1:11-13; Hosea 6:1-3.) On the third day our Lord left the grave behind and rose from among the dead. We quote a helpful paragraph on the question of the three days and nights: "So our Lord Jesus, though by Jewish reckoning three days and nights in the grave, literally lay there but the whole of Saturday, the Sabbath, with the part of Friday not yet closed, and before the dawn of Sunday. For we must always remember in these questions the Jews' method of reckoning. Part of a day regularly counted for the twenty-four hours. The evening and the morning, or any part, counted as a whole day. But the Lord, as we know, was crucified in the afternoon on Friday; His body lay all the Sabbath day in the grave; and He arose early on the Sunday morning. That space was counted three days and three nights, according to sanctioned Biblical reckoning, which no man who bows to Scripture would contest. This was asserted among the Jews, who, fertile as they have been in excuses for unbelief, have never, as far as I am aware, made difficulties on this score. The ignorance of Gentiles has exposed some of them when unfriendly to cavil at the phrase. The Jews found not a few stumbling blocks, but this is not one of them; they may know little of what is infinitely more momentous; but they know their own Bible too well to press an objection which would tell against the Hebrew Scriptures quite as much as the Greek."[1]

2. As to the Nation. The prayer for deliverance and Jonah's deliverance by the power of God foreshadows the coming experience of the remnant of Israel. There is coming the time of Jacob's trouble in the closing years of this age. Then a part of the nation will call upon the Lord. Their prayers are also pre-written in the book of Psalms, and when finally they acknowledge that "salvation is of the Lord," and He appears in His glory, to turn away ungodliness from Jacob, the Lord will bring them out of their spiritual and national death. He will speak to the fish, the nations, and they will give up the Jews. Then comes the third day of their restoration. (See Hosea 6:1-3.)

---

[1]William Kelly, *Jonah.*

CHAPTER 3

Jonah Preaching in Nineveh

1. The repeated commission and Jonah's obedience (3:1-4)
2. The repentance and salvation of Nineveh (3:4-10)

Verses 1-4. And now after Jonah's death and life experience the Word of the Lord came unto Jonah the second time, telling him to arise and go to Nineveh to preach there what the Lord would command him. And now he is obedient. Jonah arrived in the great city of three days' journey, and advancing a day's journey into it he cried out his message, 'Yet forty days, and Nineveh shall be overthrown." Following is the objection of higher criticism as to this statement: "If we were reading a historical description the narrative would be full of difficulties. A strange prophet announced the impending destruction as he traveled through the vast city for one day, and the huge populataion immediately believed and repented. The king, who is not named, heard, put on sackcloth, sitting in ashes. If this were history, Jonah did what no prophet, no apostle, what Christ Himself never did. Never did a day's preaching bring a vast strange city to repentance. But we repeat, it is not history; it is a story with a meaning, an allegory; it is the great announcement that God cares for the heathen world, and calls it to repentance, and whenever men anywhere repent, His compassion is kindled towards them" (*New Century Bible*). We reserve the answer to the supposed difficulties in this historical account for the typical unfolding of this event.

Verses 4-10. The people of Nineveh believed God. The news that a strange prophet had appeared with the message of doom must have spread like wildfire and hundreds upon hundreds must have passed it on so that in a very short time it reached every nook and corner of the great city; it reached the palace of the king and the prisoners in the dungeon. That this is real history has been confirmed by archaelogy. For just about that time Nineveh was in great trouble and facing a crisis, which made them eager to believe the message and return to God. They evidenced their faith by a universal fast and humiliation before God. The king laid aside his royal robe and humiliated himself as every one of his subjects did. He issued a proclamation to abstain from food and drink, in which the dumb creation was included. What a solemn time the great city had, when hundreds and thousands humbled themselves and when the lowing and groaning of the domestic animals was heard throughout the city. The people acknowledged all their wickedness and turned away from their evil ways and deeds of violence, expressing the hope of God's mercy. "Who can tell if God will turn and repent, and turn away from His fierce anger, that we perish not." And God answered and was merciful to them.

The Typical Application

1. As to the Lord Jesus. Jonah who typifies in his experience the death, burial and resurrection of our Lord, preached the message as one who had been in a grave and came to life out of that grave. In Luke 11:29-30, 32, our Lord makes the application: "For as Jonah was a sign unto the Ninevites, so shall also the Son of Man be to this generation . . . The men of Nineveh shall rise up in the judgment with this generation, and shall condemn it, for they repented at the preaching of Jonah, and, behold, a greater than Jonah is here." Christ was not preached as a Saviour to the Gentile world till He had died and risen from the dead. The Greeks who inquired after Him (John 12) received no answer. But the Lord spoke of Himself at that time as the corn of wheat which was to die to bring forth the abundant fruit. Christ died for the sins of His people Israel, "for that nation," but He also died as a member of the nation, from which He came according to the flesh, so that He might rise and become the Saviour of the Gentiles. Christ preached as having died for our sins, buried and risen on the third day, is the true gospel and carries with it the power of God in the salavation of sinners.

2. As to the Nation. The third day is the day of Israel's spiritual and national resurrection. When that day comes converted Israel will be, according to God's gifts and calling, a holy nation, a nation of priestly functions, a kingdom of priests. They are then fit to show forth the Lord and His glory, and to bring the message, not of judgment, but of life and glory, to the nations of heathendom. The statement in the *New Century Bible* quoted above is quite correct in one particular—that "Jonah did what no prophet, no apostle, what Christ Himself never did"—that never a day's preaching brought a vast strange city to repentance. And we might add that no preaching today, during this age, can ever bring such results. The case is unique; it never happened again, that a man who was disobedient, who turned against the divine commission, became a castaway, was miraculously preserved and delivered, led a great world city to God and to true repentance. But if we take into consideration the fact that this true history is a prophecy, all these invented higher critical difficulties vanish altogether. When the nation is reinstated in the land, filled with the Spirit, they will fulfill their calling and go forth in bringing the message to the nations of the world. Then Matthew 28:19 will be accomplished. Then and not before will the world be converted, and all the nations will be joined in the kingdom to Israel, His kingdom people.

And as for repenting Nineveh there came a day of joy and gladness, as animal creation in that city ceased its lowing and groaning, so will come the day of joy and gladness for this poor world, "in that day" when even groaning creation will be delivered of its groans and moans.

CHAPTER 4

Jonah's Discontent and Correction

1. Jonah's discontent (4:1-3)
2. The correction (4:4-11)

Verses 1-3. All that had happened displeased Jonah exceedingly and he was very angry. Did he feel that he had lost his prestige as a prophet, having announced the overthrow of Nineveh, when it did not happen? What he feared had come true; God had been merciful to this great city and they were now enjoying what he considered Israel's exclusive inheritance. Instead of rejoicing in the great exhibition of God's mercy towards such a wicked city, he was angry. Like Elijah, in the hour of despondency he requests to die. "Therefore, now, O Lord, take, I beseech Thee, my life from me; for it is better for me to die than to live." The trouble with Jonah was that he thought only of himself, and, as another has said, "the horrid selfishness of his heart hides from him the God of grace, faithful in His love for His helpless creatures."

Verses 4-11. The Lord God who had been so merciful to Nineveh is now merciful to His angry servant the Prophet. "Doest thou well to be angry?" How great is the patience and kindness of the Lord, even towards them who fail! Jonah leaves the saved city evidently in disgust, and finds on the east side a place where he constructed a booth and sat there waiting to see what would become of the city. He evidently expected still an act of judgment. Then comes the lesson. The Lord God who had prepared a fish to swallow the disobedient prophet now prepared a gourd to provide a shade for him. This gourd, a *quipayon,* is a very common plant in Palestine. The Creator whose creation is so wonderful, manifested the Creator's power in raising up this plant, for the relief of His servant, in a sudden manner. And Jonah was exceedingly glad. Then God prepared a worm which destroyed the gourd. When the morning came and the sun beat upon the head of the prophet he fainted, and once more wished in himself to die. Alas! if the prophet had been in the right place before the Lord he would have accepted the gourd as evidence of His loving care, and when the worm destroyed the plant so that it withered he would have equally acknowledged his Creator-God and not have murmured. He might have said with Job, "The Lord gave, the Lord has taken away; blessed be the name of the Lord." Jonah in his selfish impatience found fault with God. It is still the common thing amongst professing Christians.

And when God asked him, "Doest thou well to be angry for the gourd?" the poor finite creature of the dust answered the Creator, "I do well to be angry, even unto death." Then comes the lesson. Not God, Elohim, the name of Him as Creator, speaks, but it is Jehovah, the Lord: "Thou hast had pity on the gourd, for the which thou hast not laboured, neither madest it grow; which came up in a night, and perished in a night: and should not I spare Nineveh, that great city, wherein are more than six score thousand persons that cannot discern between their right hand and their left; and also much cattle?" If Jonah felt pity and was angry because of a small vine he had not planted nor made to grow, should not God with greater right have mercy upon His creatures, whom He created and sustained? Jonah is silenced; he could not reply. The last word belongs to Jehovah, who thus demonstrated that in His infinite compassion He embraces not Israel alone, but all His creation, the Gentile world and even animal creation.

"Most touching and beautiful is the last verse of the book, in which God displays the force and supreme necessity of His love; which (although the threatenings of His justice are heard, and must needs be heard and even executed if man continues in rebellion) abides in the repose of that perfect goodness which nothing can alter, and which seizes the opportunity of displaying itself, whenever man allows Him, so to speak, to bless him—the repose of an affection that nothing can escape, that observes everything, in order to act according to its own undisturbed nature—the repose of God Himself, essential to His perfection, on which depends all our blessing and all our peace" *(Synopsis of the Bible).*

THE PROPHET
MICAH

Introduction

When the prophet Jeremiah was in danger of being put to death for his faithful testimony, certain of the elders rose up and said, "Micah the Morashtite prophesied in the days of Hezekiah, King of Judah; and spake to all the people of Judah, saying, Thus saith the Lord of hosts: Zion shall be plowed like a field, and Jerusalem shall become heaps, and the mountain of the house as the high places of a forest" (Jer. 26:18). This is the testimony of the book of Jeremiah to Micah, who prophesied under the reign of Hezekiah, as well as Jotham and Ahaz. The first verse of the book of Micah gives us this information. While Jonah was a Galilean, Micah was a Judean. He came from Moresheth-Gath, which distinguishes him from another prophet of the same name, Micah the son of Imlah. (See 1 Kings 22:8; Micaiah is the same as Micah.) The name Micah means "who is like the Lord?"

Prophesying mostly in Jerusalem during the reigns of Jotham, Ahaz and Hezekiah, he was contemporaneous with Isaiah. Though his name is not mentioned in the prophecy of Isaiah, his message is the same as the message of Isaiah, in describing the moral corruption of their times, and the Messianic prophecies. The following passages will confirm this: Micah 1:9-16 and Isaiah 10:28-32; Micah 2:1-2 and Isaiah 5:8; Micah 2:6, 11 and Isaiah 30:10,11; Micah 2:12 and Isaiah 10:20-23; Micah 3:5-7 and Isaiah 29:9-12; Micah 3:12 and Isaiah 32:14; Micah 4:1 and Isaiah 2:2; Micah 4:4 and Isaiah 50:19; Micah 4:7 and Isaiah 9:7; Micah 4:10 and Isaiah 39:6; Micah 5:2-4 and Isaiah 7:14; Micah 5:6 and Isaiah 14:25; Micah 6:6-8 and Isaiah 58:6-7; Micah 7:7 and Isaiah 8:17; Micah 7:12 and Isaiah 11:11. Thus the Lord gave the same witness through the mouth of these two. Of course Isaiah was the leading figure. But Micah did not copy him, but as the Holy Spirit came upon him he uttered his prophecies bearing witness to the same truths Isaiah had spoken. The style of Micah's writings is different from the style of Isaiah. "This may be all explained by the vivacity of his own individuality, and the excited state of his mind, passing as he does rapidly from threatening to promise, from one subject to another, and from one number and gender to another." But his words are never deficient in clearness, while in other respects he comes quite near to the style of Isaiah.

The prophetic horizon of Micah is very much restricted. The magnificent sweep of Isaiah, looking forward to the great and glorious consummation in the kingdom, is lacking in Micah. The question of the exact time when Micah uttered his prophecies, what was spoken during the reign of Jotham, during the reign of Ahaz or Hezekiah, is unessential, and we do not follow it in this introduction.

His Message

The book consists of three great prophetic discourses which all begin in the same way, with the command to hear. "Hear all ye people," chapter 1:2, the first discourse. The second discourse, chapter 3:1, "Hear, I pray you." The third discourse, chapter 6:1, "Hear ye now what the Lord saith." In the first prophetic message he predicts the destruction of Samaria, the ten-tribe kingdom, and the captivity of Judah. The second message is a message of reproof of the leaders of the nation, the heads of Jacob and the princes of the house of Israel, followed by a denunciation of the false prophets. This is followed by the vision of the coming glory in the last days and the restoration of Israel. In this second discourse the coming ruler of Israel and His birthplace are announced; what He is and the kingdom He will establish in the midst of His people. Here is the message of hope and glory.

The third discourse contains a very solemn pleading with His people. Jehovah tells them again of all His loving kindness. He tells them He has a controversy with them; He speaks to them of His rightful demands. It is a most eloquent outburst. The last part contains an assurance that the Lord will surely have compassion upon His people, while their enemies will be overthrown to lick the dust. One of the greatest words of praise in the Scriptures is found in the last three verses. It contains Israel's hope and is a prophecy of the time when the Redeemer shall return and turn away ungodliness from

Jacob and remember their sins no more.

The three prophetic discourses of Micah the Morashtite give a progressive message. The book begins with the threatening judgment; it leads on towards the Messianic salvation and glory, and finally the exhortation and reproof—to return unto Him, to repent, and the assurance of His compassion and forgiveness.

Analysis and Annotations

The First Prophetic Message

CHAPTER 1

1. The introduction (1:1)
2. Judgment announced (1:2-5)
3. The destruction of Samaria (1:6-7)
4. The lamentation of the prophet over the coming judgment (1:8-16)

Verse 1. This introduction tells us two things. In the first place, we learn that this book contains the word of the Lord that came to Micah, the Morashtite; in the second place, we are told when Micah exercised his office. As stated in the introduction, he was contemporary with Isaiah, probably for about twenty-nine years. Criticism has attacked the authorship of this book also. Since criticism began, with Ewald, to question the unity of this little book, it has raged with increasing violence, until Professor Cheyne, improving on Robertson Smith in the *Encyclopedia Britannica,* concludes: "In no part of chapters 4—7 can we venture to detect the hand of Micah." There is no need to answer such statements. The unity of the book of Micah is fully demonstrated by the message it contains. If chapters 4—7 were not written by Micah, will the critics give us light on who the author is?

Verses 2-5. The opening message is sublime. It is an appeal to all the nations, the whole earth and all that is in it, to listen to the witness of the Lord Jehovah against them, the witness which comes from His holy temple. The other Micah (Micaiah, the same as Micah) the son of Imlah, uttered similar words (1 Kings 22:28). He next describes the Lord coming out of His place, the place where He dwells in mercy, to come down and tread upon the high places of the earth. He is coming to judge; He is coming in wrath. The nations are to hear it, that the judgment is for the transgression of Jacob and for the sins of the house of Israel. On verse 4 see Psalm 18:7-10; Psalm 68:8 and Judges 5:4. The near fulfillment was the double judgment which came upon the two kingdoms, the kingdom of the ten tribes, Samaria, and the kingdom of Judah. But the description of the coming of the Lord in judgment also relates to that great future event, the day of the Lord.

Verses 6-7. The sin of Israel was Samaria, it originated there and consisted of idol worship; the sins of Judah were the high places in Jerusalem. (See Jer. 32:35.) Complete destruction of Samaria would come with this announced judgment and all her graven images would be broken to pieces, and her whoredoms burned with fire (Joel 2:3; Hosea 2:7).

Verses 8-16. Here is the lamentation of Micah as directed by the Spirit of God, not only over the fate of Samaria, but over Judah as well. He weeps for both Samaria and Judah. "I will wail and howl; I will go stripped and naked; I will make a wailing like the jackals, and a mourning like the owls (ostriches)." It shows how these men of God entered in a whole-souled manner into the divine revelations they received. It created deep soul exercise. This must be the result of faith in the prophetic word with all His people at all times. In verse nine the prophet speaks of one who comes to execute the threatened judgment. "He is come unto the gate of my people, even to Jerusalem." This enemy is the Assyrian whom Micah beholds advancing and who came before the gates of Jerusalem. (See Isa. 10.) The Assyrian was used in ending the kingdom of Israel; Babylon under Nebuchadnezzar was the instrument used against Judah and Jerusalem. Sennacherib came against Jerusalem, but it was Shalmaneser, king of Assyria, who carried Israel away into captivity. Isaiah's prophecy enters more fully into this. He describes both the Assyrian and the Babylonian power. And both will appear again at the close of the times of the Gentiles. The little horn of Daniel's prophecy in chapter 7, the head of the confederated nations, the revived Roman Empire, corresponds with the final King of Babylon, while the final Assyrian is the other little horn in Daniel 8. (See annotations on Dan. 7 and 8).

Verses 10-13 correspond to Isaiah 10:28-34; it is a description of the advance of the Assyrian. The coming disaster is not to be published in Gath, that is, the Philistines are not to hear of it. (See. 2 Sam. 1:20.) There is a remarkable play of words in these statements. It may be literally rendered as follows: "Weep not in Weeptown; in Dust-town (the meaning of Aphrah) roll thyself in dust"; then a contrast, "in Beauty-town (Saphir means beauty) be in nakedness and shame; and in March-town (the meaning of Zaanan) march not forth."

The inhabitant of Maroth waited anxiously for good, but evil came from the Lord unto the gate of Jerusalem (Maroth means bitterness). In the Assyrian cylinder, known as Taylor's cylinder, Sennacherib mentions the great gate of Jerusalem.

Then follows a call to Lachish to escape. "Bind the chariot to the swift beast." Lachish was a fortified city, as the excavations have shown, and was taken by Sennacherib. Here is still another play of words in the original. Lachish means "Horse-town," so that it can be translated "Bind the chariot to the horse, O inhabitant of Horse-town." It has been suggested that the sin mentioned in connection with Lachish was that "the horses of the sun" in connection with idolatry were kept there (2 Kings 23:11).

In verse 14 the prophet mentions his home town Moresheth-gath; there is to be a parting gift for she shall go into captivity. And Achzib will not keep the invader back; Achzib means a lie—the "Lie-town" shall be a lie to the kings of Israel, a false hope.

The heir who is to possess Moreshah is the Assyrian, and "the glory of Israel shall come even unto Adullam," the nobles of Israel shall gather in the cave of Adullam, like outcasts. (See 1 Sam. 22:1.)

They were now to mourn, expressed in making themselves bald (Job 1:20; Isa. 15:2; 22:12; Jer. 16:6), for they are gone into captivity.

CHAPTER 2

1. The guilt and punishment of Israel (2:1-11)
2. The future restoration (2:12-13)

Verses 1-11. In the first two verses the special sins of Israel are mentioned, the same as in Amos—idolatry, covetousness and oppression. Therefore punishment is to fall upon them. There would be a doleful lamentation: "We be utterly spoiled: he changeth the portion of my people; how does he take it away from me!" Their fields would be divided. Nor did they listen to the true prophets; they gave ear to the false prophets who flattered them. It is interesting to note that the sentence, "Prophesy ye not, thus they prophesy," literally translated is, "Do not sputter, thus they sputter." They did not give out the real message, but they sputtered out their own words. These false prophets tried to prevent the true prophets from announcing the judgment of the Lord.

Then comes a passionate appeal: "O, thou that art named the house of Jacob, is the Spirit of the Lord straitened? Are these His doings? Do not my words do good to him that walketh uprightly?" He still appeals to their consciences. The Spirit of God does not change, nor was it His doings, when the nation drifted into idolatry and judgment was impending. Still, if they but walked uprightly His words would surely do them good. But they had risen as an enemy against Him; and yet the Lord, in spite of all, called them "My people."

Verses 12-13. In this prophecy Christ is announced as the Breaker, the One who goes before them, clears the way, and removes every obstacle out of the way. In verse 10 we read, "Arise ye, and depart; for this is not your rest." The true rest for His people Israel comes when the King comes and brings with Him the promised blessing and glory. Then the remnant of Israel will be gathered, "and their king shall pass before them, and the Lord at the head of them." It is a great prophecy of the ultimate restoration of Israel. "We must not exclude all allusion to the deliverance of the Jewish nation out of the earthly Babylon by Cyrus; at the same time, it is only in its typical significance that this comes into consideration at all, namely, as a preliminary stage and pledge of the redemption to be effected by Christ."

THE SECOND PROPHETIC MESSAGE

CHAPTER 3

1. Address to the godless princes and judges (3:1-4)
2. Address to the false prophets (3:5-8)
3. The verdict of judgment (3:9-12)

Verses 1-4. The second prophetic message of Micah contains the great Messianic prophecies. But first the prophet gives a description of the degradation of the nation, the moral corruption of the leaders and judges, as well as the false prophets. It is all summed up in one sentence, "who hate the good, and love the evil." The princes and judges robbed the people, treated them like cattle (verse 3). For these unjust deeds the Lord would not hear them when they cried in the hour of their need, and would hide His face from them.

Verses 5-8. The false prophets were mostly responsible for these abominations, just as today the false in Christendom, the deniers of the faith, destructive critics and others, are responsible for the conditions in the professing Church. They make the people err. While they bite with their teeth, that is, being fed, they cried "peace" to their patrons; and those who did not support them, by putting food in their mouths, they fought and denounced. There would be night for them, with no vision; darkness would come upon them. They would be ashamed and confounded; the covering of the lips was a sign and emblem of mourning and silence. Such will be the fate of all false prophets and teachers.

The eighth verse is a magnificent outburst of God's true prophet, Micah's confession. As the true prophet he was full of power by the Spirit of the Lord, and thus filled he declared unto Jacob his transgression and to Israel his sin.

Verses 9-12. What Micah had announced in the preceding verse he does now. He tells the heads and rulers that they build Zion with blood and Jerusalem with iniquity. He speaks of the influence of money. Judges acted for reward, priests taught for hire, and prophets prophesied for money. The verdict of judgment is mentioned in Jer. 26:18. This prophecy was fulfilled when Babylon conquered Jerusalem. And when finally the returned remnant rejected the Lord of Glory, their King, Zion and Jerusalem became once more heaps, as he announced, "Jerusalem shall be trodden down by the Gentiles until the times of the Gentiles are fulfilled."

CHAPTER 4

1. The future of glory (4:1-5)
2. The restoration and the final victory (4:6-13)

Verses 1-5. The last verse predicted the long desolation and ruin of Zion. This is followed at once by a great prophecy of the future of glory in store for Zion. Isaiah also uttered this great prediction. Not that Micah copied Isaiah, nor Isaiah Micah, but the same Spirit gave to the men the same prophecy. It concerns the latter days, which means the coming of Messiah's kingdom on earth. These days are not yet here. To apply these words, even in a spiritual way, to the present age, or to the Church, is a serious mistake. The house of the Lord is not the Church, but the house in Jerusalem, to which in the kingdom the nations will come to worship the Lord of hosts. The nation will be judged and rebuked by Him whose glorious throne will be established in Jerusalem. Then, and only then, comes the time of universal, world-wide peace. How blind Christendom is in not seeing in what connection the favoured text concerning peace on earth stands! It will be "in that day" when "they shall beat their swords into plowshares and their spears into pruning hooks." The prediction of our Lord that throughout this age, down to its end, nation would lift up sword against nation, is then ended, and another order of things begins; for then "nation shall not lift up sword against nation, neither shall they learn war any more." What peace and prosperity will then follow! It is described in the fourth verse, "But they shall sit every man under his vine and under his fig tree; and none shall make them afraid: for the mouth of the Lord hath spoken it."

Verses 6-13. The regathering of all Israel then takes place. Not the boasting, proud, infidel, portion of the nation as it is today. Reform-Judaism and the other apostates in the nation will suffer judgment in the future as they did in the past. But there is a feeble, God-fearing remnant, and to that remnant belong the promises. "In that day, saith the Lord, will I assemble her that halteth, and I will gather her that is driven out, and her that I have afflicted." In His grace He will make the remnant a strong nation and reign over them in the established kingdom. To Zion shall return "the first dominion," that is, the reign and power and glory that was manifested in the monarchy under David and Solomon; only it will be greater than David's or Solomon's kingdom.

All this is preceded by her sorrow and captivity. It must be noticed that verse 10 goes beyond the Babylonian captivity, for it could not be said that the Lord redeemed in that past captivity Israel from the hands of her enemies. Nor was it true then that many nations were gathered against her. The Babylonian captivity is a type of the greater dispersion throughout this present age. When it ends, as it will end, the Lord will then redeem His people and deal in judgment with the opposing nations which finally gather against Jerusalem. (See the annotations of the last chapters of Zechariah.) He gathers the nations for the harvest time, when the sheaves are to be threshed. The daughter of Zion is to trample on them and beat them, and the grain, the riches of the Gentiles, will be consecrated unto the Lord. In connection with verses 11-13 the following Scriptures should be read and studied with the annotations: Joel 3; Ezekiel 38; Zechariah 12.

CHAPTER 5

1. The siege and the smitten judge (5:1)
2. The smitten judge: Who he is (5:2)
3. The events of the future: (5:3)
4. The Rejected One, the Shepherd of Israel (5:4-6)
5. The remnant of Jacob and the kingdom (5:7-15)

Verse 1. This interesting chapter presents difficulties, but they all vanish if we view all in the light of the future as revealed in the prophetic Word. Here it is necessary to divide the Word of Truth rightly, or we shall never find our way through this great Messianic chapter. The daughter of troops gathers herself in troops to besiege Jerusalem. It is the Assyrian army gathering before the city. But it is not the Assyrian of the past, whose invasion both Isaiah and Micah describe prophetically, but it is the Assyrian of the future, the great troubler which invades the land of Israel at the end-time, the time of Jacob's trouble, the great time of travail and final deliverance. This last invader, the king of the north (see Joel 2), besieges Jerusalem. And the reason of it all, their long history of trouble, culminating in the great tribulation, is the rejection of the judge of Israel. It is the Messiah, our Lord. They despised Him, insulted Him, smote Him with a rod upon the cheek. He is called the Judge of Israel, because the judge held the highest official position in Israel; the king of Israel held this office. The smiting upon the cheek was considered the greatest disgrace; thus Zedekiah smote the prophet Micaiah upon the cheek and asked him, "Which way went the Spirit of the Lord from me to speak to thee?" (See 1 Kings 22:24 and Matt. 26:67, 68). In Job 16:10 we read Job's complaint, "They have gaped upon me with their mouth; they have smitten me reproachfully upon the cheek; they have gathered themselves together against me."

Verse 2. This great verse is a parenthetical statement, giving a description of the Judge of Israel. It shows forth Him who is to be the Ruler and the Judge, the Redeemer and the King. It is the passage which the chief priests and the scribes quoted to wicked Herod, when he demanded to know where Christ should be born (Matt. 2:4-6). This great prophecy was therefore known when our Lord was born to predict the birth of the Messiah, in fact, the Jews always believed this. But after He was born and lived among them and was rejected by them they attempted deliberately to explain it away, and invented fables to accomplish this. It was Tertullian, and other prominent teachers of the early Church, who argued with the Jews, that if Jesus was not the promised Messiah, the prophecy given by Micah could never be fulfilled, for none of David's descendants was left in Bethlehem.

But here is more than an announcement of the birthplace of Christ. We have a wonderful description of His Person. He is to be the Son of David, coming out of David's city, destined to be the Ruler in Israel. But He is more than a descendant of David, "His goings forth have been of old, from everlasting." Even this plain announcement has not been left unattacked by the infidel critics. Dr. R. F. Horton in his comment on this passage says the following: "We are not called on to explain away this wonderful and solemn forecast, especially when we have seen it in the Babe of Bethlehem, who came into the world out of the bosom of the Father. Micah could not understand his own deep saying; but how foolish of us to discredit it when history has made its meaning plain."

Here we have His deity fully revealed as well as His humanity; He is the God-Man. In this passage Micah's testimony harmonizes with Isaiah's in chapter 9:6, 7.

Verse 3. The meaning of this verse becomes plain if we connect it with the first verse and treat the second verse as a parenthesis. They smote the Judge of Israel upon the cheek, they rejected the Lord of Glory, and as a result God gave them up. "Therefore will He give them up, until the time when she that travaileth hath brought forth; then the remnant of His brethren shall return to the children of Israel." It is often applied to the birth of Christ and connected with Revelation 12, the birth of the man-child. There can be no question that the man-child in the chapter of Revelation is Christ, and the woman described is Israel; but its exegetical meaning is in connection with the last days, when Israel will be in travail pains to give birth to the remnant, so prominently mentioned in prophecy. Since the nation rejected the Messiah they have had nothing but suffering, but the great travail pains come in the future. "For thus saith the Lord: We have heard a voice of trembling, of fear and not of peace. Ask ye now, and see whether a man doth travail with child? Wherefore do I see every man with his hands on his loins, as a woman in travail, and all faces are turned into paleness? Alas! for that day is great, so that none is like it, it is even the time of Jacob's trouble, but he shall be saved out of it." (Jer. 30:5-7). That godly remnant turning then to the Lord, born in that future travail, are called here "His brethren." They are the same of which our Lord spoke in the description of the judgment of nations, which He executes when sitting upon the throne of His glory. (See Matt. 25:31.) That remnant will resume their place as and with Israel, not becoming a part of the true Church, which is then no longer upon the earth, but having all the earthly Jewish hopes realized in the kingdom, of which they are the nucleus.

Verses 4-6. This refers to His second coming. He will stand and feed in the strength of Jehovah, for He is the Lord; and they (saved Israel) shall abide. Yea, more than that, "He shall be great unto the ends of the earth."

How beautiful is the opening sentence of the fifth verse! "This Man shall be peace (or our peace)." Of Him Isaiah spoke, too, as "the Prince of Peace," and that "of the increase of His government and peace there shall be no end." David in his great prophetic psalm (72:7) concerning these coming days speaks of "abundance of peace." Zechariah likewise in predicting the future says, "He shall speak peace to the nations" (Zech. 9:10). He made peace in the blood of His cross and for all who trust in Him He is peace, "for He is our Peace."

Here it concerns the peace He has and gives to His restored people Israel. He will be the peace for them, when the Assyrian, the king of the north, enters their land, and by His power will strike down the invader. Who are the seven shepherds and the eight principal men? They will be those who will be used in that day to stem back the invading hosts. Who they are is unknown, but it will be known at the time of fulfillment. Then Assyria, the land of Nimrod, as well as all opposing world powers will be completely ended.

Verses 7-15. The restored and blessed remnant of Jacob will possess a double character. They will be used in blessing and refreshing among the nations, "as dew from the Lord, as the showers upon the grass." On the other hand, they will be in the midst of many people as a lion and as a young lion, to avenge unrighteousness and opposition. All the adversaries and enemies of Israel will be cut down and cut off (Num. 24:9; see exposition of Balaam's parables at the close of annotations on Numbers). All the instruments of war will be done away with, as well as witchcrafts and the soothsayers. Spiritism, Christian Science, theosophy and all the other demon cults flourishing now, and still more before He comes, will find their ignominous end. Idolatry, the graven images, and the standing images will be abolished. Before the Lord comes the evil spirit of idolatry will once more seize hold on Israel, that is, among the apostates. (See annotations on Matt. 12:43-45.) While all this refers to Israel it also includes the rest of the world. All offences will be gathered out of His kingdom. The better rendering of verse 15 is, "And I will execute vengeance in anger and fury upon the nations which hearkened not." That is, during the end of the age God sent forth a testimony to the nations and those who hearkened not will fall under the wrath of the lion of the tribe of Judah.

THE THIRD PROPHETIC DISCOURSE (6—7)

CHAPTER 6

1. The words of Jehovah to His people (6:1-5)
2. Israel's answer (6:6-7)
3. The moral demands of Jehovah (6:8)
4. The Lord must judge them (6:9-16)

Verses 1-5. This chapter is cast in the form of a controversy. The utterance has been called by some the most important in the prophetic literature. It is hardly this, nor is, as critics claim, the eighth verse a definition of religion, "the greatest saying in the Old Testament."

The beginning is sublime, "Hear ye now what Jehovah saith!" The prophet is to arise and contend before the mountains so that the hills may hear his voice. The mountains and the enduring foundations of the earth are to hear the controversy the Lord has with His people and how He pleads with Israel.

Then follows the tender loving pleading of Jehovah, who still loves His people, in spite of their wickedness, "O My people, what have I done to thee?" What matchless condescension! The Lord whom they had rejected, from whom they had turned away, does not denounce them for their sins, nor does He enumerate them, but He asks whether He had been at fault. Had He done anything amiss towards them? Had He wearied His people? He is willing that they should testify against Him. Had He done anything that they should get tired of Him? We may imagine a pause here, as if He were waiting for an answer. But there is no answer.

He continues to speak. He had brought them out of Egypt, redeemed them out of the house of bondage; He had given them Moses, Aaron, and Miriam, by whom He led them. He reminded them of Balak, King of Moab, and Balaam, the son of Beor, who wanted to have

Israel cursed. But what had Balaam been forced to say? "How shall I curse whom God has not cursed!" What a faithful, loving God He had been to them.

Verses 6-7. Here the people speak, but it is significant that they do not address the Lord, who had spoken to them by the prophet. They knew themselves guilty and condemned. So they address the prophet and ask what to do. "Wherewith shall I come before the Lord, and bow myself before the high God? shall I come before Him with burnt offerings, with calves of a year old? Will the Lord be pleased with thousands of rams, or with ten thousand rivers of oil? Shall I give my firsborn for my transgression, the fruit of my body for the sin of my soul?" For generations they had brought burnt offerings, thousands of rams and rivers of oil. But it was nothing but an outward worship; inwardly they remained the same. But they were willing to do more in this outward service, even to the sacrifice of the firstborn. Isaiah 1:10-18 is an interesting commentary to these questions, showing how the Lord despised these ceremonies of a people who were evil doers and corrupters. (See also Psalm 50:7-23.)

Verse 8. The prophet gives the answer of Jehovah. "He hath showed thee, O man, what is good; and what doth the Lord require of thee, but to do justly, and to love mercy, and to walk humbly with thy God?" Where has God made the demand? In the law. There is no more deadly error than to hold up this verse as the essence of the gospel and the one true, saving religion. Yet this we hear today on all sides. But the most loud-mouthed advocates of this "saving religion" practise what the Lord demands the least. And there is a good reason for it. Israel did not act in righteousness, nor did they love mercy, nor did they walk humbly in fellowship with the Lord. Why not? Because they were uncircumcised in their hearts. To do right, to love mercy, to walk in humility with God is impossible for the natural man; in order to do this there must be the new birth, and the new birth takes place when the sinner believes and expresses his faith in true repentance. Only a blind leader of the blind can say this verse is the gospel, and that faith in the deity of Christ and in His atoning, ever blessed work on the cross is not needed. Israel never has been anything like this which Jehovah demands. The day is coming when the Lord in His grace will give them a new heart and take away the stony heart, and fill them with His spirit. (See. Ezek. 36.)

Verses 9-16. The Lord speaks again and puts before them once more their moral degeneration. Wicked balances, deceitful weights, the deeds of unrighteousness. They were destitute of mercy, for they were full of violence, lies and deceit. Therefore judgment must now fall upon them.

CHAPTER 7

1. The prophet's complaint (7:1-6)
2. Confession, prayer and thanksgiving (7:7-20)

Verses 1-6. It is the prophet's voice complaining over the conditions of the people. But he is also the typical representative of the remnant during the time of travail in Zion. It is to be noted that our Lord quotes from this portion of Micah. (See Matt. 10:21, which dispensationally applies to the future remnant.) In the midst of the conditions the prophet describes we read that his refuge was prayer, looking to the Lord with the assurance that He will hear. "Therefore I will look unto the Lord; I will wait for the God of my salvation; my God will hear me." This will be the attitude of the godly Israelites during the time of trouble.

Verses 7-20. It is Israel speaking in the remnant, represented by the prophet. The enemy is addressed; at the time of Micah it was the Assyrian, the type of the end Assyrian; but it includes all the world powers in their anti-Semitic attitude. The real Israel has always had this comfort, founded on the fact that God's gifts and calling are without repentance, that they are the elect nation, that their fall must be followed by a spiritual and national resurrection (Rom. 11). Hence they say, "Rejoice not against me, mine enemy; when I fall I shall rise again; when I sit in darkness, the Lord will be a light unto me." This will be the case when their greatest darkness comes in the end of the age (Isa. 60).

It is a willing submission to the chastisement of the Lord expressed in verse 9; they acknowledge their sins and once more declare, "He will bring me forth to light, and I shall behold his righteousness."

This is followed by a prophetic declaration. The day is coming when her walls will be built again, and in that day shall the decree be far removed. The latter statement may mean the same which the prophet Jeremiah reveals in chapter 31:31 to the end of the chapter. The old decree, or law, will end, and there will be the new covenant into which Judah and Israel enter "in that day." Then the nations will gather to restored Israel in the kingdom. (Compare verse 12 with Isa. 60:3-10.)

In the meantime the land will be desolate, as it is now, the fruit of their evil doings, till the day comes when the wilderness will be a fruitful field (Isa. 32:16) when the desert shall rejoice and blossom as the rose (Isa. 35:1).

Once more the prophet's voice is heard in supplication. The prayer in verse 14 is answered by the Lord in verses 15-17. The Lord will show again in that day the marvelous things as He did in their past redemption out of Egypt. The nations, their enemies, will be witness to it; they will be humiliated in the dust.

The three concluding verses belong to the greatest in the Old Testament Scriptures. Here we listen to a great praise and outburst of adoration. "Who is a God like unto Thee, that pardoneth iniquity, and passeth by the transgression of the remnant of His heritage? He retaineth not His anger forever, because He delighted in mercy. He will turn again, He will have compassion upon us; He will subdue our iniquities; and Thou wilt cast all their sins into the depths of the sea. Thou wilt perform the truth to Jacob, and the mercy to Abraham, which Thou hast sworn unto our fathers from the days of old."

Such will be the future praise of the remnant of His heritage, when the Deliverer comes to Zion and turns away ungodliness from Jacob, when the covenant with them will be consummated and their sins will be taken away (Rom. 11:26, 27). Once a year orthodox Jews go to a running stream and scatter into it bits of paper and small articles, repeating while they do it these three verses (the so-called Tashlik ceremony). It is but an outward act, yet testifying that there is still faith in Israel. It will be a glorious day when God forgives them their sins and remembers them no more.

THE PROPHET NAHUM

Introduction

Nahum's history is unknown. All we know of him is that he was an Elkoshite. His name means "comforter." Some have identified Elkosh with a village of similar name which is in existence today, not far from the site of ancient Nineveh, on the eastern banks of the Tigris. There the grave of Nahum is shown, adored alike by nominal Christians and the followers of Mohammed. But careful research has shown this to be absolutely without any foundation whatever. No one knew anything about that grave till about the sixteenth century of our era. It is the Elkosh which existed in Galilee and which is still known as a little village. Nahum, like Jonah, was a Galilean.

The Date of Nahum

The opening verse does not give a hint as to the time Nahum lived and prophesied. Critics, on account of some Assyrian expressions found in the book have put the date later. From internal evidences we can ascertain the date without difficulty. Judah and not Israel is addressed by Nahum. There is no reason to assume that he lived in exile and uttered his prophecy in the land of Assyria. He spoke in the land of Israel, probably in Jerusalem. The most significant passage which gives us important information is chapter 1:11: "There is one come out of thee (out of Assyria) that imagineth evil against the Lord, a wicked counsellor." Who was this wicked counsellor, who imagined evil against the Lord? There can be but one answer. A wicked counsellor came out of Assyria, the mouthpiece of its reigning King Sennacherib. His name was Rab-shakeh. He blasphemed and defied the God of Israel. His vile words are recorded in 2 Kings 18:26-27. The description of Nahum fits this Assyrian villian. We are justified in placing Nahum in the period of Hezekiah; he was therefore contemporary with Isaiah and Micah.

There is an interesting link between Jonah, Micah and Nahum. Jonah was sent with the message to Nineveh about one hundred and fifty years before Nahum prophesied. Through his message Nineveh turned to the Lord. Isaiah and Micah prophesied concerning the same Assyrian power, the capital of which was Nineveh. They witnessed the Assyrian attack upon Jerusalem and Jehovah's intervention in behalf of His people. They saw the downfall of the kingdom of Israel through Assyria and were well acquainted with the wickedness of the Assyrian. And then came Nahum from Galilee, and the Spirit of God gave through him the great message of the coming complete destruction of Nineveh.

Assyrian History

A knowledge of Assyrian history, and its great capital, Nineveh, is needed for a better understanding of Nahum's prophecy. It is strange that ancient writers like Ctesias, the physician of Artaxerxes, Mnemon, and Diodorus Siculus have but little to say about Assyria, and many identified Assyria with Babylonia. The infidel critics have seen their defeat in this respect. Not believing the Bible, they trusted in the historical accounts of pagan writers, and assuming that they were right discredited the Word of God, only to find out afterward that the Bible is right and the heathen historians were wrong. For instance, Isaiah mentions in chapter 20 Sargon, king of Assyria. Because the secular historians know nothing of such a king, they sat in judgment upon the Word of God. They denied that such a king ever existed, thinking that the statement by Isaiah is an invention. It was then proven that Sargon was a great warrior, the father of Sennacherib, and that Isaiah gave a true record.

Hezekiah, the King of Judah, under whom Nahum as well as Isaiah and Micah prophesied, had paid tribute for many years to Assyria. When he revolted an Assyrian army appeared in the land, by which over forty Judean cities were captured. Jerusalem itself was saved by divine intervention (Isa. 37:36). Sennacherib, who had sent the expedition against Jerusalem, being murdered by his own sons in 681 B.C. (Isa. 37:38). His successor was Esarhaddon, who besieged Sidon and carried its treasures to Nineveh. Asshurbanipal succeeded him to the throne and made his son Shamash-shumukin regent of Babylon, for Babylon was then an insignificant power. Here we must remember that when Babylon was next to nothing in world history, Isaiah had predicted its coming greatness and conquest of Jerusalem by the Babylonian power. Under Asshurbanipal the ancient and great capital of Upper Egypt was captured, which is mentioned by Nahum in chapter 3:10; that is, No-Amon is Thebes. Asshurbanipal conquered many countries and nations; he razed Susa, and immense treasures were carried off to Nineveh. During his reign every year saw a cruel war, and ruin and carnage were spread in every direction. The captives were treated in a horrible manner, with all kinds of torture. The nations suffered terribly under this wicked monarch, so that when finally Assyria fell the nations rejoiced, as mentioned by Nahum at the conclusion of his prophecy. "All that hear the bruit of thee shall clap hands over thee; for upon whom hath not thy wickedness passed continually?" After Asshurbanipal Assyria declined. He was followed by Asshur-etil-ilani and Sin-shar-ishkun, and finally Assyria and its great and proud capital were conquered by Nabopolassar, the father of Nebuchadnezzar and Cyaxares. This happened about 625 B.C., just about ninety years after Nahum announced the destruction of Nineveh.

The Message of Nahum

His prophetic message concerns exclusively Nineveh. Critics have put question marks over against certain parts of this book, while other critics have contradicted their fellow critics. In fact, if one wishes to find theories and assumptions, wild guesses and fanciful hypotheses, the camp of the rationalist is the place. The unity and integrity of the prophecy of Nahum is beyond controversy. As the opening verse announces, it is the burden of Nineveh.

Typically Nineveh stands for the world powers to the end of the times of the Gentiles, and its overthrow foreshadows the overthrow of the final world powers.

The Division of Nahum

The three chapters of which Nahum is composed give us the correct division of his prophecy. In the first chapter we find the purpose of God is dealing in judgment with the oppressor of Israel. The second chapter describes the overthrow, the plundering, and destruction of Nineveh. The third chapter shows the guilt and the well-deserved judgment and ruin of Nineveh.

Analysis and Annotations

CHAPTER 1

The Purpose of God in Dealing with the Assyrian Oppressor

1. The superscription (1:1)
2. Jehovah's majesty in judgment (1:2-6)
3. His people conforted and assured (1:7-13)
4. The judgment of Assyria and the result (1:14-15)

Verse 1. The burden of Nineveh; it means that there is to follow a weighty prophetic oracle concerning the great world city of Nineveh whose dimensions are given by Jonah, which have been confirmed by excavations. The next sentence gives us the definite information that what follows in the book is the vision of Nahum the Elkoshite.

Verses 2-6. It is a sublime description. God is a jealous God. The jealousy of God has for its source the love of His elect people. (See Zech 1.) "For thou shalt worship no other god; for the Lord, whose name is jealous, is a jealous God." He is jealous over His people lest they serve other gods. And because He is a jealous God, a holy, a sin-hating God, He must be an avenger of what is against His character. He will take vengeance on His adversaries and reserveth wrath for His enemies. Destructive criticism has invented an infidel theory as if the God of wrath and vengeance were the product of the mind of man, and that Jehovah is some tribal deity, corresponding to the tribal gods of the surrounding heathen nations. Thus criticism rejects the Jehovah of the Bible and invents its own god, rejecting the threatenings of coming wrath and judgment as taught in the Old Testament and in the New in connection with the coming of the Lord, branding these revelations the result of the false apocalyptic teachings of the Jews. God is the God of Love, as much as He is the God of Wrath. He must be that or He would not be the God of Light and Holiness. He cannot afford to let evil go on forever. He is the Lord slow to anger. His patience is great, but He will not acquit the guilty, who continue to sin and do evil. Verses 2 and 3 describe His righteous government. Then follows a beautiful poetic description of His majesty, a description suited to the finite mind of man.

In whirlwind and storm is His way,
And clouds are the dust of His feet.
He rebuketh the sea and drieth it up

And empties all the rivers.
Carmel, Bashan, and Lebanon are thinned out,
And the Flower of Lebanon languisheth.
Mountains quake before Him
And all the hills melt away;
And the earth is consumed in His presence,
The world and all that dwell therein.
Before His indignation who can stand?
And who can abide His fierce anger?
His fury is poured out like fire.
And the rocks are thrown down by Him.

What to the mind of man is more imposing than the towering storm-clouds, and what more terrifying than the onrushing whirlwind, which lays low the forest? Man, the creature of the dust, steps upon the dust of the earth, to which man returns in the hour of death. But Jehovah has the clouds as the dust of His feet. If He arises in His righteous wrath all will be swept before Him, and the mountains, symbolical of the kingdoms of the earth, will quake before Him, and the pride of man will be humbled in the dust. (Isa. 2).

Verses 7-13. While in the foregoing section He speaks of His own character in dealing with evil, He now gives comfort and assurance to those who trust in Him, that is, to His people. He knoweth them, the comfort all His people have at all times, the Lord knoweth them that are His, and as our Lord said, "I know my sheep." For such the Lord is good and a stronghold in the day of trouble. But His enemies will feel His wrath. "But with an overrunning flood He will make an utter end of the place thereof (Nineveh) and darkness will pursue His enemies."

In the prophetic application we must look beyond the horizon of Nahum's time and the judgment of Nineveh. The day of the Lord brings the final overthrow of the proud world powers, and the remnant of His people will have in the Lord a refuge, while the judgment floods sweep over the earth (see Psa. 46).

On the ninth verse many expositors have erred in their interpretation. It is also addressed to Israel. "What do ye imagine against the Lord?" Do you imagine that the Lord is not going to do it? Will He repent of His judgment purpose? No! He who has spoken "will make an utter end," and to His people it is spoken "affliction shall not rise up the second time."

Then a description of the Assyrian in verse 10. They are entangled like thorns, so that they will find no escape when the judgment overtakes them, while they are drunk with wine in their carousings. Like the dry stubble are they to be devoured. Rab-shakeh, as mentioned in our introduction, is the one who came out of Assyria against Jerusalem with evil imaginations. The better translation of verse 12 is, "Though they be strong, and likewise many, even so shall they be cut down, and he (the Assyrian) shall pass away."

The second half of the twelfth verse concerns His people. "Though I have afflicted thee, I will afflict thee no more." One can see at once that the "no more" demands a future fulfillment. For, while it is true, the Assyrian did no longer afflict Israel, yet affliction upon affliction has been their lot. But there comes the day when all afflictions will cease. "For now I will break his yoke (the yoke of the Assyrian) from off thee (Israel) and I will burst thy bonds asunder."

Verses 14-15. The fourteenth verse gives the judgment commandment as to Assyria and Nineveh. They are vile, and the God who declared His character in the beginning of this message, is going to act accordingly.

The result is stated in the last verse of this chapter. "Behold, upon the mountains the feet of him that bringeth good tidings, that publisheth peace! O Judah, keep thy solemn feasts, perform thy vows; for the wicked shall no more pass through thee; he is utterly cut off." The prophet beholds how the messengers rush over the mountains with the good news. Judah and Jerusalem are delivered. Peace has come. Praise and thanksgiving are heard in Zion.

We must not overlook the similar passage in Isaiah 52:7. "How beautiful upon the mountains are the feet of him that bringeth good tidings, that publisheth peace, that bringeth good tidings of good, that publisheth salvation, that saith unto Zion, Thy God reigneth! . . . Break forth into joy, sing together, ye waste places of Jerusalem; for the Lord hath comforted His people, He hath redeemed Jerusalem. The Lord hath made bare His holy arm in the eyes of all the nations; and all the ends of the earth shall see the salvation of our God." This was spoken in connection with Babylon's overthrow, but its wider application and meaning is future. The overthrow of Babylon and Nineveh did not result in the glorious things spoken of by Isaiah and Nahum. Not then did the ends of the earth see the salvation of God, nor was Jerusalem redeemed, nor God as King enthroned in Zion. It is all yet to come. When that day comes, the messengers will go forth from Jerusalem and declare the good tidings to the nations of the world. The good news of the kingdom will be heralded far and wide, in the beginning of the millennium, and then the abiding, abundant peace will come, so that all the nations see the salvation of the God of Israel. The wicked, opposing powers of the world will then be no more.

CHAPTER 2

The Overthrow, Plundering, and Destruction of Nineveh

1. The capture of Nineveh announced and described (2:1-10)
2. The completeness of the judgment (2:11-13)

Verses 1-10. This great prophecy was literally fulfilled some ninety years after Nahum had spoken. When these words were spoken Nineveh was in the zenith of her glory. Who told Nahum the Elkoshite that the proud world city would undergo such a sack and be completely wiped out? Who moved his pen to give such a vivid descsription of what would take place? There is but one answer—the Spirit of God. How was the prophecy fulfilled? Cyaxares of the Medes had surrounded Nineveh in the north. Nabopolassar of Babylon entered into an alliance with Cyaxares against the Assyrians, which was sealed by the marriage of the daughter of Cyaxares, Amunia, with the son of Nabopolassar, that is, Nebuchadnezzar, who appeared then as the colleague of his father, till the Lord called him as the instrument of judgment upon Jerusalem and he became the head of the Babylonian monarchy (Dan. 11). They made an assault upon Nineveh. The Assyrian king, a son of Asshurbanipal, collected all his forces into the lower part of the immense city. Three times the forces of the Assyrian sallied forth from the city and inflicted severe punishment upon the besieging armies, and Nabopolassar had great difficulty in keeping the Median forces from flight. The Assyrians after these successes abandoned themselves to great carousings, as stated in Nahum 1:10. But during that night they were attacked by the besiegers and driven back behind the walls. Then the troops which were under the command of the brother-in-law of the Assyrian king were routed and driven into the river Tigris. The main part of Nineveh was still safe. In the third year of the siege the river which surrounded the city became its enemy. Great rains had fallen and suddenly there was a tremendous flood which broke down the walls surrounding the city. This was predicted by Nahum in this chapter in the sixth verse. The king despaired of saving his life. He had sent his family north, and when all hope was gone he shut himself up with all his treasures in the royal citadel and burned himself with them. Then the victors entered into the city, and, after securing an immense booty, which was carried to Babylon and Ecbatana, the Babylonians set fire to the sacked city, and destroyed it completely by fire.

The prophet in the beginning of this chapter addresses Nineveh; he urges that she make ready to defend herself, for he that dasheth into pieces has appeared before her walls. It was the Lord who had used the Assyrian to bring judgment upon Israel and upon Jacob, but now the time had come for the restoration of their former excellency. The Authorized Version gives the wrong sense, and the second verse is correctly rendered: "For the Lord bringeth again the excellency of Jacob, as the excellency of Israel; for the emptiers have emptied them out, and marred their vine branches." Then the besieging army is described. Here we read of their glittering arms, their fast racing chariots, which dash along like lightning.

We have heard even reputable Bible teachers make the statement that Nahum predicted the automobiles racing along our streets. Such fanciful, far-fetched and arbitrary applications of the Word of God do immense harm. Nahum does not anticipate the automobile, but gives a picture of the besiegers of Nineveh with their chariots, drawn by swift horses.

In verse 5 the Assyrian king is seen turning to his army, as he sees the chariots dashing along the highways and broadways which lead to the city; he counts his worthies, his generals and captains. And the army suddenly called, in making haste stumbled along in disorder and made haste to reach the walls. As stated above, the sixth verse was fulfilled when the river became a flood and undermined the foundations of the walls, so that the besiegers could enter in. And when Babylon fell, under the grandson of Nebuchadnezzar, the river also was the means of defeat, for the enemy had diverted the river Euphrates and through the dry river-bed entered the city.

The word "Huzzab" in the seventh verse has led to a great deal of discussion. Some claim that it is the name of the queen of Nineveh; others that it is a symbolical name of the city; archaeology throws no light upon its meaning. We believe the word "Huzzab" should be translated, "it is determined." Then the sentence reads, "It is determined; she is made bare and led away captive; and her maids moan like the doves, smiting upon their breasts."

The flight of the population of Nineveh is pictured in the eighth verse. Like as a pool of water empties when the sluices are opened, so they flee. The soldiers cry "Stand! Stand!" but there is a panic. They rush away and none looks back.

In the next two verses the plundering of the city is predicted. Silver and gold is taken away. There seems to be no end of all the glorious things which were heaped together in Nineveh. The city is emptied; hearts melt, courage is gone; there are tottering knees and pale faces.

Verses 11-13. Is it a sarcastic question which is asked, "Where is the den of lions?" What has become of her proud boastings of being the Queen-City of the nations?

Then Jehovah speaks of the completeness of her judgment and overthrow. "Behold, I am against thee, saith the Lord of hosts, and I will burn her chariots in the smoke, and I will cut off thy prey from the earth, and the voice of thy messengers shall no more be heard."

CHAPTER 3

Nineveh's Guilt and Well-Deserved Judgment

1. The great wickedness of Nineveh (3:1-7)
2. Her fate to be like the fate of No-Amon (3:8-13)
3. Her well-deserved and complete judgment (3:14-19)

Verses 1-7. Nineveh was a bloody city, for her kings never knew peace, but were constantly at war. The Hebrew *Ir-Damim* means "city of blood drops." They boasted of making the blood of their enemies run like rivers. It was a city full of lies and rapine. Her word could not be trusted; she broke truces and covenants and deceived nations with lying promises of help and protection. As stated in the second chapter, she was ferocious as a lion and the prey never departed.

But she received as she had sown. The next two verses give again the scenes of carnage during her judgment hour.

The cracking of the whip;
And the noise of the rattling wheels;
The prancing of the horses,
And the dashing chariots.

The horseman mounting;
And the flashing sword,
And the glittering of the spear;
And the multitude of the slain;
And the heaps of the corpses.
There is no end of dead bodies;
They stumble over their corpses.

And why? "Because of the multitudes of the whoredoms of the well-favored harlot, the mistress of witchcrafts, that selleth nations through her whoredoms, and families through her witchcrafts." She made herself attractive as a harlot does, to ensnare and beguile weaker nations. Like all these ancient cities she was filled with witchcrafts, that is, sorceries. The power of darkness manifested itself in the dominion of evil spirits, which Nineveh courted. Spiritism, as advocated today by men of research and culture, of the type of Oliver Lodge and Conan Doyle, and a multitude of others, is not a new thing. Egypt, Babylon, and Nineveh and other centers of paganism were filled with occultism, the practice of which hastened their doom; as the doom of our age will be consummated through the influence of the same evil powers.

Then Jehovah speaks again, as the God of retribution and judgment. These are solemn words.

Behold! I am against thee, saith the
  Lord of hosts;
And uncover thy skirts over thy face,
And display to the nations thy nakedness,
And to kingdoms thy shame!
And I will cast vileness upon thee,
And disgrace thee
And make thee a gazing-stock.

And it shall come to pass,
That all that look upon thee
Shall flee from thee,
And say, Nineveh is laid waste;
Who will lament over her?
Whence shall I seek comforters for her?

She had acted the harlot and now she receives the punishment of a harlot, which consisted in exposing her in public. She would be a gazing-stock for nations and kingdoms, as the righteous God stripped her of all and exposed her shame. There would be no one to lament over the vile mistress of witchcrafts.

Verses 8-13. "Art thou better than No-Amon that dwelt by the rivers? Waters were round about her; her bulwark was the sea and her wall was of the sea. Ethiopia and Egypt were her strength, and there was no limit; Put and Lubim were thy helpers." No-Amon was an Egyptian city, known to the Greeks by the name of Thebes. The judgment of No-Amon, or, as it is also called, "No," was announced by the prophet Jeremiah. "The Lord of Hosts, the God of Israel saith, Behold I will punish the multitude of No, and Pharaoh and Egypt, with their gods and their kings, even Pharaoh and them that trust in him" (Jer. 46:25). Ezekiel likewise had spoken of this great Egyptian city (Ezek. 30:14-16). There existed an immense temple there in honor of the god of No, the building had great facades and columns and covered a large space; the ruins which are left are still most wonderful to look upon. It was situated on the upper Nile some four hundred miles from Cairo, and was built along the river front. On the other side of the river was the city of the dead, the Necropolis, with a long line of temples, devoted to the worship of former Pharaohs, and behind these temples were thousands of tombs, many of which have been uncovered by the spade of the explorer. The cuneiform monuments tell of the fate of Thebes. Though she was defended by the strong men of Ethiopia and of Egypt and Phut, and the Libyans, nothing could avert her doom. She was carried into captivity, her young children were dashed in pieces, and her great men were bound in chains. Could then Nineveh hope to escape? The fate of No-Amon was a prophecy of Nineveh's fate. She was even more wicked than the Egyptian city. Her fate is described in verses 11-13.

Verses 14-19. Dramatically the prophet calls upon Nineveh to draw water for the siege, to secure clay for brick to repair the breaches in the wall. But all would be useless, for the Almighty had decreed her downfall. The fire would devour the proud city, the sword do its havoc in cutting them off. Let them be as numerous as the cankerworm (see annotations of Joel 1), make thyself as many as the locusts, which come in immense swarms, and it will be all to no avail. Her great commerce, her merchant-princes, were a vast host, like the stars of heaven, but all would soon be devastated, as the cankerworm spoileth and then flies away. Their crowned ones, the chiefs in authority, would all be scattered just as the sun-rise scatters the locusts and swarms of grasshoppers to a place unknown. Their shepherds, the leaders and rulers, under the King of Assyria, would sleep in death, while the population wandered homeless over the mountains, with none to gather them.

Nineveh's ruin is complete and irreparable. All who hear of her fall rejoice and clap their hands.

THE PROPHET
HABAKKUK

Introduction

There is a very interesting diversity among these minor prophets. Hosea starts with the command of the Lord for a symbolical action to show Israel her spiritual whoredoms. Joel plunges in at once to describe the judgment of the land by the locusts and leads on to the day of the Lord. Amos begins with the announcement of the judgment of the surrounding nations, while Obadiah is chiefly concerned with the judgment of Edom. Jonah is different from all the rest in his miraculous experience, while Micah has a character of his own. Nahum, as we saw, has the one great message of the doom of Nineveh, and brings comfort to God's people. Habakkuk again is different from all the rest. In nature God displays as Creator a wonderful diversity, and so in His revelation His Spirit uses every instrument in His own way, as it pleases Him.

Of Habakkuk the same holds good as with most of the other minor prophets; we know nothing of the particulars of his life. It does not matter much. God knows these holy men, whom He called to make known His will and the future, and He has kept the record of their lives, as He keeps the record of all of our lives.

His name means "to embrace," but it has the double meaning "to embrace" and "being embraced." He embraced his own people and embraced God in prayer, then "being embraced"—God answered him. Dr. Martin Luther gave a very striking definition of his name, which cannot be improved upon. "Habakkuk signifies an embracer, or one who embraces another, takes him into his arms. He embraces his people, and takes them to his arms, i.e., he comforts them and holds them up, as one embraces a weeping child, to quiet it with the assurance that if God wills it shall soon be better."

It has been assumed that he probably sprang, like Jeremiah and Ezekiel, from a priestly family, for at the end of the great ode, at the conclusion of the book, he states—"to the chief singer on my stringed instruments," from which we may gather that he was officially qualified to take part of the temple service. But Isaiah 38:20 seems to contradict this.

An apocryphal book, "Bel and the Dragon," states that Habakkuk was miraculously transported to Daniel, who had been cast a second time to the lions by Cyrus. This and other legends are without any foundation at all, and need not be examined, for they are worthless.

The Date of Habakkuk

As it is with Nahum, so it is with Habakkuk, the superscription does not fix a definite date, but the contents of the book do not leave us in doubt about the time when this man of God prophesied.

In the sixth verse of the opening chapter we read, "For, lo, I raise up the Chaldeans, that bitter and hasty nation, which shall march through the breadth of the land, to possess the dwelling places that are not theirs." He therefore prophesied at the time when the Chaldeans, or as they are also called the Babylonians, were coming into power, and soon to be used against the house of Judah, as the Assyrian was used in judgment with the house of Israel. He prophesied during the reign of Josiah, that is at the very close of his reign, and a few years before Nineveh was destroyed, which elevated the Babylonians to the place of prominence. Some have put the date into the reign of Manasseh, the father of Josiah, but this is too early. Josiah died on the battlefield, and after his son Jehoahaz had reigned three months, Pharaohnecho, who had slain Josiah, made Eliakim, the son of Josiah, king over Judah, and gave him the name of Jehoiakim. (See 2 Kings 23:28-37.)

The Message of Habakkuk

The langugae which Habakkuk used is extremely beautiful. Professor Delitzsch speaks of it as follows: "His language is classical throughout, full of rare and select turns and words, which are to some extent exclusively his own, whilst his view and mode of presentation bear the seal of independent force and finished beauty. Notwithstanding the violent rush and lofty soaring of the thoughts, his prophecy forms a finely organized and artistically rounded whole. Like Isaiah, he is, comparatively speaking, much more independent of his predecessors, both in contents and form, than any of the other prophets." "Everything reflects the time when prophecy was in its greatest glory, when the place of the sacred lyrics, in which the religious life had expressed itself, was occupied, through a still mightier interposition on the part of God, by prophetic poetry with its trumpet voice." Much in his message is in the form of communion with the Lord. He begins with the familiar heart-cry, "O Lord, how long shall I cry?" He receives an answer, which announces the coming of the Chaldeans, to which again the prophet replies. Then he said, "I will stand upon my watch, and will set me upon the tower, and will watch and see what He will say unto me" (chapter 2). Then he receives another answer. The judgment of Judah by the Chaldeans as well as the overthrow of the Chaldeans, on account of the deification of their power, is the prophetic message with which he starts.

Sublime is the great lyric ode contained in the third chapter, which begins with a prayer (chapter 3). It is one of the greatest descriptions of the theophany, the coming of the Lord, which the Spirit of God has given. He comes in glory and in wrath; the wicked are overthrown, His people are saved. It waits for its great fulfillment when our Lord Jesus Christ shall be revealed from heaven in flaming fire with His holy angels.

The Division of Habakkuk

The division is very simple. Chapter 1 forms the first part and gives the coming invasion of Judah by the Chaldeans. In chapter 2 the "woe" is pronounced upon the Chaldeans and their destruction is predicted. The third chapter contains the vision of the coming of the Lord, with which all the ungodly world powers terminate, and the dominion of the Gentiles ends.

Inasmuch as the Authorized Version contains numerous incorrect renderings, we give a complete text in a metric version.

The Prophet Habakkuk

CHAPTER 1

1. The burden, which Habakkuk, the prophet saw.
2. How long, O Lord, must I cry
   And Thou hearest not?
   I cry to Thee; Violence!
   And Thou dost not help.
3. Why dost Thou show me iniquity,
   And cause me to behold grievance?
   Oppression and violence are before me;
   There is strife, and contention ariseth.
4. Therefore the law is slacked;
   And justice doth never go forth
   For the wicked compass about the righteous;
   Therefore justice goes forth perverted.
5. Behold ye among the nations and regard!
   And wonder marvellously;
   For I work a work in your days
   Which ye will not believe, though it were told.
6. For behold! I raise up the Chaldeans,
   That bitter and impetuous nation,
   Which march through the breadth of the earth.
   To possess dwelling-places that are not theirs.
7. They are terrible and dreadful,
   Their judgment and dignity proceed from themselves.
8. Swifter than leopards are their hoses,
   And fiercer than the evening wolves.
   Their horsemen shall spread themselves,
   And their horsemen shall come from afar.
   They fly like an eagle hastening to devour.
9. All of them come for violence;
   The host of their faces is forward;
   And they gather captives like the sand.
10. Yea, he scoffeth at kings,
    And princes are a derision unto him.
    He laughs at every stronghold
    For he heapeth up earth and taketh it.
11. Then he sweepth by as a tempest
    And shall pass over and be guilty,
    He whose might is his god.
12. Art Thou not from Everlasting,
    Jehovah, my God, my Holy One?
    We shall not die!
    Jehovah! Thou has appointed them for judgment;
    And Thou, O Rock! Thou has established him for chastisement.
13. Thou art of purer eyes than to behold evil;
    Thou canst not look upon injustice.
    Why lookest Thou upon the treacherous?
    Why art Thou silent when the wicked destroys
    The man that is more righteous than he?

14. And Thou makest men like fishes of the sea,
Like reptiles that have no ruler.
15. All of them he lifts up with the hook,
He catcheth them in His net
And gathers them in his drag;
Therefore he rejoices and is glad.

16. Therefore he sacrificeth to his net,
And burneth incense to his drag,
Because by them his portion is rich,
And his food plenteous.
17. Shall he, therefore, empty his net,
And spare not to slay the nations continually?

CHAPTER 2

1. I will stand upon my watch,
And set me upon the tower,
And I will wait to see what He will say to me,
And what I shall answer as to my complaint.
2. And Jehovah answered me and said:
Write the vision and make it plain on tablets,
That he may run that reads it.
3. For the vision is yet for the appointed time,
And it hastens to the end, and shall not lie;
Though it tarry, wait for it;
Because it will surely come, it will not tarry.
4. Behold the proud:
His soul is not right within him;
But the just shall live by faith.
5. And moreover, wine is treacherous;
A haughty man, that keepeth not at home:
Who enlargeth this desire as Sheol,
As death he is and cannot be satisfied,
And gathereth all nations to himself
And heapeth unto him all peoples.
6. Will not all these take up a song against him?
And a taunting proverb against him, and say:
Woe to him who increaseth what is not his own!
How long?
And that ladeth himself with pledges.
7. Will not thy biters rise up suddenly,
And those awake that shall shake thee violently?
And thou wilt become a prey to them.
8. Because thou hast plundered many nations,
All the remnant of the peoples shall plunder thee;
Because of men's blood, and for the violence done to the land,
To the city and all that dwell therein.
9. Woe to him that procureth a wicked gain for his house,
To set his nest on high,
To secure himself from the hand of disaster.
10. Thou has devised shame for thy house,
By cutting off many peoples, and sinning against thyself.
11. For the stone crieth out from the wall,
And the beam out of the wood-work answers it.
12. Woe to him that buildeth a town with blood,
And founds a city by iniquity.
13. Behold is it not from Jehovah of hosts,
That the peoples labor for the fire,
And the nations weary themselves for vanity?
14. For the earth shall be filled
With the knowledge of the glory of Jehovah,
As the waters cover the sea.
15. Woe to him that giveth his neighbor to drink,
Pouring out thy fury, and also making drunk,
In order to look upon their nakedness.
16. Thou art filled with shame instead of glory,
Drink thou also, and be like the uncircumcised:
The cup of Jehovah's right hand shall be turned to thee,
And vile shame shall be upon thy glory.
17. For the violence done to Lebanon shall cover thee,
And the destruction of wild beasts which made them afraid,
Because of the blood of men, and the violence done to the land,
To the city and all that dwell therein.
18. What profiteth a graven image, that its maker has carved?
The molten image, and the teacher of lies,
That the maker of his image trusts therein, to make dumb idols?

19. Woe to him that saith to the wood,
Awake;
To the dumb stone, Arise!
Shall it teach? Behold it is overlaid with
gold and silver;
And there is no breath in its inside.
20. But Jehovah is in His holy temple.
Let all the earth be silent before Him.

CHAPTER 3

1. A prayer of Habakkuk, the prophet, set
to Shigionoth.
2. O Jehovah! I have heard the report of
Thee. I am afraid!
O Jehovah! revise Thy work in the midst
of the years;
In the midst of the years make it known;
In wrath remember mercy.
3. God cometh from Teman,
And the Holy One from Mount Paran.—
Selah.
His glory covereth the heavens,
And the earth is full of His glory.
4. His brightness is like the sun;
Rays are streaming from His hand;
And there is the hiding of His power.
5. Before Him goeth the pestilence;
And fiery bolts follow His feet.
6. He standeth and measureth the earth;
He looketh and maketh nations tremble;
The everlasting mountains are broken to
pieces;
The eternal hills sink down:
His goings are as of old.
7. I saw the tents of Cushan in trouble;
The tent-curtains of Midian are
trembling.
8. Was it against the rivers Thou wert
displeased, O Jehovah?
Was Thine anger against the rivers?
Was Thy fury against the sea?
That Thou didst ride upon Thy horses,
In Thy chariots of victory?
9. Thy bow is made completely bare;
Rods (of chastisement) are sworn by Thy
Word,
Thou cleavest the earth with rivers.
10. The mountains saw Thee, and trembled;
The flood of waters passeth over;
The deep uttereth its voice,
And lifteth up its hands on high.
11. The sun and moon stood still in their
habitation;
At the light of Thine arrows, which flew,
At the slinging of Thy glittering spear.
12. In wrath Thou marchest through the
earth;
In fury Thou treadest down the nations.
13. Thou goest forth for the salvation of
Thy people,
For the salvation of Thine anointed;
Thou dashest in pieces the head out of
the house of the wicked,
Laying bare the foundation even to the
neck—Selah.
14. Thou piercest with his own staves the
chief of his warriors.
That rush on like a whirlwind to scatter
me;
Their rejoicing is to devour the poor
secretly.
15. Thou treadest upon the sea with Thine
horses,
The swelling of mighty waters.
16. I heard, and my bowels trembled;
My lips quivered at the sound;
Rottenness entered my bones;
And I trembled in my place,
That I might rest in the day of trouble
When he that approaches the nation
presseth upon it.
17. For though the fig tree shall not
blossom,
Neither shall fruit be in the vines;
The fruit of the olive tree fails
And the fields shall yield no food;
The flock shall be cut off from the fold,
And there shall be no cattle in the stalls.
18. Yet I will rejoice in Jehovah,
I will joy in the God of my salvation.
19. Jehovah, the Lord, is my strength,
And makes my feet like the hinds',
And will make me to walk upon mine
high places.
(For the Chief Musician, on my stringed
instruments.)

Analysis and Annotations

CHAPTER 1

The Judgment of Judah Through the Chaldeans Announced

1. The prophet's cry to Jehovah (1:1-4)
2. The answer (1:5-11)
3. The prophet's plea (1:12-17)

Verses 1-4. The prophet begins his message with a prayer-cry to Jehovah. He whose name is "the embracer" embraces the Lord and cries to Him on account of the conditions prevailing in Judah. The Spirit of God stirred up the heart of Habakkuk on account of the moral conditions in Judah. He is jealous for Jehovah's glory, which manifested itself in hating the evil. "There is no prophetic delivery among the twelve lesser books more peculiar and characteristic than that of Habakkuk. It has no longer the occupation with the enemy as its main feature, although the enemy is referred to; but for its prominent topic we find the soul of the prophet, as representing the faithful among Judah, brought into deep exercise, and indeed a kind of colloquy between God Himself and the prophet, so as to set out not only that which gave him trouble of heart, but also divine comfort, as well as into exulting hope into which he was led by the communications of the Spirit of God."

Like Jeremiah, the weeping prophet, Habakkuk is deeply stirred on account of the declension among the people of God, and that led him to cry to Jehovah, to tell Him all about it. He begins with "How long, O Lord." It is the cry of the saints of God in all generations. We, too, in the midst of the increasing apostasy, the perilous times, cry to Him, "How long, O Lord." He had cried and there seemed to be no answer. Heaven was silent. And with him the righteous among the Jews had cried for help and for a change of conditions, under which they were suffering affliction. Wickedness and violence were evident on all sides. Strife and contention were the continued order of things. They injured each other wherever they could. The law of God was completely flouted; there was no more justice, and the wicked compassed about the righteous.

Verses 5-11. Jehovah speaks and answers the complaint of His servant. He is going to raise up the Chaldeans to chastise His wayward people. The Lord is calling on His people, that they should see now what He was going to do. "Behold ye among the nations, and regard, and wonder marvellously; for I work a work in your days, which ye will not believe though it were told you." The meaning is that they should look around among the nations, the faithless ones among the Jews, and see how the storm would gather and ultimately break over the head of the house of Judah. He would work a judgment work, which they would not believe, it would be an unparalleled occurrence, amazing and terrible. This passage is quoted by the Apostle Paul in Acts 13:41 and applied to the unbelievers and despisers of the gospel. In the quotation the Spirit of God led the Apostle to omit the address to the nations, and substituted for it "Ye despisers." While in Habakkuk's day God was about to work a work of judgment, which the unbelievers would not believe when they heard of it, we note that Paul preached the gospel; he has reference to speaking to the Jews in the synagogue; preached the gospel unto them, and they did not believe. Then He worked a work which they would not believe, in sending that gospel far hence to the Gentiles (Acts 28) while the unbelieving Jews would be dispersed among the nations.

In verse 6 the instrument of chastisement is announced, and afterward described. A new power would arise, the Chaldeans. They would make an invasion, and possess dwelling places which were not theirs, that is, they would set out for a widespread conquest and take away the dwelling place of Judah. They were to be the instrument in the hand of God to mete out judgment to the Jews and humble them, as well as other nations. The Chaldeans, called in Hebrew *Hakkadsim* were of Semitic origin, springing from Kesed, the son of Nahor, and brother of Abraham (Gen. 22:22). Jeremiah, who also announced the Chaldean invasion, speaks of them in the following manner: "Lo, I will bring a nation upon you from afar, O house of Israel, saith the Lord, it is a mighty nation, an ancient nation, a nation whose language thou knowest not, neither understandest what they say. Their quiver is an open sepulchre, they are all mighty men. And they shall eat up thine harvest, and thy bread, which thy sons and thy daughters should eat, they shall eat up thy flocks and thine herds, they shall eat up thy vines and thy fig trees; they shall impoverish thy fenced cities, wherein thou trustest, with the sword. Nevertheless, in those days, saith the Lord, I will not make an end of you" (Jer. 5:15-18). Their terrible onslaught is here compared to the swiftness of the leopards, their fierceness with the prowling evening wolves, and their horsemen in their dash with the eagle's flight. They come for violence and know no defeat, for their faces are always forward. They make prisoners like the sand, and mock all attempts to check their advance; kings and princes are ridiculed and all strongholds are quickly reduced.

But as he is victorious the Chaldean becomes proud and forgets that he was but used as an instrument in the hand of God to deal with those who had done evil. As a result, they imputed their power to their own god, and do not give God the honor and the glory. His own might is his god. Then comes the day when the Lord takes the Chaldean in hand for judgment and deals with him, as He dealt with other nations. Nebuchadnezzar, the first great king of Babylon, after his humiliating experience, acknowledged the God of heaven, but his grandson Belshazzar praised the Babylonian idol-gods, at his licentious feast, dishonoring the temple vessels. Then followed the judgment of the Chaldeans in the overthrow of Babylon.

Verses 12-17. The prophet had listened to the terrible announcement from the lips of Jehovah, what was to befall his nation. How it must have shocked the man of God! But he knows the comfort and expresses it in faith at once. "Art Thou not from everlasting, O Jehovah, my God, my Holy One? we shall not die!" He knows Jehovah as the faithful God, the covenant-keeping God. Such a God will surely not permit the nation, to whom He has pledged His Word, to be wiped out. His faith lays hold on that and he realizes that the Lord is using this enemy for correction, to chastise His people. And furthermore in his plea he says, "Thou art of purer eyes than to behold evil, Thou canst not look upon injustice." Would He, the righteous God, look on unconcerned at the wicked deeds of the Chaldeans? Can He remain silent to all their deeds of violence? If such is the case, the prophet asks next, "Why lookest Thou upon the treacherous; why art Thou silent when the wicked destroys?" It is the voice of the godly remnant here, seen suffering with the nation. It brings before us the same question concerning the suffering of the righteous.

The Chaldean took men as if they were fishes, as a fisherman puts out the net and the drag, so they catch men by the net and the drag. Gathering in the people with their wealth, he rejoices and is glad. Then the prophet takes up the statement given by the Lord that the Chaldean would offend, and fall by his pride, and the worship of his false gods, he sacrifices to his net; he burns incense; he makes the thing which prospers him his idol, his god. Is this then to go on continually? Shall he who empties his net, and throws it out to catch more, to do this again with the nations forever?

Such was the plea of Habakkuk, after the announcement of the coming chastisement of the Jews by the Chaldeans. He knows that the affliction could not continue forever, for God is a covenant-keeping God, and of purer eyes than to behold evil, a holy and a righteous God.

CHAPTER 2

The Ungodliness of the Chaldeans and Their Destruction

1. The waiting prophet and the message he received (2:1-4)
2. The five-fold woe upon the Chaldeans (2:5-20)

Verses 1-4. It seems there was no immediate answer to the plea of the prophet. He then speaks to himself and expresses his attitude. "I will stand upon my watch, and set me upon the tower, and I will wait to see what He will say to me, and what I shall answer as to my complaint." He watches like a sentinel upon a watch-tower for the answer the Lord will give him. It does not mean that the prophet actually ascended a tower, but he expresses his innermost attitude by the symbol of the watchman. He remained silent and eagerly looked for the reply.

How long he waited is not stated. But the answer came, for the Lord never disappoints His inquiring and waiting servants. He is told to write the vision and make it plain upon the tablets, that he may run that readeth it. Thus the Lord spoke to him and gave him the vision, which he was to write in plain characters upon tablets. The effect should be not that he that runneth may read (as it it sometimes misquoted) but that he that readeth may run. The prophetic Word is always plain. It is far from being the deep and complicated portion of God's truth that some make it, but it needs an ear opened by the Spirit of God. Prophecy believed is a great stimulating agent to Christian service, even as it is stated here, that the reader of the vision runs to spread the message.

In the next place we hear of the certainty of the vision. It is for the appointed time. It hastes toward the end, and shall not lie. The prophet is commanded to wait for it, though it tarry, and then receives the assurance that it will surely some and not tarry. These are important instructions by which many a believer might profit. God has an appointed time for all His purposes and their fulfillment. He cannot be hastened, for His schedule was made before the foundation of the world. When the appointed time comes all visions will be accompshed. It hastens toward the end. That end is the end of the times of the Gentiles, which began with the rising of the Babylonians, and the first great king, Nebuchadnezzar, the golden head in the prophetic image of Daniel 2. When the end of the times of the Gentiles comes, the world-power then, final Babylon as revealed in the last book of the Bible, will be judged and the Lord will be manifested in all His glory. The prophet's business is, as well as that of every believer, to wait for it and not be disturbed if there is delay, for the assurance is given that it will surely come and not tarry. And here faith can rest.

Part of this is quoted in the Epistle to the Hebrews. "For yet a little while, and He that shall come will come, and will not tarry" (Heb. 10:37). From this quotation we learn that the vision which will surely come is a person, the Lord Jesus Christ. He is the center of every vision and without Him there is no vision. The Septuagint translation is the same: "If He tarry wait for Him, for coming He will come and not delay."

In the fourth verse, which may properly be taken to be the opening statement for the vision which follows, the all importance of faith in the vision is made known. The proud one who is mentioned must primarily be applied to the haughty Chaldean, but it is equally true of the unbelieving, proud Jew, and of the nominal Christian. The proud, the puffed up one, his soul is not right within him, and God resisteth the proud, while he that humbleth himself shall be exalted.

"But the just shall live by faith." Criticism has not left this matchless sentence untouched. The higher critic Davidson labors to show that the Hebrew word for faith (Emunoh) means faithfulness, dealing in faithfulness in money matters, that is, one who deals honestly. According to his statement the verse means if an Israelite, or anybody else, does right he will live. But in Genesis we read, "Abraham believed the Lord and He counted it to him for righteousness." As every intelligent Christian knows, there was no law then, and the New Testament in the testimony of the Holy Spirit makes it plain that this is the gospel of grace in which the ungodly are justified; justified by faith. Interesting is the quotation of the sentence "the just shall live by faith" in the three passages of the New Testament Epistles.

Romans 1:17 quotes this sentence. In this passage the emphasis is upon the word "just." The theme of Romans is the righteousness of God, at least in the opening chapters. It shows how a person, a lost and guilty sinner, becomes righteous, and as such is saved. "For by grace are ye saved through faith, and that not of yourselves, it is the gift of God: not of works, lest any man should boast."

In Galatians 3:11 the emphasis is upon the word "faith." "But no man is justified by the law in the sight of God, as it is evident: for, the just shall live by faith."

In Hebrews 10:38 the emphasis is upon "live." "For yet a little while, and He that shall come will come, and will not tarry. Now the just shall *live* by faith, but if any man draw back, My soul shall have no pleasure in him."

Verses 5-20. The Lord uncovers the wicked conditions prevailing among the Chaldeans. God had allowed the people whom He loved to be chastised by an evil instrument; they were to be crushed by injustice and by the actions of the cruel invader. But the character and conduct of the oppressor, the Chaldeans, was not unknown to Him, as the prophet expressed it, "Who is of purer eyes than to behold evil." And now the righteous Lord announces the five-fold woe upon the wicked world-power. While all this applies primarily to the Chaldean, it is likewise a prophecy concerning the future. The world powers remain the same to the end of the times of the Gentiles. It was true then, as it is true now, and will be true in the future throughout this present age, "The world lieth in the Wicked One." There is no improvement to be looked for among the world powers, and as we have seen so frequently in the study of the prophets, the end of the age brings still greater opposition and defiance of God, with a corresponding moral decline. We see therefore in these verses a description of the world conditions down to its very end. The word "wine" does not need to be interpreted in a literal way, though drunkenness was one of the sins of the Babylonians. They were inflamed with an ambition for conquest, as a drunken man is inflamed with wine. This intoxication made them treacherous, haughty, restless: like death, which is never satisfied, so they are never satisfied; constantly pressing on they spoil the nations, gather prisoners, and act in violence. How can God permit this to go unjudged?

Then follows a taunting song in verses 6-7. Divine retribution is coming for them. The spoiler is going to be spoiled. It is the retribution which may be read in all history, which still continues, for of nations it is true as of individuals, "Whatsoever a man soweth that shall he also reap."

The second woe is on account of their covetousness and their self-aggrandizement. Like Edom, they were possessed by an abominable pride to make their nest high, they image self-security, thinking they can avert "the power of evil." But their proud plans were to result in shame; their security would end in collapse and confusion. It is well known how Nebuchadnezzar manifested this spirit. One day this proud monarch walked in the palace of the kingdom of Babylon. "The king spake and said, Is not this great Babylon, that I have built for the house of the kingdom, by the might of my power and for the honor of my majesty?" The humiliation which came upon the king is prophetic. Thus the Lord will humble the proud world-power into the dust (Dan. 4).

Then comes a third woe. Verses 12-14 are of special interest, for they give us a picture of a godless civilization and its appointed end. Their cruel oppression, their ungodly gains, had built up a magnificent city. Excavations have shown what a marvelous civilization was in force when Babylon was mistress of the world. But the foundations of it all were iniquity and the blood of victims. Is it any better today? We have seen the top-notch of a boasted civilization, steeped in iniquity and defiance of God, suddenly collapsing and producing a war of horrors and cruelty which makes the conquests and atrocities of the Chaldeans pale into insignificance.

And how true it is today, "The peoples labor for the fire, the nations weary themselves for vanity." The day is approaching when this civilization will be swept away, and before the better things come, the kingdom is established and He reigns whose right it is, there will be the fires of judgment. And after that it will be true, as it cannot be true before, "The earth shall be filled with the knowledge of the glory of the Lord, as the waters cover the sea."

The fourth woe shows the corruption which held sway in the Babylonian empire. Drunkenness here is a figure of the utter prostration of the nations which the Chaldeans had conquered; they stripped them in their wicked endeavors of all they possessed. They spread a shameless dissolution in every direction. For this they will have to drink the cup of fury from the hand of the Lord, and shall be covered with vile shame, so that their glory will be blotted out.

The fifth woe is on account of their idolatry. They worshipped wood and stone. Nebuchadnezzar set up his golden image in the plain of Dura and demanded worship for it. The spiritual Babylon, Rome, is a well-organized system of idolatry which goes on undiminished. Finally the age ends in idolatry, for the image of the beast of Revelation 13 is still future.

"But the Lord is in His holy temple; let all the earth keep silence before Him." First, by way of contrast, their idols are dumb; Jehovah, the God of Israel, is the living God. He is in His holy temple; from there He takes notice of the doings of men. He is the Sovereign, the only Potentate; the nations are as a drop of a bucket, and are counted as the small dust of the balance (Isa. 40:15). "It is He that sitteth upon the circle of the earth, and the inhabitants thereof are as grasshoppers; that stretcheth out the heavens as a curtain, and spreadeth them out as a tent to dwell in" (Isa. 40:22).

But this closing verse of the chapter of woe has a prophetic meaning. When at last the world-power is dethroned, when the Lord returns, He will take His place as King of Kings. He will be in His holy temple, and then all the earth will keep silence before Him.

CHAPTER 3

The Vision of the Coming of the Lord.

1. The prophet's prayer (3:1-2)
2. The coming of the Lord for judgment and redemption (3:3-15)
3. The effect upon the prophet (3:16-19)

Verses 1-2. Once more we hear the voice of the man of God in prayer. Shigionoth is the plural of Shiggaion, and is found in the superscription of Psalm 7. Its meaning is "loud crying." The connection with the seventh Psalm is interesting. In that Psalm God appeared to David as the God of judgment, the righteous God who must save His righteous people and condemn the wicked. (See Annotations on Psalm 7.) The prophet had listened to the message and penned it as we have it in the preceding chapter. It struck terror to his heart and he trembled. Therefore he pleads for a revival of the Lord's work in the midst of the years. He must have taken a hasty glance over the past history of his people, how God had worked in their behalf in Egypt, redeemed them, led them forth, and the many evidences of the display of His power in behalf of the elect nation. And now, in the midst of years, he asks a revival of this work, the interposition of Jehovah, that He may be known in His power. The text is often quoted in pleading a revival among the dead conditions of Christendom. But it is a revival of the work of the Lord in a very different sense of the word, as we have indicated.

He knows that wrath is on the way. Not only wrath for the Chaldeans, but for his people, that the unbelieving, the apostates, would also have to face the judgment. Therefore he pleads, "In wrath remember mercy." Such is the way of God always. Judgment is His strange work, and mercy is mingled with His judgments. It will be so in connection with the winding up of this present age, when judgment wrath sweeps over the earth, and especially Israel's land; He then will have mercy upon His people. The time of wrath will be His time of mercy, the covenant mercies promised to Israel. "Thou shalt arise and have mercy upon Zion, for the time to favor her, yea, the set time, is come." And when will that be? When the Lord shall build up Zion; He shall appear in His glory (Psa. 102:13-16).

The great inspired ode which follows is one of the greatest sections of prophecy. It is a wonderful theophany the Spirit of God describes. Wrath and mercy are manifested, so that it is an answer to the prophet's plea, "In wrath remember mercy."

It has been said, "The poet describes a great storm, advancing from the south, the region of Paran and Sinai. In the dark storm clouds he conceives Jehovah to be concealed; the lightning flashes which illumine heaven and earth disclose glimpses of the dazzling brightness immediately about him; the earth quakes, the hills sink, and the neighboring desert tribes look on in dismay" (Canon Driver). Thus higher criticism reduces one of the sublimest inspired prophecies, concerning the future appearing of the Lord, to the level of poetry.

The great description of His coming must be linked with similar prophecies (Deut. 33:2; Psa. 18:8-19, 33, 34; Psa. 68:8, 34; Psa. 77:17-20). The great ode, cast in the form of a Psalm, begins with the statement that God cometh from Teman and the Holy One from Mount Paran. Moses in his prophetic blessing also begins with a similar declaration. "The Lord came from Sinai, and rose from Seir unto them; He shined from Mount Paran, and He came with the thousands of His saints (angels); from His right hand went a fiery law for them." Just as he was manifested when He had redeemed them out of Egypt, and constituted them His Kingdom people at Sinai (Exod. 19), so will He appear again to deliver the remnant of His people from the dominion of the world-power, and judge them as He judged Egypt. He comes from the direction of Edom, for Teman is the southern district of Idumea, while Paran is more southward. Isaiah also beheld him advancing from the same direction. "Who is this that cometh from Edom, with dyed garments from Bozrah?" (Isa. 63:1-6). It is unfortunate that the Authorized Version has "God came from Teman," when it is "God cometh," not a past but a future event. After this opening statement the first Selah is put. This means to pause and to lift up. We are to pause and meditate, and then to lift up our hearts and voices in praise and thanksgiving. It is found seventy-one times in the Psalms and three times in this chapter of Habakkuk.

His glory covers the heavens, while the earth is filled with His praise. Heaven and earth reflect the glory of the Coming One. How all this corresponds with the divine statements concerning His coming in the New Testament does not need to be pointed out. He comes in power and great glory, in the clouds of heaven, as Daniel beheld Him in the night vision, and as our Lord testified Himself. Brightness fills the sky as He appears in person, while out of His hand glory rays emanate, the hiding of His power. The picture is evidently taken from the rising sun, which shoots forth great rays, heralding its ascending. As Delitzsch remarks, "His hand" means in a general sense, as signifying the hand generally, and not a single hand only. May we not have here a hint of His hands pierced once, but now emanating glory? Before Him goes the pestilence, indicating the trouble which precedes His coming, when the four apocalyptic riders bring war, famine, pestilence, and death in judgment for this earth.

With the sixth verse He draws nearer. Up to this point in the theophany He is described as coming forth, like the sun out of His chamber, heaven and earth reflecting His glory, but now He stands and measures the earth; He looks and the nations tremble, while all creation is affected, and earthquakes shake down the mountains.

Then the prophet sees the tents of Cushan in affliction and the curtains of Midian tremble. Cushan means the Ethiopians, and the Midianites inhabited the Arabian coast along the Red Sea. The past is seen as a prophecy of the future. As He once came at Sinai, when the mountains shook and the hills trembled, and as once the tidings of the Red Sea disaster inspired terror among the neighboring nations, so will it be, only on a larger scale, when He comes in great power and glory.

The verses which follow (verses 8-15) are in the form of an address to God. The rivers and the seas, and the mountains feel His wrath; they represent symbolically the nations and the world-powers. He is seen marching in anger through the earth and in His fury treading down the nations. It is a majestic picture the Spirit of God gives of that coming day of wrath and judgment.

But while He comes thus, executing wrath and judgment upon the ungodly, He comes in mercy. He goes forth for the salvation of His people, for the salvation of Thine anointed, that is, the elect nation and the God-fearing, waiting remnant of the last days (Psa. 105:15). And there will be on the earth in that day the head of the house of the wicked, the ungodly head, the man of sin, the heading up of all apostasy and opposition to God. His doom is predicted in verse 13, followed by another Selah, like verses 3 and 9.

Verses 16-19. The prophet now speaks of his own feeling, which reflects the feeling of the godly among the Jews when this great theophany becomes history. There is fear and trembling in view of the coming tribulation. When he heard it he trembled; he is completely prostrated. He desires rest in the day of trouble, the day when the final enemy of God's people marches through the land. Then faith is triumphant, and in one of the most magnificant outbursts the prophet declares his confidence in his God (verse 17). Such will be the faith of the godly who pass through the time of great trouble. Finally he rejoices in the God of his salvation and declares his hope that his feet will be like hinds' feet to escape to the high places. Even so the remnant of Israel will be delivered. We leave the application to the Church-saints with the reader.

THE PROPHET
ZEPHANIAH

Introduction

Zephaniah is the last of the prophets before the captivity, according to the arrangement of the Hebrew Bible. Haggai, Zechariah and Malachi are post-exilic. His name means "Jehovah hides." His genealogy is traced back for four generations. Zephaniah was the son of Cushi, the son of Gedaliah, the son of Amariah, the son of Hizkiah. We have therefore more information concerning him than of most of the other minor prophets. There must be a reason why these four generations are given. We believe the reason is to show that he was of royal descent, the great-grandson of the pious king of Judah, Hezekiah. Hizkiah is the same as Hezekiah in the Hebrew. Jewish tradition as well as the reliable rabbinical sources confirm this. The objection that the royal title is not given in connection with Hizkiah is insignificant; at any rate "king of Judah" is mentioned in connection with Josiah in the first verse of this book of Zephaniah, so that it may have been left out in connection with Hizkiah on purpose. As to his personal history we have no further information. It seems as if the Lord has hidden for a good reason these details of His chosen instruments.

The Date of Zephaniah

The date is given in the first verse. He prophesied in the days of Josiah the king of Judah. We are therefore not left in doubt about the time in which he exercised his office as prophet; he was the contemporary of Jeremiah and Micah. As to the exact time during the reign of Josiah in which Zephaniah prophesied, we can be quite sure that it was during the time of the reformation instituted by the king, that is between the twelfth and eighteenth year; yet the reformation was still in process and not yet fully completed. The temple must have been purified from the idol abominations, for Zephaniah presupposes the maintenance of the temple worship.

The Message of Zephaniah

To understand the message we must consider the character of the times in which the prophet lived, and the conditions in Judah. We have done so already in connection with the annotations on Jeremiah, but add here another description. As already stated a great reformation was in progress, which, like all reformation, ended in deformation, producing a reaction which plunged the house of Judah into the final apostasy. It seems the reformation was mostly an outward one; in their hearts the people still had a longing for the idols and the abominations connected with them (1:4). We shall point out in the annotations some of the details of the evils prevailing at that time.

Like the other minor prophets, judgment is announced first, followed by exhortations to repentance, with the promises of glory for the remnant of His people when the day of Jehovah is passed and the Lord is King over all the earth. He proclaims the judgment to come for the whole earth, as well as upon Judah and Jerusalem, and then gives a fuller description of the day in which that judgment is to be executed, the still future day of Jehovah. As we have seen, Obadiah and Joel are the earliest prophets, and both announced the day of Jehovah. The last of the prophets before the captivity bears his additional testimony to the same day, describing it as a day of wrath, of trouble and distress. This is the first chapter.

In the second chapter the exhortations begin. He exhorts the nation to repent and to seek the Lord, so that they might be hid in the day of the Lord's anger. Then he announced that the day is surely coming upon all the nations, and that the isles of the nations will not escape.

In the third chapter the prophet shows how the Lord will deal in judgment also with the ungodly among His people. He announces His purpose concerning the nations with the expectation that the godly remnant among the Jews will fear Him then, and receive instruction and wait for Him.

Then follows the joyous message of the future salvation of the elect people. It will be a poor afflicted remnant which trusts in the Lord, which, born again, will be a holy people separated from evil. This is followed by the singing times. "Sing, daughter of Zion; shout, O Israel;

be glad and rejoice with all thy heart, O daughter of Jerusalem. The Lord hath taken away thy judgments, He hath cast out thine enemy; the King of Israel, even the Lord, is in the midst of thee; thou shalt not see evil any more."

The Division of Zephaniah

Like Nahum's prophecy, Zephaniah's is one great prophetic utterance. The division into three chapters, as given in the Authorized Version, is the correct arrangement, with the exception of the first eight verses of chapter 3, which should be added to the second chapter. The subdivisions will be pointed out in the analysis and annotations.

Analysis and Annotations

CHAPTER 1

The Day of the Lord, the Day of Judgment

1. The judgment of all the world (1:1-3)
2. The judgment will destroy the evildoers in Judah (1:4-13)
3. The day of the Lord (1:14-18)

Verses 1-3. The first verse is the superscription, and tells us, as pointed out in the introduction, of the connection of Zephaniah and the date of his prophecy.

Then comes the announcement of the judgment. It is to consume all things from off the face of the land, man and beast, the fowls of heaven, the fishes of the sea, and end the stumbling blocks of the wicked, that is, their idols and idol worship. The land is not to be understood as being Israel's land exclusively; it means the earth. That the judgment vision of Zephaniah has a wider scope than the land and the people is fully confirmed by other passages. The great day comes upon men everywhere (1:17); it is universal (2:4-15); all the isles of the nations are mentioned (2:11).

Verses 4-13. It will fall especially upon the house of Judah and Jerusalem. In the verses which follow we have a description of the moral conditions of the Jews when Josiah started his reformation, which prophetically gives us a picture of the conditions among the Jews when this age closes, and a portion of them is back in the land of their fathers, as they are attempting to get it back now through political Zionism.

The hand of the Lord will be stretched out upon Judah and Jerusalem. The remnant of Baal will be cut off and the Chemarim, with the priests. Idolatry, whatever remains of it, should then be completely abolished. "Baal" was the idol of god of the Phoenicians and Canaanites; the word means "lord" or "possessor." With the worship of this god licentious practices were connected. Chemarim is the name of the idolatrous priests which conducted the high places, appointed for this service by the kings of Judah (2 Kings 23:5). In verses 5 and 6 other forms of idolatry are mentioned. They worshipped the hosts of the heavens from housetops. They worshipped the stars, and studied their movements as if they could give them help and a revelation. Astrology, so widely practiced among civilized nations today, is an old cult (2 Kings 21:3, 5; Jer. 8:2; 19:13). Others used the Holy Name of Jehovah, and at the same time they used the name of Malcham. All was a turning back from Jehovah and dishonoring His Name.

As to the future curse of idolatry among the Jews, the passage in Matthew 12:43, 45, the words of our Lord, gives us the full information. The unclean spirit there is the spirit of idolatry, from which the Jews in their dispersion are free; the unclean spirit has left the house, but it is to return, and the last state is worse than the first: "Even so shall it be also unto this wicked generation." They will worship the man of sin, the masterpiece of Satan, who in the end of the age will take his place in the temple of God (2 Thess. 2).

The day of the Lord is at hand; a statement which verifies our interpretation that this prophecy referes to the future day. The Lord has prepared His sacrifice and bidden his guests. It is the supper of the great God, to which He invites His guests. Read in connection with this Revelation 19:17-18. What that day will bring is described in verses 8-13. All the evil doers will be dealt with by the Lord.

Verses 14-18. The great day of the Lord is now more fully described. It is the day when the announced judgment will take place. Higher criticism sees nothing but some invasion of the land by hostile forces. But it is the same great day, the culmination of the past ages, when Jehovah is revealed, so vividly described in Joel 2:11. On that day the voice of the Lord will be heard (Psa. 29; Isa. 66:6). When that day comes the mighty man will cry out in bitterness, for he is unable to save himself from the judgment tempest. In two verses the prophet describes vividly the greatness of that day.

A day of wrath is that day,
A day of trouble and distress,
A day of ruin and desolation,
A day of darkness and gloom,
A day of clouds and cloudy darkness;
A day of the trumpet and the warcry
Against the fortified cities,
And against the lofty battlements.

Thomas of Celano used in 1250 the Vulgate translation of the first sentence *Dies irae, dies illa* in writing his famous judgment hymn. It is well to compare Scripture with Scripture about that day. (For instance, verse 15 with Joel 3; Amos 5:18, 20; 8:9; Isaiah 13:10, and many other passages.) When that day comes the wicked will perish; distress will be upon all. They will walk like blind men, that is, trying to find a way to escape, but not able to find one. Nothing will be able to deliver from the fury of that day, neither silver nor gold will avail anything.

CHAPTERS 2—3:8

The Call to Repentance in View of the Judgment

1. The call to repentance (2:1-3)
2. The judgment of the Philistines (2:4-7)
3. The judgment of Moab and Ammon (2:8-10)
4. The judgment of the other nations (2:11-15)
5. The woe and warning to Jerusalem and His people (3:1-8)

Verses 1-3. As we found it in Joel, so it is here. In view of the coming of the day, the call goes forth to the nation to humble themselves and to repent. On the near horizon in Joel the Assyrian invasion was threatening. In Zephaniah it is the Babylonian power. But all points to the future day of the Lord. They are to gather themselves together. The word used for "gather" has the meaning of gathering stubble or wood for burning. In their unbelief they were worthless as stubble and dry wood, fit for the burning. The phrase "not desired" has been translated "which does not turn pale." But this cannot be sustained. The better meaning is "unashamed."

The second verse gives the reason why they should humble themselves and be ashamed of all their evil doings. Because the decree of judgment has gone forth, the fierce anger of the Lord in His day is about to pass as the chaff. This is followed by the appeal to seek the Lord. This is addressed to the meek in the land, the godly remnant which fears the Lord, both in Zephaniah's day and in the end of the age, when "that day" comes. They are meek and seek to keep the statutes and judgments of the Lord in a righteous life. Still they are exhorted to seek meekness. For it is this, meekness and lowliness, that pleases the Lord. The promise is held out that they would be hid in the day of the Lord's anger. Zephaniah means "hidden by the Lord" or "whom the Lord hides;" His name comes into play as a comfort that the godly will be hid in the day of the Lord. In Isaiah we have a more direct word about this. "Come, My people, enter thou in thy chambers, and shut thy doors about thee; hide thyself as it were for a moment, until the indignation be overpast" (Isa. 26:20). This has often been used as a proof text that the true Church is not to pass through the great tribulation period. But it has nothing whatever to do with the Church, but is the promise given to the godly remnant (Rev. 12, the preservation of the seed of the woman). It is the teaching of the New Testament that the true Church will be taken to her heavenly abode by the coming of the Lord for His saints (1 Thess. 4:13-18; 2 Thess. 2).

Verses 4-7. Judgment is to come in that day upon Gaza and Ashkelon, upon Ashdod and Ekron, the chief cities of Philistia. The inhabitants of the seacoast, the nation of the Cherethites, and all the land of the Philistines, will undergo judgment. The seventh verse gives the connection with the opening message of the chapter, the call to repentance. "And the coast shall be for the remnant of the house of Judah; they shall feed thereupon; in the house of Ashkelon shall they lie down in the evening; for the Lord their God shall visit them, and turn away their captivity." Because the remnant is to possess this territory when Philistia is judged they ought to repent and seek the Lord. That this is still unaccomplished hardly needs to be pointed out. It was not fulfilled in the remnant which returned from the Babylonian captivity. Since the day of their rejection, when they rejected Christ, they have been out of the land. Here is a prophecy of ultimate blessing to the remnant in the day of the Lord, when they will be regathered.

Verses 8-10. Moab and Ammon had sinned against Israel, they reviled them and magnified themselves against their border. Their judgment is announced, as it is in the former prophets, like Joel, Amos, and Ezekiel. Moab will be overthrown like Sodom, and Ammon will become like Gomorrah. Then when the judgment of Moab and Ammon finally takes place, as it will in His day, the remnant of His people shall spoil them, and the remnant shall possess them. It is obvious this also remains to be fulfilled.

This judgment of Moab and Ammon is the harvest which their pride and self-exaltation has brought to them (verse 10).

Verses 11-15. The Lord, in that day, will be terrible unto all these nations. The idol gods will all be abolished. In their place He alone will be worshipped (Zech. 14). All the isles of the nations will turn in worship to Him. The Ethiopians, the African nations, will fall under the judgment. He will stretch out His hand against Assyria, the power of the north, including both the Assyrian which then was and the Assyrian of the end-time, still to come. It is evident from verse 13 that when Zephaniah penned these words Nineveh had not yet fallen. Her utter desolation is predicted by Zephaniah as it was predicted by Nahum. The fate of Nineveh announced was literally accomplished. And some day all the proud cities of the nations, steeped in iniquity, will also fall as Nineveh was dethroned from her place of mistress of the world.

Chapter 3:1-8. The filthy, polluted and oppressing city is Jerusalem. Four charges are laid against her. 1. She obeyed not the voice. 2. She received not correction. 3. She trusted not in the Lord. 4. She drew not near to her God. And because she was untrue to her God and Lord, oppressive cruelty and evil persisted. It was the outcome of her wrong attitude toward the Lord. Her leaders, the princes, were like roaring lions, devouring the prey. Her judges in oppressing the poor were like ravening wolves, ferocious and destructive. How all this fits Christendom today. There is disobedience to the Lord, no faith in Him, no humiliation and no repentance. Hence the moral conditions of today.

Their prophets and priests were also corrupt, as we have learned before in the former prophets. Yet the holy and just Jehovah was in the midst of them. Yet the unjust was not ashamed, but continued in evil-doing.

Then Jehovah addresses the nation: "I have cut off nations; their towers are desolate; I have made their streets waste, that none passeth by; their cities are destroyed, so that there is no man, that there is none inhabitant. I said, Surely thou wilt fear me, thou wilt receive instruction; so their dwelling should not be cut off; howsoever I punished them, they rose early, and corrupted all their doings." But they did not heed His plea. They did not take warning from what happened to other nations.

CHAPTER 3:8-20

Judgment and Glory

1. The waiting for the end (3:8)
2. The glory that follows (3:9-20)

Verse 8. "Therefore wait for me, saith Jehovah, for the day when I arise for the prey; for my determination is to gather the nations, to assemble the kingdoms, to pour upon them mine indignation, all my fierce anger; for all the earth shall be devoured with the fire of my jealousy." This verse leads us back to the opening exhortation of this chapter. They are as a nation to wait for Him, till the day comes in which He arises to execute the judgment of the nations. It has been a long waiting. Centuries have come and gone; His earthly people have been the wanderers among the nations of the world, where they have been a byword and a curse, yet witnesses for Him also. Still they are waiting for "that day," the day which closes the times of the Gentiles, when the stone strikes the great man image and becomes a mountain filling the whole earth (Daniel 2).

Verses 9-20. The opening verse of this glory section has been variously interpreted. It has been used by the "Pentecostal-delusion" as being a prophecy concerning their imagined gift of tongues restoration. In the first place it must be noticed that in the Hebrew the word people is in the plural. We read therefore this verse as follows: "For then will I turn to the nations a pure lip, that they may all call upon the name of Jehovah, to serve Him with one shoulder." Luther paraphrased this verse in the following way: "Then will I cause the nations to be preached to otherwise, with friendly lips, that they may call upon the name of the Lord." But this interpretation is not sustained by the text. It means that the nations which escaped the judgment-wrath of the day of the Lord will be converted, and as a result of their conversion they will call upon the Lord with pure lips; all idolatry will cease and all serve the Lord as one man.

While the peoples in verse 9 are the Gentiles, the suppliants in verse 10 are Jews brought back from the dispersion. They are brought back by the converted Gentiles as an offering unto the Lord (Isa. 66:20). When that takes place the restored nation will not have need to be ashamed for all their doings, for the Lord in infinite grace will have cleansed them from their iniquity, and now they are no longer proud and haughty, but a remnant humbled, trusting in the Lord. The great chapter in Ezekiel tells us of the conversion of this remnant (Ezek. 36). They will then be a righteous nation, do no iniquity, nor speak lies. The speaking of lies, the use of deceit, is one of the traits of the Jews today, and has often been responsible for their sufferings among the Gentiles. But when that day comes the deceitful tongue will not be found in their mouth. They will feed and lie down and none shall make them afraid. They have become once more "the sheep of His pastures," gathered by the Good Shepherd. The time of singing and rejoicing has come.

> Sing, O daughter of Zion!
> Shout, O Israel!
> Be glad and rejoice
> With all thy heart,
> O Daughter of Jerusalem.
>
> Jehovah has removed thy judgments;
> He has cast out thine enemy;
> The King of Israel, Jehovah,
> Is in the midst of thee,
> Thou wilt see evil no more.
>
> In that day it shall be said to
> Jerusalem,
> Fear not, Zion, let not thy hands
> be feeble.
> Jehovah, thy God is in the midst of thee,
> A mighty One who saves;
> He rejoices over thee with gladness;
> He rests in His love;
> He rejoices over thee with singing.

What a glorious day that will be! It will be glory for Him and glory for His people. The great prophetic song recorded by Isaiah (chapter 12) will then be heard in the midst of His redeemed people. The great Psalms of praise and worship will fill Jerusalem. Judgments are forever gone; no enemy will threaten them again. He Himself is in their midst, none other but He whom their fathers delivered once into the hands of the Gentiles, over whom they cried, "His blood be upon us and our children." He is King. The throne of His father David is now filled. The Mighty One saves, and rejoices over His redeemed people. He has the travail of His soul to the full and is satisfied.

Then He will make them a name and a praise among all the peoples of the earth. Thus ends the great message of Zephaniah, the great-great-grandson of the pious King Hezekiah.

THE PROPHET
HAGGAI

Introduction

Between Zephaniah and Haggai is the period of the captivity of the house of Judah in Babylon. Haggai is the first of the three post-Exilic prophets, though not the most prominent one, which is Zechariah.

Haggai means "my feast," or perhaps "the Festal one." Nothing is known of his personal history. He is mentioned in Ezra, chapter 5:1 and 6:14. The first verse of the book which bears his name gives us the date of his prophecy. It was in the second year of Darius the king. The king is Darius Hystaspes, and the year is 520 B.C. Two months later young Zechariah began to lift up his voice likewise. It seems that Haggai's prophetic office extended over four months only. Some have concluded from chapter 2:3 that he must have known the first temple. If he saw that temple he must have been at least 80 years old, if not older, when he prophesied. But the passage upon which this supposition rests does not necessarily imply this. He was probably born in the captivity, and a young man like his greater associate Zechariah.

The Times of Haggai and Zechariah

In order to understand the prophecies of Haggai as well as Zechariah, the history contained in the book of Ezra must be carefully studied. The reader will consult the introduction to the book of Ezra and the annotations on the different chapters.

We mention here but a few of the leading historical facts of this period. After the remnant had returned from Babylon the feasts commanded by the law were first of all reinstituted. Then in the second year, 535 B.C., the foundations of the new temple were laid. It was a time of rejoicing and a time of sorrow. What was this second temple in comparison with the first house? (See Ezra 3:12, 13.) There were tears of joy and tears of sorrow. Then the building of the temple was neglected for a time. There were three causes. The indifference, the faintheartedness of the people, and the oppositions from the enemy. The Samaritans, a mongrel race (Ezra 4:1, 9, 10) offered, after the foundation of the temple had been laid, to form an alliance with the Jewish remnant, and to assist them with it. When the proposal was nobly rejected they employed political means to dwarf the rebuilding of the house of the Lord, by misrepresentations at the Persian court. Their schemes, after some time, seemed to be quite successful, when in reply to their petition to Artaxerxes, 522 B.C., they were told that the building of the temple must be stopped. Artaxerxes was a pretender, known in history as Pseudo-Smerdis. During the remainder of his reign the building was completely stopped; but it lasted about a year only. His successor, Darius Hystaspes (521. B.C.) was more favorable to his Jewish subjects. It was then that Haggai and Zechariah urged the continuation of the building of the temple in their prophetic messages. But the slow progress in the building of the temple was altogether chargeable to the intrigues of the Samaritans. The remnant was negligent in this matter to a great extent. During the time when the house was unfinished many Jews had used their means in erecting fine dwellings and beautifying them; they acted in a selfish, indifferent manner.

The harvest also had turned out very poor; the blessing of the Lord was lacking in all that they did, therefore the prophet spoke then and told them that all was an expresion of the displeasure of the Lord in neglecting His house. "Ye have sown much and bring in little; ye eat but ye have not enough; ye drink, but ye are not filled with drink; ye clothe you, but there is none warm; and he that earneth wages, earneth wages to put it into a bag with holes" (1:6).

These were outward circumstances which led the Spirit of God to call Haggai to the prophetic office.

The Message of Haggai

The purpose of his message has been stated in the preceding paragraph. But the message goes far beyond his time, and like the former prophets, leads up to the time of glory. He speaks of the Messiah, our Lord, as the desire of all nations, and of the times when all nations shall be shaken; when another house is to be filled with the Lord's glory. This passage is quoted in Hebrews 12:26, 27, and will be more closely examined in the annotations. Our post-millennial brethren in their expositions have explained all these promises as being realized in the Church. The second temple is, according to their views, a prophecy concerning the Church. In the language of one: "He announces that the time is not far off when the privileges of Jehovah's worship shall be extended over all the earth, and that the treasures of all nations will then be brought to adorn this temple, and exalt its glory above the departed splendor of the former house, while peace and prosperity shall reign among the unnumbered worshippers." But inasmuch as none of the prophets knew anything whatever about the body of Christ, the Church, in which there is neither Jew nor Gentile, this interpretation is incorrect. The Church is the mystery which was not made known in former ages (Eph. 3). Hence Haggai did not describe the Church under the term of the temple, but his prophecy reaches beyond the church-age to the day of the Lord, when all nations will be shaken, and the Lord will return and bring with Him the promised glory.

The mesage of Haggai is written in a very simple style, quite different from the style of the pre-exilic prophets. He makes frequent use of interrogatives.

The Division of Haggai

The two chapters contain five addresses. The first address in chapter 1:1-11 is one of reproof and warning, to arouse the remnant from the apathy into which they had drifted in the building of the temple. The second address in chapter 1:12-15 was made when the people responded to his appeal, assuring them of the presence of the Lord in their obedience. The third address in chapter 2:1-9 contrasts the glory of the first house with the greater glory of the second house and introduces the distinctively Messianic glory. The fourth address in chapter 2:10-19 contains moral instructions and the assurance of blessing. The last address, the conclusion of the message of Haggai, points still more prominently to the day of the Lord, when heaven and earth is to be shaken and the kingdoms of the nations will be overthrown. In the last verse, Zerubbabel, the servant of Jehovah, is a prophetic type of our Lord.

Analysis and Annotations

CHAPTER 1:1-11

Haggai's First Address

1. The introduction (1:1)
2. The reproof (1:2-6)
3. Consider your ways (1:7-11)

Verse 1. Darius Hystaspes had been king one year and had entered upon the second year, 520 B.C., when, in the sixth month, in the first day of the month, the word of the Lord was given by Haggai. It was addressed to Zerubbabel, the son of Shealtiel, governor of Judah, and to Joshua, the son of Josedech, the high priest. Zerubbabel and Joshua were the prominent civic and religious leaders of that day. Zerubbabel was the son of Shealtiel (which means asking of God in prayer). Zerubabel (sown in Babylon) was of royal seed, in direct line of descent from David. In Ezra this princely leader is called by his Persian name Sheshbazzar. In the genealogy of Luke 3:27 he is called a son of Neri, a descendant of David through his son Nathan; he is also called a son of Pedaiah. These divergent statements have been satisfactorily explained by the law of the Levirate marriage (Deut. 25:10).

Joshua is mentioned several times in Zechariah. He was the first high-priest after the captivity, and is called in Ezra and Nehemiah Jeshua, the name Joshua transcribed into Greek. He and Zerubbabel are prophetic types of our Lord as the King-Priest. Joshua was the son of Josedech (Jehozadak) the high-priest who was taken by the Babylonians into captivity (1 Chron. 6:15), and was the grandson of Seraiah, who was put to death by Nebuchadnezzar at Riblah, after the capture of Jerusalem.

Verses 2-6. His message starts with the excuse which the people offered for the apathy in the things of God. "This people say, The time is not come, the time that the Lord's house should be built." The Lord does not address them as "My people," but in a way which is deprecatory. It was an empty excuse, that His time had not yet come; in reality they were cold towards the cause of the Lord, and sought their own things in place of it. In their indifferent spirit they probably took the relation to Persia, produced by the Samaritan interference, as the ground of their opinion, that it was not the time to come and finish the task. They were an ungrateful people and should have known better. The Lord, who had announced through Isaiah that Cyrus should be born and say, "Let Jerusalem be built," who raised up Cyrus, whom the prophet had named so many years before he was born; the Lord who had brought them back to the land and prospered them, would certainly give them the victory over all their enemies and make the building of the house possible. They hid behind the unreasonable excuse, it is not the time. How often the same excuse has been used by the professing people of God in our age!

Then the Lord answers them. "Is it a time for you yourselves to dwell in your ceiled houses, while this house lieth waste?" They had begun well, as we read in Ezra 3, when they set the altar upon its bases. But now they had departed from their endeavor; the interest in the one thing had waned, and selfish aims were substituted. They were living in luxurious houses, while His house was completely neglected, it was in a waste condition. The insincerity of their vain excuse was therefore exposed.

Then comes the exhortation to consider their ways (literally: set your heart upon your ways). Had it been profitable for them? No. Ever since they left off building His house bitter disappointment had been their lot. All their self-seeking brought them no gain, but steady loss. The Lord's blessing, given to His earthly people concerning earthly things, had been withholden. They had sown much seed; there was a scanty return. They had not been satisfied in eating or drinking. Their clothing was insufficient. The wages they earned may have been good wages, but it was as if they put them in a bag with holes; the great part of them was lost. While all this must be considered on the ground of the Jew, the principle nevertheless holds good for us as well. "But seek ye first the kingdom of God and His righteousness; and all these things shall be added unto you" (Matt. 6:33), also refers primarily to the believing Jew, yet it has its application for us. The heart of the believer must always seek Him first. The life of a child of God must always be devoted to Him and the things of God. Our business is to care for His things; His gracious business is to care for us in all things. Neglect of the things of God always brings the same bitter disappointment.

Verses 7-11. Consider your ways; the Lord spoke again. And now He commands them to go to the mountains and fetch wood and to build the house. He declares that He will take pleasure in it and that He will be glorified. How graciously He craves the whole-heartedness of His people and their full devotion to Himself. It is in worship, indicated by the building of the house, that we glorify Him. It is worshippers the Father seeketh, worshippers in spirit and in truth (John 4).

On account of their neglect, neglect of Himself and the honor of His Name, as centered in the house, He could not give the blessing He is so willing to bestow upon His people. He withheld the dew and the rain; He prevented the fruitfulness of the fields, and all else was stunted, on account of their attitude toward Him.

"It was Jehovah who blighted their selfish efforts. He was dealing with them on account of their unbelief and neglect. It was not because He loved them not, but because He did. 'Whom the Lord loveth He chasteneth, and scourgeth every son whom He receiveth.' When the Lord allows persons to go away without rebuke, it is the sure sign that all practical bond is broken—if any bond did exist—that He now disowns them, for a time at least. Hence these very chastenings of the Jewish remnant were the proof that His eyes were still over them, and that He felt their negligence of Him and resented—in divine faithfulness—the failure of His people in the care of His glory" (William Kelly).

CHAPTER 1:12-15

The Second Address

The spirit of God carried home the burning message of rebuke, and that happened which did not happen with the generation before the captivity. They considered their ways. They took it to heart. They knew the Lord had spoken, and that He was right, the rebuke well earned. Happy are all those who act always in this way, who humble themselves and are obedient to the Lord. It is a refreshing scene which the twelfth verse records. They all united, Zerubbabel, Joshua, and all the remnant of the people. There was not one dissenting voice. They all obeyed the Lord and the words of the prophet.

"Then Haggai, the Lord's messenger, spoke again in the Lord's message unto the people." It is striking how it is made prominent that he did not speak of himself, but was the Lord's messenger and brought the Lord's message. Would to God that all those who claim the dignity of a minister of the gospel were all the Lord's messengers, and spake nothing but the

Lord's message. The greatest curse in Christendom today is the man who claims to be the Lord's servant, but has no message from the Lord, for the reason that he has lost faith in the Word of God.

Another has pointed out the fact that Haggai is the one prophet who is directly called Jehovah's messenger. He is the least of the post-exilic prophets, yet the Lord puts this honor upon him. In spite of his inferior style, according to the critics, the Lord owns him by this title of distinction.

And what was his message at this time? "I am with you, saith the Lord." That is the content of the second address; just one sentence. But what a sentence it is! What assurance it brings to the heart, and how it inspires faith to action. "I am with you, saith the Lord." Such is our blessed assurance. "Lo, I am with you always, even unto the end of the age." And as we look to Him and trust Him there is power.

The result was a mighty revival in the good work. The Lord stirred them up through His Word, the brief message He sent. Every true revival begins the same way. It has been well said, "I am with you, is the saving principle for faith in the weakest possible day, and let me add, what had they better in the brightest day?"

CHAPTER 2:1-9

The Third Address

Over a month later, after a good deal of work had been done, the prophet delivered his third message. He is commanded to speak to the same company, headed by Zerubbabel and Joshua; but here the remnant of the people, the exiles who had returned, is also included. If we consult Ezra 3:12 we find that many old men, who had seen the temple of Solomon, burst out in weeping when the small foundation was laid for the new temple. A similar feeling possessed the people when they resumed the temple work after Haggai's first message. In comparison with the former temple, so grand and glorious, the new temple was a feeble and insignificant affair. The prophet begins his message by asking, "Who is left among you that saw this house in its former glory, and how do you see it now? Is it not in your eyes as nothing?" No doubt there was additional weeping when the prophet asked these questions.

Haggai then becomes the prophet of comfort and of hope. "Yet now be strong" is in literal translation, "And now be comforted, O Zerubbabel, saith Jehovah; be comforted all the people of the land, saith Jehovah; for I am with you saith the Lord of Hosts." They were discouraged on account of the smallness of their cause. It is then when the Lord delights to comfort and to cheer his trusting people. He was with His people, though now no longer a mighty host as of old, but only a small remnant; yet had He not forgotten the Word which He covenanted with them, when He brought them out of Egypt with an outstretched arm. "My Spirit abideth among you; fear ye not." And that should be enough. His Spirit was dwelling with them to execute His work, and be their strength. The gift of the Spirit in New Testament times is something greater than this. After the finished work of our Lord and His glorification, the third Person of the Godhead came in person to indwell every member of the Body of Christ.

Verses 6-9 contain the great prophecy concerning the future. It takes us beyond the time of Haggai, past this present age, and puts before our hearts the same great and glorious day when Christ comes again, when there shall be greater glory and peace. The question is, who is the desire of all nations? It merits a closer examination, for the critics have labored to explain away the Messianic meaning of this sentence and rob it of its true meaning. For instance, Canon Driver, in *The New Century Bible* makes the following comment: "The desirable things of all nations shall come, i. e., their costly treasures will be brought to beautify the temple." The Hebrew is a peculiar phrase; the subject is a noun, feminine, singular; the predicate is a plural masculine. The word "chemdath"—desire, is the same as used in Daniel 11:37, the desire of women. If literally translated it would read thus: "And the desire of all nations, they shall come." The Septuagint therefore translates it, "the choice things of all nations shall come;" others have rendered it in the following ways: "The things desired by all nations shall come," with the interpretation that it is the gospel; "all the Gentiles shall come with their delightful things;" "the beauty of all the heathen;" "they shall come to the desire of all nations;" "with the desire of all nations;" the "choicest of all nations (that is the best of them) will come," etc. With all these suggested renderings of the difficult phrase there can be no question that it points to Christ, and must be interpreted as a great Messianic prophecy. The most ancient comments are on this line altogether. Christ is the object of the desire of all nations. This does not necessarily mean that He is subjectively the desire of the nations, but He is objectively, for through Him alone the nations can be blest and receive the righteousness and peace which they need.

First, the announcement is made, "I will shake the heavens, and the earth, and the sea, and the dry land." Have these convulsions been? While there have been shakings of kingdoms in the political sense, and the earth has often been shaken physically and otherwise, this prophecy is yet to be fulfilled. The Holy Spirit bears witness to it in the New Testament, for we read in Hebrews 12:26-28, "Whose voice then (at Sinai in a physical manifestation) shook the earth; but now He hath promised, saying, Yet once more I shake not the earth only but also heaven. And the word, Yet once more, signifieth the removing of those things that are shaken, as of things that are made, that those things which cannot be shaken may remain. Wherefore, we receiving a kingdom which cannot be moved (the coming kingdom and not the church) let us have grace, whereby we may serve God acceptably with reverence and godly fear." This settles the question as to the futurity of this prophecy. Critics have objected to this interpretation on account of the statement that this universal shaking is to be in "a little while." They apply it therefore to the nearer political events of that period. But the future in prophecy is often fore-shortened, and besides this, the little while is not man's little while, but God's; with Him a thousand years is as a day. Furthermore, in the political events of the times which followed the restoration of the Jews from Babylon not all nations were involved. The prophecy before us declares, "I will shake all nations;" this, too, is future. The Messiah, spoken of next as "the desire of all nations," came the first time, but His coming did not bring the blessing and glory to nations as predicted here, nor did the promised peace come. He made peace in His sacrificial death; the foundation for "peace on earth" was then laid, as well as for the great future blessing of all the nations. But the Jews delivered Him into the hands of the Gentiles, and the Gentiles treated Him as did the Jews. In anticipation of His rejection He said, "Think not that I am come to bring peace, but the sword." Then followed the present age, unknown with its mystery, the church, to the prophets. It will close with the shaking of all nations, when the King-Messiah will appear again and bring the promised blessing to all nations. The silver and gold, which belong to the Lord, will then be brought by the nations. (Isa. 60:5).

It is important to read the ninth verse in the right way, as our Authorized Version is incorrect. It does not say in the Hebrew, "The glory of this latter house shall be greater than the former," but the Hebrew is, "The latter glory of this house shall be greater than the former, saith the Lord of hosts; and in this place will I give peace, saith the Lord of hosts." The house of course is the temple. The visible glory dwelt once in the former house; the day is coming when there will be greater glory, the day of His glorious manifestation; then in connection with His coming and that coming restoration, He will give peace.

CHAPTER 2:10-19

The Fourth Address

A few months later Haggai delivered another address of moral instruction and admonition. The question the prophet asks first is answered by the priests negatively. This is followed by a second question, "If one that is unclean by a dead body touch any of these, shall it be unclean?" This they answered affirmatively; for he that is defiled puts defilement upon everything he handles. When they had given the right answers, the prophet makes the moral application. "So is this people, and so is this nation before me, saith Jehovah; and so is every work of their hands; and that which they offer thereon is unclean." All their works and offerings were unclean, because they were in that condition. They had to be cleansed first. Separation from evil, from that which defiles, was therefore demanded. So it is today. The order is "cease to do evil" and then "learn to do well." We are, as Christians, no less exhorted to purge ourselves, to separate from evil, and then to become fit vessels for the Master's use.

And then the Lord challenges them to prove Him, to see if they separate from evil, are wholly for Him, how faithful He is going to be to them. "From this day," the day of a true return to the Lord followed by obedience and separation, "I will bless you."

CHAPTER 2:20-23

The Fifth Address

The final address of Jehovah's messenger is altogether prophetic. It is addressed exclusively to Zerubbabel, the governor, a son of David.

He tells the princely leader that the heavens and the earth will be shaken; it is the same as in verse 6. When that comes the throne of the kingdoms will be overthrown; the power of the kingdoms of the nations (the ten kingdoms; Dan. 2) will be destroyed, for in that day, the falling stone, typifying the second coming of Christ, will make an end of Gentile dominion. The battle of Armageddon will take place and end the military power of these nations. Zerubbabel, the son of David, is the type of Christ, the Son of David. He will then receive the throne of His father David. He will be made a signet. The signet-ring was among those nations a mark of honor. It was given by monarchs to their prime-ministers, conferring all authority upon them. Thus the Lord Jesus Christ is pictured as receiving from God the rule and authority.

THE PROPHET

ZECHARIAH

Introduction

Zechariah is the great prophet of the restoration, and, as stated in the introduction to Haggai, was contemporary with him. The prophecies in both books are dated. These are as follows:

In the sixth month of Darius's second year	Haggai 1
In the seventh month of the same year	Haggai 2
In the eighth month, the same year	Zechariah 1
In the ninth month, the same year	Haggai 2
In the eleventh month, the same year	Zechariah 1—6
In the fourth year of Darius, ninth month	Zechariah 7—14

Zechariah is named in Ezra 5:1 and 6:14; he was of priestly descent, which we learn by consulting Nehemiah 12:4, 16. His name means "Jehovah remembers." He was the son of Berechiah, which means "Jehovah will bless;" and his grandfather's name was Iddo; Iddo means "the appointed time." These are significant names; one might say the great prophetic message of Zechariah is given in these three names in a nutshell. For the covenant-keeping God remembers His people, which the visions and messages of Zechariah show. When He remembers them He will bless them, but it will be at the appointed time, and the appointed time has not yet come, hence the greater part of Zechariah remains unfulfilled.

He was born in Babylon, and when he returned to the land of his fathers he was a child. In his vision he is addressed as a young man, so that he was quite young when called into the responsible position of a prophet. As to the historical setting of his prophecies, it is the same as Haggai's, and we refer the reader to what we have said there.

According to ancient sources he lived to be a very old man, and was buried alongside of Haggai in Jerusalem; but this cannot be verified. Jewish tradition says that he was a member of the great synagogue, and took an active part in providing for the liturgical service of the new temple. The Septuagint version of the Old Testament ascribes to him the composition of Psalms 137 and 138, and to Haggai and Zachariah Psalms 145—148; and the same do other versions like the Peshito and the Vulgate. Some expositors have been so superficial in their statements that they identified him with the Zechariah who was slain by Joash of Judah, between the temple and the altar, as mentioned in 2 Chronicles 24:20-23.

His Great Message

Zechariah in his message does not rebuke the people on account of their slackness in building the house of the Lord, as we learned Haggai did, though his great prophecies were given to encourage the remnant in their work. The horizon of Zechariah's visions and prophecies is far more extended than the horizon of the other minor prophets. He covers the entire future of Israel and leads onward from his days to the time when Messiah comes to Jerusalem, when His own received Him not. He pictures the condition of the nation after the rejection of Christ, and then leads up to the time of His return and the happy results which follow the repentance of the remnant, when they shall look upon Him whom they pierced.

The Gentile world-powers, as prophetically announced in Daniel's great visions, are seen by him as domineering over Jerusalem; and how the Lord will finally deal with these powers. The last siege of Jerusalem, and what is connected with that siege, the tribulation, the deliverance by the visible coming of the Lord, and the resultant kingdom, concludes his book. It is indeed a complete prophetic history of Israel and the times of the Gentiles from the captivity to the end of these times. His book has rightly been called by the same name as the last book of the Bible, the Apocalypse—an unveiling. And there are certain features which identify Zechariah in some measure with the book of Revelation. Zechariah may well be placed alongside of Isaiah and Daniel.

The Messianic Predictions in Zechariah

Zechariah has more to say about Christ, His person, His work and His glory than all the other minor prophets combined. We mention here the more direct predictions found in the book; there are others, which will be pointed out in the annotations.

I. He speaks of Christ as "the Branch." This is one of the names of our Lord revealed to Isaiah and Jeremiah (Isa. 4:2; Jer. 23:5). Zechariah speaks of Him twice under this title, in chapters 3 and 4.

II. A great prediction concerning Christ is found in the sixth chapter, when the prophet is commanded to order the crowning of the high-priest, symbolical of our Lord, who is the crowned King-Priest.

III. In chapter 9:9-10 we have the familiar passage quoted in the New Testament concerning Christ's entrance into Jerusalem. In this passage the first and the second coming of our Lord are blended together.

IV. He speaks of Him as the Shepherd, and the price of His betrayal, the thirty pieces of silver, also quoted in the New Testament. Chapter 11:12, 13 and Matt. 27:9, 10.

V. Another great Messianic prophecy is recorded in chapter 12:10. Here His death on the cross is predicted, and that He is the pierced One, on whom they shall look, on account of whom they shall yet mourn. (See John 19, and Revelation 1.)

VI. Still another prophecy relating to the sufferings of Christ is chapter 13:7. The sword is to awake against the Man, who is the fellow of God; that sword is to smite Him.

VII. Finally, we mention the passage in the last chapter, where the prophet describes Him as coming for the salvation of His waiting people, and that His feet in that day shall stand on the Mount of Olives. It is He who was seen last standing on the Mount of Olives, with the promise of His return "in like manner." As stated before, these passages are the prominent ones, but not by any means all the predictions concerning Israel's Messiah.

There is an interesting Jewish work on Zechariah, the Yalkut of Zechariah. It gives interesting comment on his prophecies. The great teacher Abarbanel confessed his inability to interpret these visions. How could he with his denials that Jesus of Nazareth is the Christ? And the much honored Jewish exegete, Solomon Ben Jarchi, declared "his prophecy is very abstruse, for it contains visions resembling dreams, which want interpreting; and we shall never be able to discover the true interpretation until the teacher of righteousness arrives."

That teacher, the Holy spirit, has come. He guides us now into all truth; He makes plain things to come, as revealed in the prophetic Word. By comparing Scripture with Scripture, and avoiding the "private interpretation" against which Peter warns (2 Peter 1) we understand the visions, which two of the greatest Hebrew scholars and teachers declared unexplainable.

The Division of Zechariah

For a correct understanding of the book, the correct divisions must be first of all ascertained. We give, therefore, first the scope of the book. After an introduction comprising the first six verses of the first chapter, we have the record of his great night-visions.

1. **The Vision of the Man upon the Red Horse Among the Myrtles** (1:7-17)
2. **The Four Horns and the Four Smiths** (1:18-21)
3. **The Man with the Measuring Line** (Chapter 2)
4. **The Vision concerning the Cleansing of the High-Priest** (Chapter 3)
5. **The Vision of the Candlestick with the Two Olive Trees** (Chapter 4)
6. **The Vision of the Flying Roll** (5:1-4)
7. **The Woman in the Ephah** (5:5-11)
8. **The Vision of the Four Chariots** (6:1-8)

Some have made ten visions out of it instead of eight; there is no need for that. The vision which they divided is the one in chapter 1:18-21. But this is one vision; and so is the vision in chapter 4. After these visions had been given the young prophet was commanded to make crowns of silver and gold and crown the high-priest. It was a great symbolical action, foretelling Him, who wore on earth the crown of thorns, and who will be crowned with many crowns when the night is gone and the day breaks.

This is the first section of the book. The second section is contained in chapters 7 and 8. It is a kind of parenthesis. Questions concerning certain fasts had been asked by the prophet; they were answered by the Lord and their interesting answers are recorded in these two chapters.

The third section is contained in chapters 9—14; it is the most majestic part of the book. It is arranged in two parts, each beginning with the phrase "The Burden of the Word of the Lord." The first burden is chapter 9:1 and the second is chapter 12:1. It reveals in a remarkable manner the future of Jerusalem, so intensely interesting to every true believer in our significant times. We follow this threefold division in our analysis and annotations.

Analysis and Annotations

I. The Night Visions

CHAPTER 1

1. The introduction (1:1-6)
2. The first night vision (1:7-17)
3. The second night vision (1:18-21)

Verses 1-6. The first utterance of Zechariah concerns the past. "The Lord hath been sore displeased with your fathers." They were a disobedient, stiff-necked people. The pre-exilic prophets had called them to repentance, but they did not hearken. Then he gives the message to turn to the Lord, with the promise that He will turn to them; they should not be like their fathers. And their fathers, where were they? They had passed away like the disobedient ones in the wilderness; God's judgment and displeasure had overtaken them and they perished.

Verses 7-17. After this opening message with its call to return, delivered probably before the assembled congregation, the prophet received his great night-visions. These were not mere dreams, but the things he describes passed before him in divine vision. He beheld them in one night. They were not only given in one night, but just as one followed the other without interval, so are they closely connected, giving progressively coming events. There is, of course, to a certain extent in some of these visions the message of hope for the Jewish remnant of that day, but the visions concern the future, and can only be understood in the light of other prophecies concerning the end of the age and the glorious future of Israel and Jerusalem. To apply them to the Church produces the greatest possible confusion. We shall see how these visions concern the Gentiles first and the overthrow of the world-powers, followed by the blessings and glory promised to Israel, which all will be given to the nation in the day when Gentile dominion ceases forever. When the visions end, the morning comes after that memorable night of revelation, the command to crown the high-priest is given.

Without quoting the text in full we give the interpretation of each vision. He beheld an army of riders upon different colored horses, led by a man riding a red horse, who is the center of the vision. There is an interpreting heavenly messenger, to whom the prophet turns to find out who the riders are. They do not represent the Persians, as some expositors have stated; they are angels. It is the man upon the red horse who speaks. "These are they whom the Lord hath sent to walk to and fro through the earth." The riders upon the horses give their report to the man in the middle. "Behold, all the earth sitteth still and is at rest."

Who is the rider upon the red horse? He is called the "Angel of the Lord." There is no question but that the rider and the Angel of the Lord are the same person. And the Angel of the Lord in the Old Testament is an uncreated Being; He is the Son of God in His pre-incarnation glory. There are three very good reasons for this interpretation. 1. The color red identifies him with our Lord. He is the Lamb of God who shed His blood in redemption; He is the Lion of the tribe of Judah (Rev. 5) who will arise in judgment upon the nation in the coming days of vengeance and trample His enemies under foot (Isa. 63). 2. He is the Leader as well as the Center of the heavenly hosts; they are subject unto Him; all things are in His hands. 3. He makes intercession, which marks Him as the one who is the intercessor before God in behalf of His people. Our larger exposition of Zechariah quotes the Jewish interpretation *(Studies in Zechariah,* pp. 11-12).

The report of the angelic hosts was that the earth sitteth still and is at rest. The nations were at rest, in the state of prosperity; but His people is in trouble, the land of promise under Gentile rule and dominion. While the cities of the nations were increased and had plenty, the city of the King was under the hoof of the Gentiles; His people suffered. Such is the condition of things throughout the time of the Gentiles. In our comment, written in 1899 we made the following remarks:

"Prosperity, universal prosperity, and with it universal peace, is the cry at the close of another century, and will be more so as we advance towards the end of this age. Civilization, world conquest, commercial extension, and a universal peace, seem to be the leading thoughts among the nations of our times. Truly it is realized by some that our boasted civilization, liberty and prosperity, is nothing but a smouldering volcano which may burst open at any moment and make an end of all boasting; but the majority of the people even in Christendom are sadly deluding themselves with idle dreams. And what of God's thoughts and His eternal purposes? What of His oath-bound covenant promises? They are being misinterpreted, set aside and forgotten. Thus it will continue till the climax is reached, so clearly foretold in the Second Psalm."

This forecast has come true; the great war has come and gone and now the age is rapidly approaching its predicted end.

Then follows in the vision the intercessory cry of the Angel of the Lord. It concerns in the first place the indignation of the seventy years. But that dispersion is the prophetic type of their greater dispersion. What was true then concerning the nations and the state of Jerusalem, is true of the present and future. The nations helped forward their affliction by hating the Jew. The great sin of the nations is Anti-Semitism, which is the result of not believing the Word of God. The hatred of the Gentiles will culminate in the end of the age in coming against the partially restored nation, as we shall learn at the close of our prophecy. Then the assurance is given that the Lord in His jealousy will remember His people and Jerusalem will be chosen and Zion comforted.

Verses 18-21. He saw next four powerful horns, the emblems of the powerful Gentile nations who have scattered Judah, Israel, and Jerusalem. The four horns are the same four world-powers announced in Nebuchadnezzar's dream and in Daniel's vision (Daniel 2, and 7). They are symbolized by the locusts in their four stages (Joel 1). Four smiths appear in the vision to fray them and to cast them out. The vision teaches two facts: first, the horns will be broken and cast down; and in the second place, God has for every power which has sinned against His people a corresponding instrument, to overcome and to break into pieces.

CHAPTER 2

1. The man with the measuring line (2:1-2)
2. The message of the third night vision (2:3-9)
3. The glorious kingdom (2:10-12)

Verses 1-2. The third night vision is one of the coming glory. The number three stands in the Word of God for resurrection, life from the dead. Thus in Hosea, concerning Israel, "After two days Thou wilt revive us, and on the third day Thou wilt raise us up" (Hosea 6:2). In this third vision Zechariah sees the glorious restoration of Israel, which has been the burden of so many prophecies, and the glory which is connected with that restoration. In this night vision Zechariah hears of a restoration and of a glory which has never yet been fulfilled in the history of God's people. Those teachers of the Word who see in Zechariah's night visions nothing but fulfilled prophecy, cannot answer certain questions satisfactorily, and their only refuge must be a spiritualizing of this restoration. Another thought before we take up this third vision. The vision of restoration comes after the enemies of Israel have been cast down. That prophecy might be fulfilled; prophecy about a believing, suffering Jewish remnant; prophecy concerning Jacob's trouble, etc., a mock restoration, generally termed a restoration in unbelief, is to take place. There can be no doubt whatever that we are privileged to see the beginning of this restoration of part of the Jewish nation to the land of the fathers in unbelief. It is one of the signs of the nearness of that event for which the Church hopes, prays and waits: "our gathering together unto Him." The world and the lukewarm Christian do not see it, but he who loves the Word and lives in the Word, has eyes to see and a hearing ear, and knows what is soon coming. The true restoration, however, will only come as it is seen so clearly in these night visions after the enemies have been overcome, the horns cast down, the image smashed—in other words, after the Lord has come.

First stands the man with the measuring line. He is to bear witness to the coming enlargement of Jerusalem. Similar visions where measuring takes place are found in Ezekiel 41, where the future temple is measured, and in Revelation 11 a reed is given to John to measure the temple of God, which is the temple erected by the Jews in unbelief during the tribulation period. Here it is the measuring of the city.

Verses 3-9. The angel who had talked with Zechariah was met by another angel. He brings the message to Zechariah, who is addressed as "this young man." The coming restoration and enlargement of Jerusalem is announced. The city is to be inhabited as villages, which denotes the peace and safety which Jerusalem will enjoy in the day of her true restoration. It will be the temptation for the enemy, Gog and Magog, to invade the land. (See Ezek. 38, and 39.) The invasion of Gog and Magog in Revelation 20 is after the millennium; the one in Ezekiel is in the beginning of the millennium. Then Zechariah hears in the message that the Lord will be Himself a wall of fire unto Jerusalem; He will be the glory in the midst of her. Glory and defence are combined, they always go together (Isa. 4). This was not the case in the restored Jerusalem after the captivity. It is altogether future. What a glory it will be when every eye sees Him, when His visible glory will be once more established in the land, from which its knowledge spreads over the earth till it covers all, like the waters cover the deep! (Habakkuk 2:14). Then they are summoned to return from the land of the North. Millions of Jews are living and suffering in the great land of the north, Russia. In that day they will return to the old homeland. They will escape out of the clutches of Babylon, the final Babylon. He calls the believing remnant the "apple of His eye." He will guard and keep them.

Verses 10-12. The singing times have come (Zeph. 3). Zion rejoices for He dwells in their midst (Isa. 12). Then the nations are joined to the Lord in that day, not to the Church, for the true Church is in glory, but they will be joined to Israel in the kingdom. The third vision closes with an exhortation similar to the one in Habakkuk 2. All flesh is to be silent before the Lord. Now is the time when God is silent. The flesh speaks now, for it is man's day. But our God shall come and not keep silent (Psa. 60). Then all the flesh, with its fruits, will have to be silent before Him in that day.

CHAPTER 3

1. The fourth night vision (3:1-5)
2. The message of the vision (3:6-10)

Verses 1-5. The fourth vision is like the first and second, closely connected with the foregoing one. It gives the crowning event of Israel's restoration. The prophet recognizes in the figure, which is seen by him, Joshua the high priest, who is standing before the angel of the Lord, while at his right hand stands Satan to oppose him. Joshua was not clothed with his clean, priestly robes, but he wears filthy garments. Jehovah rebukes Satan and terms Jerusalem a brand plucked from the fire. After the accuser is rebuked, the filthy garments of the high priest are removed, his iniquity is forgiven, and he is clothed with festal raiment. The prophet is so carried away with the vision that he asks that a clean mitre is to be put upon his head. And now, after the high priest is thus clothed, the Angel of the Lord charges him with an important message: If thou wilt walk in My ways and keep My charge, thou shalt judge My house and also keep My courts. I will give thee access among those standing here, etc. The servant—the branch—is promised, and the stone which is laid before Joshua is to have seven eyes. The iniquity of this land is to be removed in one day, and the vision closes with the peaceful scene, every man inviting his neighbor under the vine and under the fig tree.

The high-priest Joshua in this vision stands as a type of the sinful nation and her priestly calling. Like Joshua in filthy garments, the nation is unclean and defiled. Yet in spite of his filthy garments Joshua was still the high-priest. The gifts and calling of God are without repentance; Israel, in the purposes of God, is still the priest. In the vision Satan is seen, true to his name, the accuser.

He is the enemy of Israel. He has tried in the past to hurt and to destroy the nation of destiny. He knows the purposes of God concerning Israel better than many a learned doctor of divinity, and therefore, he has opposed that people and opposes them still. His opposition has been mostly through nations. How much could be said on this topic! The end of this age will reveal the enemy of Israel, the adversary, as never before in the history of the world. There is to be war in heaven; Michael and his angels going forth to war with the dragon; and the dragon warred, and his angels, and they prevailed not, neither was their place found any more in heaven. And the great dragon was cast down, the old Serpent, he that is called the Devil and Satan, the Deceiver of the whole world, he was cast down to the earth and his angels were cast down with him (Rev. 12:7-9). His wrath will be directed against Israel and Jerusalem. It is the time of which Daniel spoke. "And at that time shall Michael stand up, the great prince which standeth for the children of Thy people; and there shall be a time of trouble such as never was since there was a nation, even to that same time (Dan. 12:1)." Once more Satan will try to destroy the people, but the Lord shall rebuke him. Israel will be again, as so often before, like a brand plucked out of the fire. So it has been in the past. Way back when Israel was in Egypt and God was about to send the deliverer, He called Moses from out of the burning bush—Israel's true type, burning, but never consumed. Oh, how the fire of persecution and adversity has been raging, but again and again the hand of God snatched the burning brand out of the fire at the right moment. The Lord who hath chosen Jerusalem will rebuke Satan. This has not yet come. The coming Lord will commission an angel out of heaven, having the key of the abyss and a great chain in his hand. And he will lay hold on the dragon—the old serpent which is the Devil and Satan—and bind him for a thousand years, and cast him into the abyss and shut it and seal it over him (Rev. 20:1, 2). Then follows the cleansing of Israel and the new charge, all so clearly given in this vision.

The filthy garments are removed by those that stand before the angel of the Lord. The iniquity is taken away, and in place of the filthy garments there is the rich apparel and the fair mitre upon the head. How blessedly all this is waiting for its fulfillment in Israel's regeneration! When He appears after the times of overturning, He whose right it is, His people Israel will be found by Him in true penitence, acknowledging their offence. It will be a national repentance, a mourning on account of Him, which Zechariah describes in detail in the twelfth chapter.

Verses 6-10. Israel was disobedient and did not keep the first charge. It is now repeated, and gives Israel's future calling after their cleansing. It will be threefold. 1. Judging in the house of the Lord, and from there ruling and judging nations, for Israel will be the head of the nations. The Church will then not be on earth, but occupy her glorious place in the new Jerusalem above the earth. 2. Israel will keep His courts. That is, Israel will attend to the millennial temple, which will become the house of prayer for all nations, which all the former temples were not. 3. Israel will have places to walk amongst those who stand by, that is, among the nations, in priestly ministry. The saved remnant will then be "men which are a wonder," the miracles of His grace and power. Then the servant, the Branch is announced; a definite Messianic prediction. The stone engraven, with seven eyes upon it, must also mean the redeemed nation, the foundation of the kingdom, filled with His Spirit, for we read in connection with it, "I will remove the iniquity of that land in one day." A picture of the conditions of peace and prosperity in the kingdom concludes the fourth night vision.

CHAPTER 4

1. The fifth night vision (4:1-10)
2. The questions of the prophet answered (4:11-14)

Verses 1-10. There was a rest for the prophet between the fourth and fifth night vision. He had fallen into a deep sleep. He may have been overcome by the grand and important visions, and is now awakened by the angel with the question, "What seest thou?" The new vision is a very striking one. A golden candlestick appears before the seer. An oil receiver is seen on top, from which the oil flows to the seven lamps of the candlestick through seven pipes. Two olive trees stand alongside of the candlestick and hang their fruit-laden branches over the golden bowl, filling it with oil, which flows through the seven pipes into the seven lamps. The question of the prophet, "What are these, my Lord?" is answered by the angel with this statement, "This is the word of Jehovah to Zerubbabel, saying, Not by might and not by power but by My Spirit, saith the Lord of Hosts. Who art thou, oh great mountain, before Zerubbabel? Be a plain! He shall bring forth the topstone with shoutings of grace, grace unto it. The hands of Zerubbabel who have laid the foundation shall also finish it, and they shall rejoice and see the plummet in the hand of Zerubbabel—even the seven. The eyes of the Lord shall run to and fro through the entire earth."

The Church in the New Testament is typified by a candlestick. The oil is the emblem of the Holy Spirit. But this is not in view in this vision.

We call attention to the fact that the vision is one which speaks of perfection, completion, fullness. The perfect and divine number seven is found three times in the vision, seven lamps, seven pipes and seven eyes. The seven lamps are united to one stem, this is union, and above it, is a golden bowl. The Spirit conquers, and not power or might does it, but His power. The great mountain becomes a plain. The topstone is brought forth and crowns the building which is finished by Zerubbabel. Shoutings, "Grace, grace, unto it," are heard, and the seven eyes run to and fro the whole earth. It is a vision of fullness and accomplishment. The candlestick shines and sheds its glorious light, its pure gold glitters and reflects the light of the seven lamps. The bowl is filled with oil, and the two olive trees give a continual supply. The high mountain removed, the temple finished, joy and victory abound. The candlestick in the vision is exactly like the one in the tabernacle, only the two olive trees are something new. The candlestick in the tabernacle represents Christ, the Light of the world, and is likewise a type of the Jewish theocracy. Theocracy, the government of this earth by the immediate direction of God, is once to be established, and when it is, it will be like a bright and glorious candlestick shedding light and dispersing the darkness. We think the *Yalkut* on Zechariah (a Hebrew commentary), is not so very far out of the way when it says, "the golden candlestick is Israel." It seems to us very clear that the vision represents the Jewish theocracy restored, Israel in their glorious inheritance as the light of the world.

Verses 11-14. The prophet asks two questions concerning the two olive trees and the branches which gave the oil through the golden pipe. The two olive trees, filled with the supply of the Spirit, are in all probability the two witnesses of Revelation 11. Their testimony is given during the second half of the last seven years of the times of the Gentiles, Daniel's seventieth week (Dan. 9). It is the time of the great tribulation and these two witnesses stand in close relation with the establishment of the kingdom. See annotations on Relevation.

CHAPTER 5

1. The sixth vision (5:1-4)
2. The seventh vision (5:5-11)

Verses 1-4. The three remaining night visions are of a different character. The first visions the prophet had were visions of comfort for Jerusalem and the dispersed nation, the overthrow of Babylon and all their enemies, divine forgiveness and the theocracy restored. Now follow the last three visions, and these are visions of judgment. Judgment precedes Israel's restoration, and is very prominently connected with it.

The sixth night vision is the one of the flying roll. The prophet's eyes seem to have been closed after the fifth vision, for we read, "And I lifted up my eyes again." The flying roll he sees is twenty cubits long and ten cubits broad. The interpreting angel tells the prophet that it is the curse that goeth forth over the face of the whole land; for every one that stealeth shall be cut off on this side according to it, and every one that sweareth shall be cut off on that side according to it. The Lord of hosts has brought it forth and it is to enter into the house of the thief, and into the house of him that sweareth by His Name to a falsehood, and it shall lodge in the midst of His house and consume it, both its wood and its stone.

That this vision means judgment is evident at the first glance. Ezekiel had a similar vision. "And when I looked, behold, an hand was sent unto me; and, lo, a roll of a book was therein; And he spread it before me; and it was written within and without: and there was written therein lamentations, and mourning, and woe (Ezek. 2:9, 10)." Ezekiel was to eat that book. This reminds us at once of the books in Revelation (chapters 5 and 10), which are likewise connected with God's judgments in the earth. The flying roll is written on both sides, signifying the two tables of stone, the law of God. Stealing and swearing falsely are mentioned because the one is found on the one side of the two tables of stone, and the other on the other side. However, it is no longer "Thou shalt not," but on the flying roll are written the curses, the awful curses against the transgressors of God's law which are now about to be put into execution. The curse is found in its awful details, as it refers to an apostate people in Deuteronomy 27 and 28. The roll is of immense size, and on it are the dreadful curses of an angry God. The vision must have been one of exceeding great terror. Imagine a roll, probably illumined at night with fire, moving over the heavens, and on it the curses of an eternal God—wherever it moves its awful message is seen; nothing is hid from its awe-inspiring presence. It reminds one of the fiery handwriting on the wall in the king's palace. Surely such an awful judgment is coming by and by, when our God will keep silence no longer. One of the sublimest judgment Psalms, the Fiftieth, mentions something similar to this flying roll. "When thou sawest a *thief,* then thou consentedst with him, and hast been partaker with adulterers. Thou givest thy mouth to evil, and thy tongue frameth deceit. Thou sittest and speaketh against thy brother; thou slanderest thine own mother's son. These things hast thou done, and I kept silence; thou thoughtest that I was altogether such a one as thyself: but I will reprove thee, and set them in order before thine eyes" (Psalm 50:18-21). The flying roll stands undoubtedly in connection with wickedness, theft, and false swearing, as it is found in so many forms in unbelieving Israel, but it finds also a large application in the judgment of wickedness throughout the earth in the glorious day of His appearing.

Verses 5-11. The angel commands the prophet

to lift up his eyes to behold another startling vision. What are the leading figures in the vision? An ephah—which is a Jewish measure standing here for commerce. The eyes of all the land (or earth) are upon it. Commercialism is very prominent in Revelation in connection with the full measure of wickedness, the climax of ungodliness. In Revelation 18 merchants are mentioned who have grown rich through the abundance of her delicacies. Then the merchants are seen weeping, for no man buys their merchandise any more. And then a long list follows, including *all the articles of modern commerce.* Compare this with the awful description of the last times in James 5. Rich men are commanded to weep and howl, for miseries are come upon them. They heaped treasure together for the *last days,* and it was a heaping together by fraud, dishonesty in keeping back the hire of the laborers. They lived in pleasure (luxuriously) and were wanton. Indeed, here is that burning question of the day, capital and labor, and its final outcome, misery and judgment upon commercialism, riches heaped up, and all in wickedness. In Habakkuk 2:12 the woe of judgment of that coming glory of the Lord is pronounced upon him that buildeth a town with blood and established a city by iniquity! The people are seen laboring for the fire and wearying themselves for vanity. Luxuries, increase, riches, etc., are mentioned in the second and third chapters of Isaiah, chapters of judgment. Other passages could be quoted, but these are sufficient for our purpose. They show us that the climax of wickedness as it is in the earth when judgment will come, and Israel's time commences once more, will be connected with commerce, riches and luxuries. The ephah points to this.

In the second place let us notice that in the *midst* of the ephah there is seen a *woman.* She is called wickedness. The Hebrew word wickedness is translated by the Septuagint with *"avouia".* We find that the Holy Spirit uses the same word in 2 Thess. 2:8, and then shall be revealed in the wicked one *(avouia)* whom the Lord Jesus will slay with the Spirit of His mouth. The woman in the ephah personifies wickedness. She has surrounded herself with the ephah and sits in the midst of it. Have we not here the great whore having a golden cup in her hand full of abominations and filthiness of her fornication? Undoubtedly. This woman is the type of evil and wickedness in its highest form. Let us glance at that wonderful description of that woman in Revelation. She is the great whore sitting upon many waters. She sits upon a scarlet colored beast, full of names of blasphemy, having seven heads and ten horns. The woman is arrayed in purple and scarlet decked with gold, precious stones and pearls. Upon her forehead is seen her name, Mystery, Babylon the Great, the mother of harlots and abominations in the earth. She is drunk with the blood of the saints. The woman in the ephah represents the same great whore, Babylon the Great. This becomes at once clear when we take into consideration that the woman in the ephah is carried swiftly away an a house is built for her in the land of *Shinar,* and it shall be established, and set there upon her own *base.* Now the land of Shinar is *Babylonia..* But while in Revelation 17 the mystical Babylon is seen, in the eighteenth chapter there is another Babylon, the final great political-commercial world system; it is still future, not very far away, for we see that the trend of modern events is towards such a combination. The vision of the ephah and the woman evidently sealed up in it may denote the overthrow and judgment of the final Babylon.

CHAPTER 6

1. The eighth vision (6:1-8)
2. The crowning of Joshua, the High-Priest (6:9-15)

Verses 1-8. The last vision is the vision of the four chariots. We notice the similarity with the first night-vision. The visions opened with the hosts of heaven upon red, speckled, and white horses. It was a vision of judgment for the Gentiles and a vision of comfort to Israel. In this last vision the chariots of judgment are seen sweeping over the earth. It seems to denote judgment in its final accomplishment. The riders of the first vision may be termed the beginning of God's dealing with the nations, but the chariots put the divine judgment decrees into operation.

The riders halted in a valley amidst a myrtle grove, but the chariots rush forth to execute their terrible work from between two mountains of brass. These mountains mean undoubtedly Mount Moriah and the Mount of Olives. They rush through the Valley of Jehoshaphat. The brass is mentioned to denote the firmness and stability of these mountains, which shall never be moved. We do not think that in the four chariots there is an allusion to the four world-powers. The judgment of them is now come. The stone is falling and smiting the image at its feet and pulverizing it, putting it completely out of existence. The chariots are God's powers, agencies for judgment in the earth, which will pass swiftly along, shown by the fast running chariots. In Rev. 6 the seven seals are opened, and there go forth the four terrible riders upon white, red, black, and pale horses. The riders in the Apocalypse are the riders which go through the earth during the great tribulation, but in the eighth night vision of Zechariah we see the chariots of God's wrath. The vision falls in the time when the heaven opens and He appears riding upon a white horse, His name Faithful and True, coming in righteousness to judge and to make war. Wonderful vision of Him who is clothed with a vesture dipped in blood! He is followed by the armies of heaven upon white horses, all clothed in fine linen white and clean. "And out of His mouth goeth a sharp sword, that with it He should smite the nations, and He shall rule them with a rod of iron, and he treadeth the winepress of the fierceness and wrath of almighty God" (Rev. 19).

The angel interprets to the prophet that the chariots are the four spirits of the heavens which go forth from standing before the Lord of the earth. These agencies for wrath were with God, standing before Him, the Lord of all the earth, but now at His command they descend to scatter death and destruction. They go forth in sets, and the north country and south country both so prominent in the prophetic word are mentioned. The bay horses, hwoever, are not confined to one direction, they go through the entire earth. At last in the judgment of the land of the north the Spirit is caused to rest. The overthrow of the enemies of Israel is complete and the spirit is quieted. How long may the wrath last and for how long may the chariots do their deadly work? Perhaps longer than we think. The millennial reign of Christ, as foreshadowed in the bloody rule of David, followed by the peaceful reign of Solomon, may teach us lessons in this direction. The night visions have ended. They may be termed the Apocalypse of Zechariah. Daniel, Zechariah, and Revelation go together in a wonderful harmony and explain each other. Alas! that just these three parts of the Bible should be so little studied and so little understood.

Verses 9-15. The merable night with its great visions was gone. The first streaks of the morning heralded the coming dawn. Then the Word of the Lord came to the young prophet commanding him to make crowns of silver and gold and crown Joshua, the High-Priest.

Some consider this to be the ninth vision of the prophet. It is, however, the word of the Lord which comes to the prophet. There can be no doubt but the command was actually carried out and Cheldai (robust), Tobiah (God's goodness), and Jedaiah (God knows), gave their silver and gold, and crowns were made out of it and placed upon the head of Joshua the high-priest. But the action had a much deeper meaning. It was a highly typical one. It must have astonished Joshua and the people to hear such a command, for the royal crown did not belong to the high-priest but to the descendant of David. He must have understood that the whole command had a symbolical bearing. Joshua hears it from the Word of the Lord that another person is only typified by him, "Behold the man whose name is the Branch." It is this man the Branch who will be a priest upon the throne. This, of course, is our Lord Jesus Christ. The name of the high-priest Joshua is in itself very significant, for the meaning is, God is salvation, Saviour, Jesus. Pontius Pilate was fulfilling prophecy when he stood there leading out Jesus of Nazareth before that tumultuous multitude, and when he said "Behold the man." If the assembled Jews had known the Scriptures they would have recognized the phrase. But how did He then come forth? He wore a crown of thorns upon His meek and loving brow, and the people gazed into the blood-stained face of the Lamb of God now ready to be placed upon the altar and slain. But once again it will sound forth, "Behold the man," for when He appears it will be after He has gathered His saints, and then He will come as the Son of Man in the heavens, and the sign of the Son of Man will be seen there. He will be crowned again, too, but not with the crown of suffering and shame, but with the crowns of glory. Thus He is seen in Revelation 19:12 as wearing many crowns.

He comes to build the temple of Jehovah, bearing majesty, sitting and ruling upon His throne. He is now the builder of the spiritual temple, which is composed of living stones (Eph. 2:21, 1 Peter 2:5). But when He comes again there will be the building of another temple. It is now no longer His Father's throne but His own, upon which He is a priest as well. The King of Kings and the Lord of Lords has now taken possession of His inheritance. The times of overturning are over and He whose right it is has come. There is a very instructive thought in the fact that the persons of the exile, as mentioned above, were to bring the silver and the gold out of which the crowns were to be made. The time will come when the whole exiled nation, so long scattered and peeled, though even in dispersion, the richest nation of the earth, will bring their silver and gold, their glory and their all and lay it at the feet of the King.

II. Questions Concerning Certain Fasts

CHAPTER 7

1. The question (7:1-3)
2. The reproof (7:4-7)
3. The lessons of the past (7:8-14)

Verses 1-3. Nearly two years had passed since Zechariah's great visions, and during that time the people had been obedient to the vision and built the house. Soon the ancient worship was to be resumed. A question arose in the minds of the people concerning certain Jewish days of fasting. The principal day was the day set apart in memory of the destruction of Jerusalem by the Babylonians. It was kept on the ninth day of the fifth month (the ninth of Ab, still kept by the Jews). The question came to the prophet through two men who bear foreign names—Sherezer (Prince of the Treasury) and Regemelech (the official of the king). The question was, "Should I weep in the fifth month, separating myself, as I have done these many years?" They had wept in Babylon on that day (Psalm 137).

Verses 4-7. The word of the Lord comes now to the prophet. The message is for all the people and for the priests. The two fasts are mentioned. The one in the fifth month as already stated was the one in remembrance of the destruction of the city. The fast of the seventh month was kept on the anniversary of the murder of Gedaliah at Mizpah (Jeremiah 41). But why did they keep these fast days? Why do they keep these days indeed still? The Lord asks, "Is it unto Me, unto Me?" No, it was not for the honor and glory of God, but their own selfish interests were at the bottom of it. Indeed God had never asked them to fast. These institutions were man-made, and highly displeasing to Jehovah. And is it not so now, not alone with the Jews but with Christendom? Oh, the man-made institutions and outward observances which only dishonor God and are for the selfish interests of the people! The eating and drinking, the fast being over, was not unto the Lord, but unto themselves. It was obedience the Lord required. Had they listened to the words spoken by the prophets they would not have been in captivity, there would have been no need for a solemn fast. Unbelief was at the bottom of it all, and so it is still with the nation in dispersion.

Verses 8-14. Here are moral lessons and instructions. They were to execute true judgment, show mercy and compassion, oppress not the widow nor the fatherless, the poor or the stranger. These were His demands in the past, but their fathers did not listen, and as a result the judgment of the Lord came upon them and they were scattered with a whirlwind. History has repeated itself. What happened in the past happened again.

CHAPTER 8

1. The restoration announced (8:1-3)
2. The peace of Jerusalem (8:4-5)
3. The return to the land (8:6-8)
4. The blessing of the land and the people (8:9-23)

Verses 1-3. The answer is now given to the question, and it is an answer which none of the petitioners expected. The answer is closely linked with the third night vision in chapter 2, for here is an enlarged prophecy concerning the restoration of Jerusalem. Jehovah was jealous for Jerusalem. The wrath fell upon the Gentiles and He poured out His fury upon them (which of course is future). When that has taken place He returns unto Zion and establishes His dwelling place in the midst of His people. Then Jerusalem is no longer trodden down by the Gentiles. Her name is a new name, "the City of Truth." How different from the other names she bore in her humiliation! She was called an unclean woman (Lam. 1:8, 17); a harlot and a murderer (Isa. 1:21); Sodom and Egypt (Rev. 11).

Verses 4-5. The misery of Jerusalem was great while under judgment. All will be changed "in that day." The city will have peace and prosperity and be largely inhabited. Hence there will be no more need to weep over her past fate and desolation, for greater glory has come.

Verses 6-8. They all return to the land. In the second chapter the north country was mentioned (Russia); and their return announced. Here the east and the west are named, the far east, India, China, Japan; and the West, the European countries and America.

Verses 9-23. What a contrast with the former days of judgment and dispersion and misery! For before these days there was no hire for man, nor any hire for beast. . . . Little fruit was had from the ground; there was nothing for man and beast. . . . Neither was there any peace to him that went out or came in on account of the affliction. . . . There was no rest, no peace, but uncertainty and affliction. Those that went out from the land had no peace, and they that came into the land found no peace. The curse said, No rest for the sole of their feet, and how literally it has been fulfilled. Again the people seek a resting place in the land without their God and their Saviour, all in the confidence of the flesh. They will succeed in their restoration plans only to find themselves at last in greater difficulties and facing worse afflictions than ever before. Then every one will be against his neighbor (verse 10). Money spent by the millions in building channels for irrigation, planting of trees and vines, building railroads, etc. (just what modern Zionism proposes and has undertaken to do), may succeed in transforming the land in spots into a fruitful garden, but the time of Jacob's trouble will sweep that all away. The Lord will be gracious to the very land in the day of His manifestation. There will be a time of peace, the vine will give her fruit, the ground her increase, the heavens their dew.

The curse will then be changed into a blessing and the remnant will be a holy people. Fast days become feast days; national calamities of the past are forgotten, and in the place of weeping there is praise and worship. The songs of praise with which the book of Psalms closes will undoubtedly then be sung by the restored nation. This great restoration chapter closes with a vision of the conversion of the whole world (verses 20-23). The nations are seeking the Lord of Hosts in Jerusalem to pray before Him. Then the Jew will no longer be a dishonored person among the Gentiles, but they will be the messengers of the King among the nations; and they will gladly take hold of the skirt of the Jew to be taken by him to Jerusalem.

III. The Two Prophetic Burdens— The Great Prophecies of the Future

1. The First Burden (9—11)

CHAPTER 9

1. The burden of the land of Hadrach (9:1-8)
2. Zion's King of Peace (9:9-12)
3. The near-event of the invasion by Antiochus Ephiphanes (9:13-17)

Verses 1-8. The final section of Zechariah is of still greater interest. The Deliverer, King Messiah, is revealed in this section as suffering, rejected, pierced, slain. The great finale leads us up to the great conflict and final siege of Jerusalem. We do not enter into the inventions of criticism, which claim that these great prophecies are less authentic than the first part of Zechariah.

The land of Hadrach against which the first burden in chapter 9 commences cannot be correctly located. Its closer connection with Damascus and Hamath shows that the land of Hadrach must have been a province of the Syrian kingdom then in existence. The Phoenician cities Tyre and Sidon are next, and then mention is made of four Philistine cities. Against these, Syria, Phoenicia and the cities of the Philistines a great calamity and overthrow is prophesied by Zechariah. They are conquered by the hosts of an enemy, and the rich reasures of Tyre are heaped together in the streets—silver as the dust and gold as the mire—the bulwarks are smitten, and she herself consumed by fire. From there the conquest goes on rapidly to the Philistinian cities, and the King of Gaza perishes. The question arises, What conquest and calamity is this? Is it accomplished or is it still future? History records one great conqueror who rapidly overthrew the countries and cities mentioned in this burden. Alexander the Great and his expedition so successfully carried on is undoubtedly meant here. All students of the prophetic Scriptures know how prominently he likewise stands out in the book of Daniel. The young monarch, after the battle of Issus, besieged and quickly captured Damascus. Sidon was easily taken, but Tyre resisted him some seven months and was burned to the ground. Gaza and the other cities came next. Thus the burden of the word of Jehovah as uttered here by Zechariah was literally fulfilled in the Syrian conquest of Alexander the Great. However, history tells us that the armies of the youthful monarch passed by Jerusalem a number of times without doing harm to the city. This is remarkable, and in accord with the prophecy of Zechariah, for we read in the eighth verse, "And I will encamp against mine house, against the army, against him that passes through and returns, and no oppressor shall come over them any more, for now I have seen it with mine eyes."

But this prophetic burden leads us up also to the final days, for we read here the promise that "no oppressor shall come over them any more." This brings it in connection with the final coming deliverance of Israel, and the final destructive visitation upon their enemies.

Verses 9-12. A great prophecy follows. The true King of Israel comes here before us in His humiliation, and coming exaltation.

> Rejoice greatly, daughter of Zion,
> Shout aloud, daughter of Jerusalem;
> Behold thy king cometh to thee,
> Just and having salvation;
> Meek and riding upon an ass,
> Even upon a colt, the she-ass's foal;
> And I will cut off the chariot from Ephraim,
> And the horse from Jerusalem,
> And the battle bow shall be cut off,
> And He shall speak peace unto the nations,
> And His dominion shall be from sea to sea,
> And from the river to the ends of the earth.
> As for thee also, for the sake of thy
> covenant blood,
> I send forth thy prisoners from the
> waterless pit,
> Return to the stronghold—Prisoners of hope
> Even today I declare I will render double
> unto thee.

This stands in contrast to the Grecian conqueror, and it needs no proofs that the coming King whom Zechariah beholds is the King Messiah. The Jews acknowledge it as such. One of the greatest Jewish commentators (Rashi) says: It is impossible to interpret it of any other than King Messiah. An interesting fable is based upon this prophecy, and well known among orthodox Jews. Rabbi Eliezer says, commenting on the words lowly and riding upon an ass, "This is the ass, the foal of that she-ass which was created in the twilight. This is the ass which Abraham our father saddled for the binding of Isaac his son. This is the ass upon which Moses our teacher rode when He came to Egypt, as it is said, And he made them ride upon the ass (Exod. 4:20). This is the ass upon which the Son of David shall ride." Other interesting quotations could be given from Jewish writings, but this is sufficient to show that the Jews believe it to be a Messianic prophecy. And what blindness that they do not see Him who is the Messiah; but is not the so-called "higher criticism" existing today in Christendom being taught in churches and schools, and that there are no Messianic prophecies in the Old Testament, much greater blindness? Alas! so it is, and the outcome can be nothing else in the end than the denial of the divinity of our Lord, or Unitarianism.

Every reader of the New Testament knows that this prophecy is quoted in the Gospels. In the Gospel of Matthew we read (chapter 21:5): "All this was done that it might be fulfilled which was spoken by the prophet, saying, Tell the daughter of Sion, Behold thy King cometh unto thee, meek, and sitting upon an ass, upon a colt the foal of an ass." The context shows a great multitude crying, Hosanna to the Son of David: Blessed is He that cometh in the name of the Lord; Hosanna in the highest. But soon the cry is changed unto, This is Jesus the prophet from Nazareth of Galilee. Notice the Holy Spirit quoting from Zechariah leaves out the sentence, *"He is just, having salvation."* This is not an error, but it is the divine right of the Spirit who gave the prophecies in olden times to apply them correctly in the New Testament. In the Gospel of Mark in the eleventh chapter there is likewise the description of Christ's entry into Jerusalem, but Zechariah is not quoted. The same is true of the account given by Luke, chapter 19, and here He is mentioned as the King that cometh in the name of Jehovah, peace in heaven, and glory in the highest. In the fourth Gospel, chapter 12:15, the account of His coming to Jerusalem is much shorter than in the other Gospels. It says there, "Fear not, daughter of Zion; behold, thy King cometh, sitting upon an ass's colt."

We see from this that the four Gospels give each an account of the entry of the Lord into Jerusalem; two of them quote from Zechariah and the other two do not. The quotations themselves are different from the prophecy in Zechariah 9 in two respects. The first words, Rejoice greatly, are not at all used. In Matthew it is, Tell the daughter of Zion, and in John, Fear not, daughter of Zion. The sentence, He is just and having salvation, is left out in both.

A superficial exposition of the Word claims that Zechariah's prophecy was fulfilled in the event recorded by the Gospels. As far as His entry into Jerusalem is concerned, riding upon the colt the foal of an ass (and note in Matthew it is shown that both the colt and the ass are brought to Him. He could ride, of course, only upon one, but the she-ass had to go along in fulfillment of prophecy), and the way He came, meekly, in this respect the prophecy was fulfilled. This entry of the Son of Man into Jerusalem was His formal presentation to Jerusalem as its King, but, as stated above, the Messianic cry of welcome, Blessed is He, soon changed into, Jesus the prophet from Nazareth in Galilee, and that again in the final cry of rejection, Crucify Him, crucify Him! There was no salvation for Israel then, and no kingdom for Him, hence no rejoicing is mentioned in the quotations.

It is His second coming to Jerusalem as the Son of Man in His glory which will bring the fulfillment of Zechariah 9:9-11. True, the colt, the she ass's foal, will not be the animal He rides, but He will come upon a white horse followed by the armies of heaven. He comes then truly for Jerusalem, fulfilling the prophecy, "Just is He having salvation" (marginal reading, victory). There will be again the welcome cry of the one hundred eighteenth Psalm, "Blessed is He that cometh in the name of Jehovah," preceded by the plea, "Hosanna, save now."

The tenth and eleventh verses show clearly that the prophecy is yet to be fulfilled and can be only fulfilled in the coming of the Son of Man in His glory. One of the reasons why modern Judaism rejects Jesus of Nazareth, and does not believe Him to be the promised Redeemer, is in this prophecy. Rabbi F. De Sola Mendes, of New York, brings in a little book, "A Hebrew's Reply to the Missionaries," the following argument: "We reject Jesus of Nazareth as our Messiah on account of His deeds. He says of Himself: 'Think not that I am come to send peace on the earth; I came not to send peace but a sword,' etc. But we find that our prophets ascribed to the true Messiah quite different actions. Zechariah says (9:10), He shall speak peace to the nations. Jesus says He came to send the sword on the earth; whereas, Isaiah says of the true Messianic time, 'They shall beat their swords into ploughshares, and their spears into pruning-hooks; nation shall not lift up sword against nation; neither shall they learn war any more.' "

Of course the Jew is right in expecting the literal fulfillment of this prophecy, and it will be fulfilled when He comes again and the restoration of all things will follow, as spoken by the mouth of all His holy prophets.

When He appears again, in like manner as He went into heaven, that is not for His saints but with His saints, there will be peace for Ephraim and for Jerusalem, and the kingdom is then restored to Israel, that is, to the house of Judah and the house of Israel. The chariot, the horse, and the battlebow will be cut off.

Not alone will He bring peace to the covenant people but to the nations. He will speak peace. "And He shall stand, and shall feed His flock in the strength of the Lord, in the majesty of the name of Jehovah His God, and they shall abide; for now shall He be great unto the ends of the earth. And this man shall be our peace" (Micah 5:4, 5). There will be abundance of peace (Psa. 72:7). His dominion will be from sea to sea and to the ends of the earth.

The prisoners of hope to be released, by the blood of the covenant, from the pit wherein there is no water, is the nation whose captivity is now ended. How strange that people should take a passage like this and interpret it as meaning the restitution of the wicked and the ungodly from the pit. There is nothing taught in the Word like that which some people term a larger hope. The restitution (restoration) of all things is not left to the fanciful interpretation of the human mind, but is clearly defined by the Word itself, as spoken by the prophets. In the vision of the dry bones in Ezekiel 37, Israel's complaint is, Our hope is lost. But when He is manifested, who is indeed the Hope of Israel, the prisoners (the captives), will be released and cleansed. "Refrain thy voice from weeping and thine eyes from tears, . . . there is hope for thy latter end, saith the Lord, and thy children shall come again to their own border" (Jer. 31:17). The exhortation to return to the stronghold follows. Israel will then sing. "He brought me up out of an horrible pit, out of the miry clay, and He set my feet upon a rock, and established my goings" (Psa. 40:2). Double will be rendered unto them, as promised, "Speak to the heart of Jerusalem, and cry unto her that her warfare is accomplished, that her iniquity is pardoned, that she has received of the Lord's hand double for all her sins" (Isa. 40:2). "For your shame ye shall have double, and for confusion they shall rejoice in that portion; therefore in their land they shall possess double; everlasting joy shall be unto them" (Isa. 41:7).

Verses 13-17. The scene changes once more. One of Alexander's successors, Antiochus Epiphanes, and the Maccabean victory is the topic of these verses. On this invader see Daniel 8, where he is predicted as the little horn and his abominable work there is fully described. He entered "the pleasant land," the land of Israel. A bitter struggle commenced, for Antiochus tried to exterminate the Jews, and their religion as well. Every observance of the Jewish religion was forbidden, the Sabbath had to be profaned, and unclean food had to be eaten. Idols were set up in the temple. Instead of the Jewish feasts, the feasts of idols, with all their shocking abominations and immoralities, were introduced, and the Jews were forced to join in them. Thousands suffered martyrdom. But all at once a few people stood up against the abominations, the Maccabeans, and in a struggle lasting about twenty-five years, they fought successfully against the enemies.

This terrible visitation of the land and the

wonderful victory of the Maccabeans are foretold by the prophet in the closing verses of the ninth chapter. We will quote the passage:

> I bend for me Judah and fill the bow with
> Ephraim,
> And I will stir up thy sons, Zion, against
> thy sons, Greece,
> And make thee like the sword of a mighty
> man.
> Jehovah shall be seen over them,
> And His arrow shall go forth like lightning.
> And the Lord Jehovah shall blow the trumpet.
> He shall go with whirlwinds of the South.
> The Lord of Hosts shall cover them;
> They shall devour and tread down slingstones,
> And they drink and make a noise as from wine,
> And they shall be filled like bowls, as the
> corners of the altar.
> And Jehovah their God saves them in that
> day, as the flock of His people;
> For jewels of a crown shall they be, glittering
> over His land,
> For how great is His goodness and how
> great His beauty!
> Corn shall make the young men flourish,
> and new wine maidens.

But again we have to remark that this prophecy is only partially fulfilled. The terrible tribulation of the land of Judah when Antiochus Epiphanes invaded the land is but a type of the great tribulation, the time of Jacob's trouble. The remnant of Israel will then be victorious. Thus everything is seen in this chapter in a past fulfillment, but only partial, and in it a future fulillment, which will be complete.

We cannot leave this chapter without calling attention to the blessed statement:

> For jewels of a crown they shall be, glittering over His land.

The slain who suffered martyrdom are meant, and all those who fought for Jehovah's name and honor. May not the statement in Hebrews 11 refer to this time? "Others had trials of mockings and scourgings, yea, moreover of bonds and imprisonment: they were stoned, they were sawn asunder, they were tempted, they were slain with the sword; they went about in sheepskins, in goatskins: being destitute, afflicted, evil entreated, of whom the world was not worthy, wandering in deserts and in mountains and caves and the holes of the earth" (Heb. 11:36-38).

And all will find a repetition during the coming tribulation. But the time for reward has not yet come. The throne of glory is not yet revealed, and the jewels, the saints made up in a crown, glittering over the land, are not yet seen. But the assurance is given, "They shall be Mine, saith the Lord of Hosts, in that day when I make up my jewels" (Mal. 3:17).

The first verse of the next chapter is misplaced; it belongs to the close of chapter 9. When the time of blessing comes, the latter rain will fall upon the land and produce the promised fruitfulness.

CHAPTER 10:2-12

1. The apostatsy of Israel in the last days (10:2-4)
2. The victory over the enemies (20:5-7)
3. Deliverance and restoration (10:8-12)

Verses 2-4. Idolatry was the great sin of both Judah and Israel. They practiced the occult things of heathendom and worshipped their false gods; they had teraphim used for divination. On account of this the wrath fell upon the former generations, and the Lord's anger was kindled against their leaders, the shepherds, and they were dispersed. We have called attention before to Matthew 12:43-35, the passage in which the Lord Jesus announces that the unbelieving part of the nation will return in the last days to the unclean spirit of idolatry, only in a worse form than before. Many of the unbelievers amongst the Jews in our days turn to the witchery of Christian Science; they adopt also that Satanic system known as spiritism. But the apostates will go beyond that. They will finally accept the Devil's master production, the man of sin, and worship him (2 Thess. 2; Rev. 13; Dan. 9:27). Then the Lord will punish these goats. At the same time there is a remnant which will stand aside from these future idolatries; they will fear the Lord and not enter into a covenant with the beast (see annotations Daniel 9:27). The second half of the third verse in this chapter belongs to this remnant: "The Lord of hosts visits His flock, the house of Judah, and makes it like His state-horse in the war." He will use them and finally deliver them.

The fourth verse is of much interest. "From him will be the cornerstone, from him the nail, from him the battle-bow, from him every ruler goeth forth at once" (corrected translation). The nail in the oriental house is a large pin, often very beautifully ornamented, and the most costly things are hanged thereupon. "And I will fasten him as a nail in a sure place and he shall be for a glorious throne to his father's house. And they shall hang upon him all the glory of his father's house" (Isa. 22:23, 24). The Shemoth rabbah, a Jewish interpretation, says on this verse, "this is King David; as it is said, the stone which the builders rejected is become the chief cornerstone." Some say it is spoken concerning the Lord, that He is the cornerstone and the nail. It refers to Him, no doubt, but what is spoken of Him finds also a fulfillment in restored Israel. Thus Israel is yet to be the cornerstone upon which everything rests in the earth, and the nail upon which hangs the glory.

Verses 5-7. The great final victory is announced in this section. They shall fight and conquer, for the Lord of hosts is with them as of old. They will be saved out of the time of Jacob's trouble, "For I have mercy upon them; and they shall be as though I had not cast them off; for I am the Lord their God, and I will hear them." Ephraim will be there, the restored ten tribes.

Verses 8-12. They will be delivered in that day, redeemed and restored. Let us notice that the eleventh verse must be applied to the Lord. He is with them in the sea of affliction, as He was with them in Egypt and went before them in the pillar of cloud.

CHAPTER 11

1. The judgment of the land, the temple and the slaughter of the flock (11:1-6)
2. The true shepherd set aside and rejected (11:7-14)
3. The foolish shepherd (11:15-17)

Verses 1-6. This chapter presents a dark prophetic picture. We have seen in the preceding chapters the blessings and mercies in store for the Israel of the future. The visions and prophecies have revealed their national and spiritual restoration, the overthrow of their enemies, the destruction of the world-powers, the establishment of the theocracy and the blessings of the kingdom. What precedes this coming glory is now more fully unfolded, and the rejection of the Shepherd of Israel is predicted. The first six verses concern the judgment as the result of that rejection. For a complete exposition see our "Studies in Zechariah," where we also give the interesting Jewish comments on this passage. They apply it mostly to the destruction of the temple.

The correct interpretation is that it includes all the devastation of the land, the burning of the temple, the slaughter of the flock, the spoiling of the shepherds, the Jewish leaders and the complete overthrow of the land and of the people. How awful the fulfillment of the prophecy has been! The Lord's voice, full of tears cried, long after Zechariah's mournful vision, "If thou hadst known, at least in this thy day, the things which belong to thy peace, but now they are hid from thine eyes! For the days shall come upon thee that thine enemies shall cast a trench about thee and compass thee round, and keep thee in on every side. And shall lay thee even with the ground, and thy children within thee, and they shall not leave in thee one stone upon another." The measure was full. After terrible wars amongst themselves, the fire advanced in the direction of Lebanon, in the form of the Roman army full of vengeance, spreading ruin and misery wherever they went, till after a long and dreadful siege Jerusalem fell, the temple was burnt, and over a million human beings were slain. Not one stone was left upon another. Up to now this judgment has been the most appalling, the tribulation then the greatest; but there is another tribulation coming of which the former destruction of Jerusalem is but a faint type, and that tribulation which is even now so close at hand will find a climax in the day of wrath, the day of vengeance of our God. The next verses (4-6) speak of the flock of slaughter and the last attempt divine love made to save the doomed nation.

Verses 7-14. The prophet acts again symbolically in taking two staves, one called Beauty, the other Bands. Much has been written on this interesting but difficult passage. The first sentence speaks of divine love. The true Shepherd came, the Messiah, and He fed the flock of slaughter, the poor of the flock. He looked on the multitudes and was moved with compassion, for they were scattered, like sheep without a shepherd. The prophet as representing the true Shepherd has two staves. The one is named Beauty; or, as we read in the margin, graciousness. The second one is named Bands. The Shepherd carries a staff to protect and to guide His flock. God's mercy and favor are clearly indicated in these two staves. The first one, Beauty, which is cut asunder first, and that before the wages of the Shepherd, the thirty pieces of silver, are given, stands no doubt for the gracious offer with which the King, preaching the kingdom, came among His people, to His own. He proclaimed that which prophets had spoken before, God's mercy and love, long promised, now to be carried out. He Himself had come to redeem His people and deliver them from their mighty enemies as well as from the false leaders. But the offer, the kingdom preaching, is rejected, the staff, Beauty, is cut asunder, the covenant with the peoples (Amim in Hebrew), His own, is now broken. The kingdom is to be taken away and given to another nation. After the breaking of the staff, Beauty, there comes the giving of the wages, the thirty pieces of silver. The Shepherd who broke the staff is treated like a slave.

The second staff in His hands, Bands, speaks of union, binding together, bringing into fellowship. It typifies the priestly side of the good Shepherd who died for the flock. This staff is broken after the thirty pieces of silver were given for Him, and cast into the temple. They cried, Away with Him! we have no King save Caesar! Crucify Him! His blood be upon us and upon our children! The cross bears the superscription, This is Jesus of Nazareth, the King of the Jews, and from the lips of the rejected King and Shepherd there came the prayer for His people, Father, forgive them, for they know not what they do. The doom came not at once upon the nation. Once more the love of the Shepherd is preached to the miserable sheep, and the remission of sins offered in the name of the Lord Jesus Christ, but it ends in rejection too; no bringing together into One followed. The foolish shepherd appears next, and after him the good Shepherd will appear again with His two staves, Beauty and Bands, kingdom and mercy, bringing and binding together. He will then be a Priest upon His throne. This interpretation is the most satisfactory one, and in harmony with the entire scope of Zechariah's visions and prophecies.

Who are the three shepherds to be cut off in one month by the Shepherd? The three shepherds are not persons, but they stand for the three classes of rulers which governed Israel, and were in that sense shepherds. We read of these shepheards in Jeremiah 2:8, priests, rulers and prophets. The Lord likewise mentions them in Matthew 16:21, elders, chief priests and scribes. When He came He was indeed weary with them, and denounced their hypocrisies and wickedness. They in turn hated and abhorred Him, and conspired to put Him to death. The Lord Himself cut them off. He pronounced His woes and judgments upon them, but the judgment was not at once carried out. When Jerusalem was taken, their rule came to an end and they were cut off.

But there are mentioned the wretched of the flock that gave heed unto the Shepherd, and they knew that it was the word of Jehovah. These wretched ones are the faithful ones who followed the Shepherd, the small remnant (compare with chapter 13:7). The others who rejected the King and the Shepherd were indeed not fed, but were dying and cut off.

The wages of the good Shepherd, thirty pieces of silver, and these thrown into the house of Jehovah to the potter is to be considered next. Thirty pieces of silver was the price of a slave who had been killed. If the ox gore a manservant or a maidservant, the owner shall give unto their master thirty shekels of silver (Exodus 21:32). Oh, what unfathomable love! The Lord from heaven became like a slave. The love He looked for He found not. It was refused to Him, and instead He was insulted, mocked, and treated like a miserable slave. There was one of the twelve who was called Judas Iscariot. He went to the chief priests and said, What are you willing to give me, and I will deliver Him unto you? And they weighed unto him thirty pieces of silver (Matt. 26:15). The money at the command of Jehovah is thrown away by the prophet with indignation into the house of Jehovah, to the potter. Perhaps the prophet never knew the real significance of his act, but we know it from the New Testament. "Then Judas which betrayed Him, when he saw that He was condemned, repented himself and brought back the thirty pieces of silver to the chief priests and elders, saying, I have sinned in that I betrayed innocent blood. But they said, What is this to us? See thou to it. And he cast down the pieces of silver into the sanctuary, and departed and hanged himself. And the chief priests took the pieces of silver and said, It is not lawful to put them into the treasury since it is the price of blood. And they took counsel and bought with them the potters' field to bury strangers in. Wherefore that field was called the field of blood unto this day. Then was fulfilled that which was spoken by Jeremiah, the prophet, saying, And they took the thirty pieces of silver, the price of Him that was priced, whom certain of the children of Israel did price, and they gave them for the potters' field, as the Lord appointed me" (Matt. 27:3-10). How striking the fulfillment. However, here is a difficulty. In Matthew it is stated that Jeremiah spoke the prophecy, and Zechariah's name is not mentioned at all. How can this be explained?

The prophecy certainly as it was fulfilled was not given by Jeremiah at all, but through Zechariah. There can be no doubt that his name should appear here instead of Jeremiah, but that Jeremiah's name is quoted must have a meaning. Let us notice that it does say not in Matthew 27 that it was *written* by Jeremiah, but it is stated that it was *spoken* by Jeremiah. Is there anything in Jeremiah which can be linked with this prophecy? We have indeed in Jeremiah a similar action of the prophet, corresponding to Zechariah 11:13, and which is seen fulfilled in the gospel. Read Jeremiah 18 and 19. The word "Tophet" used there means an unclean place, a burial ground. Jeremiah's name appears in Matthew's Gospel, to call attention to the fact that Jeremiah also spoke of the same event, the rejection of the true Shepherd.

Verses 15-17. The foolish shepherd is the false Messiah, the man of sin, the son of perdition. The prophet impersonates him likewise. He no longer holds the staves of Beauty and Bands, but has the instrument of the foolish shepherd to wound and to hurt. This false Christ is the opposite from the true Christ. The true Shepherd came to see, to save, to feed, to heal, and to gather; the false shepherd does the opposite.

The True One rejected, the nation becomes the prey of the foolish shepherds. Poor, blinded Israel! How many wicked shepherds they have had, and how often the prey of wicked leaders. False Messiahs appeared among them again and again to find strong and numerous following. Still the foolish shepherd, the last one, the very embodiment of Satan himself, the accuser, has not yet come. Forerunners there have been many. Herod was one of them, but not that man of sin, the son of perdition who will appear and be worshipped as a God, right before the King of Kings and the true Shepherd of His flock appears to slay that wicked one with the breath of His mouth and the brightness of His coming (2 Thess. 2). The Lord said, I am come in My Father's name, and ye receive Me not; if another shall come in his own name, him ye will receive (John 5:43). That one who comes in his own name has not yet come, and when at last he is here, it will be for Israel the time of greatest trouble and tribulation for all them that inhabit the earth. During the war interpretation of prophecy went to seed with some who saw in the deluded German Kaiser a fulfillment of this passage, because he had a withered arm. Such foolish inventions are deplorable, for they bring the study of prophecy into disrepute. The third section of our chapter finds its complete fulfillment in the Antichrist, the false Messiah, the beast, the little horn, the leader of the enemy, the false prince of Israel; thus the foolish shepherd is called throughout the prophetic word. The dreadful punishment will be executed upon the foolish shepherd in the day of the Lord's coming with His saints for the salvation of his people Israel.

The eleventh chapter in Zechariah is the darkest in Israel's history. The night began with their apostasy and rejection of the Lord of Glory, their own brother, their loving Shepherd, the Lord Jesus Christ. It ends in darkness greater still under the regime of the foolish shepherd. But the morning cometh after that dark night, and Israel's sun will never set again.

II. The Second Burden of Zechariah
(12—14)

CHAPTER 12

1. Jerusalem's conflict and victory (12:1-9)
2. The vision of the Pierced One and its results (12:10-14)

Verses 1-9. The second burden begins with this chapter. It is wholly unfulfilled with the exception of the prophecy at the end of chapter 13 concerning the Shepherd who was smitten. The great future events recorded in these closing chapters of Zechariah are the following: The victory of Jerusalem, the overthrow of the hostile nations from the west (the nations which constitute the revived Roman Empire), the outpouring of the Spirit upon the remnant, the appearing and the vision of the Pierced One, the national repentance, the cleansing of the people, the invasion from the north, the appearing of Christ standing upon the Mount of Olives, the establishment of the kingdom and the glory of Jerusalem. Historically no such gathering of all nations against Jerusalem can be located. It is all prophetic, and so intensely interesting in the days we write, for these things are "about to come to pass."

> Behold, I make Jerusalem a cup of
> reeling
> To all the nations round about:
> Upon Judah also shall it be,
> In the siege against Jerusalem.
> And it shall come in that day, I make
> Jerusalem
> A burdensome stone for all the peoples;
> All that are burdened with it shall
> be wounded;
> All the nations of the earth shall
> gather against it.

This does not take place till the end of the age is reached, the end which begins after the true Church is taken to glory. Then the nations satanically blinded will form the confederacy which in prophecy is the reconstruction of the Roman Empire, seen in the second chapter of Daniel under the symbol of the two feet and ten toes, and in Daniel 7 under the symbol of the ten horns with the little horn. In Revelation 13 it is the beast with the ten horns. The Jews will have to return first, at least a goodly number of them, and repossess the city.

In 1899 the author wrote as follows: "An exodus of Jews will take place, the land will become theirs, and the well laid plans and schemes of the present time will be carried out. Political combinations will be their chief hopes for success." This anticipated return is now a historic fact as one of the chief results of the great war. When finally the Jews think that they have reached the goal of their fleshly, unbelieving hopes, their greatest trouble begins. There is yet to appear the beast who makes a covenant with them. But according to Daniel's great prophecy (Dan. 9) the covenant will be broken in the middle of the seventieth week. Then the beast heads the armies of the nations to come up against the land and against Jerusalem (see Rev. 19:19). They will lay siege to the city, but the Lord announces that these nations shall be cut to pieces. It is the time when the stone strikes the feet of the prophetic image in the second chapter of Daniel, the great battle of Armageddon. Verses 4-9 describe that day. Jehovah will smite these nations and all these hostile forces will be overthrown.

Here also is given the order of how the Lord will save the remnant of His people. Those who live in tents outside the city will be saved first; Jerusalem comes next. The purpose is that the house of David and the inhabitants of Jerusalem may not exalt themselves over the rest of Judah. The house of David in this vision is mentioned five times. We have the glory of the house of David in verse seven, the strength of David and the supremacy of it in verse eight. The spirit of grace and supplication is given to the house of David, and the family of the house of David will mourn. Jews have a tradition which states that the last descendant of the house of David died in Spain centuries ago. There are no genealogies at present to prove that the kingly house of David is extinct or not, but the prophecies like the one we have in consideration, and many others which speak of the prominence of David and the house of David in the day when Jehovah will be manifested, make it very clear that among the wandering sons of Israel there are yet lineal descendants of the house of David. If they do not know it themselves, Jehovah knows it, and they will know it through Him. The feeble ones, literally the stumblers, among His people in that day of manifestation will be like David. What a hero David was! A man of war and strength conquering always and never conquered. And now the stumbler in Israel, the weakest one, will have strength and courage like David. And David shall be as God, as the angel of Jehovah before them.

Verses 10-14. This is another great Messianic prophecy mentioned in the New Testament. In John 19:37 it is written, after the blessed side of our Lord had been pierced, "And again another Scripture saith, They shall look on Him whom they pierced." It is significant that the Holy Spirit speaking in the preceding verse, "that the Scripture be fulfilled," avoids this well known phrase in the verse we quoted and does not say that the looking on Him has been fulfilled. It was not then fulfilled, nor is it fulfilled during the age of Gospel preaching, but its fulfillment comes in the day which is prophetically described in the verses before us. Matthew 24:30 and Revelation 1:7 refer also to this portion of our chapter.

We do not follow the rationalistic reasonings of the school of criticism on this passage, nor do we mention the many question marks which these modern infidels have put over against this great prophecy. One of the mildest critics, Canon Driver, says: "The passage is, however, one of those which our ignorance of the circumstances of the time makes it impossible to interpret as a whole satisfactorily or completely. As the text stands the speaker must be, of course, Yahweh, and it is, no doubt, true that the Jews had pierced Him metaphorically by their rebellion and ingratitude throughout their history. . . . 'They pierced Him literally as the crowning act of their contumacy, in the Person of His Son on the cross' (T. T. Perowne; quoted by Driver), but these considerations do not explain the passage here." The New Testament quotations as given above are to any believer sufficient evidence that the Lord Jesus Christ is meant, and therefore explain the passage fully.

What a day it will be when the Spirit of grace and supplication comes upon the remnant of His people, when He appears in the clouds of heaven, when they shall see Him and know Him by the pierced side. The great vision of Saul on the road to Damascus will then be repeated; the young Pharisee saw Him as one "born out of due season." He was in his experience the earnest that the remnant of the nation to which Paul belonged would some day pass through the same experience. (See *Studies in Zechariah,* pp. 120-125.) A great mourning follows. It will be like the mourning in Hadadrimmon in the valley of Megiddon (2 Chron. 35:22-27 and 2 Kings 23:29). What a day of repentance it will be when this takes place.

CHAPTER 13

1. The cleansing (13:1)
2. The blessed results of the cleansing (13:2-6)
3. The smitten Shepherd (13:7)
4. Salvation and condemnation (13:8-9)

Verse 1. This verse is misplaced; it belongs to the preceding chapter. It is a prophecy of the cleansing of the repenting portion of God's earthly people. The fountain of cleansing, so beautifully expressed by Cowper:

> There is a fountain filled with blood,
> Drawn from Immanuel's veins,
> And sinners plunged beneath that flood,
> Lose all their guilty stains—

was in existence through all the centuries of Israel's long dispersion. But the nation in blindness did not believe. Now all is changed. Their guilt is pardoned; all unrighteousness and iniquity is taken away. The Redeemer has come and turned away ungodliness from Jacob (Rom. 11: 26, 27). The prophetic Word is filled with promises concerning this future cleansing of the remnant of the nation (Psa. 103:1-4; Isa. 33:24; Ezek. 39:29; Isa. 59:20, 21; Isa. 45:19).

Verses 2-6. The cleansing is followed by the cutting off of the names of the idols, so that they will no longer be remembered. The false prophets and the unclean spirits, which had control during the great tribulation will be cast out and forever pass away.

We have seen before in the 10th chapter that Israel will return to idolatry in the last days. The unclean spirit of idolatry which was cast out will at last return with seven others and will find the house empty, swept, and garnished. And the evil spirit, with the seven others more evil than himself, will enter in and dwell there, so that the last state of Israel becometh worse than the first. This will happen to this evil generation. This section of the 13th chapter makes it very clear that when the fountain is opened against sin and uncleanness, that idols will have been in the land, and false prophets prophesy there immediately before the manifestation of the Lord from heaven; for how could the names of the idols be cut off from the land if there were none there? Palestine may well be put down now as the great centre of false worship. Greek and Latin crosses are seen on all sides in Jerusalem and other places, while saints, holy houses, and places are worshipped and adored.

On the spot where the Lord's house stood, there stands to-day the mosque of the false prophet. All is idolatry. Of course when the Lord returns these false temples will be destroyed, and the Greek and Latin idolatries, as well as Islam, will forever pass out of existence. There will be a purging of the land from these abominations. This may be included in the prophecy here. Still, it is the people of Israel who are especially concerned in the prophecy before us. The land has often been the scene of idol worship, and the people engaged in that which Jehovah despises. It will be so again, only in a much worse form, when false prophets who are inspired by the unclean spirit and demons themselves will be their guides.

We must look to Revelation for a key. It is well known to all students of the prophetic word that all which comes after the third chapter in the last book of the Bible is future still. We are yet in the things which are present. When the Lord has taken the Church to Himself then the great visions, tribulations, wrath, and judgment will be fulfilled. Aside from the scenes in heaven we learn from Revelation the events in the earth during the great tribulation which ends with the wrath from heaven.

Now in the 9th chapter and the 20th verse of Revelation we read, And the rest of mankind which were not killed with these plagues repented not of the works of their hands that they should not worship demons and the idols of gold, and of silver, and of brass, and of stone, and of wood, which can neither see nor hear nor walk.

Who is the person mentioned in verse six? In *Studies in Zechariah* we speak of this man as representing the counterfeit Christ, imitating the true Christ. But after more careful consideration we have come to the conclusion that this view is untenable. It is Christ Himself. He is here contrasted with the false prophets. It is the Pierced One. After they look upon Him they will inquire about those wounds in His hands and He will answer them, revealing the story of His rejection. This leads to the prophecy in the next verse.

Verse 7. This certainly is Christ, whose rejection, more than His rejection by His own, is here revealed. It is the same as in Isaiah 53, the suffering One, who is a man, and called My Fellow, the fellow of Jehovah of Hosts, Jehovah Himself, who speaks here, and what does He speak? The sword is to work against His Shepherd and against His own Fellow. The blessed mystery of the atonement is thus brought out. Indeed it is the heart of the Gospel here. For God so loved the world that He gave His only begotten Son, that whosoever believeth on Him should not perish but have life eternal. The Lord laid on Him the iniquity of us all. It speaks of Him, the forsaken One, the Son of God, forsaken in the hour of His agony, the sword upon Him and against Him. In the New Testament we find the passage quoted in the Gospel of Matthew, 26th chapter and 31st verse: Then saith Jesus unto them, all ye shall be offended because of Me this night; for it is written, I will smite the Shepherd and the sheep of the flock shall be scattered abroad.

Verses 8-9. There is a very misleading idea among many students of prophecy as if the statement of Romans 11:26, "all Israel shall be saved," meant that all the Jews will receive the blessing and the glory on that coming day of salvation. Some of the evil systems, like the Russell cult (International Bible Student Association), go so far as to teach that there will be a resurrection of all the ungodly Jews of past generations for a second chance. This passage silences these unscriptural theories. The promise of restoration and glory belongs to the godly, the believing and repenting remnant. The mass of Jews, who call themselves "Reform Jews," who in reality are infidels, because they deny the Word of God and have comletely discarded the faith in a coming Messiah, will be cut off. The third part (the remnant) only will be saved.

CHAPTER 14

1. The last conflict and the manifestation of the Lord (14:1-5)
2. The complete salvation (14:6-11)
3. The punishment of the enemies (14:12-15)
4. The conversion of the world (14:16-19)
5. The holiness of Jerusalem (14:20-21)

Verses 1-5. Post-millennialism has tried to find some explanation of this chapter, but has failed. The common view that the destruction of Jerusalem by the Romans in the year 70 A.D. is the burden of this prophecy is ridiculous. We read that "all nations will be gathered against Jerusalem." Is this true of the destruction of Jerusalem under Titus? It was only one nation. Did the Lord then go forth and fight against the Romans? No! He used the Romans in judgment. Did His feet stand at that time upon the Mount of Olives? Did He come and all the saints with Him? Were the results of the year 70 the results predicted in the rest of this chapter? Any intelligent Christian must see how foolish it is to interpret this passage as having seen its fulfillment in the destruction of Jerusalem.

Nor is it true that previous sieges have fulfilled this chapter. Ptolemy Soter took Jerusalem about 315 B.C.; Antiochus the Great took the city in 203 B.C.; the Egyptian Scopus in 199 B.C.; Antiochus Epiphanes in 170 B.C. There were other sieges besides. But none of these sieges is predicted here. It is future.

What siege then is it? Some premillennial expositors have a very convenient way of calling everything "the battle of Armageddon" and claim that the twelfth and the fourteenth chapters predict one and the same event. But this is erroneous. It is not the beast, the head of the ten kingdoms, the Roman revived Empire. The details of prophecy concerning the last events can only be understood by distinguishing between the leaders of opposition. There is the beast, the political head of the western nations, the little horn of Daniel 7. He is in league with the second beast, coming out of the earth, with two horns like a lamb (Rev. 13). This is the false Christ, the man of sin, who is also called in Revelation the false prophet. He has his seat in Jerusalem, where he poses as Israel's Messiah-King and is worshipped as such. Then there is another, the king of the north, typified by the Assyrian, the great invader whom Ezekiel also describes. This king of the north is the sworn enemy of the one who is in Jerusalem, that is the false Messiah; they hate each other. The king of the north heads the confederacy of nations from the East, Russia, Persia, Gomer and different Asiatic nations. Then Jerusalem is finally attacked by these nations. It is this final attack which is described in this chapter (see Joel 2). But then the Lord goes forth, and fights against those nations, as when He fought in the day of battle (Exodus 14; 2 Chronicles 20:15-17). He manifests His kingly power and glory in the defense of His city and His people. His feet stand in that day upon the Mount of Olives, the place so well known in His earthly life, the place from which He departed to go back to the Father. A great physical upheaval takes place, for the mountain splits in the center, toward the east and west, forming a great valley between. The earthquake mentioned is the same to which Amos refers (Amos 1:1). All this has never been; it is future, and the details of it will probably only be understood at the time of its fulfillment. The valley will be the avenue of escape, and the divided Olivet mountain will be ever after a witness to the literal fulfillment of God's Word.

"And Jehovah my God shall come, and all the saints with Thee." Different manuscripts and versions have instead of "with Thee"—"with Him." But the difficulty is cleared up when we consider that it is the Seer who addresses Jehovah, whose feet shall stand on the Mount of Olives. Zechariah bursts out in speaking to Him, "And Jehovah my God shall come, and all the saints with Thee." What a glorious manifestation it will be when He is present and all His holy angels with Him!

Verses 6-11. Verses six and seven have been rendered in different ways, and have been differently interpreted.

> And it shall come to pass in that day
> That the light shall not be with
> brightness and with gloom,
> And the day shall be One.
> It shall be known unto Jehovah.
> Not day and not night.
> And at evening time there shall be
> light.

We believe that this passage means the physical phenomena in nature which are always connected with the day of the Lord (Amos 5:18; 8:9; Joel 2:31; Matt. 24:30, and other passages). Changes will then occur which will mean that the present order of day and night are superseded by another order, so that when the evening time comes it will be light. That day will just be one day of light and glory. The glory light will probably be shining throughout the thousand years, and cover the earth as the waters cover the deep.

From verse eight we learn that living waters shall go out from Jerusalem (Ezek. 47). This must be interpreted as a literal fact, and likewise as a symbol of the great spiritual blessings. "From the holy city go forth westward and eastward the waters which are destined to heal the long miseries of a world groaning under Satan's thralldom, themselves the effect and symbol of the rich blessing which Jehovah then diffuses far and wide, and this above all the changes ordinary in nature; in summer and in winter it shall be. Drought and frost will not affect them; neither will the obstruction of the hilly ground toward the west; the waters shall flow as steadily toward the great sea on the west as to the Dead Sea on the east." The Lord Jesus Christ, Jehovah, then shall be King over all the earth; and His Name shall be one. His throne is established over the earth and He rules the nations in righteousness. In that day of His glorious manifestation His Name will be revealed as the One who on earth declared "I and the Father are One"; He will be known as the One Lord and God, and worshipped as such. All idolatry is at an end and the abominations connected with it are abolished. Confusion is forever ended (Zeph. 3:9).

Other physical changes in the land are indicated in verse ten, and from verse eleven we learn that there shall be no more curse and that Jerusalem shall dwell safely.

Verses 12-15. This is the description of the dreadful punishment which will befall the enemies in that day. It is to be read in connection with the third verse, the Lord fighting against those nations, and the punishment will be upon them when He appears. Thus it is seen in Revelation 19. He appears, and after His appearing there is the scene of punishment of the enemies. "And I saw an angel standing in the sun; and he cried with a loud voice to all the birds that fly in midheaven, Come and be gathered unto the great supper of God; that ye may eat the flesh of kings, and the flesh of captains, and the flesh of mighty men, and the flesh of horses and them that sit thereon, and the flesh of all men, both free and bond and small and great" (Rev. 19:17, 18).

"And they shall go forth, and look upon the carcasses of the men that have transgressed against me; for their worm shall not die, neither shall their fire be quenched; and they shall be an abhorring unto all flesh" (Isa. 66:24).

Verses 16-19. It is clear from this passage that some nations, or representatives of nations, will be left of those who came against Jerusalem. They, with all the other nations of the world, will then know the Lord and worship Him. The temple will then stand in Jerusalem as the house of glory and a house of prayer for all nations. There will be a perfect worship, grand and glorious, and it will not be confined to Israel, but the nations will join it. We may learn perhaps from this verse that the Lord will leave every year once His place on His throne over the earth and come down to Jerusalem and show Himself in His glory before the worshipping multitudes in the earth, as He is seen in the

New Jerusalem above. The occasion is the feast of tabernacles. It is the millennial feast. It is a feast kept in remembrance of Israel's journey through the wilderness for forty years and all their subsequent wanderings. It stands also for the ingathering of the full harvest. It is a feast of joy, praise, and thanksgiving. The Jews keep it to the present day, though few know the full meaning of it. Every year when it comes again they read this 14th chapter of Zechariah. It is strange indeed. What a glorious feast that will be, kept there in Jerusalem, when the fullness at last has come! The fullness of the Gentiles has been gathered in, and is in the New Jerusalem; the fullness of Israel has come in the earth, and their receiving has been life from the dead, and Gentiles know the glory of the Lord. Some find a difficulty here in the fact that it is stated that the nations, the residue of men, are to come up to Jerusalem, and the difficulty is that it will be impossible for all of them to do that. It is not at all necessary that every individual must go up to Jerusalem once in a year. Perhaps every nation will send representatives to the feast of tabernacles, and they come in the name of the different nations and bring their presents. This seems to be indicated in the visit of the wise men from the East, who came to Bethlehem to worship the new-born King (Matthew 2). They brought gold, frankincense and myrrh. In Isaiah 60:6 we read of the coming of the Gentiles to Jerusalem when the Lord has come again. They shall come from Sheba; they shall bring gold and frankincense (the myrrh is left out here, for it speaks of suffering), and shall proclaim the praises of the Lord. As the wise men who came to Bethlehem were representatives of nations, so during the Millennium the nations will send delegations to the feast of tabernacles. What a scene that must be! How crowded Jerusalem will be by those from Greenland and from the interior of Africa, from India and the islands of the sea, as well as from the nations which composed the Roman empire. The ends of the earth have seen the salvation of God, and now their praise is heard in the city and mingling with the psalms sung by His own redeemed people.

On the other hand verses 17-19 acquaint us with the fact that even during the coming age of the kingdom-glory there will be disobedience among the nations, which will be fully demonstrated at the close of the Millennium, when a final revolt takes place.

Verses 20-21. The most holy person in Israel, the high-priest, carried the inscription, "Holiness to Jehovah" around his mitre, but now even the little bells of the horses bear that inscription. In that temple which stands during the Millennium, sacrifices will be brought, but there will be no difference in the vessels which are used in Jerusalem, the meanest and smallest will be holy. In one word, all will be holy, all will be consecrated to Jehovah. What a perfect service that will be of the people which are then, in truth, a holy people. Application can be made of this to believers now. Surely everything the saint has, and his whole life, must be thus consecrated to Jehovah, to the Lord. No Canaanite will be there, nothing unclean. The Vulgate translates the word Canaanite with merchant. It stands, however, for everything that is unclean and an abomination. The city will be completely purged from it.

And of the New Jerusalem it is written, "There shall in no wise enter into it any thing unclean, or he that maketh an abomination and a lie, but only they that are written in the Lamb's book of life. . . . Without are the dogs, and the sorcerers, and the fornicators, and the murderers, and the idolaters, and every one that loveth and maketh a lie" (Rev. 21:27 and 22:15).

THE PROPHET
MALACHI

We know nothing of the person of this prophet. His name only is given in the record. Critics have therefore doubted whether Malachi is really the personal name of the prophet, and many believe that it is merely an ideal name, given to the unknown person, on account of his message. Malachi means "my messenger" or "the messenger of Jehovah." The Targum Jonathan, an Aramaic paraphrase, adds after the name of Malachi, *"Cujus nomen appelatur Ezra scriba,"* whose name is called Ezra the Scribe, thus claiming that the great and good Ezra is Malachi. But why should Ezra hide behind an assumed name? This is unworthy of the man, and more so of the Holy Spirit. Many of the leading expositors have accepted the theory that Malachi is the official name of the prophet, whoever he may have been. One of the reasons for this theory is that "the first verse does not contain any further personal description, and that nothing is said about his father or place of birth." But Obadiah and Habakkuk show the same omissions. Nor is it true that nothing was known historically of a person by name of Malachi. The Talmud has a statement which makes Malachi a member of the great synagogue, to which also the two post-exilic prophets Haggai and Zechariah belonged. Other traditions claim that he was of the tribe of Zebulun, born in Supha. There is no reason to doubt that Malachi is the real name of the prophet.

The Date of His Prophecy

This also has caused a great deal of dispute. That he prophesied after the captivity has never been doubted. Furthermore, the reading of his utterances makes it clear that he prophesied after Haggai and Zechariah. We learn that the temple has been completely finished, and the temple worship with priests has been restored for a number of years. After Ezra and Nehemiah's beneficient influence had passed the people went into a decline, and the conditions which the prophet rebukes were the results of backsliding. The abuses which were corrected by Ezra and Nehemiah had taken hold upon the people again. The exact time can hardly be fixed. It seems by comparing Malachi 1:8 with Nehemiah 5:15 and 18 that Nehemiah was no longer governor when Malachi exercised his office.

The Message of Malachi

As the last prophetic voice of the Old Testament, Malachi, in unison with all other prophets, announces the coming of the Messiah and points once more to Him. The next prophetic voice, after the four hundred silent years, is the voice in the wilderness, the herald of the King, of whom Malachi predicted that he should come. But the message of Malachi is overwhelmingly condemnatory. "The great moral principle unfolded in this book is the insensibility of the people to that which Jehovah was for them, and to their own iniquity with respect to Jehovah—their want of reverence for God, their despisal of Jehovah. Alas! this insensibility had reached such a point that, when the very actions which proved their contempt were laid before their consciences, they saw no harm in them. Nevertheless, this did not alter the purposes and counsels of God, although it brought judgment upon those who were guilty of it" (chapter 1:2, 6, 2:14, 3:7, 13, *Synopsis of the Bible.*).

It is unquestionably true that the spirit manifested by the people in Malachi's day assumed later the concrete forms expressed by the two leading sects of Judaism, when our Lord was on earth, the Pharisees and the Sadducees. "The outward or grosser kind of idolatry had been rendered thoroughly distasteful to the people by the sufferings of the exile; and its place was taken by the more refined idolatry of dead-work righteousness, and trust in the outward fulfillment of the letter of the divine commands without any deeper confession of sins, or humiliation under the Word and the will of God." It has been well stated that "Malachi is like a late evening, which brings a long day to a close; but he is also the morning dawn, which bears a glorious day in its womb." The shadows are dark, but there is the rising of the Sun of Righteousness, still to take place, when all shadows flee away.

But beside the apostate masses of the people, steeped in a dead formalism, there is seen in the book of Malachi the faithful remnant. It is interesting to follow this remnant, we have so often mentioned in our annotations, through the entire Jewish history, past, present and future. There was always a godly remnant. We see that remnant in the wilderness wandering of Israel; there was a remnant during the period of the Judges, and in every other period, like the sad days of Ahab's wicked rule, when despondent Elijah desired to die, and the Lord informed him that there were seven thousand who had not bowed the knee to the image of Baal. There was a remnant when Jerusalem was captured by Nebuchadnezzar: a remnant returned from the captivity, and when the returned exiles degenerated, as seen in Malachi, there were still the few left who assembled together and whom the Lord owned.

In Romans 11 we read that at the present time, during this age, there is likewise a remnant according to the election of grace. It is not a small remnant, who, during this age, turn to the Lord, believe on Christ and thus become members of the Body of Christ, in which there is neither Jew nor Gentile. And when the age closes, and the nation faces the final calamity in the great tribulation, and the acceptance of the false Christ, there will be that godly remnant, as we have so often shown in our comments on the prophetic word.

The Lessons for Our Age

The Jewish age with all its glorious manifestations of the Lord in behalf of His people Israel, and the great revelations given by the prophets of the Lord, did not improve in its development and become a better age. Neither does our age improve and become better, the age in which God has revealed His best and offers to man the riches of His graces in the Person of His blessed Son our Lord. It ends as Old Testament times ended, in failure and apostasy. The moral conditions of the Jews in the days of Malachi are the moral conditions of Christendom. But as then, so there is now, a remnant of God's own, who are faithful to Him, and whom He acknowledges as His true Church.

The Division of Malachi

We divide the prophecy of Malachi in six sections: 1. Jehovah's Love for His People (1:1-5). 2. The Rebuke of the Priests (1:6-2:9). 3. Rebuke of the Social Conditions (2:10-16). 4. The Announcement of the Messenger and the Day of the Lord (3:1-6). 5. Rebuke for Defrauding the Lord (3:7-15). 6. The Remnant and the Concluding Prophecy (3:16—4:6).

Analysis and Annotations

1. Jehovah's Love for His People

CHAPTER 1:1-5

The message of Malachi begins with the sublime statement, "I have loved you, saith Jehovah." It is the message to Israel. This love is written large on every page of their history. A former prophet gave the message from the Lord, "You only have I known of all the families of the earth" (Amos 3:2). And long before that Moses had told them, "Only the Lord had a delight in thy fathers to love them, and He chose their seed after them, even you above all people, as it is this day" (Deut 10:15). And the man of God in his final utterance burst out in praise, "Yea, He loved the people" (Deut. 33:3). And this generation, brought back through His mercy from Babylon, the generation that had listened to the marvelous words of Haggai and Zechariah, could brazenly answer back, "Wherein hast Thou loved us?" How deep they had sunk! Greater still is the insensibility of nominal Christendom which rejects, yea, despises, the great love wherewith He has loved us in the gift of His Son.

Then the Lord in infinite patience answered them, "Was not Esau Jacob's brother? saith Jehovah: yet I loved Jacob, and hated Esau, and laid his mountains and his heritage waste for the dragons of the wilderness." This takes us back to Genesis, but in vain do we look for this statement in that first book of the Bible. Though it is quoted also in Romans 9, it is nowhere to be found in connection with the story of the birth of the twins. The late scholar, William Kelly, has expressed the whole matter so well that we can do nothing better than to quote his excellent comment. "It is only in Malachi that He says 'Esau have I hated.' I could conceive nothing more dreadful than to say so in Genesis. Never does Scripture represent God as saying before the child was born and had manifested his iniquity and proud malice, 'Esau have I hated.' There is where the mind of man is so erroneous. It is not meant, however, that God's *choice* was determined by the character of the individual. This would make man the ruler rather than God. Not so; God's choice flows out of His own wisdom and nature. It suits and is worthy of Himself; but the reprobation of any man and of every unbeliever is never a question of the sovereignty of God. It is the choice of God to do good where and how He pleases; it is *never* the purpose of His will to hate any man. There is no such doctrine in the Bible. I hold, therefore, that, while election is most clearly taught in the Scriptures, the consequences that men draw from election, namely, the reprobation of the non-elect, is a mere reproduction of fatalism, common to some heathen and to all Mohammedans, the unfounded deduction of man's reasoning in divine things." With these good words we agree perfectly. The hatred against Esau is mentioned in this last book, because it was well-deserved, after all the opposition and defiance of God the descendants of Esau, Edom, had manifested. But the love wherewith Jacob was loved was undeserved. His love for His people had been fully manifested, as well as His displeasure against Edom by laying his mountains and heritage waste, and all their attempts at reconstruction failed. God was against him on account of Edom's wicked ways.

2. The Rebuke of the Priests

CHAPTER 1:6—2:9

The priests, the religious leaders of the people, are described first in their evil ways, and rebuked. But the rebuke includes the entire people, for it is true, "like priests like people." The Lord called Israel to be His firstborn son, and therefore, nationally, He is their Father. He is the Lord, and Israel called to be His servant. But they had not honored Him, as a son should honor the father by obedience; they did not fear Him, but despised His Name. This charge brought forth from the side of the priests another brazen statement, the result of their hypocritical self-righteousness. They answered back, demanding proof of the charge by saying, "Wherein have we despised Thy Name?" They seemed to be hardened in their consciences, though they kept up outward appearances. Such, too, is the religious condition in much of Christendom. Another charge follows, the charge that they offer polluted bread, which brought forth the retort, "Wherein have we polluted Thee?" They had considered the table of the Lord contemptible; instead of offering upon the altar the very best, as demanded in the law, they showed their contempt by bringing the blind, the lame and the sick, a thing which they would never have done to an earthly governor, who would have been sorely displeased at such an insult and rejected their person on account of it. They had treated the Lord of Hosts shamefully in their worship. Is it different in Christendom? Under such conditions, even if they were to pray to Him to be gracious, would He, or could He, regard their persons and listen to their prayers (verse 9)?

Verse 10 has often been interpreted to mean that the priests were covetous and demanded money for every little service, the opening of doors and the kindling of a fire. It has another meaning. The better rendering is, "O, that some among you would even shut the doors of the temple." The doors are the doors which lead from the outer court into the holy part. The Lord declares that it would be more profitable if they would shut these doors, and kindle no longer a fire upon the altar for nought; in other words, He wishes that the whole outward worship might be stopped. The last sentence of this verse shows this is the correct interpretation. "I have no pleasure in you, saith the Lord of Hosts, neither will I accept an offering at your hand." Nor has He today any pleasure in the unscriptural worship of ritualistic Christendom, or the dead, Spiritless worship of an apostate Protestantism.

The next verse (verse 11) is a prophecy. Is it fulfilled today, during this age? We think not; it refers to the millennial age. Critics say that the passage refers to the worship of God among the heathen, under different names, as expressed lines by a poet (Pope):

> Father of all! in every age,
> In every clime adored,
> By saint, by savage, and by sage,
> Jehovah, Jove or Lord.

Canon S.D.Driver says on this passage, "It is a tribute to the truer and better side of heathen religion." It is no such thing. But why should it not be applied to this gospel age, in which among all nations His Name is known and called upon? There is a statement which excludes this interpretation: "and in every place incense shall be offered unto My Name, and a pure offering." The Romish Catholic Church uses this passage as one of her proof texts for that abomination, the Mass. In the canons of the Council of Trent we read that "the Mass is that pure sacrifice which the Lord predicted by Malachi should be offered to His Name in every place." Another prominent writer declares that it is "the bloodless sacrifice of the New Testament, the holy sacrifice of the mass." All this is Satanic invention. It is true the Name of the Lord is known among the nations, but no incense, sacrifice or offering is connected with the worship of the Lord in the true Church. For His heavenly people the earthly sacrifices and incense, offering and priesthood, are all passed; and more than that, these things would be inconsistent with their heavenly standing and calling. It will be different during the age to come, the Millennium. The last chapters of Ezekiel reveal the fact that with the millennial worship in the millennial temple incense and offerings are connected. The prophecy of the eleventh verse will be fulfilled during the millennium. Now His Name is not universally great among the Gentiles; it will be otherwise when the Lord Jesus Christ has come back.

Then follow additional expostulations on account of these conditions.

In the second chapter the priests are again addressed. If they do not hear, do not lay it to heart, if their consciences are not aroused, to give glory unto His Name, He would curse their blessings; yea, they had been cursed already; He would punish them severely for their contempt. Levi and the covenant with him is especially mentioned, on account of his faithfulness at the time when the golden calf had been set up by Israel in the wilderness, in contrast with Aaron who gave way to the demand of the people. But what a contrast between Levi and the priests in Malachi's day! For the priests' lips should keep knowledge, and they should seek the law at his mouth, for he is the messenger of the Lord of Hosts. Such is the calling of the priest. But they had departed out of the way; they caused many to stumble at the law; they had corrupted the covenant of Levi. Therefore the Lord made them contemptible and base before all the people.

3. The Rebuke of the Social Conditions

CHAPTER 2:10-16

The priests were corrupt, and with their bad example the people were likewise corrupt. It is the prophet who speaks in verse 10. The One Father was Jehovah, with whom the nation was in covenant relation. They had one Father, and they were one as a nation. By profaning that covenant they dealt treacherously every man against his brother. The abomination in social life, by which the covenant was profaned, and the holiness of the Lord outraged, was the marriage with the daughters of the heathen. They had put away their own Israelitish wives in order to enter into these unholy alliances. The Jew acted faithlessly toward his brother, both when he contracted a marriage with a heathen woman, and when he put away his legitimate wife, and thereby desecrated the covenant of the fathers, i.e., the covenant that Jehovah made with their fathers when He chose them to be a separated people. Those who have done this will surely be cut off. Verse 13 describes the weeping and the tears of the abandoned Jewish wives; it is the same condition, only worse, which is recorded in Ezra and Nehemiah. All was an abomination unto the Lord. Over fifty years ago a writer called attention to the divorce evil in the United States. He wrote then:

> The frequency of *divorce* in the United States, so that in one of the States divorce is allowed for "misconduct," reveals the same state of things existing now, as was here condemned by Jehovah, and must bring with it the same evils, and the same punishment. What tongue can adequately tell, what heart conceive, the untold misery from this cause, especially to the deserted wives, and the children left without a mother's care! How little is the indissoluble nature of the marriage relation regarded! and the fact, that the Lord was the witness of it, and will be a swift witness against those who violate it! The Saviour only allows of one cause of divorce, and regards divorce for any other as adultery.

Since then this evil has increased a hundredfold or more among professing Christians, so that it threatens to undermine the home and all family life. It is the sign of the rapid disintegration of our nation.

And yet rebuked for these social conditions and wicked deeds, they could ask another, "Wherefore?" They were so hardened that they could not see why they were to blame. The difficult fifteenth verse refers to the marriage relation, in which God makes of twain one. He made the woman for man, though He had the residue of the Spirit, the creative power by which He might have made many women for one man. And wherefore one? that is, one woman for the man—that He might seek a godly seed, to perpetuate those who are godly, which is counteracted by divorce, such as they had practiced. It seemed as if the remnant who feared Him were being influenced by these corrupt practices, hence the warning. "Therefore take heed to your spirit, and let none deal treacherously against the wife of his youth."

4. The Announcement of the Messenger and the Day of the Lord

CHAPTER 3:1-6

In this chapter and in the next we have the prophecies of Malachi as to the Messiah and His forerunner. The last verse of the preceding chapter belongs rightly to this chapter. "Ye have wearied the Lord with your words. Yet ye say, Wherein have we wearied Him? When ye say, Every one that doeth evil is good in the sight of the Lord, and He delighteth in them; or, Where is the God of judgment?" It is this last bold question, produced by their arrogant pride and self-security which opens the way for the prophetic message in this chapter. "Where is the God of judgment?" The answer is, "Behold, I will send My messenger, and he shall prepare the way before Me; and the Lord, whom ye seek, shall suddenly come to His temple, even the messenger of the covenant, whom ye delight in; behold, He shall come, saith the Lord of hosts." The first announcement of the messenger, who goes before the Lord, is quoted in Matthew 11:10; Mark 1:2; Luke 1:76 and 7:27. Isaiah, too, had spoken a similar prophecy in chapter 40:3. This prophecy was fulfilled in the person of John the Baptist, as the herald of His first coming; still this prophecy considered in the light of the prophecy in the next chapter, concerning the coming of Elijah, remains yet to be fully accomplished. John the Baptist was not Elijah; Elijah is still to come and do his work preceding the coming of the Lord. The messenger is followed by the Lord, the Messenger, or Angel (the meaning of the Hebrew word) of the Covenant. The word Lord is here the word *Adon* with the article, always used of God. It is the Lord God who comes, and His official title is "The Angel of the Covenant." Many expositors have blundered here in that they imagined the word covenant means the new covenant of which the Lord Jesus is the Mediator (Heb. 9:15). But it is not the truth. The Messenger of the Covenant is the same "Angel of the Lord" who appeared frequently in Israel's past history, and generally in the form of a human being. The Angel of the Lord is the Son of God in His preincarnation manifestations, and He is announced here as the Angel of the Covenant. The nation believed in His coming, and in the question "Where is the God of judgment?" they had asked for Him. That there was a partial fulfillment of this prophecy when our Lord, the Messiah of Israel, came unexpectedly in the temple, must not be overlooked, but that it was *the* fulfillment of these words is not true. It will be accomplished in the day of His Return, preceded by another messenger. Their question "Where is the God of judgment?" will then be fully answered, and what it will be we read in the next two verses (verses 2 and 3). He will purge the nation of the dross, beginning with the sons of Levi. It is the same as in Zechariah 13:9. John the Baptist announced the same also, and when he gave his inspired testimony of the purging of the threshing floor and the burning of the chaff with unquenchable fire (Matt. 3:12) he referred not to the first coming of Christ, but to His second coming.

As the result of this judgment in store for the nation, when the sorcerers, the adulterers, the false swearers, and the oppressors will be dealt with, we read in the fourth verse "Then shall the offering of Judah and Jerusalem be pleasant unto the Lord, as in the days of old, and as in former years."

5. Rebuke for Defrauding the Lord

CHAPTER 3:7-15

Another rebuke is administered. They were alway a stiff-necked people, never obedient to His ordinances. His gracious call to return unto Him, and the promise that He will return unto them is answered by "Wherein shall we return?" They had robbed God of what was His right. The tithes and offerings which He demanded in the law covenant had been withheld. On account of it the blessing was lacking and curse was upon the nation. Then follows a command to bring all the tithes into the storehouse, the challenge to prove Him, the assurance of abundant blessing. It is strange that even those who have a good knowledge of the truth, the dispensations and the heavenly position of a Christian, should fall back upon this verse and claim that it is binding and should be practiced among believers. For a system like Seventh Day Adventism, a system which has perverted the gospel of grace, which denies God's oathbound covenants with Israel, which claims to be the true Israel, the system to which applies the term "the synagogue of Satan, who say that they are Jews and are not;" for such a cult to make this command a binding law is not surprising. But well taught believers should never look upon this passage as in any way in force today. True Christian giving, like everything else in the life and service of a true believer, must be done, not by law but through grace, under the direction of the Holy Spirit. Nowhere in the New Testament is there anything said about tithing. A believer must be a cheerful giver, giving as the Lord has prospered him, communicating to others, doing good, remembering the poor, ministering in temporal things to those who minister in spiritual things; but all this giving must be under the direction of the Spirit of God.

The day will come when His earthly people will minister to the wants of the Lord's house (a Jewish term), so that there will be an abundant supply for sacrifices. That will be in the future day of their restoration, when the devourer will be rebuked (verse 11). It is at that time, when the millennium has come, that all nations will call them blessed, when they shall be a delightsome land (Isa. 62:4). This has never been since it was written by the pen of Malachi.

6. The Remnant and the Concluding Prophecy

CHAPTER 3:16—4:6

In the midst of all these moral conditions, the apostasy of the masses, we find a pleasing picture of a godly portion, whom the Lord mentions in a special manner. There were those who feared the Lord. They had no sympathy with the wicked practices of their brethren; they did not share the contempt and unbelief manifested by the rank and file of the people. They were drawn together by the Spirit of God; they had fellowship one with another. They came together to think upon His Name, to honor Him, to read His Word, to call unto the Lord. And the Lord heard; He was pleased with them, and He is represented as recording their names in the Book of Remembrance, the bookkeeping in glory (Psa. 56:8). He has a special promise for such. "And they shall be Mine, saith the Lord of hosts, in that day when I make up My jewels; and I will spare them, as a man spareth his own son that serveth him."

Such a remnant of godly ones was in existence in Malachi's day, and when they passed away others took their places. The Lord preserved such a godly seed in every generation throughout the four hundred silent years. And when that silence was broken, by the Angel's message to the ministering priest Zechariah, we see such a remnant on the threshold of the New Testament. Good old Anna and Simeon, the shepherds and others belonged to this waiting, God-fearing remnant. And so it will be before His second coming. A similar remnant will then be on earth awaiting His glorious return.

It is so in Christendom. Departure from the faith soon manifested itself in the professing church. Decline followed decline, till the awful Romish apostasy was consummated. But in every generation the Lord kept a people separated unto Himself. The Reformation came, followed by revivals and recovery of truth. But the Spirit of God does not predict that this age ends in universal acceptance of the truth and universal righteousness and peace, but He predicts a universal apostasy. But even then He has a remnant true to Him. That remnant is seen prophetically in the Church message to Philadelphia (Rev. 3).

In the fourth chapter is the final message of the Old Testament Prophetic Word. The day, that coming day of the Lord, so often mentioned in every portion of the Old Testament, is once more brought before us. It is the day of fire, the day of reckoning with the wicked, who will be consumed like stubble. But that day brings not only the fire of judgment, the winding up of "man's day," the dethronement of evil, but it will be the day of the sunrise. "The Sun of Righteousness shall arise with healing in His wings." The Sun of Righteousness is the Lord Jesus Christ. It is the beautiful symbol of His personal, visible, and glorious coming to usher in that day, which will last for a thousand years, in which He will rule in power and glory. The Old Testament knows nothing of His coming as the Morning Star. That coming is exclusively revealed in the New Testament in relation with the Church. The Morning Star precedes the sunrise. Even so, before that day comes, before the great tribulation, with wrath poured out, He comes for His saints as the Morning Star. The Church does not wait for the rising of the sun, but for the rising of the Morning Star. While the world sleeps, and the world-church dreams its idle dreams, true believers look for the Morning Star. Some day we shall see that glorious Morning Star, when suddenly He descends with that long promised shout.

When the Sun of Righteousness arises, He

will bring healing and blessing. His waiting earthly people, the remnant, will be filled with joy and gambol as calves, while the wicked will be trodden under foot.

The whole chapter is a future prophecy. While there has been a partial fulfillment of the first verse of the third chapter, everything in this concluding chapter awaits its fulfillment. Elijah the prophet is announced. John the Baptist came in the Spirit and power of Elijah, but he was not the Elijah promised here. If ye will receive it, said our Lord, this is Elijah who should come. It was a testimony to faith and not the fulfillment of Malachi's prophecy. If the Jews had accepted Christ, John would have been Elijah. Our Lord bears witness to this. "Elias truly shall come first and restore all things. But I say unto you, That Elias is come already, and they knew him not, but have done unto him whatsoever they listed. Likewise shall also the Son of man suffer of them." When the age closes another one will appear, the Elijah announced by Malachi, who does his work of restoration before the coming of the great and dreadful day of the Lord. His work will be carried on among the people Israel. Deceivers and imposters have occasionally arisen who claimed to be this Elijah; the most prominent in recent years is the Dowieite delusion of Zion City. Such is the havoc produced by not dividing the Word of Truth rightly.

The close of the Old Testament prophetic Word is majestically solemn. In the beginning of the Old Testament stands written the sin and the curse which came upon the race through the fall of man. The final testimony in Malachi speaks of Him who comes to take the curse upon Himself, the promised Christ; who comes to deal with the wicked, who comes to bless and to remove that curse. The New Testament which follows tells us of Him and of His matchless work, the fullness of redemption and the all-sufficiency of Grace. And the final New Testament book shows the consummation, the coming judgments, the righteous judgments of the Lord, and the fulfillment of all "which was spoken by His holy prophets;" ending with the great words, "Surely I come quickly! Amen. Even so, come, Lord Jesus!"

THE GOSPEL OF
MATTHEW

The Key to the Gospel of Matthew

The Gospel of Matthew stands first among the Gospels and in the New Testament, because it belongs in the first place and may be rightly termed the Genesis of the New Testament. Genesis, the first book of the Bible, contains in itself the entire Bible. Matthew is the book of the beginnings of a new dispensation. It may be compared to a mighty tree. The roots are deeply sunk in massive rocks while its uncountable branches and twigs extend upward higher and higher in perfect symmetry and beauty. The foundation is the Old Testament with its Messianic and kingdom promises. Out of this all springs forth in perfect harmony, reaching higher and higher into the new dispensation and to the end of the millennial age.

The instrument chosen by the Holy Spirit to write this Gospel was Matthew. He was a Jew. However, he did not belong to the religious, educated class, to the scribes, but he belonged to the class which was most bitterly hated. He was a publican, that is, a tax gatherer. The Roman government had appointed officials whose duty it was to have the legal tax gathered, and these officials, mostly, if not all Gentiles, appointed the actual collectors, who were generally Jews. Only the most unscrupulous among the Jews would hire themselves out for the sake of gain to the avowed enemy of Jerusalem. Wherever there was still a ray of hope for Messiah's coming, the Jew would naturally shrink from being associated with the Gentiles, who were to be swept away from the land with the coming of the King. For this reason the tax gatherers, being Roman employees, were hated by the Jews even more bitterly than the Gentiles themselves. Such a hated tax gatherer was the writer of the first Gospel. How the grace of God is revealed in his call is seen in the record itself. That he was chosen to write this first gospel is in itself significant, for it speaks of a new order of things about to be introduced, namely, the call of the despised Gentiles.

Internal evidences seem to show that most likely originally Matthew wrote the Gospel in Aramaic, the Semitic dialect then spoken in Palestine. The Gospel was later translated into Greek. This, however, is certain, that the Gospel of Matthew is pre-eminently the *Jewish* Gospel. There are many passages in it, which in their fundamental meaning can only be correctly understood by one who is quite familiar with Jewish customs and the traditional teachings of the elders. Because it is the Jewish Gospel, it is *dispensational* throughout. It is safe to say that a person, no matter how learned or devoted, who does not hold the clearly revealed dispensational truths concerning the Jews, the Gentiles and the Church of God, will fail to understand Matthew. This is, alas, too much the case, and well it would be if it were not more than individual failure to understand; but it is more than that. Confusion, error, false doctrine are the final outcome, when the right key to any part of God's Word is lacking. If the dispensational character of Matthew were understood, no ethical teaching from the so-called Sermon on the Mount at the expense of the atonement of our Lord Jesus Christ would be possible, nor would there be room for the subtle, modern delusion, so universal now, of a "social Christianity" which aims at lifting up the masses and the conversion of the world.

How different matters would be in Christendom if its leading teachers and preachers, commentators and professors, had understood and would understand the meaning of the seven parables in Matthew 13, with their deep and solemn lessons. When we think how many of the leaders of religious thought reject and even oppose all dispensational teachings, who never knew how to divide the Word of Truth rightly, it is not strange that so many of these men dare to stand up and say that the Gospel of Matthew, as well as the other Gospels and the different parts of the New Testament, contain numerous contradictions and errors. Out of this failure to discern dispensational truths has likewise arisen the attempt, by a very well meaning class, to harmonize the Gospel records and to arrange the events in the life of our Lord in a chronological order, and thus produce a life of Jesus Christ, our Lord, as we have a descriptive life of Napoleon or other great men. The Holy Spirit has never undertaken to produce a life of Christ. That is very evident by the fact that the greater part of the life of our Lord is passed over in silence; nor was it in the mind of the Spirit to report all the words and miracles and movements of our Lord, nor to record all the events which took place during His public ministry, and to arrange it all in a chronological order. What presumption, then, to attempt to do that which the Holy Spirit never attempted! If the Holy Spirit never intended that the recorded events in the life of our Saviour should be strictly chronological, how vain and foolish then, if not more, the attempt to bring out a harmony of the different Gospels! One has correctly said, "The Holy Spirit is not a reporter, but an editor." This is well said. A reporter's business is to report events as they happen. The editor arranges the material in a way to suit himself, and leaves out or makes comment just as he thinks best. This the Holy Spirit has done in giving four Gospels, which are not a mechanical reporting of the doings of a person called Jesus of Nazareth, but the spiritual unfoldings of the blessed person and work of our Saviour and Lord, as King of the Jews, servant in obedience, Son of Man and the only-begotten of the Father. We cannot enter more deeply into this now, but in the annotation of the Gospel we shall illustrate this fact.

In the Gospel of Matthew, as the Jewish Gospel, speaking of the King and the kingdom, dispensational throughout, treating of the Jews, the Gentiles and even the church of God in anticipation, as no other Gospel does, everything must be looked upon from the dispensational point of view. All the miracles recorded, the words spoken, the events which are given in their peculiar setting, every parable, every chapter from beginning to end, are first of all to be looked upon as foreshadowing and teaching dispensational truths. This is the right key to the Gospel of Matthew. It is likewise a significant fact that in the condition of the people Israel, with their proud religious leaders rejecting the Lord, their King and the threatened judgment in consequence of it, we may see a true photograph of the end of the present dispensation, and the coming doom of apostate Christendom. The characteristics of the times, when our Lord appeared among His people, who were so religious, self-righteous, being divided into different sects, ritualists (Pharisees) and rationalists (Sadducees—higher critics), following the teachings of men, occupied with man-made creeds and doctrines, etc., are exactly reproduced in Christendom, with its man-made ordinances, rituals and rationalistic teachings.

There are seven great facts which are prominent in this Gospel and around which everything is grouped. We will briefly review them.

1. *The King.* The Old Testament is full of promises which speak of the coming, not alone of a deliverer, a sin-bearer, but of the coming of a King, King Messiah as He is still called by orthodox Jews. This King was eagerly expected, hoped for and prayed for by the pious in Israel. The Gospel of Matthew proves that our Lord Jesus Christ is truly this promised King. In it we see Him as King of the Jews, everything shows that He is in truth the royal person, of whom seers and prophets wrote. First it would be necessary to prove that He is legally the King. This is seen in the first chapter, where a genealogy is given which proves His royal descent. The beginning is, "The book of the generation of Jesus Christ, Son of David, Son of Abraham." It goes back to Abraham and there it stops, while in Luke the genealogy reaches up to Adam. In the Gospel of Matthew He is seen as Son of David, His royal descent, and as Son of Abraham, according to the flesh from the seed of Abraham.

The coming of the wise men is only recorded in Matthew. They came to worship the new born King of the Jews. His royal birthplace, David's city, is given. The infant is worshipped by the representatives of the Gentiles and they do homage indeed before a true King, though the marks of poverty were around Him. The gold they gave speaks of His deity. Every true King has a herald, so has the King Messiah. The forerunner appears and in Matthew his message to the nation is that "The kingdom of heaven has drawn nigh"; the royal person so long foretold is about to appear and to preach that kingdom likewise. When the King who was rejected comes again to set up the kingdom, He will be preceded once more by a herald who will declare His coming among His people Israel, even Elijah the prophet. In the fourth chapter we see the King tested and proven that He is the King. He is tested thrice, once as Son of Man, as Son of God and as the King Messiah. After the testing, out of which He comes forth a complete victor, He begins His ministry. The Sermon on the Mount is given in Matthew in full. Mark and Luke report it only in fragments and John has not a word of it. This should at once determine the status of the three chapters which contain this discourse. It is a teaching concerning the kingdom, the magna charta of the kingdom and all its principles. Such a kingdom in the earth, with subjects who have all the characteristics of the royal requirements laid down in this discourse, will yet be. If Israel had accepted the King it would have come, but the kingdom has been postponed. The kingdom will at least come with a righteous nation as a center, but the church is not that kingdom. In this wonderful discourse the Lord speaks as the King and as the Lawgiver, who expounds the law which is to rule His kingdom. From the eighth to the twelfth chapters, we see the royal manifestations of Him who is Jehovah manifested in the flesh. This part especially is interesting and very instructive, because it gives in a series of miracles, the dispensational hints concerning Jew and Gentile, and what comes after the present age is past.

As King He sends out His servants and endues them with kingdom power, preaching likewise the nearness of the kingdom. After the tenth chapter the rejection begins, followed by His teachings in parables, the revealing of secrets. He is presented to Jerusalem as King, and the Messianic welcome is heard, "Blessed is He who cometh in the name of Jehovah." After that His suffering and His death. In all His kingly character is brought out, and the Gospel closes abruptly, and has nothing to say of His ascension to heaven; but the Lord is, so to speak, left on the earth with power, all power in heaven and on earth. In this closing it is seen that He is the King. He rules in heaven now and on the earth when He comes again.

2. *The Kingdom.* The phrase "kingdom of heaven" occurs *only* in the Gospel of Matthew. We find it thirty-two times. What does it mean? Here is the failure of the interpretation of the Word; all error and confusion around us spring from the false conception of the kingdom of heaven. It is generally taught and understood that the term kingdom of heaven means the Church, and thus the Church is thought to be the true kingdom of heaven, established in the earth, and conquering the nations and the world. The kingdom of heaven is *not* the Church, and the Church is *not* the kingdom of the heavens. This is a very vital truth. May the annotations of this Gospel be used in making this distinction very clear in the minds of our readers. When our Lord speaks of the kingdom of heaven up to the twelfth chapter He does not mean the Church, but the kingdom of heaven in its Old Testament sense, as it is promised to Israel, to be established in the land, with Jerusalem for a center, and from there to spread over all the nations and the entire earth. What did the pious, believing Jew expect according to the Scriptures? He expected (and still expects) the coming of the King Messiah, who is to occupy the throne of His father David. He was expected to bring judgment for the enemies of Jerusalem, and to bring together the outcasts of Israel. The land would flourish as never before; universal peace would be established; righteousness and peace in the knowledge of the glory of the Lord to cover the earth as the waters cover the deep. All this in the earth with the land, which is Jehovah's land, as fountain head, from which all the blessings, the streams of living waters, flow. A temple, a house of worship, for all nations was expected to stand in Jerusalem, to which the nations would come to worship the Lord. This is the kingdom of the heavens as promised to Israel and as expected by them. It is all to be on the earth. The Church, however, is something entirely different. The hope of the Church, the place of the Church, the calling of the Church, the destiny of the Church, the reigning and ruling of the Church is not earthly, but it is heavenly. Now the King long expected had appeared, and He preached the kingdom of the heavens having drawn nigh, that is, this promised earthly kingdom for Israel. When John the Baptist preached, Repent ye, for the kingdom of the heavens has drawn nigh, he meant the same. It is all wrong to preach the gospel from such a text and state that the sinner is to repent and then the kingdom will come to him. A very well known English teacher of spiritual truths gave not long ago in this country a discourse on the mistranslated text, "The kingdom of God is within you," and dwelt largely on the fact that the kingdom is within the believer. The context shows that this is erroneous; the true translation is "The kingdom is *among you*"; that is, in the person of the King.

Now if Israel had accepted the testimony of John, and had repented, and if they had accepted the King, the kingdom would have come, but now it has been postponed till Jewish disciples will pray again in preaching the coming of the kingdom, "Thy kingdom come. Thy will be done in earth as it is done in heaven." That will be after the church has been removed to the heavenly places.

3. *The King and the Kingdom Are Rejected.* This is likewise foretold in the Old Testament, Isaiah 53, Daniel 9:26, Psalm 22, etc. It is also seen in types, Joseph, David and others. The herald of the King is first rejected and ends in the prison, being murdered. This speaks of the rejection of the King Himself. In no other Gospel is the

story of the rejection so completely told as here. It begins in Galilee, in His own city, and ends in Jerusalem. The rejection is not human but it is *satanic.* All the wickedness and depravity of the heart is uncovered and Satan revealed throughout. All classes are concerned in the rejection. The crowd who had followed Him and were fed by Him, the Pharisees, the Sadducees, the Herodians, the priests, the chief priests, the high priest, the elders. At least it becomes evident that they knew Him who He was, their Lord and their King, and wilfully they delivered Him into the hands of the Gentiles. The story of the cross in Matthew, too, brings out the darkest side of the rejection. Thus prophecy is seen fulfilled in the rejection of the King.

4. *The Rejection of His Earthly People and Their Judgment.* This is another theme of the Old Testament which is very prominent in the Gospel of Matthew. They rejected Him and He leaves them, and judgment falls upon them. In the eleventh chapter He reproaches the cities in which most of His works of power had taken place, because they had not repented. At the end of the twelfth chapter He denies His relations and refuses to see His own, while in the beginning of the thirteenth He leaves the house and goes down to the sea, the latter typifies the nations. After His royal presentation to Jerusalem, the next day early in the morning, He curses the fig trees, which foreshadows Israel's national death, and after He uttered His two parables to the chief priests and elders, He declares that the kingdom of God is to be taken away from them and is to be given to a nation which is to bring the fruit thereof. The whole twenty-third chapter contains the woes upon the Pharisees, and at the end He speaks of Jerusalem and declares that their house is to be left desolate till they shall say, Blessed is He who comes in the name of the Lord.

5. *The Mysteries of the Kingdom of the Heavens.* The kingdom has been rejected by the people of the kingdom and the King Himself has left the earth. During His absence the kingdom of the heavens is in the hands of men. There is then the kingdom in the earth in an entirely different form as it was revealed in the Old Testament; the mysteries of the kingdom hidden from the world's foundation are now made known. This we learn in Matthew 13, and here, too, we have at least a glimpse of the church. Again, it is to be understood that both are not identical. But what is the kingdom in its mystery form? The seven parables teach this. It is seen there is an evil mixed condition. The Church, the one body, is not evil, for the Church is composed of those who are beloved of God, called saints, but Christendom, including all professors, is properly that kingdom of the heavens in the thirteenth chapter. The parables bring out what may be termed the history of Christendom. It is a history of failure, becoming that which the King never meant it to be, the leaven of evil, indeed, leavening the whole lump, and thus it continues till the King comes back, when all the offences will be gathered out of the kingdom. The parable of the pearl alone speaks of the Church.

6. *The Church.* In no other Gospel is anything said of the Church except in the Gospel of Matthew. In the sixteenth chapter Peter gives his testimony concerning the Lord, revealed to him from the Father, who is in the heavens. The Lord tells him that on "this rock I will build my assembly—Church—and hades' gates shall not prevail against it." It is not I *have built,* but I *will* build My Church. Right after this promise He speaks of His suffering and death. The transfiguration which follows the first declaration of His coming death, speaks of the glory which will follow, and is a type of the power and coming of our Lord Jesus Christ (2 Peter 1:16). Much that follows the declaration of the Lord concerning the building of the Church is to be applied to the Church.

7. *The Mount of Olivet Discourse and Prophetic Teachings Concerning the End of the Age.* This discourse was given to the disciples after the Lord had spoken His last word to Jerusalem. It is one of the most remarkable sections of the entire Gospel. We find it in the twenty-fourth and twenty-fifth chapters. In it the Lord teaches concerning the Jews, the Gentiles and Christendom, including the true Church. The order is different. The Gentiles stand last. The reason for that is that the Church will be removed first from the earth and the professors of Christendom will be left, who are nothing but Gentiles concerned in the judgment of nations as made known by the Lord. The first part of Matthew 24 is Jewish throughout. From the fourth to the forty-fifth verse we have a most important prophecy, which gives the events which follow after the Church is taken from the earth. The Lord takes here many of the Old Testament prophecies and blends them in one great prophecy. Three parables follow in which the saved and unsaved are seen. Waiting and serving is the leading thought. Reward and casting out into outward darkness the twofold outcome. This, then, finds an application in Christendom and

the Church. The ending of Matthew 25 is the judgment of nations. This is not the universal judgment, a popular term in Christendom, but it is the judgment of the nations at the time when our Lord as Son of Man sits upon the throne of His glory.

The Scope and Division of Matthew

The characteristic keyword of the Gospel of Matthew is the word "kingdom." As stated before, the phrase "kingdom of heaven" is found thirty-two times in this Gospel. In the third chapter the herald of the King, John the Baptist, announced the kingdom of heaven at hand. The King in beginning His ministry preached the same message and when He sent forth His disciples He gave them this instruction: "And as ye go, preach, saying, The kingdom of heaven is at hand" (chapter 10:7). But this preaching suddenly ended. John the Baptist was cast into prison. The Pharisees and Sadducees opposed the King and the kingdom He preached. After the twelfth chapter we hear no longer the kingdom announced as being at hand. Instead of the nation-wide proclamation of the kingdom, the Lord begins to teach the mysteries of the kingdom, announces His rejection and His death; then goes up to Jerusalem where He was presented as King, suffered, died and was raised from the dead.

The Gospel has therefore two main divisions: The first, chapters 1—12, and the second, chapters 13—28.

I. THE KING AND THE OFFER OF THE KINGDOM (1—12)

1. **The King, His Genealogy and His Birth** (1)
2. **The King Worshiped by Gentiles, Jerusalem in Ignorance of Him, and the Child Persecuted** (2)
3. **The Herald of the King: the King Enters Upon His Public Ministry** (3)
4. **The Testing of the King and His Testimony** (4)
5. **The Proclamation of the King** (5—7)
6. **The King Manifested by Signs of Divine Power** (8—9)
7. **The Messengers of the King** (10)
8. **The Forerunner in Prison and the Rejection of the Kingdom** (11)
9. **The Rejection Consummated and the Broken Relationship** (12)

II. THE REJECTED KINGDOM AND THE REJECTION OF THE KING; HIS DEATH AND RESURRECTION (13—28)

1. **The King at the Seashore and the Mysteries of the Kingdom** (13)
2. **John's Martyrdom and the Fourfold Attitude of the Rejected King** (14)
3. **The Corruption of the Scribes and Pharisees, the Canaanitish Woman, and the Multitudes Healed** (15)
4. **The Predictions of the Rejected King Concerning Himself** (16)
5. **The Coming Glory, the Helpless Disciples, and the Power of the King** (17)
6. **Instructions to His Disciples and Concerning Forgiveness** (18)
7. **Departure from Galilee, Concerning Divorce, The Little Children Blessed, and the Rich Young Man** (19)
8. **The Parable of the Laborers in the Vineyard and the Healing of the Two Blind Men** (20)
9. **The King's Entry into Jerusalem, the Parables of the Two Sons and the Householders** (21)
10. **The Parable of the Marriage Feast, Questions Answered, and the Unanswered Question** (22)
11. **The Woes of the King and the Lamentation over Jerusalem** (23)
12. **The Olivet Discourse** (24—25)
13. **The Passion of the King** (26—27)
14. **The Resurrection and the Great Commission (28)**

Analysis and Annotations

I. The King and the Offer of the Kingdom (1—12)

CHAPTER 1

1. Jesus Christ, the Son of David, the Son of Abraham (1:1)
2. From Abraham to David (1:2-6)
3. From David to the captivity (1:6-11)
4. From the captivity to the birth of Christ (1:12-17)
5. The birth of Jesus Christ (1:18-25)

The first two words in the Greek *(biblos geneseos),* "the book of generation," corresponds to the same term in the book of Genesis (Gen 2:4, etc.). The question of a genealogy is an important one with the Jew. The legal right to the throne of David must be first of all proven so that no doubt can be attached to His claim of being the promised King. Because it is the question of kingship, "Son of David" precedes "Son of Abraham." An uninspired writer would have put "Son of Abraham" in the first place. As He is the promised King who comes to the nation Israel, the fact that He is the Son of David is put into the foreground. But He is also the Son of Abraham through whom the promises of blessing to the Gentiles are to be fulfilled.

The genealogy of our Lord in Matthew differs from the one in Luke. The one in the Gospel of Luke (chapter 3) proves that Mary, the mother of Jesus, is of David through the house of Nathan. The genealogy of Matthew shows Joseph, who was supposed to be the father of Jesus (Luke 3:23), is a descendant of David through the line of Solomon. The descendants of Solomon have the legal right to the throne. But the last King of Judah, Jeconias, a son of Solomon, was so wicked that a curse was pronounced upon him and he was to be childless, "no man of his seed shall prosper, sitting upon the throne of David" (Jer. 22:30). However, this curse did not affect the *legal* claim to the throne. But Jesus was not the son of David through Joseph, but through Mary the virgin, who came of David through the line of Nathan. No curse rested upon that line. As the supposed son of Joseph, He inherited the legal title to the throne through Joseph, but being the son of David through Mary, the curse which rested upon Jeconias was not upon Him. The genealogy in Matthew shows, therefore, that Joseph, the supposed father of Jesus, is in point of law entitled to the throne, therefore Jesus is legally heir to the throne of David. If Mary, the mother of our Lord, had not been legally the wife of Joseph, a son of David, the Jews could have rejected the claims of Jesus to the throne. We see, then, that legally He was the son of Joseph with the full crown rights upon Him; in His true humanity, He is of Mary the virgin, also of David; then at the close of the chapter we read that He is the Son of God.

The genealogy tells the story of decadence. Corruption, ruin and hopelessness are written therein. As generation after generation is given, we follow the shameful history of Israel, a history of unbelief and judgment. At last all is dark and hopeless. Like Sarah's womb (the type of the nation) the nation is dead. But God can bring life from the dead. "When the fulness of time was come, God sent forth His Son, come of woman, come under the law" (Gal. 4:4). The genealogy has three divisions, each division has fourteen generations. David alone has the title, the king (verse 6). Solomon's name is not given as king, to show the promises made to David concerning a son to come from his loins (2 Sam. 7:8-16) were not fulfilled in Solomon.

Notice the four Gentile women in the genealogy of the King. *Tamar* (telling out the ravages of sin); *Rahab* (she was saved by faith); *Ruth* (under the curse of the law, but brought into relation with Israel); then the one of *Uriah,* that is Bath-Sheba (David's sin brought into remembrance). These four women tell out beforehand the story of the gospel and how the promised King would also be the Saviour of the Gentiles.

The story of His birth concludes this chapter. The virgin birth is here fully revealed and this birth is given as the fulfillment of Isaiah 7:14. The two Gospels, which mention His birth, Matthew and Luke, show in the most perfect way that the Son of God, the eternal Word, became man, born of the virgin, a true human being, yet "that holy thing," absolutely without sin. His human nature proceeded directly from the Spirit of God. The early Jews never attacked the accounts of the birth of our Lord. Many, many years later wicked hands wrote a vulgar and blasphemous account of the birth of our Lord. Apostate Christendom has sided with the wicked denials of Jewish and Gentile infidels of the past. Can there be anything more blasphemous, more wicked, more immoral, than the teaching, so widespread to-day, that our Lord as to His human nature was not "conceived by the Holy Spirit?"

CHAPTER 2

1. The visit of the wise men (2:1-12)
2. The flight into Egypt (2:13-18)
3. The return from Egypt (2:19-25)

The authenticity of the story of the visit of the wise men seeking the new-born King of the Jews has been doubted, because no other Evangelist reports this incident. It belongs properly in the Gospel in which our Lord is portrayed as the King. This is the reason of its being reported only in Matthew's Gospel. The wise men were not three persons, nor were they kings. It must have been a larger company, for it troubled Herod and all Jerusalem with him. Nor did the visit take place immediately after the birth of our Lord. The correct rendering of the first verse is, "But Jesus having been born," that is, some time after and not immediately after. The pictures which portray the wise men worshipping the child in a stable are unscriptural, for it says they found the young child in a house. It was most likely a year after His birth, that the wise men from the East appeared. Luke 2:41 shows that His parents went to Jerusalem every year; they must then also have visited Bethlehem again.

The promised King is unknown in His own city, Jerusalem. His own people are ignorant of Him. Gentiles come first to do Him homage. The ecclesiastical authorities are indifferent to His claims, the civil ruler, Herod, the King, hates Him, and as Satan's instrument seeks His life. The history of the King and His kingdom is outlined in this story. His own are not going to receive Him. The indifference of the chief priests and scribes points to their coming antagonism. But Gentiles seek Him first. Simeon's prophetic song is seen here in its coming fulfillment, "A light to lighten the Gentiles," but in the end also, after God's purpose in this age is accomplished, "the glory of Thy people Israel" (Luke 2:32). They bring gold, typical of divinity; frankincense, indicating the fragrance of His life and worship; and myrrh, that which is used in burial, a hint as to His death. Note that this is not a fulfillment of Isaiah 60:6. That passage refers to the time when the Kingdom is set up on earth. Myrrh in Isaiah is not mentioned.

Throughout the chapter the child always occupies the first and prominent place. It is never "Mary and the child," or "the mother and the child," but "the little child and His mother"—the child is above the mother. What a rebuke to the Romish church, which in idolatry puts the mother above the child.

See Hosea 11:1 on the flight to Egypt and the return. All indicates what is to be done to Him, who is the King.

CHAPTER 3

1. The herald of the King (3:1-6)
2. His message and His baptism (3:7-12)
3. The King in Jordan's waters (3:13-17)

John the Baptist, the herald of the King, is now introduced. See Luke 1:15-17 for the angelic announcement of his birth and mission. He is predicted in the Old Testament (Isaiah 40:3-5, Mal. 3:1). He appeared like Elijah the Prophet (2 Kings 1:8). But He was not Elijah. See also Matthew 17:12. And before the King comes the second time there will be once more a forerunner. Mal. 4:5-6 will then be fulfilled. John knew his mission (John 1:23). His testimony as reported by Matthew concerns the nation. In the Gospel of John we find the record of another testimony given by the forerunner. He knew the King also as the Lamb of God.

He calls the nation to repentance, because the kingdom of heaven is at hand. The phrase "kingdom of heaven" (literally "of the heavens") occurs here for the first time. It does not mean the offer of salvation, nor does it mean the Church, nor the social betterment of the people, but it signifies the Messianic kingdom as promised by the prophets of God, a kingdom which is to be set up on earth and over which the Son of David is to be King. This the forerunner announced. This kingdom the Lord Jesus and His disciples preached, till it became evident that Israel would not have this kingdom. Then the preaching ceased.

In verses 11 and 12 there is a blending together of the first and second coming of Christ. As a result of the first coming of Christ the baptism with the Holy Spirit took place. The fire baptism refers to judgment. The twelfth verse describes the fire baptism of judgment when the King comes again.

The baptism of John has nothing to do with Christian baptism. It was baptism unto repentance only. By being baptized in Jordan (the type of death) they confessed that they had deserved death.

Then the King entered upon His public ministry. He too entered the waters of Jordan and was baptized; not that He needed it, but to signify He came to be the substitute of sinners and to take the sinners' place in death. In the baptismal scene we have His whole blessed work foreshadowed. He is the Holy One, who needed no baptism for He had no sin. His *death* is foreshadowed when He went into Jordan; His *resurrection,* when He came out of the water; His *ascension,* when heaven was opened unto Him. The gift of the Holy Spirit is seen next and this is followed by the declaration of Sonship. Into this the believer enters. We are dead and risen with Him; Heaven too is opened unto us and we have received the Spirit of Sonship.

CHAPTER 4

1. The testing by the devil (4:1-11)
2. His testimony and His disciples (4:12-22)
3. The powers of the kingdom (4:23-25)

Then He was led (literally: carried) by the Spirit into the wilderness to be tempted of the devil. "And immediately the Spirit drives Him out into the wilderness" (Mark 1:12). And He was there with the wild beasts (Mark 1:13). After He had fasted for forty days, the tempter came to Him. What a contrast with the first man, Adam, in the garden of Eden!

The devil is a person and not an evil influence. The "new theology" invented by the father of lies has no use for a personal devil. The Lord's temptations, according to that theology, were only imaginations. The denial of the personality of the devil is a serious thing.

In studying this chapter it must be remembered that the Lord Jesus was absolutely holy. Therefore He could not fall nor be tempted by sin. If He could have fallen into sin He would have needed a Saviour and could not have been our Saviour. He was tempted in all things as we are "apart from sin." A better word for tempting is "testing." The devil came to test Him. He was tested as to His ability to do that for which He came. The test proves that He is pure gold, the Holy and Spotless One, who is fit to put away sin by the sacrifice of Himself. Satan makes three tests. Each test is met by the Lord Jesus with the Word of God, with an "It is written." And He quotes the Word exclusively from Deuteronomy, the book of obedience. The devil with his three temptations tried to keep Him back from doing the will of God. He wanted Christ to act independently from His Father. If He had acted thus for Himself He would have proven His unfitness to suffer and to die. If He had been disobedient in the smallest matter, He could not have been obedient unto death. The first two temptations were a challenge to prove Himself the Son of God. The last was the presumptuous offer of the usurping prince of this world to give to Christ the kingdoms of the world, if He would fall down before him. He knew that eventually, by the way of the cross, the Son of God would obtain the kingdoms, that they would become His and he, the proud usurper, would be spoiled of all, stripped of his power and cast into the lake of fire. He wanted Christ to be disobedient to the Word as he led the first man to disobedience. He tried to keep Him from going to the cross. The Lord defeated the devil completely and he left Him for a season. (For a complete exegesis of the temptation see our larger commentary on Matthew, pages 79-96.)

The report reached Him that John, the forerunner, had been cast into prison. He then departed into Galilee. It is His Galilean ministry which Matthew reports; the events of the Judean ministry are not given by him. These we find in the Gospel of John. He preached in Nazareth and dwelt in Capernaum. What happened in Nazareth is more fully reported by Luke (4:14-32). His own townspeople were filled with wrath and thrust Him out of the city, trying to cast Him down a hill. The first murderous attempt was made in Nazareth.

He preached the message of the kingdom throughout that region. Peter, Andrew and the two sons of Zebedee, James and John, are called by Him into service. They left all, the nets, the ship and even the father to follow Him and became fishers of men.

For the first time in Matthew we read of the signs which were linked with the preaching of the gospel of the kingdom. The healing of the sick and the demon-possessed were truly signs that the King is Jehovah manifested in the flesh and that the kingdom had drawn nigh.

CHAPTER 5

1. The characteristics of the heirs of the kingdom (5:1-16)
2. The confirmation of the law and its expansion (5:17-48)

In chapters 5—7 we have the full report of the so-called Sermon on the Mount. Mark and Luke give fragments of this discourse, but the complete discourse is found only in Matthew. The Sermon on the Mount is the proclamation of the King concerning His kingdom, and may well be called the "Magna Charta of the kingdom of heaven." This discourse does not expound the gospel of grace, the way of salvation, the privileges and blessings of true Christianity. The teachers who say that the Sermon on the Mount is the gospel are ignorant of what the gospel is. We mention three wrong applications which are being made of this discourse.

1. The application to the unsaved, as if in this discourse the way to righteousness is shown, which man by his own effort is to attain. The discourse in the beginning speaks of saved persons, of disciples. The Lord does not address sinners. He taught His disciples. As the great

unfolding of the salvation of God as revealed in the Epistle to the Romans is abandoned in Christendom, the false application of this discourse is increasingly followed. There is little preaching of the lost and helpless condition of man, the necessity of the new birth and the reception of eternal life. What is put in the place of the true gospel is ethical teaching; and this has culminated in a Christian-socialistic attempt to save society. The Sermon on the Mount is taken as the program for this. But it condemns this spurious gospel of works and evolution.

2. The second wrong application is the one which makes this discourse exclusively Christian and applies it to the Church. The magna charta of the Church is in the Epistles of Paul, to whom the full revelation of the Church was given. Christian position is not revealed in the Sermon on the Mount. The Sermon on the Mount is not given as the standard of Christian experience and walk.

3. The third false application is the one which makes this discourse exclusively Jewish. Some Christians refuse to consider these chapters as having any message or instruction for them at all. This is the other extreme and equally wrong. We repeat, the Sermon on the Mount is the proclamation of the King concerning His kingdom. That kingdom is not the Church, nor is it a state of righteousness of the earth brought about through the agency of the Church. It is the kingdom as it will be set up by the King with the coming age. While in the Old Testament we have the outward manifestations of that earthly kingdom revealed, we have here from the lips of the King the inner principles of that kingdom. When the Lord Jesus Christ comes again the Old Testament predictions concerning the kingdom will be literally fulfilled and the kingdom itself will be a kingdom of righteousness according to this proclamation. However, this does not exclude application to us, the heirs of the kingdom.

The beatitudes give the character of the heirs who enter the kingdom. They do not speak of what a person should be, or strive to be, but what *they are.* Only the grace of God can produce such a character. The blessings are in possession of those, who have believed on the Son of God. And the Lord Jesus manifested all these characteristics in His humiliation. But these beatitudes have also a significance in connection with the future believing remnant of Israel, waiting amidst the great tribulations and under the severest persecutions at the end of the age for the return of the King. See Zephaniah 3:12 and Isaiah 66:2; Micah 7:1-7.

The law is then taken up by the King in this proclamation. He is the Lawgiver and therefore He confirms, expands and supplements the law. Here we are on Jewish ground. Believers in Christ have nothing to do with the law. We are dead to the law (Rom. 7:4; Gal. 3:24-25). The better righteousness needed to enter the kingdom is not man's own righteousness, but that which is by faith in Jesus Christ.

As He speaks with authority He uncovers the heart of man and shows the depths of corruption and the hopelessness that the natural man could ever attain such a righteousness. The words of the King condemn every man and prove him lost. The condemnation of the natural man is written there.

CHAPTER 6

1. The better righteousness (6:1-18)
2. Kept in the world, single-eyed, and trusting God (6:19-34)

He makes now known the motive of the true righteousness, which the heirs of the kingdom are not only to possess, but also to practice. The motive is to act in the presence of the Father. The word Father is found ten times in the beginning of this chapter. The Father sees, the Father knows. Here a relationship is acknowledged and made prominent, which is unknown in the Old Testament. How the heirs of the kingdom are brought into this relationship is not taught in Matthew. The Gospel of John reveals this.

In verses 1-4 we see the motive of the true righteousness in relation to man; in verses 5-15 in relation to God and in verses 16-18 in relation to self.

In verses 9-13 the King gives to His disciples a model prayer. It has been called "the Lord's prayer." A better name would be "the disciples' prayer." The Lord had no need to use it Himself. The ritualistic use of this form of prayer, its repetition at many occasions, as if it were a meritorious act, must be condemned. It was given to His Jewish disciples. In connection with the announcement of His departure and the coming of the Holy Spirit, our Lord did not teach His disciples the continued use of this form of prayer, but He said, "Hitherto ye have asked nothing in My name; ask and ye shall receive, that your joy may be full" (John 16-24).

We do not find this prayer used in Acts of the Apostles; nor do we find in the Epistles an exhortation that it should be used by the Church. It had a special meaning to the disciples, as it will have again for the remnant of Israel at the close of the age. Yet the prayer is perfect, beautiful and embodies heavenly wisdom. The Christian believer finds under the guidance of the Spirit the deeper meaning and can enter into all the petitions.

In the second half of this chapter the heirs of the kingdom are seen as in the world, subject to its cares and temptations. Our Lord tells us how to behave in the midst of the world and what are our privileges and comforts. The natural man lives for the earthly things; his delight is in treasures which are here below. It is to be different with the true disciple (verses 19-21). In connection with His exhortation, "lay not up for yourselves treasures, which are on earth," read the following passages: Col. 3:2-3; 2 Cor. 4:18; 1 Tim. 6:9-11, 6:17-18; Heb. 13:5. May we heed these words in a day when professing Christians heap together treasures in the last days (Jas. 5:1-3). And how great is the comfort that we have a Father, who careth! "Be not careful"—oh, how blessed it sounds, how full and rich it comes to the heart of the believer! And it is the Son of God who exhorts us to trust the Father, who gives us the assurance if we seek first the kingdom of God and His righteousness, that all these things shall be added unto us.

CHAPTER 7

1. The judgment of righteousness (7:1-14)
2. Warning against false prophets (7:15-20)
3. Warning against false professors (7:21-29)

The first few verses are warning against judging. The attention is called to the conduct of a disciple toward another disciple. The Lord does not forbid here the righteous judgment and condemnation of what is evil. We are told elsewhere to do this (1 Cor. 5:12, 13). The judgment of motives is forbidden. These are known to God alone. Verse 6 must be compared with 2 Pet. 2:22. The dogs and the swine represent mere outward profession, who were never born again.

"Christendom has in fact done shamelessly what the Lord here forbids, and has proved the truth of His words in consequence. Baptism and the Lord's Supper, perverted from their original meaning and application, have been used above all to give the grossest evils tolerance in the house of God, and to make Babylon the great "a cage of every unclean and hateful bird." They have thus been trampled under foot by the profane, and Christianity been rent and mangled fearfully, as all the centuries bear witness. The "judgment of charity" is continually invoked to take darkness to be light, and credit the most barren profession with what it dares not even claim for itself. But the false judgment of laxity has here its woe upon it, as much as the false judgment of censoriousness: upon that which puts good for evil, and that which puts evil for good alike" *(Numerical Bible).*

The great proclamation of the King closes with warnings against false prophets and false, religious professors. The warning of verse 15 is for our age as well and has a special significance in the end of the age. False teachers and false spirits are on all sides, and false prophets increase. See Acts 20:29, 30: Col. 2:8; 1 Tim. 4:1; 6:20; 2 Pet. 2:1; 1 John 4:1-3; 2 Cor. 2:17, 11:13-15. How different these divine warnings are in comparison with the optimistic vision of Christendom of an age which increases in righteousness. When the King comes again "in that day" the false prophets and false professors will be discovered. The false prophets, though they used His Name (like "Christian Science" and the "Russell Cult"), will be disowned by Him. The house built upon the sand of a mere profession and not the rock of ages will be swept away by the judgment.

CHAPTER 8

1. The healing of the leper (8:1-4)
2. The healing of the centurion's servant (8:5-13)
3. The healing of Peter's wife's mother (8:14-15)
4. The healing of all (8:16-17)
5. The self-seeking scribe and the test of true discipleship (8:18-22)
6. His power over nature (8:23-27)
7. His power over the demons (8:28-34)

The King who had uttered this great proclamation now manifests more fully His divine power by signs and miracles. These signs showed Israel that the kingdom was at hand. In Isaiah 35 we find a prophetic description of the kingdom powers; and the King shows that He has come to make good these promises. The arrangement in Matthew shows that these miracles are taken out of their chronological order. They are found in Mark and Luke in a different setting. This is not a discrepancy as so often claimed by the deniers of inspiration. The Holy Spirit has grouped them together in such a way to show first of all that the King proved Himself as the promised Messiah-King. In the second place the Spirit of God put them in the order, in which they appear in these two chapters to teach thereby certain dispensational purposes of God.

The first four miracles show His dispensational dealings with the Jews and the Gentiles in a most striking manner. The leper is a type of the sinner and also a type of the nation Israel (Is. 1:5-6). Jehovah alone can heal this awful disease (Num. 12:13; 2 Kings 5:1-15). The attitude and faith of this leper should have been Israel's. He had come to heal the nation. The leper was healed and is sent by the King to the priest. The priest, however, does not proclaim the good news that Jehovah had appeared in the midst of His people. Thus Israel's failure to recognize and receive the Messiah and be healed is seen in the first miracle. The centurion was a Gentile. The Lord found there greater faith than among His own people. He healed the servant not by touch, but He was absent from the place where he was. This miracle stands for the fact that Gentiles would believe on Him during this age, while He is absent.

Then He healed Peter's wife's mother by going to the house and touching her. After this present dispensation is passed He will restore His relationship with His people Israel and heal and restore her to service. Then follows the healing of all. Verses 16-17 show the kingdom blessings for the world after His second coming. And the King manifests power as the Lord of Creation, by rebuking the winds and the sea. He has power over demons, who acknowledge Him as Son of God and tremble in His presence.

CHAPTER 9

1. A man sick of the palsy healed (9:1-8)
2. The call of Matthew (9:9)
3. With the publicans and the sinners (9:10-13)
4. The question of John's disciples (9:14-17)
5. The ruler's request (9:18-19)
6. The woman healed of an issue of blood (9:20-22)
7. The maid raised from the dead (9:23-26)
8. The two blind men healed (9:27-31)
9. The dumb man with a demon healed (9:32-33)
10. The blaspheming Pharisees and the compassionate Shepherd of Israel (9:34-38)

The King next manifests His power to forgive sins and when that power is questioned by the scribes and He is accused of blasphemy He healed the paralytic so that he arose. By this miracle full proof was given that the Son of Man has power on earth to forgive sins. Well did the scribes and Pharisees say, "Who is able to forgive sins but God alone?" (Luke 5:21). By healing the paralytic they received the conclusive evidence that He who had spoken "thy sins are forgiven" is God manifested in the flesh. The miracle foreshadows His gracious work for every sinner who believes on Him. Our bodies, too, are redeemed, but we still wait for that redemption (Rom. 8:21). The miracle foreshadows likewise the healing of Israel. The day will come when the remnant of His earthly people will have forgiveness of their sins and be healed (Isa. 33:24). It will be when He comes again (Isa. 59:20; Rom. 11:26-27). Thus will they witness in reality to the truth expressed in Ps. 103:1-5.

The call of Matthew follows next. He left his office as taxgatherer and yielded ready obedience. And then the King eats and drinks with the publicans and the sinners, showing that He came to call sinners to repentance. A change of dispensation is indicated by Him in verses 16-17. The old garment and the old bottles (literal: wine-skins) stand for the law with its ordinances. The piece of the new cloth and the new wine stand for the better righteousness, the gospel. The old wine-skins and the new wine do not go together; neither do law and grace.

The daughter which had died is the type of the daughter of Zion, spiritually and nationally dead. The Lord is on the way to raise her up. The woman, who touches Him and is healed represents Gentiles, who touch Him in faith. This miracle is a parenthetical event, just as the present age with its era of salvation to the Gentiles is a great parenthesis. And as He raised the daughter of the ruler, so will He in the future raise up Israel. For the first time in this Gospel we find here the awful blasphemy of the religious leaders of the people. They accused the Lord from heaven of using satanic power in casting out demons. But the King continued in His minstry of preaching the Kingdom and healing the sick. Then He beheld His poor scattered sheep in their deplorable condition. His loving heart was moved with compassion (Ezek. 34:7-31).

CHAPTER 10

1. The twelve disciples (10:1-4)
2. Their commission (10:5-15)
3. Persecutions promised (10:16-23)
4. Words of encouragement (10:24-33)
5. Not peace but the sword (10:34-36)
6. True discipleship and rewards (10:37-42)

The King now calls His disciples to go forth as the messengers of the kingdom. The commission He gives them was temporary and ended with the complete rejection of the kingdom by Israel. He told them not to carry the kingdom message to the Gentiles, not even to the Samaritans. It was a message for the lost sheep of the house of Israel. They were to preach the good news of the kingdom and the King conferred upon them His own Messianic power to heal the sick, cleanse the lepers and to raise the dead. Freely they had received it and freely they were to give. All this has nothing whatever to do with the preaching of the gospel of grace among all the nations. We have here not the commission of the Church, but the ministry of a transition period. Christian Science and other cults claim that they are obedient to this commission and that they practice the healing of the sick. They, however, know nothing of raising the dead. Neither are they obedient to the command "freely ye have received, freely give." Their cults are for filthy lucre sake and are the cults of deception.

Persecutions and severe sufferings are predicted by the King. His messengers were to suffer, to be delivered to councils, to be scourged and put to death. Part of the fulfillment of all this is recorded in the book of Acts, where in the beginning the gospel of the kingdom is still preached.

Verse 23 tells us of an unfinished testimony. "For verily I say unto you, Ye shall not have gone over the cities of Israel, till the Son of Man be come." The coming of the Son of Man is His second coming. Before He comes again the gospel of the kingdom will be preached once more both in Israel's land and also among all nations (Matt. 24:14). The heralds in the future will again be a company of believing Jewish disciples. The predictions concerning persecution and tribulation will then all be finally fulfilled in that period of time, which is called in the Word of God "the great tribulation" (24:21). The true Church will then be no longer on earth. Before that time of trouble comes, preceding the second visible coming of Christ, the Church will be gathered home to be with Christ (1 Thess. 4:13-18).

Verse 34 describes the present age. There is no peace on earth while the King and His kingdom are rejected. When He comes again He will establish the promised peace (Ps. 46:9; Zech. 9:10).

CHAPTER 11

1. John imprisoned sends His disciples (11:1-6)
2. The King's testimony concerning John (11:7-19)
3. The King announces judgment (11:20-24)
4. The greater invitation (11:25-28)

Once more the King takes up the work of teaching and preaching in the cities of Galilee. It is now becoming increasingly evident that Israel is not going to repent and accept the offered kingdom. The present chapter is the beginning of the crisis, the rejection is consummated in the chapter which follows.

John the Baptist imprisoned is assailed with doubt; he was but human. He did not send to the Lord for the sake of His disciples, but wanted comfort and assurance for himself. Beautiful it is to see how the Lord speaks of him.

Verse 12 needs some comment. "And from the days of John the Baptist until now the kingdom of heaven suffereth violence, and the violent take it by force." The wrong interpretation is that which makes the violent, who seize the kingdom of heaven, unsaved sinners. According to this the sinner must exert his own strength and by force lay hold on the kingdom of heaven. It means, however, the opposite. The Pharisees and scribes, who listened to the words of the Lord, are the violent who used force in connection with the kingdom of heaven. (The student must remember that the kingdom of heaven does not mean the gospel at all, but is still the literal kingdom promised to Israel.) They rejected the kingdom. In this sense the kingdom of heaven suffered violence. No sooner did John the Baptist preach "the kingdom of heaven is at hand," than the leaders of the nation raised their opposition. It increased till it culminated in the rejection and crucifixion of the King.

Then the King pronounced His woe upon the unbelieving cities. But more than that, upon the evident rejection of the kingdom message, the King lifts His eyes to heaven and addresses the Father. For the first time He announces the greater invitation of the gospel of His grace. It is now "Come unto Me *all*"; the message of the kingdom will cease and the message of His love will be sent forth into all the world. That message comes from the cross.

CHAPTER 12

1. The hungry disciples and the accusing Pharisees (12:1-9)
2. The man with the withered hand healed (12:10-13)
3. The hatred of the Pharisees (12:14)
4. The King in rejection (12:15-21)
5. The demon-possessed man healed (12:22-23)
6. The blasphemy of the Pharisees and the King's answer (12:24-37)
7. The sign of Jonas and his warning prediction (12:38-45)
8. The broken relationship (12:46-50)

This chapter is the great turning point in this Gospel. It brings before us the full rejection of the kingdom. After this chapter we hear no longer the kingdom preached to Israel.

The King manifests Himself as the Lord of the Sabbath and answered the charge of the accusing Pharisees. That the disciples, the messengers of the kingdom, were hungry shows that the people had no sympathy for the messengers and the message. To pluck ears of corn on the Sabbath is nowhere forbidden. The tradition of the elders had added the commandment on account of which the Pharisees brought their accusation. He silences them with David's action, who, though he was God's anointed, yet rejected, entered the house of the Lord and did what was not lawful for him to do (1 Sam. 21).

Their first attempt to accuse Him and His disciples failed. They tried again by the man with the withered hand. He silenced them again and healed the man, who obeyed His Word. He, too, is a picture of Israel in their spiritual and national withered condition. Then they held a council to plan the destruction of the King. And after He healed the man who was possessed with a demon, who had robbed him of his sight and his speech, the Pharisees charged the Lord with driving out the demons by Beelzebub, the prince of demons. This was the crowning sin of the unbelieving Pharisees. It is the blasphemy against the Holy Spirit. That is the sin against the Holy Spirit for which there is no forgiveness in this age nor in that to come.

Interesting are His words in verses 43-45. The nation Israel is here again in view. The unclean spirit which left Israel was the spirit of idolatry. But that unclean spirit will return with seven others and take possession again of that house, and the last condition, the end, becomes worse than the beginning. This condition will yet be reached among the apostate Jews during the time of the Antichrist.

In the end of this chapter the King refuses to see His own. This action was symbolical. He declared through it that the relationship with His own nation, to whom He came as the promised King, was now broken off. He announces a new relationship (verses 49-50). As stated already after this event He announces no longer the kingdom at hand. The message of the kingdom had been given and had been rejected. The first part of the Gospel of Matthew ends here.

II. The Rejected Kingdom and the Rejected King (13—28)

CHAPTER 13

1. The King at the seaside (13:1-2)
2. The parable of the sower (13:3-9)
3. The question of the disciples and His answer (13:10-17)
4. The parable of the sower explained (13:18-23)
5. The parable of the good seed and the tares (13:24-30)
6. The parable of the mustard seed (13:31-32)
7. The parable of the leaven (13:33-35)
8. The parable of the good seed and of the tares explained (13:36-42)
9. The parable of the treasure in the field (13:44)
10. The parable of the pearl of great price (13:45-46)
11. The parable of the drag-net (13:47-52)
12. Rejected in His own country (13:53-58)

This is an important and most interesting chapter. It is perhaps the most misinterpreted chapter in the entire Gospel. Precisely that which our Lord did not teach has been read into it. If the parables were correctly understood the consequences would be the most far-reaching. The King having declared the relationship with His people broken left the house (symbolical of this fact) and sat by the seaside. Then He began to teach in parables. These parables, repeated in full only in Matthew, concern the mysteries of the kingdom of heaven. He makes known things hidden from the foundation of the world (verses 11, 34-35). The kingdom of heaven is now no longer that Old Testament kingdom promised to Israel, for that kingdom was not an unrevealed secret. The parables of the mysteries of the kingdom of heaven give a description of what is to be on the earth religiously after Israel's rejection of the kingdom. The parables contain a wonderful revelation of the present age, beginning with the sowing of the good seed by the Son of Man and ending with the harvest, the end of the age, when He comes the second time. To say that our Lord speaks of the Church in these parables would be incorrect. He speaks of what we term to-day "Christendom," the sphere of Christian profession.

The first four parables were spoken by Him before the multitudes. After He sent the people away (verse 36) the Lord spoke the last three to His disciples. The first two parables our Lord explained to the disciples and gives the key to the entire seven. The field mentioned in different parables means "the world." The Man (sower; the man who buys the field; the merchantman) is the Lord Himself. Birds (picking up the seed; flocking into the mustard-tree) are unclean beings. Wheat (sown by Him; the wheat in the three measures) stands for the doctrine of Christ and what it produces, the children of the kingdom.

The first two parables go together. They refer to the beginning of the present age and reveal the conditions which continue to the time of the harvest, the end of the age. (The word "world" in verses 39, 40, and 49 is "age." The same is true of 24:3.) The good seed, the gospel, is now to be scattered in the field, that is, the world. It is a different work from the work of the vineyard (Israel is the vineyard, Isa. 5:1-7). But only the fourth part of the sown seed springs up. The devil, the flesh and the world are the three things which make the universal success of the gospel impossible in this present age. World conversion is not to be expected in the age when the King is absent. The second parable shows the mixed conditions. Wheat and tares grow together till the harvest comes. Then the wheat will be gathered and the tares burned up. The parables of the mustard seed and of the women who hid leaven in the three measures of meal foretell the external development and the internal corruption of the kingdom of heaven in its form during this present age. The mustard seed shows an unnatural, an abnormal growth and the birds lodging there bring defilement. Such is Christendom with its worldly ambitions and its unsaved masses.

The parable of the woman with the leaven is the most misunderstood. The woman does not mean the Church, nor does the leaven stand for the gospel and the doctrine of Christ. Leaven is *always* in the Word of God the type of evil (Matt. 16:11-12; Mark 8:15; 1 Cor. 5:6; Gal. 5:9). If our Lord taught here (as almost universally claimed) that leaven is something good and that the "gospel-leaven" is leavening the whole lump of unconverted humanity, etc., then would He contradict Himself, for the first two parables teach the opposite. Leaven stands for a corrupting process of evil, which is introduced by woman under the control of satanic influence, to corrupt the doctrine of Christ. Here is, no doubt, a prophecy, which has been abundantly fulfilled. The woman "Jezebel" in Rev. 2:20 is the same as the "mother of harlots" in Rev. 17; it is the Romish apostasy. Rome speaks of "Mother church" and *she* is the corrupteress of true Christianity. We may well think here of other wicked corruptions of the doctrine of Christ. Christian Science (Mrs. Eddy); Seventh Day Adventism (Mrs. White); spiritism (Fox sisters); theosophy (Mrs. Blavatsky) and other systems, which originated with women (1 Tim. 2:14). This process of corruption in this present age is also witnessed to by the Holy Spirit in 1 Tim. 4:1-3; 2 Tim. 2:17-18, 3:1-5, 4:3-4; 2 Pet. 2:1-3; Jude. The fire of judgment will arrest it all, as the fire arrests the working of the natural leaven.

The parable of the treasure and of the pearl also go together. The man in both is not the sinner who seeks a treasure and a pearl, who gives up all in order to get all. The man is our Lord, who buys the field. He gave all He had to have the treasure (Israel) hid in the field, who sold all to have the one pearl of great price (the Church). The parable of the drag-net brings us to the end of the age. The net is cast into the sea (nations) and in that net (Christendom) the good and the bad, the true and the false are gathered. They remain there till the end of the age, when they will be separated.

CHAPTER 14

1. John's martyrdom (14:1-11)
2. The disciples of John with the Lord Jesus (14:12)
3. Feeding the five thousand (14:13-21)
4. Praying on the mountain-top (14:22-23)
5. Walking on the sea and coming to His disciples (14:24-35)

The details of the martyrdom of John are given first. It is the story of lust, crime and bloodshed. Such is the entire age in which the King is absent. We see Him in a fourfold attitude, an attitude which teaches us much. First the disciples of John seek Him for comfort—"they came and told Jesus." Then He fed miraculously the multitudes, who had followed Him into the desert place. He used His own. They put the little they possessed in His hands. Next we behold Him praying on the mountain (typical of His presence with the Father in glory) and the final scene in this chapter is the storm on the sea, the wind contrary (a perfect picture of this age), the disciples in danger and He coming across the stormy seas to bring salvation and peace. Then follows a still greater manifestation of His kingly power. We can come to Him for comfort and help; He will feed those who follow Him; He prays and intercedes for His own and at last comes again. With that blessed event the time of peace and blessing for this world will come.

CHAPTER 15

1. The question of the scribes and Pharisees (15:1-2)
2. His answer (15:3-9)
3. The multitude called (15:10-11)
4. The disciples instructed (15:12-20)
5. The Canaanitish woman (15:21-28)
6. The multitudes healed (15:29-31)

The events which follow the rejection of the offered kingdom by Israel, revealing their enmity, are now brought more fully in view. The scribes, the Pharisees and the Sadducees take a leading part. They test Him and bring their questions, but He silences them all. His wisdom is gloriously manifested. A delegation came from Jerusalem. The question concerned a mere traditional law of the elders. Nothing is said whatever in the Old Testament about washing the hands before eating. He uncovers their hypocrisies and shows their corruption.

(Several years ago we read in a Jewish volume printed in Poland, that evil spirits alight overnight on the hands and if hands are not washed as prescribed by the traditional law those evil spirits find their way into the mouth and the stomach of the transgressor and defile him. This foolish superstition is founded upon a talmudical statement of great antiquity. It will throw light on the above passage.)

The Canaanitish woman addressed Him as "Son of David." She had no claim on Him as Son of David. But when she took the place He gave to her and appealed to Him as "Lord" He healed her daughter. Thus the rejected King ministered to a Gentile. The first part of this chapter reveals the desperate condition of Israel. The second part, the healing of the daughter of the Canaanitish woman, shows typically the call of the Gentiles and the salvation in store for them, if they believe. The last part, the healing of the multitude, reveals the dispensation to come, the kingdom age.

CHAPTER 16

1. Pharisees and Sadducees asking a sign (16:1-4)
2. Instructions concerning the leaven (16:5-12)
3. Peter's confession (16:13-16)
4. The future building of the Church announced (16:17-20)
5. The announcement of His death and resurrection (16:21)
6. Peter's rebuke and the Lord's answer (16:22-23)
7. The path of the disciple (16:24-26)
8. His second coming announced (16:27-28)

Seven things are seen in this chapter, the center being the predictions of the King concerning Himself: 1. The rejection of the Lord; Pharisees and Sadducees making common cause to tempt Him. 2. The confession of Him as the Christ, the Son of the living God. 3. The building of His Church. 4. His death. 5. His resurrection. 6. The path of the disciple. 7. His return.

Of greatest interest is the fact that we find the word "Church" mentioned in this chapter for the first time in the Bible. The King had not said a word about a Church, an outcalled company (this is the meaning of the Greek word), when He preached "the kingdom of heaven is at hand." No prophet ever mentioned the Church. When the Lord mentioned the Church, that body was not yet in existence, for He said, "I *will* build My Church." The Church therefore did not exist in the Old Testament; at the time the Lord spoke these words the Church was still future. The rock upon which this Church is to be built is Christ the Son of God (not the Son of David, the promised King). Christ raised from the dead is the great rock foundation. Peter is not the rock. Peter means in the Greek "petros," a stone; the word rock in Greek is "petra." This word is used in Matt. 7:24, 25. Therefore Christ is *the* rock and Peter a part of the rock. This brings out the blessed truth that every true believer in possession of eternal life is one with Christ. The testimony of Peter in 1 Pet. 2:4-6 must be read in connection with this first announcement of the Church.

The keys of the kingdom of heaven do not mean that Peter (and his alleged successors) have a supremacy in the Church. The kingdom of heaven is not the Church, but it is the professing sphere of Christendom. Peter used the authority conferred upon him on the day of Pentecost, when preaching to the Jews and again in the house of Cornelius, preaching to the Gentiles. See what Peter said of himself (1 Pet. 1:1, 5:1). The power to bind and to loose has nothing whatever to do with salvation. It refers only to discipline on earth. The same power was conferred upon all the other disciples (Matt. 18:18; John 20:23). And they represent the Church which was to come into existence.

For the first time the rejected King announces His coming suffering, His death, His resurrection and His second coming in glory. The break in the chapter at verse 28 is unfortunate. The Transfiguration which follows solves the difficulty of the last verse of this chapter.

CHAPTER 17

1. The Transfiguration (17:1-13)
2. The helpless disciples and the power of the King (17:14-21)
3. The second announcement of His death and resurrection (17:22-23)
4. The tribute money (17:24-27)

At the close of the previous chapter the Lord announced His coming in glory. This means His personal and glorious return. Some, He predicted, who were standing there would not taste death till they would see the Son of Man coming in His kingdom. The Transfiguration, which took place a week later, witnessed to the yet future coming of the Son of Man in the glory of the Father to receive the kingdom. Three of His disciples saw this startling occurrence. The Transfiguration scene is typical of the second, visible and glorious coming of our Lord (2 Pet. 1:16-21). The Man of Humiliation is transfigured and thus a glimpse of His coming glory is given. Moses glorified represents the saints of God who died; Elijah represents the saints caught up to meet the Lord in the air (1 Thess. 4:16-18). The saints come with Him in glory (Col. 3:4; 1 Thess. 4:14). The three disciples seeing the Transfiguration represent here the Jewish remnant awaiting the coming kingdom. The desperate condition the Lord finds coming down is a little picture of the condition of the world under Satan's power. He will bring deliverance with His return. The tribute money brings out His glory. He is the Omniscient One, who knows all and the Omnipotent One, who commands the fish to take up a coin in the bottom of the sea and bring that fish to Peter's hook. He provided what was needed. "For Me and thee" shows the most blessed identification of the Lord and the disciples. All is His and into the riches of Himself He brings His own.

CHAPTER 18

1. Concerning the little ones and offences (18:1-10)
2. The Son of Man to save what is lost (18:11-14)
3. The Church anticipated and instructions concerning it (18:15-20)
4. Concerning forgiveness (18:21-35)

The question of the disciples may have been occasioned by the words of the Lord to Peter in chapter 16. When He had announced twice His coming passion and set His face like a flint to go up to Jerusalem, they were reasoning among themselves who should be the greatest (Luke 9:46). With what patience and tenderness He instructs them! The object lesson is a little child. He gives them the characteristics of those who have entered the kingdom in reality and the principles which are to govern them. The kingdom must be entered in. It is the same truth, which Nicodemus heard from His lips. A new life is given; the believing sinner is born again and enters the kingdom as a little child, as the child enters the world by the natural birth. The characteristics of the child are lowliness and dependence. Such must be the leading characteristic of the heir of the kingdom. And the Lord teaches His identification with every one, who is born again, who has become a little child. Honor done to one of these little ones is done unto Him; and injury done to one of them is done unto Him.

Then He gives additional instructions concerning the Church. It relates to discipline and gives the true way how offences are to be dealt with in the new relationship about to come into existence (verses 15-19). But it must be remembered that the true meaning of the Church as the body of Christ, etc., is not revealed here at all. Nor was it fully made known on the day of Pentecost when the Church began on earth. Through the Apostle Paul the full revelation of the Church was given. But verse 20 gives us the center around which the Church is gathered. "Where two or three are gathered unto My name (not *in* My name) there I am in the midst of them." Not the name of a man, but unto the name of the Lord Jesus Christ, who is the Head of the body, the Church. Connected with this is the blessed assurance of prayer to be heard and answered.

CHAPTER 19

1. The departure from Galilee (19:1-2)
2. Concerning divorce (19:3-12)

3. The blessing of little children (19:13-15)
4. The rich young man (19:16-26)
5. The rewards in the kingdom (19:27-30)

The Pharisees appear to tempt the Lord, this time concerning divorcing a wife. It is again a question which had to do with their traditional laws and sayings of the elders. The ritualists in Christendom like the legal, ritualistic Pharisees, are also much more occupied with their man-made rules than with the Word of God. Perhaps their question was the result of the Lord's teaching in chapter 5:31-32. This statement of our Lord in the Sermon on the Mount dealt a severe blow to the rabbinical traditions held by the Pharisees concerning divorce. They were divided among themselves. Some had adopted the views of Hillel, that a wife may be put away for almost any cause. Others again held with the teaching of Shammai, another rabbinical authority, that divorce was only permissible in cases of adultery. He answers them in His divine wisdom. He calls their attention to the beginning. Marriage as instituted by the Creator is an argument against polygamy and divorce. In the new creation this relationship has a still deeper meaning (Eph. 5:21-33). The answer of the Pharisees reveals their ignorance (verse 7). Moses did not command divorce; he allowed it because of the hardness of their hearts (Deut. 24:1). The scandalous thing Moses mentioned is explained by our Lord to be fornication. This is the only ground for divorce. Professing Christendom pays no heed to this instruction. The increase of unlawful divorces is alarming and a sign of the last days.

The relation of little children is next seen in this chapter. They belong to the kingdom of heaven, are subjects of it and therefore He blessed them. The young man who asks the Lord, "What good thing shall I do that I may have eternal life?" pictures the condition of thousands in the professing Christendom. He was a religious and moral young man. But all his morality and religiousness had not given him the assurance of eternal life. He wanted to do something in order to get eternal life. Eternal life is the gift of God through Jesus Christ our Lord. The Lord did not promise him eternal life if he were to sell all he had and give it to the poor. He wanted to convince him that his profession of loving his neighbor as himself was spurious. That law demanded that he should sell all and give it to the poor. He did not understand the lesson and went away sorrowful from the Lord.

Verse 28 is often misunderstood. It must be read in the following way: "Verily I say unto you, that ye who have followed Me—In the regeneration, when the Son of Man shall sit upon the throne of His glory," etc. The word "regeneration" *(paliggenesia)* means here the re-creation promised in the Word of God, when all things will be made new and groaning creation put back in its right place, where it was before the fall of man. This regeneration comes when the Son of Man comes the second time. Then the rewards are given.

CHAPTER 20

1. The parable of the laborers in the vineyard (20:1-16)
2. The third prediction of His death and resurrection (20:17-19)
3. The ambitiousness of the disciples (20:20-28)
4. The healing of the two blind men (20:29-34)

Notice verse 30 of the preceding chapter and the same statement contained therein repeated in verse 16: "*So* the last shall be first and the first last." The parable which comes in between these two verses illustrates this fact, that many who are first shall be last; and the last shall be first. The parable speaks of rewards. The great principle of the parable is, that God will distribute rewards as He chooses in fullest accord with justice. While God owns every service and loss for the sake of Christ, yet He maintains His sovereignty to do as He will. The Lord wants us to leave the rewards with Him and not to think anything of our service. The parable appears to correct Peter's self-occupation (19:27). Jew and Gentile are also in view here in a dispensational way. Then after the third prediction of His death and resurrection, and the ambitiousness of the sons of Zebedee, He healed the two blind men.

Here we have again a dispensational foreshadowing, the importance of which should not be overlooked. These two blind men sitting at the wayside, groping in the dark, crying to the Son of David for deliverance, are types of the poor and feeble remnant of Israel in the end of this age, after the testimony of the Church for Christ the Son of God by resurrection from the dead, has been finished and the Church is no longer upon this scene. The remnant of Israel will cry to Him as Son of David and call upon Him for deliverance. The entrance into Jerusalem, which follows in the next chapter, foreshadows also that coming of the Son of David to Jerusalem, when He comes as King crowned with honor and glory. And as the two blind ones called upon Him when He was on the way to Jerusalem, and He heard and delivered them, so will that remnant of His earthly people seek Him, and in that darkness which precedes His return to Jerusalem cry to the Son of David, without seeing Him in person, though they believe on Him, that He is the promised One. And as the cry of the blind men was the work of the Holy Spirit, so will the seeking, the longing, the prayer of that future remnant be produced by the Spirit of God.

CHAPTER 21

1. The King enters Jerusalem (21:1-11)
2. The second cleansing of the temple (21:12-17)
3. The fig tree cursed (21:18-22)
4. His authority impeached and His question (21:23-27)
5. The parable of the two sons (21:28-32)
6. The parable of the householder (21:33-39)
7. The Lord's question and the King's sentence (21:40-46)

The King with His disciples draws near to Jerusalem to hold His royal entrance into His city.

Criticism has given a strange motive for the Lord's entrance into Jerusalem. It has been said that He was carried away by enthusiasm and expected that the people would now surely receive Him as the Messiah-King; while other critics explained His entry to the city as a kind of a concession to the messianic expectations of His disciples. How dishonoring to Him are all such foolish speculations. The simple fact is that He is the King and as such He had to come to Jerusalem and fulfill that which had been predicted by Zechariah, the prophet (Zech. 9:9).

What a sight it must have been the thousands coming to meet Him with palm branches in their hands, waving them over their heads, while the multitudes which followed did the same. And then they broke out in the glad shouts, quoting partly from the One Hundred Eighteenth Psalm, "Hosanna to the Son of David! Blessed is He that cometh in the name of the Lord; Hosanna in the highest." Hosanna means "save now."

What a triumph it was! The King entering Jerusalem. And in all He is undisturbed. Others might have been swept away by this enthusiasm; but He is calm in all His kingly majesty. Luke's Gospel tells us that He wept. "And when He was come near, He beheld the city, and wept over it." And what kind of weeping was this? He wept at the grave of Lazarus and that was a still, a silent weeping. But before Jerusalem He broke out in loud and deep lamentations. This is clearly proven by the different words used in the original.

The King knew what was soon to be, and on yonder hill He saw looming up the cross. True, they were crying, "Son of David, save now!" But the question, "Who is this?" is answered in the terms of rejection. Instead of "the King, Jehovah-Jesus, the Messiah," the multitude answers "Jesus, the Prophet of Nazareth of Galilee."

Then He cleansed the temple. This is the second time that the Lord acted in cleansing the temple. The first is recorded in the Gospel of John (2:13-17), and it took place at the beginning of His ministry. There it is the zeal for God's house, but here He acts in all His kingly authority.

But a more refreshing scene follows. The temple is cleansed. The noise and confusion are at an end. Nothing is said of the return of these evil occupants. But instead of them, there came the blind and the lame to Him in the temple and He healed them. The vacancy was filled by the crowd of poor, stricken suffering ones, who were delivered of their pains and diseases. Blessed and glorious foreshadowing of what will be when He comes again and when by His life-giving, healing touch, He will cure "all diseases" and make perfectly whole.

Then followed the cursing of the fig tree. The King was hungry. He who was rich, had indeed become poor. There by the wayside is a fig tree bearing many leaves; there He looked for some of the old fruit, or perhaps some of the unripe figs. He finds nothing and a curse follows, which withers the tree. It is well known that the fig tree is the type of Israel. The cursing of the fig tree stands for the national rejection of the people.

The mountain mentioned in verse 21 is a type of Israel in unbelief. The nation was a mountain and by its disobedience and rejection of the Lord, the nation was an obstacle in the path of the gospel. But on account of faith this mountain was indeed cast into the sea, the type of the nations. Precious to faith has ever been and ever will be the word, the author and finisher of the faith speaks here. "And all things whatsoever ye shall ask in prayer, believing, ye shall receive."

The two parables need no comment. Even

the chief priests and the Pharisees understood that He spoke of them (verse 45). Their hatred rose high. Verse 44 is of a deeper meaning. The Jews at this first coming fell on this stone (He is the stone) and were nationally broken. At His second coming, He, the stone, will fall on the Gentiles, deal with them and their dominion in judgment (Dan. 2:37-45).

CHAPTER 22

1. The parable of the marriage feast (22:1-14)
2. The Herodians answered (22:15-22)
3. The Sadducees answered (22:23-33)
4. The Pharisees answered (22:34-40)
5. The unanswered question (22:41-46)

A significant parable follows. The same parable appears in the Gospel of Luke. A comparison will show that in Matthew the dispensational features stand out more prominently. The third verse speaks of the offer of the kingdom as made to Israel by the King and His disciples. It was refused. In verses 4-6 there is a repeated offer and how this second offer was treated. This took place after the cross ("all things are ready"; the cross of Christ has done that). The beginning of the book of Acts reveals that offer made exclusively to Jerusalem. Those who had rejected Christ and crucified Him had a chance to repent. They did exactly with the message and the messengers what our Lord predicts in this parable. Verse 7 is a prediction of what should befall Jerusalem. This was fulfilled in the year 70. The city, which had become a city of murderers (Isa. 1:21) was burned. Then the King predicts the world-wide offer made to the Gentiles (verses 8-10).

The wedding garment corresponds to "the best robe" in the parable of the prodigal. The Lord Jesus Christ Himself is the wedding garment and all who are mere professors of Christ, without having put on the Lord Jesus Christ, will share the fate of which the Lord speaks in the parable.

Then He answered the questions of the Herodians (politicians), the Pharisees (ritualists) and the Sadducees (rationalists). They all tried to entangle Him, but failed miserably. The Herodians had to marvel and the Sadducees were astonished. Then He asked the Pharisees a question, which they failed to answer.

It is from Psalm 110 the Lord draws His question. This Psalm is one of the great messianic prophecies in the Old Testament. It is very prominent in the Epistle to the Hebrews, where it is quoted a number of times as being fulfilled in Him, who is now the man of glory, seated at the right hand of the majesty on high, waiting till His enemies are made His footstool. This will be done when He comes again. In sending Him, the First-Begotten, into the world, God will put down all His enemies. It is almost impossible to believe that, with the evidences from Scripture, such as the word of our Lord and the testimony of the Holy Spirit in the Epistle to the Hebrews, certain men who call themselves "scholars" and assume the place of "critics" can deny the One Hundred Tenth Psalm was composed by David and that the Psalm has any messianic reference at all. This surely is wicked unbelief, as pronounced, perhaps more so, than the unbelief of the Pharisees.

Well, the Pharisees here answer that Messiah is to be the Son of David. They were professed teachers of Israel and still they did not understand the Scriptures. The question the Lord now puts to them, David calling Him who is to be a son of his, Lord, that is Jehovah, they could not, perhaps would not, answer. The passage teaches clearly who Messiah is. He is Jehovah incarnate, the Son of David and David's Lord. And the interrogator is He. His Davidic descent could not be denied; that He has a legal title to the throne of David is clearly proven by the genealogy. In His ministry throughout these years, He had manifested Himself in His mighty works as Jehovah. They could give Him no answer. Solemn moment it was. No answer! No repentance! They are silenced, and when they open their lips again it is to cry "Crucify Him!" The end is now coming on rapidly. In the next chapter He speaks as Judge pronouncing His judgment upon the leaders of the nation.

CHAPTER 23

1. The hypocrisy of the Pharisees (23:1-12)
2. The woes of the King upon them (23:13-36)
3. The lamentation over Jerusalem (23:37-39)

The chapter which is before us contains the "woes" of the King upon the Pharisees. It is one of the most solemn ones in Matthew. Pharisaism is still on the earth; ritualism, traditionalism and with it the rejection of the authority of the Lord and His written Word, is Pharisaism, that evil leaven against which the Lord warns. This Christian Pharisaism is far worse than the old Jewish system. And where in Christendom is a little of that leaven lacking? Only the grace of God, an unbroken fellowship with the Father and His Son in the power of the Holy Spirit, can keep the individual believer from manifesting a Pharisaical spirit.

And now the Lord takes up His "woes." It is a fearful uncovering of the hearts of the Pharisees and their corruption. And thus He lays bare the hidden things. He will do so again. There are eight woes given in this chapter, though it has been claimed that the fourteenth verse does not belong to this chapter. It is, however, found in both the Gospels of Mark and Luke, so that it is evident the Lord also uttered these words.

He now pronounces judgment upon them and uncovers all they are. Pharisaism keeps the outside clean, while inside there is corruption and death. There is a self-righteous religious boasting of being more advanced than the fathers and more tolerant than they were. But the Omniscient One reads their hearts and declares that they fill up the measure of the fathers. They were unsaved men, not the offspring of God, but of vipers; their father, the devil; and they were facing judgment of Gehenna.

And then His lamentation, how He must leave the house desolate and turn away from His beloved city. The King is the King of love and His heart yearns over Jerusalem.

But the discourse which has nothing but woes ends with a "blessed," and here comes in the bright ray of hope for Israel. "Ye shall in no wise see Me henceforth until ye say, Blessed be He that comes in the name of the Lord." This is the promise of His second coming, and when He comes He will find a believing remnant of that very people, welcoming Him with the messianic greeting of the One Hundred Eighteenth Psalm. Then the Shekinah-Glory will spread over Jerusalem and Israel's land, and He that scattered Israel will gather them from the four corners of the earth. It is a strange and evil doctrine which maintains that inasmuch as the woes were spoken upon these Pharisees, that they are also to see Him again. It is claimed that these wicked Pharisees, the offspring of vipers, who could not escape the judgment of hell, are all to be raised from the dead when Christ comes again and have "a second chance" to see Him, and that then they will receive Him. Such Jewish universalism has no Scripture foundation whatever. It is a remnant which will behold the King coming out of the opened heavens in the day of His manifestation.

CHAPTER 24

1. The destruction of the temple foretold (24:1-2)
2. The questions of the disciples (24:3)
3. The end of the age and events preceding His coming (24:4-14)
4. The great tribulation and what will happen (24:15-26)
5. The visible and glorious return of the King (24:27-31)
6. The exhortations of the King (24:32-44)
7. The parable of the faithful and evil servant (24:45-51)

The Olivet discourse is the last great utterance of the King. It was delivered to the disciples and concerns the future. It is divided into thee parts: First, He answers the three questions of His disciples (24:4-44); then He speaks three parables (24:45—25:30); the last part contains a great judgment prophecy (25:31-46). The first part concerns the end of the age, and in it the King describes what will take place on earth immediately before His visible return. The second part reveals the conditions in the kingdom of heaven (Christendom) and how He as King and Judge will deal with those conditions. The third part is a prophecy concerning the judgment of the nations the King finds on His return to this earth. (It is impossible to give satisfactory annotations of this great and important discourse here. The readers will find the complete exposition in our commentary on Matthew.)

The first part has nothing to do with the destruction of the temple and Jerusalem. Jerusalem and the temple are not even mentioned by Him. The interpretation that all His predictions in verses 4-44 found their fulfillment during the siege of Jerusalm in the year 70 is totally wrong. The destruction of the temple is foretold by Him in verse 2 before the disciples asked the questions, which resulted in His discourse. Luke reports the destruction of Jerusalem and the scattering of the nation (Luke 21:20-24). But in Matthew the Holy Spirit records the regathering of His elect, earthly people (verse 31). Nor does the answer of the Lord to His disciples have anything to do with this Christian age. The Church is not mentioned by Him at all. The disciples had asked about the end of the age. (Again we remind the students of this Gospel that the word "world" is incorrect. The end of the world cannot come for a long time. Before the end of the world can come this earth must first be put in order and delivered from the curse.) They only knew their Jewish age and were ignorant of this Christian age. The Jewish age did not fully terminate with the rejection of the Messiah and the worldwide dispersion of the nation. It was only interrupted in its course. The interruption is this present Christian age during which the Church is gathered out. When that purpose is accomplished, the true Church will be removed from the earth to be joined to the Head in glory. Then the dealings of God with His ancient people Israel will be resumed. The end of their age of unbelief ends. It will last seven years, the last week of the great prophecy of Daniel (chapter 9; see our commentary on Daniel).

It is this end, these seven years still future which our Lord describes in the first part of His discourse. True it is that throughout the age in which we live all these things He mentions, wars, earthquakes, famines, pestilences, persecutions of the godly have taken place. All these will occur in a more intensified form during the end of the age, when the true Church is no longer on earth. Then the remnant of Jews who believe, like the disciples of the King when He appeared the first time, will preach the gospel of the kingdom among all nations. In Revelation 7 we find this remnant sealed and in the second half the result of the preached testimony, a multitude which comes out of the great tribulation.

When these seven years are ended the King appears in all His glory in the clouds of heaven. For the Church and His saints there is another coming (1 Thess. 4:13-18). The saints come with Him in that day (Zech. 14:1-5).

Verse 34 has been a difficulty with many. The word generation does not mean the people who were then living; it has the meaning of "this race." It is the same as 1 Pet. 2:9, "a chosen generation," i.e., class of peoples. The Jewish race cannot pass away till these things be fulfilled.

With verse 45 the second part beings. It concerns Christendom. While the seven parables of the kingdom (Matthew 13) teach the beginning, the development and end of Christendom, the three parables of the Olivet discourse show the moral aspect of those who profess Christianity. The true and the false, the faithful and the unfaithful are uncovered and dealt with.

CHAPTER 25

1. The parable of the ten virgins (25:1-13)
2. The parable of the servants and the talents (25:14-30)
3. The judgment of nations (25:31-46)

The parable of the ten virgins describes Christendom and what will take place some day. In the beginning of this age the entire Christian profession expected the promised return. He delayed and they all slumbered and slept. They gave up the hope which energized them in the beginning. The midnight cry aroused entire Christendom again. This is now an accomplished fact. Many years ago during the first half of the nineteenth century the Spirit of God revived the blessed hope. And still the cry is heard and will be heard till He comes. The next is He comes. His true people who have the oil enter in with Him. Those who possess not the oil (the Holy Spirit), because they have never believed on Him, face a shut door and hear the awful word, "I know ye not." (Some teach on this an invention. They say the foolish virgins represent worldly minded believers, who will pass through the great tribulation. The Lord will never say to any one who trusts in Him, "I know ye not.") Then an account must be given how His gifts were used. The man with one talent unused represents an unsaved soul.

The third section is a prophecy. The King returned will occupy the throne of His glory. The judgment is not a judgment of the entire human race. None of the dead are here. The dead saints are raised when He comes in the air to receive His own and the dead martyrs of the tribulation period will also have been raised at the close of that period. The rest of the dead does not live till the thousand years of the kingdom are ended (Rev. 20:5). Here the living nations are seen judged. The standard is the treatment they accorded to the last messengers of the King, these are "the brethren" of the King, of the Jewish race. If these nations believed that testimony they treated the messengers with kindness; if they rejected this final message they refused help to the messengers. The righteous nations who believed will remain on the earth for the kingdom. The unrighteous will go into everlasting punishment.

CHAPTER 26

1. His death planned (26:1-5)
2. Mary of Bethany anointing the King (26:6-13)
3. The betrayal (26:14-16)
4. The last Passover (26:17-25)
5. The Lord's Supper instituted (26:26-29)
6. Peter's denial announced and the scattered sheep (26:30-35)

7. In Gethsemane (26:36-46)
8. Judas and his deed: The arrest of the King (26:47-56)
9. Before Caiaphas and the Sanhedrin (26:57-68)
10. Peter's denial (26:69-75)

The great last discourse of the King being ended, there remains now nothing else to record than the story of His passion, His suffering, death and resurrection. This is the record of the remaining three chapters of the first Gospel. Two of these are the longest in the whole book. He had foretold in His great prophecy in the Olivet discourse the future of the Jews, the Christian profession, and the future of the nations. Now He is to go and fulfill all the predictions concerning His suffering and death, as written in Moses, the prophets and the Psalms. The twenty-sixth chapter is one of contrasts. Here we behold Him in all His wonderful perfection again. With what calmness and dignity He enters upon that great work, which the Father gave Him to do. On the other hand we see wickedness and satanic powers revealed which now cast themselves in all their fury upon the Holy One. What a wonderful story it is which we have followed in this first Gospel. How marvelous the events and how perfect and divine the entire arrangement! Man could never have written such an account.

Notice the last prediction of His death. This is the fourth time He predicts His death in this Gospel. He not only predicts the manner of His death, but now also the time; He is to be crucified at the time of the Passover. All this manifests His deity. He knew all beforehand. Let none think that all that which was before Him dawned upon Him gradually; He knew every one of the sufferings and all that which was now to come upon His holy head. But what calmness breathes in these words, in which He predicted His coming crucifixion! There is no anxiety, no concern about anything, but to do the will of Him that sent Him and to give Himself as the true Passover Lamb.

How beautiful the scene in Simon's house! Mary was fully devoted to her Lord. We first see her at His feet listening to His words. "One thing is needful, and Mary hath chosen that good part." She acknowledged Him in His office as Prophet. In John 11 we see her again at His feet. There she is weeping on account of the death of Lazarus; a little while later He weeps with her. She knew Him as the Sympathizing One, as He is now our Priest. And here she anoints Him, and does it for His burying. In faith she realizes the near approach of that death, of which He had spoken. She believed He, the Lamb of God, would soon die; she understood more of that death than all the other disciples. Perhaps when she sat at His feet He had spoken to her about His coming death and burial and resurrection. But some readers of the Bible have a difficulty. Here in our Gospel she anoints His head, but in the Gospel of John she is at His feet and anoints them, wiping His feet with her hair. Critics and infidels who deny the inspiration of the Bible have pointed out this as one of the glaring contradictions, while others have thought of two different occasions when the anointing took place. There is, however, no difficulty here at all. She anointed both His feet and His head. The Holy Spirit reports the anointing of the head of the Lord in Matthew, because this is in harmony with the object of the Gospel. He is the King, and while He is the rejected King, her faith no doubt looked beyond death and burial. In John the Holy Spirit gives the anointing of the feet and leaves out the anointing of the head, because the King is the Son of God; as such He is described in the Gospel of John, and that attitude of Mary before His feet anointing them is in fullest harmony with the fourth Gospel.

And after the Passover and the institution of that blessed and most precious memorial feast which we call "the Lord's Supper" we see Him in the garden. Who can fathom the deep anguish of His soul, who can understand the agony of those midnight hours? Worship is demanded here. He looked on toward the cross, where He who knew no sin was now to be made sin. From this His holy soul shrank. But it had to be. He knew all the depths into which He had to plunge.

Then after His willing arrest we see Him first before Caiaphas and the elders. Before that council He had to appear first. But all their schemes failed. They found nothing in Him. The question of the high priest concerning His Sonship is answered by the King. The Blessed One could not be condemned by false witnesses. His own confession of who He is could alone bring about His unjust condemnation. The King is condemned.

"What think ye?" And they answering said, "He is liable of the penalty of death" (verse 66). What a justice! Satanic, fiendish injustice rather. But there He stands, the silent Lamb of God. What a picture! Oh, that we might behold Him once more as He stood before this company of His enemies. What calmness! "Majestic in His silence, majestic in His speech; unmoved by threats to speak, unmoved by threats when He had spoken."

And how affecting the scene which follows. His confession set the powers of darkness loose and the undefending Christ, the Son of God, is tasting a little of the cup He had to drink. Oh, to think of it! They spit in His face! That face, which in loving tenderness had gazed with compassion upon the multitudes, yea, that face, the image of the invisible God, was covered with the vile spittle of men. How He must have suffered! They buffeted Him, struck Him with the palms of their hands, mocked Him. And not a word, not a murmur came from His blessed lips. "When reviled, He reviled not again, when suffering, He threatened not." And reader! it was all for such vile sinners as we are! He loved us and gave Himself for us. What a Saviour!

CHAPTER 27

1. Delivered unto Pilate (27:1-2)
2. The suicide of Judas (27:3-10)
3. Before Pilate (27:11-14)
4. The awful choice (27:15-26)
5. Crowned with thorns and crucified (27:27-44)
6. The death of the King (27:45-50)
7. The rent veil and the earthquake (27:51-56)
8. The burial (27:57-66)

In this chapter we follow Him to the cross. What a journey it was! He, who had lived that wonderful life, preached the kingdom, had healed the sick, cast out the demons, raised the dead, He, who is announced in the beginning of this Gospel to be Immanuel, God manifested in flesh, the Beloved of the Father is in the hands of men, led away to the cross. What sufferings were His! Who is able to follow the depths of that shame, which He despised, the cross which He endured!

Judas filled with remorse ends his life by hanging himself. What is written in Acts 1:18 is not a discrepancy. The rope must have broken and the terrible thing described in Acts must have happened. Judas was a disciple, yet not born again. He never called the King "Lord."

The silver pieces he cast into the temple and the priests, as covetous as Judas, stoop down to pick them up. That which follows is only reported in this Gospel, in the other Gospel records no mention is made of the fate of Judas. It is put only in the Gospel of Matthew on account of its dispensational bearing. The priests judge very religiously that it is not lawful to put the money into the *Corban,* the treasury of the temple. They decide to buy with the pieces of silver, the field of the potter for a burying ground for strangers. This was in partial fulfillment of what was spoken by Jeremias. The full prophecy is found in Zechariah, but the Spirit calls here attention to what is also spoken by Jeremias. We read in that book (Jeremiah 18 and 19) of a potter's field, which was situated on the side of the valley of Hinnom. That valley is also called "Tophet," a fearful type with its awful memories of Gehenna.

And then we see the Lord in fulfillment of His own words, delivered into the hands of the Gentiles. Then the people have their choice between Him, their King and Barabbas (son of the father), the child of the devil.

And now Pilate puts the important question: "Which of the two will ye that I release unto you?" It does not take long to bring forth the answer. Barabbas is the people's choice. Barabbas! Barabbas! Not a voice was heard for the Lord. Where were now the multitudes who had followed Him? Where they who had cried "Hosanna"? But Pilate convinced of the awful choice, which had been made, against the authority which he had, makes another attempt: "What then shall I do with Jesus, who is called Christ?" What a solemn question it was; and it is so still. The question was answered there and it must also be answered by every person to whom the Lord Jesus Christ is offered. He must either be accepted as Saviour and Lord or rejected. The choice decides the eternal destiny; those who accept Him and own Him as their Saviour are saved and all who reject Him as Son of God and Saviour are lost. Pilate's second question is answered by a great cry, that fearful cry: "Let Him be crucified." Again Pilate asks: "What evil then has He done?" But his voice is drowned in a greater demand: "Let Him be crucified." Pilate was fully convinced of the innocence of the silent victim before him, but miserable coward he was, he would not act. When he saw he availed nothing and a great tumult was rising, he took water, washed his hands before the crowd and said: "I am guiltless of the blood of this righteous one, see ye to it." And what did they answer to the governor's action and "see ye to it" his word to them? And all the people answering said, "His blood be on us and our children. Then he released unto them Barabbas; but Jesus, having scourged Him, he delivered up that He might be crucified."

Terrible answer it was. Barabbas is the nation's choice and the blood of the Holy One is wished by them upon their heads and the heads of their children. Has that awful wish been granted? Let the history of the Jews answer down to the present day, how His blood came upon them and their children; the end is not yet. Barabbas has been their choice and there is still that false Christ to come, who comes in his own name and whom they will receive. Crowned with thorns, mocked, spit upon and dishonored the King is led away to Golgotha. And they crucified Him.

It may be well to group together the different events of the cross. 1. They brought Him to Golgotha (Matt. 27:33; Mark 15:22; Luke 23:33; John 19:17). 2. The refusal of the vinegar and the gall (Matt. 27:34; Mark 15:23). 3. Crucified between the two thieves (Matt. 27:35-38; Mark 15:24-28; Luke 23:33-38; John 19:18-24). 4. The first word from the cross, "Father, forgive," (Luke 23:34). 5. The soldiers part His garments (Matt. 27:35; Mark 15:24; Luke 23:34; John 19:23). 6. The Jews mock their King (Matt. 27:39-44; Mark 15:29-32: Luke 23:35-38). 7. The thieves rail on Him, but one repents and believes (Matt. 27:44; Mark 15:32; Luke 23:39-43). 8. The second word from the cross, "Today shalt thou be with Me," etc. (Luke 23:43). 9. The third word, "Woman, behold thy son" (John 19:26, 27). 10. The darkness (Matt. 27:45; Mark 15:33; Luke 23:44). 11. The fourth word, "My God, My God, why hast Thou forsaken Me?" (Matt. 27:46, 47; Mark 15:34-36). 12. The fifth word, "I thirst" (John 19:28). 13. The sixth word, "It is finished" (John 19:30). 14. The seventh word, "Father into Thy hands I commend My Spirit" and the dismissal of His Spirit (Matt. 27:50; Mark 15:37; Luke 23:46; John 19:30). The rent veil was the first testimony from God's side that the work of the sinbearer is done, that the great work is finished and the new and living way into the Holiest is made by the blood of the Lamb of God (Heb. 10:19-20). His resurrection is the second testimony. But the resurrection mentioned in verse 52 did not take place immediately upon His death on the cross, but those graves were opened "after His resurrection" (verse 53).

And He was buried. Isaiah 53:9 was fulfilled. The literal translation reads: "And men appointed His grave with the wicked, but He was with the rich in His death." The enemy, who could not frustrate His death, is at work to make all secure, but instead he makes his own defeat a perfect defeat. They remembered His promise of resurrection. The disciples had forgotten that promise completely. The stone is sealed, the guard is placed there to make fraud and illusion impossible. Little did they realize that they were even then working to make the glorious resurrection of the Son of God a fact, which is secure beyond all controversy.

CHAPTER 28

1. His resurrection (28:1-10)
2. The lying report of the Jews (28:11-15)
3. The great commission (28:16-20)

We have reached the last portion of our Gospel. The end is brief and very abrupt. The account of the resurrection of the Lord as given by Matthew is the briefest of all the Gospels. Only a few of the facts are mentioned. Then the characteristic feature of this last chapter is that no mention is made of the ascension of the Lord. However, the fact of His ascension is implied in numerous places in this Gospel. In the Gospel of Mark we find the statement that He was taken up into heaven and sat at the right hand of God. In Luke we read that He was "carried into heaven," but in Matthew no such statement is made. The Gospel ends as if He were still on the earth, all power in heaven and on earth in His hands and with His own to the end of the age. All this is in perfect harmony with the scope of this Gospel.

The resurrection account needs no further comment. In our annotations on the Gospel of Luke the reader will find a brief review of the resurrection as reported by the synoptics.

Three classes are seen in connection with the resurrection of the Lord in Matthew. The soldiers represent unbelieving Gentiles, the women, believers and then the Jews. The soldiers are terror-stricken. They were lying around on the ground as if they were dead. It is the effect upon the natural man of God's power made known. On what greater scale this will be repeated when He comes again in resurrection glory, as King of Kings and Lord of Lords.

Then the resurrection of Him who was dead, that glorious and unassailable fact, was officially reported to the chief priests. The Sanhedrin is once more assembled. Lying, fraud of the most ridiculous nature is resorted to, to deny what had taken place.

The whole story they invented is, of course, incredible. It is far easier to believe He arose from the dead than to believe what the Jews invented about His resurrection. If His disciples could have stolen the body, if it had been possible, they surely would not have done it. But if they had a desire to steal the body, they could not have done so, for with the guard placed at the tomb, it was an impossibility. The disciples had forgotten all about the resurrection promise; they were a scattered, poor and timid lot of people. But even if they had been anxious to steal the body, how could they have done it? Here was the company of armed men. They were experienced guards and careful watchers, trained in that profession. Then there was the sealed, heavy stone. How could they have rolled away the stone and carried away the body without being detected? Impossible. But the utterly ridiculous side of the whole lie came out with the report which these soldiers were to circulate, being well paid for it by the Sanhedrin. The disciples came and stole the body, while they were sleeping! In the first place, it is incredible that all these men had fallen asleep at the same time. All were fast asleep, so fast asleep that the commotion of rolling away the stone and the carrying away of a dead one did not disturb them. Furthermore, sleeping at a post meant death for the Roman soldier. One might have nodded and thus risked his life, but that all slept is an impossibility. But the report is foolish; they were asleep, and while they were asleep they witnessed how the disciples stole the body of Jesus. How ridiculous! The whole proceedings were out and out fraud and falsehood. And this was indeed the only statement they could possibly bring against the resurrection of the Lord Jesus Christ.

Then follows the great commission.

This is the kingdom commission. In Luke 24 we have the proper Christian commission. A time is coming when this great commission here will be carried out by a remnant of Jewish disciples, who are represented by the eleven. It is the same remnant as in Matthew 24.

All power is His; all power in heaven and on earth. Soon the day will come when indeed He will have all things put under His feet. And the last word, "And behold, I am with you all the days until the completion of the age." Precious promise of faith! He will never leave nor forsake, and He who is with us is the "I am," the mighty Jehovah, the Immanuel, having all power in heaven and on earth.

The Gospel of Matthew begins with Immanuel, "God with us," it ends with Immanuel. With Him, our Saviour and Lord, we shall be in all eternity. Forever with the Lord. With all our hearts we praise God for such a Saviour, for such a Lord, for such a Gospel and for such a future with HIMSELF, the King of Kings and Lord of Lords.

THE GOSPEL OF

MARK

The Gospel of Mark is the briefest of the four Gospels. The traditional view, which holds that the Apostle Peter dictated this record into the pen of Mark, so that he was only an amanuensis, has been proven erroneous. Equally incorrect are other theories, that the Gospel of Mark was written first and served Matthew and Luke in giving their account, copying from it and making additions, or, the hypothesis that there was an original record, a common source, which the Evangelists used. All these opinions are mostly the inventions of men who disbelieve the inspiration of the chosen instruments of God in giving a fourfold picture of His blessed Son on earth. An unswerving faith in the inspiration of the four Evangelists solves all the supposed difficulties and discrepancies of which we hear so much in our days. Inspiration makes error impossible.

Mark was not an apostle. Two apostles were chosen to write Gospel records, Matthew and John. The other two, Mark and Luke, did not belong to the twelve. Mark's and John's Gospels give us the chronological account, while Matthew and Luke were led under the guidance of the Holy Spirit not to pen the events chronologically, but to arrange them in such a way as to bring out the distinctive features of their respective Gospels.

While Matthew describes the Lord Jesus Christ as the King, Luke as the Son of Man in his perfection, John as the true God and the eternal life, Mark was chosen to write the account of our Lord as the obedient Servant. It was announced by the prophets that He would appear as a servant. Isaiah beheld Him as the Servant of God. Through Zechariah the Spirit of God announced, "Behold, I will bring forth My Servant, the Branch" (Zech. 3:8). And after He had been on earth in the form of a servant, the Holy Spirit in the Epistle to the Philippians tells us again that He who ever existed in the form of God "made Himself of no reputation, and took upon Him the form of a servant, and was made in the likeness of men" (Phil. 2:7). Mark, himself a servant, was graciously called to give a pen picture of this blessed Servant and to record His toil, His service of love and patience, as well as His mighty works. All which does not stand in definite relation to our Lord as the Servant is carefully omitted, and many other things omitted by the other Evangelists are added, to describe the manner and perfection of the Servant's work.

The purpose of the Gospel of Mark must never be lost sight of in studying it. Well may we call it the neglected Gospel, for it is the least studied. God gave it that we His redeemed people might as His servants have a pattern in our service. One thing, however, is absolutely necessary in the intelligent and spiritual study of Mark and that is a constant comparison with the Gospel of Matthew. Such a comparison will bring out the beauties of the record given by Mark and shows the divine power which guided infallibly these men of God.

We have therefore given in the analysis the parallel passages from the Gospel of Matthew and from the Gospel of Luke. The analysis contains many hints and annotations, which will help in a closer study. At the close of the analyzed Gospel the reader will find several articles on the personality of Mark, the characteristic featues of this Gospel and other information, which, we hope, will prove of help to all students of this part of God's Holy Word.

The Division of the Book of Mark

"For even the Son of Man came not to be ministered unto, but to minister, and to give His life a ransom for many" (Mark 10:45)

I. **THE SERVANT: WHO HE IS AND HOW HE CAME** (1:1-13)

II. **THE SERVANT'S WORK: NOT TO BE MINISTERED UNTO, BUT TO MINISTER** (1:14—10:52)

III. **THE SERVANT IN JERUSALEM: PRESENTED AS KING AND REJECTED** (11—13)

IV. GIVING HIS LIFE A RANSOM FOR MANY (14:1—15:47)

V. THE SERVANT HIGHLY EXALTED, RISEN AND ASCENDED: HIS COMMISSION TO HIS SERVANTS AND WORKING WITH THEM (16)

Analysis and Annotations

I. The Servant: Who He Is and How He Came (1:1-13)

CHAPTER 1:1-13

1. The Servant, the Son of God (1:1)
2. His coming promised and announced (1:2-8); Matthew 3:1-11; Luke 3:1-18; John 1:19-30
3. The Servant comes forth (1:9-11); Matthew 3:13-17; Luke 3:21-22; John 1:31-34
4. The Servant in the wilderness (1:12-13); Matthew 4:1-11; Luke 4:1-13

Verse 1. No other Gospel begins in this way. The deity of our Lord is first of all emphasized. Nothing is said about the virgin birth, nor is a genealogy given. The miraculous birth is most fully brought out in Luke's Gospel, the Gospel of our Lord's humanity. No genealogy appears in Mark; a servant does not need such. Nor do we find Bethlehem mentioned, or the event, which is characteristic of the Gospel of Matthew, the visit of the wise men seeking the newborn King of the Jews. All these and other matters are omitted because they do not fall within the scope and purpose of the Gospel of Mark. The Servant is the Son of God. This great truth is fully attested by His obedience in always doing the will of Him that sent Him and by His mighty miracles which accompanied His loving service. If He were not the Son of God He could not have rendered the perfect service. Sonship and service always go together. Only a Son of God can be a servant of God. Grace makes us, if we believe on the Lord Jesus Christ, sons of God. True service for God is the result of the enjoyment of our sonplace in Christ Jesus. A deeper realization and enjoyment of our sonship will be followed by a more obedient and constant service. The Gospel of John gives the fullest witness that Jesus is the Christ, the Son of God (John 20:31). The Gospel of Mark shows that He is the Son of God by His wonderful character as Servant.

Verses 2-8. Prophets promised His coming (Malachi 3:1). The passage proves Him to be Jehovah. In Malachi we read that Jehovah says "he shall prepare the way before Me." The Spirit of God changes the "Me" to "Thy Face." The servant is none other than Jehovah, who spoke to the Prophets. Isaiah 40:3 is likewise quoted. Here too we find the same testimony that Jesus the Servant is Jehovah. "Prepare ye the way of Jehovah."

The account of the ministry of John the Baptist is the briefest in the Gospel of Mark. A few sentences only describe his testimony in the wilderness and his person. All the land of Judea and they of Jerusalem went out to him. The baptism of John in the river of Jordan was the outward sign of repentance. They confessed their sins. A comparison with the record of the Baptist's ministry in Matthew, Luke and John is very instructive. In Mark all the preaching of John concerning the state of the nation is omitted, for the Holy Spirit describes in Mark John's ministry only as a necessary preliminary to introduce the Servant and His ministry. Of the baptism which Christ is to bring Mark mentions "the Holy Spirit"; "and with fire" is left out. The fire baptism is His judgment work stated in Matthew and Luke. Christ as the humble Servant does not execute judgment, but the coming King (Matthew) and the Son of Man coming again (Luke) will judge and burn the chaff with unquenchable fire.

Verses 9-11. The Servant appears to begin His service. From Nazareth of Galilee He came forth. There too during the hidden years He had served. The Servant was absolutely sinless and yet He was baptized in Jordan. He showed His perfect willingness to take, in obedience to the Father's will, the sinner's place in death. In verse 10 the word "straightway" is found for the first time in Mark. It is the characteristic word of this Gospel describing the promptness of His service. The anointing by the reception of the Spirit follows. In Matthew we read "heaven was opened unto Him." In Luke, "heaven was opened." In Mark "He saw the heavens opened." Encouraging sight for Him, who had taken the lowest place! All God's servants need the vision of the opened heavens. The Father's voice proclaimed Him then as His beloved Son.

Verses 12-13. Upon this He was driven immediately into the wilderness to be tempted of Satan. His fitness to be the Servant to minister and give His life for a ransom was fully proven in His victorious conflict. The different temptations are not reported by Mark; they belong to the Gospels of Matthew and Luke, where we find them. But here we have a statement which is peculiar to Mark. "And was with the wild beasts." It tells of His deep humiliation. Moses and Elijah were in the wilderness being prepared for service. David also had been alone in the solitary places. None, however, was in the place which He took, whose eternal abode was the Father's bosom. The wilderness and the wild beasts are the witnesses of a marred creation; the mighty Creator had come in the form of the creature to meet and overcome under such conditions the fallen being, Satan. Some have taught that He was in danger of being attacked by wild beasts. This was impossible (Psalm 91:9-13).

II. The Servant's Work: Not To Be Ministered Unto but To Minister (1:14—10:52)

CHAPTER 1:14-45

The Ministry in Galilee after John's Imprisonment

1. The Servant in Galilee preaching the gospel of the kingdom (1:14-15); Matthew 4:12-17; Luke 4:14-15
2. The calling of fellow servants (1:16-20); Matthew 4:18-22; Luke 5:1-11
3. The Servant in Capernaum (1:21-18); Luke 4:31-37
4. Peter's mother-in-law raised up (1:29-31); Matthew 8:14-15; Luke 4:38-39
5. The Servant heals many and casts out demons (1:32-34); Luke 4:31-37; Matthew 8:16-18; Luke 4:40-41
6. The Servant in prayer (1:35)
7. The interruption and the renewed service (1:36-39); Luke 4:42-44
8. The leper healed (1:40-45); Matthew 8:1-4; Luke 5:12-16

Verses 14-15. The Servant begins His blessed service in Galilee immediately after John had been put into prison. And now the Lord takes up the hushed testimony of the forerunner. The heralding of the kingdom at hand through the presence of Him who came to His own is less prominent in Mark. In the first twelve chapters of the Gospel of Matthew it is one of the leading features. The time, indeed, was fulfilled. While Matthew and Luke report the preaching of the gospel of the kingdom with the demand to repent, here in Mark the words are added "and believe the gospel." This gospel is of course not the gospel of our salvation. That was not preached till after He had finished the work the Father gave Him to do.

Verses 16-20. It is a blessed scene which we have before us. The Servant of God calls fellow servants, weak and sinful men, to become fishers of men. These are Simon and Andrew, James and John. They knew Him and had believed in Him. They were His disciples. But now He calls them into service. "Come ye after Me." The grace which called them gave them power to forsake earthly things and to come after Him. Boats and nets, their trade as fishermen and even their father, Zebedee, were left behind. Oh! blessed place to serve the Lord Christ and yield obedience to His call. We must own Him as Lord and follow Him in His own path of faith, obedience and humility. To seek others and bring them to Himself is the service to which He still calls. Note the word "straightway" in verses 18 and 20.

Verses 21-28. The Servant and His fellow servants went to Capernaum. Straightway He entered the synagogue on the Sabbath to teach. His first preaching in Nazareth (Luke 4:16-30) is not reported by Mark. It is after they thrust Him out of the city where He had been brought up, that He went to Capernaum. The blessed Servant knew no discouragement nor self-pity. They laid their wicked hands on Him in Nazareth, then He went on to Capernaum and straightway taught there. His doctrine uttered with authority and power astonished all, yet He ever was the meek and lowly One. But the Word had another effect. A man with an unclean spirit interrupted Him in the synagogue. Satan's power was present and the demons were forced to confess "Jesus of Nazareth" as "the Holy One of God." Then the Servant's power is manifested. He rebuked him and commanded the demon to come out of him. The Servant's fame spread abroad throughout all that region.

Verses 29-31. This miracle is found in the Gospel of Matthew in a different setting. (For the dispensational setting see *The Gospel of Matthew,* chapter 8.) The place given to this miracle here is equally significant. The first healing of disease in the Gospel of Mark follows the casting out of the demon, the defeat of Satan's power. This order will be followed when He comes again, not as the lowly Servant, but as the mighty King. Then Satan will be bound first and the greatest spiritual and physical blessings will come to this poor world at last. Concerning the healing of Peter's wife's mother, Matthew tells us "He touched her hand;" Luke "He stood over her and rebuked the fever." Mark's testimony by the Holy Spirit is "He took her by the hand

and lifted her up." How beautiful! It reveals the tenderness, the loving sympathy of the blessed One. With what gentleness He must have lifted her up so as to avoid another pang of pain in her feverish body; but immediately she was healed. And He is still the same.

Verses 32-34. Deliverance from demons and divers diseases came to many on that memorable day "when the sun did set." We must view these deliverances and healings in Mark's Gospel not so much as the evidences of His power as the manifestations of the great love and goodness of the Servant. Then He suffered the demons not to speak, because they knew Him. He loved to be unknown and did not want the applause of men nor the witness of the unclean spirits. Of His unostentatiousness we shall find further evidences.

Verse 35. And after such a day of uninterrupted toil, preaching, healing diseases, driving out demons, occupied from early morning till the sun did set, we find Him, rising a great while before day, in a solitary place, praying. He is alone in the presence of the Father. Thus it was fulfilled, "He wakeneth morning by morning, He wakeneth mine ear as the instructed" (Isaiah 50:4). Only Mark gives us this precious information. It tells us that the Servant, though the Son of God, walked in complete dependence on God His Father. Prayer is the expression of such dependence. He had been anointed with the Spirit for His work, heard the Father's loving approval, defeated Satan, cast out demons, healed divers diseases, yet He is still the dependent One. Independence in service for God is a snare, the very spirit of Satan. The perfect Servant had His times for quietness, retirement and prayer, in which He cast Himself anew upon Him, whom to glorify He had come to earth. "And if He thus retired to be with God, Himself the Lord God, before He entered upon the work of the day, can we wonder that we fail so much in outward labor, who fail yet more in this inward intimacy with our Father? Be assured, the secret of holy strength and endurance in service is found there alone."[1] What child of God does not feel the deep necessity of this and deplores the neglect of this blessed privilege?

Verses 36-39. But He is followed by His disciples and is interrupted even in prayer. No rebuke comes from His lips. Willing He responds to the new demands. For that He came "not to be ministered unto, but to minister."

Verses 40-45. Leprosy, that vile and loathsome disease, is a type of sin. Like sin it is incurable and only Jehovah could cure leprosy. When Jehovah had healed the disease the priest had to pronounce the leper clean. This leper recognized in the humble Servant the mighty Jehovah. He kneeled in His presence and expressed his faith in His power and implored Him to make him clean. Here again Mark tells us something of our blessed Lord, which we find neither in Matthew or Luke's account. He was moved with compassion. Thus the Spirit of God in some brief additions portrays the Servant in His loving service. The leper is healed. The Servant is Jehovah and both His love and His power are revealed. He charged him to say nothing to any man. In this the Servant once more manifests His humility, that He served in an unostentatious way. He did not want honor from man. His Father knew all His service; that was enough for Him. Yet the enemy through the cleansed leper attempted the popularity of the Servant. He sought the desert places once more to hide Himself. May we serve after this great pattern Servant.

CHAPTER 2

1. The Servant again in Capernaum and the healing of the paralytic (2:1-12); Matthew 9:1-8: Luke 5:17-26
2. Levi called and with the Publicans and Sinners (2:13-17); Matthew 9:9-13; Luke 5:27-32
3. The question concerning fasting (2:18-22); Matthew 9:14-15; Luke 5:33-39
4. The question concerning the Sabbath (2:23-28); Matthew 12:1-8; Luke 6:1-5

Verses 1-12. His second visit to Capernaum brought out a large multitude. We see Him occupied with preaching the Word. He always preached the Word first, to make known the Truth; for this He had come (1:38). Then in the next place He confirmed His Word by His mighty works. The paralytic tells of man's impotence; leprosy is the type of sin as a defiling, incurable disease, paralysis shows man's helpless condition. The paralytic is likewise the picture of Israel. The helpless paralytic is brought into the presence of the Lord. Mark alone tells us that four carried him and describes fully the obstacles in the way. They had faith in His love and in His power. How it must have refreshed His heart! As His servants we can still bring sinners into His presence and honor Him by our confidence. "Son, thy sins be forgiven thee."

---

[1]W. Kelly, *Gospel of Mark.*

With this blessed Word He touches the root of all evil. To deal with it He had come. The proof that He is Jehovah and has power to forgive sins is the healing of the paralytic. Love and power are here blessedly manifested. Love in forgiveness, power in healing and restoration. It is ever repeated in the case of every believing sinner. The two great elements of the gospel are here. In some future day converted Israel will know this (Ps. 103:1-3).

Verses 13-17. Levi, the son of Alphaeus, is Matthew, the writer of the first Gospel. He was a tax gatherer. As such he was despised by the nation Israel. Not alone were they considered thieves, but they were the miserable hirelings of the Romans and as such hated as apostates. What grace to call such an one to the office of an apostle! And the feast which followed reveals both the loving condescension of the Servant-Son and His grace to seek that which is lost. The Servant had taken a low place by associating with the tax-gatherers. In the eyes of the self-righteous Pharisees it was an abomination. God in the person of His Son had come in love and grace seeking man.

Verses 18-22. The disciples of John approach Him next with a question. The Servant's ear was always ready to listen to the perplexities, difficulties and sorrows of others. He was always approachable. Under the law they fasted. The grace of God had now appeared and grace was soon to take the place of the law. He Himself is the Bridegroom. No need of fasting and mourning while He was with them. His rejection would come and with it their fasting. A significant parable follows. The old garment and the old wineskins are symbolic of Judaism with its laws and ceremonies. The new piece and the new wine stand for the gospel. Law and grace must not be mixed. If the gospel of grace, the new wine, is put into the old wineskins, Judaism with its laws, the wineskins go to pieces and the new wine is spilled. Much in Christendom to-day is neither law nor grace. The Servant announced a change of dispensations.

Verses 23-28. The question concerning the Sabbath is closely connected with the preceding parable. The Sabbath, not a seventh day, but the seventh day, was the day on which God rested in creation. It was also the sign of His covenant with His people Israel. Plucking ears of corn on the Sabbath to eat them is nowhere forbidden in the law. It was one of the hard and burdensome man-made traditional injunctions. The Lord cites David's case. Mark adds that David was not alone hungry, but "he had need." David, though anointed king, was despised and in need. His greater Son and His disciples were in the same condition. What is greater with God, the maintenance of an ordinance or the need of man? Surely the latter. He, the humble Servant, was none other than the Lord of the Sabbath. He had rested in His creation work and instituted the Sabbath for His people. He had become the Son of Man for the need of man. As the Lord of the Sabbath He speaks, "The Sabbath was made for man and not man for the Sabbath." On the ground of grace the Sabbath no longer exists. We have the Lord's day, the first day of the week to enjoy communion with our risen and glorified Lord, resting from our daily occupation. Blessed privilege to adore Him on that day and to follow His own example of doing good.

CHAPTER 3

1. In the synagogue and the man with the withered hand healed (3:1-6); Matthew 12:9-14; Luke 6:6-11
2. The withdrawal of the Servant and many healed (3:7-12); Matthew 12:15-21; Luke 6:17-19.
3. On the mountain calling the twelve (3:13-19); Matthew 10:1-4; Luke 6:12-16
4. The interrupted meal (3:20)
5. The Servant charged with madness (3:21)
6. The blasphemy of the scribes and His warning (3:22-30); Matthew 12:22-32; Luke 11:14-23
7. Old relationship disowned and a new relationship announced (3:31-35); Matthew 13:46-50; Luke 8:19-21

Verses 1-6. This incident stands in closest relation to the preceding chapter. In their blindness they watched Him, if He would heal on the Sabbath. "Is it lawful to do good on the Sabbath day, or to do evil; to save life or to kill?" He answered the question by healing the sufferer. Note the addition by Mark, which is not found elsewhere. "When He had looked round about them with anger, being grieved for the hardness of their hearts." It was a righteous wrath when He saw them in their wicked and willful hardness. His service was rendered in the deepest emotions of His holy soul. He did good, but Pharisees and Herodians were ready to destroy Him.

Verses 7-12. The sudden departure of the Lord is not without meaning. Not alone did He withdraw Himself from the hatred of the Pharisees and Herodians to continue His ministry of love and power elsewhere, but His withdrawal indicates that the nation Israel was to be set aside dispensationally. He withdrew Himself to the sea. The sea is symbolical of the Gentile nations. Again they crowd about Him—a great multitude from the border land of the Gentiles (Tyre and Sidon). Satan's power was likewise manifested. Unclean spirits, when they saw Him, fell down before Him. These were demon possessed persons. They had to own and confess the glory of the Servant. But He did not want their witness and forbade them to make Him known.

Verses 13-15. In Matthew we find all these events and actions of our Lord in a different setting. In vain do we look in our Gospel for the Sermon on the Mount. It is not reported and only given in full in the Gospel of Matthew. The Sermon on the Mount is the proclamation of the King concerning His Kingdom. Mark, describing Him as the Ministering One, had to omit the utterances of the King. If we look for a place in Mark where the Sermon on the Mount belongs chronologically, it is at this point. (For the peculiar arrangement of the events in the Gospel of Matthew see *Exposition of Matthew.*) He ordained the twelve to be with Him and endowed with supernatural power to be sent forth by Him. In Luke we read He prayed all night. The calling of the twelve was for the extension of His loving ministry. Notice also the giving of names. "Boanerges" for the sons of Zebedee is only found here.

Verse 20. This is likewise mentioned by Mark exclusively (6:31). It shows that the Servant was ever ready to minister, forgetting his own physical need.

Verse 21. This is also a characteristic statement in Mark's Gospel. It shows that His own relations were ashamed of Him. They looked upon Him as being out of His mind. Thus His perfect service of love, the untiring labor, never ceasing toil, was judged by them.

Verses 23-30. Still worse, the Jerusalem scribes attributed His divine power to Satan. What an awful accusation! They could not deny the power, but refused to believe that it was the power of God. Under satanic impulses they called the Holy Spirit a demon power. But the perfect wisdom of the Lord silenced their blasphemy. The power He manifested was a power in the most blessed mercy to man, the prey of Satan and his demons. If it were Satan's power then his kingdom is divided. This is the unpardonable sin. No forgiveness for this sin. The words "is in danger of eternal damnation" are better rendered by "is guilty of an eternal sin." (See the 1911 Bible.)

Verses 31-35. He refused to see His relations. This refusal indicates the broken relationship with Israel. He no longer recognizes His own, and speaks of a new relationship, founded upon obedience to the will of His Father. It was spoken in anticipation of the present dispensation.

CHAPTER 4

1. Teaching by the seaside and the parable of the sower (4:1-20); Matthew 13:1-12; Luke 8:4-15
2. The Word to shine forth in testimony (4:21-25); Luke 8:16-18
3. The parable of the growth of the seed and the harvest (4:26-29)
4. The parable of the mustard seed (4:30-34); Matthew 13:31-35; Luke 13:18-19
5. The storm on the sea and the wind rebuked (4:35-41); Matthew 8:23-27; Luke 8:22-25

Verses 1-20. In the Gospel of Matthew the scene which closes the preceding chapter is followed by the seven parables (Matthew 13). In the seven parable discourse the Lord teaches the mystery of the kingdom of heaven in its present form. These parables belong into the first Gospel because it is the Gospel of the King. First He proclaimed the principles of the kingdom (Matt. 5—7); then after His rejection He taught in parables the kingdom in mystery. Only two of these parables are reported by Mark, the parable of the sower and of the mustard seed. Both relate to His work of ministry. Another parable, however, is added, which is found nowhere else in the Gospels.

The parable of the sower is explained by Himself (verses 13-20). He Himself is the great Sower and His fellow servants sow after Him. That which is sown is the Word, even as He came to preach the Word. The Devil, the flesh and the world are the hindering forces.

The parable of the sower is very simple. It is also noteworthy that Mark adds a sentence, which is not found elsewhere. "Know ye not this parable? And how then will ye be acquainted with all parables?" It is a fundamental parable and a key to other parables. He graciously explains it. What patience He had with His dull fellow servants! He is the Sower. That which is sown is the Word; for this He came. Man cannot bring any fruit. That which He sows can produce fruit. The devil, the flesh and the world are antagonistic to the Word and the causes of failure and unfruitfulness. Those who hear the Word and receive it (believe) yield fruit. But the devil, the flesh and the world are even then active and influence fruitbearing.

Verses 21-25. The Word received in faith gives life and yields fruit. It must also shine forth in testimony. This testimony may be obscured by the "bushel and the bed." The bushel stands for the cares and material things of this present age; the bed for ease and comfort. The cure of occupation with earthly things and for an ease-loving life, the hindrances of a bright shining testimony, is to remember the coming day of manifestation (verse 11). How bright and perfect the example of the Servant. He did not know the bushel nor the bed.

Verses 26-29. This parable is not recorded by any of the other evangelists. It is closely linked with the words which precede. The day of manifestation is the day of the harvest. The seed sown grows in secret. None knows how. Life is in the Word. The blade, the ear and the full corn, after that the harvest. This is the comforting assurance of the Servant. He sowed the seed and then "slept and rose"—He died and rose from the dead. In view of it He could rejoice in the knowledge that the seed would spring up, increase and bring a harvest. And the sower will put in the sickle. The harvest (the end of the age) is more fully revealed in Matthew 13. What was His comfort is the comfort of all His true servants who sow the Word.

Verses 30-34. The unexpected growth of the kingdom during the absence of the Sower is taught in this parable. In Matthew it is linked with the parable of the leaven. The external growth (mustard seed) and the internal corruption (leaven) of Christianity are foretold by Him. Christendom has developed into a powerful world institution and become the lodging place of the fowls of the air. These typify unclean beings (4:4, 15). The humble Servant never meant the Word to produce such an abnormal growth.

Verses 35-41. The close of the chapter fits in beautifully with the whole. The Servant is seen in chapter 4 as the rejected One. He is sowing the seed. He leaves the earth while the seed groweth unto the harvest. The storm on the lake gives the picture of the trials and dangers of His own during this age; but He is in the ship. Note a statement peculiar to Mark. "They took Him even as He was in the ship." The Servant, though Lord of all, had a real human body. Here we have a little picture of His weariness as Servant. Yet what a scene! He had perfect rest in the midst of the storm while His disciples were unbelieving. And then He manifested His power in rebuking the wind.

"Reader, do you think that the power of the Son of God and God's counsels could have failed because of an unexpected storm? Impossible! The disciples were in the same boat with Jesus. Here is a lesson for us. In all the difficulties and dangers of the Christian life, during the whole journey upon the waves, often agitated by the tempestuous sea of life, we are always in the same boat with Jesus, if we are doing His will. It may seem to us that He is sleeping; nevertheless, if He allows the tempest to rise in order to prove our faith, we shall not perish since we are *with Him* in the storm; evidently neither He or we can perish. His security is our own."

CHAPTER 5

1. The Servant's power over Satan's work (5:1-20); Matthew 8:28-34; Luke 8:26-39
2. The Servant's power over disease and death (5:21-43); Matthew 9:18-26; Luke 8:40-58

Verses 1-20. The storm on the lake was the work of Satan, but here the power of the enemy is more prominent. The description of the demoniac differs from Matthew's and Luke's account. His condition is described in the fullest detail. He dwelt in the place of the dead. No one could chain him; Satan's dominion and power cannot be conquered by the effort of man. Then there is self-torture and delusion in thinking of Christ as a tormentor. The complete identification of the legion of demons with this poor victim in seen in verse 9. The power of the Lord delivers the man. This miserable world is still in the thraldom of Satan and his legion of demons. Demon possessions have not ceased. And the Lord Jesus Christ is still the same. The demons enter the swine by their own request and when granted the herd of swine rushed to destruction. This is an evidence of the character of the devil. He is the murderer from the beginning. But oh! the blessed change which had come for the demoniac. Delivered completely, in the attitude of rest, no longer rushing to and fro in torment, his nakedness covered and in his right mind. These are still the results of salvation. He would remain in constant fellowship with His deliverer. But the Servant demands service—and he announces directly what the Lord had done for him. This is still the blessed privilege of all who have been delivered. They asked the Servant, with His loving power to save to the uttermost, to leave their coast. "When the presence of God is felt, it is more terrible than that of Satan. Man would wish to free himself from the latter, but cannot; but the presence of God is insupportable when it makes itself felt, and indeed man has driven God (in the person of Christ) out of this world." It shows once more the rejection of the Servant.

Verses 21-43. And now He manifests power over disease and death. The daughter of Jairus was sick unto death. The willing Servant responds at once to the request of her father. While on the way the poor, suffering woman touches the hem of His garment. Verse 26 is found only in Mark. The Lord knows the touch of faith and heaing power goes forth from Him. She is healed. The sick daughter had died, but the Lord raised her up. All has its blessed spiritual and dispensational lessons. Man is dead in trespasses and sins but One has power to give life and raise the dead. Faith is beautifully illustrated in the woman who touched Him. Jairus' daughter represents Israel. The Lord will come again into this earthly scene and then will call the remnant of Israel to spiritual and national life. The woman, so hopeless, so helpless, suffering and getting worse, is typical of the Gentiles. The hand of faith can touch Him still. In verse 43 we see once more how the Servant loved secrecy and despised ostentatiousness.

CHAPTER 6

1. The Servant rejected in Nazareth (6:1-6); Matthew 13:54-58; Luke 4:16-30
2. The Servant sends forth the twelve (6:7-13); Matthew 10:5-15; Luke 9:1-6
3. King Herod troubled (6:14-16); Matthew 14:1-2; Luke 9:7-9
4. The martyrdom of John (6:17-29); Matthew 14:3-12
5. The Servant's withdrawal for rest (6:30-31); Luke 9:10-11
6. The feeding of the five thousand (6:32-44); Matthew 14:13-21; Luke 9:12-17; John 6:1-13
7. The Servant alone and His return walking on the waters (6:45-52); Matthew 14:22-32; John 6:15-21
8. New manifestations of His love and power (6:53-56); Matthew 14:34-36

Verses 1-6. Once more we find Him in Nazareth. The first thing is teaching, and though they were astonished at His wisdom and power, they did not own Him as the Lord, but called Him the Carpenter and were offended in Him. Such is the heart of man. Unbelief tied His hands, yet in love He healed a few and marvelled because of their unbelief. But did He abandon them? Oh! the infinite patience and seeking grace of this perfect Servant! "He went round about the villages teaching," if perchance faith might yet respond to His willingness and power to heal.

Verses 7-13. Now He sends His Apostles forth and endows them with power. They are to depend in their ministry upon Himself. Thus they were to be His followers for He was ever dependent on God. Blessed principles are here which still hold good, though the sending forth had a special meaning for Israel. (See Matthew 10:5-15.)

Verses 14-16. It is the story of a troubled conscience and fear produces the thought that it is John the Baptist risen from the dead.

Verses 17-29. The faithful herald of the Servant suffered martyrdom. In the whole sickening scene of lust and bloodshed the prince of this world, the god of this age is manifested in this awful rule and power. It is a picture of the present age in opposition to God. The lust of the flesh, the lust of the eyes and the pride of the life hold sway. And this evil age is not gradually improved and getting better. It is not abandoning its lusts and pride, its hatred of God and His Christ. As long as Satan is the ruler the age must be evil. In such a scene the Holy One came to minister and to give His life.

Verses 30-31. We have noticed different withdrawals of the Lord. He withdrew for prayer and to the sea and now when the Apostles gathered unto Him, the One to whom the fellow servants must ever gather, to give a report of what they had done and taught, He withdrew with them into a desert place. The Lord does not say anything about their success (verse 13). There was danger of the self-exaltation of the messengers. The silence of the Lord puts a check upon it. It was His own power, which in goodness and mercy had done all this. Instead we hear Him say, "Come ye yourselves apart into a desert place and rest awhile." This again is found nowhere but in Mark. How needful for all servants it is to heed this loving word. How easily in constant service a servant can be lifted up and attribute something to himself. True service only is possible by being occupied with the Lord. And therefore we must ever learn to seek the presence of God. He remembered the need of His messengers and the time of rest with Him gave them new strength.

Verses 32-44. Here we have the compassion of the Servant in remembering the physical need of the people. But before He supplied that need, "He began to teach them many things." The Word stands always first. He came to serve. The giving of the Word followed by the works of goodness and power is the order maintained in His service. Note the contrast between Him and the request of the disciples. How untiring, loving, gracious He was in all His service for man. May we learn of Him. A comparison of the account of this miracle in the four Gospels will teach us many lessons. He feeds the poor with bread (Ps. 132:15) as the true Shepherd of His people. He is the miraculous giver, but He uses His disciples in dispensing His blessing. His power for the good of others is at the believer's disposal. And the little put into His hands was not only sufficient for all but more was left over than they had given to Him. And still He delights to take the little things and manifest through them His power, if we but trust Him.

Verses 45-52. All is full of blessed meaning. He is once more alone in the mountain to pray. His disciples are alone on the stormy sea. He is absent now and has sent the people (Israel) away. He is in the presence of God as our intercessor. The stormy sea with the contrary wind is a type of this present age. Trouble and perplexity is the lot of His disciples during His absence. About the fourth watch of the night He came unto them walking upon the sea. Mark does not mention Peter going forth to meet Him. They see Him coming, but do not recognize Him, believing Him a spirit. His loving voice soon assures them, "Be of good cheer; it is I, be not afraid." Thus He will return across the stormy sea to meet and deliver His own. Blessed are we if we ever behold Him as the Mighty One, who is above all circumstances and if we hear His words of comfort. How He cares for us. And when He comes the wind will cease.

Verses 53-56. What a scene of toil! What ministry in doing good! Dispensationally it stands for all the blessed time, yet in store for this world, when He comes again. Then He who was the Son of Man in humiliation will, as Son of Man, with power and glory, be known to all. Then the earth will be blessed as Gennesaret was.

CHAPTER 7

1. The opposition of the Pharisees (7:1-23); Matthew 15:1-20
2. Grace shown to the Syrophenician woman (7:24-30); Matthew 15:21-28
3. The healing of the deaf man (7:31-37); Matthew 15:29-31

Verses 1-23. This paragraph is of much importance. The scope of the analysis forbids a full annotation, but we refer the reader to the exposition of Matthew 15:1-20, the parallel passage. The Servant in His divine wisdom uncovers the hypocrisy which lies underneath the traditions of the elders. He shows that the Pharisees had rejected the commandment of God for the sake of men-made inventions and traditions. Their ritualistic service founded upon tradition was dishonoring to God and His Word. Such ritualism springing from tradition must always be. He condemns religiousness, which knows nothing of heart obedience and holiness of life. And this outward, human, man-made religion, which boasts of being something and doing something, He condemns. Then He shows that man's defilement does not consist in what enters into him, but the things which come out of him. He shows what man is within (verses 21-23). No, mere religiousness cannot take away this defilement. Thus He uncovers the hypocrisy of an outward religion and the true state of the heart of man. The product of the natural heart of man, though it may delight in religious observances, is nothing but vileness.

Verses 24-30. While the omniscient Lord in the form of the Servant showed what the heart of man is, He now also uncovers His own heart in showing grace to one, who belonged to the Gentiles. In the borders of Tyre and Sidon the blessed Servant sought quietness and entered a house; but He could not be hid. Note again that Mark mentions this exclusively, because it brings out His character as Servant. He also informs us that she was a Gentile, a Syrophenician, belonging to the enemies of God's people, Israel. But Mark leaves out Matthew's statement, that she appealed to Him as "Son of David." Matthew's Gospel is the proper place for that. What evidences all along we find of the inspiration of these records. She had no claim on His mercy and power, for she was under the curse. Her daughter had a demon. And though she had no claim on His power and no promise, she believed in His love. She takes the place He gave to her and the daughter was restored. What a manifestation of grace! And how it must have cheered the Servant's heart! In that moment His omniscient eye must have beheld the multitudes of Gentiles, who, after His death on the cross, as lost sinners, with no promise, aliens from the commonwealth of Israel, would believe in His love.

Verses 31-37. A comparison with Matthew shows that the account here is peculiar to Mark's Gospel. In Matthew 15:29-31 we find the dumb man mentioned among others whom He healed. He represents Israel. Altogether deaf, unable to hear God's voice, which spoke through the One who had come and an impediment in speech. They attempted to speak of God and praise God. And such is the man's natural state. And such He came to heal. Israel might have had the ear opened by Him, the Servant, whose ear was always open, and Israel might have the tongue loosed, to praise His Name. He heals the afflicted one. And how the Servant looked to heaven and groaned. What must He have felt!

CHAPTER 8

1. The feeding of the four thousand (8:1-9); Matthew 15:32-39
2. The Pharisees ask a sign (8:10-13); Matthew 16:1-4
3. The warning against the leaven of the Pharisees (8:14-21); Matthew 16:5-12
4. The healing of the blind man (8:22-26)
5. Peter's confession (8:27-30); Matthew 16:12-16; Luke 9:18-20
6. The first announcement of His coming, rejection and death (8:31-33); Matthew 16:21-23: Luke 9:22
7. His disciples to follow in His path, and the coming glory (8:34-38); Matthew 16:24-28; Luke 9:23-27

Verses 1-9. The compassion and loving care of Him who came to minister is once more seen. Again He meets the need of the multitude in a miraculous way. But here we have seven loaves and seven baskets are left over. It points clearly to the manifestation of divine power, for the number seven occurs twice. He in His great goodness and great power is sufficient to meet all human need. The miracle foreshadows the great and perfect blessings of the coming Kingdom age.

Verses 10-13. Though the religious leaders had seen so many signs and display of divine goodness and power they asked for a sign from heaven. Unbelief ever looks for something new and is never satisfied. Their request may be looked upon as a temptation. He could have shown a sign from heaven, but with it He would have left the humble path of the Servant. "He sighed deeply," which is another phrase peculiar to Mark's account, showing His deep emotion. He refused the sign. The next sign will be "the sign of the Son of Man in heaven" at the time of His glorious return. Then a believing remnant of His people will welcome Him.

Verses 14-21. He warns against the leaven of the Pharisees and Herodians. It is the only time the word leaven is found in Mark. It means, as elsewhere in the Word of God, evil. The leaven of the Pharisees is hypocrisy, insincerity of an unbelieving heart in opposition to God. The expression of it is self-righteousness in pride. The leaven of the Herodians is worldliness. He warns His disciples to beware of it for the leaven of the Pharisees was in them too. They did not fully see His glory, though they believed in Him as the promised Messiah. Their state and the Lord's power and patience towards them is beautifully brought out in the healing of the blind man.

Verses 22-26. This healing at Bethsaida is only recorded by Mark. It reveals the tender, patient and successful method of the Servant in His ministry. The disciples' case is illustrated. They saw "men as if they were trees." Their sight was imperfect. But He did not leave them in that condition. Their clear sight came, when the promise of the Father, the Holy Spirit, was given to them. But many other lessons are found here. See how He led the blind man outside and what pains He took, and though He knew all about the effect of putting His hands upon his eyes, yet He inquired lovingly "if he beheld anything." If we are in His loving hands, separated from Bethsaida ("place of snares," a picture of the world), He will deal with us in the same tenderness and patience. Verse 26 tells us once more how He did not seek honor from man.

Verses 27-30. How perfectly all is linked together. Though the disciples were imperfect in their sight yet they knew that He was the Christ. That is true faith, which they all possessed, with the exception of Judas, who never addressed Him as Lord. Mark gives the briefest account of Peter's confession. Matthew contains the completest record. The church, as a future thing, is announced in Matthew as well as the kingdom. The church is not mentioned by Mark. All shows the divine hand which guided the pens of these instruments. What is dispensational is always fully given in the kingly, dispensational Gospel by Matthew and omitted by Mark.

Verses 31-33. The Servant now speaks of Himself as the Son of Man, the title both of His rejection and of His exaltation. For the first time He announces His coming death. He knew all from the beginning. He knew it when He went into the dark waters of Jordan. He knew it all along in His ministry of toil. Yet with the vision of His rejection, of His suffering on the cross, constantly before Him, He continued uninterruptedly in His ministry of love. Nothing could swerve Him from it. What perfection and beauty! But He also spoke of His resurrection. He knew the glory that should follow. For the joy set before Him He endured the cross and despised the shame. In our service for God the cross and the glory should ever be seen. We, too, must be willing to share His reproach and look forward to the crowning day, the day of His glory and ours as well. Peter becomes, on account of his blindness, the mouthpiece of Satan, rebuking the Lord. Then "He looked on His disciples," an addition in Mark. What a look it must have been! He rebuked Peter in the words He used when Satan made the same suggestion to avoid the cross.

Verses 34-38; 9:1. Well may God's people ponder over these words. Salvation is by grace. Nothing can save but grace. Eternal salvation is not dependent on our walk. But the way which leads to glory is the way of self-denial and suffering. It is His own path. "Is it not true that we naturally like to escape trial, shame and rejection; that we shrink from the suffering which, doing God's will, in such a world as this, must ever entail; that we prefer to have a quiet, respectable path in the earth—in short, the best of both worlds? How easily one may be ensnared into this!" (W. Kelly.) We may not be called upon to lose the life for His sake, but "let him deny himself" we can always do, enabled by His grace. All the words our ever blessed Lord spoke to His disciples hold good in this dispensation of grace. He announces His coming glory. It is His second coming in the glory of His Father.

CHAPTER 9

1. The glory to come foreshadowed in the Transfiguration (9:1-13); Matthew 17:1-13; Luke 9:28-36
2. The helpless disciples and the secret of failure (9:14-29); Matthew 17:14-20; Luke 9:37-42
3. The second announcement of His death (9:30-32); Matthew 17:22-23; Luke 9:43-45
4. The self-seeking disciples (9:33-37); Matthew 18:1-5; Luke 9:46-48
5. The Servant's gentleness and tolerance (9:38-41); Luke 9:49-50
6. The solemn warning (9:42-50); Matthew 18:6-9

Verses 1-13. The Lord has the transfiguration in mind when He spoke of some standing there and not tasting death. 2 Peter 1:16 gives the meaning of the transfiguration as a type and earnest of His coming into His kingdom. On that mountain the three disciples saw the kingdom of God come with power. The Servant appears in glory. The saints are represented by Moses and Elias, those who have died and those changed in the twinkling of an eye. The three disciples represented the saints on earth, when He comes into His kingdom; the Shekinah cloud was there. And Peter blundered again when He lowered the dignity of the Lord by putting Him alongside of the two Old Testament servants of God. The Father's voice is heard once more, vindicating the honor of His Son. What an encouragement the transfiguration must have been for the Servant-Son.

Verses 14-29. The whole scene is of greatest importance. The conditions He finds returning from the mount of transfiguration are typical of the conditions on the earth when He comes again. Here are helpless disciples, triumphant, unbelieving scribes and the manifestation of Satan's power. All this we cannot follow in detail. Notice the additions in Mark's account. They had no power to cast out the demon, because they were "faithless." The Lord told them that lack of prayer and fasting were the causes of their failure. Dependence on God and denial of self are meant. How gracious was the complete deliverance of the afflicted boy. If God's people knew more of a real prayer and real denial of self, there would be a greater manifestation of His power through them.

Verses 30-32. Passing again through Galilee He announced His death and resurrection the second time. They understood not and were afraid to ask Him. The cross was foreign to them. Other thoughts occupied their hearts.

Verses 33-37. And while He who had made of Himself no reputation, who came to be the Servant of all, was looking towards the goal of His earthly ministry, the cross and its shame, they disputed all the way who should be the greatest. Vain glory filled their hearts in expectation of the earthly kingdom for which they waited. They were unable to enter into His thoughts. They were silent because they realized that their dispute was wrong. Then He taught them. The desire of being first shows only fitness to be last. Such a desire reveals nothing but self. Humility must ever be a leading characteristic of the disciple. Then He illustrates it by the small child He took in His arms. Such in dependence, humbleness in mind and confidence, the disciples must be to enjoy His fellowship. With such He can identify Himself.

Verses 38-41. Another form of self appears among the disciples. John would have the Lord rebuke those who used His name effectually and belonged not to their company. It was a narrow sectarianism. Of all the manifestations of self the religious sectarian self, as expressed in exclusivism, rejecting those who do not fellowship with them—is by far the worst, and in the Epistles by the Spirit of God is designated as a work of the flesh. How very offensive it must have been to God's perfect Servant. Yet what a gentle answer He gives. How we all can learn from Him. The smallest service in doing honor to His name would not be forgotten of God.

Verses 42-50. The words are for both saint and sinner. We quote from another on this solemn word. "Nevertheless, as regards themselves, all depends on the faithfulness of Christ; and on this account they need to free themselves from all the things which tend to separate from Christ, which led into sin, and bring on apostasy in the heart as well as outward apostasy. God will keep His own, but He will keep them in making them obedient to His Word. Besides this, God puts all to the proof; the fire of His judgment is applied to all, both to saints and sinners. In the saints it consumes the dross, in order that the pure gold may shine in its true lustre; in the case of sinners it is the fire of eternal judgment that is not quenched.

" 'Every sacrifice must be salted with salt' refers to Levit. 2:13. The salt represents the power of the Holy Spirit to keep us from all that is impure and produce holiness in a heart devoted to God, to keep us from all corruption. 'Have salt in yourselves.' He wishes us to exercise diligence in order that our souls, in our walk, may be thus sanctified before God, and then manifest it before the world and that we should walk with others in peace."[2]

"The burden" where the worm dieth not, and the fire is not quenched, "falls on the conscience stricken like the bell that tolls the felon to his doom. Would that it might kindle our hearts who believe into an unwonted earnestness on behalf of perishing souls!" Many attempts are made to deny that solemn warning in its fearful meaning, but they are eternal truth. The Son of God came from Heaven's glory, walked on earth as the Servant and tasted death, yea, forsaken of God on the cross, to save man from the unquenchable fire.

CHAPTER 10

In Judea

1. The question concerning divorce (10:1-12); Matthew 19:1-9
2. Children are blessed by Him (10:13-16); Matthew 19:13-15; Luke 18:15-17
3. The rich young ruler and warning against riches (10:17-27); Matthew 19:16-26; Luke 18:18-27
4. Concerning rewards (10:28-31); Matthew 19:27-30; Luke 18:28-30
5. On to Jerusalem and the third announcement of His death and resurrection (10:32-34); Matthew 20:17-19; Luke 18:31-34
6. The desire of James and John (10:35-45); Matthew 20:20-28; Luke 22:24-27
7. At Jericho and the healing of Bartimaeus (10:46-52); Matthew 20:29-34; Luke 18:35-43)

Verses 1-12. The Lord restores in teaching the original meaning of marriage and speaks against divorce Moses had permitted on account of the hardness of their hearts. Thus He restored the original institution of marriage. His ministry is now almost ended and He is on His way to Jerusalem to go to the cross.

Verses 13-16. Again the disciples failed. They showed a kind of self-importance and dignity in rebuking those who brought the little children. He was indignant. They had no right whatever to rebuke and to shut out from His presence. They usurped His place and by their domineering attitude misrepresented Him. And priest-craft has brought this to perfection. But oh! the contrast. He received them and tenderly took them into His arms to bless them. Such is the kingdom of God. Sin is in them. But the little children present some characteristics of uncorrupted nature. The way into the kingdom is the new birth; and that must be received as a little child.

Verses 17-27. Here is one, who would inherit eternal life by doing. He "kneeled" (mentioned only by Mark) and showed reverence, and yet he called Him only "Good Master." He was a moral young man but unsaved. The reply of the Lord is significant. He refuses the address "Good Master." The young man did not believe on Him as Son of God. The logic is perfect. If He is not God, He could not be good, and if He is good, then He is God. Yet "Jesus, beholding him, loved him;" a statement found only in Mark. He did not see the truth that man is not good, but a sinner, and salvation cannot be by works but it is by grace. Note the beautiful answer the Lord gave to His disciples. "Who then can be saved?" And Jesus looking upon them saith, "With men it is impossible, but not with God; for with God all things are possible." Man cannot be saved by what he is or does. Blessed truth. But God has accomplished salva-

[2]J. N. Darby, *Mark.*

tion by the gift of His Son and this salvation is received by faith in Him.

Verses 28-31. It was a selfish question, which Peter asked. Somehow he would remind the Lord that while the young man refused to part with his riches, they had left all. And the meek and lowly One answers graciously and gives the promise of rewards in this life and in the age to come. But it is reward only if it is done for His sake and the gospel's. It is a blessed thing to leave the rewards with Him.

Verses 32-34. But were they willing to leave all for His sake? As the Servant now at the close of His ministry went up to Jerusalem they were amazed at His calmness and determination to go to the place, where death awaited Him, according to His own predictions. They were afraid of their own lives as they followed Him. The Servant went before them in the lead; the frightened group came behind. The third prediction of His death is the completest.

Verses 35-45. Their fear was short-lived. They did not grasp the solemn announcement that the Son of Man would have to die and did not understand that all the promised blessings could only be realized through His death on the cross. They had faith in a coming kingdom of glory, faith in the Servant so lowly to be the King and that they were to reign with Him. The request is stated and answered graciously by the Lord. And the two who were afraid when He turned towards Jerusalem now say that they are able to drink the cup with Him and be baptized with the baptism, which awaited Him, the inward and outward sufferings of the cross. But these two forsook Him a few days later and fled. The others were much displeased, no doubt for selfish reasons, and then still other words of instruction came from His lips.

Verses 46-52. This healing stands at the beginning of the end of that blessed life lived on the earth. Up to verse 45 He speaks of Himself as "Son of Man." The phrase "Son of David" appears only once in Mark's Gospel. Bartimaeus calls upon Him by that name and is healed. It is the prelude to the great events in Jerusalem, His presentation as King, rejection, suffering and death. The miracle of Jericho holds the same place in the three Gospels. Israel's condition is easily seen in Bartimaeus' blindness. The Son of David had come to give sight to the blind and in Jericho (the place of curse) He shows His gracious power. Bartimaeus followed Him as the blessed witness of His power.

III. The Servant in Jerusalem: Presented as King and Rejected (11—13)

CHAPTER 11

1. The Servant enters into Jerusalem (11:1-11); Matthew 21:1-11; Luke 19:28-40; John 12:12-16
2. The fig tree cursed (11:12-14); compare with Matthew 21:19-21
3. The cleansing of the temple (11:15-18); Matthew 21:12-19; Luke 19:45-48
4. The withered fig tree (11:19-26); Matthew 21:20-22
5. Again in the city: His authority questioned (11:27-33); Matthew 21:23-27; Luke 20:1-8

Verses 1-11. He presents Himself as the promised Son of David to the nation as written in the prophecy of Zechariah (9:9). As King the multitudes welcome Him. Hosanna (save now); Blessed is He that cometh in the Name of the Lord. "Blessed be the kingdom of our Father David, that cometh in the Name of the Lord: Hosanna in the highest." They expected the promised kingdom and they welcomed Him as Son of David with power to save. But He knew what it all meant. He is silent, according to Mark, but enters into the temple and looked around upon all things without uttering a word. There is nothing for Him there. He then left the city and returned to Bethany (meaning: house of affliction). When He comes the second time with glory, He will be greeted by a remnant of His people and set up the kingdom of David.

Verses 12-14. He was hungry. In all the enthusiasm no one had thought of His need. The rejection of the Servant-Son is evident in this. The fig tree is the emblem of the Jewish nation. He came looking for fruit and found none. "The fig tree was punished not for being without fruit, but for proclaiming by the voice of those leaves that it had fruit; not for being barren, but for being false; and this was the guilt of Israel, so much deeper than the guilt of the nations" (Trench).

Verses 15-19. Twice He cleansed the temple, in the beginning of His ministry (John 2:13-16) and at the close. Most likely the desecration of the house was worse at the end than in the beginning. The greed for money is the prominent feature in the defilement of the temple. The actions of the Lord bring out the satanic hatred of the scribes and chief priests. He was hated as the Servant without a cause and hated unto death. Again He went out of the city.

Verses 20-26. The dried up fig tree is made the occasion to teach the disciples the power of faith in God. The fig tree typifies the religious condition of the people. The mountain, the nation as such, thinking themselves firmly established. But soon that mountain was to be removed and cast into the sea (the sea of nations). Faith was exercised by the Servant and He calls upon His own to have faith in God. Faith can remove every obstacle. For the disciples it meant the obstacle of that mountain, the nation. Verse 24 is precious and has the same meaning to-day as it had when the words were spoken. God ever answers faith. But that faith must be paired with forgiveness.

Verses 27-33. Visiting the temple again He met His enemies, who questioned Him concerning His authority. His authority was completely established by the mighty works He had done. The Omniscient One knew their hatred and asked them a question, which they did not dare to answer. He, the perfect Servant, had zeal for God and for His house; they, the religious leaders, had only zeal for their own authority. This is still the mark of all ritualism.

CHAPTER 12

1. The parable of the vineyard (12:1-12); Matthew 21:33-46; Luke 20:9-19
2. The question concerning the tribute money (12:13-17); Matthew 22:15-22; Luke 20:20-26
3. The Sadducees questioning concerning resurrection (12:18-27); Matthew 22:23-33; Luke 20:27-38
4. The question of the scribe (12:28-34); Matthew 22:34-40
5. His question (12:35-37); Matthew 22:41-46: Luke 20:41-44
6. Beware of the scribes (12:28-40); Matthew 23; Luke 20:45-47
7. The Servant's loving sympathy and praise (12:41-44); Luke 21:1-4

Verses 1-12. The parable is a review of the history of Israel and its culmination in the rejection of the Son. With what calmness the Perfect One relates it all. He is ready to have all done unto Him of which He speaks. A comparison with the Gospel of Matthew will show that Mark is brief and passes on rapidly, omitting utterances of the Lord which are not needed in his description of the Servant.

Verses 13-17. With this paragraph we have the different classes of Jews approaching the Lord to tempt Him. Pharisees and Herodians, Sadducees and a scribe. The Lord manifests His wisdom and they are defeated. Then He turns questioner and warns against the scribes. His authority they could no longer question and now they tried to catch Him in His words. Pharisees and Herodians, so opposed to each other, could make a common cause in hating God's Servant. If He had answered "yes" the Pharisees would have condemned Him for favoring the Gentile yoke. If He had said "no," the Herodians would have accused Him as an enemy of Caesar. How wonderful His answer! They even had to marvel and yet it only intensified their hate. Caesar's image told out the story of their sin.

Verses 18-27. The Sadducees were rationalists and denied the existence of angels and the resurrection. They only believed in the giving of the law and accepted the Pentateuch. It was a fine spun argument. The Lord silences them from the portion of the Scriptures they endorsed.

Verses 28-34. A scribe now makes the last attempt. But he was indeed "not far from the kingdom of God." The one step was the acceptance of Christ, whose wisdom he had owned.

Verses 35-37. Then the Lord turned questioner. His wisdom had closed their mouths. In Matthew's Gospel this significant question is more fully given. He refers to Psalm 110. In connection with Matthew four great facts are stated by the Lord. 1. This Psalm was written by David. 2. It was written by inspiration. 3. It is a Messianic Psalm. 4. Christ is David's Lord and David's Son. While it silenced the scribes it also silences the present day Sadducees, the higher critics, with their inventions. They claim that Psalm 110 was not written by David and Christ is not foretold in it.

Verses 38-40. In Matthew the Holy Spirit reports the full discourse against the scribes and Pharisees (chapter 23) ending with the solemn statement, "Behold your house is left unto you desolate." In Mark, where the divine design is to give us the picture of the Servant, only a few sentences are given. Yet they contain the chief characteristics of the corrupt leaders of the nation. Love of being seen, love of applause, love of pre-eminence, assumed religiousness and the devouring of the poor are all mentioned. These hireling servants shall have greater damnation.

Verses 41-44. He had rendered such perfect service free from seeking applause or pre-eminence and now He shows His loving sympathy to one of the poor widows who were being spoiled by the greed of the Pharisees. That poor, yet rich, widow had two mites. It was her all and she gave it. She might have given one mite and retained the other. She cast in all she had. And He saw it and His sympathy was towards her for she reminded Him of His own service in giving all. How it must have refreshed His heart. May we remember that nothing escapes His eye.

CHAPTER 13

1. The destruction of the temple predicted (13:1-2); Matthew 24:1-2; Luke 21:5-6
2. The questions of the disciples (13:3-4); Matthew 24:3; Luke 21:7
3. The Olivet Discourse (13:5-37); Matthew 24:4-42; Luke 21:8-38

Verses 1-2. He went out of the temple for the last time, when one of His disciples called attention to the temple buildings. They were of the most massive construction, some of them still in process of erection. He predicted a complete destruction, which was fulfilled later in the year 70. The destruction of Jerusalem is more fully foretold in Luke 21:20-24.

Verses 3-4. Mark gives us their names, which are omitted by Matthew and Luke. What follows is the answer.

Verses 5-37. Mark's report is the briefest, Matthew's the longest. Omitted in Mark are the parables, which have special reference to the Christian profession (Matthew 25) and the judgment of living nations (chapter 25:31-46). These belong in Matthew, but would be out of keeping with the purpose of the Gospel of Mark. The service of our Lord, as we have seen, is in the foreground. The three characteristic discourses in Matthew nowhere else reported in full are: 1. The Sermon on the Mount, which is the Proclamation of the King. 2. The Parable Discourse in Matthew 13, the mysteries of the kingdom. 3. The Olivet Discourse, Matthew 24—25, the future of the kingdom. But why should there be anything at all in the Gospel of Mark about the future things, such as the end of the age and His return in glory, if only the Servant is described? It will be seen that the predictions are in part at least in view of their service. He forewarned them as His servants of what was to come after His departure.

It is not the purpose of this annotated analysis to give an exposition of this discourse. We must ask the reader to turn to our commentary on Matthew. We give here a subdivision of the discourse as contained in Mark: 1. The characteristics of the present age and the end of the age (13:5-13). 2. The abomination of desolation or the great tribulation which precedes the second coming of Christ (13:14-23). 3. The visible manifestation of Christ. He will come again in clouds as Son of Man, not as an humble Servant but as the King of Glory; the regathering of the elect Israel then takes place (13:24-27). 4. The signs of His coming; the budding fig tree is Israel awakening to new national life (13:28-33). Note that in verse 32 "neither the Son" is added. This statement of our Lord that even He the Son does not know the hour of His return has been used to deny His deity. All kinds of theories have been invented to explain it. It is explained by the Lord having taken the place of humiliation as a Servant for "the servant knoweth not what his lord doeth." This is why the statement appears only in Mark. It does not affect the truth of His Person. 5. The solemn exhortation to watch. It behooves the servants to watch during the absence of the Lord.

IV. Giving His Life a Ransom For Many (14—15)

CHAPTER 14

1. Seeking by craft to put Him to death (14:1-2); Matthew 26:2-5; Luke 22:1-2
2. The anointing (14:3-9); Matthew 26:6-13; John 12:1-8
3. Judas offers to betray Him (14:10-11); Matthew 26:14-16; Luke 22:3-6
4. The last Paschal feast (14:12-21); Matthew 26:17-24: Luke 22:7-18, 21-23
5. The Lord's Supper instituted (14:22-25); Matthew 26:26-29; Luke 22:17-20
6. Peter's denial predicted (14:26-31); Matthew 26:31-35; Luke 22:31-34; John 13:36-38
7. The suffering in the garden (14:32-42); Matthew 26:36-46; Luke 22:39-46
8. The betrayal and arrest of the Lord Jesus (14:43-52); Matthew 26:47-56; Luke 22:47-53
9. Before the High Priest and the Sandedrin (14:53-65); Matthew 26:47-68; Luke 22:47-55; John 18:2-24
10. Peter's denial (14:66-72); Matthew 26:69-75; Luke 22:56-62; John 18:17, 25-27

Verses 1-2. His enemies were plotting, but over all was God and His eternal counsels. They were now ready "to do whatsoever Thy hand and Thy counsel determined before to be done" (Acts 4:28). The Servant is to die as the true Passover Lamb and He who had ministered in such a perfect way is to give His life a ransom for many. They had resolved it should not be on the feast day. But God's will demanded that it should be on that day; and so it was.

Verses 3-9. The woman is not mentioned by Mark. It was Mary of Bethany, who sat at His feet when He had come to her house and who wept at His feet when Lazarus had died. She alone had grasped the meaning of the Lord's announcement concerning His death and resurrection. She did not go to the grave as others did. She anointed His body for the burial. What love there was in her heart! How it must have delighted His heart when she did this act of faith and love.

Verses 10-11. The anointing hastened Judas to betray Him. (See John 12:5-6.)

Verses 12-21. First there was the preparation (verses 12-16) and then the feast itself (verses 17-21). What calmness and dignity is seen in all He does! He knew all what awaited Him. During the feast He announced the coming betrayal. Awful are the words coming from such lips, "Good were it for that man if he had never been born." The same is true of every human being who rejects the Lord Jesus Christ and dies in sin.

Verses 22-25. It is His own supper, the blessed memorial feast. "Do this in remembrance of Me." They did not know then what it meant. But when the Holy Spirit had come they broke the bread. The Passover was the memorial of the deliverance of the people out of Egypt and reminded them of the blood that was sprinkled. A better blood was soon to be shed and a greater deliverance wrought by the Lamb of God. A blessed privilege to carry out His request (1 Cor. 11:23-26).

Verses 26-31. The hymn they sang was composed of Psalms 115—118. With what emotion of soul He must have sung with His disciples! The shadow of deepest agony and death was upon Him and yet the fullest praise flowed from His lips. He announced the scattering of the sheep and His own smiting by the hand of God. What must it have meant for Him, when He said with His perfect knowledge, "I will smite the shepherd." That smiting, which took place on the cross, is the heart and mystery of the atonement. Peter's denial is then predicted.

Verses 32-42. In Gethsemane we are face to face with the most solemn event in the life of the Servant-Son, save that hour, when He hung on the cross, forsaken of God. What was His suffering there? No saint can ever fathom its depths. He did not shrink from death, nor was the agony on account of the physical sufferings He knew were to be His lot; nor was Satan, as some foolishly teach, ready to slay Him. All such statements are dishonoring to Him. He was not in danger of death in Gethsemane. What was the cup He dreaded? The Sinless One, who knew no sin, was now soon to be made sin for us. God's face upon which He had ever looked was soon to be hid. And what was it when at last He was made sin for us on the cross? One sentence gives us the answer, "My God, My God, why hast Thou forsaken Me?"

Verses 43-52. He surrenders Himself as the willing victim. Peter was ready to fight and cut off the ear of the high priest's servant. Mark omits the healing for he is to picture the Servant in His suffering and all relating to power is now out of place. In John's Gospel the Lord said one word, "I am," and those who came to arrest Him fell backward to the ground. John was guided by the Spirit of God to make a record of it. It could have no place in Mark's Gospel. They all forsook Him and fled. But only Mark tells of a certain young man, who followed and then fled naked. The young man may have been Mark himself.

Verses 53-65. We behold the Servant now delivered into the hands of man and behind man stood Satan. Man's wickedness and Satan's power are there, and in the midst, in solitary grandeur, stands the perfect Servant-Son. Mark tells us exclusively that the witnesses brought against Him did not agree. The Holy Spirit continues to hold Him up as the perfect Servant, in whose character and service not a flaw could be detected. But He witnesses the good confession and upon that blessed Word of Truth as it came from His lips He is condemned. Then they condemned Him to death and man's vile hatred energized by Satan cast itself upon the Blessed One.

Verses 66-72. The Lord had given the true testimony and Peter followed with his shameful denial. Mark gives what the other two evangelists omit, the cock crowing twice. The lessons from Peter's fall are simple. He had to pass through this terrible experience to become broken down and learn to know his own weakness. And how we all need to know that we are in ourselves good for nothing; "in my flesh there dwelleth no good thing."

CHAPTER 15

1. Before Pilate (15:1-5); Matthew 27:1-14; Luke 23:1-4: John 18:28-38
2. Barabbas released and the Servant condemned (15:6-15); Matthew 27:15-26; Luke 23:16-25; John 18:39-40
3. Crowned with thorns and mocked (15:16-21); Matthew 27:27-32; Luke 23:26-43; John 19:1-16

4. Crucified (15:23-32); Matthew 27:33-44; Luke 23:26-43; John 19:17-27
5. Obedient unto death, the death of the Cross (15:33-41); Matthew 27:45-56; Luke 23:44-49; John 19:28-37
6. The Burial (15:42-47); Matthew 27:57-61; Luke 23:50-56; John 19:38-42

Verses 1-5. The council had condemned Him to death and now the whole council delivered Him into the hands of the Gentiles. First the religious power had condemned the blessed Servant and the civil power had to do the same. It will be seen that Mark's account of our Lord's trial before Pilate is the briefest, while Matthew's is the longest. Again the Servant witnesses a good confession. But when accused by the chief priests His blessed lips were sealed. He stood there to witness and not to defend Himself. What a gracious example He gives to all His servants. The hatred of the religious leaders of the people is especially emphasized by Mark. (For the complete exposition of this trial before Pilate see *Exposition of Matthew.*)

Verses 6-15. The story of Barabbas and his release is full of helpful instruction. "So true it was that, even in this last scene, Jesus delivers others at His own cost and in every sense. He had just before delivered the disciples from being taken; He is now the means of delivering Barabbas, wicked as he was. He never saved Himself. It was the very perfection of the moral glory of Christ to deliver, bless, save, and in all at the expense of Himself."[3] Barabbas was released, though guilty and condemned, because the Lord Jesus took his place. Christ was his substitute. Barabbas released might have gone out and looked up to Him, who hung on the cross and said, "He died for me; He paid my penalty." It is a blessed illustration of the atonement. They ask for the murderer Barabbas and demand the horrible death by crucifixion for God's perfect Servant and their King. The chief priests had moved the people to make this final choice. See the interesting additions in Matthew's Gospel on account of its Jewish-dispensational character.

Verses 16-21. Oh! the heart piercing scenes of this section of our Gospel! They led Him away to heap the greatest indignities upon the Holy One. That is man's answer to that service of love and power He so unceasingly had rendered. After the cruel scourging they clothed Him with a purple robe in mockery. Matthew reports a scarlet cloak. This is not a discrepancy. "A scarlet military robe was made to represent the imperial purple, hence the designation, a purple robe. And because this is the symbolic import of the robe, there is no discrepancy" (Lange). The scarlet cloak was used to represent in mockery the imperial purple robe. The crown of thorns was made to inflict cruel pain upon His brow. Thorns came on account of man's sin; they are the signs of the curse. He took the curse upon His own head. Mark tells us most definitely who Simon the Cyrenian was, who was compelled to bear His cross, the father of Alexander and Rufus. (See Romans 16:13.) God did not forget this service; Simon's sons became believers.

Verses 22-32. It is interesting to note here that Mark speaks of bringing Him to Golgotha. The word translated "bring" really means "bear" (translated thus in Mark 2:3 and Luke 23:26). "And they bear Him unto the place Golgotha." They had to hold Him up. The blessed Servant had spent His strength. What appearance He must have presented after all the scourging and cruel indignities! His face from the awful blows was marred. No wonder that His real human body was weak. But could He succumb? Never. No one could take His life. It could not be touched by man or Satan; death (the result of sin) had no claim on Him. He *gave* His life for a ransom. Mark also reports exclusively that the wine they offered Him was mingled with myrrh. This was considered an anodyne, to relieve and deaden the pain. The Servant who had come to spend all He had and to give Himself did not need it, but refused the concoction. Mark gives the hour of crucifixion as "the third hour." In John's Gospel (19:14) the sixth hour is mentioned when Pilate said, "Behold your King." The critics triumphantly point to this as a discrepancy. But John gives the Roman way of reckoning the civil day and Mark adheres to the Jewish timekeeping.

The superscription on the cross is the briefest in Mark. He gives the substance of the accusation and not the full wording of it. The perfect Servant who had so fully glorified God and given Himself in all His service, hangs between the two thieves, who had robbed God and man. How true it was (though they knew it not), "He saved others; Himself He cannot save." He did not save Himself for He came to die. He was obedient unto death.

Verses 33-41. What hours those were! What heart can penetrate its deep mysteries or fathom the depth of the sufferings of the Lamb of God,

---

[3] *Gospel of Mark,* W. Kelly.

when He was obedient unto death, the death of the Cross! Nature bears witness to it by the supernatural darkness, for the One who created all things suffers for the creature's sin. And what a scene in heaven, when God's own hand rested upon that One! Worship, praise and adoration is here more in order than an attempt of explanation. He was forsaken of God; and then He paid our penalty and stood in our stead in the presence of a holy God. Never say He was forsaken by His Father. Read John 16:32. The Servant's cry with a loud voice shows that no one took His life, but that He gave "Himself." And there was the rent veil from top to bottom (rent by God's own hand). Then came the utterance of the centurion: a Gentile confessing Him as Son of God. And the women are mentioned, who had ministered unto Him. The men had fled, the feeble women were there. All service now after the great victory He won, must be in weakness, depending on Him alone.

Verses 42-47. Joseph of Arimathea, like Nicodemus, identified himself with Him, who had died on a cross and confessed Him boldly by this action. In Pilate's astonishment that He had died so soon we have additional evidence that the Servant "gave His life." Death by crucifixion, perhaps so often witnessed by the centurion, is a lingering death. They would have given Him the grave of the wicked, but God had predicted it otherwise. (Isaiah 53:9 reads, "they appointed His grave with the wicked, but with the rich He was when He had died.") The tomb was one in which no other dead had ever been. "The one born of a virgin-womb could only be fittingly honored in a virgin tomb. He who could not see corruption, could not lie in a tomb which corruption had defiled."

V. The Servant Highly Exalted. Risen and Ascended; His Commission To His Servants and Working With Them (16)

CHAPTER 16

1. The resurrection and His manifestation (16:1-13); Matthew 28:1-8; Luke 24:1-35; John 20:1-18
2. The commission (16:9-18); Luke 24:36-49; John 20:19-29
3. The ascension (16:19-20); Luke 24:50-53

Verses 1-8. Again we notice the brevity of Mark's account of the resurrection of the Lord. The resurrection of Him who saved and toiled so patiently, who was cast out of His own city and suffered and died on the cross, was the fullest vindication of His person. A still greater vindication lies in the future, when He returns in power and glory. By His resurrection He was declared the Son of God (Romans 1:4). Had He not risen in the same body He had taken on in incarnation, His death on the cross would have no more power for redemption than the death of any other human being (1 Cor. 15:12-20). His resurrection is also the completest proof that His work on the cross is accepted by God. The women last mentioned at the cross are the first at the tomb. In the first eight verses the Lord Himself is not mentioned as being seen. The stone rolled away, the empty tomb and the angel's words declare that He is risen indeed. In Mark, Peter is specially mentioned, "but go your way, tell His disciples and Peter." Peter's denial is descibed by Mark in the fullest way. How fitting that he should record the divinely sent message to Peter. What comfort and peace it must have brought to sorrowing Peter.

Higher criticism declares that the proper ending of the Gospel of Mark is verse 8. They disputed the genuineness of verses 9-20. Another hand, they claim, added later these verses. That spurious translation, which goes under the name of *The Twentieth Century New Testament* (wholly unsatisfactory) also gives this portion as "a late appendix." It is not. Mark wrote it and some of the best scholars have declared that it is genuine. How foolish to assume that the blessed document, which begins with the sublime statement "The gospel of Jesus Christ, the Son of God" could end with "they were afraid!" The trouble with these critics is that they approach the Word of God with doubt and reject its inspiration.

Verses 9-18. To her who came to the tomb very early in the morning He appeared first. Mary Magdalen had been under the control of demons in a most awful way. She is there as a trophy of His power over Satan; as the mighty victor over Satan He appeared first to her. Knowing Him and His power as well as the Risen One, He sends her forth with the glad message. This is fully given in the Gospel of John. The disciples did not believe. Then He appeared to the disciples on the way to Emmaus so fully reported in Luke. Even then they did not believe their testimony. He appeared unto the eleven as they were at meat and at that time He gave them the commission. But before He upbraided them with their unbelief. How it must have humbled them. And such weak, unbelieving, doubting men the perfect Servant sent forth to preach the gospel to every creature. The commission differs in many ways from that given in the Kingdom Gospel of Matthew. In Mark the kingdom is not in view, the Servant has served, He has given His life for a ransom and upon that the good news goes forth. The message is to be believed and faith confessed. He that believeth not shall be damned. Signs were to follow them (but not all) that believe and signs did follow. Signs were never universal, not even in the days of the apostles. The Lord's own sovereign will is over this.

Verses 19-20. The Gospel of Matthew makes no record of the ascension. If we had only Matthew we would think the Lord still on the earth even as some day He will be earth's glorious King. The Holy Spirit gives through Mark a brief word on the return of the Servant-Son to the glory from where He had come. The Servant who had stooped so low is lifted so high. There at the right hand of God He has taken His place—the Man in glory. The work is finished. But the word "work" appears once more in this Gospel. "And they went forth and preached everywhere, the Lord working with them, and confirming the Word with signs following." Nowhere else in the Gospels is the statement given that the risen One works with His servants. How fitting that the Holy Spirit put it at the close of the Gospel of the Servant. He came from God to take the Servant's place; He served on earth; He sacrificed Himself for our sins, and now as His servants go forth to serve in His name He still works with them. What joy it ought to be for all who love and adore Him to be obedient to such a Lord, who was such a Servant on earth and whose delight is still to serve.

MARK, THE WRITER OF THIS GOSPEL

Were we to give even the gist of theories on the Gospel of Mark and how it was written, we would have to fill many pages. That is needless and even unprofitable. The chosen instrument to write this Gospel in which the Lord Jesus Christ is so beautifully pictured as the Servant of God on earth, was not an Apostle, but himself a servant. We find his name mentioned for the first time in Acts 12:12-15. His full name was John Mark and his mother's name Mary. In Acts 13:5, 13 he is called by the first name John, while in 15:39 we read of him as Mark. He accompanied Barnabas and Paul on their first missionary journey as a helper. We read nowhere that he addressed a single gathering. When they reached Perga he left the apostles and returned to Jerusalem (Acts 13:13). The reason of this abrupt departure was failure on Mark's side. He did not want to work and had become unprofitable (Acts 15:28, compare with 2 Tim. 4:11). On account of his failure Paul and Barnabas had a falling out and separated from each other. Paul refused him as a companion on the second journey, but Barnabas wanted to take him again (Acts 15:37-40). He went with Barnabas to Cyprus (Acts 15:39). The Holy Spirit has nothing to report of this journey. A period of unprofitableness followed for John Mark till he was restored to service. That such was the case we learn from Col. 4:10; Phile. 24; 2 Tim. 4:11. He had become Paul's fellow laborer. This personal history of John Mark is of blessed encouragement. He who had such a humble place as a servant of the two mighty men of God and who even failed in that, when restored became the divinely chosen and inspired instrument to pen the perfect Servant's path down here. Have we failed as servants? Let us go and tell Him all about it. He will have better service for us.

Tradition linked him with Peter and makes him a Bishop in Alexandria. There is no truth in it. All we know is that he was led to Christ by the Apostle Peter and was with him in Babylon (1 Peter 5:13).

THE CHARACTERISTIC FEATURES OF MARK[4]

A careful study of the preceding analysis and comparison with the other Gospel records will bring out the characteristic features of this Gospel. Many events recorded in Matthew, Luke and John are omitted in Mark because they have no bearing upon the Servant's work. We find not a word about a genealogy, nor is there any reference to Bethlehem, David's city. The Lord is called but once the Son of David in Mark's Gospel. Nor do we find a word about His childhood spent in Nazareth and the details of His temptations in the wilderness. The Sermon on the Mount so fully reported in Matthew is altogether omitted, because He spoke it as the King, proclaiming the principles of the kingdom. Many of the parables are omitted by

---

[4]We can heartily recommend *The Gospel of Mark* by W. Kelly. The excellent notes and hints by the editor of this volume, Mr. Whitefield, make the book still more valuable. Also A. Jukes on the four Gospels. We acknowledge our indebtedness to both.

Mark, for instance, five of those which appear in Matthew 13; also a number of others found in Matthew, notably those of Matthew 25, and the description of the judgment of the nations, when He comes again. The lengthy woes pronounced upon the religious leaders of the nation (Matt. 23) are likewise nearly all absent. All these omissions are the evidences of the verbal inspiration of this Gospel and if closely studied will show the divine wisdom. The word "Lord" as applying to Him is carefully omitted by Mark. Textual investigation has shown that "Lord" in Mark 9:24 does not belong there. But in the resurrection chapter He is called "Lord." In a number of psasages in the analysis attention has been called to additions, sentences, verses and sections not found in other Gospels. Many have not been mentioned, but the most prominent are pointed out. These additions reveal the quality of His service and give us descriptions of His moral glory. We ask our readers to look up once more the following passages and compare them with the Gospel of Matthew. Chapters 1:13, 1:31, compare Luke 4:39; 3:5 comp. Matt. 12:13; 3:34 comp. Matt. 12:47 and Luke 8:21; 4:33; 6:31 comp. Matt. 14:15; 4:36; 8:33 comp. Matt. 16:23; 9:36 comp. Matt. 18:2; 8:23; 8:33; 9:27 comp. with Matt. 17:18; 10:16 comp. Matt. 19:13, 15; 10:21, 23 comp. Matt. 19:21-23; 16:7 comp. Matt. 28:7, etc.

The parable in chapter 4:26-27 is found only in Mark. Then there are two miracles which are exclusively reported by Mark. They are characteristic of true ministry. These are the deaf man in 7:32-37 and the blind man at Bethsaida, 8:22-26.

The characteristic word of the Gospel of Mark is the word "straightway." The Greek word "ευθέωϛ" has also been translated "forthwith" and "immediately." It occurs some 40 times in this little Gospel and is the Servant's word.

"But enough. Blessed be God that such service has been seen on earth; that there has been such a hand, such an eye, and such a heart here, among the sons of men. And blessed be God, that by the same Spirit He waits to mold us to His pattern, yea, that He has predestinated us to be conformed to the image of His beloved Son. And if the Head was content to serve thus—if, while He tarried here, He lived to meet the need of all who sought succour—if, now risen, He is yet the same, still the loving Worker, interceding within the veil, and working here too for us—if He shall yet serve us, 'for the less is blessed of the greater,' when in the coming kingdom He shall still lead His flock to living fountains, and wipe away their tears—shall not we whom He has purchased, in whom He seeks to dwell, who are His witnesses in a world which knows Him not, wait upon Him until His mantle fall on us, and His Spirit, 'the oil which was upon the Head,' run down even to us also; till we catch the mind of heaven, and are made like unto the angels, children of God and children of resurrection, called to stand in the presence of God, and yet to serve, as ministering spirits to them who shall be heirs of salvation? God is serving,—'the Father worketh,'—Oh! what works of love, from the rain and fruitful seasons up to the mighty work of raising man from earth to highest heaven; and Christ has served and is serving; and the Holy Ghost is serving, taking of the things of Christ, to reveal them to us, and then to work them in us; and angels are serving, and saints are serving, and the Church proclaims her call, that she too because redeemed must be a servant here, and that her rulers are but servants, yea, servants of servants; and heaven is serving earth, and earth the creatures on it. So let us, after our Pattern, being redeemed, go forth to serve also. 'Blessed are those servants whom the Lord when He cometh shall find so doing. Verily, He shall gird Himself, and make them sit down to meat, and He will come forth and serve them.' O Lord, Thou canst perform it; perform it to Thy praise; Oh! shew us the glory of Thy service, full of grace and truth, that in its presence we may be changed; and as we have borne the image of the earthly, may even here bear to Thy glory the image of the heavenly. Amen" (A. Jukes).

THE GOSPEL OF
LUKE

The Gospel of Luke is the third of the so-called synoptics. The word synoptic means "seeing the whole together or at a glance." Matthew, Mark and Luke are called the synoptic Gospels, because they present a common narrative, relate the same incidents of our Lord, with much the same words, though characteristic differences, omissions, and additions are equally apparent. Various theories have been advanced to explain the similarity and differences, so often called discrepancies, of these three Gospels. One is the theory that originally there existed a primitive Gospel, which has been lost. Out of this primitive Gospel, it is claimed, the three Gospels were constructed. Another theory is that they grew out of one another; that one wrote first and the others followed to add to it and omit what they thought best to omit. It is beyond the scope of our Bible study work to take up these attempted explanations of how the Gospels came into existence. Nor can we follow in detail the intensely interesting historical evidences, which so wonderfully demonstrate their authenticity. However, we desire to say that the last word in the controversy of the Gospels and their genuineness has been spoken. The attacks upon the historicity of the narrative, the denials which have been made, have been silenced, though infidelity cannot completely be silenced, at least not in the present age.

The well-known scholar, Dr. Phillip Schaff, made the statement, "The essential identity of the Christ of the synoptics is now universally conceded." This is true. But the differences, the divergencies in numerous things of the story of the Synoptic Gospels reveal, how are they to be explained? There can be but one answer. The three persons who have written were chosen by the Spirit of God to write the narrative in exactly the way in which they did. The characteristic differences of their work is not man-made, but God-breathed. They wrote independently of each other. They did not try to improve upon a record already in existence. The Holy Spirit guided the pen of each, so that we possess in these three Gospels the testimony of the Holy Spirit concerning the Lord Jesus in a threefold aspect. The proof of this will soon be found in the careful and prayerful study of the Gospels. The truth is not discovered by learning and research in linguistic or historical lines, but by earnest searching in the Word itself. The three Gospels make the humanity of the Lord Jesus prominent, but not to the exclusion of His deity. The full revelation of His deity is given in the fourth Gospel, the Gospel of John, but not excluding His true humanity. The Transfiguration is given by each of the synoptics, but it is not found in the fourth Gospel. There is no room for it in the Gospel of John. Of the characteristic features of the Gospel of John and the contrast with the synoptics, we have more to say in our introduction to that Gospel.

We have already seen that Matthew describes the Lord Jesus as the King and Mark pictures Him as the obedient servant, who came not to be ministered unto, but to minister and to give His life a ransom for many. The Gospel of Luke is the Gospel of His manhood; we behold Him in this Gospel as the Son of Man. It has often been pointed out that the early Church possessed these fundamental facts concerning the synoptic Gospels and the Gospel of John and that knowledge may be traced in an outward form through centuries. It was Irenaeus who, as far as we know, called first the attention to the fourfold appearances of the cherubim and the four Gospels. He declared that the four faces of the cherubim are images of the activity of the Son of God. The cherubim had the faces of the lion, the ox, the man, and the eagle. The application to the four Gospels of the four faces of the cherubim has been maintained for many centuries as the true application. Ancient manuscripts, illuminated missals, etc., bear witness to it. The lion, the kingly animal, represents Matthew's Gospel. Mark, the Gospel of the Servant, is represented by the ox, the burden-bearing animal. In Luke we see the face of a man and the eagle, sweeping the heavens coming from above and returning there, represents Him, who came from the Father and has gone back to the Father.

We turn now our attention to the Gospel of Luke, the Gospel of Manhood.

The Writer of the Third Gospel

The writer of the third Gospel does not mention his name, though he speaks of himself in the opening verses of the first chapter. The first verse in the book of Acts makes known that the same writer who wrote the book of Acts also wrote the third Gospel and that both mention the same person, who is addressed, that is, Theophilus. Furthermore, we learn from Acts 1:1, that the third Gospel had been written, when the writer of Acts began his work. Inasmuch as Luke is undoubtedly the writer of the book of Acts, he is also the penman of the third Gospel. "It has been generally and almost unanimously acknowledged that the Gospel, which we now possess is that written by Luke" (Dean Alford).

Luke did not belong, as some hold, to the seventy our Lord sent forth to minister. His own words answer this statement. (Read Luke 1:2.) The Epistles give us the only reliable information about his person. In Colossians 4:14 we read of him as "the beloved physician." In the Epistle to Philemon he is called a fellow laborer of the Apostle Paul. From Second Timothy we learn that he was in Rome when Paul was a prisoner and remained faithful to him when others forsook the Apostle. He had also joined the Apostle during his second missionary journey at Troas (Acts 16:10). The evidence of it is found in the little word "we." He went with Paul to Macedonia and remained some time in Philippi. In Colossians, chapter 4, we find also the fact brought out that he was a Gentile. First Paul mentions those of the circumcision (Col. 4:11). Then Epaphras, a Colossian Gentile, is mentioned, followed by the names of Luke and Demas, both undoubtedly Gentiles. He is therefore the only writer in the Bible who was a Gentile. The reason that he was selected to write the Gospel, which pictures the Lord Christ, as the perfect Man, and the book of Acts is more than interesting. The Gospel of Luke, a Gentile, addressed to a Gentile (Theophilus) is the Gospel for the Gentiles. And the same Gentile instrument was chosen to relate the history of the Gospel going forth from Jerusalem to the Gentiles. Other critical questions, such as the time it was written, where it was written, etc., we are obliged to pass by.

The Characteristic Features of the Gospel of Luke

We have seen from the study of Matthew that our Lord is seen in it as the King and in Mark as the Servant. The Gospel of Luke has even more characteristic features which bring out the great purpose of the last synoptic Gospel. The perfect Manhood of the Lord Jesus Christ, His moral perfections, His tender sympathies as the Saviour of man, are written here in a most precious way. The Priesthood the glorified Son of Man exercises now in behalf of His people, being touched with a feeling of our infirmities has for its foundation His true Manhood. "For every high priest taken from among men is appointed in behalf of men in things Godward, that he may offer both gifts and sacrifices for sins; Who can have compassion on the ignorant, and on them that are out of the way; since he himself also is compassed with infirmity" (Heb. 5:1-2). That He was the true and perfect Man, tempted in all points like as we are, apart from sin; holy, blameless, undefiled and separate from sinners, is fully seen in the Gospel of Luke.

A glance at the beginning of the Gospel of Luke reveals at once its object. Matthew's Gospel begins with a genealogy; the genealogy of the King and is followed by the account of the wise men coming to Jerusalem looking for the new born King of the Jews. Mark begins abruptly, one might say in a hurried way, as if the writer is anxious to introduce the untiring ministry of the perfect Servant at once. And so he does.

How different is the beginning of the third Gospel! It is perfectly human. A friend writes to a friend and when he begins to tell the story he starts also in a very human way, "There was in the days of Herod the King." The two opening chapters are peculiar to Luke. All is new. We do not find anywhere else the details of John's birth, Gabriel's visit to Mary and the announcement of the coming birth of Christ, and the beautiful outbursts of praise of the two women and Zacharias. The Gospel, which is to reveal "the face of a Man" had to give these blessed facts. The second chapter, containing the most beautiful description of the birth of our Lord; bringing out the facts that He entered the world, whose Creator He is, like every other son of man, born of a woman, no room in the inn, His first resting place a manger, known to Matthew, Mark and John, were omitted by them. Luke, chosen to describe the perfect Man, had to embody these blessed details in his narrative. The babe, the child growing, the twelve year old boy in the temple, His increase in wisdom and stature, in favour with God and man, all related in the second chapter of Luke show Him forth in His true humanity. The authenticity of these two chapters has often been doubted. There can be no valid reason for it; on the contrary their genuineness are as completely proven as the rest of the Gospel. Another beautiful feature of this Gospel is that Luke speaks more of the prayers of our Lord than the others. Prayer is the expression of human dependence upon God. Inasmuch as the Son of God had taken the Creator's place, He prayed and was cast upon God. Being baptized "and praying" heaven was opened (Luke 3:21). Before He called the twelve apostles He continued all night in prayer (6:12-13). "As He was praying" He asked the disciples, "whom say the people that I am," (9:18). According to Luke He was transfigured "as He was praying." He also said to Peter "I have prayed for thee." All this is peculiar to this Gospel and is needed to bring out His true humanity. When Luke speaks of Him more than the other evangelists, that "He sat down to eat meat" we have the picture of a true man among men. And what more do we find in the Gospel of the beloved physician, which brings out His tender human sympathy. The story of the raising up of the widow's son at Nain is alive with tenderness and sympathy. Then there are the parables peculiar to Luke. The parable of the lost coin, the prodigal son, the parable of the importunate friend, the unjust steward, the good Samaritan, the Pharisee and the Publican praying in the temple and others are reported only by Luke. In this Gospel only we have the record of the story of the rich man and Lazarus, their life on earth, their death and their state after death; the conversion of Zacchaeus; the dying thief and his salvation; the walk to Emmaus and other incidents. How fitting that Luke, the Gentile, should also tell us what the others were not commissioned to write in reporting the prophetic utterances of our Lord, that Jerusalem should be trodden down by the Gentiles, till the times of the Gentiles are fulfilled.

All these characteristic features and many others, such as the genealogy in chapter 3, His ministry as reported by Luke, the description of His suffering, His death, and His resurrection are pointed out in the annotations. May it please the Holy Spirit to give us through the study of this Gospel a new vision of Him who was rich and who became poor for our sakes, that we through His poverty might be rich.

Events and Principal Circumstances Reported Exclusively by Luke

It will be of much help to the student of the Gospels to possess a list of events and a number of circumstances, which are not reported by Matthew, Mark, and John, but only by Luke. These interesting peculiarities of the third Gospel shed much light upon the Gospel itself. We give the list of fifty-eight items.

	CHAP.	VER.
1. The vision of Zacharias and conception of Elisabeth	1	5—25
2. The salutation of the Virgin Mary		26—38
3. Mary's visit to Elisabeth		39—56
4. The birth of John the Baptist and hymn of Zacharias		57—80
5. The decree of Caesar Augustus	2	1—3
6. The birth of Christ at Bethlehem		4—7
7. The appearance of angels to the shepherds		8—20
8. The circumcision of Christ		21
9. The presentation of Christ in the temple		22—24
10. The account of Simeon and Anna		25—38
11. Christ found among the doctors		41—52
12. Date of beginning of John's ministry	3	1—2
13. Success of John's ministry		10—15
14. Genealogy of Mary		23—38
15. Christ preaching and rejected at Nazareth	4	15—30
16. Particulars in the call of Simon, James and John	5	1—10
17. Christ's discourse in the plain	6	17—49
18. Raising of the widow's son at Nain	7	11—17
19. Woman in Simon's house		36—50
20. Women who ministered to Christ	8	1—3
21. James and John desiring fire to come down	9	51—56
22. Mission of seventy disciples	10	1—16
23. Return of seventy disciples		17—24
24. Parable of the good Samaritan		25—37
25. Christ in the house of Martha and Mary		38—42
26. Parable of friend at midnight	11	5—8
27. Christ in a Pharisee's house		37—54
28. Discourse to an innumerable multitude	12	1—53
29. Murder of the Galileans	13	1—5
30. Parable of the barren fig tree		6—9
31. Case of the woman diseased 18 years		10—20
32. Question on the few that be saved		22—30
33. Reply to the Pharisees' warning about Herod		31—33
34. Case of a dropsical man	14	1—6

35.	Parable of the lowest room		7—14
36.	Parable of the great supper		15—24
37.	Difficulties of Christ's service		25—35
38.	Parable of the lost sheep and piece of money	15	1—10
39.	Parable of the prodigal son		11—22
40.	Parable of the unjust steward	16	1—18
41.	The rich man and Lazarus		19—31
42.	Instruction to disciples	17	1—10
43.	Healing of ten lepers		12—19
44.	Question and answer about the coming of God's kingdom		20—37
45.	Parable of the importunate widow.	18	1—8
46.	Parable of the Pharisee and Publican		9—14
47.	Calling of Zacchaeus	19	2—10
48.	Parable of the pounds		11—28
49.	Christ weeping over Jerusalem		41—44
50.	Special warning to Peter	22	31—32
51.	Direction to buy sword		35—38
52.	Appearance of an angel, and bloody sweat in garden		43—44
53.	Pilate sends Christ to Herod	23	6—16
54.	Women deplore Christ's sufferings		27—32
55.	The penitent thief		39—43
56.	The appearance of Christ to two disciples going to Emmaus	24	13—35
57.	Circumstances attending Christ's appearance to the eleven		37—49
58.	Christ's departure in the act of blessing		50—53

The Division of the Gospel of Luke

As already stated, the Gospel of Luke in its beginning gives the birth and childhood of our Lord; then reveals His perfect manhood, ministering, suffering and dying as the Saviour of men. The last chapter reveals the second Man in His resurrection glory and His ascension. All is cast in such a way as to bring out His true and perfect humanity. The best verse to quote as key for this Gospel is found in the nineteenth chapter: "For the Son of Man is come to seek and to save that which was lost" (19:10). Various divisions have been made. Seven great parts, however, are clearly marked.

I. **THE BIRTH AND CHILDHOOD** (1—2)

II. **THE BEGINNINGS OF HIS MINISTRY** (3—4:13)

III. **THE MINISTRY IN GALILEE** (4:14—9:50)

IV. **THE JOURNEY TO JERUSALEM** (9:51—19:27)

V. **IN JERUSALEM** (19:28—21:38)

VI. **HIS REJECTION, SUFFERING AND DEATH** (22—23)

VII. **HIS RESURRECTION AND ASCENSION** (24)

We give the different chapters with their contents in the analysis.

Analysis and Annotations

I. The Birth and Childhood (1—2)

CHAPTER 1

1. The introduction (1:1-4)
2. Zacharias and Elisabeth: the vision (1:5-12)
3. John the Baptist, his birth and ministry announced (1:13-17)
4. Zacharias' unbelief and punishment (1:18-26)
5. The angel's announcement to the Virgin Mary (1:27-33)
6. Mary's question and the answer (1:34-38)
7. Mary visits Elisabeth (1:39-45)
8. The Virgin Mary's hymn of praise (1:46-56)
9. The birth of John (1:57-66)
10. The prophetic song of Zacharias (1:67-88)

Verses 1-4. The third Gospel begins in a way that no other Gospel does. It begins in a very human and humble way corresponding beautifully with the purpose of the Gospel. Yet it is couched in the choicest language. "Not only is it written in most classical Greek, but it reminds us by its contents of the similar preambles of the most illustrious Greek historians, especially those of Herodotus and Thucydides" (Professor F. Godet). From the introduction we learn that Luke was not an eye-witness and minister of the Word; he did not belong to those who walked with the Lord during His earthly ministry. We do not know who the "many" were, who had written on the great things, which had taken place on earth and which all Christians believed. The remark has no reference to Matthew or Mark. Some have found in this simple introduction, in which Luke has nothing to say about a divine commission to write, an evidence that he did not write by inspiration. Others have pointed out the fact that the words "from the very first" mean literally "from above" (so rendered in John 3:3) and found in these words an evidence that Luke was inspired. This, however, is incorrect; Luke does not assert his own inspiration. The entire introduction rather shows the guidance of the Spirit of God.

It is a beautiful example of how naturally the Spirit of God works, or may work, in what we term inspiration. The instrument He uses is not like a mere pen in the hand of another. He is a man acting freely—for "where the Spirit of the Lord is there is liberty"—as if from his own heart and mind alone. He uses all the means he has got, and uses them diligently. You are quite prepared to find in his work the character of the writer: why should not He who has prepared the instrument, use it according to the quality of that which He has prepared? Why should He set aside the mind which He has furnished, any more than the affections of the heart which He has endowed? (*Numerical Bible*)

Verses 5-12. For about 400 years the Lord had sent no communication to His people Israel. The silence of heaven is at last broken. The ministering priest Zacharias beholds the angel Gabriel, the same wonderful being, who brought heaven's messages to Daniel. The names of the aged and pious couple are significant. Zacharias means "Jehovah remembers," and Elisabeth is translated "the oath of God." If we join them together we have the sentence "Jehovah remembers the oath of God." The time of remembrance had come. Prophecy is about to be fulfilled.

Verses 13-17. John's birth and ministry are announced. "John" means "favor of Jehovah." It fits in beautifully with the names of Zacharias and Elisabeth. "Jehovah remembers the oath of God" and the blessed result of the remembrance is "the favor of Jehovah." Gabriel (which means "God is mighty") announces that Zacharias' prayer had been heard and the answer was now given. The prayers of many years had not been forgotten. God's time for the answer had come. John is not Elias, but he came in the spirit and power of Elias. Malachi 4:5-6 is yet to see its fulfillment before the coming of the great and dreadful day of the Lord.

Verses 18-26. The announcement of the birth of a son was not believed by Zacharias. Like Abraham and Sarah he looked to earthly circumstances. He did not reckon with the power of God. Disbelieving the words of Gabriel he was struck dumb. He should have shouted praises; instead, he expressed his doubt. Unbelief insults God; the character of God demands judgment upon unbelief.

Verses 27-33. Next God's messenger is sent to Nazareth of Galilee to carry the greatest message, which was ever given to an angel. He appears in Nazareth and came in to the Virgin Mary. How simple and beautiful is the narrative! Here is the woman, the Virgin of prophecy, who is to bring forth the long promised Son. She is to conceive, bring forth a Son; His name is to be called Jesus; He shall be great and shall be called the Son of the Highest. Even so it came to pass. Then we have an unfulfilled part of the announcement. "The Lord God shall give unto Him the throne of His father David; and He shall reign over the house of Jacob forever; and of His kingdom there shall be no end." When He comes the second time, not in humiliation, but in power and great glory, He will receive the throne of His father David and the promised kingdom. "Let us beware of spiritualizing away the full meaning of these words. The house of Jacob does not mean 'all Christians.' The throne of David does not mean the office of a Saviour to Gentile believers. These words will yet receive a literal fulfillment, when the Lord Jesus comes a second time. The kingdom of which he speaks is the glorious kingdom of Daniel 7:27" (Bishop Ryle).

Verses 34-38. The Virgin's question "How shall this be, seeing that I know not a man?"—is not the result of unbelief. She believed, presupposing the absolute reality of the promise, in asking the exact manner of its fulfillment. The blessed mystery of the incarnation, how the Son of God should take on the human form and become man, is made known. It is a great mystery. "The Holy Spirit shall come upon thee" means that the human nature of our Lord was produced in the Virgin by a creative act of the Holy Spirit (Matt. 1:18-20). And therefore He possessed an absolutely holy nature. "And the Power of the Most High shall overshadow thee." This is not a repetition of the first statement. It means that the Son of God, who is the Most High, overshadowed the Virgin, uniting Himself with the miraculously prepared human nature. He is designated in His Being "that holy thing" because He cannot be classified. And because He *is* holy there could be nothing in Him, who was born of the Virgin, which is unholy. And beautiful is the submission of the Virgin to the will of God.

Verses 39-45. Mary then visited her cousin Elisabeth. How perfectly human is the whole account! And how beautiful the language of the elder woman calling the Virgin "the mother of my Lord." Surely this was a great revelation she received. With holy reverence we also should use that worthy Name. Well has it been said, "Let us remember the deep meaning of the words 'the Lord' and beware of using them lightly and carelessly." Then she blessed Mary. "Blessed is she that believed."

Verses 46-56. The marvellous outburst of praise which comes from Mary's lips is a beautiful echo of the Old Testament Scriptures. The pious Virgin knew the Word of God; her heart was filled with it and the Holy Spirit used the Word in the expression of her praise. Many Psalms are touched upon, but especially are we reminded of Hannah's inspired song (1 Sam. 2). Notice also Mary's deep humility and her acknowledgment of the need of a Saviour. The invention of Rome, of the sinless and immaculate person of Mary, is disproved by everything in the Word of God.

Verses 57-66. When John is born Zacharias' tongue is loosed. He is a type of Israel. Now that people is dumb; some future day when "the grace of Jehovah" is acknowledged by them, when they see and believe, the remnant of Israel will praise and bless God. No doubt Zacharias was also afflicted with deafness. The last written word of the Old Testament is a curse, Malachi 4:6, the first written word of the New Testament is "grace" (Bengel, "gnomen"; John: grace of Jehovah).

Verses 67-88. Zacharias prophesies. He praises God for the fulfillment of His promises spoken by the mouth of His holy prophets. The Lord of salvation is Messiah. It denotes strength and power. He brings deliverance, salvation from enemies and the promised covenant mercies (Ps. 132:17-18). He beholds the blessings of the promised kingdom and beholds the blessed results of the visit of the day spring from on high. The Septuagint (Greek translation of the Old Testament) translates the word branch with "day spring." Christ, the Branch, is also the day spring from on high. The fulfillment of Zacharias' prophecy takes place with the coming of the Lord.

CHAPTER 2

1. The birth of Christ at Bethlehem (2:1-7)
2. The glad tidings announced to shepherds (2:8-20)
3. The circumcision and presentation (2:21-24)
4. Simeon and his prophecy (2:25-35)
5. Anna the prophetess (2:36-38)
6. In Nazareth (2:39-40)
7. In the temple (2:41-51)
8. The increase (2:52)

Verses 1-7. The appointed time (Gal. 4:4) had come. According to prophecy the Saviour had to be born in Bethlehem (Micah 5:2). But Mary lived in Nazareth. God in His own marvellous way ordered everything and Caesar Augustus was directed to issue the decree of taxation at such a time and in such a way and also the journey of Joseph and his espoused wife, Mary, that she had to be in Bethlehem when the days were accomplished that she should be delivered. The great Roman Emperor knew nothing of what God was accomplishing by his decree. Then He was born, who left the glory of Heaven and became poor for our sakes. What condescension we behold here! The Maker of Heaven and Earth, born of a woman, taking the creature's place! The first resting place of Him, who came from the bosom of the Father is a manger! There was no room for Him in the inn.

Verses 8-20. Here not the birth of a King is announced as in Matthew, but the birth of a Saviour. The wise men from the east looking for the new-born King are not mentioned by Luke. Poor shepherds hear the glad tidings first. Heaven is opened. The glory of the Lord shines round about; angels' voices are heard, telling out in heavenly praise, what will be the ultimate result of the work of the Second Man. "Glory to God in the highest, peace on Earth, good will toward men." But the world rejected Him. Good will toward men sounds forth in the glad tidings, but "glory to God in the highest and peace on earth" is yet to come, when He, the Son of Man, appears again. The shepherds were obedient. They made haste. How simple their faith; how great their reward!

Verses 21-24. And now we find that He, who came of a woman also was made under the law. The circumcision made Him "debtor to do the whole law" which He alone could fulfill; and then to redeem those upon whom the curse of the law rests, by being made a curse for us (Gal. 3:13). The name announced before His birth is then given to the child (Matthew 1:21). Five other persons in the Bible were named before their birth: Isaac, Genesis 17:19; Ishmael, Genesis 16:11; Josiah, 1 Kings 13:2; Cyrus, Isaiah 44:28, and John the Baptist. As the first-born, according to His own law, He is presented unto the Lord. The required sacrifice is brought, in which is written the story of the cross. The sacrifice tells the story of poverty, for the sacrificial birds were only for the poor. "If she be not able to bring a lamb, then she shall bring two turtle doves, or two young pigeons" (Lev. 12:6).

Verses 25-35. Simeon had the divine revelation that he should not see death before he had seen the Lord's Anointed. He belonged to the faithful remnant of Israel, who in the dark days of decline and apostasy held fast the Word and waited for its promised fulfillment. The Lord had then a faithful remnant, who waited for His first coming; and His faithful people wait for the blessed hope, His coming again to receive them unto Himself. Simeon had the revelation that he should not see death, till He had come. This corresponds to the greater promises in 1 Cor. 15:51 and 1 Thess. 4:17. The Spirit led him into the temple at the right moment. His waiting ended when he held the child in his arms. It was a babe, like any other babe. Yet faith saw in Him what He is, the Lord's salvation for His people; He who had come to do the great work. "A light to lighten the Gentiles, and the glory of Thy people, Israel." This is prophetic. The Gentiles are put first. Even so it has come to pass; after the fulness of the Gentiles has come in all Israel will be saved. See Isaiah 49:5-6; Rom. 11:25-26. And Simeon, holding the babe in his arms, blest the mother and Joseph, not the child, for he knew He was the Blesser.

Verse 36. Then a daughter of Phanuel, Anna, appeared to add her testimony. What a beautiful woman she must have been in her self-denying service! No sooner had she seen the Lord than she spake at once of Him to all them that looked for redemption in Jerusalem. In the midst of the wicked city, soon to become a city of murderers (Is. 1:21), there was a company of men and women who looked for redemption.

Verses 39-40. They returned to Nazareth. The visit of the wise men, the flight into Egypt and the return are omitted. Twelve years passed and it did not please the Holy Spirit to give us a report of them. Spurious gospels of the infancy were circulated later; they are all legendary and unreliable. As the true Man He grew from infancy to boyhood. Of all the sinless conditions of the human body He was partaker. He grew both mentally and physically. His heart ever seeking God and being in subjection unto Him.

Verses 41-50. Every Jewish boy of twelve years visited Jerusalem at the time of the great festivals. He stayed behind and His anxious mother and Joseph found Him in the temple three days later. For three days He was lost to them. May this not be a reminder of the three days He was thought lost by His disciples? (24:21). Here the human infirmity of Mary comes to light. She was nervously anxious. Her words have an accusing tone. The greatest mistake she committed was the mentioning of Joseph as "Thy father." In all this her human failure is in evidence. But how sublime the answer of the twelve year old boy! He is astonished that they should have sought Him; He came to seek them. He is astonished that they did not know that He had to be about His Father's business. What an answer it is! These are His first words recorded in the Gospels. He corrects His fallible mother, who had said, "Thy father and I." His Father, He declares, is He in whose house He had gone. It is the first self-witness to His deity.

Verses 51-52. And He went down with them to Nazareth and was subject unto them. He was obedient in all things.

II. The Beginnings of His Ministry (3—4:13)

CHAPTER 3

1. The ministry of John the Baptist (3:1-14)
2. His testimony of Christ and his imprisonment (3:15-20)
3. The baptism of the Lord Jesus (3:21-22)
4. The genealogy of Mary, the Mother of our Lord (3:23-38)

Verses 1-14. Eighteen more years of silence follow. It is broken by the voice of the forerunner, John, who preached at Jordan the baptism of repentance for the remission of sins. He is not reported here preaching "the kingdom of heaven is at hand." He preached thus as the witness for the King and the kingdom about to come. Matthew had to give the report of this preaching. Here we read that "all flesh should see His salvation." This awaits still its great fulfillment when He comes the second time. John's call to repentance is answered by the people, by the publicans and by the soldiers. They asked "What shall we do?" How different, however, the question concerning salvation and the answer (Acts 16:30-31).

Verses 15-20. Then he gave witness concerning Christ. The expectation among the people was great and some thought that John might be the Messiah. The answer he gives directs the people to the Coming One. Verses 16 and 17 blend together the first and second Coming of Christ. The fire-baptism takes place when He comes again; it is the fire of judgment. His first coming has brought for all who believe in Him the baptism with the Holy Spirit.

Verses 21-22. We request the reader to turn

at this point to the remarks made in our annotations on Matthew and Mark. Luke omits, however, the conversation which took place between our Lord and John; then there is the additional information that our Lord was praying, when heaven opened and the Holy Spirit came upon Him. The descent into the water signified His death and as the result of His death, heaven was opened and the Holy Spirit came down. As He prayed in Jordan so He prayed in Gethsemane as He approached the cross. "Who in the days of His flesh, when He had offered up prayers and supplications with strong crying and tears unto Him that was able to save Him out of death and was heard in that He feared" (Heb. 5:7).

Verses 23-38. The age of our Lord, about thirty years, is only given by Luke. In the Gospel of Manhood this properly belongs. The annotations on the first chapter in Matthew should be carefully considered here and the two genealogies compared. The genealogy in Matthew is that of the King; Luke's genealogy is that of the Son of Man. Matthew's genealogy begins with David and Abraham and leads up to Joseph; Luke's genealogy begins with Joseph and leads up to Adam, the first man. It is a tracing backward to the head of the human race, Adam; and back of Adam is God Himself. So He who is God had come and became the Son of Man, the Second Man, the last Adam. The genealogy in Matthew is that of Joseph, a son of David, through the line of Solomon; Luke's genealogy is that of Mary, the mother of our Lord. who is also of David through the line of Nathan. Joseph is called in Luke's genealogy the son of Heli, because Mary was a daughter of Heli. Matthew's Gospel tells us that Jacob begat Joseph, the husband of Mary.

CHAPTER 4:1-13

1. The temptation in the wilderness (4:1-12)
2. The devil defeated (4:13)

Verses 1-13. What interests us most is the different order in which the three temptations of the Lord are reported by Luke. The second temptation the devil brings to bear upon Him (in the high mountain) is the last in the Gospel of Matthew. Why did Luke change the order and put the second temptation last and the last temptation into the second place? Matthew gives, no doubt, the correct order. The Lord's word to Satan, "Get thee behind Me, Satan," proves this. (These words must be omitted in the 8th verse. They are not found in the best manuscripts.) The order in Luke corresponds to the nature of man. Man is composed of body, soul and spirit. The first temptation concerns the body; the second the soul; and the third the spirit. The temptations man has to go through in life are clearly seen here. In youth it is the lust of the flesh; in manhood the lust of the eyes, to possess and to enjoy; in old age the pride of life. The change in the order is made to correspond to this. But "the holy thing," the holy Son of God, had nothing in Him which could ever respond to this trinity of evil. He did not sin, nor could He ever sin. The devil departed from Him for a season.

III. The Ministry in Galilee (4:14—9:50)

CHAPTER 4:14-44

1. In the synagogue of Nazareth (4:14-21)
2. Unbelief and rejection of Christ (4:22-32)
3. A demon cast out in Capernaum (4:33-37)
4. Peter's wife's mother healed, many healed (4:38-44)

Verses 14-21. And now the description of the ministry of the Son of Man begins. The beginning is in His own city. How all written here is again in a very human manner. He had been brought up in that city and as His custom was "He went into the synagogue," and as He had done, no doubt, before, He stood up to read and like a man finds the place in the scroll which the servant had handed Him. Isaiah 61:1-2 is read by Him and then applied to Himself. The Spirit of the Lord was indeed upon Him to preach the gospel to the poor. But He stopped in the middle of a sentence. The acceptable year of the Lord, is the last word He read. In His Person this had appeared. He came to preach the gospel, to heal the broken-hearted, to preach deliverance to the captives, recovering of sight to the blind and to set at liberty them that are bruised. He did not read "the day of vengeance of our God." That too is His work, but not as long as the acceptable year of the Lord lasts.

Verses 22-32. "Is not this Joseph's son?" It is the first hint of the coming rejection. Then when He declared that God's grace is not to be confined to Israel, but that it will, as in days of old, in the case of the widow of Sarepta and Naaman, go out to the Gentiles, they were filled with wrath. They were ready to kill Him. What happened? "But He, passing through the midst of them, went His way." Was it a miracle? Is it the same as when He passed through shut doors? It was the result of His own dignity as the perfect Man, which awed the crowds, so that no one dared to touch Him.

Verses 33-37. The same incident is reported in Mark 1:21-28. The demons knew Him but He had come to spoil the enemy and here He manifested His power.

Verses 38-44. Many works of power followed. As the seeker of the lost to preach the good tidings, He went from city to city.

CHAPTER 5

1. The miraculous draught of fishes (5:1-11)
2. The leper healed (5:12-16)
3. The paralytic healed (5:17-26)
4. The call of Matthew and the feast (5:27-29)
5. The scribes and Pharisees answered (5:30-35)
6. The parable of the garment and the bottle (5:36-39)

Verses 1-11. Two miraculous draughts of fishes are found in the Gospels. The one here at the beginning of His ministry; the other after His resurrection (John 21). Both demonstrate His power as Lord over the animal creation. Here the net broke (or began to break), in the other miracle it did not break. Peter is prominent in both. Here he falls at His feet crying out, "Depart from me, for I am a sinful man, O Lord." The divine presence, made known by the miracle, showed Peter his own condition. The Lord graciously calms his fear. The soul that sinks down at the blessed feet of the Lord and owns his sinfulness is safe. He came to seek and to save what is lost. And more than that. He calls into service. "Fear not, from henceforth thou shalt catch men." They left all and followed Him. It would have been strange if they had done anything else. The highest and best besides knowing the Lord as our Saviour is to follow Him and to be obedient to His call.

Verses 12-16. Luke describes the leper as being full of leprosy. The terrible disease had advanced so as to cover the entire body. Leprosy is the most awful, incurable disease. It is a living death and one of the best illustrations of sin and its ravages. He has the power, and He alone, to heal the leper, as He is the only One who can heal the spiritual leprosy. Then great multitudes came together to hear and to be healed. How men were attracted to Him and sought Him! But He went instead into the wilderness to pray. He felt the need as the perfect man to seek the Father's presence. He has given us an example. It is the pattern we should follow.

> Why is it that there is so much apparent religious working, and yet so little result in the positive conversions to God,—so many sermons, and so few souls saved,—so much machinery, and so little effect produced,—so much running hither and thither, and yet so few brought to Christ? Why is all this? The reply is short and simple. There is not enough private prayer. The cause of Christ does not need less working, but it does need among the workers more praying. Let us each examine ourselves, and amend our ways. The most successful workmen in the Lord's vineyard, are those who are like their Master, often and much upon their knees (Bishop Ryle).

Verses 17-26. The same miracle is reported by Matthew and Mark (Matthew 9:2-8; Mark 2:1-12). See annotations there.

Verses 27-29. The publican Levi is Matthew, the writer of the Gospel of Matthew. He was a taxgatherer and as such despised by his own brethren, because he was serving the hated Roman government. Taxgatherers and sinners the Son of Man came to call. Levi left all and followed him. That he became at once a witness for the Lord is seen by the feast he made and the large number of taxgatherers he had invited.

The concluding verses of this chapter we have already considered in the preceding Gospels.

CHAPTER 6

1. The Son of Man, the Lord of the Sabbath (6:1-5)
2. The man with the withered hand healed (6:6-11)
3. The twelve apostles chosen (6:12-19)
4. Blessing and woe (6:20-26)
5. Good for evil (6:27-31)
6. Instructions to disciples (6:32-38)
7. Warnings (6:39-45)

Verses 1-11. The opening verses of the chapter are nearly alike in the three Gospels. The arrangement in Matthew is different. It is used there to bring out the consummation of the rejection of the King (Matt. 12:1-8). Then He healed the man with the withered hand. The healing was done in their midst; it was a miracle done before their eyes. How different from the pretended healings of Christian Science and other cults. They were filled with madness and began their plotting.

Verses 12-19. Before He chose the twelve apostles He spent the whole night in prayer. It was "in those days," the days when they were rejecting Him. The refuge of the perfect Man was then in God. He sought His presence and cast Himself upon Him for guidance. The Gospel of Luke has much to say about the prayers of the Lord Jesus. His prayers are the expression of dependence of His perfect humanity. Among the twelve is Judas the traitor. He was called to be an apostle that the Scriptures might be fulfilled. The Lord knew him from the beginning. He was not a believer in the deity of our Lord; Judas never called Him, Lord. A very old commentary gives the following suggestion: "Judas is chosen that the Lord might have an enemy among His attendants, for that man is perfect who has no cause to shrink from observation of a wicked man, conversant with all his ways" (Anselim, 1033-1109 A.D.).

Verses 20-45. Certain parts of the Sermon on the Mount. In Matthew it occupies the most prominent place, for in the Gospel of the King it is the great proclamation He utters in the beginning of His ministry. (See the annotations on Matthew.) Luke reports only a part of the great discourse. A comparison will show that Luke gives a number of additions, which are all in line with the purpose of the Gospel. There is no allusion made as in the Gospel of Matthew to the law, nor is there given in Luke the expansion of the law. The instructions concerning alms and prayer are likewise omitted. In Luke's Gospel the words are reported which touch upon the wants of the disciples as men, who are in the world. Their separation from the world, their conduct, besides warnings are fully given. In Matthew we read, "Be ye therefore perfect as your Father in heaven is perfect." Luke changes by divine guidance the word perfect to "merciful." The correct rendering is "become ye merciful." The Son of Man came to this earth in mercy to meet man; the disciple is to manifest the same mercy. The word "perfect" given by Matthew is the larger description; it includes "mercifulness," which Luke is led by the Spirit of God to emphasize.

CHAPTER 7

1. The centurion's servant healed (7:1-10)
2. The widow's son raised from the dead (7:11-17)
3. John's questions and the answer (7:18-23)
4. The testimony concerning John (7:24-29)
5. The unreasonableness of unbelief (7:30-35)
6. The woman with the alabaster box (7:36-40)
7. The parable of the two debtors (7:41-50)

Verses 1-10. In Matthew the healing of the centurion's servant comes after the healing of the leper. It teaches there the dispensational lesson, that the Gentiles would enter the kingdom and the children of the kingdom would be cast out into the outer darkness. As Luke writes for another purpose he omits Matthew 8:11-12. Luke tells us that the centurion sent the Jewish elders first; when on the road to the centurion's house, the friends of the centurion with the message of unworthiness, met the Lord. Some have tried to explain these differences by making the two accounts, two different miracles. This is not the case at all. The account given by Matthew is more fully explained by Luke. The centurion first sent messengers to our Lord, and afterwards he came to speak to Him in person. Matthew relates the personal interview and Luke the message. "Speak the word only, and my servant shall be healed," is a marvellous utterance of faith. The centurion owned Him as Lord of all, with power over all. To him He is the Creator with omnipotent power. And the Lord marvelled at him. It is an evidence of His true humanity. Twice He marvelled; here at faith and in Mark 6:6 at unbelief.

Verses 11-17. The account of the raising of the widow's son is peculiar to Luke. The story brings out the deep compassion of the Son of Man and that is why it is exclusively reported in the third Gospel. The only son of a widow had died. Here is human sorrow in the fullest sense. A widow losing her only son, her only support. He had compassion on her. How human and filled with sympathy were His words "Weep not!" the word of His sympathy; "Arise" the word of His power. No wonder that the people declared, "God hath visited His people." Elijah raised the son of a widow, but he had to humble himself and had to cry to the Lord. Elisha also raised the son of the Shunamite, but only after having stretched himself over the child. But the Lord commands and death has to release its prey at the one word. The Second Man has power to deal with sin and death and man's need is fully met.

Verses 18-35. John, perplexed with doubt, sends to Him two of his disciples. "Honest doubt never stays away from Christ, but comes to Him for solution." The disciples beheld the miracles the Lord did at that time. Then when John had evidently made shipwreck of his witness bearing, the Lord bears witness to him. He declares the greatness of His person (verses 27-28). All this is recorded in Matthew 11:2-15; but Luke gives an interesting addition. Two classes of people stood there. The people who had heard John, accepted his message of repentance and who had been baptized. They and the taxgatherers justified God. The leaders of the nation rejected the counsels of God against them, they had testified to that by not being baptized by John.

Verses 36-50. The balance of this chapter is again peculiar to Luke. He is seen as the friend of sinners, who had come to seek and save that which is lost. Beautiful sight this woman so sinful, standing behind Him at His feet, weeping, so that she wet His feet with her tears! This incident must not be confounded with the similar one reported by Matthew, Mark and John; nor was the woman Mary Magdalene. She seeks shelter with her burdened soul at the feet of Him, whom the proud Pharisees called "a friend of publicans and sinners." How great must have been His compassion, how marvellous His lovingkindness, that a woman could come thus in His presence. The loveliness and attractiveness of the perfect Man as the friend of sinners is here fully seen. And the proud host, the Pharisee Simon, doubts that He is a prophet, for would He then not know what kind of woman she is! The Son of Man at once gives him the evidence of His omniscience. Not alone does He know who the woman is, but He also knows the unspoken thoughts of Simon. The parable the Lord gives to Simon explains the great love of the woman, much had been forgiven her. The consciousness of that forgiveness had produced these blessed actions of the woman. And once more she hears from the lips of the Friend of Sinners, what countless thousands have heard spoken to their hearts by His Spirit: "Thy faith hath saved thee; go in peace."

CHAPTER 8

1. The ministering company (8:1-3)
2. The parable of the sower (8:4-15)
3. The parable of the lighted candle (8:16-18)
4. The declaration of a new relationship (8:19-21)
5. The storm on the lake (8:22-25)
6. In the country of the Gadarenes and the maniac healed (8:26-36)
7. His rejection by the Gadarenes (8:37-40)
8. The woman with the issue of blood healed (8:41-48)
9. The daughter of Jairus raised (8:49-56)

Verses 1-3. This also is reported exclusively by Luke. What wonderful preaching it must have been when He with the apostles went about preaching! And the trophies of His power and grace were also with Him. Here we read that women ministered unto Him of their substance. What privilege was theirs to minister to Him!

Verses 4-18. The parables which follow are known to us from the Gospels of Matthew and Mark. The parable of the sower is here not in the dispensational setting in which it appears in Matthew (chapter 13). The parables of the mustard seed and the leaven are reported later by Luke. The parable of the sower is linked here with the preaching of the Word in verses 1-3.

Verses 19-56. The events which follow are also found in the synoptics. The storm on the lake shows His true humanity. He is asleep. But in the threatening danger, when the helpless vessel fills with water, He knows no fear. They have to wake Him. The wind and waves obey His Word. And blessed be His Name! He is still the same. Then there is the man in his fallen, pitiful condition, under the complete dominion of Satan, both in body and in soul. And once more the Son of Man shows His absolute power over Satan. The sufferer is completely healed. What a transformation took place! "The 'many devils' by whom he had been possessed were compelled to leave him. Nor is this all. Cast forth from their abode in the man's heart, we see these malignant spirits beseeching our Lord that He would 'not torment' them, or 'command them to go out into the deep,' and so confessing His supremacy over them. Mighty as they were, they plainly felt themselves in the presence of One mightier than themselves. Full of malice as they were, they could not even hurt the 'swine' of the Gadarenes until our Lord granted them permission."

CHAPTER 9:1-50

1. Christ sends forth the twelve apostles (9:1-6)
2. Herod perplexed (9:7-9)
3. The return of the apostles (9:10)
4. The feeding of the five thousand (9:11-17)
5. Peter's confession of Christ (9:18-21)
6. The Son of Man announces His death and resurrection (9:22)
7. Necessity of self-denial (9:23-26)
8. The Transfiguration (9:27-36)
9. The demon cast out (9:37-43)
10. The second prediction of His rejection (9:44-45)
11. Disciples rebuked (9:46-50)

Verses 1-9. The sending out of the twelve is briefly given by Luke. The full account is in

Matthew. All this shows the guidance of the Holy Spirit. Matthew writing concerning the King must needs give all the details of the sending out of the kingdom messengers. In the foreground is put here the power and authority which the Lord gave to the apostles over all demons and to cure all diseases. Did Judas also have this power? Assuredly, for he was an apostle. The authority and power was conferred upon them and not for any faith, virtue or merit on the apostle's side. They went forth preaching the gospel and healing everywhere. They are the messengers of the compassionate friend of sinners. Herod here fears Him and desires to see Him, who was greater than John, whom he had beheaded. Herod saw Him later. He had desired to see Him for a long time. At last He stood before Him bound, the willing sacrifice to be led away to the cross. Herod never heard a single word from His lips. Then the wicked King mocked (23:8).

Verses 10-26. The compassion and tenderness of the Lord is blessedly revealed throughout these verses. The apostles returned and He took them away for rest. The multitude followed Him "and He received them, and spake unto them of the kingdom of God, and healed them that had need of healing." The miracle of the feeding of the five thousand is reported in all the Gospels including John. He graciously supplied their need. Peter's confession is preceded by prayer. In Matthew we read the fuller confession, "Thou art the Christ, the Son of the living God." There also the Lord saith that it was revealed unto Peter by His Father. Luke alone tells us He prayed before. May we then not look upon the confession as an answer to the Lord's prayer?

Verses 27-50. In the transfiguration scene we see Him again in prayer. "And as He prayed the fashion of His countenance was altered, and His raiment was white and glistening." Luke tells us of the subject of the conversation between the Lord, Moses, and Elijah. They spoke of His decease, which He should accomplish in Jerusalem. He had announced for the first time His coming suffering and death (verse 22) and that death demanded by the Law (Moses) and predicted by the prophets (Elijah), which must needs be and precede His glory, is the great theme. Another statement is found in Luke, which is absent in Matthew and Mark. Moses and Elijah "appeared in glory"; not their own glory, but His glory. Luke also informs us that when they entered the overshadowing cloud, they feared. The Transfiguration is prophetic. Some day the Second Man, the last Adam, the head of the new creation, will appear in His glory, and all His saints will share that coming glory.

IV. The Journey to Jerusalem (9:51—19:27)

CHAPTER 9:51-62

1. His face set toward Jerusalem (9:51-52)
2. The rejected messengers and His rebuke (9:53-56)
3. Tests of discipleship (9:57-62)

The fifty-first verse marks a new part in this Gospel. The time was come; His hour was approaching. As the perfect Man we have seen Him. As babe, as child, as man in all His loveliness we have seen Him and now the compassionate, Loving One, He, who always pleased God in a perfect obedience "steadfastly set His face to go up to Jerusalem." Coming from Galilee the messengers entered into a village of the Samaritans, who would not receive Him because His face was set toward Jerusalem, the city the Samaritans hated. James and John asked the Lord to command fire to come down from heaven to consume them as Elias did. They believed the Lord had the power to do this. They had been with Him and had seen His deeds of love and kindness and yet they could make so strange a request. He then rebuked them. Later John went again into Samaria, but manifested a far different spirit (Acts 8).

CHAPTER 10

1. The seventy appointed (10:1-16)
2. The return of the seventy and the true rejoicing (10:17-20)
3. Jesus rejoiced in spirit (10:21-24)
4. The question of the lawyer (10:25-29)
5. The parable of the good Samaritan (10:30-37)
6. Martha and Mary (10:38-42)

Verses 1-24. Seventy others are commissioned by Him to be His heralds. They were to visit every city and place, which He would visit. How great and extended the labors of the Son of Man must have been. The gospel of the kingdom was then heralded as a witness. And He knew that the message would be rejected. The meek and lowly One, the friend of sinners pronounces as Judge the woes upon the cities, who had already rejected the message. When the messengers returned He said unto them, "I beheld Satan as lightning fall from heaven." According to Revelation 12, He is still occupying the heavens and the casting out of Satan is still future. The Lord beheld this complete downfall of Satan; the work the seventy had done was but a little anticipation of that which is yet to come. Then He rejoiced. Three times we read of Him that He wept, but only once that He rejoiced. He uttered concerning Himself a great declaration, which reveals His glory. "All things are delivered to Me of My Father: and no man knoweth who the Son is but the Father, and who the Father is but the Son, and he to whom the Son will reveal Him." Only He who is very God could utter such a declaration.

Verses 25-37. The lawyer's question leads to the utterance of the parable of the good Samaritan, to answer the question, "Who is my neighbour?" The parable answers the question fully, but it also contains the most blessed Gospel truths. Jerusalem is the city of God; Jericho represents the world. The traveller is the type of humanity. Man has fallen in the awful road which leads down, fallen among thieves, naked, wounded, helpless and hopeless. The failure of the priest and the scribe to help illustrates the inability of the law and the ordinances to save man out of his deplorable condition. The good Samaritan is the Lord Jesus Christ. He came to the place where the lost are and He alone could have compassion on him. The wine typifies His precious blood He shed to save us. The oil is the type of the Holy Spirit, who applies the blood. He takes care of fallen man found by Him. The inn is typical of the Church, where the Lord through His Spirit cares for His own. The two pence are not typical of "two sacraments" but speak of the reward, which those receive, who, under the Holy Spirit, care for souls. The promised coming again with a greater reward offered is the second coming of our Lord. The Gospel of the Manhood records this parable exclusively.

In *Verses 38-42* we find another incident reported exclusively by Luke. The story of Martha and Mary is closely linked with the preceding paragraph. Martha and Mary were both disciples. Martha was busy serving the Lord, while Mary took her place at His feet and let the Lord serve her. In this He delights.

> Martha has received Christ into her house, and surely into her heart. If she is busy, she is busy serving *Him;* yet that does not prevent her being distracted by it. She is more: she is vexed and irritated. Mary her sister is sitting quietly at the feet of Jesus, listening to His word; and she blames even the Lord for permitting it, while she needs her help so much. But the Lord asserts that Mary has chosen the good part, and it is moreover the only needful thing: it shall not be taken from her.
>
> But is learning of Jesus, then, the one needful thing? Is activity nothing? is service nothing? We may be sure the Lord is very far from meaning that. But if a man brings me, let us say, an apple, I do not despise it when I say, "The one thing is the tree that bears the apples" (*Numerical Bible*).

Twice more we find in the Gospels Mary at the feet of the Lord. When her brother Lazarus had died, she wept at His feet and He comforted her. When she anointed Him, Mary again was at His feet. She owned Him as Prophet (Luke 10); as Priest (John 11) and as King (John 12).

CHAPTER 11

1. The prayer given to the disciples (11:1-4)
2. The friend at midnight (11:5-10)
3. Encouragement to pray (11:11-13)
4. A demon cast out and the blasphemous accusation (11:14-23)
5. The return of the unclean spirit (11:24-26)
6. The blessedness of hearing the Word (11:27-28)
7. The sign of Jonas (11:29-32)
8. The single eye (11:33-36)
9. The Pharisees exposed and denounced (11:37-44)
10. The lawyers exposed and denounced (11:45-54)

Verses 1-13. Prayer is here more fully dealt with. We have learned how the perfect Man, the Son of God, who had taken the creature's place, made use of prayer. Again we see Him praying and when His disciples request Him to teach them to pray, He gives them the form of prayer, commonly known as "the Lord's Prayer." But the better name is "the Disciples' Prayer," for the Lord Jesus had no need to pray, "forgive us our sins." Many teach that this form of prayer was given twice, once in the Sermon on the Mount and the second time here. This is of course not impossible, but far from probable. If the prayer had been previously given, why should the request be made again? The ending which appears in Matthew, "For thine is the kingdom, etc.," is omitted here as it ought to be in the Gospel of Matthew, for it was undoubtedly added by someone else. The parable which follows is peculiar to Luke. The parable was spoken to encourage perseverance in prayer, to pray without ceasing, continue in prayer, to always pray and not faint, which are all exhortations to His people. The promise contained in the thirteenth verse was fulfilled when the Holy Spirit was given on the day of Pentecost. To plead this promise now is unscriptural. The Holy Spirit has been given; He has come and dwells in the believer.

The story of His rejection is followed much in the same way as in Matthew. Verses 24-26 are in Matthew's Gospel applied to the nation. The unclean spirit of idolatry had left them and is to return with seven others. But here the words of the Lord have a wider application, for He speaks of the state of a man. Outward reformation without true conversion and the reception of the nature from above, but brings Satan back with seven other spirits. Self-reformation cannot save.

The chapter closes with the judgments pronounced upon the Pharisees and lawyers (verses 37-54). He had entered the lawyers' house as his guest. When the Pharisee marvelled, that He had not washed His hands in the ceremonial way, as commanded by the traditional law, the Lord uttered these solemn woes. They remind us of Matthew 23, but a closer study reveals the fact that the words of judgment Luke reports here were uttered at another occasion entirely. The words in Matthew were uttered in Jerusalem, while the words in Luke were spoken when He was journeying toward Jerusalem.

CHAPTER 12

1. Warning against hyprocrisy (12:1-3)
2. Encouragements (12:4-14)
3. Warning against covetousness (12:15-21)
4. Warning against anxiety (12:22-31)
5. The disciples comfort and hope (12:32-40)
6. The parable of the steward (12:41-48)
7. The purpose of God and the resulting division (12:49-53)
8. Concerning signs (12:54-57)
9. The failure of Israel (12:58-59)

Verses 1-31. Nearly all of the entire twelfth chapter is not found in the other Gospels. Perhaps the largest multitude, which ever gathered to hear the Lord, is seen here. He speaks to His disciples first of all and warns of the leaven of the Pharisees. But the warning was also meant for all who heard Him. He declares a coming day, when the hidden things shall be uncovered. Then He gives encouragement to His friends, "Be not afraid." What meaning these words have, coming from such lips! The entire first half of the chapter is taken up with warnings and encouragements to those who heed the warnings and are His friends.

Verses 32-48. He speaks of His own coming again. The little flock is assured of the kingdom. Everything else is uncertain, insecure and passing away. He is coming again and His return will bring the reward to His friends, who are obedient to His Word. They are to wait for Him. "From the wedding" is better rendered by "because of the wedding." The wedding, the marriage-feast does not precede His return, but follows that event. "He shall gird Himself, and make them to sit down to meat, and will come forth and serve them." This is a wonderful statement. What service that will be, when He has His faithful people with Him! The Romans divided the night into four watches. The Lord speaks of the second and third watches, but does not mention the fourth. However in Matthew 14 we read that He came to His toiling servants in the fourth watch.

> He says nothing of the fourth, simply for the reason that the disciples, from that, should note that His return was by no means to be expected as late as possible; even as He does not name the first, because it would weaken the whole representation of the watchful servants. The Parousia does not come so quickly as impatience, nor yet so late as carelessness supposes, but in the very middle of the night, when the temptation to fall asleep is great and therefore must be most vigorously combated. It may even tarry longer than the servants think; but, grant that it should not take place even till the third, or should come even in the second watch of the night, whosoever perseveres faithfully at his post shall in no wise lose his reward (Van Oosterzee).

He assures them that He will come "at an hour when ye think not." The parable of the steward is closely linked with all this. A solemn declaration is made, found only in Luke, concerning the penalties (verses 47-48). The punishment is according to the knowledge of the Lord's will. His rejection by Israel has brought for the world the results of which He speaks next.

CHAPTER 13

1. The necessity of repentance (13:1-5)
2. The barren fig-tree (13:6-9)
3. The healing of a daughter of Abraham (13:10-17)
4. Parable of the mustard-seed (13:18-19)
5. Parable of the leaven (13:20-21)
6. Solemn teachings (13:22-30)
7. The answer to Herod (13:31-33)
8. Lament over Jerusalem (13:34-35)

Verses 1-9. Luke alone gives the parable of the fig tree as well as the historical incidents preceding the parable. The absolute necessity of repentance is emphasized by the Lord. The fig tree is the nation Israel; but the individual application must not be eliminated. When there is no repentance, after God's merciful patience, the delayed judgment will be executed. Israel illustrates this fully. The tree was hewn down, though the root remains. In Matthew we read of the budding fig tree, the sign that the summer is nigh.

Verses 10-17. The healing of the daughter of Abraham, whom Satan had bound for eighteen years, is reported only by Luke. Attention has been called to the significance of the number 18. Upon 18 fell the tower of Siloam and the woman, who was bound for 18 years. "The number 18, which is 3 x 6 (six the number of man) speaks of evil manifested in its highest uprise" (*Numerical Bible*). Satan had manifested his dreadful power over this daughter of Abraham but the Son of Man, who came to seek and to save that which is lost, has the power to deliver her. She was made straight and glorified God. The expression "daughter of Abraham" signifies that she was a believer. Satan was permitted to afflict her body; it was the same with Job. See also 1 Cor. 5:5.

Verses 18-21. The parables of the mustard seed and the leaven appear in Luke in an entirely different setting than in Matthew. We have already seen in our annotations of Matthew 13, what these two parables teach. Here in Luke they are evidently closely linked with the parable of the barren fig tree, showing that when Israel has failed and passed uner the national judgment, the kingdom of God, as resting in the hands of man, becomes like any other kingdom of the world, sheltering the unclean (fowls), and internally it is corrupted by leaven.

Solemn teachings follow in answer to the question "Lord, are there few to be saved?" The door is open, but narrow. And the door to salvation will one day be shut for those who refused to enter in. And here we find the words which were omitted by Luke in the account of the healing of the centurion's servant. The application to the Jews, who rejected Him, and the acceptance of the gospel by the Gentiles is self-evident. The person, whom our Lord calls "fox," most likely was Herod himself. The "today and to-morrow" refer to His great work in bearing testimony and working miracles; the third day, when He would be perfected, is the day of resurrection. Then follows His lament over Jerusalem. The consecutive teachings of this chapter, beginning with the necessity of repentance, Israel's failure, the demonstration of His power, His solemn words and finally His lament over Jerusalem are intensely interesting.

CHAPTER 14

1. The man with the dropsy healed on the Sabbath (14:1-6)
2. The wisdom of humility (14:7-11)
3. Recompensed in resurrection (14:12-14)
4. The parable of the great supper (14:15-24)
5. Conditions of discipleship (14:25-35)

Verses 1-6. Again He heals on the Sabbath. In the house of a ruler, a Pharisee, they were watching Him. He had gone there to eat bread. What condescension! They were His enemies, yet He loved them. He healed the man with dropsy. The question, "Is it lawful to heal on the Sabbath day?" was answered by the very power of God.

Verses 7-14. The parable which follows, also peculiar to Luke, emphasizes the wisdom of humility. The natural man with the pride of life as a governing principle loves self-exaltation. Abasement for him follows in judgment to come; but if man humbleth himself before God, exaltation will follow. He, the Son of Man, had humbled Himself and taken the lowest place. How great is His exaltation! Then He exhorts to seek recompense at the resurrection of the just. Here is a hint on the two resurrections, which are so clearly distinguished in Scripture. The first resurrection is the resurrection of the just and includes all the saints of God. In that resurrection there will be a reward according to works, but no sinner can work to make himself worthy of that resurrection.

Verses 15-24. The parable of the great supper is distinct from the similar one in Matthew 22:1-14. They were spoken at different occasions. The parable in Matthew has clearly marked dispensational aspects, such as the twofold offer to Israel, before and after the cross, the judgment upon Jerusalem and the calling of the Gentiles, etc. The primary object of the parable in Luke is also to show the unbelief of the Jews, especially the self-righteous Pharisees and the call of the publicans and harlots. God has mercifully provided the feast. The kingdom had come nigh. All things are now ready. The Son of God had come in their midst. But the parable also looks forward to the finished work of the cross. That work has made all things ready. The self-righteous among the Jews refused and brought their excuses. Then exactly that came to pass of which the Lord had spoken (verses 12-14). The publicans and harlots, the poor, maimed, blind and lame came. They could not have the excuses of the self-righteous of the nation. The call of the Gentiles is also seen in this parable: "Go out into the highways and hedges, and compel them to come in, that my house may be filled." The doom of the rejectors is seen in verse 24. The great multitude, which followed Him then hears from His lips the conditions of true discipleship. Let no one say, as it has been said, that they are not binding to-day.

CHAPTER 15

1. The murmuring Pharisees (15:1-2)
2. The parable of the lost sheep (15:3-7)
3. The parable of the lost coin (15:8-10)
4. The parable of the prodigal son and the elder brother (15:11-32)

Verses 1-10. A blessed climax of the teaching of our Lord as the Saviour and the friend of sinners is reached with this chapter, a chapter which the saints of God have always loved and will always love. Here we find the completest illustration of the key text of Luke "For the Son of Man is come to seek and to save that which is lost." The taxgatherers and sinners, after hearing His words and knowing the welcome which awaited them, drew near to Him in large numbers. The murmuring of the Pharisees and scribes and their words "This man receiveth sinners and eateth with them" is answered by the Lord with three parables. The parables of the lost sheep, of the lost coin and of the prodigal son belong together. The lost coin parable and the parable of the prodigal are peculiar to Luke. The Trinity is revealed in these parables seeking that which is lost. The Son is seen in the shepherd; the Holy Spirit in the parable of the lost coin and the Father in the parable of the prodigal.

In the study of these parables it must not be overlooked that the Lord answers in the first place the murmuring Pharisees. This however does not exclude the wider application on gospel lines. Bengel states that in the first parable the sinner is seen as stupid; in the second as totally ignorant of himself and in the third as the daring, wilful sinner. In the parable of the shepherd the ninety and nine do not represent the unfallen angels, nor, as it has been suggested, inhabitants of other worlds, but the self-righteous Pharisees, who think they need no repentance. The one sheep, lost and helpless, pictures the taxgatherers and sinners, who owned the lost condition. All must first be applied on this ground. The Son of Man had come to seek and to save. He looked for the lost; He followed them and sought them out at their tables; He ate and drank with them, so that He was called a wine-bibber. The found sheep He puts on His own shoulders; He would not leave this to a servant. The care of the saved sheep is all His own. And there is joy in heaven over one repenting sinner. It was a severe rebuke to the Pharisees, who did not rejoice when the taxgatherers and sinners came, but murmured. The second parable is of much interest and has been interpreted in various ways. We quote here the exposition as given in the *Numerical Bible* as the most satisfactory one.

> The second parable is that of the woman, in the Scripture the figure of the Church, the instrument of the Spirit. The lamp of the Word is in her hand, and she needs it in the darkness of the night, while Christ is absent. The 'house' is the circle of natural ties and relationships; for it is not just a question of public preaching, but of that testimony upon which the success of the preacher after all so much depends, and for which the whole Church, and not any class or section of it, is responsible. Good it is to realize that every soul of man, covered with the dust of sin as he may be, and hidden in the darkness of the world, belongs of right to the King's treasury, and has the King's image stamped on him, though with sore disfigurement. Claim him we may, wherever we may find him, for God to whom he belongs. This general evangelism, we may learn from the parable here, is what is the mind of the Spirit for the Church indwelt of Him. Here too there must be friends and neighbors summoned to rejoice,—angelic onlookers who are in sympathy with Him who is always the glorious Seeker, and who sets in motion all the springs of love and pity that flow anywhere in unison with His own.

In the parable of the prodigal son is brought out again the two classes of men before whom the Lord spoke these parables. The prodigal represents the publicans, the elder son the ritualistic Pharisees. The application in the gospel, which this parable so blessedly reveals, the condition of man as a sinner, the true repentance, the Father's joy, the welcome the returning one receives, etc., all is so well known that we need to make no further annotations. The elder son's character clearly shows that the Pharisee, self-righteous and self-sufficient, is completely in view. He has never transgressed a commandment and therefore considers himself above the poor, lost wanderer, who has returned home; he was angry. Thus the Pharisees were angry, when the Lord received the outcasts. It is strange that this parable should have been explained to mean that our Lord endorses worldly amusements and that a Christian may dance and make merry. There is no reason whatever that He has done so. The parable has, no doubt, a national meaning as well. The elder son represents the Jews and their unwillingness to see the Gentiles converted. The prodigal then is a picture of the degradation of the Gentiles.

CHAPTER 16

1. The unjust steward (16:1-12)
2. The impossible service (16:13)
3. The deriding Pharisees answered (16:14-17)
4. Concerning divorce (16:18)
5. The rich man and Lazarus (16:19-31)

Verses 1-12. Let us notice that this story was spoken to the disciples. It contains a number of difficulties. It has well been said "there are knots in it which perhaps will never be untied, until the Lord comes again. We might reaasonably expect that a book written by inspiration, as the Bible is, would contain things hard to be understood. The fault lies not in the Book, but in ourselves." The story of the unjust steward is used to teach wisdom in the use of earthly things. What the steward did was an unjust thing, but he acted wisely. "The lord commended the unjust steward because he had done wisely." Then our Lord makes the statement that "the children of this world are in their generation wiser than the children of light."

But what is the application? "And I say unto you, Make yourselves friends of the mammon of unrighteousness; that when it (not ye) fails, they may receive you into everlasting habitations." Pages could be filled with interpretations which have been given of this statement. Many of these have been made at the expense of the grace of God, which alone fits a sinner for glory. (Godet gives a novel interpretation: "May not the disciple who reaches heaven without having gained here below the degree of development which is the condition of full communion with God, receive the increase of spiritual life, which is yet wanting to him, by means of those grateful spirits with whom he shared his temporal goods here below?") Heaven cannot be bought by the rightful use of earthly things. Man as God's steward has failed and has wasted His goods. But the disciple is to use earthly things, the mammon of unrighteousness, to a wise and advantageous purpose. The Lord's word may be paraphrased in this wise: "Use the temporal things, the mammon of unrighteousness with an eye to the future, as the steward did his, so that it will be like friends you have made." "That they may receive you." is indefinite and must be regarded to signify rather "Ye may be received." We leave this difficult passage by quoting a valuable comment on it: "On the one hand let us beware of supposing that by any use of money we can purchase to ourselves God's favor and the pardon of our sins. Heaven is not to be bought. Any such interpretation of the verse is most unscriptural. On the other hand, let us beware of shutting our eyes against the doctrine which the verse unmistakably contains. That doctrine plainly is, that a right use of our money in this world, from right motives, will be for our benefit in the world to come. It will not justify us. It will not bear the severity of God's judgment, any more than other good works. But it shall be an evidence of our grace, which shall befriend our souls. There is such a thing as 'laying up treasure in heaven,' and 'laying up a good foundation against the time to come' (Matt. 6:20: 1 Tim. 6:19)" (Bishop Ryle). That the whole story has a meaning connected with the elder son the Pharisee in the preceding parable must not be overlooked. The Pharisees were avaricious. After the Lord had declared the impossible service, not alone then, but in all times, "Ye cannot serve God and mammon," the Pharisees, who heard all these things and who were covetous, derided him.

Verses 19-31. A solemn paragraph closes the chapter. Avoid the use of the word "parable" in connection with these verses. The Lord said, "There was a certain rich man." It is history and not a parable. The derision of the Pharisees on account of the Lord's words about the unjust steward must have been based upon their trust in the law and the promise of the law, that temporal blessings and riches were in store for all who keep the law. The story our Lord relates is aimed once more at the sneering, unbelieving, self-righteous Pharisees. The rich man had great riches. But his riches were not the evidences of divine favor and blessing. Lazarus, the poor man, had no earthly possessions. Was his poverty an evidence of divine displeasure? Then the Lord, the omniscient Lord, draws aside the veil and reveals what is hidden from the sight of man. Both die. Lazarus is carried by the angels into Abraham's bosom. He had no means to make friends for himself by using the mammon of unrighteousness, so as to be welcomed in the everlasting habitations. And yet he is there. God had in His infinite grace carried him so high. Lazarus' name means "God is Helper." The rich man also died and is in Hades (not in hell; the lake of fire opens after the judgment). He is in torment and sees Lazarus in Abraham's bosom. He hears that there is no relief, no hope. An impassable gulf is fixed, which separates *forever* the lost and the saved. Not a ray of hope is given by the Lord, that there is the slightest possibility after death for another chance. Death fixes forever the eternal condition of every human being. Whoever meddles with this solemn truth, whether a Russellite, or restorationist or whatever name he may bear, rejects the testimony of the Son of God and charges Him with not having spoken the truth. We cannot follow the solemn story in all its details. Future punishment of the wicked, the future conscious punishment of the wicked, the future conscious and *eternal* punishment of the wicked is denied and sneered at to-day by the majority of professing Christians. But the Lord Jesus, the friend of sinners, the One who came to seek and to save what is lost, teaches *beyond controversy* in this solemn story, the future, conscious and eternal punishment of the wicked.

Of late one hears much that the story is a parable, that the rich man typifies the Jew, his torment, their persecutions; the poor man is the Gentile. It is an invention. The story must be forced to mean this. The careful student will soon see how impossible such an application is. Nor is the view new. It was taught by many errorists of past generations.

CHAPTER 17

1. Concerning offences and forgiveness (17:1-4)
2. Increase of faith and lowly service (17:5-10)
3. The ten lepers (17:11-19)
4. Concerning the kingdom and His second coming (17:20-37)

Verses 1-19. The story of the ten lepers is only found in Luke. All were cleansed by the power of God and the nine obeyed the Word of the Lord and went to the priests (Leviticus 13—14). But the tenth did not go but instead turned back and glorified God with a loud voice and fell on his face at the feet of the Lord. He took the attitude of a worshipper; and he was a Samaritan. He turned his back upon the ceremonial law and owned the Giver of the blessing he had received. We have in this healed, worshipping Samaritan, who does not worship in the mountain of Samaria, nor in the temple in Jerusalem, an earnest of the new dispensation to come (John 4:22-24).

Verses 20-37. The question "when the kingdom of God should come" is answered by the statement "the kingdom of God is within you." The translation is faulty. The "within" means "among"; so that we read "the kingdom of God is among you." It had appeared in their midst in the Person of the King. Then He spoke of His second coming. He reminds them of the days of Noah and the days of Lot. His coming here is His visible coming at the end of the age and not His coming for His saints, which is a subsequent revelation (1 Thess. 4:13-18). Then one will be taken (in judgment as the people perished in Noah's and Lot's day) and the other left (on earth to be in the kingdom).

CHAPTER 18

1. The unjust judge and the avenging of His elect (18:1-8)
2. The parable of the Pharisee and the publican (18:9-14)
3. The little children and the required lowliness (18:15-17)
4. The rich young ruler (18:18-27)
5. Rewards promised (18:28-30)
6. The renewed prediction of His suffering, death and resurrection (18:31-34)
7. The blind man near Jericho healed (18:35-43)

Verses 1-8. The parable of the unjust judge is closely connected with the preceding announcement of His second coming. "When the Son of Man cometh, shall He find faith on the earth?" Apostasy and darkness will rule the day. But a faithful remnant of His people, His elect, will suffer and cry day and night to Him for help and deliverance. His coming will avenge them. The resources in those days will be prayer, as prayer is always the resource of the saints of God. In the Psalms the Spirit of God has recorded the prayers of the suffering Jewish saints during the great tribulation.

Verses 9-14. This parable also is found only in Luke. It is a continuation of the great subject of this Gospel, that the lost are saved and the self-righteous rejected. "Every one that exalteth himself shall be abased; and he that humbleth himself shall be exalted." The self-righteous Pharisee trusted in himself; pride and self-conceit are expressed in his prayer. He speaks of a negative goodness "not as other men" and then speaks of his good works, which are even more than God demanded in His law. God did not demand tithes of all possessions. The Publican did not lift his eyes to heaven. His prayer was more than asking for mercy. It means literally translated, "God be propitiated towards me, the sinner." He felt the need of a sacrifice. It is interesting to note that the Greek word "be merciful to" is found only once more in the New Testament. In Heb. 2:17 it is applied to our Lord "making reconciliation."

CHAPTER 19:1-27

1. The salvation of Zacchaeus (19:1-10)
2. The parable of the ten pounds (19:11-27)

Verses 1-10. When He drew near to Jericho the Lord healed the blind beggar. The reader will find hints on the meaning of this miracle in the annotations of the Gospel of Mark (10:46-52). The story of Zacchaeus is not found in the other synoptics. The Lord is now in Jericho. Zacchaeus (clean) was the chief taxgatherer and a rich man. "He sought to see Jesus"; his desire and faith overcame all hindrances which were in his way. The rich man climbing into a sycamore tree must have brought him ridicule. Little did he know that He, whom he sought, was seeking him. The Lord knew him and called him by name. And so Zacchaeus received Him joyfully into his house, while others murmured because He was to be a guest of a sinner. But Zacchaeus, though the chief publican, was an honest man. His confession shows that. He did not say what he intended to do, but what he had done already in his past life. It was not the result of having received the Lord in his house, but Zacchaeus answered by it the accusation of those who had murmured. He was a son of Abraham, yet destitute of salvation, which he knew not with all his honesty. But the Lord had brought now salvation to his house. Zacchaeus was lost but the Son of Man had found him.

Verses 11-27. The parable of the ten pounds was occasioned because they that heard Him thought the kingdom of God should immediately appear. He speaks of Himself in the parable as going to a far country to receive a kingdom and to return. In the interval His servants are to be faithful with the entrusted pounds. "Occupy till I come." The ten servants represent Christendom in the same way as the ten virgins. The one who had hidden the pound in the sweat cloth *(soudarion)* is called a wicked servant and represents a mere professing believer, an unsaved person. The citizens mentioned in the parable, who hated the nobleman are the Jews (verse 14). The parable teaches definitely that when the Lord returns He will reward His faithful servants for their faithfulness. May it be an incentive for us to occupy till He comes.

V. In Jerusalem (19:27—21:38)

CHAPTER 19:28-48

1. The triumphal entry in Jerusalem (19:28-40)
2. Weeping over Jerusalem (19:41-44)
3. The purification of the temple (19:45-48)

Verses 28-40. The triumphal entry of the Lord into Jerusalem has been before us already in Matthew and Mark. He is presented as King. Luke gives an interesting addition. The multitude of disciples rejoiced and praised God for all the mighty works they had seen. "Blessed be the King that cometh in the name of the Lord; peace in heaven and glory in the highest." The angelic announcement was "peace on earth"; here the disciples say "peace in heaven." Such will be the ultimate and glorious effect of the work of Christ, when Satan will be cast out of heaven, the heavenly inheritance redeemed (Ephes. 1:13), and the reconciliation of things in heaven (Col. 1:20) accomplished. All this and much more will surely come, when the King-Messiah comes again. Then there will be peace on earth, peace in heaven and glory in the highest.

Verses 41-48. What a scene it must have been when He saw the great city and wept over it! Before He utters the great prophecy announcing the doom of the city, He weeps. What a glimpse it gives of the loving heart of the Saviour-King, the friend of sinners! And all came as He announced. The second cleansing of the temple took place after that. See annotations on Mark 11:15-18.

CHAPTER 20

1. His authority demanded and His answer (20:1-8)
2. Parable of the wicked husbandmen (20:9-19)
3. Question about tribute to Caesar (20:20-26)
4. The question concerning resurrection (20:27-40)

5. The question Christ asked (20:41-44)
6. Beware of the scribes! (20:45-47)

The events in this chapter are found in both Matthew's and Mark's Gospels. The parable of the vineyard foretells His death. He is the son, the beloved son, whom the husbandman cast out of the vineyard and killed. The rejected stone, which becomes the head of the corner (Psalm 118:22) is likewise Christ. Verse 18 shows the judgment which came upon the Jews nationally. Rejecting Christ, stumbling and falling upon that stone they were broken. It also shows the future judgment which will strike the Gentile world-powers at the close of the times of the Gentiles, when the stone shall fall out of heaven and smite the image, which represents Gentile dominion (Daniel 2). Inasmuch as we have followed the different questions in Matthew and Mark, put to the Lord by the chief priests, scribes, Sadducees and Pharisees, to ensnare Him, no further annotations are needed here.

CHAPTER 21

1. The widow's mite (21:1-4)
2. The destruction of the temple predicted (21:5-6)
3. The disciple's question concerning the future (21:7)
4. Things to come (21:8-19)
5. The destruction of Jerusalem and the world-wide dispersion of Israel (21:20-24)
6. The return of the Lord with power and great glory (21:25-28)
7. The fig tree and warnings (21:29-38)

This entire chapter with the exception of the incident of the widow's mite is prophetic. Luke's account however differs in many ways from the account given of the prophetic Olivet discourse in Matthew and also that in Mark. Matthew gives the Olivet discourse in its completest form. (See Matthew 24 and 25.) He reports what the Lord had to say concerning the end of the age, the great tribulation, which concerns the Jewish believers living at that time; then in three parables He revealed the moral conditions existing in Christendom and how He will deal with them and finally He revealed, as reported by Matthew, the judgment of the Gentile nations. The characteristic feature of Luke's report is that he has little to say about the details of the end of the age, such as the great tribulation and what will take place during that period of time (Matthew 24:4-42). Instead of this he was led by the Spirit of God to record in the fullest way what our Lord had said concerning the fall of Jerusalem, the fate of Jerusalem, the dispersion of the nation and the duration of all this. The Lord announced that Jerusalem would be compassed by armies and that the days of vengeance would come (verses 20-23). There would then be great distress in the land and wrath upon this people. This great prophecy was fulfilled in the year 70 A.D., when the Romans besieged Jerusalem and a million perished, besides 100,000 who were made slaves. It is one of the most awful pages in human history. So has verse 24 been fulfilled. The Jewish nation has been scattered among all the nations; Jerusalem has been trodden down by the Gentiles and is still in that state. But the times of the Gentiles will be fulfilled in the future and when that comes, deliverance and restoration for Jerusalem and the nation are promised. Luke significantly tells us about the fig tree, "and all the trees" (verse 29). They are to shoot forth and that would be a sign of His return. The fig tree is Israel. Who are the other trees? Other nations, who are to see a revival before the Lord comes, such as the centers of the Roman empire, Italy, Greece and Egypt. Israel and these other nations indeed "shoot forth"; from this we are to learn that great events in connection with the kingdom of God are at hand. May we also heed the warnings with which this chapter closes.

VI. His Rejection, Suffering and Death (22—23)

CHAPTER 22

1. The betrayer (22:1-6)
2. Preparation for the Passover (22:7-13)
3. The last Passover (22:14-18)
4. The Lord's Supper instituted (22:19-20)
5. The betrayal announced (22:21-23)
6. Strife for honor and true greatness (22:24-27)
7. Rewards promised (22:28-30)
8. Peter and the disciples warned (22:31-38)
9. The agony in the garden (22:39-46)
10. The betrayal and the arrest (22:47-53)
11. Peter's denial (22:54-62)
12. The Son of Man buffeted and before the council (22:63-71)

And now we read the story of His rejection, suffering and death. What pen is able to describe it all! What mind can fathom it! We shall again confine ourselves to those things which are peculiar to Luke and not repeat annotations as given in Matthew and Mark. Notice the difference in the words of the institution of the

Lord's supper. Matthew and Mark have "My blood shed for many." In Luke we find the words "My body which is given for *you*"; "My blood which is shed for *you.*" His love shines out fully in these words. In Luke alone we have His loving request "this do in remembrance of Me." Oh! that His people for whom He shed His blood may never forget this beautiful word and remember Him in this simple way.

And Luke shows us the contrast between Himself and His disciples. He was about descending into the deepest depths of humiliation; sorrow and shame were before the willing victim, yea the greatest agony and death. Among them was strife, who of them should be accounted the greatest. This was the second instance of contention of pre-eminence recorded by Luke. (See 9:46.) Then He announced the denial of Peter. Verses 31-32 are peculiar to Luke. Satan was to sift him as wheat, but the Lord knew all about it and had prayed for him and therefore Peter could not succumb and be lost. And the Lord is the same to-day. He knows His own and prays for them before Satan can ever come near you with his temptations. The word "when thou art converted" does not mean that Peter was unconverted. It has the meaning "when thou hast returned back."

There is also a marked difference in the account Luke gives of Gethsemane from the accounts in Matthew and Mark. Luke tells us of an angel who strengthened Him. How could an angel strengthen Him, who is the Creator of the angels? He certainly could not strengthen His holy soul. That an angel strengthened Him must belong to His deep humiliation.

> But the body suffers, and presently the strain upon it is seen in the 'sweat, as it were great drops of blood,' that fall down upon the ground. Laborer for God and man as He is, His labor is a warfare also: the enemy is here, as He presently says to those who come to apprehend Him: 'This is your hour, and the power of darkness.' The seed of the woman is planting His heel upon the head of the old serpent, but His heel is bruised in doing this. In the weakness of perfect Manhood He suffers, and conquers by suffering (F. W. Grant).

Then follows the betrayal with a kiss, the arrest of the Son of Man, Peter's denial. Luke alone tells us that the Lord looked upon denying Peter; what look that must have been! The chapter ends with the cruel treatment of the Son of Man, the Friend of Sinners, who had come to seek and to save that which is lost, received from man, His glorious self-witness and unjust condemnation by the council.

CHAPTER 23

1. The Son of Man before Pilate and Herod (23:1-12)
2. Pilate yields to the people's will, Barabbas freed and the Son of Man condemned (23:13-26)
3. The crucifixion of the Son of Man (23:27-38)
4. The penitent thief (23:39-43)
5. The death of the Son of Man (23:44-46)
6. The testimony of the centurion (23:47-49)
7. The burial (23:50-56)

Verses 1-12. Before Pilate the Son of Man is accused as a perverter of the nation and as an enemy of the Roman government. They had attempted to ensnare Him with the question of the tribute money and failed so miserably in it. Their motive stands now uncovered. Pilate asks Him concerning His Kingship, which the Lord answered affirmatively. Thus He witnessed to two facts, His Sonship and His Kingship. Luke tells us what Matthew and Mark omit, that Pilate sent Him to Herod. The silence of the Son of Man standing before that wicked king is very solemn. Then He is mocked by Herod and his soldiers. Herod and Pilate became united in rejecting Christ. See how this fact is used in the first prayer meeting after the church had been formed (Acts 4:23-30).

Verses 13-38. The weakling Pilate is helpless. Their words prevail. "Away with this man!"; "Release unto us Barabbas!"—"Crucify Him! Crucify Him!" These are the cries now heard. Pilate then gave the awful sentence, that it should be done to Him as they required. The lamenting women and the Lord's answer are peculiar to Luke. "Weep not for me!" Blessed words of His great love. He looked for no sympathy from man. Frail women were moved to pity. He is the green tree; they were the dry wood. The people's wrath fanned by Satan's power was spending itself upon Him, the green and fruitful tree. How awful it would be when the dry wood, the unsaved masses, would be exposed to the fires of wrath and persecution. Forty years later the "dry wood" burned fiercely in the siege of Jerusalem. When they reach the place called "Calvary" (the skull), the Latin, Gentile name for Golgotha, they crucified Him. (Luke only gives the name "Calvary" because it is the Gentile Gospel.) Luke omits much which is more fully given in the other synoptics; we read nothing of the cry of the Forsaken One. But Luke tells us of the blessed prayer which Matthew and Mark omit, "Father, forgive them for they know not what they do." And His last word, "Father, into Thy hands I commit My Spirit," is also given exclusively by Luke. All this is in blessed keeping with the character of this Gospel.

Verses 39-56. The story of the dying thief and his salvation is also characteristic to Luke. The great lesson of the three crosses is so familiar that it needs no lengthy annotations. The two classes, the saved and the unsaved, are represented by the two thieves. He, the Lamb of God paying the penalty of sinners, is in the midst. The way the penitent was saved is the only way in which man can be saved. He could do no good works; he could not get baptized or perform anything else. All he could do was cast himself in faith as a lost sinner upon the Lord. Nor was his salvation a life-long, progressive work (as some teach on salvation); it was instantaneous. Nor was there any "purgatory" for him. He expected to be remembered in the kingdom to come. Instead of that he hears, "Verily I say unto thee, to-day thou shalt be with Me in paradise." The attempt by soul-sleepers, restorationists and others to put the comma after "to-day" is a deceptive invention to bring the Word of God into line with their evil doctrines.

> This short prayer contained a very large and long creed, the articles whereof are these. 1. He believed that the soul died not with the body of man; 2. That there is a world to come for rewarding the pious and penitent, and for punishing the impious and impenitent; 3. That Christ, though now under crucifying and killing tortures, yet had right to a kingdom; 4. That this kingdom was in a better world than the present evil world; 5. That Christ would not keep this kingdom all to Himself; 6. That He would bestow a part and portion hereof on those that are truly penitent; 7. That the key of this kingdom did hang at Christ's girdle, though He now hung dying on the cross; 8. That he does roll his whole soul for eternal salvation upon a dying Saviour" (Ness).

Then the Son of Man cried with a loud voice ere He dismissed His spirit and the centurion, in keeping with this Gospel, bears witness, that He was a righteous man.

VI. His Resurrection and Ascension (24)

CHAPTER 24

1. The resurrection (24:1-12)
2. The walk to Emmaus; the appearance of the risen Son of Man (24:13-35)
3. The appearance to the eleven (24:36-45)
4. The Commission (24:46-48)
5. The Ascension (24:49-53)

The account of the resurrection in Luke's Gospel has also its characteristic features. He alone reports the full account of the walk to Emmaus. It is a precious story showing forth the fact that the Risen One is the same tender, loving, sympathizing friend of His own. He joined Himself to the two disciples, who had left Jerusalem. Their hearts were filled with sadness and perplexity. He Himself drew near and their eyes were holden that they could not recognize Him. In a perfectly human way He joined Himself to them and asked them about their troubles. Then He reproved them for their unbelief and opened the Scriptures unto them. Constrained by them, He abides with them, as He always will with those who belong to Him. In the breaking of bread, their eyes were opened and they knew Him and He vanished from them. They returned to Jerusalem where they found abundant proof that the Lord is risen indeed. The appearance to Simon is not fully made known. What took place between the Lord and the disciple who failed Him is a blessed secret between them. He then appeared again with His gracious "Peace be unto you." He showed them His hands and feet. He had a body of flesh and bones. He was not a phantom, but a real man. His body was real for He ate fish and honeycomb. All this belongs properly to the Gospel of the Manhood. It is the fullest demonstration of His physical resurrection. All the wicked "isms," including Russellism and Christian Science, which deny His physical resurrection, stand here fully convicted.

It may be well to mention here the twelve distinct appearances of our Lord after His resurrection. He appeared:

1. To Mary Magdalene alone. Mark 16; John 20:14.
2. To the women returning from the sepulcher. Matt. 28:9, 10.
3. To Simon Peter alone. Luke 24:34.
4. To the two disciples going to Emmaus. Luke 24:13, etc.
5. To the apostles at Jerusalem, except Thomas who was absent. John 20:19.
6. To the apostles at Jerusalem, a second time, when Thomas was present. John 20:26, 29.
7. At the sea of Tiberias, when seven disciples were fishing. John 21:1.
8. To the eleven disciples, on a mountain in Galilee. Matt. 28:16.
9. To above five hundred brethren at once. 1 Cor. 15:6.

10. To James only. 1 Cor. 15:7.

11. To all the apostles on Mount Olivet at His ascension. Luke 24:51.

12. To Paul as an untimely birth. 1 Cor. 15:8-9.

Three times we are told that His disciples touched Him after He rose. Matt. 28:9; Luke 24:39; John 20:27. Twice we are told that He ate with them. Luke 24:42; John 21:12, 13.

The Gospel of Luke ends with the commission given to His disciples and the ascension of the Lord "while He blest them."

THE GOSPEL OF
JOHN

Introduction

The fourth Gospel has always been ascribed to the beloved disciple, the Apostle John. He was one of the sons of Zebedee. His mother Salome was especially devoted to the Lord. (See Luke 8:3; 23:55 and Mark 16:1.) He knew Him from the beginning of His ministry and had followed Him with much love and faithfulness, and seems to have been the most beloved of the Lord. He never mentions himself in the Gospel by name, but nevertheless speaks of himself, as the disciple whom Jesus loved (chapters 13:23; 19:26; 20:2; 21:7, 20, 24). With James and Peter he was singled out to witness the Transfiguration and to go with the Lord to the garden of Gethsemane. The three also were present when the Lord raised the daughter of Jairus from the dead (Mark 5:37). John was likewise an eye-witness of the sufferings of Christ (19:26,35).

The Johannine Authorship

The Johannine authorship of the fourth Gospel is proven by the testimony of the so-called church-fathers. Theophilus of Antioch, Tertullian, Clement of Alexandria, Hippolytus, Origen, Dionysius of Alexandria, Eusebius, and above all, Irenaeus, all speak of this Gospel as the work of the Apostle John. Other ancient authorities might be added. Of great value is the testimony of the two most pronounced enemies of Christianity, Porphyry and Julian. Both speak of the Gospel of John and neither one doubted that the Apostle John wrote this last Gospel. Had there been any evidence against the Johannine authorship we may rest assured that these two prominent adversaries would have made good use of it to reject the authenticity of the Gospel which emphasizes the absolute deity of Christ.

The most interesting and conclusive evidence for the Johannine authorship is furnished by Irenaeus and Polycarp. Polycarp had known the Apostle John personally and Irenaeus knew Polycarp. In a letter to his friend Florinus, Irenaeus wrote as follows:

> I can describe the very place in which the blessed Polycarp used to sit when he discoursed, and his goings out and his comings in, and his manner of life, and his personal appearance, and the discourse which he held before the people, and how he would describe his intercourse with John and with the rest who had seen the Lord, and about His miracles, and about His teaching, Polycarp as having received them from eye-witnesses of the life of the Word, would relate altogether in accordance with the Scriptures.

Now Irenaeus who had known Polycarp the friend and companion of the Apostle John, speaks of the Gospel of John as the work of the Apostle John; he treats the entire fourth Gospel as a well-known and long-used book in the church. He does not mention what authority he had for doing this. There was no need for it in his day, for everybody knew that this Gospel had been written by John. "When Irenaeus who had conversed with Polycarp, the friend of the Apostle John, quotes this Gospel as the work of the Apostle, we may fairly presume that he had assured himself of this by the testimony of one so well capable of informing him."[1] This strongest evidence for the Johannine authorship has been ably stated by R. W. Dale of Birmingham in the following words:—"Irenaeus had heard Polycarp describe his intercourse with John and the rest who had seen the Lord; this must have been long after John's death, perhaps as late as A.D. 145, or even A.D. 150, for Irenaeus lived into the third century. Was the fourth Gospel published before that time? Then Polycarp must have spoken of it; if John had not written it, Polycarp would have denied that it was genuine; and Irenaeus, who reverenced Polycarp, would never have received it. But if it was not published before that time, if it was unknown to John's friend and disciple forty or fifty years after John's death, then, again, it is incredible that Irenaeus should have received it.

"Polycarp's martydom was in the year A.D. 144 or A.D. 156. He had known John; and for more than fifty years after the death of John he was one of the trustees and guardians of John's

[1]Dean Alford, *Greek New Testament.*

memory. During a great part of that time he was the most conspicuous personage among the churches of Asia Minor. Nor did he stand alone. He lived to such an advanced age, that he probably survived all the men who had listened with him to John's teaching; but for thirty or forty years after John's death there must have been a large number of other persons who would have associated themelves with him in rejecting a Gospel which falsely claimed John's authority. While these persons lived, such a Gospel would have had no chance of reception; and for thirty years after their death, their personal friends, who had heard them speak of their intercourse with John, would have raised a great controversy if they had been asked to receive as John's a Gospel of which the men who had listened to John himself had never heard, and which contained a different account of our Lord from that which John had given. But within thirty years after the martydom of Polycarp our fourth Gospel was universally regarded by the church as having a place among the Christian Scriptures, and as the work of the Apostle John. The conclusion seems irresistible; John must have written it."

The Defeat of the Critics

The Johannine authorship of this Gospel was first doubted by an English clergyman by name of Evanson, who wrote on it in 1792. In 1820 Prof. Bretschneider followed in the history of the attack upon the authorship of this Gospel. Then came the Tübingen school, Strauss and Baur. Baur, the head of the Tübingen school gave the year 170 as the date when the Gospel of John was written; others put the date at 140; Keim, another critic, at 130; Renan between 116 and 138 A.D. But some of these rationalists were forced to modify their views. The Tübingen school was completely defeated and is now the dead thing of the past. We could fill many pages with the views and opinions of these critics and the answers, which able scholars who maintain the orthodox view, have given to them. This, we are sure, is not needed for true believers. The ripest and the best scholarship declares now that the fourth Gospel was written by John. Well said Neander, "this Gospel, if it be not the work of the Apostle John, is an insoluble enigma."

While the correct year in which the Gospel of John was written cannot be given, it seems quite evident that it was about the year 90 A.D.

The Purpose of the Gospel of John

Modern critics of this Gospel have opposed the genuineness of it on the ground of the radical diversity between the views of the Person of Christ and His teachings as presented in the Gospel of John and the Synoptics. Such a diversity certainly exists, but it is far from being an evidence against the genuineness of this Gospel. It is an argument for it.

The synoptic Gospels, Matthew, Mark and Luke, were already in existence for several decades and their contents known throughout the church. If an uninspired writer, some other one than John the Apostle, had undertaken to write another Gospel, such a writer would, in some way at least, have followed the story, which the synoptics so closely follow. But the Gospel of John is, as already stated, radically different from the three preceding Gospels, and yet no critic can deny that the Gospel of John reveals the same wonderful Person who is the theme of the other Gospel records. As we have seen Matthew wrote the Jewish Gospel, describing our Lord as the King; Mark makes Him known as the true Servant, and Luke pictures the Lord as the perfect Man. Thus the Synoptics emphasize His true humanity and show Him forth as the minister of the circumcision. The first two Gospels at least belong as much to the Old Testament as they belong to the New. True Christianity is not fully revealed in these Gospels. They move on Jewish ground. And what had taken place when finally the Holy Spirit moved the Apostle John to write his Gospel? The nation had completely rejected their Lord and King. The doom predicted by the Lord Jesus had fallen upon Jerusalem. The Roman army had burned the city and the temple. The Gentiles had come into the vineyard and the nation's dispersion among all the nations had begun. These facts are fully recognized by the Spirit of God in John's Gospel. This we find on the very threshold of this Gospel. "He came unto His own, and His own received Him not" (John 1:11). That Judaism was now a thing of the past is learned from the peculiar way in which the Passover is mentioned. "And the Passover, a feast of the Jews, was nigh" (6:4; also 2:13; 11:55). The Sabbath and the Feast of Tabernacles are spoken of in the same way (5:1; 7:2). Such statements, that the divinely given feasts were but "feasts of the Jews," are not found in the Synoptics. In John's Gospel these statements show that we are outside of Judaism. Hebrew names and titles are translated also and the Gentile meaning is given (Messiah, which is interpreted Christ. 1:41. Rabbi, which is to say, being interpreted, Master. 1:38. The place of a skull, which is called in Hebrew, Golgotha. 19:17, etc.). This is another evidence that Judaism is no longer in view.

But something else had happened since the three first Gospels had been written. The enemy had come in perverting the truth. Wicked apostates and anti-Christian teachers asserted themselves. They denied the Person of the Lord, His essential deity, the virgin birth, His finished work, His physical resurrection, in one word, "the doctrine of Christ." A flood of error swept over the Church.

(The Epistles of John, besides the early Christian literature, bear witness to this fact. See 1 John 2:18-23; 4:1-6. Men were scattering the anti-Christian doctrines everywhere so that the Spirit of God demanded the severest separation from such. "If there come any unto you, and bring not this doctrine, receive him not in your house, neither bid him God speed. For he that biddeth him God speed is partaker of his evil deeds" (2 John 10-11). An exhortation which is in force for all times.)

"Gnosticism" was corrupting the professing Church everywhere. This system spoke of the Lord Jesus as occupying the highest rank in the order of spirits; they also denied the redemption by His blood and the gift of God to believing sinners, that is, eternal life. God in His infinite wisdom held back the pen of the Apostle John till these denials had matured and then he wrote under divine guidance the final Gospel in which the Lord Jesus Christ, the Son of God, the Only-Begotten, the Second Person of the Godhead, is made known in the fulness of His glory. Linked with this marvellous picture of Him, Who is the true God and the eternal life, is the other great truth made known in the fourth Gospel. Man is dead, destitute of life; he must be born again and receive life. And this eternal life is given by the Son of God to all who believe on Him. It is communicated as a present and abiding possession, dependent on Him, Who is the source and the life as well. At the same time the Third Person of the Godhead, the Holy Spirit, is revealed in this Gospel as He is not revealed in the Synoptics. The Gospel which reveals the eternal life is necessarily the Gospel in which the Holy Spirit as the Communicator, Sustainer and Perfecter is fully made known. The Gospel of John is therefore the New Testament Gospel, the good news that grace and truth have come by Jesus Christ. It makes known what is more fully revealed in the doctrinal Epistles.

The last chapter in which we hear the Lord Jesus Christ speak, before His passion, is the seventeenth chapter. He speaks to the Father in the great prayer rightly called "the high-priestly prayer." In it He touches upon all the great truths concerning Himself and His own made known in this Gospel, and we shall also find that all the great redemption truths given in their fulness by the Holy Spirit in the Epistles, are clearly revealed in this prayer.

John's Own Testimony

At the close of the twentieth chapter of this Gospel we find John's own testimony concerning the purpose of this Gospel. "And many other signs truly did Jesus in the presence of His disciples, which are not written in this book. But these are written that ye might believe that Jesus is the Christ, the Son of God, and that believing ye might have life through (in) His Name." Thus the twofold purpose of the fourth Gospel is given by the apostle: Christ the Son of God and the life He gives to all who believe.

The characteristic features of this Gospel are too numerous to mention in this introductory word. We shall point them out in the annotations.

The Division of the Gospel of John

"For God so loved the world that He gave His only begotten Son, that whosoever believeth in Him should not perish, but have everlasting life" (3:16). This verse may be given as the key-text of this Gospel, while the prominent words are: life; believe; verily.

Different divisions of this Gospel have been suggested. In its structure it has been compared to the three divisions of the temple. The outer court (1—12); the Holy Part (13—16); the Holiest (17—21). Others have used chapter 16:28 to divide the Gospel; "I came forth from the Father, and am come into the world; again I leave the world and go to the Father." This is unquestionably the order of events in the Gospel of John. He came forth from the Father (1:1-18); He came into the world (1:19—12); He left the world and has returned to the Father (13—21). Keeping the great purpose of this Gospel in view we make a three-fold division.

I. **THE ONLY-BEGOTTEN, THE ETERNAL WORD, HIS GLORY AND HIS MANIFESTATION** (1:1—2:22)

II. **ETERNAL LIFE IMPARTED: WHAT IT IS AND WHAT IT INCLUDES** (2:23—17)

III. **"I LAY DOWN MY LIFE, THAT I MIGHT TAKE IT AGAIN"** (18—21)

First then we behold Him, the Only-Begotten, the Creator of all things, the Life and the Light of men, in His full glory. The Eternal Word was made flesh and manifested Himself among men. This is followed by the main section of the Gospel. It begins with the story of Nicodemus in which the absolute necessity of the new birth, the reception of eternal life by faith in the Son of God, is emphasized; it ends with the great summing up of all He taught concerning eternal life and salvation, in the great prayer of chapter 17. Chapters 3—17 contain the progressive revelation concerning eternal life. The reception and assurance of it, the Holy Spirit as the Communicator, the provisions for that life, the fruits of it, the goal of it, etc., we can trace in these chapters. In the third part we find the description of how He laid down His life and took it again in resurrection.

Analysis and Annotations

I. The Only-begotten, the Eternal Word, His Glory and His Manifestation (1:1—2:22)

CHAPTER 1

1. The Word: the Creator, the Life and the Light (1:1-4)
2. The Light and the darkness: The Light not known (1:5-11)
3. The word made flesh and Its gracious results (1:12-18)
4. The witness of John (1:19-34)
5. Following Him and dwelling with Him (1:35-42)
6. The next day: Nathanael's unbelief and confession (1:43-49)
7. The promise of greater things (1:50-51)

Majestic is the beginning of this Gospel. Hundreds of pages might be written on the opening verses and their meaning would not be exhausted. They are inexhaustible. The name of our Lord as "the Word" (Logos) is exclusively used by the Apostle John. The Jewish philosopher Philo of Alexandria, who lived in the days of the Apostle John, also speaks of the Word. Critics have therefore claimed that the Apostle copied from Philo and reproduced his mystical Jewish philosophy. However, this theory has been exploded. Prof. Harnack, the eminent German scholar, states "the Logos of John has little more in common with the Logos of Philo than the name." It is significant that the rabbinical paraphrases on the Old Testament (Targumim) speak hundreds of times of the Lord as "the Word" (Memra). These ancient Jewish paraphrases describe Jehovah, when He reveals Himself, by the term "Memra," which is the same as the Greek "Logos"—"the Word." Genesis 3:8 they paraphrased "they heard the Word walking in the garden." These Jewish comments ascribe the creation of the world to the Word. It was "the Word" which communed with the Patriarchs. According to them "the Word" redeemed Israel out of Egypt; "the Word" was dwelling in the tabernacle; "the Word" spake out of the fire of Horeb; "the Word" brought them into the promised land. All the relationship of the Lord with Israel is explained by them as having been through "the Word." In the light of the opening verses of the Gospel of John these Jewish statements appear more than interesting. (These paraphrases in the form we possess them were written in Aramaic about 300 A.D. But long before they were written they must have existed as traditions among the Jewish people.) The Only-Begotten is called "the Word" because He is the express image of God, as the invisible thought is expressed by the corresponding word. He is the revealer and interpreter of the mind and will of God.

"In (the) beginning was the Word, and the Word was with God, and the Word was God." Three great facts are made known concerning our Lord. 1. He is eternal. He did not begin to exist. He has no beginning, for "in the beginning *was* the Word." He ever was. Before time began and matter was created, He was. 2. He was and is a Person distinct from God the Father, yet one with Him. "The Word was with God." 3. The Lord Jesus *is* God, for we read "The Word was God." He could therefore not be a being, a creature like the angels. The verses which follow add to this the fact that He is the Creator of all things and the Source of all light and life. Here is the most complete refutation of the wicked teachings concerning the Person of our Lord, which were current in the days of the Apostle, which have been in the world ever since and which will continue to exist till the Lord comes. Arianism, which makes our Lord a Being inferior to God, is answered. So is Socinianism, Unitarianism, Russellism, International Bible Student Assoc., which teach that Christ was not very God, but a man. Well has it been said in view of the revelation contained in the first verse: "to maintain in the face of such a text, as some so called 'Christians' do, that our Lord Christ was only a man, is a mournful proof of the perversity of the human heart." And in Him was life, which must be applied to spiritual life. Spiritual life and light is impossible apart from the Second Person of the Godhead. The commentator Bengel makes a helpful statement on the opening verses of this chapter. "In the first and second verses of this chapter mention is made of a state before the creation of the world; in the third verse, the world's creation; in the fourth, the time of man's uprightness; in the fifth, the time of man's decline and fall."

John the forerunner is in this Gospel presented to bear witness of the Light. How this reveals the darkness which is in the world that He, Who is the Life and the Light, needed one to announce His coming! "The true light was that which, coming into the world, lighteth every man" (verse 9; correct translation). And when He came into the world He had made, the world knew Him not. Even His own, to whom He came, received Him not. This is His rejection by Israel, which in detail is described in the first three Gospels.

Verses 12 and 13 make known the gracious results for those, who receive Him, who believe on His name. The world had not known its Creator; Israel had rejected Him. After the great work of the cross had been accomplished, the work done for guilty man, the good news is made known. As many as receive Him, to them He gives the right to be the children of God. The new birth is here mentioned for the first time; it is the communication of the divine nature by believing on His name. Believing on Him, receiving Him, we are begotten again and are therefore the children of God. Of this nothing is said in the preceding Gospels. The Gospel of John begins where the others end. The authorized version is incorrect in having "sons of God." (The same error appears in 1 John 3:2.) John always speaks of "children" not of "sons." The expression "children of God" denotes the fact that we are God's born ones, born by the new birth into the family of God. "Sons of God" we are called in view of our destiny in Christ and with Him. As sons of God we are also the heirs of God and fellowheirs of Jesus Christ. Nowhere is it said that we are heirs of God because we are children of God. Our Lord is never called a child of God, for He is not born of God as we are; He is "Son." (Acts 4:30 is incorrect; not "holy child Jesus," but "holy servant.") Verse 14 gives the fact of His incarnation. Here then we read what the Word became. It is almost impossible to believe that men who claim scholarship, who deny the fact of the incarnation, can state as they do, that the Gospel of John has nothing to say on this great foundation truth of our faith. These apostates must be blinded. The great mystery is made known here as it is in Matthew and in Luke. The Eternal Word, the Word which ever was, the Word which is God, became flesh. He became so by the union of two perfect and distinct natures in one Person. His Person however cannot be divided. And when He became flesh, took on the creature's form, He did not cease to be very God; He emptied Himself of His outward glory, but not of His deity. He became truly man, but He was holy, sinless; not alone did He not sin, but He could not sin. There is an ancient Latin statement which is worth repeating. It represents "the Word having become flesh as saying: "I am what I was, that is *God*"—"I was not what I am, that is *Man*—"I am now called both, *God and Man.*" In Him they beheld His glory, the glory of the Only-Begotten, full of grace and truth. Grace and truth came by Him. The only begotten Son, who is in the bosom of the Father, declared Him, whom no one hath seen at any time. These are great statements. The word "grace" is found here for the first time in the New Testament. And He, the Incarnate Word, and He alone is full of grace and truth. Out of His fulness have we all received, and grace upon grace. It is all grace, that those receive from Him who believe on His name.

The witness of John the forerunner is different from his witness and preaching as given by the synoptics. They report mostly his testimony to the nation. Here we read when he saw Jesus coming to him, he saith, "Behold the Lamb of God who taketh away the sin of the world." (Often Christians quote "sins of the world." If our Lord had taken away the *sins* of the world, the whole world would be saved. Our Lord only bore the *sins* of those who believe on Him. All who do not believe die in their sins and are lost.) He knew that He Who came to him was to be the Sin-Bearer. He knew that He is the true Sacrifice for sin, the true Passover-Lamb, the Lamb which Isaiah predicted. And he testified that the Lamb of God was to take away (not taking away then, or has taken away) the sin of the world. The Lamb of God had to die and the ultimate results of His death are announced in this testimony. They have not yet come, but will be realized in the new heaven and the new earth, when all things are made new.

Beginning with *verse 35* we read what happened the next day after John had given his testimony concerning the Lamb of God. The results of that testimony now appear. Once more John points to Him: "Behold the Lamb of God." He, who was the greatest prophet of the Old Testament, directs his disciples to the Lord. The two disciples heard him speak and followed Jesus. These are the blessed steps: speaking the message, hearing (and in hearing believing) then following the Lord. And He knew them and their hearts' desire. His grace was drawing them to Himself. Their question, "Rabbi, where dwellest Thou?" is answered by that most blessed invitation, "Come and see." These are the first words of our Lord besides His question, written in this Gospel. He wanted them to know Him, to be in communion with Himself. They abode with Him that day. It foreshadows the results of the gospel of grace. The unmentioned place where they dwelt with Him is typical of the heavenly place where He is now. In faith we see where He abides, and by faith we know we are there in Him. It is a beautiful picture of the gathering which takes place throughout this gospel-age. He is the center, and "Come and see" are still His gracious words to all who hear and believe. And how Andrew at once testified and brought his brother Simon to Jesus!

Verses 43-49 unfold another picture. Nathanael (gift of God) would not believe. Philip had testified to him "We have found Him of whom Moses in the law, and the prophets did write, Jesus of Nazareth, the son of Joseph." Nathanael under the fig-tree, where the Lord had seen him, is the type of the remnant of Israel. When the Lord spoke to him he owned Him as the Son of God, the King of Israel. So all Israel in a future day will confess Him. Notice the first day, when the first company is gathered to abide with Him (typical of this age and the gathering of a heavenly company); then the second day, when the Lord reveals Himself to unbelieving Nathanael (typical of the conversion of the remnant of Israel).

The last two verses of this marvellous chapter will find their fulfillment in that day when heaven is opened. Then greater things will take place. The angels of God will be seen ascending and descending upon the Son of Man. It will take place when He comes the second time, when Israel acknowledges Him as their King and as the Son of God.

CHAPTER 2:1-22

1. The marriage in Cana (2:1-11)
2. The temple cleansed (2:12-22)

The second chapter gives the record of the first miracle reported in this Gospel. He manifested His omniscience in the previous chapter and here, in turning water into wine, He reveals Himself as the omnipotent Creator. What harmony there is between the opening of the first two chapters of the Gospel of John. The first chapter speaks of Him as the Creator of all things and in the second chapter He manifests the power of the Creator. He needed no wine, no grapes, no mellowing process, to furnish the best wine. He but commanded and it was so. This is omnipotence. In verse 17 of the previous chapter there is a contrast between Moses representing the law dispensation and our Lord Jesus Christ through whom grace and truth have come. The first miracle Moses did, was turning water into blood, typical of the ministration of the law unto death; the first miracle of our Lord turns water into wine, which is typical of joy and the ministration of grace which is unto life.

The many applications and lessons of the marriage in Cana and the changing of water into wine we have to omit. But we call attention to the dispensational aspect. (The numbers 3 and 7 are prominent in this Gospel. Three times the Lord went into Galilee, three times into Judea; three Passovers are mentioned, etc. There are seven signs or miracles, seven times the Lord speaks 'I am"; seven times the phrase "These things have I spoken unto you, etc." is used.) The third day mentioned connects with the preceding chapter. On the first day the two disciples abode with the Lord. On the second day unbelieving Nathanael confessed Him as

Son of God and King of Israel. On the third day there was a marriage. The third day clearly indicates the time of Israel's blessing and restoration. Beautiful is the predicted and still future confession of Israel: "After two days will He revive us, in the third day He will raise us up and we shall live in His sight." (Hos. 6:1-3). The marriage typifies the restored relationship of the Lord with Israel. That is why the mother of Jesus (type of Israel) and His disciples (those who come with Him to the marriage) are mentioned. And this miracle is spoken of as the "beginning of miracles," when He manifested His glory. When He comes again and changes existing conditions, when Israel enters into the promised and blessed relationship, when He manifests His glory, then the wine of joy will not fail. Better things are promised and better things will come, when that blessed day appears. But "His hour is not yet come." It will surely come.

The words of rebuke to Mary clearly show that she erred and was as fallible as any other woman. The Lord rebuked her because He did not want her to interfere with Him and His work. "She erred here, perhaps from an affectionate desire to bring honour to her Son, as she erred on other occasions. The words before us were meant to remind her that she must henceforth leave our Lord to choose His own times and modes of acting. The season of subjection to her and Joseph was over. The season of His public ministry had at length begun. In carrying on that ministry, she must not presume to suggest to Him. The utter contrariety of this verse to the teaching of the Roman Catholic Church about the Virgin Mary is too palpable to be explained away. She was not without error and sin, as Romish writers have dared to assert, and was not meant to be prayed to and adored. If our Lord would not allow His mother even to suggest to Him the working of a miracle, we may well suppose that all Roman Catholic prayers to the Virgin Mary, and especially prayers entreating her to 'command her Son,' are most offensive and blasphemous in His eyes" (J. C. Ryle).

The purging of the temple is closely connected with the marriage and miracle of Cana. When He comes again the Father's house, the temple, will be cleansed. "Yea every pot in Jerusalem shall be holiness unto the Lord of hosts . . . and in that day there shall be no more the Canaanite (which means "merchantman") in the first cleansing of the temple, mentioned exclusively by John. The synoptic Gospels report the cleansing which occurred at the close of His ministry. He manifested in it His authority as the Son of God, and Psalm 69:9 was fulfilled in His action.

> The whole transaction is a remarkable one, as exhibiting our Lord using more physical exertion, and energetic bodily action, than we see Him using at any other period of His ministry. A word, a touch, or the reaching forth of a hand, are the ordinary limits of His actions. Here we see Him doing no less than four things: (1) Making the scourge; (2) Driving out the animals; (3) Pouring out on the ground the changers' money; (4) Overthrowing the tables. On no occasion do we find Him showing such strong outward marks of indignation, as at the sight of the profanation of the temple. Remembering that the whole transaction is a striking type of what Christ will do at His second coming, we may get some idea of the deep meaning of that remarkable expression, "The wrath of the Lamb (Rev. 6:16) *Expository Thoughts on John.*

Then He spoke of His coming death and resurrection in a veiled form. The Jews and His disciples did not understand what temple He meant. He spoke of His own body. "In three days I will raise it up." His resurrection was both through the power of God and by Himself. God raised Him up and He raised Himself up. This statement properly belongs to this Gospel in which we behold Him as the Son of God. The same statement we find in chapter 10:18: "I have power to lay down My life, and I have power to take it again."

II. Eternal Life Imparted: What It Is and What It Includes (2:23—17)

The second part of this Gospel contains the blessed teachings the Son of God gave concerning eternal life, how it is imparted and what it includes. Everything in these chapters is new. The story of Nicodemus, the woman at Sychar's well, the healing of the impotent man, the discourses of our Lord, etc., are not reported by the synoptic Gospels. There is not a word of the Sermon on the Mount reported by John; the many miracles, so significantly arranged in Matthew, are omitted (except the feeding of the 5000); nor do we find a single parable concerning the kingdom of Heaven. The progressive revelation concerning eternal life will be brought out in the annotations. As already stated the teachings begin with the new birth, in which eternal life is imparted, and end with the destiny of those who are born again. This is revealed in His high priestly prayer, "Father, I will that they also whom Thou hast given Me be with Me where I am, that they may behold My glory."

CHAPTERS 2:23—3:36

1. The many who believed on Him (2:23-25)
2. Nicodemus and the new birth (3:1-8)
3. How the new birth is accomplished (3:9-21)
4. The last testimony of John (3:22-36)

He worked many miracles in Jerusalem, which are unreported by John. Many therefore believed in His name, but the Omniscient One knew that they were only convinced, but their hearts had not been touched and so they did not receive Him as the Son of God. But there was one who was more deeply exercised, an earnest, seeking soul, Nicodemus. He came to Jesus by night and addressed Him as Rabbi, acknowledging that He was a teacher come from God. The Lord did not permit him to go on with his address nor to state the object of his visit. The Lord treated him in an abrupt, almost discourteous, way and informed him at once of the absolute necessity of the new birth. "Verily, verily, I say unto thee, except a man be born again (literally: born from above) he cannot see the kingdom of God." Not teaching, mere knowledge, was the need Nicodemus had to see the kingdom, but to be born from above.

But what kingdom does our Lord mean? It refers primarily to the kingdom of the Old Testament, promised Israel. When that kingdom comes, with the return of the Lord, only those of Israel will enter in who are born again. The unbelieving and apostate mass of Jews will be excluded from that earthly, millennial kingdom. Only the believing remnant inherits that kingdom to come. This may be learned from Ezekiel 36 and Isaiah 4:3, and other passages. That is why the Lord said to Nicodemus: "Art thou the teacher of Israel, and knowest not these things?"

But the truth our Lord gave to Nicodemus has a wider application. Man is spiritually dead, destitute of spiritual life. In order to enter the kingdom of God, to be in the presence of God, man must be born anew. Such a statement is nowhere found in the preceding Gospels. In the Gospel of John, the Gospel of Eternal Life, it is put into the foreground. Nicodemus is the only person to whom the Lord spoke of the absolute necessity of the new birth. He never made such a statement to the publicans and the harlots. And who was Nicodemus? A Pharisee, and therefore an extremely religious man. A ruler of the Jews, which necessitated a moral life. The teacher of Israel, one who possessed much learning. Religiousness, morality, education and culture are insufficient to save man and give him a place in the kingdom of God. The new birth is the one thing needed. "That which is born of the flesh is flesh." The flesh is the old nature which every human being brings into the world; it is a fallen, a corrupt nature and can never be anything else. And "they that are in the flesh cannot please God" (Rom. 8:8). The natural man may do anything he pleases, become religious and philanthropic, but he cannot please God. What then is the new birth? It is not reformation. Nor is it, as so often stated, an action of the Holy Spirit to make an evil nature good. The flesh cannot be changed into something better. The new birth is the impartation of a new nature, the divine nature, by the Holy Spirit. "That which is born of the Spirit is spirit." This new nature is absolutely holy, as the old nature is absolutely corrupt. This new nature is the only thing which fits man to be in the presence of God.

But what is the meaning of "water" in verse 5? "Except a man be born of water and of the Spirit, he cannot enter the kingdom of God." The water is claimed by ritualists to mean baptism. If a little water is put upon the head of an infant, they would have us believe, regeneration takes place. Others hold upon this statement of our Lord that the water is Christian baptism, and that therefore water-baptism is necessary to salvation. But the words of our Lord have nothing whatever to do with baptism. (Ezekiel 36:25-27 must be linked with John 3:5 and must be considered here as a national promise to Israel, how they will enter the kingdom. But the verses in Ezekiel have absolutely nothing whatever to do with baptism. To apply them thus is ridiculous.) The water cannot mean Christian baptism. Christian baptism (an entirely different thing from the Jewish baptism of John) was not instituted till after His death and resurrection. If it meant Christian baptism, the Lord's rebuke to Nicodemus would be unjust. How could he know something that was still undivulged? Water in this passage is the figure of the Word of God, which the Spirit of God uses for the quickening of souls. The following passages will demonstrate this fact: Eph. 5:25-26; 1 Cor. 4:15; 1 Peter 1:23; James 1:18. Begotten again by the Word of God, and water is the figure of that Word.

The Lord speaks next of revealing heavenly things (in distinction from earthly things relating to Israel). Then the cross is revealed by which the heavenly things are realized, and how lost man is to be saved and receive eternal life (the new nature). The Son of Man must be lifted up. He Who knew no sin was made sin for us. "God so loved the world that He gave His Only-Begotten Son, that whosoever believeth on Him should not perish but have everlasting life." "In this was manifested the love of God toward us, because God sent His Only-Begotten Son into the world, that we might live through Him. Herein is love; not that we loved God, but that He loved us, and sent His Son to be the propitiation for our sins" (1 John 4:9-10). Blessed words these! It is by believing on the Son of God, who died for our sins, that we are saved and are born again.

John bears his final testimony in verses 23-26. He testifies of Christ as the bridegroom, who is to have the bride. John calls himself the friend of the bridegroom. "He must increase, but I must decrease." Note the three "musts" in this chapter. "Ye must be born again"; the necessity of the new birth. "The Son of Man must be lifted up"; the necessity of the death of the Lord to make salvation possible. "He must increase, but I must decrease"; the result of salvation. The final testimony of John the Baptist takes us beyond the cross (verses 35-36). Blessed assurance! He that believeth on the Son hath everlasting life. Solemn declaration! He that believeth not the Son shall not see life; but the wrath of God *abideth* on him.

CHAPTER 4

1. He must needs pass through Samaria (4:1-5)
2. At Sychar's Well: Jesus and the Samaritan woman (4:6-26)
3. The woman's witness and the believing Samaritans (4:27-42)
4. His return to Galilee (4:43-45)
5. The second miracle, the healing of the nobleman's son (4:46-54)

In the Gospel of Matthew the Lord told His disciples not to go into the way of the Gentiles and not to enter into any city of the Samaritans (10:5). He sent them to preach the nearness of the kingdom. Here He must needs go through Samaria. He had left Jerusalem and was on His way to Galilee and passing through Samaria He manifested His marvellous grace. Tired on account of the way, an evidence of His true humanity, "He sat thus on the well." There He rested in unwearied love, waiting for the poor, fallen woman, whose sad story He knew so well.

To follow the beautiful account of His dealings with the Samaritan woman in all its blessed details is impossible in our brief annotations. What mercy and grace He exhibited in seeking such a one! What wisdom and patience in dealing with her, bearing with her ignorance! And what power in drawing her to Himself and making her a messenger to bring others to Him! How different He treated her in comparison with Nicodemus in the preceding chapter.

The Lord speaks to the Samaritan woman concerning the living water, which He can give to all that ask Him. The central verse of His teaching is the fourteenth, "But whosoever drinketh of the water that I shall give him shall never thirst; but the water that I shall give him shall be in him a well of water springing up into everlasting life." The well or fountain of water in the believer is the indwelling Spirit. In chapter 7:37-39 the Lord speaks also of living water and there the interpretation of it is given. "This He spake of the Spirit, whom they that believe on Him should receive; for the Holy Spirit was not yet given, because Jesus was not yet glorified." The believer has therefore not only eternal life, but also the gift of the Spirit, Who dwells in him as the spring of living water.

The new worship is next revealed in answer to the question of the woman (verses 21-24). The Samaritans worshipped on a mountain (Gerizim); the Jews in the temple, but the hour was coming when the true worshippers would worship the Father in the Spirit. No longer would true believers worship God as the God of Israel, but as Father. It is to be a worship in the Spirit and not confined to a locality. Christian worship has for its foundation the possession of eternal life; the indwelling Spirit is the power of that worship. Only true believers, such who are born again and possess the gift of the Spirit, can be worshippers. "For we are the circumcision who worship God in the Spirit and rejoice in Christ Jesus, and have no confidence in the flesh" (Phil 3:3). And such worshippers the Father seeketh. In Old Testament times the Jews worshipped in an earthly place. In the coming, the millennial age, nations will go up to Jerusalem to worship the Lord of hosts in the great millennial temple (Is. 2:1-4; Zech. 14:16, etc.). This present dispensation is the dispensation of grace, and the Father seeketh worshippers who worship Him in spirit and in truth. Thus we are brought in the Gospel of John altogether upon the ground of grace.

Then He revealed Himself to the woman. "Jesus saith to her, I that speak to thee am He." She was face to face with the Messiah; she stood in the presence of Jehovah. She left her water-pot to tell others the good news of the living water. The earthly things were forgotten. And what a messenger she became! How her simple testimony was blessed in the conversion of souls! He abode there two days and is owned and proclaimed not alone as the promised Messiah but as the Saviour of the world (verse 42).

Once more we see Him at Cana of Galilee, and the nobleman's son, who was sick at Capernaum, is healed by the Lord. The nobleman represents typically Israel. The word the Lord addressed to him fits that nation. "Except ye see signs and wonders, ye will not believe." How different from Samaria, where He did no miracle and yet they believed. And as the nobleman and his whole house believed, so will Israel believe in a future day.

CHAPTER 5

1. The healing of the impotent man (5:1-9)
2. The opposition of the Jews (5:10-18)
3. His unity with the Father (5:19-23)
4. The present hour: Believers delivered from death and judgment (5:24-25)
5. The future hour: His power to raise the dead (5:26-29)
6. Witness concerning Himself (5:30-32)
7. The witness of John (5:33-35)
8. The witness of His Works (5:36)
9. The witness of the Father (5:37)
10. The witness of the Scriptures and the unbelief of the Jews (5:39-46)

The teachings contained in this chapter are closely linked with the third and fourth chapters. He went up to Jerusalem again. In the foreground stands the healing of the impotent man at the pool of Bethesda with its five porches. An angel troubled the water at certain seasons, so that some were healed. We believe that it was actually so, though we cannot explain it. Many critics attack this occurrence and reject its genuineness. But the impotent man could not avail himself of the opportunity for he was helpless. Such was Israel's condition under the law. The thirty-eight years point back to Israel's wandering in the wilderness. Furthermore the impotent man presents a striking picture of the utter helplessness of man as a sinner. By His word the Lord Jesus made him perfectly whole, so that he took up his bed and walked.

(After all there is no more real difficulty in the account before us, than in the history of our Lord's temptation in the wilderness, the various cases of Satanic possession, or the release of Peter from prison by an angel. Once admit the existence of angels, their ministry on earth, and the possibility of their interposition to carry out God's designs, and there is nothing that ought to stumble us in the passage. The true secret of some of the objections to it, is the modern tendency to regard all miracles as useless lumber, which must be thrown overboard, if possible, and cast out of the Sacred Narrative on every occasion. Against this tendency we must watch and be on our guard.)

Opposition and objection from the Jews followed at once. They accused the healed man of breaking the Sabbath. He evidently did not know the Lord at all; only after He had spoken to him (verse 14) did he find out that it was Jesus. Then he told the Jews. Their hatred was turned at once against the Lord. They persecuted Him and sought to slay Him because He had done this miracle on the Sabbath. The Lord's answer is most blessed. "My Father worketh hitherto, and I work." It is the first time in this Gospel that He speaks of God as "My Father." He, the Son, was in their midst to make the Father known. He told them that His Father works and that the Son works. Sin made this work necessary. He stood in their presence and claimed perfect and unspoken fellowship with His Father.

The Jews knew what He meant. Had He said "Our Father" instead of "My Father" no word of protest would have escaped their lips. They knew His words could mean but one thing, that He is equal with God, by saying that God was His Father. Augustine remarked on this verse; "Behold the Jews understood what the Arians (deniers of His deity) would not understand." And He accepted the charge of the Jews as a correct one. "He thought it not robbery to be equal with God" (Phil. 2: 6). His words which follow declare His perfect unity with the Father in His work; He is the Beloved of the Father; the Father raiseth up the dead, so does He; judgment is committed unto the Son; He is to be honoured as the Father is honoured. "Whosoever does not honour the Son with equal honour to that which he pays to the Father, however he may imagine that he honours or approaches God, does not honour Him at all; because He can only be known by us as 'the Father who sent His Son' " (Dean Alford). Unitarianism, Russellism, the new theology and a host of other "isms," which deny the absolute deity of our Lord, stand condemned and convicted in the presence of these wonderful words, "He that honoureth not the Son honoureth not the Father." All worship apart from the Son of

God is idolatry. He claims the unity in Godhead; and such belongs to Him.

Verse 24 is a blessed gospel text. Hearing and believing are the conditions to receive eternal life. There is no mention made of repentance. The word "repent" so prominent in the Gospel of Matthew in the kingdom offer is not found once in the fourth Gospel. Faith and repentance, however, are inseparable. He that hears His words and believeth Him that sent the Son also repents. Again eternal life is spoken of as a present possession, "hath" not "shall have" or "shall receive later," but "hath eternal life." And with that gift comes deliverance from judgment. The reception of eternal life is a full acquittal; passed from death and all it means, into life.

"The coming hour" in verse 25 is the present dispensation. The dead are the spiritually dead. They that hear the voice of the Son of God shall live; they receive His life. Then He speaks of an hour which was to come and which has not yet come. Two resurrections are revealed by Him; the resurrection of life and the resurrection of judgment. This does not mean that these two resurrections are to take place the same time, in, what is termed, a general resurrection. Elsewhere we find the full revelation concerning these two resurrections. There is the first resurrection, the resurrection of the just, and a thousand years later the resurrection of the wicked dead (Rev. 20). All the wrong teachings concerning the wicked dead, such as annihilation, restitution, restoration, second chance, etc., as taught by Seventh Day Adventism, Millennial Dawnism, Universalism and others, are completely refuted by the words of our Lord in verse 29.

The five witnesses who testify concerning Himself, that He is the Son of God, are of much importance and should be carefully studied.

CHAPTER 6

1. The feeding of the five thousand men (6:1-14)
2. The attempt to make Him king (6:15)
3. The Stormy Sea: "It is I, be not afraid" (6:16-21)
4. The discourse on the bread of life, the food of the believer (6:22-59)
5. The falling away of disciples (6:60-66)
6. Peter's confession (6:67-71)

The events which are recorded in this chapter happened at the Sea of Galilee, the Sea of Tiberias. John exclusively uses this name, an evidence that he wrote after the fall of Jerusalem. By this name the lake had become known to the Gentiles. The feeding of the five thousand is the same mentioned by the Synoptics. This great sign showed that Jehovah was in their midst, He Who had fed His Israel with manna in the wilderness and promised to satisfy the poor with bread (Ps. 132:15). When they had seen the great sign they acknowledged Him to be the promised Prophet who should come (Deut. 18:15) and wanted to make Him King. But He departed into a mountain. He knew that all they meant by making Him King was to become the leader of a carnal movement to overthrow the hated Roman government.

The storm on the sea and His coming across the stormy sea we have had in the other Gospels.

The great discourse on the Bread of Life follows. It is connected with the sign of the feeding of the multitude. When He speaks of being the Bread from Heaven He refers to His incarnation. "For the bread of God is He which cometh down from heaven, and giveth His life for the world." They rejected that Bread. Then He speaks of eating His flesh and drinking His blood both for the reception of life and for the sustenance of that life. These words have nothing whatever to do with the Lord's Supper. Bishop Ryle, who was a leader in a ritualistic church, repudiated this wrong interpretation in the following words: "For one thing, a literal 'eating and drinking' of Christ's body and blood would have been an idea utterly revolting to all Jews, and flatly contradictory to an often-repeated precept of their law. For another thing, to take a literal view of 'eating and drinking,' is to interpose a bodily act between the soul of man and salvation. This is a thing for which there is no precedent in Scripture. The only things without which we cannot be saved are repentance and faith. Last, but not least, to take a literal view of 'eating and drinking,' would involve most blasphemous and profane consequences. It would shut out of heaven the penitent thief. He died long after these words were spoken, without any literal eating and drinking. Will any dare to say he had 'no life' in Him? It would admit to heaven thousands of ignorant, godless communicants in the present day. They literally eat and drink, no doubt! But they have no eternal life, and will not be raised to glory. Let these reasons be carefully pondered.

"The plain truth is, there is a morbid anxiety in fallen man to put a carnal sense on Scriptural expressions, wherever he possibly can. He struggles hard to make religion a matter of forms and ceremonies, of doing and performing, of sacraments and ordinances, of sense and of sight."

The Bread of God, He Himself, gave His life for the world. He gave His body and shed His blood on the cross. It is His sacrificial, atoning death. By faith we partake of it. Without it there is no life. Note the difference in verses 53 and 54. In verse 53 He speaks of those who have eaten His flesh and drunk His blood, apart from which there is no life. By faith the sinner appropriates Him, Who gave His body and shed His blood, and then receives eternal life. In verse 54 He speaks of a continuous eating and drinking. He is the source of eternal life. The believer feeds on Him; the eternal life the believer has must be sustained, nourished and kept by Himself, by ever feeding on His dying love. "The life that I now live in the flesh I live by the faith of the Son of God, who loved me and gave Himself for me" (Gal. 2:20). And the believer eating and drinking becomes one with Him. "He that eateth My flesh and drinketh My blood dwelleth (literally: abideth) in Me and I in him." It is a wonderful discourse on His incarnation, His sacrificial, atoning death, and the blessed assurances given to those who believe on Him. Precious are the promises of this great chapter. "He that cometh to Me shall never hunger, and he that believeth on Me shall never thirst" (verse 35). "Him that cometh unto Me I will in no wise cast out (verse 37). "Every one who seeth the Son, and believeth on Him, may have everlasting life; and I will raise him up at the last day" (verse 40). "Verily, verily, I say unto you, he that believeth on Me hath everlasting life" (verse 47).

("The last day" does not mean a day of a final and universal judgment followed by the end of the world. It is the end of the Jewish age to which our Lord refers (the age which is yet to be completed in great tribulation. Matt. 24). The first resurrection includes Old Testament saints, New Testament saints and the Jewish believers, who are martyred during the great tribulation. The first resurrection will be completed at the close of the tribulation period and followed by the setting up of the kingdom.)

CHAPTER 7

1. My time is not yet come (7:1-9)
2. Departure from Galilee: Sought by the Jews (7:10-13)
3. In the temple teaching (7:14-29)
4. Opposition to Him (7:30-36)
5. The indwelling Spirit promised (7:37-39)
6. The division among the people because of Him (7:40-44)
7. The returning officers and the defence of Nicodemus (7:45-53)

The Lord tarried in Galilee. How He must have sought souls there as He walked in Galilee! He would not walk in Judea (not "Jewry," as in the *Authorized Version*) because the Jews, that is the leaders of the people, sought to kill Him. The Feast of Tabernacles was at hand and what we find written in this chapter happened during that Feast. His brethren, no doubt sons born to Mary after His own birth, urged Him to go to Judea. Their motives were selfish. They did not believe on Him. However, later they believed, for we find them among those who waited in Jerusalem for the promise of the Father (Acts 1:14). The Feast of Tabernacles typifies the millennial blessings for Israel and the Gentiles, the great consummation. The world hated Him and He declared that His time had not yet come. We cannot follow at length the interesting account of His coming to Jerusalem, the words He spake, the answers He gave to those who hated Him. He taught and they marvelled. He declared that the doctrine He preached was of Him that sent Him. What a challenge He gave them! "If any man will do His will, he shall know of the doctrine, whether it be of God, or whether I speak of Myself." When He told them that they tried to kill Him. "Thou hast a demon," was their reply, while others said: "It not this He whom they seek to kill?" They sought to take Him and the Pharisees and Chief Priest sent officers to arrest Him. Thus the hatred against Him is manifested. His hour had not yet come; no one could touch Him. When the hour came He yielded Himself.

The great center of this chapter is found in verses 37-39. The last day of the Feast of Tabernacles was the greatest. It was the eighth day, a day of rest and holy gathering together. During the seven days of the feast water was daily drawn from the pool of Siloam and then poured out. On the last day this ceremony did not take place. The seven days typified their wilderness journey; the eighth day the entrance into the land. For seven days they drew the water and poured it out, commemorating the water the Lord had supplied to Israel during the wilderness journey. On the eighth day they enjoyed the springs of the land itself; an emblem of the living waters which the Lord had promised to

His people. Israel has three promises. "And it shall be in that day that living waters shall go out from Jerusalem" (Zech. 14:8). The same promise we find elsewhere. (See Ezek. 47; Isaiah 12.) And He Who had given to His people these promises, Who had come to fulfill them, stood in their midst. They hate Him. They tell Him to His face, "Thou hast a demon." They seek to kill Him.

On the last day of the feast, typical of Israel's promised blessing and glory, He stood and cried: "If any man thirst let him come unto Me and drink." He offers now upon the rejection of Himself something new to "any man who thirsts"; the national promises of living water pouring forth from Jerusalem cannot be fulfilled now. They will be fulfilled when He comes again. It is an individual invitation, an individual promise, He gives. "He that believeth on Me, as the Scripture hath said, out of his belly shall flow rivers of living water." We are then told that this means the gift of the Holy Spirit, which they were to receive who came to Him and believed on Him. The promise was fulfilled on the day of Pentecost. Then the Holy Spirit came to dwell in believers. The overflow, the streams of living water to flow from the believer, is the type of the Spirit, the Spirit of power manifesting Himself through the believer in bearing testimony for Christ. In the third chapter we saw the Holy Spirit communicating life; He is the Life-giving Spirit. In the fourth chapter the Lord spoke of the Spirit as the well of living water; He indwells the one who is born again to make communion and worship possible. Then followed His teaching in chapters 5 and 6, again concerning the life the believer hath in Him and how it is sustained. In the present chapter the indwelling Spirit, Who is the well of living water in the believer, is seen flowing forth to others, just as a spring will overflow.

CHAPTER 8

1. The woman taken in adultery (8:1-11)
2. The Light of the World (8:12)
3. His testimony concerning Himself and the Father (8:13-20)
4. His solemn declarations (8:21-47)
5. Before Abraham was, I am (8:48-59)

The first verse belongs to the preceding chapter. The officers returned without Him, bearing their testimony that "never man spake like this man." Nicodemus ventured his timid defence. Then every man went to his own house while the Lord went to the Mount of Olives.

The story of the woman taken in adultery has been rejected by many leading scholars. It is claimed that it is nothing less than a forgery. The chief arguments against it are the following: That the story is missing in some of the oldest manuscripts and earlier translations: that some of the Greek Fathers never refer to it; that it differs in style from the rest of the Gospel of John, and that the incident ought to be discredited on moral ground. However all these arguments have been proven invalid. Many old manuscripts have the story as well as some of the oldest translations. Others of the so-called Church Fathers speak of it. There can be no question whatever of its genuineness. It was omitted on purpose in certain manuscripts. The grace, which shines forth so marvellously in the Lord's dealing with the woman, was unpalatable to teachers who mixed law and grace. They left it out for a purpose.

(The argument from alleged discrepancies between the style and language of this passage, and the usual style of St. John's writing, is one which should be received with much caution. We are not dealing with an uninspired but with an inspired writer. Surely it is not too much to say that an inspired writer may occasionally use words and constructions and modes of expression which he generally does not use, and that it is no proof that he did not write a passage because he wrote it in a peculiar way.)

It was a clever scheme from the side of the scribes and Pharisees to tempt Him. The law of Moses demanded her death by stoning. If He gave as an answer, "let her be stoned!" He would contradict His own testimony that He came not to judge, but to save. If He declared that the guilty woman was not to be stoned, then would He break the law. They appealed to Him as teacher, not as judge. He was silent and stooped down and wrote with His finger in the ground. (The words "as though He heard them not" are in italics and must be omitted.) It is the only time we read of our Lord that He wrote. The finger which wrote in the ground was the same which had written the law in the tables of stone. What He wrote we do not know; but it was symbolical of the fact that the law against man is written in the dust, the dust of death. Not alone had the woman deserved death, but all were equally guilty. After His demand, "He that is without sin among you, let him first cast a stone at her," the oldest in the company left first till the Lord was alone with the guilty woman. He did not set aside the law, and yet He manifested His marvellous grace. The self-righteous accusers were condemned and sneaked into darkness, away from Him Who is the Light. The woman addressed Him as Lord, showing she believed on Him; and He told her to go and sin no more. The grace He shows demands holiness.

The scene occurred in the temple and the words He spoke following this incident were likewise spoken there. A great testimony again follows, which He gives concerning Himself. He is the Light of the world; it is not confined to Israel, but the light is to reach the Gentile nations. This is revealed in the Prophet Isaiah. After Messiah's complaint, "I have laboured in vain," the Rejected One is to be the light to the Gentiles. "I will also give Thee for a light to the Gentiles that Thou mayest be My salvation unto the ends of the earth" (Is. 49:1-6). Then follows an individual promise. He that followeth Him walks not in darkness, but has the light of life. In Him is life as well as light; there is then fellowship with God for the child of life, fellowship one with another if we walk in the light.

He then bore additional testimony concerning Himself. He knew where He came from and whither He went. The blind Pharisees did not. And when He spoke of the fellowship of Himself and the Father, they asked, "Where is Thy Father?" They were blind and blinded, and knew neither Him nor the Father.

Very solemn are the declarations in verses 21-29. They are as solemn and as true to-day as when they were uttered by the lips of the Son of God. "I said therefore unto you that ye shall die in your sins; for if ye believe not that I am He, ye shall die in your sins." Rejecting Christ, not believing on Him, means to die in sin. When they ask Him again, "Who art Thou?" He answered, "Absolutely what I am also speaking to you." (The rendering of the *Authorized Version* is incorrect.) He is the Word, the Truth, the Life, the Light. He is, in the principle of His being, what also He speaks. Essentially, precisely, what He is, He also speaks. The phrase "lifting up" means His crucifixion. (See 3:14 and 12:32.) After that event His vindication would come. He is the "I am." Many believed on Him. Were they true believers or the same class as we find at the close of the second chapter? Most likely they misunderstood His statement of being lifted up. They may have thought of Him becoming King; they certainly knew nothing of the cross.

More teaching follows. To be a true disciple means to abide in His Word. By the Word and the Spirit we are begotten, and to live as a disciple needs abiding in His Word. The Son is the Deliverer Who makes free from the power of Satan and of sin, of which He bears witness.

This interesting chapter ends with a startling self-revelation of His absolute deity, that He is the eternal Jehovah. Eleven times the name "Abraham" is found in the eighth chapter of John. At the close the Lord speaks of Abraham having seen His day and rejoiced. He saw it in faith. Then when the Jews expressed their astonishment He answered, 'Before Abraham was, *I AM!"* It is the most positive, the clearest declaration of our Lord of His Eternity, that He is God. He is the "I AM"—Jehovah. Thus this great testimony has always been received. We let a few of the ancient teachers speak:

> Chrysostom observes: "He said not before Abraham was, I was, but, I AM. As the Father useth this expression I AM, so also doth Christ, for it signifieth continuous being, irrespective of all time. On which account the expression seemed to the Jews blasphemous."
>
> Augustine says: "In these words acknowledge the Creator and discern the creature. He that spake was made of the Seed of Abraham; and that Abraham might be, He was before Abraham."
>
> Gregory remarks: "Divinity has no past or future, but always the present; and therefore Jesus does not say before Abraham was I *was,* but I *am."*

The unitarians try to explain this away by saying, "Jesus only meant that He existed as Messiah in God's counsels before Abraham." Astonishing! How do they know what He meant? It is a satanic invention. The Jews knew better. They understood what He meant. They took up stones to stone Him, because they knew He claimed absolute deity. A miracle followed. The Greek means literally "He was hid." Their eyes must have been holden as He went out of the temple and passed by.

CHAPTER 9

1. The man born blind, healed (9:1-7)
2. The healed man questioned (9:8-26)
3. Reviled and cast out (9:27-34)
4. Jesus reveals Himself to him (9:35-41)

The healing of the man born blind is a type and an illustration of how Christ, the Light, communicates light and how he who follows the Light walks no more in darkness, but has the light of life (8:12). And before He healed the man He testified that His day of activity on earth as Man was rapidly drawing to its close (verses 4 and 5). The clay and the spittle did not effect the opening of the eyes; it was the power of Christ. The blind man went and washed in the pool of Siloam and came seeing.

The conflict the blind man had is interesting and instructive, but too lengthy to follow in our annotations. The Pharisees exhibit their hatred against Him Who healed the blind man and they did all in their power to discredit the miracle and Him Who performed it. They questioned the man to confound him, but did not succeed. Then they questioned the parents, but they were afraid to say how their son had received his sight, for the Jews had agreed that if any man confessed Him as Christ he should be put out of the synagogue. Then they questioned the man again and he gave them an excellent testimony. "Whether He be a sinner or no, I know not; one thing I know, that, whereas I was blind, now I see." And when after repeated questionings the healed one expressed his firm belief that He Who gave him sight was of God, they cast him out.

But they only cast him into the arms of the loving Lord. He heard of what had been done to the man, and He sought for him. Then He revealed Himself to him as the Son of God. The man believed and worshipped Him. He was thrust outside of Judaism: and in that outside place Christ found him, and he believed on Christ. Like everything else in the Gospel of John this anticipates the position of true Christianity. It is outside of the camp of Judaism, outside of that which has rejected Christ. "Let us go forth therefore unto Him without the camp, bearing His reproach" (Heb. 13:31).

CHAPTER 10

1. The Shepherd of the sheep (10:1-5)
2. The Good Shepherd, His sheep and His work (10:6-21)
3. At the Feast of Dedication: the repeated testimony (10:22-30)
4. Accused of blasphemy and His answer (10:31-39)
5. Beyond Jordan, and many believed on Him (10:40-42)

The teaching of this chapter is closely linked with the preceding event. It has become evident that the true sheep of Christ, belonging to His flock, would be cast out of the Jewish fold. The healed man cast out had become one of His sheep. Therefore He teaches now more fully concerning Himself as the Shepherd and about His sheep. The Old Testament speaks often of Israel as the sheep of Jehovah, and of Jehovah as the Shepherd (Ps. 80:1; 95:7; 23:1; Ezekiel 34: Zech. 11:7-9; 13:7). The true Shepherd had come through the appointed door into the sheepfold, that is, among Israel. He is the only One, and the porter (the Holy Spirit) opened to Him. He came and called His own sheep by name to lead them out. And the sheep hear His voice and follow Him. All is Jewish. He came, the true Shepherd, into the sheepfold to lead them out to become His flock.

It was a parable He spoke in these opening verses, but they did not understand it. What follows is a fuller revelation of Himself as the Good Shepherd, and the sheep who belong to His flock. Judaism was a fold out of which the Shepherd leads His flock. He is the Door of the sheep. He is the means of getting into the flock, as a door is the means of getting into a house. Through Him all His sheep must enter by faith into the flock. There is no other door and no other way. He came into the fold by God's appointed way and He is God's appointed way. "I am the door, by Me if any man enter in, he shall be saved, and shall go in and out and find pasture." A most blessed promise. He is the door. Any man, it does not matter who it is, any man may enter in by Him and then having entered in by Him, that is believed on Him, He promises salvation, liberty and food. These three things are bestowed upon all who believe on Him. Salvation is in Him and it is a present and a perfect salvation; liberty, freed from bondage of the law which condemned the sinner, a perfect liberty; pasture, food, which He supplies; He Himself is the food, a perfect food. It is all found outside of the fold, the fold of Judaism, and in Christ. He came that they might have life and that they might have it more abundantly. The abundant life He speaks of here is the life which comes from His death and resurrection. The good Shepherd had to give His life for the sheep. How different from the hireling, who fleeth and careth not for the sheep. The hirelings were the faithless shepherds (Ezek. 34:1-6). Again He said: "I lay down My life for the sheep."

The expression, "laying down the soul or life" for any one, does not occur anywhere else independently in the New Testament. It is never found in profane writers. It must be referred back to the Old Testament, and specially to Isa. 53:10, where it is said of Messiah, "He shall make, or place, His soul an offering for sin. *Hengstenberg*.

In verse 16 our Lord speaks of other sheep, which are not of this fold. These are the Gentiles. He leads out first from the Jewish fold His sheep; then there are the other sheep whom He will bring and who will hear His voice. The result will be one flock and one Shepherd. The Authorized Version is incorrect in using the word "fold." Judaism was a fold, the Church is not. The ecclesiastical folds in which Christendom is divided have been brought about by the Judaizing of the Church. The fold no longer exists. There is one flock and there is one Shepherd; one body, as there is one Lord. All who have heard His voice, believed on Him, entered in by Him, are members of the one flock.

At the Feast of Dedication, commemorating the cleansing of the temple and re-dedication by Judas Maccabaeus after the desecration by Antiochus (Daniel 8:9-14), the Lord continued His blessed teaching, ending it once more with a great revelation of Himself. He makes a most blessed addition to His previous instructions concerning Himself and His sheep. "I give unto them eternal life and they shall never perish, neither shall any man pluck them out of My hand. My Father, which gave them Me, is greater than all; and no man is able to pluck them out of My Father's hand." Here we have the comforting assurance of the absolute security of every sheep of Christ. Eternal life is a present and personal possession, not something which comes after death. It is therefore an abiding possession and cannot be lost. Then He Who is the Life and the Light, the Way and the Truth, assures us that His sheep shall never perish. Some say that He said "no one can pluck them out of His hand" but we can do it ourselves by living in sin, etc. This is fully answered by the correct rendering of His words, "they shall never perish." It means literally: "they shall in no wise ever perish." This is absolute; it covers everything.

Then His great revelation: "I and the Father are one." Again the Jews understood what He meant, for they wanted to stone Him. After His answer they wanted to take Him, but He escaped out of their hands. His hour had not yet come.

CHAPTER 11

1. The sickness of Lazarus announced (11:1-4)
2. The delayed departure and the death of Lazarus (11:5-16)
3. The arrival at Bethany (11:17-27)
4. Weeping with them that weep (11:28-38)
5. The resurrection of Lazarus (11:39-46)
6. The prophecy of Caiaphas (11:47-52)
7. Seeking to kill Him (11:53-57)

The resurrection of Lazarus is the final great sign or miracle in this Gospel. It is the greatest of all. Some critics have discredited it by saying that, if it had really taken place the Synoptics would have something to say about it. The Gospel of John is the Gospel in which this miracle properly belongs. As we have seen, the Gospel of John is the Gospel in which our Lord as Son of God is fully revealed. The resurrection of Lazarus proves Him the Son of God, Who can raise the dead. The philosopher and sceptic Spinoza declared that if he could be persuaded of the historicity of this miracle he would embrace Christianity. The miracle is supported by the most incontrovertible evidence; it requires more credulity to deny it than to believe it.

A German Expositor, Dr. Tillman, put together the evidences of this great miracle in the following way.:

> The whole story is of a nature calculated to exclude all suspicion of imposture, and to confirm the truth of the miracle. A well-known person of Bethany, named Lazarus, falls sick in the absence of Jesus. His sisters send a message to Jesus, announcing it; but while He is yet absent Lazarus dies, is buried, and kept in the tomb for four days, during which Jesus is still absent. Martha, Mary, and all his friends are convinced of his death. Our Lord, while yet remaining in the place where He had been staying, tells His disciples in plain terms that He means to go to Bethany, to raise Lazarus from the dead, that the glory of God may be illustrated, and their faith confirmed. At our Lord's approach, Martha goes to meet Him, and announces her brother's death, laments the absence of Jesus before the event took place, and yet expresses a faint hope that by some means Jesus might yet render help. Our Lord declares that her brother shall be raised again, and assures her that He has the power of granting life to the dead. Mary approaches, accompanied by weeping friends from Jerusalem. Our Lord Himself is moved, and weeps, and goes to the sepulchre, attended by a crowd. The stone is removed. The stench of the corpse is perceived. Our Lord, after pouring forth audible prayer to His Father, calls forth Lazarus from the grave, in the hearing of all. The dead man obeys the call, comes forth to public view in the same dress that he was buried in, alive and well, and returns home without assistance. All persons present agree that Lazarus is raised to life, and that a great miracle has been worked, though not all believe the person who worked it to be the Messiah. Some go away and tell the rulers at Jerusalem what Jesus had done. Even these do not doubt the truth of the fact; on the contrary, they

confess that our Lord by His works is becoming every day more famous, and that He would probably be soon received as Messiah by the whole nation. And *therefore* the rulers at once take counsel how they may put to death both Jesus and Lazarus. The people, in the meantime hearing of this prodigious transaction, flock in multitudes to Bethany, partly to see Jesus, and partly to view Lazarus. And the consequence is that by and by, when our Lord comes to Jerusalem, the population goes forth in crowds to meet Him and show Him honour, and chiefly because of His work at Bethany. Now, if all these circumstances do not establish the truth of the miracle, there is no truth in history.

To follow the historical account in all its detail would take many pages. It reveals the glory, the sympathy and the power of our Lord as perhaps no other Scripture does.

The heart of the chapter is found in His words to Martha: "I am the resurrection, and the life: he that believeth in Me, though he were dead, yet shall he live. And whosoever liveth and believeth in Me shall never die" (verses 25-36). In the first place these words anticipate His death and resurrection. He Who laid down His life and took it again, *is* the resurrection, and the life. He can raise the dead, the spiritually and physically dead. But these words take us also forward to His coming again, when they will find their great fulfillment, and when the crowning proof is given that He is the resurrection and the life. The saints, who believe on Him and died in Christ, will be raised first. This truth is expressed in His words: "He that believeth in Me, though he were dead, yet shall he live." And all who live when He comes for His saints, when His shout opens the graves, will be caught up in clouds, changed in a moment, in the twinkling of an eye, passing into His presence without dying. Of this He speaks in His last statement: "He that liveth (when He comes) and believeth on Me shall never die" (1 Cor. 15:51; 1 Thess. 4:16-18).

Who is able to describe the scene as He goes to the cave where His friend Lazarus had been laid away four days previous! Mary sank weeping at His feet. When He saw her weeping, the Jews weeping, then He groaned in the spirit and was troubled. Jesus wept! Oh, precious words! Conscious of His deity and of His power, He enters with deepest sympathy into the sorrows and afflictions of His people. Such He is still, our great High-Priest, Who is touched with the feeling of our infirmities. The cave was covered with a stone. When He commands that stone to be removed, Martha interrupted Him by saying, "By this time he stinketh, for he has been dead four days." It was unbelief. After He had lifted His eyes to heaven and had spoken to the Father, He uttered His majestic "Lazarus, come forth!" It was the word of omnipotence to manifest now fully that He is the Son of God, Who hath the power to raise the dead. Who can describe the solemn moment and what happened immediately! Perhaps there was a faint echo out of the cave, for He had cried his command with a loud voice. All eyes were looking towards the dark entrance of the cave, when lo! the dead man was seen struggling forward, bound by the grave clothes. Lazarus, who had been dead four days, whose body had already entered into decomposition, came forth a living man.

A more plain, distinct, and unmistakable miracle it would be impossible for man to imagine. That a dead man should hear a voice, obey it, rise up, and move forth from his grave alive is utterly contrary to nature. God alone could cause such a thing. What first began life in him, how lungs and heart began to act again, suddenly and instantaneously, it would be waste of time to speculate. It was a miracle and there we must leave it *(C. Ryle).*

"He came back, a challenge thrown in the face of Christ's would-be murderers, of the possibility of success against One to Whom death and grave are subject" (*Numerical Bible*). A second word He spoke: "Loose him and let him go." Lazarus is the type of a sinner who hears His Word. We are dead in trespasses and sins. Spiritually man is in the grave, in death and in darkness. He is in corruption. The Lord of Life gives life. And besides this He gives with that life—liberty. He looses from the bondage of the law and of sin. In the next chapter we read of Lazarus again. He is in fellowship with the Lord Who raised him from the dead. Life, liberty and fellowship are the three blessed things which he receives who hears and believes. Compare this great chapter with the teachings of the fifth chapter. And Lazarus is also a fit type of Israel and her coming national resurrection.

Then many believed on Him, while the Pharisees and chief priests, acknowledging the fact that He did many miracles, plan His death. Remarkable is the prophecy of Caiaphas. He was used as an instrument to utter a great truth. Christ was indeed to die for that nation, and also that He should gather together in one the children of God that were scattered abroad.

CHAPTER 12

1. The feast at Bethany (12:1-8)
2. The entrance into Jerusalem (12:9-19)
3. The inquiring Greeks and His answer (12:20-33)
4. His final words (12:34-50)

From the close of the previous chapter we learn that the Lord had gone with His disciples to a city called Ephraim. Six days before the Passover He came to Bethany again. They made Him a feast. Lazarus is especially mentioned as well as Martha, who served; Mary also was present with others who were of His disciples. It is a beautiful type of the Marriage Supper of the Lamb, when He will have His own with Him. Lazarus represents the saints risen from the dead, the others represent the saints who never died, but are changed in a moment. Service is represented in Martha. Fellowship they had together in the feast with the Lord, and worship in Mary, who anointed His feet. The Synoptics record the fact that she also anointed His head; she did both and there is no discrepancy. She was deeply attached to Him and knew of the threatening danger which hung over Him as Man. She did not know the full meaning of her beautiful act, but the Lord knew and said: "Against the day of My burying hath she kept this." And how He appreciated her love and devotion, though she had not the full intelligence of all it meant. It is devotion to Himself our Lord appreciates most in His people. Well has it been said, "She learned at His feet what she poured out there."

A large number of Jews came to Bethany to see Him, while others came out of curiosity to see Lazarus. Then the wicked chief priests held a consultation that they might put Lazarus to death. We do not hear another word about Lazarus after this.

His triumphant entrance into Jerusalem followed. The account of it in John's Gospel is very brief. The people welcome Him with the Messianic welcome, "Hosanna! (save now). Blessed is the King of Israel that cometh in the name of the Lord." That shout will be heard again in Jerusalem and then it will not be followed by the awful cry, "Crucify Him!" When He comes in power and glory as Israel's King the believing remnant of His people will welcome Him by the same word. (See Matthew 23:39.) Zechariah's prophecy (Zech. 9:9) is quoted in part, and that which was unfulfilled is omitted. But the disciples did not understand it, nor did they know that they were fulfilling prophecy. Only after "Jesus was glorified" (John 12:16) did they remember these things. The resurrection of Lazarus played an important part in His triumphant entrance into Jerualem. Those who stood by and saw the miracle done, bore witness, and others met Him because they heard of the miracle. The testimony of His enemies was: "Behold the world is gone after Him."

Then Greeks (Gentiles) inquired after Him, "Sir, we would see Jesus." How great was His triumph! There was no answer to those Greeks. Before the Gentiles could come to Him, He would have to die. The hour then had come when He, the Son of Man, should be glorified. He meant the cross and that which follows the suffering, His resurrection and ascension. By His death as Son of Man He acquired glory and receives ultimately the kingdoms of this world, the nations and the uttermost parts of the earth for His inheritance. He, therefore, speaks of Himself as the grain of wheat. If there is to be fruit from the one grain of wheat it must fall into the ground and die. The grain of wheat has life in itself and when it is put into the ground that life is carried through death, to be reproduced in the many grains of wheat. The life had to pass through death so that it might be communicated to others. The fruit springs from His death and resurrection. What a wonderful sacrifice he brought in giving His life! Believers possess the life of the grain of wheat, which passed through death and therefore are to follow Him and manifest it in a practical way. That is why He adds: "He that loveth his life shall lose it; and he that hateth his life in this world shall keep it unto life eternal. If any man serve Me, let him follow Me; and where I am, there shall also My servant be; if any man serve Me, him will My Father honour." Giving up, self-denial, the path He went is our path. But how glorious the promised reward!

Then He looked forward to the cross and His soul was troubled. "Father, save Me from this hour!" This was His prayer, much like that in Gethsemane. But He also adds at once, "for this cause came I unto this hour." He had come to die. The next request, "Father, glorify Thy Name," is at once answered by the voice from heaven. The Father's Name had been glorified by the Son, in a special manner the Father's Name was glorified in the resurrection of Lazarus. The glorification in the future, "and will glorify it," took place "when Christ was raised up from the dead through the glory of the Father" (Rom. 6:4).

The chapter closes with the final word of our Lord to the people. Many of the chief-rulers believed on Him without making an open confession. The last words He speaks before He gathers His own around Himself are concerning the Father Who sent Him.

CHAPTER 13

1. The washing of the disciples' feet (13:1-11)
2. Instructions given to wash one another's feet (13:12-17)
3. The betrayal foretold (13:18-30)
4. His own departure and the new commandment (13:31-35)
5. The denial of Peter foretold (13:36-38)

We reach with this chapter the most precious portion of this Gospel. The multitudes are left behind. Israel has completely rejected Him and now He gathered His own beloved disciples around Himself and gave them the sweet and blessed words of instruction, of comfort and cheer, His farewell. A little while and He would leave them to return to the glory from which He came.

> He is leaving upon earth the chosen companions of His path; those indeed that have hardly ever understood Him, whose lack of sympathy has been itself one of the bitterest trials, of those that made Him the "Man of Sorrows" that He was. Yet they are His hard-won spoils from the hand of the enemy, the first-fruits of the spiritual harvest coming in. They are His own, the gift of His Father, the work of His Spirit, the purchase of His blood, by and by to tell out, and, for the ages to come, divine love and power to all His intelligent creation. Nor, spite of their feebleness, can He forget how their hearts awakened by His call, have clung to Him in the scene of His rejection, how they have left their little all to follow Him. Now He is going to leave them in that world whose enmity they must for His sake incur, and in which they would fill up that which was behind of His afflictions for His body's sake, which is the Church (Col. 1:24). In human tenderness His heart overflows towards them, while in divine fulness; and this is what we find before us now. It is peculiar to John, and furnishes them for the way, and arms them for the impending conflict (F. W. Grant).

Our brief annotations are not sufficient to cover all the blessed teachings of these chapters. What a great assurance is given in the first verse of this chapter! He knew that His hour had come to depart out of this world. He knew because He is the Son of God. Then follows the assurance of His love for His own; even unto the end. His love knows no change. His tender, loving words addressed to His own in these chapters fully manifest that love which passeth knowledge.

The washing of the disciples' feet was a great symbolical action to teach His own the gracious provision made for them during His absence. Some well meaning Christians have applied the words of our Lord, "ye also ought to wash one another's feet," in a literal way, and teach that the Lord meant this to be done literally. The words of our Lord to Peter, "What I do thou knowest not now; but thou shalt know hereafter" (verse 7), show that underneath the outward action of the Lord in washing the disciples' feet there is a deeper spiritual meaning. We see Him girded, with a basin of water in His blessed hands, to wash the disciples' feet. The water explains the spiritual meaning. We have seen that the water in the third chapter is the type of the Word of God. It has the same meaning in this chapter. Peter first refused to have his feet washed; then when the Lord had said unto him, "If I wash thee not thou hast no part with Me," he asked Him to wash his hands and his head as well. "Jesus saith to him, He that hath been bathed needeth not save to wash his feet, but is clean every whit: and ye are clean, but not all." (Verse 10 contains two different words for washing; the one is "bathed" and the other "wash." This difference is not made in the Authorized Version.) When the Lord spoke of His disciples being bathed and clean every whit, He had references to the new birth by the water and the Spirit. They were all bathed, born again, except Judas, whom the Lord meant when He said "but not all." Titus 3:5 reads, literally translated: "Not by works of righteousness which we have done, but according to His mercy He saved us by the *bath of regeneration* and renewing of the Holy Spirit." This great work is done once for all and cannot be repeated, just as the natural birth cannot be repeated with the same individual.

The Lord washed the disciples' feet, not their hands. Hands are for work and the feet for walking. His action has a meaning in connection with our walk in the world. We contract defilement as we pass on through this world. And defilement severs communion with the Lord. We need therefore cleansing. All disciples need it. This He has graciously provided, and the washing of the disciples' feet typifies that needed cleansing. He uses His Word to bring this about. This is "the washing of water by the Word." He is the Advocate with the Father to restore us to fellowship. We must come to Him with our failures, our stumbling, imperfect walk, our defilement, and place ourselves into His hands as the disciples placed their soiled feet in His loving hands. His own perfect light will then search our innermost beings and bring to light what has defiled us, so that, after cleansing, we can enjoy His fellowship and have part with Him. This necessitates confession and self-judgment from our side. If this blessed truth is not realized and enjoyed in faith, if we do not come to Him for this service of love, we are at a distance from Him.

And we are also to walk in the same spirit of serving and wash one another's feet. As He lovingly deals with us, so we are to deal with one another. The one that is overtaken in a fault is to be restored by him that is spiritual in the spirit of meekness. "He that would cleanse another's feet must be at his feet to cleanse them." How little of all this in a practical way is known among God's people.

The betrayal by Judas is announced, and he goes into the night. The Lord announces also His imminent departure and gives them the new commandment " love one another." The chapter closes with the prediction of Peter's denial.

CHAPTER 14

1. Let not your heart be troubled! (14:1-7)
2. I am in the Father and the Father in Me (14:8-14)
3. The other Comforter promised (14:15-27)
4. I go unto the Father (14:28-31)

There is no break between these two chapters. The Lord continues His discourse to the eleven disciples. "Let not your heart be troubled!" What precious words of comfort! How many hearts have been soothed by them and how many tears they have dried! And after His loving words He said again: "Let not your heart be troubled, neither let it be afraid" (verse 27). He speaks first of all of the Father's house with its many abodes. The Father's house is no longer the temple, but the blessed home where the loving Father dwells and to which the Son of God was about to return in the form of man, after His death and resurrection. And the Father's house with its many abodes belongs to all who belong to Him; and all who are His, whom He is not ashamed to call brethren (John 20:17; Hebrews 2:11 and Psalm 22:22) belong to the Father's house. He has gone there to prepare a place. The ark of the covenant of the Lord went before Israel to search out a resting place for them (Numbers 10:33) and so He has gone before as our forerunner. What it all means "to prepare a place for you" we cannot fully know, but we know that His great work has removed every barrier for all who believe on Him, and in God's own time the full redemption of the purchased possession by the power of God will be accomplished (Eph. 1:14). Then His unfulfilled promise, "I will come again and receive you to Myself, that where I am ye may be also," will be fulfilled. He did not mean the death of His disciples. The death of the believer is not the coming of Himself to the child of God, but when the believer dies he goes to be with Christ. "I will come again" means His coming for those who belong to Him, His saints. How He will redeem this gracious promise and lead His own into the blessed home, is not revealed here. But He gave it in the form of a special revelation to the Apostle of the Gentiles (1 Thess. 4:13-18). Thomas speaks first. He misunderstood the words of the Lord and as troubled with unbelief. Yet Thomas loved the Lord and was greatly attached to Him, as we learn from chapter 11:16. Blessed answer he received. "I am the way"; He is the only way to God and to the Father's house; "the truth"; the revelation of the Father; and "the life" as well.

His answer to Philip's question shows that He was grieved. Yet how gentle the rebuke, "Have I been so long time with you, and yet hast thou not known Me, Philip? He that hath seen Me hath seen the Father." It is another great witness of His oneness with the Father. "I am in the Father and the Father in Me." And His own belonging to Him, know the Father in Christ and are His. (Solemn truth it is: "Whosoever denieth the Son, the same hath not the Father" 1 John 2:23). "And ye are Christ's and Christ is God's" (1 Cor. 3:23). Verse 12 has been a difficulty to many. What did our Lord mean when He said: "He that believeth on Me, the works that I do shall he do also, and greater works than these shall he do; because I go unto My Father"? Christian Scientists and extreme faith-healers claim that He meant His actual works of healing and Christians should do now the same works and even greataer works. But how could a believer do a greater work than the raising of Lazarus from the dead? The promise "the works that I do shall he do also" was fulfilled immediately after the day of Pentecost. The sick were healed by Peter's shadow, the lame man was healed, demons were driven out, and the dead were raised. Were these miracles to continue to the end of the dispensation? There is nowhere a statement in Scripture that this should be the case. "If miracles were continually in the Church, they would cease to be miracles. We never see them in the Bible except at some great crisis in the Church's history" (*Thoughts on the Gospel of John*). The "greater works" are spiritual works. The thousands saved in the beginning of the dispensation, the preaching of the gospel far hence among the Gentiles and the gracious results, are these greater works.

The promise of prayer in His Name follows. This is something new. It is to be addressed to the Father and the Son, and He promises, "If ye shall ask anything in My name I will do it." So far He had spoken of Himself and the Father. God the Father had been revealed in the Son, and now He speaks of the other Person of the Godhead, the Holy Spirit. He is promised to come, not to the world, but to His own as the other Comforter. (In Greek "Parakletos," one who is alongside to help. The same word as in 1 John 2:1 "Advocate.") He would come to abide in them, dwell with them and be in them. Verse 18, "I will come to you," does not mean His second coming as in verse 3. It is Christ Himself in Spirit. The result of the coming and abiding of the Comforter is a blessed knowledge for the believer. "Ye shall know that I am in My Father, and ye in Me, and I in you." Love to Him in the power of the Spirit must be expressed in obedience. Then there is the blessed legacy: "Peace I leave with you, My peace I give unto you." It is not peace with God, but the peace of Himself which He has left us. And that peace will ever be enjoyed if we believe and obey His words.

CHAPTER 15

1. The Vine and the Branch (15:1-18)
2. Communion with Him and its conditions (15:9-16)
3. Love one another! and the hatred of the world (15:17-27)

Israel is called a vine in the Old Testament (Ps. 80:8; Isaiah 5:1-8; Jerem. 2:21; Hosea 10:1) and Christ here in this parable takes the place of Israel and is the true vine. His disciples are the branches. Israel under the law covenant could not bear fruit for God, as the law cannot be the source of fruit-bearing. Fruit unto God can only spring from union with Christ. (See Romans 7:4.) He as the true vine on earth brought fruit unto God. The true believer is as closely united to Him as the branch. The life-sap of the vine circulates in the branch. And this life and nature in the believer produces the fruit. Our Lord said: "The Father who abideth in Me, He doeth the works." And believers should confess: The Lord Jesus Christ Who abideth in me and I in Him, He produces the fruit. Apart from Him we can do nothing. This vital union with Christ, dependence on Him, the result, fruit unto God, is more fully revealed in the Epistles.

He told His disciples, "now ye are clean (purged) through the word that I have spoken unto you." In chapter 13 He said, "ye are clean, but not all." Judas was then present, but he had gone out to betray Him. But what does it mean: "Every branch in Me that beareth not fruit He taketh away," and again, "if a man abide not in Me, he is cast forth as a branch, and is withered; and men gather them and cast them into the fire, and they are burned"? These words are often taken to teach that a believer's salvation and safety depends upon his fruit-bearing and his faithfulness. These two statements have been much perverted and misapplied as if they taught that a true branch in the vine, one who is really in Christ, may be cut off and be cast away to perish forever. If this were the meaning of these words our Lord would contradict His previous teachings. The branch in the vine which beareth not fruit is not a true believer at all, but one who by profession claims to be a branch in the vine. Note in verse 6 the change from "ye" to "a man." If our Lord had said "if *ye* abide in Me, *ye* shall be cast forth as a branch, etc.," it would mean a true believer. But the change makes it clear that no true disciple is meant, but one who makes a profession without being born again.

> These are awful words. They seem, however, to apply specially to backsliders and apostates, like Judas Iscariot. There must be about a man some *appearance* of professed faith in Christ, before he can come to the state described here. Doubtless there are those who seem to depart from grace, and to back from union with Christ; but we need not doubt in such cases that the grace was not real, but seeming, and the union was not true, but fictitious. Once more we must remember that we are reading a parable.
>
> After all, the final, miserable ruin and punishment of false professors, is the great lesson which the verse teaches. Abiding in Christ leads to fruitfulness in this life and everlasting happiness in the life to come. Departure from Christ leads to the everlasting fire of hell (J. C. Ryle).

The secret of true fruit-bearing (the manifestation of the new nature in our life) is abiding in Christ and Christ in us. "He that saith he abideth in Him ought himself also so to walk as He walked." The vine reproduces itself in the branch. And abiding in Christ means to walk in communion with Him and in utter dependence on Himself.

Then He declared: "As the Father hath loved Me, so have I loved you; continue ye in My love." Who is able to fathom the depths of these words! As the Father loved Him so He loveth us. Continue in My love means "abide in My love." "If ye keep My commandments, ye shall abide in My love; even as I have kept My Father's commandments and abide in His love." A blessed and equally solemn contrast! When we walk in fellowship with Him, when we are obedient to Him, as He was obedient to His Father in His path down here, then we abide in His love. Obedience to His words proves our love to Him, and walking in obedience we abide in His love "and hereby we know that we know Him, if we keep His commandments" (1 John 2:3). Then He declares, "that My joy might remain in you" and "that your joy might be full." For the knowledge of His joy and the fullness of joy we need to walk in obedience.

Once more He mentions the new commandment (13:34) "love one another." The Holy Spirit in the first Epistle of John enlarges upon this. In the world there is no love, but hatred. It hates the true believers, as the world hated Him. The true disciple must expect the same treatment which He receives in this world. "If they have persecuted me, they will also persecute you." Israel is in view in verse 24. They had seen and hated both Him and the Father.

Once more He announces the coming of the Paraclete, the Comforter. In chapter 14 our Lord said, "I will pray the Father and He shall send you another Comforter." Here He promises to send Him from the Father. He is to testify of Himself, witnessing to Him as glorified in the presence of the Father. They were to be witnesses of Him.

CHAPTER 16

1. Persecutions predicted (16:1-6)
2. The Comforter and His demonstration (16:7-15)
3. Sorrow and joy (16:16-22)
4. The Father Himself loveth you (16:23-27)
5. His final word before His prayer (16:28-33)

Again He announced coming persecutions. The world is the same to-day as then, and before this age ends these predictions of our Lord will be again fulfilled, during the great tribulation.

The coming of the Comforter is once more announced by Him. He could not come unless the Lord departed. He is to be sent to His own and when He comes He will make a great demonstration to the world. The word "reprove" in verse 8 is incorrect; the Greek word is difficult to express in its full meaning. Some have translated it by "rebuke," others use the word "convince" or "convict." The word "demonstrate" seems to be the nearest to the original. "And when He is come He will bring demonstration to the world of sin, and of righteousness and of judgment." The presence of the Holy Spirit in believers is the proof to the world that the whole world is guilty of the death of Christ; the whole world is under sin and therefore not on probation but under condemnation. The Holy Spirit is also the demonstration to the world of righteousness. This does not mean that He brings righteousness to the world, or makes the world righteous, as so many erroneously believe. Our Lord adds: "Of righteousness, because I go to My Father and ye see Me no more." The Holy One was rejected by the world, cast out as an unrighteous One. But He, Who owned and satisfied God's righteousness in dying as the substitute of sinners, is now exalted to the right hand of God; there He is the witness of righteousness. The presence of the Holy Spirit on earth demonstrates this fact. God raised Him from the dead and gave Him glory; the world sees Him no more as a Saviour personally on earth; but will see Him again as Judge, when He comes to judge the world in righteousness. Righteousness is fully displayed in the glory, where He is. The hope of righteousness is to be with Him there (Gal. 5:5). The Holy Spirit also brings demonstration to the world of judgment "because the prince of this world is judged." Sentence of judgment is pronounced against Satan, but not yet executed. He is the god of this age, but he was judged in His cross. Judgment must come upon the world and its prince. The Holy Spirit now present upon the earth in the believers demonstrates this fact.

Many things He had to say unto His disciples, which they could not bear. The many things He mentioned were made known in due time by the Holy Spirit come down from heaven. Of this He speaks in the verses which follow. Note the seven things spoken of the Spirit of truth: 1. He will guide you into all truth. 2. He shall not speak of Himself. 3. Whatsoever He shall hear that shall He speak. 4. He will show you things to come. 5. He shall glorify Me. 6. He shall receive of Mine. 7. He shall show it unto you. This is the work He does now among and in the saints. In all His work His gracious aim is to glorify Christ. When we glorify Christ, exalt Him, obey Him, follow Him and are devoted to Him, the Holy Spirit fills and uses us.

Then He spoke of the little while; the little while when they would see Him not; the little while, when they would see Him again. His final words before His great prayer are full of comfort and assurance. "Verily, verily, I say unto you, Whatsoever ye shall ask the Father in My name, He will give it you." "For the Father Himself loveth you, because ye have loved Me, and have believed that I came out from God." These are words precious to faith. Once more He speaks of His leaving the world to go back to the Father. But before that homegoing takes place they all were to be scattered and leave Him alone. He added: "Yet I am not alone, because the Father is with Me." Our Lord was never forsaken by His Father; He was forsaken of God, the Holy God, when He stood in the sinner's place.

The last utterance to His own is the assurance of peace in Him, the tribulation in the world, and the shout of victory: "Be of good cheer: I have overcome the world." And then His prayer.

CHAPTER 17

1. The finished work (17:1-5)
2. The Father's Name and the Father's gift (17:6-10)
3. Not of the world but kept in it (17:11-16)
4. Sanctification of Himself for His own (17:17-21)
5. The glorification (17:22-26)

His words were ended to the eleven disciples and next He spoke to the Father, and His disciples listened to all His blessed words. What moments these must have been! His words to the Father told them once more how He loved them, how He cared for them, what He had done and what He would do for them. Whenever we read this great Lord's prayer we can still hear Him pray for His beloved people. What a glimpse it gives of His loving heart! The prayer is His high-priestly prayer. He is in anticipation on the other side of the cross. He knows the work is finished, atonement is made; He is back with the Father and has received the glory. This anticipation is seen in His words, "I have finished the work Thou gavest Me to do"; "and now I am no more in the world";—"the glory Thou hast given Me I have given to them." It is impossible to give an exposition of this great chapter. Blessed depths are here which we shall fathom when we are with Him.

All He taught concerning Himself and eternal life, what believers are and have in Him, He mentions in His prayer. All the great redemption truths more fully revealed in the New Testament Epistles may be traced in this high-priestly prayer of our Lord. We mention seven of these great truths as made known by Him in addressing the Father.

1. *Salvation.* He has power to give eternal life to as many as the Father has given Him. "I have glorified Thee on the earth: I have finished the work Thou gavest Me to do." He glorified the Father in His life and He finished the work He came to do on the cross. There alone is redemption and salvation.

2. *Manifestation.* "I have manifested Thy name unto the men which Thou gavest Me out of the world" (verse 6). The Name of God, He, the Son, has made known to those who believe on Him is His Name as "Father." Such a name and relationship of the believer to God was not known in the Old Testament. The Son of God had to come from heaven's glory and declare the Father. After He gave His life and rose from the dead He spoke of "My Father and your Father." The Spirit of Sonship was given by Whom we cry: "Abba—Father."

3. *Representation.* He is our Priest and Advocate. He appears in the presence of God for us. "I pray for them; I pray not for the world but for them which Thou hast given Me; for they are Thine" (verse 9). Like the High Priest He carries only the names of His people upon His shoulders and upon His heart. He prays now for His church, His body, for every member. When the Church is complete and the body is united to Himself in glory, He will pray for the world. "Ask of Me," the Father has told Him, "and I will give Thee the nations for thine inheritance" (Ps. 2:8). When He asks this, He will receive the kingdoms of this world. What comfort it should be to all His people to know He prays for us individually! His love and His power are for us.

4. *Identification.* We are one with Him, and all His saints are one. The Church is His body, an organism and not an organization. He did not pray for a unity in organization, but for a spiritual unity, which exists. "That they also may be one in Us" is not an unanswered petition. The Spirit Who has come unites believers to Him and baptizes them into one body. "I in them, and Thou in Me, that they may be made perfect in one, that the world may know that Thou

hast sent Me, and hast loved them as Thou hast loved Me"—this looks on towards the blessed consummation, when the saints will appear with Christ in glory; then the world will know.

5. *Preservation.* He prayed for the keeping of His own. He commits them into His Father's hands. The believers' keeping for eternal life and glory rests not in their own hands but in His hands. Judas is mentioned as the son of perdition; he was never born again.

6. *Sanctification.* (See verses 17-19.) He is our Sanctification. In Him we are sanctified. We are sanctified by the truth, by walking in obedience. Believers are constituted saints in Christ and are called to walk in separaion. The separating power is the Word and the Spirit.

7. *Glorification.* "And the glory which Thou gavest Me I have given them, that they may be one as We are one"—"Father, I will that they also, whom Thou hast given Me, be with Me where I am; that they may behold My glory, which Thou hast given Me, for Thou lovest Me before the foundation of the world." This is His unanswered prayer. Some day it will be answered and all His saints will be with Him and share His glory.

And oh! the wealth of grace and truth in His wonderful words we must pass by! May His own Spirit lead us deeper and fill our hearts with joy unspeakable and full of glory.

III. "I Lay Down My Life, That I Might Take it Again" (18—21)

CHAPTER 18

1. The arrest in the garden (18:1-11)
2. Before Annas and Caiaphas and Peter's denial (18:12-27)
3. Before Pilate (18:28-38)
4. Not this Man, but Barabbas (18:39-40)

The hour of His suffering had now come. With His disciples He went across the brook Cedron into the garden. It is the Kidron mentioned frequently in Old Testament history. When David fled from his own son Absalom, he passed weeping over this brook (2 Sam. 15:23). See also 2 Chronicles 15:16 and 2 Kings 23:12. It is claimed that the way by which our Lord left the city was the way by which the scapegoat was yearly, on the great day of atonement, sent into the wilderness. The garden, though not named here, is Gethsemane. Judas knew the place, and the Lord knowing that Judas would betray Him, went deliberately there to be delivered into the hands of man. Nothing is said at all by John about the agony, the deep soul-exercise, through which our Lord passed in that night; nor is there a word about His sweat, as it were great drops of blood.

All these things are recorded in the Synoptic Gospels, in which His perfect humanity is described, they are passed over in the Gospel of His deity. But John describes a scene which the other Gospels omit. He manifests His power. When the band of men said that they sought Jesus of Nazareth, He said unto them, "I am He." Then the whole company went backward and fell to the ground. What a scene that must have been! Several hundred men with their lanterns, torches and weapons all prostrate on the ground before the One Man. They stood in the presence of Jehovah and His power and majesty was present so that the one word was sufficient to prostrate them all. It was a striking evidence that neither the treachery of Judas, nor the wicked hatred of Jews, nor the power of Rome, could touch our Lord. But the hour had now arrived when He was ready to give Himself up. Augustine made the following comment: "What shall He do when He comes to judge, Who did this when He was about to be judged? What shall be His might when He comes to reign, Who had this might when He was about to die?" Then after His second answer He said, "If therefore ye seek Me, let these go their way." Willingly He allows Himself bound, on the condition that His own must be free. It is a blessed illustration of the gospel. The Good Shepherd gives His life for the sheep. Substitution is fully revealed in this gracious statement. He gives Himself up that His people might be free.

Then Simon Peter drew the sword and cut off the right ear of Malchus. Peter had slept; had he been watching and praying it would not have occurred. And how beautiful the words of the Lord: "The cup which My Father hath given Me, shall I drink it?" Perfect willingness and readiness to drink the bitter cup were thus expressed in the presence of His disciples and His enemies.

Then follows the account of Peter's denial, the questioning before Annas, which is only reported by John, and finally He was taken into the judgment hall before Pilate. The miserable character of the Roman Governor is brought fully to light in this Gospel. He was destitute of all moral courage; he acted against better knowledge; he knew the Lord was innocent, yet he dared not to acquit Him for fear of displeasing the Jews. Verse 32 refers to the Lord's death by crucifixion, from the hands of the Gentiles. Note the four questions of Pilate. "Art Thou the King of the Jews?"—"What hast Thou done?"—"Art Thou a King then?" "What is truth?" The Roman historian Suetonius states that many rumors were then prevalent that a king was about to rise among the Jews who would have dominion over the whole world. No doubt Pilate knew of these rumors and therefore asked the Lord about His kingship. The answer of our Lord, "My kingdom is not of this world," has often been misconstrued to mean that the Lord never will have a kingdom in this world in the sense of a literal kingdom. Our post-millennial friends use it against a literal interpretation of the prophecies relating to the coming of an earthly kingdom of Christ. What our Lord meant by saying "My kingdom is not of this world" is, that His kingdom has not its origin or nature from the world. He will receive the kingdom promised unto Him from the Father's hands (Daniel 7:14).

CHAPTER 19

1. Behold the Man! (19:1-7)
2. The last question of Pilate and Christ's last word (19:8-11)
3. Delivered up and crucified (19:12-18)
4. The title upon the cross (19:19-22)
5. The parted garments (19:23-24)
6. Behold thy Son! Behold thy mother! (19:25-27)
7. It is finished! (19:28-30)
8. His legs not broken (19:31-33)
9. The testimony of the Scriptures (19:34-47)
10. The burial in the garden (19:38-42)

The cruel scourging, such as cruel Rome had invented, then took place. It often was so severe that prisoners died under the awful blows. What pen can ever describe the suffering and the shame He endured! Perhaps Pilate thought this awful scourging would satisfy the Jews, so that the Lord would be released. Then the mockery followed. The crown of thorns, the emblem of the curse of sin, was put upon His holy brow. The sin-bearer wore that crown for us, that we might wear a crown of glory. When He comes again He comes with many crowns (Rev. 19:12). They put the robe of purple, the imperial color, upon Him; ridiculed and smote Him. Then Pilate led Him forth and said: "Behold the Man." Was it pity or contempt? Most likely both. But oh! the sight! To see Him, Who is the Life and the Light, the Holy One, the Creator, treated thus by the creature of the dust! Satan's power energized the chief priests and officers, and the answer they give as they behold "the Man of Sorrows" is "Crucify Him!" "He made Himself the Son of God" was their wicked accusation. He is the Son of God and because He had come in marvellous love to this poor lost world, He was condemned to die.

The last word the Lord Jesus spoke to Pilate is found in verse 11. The authority given from above is from God, Who spared not His own Son; but the Jews, who delivered Him up to Pilate, have the greater sin. Once more we hear Pilate's voice, "Behold your King!" They answer : "Away with Him! Crucify Him!" And then again: "Shall I crucify your King?" The answer of complete apostasy follows: "We have no King but Caesar." Pilate is lost; he delivered Him to be crucified. We see the Lord bearing His cross to the place of the skull, Golgotha. Who can describe His agony and His sufferings as He was lifted up! Two others were crucified with Him. "He was numbered with transgressors" (Isaiah 53:12).

Above His cross was the title written by Pilate himself. It was written in Hebrew, Latin and Greek. There is no discrepancy between the different Gospels, because they give the inscriptions in different words. Pilate worded them differently in the three languages. Matthew and John report the Hebrew title; Mark gives the Latin and Luke the Greek inscription. (Matthew was guided to leave out "of Nazareth." This is in full accord with the purpose of his Gospel.)

The coat (robe) without seam, woven from the top throughout, is only mentioned by John. The German expositor Bengal calls attention to the fact that our Lord never "rent" His garments in sorrow like Job, Jacob, Joshua, Caleb, Jephthah, Hezekiah, Mordecai, Ezra, Paul and Barnabas. The seamless robe is typical of His perfect righteousness, which now was stripped from Him by man's hand and thus He received the place as the evildoer. Then the prophecy of Psalm 22:18 was literally fulfilled. Could there be anything else but a *literal* fulfillment of prophecy?

The importance of interpreting prophecy literally, and not figuratively, is strongly shown in this verse. The system of interpretation which unhappily prevails among many Christians—I mean the system of spiritualizing away all the plain statements of the prophets, and accommodating them to the Church of Christ—can never be reconciled with such a verse as this. The plain, literal meaning of words should evidently be the meaning placed on all the statements of Old Testament prophecy. This remark of course does not apply to symbolical prophecies, such as those of the seals, trumpets, and vials in Revelation.

And then the loving tenderness He manifested towards His mother.

Here, with one exception in the first chapter of Acts, we part with Mary; she is not mentioned in the after-books. In all the doctrine of the Epistles she has no place. Blessed among women as she is surely by her connection with the human nature of our Lord, the entire silence of Scripture as to her in that fulness of Christian truth which it was the office of the Spirit of truth to communicate is the decisive overthrow of the whole Babel-structure of Mariolatry which Romanism has built up upon a mere sand-foundation. She remains for us in the Word of God, a simple woman rejoicing in God her Saviour,—a stone in the temple to His praise, and with no temple of her own. To use the grace of the Redeemer in taking flesh among us by her means to exalt the mother to the dishonor of Christ her Lord is truly a refined wickedness worthy of the arch-deceiver of mankind (*Numerical Bible*).

John has nothing to say of the darkness which enshrouded the cross. Nor do we find here the cry of the forsaken One: "My God, My God, why hast Thou forsaken Me?" The Father did not forsake the Son; this was His statement in chapter 16:32. "After this, Jesus knowing that all things were now accomplished, that the Scriptures might be fulfilled, saith, I thirst." It is not so much the awful thirst connected with crucifixion which is viewed here, as it is His perfect obedience to do the Father's will and that the Scriptures might be fulfilled. "He bowed His head and gave up the spirit." In Luke's Gospel we read that He said: "Father, into Thy hands I commend My spirit" (23:46); John says nothing of Him commending His spirit, for as the Son of God He did not need to commend Himself to the Father. The final word preceding the giving up of His spirit is the majestic "It is finished." In the Greek it is but one word, "tetelestai." Never before and never after was ever spoken one word which contains and means so much. It is the shout of the mighty Victor. And who can measure the depths of this one word!

Psalm 34:20 was fulfilled; "A bone of Him shall not be broken." Scripture had to be fulfilled. The spear, which pierced His blessed side, fully evidenced that He had died. The blood and water have a most precious meaning. That it was a supernatural thing we do not doubt. The blood stands for the atonement, which had been made; the water for cleansing. The Jews have a strange tradition that from the rock which was smitten by Moses in the wilderness there flowed, when first smitten, blood and water (*Shamoth Rabba*). John alone mentions this blessed fact. "It is a beautiful testimony of divine grace, answering the last insult man could heap upon Him. They drove Him outside the camp, put Him to death on the Cross, and then, to make His death doubly sure, the soldier pierced His side. Salvation was God's answer to man's insult, for the blood and water were the signs of it." John speaks of this never to be forgotten occurrence in his first Epistle (5:6). There he mentions water first. It denotes purifying which man needs, and that has come with all its attending blessings by His precious blood. But notice John writes: "And again another scripture saith, They shall look on Him whom they pierced." He does not say, another Scripture was fulfilled. Zech. 12:10 was not fulfilled when He died, but will be fulfilled when He comes again and the believing remnant of Israel mourns for Him.

Nicodemus is mentioned for the third and last time in the Gospel. He came to Jesus by night and heard the Gospel message from His lips. Later he ventured a weak and timid defence (7:48-53); here he comes out boldly honouring the body of Jesus. Surely he believed and therefore confessed the Lord.

CHAPTER 20

1. The empty sepulchre (20:1-10)
2. The Risen One and Mary of Magdala (20:11-18)
3. The gathered company and He in the midst (20:19-23)
4. The second time (20:24-29)
5. The purpose of John's record (20:30-31)

"I lay down My life that I might take it up again." The sufferings were accomplished. The Good Shepherd laid down His life for the sheep and now we learn how He arose from the dead. Chapter 2:19 was fulfilled. "Destroy this temple and in three days I will raise it up." The stone is rolled away; the sepulchre is empty. Mary of Magdala carried the good news to Peter and John. Peter and John ran together to the sepulchre, and John outran Peter. In the sepulchre all is in order. If a thief had stolen the body he would have acted in fear and haste. A thief would not have gone about in such an orderly way. The linen clothes were lying in the proper place; the napkin (soudarion—sweatcloth) was folded inwards (this is the meaning of "entetuligmenon") in a place by itself. He had detached Himself in a miraculous way without disturbing them at all. It is an evidence of His resurrection in His own power as Son of God.

And how beautiful is the incident when Mary stood weeping and looking into the sepulchre! She beheld two angels there, yet she was not frightened when she beheld these mysterious Beings. Her heart was so occupied with her Lord that she did not even inquire of the angels. But they addressed her: "Woman, why weepest thou?" Then He came Himself. Her tears of ignorance and unbelief held her eyes that she did not recognize Him till He, Who in resurrection is the great Shepherd of the sheep, called her by name. What sound that one word "Mary" must have had in her ears and heart! She would fall at His feet and hold Him, as the other women held Him by the feet and worshipped Him (Matt. 28:9). But He told her: "Touch me not; for I am not yet ascended to My Father; but go to My brethren and say unto them, I ascend unto My Father and your Father; and to My God and your God." Matthew reports how they touched Him and held Him by the feet. He is presented in that Gospel as Israel's King. Not a word is said in the first Gospel of His ascension. He is presented in Matthew as if He were to remain on earth, in an earthly relationship with His people. This is why He permitted the holding of His feet. It is symbolical of how the remnant of Israel will enjoy His presence on earth as King in the day of His return.

But John's Gospel reveals a new relationship. He is to ascend into heaven to His Father. She must not hold Him as to keep Him here. (The word "touch" really means: to fasten oneself to, to hang on, to lay hold of.) As true believers we are linked with the glorified Lord. This higher relationship He makes known and she becomes the bearer of the great message. The relationship centers in the word "brethren." Risen from the dead He calls His own "brethren" and speaks of "My Father and your Father, My God and your God." He is not ashamed to call us brethren, because He that sanctifieth and they that are sanctified are all of one (Ps. 22:21-22; Hebrews 2:11-12). Thus He, the Son of God, Who laid down His life and took it again has brought us to God, His God and His Father. The grain of wheat has brought forth its blessed and gracious fruit in resurrection.

The evening scene of that wonderful day, when He stood in their midst, is very suggestive. In a measure the assembled disciples correspond to the two who, in the first chapter, on the first day abode with Him. Though John does not mention the Church, here is a beautiful picture of what the Church is. They are shut in and Judaism is shut out. He is in the midst. "Where two or three are gathered together in unto My name, there am I in the midst." Here it is fulfilled for the first time. There is the message of peace; the sending forth; the Holy Spirit, Who comes from Him, Who as the last Adam is the quickening Spirit. He communicates spiritual life, which is divine life. And the authority of the church in discipline on earth, representing Himself, is made known by Him in verse 23. This authority is not conferred upon a priestly class, a doctrine which has produced the most obnoxious corruption of Christianity, but upon believers, who constitute a church.

Thomas corresponds to Nathanael at the close of the first chapter. Both are unbelieving. Both see first and then believe. Both acknowledge Him as God. Thomas, like Nathanael, is the type of the unbelieving Jewish remnant. The Lord comes the second time and then the remnant of His earthly people will fall at His feet and say, "My Lord and my God."

CHAPTER 21

1. At the sea of Tiberias and the third manifestation (21:1-14)
2. Peter's restoration and ministry and the manner of His death predicted (21:15-19)
3. Tarry till I come! (21:20-23)
4. Conclusion (21:24-25)

This chapter has often been looked upon as an appendix to the Gospel of John. It is not. Quite true, John states in the last two verses of the preceding chapter the purpose of this Gospel, but that does not mean that the twenty-first chapter has no connection with the Gospel itself. Verse 14 shows that it belongs to the Gospel proper.

The third time that He showed Himself after His resurrection:—The first time on the first day of the week (20:19); this is typical of the present age, when He is in the midst of His people. The second time, when Thomas was present; typical of His second coming and manifestation to Israel. The third time on the Lake of Tiberias; typical of the future blessings through Israel, and corresponding to the third day in chapter 2, when there was a marriage in Cana of Galilee. The miraculous draught of fishes took place by His power, but the net did not go to pieces. It was different before His death and resurrection; then the net broke. The scene on the lake of Tiberias foreshadows the ingathering of the nations into His kingdom when He returns. The number of the fish caught is given, one hundred and fifty-three. The number of the nations of the world known at that time was exactly 153. How significant this is! Thus all the nations of the world will be gathered into His kingdom.

But there are blessed spiritual lessons here. He is seen as Lord over His own. He can direct our service as He directed the disciples in casting the net at the right side of the ship. He provides for the need of His servants, as He did then in preparing a breakfast for them (verse 9). He restored Peter, and gives a higher and a better service. He also appoints the time and the manner of the servant's departure out of this life; He told Peter when and how he was to die. He said of John, "If I will that he tarry till I come, what is that to thee?" The Lord did not say that he should not die. John lived the longest of the disciples, and on the Isle of Patmos he beheld the events of the future and heard the voice, "Come up hither" and immediately he was in the Spirit and beheld heavenly things. The words of our Lord find likewise an application in connection with John's writings.

"It is simple enough to say that John lives on in his writings. But then it might be urged, that is only what all the inspired writers will; still it cannot but come to mind that, in fact, John's writings not only predict circumstantially the Lord's return, but stretch over all the intervening time till then. While he does not take us up into heaven, as Paul does, and show us our place in the glorified Man up there, yet all the more he seems to abide with the people of God on earth until Christ's return, as a human presence watching and caring for them. John may be thus truly said to be waiting with those on earth for his absent Lord in a way in which we could not speak of any other inspired writer" (F. W. Grant).

The last word John reports in His Gospel, coming from lips of our Lord, is "Follow thou Me." And thus He speaks to all of His people. Wonderful Gospel it is, this Gospel of the Son of God and the eternal life! How full and rich each portion of it! And oh! the grace which has sought us, saved us, made us one with Him, keeps us and which will soon bring us home to the Father's house with its many mansions. May we follow Him in loving obedience, till He comes.

THE ACTS
OF THE APOSTLES

Introduction

The book known by the name "The Acts of the Apostles" (the oldest manuscript, the *Sinaiticus,* dating from the 4th century, gives the title simply as "The Acts," which is, no doubt, the better name for the book) follows the four Gospel records. This is its proper place. The books of the New Testament have been correctly divided into five sections, corresponding to the first five books, with which the Bible begins, that is the Pentateuch. The four Gospels are the *Genesis* of the New Testament. Here we have the great beginning, the foundation upon which the subsequently revealed Christian doctrines rest. The book of Acts is in the *Exodus*; God leads out from bondage a heavenly people and sets them free. It is the great historical book of the New Testament given by inspiration, the beginning of the church on earth. The Pauline Epistles are the *Leviticus* portion. Holiness unto the Lord, the believer's separation and standing in Christ; what the believer has and is in Christ, by whose blood redemption has been purchased, are the core truths of these Epistles. The Epistles of Peter, James, John and Jude, known by the name of the Catholic Epistles, are for the wilderness journey of God's people, telling us of trials and suffering; these correspond to the Book of *Numbers.* The book of Revelation in which God's ways are rehearsed, and, so to speak, a review is given of the entire prophetic Word concerning the Jews, the Gentiles and the Church of God has therefore the same character as *Deuteronomy.*

By Whom Was This Book Written

There is no doubt that the writer of the third Gospel record is the one whom the Holy Spirit selected to write this account of the establishment of the Church on earth and the events connected with it. This becomes clear if we read the beginning of that Gospel and compare it with the beginning of Acts. The writer in the third Gospel says: "It seemed good to me also, having had perfect understanding of all things from the first, to write unto thee in order, most excellent *Theophilus,* that thou mightest know the certainty of those things, wherein thou hast been instructed" (Luke 1:3-4). The Acts of the Apostles begin: "The *former* treatise have I made, O *Theophilus,* of all that Jesus began both to do and teach." The former treatise known to Theophilus is the third Gospel, called the Gospel of Luke. The writer of that Gospel must therefore be the penman of the book of Acts. Though we do not find Luke's name mentioned in the Gospel, nor in the second book, he was entrusted to write by inspiration, there is no doubt that he wrote them both. We find his name mentioned a number of times in the Epistles, and these references give us the only reliable information we have. In Colossians 4:14 we read of him as "the beloved physician." In the Epistle of Philemon he is called a fellow laborer of the Apostle Paul and from the last Epistle the great Apostle wrote, the second Epistle to Timothy, we learn that Luke was in Rome with Paul and was faithful to him, while others had forsaken the prisoner of the Lord. From Colossians 4 we also may gather that he was not a Jew, but a Gentile, for with the eleventh verse Paul had mentioned those of the circumcision. Epaphras was one of the Colossians, a Gentile, and then follow the names of Luke and Demas, both of them undoubtedly Gentiles. The reason that the Holy Spirit selected a Gentile to write the Gospel which pictures our Lord as the Man and the Saviour and the book of Acts, is as obvious as it is interesting. Israel had rejected God's gift, and the glad news of salvation was now to go to the Gentiles. The Gospel of Luke addressed by a Gentile to a Gentile (Theophilus) is the Gospel for the Gentiles, and Luke the Gentile was chosen to give the history of the Gospel going forth from Jerusalem to the Gentiles.

Internal Evidences

There are numerous internal evidences which show likewise that the writer of the third Gospel is the instrument through whom the book of Acts was given. For instance, there are about fifty peculiar phrases and words in both books which are rarely found elsewhere; they prove the same author.

Then we learn from the book of Acts that

Luke was an eyewitness of some of the events recorded by him in that book. He joined the Apostle during his second missionary journey to Troas (16:10). This evidence is found in the little word *"we."* The writer was now in company of the Apostle, whose fellow laborer he was. He went with Paul to Macedonia and remained some time in Philippi. He was Paul's fellow traveler to Asia and Jerusalem (21:17). He likewise was with him in his imprisonment in Caesarea, and then on to Rome. There is no doubt that Luke had completely written and sent forth the Book of the Acts of the Apostles at the end of the two years mentioned in Acts 28:30, though the critics claim a much later period.

The Contents and Scope of the Book

The first verse gives us an important hint. The former treatise, the Gospel of Luke, contains that which Jesus *began* to do and teach. The book of Acts contains therefore the continuation of the Lord's actions, no longer on earth, but from the glory. The actions of the risen and glorified Christ can easily be traced through the entire book. We give a few illustrations. In the first chapter He acts in the selection of the twelfth Apostle, who was to take the place of Judas. In the second chapter He himself poured forth the Holy Spirit, for Peter made the declaration "therefore, being by the right hand of God exalted, and having received of the Father the promise of the Holy Spirit, *He* has poured out this which ye behold and hear." And in the close of the second chapter we behold another action of the risen Lord, "the Lord added to the assembly daily those that were to be saved." In the third chapter He manifested His power in the healing of the lame man. Throughout this book we behold Him acting from the glory, guiding, directing, comforting and encouraging His servants. These beautiful and manifold evidences of Himself being with His own and manifesting His power in their behalf can easily be traced in the different chapters.

Then on the very threshold of the book we have the historical account of the coming of that other Comforter, whom the Lord had promised, the Holy Spirit. On the day of Pentecost the third Person of the Trinity, the Holy Spirit, came. His coming marks the birthday of the Church. After that event we see Him present with His people as well as in them. In connection with the Lord's servants in filling them, guiding them, fitting them, sustaining them in trials and persecutions, in the affairs of the Church, we behold the actions of the Holy Spirit on earth. He is the great administrator in the Church. Over fifty times we find Him mentioned, so that some have called this book, "the Acts of the Holy Spirit." There are no doctrines about the Holy Spirit and His work in the book of Acts. But we find the practical illustrations of the doctrines of the Holy Spirit found elsewhere in the New Testament.

In the third place another supernatural being is seen acting in this book. It is the enemy, Satan, the hinderer and the accuser of the brethren. We behold him coming upon the scene and acting through his different instruments, either as the roaring lion, or as the cunning deceiver with his wiles. Wherever he can, he attempts to hinder the progress of the Gospel. This is a most important aspect of this book, and indeed very instructive. Aside from the human instruments prominent in this book of Acts, we behold three supernatural beings acting. The risen and glorified Christ, the Holy Spirit, and Satan.

Another hint about the contents of this book and its scope we find at the close of the Gospel of Luke. There the risen Christ said "that repentance and remission of sins should be preached in His Name to all the nations beginning at Jerusalem." In the first chapter of Acts the Spirit of God reports the commission of the Lord, about to ascend, in full. "Ye shall be my witnesses both in Jerusalem and in all Judea and Samaria, and to the end of the earth." The book of Acts shows us how this mission, beginning in Jerusalem, was carried out. The witness begins in the city where our Lord was crucified. Once more an offer was made to the nation Israel. Then we behold the gospel going forth from Jerusalem and all Judea to Samaria, and after that to the Gentiles, and through the Apostle Paul it is heralded in the different countries of the Roman empire. The parable of our Lord in Matthew 22:1-10 gives us prophetically the history of these events. First the guests were called to the wedding and they would not come. This was the invitation given by the Lord to His earthly people when He moved among them. They received Him not. Then came a renewed offer with the assurance that all things are ready. This is exactly what we find in the beginning in the book of the Acts. Once more to Jerusalem and to the Jewish nation is offered the kingdom, and signs and miracles take place to show that Jesus is the Christ risen from the dead. In the above parable our Lord predicted what the people would do with the servants, who bring the second offer. They would ignore the message and treat the servants spitefully and kill them. This we find fulfilled in the persecution which broke out in Jerusalem, when Apostles were imprisoned and others were killed. The Lord also predicted in His parable the fate of the wicked city. It was to be burned. Thus it happened to Jerusalem. And after the second offer had been rejected the servants were to go to the highways to invite the guests. And this shows that the invitation was to go out to the Gentiles.

Jerusalem is in the foreground in this book, for the beginning was to be in Jerusalem, "to the Jew first." The end of the book takes us to Rome, and we see the great Apostle a prisoner there, a most significant, prophetic circumstance.

The Division of the Book of Acts

"But ye shall receive power after that the Holy Spirit is come upon you, and ye shall be My witnesses both in Jerusalem and in all Judea and in Samaria and unto the uttermost part of the earth" (Acts 1:8). This verse in the beginning of the book is the key to the historical account it contains. The Holy Spirit came on the day of Pentecost and the witness to Christ began. We make a threefold division.

I. THE WITNESS TO JERUSALEM, THE ADVENT OF THE SPIRIT AND THE FORMATION OF THE CHURCH, THE OFFER TO ISRAEL AND ITS REJECTION (1—7)

II. THE WITNESS TO SAMARIA, SAUL'S CONVERSION AND PETER'S WITNESS IN CAESAREA (8—12)

III. THE WITNESS TO THE GENTILES, THE APOSTLE TO THE GENTILES, AND HIS MINISTRY AND CAPTIVITY (13—18)

While undoubtedly all witnessed, the book of Acts reports mostly the acts of Peter and Paul. The Apostle Peter is in the foreground in the first part of the book. After the twelfth chapter he is mentioned but once more. Then Paul comes upon the scene with his great testimony concerning "The Gospel of Christ, the power of God unto salvation to every one that believeth." Jerusalem is prominent in the start. Antioch, the Gentile center of Christian activity, follows, and Rome is seen at the close of the book. The witness of which the risen Lord spoke was therefore given to Jerusalem, in all Judea, in Samaria. Then to the uttermost part of the earth. Africa received a witness in the conversion of the Ethiopian Eunuch. Then followed the witness to Asia and Europe. The book of Acts ends, so to speak, in an unfinished way.

Analysis and Annotations

I. The Witness to Jerusalem, the Advent of the Spirit and the Formation of the Church, the Offer to Israel and its Rejection (1—7)

CHAPTER 1

1. The introduction (1:1-3)
2. The final words of the risen Lord (1:4-8)
3. The ascension (1:9-11)
4. The waiting company (1:12-14)
5. Matthias chosen in the place of Judas (1:15-26)

The introductory words prove that Luke is the writer. In the former treatise, Luke had addressed to Theophilus (the Gospel of Luke) the beginning of the teaching, and acts of our Lord were reported. The book of Acts reveals the same wonderful person witnessed to by the Holy Spirit. Eight things are mentioned concerning our Lord in the beginning of this book. 1. His earthly life of doing and teaching. 2. He gave them commandments. 3. He had suffered. 4. He had showed Himself after His passion by many infallible proofs. 5. He was seen by them for forty days. 6. He spoke of the things which concern the kingdom of God. 7. He was taken up. 8. He will come again. Once more He gave to them the promise of the coming of the Holy Spirit. In verse 5 we read "ye shall be baptized with the Holy Spirit not many days hence." John the Baptist had spoken also of a baptism with fire. The Lord omits the word fire, because the baptism with fire is a judgment act linked with His second coming (Matthew 3:12).

The question they asked of Him concerning the restoration of the kingdom to Israel was perfectly in order. This is the Hope of Israel; the hope of the Church is not an earthly kingdom, but a heavenly glory; not to be subjects in the kingdom on earth, but to reign and rule with the King. The answer they received assured them that the kingdom was to be restored to Israel; the times and seasons for that, however, rested with the Father.

Then they saw Him ascending. What a sight it must have been! Their Lord was "received into glory." Gradually in majestic silence He must have been lifted out of their midst. Lovingly His eyes must have rested upon them, while their eyes saw only Him. Then a cloud received Him out of their sight. "And then a cloud took Him in (the literal rendering) out of their sight." The cloud was not a common cloud of vapor, but the glory-cloud. It was the cloud of glory which had filled Solomon's temple, which so often in Israel's past history had appeared as an outward sign of Jehovah's presence. Then angels announced His coming in like manner. And thus He will come, even back to the Mount of Olives (Zech. 14:4).

However, we must beware of confounding this event given here with that blessed hope, which is the hope of the Church. The coming of the Lord here is His visible coming as described in the prophetic books of the Old Testament; it is His coming to establish His rule upon the earth. It is the event spoken of in Daniel 7:14 and Rev. 1:7. When He comes in like manner as He went up, His saints come with Him (Col. 3:4; 1 Thess. 3:13). The hope of the church is to meet Him in the air, and not to see Him coming in the clouds of heaven. The coming here "in like manner" is His coming for Israel and the nations. The coming of the Lord for His Church, before His visible and glorious manifestation, is revealed in 1 Thess. 4:16-18. It is well to keep these important truths in mind. Confusion between these is disastrous. He left them to enter into the holy of holies, to exercise the priesthood which Aaron exercised on the day of atonement, though our Lord is a priest after the order of Melchisedec. And when this promise of the two men in white garments is fulfilled, he will come forth to be a priest upon His throne.

Then we see them as a waiting company. They are not the Church. Their waiting for the coming of the Holy Spirit ended ten days after, when the Holy Spirit came. Since then He is here. To wait for another outpouring of the Holy Spirit, as so often done by well-meaning people, is unscriptural. Among the waiting ones were "Mary the mother of Jesus and His brethren." The one chosen by God's grace to be the mother of our Lord, Mary, who had conceived by the Holy Spirit, is waiting with the other disciples. This proves that she has no place of superiority among God's people. When the Holy Spirit came she too was baptized by the Spirit into the one body of which, through the grace of God, she is a member like any other believer in our Lord. After this she is not mentioned again in the Word of God. Mary, the mother of Jesus, has absolutely no relation with the redemption work of the Son of God. His brethren, according to John 7:5, were unbelieving. Since then they had also believed on Him.

The action of Peter in proposing to place another in Judas's place was not a mistake as some claim. Peter acted upon the Scriptures and was guided by the Lord. Some hold that Paul was meant to be the twelfth apostle. This is incorrect. Paul's apostleship was of an entirely different nature than that of the twelve. Not till Israel's complete failure had been demonstrated in the stoning of Stephen was he called, and then not of men, but by revelation of Jesus Christ. There is positive proof that the Holy Spirit sanctioned this action of the disciples. See 1 Cor. 15:5-8. Furthermore, twelve apostles were needed as a body of witnesses to the entire nation. How strange it would have been if Peter and the ten, eleven men in all, instead of twelve, had stood up on the day of Pentecost to witness to Christ in the presence of the assembled multitude.

CHAPTER 2

1. The outpouring of the Holy Spirit (2:1-4)
2. The immediate effect of His presence (2:5-13)
3. Peter's address (2:14-36)
4. The result of the witness (2:37-41)
5. The gathered company in fellowship (2:42-47)

This is an important chapter. The promise of the Father was fulfilled, the Holy Spirit, the third person of the Trinity came down to earth, to be the other Comforter. He came on that blessed day.

Two things are at once apparent. He came upon the assembled believers individually, and also did a work in a corporate way. Each believer on that day was filled with the Holy Spirit. He came as the indweller to each. But He also was present as the mighty rushing wind which filled all the house. He did not only come upon each, but all were baptized with the Holy Spirit, and united into a body. In 1 Corinthians 12:13 the more complete revelation is given concerning this fact. "For by one Spirit are we all baptized into one body, whether we be Jews or Gentiles, whether we be bond or free, and have been all made to drink into one Spirit." The one Spirit is the Holy Spirit as He came on the day of Pentecost, the one body is the Church. All believers were on that day united by the Spirit into the one body, and since then, whenever and wherever a sinner believes in the finished work of Christ, he shares in that baptism and is joined by the same Spirit to that one body. A believer may be in dense ignorance about all this, as indeed a great many are; but this does not alter the gracious fact of what God has done. The believing company was then formed on the day of Pentecost into one body. *It was the birthday of the Church.*

There is an interesting correspondency between the second chapter of Luke and the second chapter of Acts which we cannot pass by. In the first chapter of Luke we have the announcement of the birth of the Saviour. In the second chapter of the Gospel of Luke we read of the accomplishment of that promise given to the Virgin. And so the second chapter of Acts contains the fulfillment of a similar promise. The Holy Spirit came and the Church, the mystical body of Christ, began.

But the truth concerning the Church was not revealed on the day of Pentecost. The twelve apostles were ignorant of what had taken place, and that the Church formed would be composed of believing Gentiles as well as believing Jews; nor did they know anything of the different relationships of the Church. Through the Apostle Paul the full truth concerning the Church was made known.

The coming of the Holy Spirit was accompanied with visible signs. A new dispensation was inaugurated with outward signs, just as the giving of the law for that dispensation was accompanied with similar signs (Hebrews 12:18-19). The rushing mighty wind filled the house, "and there appeared unto them cloven tongues like as of fire and it sat upon each of them." The filling of the house indicated the fact that His abode would be the house; the Church and the parted tongues upon each head testified to the fact that each had received Him. The Person, not a power or influence given by measure, had filled each believer. He came as the gift of God.

Then they spoke in different languages. The speaking in other languages was a miracle produced by the Holy Spirit, who had come upon them in mighty power. These Galileans spoke in different tongues, sixteen at least, if not more. "By a sudden and powerful inspiration of the Holy Spirit, these disciples uttered, not of their own minds, but as mouthpieces of the Holy Spirit, the praises of God in various languages hitherto, and possibly at the time itself, unknown to them."[1]

The significance of this miracle speaking in other tongues is not hard to discover. It was the oral manifestation of the parted tongues of fire, which had come upon each. Besides this it proclaimed the great fact that the Holy Spirit had come to make known the blessed gospel to all nations under heaven, and though no Gentiles were present when this took place, the languages of the Gentiles were heard, and that from Jewish lips, showing that the gospel should go forth unto the uttermost parts of the earth. But did they all utter an orderly discourse, preaching the truth concerning Christ, or was their speech of an ecstatic nature, in the form of praising God? We believe the latter was the case. We look in vain through this book for the evidences that these believers continued speaking these different languages.

Now, while it is true that there was such a gift as speaking in an unknown tongue in the apostolic age, and no Christian believer would doubt the power of God to impart to a person the gift to preach the gospel in a foreign tongue, we do not believe that this gift of speaking in an unknown tongue was to abide in the Church. Repeatedly claims were made in years gone by that it had been restored (for instance during the Irvingite delusion in England), but in every case it was found to be spurious or emanating from the enemy. The present day "apostolic or pentecostal movement" with its high pretensions and false doctrines, lacking true scriptural knowledge and wisdom, creating new schisms in the body, with its women leaders and teachers, has all the marks of the same great counterfeiter upon it. (For a closer examination of the speaking in tongues see our larger work on this book, *The Acts of the Apostles.*)

Then Peter stood up with the eleven and gave his great testimony. What boldness he manifested! What a change from the Peter before Pentecost! It was the result of the Holy Spirit he had received. His address dealt with the great historical facts of the gospel, bearing

---

[1]Dean Alford, *Greek Testament.*

witness to the resurrection and exaltation of the Lord Jesus. In its scope and pointedness it is a remarkable production. It has three parts. 1. He refutes the charge of drunkenness and quotes from Joel, avoiding, however, the statement that Joel's prophecy was fulfilled (verses 14-22). (Joel's prophecy will be fulfilled in connection with the second coming of Christ. Then the Holy Spirit, after the predicted judgments are passed, will be poured out upon all flesh. To put the fulfilment in our day is erroneous. See our exposition of Joel.) 2. Next he gives a brief testimony of the life and the resurrection of the Lord Jesus. He quotes from the Sixteenth Psalm (verses 23-28). 3. The last part of his address shows that the Holy Spirit had come as the result of the resurrection and exaltation of the Lord Jesus Christ. The briefest but deepest Messianic Psalm is quoted in this section (Psalm 110). The address as reported closes with the significant word: "Let the whole house of Israel, therefore, assuredly know that God has made Him, this Jesus whom you have crucified, both Lord and Christ" (verses 29-36). Notice how the Holy Spirit uses through Peter the Word of God. The Holy Spirit testifies in and through the written Word. The aim of Peter's address was to prove to the house of Israel that the Crucified One is raised from the dead and that God made Him Lord and Christ, witnessed to by the presence of the Holy Spirit. The Person of Christ and His work is still the great theme. Whenever He is preached the power of God will accompany the message.

Wonderful results followed. The Word had been preached and the power of the Holy Spirit brought the great truths to the hearts and consciences of the hearers. Their guilt in having crucified Jesus had been fully demonstrated, and now they asked, "Now, brethren, what shall we do?" Peter gives the needed answer. Repentance and baptism are the conditions. If these are fulfilled remission of sins and the gift of the Holy Spirit are promised to follow. Peter's words wrongly interpreted have led to much confusion. Upon these words doctrines, especially concerning water baptism, have been built, which are not only nowhere else taught in the Bible, but which are opposed to the gospel. The words of Peter to his Jewish brethren have been used to make water baptism a saving ordinance, that only by submission to water baptism, with repentance and faith in the Lord Jesus, can remission of sins and the gift of the Holy Spirit be obtained. We do not enlarge upon these unscriptural conceptions nor answer the utterly false doctrine of "baptismal regeneration," but rather point out briefly what these words of Peter mean. We must bear in mind that Peter addressed those who had *openly* rejected Jesus. They had, therefore, also openly to acknowledge their wrong and thus openly own Him as Messiah, whom they had disowned by delivering Him into the hands of lawless men. Repentance meant for them to own their guilt in having opposed and rejected Jesus. Baptism in the name of Jesus Christ (in which it differs from the baptism of John) was the outward expression of that repentance. It was for these Jews, therefore, a preliminary necessity. And here we must not forget that Peter's preaching on the day of Pentecost still had to do with the kingdom, as we shall more fully learn from his second address in the third chapter. Another offer of the kingdom was made to the nation. The great fact that the Holy Spirit had begun to form the body of Christ, the Church, as stated before, was not revealed then. In this national testimony the word "repent" stands in the foreground, and their baptism in the name of Him whom they had crucified was a witness that they owned Him now and believed on Him.

About three thousand souls were added, who repented and were baptized. Then we behold them in blessed fellowship. Doctrine stands first. It is the prominent thing. They continued steadfastly in the apostle's doctrine. In the doctrine of the apostles they were in fellowship together, and that fellowship was expressed in "the breaking of bread." It was not a common meal, but the carrying out of the request the Lord had made in the night He was betrayed, when He instituted what we call "the Lord's supper." Prayer is also mentioned. They had all things in common. They were like a great family, which in reality they were through the grace of God.

And how happy they were! They had Christ, and that was enough. No system of theology, creeds, set of forms or any such thing, with which historical Christianity abounds—"Nothing but Christ." They received their food with gladness and singleness of heart, praising God and having favor with all the people. Joy and singleness of heart are two great characteristics of the true believer.

CHAPTER 3

1. The healing of the lame man (3:1-11)
2. Peter's address and appeal (3:12-26)

The lame man, forty years old, at the gate called Beautiful is the type of the moral condition of the nation, like the impotent man whom the Lord healed (John 5). Israel with all its beautiful religious ceremonies was helpless, laying outside with no strength to enter in. Peter commands the lame man in the name of Jesus Christ of Nazareth to rise up and to walk. He is instantly healed. He then walked and leaped and entered through the gate as a worshipper into the temple, praising God. This great miracle was wrought as another evidence to the unbelieving nation that Jesus of Nazareth, whom they had rejected and crucified, is their Messiah and King. It was a proof that the Rejected One, who had died on a cross and had been buried, is living in glory, and that God's omnipotent power had been revealed in answer to that name. The miracle also denoted that the promised kingdom was once more offered to the nation. Concerning that kingdom, when it comes, it is written that "the lame man shall leap as an hart" (Isaiah 35:6). But the lame man, so wonderfully healed, leaping and praising God, is likewise a picture of what the nation will be in a future day, when they will look upon Him whom they have pierced. (See Zech. 12:10; Ezek. 36:27; Isaiah 12:1-6; 35:10.) Peter delivers his second address. Interesting and of much importance are verses 19-21. They can only be understood in the right way if we do not lose sight of the fact to whom they were addressed, that is to Jews, and not to Gentiles. They are the heart of this discourse, and as such a God-given appeal and promise to the nation. If this is lost sight of, the words must lose their right meaning. The repentance which is demanded of them is an acknowledgment of the wrong they had done in denying the Holy and Righteous One, a confession of their blood-guiltiness in having slain the author of life. This, of course, would result in their conversion and the blotting out of their sins as a nation. This God had promised before to the nation (Isaiah 43:25; 44:22-23).

The "times of refreshing" and "restitution of all things" are expressions in which the Holy Spirit gathers together the hundreds of promises He gave through the different prophets of God concerning a time of great blessing for His people, and through them for the nations of the world. It would be impossible to mention all these promises and in what the times of refreshing and restoration of all things consist. These days of a coming age, the kingdom age, or as we call it because its duration will be a thousand years, the millennium, are fully described on pages of Old Testament prophecy. Not alone will the nation be blessed, but Jerusalem will be a great city; the land will be restored and become the great center for blessing; the nations of the earth will receive blessings, and groaning creation will be delivered from its groans and the curse which rests upon it. If we interpret the Word of Prophecy literally and cease spiritualizing it, we shall have no difficulty to behold the full meaning of the times of refreshing and the restitution of all things. The latter word does not include a restoration of the wicked dead, a second chance for those who passed out of this life in an unsaved condition. And these glorious times cannot come till the Lord Jesus Christ comes again.

CHAPTER 4

1. Their arrest (4:1-3)
2. The result of the testimony (4:4)
3. Peter and John before the rulers and elders (4:5-7)
4. Peter's bold witness (4:8-12)
5. The astonished Sanhedrin and their release (4:13-22)
6. With their own company (4:23-31)
7. The saved multitude (4:32-37)

The enemy begins now his acts, and the first indication is given that the offer God's mercy was making to the nation would not be accepted. The Holy Spirit was acting mightily through the spoken Word, but these ecclesiastical leaders were hardening their hearts against the Word and the Spirit of God. The hate against that blessed Name broke out anew under the satanic power to which they had yielded. And the Sadducees came too. Though not much had been said on the resurrection, yet these rationalists, or as we would call them to-day, "higher critics," were much distressed because they preached Jesus and the resurrection. The next step is the arrest and imprisonment of the two apostles. Rough hands seize them. Of the apostles we read nothing else. They submitted. The power of the Holy Spirit now manifested itself in a new way with them. They could suffer, and perhaps with great joy; in perfect peace they allowed themselves to be taken away.

We have here also the first fulfillment of the many predictions given by our Lord that His own were to suffer persecution (Matt. 10:16-17; Mark 13:9; John 15:20). In Peter's witness we see the effect of the filling with the Spirit. What holy boldness he exhibited! He quotes the same

Scripture passage to the assembled Sanhedrin, which the Lord had mentioned in their presence (Matt. 22:23-41).

They knew that the Lord meant them when He quoted that verse, that they were the builders, who were to reject Him. They had done so in fulfillment of that prophecy. Peter's words are directed straight at them, "He *is* the stone which has been set at naught by you, the builders."

The rejected stone had become the corner stone. The One whom they had delivered up and cast out had been given the prominent place of the corner stone upon whom, as the foundation stone, everything rests, and who unites the building.

Peter closes with the statement that salvation is only in Him whom they had set at naught. There is no other Name given to men by which man can be saved, and that is the Name of Him who had made this lame man whole. Salvation they all needed. They, too, rulers, elders, chief priests must be saved. But only in Him God had procured salvation free and complete for all, who will have it by believing on Him. This salvation was offered to these rulers, the builders who had rejected the Lord.

They were then threatened by the astonished rulers and elders and set at liberty. We find them in their own company and after praise and prayer new manifestations of the Holy Spirit follow. In the closing verses we have another glimpse of the assembly in Jerusalem.

CHAPTER 5

1. Ananias and Sapphira (5:1-10)
2. Signs and wonders by the apostles (5:11-16)
3. The second arrest of the apostles and their deliverance (5:17-25)
4. Before the council (5:26-33)
5. Gamaliel's advice (5:34-39)
6. The apostles beaten and dismissed (5:40-42)

With this chapter the scene changes. Beautiful is the ending of the previous chapter, Barnabas having sold his land, laid the money at the feet of the Apostles. He gave by it a striking testimony how he realized as a believing Jew his heavenly portion, by giving up that which is promised to the Jew, earthly possessions.

Our chapter begins with the significant word "But." It is the word of failure and decline. All was evidently perfect; nothing marred the precious scenes of fellowship—"but," and with this little word the story of evil begins. The enemy seeing himself so completely defeated by his attacks from the outside now enters among the flock and begins his work within.

Ananias and Sapphira were lying to the Holy Spirit. Swift judgment followed as to their earthly existence. They were cut off by death. The sin they had done was "a sin unto death" and the sentence, physical death, was immediately carried out. Peter is still in the foreground. We must remember here the words of the Lord which He spake to Peter, after this disciple had confessed Him as Son of God. "And I will give unto thee the keys of the kingdom of heaven, and whatsoever thou shalt bind upon earth shall be bound in heaven, and whatsoever thou shalt loose on earth shall be loosed in heaven" (Matthew 16:19). The same words concerning binding and loosing, the Lord addressed to all the disciples (Matthew 18:18). The binding and loosing refers to discipline on earth. It has nothing whatever to do with forgiveness of sins or eternal salvation. Peter here exercises this authority, it was the first discipline. We must likewise remember that these events happened on Jewish, on kingdom ground. The witness was still to the nation. The sudden judgment which came upon Ananias and Sapphira was a strong witness to the nation that the Holy One of Israel, Jehovah, dwelt in the midst of this remnant, who believed in the One whom the nation had rejected. When the kingdom is established on earth and the Lord Jesus Christ rules in righteousness, then, no doubt, every sin will be swiftly judged by death.

Great things followed. Their habitual place seems to have been in Solomon's porch. No one dared to join them. They held the position of authority. Though they had been forbidden the public ministry they are back in a prominent place. The people magnified them too. Then another result was that more believers were added. Added to what? The First Hebrew Christian Church of Jerusalem? The First Jewish Christian Society? No. They were added to the Lord. The sinner believing is saved, receives the Holy Spirit, is joined to the Lord, becomes one spirit with the Lord, a member of the body of which He is the Head. Signs and wonders were done by the apostles. The sick were healed, unclean spirits were driven out. Multitudes of people from the surrounding country flocked to Jerusalem, bringing their sick, and they were all healed. They waited even in the streets for the time when Peter walked along so that his shadow might fall on some of them. These were great manifestations of the power of God. The words spoken by the Lord were then fulfilled. They did the works He did. These signs and wonders, however, are nowhere mentioned as to their permanency throughout this age. They were only for the beginning of this age; after the gospel of grace and the mystery hidden in former ages had been fully made known they disappeared.

All the Apostles were then arrested and put into the common prison. During the night an angel of the Lord opened the prison door and led them out. Such a manifestation was perfectly in order at that time, and fully corresponds with the other kingdom characteristics in the beginning of this book. But these supernatural manifestations have ceased. Peter once more with the other apostles bears witness to the resurrection and exaltation of the rejected Christ. On the advice of Gamaliel they were released after they had been beaten. With rejoicing that they had been counted worthy to suffer shame for His Name, they departed and continued in their great ministry.

CHAPTER 6

1. The murmuring of the Grecians against the Hebrews (6:1-7)
2. Stephen: His ministry and arrest (6:8-15)

Another failure is brought before us. The enemy acts again. From without and from within Satan pressed upon that which was of God. While the Lord Jesus Christ and the Holy Spirit acted in grace and power, the enemy came in to disturb. It is still so. Whenever there is a door opened there are also many adversaries (1 Cor. 16:9).

The flesh manifested itself in murmuring. The assembly took care of the poor; widows being specially helpless, were the objects of daily ministrations. The Jews themselves in connection with the synagogue had special funds for them. They must have also formed a recognized group in the early church (1 Tim. 5:9, 10). The ministration is the distribution mentioned in chapter 4:35, and as the multitude was very great, including, perhaps, hundreds of widows, this work was quite a task. Murmurings arose and these were born of jealousy, the result of unbelief. It is the first indication of weakness and failure. This reminds us of the murmurings of Israel as recorded in the book of Exodus. The same old thing, the changeless flesh, shows itself among the saved and united company of believers, indwelt by the Holy Spirit. The murmurings were on the side of the Grecians. Their complaint was against the Hebrews that the Grecian widows were being overlooked. The Grecians were not, as some teach, Gentiles, but they were Greek-speaking Jews, born in countries outside of Palestine, and therefore called Hellenists, or Grecians.

The murmuring is at once arrested. Seven men are chosen under the direction of the Holy Spirit. The apostles declared "we will give ourselves continually to prayer, and to the ministry of the Word." The Holy Spirit thus separated the gifts called to minister in spiritual things from those in temporal matters. Note how prayer is put before the ministry of the Word. There can be no effectual ministry, no successful preaching and teaching of the Word, unless it is preceded by prayer.

The seven chosen ones are then named.

While we know little of these men and the service they rendered, with the exception of Stephen and Philip, it is an interesting fact that their names are all Greek. In this the grace of God is beautifully exhibited. The Grecians were the murmurers, and no doubt they were fewer in number than the Hebrews. A modern day church meeting would have proposed to elect a committee composed of equal numbers of the two parties. But not so here.

Grace and wisdom from above are manifested in this action. The entire seven were chosen from those who had complained. This was the blessed rebuke of grace.

The seven were then set before the Apostles, and when they had prayed they laid their hands on them. As this "laying on of hands" is so much misunderstood, and has been made an act by which authority, power and blessing is claimed to be conferred, we must say a brief word on it. It is always proper in reading and interpreting the Word of God, to see if not elsewhere in the Bible the terms or things to be interpreted are used, so that through them the right meaning can be ascertained. The laying on of hands is first mentioned in the book of Leviticus. In the opening chapters of that book we read how the offerer was to lay his hand upon the head of the offering. Thus we read of the peace offering: "He shall lay his hand upon the head of his offering" (Lev. 3:2). This meant the identification of the Israelite with the offering itself. And this is the meaning of the laying on of hands from the side of the apostles. They identified themselves and the assembly with them in their work for which they had been chosen. It was a very simple and appropriate act to show their fellowship with them. All else which has been made of the laying on of hands is an invention. There is no Scripture for the present day usage in Christendom, that a man in order to preach the gospel or teach the Word of God must be "ordained."

Stephen, full of faith and power, did great wonders and miracles among the people. Certain of the synagogue of the Libertines and others disputed with Stephen. (It is wrong to call these "Libertines" free thinkers. Jews had been taken to Rome as slaves. Their descendants who had been liberated were called Libertines, that is, freed men. They were known as such in Jerusalem and hence the name "synagogue of the Libertines.") And they were not able to resist the wisdom and the spirit by which he spake. Stephen is accused of blasphemy. The charge is "blasphemy against Moses and against God." They succeeded in their satanic work by stirring up the people, the elders and the scribes. Three things are mentioned by them. He ceaseth not to speak words against this holy place, against the law, and that he should have said: "This Jesus of Nazareth shall destroy this place and shall change the customs which Moses delivered us." And then they looked upon him, and behold his face was like the face of an angel. All eyes were attracted to this wonderful sight. Steadfastly they looked upon a face of glory; a face reflecting heaven's light, heaven's glory; a face reflecting the glory of Him into whose presence he soon would be called. And may not that young man named Saul also have been there and seen that face? And that dark countenance of that young Pharisee of Tarsus was soon to behold that same glory-light, and then tell the world of the gospel of the glory and that "we all, with open face beholding as in a glass the glory of the Lord, are changed into the same image from glory unto glory."

CHAPTER 7

1. The address of Stephen (7:1-53)
2. The martyrdom of Stephen (7:54-60)

This is the largest chapter in this book and concludes the first section. Stephen is the chosen instrument to deliver the final testimony to the nation. He was not permitted to finish it.

We notice at once a marked difference between the previous preaching by the Apostle Peter and the address of Stephen. The testimony of Peter was marked on the day of Pentecost and at the other occasions by great brevity. Stephen's address is the longest discourse reported in the New Testament. The name of Jesus is prominent in all the addresses of Peter. The fact that He was rejected by the people, crucified and that He rose from the dead, and the call to repentance, were the leading features of Peter's preaching. Stephen does not mention the name of Jesus at all, though he has the person of Christ and His rejection as the theme of his testimony. (The name "Jesus" appears in the A. V. in verse 45; but it should be "Joshua" instead.) At the close of his address he speaks of the Just One of whom they had become betrayers and murderers.

Stephen had been accused of speaking against Moses and against God, also against the temple and the law. These accusations he is asked to answer. What he declared before the council shows plainly that the accusations are utterly false. His speech is, therefore, partly apologetic; but it is also teaching, in that it shows certain truths from the historic events he cites. And before he finishes his testimony the accused becomes the accuser of the nation; the one to be judged becomes the judge. Indeed his whole testimony, as he rapidly speaks of past history in his great and divinely arranged retrospect, is a most powerful testimony to the nation as well as against the nation.

The great address falls into the following sections: 1. Abraham's history (verses 2-8). 2. Joseph and his brethren (verses 9-16). 3. The rejection of Moses. The rejected one became their deliverer and ruler (verses 17-38). 4. The story of the nation's apostasy and shame (verses 39-50). Then Stephen ceased his historical retrospect, he addressed them directly. The accused witness becomes the mouthpiece of the Judge, who pronounces the sentence upon the nation. This is found in verses 51-53. His matyrdom followed.

Three things are mentioned of this first martyr. He was full of the Holy Spirit; he looked steadfastly into heaven, seeing the glory of God; he saw Jesus standing on the right hand of God.

This is the first manifestation of the glorified Christ, which we have on record. There are three of them only. He appeared here to Stephen. Then He appeared unto Saul, who consented unto Stephen's death. Saul beheld Him in that glory, brighter than the noon-day sun, and heard His voice. The last time the glorified Christ manifested Himself was to John in the island of Patmos. These three appearings of the glorified Christ present to our view the three aspects of His second coming. First He comes to welcome His own into His presence. He will arise and come into the air to meet His beloved co-heirs there. This is represented by the first appearing to Stephen, standing to receive him. Then Israel will behold Him, they who pierced Him will see Him, as Saul of Tarsus beheld the Lord. Then He will appear as John saw Him, the One who judges the earth in righteousness.

And now after this great and glorious vision, Stephen bears testimony to it. "Behold, I see the heavens opened, and the Son of Man standing on the right hand of God." He speaks of the Lord as "Son of Man." This is the only time outside of the Gospel records that we find this title of the Lord (aside from the Old Testament reference in Hebews 2).

They stoned him and Stephen, the mighty witness and mouthpiece of the Holy Spirit, fell asleep.

God's gracious offer and Christ had now been fully rejected by the nation. Stephen, who bore this last witness, is a striking evidence of the transforming power of Christ. How much like the Lord he was!

He was filled with the Spirit, full of faith and power, and like the Lord he did great wonders and miracles among the people. Like Christ, he was falsely accused of speaking against Moses, the law and the temple, and of being a blasphemer. They brought him before the same council and did what they did with the Lord, bringing false witness against him. He gave witness to the truth of the confession the Lord had given before the council, that He was to sit at the right hand of God. He beheld Him there. The Lord Jesus committed His spirit in the Father's hands, and Stephen prayed that the Lord Jesus receive his spirit; and like the Lord he prayed for the forgiveness of his enemies. May the same power transform us all into the same image.

II. The Witness to Samaria, Saul's Conversion, and Peter's Witness in Caesarea (8—12)

CHAPTER 8

1. The first great persecution (8:1-3)
2. The preaching of the scattered believers and Philip in Samaria (8:4-8)
3. Events in Samaria (8:9-24)
4. The gospel in many villages of Samaria (8:25)
5. Philip and the eunuch (8:26-40)

The final testimony to the rulers of the people had been given. It was rejected, and the Spirit filled messenger killed. The last offer had therefore been completely rejected. The gospel is now to be sent to the Gentiles. The eighth chapter gives the record how Samaria heard the gospel.

Saul, the young Pharisee, was consenting unto Stephen's death. Later he refers to the scene, which must have been impossible for him to erase from his memory. "When the blood of Stephen was shed, I was standing by and keeping the garments of them that slew him" (Acts 22:20). Concerning Saul the Lord said to Ananias, "I will shew him how great things he must suffer for My name's sake" (9:16). What was done unto Stephen was done unto Paul. The Jews and Saul with them, as we believe, disputed and resisted Stephen in the synagogue. The Jews disputed with Paul, resisted him, and rejected his testimony. Stephen was accused of blasphemy; so was Paul (Acts 19:37). Stephen was accused of speaking against Moses, the holy place and the customs; so was Paul (Acts 21:28; 24:6; 25:8; 28:17). They rushed upon Stephen with one accord and seized him. The same happened to Paul (Acts 19:29). Stephen was dragged out of the city. So was Paul (Acts 14:19). Stephen was tried before the Sanhedrin; so did Paul appear before the Sanhedrin. Stephen was stoned and Paul was stoned at Lystra. Stephen suffered martyrdom; so did Paul in Rome. And yet, with all the sufferings that Paul had to undergo, he rejoiced. His eyes rested constantly upon that Glorious One, whom Stephen, filled with the Holy Spirit, beheld in glory. Later we hear him crying out from the prison in Rome, "That I may know Him, and the power of His resurrection, and the fellowship of His sufferings, being made comformable unto His death" (Phil. 3:10).

The first great persecution then broke out against the Church in Jerusalem. Saul was evidently the leader (Acts 26:10-11; 1 Cor. 15:9; Gal. 1:13). But "the blood of the martyrs is the seed of the Church." God permitted this persecution that His Word might now be scattered abroad by the suffering saints. Philip, the Grecian Jew, one of the chosen seven, not an apostle, is mightily used in preaching the gospel in Samaria. The first missionary move to extend the gospel was, therefore, not brought about under apostolic leadership, nor by the decree of an apostolic council, but by the Lord Himself. He led Philip to Samaria, where He Himself had been, yea to the very city of Samaria, Sychar (John 4). Great results followed the preaching of the gospel. Miracles took place. Unclean spirits were driven out, many taken with palsies, and those who were lame were healed, so that there was great joy in that city. Simon Magus was a sinister instrument of Satan. He bewitched the people of Samaria, claiming to be some great one.

The hour of deliverance came for the Samaritans when Philip preached the Word, concerning the kingdom of God and the name of Jesus Christ. Signs and great miracles followed, and the Samaritans believed and were baptized. The miracles were done to show the power of God, to attest the preaching of the gospel by Philip, and to expose the counterfeit powers of Simon. And he, like the sorcerers of Egypt, had to own that this was the power of God. He was amazed when he beheld the great miracles. But more than that, he also believed, was baptized, and then continued with Philip. But his faith was not through the Word of God. God's Word alone can produce faith in man, for faith cometh by hearing, and hearing by the Word of God. Simon was captivated by the miracles he had seen. Philip was deceived by him, but not Peter, who uncovered his wickedness.

That the Holy Spirit had not been given to the Samaritans and that He was received by them after Peter and John had come from Jerusalem and laid hands on them, has puzzled many earnest students of the Word. It has also led to erroneous teachings, as if the Holy Spirit must be received in a special manner after conversion.

The Samaritan believers had to be identified with those in Jerusalem, so much the more because there was a schism between Samaria and Jerusalem. Samaria had denied both the city of Jerusalem and the temple. This had to be ended and could no longer be tolerated. It was therefore divinely ordered that the gift of the Spirit in *their* case should be withheld till the two apostles came from Jerusalem. This meant an acknowledgment of Jerusalem; if the Holy Spirit had been imparted unto them at once it might have resulted in a continuance of the existing rivalry. And Peter is in the foreground and uses the keys of the kingdom of heaven here with the Samaritans as he did on the day of Pentecost with the Jews, and later with the Gentiles. Nowhere in the Church Epistles, in which the great salvation truths and blessings of Christ Jesus are revealed, is there a word said about receiving the Holy Spirit by the laying on of hands, or that one who has trusted in Christ and is born again should seek the gift of the Holy Spirit afterward.

The conversion of the Eunuch is full of blessed lessons. Philip was obedient to the call of the Lord and the eunuch, the prominent Ethiopian, Queen Candace's treasurer, who had returned from Jerusalem, an unsatisfied seeker, believed on the Lord Jesus and went on his way rejoicing. Verse 37 is an interpolation and should be omitted. Philip was caught away and was found some twenty miles north of Gaza, at Azotus. From there he started out anew preaching the gospel. In many cities his voice was heard. These coast cities were inhabited by many Gentiles and included larger places like Jamnia, Lydda, Joppa and Antipatris. The day of Christ will make known the labors and also the reward of this great evangelist. Then he came to Caesarea. But did he stop with that? We do not know. Twenty years later we find him there and Paul was then his guest.

CHAPTER 9

1. The vision of glory on the road to Damascus (9:1-9)
2. Instructions given to Ananias (9:10-16)
3. Saul filled with the Spirit, is baptized and preaches that Jesus is the Son of God (9:17-22)
4. Saul persecuted and back in Jerusalem (9:23-30)
5. Further acts of Peter.

The previous chapter must be looked upon in its main part as a parenthesis. The record now leads us back to the close of the seventh, and the person who was connected with the great tragedy enacted there is prominently brought now before us. The witnesses of the wicked deed had laid down their clothes at a young man's feet, whose name was Saul. This is the first time this remarkable man is mentioned. We also learned that he was consenting unto Stephen's death; he made havoc of the Church and committed men and women to prison. While the scattered believers had carried the gospel throughout Judea, Philip had gone down to Samaria and with great results preached the gospel, and during the same time Peter and John preached in the Samaritan villages, Saul carried on his work of persecution. This we learn from the opening verse of the present chapter. "And Saul, yet breathing out threatenings and slaughter against the disciples of the Lord, went unto the high priest." The conversion of this great persecutor and his call by the risen and glorified Lord to be the apostle to the Gentiles is the event which is next described. It is the greatest event recorded in Acts next to the outpouring of the Holy Spirit on the day of Pentecost.

Saul was from Tarsus in Cilicia, where he had become acquainted with Greek life, literature, art and philosophy. The chief industry of Tarsus was tent making. This trade the young Saul learned. He had a married sister living in Jerusalem (Acts 23:16). He also was a Roman citizen.

Saul received his religious education in Jerusalem. We find this from his own words, "I am verily a man, a Jew, born in Tarsus, a city in Cilicia, yet brought up in this city (Jerusalem) at the feet of Gamaliel, and taught according to the perfect manner of the law of the fathers, and was zealous toward God, as ye are all this day" (Acts 22:3).

That Saul was highly respected in Jerusalem and close to the leaders of the people, is seen by letters entrusted to him and the commission to Damascus. He may have been even a member of the council, for "he voted." "When they (Christians) were put to death, I gave my voice (lit., my vote) against them" (Acts 26:10).

And now God's marvelous grace and power in salvation is to be manifested. Israel as a nation had rejected the offer and Stephen's death marked the end of that gracious offer. But God can manifest even greater riches of His grace and display His great love. Saul not alone belonged to the nation, which had rejected Christ, but shared in that rejection, but he was, so to speak, the heading up of all the hatred and malignity against the Christ of God. He personified the blindness, unbelief and hatred of the whole nation. He was indeed an enemy, the greatest enemy, the chief of sinners. Surely only grace could save such a one, and grace it is, which is now to be manifested in the conversion of Saul of Tarsus, the grace which he was to know first by the vision of the glorified Christ, and which he, ever after, was to proclaim and make known to others.

The vision itself which burst upon Saul on the road to Damascus is one of the greatest in the whole Bible. It has baffled unbelief. Infidels of all descriptions, French rationalists like Renan, reformed rationalistic Jews, and the worst of all, the advocates of the destructive Bible Criticism, have tried to explain the occurrence in some natural way.

Renan said that it was an uneasy conscience with unstrung nerves, fatigue of the journey, eyes inflamed by the hot sun, a sudden stroke of fever, which produced the hallucination. And this nonsense is repeated to this day. Others of the critics have stated that it was a thunderstorm which overtook him, and that a flash of lightning blinded him. In that lightning flash he imagined that he saw Christ. Again, others have tried to explain his vision by some physical disease. Jews and others have declared that he suffered from epilepsy, which the Greeks called "the holy disease." This disease, they say, put him into a state of ecstasy, which may have greatly impressed his Gentile hearers. In such an attack he imagined to have seen a vision and heard a voice. All these and other opinions are puerile inventions. The fact is, the conversion of Saul is one of the great miracles and evidences of Christianity.

The ninth chapter does not contain the full record of what happened on the road to Damascus. The Apostle Paul himself relates twice his own experience in chapter 22:5-16 and in chapter 26:12-18. He also mentions his conversion briefly in 1 Corinth. 15:8; Gal. 1:15-16 and 1 Tim. 1:12-13. The three accounts of Saul's conversion are not without meaning. The one before us in the ninth chapter is the briefest, and is simply the historical account of the event as it had to be embodied in the book of the Acts, as history. The account in the twenty-second chapter was given by Paul in the Hebrew tongue; it is the longest statement and was addressed to the Jews. The account in the twenty-sixth chapter was given in presence of the Roman governor Festus and the Jewish king Agrippa, therefore addressed to both Jews and Gentiles. But are there not discrepancies and disagreements in these three accounts? Such has been the claim from the side of men who reject the inspiration of the Bible. There are differences, but no disagreements. These differences in themselves are the evidences of inspiration. The differences, however, are simply in the manner in which the facts of the event are presented.

He saw then the Glorified One and heard His voice. This great vision became the great turning point of his life. He received perfect knowledge and assurance, that the rejected Jesus of Nazareth is the Son of God. The great event is prophetic. It will be repeated on a larger scale when the Lord Jesus comes again and the remnant of Israel sees Him coming in the clouds of heaven.

The words which the Lord addressed to Saul:—"Saul, Saul, why persecutest thou Me?" contain the blessed gospel he was soon to proclaim. He did not persecute Christ, but those who had believed on Him.

Every believing sinner is a member of the body of Christ. Christ in glory, the Lord, who spoke to Saul in the way, is the Head of that body, the Church. Christ is in each member of His body, His life is there; and every believer is in Christ. "Ye in Me and I in you." And this great hidden mystery flashes forth in this wonderful event for the first time "Saul, Saul, why persecutest thou *Me*." "I am Jesus whom thou persecutest." The poor, hated, despised Nazarenes, whom the mad, Jewish zealot Saul of Tarsus had driven out of Jerusalem, put into prison and delivered unto death, were one with the Lord in glory. They were identified with Him and He with them. Their persecution meant His persecution, in their affliction He was afflicted. They were members of His body and that body was in existence.

Soon after we see the erstwhile persecutor preaching Jesus, that He is the Son of God. Persecution soon followed. He also spent a time in Arabia and then paid a visit to Jerusalem for fifteen days (Gal. 1:17-42). Further acts of Peter by divine power conclude this chapter.

CHAPTER 10

1. Cornelius of Caesarea and his preparation (10:1-8)
2. The trance-vision of Peter (10:9-16)
3. Peter with Cornelius at Caesarea (10:17-33)
4. Peter preaching to the Gentiles (10:34-43)
5. The interrupted message (10:44-48)

The ending of the preceding chapter tells us that Peter tarried in Joppa in the house of Simon the tanner. Was he breaking with his Jewish law and customs? Tanning as a trade was considered unclean by the Jews.

In Ephesians 2:11-18 we read of the grace of God to the Gentiles.

Up to this time in the book of Acts we have seen nothing of this gracious purpose, the blessed result of the finished work of Christ on the cross. Jerusalem heard the gospel first. Once more the good news of the kingdom was preached with a full offer of forgiveness to the Jews. God was willing to blot out their transgressions and to make good all He had promised to the nation. Many signs and miracles had been done in Jerusalem in demonstration of the resurrection from the dead of the Prince of Life, whom they had crucified. We have seen how the seventh chapter in this book marks the close of that special offer to Jerusalem. Immediately after the death of Stephen, the gospel was carried into Judea and Samaria. In Samaria a people heard and accepted the glad tidings. They were a mixed race and practiced circumcision and obeyed parts of the law. In the ninth chapter the conversion of Paul is recorded and the Lord makes known that the persecutor of the Church is to be the chosen vessel to bear His name before the Gentiles. Paul, however, was not chosen to open first the door to the Gentiles as such, but Peter, the apostle of the circumcision. A new work is given him to do, which was indeed a strange work for a Jew. He was to go to the Gentiles, whom the Jews considered unclean. It was unlawful for a Jew to join himself to any Gentile; an insurmountable barrier divided them. For this reason the Jews considered the Gentiles as unclean, common, spoke of them as dogs, and had no intercourse with them. It is of interest to notice that Peter tarried in Joppa; from this old city he is to be sent forth to preach the gospel to Cornelius and his household. Centuries ago another Jew had come to Joppa with a solemn message from his God, which he was commissioned to bear far hence to the Gentiles. Jonah, the prophet, took a ship from Joppa and refused obedience to the divine call.

But here is one who is obedient to the heavenly vision and who is to bring a higher message to the Gentiles, the good news of a free and full salvation. That Peter, the apostle of the circumcision, was chosen for this great errand, was an important hint that the middle wall of partition had been broken down and that believing Jews and Gentiles were to form one new man.

Cornelius belonged to that class of Gentiles who, illumined by the Holy Spirit, had turned to God from idols, to serve the true and living God. He was therefore a converted man, for God acknowledged him as such. Of salvation through the Lord Jesus Christ and the blessed assurance of that salvation he knew nothing. His prayers had been heard. The angel who appeared gave Cornelius the full directions where Peter was to be found. While the messengers were hastening to Joppa, Peter had his vision.

And what is the meaning of the vision? The vessel is the type of the Church. The four corners represent the four corners of the earth. The clean animals it contained, the Jews; the unclean, the Gentiles. But all in that vessel are cleansed. The grace of God in the Lord Jesus Christ has cleansed those who are in Christ. "But ye are washed, but ye are sanctified, but ye are justified in the name of the Lord Jesus, and by the Spirit of our God" (1 Cor. 6:11). Jew and Gentile believing, redeemed by blood, saved by grace, washed and sanctified, are to be put into one body.

Then Peter reached Caesarea and preached to Cornelius and those who were gathered together. How different this message from those he delivered in Jerusalem. There are a few introductory remarks followed by a declaration of the facts concerning Jesus of Nazareth. Then he pressed the message home to their hearts. "To Him give all the prophets witness that through His Name whosoever believeth on Him shall receive remission of sins." This was his last word to the assembled company. It is the first time we find the word "whosoever" in this book. He had nothing to say to this Gentile company about repentance and baptism. His message was interrupted. They believed and the Holy Spirit fell on them.

Something new had taken place. On Pentecost it meant water baptism as a condition of receiving the Holy Spirit (Acts 2:38) and the remission of sins; in Samaria the Apostles Peter and John, according to the wisdom of God, had to lay on hands, but here without water baptism and laying on of hands the Holy Spirit came upon the Gentiles. Nor was there any process of seeking, surrendering, examining themselves, giving up, praying for it, but by hearing of faith, in believing the message of the Gospel the Holy Spirit fell on them. And to show that every barrier between Jew and Gentile had been removed, that nothing inferior had been bestowed upon Gentiles, than that which came upon the believing Jews on the day of Pentecost, Cornelius, his kinsmen and friends spoke with tongues and magnified God. It was the conclusive evidence that Gentiles, uncircumcised and unbaptized, received the Holy Spirit like the Jews.

Water baptism follows. Up to this chapter water baptism preceded the gift of the Holy Spirit. This shows the place water baptism holds on the ground of grace. Water baptism has no place in the proclamation of the gospel of Grace. It is not a means of grace, nor a sacrament. Peter, however, does not slight nor ignore baptism. "Can any man forbid water?" Then he commanded them to be baptized in the name of the Lord.

CHAPTER 11

1. Peter's defence in Jerusalem (11:1-18)
2. The beginning of the Church in Antioch (11:19-21)
3. Barnabas sent to Antioch (11:22-26)
4. The prophecy of Agabus (11:27-30)

Peter silenced the objections of his brethren in Jerusalem by a rehearsal of his experience. Verse 19 connects with chapter 8:4. Antioch comes now into prominence as the great Gentile center of Christianity. A great number believed and turned unto the Lord. Then Barnabas was sent to Antioch to inspect the great work. They wanted to know in Jerusalem if the reports were true, and if true the assembly had to be recognized as such. This shows that the oneness of the church, though not yet *fully* made known by revelation, was nevertheless realized through the Holy Spirit. And that a blessed relationship existed between the assembly in Jerusalem and the one in Antioch, is seen by Peter's visit in that city, when in the liberty wherewith Christ has made us free, he ate with these believing Gentiles and enjoyed fellowship with them (Gal. 2:11-12).

The movement also attracted the attention of the outsiders. They called them "Christians." The Jews, it is certain, did not give this name, but the Gentiles invented it. Antioch was famous for its readiness to jeer and call names; it was known by its witty epigrams. So they coined a new word, "*Christianoi*"—Christians. It is used exclusively by outsiders, as seen in the case of Agrippa; also see 1 Peter 4:16. Jews and Gentiles alike were called by this name, "Christians," so that it bears testimony to the oneness of Jew and Gentile in Christ.

CHAPTER 12

1. The great persecution by Herod Agrippa I (12:1-5)
2. The miraculous deliverance of Peter (12:6-17)
3. The presumption and judgment of Herod (12:18-23)
4. Barnabas and Saul returning to Jerusalem (12:24-25)

With this chapter we reach the conclusion of the second part of this book. Jerusalem had heard the second offer concerning the kingdom, and mercy was ready even for the murderers of the Prince of Life. But that offer was rejected. Stephen's testimony followed by his martyrdom marked the close of that second offer to the city where our Lord had been crucified. Then broke out a great persecution, and they were scattered abroad except the apostles. From our last chapter we learned that others who were driven out of Jerusalem preached the Word in Phenice, Cyprus and Antioch. The twelfth chapter, with which this part of Acts closes, in an interesting one. It is not only interesting on account of the historical information it contains, but also because of its dispensational foreshadowing. Once more we are introduced to Jerusalem and see another great persecution. The wicked king is reigning over the city. James is killed with the sword, while Peter is imprisoned but wonderfully delivered; the evil king, who claimed divine power and worship, is suddenly smitten by the judgment of the Lord. Then the Word grew and multiplied, Barnabas and Saul returned from Jerusalem to Antioch, from where the great missionary operations were soon to be conducted. The events in Jerusalem, James' martyrdom under King Herod, Peter's imprisonment and deliverance, as well as the fate of the persecuting king, foreshadow the events with which this present age will close. After the true Church is taken from the earth, that is when 1 Thess. 4:16-17 is fulfilled, the great tribulation will take place. While great tribulation and judgment will come upon the whole world, *the* great tribulation will come upon the Jewish people who have returned in part to their own land. In the midst of the masses of unbelieving Jews, there will be found a remnant of God-fearing Jews, who are converted and bear testimony to the truth. A wicked king, the man of sin, the false messiah, will then be in power in Jerusalem. Part of that Jewish remnant will suffer martyrdom; these are represented by James, whom Herod, the type of the Antichrist, slew. Another part will be delivered as Peter was delivered. Herod's presumption and fate clearly points to that of the Antichrist (2 Thess. 2:3-8). All this may well be kept in mind in the study of this chapter in detail.

Interesting is the account of the prayer meeting held in behalf of Peter. When God had answered their prayers they were reluctant to believe it. Not one of the company believed that Peter had been released. Rhoda was the one who believed that it was Peter. And this is undoubtedly the reason why her name is mentioned in this book. The poor maid, perhaps a slave girl, pleased God because she had faith. While there was great earnestness in that prayer meeting, when the prayer was answered, unbelief manifested itself.

III. The Witness to the Gentiles, the Apostle to the Gentiles, and His Ministry and Captivity (13—28)

CHAPTER 13

1. The divine choice, Barnabas and Saul separated unto the work (13:1-3)
2. The beginning of the journey and the events in Cyprus (13:4-12)
3. The gospel in Galatia and Paul's address (13:13-41)
4. The gospel rejected by the Jews (13:42-52)

The thirteenth chapter is the beginning of the third part of this book. The second great center of Christianity comes to the front. It is no longer Jerusalem, but the city of Antioch. The gospel which had been preached in Jerusalem, in Judea and Samaria, which Cornelius and his house had heard and accepted, is now in a special manner to go far hence to the Gentiles. The city in which the first great Gentile Church had been established is the starting point. Peter, so prominent in the first twelve chapters of our book, is no longer the leading actor. He is mentioned only once in this second part of the book of Acts. In the fifteenth chapter, in connection with the council in Jerusalem, his voice is heard once more. The special work in connection with the kingdom of heaven, in opening the door to the Jews and Gentiles (Acts 2 and chapter 10) had been accomplished by him. Now he disappears from our view, though he continued to exercise his apostleship in connection with the circumcision (Galatians 2:7). Paul, the great apostle of the Gentiles, instead appears upon the scene, and his wonderful activity is described in the remaining part of the book. The opposition and blindness of the Jews in a continued rejection of the gospel becomes fully evident throughout this section, and the book itself closes with the testimony against them: "Be it known therefore unto you, that the salvation of God is sent unto the Gentiles, and that they will hear it" (Acts 28:28). Besides this we shall find in these chapters the acts of the Holy Spirit in the call and sending forth of the chosen instruments in the way He guided them, how He filled them, opened doors, and manifested His gracious power in the salvation of sinners.

The beginning of the great movement to send now the gospel far hence to the Gentiles was inaugurated by the Holy Spirit. The assembled prophets and teachers ministered to the Lord in praise and prayer, when the Holy Spirit's voice was heard demanding the separation of Barnabas and Paul unto a work He had called them. The personality of the Holy Spirit is here fully demonstrated. They were thus sent forth not by the Church, nor by a missionary society or committee, but by the Holy Spirit.

Accompanied by John Mark as a helper they sailed to Cyprus. Here at Paphos they found a Jew, a sorcerer and false prophet by name of Bar-Jesus (son Jesus). Such evil persons, special instruments of Satan, appear repeatedly in this book, and generally when the Gospel was carried into some new regions. In Samaria it was Simon Magus; in Macedonia the damsel with the familiar spirit, and here this demon-possessed Jew. He was an enemy of all righteousness. He tried to keep the Word from the Roman Sergius Paulus. Thus the Jews tried to keep the gospel from reaching the Gentiles. The judgment which fell upon this wicked Jew is typical of the judicial blindness which has come upon the Jews. But as this sorcerer who opposed the gospel was not to see the sun for a season, even so, the blindness of the Jews is not permanent.

For the first time, and that in connection with this incident, the name of Paul is mentioned. Some have suggested that he took the name in honor of Sergius Paulus, but that is incorrect. Paul is a Roman name, and means "little." Later he writes of himself as "less than the least of all saints." He took the lowest place, and the name which signifies this comes now into prominence. Barnabas is taking the second place; not Barnabas and Saul, but Paul and Barnabas is now the order.

John Mark left them when they had come to Perga in Pamphylia. It was on account of the work (chapter 15:38). It was a failure and for a time he was unprofitable. See 2 Tim. 4:11 where we read of his restoration. He is the one who wrote the gospel of the obedient servant, the gospel of Mark.

In verses 16-41 Paul's great address in Antioch of Pisidia is reported. Then the Jews rejected the Gospel, and when they preached to the Gentiles they contradicted and blasphemed.

CHAPTER 14

1. The work in Iconium and the persecution of the Apostles (14:1-6)
2. In Derbe and Lystra: the impotent man healed (14:7-18)
3. The stoning of Paul and further ministries (14:19-24)
4. The return to Antioch (14:25-28)

Iconium was a Phrygian town, bordering on Lycaonia. Here again the unbelieving Jews stirred up the Gentiles. They abode there a long time, and in spite of opposition and persecution they spoke with much boldness the Word of God. Signs and wonders were also done by their hands. When their lives were threatened by the unbelieving Jews and Gentiles, they fled to Lystra and Derbe.

Derbe was the home of a pious Jewess by name of Eunice. She had married a Greek, who had died. Her son was Timotheus and she lived with her mother Lois (Acts 16:1-2; 2 Tim. 1:5). In Lystra another lame man is healed by the power of God. The ignorant heathen, seeing the miracle, thought the two apostles were gods and attempted to worship them. They abhorred their proceedings and refused the honor of men.

The enemy lurked behind this, no doubt, but the grace of God gave to the apostles the power to act as they did. How much of such idolizing is going on in modern days; how men, professedly the servants of the Lord, seek and love the honor and praise of men, is too evident to be mentioned. Seeking honor from men and having delight in the applause of the "religious world" is a deadly thing, for it dishonors Christ, to whom all honor and glory is due. And how much of all this there is in the present day! It is but the result of not giving the Lord Jesus Christ the pre-eminence.

Jews then appeared coming from Iconium and Antioch and stirred up the people against them. The mass of people who were ready to worship Barnabas and Paul changed quickly and stoned Paul. Most likely the fury turned against him because he had been instrumental in healing the crippled man. As the stones fell upon him, must he not have remembered Stephen? And may he not have prayed as Stephen did? And after they thought him dead, they dragged his body out of the city. But the Lord, who had announced such suffering for him, had watched over His servant. He was in His own hands, as every child of God is in His care. The enemy who stood behind the furious mob, as he stood behind the attempt to sacrifice unto them, would have killed Paul. But he could not touch Paul's life, as he was not permitted to touch the life of another servant of God, Job (Job 2:6). His sudden recovery was supernatural. He refers in 2 Cor. 11:25 to this stoning, "Once I was stoned." Another reference to

Lystra we find in his second Epistle to Timothy; "Persecutions, afflictions, which came unto me at Antioch, at Iconium, at Lystra, what persecutions I endured; but out of them all *the Lord delivered me*" (2 Tim. 3:11). Blessed be His name, He is the same Lord still and will deliver them that trust in Him.

Then after additional testimony in Lystra and a visit to Iconium and Antioch in Pisidia, to build up the disciples and to strengthen them, they terminate this first great journey by returning to the place from which they had started.

CHAPTER 15

1. The false teachers from Judea and Paul and Barnabas sent to Jerusalem (15:1-5)
2. The council in Jerusalem (15:6-21)
3. The result made known (15:22-29)
4. The consolation brought to Antioch (15:30-35)
5. Paul and Barnabas separate (15:36-41)

A very critical time had now arrived for the Church. An important question had to be settled. That Gentiles can be saved and salvation must be extended to the Gentiles had been fully demonstrated. The apostle of the circumcision, Peter, had been used to preach the gospel to a company of God-fearing Gentiles. Evangelists had gone to Antioch and the great Gentile center had there been founded. Paul and Barnabas had completed their great missionary journey and numerous assemblies of Gentiles, saved by grace, were formed. The question of the salvation of Gentiles could no longer be raised. But we remember from the eleventh chapter of this book, that when Peter returned to Jerusalem, they that were of the circumcision contended with him. They objected to Peter going to men uncircumcised and eating with them. But those of the circumcision had not been fully satisfied with the status of the believing Gentiles. What about circumcision in their case? Should they not also keep the law? In other words, the question of the relation of the believing Gentile to the law and to circumcision had to be determined.

These teachers which taught that Gentiles, in order to be saved, had to be circumcised after the manner of Moses, disturbed greatly the church in Antioch. Paul and Barnabas with others were therefore delegated to go with this question to Jerusalem. Galatians 2:1-10 must be carefully read for interesting and additional information. The question was settled in favor of the gospel Paul had preached. James declared: "Wherefore my sentence is, that we trouble not them, which from among the Gentiles are turned to God." They were to abstain from pollution of idols, from fornication, from things strangled and from blood. Of great importance are the words which James uttered by inspiration at this occasion. It was the first church-council, and here the Holy Spirit revealed God's gracious purposes concerning the age that is and the age to come.

Note in verses 14-18 the four important steps: 1. God visits the Gentiles, to take out of them a people for His Name. This is the purpose of the present age. The called people constitute the Church, the body of Christ. 2. After this I will return. This means the second coming of Christ. When the Church is completed and all the members added to that body, Christ comes again, first, as subsequently revealed, for His saints and then with them. 3. The restoration of Israel follows after His return. The tabernacle of David will be built again and will be set up. 4. Then all the Gentiles will seek after the Lord. This is the world-conversion. How strange that this divinely revealed program should be entirely ignored by all church-councils at the present time.

Then after the results of the council and the decision concerning the Gentiles had been made known by a letter, Antioch received consolation.

The beginning of the second missionary journey of Paul is described in the closing paragraph of this chapter. We read nothing of prayer or waiting on God for guidance. Paul said to Barnabas, "Let us go again." He wanted to go over the same territory. This was not the plan of the Spirit. Failure follows on account of self-will and self-choosing. Paul and Barnabas separate on account of John Mark. Barnabas took Mark and Paul chose Silas.

CHAPTER 16

1. In Derbe and Lystra again. Timotheus (16:1-5)
2. The preaching forbidden in Asia (16:6-8)
3. The vision of the man from Macedonia (16:9-12)
4. The gospel in Europe (16:13-40)

Read in connection with the first verses of this chapter 1 Tim. 1:18, 4:14; 2 Tim. 1:5-6, 3:15. The circumcision of Timothy, the offspring of a mixed marriage, was not demanded by the law. Paul in circumcising Timothy manifested his liberty; he acted graciously, not wishing to put a stumbling block in the way of the Jews (1 Cor. 9:20).

They travel on through Phrygia and Galatia but were forbidden to preach in Asia. This was at that time a large province in Asia Minor with many flourishing cities. It was not God's purpose to have work done at that time. They followed divine guidance obediently. Later Paul spent three years in Ephesus, the capital of that province, and all Asia heard the Word. They also wanted to visit Bithynia, but were not allowed to do so. Bithynia heard the Word at another time, perhaps through Peter (1 Peter 1:1-2). All this shows clearly how the Holy Spirit is an infallible guide in Christian service. He must point out the way and the places as well as the time when and where the Word is to be spoken. Then follows the vision of the man from Macedonia. This Macedonian cry is answered at once. From the tenth verse we learn that Luke, the author of this record, joined the party. This is seen by the changed pronoun from "they" to "we." Then they reached Philippi. On the small river Gangites the first opportunity to minister is given. We wonder if Paul looked for the man he had seen in his vision. There was no man present. A company of women had gathered in the place "where prayer was wont to be made." Lydia of Thyatira is the first convert of Europe. She was a true worshipper of God like Cornelius. And it was the Lord who opened her heart. Satan's opposition is seen once more in the demon-possessed damsel. Satan is a cunning being full of wisdom. He tried through this damsel to establish a friendly relation with the servants of the Lord. But the gospel does not need such support. After her conversion Satan changed his tactics. They were beaten with many stripes and cast into prison, their feet held in the stocks. What followed is familiar to all. God had worked in mighty power delivering His servants and saving the jailer and his household.

CHAPTER 17

1. The gospel in Thessalonica (17:1-9)
2. The gospel in Berea (17:10-14)
3. Paul in Athens (17:15-34)

Three cities in which the gospel is next preached are before us in this chapter. But there is a marked difference between these three places. In Thessalonica there was much hostility, the result of the success of the gospel. In Berea a more noble class of Jews was found. Their nobility consisted in submission to the Scriptures, the oracles of God, and in a ready mind. There was a still greater blessing among the Jews and Gentiles. In Athens the Apostle Paul met idolatry, indifference and ridicule.

An interesting fact is learned concerning the activity of the apostle in Thessalonica from the two Epistles, which he addressed some time after to the Thessalonians. These were the first Epistles Paul wrote. From these we learn that the Apostle not only preached the gospel, but also taught the Thessalonian believers prophetic truths and emphasized the second coming of Christ and the events connected with it. In the second Epistle he reminds them of his oral teaching (2 Thess. 2:5).

The address Paul gave in Athens has three sections: 1. The introduction (verses 22-23) in which he refers to the altar with the strange inscription "to the unknown God." Then he uttered the words, "Him I declare unto you." 2. Who the unknown God is (verses 24-29). He is a personal God who made the world and all that is in it. He answered the Epicurean and Stoic schools of philosophy. Materialism and pantheism were thus swept aside. 3. He closes with the message from God (verses 30-31).

He aims at their conscience to awaken them to the sense of need to turn away from idols to the true God. God sends to all one message, be they Jew or Gentiles, Greeks or Barbarians, to repent. And then he states the reason. A day is appointed in which He will judge the world in righteousness. The one through whom God will judge is a Man ordained by Him; then follows the declaration of the resurrection of this Man. The day of judgment here does not mean a universal judgment (a term not known in Scripture) nor the great white throne judgment. The judgment here does not concern the dead at all, but it is the judgment of the habitable world. It is the judgment which will take place when the Man whom God raised from the dead, our Lord Jesus Christ, comes the second time. His resurrection is the assurance of it.

CHAPTER 18

1. In Corinth with Aquila and Priscilla, his testimony and separation from the Jews (18:1-8)
2. Encouragement from the Lord in a vision (18:9-11)
3. Paul and Gallio (18:12-17)
4. From Corinth to Ephesus and Antioch: The second journey ended (18:18-22)
5. Establishing disciples in Galatia and Phrygia (18:23)
6. Apollos, the Alexandrian (18:24-28)

Aquila and Priscilla are mentioned here for the first time. This interesting couple had established themselves in Corinth, and what a joy it must have been to the apostle when he was led to their home. How sweet their fellowship must have been as they toiled together in their trade as tent-makers and spoke one to another about the Lord. From the same chapter we learn that after Paul's ministry had terminated they went to Ephesus (verse 19). From 1 Cor. 16:19 we learn that they were still there when that epistle was written. But in writing to the Romans Paul says, "Greet Priscilla and Aquila, my helpers in Christ Jesus" (Rom. 16:3), so that they had wandered back to Rome and were in happy fellowship with the Roman assembly. 2 Tim. 4:19 tells how once more they were back in Ephesus where Timothy had his abode. "Salute Prisca (an abbreviation of Priscilla) and Aquila." They were indeed strangers and pilgrims, but blessed to know that their wanderings were directed by the Lord. Priscilla is mostly mentioned before Aquila, from which we may learn that she, like other notable women of apostolic days, "labored for the gospel."

It seems that Paul followed the same method of work as he did in Thessalonica. First, he reasoned in the synagogue every Sabbath and persuaded the Jews and the Greeks (verse 4). This must have been altogether on Old Testament ground, showing the divine predictions concerning Christ. When Silas and Timotheus arrived, then he was greatly pressed in spirit and testified to the Jews more fully that Jesus is the Christ. That there was blessed fruit we learn from his Epistles to the Corinthians. He himself baptized Crispus and Gaius and the household of Stephanas (1 Cor. 1:14-16). And he was with them in weakness, and in fear, and in much trembling. His speech was far different from the one he had used in addressing the philosophers of Athens. "My speech was not with enticing words of man's wisdom, but in demonstration of the Spirit and of power" (1 Cor. 2:3-4). His presence was base unto them. "Who in presence am base among you" (2 Cor. 10:1). His bodily presence, these Corinthians said, is weak, and his speech contemptible (2 Cor. 10:10).

The Lord encouraged His servant in a vision. The Jews' attempt to harm Paul through Gallio failed. Sosthenes the chief ruler received a beating instead of the apostle.

If the Sosthenes who is mentioned in the opening verse of the first Epistle of the Corinthians is the same, then he profited immensely by his experience. Paul addresses him as a brother. We believe he is the same person, for the grace of God delights to take up such characters and show in them what grace can do.

From Corinth he went to Ephesus, then to Jerusalem and back to Antioch. Thus ended the second missionary journey. After this he established the disciples in Galatia and Phrygia. An extremely beautiful incident closes this chapter. A new preacher appeared among the Jews in Ephesus, Apollos the Alexandrian. He is described as an eloquent man and mighty in the Scriptures. In Alexandria, Philo, the great Hellenistic Jewish Philosopher, had flourished. He was born about 20 B.C. and died after the year 40 A.D. He introduced Platonism into Judaism. In all probability Apollos was one of his disciples, but he accepted that which Philo did not believe. He had come most likely in touch with disciples of John the Baptist, and had been baptized with John's baptism unto repentance. He knew that Jesus is the Messiah, knew the facts of His earthly life and the miracles He did. Of the meaning of His death and resurrection Apollos knew nothing, nor had he any knowledge of the Holy Spirit. The entire truth of the gospel of grace was unknown to Him. The text in the authorized version that he "taught diligently the things of the Lord" is incorrect. The correct translation is "he taught diligently the things concerning Jesus."

Aquila and Priscilla were then used to expound unto him the way of God more perfectly.

CHAPTER 19

1. The second visit of Paul to Ephesus and the twelve disciples of John (19:1-7)
2. The Apostle's continued labors, the separation of the disciples, and the province Asia evangelized (19:8-10)
3. The power of God and the power of Satan (19:11-20)
4. Paul plans to go to Jerusalem and to visit Rome (19:21-22)
5. The opposition and a riot at Ephesus (19:23-41)

The disciples whom Paul found at Ephesus were disciples of John. The question the apostle asked them has often been made the foundation of wrong teaching concerning the Holy Spirit. It is claimed that the Holy Spirit must be received in a special manner after conversion. The little word "since" in Paul's question must be changed into "when," for it is mistranslated.

"Did ye receive the Holy Spirit when ye believed?"

Paul makes the gift of the Spirit a test of true discipleship. If they were true believers they received the Holy Spirit *when* they believed, that is when they accepted the Lord Jesus Christ as their Saviour. If they did not receive the Holy Spirit then it is an evidence that they did not believe. "Now if any man have not the Spirit of Christ, he is none of His" (Rom. 8:9).

They heard next the full truth of the gospel and believed, therefore they received the gift of the Spirit. Ephesus was the stronghold of Satan. When the power of God was manifested in the special miracles of Paul and the demons were driven out, then Satan also began to work. A great victory over the power of darkness followed.

Then Paul purposed in the spirit (verse 21) to go to Jerusalem. This verse marks an important change, which introduces us to the last stage of the recorded acts of Paul in this historical account. *Rome* is the goal which looms up before him. "I must also see Rome." And he saw Rome, but not in the way as he purposed in his spirit, but as the prisoner of the Lord. His journey begins now towards that great city, and at the close of the book we find him there a prisoner. The story of his journey to Jerusalem, a journey in which he perseveres though repeatedly warned by the Spirit of God, his arrest in Jerusalem, his trials and addresses before the Jews, before Felix, Festus and King Agrippa, his voyage to Rome and shipwreck and arrival in Rome, are the contents of the remaining part of our book.

The question has often been raised how the purposing of Paul in the spirit to go again to Jerusalem is to be understood. Is the word "spirit" to be written with a capital "S" or not? In other words, did he purpose in the Spirit of God, after prolonged prayer, to go up to Jerusalem? Did the Holy Spirit guide him to take up to the city of his fathers the contributions from Achaia and Macedonia for the poor saints? (Romans 15:25-26). It could not have been the Spirit of God who prompted him to go once more to Jerusalem, for we find that during the journey the Holy Spirit warned him a number of times not to go to Jerusalem.

He was called to evangelize; to continue to preach the glorious gospel, and it was a turning aside from the great ministry committed unto him. But behind his burning desire to go up to Jerusalem stood the mighty constraint of love for his own beloved brethren. How he did love them and how his heart, filled with the love of God, yearned over them! This love is so fully expressed in his epistle to the Romans. "I say the truth in Christ, I lie not, my conscience also bearing me witness in the Holy Spirit, that I have great heaviness and continual sorrow in my heart. For I could wish that myself were accursed (or separated) from Christ for my brethren, my kinsmen according to the flesh" (Rom. 9:1-2). "Brethren, my heart's desire and prayer to God for Israel is, that they might be saved" (Rom. 10:1). This holy love and courage prompted him to say, when once more his brethren had besought him by the Spirit not to go up to Jerusalem, "What mean ye to weep and break my heart? for I am ready not to be bound only, but also to die at Jerusalem for the name of the Lord Jesus" (Acts 21:13).

At the close of this chapter we read of the great opposition and riot in Ephesus and the apostle's persecution.

CHAPTER 20

1. Paul in Macedonia (10:1-2)
2. His abode in Greece, the visit to Troas and what transpired there (20:3-12)
3. The journey from Troas to Miletus (20:13-16)
4. The farewell to the Ephesian elders (20:17-38)

The record before us is very brief. Some have thought the reason is the fact that the apostle had turned aside from His given ministry, and therefore the Holy Spirit had nothing to report. We believe that this is correct. The object of the Spirit of God is now to lead us rapidly forward to the last visit of the apostle to Jerusalem, therefore much is passed over in the untiring service and labors of the great man of God. After the uproar was over in Ephesus Paul embraced the disciples and departed to go into Macedonia. It is the first farewell scene on this memorable journey. He must have visited Philippi, Thessalonica, Berea and perhaps other cities. Besides giving them much exhortation, he received their fellowship for the poor saints in Jerusalem.

Then there is the record of a blessed scene on the first day of the week in Troas. They remembered the Lord in the breaking of bread (1 Cor. 11:23-26).

The company then took ship to sail to Assos, but Paul made the journey of over twenty miles on foot. He wanted to be alone like Elijah as well as others. What thoughts must have passed through his mind! What burdens must have been upon his heart! What anxieties in connection with that coming visit to Jerusalem!

From Miletus Paul sent to Ephesus and called the elders of the church. The remaining part of this chapter contains his great farewell address to the Ephesian elders and through them to the church located there. Two great speeches by the apostle have so far been reported in this book. The first was addressed to the *Jews* in Antioch of Pisidia (Acts 13:16-41). The second was addressed to the *Gentiles* in Athens (chapter 17). The address here in our chapter is to the *Church.* It is of very great and unusual interest and importance. He speaks of himself, his own integrity and recalls to them his ministry. He declares his own coming sufferings and his determination not to count his life dear, but to finish his course with joy. He warns the Church concerning the future apostasy and the appearance in their midst of false teachers.

CHAPTER 21

1. The journey from Miletus to Tyre and Ptolemais (21:1-7)
2. In Caesarea (21:8-14)
3. The apostle's arrival in Jerusalem and his visit to the temple (21:15-26)
4. The uproar in the temple and Paul taken prisoner (21:27-40)

Coos, Rhodes, and Patara are mentioned. Then they sailed over to Phoenicia and landed in Tyre. Here they found disciples.

And the Holy Spirit through these disciples warned the Apostle at once that he should not go to Jerusalem. This, indeed, was very solemn. If these disciples had spoken of themselves, if it said that they were in anxiety over Paul's journey to that city, one might say that they were simply speaking as men; but the record makes it clear that the *Holy Spirit* spoke through them. Could then the Apostle Paul have been under the guidance of that same Spirit in going to Jerusalem? As stated before, the great love for his brethren, his kinsmen, burned in his heart, and so great was his desire to be in Jerusalem that he ignored the voice of the Spirit.

In Caesarea they were the guests of Philip the evangelist. Here Agabus, who had given a prediction of a great dearth years ago (11:28) comes once more upon the scene. When he had come he took Paul's girdle and with it bound his own hands and feet, and then he said: "Thus saith the Holy Spirit, So shall the Jews at Jerusalem bind the man that owneth this girdle, and shall deliver him into the hands of the Gentiles." Here then another warning was given. It was the last and by far the strongest. Did Agabus really speak by the Spirit? The literal fulfilment of his predictive action furnishes the answer. The whole company, both his fellow travelers and the believers in Caesarea, began to beseech him not to go up to Jerusalem.

Then they reached Jerusalem. On the next day the company paid a visit to James, in whose house all the elders had assembled for the purpose of meeting with Paul and his friends. And now once more the apostle relates what no doubt was dearest to the hearts of James and the elders, what God had wrought through his God-given ministry among the Gentiles. It must have been a very lengthy account; for he rehearsed particularly, "or one by one," the things which had happened in his great activity. After Paul had spoken, "they glorified God."

All had progressed nicely up to this point. But now the great crisis is rapidly reached. The meeting had been called in the house of James, and only the elders had been invited for a very good reason. Reports had reached Jerusalem that Paul had taught the Jews among the Gentiles to forsake Moses, and even to deny children the covenant sign, circumcision. Most likely the Judaizing element in the assembly of Jerusalem, the men who were so successfully overcome by the bold arguments of the Apostle at the council in Jerusalem (Acts 15, Gal. 2), the men who so strenuously taught, that unless the Gentiles became circumcised, they could not be saved—these men were responsible for the rumors. What could be done to convince the multitude that all this was incorrect, that Paul after all was a good Jew?

The elders suggest to him that there were four men who had a vow on them. These he should take and purify himself with them as well as pay the charges. This action, they reasoned, would not only demonstrate that the reports were untrue, but that he, the apostle of Gentiles, "walketh orderly and keepeth the law." To make this temptation stronger, they restated that which had been agreed concerning the status of the believing Gentiles, according to the decision of the church council years ago. All was a most subtle snare. He was by that action to show that, with all his preaching to the Gentiles, he was still a good Jew, faithful to all the traditions of the fathers, and attached to the temple.

And a strange sight it is to see the Apostle Paul back in the temple, going through these dead ceremonies, which had been ended by the death of the cross. A strange sight to see him, who disclaimed all earthly authority and taught deliverance from the law and a union with an unseen Christ, submitting once more to the elementary things, as he calls them in his Epistle to the Galatians, "the beggarly elements!" And has not the whole professing Church fallen into the same snare?

His arrest followed and he is taken prisoner. A great tumult followed. They would have killed him if the chief captain had not rescued him. He then was bound with two chains. Agabus' prophecy is fulfilled.

Paul gives the Roman officer his pedigree. "I am a man, a Jew of Tarsus," and then requests the privilege of addressing the furious mob. This was permitted, and taking a prominent place on the stairs, where he could be seen by all below, and when after beckoning to the people, silence had been secured, he addressed them in Hebrew. The break of the chapter at this point is unfortunate. The next chapter contains the first address of defence of the prisoner Paul.

CHAPTER 22

1. The address of the Apostle (22:1-21)
2. The answer from the mob, and Paul's appeal to his Roman citizenship (22:22-30)

What a scene it was! On the stairs, midway between the temple-court and the fortress, stood the apostle in chains, his person showing the effects of the beating he had received. Around him were the well-armed Roman soldiers, and below the multitude, with up-turned faces, still wildly gesticulating and only becoming more silent when they heard the first words from Paul's lips in the Hebrew tongue.

He relates his great experience. They were impatient listeners; the storm broke with the word "Gentiles." Another great tumult resulted and the many voices demanded that such a fellow should not live. It was a scene of utmost confusion.

The chief captain seems to have been ignorant of the Aramaic dialect. He gave orders that Paul be now removed into the castle itself, and be examined by scourging so that he might find out why they cried so against him. He was led away, and everything made ready for the cruel treatment, when the prisoner spoke: "Is it lawful for you to scourge a man that is a Roman, and uncondemned?" The centurion reported this to the chiliarch, the chief officer, who at once appeared on the scene. When he discovered that Paul was indeed a Roman by birth, they left their hands off of his person, and even the chiliarch was afraid. It was a highly illegal act to bind a Roman.

Not a few had pointed to this as a prominent failure in the career of the apostle. According to these critics he made a grave mistake when he pleaded his Roman citizenship; he should have been silent and taken the unjust and cruel treatment without a murmur. If some of these harsh critics of the beloved apostle were placed in the same condition, what would they do? As one has truly said: "It is easy to be a martyr in theory, and such are seldom martyrs in practice." He had a perfect right to tell the ignorant officers of the law who he was, and thus prevent a flagrant and cruel transgression of the law. And yet his conduct in Philippi was far different. Why did he not announce his Roman citizenship there? The power of the Spirit rested then upon him; it is different here.

CHAPTER 23

1. Paul before the Sanhedrin (13:1-10)
2. The vision of the Lord (23:11)
3. The conspiracy against Paul (23:12-22)
4. Paul taken to Caesarea (23:23-25)

And now we find him addressing the Sanhedrin.

For the last time the Jewish council is mentioned in this book. Three times before the Sanhedrin had been called together in connection with those who believed in the Lord Jesus (4:5, 5:21 and 6:12-15). Looking straight at the council, Paul did not wait for the formalities connected with the proceedings, but addressed the gathered Sanhedrin as men and brethren. And strange are the words with which he opened his defence: "I have lived in all good conscience before God until this day." In this he made a public declaration of his righteousness, which reminds us of his confession as a Pharisee (Phil. 3:4-6). This self-justification shows that he was not acting under the leading of the Holy Spirit. This bold language resulted in stirring up the anger of the high priest Ananias, who commanded that the bystanders should smite the apostle on the mouth. And Paul was not slow to reply with a harsh word, calling the high priest "a whited wall" and demanding of God to smite him. No doubt the high priest was indeed a "whited wall" and fully deserved the judgment from God. But did Paul in speaking thus show the meekness of Him, whose servant he was?

In a clever way he tries to bring in dissension by his statement of being a Pharisee and the son of a Pharisee. A big commotion followed. Some of the scribes belonging to the Pharisees cried loudly indefence of the prisoner—"We find no evil in this man; but if a spirit or an angel has spoken to him, let us not fight against God." The latter sentence was a faint echo of the advice given by Gamaliel. The scene which follows beggars description. The shouting must have been terrific and Paul was in danger of being pulled to pieces by the council mob. Lysias, the chief captain, was obliged to interfere. The soldiers, at his command, came down and rescued Paul and brought him into the castle. The cleverness of Paul had been the means of liberating him from the hands of the Sanhedrin.

The night following the Lord appeared unto him and comforted him. No doubt he had sought before His face in confession and self-judgment. He is in the Lord's hands. Forty men had made a conspiracy not to eat and to drink till they had killed him.

The prisoner of the Lord is now delivered into the hands of the Gentiles. A large force of soldiers accompanied Paul for his protection. The danger was great, hence the great precaution the chief officer, whose name is now mentioned, Claudius Lysias, had taken. Could we have read in Paul's own heart we would have seen there the peace of Christ; the words of His Lord still resounded in that faithful and devoted heart—"Be of good cheer."

The letter of Claudius Lysias to the governor Felix is interesting. It shows how Lysias claims the full credit of having rescued Paul, because he was a Roman. He declares him innocent, yet delivers him into the hands of the governor.

One would also like to know what had become of the forty conspirators. If they were true to their vow not to eat or drink till Paul had been killed, they must have starved to death, which, we are sure, did not happen. Caesarea is reached in safety and Paul is delivered into the hands of the governor, who promised him a hearing as soon as the accusers would arrive. Jerusalem now laid forever behind him. Rome was before him.

CHAPTER 24

1. The indictment of Paul (24:1-9)
2. The defence of the apostle (24:10-21)
3. How Felix disposed of the case (24:22-23)
4. Paul addresses Felix (24:24-27)

If the Jews, after Paul's removal from Jerusalem, had not pressed the case against him, he would have been liberated. As he had gone years ago to Damascus to persecute the Christians there, so now the Jews follow him to Caesarea to accuse him before the Roman governor. They evidently did not lose any time. Only a few days had elapsed when a strong deputation from Jerusalem appeared in Caesarea. The high priest filled with much hatred against Paul had taken it upon himself to come in person. This must have been an unusual occurrence for a person of Ananias' standing to leave Jerusalem.

They brought along a certain orator named Tertullus, who accused Paul in the presence of Felix. The words Tertullus used against the great man of God are extremely vile and manifest the hiss of the serpent. He calls him "a pestilent fellow," a person whom society may well be rid of. The indictment contains three counts. First stands a political accusation. This, in presence of the high Roman officer, was of the greatest importance. Any conspiracy against the Roman government was a capital offence. The charge of sedition or treason was thus at once laid at the door of the apostle. The second offence Tertullus brought against Paul was of a religious nature. As ringleader of the Nazarenes, presented by him as a sect of the Jews, he had abetted that which was against the peace of Judaism and intoduced not alone a disturbing element, but had transgressed another Roman law, which forbade the introduction of an unrecognized religion. The third charge was the profanation of the temple. Paul answers the indictment in a masterly way. His address contains a denial of the first charge; a confession and admission concerning the second, and a complete vindication of the accusation of the temple profanation.

Felix knew the accusations were not true, but he refused decision. Paul should have been set at liberty. Felix defers it till Lysias the chief-captain came to Caesarea. But he never came and Paul was kept a prisoner. Felix and his wife, Drusilla, a wicked woman, the daughter of Herod Agrippa I, heard Paul and Felix trembled. Later Felix left Paul behind a prisoner, when Porcius Festus became governor.

CHAPTER 25

1. Festus and the Jews: Paul appeals to Caesar (25:1-12)
2. King Agrippa visits Festus (25:13-22)
3. Paul brought before the king (25:23-27)

The new governor, Festus, had arrived at Caesarea, and then went up to Jerusalem, the capital of the province. The Jews had not forgotten Paul, though they had not attempted another accusation before Felix, knowing that the case was hopeless. But they made at once an effort with the new governor. No sooner had this official made his appearance in Jerusalem than the high priest and the chief of the Jews made a report about Paul. Most likely Festus had not even heard of Paul up to that time. What really took place in Jerusalem, Festus later relates to Agrippa. When Paul was presented to Agrippa, Festus introduced him by saying, "Ye see this man, about whom all the multitude of the Jews have dealt with me both at Jerusalem and also here, crying that he ought not to live any longer" (verse 24). A scene of tumult must have been enacted in Jerusalem when Festus showed himself. The mob clamored for the life of Paul. When they noticed the reluctance of the governor, they concocted another plan. They requested that Paul be brought to Jerusalem. On the way there they intended to murder him.

But Festus was divinely guided in it all, and when he asked Paul if he would go to Jerusalem, Paul appealed to Caesar. This settled his journey to Rome.

King Agrippa and Bernice paid a visit to the new governor. The father of this king was known as Herod Agrippa, and died under awful circumstances (chapter 12) in the year 44. When his father died Agrippa was in Rome. He was too young to receive the kingdom of his father Herod. Eight years later, Herod, King of Chalcis, the uncle of Agrippa, died. He had married Agrippa's sister Bernice, and Caesar gave Chalcis to Agrippa. Later Agrippa received the title as king. Agrippa I had left three daughters besides this son—Bernice, Marianne and Drusilla, the wife of Felix. Bernice, who was the wife of her uncle, after his death joined her brother Agrippa in Rome. She married a Celician ruler, but deserted him and joined again her brother, in whose company she paid this visit to Caesarea. And Paul appeared before the King. A great audience had gathered and much pomp was displayed. Then the prisoner was brought in. What a contrast! Perhaps they looked upon him with pity as they saw the chain. But more pity must have filled the heart of the great servant of Christ as he saw the poor lost souls bedecked with the miserable tinsel of earth. Festus addressed the king and the whole company. He frankly states what troubled him and that he expects the king to furnish the material for the statements he had, as governor, to send to Rome.

CHAPTER 26

1. The address of the Apostle Paul (26:2-23)
2. The interruption by Festus and the appeal to the king (26:24-29)
3. The verdict (26:30-32)

The opening words of the apostle are indeed gracious. Even as he stands in chains the great apostle counts himself happy. His happiness consisted in the knowledge that he was now privileged to bear witness of His Lord and the gospel committed to him before such an audience. What an opportunity it was to him, and how he rejoiced that he could speak of Him, whom he served. He also honored the King by a brief remark in which he expressed his delight in speaking before one who was so well acquainted with Jewish customs and questions. Then he restates his life as a Pharisee.

At once he touches upon the resurrection of the Lord Jesus Christ. Why should it be thought a thing incredible with you, that God should raise the dead? The whole history of Israel bears witness to the fact that God can bring life from the dead. The very origin of the nation demonstrates this, for Sarah's womb was a grave, and God brought life out of that grave. Many promises of the past vouched for God's power to raise the dead. The nation had this promise that spiritual and national death is to give way to spiritual and national life (Ezek. 37:1-15; Hosea 6:1-3). The resurrection of the Lord Jesus Christ proved Him to be the Holy One and the hope of Israel. In this sense Peter speaks of His resurrection. "Blessed be the God and Father of our Lord Jesus Christ, who according to His abundant mercy hath begotten us again to a living hope by the resurrection of Jesus Christ from the dead" (1 Pet. 1:3). The grave of the Lord Jesus was for the disciples the grave of their national hope, but His resurrection from the dead the revival of that hope. Once more he also relates the sad story of how he persecuted the saints. Upon that dark background he can now flash forth again the story of his conversion.

Then the proper moment had arrived to state the gospel message before this company. It is a terse statement of the message which the Lord had committed unto him. All the elements of the gospel are contained in the eighteenth verse. There is first the condition of man by nature. Eyes, which are blind, in darkness, under the power of Satan. The eyes are to be opened and through the gospel man is turned from darkness to light, from the power of Satan unto God. In Colossians 1:12 the same is stated. Then the blessings of conversion. Forgiveness of sins and an inheritance. Faith is the means of all this; sanctification, that is separation, in conversion "by faith that is in Me." One wonders if the Holy Spirit even then did not bless the message to some heart, and the grace of God bestowed these blessings upon some believing sinners. It may have been so. The day will make it known.

Festus interrupted him, and when Paul addressed the king directly, he answered him by saying: "Almost persuadest thou me to become a Christian." The meaning is rather "by a little more persuasion you might make me a Christian." No doubt conviction had taken hold on him. In this half-mocking way he answers the apostle. How many after him have acted in the same way and rejected the grace, which stood ready to save.

The verdict of a private consultation is "This man doeth nothing worthy of death." Herod Agrippa said unto Festus "This man might have been set at liberty, if he had not appealed unto Caesar." If Paul had not made his appeal to Caesar he might have then been freed. We have seen before that his appeal to Rome was according to the will of the Lord. To Rome then he goes. All is ordered by a gracious Lord.

CHAPTER 27

1. From Caesarea to fair havens (27:1-8)
2. The unheeded warning, the storm, Paul's vision and assurance of safety (27:9-26)
3. The shipwreck (27:27-44)

Much has been written on this chapter. The voyage of the Apostle Paul to Rome and the shipwreck is often explained as being typical of the stormy voyage of the professing church, her adversities and shipwreck.

However, such an application needs caution. It is easy to make fanciful and far-fetched allegorical applications. Besides Church history other lessons have been drawn from this narrative. A recent commentator claims that the keynote to the interpretation is given in verse 34 in the word *salvation.* "This and cognate words occur seven times in the chapter: *Hope to be saved; ye cannot be saved; to be completely saved.* While the contrary fate is no less richly depicted—*injury, loss, throwing away, perish, kill* and *to be cast away.* The history, then, is a parable of the great salvation, by which man is brought through death to life."

We shall not attempt to seek for an outline of Church history in the events of this chapter. The central figure, the prisoner of the Lord, must occupy us more than anything else. It is said that in all the classical literature there is nothing found which gives so much information on the working of an ancient ship as this chapter does. Even the critics have acknowledged that this chapter "bears the most indisputable marks of authenticity." "Historical research and inscriptions have confirmed the facts given in this chapter, while the accuracy of Luke's nautical observations is shown by the great help he has given to our understanding of ancient seamanship. None have impugned the correctness of his phrases; on the contrary, from his description contained in a few sentences, the scene of the wreck has been identified."

The apostle is courteously treated by the centurian Julius. Paul may have been in a physically weakened condition. The Lord's gracious and loving care for His faithful servant shines out in this. How clearly the whole narrative shows that all is in His hands: Officers, winds and waves, all circumstances, are under His control. So far all seemed to go well; but contrary winds now trouble the voyagers. The ship is tossed to and fro. If we look upon the ship as a type of the professing church and the little company, headed by Paul, as the true church, then there is no difficulty in seeing the issue. Winds which drive hither and thither trouble those who hold the truth and live in fellowship with the Lord, while the professing church is cast about. Then Myra was reached. Here they took a ship of Alexandria. Danger then threatened. Most likely a consultation of the commander of the ship and the owner, who was on board, and the centurion, was held, and Paul was present. He gives them a solemn warning and cautions them to beware. This shows his close fellowship with the Lord. In prayer, no doubt, he had laid the whole matter before the Lord and received the answer, which he communicates to the persons in authority. They looked upon it as a mere guess, and the centurion rather trusted in the judgment of the captain and the owner.

And here we can think of other warnings given through the great apostle. Warnings concerning the spiritual dangers, the apostasy of the last days, the perilous times, warnings against the seducing spirits and doctrines of demons. The professing Church has forgotten these divinely-given predictions. The world does not heed them. Like these mariners, who believed in their own wisdom and disregarded the warning given, Christendom has paid no attention to these warnings. For this reason the ship is drifting, cast about by every wind of doctrine and rapidly nearing the long predicted shipwreck. Then there came the terrific tempest. Sun and stars were hidden for many days.

When despair had reached its heights, Paul appears once more upon the scene. When all was hopeless the prisoner of the Lord spoke the words of hope and cheer. He reminds them first of their refusal and disobedience. What had come upon them was the result of having not heeded the warning. He then assures them that an angel of God had assured him once more that he would have to stand before Caesar; but God had given to him all that sail with him. Only the ship is to go down, the lives of all who sail with him will be preserved. "Wherefore, sirs, be of good cheer; for I believe God, that it shall be even so as it hath been spoken unto me." And now they were willing to listen to him. They had to acknowledge their disobedience and believe the message of cheer as it came from the divinely instructed messenger, assuring them of their ultimate salvation.

And so, at least in part, drifting Christendom can listen to the Apostle Paul, and if the mistake, the wrong course, is acknowledged, the heavenly-sent message is accepted, salvation is assured.

How calm the apostle and his companions must have been after this assurance of their safety. The dreadful winds might continue and the ship drift still further. They knew they were safe, for God had spoken. Different it was with the crew of the ship. In great distress they feared the coming disaster and cast out four anchors. The shipmen attempted flight by a clever scheme. Paul discovered their plan and said to the centurion and soldiers, "Except these abide in the ship, ye (not *we*) cannot be saved." God had given him all who were in the ship. The work of the sailors was needed when the daybreak came. And the soldiers believed the word of Paul, for they cut the ropes, which set the boat adrift the sailors tried to use. Then Paul exhorted them to eat. Once more he assured them that not a hair should fall from the head of any one. Before the whole company, two hundred and seventy-six persons, Paul took bread and gave thanks to God. The Lord had exalted the prisoner, and he really stands out as the leader of the distressed company. They all became encouraged by the words and action. All has its lessons. However the meal has nothing to do with the Lord's Supper. It tells us typically how necessary it is that we must feed on the bread of life in the days of danger, the times when everything breaks up. "And so it came to pass, that they escaped all safe to land."

CHAPTER 28

1. In the island of Melita (28:1-10)
2. The arrival in Rome (28:11-16)
3. Paul calling the chief of the Jews and his message (28:17-29)

Melita, which means "honey," is the island of Malta. It was even then a prominent place for navigation where many vessels wintered. Luke calls the inhabitants barbarians, a term used by the Greeks for all peoples who did not speak their language. The wrecked company was not plundered by the people of the island, but instead received much kindness and were made comfortable in the cold rain which fell.

It was God who moved the hearts of these islanders to show such hospitality to the shipwrecked company for the sake of His servants. Paul is active even then. The shipwreck and privations must have told on the great man of God physically, yet we see him going about gathering a bundle of sticks for the fire. This labor must have been difficult, since as a prisoner he wore a chain on his hands. A viper, which had been benumbed by the cold and revived by the heat of the fire, fastened on his hand. We doubt not it was a poisonous viper. This is denied by some critics on the plea that poisonous snakes are not found in the island of Malta. However, that is no proof that such did not exist at that time. The inhabitants of the island expected Paul to fall dead. If it had been a harmless snake, why such an expectation? God's power was manifested in his behalf. It was a fulfillment of the promise in Mark 16:18: "they shall take up serpents and it shall not hurt them." The viper also reminds us of Satan and his fate. As Paul cast the viper into the fire, so Satan will be cast into the lake of fire. Then there was a manifestation of the gracious power of the Lord towards the inhabitants of the island.

And then they reached Rome at last. What joy must have filled Paul's heart and the hearts of the believers in Rome! How often they must have read his words, in the beginning of his letter: "I long to see you, that I may impart unto you some spiritual gift, to the end ye may be established; that is, that I may be comforted together with you by the mutual faith both of you and me. Now, I would not have you ignorant, brethren, that ofttimes I proposed to come unto you (but was hindered hitherto), that I might have some fruit among you also, even as the rest of the Gentiles" (Rom. 1:11-13). He had never been in Rome. The Roman assembly was not founded by Paul and certainly not by Peter. The origin of that church is obscure, and the Holy Spirit has not given us a history of the beginning of the church of Rome. And now he whom they all loved, whose face they longed to see, was actually on the way to visit Rome. But in a far different way did he come than he expected when he wrote his Epistle. He came as the prisoner of the Lord. What a meeting it must have been!

And now it is for the very last time in this book, "to the Jew first." The first service the great apostle rendered in Rome was not in the assembly, but he called the chief of the Jews together. He knew no bitterness in his heart against the Jews. In writing the letter to the Romans he had written, "I say the truth in Christ, I lie not, my conscience also testifying with me in the Holy Spirit, that I have great heaviness and continual sorrow in my heart. For I could wish that myself were accursed from Christ for my brethren, my kinsmen according to the flesh" (Rom. 9:1-2). "Brethren, my heart's desire and prayer to God for them is, that they might be saved" (10:1). And now, after all the sad experience he had made, the treatment he had received from his kinsmen, after he had found out their malice and deep hatred, the same love burns in his heart and the same yearning for their salvation possesses him.

In Rome Paul manifests first of all his loving interest in his Jewish brethren. To these leading Jews he testified once more that he was innocent of any wrong doing. Briefly, he rehearsed his whole case and why he had been compelled to appeal to Caesar. For this purpose—to talk to them about this matter—he had called them. Then most likely he must have lifted his hands, from which the prisoner's chain dangled, and said, "because for the hope of Israel I am bound with this chain." The Jews, however, wanted to hear more from his lips of—"what thou thinkest; for as concerning this sect, we know that everywhere it is spoken against." They knew he believed in Christ.

A great meeting took place a short time later. Many Jews assembled in Paul's lodging. The meeting lasted from morning till evening. Once more he testified of the kingdom of God to a large company of Jews. He also persuaded them concerning Jesus both out of the laws of Moses and out of the Prophets. What a wonderful message must have came from his lips as he unfolded the prophetic testimony concerning the Messiah in the power of the Spirit of God! But what was the result? Some believed and some believed not. They did not agree amongst themselves. The end of God's gracious way with the Jews is reached. We repeat, for the last time, it was to the Jew first. The final crisis is reached. Judgment must now be executed upon the nation and the blindness is now to come, which has lasted so long and will continue till the fullness of the Gentiles is come in (Rom. 11:25). Stephen, whose death young Saul had witnessed and approved (8:1), had pronounced judgment upon the nation, in Jerusalem. God's mercy had still waited. Marvelous grace, which took up the young Pharisee, Saul, and made him the apostle to the Gentiles! Through him, the chosen instrument, the Lord still sought His beloved Israel, even after Jerusalem had so completely rejected the offered mercy. We have seen how the apostle's intense love for his brethren had led him back to Jerusalem, though warned repeatedly by the Holy Spirit. And now he is used to give the very last message to the Jews and speak the final word of condemnation.

The salvation of God is now to go far hence to the Gentiles.

A prisoner in Rome and yet active. He preached the kingdom of God (not of heaven, the Jewish, earthly aspect of it), and ever speaking of that worthy name, that blessed and adorable Person, the Lord Jesus Christ. The ending of the book is sad and it is joyous. Sad to see the great apostle, a prisoner, shut up in Rome with his God-given gospel. Joyous because the last verse mentions the Lord Jesus Christ and an unhindered ministry of the gospel. The Book begins with Jerusalem and ends with Rome. It is a prophecy of the course of the professing Church. The book closes in an unfinished way, because the acts of Christ, the Spirit of God, and Satan, recorded in this book, are not finished. We hear nothing more of Paul, though we know that from the prison the Holy Spirit of God sent forth through him the blessed Epistles, in which He has been pleased to give us the highest revelation. And how much more might be written on all this!

THE EPISTLE TO THE
ROMANS

Introduction

The Epistle to the Romans is not the first Epistle which the Apostle Paul wrote. The First Epistle to the Thessalonians was written six years prior to the Epistle to the Romans, that is in 52 A. D. and the Second Thessalonian Epistle a few months later. The place given to this great document, immediately after the book of Acts, is the right place, for the Epistle to the Romans has for its leading theme the gospel of God, and that needs to be unfolded first of all. This Epistle was written by Paul in the year 58. Paul was staying in the house of Gaius (Rom. 16:23). He was a wealthy Corinthian whom Paul had baptized (1 Cor. 1:14). His amanuensis was Tertius, who makes the statement himself, "I Tertius, who wrote this Epistle, salute you in the Lord" (16:22). It was during the brief visit to Corinth (Acts 20:3) when the Apostle wrote the Epistle. He was on his way to Jerusalem, with the great desire in his heart "I must also see Rome" (Acts 19:21). Of this he speaks in the Epistle. "But now having no more place in these parts, and having a great desire these many years to come unto you; whensoever I take my journey into Spain, I will come to you, for I trust to see you in my journey, and to be brought on my way thitherward by you, if first I be somewhat filled with your company. But I go unto Jerusalem to minister unto the Saints" (15:23-25). And in the beginning of the Epistle he expressed the same wish. "Making request, if by any means now at length I might have a prosperous journey by the will of God to come unto you. For I long to see you, that I may impart some spiritual gift, to the end ye may be established" (1:10-11). When a Greek Christian woman, Phoebe, was about to visit Rome, he was constrained to write this letter and she was undoubtedly the bearer of this Epistle. This we learn from Chapter 16:1-2. "I commend unto you Phoebe our sister, which is a servant of the church which is at Cenchrea (the port of Corinth); that ye receive her in the Lord, as becomes the saints, and that ye assist her in whatsoever business she hath need of you; for she hath been a succorer of many, and of myself also." The genuineness of this Epistle has never been doubted. The critics have never been able to attack its authenticity. Universally it has been believed, and that from earliest time, to be the production of the Apostle Paul.

To Whom the Epistle Was Written

The Epistle is addressed "to all that be in Rome, beloved of God, called saints." There was then a church, a local assembly of believers in the great world city Rome. We do not know the facts of its origin. The wicked system which goes by the name "the church of Rome" claims that Peter had much to do with the church there and was the first bishop in Rome. This is done to uphold the claims of the papacy. But it is a mere invention, lacking all historical support. Long before Paul ever addressed the saints in Rome, Peter had made in Jerusalem declaration which confined his ministry to the circumcision (to Jews) while the Gentile field was left to Paul. "And when James, Cephas (Peter), and John who seemed to be pillars, perceived the grace that was given unto me, they gave to me (Paul) and Barnabas the right hands of fellowship, that we should go unto the Gentiles and they unto the circumcision" (Gal. 2:9). Peter wrote two Epistles addressed to scattered Jewish believers. He does what the Lord told him "to strengthen his brethren," and nowhere does he claim the exalted position into which the Romish apostate system has put him. That no apostle had anything to do with the foundation of the local assembly in Rome seems fully established by Paul's statement in chapter 15:20. If Peter had anything to do with the church in Rome, if he had founded the church there, Paul would have certainly made some mention of him. And when later the Apostle Paul wrote his great prison Epistles, not a word did he say about Peter's presence and activity in Rome. These and other evidences are conclusive. Perhaps Jewish believers were used in carrying the gospel to the capital of the Roman Empire; or Gentile believers may have been the means of proclaiming first the good news there. While the assembly in Rome was composed of Jews and Gentiles, the latter were predominant, for the names mentioned in chapter 16 are nearly all Gentiles. Many of these may have been Jewish proselytes. That this church was also troubled with a Judaizing element, teachers who demanded the keeping of the law and circumcision as a means of salvation, may be learned from the warning exhortation at the close of the Epistle: "Now I beseech you, brethren, mark them which cause divisions and offences contrary to the doctrine which ye have learned; and avoid them." (16:17). This may explain the different objections raised and answered in the Epistle, objections which would come mostly from a Jewish mind. See 3:1, 5, 7, 31; 4:1, 6:1, 15; 7:7; 9:14, 19, 30; 11:1, 11. However, there are conclusive proofs in the Epistle itself which show that the Gentiles were the more numerous in the Roman assembly. Paul addresses them as the Apostle of the Gentiles and in chapter 15:16 he writes, "that I should be the minister of Jesus Christ to the Gentiles, ministering the gospel of God, that the offering up of the Gentiles might be acceptable, being sanctified by the Holy Spirit."

The Great Theme of the Epistle

The great theme of Romans is the gospel of God, that is the good news concerning the way which God, in His infinite love, has provided by which sinners are saved and all which this free and full salvation includes. While this great theme has been recognized by all intelligent writers on this Epistle, various estimates have been given of the doctrinal unfoldings, which often miss the mark. Some have called Romans a religious treatise written by a man with a wonderful, logical mind, in which he explains his views concerning salvation. Others state that the letter is "the foundation document of the Pauline system of teaching" or they call it "the explanation of the Pauline theology." Still others have suggested that the Epistle to the Romans is "the personal mental history of the Apostle, in which, after his conversion, he worked his way from the old Jewish standpoint to his standpoint under the gospel." But there is a far better statement which explains it all. In the sister Epistle of Romans, the Epistle to the Galatians, in which he gives the defence of the gospel, Paul acquaints us with the origin of the gospel, which he called so peculiarly "My gospel."—"But I certify you brethren that the gospel which was preached of me is not after man. For I neither received it of man, neither was I taught it, but by the revelation of Jesus Christ" (Gal. 1:11-12). The gospel he preached and which is so wonderfully taught in the Epistle to Romans was given to him by revelation. It was not the product of a logical mind, a system of theology which he had thought out, or which some one else had taught him. It is revelation. And the proof of it is the gospel itself. The mind of man could not have invented or discovered such a scheme. God Himself had to reveal it. The more a Christian studies this great Epistle concerning the gospel of God, the more he will find out the truth that all is of God and not of man. A great thinker called Romans the profoundest document which has ever been written. It is that, because it is of God. And all that comes from Him is as inexhaustible as His Person. The things revealed in this gospel of God are deep; no saint has ever sounded the depths. Yet it is simple at the same time. This is always the mark of divine revelation, profundity and simplicity.

We shall point out more fully in the analysis the scope and division of this Epistle, how this great theme is unfolded. God reveals man's true condition, destitute of all righteousness, positively and negatively bad, the whole world guilty before God, Jew and Gentile lost. Upon that dark background God writes the story of His great love. The source and center of all is the sacrificial work of Christ in which the righteousness of God is now manifested, no longer condemning the guilty sinner, but covering every sinner who believes in Jesus. Justification is by faith, and this faith which trusteth in Jesus is counted for righteousness. "But to him that worketh not, but believeth on Him that justifieth the ungodly, his faith is counted for righteousness" (4:5). And the resurrection of Jesus from the dead is also our justification; the blessed results of all this are seen in the opening verses of the fifth chapter. Being justified by faith we have peace with God, a secure standing in grace and the hope of the glory of God. The justification of the sinner is the great foundation of the gospel of God. Then follows an equally blessed revelation, which is another part of the gospel. The justified sinner is constituted a saint, and as such he needs deliverance from sin and its power. Up to chapter 5:11 we learn how God has dealt with our sins and after that how He has dealt wih sin. The believing sinner is no longer in Adam, the first man, but in Christ, the second man. What we have by nature through Adam and what we receive through grace in being in Christ (by the new birth), this most wonderful contrast, is the subject in chapter 5:12-21. God therefore does no longer behold the believer as in Adam, but he sees him in Christ; the old man has been put to death in the death of Christ "that the body of sin might be annulled that henceforth we should not serve sin." God looks upon the believer as being dead with Christ to sin. He is therefore no longer to live in sin. The assurance is given "sin shall not have dominion over you." And faith is to act upon it as being dead to sin and alive unto God (6:11-13). In the seventh chapter the question of the law is raised and the gospel of God declares that the justified believer, in Christ, dead with Him and delivered from the sin principle is also dead to the law. The eighth chapter leads us into the full place of deliverance. What was impossible to the law, to produce the righteous requirements of the law, is made possible by the law of the spirit of life in Christ Jesus. The Spirit of God and His work in the believer is now revealed as a part of the gospel. Furthermore the believer saved by grace is a child of God and an heir of God. Glory is his eternal destiny and nothing can separate him from the love of God which is in Christ Jesus our Lord. Then follow three chapters which deal with dispensational matters, Israel's fall and coming restoratin to the place of blessing as His earthly people. The final chapters contain exhortations to walk in the power of this blessed gospel.

The Importance of Romans

If we are asked what portion of the New Testament should a Christian study the most, we answer always, unhesitatingly, the Epistle to the Romans. Dr. Martin Luther found his great message and deliverance in this Epistle. No better testimony about this Epistle could be given than his. He said, "It is the true masterpiece of the New Testament, and the very purest Gospel, which is well worth and deserving that a Christian man should not only learn it by heart, word for word, but also that he should daily deal with it as the daily bread of men's souls. For it can never be too much or too well read or studied; and the more it is handled the more precious it becomes, and the better it tastes." John Wesley, the godly preacher of the eighteenth century, found peace and deliverance while listening to the reading of Luther's introduction to Romans. No Christian can enjoy the gospel and know true deliverance unless he knows the precious arguments of the first eight chapters of this Epistle. It is the great need at the present time. So many professing Christians are ignorant of what redemption is and what it includes. Many have but a hazy view of justification and have little or no knowledge of a settled peace with God and lack the assurance of salvation. They are constantly striving to be something and to attain something, which God in infinite grace has already supplied in the gospel of His Son. And the ignorance about deliverance from the power of indwelling sin! Most Christians live constantly in the experience of the wretched man in chapter 7:15-24. The teaching of the gospel of God according to Romans is therefore of the greatest importance. It brings assurance and peace; its teachings lead the believer into a life of victory. So many sincere, but untaught believers become ensnared in all kinds of strange doctrines, taught by different cults, because they are deplorably ignorant of the salvation of God. Luther was right, "it can never be too much or too well read or studied." Even if we have grasped the great doctrines of salvation as revealed in this Epistle it is needful that we go over them again and again. And it must be done with prayer. There are many Christians who hold the correct doctrines concerning justification and sanctification as made known in Romans, but they lack the power of these truths in their lives.

Nor must we forget that these blessed truths are increasingly denied as well as perverted in our days. We must therefore keep in constant touch with them, lest they slip away from us and we lose the reality and power of the blessed gospel in our lives.

Division of the Epistle to the Romans

The division of the Epistle is very simple and presents no difficulty. There are three very clearly defined parts. The first eight chapters contain the doctrine of the gospel of God, what salvation is and what it includes. Justification, sanctification and glorification are revealed and the believer's deliverance from the guilt of sin, the power of sin and the future deliverance from the presence of sin is made known in these eight chapters. Chapters 9—11 form the second part. God's sovereign dealings with Israel is the theme of these chapters, which have a parenthetical character. Here we learn of Israel's election, rejection and coming restoration. God's righteousness is demonstrated in this second part as it is in the doctrinal section of this

Epistle. Chapters 12—16 constitute the third part. Here we find the exhortations for the justified and sanctified believer, who waits for the coming glory, how he is to live on earth in the power of the gospel and manifest practically the righteousness of God.

I. DOCTRINAL: THE SALVATION OF GOD (1—8)

1. **Introduction** (1:1-17)
2. **The Need of Salvation Demonstrated: The Whole World Guilty and Lost** (1:18—3:20)
3. **The Righteousness of God Revealed and Justification, What it is and What it Includes** (3:21—5:11)
4. **In Christ: The Sanctification of the Believer, his Deliverance from Sin and the Law, Children and Heirs** (5:12—8)

II. DISPENSATIONAL: GOD'S DEALINGS WITH ISRAEL(9—11)

1. **Israel and God's Sovereignty** (9)
2. **Israel's Failure and Unbelief** (10)
3. **Israel's Future** (11)

III. EXHORTATIONS AND THE CONCLUSION (12—16)

1. **The Exhortations** (13—15:13)
2. **The Conclusion** (15:14—16)

The Epistle to the Romans demands the closest study. "Its texture is so fine, its very vein so full, its very fibres and ligatures so fine and yet strong, that it requires not only to be again and again surveyed as a whole, and mastered in its primary ideas, but to be dissected in detail, and with unwearying patience studied in its minutest features, before we can be said to have done it justice. Not only every sentence teems with thought, but every clause; while in some places every word may be said either to suggest some weighty thought, or to indicate some deep emotion" (D. Brown). In the analysis and annotations we point out the way to the deeper study of the Epistle. But the most successful learners of these great truths are the men and women who walk in the truth and learn daily anew that the gospel is the power of God unto salvation, who rejoice in God through the Lord Jesus Christ.

Analysis and Annotations

I. DOCTRINAL: THE SALVATION OF GOD (1—8)

1. Introduction

1. The apostle and the Gospel of God (1:1-6)
2. The greeting (1:7)
3. The apostle's prayer and desire (1:8-15)
4. The great theme introduced (1:16-17)

Verses 1-6. The introduction to the Epistle is unsurpassed by any other Epistle. Every word should be carefully studied. The writer introduces himself first of all as a servant (literally: slave) of Jesus Christ and called an apostle. Notice that in verses 1-7 two little words are found three times in italics, the words "to be." They are supplied by the translators and should be omitted. Paul was not called *to be* an apostle, but he was called an apostle. The Lord Jesus Christ was not declared *to be* Son of God, but He was declared Son of God; believers are not called *to be* saints, but they are called saints. Paul loved to call himself bondman of Jesus Christ. He knew the Lord had redeemed him and now he was no longer his own, but belonged to Him who had purchased him and made him one with Himself. His highest ambition was to serve the Lord Jesus Christ. His apostleship he puts in the second place. The highest and best is to be in reality a willing, devoted servant of the Lord. How did he become an apostle? "Not of men, neither by man, but by Jesus Christ" (Gal. 1:1). The exalted Christ in glory had called him and sent him forth. And next we find in the opening verse the specific work unto which the Lord had separated him—"separated unto the gospel of God." The gospel was his great commission and therefore is the great theme of his Epistle. The Holy Spirit who guided his mind, as well as his pen, now unfolds this gospel. The highest and the best, after all, in God's whole revelation is the gospel. And the gospel is not confined in the Pauline Epistles to Romans. We read Colossians and find there still the gospel. The highest revelation which ever flowed through this chosen vessel is contained in the Epistle to the Ephesians; it is still the gospel. Oh! the blessed gospel! it can never be exhausted; it will be the object of eternal praise. In His presence, conformed into His image we shall know its heights and its depths.

Notice after Paul mentioned the gospel of God there follows a parenthetical statement about that gospel. Verse 5 is the continuation of what he saith about his apostleship. The word gospel means "good news." It is the good news of God, for it has its source in Himself and in His eternal counsel. The gospel is also called the gospel of Christ, because it centers in Him, and is proclaimed through His finished work on the cross. This gospel was promised by God's prophets in the Old Testament Scriptures. In many ways, in types, in the sacrifices, in direct predictions this gospel has been announced and Jewish believers looked forward to its accomplishment. Throughout the Old Testament from Genesis 3 to the Prophet Malachi the promises and predictions of the gospel are found. The Old Testament is the foundation of the gospel. The rejection of the Old Testament as the inspired Word of God is therefore a very serious matter. And the gospel of God we learn next is a person. It is "concerning His Son Jesus Christ our Lord." Jesus is the name of the Son of God in humiliation, living on the earth; Christ is His official name in resurrection and He is the Lord of all. The Lord Jesus Christ is the proper way to address Him. "Made of the seed of David according to the flesh." This brings before us His incarnation "made of a woman, made under law" (Gal. 4:4). He came of the seed of Abraham and from the house of David, according to divine promise. He was both David's Son and David's Lord, the root and offspring of David. To Him belongs a throne for He is the King of the Jews. But "He came to His own and His own received Him not." He came to go to the cross and finish the mighty work there which enables God to be just and a Justifier, as we shall find later. He will receive the throne when He comes again in great power and glory. And He is declared (marked out) the Son of God with power, according to the Spirit of holiness by the resurrection from the dead. He lived in perfect holiness on earth and the Spirit of holiness was upon Him. He raised the dead and thereby demonstrated that He is the Son of God. But it is equally true that His own resurrection must be included in this statement, for His resurrection is the effectual justification of Himself as the Son of God. Trace in these opening verses all the great facts of Christ—Son of God—Son of Man—incarnation—His death—His resurrection—His lordship.

Verse 7. Precious is the word of greeting to all the believers, not only in Rome, but everywhere. "Beloved of God called saints." Such are all who have accepted Christ as their Saviour. They are justified, sanctified, and accepted in the Beloved. Blessed truth! In Christ, one with Him, we are the objects of the love of God. The love wherewith God loves His Son is the love with which He loves all who belong to Christ (John 17:23). And then we are saints, not called to be, or to become saints, by a separated life; but we are constituted saints in Christ, sanctified, that is separated unto Himself. God loves us and in Christ has set us apart to Himself. Nothing that we do could ever make us the Beloved of God. No effort of ours to live consistently, apart from evil, could make us saints of God. God has done it for us in Christ. And because we are saints we can live saintly lives. The greeting is from the Father and the Lord Jesus Christ. The third person of the Trinity, the Holy Spirit, is not mentioned, for He is in and with the saints of God, both individually and also collectively forming the body, the Church.

Verses 8-15. In addressing them the apostle has no rebuke, no evil to correct, no exhortation. Instead he thanked God that their faith was spoken of throughout the whole world. They let their light shine brightly in the darkness of paganism. And His heart was filled with love for them. He thanked God for them, He prayed for His blessing upon them and that "by the will of God" he might be enabled to be with them. He longed to see them for mutual blessing. Here we have an illustration of Christian fellowship. Oftentimes he had purposed to come unto them, but was hindered. "The thwarted desires of Paul gave occasion to the Spirit of God to indite and publish, by his hand, this invaluable Epistle; to present to the Church a gift, not of present and passing effect, but which should build up and feed, and instruct, the saints to the end of the time of the Church's patience in the wilderness of this world." He felt, what every sinner, saved by grace should feel, that he was a debtor to all. The possession of the gospel makes us debtors to all. He had constantly discharged his debt by preaching the gospel to the Jews and Gentiles and now he is eager "to preach the gospel to you that are in Rome also." And can there be anything more blessed for the saints than the gospel? To be reminded of it and to be led deeper into the story of God's love and redemption is one of the great needs of God's people. Only as we do this can we be maintained in the reality and freshness of the gospel. Therefore Paul longed to visit Rome to preach the Gospel to "the Beloved of God called saints."

Verses 16-17. These two verses are the key verses of the Epistle. The great words of the doctrinal part of the Epistle are found here. Righteousness and faith are these words; Paul declared that he is not ashamed of the gospel of Christ. It cannot mean, what it is often said to mean, that Paul was not ashamed to confess Christ. It means that he had the utmost confidence in the gospel of Christ; he knew it would not make him ashamed; he was not ashamed of it because of its intrinsic character. The world sneered at the gospel he preached "for the preaching of the cross is to them that perish foolishness" (1 Cor. 1:18). He knew that in the gospel was embodied the highest wisdom, that God Himself was its author, that it came from God and leads to God; he knew that through the gospel the Greek, the Jew, the Barbarian could be saved out of the horrible pit and the miry clay and become a child of God and an heir of God. He was not ashamed of it for "the gospel of Christ is the power of God unto salvation." What weighty words these are! The power of God is needed to save man. And that power God has, to save the vilest sinner through the gospel of Christ. God is omnipotent, but in one thing God is powerless, He cannot save sinners apart from the gospel of Christ, for the Gospel of Christ *is* the power of God unto salvation. The spurious gospel of today, which denies the cross of Christ and the blood, which substitutes character, good works or something else for faith in the work of Christ as sin-bearer, has no power to save. God cannot save in any other way than the way made known in the gospel of Christ, who died for our sins. And what is salvation? It includes the whole of Christ's redemption work. It includes justification, sanctification, and glorification. Saved from the guilt of sins; saved from the power of sin; saved from the presence of sin. Salvation from wrath and eternal damnation; salvation from the power of darkness and sin's awful dominion; salvation unto eternal glory. The word includes all the sinner needs. The cross of Christ has supplied every need. If man had to do something with it and could help along in his salvation, it would be an imperfect and insecure salvation. But God being the author, it is His salvation and thus (Acts 28:28) it is a perfect salvation, a salvation which is both deliverance and safety forever. (Phil. 2:12 "Work out your own salvation" is often quoted as meaning that we must work to be saved and to stay saved. It means that we are to work out with results the salvation which is ours by faith in Jesus Christ.) And this salvation is to any one that believeth, to the Jew first and also to the Greek. Faith is the means of obtaining this salvation. Of this we shall hear more in the third and fourth chapters. Furthermore, in the gospel "the righteousness of God" is revealed. This great word will receive our closest attention in the annotations of the third chapter. Here we briefly state that the gospel of Christ makes known that the very righteousness of God, which condemns a sinner, is now on the side of the believing sinner. It is revealed from faith to faith, which means that it is not on the principle of works, but on the principle of faith.

2. The Need of Salvation Demonstrated: The Whole World Guilty and Lost

(1:18—3:20)

CHAPTER 1:18-32

1. Wrath revealed from heaven (1:18)
2. Gentile knowledge of God (1:19-20)
3. Turning from God to idolatry (1:21-23)
4. God gave them up to corruption (1:24-32)

Verse 18. God now demonstrates that the whole world is destitute of righteousness and needs salvation. Verses 18—3:20 are parenthetical, showing the moral condition of the whole race, away from God and lost and therefore under wrath. In this verse we read that wrath is revealed from heaven against all ungodliness and unrighteousness of men, who hold the truth in unrighteousness. It is a solemn declaration. All who are ungodly and unrighteous, who oppose the truth by living in sin are under wrath. And this is now shown to be the actual condition of the entire race, Gentiles and Jews. All are by nature the children of wrath (Eph. 2:3). A holy God must forever exclude from His presence those who are His enemies by wicked works.

Verses 19-20. The heathen world in its moral history is first described. The heathen darkness which prevails now in idolatry and its attending degradations was preceded by the knowledge of God and produced by turning from God. Man can know God, in and through creation; His eternal power and Godhead are clearly seen in the things that are made. "The heavens declare the glory of God, and the firmament showeth His handiwork. Day unto day uttereth speech and night unto night showeth knowledge. There is no speech nor language where their voice is not heard" (Ps. 19:1-3). And there was no doubt also a primeval revelation, though unwritten, so that the Gentiles could know God.

Verses 21-23. They knew God and glorified Him not. They turned away from the light. Here is the true law of evolution, not an evolution upward as taught so much at the present time, but an evolution downward. The ascent of man is a delusion; the descent of man is the truth. The only possible way of lifting man, who has fallen so low, yea beneath the beast, is the gospel of Jesus Christ. "They became vain in their imaginations." The word imagination means, perverse, self-willed reasonings revealing the evil heart beneath from which they spring. Then their foolish heart was darkened. The next step down is that they professed themselves wise and became fools. Rejecting the light and turning away from God, they became philosophers and thought to find out things by searching. Idolatry was the next step. "A god, in some shape, is a natural necessity of man. His natural desire, in his first apostasy from truth, is a god after his own heart." A brief history of idolatry is given. First they changed the glory of the incorruptible God into a likeness of an image of corruptible man. But they did not stop with this, but they worshipped birds, four-footed beasts and creeping things. Birds, flying through the air, therefore considered nearer heaven, are put above the quadrupeds, which walk on the earth and the creeping things, which cannot rise out of the dust and mire of the earth are the lowest form. They worshipped the serpent, as it is still done by the Indians in Arizona. And idolatry is not confined to the heathen nations, it is practised in that great apostate system Romanism. A piece of bread, under an elaborate ritual, is lifted up and claimed to be changed by a few words of a sinful man, into the body and soul of the Son of God; then they fall down and worship. The mass is a blasphemous idolatry.

Verses 24-32. Then moral corruption of the worst kind follows. They had given Him up and now He gives them up. Three times we read that God gave them up. But why should there be a threefold repetition of the fact that He gave them up? Man is composed of body, soul and spirit. The first giving up is as to the body; this is found in verses 24-25. Then He gave them up to vile passions; this concerns the soul and the horrible things stated in verses 26-27 are the results. These were practised openly in the Greek and Roman world in the days of the Apostle Paul. Ancient literature bears abundant witness to that effect. These vile things are still going on in heathen India, China, Africa and elsewhere. They are found likewise in the midst of Christendom. Whenever and wherever the truth of God is abandoned, degradation in every way follows, for the truth of God alone can restrain evil. The third giving up is found in verse 29. Given up to a reprobate mind, which involves the spirit of man. "All these things spoken of here are clearly regarded as the recompense" even now, of the error of the creature, in departing from the Creator. "The world is thus regarded as under a judicial bondage of sin and dishonour. Men eat the fruit of their own ways, sometimes pleasant to the taste of corrupted nature, but with prospect of divine and eternal judgment at the end. The very lusts which govern and torment the slaves of sin are, as it were, the earnest and token of that wrath of God, which, now revealed from heaven, will yet deal with ungodliness and unrighteousness of unrepentant sinners after death" (Heb. 9:27).[1]

Then follows a description of the sins, the fruits of a corrupt human nature, sins which were the characteristic features of heathendom when this Epistle was written. If we turn to 2 Tim. 3:1-5 we find a similar list, which corresponds in a striking way with the list at the close of the first chapter of Romans. There is, however, an important difference. As already stated Romans 1:29-31 describes the moral condition of the heathen world in Paul's day, but 2 Tim. 3:1-5 describes the moral condition of the professing Christian masses of the last times, church members who have the form of godliness and who deny the power thereof. They make an empty profession, their hearts are away from God and the last days of this age revert to the moral conditions in which the heathen world was in the days of the apostle. And these characteristics prevail everywhere in Christendom. The last verse of our chapter tells us, that they know that they are worthy of death, yet they keep on in their evil ways.

CHAPTER 2

1. The Gentile moralist and reformer and his condemnation (2:1-6)
2. The two classes (2:7-16)
3. The state of the Jew (2:17-29)

---

[1]Pridham on Romans.

Verses 1-6. But in the heathen world there were such who gave witness against the immoral condition, the different vices. There were moralists, reformers and philosophers like Socrates, Seneca and others. They judged and condemned certain evils. But God declares that they were not a whit better than the rest. The very things they condemned they were guilty of themselves. One of their own writers declared, "I see the good and approve of it and follow the evil." Thus they practiced evil, because the same evil heart was in them; in spite of their ethical writings, they were corrupt. And this is not confined to heathen moralists in the past, the same is true of others during this age, who judged existing evils and condemned them, while later they were found out to do the very things they condemned. Such is the unregenerated heart of man. They cannot escape the judgment of God. They were impenitent, despising the riches of His goodness and were treasuring up unto themselves wrath against the days of wrath.

Verses 7-16. God is righteous and He will render every man according to his deeds. Then two classes are mentioned. The first are those who by patient continuance in well-doing seek for glory and honour and immortality, and to that class God will give eternal life. (Eternal life is here not, as in John's Gospel a present possession, but is that to be entered in after death.) How is this to be applied? Does this answer the question how man is to be saved? It does not, but it is the question of God's moral government. Man in his unconverted state cannot obtain eternal life by patient continuance in well-doing, for we read later that God's Word declares "there is none that doeth good, no, not one." Man cannot seek for glory for it is written "there is none that understandeth, there is none that seeketh after God" (3:11). On these terms no human being can obtain eternal life. Man is a sinner and all the wages he can earn is death, but the gift of God is eternal life through Jesus Christ our Lord (6:23). If eternal life is received by faith in Jesus Christ, man is able to do right and live the life that pleases God. Then there is the other class; those who obey not the truth, who live in unrighteousness, who reject His Word. Indignation and wrath are in store for such and this is the condition in which Jews and Gentiles are by nature "Among whom also we (Jews) all had our conversation in times past in the lusts of our flesh, fulfilling the desires of the flesh and of the mind; and were by nature the children of wrath even as others (Gentiles)" (Eph. 2:3). God states in these verses the principles on which He judges according to man's works, and as man is a sinner and cannot do good works, man is therefore under condemnation.

And likewise there is no respect of persons with God. The Jew may boast of a higher place than the Gentile, but God deals with all alike. The Gentiles had not the law and therefore sinned without law and they cannot escape the righteous judgment of God. They had the witness in creation, as seen from the first chapter, and besides this there is conscience and that witnesses of what is sin; they have the knowledge of good and evil and are therefore morally responsible. They turned from God and they will be judged apart from the law; but it is more than that "they shall *perish* without the law." That completely answers the teaching that the mercy of God covers in some way the heathen world and that the heathen are not lost. And the Jews had the law and did not keep it. Could the possession of the law make them just before God? Certainly not, "for not the hearers of the law are just before God, but the doers of the law shall be justified." "For as many as are of the works of the law are under the curse, for it is written, Cursed is every one that continueth not in all things which are written in the law to do them" (Gal. 3:10). And theirs will be the greater judgment, for they knew His will and did not according to His will and shall be beaten with many stripes (Luke 12:47). The entire passage deals with the judgment of a righteous God and that neither the Gentile without the law nor the Jew with the law is righteous before God, but that both classes must fall under the judgment of God. And there is a day appointed when this righteous judgment will be executed by the Son of Man, our Lord. And that none can be just by doing is seen in Paul's defence of the gospel.

Verses 17-29. Then the case of the Jew is more specially considered. He possessed the law, the Holy Scriptures. And he rested in the law; the apostle knew something of that in his own experience for he had declared "that touching the righteousness which is in the law" he thought himself "blameless" (Phil. 3:6). The Jew still does the same thing. He rests in the law and in the obedience to it for righteousness. But the law was never given for man to obtain righteousness. "For by the works of the law shall no flesh be justified" (Gal. 2:16). The law was given to convict of sin and not as a means to obtain righteousness. All the outward righteousness of which the Jew boasted, especially in the strictest sect of the Pharisees, was but an attempt to cover the inward corruption of a heart which cannot bring forth the fruits of righteousness. The Scribes and Pharisees were "like unto white sepulchres, which indeed appear beautiful outward, but are within full of dead bones, and of all uncleanness" (Matth. 23:27). Self-righteous, despising others, condemning others—such was the state of the Jew, as he rested in the law, boasted of God and as being instructed out of the law. But the Spirit of God now uncovers his true condition. They violated that law. All the sins forbidden by the law were secretly and publicly committed by them. They dishonoured God so much so that the name of God was blasphemed among Gentiles through them. Their whole history bears witness to all which is written in these verses. In Ezekiel's message we read that they profaned His name among the heathen (Ez. 36:20-23). And this condition is the same among ritualistic, law and ordinance keeping, professing Christians, who are religious, but unsaved. They boast in what they do and what they possess and yet they live in sin, and their conduct belies their profession.

Especially did the Jew boast of his circumcision as a means of having favor with God, as nominal Christians trust in the sacraments as the means of salvation. But circumcision or ordinances cannot save man and make him right before God. And besides this, circumcision had become a reproach among the Gentiles, because the Jews had dishonoured God and denied the true meaning of circumcision (separation). "Was circumcision of no use because of the dishonour put upon it? No, but that could not be counted such which was united with the transgression of that which it pledged one to keep. And the uncircumcised person keeping the commandments of the law would before Him be counted as circumcised. Israel, in fact, never contained all the sheep of the Lord's flock, as we know; and the apostle will presently remind us that Abraham himself was an example of the faith that might be in one uncircumcised. How indeed would the obedience of the uncircumcised condemn the man who, having both the letter of the law and circumcision also, yet violated the law! Plainly then, one must place what is internal and spiritual before what is external in the flesh. The true circumcision is spiritual and of the heart, and constitutes the true Jew, whose 'praise' (the word Jew means 'praise') is found with Him who sees the heart" (*Numerical Bible*).

Outward observances have no value; it is the heart which needs circumcision. They boasted in circumcision and all the time denied and broke the law. Verse 29 is often misused by certain sects who claim that all the Jewish promises are now fulfilled in those who are Jews inwardly, that is Christians, and that Christians are the spiritual Israel and should keep the seventh day as Sabbath, etc. These arguments reveal ignorance in the scope of this Epistle. It is simply to prove the Jew with his boast in circumcision is lost. There is a circumcision of the heart, in the Spirit. Of this Paul wrote to the Philippians, "We are the circumcision, who worship by the Spirit of God, and rejoice in Christ Jesus, and have no confidence in the flesh."

CHAPTER 3:1-20

1. Objections and their answers (3:1-8)
2. The whole world under sin (3:9-20)

Verses 1-8. A number of objections are next raised and answered. "What advantage then hath the Jew? or what profit is there of circumcision?" Such would be the natural question of the Jew after reading the argument that the Jew is on the same level with the Gentile. This objection is stated here for the first time. It is important, for the Jews are God's chosen people and as the apostle states later, to them belongs "the adoption, and the glory, and the covenants, and the giving of the law, and the service of God and the promises" (9:4). If God puts Jews and Gentiles upon the same footing, what then becomes of all these peculiar blessings promised to the Jews? And in chapter 11 the question comes up again. "I say then hath God cast away His people?" What superiority then hath the Jew? This question of a supposed objection is at once answered. The advantage of the Jew is "much every way." The chief advantage is stated "unto them were committed the oracles of God." They possessed what the Gentiles did not have, the Holy Scriptures, the Word of God. What we call now the Old Testament is therefore the Word of God, in which God spoke to His covenant people. And in these oracles of God are found the great promises for that race, which await their glorious fulfillment in the day of their national restoration.

Another objection comes next. And this is also met and answered (verses 3-4). All did not believe, but that does not make the faithfulness of God void for those who do believe. God does not fail those who put their trust in Him, because others did not believe. Part of the answer is from David's penitential Psalm (Ps. 51:4). David justified God, declared that He was true and then condemned himself. In the day of judgment it will be found that God is true and every man a liar. But this second objection leads to still another one, which is also answered by the apostle (verses 5-6). But if our unrighteousness commends God's righteousness, what shall we say? Is God unrighteous who inflicteth wrath? If that were true, that He needs our sins for the praise of His righteousness "then how shall God judge the world?" But more than that. They had accused the apostle and others of saying, "Let us do evil, that good may come." If it were true that our unrighteousness commends God's righteousness, then this slanderous statement would be perfectly right. For if our sins help to glorify God, why should we be judged for them? But the apostle brands it as utterly false. For those who sin on such a principle await a damnation (judgment) which is just.

Verses 9-20. We have seen that the previous verses considered possible objections to the arguments of the preceding chapter. Verses 1-8 have therefore a parenthetical character. And now we come to the summary. Gentiles and Jews were proved to be absolutely unrighteous and therefore guilty and lost. The judgment wrath of a righteous God is upon them who had no law and upon them who possessed the law. The verdict of the oracles of God is given. The following Scripture passages are quoted to confirm all that has been said: Psalm 14:1-3, 53:1-3; 5:9; 140:3; 10:7; Isaiah 59:7-8; Ps. 36:1. The whole human race is proved to be negatively and positively bad; nothing good and everything bad is in man. Read carefully these positive statements. We need to be reminded of them in a day when almost universally the truth of man's lost condition is disbelieved, and when religious teachers constantly speak of "a better self," "a divine spark," "the germ of good"; when thousands follow the unscriptural teaching of a fatherhood of God apart from true and saving faith in the Lord Jesus. Therefore read what God saith about the condition of his fallen creature. "There is *none* righteous, no, not one"; "There is *none* that understandeth, there is *none* that seeketh after God"; "There is *none* that doeth good, no, not one." How positive are these statements. And it is blessed to read in the Scriptures that God knows all the depths of sin into which we have been plunged. God knows all, and here He shows us the true picture of ourselves. "Wherefore by works of law shall no flesh be justified before Him; for through law is knowledge of sin." Men try to do something to meet God's requirements, but they cannot do that. All human efforts in doing good works are futile. That which is born of the flesh is flesh. And they that are in the flesh cannot please God. By deeds of law, all kinds of religious observances and good works, no flesh shall be justified before Him. Thus ends the revelation concerning man guilty and lost. The whole world is proved under sin. Man cannot save himself. If there is salvation, it must come from God. Upon this dark, dreary background a righteous God now flashes forth the wonderful story of redeeming love.

3. The Righteousness of God Revealed and Justification, what it is and what it Includes. (3:21—5:11)

CHAPTER 3:21-37

1. The righteousness of God manifested (3:21-22)
2. Just and Justifier (3:23-26)
3. Not of works but of faith (3:27-31)

Verses 21-22. And now God comes forward and manifests His righteousness. Verse 21 must be connected with chapter 1:17. As previously stated chapter 1:18—3:20 is a parenthesis proving all the world destitute of righteousness and therefore guilty. Righteousness of God as revealed in the gospel was the statement in chapter 1:17 and it is this which is brought more fully in view. The term "righteousness of God" is much misunderstood. Not a few think it is the righteousness of Christ (a term nowhere used in Scripture) which is attributed to the believing sinner. They teach that Christ fulfilled the law, lived a perfect life on earth and that this righteousness is given to the sinner. All this is unscriptural. Righteousness cannot be bestowed by the law in any sense of the word. If the holy life of the Son of God, lived on earth in perfect righteousness, could have saved man and given him righteousness, there was no need for Him to die. "If righteousness came by the law then Christ is dead in vain" (Gal. 2:21). It is God's righteousness which is now on the side of the believing sinner; the same righteousness which condemns the sinner, covers all who believe. And this righteousness is revealed in the gospel.

God's righteousness has been fully met and

maintained in the atoning work of Christ on the cross. By that wonderful work God is now enabled to save sinners and to save them righteously. The righteousness of God is therefore first of all revealed in the gospel of Christ. Apart then from the law, righteousness of God is manifested, the righteousness of God by faith of Jesus Christ. And this righteousness now revealed was also witnessed to by the law and the prophets. The law of the different sacrifices, insufficient in themselves to take away sins, pointed to the great sacrifice, in which God would be fully glorified as well as His righteousness satisfied. There were many types and shadows. Now since the righteousness of God is fully made known in the gospel we can trace God's wonderful thoughts and purposes in the types and histories of the Old Testament. To deny that the law testified to the coming redemption by the blood of Jesus Christ is to deny the gospel itself. And this is done in the camp of higher criticism. But the prophets also witnessed to it (Isaiah 41:10, 46:13; 51:5, 6, 8; 56:8).

It is blessed to see that the Prophet Isaiah who has the most to say concerning the sufferings of Christ, also witnesses to the righteousness which should follow. "Though your sins be as scarlet, they shall be white as snow; though they be red like crimson, they shall be as wool" (Is. 1:18). "Thou hast made Me to serve with thy sins, thou hast wearied Me with thine iniquities. I, I am He that blotteth out thy transgressions for Mine own sake and will not remember thy sins" (Is. 43:24-25). "A just God and a Saviour" (Is. 45:21). "His Name . . . the Lord our righteousness" (Jer. 33:6). The old, old question never fully answered "how should man be just with God?" is now solved. Thus the oracles of God witness to the righteousness of God. And this righteousness of God by faith of Jesus Christ is "unto all and upon all them that believe." It is unto all, which means that the propitiatory sacrifice of Christ is sufficient to save all. The whole world may be saved. It is "upon all that believe," which means that only those who believe on Christ are covered by the righteousness of God and are justified.

Verses 23-26. "Being justified freely by His grace through the redemption that is in Christ Jesus." Christ has met all, He paid for all our sins. If we believe on Jesus we are justified freely by His grace, that is, as a free gift. And justification is acquittal; we are acquitted from sin and from any charge of it. "It is divine righteousness that acts in justifying; righteousness is just that attribute of God which is concerned in it. It is like a broad, effectual shield stretched *over the believer,* and *for all* like a house that with its open door invites men to take shelter from the coming storm of judgment." The redemptive work of the Lord Jesus Christ has satisfied every claim forever. Christ has paid the price and all who believe are fully acquitted from every charge and penalty. "Whom God hath set forth a mercy seat through faith by His blood." On the day of atonement on the mercy seat, overshadowed by the cherubim, the blood was sprinkled. And now the better blood, that which alone can take away sin, is upon the mercy seat, and God is faithful and just on account of that blood, to justify the believer.

"To declare His righteousness in respect of the passing by the sins that had taken place before, through the forbearance of God." The sins that had taken place before, does not mean the sins committed before the conversion of an individual believer. It means the sins of believers before Christ had come and died. When sins were forgiven in Old Testament times God's gracious forbearance was manifested, but when Christ had paid the great redemption price, when His blood had been shed, then God's righteousness was made manifest in having declared righteous believers, who lived before Christ had died. In view of what God's blessed Son would do, a righteous God forgave the sins of all who believed. And now God is just; His righteousness is unchanged and fully maintained and as the just God He is the justifier of Him that believes on Jesus. The justification of the believer is fully consistent with the righteousness of God. Negatively stated "what if God were not to justify, declare free, a sinner who believes in Jesus?" Then God would not be just to the blood of Christ. And in view of these wonderful revelations of the gospel of Christ, so far above man's wisdom, God-like from the start to finish, how awful the rejection of this blessed gospel, as well as the perversion of it! Surely a righteous God must deal with such in judgment of eternal wrath.

Verses 27-31. Boasting from man's side is excluded. The law could do nothing but condemn man. The principle of simple faith excludes all boasting. "Not of works lest any man should boast." It is all of God and therefore all the praise belongs to Him. And there is another question. God justifies the circumcision (the Jews); He justifies the uncircumcision by faith (Gentiles). "Do not we then make void the law by faith? Far be the thought! No, but we establish the law." The law is not made void but established by the gospel, not in the sense that it is to help the sinner. The broken law and its curse were borne by Christ; therefore the law has been vindicated as well as the holiness and righteousness of God. The man who tries to be right with God by the works of the law makes the law void, for he will not live up to the letter of the law, as the law demands and excuses his failures at the expense of the law, which is holy and good.

CHAPTER 4

1. The witness of Abraham to justification (4:1-5)
2. As confirmed also by David (4:6-8)
3. Circumcision the sign of the covenant (4:9-12)
4. Faith in Him who raiseth the dead. (4:13-25)

Verses 1-5. Two witnesses are summoned next in whose lives the truth of justification by faith is illustrated. The Jews boasted of Abraham as the father of their nation. "Abraham our father" is still the common phrase used by all orthodox Jews as it was in the days of John the Baptist, as he declared, "Say not within yourselves, We have Abraham to our Father." How then was Abraham counted righteous before God? Was he justified by keeping the law? That was impossible, for the law was 430 years after Abraham. He was not justified by works. He was a sinner like every other human being. He had no works to justify him. But what saith the Scripture? "Abraham believed God and it was counted unto him for righteousness." Abraham simply believed God when He gave him a promise (Gen. 15:5-6) and God said, you have no righteousness, but I take your faith instead of righteousness. Faith was reckoned to him for righteousness.

There is then a difference between the righteousness of God in the previous chapter and the righteousness imputed in this chapter. And a blessed statement it is "But to him that worketh not, but believeth on Him that justifieth the ungodly, his faith is reckoned for righteousness." Abraham did not work. To him that worketh not, God reckons a reward. And what a reward. What God puts on the side of him, who believeth on Him that justifieth the ungodly, will only be fully known when redeemed sinners are in His presence. "The glory which Thou has given me I have given Them" (John 17:22). This wonderful utterance of our Lord tells us of the great reward in store for him that worketh not, who, as ungodly, believes on Christ, who died for the ungodly. Thus faith is reckoned for righteousness and has its reward of glory through grace. The statement in Galatians 3:6-9 must be studied in connection with these verses. "Even as Abraham believed God, and it was reckoned to him for righteousness. Know ye therefore that they which are of faith, the same are the children of Abraham. And the Scripture, foreseeing that God would justify the heathen through faith, preached before the gospel unto Abraham, saying, In thee shall all nations be blessed. So then they which be of faith are blessed with believing Abraham." (In the Galatians annotations this statement is more fully explained.)

Verses 6-8. And David is the second witness. David and Abraham are mentioned in the first verse of the New Testament. The covenant God made with Abraham and with David make these two men the leading men of the nation. Now Abraham had no law, but David was under the law. David describeth the blessedness of the man (whosoever he may be) to whom God imputes the righteousness without works. The beautiful thirty-second Psalm is quoted. The blessedness of the believer is there described. Iniquities forgiven; sins covered; sin no longer imputed. He does not impute sin, but imputes righteousness. Forgiveness takes the place of sin, and everlasting righteousness has covered the believer's iniquity, hiding it alike from the eyes of divine glory, and from the conscience of the justified vessel of His grace; and significantly it is stated in that Psalm "for this cause shall *every one that is godly* pray unto Thee in the time when Thou mayest be found." This is the way to be godly, confessing ourself a sinner, confessing sin and believing on Him, who justifieth the ungodly.

Verses 9-12. The question of circumcision is raised again. The Jew boasted in circumcision as placing him into a position of favour and blessing before God. Is this blessedness, justification by faith, sins put away, righteousness imputed, for the circumcision, the Jews, only, or does it come also upon the uncircumcision, the Gentiles? When Abraham was declared righteous he was still in uncircumcision. The historical account in Genesis shows that circumcision followed the declaration "he believed God and it was counted to him for righteousness;" circumcision did not precede his faith which was reckoned to him for righteousness. He was in uncircumcision, practically a Gentile, and circumcision was a sign and seal of the righteousness of faith. All this manifests the wisdom of

God. It was divinely arranged so that Abraham "might be the father of all them that believe, though they be not circumcised (Gentiles) that righteousness might be imputed unto them also; and the father of circumcision to them who are not of the circumcision only, but who also walk in the steps of the faith of our father Abraham, which he had being uncircumcised." Here we have the best possible argument that ordinances, or sacraments so called by man, have no part in bestowing salvation upon man. Baptism is called "a sacrament" and ritualistic Christians hold that it is necessary to receive the blessing of forgiveness. Others who do not hold to corrupt ritualism, also teach that baptism as an ordinance is necessary for salvation. This portion of the Epistle answers completely these unscriptural claims. "For by grace are ye saved through faith, and that not of yourselves; it is the gift of God. Not of works lest any man should boast" (Eph. 2:8-9).

Verses 13-25. This section is of deep interest and must be carefully studied. While we had the atoning death of Christ so far before us, resurrection is now brought to the foregound as another important fact of the gospel. The faith of Abraham is defined. How did he believe? When the promise was given that he should have a son and numerous offspring (Gen. 15:4-5), he believed God, who quickeneth the dead (resurrection) and calleth those things which be not as though they were. Abraham was an old man and Sarah was far beyond the time of childbirth; their case was humanly impossible. But Abraham believed that God could bring life from the dead, that He had the power to touch a grave and bring life out of it. "Against hope he believed in hope—and being not weak in faith he considered not his own body now dead, when he was about an hundred years old, neither yet the deadness of Sarah's womb; he staggered not at the promise of God through unbelief, but was strong in faith, giving glory to God; and being fully persuaded that what He had promised, He was able to perform. And therefore it was imputed to him for righteousness." From Genesis we know that he was also weak in faith and that he acted in unbelief. But this is graciously passed by. God, so to speak, had forgotten his unbelief and remembered it no more.

The application of all this is found in verses 23-25. The promised seed was more than Isaac, it was Christ; so that Abraham believed the God who raised the Lord Jesus from the dead. And we believe on Him also. Our Lord was delivered for our offences and has been raised for our justification. His resurrection is the blessed and positive proof that our sins are completely put away. For this reason the resurrection of Jesus, our Lord, is the justification of the believer. We have then a threefold justification of the believer. We are justified by His blood; He bore our guilt and penalty. We are justified by His resurrection, because this assures us that the work is done and we are accepted, and we are justified by faith, which is reckoned for righteousness.

CHAPTER 5:1-11

1. What justification includes (5:1-11)

The blessed results of justification are next revealed. What justified believers possess and what they may enjoy is the theme of the opening verses of this chapter. The first thing mentioned is that all who are justified by faith have peace with God through our Lord Jesus Christ. Peace was made in the blood of the cross, He who died for our sins is our peace. His greeting to the assembled disciples on the resurrection day was "Peace be unto you," and then He showed unto them His hands and His side, and again He said, "Peace be unto you." This peace with God we have as believers in Christ. It is settled forever and can never be disturbed. Some times Christians ask others if they made their peace with God. They mean by it, turning away from sin, repentance, conversion, surrender, etc., as if those actions from our side could make peace with God. This is incorrect and the reason why so many professing Christians lack the assurance that they have peace with God is in this very fact, that they are constantly trying what they term "to be right with God." Peace does not need to be made, it was made when Christ died for our sins. And into this peace we enter when we believe on the Lord Jesus and are justified freely of all things. We may live sober, earnest and useful Christian lives for fifty years or longer and at the end of such a devoted life we have not more of the peace with God than we had the moment we trusted in Christ. And our failures and stumbling walk as the "beloved of God, called saints" our sinning, can never disturb and undo that peace.

The second result is that we have access by faith into this grace in which we stand. We have a perfect standing before God in Christ, and perfect access. We stand in grace, accepted in the Beloved One and this grace keeps and sustains. We are the children of God made nigh by blood. Grace makes us nigh. We can draw near with a true heart in full assurance of faith. Our faithfulness cannot increase this standing in grace, nor can our unfaithfulness decrease it, for the simple reason that it is grace. The third result of justification is "the hope of the glory of God" in which we can now boast. The only title to glory is the blood of our Lord Jesus Christ. Christ has secured the glory for us and has made us sharers of His own glory He received from God, who raised Him from the dead and gave Him glory.

People speak of fitting themselves for heaven by living good lives. No one can be fitted for heaven. The only fitness is the new nature, received in the new birth. And that nature is given to the justified believer when he is justified by faith. That there are special rewards for sacrificing service is very true, but to be in glory is a matter of grace and is given along with justification. The glory of God is the hope of righteousness (Gal. 5:5). These three things cover the past, the present and the future. Past: Peace was made. Present: Standing in this Grace. Future: The hope of the glory of God. The approach to God in the tabernacle illustrates this beautifully. First the brazen altar, the type of the sacrifice of Christ; then the laver for washing, the candlestick, the table—typifying the cleansing, light, food and fellowship, the grace wherein we stand. Then behind the veil the glory of Jehovah, which ere long God's people shall reach when He calls them home. How happy God's people should be in possession of such precious things with the knowledge of sins forever put away!

But we are still in the wilderness and there are tribulations. And in tribulations, as justified and assured of the glory of God, we can even boast (the word used in the Greek) in them. Tribulation worketh patience; and patience experience; and experience, hope; and hope maketh not ashamed. "Here is how that which is against us works for us; and notice that the very first thing effected is the breaking down of our own wills, those wills, that Jacob-like struggle so much with the will of God. Sovereign He must be; and in spite of all that we have known of Him, it is what in practical detail we so little want Him to be. Amid the clouds and darkness that encompass Him in His providential dealings, faith that should find its opportunity finds oftentimes bewilderment and perplexity; yet in it we are forced to recognize our nothingness, and creep close to the side of Him who yet goes with us. Forced to let God be God, it is then that we get experience of a moral government which is that of a Father. The *forcing* of outward things comes to be read as *drawings* of omnipotent Love that seeks us for its own delight. His ways, if still they may be beyond us, are not strange and still less adverse. They beget, not fear or misgiving, but a brightening hope, that steadies as it brightens" (F. W. Grant).

In verse 5 the Holy Spirit is mentioned for the first time in this Epistle. The highest truth is not the work of the Spirit in the believer, but the work of Christ for the believer. The Holy Spirit is here to take of the things of Christ and to show them unto us. Once more therefore Christ and His finished work and the outflow from it are mentioned. God commending His love toward us, in that while we were yet sinners Christ died for us. Justified by His blood we shall be much more saved from wrath through Him. All believers are exempt from the wrath to come because they are one with Him who is the administrator of the judgments of God. And there is a second much more. Reconciled by the death of His Son, much more being reconciled we shall be saved by His life, the life which is in God's own presence and which is in us, for He is our life. And the very highest result, the joy in God through our Lord Jesus Christ, by whom we have received the reconciliation.

4. In Christ: The Sanctification of the Believer, his Deliverance from Sin and the Law, Children and Heirs (5:12—8)

CHAPTER 5:12-21

1. Sin and death through the first Adam (5:12-14)
2. In Adam by nature, in Christ through grace (5:15-21)

So far the subject of this Epistle has been our sins and how God has dealt with them in the cross of Christ. The guilt and penalty of the sins of the believer are forever gone. With this section the question of sin itself is taken up and we learn how the justified believer is also sanctified in Christ and as such delivered from the dominion of sin and from the law. Furthermore we learn it also includes that believers are children and heirs of God. To distinguish between sins and sin is important. Sin is that evil principle in us, as fallen creatures, and sins are the fruits which spring from the evil root in us. Sin, the old nature, and how God deals with it in virtue of the redemption of Jesus Christ, is now, first of all, revealed. What we were in Adam and what we are through grace in Christ, how as identified with Christ we may be delivered from the power of indwelling sin, are truths unknown to many believers. Without this knowledge a true Christian experience, such which a believer should constantly enjoy, is impossible. One of the chief reasons why true believers are carried about with divers and strange doctrines, is the ignorance of these great facts of our redemption in Christ as unfolded in this part of Romans. How many others are constantly striving and struggling to lead a spiritual life and fail in it because they know not the great principles of sanctification and deliverance in Christ.

Verses 12-14. "Wherefore as by one man sin entered into the world, and by sin death and thus death passed upon all men, for that all have sinned." By one man, the first Adam, sin entered into the world (not sins, but *sin*). And death followed, which is physical death. "Dust thou art, and unto dust shalt thou return," and this death has passed upon the race because of sin. The margin of the Authorized Version contains a statement which is responsible for a very unscriptural teaching. The margin states "in whom all have sinned"; upon this it has been taught that the guilt of Adam has been imputed to all. This is not correct. We are not responsible for the sin of Adam nor are we held responsible by God for a sinful nature; we are responsible for the outworking of that nature, that is, for our own sins. The wicked dead, those whose sins were not taken away, because they believed not, will not be judged for having had a sinful nature, but solely according to their works (Rev. 20:12). Death comes upon us on account of our sins, as it is stated in this verse "death passed upon all men for that all have sinned."

"For until the law sin was in the world, but sin is not imputed when there is no law; nevertheless death reigned from Adam to Moses, even over them that had not sinned after the similitude of Adam's transgression, who is the figure of Him to come." This looks difficult, but it is simple after all. The law was given by Moses; from Adam to Moses there was no law, men were left to conscience, by which they knew good and evil. But death reigned nevertheless from Adam to Moses, even over them that had not sinned after the similitude of Adam's transgression. Adam had a commandment which he transgressed, inasmuch as there was no law till Moses, the generations could not sin after the similitude of Adam's transgression. Sin is lawlessness and not as the faulty translation of 1 John 3:4 states, "sin is the transgression of the law." However, sin becomes transgression when there is a law. As there was no law from Adam to Moses, sin was therefore not imputed as transgression. But as they all sinned, death reigned and there is also judgment afterwards for them. The last sentence of verse 14 "who is the figure of Him that was to come" is the important statement which is fully developed in the verses which follow and upon which the whole argument rests.

Verses 15-21. The first Adam is the type of the last Adam, the Lord Jesus Christ. The same comparison is also found in 1 Cor. 15. "For as all in Adam die, even so all in Christ shall be made alive" (verse 22). This passage has often been used by those who teach the ultimate, universal salvation of the whole race. It has nothing whatever to do with salvation from the penalty of sin, but it applies to the resurrection of the bodies of the redeemed. Here in Romans the contrast is of a different nature. Adam and Christ are viewed as two heads, having each his offspring to whom they communicate something. The first Adam bestows upon his offspring the results of his sin; Christ, the last Adam, bestows upon those who belong to Him, by personal faith in Him, the blessed consequences of His great work. (Christ is never called the second Adam, but the last Adam, as there will not be another after Him.) A sinful nature and physical death is what we have as the children of the first Adam. In Christ the believer receives a sinless nature, eternal life and glory. In this sense Adam is the figure of Him to come.

"But shall not the free gift be as the offense?" (The first sentence of verses 15 and 16 is best put in the form of a question. This helps much in understanding this deep portion of the Epistle.) By the offence of Adam the many died, his offspring has been affected by his offence. In like manner the grace of God and the gift of grace, which is by the other Adam, Jesus Christ abounds also to the many. The question asked must therefore be answered in the affirmative. This and the following verses have also been used to teach that there is universal salvation. But it does not mean that. The condition "faith in Christ" must not be lost sight of. We are all in the first Adam by the natural birth; identification with the second Man is only possible by the new birth and that takes place when a sinner believes on Christ and in His finished work. Those who do not believe are in Adam and are dead in trespasses and sins.

"And shall not as by one that has sinned be the gift? For the judgment was of one to condemnation, but the free gift is of many offences unto justification" (verse 16). The sins committed are here in view. Our sin brought judgment. The free gift of justification, on account of Christ's atoning sacrifice, is blessedly sufficient to deliver from the guilt of many offences. "For if by the offence of one death reigned by the one; much more shall those who receive the abundance of grace, and of the free gift of righteousness, reign in life by the one, Jesus Christ" (verse 17). The previous verse spoke of the guilt of sins, which rests upon all those who are in Adam and this guilt is met in Christ by justification.

In verse 17 death which reigns in the first man is met by reign of life in Jesus Christ. Those who believe on Him have life now and are delivered from the reign of death. When He comes, the bodies of His Saints will be raised in incorruption and we who remain shall be changed in a moment and be caught up into His presence without dying. Verse 18 in the Authorized Version is poorly translated and misleading. "So then as it was by one offence towards all men to condemnation, so by one righteousness towards all men to justification of life." This blessed contrast between Adam and Christ is made again in verse 19. "For as indeed by the disobedience of the one man (Adam) the many have been constituted sinners, so also by the obedience of the one the many shall be constituted righteous." Here it is the contrast between Adam's disobedience and Christ's obedience. And the obedience of Christ which constitutes all who believe on Him righteous, is not His obedient life, but His obedience in the death of the cross.

"But law came in in order that the offence might abound; but where sin abounded grace overabounded, in order that, even as sin has reigned in the power of death, so also grace might reign through righteousness to eternal life through Jesus Christ our Lord." Here for the first time a reason is given why God gave the law. The Epistle to the Galatians will bring the subject of law and grace more fully to our attention. Law came in that the offence might abound; it has constituted man a transgressor and in this sense the offence abounds. But grace overbounds. It deals with the transgressions and reigns through righteousness to eternal life through Jesus Christ our Lord. Wonderful and preciously deep contrast! In Adam sin, condemnation and death. In Christ righteousness, justification and eternal life; yea much more, eternal glory. In Adam we have his constitution; in Christ we possess through grace His life and glory.

CHAPTER 6

1. Dead with Christ to sin (6:1-7)
2. Risen with Christ and alive to God (6:8-11)
3. Sin shall not have dominion (6:12-14)
4. Servants to righteousness (6:15-23)

Verses 1-7. We have learned from the previous chapter that the justified believer is in Christ and fully identified with Him. God sees the believer in the Lord Jesus Christ, no longer in Adam, but in Christ, the head of a new creation. "So if any one be in Christ, it is a new creation; the old things have passed away, behold all things have become new" (2 Cor. 5:17). Judicially the believer therefore is dead to sin, the old man was crucified, put completely to death in the death of Christ, and the believer is alive to God in Him. But this wonderful part of the gospel must become a reality in the life and experience of the believer. God beholds us as dead to sin in Christ and alive in Himself, this must be lived out. This is the solemn responsibility of the justified believer. And we are not to do this in our own strength, but in the power of the indwelling Spirit, who is also given to the believer. All this is unfolded in this chapter.

"What shall we say then? Shall we continue in sin that grace may abound? God forbid. How shall we, that are dead to sin, live any longer therein?" Inasmuch as we have died to sin in the death of Christ, the practical deliverance of sin and its dominion must be manifested in our lives. As we find later the old nature, the flesh, is still in the justified believer, but he has also another nature, another life, and he is therefore enabled in the power of that new life and his identification with Christ, to continue no longer in sin. It is a most positive fact "dead to sin" and this is true of all believers positionally in Christ, and therefore the Holy Spirit tells us that we should no longer live therein.

This truth is illustrated in Christian baptism; it is into Christ's death and illustrates the truth of death and burial in Christ. Baptism therefore does not save. It has no power to put a sinner in Christ, nor can it convey forgiveness of sins and impart the new life. Faith alone is needed for that, and when the sinner believes, the grace of God saves and accomplishes identification with Christ. And furthermore we are more than dead and buried with Christ "as Christ was raised up by the glory of the Father, even so we also should walk in newness of life." We share in His resurrection. What the Father of our Lord Jesus Christ did to Him, raising Him from the dead, He does to all who believe on Him. "He hath raised us up together" (Eph. 2:6). We possess His life, the risen life and therefore we should also walk in the power of this life. Our old man (what we are in Adam), was crucified with Christ. When He died we also died. Our old man was crucified with Christ "that the body of sin might be annulled, so that we should be slaves to sin no longer."

Many have been misled by the mistranslation which states "that the body of sin might be destroyed" and teach that the old nature is completely eradicated. But it does not say destroyed, but annulled, or cancelled. The body of sin is our mortal body with the law of sin in its members. And as long as we have this mortal body, the law of sin is in its members. But the operation of that law is annulled for the believer, who in faith, as we shall see later, reckons himself to be dead unto sin and alive unto God in Christ Jesus. And therefore the believer is enabled to be no longer a slave to sin, as the natural man is. A dead man is justified or discharged from sin; the tyrant's power is at an end when the subject over which he domineers is dead. And so we being crucified with Christ escape the tyrant's power, and ultimately when the Lord comes this mortal body will be changed and sin itself will be forever gone.

Verses 8-11. Inasmuch as we have died with Christ we shall also live with Him. Death hath no more dominion over Him; He liveth unto God. And all this is true of the believer. Then comes the most important answer to the question raised, in the beginning of the chapter. "Shall we continue in sin, that grace may abound?" "In the same manner reckon yourselves to be dead indeed unto sin, but alive unto God in Christ Jesus." This is an exhortation to take hold of this great and deep truth, the identification of the believer with Christ in death and resurrection. To reckon is an act of faith. It means to believe all this and to appropriate in faith what God has put on our side in Christ Jesus. We must reckon that we are dead and in possession of the life which empowers us to live unto God.

"We reckon this is so, not feel it to be so. It is an entire mistake, and fraught with important consequences, to imagine this being dead to sin to be a feeling or an experience. We cannot *feel* Christ's death on the cross, and it was there He died to sin, and *we* because He died. If it were experience, it would be an absolute perfect one, no evil thought, feeling, or desire, ever in the heart; and this true not only of some of the more advanced, but of all Christians and that always. But this is contrary to the experience of all. The attempt to produce such a condition in ourself ends either in the misery of utter failure, or, still worse, in self-satisfaction, indeed, the well-nigh incredible delusion for a Christian, that he is as impassive to sin as Christ Himself! The words do not express such an experience (as claimed by perfectionists and holiness sects). In every way, it is plain that it is not an experience of which the apostle is speaking here. We could not be told to reckon what we experience. What we reckon is a fact for faith, the fruit of the work done for us, not of that done in us. Because Christ died unto sin once for all, and in that He liveth, liveth unto God, thus also do we reckon ourselves dead indeed unto sin, and alive unto God in Christ Jesus" *(Numerical Bible).*

Verses 12-14. The exhortation which follows in verse 12 addressed not to the world, but to justified believers, proves that sin is still in the mortal body of the believer. It is not destroyed. But while sin is in our mortal body, it has no more right to reign there. However it will reign, if we yield to the desires of the old nature. If a believer obeys the old nature in its lusts, he walks not in the Spirit but in the flesh. Whenever temptation comes, the believer must take refuge in prayer, in self-judgment and self-surrender and yield (or present) his members afresh as instruments of righteousness unto God.

As long as the believer is in the mortal body there is the conflict between the flesh and the Spirit (Gal. 5:17). And if we walk in the Spirit we shall not fulfil the lust of the flesh; this necessitates that we make no provision for the flesh to fulfil the lusts thereof (Rom. 13:14). Furthermore, the promise is given to the believer in Christ that sin shall not have dominion over him because he is not under the law, but under grace. The grace which has saved the believing sinner and made Him nigh unto God, teaches also to deny ungodliness and worldly lusts and to live soberly, righteously and godly in this present age (Titus 2:12). And more than that; grace supplies the power to live godly. Therefore sin shall not have dominion over a believer because he is under grace. But this promise must be appropriated in faith.

Verses 15-23. Another question is asked. "What then, shall we sin because we are not under the law, but under grace?" Another, "God forbid"—perish the very thought of it—is the answer. Whoever yields to sin falls under the mastery of sin. Then follows a word of praise. He thanks God that the believers to whom he writes, once servants of sin, but having obeyed from the heart (and true faith is obedience), they were made free from sin and became servants of righteousness. "Free from sin" does not mean, as often taught, free from the old nature, but free from the domineering power of indwelling sin. Then there is the contrast between the former state in sin and the place of deliverance into which grace has brought the believer. In the former life as unsaved, slaves of sin, there was an awful fruit and the end of it is death. But now as servants of God, freed from sin's awful slavery, there is another fruit, the fruit of holiness and the end of it is eternal life. How this fruit of the justified believer is to be produced we shall learn in the next chapter. Sin's wages is death; that is what man receives in payment for sin. Eternal life, the great and inestimable gift of God is bestowed through Jesus Christ our Lord.

CHAPTER 7

1. The law and its dominion (7:1-3)
2. Dead to the law and married to another (7:4-6)
3. Concerning the law: Its activities and purpose (7:7-13)
4. The experience of a believer in bondage to the law (7:14-24)
5. The triumphant note of deliverance (7:25)

Verses 1-3. The law is now more fully taken up. We have learned before that by the works of the law no man can be justified before God. But when the sinner is justified by faith, does he need the law to please God? Can obedience to the law produce in him the fruit of holiness unto God? What is the relation of the justified believer to the law? Is he still under the dominion of the law or is he also delivered from the law and its bondage? These questions are answered in this chapter. An important principle is stated in the first verse. The law has dominion over a man as long as he lives. The law has dominion over man (both Jews and Gentiles). The law, which is holy, just and good (verse 12) condemns man, his sinful nature and the fruits of that sinful nature, and in this sense it has dominion over every man and holds him in its grasp. But when death takes place, the rule of the law is broken. It cannot touch a dead man. The penalty of the broken law is death, when that sentence is executed, the law can have no longer dominion.

An illustration from the marriage law as instituted by God is given to make this clear. Husband and wife are united in a union till death dissolves it. The married woman is bound by that law to her husband as long as he lives. When he dies she is free and can be married to another. And we are become dead to the law by the body of Christ. The body of Christ means the death of Christ on the cross. On the cross He bore the judgment which is our due. He bore the penalty and the curse of the law for us. "Christ hath redeemed us from the curse of the law, being made a curse for us, for it is written, Cursed is every one that hangeth on a tree" (Gal. 3:13). The penalty of the broken law has been met and the law is vindicated. Inasmuch, then as His death is our death, in that we died with Christ, the law can have no more dominion over us; "we are dead to the law by the body of Christ."

Verses 4-6. The old union is dissolved. Death has done its work and it is now possible after being freed from the law to be married to another. In Galatians the question about the law and its authority is viewed from another side. The law was the schoolmaster unto Christ; now after faith is come, the full truth concerning redemption by the death of Christ is made known, we are no longer under a schoolmaster (Gal. 3:23-25). Being then dead to the law by the body of Christ we are married to another. And this other One is He who died for us and who is risen from the dead. Justified believers are in a living union with a risen Christ; He lives in us and we live in Him. And the result of this most blessed union is fruit unto God. The law could not produce any fruit whatever but only death; nor can the legal principle bring forth fruit unto God in a believer. Ephraim was joined to idols as we read in Hosea. But Ephraim observed the Lord, heard Him and became like a green fir tree. And the Lord adds, "From Me is thy fruit found" (Hosea 14:8). The parable of the vine and the branches (John 15) illustrates in a simple and blessed way the apostolic statement, "Married unto another—that we should bring forth fruit unto God." As the branch is in closest union with the vine and the sap of the vine produces the fruit, so are we one with Christ, and abiding in Him we bring forth the fruit unto holiness, the fruit which pleases God.

And "when we were in the flesh" (our former state) the passions of sins were by the law. The law by its holy character brings out what the natural man is and stirs up the passions of sins. But it is different now. We are delivered from the law and we can serve in newness of Spirit. We have a new nature, even eternal life, and in that we can render a true spiritual service.

Verses 7-13. "Is the law sin?" is the next question raised. It springs logically from the statement that the passions of sins, coming out of an evil, sinful heart, were by the law and bringing forth fruit unto death. Still another "God forbid" is the answer. The law was given that we might have through that law the knowledge of sin. "I had not known sin, but by the law." I would not be conscious of lust, unless the law said, "Thou shalt not covet." The law given by a holy God is God's detective. The law forbids and the commandment at once brings out what is in the heart of man. Therefore, no blame can be put upon the law. Sin is that which must be blamed. Sin is lawlessness, rebellion against God and the law brings out that rebellion. Therefore apart from the law sin was dead, that is, dormant. But as soon as the commandment is given, the evil heart rebels against it and man is detected to be a sinner and a transgressor. Let us notice the change of the pronoun "we" to "I." Some thirty times this little word "I" is found in verses 7-25. We are brought upon the ground of personal experience; it has to be discovered and learned experimentally. The apostle personifies this experience and speaks thus personally describing how a believer learns the lessons about the law, how the law cannot help a justified believer, and but makes of him a wretched man. It must also have been his own experience.

"For I was alive without the law once, but when the commandment came, sin revived, and I died." This is the experience of a man who is ignorant of the spirituality of the law. He thinks himself alive, but when the commandment came, its spiritual demands realized (the law is spiritual, verse 14), the false notion of being alive was detected, for sin revived and he died, which means that sin, discovered by the law, condemned him to death. "And the commandment which was unto life was found for me to be unto death."

In connection with the commandment, the law, it is written, "This do, and thou shalt live." And so in this experience—he tries next to get life by the law, but he found it was unto death, for the declaration of the law is "Cursed is every one that continueth not in all things which are written in the book of the law to do them" (Gal. 3:10; Deut. 27:26). He speaks of sin, his evil nature, as one who had deceived him into all this, so that the law could manifest its power in slaying him. Verse 12 is the real answer to the question, "Is the law sin?" The law is holy, and the commandment holy, and just and good. And because the law is holy it gives knowledge of sin and detects sin, bringing it to light in all its hideousness and then pronounces the sentence of death. One other question is asked, "Was then that which is good (the law) made death unto me?" God forbid. But sin, that it might appear sin, working death in me by that which is good; that sin by the commandment might become exceedingly sinful." It all comes back upon sin (the evil nature, the flesh). Thus by the commandment sin becomes exceeding sinful.

Verses 14-24. But all this must be learned by experience especially the fact "I am carnal," the knowledge that in my flesh there dwelleth no good thing and that I have no power, I am powerless against indwelling sin. What person is it who describes his experience in these words? Some have applied it exclusively to the apostle. Others state that it pictures an awakened sinner and not a converted man. The man described is born again, but is in bondage to the law and is ignorant of his deliverance in Christ. We find first the statement "we know that the law is spiritual." This is the knowledge which a true Christian possesses concerning the law. And the Christian who knows this great truth, that the law is spiritual, also has learned another truth. "I am carnal and sold under sin." Here then it is where experience begins.

True Christian experience is to know our full deliverance in Christ and to walk in the Spirit; the experience of a Christian in struggling with the old nature and discovering what is that old nature, the flesh, is put before us in verses 15-24. That we have here a converted person is seen by the fact first of all, that he does not want to do evil, he wants to do good and cannot do it and therefore hates what he does. The carnal nature, the flesh, which is still in a converted person, is thus demonstrated as enslaving him, however, he is no longer a willing slave, but he hates that old thing which has the mastery over him. In hating it and condemning sin, he does the same what the law does, for it also condemns sin. In this way he consents to the law that it is good.

The seventeenth verse is of much importance. "Now then it is no more I that really do it, but sin that dwelleth in me." He learns the difference between himself as born again, in possession of a new nature, and the old nature. He begins to distinguish himself as in possession of a new nature that wills to do good, hating evil, and sin in him, the flesh in which dwells nothing good, but all that is evil. "For I know that in me, that is, in my flesh dwelleth no good thing, for to will is present with me; but how to perform that which is good I find not." It is a great discovery to find out by experience, that although the believer is born again, he has a nature in him which is evil, which cannot bring forth a good thing. But the will is present with him to do good, because he is born again; however, he finds not the power in himself to perform what is good.

Now the conflict between the two natures is on. It brings out some important facts. "It is no more I that do it, but sin that dwells in me." He as born again, no longer loves sin; he hates it. Because he does that, which he does not want to do he can truthfully say "it is no more I that do it." Furthermore he delights in the law of God after the inward man. This can never be said of an unconverted man, but only he who has a new nature can delight in the law of God. But he finds himself in helpless captivity to the law of sin which is at work in his members. He finds out that while he has a new nature to will good and to hate evil, he has no power; sin is too strong for him. And this is to teach the believer that he must get power to overcome outside of himself. All his resolutions and good wishes cannot supply the strength to do. That he is self-occupied, seeking power by what he does and tries to do, is seen from the use of the little word "I." The name of the One in whom we have deliverance, Christ, is not mentioned once.

The case is clear, it is the description of the experience of a believer, who is justified, born again, in union with Christ, dead with Him, risen with Him and indwelt by the Holy Spirit; but he lacks the knowledge of this and tries by his own efforts and in his own strength, through keeping the law, to obtain holiness. Having discovered that nothing good dwells in his flesh; that the flesh is not himself, but sin in him and that, because it is too strong for him, he is powerless, the cry of despair is uttered by him. "O wretched man that I am! Who shall deliver me from the body of this death?" He has reached the end of self. He looks now for deliverance from another source, outside of himself. The answer comes at once. "I thank God through Jesus Christ our Lord." In Him there is deliverance and what that deliverance is, we shall learn from the first four verses of the eighth chapter. The two laws are mentioned once more in the last verse of this chapter. With the mind, as born again, he serves the law and the law gives him no power; in the struggle with the old nature he is enslaved by the law of sin.

CHAPTER 8

1. In Christ: no condemnation but deliverance (8:1-4)
2. Flesh and spirit (8:5-8)
3. The body and the spirit (8:9-11)
4. Sons and heirs of God (8:12-14)
5. The time of travail and groaning; the Future Redemption (8:18-25)
6. The intercession of the Spirit (8:26-27)
7. The saints calling, the challenge and the assurance (8:28-39)

Verses 1-4. We have reached the mountaintop of this great Epistle. What man is in the flesh and under the law has been fully demonstrated. "The flesh profiteth nothing" (John 6:63). The law cannot give power to deliver, but only produces wretchedness, and, as we saw, deliverance must come from another. "Power belongeth unto God" (Ps. 62:11); the power of deliverance must come from God. And this was the triumphant note in the previous chapter. "I thank God through Jesus Christ our Lord." And now we see the believer in Christ Jesus, free from all condemnation, free from the law of sin and death, indwelt by the Holy Spirit, a child of God, an heir of God and joint heir with the Lord Jesus Christ." It is the contrasted statement of the privileges, the capacities, the security, and the prospects of the Christians as having the Spirit, that is here presented as the divinely wrought counterpart of the preceding description of man "as carnal, sold under sin." The proof and witness of human wretchedness is the law. The title and measure of Christian blessedness is Christ. As alive in Christ the believer is estimated, not according to the variable standard of his own emotions, but according to the eternal fixedness of divine truth now realized and established in the person of Christ before God."[2]

---

[2]Pridham on Romans.

The first statement assures the believer in Christ that there is for him no more condemnation. In Christ Jesus, in identification with Him who died for our sins and is risen from the dead, in whom we have died and have life, in such a position condemnation is no longer possible, because nothing is left to be condemned. There can be no condemnation for those who are united to a risen Christ; as He is so are we. And this most blessed assurance is unconditional. The words "who walk not after the flesh, but after the Spirit" as they appear in the Authorized Version must be omitted here; they have been proven to be an interpolation. We find them at the close of the fourth verse, which is the proper place for them. But what makes the believer in Christ Jesus free from the law of sin and death, which is in his members? The second verse answers this question. "For the law of the Spirit, of life in Christ Jesus, hath set me free from the law of sin and death."

The law of sin and death has lost its power by another law; the law of the Spirit is, that of life in Christ Jesus. It means that the Spirit's law is that we are, as believers, for everything, for all things, dependent on Christ. In Him are all our springs and resources. He is our life and His life is in us. We are one with Him. To appropriate this in faith, identifying ourselves with Christ as God has done it, giving Him the pre-eminence, glorifying Him—this gives power and deliverance. And the Spirit, the Spirit of holiness and power is also given to the believer; He dwells in Him. If the believer then walks according to the law of the Spirit, that is in Christ, we are made free from the law of sin and death. The righteousness of the law can in this way be fulfilled in us. But there is a condition. We must walk not according to the flesh but according to the Spirit.

What is the walk according to the Spirit? It is not self-occupation, nor even occupation with the Holy Spirit. Walking according to the Spirit is occupation with the Lord Jesus Christ. If the believer ever looks to Christ, depends on Him, draws all he needs from Him, if Christ is His all—then the believer walks according to the Spirit. Then there is power over the old nature and the righteousness, demanded by the law is being fulfilled. And we must not overlook the fact that God's love is mentioned in this blessed unfolding of our deliverance in Christ. The law was weak, it could not get its righteous requirements fulfilled, on account of the flesh, the fallen nature of man. Then God came in. "God sending His own Son in likeness of sinful flesh, and for sin condemned sin in the flesh." It points us once more to the cross.

"He has sent His own Son in 'the likeness of sinful flesh' as the cross manifests Him, but there for sin, our sin, putting it completely away, while, at the same time condemning it utterly. Sin in the flesh is condemned,—I myself, with all that is in me, my own thoughts, my will, my wisdom, my ways,—in the cross, I see the end of it all, but the end of it in the love which has come in fully for me and which now fulfills in me the righteous requirement of the law when it is no longer simply requirement, but the Spirit of God has filled my heart with the joy of Christ. 'The joy of the Lord is your strength.' I am free to give myself up to drink in this love which God has shown me and which rests upon me in Christ, in all the fulness of God's delight in Him. I have no cause now to ask: Must not God condemn the evil in me? He *has* condemned it, and I read the condemnation there where I find also Himself for me in a grace which knows no conditions, and which holds me fast, therefore, forever" (*Numerical Bible*).

Notice that the opening verses of the eighth chapter refer us back to the fifth, sixth and seventh chapters. The believer is in Christ the last Adam and therefore beyond condemnation (chapter 5:12-21). Sin is not to have dominion over us (chapter 6). Sin in the flesh has been condemned and the righteousness of the law is fulfilled by a walk according to the Spirit (chapter 7).

Verses 5-8. Next we find a contrast between the flesh and the Spirit. While the believer is no longer in the eyes of God in the flesh, the flesh, however, is still in him as long as he has this mortal body. There is therefore a conflict between the Spirit and the flesh. Humanity falls into two classes, those who are according to the flesh, the unsaved; and those who are according to the Spirit, believers in Christ. A believer is called to walk according to the Spirit, in the sphere into which he is brought through grace. He may walk according to the flesh, but that does not put him back into his former state, when unsaved, he was in the flesh.

The mind of the flesh, the condition in which man is by nature, is described in a fourfold way: 1. It is death. 2. It is enmity against God. 3. The flesh is not subject to the law of God, neither indeed can be. 4. They that are in the flesh cannot please God. Such is the state of all who are not born again. But the believer is no longer in the flesh, but is in Christ and the mind of the Spirit is life and peace, which the believer possesses. The believer who walks carnally cannot please God, just as a man who is not born of the Spirit, cannot please God. The carnal walk of the believer results in a broken fellowship with God. But Christ is our Advocate with the Father and He restores while the indwelling Spirit leads to confession and self-judgment. The standing of a believer before God is always in Christ; God beholds us in Him and no longer in the flesh, the sphere of sin and death. The practical state of a believer is often varying. But our failures and shortcomings can never affect our standing before God in Christ. This is an important truth. Many true believers are in a miserable bondage, in doubts and fears, lacking assurance and the joy of salvation, because they do not know the fixed and unalterable standing a believer hath in Christ.

Verses 9-11. The believer's standing is, therefore, emphasized. "But ye are not in the flesh, but in the Spirit, if so that the Spirit of God dwell in you; but if any one have not the Spirit of Christ, he is none of His." The believer is no longer in the flesh, but in the Spirit because the Spirit of God dwells in him. For the first time we have the blessed truth declared that the Spirit of God is in the believer. As the Spirit of God, He marks the new standing before God; as the Spirit of Christ, He is evidencing the fact that the believer belongs to Christ, and that He produces in him Christ-likeness. Sometimes true believers ask the question, "How can I get the Holy Spirit?" Certain teachers say that a believer, after being saved, should seek the gift and sealing of the Spirit. To teach this is altogether unscriptural. The gift and sealing of the Spirit are at once bestowed upon all who are in Christ, and every true believer is in Christ.

"In whom ye also trusted, having heard the word of truth, the gospel of your salvation; in whom also believing, ye were sealed with the Holy Spirit of promise" (Eph. 1:13). "He that hath sealed us with the Holy Spirit is God" (2 Cor. 1:22). The sealing with the Spirit does not put a believer in Christ; but because we have trusted on Him we are sealed. This verse here in Romans is conclusive. The Spirit given to us marks off the believer as belonging to Christ. Acts 19:2 is frequently quoted to back up the erroneous teaching that the Spirit must be received in a definite experience after conversion. One little word is responsible for the error. The word "since" is mistranslated; it is "when." "Have ye received the Spirit when ye believed?"

Occupation with the Spirit of God and His indwelling is nowhere demanded of the believer. He has come not to testify of Himself, but to glorify Christ. Therefore He testifies of the blessed fact that "Christ is in you." The Spirit is life on account of righteousness. It means that the spirit of the believer is energized by the Holy Spirit and the Holy Spirit is the power of life in the believer. What about the body of the believer? It is dead on account of sin. The body has not yet the effects of redemption in it; it is not yet quickened. But the mortal body of the believer has the promise of redemption. The Holy Spirit dwells in that body and He is the earnest of our inheritance. "If the Spirit of Him who raised up Jesus from the dead dwell in you, He who raised up Christ from the dead shall also quicken your mortal bodies on account of His Spirit who dwelleth in you." This is the redemption for which we wait (verse 23). It will come when the Lord comes for His saints.

The believer is nowhere taught to look for the death of the mortal body he has, but for the coming of the Lord, who "shall change our body of humiliation that it may be fashioned like unto His glorious body, according to the working whereby He is able to subdue all things unto Himself" (Phil. 3:21). "Behold, I show you a mystery; we *shall* not all sleep, but we shall all be changed, in a moment, in the twinkling of an eye" (1 Cor. 15:51-52; 1 Thess. 4:17). Here we have a blessed answer to the question asked in the previous chapter. "Who shall deliver me from the body of this death?" The answer is "the Lord Jesus Christ." And while the believer waits for that promised, coming deliverance, deliverance from the presence of sin, he walks in the Spirit, freed from the power of sin.

Verses 12-17. Believers are therefore no longer debtors to the flesh, to live after the flesh. We owe the flesh nothing, for it has never done anything for us. If a person lives according to the flesh, if this is the sphere in which he moves, he is "about to die," on the road to death. But if by the Spirit ye mortify the deeds of the body, ye shall live." "Death and life are here set in prospect before the soul as the results, respectively, of the path now chosen. As to the believer, he is characteristically one who is not in the flesh. This he is, not as the result of attainment, but by the grace of God.

The appeal which the apostle here makes is to the Christian conscience. Where there is life, there will be an answer to that appeal. The mortification of the deeds of the body is the result of the Spirit's energy, the energy of that Spirit, who produces in him the fruits of life, when unhindered in the gracious operations of His love. Mortification of the deeds of the body is looked for only from believers who are indwelt by the Spirit. There is, therefore, nothing in verse 13 that need chill in the least the confidence of the poor weak-spirited self-judging Christian. Those who are most given to self-judgment are they to whom the warning here expressed has the least application." The mortification of the deeds of the body does not mean asceticism. It is that which is more fully mentioned in Col. 3:5-7.

(If men live according to the flesh, they are on the way to death. It does not say that they will die. God's grace is always free to come in, but then if it comes in it takes one off the road to death; it does not speak in such a manner as if sin were of no consequence. *Numerical Bible*)

For as many as are led by the Spirit of God, they are the sons of God. This proves the believer to be in this blessed relationship. The life and walk in the Spirit is the outward evidence of sonship. And the Spirit we have received is not the Spirit of bondage, to fear and to doubt, but it is the gracious Spirit of adoption, whereby we cry, Abba, Father. Abba is the Aramaic (the language spoken by Jews in Palestine). Father is the word the Gentile uses. Both Jews and Gentiles believing receive the Spirit of sonship. They both have access by one Spirit unto the Father (Eph. 2:18). "And because ye are sons, God hath sent forth the Spirit of His Son into your hearts, crying, Abba, Father" (Gal. 4:6). The marks and evidences of the sonship of the believer are more fully given in the first Epistle of John (1:5-7, 2:1-3, 9, 10, 27, 28, 3:1-6, 14, 19, 24, 4:1-4, 7, 8, 15, 20, 21, 5:1-4, 10-12, 13).

Furthermore, the Spirit beareth witness with our spirit that we are the children of God. This witness is not a mere good feeling, which is subject to fluctuations, but the witness of the Spirit is in the Word of God. We know that we are the children of God, because the Word assures us that it is so; this is the witness of the Spirit. And our own spirit bears the same witness, for we know that we have passed from death unto life. "Hereby know we that we dwell in Him, and He in us, because He hath given us His Spirit" (1 John 4:13). We have the blessed consciousness of our relationship as children in our own spirit, the highest intelligence we possess in ourselves. "Behold what manner of love the Father hath bestowed upon us, that we should be called the children of God. . . . Beloved, now are we the children of God, and it doth not appear what we shall be, but we know, when He shall appear, we shall be like Him; for we shall see Him as He is" (1 John 3:1-2). We are heirs of God and joint heirs with Christ. And we suffer with Him—for the world knoweth us not as it knew Him not—and shall be glorified with Him, in the coming day of His glorious manifestation. Our fellowship with Him as God's children is now in suffering, and afterward in glory.

Verses 18-25. The highest summit of the Epistle has been reached. In Christ; no condemnation; free from the law of sin and death; indwelt by the Spirit of God; led by the Spirit of God; children of God; heirs of God; joint heirs with Christ—this is the blessed and sublime culmination. And as it is when we stand on some mountain-peak, a great vision now bursts upon us. It concerns the future. A wonderful glory is in store for the children of God. The sons of God are going to be manifested (verse 19). That will be when Christ, the head of the new creation is manifested; then we shall also be manifested with Him in glory (Col. 3:4). Then He will occupy the throne of His glory and "we shall reign with Him over the earth."

All creation groaneth and travaileth until now, anxiously looking forward to that coming day when the creature itself also shall be delivered from the bondage of corruption into the liberty of the glory of the children of God. For creation was put into the place of corruption and death through the fall of man. But it was subjected to this not without hope. The hope of a ruined creation is the coming of the Lord Jesus Christ, who is both the Creator of all things and the Redeemer. Upon His blessed brow He bore the thorns, the emblem of the curse which rests upon creation. And when He comes, groaning creation will be delivered. Then "the wolf shall dwell with the lamb, and the leopard shall lie down with the kid, and the calf and the young lion and fatling together; and the lion shall eat straw like the ox" (Isa. 11:6-9). It is the glorious vision of the coming age, the dispensation of the fulness of times, when all things will be gathered together in Christ. The prophets and the Psalms tell out more fully the story of a restored creation, blest through Him who paid for it by His own precious blood. And we, who have the first fruits of the Spirit also groan within ourselves, awaiting that blessed consummation, when we shall come into our full inheritance, the redemption of our body. Our salvation is in hope of this future redemption and glorification. We wait patiently for it.

Verses 26-27. Prayer is now mentioned. We need it in the midst of the groans, the sorrows and sufferings with which we are surrounded and which is our lot as long as we are in this mortal body. And prayer is our refuge, the expression of our dependence upon God and our utmost confidence in Him. But while we know how to pray, we often do not know "what we should pray for as we ought." Then the Spirit Himself maketh intercession with groanings that cannot be uttered. "Prayer is most commonly the witness of our infirmities. The burdened heart may find itself too full for speech, too much perplexed, for the ordering of its thoughts. But there is an utterance of supplication that makes no sound. It is the Spirit, as the helper of our infirmities, who makes these desires known to the God. Groaning in sympathy with the tried and longing heart, He makes His intercession for the Saints according to the will of God." Thus the mind of the Spirit in us is known of God—and heard by Him. And then we must remember that besides this intercession of the Spirit there is the intercession of Christ at the right hand of God (verse 34). The believer is therefore hedged about and made secure and if he walks in the Spirit, constant peace and joy will be his daily portion.

Verses 28-39. Therefore we know that to those who love God all things work together for good, to those who are called according to purpose. We can rest in God and commit all to Him. The purpose of God for His own, from eternity to eternity is blessedly revealed. "From God's foreknowledge of us in the past eternity to the accomplished glory of the future, there is a perfectly linked chain of blessing, no link of which can ever be sundered. God's purpose is that Christ His Son, should be a First-born among many brethren." (*Numerical Bible*). And the chain of blessing is—foreknown—predestinated—called—justified and glorified. We do not enter into the controversies of the past concerning predestination, but repudiate that unscriptural conception that God has predestinated a part of the human race to be lost. This is incorrect in view of the statement of Scripture that God "will have all men to be saved and come unto the knowledge of the truth" (1 Tim. 2:4). But all are not saved because they believe not. God knows all who would believe and these are predestinated, called, justified and will be ultimately glorified. And His eternal purpose will not fail and all who are in Christ will be conformed to the image of His Son. This is the hope of God's calling (Ephes. 1:18).

Foreknowledge expresses the original operation of the divine mind, considered with reference to the pure and unapproachable majesty of the blessed and only Potentate. Predestination respects rather the condition of that which is thus foreknown, objectively regarded as a vessel of His will (Pridham).

And what a blessed, most precious and glorious ending of this great chapter and the entire doctrinal section of this great Epistle! What shall we say then to these things? Our answer must be worship and adoration of the God who hath loved us so in giving His only begotten Son, who reached down to our misery and shame and who hath lifted us so high. The great truths of the gospel are once more reviewed. God is for us. Who can be against us? The proof of it is that He spared not His own Son, but delivered Him up for us all. With Him He has given us freely all things. God is the justifier; therefore "Who shall lay anything to the charge of God's elect?" Christ died, Christ is risen, Christ is at the right hand of God making intercession for us—who then is he that shall condemn? And nothing can separate us from the love of Christ and the love of God which is in Christ Jesus our Lord. No condemnation and no separation! No more wrath but eternal glory! Such is the salvation of God.

II. Dispensational: God's Dealings with Israel (9—11)

1. Israel and God's Sovereignty

CHAPTER 9

1. Paul's yearning over Israel (9:1-3)
2. What Israel possesseth (9:4-5)
3. God's unconditional election (9:6-13)
4. God's sovereignty and the vindication of His justice and mercy (9:14-26)
5. Mercy for the remnant (9:27-29)
6. Israel's rejection of God's righteousness (9:30-33)

This second division brings before us Israel and shows that the principles of the Gospel, as unfolded in the first eight chapters are in harmony with God's ways with Israel. Jews and Gentiles, those who have the law and those who had no law, were proved guilty before God. All have sinned and are equally lost. Both Jews and Gentiles are all under sin. The same God justifies the circumcision by faith, and also the uncircumcision. Jews were thus brought upon the same level with the Gentiles. There is no difference. Grace goes forth alike to Jews and

Gentiles who believe. But this fact raises a most important question. How can all this be reconciled with the promises made in a special manner to the Jews? How can the principles be harmonized with God's faithfulness? Has God gone back on His Word and covenants? Hath God cast away His people? The answer to these questions and the demonstration that God is just and faithful in all His dealings with Jews and Gentiles is given in these three chapters.

(Godet states that the problem "how can God set aside those He elected," is answered in three ways: 1. God preserves His entire liberty (9). 2. He shows that Israel's sin is the true explanation (10). 3. God vindicates His action by foretelling future consequences (11).)

Verses 1-3. Paul speaks of himself in each of these three chapters. Knowing that they rejected the salvation of God, he yearns and sorrows over his kinsmen. In the next chapter he expresses his heart's desire and prayer for their salvation, and in the eleventh chapter he mentions himself as an evidence that God has not cast away His people. The Jews, because he preached salvation to the Gentiles, looked upon him as an enemy of their nation and as a traitor. "Forbidding us to speak to the Gentiles that they might be saved, to fill up their sins always, for the wrath is come upon them to the uppermost." Thus he wrote to the Thessalonians (1 Thess. 2:16). In Jerusalem the Jewish mob cried, "Away with such a fellow from the earth." They hated him, but he loved his brethren, his kinsmen according to the flesh. It was this mighty love which burned in his soul which constrained him to go up to Jerusalem, in spite of the warnings given by the Holy Spirit. So intense was his yearning for them that he had wished to be cut off from Christ for them, if that were possible. He was like Moses, when he prayed, "If Thou wilt forgive their sin; and if not blot me, I pray Thee, out of Thy book, which thou hast written" (Exod. 32:32).

Verses 4-5. And what is this people in the purpose of God? What are their possessions and privileges? It is the most favored nation on the earth. "What nation is there so great, who hath God so nigh unto them, as the Lord our God is in all things that we call upon Him for?" (Deut. 4:7). The *adoption* is theirs, as His family on earth, destined for earthly blessings (Amos 3:2). And God had said, "I am a Father to Israel" and "Israel is my son, my Firstborn." They had the *glory.* In visible glory Jehovah dwelt in their midst. While absent now, the promise is, that in the future day of their restoration, that glory will return with the coming of the Lord (Isa. 4; Ezek. 43:4). Theirs are also the *covenants;* they were made with the nation; and the giving of the *law.* Furthermore, theirs is the *service* of God, that divinely instituted levitical ritual, so full of blessed and prophetic meaning. All other rituals are unauthorized counterfeits. They also have the *promises.* "Whose are the fathers, and of whom, concerning the flesh, Christ came, He, who is God over all blessed forever. Amen." (More than once the attempt has been made to change those wonderful words, bearing testimony to the deity of our Lord. The revised version, in its marginal reading, is one of the latest attempts to rob our Lord of this great and true tribute.) And all these great things belong to Israel. They still belong to them. When the time of their national conversion and restoration comes, all these things will be manifested in their fulness, even to a restored, glorious service in the millennial temple (Ezek. 40—47). And these statements show that the apostle to the Gentiles did not despise the nation Israel and its privileges.

Verses 6-13. Now if the nation as such had failed, as we find later, on account of unbelief, and they were rejected for the present, the Word of God had not failed on that account. If God had called the Gentiles and they received now the blessing of righteousness, it does not mean that the Word of God has come to naught. God's purpose concerning Israel cannot fail. But they prided themselves that they were of the seed of Abraham and therefore exclusively entitled to the promises. "We have Abraham to our father" (Luke 3:8), was their boast, and the Lord had told them "If ye were Abraham's children, ye would do the works of Abraham" (John 8:39). They forgot in their blind antagonism to the gospel that the Scriptures showed that blessing had its source with the choice of God, that blessing is the result of elective mercy and the title to it must be of faith. Divine election is the only ground of blessing.

They are not all Israel, which are of Israel; neither because they are the seed of Abraham are they all children. If such were the case, then the children of the flesh, Ishmael and his offspring, were on the same ground with them. There was a promise made "At this time will I come, and Sarah shall have a son." In that promised son, in Isaac alone, the seed was called, therefore the children of the promise are counted for the seed. This showed that they had no right to expect divine blessing simply on the ground of natural descent. And in the choice of Isaac, God's sovereignty and election is seen. They might therefore be Abraham's seed and yet not be Abraham's children; only those that are of faith are the children of Abraham (Gal. 3:7). The case of Jacob and Esau is next cited. Rebecca was their mother. Before the children were even born, and therefore had done neither good nor evil, to merit anything, it was said unto her, "the elder shall serve the younger." It was so ordered "that the purpose of God according to election might stand, not of works, but of Him that calleth." If they claim and expect blessing merely on the ground of natural descent, then the descendants of Esau, the Edomites, must be admitted to the same blessings with them. This they would not admit. Inasmuch as all rests upon God's unconditional election, their objections to the blessing of the Gentiles through the gospel, God dealing with them in grace, were disproved by their own history.

("Jacob have I loved, but Esau have I hated." The love for Jacob was unmerited. "Esau have I hated" stands written at the close of the Old Testament, after the continued wickedness of Edom had been fully demonstrated and merited God's indignation.)

Verses 14-26. God can choose whom He will. This is His sovereignty. Is then God unrighteous in doing this? God forbid. Two examples of God's sovereignty in mercy and in judgment are given. Had God dealt with Israel according to His righteousness, they would have been cut off. Then the sovereignty of God was displayed and Israel was spared. All rests upon that sovereign mercy—"So then it is not of him that willeth, nor of him that runneth, but of God that showeth mercy." And Pharaoh illustrates God's sovereignty in judgment. Pharaoh was a wicked, God-hating man. God had shown him mercy, but he hardened his heart and defied the Lord. In arrogant pride he said, "Who is Jehovah that I should obey Him? I know not Jehovah." Then He hardened his heart and made him a monument of His wrath. "Both were wicked—Israel and Pharaoh. Righteousness would have condemned both. He has mercy on one, and hardens the other. He has mercy on whom He will have mercy, and whom He will He hardens, when simple righteousness would have condemned both. This is sovereignty. He proves Himself not merely righteous (the day of judgment will prove that), but proves Himself God." But man, the creature of the dust, replies to God and brings his finite thoughts to judge God. The questions in verse 19 are severely rebuked. What is man that he should speak to his Creator! The thing formed speaks to Him that formed it. "Why hast Thou made us thus?" The potter can take a lump of clay and form out of it two vessels, one unto honor and another unto dishonor. It is his right. God can do this according to His sovereign will, and none can say, What doest Thou? However, while this is God's right, that He can do so, if He chooses to do it, there is nothing said, that He has done so.

"God's sovereignty is the first of all rights, the foundation of all rights, the foundation of all morality. If God is not God, what will He be? The root of the question is this; is God to judge man, or man God? God can do whatsoever He pleases. He is not the object for judgment. Such is His title: But when in fact the apostle presents the two cases, wrath and grace, he puts the case of God showing *longsuffering* towards one already fitted for wrath, in order to give at last an example to men of His wrath in the execution of His justice; and then of God displaying His glory in vessels of mercy whom *He* has prepared for glory. There are then these three points established with marvellous exactitude; the power to do all things, no one having the right to say a word; wonderful endurance with the wicked, in whom at length His wrath is manifested; demonstration of His glory in vessels, whom He has Himself prepared by mercy for glory, and whom He has called, whether from among the Jews or Gentiles, according to the declaration of Hosea."[3] The objections which were raised against God's dealings in grace with Gentiles are completely met and answered. He calls whom He will and calling the Gentiles and showing them mercy has not cancelled the promises made to Israel.

Verses 27-29. Now while grace goes forth to the Gentiles, mercy is also in store for Israel. Ultimately a remnant will be saved—not the whole nation, but a remnant. It refers us to a specific time, "When He will finish the work, and cut it short in righteousness, because a short work will the Lord make upon the earth" (Isa. 10:22-23). It is a prediction concerning the future. They will, when this age closes, pass through a time of judgment; in that period God in sovereign power and mercy will call a remnant of His people, the remnant so often seen in the prophetic Word and in the book of Revelation. That remnant will be saved and will become the nucleus of the coming kingdom;

[3]J. N. Darby, *Synopsis.*

the unbelieving apostate Israel will be swept away in judgment.

Verses 30-33. The conclusion of this intensely interesting and often misunderstood chapter puts before us the fact of God's merciful dealings with Gentiles and Israel's failure. The Gentiles, who did not follow after righteousness, have attained to the righteousness, which is of faith. They believe the gospel and enjoy the blessings of the gospel. Israel failed. Why? They sought it not by faith, but as it were by the works of the law, the way of failure and death. They rejected the principle of faith, even declared in their own Scriptures, "the just shall live by faith." They stumbled at the stumbling stone (1 Peter 2:8).

2. Israel's Failure and Unbelief

CHAPTER 10

1. Israel's condition. (10:1-4)
2. Righteousness by works and by faith (10:5-13)
3. The gospel published abroad (10:14-17)
4. Israel's unbelief (10:18-21)

Verses 1-4. For His beloved people Israel, the great apostle of the Gentiles, prayed to God, that they might be saved. What an example he has given to us believers of the Gentiles. We owe a great debt to Israel; but how little prayer there is among Gentile Christians for the salvation of the Jews! Paul bears witness that they had zeal for God, but not according to knowledge. Their ignorance consisted in not knowing God's righteousness, that which is found in the first part of the Epistle, seeking therefore to establish their own righteousness; in doing this, they did not submit themselves unto the righteousness of God. They were religious, kept the law outwardly, and Christ, who is the end of the law for righteousness to every one that believeth, they rejected. Alas! The same is still the condition of the Jews.

Verses 5-13. Righteousness by works and by faith is contrasted. Moses, in whom they trusted as their great teacher, describes the righteousness which is of the law in these words, "the man who doeth those things shall live by them." But the righteousness by faith is likewise mentioned by Moses; but for the Holy Spirit calling attention to it in this passage, it would never have been known. Deut. 30, where these words are found, speaks of the time, when Israel in a world-wide dispersion, will return with the heart to God and when He will have compassion upon them. Then their heart will be circumcised and grace will be manifested towards them. Driven out of the land for having broken the law, they will hearken to the Word and obey in faith.

"The Apostle therefore quotes such terms as exclude 'doing' on the part of man. Righteousness springs out of the finished work of Christ (verses 3, 4), and there can be no 'finished' work while man is endeavoring to be saved by law, for this would be virtually to undo what Christ has done. That which would be impossible to man, God has already done in Christ. All the 'doing' required by the law, has been accomplished by Jesus Christ, and everything that is required now from men is to believe what Christ has done. Christ has neither to be brought down from heaven, nor to be raised again from the dead; everything has been accomplished, and all that is left is to accept in trustful thankfulness. Faith has not to acquire or win a Saviour, but to accept One Who has already accomplished the work of redemption. God's righteousness is not distant and difficult, but near and easy" (W. A. Griffith Thomas).

This word, which is nigh, the Apostle saith "is the word of faith which we preach." And this it is "if thou shalt confess with thy mouth Jesus as Lord, and shall believe in thy heart that God hath raised Him from the dead, thou shalt be saved. For with the heart man believeth unto righteousness and with the mouth confession is made unto salvation." How blessedly simple all this is. Jesus must be owned as Lord; He, who died for our sins, and whom God raised from the dead. Blessed assurance, "thou shalt be saved!" Saved by grace, through faith, and that not of yourselves, it is the gift of God.

"Moreover, this faith is manifested by the proof it gives of its sincerity—by confession of the name of Christ. If some one were convinced that Jesus is the Christ, and refused to confess Him, his conviction would evidently be his greater condemnation. The faith of the heart produces the confession of the mouth; the confession of the mouth is the counterproof of the sincerity of the faith, and of honesty, in the sense of the claim which the Lord has upon us in grace. It is the testimony which God requires at the outset. It is to sound the trumpet on earth in face of the enemy. It is to say that Christ has conquered, and that everything belongs in right to Him. It is a confession which brings in God in answer to the name of Jesus. It is not that which brings in righteousness, but it is the public acknowledgment of Christ, and thus gives expression to the faith by which there is participation in the righteousness of God, so that it may be said, 'He believes in Christ unto salvation; he has the faith that justifies.' "

Then twice the word "whosoever" is mentioned, that precious gospel word, which includes all, Jews and Gentiles, for there is no difference between the Jew and the Gentile, for the same Lord over all is such unto all that call upon Him. "For whosoever shall call upon the name of the Lord shall be saved" (Joel 2:32; Acts 2:21). All proves that righteousness is by faith and is offered to all. The statement in Joel also refers to a future day in connection with the coming deliverance of the remnant and the coming of the Lord.

Verses 14-17. And this good news for Jews and Gentiles must be proclaimed, for how can they call on Him, in whom they have not believed? And how shall they believe on Him of whom they have not heard? And how shall they hear without a preacher? And how shall they preach unless they have been sent? Of such a gracious world-wide mission the law had nothing to say. Its message and the promises were confined to the nation Israel. The Lord Jesus as the minister of the circumcision sent His messengers only to the lost sheep of the house of Israel (Matt. 10); but after His death and resurrection He gave the commission "that repentance and remission of sins should be preached unto all nations, beginning in Jerusalem" (Luke 24:47). And the Lord sends forth His messengers; even so it was written before in Isa. 52:7. (A careful study of this passage and the context shows its future meaning likewise, at the time, when the Lord reigneth, "when the Lord shall bring again Zion.") All is of Him, the righteousness, the salvation as well as the proclamation. But not all obeyed the gospel, nor do all obey the gospel call now. This also was foretold by Isaiah, in the great chapter (53) in which Israel's rejection of the Messiah is foretold, as well as the future confession of that rejection. "So then faith cometh by hearing, and hearing by the Word of God."

Verses 18-21. Israel is unbelieving. They heard and believed not. The law and the prophets had borne witness to the fact that the Gentiles would believe (Deut. 32:21; Isa. 65:1). And in infinite patience and longsuffering the Lord had stretched forth His hands unto Israel as a disobedient and gainsaying people. They were unbelieving and set aside. Their future restoration is the theme of the next chapter.

3. Israel's Restoration[4]

CHAPTER 11

1. God hath not cast away His people (11:1)
2. Israel's apostasy not complete: a Remnant Saved (11:2-6)
3. Israel's blindness for a season (11:7-10)
4. To provoke them to jealousy (11:11)
5. Their fulness and reception life from the dead (11:12-15)
6. The parable of the two olive trees (11:16-24)
7. A mystery made known, and All Israel Saved (11:25-32)
8. The doxology (11:33-36)

Verse 1. In view of the preceding chapter on Israel's rejection, the question is asked "Hath God cast away His people?" Is there nothing more in store for national Israel? God forbid. If it were so, God's gifts and calling would be subject to repentance and He would not be the faithful, covenant-keeping God. He foreknew His people Israel and that foreknowledge embraced all their sad history of failure and apostasy. The Apostle Paul speaks of himself as an Israelite of the seed of Abraham. He demonstrates in his own experience the fact that God hath not cast away His people. Hating Christ, having zeal for God without knowledge, a persecutor of the church, he had obtained mercy that in him Jesus Christ might show forth all long-suffering, for a pattern to them which should hereafter believe on Him (1 Tim. 1:16). His unique conversion must be looked upon as a prophetic type of the conversion of the remnant of Israel, when the Lord comes. As Saul of Tarsus saw Him in the glory-light, so the Israel living in the day of the second coming of Christ will behold Him (Zech. 12:10; Rev. 1:7). This vision will result in their national conversion.

Verses 2-6. The time of Elias was one of the darkest periods of their history. It seemed as if the whole nation had apostatized from God. Elias had this conception when he complained in his despondency. "They have killed Thy prophets, and digged down Thine altars; and I am left alone, and they seek my life." The Lord told him then that there were seven thousand men who had not bowed the knee to the image of Baal. The apostasy of Israel was not a complete apostasy. The Lord had preserved a faithful remnant. Even so at this present time

[4] *The Jewish Question,* by A. C. G., gives a complete exposition of this great chapter.

there is a remnant according to the election of grace. In the beginning of this present age there was in existence a distinctive Jewish remnant. This Jewish-Christian remnant in the beginning of the dispensation was an evidence that God had not cast away His people. A similar remnant of believing Jews will be called for a definite work and testimony during the end of the age. And throughout this Christian dispensation it has been abundantly demonstrated that God has not cast away His ancient people, for thousands of them have been saved by grace and have become members of the body of Christ.

Verses 7-10. When the apostle speaks here of the election he has in view the believing part of the nation at all times, the remnant past, the future remnant and all those who believe in Christ now. When he speaks of the rest being blinded he means the unbelieving part of the nation. Judicial blindness has come upon them for their unbelief. Three quotations are given from the Old Testament showing that the Lord foreknew their unbelief and predicted the judgment which was to come upon the nation (Deut. 29:4; Isa. 29:10 and Psalm 69:22-24). A careful study of these chapters will show that the threatened judgments and the judicial blindness are not permanent. All the prophets and many of the prophetic Psalms reveal the fact that the judgments which have come upon the people are for a season only and that there is glory and blessing in store for them. The curses pronounced upon them have found their literal fulfilment; the unfulfilled promises of blessing and glory will also be literally fulfilled and Israel will be saved and restored to their land.

Verse 11. The setting aside of Israel is not final; their present blindness is not their permanent condition. But have they stumbled that they should fall? God forbid. They stumbled over Him in whom they saw no beauty and whom they did not desire. They received Him not, who had come to His own. But this did not result in their complete fall. God in His infinite wisdom and all-wise purpose brought by their fall salvation to the Gentiles to provoke them to jealousy. In this statement we see again that God has not cast away His people Israel. If He had cast them away, why should He wish to provoke them to jealousy? And this provoking to jealousy is with the intent that some of them might be saved (verse 14).

Verses 12-15. And now the apostle of the Gentiles addresses us Gentiles. "I speak to you Gentiles." It is a message of much importance. The fall of Israel was the riches of the world, the diminishing of them the riches of the Gentiles (verse 13); the casting away was the reconciling of the world. Thus blessing, great blessing came to the Gentiles by Israel's unbelief and fall. But this is not all. All this is far from accomplishing the promise made to the father of the nation, when God said to Abraham "In thy seed all the nations of the earth shall be blest." Israel's fall, the means in God's purpose to bring salvation to the Gentiles, is not the final thing, and the blessing the Gentiles received by their fall is not the fullest blessing which God has in store for the world.

Much more is in store for the world in blessing through Israel's restoration. To Israel is promised in the Old Testament a time of fulness, a time when they shall be taken back. Their time of fulness comes when Christ returns in power and in glory. If then God brought blessing to the Gentiles by their fall, how far greater will be the blessings for the world, when their time of fulness has come. It will be life from the dead. Israel is now nationally and spiritually dead. They will be nationally and spiritually made alive (Ezek. 37:1-17, 39:25-29; Hosea 5:15—6:3). And the whole world comes in for blessing then. The nations will be converted and the kingdom will be set up on earth (Zech. 2:10-13).

Verses 16-24. The parable of the two olive trees illustrates great dispensational facts and contains solemn warnings for Christendom. The good olive tree typifies Israel in covenant relation with God in the Abrahamic covenant. The olive tree is evergreen; and so is the covenant, unchangeable. Israel's faithlessness and disobedience cannot annul it. The root is Abraham, who was holy, separated unto God. On account of unbelief some of the branches were broken off. They are now separated from the good olive tree and are withered.

The wild olive tree is a picture of the Gentiles. The branches of this wild olive tree are grafted among the branches of the good olive tree to partake of the root and fatness of the good olive tree. The wild olive tree branches grafted upon the good olive tree do not represent the true church. The Gentiles are meant by it, who are, after Israel's unbelief, put upon the ground of responsibility which Israel had, to partake now of the promised covenant blessings. The grafted-in branches represent the Christian profession, Christendom, as we call it. The grafted-in branches are solemnly warned. They are not to boast, not to be high-minded; they must abide in goodness. If the warning is unheeded they will not be spared but cut off. And when that happens God will graft in again the natural branches into their own olive tree if they no longer abide in unbelief. God is able to do this. He can and will put back Israel into their former relation. It is prophetic.

Christendom is exactly that which is here warned against—boasting, high-minded, not abiding in goodness, in one word, apostate. The unbelief and failure of professing Christendom is as great, if not greater than the unbelief and failure of Israel. The time will come when God will not spare, but execute judgment upon Christendom. He will spew Laodicea out of His mouth (Rev. 3:16). Then the hour of Israel's restoration has come.

Verses 25-32. A mystery is made known. Blindness in part has happened to Israel, until the fulness of the Gentiles be come in. The fulness of the Gentiles means, the full number of the saved, gathered out from among the Gentiles, who constitute the Church, the body of Christ. And when the body is joined to the Head in glory, the time of the coming of the Lord for His saints (1 Thess. 4:17), the Lord will turn again to Israel. All Israel, that is, the all Israel living in the day will be saved, when the Deliverer comes out of Zion (Isa. 59:20; Psalm 14:7). It is the second, visible, personal and glorious coming of the Lord Jesus Christ. He will turn away ungodliness from Jacob and take away their sins. Between the coming of the Lord for the saints, who will meet Him in the air, and His coming in great power and glory, are the days of Jacob's trouble, when the nation will have to pass through the fires of tribulation and the wicked among Israel will be cut off. And after He has come and has taken away their sins, all the great prophecies of Israel's earthly glory will be fulfilled.

Verses 33-36. A doxology closes this dispensational section of the epistle. What depths of riches, both of wisdom and knowledge of God, in His merciful dealings with the Gentiles and the Jews! How unsearchable His judgments! How untraceable His ways! For of Him, and through Him and to Him are all things to whom be glory forever. Amen.

III. Exhortations and the Conclusion (12—16)

CHAPTER 12

1. The body as a willing sacrifice (12:1-2)
2. Service (12:3-8)
3. The daily walk in holiness (12:9-21)

Verses 1-2. Grace calls for obedience. After God has made known the riches of His grace, the fulness of the gospel, His Spirit shows how believers should walk in a world of sin and tribulation. The first thing is to present the body a living sacrifice, holy, acceptable to God. This connects with the truth of chapter 6:19, "yield your members servants to righteousness unto holiness." "The body is the instrument of the spirit; and this so completely, that, if it be laid hold for Him, there is no part of the practical life but must, of necessity, be His. The feet are used to walk at His bidding, the hands to employ ourselves in His things, the tongue to speak for Him and nothing else, the ear to hear His words; the eye also, so that whatever it looks upon, it will look upon as being under His control (*Numerical Bible*). It is plain that the whole life thus finds its government."

This yielding of the body, giving it as a living sacrifice, is our intelligent service. It is the needful thing so that all which is written in the sixth chapter may become a practical thing in our lives. Is this presentation of the body as a living sacrifice an act done once for all (as some teach), or is it a daily yielding? It must be done continually. And it becomes possible to go on presenting the body thus, under all circumstances, if we remember the mercies of God, what God in Christ has done for us and in what a wonderful position He has put us in His own Son. But it needs constant watchfulness, prayer, meditation on the Word and self-judgment.

In doing this the believer will be able to carry out the exhortation, "be not conformed to this world (age)." A soul in touch with Christ, knowing the mercies of God in redemption, cannot enjoy the world. Well has it been said "true joy in the Lord renders the soul in which it dwells incapable of enjoying what the world esteems pleasure. Natural pleasures are the solace of that which is essentially alien of God." The present age is evil and Christ died to deliver us from this present evil age. Satan is the god of this age. It is not controlled by the Spirit of God. Therefore friendship with the world, conformity to it, is enmity to the cross of Christ. Separation from it is God's demand, for the cross of Christ has made us dead to the world and the world dead unto us. We must be transformed by the renewing of our mind. This is the work of the Spirit of God in us. The inward man is to be renewed day by day (2 Cor. 4:16); and this will be so as we daily present our bodies as the living sacrifice.

Verses 3-8. Service is mentioned next. This is to be rendered in humility and according to the measure of faith as God has dealt to every man, who is a believer. Here the body, that is, the church, is touched upon. In First Corinthians and Ephesians the truth concerning the church and the different gifts is more fully revealed. All believers are members of that body, and as in the human body not all members have the same office, so in the one body there are different gifts bestowed by grace. Each must take his place given to him in that body and render the service unto which he is called and thus demonstrate the divine truth, that we are one body in Christ, and individually members one of the other. Ministry in the Word stands first and there is also ministry in other ways. The latter are, giving, ruling (or leading) and showing mercy. Giving is to be in simplicity (or liberality); ruling is to be in diligence and showing mercy in cheerfulness. The emphasis here is not so much upon the different gifts as it is upon the faithful exercise of the gift.

Verses 19-21. The daily walk in holiness is unfolded in these verses. These are precious exhortations and every Christian should read them often and order his daily life accordingly. Love stands first, for it is the great essential of the divine nature. He that dwelleth in love dwelleth in God, and God in him (1 John 4:16). It is to be unfeigned. Love seeketh not her own and therefore we are to prefer in honor one another. "Not slothful in business" is often misunderstood and many have thought it means devotion to a secular business. But the correct translation is, "In diligence, not slothful." Then there is rejoicing in hope, patience in suffering, prayer, sympathy with others and many other blessed things into which we cannot enter in detail. The child of God desires all these things and the Spirit of God is with us to produce these blessed fruits in our lives.

CHAPTER 13

1. Obedience to authorities (13:1-7)
2. Love the fulfilling of the law (13:8-10)
3. The day is at hand (13:11-14)

Verses 1-7. The children of God are strangers and pilgrims in the world. Our citizenship is in heaven. But what is the Christian to do as living under different forms of government? The Christian is to be in subjection to these, for the powers that exist are ordained by Him. Resisting these powers would mean resistance to God who has ordained them. They are God's ministers to maintain order. "Render therefore to all their dues, tribute to whom tribute is due; custom to whom custom; fear to whom fear; honor to whom honor." If Christians had always obeyed these injunctions, how well it would have been. But often they are forgotten and an attempt is made to control the politics of this age and to rule.

Verses 8-10. "Owe no man anything, but to love one another, for he that loveth another hath fulfilled the law." The first sentence does not mean that it is wrong to borrow money. The question is about paying. If a debt is due it should be paid exactly on time. Borrowing money in a reckless way, without any prospect of returning the amount, is sinful, and often great dishonor has been brought upon the name of our Lord on account of it. But there is another debt which always remains. The Christian owes the debt of love to all. And this love is the fulfilling of the law. Love does not work ill to his neighbor. The natural man may claim that he keeps the sum of the other commandments, "Thou shalt love thy neighbor as thyself," but he cannot do it. Only one who is born again, in whose heart there is love, has the power to do this.

Verses 11-14. The coming of the Lord is brought before us in these verses as a motive to holy living. The final salvation is nearing, for the night is far spent and the day is at hand. The blessed hope is to be always before the Christian's heart; it is a purifying hope. "He that hath this hope set upon him purifieth himself as He is pure." In view of that approaching day, when we shall see Him face to face and be with Him in glory, the exhortations are given to awake out of sleep, to cast off the works of darkness, to put on the armor of light, to walk becomingly as in the day, to abstain from the things of the flesh, putting on the Lord Jesus and making no provisions for the flesh. We are to walk in the light as the children of the day, with faces set towards the coming glory. And never before were those exhortations more needed than now. The night is far spent, the day is at hand. The signs of the end of the age are seen everywhere, and yet in these solemn days how few of God's people walk as the children of the day in the path of separation.

CHAPTER 14

1. Strong and weak brethren are the Lord's servants (14:1-12)
2. The true way of love (14:13-23)

Verses 1-12. The question concerning brethren who were weak in faith, how they are to be treated by those who are strong is now taken up. Those weak in the faith had not the complete knowledge of their position in Christ, though they knew Christ and loved Him. They did not realize that certain observances of days, or abstinences from meats and drinks, could not affect their salvation in any way. There were scruples and conscientious difficulties, as there are still among God's people. One believeth he may eat all things, he knew his full Christian freedom—another who is weak eateth herbs. How are these two to treat each other? Were they to criticize and condemn one the other? "Let not him that eateth despise him that eateth not; and let not him that eateth not judge him that eateth, for God hath received him."

The weak in faith are to be received, but not to doubtful points of reasonings; these questions are not to be brought up for discussion, or worse, to make them a test of Christian fellowship. Judging a brother, or condemning him on such matters is forbidden, for inasmuch as God hath received him, he is the Lord's servant and not ours. The rebuke is "Who art thou that thou judgest another's servant? to his own Lord he standeth or falleth." More than that, the Lord in His gracious power shall keep him in all his weakness. He bears with him, "the Lord is able to make him stand." Each is responsible to the Lord. Each does it as unto the Lord. No one lives to himself, and no one dies to himself, we are all the Lord's. There is also a day coming when we all must stand before His judgment seat and then He will judge, who knows the secrets of every heart. Therefore we must not judge. Every one, as stated in all these cases, should be fully persuaded in his own mind and should not judge another, but look forward to the judgment seat of Christ.

Verses 13-23. But more than that there should be loving tolerance for the brother. Let the harsh judgment of the brother, whom God has received be abandoned; but judge this rather, "not to put a stumbling block or an occasion to fall in his brother's way." There is nothing unclean in itself. Yet a brother may account something unclean, his conscience so judges, then it is unclean for him. The brother with the weak conscience must be considered. The law of love demands this. "If thy brother is grieved on account of thy food, thou walkest no longer in love; destroy not with thy food him for whom Christ died." Therefore "it is good not to eat flesh, nor to drink wine, nor to do anything, whereby thy brother stumbleth or is offended, or is made weak."

"He that serves Christ in these things is acceptable and approved of men. We are to follow what makes for peace and edifies others. To the pure all things are pure; but if a person defiles his conscience, even though an unfounded scruple, to him it is unclean. Happy for him who, in boasting of his liberty by faith, does not go beyond his faith in what he does; and does not offend in what he allows himself to do; for whatsoever is not of faith is sin. If a man thinks he ought to honor a certain day, or abstain from a certain food, and then, for the sake of showing his liberty, does not do it, to him it is sin. It is not faith before God" (*Synopsis of the Bible*).

CHAPTER 15

1. The example of Christ (15:1-7)
2. The ministry of Christ (15:8-13)
3. Paul's personal ministry (15:14-38)

Verses 1-7. An additional motive is brought in why the strong should bear the infirmities of the weak and not please themselves. It is Christ. He did not please Himself, but bore in great meekness and patience the reproaches with which men reproached God, and these reproaches fell on Christ Himself. It was the reproach of God He bore in perfect meekness. We are therefore to be likeminded one to another according to Christ Jesus. Wherefore receive ye one another even as Christ also received you to the glory of God. We have then three instructions concerning the weak brother: 1. To receive the weak, but not to doubtful disputations. 2. Not to judge a brother in those things, because he is Christ's servant, and any one must give an account of himself. 3. To bear the infirmities of the weak, to put no stumbling block in their way, not to please ourselves. We are to walk in love and manifest that love by receiving one another as Christ has received us to the glory of God. And blessed are we if we also walk according to those rules and manifest the mind of Christ.

Verses 8-13. The exhortations are ended, and what we find in the rest of this chapter is supplementary to the whole Epistle and touches once more on the question concerning the Jews and the Gentiles. Christ was the minister of the circumcision for the truth of God to confirm the promises to the fathers. Thus He appeared in the midst of His people. But the Gentiles also were to receive mercy through Him. Four Scriptures are quoted to prove that it is the purpose of God to bless the Gentiles in mercy with His people Israel (Psalm 18:49; Deut. 32:43 in Moses' great prophetic song; Psalm 117:1 and Isa. 11:10). But it must not be overlooked that these quotations do not teach that Gentiles are as fellow heirs put into the same body with believing Jews. They show that God had announced that Gentiles would rejoice in salvation and trust in Christ. The fulfilment of the passages quoted awaits the second coming of our Lord "when He shall rise to reign over the Gentiles," when Gentiles will rejoice with the saved remnant of Israel. "Now the God of hope fill you with all joy and peace in believing, that ye may abound in hope, through the power of the Holy Spirit." This is our most blessed inheritance. The Holy Spirit indwells the child of God and in believing He manifests His power, the God of hope filling us with all joy and peace, so that we abound in hope, looking forward to that blessed day, the realization of our blessed hope, when we shall be like Him and see Him as He is.

Verses 14-33. Then the great man of God speaks lastly of His own ministry. Much might be written on this interesting paragraph. He had a special ministry conferred upon himself. It was grace which had given it to him. His ministry he describes as being "the minister of Jesus Christ to the Gentiles, ministering the gospel of God, that the offering of the Gentiles might be acceptable, sanctified by the Holy Spirit." A closer study of his statements, which tell of his humility, his marvellous service in power, his confidence, as well as other things, will be found helpful and instructive. He looked forward to his coming visit to Rome and requested the prayers of the brethren. And when he came there at last, he came as the prisoner of the Lord, and from Rome he sent forth the greatest of his Epistles.

CHAPTER 16

1. Greetings to individuals (16:1-16)
2. Warning and comfort (16:17-20)
3. The final salutations (16:21-24)
4. The conclusion (16:25-27)

Verses 1-16. Phoebe (which means "radiant") is first mentioned. She was probably a person of great influence and wealth, for she had been a succourer of many, including the apostle. She is heartily commended to the assembly in Rome, to be received in the Lord, worthily of the saints. Then that interesting pair of fellow workers of the Apostle Paul, Priscilla and Aquila, are saluted. To follow their wanderings and interest in the gospel we have to omit here. See Acts 18:1-3, 18-19, 26; 1 Cor. 16:19; 2 Tim. 4:19. At what time they laid down their necks for the life of the apostle we do not know. The assembly met in their house. Then the first convert of the province of Asia, the beloved Epaenetus is greeted. Many, who had labored much; Andronicus and Junius, who were in the Lord before Paul, and others are greeted. Little do we know of all these names, but their records are on high and at the judgment seat of Christ they and their abundant labors and sufferings will be made manifest.

(Not till the third century have we any proofs of the existence of buildings set apart for Christian worship. Not only were most of the churches too poor to build meeting-places, but, until Christianity became the religion of the empire, the privacy and secrecy possible in a meeting held in a dwelling-house were important considerations. The wealthier members of a church seem to have put one of their rooms at the disposal of the brethren for this purpose. First comes the upper room, in which our Lord held his Last Supper with his disciples (Matt. 26:18), and then the house of Mary in Jerusalem (Acts 12:12), although this may have been the same place. In Ephesus the house of Aquila and Priscilla was a meeting-place (1 Cor. 16:19), as it was in Rome also. At Laodicea the church met in the house of Nymphas (Col. 4:15), and at Colosse in the house of Philemon (verse 2). Although there may have been in Rome one house in which the whole body of Christians met, yet it would seem that it was unusual to hold meetings in a number of houses. The phrases, "and the brethren that are with them" (verse 14), and "all the saints that are with them" (15), seem to imply separate groups of believers (A. E. Garvie).

Verses 17-20. There is a warning against those who create divisions and give occasions to stumbling, contrary to the doctrine they had learned. These were probably teachers like those who disturbed the Galatians and these teachers were to be shunned—"turn away from them." To create divisions in the body of Christ is a work of the flesh and a serious matter. "For they that are such serve not our Lord Jesus Christ but their own belly, and by kind and fair speeches deceive the hearts of the guileless." How often this is the case with false teachers in our own times. Destructive critics, false teachers, deniers of the gospel of grace are often in character very amiable and kind. Such is especially true of Christian Science with their leaders; the blasphemies of that cult are generally covered up by kind and fair speeches. And Satan, who is behind all these things, will shortly be bruised under the feet of His people. Complete victory over all evil is promised for His people and will surely come.

Verses 21-27. And now the final salutations and the conclusion in praise. "Now to Him who is able to establish you according to my gospel and the preaching of Jesus Christ, according to the revelation of the mystery, which was kept secret since the world began, but now is made manifest, and by the prophetic Scriptures, according to the commandment of the everlasting God, made known to all nations for the obedience of faith. To God only wise, be glory through Jesus Christ forever. Amen."

THE FIRST EPISTLE TO THE CORINTHIANS

Introduction

The two Epistles addressed to the Corinthians follow, in our New Testament, the Epistle to the Romans. A more logical arrangement would be to put the Epistle to the Galatians next to Romans, for the Galatian Epistle contains the defence of the gospel and its message is closely linked with the truths unfolded in Romans. Ephesians and Colossians lead upon still higher ground, and if the arrangement of the Pauline Epistles is to be made according to progressive revelation, these two documents should follow the Epistle to the Galatians. While Romans, Galatians, Ephesians and Colossians are pre-eminently doctrinal Epistles, the Epistles to the Corinthians, while not excluding Christian doctrines, are more of a practical character, dealing with very grave and serious conditions which had arisen in the church at Corinth.

The Church at Corinth

Corinth was one of the foremost Grecian cities, the capital of the Province of Achaia. The Roman pro-consul resided there (Acts 18:12). Corinth had a very excellent situation, which gave to the city commercially a great advantage and was therefore known for its vast commerce and great wealth. Its large population had a cosmopolitan character, thousands of traders and mariners of all nations visited the far-famed city. Greek civilization flourished here in all its branches. The fine arts were cultivated, athletic games as well as schools of philosophy and rhetoric flourished in this proud city. But the worst feature was an open and very gross licentiousness. The whole city was steeped in immoralities of various kind. Drunkenness, gluttony, and above all religiously licensed prostitution were at their worst in Corinth. The Greek worship of Aphrodite was of the most degraded nature. So great was the moral corruption that the Greek word *"Corinthiazesthai,"* which means "to live like a Corinthian," had become a byword of shame and vileness among the profligate heathen of that time. The horrible picture of vileness as given in the Epistle to the Romans (chapter 1), written by the apostle in Corinth, describes some of these moral conditions prevailing in Corinth. It has well been said, "The geographical position of Corinth was its weal and its woe."

The Apostle Paul had been in Athens first and then came to Corinth (Acts 18:1). While the origin of the church in Rome is obscure, we know that the Corinthian assembly was founded by the Apostle. The record of it we find in Acts 18. He labored there under great blessing for a year and six months. Jews and Gentiles were saved, among the former was Crispus, the chief ruler of the synagogue. But the majority of those who believed were Gentiles, and these belonged to the poorer classes (1 Cor. 1:26) with at least two exceptions, Erastus, the chamberlain of the city, and Gaius, a wealthy man, whom Paul had baptized. The historical account of Paul's ministry in Corinth and what happened there should be carefully read, for it throws light upon the Epistles he sent to that church.

What he preached in that wealthy and wicked city, boasting of culture and much learning, filled with an arrogant pride, we learn from his own words in the first Epistle. "And I, brethren, when I came unto you, came not with excellency of speech or of wisdom, declaring unto you the testimony of God. For I determined not to know anything among you, save Jesus Christ, and Him crucified" (2:1-2). He was greatly pressed in spirit while there (Acts 18:5), yea, in fear and trembling (1 Cor. 2:3). He knew this was one of Satan's strongholds. But God stood by His servant, and while his preaching was not with enticing words of man's wisdom, it was in the demonstration of the Spirit and of power (1 Cor. 2:4).

Both Epistles reveal the deplorable state of the Corinthians and these conditions called forth through the energy of the Holy Spirit this first Epistle. The evil things which had sprung up among the Corinthians had been reported to the apostle. The house of Chloe (1:11) is mentioned, as informing him about the contentious spirit which was manifesting itself. Probably from the same source, as well as from others, he heard even of worse things which were making headway among the believers. Gross immorality was being tolerated in their midst; lawsuits of Christians were being submitted to courts over which pagan judges presided; they had degraded the blessed memorial feast, the Lord's Supper, on account of which some had been dealt with by the Lord. Then there were other matters, such as disorder in public worship, abuse of certain gifts, the forwardness of women. Controversies must have also agitated the Corinthian assembly about the marriage state, certain church matters, such as collections, the exercise of gifts, etc. They had not been brought up Christians, and had everything to learn. This fully explains the character of this first Epistle.

When and Where Was the Epistle Written?

Attempts have been made to question the authenticity of the first Corinthian Epistle. They have not, however, been successful. Testimonies to the authorship of this document are found in the writings of Clement of Rome, Polycarp, Irenaeus, Clement of Alexandria, Tertullian and others. Dean Alford states, "As far as I am aware, the authorship of the First Epistle to the Corinthians has never been doubted by any critic of note. Indeed, he who would do so must be prepared to dispute the historical truth of the character of St. Paul." The Epistle itself answers our question concerning the place and the time when it was written by the apostle. The statement at the close of the Epistle, printed in some editions of the Bible "written from Philippi," is incorrect. In chapter 16:8 we read the writer's statement, "But I will tarry in Ephesus until Pentecost." The Apostle Paul was therefore in Ephesus and intended to leave about Pentecost. The book of Acts shows that he left that city about the time of Pentecost in the year 57. It is quite certain that this first Epistle to the Corinthians was written during the first part of the year 57, probably around the time of Easter. (See 1 Cor. 5:7-8). From Acts 19:22 we learn that the apostle, while still in Ephesus, had sent Timotheus and Erastus to Macedonia. He had given commission to Timotheus to go to Corinth (1 Cor. 4:17; 16:10). No doubt Timotheus was to prepare the way for the visit of the Apostle (1 Cor. 4:17-19). In all probability the Epistle was taken to Corinth by Stephanas, Fortunatus and Achaicus (1 Cor. 16:17).

But are the two Corinthian Epistles the only epistles Paul wrote to them? In chapter 5:9 Paul says: "I wrote unto you in an epistle not to company with fornicators." From this we learn that he had written them a previous letter. Commentators have spoken of this letter as a lost epistle. If it was an inspired document, like these two Epistles and the other Pauline Epistles, it would certainly have been preserved. But the Apostle also wrote letters which were not meant to form parts of the Word of God, which were not inspired, as Romans, Ephesians and the other epistles are. The Epistle therefore mentioned in chapter 5:9 was a private letter of the Apostle.

Important and Practical Truths

The Church, constituting the fellowship of the saints on earth, its place and testimony in the world; the Church, its order, membership, spiritual gifts and manifestations, discipline and other important matters, are the truths dealt with in this first Epistle. Then, after the Church is viewed as on earth, as His witness, the great truth of the resurrection of the body is made known as well as the fact that when the Lord comes "we shall not all sleep, but shall be changed in a moment." This puts before us the blessed hope, the great consummation, when the Church will leave this earthly scene of conflict and failure and become, according to promise, the glorious Church.

All about us in the professing Church manifests the fullest failure and ruin. The evils which were in the Corinthian church such as sectarianism, self-indulgence and worldliness have become the prominent features of the institution which claims to be the Church. For the true believer whose aim it is to be obedient to the Lord in all things, this Epistle has a message and shows him the way which he can follow, though failure and confusion is about him.

The Division of First Corinthians

On account of the different topics and questions treated in this Epistle, a division into well defined sections is rather difficult to make. The Epistle is a Church Epistle, dealing throughout with matters concerning the church. A careful reading of the Epistle will disclose the fact that first, the church is viewed as the temple of God indwelt by His Spirit. As such the Church is in the world, though not of the world, and is called to be separated from the world and all its wisdom. The world is hostile to the Church; the activities of the enemy of the truth, through the wisdom of this world and the lusts of the flesh are learned from the state of the church in Corinth. The Church and her relation to the world, and the testimony for Christ, the Chruch is to give and to maintain in the world, are unfolded in the first ten chapters of this epistle. After that, the Church is viewed as the body of Christ. In chapters 11—14 no more mention is made of the world and the believer's conduct in the world. We are introduced to Church order, the activities of the Church, the body and its members, the ministries and the exercise of the different gifts, bestowed upon the body. Then follows the great chapter which deals with resurrection. The doctrine of resurrection is unfolded in chapter 15; first, the resurrection of the Lord Jesus Christ, who is Himself the head of the body, and also the resurrection and translation of His people. The glorious destiny of the church is therefore revealed at the close of the epistle. The concluding chapter contains an instruction concerning collection and the greetings. This brief survey of the Epistle, showing its scope, gives us three main divisions:

I. THE CHURCH AND THE WORLD: SEPARATION AND TESTIMONY (Chapters 1—10)

1. **What Grace Has Done and the Assurance which Grace Gives** (1:1-9)
2. **Contrasts** (1:10—4)
3. **Corinthian Failures** (5—6)
4. **Concerning the Relationship of Man and Woman** (7)
5. **Concerning Meats Offered to Idols: Christian Liberty Governed by Love** (8)
6. **Paul's Gracious Example** (9)
7. **Concluding Warnings and Exhortations** (10)

II. THE CHURCH AS THE BODY OF CHRIST (Chapters 11—14)

1. **The Headship of Christ and of Man and the Lord's Supper** (11)
2. **The Body and the Members of the Body** (12)
3. **The Need and Superiority of Love** (13)
4. **Prophecy and Speaking with Tongues** (14)

III. RESURRECTION AND THE HOPE OF THE CHURCH AND CONCLUSIONS (Chapters 15—16)

1. **The Doctrine of Resurrection and the Hope of the Church** (15)
2. **Instruction and Greetings** (16)

Analysis and Annotations

I. The Church and the World: Separation and Testimony (1—10)

What Grace has Done and the Assurance Grace Gives (1:1-9)

In the opening verse of this Epistle the Apostle Paul associates with himself the name of Sosthenes. There can be little doubt that he is the same Sosthenes mentioned in Acts 18:17. Like the great apostle he was once "a persecutor and injurious." The experience through which he passed, when, as an enemy of Christ he received the deserved beating was instrumental to bring him to Christ. When he was the chief ruler of the synagogue he was an enemy, but now through the grace of God he had become "a brother beloved." It was to call to the remembrance of the sadly drifting Corinthians the former days, as well as the power of God in salvation. Then Paul addresses them as "the Church of God which is at Corinth"; and this Church of God is composed of those who are sanctified in Christ Jesus, called saints. All believers are set apart to God in Christ. Grace has constituted them saints; but with the gifts grace bestows, there also goes the responsibility of manifesting that separation from the world, from which the church is called out.

To the saints, true believers, sanctified in Christ, set apart to God, the Epistle is addressed. Then follows another sentence, which goes beyond the church at Corinth. "With all that in every place call upon the name of Jesus Christ our Lord, both theirs and ours." Thus the true circle of fellowship was laid down, for every local church to observe. As we shall find later in this Epistle, the party spirit, sectarianism, was manifesting itself in Corinth and these words of address may be looked upon as a protest against that unchristian spirit. All who acknowledge Christ as Lord and call upon His name belong to the Church. He is their Lord as He is our Lord. Futhermore we learn from these words that the messages of this Epistle are for God's people at all times. "In every place" means every place where believers are found to-day. The truths unfolded, the exhortations given, have therefore a universal application; they are the commandments of the Lord to all His people (14:37).

Before the apostle begins to mention the evils which the Corinthian assembly tolerated and which burdened his spirit, he speaks first of all of the grace of God given to them by Jesus Christ. They had been saved and were enriched by Him. The truth they had received, they also communicated "in all utterance and knowledge" to others. They had all the gifts in their midst, and were waiting for the revelation of our Lord Jesus Christ. Grace had bestowed all these gifts, and yet they failed to manifest His grace. In possession of such grace and the gifts of grace, they should have walked in humility and should have lived soberly, righteously and godly. But they were walking in an evil way.

The Apostle knew all the evil which was among them as an assembly (and more so did the Holy Spirit know), but before he uncovers their condition, he gives a most precious assurance. He speaks of the faithfulness of God, who had called them into that wonderful fellowship of His Son, Jesus Christ. God is faithful! He reckons on God's faithfulness to do in the end all for them which He had promised, so that they would be blameless in the day of the Lord Jesus Christ. God does not repent of His gifts and calling. The same assurance is found in other epistles. "And the very God of peace sanctify you wholly, and your whole spirit, soul and body be preserved blameless unto the coming of our Lord Jesus Christ. Faithful is He that calleth you, who also will do it" (1 Thess. 5:23-24). Such a loving and gracious assurance to those who are called according to His purpose, that He is faithful and will bring it about that His people shall be blameless in that coming day of Christ, leads to self-judgment and repentance.

2. **Contrasts** (1:10—4)

CHAPTER 1:10-31

1. Divisions rebuked (1:10-16)
2. The cross of Christ, the power of God (1:17-31)

The section which begins, after the introductory words, with the tenth verse and ends with the fourth chapter, shows a number of contrasts. There is the contrast of the fact that they were called into the one fellowship. The fact of being called into the fellowship of God's Son, as members of the one body is contrasted with their divisions. There is the contrast of the preaching of the cross, which is foolishness to them that perish, but the power of God to those who are saved. The wisdom of God and the wisdom of the world are likewise contrasted. Jews and Gentiles, what they require and seek are seen in their contrast with those who believe. Every chapter makes these contrasts and through them the blessed truth of the gospel and the walk of the saints of God are fully brought out.

As the introduction to the Epistle reveals, all believers have one Lord to whom they belong, and God has called all into the one fellowship, the fellowship of His Son, Jesus Christ our Lord. No other name is to be owned by His people, but all must be united in that blessed name, and obedience yielded to Him. He therefore beseeches them in that name to present a united confession and testimony "that ye all speak the same thing"; an unmarred fellowship in the Spirit "that there be no divisions among you"; and such a oneness of mind and judgment which becomes those who are one in Christ "that ye be perfectly joined together in the same mind and in the same judgment." And why this exhortation? Because those of the house of Chloe had given to Paul the information that contentions had arisen among them. He mentioned the source without giving the names of the individuals. Those of the house of Chloe were no doubt deeply spiritual and much exercised over these contentions and the dishonor done to the name of the Lord Jesus.

These contentions, which threatened serious schisms in the one body were connected with teachers, the chosen instruments of the Lord. Some said, "I am of Paul"; others, "I of Apollos"; another party, "I of Cephas." Instead of sitting at the feet of the one who alone is worthy and is the teacher of His people they scattered and divided themselves among the different teachers, given by the Lord to the church. It was the beginning of sectarianism, which has been such a curse to the people of God. It did not begin in the blessed assembly of Philippi, nor among the saints in Ephesus, but among the puffed up, worldly-minded Corinthians. Partyism, sectarianism, is the fruit of the flesh (Gal. 5:20). How it has multiplied in Christendom, the evil fruit it has borne, the apostasy which is fostered by it, we need not point out, for all spiritually minded Christians are acquainted with it.

But a fourth party said, "I of Christ." Piously they said, we do not acknowledge Paul, Apollos or Cephas; we call ourselves after Christ. They made Him the head of a party, and put His teaching in contrast with the teachings of the chosen vessels of the Lord, through whom He made known His will. It was only a pretext to discredit the ministry of Paul and the other apostles. That last named contention was perhaps the worst.

And so the inspired apostle asks, "Is Christ divided? Was Paul crucified for you? Or were ye baptized in the name of Paul?" Christ was crucified for them and in His Name they had been baptized. In their contentions they were doing wrong to the Person of Christ and to His blessed work. And water baptism is especially mentioned by him. He thanked God, that he had baptized none of them, but Crispus and Gaius, as well as the household of Stephanas. Baptism has been and is a prominent source of the division of the body of Christ. Ritualism has made of it a sacrament which saves and none can go to heaven without it. Other sects make it likewise a necessary act for salvation. Still others teach that water-baptism is the appointed means by which a believer becomes a member of the church, the body of Christ. It is not water-baptism by which a believer becomes a member of the body of Christ; the Holy Spirit alone can do this and does it with every believer (1 Cor. 12:13).

Others have gone into the other extreme and reject water-baptism entirely. The apostle did not do this. "The solemn assumption, by the newly born believer, of the name of Jesus as his Lord (as it is done in baptism) was an act both too important and of too solemn and precious a significance to be regarded lightly by an inspired apostle." Then the apostle states his commission. He was not sent by His Lord to baptize. His great mission was to preach the gospel. "Baptism would surely follow a true reception of his testimony, but that, with all other resulting effects, is kept distinct from the positive and vital work of God by His own Word. We may notice a real difference between the apostolate of Paul and that of the eleven, as defined at the close of Matthew. The latter were sent expressly to baptize. Paul was not."[1]

Verses 17-31 unfold the gospel which he was sent to preach, the cross of Christ and the power of God to salvation made known by that cross. He preached that gospel "not with wisdom of words." All that was attractive to the natural man, such as rhetoric, beautiful language, enticing words, was avoided by the apostle. He was "rude in speech" (2 Cor. 11:6); he did not preach with enticing words (1 Cor. 2:4). He feared that in any way the power of the cross of Christ should be made void. He had a complete, a perfect confidence in the gospel and knew it needed not human embellishment and human schemes to make it effective. All human efforts by rhetoric, sentimental claptrap methods, aim to stir up and to direct the emotions and sympathies of the natural man.

The preaching of the cross is foolishness to those that are perishing. Unto us who are being saved it is the power of God, for it saves us from the guilt of sins, the power of sin itself and ere long from the presence of sin, in our homegoing. And those who are perishing in rejecting the cross of Christ were never so numerous as to-day. To the "Christian Scientist"—the Unitarian—the destructive critic—the new Religionist and others, the preaching of the cross is foolishness. And the world with all its boasted learning and wisdom did not think of the gospel and its wonderful plan and power. The nations who boasted of culture and wisdom even in their highest form groped in the dark, and instead of discovering how man can be saved and brought back to God, were dragged down deeper and deeper into sin and despair. And thus God made foolish the wisdom of this world. Therefore the men who today turn their backs upon the gospel and speak of philosophy, science and wisdom, turn to foolishness once more, which will lead them into the blackness and darkness forever.

The preaching of Christ crucified was to the Jews a stumbling block, and to the Greeks foolishness, because the Jews required a sign and the Greeks sought after wisdom, but the cross puts human pride and glory into the dust. And what Jews and Greeks rejected and treated as foolishness is the power and wisdom of God. What men considered foolishness, a crucified Christ, is therefore wiser than men, for it gives to the believer what the wisdom of the world cannot supply. And the "weakness of God," which is Christ crucified through weakness, is more powerful than men; man is saved by it. Thus the charge of Jews and Gentiles, that the cross is foolishness, that it is weakness, is repudiated and the foolishness and weakness of man is thereby demonstrated and laid bare.

And that no flesh should glory in His presence, God hath chosen the foolish things of the world to confound the wise, and the weak things to confound the things which are mighty. He hath chosen the base things, the despised things and the things which are not to bring to naught the things that are. Therefore not many wise men after the flesh, not many mighty, not many noble are called. God in His sovereignty takes up that which is foolish and weak to manifest

[1]Pridham on Corinthians.

His power. How fully this is evidenced by experience. And the believer is always in the safe place, if he is in the place of self-abasement, self-effacement and weakness. "Of Him are we in Christ Jesus who of God is made unto us wisdom, and righteousness, and sanctification, and redemption; that according as it is written, he that glorieth, let him glory in the Lord." It is all of God, and all in Christ, and nothing of us or in ourselves. Christ is the wisdom of God.

"Christ is made unto us wisdom from God; and thus with Christianity, for faith, every cloud is lifted. The wisdom that is from God is a casket of priceless jewels; in which the redeemed one finds, not only liberty, but marvelous enrichment. How much is contained in just those three words, 'righteousness, sanctification and redemption!' And they are in an order of progressive fulness, by which we enter more and more into the heart of God" (*Numerical Bible*).

Righteousness in Christ is that of which Romans so fully speaks. Our guilt is gone. Righteousness is on our side, covering the believer. The believer is justified by His blood and by faith in Him and fully accepted in the Beloved. And Christ is the believer's sanctification. The work of Christ has separated us unto God; but the believer is also sanctified by the Spirit of God, the Spirit of holiness. In Christ we are holy and walking in the Spirit, obedient to His Word, the believer manifests in his conduct the fact that he is set apart to God. Redemption looks forward to the future, when the believer shall be glorified, and be conformed to the image of the Lord. "Of Him are ye in Christ Jesus." Therefore the believer has nothing to glory in himself, but he glories in the Lord. And all this put to shame the Corinthians who made so much of the wisdom of this world and were puffed up.

CHAPTER 2

1. The apostle's preaching (2:1-5)
2. The revelation of the Spirit (2:6-13)
3. The helplessness and ignorance of the natural man (2:14-16)

The apostle had been among them and declared unto them the testimony of God. This he had not done with excellency of speech or wisdom. He preached unto them the person of Jesus Christ and Him crucified. He, who is the wisdom of God, in whom are hid all the treasures of wisdom and knowledge (Col. 2:3), was his one theme; he determined not to know anything among them but the person and work of Christ. He had not come with a system of philosophy, to tickle their ears, but with the highest wisdom made known by revelation. He well knew that in Christ, His blessed person and in His cross all their unanswered questions, seeking for light, were answered, and more than that, the power of God through His Spirit would be active in their salvation. When he was with them he had a sense of weakness; he was in fear and much trembling. It shows the deep exercise of his soul.

But Paul also had the special encouragement from the Lord, who spoke to him by a vision (Acts 18:9-10). He avoided all human eloquence, to which the Corinthians were specially given and attracted, so as not to flatter them. And therefore the Spirit of God manifested power; his preaching was in demonstration of the Spirit and of power. Their faith, as a result, rested not on the beautiful, persuasive and eloquent words of a man, but on the power of God. Here is the pattern for every preacher of the gospel of Jesus Christ. What unworthy methods are used in our day by some professional evangelists! What sentimental trash is preached by those who are men-pleasers and under the guise of gospel-preaching aim at their own popularity!

("For just so far as preachers fill men with admiration for their peculiar style of thought or language, is it evident they are weak in the Spirit, and attract to themselves instead of clearing and establishing souls in the truth whereby the Spirit works in power" W. Kelly.)

Among them that are perfect he spoke wisdom. The perfect are those who have believed the gospel, experienced its power and are in Christ, accepted in the perfect One; they know the truth as it is in Christ. But the wisdom Paul spoke was not the wisdom of the world (literally: age), but God's wisdom in a mystery, the hidden wisdom ordained by God before the world unto our glory. And what is this hidden wisdom, God's wisdom in a mystery which Paul preached to those who had accepted Christ? It is more than Christ crucified. It is Christ glorified, seated at the right hand of God, given as head over all things to the church which is His body. This wisdom of God in a mystery (but now made known) is fully revealed in the Epistle to the Ephesians. It was unrevealed in the Old Testament. The rulers of this age did not know it, for had they known the wonderful wisdom of God they would not have crucified the Lord of Glory. But the very deed they committed (ignorantly as Peter declared, Acts 3:17) fulfilled the Scriptures, and the Lord of Glory whom they crucified is now the Glorified Man filling the throne of God, and believers are one with Him. This is the manifold wisdom of God which is made known by the Church (Christ as glorified head and the Church, His body) to the principalities and powers in heavenly places (Ephes. 3:10).

Interesting is the quotation from Isaiah 64:4. The prophet speaks of the inability of man to know what God hath prepared in His infinite grace and love for them that love Him. It was hidden from the prophet. None of them beheld the great truths of the Church as the body of Christ nor the glory connected with it. But now this is changed. God hath revealed it through His Spirit. The Spirit has come and He has made known the hidden wisdom of God. Through Him and His blessed testimony in the Word we know "the things which God hath prepared for them that love Him." And these things are in Christ. The Church is going to share with Him the glory which He has received. And the Spirit in the believer is searching all things, yea, the deep things of God. So the Spirit of God Himself leads the child of God deeper and deeper into this wisdom of God. The more we learn of it, the more we enter into the deep things in blessed fellowship with the Father and the Son, the more we desire to know. This should be for the child of God, the greatest thing—the Spirit in him searching out the deep things of God. The excuse some Christians make of their inability to grasp certain truths, when they say "it is too deep for me," dishonors the indwelling Spirit. For our poor, little minds all is "too deep"; but not for the Spirit of God.

The things of God cannot be known, save by the Spirit of God. This blessed gift is bestowed upon the believer, so that he can know the things which are freely given to him of God. And these deep and spiritual revelations were transmitted by chosen instruments. "Which things also we speak, not in the words which man's wisdom teacheth, but which the Holy Spirit teacheth, comparing (or communicating) spiritual things with spiritual" (verse 13). Here is a definition of verbal inspiration. The thoughts and revelations of God have been given to us through human instruments, in the words which the Spirit teacheth. We have therefore an inerrant Bible.

A contrast between the natural (psychical) man and the spiritual man concludes this chapter. The natural man, no matter what his mental attainments are, cannot receive the things of the Spirit of God. He must be born again and receive the Spirit before he can discern spiritual things. Why do men criticize the Bible, reject its great truths, ignorant in spiritual things, though learned in the wisdom of the world? They are natural men, not having the Spirit (Jude verse 19).

CHAPTER 3

1. The carnal state of the Corinthians (3:1-9)
2. The workmen and their work (3:10-15)
3. The Church the temple of God (3:16-17)
4. Warning against deception and glorying in Men (3:18-23)

Their condition is next uncovered. They did not depend on the Spirit of God and did not enjoy the hidden wisdom and walk in it. They were carnal, mere babes in Christ, in the sense that their growth, their spiritual development had been arrested. Carnal (fleshly) is not equivalent to "natural." The believer is no longer a natural man, for he is born again. Carnal describes a condition in which the believer walks when he is not subject to the Spirit of God, but is led and governed by natural instincts and motions. Such was their condition. What was merely of man; wisdom, learning, intellect, eloquence and other things, were highly esteemed by them. They were wise in their own conceits and gloried in men. They delighted in and longed for that which is of man, and admired it, therefore the real spiritual truths communicated by the Spirit were unknown to them.

The evidence that they walked not according to the Spirit and the wisdom of God, was the strife and fractions which existed among them. They were carnal and walked according to man. This party spirit among them had its source not in the Spirit of God, but in the flesh. In it, not the Lord was glorified, but man was exalted. They were more occupied with Paul and Apollos, their persons and talents, than with the Lord Jesus Christ. In this way sectarianism began, as the fruit of the flesh. And the remedy for it is "seeing no man but Jesus only." If the Lord Jesus Christ is owned in His glory, and union with Him is enjoyed, then the carnal condition ends and the believer walks in the Spirit and glories no longer in man. Paul and Apollos were but servants by whom they had believed. It is true Paul planted; Apollos coming after him, watered, but God gave the increase. God is all. And any man, whether he planteth or watereth, shall receive his own reward according to his own labour. They were God's fellow-workmen and the saints are God's husbandry (tillage), God's building. And so all true servants of the Lord, though differing in gifts, are one in this that they are instruments in God's hand.

Next (*verses 10-15*), God's fellow-workmen and their work is considered in view of the time "when each shall receive his own reward according to his own labour." Paul here calls himself a wise master-builder (an architect). It was not of himself. He did not plan the great building, the Church, but it was according to the grace bestowed upon him. The Lord had chosen him for that. The mystery concerning the Church which was hidden in former ages, had been made known to him by revelation. Laboring in Corinth, by preaching the gospel, he was used by the will and the grace of God to establish the church there. The foundation was laid by him in sound doctrine, according to the revelation given to him. But neither Paul nor Peter nor any other man is the foundation upon which the building rests; there is but one foundation, Jesus Christ, the Son of God. The Church is "built upon the foundation of the apostles and prophets, Jesus Christ Himself being the chief corner stone; in whom all the building fitly framed together groweth unto an holy temple in the Lord" (Eph. 2:20-21). The foundation is laid, but the question is what fellow-workmen are going to build upon this one foundation.

Those who are not at all building upon the one foundation, Jesus Christ the Son of God, are of course, not considered. (The different anti-Christian cults, like Christian Science, spiritism, New Thought, theosophy, etc., all lay claim to the name of Christ, but they reject Him and belong therefore to that class who destroy the temple of God.) Those who own the one foundation may build upon it either gold, silver, precious stones; or wood, hay, stubble. The first three things mentioned are precious and durable; the other three things are worthless and perishable. Gold, silver and precious stones are the fit adornment of the church as the temple of God, but wood, hay and stubble are worthless material fit not for a temple, but for a mud hovel. Gold, silver and precious stones typify the service of the workmen which is of faith, done in obedience to the Word and manifesting the character of the Lord Jesus Christ; while wood, hay and stubble represent what is not of faith, the work and service done in self-will, exalting man instead of the Lord, and therefore disfiguring the temple of God.

The workman whose aim is to please God and not men, whose one ambition is to exalt Christ in all his service, who labors for the perfecting of the saints, the edifying of the body of Christ (Eph. 4:12), builds that which is durable and which can never perish. The workman who pleases men, seeks the applause of man, uses the means and schemes of the world to carry on what is called "Christian work" and in it all is not obedient to the Word of God, builds that which is worthless and his work will perish.

A day is coming in which each man's work shall be made manifest. The day is the day of Christ when all believers shall appear before the judgment seat of Christ. He is a consuming fire; and before Him whatever is of man and not of Himself will be burned up. That fire shall try every man's (who is a believer saved by grace) work of what sort it is. Then those who toiled in an unostentatious way, who built upon the one foundation that which glorifies Him, whose work was done in faith, shall find that their work abides and they will receive their own reward. The others will see all their work go up in smoke. They shall suffer loss. There is no reward for them. They shall be saved, yet so as by fire. Like Lot who escaped out of Sodom; but all that he had wrought in Sodom, his righteous soul being vexed, was burned up. But the salvation the believer has is independent of his service and work. Every believer will be saved and live, though what he wrought may be found in that day only fit for the fire.

The building of which the apostle speaks is the Church, the temple of God, the habitation of God through the Spirit. God's Holy Spirit is dwelling in every member of the body. The temple of God is holy and such are ye. Then the solemn warning "if any man destroy (not defile) the temple of God, him shall God destroy." God's temple in which He dwells, the Church, is founded on His truth. The destruction of that temple means therefore the denial of the truth of God or the introduction of false doctrines; critics of the Word, who deny the fundamentals of the faith have well been called "destructive." They are the enemies of the cross, whose end is perdition. They are not saved as by fire, but God is going to deal with them in an awful judgment.

In the professing Church today are uncountable numbers, who have crept in unawares: they were never born again and therefore they work corruption and will perish. Therefore "let no man deceive himself." The Corinthians were setting aside the wisdom of the Spirit and were being seduced by the wisdom of the world, which is foolishness with God. They marred the temple of God by their carnal spirit, trusting in men and glorying in men. In God's gracious purpose as revealed by the Spirit of God all things were theirs. Paul, Apollos and Cephas were the chosen instruments of God for blessing them. As believers they had all things and belong to none but Christ and through Christ to God Himself.

CHAPTER 4

1. Servants of Christ and stewards of the mysteries of God (4:1-5)
2. Contrast between self-glorification and humiliation (4:6-13)
3. Admonition to beloved children (4:14-21)

Paul speaks of himself and the fellow workmen as servants of Christ and the stewards of the mysteries of God. They were serving under Christ. Apollos, though not an apostle, is included by Paul. Apollos with his great eloquence probably appealed strongly to the Corinthians and thus the party spirit had been fostered among them. But Paul classes Apollos with himself; he might have told the Corinthians that Apollos was not an apostle and by this belittle him in their eyes. All were servants of Christ to serve the household of faith and to give meat in due season.

The "mysteries of God" are not, as claimed by ritualistic Christendom, the sacraments in their invented "mysterious" actions. The mysteries of God are those blessed hidden things, which were not revealed in former dispensations; but now they are made known and the servants of Christ are the stewards of the blessed truths of Christianity, to guard and to dispense them. Paul, who may be called "the chief steward" of these mysteries, had been judged by them, but he expresses his independence of all their judgment. He is responsible to the Lord although he was not aware of anything against himself yet he was not thereby justified, for the Lord might know something, that he had overlooked. He then points to that day (the day of Christ) when He comes and all His people will have to appear before the judgment seat of Christ. Then the hidden things will come to light, the counsels of the hearts will be manifest and each man have his praise from God. To that day the servant of Christ, the steward of God's mysteries, yea, every Christian, must look, and serve in anticipation of it. Then all our acts and ways will be examined and judged by the Lord Himself. Paul therefore declared that any judgment now was a judgment "before the time."

And all this he wrote by the Spirit to uncover their foolishness and to counteract their party-spirit. "That ye might learn not to go beyond the things which are written, that no one of you be puffed up the one against the other. For who maketh thee to differ? and what hast thou that thou hast not received? But, if thou hast received it, why dost thou glory, as if thou hadst not received it?" Thus the Spirit of God exposed the folly of the Corinthian party spirit in which they were puffed up and had lost sight of Christ.

Where they had drifted in their carnal spirit by glorying in men and not in Christ is made known by the contrast between their self-glorification, self-exaltation, and self-sufficiency and the path of humiliation, suffering, and contempt, which is marked out for the true follower of the Lord and the servant of Christ. Here is solemn food for reflection. They were full and rich, reigned as kings, but without the apostles, who were blessedly sharing the sufferings of Christ and were a spectacle unto the world, to angels and to men. By their profession the Corinthians were waiting for the coming of the Lord, yet in His absence they reigned as kings. They enjoyed prosperity, had all things in abundance, they gloried in all these things while the true servants of Christ were suffering, were in want, following in the path of His blessed life on earth, bearing His reproach, despised and rejected by the world. And so it is today that the professing Church has fully gone the Corinthian way; an outward profession, a seeking after the honor of men, the applause of the world, glorying in earthly attainments, rich, increased in goods. With it the offence of the cross has ceased. The cross which has written the sentence of death upon the flesh, which has made the believer dead to the world and the world dead to him; the cross, which demands separation, self-denial, self-surrender and self-sacrifice is denied.

What a record of suffering and privation, persecution, reproach, and shame the apostle gives! The Corinthians knew nothing of that; nor does the professing Church of today. But has not the world changed since then? Is not the age becoming better? Is not the leaven of Christianity changing existing conditions so that the reproach of Christ ceases and suffering is changed into worldly honor and glory? A thousand times, No! These are the spurious claims. The world, this present age, man's day, does not change. The world is the same to-day as it was in the days of the apostle. It is still true and will be true till the Lord comes "all that will live godly in Christ Jesus shall suffer persecutions." The applause and approval of the world, the recognition by the world of that which is called "religion"—"Christian work and service," is an evidence that that service and religion is not according to the truth of God.

Paul sent Timothy to remind them "of my ways which are in Christ, as I teach everywhere in every church." And he was also coming in person. He was not afraid to visit them and meet them face to face; he would come in power. "What will ye? Shall I come unto you with a rod, or in love, and in the spirit of meekness?" It was his loving call for them to repent and humble themselves.

3. Corinthian Failures (5—6)

CHAPTER 5

1. The tolerated case of gross immorality (5:1-5)
2. The call to separation (5:6-13)

The spiritual declension, the carnal spirit which prevailed among them, had brought forth fruit. One of their members had committed an act of the grossest immorality, which was an unspeakable outrage, such as was not even named in a licentious city like Corinth, where licentiousness of life was a broadly marked feature of society. It was a case of lawlessness and vileness, which was unknown among the heathen. And this case was tolerated in their midst. Instead of mourning over their sin they were puffed up and did not put away the evil-doer from the assembly. If they lacked the personal instruction of the apostle what to do in such a case, they should have turned to the Lord in sorrow of heart and asked Him for guidance. But they were indifferent. The apostle now tells them what had to be done. He was among them in spirit, and exercises his apostolic authority in the name and power of the Lord Jesus Christ, to deliver such an one to Satan for the destruction of the flesh, that his spirit may be saved in the day of the Lord Jesus.

"If the enemy had succeeded in drawing aside by the flesh a member of Christ, so that he dishonors the Lord by walking after the flesh as men of the world do, he is put outside, and by the power of the Spirit, as then exercised in their midst by the apostle, delivered up to the enemy, who is in spite of himself the servant of the purposes of God (as in the case of Job), in order that the flesh of the Christian (which, from his failure to reckon himself dead to sin, had brought him morally under the power of Satan) should be physically destroyed and broken down. Thus would he be set free from the illusions in which the flesh held him captive. His mind would learn how to discern the difference between good and evil, to know what sin is. The judgment of God would be realized within him, and would not be executed upon him at that day when it would be definitely for the condemnation of those who should undergo it. This was a great blessing! although its form was terrible. Marvellous example of the government of God, which uses the adversary's enmity against the saints as an instrument for their spiritual blessing! We have such a case fully set before us in the history of Job. Only we have here, in addition, the proof that in its normal state, apostolic power being there, the assembly exercised this judgment itself, having discernment by the Spirit and the authority of Christ to do it. Moreover, whatever may be the spiritual capacity of the assembly to wield this sword of the Lord (for this is power), her positive and ordinary duty is stated at the end of the chapter" (*Synopsis of the Bible*).

The second Epistle will show us how this discipline was greatly blessed to this wicked person upon whom this sentence was pronounced and who was put out of fellowship with God's people. But not only was there individual evil, but the sin affected the whole Corinthian assembly. As Achan's sin was a curse to Israel (Joshua 7), so the leaven of this wickedness was corrupting the whole church. Leaven is seen here once more as a type of evil. A little leaven, a little evil allowed, leavens the whole lump both individually and collectively. The apostle demands that no evil in any form, whether moral or doctrinal, is to be tolerated among those who are Christ's. Christ is our Passover Lamb sacrificed for us. In Him all believers are constituted holy.

With the Passover there was inseparably linked the feast of unleavened bread, showing that redemption is holiness. As the Jew had to put away all leaven in eating the Passover, so the Christian must purge out all leaven and be in an unleavened condition, in sincerity and in truth before God. Even the smallest bit of leaven, the least deviation from the truth of God, in holding some unscriptural doctrine, or any other evil, will, if not purged, ultimately leaven the whole lump. Christendom today is a solemn witness to this truth. The whole professing Church is leavened by the leaven of the Pharisees (ritualism); the leaven of the Sadducees (higher criticism or infidelity); the Corinthian leaven (vain glory and worldliness) and the Galatian leaven (legalism). Then follows the command, "therefore put away from among yourselves that wicked person." Such discipline demanded by the Holy Spirit is almost unknown today in that which professes to be the church of God. It has been said that it is uncharitable and harsh to deal in this way with those who are evil in doctrine or practice. It is not that, but rather a gracious measure, to humble such an one and bring him back to the place of blessing.

CHAPTER 6

1. Concerning disputes before heathen courts (6:1-7)
2. The holiness of believers: Their bodies the temples of the Holy Spirit (6:8-20)

Instead of settling their disputes amongst themselves, as it becomes the saints of God, they brought their difficulties before a heathen court. In doing this they had lost sight of the dignity of their calling. The saints of God are to reign with Christ and share His glory; they shall judge the world and angels in that day. Going to a heathen court to have these matters settled by one who was not a child of God, but unrighteous, was unworthy of them; they were making known their own shame before the world. If they had remembered that coming day of glory, when as saints they were to participate in the judgment of the world, they would not have acted in such a way. They would have gladly suffered wrong themselves and permitted themselves to be defrauded instead of rushing with their grievances before a heathen court. Matthew 18:15-18 shows the true way for believers to settle such matters. They were doing wrong and defrauding their own brethren. In all this they dishonored God and denied their relationship to Him. And these Corinthian failures are today in professing Christendom fully developed.

The unrighteous shall not inherit the kingdom of God. He reminds them what some of them had been in their unconverted state. They had practised the vile things of the flesh, which were so common in Corinth. And connected with this there is a warning. If the little leaven was allowed to work, if they continued in the evil ways they were following, they would surely relapse into their former state. But even more, the apostle reminds them what the grace of God had done for them in saving them from such a life. They had been translated from the power of darkness into the Kingdom of the Son of His love. "And such were some of you, but ye are washed, but ye are sanctified, but ye are justified in the name of the Lord Jesus, and by the Spirit of our God." The washing has nothing to do with baptism, as some claim. Through regeneration (called in Titus 3:5, "the washing of regeneration"), the believing sinner becomes clean every whit (John 13:10). Then he is also sanctified in Christ, set apart unto God. And the Holy Spirit takes possession of the believer as His own temple. This is the meaning here of "justified in the name of the Lord Jesus, and by the Spirit of our God." He is the seal.

Then the question concerning the believer's body is introduced. A believer is no longer under the law as to meats and foods, as the Jews were. "All things are lawful unto me, but all things are not profitable." A believer is not to be brought under the power of any of these things. He is not in bondage to anything, but is to have perfect liberty. To be a slave to anything, for instance, a habit, would be wrong. Meats are for the belly; they are but temporary and will pass away. "God will bring to nought both it (the belly) and them (the meats)." But the body itself is something different. In the body of the believer the Holy Spirit is the abiding guest, the divine indweller. The body is therefore for the Lord and the Lord for the body. The body has the promise of redemption. God, who raised up the Lord, will also raise us up by His own power. And the bodies of believers are members of Christ, joined to Himself by the Spirit of God. "For he that is joined unto the Lord is one Spirit." And all is in warning against the horrible sin, which was so prominent in Corinth, fornication. The bodies of believers belong to the Lord. They are the temples of the Holy Spirit. Therefore we are not our own. Furthermore, all this has been accomplished by the great redemption price, the price paid upon Calvary's cross. The body must be yielded to God as a living sacrifice. "For ye are bought with a price; therefore glorify God in your body . . . ."

4. Concerning the Relationship of Man and Woman

CHAPTER 7

1. The single and the married life (7:1-9)
2. Separation and divorce (7:10-16)
3. Abiding in the different callings (7:17-24)
4. The unmarried and married in contrast (7:25-40)

It is evident from the first verse that the Corinthians had inquired of the apostle about marriage and the relationship of man and woman. It was an important question in a city of the character of Corinth, so full of immorality. This chapter answers their question and gives instructions concerning the unmarried and those who are joined together in marriage. "It is good for man not to touch a woman" has been used as sanctioning celibacy and discrediting the marriage union. Such is not the case. The unmarried state has for the Christian, who is fully devoted to the Lord, certain spiritual advantages. "He that is unmarried careth for the things that belong to the Lord, how he may please the Lord" (verse 32). Compare this also with the words of our Lord in Matthew 19:4-12.

The Apostle Paul was unmarried (verse 8) and denied himself the lawful privilege of having a wife (9:5) to be free in all things to serve the Lord. But there were great dangers, especially in heathen Corinth, where fornication was religiously sanctioned. Therefore the Apostle enjoins them that every man should have his own wife and every woman have her own husband. And in this relationship, fully approved by the Lord both must be true to its natural claims. As to the body, the husband belongs to the wife and the wife to the husband. They are not to defraud each other. However, by mutual consent they may be apart for a season to give themselves unto prayer. And this he wrote not as a command, but as a permission. "The apostle gives his thoughts and judgment as a spiritual man, his mind animated and guided by the Spirit, and contrasts it with inspiration and what the Lord said."

Then the question of separation and divorce is taken up. The indissolubleness of the marriage tie had been declared by the Lord and is here confirmed. "What therefore God hath joined together, let no man put asunder." "And I say unto you, Whosoever shall put away his wife, except it be for fornication, and shall marry another, committeth adultery; and whoso marrieth her which is put away doth commit adultery" (Matthew 19:6, 9). And so the apostle writes that which is a command not coming from himself but from the Lord, that if a separation takes place between husband and wife, she is to remain unmarried, or be reconciled. The husband is not to put away his wife. How little heed is paid to all this among professing Christians in our days. The increase of unscriptural divorces is appalling.

Next the case of mixed marriages is considered. Most likely many such cases were in existence in Corinth. "According to the law a man who had married a woman of the Gentiles (and was consequently profane or unclean) defiled himself, and was compelled to send her away; and their children had no right to Jewish privileges; they were rejected as unclean. (See Ezra 10:3). But under grace it was quite the contrary. The converted husband sanctified the wife, and *vice versa,* and their children were reckoned clean before God; they had part in the ecclesiastical rights of their parent. This is the sense of the word "holy," in connection with the question of order and of outward relationship towards God, which was suggested by the obligation under the law to send away wife and children in a similar case. Thus the believer was not to send away his wife, nor to forsake an unbelieving husband. If the unbeliever forsook the believer definitively, the latter (man or woman) was free—"let him depart." The brother was no longer bound to consider the one who had forsaken him as his wife, nor the sister the man who had forsaken her as her husband. But they were called to peace, and not to seek this separation; for how did the believer know if he should not be the means of the unbeliever's conversion? For we are under grace" (*Synopsis of the Bible*).

Of course the unbelieving husband by being united to a believing wife was not actually sanctified. This requires faith in the Lord Jesus Christ. But the unbelieving husband of a Corinthian household, whose wife was a believer, was no longer in the darkness of heathendom; he was surrounded by the light of Christianity and had come through being linked with a believer under its blessed influence. And so the offspring of such a union. Grace sought both the unbelieving husband and the children. But mixed marriages are never to be encouraged. 2 Corinthians 6:14 forbids them.

Verses 17-24 are parenthetical. And every man is to abide in the calling wherein he is called. Each is to abide with God (verse 24) in his own particular calling and thus glorify God in it. A believer is to be above all earthly circumstances. Yielding obedience to God is the one great thing. "Ye are bought with a price; be not ye the servants of men."

The final paragraph of this chapter (verses 25-40) gives the contrasts between those who marry and those who do not. Let us heed these blessed exhortations of such importance to God's people. "I say, brethren the time is short." If that was true then, how much more so is it in the significant days in which our lot is cast. With the ever increasing signs of the ending of the age and the coming of the Lord about us, we know that the time is short. In view of this fact those who have wives are to be as though they had none; they who weep, who pass through suffering, as though they wept not; they that rejoice, as though they rejoiced not; they that buy, as though they possessed not; and they that use the world as not abusing it, for the fashion of this world passeth away. We are to be without carefulness and distraction, so that we can serve the Lord. Much here is the advice of the apostle concerning yielding to nature, which is perfectly lawful, or not yielding to it as to marriage. It is not the commandment of the Lord. Nevertheless we must remember that if he gives his apostolic advice, it is inspired advice, the advice of the Holy Spirit.

5. Concerning Meats Offered to Idols: Christian Liberty Governed by Love

CHAPTER 8

1. Concerning things sacrificed to idols and knowledge (8:1-6)
2. True knowledge and liberty governed by love (8:7-13)

Another question is raised concerning things offered to idols. Should Christians eat what had been offered in sacrifice to idols? These idol-offered meats were generally sold in the meat market. Would a believer be defiled by using such meats? They all had knowledge concerning these matters. But mere knowledge without love only puffeth up. Love is better than knowledge, for it edifieth, and this love they had to manifest in the matter of eating things sacrificed to idols. As to knowledge, how little man knoweth. How true it is "if any man think he knoweth anything, he knoweth nothing yet as he ought to know." Pride because of knowledge is a dangerous thing, and much of this we see among Christians. True knowledge of God produces love for Him and such a one is known of God. Then the question is taken up. They had the knowledge that an idol is nothing in the world. There is none other God but one, "the Father, of whom are all things and we for Him, and one Lord, Jesus Christ, by whom are all things and we by Him."

But not all had this perfect knowledge. Some had the conception that the idol is a reality, a god, though a false one; they did not grasp the fact that an idol is nothing. They ate of the meat, feeling that it had been an idol sacrifice, and their conscience in these scruples being weak is defiled. They were therefore in bondage and did not enjoy the liberty in Christ.

Verse 8 shows that eating meat or not eating meat has no advantage whatever before God. The important thing then is stated. "But take heed lest by any means this liberty of yours becomes a stumbling block to them that are weak." One who is weak in faith (not possessing true knowledge) sees a brother eating meat in the idol's temple and by it he will become emboldened to do violence to his conscience and do the same thing, and in doing it he sins. He acts not in faith, but imitates another and worse things may follow. By his act the brother who has knowledge may be more than a stumbling block. The weak brother may perish, for whom Christ died, through such an example. The disastrous effect is put in the strongest term. Of course the weak brother will not actually perish, but in his conscience he will be guilty. However grace will step in and prevent this threatening danger. No sheep or lamb of His shall perish; for none can pluck them out of His hand. We are our brother's keepers, not their Saviour. Well has it been said, "out of our careless hands they fall for safety into His." But sinning against brethren and wounding their weak consciences is sinning against Christ. "Knowledge puffeth up, but love edifieth" (verse 1). The apostle then states that he will relinquish his knowledge and liberty in case it would offend his brother, "Lest I make my brother offend." Christian liberty is to be governed by love for the brethren.

The liberty of God's children is absolute, but they are expected to use it as imitators of God. We have to consider not ourselves only, but both our brethren and the world. A saint may be walking without circumspection, and yet with an unruffled conscience. But this is dangerous. Heed must be taken lest, while enjoying, in one sense blamelessly, our liberty, we become unwittingly a stumbling block to others. An ostentatious use of liberty rarely fails to injure the boaster and those who may observe his ways. True grace, because it is free and knows its happiness in fellowship with God, makes no effort to *seem* free. Rather it will seek to use its liberty in love, considering the weak, and neither despising them, nor tempting them by wrong example to act in anything beyond their faith (Pridham).

All this is practical truth and much needed in our days of worldliness and laxity in the Christian walk. It is a good rule to ask in all our walk and in the use of our liberty, how will it affect the fellow-members of the body? We refer the reader to Romans 14 where the same truth is treated. (See the annotations there.)

6. Paul's Gracious Example

CHAPTER 9

1. The apostle's rights (9:1-14)
2. He waives his rights for the gospel's sake (9:15-27)
3. The race-course and the crown (9:24-27)

The great principle laid down in the previous chapter to forego one's Christian liberty, the Apostle Paul enforced by his own example. He was an Apostle and had seen the Lord Jesus, from whom he had received his apostleship (Gal. 1:1). From the second verse we learn that some had not recognized him as an apostle; these must have been false teachers. But the Corinthians knew he was an apostle. Through his testimony they had been converted so that he could say "for the seal of mine apostleship are ye in the Lord." As an apostle he had certain rights, but he did not make use of them. All his rights and his privileges had been given up by him. The law also affirmed his claim, for it forbad the muzzling of the oxen that treadeth the corn. Those that sow spiritual things are perfectly entitled to reap carnal (material) things. Other teachers used this God-given right and accepted their material things; and he had a greater claim for this upon the Corinthians, for he taught them first.

"Nevertheless we have not used this power, but suffer all things, lest we should hinder the gospel of Christ." The Lord certainly had ordained that they who preach the gospel should live of the gospel. All this he had not used; he had not made use of what was his right. Nor did he write these words that his claims might be satisfied. He did not want his glorying made void. What was his glory? Not the preaching of the gospel in itself. Necessity was laid upon him and "Woe is unto me, if I preach not the gospel!" "For if I do this of mine own will, I have a reward; but if not of mine own will, I am entrusted with a stewardship." (The translation of verse 17 in the Authorized Version is faulty.)

What is his reward? In what does he glory? His answer is "that when I preach the gospel without charge, so as not to use, as belonging to me, my right in the gospel." In this way the gospel was not hindered; it was made more effective. For being free from all, free from the control of any person, he had made himself the servant of all, that he might win as many as he could. This was his reward, to preach the gospel gratuitously. Governed by love he had become a servant of all. His rights were given up, but he did not insist upon his Christian freedom, but gave up his liberty in order "that I might by all means save some." He did not seek his own things but the things of Christ. The most blessed self-sacrifice on behalf of Christ and the gospel of Christ marked his service. How few such servants, who give up, self-denying, self-sacrificing, waiving their rights for the gospel's sake, are found today in Christendom. But how many are seeking their own!

The concluding paragraph is fully in line with these statements of the apostle. He uses as an illustration the Greek stadium, the race-course, well known to the Corinthians on account of the games on the isthmus of Corinth. In order to run successfully and obtain the prize, self-denial was necessary. There was a prize for him who won. Spiritually, not one, but all may obtain the prize, if all run well. And in the race every man that striveth for the mastery, to obtain the victory, is temperate in all things. They do it to obtain a fading crown, a wreath; but we have the promise of a crown that fadeth not away, an everlasting crown.

And if those who strive for earthly honor deny themselves, how much more should we practice self-denial in view of the crown of glory! "I therefore so run not as uncertainly; so fight I, not as one that beateth the air; but I keep under my body, and bring it into subjection, lest that by any means, having preached to others, I myself should be a castaway." What did the apostle mean by the latter statement? The word "castaway" is found also in the following passages: Rom. 1:28; 2 Cor. 13:5, 6, 7; 2 Tim. 3:8; and Titus 1:16. In these passages it is translated by "reprobate." In Heb. 6:8 it is translated "rejected." Did he mean that he feared to be lost himself? Or did he only fear disapproval as a workman, whose service is rejected and to be counted unworthy of a crown? The statement does not clash with the teaching of the eternal security of the believer. The apostle personally does not fear for himself, as no true believer need to fear, but he applies an important principle to himself. Salvation and a holy walk are inseparably connected. Preaching alone will not do, but the truth must be lived.

"There would be difficulty indeed, if the apostle spoke of having been born again and afterwards becoming a castaway: in this case life would not be eternal. But he says nothing of the sort. He only shows the solemn danger and certain ruin of preaching without a practice according to it. This the Corinthians needed to hear. Preaching or teaching truth to men without reality, self-judgment and self-denial before God, is ruinous. It is to deceive ourselves, not Him who is not mocked. Nor do any Christians more deeply need to watch and pray than those who are much occupied with handling the word of God or guiding others in the ways of the Lord. How easy for such to forget that *doing* the truth is the common responsibility of all, and that speaking it to others ever so earnestly is no substitute for their own obeying it as in the sight of God!" (W. Kelly)

It is a warning against an empty profession of Christianity without the manifestation of the power. Where there is true salvation and eternal life, it is proved by a godly walk. The apostle in these personal statements shows that all the blessed knowledge he had and with it the most positive assurance of eternal glory, did not make him careless, but prompted him to still greater earnestness and continued self-denial. He knew nothing in his life of the self-indulgence which characterized so many in the Corinthian assembly; he kept his body under. But he also knew, as every Christian should know, that the grace which had saved him, which taught him to live soberly, righteously and godly, would also keep him and enable him to persevere through all hindrances.

7. Warnings and Exhortations

CHAPTER 10

1. Warnings from Israel's past history (10:4-7)
2. Exhortations (10:15-33)

The same subject is continued with this chapter. The concluding paragraph of the previous chapter is illustrated from Israel's history, as the professing people of God. What happened unto them has a typical meaning for us. "Now all these things happened unto them for ensamples (types), and they are written for our admonition, upon whom the ends of the world (ages) are come." He speaks of "our fathers (Israel's fathers) were under the cloud, and all passed through the sea, and were all baptized unto Moses in the cloud and in the sea."

God had delivered them out of Egypt; the cloud covered them and the sea divided, for their salvation and for the judgment upon the Egyptian hosts. The Lord had made them free to serve Him and it is written "they believed the Lord and His servant Moses." In this sense they were baptized, or set apart, unto Moses as his disciples. And the person who accepts and professes Christianity is set apart to Christ.

All who were under the covering and protecting cloud and who had passed through the sea, ate the same spiritual food, and drank the same spiritual drink, of the rock which followed them, and the rock was Christ. The Lord in infinite love provided for them by giving them food and water, which both are typical of Christ. All ate and drank of the miraculous supply. But what became of the great mass of this people? "But with many of them God was not well pleased, for they were overthrown in the wilderness." They lusted after evil things; some became idolators; some fornicators; some tempted the Lord by trying His patience and murmuring. Judgment followed. In one day 23,000 fell; others were destroyed by serpents and perished by the destroyer. (See Numb. 25:9; when 24,000 are mentioned. See for an explanation of this alleged discrepancy annotations on Numb. 25.)

All this was written for the admonition and warning of the Corinthians. It shows how those who enjoy divine privileges and lay claim to the title of being God's people, but do not live in separation, do not please God. They that are in the flesh cannot please God, though they may profess Christianity and partake of divine things. Many of the Corinthians were in this dangerous condition. And the admonition and warning is for us as well.

"The warning is for us all. We have no right to say, 'Well, but we are true Christians, and therefore we need not trouble about these things.' These are things which as principles are of the greatest importance for us to realize. There are evil things for which we may lust as they lusted. If God prevents the extreme result for us, that is His mercy, but the effect of our disregarding the warnings may be that our lives may be alas, how greatly spoiled and disfigured and made quite other than He would have them, by our laxity!" (*Numerical Bible*)

Two important statements follow. "Let him that thinketh he standeth take heed lest he fall." This is our responsibility. But how can a believer stand in this world, so dangerous and full of evil? Only by faith can we stand, and faith is confidence in God. As we have no self-confidence, but trust in Him alone and walk in fellowship with Him we shall stand and be upheld. Then there is the blessed comforting statement: "God is faithful." He does not allow that we are tempted above that we are able, but he provides a way to escape. "Wherefore, dearly beloved, flee from idolatry." It meant for the Corinthians the idolatry of heathendom. But there is also a more subtle idolatry. That believer is kept from all idolatry who is wholly devoted to the Lord and who gives to Him constantly the *pre-eminence. Devotedness* to God keeps from idols.

The second half of this chapter contains exhortations about idolatry and the believer's walk in the midst of the corruption which is in the world. The Lord's Supper is significantly introduced at this point. As we find in the next chapter, it is the memorial feast of what the Lord Jesus Christ has done for us. Blessed and precious is this feast of communion. And in eating of it there is identification with the body of Christ, for "we are all partakers of that one bread." In the Lord's supper, many of the essential truths of Christianity are revealed and enjoyed by faith, in the power of the Spirit, as an act of true worship. If the believer then realizes that he is a partaker of Christ and tastes afresh of His love and gazes in hope towards the coming glory, he will have nothing to do with idols, nor have any fellowship with darkness. As he has written before, the idol is nothing, meaning the supposed gods of the heathen.

However, idolatry was a horrible reality, by which the souls and bodies of men were corrupted. The heathen sacrificed in idol-worship to demons and not to God. And how can he who drinks the cup of the Lord, the Lord of all, drink also the cup of demons? Ye cannot be partakers of the Lord's table, and of the table of demons. In doing this they would provoke the Lord to jealousy. Every wicked doctrine and false worship is backed by demons and participation in it means identification. This is especially true of the anti-Christian movements of our times, such as Christian Science, theosophy, and others (1 Tim. 4:1). The instructions call for a cautious and separated walk, as it becometh those who are the Lord's. God is to be before the heart of the believer in all things. "Whether therefore ye eat, or drink, or whatsoever ye do, do all to the glory of God."

II. The Church, the Body of Christ (11—14)

1. Headship of Christ and of Man and the Lord's Supper

CHAPTER 11

1. The headship of Christ and of the man, the position of woman (11:1-16)
2. The Lord's Supper (11:17-31)

The opening verse belongs to the preceding chapter. And now after the church in relation to the world had been treated by the apostle in the first part of this Epistle, he takes up next the affairs of the church itself. Here, too, much had to be corrected into which the Corinthian assembly had drifted. After the brief and excellent word of praise by which he expressed his confidence in them (verse 2), he calls their attention to an important truth, which in our times is not only overlooked, but often belittled and altogether set aside. It concerns the headship of Christ, of the man, and the position of woman. It is evident that Corinthian women had assumed in the church a position which was not according to God's order in creation. They had not yet learned it. God's order in creation has to be manifested in the Church. This order is unaltered by redemption, though in Christ there is neither male nor female, yet has God assigned to man and to woman their respective places which must be maintained.

This divine order the apostle states. "But I would have you know, that the head of every man is Christ, and the head of the woman is the man; and the head of Christ is God." These are weighty and blessed statements. Christ is the Creator, the Lord of all, but He also became man and is the "First born of all Creation" (Col. 1:15-16). He is therefore in possession of the headship in creation, and head of man as the Man, as He is also the head of the Church. God has given Him the pre-eminence in all things. And the head of the woman is the man; this is the place which God has given to woman on earth. In creation the head of the woman is man. Yet what would man be without the woman!—she is necessary to him.

"The woman is the glory of man. For the man is not of the woman; but the woman of the man. Neither was the man created for the woman, but the woman for the man." To these statements about the headship of Christ, the headship of man, he being head of the woman, the apostle adds "and the head of Christ is God." Christ is the eternal Son of God, co-equal in Godhead in every way. He is God. But the Only-Begotten humbled Himself; He took on the creature's form and "was made of a woman." And as Man He has taken the place under God, yielding perfect obedience in all things. In all His redemption work He is under God, not only on earth, but now in glory, as the Glorified Man at the right hand of God, who raised Him from the dead and gave Him glory.

The purpose of the declaration of this order of the ways of God in creation was to set them right on a matter which in our days is often sneered at. Man praying or prophesying is not to cover his head. Woman praying and prophesying is to have a covering on her head. The man who covereth his head in praying dishonoreth his head. Woman uncovered dishonoreth her head. A covering on the head is the outward sign of being in the place of subjection. An uncovered head signifies the opposite. The order which God has instituted as to the place of man and woman, His people are bound to respect. It may appear a little thing, yet if disobeyed, as it was in Corinth (where women seemed to be puffed up and refused to follow this order), it becomes a stepping stone towards more serious evil. Woman is to testify to her place of subjection by covering her head in praying and testifying. Man similarly engaged does not cover his head, for the authority is vested in man "for as much as he is the image and glory of God, but the woman is the glory of man." How all this is denied and woman aims to take leadership and rulership in place of man, we need not to enlarge upon.

> If woman persists in leaving the place (in subjection) where her glory shines, if she will persist in pushing out into the glare of public life and thrust herself into the struggle and grinding competition that wears out men's lives and tenderer instincts, let her not be astonished if she lose her distinctive grace—the delicate sheen that cannot bear the world's rough, unhallowed ways (Prof. Moorehead).

Another reason is given why praying women should wear outwardly a sign of subjection—because of the angels. Angels are watchers and attendants of the heirs of salvation. As the Church is known to them and by it they know the manifold wisdom of God (Eph. 3:10), so are they observers of Christian worship and the order and behavior of God's people in His house. And angels themselves are in subjection and yield perfect obedience.

Then the Church itself is brought into view. The first thing is not the fact that Christians are the members of Christ, who constituted the body of Christ, the gifts of the body and the exercise of these gifts. The Lord's Supper, that blessed memorial of His love in His sacrificial death, the love which passeth knowledge, is the first thing mentioned. "Do this in remembrance of Me" was His request in the night in which He was betrayed. When the Holy Spirit came and the company gathered in fellowship we read at once of "the breaking of bread," to remember Him (Acts 2:46).

The first thing in the assembly must be to remember Christ, His death, His presence in glory, His coming again. But before the Apostle tells them what he had received of the Lord, he had to reprove them for their disorder and their divisions. In these sects and parties they denied the very truth of the Church as the one body, the body of Christ. They had a custom of eating a meal in connection with the Lord's Supper. And at this meal some drank to excess, while it seems this custom of a preliminary meal led to a complete neglect or unworthy observance of the Supper itself. Then he writes of what he had received of the Lord. How simple it all is! "This do ye, as oft as ye drink it, in remembrance of Me. For as oft as ye eat this bread, and drink this cup, ye do show the Lord's death till He come." The Lord's Supper is to remember Him, to show the Lord's death till He come. And all else that man has made of it is pure invention, if not wicked blasphemy, like the idolatrous mass of Romanism. And how often shall this feast, which delights His heart, where God's children worship and adore, be kept? In apostolic days it was evidently kept every Lord's day (Acts 20:7).

All God's children, whom the Lord has received, have a right to the Lord's table and gather thus around His blessed Person. The only things which bar from the Lord's table are evil doctrines and an evil walk. And the Lord's Supper may be eaten unworthily. He, who comes to the Lord's table without self-judgment, eats and drinks of it unworthily. We eat and drink unworthily when we partake without discerning the Lord's body and blood represented by the bread and the wine, for we do not then shew to God the death of Christ. Let a man examine (judge) himself before eating or else he eats for his own judgment. This is God's way of producing and maintaining holiness in the Church. And the Corinthians had experienced that the Lord dealt with a number of them in judgment. Upon many the Lord had laid His hand, many were weak and stricken with disease, while others had fallen asleep. It was mercy, "but when we are judged we are chastened of the Lord, that we should not be condemned with the world."

The world is condemned. Sin in the Christian is judged; it escapes neither the eye nor the judgment of God. He never permits it; He cleanses the believer from it by chastening him, although He does not condemn, because Christ has borne his sins, and been made sin for him. The death of Christ forms then the centre of communion in the assembly, and the touchstone of conscience, and that, with respect to the assembly, in the Lord's Supper *(Synopsis of the Bible)*.

2. The Body and the Members of the Body

CHAPTER 12

1. Concerning spiritual manifestations and diversities of gifts (12:1-11)
2. The body and its members (12:12-31)

In this interesting, important chapter, spiritual manifestations are first mentioned. The Church is the body of Christ, the habitation of God through the Spirit. The Holy Spirit dwells in the Church. And first the distinctive mark of the Spirit is stated. As heathen they had been under the control of evil spirits, who had deluded them with idolatrous worship. And these evil spirits were still active, creeping in among Christians, pretending to be the Spirit of God and counterfeiting His manifestations. It was so then and it is so now. Seducing spirits and doctrines of demons are in fullest evidence in the professing Church. Satan transforms himself into an angel of light; he imitates and produces certain manifestations, as he must have done among the Corinthians; but Satan never owns Jesus as Lord. The work of the Holy Spirit is to exalt the Lord Jesus. The Spirit does not even speak of Himself, but always glorifies Christ, giving Him the right place. The evil spirits do the opposite; they degrade Him and attempt to rob Him of His glory. This they do through evil doctrines. It amounts to the same as saying "anathema" (curse) "Jesus" as Jews and Gentiles did in rejecting Jesus as Lord. No man speaking by the Spirit of God would say that. And all who own Him as Lord do so by the bidding and the teaching of the Holy Spirit.

If the highest honor is not freely and sincerely given to the name of Jesus, its only other place is utter degradation. Between 'anathema' and 'Lord' there is no other place which it can justly occupy. The wide space which seems morally to intervene between a living and adoring faith and a deliberate and positive denial of that name, is ignored by the Spirit, in His estimate of human character, as a nullity and a deception. With Him men are either believers or unbelievers, confessors or deniers of the Lord. Now, by the Apostle's testimony, to confess Him truly is impossible but by the Holy Ghost (Pridham).

The Holy Spirit, the divine Person, is on earth and manifests His power in the body of Christ, the Church. The Lord Jesus having accomplished redemption, believers on His name are ransomed and cleansed by His blood, and united to Him, as His body, and the Holy Spirit dwells in each member of this body. It is through the Spirit that communion with the Head is realized and maintained. In His gifts the presence of the Spirit of God is therefore manifested in the members of the body. This is now more fully treated in this chapter. In verses 4-6 we hear of the Spirit, the Lord, and God; the same Spirit—the same Lord, and the same God. Yet there is not a division into three classes of gifts, but the same thing is seen in three relations. The diversities of gifts are by the same Spirit; through Him they are bestowed. These gifts are in relation to the Lord; they are to be used in ministries, that is, in service for the Lord, under whom and for whose glory these gifts are to be used. And the whole operations are of God, who worketh all in all. All this is of course confined to the members of the body of Christ.

"But the manifestation of the Spirit is given to every man (a true believer) for profit." The gift bestowed upon one member is for the whole body, all are to profit by it. The possession of a gift makes the believer a debtor to the other members of Christ. Nine gifts by the same Spirit are mentioned. They are the following: The word of wisdom; the word of knowledge; faith; the gift of healing; the working of miracles; prophecy; discerning of spirits; tongues and interpretations of tongues.

It will be seen that the miraculous sign-gifts hold a secondary place, the last being speaking in tongues and their interpretations. The word of wisdom stands at the head of these gifts and is followed by the word of knowledge. They stand for the gifts to understand the deep things of God and to impart them unto others. It means a spiritual apprehension of the truth of God in all its phases and the power to communicate this truth to others. The gift of faith is a special endowment of confidence in God and His promises, which enables the possessor to lay hold on God and accomplish great things. All believers have faith and live by faith. The gift of healing and the working of miracles, were sign-gifts for the inauguration of the Christian dispensation. There is no intimation that these miraculous gifts were to continue in the Church throughout this age.

In Ephesians, the highest revelation concerning the body of Christ, the permanent gifts for the edifying of the body are mentioned, but gifts of healing, working miracles or speaking in tongues are omitted. Nor is there a promise in the Word that those extraordinary gifts are to be restored by the Spirit of God to the Church before the Lord comes for His saints. Signs and miracles will take place at the close of this age, but they are the lying things of Satan (2 Thess. 2).

Anything which claims to be a restoration of miraculous gifts, as it is the case among certain sects, must be looked upon with grave suspicion. Besides prophecy and the discerning of spirits (trying the spirits whether they are of God) the gift of tongues and their interpretation are mentioned. As we find later the Corinthians, in their bad spiritual state, esteemed the gift of tongues the highest; the Spirit of God, however, gives to it an inferior place. They were almost destitute of the exercise of the highest gift of wisdom and knowledge and magnified what was for outward demonstration, because it exalted themselves.

The exercise of the gift of healing and similar gifts was never discretional. They were manifested only in their fitting season, and could only work effectually by the immediate will of God. Power is His, and always in His hands. If Trophimus was sick, the wish of Paul could not restore him. Yet the believer can come to the Lord in prayer and claim His power. Our refuge in time of need must be sought, not in God's gifts, but in the faithfulness of the Giver.

Of much importance is verse 13. "For in one Spirit are we all baptised into one body, whether we be Jews or Gentiles, whether we be bond or free; and have been all made to drink into one Spirit." This refers to the formation of the body. The baptism mentioned in this verse is not water-baptism. Water baptism does not save nor can this ordinance put any one as a member into the true Church, the one body. The baptism is the baptism of the Spirit. It took place on the day of Pentecost. On that day the Spirit was poured out and while He filled every believer, He also united them into one body. Then the body of Christ was formed once for all by this baptism. Since that day whenever a sinner trusts in Christ he is at once joined to that body and shares in the one Spirit. Many Christians speak of repeated baptisms by the Spirit and refer to certain experiences as being new baptisms. In the light of this verse all this is incorrect. Scripture knows only one baptism. And all believers drink of one Spirit; they are all made partakers of one and the same Spirit.

This body which was called into existence by the Spirit on the day of Pentecost is not one member, but many. There are many members, yet but one body. And the different members in that body are dependent the one on the other, and have need of each other, just as it is in the human body. And God hath set the members every one of them in the body as it hath pleased Him. Each member has his own place with a gift, a function, which is suitable for it. Nothing in this body is left to man himself. It is His Church and God orders the place of each and of all in that body. Therefore, self-choosing is excluded. How all this is marred, if not wholly forgotten, in the professing Church, is only too evident. The conditions to-day, the divisions in the body, the false doctrines and unscriptural practices throughout Christendom, are plainly the result of having set aside the truth concerning the one body.

And those members of the body, which seem to be more feeble, are necessary. "And those members of the body which we think to be less honorable, upon these we bestow more abundant honor; and our comely parts have more abundant comeliness. For our comely parts have no need; but God has tempered the body together, having given more abundant honor to that part which lacked." As it is in the human body, so also is it in the body of Christ. There was to be no self-exaltation, as it undoubtedly was among the Corinthians on account of the gifts which they had so abundantly, especially the sign-gifts. They looked down upon other members who were less prominent. And this was responsible for the threatening division in the body. The blessed injunction is that the members should have the same care one for another, then there would be no schism in the body.

If one member suffers, all suffer, because they are in one body indwelt and united by the same Spirit; and if one member be honored, all rejoice with it. And this body is the body of Christ; He is the head of the body and wants to manifest Himself through His body. This is the Church collectively, but the same are the members severally. The order of how God has bestowed gifts follows (verse 28). Again the gift of tongues, in which the Corinthians abounded, on account of which grave disorders and disturbances had come in, is put last.

"And the Corinthians then, as others of late, had to hear, whether they heeded or not, that those striking displays of power in which they found their childish surprise and delight, like the world without, were not the highest, that there were gifts relatively first and second and third, the last-named being the very one they had been abusing to no small disorder and hindrance of edification in the assembly."

Verses 29-30 show another important principle. All cannot be apostles, prophets, leaders, workers of miracles, etc. God does not bestow all these different gifts upon one individual. They are distributed as it pleases Him, to each member as He sees fit. Ministry in the body of Christ is the exercise of a gift. The Corinthians in their puffed up condition had a selfish ambition to have all these gifts concentrated in every member.

"The Corinthians' folly was not greater in wishing all the gifts to be in each and all the saints, than the modern theory of arrogating all, as far as public ministration goes, to a single official. The one was ignorant vanity before the truth was fully revealed in a written form; the other is more guilty presumption in presence of the acknowledged word of God, which condemns every departure from His principles, and the great fact of the one body with its many members, wherein the Holy Spirit works to glorify the Lord Jesus" (W. Kelly).

He tells them to covet earnestly the best gifts and he would show unto them a more excellent way. This more excellent way is the way of love of which we hear in the next chapter.

3. The Need and Superiority of Love

CHAPTER 13

1. The pre-eminence of love (13:1-3)
2. Love described in its characteristics (13:4-7)
3. Love never faileth: its permanence (13:8-13)

This chapter is a most blessed exaltation of love. The word "charity" is an unfortunate mistranslation. The Greek word for love used in the New Testament was never used by the Greek heathen classical writers. In its meaning it was unknown among the Gentiles. God is love. As His people, members of His body, we know the love of God manifested in the gift of God's well-beloved Son. And this love is shed abroad in the hearts of the children of God. "Beloved, let us love one another, for love is of God; and every one that loveth is born of God and knoweth God." "Beloved, if God so loved us, we ought also to love one another . . . if we love one another, God dwelleth in us, and His love is perfected in us" (1 John 4:7, 11-12).

The divine nature bestowed by the Spirit of God is a holy nature and a nature which posseseth in it the love of God. Love is therefore the divine nature in its manifestation. And this wonderful love, the divine love, is to be manifested in the body of Christ. It is the true motive for all ministry. The Corinthians in their worldly, self-seeking, ambitious spirit, in their use of the gifts, had not followed this more excellent way. The divisions among them and their self-exaltation and self-confidence were the result of not being governed by love. If love had been supreme in the Corinthian church, neither sectarianism, nor careless walk, nor indifference to sin of others and toleration of evil, nor going before a heathen judge, nor high-minded pretensions, nor the desecration of the Lord's Supper, nor a false practise of Christian liberty, could have prospered. Love surpasses everything. It is a far better thing than any gift. Very significantly the apostle begins with the gift, as already pointed out, of the smallest value. Speaking with the tongues of men and of angels without love is like sounding brass, or a tinkling cymbal.

(For a number of years movements have started which claim to be a new Pentecost. The gift of tongues is the leading feature. They go by different names—Apostolic Faith—Pentecostal Faith—Latter-Day Reign, etc. But is it the work of the Holy Spirit? The divisions which exist in these movements, the unscriptural teachings which are held by some of them and the lack of love, besides other characteristics are not the marks of the energy and power of God's Spirit.)

Prophecy, the understanding of all mysteries, all knowledge, all wonder-working faith and even the giving up of all things and martyrdom, are valueless without love. God looks for love; it is of God, and loving is conformity to God. It is a solemn warning that true gifts may be possessed without a manifestation of love.

Many pages could be filled with a closer examination of the different characteristics of divine love as given by the apostle. If we study the blessed life the Son of God lived down here we shall find how He manifested this love in His life among the children of men. The fifteen brief, but deep, descriptions of love should be the standing mirror of self-judgment for all God's children. To read these pithy sentences in His presence at the close of each day and apply them as a test, is a wholesome exercise.

The opening descriptions are all of a passive character, and show that love demands the renunciation of self. Longsuffering and kindness head the list. These are the attributes of our loving God and Father, and we are to imitate Him as His children and forbear one another in love. Love does not envy. God does not envy. Envy is of Satan; all self-seeking has its origin in pride, which is the crime of the devil (1 Tim. 3:6). Love vaunteth not itself. It never seeks the applause of men. Self-display is self-love. True love is not puffed up. Love doth not behave itself unseemly. Its ornaments are meekness, modesty and unobtrusiveness. It seeketh not its own; it is self-neglect and is expressed in devotion to others. Nor is it easily provoked, for self-consciousness and self-seeking being absent, sensitiveness becomes impossible. Love thinketh no evil. The better translation is, "does not impute evil." It rather hides than exposes. Furthermore, love "rejoiceth not in iniquity but rejoiceth with the truth." The last four characteristics show its positive energy. It beareth all things—it puts up with anything but that which is wrong and sinful; believeth all things; it does not suspect, therefore it hopeth all things and also endureth all things. Finally the permanence of love is stated. Prophecies, tongues and knowledge will fail, cease and pass away. Love never. It is abiding eternal, the greatest of all.

4. Prophecy and Speaking with a Tongue

CHAPTER 14

1. Prophecy the better gift (14:1-13)
2. Intelligibility demanded (14:14-25)
3. Practical instructions for the public use of these gifts (14:26-40)

It is evident from the contents of this chapter that the Corinthians had unduly magnified the gift of speaking in a strange tongue. It had a spectacular aspect which they enjoyed. He therefore shows them that the gift of prophecy is more to be coveted than speaking in an unknown tongue. The speaking in an unknown tongue is intelligible to God, but he that prophesieth speaketh unto men to edification, exhortation and comfort. While the apostle does not deny the value of speaking with tongues, he would rather that they prophesied "for greater is he that prophesieth than he that speaketh with tongues." Speaking with tongues edifies the speaker alone but prophecy edifies the church. What is the profit in speaking with an unknown tongue to believers unless the tongue has a real meaning? Musical instruments, which give forth sound, like a pipe or an harp, have no meaning whatever unless there be distinction in the tunes. Thus he shows the uselessness of the gift of tongues for edification unless the tongue is intelligible to all. "Even so ye, for as much as ye are zealous of spiritual gifts, seek that ye may excel to the edifying of the church. Wherefore let him that speaketh in an unknown tongue pray that he may interpret."

What the speaking in tongues really was we do not know positively. It was probably an ecstatic form of speech, or some foreign language. As a distinctive gift it has passed away, notwithstanding the fact that from time to time the restoration of this sign-gift has been claimed. (During the Middle Ages, at the time of the Wesley's, during the days of Edward Irving, when it was proven to emanate from evil spirits, and in our own days, thousands claim to possess it.) But what is prophesying? In the Old Testament prophecy, it was foretelling coming events. In the New Testament, it has a different meaning. It is not foretelling, but forthtelling. It is one who is speaking as from God and for God; the one who possesses this gift must therefore be in communication with God through the Spirit so as to be able to communicate to others His mind and His will. The exercise of this gift necessitates a close walk with God. This gift the apostle desired the Corinthians to have. Instead the Corinthians had the inferior gift, which they valued on account of the display and perhaps the mysteriousness of it.

(The people in our own times who profess to have received this sign-gift claim that it is an evidence of having received the "baptism" of the Spirit, which, as we have already pointed out, is in itself unscriptural. They are on ground on which they are open to the subtle influences of Satan's power.

The apostle also states that he spoke with tongues more than they did. "Yet in the church I had rather speak five words with understanding, that by my voice I might teach others also, than ten thousand words in an unknown tongue." From all these regulations and statements we learn that the use of this gift was rather tolerated than commended (verse 39) to the churches because it was a hindrance rather than a help to the needed thing, which is edification in love. Futhermore, tongues were for a sign to the unbelievers. Prophesying is for the believers. "If therefore the whole church be come together into one place and all speak with tongues and there come in those that are unlearned, or unbelievers, will they not say that you are mad?"

It is a fact that in the meetings of the modern advocates of the gift of tongues often the greatest disorder prevails. Men and women falling down in convulsions, hysterical laughter, unpleasant shrieks, and other demonstrations have not been uncommon, so that an unbeliever would be perfectly right to pass the verdict "they are mad." It is different with prophesying. "But if all prophesy, and there come in one that believeth not, or is unlearned, he is convinced of all, he is judged of all. And thus are the secrets of his heart made manifest; and so falling down on his face he will worship God, declaring that God is truly among you."

The meetings of the saints of God coming together in His Name and gathered to that name must be characterized by quietness and order. "For God is not the author of confusion (tumult, unquietness), but of peace, as in all churches of the saints." All things must be done decently and in order (verse 40). Another important instruction is given in verses 34-35. "Let your women keep silence in the churches, for it is not permitted unto them to speak; but they are commanded to be under obedience, as also saith the law. And if they will learn anything, let them ask their husbands at home, for it is shame for women to speak in the church." Some have said that this demand of the apostle was given solely to the Corinthians, because women were forward in the church and that it does not apply to our days. This is a serious mistake. Nor are these words merely the words of the Apostle Paul, as some have claimed. It is God's Word and the command is the command of the Holy Spirit. The public ministry of women is not permitted by the Spirit of God.

The Word of God discountenances a prominent public ministry of women as inconsistent with the original law of creation, and with the modesty and meekness which are the woman's chief adorning in the sight of God. What mischief, confusion, and worse things have resulted from disobeying this divine command. Woman leaving the sphere assigned to her by the Creator and the Redeemer is stepping on dangerous ground. In connection with the statement, "A woman suffer not to teach, nor to usurp authority over the man, but to be in silence," the apostle calls attention to the fact "Adam was not deceived, but the woman being deceived was in transgression" (1 Tim. 2:12-13). The originators and leaders of the most damnable heresies of the latter times such as Christian Science, theosophy, and spiritism are women. But woman has a ministry and can exercise her gifts as a member of the body of Christ.

(Again we call attention to the modern gift of tongues, the Pentecostal movements. Women are prominent among them. The divine command "let your women keep silence in the churches" is disregarded by them, while they claim obedience to the Word and a return to apostolic faith and practice.)

"The woman's sphere of liberty, and, one may say, sovereignty, is at home; that is to say, it is private and not public. It must not be thought that this does not give ample scope for the exercise of gifts of whatever kind. If there were only more of the cultivation on the woman's part of that which belongs really to her sphere, how fruitful would be the exercise of the gift with which God has endowed her and how many places would be open to her which men, by reason of their being men, could not in the same way fill! This in relation to children, it is at once evident; with the younger children, the woman is still the best and the nature-ordained teacher. God has placed the babe in its mother's arms and not its father's; and this does not mean that the woman's sphere is only in her own family. There are countless families to which her sex will introduce her, and where she may find herself fully at home and abundant profit and recompense of her work. So, through the wives, women have access in this way to an indefinite sphere of occupation for varied blessing. The wife is the heart-centre of the household, and the ability thus to reach the wife in a way that women certainly can do far beyond others is an immense privilege and responsibility entrusted to her. Would that there were more realization of this!" (*Numerical Bible*)

III. Resurrection and the Hope of the Church and Conclusion (15—16)

1. Resurrection and the Hope of the Church

CHAPTER 15

1. The gospel and the resurrection of Christ (15:1-11)
2. If Christ were not raised—then what? (15:12-19)
3. Christ, the first-fruits and what follows (15:20-28)
4. Further practical arguments about resurrection (15:29-34)
5. Concerning the resurrection of the body (15:35-49)
6. The coming of the Lord and the victory (15:50-58)

The third section lifts us higher and brings us to the summit of this Epistle. We have seen the Church in relation to the world, the Church as the body of Christ and now we see the consummation, the destiny of the Church in resurrection glory. From this chapter we learn that some members of the Corinthian church said "there is no resurrection of the dead" (verse 12). The denial of this fundamental doctrine of the faith brought forth this blessed portion of the Epistle concerning resurrection and the coming of the Lord.

The first thing mentioned in opening up this subject is the gospel which Paul had preached to the Corinthians, which they had received and wherein they stood. This is the order: The preaching of the gospel, the good news, its reception by faith, followed by the standing in salvation and the enjoyment of it. By this gospel is salvation as it is so fully revealed in the Epistle to the Romans. The Apostle Paul had delivered unto them, which he himself had received from the Lord (Gal. 1:11-12). The three great facts according to the Scriptures (the Old Testament Scriptures) are: (1) Christ died for our sins. The death of Christ, the cross and the mighty work accomplished there, is the great foundation. The entire Old Testament revealed in many ways this fundamental fact without which there would be and could be no redemption. (2) He was buried. He expired as to the body on the cross. The death of Christ was real and not a deception. And His burial also has a meaning in the gospel (Romans 6:4). And the third great fact of the gospel, "He rose again the third day according to the Scriptures." This is the great truth of this chapter, a truth, if denied, must result in the complete collapse of the gospel. And His resurrection had been foretold by Himself as well as by the Scriptures. (See Genesis 22:4 and Hebrews 11:17-19; Psalm 16.) This great truth, the enemy has always hated. The lying inventions of the Jews are well known to every reader of the gospel (Matt. 28:11-15). In Corinth this truth was being denied, and in our own days those who deny the physical resurrection of the Lord Jesus are ever on the increase in the professing Church. They occupy leading pulpits and are prominent in institutions of learning.

The apostle brings forth a number of witnesses, but he does not mention the women who play such an important part in the resurrection account of the Gospel. He gives only a number of witnesses, all men, who furnish an unanswerable evidence. Unbelievers have often attempted to trace the belief in the resurrection of our Lord to the women. Cephas is mentioned first. "But go your way, tell His disciples and Peter," had been the angelic instruction on the resurrection morning. And Peter who had so shamefully denied Him had seen the Risen One. "The Lord is risen indeed and hath appeared unto Simon" (Luke 24:34). On the day of Pentecost he became the wonderful witness of the risen Christ. That He appeared first to Simon Peter shows His infinite grace.

Then He was seen of the twelve. Luke 24:36-48 speaks of the eleven; the twelfth had gone to his awful place. But the passage in Luke also informs us that others were with them when the Lord appeared. The eleven were gathered together, and those that were with them (Luke 24:33). Probably Matthias, the one added to the apostolate (Acts 1:26), was in that company. "After that He was seen of above five hundred brethren at once, of whom the greater part remain unto the present, but some are fallen asleep." This was probably in Galilee. And how could such a large number of men be deceived together, or concoct a falsehood? It is an impossibility. Sooner or later, if they had all agreed to deceive the world, the fraud would have been discovered. He was also seen by James and by all the apostles. Last of all he was seen by the Apostle Paul on the road to Damascus, where as the blind persecutor of the Church, the chief of sinners, he beheld Him in the glory light. He was like one born out of due season. He was an untimely birth. He was in his experience a type of the nation to which he belonged. As he saw Christ in glory so will the remnant of Israel behold Him at the time of His second coming. He was therefore a firstfruit of the nation.

(The correct meaning of the Greek word "ektroma" seems to point to a child born from a dead mother, by what is called the Caesarian operation. The dead Jewish system gave birth to the chosen vessel who was to become what Israel should have been, and yet will be, when the mystery of the present dispensation is complete. (Rom. 11:25-27)

The Apostle Paul is one of the greatest witnesses to the resurrection of the Lord Jesus. The argument which follows (verses 12-19) is so clear and powerful that no comment is needed. If Christ is not risen from the dead, if it were true what some said in Corinth "there is no resurrection of the dead"—then what? The answer is fearful, for it strips the Christian of everything. "Your faith is vain; you are yet in your sins; your loved ones who died in Christ are perished, gone forever; we are of all men most miserable." And into this terrible pit the men who deny this fundamental doctrine are leading those who accept this damnable heresy (2 Peter 2:1).

But triumphant is the incontrovertible fact, "Christ is risen from among the dead"; and more than that, "He is become the firstfruit of them that slept." As He was raised, not as we have it in the authorized version "from the dead," but "from among the dead," so will there be in the future an "out-resurrection from among the dead," which is the first resurrection of all those who are Christ's. A general resurrection is no more taught in the Bible than a general judgment. By man came death (the first Adam) by man also is the resurrection of the dead (by the last Adam, Christ). Verse 22 does not teach a universal salvation. Those who will be made alive are those who are "in Christ." But only such are in Christ, who have believed on Him and were born again. Verses 20-28, unfold the successive stages in the accomplishment of God's purposes. (1) The resurrection of Christ, then after the purpose of the present age is accomplished. (2) His second coming (verse 23). (3) The resurrection of those who belong to Him. (4) The overthrow of all His enemies and the establishment of His kingly and glorious rule over the earth. (5) His delivering up the kingdom to God that God may be all in all.

Verses 29-34 continue the reasoning on the fatal results if there were no resurrection. Verse 29 connects with verse 19 and what is between, verses 20-28, form a parenthesis. What then is the value of Christian suffering, self-denial, trial and persecution if there were no resurrection? This connection with the previous argument helps us to understand the much disputed statement "else what shall they do which are baptized for the dead, if the dead rise not at all? Why are they then baptized for the dead?" It is said that some thirty different interpretations of this statement are in existence, most of them so fanciful and strained that they merit no further mention. Some say it meant those who were about to be baptized and others believe it has a meaning concerning those who had relatives who had died unbaptized. There is no need of inventing these theories. If we look at it in the most simple way the difficulty disappears. They had been baptized and taken the place as being dead with Christ. In this sense they had been baptized for the dead. But if the dead rise not, then this ordinance, which is so closely connected in a symbolical way with death and resurrection, has no meaning and value at all.

"Baptized, then, for the dead is to become a Christian with the view fixed on those who have fallen asleep in Christ, and particularly as being slain for Him, taking one's portion with the dead, yea, with the dead Christ; it is the very meaning of baptism (Rom. 6). How senseless if they do not rise! As in 1 Thessalonians 4, the subject, while speaking of all Christians, is looked at in the same way. The word translated 'for' is frequently used in these epistles for 'in view of,' 'with reference to' " (*Synopsis of the Bible*).

Then those who had been affected by these doubts about resurrection asked questions concerning the resurrection of the body and the process of resurrection. How are the dead raised? And with what body do they come? But he brands as folly their doubting reasonings. There are of course, difficulties for reason but none for faith. If God's omnipotent power is admitted and believed every difficulty vanishes. Their difficulties and objections were not of faith. Nature and God's works give abundant evidence of the resurrection of the body. There will be in resurrection a continuity of identity.

"They sowed but bare grain, whether wheat or any other, but they knew quite well that that grain was not to continue grain, but that it would soon be clothed with a body very different from that which it had when sown in the earth. God gave it the body that He had willed for it, and to every seed its own kind of body. Thus, the individuality of what was sown was maintained all through, in spite of disorganization. God in it, as in innumerable cases in nature, has stamped things everywhere with His own stamp of resurrection. Things are in His hand. You may call the process natural because you are so familiar with it, because it is so constantly taking place under your eyes. All the same, God is working in it and through it.

"And what advantage would it have, if there were no resurrection, by dying daily, denying self, passing through all kinds of trials, suffering persecution and fighting, as Paul had done at Ephesus, with wild beasts? If there were no resurrection, then man is like the beast: let us eat and drink, for tomorrow we die. That which looks so merely lifeless has, nevertheless, in itself the determination of its future life. No seed produces anything else, but its own kind, and yet how different is that which springs out of it from the seed out of which it springs!" (*Numerical Bible*)

True from all this we learn that the resurrection of the same body is promised and while its identity is preserved it will be a different body at the same time. So then is the resurrection of the dead.

(All through this resurrection chapter only the resurrection of believers is in view. Nothing is said about the resurrection of the wicked dead. They too will be raised as to the body to exist forever in the dreadful condition of eternal punishment.)

It is sown in corruption; it is raised in incorruption. It is sown in dishonor; it is raised in glory; it is sown in weakness; it is raised in power; it is sown a natural body; it is raised a spiritual body. What kind of a body will it be, this spiritual body? Scripture gives the answer. "Who shall change our body of humiliation that it may be fashioned like unto His glorious body, according to the working whereby He is able even to subdue all things unto Himself" (Phil. 3:21). We shall be like Him for we shall see Him as He is.

Now our blessed Lord was not raised from the dead with an ethereal, airy body. His was a real human body of flesh and bones. He ate in the presence of His disciples; He was able to take food, though He needed none. He was capable of passing through closed doors and was in nowise limited by earthly conditions, such as space. And even so will be the spiritual body of the risen believers. Not a spirit phantom, but a spiritual body in its adaptation to the spirit. As we have now a natural body which is suited for an earth-life, so the believer shall have a body suited for a glory-life. We shall be like Him to be with Him in eternal glory and in these wonderful bodies we shall rule and reign with Him.

"Now this I say, brethren, that flesh and blood cannot inherit the kingdom of God; neither doth corruption inherit incorruption" (verse 50). It simply means that man as he is here below cannot inherit God's kingdom. It does not mean the kingdom which will some day be established on earth in which converted Israel and converted nations will be the subjects. It means the kingdom of God on the other side of death. The kingdom on earth for a thousand years will be an earthly thing; the kingdom mentioned in this verse is the kingdom of God in glory.

"The blood applies to the present life. It is the vehicle of change. It is that which implies the need of continual sustenance and renewal. A body which needs no renewal cannot need blood to renew it, and thus the Lord speaks of Himself as risen from the dead, not as having flesh and blood, but as having flesh and bones. "A spirit hath not flesh and bones," He says, "as ye see Me have." He has poured out His blood and left it with the earthly life that He had lived. He has entered upon a new sphere, retaining all that makes Him truly man, but not the conditions of the old earthly life. The conditions are changed. Flesh and blood are not suited for the kingdom of God in this sense of it. He is not, of course, in the least implying that there is any evil in flesh and blood."

And what a change it will be for God's redeemed people to receive these wonderful bodies of glory and enter into the kingdom of God in glory! And when will it come? Paul writes of a mystery.

(The teachers who say that there is no such thing as a coming of the Lord for His saints may well pause at this word "mystery." They teach that this coming here, when the dead shall be raised and living believers shall be changed, is the visible coming of Christ at the end of the great tribulation. But this visible coming is the revelation which is found in the entire Old Testament prophetic Word. It was and is not a mystery. But the coming of the Lord for His saints, who are to be caught up in clouds to meet Him in the air, is a *new* revelation, unknown in former ages.)

We shall not all sleep (die), but we shall be changed. It will be a sudden thing. In a moment, in the twinkling of an eye. It will be at the last trump. This trumpet has nothing whatever to do with the seventh trumpet in Revelation. Before any trumpet has sounded, before the Lamb of God, the Lion of the Tribe of Judah, opens the seals, He comes for His saints "in a moment, in the twinkling of an eye."

The trumpet is a military term. The first trumpet bade the armies to arise and be ready; the last trumpet commanded them to depart, it was the signal to march. When that shout (1 Thess. 4:13-18) comes from the air and He comes for His saints, the dead (the dead in Christ, only those who believed) will be raised incorruptible. And "*we* shall be changed." The apostle did not write "*they*" shall be changed. He expected not death, but the blessed Hope for himself and the Corinthians was the change in a moment, in the twinkling of an eye, which means translation and not death. He speaks of the dead when he writes "for this corruption must put on incorruption." He speaks of living believers in these words: "this mortal must put on immortality." This gives the true meaning of Romans 8:11. The coming of the Lord is the hope of the Church. And then we have the shout of victory. And what manner of lives we should live and what manner of service should be ours in view of such a destiny, such glory, which in a moment, in the twinkling of an eye, may burst upon us! "Therefore, my beloved brethren, be ye stedfast, unmoveable, always abounding in the work of the Lord, forasmuch as ye know that your labor is not vain in the Lord."

2. Exhortations and Conclusion

CHAPTER 16

1. Concerning collections (16:1-4)
2. Ministry (16:5-18)
3. Greetings (16:19-24)

First, in concluding this Epistle, he writes them about collections for the saints. The same directions, he has given to the assemblies in Galatia. The collection for the saints was to be taken on the first day of the week in connection with the remembrance of Him who had said, "it is more blessed to give than to receive." He did not want to have any collections when he came, His presence might have influenced them in some way and he wanted to avoid this. How different is the collection-system in the professing church of to-day! No unsaved person should be permitted to give anything for the Lord's work; only the saints can give acceptably. It is an unscriptural thing to go to the world, which lieth in the wicked one, and ask support and help from the unregenerated. God's blessing cannot rest upon this.

(Other unscriptural methods are those which raise funds by entertainments, suppers, etc., and then the appeals which are often made by evangelists and others, the influences which are used to obtain the largest results! All this is condemned by the simple and brief instruction about collections in this chapter.)

Then he writes of his plans. He was tarrying in Ephesus until Pentecost. A great and effectual door had been opened unto him and there were many adversaries. It is still so. Whenever the Lord opens a door and His Spirit works we may well expect the opposition of the adversary. But may we also remember His gracious promise to those who are in Philadelphian condition of soul (Rev. 3:7). If we have a little strength, if we keep His Word and do not deny His Name, He will still open doors and no power can shut them. He will keep the door of service open as long as it pleases Him.

Solemn is the final statement after the greetings. "If any man love not the Lord Jesus, let him be Anathema Maranatha. The words "Anathema Maranatha" mean "Accursed—Our Lord cometh." And accursed will be any man who has rejected the love and the gospel of the Lord Jesus Christ. It shows that some in the Corinthian assembly may have been mere professing Christians without ever having tasted the love of Christ. Then the final word "The grace of our Lord Jesus be with you. My love be with you all in Christ Jesus."

THE SECOND EPISTLE TO THE
CORINTHIANS

Introduction

This second Epistle is inseparably connected with the first Paul had written to the Corinthians. Its authorship is undoubted, for no other Epistle bears such distinctive marks of the author and brings out all which characterized him as a servant of the Lord Jesus Christ. From critical sides it is claimed that between the first and second Epistles, there must have been another letter of the Apostle, more severe in tone than the first Epistle. This letter the critics maintain was lost. This supposition is mostly founded on chapter 2:3-4 and chapter 7:8. The statements made by the apostle in these passages, it is argued, cannot be explained by the message of the first Epistle and the situation described is altogether too strong to have been created by the first Epistle. But there is no need to invent an intermediate letter to explain the tone and burden of this second Epistle. The first Epistle contains sufficient material to produce the effects in the Corinthians and also in the mind and heart of the apostle of which he writes in the above passages. 1 Cor. 4:18-21; 5:1-8; 6:5-8; 11:17-22; and 15:35-36, account fully for the great apostle's solicitude and emotions.

How the Second Epistle Originated

After the first Epistle had been written and delivered to the Corinthians, Paul seemed to have been greatly troubled in his mind about how the church in Corinth would receive and treat his inspired communication. The first Epistle had been written with many tears and deep soul-exercise. He knew that it would make them sorry, yet he was in doubt and unrest about it all. Titus had evidently been sent by the apostle to Corinth to ascertain the truth about this matter and to find out what effect the first Epistle had upon the Corinthians. Others think that Timotheus had first returned from Corinth and had brought very painful news, which greatly increased the anxiety of Paul and he sent, therefore, another letter through Titus to the Corinthians (the letter which it is claimed was lost). However, this is only a conjecture.

At the time of writing this Epistle, Paul had left the province Asia (2 Cor. 1:8) where he had been in some great peril. In leaving Asia he had come by Troas, where the Lord had opened a door for him to preach the Gospel (2 Cor. 2:12). In Troas he fully expected to meet Titus and receive the much longed for report from the Corinthian Church. "I had no rest in my spirit, because I found not Titus my brother" (2:13). He therefore sailed to Macedonia. It was in Macedonia where Titus met him and told Paul about his visit to Corinth. "For when we were come into Macedonia, our flesh had no rest, but we were troubled on every side; without were fightings, within were fears. Nevertheless God, that comforteth those that are cast down, comforted us by the coming of Titus; and not by his coming only, but by the consolation wherewith he was comforted in you, when he told us of your earnest desire, your mourning, your fervent mind toward me; so that I rejoiced the more" (2 Cor. 7:5-7). The tidings which Titus brought were in the main good tidings. They had mourned over the wrong which the first letter had pointed out and they had repented; however, it is also clear that not all had been settled. There were still his enemies who attacked him and they became evidently more bitter against him on account of the strong letter he had written to the church. He wrote therefore, this second Epistle in which he expresses the comfort which the news of their repentance had brought him, but in which he also very strongly defends his personal character and his apostolic authority.

This establishes beyond controversy the fact that the Epistle was written in Macedonia. The exact place can hardly be ascertained. The note at the end of the Epistle "written from Philippi" is simply traditional. It is more likely that he spent some time in Thessalonica. The time when this second Epistle was written must have been the early autumn of 57, A.D.

The Contents and Characteristics

That in many ways there is a vast difference in the two Epistles to the Corinthians cannot escape even a superficial reader. The second epistle is a far more personal one than the first and there is less doctrinal matter mentioned. One of the leading characteristics is the rapid transitions, which emanated not from the moods of the great man of God, but from the deep exercises of his soul. Anxiety, indignation, resentment, trust and love are linked together in rapid succession. A critic begins his remarks on this Epistle with the following words "Of all Paul's Epistles this is the most obscure. It is a veritable cloudland." But another writer expresses the value of this Epistle in a true way, when he says "What an admirable Epistle is the second to the Corinthians! How full of affections! He joys and is sorry; he grieves and he glories: never was there such care of a flock expressed, save by the great Shepherd, who first shed tears over Jerusalem and afterward blood." Dean Alford remarks on this grand document: "In no other Epistle are matter and style so various, and so rapidly shifting from one character to another. Consolation and rebuke, gentleness and severity, earnestness and irony, succeed one another at very short intervals and without notice." Still another gives a good summary of the contents of this Epistle.

"Personal experience, and this used for the help of others in their trials; the work of the Lord in all its varieties, with the action of the Holy Ghost answering to it; the truth of God in its distinctive shape and highest forms, or the glory of Christ contrasted with the Spirit, in former days hidden under the letter; the walk and service which befit such revelations of grace; the affections called into action by all this in the midst of sorrow and suffering, with evil abounding and grace much more abounding; the trials and wants of saints, calling out the loving remembrance of others; the opposition of self-seeking men, employed of the enemy to hinder the blessing of saints and to lower the glory of Christ, to distract the weak and give scope for unscrupulous activity; but on the other hand the energy of the Holy Ghost working not only to vouchsafe heavenly visions, and so give faith its object, but to manifest Christ in weakness and suffering where the power of Christ may rest, are all brought out with remarkable force and fulness."

The Apostle's Self-Defence

While the Epistle to the Galatians is the defence of the doctrine of the gospel against false teachers, the second Epistle to the Corinthians is the defence of his own personal character, his apostolic authority, his motives and his ministry. His adversaries, judaizing teachers and others, who were continuing the sectarian spirit, had charged him with many things, slandering his character and belittling his apostolic authority and efficiency. What they had spoken against him we learn from the Epistle itself. They depreciated his person. "For his letters, they say, are weighty and powerful, but his bodily presence is weak, and his speech contemptible" (10:10). "Though I be rude in speech (as they had accused him) yet not in knowledge" (11:6). The reason why he speaks in this Epistle so much of his self-sacrifice, his zeal, his sincerity, his manly courage, his untiring service and his many sufferings, is that he had been attacked and belittled in all these things. It is well known that Paul means "little." Saul had been changed to Paul, the little one. Unlike his namesake in the Old Testament, King Saul, whom Samuel had rebuked, with the words "when thou wast little in thine own eyes," the great apostle was little and remained little in his own estimation, the mark of every true servant of Christ. He called himself "less than the least of all saints" (Ephes. 3:8). Yet in this Epistle he is forced to boast in order to vindicate his character and ministry. In chapter 12:11 we read "I am become a fool in glorying; ye have compelled me; for I ought to have been commanded of you; for in nothing am I behind the very chiefest apostle, though I be nothing." Thirty-one times he speaks of glorying or boasting and that because he was compelled to do so. In this way we learn of some new things which happened in the life of the Apostle Paul which are unrecorded elsewhere. These are: his escape from Damascus in a basket (11:32-33); his great experience in being caught up to the third heaven (12:1-4); his thorn in the flesh (12:7, etc.); his remarkable sufferings and privations (11:23-27). The fact that these experiences were not mentioned by him till he was compelled to do so and to show that, if he wanted to boast in something, he had abundant reasons for doing so, manifests his great humility.

True Ministry

The Epistle is a wonderful mine in spiritual and practical truths. The one great truth which may be traced throughout the entire Epistle is the ministry in the body of Christ, the Church. And the apostle himself in making his self-defence is a pattern of what true ministry in the body of Christ is and what it means. Here are blessed, spiritual lessons and principles which apply to God's true children at all times. All who desire to be devoted to the Lord Jesus Christ in these days, need these practical truths. May it please God to lead us into them and enable us by His grace to walk in His truth.

The Division of Second Corinthians

We divide this Epistle into three parts, which is the most satisfactory division.

I. TRUE MINISTRY AS MANIFESTED IN THE LIFE AND CHARACTER OF THE APOSTLE (Chapters 1—7)

1. **The Introduction** (1:1-7)
2. **Paul's Experience and Explanations** (1:8-24)
3. **His Deep Exercise Concerning Them** (2)
4. **The Ministry of the New Covenant as Contrasted with the Old** (3)
5. **The Character of the True Ministry** (4)
6. **Concerning the Future: The Ministry of Reconciliation** (5)
7. **Ministry in Connection with Testings and Trials** (6:1-13)
8. **The Apostle's Appeals and Rejoicing** (6:14—7)

II. THE MINISTRY OF GIVING (Chapters 8—9)

1. **The Examples and Principles of Giving** (8)
2. **Exhortation and Encouragement** (9)

III. THE APOSTLE'S SELF-DEFENCE AND VINDICATION (Chapters 10—13)

1. **The Defence of His Authority** (10)
2. **Answering His Adversaries and His Boasting** (11)
3. **Revelations in which He Might Glory and the Marks of His Apostleship** (12)
4. **Still Absent, Yet Coming and the Conclusion** (13)

Analysis and Annotations

I. True Ministry as Manifested in the Life and Character of the Apostle (1—7)

1. The Introduction

CHAPTER 1:1-7

1. The salutation (1:1-2)
2. The thanksgiving (1:3-7)

After the opening words of salutation, the apostle blesses God, the God and Father of our Lord Jesus Christ, the Father of mercies and the God of all comfort. The apostle had many trials and testings, as well as much suffering, and in all these depressing experiences, God had graciously ministered unto him. Therefore he blessed God in this outburst of praise. We can only bless God as we know Him. Trials, afflictions, sorrows and sufferings make God a greater reality to the believer and display His gracious favor towards His beloved people. The apostle had made this experience, "Who comforteth (or encourageth) us in all our tribulation, that we may be able to comfort them which are in any trouble, by the comfort wherewith we ourselves are comforted of God." In all his distress and tribulation he had drawn near to God, and God had not failed him, but ministered to his need. The blessing and encouragement he had received from God fitted him to comfort those who are in trouble.

An important principle concerning true ministry in the body of Christ is made known in these words of thanksgiving. God must minister to our hearts first, and, through what we receive, we can minister to others. And so all true ministry is of Him. He knew the sufferings of Christ in an abundant measure, but while the sufferings of Christ abounded toward him, so did his consolation abound through Christ also. All he passed through and suffered as a devoted servant of Christ in an antagonistic world, were the sufferings of Christ. Of these sufferings, he speaks more fully elsewhere in this Epistle. And both, the trouble and the comfort, were not exclusively for him, but for all Christians likewise. All was for their benefit and blessing. The apostle states, that whether afflicted or comforted, it is for their consolation and salvation, and that the same result is wrought in them by their own participation in a like experience. The Lord in His gracious dealing would turn affliction to their blessing as well as the consolation. His heart had been encouraged by what he had heard from Titus about their godly sorrow and therefore he could express his confidence "and our hope of you is steadfast, knowing that as ye are partakers of the sufferings, so are ye also of the consolation."

2. Paul's Experience and Explanations

CHAPTER 1:8-24

1. His experience (1:8-14)
2. His explanations (1:15-24)

The apostle speaks, first of all, of the trouble he had when he was pressed out of measure, (or "weighed down exceedingly, beyond our power"), in so much that he despaired of his life. What experience did he mean? The question cannot be positively answered. It may have been the trouble in Ephesus (Acts 19) to which he refers in 1 Cor. 15:32, "If after the manner of men I have fought with beasts in Ephesus." Others think that it was some severe attack of sickness or a powerful assault upon his life from some other source. Whatever it was, he had been in such a peril that he almost lost his life. "But we had the sentence of death within ourselves, that we should not trust in ourselves, but in God who raiseth the dead: who delivered us from so great a death and doth deliver; in whom we trust that He will yet deliver us." It was all permitted to come upon him for his own good. He learned by it his own utter helplessness; it destroyed in him all self-reliance; he had to cast himself upon God, whose power and faithfulness as a deliverer were blessedly manifested in this experience. It showed him his nothingness and God's power in deliverance. Every true believer will welcome any affliction or tribulation which produces such precious results.

In the tenth verse, he groups together the fact of God's deliverance past, present, and future. "Who delivered us from so great a death." This undoubtedly refers to the danger he was exposed to and out of which He had been delivered, but it may also be applied in a more general way. We are as believers delivered from so great a death, that is, eternal death. Then there is a present deliverance "who doth deliver." These are the trials and testings in the way, in which the believer learns anew that He is the God of our salvation. "Salvation through a work wrought already for eternity is the daily lesson of a growing faith. Sickness, privation and trouble of any kind are, with outward persecution, permitted as occasions of sustaining and delivering love. Grace knows how to deliver even from those snares in which our own folly or carelessness may have entangled our feet" (Pridham). And the apostle expressed his confidence in a future deliverance. He who has delivered His people, saved them by grace, who constantly delivers and keeps, will do so in the future till the final great deliverance comes and all His redeemed people will be gathered home.

But while the apostle trusted in God for all this, as all true believers do, he also recognized the value of the prayers of others. God's children can be fellow-helpers in prayer for the servants of God "helping together by prayer for us." Prayer is therefore a very important part of true ministry in the body of Christ. And what had been bestowed upon him, would lead many to praise God in giving thanks on his behalf. He was rejoicing (that is, "glorying" or "boasting") in the testimony of his own conscience, that in holiness (not "simplicity" as in the *Authorized Version*) and sincerity before God he had acted in the world and more abundantly towards them. Only partly had they recognized him. He mentions "the day of our Lord Jesus." In that day the Corinthian saints would be the apostle's glorying, and the apostle was their glorying. The day of the Lord Jesus is not the Old Testament day of God. The day of the Lord will bring the visible manifestation of the Lord in great power and glory. Judgment for this earth follows as well as mercy in bringing righteousness, peace and the kingdom. The day of the Lord Jesus is for the saints of God and is celebrated not on earth but in glory. Often the apostle refers to that blessed coming day when the saints shall be gathered home. As a doctrine it is impressed continually on the memory of the Church, while as a moral power it is a constant endeavor of the Spirit to bring to bear directly on the daily walk of the believer, both as a regulator of conscience, an argument of patience, and an efficient stimulant of all true spiritual affection (Rom. 13:12-13; 1 Pet. 1:7; 1 John 3:1-3).

His explanations follow. He intended to come to them long before this. His plan was to pass by them into Macedonia, and to come again out of Macedonia unto them, so that they might bring him on his way toward Judea. He had not done so. They might accuse him therefore of having failed. The word "lightness" in verse 17 means fickleness. Was he fickle-minded? Was it merely the lightness and fickleness, a changing yea, yea, followed by nay, nay? He had stayed away from Corinth for other reasons; it was to spare them that he did not go there. Therefore, it was not fickleness on his part at all.

He did not purpose according to the flesh. What he earnestly desired was from love for them, and all his plans were under the guidance of the Lord. "But as God is true, our word toward you is not yea and nay. For the Son of God, Jesus Christ, who was preached among you by us, even by me and Silvanus and Timotheus, was not yea and nay, but in Him is yea. For whatever may be the promises of God, in Him is the yea, wherefore also through Him is the amen, unto the glory of God through us." They had been suspicious of him and his motives, and now after having denied the false charge of being fickle-minded he reminds them of his preaching among them which was not yea and nay. He turns from the accusations against him, to what he had preached. The positive doctrines of the gospel had moulded his character and controlled all his motives. He and his companions, Silvanus and Timotheus, had preached among them the Son of God, Jesus Christ, and the blessed truths of salvation and redemption which centre in Him and flow forth from His person.

The preaching of the Son of God has no doubt and uncertainty in it; it is the declaration of positive and final truth. Men doubt and are fickle-minded about the person of Christ and the gospel in our days, but God's Word speaks in positive terms, which do not permit any uncertainty whatever. It is a wonderfully deep statement that all the promises of God, whatever they may be, are in Christ—in Him is the yea and through Him the amen likewise. All promises are made to Christ and are in Him and those who trust in Christ share them in Him. All came by Him, all is in Him, all will be accomplished through Him. "Whatever promises there had been on God's part, the yea was in Him, and the amen in Him. God has established—deposited, so to speak—the fulfillment of all His promises in the person of Christ. Life, glory, righteousness, pardon, the gift of the Spirit, all is in Him: it is in Him that all is true—yea and amen. We cannot have the effect of any promise whatsoever apart from Him. But this is not all: we, believers, are the objects of these counsels of God. They are to the glory of God by us" (*Synopsis of the Bible*).

But how can we participate in it, if all is in Christ? Here is the blessed answer. God Himself establishes the believer in Christ, in whom all the promises subsist, so that the true Christian securely possesses in Him all that is promised. We have it all through God in Christ and can enjoy it in Him. And furthermore, God hath anointed us. We possess in Christ the gift of the Holy Spirit. We are sealed by that Spirit; God has put His seal upon us. And finally the Spirit also is in us the earnest of that which we shall possess with Christ in the coming day of His glory. "In whom ye also, after that ye heard the word of truth, the gospel of your salvation; in whom also believing, ye were sealed with the Holy Spirit of promise, which is the earnest of an inheritance until the redemption of the purchased possession, to the praise of His glory" (Eph. 1:13-14).

3. His Deep Exercise Concerning Them

CHAPTER 2

1. The burden of his soul (2:1-4)
2. Concerning the brother who had been disciplined (2:5-11)
3. Overcoming (2:12-17)

In the previous chapter we read the reason why he had not gone to Corinth. "To spare you I came not to Corinth" (verse 23). He feared, that on account of their deplorable condition; exercising his God-given apostolic authority, he might appear as dominating over them. He had determined that he would not come again to them with sorrow. He might have hastened to Corinth with a rod (1 Cor. 4:21), but he exercised patience and had waited, no doubt with much prayer to God, for the gracious effect of the first Epistle he had sent unto them. In all these statements so humble, so loving and so patient, we have the love exemplified which is described in the previous epistle (chapter 13). He was not easily provoked; he hoped all things and endured all things. He also tells them in what state of mind he was in when he wrote his first Epistle. What deep soul exercise the fourth verse reveals! He was so much concerned that he wrote out of much affliction and agony of heart, while his tears flowed freely. But it was not done to grieve them; love for them was the only motive, "that ye might know the love which I have more abundantly towards you."

The case of the transgressor whose wicked deed had been exposed and rebuked in the first Epistle (1 Cor. 5), whose discipline had been demanded by the Apostle, is taken up first. What had grieved him had grieved them also. This they had shown by the way in which they had treated this brother. Titus had brought him the information that they had acted and the transgressor had been put away from fellowship. He also must have told Paul of his deep and true repentance. He therefore exhorts them to receive him again and comfort him, who was in grave danger of being swallowed up with much sorrow on account of the discipline from the side of the mass of Christians. He tells them to assure this weak brother, who had been restored, of their own love, and while they had forgiven him, he also forgave. In assuring the disciplined brother of their love they would thereby prove their obedience in all things. They had previously shown their obedience by judging the evil doer for his sin. "Lest Satan should get an advantage of us, for we are not ignorant of his devices." The brother in question who had been delivered to Satan was in danger of being driven to despair, and in this way Satan might get an advantage over them. This might have resulted in bringing about a division between the apostle and the Corinthians. The course pursued by the apostle in forgiving love, prevented this.

When the apostle came to Troas to preach the gospel of Christ, there was a door opened unto him by the Lord. His great business was to preach the gospel, and the Lord had manifested His approval by opening a door. Yet Paul was restless. He had expected to meet Titus to receive the anxiously awaited news from Corinth. So he did not enter the door which the Lord opened to preach the gospel, but he hastened to Macedonia. His own anxiety and restless haste were weaknesses. The door opened for service should have made him tarry at Troas to preach that gospel, which he loved so well. Then, in due time, the Lord would have led Titus to him. From all this the Corinthians could learn his great love for them and his deep anxiety and concern. And yet his conscience must have been troubled in having lost so great an opportunity to preach the gospel. Surely he was in a very trying position as a servant of Christ. On the one hand he valued the gospel and loved to preach it, and on the other hand was his burdened heart for the saints of God. And therefore he comforts and encourages himself by an outburst of thanksgiving. He knows that God is in it all; not he himself leads, but God always leadeth him in triumph in Christ "and maketh manifest the odor of His knowledge through us in every place." It is an allusion to a Roman triumphal procession after the victory. Captives were led in these processions, but the victors were the prominent figures. So Paul declares, "God always leadeth us in triumph in Christ." He gives us the victory. All his anxiety for the Corinthians ended in triumph. This was always so.

In connection with a Roman triumph incense was burned upon every altar. These aromatics pervaded the whole procession. Through the apostle the sweet smell of His knowledge was spread about. But he also applies this to the gospel. The two classes are mentioned by him, those who are now being saved and those who are perishing. Let us also notice the beautiful thought that the preaching of the gospel is a sweet incense of Christ unto God. Independent of the results of the preaching of the Gospel, whenever that precious name is preached, which is an ointment poured forth (Sol. Song 1:3), it delights the heart of God and is a sweet savor unto Him. But as to men, to some it is a savor (or odor) of death unto death and to others a savor of life unto life. (In the Roman triumphal procession were captives to whom the burning incense was a token of death; to others it was a token of life.)

Who is sufficient for these things? What great issues the gospel ministry involves and how great the responsibility! The question is answered in the next chapter. "Our sufficiency is of God" (3:5). Upon Him the true minister of the gospel is solely cast. And because Paul had his sufficiency of God as well as those who were associated with him, he could say, "for we are not as the many, corrupting the Word of God; but as of sincerity, but as of God, in the sight of God, speak we in Christ." The word "corrupt" has the meaning of adulterating, trading. It has been strikingly translated "driving a traffic in the Word of God" and with this making merchandise of the truth of God, the adulterating is closely connected. It began with apostolic days. How much worse is it in our times! Many who lay claim to the name of ministers of the gospel are men-pleasers, covetous, aiming at their own popularity, seeking their own and not the things of Christ; and therefore they trade in these truths and handle the Word of God deceitfully as well as diluting it. A solemn description of a true servant of Christ is the concluding sentence of this chapter. He is of God, with a God-given message, and he speaks of God in the sight of God.

4. The Ministry of the New Covenant in Contrast with the Old

CHAPTER 3

1. The epistle of Christ (3:1-3)
2. The true sufficiency (3:4-6)
3. The old and new ministry contrasted (3:7-11)
4. The glory in the face of Moses and the glory in the face of Christ (3:12-18)

It was customary in the church to give letters of commendation (Acts 18:27; Rom. 16:1). Did the Apostle need, as some others, epistles of commendation to the Corinthians, or such letters from them? Probably his enemies, the Judaizing teachers, who upheld the law and its ordinances, demanded such letters. They may have said, he did not come from Jerusalem; who then is Paul? Why has he not letters of commendation? His answer is, "Ye are our epistle, written in our hearts, known and read of all men; being made manifest that ye are the epistle of Christ, ministered by us, written not with ink, but with the Spirit of the living God; not on tables of stone, but on fleshly tables of the heart." It is a most beautiful and tender statement. The Corinthians were his letter of commendation, the proof of his blessed ministry, because under his preaching they had been saved and were walking well. After their obedience, he could rightly say so. It would have been impossible for him to make such a statement in the first Epistle. Let all men read you as an epistle, and they will know what kind of a man I am. What confidence and love this expresses! It would also lead them to earnest inquiry if they were really such a letter of commendation. When he speaks of "ye are the epistle of Christ" he describes the general character of the Church and her responsibility. The Church is the representative of Christ, or Christ's letter of commendation to the world.

What a solemn responsibility to recommend in life and walk Christ to the world! Just as God had written once the law on tables of stone exclusively for Israel, so now the Spirit of the living God writes Christ on the hearts of believers, that the world may read Christ in the Church composed of all believers.[1] And this is true ministry, witnessing to Christ not alone in the proclamation of the gospel, but in life and walk. "That ye may be blameless and harmless, the children of God, without rebuke in the midst of a crooked and perverse generation, among whom ye shine as lights in the world" (Phil. 2:15). And such was Paul's confidence through Christ to Godward. He trusted the grace of the Lord Jesus Christ to accomplish this. In himself, he acknowledges, there is no sufficiency for anything, "all our sufficiency is of God, who also made us sufficient as ministers of a new covenant, not of letter, but of spirit; for the letter killeth, but the spirit giveth life." The latter statement is often wrongly interpreted. The word "letter" does not mean the entire written Word of God. Many have taken this view and declare that the Bible must not be taken literally, just as it says. (This is mostly said in connection with prophecy, the second coming of Christ, etc. More than once the word "the letter killeth" has been used to explain away the literal meaning of things to come.) It is not the question at all between the literal words and meaning of the Scriptures and the spiritual meaning, but it is a contrast between the old covenant and the new covenant, between the law and the gospel. The word "letter" stands for the law, which in its ministration kills and cannot give life. What the purpose of the law is and what it can do and cannot do is learned from the following passages: Rom. 3:20, 5:20, 7:5-11, 8:3; Gal. 3:10, 19.

By the law no flesh can be justified; by the law the offence abounded; the law means death to man (Rom. 7:10-11). It is weak and has no power to help man, and it curses man. In this sense the letter, the law, killeth. But the spirit giveth life. It means that the spirit of the gospel is different from the law, for the Holy Spirit

---

[1]"Ex. 34:1; John 13:35; 17:21. The analogy is obvious. Jehovah was 'the God of Israel,' Christ is 'the Saviour of the world.' The tables were Jehovah's witness to His people, the Church is Christ's living epistle to the world. Israel heard but turned away; the world saw and read but refused, and yet refuses Him who thus speaks from heaven. Lastly, in the former case, the law was made void by the commandments of men; in the latter, the Church, the power of whose testimony consists in her separation from the world, has by mingling with it become the betrayer, rather than the witness of the name by which she is called."

operates through the gospel and quickens the sinner who is dead and under the curse. Here then we have the absolute incompatibility of law and gospel. The epistle to the Galatians makes this fact fully known. The contrast between law and gospel, the old and the new covenant, is introduced in this epistle because the teachers who magnified the law and preached the keeping of the law for righteousness, were also at work in Corinth (11:22). And the glory of the gospel and its ministry cannot be fully demonstrated except in its relation to the law. The contrast made is fivefold:

Law	**Gospel**
Letter	Spirit
Ministration of death	Ministration of the Spirit (life)
Ministration of condemnation	Ministration of righteousness
Vanishing glory	Abiding glory
Veiled glory	Unveiled glory

The law ministers death. It was written and engraved and came with glory. This refers us to the second giving of the law. Glory was connected with that, for Moses' face shone. Because grace and mercy were mingled with the second giving of the law (Exodus 34:1-7), glory was seen upon the face of Moses. They could not look upon that glory, and Moses, the mediator, had to cover his face with a veil. It was a brightness which dazzled and repelled, but had no power to attract or to bring light, warmth and joy to the hearts of the people. But if glory was connected with the ministration which is death, how shall not the ministration of the Spirit be rather glorious?

The gospel is all-glorious and abiding; it is the ministration of righteousness which abounds in glory. The glory on the face of Moses has given way to the glory in another face, even in the face of the Lord, Jesus Christ. The glory on Moses' face was but the reflection of His glory who came and dwelt among men. It is now a remaining glory as well as a surpassing glory, "the glory that excelleth." And the sinner can behold that glory. "Righteousness is now ministered unto us, not worked out by us; and thus, indeed, the glory of God is revealed as nothing else could reveal it. His inmost heart is told out in righteousness, but love is righteousness, and love, how marvelous, as shown in the gift of Christ for men! So that which was made glorious in the time past had, in itself, no glory compared with this surpassing glory" (*Numerical Bible*).

"Seeing then that we have such hope, we use great plainness (literally: boldness and confidence) of speech." With such blessed assurance and knowledge of the ministration of righteousness and the Spirit, the true minister can use great plainness of speech in the proclamation of the gospel. "To make the marvelous truth of God's gospel as clear as daylight to the human conscience is the first duty of those whom the Lord now sends forth as heralds of His grace. Whatever is recondite or enigmatic is not now of God. Babes receive that which, when digested, makes them men. It could not be thus with Moses, who was indeed the open minister of the law, but the veiled prophet of grace. The action of Moses in covering his face is here described as something intentional, and in keeping with his office as the minister of that which he knew to be imperfect in character, and therefore not of permanent effect. The lawgiver was a witness also of a better thing than law. To deliver his present message to the people he lifted the veil, which was again replaced when the commandment was uttered. Before God he was unveiled, and looked with open vision on the mystery of Jehovah's ways, but to Israel his covered face was an emblem of the incomplete and unsatisfying nature of the ministry committed to his charge" (A. Pridham).

But Israel has been blinded. The people who boast in the ministration of the law did not believe, and as a result their minds were blinded (Isaiah 6:9, 10; Matthew 13:14; John 12:40; Acts 28:26; Rom. 11:8). They read the Old Testament, but the veil is unremoved; yet the day of grace is coming when the veil shall be taken away, and that will be when they turn to the Lord during the coming time of great tribulation, ending with the glorious coming of Him whom they once rejected (Hosea 5:15; 6:1-3).

And those who believe look upon the unveiled, the unhidden glories of the Lord, and are transformed into the same image from glory to glory. It is through faith. And all is through the blessed life-giving Spirit of Christ, who works in believers as the Epistle of Christ. "The power to enjoy Him is the power to reflect Him. The reflection is no effort, but the necessary effect of enjoyment." May we enjoy Christ by being more and more occupied with Him through His Word and then make Him known by walking even as He walked. This is a part of true ministry so much needed.

5. The Character of the True Ministry

CHAPTER 4

1. The gospel of the glory of Christ (4:1-6)
2. The treasure in earthen vessels: Weakness and Power (4:7-12)
3. Resurrection and coming glory (4:13-18)

This ministry which the apostle mentions is the ministry of the gospel. And those who know it by having received mercy are to be the witnesses. Every Christian who has obtained mercy, who is saved by grace, is called to witness to this blessed fact in some way. "We faint not"—we are not discouraged, but encouraged to go on in its proclamation, knowing that it is a sweet savor unto God and the power of God unto salvation to every one that believeth. The hidden things of shame, the methods of the flesh, craftiness, the deceitful handling of the Word of God, were renounced by the apostle: he avoided those things.

All carnal things, all artifices, human wisdom and rhetoric, by which men's minds might be captivated and their applause gained, were unknown to the apostle. His commendation to every man's conscience in the sight of God was by the manifestation of the truth. He had implicit confidence in God's Word and in the gospel of the glory of Christ. This confidence is sadly lacking in our days among the professed preachers of the Word. As a result the methods of the flesh are used and the holy things are dragged down into the gutter. What abominable methods are used by professional "evangelists" to gain notoriety, secure large crowds and large collections! And the falsifying of the Word, the deceitful handling of the Scriptures, which go along with those methods! No wonder the world applauds such methods and the defence of the cross has ceased.

The gospel is here called "the gospel of the glory of Christ, who is the image of God." And this gospel shines in all its radiancy. In the first Epistle we had a blessed definition of what the gospel is (1 Cor. 15:1-4). There we read of His death for our sins, His burial and His resurrection. But here we are lifted higher; the Christ who died and rose again is in heaven crowned with glory and honor. He is there at the right hand of God as our representative, and all the love, the grace and power which are for His people shine out in His blessed face. A glorified Christ in all His fulness and glory, is the gospel in its highest meaning. But if this gospel, which Paul calls "my gospel" is hid, that is, veiled, it is in those that are perishing. They are unbelieving, and unbelief puts them under Satan's power. He is called here the god of this age (the word world means age), that is our age.

The age rejected Christ, and that has made Satan the god of the age, a title which he did not possess in the previous age. And he blinds the eyes of them that believe not. As they refuse to see the light which now shines in the gospel of the glory of Christ, they become blinded by the father of lies by various methods and means. He blinds the eyes by the age itself over which he domineers. He makes it appear as if this age is fast making for better things. Righteousness and peace are impossible during the present evil age; this age is one of darkness, ending in a complete manifestation of the mystery of iniquity in the person of Satan's man, the Antichrist. Righteousness and peace can only come through the return of the Lord Jesus Christ and by His enthronement as king over this world. Satan hides the real character of this age and this is one of the ways by which he blinds the eyes of them that believe not. He leads man to exalt himself, and nourishes self-trust and self-exaltation.

But what is the message of the true servants of Christ? Do they exalt man, or themselves, or the age with its boasted progress? "We preach not ourselves, but Christ Jesus as Lord, and ourselves your servants for Jesus' sake. Because it is God who commanded the light to shine out of darkness, who hath shined in our hearts for the shining forth of the knowledge of the glory of God in the face of Jesus Christ." As it was in the hour of creation when darkness covered all, so it is in redemption. God hath shined in His grace into the hearts of them who believe. And He hath shined, in that, through us, the knowledge of the glory of God in the face of Jesus Christ may shine forth to others.

This unspeakable treasure and glory is in earthen vessels that the exceeding greatness of the power may be of God and not of us. As the ancients kept the most valued treasures in earthen jars, so all those glorious things God has given in the gospel, as well as the ministry of it, are deposited in earthen vessels. The believer, with a body of humiliation, weak and frail, though no longer in the flesh, yet the flesh, the old nature, still in him, is the earthen vessel. The term reminds us of Gideon and his men with the torches in earthen pitchers (Judges 7:16-22). The pitchers had to be broken to pieces so that the light could shine, and thus in that dark night the victory was won. The old man has to be kept constantly in the place of death, self must be judged and broken to pieces, that the light may shine forth. This is a truth which is more than suggested by this statement, though the outward man in his weakness and frailty, subject to affliction and suffering in the world is principally in view.

Then follow statements which illustrate the earthen vessels in their weak and helpless condition, and the exceeding greatness of the power of God. The power is manifested through the earthen vessels in trial and affliction. The earthen vessels may be troubled, afflicted on every side, but the power keeps them from being straitened or distressed. Perplexed, persecuted, smitten down—such is the condition of the earthen vessels. But God's gracious power is manifested in all these earthly and trying circumstances.

"Always bearing about in his body the dying of the Lord Jesus (made like Him, in that the man as such was reduced to nothing), in order that the life of Jesus, which death could not touch, which has triumphed over death, should be manifested in his body, mortal as it was. The more the natural man was annihilated, the more was it evident that a power was there which was not of man. This was the principle, but it was morally realized in the heart by faith. As the Lord's servant, Paul realized in his heart the death of all that was human life, in order that the power might be purely of God through Jesus risen. But besides this, God made him realize these things by the circumstances through which he had to pass; for, as living in this world, he was always delivered unto death for Jesus' sake, in order that the life of Jesus might be manifested in his mortal flesh. Thus death wrought in the apostle; what was merely of man, of nature and natural life, disappeared, in order that life in Christ, developing itself in him on the part of God and by His power, should work in the Corinthians by his means. A thorough trial of the human heart, a glorious calling, for a man to be thus assimilated to Christ, to be the vessel of the power of His pure life, and by means of an entire self-renunciation, even that of life itself, to be morally like unto Jesus. What a position by grace! What a conformity to Christ" (*Synopsis of the Bible*).

How little of all this is known experimentally in our easy-going days among God's people! In verse 12 we read, "So then death worketh in us, but life in you." Different explanations have been given of this statement. True ministry in self-denial and self-forgetfulness works death to the servant. His self-forgetting love brought him constantly hardships and suffering; he followed the Lord in all this and knew the fellowship of His sufferings. But through it the people of God were helped, comforted and blessed. In this sense life worked in them through the self-sacrifice of the apostle.

And what sustains in all this? It is faith. And faith reckons on God who raiseth the dead. "Knowing that He who raised up the Lord Jesus shall raise us up also with Jesus, and shall present us with you." The faith of the believer and the servant looks forward to the glorious consummation when Christ comes for His saints and the great presentation (Jude 24) takes place. This is the glorious goal when we shall no longer see in the glass darkly, when we shall know as we are known, when we shall see Him as He is and be like Him. Therefore, "we faint not; but if our outward man be consumed, yet the inward man is renewed day by day. For our light affliction, which is but for a moment, worketh for us a far more exceeding and eternal weight of glory." Faith always looks upon things seen as temporal. Unseen things, the things above, where Christ sitteth on the right hand of God, are eternal; with these faith is to be occupied. But who is able to say what awaits us there? Who is able to tell out the meaning of that wonderful sentence, "A far more exceeding and eternal weight of glory?" There is a surpassing, an unspeakable, an indescribable, an unfathomable and eternal glory for the saints of God. In ages to come God will display the surpassing riches of His grace in kindness towards us in Christ Jesus" (Eph. 2:7).

6. Concerning the Future and the Ministry of Reconciliation

CHAPTER 5

1. The earthly and the heavenly house (5:1-8)
2. The judgment seat of Christ (5:9-12)
3. The constraint of love (5:13-16)
4. The ministry of reconciliation (5:17-21)

The certainty of the future things is brought more fully in view. The apostle had given the great doctrines concerning the resurrection of the body, the coming of the Lord and the blessed hope in his first epistle (chapter 15). In the closing verses of the preceding chapter, he mentioned again the fact of the believer's resurrection and presentation in the presence of the Lord (verse 14) and spoke of the eternal things, the coming glory. And so he continues: "For we know that if our earthly house of this tabernacle were dissolved, we have a building of God, an house not made with hands, eternal in the heavens."

The earthly house of this tabernacle is the body of the believer, the earthen vessel in the previous chapter. It is called a tabernacle (a tent) because it is only the temporary lodging of those who are by grace but strangers and pilgrims on the earth. Yet in this earthen vessel, this frail tabernacle, there is a divine indweller, the Holy Spirit. The apostle speaks of the dissolution of our earthly house, "if our earthly house of this tabernacle were dissolved." He does not say "when we die," but only states the possibility that the tabernacle might be dissolved. The dissolution of the mortal body of the believer is not presented therefore by the apostle as a certainty, but only as a possibility. "We shall not all sleep, but we shall all be changed" was the blessed mystery revealed through the apostle in his first epistle (1 Cor. 15:51). The change of the body of the believer is the certainty, but its dissolution is not. But if our earthly house of this tabernacle were dissolved "we know we have a building of God, an house not made with hands, eternal in the heavens." What do these terms mean?

What is the building of God, the eternal house in the heavens? Some have identified it with the Father's house and its many mansions of which our Lord speaks. But this house of which the apostle writes cannot be heaven, the Father's house, for it is said to be from heaven and in the heavens. Others have invented a temporary body. They teach that when the believer dies he gets at once a kind of an ethereal body which he will possess between death and resurrection. This is a speculation contradicted by the word "eternal." Nowhere in the Word of God is it taught that the disembodied spirits of the redeemed are to be clothed with a body before resurrection takes place. The body of the believer in its present state is compared to a tabernacle; the building of God, the house not made with hands, refers to that which the believer shall possess in the future, no longer an earthly house, a tabernacle, but something permanent, of supernatural origin. It is quite evident that the apostle means by way of contrast the spiritual body (1 Cor. 15:44), which is in store for the believer. This fact is stated once more, but the purpose of these words is not to convey the thought that this house is to be possessed immediately after death: the emphasis is upon "we know" and "we have." The Spirit of God assures us of the certainty of it. Thus positively every child of God can speak.

"For in this we groan, longing to be clothed upon with our house which is from heaven." The groaning is not on account of infirmities, hardship, privations or unsatisfied desires. It is deeper than that. It is the longing for the promised glorified condition with which we shall be invested. "It is the groaning not of a disappointed sinner, nor of an undelivered saint, but of those who, assured of life and victory in Christ, feel the wretched contrast of the present with the glory of the future." If we, beloved fellow-believer, live close to God, enjoy the fellowship with His Son into which grace has called us, then even in the fairest scenes and in the most attractive earthly conditions, we shall know something of this groaning and longing to be clothed upon with that which is from above and which will fit us to be the vessels of the exceeding great and eternal weight of glory. (The knowledge that at any moment one may change the prison-garments of mortality, and as a chosen companion of the King of Kings be found in the likeness of the Lord of Life, must generate a longing for that moment to arrive. "Even so, come, Lord Jesus.")

"If so be that being clothed upon we shall not be found naked." This again is another warning corresponding to the one at the close of 1 Corinthians 9. All human beings will be clothed upon with a body, for there is a resurrection of the bodies of the just and the unjust. The wicked dead, standing before the great white throne, will be clothed upon, but, not having Christ, they will be found naked for their eternal shame. And so the apostle warned of the possibility that even among the Corinthians there may be some who, destitute of Christ, only professing to be Christ's, would then be found naked.

Then again the apostle speaks of the groaning in this tabernacle, the body of our humiliation. His desire is not to be unclothed, that is, unclothed in death, when the body is put into the grave; he desires to be clothed upon, to be changed in a moment, in the twinkling of an eye. For this the apostle groaned; and this is what we wait for and not for death. When the shout comes from the air and His voice opens the graves of His saints, we who are alive and remain shall be changed (1 Thess. 4:13-18). No death then but mortality will be swallowed up in life. Then our mortal bodies will be quickened. And God has wrought us for this very thing; the evidence of it is the indwelling Spirit, who has made the body of the believer His temple. Then the apostle describes a twofold condition, "at home in the body (the tabernacle) we are absent from the Lord"; and "absent from the body, present with the Lord." The latter statement is a complete refutation of that evil doctrine called "soul-sleep," *i.e.,* an unconscious state between death and resurrection. The believer who dies goes into the presence of the Lord and is consciously present there, waiting with the redeemed of all ages, "to be clothed upon with the house from heaven."

Linked with all this blessed teaching is the judgment seat of Christ (verse 10). All, whether saints or sinners, will have to appear before the judgment seat of Christ; certainly not at the same time. There is no universal judgment taught in the Bible, when the righteous and the unrighteous appear together before the judgment seat of Christ. The saints of God will appear before the judgment seat of Christ, when He has taken them from earth to glory, not at death, but when He comes with the shout in the air. But for His blood-bought people, who constitute His body, who will then be clothed with the house from heaven (the glorified body), there is no more judgment in the sense of condemnation. His own blessed lips have given us the assurance of this. (See John 5:24—that blessed word!) Nevertheless, there is a judgment seat of Christ for believers. The word "appear" in verse 10 is "manifested." We must all be manifested before the judgment seat of Christ. Our works and our ways as Christians will then be brought fully into view; all will be brought into the light. Nothing can be concealed, and the believer receives the things done in the body.

"But there is more than this. When the Christian is thus manifested, he is already glorified, and, perfectly like Christ, has then no remains of the evil nature in which he sinned. And he now can look back at all the way God has led him in grace, helped, lifted up, kept from falling, not withdrawn His eyes from the righteous. He knows as he is known. What a tale of grace and mercy! If I look back now, my sins do not rest on my conscience; though I have horror of them, they are put away behind God's back. I am the righteousness of God in Christ, but what a sense of love and patience, and goodness and grace! How much more perfect then, when all is before me! Surely there is great gain as to light and love, in giving an account of ourselves to God; and not a trace remains of the evil in us. We are like Christ. If a person fears to have all out thus before God, I do not believe he is free in soul as to righteousness—being the righteousness of God in Christ, not fully in the light. And we have not to be judged for anything: Christ has put it all away" (*Synopsis of the Bible*).

Thus the believer has no more fear of death, for he knows what awaits Him; and the judgment seat of Christ has also no terror for him. But the words of the apostle apply equally to unbelievers. The occupant of the great white throne (Rev. 20) before which the wicked dead appear and will be manifested, is the Lord Jesus Christ. They will be judged according to their works and condemned to eternal darkness and conscious punishment. In view of this the apostle states, "Knowing, therefore, the terror of the Lord, we persuade men."

And how can we persuade men to flee the wrath to come, unless we preach the gospel to them? Beautifully linked with this is the constraining power of the love of Christ (verse 14). In his ministry, service, walk and everything else, the great apostle knew this mighty constraint of love. And the cross and its glorious work looms up before his vision, in view of that love manifested there. In Him who died and who liveth, we are called as well as equipped with power to live unto Him. In faith, as dead with Christ and risen with Him, we look to a risen and glorified Christ in whom we are a new creation, "old things have passed, behold all things are become new."

Having reconciled us unto Himself by Jesus Christ, He has also given to us the ministry of reconciliation. Having brought us into this blessed position through grace, He calls us to make it known to others and lead others to Him. What we have received we are to use in our ministry. And every reconciled one is called into this service to exercise the ministry of reconciliation and be a soul-winner. "We are ambassadors for Christ, as though God did beseech you by us, we pray you in Christ's stead, be ye reconciled to God. Him who knew no sin, He hath made Him to be sin for us, that we might become the righteousness of God in Him." This is the great message of the true minister, and all believers can be true ministers and proclaim the message in Christ's stead and point sinners to the cross, where He who knew no sin was made sin for us, where redemption full and free is offered to all.

7. The Example of the Apostle Paul: His Testings and Trials

CHAPTER 6:1-13

He beseeches the Corinthians as co-workers, in view of the ministry of reconciliation, not to receive this grace of God in vain. This is not a contradiction of the doctrine of the security of a true believer. The apostle evidently was uneasy about some of these Corinthian Christians and feared that some had not received the grace of God in their hearts. Their conduct led him to this questioning. If the grace of God comes to man it may be received in vain and lead not to the blessed results in quickening power and real salvation for which it is given. "The security of His children is unquestionable, not so much through their perseverance, as many say, but by His power through faith; but the Corinthians needed and received faithful entreaty, for their ways were not such as became the gospel. They were compromising His glory, who had called them to the fellowship of His Son; and the apostle instead of comforting them with the blessed assurance of the close of Romans 8, would here exercise conscience as well as affection in presence of God's grace" (W. Kelly).

Interesting is the quotation from Isaiah 49. A careful examination of Isaiah 49:4-8 is suggested. It is a prophecy concerning the Messiah. His rejection by Israel is there predicted, and the words of the eighth verse, quoted here, "I have heard Thee in a time accepted and in the day of salvation I have succoured Thee" are addressed to Christ, whom Israel rejected. God raised Him from the dead, and though Israel is not gathered, He becomes the power of salvation for the Gentiles. This is the meaning of "behold now is the accepted time; behold now is the day of salvation." "Now" means this present dispensation when salvation is offered to the Gentiles. But grace rejected, neglected or perverted, as it is the case in this age in which grace reigns through righteousness, will bring judgment, followed by the blessings for Israel and the earth.

The apostle speaks once more of himself and describes negatively and positively the moral features which he manifested in his life as a true minister of God. He knew nothing of inconsistency in life, which is so detrimental to the ministry of the Word. "Giving no offence in anything that the ministry be not blamed." Well has it been said, "Christianity is real and living, not dogmatic only, still less official, else it becomes of all things the most contemptible." The apostle's life in every detail was a comment on his ministry. He practiced what he preached. The opposite undermines any preaching or teaching.

"But in everything commending ourselves as the ministers of God." There was more than the avoidance of offence; in anything, in all conditions and under all circumstances he behaved himself as becomes the minister of God, the ambassador of Christ. In much patience, never impatient, but always enduring in afflictions of various kinds when the world and the god of this age pressed him hard; in necessities and straits, when there seemed to be no escape. Then there were sufferings: in stripes, in prisons, in tumults. Of these we read more in chapter 11. Then there are named things he took upon himself willingly and gladly as the minister of God, namely: labors, watchings, and fastings. By these he manifested his devotedness. Well may we ponder over each as they are given in verses 6 and 7. Then follows a series of contrasts: glory and dishonor. He experienced these opposite extremes, both among the saints, and also in the world. He was shamefully entreated and also revered. He was beloved and honored by God's people and dishonored by the slandering tongue of false teachers. But throughout he proved himself as the minister of God. By evil report and good report, as deceivers and yet true. "Woe unto you if all men speak well of you."

If the servant of Christ follows Him, the world will hate him and brand him a deceiver as it was done with the Lord (Matt. 27:63). It would take many pages to follow the paradoxes as given by this model and master servant. Nothing more beautiful and attractive than verse 10, "As sorrowful, yet always rejoicing; as poor, yet making many rich; as having nothing, yet possessing all things." Oh, blessed life! May God's grace and God's Spirit enable us to manifest Christ as this servant of Christ did.

8. The Apostle's Exhortations and Rejoicings

CHAPTER 6:14—7

1. His exhortations (6:14—7:1)
2. His rejoicing and confidence (7:2-16)

The first exhortation is to separation from evil, without which no true fellowship with God can be enjoyed. It is one of the most important exhortations in the Pauline Epistles, and greatly needed in our days of laxity and worldliness among Christians. God calls His people to holiness. "But as He who hath called you is holy, so be ye holy in all manner of conversation; because it is written, Be ye holy; for I am holy." He has separated us from the world which lieth in the wicked one and separated us in Christ to Himself. Believers are not of the world as He is not of the world (John 27:14). The cross of Christ makes us dead to the world and the world dead unto us (Gal. 6:14). Furthermore God's Word tells us not to love the world, neither the things that are in the world (1 John 2:15), and "that the friendship of the world is enmity with God; whosoever therefore will be a friend of the world is the enemy of God" (James 4:4). And the world is that great system over which Satan domineers, built up and developed by him, to give the natural man a sphere of enjoyment. True faith not only joins the believer to the Lord, but also separates him in heart and practice from the world which crucified the Lord and still rejects Him.

"Be ye not unequally yoked together with unbelievers" is often quoted as a prohibition of a mixed marriage. This is no doubt included, but the exhortation means more and includes every form of alliance with the world and ungodly principles. It also includes the so-called "religious world" with its unscriptural practices and denials of the truth. The apostle shows that the believer going along with unbelievers and the world, is indeed in an unequal, a strange, yoke. What fellowship can there be between righteousness and unrighteousness? What fellowship hath light with darkness? Each has a different head; Christ is over His people, they belong to Him; Belial is the head of those who believe not. What could there be for a believer to enjoy with an unbeliever? And believers are the temple of God. How then is association with idols possible? "For ye are the temple of the living God; as God hath said, I will dwell in them, and walk in them, and I will be their God, and they shall be my people." Blessed statement! But God's presence demands holiness, separation from evil. Fellowship with evil shuts out God in His gracious manifestations. "Wherefore come out from among them, and be ye separate saith the Lord and touch not the unclean thing."

"God must have His own holy, for He is holy; and this not only in an inward way, without which all would be hypocrisy, but in outward ways also to His own glory, unless He would be a partner with us to His own dishonor. He will have us clear from associations which are worldly and defiling; He will exercise our souls in order to free them from all that denies or despises His will. He commands those that believe to come out from those that believe not, and to be separated. Indeed the union of the two is so monstrous that it never could be defended for a moment by a true heart. It is only when selfish interests or strong prejudices work, that men gradually accustom and harden themselves to disobedience so flagrant and in every way disastrous. For as the man of the world cannot rise to the level of Christ to be together with His own, the Christian must descend to the level of the world. God is thus and ever more and more put to shame in what claims to be His house, with a loudness proportioned to its departure from His Word" (W. Kelly).

And in connection with this exhortation to separation from unbelievers the Lord declares His relationship to us. Interesting is the use of the name Lord Almighty in verse 18. "And I will receive you, and will be a Father unto you, and ye shall be my sons and daughters, saith the Lord Almighty." In the Greek the definite article before "Lord" is missing. It is simply *"Kyrios,"* Lord. It is the same as "Jehovah." By that name He revealed Himself to Israel. To Abraham he spoke as the *El Shaddai,* the Almighty. The Lord who revealed Himself to Abraham, called him to separation, "Get thee out from thy country." To Israel God spoke as Jehovah and they became His people, separated by Him and to Him. And the same Jehovah-Shaddai declares now a new relationship, He will be a Father and we His sons and daughters. In Christ we know God as our Father; "we are all the sons of God by faith in Jesus Christ." But to enjoy this relationship practically is only possible if the believer walks in separation. Real communion with God as Father without separating from evil is an impossibility.

"God will not have worldlings in relation with Himself as sons and daughters; they have not entered into this position with regard to Him. Nor will He recognize those who remain identified with the world, as having this position; for the world has rejected His Son, and the friendship of the world is enmity against God, and he who is the friend of the world is the enemy of God. It is not being His child in a practical sense. God says, therefore, "Come out from among them, and be separate, and ye shall be to me for sons and daughters" (*Synopsis of the Bible*).

May we heed these important truths. God cannot compromise His own holy and righteous character. His demands upon His people are the demands of separation. And, as we are obedient, we enjoy in faith the blessed relationship into which His grace has brought us.

The second exhortation is closely linked with this. "Having therefore these promises, dearly beloved, let us cleanse ourselves from all defilement of the flesh and spirit, perfecting holiness in the fear of God." Holiness in our walk is God's demand. God looks for practical holiness in His people. If we walk thus, habitually cleansing ourselves from all defilement of the flesh and spirit, we perfect holiness, a practical daily separation, in the fear of God. While we are, as born again, "clean every whit" (John 13:10), our calling is equally to purify ourselves as He is pure. The defilements of the flesh are the things mentioned in Col. 3:5, Gal. 5:19, and elsewhere. What are the defilements of the spirit? It means the license of the natural mind, the whole sphere of thought and will, when unregulated by the truth and fear of God. Read Chapter 10:5. Every thought must be brought into captivity to the obedience of Christ.

The words which follow tell us again of the affectionate concern which the apostle had for the Corinthians! How he loved them and how considerate he was. His whole soul yearned for them. He had wronged no one, nor had he corrupted any, nor did he make personal gain through them. He was filled with comfort. He had fightings without and fears within, but now all was changed. He had met Titus in Macedonia, and through his report and the encouraging news he brought from Corinth, God had comforted him. He knew his former letter (the first Epistle) had grieved them, but it had worked for them the godly sorrow which was the aim of the messages sent to them through his inspired pen. "Now I rejoice, not that ye were made sorry, but that ye sorrowed to repentance, for ye were made sorry after a godly manner, that in nothing ye might be injured by us." But he also states that for a moment at least he regretted that he had written his first Epistle of rebuke (verse 8). But was not that letter inspired? The power behind his pen was the Holy Spirit, yet he regretted for a time that he had written. How is this to be understood? It shows the difference between the individuality of the apostle and divine inspiration.

His heart was filled with so much love, that it obscured his spiritual discernment and he forgot for a moment the character of his Epistle, that not he was responsible for what he had written, but that the Spirit of God was the author. The regret was an evidence of weakness at the time when no tidings reached him from Corinth and when his loving heart was so burdened for the Corinthians. (The same weakness is manifested in his journey to Jerusalem. He loved Jerusalem and Israel in such a way that he went there even against the solemn warnings given by the Holy Spirit.) And what he writes now is a loving apology and great joy over what the Epistle had wrought, an earnestness to clear themselves of the reproach, indignation on account of sin permitted, yea, zeal for God, and what revenge (or vengeance—righteous wrath)! And so he rejoiced therefore that his confidence had been restored in them in all things.

II. The Ministry of Giving (8—9)

1. The Examples and Principles of Giving

CHAPTER 8

1. The grace of God manifested in the churches of Macedonia (8:1-7)
2. The great example (8:8)
3. The advice, principles and administration (8:9-24)

There is to be a practical ministry in giving, especially in remembering the poor of the flock. He is anxious now to lay this responsibility upon their hearts. In the first epistle he had written them that his glory was in giving the gospel gratuitously. He would not take anything from the Corinthians for himself, but he wants their gifts for others. He was making up a collection for the poor saints in Judea and Jerusalem; of this he writes to them. Thus Gentile believers were to show their appreciation for the blessing which they had received through the Jews, for salvation is of the Jews.

We also see in this an illustration of the oneness of the body of Christ, how the members are to minister to each other. Great grace in this ministry had been bestowed upon and manifested by the churches in Macedonia. They were themselves stricken with great affliction. They were very poor, but their deep poverty did not stint their gifts; they joyfully gave and abounded in the riches of liberality. These poor, afflicted Macedonian saints had even prayed the apostle with much entreaty to receive the gift from their hands. And the secret of it was that they had given themselves first to the Lord. All else was the outflow of this self-surrender.

In all this the apostle rejoiced greatly, and therefore he exhorts the Corinthians to abound in this grace also. But the greatest example, which should constrain to abundant giving is the Lord Jesus Himself. He was rich and became poor, even for such as the Corinthians were, "that through His poverty ye might be rich."[2]

What confidence the apostle had in the Corinthians that they would indeed abound in this grace. They had begun a year before not only to do, but to go forward also. He urges them to act now in performing what they had begun. It depends upon the willing mind: without this giving has no value at all. But if there is the willing mind, one is accepted according to what he has, and not according to that he hath not.

And in all this ministration Paul exercised great caution, "avoiding this, that no man should blame us in this abundance which is administered by us, providing for honest things, not only in the sight of the Lord, but also in the sight of men." There is always danger of reproach in these matters. Messengers were chosen to travel with the apostle "with this grace (the collections) which is administered by us to the glory of the self-same Lord, and for a witness of your ready mind." The apostle knew the devices of the enemy and therefore watchfully guards against suspicion and mischievous insinuations. Alas! what havoc the filthy lucre, the love of money, covetousness, which is idolatry, has worked in the professing Church, and what offences have been given by it to unbelievers.

2. Exhortation and Encouragement

CHAPTER 9

1. Further exhortations to liberality (9:1-5)
2. The blessings connected with giving (9:6-15)

Again he exhorts them to liberality in giving. He knew their willing mind and had boasted of it to them in Macedonia and told them they were ready a year ago. (This had stimulated many. He hoped that they would measure up to this report and fall not behind in this expectation "lest our boasting should be in vain in this behalf." To encourage them in giving and carrying out what they had purposed, he speaks of the blessing: "He which soweth sparingly shall reap also sparingly; and he which soweth bountifully, shall reap also bountifully." There is, then, blessing according to faithfulness in this ministry; as any other faithful ministry is not forgotten of God. Giving must not be grudgingly or of necessity, for God loveth a cheerful giver. God Himself delights to give. In infinite love He gave His only begotten Son, and He delights in all who imitate Him in His ways. There is no compulsion in giving save the constraint of His love.

"And God is able to make all grace abound toward you, that ye always having all sufficiency in all things, may abound to every good work." Such a loving ministry is not an unremunerative service. He is able to make up to all who, out of love, minister to the needs of poor and suffering and afflicted brethren. The apostle shows that thanksgiving to God would be the result of their loving ministry in giving. Three causes are specified: 1. Their subjection to the gospel. 2. Their liberal gifts to the Saints of God. 3. "By their prayer for you, which long after you for the exceeding grace of God in you"—that thanksgiving and glory to God for the fervent and longing prayers of other saints, who received their ministry.

This section ends with thanksgiving unto God, "for His unspeakable gift." There is no need to add what that gift is, for every saint knows, God's unspeakable gift is His Son, the Lord Jesus Christ.

III. The Apostle's Self-Defence and Vindication (10—13)

1. The Vindication of His Authority

CHAPTER 10

The apostle now turns to vindicate the authority, which he had received from the Lord. This had been brought into question by the enemy. In doing this Satan aimed at three things: he attempted to discredit him as a true minister of God; he tried to damage the great truths the apostle preached, and he endeavored also to bring about a separation between the apostle and the Corinthians. Assuredly the great man of God was troubled and did not want to speak much of himself and his authority. But he was forced to do so in this Epistle and also in the Epistle to the Galatians, for the truth of God and the honor of the Lord were at stake. The defence of his apostolic authority stands in the

---

[2] *His Riches—Our Riches,* by A. C. G., unfolds the three leading truths of this precious word. The eternal riches of the Son of God; His deep poverty in our behalf, and His riches in resurrection-glory.

foreground in Galatians; here he puts it at the close of his letter, for it was necessary to deal with other matters first, and to assure the Corinthians of his deep concern for them and thus pave the way for an answer to the accusations brought against him.

The apostle begins by entreating them by the meekness and gentleness of Christ. The three words "Now I, Paul," were to remind them of his own person. It was the Paul who had come amongst them to preach the gospel, and through his preaching wonderful results had been brought about. And now attacked and belittled among the same people, who, next to God, had to thank him for everything, he begins to entreat them and vindicate his authority and character. He states, "Who in presence am base among you, but being absent am bold toward you." These words make partial reference to his personal appearance, which was not of a character which appealed to the Corinthians, who admired the athletic physique of the Greeks. Not alone was his outward form lowly, but he was equally so in his manner and conduct. From this we learn that his accusers, who tried to influence the Corinthians against him, had thrown contempt on his person and character. We shall find that he takes up repeatedly their false charges and insinuations, to meet and refute them. When he writes, "but being absent am bold toward you," he has in mind what his enemies had said about the Epistle he had written them; they belittled his personal appearance and his character, and sneeringly said, he is bold when he is absent; he knows how to write strong letters when he is away, but otherwise he is a coward. He answers by saying, "But I beseech you that I may not be bold when I am present with the confidence with which I think to be bold against some, who think of us as if we walk according to the flesh." He beseeches them that he may not be obliged to use his authority as an apostle when among them, against those who had wronged him by their false charges.

The apostle had written in boldness, yet he could also act in boldness and with authority when he was present with them. They had accused him that he was walking on the same level with them, that is, "according to the flesh." This he repudiates by saying that he walks in flesh, which is quite a different thing. (Note in the Greek the word flesh is without the definite article; not "in *the* flesh." but "in flesh.") He was a man like other men; but when it came to warfare, he waged no fleshly conflict. He acknowledges that he has no wisdom in himself; as to flesh he is powerless, he is cast upon God. How different from these false teachers, his accusers who walked in pride and boasted of wisdom and were governed by selfish motives. The weapons he used were not fleshly, but mighty through God; the weapons which the Holy Spirit supplies. And this spiritual warfare means "the pulling down of strongholds, casting down imaginations, and every high thing that exalts itself against the knowledge of God, and bringing into captivity every thought to the obedience of Christ."

Well has it been said, "repression of the natural will, which is the seat and vehicle of Satan's machinations, is the true aim of spiritual warfare." Mere fleshly, independent "reasonings" and "imaginations" are inconsistent with a real subjection to God. The natural man thinks his own thoughts and follows his own imaginations, but not so the believer: he abandons his own thoughts and imaginations; he casts down all that exalteth itself against the true knowledge of God, and brings into captivity every thought to the obedience of Christ. The Corinthians had not done this; they walked in a carnal way and the enemy got an advantage over them. And so it is largely today among God's people.

After stating that he was ready to avenge all disobedience, in virtue of his apostolic authority, when their obedience was fulfilled, he asks, "Do ye look on things after the outward appearance?" This is what they had done. "For his letters," say they, "are weighty and powerful, but his bodily presence is weak, and his speech contemptible." But he answers that just what he was in his letters when not with them, so would he also be when he is present with them. He speaks of his authority given to him by the Lord for edification and not for their destruction; he wanted them to know that he was not terrifying them by his letters. He did not dare to do as others did, commending himself. Those who opposed him constantly measured themselves among themselves, and not in God's presence. He acted differently. "But we will not boast of things without measure, but according to the measure of the rule which God hath distributed to us, a measure to reach even unto you." He disavowed all connection and comparison with those whose glory was of themselves, and though he had greater gifts bestowed upon himself than others, yet he would not boast of it. The measure which God had given to him had reached unto the Corinthians, for they were the fruit of his labors. He did not boast of other men's labors, and hoped that with an increase of their faith there would also be an increase of his labors even to the regions beyond.

"But he that glorieth, let him glory in the Lord." If there is any glorying it must be in Him, who is the only proper object. He must be glorified by the true minister; He must be praised and exalted, and not the instrument. Self-praise and self-commendation do not mean approval from the Lord, but the opposite. "For not he that commendeth himself is approved, but whom the Lord commendeth." Self-commendation, the love of human praise in some form, disguised or undisguised, are prominent characteristics with many who preach and teach a great deal of truth in our days of boasting. Happy is the servant who hides himself, whose aim is to please the Lord and who looks to Him for approval.

2. Answering His Adversaries and His Boastings

CHAPTER 11

1. The danger through false teachers (11:1-6)
2. Answering his adversaries (11:7-15)
3. His boastings of labors and sufferings (11:16-33)

Inasmuch as he did not want to boast, the apostle tells the Corinthians to bear with him a little while he acts foolishly in speaking of himself. It had become necessary to do so in order to answer his adversaries, who were making havoc among the Corinthians, but he looks upon his vindication and boasting as nothing less than folly. He is about to do what he had exposed in others in the previous chapter (verse 12). He therefore asks their indulgence. What he did he asked them to look upon as being folly, but to remember that it was for their sakes. He was jealous over them, not with a jealousy which originated in the spirit of a natural emulation, but with godly jealousy. He had espoused them to one husband, so that he might present them a chaste virgin to Christ.

The Church is the bride of Christ. He as God's messenger by the preaching of the Gospel of Grace, and the acceptance of it by the Corinthians, had betrothed them as an assembly to the Lord. His jealous desire was to present the Corinthian church to the bridegroom in the coming day. He had his grave fears that as the serpent had beguiled Eve through his subtilty, so their minds might also be corrupted from the simplicity that is in Christ. Eve was for Adam, and so the Church is for Christ and for Him alone. Eve was deceived by listening to another voice. Even so the Corinthians were listening to other voices and their simple faith was being corrupted by false teachings. Behind it stood the same enemy who had deceived Eve. Was there another Christ, which these teachers preached, than the Christ he preached? Or were they receiving another and a better Comforter, another Holy Spirit, than the One they had received, in believing the gospel Paul had preached unto them? Or, have these men brought you a better gospel? If such were the case, they could bear with it. But how could there be another Jesus, or a better Comforter or a better gospel? He was not a whit behind the very chiefest apostles; though he had, for the gospel's sake, abstained from excellency of speech, yet in all things had he been manifest among them.

Evidently the great apostle searched his heart and life to discover the cause of the alienation of the Corinthians. Was the offence perhaps in taking nothing from them and preaching the gospel freely, without money? It was his boast that he took nothing from them, as the brethren in Macedonia had ministered to his needs. But his boast was that he had preached the gospel in Achaia gratuitously. But why? Because he loved them not? God was his witness that such was not the case. It was to take away from these false teachers the boasting of preaching for nothing, so that they could not say, we labor gratuitously while the apostle receives money for his services.

Who were these teachers? The Holy Spirit now exposes the true character of these men. They were not apostles at all, but deceitful workers, who transformed themselves into the apostles of Christ. They were the instruments of that sinister being who was once an angel of light and whose most powerful tactic is to assume this character, to which he had lost all claim by his fall. These false teachers posed as ministers of righteousness. They made high pretensions, yet denied the true righteousness of God. We see much of this in our own days, especially in systems like Christian Science and others.

From dealing with the deceivers, he turns now to those who had become ensnared by them (verse 16). Reluctantly he speaks of himself again. To boast of anything except the Lord was a foolish thing to Paul. "That which I speak,

I speak it not after the Lord, but as it were foolishly, in this confidence of boasting. Seeing that many glory after the flesh, I will glory also." Inasmuch as they compelled him to glory (12:11), he is therefore ready to show what reasons he had for boasting. These Judaizing teachers boasted much of being Hebrews, of the seed of Abraham. But so was Paul. They boasted of being ministers of Christ.

Here the apostle marshals his wonderful proofs of how much he excels in his ministries and labor. What other one could say what he rightfully said of himself? "In labors exceedingly abundant, in stripes above measure, in prisons more frequent, in deaths oft." Then follows the remarkable record. If it had not been for these evil teachers who had invaded the Corinthian church, we would never have known of these experiences of the great man of God, for the historical record, the book of Acts, does not give us a full account of his devotedness and trials. And most likely even this list is not complete.

"Troubles and dangers without, incessant anxieties within, a courage that quailed before no peril, a love for poor sinners and for the assembly that nothing chilled—these few lines sketch the picture of a life of such absolute devotedness that it touches the coldest heart; it makes us feel all our selfishness, and bend the knee before Him who was the living source of the blessed apostle's devotedness, before Him whose glory inspired it" (*Synopsis of the Bible*).

And if he must needs glory, he would glory in his infirmities, in his helplessness. Why should he mention the otherwise unrecorded incident of his escape from Damascus? It was an inglorious experience. There was nothing to glory in, for no miracle took place to preserve him, nor angelic interference. Anyone who gloried in himself would never have mentioned so humiliating an experience.

3. Revelation in which He Might Glory and the Marks of His Apostleship

CHAPTER 12

1. Caught up to the third heaven (12:1-6)
2. The thorn in the flesh (12:7-10)
3. The marks of his apostleship (12:11-15)
4. His continued deep concern (12:16-21)

In the previous chapter the apostle gloried in that which in the eyes of man has no glory at all. From the ignominious experience of being let down in a basket he turns to another experience in which he was caught into the third heaven. "I will come to visions and revelations of the Lord." Of these he undoubtedly had many, given to him by the Lord, to comfort and strengthen him. We would never have heard of this great spiritual experience he speaks of now, if he had not felt the need of boasting on account of the deceiving teachers among the Corinthians. He had kept it as a secret to himself for fourteen years; an evidence of his humility. In telling us of this experience he does not speak of himself as the apostle, but "as a man in Christ." It was therefore not a distinction put upon him on account of his calling as an apostle. As a man in Christ, that is, a heavenly man, for such every believer is, he was taken up in a marvellous, unaccountable way, into the heavenly sphere.

"Paul was in a state neither intelligible to himself nor explicable to his brethren. Yet he knows well the man, and can attest the visions which he is unable to describe. It was himself, but in a condition equally distinct from nature and from ordinary spiritual experience. He had while in this state a faculty of perception independent of both bodily and mental organs." He was in this state, undefined by himself, caught up into the third heaven and being caught up into paradise, he heard unspeakable words, which it is not allowed to man to utter. The word "paradise" is found but three times in the New Testament. The Lord used it first in speaking to the dying thief (Luke 23:43) promising him that he would be with Him in that blessed place that very day. Once more our Lord uses this word, promising the overcomer to eat of the tree of life which is in the midst of the paradise of God (Rev. 2:7).

The passage here is the third in which this word is used. It is the wonderful place above in His glorious presence, and Paul, being caught up to that place, had a foretaste of the joys and blessings of the redeemed. But he does not tell us anything he saw, but only what he heard. And the words he heard were unspeakable; they were unutterable—he had not the ability nor the permission to make them known. Thus the apostle, to whom the great truth concerning the Church and her heavenly destiny was especially committed, passed through this great experience. And all who are "in Christ," who constitute the body of Christ, will ultimately be caught up in clouds to meet the Lord in the air and be forever with the Lord.

Then we shall know the unspeakable words.

Surely the heart burns within us when we think of such a destiny. And Paul saith, "Of such a one will I glory, but of myself will I not glory." It was of himself as in Christ he gloried; as he looked to himself as a man, the earthen vessel, he could not glory, save in his infirmities. But was there not danger of being exalted on account of this great experience? Linked with the revelation, is the thorn in the flesh. "And lest I should be exalted above measure through this abundance of the revelations, there was given to me a thorn in the flesh, the messenger of Satan, to buffet me, lest I should be exalted above measure." There was a danger of pride of heart after such a vision, and so the Lord permitted a messenger of Satan to buffet the apostle for his own good. Here we have one of the most interesting evidences, that the flesh, the proud, old nature, is still in the believer and not eradicated as some claim. He had perhaps the greatest experience a human being ever had, and yet, though he did not exalt himself, in view of the tendency of the old nature to lift itself up, there was given him this thorn in the flesh.[3]

What was this thorn in the flesh? Numerous answers have been given to this question. It is evident that it was not something sinful as some suggested, but it must have been some affliction in his body, which made him contemptible in the eyes of others and in his preaching. The exact nature of his affliction in the flesh cannot be determined. And he had gone to the Lord with this thorn in his flesh. "For this thing I besought the Lord thrice, that it might depart from me." And the answer came to him. The thorn was not taken away but something better he hears from his Lord. "My grace is sufficient for thee; for my strength is made perfect in weakness." The assurance of the sufficiency of divine grace was to comfort his heart in the affliction, and that the power of God needed his weakness for its display, was to encourage him as the servant of the Lord. He at once understood the divine message. It enabled him not only to bear with infirmities, reproaches, necessities, persecutions and distresses for Christ's sake, but to take pleasure in them, for he knew all these things were the things which enable God to manifest His power. He therefore gloried most gladly in infirmities.

They had compelled him to become a fool in glorying. It should have been different. Instead of his self-defence and vindication in writing all these things to them they should have commended him, for in nothing he was behind the very chiefest of the apostles, yet he adds "though I be nothing." He speaks of the signs of an apostle which were wrought among them by himself. What love and tenderness he manifests once more towards his weak and wavering Corinthian brethren! And still he has deep concern about them. "For I fear lest, perhaps when I come, I find you not such as I would, and that I shall be found unto you such as ye would not; lest there be strifes, emulations, wraths, contentions, back-bitings, whisperings, swellings, tumults; and lest when I come again, my God should humble me with regard to you, and that I shall bewail many who have sinned before, and have not repented of the uncleanness and fornication and lasciviousness which they have committed." What a Christ-like servant he was!

4. Still Absent—Yet Coming and the Conclusion

CHAPTER 13

1. Being absent and expecting to come (13:1-10)
2. The conclusion (13:11-14)

He speaks in the conclusion of his coming to them. "This third time I am coming to you." And when he comes again he will not spare them. He reminds them once more of their doubtings about Christ speaking in him and using him as an apostle. They themselves were proof of this. If it were that Christ had not spoken to them through him (by preaching the gospel), then Christ also did not dwell in them. But if Christ really was in them then it was an evidence that Christ had spoken by him. Notice that part of the third verse and the fourth verse are parenthetical. Leaving out the parenthetical words gives us the correct argument. "Since ye seek a proof of Christ speaking in me—examine yourselves, whether ye be in the faith, prove your ownselves. Do ye not know yourselves

---

[3]"Alas! what is man? But God is watchful; in His grace He provided for the danger of His poor servant. To have taken him up to a fourth heaven—so to speak—would only have increased the danger. There is no way of amending the flesh; the presence of God silences it. It will boast of it as soon as it is no longer there. To walk safely, it must be held in check, such as it is. We have to reckon it dead; but it often requires to be bridled, that the heart be not drawn away from God by its means, and that it may neither impede our walk nor spoil our testimony" *Synopsis of the Bible.*

that Jesus Christ is in you, except ye be reprobates?" What he wished was their perfecting. Why had he written this second Epistle? "I write these things being absent, but being present I should use sharpness, according to the power which the Lord hath given me to edification, and not to destruction." "Finally, brethren, rejoice" (not farewell, but rejoice). And the believers' joy as well as glorying is in the Lord. "Be perfected; be of good comfort; be of one mind; be at peace; and the God of love and peace shall be with you."

THE EPISTLE TO THE
GALATIANS

Introduction

This Epistle was addressed to the churches in Galatia. The authorship of this document has never been doubted and it has been well stated that "whoever is prepared to deny the genuineness of this Epistle, would pronounce on himself the sentence of incapacity to distinguish true from false." Like the Corinthian Epistle this Galation Epistle has in every way the characteristic marks of the Apostle Paul.

Galatia was a prominent province of Asia Minor. The leading cities were Ancyra, Pessinus and Tavium. The inhabitants of Galatia were not Orientals, but Gauls or Celts. They had pillaged Delphi in the third century before Christ and had settled in the central parts of Asia Minor, which was then named Gallograecia or Galatia. Classical writers give a description of their character. "The infirmity of the Gauls is that they are fickle in their resolves and fond of change, and not to be trusted." The leading characteristic seems to have been fickleness, which is also prominent in the opening chapter of this Epistle. The apostle was greatly surprised by it. "I marvel that ye are so quickly changing from him who called you in the power of the grace of Christ unto another gospel."

When the apostle had visited them for the first time, they had received him with open arms and had shown him much kindness. But when afterwards false teachers appeared amongst them, who preached another gospel, they listened willingly to them and became cold and indifferent towards the Apostle Paul and the gospel he had brought to them. They had received the gospel and experienced its blessed power, but they were so unstable that they were about ready to give up the gospel of grace and to turn back to the weak and beggarly elements, to the law and its ordinances.

Paul had been in Galatia (Acts 16:6). He had preached the gospel in this province and God had blessed the preaching, so that many were saved and a number of churches founded. From chapter 4:13, 14 in this Epistle, we learn something additional. "Ye know how through infirmity of the flesh I preached the gospel unto you, at the first. And my temptation which was in my flesh ye despised not, nor rejected, but received me as an angel of God, even as Christ Jesus." It seems he was then troubled with the thorn in the flesh. They had received him as a messenger of God and sympathized with his affliction that if it had been possible, they would have plucked out their own eyes and given them to Paul (4:15). From this statement some have concluded that Paul's affliction was the well-known oriental eye-disease, ophthalmia. Later he visited Galatia again and strengthened the disciples (Acts 18:23).

The Work of Judaizing Teachers

The men who had gone to the Galatian churches and disturbed them were Judaizing teachers. Their evil teaching consisted in a denial of the gospel of grace, so blessedly unfolded in the Epistle to the Romans. They taught that a simple faith in the Lord Jeus Christ is not sufficient for salvation, that in order to be saved the keeping of the law is necessary and that a Christian must observe the precepts of the law of Moses. Circumcision was especially emphasized by them. They had been to Antioch and taught "except ye be circumcised after the manner of Moses ye cannot be saved" (Acts 15:1). They had also constrained the Galatians to submit to circumcision (5:2; 6:12). In order to establish themselves, they tried to undermine the apostleship of Paul and they attacked his authority. Peter evidently was in their eyes the great apostle of authority and as Paul was independent of Peter in his ministry and apostleship, as he had not been sent by Peter, they belittled him. It seems as if the fable of an apostolic succession was invented by these perverters of the gospel of grace.

The Object of the Epistle

The object of this Epistle is the defence of the gospel which Paul had received by the revelation of Jesus Christ. In order to do this successfully the apostle had first of all to defend his own apostolic authority. After he had done so he fully exposed the evil teachings by which the Galatians were being deceived and showed them the perniciousness of the doctrine to which they had listened. The work of Christ on the cross was at stake, "for if righteousness come by the law, then Christ is dead in vain." The exposure is made by a number of contrasts between law and grace in which the apostle shows what the law could not do and what grace has done. The object of the Epistle therefore is to defend the gospel, as he writes in the second chapter "that the truth of the gospel might continue with you"; to point out the seriousness of the false teaching which was, through Satan's power, bewitching them, and in warning them to lead them back upon the foundation of grace from which they had fallen.

The Practical Value and Importance

From critical sides it has repeatedly been stated that the Epistle to the Galatians contains a controversy of the Church in the first century which has no longer interest for us, as there is no danger of Christians becoming Jews. Who would think in the twentieth century of submitting to circumcision in order to be saved? Or who would keep the ordinances of the law and Jewish holidays to obtain righteousness? And so this Epistle is looked upon by some as having little value for our times. But the opposite is true. The perverted gospel, which is so severely condemned in this Epistle, upon which the anathema is pronounced, is the very gospel which is almost universally preached and accepted in our days. Christendom is thoroughly leavened with the leaven of legalism. And even a little leaven of it leaveneth the whole lump (5:9). To begin with, ritualism, so prominent in Christendom, is Galatianism. In fact ritualism had its beginning in the Judaizing teachers, who mixed law and grace and taught that ordinances are necessary for salvation. Their fatal error was the principle that works are needed to justify a sinner before God and that blessings can only come through ordinances. And this is the error in ritualistic Christendom. These Judaizing teachers looked to man and human authority; they acknowledged Peter as the apostle of authority. Ritualism, teaches human authority and believes in a succession which has its source in Peter. Ritualism, in denying the gospel of grace and teaching the necessity of law-keeping ordinances, keeping of holidays, has become corrupt in doctrine and practice. The all-sufficiency of the work of Christ is no longer believed and Christ Himself is dishonored. Romanism is the great and powerful Galatian system. It is branded in Revelation as the great whore, the mother of harlots and abominations of the earth. Protestantism also is leavened by this evil leaven of legalism. Works and ordinances are in many denominations looked upon as being necessary to obtain righteousness and blessings from God. There is hardly any denomination which is free from the Galatian error. It is often present in a very subtle form. Most prominent to-day is that evil doctrine which maintains that salvation is by character. They speak of Christ and believe in Christ helping man, but that salvation is by grace, and that an eternal and perfect salvation is the free gift of God bestowed upon the believing sinner, on account of the finished work on the cross, is denied. This also is a perverted gospel, which is exposed in this Epistle. We shall point out more fully in the exposition of the text the different errors and phases of legalism. The Epistle, in view of the present day drift away from the gospel of grace, is of great importance. This great defence of the gospel should be much studied and obeyed by all who stand for and love the faith delivered unto the saints.

The time when the Epistle was written and where it was written cannot be positively determined. It is probable that Paul wrote the Epistle while he as at Ephesus (Acts 19) from autumn 54 till Pentecost 57. The subscription "written from Rome" is incorrect.

The Division of Galatians

The Epistle consists of three parts. In the first part (chapters 1 and 2) the apostle defends his apostolic authority and that he was absolutely independent of those who were apostles before him. He shows how he became an apostle and traces his own experience. Then he speaks of his visit to Jerusalem and what took place there at that time. The gospel he preached had been acknowledged by James, Peter and John, a fact which these Judaizing teachers had kept from the Galatians. A third fact is brought by Paul to their attention. Peter had been made prominent by these false teachers; they made it appear as if all the authority was invested in Peter. Perhaps they spoke of him as almost perfect. But Paul shows that Peter had no authority whatever over him. Paul had rebuked him when he had done wrong and committed a most serious mistake.

The second part (chapters 3 and 4) contains the defence of the truth of the gospel itself. The Holy Spirit leads deep into the blessed truths of Christianity, and by a number of vital contrasts between law and grace shows what the law cannot do and what grace has done. Not ordinances, the works of the law make a sinner righteous before God, but it is faith which justifies. Why the law was given and how the limit of the law is reached when faith has come, as well as the blessed fact that those who are of faith are sons and heirs of God, indwelt by the Spirit of sonship, is all unfolded in this section. Here we learn that the law cannot give righteousness and that the justified believer is no longer under the law. "We are no longer under the schoolmaster." The third part (chapters 5 and 6) shows how a believer who is justified by faith, no longer under the law, but under grace, should walk. It is the walk in the Spirit and the manifestation of the fruits of the Spirit. The division of this Epistle is therefore as follows:

I. **THE TESTIMONY OF PAUL CONCERNING HIS APOSTOLIC AUTHORITY** (1—2)

II. **CONTRASTS BETWEEN LAW AND GRACE** (3—4)

III. **THE WALK OF THE JUSTIFIED BELIEVER, AS NOT UNDER THE LAW BUT UNDER GRACE** (5—6)

Analysis and Annotations

I. The Testimony of Paul Concerning His Apostolic Authority and the Gospel

CHAPTER 1

1. The introduction (1:1-5)
2. The rebuke (1:6-10)
3. Paul's gospel given by revelation (1:11-12)
4. How Paul became an apostle independent of Jerusalem (1:13-24)

The introductory words of this Epistle are brief and of deep significance. He speaks of himself as an apostle not from men, nor through man, but through Jesus Christ and God the Father. His apostleship had been called in question and the gospel he preached branded as lacking authority. This opening statement of how Paul became an apostle is more fully developed in the main part of this chapter (verses 11-24). He did not receive his apostleship through any man; his authority was neither successional nor derived. The Judaizing teachers who had sown their evil seed among the Galatians, had spoken of Peter as the apostle with authority and probably demanded that he should be recognized as the ecclesiastical head. Inasmuch as Paul had not been constituted an apostle through Peter's authority, they said that he was no apostle at all. With their wrong doctrines about the law as a means to obtain righteousness, they evidently attempted to foster upon Christian ground an ecclesiastical authority, corresponding to the successional priesthood of the law covenant. What was begun by these false teachers has become the curse of Christianity, for any priestly assumption in the Church is the corruption of Christian doctrine.

The Apostle Paul declares therefore that the source of his authority and his ministry was higher than man. He received his commission "through Jesus Christ and God the Father, who raised Him from among the dead." On the way to Damascus the risen Christ appeared to him in glory and made him an apostle. God the Father, who had raised His Son from the dead and gave Him glory (1 Peter 1:21) also made Paul an apostle. To be one of the twelve apostles it was necessary to have been an eyewitness of His deeds and a listener to His words (Acts 1:21). Matthias met this requirement and was therefore divinely chosen to fill the place of Judas. Some teach that Paul should have been put in the apostolate as the twelfth. But Paul could not have been one of the twelve apostles for he did not follow the Lord Jesus during the days of His earthly ministry. He did not know Christ after the flesh, but his acquaintance with Him began when he beheld Him in resurrection-glory. All his ministry, the gospel he preached, the glorious truths he taught, had their blessed source in the risen and exalted Christ. He therefore owned no other source, no other authority, but God the Father and the Lord Jesus Christ.

And he mentions in these introductory words "all the brethren which are with me." This means that the brethren with him endorsed all he was about to write to the Galatians in his great, God-given defence of the gospel. None of them could have any sympathy whatever with the most serious errors, aiming at the very heart of true Christianity, to which the Galatians had been willing listeners.

Another important fact is that the Epistle is

not addressed "to the church in Galatia" but "to the churches." The Spirit of God in the Corinthian Epistles addressed the Corinthians as "the church of God, the sanctified in Christ, called Saints" (1 Cor. 1:2). In spite of their carnal walk and their spiritual declension the church in Corinth is recognized as being the Church of God and its members as saints. In writing to the Galatians, who were relinquishing the essential truths of the gospel of grace, departing from it and going back to the law as a means of justification, the Spirit of God does not make use of these distinguishing terms. He does not recognize as the Church of God those who fall away from grace. From this we may learn that doctrinal evil is even a more serious matter than moral evil. How serious a thing a perverted gospel is we shall soon discover. "Grace be to you and peace from God the Father, and our Lord Jesus Christ, who gave Himself for our sins, that He might deliver us from this present evil age, according to the will of our God and Father, to Whom be glory forever and ever, Amen." The great truth in these concluding introductory words the Galatians had forgotten. Righteousness cannot come by the law, to which the Galatians were turning again. Man destitute of all righteousness, helpless to obtain any kind of righteousness, is a lost and condemned sinner. But Christ came and gave Himself for our sins and to deliver us from this present evil age.

The words of introduction are followed by words of rebuke and painful surprise. The apostle marvelled at their strange behaviour, that they were so quickly changing from him who had called them in the grace of Christ unto a different gospel. From his lips they had heard the glad tidings of the grace of Christ when they were serving idols (4:8). And now suddenly they were abandoning the gospel which had brought them such blessing, peace and power, and had saved them from the degradation of idolatry. They were accepting a different gospel, which was not another. Though another gospel was preached unto them, it was no gospel at all, for there can be no other gospel.

There is but one gospel and that is the gospel of God concerning His Son Jesus Christ our Lord, the love-gift of God, who became incarnate in order to die for sinners and be the propitiation for our sins. He finished the great work on the cross, a work which has glorified God and which enables Him to be a just God and a justifier (Romans 3:26) of all them that believe in Jesus. And He who finished this work is at the right hand of God. Therefore God has not another gospel, nor can He tolerate the perversion of His gospel. This is what the false teachers among the Galatians were doing as Paul writes: "but there be some that trouble you, and would pervert the gospel of Christ." They were perverting the gospel by teaching that the finished work of Christ was not sufficient for salvation, but that man must add his works, keep the law, and become circumcised. It was a God-dishonoring denial of the completeness and perfection of the work of Christ. And this perversion of the gospel, and more than that, the setting aside of that gospel altogether, is the almost universal thing in Christendom in our times.

We hear much of "salvation by character," which is Satan's invention. Ritualism which makes ordinances the necessary means of salvation is another perversion of the gospel of grace; and so is the teaching of Seventh Day Adventism. The phrase one hears so much, "God has done His part and we must do our part," is another phrase of a perverted gospel. Man is a lost sinner, helpless and hopeless in himself; he can do nothing, for he is without strength (Rom. 5:6). The doing is all on God's side; all the sinner can do is to accept what the grace of God in Christ offers to him. "For by grace are ye saved through faith; and that not of yourselves: it is the gift of God. Not of works, lest any man should boast" (Eph. 2:8-9).

"But though we, or an angel from heaven should preach unto you any other gospel than that we have preached unto you, let him be accursed (anathema). As we said before, so say I now again, if any man preacheth unto you any other gospel than that ye did receive, let him be accursed." These are strong and solemn words. Some have suggested that Paul was carried away by his passion, when he heard that his authority had been impeached, and that he wrote unwisely. They forget that it was not Paul who penned these words but the Spirit of God. The anathema upon the perverters of the gospel of Christ is fully justified when we consider what is at stake. The perversion of the gospel touches the unspeakably blessed work of Christ on Calvary's cross. If in any way righteousness is through the law, by what man does, then Christ died in vain (2:21).

Behind every perversion of the gospel, be it ritualism, Christian Science, Seventh-Day keeping, the new theology and other systems, stands the enemy of the truth of God, who always aims at the person and work of Christ. God, and it is a solemn truth, can do nothing else than put His curse upon those who reject, pervert and falsify the gospel of His Son. The ardent words of the apostle are very remarkable. The Holy Spirit has given us God's own testimony, that if an angel came to teach what the apostle had not taught, he would be anathema. It little mattered who he might be, if he contradicted the testimony of God. Paul well knew that he had received it from God Himself, and he who opposed or falsified it, opposed the authority of God, and the truth which He in His grace made known.

Let Christians take heed to the solemn words of the apostle. We possess them in this Epistle, as well as in others which he wrote. They are the touchstone for all teaching; and we need to study them in order to know if he who speaks, tells us the truth of God. So solemn was this point, so deeply was it felt by the apostle, that he again repeats what he had before said—that whoever should preach any other gospel than that which the Galatians had received from himself, should be anathema (J. N. Darby).

Nor must we forget that a day is coming when the divine anathema pronounced here will be executed. God will surely not tolerate forever the rejection of His Son and the work He accomplished. The vengeance of God is in store for all who do not obey the gospel (2 Thess. 1:8). The doom of an apostate Christendom is pre-written in God's word; and the apostasy is the rejection and perversion of the gospel. Let God's people everywhere witness against the spurious gospel as positively and solemnly as the great servant of Christ did in these words.

In his testimony and service he was not a man-pleaser, "for if I were pleasing men, I should not be the servant of Christ." He did not seek the applause of men and of the world. If he accommodated himself to men, seeking to please them, he would not be Christ's servant. Characteristic of the preachers of a perverted gospel is that they are catering to the wishes of men. When sound doctrine is no longer endured, then after their own lusts do they heap to themselves teachers, having itching ears (2 Tim. 4:3). And Jude describes these "men-pleasers" as follows: "Their mouth speaketh great swelling words, having men's persons in admiration because of advantage" (Jude 16).

The words of rebuke are followed by an historical account of his ministry, how he received the gospel and how he became an apostle independent of Jerusalem. The gospel he preached was not according to man, by which he meant, that he had not received it from any man, nor had somebody taught it to him. He did not get his instructions from those who were apostles before him. He had received it all by the immediate revelation of Jesus Christ. It is then incorrect to speak of a "Pauline theology" and "Pauline gospel" as if his mind had somehow put it all together and constructed a gospel-scheme. No mind of man could have ever invented or discovered the marvellous truths of the gospel. It is supernatural in its revelation and in its power. He then traces his remarkable experience once more, what a religious, zealous, law-keeping Jew he was. And where did all his zeal, his law-keeping lead him? It made him a persecutor of the church of God. (Legalism is harsh like the law which can only curse man. The great legalistic and ritualistic system, Rome, is the persecutor of the Saints of God. Wherever grace is denied and the legal principle is made prominent harshness and intolerance are the results, if not actual persecution.)

On the road to Damascus the God who had separated Paul called him by His grace, and the Son of God in His glory was revealed to him as well as in him, so that He might preach Him to the Gentiles. And he did not confer with flesh and blood after his conversion, neither did he go to Jerusalem to them which were apostles before him. To go up to Jerusalem would have been for him a natural thing; to go back to the city where he had wrought such havoc as a persecutor and there to confess his guilt and testify of Christ, may have appealed to him as manly. But he did not confer with flesh and blood; he did not follow his own reasonings. And why should he go to Jerusalem to consult with the other apostles? Should he go there to report to them of what had happened, ask their counsel and gain their sanction? All this was unnecessary for he had received his call and commission from the Lord, and there was no need to go and consult any man about it. His independence of Jerusalem and his dependence on the Lord as His servant is thereby established.

Jerusalem did not make Paul an apostle; the Lord had done this. Instead of going to see the apostles and put himself under them he went under the Lord, into Arabia and returned to Damascus. After three years he went up to Jerusalem to visit with Peter. What happened during that visit? The apostles did not meet in council to examine Paul about his experience and fitness to preach the gospel. He did not seek the sanction or authority of Jerusalem, but he abode there with Peter for only fifteen days, to become acquainted with him. The other apostles he did not see at all, not even the beloved disciple, save James, the Lord's brother. All this proves his claim "an apostle not from men, nor through man." Afterwards he went into the regions of Syria and Cilicia, everywhere preaching and teaching his God-given gospel. The many churches of Judea did not know him by face, but heard that the erstwhile persecutor now preached the faith he once destroyed. He tells the Galatians how little he had to do with Peter and the other apostles. The false teachers had brought this against him and had challenged his authority as an apostle on account of not being linked with Peter. He fully avows all this and shows that his apostleship was entirely independent of Jerusalem and the twelve apostles. And here we have the character of true New Testament ministry. It is from the Lord, independent of man and human, ecclesiastical authority. Its message is the message of God.

CHAPTER 2

1. How Jerusalem had confirmed the gospel Paul preached (2:1-10)
2. Peter's failure, Paul's rebuke and testimony (2:11-21)

Fourteen years passed by before he ever saw Jerusalem again. What wonderful years of service these years were! The great servant of Christ had preached the divine message in demonstration of the Spirit and of power. The day of Christ will reveal the blessed results of these years. Acts 15 must be read to see why Paul and Barnabas went up to Jerusalem. The same false teachers had visited the great Gentile center, Antioch, and taught "except ye be circumcised after the manner of Moses, ye cannot be saved." Then Paul and Barnabas were appointed to go to Jerusalem to lay this question before the apostles and elders. Here the additional information is given that Paul went up by a direct revelation from God. It shows his dependence on the Lord. They also took Titus with them, who was a Gentile believer and not circumcised. He was acknowledged as in Christian fellowship and not compelled to be circumcised. This, in itself, was sufficient evidence that the apostles in Jerusalem did not sanction the teaching that circumcision is necessary for salvation.

Paul communicated to the leaders in Jerusalem the Gospel which he preached among the Gentiles. He did so privately first, for there was grave danger of a division in the body of Christ which he wanted to avoid; he did this so that he might not run in vain. In all this he manifested a gracious spirit. But when the false brethren introduced their perverted gospel to bring him and his fellow-laborers into bondage, he did not yield to them for a moment, but contended earnestly for the faith "that the truth of the gospel might continue with you." The result was the full confirmation of the gospel Paul preached, by James, Cephas and John, who gave to him and Barnabas the right hand of fellowship. The pillars of the church, as these three apostles are called, recognized the fact that the gospel of the uncircumcision had been committed unto Paul, as the gospel to the circumcision was Peter's calling and ministry. Both apostleships were from God and depended upon His gift. Thus the Apostle Paul is the apostle to the Gentiles, to whom was also committed the truth concerning the church, in which there is neither Jew nor Gentile, one body with Christ as the Head.

"It is evident that these facts are of great importance in the history of the church of God. How often have we not heard Peter spoken of as head of the Church. That Peter, ardent and full of zeal, began the work at Jerusalem, the Lord working mightily by his means, is certain; we see it plainly in Scripture. But he had nothing to do with the work carried on among the Gentiles. That work was done by Paul, who was sent by the Lord, Himself, and Paul entirely rejected the authority of Peter. For him, Peter was but a man; and he, sent by Christ, was independent of men. The Church among the Gentiles is the fruit of Paul's, not of Peter's work; it owed its origin to Paul and to his labor, and in no way to Peter, whom Paul had to resist with all his strength, in order to keep the assemblies among the Gentiles free from the influence of that spirit which ruled Christians, who were the fruit of Peter's work. God maintained unity by His grace; had He not kept the Church, it would have been divided into two parts, even in the days of the apostles themselves."[1]

This confirmation of Paul and the gospel he preached was a complete answer to the false claims and accusations of the enemies of the apostle.

A more serious matter is next brought to our attention. It shows the failure of Peter and how he had compromised the truth of the gospel. This exposure was necessary, for the false teach-

[1] J. N. Darby, *Epistle to the Galatians.*

ers claimed for Peter a special place of authority as if he were the perfect apostle, whose words and actions were next to infallible. The perverted gospel which teaches law-keeping and ordinances as necessary means for salvation, puts up man as authority and looks to man and not to the risen and glorified Lord. The Judaistic claims of Peter's superiority were the starting point of the Romish system, which asserts that Peter occupied a place as the visible head of the church in Rome, and which has culminated in the wicked assumption that the popes are the infallible vice-regents of Christ on earth.

Peter had visited Antioch and Paul had to withstand him to the face, for he was blameworthy.

Coming to Antioch, where Peter found a large Gentile church he there enjoyed his liberty in Christ; he ate with the Gentiles, realizing that the middle wall of partition was broken down (Eph. 2:14) and that believing Jews and Gentiles were one in Christ. All went well till some from James in Jerusalem showed themselves in Antioch. Then Peter, afraid of opposition, not because he thought in the least that he was wrong, separated himself, leaving them which were of the circumcision. His example led the other Jewish believers to dissemble likewise with him and even Barnabas joined in and, as a result, the unity of the Spirit was given up and the truth of the gospel marred. And Paul when he saw that they walked not uprightly, according to the truth of the gospel, rebuked Peter before them all. The leaven of the Pharisee, hypocrisy, is manifest in Peter's action. He wanted to appear before those who were still Jewish in their customs and sentiments as being in sympathy with them, and therefore he gave up his liberty in Christ, which he knew was according to the truth of the gospel. Paul rebuking Peter in public shows that Peter had not the least authority over Paul.

"If thou, being a Jew, livest as do the Gentiles, and not as do the Jews, why compellest thou the Gentiles to live as do the Jews?" These are the words Paul addressed to Peter. Why should Gentiles be forced to live as Jews, when Peter, being a Jew, had lived as the Gentiles? Verses 15-18 reveal the fatal consequences of Peter's action. He shows that Peter was a transgressor by building again what he had destroyed (verse 18). How had Peter done so and what suggested the question "Is, therefore, Christ the minister of sin?" (verse 17). When Peter refused to eat with the Gentiles he went back to the law and was thereby attempting to be justified by works; he was building again the law. But, previous to that, he had abandoned the law as a means of justification before God and he had believed in Jesus Christ to be justified by faith in Christ, and not by the works of the law. He had found out that "by the works of the law shall no flesh be justified." By building again the system of the law, which he had given up as unable to justify him, he made himself a transgressor, because he had left it. Inasmuch as it was Christ who had led him to do this—was, then, Christ a minister of sin? God forbid. It was the doctrine of Christ which had made him a transgressor in giving up the law; for in building it again and going back to it he acknowledged that he was wrong when he had rejected it as a means of justification. This is the argument of these verses.

The concluding verses of this chapter give the truth of the position of a believer in Christ who is justified by faith. It is Paul's individual testimony which every believer in Christ may repeat, for what was the apostle's position is ours also. "For I through the law died to the law, that I might live unto God." The law had pronounced the sentence of death and condemnation upon him and, through the law he had died to the law. But the sentence of the law was executed upon him in the person of Christ, who took the curse of the law, the condemnation, upon Himself, and believing in Christ he had died as to the old man. The law had slain him, but Christ had died in his stead, and thus he had died to the law, for the law only has dominion over a man as long as he lives. Death, the death of Christ, had freed him from the dominion of the law. As having died with Christ, he was dead to the law. (Romans 6—7 gives us the doctrine concerning these blessed facts of being dead to the law and delivered from the power of sin.)

All this is true of every believer. The great and precious truth of being dead with Christ and living unto God is blessedly stated in Paul's triumphant declaration, "I was crucified with Christ." (Not "I am crucified"; not in the sense of living as crucified with Christ, etc., but "I was crucified," put to death as to the old man, when Christ died.) The death of Christ has not only set the believer free from the guilt of sins, but has also put him to death as to the old man and delivered him from the power of sin in the flesh. "Knowing this, that our old man was crucified with Him, that the body of sin might be annulled, that we should no longer serve sin" (Rom 6:6). Then follow the other equally blessed statements: "Nevertheless, I live; yet not I, but Christ liveth in me; and the life which I now live in the flesh I live by the faith of the Son of God, who loved me and gave Himself for me." Dead to sin and the law, the believer no longer lives in his old life, but he has another life, which is Christ—"Christ liveth in me." It is that life which we receive, believing on Him.

The principle which governs this life is not the law principle, but it is a life lived in the faith of the Son of God. "All life in the creature has an object—we cannot walk without one. If the Lord Jesus is our life, He is also, personally, the object of the life, and we live by faith in Him. The heart sees Him, looks to Him, feeds upon Him, is assured of His love, for He gave Himself for us. The life that we live in the flesh, we live by the faith of the Son of God, who loved us and gave Himself for us. Happy certainty! Blessed assurance! It is a new life, the old man is crucified, and Christ, whose perfect love we know, is the sole object of faith and of the heart."

"It is this which always characterizes the life of Christ in us: He Himself is its object—He alone. The fact, that it is by dying for us in love that He—who was capable of it, the Son of God—has given us thus freed from sin this life as our own, being ever before the mind, in our eyes He is clothed with the love He has thus shewn us. We live by faith of the Son of God, who has loved us, and given Himself for us. And here it is personal life, the individual faith that attaches us to Christ, and makes Him precious to us as the object of the soul's intimate faith" (*Synopsis of the Bible*).

And then the conclusion. "I do not frustrate (set aside) the grace of God; for if righteousness is by the law, then Christ is dead in vain" (or: has died for nothing). If righteousness can be obtained by works, by a self-made character, or through keeping ordinances, then the death of Christ was superfluous and the grace of God is set aside. Christ is dead in vain if there is any other way to obtain righteousness than by faith in Him and through the grace of God.

II. Contrasts Between Law and Grace (3—4)

CHAPTER 3

1. The gift of the Spirit not by the works of the law, but by hearing of faith (3:1-5)
2. Righteousness not bestowed by the law, but by faith (3:6-9)
3. The law curses and the curse born by Christ (3:10-14)
4. The law cannot annul the covenant of promise (3:15-18)
5. Wherefore serveth the law? (3:19-22)
6. Faith having come—no longer under the law (3:23-25)
7. Sons of God by faith in Christ Jesus (3:26-29)

What the law could not do and what grace has done for the believer in Christ is now unfolded. Paul addresses them as foolish, and asks, "Who hath bewitched you, that ye should not obey the truth?" Who was responsible for the awful error they were following so destructive to the whole truth of the gospel? It was the witchery of Satan; as he tells them later, "Ye did run well; who did hinder you that ye should not obey the truth? This persuasion cometh not of Him that calleth you" (5:7-8). As Christians, they possessed the Holy Spirit, as all true Christians receive Him and are sealed by the Spirit. They also enjoyed the ministry of the Spirit through the different gifts.

Now he asks the question, "Received ye the Spirit by the works of the law, or by the hearing of faith?" There is no promise in the law that if it is kept in obedience, that God would send His Spirit to the heart of man to be the indwelling guest and make the obedient keeper of the law the temple of the Holy Spirit. The law does not promise even the Spirit. In Ezekiel 36:27 the promise is made, "I will put My Spirit within you," but, as the context shows, this promise refers to the future when the remnant of Israel will turn to the Lord and the promised spiritual and national blessings are given to them through grace. The Galatians knew nothing of the law and were not under the law, for they were, by nature, idolators. They had received the Spirit by hearing of faith. Before this great gift could ever be bestowed the Son of God had to die on the cross and be glorified (John 7:39). And all who receive the Lord Jesus Christ by faith, also receive the great gift of grace, the Holy Spirit, the Spirit of Sonship. They had received the Holy Spirit by simply believing. They were sealed by that Spirit and knew thereby that they were redeemed and the sons of God. If they possessed this seal of divine righteousness why should they add to it the works of the law? They acted, indeed, foolishly.

(Strange, unscriptural doctrines concerning the Holy Spirit are taught in different sects and parties. Some teach that the Christian should earnestly seek this gift, and the baptism with the Spirit. They claim that each individual must make a definite experience of receiving the baptism with the Spirit. This seeking includes, what they term, a full surrender, etc., and after enough seeking, surrender, giving up and praying, they claim to have received the power of the Holy Spirit. The argument here refutes this teaching. The Holy Spirit is given to every believer in Christ.)

The second argument is concerning righteousness. These false teachers made much of Abraham and the Jews honored him as the father of the nation. How did he obtain righteousness? It was not by the works of the law, for there was no law and no ordinances. "Abraham believed God, and it was reckoned to him for righteousness." He believed and grace imputed this to him for righteousness.

This took place before his circumcision. "How was it, then, reckoned? When he was in circumcision, or in uncircumcision? Not in circumcision, but in uncircumcision. And he received the sign of circumcision, a seal of the righteousness of the faith which he had, being yet uncircumcised; that he might be the father of all them that believe, though they be not circumcised; that righteousness might be imputed unto them also" (Rom. 4:10-13). Thus, righteousness is apart from the law and circumcision has nothing whatever to do with salvation; neither has baptism or any other ordinance. These Judaizing teachers and perverters of the gospel probably told the Galatians about being linked with Abraham and the privilege of being the children of Abraham. Paul writes them that, as believers, they are without the works of the law and circumcision, the children of Abraham. "Know ye, therefore, that they which are of faith, the same are the children of Abraham." And the Scriptures, the Word of God, had anticipated this. The Word of God foresaw that, ultimately, in God's gracious purpose, the Gentiles were to be justified by faith. The Word of God had, so to speak, preached the gospel unto Abraham, the very gospel Paul was heralding among the Gentiles. This gospel-message, preached by the Scriptures, is the announcement, "In thee shall all nations be blessed." The logical conclusion, therefore, is "they which be of faith are blessed with believing Abraham."

The law cannot give righteousness, but it gives man something and that is the curse. "For as many as are of the works of the law are under the curse, for it is written, cursed is everything that continueth not in all things which are written in the book of the law to do them." The law demands obedience, but it has no power to give a nature which delights in the law to keep it, nor can it bestow the power to fulfill its demands. Nothing can the law give to the sinner, but the curse.[2] But grace had also stated the faith principle in the Old Testament. "But that no man is justified by the law in the sight of God, is manifest, for the just shall live by faith." But redemption has come. Christ hath redeemed us from the curse of the law, being made a curse for us, for it is written "Cursed is everyone that hangeth on a tree." If a believer then goes back to the law and puts himself under the law, tries to live by it, he puts himself under the curse. He slights the precious work of Christ, who took the curse upon Himself, so that it can no longer fall upon us. And the result of Christ having removed the curse of the law is that the blessing of Abraham might be extended to the Gentiles through Him, so that all believers, both Jews and Gentiles, should receive the promised Spirit.

In verses 15-18, the priority of the grace-covenant is shown and that the law-covenant which came 430 years after cannot disannul the former covenant nor make the promise of none effect. If a covenant is made and confirmed, it cannot be rightly disannulled nor can anything be added to the same. The promises were made to Abraham; they were unconditional promises with no "if" attached to them, grace is the foundation of them. These promises were, afterward, confirmed to his seed. And that one seed (not seeds) is Christ. Isaac was a type of Him. And the original promise that all nations should be blessed in Abraham (Gen. 12:1-3) had been confirmed after the promised seed, Isaac, had been upon the altar (Gen. 22:18). Isaac, upon the altar and taken from the altar, was a type of Christ, His death and resurrection (Heb. 11:19). The law-covenant can, therefore, not disannul the promise nor add to it. If the inheritance is of the law, it is no more of promise, but God gave it to Abraham by promise.

If, then, the law cannot give the Spirit of God, if it cannot give righteousness, if the law has no blessing for man, but pronounces a curse upon him, if it cannot, in any way, affect the original grace-covenant made with Abraham, confirmed in Isaac, then the logical question

---

[2]See quotation from Deut. 27:11-26. Six tribes were put on Mt. Gerizim to bless and six upon Mt. Ebal to curse. The six tribes on Gerizim were silent; they could utter no blessing, for the law cannot bless. But the tribes on Mt. Ebal uttered twelve times the word "cursed." This is what the law does.

which follows is "Why did God give the law?"—"Wherefore, then, serveth the law?" (verse 19). The answer is "It was added because of transgressions." It was added not that sin might be curbed, or man might be saved by it, but that man might be constituted a transgressor and his hopeless and guilty condition fully demonstrated. It was introduced as a parenthetical thing, between the original promise and its fulfillment in Christ, in order that the moral condition of man might be manifested. (See also Rom. 3:20; 5:13; 5:20; 7:7-9.) Therefore, it was a mere addition "till the seed (Christ) should come, to whom the promise was made."

The law was ordained by angels in the hand of a mediator. "Now, a mediator is not of one, but God is one." Angels in glory were present at Sinai (Ps. 68:17); God did not reveal Himself in His glory and a mediator was needed, that is Moses. The statement "a mediator is not of one" means that mediatorship necessitates two parties. So there were God and Israel, Moses between as the mediator. But in the promise, the covenant made with Abraham and his seed, God was the only One who spoke. Its fulfillment is not (as in the law-covenant) dependent upon a faithful God and Israel's obedience, but on God's faithfulness alone; all depended upon God Himself. The mediatorship of the Lord Jesus Christ is a different thing and not in view here at all. But the law is not against the promises of God. Man needed life; the law could not give that, neither can it give righteousness. All—Jews and Gentiles—were shut up under sin, so that the promise made to Abraham might be fulfilled to all believers through faith in Jesus Christ.

"Before faith came—that is, before Christ had died and faith, as the great principle for the fullest blessing, had been made known—we, the Jews, were kept under the law, shut up to the faith which should, afterwards, be revealed." The apostle writes of the condition of the Jews before the cross of Christ and before the faith in Him was fully revealed. Therefore, the law was their schoolmaster unto Christ, that they might be justified by faith. The law was, for the Jews, a pedagogue, just as a pedagogue in a Greek household had charge of the children during their minority. The authorized version, "the law was our schoolmaster to bring us to Christ," is not correct. Upon this the statement is often made that the law is like a whip to bring us to accept Christ. But that is not the meaning. The law was the schoolmaster for the Jews unto Christ, until Christ came—the schoolmaster up to the time of Christ. Verse 25 makes this clear. "But after that faith is come"—faith being fully made known after the finished work of Christ and preached in the gospel—"we are no longer under the schoolmaster."

A great change has come since the faith has been made known through the gospel. Not alone are believers no longer under the schoolmaster, but they are sons of God. "For ye are all the sons of God by faith in Jesus Christ." Life and righteousness, the life from above and the righteousness of God are needed for divine sonship. The law cannot give life and righteousness, but grace bestows both on the believer and makes him a son of God. Being baptized unto Christ, they had put on Christ and had assumed in profession the name of Christ; a new place given to all, "there is neither Jew nor Gentile, there is neither bond nor free, there is neither male nor female; for ye are all one in Christ Jesus." Inasmuch as they were Christ's, heirs of the promise, they could not be under the law. "And if ye be Christ's, then are ye Abraham's seed, and heirs according to the promise."

CHAPTER 4

1. Under the law in the state of minority (4:1-3)
2. The Son revealed to redeem (4:4-5)
3. Because ye are Sons: the Spirit of sonship (4:6-7)
4. The backsliding Galatians (4:8-20)
5. The sons of the bondwoman and of the free woman (4:21-31)

Jewish believers were, before Christ had died, the children of God, and as such they did not differ from servants. They were in a state of minority, as children who do not know the father's thoughts, nor could they fully know God as Father.

"He compares the believer before the coming of Christ to a child under age, who has no direct relation with his father as to his thoughts, but who receives his father's orders, without his accounting for them to him, as a servant would receive them. He is under tutors and governors until the time appointed of the father. Thus the Jews, although they were heirs of the promises, were not in connection with the Father and His counsels in Jesus, but were in tutelage to principles that appertained to the system of the present world, which is but a corrupt and fallen creation. Their walk was ordained of God in this system, but did not go beyond it. We speak of the system by which they were guided, whatever divine light they might receive, from time to time, to reveal heaven to them, to encourage them in hope, while making the system under the rule of which they were placed yet darker. Under the law then, heirs as they were, they were still in bondage" (*Synopsis of the Bible*).

But a great change has taken place. "But when the fullness of time had come, God sent forth His Son, made of a woman, made under the law, that He might redeem those under the law, that we might receive the adoption of sons." God sent His Son from His bosom to become man and "made under the law." He took His place down here in two relationships. First with man, through the woman, and with the Jews, as born under the law. Sin and death came in by the woman; Christ came into this world by woman also. Through the law, man is under condemnation and Christ came as under that law. But that law was no bondage for Him. He fully worked out the righteousness of the law. Yet His righteous and holy life could not redeem those under the law. Redemption from the curse of the law was accomplished in the death of the cross. And the glorious result of the coming of the Son of God and His finished work is for all believers in Him "the adoption of sons"—that is, placed, through grace, before God as sons. And because believing Jews and Gentiles are sons, through the efficacy of the redemption wrought by the Lord Jesus Christ, God sent the blessed proof and power of sonship. "He sent forth the Spirit of His Son into your hearts, crying, Abba, Father." The Holy Spirit was given as the seal of redemption, and as the joy of sonship. "Wherefore, thou art no more a servant, but a son; and if a son, then an heir of God through Christ."

"Was it possible, then, that any could desire to put the Gentiles under the law, when they (the Jews) had been brought out from it themselves by the will of God, the work of Christ, and the witness of the Holy Spirit? What a gross inconsistency! What a subversion, not only of the truth of God revealed in the gospel, but also of redemption, which is its basis! For Christ bought off those that were under the law, that we might receive the adoption of sons, bringing them, by grace, into a place of known salvation and intelligent joy in relation with our God and Father, out of that bondage and nonage which the law supposes" (W. Kelly).

Then follows the appeal of the apostle to the backsliding Galatians, who were fast falling away from grace and turning to the weak and beggarly elements. Verses 8-10 are of much interest and significance. They were heathen, and knowing not God, they served idols. Now, as being converted, they had known God, or rather God had known them. Turning to Judaism, to the law with its ordinances, meant, for them, a turning back to the weak and beggarly elementary things in which they were as heathen. They were, practically, turning again to that which they had left—"how turn ye again?" As heathen they had ceremonies, different offerings, and they observed different days by which they tried to please their supposed gods. Ritualistic observances upon Christian ground are more than a perverted gospel: they are heathenish in principle. Some African fetish-priest attires himself in a fantastic costume. He takes a rattle, dances and mumbles something in an unintelligible way. Then he declares what he does will induce the gods to send rain. In a magnificent edifice called "church" stands a man who wears different colored robes. This man goes through different ceremonies, bows and crosses himself, mumbles something in a foreign language, then lifts up a receptacle before which the people bow in worship. He claims that, through him, blessing comes upon the people.

Both, the African heathen-priest and the ritualistic-priest follow the same principle, and the practice of the so-called "Christian priest" is as much heathenish as the practice of the other. And so as to the obesrvance of special holy days, months and years. "Ye observe days, and months, and times, and years. I am afraid of you, lest I have bestowed upon you labor in vain." The gospel knows nothing of the observance of days and seasons such as saint-days, Lent, etc. All these special saint-days and most of the feast-days kept in Christendom were taken from the heathen.

Then what a tender appeal follows! He reminds them of the former days when he preached first the gospel unto them. In the infirmity of the flesh, physical weakness, they had not despised nor rejected him, but received him as an angel of God, as the Christ whose blessed ambassador he was. Then they enjoyed great blessedness and would have plucked out their own eyes and given them to him. But where was their blessedness now? Had he become their enemy in speaking the truth to them? He addresses them as His little children "of whom I travail in birth again."

He needed, so to speak, to travail in birth afresh with them till Christ should be formed in them. Nevertheless, he calls them his children: his love inspired him with confidence, and yet filled his heart with uneasiness. He would have desired to be with them that he might change his voice, suiting it to their state; not only teaching them the truth, but doing whatever their need required. Mark here the deep love of the apostle. Moses, faithful as he was, grew weary of the burden of the people and said: Have I conceived all this people? have I begotten them, that thou shouldest say unto me, Carry them in thy bosom, as a nursing father beareth the sucking child, unto the land which thou swearest unto their fathers? (Num. 11:12); but the apostle is willing to travail in birth with them as his children a second time, in order that their souls might be saved.

Verses 21-31 give an interesting, typical foreshadowing and contrast. As they were abandoning grace, he wants the law to speak to them. Abraham had two sons, one by Hagar, the bondmaid, born after the flesh; the other son was Isaac, the son of promise, born by Sarah, the free woman. Both illustrate the covenants of God. Mount Sinai, the law covenant, which gendereth to bondage, is represented in Hagar and her son; the other, the covenant of promise, "Jerusalem which is above"—the mother of us all—it is the true church of God viewed in her heavenly state; she is free. He quotes Isaiah 54:1, "Rejoice thou, barren, that bearest not; break forth and cry, thou that travailest not, for the desolate has many more children than she which hath an husband." These words are addressed to Jerusalem during the millennial kingdom, in the time of her promised restoration. Then Israel, redeemed and blessed, will look back and find that, during our age, this gospel-age, many more children were begotten by the gospel, during the time when Israel was cast off and Jerusalem trodden down by the Gentiles than at the time when Jerusalem flourished and enjoyed the favor of Jehovah. "Now, we, brethren, as Isaac was, are the children of promise." Those who believe and are saved by grace are, therefore, the true children of promise.

But, as then, he that was born after the flesh persecuted "him that was after the Spirit, even so it is now." The Jews persecuted Paul for preaching the gospel. They opposed the gospel and all those who believed in Christ. But what was said about the bondwoman and her son? "Cast out the bondwoman and her son, for the son of the bondwoman shall not be heir with the free woman." This has happened to Israel; she, for a time, is disowned and their house is left desolate. "So then, therefore, we are not children of the bondwoman, but of the free." It would be impossible to be children of both. Equally impossible is it to be under law and under grace. The two cannot exist together. We are children of the free woman and of her only and have nothing whatever to do with the law-covenant. We belong to a risen Christ, with whom we have died, who has borne the curse for us and bestowed upon us life and righteousness, and, therefore, we are free from the law, from its service and ceremonies.

III. The Walk of the Justified Believer, As Not Under The Law, But Under Grace (5—6)

CHAPTER 5

1. Stand fast! Be not entangled! (5:1-6)
2. Exhortations and the law of love (5:7-15)
3. Flesh and Spirit (5:16-21)
4. The fruits of the Spirit (5:22-26)

The first exhortation is to maintain, by faith, the liberty which is found in Christ, to stand fast in that liberty where with Christ has made the believer free and not to be entangled again with the yoke of bondage. The believer has perfect liberty in Christ; he is absolutely dead to the law and the law is not to be used by him in any way. But verse 13, where the apostle speaks again of this liberty, must be brought in connection with the opening statement of this chapter. "For, brethren, ye have been called into liberty; only use not liberty for an occasion to the flesh, but by love serve one another." The liberty the believer has in Christ is to be used for holiness. When God redeems from the curse of the law it is a redemption unto holiness, to live a righteous and holy life; the Holy Spirit indwellin the believer does not give license to live fter the flesh.

But as being in Christ, dead to the law, if they become circumcised Christ would profit them nothing and they were bound to fulfill the whole law. Going back to the law for righteousness, they had fallen from grace. This is the only time "fallen from grace" is used in the Bible. It has been strangely misapplied by a certain system of theology to deny the security of the believer in Christ. It is generally used to describe a Christian who has fallen in sin and, as it is claimed, lost his relationship as a child of God and is, therefore, once more under judgment. Falling from grace does not mean this; it means to give up the grace of the gospel in order to satisfy the requirements of the law. To go back under the law and its bondage is falling from grace. Verse 5 does not mean that a believer hopes for righteousness; he possesses righteousness by faith. Indwelt by the Spirit, the believer waits not for righteousness, but for the hope of righteousness by faith. And the hope of the righteousness is the coming glory, when all those who are saved by grace will be glorified and be like Christ.

Then the earnest pleadings and warnings. They had run well; who hindered them? It was Satan who had led them astray. Once more leaven is used. A little leaven leaveneth the whole lump. Even so it is today in Christendom. The leaven of a perverted gospel has well nigh leavened everything. He was deeply concerned about the spiritual condition of these Galatian Christians. But while he was in doubt about them and he was overwhelmed with grief because they abandoned grace, his heart, after all, was also in peace about them. "I have confidence in you through the Lord that ye will be now otherwise minded." He cast them as his burden upon the Lord and he knew the Lord, who loveth His own, would after all bring it about that they would surely not be otherwise minded.

He who troubled them and bewitched them with that spurious gospel, whosoever he would be, would bear his judgment; and he wishes that these troublers were cut off. "And I, brethren, if I preach yet circumcision, why am I still persecuted? Then is the offence of the cross ceased." He had probably been charged by some of endorsing circumcision and preaching it. If such were the case, what further excuse was there for the Jews to persecute him? If he were still preaching circumcision the offence of the cross would have been done away. Circumcision stands for the religion of the natural man. The religious spirit of the natural man is always in opposition to the true gospel. Difficulties will cease and the world will even applaud the preaching if the religion of the flesh, the "do-religion"—"observe"—"keep"—"reform", etc., is proclaimed. Of this we see much today. The true gospel of grace, proclaimed upon the finished work of Christ, with nothing to do and nothing to pay, is still the same stumbling-block.

The believer possesses in Christ true liberty (verse 13); a liberty, as already stated, not to sin, but to walk and serve God in holiness. It is the liberty of the new nature, the divine nature, which gives power over sin. The law seeks to constrain the old nature, which is impossible; but it is the mighty constraint of love, given by the Holy Spirit. And that love is the fulfillment of the law. The law, as a rule, for the believer's life is, therefore, not needed. The gospel of grace sets the believer free and makes him happy in the assurance of God's love and his own salvation; and the Holy Spirit is there. Under His guidance and power, walking in the Spirit, the lust of the flesh will not be fulfilled. And the believer, walking thus, has the blessed assurance that sin shall not have dominion over him. "For sin shall not have dominion over you, for ye are not under the law, but under grace" (Rom. 6:14). The law had not the power to do this, but grace has delivered us from the law of sin and death (Rom. 8:1-4).

In the preceding part of the Epistle he had set forth Christian justification by faith, in contrast with works of the law. He here shows that God produces holiness. Instead of exacting it, as did the law with regard to human righteousness, from the nature which loves sin, He produces it in the human heart, as wrought by the Spirit.

"This life, produced in us by the operation of the Holy Ghost through the word, is led by the Spirit who is given to believers; its rule is also in the word. Its fruits are the fruits of the Spirit. The Christian walk is the manifestation of this new life, of Christ our life, in the midst of the world. If we follow this path—Christ Himself—if we walk in His steps, we shall not fulfill the lusts of the flesh. It is thus sin is avoided, not by taking the law to compel man to do what he does not like; the law has no power to compel the flesh to obey, for it is not subject to the law of God, neither, indeed, can be. The new life loves to obey, loves holiness, and Christ is its strength and wisdom by the Holy Ghost. The flesh is indeed there; it lusts against the Spirit, and the Spirit lusts against the flesh, to prevent man from walking as he would. But if we walk in the Spirit, we are not under the law."[3]

The works of the flesh and the fruit of the Spirit are given in verses 19-23. In a more literal rendering, the works of the flesh, sixteen in number, are as follows: Fornication, uncleanness, licentiousness, idolatry, sorcery, hatred, strifes, jealousies, angers, contentions, disputes, factions, envyings, murders, drunken-

[3]J. N. Darby, *Notes on Galatians.*

ness, revels and things like these. Such is the old nature of man and such the fruit it bears. They that do such things, living according to the flesh, shall not inherit God's kingdom. And only the power of the Spirit of God can deliver from the outworking of this fallen nature, the flesh, which is still in the believer. The Holy Spirit is in the child of God to manifest this power, but it means subjection to Himself.

The Spirit also produces His own blessed fruit in the life of the believer. The first three are: Love, joy and peace. These give the blessed consciousness the believer has in his heart of his relationship to God, which consciousness comes through the Spirit. The other six fruits: "long-suffering, kindness, goodness, fidelity, meekness, self-control," witness in the believer's walk to the fact that the love, the joy and peace of God are realities in the soul. The believer who walks according to the Spirit manifests in his walk the fruits of the indwelling Spirit and against such there is no law. And they that are Christ's have crucified the flesh and its lusts. They have accepted the sentence of the cross which has put the old man with its lusts into the place of death. God declares us as dead with Christ and looks upon us thus (Col. 3:3). And this great truth must be lived. The believer lives in the Spirit and is called upon to walk in the Spirit so that the righteousness of the law may be fulfilled in him. "Let us not be desirous of vain-glory (the law fosters such a spirit, but grace humbles), provoking one another, envying one another"—which is the sad effect of vain-glory, provocation and envy.

CHAPTER 6

1. Concerning the restoration of a brother (6:1-5)
2. Concerning reaping and sowing (6:6-10)
3. The conclusion (6:11-18)

Practical exhortations conclude the defence of the gospel. The previous chapter stated that they that are Christ's have crucified the flesh and its lusts. In the beginning of this chapter the treatment to be accorded to a man (a brother) who has been overtaken in a fault is given. The law would demand the cutting off of such a one. It is harsh and merciless. But grace bears a different message. "Brethren, if a man be overtaken in a fault, ye which are spiritual, restore such a one in the spirit of meekness; considering thyself, lest thou also be tempted." The sin of a believer does not put him out of the true Church, the body of Christ, but it interrupts communion with God. The erring brother is to be treated in a spirit of meekness and to be restored. Then law is mentioned, but not the law of Moses, but the law of Christ. "Bear ye one another's burdens, and so fulfill the law of Christ." He is the great burden-bearer for His people and to bear the burdens of others is to act as the Lord Jesus does. None is to think of himself to be something when he is nothing; the legal spirit puffs up. Every man is to prove his own work, and then shall he have rejoicing in himself alone, and not in another. "For every man shall bear his own burden"—this is in reference to the judgment-seat of Christ when each must give an account of himself.

Another instruction is concerning ministry to those who teach. "Let him that is taught in the Word communicate unto him that teacheth in all good things." This is the way a loving and gracious Lord has appointed. The believer who receives the ministry of the Word through one of the gifts in the body of Christ has a personal responsibility towards him who ministers. He is to communicate to him in earthly things, and thus have a part in his ministry. How different in Christendom, with its fixed salaries, pew-rents and, worse still, when evangelists appeal to the unsaved, to Catholics and Jews, to swell the collection. Important is the principle of verses 7-9. We quote from another:

"We may repeat again that the toleration of evil is never grace. It would be a perversion of the very thought of grace to imagine this. 'Be not deceived,' he says, therefore, 'God is not mocked, for whatsoever a man soweth, that shall he also reap, for he that soweth to his flesh shall of the flesh reap corruption and he that soweth to the Spirit, shall of the Spirit reap life everlasting.' These are principles of absolute necessity. Nothing can alter them. If a man sows a certain seed, he knows, or he should know, that he can get of that seed nothing but what is proper to it. If a man sows to his flesh, he sows, in fact, the corruption which he reaps. The very principle of self-will which must, of necessity, be in it, is a principle which is essentially that of sin. Every form of sin will come under this, and God may allow, in fact, such seed to come to harvest, in order that we may recognize its character, as we otherwise would not do. In the opposite way to that of the man who, bearing good seed, goes forth even weeping, but returns with joy, a man in this way may sow his seed rejoicing, but it will be the return that will be sorrowful.

"It does not follow that God cannot come in and deliver us from what would otherwise be the necessary fruit of such sowing, if only there be the true self-judgment of it in the soul; for to a Christian, the reaping of it is but in order to self-judgment, and if we will judge it first, there may be no need of reaping at all. Judge it first or last we surely must, or the thing will develop for what it is and be manifest, not to ourselves alone it may be, but to others also. On the other hand, 'He that soweth to the Spirit, shall of the Spirit reap life everlasting.' Blessed and wonderful reaping! The life is looked at here, of course, in its practical character, in its fruits and activities. The life itself, the life which produces this, is no matter of reaping at all, it is what we must have to be Christians. Nevertheless, we can reap it as a practical thing, and the witness of it is that, even though reaped here upon earth, it is something which has eternity in it" (*Numerical Bible*).

Verse 11 tells us that he had written this letter with his own hand and that in large letters. It seems as if the energy of the Holy Spirit came upon him in such a degree that he had to dispense with the usual amanuensis he employed. Then he reverts to the great controversy once more. These false teachers, the proselyting teachers, wanted to boast with the Galatians, but he knew only one boasting or glorying, "in the cross of our Lord Jesus, whereby the world is crucified unto me, and I unto the world." The cross meant everything to him and thus it should be with every believer, saved by grace.

But what does he mean when he speaks of bearing in his body the marks—the stigmata—of the Lord Jesus? The Romish conception of the supernaturally imprinted scars of the nails in the apostle's body does not need to be investigated, for it is a superstition. The expression simply means the trials and sufferings he underwent for Christ's sake and which left their marks on his frail body (2 Cor. 11:24-33). What the Galatians needed the most is the final word of Paul to the Galatians. "The grace of our Lord Jesus Christ be with your Spirit, brethren."

THE EPISTLE TO THE
EPHESIANS

Introduction

The city of Ephesus was situated in Lydia on the River Cayster, about forty miles from Smyrna. It was a place of considerable commerce and also noted for its magnificent temple of Artemis, which was from very ancient times the centre of the worship of that goddess. This temple was burnt down by Herostratus 355 B.C., but rebuilt at immense cost, and was one of the wonders of the ancient world. Pliny tells us that it was 425 feet long and 220 feet in breadth. All Asia contributed to its erection, and 127 magnificent columns were bestowed by so many kings. Little models of the temple in silver, with the image of the goddess enshrined in them, were made for sale, and sold in large quantities (Acts 19:24-29).

From Acts 18:19-21 we learn of Paul's first brief visit to that city. He was then hastening to Jerusalem to be there at Pentecost. After his visit to Jerusalem he returned to Ephesus (Acts 19:1) and remained there laboring for about three years, so that he could say later to the elders of Ephesus, "therefore watch, and remember, that by the space of three years I ceased not to warn every one night and day with tears" (Acts 20:31). During this time the Ephesian assembly was founded, composed of Jews and Gentiles, who heard and believed the gospel. On his last journey to Jerusalem he did not visit Ephesus, but called the elders of the church to meet him at Miletus, where he said farewell and exhorted them (Acts 20:18-35).

The Epistle Written by Paul

The Epistle to the Ephesians was written by the Apostle Paul when he was a prisoner (chapter 3:1; 4:1; 6:20). There can be no doubt that the Colossian Epistle and the Epistle to Philemon were sent by Paul the same time as the Ephesian Epistle. The date was about 62 A.D. Tychicus and Onesimus, the runaway slave, but now through grace "a brother beloved" (Philemon 16) were sent to Colossae by Paul (Col. 4:7-9). Tychicus carried the letter addressed to the Colossians to correct the evils which had arisen in that church, and to warn them against the wicked doctrines which were being promulgated amongst them. Onesimus the slave carried that beautiful little Epistle addressed to his master Philemon. And at the same time when Tychicus and Onesimus left Rome, Paul handed to Tychicus the Epistle to the Ephesians. Never before and never after were such weighty and blessed documents entrusted to human messengers. The reception of the authorship of Paul has been almost universal; only in very recent times has the Pauline authorship been foolishly questioned by some rationalistic critics.

Some scholars claim that the words "at Ephesus" should be omitted and that the Epistle was not addressed to the Ephesians at all. The chief objection is, that if this Epistle is addressed to the church at Ephesus, it would be inexplicable that Paul should not have sent a single message of personal greeting to the Ephesians, amongst whom he had spent so long a time, and to whom he was bound by ties of such close affection. But there are also other Epistles written by Paul which do not contain such personal greetings; for instance, first and second Corinthians, Galatians, Philippians, first and second Thessalonians and first Timothy. Other objections have been raised. Dean Alford states rightly "there is nothing in its contents inconsistent with such an address" (to the Ephesians). We find in it clear indications that its readers were mixed Jews and Gentiles (2:14; compare with Acts 19:10). It would seem quite improbable that the apostle should not have sent an epistle to Ephesus, where the Lord had so largely owned his testimony and where the Lord had so miraculously delivered him when he fought with beasts (1 Cor. 15:32). But while this Epistle was undoubtedly first sent to Ephesus, it may have been used as a kind of circular letter, being sent to and read by other assemblies. The Epistle mentioned in Col. 4:16 was probably this Epistle.

Its Deep and Blessed Message

In the Epistle to the Colossians Paul makes the statement, "Whereof I am made a minister, according to the dispensation of God which is given to me for you, to fulfill the Word of God" (Col. 1:25). To fulfill the Word of God does not mean, as often stated, that Paul fulfilled his ministry and was faithful in it. It means rather that to him was given the revelation which makes full, or completes, the Word of God. The highest and most glorious revelation, which the God and Father of our Lord Jesus Christ has been pleased to give, He has given through the Apostle Paul. The two prison Epistles to the Ephesians and Colossians embody this completion of the Word of God. The Ephesian Epistle holds the place of pre-eminence. The revelation which is given in this Epistle concerning believing sinners, whom God has redeemed by the blood of His Son, and exalted in Him into the highest possible position, is by far the greatest revelation. God is revealing His own loving heart and tells out by His Spirit how He loved us and thought of us before the foundation of the world. He shows forth the riches of His grace and now makes known the secret He held back in former ages. How rich it all is! Like God Himself, so this revelation, coming from His loving heart, is inexhaustible. We may speak of Ephesians as the rich Epistle of the God and Father of our Lord Jesus Christ, who, rich in mercy, tells us of the exceeding riches of His grace in kindness towards us through Christ Jesus. But even this definition does not tell out half of all the glory this wonderful document contains. It is God's highest and God's best. Even God cannot say more than what He has said in this filling full of His Word.

In the Psalms we read: "The heavens declare the glory of God and the firmament showeth His handiwork" (Psalm 19:1). We lift up our eyes and behold the wonders of God's creation, which He called into existence by His Son and for Him (Col. 1:16). Here in this Epistle another heaven is opened. If the heavens of creation are so wonderful and their depths unfathomable, how much more wonderful are the heavenlies into which Christ has entered, where He now is seated, far above all principality and power and might, and into which God's grace has brought us in Christ! The first three chapters contain this great revelation. What God has accomplished in His Son, to the praise of the glory of His grace; how He makes believers one with His Son, sharers of His glory, is told out in these chapters. The church, the body of Christ, the fulness of Him that filleth all in all; the one body in which believing Jews and Gentiles are united; the building growing into an holy temple, the habitation of God by the Spirit, and the ultimate destiny of that body, are further revelations in these great chapters.

The central verse of the first three chapters is found in chapter 2:10, "For we are His workmanship created in Christ Jesus unto good works, which God has before ordained, that we should walk in them." The word "workmanship" is in the Greek "poiema," from which our word "poem" is derived. It is a beautiful thought in itself to think of those who are saved by grace, and united to Christ, as "the poem of God." But the word "poiema" may also be rendered "masterpiece" or "masterwork."

Only once more is the same word found in the original language of the New Testament Scriptures. In Rom. 1:20 it is used in connection with the physical creation. God has produced two great masterworks in which He manifests His power. He called the universe into existence out of nothing. What He, as the omnipotent One can do, is seen in the creation of the heavens and the earth and in the sustenance of His creation. His eternal power and Godhead are revealed in creation (Rom. 1:19-20). But the creation of the universe out of nothing is not the greatest masterpiece of God. God has done something greater. He has produced a work, which reveals Him in a far higher degree. That greater masterpiece is the redemption of sinners. God took only six days to bring order out of the chaos of the disturbed original creation and to call into existence the present earth and heavens, but He spent forty days with Moses in directing him to build the tabernacle, because the work of redemption is more glorious than the work of creation.

God's creation and also the Bible, His revelation, may be studied by the telescope and the microscope. A telescopic sweep of this wonderful Epistle is hardly sufficient. The miscroscopic examination brings out its wonders. "The student of Ephesians must not expect to go over his ground too rapidly; must not be disappointed, if the week's end finds him still on the same paragraph, or even on the same verse, weighing and judging—penetrating gradually, by the power of the mind of the Spirit, through one outer surface after another, getting in his hand one and another ramifying thread, till at last he grasps the main cord whence they are diverged, and where they all unite—and stands rejoicing in his prize, deeper rooted in the faith, and with a firmer hold on the truth as it is in Christ. And as the wonderful effect of the spirit of inspiration on the mind of man is nowhere in Scripture more evident than in this Epistle, so, to discern those things of the Spirit, is the spiritual mind here more than anywhere else required."[1]

And the more we read and study this Epistle, the more we will be impressed with the greatness and the glory of the revelation it brings to our hearts. It is a theme for eternity. How needful the study of this Epistle is for us in these days! The truths revealed will keep us in the days of apostasy and lift us above the materialistic spirit of the times. Without earnest and continued meditation on the great truths made known in this Epistle, spiritual growth and enjoyment are impossible. May it please the Holy Spirit to lead the writer and the reader into a better and deeper heart knowledge of His wonderful grace.

The Division of Ephesians

The Epistle to the Ephesians has two clearly defined sections. Chapter 4 begins with the following words: "I therefore, the prisoner of the Lord, beseech you that ye walk worthy of the calling wherewith ye are called." What the calling is wherewith the God and Father of our Lord Jesus Christ has called those who believe in His Son, is revealed in the first three chapters. As stated in the introduction, God's great masterwork, the redemption of sinners, is blessedly told out in the opening chapters of this Epistle. The last three chapters contain exhortations and instructions to walk worthy of this high calling, to manifest in every way the great Work of God.

I. THE MASTERWORK OF GOD (1—3)

1. **The Godhead at Work** (1)
2. **The Production of the Masterwork and its Destiny** (2:1-10)
3. **The Mystery now made Known** (2:11—3:21)

II. THE PRACTICAL MANIFESTATION IN THE LIFE OF THE BELIEVER (4—6)

1. **Walking worthy of the Calling** (4:1-6)
2. **The Ministry and its Purpose** (4:7-16)
3. **The Walk in Holiness and Righteousness** (4:17—5:21)
4. **Manifestation in the Family Relationship** (5:22—6:4)
5. **Exhortations to Servants and Masters** (6:5-9)
6. **The Warfare and the Panoply of God** (6:10-20)
7. **The Conclusions (6:21-24)**

[1]Dean Alford, *Prolegomena*.

Analysis and Annotations

I. The Masterwork of God (1—3)

1. The Godhead at Work

CHAPTER 1

1. The introduction (1:1-2)
2. The great doxology (1:3)
3. The work of the Father (1:4-6)
4. The work of the Son (1:7-12)
5. The work of the Holy Spirit (1:13-14)
6. The parenthetical prayer to the God of our Lord Jesus Christ, the Father of glory (1:15-23)

In the brief introductory words to this Epistle, Paul speaks of himself as an apostle of Jesus Christ by the will of God. It is to be noticed that the will of God is repeatedly mentioned in this first chapter. All blessings mentioned in this Epistle flow from the will of God. What God hath done for us in Christ is "according to the good pleasure of His will" (verse 5). Then we read also of "having made known unto us the mystery of His will" (verse 9) and "who worketh all things after the counsel of His own will" (verse 11). This will of God goes back to eternity, before the foundation of the world. This will made the erstwhile persecutor of the Church, the apostle of Jesus Christ, the instrument through whom that blessed will of God is now fully revealed. The Epistle is addressed "to the saints and to the faithful in Christ Jesus." This does not mean two classes of believers. All believers are saints—separated ones. Yet a saint may not be faithful. Many who are saved by grace and are constituted saints in Christ are unfaithful in their walk and testimony. The words "to the saints and to the faithful in Christ Jesus" correspond to the two divisions of the Epistle. In the first three chapters we learn that God has made us His saints in Christ; in the last three chapters we are exhorted to walk in obedience and be faithful.

The doxology (verse 3) marks the beginning

of the epistle. When we reach the end of this first section we find another doxology (3:20-21). Between these two doxologies are found the unsearchable riches of God's grace in Christ. The third verse is in itself the key to the great and deep revelation which follows in this chapter. It is the bud which the Holy Spirit gradually unfolds. The Godhead in blessing believers is revealed in the doxology. First we find the God and Father of our Lord Jesus Christ. He is the author of all blessings. In the second place we learn that the blessings are in the Son of God, in Christ. Then thirdly, we read what kind of blessings we receive in Christ, "every spiritual blessing," that is, blessings communicated by the third person of the Godhead, God the Holy Spirit.

The phrase "in the heavenly places" (or heavenlies) is peculiar to this Epistle. We find it five times: chapters 1:3, 20; 2:6; 3:10 and 6:12. It means both the nature of the blessings which we have in a risen and glorified Christ, and the locality, where our Lord is in glory. The three persons of the Godhead are mentioned in the third verse. The God and Father of our Lord Jesus Christ has blessed us; these blessings are in the Son and are communicated by the Holy Spirit. What follows is very interesting. In verses 4-14 we have the three persons of the Godhead revealed and their work in the redemption of sinners. Read verses 6, 12 and 14. Each is an utterance of praise—"to the praise of the glory of His grace" (verse 6); "that we should be to the praise of His glory" (verse 12); "unto the praise of His glory" (verse 14). Each of these verses marks the close of what is said about the Father, the Son and the Holy Spirit. In verses 4-6 we read what the Father has done; verses 7-12 reveal what we have and are in the Son, in Christ; verses 13-14 reveal the work of God, the Holy Spirit.

Three great facts are mentioned of the God and Father of our Lord Jesus Christ.

1. He hath chosen us in Christ before the foundation of the world.

2. He hath predestinated us unto the Son-place in Christ.

3. He hath made us accepted in the Beloved.

What wonderful statements these are! We are in them face to face with the deepest revelation. To deny this would stamp these words as the imaginations of a deceiver. Only revelation can make known that which happened before the foundation of the world. Whatever is in God's eternity, that unfathomable existence without beginning, is beyond man's ability to grasp and therefore unrevealed. But here the great truth is made known that God, before there was a world, planned His masterwork. With Him in His bosom was His blessed Son, the Son of His love. In Him, by Him and for Him all things were called into existence. Yet before this creation was effected, God knew the outcome. Surprise is an impossibility with God. He knows the end from the beginning. The whole story of man's fall and its results were not hidden from Him. And before it ever came to pass God made provision. And those who would accept Christ, as their Saviour, He willed should be before Him holy and without blame, become partakers of His own divine nature. This God willed before the foundation of the world, and this is now, through grace, the portion of every believer in the Lord Jesus Christ. And, furthermore, He predestinated all who believe in Christ to the Son-place.

A brief word on "predestination." This word, which means "marked out" is nowhere found in connection with the Gospel, nor does it say anywhere in the Word, what some have said, that God has predestinated human beings to be lost. But while we do not read that He ever predestinated any one to be lost we read "God would have all men to be saved" (1 Tim. 2:4). God has nothing to say to a lost world about predestination. His grace, bringing salvation has appeared unto all men. God's offer of salvation is therefore to all.

The *Authorized Version* speaks of "adoption of children." This hardly expresses it correctly. Believers in the Lord Jesus Christ are not adopted into the family of God; they are born into the family. The Greek has only one word "Son-place." We are placed into the position of Sons. Not alone hath God given to us His own nature, but He gives us, because we have that nature in and through His Son, the place as Sons. Think of what God might have done for those, who by wicked works are His enemies. He might have given us the place of unfallen angels, the wonderful ministers of heaven. What mercy that would have been! Or He might have lifted us to the dignity of an archangel, full of beauty and power. But even that would not have been the very best He could have done in the riches of His grace and love. He has made us Sons, like *the* Son, whom He raised from the dead and seated at His own right hand.

And then He hath accepted us in the Beloved One. All this God planned and willed before the foundation of the world.

The Beloved One having been mentioned,

we read at once of His work. Three facts are given of the work of the Son of God:

1. He redeemed us by His blood.
2. In Him we received the revelation of the mystery of His will.
3. In Him we obtain an inheritance (verses 7-12).

He came from the bosom of the Father to this earth to redeem us, so that God's eternal will might be accomplished. Redemption, the taking out of the condition in which we are by nature, is a necessity, and has been accomplished by the blood of the Son of God, which was shed on the cross. He paid the price and has set us free. The riches of His grace by the redemption through His blood includes all our needs as sinners; the forgiveness of sins, mentioned here, is, so to speak, the foundation.

"Whosoever will" and "whosoever believeth" are the glorious terms of God's good news to all alike. But when we believe, we *know* that we are chosen and predestinated. Those who have believed on Christ are predestinated and they possess the Son-place. Then having believed, we know that we were chosen in Him before the foundation of the world.

The words which follow put before us some blessed and deep truths. Redeemed through His blood, having redemption, the forgiveness of sins, according to the riches of grace, He hath made known unto us the mystery of His will. God wants His elect, His Church, to know the secret things of His will and what He hath purposed in Himself. Therefore He hath made the riches of His grace abound towards us in all wisdom and intelligence. God has been pleased to make known in Christ the mystery of His will. It is the revelation of the mystery, which was kept secret since the world began (Rom. 16:25), so that we know in Christ and through Christ the fulness of His purpose. That mystery of God is Christ, in which are hid all the treasures of wisdom and knowledge (Col. 2:3).

Christ, who has redeemed us by His blood, was raised from the dead. God "set Him at His own right hand in the heavenlies"—"He hath put all things under His feet, and gave Him to be the head over all things to the Church, which is His body, the fulness of Him that filleth all in all" (1:21-23). This is the mystery: that Christ risen from the dead, seated at the right hand of God, is the Head and those who believe on Him constitute the Church, His body. This body is destined, according to the eternal purpose of God, to share the glory of the Head. This purpose is still in the future. The administration (or dispensation) of the fulness of times has not yet come. When it comes all things, both which are in heaven and which are on earth, will be headed up in Christ.

And in Christ we have an inheritance. In Him we have obtained an inheritance; it is equally true, that we are redeemed by His blood, His inheritance. And our inheritance in Christ is that we shall be like Him; be joint-heirs with Him and be forever with the Lord.

The work of the Holy Spirit is revealed in verses 13 and 14. Three things are also mentioned of Him and His work:

1. Hearing and believing resulting in the quickening by the Spirit.
2. The sealing by the Holy Spirit of Promise.
3. The Holy Spirit the earnest of our inheritance.

These words are of great importance. The Son of God came to this earth to redeem us and because He has finished the work the Father gave Him to do, the Holy Spirit, the third person of the Godhead, has come to do His work.

Three words are prominent in the thirteenth verse, the words "heard," "believed," and "sealed." They go together. The Word of Truth, the gospel of salvation must be heard and believed; the hearing and believing results in the sealing with the Holy Spirit of promise. The Holy Spirit indwelling the believer is the earnest of the inheritance until the redemption of the purchased possession takes place. (For a more complete exposition we refer the reader to our larger work *The Masterpiece of God.*)

A brief restatement of the work of the Godhead will be helpful:

1. We found *God the Father* has chosen us in Christ before the foundation of the world. *God the Son* came down from Heaven's glory and redeemed us by His blood. *God the Holy Spirit* quickens those who hear and believe. He is here because Christ finished His work on the cross.

2. *God the Father* has predestinated us unto the Son-place. *God the Son* reveals, to all who are sons with Him, the mystery of His will, concerning the future of the new creation. *God the Holy Spirit* because we are sons, possesses us and keeps those whom He possesses. He is the Spirit of Sonship.

3. *God the Father* has accepted us in the Beloved. *God the Son* has given us in Himself an inheritance. *God the Holy Spirit* is the earnest of that inheritance.

Surely this is revelation from God. So blessedly simple, so profound that all the eternal ages will not suffice to sound its depths. No man could have ever discovered or invented such a plan. Let us bow before it in worship and yield our lives "to the Praise of the glory of His grace."

In verses 15-23 we have the first prayer in this Epistle; the second prayer is found at the close of the third chapter. Let us notice that the greatest revelation of God as given in this Epistle has two prayers connected with it. The revelation is given to His people that they might know it and enjoy it. Prayer is needed for this. First, there is thanksgiving (verses 15-16).

The prayer here is addressed to "the God of our Lord Jesus Christ, the Father of glory." The prayer in the third chapter is made to "the Father of our Lord Jesus Christ." This corresponds most beautifully to the blessed revelation in the first fourteen verses of this chapter. "God and Father" are the blessed words, which stand in the foreground of this Epistle. God is light and God is love. The first prayer is a prayer for light, that His redeemed people may know, be enlightened; therefore it is addressed to the God of our Lord Jesus Christ. The second prayer in the third chapter is for love, and therefore addressed to the Father of our Lord Jesus Christ.

Then we find three petitions: 1. "That ye may know what is the hope of His calling." The hope of God's calling is that we shall be one with Him, whom He raised from the dead and to whom He gave glory. 2. That we may know "the riches of the glory of His inheritance in the saints." The riches into which God, the Father of glory, has brought us through Him, who laid His glory by, is told out in this Epistle. It is the rich Epistle of our riches in Christ. "The riches of His grace" (Eph. 1:7); "the riches of the glory of His inheritance" (1:18); "rich in mercy" (2:4); "the exceeding riches of His grace" (2:7); "the unsearchable riches of Christ" (3:8); "according to the riches of His glory" (3:16); these are the passages in which we read of His riches towards us and our riches in Him.

And what is the meaning "the riches of the glory of His inheritance in the saints"? We have an inheritance, and He has us for His inheritance. He is our inheritance, and we are His inheritance. The glory of Christ's inheritance are the saints, for whom He died, the many sons He brings to glory. The Church is the fulness of Him, who filleth all in all.

3. And the third petition is that we may know "the exceeding greatness of His power which is to us-ward who believe." It is resurrection power, the power which raised Him from the dead and seated Him on God's right hand, which is to us-ward who believe. We can count on it. Ultimately the same power which raised Him up and carried Him through the heavens, will bring all the redeemed into glory.

In the presence of the words of verse 23 one feels more like worshipping than trying to expound their meaning. Marvellous words! They tell out the blessed masterpiece of God. Christ the Head; the Church, chosen in Him before the foundation of the world, the body. The Head is in glory; the body not yet joined to the Head. He waits in glory; the saints wait on earth. The body needs the Head, but the Head also needs the body. "The Christ" will be complete when the body is joined to the Head by the mighty power of God. The Church as His body is His fulness; it makes Him complete. And when that is reached, when Head and body, Christ and the Church, are united in glory, then will the hope of His calling be realized and He will have the glory of His inheritance in the saints, and we shall know the exceeding greatness of His power to us-ward.

2. The Production of the Masterwork and its Destiny

CHAPTER 2:1-10

1. What we are by nature (2:1-3)
2. What God does—rich in mercy (2:4-6)
3. The destiny of the masterwork (2:7)
4. Saved by grace (2:8-10)

After the great revelation of the first chapter and the prayer which followed, the production of the masterpiece itself is now brought more fully into view. We have before us a revelation concerning our state by nature and how God takes us up and produces out of such material His masterpiece. The first ten verses of this chapter give us this story. They contain one of the richest portions of the whole Word of God.

The first verse tells us that we are by nature in the state of death—"dead in trespasses and sins." Man is dead spiritually; he is dead towards God (John 5:24-25). This fact that the unregenerated man is dead is much denied in our days. We hear of "the better self," or "the good spark" which is in everybody, and the truth God has revealed concerning man, that he is dead in trespasses and sins is but little believed. The next verse states the walk of the natural man.

It fully shows the awful place in which man

is as dead in trespasses and sins. The walk is according to his fallen nature; the lust of the flesh, the lust of the eyes and the pride of life are the governing principles of this walk. We are enemies of God by wicked works. And behind all there stands the prince of the power of the air, Satan. He works in the children of disobedience, which here means the Jews. Of this our Lord spake when He said, "Ye are of your father, the devil, and the lusts of your father ye will do" (John 8:44). And again it is written, "He that committeth sin is of the devil; for the devil sinneth from the beginning. (1 John 3:8). It is a solemn truth, which God has revealed concerning our condition as fallen beings, that we are in the grasp of the prince of the power of the air; that man is under this mighty being of darkness. To what a place of degradation man has been brought by sin! This likewise is disbelieved by the great majority of professing Christians. A personal devil is ridiculed and his existence is denied.

In the third verse another description is added, "children of wrath." The "you" of the first verse is addressed to the Ephesians, showing what they were in their former condition. The "we" in the third verse means the Jews "among whom *we* also had our conversation." The apostle shows that the Jews were in the same condition; and he adds "and were by nature the children of wrath, even as others." Jews and Gentiles are dead in trespasses and sins, are the enemies of God and children of wrath. And this truth is also increasingly denied. The Word of God is most positive, and tells us "that he that believeth not the Son shall not see life, but the wrath of God abideth on him" (John 3:36). The denial of a future, conscious and eternal punishment of the wicked is becoming wide-spread; it is one of the marks of the latter day cults like Christian Science, Russellism, the New Theology, Spiritism and others. But the believer who knows the gospel and knows that he is "saved by grace" does not deny the truth of these first three verses of this chapter. It is our true photograph. Such material, God has to produce out of it His great masterwork.

After this dark picture of death, ruin and wrath, we read what God has done and does, for all who believe on His Son, our Lord Jesus Christ. "But God who is rich in mercy, for the great love, wherewith He loved us" (verse 4). This is the blessed bridge, which leads out of the dark and dreary, hopeless condition. *But God!* Man is guilty and lost. But God! God now comes in and makes known the riches of His mercy. Yet a righteous, holy God cannot be rich in mercy unless His righteousness is fully met and maintained. His mercy must have for a foundation His righteousness. And this is blessedly the case. He is rich in mercy for the great love wherewith He loved us. He gave His only begotten Son. He made Him who knew no sin, sin for us. He made full atonement on the cross and now God can be rich in mercy. And what does He do with such as we are? Verses 5-6 tell the blessed story.

These verses in which we read of the believer's quickening, his resurrection with Christ and being seated in Christ in the heavenlies, take us back to the time when our blessed Saviour Lord was quickened and raised from the dead and seated in glory. It is plain what God did for Him, who died on the cross, He has done for all, who believe on His Son. Many Christians are ignorant of this great truth, while others have difficulty in grasping it. Yet it is quite simple. Every Christian believes that when the Lord Jesus suffered on the cross He bore our sins in His own body on the tree. With the Apostle Paul every believer is entitled to say in looking back to the cross, "He loved me, He gave Himself for me." We know all our sins were paid for by Him; all the punishment we deserved fell upon Him, our substitute. In Him we died. All this happened when we were not in existence at all. The sins He bore were not yet committed. God knew all about us and all about our sins and shame, the punishment we deserved, and His ever-blessed Son took all upon Himself.

In the same sense God hath quickened us with Christ, raised us up and seated us in Him, when He did this for His Son our Lord Jesus Christ. This is simple, yet so wonderful and deep, that it is incomprehensible. It was all done for us, who believe, when it was done for Him. God in His marvellous counsels in redemption has associated us with Christ. He has made all, who believe on Him, sharers of His life and nature; He brings us into the same relationship as sons, and finally into the same glory and inheritance. Let us bear in mind that all this was done for us in Christ. He is the first one who was quickened, raised up and exalted in glory, and associated with Him are all His members; we share it with Him.

And all this becomes our blessed portion by faith in Jesus Christ. As we believe on Him, we are quickened, that is, we receive life, even eternal life and are saved by grace. Then we are risen with Him. We are now in Him, risen from the dead, the sons of God. Likewise in Christ (not with Christ) we are seated in the heavenly places. Now it is "in Him"; when He comes again we shall be "with Him" and share His glory. Here we have the summit of Christian position. We are not along representatively, but also virtually seated in Christ in the highest glory.

It is worth the while to review in a brief word the blessed revelations given in the first six verses of this chapter.

We saw first what man is by nature. Dead in trespasses and sins. Enemies of God under the prince of the power of the air; this is the result of such a condition. Children of wrath, because we are dead, His enemies and linked with Satan.

And now God has come in with His mighty power in the production of His masterwork. He gives life so that the dead condition is ended. Instead of enemies, we are constituted, by the resurrection of His Son, beloved sons of Himself. And in Christ Jesus, He makes of us children of glory, instead of children of wrath. Marvellous masterwork of God! May we praise Him for it all.

But one must ask in view of such riches of grace, as revealed in the preceding verses, What is the purpose of all this? The verse which follows gives the answer. We find ourselves face to face with the destiny of His masterpiece.

"That in the ages to come He might show (or display) the exceeding (surpassing) riches of His grace in kindness towards us in Christ Jesus" (verse 7). This is one of the richest and deepest statements in the Bible. Two ages follow the present age. The millennial age, and after that has lasted for a thousand years, the eternal state begins. In the coming age and in all eternity, God is going to make known His glory through and in His masterwork. All His redeemed will be with Him in glory. When He comes again He brings many sons to glory; and we shall reign and rule with Him over the earth.

But this is not all. In the eternal age, from eternity to eternity, God is continuing in this. He will bring forth something new in glory, new riches of Himself for those who are one with His well-beloved Son. From eternity to eternity He displays the surpassing riches of His grace in kindness towards us in Christ Jesus. How one is overwhelmed in the presence of such a statement! And how little after all we can understand all those coming riches in glory. What a destiny! The heart may well cry—nothing but glory! What is the little suffering, the little while down here, in comparison with such never ending glory!

Fittingly this great revelation ends with the blessed statement that we are saved by grace through faith, and that not of ourselves, it is the gift of God; and that we are His workmanship, created in Christ Jesus unto good works, which God hath before ordained that we should walk in them.

3. The Mystery Made Known

CHAPTERS 2:11—3:21

1. The condition of the Gentiles (2:11-12)
2. But now in Christ Jesus (2:13-18)
3. The new and great relationship (2:19-22)
4. The Mystery made known and Paul's ministry (3:1-13)
5. The prayer (3:14-19)
6. The doxology (3:20-21)

With the eleventh verse of the second chapter we reach a new division in this Epistle. The great mystery of the masterwork of God, the Church, is next revealed by the Holy Spirit. We saw in the first chapter of this wonderful Epistle how God planned His masterpiece. Then we learned in the first ten verses of the second chapter how God deals with us individually and fashions lost sinners, who trust in Christ, into His masterwork. And now we are led higher, and the fact is made known that all believers are united into one body. This truth was briefly mentioned at the close of the preceding chapter (1:22, 23).

First, the condition of the Gentiles, the uncircumcision, as called by the Jews, is briefly described. They were without Christ; aliens from the commonwealth of Israel; strangers from the covenants; and without hope and without God. Such was the condition of the great Gentile world.

Well may we remember in the dreadful days of apostasy, which are upon us, that Gentiles, who have had the gospel preached unto them, are turned once more from the light, yea, from God's best. Christendom in denying Christ is rapidly waning, and must eventually plunge into a greater darkness than the darkness of the Gentile world before the cross. Without Christ, without hope, and without God! Fearful and solemn words these are! When Christ is given up, His deity and His blood rejected, when men deliberately turn away from Him, and deny His person and His glory, they rush into the outer and eternal darkness "without hope and without God."

But now Christ being preached and believed in, Gentiles who were once far off are made nigh by the blood of Christ. The little word "now" is of importance.

This present dispensation of grace in which He makes known the mystery, which in other ages was not made known, that the Gentiles, once without Christ and without God, should be fellow-heirs and of the same body, is the *"now"* in which the surpassing riches of God's grace are made known. *Now,* after Israel rejected the King and the Saviour, *now,* when He is upon the Father's throne, *now,* when the Holy Spirit is on earth to do His appointed work, *now,* during the present age, God makes fully known what He had planned before the foundation of the world. He is producing His masterwork, taking the material from Israel, and reaching out with His mighty power after the Gentiles, to put them into one body. The poor, miserable, naked beggar upon the dunghill, the Gentile, is taken up to sit among princes and inherit the throne of glory.

And all who believe are made nigh by the blood of Christ. Then we find three statements in verses 14 and 15: 1. He is our peace, making of both one. The parties mentioned here as made one are Jews and Gentiles. 2. Broken down the middle wall and abolished the law of commandments. Between these two there stood a middle wall of partition, which separated them. This wall is the law. God Himself had put it up. But now in the cross of Christ, God has broken down this middle wall and made an end of the enmity which existed between Jews and Gentiles. And the law of commandments and ordinances finds its end in the cross. 3. Making in Himself one new man.

Jews and Gentiles, believing, trusting in Christ, made nigh by His blood, are made both one and constitute one new man. This is what God has accomplished, taking believing Jews and believing Gentiles, gathering them into one. This is the masterwork of God, He does during this age. When the kingdom age comes the Jews will receive their place of blessing and glory in their land, and the Gentiles will be greatly blessed and enjoy righteousness and peace. Both Jews and Gentiles will be in the kingdom then, but not as *one body.* In the present age a body is forming "where there is neither Greek nor Jew, circumcision nor uncircumcision, Barbarian, Scythian, bond nor free, but Christ is all and in all" (Col. 3:11). This new man is the church, and Christ is the Head of that new man. Grace flowing from the cross of Christ, where peace was made in the blood, takes up Jews and Gentiles and makes them one. When our Lord prayed in His high priestly prayer "that they may all be one as we are one," He must have thought of this great truth, now fully revealed in this Epistle by the Spirit of God.

In verse 16 we have two similar statements as in the preceding verses: 1. Both (Jews and Gentiles believing) reconciled unto God in one body. 2. The enmity slain by the cross. And furthermore He came and preached peace to both, to those afar off (Gentiles) and to those that were nigh (the Jews). Then follows the blessed result. "For through Him we both (believing Jews and Gentiles) have access by one Spirit unto the Father." The Jew did not know anything in Old Testament times about "access unto the Father." He had a tabernacle and the way into the holiest was not yet made known. And the Gentile was without God altogether. But now believing Jews and Gentiles belong to the family of God, indwelt by the same Spirit, the Spirit of Sonship.

In verse 19 we hear of the new relationship into which believing Gentiles are brought in Christ. "Now therefore, ye are no more strangers and foreigners, but fellow-citizens with the saints, and of the household of God." In verse 20 the Church comes into view, and we hear that Gentiles saved by grace and made nigh by blood "are built upon the foundation of the apostles and prophets, Jesus Christ being the chief corner stone." The Church is compared to a building.

In the Old Testament God had a building in which He manifested His presence and His glory. The tabernacle in the wilderness and the temple of Solomon were shadows of the Church, which God is now building. The foundation upon which the Church as the house is built, we find mentioned first. One of the common mistakes concerning the foundation upon which the Church is built, is that, which claims that the foundation are the prophets of the Old Testament. According to this view the Old Testament saints belonged to the Church, and the Church itself was therefore in existence throughout the previous dispensations. This view is often based upon the words we have under consideration, that the Church is built upon the foundation of the apostles and prophets. Now if the prophets were mentioned before the apostles, there might be a possibility that the prophets of the Old Testament are meant. But it says "apostles and prophets." They are the New

Testament apostles and prophets. Chapter 3:5 gives positive evidence on this whole question. The Church is called a mystery "which in other ages was not made known unto the sons of men, as it is now revealed unto His holy apostles and prophets by the Spirit."

"Built upon the foundation of the apostles and prophets" does not mean that the apostles are the foundation. The apostles are the foundation through their inspired teachings as Paul wrote, "I have laid the foundation." But he also adds "for other foundation can no man lay than that is laid, which is Jesus Christ." (1 Cor. 3:9-11). The Lord Jesus Christ and the doctrine of Christ is the foundation. This the apostles taught. And the Lord Jesus Christ is the chief corner stone (Isa. 28:16; Psalm 118:22; Matt. 21:44; Acts 4:11; 1 Peter 2:4-5). "In whom all the building fitly framed together groweth unto a holy temple in the Lord" (verse 21). The building, the true Church is fitly framed together, which means that God puts it together in His own marvellous way.

Solomon's temple gives a little illustration of this. When that temple was building, hammer, axe and tools of iron were not heard. "And the house, when it was building, was built of stone made ready before it was brought thither, so that there was neither hammer nor axe, nor any tool of iron heard in the house, while it was building." Every stone was prepared beforehand and fitted into the place where it belonged. How beautifully it illustrates the fitting together of the house, His Church! He chooses and prepares the material and puts each in its proper place (1 Cor. 12). What a contrast with man's methods in trying to increase "church-membership"! The divine revelation is forgotten. Christendom has departed from the faith in these revelations concerning the one Church and its architect. But all the confusion, the wrong conceptions and attending evils, cannot frustrate the purpose of the Lord. He is building His Church. He takes the material and puts it as living stones in the place where it belongs. This is the work of His Spirit.

And the Holy Spirit dwells there. He dwells in the true Church, because He indwells every individual member of the body of Christ. We are the habitation of God. As He dwelt of old in the tabernacle, so He dwells in the Church through the Spirit. God does no longer dwell in an earthly house. The conception of a church building being a "holy place" which we must call "the house of the Lord" or "a temple" is absolutely wrong. It is the Jewish idea. God does no longer dwell in an earthly house and yet He has His habitation here. Wherever two or three are gathered together in His name, there He is in the midst; that is a Church and the habitation of God through the Spirit. "Even now in the state of imperfection, by the Spirit dwelling in the hearts of believers, that God has His habitation in the Church; and then when the growth and increase of that Church shall be completed, it will be still in and by the Holy Spirit, fully penetrating and possessing the whole glorified church, that the Father will dwell in it forever."[2]

In the first verse of the *third* chapter Paul speaks of himself as "the prisoner of the Jesus Christ, for you Gentiles." He became a prisoner on account of the Gentiles, when on his last visit to Jeruslem (Acts 22:21-22). And to him was made known the mystery which was hidden in other generations. And the mystery is "that the Gentiles should be fellow-heirs, and of the same body, and partakers of His promise in Christ by the gospel."

That Gentiles should be fellow-heirs with Jewish believers in a distinct body is a new revelation. The Old Testament abounds in promises for the Gentile nations. These promises speak of righteousness and peace, which the nations of the earth are to enjoy. But they all stand connected with the age which is yet to come. That age is introduced by the visible manifestation of the Lord. At that time the people Israel will receive the place of headship among the nations. The Gentiles will join themselves to Israel, and Israel has the promise that the nations will seek the light and glory revealed in their midst. "And the nations shall come to thy light, and kings to the brightness of thy rising. Lift up thine eyes round about and see; all they gather themselves together, they come to thee. Thy sons shall come from far, and thy daughters shall be nursed at thy side. Then shalt thou see, and be filled with delight; and thine heart shall thrill, and be enlarged; because the abundance of the sea shall be converted unto thee, the forces of the nations shall come unto thee" (Isa. 60:3-5).

Many other passages could be quoted, but in not one of them is it said that Gentiles should be joint-heirs. In this mystery of the Church there is revealed an inheritance which is far greater than any blessing promised to earthly Israel during the coming kingdom. Both, believing Jews and Gentiles are joint-heirs of Christ,

---

[2]Dean Alford, *Greek New Testament.*

and in the coming day of glory they will reign and rule with Him.

Then "of the same body" joint-members. The believing Jews on the day of Pentecost were formed into one body by the Holy Spirit. They became then one spirit with the Lord, and that marvellous organism, the body of Christ, had its beginning. Gentiles are joint-members of the same body; they are united with all the saints in one body. And therefore believing Gentiles are joint-partakers of His promises in Christ by the gospel. These promises do not concern the earth, but they concern the glory to come. Israel's promises will be fulfilled, and they will be under Christ as King, when He comes to reign. But the body of Christ has far greater promises in Christ. The body will be joined to the head, share the glory of the head and be where the head is. The Head, Christ, and the body, the Church, composed of believing Jews and Gentiles, joint-heirs, joint-members, joint-partakers—this is the mystery.

And of all this the Apostle Paul was the minister. Beautiful words, "Unto me, whom are less than the least of all saints, is this grace given, that I should preach among the Gentiles the unsearchable riches of Christ." The great revelation had made him very humble.

He might have made much of his superior knowledge, of the great revelation given to him, and he might have paraded a kind of an official pride as the apostle to the Gentiles. But the high calling, the mystery made known unto him, the blessed ministry given to him, produced far different results. It humbled him into the dust before God. It could not be otherwise. Grace, such wondrous grace, as revealed through Paul, reaching down to such as we are, lifting so high with such an unspeakable calling and destiny, will ever humble us into the dust to give Him the glory. Grace necessitates this. The more we know of the blessed mystery of God's masterpiece, the less we shall think of ourselves and delight to take the lowest place. Truth learned or knowledge gained in spiritual things, which does not humble us and make us think less and less of ourselves, is a dangerous thing. Truth, must ever break us down and lead into self-judgment and self-abasement.

The purpose of preaching the mystery concerning the church (verse 9-13) is twofold: 1. To make all men see what is the fellowship of the mystery; to make it known among men. 2. To the intent that now unto the principalities and powers in heavenly places might be known by the church the manifold wisdom of God. The heavenly hosts look on (1 Cor. 11:10) and behold by the Church the manifold wisdom of God.

That which no prophet ever saw, what no human being could have imagined, what no angel ever knew, what was known alone to God, took place. The Church, the body of Christ, the fullness of Him that filleth all in all, began on earth with the coming of the Holy Spirit on Pentecost. They see how this body is being built, fitly framed together, and they know the glory which awaits that body. Therefore *now* is made known unto angels by the Church the manifold wisdom of God.

And because the angels possess this knowledge, they rejoice over one repenting sinner (Luke 15:7). They know what it means to the sinner, and more so to Christ, when another member is added to His body. Nor must we lose sight of another statement. "Are they not all ministering spirits, sent forth to minister to them who shall be heirs of salvation?" (Heb. 1:14). We do not know how they minister to our need, but we know they do minister.

The second prayer in this epistle (verses 14-21) is addressed to the Father of our Lord Jesus Christ. The petitions of the prayer are five: 1. To be strengthened with might by His Spirit in the inner man. 2. That Christ may dwell in your heart. 3. To comprehend with all saints what is the breadth and length and depth and height. 4. To know the love of Christ which passeth knowledge. 5. To be filled with all the fullness of God. The Holy Spirit who gave this prayer wants God's people to know more of Christ, to feed on Him and by knowing the love of Christ, which passeth knowledge, to be filled unto all the fullness of God. Think of the dimensions of this love! We are to comprehend with all the saints, what is the breadth and length and depth and height. But who can know all this? It will take eternity to comprehend it all. Look at the outstretched arms of the blessed One on the cross! Here we behold the breadth. "Come unto Me all"—that is the breadth of His love. The length is from eternity to eternity. The first chapter told us of the fact that before the foundation of the world He thought of us. He loved us before we ever existed. His love has no beginning and no end. It is an eternal love with which He loveth us.

And the depth! How deep, oh! how deep did He go down! The manger? The boyhood days in Nazareth? The manhood when He had not where to lay His head? The life that spent and was spent? Ah! the depths are far deeper. Let the hours of darkness give the answer, when He descended into the deep, dark waters of judgment and God's face was hidden from Him. Shall we ever know the depths of His love?

The height takes us into the heaven of heavens. Look into an opened heaven! See the glory-light! Behold there on that throne, there sits, not an angel, but a man! "We see Jesus who was made a little lower than the angels for the suffering of death, crowned with glory and honor." And into that glory He has taken us. His love could never stop short of that. Where He is there the objects of His love shall ever be with Him. "The glory Thou hast given me I have given them." Oh! the breadth, the length, the depth, the height!

"To know the love of Christ that passeth knowledge." We are to know something which passeth knowledge. It is a paradox. We know that love, and the more we know it the more it passeth our knowledge. Shall we ever know fully the love that passeth knowledge? This ever must be our blessed occupation to know the love of Christ, which passeth knowledge. And what are the consequences? "That ye may be filled unto (not with) all the fullness of God." In the measure in which we know the love of Christ and comprehend the dimensions of this love, in the measure in which we have Christ dwelling in our hearts by faith and are rooted and grounded in love, in that measure shall we be filled unto all the fullness of God.

The blessed doxology ends this wonderful section of God's highest revelation. "Now unto Him that is able to do exceeding abundantly above all that we ask or think, according to the power that worketh in us, unto Him be glory in the church, in Christ Jesus throughout all ages, world without end, Amen." What assurance and what encouragement to pray. Let us ask much in spiritual things and He will do exceeding abundantly above all that we ask or think.

II. The Practical Manifestation in the Life of the Believer (4—6)

1. Walking worthy of the Calling

CHAPTER 4:1-6

1. The walk in lowliness and meekness (4:1-2)
2. Keeping the unity of the Spirit (4:3-6)

"I therefore, the prisoner of the Lord, beseech you that ye walk worthy of the calling wherewith ye are called." This marks the beginning of the second part of the epistle. It is obvious then, to walk worthy as a Christian, one has to know the calling wherewith God has called us. This calling, as we have seen, is revealed in the first three chapters. The first exhortation is to walk "with all lowliness and meekness." He does not speak of doing some great work, or to seek special gifts and special power. Lowliness and meekness are to be manifested by the members of the body of Christ. These two words remind us of the Lord Jesus and the words which came from His blessed lips. "Take my yoke upon you and learn of Me, for I am meek and lowly in heart" (Matt. 11:29). He who had laid His glory by, thus emptying Himself, lived down here in lowliness and meekness. And we are called to walk even as He walked (1 John 2:6). "Let this mind be in you, which was also in Christ Jesus" (Phil. 2:5). The Holy Spirit tells us then that the first thing in the walk of the believer is to manifest the lowliness and meekness of the Lord Jesus. Walking in meekness produces gentleness towards the brethren, the fellow-saints. And as we walk "with long-suffering, forbearing one another in love" we manifest practically that we are members of the one body. Love is to be the governing principle towards all the saints of God.

In the second place we are to give "diligence to keep the unity of the Spirit in the bond of peace." We are not told to produce the unity of the Spirit, but to keep it. What is this unity of the Spirit? It is the unity which God in His infinite grace has made Himself. All believers are members of the body of Christ, the Church. The Holy Spirit dwells in each and He has put us into that body as members; the one body, and believers members of that body, constitutes the unity of the Spirit. We are to own it by keeping it in the bond of peace. This unity can never be destroyed for it is the work of God. But it may be denied and the expression of it completely lost. Alas! this is the common thing about us. Sectarianism is a denial of this unity of the Spirit. We keep the unity of the Spirit when we recognize in every true believer a member of Christ and of His body. What will enable us to keep this unity and this walk worthy of our calling? We must constantly feed on the glorious realities of our redemption in Christ. What God has wrought for us and for all His saints, the fact that all are indwelt by the same Spirit, and that all have the same glorious destiny, must never be lost sight of.

The unity of the Spirit is revealed in verses

4-6. Again, the three persons of the Godhead are seen only in reverse order, the Holy Spirit first, the Son of God the second, and the God and Father third.

The Holy Spirit
1. One Body
2. One Spirit
3. One Hope

The Son of God, the Lord
4. One Lord
5. One Faith
6. One Baptism

The God and Father
7. One God and Father of all, who is above all and through all and in all

The one body, which stands first, is the Church, the body of Christ. The fullness of Him that filleth all in all. The one Spirit is the Holy Spirit. He came on the day of Pentecost and the Baptism of the Spirit then took place, by which the body of Christ is formed. "For by one Spirit we are all baptized into one body" (1 Cor. 12:13). The one hope is the hope of the Church, to be with the Lord in glory, to be like Him and share His glory. The next three linked with the Lord and are likewise connected with the Church. One Lord, one faith, one baptism, presents the aspect of public profession. The one Lord, is Christ; all Christians own Him professedly as Lord. The "one faith" is the faith in the Lord and the "one baptism" is water-baptism, which is both, the initiatory rite of Christian profession and an expression of that faith in the one Lord. And God is the "one God and Father of all, who is above all, and through all, and in all." Of course this applies only to believers.

2. The Ministry and Its Purpose

CHAPTER 4:7-16

1. Ministry according to the measure of the gift of Christ (4:7-10)
2. The needed and permanent gifts (4:11)
3. The purpose and the goal (4:12-16)

Each member in the body of Christ has a specific place for a specific work. See Romans 12:4-5 and 1 Cor. 12:4-5. And the bestowal of gifts for service in the body is in His hands. He ascended upon high and triumphed over all enemies. He led captivity captive and gave gifts unto men. He triumphed over the devil, who has the power of death and stripped him of that power. And all who constitute His body share in His triumph. They are no longer under the power of Satan, but delivered from the power of darkness, they are His trophies. "He led captivity captive," *i.e.,* those who were in captivity, or "a troop, a multitude of captives." The view held by some that the Old Testament saints are meant, whom He led forth from Hades is incorrect.

Psalm 68 is quoted. But we discover an omission. Psalm 68:18 reads, "Thou has received gifts for men, yea, for the rebellious also, that the Lord God might dwell among them." The last sentence is omitted, for the rebellious are the Jews; they are as the rebellious nation not in view in Ephesians, though the day will come when Israel will be converted and the promised gifts will be bestowed upon that nation. And He who ascended also descended first into the lower parts of the earth. It means the deepest depths of suffering, the shameful death of the cross and that He was buried. (This passage has nothing to do with 1 Peter 3:18. The meaning of this Scripture will be fully explained in our annotations of the First Epistle of Peter.) As the Ascended One He has given gifts for the ministry in the body. These gifts are "apostles, prophets, evangelists, pastors and teachers." Other gifts are mentioned in First Corinthians such as the gift of healing, the gift of tongues, etc. These were not permanent gifts, and not absolutely necessary for the perfecting of the saints and the building up of the body of Christ.

The gifts mentioned here in Ephesians abide to the end until the Church is complete and removed from the earth. The apostles are the apostles of the beginning. The apostolate of Mormonism and similar cults is an invention. Nowhere does it say that Paul, Peter or John should have successors; all who lay claim to the title of apostle in the church are deceivers (Rev. 2:2). The doctrines of the apostles are in our possession as the supreme gifts of the exalted Lord to His body. New Testament prophets are such who speak the message of God for the comfort and exhortation of God's people. The evangelist preaches the gospel. The pastor and teacher are practically one. The teacher expounds the Word and teaches the doctrines of the Bible. And these gifts remain till the Lord comes for His saints. The gifts are for the perfecting of the saints, unto the work of the ministry for the building up of the body of Christ. And each gift is not for a certain part of the church, but for the whole body. "Till we all come unto the unity of the faith, and of the knowledge of the Son of God, unto a full-grown man, unto the measure of the stature of the fullness of Christ." This measure of the stature of the fullness of Christ will be reached when the body is joined to the Head. When the Church enters into His presence and He presents the church to Himself (Eph. 5:27), then this completion has come. Till then He will give the gifts to the Church, His body, for the upbuilding of that body. And He puts this body together and ministers unto its needs (verse 16).

3. The Walk in Holiness and Righteousness

CHAPTERS 4:17—5:21

1. Not as the Gentiles walk (4:17-19)
2. The putting off and putting on (4:20-32) 3. Followers of God (5:1-2)
4. Exhortations (5:3-21)

At this point the exhortations to walk in separation begin. The "therefore" of verse 17 refers us to the "wherefore" of chapter 2:11-12. What Gentiles are in their natural condition is here once more put before us. The grace of God takes the believer out of these conditions and puts power on our side to walk "no longer as the Gentiles walk." And how solemn is the description of what Gentiles are by nature! Nor must we overlook the fact, that beneath the thin veneer of our boasted civilization, which rejects Christ and the gospel, there is the same darkened understanding, the same alienation from God, the same blindness and the uncleanness of which these words speak.

Saved by grace these Gentiles had heard Christ and had been taught by Him. To walk according as the truth is in Jesus is the responsibility of all who know and follow Him. He is our pattern. The old man is put off and the new man is put on. We are not told to put off the old man by all kinds of endeavors and resolutions; it is already done. The old man was put away by the cross of Christ (Rom. 6:6). This is the blessed truth which delivers from doubt and bondage. And then we receive something in Christ, the new man, the new nature. Grace unclothed us and clothed us. Grace made an end of the old man and put upon us the new man. And this new man, after God, is created in righteousness and true holiness, which calls for a corresponding walk. But there is also a practical putting off and putting on. Of this we read in verses 25-29. In verse 26 there is a command to be angry and sin not. There is a righteous anger which is not sinful. The Lord Jesus exhibited that (Mark 3:5). When truth is perverted, or that blessed and worthy name is dishonored, a righteous feeling of displeasure arises in the heart, which is indwelt by the Holy Spirit. Such a feeling is not sin. But we are warned "let not the sun go down upon your wrath." The wrath of man, if nourished, worketh not the righteousness of God (Jas. 1:20). How easy it is to harbor feelings which are sinful, and in doing so give place to the devil. Corrupt communications are not to proceed out of the mouth of a member of the body of Christ, "but that which is good for needful building up, that it may minister grace unto the hearers." Speech is always to be with grace, seasoned with salt (Col. 4:6). In view of such exhortations, the practice of certain evangelists to use "slang," vulgar and common expressions in public speech stands condemned.

"And grieve not the Holy Spirit of God, by whom ye have been sealed unto the day of redemption." We are His temple and all must be avoided which displeases the holy guest. That He dwells in us and we are sealed by Him is the evidence of our eternal security. We are sealed by Him unto the day of redemption. We may grieve Him, but He will never leave those who are washed in the blood of the Lamb. He abides with us forever. In verse 32 we find another exhortation how the members of the body of Christ should act towards each other.

We are to be imitators of God, as dear children and walk in love as Christ also hath loved us and hath given Himself for us an offering and a sacrifice to God for a sweet-smelling savour. Then there are additional exhortations about fornication, all uncleanness, or covetousness, as well as other things. It shows the possibility of a child of God falling into these things. The true believer knows that in his flesh dwelleth no good thing, and that only the power of the Holy Spirit can deliver him from the power of the flesh; therefore he walks in the Spirit. There can be no inheritance in the kingdom of Christ and of God for such whose life is in these things. A child of God may fall and commit some of these things, but no true believer will continue to live in them.

"And have no fellowship with the unfruitful works of darkness, but rather reprove them" (5:11). When our Lord was on earth He reproved the unfruitful works of darkness. His condemnation was aimed at the religious Pharisees and rationalistic Sadducees. He pronounced His solemn "woes" upon them. Walking as the children of light, therefore, means separation from evil, moral and religious, and a definite witness against it.

The exhortation in verse 14, to awake and arise, is not addressed to an unsaved person, but to a Christian. Many believers are in the state of spiritual sleep among the spiritually dead in the world; but the promise is given, that Christ will give light when the awakening comes. Another important exhortation is found in verse 18: "And be not drunken with wine, wherein is excess, but be filled with the Spirit." "Be filled with the Spirit" does not mean another outpouring of the Holy Spirit, another Pentecost. The Holy Spirit dwells in every child of God; He is the abiding guest. He is in us to fill us, and He will do so if we walk in the Spirit. May we open our whole heart to Him and walk in obedience, abiding in Christ, occupied with Christ, exalting Christ, and we shall know what it means to be filled with the Spirit. Some of the effects of it are mentioned in the verses which follow (verses 19-21). There is worship and thanksgiving. He is also the Spirit of love and grace—"submitting yourselves one to another in the fear of God."

4. Manifestation in the Family-relationship

CHAPTERS 5:22—6:4

1. Wives representative of the Church (5:22-24)
2. Husbands representative of Christ (5:25-29)
3. The mystery: concerning Christ and the Church (5:30-33)
4. Exhortations to children and parents (6:1-4)

The exhortations which follow concern the Christian family. The mystery concerning Christ and the Church (verse 32) is to be manifested in the family relationship. While before we have seen the Church as the body of Christ, here in these verses we see the Church in her love-relation to Christ. He loved the Church and gave Himself for it. The union of husband and wife is used as a type of the union of Christ and the Church. Wives are mentioned first: "Wives submit yourselves unto your own husbands, as unto the Lord." And why? For the husband is head of the wife, even as Christ is head of the Church; and "He is saviour of the body." The wife is therefore to be in submission to her own husband in everything, as the Church is subject unto Christ. Thus the wife in her submission is to bear witness to the blessed relationship of Christ and the Church. She has the blessed portion of being in subjection. The question arises, What, if the husband is not a believer? Is she to submit in such a case? The Word of God gives definite instructions covering such a case, and adds a promise (See 1 Peter 3:1-2).

The husband is not to demand of the wife this submission, which is her place. Husbands are to love their wives as Christ loved the Church. He stands in the Christian family as the representative of Christ and is called to love his wife. And how did Christ love the Church? He came from heaven's glory to be a servant. He served and is serving the Church. The husband's love towards the wife is to be expressed in loving service in her behalf and giving unto her, as unto the weaker vessel (1 Peter 3:7). Not the wife is to serve the husband, but the husband is to serve her in love, thus manifesting in a little measure the love of Christ for the Church. Beautiful is the description of the love of Christ for the Church. It is a love in the past: "He loved the Church and gave Himself for it." Thus there is a present love: "That He might sanctify and cleanse it with the washing of water by the Word." Then there is His future love: "That He might present it to Himself a glorious Church not having spot or wrinkle or any such thing; but that it should be holy and without blemish." It is the love which passeth knowledge, the love which never changeth; the love which is eternal. Equally blessed is the truth contained in verses 30-33. We are members of His body, and of His flesh and His bones.

That we have here a reference to Adam and Eve as the types of Christ and the Church is obvious. While Adam slept God built the woman out of his side and then presented her to him. "This is now bone of my bones, and flesh of my flesh," were Adam's words. She was taken out of his body, shared the same life and was also Adam's wife. Adam is the figure of Him that was to come (Rom. 5:14). Eve is the type of the Church. We possess His life and are of Himself, bone of His bone and flesh of His flesh. And the Church's destiny is to have dominion with Him over the new creation.

Children are to obey their parents in the Lord. And the fathers are not to provoke the children to wrath, "but bring them up in the nurture and admonition of the Lord." And how much wisdom this takes! Parents must show constantly to the children the love and patience of Christ and bring them up in the nurture and admonition of the Lord. Then the promise will be made good. "Believe on the Lord Jesus Christ, and thou shalt be saved, and thy house" (Acts 16:31).

5. Exhortations to Servants and Masters

CHAPTER 6:5-9

The servants exhorted were slaves. Slavery existed throughout the Roman Empire at that time. Nowhere is slavery attacked in the New Testament, nor is there a statement telling believers that it was a sin to own slaves and incompatible with the gospel. Paul wrote a courteous letter to Philemon and sent it by Onesimus, the runaway slave, who probably had stolen money from Philemon, his master. The gospel is not here to reform the world, to meddle with social conditions and politics.

The slaves here exhorted were Christians. They all belonged to the one body where there is neither Greek nor Jew, bond nor free. They were in Christ, saved by grace and seated in Christ in the heavenly places. What did it matter if they were but slaves! Did not God's well beloved Son walk on this earth as a servant, yea, the servant of all! In all their bonds they were the servants of Christ. Their service was to be rendered as unto the Lord and not unto men. The Lord would give them their reward. How happy these believing slaves must have been! And the Christian masters were to remember the one Master in heaven, with whom there is no respect of persons.

6. The Warfare and the Panoply of God

CHAPTER 6:10-20

1. The warfare (6:10-12)
2. The panoply of God (6:13-20)

Christian warfare or conflict is with the devil and his wiles, with the principalities, the powers, the rulers of the darkness of this world, and with the spiritual armies of wickedness in the heavenly places (literal translation).

This revelation given here concerning the powers of darkness, the principalities, the rulers of the darkness of this world and the wicked spirits in the heavenly places, is important and demands a closer attention. The Scriptures clearly teach that there is a vast dominion of darkness over which Satan is the head and that, as the god of this present age, he has rulers over this world and a large army of wicked spirits in the heavenlies. He is the prince of the power in the air. The sphere above the earth, the aerial heavens and beyond are tenanted by these wicked spirits, which under the headship of Satan form with principalities and powers, his kingdom. How mighty this being is, what powers are at his disposal how vast his dominion, how numerous the fallen angels, the wicked spirits which possess the heavenly places, no saint has ever fully realized, nor can it be all known, till the day comes in which the God of peace shall bruise Satan completely under our feet. Satan has even access into heaven itself. The first two chapters of the book of Job acquaint us with this fact. See also 1 Kings 22:19-23.

But a day is coming when the old serpent, called the devil and Satan, will be cast out into the earth and his angels with him. This will happen according to the Apocalypse (Rev. 12), when the saints of God are taken into glory and Michael begins his great war against Satan. Then the heavenlies will be cleared of their wicked and unlawful occupants. They will be forced to the earth, where Satan for a brief period will exhibit his great wrath and institute the great tribulation. The devil and his angels will finally be cast into the lake of fire prepared for them (Matt. 25:41). All this we know from God's revelation, and it is a solemn revelation.

In our days the masses of professing Christendom are wholly indifferent to these truths. Others openly oppose them, sneer at them and reject them as superstitions. Well has it been said, "No one but an unbeliever can overlook and despise them." Behind all these denials and sneers, coming from the camps of higher criticism and the new theology stands the dark shadow of Satan. The rulers of darkness of this world, the wicked spirits, do all in their power to keep a lost world, with its supposed progress and scientific discoveries, in ignorance and darkness about themselves. And occultism, known by the names of spiritualism and psychical research, tries to establish communion with departed spirits. In reality it is communion with the wicked spirits in the heavenlies, who use this unlawful intrusion to delude their victims and make them doubly secure for the impending doom.

And these wicked spirits are against the masterpiece of God. Those who are in Christ and lay hold in the power of His Spirit of the great and ever blessed truths revealed in this epistle, who know the hope of His calling, who rejoice in God and the glory to come, who walk worthy of the calling, come face to face with these powers of darkness. They hate us as they hate Christ.

The wiles of the devil, not his power, we are exhorted to stand against. His wiles are all aimed at getting us away from the enjoyment of the fellowship into which God has called us, the fellowship of His Son Jesus Christ our Lord. If he succeeds in that he has dislodged us from our stronghold and then is able to attack us. The world over which he rules is at his disposal and he uses it to accomplish his sinister purpose. Many pages could be written on his tactics and not the half would be told. It is not so much by the gross things of the flesh and the world he works, though he also uses them; errors of all descriptions becoming more subtle and more cunning, are the chiefest wiles of this great being and the wicked spirits under his control. And how well he succeeds in our present time!

And we must put on the whole armor of God, the panoply of God. It is the only way that we can get the victory and stand and withstand. First, *the loins are to be girt about with truth.* Even so our Lord exhorted, "Let your loins be girded about" (Luke 12:35).

It is the girdle around the loins, which holds all things together. The girdle is the truth. What truth? The truth of heavenly things, heavenly blessings, acceptance in Christ, oneness with Him, the truth so fully revealed in this Epistle. This we need as a girdle to hold up our garments, our habits, so that in the warfare and conflict we may not be entangled with the affairs of this life (2 Tim. 2:4). The truth is to govern our conduct, our affections.

The breastplate of righteousness. This covers the heart. It means having a good conscience. Not merely knowing that we are the righteousness of God in Christ, that we are righteous because we believe on Him, but it means a consistent walk with our position in Christ and the relationship into which the grace of God has brought us. It is again the walk, worthy of our vocation, obedience to the exhortations of the preceding chapters. Covered by this the devil cannot touch us. Such practical righteousness "love out of a pure heart and of a good conscience and of faith unfeigned" keeps us in the realization and enjoyment of our relationship to God, in the fellowship with the Father and the Son. How often we fail in having on the breastplate of righteousness. Then we must seek restoration by confessing our sins (1 John 1).

The feet shod with the preparation of the gospel of peace. This does not mean the preaching of the gospel to others, Christian service or soul winning. We have through the gospel perfect peace with God. We know that God is for us, who then can be against us? This perfect peace we have, in which we stand is our preparation. And we have the peace of God as well, yea, the legacy our Lord left unto us, "My peace I give unto you." Therefore we are not terrified by our adversaries (Phil. 1:28). Israel wandered over the desert rocks and desert sands for forty years with shoes, which did not wear out. We too wander through the wilderness, the feet shod with the preparation of the gospel of peace, a peace which will last as long as God Himself. Knowing this Peace, knowing we are in God's hands, knowing that we are Christ's and Christ is God's, knowing that all things are ours, we can stand and withstand the wiles of the devil. He cannot touch one who rests in the peace of God and who trusts in the God of peace.

The shield of faith. This is to be "over all" (not "above all" as in the *Authorized Version*). Faith in God, faith in His promises, faith in His Word, simple child-like faith is to cover the head and the body like a great shield. It is the exercise of an unwavering confidence in God. The fiery darts will thus be quenched. These "fiery darts" are indeed terrible weapons. The fire speaks of the wrath of God, of judgment, at least, from Him, and it is with this that the enemy would assail us. He is, we must remember, the accuser. His aim, as already said, is to bring distance in some sense between our souls and God. How great a necessity, therefore, to maintain this happy confidence in Him, which, while it does not excuse failure in the least, yet, in utter weakness, finds all its confidence in Him who has undertaken for us. "All the fiery darts of the wicked one" can thus be "quenched" by the "shield of faith" (F. W. Grant).

The helmet of salvation. The helmet rests upon the head. It covers the head, the seat of intelligence. Assurance of salvation past, present and future is this helmet. As we wear it and as it governs our mind and heart as well, the wiles of the devil cannot fall upon us. We are in possession of a salvation which is secure. No power in earth or heaven the devil with all his demon powers cannot spoil us of it. This gives not alone confidence, but boldness in the conflict. Sad it is to see the thousands of believers without the helmet of salvation, destitute of the assurance of salvation and therefore the easy prey of the devil's wiles, driven about by every wind of doctrine. Well has it been said: "Girded by the truth applies to the judgment of the inner man. Practical righteousness guards the conscience from the assaults of the enemy; the power of peace gives a character to our walk; confidence in the love of God quenches the poisoned arrows of doubt; the assurance of salvation gives us boldness to go onward."

The sword of the Spirit. It is the Word of God, the only offensive weapon mentioned in the armor of God. It is to meet the devil and to make him flee from us. How our blessed Lord wielded this sword in the wilderness, how He met the devil by a "It is written" is well known to every Christian. Was there ever a time when God's people had greater need of laying hold with a firm grasp of the sword of the Spirit? Satan has succeeded by his wiles to dull the edge of that sword. The enemy also perverts and counterfeits the Word. What need then that as never before we go "to the law and to the testimonies." We must search the Word and have the Word search us. We must have the Word in our hearts and our hearts in the Word, and thus alone can we meet the enemy.

Praying always. We do not detach this from the armor of God. It belongs to it. Prayer always with all prayer and supplication in the Spirit, is next to the sword of the Spirit the most powerful weapon against the devil and his wicked hosts. We must read the Word and pray. Prayer and the Word cannot be separated. The searching of the Word must be done with prayer and prayer will be effectual through knowing the Word. Prayer is dependence on God; we lean on Him. And as we pray in the Spirit (not for the Spirit) we are to watch also and remember all the saints of God, the blessed members of the body of Christ, the masterpiece of God.

7. The Conclusion

CHAPTER 6:21-24

In the preceding verses the great apostle asked the prayers of the saints for himself. Thereby he testified in a practical way to the great truth of the body of Christ, the church. The conclusions are brief. Tychicus, a beloved brother and faithful minister in Christ, would make known to them all things, and he was sent also by the loving apostle to comfort their hearts. What a marvellous document this epistle is! What a solid rock to stand upon! What revelations concerning God, and ourselves as redeemed by the blood of His Son! God grant that all His people may increasingly enjoy the riches of this richest portion of His Holy Word.

THE EPISTLE TO THE
PHILIPPIANS

Introduction

The city of Philippi was built as a military position by Philip the Great of Macedon to keep the wild Thracians in check, which were the neighbors of the Macedonians. Later it became a Roman colony by Augustus, as a memorial of his victory over Brutus and Cassius. It was not a very important city. The Jews had not settled there at all, so that the city did not contain a synagogue. In Acts 16:12 Philippi is called "the chief city of that part of Macedonia." This does not mean that Philippi was the chief city of all Macedonia, which Thessalonica was; but Philippi was the chief city of that district and the first city to which Paul and his companions came. The historical record of the apostle's visit to Philippi and how the gospel was preached there, for the first time on European ground, is found in the book of Acts (chapter 16). The conversion of Lydia, her hospitality to the servants of Christ, the demon possessed girl and her deliverance, the suffering of Paul and Silas on account of it, their prayer and praise in the prison, the earthquake, the conversion of the jailer and of his house, are the interesting and blessed incidents connected with the beginning of the church in Philippi. The apostle probably visited this city twice after this (Acts 20:1 and 6), though the details of these visits are not reported in the book of Acts.

The church in Philippi was greatly attached to the Apostle Paul. He had no need to defend his apostleship and authority, for the Philippians had not been affected by the false Judaizing teachers, who had wrought such havoc in Galatia and Corinth. This must have been due to the fact that there were few Jews in that city. But the apostle evidently feared the invasion of the Philippian assembly by these false teachers. This we learn from the warning given in chapter 3:2. The church itself was poor and had much trial and affliction; yet did they minister out of their deep poverty to other needy saints (2 Cor. 8:1-2; Phil. 1:28-30). They had also ministered liberally to the apostle twice shortly after he had left them (Phil. 4:15-16); he received their fellowship in Thessalonica. The third time they had remembered him. Epaphroditus was their messenger who brought the love-gift to the prisoner of the Lord. In return the apostle sent to the beloved Philippians another gift, this beautiful Epistle, dictated by the Spirit of God.

Written From Rome

That this Epistle to the Philippians was written by Paul seems almost impossible to doubt. "Indeed, considering its peculiarly Pauline psychological character, the total absence from it of all assignable motive for falsification, the spontaneity and fervor of its effusions of feeling—he must be a bold man who would call its authorship in question" (Alford). Yet the critics are bold and leave nothing unquestioned and some have questioned the genuineness of this document. Needless to say the Epistle has not suffered by this foolish criticism. The ancient testimony of Polycarp, Irenaeus, Clement of Alexandria and others mentions this epistle as being Pauline and written by him in Rome, during his imprisonment, of which we read in Acts 28:30-31. The question arises at what time of his prison life he wrote this letter. It was not in the very beginning, but must have been towards the end. The Philippians had heard of his imprisonment and had made up a sum of money which Epaphroditus carried in person to Rome. And Epaphroditus had fallen sick and the Philippians had heard of his severe illness "nigh unto death" (Phil. 2:30). This sickness of their beloved Epaphroditus had been in turn reported to them (Phil. 2:26) and the apostle heard how they had been grieved on account of it. All this necessitated a number of journeys from Rome to Philippi and back. This took a good many months. And furthermore, in the beginning of his stay in Rome he dwelt for two years in his own hired house and seemed to have perfect liberty (Acts 28:30). In his epistle to the Philippians he writes that he is in the praetorium and no longer in his own house. "But I would have you know, brethren, that the circumstances in which I am here turned out rather to the furtherance of the gospel, so that my bonds have become manifest as being in Christ in all the praetorium and to all others" (Phil. 1:12-13, revised translation). The praetorium was the place where the praetorium guards were kept, next to the palace of the Emperor Nero. He had now been put in stricter confinement and felt his bonds more severely (Phil. 1:18). The Epistle must therefore have been written by him after the Epistles to the Ephesians, Colossians and Philemon, that is, about the middle of the year 63 A.D.

The Epistle of Christian Experience

Philippians is put in our Bibles between Ephesians and Colossians. A better arrangement is to put this Epistle after Colossians. The Epistle to the Ephesians shows the believer's position in Christ and what he possesses in Him; Colossians reveals the glory of Christ as the Head of the body in whom all the fullness of the Godhead dwells bodily. Philippians also speaks of Christ, but not in a doctrinal way. It is an Epistle which describes the walk and the life of one who has apprehended his position in Christ and walks therefore in the power of the Spirit of God. It shows what manner of lives those should live on earth who are saved by grace and who are waiting for glory. The epistle assumes the knowledge of what the salvation of God is. We therefore find nothing said about justification, peace with God or assurance of salvation. The word "salvation" as used in Philippians has nowhere the meaning of salvation by grace in the sense of deliverance from guilt and condemnation. Philippians shows us what true Christian experience is in the power of the Spirit of God. The words "sins" and "sin" are not found in this Epistle. The true believer knows that his sins are put away and that the old man was crucified with Christ. The question of deliverance from the guilt of sin and from the power of sin, as so blessedly revealed in Romans, does not enter into true Christian experience. True Christian experience is to walk in the power of the Holy Spirit and to manifest Christ in that walk. This the Epistle to the Philippians reveals from beginning to end. The name of our Lord is used over fifty times in the four chapters. He is the believer's life; Christ must be always before the heart and He must be made known by the believer in his life, following Him as the pattern and looking to Him as the goal.

The words "joy" and "rejoicing" are used eighteen times in Philippians. It is the Epistle of rejoicing. "He went on his way rejoicing" is the description of the experience of the eunuch after he had believed on the Lord. The true believer's way should be one of constant rejoicing. The whole atmosphere of this Epistle is that of joy, and so the believer in whatever earthly circumstances he may be placed should manifest the joy of the Lord. Paul, the great apostle, and now the prisoner of the Lord, as years before in the Philippian prison, sends forth from the Roman prison the triumphant song of faith and holy joy. There is not a word of murmur or complaint. It is "counting it all joy" and "glorying in tribulation." He had Christ; He knew Christ; Christ was his all; he knew himself in His hands and the glorious goal was ever before him and the Holy Spirit filled him therefore with joy. And such should be the experience of every believer. The word Philippians means "those who love horses." The racehorse in fullest energy stretches its neck to reach the goal. This epistle describes also the Christian race. This is especially seen in the third chapter where the energy and holy ambition of the new life to win Christ, to attain and to reach the goal is given. The Epistle likewise reveals the real affection and fellowship which exists between the servant of the Lord and those who have received blessing through his ministry. The annotations of this precious little Epistle contain many hints on the true Christian experience and walk.

The Division of Philippians

The division into four chapters is the correct one. As stated in the introduction it is true Christian experience which this little Epistle unfolds, showing the motives which should govern the believer in his life, the energy he should manifest, the resources which are at his disposal and the victory over all circumstances through Christ. The Christian in a normal, spiritual condition as seen in this Epistle has been aptly described as on a journey with an object before him, which is Christ. The Lord Jesus Christ is therefore the theme of each chapter. Hence we have four aspects of the true Christian life and experience.

In the *first* chapter Christ is made known as the all-controlling principle of the life of the believer. Christ is our life; He indwells the believer, and true Christian life and experience is to live for Him and be fully controlled by the Lord. "For to me to live is Christ and to die is gain" (1:21). In the *second* chapter Christ is seen in His humiliation and obedience as the believer's pattern. The One who passed through this life, who left the glory to humble Himself, who was obedient unto death, the death of the cross; He who endured the cross and despised the shame, who is now exalted at the right hand of God and has a name which is above every name, is to be constantly before the believer's heart. "Let this mind be in you, which was also in Christ Jesus" (2:5). In the *third* chapter Christ is the bright object and the final goal before the believer. In the energy of the new life the believer reaches out after that goal, never satisfied with anything else. It is the desire to win actually Christ, to lay hold of that for which he has been laid hold of by Christ. "That I may know Him, and the power of His resurrection, and the fellowship of His sufferings, being made conformable unto His death; if by any means I might attain unto the resurrection from the dead" (3:10-11). In the *fourth* chapter we learn that Christ is enough for all circumstances. The believer, who, like the great apostle, can say, "for me to live is Christ"; who ever follows His path of self-humiliation and obedience, constantly reaching out for the goal, will find that Christ is sufficient for all earthly circumstances. "I can do all things through Christ who strengtheneth me" (4:13). This then is the division of this brief but most important and practical Epistle:

I. **CHRIST, THE CONTROLLING PRINCIPLE OF THE BELIEVER'S LIFE** (1)

II. **CHRIST, THE BELIEVER'S PATTERN** (2)

III. **CHRIST, THE OBJECT AND THE GOAL** (3)

IV. **CHRIST, THE BELIEVER'S STRENGTH, SUFFICIENT FOR ALL CIRCUMSTANCES** (4)

Analysis and Annotations

I. Christ, the Controlling Principle of the Believer's Life

CHAPTER 1

1. The introduction (1:1-2)
2. The fellowship in the gospel (1:3-8)
3. The apostle's prayer (1:9-11)
4. Paul's victory (1:12-20)
5. Paul's life and confidence (1:21-26)
6. Exhortation to walk worthy of the gospel (1:27-30)

Verses 1-2. The introductory words to this Epistle differ from those of the preceding epistles in that he does not mention his apostleship. The reason for this omission is because his letter to the Philippians does not unfold the great doctrines of the gospel, nor does it correct evil teachings. In writing to them about his own experience as illustrating Christian experience, he does so as a member of the body of Christ. Associating Timotheus, his son in the gospel, with himself as servant of Christ Jesus, he addresses all the saints in Philippi with the bishops and deacons.

Notice the way the name of our Lord is used in this opening verse of the Epistle: "Servants of Christ Jesus" (not Jesus Christ as in the authorized version) and "saints in Christ Jesus." Christ is His name as the Risen One, as Peter declared on the day of Pentecost, "God has made Him both Lord and Christ." The attention is directed at once to Him as the Risen, Glorified One by putting His title "Christ" first.

Believers are saints, that is, separated ones, and servants in the risen, exalted Lord; He must ever be before the heart in life and walk down here and all service must come from Himself. All the saints are mentioned first and then the bishops and deacons. The bishops are the overseers, who are also called elders; the deacons were ministers. The custom of ritualistic Christendom in electing a man a bishop, who has charge over a diocese, the oversight of so many churches, with certain functions of authority, is not according to Scripture. They had a number of bishops, overseers, in the small assembly in Philippi as well as in Ephesus. Acts 20:28 gives their work and responsibility. "Take heed therefore unto yourselves, and to all the flock, over which the Holy Spirit hath made you overseers (bishops), to feed the Church of God, which He hath purchased with His own blood." And these chosen ones who labor for the flock are to be recognized and esteemed. "And we beseech you, brethren, to know them which labor among you, and are over you in the Lord, and admonish you. And to esteem them very highly in love for their work's sake" (1 Thess. 5:12-13). The deacons probably ministered more in temporal affairs. Of bishops and deacons and their qualifications the apostle writes more fully in 1 Tim. 3.

Verses 3-8. And as he remembered them all

and thought of their love and devotion he thanked God for them. "I thank my God upon every remembrance of you, always in every prayer of mine making request for you all with joy, because of your fellowship in the gospel from the first day until now." He remembers with praise to God their fellowship in the gospel, how they took part in the trials, labors, conflicts occasioned by the preaching of that gospel. They had taken a zealous part in the gospel Paul preached and manifested a loving interest by ministering to the needs of the Lord's servant. The remembrance of all which had happened when he was in Philippi and their combined fellowship and steadfastness filled the prisoner of the Lord with gratitude and joy. Therefore he prayed for them continually; he carried them upon his heart and in the prayer of intercession mentioned their names before the throne of grace. How Christ-like this was. He ever carries His dear people upon His heart and intercedes for them.

If we love the saints of God we also will pray for them. This gives joy, courage and confidence. "Being confident of this very thing, that He who hath begun a good work in you will perform it until the day of Jesus Christ. Even as it is meet for me to think of you all because ye have me in your hearts, and that, both in my bonds and in the defence and confirmation of the gospel, ye all are partakers of my grace." (The Authorized Version has it "because I have you in my heart"; the correct translation is "Ye have me in your hearts.") The grace of God had wrought this loving spirit in the Philippians; the Lord had produced all this interest in the gospel and their whole-hearted devotion. And so the apostle is confident that He who had done all this in them, who had begun the good work, would surely complete it until the day of Jesus Christ, when all His saints meet Him face to face. They had him in their hearts, not merely as a fellow-saint, but they had loving sympathy for him in his sufferings and as the one who suffered for the defence and confirmation of the gospel. And Paul, knowing their love and heart-fellowship, in return longed after them. The response to their affection was his affectionate desire. What a blessed illustration of the command of our Lord, "A new commandment I give unto you, that ye love one another, as I have loved you, that ye also love one another" (John 13:34). How little of this real affection there is among the children of God! How much faultfinding, sectarian exclusion from fellowship, especially among those who claim deliverance from sectarianism, and how little real manifestation of love towards all the saints! It is one of the leading characteristics of the Laodicean condition.

Verses 9-11. The apostle now utters his inspired prayer for them. It is still the prayer of the Holy Spirit for God's people. They had love, but he prays that their love may abound yet more and more. But this abounding love is to be "in knowledge and all intelligence." Love must not and will not tolerate evil. If the heart is fixed on the Lord Jesus Christ, then the Christian will manifest this love in knowledge and all intelligence, having discernment of good and evil. As Christ is before the heart the believer will abound yet more and more in love and also "judge of and approve the things that are excellent." Walking after this rule means to be "pure and without offence till the day of Christ." That day is not the Old Testament day of the Lord, when He is revealed on earth in power and glory to judge and to establish His kingdom, but it is the day for the saints when they meet Him in the air and then appear before His judgment seat. And such a walk produces the fruits of righteousness which are by Jesus Christ, unto the glory and praise of God. Thus it is seen that love is the source of everything in the life of the believer.

Verses 12-20. After the words of love and prayer Paul speaks of himself and his circumstances. But how does he speak of that which had happened unto him? There is not a word of murmur or complaint. Not a word of uncertainty or doubt. Not even a thought of self-pity or discontent. He might have accused himself about having gone to Jerusalem; to create sympathy he might have complained and described his bonds and the sufferings. But he rises above all. Christ is in his life the controlling principle. His own self is out of sight and he bears joyful testimony how all turned out for good, for the furtherance of the gospel. He had written to the Romans years before that all things work together for good to them that love God. In Rome, a prisoner, he shows practically the truth of that statement. The overruling hand of the Lord was manifested in the furtherance of the gospel, even in the praetorium, adjoining Nero's palace. It was enough for him who was so devoted to Christ and the gospel of grace. And his bonds encouraged many in becoming more bold to speak the word without fear. Who were they who preached Christ out of envy and strife, who tried to add still more affliction to his bonds? They were such who were selfish, envying the great apostle for his gifts and power. They were jealous of him. And now when he was in prison, his widespread activities completely arrested, they began to speak against his person and perhaps used his imprisonment as an evidence against him, that claiming too much authority, the Lord had set him aside. By their envy and strife, they would add affliction to the apostle. And yet they preached Christ. The prisoner of the Lord rises above it all. He is not self-controlled, but Christ controls him. And so he writes, "What then? notwithstanding every way, whether in pretence or in truth, Christ is preached; and I therein do rejoice, yea, and will rejoice." God was with His servant; and instead of the self-seeking which instigated these sorry preachers of the truth, there was found in Paul the pure desire for the proclamation of the gospel of Christ, the whole value of which he deeply felt, and which he desired above all, be it in what way it might." His own self was completely out of sight. Christ was his all; in Him he rejoiced and though he was in prison he was filled with joy and the worthy Name was being proclaimed.

He speaks next of his confidence that this will turn out to his salvation through their prayer and the supply of the Spirit of Jesus Christ. What salvation is it he means? It is not salvation in the sense of deliverance from guilt and condemnation. Of this the Apostle Paul was not in doubt; for this he did not need the prayers of others. Deliverance from the guilt of sins and from condemnation is the gift of God in Christ Jesus. We are saved once for all by the finished work of the cross. To this salvation nothing can be added. Believers are saved and forever safe in Christ. "There is therefore now no condemnation to them that are in Christ Jesus" (Rom. 8:1). Salvation in the New Testament has two more meanings. There is a salvation for the believer when the Lord Jesus comes again. "We are saved in hope" (Rom. 8:24). And there is a present salvation which the believer needs day by day as he journeys towards the blessed goal. In the midst of trials, temptations, hardships and other perils, victory over all these things is to be gained and Christ's name to be exalted and glorified. The salvation we have in Christ through Christ is to be practically manifested. For this the apostle desired the prayers of the Philippians; for this he needed, and we also, the supply of the Spirit. The latter certainly not in the sense, as some teach, of a new baptism of the Spirit. The Holy Spirit indwells the believer and if the heart is set upon Christ and controlled by Him, the supply of the Spirit will not be lacking. Therefore the apostle's earnest expectation and hope was that he would be ashamed in nothing, that he would be victor in all these circumstances. Christ would be magnified in his body whether by life or by death.

Verses 21-26. The great principle of his life, the all governing principle, was Christ. He was all in Paul's life. "For me to live is Christ" means that Christ lived in him (Gal. 2:20); he lived by Him and for Him. If death should come it would be gain, for it would bring him to Christ. But he finds himself in a strait betwixt two things. He has a desire to depart and to be with Christ, which would be far better and yet, if he was to live still down here, it was worth his while. Far better for him personally to depart and be delivered from all the conflicts, trials and sufferings; but, on the other hand, the needs down here, the saints who needed him and his labors, induce him to decide to choose "to abide in the flesh," for it was more needful for them. So he decides to remain, no matter what sufferings were still in store for him, so that he might minister unto their spiritual needs. How unselfish! How very much like Christ! Self again is all out of sight. And there is no mention made of Nero and his power. Through faith Paul knew himself not in the hands of Rome but in the hands of Christ.

We must not overlook the argument against the false doctrine of soul-sleep, which is contained in the words of the apostle, "to depart and be with Christ, which is far better." This false doctrine claims that when the believer dies he passeth into a state of unconsciousness. If this were true it would certainly not be "far better" to depart, or as the original states, "much more better." Enjoying the fellowship with the Lord is a good and blessed thing. To pass out of the body and to be with Him is "much more better," for in the disembodied state, the saints of God enjoy and know the Lord in a degree that is impossible down here. And the best of all is when the Lord comes and all the redeemed receive their glorified bodies.

Verses 27-30. And now he desires that their life should be worthy of the gospel he loved so well. He wants them to stand fast in one spirit and with one mind striving together for the gospel; this was to be their attitude whether he was present with them or absent. Only the Holy Spirit could accomplish this; He only can give to believers oneness in all things and power to strive together for the gospel. Walking thus believers need not to be terrified by the adversaries, those who oppose and reject the gospel. These adversaries always try to inspire fear, like the enemies of Israel in the land. But looking to the Lord, letting Him govern all things, walking in the Spirit, was an evident testimony of their own promised salvation (which here means the final deliverance) and to their enemies an evident token of perdition. And suffering through which they passed in Philippi, as well as that of the apostle in the prison of Rome, is viewed as a gift of God, just as much as believing on Christ. It is then a gracious, God-given privilege to suffer for His sake. Murmuring and complaining will be completely silenced when suffering for Christ's sake is looked upon as a gift of grace. "Blessed are ye when men shall revile you and persecute you and shall say all manner of evil against you falsely for My sake. Rejoice and be exceeding glad, for great is your reward in heaven, for so persecuted they the prophets, which were before you."

II. Christ, the Believer's Pattern

CHAPTER 2

1. Oneness of mind through self-effacement (2:1-4)
2. The humiliation and exaltation of Christ (2:5-11)
3. Work out your own salvation (2:12-13)
4. As lights in the world (2:14-16)
5. The example of Paul (2:17-18)
6. The example of Timotheus (2:19-24)
7. The example of Epaphroditus (2:25-30)

Verses 1-4. This chapter puts before us Christ as our pattern. The path He went is to be the believer's path. He trod the way, and the many sons He brings ere long with Himself to glory are called upon to follow Him in the same way. And what honor, what glory, to be called to follow in the same path! The chapter begins with a loving appeal of the prisoner of the Lord. He reminds them of the comfort in Christ which was their blessed portion, of the comfort of love and the fellowship of the Spirit and the bowels of mercies, the result of these precious possessions of the gospel. And now while they had manifested all this in a practical way among themselves and towards the apostle, he tells them that they would fulfill his joy by being of the same mind, having the same love, united in soul and thinking one thing. That they had difficulties among themselves may be learned from the fourth chapter. And so he desired that all might be one. It is a precious echo of our Lord's prayer in John 17. Nothing is to be done among His people in the self-seeking spirit of strife or vain-glory. This is the spirit of the natural man and of the world.

The true way which becomes the followers of the Lord Jesus Christ, who live by Him and for Him, is to esteem the other better than himself in lowliness of mind, regarding not each his own things (or qualities) but each the things of others also. To walk in such a manner is only possible with those who have received, by being born again, a new nature and walk in the power of the Spirit of God. To be utterly forgetful of self, complete self-effacement and self-denial and thus the absence of strife and vain-glory and the manifestation of true humility, is the manifestation of the mind of Christ. But is it possible at all times to esteem each other better than himself?

We let another answer: "There will be no difficulty in this if we are really walking before God; we shall be occupied with each other's good, and the one will esteem the other better than himself, because when the soul is really before the Lord, it will see its own short-comings and imperfections, and will be in self-judgment; and according to the love and spirit of Christ see all the good that is from Him in a brother and one dear to Him, and will therefore look upon his fellow-Christian as better than himself, and so all would be in beautiful harmony; and we should be looking after each other's interests too."[1] How true it is, love likes to be a servant; selfishness likes to be served.

Verses 5-11. With the fifth verse begins that portion of the chapter which reveals Christ as our pattern. Christ in His humiliation and His exaltation; Christ who did not please Himself, who was obedient unto death, the death of the cross; Christ, who is now exalted and has a name which is above every other name, is blessedly before us in these verses. There are seven steps which lead down deeper and deeper, even to the death of the cross. And there are seven steps which lead up higher and higher.

His Humiliation

1. He thought it not robbery to be equal with God.
2. He humbled Himself.
3. He became a servant.
4. He was made in the likeness of man.

---

[1]J. N. Darby, *Philippians.*

5. He was found in fashion as a man.
6. He became obedient.
7. Obedient to the death of the cross.

His Exaltation

1. God highly exalted Him.
2. Gave Him the Name above every name.
3. Every knee is to bow at His name.
4. Things in heaven must acknowledge Him.
5. Things on earth.
6. Things under the earth.
7. Every tongue must confess Him as Lord.

"Let this mind be in you which was also in Christ Jesus." The Spirit of Christ is in the believer for this very purpose, not that we should be imitators of Christ, but that His own life may be reproduced in us. We have this mind of Christ in the divine nature. What wonderful grace that we are called with such a calling, to be in His fellowship and follow His own path! Having delivered us from guilt and condemnation we are called to walk even as He walked down here, the author and finisher of the faith.

We trace briefly His path. We behold Him first in His absolute deity, "subsisting in the form of God." He ever was and is God; as we know from the opening of the gospel of John, "In the beginning was the Word, and the Word was with God and the Word was God." Who can describe what glory was His? And the equality with God which is His He did not esteem an object to be grasped at, but He emptied Himself. (This is the correct translation and better than the King James version, "He made of Himself no reputation.") He gave up something which was His; He laid aside His outward glory. Some teach that He laid aside His deity. This is positively an unscriptural and evil doctrine. It is widely known in theological circles as the kenosis-theory, which is so dishonoring to our adorable Lord. He could never be anything else but the true God and the eternal life. He came down from the heights of eternal and unfathomable glory and took on a body prepared for Him, yet in that body He was very God. John 17:5 shows of what He emptied Himself.

The next step tells us that He who gave up, came down. "He took upon Him the form of a servant, taking His place in the likeness of men." Had He taken upon Himself the form of an angel, it would have been a humiliation, for He created the angels. But He was made a little lower than the angels. He took on the servant's form in the likeness of men. But in Him was no sin, so that it was impossible for Him to sin, for He knew no sin and was in all points tempted as we are, apart from sin.

But the path did not end with this. He who gave up the glory, He who came down and became a servant also became obedient. It was an obedience unto death, the death of the cross. Wonderful condescension and love. It was all for our sake. And redeemed by His precious blood, called into His own fellowship, His way must become ours; we are to follow Him. If we then consider Him and let this mind be in us which was also in Christ Jesus, self will have nothing more to say; all strife and vain-glory will be at an end. And this path of giving up, coming down, true humility, self-denial and true obedience is the only one in which there is perfect peace and rest for the child of God. "Learn of Me, for I am meek and lowly in heart and you shall find rest for your souls."

The description of His exaltation follows. God has highly exalted Him and given Him a name which is above every name. God raised Him from the dead and gave Him glory. What glory it is! In the first chapter of Hebrews we read that the risen man Christ Jesus is the heir of all things, "made so much better than the angels, as He hath by inheritance obtained a more excellent name than they" (Heb 1:4). In Him we have also obtained an inheritance. Before He ever received that glory He prayed to the Father "the glory Thou hast given me I have given to them" (John 17:22). In His glorious exaltation He is likewise our pattern. We shall see Him as He is and shall be like Him, His fellow-heirs. And while we follow in His steps down here we can look upon Him seated in the highest heaven and rejoice that we shall someday be with Him and share His glory. Every knee must ultimately bow at the name of Jesus, even beings under the earth, infernal beings. They must own His title in glory. Yet this does not make them saved beings. Nor does this passage teach that ultimately all the lost will be saved, as claimed by restitutionists and others. The fact that every tongue will have to confess that Jesus Christ is Lord does not mean the salvation of the lost. In Col. 1:20 things, or beings in heaven and on earth are also mentioned in connection with reconciliation, but then the things under the earth are omitted. See our annotations on that passage.

Verses 12-13. Words of exhortation come after this blessed paragraph in which the Lord Jesus is put before us as our pattern. "Work out your own salvation with fear and trembling, for it is God who worketh in you both to will and to do according to His good pleasure." These words are misunderstood by many Christians. It is being taught that Christians should work for their own salvation. This is the grossest perversion of this exhortation. Every true believer has salvation which is given to Him by grace. It is his own salvation; he does not need to work for it. Others say that one who is really saved by grace must work in order to stay saved, and work with fear and trembling. They tell us, if a believer does not keep on working, if he fails and sins, he will fall from grace and is in danger to be unsaved and lost again. This also is unscriptural; the Word of God teaches the eternal security of all who have received eternal life, the gift of God in Christ Jesus our Lord. The exhortation does not mean that we must work to keep ourselves saved, but it means that our *own* salvation which we *have* in Christ is to be worked out into result. Salvation is to be practically manifested in the life and walk by glorifying Christ. We are to work it out after the blessed pattern of Christ with fear and trembling, not the fear of being lost, but the fear of failure in not walking in lowliness of mind, in true humility and in obedience. This will ever be the chiefest concern of the believer who walks in the Spirit. "It is this, therefore, which is to induce the fear and trembling; not in selfish dread, but the sense of our responsibility to Him to whom we owe our all and whose our life is. Plenty there is to make us serious in such work as this, but nothing to dishearten us. If God has taken in hand to work in us after this fashion, that is ample security for our success. The fact that the apostle was now absent from them, he whose presence had been so great a comfort and blessing to their souls, was only to make them more completely realize this divine power which was carrying them on to the full blessing beyond" (*Numerical Bible*).

Verses 14-16. If we thus work out our own salvation, with Christ ever before us as our pattern, following after Him in the same path, we shall do all things without murmurings and reasonings. These are the fruits of the old self. But following Him as our pattern there will be no more strife and vain-glory; we shall esteem the other better than ourselves and consequently there will be no murmurings. Furthermore, like our Lord was "harmless and sincere," we shall be harmless and sincere, irreproachable children of God in the midst of a crooked and perverted generation, without any self-assertion whatever. And as He was the light down here, so are believers now to shine as lights. As He on earth was the Word of life, holding it forth is what the apostle writes believers should also do, "holding forth the Word of life, that I may rejoice in the day of Christ, that I have not run in vain, neither labored in vain." (See 1 Thess. 2:20.)

Verses 17-18. Three witnesses follow whose experiences tell us that the grace of God can produce such a character after the pattern of Christ in the believer. First, the apostle speaks of himself. "Yea and if I am poured out as a libation on the sacrifice and ministration of your faith I rejoice in common with you all. For the same cause also do ye joy and rejoice with me." With death threatening, the prisoner of the Lord expresses His joy. Paul speaks of what the Philippians did, their ministrations of faith as the greater thing; he looks upon it all as a sacrifice and himself and his service only as a libation; that is, he views his own life poured out upon it. Thus he manifested lowliness of mind in regarding the devotion of the Philippians as the sacrifice, and the devotion of his own life he regards only as poured out as a drink offering (the symbol of joy) upon their sacrifice.

Verses 19-24. Timotheus is the next witness. Of him Paul writes, "For I have no one like-minded who will care naturally for your state (or, who will care with genuine feeling how ye get on). For all seek their own things and not the things of Christ." Many already there lived selfishly, seeking in service their own things and not serving and walking, glorifying Christ. So it is today in the Laodicean condition into which Christendom is fast sinking. But Timotheus, Paul's spiritual son (1 Tim. 1:2) was a blessed exception. He was in fullest fellowship with the apostle, like-minded, who forgot himself completely and cared genuinely for the Philippians. They knew the proof of him, for as a son with the father, he served with the apostle in the gospel. The two, Paul and Timothy, illustrate what it means "to be like-minded, having the same love, being of one accord, of one mind" (verse 2). And thus it ought to be among all the members of the body of Christ. What a comfort Timotheus must have been to Paul in the Roman prison! What cheer and joy to have such a one with him! What refreshment to his soul! But he is willing to give him up. "But I trust in the Lord Jesus to send Timotheus shortly unto you, that I also may be of good comfort, when I know your state." Not seeking his own, in self-denying devotion, he is willing to part with him, so that the Philippians might enjoy his fellowship.

Verses 25-30. Another gracious witness is Epaphroditus. He also manifests the mind of Christ. Epaphroditus was the messenger of the Philippians. He brought to Rome the collection, expressing the fellowship of the church in Philippi. But he had been taken violently ill in the exercise of his service, "for the work of Christ he was nigh unto death." He did not regard his own life and in this he exemplified the Lord Jesus Christ. "Greater love can no one show than that he lays down his life for his friends." His was a service in entire forgetfulness of self. And when he was sick nigh unto death "God had mercy on him." The Philippians also heard of the dangerous illness of their beloved messenger. They must have been deeply grieved. Then unselfish Epaphroditus was greatly distressed because the Philippians had heard of his illness. In his suffering, nigh unto death, his thoughts were with the saints in Philippi, and he was grieved that they had anxiety for him. It all shows the mind of Christ.

III. Christ, the Object and the Goal

CHAPTER 3

1. The true circumcision (3:1-3)
2. Paul's past experience (3:4-7)
3. The one passion (3:8-11)
4. Pressing towards the mark (3:12-16)
5. The goal of glory (3:17-21)

Verses 1-3. Finally (or, for the rest), my brethren, rejoice in the "Lord." Rejoicing in the Lord, not merely in the salvation which is ours, nor in His mercies, in His gifts or in our service, but in Him, is what gives strength and victory down here. He rejoiced in Him because He knew the Lord was controlling all and that he was in His hands; he followed the same path in humiliation, which he knew would lead him to the glory where He is. And the prisoner of the Lord enjoying the blessedness of fellowship with Christ, following Christ, looking to Him and not to earthly circumstances, exhorts the beloved Philippians to find their joy in nothing less than the Person Christ. It was not a grievous thing for him to write them the same things, but it was safe for them. They needed the exhortation in the midst of spiritual dangers, for nothing else keeps from evil as heart occupation with the Lord Jesus Christ. He warns "beware of dogs, beware of evil workers, beware of the concision." By these terms the same false teachers are meant which disturbed the Galatian churches, which did such evil work also among the Corinthians. He speaks of these perverters of the gospel in severe terms, but not too severe. They boasted of religiousness, of righteousness by the observance of ordinances and the keeping of the law; they trusted in the flesh and set aside Christ. They, with their religion of the flesh, are branded by the apostle as dogs, unclean and outside, therefore unworthy of fellowship. They called the Gentiles dogs, but now the Spirit of God shows that they are not better than the Gentiles. (See Gal. 4:8-10.) They were evil workmen who led souls away, as the havoc they had wrought shows. They gloried in ceremonies, the circumcision of the flesh; in reality they were the concision, the mutilators of the flesh, who knew nothing of the true separation through the cross of Christ and union with a risen Christ in whom the believer is complete.

Dogs, evil workers and the concision, are terms which fit the many cults today, including "Christian Science," the "new thought," the "new religion and modern theology," all of which deny the gospel of Jesus Christ. True believers are the circumcision, not a circumcision made by hands, but a spiritual circumcision, the putting off of the body of the flesh by the death of Christ (Col. 2:11). The cross of Christ separates the believer from the flesh, the religious forms, and self-improvement, and separates him unto God. And knowing that Christ is all, glorying in Him with no more confidence in the flesh, the believer worships by the Spirit of God, and no longer in ordinances. The indwelling Spirit fills the heart with Christ, glorifies Him, and true worship by the Spirit is the result. To have no more confidence in the flesh, to expect nothing whatever from ourselves, to glory only in Christ Jesus is true Christian attainment and experience.

Verses 4-7. And this blessed servant of the Lord Jesus speaks of his experience as a Hebrew. He might have had abundant reason to place confidence in the flesh. We had something as a natural, religious man to glory in. What fleshly advantages were his! He was circumcised the eighth day, of the stock of Israel, of the tribe of Benjamin, an Hebrew of the Hebrews; as touching the law a Pharisee; concerning zeal persecuting the Church; touching the righteousness which is in the law blameless. He had indeed, as he testified before, "profited in the Jews' religion above many my equals in mine own nation, being more exceedingly zealous of the traditions of my father" (Gal. 1:14).

He was a very religious man, for he belonged to the most religious sect of his day, with a blind zeal which led him to persecute the church, yet touching the righteousness in the law, he knew himself blameless.

And all this religiousness and zeal for God, his law keeping and blamelessness he looked upon as being of value and gain for him, though they did not give him peace or fellowship with God. A change came. The things which were religious gain to him he now counted loss for Christ. On the road to Damascus he had seen the glorified Christ and that vision had laid him in the dust so that he saw himself as the chief of sinners.

Verses 8-11. From that moment when it pleased God to reveal His Son to him the self-righteous Pharisee could say, "I count all things[2] loss on account of the excellency of the knowledge of Christ Jesus my Lord, for whom I suffered the loss of all things, and do count them refuse that I may win Christ and be found in Him." What had been gain to him he cast aside. He had seen Christ and that was enough, he would have nothing else after that. Christ had become his all. The excellency of the knowledge of Christ Jesus, whom the erstwhile persecutor now blessedly calls "my Lord," made it a joy to suffer the loss of all things, yea, to count them refuse. How he suffered the loss of all things, things needful in life, suffering, hunger, stripes; giving up all earthly distinction and advantage, we know from his own testimony (2 Cor. 11:22-31). He suffered the loss of all things and counted them refuse. "This is the marvelous estimate of one who had all the advantages in the world; and then had known all sufferings from it in behalf of Christ, looking upon the former as worse than nothing, as a detriment, and the latter to be nothing, because the knowledge he had already gained of Christ outweighed them all." All earthly things, all human attainments, everything which exalts man were counted as loathsome things in comparison with Him whom He had beheld in the glory light.

[2]"He does not say: When I was converted I counted all things loss. When a person is truly converted, Christ becomes and is everything; the world then appears as nothing. It has passed from the mind and the unseen things fill the heart. Afterwards as the convert goes on with his duties and with his friends, though Christ is still precious, he does generally not continue to count all things loss. But Paul could say, 'I count all things loss' not 'I did.' It is a great thing to be able to say that."

But what does he mean when he expresses the desire "that I may win (or gain) Christ and be found in Him"? Did he not possess Christ already? Was he not in Him and Christ in him? He possessed Christ. He was in Him. Nor does the apostle mean that he reaches out, as some teach, after a "deeper life" experience or some such thing. He had perfect assurance of his standing before God in Christ; no doubt whatever as to that could be in the apostle's heart. Nor did he need some kind of an experience, as some claim, a holiness-perfection experience, to give him greater assurance. His wish to win Christ, to gain Christ, is his longing desire for the actual possession of Christ in glory. Christ in glory is the great object and goal for the believer down here. This object and goal must ever be before the heart in the Christian's race. Like the racer who has no eyes for his surroundings, but whose eye is steadily fixed upon the goal, so the believer is to look to the glorified Christ and press forward toward the mark. This is the truth unfolded in this chapter.

Paul knew that Christ belonged to him, that his destiny was to be forever with Him, and then his passion was to be worthy of all this. And when Christ is gained in glory and the goal is reached then he would be "found in Him, not having mine own righteousness which is of the law (the righteousness which is nothing but filthy rags), but that which is through faith of Christ, the righteousness which is of God by faith." How he emphasizes this righteousness in which he delighted! And this great servant of the Lord, who knew Him so well, wants to know Him and the power of His resurrection and the fellowship of His suffering "being made conformable unto His death, if by any means I might arrive at the resurrection from among the dead." The power of His resurrection he desires to know is more than a spiritual power, for he knew that power in practical experience. Of this he had written to the Ephesians (1:15—2:10). It is again the goal of the Christian's life towards which he reaches out. He wants to arrive at the resurrection from among the dead by any means and to get there though it means fellowship with His suffering being made conformable to His death. And this was before him in the Roman prison. He wanted to be with Christ, and to arrive there he desired to be like Christ in participating in His suffering even to be made conformable to His death.

It is important to note here the difference between "resurrection *of* the dead" and "the resurrection *from among* the dead." The latter is the correct translation of verse 11. There is a resurrection of the dead, of all the dead. But there is a resurrection from among the dead, which elsewhere in the Word is called the first resurrection. The Lord Jesus was raised *from* the dead. When the Lord spoke to His disciples of His resurrection from among the dead they were astonished and spoke among themselves "what the rising of the dead should mean." They did not know what it meant. When the Lord was raised He became the first fruits of them that slept, that is, the righteous dead. And God raised Him from the dead, because His delight was in Him, for He had glorified Him and finished the Work the Father gave Him to do.

The first resurrection, the resurrection from the dead, is the expression of God's delight and satisfaction in those raised; it is His seal on Christ's work. Because He finished that great work which glorified God, all who are in Christ will be raised from among the dead, while those who live when the Lord comes, will not die, but be changed in a moment, in the twinkling of an eye (1 Cor. 15:51-52). But it is not on account of the believer's attainment, but because of Christ that the power of God will take His own out. The rest of the dead will be left until the second resurrection.

The Apostle knew that through grace he belonged to this out-resurrection from among the dead. He had an absolute certainty of it. But in divine energy he presses on towards it. All in him wants to get there where the grace of God in Christ had put him. He reaches out for this blessed goal and when he speaks of attaining "by any means" he gives us to understand that nothing shall hinder him in the race. May the cost be what it will, I want it; I want it because I have it in Christ and through Christ and I want to be worthy of it. And therefore he despised the loss of all things and was ready to suffer and die the martyr's death.

Verses 12-16. The words which follow show that this is the true meaning of the desire he expressed. "Not as though I had already attained (obtained), or am already made perfect, but I press on if so be that I may apprehend that for which also I am apprehended of Christ Jesus. Brethren, I do not count myself yet to have apprehended; but one thing I do, forgetting the things which are behind, and stretching forward to the things which are before, I press towards the goal for the prize of the calling on high of God in Christ Jesus." The goal had not yet been reached, he was still on the way and had not yet obtained nor was he made perfect. He constantly presses on towards the goal, Christ in glory. He knew that he had been apprehended, taken possession of, by Christ Jesus and for Christ and therefore he also wants to take possession, to apprehend it. He forgets what is behind and even stretches forward to the things which are before, the blessed goal. This was his constant attitude, ever occupied with the Lord Jesus Christ to be like Him and with Him in glory.

"The whole of Paul's life was founded on that and completely formed by that. The Son of God was forming his soul day by day, and he was always running towards Him and never doing anything else. It was not merely as an apostle that he entered into the fellowship of His sufferings, and conformity to His death, but every Christian should do the same. A person may say he has forgiveness of sins. But I say, What is governing your heart now? Is your eye resting on Christ in glory? Is the excellency of knowledge of Christ Jesus so before your soul as to govern everything else, and make you count everything loss? Is that where you are? Has this excellent knowledge put out all other things? Not only an outwardly blameless walk, but has the thought of Christ in glory put out all other things? If it were so, we would not be governed by everyday nothings" (J. N. Darby). Some teach that these words of Paul, speaking of attaining and not yet perfect, mean that he was still in doubt as to having a share in the first resurrection. We quote the words of a leading advocate of this interpretation:

> But what was the goal towards which Paul was thus directing his efforts? 'If by any means,' he continues, 'I may attain to the select (?) resurrection out from among the dead.' In other words, his aim was to be numbered with those blessed and holy ones who shall have part in the first resurrection. But we must notice that he had, at the time, *no certain assurance* (italics ours) that he would compass the desire of his heart. . . . Just before his death, however, it was graciously revealed unto him that he was one of the approved.[3]

Think of it! The prisoner of the Lord who suffered joyfully the loss of all things, who counted all but dung, who walked in such separation and devotion, still uncertain about his share in the first resurrection! This interpretation is not only wrong, but it denies the grace

[3]Pember, *The Church, the Churches and the Mysteries.*

of God in the Lord Jesus Christ, by making the first resurrection a question of attainment when it is purely the matter of divine grace. This teaching aims at the very vitals of the gospel of grace and glory.

An exhortation follows. He exhorts all who are perfect to be thus minded. What does the word perfect mean and who are the perfect? Above, when he said he was not yet made perfect, it applies to Christ-likeness in glory by being conformed to His image. True Christian perfection will be reached when the Lord comes and we shall see Him as He is and be like Him. Now those are the perfect down here who have no confidence in the flesh, who glory in Christ and who know He is all in all, that by one offering He has perfected forever them that are sanctified, that they are accepted in the Beloved and complete in Him in whom the fullness of the Godhead dwells bodily. And they are all to be "thus minded" like he was, ever occupied with Christ in glory, doing this one thing—pressing on towards the goal for the prize of the calling on high of God in Christ Jesus.

Verses 17-21. "Brethren, be followers (imitators) together of me, and mark them which walk so as ye have us for an ensample." What a blessed thing that Paul could write this! Grace had enabled him to follow Christ fully. But even then there were those over whom Paul wept because their walk showed that they were the enemies of the cross. "For many walk, of whom I have told you often, and now tell you even weeping, that they are the enemies of the cross of Christ, whose end is destruction, whose God is their belly, and whose glory is in their shame, who mind earthly things." Were these real believers? The statement "whose end is destruction" answers this question. They could not be true children of God, but were such who had professed Christianity, having the form of godliness, but denying the power thereof (2 Tim. 3:5). They turned the grace of God into lasciviousness. "Their god was really their belly; that is to say, the fleshly craving in them had never been set aside by any satisfaction that they had found for themselves in Christ. The craving of the old nature led and governed them." Instead of minding heavenly things, seeking the things which are above where Christ sitteth, they minded earthly things, showing thereby that they had never really known Christ. If there were "many" then among God's people who were enemies of the cross, who had with all their profession no desire for the heavenly calling, how much larger is their number now at the end of the age. They are religious, yet they cling to the world, love the world and thus deny the cross of Christ, which makes them the enemies of the cross.

"There is nothing like the cross. It is both the righteousness of God against sin, and the righteousness of God in pardoning sin. It is the end of the world of judgment, and the beginning of the world of life. It is the work that put away sin, and yet it is the greatest sin that ever was committed. The more we think of it, the more we see it is the turning point of everything. So, if a person follows the world, he is an enemy of the cross of Christ. If I take the glory of the world that crucified Christ, I am glorying in my shame" (J. N. Darby).

"They walked according to the flesh, minding earthly things instead of the heavenly, the heavens being the proper and only sphere of spiritual life, demonstrated that they knew nothing of the matter as to the heart, and for the truth of resurrection and life in a risen Christ, were walking according to their own religious feelings, making this their god. And surely there is enough of this everywhere, a bringing down revelation of the truth to the standard of human feelings and experiences, making these the umpire instead of God. It is a religious appetite ruling and hungry, and satisfied with its own sensations when filled. Israel was charged to take heed lest when they had eaten and were full, they should forget Jehovah (Deut. 8:14) and the prayer of Agur in Prov. 30:9 is, 'lest I be full and deny Thee.' The grand object, Christ Himself, is ignored, and religious excitement, like any other intoxication, displaces Him and occupies the soul to its damage and peril. It is the belly, not Christ. It is religious emotion, it is not Christ. It is perfection in and of the flesh; it is having no confidence in the flesh. The flesh may find its satisfaction and growth as much in religion as in the lower passions and the more secular world. The cross came in to put all this to death. Hence these are enemies to the cross of Christ, even though much mention may be made of the cross, and even continual prostrations before it practiced" (M. Taylor).

In the last two verses the blessed goal itself is fully revealed. "For our conversation is in heaven (or commonwealth-citizenship)[4] from whence also we look for the Saviour, the Lord

---

[4]The Greek word is "*politeuma*," from which we have our English "politics." Hence one might say "our politics are in heaven."

Jesus Christ, who shall transform our body of humiliation into conformity to His body of glory, according to the working whereby He is able even to subdue all things unto Himself." This is the blessed hope and the blessed goal. All we have as Christians, our relationships, rights and possessions are in heaven. Some blessed day He, for whom we wait, will come and take us to the place where He is transforming our body of humiliation into conformity to His body of glory. Then we shall have attained that for which down here we hope and pray (1 Thess. 4).

IV. Christ, the Believer's Strength, Sufficient For All Circumstances

CHAPTER 4

1. Stand fast and rejoice (4:1-4)
2. Dependence on God and true heart occupation (4:5-9)
3. I can do all things through Christ (4:10-13)
4. The fellowship of the Philippians (4:14-20)
5. The greeting (4:21-23)

Verses 1-4. And now the final testimony of the prisoner of the Lord, telling us from his own experience that Christ is sufficient for all circumstances down here. The first verse is filled with the precious fragrance of the great apostle's affection. What refreshment there is for all His dear saints in these opening words of this chapter! "Therefore my brethren dearly beloved and longed for, my joy and crown, so stand fast in the Lord, dearly beloved." How he loved the saints and longed for them. He looked upon them as his joy and crown; his joy down here and his crown in the day of Christ. So the aged John testified, "I have no greater joy than to hear that my children walk in truth" (3 John 4). They were to stand fast in the Lord, for this gives strength and the Lord constantly before the heart and mind gives victory. Euodias and Syntyche, two sisters in the Lord, are exhorted to be of the same mind in the Lord. They had difficulties and had become separated. How graciously and tenderly they are exhorted to overcome their differences. The true yokefellow is probably Epaphroditus, who was now fully restored and carried this letter to the Philippians. Paul requests him to assist those women who had contended with him in the gospel, of course in the sphere which belongs to woman. And there were Clement and other fellow laborers, whose names are in the book of life. These names are known to Him and in His day their labors will come to light and they will receive their reward. It is enough for the laborers to know that his name, though unknown to the world, is in the book of life, and his service, through unapplauded by the world, has His approval. Once more he exhorts to rejoice in the Lord alway, under all circumstances, at all times. And again I say, Rejoice. He did not write such words when he was taken up into the third heaven, but these blessed words come from the prison in Rome. When the Lord is before the heart, if He is the controlling principle of our life, the pattern and the goal, never lost sight of, then He giveth songs in the night.

"Were a light at the end of a long straight alley, I would not have the light itself till I get to it; but I have ever increasing light in proportion as I go forward; I know it better. I am more in the light myself. Thus it is with a glorified Christ, and such is the Christian life."

Verses 5-9. And this walk in Christ and with Christ must be characterized by dependence on God. "Let your moderation be known to all men. The Lord is at hand." Walking thus means to walk in meekness, not reaching out after the things which are but for a moment, content with such things as we have, never asserting one's right. Moderation means to put a check upon our own will. How easy all this becomes if we just have it as a present reality that the Lord is nigh and that when He comes all will be made right. A little while longer and all will be changed. And while we walk here in His fellowship, His command to us is, "Be anxious for nothing." All rests in His loving hands. His people have tribulation down here. He told us so. "In the world ye shall have tribulation; be of good cheer, I have overcome the world" (John 16:33). And prayer is our refuge. Most blessed words! How the child of God loves, appreciates and makes use of them! "Be anxious for nothing, but in everything by prayer and supplication with thanksgiving let your requests be made known to God. And the peace of God, which passeth all understanding, shall keep your hearts and minds through Christ Jesus." We can cast all our cares upon Him, for we know He careth for us. He is our burden bearer. We may look upon all our burdens as being permitted by Him so that we may give them back to Him and find out His love and power.

"We are in relationship with God; in all things He is our refuge; and events do not disturb Him. He knows the end from the beginning.

He knows everything, He knows it beforehand; events shake neither His throne, nor His heart; they always accomplish His purposes. But to us He is love; we are through grace the objects of His tender care. He listens to us and bows down His ear to hear us. In all things therefore, instead of disquieting ourselves and weighing everything in our hearts, we ought to present our requests to God with prayer, with supplication, with a heart that makes itself known (for we are human beings) but with the knowledge of the heart of God (for He loves us perfectly); so that, even while making our petition to Him, we can already give thanks, because we are sure of the answer of His grace, be it what it may; and it is *our* requests that we are to present to Him. Nor is it a cold commandment to find out His will and then come: we are to go with our requests. Hence it does not say, you will have what you ask; but God's peace will keep your hearts. This is trust; and His peace, the peace of God Himself, shall keep our hearts. It does not say that our hearts shall keep the peace of God; but, having cast our burden on Him whose peace nothing can disturb, His peace keeps our hearts. Our trouble is before Him, and the constant peace of the God of love, who takes charge of everything and knows all beforehand, quiets our disburdened hearts, and imparts to us the peace which is in Himself and which is above all understanding (or at least keeps our hearts by it), even as He Himself is above all the circumstances that can disquiet us, and above the poor human heart that is troubled by them. Oh, what grace! that even our anxieties are a means of our being filled with this marvellous peace, if we know how to bring them to God, and true He is. May we learn indeed how to maintain this intercourse with God and its reality, in order that we may converse with Him and understand His ways with believers!" (*Synopsis of the Bible*).

Our prayers may not always be answered as we want to have them answered, for He alone knows what is best. We speak to Him about our cares and put them thus into His heart and He puts His own peace into our hearts.

What are thy wants to-day? Whate'er they be
Lift up thy heart and pray: God heareth thee,
Then trustfully rely that all thy need
He surely will supply in every deed.
But every prayer of thine, and every want
Of either thine or mine, He may not grant,
Yet all our prayers God hears, and He will show
Some day, in coming years, He best did know.
C. Murray

And in the life down here, surrounded by every form of evil, we are to be occupied with only that which is good, things true, things noble, just, pure, lovely, things of good report; if there be any virtue or any praise, think on these things. This is the way how peace of mind and blessing, happiness and joy may be maintained, not being occupied with the evil which surrounds us, or the evil in others, but with the very opposite. The Word of God is given to us for this purpose. As we read it prayerfully and meditate on it we are kept in that which is good, true, noble, just and lovely. Walking according to these exhortations they would find that the God of peace is with them. And so shall we.

Verses 10-13. Paul also rejoiced in the Lord greatly because their care for him had flourished again, and added "wherein ye were also careful, but ye lacked opportunity." They had ministered to him as the Lord's servant, in temporal things. The words, "now at last your care of me hath flourished again," indicates that they had delayed their ministration, but he puts another meaning upon it. He does not insinuate that it was a failure and neglect on their side, "but ye lacked opportunity." He did not mention this in respect of want. "For I have learned in whatsoever state I am, therewith to be content." He had learned it all practically and knew about being abased and abounding—"everywhere and in all things I have learned the secret, both to be full and to be hungry, both to abound and to suffer want. I can do all things through Christ who strengtheneth me." The secret of this victory over all circumstances, whether good or evil, was Christ. It was "not I but Christ." In himself he had no strength, but all His strength to be abased and to abound, to be full or hungry, in abounding and in suffering want, was the Lord Jesus Christ. And this strength continually flows from and is supplied by our relationship with Christ as it is maintained by faith in a close walk with Him. He had learnt to trust Him fully; he trusted Him and walked in fellowship with Him in adversity, and, also, which is more difficult, in prosperity. His faith always reckoned on Christ. He kept him from being careless and indifferent, when he was full and abounded in all things and He kept him from being discouraged and dissatisfied when he suffered privations. He had found Christ sufficient in every circumstance. This is the happy life, which, too, we may live if Christ is our object and our all.

(Prosperity in earthly things is for many children of God a snare. The person who requested prayer for a brother who was getting rich made a good request. We need more prayer and need more watching when all goes well and when we abound. Then the danger to become unspiritual and indifferent is great.)

Verses 14-20. He reminds them of their faithfulness to himself; he had not forgotten their love and what they had done in the past. He delighted in the remembrance of it, nor does God forget the ministries to His servants. "But to do good and communicate forget not, for with such sacrifices God is well pleased" (Heb. 13:16). "For God is not unrighteous to forget your work and labor of love, which you have showed toward His name, in that ye have ministered to the saints, and do minister" (Heb. 6:10). Yet he does not want them to misunderstand him, as if he was anxious to receive further fellowship from them for his personal need. Therefore he adds, "Not because I desire a gift, but I desire fruit that may abound to your account. But I have all, and abound; I am full, having received of Epaphroditus the things which were sent from you, an odor of a sweet smell, a sacrifice acceptable, well pleasing to God." In reminding them and himself of their love he did not desire more gifts for the sake of having them, but he desired the fruit which would result from their faithfulness and liberality, which would abound to their account in the day of Christ. All ministry to God's servants and to the saints should be done from this viewpoint.

"But my God shall supply all your need according to His riches in glory in Christ Jesus. Now unto God and our Father be glory for ever and ever. Amen." The God whom He had learnt to know so well in all circumstances—my God, as he called Him—would supply all their need. It is not a wish that He may do so, nor a prayer that he prays, but it is an assured fact. He knows his God so well that he counts on Him for the supply of all the need of the beloved saints according to His riches in glory in Christ Jesus.

Verses 21-23. The greetings close this blessed little Epistle of love and joy, so full of the realities of true Christian experience, made possible for every child of God through the indwelling Spirit. He sends his greetings to every saint and conveys the greetings of the saints with him, chiefly they that are of Caesar's household. Blessed hint that even there the gospel had manifested its power in the salvation of some.

THE EPISTLE TO THE
COLOSSIANS

Introduction

Colossae was a city of Phrygia, a district in Asia Minor. It was pleasantly located in the valley of the Lycus, a branch of the Meander. Two other cities are also mentioned in this Epistle to the Colossians, the cities of Laodicea and Hierapolis (4:13). Laodicea was only nine miles and Hierapolis, thirteen miles from Colossae. Laodicea was a very rich and influential city. Hierapolis was famous for its hot springs. Colossae was the smallest of these three cities. Christian believers lived in all three cities and later the Lord selected the church of the Laodiceans and addressed to it the final message of the seven churches (Rev. 3). The region of Phrygia was well settled by Jews, some of whom were in Jerusalem on the day of Pentecost (Acts 2:10). We shall find through the study of this Epistle that a Jewish sect which held evil doctrines flourished in the whole region; this sect was known as the Essenes, and the Spirit of God warns against their false teachings in the Epistle. Phrygia also was known as the seat of other heresies, especially an oriental-philosophical mysticism.

The Church in Colossae

It seems that the church in Colossae was preeminently a Gentile church (2:13). How did it come into existence? Paul evidently did not visit the city, though he passed through Phrygia (Acts 16:6; 18:23), for he writes in this Epistle, "For I would that ye know what great conflict I have for you, and for them in Laodicea, and for as many as have not seen my face in the flesh" (1:1). It seems also clear that the church in Colossae came into existence after Paul had passed through that region the second time as stated in Acts 18:23, for if a church had existed then in that city, he would probably have visited Colossae. If we turn to the nineteenth chapter of the book of Acts, which records the long sojourn of the Apostle Paul in Ephesus, we find a hint on how the gospel was made known to the Colossians. First we read that Paul continued for two years, "so that all they which dwelt in Asia heard the word of the Lord Jesus, both Jews and Greeks" (Acts 19:10). And then Demetrius the silversmith witnessed to the extension work of Paul while being in Ephesus. "Moreover ye see and hear, that not only in Ephesus, but almost throughout Asia, this Paul hath persuaded and turned away much people . . ." (Acts 19:26). Asia does not mean the continent, but a province of Asia Minor, of which Phrygia was a part. The whole region heard the gospel during his stay in the prominent city of Ephesus; among the visitors who listened to the messages of Paul were people from Colossae, Laodicea and Hierapolis. These carried the gospel back to their homes and thus churches were formed. Philemon and Epaphras of Colossae must in this way have heard the gospel from the apostle and became the instruments through whom the church in their home-city was founded. That Epaphras was the more prominent one becomes certain from chapter 1:7 and 4:12-13.

The Occasion and Object of the Epistle

Paul in Rome had received, probably through Epaphras, the information that the Colossian Christians were facing great dangers as to their faith. What the danger was the text of the Epistle will show us more fully. A number of false doctrines emanating from philosophical speculations, oriental mysticism, asceticism and Judaism, were being advocated amongst them and threatened the complete corruption of the church. Later a system known by the name of Gnosticism (from the Greek word *"gnosis"*—knowledge) wrought great havoc in the Church; the beginning of it was troubling the Colossians, who seemed to have been an intellectual class to whom the philosophical, mystical and ascetic teachings appealed in a special way. Gnosticism attempted to explain creation, the origin of evil, God, etc., apart from the revelation God has given in His Word. Besides speaking of a certain class of beings, half-gods of different rank, they denied that God had created the world, but that an inferior being had called it into existence. This system taught that matter is evil and that the only way to escape from evil would be to repudiate matter completely.

The worst feature of these Gnostic teachings was a denial of the deity of the Lord Jesus

Christ and His work of redemption. It was a philosophical, theosophical speculation, antichristian throughout. Well did Polycarp say to the Gnostic Marcion, "I know thee, thou first-born of Satan." While this evil system had not yet fully developed in the Colossian church, the foundation for it had been laid and the Holy Spirit anticipated its coming, and in sending this document to the Colossians answers the false teachings of Gnosticism. This is of equal interest and importance to the Church in the twentieth century. "Christian Science," so called, that philosophical-theosophical-mystical cult, is a satanic revival of ancient Gnosticism. The Epistle to the Colossians must, therefore, be an effectual weapon against this cult, which denies the two pillars of Christianity, the Son of God and the finished work of the cross. The Colossians were also being misled, as the second chapter shows us, by other false teachers. Judaizers were at work among them. We are not left to infer respecting the class of religionists to which these teachers belonged, for the mention of "new moon and Sabbath" in chapter 2:16, at once characterizes them as Judaizers, and leads us to the then prevalent forms of Jewish philosophy to trace them. Not that these teachers were merely Jews; they were Christians (by profession), but they attempted to mix with the gospel of Christ the theosophy and angelology of the Jews of their times. They became infected with theosophic and ascetic principles and were gradually being drawn away from the simple doctrine of Christ. This false system of philosophy and ascetic mysticism, attempting to intrude into unseen things, with which was linked angel-worship, limited the superiority and greatness of the Lord Jesus Christ and more so the sufficiency of His work of redemption.

The occasion of the Epistle was the existence of these evil things among them. The object in writing was more than counteracting the false doctrines. The Holy Spirit unfolds the truth of the gospel, showing in this Epistle the majesty and glory of Christ, that He has the pre-eminence in all things, head of creation and head of the Church; it unfolds the completeness of His redemption and the believer's completeness in Christ as risen with Christ and in living union with Him, in whom the fullness of the Godhead dwells bodily. Like all the great Pauline Epistles, containing the revelation of God to man, the Colossian Epistle with its vital and glorious truths, is meat in due season for God's people, especially in these days when we are confronted by the same errors in modern movements and energized by the power of Satan to destroy the very foundations of the faith.

Colossians in Contrast with Ephesians

Colossians was written by Paul about the year 62 A.D., from the Roman prison, and, as stated in the introduction to the Epistle to the Ephesians was carried by the same messenger who also received the Ephesian Epistle from the hands of the Apostle. Tychicus was this messenger (Ephes. 6:21; Col. 4:7-9). There is a striking resemblance between these two Epistles, which have been called "twins." Dean Alford speaks of it as follows: "In writing both, the apostle's mind was in the same frame—full of the glories of Christ and the consequent glorious privileges of His Church, which is built on Him, and vitally knit to Him. This mighty subject, as he looked with indignation on the beggarly system of meats and drinks and hallowed days and angelic mediations to which his Colossians were being drawn down, rose before him in all its length and breadth and height, but as writing to *them,* he was confined to one portion of it, and to setting forth that one portion pointedly and controversially. He could not, consistently with the effect which he would produce on them, dive into the depths of the divine counsels in Christ with regard to them." Ephesians and Colossians embody the highest revelations God has given to man. Colossians is the counterpart of the Ephesian Epistle; each may be viewed as a supplement to the other. In Ephesians the revelation concerns mostly the body of Christ (the Church), the fullness of that body, its rich privileges and heavenly destiny; in Colossians the head of that body in His fullness and glory is blessedly revealed. In Ephesians we find repeatedly the blessed position of the believer stated "in Christ Jesus"; in Colossians we read of Christ in the believer, "Christ in you." Ephesians reveals the calling of God and exhorts believers "to walk worthy of the vocation wherewith we are called"; Colossians making known the Lord and His glory, exhorts "to walk worthy of the Lord." Controversy concerning evil doctrines and errors is absent in Ephesians; it is prominent in Colossians. In Ephesians the Holy Spirit and His work in the believer is fully brought out. Then we read of the quickening, the sealing, the filling of the Spirit and are warned against quenching and grieving the Spirit; in Colossians nothing is said about the Holy Spirit, the doctrine concerning the Spirit is absent.

The annotations will point out the reason for this. At the same time the redemption truths of Ephesians as well as Romans and Galatians are all touched upon in Colossians. The great truths contained in these wonderful Epistles must ever be kept in freshness and in power by the Spirit of God before the heart and mind of God's people, so that they can live and walk as those who are redeemed and be kept in the enjoyment of salvation. The more these deep and precious documents are studied the greater the blessedness for God's people. May God the Holy Spirit, the author of this Epistle, fill, through His message, our eyes and hearts with Him who is our Lord and the Head of His body.

The Division of Colossians

Chapter 2:9-10 is the center of the Epistle. "For in Him dwelleth all the fullness of the Godhead bodily. And ye are complete in Him who is the head of all principality and power." It is the very heart of the Epistle, the key which unlocks its heavenly treasures. We get in this verse the scope of the Epistle. The apostle does not begin by warning the Colossians of the danger and by exposing the fatal errors which were creeping in among them. He writes first of Him and His glory. The Spirit of God wants the Colossians to get the right estimate of the Person and glory of the Lord Jesus Christ, of His dignity and pre-eminence in all things, of the great work of reconciliation, the peace which was made in the blood of the cross and the present and future results of this work. Then He shows that the believer is in Christ, that He who is bodily in glory, in whom all the fullness of the Godhead dwells is the fullness of the believer. Each is complete in Him. And therefore ordinances, philosophy, traditions of men, intruding in mysterious things, angel-worship, cannot add anything to the believer's knowledge or perfection. His perfection is Christ. Then follow exhortations, how a believer who is risen with Christ and one with Him should walk down here. We divide, therefore, this Epistle into three parts.

I. THE PERSON OF CHRIST, HIS GLORY AND HIS WORK (1)

II. COMPLETE IN HIM, IN WHOM ALL THE FULLNESS DWELLS (2)

III. THE PRACTICAL RESULTS, LIVING AS RISEN WITH CHRIST (3:4—4:18)

Analysis and Annotations

I. The Person of Christ, His Glory and His Work

CHAPTER 1

1. The introduction (1:1-8)
2. The prayer (1:9-14)
3. The person and glory of Christ, Head of creation and Head of the Church (1:15-18)
4. The work of reconciliation and the double ministry (1:19-29)

Verses 1-8. This Epistle unfolds the doctrine of Christ and therefore Paul speaks of himself as an apostle of Christ Jesus by the will of God; Timotheus is spoken of as a brother. In addressing the Philippians, the apostle spoke of himself and of Timotheus as servants and did not mention his apostleship at all. In addressing the Colossians, when error is to be refuted and truth to be revealed, he uses his title as apostle. He addresses them as saints and faithful brethren in Christ and the precious greeting to such whom God has separated from evil and unto Himself follows: "Grace be unto you and peace, from God our Father and the Lord Jesus Christ." Grace and peace belonged to them, as it belongs to all who are in Christ. Their state could not affect what God has bestowed upon them in His Son. Then he gives thanks "to God and the Father of our Lord Jesus Christ, praying always for you." He had heard of their faith in Christ Jesus; of the love which they had towards all the saints and then mentions the hope which is laid up for them in heaven.

Faith, love and hope are the blessed marks of all true believers, produced in them by the Spirit of God. Their faith in Christ Jesus was manifested in love for all the saints. "This is His commandment, that we should believe on the name of His Son Jesus Christ, and love one another, as He gave us commandment" (1 John 3:23). "We know that we have passed from death unto life, because we love the brethren" (1 John 3:14). And they also know the blessed hope which they had heard and learned in the word of the truth of the gospel. The gospel then had produced these blessings among the Colossians, who were once heathen; and the same gospel was also going out in all the world bringing forth fruit wherever it was received in faith. Could this be said of the various philosophical systems which were being introduced among the Colossians? Or could mysticism and law-keeping show such results? Only those who hear and believe the gospel know the grace of God in truth.

Then Paul mentions Epaphras, the beloved fellow servant, who was for them a faithful minister. Through his ministry they had learned these things, while Epaphras had declared unto Paul their love in the Spirit. This is the only time the Spirit of God is mentioned in this Epistle. It is different in the Epistle to the Ephesians. There the fullest teachings concerning the Holy Spirit are given. Every chapter in Ephesians speaks of the Holy Spirit. We read there that He is the seal and the earnest; He is the Spirit of wisdom and revelation; access is through Him unto the Father; the church is described as the habitation of God through the Spirit, who has also made known the mystery hid in former ages. Furthermore He strengthens the inner man that Christ may dwell in the heart by faith. Then the unity of the Spirit is spoken of in Ephesians; believers are not to grieve the Spirit by whom they are sealed unto the day of redemption; the filling with the Spirit, spiritual songs as the result, the sword of the Spirit and prayer in the Spirit are likewise mentioned in the Epistle to the Ephesians.

Why is all this omitted in Colossians? Why is this Epistle silent about the work of the Spirit in the believer? The reason is of much interest. Our Lord said concerning the coming of the Spirit of truth, "He shall not speak of Himself," and again He said, "He shall glorify Me" (John 16:13, 14). While the Ephesians knew Christ, owned Him and His glory, the Colossian Christians, through false teachers, were being turned away from Christ; they began to lose sight of the glory of Christ by listening to philosophy (2:8); their eyes were no longer only on Christ. He therefore aims in this Epistle to glorify Christ, to lead the Colossians back to a full realization of the Person and Glory of Christ and their completeness in Him. He directs their hearts to the Lord Jesus Christ and thus fulfills his mission, speaking not of himself and glorifying Christ.

(Certain sects which claim a restoration of Pentecostal power and gifts are constantly occupied with the Holy Spirit, His work in the believer; they speak much of the Spirit, the feelings He produces, the energy He gives, etc. Nowhere in the Word are believers told to be occupied with the Spirit. The one object given to the believer to have ever before the heart is the Lord Jesus Christ and His glory. One finds among these people who claim a restoration of apostolic gifts (notably the smallest, speaking in tongues) those who are quite ignorant of the work of Christ, and the glory of Christ.)

Verses 9-14. Next follows a prayer, Paul being only the instrument of the utterance of the Spirit of God. And it is a prayer fully adapted to the conditions of the Colossian Christians. It is still the prayer of the Holy Spirit for all the people of God. The leading petition in this prayer is for the knowledge of the will of God—"that ye might be filled with the knowledge of His will in all wisdom and spiritual understanding." All the other requests may be looked upon as the results of a spiritual understanding of the will of God. What is the meaning of the will of God? It is that will of God of which we read so much in the first chapter of Ephesians and concerns those who are in Christ. What we possess in Christ, what God has made us in Him and given to us with Him, according to the good pleasure of His will, is that which believers need to know. What God has willed for those who are redeemed by the blood of His Son, how they are constituted in Him holy, put into the place of sons, accepted in the Beloved, heirs of God, sealed and indwelt by His Spirit, is the knowledge with which Christians should be filled. This the Colossians lacked. The full knowledge of that will would have kept them from listening to the enticing words of false teachers, who promised them wisdom, knowledge and other benefits, which are only found in Christ and which the believer possesses in Him. And this knowledge of His will is a growing knowledge and must govern the walk of the believer. It is needed "to walk worthy of the Lord unto all pleasing." Such a walk is only possible by enjoying constantly the relationship into which the gracious will of God has brought the believer; the more we enter into all grace has done for us and lay hold of it, the more we shall walk worthy of the Lord. And this walk is "unto all pleasing." With a true Christian, God may be displeased, though He condemn not; and there is a lack of felt fellowship. Only as walking worthily of Christ can we abound in obedience to God, and be as children intimate with their father. Every Christian's habitual question should be, not, "What must I do to escape censure, or win wages?" But "What will please God?" It produces also fruit bearing in every good work and growth by the true knowledge of God. And this gives strength in the way down here.

"Strengthened with all power, according to the might of His glory, unto all patience and long suffering with joy." In the midst of tribulation and suffering strength is supplied through the might of His glory. It is the glory of Christ and Christ in glory which strengthens the believer, gives power to endure and to pass through every trial and hardship with joy. To know this will of God in Christ and Christ and His glory constantly before the soul, this is what leads to Christlikeness and what gives victory as we walk through a world to which the believer no longer belongs. "For, with our feet outside of the land, our way must be a toilsome and afflicting one, dreary enough and a perpetual outrage to the soul strung to heavenly purity and peace and worship. But He who was from heaven and is now its attractiveness went through it all with a glow of gladness that broke out in a rapture at times of greatest neglect and misapprehension and hatred from without (Matt. 11:25-27). He was as a weaned child, desiring nothing here. There has been no promise of making things smooth here, but the opposite, and if we nestle we must have made the nest by gathering worldly materials, by accepting a friendship where He would get hate. God brings nothing before us to hold the heart in comfort, peace, and joy, but the glory to be revealed. And is it not enough for that and enough to wait for?"[1]

Being filled with the knowledge of His will produces likewise worship. "Giving thanks unto the Father who hath made us meet to be partakers of the inheritance of the saints in light; who hath delivered us from the power of darkness and translated us into the kingdom of the Son of His love; in whom we have redemption, the forgiveness of sins." It is a part of the prayer that Christians might give thanks to the Father in spiritual worship. And these things mentioned are known to the believer if he is filled with the knowledge of His will, for they tell us what God *hath done* for the sinner who believes on His Son. Here are the most assuring statements, the things forever settled for those who have accepted the Lord Jesus Christ. There is an inheritance of the saints in light and the Father hath made us meet to be partakers of it through the work of His Son. From the Father we receive this inheritance. The title to that inheritance, which every true child of God fully owns, is the blood of the Lord Jesus Christ, and the fitness to be there is the new nature bestowed upon the believer. It is therefore not, as so often stated, that we try to fit ourselves for heaven; this is impossible. The moment a sinner accepts the Lord Jesus Christ, he is made meet to be a partaker of that inheritance. All the glory of that inheritance is at once put on the side of him who trusts on Christ. All was done for us once for all when Christ died; in Him we are sons and if sons, heirs of God, the fellow heirs of Christ.

"There can be no greater acceptance of us in heaven than God gives us now in Christ, for even there we shall stand accepted in Him alone. Our Father will not more fully rejoice over us there than He does here; for then, as now, He will see us only as in Christ. Our meetness, then, for the one part of the inheritance is just our meetness for the other part. And so, when some eminent saint comes to his death-bed, what is it that gives him his comfort, his serene triumph, in that critical hour? Is it his progressive practical sanctification? Indeed, no. He is too conscious of many failures, that he should rely on that as his passport through the gates into the city. Thankful he is to God, that He has enabled him to serve Him with whatever degree of faithfulness, and he may speak of it to the praise of the glory of His grace; but he rests not his destination on so imperfect a prop as that. What is it then? Just this: the infinite value of the blood which sprinkled him. On that he rests, as on the Rock of Ages. Yes, Christ Himself is our only meetness for the inheritance, and our believing on Christ is our having the meetness" (Bishop W. Nicholson).

And more than that, "He *hath* delivered us (not a gradual deliverance, but a deliverance accomplished) from the power of darkness and hath translated us into the kingdom of the Son of His love." And the deliverance takes place as well as the translation into His kingdom, when we believe on Christ. There is a power of darkness. Satan is the ruler of darkness and to this power of darkness the unsaved sinner belongs. We are by nature the complete subjects of this power and also the children of wrath (Eph. 2:1-3). As such we are in a helpless condition and if deliverance is to take place it must come from the side of God. And it has come for all believers. All who are in Christ are no longer under the authority of Satan, the prince of the power of the air, they are taken from his domain and rule and are translated into another kingdom, the kingdom of the Son of his love.

[1]M. Taylor, *Colossians.*

My chains are snapped, the bonds
of sin are broken,
And I am free.
Oh! let the triumphs of His
grace be spoken
Who died for me.

The expression "kingdom of the Son of His love" has been identified with the Church, while others make it to mean the coming kingdom, which will be set up when the Lord Jesus Christ comes again. But it does not mean the body of Christ and much less the kingdom on earth, which is termed the kingdom of the Son of man. We quote from the *Synopsis* by Darby, who gives the correct meaning of this term.

"Here alone, I believe, is the kingdom called the kingdom of the Son; and, I think, it is only as introducing His Person as the centre of everything and giving us the measure of the greatness of the blessing. It is the kingdom of One who has this place, the Son of His love, into which we are introduced. It is indeed His kingdom; and in order that we may apprehend the character of this kingdom as it is now for us, and our nearness to God as having part in it, it is called the kingdom of the Son of His love. It is this which is the present foundation and characteristic of the relationship with God of those who are truly in and of it. As the kingdom of the Son of man, it is His manifestation hereafter in glory and in government. Here it is characterized by the relationship of the Son Himself to the Father, in His person, with the addition of that which gives us a full title to share it—redemption through His blood, the forgiveness of sins."

Blessed possessions! Blessed assurance! In Christ, fit for glory; in Christ, delivered from the power of darkness and near to God now as He, the Son of His love, is near, belonging to same realm of glory; in Christ redemption, the forgiveness of sins. There are no "ifs" and no questionings. All is positive. For all this we should give thanks to the Father and praise Him for what He has done for us. Such worshippers the Father seeketh (John 4) for they delight in His Son, in whom all His delight is. Yet how little such true worship is rendered! And why? Because Christians are so little filled with the knowledge of His will, with that which grace has accomplished in Christ. (The spiritual condition of a Christian may be learned by his prayer. One who knows what God has done, who has looked deep into the gospel of God, whose heart knows and enjoys Christ will praise much and thank the Father for all these blessed realities. But how many ask God constantly to give to them that, which they already possess; and there is no real worship possible unless we know and enjoy His grace. Bye and bye all our prayers will cease and it will be all praise and worship—when we are with Him in glory and know what grace has done for us forever.)

Verses 15-18. With these verses we reach the heart of this chapter. Christ, the Son of His love, having been named in the prayer, the Holy Spirit reveals Him now in His Person and glory as well as the work of redemption accomplished by Him. It is a remarkable portion of this Epistle in which all the errors about the Person of Christ are refuted and silenced. Arianism, Socianism, Unitarianism, Russellism, Christian Science and other "isms" which rob the Lord Jesus Christ of His full glory and deny His deity, are completely answered in the brief words which unfold His glory. It was Arius of Alexandria who taught in the beginning of the fourth century that the Lord Jesus was a creature, the first of all created beings, though superangelic, yet not eternal in His being nor a partaker of the divine essence. The council of Nice (325 A.D.) condemned the wicked theory of Arius. Socinus in the Reformation period revived this error, as did Priestly and Martineau in England and Channing and others in America.

It remained for one Charles T. Russell, whose system is known by different names, to popularize these false and corrupt views and spread them throughout Christendom. Russell with Arius asserts that in His pre-existent state Jesus was a pure spirit, higher than the angels, yet only a creature. When born of the Virgin Mary, He dropped His spirit nature while on earth. He teaches that the atonement offered by our Lord was only human, having nothing divine about it. Russellism also denies that the human body of our Lord was raised from the dead. The whole system is a conglomerate of Arianism, Ebioniteism and Rationalism. Christian Science equally denies the deity of Christ and contains in itself all the fatal errors of Gnosticism, which the Colossians were facing in their day.

1. The first statement concerns His absolute deity—*"Who is the image of the invisible God."* He is the image of God in all His fulness and perfection. As the image of God, the invisible God, He therefore is God. "He is the effulgence of His glory and the expression of His substance" (Heb. 1:3). He has made known God to man; in Him we see what God is. "No man hath seen God at any time; the only begotten Son, who

is in the bosom of the Father, hath declared Him" (John 1:18). Were He not the essential image of God in His own person, one with God in eternity and glory, He could not be the representative image of God by incarnation.

2. *"Firstborn of all Creation"*—not as the Authorized Version has it "the firstborn of every creature." It is here where the false teaching originates, which claims that our Lord was after all only a creature, called into existence by God, and not very God. This passage teaches no such thing. The title "Firstborn" denotes His priority to creation, for He is creation's head; the headship of all creation belongs to Him. When He who is the image of the invisible God takes His place in creation, as He did in incarnation, it can only be as the Firstborn, as the beginning of the creation of God, the head of all. He, who became man, under whose feet as the second Man all things will be put in subjection (Ps. 8; Heb. 2), is the Lord from Heaven, the Creator of all things.

3. That He is not a creature, though He took on the creature's form, is at once demonstrated by the words which follow. The Holy Spirit anticipated the errors which would deny His glory and therefore we read of Him as the Creator. *"For by Him were all things created, in the heavens and upon the earth, things visible and invisible, whether they be thrones or dominions, or principalities, or powers, all things were created by Him and for Him."* It is therefore absolutely certain that the "Firstborn" does not mean that our Lord is a creature, but the Creator. These words which were written by the apostle are revelation. Nor is Paul the only instrument through whom the Spirit of God makes known His glory. John wrote in the beginning of his Gospel the same truth. "All things were made by Him; and without Him was not anything made that was made" (John 1:3).

The Son of God is therefore the Creator, yet not to the exclusion of the power of the Father, nor the operation of the Spirit. The three are one, in character and in their work; in creation and in redemption the three persons of the Godhead are active. What a dignity and glory is His! All things visible were created by Him and for Him; all life, vegetable and animal, all matter and all physical forces, the small things and the big things, everything was called into existence by Him. The heavens are the work of His fingers (Ps. 8:3); the firmament showeth His handiwork (Ps. 19:1). The millions of stars with their suns, the planets and comets, the whole universe, unfathomable and incomprehensible for the creature, were all called forth by His omnipotent word. Not by science, nor by searching do we know of this, but "through faith we understand that the worlds were framed by the Word of God, so that things which are seen were not made of things which do appear" (Heb. 11:3). And then things invisible—how little we know of these!

The innumerable company of angels, this vast and wonderful world of the unseen, are also created by Him. It is all "by Him" and "for Him"; He is the primal cause of it, as well as the final cause. In the presence of such deep and blessed revelations, which man's mind could never discover, in the presence of the infinite, the reasonings of Unitarianism and Darwinianism and all other reasonings crumble into dust. The evolutionary hypothesis of the creation of a cell or of "primordial germs" from which, through millions of years, all things were developed is an invention of man and completely silenced by this passage and other portions of the Word. "And what a wonderful light do these words throw upon creation itself and upon its destiny! Christ is not only the One under whom it is; He is not only the One who will bring it all into blessing, but He, the One who has become the man Christ Jesus, is the One for whom it all exists!" And such a One, the Lord of creation, by whom and for whom are all things is our Lord, with whom all who have accepted Him are one. How blessed, how safe we are in Him and with Him, sheltered and kept by His mighty arms! And when all things are put under His feet, when in the dispensation of the fullness of times, all things in heaven and on earth are headed up in Christ, when the glories of the new creation are manifested, what glory will be ours in Him and with Him!

4. *"And He is before all things and by Him all things consist."* Everything depends upon Him; all things are held together by Him. Without Him all would cease to be. Four times in these two verses we read of "all things." All things created by Him; all things for Him; He is before all things; all things consist by Him.

Verse 18 reveals another headship and glory. *"And He is the head of the body, the Church, who is the beginning, the firstborn from among the dead, that in all things He might have the pre-eminence."*

From creation the Holy Spirit now leads us to another sphere, that of Redemption. Creation became marred and ruined by sin and He who is the head of all things in creation had to come to earth in the form of man to redeem. He died, and, raised from among the dead, He is the Firstborn, the head of the body, the Church, and as such the Beginning, that is, a new Beginning. The Church was not in existence before His death and resurrection from the dead. He could not be the Head of the Church till He had become the Firstborn by resurrection. And now He has a body, composed of all who have believed on Him as Saviour and Lord, born again and one Spirit with Him. This body is one with Him in life, in position and in glory. This body is the new creation, completely identified with Him, who is the Head, the fullness of Him who filleth all in all (Eph. 1:23).

"He is the First-born of creation, He is the First-born according to the power of resurrection, in this new order of things in which man is predestined to an entirely new position, gained by redemption, and in which he participates in the glory of God (as far as that which is created can do so), and that by participating in divine life in Jesus Christ, the Son of God and everlasting life; and, as regards the Church, as members of His body. He is the First-born of creation, the First-born from among the dead; the Creator, and the conqueror of death and the enemy's power. These are the two spheres of the display of the glory of God. The special position of the Church, the body of Christ, forms a part of the latter. He must have this resurrection-glory, this universal pre-eminence and superiority also, as being man, for all the fulness was pleased to dwell in Him" *(Synopsis of the Bible).*

Thus in all things He has the pre-eminence. And we also must give Him in all things the first place. As we lay hold on the glory of Christ, the head of creation, the Risen One now, the head of the body in glory, and look forward to the day of consummation and glory to come, when we shall see Him as He is, and participate in the glory, which His grace has bestowed upon us, we shall indeed walk worthily of the Lord and be strengthened according to the power of His glory.

Verses 19-29. His great work of redemption and the ministry connected with it is the theme of the remaining verses of this chapter. "For it pleased the Father that in Him should all fullness dwell." It is to be noticed that the words "the Father" are supplied. If a word is to be used it must be the word "Godhead" (2:9). But there is no need to do that. The correct rendering of the verse is "In Him all the fullness was pleased to dwell," and that is the fullness of the Godhead. It is a blessed and deep truth that the whole Godhead manifested itself in Him for the great purpose of redemption. The Father, the Son and the Holy Spirit dwelled in all fullness in the blessed One who walked among men. He could say of Himself that the Father dwelleth in Him (John 14:10); he that hath seen Me hath seen the Father (John 14:9) and again, "I am in the Father and the Father in Me." And He who spoke thus was and is the Son of God. And the third person of the trinity, the Holy Spirit, was not given to Him by measure (John 3:34) but He was in Him in all His fullness. The fullness of the Godhead was pleased to dwell in the incarnate One. The Gnostic teachers, which began then to sow their evil seed in the early Church, used the word "fullness" (*pleroma*) very much, and meant by it the absolute perfection of deity. But they taught that portions of this fullness were given to various divine incarnations and angels, who were generated by a supreme being. Christ, according to their philosophy, was an inferior being, who did not possess the pleroma of the Godhead.

In answer to this perversion the Holy Spirit witnesses to the truth that in Him all the fullness, the pleroma, was pleased to dwell. The fullness of the Godhead dwelt in Him and was manifested through Him, yet man, His creation, would not have Him. Man gave Him a cross which showed that man was irreconcilable as far as he was concerned. "He in whom all fullness dwelt, who was the one altogether lovely, who manifested the very character of God and brought among men unimagined goodness and power, who dealt with every need, going about doing good, who never refused a single soul, He was despised and rejected by man, hated without a cause. They crucified the Lord of glory, the Creator of all things.

"And what was to be done? Ah! this was the serious question, and this it was which God was waiting to solve. He meant to reconcile man in spite of himself; He would prove His own love to be the conqueror of his hatred. Let man be unmendable, let his enemy be beyond all thought, God, in the calmness of His own wisdom, and in the strength of His unwearied grace, accomplishes His purpose of redeeming love at the very moment when man consummates his wickedness. It was at the cross of Christ. And so it was that, when all seemed to fail, all was won. The fulness of the Godhead dwelt in Jesus; but man would have none of it, and proved it above all in the cross. Yet the cross was the precise and only place where the foundation that cannot be moved was laid. As he says, 'having made peace through the blood of His cross, by Him to reconcile all things unto Himself; by Him, I say, whether it be things on earth or things in heaven' " (W. Kelly).

He made peace in the blood of His cross. Then the great work of redemption was accomplished. And through the blood of the cross, all things are to be reconciled by Him to the Godhead, whether things on earth or things in heaven. What reconciliation is this? It is a reconciliation which is not yet accomplished. It includes all creation and the universe. The heavens and the earth will be completely delivered from the power of evil. This reconciliation of all things in virtue of the blood of His cross will take place when He comes again, when all things are put in subjection under His feet. All is in disorder in creation; it is a groaning creation. Satan with his wicked spirit is in the heavenlies and defilement is there. Yet the purchase price has been paid in the blood of His cross. The reconciliation of all things yet to come is the same which Peter preached as "the restitution of all things of which God has spoken by the mouth of His holy prophets since time began" (Acts 3:19-21). Therefore the prophets in the Old Testament give us the meaning of this coming reconciliation. We find it predicted in portions of the prophetic Word, concerning the coming age, when righteousness reigns, peace is established, the knowledge of the glory of the Lord covers the earth and the earth is full of His glory, when Israel has received the promised blessing and glory, and groaning creation no longer groans under the curse (Isaiah 11:6-9; Rom. 8:19-22). It will all be accomplished when He returns, whose right it is to reign and who paid for all in the blood of His cross. Then all present disorder will cease, the curse will be removed, Satan will be bound. This dispensation of the fullness of times will have come and Christ will reign and His saints with Him.

Does this reconciliation include the unsaved, the unregenerated, who reject Christ and remain in their sins? Does it include Satan and the fallen angels? Some, who call themselves "Reconciliationists" or "Restitutionists" teach this; and so does Russellism and other cults. But it is not so. The Scriptures do not teach such a universal reconciliation which reaches the wicked dead and wicked spirits. The best proof is when we compare the statement here with a similar on in Phil. 2:10. In this passage Paul speaks of the things under the earth, which are the lost. It is there the question of acknowledging the supreme authority of the Lord. But here in Colossians where it is the question of reconciliation, things on earth and things in heaven are mentioned, but the things under the earth are omitted, because there is not reconciliation for such. "These shall go away into everlasting punishment"; no future reconciliation is anywhere promised in the Word of God for the lost. There is no new birth, no repentance, no faith in hell. Not a drop of the living water will ever reach there to quench the spiritual thirst of the damned.

But while the reconciliation of all things awaits the return of our Lord to put all things in order, there is another reconciliation which is already effected. "And you being in time past alienated and enemies in mind by wicked works, yet now hath He reconciled in the body of His flesh, through death, to present you holy and unblamable and irreproachable before Him; if indeed ye abide in the faith, grounded and firm, and not moved away from the gospel which ye heard, which hath been preached in the whole creation which is under heaven, whereof I Paul was made a minister" (verses 21-23). This is spoken of those who have believed on the Son of God. All were once estranged from God and enemies in mind by wicked works, but having believed His work, His sacrificial death on the cross hath reconciled them. In virtue of this reconciliation believers are no longer enemies but made nigh, accepted in the Beloved and presented holy, unblamable, and irreproachable before God. What a change! And it is not of man, by his work, or having become a believer by living a fully separated life, but it is all through His death. In Him we are constituted holy, unblamable and irreproachable; this is the believer's standing before God. The words "if ye continue in the faith," etc., are words of caution. They do not touch the election and perseverance of the saints who are members of the body of which He is the head. A believer thus reconciled will continue in the faith and will not be moved away from the hope of the gospel; this is one of the tests of salvation. There was danger for the Colossians to abandon the great fundamentals of Christianity; if they did so they rejected the grace which presented them to God and in doing this they showed that they had never received the reconciliation, for one who is reconciled continues in the faith and remains upon the sure foundation.

"All the blessedness that Christ has procured is for those that believe; but this of course supposes that they hold Him fast. The language does not in the smallest degree insinuate that there is any uncertainty for a believer. We must never allow one truth to be either shut out or enfeebled by another; but then we need also to remember that there are, and have always been, those that, having begun seemingly well, have ended by becoming the enemies of Christ and the Church. Even antichrists are not from without in their origin. "They went out *from* us, because they were not *of* us." There are no enemies so deadly as those who, having received enough truth to overbalance them and to abuse to their own self-exaltation, turn again, and would rend the church of God, wherein they learnt all that gives them power to be specially mischievous. They apostle could not but dread the slide on which the Colossians found themselves; and the more so as they themselves had no fears, but on the contrary thought highly of that which had attracted their minds. If there was danger, certainly it was love to admonish them; and in this spirit he therefore says, 'If ye continue in the faith, grounded and settled.' "

(If thousands and tens of thousands of members of the professing church turn to "Christian Science" or accept the teachings of the "New Theology" and in doing so abandon the gospel and deny the doctrine of Christ, they show thereby that all their profession was only a sham, that they never received the love of the truth, were never real believers who have been reconciled. They were at least the enemies of the cross who more openly deny Christ.)

Then Paul speaks of himself as being the minister of that gospel which hath been preached in the whole creation. How he termed this gospel "my gospel" and received it by revelation, and the meaning of all this we learned from Romans and Galatians. And the sound of this gospel goes forth into all creation.

We must notice here that up to this point in this Epistle we have learned of the two headships of Christ. He is Head of Creation and Head of the Church. Then followed a twofold reconciliation. The reconciliation of all things which includes all creation over which He is the head, and the reconciliation of believers, who are in that body over which He is the head. All these wonderful revelations fully answered the teachers who brought among the Colossians the most deadly errors, denying the deity of Christ, as if some demiurge had created the world, etc. And these great statements of verses 15-23 also answer all heresies of to-day.

To the two headships of Christ and the two reconciliations there is now added a twofold ministry. The ministry of the gospel and the ministry of the church. Twice Paul writes he was made a minister, the minister of the gospel (verse 23) and the Church, whereof he was also made a minister (verse 25). It means that to him was given the revelation concerning the gospel of grace and glory and through him was also made known the truth concerning the Church, the body of Christ. There is then a blessed harmony in these statements.

1. The twofold Headship of Christ: *Head of Creation and Head of the Church*

2. The twofold Reconciliation: *Reconciliation of all things* (creation) and *our reconciliation* (the Church)

3. The twofold Ministry: *The gospel.* (preached in all creation) and *The Church* (to present every man perfect in Christ)

Paul, to whom the Spirit of God revealed these great truths, fulfilled in this way the Word of God, for the truth about the Church, the body of Christ, is the highest revelation. He was shut up in a prison and was suffering "for His body's sake," which sufferings he looks upon as filling up that which remained of the sufferings of Christ in them. He rejoiced in these sufferings for he knew they were "for His body's sake." He knew and declared "the mystery which hath been hid from ages and generations, but now hath been made manifested to His saints, to whom God would make known what are the riches of the glory of this mystery among the Gentiles, which is Christ in you the hope of glory." The mystery of which he writes is not the coming of Christ to this earth, His incarnation, death, resurrection, ascension and coming again.

All this was not a mystery, for it was revealed in the Old Testament. The mystery made known through him and of which he writes is a glorified Christ who unites all in His person, the Head in glory, who has a body composed of saved Jews and Gentiles, who are one in Him, and "Christ in (or among) you the hope of glory"— which looks forward to the consummation, when this body which is now forming, through the preaching of the gospel, is to be with the Head in glory. This is the mystery which was hid in former ages. It is unrevealed in the Old Testament and therefore exclusively a New Testament revelation. With such a revelation and ministry he preached, "warning every man, and teaching every man in all wisdom that we may present every man perfect in Christ Jesus; whereunto I also labor, striving according to His working which worketh in me in power." Every man "perfect" means full-grown. (See Phil. 3:15 and Heb. 5:14.) It is the believing apprehension of what Christ is for us and what we are in Him. Through this knowledge and heart occupation with the Lord of glory the believer becomes full grown and true Christian character is formed. And what toil and energy the great apostle manifested that this might be accomplished!

II. Complete In Him, In Whom All the Fullness Dwells

CHAPTER 2

1. The mystery of God (2:1-8)
2. Complete in Christ (2:9-15)
3. Exhortations and warnings (2:16-23)

Verses 1-8. In view of the last verses of the preceding chapter we can understand his anxiety and the great conflict he had for the Colossians and for those living in nearby Laodicea, and for as many who had not seen his face in the flesh. He was deeply concerned about them after he heard of their danger of going into error. It was a spiritual conflict. He was greatly exercised in his thoughts and feelings. He knew the powers of evil so well; hence the burden for the Colossians, for the Laodiceans and for all others. In writing to them about his great conflict for them, and therefore his prayerful interest in them, he did so that their hearts might be comforted thereby and then, being knit together in love for this purpose: "unto all riches of the full assurance of understanding to the full knowledge of the mystery of God in which are hid all the treasures of wisdom and knowledge." (The translation in the Authorized Version is not correct. The words "of the Father and of Christ" must be omitted. It is "The mystery of God, in which are hid all the treasures of wisdom and knowledge.")

And what is this mystery of God in which the treasures, yea all the treasures of wisdom and knowledge are hidden? The mystery of God is *Christ.* But it is not Christ in incarnation, in His life on earth, His death on the cross and His resurrection. Nor is it Christ at the right hand of God, or Christ coming again to rule over the nations on earth and establish His kingdom of glory. All these things are subjects of divine revelation in the Old Testament. They are not a mystery. It is Christ, the Head of the body and believers in union with the glorious Head, joined to Him by His Spirit, possessing His life, one with Him, destined to share His glory. This is the mystery of God in which are hid all the treasures of wisdom and knowledge. And what treasures these are! How little His people know of all this mystery of God contains! It will take eternity to know and enjoy these treasures, the unsearchable riches.

The Greek word for knowledge is "gnosis"; the false teachers called themselves, after this word, "gnostics," boasting of superior knowledge and as if they possessed mysteries unknown to those who believed on Christ. We understand in this light the brief exhortation which follows: "And this I say, lest any man should delude you with enticing words." Being in Christ they had all in Him and no human philosophy or science, falsely so called, could give a greater wisdom or knowledge, than that which God had made known by revelation. The enemy's work is to keep God's people back from fully enjoying their union with Christ and increasing in the knowledge of it. Satan does this work in the garb of an angel of light, through all kinds of theories and inventions.

Before the apostle sounds a more definite warning, he expressed his joy in seeing their order and steadfastness of their faith in Christ. No doubt a part of the Colossian church stood unwavering for the faith, while others had given ear to the delusive teachings. "As ye have therefore received Christ Jesus the Lord, so walk ye in Him, rooted and built up in Him and stablished in the faith, as ye have been taught, abounding therein with thanksgiving." This was their danger, as it is still more in these days of declension and delusion, our danger, not to walk in Him, rooted and built up in Him. They were not satisfied with Christ only. They did not realize that the secret of blessing and all a Christian needs, is to go on and know more and more of Christ. This they did not do but turned instead to other sources and listened to that which was not after Christ.

"When we have received Christ, all the rest is but a development of that which He is, and of the glory which the counsels of God have connected with His person. Knowledge, or pretended knowledge, outside this, does but turn us away from Him, withdraw our hearts from the influence of His glory, throw us into that which is false, and lead our souls into connection with the creation apart from God, and without possessing the key to His purposes. Thus, since man is incapable of fathoming that which exists, and of explaining it to himself, his efforts to do so cause him to invent a mass of ideas that have no foundation, and to endeavor to fill up the void that is found in his knowledge through his ignorance of God by speculations, in which (because he is at a distance from God) Satan plays the chief part without man's suspecting it" (*Synopsis of the Bible*).

Then follows a stronger and important warning. "Beware lest any man spoil you through philosophy and vain deceit, after the tradition of men, after the rudiments of the world, and not after Christ." It is a warning against the natural man's philosophy, and the religious man's traditions; both are not after Christ, but aim at the person, the work and the glory of Christ. Rationalism and ritualism are still the pronounced enemies of the Lord Jesus Christ, as they were when He walked on the earth. (The Sadducees were the philosophers, the rationalists. The Pharisees, the most religious sect, the ritualists. Both combined in hatred of Christ.) Both may use His name, but deny His glory and reject the great truth of His headship. Philosophy is the wisdom of this world. Well has it been said: "Philosophy is an idol of man, a blind substitute for the knowledge of God." It is false and ruinous whether it leaves Him out or tries to bring Him in, whether it denies the true God, or sets up a sham god. Atheism and pantheism are the ultimate goal and results of philosophy, and both set God and His revelation aside. This is especially true of the present day destructive Bible criticism, which claims to be "scientific" and "philosophical." It is the most subtle deception the father of lies has produced.

This destructive criticism, which denies with a show of learning the Word of God, denies with it God and His blessed Son; it is an antichrist, preparing the way for the final great delusion, the full manifestation of the mystery of iniquity, the man of sin. The evolution theory is another philosophy. Though proven to be untenable, preachers, and especially the teachers of the young, still adhere to it and thereby deny God's revelation. The evolution-philosophy has no explanation for the sin and misery of the world, but makes it all a part of the nature of things which God could not avoid when He started the world evolving. It makes God the author of sin. And evolution offers no remedy for sin and its results. Evolutionists as found in all the prominent sects or denominations of Christendom teach that sin is only animalism left in man; and then they substitute for true conversion, regeneration, for reconciliation by the death of Christ and salvation by grace—they substitute for it a development for the better by civilization and culture. Evolution-philosophies are the enemies of revelation and the cross of Christ.

"But obviously this evolutionary 'salvation' is largely or wholly a salvation of the race through the prospective future perfectibility of mankind as a whole; and it is childishly inadequate in dealing with the poor individual here and now who, under this hideous handicap, fails in the sad conflict with his inherited animalism; and it has no gospel for these present moral failures (or those of the past), unless they can be reincarnated at a higher stage of the racial development, or have 'another chance' under some less hard conditions in the future; while it goes without saying that, in the view of these theistic evolutionists, this racial culture or development can be accomplished without the intervention of a divine mediator and the help of a divine sacrifice" Professor Price.

"Christian Science" also comes under the garb of a philosophy. This wicked system with its outrageous deceptions may be termed the masterpiece of Satan. Against its blasphemous inventions the Spirit of God bears a perfect witness in the first chapter of this Epistle. Christianity is not science. Science is knowledge gained by experience, by searching. Christianity is a revelation from God. It is a faith.

The traditions of men and rudiments of the world are terms which apply to the religion of the flesh, by which we mean a religion which the natural man can lay hold of and which suits perfectly the natural, unregenerated man. This is ritualism, the Galatianized gospel which has the curse of God resting upon it. It brings in man's works, law-keeping, ceremonies, holy days, saints' days, the mass and other things. But it is not after Christ. Against these two currents, rationalism and ritualism, the Spirit of God warns. Any one who follows either must deny Christ and becomes spoiled and ruined.

Verses 9-10 introduce us to the heart of this great document. *"For in Him dwelleth all the fullness of the Godhead bodily, and in Him ye are filled full, who is the head of all principality and power."* How this blessed statement recalls our attention to the great truths of the first chapter we do not need to point out. While in the first chapter He is displayed as the Incarnate One, who walked on earth, in whom all the fullness was pleased to dwell; in this statement of the second chapter we see Him as the Risen One, who is in glory as the Glorified Man and in Him dwelleth all the fullness of the Godhead bodily. Glorious truth that there is the Man, in glory, in a real human body, the Man, who made peace in the blood of His cross. The fullness of the Godhead dwelleth in Him and out of this fullness we receive grace upon grace, and that we might also be filled with all the fullness of God (Eph. 3:19). In Him believers are filled full. In Him we possess perfection and completeness before God and are not wanting anything whatever as to our position before God. Believers are in Him before God, not in what they do or according to their service, or anything else, but in perfection of what He is. Who could add to His fullness and who can add to the fullness and completeness the believer possesseth forever in Him!

The child of God has no need of philosophy, ceremonies, asceticism, advanced thought, or any other thing. No need of the traditions of men as embodied in ritualism, a man-made priesthood which He hates (Rev. 2:15); or the mass with its terrible blasphemy, or the worship of angels! We have and are all in Christ. Our only concern must be to lay hold in a practical way of this fullness, to take more and more of Him and walk in the power of it.

This is viewed next. The literal rendering of *verses 11 and 12* is as follows:

"In whom also ye have been circumcised with circumcision not done by hand, in the putting off of the body of the flesh in the circumcision of Christ; buried with Him in baptism, in whom ye have been also raised together through faith in the operation of God, who raised Him from among the dead." Circumcision done by hand is for the Jew, the sign of separation from the Gentiles. Believers are circumcised in the circumcision of Christ, that is, "the putting off of the body of flesh" (not "putting off the body of the sins of the flesh") separated from it, by being made partakers of the efficacy of His death. In the death of Christ the old man is put to death as more fully demonstrated in Romans 6; we are dead to sin, because we are in Christ, who is our life. And having now no more confidence in ourselves we are the true circumcision, who worship God in the Spirit, and rejoice in Christ Jesus (Phil. 3:3). Baptism is the symbol of this "buried with Him in baptism." And we are raised up with Him through faith in the operation of God who raised Him from among the dead. It is "through faith" this is accomplished and not in an ordinance; we are risen with Christ in possession of life.

"It is thus that we are set free from the thought of deliverance by an ordinance, which so many hold today. We are 'raised up through the faith of the operation of God who raised Him from among the dead.' Here we see distinctly what is meant. Resurrection is the opposite of burial. In burial a dead man is put among the dead. In resurrection a now living man is given his place among the living; and it is seen that Christ, identified with us through grace in His death, has been raised up of God; that we might find, therefore, our own title and ability to take our place amongst those truly alive. But then all depends upon this identification of ourselves with Him. Our eyes are now, therefore, to be upon Christ. He is in this character our true self; and our confidence, therefore, is to be in Him. As we have had it in Galatians, we live, yet no more we, but Christ liveth in us. It is the One who is before God for us who is before us now in faith and whom we accept as now our true self, a self in whom we can have confidence, a self that we can contemplate with joy and satisfaction, and without the least tendency to such pride of heart as results naturally from what we call self-occupation. Here is One who will draw us away from self, who will, as a Heavenly Object draw us completely out of the world, and accomplish our deliverance in both senses at the same time" (*Numerical Bible*).

The truth unfolded in the Ephesian Epistle (chapter 2) is also mentioned here by the apostle. *"And you being dead in offences and the uncircumcision of your flesh hath He quickened together with Him, having forgiven you all trespasses."* Blessed truth again! What follows has a meaning for both Jewish and Gentile believers. *"Having blotted out the handwriting in ordinances that was against us, which was contrary to us, He has taken it out of the way, having nailed it to the cross."* The Colossians were Gentiles, they had not been under the law and its ordinances, therefore he writes not which were "against you" but "against us." All the ordinances were against them, for they were as Jews under obligation to keep them, as they had, so to speak, put their handwriting, their signature to it, when they said with one voice, "All the words which the Lord hath said we will do" (Exodus 24:3). And inasmuch as they did not keep these ordinances, they were against them. The work of Christ has taken it out of the way; all was nailed to the cross. Then the signature was erased and the debt paid. The ordinances are removed. This applies to Gentiles as well and also in another sense. The law and the ordinances were the middle wall of partition, which excluded the Gentiles. Christ "has broken down the middle wall of partition, having abolished in His flesh the enmity, the law of commandment in ordinances, for to make in Himself of twain one new man, so making peace" (Ephes. 2:14-15). At the same time He spoiled principalities and powers, made a show of them openly, leading them in triumph by it. This means the principalities and powers of Satan and the wicked spirits. They were against us, but He has vanquished them in His death on the cross and in it has triumphed over them. Trespasses are forgiven; ordinances blotted out, completely gone; principalities and powers triumphed over.

Verses 16-23. The chapter closes with warnings and exhortations. The first warning exhortation is against ritualistic legalism. *"Let none therefore judge you in meat or in drink, or in matter of an holy day, or new moon, or of the Sabbath, which are a shadow of things to come; but the body of Christ."* All the ceremonies of the law were shadows; the substance has come and the shadows have ceased. Ritualistic Christendom has aped the shadows and by doing so practically denies by it the truth of the gospel. It is a turning away from the substance and moving after the shadow. A religion in ordinances, so-called sacraments with mysterious powers, with an imposing ritual for the eye and the ear, which gives the flesh something to do and to boast in, is an invention of Satan. True Christianity has no holy days and feast days, saints' days, lenten days, etc.; nor does it need these "beggarly elements."

The Sabbath is also mentioned. Some keep the seventh day, Saturday, and claim that this is the day to be kept. But the church has no Sabbath to keep in the legal sense. The first day of the week, the Lord's day, is the day of worship.

The next warning is against the worship of angels and occultism. *"Let no one fraudulently deprive you of your prize, doing his own will in humility and worship of angels, entering into things which he has not seen vainly puffed up by the mind of his flesh, and not holding fast to the head, from whom all the body ministered to and united together by the joints and bands, increases with the increase of God."* Here the Romish idolatry comes into view. It began early in the church. Angels are ministering spirits who minister to the heirs of glory. Their presence with and ministry to God's people may be believed, but never must they be worshipped. Putting them between Christians and Christ as a mediatorial agency is idolatrous, sinful and a denial of the headship of Christ. The worship of angels denies the union of the believer with the Head. The Head, Christ in glory, ministers to the body in spiritual things. All looked like humility when it was in reality self-will and pride. Intruding into unseen things points to such evil systems as spiritism, theosophy, psychical research and other cults. Whoever follows these things proves thereby that Christ as the Head over all is not recognized but denied. He who knows Christ and is in conscious union with Him will never crave after any of these things.

Asceticism is the concluding thing against which the Holy Spirit warns. "If ye have died with Christ from the elements of the world, why as if alive in the world do ye subject yourselves to ordinances?" Then he gives an illustration of these "Do not handle, do not taste, do not touch." (Strange it is that these words are generally misapplied, wrested from the context, twisted and contorted to furnish a text for the drink-evil and to advocate prohibition. It has nothing to do with that.) This and the concluding words reprove asceticism "the harsh treatment of the body" not keeping the body in a certain honor and all to the satisfaction of the flesh, as he writes: "According to the injunctions and teachings of men (which have indeed an appearance of wisdom in voluntary worship, and humility, and harsh treatment of the body, not in a certain honor), to the satisfaction of the flesh." These errorists taught that matter is evil and the body is the source of sin and therefore they treated the body harshly. They denied honor to the body but it was for their own satisfaction of the flesh.

"Asceticism is utterly powerless to effect the object aimed at: it does not, it cannot sanctify the flesh. It has a show of wisdom. It is extravagant in its pretensions and loud in its promises. But it never fulfills them. The apostle here declares that it has no value against the indulgence of the flesh (5:23). It, rather, stimulates the appetites and passions it is meant to extirpate. Asceticism has often proved to be a hotbed of vice. Some of the vilest men have been found among those who advocated the strictest austerities. They denounced the holiest of human associations, and branded as sensual the purest relations. Marriage was degraded, celibacy glorified, the family disparaged, domestic life despised. And some of these foes of truth have been canonized!

"Asceticism does not touch the seat of sin. All its strength is exerted against the body. Sin is of the soul, has its seat in the soul. So long as the heart is corrupt, no bodily restraints will make the life holy. There is one remedy alone for human sin, one that reaches to its roots, that ultimately will totally destroy it, viz., the blood of Christ" (1 John 1:7) (Professor W. A. Moorhead).

And all these warnings are for our own times, for we live in the day when the tares the devil sowed in the field in the beginning of the age are ripening for the harvest. They are full grown. Legalism, ritualism, evolution, higher criticism, Christian Science, Russellism, demonism, spiritism, New Thought, New Religion, New Theology, theosophy, Unitarianism, Romanism, Mormonism, Seventh Dayism and other still more dangerous theories, because more subtle, are about us. Only a constant realization of our position in Christ and holding fast the head will keep His people in the days of apostasy. May God's people to-day, the faithful remnant, never lose sight of the two vital truths of these two chapters: In Him dwelleth the fullness of the Godhead bodily—and we are complete in Him.

III. The Practical Results: Living as Risen with Christ (3—4)

CHAPTER 3

1. The life hid with Christ in God (3:1-4)
2. The contrast: The old man and the new man (3:5-11)
3. Manifesting Christ (3:12-17)
4. Relationships (3:18—4:1)

Verses 1-4. Risen with Christ; such is the believer's position. "Ye are dead and your life is hid with Christ in God." These are the great truths of Christianity: The believer dead with Christ; risen with Christ and in possession of a life which is hid with Christ in God and therefore safe and secure. And these facts constitute the controlling motive of the believer's life on earth. If apprehended in faith they will lead the soul to seek the things which are above, where Christ sitteth at the right hand of God. The mind will then be constantly set on the things above and not on things which are on the earth. The more a believer enters into those blessed truths, making them his own by reckoning himself dead with Christ and risen with Him, with his life hid with Christ in God, the more will the things above be for him the great attraction and the things on earth will lose their charm. The things above are Christ and His glory. The things on earth include all the deceiving things mentioned in the previous chapter, such as the rudiments of the world, philosophy and words of vain deceit, legalism, ritualism, ordinances, as well as worldly ambitions, honors, pleasures and achievements. All these will fade away when the believer's heart is occupied with Him who fills the throne in glory. This is the true and only way of sanctification—heart occupation with the risen Christ.

When the eyes of the heart see the risen and glorified Christ and faith lays hold of the wonderful meaning for us who believe, then we learn to walk in that separation into which God has called His people. What the Christian therefore needs is an ever increasing realization in faith of his position in Christ, and then to be energized by the indwelling Spirit to seek those things which are above and not the things on earth. Such a life means joy and peace. It is a life of obedience and quietness, victorious over all earthly circumstances. And because it is a life which is hid with Christ in God, it is hidden from the world. "Therefore the world knoweth us not, because it knew Him not" (1 John 3:1). The world, which lieth in the wicked one, cannot understand nor estimate such a life of separation through faith in an unseen person, a life which reaches out after an unseen goal and which spurns worldly honors and the things which are the boast of the natural man. (Phil. 3:18-19 tells us that those who mind earthly things, though Christians in profession, are the enemies of the cross of Christ and that their end will be destruction. Such is the state of the masses of Christendom today—minding earthly things; filled with the love of the world and dead to the spiritual heavenly things.)

But it will not be always thus. A day is coming when this life, hidden now, will be fully manifested. "When Christ is manifested who is our life, then shall ye also be manifested with Him in glory." It will be a manifestation in glory. It comes when He comes again. "When He shall come to be glorified in His saints, and to be admired in all them that believe in that day" (2 Thess. 1:10). It is not the day when He comes for His saints; it is the day of His visible manifestation, when all His own share His glory and come with Him, when He brings His many sons unto glory. To look constantly in holy anticipation to this promised glory-event, is inseparably connected with the statements of the preceding verses. What blessed links these are:—dead with Christ—risen with Christ—a life hid with Christ in God—a life to be manifested when He comes again! May God's people know the reality of all this in power and be kept from a mere profession, lifeless and powerless, of these fundamental facts of the gospel.

Verses 5-11. An exhortation follows to mortify the members which are upon the earth. And what shameful and shameless things are mentioned here! "Fornication, uncleanness, inordinate affection, evil concupiscence, and coveteousness, which is idolatry." From this exhortation addressed to those who are believers, dead and risen with Christ, we learn that the old nature is not eradicated in the child of God. The believer knows that the old man is crucified with Christ (Rom. 6:6), that being in Christ he is now no longer seen by God as in the flesh; but the believer also knows that the old nature is still in him. He finds this out daily "for the flesh lusteth against the Spirit." The spiritually minded believer acknowledges freely that in his flesh there dwelleth no good thing, and that in his fallen nature are all these shameful things and that this old nature is capable of all of which the apostle writes. On account of these things the wrath of God cometh on the children of disobedience. "In the which ye also walked some time, when ye lived in them." The natural man lives in these things; but not so the believer. A child of God may commit these horrible things of the flesh, but he no longer lives in them.

And what is to be done to these members? The translation, "mortify your members which are on the earth," does not fully express the original meaning. It does not mean that we are to be doing it as it is so often attempted by resolutions, fasting and other exercises, ever trying to fight the flesh and conquer the evil things of the old nature. We are never told to fight the flesh, but to flee and abstain from fleshly lusts. Fighting the flesh, trying to put it to death ourselves leads to defeat. We cannot do it, but it has been done for us. The old man was put to death in the cross of Christ; we are now dead to sin—sin is not to have dominion over us. "Likewise reckon ye also yourselves to be dead unto sin, but alive unto God through Jesus Christ our Lord. Let not sin therefore reign in your mortal body, that ye should obey it in the lusts thereof" (Rom. 6:11-12). "Mortify your members" means keep them in the place of death where they have been put by the death of Christ. "Let it be as done"—exercise the power which redemption gives by holding in the place of death the members which are upon earth. This, however, is not possible unless the believer walks in the Spirit, is occupied with Christ and seeks those things which are above. For this reason the exhortations of verses 5-11 are the result of doing what the opening verses of this chapter put before us.

And there are other things besides the gross things of the flesh. "Anger, wrath, malice, blasphemy, filthy communications, lying one to another" are likewise the works of the flesh. They are to be put off. The same Greek tense, aorist imperative, is here also employed—"let it be as done"—have it put off, because grace in redemption has made it possible. No need, therefore, to tolerate these things any longer in your lives, "seeing that ye have put off the old man with his deeds and have put on the new man which is being renewed in knowledge after the image of Him that created him, where there is neither Greek nor Jew, circumcision nor uncircumcision, Barbarian, Scythian, bond nor free; but Christ is all, and in all."

Born again, believers have received a new nature, the nature from above; and this new man is being renewed in knowledge, not after the pattern of the first man, Adam, but after the image of Him, who created him. Christ Himself is the type of the new man; Christ is the object of the faith and the ambitions of the new nature in the believer. And in this new man all differences have ceased, all human distinctions disappear forever. Greek, Jew, circumcision, uncircumcision, barbarian, and the worst type of the barbarian, the Scythian, bond and free, are completely obliterated and gone. Having believed in Christ the new man is formed in each, and Christ is all as well as in all. He Himself is everything and all things are found in Him. The new man is independent of all earthly things and conditions and blessedly dependent upon Him, who created the new man.

It is a great truth that Christ is all and also "in all." The believer must look upon all fellow-believers as being indwelt by Christ, that He is *in all.* This brings deliverance from self; all jealousy, pride and fleshly ambitions will end among the saints of God if they look upon each other after this manner, that Christ is in all. Here is comfort and power.

Verses 12-17. Therefore, as the elect of God, who are the new man indwelt by Christ and one with Him, holy and beloved, are exhorted to put on (have it done) the things which manifest Christ. Bowels of mercy, kindness, humbleness of mind, meekness, long-suffering. It is the fruit of knowing Christ risen and seated in glory. His own character is reproduced and Christ is manifested in the believer's walk.

"As the elect of God, those who owe everything to His will, His choice as those set apart to Him, and those upon whom He has set His love, we are to put on the things which properly accompany this: "bowels of compassion, kindness, lowliness, meekness, long-suffering, forbearing one another and forgiving one another." It is striking how, in all these, there is found some form of self-denial. Power is shown by competence for stooping; God turning also the very things that are against us into the means of educating us in this. Things evil in themselves may, nevertheless, furnish us with a wholesome discipline for the way and enable us, in answer, to bring forth fruit which is according to God. We are to forbear as God has forborne. We are to forgive as Christ has forgiven us; to all which is to be added love as that which is the "bond of perfectness," which keeps everything in its place and perfects every detail of life. Think how the world, even, has to put on the appearance of love, the more if it has not the reality; but love itself has no need to put on an appearance. It will manifest itself in harmony in every tone and gesture. The manifestation of the divine nature has a unity in it which makes everything to be in harmony. If there is love in the heart, the words will not be hard or unseemly; their very tone will be affected" (*Numerical Bible*).

"And let the peace of Christ (not 'peace of God' as in the Authorized Version) preside in your hearts, to which also ye have been called in one body, and be thankful." All God's true children have peace with God and their calling in one body is also to have the peace of Christ presiding in their hearts. This blessed heritage (John 14:27) will be enjoyed by all who walk in the Spirit, who walk in love, obedient to His will and in unbroken fellowship with Him. The crown and glory of such a walk is the peace of Christ, the very peace which He possessed while down here. Blessed, unspeakable privilege!

Yet how few know this peace of Christ and enjoy it daily! If Christ is all for the believer and seen as being "in all," in every member of the body of Christ, then that peace will rule in the heart and we shall know the comfort and joy of it. Furthermore the word of Christ is to dwell richly in the believer's heart in all wisdom. And this word ever directs us to Himself. It does not teach us self-occupation but occupation with Himself, His own person and glory. It is through His word that we learn to know Him better and by which we are kept in His fellowship. And this again bears the blessed fruits of joy and praise, as well as spiritual fellowship with the saints. "Teaching, and admonishing one another; with psalms and hymns and spiritual songs, singing with grace in your hearts to God." And all the believer does in word or in deed is all to be done in His own worthy name, "giving thanks to God the Father by Him." The Lord Jesus is to be in all our thoughts; in every word and in every deed must be given Him the preeminence.

"This consciousness of relationship with Christ, in the life which is of Him in us, applies to everything. Nothing is done without Him. If He is the life, all which that life does has Him for its end and object, as far as the heart is concerned. He is present as that which is the governing motive, and gives its character to our actions, and which preoccupies our heart in performing them. Everything relates to Him: we do not eat without Him (how can we when He is our very life?); we do not drink without Him; what we say, what we do, is said and done in the name of the Lord Jesus. There is the sense of His presence; the consciousness that everything relates to Him, that we can do nothing—unless carnally—without Him, because the life which we have of Him acts with Him and in Him, does not separate from Him, and has Him for its aim in all things, even as water rises to the height from which it descended. This is what characterizes the life of the Christian. And what a life! Through Him, dwelling in the consciousness of divine love, we give thanks to our God and Father."

Verse 18—4:1. Wives, husbands, children, fathers, servants and masters are exhorted how to walk in the different relationships while still in the body. The more complete exhortations as to husband and wife are found in the Epistle to the Ephesians (5:22-23); and as to children, fathers, servants and masters in chapter 6:1-9. The same loving submission of the wives to their husbands "as is fitting in the Lord" is here stated once more. And husbands are to love their wives and be not bitter against them. God has established and sanctioned the marriage relation; sin has come in and brought its corruption, never so much in evidence as in our own days. Believers in this relationship are exhorted to give in it a lovely display of the union which exists between Christ and the Church. Children in the believer's family are to be brought up in the nurture and admonition of the Lord (Eph. 6:4), and seeing the truth that "Christ is all" exemplified in the family life they are exhorted to obey their parents in all things. The disintegration of the family life is one of the evil things of the closing days of this age.

Among the characteristics of "the perilous times" with which our age closes we find "disobedience to parents" and "without natural affection" (2 Tim. 3:1-5). And fathers must take heed so as not to provoke their children to anger by any unjust treatment, so that the children be not discouraged to obey in all things. How often a spirit of rebellion is fostered in children by the treatment of parents, who do not manifest the love of Christ. But if "Christ is all" in the family life, if the peace of Christ presides in the hearts, if the Word of Christ dwells there richly, then love will govern all.

The servants exhorted were slaves, who had believed and become in Christ true freedmen. Not a word is said about the wrong of slavery. Sin is responsible for it. But these Christian slaves are exhorted to obey their masters according to the flesh in all things. In serving them, not with eye-service, as men-pleasers, but in faithfulness, meekness and devotedness they do it as unto the Lord. The place of honor belonged to these slaves in Christ, for they could manifest in their low place the life of Christ, who was here on earth the servant who came not to be ministered to but to minister; the servant of all. In the coming day of Christ many of the slaves who believed on Christ and served in meekness and lowliness will receive a great reward.

"Two principles act in the heart of the Christian slave: his conscience in all his conduct is before God; the fear of God governs him, and not his master's eye. And he is conscious of his relationship to Christ, of the presence of Christ, which sustains and lifts him above everything. It is a secret which nothing can take from him, and which has power over everything, because it is within and on high—Christ in him, the hope of glory. Yes, how admirably does the knowledge of Christ exalt everything that it pervades; and with what consoling power does it descend into all that is desolate and cast down, all that groans, all that is humbled in this world of sin!

Three times in these two verses, while holding their conscience in the presence of God, the apostle brings in the Lord, the Lord Christ, to fill the hearts of these poor slaves, and make them feel who it was to whom they rendered service. Such is Christianity" *(Synopsis of the Bible).*

And masters are exhorted to render unto the slaves that which is just and equal. "Knowing that ye also have a Master who is in heaven." Before that Master, all will have to appear and there will be no respect of persons.

CHAPTER 4

1. Prayer and ministry (4:2-4)
2. Walking in wisdom (4:5-6)
3. The fellowship of the saints in their service (4:7-17)
4. The conclusion (4:18)

Verses 2-4. The first verse of this chapter belongs to the preceding one. Prayer is the most needed thing for those who are risen with Christ and know that they are complete in Him. Without continued prayer the full realization of the great truths unfolded in this Epistle is impossible. Communion with God makes it all real. "Continue steadfastly in prayer, and watch therein with thanksgiving." The knowledge of our position in Christ, that we are in Him and have all in Him teaches us our dependence on Him. The more we enter into all these things the greater will be our sense of the need of prayer and real communion with God. The new man yearns for this. All the exhortations to seek the things which are above, to set the mind on those things and not on earthly things, to keep in the place of death the members which are on the earth, to put on the new man and manifest Christ, are impossible without prayer. (Those who boast of being complete in Christ and treat prayer slightingly show thereby how little they know of the real spiritual meaning of being dead with Christ and risen with Him.)

Without continued prayer the reality and power of our position and blessing in Christ is on the wane and soon lost. It is through prayer that we lay hold of all; it is the means by which we enter deeper into His knowledge. Prayer is, therefore, the greatest need for those who are risen with Christ. And while we express in this way our utter dependence on Him, conscious of Himself and our union with Him, He also delights in our fellowship. We can bring all to Him, "nothing is too small to enlist His love; nothing too great for His strength, and nothing too difficult for His wisdom." And there must be perseverance in it; a broken and interrupted communion soon tells in the life of the believer. No other way to know and enjoy our portion in Christ, to advance in it and be victorious in the conflict which is ours in a world of evil, than continued, steadfast prayer, communion with God.

In prayer we are "to watch therein and be thankful"—"Watch and pray" our Lord said to His disciples in the garden, and while He prayed more earnestly they slept (Matt. 26:41). And again it is written, "Be ye therefore sober and watch unto prayer" (1 Peter 4:7). Our thoughts wander and our infirmities often become very evident in the exercise of this blessed privilege. We must watch before we pray, watch while we pray and watch after we have prayed, and watch for the answer, not impatiently, but in child-like faith. The spirit of praise and thanksgiving is needed for this watching.

The apostle next requests prayer for himself and the ministry of the mystery of Christ. "At the same time praying also for us, that God may open unto us a door of the word, to speak the mystery of Christ, for which I am also in bonds, that I may make it manifest as I ought to speak." This blessed man of God was in the prison. From the Epistle to the Philippians we learned how unselfish he was. And here is another evidence. He might have requested united prayer for his deliverance, for divine interference in his behalf as it happened to Peter when he was imprisoned; he might have asked the prayers of the saints that his needs might all be supplied. As risen with Christ he is above these earthly circumstances. His request is for prayer for the gospel, the mystery of Christ, so preciously told out in the first part of this Epistle. God must open the door for this. How humble and dependent he was! What a contrast with present day professional evangelism! And for the open door to preach the gospel; to speak the mystery of Christ effectively, the saints of God must continue to pray and watch confidently for the answer. In praying for the Word that it may have free course and be glorified (2 Thess. 3:1), we can have all boldness and expectation. Such prayers have God's approval and answer.

Verses 5-6. Towards those who are without, the unsaved, believers with the profession of being risen with Christ, for whom Christ is all, must walk in wisdom. What we are in Christ, the grace which has saved us, the love of God which is shed abroad in our hearts must be made known in our intercourse with those who know not Christ. How great is our failure! And why? Because we are not constantly occupied with our Lord and our heavenly position in Him. Lack of real communion with God and prayer for the gospel, in behalf of the unsaved about us, strips us of the power to walk in wisdom. "Redeeming the opportunity." It means to bear witness to those without when the proper time for it presents itself. And when the opportunity comes the word spoken is to be "always with grace, seasoned with salt, that ye may know how ye ought to answer each one."

Verses 7-11. The words which follow these exhortations bring out the fellowship of saints and their different services. Tychicus is mentioned first. We find his name also in Acts 20:4; Ephes. 6:21; 2 Tim. 4:12 and Titus 3:12. With Onesimus he was the bearer of this Epistle, as well as the Epistle to the Ephesians, while Onesimus carried also the letter to Philemon. Three things has Paul to say of Tychicus. He calls him the beloved brother, well known because he was a faithful minister, who preached faithfully the gospel and as such he was for the apostle a fellow-servant in the Lord. He sent him to the Colossians to tell them about his own state, and that he might know their state and comfort their hearts.

"We see how Christian love delights to communicate and to hear. It was his confidence in their love; and this is shown not merely in his desire to hear about *them,* but in the conviction that they would like to hear about *him.* Can anything be sweeter than this genuine simplicity of affection and mutual interest? In a man it would be vain and curious; it is blessed in a Christian. No right-minded man, as such, could take for granted that others would care to know about his affairs any more than he theirs, unless indeed in case of a relation, or a friend, or a public and extraordinary personage. But here writes the lowly-minded apostle, in the full assurance that, though he had never seen them, or they him, it would be real and mutual gratification to know about one another from him who went between them. What a spring of power is the love of Christ! Truly charity is 'the bond of perfectness.' 'And my state shall Tychicus declare unto you, who is a beloved brother, and a faithful minister and fellow-servant in the Lord; whom I have sent unto you for the same purpose, that he might know your state, and comfort your hearts; with Onesimus, a faithful and beloved brother, who is one of you. They shall make known unto you all things which are done here' " (W. Kelly).

Onesimus, the once good for nothing slave, the runaway also is called a faithful and beloved brother. The Epistle to Philemon will tell us more of this.

Then there was Aristarchus (Acts 19:29; 20:4) who was a fellow-prisoner of Paul and also a fellow-worker (Philemon 24). And how delightful to find Mark here, the sister's own son to Barnabas. Twelve years before, he left the work (Acts 13:13) and was the occasion of the deplorable separation between Paul and Barnabas (Acts 15:26-40). But now he is seen restored. (See also

2 Tim. 4:11.) The third fellow-worker for the kingdom of God, who was a comfort to the prisoner of the Lord, was Jesus Justus. These sent their greetings, as also did Epaphras. Him the Colossians knew well for this servant of Christ was one of them. He is an example of a praying saint. He continued steadfastly in prayer for them. He prayed, yea, he agonized (such is the Greek word) in prayer for the Colossians, that they might stand perfect and complete in all the will of God. He knew their danger; he had as a faithful minister communicated some of these things to the apostle. Knowing the Colossian condition, he prayed fervently. His ministry was the ministry of prayer. Paul adds his own word of commendation and approval.

"For I bear him record, that he hath a great zeal for you, and them that are in Laodicea, and them in Hierapolis." Though the Laodiceans were probably even then drifting into the lukewarm condition which the Lord from heaven so fully uncovered later (Rev. 3), this servant of Christ did not stand aside, but had a prayerful and loving interest in them.

Luke and Demas sent their greetings. Luke, the beloved physician, is the inspired author of the Gospel which bears his name. He also was with Paul in Rome as he was for some time his travelling companion. What a comfort the beloved physician must have been to the prisoner of the Lord! Demas is mentioned, but not a word is said about him. Was even then the evil working in his heart, which later broke out? No doubt it was. A short time afterward we read his sad story. "Demas hath forsaken me, having loved this present age" (2 Tim. 4:10).

"Salute the brethren which are in Laodicea, and Nyruphas and the church which is in his house. And when this Epistle is read among you, cause that it be also read in the church of the Laodiceans; and that ye likewise read the epistle from Laodicea" (4:15, 16). (This must have been the Epistle to the Ephesians. See our introduction to Ephesians.)

One more message is given. "And say to Archippus, take heed to the ministry which thou hast received in the Lord, that thou fulfill it." He probably had become in one of these cities the instrument for ministry. This he had received from the Lord. He alone can call into the ministry and bestow gifts. Whatever our ministry is, faithfulness in the exercise of it is the important thing.

Verse 18. "The salutation by the hand of me, Paul. Remember my bonds. Grace be with you." Like other Epistles, except Galatians (Gal. 6:11) and Philemon (verse 19), this letter was dictated to an amanuensis. But this closing verse was written with his own hand. (See also 1 Cor. 16:21; 2 Thess. 3:17.) And when he added these words the chain was upon his hand. "Remember my bonds." We may look upon it as a delicate excuse for not having written the whole letter to the Colossians, whom he knew not personally. At the same time the mentioning of his bonds were to remind them that he is the prisoner of the Lord for the Gentiles (Ephes. 3:1). Grace be with you. Blessed be God that His Grace will always be with His people.

THE FIRST EPISTLE TO THE
THESSALONIANS

Introduction

The city of Thessalonica was situated on the northern part of the Aegean Sea, on the Thermaic Gulf. It was a prominent city of the Roman province, Macedonia. Its inhabitants were mostly Thracians. Thessalonica was a wealthy and large city and for a time, the most influential centre in the northeastern part of the Roman empire. On account of its great commerce many Jews had settled there and a flourishing synagogue existed in the city.

The visit of the Apostle Paul to Thessalonica is recorded in the seventeenth chapter of the book of Acts. It took place after his ministry in Philippi. It seems that the persecution there hastened his departure. Paul had said to the magistrates, "They have beaten us openly uncondemned, being Romans, and have cast us into prison; and now would they thrust us out privily? Nay, verily; but let them come themselves and fetch us out." When this came to the ears of the authorities, they became frightened for it was illegal to scourge a Roman citizen. "And they came and besought them, and brought them out, and desired them to depart out of the city. And they went out of the prison and entered into the house of Lydia; and when they had seen the brethren, they comforted them and departed" (Acts 16:37-40). Of his experience Paul writes in his first letter to the Thessalonians. "For yourselves, brethren, know our entrance in unto you, that it was not in vain. But even after that we had suffered before, and were shamefully entreated, as ye know, at Philippi, we were bold in our God to speak unto you the gospel of God with much contention" (1 Thess. 2:1-2). Leaving then Philippi with Silas (Silvanus) and Timothy they went along the famous highway, the *Via Egnatia* and reached the city of Thessalonica. On the way they passed through Amphipolis and Apollonia. On their arrival Paul followed his usual custom and visited the synagogue.

For three Sabbaths, the record in Acts tells us, he reasoned with them out of the Scriptures. The Scriptures, of course, were the Old Testament Scriptures, for the New Testament was then not in existence. The way he dealt with his Jewish brethren is the pattern still for reaching the Jews with the gospel. He opened the Scriptures, and without mentioning the name of the Lord Jesus at all, he showed that the Old Testament teaches that the Messiah (Christ) promised to them must suffer and rise from the dead. This great truth that the sufferings of Messiah come first and the glory follows, had been forgotten by the Jews. A crucified Christ was their stumbling block (1 Cor. 1:23). They looked only to the glory-side and the accomplishment, through Him, of the national promises. And after Paul had demonstrated from the Scriptures "that Christ must needs have suffered, and risen again from the dead," then he boldly declared that "this Jesus, whom I preach unto you, is Christ." The predictions of the suffering and the resurrection of Christ were fulfilled in the Lord Jesus. But he must have preached more than that. He also taught that Christ would come again. This we learn from the fact that the unbelieving Jews, in bringing Jason, who had believed, with other brethren before the rulers, accused them of "turning the world upside down," and "that there is another King, one Jesus" (Acts 17:5-7). His second Epistle also shows that he had given them instructions in dispensational and prophetic truths (2 Thess. 2:5).

The Church in Thessalonica

As a result of his testimony a church was at once gathered out. "And some of them believed and consorted with Paul and Silas; and of the devout Greeks a great multitude, and of the chief women not a few" (Acts 17:4). From this we learn that a number of Jews were persuaded that the Lord Jesus is the Christ and accepted Him as their Saviour and Lord. But the church was mostly composed of devout Greeks. These were not heathen, but Greeks who had given up idolatry and had become Jewish proselytes. They were convinced that paganism was wrong and seeking for light attended the synagogical services. Of this class a great multitude believed. The third class mentioned are women who occupied positions of distinction. Not a few of them believed. The

Epistles Paul wrote to the church of the Thessalonians also shows the character of those gathered. That the majority of them were Gentiles is learned from the statement that they had turned to God from idols (1 Thess. 1:9). The evils against which he warns (1 Thess. 4:1-8) were mostly practised by the Greeks; and they belonged mostly to the poorer, the working class (1 Thess. 4:11).

Paul's First Epistle: When and for What it was Written

The Epistle to the Thessalonians is the first Epistle Paul wrote. Even the most outspoken critics acknowledge that it is a genuine document. Irenaeus (about 140 A.D.) bears witness to this Epistle. There are many other historical evidences, besides the contents of the Epistle, which prove conclusively that Paul is the author of it. All this is not necessary to follow in this brief introduction. The Authorized Version has a postscript "written from Athens." This claim is made on account of the apostle's statement in chapter 3:1-2. "Wherefore, when we could no longer forbear, we thought it good to be left alone at Athens. And sent Timotheus, our brother, and minister of God, and our fellow laborer in the gospel of Christ, to establish you, and to comfort you concerning your faith." It is surmised that Timotheus carried this letter to the Thessalonians. This is incorrect. The Epistle was written after Timotheus had returned from his visit to Thessalonica. The sixth verse of the third chapter furnishes this evidence. "But now when Timotheus came from you unto us, and brought us good tidings of your faith and love, and that ye have good remembrance of us always, desiring greatly to see us." Timothy came from Thessalonica with the good news of the happy state of the Thessalonian church and joined the apostle in Corinth (Acts 18:5). From Corinth Paul wrote this first Epistle about the year 52 or possibly a few months later.

The apostle had been compelled to break off suddenly his ministry in Thessalonica on account of the persecutions which had arisen in that city. "The brethren immediately sent away Paul and Silas by night unto Berea" (Acts 17:10). He must have felt that the new converts needed more instructions. Of this he writes in the Epistle. "But we, brethren, being taken from you for a short time in preference, not in heart, endeavoured the more abundantly to see your face with great desire. Wherefore we would have come unto you, even I Paul, once and again: but Satan hindered us" (2:17, 18). To comfort them in the midst of the persecution and in their sorrow, to encourage them in their conflicts, he was moved by the Holy Spirit to write this first Epistle. Timothy had brought to him the information of the tribulations they were undergoing. And they were especially distressed by the death of a number of believers. They sorrowed almost like those who had no hope, because they feared that these departed ones would have no share in the glory and in the kingdom of the returning Christ. To relieve them of their anxiety, to give them further light on the coming of the Lord in relation to those who are asleep and the reunion with them who have gone before, what will happen when the Lord comes for His saints, so that they could comfort each other, is one of the chief reasons why this letter was written.

The Coming of the Lord

The blessed hope of the coming of the Lord occupies a very prominent place in this Epistle. In our days we often hear the statement that the coming of our Lord is an unessential doctrine. Those who make such an assertion are ignorant of the fact that the blessed hope is a part of the gospel itself. Christian preaching and teaching which ignores the blessed hope, the coming of the Lord, is incomplete; it omits one of the most vital truths which the Spirit of God has linked with the gospel and with the life and service of the believer. The first Epistle the great apostle wrote is an evidence of this. In this Epistle one of the greatest revelations in the Word of God about His coming, is made known (4:13-18). It is the Epistle in which the doctrine of the coming of Christ is unfolded and shown to be practically connected with the Christian's life. Each chapter bears witness to it (1:9-10; 2:19-20; 3:13; 4:13-18; 5:1-11). Christians wait for Him; serve in anticipation of His coming when all service will be rewarded and the servant crowned; His coming is the incentive to a holy life, it is the comfort and consolation and when He comes and takes His own in clouds to meet Him in the air, it will bring the unexpected judgment for the world. The second Epistle gives additional light on the visible manifestation of the Lord, what will precede that day and what is connected with it, when He comes with His holy angels. The fate of those who obey not the gospel and who receive not the love of the truth is made known in the second Epistle.

The Division of First Thessalonians

Simplicity and deep affection are the marks of this Epistle. We find nothing about Judaizers, these perverters of the gospel of Jesus Christ against whom Paul had to warn in his later Epistles. Warnings such as we have in Colossians and other Epistles are absent. The loving apostle is not grieved in any way, but happy on account of the gracious work going on in the midst of the Thessalonians, and rejoicing in them as his beloved children. In the study of this Epistle we maintain the division in five chapters.

I. **THE CHURCH OF THE THESSALONIANS AND ITS BLESSED CONDITION** (1)

II. **TRUE SERVICE, AS MANIFESTED IN APOSTOLIC MINISTRY** (2)

III. **AFFLICTIONS AND COMFORT** (3)

IV. **THE SEPARATED WALK AND THE BLESSED HOPE** (4)

V. **THE DAY OF THE LORD AND EXHORTATIONS** (5)

Analysis and Annotations

I. The Church of the Thessalonians and Its Blessed Condition

CHAPTER 1

1. Greetings and thanksgiving (1:1-4)
2. The gospel and its blessed fruits (1:5-7)
3. The blessed condition of the Church (1:8-10)

Verses 1-4. Paul, Silvanus and Timotheus were known to the Thessalonians, for they had been with them, and were the instruments of God used in bringing the gospel to them. He does not speak of himself as an apostle. In nine of his Epistles, Paul uses his title as apostle. In Romans and Titus, he calls himself also "a servant of Jesus Christ and of God." In Philippians, he speaks of himself and of Timothy as "servants of Christ Jesus." In the Epistle to Philemon, he also omits his apostleship, because this Epistle was a private letter. He asserts his apostolic title and authority in the strongest way, when he addresses the Galatians and the Corinthians, because these churches were troubled with false teachers who impeached his apostolic calling. As this trouble did not exist in Thessalonica, he does not call to their remembrance that he is an apostle. He did not parade his title, and only mentions it when the truth he preached and which he had received from the Lord was questioned.

He addressed the church in Thessalonica as "the church of the Thessalonians, in God the Father, and the Lord Jesus Christ." The church in Thessalonica is the only one addressed in this manner. The church is looked upon as the family of God, as the children of God, and God their Father through the Lord Jesus Christ. They were the happy children of God and in simplicity of faith knew Him as their Father. What a transformation had taken place in these Thessalonians! They were idolators, worshipping idols; through believing the gospel, they were born again and now enjoyed the blessed relationship to God as Father. There is no other way into the family of God than the way by which these heathen had been brought there. We are sons of God by faith in Jesus Christ (Gal. 3:26). And John, in addressing the family of God wrote "I write unto you, little children (those born again), because ye have known the Father" (1 John 2:13). The apostle, who had declared the gospel unto them, thanked God always for them, and with his fellow laborers made mention of them in prayer. The life which they possessed manifested itself in faith, love and hope. These are the principles which form our character as Christians. Theirs was a work of faith in the Lord Jesus Christ, in the sight of God and the Father, labor undertaken by love; all their labor in service flowed from love, and they endured because they possessed hope, waiting for Him. The objects of faith, love and hope are the Lord Jesus Christ and God the Father.

Verses 5-7. The apostle mentions next the gospel and what it had wrought among them. "Our gospel came not unto you in word only, but in power and in the Holy Spirit and in much assurance." Paul, Silvanus and Timothy had preached to them the good news of a free and full salvation by faith in the Lord Jesus Christ and the gospel message came to them in power. He made the word effective in their souls and quickened them so that the great change took place by which they passed from death unto life; thus believing, the Holy Spirit was received by them, giving them full assurance. Here we have the divine order of salvation; the message of the gospel heard and believed; the Spirit of God manifesting His power in the conversion and the sealing of those who believed, and the consequence: the full assurance of the truth in all its blessed power and reality. But the gospel was not only preached by these messengers among the Thessalonians; the chosen instruments also witnessed to that gospel by their life and walk—"As ye know what manner of men we were among you for your sakes." They were living and blessed witnesses of the power of the gospel which they proclaimed. Their holy walk, their self-denial, their peace and quietness had its blessed effect on the Thessalonian believers, for they became imitators of the apostles. Inasmuch as the messengers followed closely the Lord Jesus Christ, the Thessalonians, being imitators of them, became thus imitators of the Lord, having received the Word in much affliction with joy of the Holy Spirit. And then in turn they became patterns to all that believed in Macedonia and Achaia. In these simple statements, we have a blessed manifestation of the real power of the gospel.

Verses 8-10. There was no need for Paul, Silvanus and Timothy to say anything about these Thessalonian Christians. It was not necessary to speak to others of what God had wrought in Thessalonica or to declare the genuineness of these new converts. The Thessalonian believers gave such a strong and full testimony that it was wholly unnecessary for the laborers to say anything about them. The word of the Lord was sounded forth by them with no uncertain sound. They were true lights in the world-darkness and were holding forth the word of life. Their faith toward God became widely known in every place. Throughout that region it became known through their witness of what the gospel is and what the gospel produces in the hearts and lives of those who believe.

And what was their testimony? It is stated in the last two verses of this chapter. "For they, themselves, report concerning us what manner of entrance we had unto you, and how ye turned to God from idols, to serve the living and true God, and to wait for His Son from heaven, whom He raised from among the dead, Jesus, who delivereth us from the wrath to come." In these words we have the great essentials of true Christianity. The first is true conversion. They had turned to God from idols, not, as it is sometimes quoted, from idols to God; the power of God, in believing the gospel had turned them away from idolatry. They were now serving no longer dumb idols, but the true and living God. In this service they manifested the genuineness of their conversion. And there was another prominent characteristic: they waited for His Son from heaven, Jesus, whom God had raised from among the dead. They looked earnestly for Him, in whom they had believed, who had died for them and of whom they knew He had been raised from among the dead, being now, at the right hand of God. According to His own promise to come again, they were patiently waiting for His coming from heaven, though they were ignorant of the manner of His coming. How He will come again, and what is connected with this great event, they learned fully from the two Epistles they received from the inspired pen of the apostle. To wait for the coming of the Lord is a vital characteristic of true Christianity; it is a part of the gospel. A sad testimony it is to the superficial knowledge of the gospel when men say and teach that the belief in the second coming of Christ is unessential and of no practical value. It is most essential and of the greatest value to the true believer. It presents the gloryside of the gospel of Jesus Christ. He who died for our sins, who is the glorified Man, the firstborn among many brethren, has promised to have all His own with Him to be like Him and to share His glory. This is the true object of the believer's expectation and hope. He has delivered us from the wrath to come. Therefore the Thessalonians, and all true believers as well, can wait without fear for that blessed event, for they know they are sheltered by Him from the wrath to come. Before this wrath comes He will take His own into His presence. He is our deliverer from the wrath to come.

II. True Service, As Manifested in Apostolic Ministry

CHAPTER 2

1. Apostolic conduct and service (2:1-12)
2. Thanksgiving for the reception of the message and the opposition (2:13-16)
3. Looking forward to His coming (2:17-19)

Verses 1-12. The apostle now enlarges upon the brief statement in the previous chapter "Ye know what manner of men we were among you for your sakes." His conduct and character, as well as that of his fellow laborers, corresponded fully with the holy character of the truth they preached. They walked worthy of the gospel and worthy of the Lord. First he makes mention of the sufferings he and Silas endured in Philippi. They had been shamefully treated. They had been stripped and scourged cruelly with the lictor's rods and cast into prison with their feet secured to the stocks. The physical discomfort resulting from such a punishment must have lasted for many days, but it did not hinder their going to Thessalonica with confidence in God to speak the gospel there, where they also had much conflict. And what a witness he bore of their unselfish conduct while they were among them! This exhortation was not a deceit, that is, out of error; nor was it in uncleanness, emanating from any low motives of self-interest; nor in guile. God had approved them; their ministry was God-given and they were fully conscious of this fact. Being intrusted with the gospel (and what a trust it is!) so they spoke. They had no need to employ different schemes to be successful; they had full confidence in God and in the message He had given to them to proclaim. Therefore their whole aim was to please God who trieth the hearts and not men. Nor had they used flattery to win them; nor did they resort to flattering words as a cloak of covetousness using sweet phrases to get money out of them; not alone were they witnesses of all this, but he could say, "God is witness." They had sought nothing of men, neither money nor glory. They might have been burdensome to them as the apostles of Christ. They did not use their authority, which they might have used, asserting their dignity and demanding something from them. Their whole conduct was in true humility and in great self-denial. (Many a "leading" evangelist of our day stands condemned by this beautiful example of a true servant of God. What God and gospel dishonoring schemes are used! What flatteries as a cloak of covetousness! How much man-pleasing!)

This is the negative side. On the other hand they were full of tenderness and kindness. A boisterous, unkind, impatient spirit was completely absent in their ministry. "But we were gentle among you, even as a nurse cherisheth her children. So being affectionately desirous of you, we were willing to have imparted unto you, not the gospel of God only, but also our own souls, because ye were dear unto us." What blessed fragrance is, and will ever be, in these precious words! How little of this gracious, loving interest in souls is manifested today among the Lord's servants! Then he reminds them what he had done so as not to be a burden to any one when he preached the gospel of God unto them. He and his companion had worked day and night with their own hands. Paul was a tent-maker and worked with his own hands in Thessalonica and elsewhere (Acts 18:2; 1 Cor. 4:12). And again he appeals to them as witnesses as well as to God, "how holily and justly and unblamably we behaved ourselves among you that believe; as ye know we exhorted and charged every one of you, as a father his children, that ye would walk worthy of God, who hath called you unto His own kingdom and glory." Having such a portion in the coming kingdom and being an heir of glory, the walk of every believer should indeed be worthy of God.

Verses 13-16. He thanked God without ceasing for the reception of the message which they heard from his lips. It was the Word of God, which Paul had preached, and hearing the message, they had received it not as the word of men, but as it is in truth, the Word of God. This Word received in faith saved them and also effectually worked in them that believed. It is still the same. Faith cometh by hearing and hearing by the Word of God. The believer is constantly dependent upon the Word of God; it worketh in him effectually through the power of the Holy Spirit. The believer's practical sanctification in the daily life is by the Word (John 17:17).

They also knew what suffering meant. They became followers (imitators) of the churches of God in Judea in Christ Jesus. Those churches suffered persecutions from the Jews, but the Thessalonians suffered from their own countrymen. And what a solemn charge is brought here through Paul against his kinsmen, the Jews! They had killed the Lord Jesus and their own prophets; they persecuted the apostles. And not satisfied with this, they tried to keep the gospel they hated from reaching the Gentiles that they might be saved. The measure of sins was now filled up "and wrath is come upon them to the uttermost." The great apostle of the Gentiles, called to go far hence to the Gentiles, in this his first Epistle is used to pronounce sentence upon his own nation, which has been set aside until the fulness of the Gentiles is come in (Rom. 11:25-26).

Verses 17-19. He had an affectionate desire for them. Separated and bereaved of them (the more correct rendering) for a little season in person, but not in heart, he had great longing to see their face. Once and again he wanted to visit them, but Satan had hindered him. How the enemy hindered him in carrying out his desire, whether by attacks upon his body (2 Cor. 12:7) or by wicked men, we do not know. He then speaks of that blessed time when all hindrances will cease, when God's people are no longer separated, when those who ministered the Word and the fruits of their labors are gathered in the presence of the Lord Jesus Christ at His coming. "For what is our hope, or joy, or crown of glorying? Are not even ye before our Lord Jesus Christ at His coming? for ye are our glory and joy." Here again the apostle mentions the coming of the Lord. The gathered saints before the Lord Jesus Christ will be the crown of glorying and the joy for the faithful servant, who then finds in the presence of the Lord, in the day of Christ, the fruit of his labors. To this consummation in glory Paul directed the attention of the Thessalonians and he speaks of them as his glory and joy, "for ye are our glory and our joy."

"It should be observed here, that the special fruits of our labors are not lost; they are found again at the coming of Christ. Our chief personal joy is to see the Lord Himself and to be like Him. This is the portion of all saints; but there are particular fruits in connection with the work of the Spirit in us and by us. At Thessalonica the spiritual energy of the apostle had brought a number of souls to God and to wait for His Son, and into a close union in the truth with Himself. This energy would be crowned at the coming of Christ by the presence of these believers in the glory as the fruit of his labors. God would thus crown the apostle's work by bearing a striking testimony to its faithfulness in the presence of all these saints in glory; and the love which had wrought in Paul's heart would be satisfied by seeing its object in glory and in the presence of the Lord Jesus. They would be his glory and joy. This thought drew yet closer the bonds that united them, and comforted the apostle in the midst of his toils and sufferings" (*Synopsis of the Bible*).

III. AFFLICTIONS AND COMFORT

CHAPTER 3

1. Timotheus, Paul's messenger (3:1-5)
2. His return with good tidings and the apostle's comfort and joy (3:6-10)
3. This earnest desire (3:11-13)

Verses 1-5. His longing for the beloved Thessalonians and his solicitude for them became so great that he could no longer forbear and he decided to be left alone in Athens and send Timotheus to Thessalonica. He knew they had great afflictions and that there was danger that they might not endure and then his labors among them would have been in vain. He therefore sent Timotheus whom he calls "our brother, minister of God and our fellow laborer in the gospel of Christ." The purpose of his mission was to establish the believers still more and to bring them comfort concerning their faith. This would result, under the blessing of God, in their steadfastness. "That no man should be moved by these afflictions, for yourselves know that we are appointed thereunto"—it is the lot of all true believers. In fact he had forewarned them of all this when he was in their midst. "For verily, when we were with you, we told you before that we should suffer tribulation, even as it came to pass, and ye knew." This was part of the apostolic message, as we learn from Acts 14:22. "Confirming the souls of the disciples, and exhorting them to continue in the faith, and that we must through much tribulation enter into the kingdom of God."

Tribulations had now come upon the Thessalonians and they were severely tested. He knew they were in the Lord's hands, that His watchful eye was upon them and that His power was sufficient to keep them. Yet he had deep concern and anxiety for them, for he also knew Satan's power. "For this cause, when I could no longer forbear, I sent to know your faith, lest by some means the tempter have tempted you, and our labor be in vain." The day of Christ, when the servant receives the reward and the saints are "the crown of glorying" is in his thoughts. If the tempter succeeded he would not have that crown of glorying in the presence of the Lord. (See 1 John 2:28. "And now little children, abide in Him: that when He shall appear, we [the laborers] may have confidence and not be ashamed before Him at His coming.") While Timotheus was away Paul left Athens from where he had sent him to visit Thessalonica. Paul went to Corinth; it was there he received the good tidings from Thessalonica, and, as we state in the introduction, after Timotheus' return he wrote this Epistle (Acts 18:5).

Verses 6-10. "But now when Timotheus came from you unto us, and brought good tidings of your faith and love, and that ye have good remembrance of us always, desiring greatly to see us, as we also to see you." It was good tidings Timotheus brought to Paul. They were standing fast in faith; they continued in love, nor had they forgotten Paul. Their hearts longed for him as his own soul desired to see them. In the midst of tribulations which had come upon them they were blessedly sustained.

And how all this cheered the apostle. He is comforted. "Therefore, brethren, we were comforted over you in all our affliction and distress by your faith; for now we live if ye stand fast in the Lord." He had also his sorrows, his afflictions and much distress. But the good tidings from the Thessalonians refreshed his spirit and filled him with new energy. As a servant of God he is so fully identified with those for whom he labored and whom he loved that he could say, "for now we live, if ye stand fast in the Lord." He feels as if he could not render sufficient thanks to God for them and for all the joy wherewith he now rejoiced, on their account before God. He also prayed night and day exceedingly that he might see their face and help them still more, so that which was lacking in their faith might be perfected. Then, knowing himself dependent upon God and the Lord Jesus Christ, He looks to direct his way to them.

"What a bond is the bond of the Spirit! How selfishness is forgotten, and disappears in the joy of such affections! The apostle, animated by this affection, which increased instead of growing weary by its exercise, and by the satisfaction it received in the happiness of others, desires so much the more, from the Thessalonians being thus sustained, to see them again; not now for the purpose of strengthening them, but to build upon that which was already so established, and to complete their spiritual instruction by imparting that which was yet lacking to their faith. But he is a laborer and not a master (God makes us feel this), and he depends entirely on God for his work, and for the edification of others. In fact years passed away before he saw the Thessalonians again. He remained a long time at Corinth, where the Lord had much people; he revisited Jerusalem, then all Asia Minor where he had labored earlier; thence he went to Ephesus, where he abode nearly three years; and after that he saw the Thessalonians again, when he left that city to go to Corinth, taking his journey by the way of Macedonia" (J. N. Darby).

Verses 11-13. We must not overlook the testimony to the deity of our Lord of the eleventh verse. "Now God and our Father Himself, and our Lord Jesus Christ, direct our way to you!" The verb "direct" in the Greek is in the singular. God the Father and the Lord Jesus Christ are in the thought of the apostle one, though, personally, clearly distinguished. It is a striking proof of the unity of the Father and Son.

He prayed "the Lord make you to increase and abound in love, one toward another and toward all, even as we also towards you." Love is the bond of perfectness and as such the true means of holiness "in order to establish your hearts unblamable in holiness before our God and Father at the coming of our Lord Jesus Christ with all His saints." This is the third time the coming of our Lord is mentioned by Paul in this Epistle. First he spoke of waiting for His Son from heaven as the characteristic of a true believer (1:9-10); then we read of the gatherings of the saints in the presence of the Lord, the time of glory and joy, when the faithful servant will receive the reward (2:19-20), and now another phase is added. The Lord is coming with all His saints; it is now not the coming *for* His saints, but *with* them, in the day of His manifestation as well as the manifestation of all the saints with Him. It is the same of which we read in Col. 3:4, "When Christ is manifested who is our life then shall ye also be manifested with Him in glory." He also speaks of this in his second Epistle: "When He shall come to be glorified in His saints and wondered at in all that have believed (for our testimony unto you has been believed) in that day" (2 Thess. 1:10). In view of this coming manifestation in glory the Holy Spirit urges a walk in practical holiness, so as to be unblamable in holiness before our God and Father. It is an incentive to holy living.

"In reading this passage one cannot but observe the immediate and living way in which the Lord's coming is linked with daily practical life, so that the perfect light of that day is thrown upon the hourly path of the present time. By the exercise of love they were to be established in holiness before God at the coming of Christ. From one day to another, that day was looked for as the consummation and the only term they contemplated to the ordinary life of each day here below. How this brought the soul into the presence of God! Moreover, they lived in a known relationship with God which gave room for this confidence. He was their Father; He is ours. The relationship of the saints to Jesus was equally known. The saints were "*His* saints." They were all to come with Him. They were associated with His glory. There is nothing equivocal in the expression. Jesus, the Lord, coming with all His saints, allows us to think of no other event than His return in glory. Then also will He be glorified in His saints, who will already have rejoined Him to be for ever with Him. It will be the day of their *manifestation* as of His."

IV. The Separated Walk and the Blessed Hope

CHAPTER 4

1. The separated walk (4:1-12)
2. The coming of the Lord for His saints (4:13-18)

Verses 1-12. "Furthermore, then, brethren, we beg you and exhort you in the Lord Jesus, even as ye received from us, how ye ought to walk and please God, even as ye also do walk, that ye would abound still more. For ye know what charges we gave you through the Lord Jesus. For this is the will of God, even your sanctification, that ye should abstain from fornication; that each of you know how to possess his own vessel in sanctification and honor (not in passionate desire, even as the Gentiles who know not God), not overstepping the rights of and wronging his brother in the matter, because the Lord is the avenger of all these things, even as we also told you before, and have fully testified. For God has not called us to uncleanness, but in sanctification. He therefore that (in this) disregards (his brother), disregards, not man, but God, who has also given His Holy Spirit to you" (corrected translation).

Having spoken of being unblamable in holiness at the coming of the Lord he exhorts them to live now in sanctification. The motive is to please God. The believer should constantly in his daily life ask himself this question, "Do I please God?" Exhortation to purity in abstaining from fleshly lusts follows. Fornication, licentiousness in various forms were closely connected with the idolatrous worship from which these Thessalonians had been saved. The lust of the flesh was a part of this former religion, as it is still today among different heathen religions. But why these exhortations? Because they were surrounded by these things on all sides, and because the old nature with its tendencies towards these evils was still present with them, as it is with all true believers. No circumstances or position can make the believer secure against these things, without exercise of conscience and self-judgment, and hence these solemn admonitions from the Lord. Each was to possess his own vessel (his own wife) in sanctification and honor, this would be a safeguard against the numerous immoralities practised among the heathen. If in this matter any one overstepped the rights of another and thus wronged his brother by committing adultery, the Lord would be the avenger; it would be a complete disregard of God who has not called His people to uncleanness, but unto sanctification, to be separated from all these things. Needful were these exhortations for the Thessalonians as they are still to all of us.

And the best remedy against these evil things is brotherly love. He had no need to say much about it, for they themselves were taught of God to love one another. But he exhorts them to be quiet and to mind their own affairs, working with their own hands, as he their leader had exemplified it when he was among them.

Verses 13-18. "But we do not wish you to be ignorant, brethren, concerning them that are fallen asleep, to the end that ye sorrow not, even as others who have no hope. For if we believe that Jesus died and rose again, so also God will bring with Him those who have fallen asleep through Jesus. For this we say to you in the Word of the Lord, that we, the living, who remain to the coming of the Lord, are in no way to anticipate these who have fallen asleep; for the Lord Himself will descend from heaven with an assembling shout, with the voice of the archangel and with the trump of God; and the dead in Christ shall rise first; then we, the living who remain, shall be caught up together with them in clouds, to meet the Lord in the air; and so shall we ever be with the Lord. Wherefore comfort one another with these words."

These words contain one of the great revelations of the Bible and require therefore closer attention. It is a special and unique revelation which he gives to the sorrowing Thessalonians, occasioned by the mistake they had made when some of their fellow believers had died, and they feared that these departed ones had lost their share in the coming glorious meeting between the Lord and His saints. They sorrowed on their account like those who have no hope. (Their pagan neighbors had no hope of meeting loved ones again after death. Classic Greek and Roman writers abound with dreary expressions of the hopelessness of death.) We must remember that the New Testament was not yet in existence; only one of the gospels, was written; and not one of the epistles. And so the Lord gave to the apostle the special revelation which would quiet their fears and put before them the details of the coming of the Lord for all His saints, those who had fallen asleep and those alive when He comes.

Our Lord spoke that blessed word to His eleven disciples, "I will come again and receive you unto myself, that where I am ye may be also" (John 14:3). It is the only time He mentioned His coming for His own, and in speaking of it He did not tell them of signs to precede that coming, such as wars, false Christs and the great tribulation. It was the simple announcement that He would come again and receive those who are His to Himself. He did not say a word about the manner of that coming and how He would receive His own into glory to be with Him. Nor did the Thessalonians hear definite teaching on this from the lips of Paul. They knew He would come again; they waited for Him. But as to the manner of His coming and concerning those who had already fallen asleep and their relation to that event they were in ignorance. Beautiful it is to see how graciously the Lord answered the question of these sorrowing ones and how much more He adds for the comfort of all His people.

The first statement is in verse 14. "For if we believe that Jesus died and rose again, so also God will bring with Him those who have fallen asleep through Jesus." Let us first notice that blessed statement that "Jesus died." Of the saints it is said that they have fallen asleep; but never is it said that Jesus slept. He tasted death, the death in all its unfathomable meaning as the judgment upon sin. For the saints the physical death is but sleep. (Some have perverted the meaning of "sleep," and instead of applying it, as Scripture does, to the body, they apply it to the soul. Soul-sleep is nowhere taught in the Bible and is therefore an invention by those who handle the Word deceitfully.) And He who died also rose again; as certainly as He died and rose again, so surely shall all believers rise. God will bring all those who have fallen asleep through Jesus with Him, that is with the Lord when He comes in the day of His glorious manifestation. It does not mean the receiving of them by the Lord, nor does it mean that He brings their disembodied spirits with Him to be united to their bodies from the graves, but it means that those who have fallen asleep will God bring with His Son when He comes with all His saints; they will all be in that glorified company. When the Lord comes back from glory all the departed saints will be with Him. This is what the Thessalonians needed to know first of all. Before we follow this blessed revelation in its unfolding we call attention to the phrase "fallen asleep through (not in) Jesus"; it may also be rendered by "those who were put to sleep by Jesus." His saints in life and death are in His hands. When saints put their bodies aside, it is because their Lord has willed it so. "Precious in the sight of the Lord is the death of His saints" (Ps. 116:15). When our loved ones leave us, may we think of their departure as being "put to sleep by Jesus."

But blessed as this answer to their question is, it produced another difficulty. Hearing that the saints who had fallen asleep would come with the Lord on the day of His glorious manifestation, they would ask, "How is it possible that they can come with Him?" Are they coming as disembodied spirits? What about their bodies in the graves? How shall they come with Him? To answer these questions the special revelation "by the Word of the Lord" is given, by which they learned, and we also, how they would all be with Him so as to come with Him at His appearing. "For this we say to you by the Word of the Lord, that we, the living, who remain unto the coming of the Lord, are in no wise to anticipate those who have fallen asleep." He tells them that when the Lord comes for His saints, those who have fallen asleep will not have an inferior place and that, we, the living, who remain to the coming of the Lord, will not precede those who have fallen asleep. When Paul wrote these words and said, "We, the living, who remain," he certainly considered himself as included in that class. The two companies who will meet the Lord when He comes, those who have fallen asleep and those who are living, are mentioned here for the first time. How the living saints will not precede those who have departed and the order in which the coming of the Lord for His saints will be executed is next made known in this wonderful revelation.

"For the Lord Himself will descend from heaven with an assembling shout, with the voice of the archangel and with the trump of God; and the dead in Christ shall rise first, then, we, the living, who remain, shall be caught up together with them in clouds, to meet the Lord in the air, and so shall we ever be with the Lord. Wherefore comfort one another with these words." This is an altogether new revelation. Nothing like it is found anywhere in the Old Testament Scriptures. In writing later to the Corinthians Paul mentioned it again. "Behold I show you a mystery; we shall not all sleep, but we shall all be changed. In a moment, in the twinkling of an eye, at the last trump; for the trumpet shall sound, and the dead shall be raised incorruptible, and we shall be changed" (1 Cor. 15:51-52).

The Lord *Himself* will descend from heaven. He is now at the right hand of God in glory, crowned with honor and glory. There He exercises His Priesthood and Advocacy in behalf of His people, by which He keeps, sustains and restores them. When the last member has been added to the Church, which is His body, and that body is to be with Him, who is the head, He will leave the place at the right hand and descend from heaven. He will not descend to the earth, for, as we read later, the meeting-place for Him and His saints is in the air and not the earth. When He comes with His saints in His visible manifestation, He will descend to the earth. He descends with a shout. It denotes His supreme authority. The Greek word is "kelusma," which means literally "a shout of command," used in classical Greek for the hero's shout to his followers in battle, the commanding voice to gather together. He ascended with a shout (Ps. 47:5), and with the victor's shout He returns.

The shout may be the single word "Come!" "Come and see" He spoke to the disciples who followed Him and inquired for His dwelling place. Before Lazarus' tomb He spoke with a loud voice, "Come forth." John, in the isle of Patmos, after the throne messages to the churches had been given, saw a door opened in heaven and the voice said "Come up hither" (Rev. 4:1). "Come" is the royal word of grace, and grace will do its supreme work when He comes for His own. But there will also be the voice of the archangel (Michael) and the trump of God. The archangel is the leader of the angelic hosts. As He was seen of angels (1 Tim. 3:16) when He ascended into the highest heaven, so will the archangel be connected with His descent out of heaven. All heaven will be in commotion when the heirs of glory, sinners saved by grace, are about to be brought with glorified bodies into the Father's house. Some teach that the voice of the archangel may be employed to summon the heavenly hosts and marshal the innumerable company of the redeemed, for "They shall gather His elect together from the four winds, from one end of heaven to the other" (Matthew 24:30-31).[1] But this is incorrect. The elect in Matthew 24 are not the Church, but Israel. Dispersed Israel will be regathered and angels will be used in this work. Furthermore the angels will do this gathering after the great tribulation and after the visible manifestation of the Lord with His saints. The coming of the Lord for His saints takes place before the great tribulation.

The trump of God is also mentioned. This trumpet has nothing to do with the judgment trumpets of Revelation, nor with the Jewish feasts of trumpets. It is a symbolical term and like the shout stands for the gathering together. In Numbers 10:4 we read, "And if they blow with one trumpet, then the princes, the heads of the thousands of Israel, shall gather themselves unto thee." The shout and the trump of God will gather the fellow-heirs of Christ. "The dead in Christ shall rise first." This is the resurrection from among all the dead of those who believed on Christ, the righteous dead. All saints of all ages, Old and New Testament saints, are included. This statement of the resurrection of the dead in Christ first disposes completely of the unscriptural view of a general resurrection. As we know from Rev. 20:5 the rest of the dead (the wicked dead) will be raised up later. He comes in person to open the graves of all who belong to Him and manifests His authority over death which He has conquered.

The dead in Christ will hear the shout first and experience His quickening power; they shall be raised incorruptible. What power will then be manifested! "Then we, the living, who remain, shall be caught up together with them in clouds to meet the Lord in the air; and so shall we ever be with the Lord." All believers who live on earth when the Lord comes will hear that commanding, gathering shout. It does not include those who only profess to be Christians and are nominal church-members, nor are any excluded who really are the Lord's. (The so-called first-fruit rapture, which teaches that only the most spiritual of all true believers, who have made a deeper experience, etc., will be caught up, and the other believers, though they are true believers of God, will be left behind to pass "through the great tribulation," has no spiritual foundation and is wrong.) The question, "Who will be caught up into glory?" is answered in 1 Cor. 15:23—"All who are Christ's." The change will be "in a moment, in the twinkling of an eye" (1 Cor. 15:52). Then this mortal will put on immortality. It will be the blessed "clothed upon" of which the apostle wrote to the Corinthians: "For in this tabernacle we groan, being burdened; not for that we would be unclothed (death) but clothed upon, that mortality might be swallowed up of life"

[1]Prof. W. G. Moorehead, *Outline Studies.*

(2 Cor. 5:4). Then our body of humiliation will be fashioned like unto His own glorious body. It is the blessed, glorious hope, not death and the grave, but the coming of the Lord, when we shall be changed. And it is our imminent hope; believers must wait daily for it and some blessed day the shout will surely come.

When He descends from heaven with the shout and the dead in Christ are raised and we are changed, then "we shall be caught up together with them in clouds to meet the Lord in the air." It will be the blessed time of reunion with the loved ones who have gone before. What joy and comfort it must have brought to the sorrowing Thessalonians when they read these blessed words for the first time! And they are still the words of comfort and hope to all His people, when they stand at the open graves of loved ones who fell asleep as believers.

Often the question is asked, "Shall we not alone meet our loved ones but also recognize them?" Here is the answer: "Together with them" implies both reunion and recognition. These words would indeed mean *nothing* did they not mean recognition. We shall surely see the faces of our loved ones again and all the saints of God on that blessed day when this great event takes place. The clouds will be heaven's chariots to take the heirs of God and the joint-heirs of the Lord Jesus Christ into His own presence. As He ascended so His redeemed ones will be taken up. Caught up in clouds to meet the Lord in the air; all laws of gravitation are set aside, for it is the power of God, the same power which raised up the Lord Jesus from the dead and seated Him in glory, which will be displayed in behalf of His saints (Eph. 1:19-23). Surely this is a divine revelation.

"How foolish it must sound to our learned scientists. But, beloved, I would want nothing but that one sentence, 'caught up in clouds to meet the Lord in the air,' to prove the divinity of Christianity. Its very boldness is assurance of its truth. No speculation, no argument, no reasoning; but a bare authoritative statement startling in its boldness. Not a syllable of Scripture on which to build, and yet when spoken, in perfect harmony with all Scripture. How absolutely impossible for any man to have conceived that the Lord's saints should be caught up to meet Him in the air. Were it not true its very boldness and apparent foolishness would be its refutation. And what would be the character of mind that could invent such a thought? What depths of wickedness! What cruelty! What callousness! The spring from which such a statement, if false, could rise must be corrupt indeed. But how different in fact! What severe righteousness! What depths of holiness! What elevated morality! What warmth of tender affection! What clear reasoning! Every word that he has written testifies that he has *not* attempted to deceive. Paul was no deceiver, and it is equally impossible for him to have been deceived" ("Our Hope," February 1902).

And the blessedness "to meet the Lord in the air"! We shall see Him then as He is and gaze for the first time upon the face of the Beloved, that face of glory, which was once marred and smitten on account of our sins. And seeing Him as He is we shall be like Him. How long will be the meeting in the air? It has been said that the stay in that meeting place will be but momentary and that the Lord will at once resume His descent to the earth. We know from other Scriptures that this cannot be. Between the coming of the Lord for His saints and with His saints there is an interval of at least seven years before the visible coming of the Lord and His saints with Him. The judgment of the saints, by which their works and labors become manifest must take place. There is also to be the presentation of the church in glory (Ephes. 5:27; Jude 24). Furthermore the marriage of the Lamb takes place not in the meeting place in the air, but in heaven (Rev. 19:1-10). He will take His saints into the Father's house that they may behold His glory (John 17:22). But what will it mean, "So shall we be forever with the Lord!"

"In this part of the passage, where he explains the details of our ascension to the Lord in the air, nothing is said of His coming down to the earth; it is our going up (as He went up) to be with Him. Neither, as far as concerns us, does the apostle go farther than our gathering together to be for ever with Him. Nothing is said either of judgment or of manifestation; but only the fact of our heavenly association with Him in that we leave the earth precisely as He left it. This is very precious. There is this difference: He went up in His own full right, He ascended; as to us, His voice calls the dead, and they come forth from the grave, and, the living being changed, all are caught up together. It is a solemn act of God's power, which seals the Christians' life and work of God, and brings the former into the glory of Christ as His heavenly companions. Glorious privilege! Precious grace! To lose sight of it destroys the proper character of our joy and of our hope" *(Synopsis of the Bible).*

V. The Day of the Lord and Exhortations

CHAPTER 5

1. The day of the Lord (5:1-11)
2. Exhortations (5:12-22)
3. Conclusions (5:23-28)

Verses 1-11. "But concerning the times and seasons, brethren, ye have no need that I write unto you. For yourselves know perfectly that the day of the Lord so cometh as a thief in the night. For when they shall say, Peace and safety, then sudden destruction cometh upon them, as travail upon a woman with child, and they shall not escape." The apostle next mentions the day of the Lord. This is the day when the Lord is revealed from heaven, the day of His visible manifestation. It is the day when judgment will be executed upon the world. While the coming of the Lord for His saints, as made known in the previous chapter, is unrevealed in the Old Testament, the day of the Lord of which the apostle now writes, is fully revealed by the prophets. (See Isaiah 2:12-22; Joel 2—3; Zeph. 1:14-18; Zech. 14:1-9, etc.)

Our Lord spoke often of that day as the day "when the Son of Man cometh," that is His own visible glorious manifestation. What precedes this day is also made known in the Old Testament prophetic Word; and our Lord gives us likewise the same information. "And there shall be signs in the sun and in the moon, and in the stars; and upon earth distress of nations, with perplexity; the sea and the waves roaring; men's hearts failing them for fear, and for looking after those things which are coming on the earth, for the powers of heaven shall be shaken. And then shall they see the Son of Man coming in a cloud with power and great glory" (Luke 21:25-27). See Matthew 24:21-31. Judgment is in store for the world when that day comes, as judgments and tribulation are the forerunners which usher in that day. The world does not believe in such a day, but dreams of peace and safety, in a continuance of prosperity, of expansion, universal peace and a constant improvement of earthly conditions.

"There shall come in the last days scoffers, walking after their own lusts, and saying, Where is the promise of His coming? for since the fathers fell asleep, all things continue as they were from the beginning of the creation" (2 Peter 3:3-4). But while the world saith, Peace and safety, their hearts are failing them for fear and they tremble in anticipation of the future. Much of all this we see clearly in our times, so ominous and so solemn. There is a false hope, a false optimism; we hear of what this world war will accomplish, how peace and safety will come to the whole world; yet underneath it all there are hearts failing for fear. And when that day has come, when He has been "revealed from heaven with His mighty angels, in flaming fire taking vengeance on them that know not God, and that obey not the gospel of our Lord Jesus Christ," the Lord Jesus Christ will reign over the earth with His saints for a thousand years (Rev. 20). That will be the day of the Lord, as the present age is "man's day."

Before that day comes with its preceding judgments and the great tribulation, the coming of the Lord, for His saints, the fulfilment of chapter 4:16-18 must take place. Of this we shall find much more in the second Epistle. When the Lord comes for His saints, the world and those who were Christians only in name, will face that coming day. It is the beginning of it. After God's true children, the praying people of God, have been removed, the age will take its final plunge into apostasy and iniquity; judgment upon judgment from above will then be poured out, as we learn from the book of Revelation.

Because these judgments, the forerunners of the day of His visible manifestation, the times and seasons connected with these events, do not concern those who are the Lord's, the apostle states that there was no need to write them about it. The Lord had told His disciples before He ascended into heaven that it was not for them to know the times and the seasons. It shows that we are not to be occupied with the times and seasons, when the times of the Gentiles end, etc., but to wait and watch for Him, who will surely come suddenly for His own, as a thief in the night.

"Had it been possible in the apostle's day to predict the centuries of delay that have, in fact, elapsed, disciples might indeed still have waited for their Lord, but *watched* they could not, and no 'thief in the night' could have troubled their slumbers. But for the heart, expectancy was needed; and they were to watch *because* they knew not. Thus for these watchers the times could not speak; and in fact when they do it will be for another people than the present Christian Church, and when this is already removed to be with the Lord in the manner which we have just had before us.

"For mere formal and worldly Christendom, the coming of the thief will then in a sense have taken place. Shut out in the outside darkness, when others have entered the chambers of light, no place of repentance will be left for the despisers of God's present grace. In a world which, having rejected the true King, will be left for that awful time to experience fully what Satan's rule is, they will fall under the power of his deception. Not having received the love of the truth that they might be saved, they will believe a lie; and comforting themselves with the cry of 'peace and safety,' sudden destruction will come upon them as upon a women with child, and they shall not escape!" (*Numerical Bible*)

The words "they" and "you" make it still more clear that the day of the Lord is for the world. He does not say "When you shall say, Peace and safety" but when "they shall say." The apostle excludes the believer completely from that day when sudden destruction falls, for he says, "Ye, brethren, are not in darkness, that that day overtake you as a thief." And why? Ye are all the children of light, and the children of the day; we are not of the night, nor of darkness. Therefore let us not sleep, as do others; but let us watch and be sober. For that they sleep in the night; and they that be drunken are drunken in the night. This is the character of true Christians, no longer in darkness, but children of light and of the day, and therefore belonging to that coming day to be with the Lord when He comes to judge, it cannot overtake them as a thief.

Being the children of the day we must watch and be sober; it is that which distinguishes true Christians from the mass of professing church-members and the world. The world and those who have a form of godliness, but deny the power thereof, do not watch, nor are they sober; and being sober, walking in separation from the world, its lusts and pleasures, the believer, having on the breastplate of faith and love, can advance against the enemy. He has also for an helmet, to protect him, this promised glorious salvation. Thus we can look always up, without fear, in the midst of danger when the judgment clouds are gathering over this present evil age. "For God hath not appointed us to wrath, but to the obtaining of salvation through our Lord Jesus Christ." Blessed knowledge and twice blessed assurance! that we might be delivered from the wrath to come and share with Him eternal glory. He died for us. "Who died for us, that, whether we wake or sleep (as to the body) we should live together with Him."

Verses 12-22. Exhortations follow. He wishes that those who labored among them should be acknowledged by them and very highly esteemed in love for their work's sake. If the apostle and his co-laborers looked upon them as their crown of rejoicing, their glory and joy (2:19-20,) they should very highly esteem them as the instruments of the Spirit of God for their edification. Be in peace among yourselves. All self-will is put aside when the heart looks forward to that coming day, when laborers and the fruits of their labors are in His presence. Then peace among His own will not be disturbed. The disorderly are to be admonished; the faint-hearted comforted; the weak sustained, and patience to be manifested towards all. Then we have joy, prayer and thanksgiving as the characteristics of those who wait for His Son from heaven and look for that blessed hope. "Rejoice evermore"—our joy is in Him. The joy of the Lord is our strength. And what joy will indeed be ours when we remember that we shall see Him as He is!

"Pray without ceasing." Prayer is constantly needed, including the forgotten prayer, "Even so, Come, Lord Jesus." If this petition is never wanting, His coming for us will never lack reality. "In everything give thanks, for this is the will of God in Christ Jesus concerning you." As we pray and ever take afresh from His own fulness grace upon grace, and remember all the abundant provision made for us in Him, and that the glorious future which awaits His own may burst at any moment upon us, then shall we give thanks in everything. "Quench not the Spirit." The Holy Spirit is not to be hindered in His action in the midst of His people. What sad consequences when He is quenched and how great the responsibility! Do not despise prophesyings—the forthtelling of the truth of God, speaking out of the fulness of the Spirit. "Prove all things; hold fast that which is good. Abstain from all appearance of evil," or, as it is better rendered, "Keep aloof from every form of wickedness."

Verses 23-28. The conclusion of the Epistle begins with a prayer. "Now the God of peace Himself sanctify you wholly; and I pray God your whole spirit and soul and body be preserved blameless at the coming of our Lord Jesus Christ. He is faithful that calls you, who will also do it." God is for all who have believed in Christ the God of peace. Peace was made in the blood of the cross; believers are both reconciled and sanctified through the peace that God has made for us in the work of His Son. We stand therefore in a blessed relationship with the God of peace, have communion with Him, and from this flows practical devotedness of life and walk to God. Believers are sanctified by the three persons of the Godhead; by God the Father, by the blood of Jesus Christ, the offering of His body, and by the Holy Spirit.

We are in Christ completely set apart for God, bought with a price and no longer our own. We possess a new nature and are indwelt by the Holy Spirit. This demands of us that we be wholly set apart to God in every faculty, whether of mind or body. This is our pactical sanctification, which springs from our increasing knowledge of God. This practical sanctification is wrought in the believer by the power of the Holy Spirit, who attaches the heart to God, revealing God more and more, as well as unfolding the glory of Christ. This devotedness to God in spirit, soul and body, depends upon the believer's apprehension of his relationship to the God of peace and his communion with Him. And this is progressive. Entire sanctification will be the blessed and eternal portion of all who are Christ's, when He comes, and we shall be like Him, "conformed to the image of His Son." The perfection comes with the coming of the Lord; in the power of this blessed hope shall we be preserved blameless even down here in this evil age. He is faithful who calls you, who will also perform it. Blessed assurance! He has called us to this life of blessed separation with Himself. He is faithful and will accomplish it. May we trust Him daily and stay close to Him.

"Observe again here, how the coming of Christ is introduced, and the expectation of this coming, as an integral part of Christian life. "Blameless," it says, "at the coming of our Lord Jesus Christ." The life which had developed itself in obedience and holiness meets the Lord at His coming. Death is not in question. The life which we have found is to be such when He appears. The man, in every part of his being, moved by this life, is found there blameless when He comes. This life, and the man living this life, are found, with their Head and Source, in the glory. Then will the weakness disappear which is connected with his present condition. That which is mortal shall be swallowed up of life: that is all. We are Christ's: He is our life. We wait for Him, that we may be with Him, and that He may perfect all things in the glory" (*Synopsis of the Bible*).

The apostle closes this First Epistle by requesting the brethren to pray for him and his co-laborers. With all the deep knowledge of the truth and the great revelations from the Lord, he felt his dependence and knew the blessing which comes from the prayers of fellow saints. He asks for the expression of affection among themselves and adjures them to have this letter read to all the holy brethren. And the final word "The grace of our Lord Jesus Christ be with you."

THE SECOND EPISTLE TO THE
THESSALONIANS

Introduction

This second Epistle to the Thessalonians was written at Corinth by the Apostle Paul and in the joint names of Silvanus and Timotheus. How long after the first epistle cannot be correctly ascertained. It was probably a year after they had received the first document.

What Occasioned This Epistle

From the second chapter we learn that they were greatly troubled about something else. The first Epistle was written to comfort them on account of those who had fallen asleep and to make known the great revelation concerning the coming of the Lord for His saints. And now the apostle writes: "Now we beseech ye, brethren, by the coming of our Lord Jesus Christ and by our gathering together unto Him, that ye be not soon shaken in mind, or troubled, neither by spirit, nor by word, nor by letter, as if it were by us, as that the day of the Lord is present" (2:1-2). Evidently some one had troubled them and tried to convince them that the day of the Lord, with its threatened judgments, was actually present. When they had received the comforting first epistle, we can imagine how their waiting for the Lord was stimulated. With what simple, child-like faith they must have taken hold of the words, "We who are alive and remain shall be caught up in clouds to meet the Lord in the air, and so shall we ever be with the Lord." Daily, no doubt, they expected this blessed promise to be fulfilled.

Certain false teachers then appeared on the scene, telling them that their hope was vain and that the day of the Lord was actually upon them, that the threatened tribulation and judgment had begun and that they had to pass through all the horrors of the times preceding the visible manifestation of the Lord. They were passing through fearful persecutions and tribulations that these teachers probably told them that these sufferings were the indication of the beginning of the day of the Lord. It was this which greatly agitated them and robbed them of the blessed hope. If they were to pass through the tribulation and judgment which is in store for the world and be on the earth when wrath is poured out, then the blessed hope ceases to be that. And it seems these false teachers had gone so far as to produce a document, which they pretended was a letter from Paul, in which he confirmed their false teaching. For this reason, that they might know that the letter they received now was really his, he added, "The salutation of Paul with mine own hand, which is the token in every epistle, so I write" (3:17).

But who were these teachers who aimed at the joy and hope of these earnest believers and troubled them with their false message that the day of the Lord was present? They belonged unquestionably to the same class of Judaizers who had sneaked among the Galatian churches. They attacked the blessed hope given to the Church and put in its place the judgment and tribulation of the day of the Lord. They swept aside the comforting revelation of the coming of the Lord and the gathering of the saints unto Him and put the Church on earthly, Jewish ground. What is in store for the ungodly nations and for the Jews, they taught would also be shared by true Christians; it would all come before the Lord comes for His own. To correct this error the Spirit of God moved the apostle to write this second epistle.

A Fundamental Prophecy

Chapter 2:1-12 contains the words of instruction to show that the day of the Lord was then not present. It furthermore tells us what must precede that day, which is nowhere related to the Church of God. It is a great unfolding of prophecy, fundamental and most important. It is needed for the correct understanding of what will take place when the Lord has taken away His true Church. Here is the prediction of the apostasy, which will have for its head and climax the man of sin, the final, personal Antichrist, the same person of whom Daniel speaks (Dan. 11:36, etc.), who is described in Rev. 13:11-18 and in other portions of the prophetic Word. Here we read of the necessary condition before this apostasy can come and that lawless one is revealed, and what will be the fate of all who received not the love of the truth. The strong delusion of him, whose coming is, according to the working of Satan, with all power and signs and lying wonders, will be believed and accepted by the apostates of Christendom. We have given to this portion of the epistle in our annotations the attention it deserves, and we trust it will be, under God, a help, and comfort to His people.

The Division of Second Thessalonians

The scope and divisions of this Epistle are very simple. In the first chapter the Apostle shows that while the Thessalonians had tribulation, they suffered not in a punitive sense, but for the kingdom of God, and that God would recompense tribulation to those who troubled them. The punishment for the world comes when the Lord Jesus is revealed from heaven. While that day brings this for the world, it will bring glory for those who have believed. As already stated in the second chapter, the day of the Lord, what must take place before that day comes is made known. Words of comfort, prayer and exhortations conclude the Epistle. This gives us three divisions.

I. **THE REVELATION OF THE LORD JESUS FROM HEAVEN** (1)

II. **WHAT PRECEDES THE MANIFESTATION OF THE LORD** (2:1-12)

III. **THANKSGIVING, PRAYER, EXHORTATIONS AND CONCLUSION** (2:3—3:18)

Analysis and Annotations

I. The Revelation of the Lord Jesus From Heaven

CHAPTER 1

1. Salutation and thanksgiving (1:1-4)
2. The revelation of the Lord Jesus from heaven (1:5-10)
3. The prayer (1:11-12)

Verses 1-4. The opening words of salutation are the same as in the first Epistle. Once more he gives thanks to God for them, because their faith increased exceedingly and love abounded, the result of an increasing faith. On account of this progress and spiritual condition he wrote, "So that we ourselves glory in you in the churches for your patience and faith in all your persecutions and tribulations that ye endure." The patience of hope, which was mentioned in the first Epistle, is omitted by him. Their hope had been dimmed through the false teachers and alarmists, who would have them believe that they were heading for all the tribulations of the day of the Lord. They endured persecutions and tribulations on account of which they were greatly disturbed, because of the insinuation that these were the judgments of the day of the Lord. They looked more to what was happening to them than to the Lord. They were more occupied with these conditions than with the blessed hope.

Verses 5-10. He quiets these fears. Satan was pressing upon them, terrifying their minds, and they were fearing everything, the enemy taking advantage of the persecutions and sufferings he had instigated to distress them. The Apostle tells them that all their persecutions and tribulations, far from having a punitive character, were "a manifest token of the righteous judgment of God" with this purpose, "to the end that ye should be counted worthy of the kingdom of God, for the sake of which ye also suffer."

They were children of God, heirs of God and joint heirs with Christ, and their path was to suffer with Him, that they also might be glorified together (Rom. 8:17). A similar word he wrote later to the Philippians. "In nothing terrified by your adversaries, which is to them an evident token of perdition, but to you of salvation, and that of God" (Phil 1:28). What was happening to them was a seal upon them of their being worthy of the coming kingdom. The persecutions they endured showed they were identified with the Lord, who was "despised and rejected of men." Their sufferings were the sufferings of Christ.

And then the contrast. When the day of the Lord comes with the revelation of the Lord Jesus from heaven, it will bring the punishment of the wicked. Their persecutions were from the ungodly, who inflicted suffering on them because they believed on the Lord. But when the day of the Lord comes God will change all by recompensing those that troubled them. "Seeing it is a righteous thing with God to recompense tribulation to them that trouble you, and to you who are troubled rest with us, when the Lord Jesus shall be revealed from heaven with His mighty angels." In other words, in His day they would have rest and peace, while their wicked enemies will suffer the well deserved judgment. From this inspired declaration they learned that the day of the Lord had not come.

The day of the Lord brings the revelation of the Lord from heaven with His mighty angels, "in flaming fire taking vengeance on them that know not God, and that obey not the gospel of our Lord Jesus Christ, who shall suffer the penalty of everlasting destruction from the presence of the Lord and from the glory of His might, when He shall come to be glorified in His saints, and to be wondered at in all who have believed (because our testimony among you was believed) in that day." "In that day" is a phrase which we find many times in the Old Testament prophetic Word. In most cases it means the day of the visible manifestation of Jehovah to deal in judgment with His enemies and to deliver those of His earthly people Israel who wait for Him. "And it shall come to pass in that day, that the Lord shall punish the host of the high ones that are as high and the kings of the earth upon the earth" (Is. 24:21). "And it shall be said in that day, Lo, this is our God, we have waited for Him, and He will save us" (Is. 25:9).

Judgment for the world is always connected with that coming day. Our Lord, in His earthly ministry, also spoke of that day, the day of the coming of the Son of man. "For the Son of man shall come in the glory of His Father with His angels, and then shall He reward every man according to His works" (Matt. 16:27). His visible coming out of heaven and bringing judgment is still more fully described in Rev. 19:11-21. It will be the day of vengeance after the acceptable year of the Lord is ended (Isaiah 61:1-2). The apostle's testimony tells us the same. Two classes are mentioned by him. Those that know not God, which means the idolatrous Gentiles and sinners in general, "and those that obey not the gospel of our Lord Jesus Christ." (The text of the Authorized Version having omitted the word "those" makes it appear as if it were only one class; but that is incorrect.) These are the Jews and also nominal and apostate Christians. The latter class will suffer the great punishment. The destruction mentioned has been explained as meaning annihilation. But that is not true. It is banishment from the presence of that glory upon which man has turned his back and which he despised—hardening himself into a final, awful incapacity for it and for communion with Him. What else is it but the destruction "of one who was made at the first in the image of God?" They will live on in eternal separation from God.

The apostle mentions something else which is not found in the Old Testament prophetic Word. When the Lord comes in that day He will be glorified in His saints and then wondered at in all who have believed. When He comes thus in judgment upon the world the true Church is no longer on earth, but the saints, having been previously caught up to meet Him in the air, come with Him in glory. It is the time of the manifestation of the sons of God, transformed into His image, each reflecting His glory, who is the leader and the first begotten. And so these poor, persecuted, despised Thessalonians would then be the marvels for the inhabitants of the earth when they appear with Him. Blessed future for all the redeemed to come with the Lord in glory and to be like Him!

These explanations concerning the day of the manifestation of the Lord bringing judgment upon their enemies and glory to them, delivered them from the confusion into which the false teachers were leading them, and they were now ready, after being put at rest in their mind, to receive the needed additional instruction about that coming day. A prayer concludes this chapter that, called with such a calling, God may count them worthy of it, that their walk may be of such a nature as to correspond with that calling and that the Lord might be glorified in them by the power of faith, and that afterwards they might be glorified in Him, "according to the grace of our God and the Lord Jesus Christ."

II. What Precedes the Manifestation of the Lord

CHAPTER 2

1. The gathering of the saints preceding that day (2:1-2)
2. The apostasy and the man of sin (2:3-4)
3. The revelation of the man of sin and his fate (2:5-8)
4. His deceptions and the fate of Christendom (2:9-12)

As this section of the Epistle is one of the most important of the New Testament, we give it first of all in a corrected translation.

"Now we beg you, brethren, by the coming of our Lord Jesus Christ and our gathering together unto Him, that ye be not soon shaken in mind, nor troubled, neither by spirit, not by word, nor by letter, as (if it were) by us, as that the day of the Lord is present. Let not any one deceive you in any manner, because it will not be unless the apostasy have come first and the man of sin have been revealed, the son of perdition, who opposes and exalts himself on high against all called God or object of worship; so that he himself sits down in the temple of God, showing himself that he is God. Do ye not remember that, being yet with you, I said these things to you? And now ye know that which restrains, that he should be revealed in his own time. For the mystery of lawlessness already works; only there is He who restrains it until He be gone, and then the lawless one shall be revealed, whom the Lord Jesus shall consume with the breath of His mouth, and shall annul by the brightness of His coming; whose coming is according to the working of Satan in all power and signs and wonders of falsehood, and in all deceit of unrighteousness to them that perish, because they have not received the love of the truth that they might be saved. And for this reason God sendeth them an energy of error, that they may believe the lie; that they all might be judged who believed not the truth, but had pleasure in unrighteousness."

Verses 1-2. He begs them "by the coming of the Lord and our gathering together unto Him" not to be disturbed by the rumours these false teachers were circulating, as if the day of the Lord is present. The Authorized Version has the misleading translation, "the day of Christ." (Equally incorrect is the translation, "the day of the Lord is *at hand.*" The meaning is "present," that it had actually come. The same Greek word is also used in Rom. 8:38, "things present.") There is an important difference between the day of Christ and the day of the Lord. The day of Christ concerns the Church, the saints of God. The day of the Lord concerns the earth—Israel and the nations. The day of Christ begins when He takes His saints in glory and they are with Him. The day of the Lord will bring, as stated before, the visible manifestation of the Lord from heaven. The day of Christ comes first and the day of the Lord follows at least seven years later. The following passages speak of the day of Christ, and it will be seen that that day is for God's people only (1 Cor. 1:8; 2 Cor. 1:14; Phil. 1:6-10, 2:16). The day of the Lord does not concern the saints at all; it falls on the world. Before the day of the Lord can come, His saints have to be gathered together unto Him. The promise of 1 Thess. 4:16-18 needs first to be fulfilled. He uses this hope of being gathered to Christ, when He comes for His saints, as a motive why they should not listen to those who said the day of the Lord is present. He reminds them of the fact that their gathering unto Him had not yet taken place. How, then, could the day of the Lord be present? And this opens the way for still more important teaching.

Verses 3-4. The false teachers were deceiving them. Before the day of the Lord can come there must be the falling away first and the man of sin, the son of perdition, must be revealed. No such conditions need to be fulfilled before the Lord comes for His saints. But before the age closes with the visible manifestation of the Lord from heaven these two solemn things must be on the earth. A falling away from the God-given faith has been going on throughout this Christian age. But that is not *the* apostasy of which the apostle speaks. The complete apostasy means that the entire faith will be abandoned by Christendom, even as our Lord indicated when He said, "Nevertheless, when the Son of man cometh, shall He find the faith on the earth?" That this present age closes in apostasy is more than once mentioned by the Spirit of God. See 1 Tim. 4:1-3; 2 Tim. 3:1-5; 2 Peter 2; Jude. Evidences to that effect are abundant in our own days. The destructive Bible criticism rejecting inspiration and revelation, the denial of the person and work of Christ and of every other article, denials which are rapidly increasing, made the way for this final apostasy. The many cults in which Satanic powers are manifested, under the garb of angels of light, such as Christian Science, spiritism, theosophy, etc., are also harbingers of the time of which the apostle writes. Satan is surely actively at work to bring about this apostasy, and his ministers are transformed as the ministers of righteousness (2 Cor. 11:15), advocating reform, better living, but denying and antagonizing the doctrines of Christ. We shall hear later that this final apostasy is held back from its full manifestation by One who restraineth; only when He is taken out of the way can this predicted apostasy and renunciation of Christianity come with its leader, the man of sin.

Who is the person whom Paul mentions as the man of sin? It would take many pages to give the views and opinions of expositors as to who is meant. The Roman Empire, the Roman

Emperors, Mohammed, the Pope and the Romish Hierarchy have been given as being the man of sin. During the French revolution many thought it was Napoleon, as some to-day say the German Emperor is the man of sin. Inasmuch as the great apostasy is not yet here, the person whom Paul describes has also not yet come. First there must be the apostasy before there can be the leader and head of that apostasy. And before the revelation of Christ comes from heaven the world, which rejected Christ, will get its Antichrist. John mentions the man of sin. "Who is the liar but he that denieth that Jesus is the Christ? He is Antichrist that denieth the Father and the Son" (1 John 2:22). It may be learned from this description that he will be the leader of Jewish unbelief and the unbelief of Christendom. Denying that Jesus is the Christ—that is Jewish; denying the Father and the Son, that is rejection of the Christian revelation. He will therefore take the leadership of Jewish and Christian apostasy. The most common interpretation that the Pope and the Papal system is this man of sin is incorrect, for the Pope does not deny that Jesus is the Christ, nor does the Pope claim to be the Christ. That the Pope has certain marks of the Antichrist about him no one can deny; but that he is *the* Antichrist is not true. (Certain Roman Catholic writers have charged Protestantism with being Babylon and anti-Christian. A so-called Protestant who denies the Virgin birth, the deity of Christ, surely is an antichrist.)

The final Antichrist, the man of sin, the son of perdition, is the heading up of the apostasy. He fills up the measure of the apostasy of humanity. He opposeth and exalteth himself against all that is called God or object of worship. He takes the place of God on earth. He will be the superman who is expected by the world to make his appearance in the near future. In the book of Revelation his number is given as 666. "For it is a man's number; and the number is six hundred and sixty-six" (Rev. 13:18). There is no need to speculate on this number. The meaning is very simple. Seven, in Scripture, is the complete number, used in connection with what is divine and perfect. Six is incomplete, and is man's number. The number 666 signifies man's day and man's defiance of God under Satan's power reaching its climax. This "superman" takes a seat in the temple of God and sets himself forth that he is God. From this we learn that he claims a religious character. He must therefore not be identified with the little horn in Daniel's prophecy (Daniel 7).

This little horn is another Satan-possessed person who takes the leadership politically of the coming federation of nations, the revived Roman Empire. He is "the prince that shall come" of Daniel 9:26. The beast out of the sea in Rev. 13:1-10 is the revived Roman Empire; the ten horns on that beastly empire correspond to the ten horns on Nebuchadnezzar's prophetic dream image and the ten horns on the fourth beast of Daniel's vision. The little horn, the domineering head of the revived Roman Empire, comes first into prominence and is soon followed by the second beast out of the earth, having two horns like a lamb, but speaking as a dragon. Rev. 13:11-18 describes this second beast and the work he does, in which he is helped by the first beast. This second beast is the man of sin, the son of perdition. Read now Daniel 11:36-39. This is another description of the same person. He is called a king because, as the false Christ, he will claim kingship among the Jews. He is also called in Revelation "the false prophet." He is the one of whom our Lord spoke in John 5:43, "I am come in My Father's name and ye received Me not; if another shall come in his own name, him ye will receive."

But what is the meaning of "he sitteth in the temple of God, setting himself forth that he is God?" The temple of God does not mean the Church. It is a Jewish temple. When the true Church is gone the Jewish people, restored once more to their own land, established there as a nation, though still in unbelief, will erect another temple and institute once more the temple worship. (See Isaiah 66:1-4). God will despise their worship. The man of sin will sit in that temple, demanding worship for the image he will set up for himself. This will be during the time of Jacob's trouble, the great tribulation. The man of sin, the Antichrist, will be undoubtedly a Jew. He will be filled with the energy and power of Satan. The nearness of the re-establishment of the Jewish people in Palestine in unbelief is an indication that all these prophecies are about to be fulfilled.

(For a closer study of the interesting details of the tribulation we refer our readers to "Exposition of Matthew," "Daniel," and "Exposition of Revelation," all by the author of *The Annotated Bible.*)

Verses 5-8. When the apostle was with them he had spoken to them about those things. "The mystery of lawlessness (not iniquity) already worketh," he informed the Thessalonians. Sin is lawlessness, and that has been at work from the beginning, man having forsaken God and exalted himself in self-will. This works on till it works out into open lawlessness in an out-and-out opposition to God and His Son, culminating in the man of sin, the false Christ, "to give the world its long-sought liberty from divine restraint and bring its vaunted progress to perfection, which under Christianity it has found impossible to attain." The mystery of lawlessness will cease to be a mystery when *the* lawless one, *the* man of sin, is manifested. But what keeps back the manifestation of this lawless one? Who or what is it that restrains it? Who is to be taken out of the way before the lawless one can be revealed? Many answers have been given to this question which we do not need to investigate. It is self-evident that that which restraineth must be a power superior to man and Satan and of a nature totally different to the man of sin. The restraining one is a power and a person. It is the Holy Spirit of God.[1]

When the Church leaves the earth then this restraining power and person, who dwells in the Church and therefore is here on earth, will be taken out of the way. As the result, in due time, the lawless one will be revealed. The Holy Spirit, who came down from heaven on the day of Pentecost to form the Church, the body of Christ, will be withdrawn when that body is complete and taken to glory to be joined to the Head, the Lord Jesus Christ. The light being gone, gross darkness will settle upon the nations, the apostasy will be here, the enemy comes in like a flood and the lawless one appears. Here we have the best evidence that the true Church cannot be on the earth during the final years with which this age closes. No true believer will be in the final apostasy under the lawless one, nor will the Church pass through the great tribulation. How this should fill our hearts with holy joy and our lips with praises!

Before he speaks of the lawless one with his lying wonders, he tells us at once of his fate. The Lord Jesus, in His visible manifestation, will consume him with the breath of his mouth and annul him with the brightness of His coming (Isaiah 11:1-5 and Rev. 19:11-21).

Verses 9-12. This lawless one, the Antichrist, will come in the energy of Satan with all power and signs and wonders of falsehood and in all deceit of unrighteousness to them that perish, because they have not received the love of the truth that they might be saved. And for this reason God sendeth them an energy of error, that they may believe the lie, that they all might be judged who believed not the truth, but had pleasure in unrighteousness. This shows us what is coming upon the so-called "Christian nations," with their boast of progress and civilization. This is the future of the destructive critics, the Bible-rejecting, gospel-neglecting masses of Christendom, as well as of apostate Judaism.

"Scientific infidelity now avouches with a sneer that we never see a miracle, and Hume's argument against all evidence in favor of such is its contradiction of universal experience. But it is soon to be matter of extensive experience that miracles there are; only in a very opposite interest to that of Christianity. These things are even now showing themselves in a more or less tentative and doubtful way; they are yet to throw off all reserve and challenge the faith of the world. 'Powers and signs and wonders' are the threefold designation of miracles in Scripture: 'wonders,' which excite attention and admiration; 'signs,' or things that have meaning and doctrine; 'powers,' that are evidently beyond human. These have borne witness in past time to the truth—never proved it, apart from the truth itself with which they were connected; and this is the mistake of so many at all times that a real miracle—something that could be rightly spoken of as all these—is an absolute guarantee of the message that it brings. Thus they are ready at any time to follow what is thus supported. Yet, if there are heavenly beings—'angels that excel in strength'—it is evident that, if permitted, and if evil enough to attempt it, they could at any time lead us thus according to their mind. Now that is the very thing which God has declared He will permit, when the time shall have arrived. When men

[1]"The Holy Ghost was here below; the Church, be its condition what it might, was still on earth, and God maintained the barrier. And as the porter had opened the door to Jesus in spite of all obstacles, so He sustains everything, however great the energy and progress of evil. The evil is bridled: God is the source of authority on earth. There is one who hinders until he be taken out of the way. Now, when the Church (the Church, that is, as composed of the true members of Christ) is gone, and consequently the Holy Ghost as the Comforter is no longer dwelling here below, then the apostasy takes place, the time to remove the hindrance is come, the evil is unbridled, and at length (without saying how much time it will take) the evil assumes a definite shape in him who is its head. The beast comes up from the abyss. Satan—not God—gives him his authority; and in the second beast all the energy of Satan is present. The man of sin is there" *(Synopsis of the Bible).*

have shown that they desire the truth no longer and the patient, long-suffering God has at last no justification further, that will have come to pass for the professing Christian world which we recognize as coming to pass in the history of individuals: God will say again, 'Ephraim is joined to his idols; let him alone.' And then will rise up one 'whose coming is according to the energy of Satan, with all power and signs and wonders of falsehood'—no longer in the interest of truth, but of a lie—and in all deceit of unrighteousness for those that perish; because they received not the love of the truth, that they might be saved.

"Dangerous would it be, as well as foolish, to assert that this is of the past, and not the future; that it has been fulfilled in Romanism, or in any like way. Has the power of Rome, whatever its pretension to fabulous miracle may be, exhibited itself after this fashion? No doubt, there is a class at all times ready to be duped in this way, as we see in the rapid progress of such transparent absurdities, as, for instance, 'Christian Science'; but in all this there is only the feeble anticipation of a delusion which will yet carry away the multitudes of unbelieving profession. The arch deceiver is not in the Vatican, nor elsewhere at the present time; he is to be revealed in his time. And yet we may indeed discern the foreshadows of this tremendous iniquity and realize that his way is being prepared in many events and movements that are taking place under our eyes" (*Numerical Bible*).

Then the rejectors of the truth will receive their judgment. No one can even imagine what will be the fate of the millions who received not the love of the truth, but had pleasure in unrighteousness. Horrible as the events are today, that coming time of Antichrist, the time when the lawless one reigns, energized by Satan, will be far worse. As it has been said, "Sin will be allowed to be its own terrible witness against itself, a witness at which eternity will shudder."

III. Thanksgiving, Prayer, Exhortations and Conclusions

CHAPTERS 2:13—3:18

1. Thanksgiving and prayer (2:13-17)
2. Prayer for the Word and for deliverance (3:1-5)
3. Exhortations (3:6-15)
4. Conclusions (3:16-18)

Verses 13-17. What blessed reasons are stated here to give thanks to God for what He has done for us and for all who believe! Brethren, beloved of the Lord, this is what believers are. Chosen we are to salvation through sanctification of the Spirit and belief of the truth. And glory is before all who have believed "the obtaining of the glory of our Lord Jesus Christ." And that glory may burst upon us at any time. For this God's people wait. Therefore we are "to stand fast and hold fast." The word "traditions" means the instructions they had received from the apostle; that is, the truth of God. To stand fast and to hold fast the truth are the two necessary things for God's people. He also prays for them that their hearts might be comforted and that they might be established in every good word and work.

Chapter 3:1-5. As in other Epistles, so here the apostle requests prayer for himself, "that the Word of the Lord may run and be glorified." His great ambition was to spread the gospel and the Word of God everywhere. When sinners are saved by grace, are added as members to the body of Christ and walk in the Spirit, then the Word is glorified. Enemies were on all sides then, as they are now, obstructing and hindering the word, "for faith is not the portion of all." He counted on the faithfulness of God to establish and keep them. It is a comfort for His people to know that their keeping rests in His hands. If God be for us, who can be against us? "And the Lord direct your hearts into the love of God and into the patience of Christ." Christ, in infinite patience, waits in heaven, and His people on earth wait for Him and with Him until the appointed time comes when His waiting and their waiting ends.

Verses 6-15. Exhortations follow. It seems there was considerable disorder among them. "For we hear that there are some which walk among you disorderly, working not at all, but are busybodies." This was no doubt the result of their unsettled condition brought about by the false teachers. He therefore exhorts them to withdraw from any brother who does not hearken to the instructions he has given and who continued in a disorderly walk. Once more he cites his own exemplary life among them (1 Thess. 2:9-10). "For we behaved not ourselves disorderly among you; neither did we eat any man's bread for nought (as charity); but wrought with labor and travail night and day, that we might not be chargeable to any of you. Not because we have not authority, but that we might give you an example to imitate us." He exhorts such who were disorderly, doing nothing but living in idleness, that with quietness they should work and no longer live from the labors of others, but each their own bread. If there is refusal from the side of such, no obedience to this rule, he is to be noted and no company kept with him. Yet he is not to be treated as an enemy, but to be admonished as a brother. How well it would be if this course would always be followed.

Verses 16-18. "And the Lord of peace Himself give you peace continually in every way." This is the final prayer in these two Epistles. It must be noticed how prominent prayer is in both of these Epistles. And the Lord, who is with His people, will give peace continually in every way, if they walk in obedience, subject to Himself.

THE FIRST EPISTLE TO
TIMOTHY

Introduction

The two Epistles to Timothy and the one to Titus are generally called the pastoral Epistles, because they were addressed to these servants of the Lord who had been put in charge of important churches. Timothy ministered in Ephesus (1 Tim. 1:3) and Titus in Crete (Titus 1:5). There never was a doubt expressed in the early Church that these epistles were written by the Apostle Paul. Quotations from them are found in the writings of Clement of Rome (96 A.D.); Polycarp of Smyrna (110 A.D.); Ignatius of Antioch (110 A.D.); Irenaeus (175 A.D.); Theophilus of Antioch (168 A.D.); Justin Martyr and others. The Syriac version, known by the name Peshito, made about 135 A.D., contains these Epistles, as well as other ancient versions. The greatest scholars of the early Church attested them as genuine. Some of the heretics, like the Gnostic Marcion, and Tatian, rejected them, and so do the destructive critics of the nineteenth and twentieth centuries. It is hardly necessary to say that the style and internal evidences establish fully the Pauline authorship.

The Personal History of Timothy

The name of Timothy is first mentioned in Acts 16:1. His mother's name was Eunice (2 Tim. 1:5); she was a Jewess, but his father was a Gentile (Acts 16:1, 3). Paul called him his son, my own son in the faith (1 Tim. 1:2), from which we conclude that he was converted by the apostle's ministry. His mother and grandmother, Lois (2 Tim. 1:5), were both Christians. They must have been, before their conversion, God-fearing Jewesses. This seems to be implied by 2 Tim. 3:14-15. Young Timothy had an excellent reputation among the brethren in Lystra and Iconium. After having him circumcised "because of the Jews," Paul took him as a fellowlaborer in the gospel (Acts 16:1-3). He must have accompanied the apostle on his journey through Macedonia, for the apostle left him at Berea with Silas (Acts 17:14). He had been in Thessalonica and Paul sent him back to ascertain the state of the Thessalonian church. After that he remained with the apostle in Corinth. He then traveled with Paul from Corinth to Ephesus. From Ephesus he was sent by the apostle with Erastus to Macedonia and Corinth (Acts 19:22; 1 Cor. 4:17). Later we find that he was with Paul, the prisoner, in Rome (Col. 1:1; Phil. 1:1, Philemon, verse 1).

When Was First Timothy Written?

Much has been written on the date of the First Epistle to Timothy. The question of one or two imprisonments of the apostle becomes important in connection with the date of the First Epistle to Timothy and the Epistle to Titus. Paul was no doubt imprisoned twice, and between the two imprisonments, when he was a free man, the First Epistle to Timothy and the Epistle to Titus were written. If only one imprisonment is maintained, the date of the writing of these Epistles is hopelessly obscure, besides other unexplainable difficulties. Paul reached Rome as a prisoner in the year 61 A.D. and remained there for two years (Acts 28:30). During this time he wrote the Epistles to the Ephesians, Colossians, Philippians, and to Philemon. In each he speaks of the fact that he was a prisoner. He does not mention himself as a prisoner when he writes the first letter to Timothy. He tells Timothy that he hoped to come unto him shortly. In writing Titus he speaks of spending the winter in Nicopolis (Tit. 3:12). This is sufficient evidence that he was no longer a prisoner. His trusting confidence to be released had been realized (Phil. 1:25; 2:24; Philemon, verse 22). The prayers in his behalf had been answered. For several years he was again at liberty, and Eusebius, a reliable source, states that it was known that Paul went forth preaching again.

Another ancient source (the Muratori fragment, 170 A.D.) gives the information that Paul after leaving Rome went to Spain. The interval between the first and second imprisonment explains fully the statement in 2 Tim. 4:20, "Trophimus have I left at Miletus sick." When Paul was at Miletus before he came to Rome (Acts 20:17), he did not leave him there sick, but Trophimus accompanied him (Acts 21:29). Therefore Paul visited Miletus and Ephesus again; this must have been between his first and final imprisonment. Nor could the statement in 1 Tim. 1:3 be explained if Paul had written this Epistle before his arrest in Jerusalem. He wrote Timothy that he had besought him to abide still at Ephesus.

The book of Acts records two visits of Paul to Ephesus. In Acts 18:19-22 we read of his brief visit, and in Acts 20:31 we have the record of his longer stay which lasted three years. At this time he did not request Timothy to stay in Ephesus, but he sent him into Macedonia (Acts 20:29, 30) he predicted the coming danger for that church, grievous wolves coming from the outside and false teachers from the inside. Some eight years later this prediction came true. He visited Ephesus again, and left Timothy there facing the different heresies which had sprung up, and bearing witness against them. A short time after he wrote this first Epistle to his beloved Timothy, beseeching him to abide still in Ephesus. The second Epistle was written from Rome after he had been thrown into prison the second time, and immediately before he suffered the martyr's death.

The Purpose of the Epistle

It is a confidential communication which Paul sent to Timothy concerning the church as the house of God. In chapter 3:14, 15 we find the words which state clearly the purpose of this Epistle, "These things write I unto thee, hoping to come unto thee shortly; but if I tarry long, that thou mayest know how thou oughtest to behave thyself in the house of God, which is the church of the living God, the pillar and ground of truth." The epistle therefore contains practical and important instructions on the order which is to be maintained in the church, as the house of God. The suitable conduct befitting to the house of God is given by the apostle. Pure doctrine, pure worship and a faithful ministry are the leading thoughts of this pastoral letter, but he also enters into the godly conduct of the individuals which are in the church of the living God. Blessed instructions! There is failure on all sides, showing, that departure from the faith, when men no longer endure sound doctrine, is upon us, according to the warning given in both Epistles. Yet individuals can always walk and live in the truth, for there is grace sufficient to lead and to maintain the members of the body of Christ in the divinely marked out path, even in the last days, the perilous times.

The Division of First Timothy

In the beginning of this Epistle unsound doctrine and all that is connected with it is rebuked, and the apostle puts a strong emphasis on true doctrine, without which no godliness is possible. This true doctrine is the gospel of grace of which Paul testifies, when he writes, "according to the glorious gospel of the blessed God which was committed to my trust" (1:11). Of this grace he was himself a witness. Prayer is the leading topic of the second chapter. In the third chapter the house of God and the holiness which becomes that house is the theme, what manner of persons overseers and deacons must be. Then in the fourth chapter we find a warning of the departure from the faith in the latter times. The last two chapters give different instructions and exhortations concerning the elder and younger women, widows, the support of elders, or overseers, as well as personal instructions to Timothy. This gives us a fivefold division.

I. **CONCERNING SOUND DOCTRINE** (1)

II. **CONCERNING PRAYER** (2)

III. **CONCERNING THE HOUSE OF GOD** (3)

IV. **CONCERNING THE LATTER-DAY APOSTASY** (4)

V. **INSTRUCTIONS AND EXHORTATIONS** (5—6)

Analysis and Annotations

I. Concerning Doctrine

CHAPTER 1

1. The salutation (1:1-2)
2. The charge concerning false doctrine (1:3-4)
3. The law, its use, and in contrast with grace (1:5-11)
4. Exceeding abundant grace (1:12-17)
5. The charge to Timothy, and the danger of shipwreck (1:18-20)

Verses 1-2. Paul writes as an apostle and mentions the fact that it is "by the commandment of God our Saviour." Necessity was laid upon him to act and write as an apostle through the energy of the Spirit of God, and therefore all he writes is of great importance, for it is not merely loving advice to his son Timothy, but by commandment of God. The expression "God our Saviour" is peculiar to the First Epistle to Timothy and to the Epistle addressed to Titus. (See 2:3; 4:10; Tit. 1:3; 2:10; 3:4.) It shows that God's character towards the world is that of a Saviour through the work of His Son. His grace, bringing salvation, has appeared unto all men, a different thing from what was under the law-dispensation. All men are now the objects of God's dealing in grace, and therefore we read in the second chapter that supplications, prayers and intercessions be made for all men (not believers only), "for this is good and acceptable in the sight of God our Saviour, who will have all men to be saved, and to come unto the knowledge of the truth." We learn from this the meaning of "God our Saviour"; it expresses His love towards the world.

This sovereign mercy of God was the true starting point of all the apostle had to declare. He then salutes his child Timothy, "grace, mercy and peace from God our Father and Jesus Christ our Lord." Here we find another interesting distinction in the use of the word "mercy." When greetings are sent by the Holy Spirit to churches, He never mentions mercy, but only "grace and peace," but when an individual is addressed "mercy" is added. It supposes the need, the constant wants, the difficulties, the trials and the dangers of individual believers. Timothy, in Ephesus, when the grievous wolves came from the outside, and false teachers from the inside, needed mercy, so that he would be kept. As the days grow darker, the departure from the faith becomes more pronounced, individual believers need mercy upon mercy to stand and to withstand. ("Mercy unto you, and peace, and love, be multiplied" is written in the beginning of the Epistle of Jude. This Epistle pictures the darkest days of departure from the faith with the church still on earth.)

Verses 3-4. The apostle had besought Timothy to abide still in Ephesus when he left that city and went to Macedonia. He was to remain behind to charge some that they teach no other doctrine. When Paul had met the elders of Ephesus at Miletus he had made this prediction, "For I know this, that after my departure shall grievous wolves enter in among you, not sparing the flock. Also of your own selves shall men arise, speaking perverse things, to draw away disciples after them" (Acts 20:29-30). Then he went to Jerusalem, where he was taken prisoner and sent to Rome. After his release he must have visited Ephesus once more and found the very things in the assembly of Ephesus against which the Holy Spirit had sounded the warning. Timothy was with him at that visit between his first and second imprisonment. He left him behind to deal with false teachers and false doctrines. (The word "doctrine" [teaching] is used eight times in this Epistle.) The better rendering of verse 4 is, "neither turn their minds to fables and interminable genealogies, which bring questionings rather than God's dispensation which is in faith."

The special warning is against fables and interminable genealogies. From the Greek word "muthos," translated fables, we have our English word "myths." The warning is undoubtedly aimed at the Gnostic emanations, the invention of "aeons" and the list of their successions. Like the church in Colosse, the church of Ephesus was also invaded by the false teachers of Gnosticism. It was not yet fully developed. That came during the post-apostolic days in the second century. These speculations were not according to sound doctrine and the truth of God. Neither are the present-day myths of evolution, the derivation of one thing from another in an interminable chain, the myths of destructive criticism, of spiritism, theosophy, Christian Science, and other vagaries. Jewish teachings on the perpetual obligation of the Mosaic law, genealogies, and other matters, are likewise included in this warning. They all lead not upon the sure foundation of the dispensation of God, (the dispensation of the grace of God [Eph. 3:2]) which is in faith, but to questionings in which there is no profit, but which open the way to a complete rejection of God's truth and God's grace made known in the gospel.

Verses 5-11. When the apostle used the word "commandment" he does not mean the Ten Commandments. It is the charge the apostle is putting upon his son and fellow-laborer Timothy. What he enjoins is, love out of a pure heart, and a good conscience, and unfeigned faith. And this is produced not by the law, nor by human imaginations and questionings, but solely by the gospel of grace. Speculative questions or anything else do not act upon the conscience nor bring into the presence of God. An unfeigned faith in Christ clears the conscience from guilt and produces love out of a pure heart. Some had swerved from this, by turning aside from the dispensation of the grace of God unto the vain talk about the law, fables and genealogies. They gave heed to Jewish fables and commandments of men (Tit. 1:14) and were consequently turned from the truth of the gospel. They aimed at being law-teachers, but they did not understand what they said and what they so strenuously affirmed. They were evidently the same Judaizers, ever insisting upon law-keeping and its ordinances, the false teachers who perverted the gospel, who continually dogged the steps of the apostle and tried to injure the work he was doing.

Then follows a parenthetical statement on the use and purpose of the law. The law is good (Rom. 7:12) if a man uses it lawfully. Its lawful application is to the lawless and disobedient, to the ungodly and sinners, who are condemned by the law. It has no application to a righteous person. A believer with unfeigned faith and love out of a pure heart and a good conscience is righteous, and has nothing to do with the law. In possession of the righteousness which is apart from the law, having the righteousness of God in Christ, the law has no power over the believer. He is dead to the law; the law can have no possible meaning or use for him. The law was never designed to be the rule for the life of the Christian. He is saved by grace, and that alone can produce godliness. It is grace which teaches to live soberly, righteously and godly in this present age, and also gives the power for it.

To use the law is for the believer a denial of grace. He continues: "And if any other thing that is contrary to sound doctrine, according to the gospel of the glory of the blessed God, which was committed to my trust." Here we see the contrast between law and gospel. The law is for condemnation, but the gospel proclaims the glory of the blessed God; and this gospel, committed to the apostle, unfolding God's counsels of glory for us in Christ, tolerates no evil. Sound doctrine is therefore not only a correct belief in the gospel of the glory of the blessed God, what is accomplished in that gospel to the glory of God, and the glory it puts on our side; but sound doctrine means also practical godliness. (See 1 Tim. 6:3, "The doctrine which is according to godliness.") A holy life is produced by sound doctrine, and sound doctrine must lead to a holy life. Unsound doctrines, profane and vain babblings, all the unscriptural teachings, the destructive criticism, and the cults "will increase unto more ungodliness" (2 Tim. 2:17) and eat like a canker.

Verses 12-17. And now he speaks of himself, thanking Christ Jesus, Who gave him power and counted him faithful, appointing him to the ministry. And who was he? A blasphemer and persecutor, and injurious. "But I obtained mercy, because I did it in unbelief. And the grace of our Lord was exceeding abundant with faith and love which is in Christ Jesus." The grace which he preached, which he defended against the attacks of Judaizing teachers, was pre-eminently witnessed to by his own case. The grace of the Lord was towards him exceeding abundant, or more literally rendered, "the grace of our Lord surpassingly overabounded." He had the most marvellous experience of this grace which saves so freely and fully. "This is a faithful saying, and worthy of all acceptation, that Christ Jesus came into the world to save sinners; of whom I am chief." He knows what he says and of what he speaks.

No fables, imaginations, vain speculations, or questionings here, but the fullest assurance, that Christ Jesus the Son of God came into the world to save sinners. And He had saved him, the chief of sinners, so that no man need to consider himself too great a sinner for this grace. He obtained mercy so that he might be a pattern of the grace that Christ would display towards all "who should hereafter believe on Him to life everlasting." In a special manner this is applicable to the nation to which Paul belonged; the Jews hereafter, at the time of our Lord's second coming, will obtain mercy. Paul in his experience is the pattern of the sovereignty of grace which in due time will save "all Israel." The chief, the most active, the most inveterate of enemies, was the best and most powerful of all witnesses that the grace of God abounded over sin, and that the work of Christ was perfect to put it away. It was the best refutation of the "other doctrines" against which Paul warns in these epistles to Timothy. He then gives utterance to the praise which filled his heart. Such praise the law could never teach the human heart. It knows no song of joy and blessing; its melody is the curse.

"Such was the foundation of Paul's ministry in contrast with the law. It was founded on the revelation of grace; but it was a revelation connected with the experience of its application to his own case. Peter, guilty of denying a living Saviour, could speak to the Jews of grace that met their case, which was his own; Paul, formerly the enemy of a glorified Saviour and the resister of the Holy Ghost, could proclaim grace that rose above even that state of sinfulness, above all that could flow from human nature—

grace that opened the door to the Gentiles according to God's own counsels, when the Jews had rejected everything, substituting the heavenly assembly for them—grace that sufficed for the future admission of that guilty nation to better privileges than those which they had forfeited" *(Synopsis of the Bible).*

Verses 18-20. He then commits a very solemn charge to Timothy. The charge is "holding faith, and a good conscience." Some put it away, that is the good conscience, and then concerning faith make shipwreck. The faith is sound doctrine, the gospel of grace, the truth of Christianity. A good conscience must be maintained in order to hold that faith in sincerity and truth. Daily self-judgment, even as to the smallest things, is absolutely necessary to keep the believer from the dangerous rocks on which his faith may be wrecked. It may be a very little sin that is allowed and not confessed and put away; but this unjudged sin becomes the starting point of something worse and may lead to terrible results. If a good conscience is put away the believer begins to drift.

"To be in communion with God, the conscience must be good, must be pure; and if we are not in communion with God, we cannot have the strength that would maintain us in the faith, that would enable us to persevere in the profession of the truth, as God gives it to us. Satan has then a hold upon us, and if the intellect of one in this state is active, he falls into heresy. The loss of a good conscience opens the door to Satan, because it deprives us of communion with God; and the active mind, under Satan's influence, invents ideas instead of confessing the truth of God. The apostle treats the fruit of this state as "blasphemies"; the will of man is at work, and the higher the subject, the more an unbridled will, possessed by the enemy, goes astray, and exalts itself against God, and against the subjection of the whole mind to the obedience of Christ, to the *authority* of the revelation of God" (J. N. Darby).

We have here an explanation why men who used to hold the faith delivered unto the saints have given up that faith. Error does not begin with the head but with the heart. Some sin was cherished; some secret sin had control. Self-judgment was not exercised; no confession made. Having no good conscience, there was no longer real communion with God and the shipwreck of faith followed in due time. Hymenaeus and Alexander, who denied resurrection, were examples of this fatal road. He delivered them over to Satan, not to be lost, but for discipline. They were to find out by sad and sorrowful experience what Satan's power is, so that broken and humbled they might be brought back. "Better surely not to need such discipline; but if we do need it, how precious to know that God turns it into account in His grace, that we might be thoroughly dealt with and exercised in the conscience" (Wm. Kelly).

II. Concerning Prayer

CHAPTER 2

1. Prayer for all men and for those in authority (2:1-7)
2. The place for the man and the woman (2:8-15)

Verses 1-7. Instructions are now given by the apostle. The first concerns prayer. "I exhort, therefore, that, first of all, supplications, prayers, intercessions, and giving of thanks be made for all men; for kings, and for all that are in authority; that we may lead a quiet and peaceable life in all godliness and honesty (literally, gravity). For this is good and acceptable in the sight of God our Saviour, who will have all men to be saved and come to the knowledge of the truth." The God who is our Father is also the Saviour-God, who acts in the gospel of His grace with love and compassion towards all men. As such He manifests a gracious willingness to have all men come to the knowledge of the truth and be saved. We must, therefore, knowing Him and the exceeding abundant grace towards us, act in love towards those who are without. God acts in grace and the household of faith must do likewise.

As the gospel of grace goeth forth to all men, and God wants all men to be saved, so are we to pray for all men. Especially are kings and all who are in authority to be mentioned in the prayers of intercession. This is the true grace-spirit; the Jewish law-spirit knew nothing of love towards all men. Gentiles and Gentile kings were looked upon as outside, and not considered to be the objects of divine love. The dispensation of the grace of God having come, salvation by grace is offered to the whole world. And how this exhortation has been neglected! How little true prayer for the salvation of all men is made! (Verse 4 disposes completely of the unscriptural idea that God has predestined a part of the human race to be lost.) We must also remember that cruel Nero was on the throne of the Roman Empire when this exhortation was written.

The house of God is to be a house of prayer for all nations, and to exercise the priestly function of intercession. Well has it been said, "Nothing but the strong sense of the infinite blessing of the place that grace has given us could lead to, or keep up, such prayer." But often we are apt to settle down in the enjoyment of grace, without reflecting on our responsibility towards those who are unreached by that grace, which is also at their disposal. Through preoccupation within, how often we forget those without! How needful to-day when thrones totter, when democracies arise, when all forms of government break down and the shadow of the coming lawless one lengthens, to be obedient to this divinely given instruction, so that even in these days of confusion God's people may lead "a quiet and peaceable life"!

"For there is one God and one mediator between God and men, the man Christ Jesus; who gave Himself a ransom for all, the testimony to be rendered in due time." Judaism was the revelation and testimony of the one God. Christianity reveals also the true God, but brings forth the equally great truth that there is but one mediator, as there is but one God. And this one mediator is the Man Christ Jesus, who came into the world and who gave Himself a ransom for all.

"Precious truth! We are in weakness, we are guilty, we could not bring ourselves near to God. We needed a mediator, who, while maintaining the glory of God, should put us into such a position that He could present us to God in righteousness according to that glory. Christ gave Himself as a ransom. But He must be a man in order to suffer for men, and to represent men. And this He was. But this is not all. We are weak—here, where we are to receive the revelation of God; and weak, with regard to the use of our resources in God and our communion with Him—even when our guilt is blotted out. And, in our weakness to receive the revelation of God, Christ has revealed God, and all that He is in His own person, in all the circumstances written wherein man could have need either in body or in soul. He came down into the lowest depths in order that there should be none, even of the most wretched, who could not feel that God in His goodness was near him and was entirely accessible to him—come down to Him—His love finding its occasion in misery; and that there was no need to which He was not present, which He could not meet.

"He came down, took part in all the sorrows of humanity, and entered into all the circumstances in which the human heart could be, and was wounded, oppressed, and discouraged, bowing down under the evil. No tenderness, no power, no sympathy, no humanity, like His; no human heart that can so understand, so feel with us, whatever the burden may be that oppresses the heart of man. It is the Man, the Christ Jesus, who is our mediator; none so near, none who has come down so low, and entered with divine power into the need, and all the need, of man. The conscience is purified by His work, the heart relieved by that which He was, and which He is for ever.

"There is but One: to think of another would be to snatch from Him His glory, and from us our perfect consolation. His coming from on high, His divine nature, His death, His life as man in heaven, all point Him out as the one and only mediator" *(Synopsis of the Bible)*.

"A ransom for all, the testimony to be rendered in due time." This statement has been perverted by some, who handle the Word of God deceitfully, to mean that the whole human race will ultimately be saved including all the wicked dead. And more than that, some of these teachers have made the astonishing statement that the testimony of their unscriptural invention was to be reserved for a certain time, and that "due time" came when they preached their "larger hope" and universal salvation. He has given Himself a ransom for all, which means that provision is made by His propitiatory sacrifice for the salvation of the whole race, but faith is necessary for the appropriation of this salvation.

All who do not accept Christ by personal faith are not covered by His substitutionary sacrifice. If they die in their sins the great ransom cannot deliver them (Job 36:18). The due time, or, its own time, when that testimony of all this was to be rendered came when the work was finished on the cross. Ever since the one mediator between God and man gave Himself a ransom for all, the message of God's love and grace has been preached. And Paul to whom the gospel of the glory of the blessed God was specially committed could therefore say, "Whereunto I was appointed a preacher (literally "herald"; also used in 2 Tim. 1:11; and of Noah in 2 Peter 2:5) and an apostle (I speak the truth, I lie not) a teacher of the Gentiles in faith and truth."

Verses 8-15. "I will therefore that men pray everywhere, lifting up holy hands, without wrath and doubting." This refers to praying in public. Audible prayer in the congregation is to be made by men, and not by women. This is apostolic teaching. (There are sects in existence today which claim to have returned to apostolic doctrines and practices, yet they ignore the apostolic commandment as to the place of women in the church. In fact in many of these sects women are the leaders.) The hands which are lifted up in public prayer must be holy hands (James 4:8). True piety and a separated walk are to characterize the man who lifts up his hands in public prayer. And it must be "without wrath," angry feeling against a brother, and without disputing or "reasoning." To harbor an ill feeling against another while praying or to introduce a dispute, a reasoning argument (as done quite often) makes prayer noneffective.

And now in regard to women he gives the charge that they "adorn themselves in modest apparel, with shamefacedness and sobriety, not with braided hair, or gold, or pearls, or costly array." She is to give her testimony in this way and show that she is not following the world, but is above these things. Immodest dress, bordering on indecency, to gratify the lust of the flesh and of the eyes, is a noticeable thing among the women of the world.

The Christian woman must bear a testimony in an outward manner that she is separated from these things. Then he gives the charge about the teaching authority of women. "Let the woman learn in silence with all subjection. But I suffer not a woman to teach, nor to usurp authority over the man, but to be in silence." This is and belongs to the wholesome, sound doctrine. Woman has her sphere of service, of laboring in the gospel and also teaching the truth, among her own sex and children. But the place of authority does not belong to her; she is not to usurp authority, nor to exercise it. This is the divine order, that the authority to teach is vested in the man. (See 1 Corinthians 11 and 14). "For Adam was first formed, then Eve." This is creation's order, which must be maintained on the ground of redemption.

And the fall teaches another lesson. "And Adam was not deceived, but the woman being deceived was in the transgression." The able expositor Bengel wrote on this: "More easily deceived, she more easily deceives." When she leaves the place given her according to this apostolic charge, she is easily deceived, and then in turn easily deceives others. The second epistle speaks of "silly women laden with sins, led away with divers lusts." Women rejecting sound doctrine, usurping authority, have become instruments of the enemy, by inventing Satanic doctrines and perverting the truth of God.

(Seventh Day Adventism had Mrs. White as prophetess; Theosophy—Mrs. Blavatsky and Annie Besant; Spiritism—the Fox sisters and the thousands of wicked and often immoral women—mediums; Christian Science—Mrs. Mary Baker Eddy and the thousands of women healers; the Irvingite movement—demon-possessed prophetess, who spoke in strange tongues; New Thoughtism has its women leaders, etc. How this bears out the divine truth stated here.)

Verse 15 refers to Genesis 3:16. She shall be preserved in child-bearing, delivered in the hour of trial and labor, if they continue in faith and love, and holiness with sobriety.

III. Concerning the House of God

CHAPTER 3

1. The overseer (3:1-7)
2. The deacon (3:8-13)
3. The house of God and the mystery of Godliness (3:14-16)

Verses 1-7. As stated before, the Church is viewed in these pastoral Epistles as the house of God. The holiness which becomes this house is to be maintained and expressed in a practical way. The different directions given as to overseers and deacons demonstrate what God esteems highly, and what He expects of those who are saved by grace, and who constitute His House. Paul wrote these instructions to his son Timothy, so that he might know how to behave himself in the house of God (verses 14-15).

Bishops (overseers) are identical with elders (presbyters). For conclusive proof see Acts 20:17 and 28; Titus 1:5 and 7. In both passages the same persons are called both bishops and elders. It is nowhere taught in the Word of God that a bishop has a place of superior authority in the body of Christ, as head of a diocese, etc. These things as practised in the Romish, Episcopal and other ritualistic churches are according to human ordinances.

The work of the overseer is learned from Paul's statement in Acts 20:28: "Take heed therefore unto yourselves, and to all the flock, over the which the Holy Spirit hath made you overseers, to feed the church of God, which He hath purchased with His own blood." The Holy Spirit called them into this work, for He is the great administrator in the church. Each local church had not one overseer or bishop, but a number of them, showing that the authority was not vested in one person only (Phil. 1:1). If anyone desired the office of an overseer, he desired a good work. It is a good work to exercise loving and patient care over souls which are beloved of God, and so dear to Him, who purchased them by His own blood. Such a desire would be the result of the Spirit of God, who laid the work of an overseer upon the heart. Paul then gives Timothy the qualities which a bishop or overseer must have. He must be blameless, that is as to his moral character irreproachable, with nothing whatever against him. "He must be the husband of one wife." This has been explained as exluding all who had been married twice. This is incorrect. It may refer to those who were as pagans married to more than one woman, for polygamy was practiced among the heathen in that day, as it is still. Converted to Christianity these pagans were in an unhappy condition, and on account of it could not exercise oversight in a local church.

On the other hand this inspired qualification of an overseer or bishop is a complete and crushing refutation of the celibacy of the Romish priesthood. He also must be vigilant, sober, of a good behavior (modest), given to hospitality and apt to teach (2 Tim. 2:24). ("Apt to teach" has also been translated "ready to learn.") Among the other qualifications we point out especially the one "not greedy of filthy lucre," that is, he must not be a lover of money. This is mentioned several times in the epistles to Timothy and to Titus. And Peter in exhorting the elders also writes, "Feed the flock of God, which is among you, taking the oversight thereof, not by constraint, but willingly, not for filthy lucre, but of a ready mind" (1 Peter 5:2). The Holy Spirit anticipated the corruption of church office and ministry through the love of money. He is also to rule well his own house and have his children in subjection, "For if a man know not how to rule his own house, how shall he take care of the Church of God?"

We see all these are moral qualifications. They are to be men of mature age, who had shown in the government of their own household their fitness for the more blessed work of having oversight in a local assembly. A new convert may begin to give a testimony for the gospel as soon as he has believed, but fitness for oversight, to be an elder, required time and a practical walk in the truth. Therefore Paul writes, "not a novice, lest being lifted up with pride he fall into condemnation of the devil." How often this has been true, that in some assembly a young convert with natural gifts was made much of, and then became lifted up and aspired, like Diotrephes (3 John) to have the pre-eminence.

Verses 8-13. "Deacon" means "a servant," one who ministers. The seven chosen in Acts 6 to serve tables were deacons. They were to be occupied with the external affairs of a local church, to serve the bodily need. Without entering into the different qualifications, which need hardly any further comment, we point out only one. "Even so must their wives be grave, not slanderers—sober, faithful in all things." As the deacons had their work in external things, in connection with the family and family life of a local church, there was danger of their wives making mischief and becoming busybodies and tale-bearers; hence the instruction to the wives of the deacons. Nothing was said to the wives of the overseers; theirs was a different sphere.

Verses 14-16. Paul expected to come shortly to be with Timothy, from which we gather that he was not then a prisoner. In the words which follow we have a threefold mention of the church on earth.

1. It is the *House of God.* God dwells in it on earth. Its leading characteristic on earth must be holiness. "Holiness becometh Thine house, O Lord, forever" (Ps. 93:5). All Paul had written, his solemn charge concerning sound doctrine, a good conscience, prayer for all men, about overseers and deacons, was to teach Timothy and to teach us also, how to behave in the house of God, as on earth. God dwells in the church on earth. And He who dwelt among Israel and said, "I am holy, be ye also holy," makes the same demand of the house in which He dwells now.

2. The second name is the *Church of the living God.* The Holy Spirit, the Spirit of the living God, dwells in the church. She is the habitation of God by the Spirit (Eph. 2:22). She is therefore set apart for Himself; not of the world, as He, who is the blessed Head of the body, is not of the world.

3. The *pillar and support of the truth.* While our Lord was on earth He said, "I am the truth." He is so still; and His Word is the truth. The church is here to maintain this truth on earth, to contend earnestly for the faith delivered unto the saints. She is the witness for Christ on earth, Christ who is hidden now with God. Therefore the true Church is the pillar of the truth, in proclaiming it. Woe! to the men who meddle with the truth of God, and by their wicked

criticism try to undermine the support of the pillar and the house of God. God shall destroy them for their evil work (1 Cor. 3:17). When the Church leaves the earth, then the truth will be abandoned, and complete apostasy has come. As long as the true Church (though it only may be a feeble remnant) the pillar and support of the truth, is on the earth, the complete apostasy cannot come (2 Thess. 2). From all this we learn that the presence of the living God and the maintenance of the truth are the foremost characteristics of the house of God.

Verse 16 brings before us the mystery of godliness (piety). It is that which the church on earth is to witness to. This mystery is the Lord Jesus Christ (Col. 2). The first fact of the mystery is, *"God was manifested in the flesh."* (The Revised Version on account of textual criticism changed this to "He who hath been manifested in the flesh." Some would therefore rule out this text as one which speaks of the deity of our Lord. But even if it were positive that the correct reading is "He" instead of "God," it does not affect the argument. The "He" could not be any one else but the Son of God.) It is the incarnation. God Himself has been manifested in the form of man. The Creator God came to be the Saviour God. He appeared on earth as man. *"Justified in the Spirit."* Upon Him, the second Man, the Spirit of God descended. He lived the holy life on earth. The power of the Holy Spirit was manifested throughout His life on earth. And having offered Himself by the eternal Spirit without spot to God, the power of the Holy Spirit marked Him out as Son of God in resurrection. "Declared the Son of God with power, according to the Spirit of holiness, by the resurrection from the dead" (Rom. 1:4). His resurrection, by God the Father and through the operation of His Spirit (Rom. 8:11) justified Him as Son of God.

"Seen of angels." Not only did man see Him as John testifies, "that which was from the beginning which we have heard, which we have seen with our eyes, which we have looked upon and our hands have handled, of the Word of Life"—but angels saw Him. The host of angels witnessed His entrance into the world, surrounded Him and were present with Him in His life on earth. He was seen of angels in His resurrection, and seen of angels when He ascended on high to take His place at the right hand of God, far above all principalities and powers, becoming the head over all things, the head of the Church. And to these heavenly principalities and powers there is now made known by the church the manifold wisdom of God (Eph. 3:10). *"Preached unto the Gentiles."* The good news is preached in the whole world. Jews and Gentiles hear the message, and especially is He preached to the Gentiles. *"Believed on in the world."* As a result of the preaching, the hearing of the Word of God, He is believed on, and those who believe on Him constitute the house, the Church of the living God. *"Received up in glory."* He ascended to the glory from which he had descended. He glorified God on earth, and now, as the Risen One, God has glorified Him in heaven. And some day all who believed on Him in the world will also be received up in glory, to be with Him where He is. And all this is the truth which is to be maintained and preached in the house of God.

IV. Concerning the Latter-day Apostasy

CHAPTER 4

1. What the Spirit has predicted (4:1-5)
2. The remedies against apostasy (4:6-16)

Verses 1-5. The mystery of godliness having been mentioned, the apostle speaks of Satan's power in opposition to the faith and truth of God (the mystery of godliness here, and the mystery of iniquity in 2 Thessalonians). "But the Spirit speaketh expressly that in the latter times some shall depart from the faith, giving heed to seducing spirits and doctrines of demons." It is a prophetic warning. Paul had given a similar warning to the Ephesian elders gathered at Miletus a number of years before, and elsewhere in the New Testament the Holy Spirit gives the same warning concerning an apostasy in the future days. Inasmuch as the faith is the foundation upon which everything rests, Satan aims to destroy this first, knowing if faith is given up and the truth of God denied, that he, the master-mind, can easily introduce his seducing spirits and substitute for the faith, demon doctrines.

All this is fully evidenced in our days, the latter times which are the perilous times (2 Tim. 3:1). The mystery of godliness, the doctrine of Christ, is being increasingly denied and rejected by seducing spirits, active in systems like the destructive criticism, Unitarianism, the New Theology and others. And in "Christian Science," Spiritism, Mormonism and other "cults" we find the very doctrines of demons. Anyone who rejects the mystery of godliness, no matter what else he may put in its place, has departed from the faith and becomes the prey of seducing spirits who lead him on to destruction and eternal ruin. And these seducers and seducing spirits, Satan's ministers, appear as ministers of righteousness (2 Cor. 11:15). They feign sanctity, "speaking lies in hypocrisy." They teach the most deadly error under the cloak of piety, devotion and of deeper religious knowledge. Evil and error put on the form of truth and godliness. All this fits the different systems which claim to be "Christian," but which are "anti-Christian." They have seared, that is branded, consciences; claiming to lead others into righteousness and holiness while their consciences are defiled.

Two things are especially mentioned, "forbidding to marry" and "commanding to abstain from meats." (The Roman Catholic Church forbids her priests to marry, and also commands her members to abstain from certain meats on certain days.) This austere asceticism was a pretension to superior piety. Men began to teach these heresies even in apostolic days. They developed later into systems like Gnosticism; and to-day we see the same principles advocated in theosophical and other occult movements. They forbid what God has established in creation, for marriage is an institution which God has sanctified, and to use that which God has created to be received with thanksgiving by them which believe and know the truth. They claimed that their superior holy character would not be consistent with marriage and eating meats.

"Forsaking the real and practical holiness of communion with God, and of His commandments by Christ, they created a false sanctity for themselves, which denied that which God had ordained from the beginning, and thus exalted themselves against the authority of Him who had ordained it, as though He was an imperfect or perhaps evil being" *(Synopsis of the Bible).*

The Spirit of God through Paul assures us that any creature of God is good, and nothing to be rejected, if it be received with thanksgiving; for it is sanctified by the Word of God and prayer. If that which God has made for the creature for its use is refused and rejected, it is sin. But all that the Creator has provided must be received from Him with thanksgiving, and the acknowledgment of a dependence upon Him. Prayer is needed for that, to sanctify to our use what He has so graciously given.

Verses 6-13. The rest of the chapter consists of exhortations in view of the threatening apostasy, how these evils may be combated and remedied. If Timothy put the saints of God in remembrance of these things, he would be a good minister (deacon) of Jesus Christ, and be continually nourished up in the words of faith and good doctrine. To remember the apostolic instructions and to maintain by them faith and good doctrine effectually counteracts error and the doctrines of demons. Then profane and old wives' fables must be avoided and refused. We have an all-sufficient revelation of God; speculative things of the human mind intruding into things unseen (Col. 2:18), following the theories, imaginations and traditions of men, only lead away from godliness, and lead from foolish questionings into that which is profane. (A believer has no business to investigate Spiritism, Theosophy, or occupy his mind with things not made known in the Word of God. We must avoid these things, refuse to have anything to do with them, else we step upon the territory of the enemy, and lay ourselves open to his attacks.)

The true exercise must be unto godliness, pious, consecrated living; and the true exercise is self-judgment, maintaining a good conscience and communion with God. Bodily exercise by erratic living, abstaining from meats and other things, profits but little. It is far different with true godliness. It is profitable for everything, both in this life and that to come. This is another faithful word and worthy of all acceptation (1:15). And for this doctrine the apostle labored and suffered reproach; but he had faith in the living God, who as Saviour-God, by His power and providence, sustains all men. He is the preserver of all men, but especially of those who believe. As Creator He is the preserver and benefactor of all men; but for those who believe He is much more than that. In this God as Creator and Saviour, preserver and keeper, the believer trusts. "These things command and teach." It is another remedy against the seducing spirits and doctrines of demons. None should despise his youth. Timothy was very young when he joined Paul (Acts 16:1-3), and now after some eleven years he was still youthful, especially in comparison with Paul the aged. He urges him to be in his life and walk a model of the believers—in word, in conduct, in faith and in purity.

These are the evidences of true piety and holding sound doctrine. Then as to himself and his service, till Paul came, he was to give himself to reading, which of course must mean the

Holy Scriptures, to exhortation and to teaching. He was not to neglect the gift that had been bestowed upon him. In his case this gift was a direct bestowal of prophecy, the voice of the Spirit making it known (as in Acts 13:1). The laying on of hands by the elders had not communicated the gift. It was the outward expression of fellowship with the gift imparted unto Timothy. This gift had to be used and developed like every other gift of the Spirit. A gift may be idle and neglected, but if rightly used it will grow and be used in blessing. To do all this and meditate in these things, be wholehearted in them, progressing constantly in godliness, is a safeguard against all error. "Take heed to thyself and the doctrine; continue in them; for in doing this thou shalt both save thyself and them that hear thee." Some have perverted this instruction as if it meant the salvation of the soul, for eternal salvation. It has nothing to do with eternal life and salvation. This the believer has in Christ through grace. "Save" has here the same meaning as in Philippians, a present salvation from the dangers in the way, being saved from error.

V. Instructions and Exhortations

CHAPTER 5

1. Concerning widows (5:1-16)
2. Concerning elders (5:17-21)
3. Responsibility and personal instructions (5:22-25)

Verses 1-16. It is not necessary to follow all these instructions in detail and explain their meaning. An elder was not to be rebuked sharply, but to be entreated as a father, and younger men as brethren. Then he speaks of widows. Those who are widows indeed are to be held in honor. Piety was to be shown at home, if they had children. "She that is a widow indeed, and desolate (left alone) trusteth in God, and continueth in supplications and prayers day and night." Happy privilege of such, with special claims upon the Saviour-God. Thus exercising trust in God and in His promises, her special ministry is the ministry of prayer and intercession (Luke 2:36-37). God hath chosen that which is weak, widows, those who are on sick-beds, "shut-ins," to use especially in the ministry of intercession.

The Day of Christ will reveal the great things which were accomplished in secret prayer. But if other widows lived in pleasure, in self-indulgence then she is dead while she liveth, that is, dead to the spiritual things. For such there could be no honor, but dishonor. And if anyone did not provide for his own house, he denied the faith and was worse than an infidel, for an unbeliever generally recognizes this duty. Then we have divinely given regulations as to those who should be given relief by the church, and those who should be refused. Practical godliness is thus to be maintained in the house of God, and manifested in every way so as "to give none occasion to the adversary to speak reproachfully."

Verses 17-21. Elders that ruled well were counted worthy of double honor, and especially those who had the gift of expounding the word of God, and teaching the truth, "who labor in the Word and teaching." And as elsewhere in his former epistles, the apostle here once more states the responsibility that "the laborer is worthy of his hire." The ox that treadeth out the corn is not to be muzzled. The Creator-God careth for the oxen, and made a merciful provision for them in His law. How much more then should those be ministered to in temporal things that labored in the Word, and with much self-sacrifice taught the truth. But the laborer must remain in dependence on the Saviour-God, for he is God's laborer. (The almost universal custom of promising a laborer in the Word, an evangelist, pastor and teacher a salary, and the laborer depending on his bargain, is nowhere sanctioned by the Word of God. It is contrary to faith which should mark the path of the servant of Christ.) Instruction is given how an elder is to be treated if charged with wrong. Before God, the Lord Jesus Christ, and the elect angels (from which we learn that angels are silent onlookers in all these things—1 Cor. 11:10), Paul charges Timothy to observe these things, to be firm in them, without showing partiality.

Verses 22-25. He was not to lay on hands hastily on any man, the outward sign of fellowship, to acknowledge them as co-laborers and become identified with them. It might result in becoming partakers of other men's sins. How little conscience there is to-day in this matter! How often believers are in fellowship with those who are not teaching the truth. "Drink no longer water, but use a little wine for thy stomach's sake and thine often infirmities." A small matter, yet not too small for the Holy Spirit. No doubt Timothy had a very scrupulous conscience, but the apostle in this God-inspired letter, sets aside his scruples and tells him to use a little wine. Much criticism has been made of this divinely given instruction. Extreme faith-healers, who reject all means in a way that is not faith, but presumption, and on the other hand extreme prohibitionists, have made the astounding statement that Paul made a mistake when he wrote these words. But if Paul made a mistake here who can convince us that he did not make a mistake when he wrote the eighth chapter of Romans? Others state that it was not wine, but "grape-juice." We give the helpful comment of another:

"Timothy's habitual temperance is here seen: weak in body, the apostle recommends him to use his liberty by taking a little wine—a pleasing instance of grace. We have here a proof of the habits of this faithful servant. The Spirit shows us how carefully he kept himself from exciting or satisfying his passions in the least thing (at the same time that there is perfect liberty to use everything that is good when there is a true reason for it), and also the apostle's tender interest in his fellow-laborer in the gospel. It is a little parenthesis attached to the expression, 'be not a partaker of other men's sins,' but it has great beauty. This affectionate watchfulness became the apostle; he desired holiness in his representative, but he well knew how to respect Timothy, and to maintain the decorum which he had enjoined, and to exhibit his heartfelt tenderness" *(Synopsis of the Bible).*

"Some men's sins," the apostle continues, "are open beforehand, going before to judgment"—they are manifested in the present life. "And some men they follow after"—unknown now, hidden away, but to be made manifest at the judgment seat of Christ.

CHAPTER 6

1. Concerning servants (6:1-2)
2. Concerning those who oppose (6:3-5)
3. Concerning contentment and temptation (6:6-10)
4. The final exhortations (6:11-21)

Verses 1-2. Servants (slaves) who had pagan masters were to count them worthy of all honor, and thus bear a good testimony for the truth, that the Name of God and the teaching be not blasphemed. Theirs was a blessed opportunity to show forth the excellencies of Him whom they served, and who once served in obedience and submission on earth. If their masters were believers, and master and slave worshipped together, there was danger that a slave might forget his place and become insolent. The apostolic exhortation guards against this.

Verses 3-5. These things Timothy was to teach and exhort. If anyone opposed these instructions, if he did not give his consent to wholesome words, the words of the Lord Jesus Christ and to the teaching which is according to godliness, he showed thereby that he knew not the real power of godliness. He gives evidence of pride of heart, that he is destitute of the truth, knowing nothing, but doting about questions and strife of words. And from such a state of soul cometh as a result envy, strife, railings, evil surmisings, perverse disputings of men of depraved minds, and destitute of the truth, supposing that gain is godliness. This is a good description of a good portion of professing Christendom.

Verses 6-10. While the class of people who have the form of godliness and deny its power, make piety a means of gain in earthly things, which is condemned, the apostle speaks of true piety, or as it is called in the Authorized Version, godliness, with contentment as a great gain. True piety, in walking with God, having a good conscience, gives contentment, no matter what earthly circumstances are. A believer who seeks the things above should no longer cling to earthly things, knowing that we brought nothing into the world nor carry anything out. If the eternal things, that promised glory, are ever real before the soul, then each will be content with having the necessary things, food and raiment. And how very true are the words which follow, as not a few have found out. "But they that desire to be rich fall into a temptation and a snare, and many foolish and hurtful lusts, which plunge men into destruction and ruin. For the love of money is the root of every evil; which, while some coveted after, they have wandered from the faith and pierced themselves with many sorrows." Money itself is not evil, but the love of it is the fearful thing. No further comment is needed on these words. Examples of this evil are all about us in the professing church, and "lovers of money" and "lovers of pleasure more than lovers of God" are constantly increasing. Surely they heap treasure together for the last days. Weeping and wailing will follow (James 5:3).

Verses 11-21. The man of God is to flee these things. If he does not it will rob him of his good conscience, his true piety and contentment. The thing to be coveted for the child of God, who belongs to the house of God, is not money, but righteousness, godliness, faith, love, patience, meekness. To covet this is to be the daily business of a Christian. While the believer has to turn his back upon the world and its filthy lucre, he is also to fight the good fight of the faith, and to lay hold on eternal life. This life is, as we have seen from the Gospel of John, a personal possession. It does therefore not mean the obtaining of eternal life; that is the gift of God. It must be laid hold on in faith, entered into and enjoyed. Many possess eternal life, but a practical laying hold on all that it implies and that is connected with it, is what they need. Timothy, in this respect, had confessed a good confession before many witnesses. Once more the charge before God, the Creator-God, who preserveth all things, and before Christ Jesus, the great and faithful Witness, to keep all spotless and irreproachable until His appearing.

The Lord Jesus is coming again. Note what is said of that coming, "which (His appearing) in its own time the blessed and only Ruler shall show, the King of those that reign, and Lord of those that exercise lordship; who only has immortality, dwelling in unapproachable light; whom no man has seen, nor is able to see; to whom be honor and eternal might. Amen" (J. N. Darby's translation). Those who deny the immortality of the human soul and who teach that man has no longer endless being, but dies like the beast, use the words that God "only has immortality" as their star-text, to affirm their error. God only hath immortality in Himself; it is His essential possession. He is the Source of it. The statement does not teach that man has not immortality, but that God only hath immortality in His Being; man has received it from Him.

We but quote the final exhortations. "Charge those that are rich in this present age not to be high-minded, nor trust in uncertain riches, but in the living God (the Creator and Preserver of all) who giveth us richly all things to enjoy; that they do good, that they be rich in good works, ready to distribute, willing to communicate; laying up in store for themselves a good foundation against the time to come, that they may lay hold on eternal life." And then another warning against the errors: "O Timothy, keep that which is committed unto thy trust, avoiding profane and vain babblings, and opposition of science falsely so-called, which some professing have erred concerning the faith" (Gnosticism—and its Satanic offspring, "Christian Science" so-called).

THE SECOND EPISTLE TO

TIMOTHY

Introduction

This is the last Epistle the Apostle Paul wrote. He was once more imprisoned in Rome, and shortly before his martyrdom he wrote this second letter to Timothy. His movements between his first and second imprisonment may be traced as follows: After having written his first Epistle to Timothy he returned to Ephesus, as he intended, by way of Troas. Then he left the books he mentions (4:13) with Carpus. From Ephesus he went to Crete, and after his return wrote the Epistle to Titus. Next he went by Miletus to Corinth (4:20), and from there to Nicopolis (Titus 3:12) and then on to Rome. If he visited Spain, as tradition claims, it must have been immediately after his release.

Timothy was evidently still in Ephesus, obedient to the charge of the Apostle delivered to him in the first Epistle. That Timothy must have been in Ephesus when he received this second letter may be learned from the persons mentioned in this Epistle. Onesiphorus is mentioned in chapter 1:16-18 as having sought out the apostle in Rome, and also having ministered to him at Ephesus. In chapter 4:19 Paul sends greetings to the household of Onesiphorus, and they lived in Ephesus. Priscilla and Aquila are also saluted, and they lived generally in that city. Hymenaeus is stigmatized as a teacher of false doctrine (2:17). There can be no doubt that he is the same person mentioned in 1 Timothy 1:20. And so is Alexander the coppersmith another evil teacher whose residence was also in that city.

The Object of the Epistle

The Apostle knew that the martyr's death was soon to be his lot. He has a great and deep desire to see his beloved Timothy once more. He therefore wrote him to that effect, "greatly desiring to see thee, being mindful of thy tears, that I may be filled with joy" (1:4). "Do thy diligence and come before winter" (4:9, 11, 21). Being uncertain how it might be with himself, whether he should live or be offered up before his arrival, he wrote this letter with his final warnings, exhortations and instructions.

The Contrast

There is a marked difference between this second Epistle and the first. In the first Epistle the house of God, the Church, is seen in order, and the fullest instructions are given how this order in all godliness is to be maintained. The house as such is no longer mentioned in the second Epistle, though we read of "a great house" in which are vessels to honor and some to dishonor; the believer is urged to purge himself from the vessels of dishonor. The professing church is foreshadowed as becoming now a great house; as the little mustard seed became a big tree, sheltering in its branches the fowls under heaven. And this great house no longer manifests the order as laid down in the first Epistle. It has become dilapidated and is in disorder. What has happened in the history of the Church is foreseen in this Epistle, in fact the beginning of it was even then noticeable when Paul wrote this last Epistle. Paul had to see before his departure the beginning of the ruin of that which as a master workman he had been used to build, and over which he watched so faithfully. He had labored more than all the other apostles, and now he had to be a witness of the decline of that which he had loved so much; departure from the faith he had preached, and with it corruption set in. The power of God had been at work and he was the channel of that power, but man fails in it.

Because the professing church, the house of God, is anticipated in its failure and disorder, not a word is said of elders and deacons. Nor is there a promise made, nor instruction given, about a recovery from these conditions. They continue to the end of the age. It is true revivals, partial recoveries there have been, but only to show that man fails again after each renewed action of the Holy Spirit. It goes from bad to worse in the professing church, till the hour strikes when the Lord takes His faithful remnant, the true Church, out of the great house (1 Thess. 4:13-18). What happens then to the great Babylon-house is written in Revelation 18:2. The house completely abandoned by the restraining Spirit becomes "the habitation of demons and the hold of every foul spirit, and a cage of every unclean and hateful bird."

Paul before his departure is alone. It is a mournful record—"all they in Asia are turned away from me"; "Demas has forsaken me, having loved this present age"; "only Luke is with me." It also foreshadows the position of the individual believer in the midst of disorder and confusion. The sure foundation of the Lord abides forever, and as we shall learn from our brief annotations, the individual believer under these conditions is to be faithful and maintain the true testimony for the Lord.

The Division of Second Timothy

The opening chapter contains the loving greeting of the apostle, and exhortations to faithfulness, especially to hold fast the form of sound words which Timothy had heard from Paul. Then follow other exhortations to be strong, to endure hardness, to strive lawfully, to labor, to consider and to remember. It is the conflict which the true servant has in the world, in which he is to be as a good soldier of Jesus. This is followed by a description of the departure from the faith, and the path the believer is to follow. In the third chapter the last days are prominently brought into view by the Spirit of God, and all that these days mean in the manifestation of evil. The fourth chapter contains the final words of the apostle; faithful to the end, and the Lord's faithfulness to him.

I. **PAUL'S PERSONAL WORD TO TIMOTHY** (1)

II. **FAITH'S CONFLICT AND THE BELIEVER'S PATH** (2)

III. **THE LAST DAYS AND THEIR PERILS** (3)

IV. **THE LAST WORDS OF THE APOSTLE** (4)

Analysis and Annotations

I. Paul's Personal Word to Timothy

CHAPTER 1

1. Paul's affectionate words and confidence (1:1-5)
2. Difficulties and assurance (1:6-12)
3. Holding the form of sound words (1:13-14)
4. Turning away and faithfulness in contrast (1:15-18)

Verses 1-5. Paul speaks in this last Epistle as an apostle of Christ Jesus, by the will of God "according to the promise of life which is in Christ Jesus." It is a blessed word and shows how the prisoner in Rome, facing now the martyr's death, had full assurance that all was well. He knew that he was in the hands of God. The promise of life in Christ Jesus was his portion; he possessed that life in Him who ever liveth. Again he addressed Timothy as his beloved son (1 Tim. 1:2) with the greeting of grace, from which all blessings flow, mercy, so constantly needed by all His own, and peace, which his people know and enjoy, who look to Him alone for grace and mercy. The apostle speaks of the past; he had served God, so had his forefathers, with a pure conscience (Acts 23:1); they had been pious, Godfearing Jews.

This also had been the case with Timothy. There was unfeigned faith in him, which dwelt first in his grandmother, Lois, and in his mother, Eunice. Both Lois, the grandmother, and his own mother, who had a Greek for a husband (Acts 16:1) had trained the child Timothy in the Holy Scriptures (the Old Testament) and he had known them from the earliest childhood (3:15). Therefore when the gospel of Christ was presented to them this unfeigned faith laid hold upon it at once. It was good ground which had been prepared to receive the gospel-seed. Thus it should be in the Christian household. The promise is "Believe on the Lord Jesus Christ and thou shalt be saved and thy house." (Acts 16:31). Unfeigned faith will be produced in the young by instructing them out of the Word of God, for "faith cometh by hearing and hearing by the Word of God" (Rom. 10:17). Without ceasing Paul remembered Timothy in his prayers night and day. He remembered his tears, occasioned no doubt by the second imprisonment. How he desired to see his beloved son to be filled with joy!

Verses 6-12. "Wherefore I put thee in remembrance that thou stir up (stir up in a "flame" or "rekindle") the gift of God, which is in thee by the laying on of my hands." God had used Paul as the instrument in bestowing a gift upon Timothy. This gift needed rekindling. The danger of decline, which began even then to be manifested, is evident by this exhortation. The rekindling of a gift needs constant use of the Word of God and fellowship with the Lord, as well as a prayerful exercise of the gift itself. And the Spirit given of God to minister is not a spirit of fear, or cowardice, fearing men and conditions, but a spirit of power, and of love, and of a sound mind. Therefore he was not to be ashamed of the testimony of our Lord, which men began to reject, nor of him, who was now the prisoner of the Lord. It was Timothy's blessed calling and privilege to be a partaker of the afflictions of the gospel according to the power of God. He was not to shrink from the reproach and difficulties which then set in, but to endure it all, enabled by His gracious power.

The gospel may be rejected and despised, so that the enemy seemingly is victorious, but finally the Lord and His truth will have the complete victory. The believer knows this amidst all present difficulties and discouragements, for God "hath saved us, and called us with an holy calling, not according to our works, but according to His own purpose and grace, which was given us in Christ Jesus, before the world began." (This refers to the first promise in Genesis 3:15, the promise of life, salvation and final victory.) "Before the world began" does not mean eternity, but the time before the dispensations, "the age-times," began. And all is now made manifest by the appearing of our Saviour Jesus Christ, who hath abolished death, and hath brought life and immortality to light through the gospel. The full accomplishment and victory comes when He who abolished death by His death on the cross, and triumphant resurrection, comes again. Paul was the herald of this gospel to all men, to Jews and Gentiles. It was for this he suffered, and he was not ashamed. He knew all he passed through, all reproach, all afflictions, would not leave him ashamed. He knew the Lord and His power. "For I know whom I believed, and am persuaded that He is able to keep that which I have committed unto Him against that day."

"The apostle does not say 'in *what* I have believed,' but *'whom,'* an important difference, which pleases us (as to our confidence) in connection with the person of Christ Himself. The apostle had spoken of the truth, but truth is allied to the person of Christ. He is the truth; and in Him truth has life, has power, is linked with the love which applies it, which maintains it in the heart and the heart by it. 'I know,' says the apostle, '*whom* I have believed,' He had committed his happiness to Christ. In Him was that life in which the apostle participated; in Him, the power that sustained it, and that preserved in heaven the inheritance of glory which was his portion where this life was developed" (J. N. Darby).

Verses 13-14. Next he exhorts Timothy to hold fast the form of sound words. "Hold fast the form of sound words which thou hast heard of me, in faith and love which is in Christ Jesus. That good thing which was committed unto thee keep by the Holy Ghost which dwelleth in us." This is one of the most important exhortations of this Epistle, and of special meaning for all believers who, in these days of departure from the truth, contend earnestly for the faith delivered once for all unto the saints. The expression "the form of sound words" is a strong argument for verbal inspiration. The truth of God is conveyed in the very words of God, and therefore the form in which the truth of God is made known is to be maintained. It is all to be held fast in faith and love, which are in Christ Jesus. It does not mean a certain creed constructed by man, but the whole truth of God as revealed by Him. And whatever good thing is committed unto the believer, in the form of a gift as a member of the body of Christ, must be kept by the energy and power of the Holy Spirit, who dwells in the believer. What we have received, the knowledge of the form of sound words and the gift imparted, must be used. "In proportion as we do not care to communicate to others the 'sound words' which we have received, we shall find their power over our own souls diminish and their sweetness for us also."

Apostasy starts with the giving up of the form of sound words. Critics and other deniers of inspiration speak of the spiritual meaning of the words of the Bible, and, that the Bible contains the Word of God, instead of *is* the Word of God. And that is the starting point of the ever increasing departure from the truth of God in our days, which will soon culminate in the predicted complete apostasy.

Verses 15-18. All in Asia (the province) had heard the Gospel in years gone by from the lips of the apostle. And now the great man of God had to write mournfully: "This thou knowest, that all they which are in Asia be turned away from me; of whom are Phygellus and Hermogenes." It would be wrong to conclude from this that they had turned their backs completely upon Christianity and abandoned the profession of it. Such was not the case. Their faith had become weak and they had withdrawn from the apostle of the Lord Jesus Christ, because he had become a despised prisoner, and with this act they showed likewise that they were departing from the great and blessed doctrines the Apostle had preached unto them. Perhaps some of those in Asia had visited Rome and had repudiated Paul the prisoner. It was an evidence of the spiritual decline which was setting in.

But there was a notable exception. Onesiphorus had also visited Rome and had diligently sought him and found him finally. There were many thousands of prisoners in Roman dungeons, and we may well imagine how day after day Onesiphorus sought for his beloved brother, going from dungeon to dungeon till he had located Paul. What a meeting that must have been! He had ministered to Paul in Ephesus, which was well known to Timothy, and now he was not ashamed to minister unto the prisoner of the Lord. He prays therefore for his house and that he may find mercy of the Lord in that day. The reward for his faithfulness to Paul will be mercy, as everything else is mercy in the believer's life.

(Stange it is that the prayer of the Apostle for the house of Onesiphorus is used as an authority to pray for the dead. The assumption that Onesiphorus had died is incorrect.)

II. Faith's Conflict and the Believer's Path

CHAPTER 2

1. The apostle's charge (2:1-2)
2. As soldier and husbandman (2:3-7)
3. Identification with Christ (2:8-13)
4. Exhortation and warning (2:14-18)
5. The great House (2:19-22)
6. The believer's path (verses 23-26)

Verses 1-2. First we find a charge of the apostle to his spiritual son Timothy. The blessed servant of the Lord knew that he was soon to depart, and therefore he charges Timothy to commit the great truths concerning the Gospel, which he had heard from the lips of the apostle in the presence of many witnesses, to faithful men, who are able to teach others. To the apostle it had been given to complete the Word of God (Col. 1:25). No new revelation is promised through Timothy, but he is charged to communicate the revealed truth to others, who would be chosen by the Lord, as His gifts to the Church, to propagate His truth. This is the only true apostolic succession, not through the church as an organization, nor through certain men who claim ecclesiastical authority, but through those who hold the form of sound words and who minister it to others in the energy of the Spirit of God. Timothy needed for this the strength of the grace that is in Christ Jesus. And so does every servant of Christ.

Verses 3-7. Here the qualities that Timothy ought to possess in order to carry on the work are given by the apostle. As a good soldier of Jesus Christ, warring a spiritual warfare, he must suffer hardships and many privations. He must beware not to be entangled with the affairs of this life. The soldier's calling is to please him who has called him, and all else, comforts and self-indulgence must be sacrificed. The soldier does this to obtain a corruptible crown, how much more then should the soldier of Jesus Christ do this to gain an incorruptible crown!

The Christian is also a laborer, a husbandman. He must labor first in order to enjoy fully the fruit of his labor. And that requires patience. He urges Timothy to consider what he tells him, with the assurance that the Lord would give him understanding in all things. These are the practical conditions for all who are engaging in service—enduring hardship, self-denial, unentangled, separated from the world and its ways, fighting lawfully and laboring first to be partaker of the fruits.

Verses 8-13. In connection with this he was to remember "that Jesus Christ of the seed of David was raised from among the dead" according to the gospel, which he calls "my gospel"—"wherein I suffer as an evildoer, even unto bonds; but the Word of God is not bound." Christ suffered, and though He is of the seed of David and has the promises of David's throne, yet it is not yet His; He waits patiently for it upon the Father's throne. In the meantime He, raised from among the dead (the seal upon His blessed work), has given His gospel of grace and glory to be preached. And suffering is connected with this (Phil. 3:10; Col. 1:24).

"The afflictions found in the path of service in the gospel assume here a high and peculiar character in the mind of the suffering and blessed apostle. It is participation in the sufferings of Christ, and, in the case of Paul, to a very remarkable degree. The expressions he uses are such as might be employed in speaking of Christ Himself as regards His love. As to the propitiation, naturally no other could take part in that: but in devotedness, and in suffering for love and for righteousness, we have the privilege of suffering with Him. And here what part had the apostle with these sufferings? 'I endure,' He says, 'all things for the elect's sake.' This is truly what the Lord did. The apostle trod closely on His footsteps, and with the same purpose of love—'that they might obtain the salvation which is in Christ Jesus, with eternal glory,' Here of course the apostle has to add, 'which is in Christ Jesus'; still, the language is marvellous in the lips of any other person than the Lord Himself. For it is what Christ did."

The servant is identified with his Lord and called upon to go in the same path. "It is a faithful saying, for if we died with Him, we shall also live with Him." While this is true positionally of all believers, all have died in Christ and live in Him, the meaning here is the practical manifestation of it in self-denial and suffering with Him. If we suffer and endure we shall also reign with Him. And if any deny Him He will also deny them before His judgment seat (Matt. 10:33). These are solemn words little heeded in our days of laxity and declension. "If we are unfaithful, yet He abideth faithful; He cannot deny Himself," that is, His own nature. "The One we serve must of necessity be served according to the reality of what He is. The Righteous One must be served in righteousness; the Holy One, in holiness; the One who is not of the world, by those who seek no place in the world. We cannot make Christ other than He is, and we cannot make the world other than it is" *(Numerical Bible).*

Verses 14-18. These things he was to remember. And if they are remembered they will bring deliverance from the strife about words, vain and unessential disputations in which there is no profit, which only subvert the hearers. It is through disputes about words, and speculations, that Satan brings in his most subtle deceptions. The true way is to strive diligently to show oneself approved of God, a workman that needeth not to be ashamed, "rightly dividing the Word of truth." What a havoc has been wrought by a wrong dividing of the Word of truth! Law and grace have been jumbled together, Israel robbed of her promises, and the church impoverished on account of it. The Word of God and the truth of God have suffered most from the hands of such unskilled workmen, who, not dividing the Word of truth rightly, have produced confusion worse confounded. The sad division of Christendom, a carnally minded, professing church, is the fruit of it, and much else. The whole truth of God has been obscured, and unbelief fostered by it. To insist upon "rightly dividing the Word of truth" and to practice it both in teaching and living is a most essential requirement of the true workman.

Profane and vain babblings are to be avoided, for they only produce ungodliness. Hymenaeus and Philetus, who held that the resurrection had taken place already and thereby overthrew the faith of some, were examples of it. How true it is that error is like a gangrene, spreading vileness and corruption everywhere.

Verses 19-22. But in the midst of the declension and perversion of the truth of God, as it began in apostolic days, and is now more fully developed in our own times, there is the foundation of God, which stands firm and unmovable. Christ is the foundation of faith, and of His church. There is a double seal. "The Lord knoweth them that are His"—this is the divine side. This statement is given for the comfort of His own, and it is a most precious comfort, "the Lord knoweth them that are His." But this comforting assurance must lead us into communion with Himself. If He knoweth us as His own, we also know Him and delight ourselves in His fellowship. And so we also know in the days of decline and departure from the truth, that the Lord knows and keeps those who belong to Him. But there is also another side, "Let every one that nameth the name of the Lord depart from iniquity." This is the solemn responsibility of every one who nameth that blessed Name, which is above every name. This is the true evidence that we walk in real fellowship with Him, that He knows us and we know Him.

The great house of which Paul speaks is Christendom. It contains vessels of gold and silver, and vessels of wood and earth, some to honor and some to dishonor. Here we have the two classes found in the professing church, those who are really the Lord's, known of Him, who know Him, who walk in His fellowship and witness to it by departing from iniquity; and the other class, which merely profess His name, who have the outward form of godliness, but deny the power thereof; more fully described in chapter 3:1-5. If the true believer is to be a vessel fit for the Master's use he must purge himself individually from such. This is demanded again by the apostle when in the above passage, describing the moral character of these vessels to dishonor, vessels of wood and earth, he writes, "from such turn away." This is the solemn responsibility of every true believer; he is not to be in fellowship with such, and when obedient to this call the believer becomes a sanctified vessel, a vessel set apart, separated, and then as such a fit vessel for the Master's use and prepared unto every good work.

The whole of that which calls itself "Christian" is looked at here as a great house. The Christian is of it outwardly, in spite of himself; for he calls himself a Christian, and the great house is all that calls itself Christian. But he cleanses himself personally from every vessel which is not to the Lord's honor. This is the rule of Christian faithfulness; and thus personally cleansed from fellowship with evil, he shall be a vessel unto honor fit for the Master's use. Whatsoever is contrary to the honor of Christ, in those who bear His Name, is that form which he is to separate himself.

By purging himself from all those who are unto dishonor, the servant of God shall be unto honor, sanctified and prepared for every good work. For this separation from evil is not merely negative; it is the effect of the realization of the word of God in the heart. I then understand what the holiness of God is, His rights over my heart, the incompatibility of His nature with evil. I feel that I dwell in Him and He in me; that Christ must be honored at all costs; that that which is like Him alone honors Him; that His nature and His rights over me are the only rule of my life. That which thus separates me unto Him, and according to what He is, separates me thereby from evil. One cannot walk with those who dishonor Him, and, at the same time, honor Him in one's own walk *(Synopsis of the Bible).*

Verses 22-26. Exhortations follow pointing out the way the servant of Christ is to walk and serve as a vessel unto honor, and fit for the Master's use. He is to flee youthful lusts and follow righteousness, faith, love and peace, in true fellowship with all who call on the Lord out of a pure heart. His service, under the direction of the Lord, must be among those who are destitute of the truth and who are ensnared by the devil, though they profess to be religious. The servant of the Lord has a solemn responsibility towards such. How he is to act in this service is given in verses 24-26. And blessed are those servants who, walking in true separation, reach out for the unsaved masses of professing Christendom and labor in love in the great house.

III. The Last Days and Their Perils

CHAPTER 3

1. The characteristics of the last days (3:1-7)
2. What the last days mean for the true believer (3:8-17)
3. The need of the Word of God (3:14-17)

Verses 1-7. Little comment is needed on these words. They are a prophecy. The apostle by the Spirit of God reveals what shall come in the last days. It is a description of the moral qualities in the vast number of professing Christians of the last days, "who have the form of godliness," that is, go "to church," profess a creed of some sect, and are outwardly religious, "but deny the power thereof." Three times they are shown to be lovers. "Lovers of themselves"—they live for themselves and know nothing of self-denial, they live and walk in the flesh. "Lovers of money"—this is what the word covetous means. Greed controls their activities so that they can enjoy themselves and live luxuriantly and in pleasure. And therefore "they are lovers of pleasure more than lovers of God."

The same class is mentioned in Phil. 3, they are the enemies of the cross of Christ, minding earthly things. Their end is destruction. Compare verses 1-4 with the last verses of the first chapter in Romans. There the characteristics, morally, of heathendom are given, and here the characteristics of the professing masses of nominal Christendom. There is no difference between the two, only the condemnation of the profession, the unsaved, religious element in Christendom is greater. There is no need to point out how this prophecy given by the aged apostle has come true. We live in the midst of these conditions, and are surrounded by them on all sides. Evil teachers began in apostolic days to creep into houses, winding about silently like a serpent, and captured silly women laden with sins, led away with divers lusts. How much more true this is to-day.

Verses 8-13. What true believers may expect in the closing days of this age, if they walk in separation and are faithful in their testimony, is the theme of these verses. Jannes and Jambres were the Egyptian sorcerers who withstood Moses. Jewish tradition gives the information that the magicians of Ex. 7:11-22 bore these names. The Spirit of God assures us here that this is correct. Another Jewish tradition claims that they were the sons of Balaam. They worked by imitations. They produced by Satanic powers certain miracles which were imitations of God's power. Such is the case in our own days. Christian Science, Spiritism and other systems are the sphere where Satan's power of imitation is manifested. Satan also imitates in a still more subtle way the work of the Holy Spirit. All this will work on till finally (after the Church has been called away) the times are reached as prophetically described in 2 Thess. 2:3-12. And like the folly and wickedness of Jannes and Jambres were manifest, so will these deceivers and perverters of the truth be uncovered. This will be when the Lord comes.

How happy in the Lord Paul must have been that he could point to himself as an example. The grace of God had enabled him to be all he writes to his beloved son Timothy. "But thou hast fully known my doctrine, manner of life, purpose, faith, long suffering, charity, patience, persecutions, afflictions, which came unto me at Antioch, at Iconium, at Lystra; what persecutions I endured; but out of them all the Lord delivered me." Paul endured persecutions because he was a faithful minister of the Lord Jesus Christ and did not shun to declare the whole counsel of God. "Yea, and all that will live godly in Christ Jesus shall suffer persecution." If the believer is true to the Lord, if he lives in separation, the world, and especially that which is called "the religious world," with its unscriptural aims and endeavors, will not applaud him, but he will have to bear the reproach of Christ and suffer persecution. Why do so few Christians suffer persecutions? Because they have not purged themselves from the vessels unto dishonor, and are consequently yoked with unbelievers.

"But evil men and seducers (juggling impostors) shall wax worse, deceiving, and being deceived." Things morally and religiously are therefore not getting better in this age. There is no hope apart from the coming of our Lord.

Verses 14-17. The inspired Scriptures of God are the need, the supreme need of the believer in the last days. Timothy had known the sacred Scriptures (the Old Testament) from a child, and of these Scriptures Paul writes, "they are able to make thee wise unto salvation, through faith that is in Christ Jesus." He exhorts him therefore, "Abide thou in the things which thou hast learned, and of which thou hast been assured, knowing of whom thou hast learned them." Then the assuring statement of the Holy Spirit, the author of the Scriptures, that all Scripture is inspired of God. It is well known that the revised version has dropped the "is," so that it reads "every Scripture given by inspiration of God." We do not accept this, for it opens the way to deny that parts of the Scriptures are given by inspiration of God.

"We are told we have to read as, 'Every Scripture inspired of God,' as if it distinguished such from other Scriptures side by side with them, and therefore we had to distinguish in like manner. At once the human mind is set in supremacy over the Scripture, and we become judges of it instead of its judging us. But the apostle has been already pointing out the sacred Scriptures of which he is speaking when he says 'all Scripture.' Nothing is Scripture in the sense he uses the word except that which is in the sacred Scriptures, and nothing that is in them is without that inspiration of God which makes it 'profitable for doctrine, for conviction, or instruction in righteousness' " *(Numerical Bible).*

How important it is to hold fast the great truth that the Bible is the Word of God, and therefore "God-breathed." All apostasy starts with the denial of this fact. The Scriptures are the permanent expression of the mind and will of God. It is not merely that the truth is given in them by inspiration, but they are inspired. They are the expression of His own thoughts. They are our only authority. Upon the constant use of them depends everything. Without adhering to the Scriptures and being obedient to them, we also would be swept along by the current of apostasy. They are the one thing profitable. Note the order: Profitable for doctrine, which we get alone from the Word of God, and which is the foundation of everything. Then follows "reproof" or conviction, and that is followed by correction and instruction for righteousness. It starts with the doctrine and leads, after conviction and correction, to righteousness. And then the man of God, obedient to the Scriptures in all things, is perfect, thoroughly furnished unto every good work.

IV. The Last Words of the Apostle

CHAPTER 4

1. The last charge (4:1-5)
2. His last testimony (4:6-8)
3. The last personal messages (4:9-22)

Verses 1-5. This last chapter is a most impressive one. It is the farewell of this great man of God. Joy and sorrow, confidence and love breathe in his final charge and message. "The sorrow that he might have in his soul was only for those he was leaving, and even that is almost swallowed up in the joyful consciousness of the thought with whom he was leaving them." And so he delivers one more charge, and that solemnly before God and the Lord Jesus Christ, who is about to judge the living and the dead, and by His appearing and His kingdom. He is as a servant to keep the coming of the Lord, His appearing and His kingdom before his heart.

"The apostle urges this upon Timothy as what would, amid all the difficulties of the way, be his strength and assurance. It is always according to Scripture, 'yet, but a little while, and He that will come shall come, and shall not tarry.' We look back and see how long it has been, and we take this to make the distance behind us put distance into that which is before us. The apostle's way for us would be rather that we should say, 'The night is far spent, and the day is at hand.' We may, after all, go to the Lord before He comes to us, but we shall not have missed the good of having been in the meanwhile 'like unto men that wait for their Lord.' The whole character of our Christianity will be affected by our 'holding fast,' or practically losing sight of His coming, as our constant expectation" *(Numerical Bible).*

With the thought of the coming of the Lord before his soul, Timothy is charged to preach the Word at all times. The blessed hope gives energy to continue in the ministry of the Word. Preach the Word! The Word, all the Word of God, the gospel and dispensational truth, is needed in the days when sound doctrine is no longer endured. And how all has come to pass! As the Apostle testified even so it is today. Sound doctrine no longer endured, "after their own lusts they heap to themselves teachers, having an itching ear." They care nothing for the message of God, but have man's person in admiration (Jude). They admire the teacher, his great swelling words (Jude). And the teachers and preachers are men-pleasers. And as a result of this their ears are turned away from the truth and are turned to fables, such as evolution, higher criticism, Christian Science and other delusions. In the midst of all this departure from the truth of God, the Lord still maintains His testimony through those who keep His Word and who do not deny His Name (Rev. 3:8).

Verses 6-8. The martyr's death now looms up, and he pens the never-to-be-forgotten words of faithfulness and assurance of the crown of righteousness. "For I am already being offered, and the time of my departure is come. I have fought the good fight, I have finished the course, I have kept the faith. Henceforth there is laid up for me the crown of righteousness which the Lord, the righteous judge, shall give me at that day; and not only to me, but also to all that love His appearing." Upon the incorrect translation of the Authorized Version "I am now ready to be offered" has been founded that strange theory that the apostle was now ready to die, and had at last the assurance that he was worthy of being a participant in the first resurrection. (See annotations on Philemon 3.) The apostle from the moment he had trusted in Christ had the fullest assurance that he belonged to Christ and was His co-heir; and so every believer knows that he is fitted for glory, not by what he does, or what he has suffered, but through grace alone. To teach that the Apostle Paul received his assurance that he would share the glory of Christ in resurrection, after, and as the result, of, his prolonged suffering, is pernicious, inasmuch as it denies all the great revelations in his Epistles concerning the standing of the believer in Christ. But he did not say he was ready; his words are, "For I am already being offered, and the time of my departure is come." Knowing the time of his departure, in which he would have fellowship with His sufferings and be made conformable unto His death (Phil. 3:10), his heart contemplated in joyful expectation the moment when he would depart to be with Christ. In this sense he was being already offered, having his heart set upon the early departure to be with His Lord. He had fought the good fight, finished the course and kept the faith. He had been faithful in all things and resisted the attacks of the enemy.

And now he looks forward to the reward. He knew that there is laid up for him the crown of righteousness. He does not say that this crown would be bestowed upon him immediately after he left the earthly tabernacle. He will receive it from the righteous Judge in that day, and that day has not yet come. At the same time "all that love His appearing" will receive the rewards. The Lord will come for His saints, as it is promised in the Word of God, and take them to Himself, and the kingdom which follows the rewards for faithful service will be enjoyed. To be in that glory with the Lord, in the Father's house is the blessed destiny of all who have accepted the Lord Jesus Christ, and who are accepted in the Beloved. No service can secure that destiny. The grace of God puts it on our side. Faithful service will be rewarded in the kingdom. How great the reward that awaits the Apostle Paul in that day! May it be an incentive to all His people to labor on, to spend and be spent.

Verses 9-22. And now the last message of the apostle. How he would have loved to have his beloved Timothy at his side and look into his face once more! "Do thy diligence to come shortly unto me." And once more at the close of the letter he writes, "Do thy diligence to come before winter." It was the cry of deepest affection of one who was deserted by others and yet not a lonely man, for the Lord was with him. Demas, a fellow worker and with Paul in his first imprisonment (Philemon 24; Col. 4:14), perhaps a Thessalonian, had forsaken the prisoner of the Lord. It is a mournful record, "having loved the present age, and is departed unto Thessalonica." It is wrong to conclude from this that Demas ceased to be a Christian and had renounced the name of the Lord. He, with love for the present age in his soul, would avoid the cross and its shame, and therefore abandoned Paul. What became of Demas? What was his after-history? The Lord alone knows this.

And Crescens had also gone away to Galatia. We know nothing else of him. Titus went to Dalmatia. It is supposed that Titus joined Paul at Nicopolis (Tit. 3:12) and accompanied him to Rome, and then went to Dalmatia to preach the gospel there. Only Luke, the beloved physician, remained with him, and no doubt he ministered in every way to the comfort of Paul. Then Mark is mentioned. It is the same John Mark mentioned in Acts 13:5 and 15:36-41. For a time after his failure in service Mark was unprofitable. His restoration had taken place, accomplished by the grace of God, and therefore the apostle desires to have him again at his side, "for he is profitable to me for the ministry." And this John Mark became the chosen instrument to write the gospel record which bears his name, in which the Spirit of God describes so blessedly the Servant of all, who never failed.

Tychicus he had sent to Ephesus. Winter approaching he feels the need of the cloak which he had left with Carpus in Troas. We see that he paid attention even to so small a matter, and that as to his earthly possessions he was poor. He also wants the books, but especially the parchments. He had opportunity as a prisoner to read and study. We do not know what these books and parchments were.

And then the sad record of Alexander the coppersmith. He warns Timothy against him, for he had done him much evil. It must be the same Alexander mentioned in 1 Tim. 1:20. It may be possible that this man became incited against Paul on account of having mentioned his name in the first Epistle, and that he persecuted him for it. "The Lord will reward him according to his works." This is according to God's righteousness. At the time of the apostle's first defence no one took his part, by standing by him; all forsook him. They left him alone and had not the courage to defend him. Beautiful is his prayer, "that it may not be laid to their charge."

But while all men had forsaken him, one had not forsaken His faithful servant. True to His promise, "I will not leave nor forsake thee," He had stood with Paul and strengthened him. And when he stood before the Roman authorities the Lord had given him another opportunity to proclaim the Gospel he loved so well, "that through me the preaching might be fully known, and all the Gentiles might hear: and I was delivered out of the mouth of the lion."

And then in simple confidence he counted on the help of the Lord to the end. "And the Lord shall deliver me from every evil work, and will preserve me unto His heavenly kingdom: to whom be glory forever and ever. Amen."

He sends his last greetings to his dearest friends and old companions, Prisca and Aquila and to the house of Onesiphorus. Erastus had remained in Corinth, where he was treasurer (Rom. 16:23). The Ephesian brother Trophimus (Acts 20:4; 21:29) he had left sick in Miletus. Then the final greetings and the last works of his inspired pen, "The Lord Jesus Christ be with thy spirit. Grace be with you."

"It is evident that this Epistle was written when the apostle thought his departure near at hand, and when the faith of Christians had grievously declined, which was proved by their having forsaken the apostle. His faith was sustained by grace. He did not hide from himself that all was going wrong: his heart felt it—was broken by it; he saw that it would grow worse and worse. But his own testimony stood firm; he was strong for the Lord through grace. The strength of the Lord was with him to confess Christ, and to exhort Timothy to so much the more diligent and devoted an exercise of his ministry, because the days were evil.

"This is very important. If we love the Lord, if we feel what He is to the assembly, we feel that in the latter all is in ruin. Personal courage is not weakened, for the Lord remains ever the same, faithful, and using His power for us: if not in the assembly which rejects it, it is in those who stand fast that He will exercise His power according to the individual need created by this state of things" *(Synopsis of the Bible).*

THE EPISTLE TO
TITUS

Introduction

Titus, to whom this Epistle is addressed, was a Greek convert of the apostle (Titus 1:4; Gal. 2:3). We have little knowledge of him. From the Epistle to the Galatians we know that he accompanied Paul and Barnabas in their journey to Jerusalem to attend the council in which the question of the relation of believing Gentiles to the law was decided (Acts 15). From the Second Epistle to the Corinthians we learn that Paul sent him to Corinth to gather the collection (2 Cor. 8:1-6) and that he discharged the duty in a zealous way. "But thanks be to God, who put the same earnest care into the heart of Titus for you. For indeed he accepted the exhortation; but being more forward, of his own accord he went unto you" (2 Cor. 8:16-17). Paul also stated in the Second Corinthian Epistle that he had no rest when he did not find Titus (2 Cor. 2:13), but when he came Paul was greatly comforted. "Nevertheless God, who comforteth those who are cast down, comforted us by the coming of Titus" (2 Cor. 7:6). The Epistle shows that he was in the island of Crete. Paul visited this island in company with Titus, leaving him there. Titus probably did not stay long in Crete, for Paul asked that he should meet him at Nicopolis (3:12). This is all that can be said on the person of Titus.

The contents of this Epistle are of the same nature as the Epistles to Timothy, though the departure from the faith so prominent in the Epistles to Timothy is less prominent in this Epistle. That the truth must be after, or according to, godliness is especially emphasized; the truth must be manifested in a godly walk.

The Division of the Epistle to Titus

The Epistle contains practical instructions. We make three divisions.

I. INSTRUCTIONS AND WARNINGS (1)

II. THINGS WHICH BECOME SOUND DOCTRINE (2)

III. IN RELATION TO THE WORLD AND FALSE TEACHERS (3)

Analysis and Annotations

I. Instructions and Warnings

CHAPTER 1

1. The salutation (1:1-4)
2. Instructions concerning elders (1:5-9)
3. Warnings against false teachers (1:10-16)

Verses 1-4. Paul calls himself in writing to Titus "a servant of God and an apostle of Jesus Christ," for he speaks in these introductory words of God's elect, and their faith in Him; and the promise of eternal life, God, who cannot lie, gave before the dispensations began; and that His Word is now manifested through preaching which was committed unto him by our Saviour-God. God's elect are those who have trusted in Christ. They have personal faith in God and know His love and are in relationship with Him. But such a faith and relationship demands godliness; therefore the statement, "The acknowledgment of the truth which is after godliness." These two, truth and godliness, belong together. If the truth is given up or not held, then godliness also is given up; the truth must be manifested in godliness. As to statement on the promise of life before the ages began, see annotations on 2 Tim. 1:9.

Verses 5-9. Paul had left Titus in Crete. From Acts 2:11 we learn that the inhabitants of Crete were present on the day of Pentecost and heard Peter preach. These Cretan Jews may have brought the gospel to the island. Titus is commissioned by Paul to set the things in order which were wanting, and to appoint elders in every city. (For discussion that bishops are elders see annotations on 1 Timothy 3.) We do not find the same intimacy between him and Titus as that intimacy and confidence which existed between Paul and Timothy. He does not open his heart to him as he did to Timothy. He invests Titus with authority to appoint elders and states the qualifications the elder must possess. These qualifications are also mentioned in the First Epistle to Timothy (1 Tim. 3:1-7). Here is added that their children must be faithful and not accused of riot or of being unruly. The bishop must also be blameless as God's steward, not self-willed (headstrong), not soon angry, not given to wine, no striker, no seeker of filthy lucre. What he is to be is given in verses 8 and 9. "But a lover of hospitality, a lover of good, sober-minded, just, holy, temperate; holding fast the faithful word according to the doctrine taught, that he may be able to exhort with sound doctrine and to convict the gainsayers." Thus we have again that godliness and sound doctrine belong together.

Verses 10-16. He states that there were many unruly and vain talkers and deceivers especially they of the circumcision. The Judaizing teachers were at work among the Cretans. Titus must have been especially distasteful to them, for he was an uncircumcised Greek. These Cretan Jews who claimed to have accepted Christianity worked evil in the assembly. The apostle demands that their mouths must be stopped, for they subverted whole houses, teaching things which they ought not, for the sake of base gain. The national traits of the Cretans are then described. One of their own prophets had said, "The Cretans are always liars, evil beasts, idle gluttons." This is a quotation from Epimenides, who lived six hundred years before Christ. The Cretans were classed with the Cappadocians and Cilicians (all beginnin in the Greek with a "K") as the most evil and corrupt in the Greek world. And Paul testifies to the truth of it, "This witness is true." They must be rebuked sharply, so that they may be sound in the faith, "not giving heed to Jewish fables, and commandments of men, that turn from the truth." These Judaizing teachers were ascetics, forbidding certain things, making rules for the outward conduct. Certain things were forbidden by their ordinances and commandments; yet though they were fasting and continent, they were, because unregenerated, inwardly defiled and unbelieving. Paul brands these Judaizers in this Epistle as "defiled and unbelieving," with a confession that they know God, but in works they denied Him. He speaks of them as abominable, disobedient, and to every good work reprobate.

I. Things Which Become Sound Doctrine

CHAPTER 2

1. Adorning the doctrine of our Saviour-God (2:1-10)
2. The grace of God and its work (2:10-15)

Verses 1-10. "But speak thou the things which become sound doctrine." The sound doctrine or healthful teaching must be accompanied and witnessed to by the right condition of soul, a godly character. The doctrine of God our Saviour must be adorned in all things. Aged men are exhorted to be temperate, grave, sober-minded, sound in faith, in love and in patience. Sound doctrine must of necessity produce such a character. Aged women are to be reverent in demeanor, not slanderers (1 Tim. 3:11) nor to be enslaved by too much wine. In the First Epistle to Timothy deacons are exhorted "not to be given to much wine." Here the exhortation is in the original in a stronger form, for the Cretans were known, and especially the women, for being slaves of strong drink. They are to be teachers of what is good. This is not contradicting 1 Cor. 14:34 and 1 Tim. 2:12. The teaching of the aged woman is here defined. She is to teach young women to be sober, to love their husbands and their children, to be discreet, chaste, busy at home, good, obedient to their own husbands; that the Word of God may not be blasphemed. These are important instructions. They show that the Christian woman's sphere is first of all at home. The disregard of this has more than once wrecked Christian families. This is the great danger in these last days to put women into a place which does not belong to her.

Young men are also to be discreet. Titus who is charged to deliver these exhortations was himself to be a pattern of good works. His example was to confirm his word. In teaching he was to show uncorruptness. Likewise gravity, setting forth the doctrines with dignity and in all seriousness, and sincerity. (What a contrast with certain evangelists and preachers of our day, who act like clowns and make sport of sacred things; instead of teaching the young reverence, they drag down holy things!) "Sound speech that cannot be condemned"—so that those who oppose may be silenced, unable to speak anything evil of the servant of God. When the preacher or teacher does not practise what he preaches it becomes a great detriment to sound doctrine. How great a stumbling block this is!

Servants (slaves) are next exhorted to be obedient to their masters. They were not to forget their place. Though they had been saved and become children of God and heirs of God, their earthly relationship was that of slaves, and as such they were to strive to please their masters in all things, not answering them in contradiction, not purloining but showing all good fidelity, "that they may adorn the doctrine of God our Saviour in all things." Chrysostom said: "The heathen do not judge of the Christian's doctrine from the doctrine, but from his actions and life." The world does the same to-day. And so even slaves in their low estate could bear a witness to the Saviour God by adorning His doctrine.

Verses 10-15. "For the grace of God, bringing salvation for all men, hath appeared, teaching us that, denying ungodliness and worldly lusts, we should live soberly, righteously and godly in the present age, awaiting the blessed hope and appearing of the glory of our great God and Saviour Jesus Christ, who gave Himself for us that He might redeem us from all lawlessness, and purify unto Himself a peculiar people zealous of good works."

This is a blessed and comprehensive statement of the gospel and Christianity. It may be looked upon as embodying all the great apostle taught in his God-revealed gospel, in a practical way. The grace of God hath appeared, and it appeared in the person of His Son, our Lord Jesus Christ. In Him His grace is made known. His finished work is the source of it. It flows from the cross. And this grace comes to man with salvation. It brings salvation, not to a certain class of men, but it brings salvation for all men. Because all men are lost, and therefore in need of salvation, unable to save themselves; the grace of God bringing an unconditional, a perfect and eternal salvation hath appeared, offering that salvation to all. And when this salvation is accepted by faith in the Son of God and the believing sinner is saved by grace, the same grace teaches how to live and walk here below in newness of life.

Grace instructs to renounce all ungodliness and all lusts that find their gratification in this age. But grace does more than that; it supplies the power to do this. It bestows upon the believer a new nature and the Holy Spirit, and walking in the power of all this, the lusts of the flesh are not fulfilled. And renouncing ungodliness and worldly lusts, the believer, saved by grace, is to walk with grace as his guide, instructor and power. That walk as concerning ourselves is to be soberly; as to our fellowmen it is to be righteously; as to God, godly. It teaches something additional. We are to await the blessed hope, "the appearing of the glory of our great God and Saviour Jesus Christ." He who gave Himself for us, to redeem us from all lawlessness,[1] who has purified us unto Himself a peculiar people, He is coming again. He will appear in glory, and grace has given us the blessed promise that we shall be with Him in glory, beholding His glory and sharing it also. And this blessed hope is the most powerful motive for a sober, a righteous and godly walk in this present age.

These things Titus was to speak, to exhort; and also to rebuke with all authority. This is still the calling of every true servant of the Lord Jesus Christ.

III. In Relation to the World and False Teachers

CHAPTER 3

1. Instructions (3:1-8)
2. Warnings (3:9-11)
3. Directions (3:12-15)

Verses 1-8. He asks Titus to remind all believers to be subject to rulers, principalities and powers (Greek: Magistracies and authorities) (Rom. 13:1), to yield obedience and to be ready for every good work. An ancient historian, Diodones Siculus, speaks of the riotous insubordination of the Cretans. They were to speak evil of no man, nor were they to be contentious, but show all gentleness and all meekness towards all men. Our own rights must be yielded, but never the rights of God. If authorities de-

---

[1]With respect to the conduct of Christians towards the world, grace has banished violence, and the spirit of rebellion and resistance which agitates the heart of those who believe not, and which has its source in the self-will that strives to maintain its own rights relatively to others. The Christian has his portion, his inheritance, elsewhere; he is tranquil and submissive here, ready to do good. Even when others are violent and unjust towards him, he bears it in remembrance that once it was no otherwise with himself: a difficult lesson, for violence and injustice stir up the heart; but the thought that it is sin, and that we also were formerly its slaves, produces patience and piety. Grace alone has made the difference, and according to that grace are we to act towards others (*Synopsis of the Bible*).

mand what is against sound doctrine then God must be obeyed more than man. This is indicated by the exhortation "to be ready for every good work." Meekness towards all men is to characterize those who are no longer of the world, but who are still in it. Such meekness towards all, not only towards fellow-believers, but towards all men, adorns the doctrine of our Saviour-God, and is a commendation of the grace of God which offers salvation to all men.

Then follows an additional reason why Christians should be gentle and meek towards all men. "For we ourselves were once foolish, disobedient, deceived, enslaved by divers lusts and pleasures, living in malice and envy, hateful and hating one another." It is a look backward, what they were in their unregenerate condition. These are the true characteristics of man in the flesh. Here is an answer to the question, What is sin? Sin is foolishness, disobedience, deception, slavery to lusts and unsatisfying pleasures, a life of malice, envy and hatred. It is lawlessness. And such is the natural man in all ages. What was true of these Cretans nineteen hundred years ago is true to-day of every unregenerated person.

And then follows a "but." (See Ephes. 2:13.) "But when the kindness and love to man[2] of our Saviour-God appeared, not by works of righteousness which we have done, but according to His mercy He saved us through the washing of regeneration and renewing of the Holy Spirit, which He has shed upon us richly through Jesus Christ our Saviour; that having been justified by His grace, we might be heirs according to the hope of eternal life." For such as the Cretans were, and we all are, the kindness and love of our Saviour-God appeared; and this Saviour-God is Christ Himself, He by whom and for whom all things were created. All who have believed and trusted in the kindness and love of God as manifested in Christ can testify in fullest assurance, "according to His mercy He saved us," and own it likewise that it is "not by works of righteousness which we have done."

And this is accomplished by the washing of regeneration and the renewing of the Holy Spirit. The washing (or bath) of regeneration is the new birth. Of this our Lord spoke to Nicodemus (John 3) and also to His disciples when He washed their feet. "He that is washed (bathed) needeth not save to wash his feet, but is clean every whit; and ye are clean, but not all" (John 13:10). He spoke in these words of the fact that His disciples, except Judas, were born again, and therefore they were clean every whit. The washing has nothing whatever to do with water-baptism; water-baptism cannot save nor help in the salvation of a sinner, nor produce regeneration. What is the renewing of the Holy Spirit? It is distinct from regeneration. The Holy Spirit is the active agent in the new birth; imparts the new nature and then indwells the believer, and as such He does His blessed work by renewing the inward man day by day (2 Cor. 4:16). He is shed upon us richly through Jesus Christ our Saviour, and gives power to all who walk in the Spirit. On the fact that the word "regeneration" is found only once more in the New Testament (Matt. 19:28) the late F. W. Grant made the following interesting comment in connection with this passage.

"The Lord promises to the twelve that 'in the regeneration, when the Son of man shall sit upon the throne of His kingdom,' they also shall 'sit upon twelve thrones, judging the twelve tribes of Israel.' 'The regeneration' is in this passage the millennial state; but thus we may see already the difference between it and the idea of new birth, whatever the connection may be between these. The millennial regeneration is not a new life infused into the world, but it is a new state of things brought about by the new government over it. Thus, the Lord speaks of the throne of the Son of man and of thrones for His disciples. The throne of the world in the hands of the Perfect Ruler is, in fact, what brings about the regeneration. Righteousness now *reigns.* In the new earth it will *dwell;* but in the millennium there is yet neither the full reality; nor, therefore, the full permanence of deliverance from evil. Righteousness reigns, and evil is not suffered any more, but the full blessing waits to be manifested in that which is eternal and not millennial. The subjugation of evil, Christ's foes put under His feet, goes on through the millennium, in different stages, towards completeness. It is the preparation for eternity, but not the eternal state itself.

"It is plain, therefore, that there is a parallel between the stages of God's preparation of the earth for blessing and that of the individual man. The present stage of the earth is that out of which the Christian has been delivered, the state of bondage to corruption, the dominion of sin. The present state of the Christian is that which the earth itself waits for, the time when the power of sin will be broken and righteous-

---

[2]"Love to man" in the Greek is "Philanthropy." Our Lord Jesus Christ is the great Lover of men, Philanthropist, as no human being could ever be.

ness will reign. For us righteousness reigns now, but the conflict with sin is not over. This, in the millennium, will be fully seen at the end, when there is once more the outbreak of evil, Satan being let loose. What follows this is the dissolution of the present heavens and earth and the coming of the new earth, in which dwelleth righteousness, just as the dissolution or the change of the body makes way for the perfect eternal state with us. Thus there is a complete parallel, which we cannot be wrong in accepting as that which will help us with the expression here. 'The washing of regeneration' is the deliverance from the power of sin, which is no more tolerated, but which is not, by any means, wholly removed. 'The renewing of the Holy Spirit' is that which is constantly needed to supplement this, although the word used does not speak of a mere reviving or refreshing constantly, but rather of a change into that which is new—thus, of ways, habits—as the light more and more penetrates, and the word of God manifests more and more its perfection and its power for the soul."

Being then saved according to His mercy by the washing of regeneration and receiving the Holy Spirit and having been justified by His grace, we become also heirs according to the hope of eternal life.

The practical side, godliness in life and walk, is once more connected with these preceding statements of sound doctrine. "This is a faithful saying, and these things I will that thou affirm constantly, that they which have believed in God might be careful to maintain good works. These things are good and profitable unto men."

Verses 9-11. Foolish questions and genealogies, contentions and striving about the law must be avoided, for they are unprofitable and vain. How many of these things are about us! Some are more occupied with the ten lost tribes and their supposed recovery, according to the Anglo-Israel hallucination, than with the grace and glory of God; and others are given to questions of law, like Seventh-day Adventism—that evil system. All these things are indeed unprofitable and vain. The heretic is one who sets up his own opinions and then causes division in the body of Christ. If such a one after a second admonition continues in his ways, he is to be rejected, for he proves that he is self-willed and not subject to the Word of God—"Knowing that he that is such is subverted, and sinneth, being condemned of himself."

Verses 12-15. In the closing directions and greetings Artemas is mentioned first; his name does not occur elsewhere. Tychicus is mentioned in 2 Tim. 4:12. He was sent by Paul to Ephesus; he probably was sent later to Crete to take the place of Titus. Zenas the lawyer and Apollos (Acts 18:24) were travelling companions, and the apostle expresses his loving care and interest in them.

"Observe also that we have the two kinds of laborers: those who were in personal connection with the apostle as fellow-laborers, who accompanied him, and whom he sent elsewhere to continue the work he had begun, when he could no longer carry it on himself; and those who labored freely and independently of him. But there was no jealousy of this double activity. He did not neglect the flock that were dear to him. He was glad that any who were sound in the faith should water the plants which he himself had planted. He encourages Titus to shew them all affection, and to provide whatever they needed in their journey. This thought suggests to him the counsel that follows: namely, that it would be well for Christians to learn how to do useful work in order to supply the wants of others as well as their own" *(Synopsis of the Bible).*

Then the final exhortations, once more "to maintain good works" and his final greeting. "All that are with me salute thee. Greet them that love us in the faith. Grace be with you all."

THE EPISTLE TO

PHILEMON

Introduction

This beautiful little letter addressed by Paul to Philemon does not occupy the right place in the New Testament. It should be put after the Epistle to the Colossians, for it was written at the same time as that Epistle. Tychicus carried from Rome the two Epistles to the Ephesians and Colossians. Onesimus, his travelling companion, received from the prisoner of the Lord this personal letter to Philemon. It was therefore written at the same time as Colossians, during the first imprisonment of the Apostle Paul, about the year 61 or 62. Its genuineness cannot be doubted, though some critics have done so. Dean Alford says: "The internal evidence of the Epistle itself is so decisive for its Pauline origin—the occasion and object of it so simple, and unassignable to any fraudulent intent, that one would imagine the impugner of so many of the Epistles would have at least spared this one, and that in modern times, as in ancient, according to Tertullian and Jerome, *'Sua illam brevitas defendisset.'* " ("Its own brevity would be its defence.") The objections raised against this Epistle we do not need to state nor investigate, for they are pure inventions and do not require an answer.

The occasion and object are both plainly indicated in the Epistle itself. Onesimus, a slave, probably a Phrygian, who were considered the lowest of all, had run away from his master, Philemon, who was a Christian. It is more than probable that he had stolen money from Philemon (verse 18). He was attracted to Rome, the great world-city, thinking perhaps he would be undetected there. What happened to him in Rome and how he came in touch with Paul is not made known in the Epistle. He may have been in dire want and destitution. Perhaps he had heard Paul's name mentioned in his master's house and learning of his presence in Rome as a prisoner, he got in touch with him. This we know, that he heard the gospel preached by the apostle, and believing, he was saved. He then told the apostle his story and Paul sent him back to his master with this precious letter. And Onesimus who returns to Philemon is no longer "unprofitable"; "not now as a servant, but above a servant, a brother beloved" (verse 16).

The Epistle itself shows the sweet and tender character of the great man of God who penned it under the guidance of the Holy Spirit. It has been remarked, "Dignity, generosity, prudence, friendship, affection, politeness, skillful address, purity are apparent. Hence it has been termed with great propriety, 'the polite Epistle.' "

Suggestive are Luther's words on this letter to Philemon: "The Epistle showeth a right noble, lovely example of Christian love. Here we see how St. Paul layeth himself out for the poor Onesimus, and with all his means pleadeth his cause with his master; and so setteth himself, as if he were Onesimus, and had himself done wrong to Philemon. Yet all this doeth he not with power or force, as if he had right thereto; but he strippeth himself of his right, and thus enforceth Philemon to forego his right also. Even as Christ did for us with God the Father, this also doth St. Paul for Onesimus with Philemon; for Christ also stripped Himself of His right, and by love and humility enforced the Father to lay aside His wrath, and to take us to His grace for the sake of Christ, who lovingly pleadeth our cause, and with all His heart layeth Himself out for us. For we are all His Onesimi, to my thinking."

Analysis and Annotations

1. The greeting (1-3)
2. Recognition of Philemon's faith and love (4-7)
3. Concerning the reception of Onesimus (8-21)
4. The conclusion (22-25)

Verses 1-3. He speaks of himself as a prisoner of Christ Jesus; the Lord had made him a prisoner. He addresses Philemon (meaning: friendly, loving), the beloved, and his fellow-laborer. Apphia was probably the wife of Philemon; Archippus is called "fellow soldier"; he ministered in the Colossian assembly (Col. 4:17). Greeting is also extended "to the church" which was gathered in the house of Philemon. While the Epistle is addressed to Philemon personally and Paul appeals to him in behalf of Onesimus, the gathered assembly was equally to be interested in this runaway slave, who was now returning as a brother beloved and therefore to be received by them in Christian fellowship. The Lord had received Onesimus and he had become through grace, a member of the body of Christ; he belonged to the Colossian assembly. Therefore in addressing the Colossians Paul had written of Onesimus as "a faithful and beloved brother, who is one of you" (Col. 4:9).

Verses 4-7. He thanked God for Philemon, making mention of him always in his prayers. He did not know Philemon personally, but had heard of his love and faith toward the Lord Jesus, and toward all saints. And he prayed for him "that the fellowship of the faith may become effectual by the acknowledgment of every good thing that is in us toward Christ Jesus." His faith was to manifest itself still more by exhibiting every good thing which Christians possess to the glory of Christ. With these words of commendation, recognition and encouragement, he opens the way to plead for Onesimus.

Verses 8-21. For this reason, because of love which was in Paul's heart for Philemon, he did not use his authority to enjoin upon him what was meet as to the reception of a good-for-nothing slave, who had been saved by grace and accepted in the Beloved. He beseeches instead, and that "for love's sake"—his love for Philemon and Philemon's love for Onesimus, for he was entitled to this love, being a saint in Christ. And he beseeches, "being such an one as Paul the aged, and now also a prisoner of the Lord." Courteously he repeats "I beseech thee," and then he mentions him who was so dear to his own heart—"I beseech thee for my child, whom I have begotten in my bonds, who in times past was to thee unprofitable, but now profitable to thee and to me." Onesimus (meaning helpful) shows the power of the gospel of Jesus Christ. A miserable, unprofitable slave, a runaway thief, had become a child of God, born again, and the loving servant of the Lord presses him to his bosom, calls him "my child" and speaks of him as being now profitable to him and to Philemon. Oh! the wonders of divine grace.

"Whom I have sent again; thou therefore receive him, that is, mine own bowels. Whom I would have retained with me, that in thy stead he might have ministered unto me in the bonds of the gospel; but without thy mind would I do nothing; that thy benefit should not be as it were of necessity, but willingly." What loving words these are! He gives Philemon to understand that Onesimus had endeared himself in such a way that he was as dear to him as his own heart. He would have liked to retain him and keep him at his side in Rome, for he would have performed all the services for Paul which Philemon would have rendered to him if he were in Rome. But without Philemon's consent he would do nothing, so that his action might not be of necessity, forced by what Paul had done, and not voluntarily.

"For perhaps he therefore departed for a season, that thou shouldest receive him forever; not now as a servant, but above a servant, a brother beloved, specially to me, but how much more unto thee, both in the flesh and in the Lord?" How delicately he expresses it all! He does not speak of Onesimus as having run away, as trying to escape forever from serfdom, but that "he departed for a season." God's providence is beautifully touched upon, when Paul thus states that he perhaps departed for a season (Greek, an hour) so that Philemon might receive him forever, not now as a slave, but above a slave, a brother beloved. And so that Philemon might not take offense at Paul asking him to receive his runaway slave as a brother beloved, he tells Philemon that he is a beloved brother especially to himself—and then how much more to Philemon who had a claim on him.

Human slavery, so universal in apostolic days, so full of misery, is indirectly dealt with in this letter to Philemon. It may be rightly called the first anti-slavery document and petition ever written and presented.

"Paul lays here broad and deep the foundation of a new relation between master and servant, a relation in which, while there is subordination of the one to the other, there is also a common brotherhood to be acknowledged and an equality before God to be maintained. Christianity would melt the fetters from the enslaved by the fervour of its love. Men's method commonly is, to strike them off by armed revolution" (Professor Moorhead).

And he continues, "If thou count me therefore a partner, receive him as myself. If he hath wronged thee, or oweth thee aught, put that on mine account." Verse 17 connects well with verse 12. If Philemon counted Paul as in Christian fellowship, he is to receive Onesimus as if he were Paul, "receive him as myself." Onesimus had probably confessed his theft to Paul, and again he uses the choicest words to approach this delicate matter. He does not call it "theft" outright, but writes "if he hath wronged thee" and that again he softens to "or oweth thee aught," then he declares himself ready to make good the loss and assume the debt in place of the slave Onesimus—"put that on mine account." These five words "put that on mine account" are translated in Rom. 5:13, by the word "impute." How blessedly this illustrates the gospel. Indeed this Epistle to Philemon is a perfect and practical illustration of the gospel of grace, the gospel Paul preached, and which is unfolded in the larger Epistles. What the gospel does for the poor slave of sin, how he becomes a son and a brother, profitable instead of unprofitable, a member of the body of Christ, may be traced in these verses.

He wrote this Epistle, not as he usually did, by an amanuensis, but with his own hand! That shows again what a fine character he was. He had full confidence in Philemon not alone that he would grant him his request, but that he would even do more than he had asked.

We do not know from Scripture what became of Onesimus. According to the "Apostolical Canons" he was emancipated by his master. Another tradition says that he became a servant of the Lord ministering in Macedonia, and that he was martyred in Rome. We shall meet him with all the other saints in glory.

Verses 22-25. Paul during his first imprisonment always anticipated his release; he and others prayed for it (Phile. 22). And so he expects to come to Colosse, and asked Philemon to prepare him a lodging. The salutations from Epaphras, Marcus, Aristarchus, Demas and Lucas, with the word of blessing, conclude the Epistle.

THE EPISTLE TO THE

HEBREWS

Introduction

This Epistle presents many problems. Some refuse to call it an Epistle and look upon it as a treatise, but the leading question is about the author of this document. It is anonymous; the writer has carefully concealed his identity. It is the only portion of the New Testament of which this can be said. What was a possible motive for doing this? We may answer that He who inspired this great message guided the pen of the instrument to put himself out of sight. Dr. Biesenthal, in a very learned work on Hebrews, advances an interesting theory why the writer did not mention himself. He shows that the teaching of Christianity that animal sacrifices, once foreshadowing the great sacrifice and now completely ended and no longer necessary, was being felt in heathendom. In consequence the many sacrifices used in heathen worship at births, marriages and different other occasions were being more and more neglected. The priestly class which lived by these sacrifices and the very large industry of cattle raising was being threatened with utter ruin, on account of which a bitter antagonism was being stirred up against Christianity and its advocates. On account of this, Dr. Biesenthal, concludes, the writer of Hebrews kept his name a secret. Furthermore, this scholarly Hebrew Christian, advancing the strongest arguments for the Pauline authorship, shows additional reason why the Apostle Paul had very valid reasons to keep himself in the background. (This work, "Das Trostschreiben an die Hebraer—The Message of Comfort to the Hebrews," has, as far as we know, never been translated into English.) His heart was filled with such burning love for his Hebrew brethren that he was constrained to send to them a special message of love and entreaty. At the same time he was deeply concerned about those who had believed. Under heathen persecution, as well as through ignorance concerning the full meaning of Christianity, a tendency towards apostasy threatened these Hebrew Christians, especially those who lived in Jerusalem before the destruction of the temple and the Jewish worship. And Paul knowing how he was disliked by the Jews, and how he had been discredited by the Judaizing teachers, whose evil work he had exposed and so severely condemned in the Epistles to the Galatians and Corinthians, feared that if his name was made prominent, the message would at once be discarded. He therefore omitted his name.

The Question of Authorship

The question of authorship of Hebrews is of much interest. Many volumes have been written on it. Origen wrote, "The thoughts are Paul's, but the phraseology and composition are by someone else. Not without reason have the ancient men handed down the Epistle as Paul's, but who wrote the Epistle is known only to God." The question is then, did Paul write Hebrews and if he did not, who wrote this Epistle? Some are very positive that Paul did not write Hebrews, as will be seen by the following statement:

"The only fact clear as to the author is that he was not the Apostle Paul. The early Fathers did not attribute the book to Paul, nor was it until the seventh century that the tendency to do this, derived from Jerome, swelled into an ecclesiastical practice. From the book itself we see that the author must have been a Jew and a Hellenist, familiar with Philo as well as with the Old Testament, a friend of Timothy and well-known to many of those whom he addressed, and not an apostle but decidedly acquainted with apostolic thoughts; and that he not only wrote before the destruction of Jerusalem but apparently himself was never in Palestine. The name of Barnabas, and also that of Priscilla, has been suggested, but in reality all these distinctive marks appear to be found only in Apollos. So that with Luther, and not a few modern scholars, we must either attribute it to him or give up in the quest" (Weymouth).

This is very sweeping, and quite incorrect and superficial. It is not the final word. To follow the controversy in our brief introduction is quite impossible. All that has ever been written on it may be condensed as follows:—1. There is no substantial evidence, external or internal, in favor of any claimant to the authorship of this Epistle, except Paul. 2. There is nothing incompatible with the supposition that Paul was the author of Hebrews. 3. The preponderance of the internal, and all the direct external evidence, go to show that the Epistle was written by Paul. The Pauline authorship can hardly be questioned after the most painstaking research.

Origen's words, that only God knows who wrote this Epistle, has been taken as final by many. But to whom did Origen refer when he said, "not without reason have the ancient men handed down the Epistle as Paul's?" He undoubtedly referred to the Greek Fathers, who, without one exception ascribed this Epistle to Paul. It appears that in no part of the Eastern church the Pauline origin of this Epistle was ever doubted or suspected. The earliest of these testimonies, that Paul wrote Hebrews, is that of Pantaenus, the chief of the catechetical school in Alexandria about the middle of the second century. This witness is found in Eusebius, the church-historian, who quotes Clement of Alexandria that Hebrews was written by Paul originally in the Hebrew language and that Luke translated it into the Greek. Clement of Alexandria was the pupil of Pantaenus and had received this information from him. Pantaenus was a Hebrew Christian and in all probability living only a hundred years after Paul, received what he taught Clement, by tradition. Apart from other similar testimonies that of Pantaenus and Clement is quite sufficient to show that the early church believed Paul to have written Hebrews.

And the internal evidences are overwhelmingly for the Pauline authorship. As to doctrine the parallels with his other Epistles are numerous and some of the peculiarities are also in full harmony with the teaching of the Apostle Paul. The personal allusions are altogether Pauline. These likewise show that Paul is the writer. The writer was a prisoner for he writes, "ye took compassion of me in my bonds" (10:34); and he hopes to be liberated "but I beseech you the rather to do this, that I may be restored to you the sooner" (13:19). Here is the same thought as expressed in Philippians (Phil. 1:25); in Philemon (verse 22). And this prisoner is in Italy for he writes "they of Italy salute you." It was probably written from Rome. The writer also was well acquainted with Timothy whom he mentions in the Epistle (13:23). All these personal words have a decided Pauline stamp.

But some have said that Christ is not mentioned in Hebrews as the head of the body, not a word is said of that union with a risen and glorified Christ, one Spirit with the Lord, that cardinal doctrine so prominent in the great Apostle's testimony. From this omission it has been argued that another than Paul must be the author. But this inference is without foundation. For though Paul alone develops the mystery concerning Christ and the Church, it is only in the Epistles to the Ephesians and Colossians, with the First to the Corinthians practically, and in that to the Romans allusively. In the rest of his Epistles we find "the body" no more than in that to the Hebrews, and this is as distinctly in the ordering of the Holy Spirit, as in those which contain it fully. Each Epistle or other book of Scripture is prepared for the purpose God had in view when He inspired each writer. As the main object is that to the Hebrews in Christ's priesthood with its necessary basis, due adjuncts, and suited results, and as this is for the Saints individually, the one body of Christ could not fall fittingly within its scope, if it were a divinely inspired composition, whether by Paul or by any other. Its central doctrine is, not as one *with Him* as members of His body, but the appearing before the face of God *for us* (William Kelly).

Peter's Significant Statement

At the close of his second Epistle the Apostle Peter wrote "and account that the long suffering of our Lord is salvation, even as our beloved brother Paul also, according to the wisdom given unto him, hath written unto you" (2 Pet. 3:15). Now Peter wrote to those of the circumcision, to believing Hebrews in the dispersion. He does what our Lord commanded him "to strengthen his brethren." And in the above words he speaks of the fact that Paul also wrote unto them. We do not hesitate to give this as an argument of the Pauline authorship of Hebrews. No other Epistle of Paul answers to this statement of Peter. There is but one Epistle addressed to the Hebrews and Peter no doubt meant this Epistle, and he also knew that Paul was the writer. So that this in itself is quite conclusive. As another has said "Where do we find beside the apostle a man who could have written this Epistle? Who beside him would have ventured to write it with such decided apostolic authority? And who had greater reason to write anonymously to Israel than the apostle who loved his people so fervently, and who was so hated by them that they refused to listen to his voice and to read his writings?" (Mallet)

His Last Visit to Jerusalem and this Epistle

It seems to the writer that Paul's last visit to Jerusalem also explains this Epistle. As we learn from the book of Acts, Paul went up to Jerusalem against the repeated warnings given by the Spirit of God. His arrest was the result of having gone into the temple to purify himself with the four men who had a vow on them. This he was asked to do and to show that he walked orderly and kept the law. He did wrong in this. It is true he acted through zeal and love for his brethren; yet he also knew that a believer, be he Jew or Gentile, is dead to the law and that all the ordinances of the law were fulfilled and ended. Yet the Jewish believers in Jerusalem still clung to the law, were zealous for the law, went to the temple and made use of the ordinances. When in Rome as prisoner the Spirit of God moved him to write this letter in which the greater glory and the better things of the new covenant are unfolded with solemn warnings not to be drawn back into Judaism. And at the close of the Epistle the final and important exhortation is given "Let us go forth therefore unto Him without the camp (Judaism), bearing His reproach" (13:13). May not this Epistle have been written in view of Paul's failure in Jerusalem, showing these Jewish-Christians the necessity of separating from the shadow things of the Old covenant?

To Jewish Christians

That this Epistle was addressed to Jews who professed the name of the Lord Jesus is shown by its contents. This fact and their peculiar state must not be lost sight of in the study of this Epistle. We may assume that the Epistle was especially addressed to the Church in Jerusalem. As already stated these Jewish believers were all zealous of the law. They observed the ordinances of the law with great zeal; they went daily into the temple and were obedient to all the ceremonial law demanded of a good Jew. Then there arose a persecution against them. Some of them were stoned and they suffered great affliction and humiliation. The Epistle speaks of this. They were made a gazing stock both by reproach and afflictions; they endured joyfully the spoiling of their goods (10:33-34).

They were being treated in a shameful way by their brethren and looked upon as apostates. They were excluded from the temple worship and the ordinances, unless they abandoned faith in the Lord Jesus Christ and forsook the assembling of themselves.

"We can scarcely realize the piercing sword which thus wounded their inmost heart. That by clinging to the Messiah they were to be severed from Messiah's people was indeed a great and perplexing trial; that for the hope of Israel's glory they were banished from the place which God had chosen, and where the divine presence was revealed, and the symbols and ordinances of His grace had been the joy and strength of their fathers; that they were to be no longer children of the covenant and of the house, but worse than Gentiles, excluded from the outer court, cut off from the commonwealth of Israel,—this was indeed a sore and mysterious trial. Cleaving to the promises made unto their fathers, cherishing the hope in constant prayer that their nation would yet accept the Messiah, it was the severest test to which their faith could be put, when their loyalty to Jesus involved separation from all the sacred rights and privileges of Jerusalem" (A. Saphir).

They were under great pressure. They loved the nation, their divinely given institutions, their traditions and their promised glory. They did not possess the full knowledge of the better things of the new covenant; that they had as believers in Christ, the substance of what the old covenant only foreshadowed. There was grave danger for them to turn back to Judaism and therefore the repeated warnings and exhortations to steadfastness. They needed instructions, teachings, to lead them on to perfection, and they needed comfort in their trying position. Both are abundantly supplied in this Epistle.

The Vision of Christ

Hebrews gives a wonderful vision of the Lord Jesus Christ. He is revealed as the Son of God, and Son of Man; as the heir of all things; higher than the angels. We can trace His path of humiliation to death and what has been accomplished by the death on the cross. All the blessings put on the side of the believer are made known in Hebrews. But above all the great message is the Priesthood of Christ. This is the great center of this sublime Epistle. It is an Epistle of contrasts. There is the contrast between the Lord Jesus Christ and the angels; between Him and Moses, between Him and Aaron, between the Priesthood of Melchisedec and that of Aaron; between the offerings of the old covenant and the one great offering of Christ. This was the supreme need of these Jewish-Christians, to know Christ in all His fullness and glory. This knowledge would make them perfect, steadfast and fill them with comfort. And this is still our need. May the Lord bless us in meditating on this wonderful document.

The Division of the Epistle to the Hebrews

"Commencing in the style of a doctrinal treatise, but constantly interrupted by fervent and affectionate admonitions, warnings, and encouragements, this grand and massive book concludes in the epistolary form, and in the last chapter the inspired author thus characterizes his work: "I beseech you, brethren, suffer the word of exhortation; for I have written a letter unto you in few words."

"We are attracted and riveted by the majestic and sabbatic style of this epistle. Nowhere in the New Testament writings do we meet language of such euphony and rhythm. A peculiar solemnity and anticipation of eternity breathe in these pages. The glow and flow of language, the stateliness and fulness of diction, are but an external manifestation of the marvellous depth and glory of spiritual truth, into which the apostolic author is eager to lead his brethren."

With these well chosen words Adolf Saphir, the Hebrew Christian scholar, begins his exposition of this Epistle.

The division of Hebrews is difficult to make because the different sections of this document often overlap and form a solid unity. It has been well said that "one feels as if he were endeavoring to dissect a living organism when he seeks to sever part from part in this marvellous Scripture."

The Lord Jesus Christ, the promised Messiah, in the fullness of the glory of His Person as the living and eternal realization of Jewish promise and type, is the most blessed theme of this Epistle or treatise. This necessitated the various contrasts in which this document abounds and which we shall point out in the annotations. The glory of Christ, all He is, as well as His sympathy, grace and power as the true high priest who has entered heaven itself, is so fully made known to help, first of all, the weak faith of the Jewish Christians who received this message, that by it they might be established in their heavenly calling and become completely separated from Judaism, which was about to pass away. The two opening chapters introduce the great theme of the Epistle and are the foundation of the doctrine developed. The first chapter reveals the glory of the Person of the Messiah, that He is the Son of God. The second chapter unfolds His glory as the Son of Man. He, who is above the angels, was made a little lower than the angels to suffer and to die. He partook of all sufferings and temptations and is now as the glorified Man in God's presence, crowned with glory and honor, awaiting the time when all things are put under His feet. The fact that He suffered, and was tempted opens the way for the development of the central truth of the Epistle, His priesthood. He is called the Apostle and High Priest and shown to be greater than Moses and Joshua. Then follows the main section of the Epistle, which reveals Him as the true priest who has opened the way into the Holiest, where He is exercising now His priesthood. The contrast is made in this portion (4:14—10) between Him and the priests and sacrifices of the Jewish dispensation. With the eleventh chapter begins the practical instructions and exhortations to walk in faith, to be steadfast and to leave the camp of Judaism. We divide, therefore, this epistle in four sections.

I. **CHRIST, THE SON OF GOD AND HIS GLORY** (1:1—2:4)

II. **CHRIST, THE SON OF MAN, HIS GLORY AND HIS SALVATION** (2:5—4:13)

III. **CHRIST AS PRIEST IN THE HEAVENLY SANCTUARY** (4:14—10)

IV. **PRACTICAL INSTRUCTIONS AND EXHORTATIONS** (11—13)

The analysis which follows shows the different subdivisions, parenthetical sections and contrasts, found in these main sections.

Analysis and Annotations

I. Christ, the Son of God and His Glory

CHAPTER 1—2:4

1. The Son in whom God hath spoken (1:1-4)

2. So much better than the angels (1:5-14)
3. Admonition and warning (2:1-4)

Verses 1-6. Sublime is the beginning of this precious document. God who in many measures and in many ways spake of old to the fathers in the prophets, at the end of these days hath spoken to us in a Son, whom He constituted heir of all things, by whom also He made the worlds; who being the effulgence of His glory and the expression of His substance, and upholding all things by the word of His power, having made (by Himself) purification of sins, sat down on the right hand of the Majesty on high, having become so much better than the angels, as He hath by inheritance a name more excellent than they."

It is an abrupt beginning with no words of introduction, no salutations or words of thanksgiving and prayer. Only one other Epistle begins in a similar way; the First Epistle of John. The foundation upon which all rests, the Word of God, is the first great statement we meet. It tells us that God has spoken of old to the fathers in the prophets. The prophets were not, as so often stated by the deniers of divine inspiration "Jewish patriots and visionaries," but they were the mouthpiece of Jehovah "holy men of God who spake as they were moved by the Holy Spirit" (2 Pet. 1:21). The words they uttered are the words of God. And this is true of Moses, the author of the Pentateuch and of all the other instruments used in the production of the Old Testament scriptures. And He spoke in many measures (or parts) and in many ways, in histories, ordinances, divinely appointed institutions, visions, dreams and direct prophetic utterances, which have a fragmentary character; they are not in themselves complete and final. And therefore we find in this epistle the law, the prophets and the Psalms more frequently quoted than in any other portion of the New Testament.

It is a striking characteristic of Hebrews that the names of the prophets, like Moses, David, Isaiah, etc., are omitted. God is the speaker. He spoke in the prophets concerning Him, who is now fully revealed in His glory, that is His Son, the promised Messiah. Our Lord declared of the Old Testament scriptures "they are they which testify of Me." (John 5:39). Before He ever came into the world He also bore witness of this fact "in the volume of the Book it is written of Me" (Heb. 10:7). God's speaking in the Old Testament culminated in the manifestation of this Person. "At the end of these days hath spoken to us in a (or the) Son." The end of these days is the present dispensation as distinguished from the preceding Jewish dispensation. The words "to us" mean primarily in this epistle the children of the fathers to whom God spake by the prophets. (In a general way it applies, of course, to all believers during this dispensation. The opinion of some that Hebrews, the Epistle of James, the Epistles of Peter have no meaning and no message to the Church is pernicious.) "Jesus Christ was a minister of the circumcision for the truth of God to confirm the promises made unto the fathers" (Rom. 15:8). It was to the Jew first. He came to the lost sheep of the house of Israel and manifested in their midst the power of the kingdom promised to that nation. The Promised One came and God spoke in Him, who is God the Son. The original has no article in connection with the word "Son." It is simply "in Son." The reason for this omission is because the character of the One in whom God hath now spoken, and not so much the person, is to be emphasized. The prophets were servants, angels were servants, but He in whom God speaks now is Son; such is His relationship, one with God.

The declaration of the glory of His Sonship follows. He is eternally Son of God, the Only-Begotten, very God in eternity. He is Son of God in incarnation, taking on the form of man, making purification of sins and He is in resurrection the first begotten, declared Son of God by resurrection from among the dead. It is a marvellous revelation of Himself, corresponding to the similar statements in the beginning of the Gospel of John and the first chapter of Colossians. He is constituted the heir of all things as He created all things and is the creator. All things in heaven and on earth are His. He possesses all things which exist. This is God's eternal purpose concerning Him. All things are by Him and for Him. By Him the worlds were made. (Literally "the ages"; Hellenists understood by it the universe. Its meaning then is equivalent to creation. It is used thus in the Greek translation of the Old Testament known as the Septuagint.) The vast universe is the work of His hands and He himself as very God is "the effulgence of His glory and the expression of His substance." He makes the invisible God visible. He is the perfect impress of God; God is fully revealed in His person who came from glory and dwelt among men. Furthermore, He is upholding all things by the Word of His power.

And He who was all this, and is all this, became man, appeared on earth, assuming manhood, to accomplish the work which He alone could do. By Himself He made purification of sins. The Son of God alone did this and none was with Him. What a blessed, sure, eternally secure foundation of our salvation! The passage shows the personal and perfect competency of the Son of God to effect this mighty work. It was done on the cross, in the death in which He glorified God and which has glorified Him forever. And therefore He arose from the dead and "sat down on the right hand of the Majesty on high." It is significant that nothing is said in the text of His resurrection, in the sense as it is spoken of in other scriptures, that God raised Him from the dead and gave Him glory (1 Pet. 1:21). Nor is it said that He was told to sit down, but He sat down and took Himself the exalted place at the right hand of God. It is presented in this way because His character as Son is here in view. The place He has taken at the right hand of the Majesty on high is only proper and possible for a divine person. The fact that He took this place and sat down attests the perfection, the completeness and acceptation of the work He undertook and finished on the cross. He is now on the throne of God. David's throne and His own throne He will receive when as the First-Begotten He returns from the glory. Such is the Messiah, the Christ, promised to Israel; He is God, the creator and upholder of all things, the heir of all things, come down from heaven, in whom God spoke on earth and is still speaking from heaven, who made purification of sins and has gone back to heaven.

Constituted now heir of all things, destined according to God's eternal decrees to be head of all things, He, as the glorified Man, has "become so much better than the angels, as He hath by inheritance a name more excellent than they." The contrast between Him and angels is now made. The Epistle being addressed to Hebrews explains this comparison and contrast on Christ with angels. In the estimation of a Hebrew, next to Jehovah Himself, angels were looked upon as the highest and holiest beings. Then furthermore the law was given through angels (Acts 7:53; Gal. 3:19), and other angelic ministrations had been prominent in Israel's history, so that these beings occupied a high place in the Jewish mind. But Christ, the man Christ Jesus, has become so much better than the angels; He is above the angels. His name is above every other name. He is on the right hand of the Majesty on high in the form and likeness of Man. As the Only-Begotten He is the creator of angels. In incarnation He was made a little lower than the angels, and now having finished the work for which He became man, He has received by inheritance that highest position and a more excellent name than angels. Into this wonderful place He takes His own people for whom He suffered and died. In Him all believers are above the angels. Angels are but servants, never said to occupy a throne, for they cannot reign. But Christ has a throne and His redeemed shall reign with Him.

Verses 5-14. Upon this the Spirit of God quotes seven passages from the Scriptures in which He speaks of Christ and His exaltation and glory in contrast with angels. All seven are taken from the book of Psalms. Psalms 2; 89; 97; 104; 45; 102 and 110. The destructive criticism declares that there are no Messianic predictions in the book of Psalms. That blessed portion of the Old Testament has suffered much from the hands of these destroyers of the faith. They say that the Second, the Forty-fifth, and the One hundred and tenth Psalms have nothing to say about Christ, that the King mentioned in these psalms was some other unknown King, but not the King Messiah. How significant that the Holy Spirit quotes now from these very psalms telling us that the Messiah, Christ, is predicted in them. The Hebrews had no difficulty in accepting this for they know these psalms speak of the promised Messiah. (The Lord Jesus used the One hundred tenth Psalm in confounding the Pharisees. He showed that that Psalm speaks of Himself and that it is the testimony of the Spirit. Such is "higher criticism"; it sets aside the testimony of the Son of God and the Spirit of God.)

The first quotation is from the Second Psalm. Never did God address angels in the way He is addressed of whom this psalm bears witness. "Thou art my Son, this day have I begotten Thee." This psalm reveals the royal glory and world-wide dominion of Christ, the one whom the people (Israel) and the nations reject. He is to be enthroned as King upon the holy hill of Zion. As Son He will receive the nations for His inheritance and the uttermost parts of the earth for His possession. The title here refers to His incarnation, and, secondarily, to His resurrection from the dead (Acts 13:33-34). It is therefore not the fact of His eternal sonship which is before us in this statement; it speaks of Him as Son of God in time. The eternal Son of God became incarnate; but this did not lower His eternal Sonship. It is therefore His birth, His entrance into the world of which this psalm bears witness. "But it is of all moment for the truth and His own personal dignity to remember that His Sonship when incarnate as well as in resurrection is based on His eternal relationship as Son, without which the other could not have been."

Psalm 89:26, 2 Sam. 7:14 and 1 Chron. 17:13 are mentioned next. It brings out the relationship in which the incarnate Son of God, the promised Messiah, is with God. God accepts and owns Him. "I will be to Him a Father and He shall be to me a Son." And this relationship was audibly declared and confirmed at His baptism and when on the mount of transfiguration. Such a relationship could never be the portion of angels. In Psalm 89:27 His future glory is made known as it is in the second psalm. "Also I will make Him, my Firstborn, higher than the Kings of the earth." He is the Firstborn; He will have the pre-eminence.

The next quotation and argument is from Psalm 97:7. "And again when He brings in the Firstborn into the habitable earth, He saith, let all the angels of God worship Him." This no longer refers to His incarnation, but to His second coming. He is to be brought into the world and then He will receive the worship of the angels of God. Some have applied this to His first coming. But then He came as the "Only-Begotten" and was sent into the world. Here it is said that as the First-Begotten (from the dead) He will be brought into the world. He, who was cast out from the world and rejected by man, will re-enter it in power and glory; God will bring Him back into the habitable earth. When this event takes place the angels will bow in worship before Him, for He comes with His holy angels. It is therefore not His first advent, but His second, which is here contemplated. When He was born, angels praised the sender and not the sent One, but when He comes again He will be the object of angelic worship. This shows His glorious superiority to all the angels.

Psalm 104 speaks of angels as servants. "He maketh His angels spirits, and His ministers a flame of fire." They are spirit and not flesh. They are made to do His will and can never be anything else but servants. And then the contrast is shown what the Son is by the quotation from the Forty-fifth Psalm. Angels are servants and cannot reign nor can they ever occupy a throne, "but unto the Son He saith, Thy throne, O God, is forever and ever, a sceptre of righteousness is the sceptre of Thy kingdom." He is addressed as God in this psalm in which He is revealed as the coming King Messiah. He has a throne which is forever and ever, and as Messiah, and the promised King, He will have an earthly throne and rule with a sceptre of righteousness. He loved righteousness and hated iniquity when down here and therefore He is anointed with the oil of gladness above His fellows. Thus we learn from this psalm His deity. He has a throne forever and ever. His humanity: He was on earth and loved righteousness and hated iniquity. Who are the fellows mentioned? Angels are not His fellows and could not be. His fellows are all they who are made one with Him through grace and who will be ultimately conformed to His image. It includes the believing remnant of Israel and all who put their trust in Him.

"This is a remarkable passage, because, while on the one hand the divinity of the Lord is fully established as well as His eternal throne, on the other hand the passage comes down to His character as the faithful man on earth, where He made pious men—the little remnant of Israel who waited for redemption, His companions; at the same time it gives Him (and it could not be otherwise) a place above them" *(Synopsis of the Bible).*

Still more remarkable is the sixth quotation from Psalm 102. Wonderful as His glory is in the Forty-fifth Psalm, the One hundred second Psalm surpasseth it. No human being would have ever known the real meaning of this psalm if it had not pleased the Spirit of God to give it in this chapter. The little word "and" shows that in verses 25-27 the Son of God is addressed by God as the creator of all things. It is Jehovah's answer to the prayer of His Son suffering as man and dying. "He weakened my strength in the way; He shortened my days. I said, O my God, take me not away in the midst of my days, Thy years are throughout all generations." These words as well as verses 1-11 in this psalm are the expressions of the Man of Sorrows, the suffering Messiah. And Jehovah answers Him and owns Him in His humiliation, approaching the death of the cross, as the Creator. He was ever the same; His years cannot fail. He, the Son of God, had laid the foundation of the earth and the heavens are the works of His hands. And He will do, as the Sovereign One, what God attributes to Him. "They shall perish, but Thou abidest; they shall grow old as doth a garment; and as a vesture shalt Thou roll them up, and they shall be changed, but Thou art the same, and Thy years shall not fail." Such is He, whose glory the Spirit of God reveals in the Holy Scriptures, who became Man, suffered and died, and risen from the dead, sits at the right hand of God. He is the unchangeable One, creator and sustainer of the universe.

The final quotation is from the One hundred and tenth Psalm, which is more frequently quoted in this Epistle than elsewhere. The preceding psalm, the One hundred and ninth, predicts His rejection by His own. In the opening verse of this psalm the Messiah is seen again in His deity and humanity. He is David's Lord and David's Son. His work is finished on earth. He has taken His place of rest (the symbol of the work done) sitting down at His right hand and waiting for the hour when God makes His enemies the footstool of his feet by bringing in again the First-begotten into the world. To no angel did God ever say, "Sit on My right hand."

Once more are angels spoken of as ministers. "Are they not all ministering spirits sent forth to minister to them who shall be heirs of salvation?" They minister now to those who are the heirs of salvation, who bear the title of sons in His Son and who possess His life. How little God's people make use of this comfort. An active and simple faith is needed to perceive in what men carelessly regard as accidents of time and place, the positive workings of angels' ministry. They minister to God's people now in a way unknown to us. "It is a truth which brings the shadow of God's majesty with a peculiar nearness over the believer's soul. That we are seen of angels is an assurance to which the Spirit elsewhere practically bids us heed (1 Cor. 11:10). A happy thought, yet one of sobering effect to be thus seen; to be the objects of near gaze, and very contact, to those holy visitants of watchful love, who, standing as the bright apparitions of heavenly majesty beside the throne on which the Son of God now rests, are sent forth to speed upon their way the pilgrim brethren of the Lord" (A. Pridham).

Chapter 2:1-4. This is the first parenthetical exhortation of this epistle, well suited to the condition of those Hebrews to whom it was first addressed. They are exhorted to give more earnest heed to the things which they had heard, that is, the gospel of salvation in this Christ, whose glory is displayed in the opening chapter. This salvation was at first spoken by the Lord when He was on earth. He began its proclamation. It was continued by those who heard Him, that is by His apostles, and finally God the Holy Spirit had put His witness to it with signs and wonders and gifts. If then the word spoken through angels (the law dispensation) was steadfast and every transgression and disobedience received a just retribution, "How shall we escape if we neglect so great a salvation?" It is a warning to Jews who were halting between two opinions and to those who had in a measure accepted outwardly the truth of Christianity without having laid hold in earnest and in faith of that salvation. If this great salvation, which God offers now not through angels, but in His Son, is rejected or neglected there can be no escape.

II. Christ, Son of Man, His Glory and His Salvation

CHAPTER 2:5-18

1. The Man crowned with glory and honor (2:5-9)
2. His humiliation, suffering and the results (2:10-18)

Verses 5-9. Angels are once more mentioned and the fact is stated first of all that angels are not called of God to reign: "Unto the angels hath He not put in subjection, the world to come whereof we speak." "The world to come" is not heaven or the eternal state. The literal translation is "the habitable world to come"; it is the existing earth, inhabited by human beings in the dispensation which will follow the present age. The world in the dispensation to come, called in Ephesians "the dispensation of the fullness of time" is not put in subjection to angels. A quotation from the Eighth Psalm follows, from which we learn that man is to have dominion and to rule over this world to come. Dominion over the earth was given to Adam (Genesis 1:28), but sin coming in, and death also, this dominion and rule was lost; the glory and honor which rested upon Adam was changed into shame and dishonor. Through man's fall Satan became the usurper, the prince of this world. Adam was the figure of Him that was to come, the Second Man in whom and through whom the lost dominion is restored.

The Eighth Psalm[1] reveals this Second Man,

---

[1]It is interesting to study the order of the psalms with which the book of psalms begins, divinely arranged by an unknown instrument. The righteous Man in Psalm 1 is the Lord Jesus; the Second Psalm shows Him as the Messiah—King. Then Psalms 3—7 show the suffering, sorrows and soul-exercise of the godly during the time when He does not yet reign, especially the suffering of the Jewish remnant during the tribulation and then comes Psalm 8, Christ, the Second Man set over all things. The *Annotated Bible* on the Psalms follows this more fully.

the Lord from heaven, the Creator in creature's form. He was made a little lower than the angels. The Son of God took the position of man to make peace in the blood of His cross "to reconcile all things unto Himself, whether they be things in earth or things in heaven" (Col. 1:20). All things are therefore put in subjection under His feet and nothing is left that is not put in subjection under Him. He will have dominion over all and His name will be excellent in all the earth. Satan knows that the dominion of the earth will not be left forever in his horrible grasp. He offered the kingdoms of the world and their glory to the Son of Man, attempting to keep Him from going to the cross, in which, through the death of Christ, the devil, who has the power of death, is brought to nought.

The work is done. Christ is the Second Man; He will have dominion over the earth in the world to come, the dispensation to come. He will reign and rule and His fellows, the partakers of His salvation, will reign with Him. "But now we see not yet all things put under Him." The time is not in this present age in which Satan is god and ruler. Only when the First-begotten is brought back from the glory, in His second coming, will all things be put under Him. Faith knows this from the unfailing promises of God. But faith also has another vision; while Satan is not yet dethroned and Christ enthroned, "We see Jesus crowned with glory and honor, who was made a little lower than the angels on account of the suffering of death; so that by the grace of God He should taste death for all things." Glorious vision! He suffered death. He perfectly glorified God on the earth where God had been dishonored. He came down and took the lowest place and now He is exalted to the highest. The Man who suffered and died fills the throne and is crowned with glory and honor. And as surely as He is there now, so will He in God's own time occupy His own throne with all things put under his feet. He tasted death for that—for all things—for a ruined creation which He has redeemed and will restore.

Verses 10-18. This salvation work is now more fully mentioned in the second part of this chapter. He is spoken of as the captain (author) of the salvation of the many sons He is bringing to glory. And as the originator and leader of their salvation He had to suffer and die. Not His person was to be perfected, for He is perfect; but He had to be perfected through suffering as a Saviour. "For it became Him for whom are all things and by whom are all things in bringing many sons unto glory to make the captain of their salvation perfect through suffering." Here God's eternal purpose is wonderfully revealed. He purposed before the foundation, knowing the coming ruin of man, to bring many sons unto glory. This is divine love. But God's holiness had to be vindicated, and therefore the Son of God became man to suffer as the captain of their (the many sons) salvation.

As disobedience had led man from life to death, so, by obedience unto death the sinless Lamb of God had to win in righteousness the path of endless life for those who trust in Him as the originator and captain of their salvation. And those who accept Him are the many sons, whom God is bringing through Him, to glory everlasting. And both He who sanctifieth and they who are sanctified are all of one. It is a wicked perversion of the truth when it is taught, that He, and all the human race are of one. This is the common error taught so much in the so-called theory of "The Fatherhood of God and Brotherhood of Man." The statement shows the wonderful relationship which divine grace has established between the captain of salvation and those who are saved by Him. He, Christ, is the sanctifier, setting those apart unto God, who accept Him as Saviour. Such are born of God and become children of God, destined to be brought by Him as sons to glory. In this sense He who sanctifieth and they who are sanctified by Him are of One, that is, of God. Higher still is the truth revealed in the Epistles to the Ephesians and Colossians, that believers are not only "of one" but are one with Him.

Again quotations from the Scriptures follow. The first is from the Twenty-second Psalm. "For this cause He is not ashamed to call them brethren, saying I will declare Thy name unto my brethren in the midst of the church will I sing praise unto Thee" (Ps. 22:22). This Psalm shows first Christ on the cross as sin-bearer. In verses 20 and 21 is the prayer of the Suffering One. And He was heard. God's answer was His resurrection from the dead. That resurrection and His exaltation are revealed in the second portion of this Psalm (verses 22-31). The beginning of this section is quoted here. And when He was risen from the dead He gave this blessed new message at once. "But go unto My brethren and say unto them, I ascend unto My Father and your Father, and My God and your God" (John 20:17).

Here we learn the blessed identification of Him that sanctifieth and with them that are sanctified, and that on the ground of resurrection. And therefore He is not ashamed to call us brethren, which, however, does not authorize believers to call Him "brother" as it is done so often. (Never before His death and resurrection did He address His disciples as "brethren." Only once did He hint before His death at this relationship to come, in Matthew 12:48-50.) And by His Spirit He is in the midst of those who are gathered unto His name, the Church, and sings praise unto God, as they praise God in His blessed and worthy name. The Twenty-second Psalm also speaks of "the great congregation," Israel, gathered unto Him and of the ends of the earth and the nations who shall remember and shall worship before Him. It is His coming glory when all things are put under Him in the age to come.

The next quotation is from Psalm 16. (It may also be brought in connection with Is. 8:17. The Septuagint has it "I will trust in Him" 2 Sam. 22:3.) "I will put my trust in Him." It is the prophetic expression of His personal faith on earth. As man He trusted in the Lord and waited for Him (Isaiah 8:17). "The Seed of David, and the object of the promises, is thus represented as awaiting, in perfect confidence, the righteous award which in due time should be made to Him who alone is worthy, by the God whom He had glorified in perfect obedience; although for an appointed season His gracious labor might seem to have been spent for nought and in vain, while man and Satan appeared only to prevail" (Isaiah 49).

The last quotation is from Isaiah 8:18. The children, which the Lord had given to Isaiah, were for signs and wonders in Israel from the Lord. The two sons of Isaiah had received their names of significant meaning from heaven. Believers are children, belong to Him and are signs and witnesses both to unbelieving Israel and the world. In a special sense this passage, no doubt, applies to the believing remnant of Israel, which owned Him, while the nation rejected Him. And some day, the day of His glory, He will declare triumphantly "Behold I and the children which God gave unto Me." Then He will be glorified and admired in all that believed (2 Thess. 1:10) and the redeemed will be for signs and wonders in a still more blessed way.

Then follows a restatement of the fact of His incarnation and its special bearing on the calling of the children, God has given Him, the many sons He brings to glory. "Forasmuch then as the children are partakers of flesh and blood, He also in like manner took part of the same (His incarnation) that through death He might bring to nought him who hath the power of death, that is the devil, and deliver as many as through fear of death were all their lifetime subject to bondage." It was for the children's sake, all who accept Him and whom God brings through Him to glory, that He took on flesh and blood and by doing so He arrayed Himself for death. He took on flesh and blood apart from sin. Satan's work is perfected in death. "That the Lord Jesus might enjoy the children as the gift of God, He must first take away the yoke of the oppressor. But because the right of Satan to destroy was founded on the victory of sin, which made man the lawful prey of death, He, who loved the children though as yet they knew Him not, took also flesh; that in their stead He might undergo that death which should forever spoil the devil of his claim" (A. Pridham). The limit of this work of the Lord Jesus to the children as its object, should be carefully observed.

Jewish saints in the Old Testament, believing the promise and expecting the Messiah, were in bondage and in fear of death. "The sting of death is sin, and the strength of sin is the law," but the death of Christ once for all to sin has received the sting and brought to nought him who has the power of death. A believer is delivered from the fear of death, for he no longer dies the sinner's death, but falls asleep in Jesus and that with the promise to awake in due time in His likeness. "For verily it is not angels upon whom He taketh hold, but He taketh hold of the seed of Abraham." And who were they whom He took hold on? Not angels, but the seed of Abraham. Those are the children for which He came, took on flesh and blood and wrought His work on the cross. The expression "seed of Abraham" is as a generic term, descriptive of the whole family of faith. Believers of Jews and Gentiles are comprehended in this term. They that are of faith are blessed with faithful Abraham.

His priesthood is next introduced for the first time in this Epistle. He was made like unto His brethren in all things "that He might be a merciful and faithful high priest in things pertaining to God to make propitiation for the sins of the people. For in that He Himself hath suffered being tempted, He is able to succor them that are tempted," and thus in suffering and temptation (apart from sin) in His humanity, He was fitted to be the priest to sympathize with His own in all their trials and conflicts.

"He suffered—never yielded. We do not suffer

when we yield to temptation: the flesh takes pleasure in the things by which it is tempted. Jesus suffered, being tempted, and He is able to succour them that are tempted. It is important to observe that the flesh, when acted upon by its desires, does not suffer. Being tempted, it, alas! enjoys. But when, according to the light of the Holy Spirit and the fidelity of obedience, the Spirit resists the attacks of the enemy, whether subtle or persecuting, then one suffers. This the Lord did, and this we have to do. That which needs succour is the new man, the faithful heart, and not the flesh. I need succour against the flesh, and in order to mortify all the members of the old man" *Synopsis of the Bible.*

CHAPTER 3

1. As Son over the house of God, greater than Moses (3:1-6)
2. The danger of unbelief (3:7-13)
3. The need of faith (3:14-19)

Verses 1-6. He now addresses believing Hebrews as "holy brethren and partakers of the heavenly calling," and exhorts them to consider the Apostle and Highpriest of our confession, Christ Jesus." Hebrews address each other as "brethren" (Acts 2:29, 7:2, 22:1). Believing Hebrews are here addressed by the Spirit of God as "holy brethren." Trusting in Christ they were sanctified and belonged to those whom He is not ashamed to call brethren. They are called "partakers of the heavenly calling" in contrast with their former "earthly calling" of Israel. The two titles of the Lord Jesus, Apostle and Highpriest, correspond to the preceding opening chapters of the Epistle. As Apostle (a Sent One), the Son of God came from God to man. And then as Man who suffered and died, He has gone from man to God as Highpriest, typified by Aaron. As the Lord Jesus Christ is in this Epistle called the Apostle, the Spirit of God may have, for this reason, kept the pen of the apostle, who wrote this document, from calling himself an apostle.

Then follows the contrast with Moses. Moses was faithful in all his house (the tabernacle) but only as a servant. Christ is over God's house, which He has built, for He is God. And in this house He is not a servant, but a Son. Both the universe and the Church, as the House of God, are here blended together. The house in the wilderness, the tabernacle, was a type of the universe. "And every house is built by some one, but He that built all things is God." Christ is the builder of the universe, the house, and the upholder of it and so He is counted worthy of greater honor than Moses, inasmuch as He who hath built it hath more honor than the house. The Apostle of our confession, the Sent One of God, the Son of God, is also the Highpriest. After His finished work on the cross, having made propitiation for the sins of the people, He passed through the heavens into the Holiest not made with hands. (The three parts of the tabernacle, the outer court, the holy part, and the Holiest typify the first, the second and the third heaven.) Ultimately in virtue of redemption, all having been cleansed by the blood, God will dwell in the house. "Behold the tabernacle of God is with men, and He will dwell with them and they shall be His people, and God Himself shall be with them, and be their God" (Rev. 21:3).

"And Moses verily was faithful in all his house as a servant, for a testimony of those things which were to be spoken after." And those things have come and are given through Christ, who is Son over His house, whose house are we. This is His spiritual house, the house of God composed of living stones, the sanctified, the holy priesthood. The Son of God, the builder of all things, has now as Highpriest, His own house, which are we "if we hold fast the confidence (boldness) and the rejoicing of the hope firm unto the end." It is a warning to those Hebrews who had confessed Christ, who were facing trials and many difficulties, not to give up the confidence and the rejoicing in the hope. They are urged to hold it fast and are solemnly warned against unbelief. They were in danger of forsaking Christianity, and turning back to Judaism. And these words of warning are also given to us, for they are needful for the exercise of the conscience. A true believer will continue in confidence firm to the end. Such a continuance is the proof of the reality of our confession.

("It is clearly not our standing which is in question; for this being wholly of God and in Christ is settled and sure and unchanging. There is no "if" either as to Christ's work or as to the gospel of God's grace. All there is unconditional grace to faith. The wilderness journey is before us (as the next verses show). Here it is that "if" has its necessary place, because it is our walk through the desert, where there are so many occasions of failure, and we need constant dependence in God.")

Verses 7-13. The danger and calamity of unbelief is next called to their remembrance. Psalm

95 is quoted. The Holy Spirit saith "Today if ye will hear His voice harden not your hearts." Such was the word of warning addressed to Israel in the past, but it also has its application in the present. The word "today" expresses God's wonderful patience and long suffering towards Israel as well as towards all during this age of grace. The "today" is now; the great morrow comes, when the "today" ends and the kingdom of power and glory with its attending judgments upon those who did not obey the gospel of Jesus Christ comes, and the once rejected King Messiah appears. The fathers of the Hebrews had tempted God in the wilderness. He was wroth with that generation and swore in His wrath "they shall not enter into My rest." It was God's solemn sentence of exclusion from His rest. They hardened their hearts, did not obey His voice and their unbelief shut them out from God's rest.

Even so these Hebrews, professing Christianity were in the same danger. "Take heed brethren, lest there be in any of you an evil heart of unbelief in falling away from the living God." But while it was "to-day," God still waited to be gracious and so they were to exhort each other daily, lest any of them be hardened through the deceitfulness of sin. Danger surrounded them on every side. "The heart of unbelief which barred the land of Canaan from their natural fathers was yet within their flesh. Not only were the lusts of nature in their ordinary shape forever combating against the will of God, they were exposed also to a more specious, and therefore a more dangerous form of evil in the still existing rivalry which they who made their boast in their traditions were opposing to the cross of Christ. Of all the evils with which Satan can afflict the heart, atheism, religion without faith in God, is by very much the worst. For it lulls the conscience, while it weaves its web of unblessed, unsanctifying exercises about the heart's affections so as effectually to exclude the light of God. It was to this peace-corroding yet seductive evil that these Hebrew Christians stood practically exposed."

"Now the remedy and safeguard of all evil is the truth of God. It is only by listening to the word of Him who speaks to us as children with a knowledge of our need, that believers can be kept in their true place. The possession of truth in the way of doctrine is not enough. God daily speaks and must be daily heard if we would really know Him" (A. Pridham).

All this is true of God's people at all times, for faith and obedience are the essential conditions of blessing and the tests of profession. God is faithful and will certainly not permit that any of His own perish. Faith reckons with this, but also heeds the warning, knowing and owning the tendency of the flesh to depart from God, and hence the need of His constant and never-failing grace is recognized and a walk in godly fear is the blessed result. There are teachers who claim that these solemn exhortations have no meaning for Christians today and even have made the statement that this epistle was not for the church at all. Such claims show a deplorable ignorance of the truth of God. All believers must heed the warning "that none of you be hardened through the deceitfulness of sin."

("Sin separates us from God in our thoughts; we have no longer the same sense either of His love, His power, or His interest in us. Confidence is lost. Hope, and the value of unseen things, diminish; while the value of things that are seen proportionately increases. The conscience is bad; one is not at ease with God. The path is hard and difficult; the will strengthens itself against Him. We no longer live by faith; visible things come in between us and God, and take possession of the heart. Where there is life, God warns by His Spirit (as in this epistle), He chastises and restores. Where it was only an outward influence, a faith devoid of life, and the conscience not reached, it is abandoned" J. N. Darby.)

Verses 14-19. The need of faith, the holding fast of the beginning of our confidence unto the end, is now more fully presented. All Israelites came out of Egypt. But with whom was he wroth for forty years? It was with them that sinned, whose carcases fell in the wilderness. Their sin was unbelief. And those who believed not were kept out of His rest. "So we see that they could not enter in because of unbelief." What the rest of God is we shall follow in the annotations of the next paragraphs.

CHAPTER 4

1. What the rest of God is (4:1-11)
2. The power of the Word of God (4:12-13)

Verses 1-11. "Let us therefore fear, lest, a promise being left of entering into His rest, any one of you might seem to come short of it. For unto us was the gospel preached as well as unto them, but the word preached did not profit them, not being mixed with faith in them that heard it." These words of exhortation belong properly to the preceding chapter.

What is the rest of which these verses speak? It is generally explained as the rest which the true believer finds and has in the Lord Jesus Christ in believing; that his conscience has rest. It is frequently identified with Matth. 11:28-29. While it is blessedly true that all who come to the Lord Jesus Christ as Saviour find rest in Him from the curse of the law and the burden of sin, while it is equally true that those who follow Him in obedience and learn of Him find rest day by day for their souls, yet it is not this present rest which is before us in these verses. The rest which is meant is called by God "My rest"; it is the rest of God and is future, the rest in coming glory, an eternal rest. It is God's rest, because He made it Himself and He will enjoy it in glory with those who have believed in Christ, in whose perfect work God has His rest, because it satisfies His holiness and His love. Into this rest the believer enters at His coming. Then work will be over and all burdens cease. Righteousness reigns and groaning creation is delivered and all the promised glory will be accomplished. God rests then in His love and rejoices (Zeph. 3:17). Till that day God works, for sin and the curse is unremoved, but all will be changed when His Son appears in glory and all things are put in subjection under Him. The perfect, complete rest of God is in the new heaven and earth, when God dwells among men and sin and death are forever gone. He then is all in all. This is the rest which remains for the people of God.

"God must rest in that which satisfies His heart. This was the case even in creation—all was very good. And now it must be in a perfect blessing that perfect love can be satisfied with, with regard to us, who will possess a heavenly portion in the blessing which we shall have in His own presence, in perfect holiness and perfect light. Accordingly all the toilsome work of faith, the exercise of faith in the wilderness, the warfare (although there are many joys), the good works practised there, labour of every kind will cease. It is not only that we shall be delivered from the power of indwelling sin; all the efforts and all the troubles of the new man will cease. We are already set free from the law of sin; then our spiritual exercise for God will cease. We shall rest from our works—not evil ones. We have already rested from our works with regard to justification, and therefore in that sense we have now rest in our consciences, but that is not the subject here—it is the Christian's rest from all his works. God rested from His works—assuredly good ones—and so shall we also then with Him.

"We are now in the wilderness; we also wrestle with wicked spirits in heavenly places. A blessed rest remains for us in which our hearts will repose in the presence of God, where nothing will trouble the perfection of our rest, where God will rest in the perfection of the blessing He has bestowed on His people.

"The great thought of the passage is, that there *remains* a rest (that is to say, that the believer is not to expect it here) without saying where it is. And it does not speak in detail of the character of the rest, because it leaves the door open to an earthly rest for the earthly people on the ground of the promises, although to Christian partakers of the heavenly calling God's rest is evidently a heavenly one" *(Synopsis of the Bible).*

The argument and exhortation of verses 3-11 is therefore easily understood. God had rested in creation on the seventh day from all His work. But that rest was broken and is also the type of another rest of God to come. Those who believe not cannot enter into that coming rest and it is shown that Joshua (verse 8, not Jesus, but Joshua) and the rest in Canaan is not the true rest of God, for if it had been why would David, long after Joshua, have spoken of it again? Nor has this rest come now for the people of God; it is still in the future. A Sabbath-keeping remaineth for the people of God. We are on the road toward it, beset by dangers and difficulties as Israel was when passing through the wilderness. And therefore the exhortation to be diligent to enter into that rest and not to be unbelieving and disobedient. Entrance into the rest is by faith. We who have believed do enter into rest. While the believer is assured of this future entrance into the rest of God, he also uses diligence and earnestness while on the way, watching and praying. True faith is evidenced by such a walk.

Verses 12-13. The Word of God and its divine living power is here introduced by the Holy Spirit. It is the method of God, to use His Word, to bring to light and judge the unbelief and workings of the heart. It judges everything in the heart which is not of Him. Its use, its constant use, is the supreme necessity of those who believe and are on the way to the rest of God, for it is His divine Word which brings us into God's presence. It is a searching Word and under its power the conscience becomes aroused and the blessed and needed work of self-judgment begins. Life, power and omniscience, three great attributes of God, are here given to His Word. The Word also gives power and spiritual energy.

("Soul and spirit" as thus named together can only be the two parts of the immaterial nature of man; which Scripture, in spite of what many think, everywhere clearly distinguishes from one another. The soul is the lower, sensitive, instinctive, emotional part, which, where not, as in man, penetrated with the light of the spirit, is simply animal; and which also, where man is not in the power of the Spirit of God, will still gravitate towards this. The spirit is intelligent and moral, that which knows human things (1 Cor. 2:11). In the "natural man," which is really the *psychic* man, the man soulled (1 Cor. 2:14), conscience, with its recognition of God, is in abeyance, and the mind itself becomes earthly. Important enough it is, therefore, to divide between "soul and spirit." "Joints and marrow" convey to us the difference between the external and the internal, the outward form and the essence hidden in it" *Numerical Bible.*)

III. Christ as Priest in the Heavenly Sanctuary

CHAPTERS 4:14—10

The Great High-Priest (4:14-16)

With this statement the main section of the Epistle begins, and the great theme, the priesthood of Christ, is introduced. This section covers six chapters, ending with the tenth. Here we learn that Christ, the true priest, has passed through the heavens and is now in a heavenly sanctuary, the way into which His own work has blessedly opened. The different contrasts with the priests and sacrifices of Judaism, the old covenant and the new, are made in these chapters. The concluding verses of the fourth chapter one might say, contain all the truth of His priesthood which the succeeding chapters develop and expand.

He is the great high priest who is passed through the heavens. He has entered heaven itself, the third heaven, the holiest. The earthly tabernacle in which Aaron and his successors ministered had three parts. Through these Aaron passed as he entered into the holiest and these parts are typical of the heavenly things. Christ also passed through, but not through the places made by hands—He passed through the heavens and into the holiest. "Christ is not entered into the holy places made with hands, which are the figure of the true, but into heaven itself, now to appear in the presence of God for us" (9:24). And He who passed through the heavens is Jesus, the Son of God; He who was made a little lower than the angels and after His sacrificial death arose, is now clothed with a glorified human body in the presence of God. His priestly ministry there is in behalf of His people. He is, as high priest, touched with the feeling of our infirmities; He was in all points tempted as we are, apart from sin. ("Yet without sin" is an incorrect translation and is responsible for the very erroneous teaching that our Lord, while He did not sin, might have sinned. It was absolutely impossible for Him to sin, for He is the Son of God and God cannot sin.) He lived on earth and passed through life; He suffered and was tempted; He experienced all the trials His people have to pass through in their lives and infinitely more than His saints can ever suffer, and therefore He sympathizes with all our infirmities. In all the difficulties, perplexities, trials and sorrows, the saint of God finds perfect sympathy in Him as priest. His heart filled with that love which passeth knowledge, is touched, beyond our finite comprehension, with the feeling of our infirmities.

As to sin, temptation from within, the lust of an evil heart, He knew absolutely nothing. He knew no sin. He was tempted in all things, apart from sin. Sin, therefore, is excluded. Nor does a child of God desire sympathy with indwelling sin. It must be judged, put into the place of death, and not sympathized with. And this fact that He is the great High Priest touched with the feeling of our infirmities, our weaknesses and our trials; the knowledge that He, who is exalted in glory, concerns Himself about us and our trials down here, gives encouragement to hold fast our confession. He will not leave, nor forsake, nor fail His saints.

We have evil temptations from within; Christ had none. Temptation from sin was absolutely incompatible with His holy person. By a miracle he was even as to humanity exempt from the taint of evil. It is of holy temptations this Epistle treats, not of our unholy ones. The Epistle of James distinguishes them very definitely in Chapter 1. Compare verses 2, 12, on the one hand, and verses 13-15 on the other. We know the latter too well. Jesus knew. But He knew the former as no other before or since. He was in all things tempted according to likeness, *i.e.* with us, with this infinite difference 'apart from sin.' He knew no sin. He is therefore the more—not the less—able to sympathize with us. For sin within, even if not yielded to, blinds the eye, and dulls the heart, and hinders from unreserved occupation with the trials of others" (J. N. Darby.)

And while we are not told to go to this great High Priest (He is constantly occupying Himself about us) we are told to come boldly to the throne of grace. We look to the Lord Jesus Christ, trust His love and sympathy, and knowing that He is there we can go with boldness to the throne of grace. And there we find all we need.

CHAPTER 5

1. What the High Priest is and represents (5:1-4)
2. The fulfillment in Christ made High Priest (5:5-10)
3. The spiritual condition of the Hebrew-Christians (5:11-14)

Verses 1-4. In developing the priesthood of Christ and showing how it excels the earthly priesthood and is more glorious than the priesthood of Judaism, the principles of priesthood of the levitical system are first stated. Upon this follows the comparison of the priesthood of Christ with that of Aaron. The transcendent priesthood of Christ is thus established by this contrast. These opening verses have nothing to do with our Lord. They show how the high priest was taken from among men and being merely a man who was to exercise forbearance toward the ignorant, himself clothed with infirmity, he was obliged not alone to offer sacrifices for the sins of the people, but also for himself. This can, of course, never apply to the Lord Jesus Christ, inasmuch as He is sinless. He therefore cannot be meant in these introductory words of this chapter. And the earthly priests did not take this honor to themselves. God's call was necessary.

Verses 5-10. How the priesthood, foreshadowed in Aaron, was first of all fulfilled in Christ is the theme of this section. Here we have His call to be priest. "So Christ also hath not glorified Himself to be made an high priest; but He that said unto Him, Thou art My Son, today I have begotten Thee" (Psalm 2). As He saith also in another place, "Thou art a priest forever after the order of Melchisedec" (Psalm 110). His call from God is to be King-Priest. The second psalm reveals Him as Son of God, King to be enthroned and to rule over the nations, and He is priest after the order of Melchisedec. This name is here mentioned for the first time. His Melchisedec priesthood the Spirit of God unfolds fully in the seventh chapter. The call of Him is according to the eternal purposes of God. He came to offer Himself as the sacrificial Lamb on the cross. This was indicated when He went into Jordan, baptized by John. It was then that the Father's voice was heard declaring His sonship. He had to pass through death and rise again to be the priest after the order of Melchisedec.

His suffering and death are therefore next mentioned in these verses: "Who in the days of His flesh having offered up prayers and supplications with strong crying and tears to Him who was able to save Him out of death and having been heard for His godly fear, though He were a Son, yet learned He obedience by the things which He suffered." These words refer chiefly to the portal of the cross, Gethsemane. There He prayed with strong crying and tears, alone with His Father in deepest agony, fallen on His face, and His sweat became as great drops of blood falling down on the ground. He went into all the anguish of death, deprecating the cup He had to drink, yet in meek and perfect submission. What a terrible weight was there upon His holy soul! And He was heard for His godly fear. He was saved, not from dying, for that would have left man in his sins and unredeemed; He was saved out of death. His prayer was answered by His resurrection. It was in that agony that He learned obedience. Though Son of God, He learned obedience from the things which He suffered. Having come to obey and to suffer (which as Son of God was unknown to Him), He obeyed in everything and submitted to everything. He did not save Himself, but drank the cup and died the sinner's death.

What He is in resurrection, the results of His sacrificial death, are next stated. "And being made perfect, He became, unto all that obey Him, author of eternal salvation; being saluted (or welcomed by God) of God as high priest after the order of Melchisedec." In the second chapter we saw that the captain of our salvation had to be made perfect through sufferings (2:10). Here we meet the same statement, that He has been made perfect. It means the completeness of His work through sufferings, in resurrection and heavenly glory. And through this finished work in which He was perfected as Saviour, He also became unto all that obey Him (all who believe on Him and own Him thus as their Saviour) the author of eternal salvation. Returning to glory, God saluted, or welcomed Him as priest after the order of Melchisedec.

Verses 11-14. Here another parenthesis begins which closes with the end of the sixth chapter. The seventh chapter resumes the instructions concerning Melchisedec and the priesthood of

Christ. Their spiritual state was that of babes as still under the ordinances and requirements of the law. They clung to Judaism and could not fully break loose from the shadow things of their system. They were dull of hearing and while they ought to have been teachers (having believed in Christ) there was need of teaching them again what are the elements of the beginning of the oracles of God. They needed milk and were not fit for the "solid food." They had not gone on in the gospel, into that maturity which the Holy Spirit has revealed as to the believer's standing and perfection in Christ. As long as they were occupied with ordinances they were but infants and in danger of apostasy.

Ritualistic Christendom today corresponds to the state of many of these Hebrew-Christians of the first century, only ritualism is worthy of greater condemnation. The fearful evil of ritualism (Romish and so-called Protestant) is that it takes and imitates Jewish forms and ordinances and through these things sets aside and corrupts true Christianity. It is the bondage of the flesh.

("We may observe that there is no greater hindrance to progress in spiritual life and intelligence than attachment to an ancient form of religion, which, being traditional and not simply personal faith in the truth, consists always in ordinances, and is consequently carnal and earthly. Without this people may be unbelievers; but under the influence of such a system piety itself—expressed in forms—makes a barrier between the soul and the light of God; and these forms which surround, pre-occupy, and hold the affections captive, prevent them from enlarging and becoming enlightened by means of divine revelation. Morally (as the apostle here expresses it) the senses are not exercised to discern both good and evil" *Synopsis of the Gospel.*)

CHAPTER 6

1. Return to Judaism the crucifixion of the Son of God afresh (6:1-8)
2. Persuaded of better things: Comfort and hope (6:9-20)

Verses 1-8. A solemn warning follows, addressed to these Hebrews who were halting and in danger of turning back to Judaism, and doing so would crucify the Son of God afresh. "Therefore leaving the word of the beginning of Christ, let us go on to full growth; not laying again a foundation of repentance from dead works and faith in God, of a teaching of baptisms, and of laying on of hands and of resurrection of the dead, and of eternal judgment." It is of much importance to see that these things are not "the principles of the doctrine of Christ" (as the authorized version erroneously states). These things mentioned are the elementary things which the Jews had before Christ came and as they were still occupied with them, He exhorts to leave the word of the beginning of Christ, the Messiah, and to go on to full growth. The full growth is Christianity as revealed in the finished work of Christ, the glory of His Person, His priesthood and the fact that the believer is in Christ and complete in Him.

While these Hebrews had believed in Christ, that He had come, they had not gone on to this maturity and lacked the spiritual knowledge of what Christ had done and the blessed results of His work and priesthood. They were therefore to leave the elementary things which they had and believed in as Jews, and abandoning them, reach the true Christian maturity. And these elementary things consisted in repentance from dead works and of faith in God. This was known and taught in Judaism. But it is faith in God, but nothing is said of faith in the Lord Jesus Christ. When baptism is mentioned and laying on of hands it has nothing whatever to do with Christian baptism, and much less does the laying on of hands mean "confirmation." (Confirmation as practiced in the Roman Catholic, Lutheran, Episcopal, and several other Protestant denominations is a merely ecclesiastical invention without the slightest scriptural foundation.) The word "baptism" is in the plural—"baptisms"—the different washings the Jews practice in connection with the ceremonial law, and so also the Jewish imposition of hands. These Jewish washings and purifications were only shadows of what was to come. It had come; and yet these Jews, though believing that Christ had come, still lingered in these things. Resurrection of the dead and eternal judgment, the things concerning the future were likewise the teachings they had in Judaism. But Christianity gives a higher truth, namely, "the resurrection from among the dead" and that the believer is passed from death unto life and shall not come into judgment.—"And this will he do if God permit"—that is in the coming unfolding of true Christianity, the full growth, as given in chapters 7—10.

Before the author of the Epistle does this he

shows what it would mean if these Hebrews turn back to Judaism altogether, and instead of going on to full growth would abandon the Christian ground they occupied as professing believers in Christ. Such a course would make it impossible to renew them again to repentance, for they, by falling away, crucified afresh for themselves the Son of God, putting Him to open shame. They committed the crime, which was done by them through ignorance (Luke 23:34; Acts 3:17), now knowingly of their own will and choice. For such a wilful falling away there was no remedy. The things mentioned in verses 4 and 5 show the possibility that a person may be enlightened, and have tested, and even participated, by listening to the testimony of the Spirit concerning Christ, and seen miracles, the powers of the age to come—without having fully accepted the offered salvation.

"The warning here has been a sore perplexity to many who are far as possible from the condition which is here contemplated. The description of these apostates, solemn as it is, does not speak of them as children of God, as justified by faith, or in any way which would imply such things as these; and the apostle, after describing them, immediately adds, as to those whom he is addressing; 'But, beloved, we are persuaded better things of you, even things that accompany *salvation,* though we thus speak.' This is the most distinct assurance that he had no thought of one who had known salvation incurring the doom of an apostate" *Numerical Bible.*

All the blessings offered upon Christian ground are to such outward professors like rain, which instead of bringing forth from the ground useful herbs, brings thorns and briers, worthless, nigh unto cursing, and then the end, to be burned. Of a true child of God this can never be said.

("When once we have understood that this passage is a comparison of the power of the spiritual system with Judaism, and that it speaks of giving up the former, after having known it, its difficulty disappears. The possession of life is not supposed, nor is that question touched. The passage speaks, not of life, but of the Holy Ghost as a power present in Christianity. To "taste the good word" is to have understood how precious that word is; and not the having been quickened by its means. Hence in speaking to the Jewish Christians he hopes better things and things which accompany salvation, so that all these things could be there and yet no salvation. Fruit there could not be. That supports life" *Synopsis of the Bible.*)

Verses 9-20. Words of comfort and hope conclude this chapter. He addresses them now as "beloved," of whom he is persuaded of better things, the things which accompany salvation. Their true faith had been manifested by works. And God is not unrighteous "to forget your work and labour of love, which ye have showed towards His name in that ye have ministered unto the saints and do minister." These are things which accompany salvation. He encourages them to be followers of them who through patience and faith inherit the promises. He calls their attention to Abraham, the father of the faithful. He endured patiently and obtained the promise. And He gave not only the promise of His Word, but also His oath. "For when God made promise to Abraham, because He could swear by no greater, He swore by Himself." What assurance therefore—God's Word and God's oath. And this makes manifest to the heirs of promise (believers) the immutability of His counsel, so that we might have strong consolation. Therefore those who trust and hope for future glory have a strong and satisfying consolation. But there is more than that. There is a personal guarantee, for the Lord Jesus as a forerunner has entered into heaven, where He now is as high priest after the order of Melchisedec. He, who is our hope, is there as a forerunner and this is the anchor of the soul; it anchors in Him who hath entered within the vail. He who is seated in glory is the promised One, the object, bearer and dispenser of all the promises of God. In Him and His work all is made secure. His presence there speaks of the ultimate realization of all the promises of glory for His people.

CHAPTER 7

1. The priesthood of Melchisedec in contrast with the Levitical priesthood (7:1-19)
2. The holy and heavenly priesthood of Christ (7:20-28)

Verses 1-19. The interrupted argument concerning the priesthood of Christ is now resumed. It connects with chapter 5:10. There we find Melchisedec mentioned for the first time, and here the historical Melchisedec is first of all described. The record is given in Genesis 14:18-20. He met Abraham, who returned from the smiting of the Kings, and blessed him. Abraham gave him the tenth of all. His name means "King of Righteousness"; but he was also King of Salem, that is, "King of Peace." First righteousness and peace afterward. This is God's order—not peace and righteousness, but righteousness and peace. It is so spiritually for the believer; it will be so in millennial times when "righteousness and peace will kiss each other."

Who was Melchisedec? Some have said he was Shem and not a few maintain that he was the Lord Himself, one of the theophanies, a pre-incarnation manifestation of the Son of God. The latter view is certainly wrong, for Scripture states that Melchisedec is "made like unto the Son of God", that is, he is a pattern, a similitude of Him; Melchisedec was therefore not the Lord Himself. It is vain to speculate on the identity of this King-Priest, for the Holy Spirit on purpose does not mention who he was. When we read, "Without father, without mother, without descent, having neither beginning of days nor end of life," it does not mean that Melchisedec had no father and no mother, etc. But it means that Scripture gives no record of these facts; Moses being divinely guided in omitting it all in the book of Genesis, and thus making Melchisedec appear as a man without father and mother, without descent, having no beginning and end of days, who has a priesthood invested in himself. And this for the purpose of furnishing a type of our Lord as the royal priest.

Melchisedec foreshadows fully the millennial glory of the Lord Jesus Christ. See Zech. 6:9-13. He will receive His own throne and be a priest upon that throne. Significantly he appeared suddenly when Abraham was returning from smiting the allied kings. (Genesis 14 gives the record of the first war of the Bible.) And then he blessed Abraham and made known to him God as the Most-High (the millennial name of God), the possessor of heaven and earth. Even so the true Melchisedec will some day appear, and after the smiting of the kings (the battle of Armageddon, Rev. 16:14-16; 19:19) will begin His glorious rule. Nor must it be overlooked that Melchisedec brought to Abraham bread and wine, the blessed emblems of the great sacrificial work of the true Melchisedec, which points us, who are by faith the children of Abraham, to the blessed memorial feast, in which His love and grace, as well as glory, are remembered. Christ is therefore now for His own the Priest after the order of Melchisedec; the full display of His Melchisedec priesthood arrives in the day of His coming glory.

The chief object of bringing forward the person of Melchisedec and his connection with Abraham is, to show first, the superiority of Melchisedec to Levi and his priesthood as better and higher than the Levitical priesthood. Abraham gave him the tenth part of all the spoil. The whole Levitical priesthood was then not in existence, inasmuch as Levi, unborn, was in the loins of Abraham; in Abraham, Levi, therefore, gave tithes to Melchisedec. Melchisedec, as priest, blessed the father of the nation, and therefore he was greater than Abraham, for "without controversy, the less is blessed of the greater." The priesthood of Melchisedec was therefore superior to that of the sons of Levi, the Aaronic priesthood.

After this argument another one is introduced. The question is concerning the Levitical priesthood, if it could give perfection. The one hundred and tenth psalm announced the coming of a priest after the order of Melchisedec and therefore superior to Aaron. If then perfection were by the Levitical priesthood, what need was there that this other priest of a higher order than Aaron should arise? Because perfection was not by that earthly priesthood, nor by the law,[2] therefore this better priest had to come to bring the needed perfection and that necessitated a change of the law also. The law in all its ordinances was a witness of imperfection, though it foreshadowed the good things to come. The law was therefore not to abide. With the cessation of the Levitical priesthood the entire law-covenant would terminate. And He of whom these things are spoken (the Lord Jesus Christ) "pertaineth to another tribe, of which no one hath given attendance at the altar (as priest). For it is certain that our Lord sprang out of Judah; of which tribe Moses spake nothing concerning priesthood." His coming, therefore, has taken from the tribe of Levi the honor and set aside their priesthood. And He who sprang out of Judah, the priest after the similitude of Melchisedec (combining priesthood and royalty) hath been made, not after a law of fleshly commandment, but after the power of an indissoluble

---

[2]"The law, doubtless, was good; but separation still existed between man and God. The law made nothing perfect. God was ever perfect, and human perfection was required; all must be according to what divine perfection required of man. But sin was there, and the law was consequently without power (save to condemn); its ceremonies and ordinances were but figures, and a heavy yoke. Even that which temporarily relieved the conscience brought sin to mind and never made the conscience perfect towards God. They were still at a distance from Him. Grace brings the soul to God, who is known in love and in a righteousness which is for us."—*J. N. D.*

life. His priesthood is not a thing of time and change, a fleshly priesthood like Aaron's but it is a priesthood in the power of an indissoluble life. He has passed through death, and now in heaven, not on earth, He is the Melchisedec priest, who has no end of days, who lives eternally.

Then follows a conclusion, a summing up of the whole argument. In the stated fact that the Lord Jesus Christ is a priest forever after the order of Melchisedec, "There is a setting aside of the commandment going before (the law and its ordinances) on account of weakness and unprofitableness (for the law made nothing perfect) and the bringing in of a better hope through which we draw near to God." The law is then set aside on account of its weakness and unprofitableness, for it could not perfect anything. All the priestly ordinances and ministrations could not make atonement, nor could bring nigh unto God. It was all imperfection. Yet perfection and bringing His children nigh unto Himself is God's gracious and eternal purpose. And God has accomplished this now in the person of His ever blessed Son, the priest after the order of Melchisedec. This is the bringing in of a better hope; by Him we draw near unto God. This truth is more fully developed later.

Verses 20-28. An additional argument is given. The priesthood of Christ was established by an oath, while that of Aaron was not. Swearing an oath God said as to Him, who sat down at His own right hand, "The Lord hath sworn, and will not repent, Thou art a priest forever, after the order of Melchisedec." How superior, then, this priesthood! By so much, also, hath Jesus become surety of a better covenant." And furthermore, they were many priests, for they were mortal men and died. But Christ continueth forever and hath the unchangeable priesthood. And this ever-living priest is able to save to the uttermost those that come unto God by Him, seeing that He always liveth to make intercession for them." He saves completely and keeps His own by His priestly, all-powerful intercession, for eternal glory. And what a high priest He is! Such a high priest! Well may His own in holy joy and praise cry out—"Such a high priest!" He is holy, harmless, undefiled, and separate from sinners. "In His official dignity and glory He is made higher than the heavens." And He has no need, day by day, as the earthly high priests, first to offer up sacrifices for His own sins, then for those of the people. This He did once for all when He offered up Himself. What a contrast with the Jewish priests. They were sinners—He, separate from sinners and absolutely holy; they with the many sacrifices, which could accomplish nothing for man—He with the one great sacrifice which has accomplished all. And so He maketh intercession for them who have believed in Him, the many sons He brings to glory. He is holy and heavenly—even so are all His own, saved by grace, holy and partakers of the heavenly calling (3:1).

CHAPTER 8

1. Christ, the High Priest (8:1-6)
2. The old covenant and the new (8:7-13)

Verses 1-6. The new priesthood which the better priest exerciseth in heaven furthermore implies also a change in the sacrifices and in the covenant. This is now more fully developed in the last three chapters of this section. There is first of all a summary. The priest we have is not ministering on earth but "we have such an high priest, who is set on the right hand of the throne of the Majesty in the heavens; a minister of the sanctuary, and of the true tabernacle, which the Lord has pitched, and not man." Every high priest had to offer gifts and sacrifices, so it was of necessity that He also should have something to offer. What He has offered is brought out in the ninth and tenth chapters. As high priest He offered up Himself on the cross and then, as the high priest who had brought this perfect offering, He passed through the heavens and into heaven itself. If He were upon the earth and His priesthood went no further than the earth, He would not be a priest. He has no place among the Levitical priests, the priests who offered according to the law, whose office and ministrations were but shadows of heavenly things; but He hath obtained a more excellent ministry, because He is the mediator of a better covenant, which has for a foundation better promises.

As Christ came not from Aaron's family He could not be a priest after that pattern; His priesthood is wholly different, for it is heavenly and exercised in glory. With this more excellent priesthood, foreshadowed in the earthly Levitical priesthood, the latter has been completely set aside. This is the truth these Hebrew believers needed more fully to lay hold on, because the earthly tabernacle was still standing and the earthly priests were still exercising their empty and meaningless functions. And that which is put away, which is gone, because the one great offering was brought, and the true high priest has entered into the holiest and is in the presence of God for His people, Satan has successfully introduced and established upon Christian ground as one of the most soul-destroying inventions. Ritualistic Christendom with a priesthood patterned after the extinct Jewish priesthood, with a worship more or less after the model of Israel's worship, is the shade of the departed shadow. It is apostasy from the truth of the gospel of grace; it is a wicked denial of the gospel of our salvation. This priestly assumption of men is the worst possible corruption of the doctrine of Christ.

Verses 7-13. The preceding verse showed that Christ is the mediator of a better covenant. This leads next to a contrast between the first (the old) and the new covenant. A covenant contains the necessary principles established by God under which man may live with God, in which He deals with man. There are only two covenants. The old covenant which was established at Sinai, the law-covenant, and the new covenant which in its fullest meaning has not yet been ratified, for it also relates to the people of Israel as we shall soon learn from this chapter. Strictly speaking the gospel, the proclamation of the salvation of God, is not a covenant. Still those who accept the gospel possess all the spiritual blessings of this new covenant, and much more than Israel can ever possess, when at last as a converted nation this new covenant will be established with them.

The argument is simple. The fact that a new covenant is promised shows that the old covenant was insufficient. "For if that first one had been faultless, then would no place have been sought for the second." It could not accomplish what was in God's heart to bring His people into the closest and nearest relationship with Himself. The first covenant, the law, could not do this, and therefore "finding fault, He saith unto them, Behold the days come, saith the Lord, when I will make a new covenant with the house of Israel and the house of Judah. Not according to the covenant that I made with their fathers in the day when I took them by the hand to lead them out of the land of Egypt, because they did not continue in my covenant, and I did not regard them, saith the Lord."

This first covenant was conditional, and the people did not keep this covenant and the Lord, because they were disobedient, did not regard them. That first covenant was unto their condemnation. And therefore the Lord had announced through the prophet Jeremiah that a new covenant was to be consummated for Israel and Judah, the same people with whom the first covenant was made. "For this is the covenant that I will make with the house of Israel after those days, saith the Lord, I will put my laws in their mind, and with them in their hearts; and I will be God unto them, and they shall be my people. And they shall not teach every man his neighbor, and every man his brother, saying, know the Lord: for all shall know me of the least to the greatest. For I will be merciful to their unrighteousness, and their sins, and their iniquities I will remember no more" (Jeremiah 31:31-34). This new covenant is unlike the old one in that it has no condition attached to it. In it the Lord speaks alone in words of soverign grace—"I will." It is the same what Jehovah promised to the nation through the prophet Ezekiel (chapter 36). And this grace covenant awaits its fulfillment for that nation in coming days.

The ground of this new covenant is the sacrificial death of Christ, His blood, as we learn from His own words when He instituted His supper. Because He died for that nation (John 6:51-52) all Israel—the house of Israel and the house of Judah—will be brought into the promised blessings through this grace covenant. In the meantime, while Israel has not yet entered into this new covenant, Gentiles, who are by nature aliens from the commonwealth of Israel, and strangers from the covenants of promise (no new covenant being promised to Gentiles), believing in Christ, are made nigh by the blood of Christ (Eph. 2:12-13), enjoy every spiritual blessing in heavenly places in Christ, become members of the body of Christ and joint heirs with the Lord Jesus Christ. When the fullness of the Gentiles has come in (Rom. 11:25) then God will turn in mercy to His people Israel, whom He hath not cast away, and this new covenant will be fully established and all the promises as to restoration, temporal blessings, as well, spiritual blessings, so richly promised throughout the Old Testament prophetic word, will through grace come upon them. Then their sins and iniquities will be remembered no more. It all comes to pass when He comes again, who alone can turn away ungodliness from Jacob. What light and joy these facts of the old covenant set aside and the promises of the new covenant must have brought to the hearts of these Hebrew believers who read first this great message.

("Modern Judaism [both rabbinical and rationalistic] is not able to account for the cessation of sacrifices and the Levitical dispensation. The former acknowledges that in the destruction of the temple and the present condition of Israel without high priest and offerings, divine judgment on the nation's sin is expressed: the idea of atonement through a vicarious sacrifice is not quite extinct, as appears in the rite of the cock performed on the eve of the day of atonement, though devoid of all Scriptural authority. Rationalistic Judaism has departed still further from the truth. Rejecting the idea of substitution and expiation in connection with sacrifices, it regards the present condition of Israel as a more spiritual development, misinterpreting the protests of David and the prophets against a mere external view of the ceremonial law (Ps. 40:7; Hos. 6:6; Jer. 7:21-23). The old has indeed vanished; but according to the will of God, because the true light now shineth, because the substance has come in Christ" A. Saphir.)

CHAPTER 9

1. The first tabernacle and its worship (9:1-10)
2. The blood and the perfect work accomplished (9:11-23)
3. The Priest in heaven (9:24-28)

Verses 1-10. The Spirit of God now brings forth the greatest and most blessed facts concerning Christ, the offering He brought, and what has been accomplished by that offering. First the worldly sanctuary, the tabernacle, which was connected with the old covenant is briefly mentioned. It was erected by divine command, exhibiting divine wisdom and foreshadowed, like the levitical priesthood, the better things to come. Yet it was a "worldly sanctuary," that is, it was tangible according to this present world and built of materials of the earth. The antithesis to worldly is heavenly, uncreated, eternal. Everything in this tabernacle had a spiritual meaning. But it is not the purpose here to explain these things, the shadows of spiritual realities, for the apostle writes "of which we cannot now speak particularly." He does not give a complete description of the tabernacle at all. Nothing is said of the outer court, nor of the brazen altar, the golden altar of incense and other details. His object is not to explain the tabernacle but to demonstrate one great fact. He speaks of the two principal parts of the tabernacle, divided by the interior veil. Into the second the highpriest entered in only once every year, not without blood—"the Holy Spirit signifying this, that the way into the holiest was not yet made manifest, while the first tabernacle had yet its standing." This is the truth he demonstrates. the way into the holiest, into God's presence was barred; the veil was in the way and concealed Him. All the gifts and sacrifices brought in that tabernacle could not give perfection as to the conscience—they could not lead the people into the holiest and give peace to the conscience.

Verses 11-23. With verse eleven begins the setting forth of the perfection which now has come. From here to the close of the tenth chapter we have the heart of this great epistle. The most blessed truth of the great work of Christ accomplished for His people is now gloriously displayed. The greatest contrast between the old things and the new is reached. Two little words of deep significance stand at the beginning of this section—"But Christ—." The gifts and offerings, the meats and drinks, the divine washings, the carnal ordinances, all and everything could not do anything for sinful man—but Christ. It is well for the understanding of what follows to give a summary of what is here taught. "But Christ having come, a highpriest of the good things that are come, by the better and more perfect tabernacle, not made with hands, that is to say, not of this building (creation)—neither by the blood of goats and bulls, but by His own blood, He hath entered in once for all into the holy places, having found an eternal redemption." Christ having come, perfection has come through His own precious blood. The blood of Jesus has opened the way into the Holiest and the believer is admitted into the presence of God by that new and living way which He has consecrated for us through the veil, that is to say, His flesh. The next chapter brings this out more fully, that believers on earth have a free, a full, a perfect access to God. The believer can now go in perfect liberty, not into an earthly tabernacle, but into heaven where His holiness dwells and be perfectly at home there in virtue of the work of Christ and His own presence there. Such is the believer's position in the presence of God through the entrance of our highpriest into the heavenly sanctuary.

And the believer can go in without doubt and fear, for he has no more conscience of sin, his conscience is made perfect before God through Christ who through the eternal Spirit offered Himself without spot to God. The question of sin is settled forever. "A perfect conscience is not an innocent conscience which, happy in its unconsciousness, does not know evil, and does not know God revealed in holiness. A perfect conscience knows God; it is cleansed, and, having the knowledge of good and evil according to light of God Himself, it knows that it is purified from all evil according to His purity.

Now the blood of bulls and goats, and the washing repeated under the law, could never make the conscience perfect. They could sanctify carnally, so as to enable the worshipper to approach God outwardly, yet only afar off, with the veil still unrent. But a real purification from sin and sins, so that the soul can be in the presence of God Himself in the light without spot, with the consciousness of being so, the offerings under the law could never produce. They were but figures. But, thanks be to God, Christ has accomplished the work; and is present for us now in the heavenly and eternal sanctuary, He is the witness there that our sins are put away; so that all conscience of sin before God is destroyed, because we know that He who bore our sins is in the presence of God, after having accomplished the work of expiation. Thus we have the consciousness of being in the light without spot. We have the purification not only of sins but of the conscience, so that we can use this access to God in full liberty and joy, presenting ourselves before Him who has so loved us *(Synopsis of the Bible)*.

And thus these Hebrews (as well as we) know that the true highpriest is in the sanctuary above, not with the blood of sacrifices, but He has put away sin by the sacrifice of Himself. As man on earth, in the perfection and value of His person, He offered Himself, by the eternal Spirit, without spot, to God. And therefore every sinner who comes to God through Him is purged from dead works to serve the living God. Being therefore perfectly cleansed, perfectly brought into God's presence, in possession of an eternal (in contrast with earthly) redemption and an eternal inheritance, the believer can serve the living God. All this was unknown in the legal covenant. It is then that through the death of Christ and the subsequent bestowal of the Holy Spirit believers are constituted true worshippers in the heavenly sanctuary, a holy priesthood. Christ is the perfect mediator. And therefore no earthly priesthood is needed. The attempt to introduce priestly mediation of sinful men between Christ and His people, whom He is not ashamed to call brethren is anti-Christian, the offspring of Satan. Adolph Saphir, the author of an able exposition of Hebrews has exposed the Romish blasphemy in aping the defunct Judaism in words, which are worthy to be quoted.

"What a marvellous confusion of Jewish, pagan, and Christian elements do we see here! Jewish things which have waxed old, and vanished away; preparatory and imperfect elements which the apostle does not scruple to call beggarly now that the fulness has come—revived without divine authority, and changed and perverted to suit circumstances for which they were never intended. Pagan things, appealing to the deep-seated and time-confirmed love of idolatry, and of sensuous and mere outward performances; the Babylonian worship of the Queen of Heaven; the intercession of saints and angels, the mechanical repetition of formulas, the superstitious regard of places, seasons, and relics. Buried among these elements are some relics of Christian truth, without which this ingenious fabric could not have existed so long, and influenced so many minds—a truth which in the merciful condescension of God is blessed to sustain the life of His chosen ones in the mystical Babylon.

"This so-called church, vast and imposing, opens its door wide, except to those who honor the Scriptures, and who magnify the Lord Jesus. It can forgive sins, and grant pardons and indulgences, extending the astounding assumption of jurisdiction even beyond the grave; yet it cannot bring peace to the wounded conscience, and renewal to the aching heart, because it never fully and simply declares the efficacy of the blood of Jesus, by which we obtain perfect remission, and the power of the Holy Ghost, who joins us to Christ. This community speaks of sacrifice, of altars, of priesthood, and stands between the people and the sanctuary above, the only High Priest, who by His sacrifice has entered for us into the holy of holies. And in our day this great apostasy has reached a point which we would fain regard as its culminating point, when it places the Virgin Mary by the side of the Lord Jesus as sinless and pure, and when it arrogates for man infallible authority over the heritage of God."

(Dr. M. Luther describes the Romish harlot in these excellent words: "The Church of Rome is not built upon the rock of the divine word, but on the sand of human reasoning." It is a rationalistic church. And Lutheranism, Episcopalianism and other sects are turning back to it and support the Satanic counterfeit of a man made priesthood.)

Verses 15-23. These verses introduce once more

the question of covenant. The covenant of which the Lord Jesus Christ is the mediator is now identified with a testament of which He is the testator. When there is a testament there must also of necessity be the death of the testator, before the rights and possessions acquired in the testament can be possessed and enjoyed. The first covenant was inaugurated by blood. "For when Moses had spoken every commandment to all the people according to the law, he took the blood of bulls and goats, with water and scarlet wool and hyssop (Lev. 14:4, Num. 19:6) and sprinkled both the book and the people, saying, this is the blood of the covenant which God hath enjoined unto you." So also the tabernacle and the vessels were sprinkled with blood. Yea, almost all things are according to the law purified with blood "and without shedding of blood is no remission." The blood was used in a threefold manner. The covenant itself is founded on the blood. Defilement is washed away by the blood and the guilt is taken away through the blood that hath been shed. And all this is only fully realized through the blood shed by the Lord Jesus Christ, He died and all the blessings of the new and better covenant are righteously willed to the believer.

Verses 24-28. "For Christ is not entered into the holy places made with hands, the figures of the true; but into heaven itself, now to appear in the presence of God for us." After His great sacrifice He entered heaven itself, where He now is, appearing in the presence of God for His people. "Nor yet that He should offer Himself often, as the high priest enters into the holy place every year with blood of others; for then must He often have suffered since the foundation of the world, but now once in the consummation of the ages hath He appeared to put away sin by the sacrifice of Himself." The sacrifice He brought needs not to be repeated, it is all-sufficient for all eternity. If He were to offer again it would be necessary also to suffer again. Both are impossible. (The Romish assumption of the Lord's Supper being a sacrifice and that the blasphemous mass is an unbloody sacrifice are completely refuted by verse 26, by this entire chapter and by the teaching of the New Testament.) At the completion of the ages of probation (the age before the law and the age under the law), when man's utter ruin and hopeless condition had been fully demonstrated, He appeared in the fullness of time (the completion of the ages) and put away sin by the sacrifice of Himself. And here let us remember that the full and complete results of this work are not yet manifested. Sin will ultimately be blotted out of God's creation. The blessed words which came from His gracious lips, when He gave Himself on the cross—"It is finished"—will find their fullest meaning when all things are made new, when the first heaven and earth are passed away and a new heaven and new earth are come, when all things are made new. Then His voice will declare once more "It is done" (Rev. 21:1-6).

But now for those who believe sin is put away. It is appointed unto men—natural men—once to die and after this the judgment. From the latter the believer is exempt. His own words "He that heareth my words, and believeth in Him that sent Me, hath everlasting life and shall not come into judgment, but is passed from death unto life" (John 5:24) assure us of this. And when the believer dies, it is no longer as penalty. A day will come at last when it will be fulfilled "Behold I show you a mystery, we shall not all sleep, but shall be changed in a moment, in the twinkling of an eye." And He who was once offered to bear the sins of many (those who believe in Him) shall appear the second time. "Unto them that look for Him shall He appear the second time, apart from sin, for salvation." It is His second coming. When He comes again He has nothing to do with sin, as far as His people are concerned. This was settled forever in His first coming. But He comes for their salvation their complete deliverance from all the results of sin, and His own will be changed into His image.

("Without sin" is in contrast with "to bear the sins of many." But it will be remarked, that the taking up of the Church is not mentioned here. It is well to notice the language. The character of His second coming is the subject. He has been *manifested* once. Now He is *seen* by those who look for Him. The expression may apply to the deliverance of the Jews who wait for Him in the last days. He will appear for their deliverance. But we expect the Lord for this deliverance, and we shall see Him when He accomplishes it even for us. The apostle does not touch the question of the difference between this and our being caught up, and does not use the word which serves to announce His public manifestation. He will appear to those who expect Him. He is not seen by all the world, nor is it consequently the judgment, although that may follow. The Holy Ghost speaks only of them that look for the Lord. To them He will appear. By them He will be seen, and it will be the time of their deliverance; so that it is true for us, and also applicable to the Jewish remnant in the last days" *Synopsis of the Bible.*)

CHAPTER 10

1. The all-sufficiency of the one offering (10:1-18)
2. Exhortations (10:19-25)
3. Warning (10:26-31)
4. Encouragements (10:32-39)

Verses 1-18. The precious truth the apostle has unfolded in the preceding chapters concerning Christ, His one offering He made, His own blood by which He entered once for all into the holy place the one all sufficient sacrifice, which has an eternal value and can never be repeated, is now still more practically applied. This one offering sanctifieth and it hath perfected forever them that are sanctified, so that the believer thus sanctified and perfected can enter into the holiest as worshipper. The sacrifices brought in the first covenant did not make the worshippers perfect. If such had been the case there would have been no need to repeat them year by year continually. The repetition of these sacrifices in the law dispensation was a memorial of sin. "In those sacrifices there is a remembrance again of sins every year." The day of atonement was repeated every year and each time the highpriest entered in the holiest with the blood of others. But the worshippers were not purged by it; the conscience as to sins remained, and those worshippers could not enter in themselves. For it was not possible that the blood of bulls and goats should take away sins. Yet the sins of Jewish believers before the cross were forgiven, not because the blood of an animal was sprinkled on the mercy-seat, but in anticipation of the one great offering, known to God in all its value and meaning.

(See Romans 3:25. The remission of sins that are past are the sins of Old Testament believers. The work of Christ on the cross declares God's righteousness in having passed over the sins of those who believed the promise.)

All is now changed. The one offering has been brought; by His own blood He entered the heavenly sanctuary, and all who believe are purged, the conscience is cleansed, we draw nigh and enter the holiest, not by the blood of bulls and goats, but by the blood of Jesus.

Verses 5-9 are of deep interest. It reveals what passed between God the Father and God the Son. When about to enter the world these words were spoken by Him to the Father; "Sacrifice and offering Thou wouldest not, but a body hast Thou prepared Me; in burnt-offerings and sacrifices for sin Thou hast had no pleasure. Then I said Lo, I come (in the volume of the book it is written of Me) to do Thy will, O God. (What a testimony the Son of God bears as to the character of the Old Testament Scriptures! As He said on earth "they testify of Me.") It is a startling revelation, the Spirit of God acquainting us with what transpired between the Father and the Son. He comes into the world to do God's eternal will.

"He is the Son of God from all eternity, and in that mysterious eternity before the creation of the world, in His pre-mundane glory, this mind was in the Son, that He would humble Himself, and take upon Himself the form of a servant, and obey the whole counsel of God concerning the redemption of fallen man. His whole life on earth, embracing His obedience and His death, His substitution for sinners, was His own voluntary resolve and act.

True, the Father sent Him; but such is the unity and harmony of the blessed Trinity, that it is equally true to say, the Son came. The love of the Lord Jesus, the sacrifice of Himself in our stead, the unspeakable humiliation of the Son of God, have their origin not in time but in eternity, in the infinite, self-subsistent, co-equal Son of the Father. He took on Him our nature. By His own will He was made flesh. From all eternity He offered Himself to accomplish the divine will concerning our salvation, He must needs be God, to have the power of freely offering Himself; He must needs take upon Him our nature to fulfil that sacrifice. Only the Son of God could undertake the work of our redemption; only as man could He accomplish it" (A. Saphir).

He speaks of "a body hast Thou prepared Me." This means His virgin-birth. The body the Son of God took on was a prepared body, called into existence by a creative act of the Holy Spirit (Luke 1:35).

The sentence, "A body hast Thou prepared Me," is the Septuagint translation, or paraphrase, of the Hebrew, "ears hast Thou digged for Me" (Ps. 40:6). This reading, or interpretation, is here fully sanctioned by the Holy Spirit. The ear is for learning, and the opened ear stands for obedience (Is. 50:5). In taking on the human body He took the form of a servant. See also Exodus 21. And thus He offered Himself, as One who had the power to do so, out of love for the glory of God, to do His will. He undertook of His own free will the accomplishment of all the will of God and He took on the prepared body in incarnation in order to accomplish the eternal will of God. In this prepared body He lived that blessed life of obedience, suffering from man for God, and then He gave that body, according to the will of God, in His death, when He suffered from God for man, in being made sin for us.

"God's rights as the Lawgiver have been fully satisfied by the unsullied and complete obedience of the Lord Jesus. He magnified the law which man had taken and dishonored. Having fulfilled it in His life, He gave Himself to death, that He might silence forever its demand on the believing sinner's life. By man and for man the will of God has been fulfilled. In the life and death of the Lord Jesus the active measure of both grace and truth has been attained. God's will was the redemption of His people. But that His grace might triumph, His holiness must first be satisfied. The cross of Christ has effected this. God's will, when finished, is thus found to be atonement. Blood has been shed, in obedience to His commandment, which is of virtue to remove all sin. It pleased Him to bruise His Son for sinners. He has laid upon Him the iniquity of all His people. By making Him an offering for sin, He has finished His intention of salvation. He has established grace in perfect righteousness" (A. Pridham). And thus "He taketh away the first (the ordinances of the law, the burnt-offerings and sacrifices) and established the second (the will of God perfectly done). "By the which will we have been sanctified through the offering of the body of Jesus Christ once for all."

This is a great and most blessed truth. His people, those who believe in Christ, are according to the will of God, to be sanctified, that is set apart to God. And this sanctification of all who believe is accomplished by the offering of the body of Jesus Christ once for all. The will of man has no part in this; the work by which believers are sanctified is absolutely and wholly of God. It was done once for all when Christ died on the Cross; before we were in existence it was all done. In this faith rests, knowing that He hath sanctified us, that His work, not ours, nor our experience, has accomplished our sanctification. Believers belong to God for ever according to the efficacy of the offering of the body of Jesus Christ once for all. And this setting aside abides; it is as settled and permanent as the peace which was made, the peace with God, the abiding possession, of all who are justified by faith. There is also for those who are sanctified in Christ, a practical sanctification which is wrought by the Spirit of God in the believer (12:14).

Once more a contrast is made between Him and the levitical priests. The priests stood ministering, always bringing the same sacrifices over and over again. And they could never take away sins. But He having offered one sacrifice for sins, sat down forever at the right hand of God. (It is not "eternal," but continuously, without interruption; He is at rest, His work is finished.) The work is accepted and believers are accepted in Him. Those who are sanctified are perfected in perpetuity by what He has done. He is forever seated, we are forever perfected by virtue of His work. And there at the right hand of God He is also waiting in patience till it pleases God to make His enemies the footstool of His feet. That will be when He comes the second time. And the Holy Spirit bears witness to it. That witness is in the Word of Go; there the Spirit of God speaks. "If we could have heard the counsel of eternity, the word of the Father to the Son, ere time began, we could have no greater certainty than now, when we listen to Scripture, the echo in time of the counsel in eternity." We see here in this chapter up to verse 15 the three persons of the Godhead in connection with redemption. The will of God is the source of the work of redemption; the Son of God accomplished it; the Holy Spirit bears witness of it. Here again is an allusion to the new covenant in verses 16-17. (See 8:10-12.) Blessed assurance which all believers have "their sins and their iniquities will I remember no more." This is the witness of the Holy Spirit.

Verses 19-25. And now the great truth is reached which the Holy Spirit wanted these Hebrew Christians to lay hold of and for which He so wonderfully prepared the way. He has shown that by the sacrifice of Christ the believers' sins are put away; a perfect and everlasting cleansing has been made, remission assured and an eternal redemption obtained. By the will of God believers are sanctified by the offering of the body of Jesus Christ once for all; they are perfected and therefore in the eyes of a holy God, believers are without sin. This gives liberty to come into God's presence. The veil is rent and we can enter in. There is no more barrier; we have a free and unfettered access. "Having therefore, brethren, boldness to enter into the holy places by the blood of Jesus, a new and living way which He hath consecrated for us through the veil, that is to say, His flesh." And we do not go in alone but we find Him in the holiest who has done the work. He is there as a great highpriest to welcome us and to minister in tenderness to our needs.

Upon this follow three exhortations. 1. "Let us draw near with a true heart in full assurance of faith, having our hearts sprinkled from an evil conscience, and our body washed with pure water (corresponding to the washing of the priests, Ex. 29:4, and typical of regeneration)." We are then a holy priesthood fit and fitted in Christ to offer up spiritual sacrifices. 2. "Let us hold fast the confession of the hope without wavering for He is faithful who hath promised." And we shall hold fast if we draw near and constantly realize our nearness, our blessings and privileges in Christ. 3. "Let us consider one another to provoke unto love and good works; not forsaking the assembling of ourselves together, as the custom is with some, but encouraging one another, and so much the more as ye see the day approaching." It is the public confession of God's people that they are one and belong together. And they saw the day approaching which is here not the day when His people will be gathered together unto Him, caught up in clouds to meet Him in the air, but the day of His appearing.

Verses 26-31. A solemn warning is now once more added. It warns against deliberate apostasy of those who have known the truth (though not regenerated). They are enemies, adversaries and for such wilful going astray there remaineth no longer any sacrifice for sins "but a certain fearful looking for judgment and fiery indignation, which shall devour the adversaries." This was the great danger for these Hebrews who had professed faith in Christ, yet lingered around the levitical institutions as the temple with its worship was still standing. If they renounced the truth of Christianity by turning back to Judaism they trampled under foot the Son of God and counted the blood of the covenant, wherewith they were sanctified an unholy thing; for such horrible, deliberate contempt there was no repentance and no remedy. They cannot escape judgment. It is a fearful thing to fall into the hands of the living God—He who hath said "Vengeance is mine, I will recompense."

("Observe here the way in which sanctification is attributed to the blood; and, also, that professors are treated as belonging to the people. The blood received by faith, consecrates the soul to God; but it is here viewed also as an outward means for setting apart the people as a people. Every individual who had owned Jesus to be the Messiah, and the blood to be the seal and foundation of an everlasting covenant available for eternal cleansing and redemption on the part of God, acknowledging himself to be set apart for God, by this means, as one of the people—every such individual would, if he renounced it, renounce it as such; and there was no other way of sanctifying him. The former system had evidently lost its power for him, and the true one he had abandoned. This is the reason why it is said, 'having received the knowledge of the truth' " *Synopsis of the Bible.*)

Verses 32-39. Words of encouragement and comfort conclude this main section of the Epistle. They had suffered for Christ's sake and he calls to their remembrance their former days. They had endured even with joy the spoiling of their goods, because they knew that they had in heaven a better and enduring substance. He exhorts them to be patient and not to cast away their confidence. The promise was sure. "For yet a little while, and He that shall come will come and will not tarry." Hab. 2:3-4 is quoted. He was sure that they are not of them who draw back unto perdition, but of them that believe (literally: of faith) to the saving of the soul. The chapter which follows describes the action of this faith through the example of their forefathers who walked and lived according to the same principle.

IV. Practical Instructions and Exhortations

CHAPTERS 11—13

1. Faith in regard to creation and salvation (11:1-7)
2. The patience of faith (11:8-22)
3. The energy of faith (11:23-40)

Verses 1-7. The disastrous effect of unbelief has been pointed out in the earlier part of this epistle (3:12, 19; 4:2) as well as the necessity of faith. After the great theme of the epistle, the sacrificial work and priesthood of Christ had been fully demonstrated, faith, in the closing verses of the previous chapter is mentioned once more "the just shall live by faith." To live and walk by faith is inseparably connected with the possession and enjoyment of the good things which have come, the perfection the believer has in Christ. And now the Spirit of God gives a remarkable record of the saints of old and shows how prominent faith was in their lives and experiences. It is one of the great and marvellous chapters not only of this epistle, but of the whole Word of God.

There is a divine order here in the way the names are mentioned as well as many and deep spiritual lessons into which we cannot fully enter. (The purpose of our work makes this impossible. Saphir, A. Pridham and others will be helpful in a more analytical study of this chapter.) First three antedeluvians are mentioned—Abel, Enoch and Noah. The main part of the chapter is devoted to Abraham and his life of faith, trust and patience, Isaac, Jacob and Joseph are also mentioned. That those who lived before the inauguration of the law covenant and the levitical institutions are prominently used in this faith-chapter is not without meaning. These illustrious heads of the Hebrew nation had the promise; the grace-covenant had been established with them, the covenant which was to remain. They had no law and carnal ordinances, no tabernacle, no priest and yet they pleased God by their faith. And now in possession of the promise, fulfilled in Christ, these Hebrew Christians were to live in faith and manifest the patience of faith, even as Abraham (whom they called "our father Abraham") did.

The first statement speaks of faith, not so much as a definition, but as a declaration of the action and power of faith. The Revised Version is better in its rendering than the King James translation. "Now faith is the assurance (or substantiation) of things hoped for, the conviction of things not seen." Faith makes real to the soul that which we hope for and is a demonstration of that which we do not see. It is therefore assurance and a settled conviction respecting things hoped for, though unseen. "It is the soul's hand that grasps the promised blessings and makes them its very own. Faith lays hold on what is future, but sure, and brings it into the life of the believer, so that in the presence and power of it he lives and walks. It is far-sightedness. It sees and foresees. It pierces into the unseen, it seizes the promised riches of God and makes them a present reality, and therefore the life of the believer may become opulent with noble deeds, because ruled and stimulated by a great motive."

It is by faith we know that the worlds were framed by the Word of God, so that things which are seen were not made of things which do appear. God called all things into existence. Matter is not eternal; the universe is not a producing cause. God has created all things by Him and for Him, who is the eternal Word (Heb. 1:2; John 1:1). Man is unable by searching to solve the mystery of creation. How ridiculous have been the cosmogonies of ancient nations. The evolution theories are equally absurd.[3] "In the beginning God created the heavens and the earth." This we believe that the worlds were famed by the Word of God. Abel is next mentioned. The truth of salvation is seen in his case. Sin and death had come in. By faith, trusting in the promise, acknowledging his true condition, he brought a more excellent sacrifice than Cain. He approached God with that more excellent sacrifice. He obtained witness that he was righteous. He was justified by faith. And Abel himself who died by the hand of his brother is a type of the Lord Jesus Christ and His sacrifice.

Enoch was translated by faith that he should not see death. In Abel the truth of righteousness by faith is illustrated. Enoch, walking with God, believing God and prophesying (Jude 14-15) went to heaven without passing through death. The power of death was destroyed in his case; the power of that life he possessed was manifested in his translation. How blessedly Abel and Enoch show forth that by faith righteousness and life are bestowed upon those who believe. The great sacrifice, typified by Abel's more excellent sacrifice and also by his death, has conquered death. Through death Christ has destroyed him who had the power of death (Heb. 2:14).

---

[3]It would be a good thing if the men of science to-day would give heed to such a text as this. Take Darwin's *Origin of the Species,* where he never gets, indeed, to the origin, and owns that he cannot prove that any species ever did originate after the fashion he decrees. And think of originating in his manner Eve out of Adam! Given even the rib, she could not have sprung out of that simply. There must have been what did not appear—the power of God. If it is not perfectly scientific to believe that in her case, we may as well give up Scripture at once, for you cannot expunge the miraculous out of it. If it be only a question of less or more, how unreasonable to measure out the power of God, and how enormous the pretence of being able to say just how much this power, or how or when it shall be fitting for it to be displayed!

After all, Scripture is at once the most scientific and rational of books, while it is, besides, a miracle of the most stupendous kind, always ready to hand, and with its own power of conviction for any who will examine it. And this one may say in the face of all the higher critics in the world, who are simply the Darwinians of theology, and who, like them, theorize after the most stupendous fashion and then talk about the credulity of faith" *Numerical Bible.*

Enoch is a type of the Church. He prophesied of coming judgment (the deluge) but did not pass through that judgment. Even so the true Church, when the Lord comes, will be taken from earth to glory without dying, before tribulation, wrath and judment come upon this age, which ends like the days of Noah. Enoch also received testimony before he was translated that he pleased God, for he walked in faith in His presence and in His fellowship. This is the walk into which all God's people are called and which faith and the power of the indwelling spirit make possible. Without faith (a faith which clings close to Him, trusts in His word and is obedient) it is impossible to please Him.

Verse 7 speaks of Noah and his faith. In this verse we find mentioned the ground of faith (warned of God); the realm of faith (things not seen); the exercise of faith (he feared); the work of faith (he prepared an ark); the result of faith (he saved his house); the testimony of faith (he condemned the world) and the reward of faith (heir to righteousness). It is the most remarkable verse in the whole chapter. Enoch was caught up to heaven before the deluge came. Noah was warned of the unseen judgment to come (which Enoch had warned would come) and was roused with godly fear. He is a type of the godly remnant of Jews at the end of this present age, who will pass through tribulation and judgment, after the true Church has left the earth, and having passed through the judgment, as Noah did, will inherit the earth. Noah represents the faith and exercise of this Jewish remnant, which will be saved out of the judgments at the close of this age.

Verses 8-22. The obedience and patience of faith is the theme of verses 8-22. Obediently Abraham went out, not knowing whether he was going. He obeyed the voice, believed the promise of God. Faith made of him a stranger in the land of promise as in a foreign country. He had no permanent place, but as a pilgrim he dwelt in tents with Isaac and Jacob—"for he waited for the city which hath foundations, whose architect and maker God is." God revealed to him the heavenly city and in patience he waited for that city, and while he waited he dwelt there content in perfect reliance on God. It was by faith that Sarah received strength to conceive seed "because she counted Him faithful that promised." And then they died in faith "not having received the promise, but having seen them (by the eyes of faith) afar off and embraced them, and confessed that they were strangers and pilgrims on earth." This faith in its power and action is exemplified. By faith Abraham offered up Isaac. He manifested in this act that absolute confidence in God, which, at His command, can renounce even God's own promises as possessed after the flesh, confident that God would restore them through the exercise of His power, overcoming death.[4] By faith Isaac and Jacob acted. And Joseph, a stranger in a strange land, yet believing the promises as to the land, reckoned in faith on their fulfillment and thus gave commandment concerning his bones (Gen. 50:25).

Verses 23-40. Faith in this section illustrates the energy connected with it which surmounts any obstacle and difficulty, and, trusting, brings forth the manifestations of God's power in deliverance. Such was the faith of the parents of Moses. They hid the child and were not afraid. "Faith does not reason; it acts from its own point of vision and leaves the result to God." And how this energy of faith is illustrated in Moses himself. His faith renounced the wealth, power, glory and splendor of Egypt. He gave up a princely position, the possibility of an earthly throne and identified himself with the people who had become slaves, because he believed them to be the people of God. Faith taught him not to fear the wrath of the king; faith fears nothing, but God and faith has nothing to fear. The secret was "he endured as seeing Him who is invisible." By faith he celebrated the passover and the sprinkling of blood, that the destroyer of the firstborn might not touch them.

And what more? The Red Sea, the walls of Jericho, the harlot Rahab.[5] God's power opened

---

[4]"Observe here that, when trusting in God and giving up all for Him, we always gain, and we learn something more of the ways of His power: for in renouncing according to His will anything already received, we ought to expect from the power of God that He will bestow something else. Abraham renounces the promise after the flesh. He sees the city which has foundations; he can desire a heavenly country. He gives up Isaac, in whom were the promises: he learns resurrection, for God is infallibly faithful. The promises were in Isaac: therefore God must restore him to Abraham, and by resurrection, if he offered him in sacrifice" *Synopsis of the Bible.*

[5]"Rahab the harlot! Those who seek for proofs of the divine authorship of Scripture may find one here. Was there ever an Israelite who would have thought of preferring that woman's name to the names of David and Samuel and the prophets, and of coupling it with the names of the great leader and prophet of the Jewish faith "whom the Lord knew face to face?" And what Jew would have dared to give expression to such a thought!" Sir R. Anderson, K.C.B.

the way to faith through the Red Sea for the salvation of His people while the unbelieving Egyptian perished. Jericho's walls fall and Rahab's house, standing upon the wall, is preserved because she believed. And then Gideon, Barak, Samson, Jephthah, David, Samuel and the prophets and the heroes of faith which follow. Their names are not given, but God knows them all as well as the countless thousands of martyrs who are constantly added to this list. "The strongest thing in the world is faith—it has an eagle's eye and lion's heart. It has a lion's heart to confront dangers and hardships, and an eagle's eye to descry the unseen glories and the sure victory. The heroism of faith is a wonderful thing. It may suffer indescribable tortures and agonies, as often it has, but it is unconquerable, invincible. Some were tortured (tympanized, i.e., stretched in a wheel as the drumhead), 'that they might obtain a better resurrection,' as were the mother and her seven sons who were put to death one after the other, and in sight of each other, by the Syrian monster, Antiochus Epiphanes (2 Macc. 7). Some were stoned, as Zechariah (2 Chron. 24) and Jeremiah, according to tradition. Some were sawn asunder, as was Isaiah under Manasseh. Some were slain with the sword, as Urijah, (Jer. 26:23), and James the brother of John (Acts 12). They might have rustled in silks and velvets and luxuriated in the palaces of princes had they denied God and believed the world's lie. Instead, they wandered about in sheepskins and goatskins, themselves accounted no better than goats or sheep, nay, they like these reckoned fit only for the slaughter. The world thought them unworthy to live here, while God thought them worthy to live with Him in glory" (Professor Moorhead).

"God having provided some better thing for us, that not apart from us should they be made perfect." The Old Testament saints who died in faith have not yet been raised from among the dead; their spirits are in His presence. New Testament saints constituting the Church, the body of Christ, have provided for themselves "some better thing." But the Spirit of God does not here enlarge upon this and only gives the information that the perfection of the Old Testament saints in resurrection from among the dead will not be apart from us, the New Testament saints. And that will be when the Lord comes for His saints with the shout (1 Thess. 4:13-18).

CHAPTER 12

1. Looking away unto Jesus (12:1-2)
2. The Contradiction of sinners (12:3-4)
3. Chastened as sons (12:5-11)
4. Exhortations (12:12-17)
5. The end of faith (12:18-24)
6. The final warning (12:25-29)

Verses 1-2. "Therefore seeing we also are compassed about with so great a cloud of witnesses, let us lay aside every weight, and the sin which doth so easily beset us, and let us run with steadfastness the race lying before us."

Some teach that the Old Testament saints are spectators of us and that they look upon us now from heaven. Dean Alford also states that they are lookers on and adds "Whosoever denies such reference, misses, it seems to me, the very point of the sense." Others have gone so far as to say that they not only look on but help the believer in his conflict on earth. But this view is unscriptural. We know that angels are spectators (1 Cor. 4:9; 11:10); angels are ministering spirits to minister unto the heirs of salvation, but the disembodied spirits of the righteous are neither spectators nor do they minister to the saints on earth. The preceding chapter contains "the cloud of witness"; they witness to us by their lives and the victory of their faith and this is the encouragement for us. The Christian's life is a race; the glory at His coming is the goal. The runner of the race does not burden himself with weights, unnecessary things. Everything that impedes spiritual progress must be laid aside, as well as the sin that so easily besets us, which is the sin of unbelief. Against this sin they had been emphatically warned. "It is a sin that easily besets us, because it is but the mind of nature acting, according to its instincts, against the will of God." And the runner's eyes are to be on the goal (Phil. 3). The believer runs the race with steadfastness and divests himself of every weight and the sin that easily besets, if he looks away from everything and looks away "unto Jesus, the author and finisher of faith (Leader and Perfecter), who, for the joy that was set before Him, endured the cross, having despised the shame and is set down at the right hand of the throne of God." He is the great exemplar of faith. He is to be constantly before us, and His people are to follow Him in the path of faith and trust. What light these words shed on His blessed life and especially His death on the cross! He endured the cross and despised the shame, connected with it, for the joy that was set before Him. See Isaiah

53:10-12. The joy set before us is to be with Him forever. Oh, for the daily vision of that goal.

"The flesh, the human heart, is occupied with cares and difficulties; and the more we think of them, the more we are burdened by them. It is enticed by the object of its desires, it does not free itself from them. The conflict is with a heart that loves the thing against which we strive; we do not separate ourselves from it in thought. When looking at Jesus, the new man is active; there is a new object, which unburdens and detaches us from every other by means of a new affection which has its place in a new nature: and in Jesus Himself, to whom we look, there is a positive power which sets us free" J. N. Darby.

Verses 3-4. The believer's life is also a conflict, trials which come from sin in the world, a world which is always, and always will be, antagonistic to Christ. Those Hebrews had their share of it; they were persecuted and hated for His Name's sake (10:32-34). Peter also wrote about these persecutions they endured. And now they are called to consider Him who endured such contradiction of sinners against Himself, lest they would be wearied, disheartened and fainting in their minds. These persecutions were the fellowship of His sufferings; and they had not yet resisted unto blood, striving against sin. Looking away unto Him gives strength to resist and to conquer.

Verses 5-11. In these verses the trials of the believer are viewed as chastenings from the Lord. As a loving father, who loves his children, He chastised them. They were not to forget this, that He speaks to them, not as to sinners, but as unto sons, "My son, despise not thou the chastening of the Lord, nor faint when reproved by Him, for whom the Lord loveth He chastiseth and scourgeth every son whom He receiveth." The chastening they were to endure. God, as Father, permits trials and tribulations to come to believers for their own good. Such experiences are not an evidence of divine displeasure, but evidences of sonship. "God dealeth with you as with sons; for who is the son whom the father chastiseth not. But if you are without chastening, of which all are made partakers, then are ye bastards and not sons." And therefore chastisements must not be despised, nor viewed as a discouraging experience; for the chastisement is for our eternal good and He does it in love. Paul's thorn in the flesh was such an experience which was needful for Him. Grace sustains in all chastisements. Then we have a contrast between the chastising of earthly fathers and that of the heavenly Father. The one is father of our flesh; God is the Father of spirits, the Creator and source of life, spiritual and ever-lasting, as well as physical and temporal. The one for a brief period; God during our whole lifetime. The one with imperfect knowledge, in much infirmity "after their own pleasure;" God with unerring wisdom, and in pure love. The aim of the one, our earthly future; the aim of God, to make us partakers of His holiness. Yet imperfect as is the earthly father's discipline, we gave it reverence, "as was right" and according to God's will, and for our safety. How much more ought we to be in subjection unto the Father of spirits, of whom is our true life.

And when we are disciplined it is not a joyous experience; it brings heart-searching, humiliation, confession, repentance and self-loathing, but afterward it yieldeth the peaceable fruit of righteousness unto them which have been exercised in this way.

Verses 12-17. Words of exhortation and encouragement follow. The first three exhortations refer to ourselves (verses 12-13); to others and to God (verse 14). To follow peace (pursue peace) with all men is to characterize those who have peace with God and who know the way of peace. Holiness must also be pursued, for without that none shall see the Lord. In Christ, believers are sanctified once for all, as this Epistle has so clearly demonstrated. The holiness which qualifies a man to see the Lord, is Christ, and His blessed finished work. Abiding in Him the believer pursues the way of holiness, practical holiness, separation from evil in all things. It does not mean a certain "holiness experience" by which a believer is fitted, by eradication of the old nature, or by something else, to see the Lord. In Christ the believer is sanctified; as Martin Luther used to say "My holiness is in Heaven." The exhortation here means to pursue that holiness into which grace has called us, which grace has given and for which grace gives daily power. Closely connected with this is the warning which follows in verses 15-17. The man who falls short of the grace of God, who lacketh that grace which is in Christ Jesus, his heart not resting in Him, is a mere professing believer and possesseth not the holiness, which grace alone can give. He is a root of bitterness and a profane, and earthly-minded person, as Esau was who sold his birthright.

(The time came when he regretted that for a paltry gratification he forfeited his right. Afterwards, when he would have inherited the blessing, he was rejected. For though he sought carefully with tears to change his father's mind he found (in Isaac) no place for change of mind. This seems to be the meaning of this difficult passage. Esau is never represented as an apostle, as one who professed and appeared to be a believer, and then fell away. So (apart from other reasons) the meaning of the apostle cannot be that Esau, as an apostate, was not able to find repentance. But we know that, notwithstanding his vehement and urgent entreaties, Isaac could not change his mind, or repent him of what he had done in conferring the blessing on Jacob, which God approved of" Saphir.)

Verses 18-24. These verses contain a great contrast. The grace of God has brought and is bringing believers to better things than those which characterize Judaism. What the end of faith will be, the goal of glory is here unfolded. Believers have nothing now to do with Sinai, the law and its terror. Then follows a marvellous enumeration of the earthly and heavenly glories to which we have come through faith and which faith beholds. First Mount Zion is mentioned. It is the place the Lord has chosen for His rest (Ps. 132:13-14). When that promised new covenant is fully established with the house of Israel and Judah, when sovereign grace has manifested its powers in the salvation and restoration of His people Israel, then Zion will be the earthly center, and God's appointed King will establish His rule there (Ps. 2). From the glory of the coming millennium we are taken to the glory above "the city of the living God, the heavenly Jerusalem." It is the city for which Abraham looked in faith, the eternal home of the saints of God.

"And to an innumerable company of angels, the universal gathering"; we shall know and behold all the tenants of the unseen world. "The Church of the firstborn ones which are written in heaven"—this is the Church in particular; there will be an unbroken and eternal fellowship with all the saints who constitute the body of Christ. "And to God the Judge of all," whose grace in Christ has put His own beyond all condemnation and who will, in His Son, judge the world in righteousness. "The spirits of just men made perfect" are the Old Testament saints, distinguished in this way from "the Church of the firstborn ones"; they receive their perfection when the Church is gathered home (11:40). "And to Jesus the mediator of the new covenant, and to the blood of sprinkling that speaketh better than Abel." Through Him and His precious blood these earthly and heavenly glories will be accomplished. And faith looks to these. It is the blessed goal for the heirs of God, the many sons He brings to glory.

Verses 25-29. A final warning follows, not to refuse Him that speaketh. (Compare with 2:3.) He that spoke on earth (giving the law) is the same that speaketh from heaven—the Son of God. To refuse Him means no escape from perdition. His voice then shook the earth. The prophetic word predicts another shaking of earth and heaven (Hag. 2:6). That will be when He comes again. Then follows the judgment of all who obeyed not the gospel of our Lord Jesus Christ. The things that can be shaken will be removed and things that cannot be shaken remain. "Therefore let us, receiving a kingdom which cannot be shaken, have grace whereby we may serve God acceptably with reverence and fear; for our God is a consuming fire."

CHAPTER 13

1. The practical walk (13:1-6)
2. The call to separation (13:7-16)
3. Conclusions (13:17-25)

Verses 1-6. No comment is needed on the simple exhortations with which this concluding chapter of this Epistle begins. Brotherly love stands in the foreground. Hospitality and loving kindness to prisoners and those who suffer adversity is especially enjoined. The great high priest in glory sympathizes with such a condition of His saints and we too are to be sympathizers as well as intercessors with Him. The life is to be clean and undefiled. Walking in faith there should be not coveteousness but happy contentment in view of His never failing promise.

Verses 7-16. The first exhortation in these verses is that they should remember their leaders who had spoken the Word of God to them, to follow their faith and to consider the issue of their walk. These leaders had passed away from the earthly service into the presence of the Lord. One abides the same. He must be exalted above everything and He alone can satisfy the hearts of His people. "Jesus Christ is the same yesterday, and today, and forever." He is the unchanging Jehovah who had spoken of old "I am the Lord who changeth not." What a One to follow and to trust. From Him and His gracious riches the enemy tries to lead away God's people and ensnare them. Christ is the person whom Satan hates and all wicked and strange doctrines are invented by him to dishonor that worthy name and to spoil God's children.

Then follows the call to separation, the great exhortation at which the Holy Spirit aimed from the beginning of this document and which He now presses upon the conscience. "We have an altar whereof they have no right to eat who are serving the tabernacle." That altar is Christ for those who have left the shadow things behind and who have found in Him their all in all.

Those who still cling to the Jewish things have no right of access; they have no right to eat if they serve the tabernacle, for everything has passed away since the substance in Christ has come. They had put Christ outside. All had been done as foreshadowed by the legal sacrifices. "Wherefore Jesus also, that He might sanctify the people with His own blood, suffered without the gate." And now all is done and the whole Jewish system has no more meaning. To remain in it and practice the old things, which are gone, is a denial of Christ and His work as the sin-bearer. The camp is the people who continued in the things of the law, who denied thereby that the new sacrifice had been brought; who still used an earthly priesthood and denied thereby that the new and living way into the holy place had been made by the blood of Jesus, the rent veil.

Ritualistic Christendom with its man-made priesthood, its so-called "saving ordinances," its legal principle, so prominent, not only in the worst form of apostate Christendom (the Romish church), but in other systems and sects, is but another camp in which the truth of Christ and His all sufficient work is denied. Outside of the camp is found the cross of Christ with all its grace and glory. And therefore the exhortation, which seems to us was the all-important message for these Hebrews (and for us as well) "let us go forth therefore unto Him without the camp, bearing His reproach. For here we have no continuing city, but we seek one to come." In other words, leave all behind, be separate from all, which denies the cross and the work accomplished there. And "outside the camp" must mean "inside the veil," to enjoy the perfection in Christ, to be in God's holy presence as a true worshipper. "For we are the circumcision who worship God in the spirit, and rejoice in Christ Jesus, and have no confidence in the flesh" (Phil. 3:3).

This priesthood of which Peter speaks (1 Pet. 2:5) is mentioned here also. "By Him therefore (not by an earthly priest or in an earthly tabernacle) let us offer up a sacrifice of praise to God continually that is the fruit of our lips, giving thanks to His name." And besides this, which is done inside the veil, there is another aspect to the sacrifice we bring in His name—"to do good and to communicate forget not, for with such sacrifices God is well pleased."

Verses 17-25. They were to obey the leaders and submit themselves. These leaders watched over their souls as those that shall give account in the coming day of Christ. And by obedience and submission they honored Him who has made them the overseers of the flock of God. Well it would be if all workers would never lose sight of the fact that they are accountable to the Lord. The writer of the Epistle, no doubt the apostle Paul, requests their prayers, "pray for us." ("The fact is that none need the prayers of God's people more than those who are active and prominent in the Lord's work. Practically occupied with preaching and teaching others, how great the danger is of going on with a conscience not good about themselves! And what can more decidedly defile or harden?") In true humility, so characteristic of Paul he writes "for we persuade ourselves that we have a good conscience, in all things desiring to live honestly." Most ask prayer because their conscience is bad. He beseeches them that they may do this, so that by their prayer of intercession he might be restored to them the sooner. (See Philemon 22.) He valued the prayers of the saints.

Then follows that blessed prayer so well suited to this epistle and its great truths. "Now the God of peace that brought up from the dead our Lord Jesus Christ, the great Shepherd of the sheep, through the blood of the everlasting covenant, perfect you in every good work to do His will, working in you what is pleasing in His sight through Jesus Christ, to whom be glory forever and ever (unto the ages of the ages). Amen."

In the final words the apostle beseeches them to bear with the word of exhortation as contained in the letter. The mention of Timothy is another evidence that Paul wrote Hebrews. Brief salutations and the benediction closes this wonderful portion of the Word of God. "Grace be with you all. Amen."

THE EPISTLE OF
JAMES

Introduction

The Epistles of James, First and Second Peter, the three Epistles of John and the Epistle of Jude constitute the so-called Catholic, or General Epistles. They were thus named in earliest days, and in the ancient manuscripts these seven Epistles are grouped together as we have them in our English version; however, they always follow the book of Acts. It is claimed that they were named General Epistles because Christians in general are addressed in them, which does not hold good with the second and third Epistles of John, for these were addressed to individuals. The first Epistle in this group, following the book of Acts in the manuscripts, is the Epistle of James.

Its Peculiar Character

That there is a great difference between the great Pauline Epistles and the Epistle of James is seen at a glance. If one reads even the Epistle to the Hebrews, addressed to the same class of people, believing Hebrews, to whom the Epistle of James is also addressed, and reads James immediately after, a great and notable change is seen at once. The character of the Epistle of James is essentially *Jewish.* In the second chapter the word synagogue is used as the place of their assembly, "If there come unto your *synagogue* a man, etc." They were then still in the synagogue. Nothing about the Church, the body of Christ is mentioned in this Epistle, nor do we find here the great doctrines of Christianity and the corresponding Christian relationship. The law is also prominent; and there are other Jewish features which will be pointed out in the annotations. The character of the entire Epistle corresponds with those to whom the Epistle was originally addressed "the twelve tribes which are scattered abroad." It is evidently a document written at an early date during the transition period and before the great doctrinal Epistles of the apostle to the Gentiles had been produced, in which the fulness of redemption, the body of Christ, the church, and its unity and other cardinal doctrines of our faith are revealed.

What do we mean by *"transition period"?* That the beginning of Christianity had a decidedly Jewish cast is known to all Bible students. For years all the believers were Jews. There was a great Jewish-Christian assembly in Jerusalem and many more throughout Judea. As we learn from the book of Acts there were many thousands of Jews who believed, but who were also zealous for the law; they still made use of the temple worship, went there at the accustomed hours of prayer. There were also many priests who at one time were obedient to the faith, believed that the Crucified One was the Messiah; they also continued undoubtedly in their priestly ministrations in the temple. They still had their great national hope of a restoration of the kingdom. That hope indeed was preached by Peter in Acts 3:19-20.

That the Epistle of James is put in all the ancient manuscripts next to the book of Acts is therefore of significance. We breathe in this Epistle the same Jewish-Christian atmosphere which we find in the beginning of the book of Acts.

James, the Author of the Epistle

What we have stated above identifies the author of this Epistle. Who is James (Greek: *Jacobos*—Jacob)? Certainly not James, the apostle, the son of Zebedee. He was martyred in the year 44, as recorded in Acts 12:2. Nor can the author be James, the son of Alphaeus, another apostle. His name is mentioned for the last time in the New Testament in Acts 1:13. We hear nothing more about him, and it is inconceivable that he should have held a position of authority which belongs to the author of this Epistle. There is another James, who is designated as "the brother of the Lord." He has been generally accepted, even by critics, as the author of the Epistle.

The Apostle Paul speaks of him in Gal. 1:19. Three years after his conversion he returned to Jerusalem to interview Peter, and Paul adds, "but of the other apostles saw I none, save James, the Lord's brother."

James, the brother of the Lord, belongs to those mentioned in John 7:5: "For neither did His brethren believe in Him." James and his brethren did not believe on Jesus, the Virgin-born Son of God, as the Messiah. But in the first chapter of Acts we find mentioned among those who waited in Jerusalem for the promise of the Father "Mary, the mother of Jesus, and His brethren." They had been converted and were now believers. How were they convinced that Jesus was the Christ? There can be no question that the James mentioned, distinct from the apostles, in 1 Cor. 15:7, to whom the risen Christ appeared, is the brother of the Lord. He saw the Lord risen from the dead; He had appeared to him and that became the great turning point in his life and he and his brethren believed.

He early held in Jerusalem the position as leader. When Peter had been miraculously led forth from prison and appeared in the midst of a company of believers, he said, "Go show these things unto James and to the brethren" (Acts 12:17). He was the acknowledged head of the Jewish-Christians in Jerusalem. He is the spokesman in the first council held in Jerusalem, in the language of our day "the presiding officer" (Acts 15:13). Through him the Holy Spirit gave a very important revelation. Years later when Paul undertook the fateful journey to Jerusalem and had reached the city, he called on James, and after salutation reported to him "what things God had wrought among the Gentiles by his ministry." And James spoke the fatal words which enticed the Apostle Paul to conform to the keeping of the law, when James told him, "Thou seest, brother, how many thousands of Jews there are which believe, and they are all zealous for the law" (Acts 21:19-26).

According to ancient sources, like Eusebius, James was a godly man and a strong observer of the ceremonial law, and, though he was ready to see the hand of God in the ministry of Paul and Barnabas among the Gentiles (confirmed by the second chapter of Galatians), he adhered closely to the law and the Judaistic form of Christianity to the end of his life. "Had not a Peter and above all Paul arisen, Christianity would perhaps never have completely emancipated from the veil of Judaism and asserted its own independence. Still, there was a necessity for the ministry of James. If any could win over the ancient covenant people it was he. It pleased God to set so high an example of Old Testament piety in its purest form among the Jews, to make conversions to the gospel, even at the eleventh hour (preceding the destruction of Jerusalem) as easy as possible for them. But when they would not listen to the voice of this last messenger of peace, then was the measure of divine patience exhausted and the fearful and long-threatened judgment broke forth. And thus the mission of James, the brother of the Lord was fulfilled. According to Hegesippus James died a year before the destruction of Jerusalem" (Dr. P. Schaff-Kirchengeschichte). The Jewish historian Josephus records this in the following paragraph: "Festus was now dead, and Albinus was but on the road, so he assembled the Sanhedrin or judges, and brought before them the brother of Jesus, who was called Christ, whose name was James, and some others. And when he had formed an accusation against them as breakers of the law, he delivered them to be stoned" (Josephus, Book 20).

For various reasons this Epistle was, even among the church fathers, treated with suspicion. It seems that the uncertainty as to the writer, and that it was addressed entirely to Jewish believers, raised these doubts. These doubts were revived during the Reformation and Luther especially called it "an Epistle of straw," meaning by it that it did not contain the wheat.

"On the whole, on any intelligent principles of canonical reception of early writings, we cannot refuse the Epistle a place in the canon. That that place was given it from the first in some parts of the church; that, in spite of many adverse circumstances, it gradually won that place in other parts; that when thoroughly considered, it is so consistent with and worthy of his character and standing whose name it bears; that it is marked off by so strong a line of distinction from the writings and Epistles which have not attained a place in the canon; all these are considerations which, though they do not in this, any more than in other cases, amount to demonstration, yet furnish when combined a proof hardly to be resisted, that the place where we do now find it in the New Testament canon is that which it ought to have, and which God in His providence has guided His church to assign to it."[1]

When Was It Written

James lived and labored in Jerusalem. There is no likelihood that he ever left the city of his fathers, hence we cannot doubt that the Epistle was written by him in Jerusalem and sent forth from there. As to the exact date scholars have been divided on that. That it was written before the destruction of Jerusalem, and not after, is

[1]Dean Alford, *Prolegomena*.

obvious, for James died before the city was taken by the Romans. But does not the Epistle of James refer to Paul's teachings in Romans as to righteousness by faith, and therefore, it is argued, James must have written the Epistle after Romans, and perhaps also Hebrews, had been written. But the argument is weak. James did not answer Paul's teaching at all; he was guided by the Spirit of God to emphasize a holy life, as a justification of real faith before man. That he cites Abraham, as Paul did in Romans, is no evidence that he had the Epistle to the Romans in his possession. "It is much more probable, that all which James saith respecting works of faith has respect to a former and different state and period of the controversy, when the Jewish Pharisaic notions (as to the boast in the law) were being carried into the adopted belief in Christianity, and the danger was not, as afterwards, of a Jewish law-righteousness being set up, antagonistic to the righteousness which is by faith of Jesus Christ, but of a Jewish reliance on exclusive purity of faith superseding the necessity of a holy life, which is inseparably bound up with any worthy holding of the Christian faith." Some of the most painstaking scholars, like Drs. Neander and Schaff have assigned to the Epistle a very early date. The absence of any mention of the decision at the church council (Acts 15) in the Epistle strengthens the early date. The date must be put around the year 45 A.D. and this makes the Epistle perhaps the earliest of the New Testament writings. Why should it not be so, considering that the Judaistic church in Jerusalem was the beginning of Christianity and the messsage of the Epistle harmonizes so fully with the character of that church?

The Twelve Tribes Scattered Abroad

As already stated James addressed the Epistle "to the twelve tribes scattered abroad." We hear much in our days about "the ten lost tribes." But were they lost when James wrote his Epistle? If they were lost how could he have addressed this Epistle to them? But furthermore he addresses also those among the twelve tribes who were believers, so that it is but logical to assume that the twelve tribes, perhaps remnants of them, were known in the days of James, and that a number of each of the tribes had accepted Christ, the Messiah. Of course, like so much else, the term "twelve tribes" has been spiritualized as if it meant "the real Israel of God," that is, all believers, Jews and Gentiles. But this cannot be done. The fact that the literal tribes of Israel are addressed has been recognized by most expositors. James as the head of the Jerusalem church came in touch with many Israelites, who, according to their age-long custom, came up to Jerusalem to the feasts. Perhaps many of these visitors becoming acquainted with James and their believing brethren were also convinced that Jesus was the promised Messiah and believed on Him. They went back to their different communities in Central Asia and beyond, in the dispersion, and formed their synagogues. Later James learned from them the spiritual conditions in these different centers in the dispersion and addressed this Epistle to them as well as to those who were not believers.

We must also remember that a similar Jewish-Christian remnant will be in existence once more in Palestine during the coming great tribulation; it is the godly remnant, which we have pointed out many times in the prophetic books and in the Psalms. Then the gospel of the kingdom will again be preached, and as it was in the Jewish beginning of the age, signs and miracles will follow, in healing (James 5:14) and otherwise. The Epistle of James will then have a special meaning for this remnant.

Is the Epistle of James for us?

The Jewish character of this Epistle has lead some to say "It is for the Jews and not for us." We have known believers who refuse to read this Epistle. But that is a serious and deplorable mistake. Here are written great and needed truths which are as needful for us as they were for those to whom the Epistle was originally addressed. The Christian who passes by the Epistle of James rejects a most important part of the Word of God and as a result he will suffer loss. We quote from another: "I am persuaded that no man, I will not say despises, but even attempts to dispense with the Epistle of James except to his own exceeding loss. Luther would have been none the worse, but all the stronger, for a real understanding of this writing of James. He needed it in many ways; and so do we. It is, therefore, a miserable cheat that any should allow their own subjective thoughts to govern them in giving up this or any portion of the Word of God; for all have an important place, each for its own object. Is it too much to ask that a document be judged by its express and manifest design? Surely we are not to take Paul's object in order to interpret James. What can be conceived more contrary, I will not say to reverence for what claims to be inspired, but even to all sense and discrimination, than such a thought? And it is thus that men have stumbled and fallen over this—it is little to say—precious and profitable, and above all, practically profitable position of the Word of God.

"At the same time we must read it as it is, or rather as God wrote it; and God has addressed it, beyond controversy, not merely to Christian Jews, nor even to Jews, but to the twelve tribes that were scattered abroad. Thus it embraces such of them as were Christians; and it gives a very true and just place to those who had the faith of the Lord Jesus Christ. Only it is a mistake to suppose that it contemplates nobody else. People may come to it with the thought that all the Epistles were addressed to Christians, but this is simply wrong. If you bring this or any other preconception to the Word of God, no wonder His Word leaves you outside its divine and holy scope. For He is ever about us, and infinitely wise. Our business is to gather what He has to teach us. No wonder, therefore, when persons approach the Scripture with preconceived thoughts, hoping to find confirmation there instead of gathering God's mind from what He has revealed—no wonder that they find disappointment. The mischief is in themselves and not in the divine Word. Let us prayerfully seek to avoid the snare" (William Kelly).

The exhortations in this Epistle are, therefore, of great value; and there are many precious gems to be found scattered throughout the Epistle of James, the brother of the Lord.

The Division of the Epistle of James

We have already pointed out that this Epistle is not a doctrinal document. Addressed as it is to the twelve tribes in the dispersion it has nothing to say about Gentile believers, nor about their place in the Church, the body of Christ. They were believers, yet distinctly Jewish believers. This is seen in the opening verse in which James calls himself "the servant of God," an Old Testament expression; but he adds "of the Lord Jesus Christ." He and those to whom he wrote were serving God, still zealous for the law, adhering to it in every way, yet they believed on the Lord Jesus Christ and served Him. Their national hope as the people of God was theirs still. The Epistle is taken up entirely with the difficulties these Jewish believers had; it refers to the trials (like Peter's first Epistle) they were undergoing, exhorts them to faith. It points out the serious errors in the lives as believers; while they believed their lives did not correspond with such a belief. The correction of the faults, while common to all believers, has a striking Jewish aspect. They had respect of persons, looked to outward circumstances, and they are reminded of the royal law of the Scriptures, and insistence is made that their faith in the Messiah must be evidenced by works. They are exhorted to be more than mere hearers of the Word, by which they had been begotten anew, but to be doers of it. Many of them evidently wanted to be teachers, had great ambitions, but their Jewish character, looseness of their tongues in speaking evil, had become prominent and that is corrected. There is a repeated reference in the Epistle to the godly of their nation, to Abraham and Isaac, to Rahab, Job and Elijah. There is also quite a little which links with the Sermon on the Mount. Finally there are exhortations to godliness, prayer, the life of trust and a reminder of the coming of the Lord. The prominent word seems to be the word "patience." We find it five times. The trying of faith is to work patience (1:3); patience is to have her perfect work (1:4); they are to be patient unto the coming of the Lord (5:7); and be like the husbandman who waits in patience, and finally they are reminded of the patience of Job. The exhortations may be grouped around this word patience. I. Exhortations to Patience in Suffering God's Will (1:1-18). II. Exhortation to Patience in Doing God's Will (1:19; 4:17). III. Exhortation to Patience in Awaiting God's Will (5:1-20). We shall follow in our analysis and annotations the chapter division as we have them in our Bibles.

I. TRIALS AND THE EXERCISE OF FAITH (1)

II. THE ROYAL LAW: FAITH AND WORKS (2)

III. THE EVILS OF THE TONGUE CORRECTED (3)

IV. FURTHER EXHORTATIONS TO RIGHT LIVING (4)

V. THE COMING OF THE LORD AND THE LIFE OF FAITH (5)

Analysis and Annotations

I. Trials and the Exercise of Faith

CHAPTER 1

1. Trials and the power of faith (1:1-4)
2. The resources of faith (1:5-8)
3. The realization of faith (1:9-11)
4. The conquest of faith (1:12-15)
5. The result of faith (1:16-27)

Verses 1-4. The first verse is the introduction. The writer is James, but he does not add, as he might have done, "the brother of the Lord." It would have identified his person at once, and being the Lord's brother, he had a perfect right to call himself thus. But he did not. His humility shines forth in this omission; others called him by that title, but he avoided it. He is "servant of God," and he served God as "servant of the Lord Jesus Christ," a godly believing Jew. He writes to the twelve tribes in the dispersion of like faith. But the beautiful words of greeting in other Epistles, "Grace and peace be unto you," are not used by him. Greetings only are sent, and in this respect it is like the Apostolic document which was issued by the council in Jerusalem in Acts 15. (See Acts 15:23.)

The practical character of his letter is at once apparent. "Count it all joy when you fall in divers temptations." They were all undergoing trials and tests as believing Jews, who had accepted the Lord Jesus Christ as the Messiah. The First Epistle of Peter, which is also addressed to believing Hebrews tells the same story. They were in heaviness through manifold temptations. Their faith was severely tried as with fire (1 Peter 1:6-7). James exhorts these sufferers not to be grieved or disturbed over these trials, but rather to count it a joy. These trials were the evidences of their sonship and that their faith was real. Faith must be tried; the trial itself worketh patience, that is, endurance. This belongs to the practical experience of a believer. "For even hereunto were ye called; because Christ also suffered for us, leaving us an example, that ye should follow His steps" (1 Peter 2:21). If endurance has its perfect work, if the believer continues steadfast and in patience he will be perfect and complete, lacking nothing. The word "perfect" has been misinterpreted by some as if it meant an assumed Christian perfection or sinlessness. It does not mean that, but it means the perfect work of patience, enduring to the end, when self-will is subdued and the will of God is fully accepted. The result is that there is no deficiency in the practical life of the believer. The Lord Jesus is an example of it. He never did His own will, but patiently waited for the will of God and yielded a perfect obedience. Faith is power to suffer and to endure trials and testings.

Verses 5-8. Such endurance is impossible without prayer. In the midst of trials and hardships, the various perplexities which come upon the believer, they, as well as we, lack wisdom; we often do not know what to do. Wisdom is needed, not human wisdom, but that wisdom which is from above. This wisdom enables us to discern His will and to follow the right guidance. It is obtained by an utter dependence on God, and the expression of that dependence is prayer. He giveth to all liberally, nor does He upbraid. We can come to Him at all times, and habitually wait on Him for guidance and direction; and as we wait on Him thus and count on Him there will be no disappointment. Often believers think they have divine guidance, but it is but following some kind of an impression, certain impulses, which may come from ourselves, or from the enemy. But constant waiting on the Lord and trusting in Him, this is wisdom. All this necessitates childlike faith, which means counting on His faithfulness and on an answer from Him. If we doubt his faithfulness or question His answer we cannot receive anything from Him. Hesitance about God, a doublemindedness, depending upon something else besides God is in reality unbelief: "For he that wavereth (is not positive in his utter confidence and dependence) is like a wave of the sea driven with the wind and tossed. For let not that man think that he shall receive anything of the Lord. A double-minded man is unstable in all his ways." If the believer is double-minded, looking to the Lord and at the same time looking elsewhere, he dishonors Him, and He cannot honor the believer and answer his prayer. How blessedly it was expressed by David, which perhaps was remembered by these believing Jews, when the inspired king wrote: "My soul, wait thou only upon God; for my expectation is from Him" (Psalm 62:5).

Verses 9-11. Faith makes things real. It lifts above the circumstances of life. The brother of low degree in the midst of his trials can glory in realizing faith that he is exalted, while the rich believer can rejoice in faith in his trials, that he is made low, that he can suffer loss, and learn from his own poverty and lowness, realizing that all his riches are but for a moment, transitory "because as the flower of the grass he will pass away." This is the realization of faith in the believer; the believer of low degree in the midst of trials realizes that he is exalted, he glories in that, while the rich learns his low estate, that riches will fade away, but that he possesses an inheritance that fadeth not away.

Verses 12-15. Here is a beatitude: "Blessed is the man that endureth temptation; for when he is proved, he shall receive the crown of life, which the Lord hath promised to them that love Him." Overcoming faith will be rewarded. As the poor believer, or the rich believer, endures temptation, is proved and overcomes through faith, the Lord will give to him the promised crown of life.

The sources of temptations are mentioned in connection with this beatitude. There are two sources of temptations. There are temptations, the trial of faith which comes from God for our own good; there is a temptation of the flesh, of inward evil, which is not of God, but of the devil. Trial of faith God permits, but when it comes to temptations of evil, to do evil, to be tempted in this fashion, God never is the author of that. God cannot be tempted with evil, nor tempteth He any man.

This passage settles the question with which so many believers are troubled: "Could the Lord Jesus Christ sin?" They generally quote in connection with this Hebrews 4:15, that He was tempted in all points as we are. They claim that "all points" includes temptation to sin coming from within. Even excellent Christians are at sea about this question. Our Lord Jesus Christ is very God. Being manifested in the flesh does not mean that He laid aside His Deity. James says, "God cannot be tempted with evil," for God is absolutely holy. Therefore our Lord could not be tempted with evil. He had nothing of fallen man in Him; the prince of this world (Satan) came and found nothing in Him. Furthermore, the correct translation of Hebrews 4:15 is as follows: But was in all points tempted like as we *are, apart from sin.* In all other points our blessed Lord was tempted, but never by indwelling sin, for He was absolutely holy in His human nature, given to Him by the Holy Spirit.

It is otherwise with man fallen, he is drawn away of his own lust and enticed. The working, as revealed in verses 14-15, is illustrated in the case of David when lust brought forth sin and death (2 Sam. 11).

Verses 16-27. Evil has been traced to its source, and now we come to the other side. From God cometh every good and perfect gift and He is a God who does not change; with Him there is no variation, neither shadow that is cast by turning. The greatest good and the greatest gift from such a God is the gift of His Only Begotten Son. Those who believe Him that sent the Son of God into the world (John 5:24) are born again by the Word of Truth (John 3:5; 1 Peter 1:23; Ephes. 1:13) to be a kind of first fruits of His creatures. His own holy nature is thus communicated to those who believe; it is the result of faith. Of that new nature, the divine nature, it is written in 1 John 3:9: "He that is born of God doth not commit sin; for his seed remaineth in him; and he can not sin, because he is born of God." It means that there is no evil, in the new nature; it is a holy nature, it will never tempt to sin. But the believer has an old nature, and that is evil, nor can it ever be anything else, "for that which is born of the flesh is flesh." Thus, begotten again by His own good and gracious will, we are the first fruits of that new creation which in God's own time will be revealed.

This new nature must produce the fruits of righteousness, hence the practical exhortation. "Wherefore, my beloved brethren, let every man be swift to hear, slow to speak, slow to wrath. For the wrath of man worketh not the righteousness of God." Hearing is the attitude of true faith, ever listening to that which God speaks in His Word; then slow to speak, because speech gives expression to what we are; and it needs caution not to let the old nature express itself; and slow to wrath, which is the flesh. Wrath does not work that practical righteousness which is pleasing to God. Then there is to be, as a result of true faith, a laying aside of all filthiness, all superfluity of naughtiness; this is the same putting off of which we read in the Pauline Epistles (Col. 3, etc). This putting off is not the working of the law, but it is the result of the implanted Word, which received in meekness, saves; it is both the means of true salvation and the working out of that salvation into results of righteousness. But it needs more than hearers of the Word; we must be doers of it.

"But whoso looketh into the perfect law of liberty, and continueth, he being not a forgetful hearer, but a doer that worketh, this man shall be blessed indeed." What is the law of liberty? It is not the law of Moses as some have imagined. The perfect law of liberty is explained in the context. It is the Word of God by which the believer is begotten again, it is the implanted

Word, which teaches, instructs, guides and directs; it is the life which flows from the new nature, subject to the Word of God. It has often been aptly described as a loving parent who tells his child that he must go here or there; that is, the very places which he knows perfectly the child would be gratified to visit. Such is the law of liberty; as if one said to the child: 'Now, my child, you must go and do such and such a thing,' all the while knowing you cannot confer a greater favor on the child. It has not at all the character of resisting the will of the child, but rather of directing his affection in the will of the object dearest to him. The child is regarded and led according to the love of the parent, who knows what the desire of the child is—a desire that has been, in virtue of a new nature, implanted by God Himself in the child. He has given him a life that loves His ways and His Word, that hates and revolts from evil, and is pained most of all by falling through unwatchfulness into sin, if it seemed ever so little. The law of liberty therefore consists not so much in a restraint of gratifying the old man, as in guiding and guarding the new; for the heart's delight is in what is good and holy and true; the Word of God on the one hand exercises us in cleaving to that which is the joy of the Christian's heart, and strengthens us in our detestation of all that we know to be offensive to the Lord" (Wm. Kelly).

This is the law of perfect liberty and in doing this there in blessedness. Then follows a definition of pure and undefiled religion before God and the Father. Religion does not mean here the inner life, but the outward manifestation of it. The fatherless and the widows are God's special objects of love and care; to visit such in their affliction is Christlike. How often this is quoted by those who do not believe in the gospel of grace and in the cross of Christ, as if works of kindness were the true religion, by which man is saved and pleasing to God. The whole chapter shows how erroneous such an application is. And the other definition "to keep himself unspotted from the world," a true life of self surrender and separation, is generally overlooked.

II. The Royal Law: Faith and Works

CHAPTER 2

1. The faith of Christ with respect to persons (2:1-5)
2. The royal law (2:6-13)
3. Faith must be manifested by works (2:14-26)

Verses 1-5. Here we have the synagogue mentioned, sufficient evidence that these Jewish believers were still gathering together in the Jewish fashion, and were not an ecclesia, an assembly, gathered out. The Epistle to the Hebrews, written many years after the Epistle of James, exhorted them to leave the camp behind and go outside of it (Hebrews 13:13). Now in the synagogue among unbelieving Jews the rich man with his gold ring and fine clothing was accorded all honor, received the foremost place, while the poor man was told to stand up. (The same spirit prevails in many "churches" too, with their pew rents, sometimes auctioned off to the highest bidder, while the poor are not welcomed in such aristocratic surroundings.) Such a practice is not according to the faith of our Lord Jesus Christ, the Lord of glory, who Himself became poor so that by His poverty we might be rich. Faith, so prominent in the opening chapter of this Epistle, is here again insisted upon. Their action, even, in so small a matter as preference of the rich and influential, was not according to that faith, which worketh by love. "Hearken, my beloved brethren, Hath not God chosen the poor of this world, rich in faith, heirs of the kingdom which He hath promised to them that love Him?"

Verses 6-13. They had despised the poor, who were believers and walked in faith, while the rich oppressed them and dragged them before the judgment-seats. These of course were not believers, but mere professors, which again shows the mixed conditions of their gatherings. Furthermore, these rich people with their shameful behavior had blasphemed "that worthy Name" by which they were called, the name of the Lord of glory. This respect of persons was a sin against the royal law: "Thou shalt love thy neighbor as thyself." "If ye have respect to persons ye commit sin, and are convicted by the law as transgressors." If it is the matter of keeping the law, it must be kept in every detail and the entire law "for whosoever shall keep the whole law, and yet offend in one point, he is guilty of all." They were in their consciences still under the law, not having fully seen "the law of liberty" which is the perfect law, flowing as we have learned from the first chapter, from the new nature guided by the Holy Spirit, producing the walk in the Spirit, thus fulfilling the righteousness of the law. James, therefore, appeals to the Ten Commandments as a witness to arouse their consciences. Then he mentions once more the law of liberty. "So speak ye, and so do, as they that be judged by the law of liberty. For judgment shall be without mercy to him that hath shown no mercy. Mercy rejoiceth over judgment." The perfect law of liberty produces mercy in the believer, but where no mercy is shown, no mercy can be expected, but judgment. "With what measure ye mete, it shall be measured to you again" (Matthew 7:2).

Verses 14-26. This section of the Epistle has produced much perplexity in the minds of some and led to a great deal of controversy. As it is well known, Dr. Martin Luther, thinking that James tried to answer and contradict Paul's statement in Romans, called James "an Epistle of straw." Others also hold that James corrects the Epistles to the Romans and Galatians, the one being the inspired statement unfolding the gospel of grace, the other the defense of that gospel. But how could James answer either Epistle when they were not at all in existence, but written years later? When Paul wrote Romans and Galatians he knew James' Epistle. But did Paul try to correct James' argument? Not by any means. Both James and Paul wrote under the guidance of the Holy Spirit. Any thought of correcting a mistake impeaches the inerrancy of the Word of God.

There is no difficulty at all connected with this passage. The Holy Spirit through James shows that true faith which justifies before God must be evidenced by works. "What should it profit, my brethren, though a man say that he hath faith, and have not works? Can faith save?" What kind of faith does he mean? It is a faith which assents to certain dogmas, consisting in a mental, intellectual assent, but it is not the living faith. A living faith manifests itself in works. That is what James insists upon. In their synagogue were those who professed to believe, but they did not show by their actions that they had the faith given by God; they only said that they had faith; works, as the proof of true faith were absent. "If a brother or a sister be naked (the fatherless and widows of the closing verse of the previous chapter), and destitute of daily food, and one of you say unto them, Depart in peace, be ye warmed and filled; notwithstanding ye give them not those things which are needful to the body; what doth it profit?" The answer to this question is, it certainly profits nothing. Such a behavior shows that the professed faith is dead. "So also faith, if it have not works, is dead in itself." The quality of faith is defined in the nineteenth verse. "Thou believest there is one God"—that which the Jew boasts of, that he believes in one God, and not like the heathen in many gods—"thou doest well; the demons also believe and tremble." Demons who also believe are still demons; so a man may believe and still be the natural man, live and act as such. The seal of true faith is works.

This the Holy Spirit now illustrates through the case of Abraham and Rahab, so different from each other, the one the Father of the faithful, the other the harlot of Jericho. The works of both bear witness to the character of true faith which produced the. In the case of Abraham he offered up his only son. Of Abraham it was said "he believed God." That he acted as he did, in unquestioning and unhesitating obedience, was the proof that he believed God. What he did was the seal put on his faith, by which he was justified before God. Rahab also believed, and her faith was demonstrated when she received the spies, hid them and associated herself with the people of God, while she separated herself from her own people. Thus faith was seen as a perfect faith, as the true faith, by works. This is what the Holy Spirit teaches through James. In Romans justification before God is taught, which is by faith only. James does not say that our works justify us before God; such are not needed before an omniscient God, for He sees the faith of the heart, which man does not see. It is in exercise with regard to Him, by trust in His Word, in Himself, by receiving His testimony in spite of everything within and without—this true faith God sees and knows. But when our fellow-men ask, show me, then that faith shows itself by works. It is our justification before man. The argument is concluded by the terse comparison: "For as the body without the spirit is dead, so faith without works is dead also."

III. The Evils of the Tongue Corrected

CHAPTER 3

1. The tongue and its work (3:1-12)
2. The wisdom which is earthly and the wisdom that is from above (3:13-18)

Verses 1-12. The practical character of this Epistle is still more evidenced by the contents of this chapter. The tongue is the member of the human body which is made prominent. The human tongue is a great and wonderful gift of the Creator; with which no other earthly creature is endowed. It is written: "Out of the abundance of the heart the mouth speaketh." It therefore reveals the real condition of the heart and by what it is governed.

The opening verse exhorts to caution as to teaching: "My brethren, be not many teachers, knowing that we shall receive a greater judgment." Here another Jewish characteristic is mentioned. They are naturally forward and love to be heard, taking leadership. It seems as if many wanted to be teachers and exercise public ministry. Perhaps this may refer to the "speaking in tongues" also, and the abuse of it as mentioned in 1 Corinthians 14:20-33. In the first chapter the exhortation was given "slow to speak"; here it is applied to teaching. The exhortation is interesting in its bearing. First, is the warning not to assume leadership in teaching for self-display; even teaching as given to the members of the body of Christ must be carefully exercised, for it carries with it great responsibility, for one may preach to others and be himself disapproved (1 Cor. 9:27). If one is a teacher he must also practice what he teaches, otherwise he shall receive a greater judgment, not as to salvation, but as to disapproval before the award seat of Christ.

In the second place, the exhortation shows that ministry among these Jewish Christians was in perfect liberty; they did not possess among themselves a special class in whom public teaching was vested. The next verse broadens and refers to speaking in general. The perfect man is he who does not offend in a word and therefore is able to govern the whole body. This introduces the tongue and its twofold possibility. "Behold we put bits in the horses mouths, that they may obey us; and we turn about their whole body. Behold also the ships, which though they be so great, and are driven of fierce winds, yet are they turned about with a very small helm, whithersoever the governor listeth. Even so the tongue is a little member, and boasteth great things. Behold how great a matter a little fire kindleth! And the tongue is a fire, a world of iniquity; so is the tongue among our members, that it defileth the whole body, and setteth on fire the course of nature when it is set on fire by Gehenna." Horses, with their powerful bodies, are governed, led about and directed by the bit in their mouths; great ships which are driven about by gales and hurricanes, are steered by a small rudder, and so the human tongue is a little member which controls the whole man. It is like a tiny spark, yet that spark can set everything on fire and produce a disastrous conflagration. "Behold how much wood is kindled by how small a fire"—this is the correct rendering of the text. The tongue of the natural man, unrestrained by anything, is a fire. It defiles the whole body. Our Lord speaks of this. "That which cometh out of the man, that defileth the man. For from within, out of the heart of men, proceed evil thoughts, adulteries, fornications, murders, thefts, covetousness, deceit, lasciviousness, an evil eye, blasphemy, pride, foolishness; all these evil things come from within, and defile the man" (Mark 7:20-23).

The tongue is the medium to reveal all these evils of the heart, and by its use for evil becomes the seducer of others. It can set everything on fire, if it is set on fire by Gehenna, (translated, hell); when it is under the control of the author of sin.

"For every kind of beasts and birds, of creeping things and things in the sea, is tamed and hath been tamed of mankind; but the tongue can no man tame; it is a restless evil, full of deadly poison. Therewith bless we the Lord and Father, and therewith curse we men, made after the likeness of God. Out of the same mouth cometh forth blessing and cursing. My brethren, these things ought not so to be. Doth the fountain send forth out of the same opening sweet and bitter? Can a fig-tree, my brethren, yield olives, or a vine figs? Neither can salt water yield sweet."

James vehemently attacks this evil, yet in the spirit of love, as seen by the repeated address, "My brethren." Sins of the tongue are especially prominent among Jews; evil speaking, backbiting and lying, so frequently mentioned in their own Scriptures. He speaks of the power man has to tame every kind of beasts and birds, even the creeping things, as serpents and things in the sea; but man, the conqueror of the brute creation, is helpless when it comes to the taming of the tongue; the tongue can no man tame. David knew of this, for he wrote: "I said, I will take heed of my ways, that I sin not with my tongue; I will keep my mouth with a bridle, while the wicked is before me" (Psa. 39:1). All resolutions man makes to keep his tongue in subjection are unsuccessful. But if man has a new nature with the Holy Spirit dwelling there, the tongue can be governed and its evils overcome. Yet what sin is more frequently found among God's people than the sins of the tongue? It needs a constant watching and words must be weighed. Idle words, words which are not according to truth, or which reflect upon the character of another child of God, insinuating evil, magnifying faults, or words which belittle, words of envy and strife—are the sins of the tongue prevalent among God's people. How well then to consider constantly the exhortation of the first chapter of this Epistle: "Let every man be swift to hear, slow to speak, slow to wrath" (1:19). The tongue is a restless evil; it is unceasingly at it and carries in its sinful use deadly poison.

Blessing and curse may be expressed by the tongue. While on the one hand, the tongue is an instrument of evil and for evil, the tongue of the believer, on the other hand, should be an instrument of righteousness and for the glory of God. What greater occupation on earth is possible than true worship in Spirit and truth! Through the tongue we can praise and exalt the Lord, bear testimony to that worthy Name, tell others of Him and become channels for eternal blessing. But how quickly, if uncontrolled, it may be used in the service of sin. Peter uttered with his tongue his great, God-given confession, "Thou are the Christ, the Son of the living God." But a short time after, that same tongue became the mouthpiece of Satan, when he rebuked the Lord for saying that He would go to Jerusalem to suffer and to die. What an inconsistency the tongue of man reveals! No such thing is found in nature anywhere. A tree does not produce two kinds of fruit; a fig tree bears no olives; a vine does not produce figs; nor does the same fountain gush forth salt water and sweet water.

Verses 13-18. "Who is wise and understanding among you? Let him shew out of a good behavior his works in meekness of wisdom. But if you have bitter envying and strife in your heart, boast not and lie not against the truth. This is not the wisdom which cometh down from above, but it is earthly, sensual, demoniacal. For where envying and strife is, there is disorder and every evil thing." This exhortation, also, is suited to the Jewish believers to whom it was originally addressed. They are noted still for their jealousies, their strife and self-exaltation, these fruits of the fallen nature of man, the works of the flesh; they are, of course, also found among Gentile believers. Envyings, the sectarian spirit, the party spirit, producing bitterness and contentions, these things are not the manifestations of the wisdom which is from above, the fruit of the new nature and of the Spirit, but it is the earthly wisdom, springing from the natural man, behind which stands the author of sin.

"But the wisdom which is from above is first pure, then peaceable, gentle and easy to be entreated, full of mercy and good fruits, without contention, without hypocrisy; and the fruit of righteousness is sown in peace for those who make peace." This is the other side, the manifestation of the wisdom from above, the true fruits of the new nature and of the Spirit of God. It is first pure and then peaceable. It is pure, because it comes from God and leads to God. That which is from God cannot tolerate evil; it repudiates it. It aims at the glory of God and maintains His holy character. As a result it is peaceable, it seeks the fruits of peace among men, through the exercise of that love which the Holy Spirit describes in 1 Corinthians 13. It is gentle: "Let your gentleness be known to all men" (Phil. 4:5); it is easy to be entreated, ready to yield. It knows nothing of stubbornness, prejudice and opinionativeness, the sources of so much strife and contention among believers. When a man is conscious that his wisdom is of a superior kind, one can understand his unwillingness to have his mind or will disputed; but the truth is, that there is nothing which so marks the superiority of grace and truth and wisdom, that God gives, as patience, and the absence of anxiety to push what one knows is right and true. It is an inherent and sure sign of weakness somewhere, when a man is ever urgent in pressing the value of his own words and opinions, or caviling habitually at others. The fruit of righteousness is sown in peace, and produces peace.

IV. Further Exhortations to Right Living

CHAPTER 4

1. Fightings and worldliness rebuked (4:1-6)
2. The Godly walk (4:7-17)

Verses 1-6. A strong rebuke follows the statements concerning the wisdom from beneath and the wisdom from above. It must be borne in mind that these exhortations are addressed to the twelve tribes scattered abroad; to say that these words mean believers only would be a serious mistake; while Christians are contemplated, those of the tribes of Israel who are not believers are equally in view. It applies therefore to those who were born of God, real believers, and to those who were not, an entirely different matter from the Pauline Epistles, which are exclusively addressed to the saints.

There was much strife and contention amongst them. Whence come wars and fightings? Certainly not from the wisdom which is above, which is first pure and then peaceable.

But wars and fightings are the fruits of the old nature, the flesh. They come from the pleasures which war in the members. The gratification of the lusts of the natural man produces fightings and not the new nature, that which is from above; this includes all forms of lusts, not only those of the flesh, but the lust for power, the lust for pre-eminence and leadership, the lusts of the mind. "Ye lust and have not"; there is nothing that can satisfy the heart of man; any kind of lust will end in disappointment and remorse. "Ye kill and covet and cannot obtain." This is the way of the world in sin and away from God; it shows that James speaks to the unbelieving of the twelve tribes, and pictures their condition. "Ye fight and war. Ye have not because ye ask not. Ye ask and receive not because ye ask amiss, that ye may consume it in your pleasures." The natural man is also religious and as such prays. But their prayers sprang from the old nature, the desires of the flesh; they received not because they asked amiss. They prayed for selfish things, incited by selfish motives, so that they might gratify their sinful natures. Even true believers often ask and receive not, because they ask amiss, out of selfish reasons, to minister to their own pleasures and gratification. If the Lord would answer such prayers He would minister to that which is evil.

The world and its unsatisfying pleasures controlled those described in the foregoing words, some of whom may have been professing believers. The wisdom which is earthly, sensual and demoniac, they followed. And now the writer breaks out in a passionate exclamation: "Ye adulteresses, know ye not that the friendship of the world is enmity with God? whosoever therefore would be the friend of the world maketh himself an enemy of God." Here others than unbelievers are contemplated. The sphere of the natural man is the world; his walk is according to the course of this world; he is governed by the lust of the flesh, the lust of eyes and the pride of life. As such he is an enemy of God by wicked works and by nature a child of wrath (Ephesians 2:1-3).

The true believer, saved by grace, is not of the world, even as our Lord was not of the world (John 17:16). Grace has severed the believer from the world; the cross of Christ has made him dead to the world and the world dead unto him. Hence the exhortation in John's Epistle "Love not the world, neither the things of the world. If any man love the world, the love of the Father is not in him. For all that is in the world, the lust of the flesh, and the lust of the eyes, and the pride of life, is not of the Father, but is of the world" (1 John 2:15-16). And believers may turn back to the world, like Demas, and love it for a time. James calls such adulteresses; they leave Him to whom they are espoused, even Christ, and turn to another. The term must have reminded the Israelites of the Old Testament passages in which unfaithful, apostate Israel is pictured as an adulteress and playing the harlot (Jeremiah 3:9; Ezekiel 16:23; Hosea 2). It is a solemn exhortation which every true believer should consider carefully; friendship with the world means enmity against God. Verse 5 should be rendered as follows: "Or think ye that the Scripture speaketh in vain? Doth the Spirit, who dwelleth in us, long unto envying?" All the Scriptures testify that worldliness and godliness cannot exist together; think ye then that these Scriptures speak in vain? And the Holy Spirit, who dwells in the believer, does not lust unto envy, for He opposes the flesh and those who walk in the Spirit do not fulfill the lusts of the flesh. But he giveth more grace, yea grace sufficient to overcome by faith the world, for faith is the victory that overcomes the world. He quotes Proverbs 3:34. God resisteth the proud, but giveth grace unto the humble.

Verses 6-17. Exhortations to a godly, holy walk follow. Submit yourselves, therefore to God; be subject unto Him, have no friendship with the world, but be His friend. There is one who would drag the believer back into the world, as Pharaoh tried to get Israel back to Egypt. Guard against it by resisting the devil and he will flee from you. This is a blessed promise which all His faithful people have tested at all times. We are not to flee from the devil, but to resist him as we do so in the name of our Lord, the enemy will be helpless and flee from us. Another blessed exhortation follows. "Draw nigh to God and He will draw nigh to you." Next James addresses again those who had not yet fully turned to the Lord. It is called to repentance. "Cleanse your hands, ye sinners; and purify your hearts, ye doubleminded. Be afflicted, and mourn, and weep; let your laughter be turned to mourning, and your joy to heaviness. Humble yourselves in the sight of the Lord, and He shall exalt you."

The attitude towards other brethren is made clear in verses 11 and 12: "Speak not one against another, brethren." Speaking evil, the sin of the tongue is once more mentioned by James. There are seven verses in which exhortations to guard the tongue and speech are given: 1:19, 26, 2:12,

3:9, 16, 4:11 and 5:9. It seems that this must have been the besetting sin of these believing Jews. Evil, of course, must always be judged, whether it is unsound doctrine or an evil conduct; this belongs to the responsibility of a believer. But God alone, the Righteous Judge, knows the heart and its motives. Speaking against a brother and judging him, that is, pronouncing a sentence of condemnation upon him, is the same as speaking against the law and judging the law. But if one judges the law, the same is not a doer of the law, but a judge; doing this we take the place of Him who is both, the lawgiver and the judge, that is the Lord.

The final paragraph urges dependence on the Lord and warns against making plans for the future without looking to the Lord and His will concerning His people. "Go to now, ye that say, Today or tomorrow we will go into this city, and spend a year there, and buy and sell, and get gain; whereas ye know not what shall be on the morrow." Such a language shows self-will, forgetfulness of God, and self-confidence. It is planning with God left out. No one knows what the morrow may bring forth; but God knows. "For what is your life? It is even a vapor, that appeareth for a little time, and then vanisheth away. For that ye ought to say, If the Lord will and we live, we will also do this or that."

The child of God who walks in godly fear, trusting the Lord, planning as under Him, will constantly remember that all depends on the Lord and on His will. It is a wholesome habit to add always, when we speak of the future, "if the Lord will and we live"; this is pleasing in His sight and a testimony of our submission to Him and dependence on Him. Otherwise it is the boasting, vain-gloriousness of the self-secure world, which boasts and plans, without thinking of God and His will. The last verse must not be detached from what goes on before. "To him, therefore, that knoweth to do good and doeth it not, to him it is sin." Sin does not consist only in doing evil, but if we do not the good we know, it is also sin. If we do not act according to the fact that we are entirely dependent on God as to the future, we sin.

"This verse should forever settle the question of sinless perfection for a Christian: 'To him who knoweth to do good, and doeth it not, to him it is sin.' This is much more, of course, than the prohibition of positive evil. There is a negative evil which we have carefully to keep before us. The responsibility of knowing what it is good to do is one that, while we may in a general way allow it, yet deserves far deeper consideration than we often would even desire to give it. How solemn it is to think of all the good that we *might* do, and yet have *not* done! How slow we are to recognize that this, too, is sin! We are so apt to claim for ourselves a kind of freedom here which is not Scriptural freedom; and there is no doubt, also, that we may abuse a text like this to legality, if there be legality in our hearts. We are to be drawn, not driven. Yet the neglect of that which is in our hand to do—which we, perhaps, do not realize our capacity for, and that only through a spirit of self-indulgence or a timidity which is not far removed from this—such neglect, how hard it is to free ourselves of it, and how much do we miss in this way of that which would be fruitful in blessing for ourselves as well as for others! for, indeed, we can never sow fruit of this kind without reaping what we have sown; and the good that we can do to others, even if it requires the most thorough self-sacrifice, yet will be found in the end to have yielded more than it cost, and to have wrought in the interests of him who has not considered even or sought this" *(Numerical Bible)*.

V. THE COMING OF THE LORD AND THE LIFE OF FAITH

CHAPTER 5

1. The oppression by the rich and their coming doom (5:1-6)
2. Be patient unto the coming of the Lord (5:7-12)
3. The prayers of faith and the life of faith (5:13-20)

Verses 1-6. The two classes whom James addresses stand out very prominently in this final chapter of his Epistle. The rich oppressors certainly are not believers but the unbelieving rich; they are not addressed as "brethren"; but others are in verse 7 and exhorted to patience. Both classes, the unbelieving rich and the believing remnant are confronted by the coming of the Lord. "Go to now, ye rich, weep and howl for your miseries that are coming upon you. Your riches are corrupted and your garments are moth-eaten. Your gold and your silver are rusted; and their rust shall be for a testimony against you, and shall eat your flesh as fire. Ye have heaped together treasures in the last days."

The present age, which began with the death and resurrection of our Lord, and the coming of the Holy Spirit, is spoken of as "the last days" and "the last time" (Heb. 1:2 and 1 John

2:18); this age will be followed by the dispensation of the fullness of times, the times of restoration as promised by God's holy prophets (Eph. 1:10; Acts 3:19-20), the age of the kingdom when Christ reigns and His saints with Him. And this present age will end with the coming of the Lord to execute judgment, to right all wrong and judge all unrighteousness. These rich Israelites heaped treasures together, and, as we shall see later, acted outrageously, thereby showing that they did not believe in the day of the Lord, when He will be manifested in judgment glory. Yet their own Scriptures announced exactly that which James here states. See Isaiah 2:10-20 and especially Zephaniah 1:14-18. In anticipation of that coming day he calls on them to weep and howl, and announces the fate of their treasures.

Let us remember that the Epistle was written years before the destruction of Jerusalem. When Jerusalem fell, and even before its fall, many of the rich Jews became paupers; they were ruined, tortured and murdered, as Josephus tells us. The fall of Jerusalem with its awful horrors, in the year 70 A.D., was a judgment of the Lord, but not the day of the Lord and the coming of the Lord. What happened then to the stubborn unbelieving masses will happen again, only on a larger scale during the coming great tribulation and when the Lord returns in power and in great glory. We believe therefore, that this exhortation to the rich has a special bearing for the future, during the very end of the age.

But they were oppressing the poor as well. "Behold, the hire of the laborers who mowed your fields, which is of you kept back by fraud, crieth out; and the cries of them that reaped have entered into the ears of the Lord of Sabaoth. Ye have lived delicately on the earth, and taken your pleasure; ye have nourished your hearts in a day of slaughter. Ye have condemned, ye have killed the Just One; he doth not resist you." Oppression of the poor, yea, the poor of their own people is another characteristic of the Jewish people. The prophet Amos rebuked it in his day, when the poor were downtrodden and robbed by the rich. It is so today and will be so in the future. And the money which was taken from the poor was used by the rich to live in luxury and wanton pleasures. The spirit they manifested in heaping treasures together, oppressing the poor and needy, robbing them, and living in pleasure, is the same which condemned and killed the Just One, the Lord Jesus Christ, who did not resist. To apply these words primarily and altogether to our Lord can hardly be done. What was done to the Lord of glory these unbelievers did to His true followers. It will be so again during the great tribulation, under Antichrist, when the godly remnant will be persecuted by those who side with the false Messiah. See Psalm 79:1-3; Daniel 12:1; Matthew 24:9-25; Revelation 11, 12 and 13.

Verses 7-12. "Be patient therefore, brethren, until the coming of the Lord. Behold the husbandman waiteth for the precious fruit of the earth, being patient over it, until it receive the early and latter rain. Be ye also patient; stablish your hearts; for the coming of the Lord is at hand." He addresses in these words the believers, the suffering remnant amongst the unbelieving masses which attended the synagogue. They are to be patient and suffer in patience, without resisting. The coming of the Lord, which is mentioned twice in these verses, is His visible and glorious manifestation, the same which our Lord speaks of in Matthew 24:30-31. The first Epistle to the Thessalonians, which contains that unique revelation of the coming of the Lord for His saints, the resurrection of the holy dead and the sudden transformation of the living saints, to be caught up together in clouds to meet Him in the air (1 Thess. 4:13-18) had not yet been given. The mystery "we shall not all sleep but be changed in a moment, in the twinkling of an eye" (1 Corinth. 15:51-52), was then unknown. And let us note here, that this is one of the mysteries nowhere made known in the Old Testament.

The coming of the Lord, we repeat, is that coming which is so many times announced in the Prophetic Word of the Scriptures. "The first generation of Christians expected to witness in the near future the personal reappearance of Christ on earth to close the old dispensation by punishing unbelievers, and delivering the Christians. These expectations were partly realized when the fall of Jerusalem closed the old Jewish dispensation by the destruction of the temple and the final cessation of the Levitical worship of Jehovah. At the same time misery and ruin befell the Jewish nation which had rejected and crucified our Lord. As regards any more exact fulfilment, the statements of the New Testament must be interpreted according to the principle laid down in 2 Peter 3:8 and 1 John 2:18." (This passage is from the *New Century Bible.* One is grateful to find this paragraph in a work which is more or less on the side of the destructive criticism.) That the destruction of Jerusalem and the judgment of the nation was predicted by our Lord is known to all, that the event when it came in the year 70 is the coming of the Lord, is not true.

James exhorts his suffering brethren to be like the husbandman who has to wait between the sowing time and the harvest. But here is another wrong interpretation. The latter rain of which James speaks has been foolishly interpreted as meaning a spiritual latter rain, another Pentecost. This is one of the star arguments of present day Pentecostalism with its supposed revival of apostolic gifts. The former and latter rain of which James speaks has no such meaning; it is purely the rainfall in nature. In Palestine there are two distinct rainy seasons, one in the spring, the other in the fall. (See Deut. 11:14.)

Then follow other words of encouragement. "Murmur not, brethren, one against the other, that ye be not judged; behold the judge standeth before the door." Among themselves they were to guard against any friction and fretfulness, always remembering Him who is the Judge, and who standeth before the door. They were also to remember the examples in suffering and patience of the prophets, who spoke in the name of the Lord, the patience of Job, and how blessedly his suffering ended through the pity and mercy of the Lord. There is a warning also against oath making, such a common thing amongst the Jews. (See our Lord's warning in the Sermon on the Mount, Matthew 5:33-37).

Verses 13-20. The Epistle closes with practical exhortations to prayer and the exercise of faith. "Is any among you suffering? Let him pray." A short but weighty instruction. Instead of murmuring, as their forefathers did, instead of complaining in suffering, prayer must be exercised. The godly in Israel always made prayer their refuge and especially are the Psalms rich in this direction. "Is any cheerful? Let him sing psalms." The Psalms were used extensively in the synagogue. To teach upon this statement, as had been done, that the church should sing nothing but the Psalms, and reject the great hymns of the saints of God of all ages, born often in adversity and in deep soul exercise, is far fetched. Much in the Psalms does not express true Christianity at all. "Is any among you sick? Let him call for the elders of the assembly; and let them pray over him, anointing him with oil in the name of the Lord; and the prayer of faith shall save him that is sick, and the Lord shall raise him up; and if he have committed sins, they shall be forgiven him." This exhortation demands a closer scrutiny and examination. Of late this instruction by James has been greatly misapplied by faith-healers. There are many extremists who teach that here is a commandment to the church how sickness among the saints should be dealt with; that means, to alleviate bodily ills, must be fully discarded and if they are used, it is unbelief in the power of God and a hindrance to faith.

There are men and women all over Christendom, who go about with a message of healing of diseases, who anoint the sick by the hundreds and thousands, claiming that this is the only way that illness is to be treated. Then these same healers claim miraculous cures which are, after careful investigation, mostly found to be falsehoods. Some of these advocates of this method of healing, denouncing means and the use of physicians, were taken sick and had to use means to overcome their bodily ills. The entire subject of "faith-healing" we cannot examine here; nor can we enlarge upon the claims of "Christian Science" and other metaphysical cults and systems. Supernatural healing of diseases is claimed by Romish Catholicism, by the shrines and holy places of the Greek Orthodox church, by Spiritism, Mormonism and in many pagan systems. We confine our remarks to the passage before us.

It has been explained by some that the words of James mean that which should be done in case sickness unto death has seized upon a believer. It is then interpreted to mean "Prayer shall save the dying man from the punishment of his sins; and after his death, the Lord will raise him up in resurrection." This view we reject. No prayer of faith is needed for the coming physical resurrection of a believer. Romanism has made out of it "the sacrament of extreme unction" which is another invention.

Inasmuch as "the anointing with oil" seems to be the point most stressed by divine healers, we shall examine this first. What does it mean? Here we must remember the Jewish character of the Epistle. We have shown before that the believers whom James addresses were still closely identified with Judaism, hence they practised many things peculiar to Judaism. Anointing with oil was extensively used in the ceremonies of the Jews. Kings and priests were anointed, oil being liberally poured upon the head, denoting outwardly the fact of consecration to office, and symbolically the Spirit of God, which they needed for the exercise of their functions. Furthermore, oil was also very widely used for health and comfort. It was and is still a great remedial agent in the Orient.

The Good Samaritan poured into the wounds of the man who had fallen among the thieves oil and wine. Oil was used in cases of fever and most generally in skin diseases. Anointing the sick with oil was a general practice, as can be shown from talmudical literature. In Mark 6:13, we read, "And they cast out many demons, and anointed with oil many that were sick, and healed them." Would they not have been healed if they had not been anointed with oil? The anointing with oil was an old custom which the disciples made use of, but the Lord in commissioning them in connection with the kingdom message did not tell them that they should anoint the sick with oil; the did it, for such was the universal practice. If James commands these Jewish believers who were sick to be anointed with oil he re-affirmed therefore this old Jewish custom. Oil is something beneficial to the body, a remedy, just as wine is recommended by the Spirit of God as a remedy for the ills of the body (1 Timothy 5:23). It is therefore an open question whether oil may not stand here also for legitimate means to be used in case of illness. Divine healers carry with them a small bottle of oil and daub the forehead with a drop of oil, but this is not the anointing commanded here. Where is the authority to say that a drop of oil must be put on the forehead?

But it is very striking that apart from this passage, in this transition Epistle, nowhere else in the New Testament (except in Mark 6:13), do we read anything about this anointing with oil in case of sickness. Why did not Paul write to Timothy, who often had infirmities, "Call the elders, let them anoint you with oil," but instead of it, the divinely given remedy, "a little wine," is urged upon him. And Paul was sick himself, suffered with his eyes, which probably was the thorn in the flesh. Trophimus was sick in Miletus. But nowhere this Jewish ceremony, anointing with oil, is mentioned. The Epistles which are the highwater mark of divine revelation, are the Epistles to the Ephesians and Colossians; we find nothing in these Epistles about healing of diseases by anointing and prayer. Nor is it mentioned in any of the other Pauline Epistles. In Corinthians the gift of healing is found among the gifts of the Spirit, but he who possessed that gift had no need of using oil besides. Our conclusion, then, is that the anointing with oil in this passage is something customary with the Jews, which is not meant to be perpetuated in the Church, for if such were the fact the Holy Spirit would have stated it elsewhere.

We pass over the question as to true elders, which are to be called. Many of those who go about as divine healers are women. Who has ever heard of "women elders"? In fact, in the public healing services which have become such a common thing in our days, the question of elders is entirely ignored. Big advertisements appear in the papers that services for the healing of the sick are to be held. As a result hundreds come and are ready to do anything, to believe anything, if only some hope is held out that they might be cured. They readily submit to the ceremony of having a little oil put on their foreheads, but the command, that the sick person, is to call for the elders of the church, those of authority, is ignored. The question is, "Do we still have the elders in the apostolic sense?" These are matters which are completely set aside by modern faith healers.

But the emphasis in the passage is on "the prayer of faith." The prayer of faith, not the anointing with oil, shall save the sick. No believer denies the efficacy of believing prayer, yet always guarded by the condition of "if it be His will." In case of sickness the child of God will not send for a physician in the first place, but the believer turns to the Lord and puts himself in His gracious and merciful hands. The passage here seems to be the matter of sickness as a chastening from the Lord on account of specific sins committed. In such a case when self-judgment has brought the matter into His light, the promise can be claimed "the prayer of faith shall save the sick."

"Was it intended to be a direction universally applicable to all cases, and to be carried out at all times, in all places, and under all conditions? Surely—most surely not. For note that there is no question at all as to the result: 'the prayer of faith *shall save* (it is certain) the sick and the Lord will raise him up.'

"Now, we know perfectly well that this is not and *cannot* be the invariable outcome of all sickness. The vast majority of mankind—yes, of Christians—has died as the result of some sickness: has this been because 'elders' have not been called? Have they come to the end of that life here because they were not anointed with oil, and the prayer that always goes up from loving hearts was not the prayer of faith, and since not of faith, was sin? Who would not reject such conclusions with abhorrence? Yet are they inevitable, if this Scripture be pressed as being the one divinely given direction in the case of all sickness.

"In it every act, every movement, must be in

faith: that is recognizing the Lord's hand in the sickness, and the Lord's mind in removing it. But where is the great and precious promise on which faith can always rest, that shall make healing sure? In one case only, and that is if the sickness does not come from constitutional weakness, as with Timothy, or the hardship of a Christian devotion as with Epaphroditus, or any other natural cause—but as *a chastening of the Lord* for some specific sins committed, and this confessed and put away, the chastening ceases.

"And this is naturally enough the point of view of such a writer as James. Freedom from sickness consequent on obedience was interwoven in the first covenant: 'And the Lord will take away from thee all sickness, and will put none of the diseases of Egypt, which thou knowest upon thee; but will lay them upon all that hate thee'—is that what the Christian desires today: his diseases put on anyone else who may hate him? yet is that involved in that covenant.

"What, then, more natural than that this writer, who, although Christian, is still on the ground of a regenerate and sincerely pious Jew, should regard sickness in a light that is common to both Christian and Jew—as a chastening for sin."[2]

With this we leave this portion of the Epistle, which has led to so much misunderstanding. To help the reader in getting the true conception we add in a brief appendix, at the close of these annotations, the comment as it is given in the *Numerical Bible.*

"Confess, therefore, your sins one to another, that ye may be healed." This brings out fully the fact that the sickness in view is on account of specific sins. When the sins are confessed and judged, grace intervenes, and God in mercy heals. Rome builds upon this passage the miserable invention of the confessional. But it does not mean confession to a man-made "priest," but a simple confiding of believers among themselves.

The great value of prayer is next pointed out by James. "The supplication of a righteous man availeth much in its working"; this is a rendering adopted by many. He cites the case of Elijah. He was a man "of like passions with us" as we learn from the historical record of the Scriptures, which tells us of his great infirmities, as well as of his remarkable faith. He prayed fervently and rain was withheld, he prayed again and God answered his faith. The God of Elijah is our God still, who delights to answer the fervent prayer of the righteous man; the power of prayer can never be separated from the character of him who prays.

"My brethren, if any among you do err from the truth, and one convert him; let him know, that he which converteth a sinner from the error of his way shall save a soul from death, and shall cover a multitude of sins." With this the Epistle ends abruptly. Faith must be manifested by love towards those who err. The exhortation finds an application in a general way, but primarily to those who know the truth and have backslidden. This is learned from the words "if any among you"; the application in a general way is also fully warranted. The ending without greeting has led some critics to assume, that the Epistle is made up of passages from sermons, compiled quite late, by a man by the name of James. The internal as well as the historical evidences refute this assumption.

APPENDIX

James 5:14-16

By F. W. Grant

The anointing with oil in the name of the Lord seems to be the claim of an authority which those of whom we are speaking would be the last to assert. No doubt the emphasis is laid here upon the "prayer of faith," to save the sick; and the prayer of faith certainly should not be lacking with us. We need not doubt how much we should gain if there were a more simple and constant reference to the Lord in these matters, and we cannot but remember the example of old of one who sought not to the Lord, but to the physicians, and died. The use of means that are in our hand may easily be perverted to the slighting of this way of faith; and it would certainly be far better to leave out the means in any case rather than to leave out the Lord. The distinct and united acknowledgment of our dependence upon Him in all these cases is due from us, and we suffer loss if God is not acknowledged; but then for this, no elders or anointing can be needed, and the prescription of these things makes it evident that something more is contemplated here than simply the prayer of faith. Even so, there is no *prohibition* of means, if there be no *prescription* of them; and in God's ordinary way of working He certainly works by them. He could sustain us at any time without food, but we do not ordinarily expect Him to do this, although

[2]F. C. Jennings, *Our Hope.*

the food may profit nothing except the Lord please to use it. We cannot but remember in this way the prescription of a little wine to Timothy, while at the same time he was in the very midst of an assembly which had its regularly appointed elders.

In Judaism let us remember how, at the beginning of it, God was pleased to act miraculously in a marked way; and in the beginning of Christianity in Jerusalem, we find the same signs and miracles accompanying the Word. This was a most suited testimony to the new doctrine being published, a testimony which was also recognized in our Lord's case by the Jews as that which was to establish a new doctrine (Mark 1:27). The waning of all miraculous powers when once the testimony was established is marked, and cannot be denied. People may impute it, as they do impute it, to a lack of faith on the part of Christians; but with regard to such things one might certainly expect faith to be manifested as much as in other things. In fact, they would be things most earnestly clung to, for the manifest benefit and the display of power in them.

On the other hand, the prevalence of corruption which, whatever may be our own individual views of truth, cannot be but acknowledged, would naturally make it less suited that the Church so failing should still preserve her ornaments; but the reason for the decline of miracles is evidently other than this. In the history of the Acts we find an apparent absence of such things, where, for instance, as in Berea, men were employed with the Word itself to test the doctrine by it. Although in general, as the Lord promised, miraculous signs did follow at the beginning those who believed, yet even then this was never universally true. It could not be pleaded as the necessary mark of Christian faith. "Are all workers of miracles?" says the apostle; and the question in itself supposes a negative answer. Thus, if a whole assembly lacked, there was no *necessary* failure, and need be no disappointment in this case; while in Corinth their "coming behind in no gift" was no necessary evidence of a right state of soul. It seems even, one would say, a matter of course that God never meant our daily lives to be full of manifest miracles. He never meant to demonstrate the truth after that fashion. He would leave it, rather, to its own inherent and spiritual power.

Men easily crave miracles; but the whole generation in the wilderness, the constant witness of these, nevertheless perished for their unbelief. The miracles work no faith, although they might, and would, awaken attention to that which God presented as an object for faith; yet to those who believe in Christ, when they saw the miracles, He did not commit Himself (John 2:23-25). Every way it should be plain to-day that what goes for such amongst men commonly is no longer the mark upon true faith or the truth itself which calls for faith. The same things exactly can be wrought by those who deny Christian fundamentals as by those who profess them; and where is the evidence then? No set of men in the present day can be found who can adjust broken bones without surgery. If God wanted to show what He was doing, do we think that a broken bone would be a greater difficulty to Him than anything else?

Moreover, the signs and wonders of the time of the end are spoken of as rather giving evidence to falsity than to truth, to Antichrist than to Christ; and there will be signs and wonders wrought yet, which, as the Lord has said, would deceive, if it were possible, even the very elect. Thus, then we can easily understand (and especially in such an Epistle as the present—an Epistle to that nation to whom God had testified by signs and wonders of old, and would repeat to them now, in evidence that Christ was in nothing behind Moses) how we should find a reference of this kind to powers which might connect themselves with the elders of the Christian assembly, and yet understand why James should leave us, as it were, at a loss how to apply these things to ourselves. We can never be wrong in believing that the prayer of faith is still really the power that will save the sick, let means be used or not used; but the use of means seems in general rather according to the Lord's mind than against it. His common way is to work through that which He has Himself ordained, and there are plainly herbs for the healing of men. The very presence of such powers is proof that the Lord has given them; and if He has given them, it is for us. Faith can acknowledge Him in these, as well as be perfectly happy in trusting Him apart from all consideration of these. The prohibition of them, if God designed it, would surely be furnished to us.

Moreover, God at no time intended that things should be left, as it were, absolutely in man's hands, even though it were the hand of faith, as the doctrines taught suppose. The prayer of faith may be that which saves the sick, and yet, after all, that be far from meaning that we can find in every case a faith which should do so. God has His own will and His own way; and while we can always reckon upon Him to answer the soul that looks to Him, yet the way of His answer we do not always know. The apostle prays that the thorn in the flesh might depart from him, but it did not depart. God turned it to greater blessing. That was an answer to the prayer, but it was not such an answer as men usually count as that. Could any one suppose that among Christians, if everything were absolutely right, the sick would always be raised up, that death would hardly obtain at all, except in the extremest old age? We may imagine any such fancies, but fancies they are, and nothing else. Yet it is plain there is an appeal to God advocated here which we are always right in making, and from which we may always expect an answer in the goodness of Him whom we address. More than this, the Lord may give distinct light as to His mind that will will enable one, as to anything, to ask with assurance, without the possibility of denial. If we are near enough to God for this we have cause indeed to be thankful; but we had better be humble about it, and be very sure that we have it before we claim it.

THE FIRST EPISTLE OF
PETER

Introduction

The genuineness of this Epistle is confirmed by the most ancient sources. Polycarp, who was personally acquainted with the Apostle John, cites the Epistle of Peter. Papias of Hierapolis made use of the Epistle likewise. This was about the middle of the second century. Two quotations of Peter's Epistle are found in a very ancient source, "The Teaching of the Twelve Apostles," a kind of manual going back to 100 A.D. All the other documents of the first and second centuries show that the Epistle was unanimously known and accepted as Peter's.

The critics have not left it unattacked. We do not need to quote the different theories advanced by Cludius, Eichhorn (the man who coined the phrase "higher criticism"), De Wette, Bauer, Davidson, Pfleiderer, Harnack, and others. The main objection seems to be that the expressions used in this Epistle are too much like the thoughts and expressions of the Apostle Paul as used in his Epistles, so, as it is assumed, Peter could not have written it. This theory was expanded into the hypothesis that some one must have written it who had spent considerable time with Paul, so that he adopted Pauline ideas and phrases; John Mark has been suggested by some to be that person. Critics have pointed out many parallels with different Pauline Epistles. "In considering these parallels, allowance must be made for ideas and phraseology, hymns, prayers, confessions of faith, and other matter, which were the common property of the primitive Church; and would introduce a degree of similarity into the writings of different authors. But much of the thought and language of First Peter belongs to what was characteristic of the teaching of Paul and his followers as distinct from that of the Palestinian or Jewish churches. The parallels in any case, show a dependence upon Pauline teaching.

But we may go further. There is a great variety of opinion as to the precise character and extent of the dependence of First Peter on the writings of Paul. It has been suggested that it is just possible that Paul himself was the author of First Peter, the passages in which Peter's name occurs being later insertions; and again that this Epistle and Ephesians were the work of one author. But that dependence, especially on Romans, is very widely recognized" *(New Century Bible).* All these objections, speculations, and theories denying the Petrine authorship are answered by the fact of inspiration. Peter no doubt knew and read the Epistles of Paul; in fact he speaks of them in his second letter (2 Peter 3:15-16). But that does not mean that he copied and reproduced the statements found in some of Paul's Epistles; nor does it mean that he depended on Paul when he wrote his Epistle. The Holy Spirit who guided Paul's pen guided also the hand of Peter; all is the direct work of the Holy Spirit.

If Peter uses some of the great truths found in the Epistles of Paul it was because the Spirit of God desired to have them restated. If we examine these parallels closely we discover that they cover the most essential truths of Christianity and are used for practical exhortations. Those whom Peter addressed needed these truths and the practical application. On the other hand there are many internal evidences which prove that none but Peter wrote this Epistle. It has been pointed out that there is a similarity between Peter's statements in the book of Acts and in this first Epistle. Compare Acts 4:11; 2:32, 3:15 with 1 Peter 2:7; 1:3, 4, 8 and 5:1. He also uses a peculiar word for the cross. It is the word *"tree"* (the Greek word *xulon*). See Acts 5:30; 10:39; 1 Peter 2:24. Furthermore, the writer speaks of having been an eyewitness of the Lord's sufferings (5:1). He describes these sufferings, how He was reviled and reviled not, how He suffered and threatened not. And Peter was an eyewitness of all this. Nor is it without significance that in this Epistle alone the Lord Jesus Christ is called "the chief Shepherd." On the shores of Lake Tiberias the risen Lord restored Simon Peter to service and told him "shepherd My sheep," hence Peter speaks of the Lord as the chief Shepherd, and also exhorts the elders to be faithful in feeding the flock of God. As it is with all other critical objections to the traditional belief as to the inspired authorship of the different Bible books, the objections against the Petrine authorship of this Epistle are wholly worthless. Peter wrote this Epistle. The date cannot be definitely settled, but must be placed between 62 and 65 A.D.

SIMON PETER

A brief review of the life and service of the Apostle Peter will be helpful in understanding his writings. He was born at Bethsaida in Galilee, from which Philip came also (John 1:44, 45). His name was Simon (or Simeon, Acts 15:14) and his father's name was Jonas. He had a brother by name of Andrew, and the three, the father, Simon and Andrew were fishermen at Capernaum. There Simon Peter had his home, as he was a married man (Matthew 8:14; 1 Cor. 9:5). His brother Andrew was a disciple of John the Baptist and when he pointed out the Lord Jesus as the Lamb of God, Andrew followed Him. Andrew brought Peter to the Lord (John 1:35-43).

When the Lord beheld him He revealed His omniscience, for He said: "Thou art Simon the son of Jona, thou shalt be called Cephas," which is the Aramaic word for stone. When later Peter, in answer to the question "Whom say ye that I am?" said: "Thou art the Christ the Son of the living God," the Lord Jesus said to him, "Thou art Peter, and upon this rock I will build My church; and the gates of Hades shall not prevail against it" (Matthew 16:17-18). The Greek word *petros* means a small rock, or piece of a rock; the Greek for rock is *petra,* the word our Lord used when He designated the foundation of the Church. It is not Peter, but Christ Himself, who is the rock. In his Epistle Peter contradicts by the Spirit of God the miserable invention that he is the rock upon which the Church is built, as claimed by Rome and even by Protestant expositors. (See 1 Peter 2:4-8). The Gospel records, as well as the Epistle to the Galatians, give us a good description of his peculiar character. He was impulsive, forward and self-confident, yet he was true, loving and faithful. Before he denied the Lord, the Lord Jesus announced Peter's great failure and assured His disciple of His prayer, when Satan would sift him as wheat. In connection with this our Lord gave him a commission. "When thou art converted, strengthen thy brethren." His denial, his bitter repentance, his restoration at the lake of Tiberias, the still greater commission to shepherd the sheep and the lambs of the flock of God, are so well known, that we need not to enlarge on them.

The Lord also committed to him the "keys of the kingdom of the heavens," not to Heaven, nor to the Church, but to the kingdom of the heavens, that is to that which is now on earth. The book of Acts gives us the history of the use of the keys. He used the keys in connection with the Jews on the day of Pentecost, when he preached to them and, in preaching, opened the door to those who heard him; then he used the keys once more in the household of Cornelius (Acts 10) and then by preaching he opened the door to the Gentiles. This is what our Lord meant.

Here is another significant fact, in writing his Epistles Peter never mentioned this commission of the keys. According to Rome and other ritualistic churches he should have stated in the beginning of his Epistle that he is the supreme holder of the keys of the kingdom of heaven. But not Peter was to be the great apostle to the Gentiles; the Lord called Paul to this position. Peter is the prominent actor in the beginning of the book of Acts, when the gospel was preached "to the Jew first." After Jerusalem rejected that gospel and the apostle to the Gentiles had been called, Paul becomes the prominent figure in Acts. Peter is mentioned only once more in connection with the council held in Jerusalem (Acts 15). In Galatians chapter 2 his Jewish character in withdrawing from the Gentile believers after he fellowshipped with them is rebuked by Paul. In that chapter we also read that Peter with James and John were to minister to those of the circumcision, that is the Jews; while Paul and Barnabas were to go to the Gentiles.

After this incident we hear nothing more about Peter. The Spirit of God might have given us a complete account of what he did, where he went, but all is passed over in silence. The omniscient Spirit saw what would come in Christendom. He knew that ritualism would give to Peter a place of supremacy in the body of Christ which does not belong to him at all. Therefore Peter's life and service are passed over by the Holy Spirit and we hear nothing more about him in the inspired records. But we hear from him in the two Epistles which bear his name and which he wrote.

But while Scripture is silent, tradition is not. It is claimed by the historian Eusebius that he was Bishop of Antioch, the church which he founded. But the latter statement is contradicted by Acts 11:19-21 and the former is equally incorrect. Other ancient sources declare that he was very active in Asia Minor. That he must have ministered widely may be gained from 1

Corinthians 9:5: "Have we not power to lead about a sister, a wife, as well as other apostles, and as the brethren of the Lord, and Cephas?" But the entire ministry he rendered is not revealed.

Another tradition claims that he settled in Rome to oppose the Samaritan sorcerer Simon Magus (Acts 8). Justin Martyr in his writings states that Simon Magus was worshipped in Rome as a god on account of his magical powers. On account of it they erected a statue on an island in the River Tiber inscribed *"Simoni Deo Sancto."* Actually there was found in the year 1574 in the Tiber a stone with the inscription *"Semoni Sanco Deo Fidio Sacrumi"* i.e. "to the god Semo Sancus," the Sabine Hercules, which is definite proof that Justin Martyr was mistaken. Upon this rests the legend that Peter went to Rome to oppose Simon Magus. It is claimed that Peter was Bishop in Rome for 25 years and founded what is called "the Holy See," which later developed into the abominable papacy with its lies. Peter never saw Rome. As we shall show later in this introduction, there is sufficient Scriptural authority to contradict this legend. Another legend states that he was martyred in Rome, where the Lord appeared to him, when Peter had left the city to escape death. That he should die the martyr's death had been announced by our Lord, as well as the manner of his death by crucifixion. Nobody knows where that death took place. When he wrote his second Epistle it was a brief time before his death (2 Peter 1:14); but that Epistle was not written from Rome.

Did Peter Write from Babylon or from Rome?

At the close of the Epistle we read the following salutation: "The church that is in Babylon, elect together with you, saluteth you, and so does Marcus my son." *"The church that is"* does not appear in the original text; it has, therefore, been explained that Peter meant his wife, though it appears more probable that he meant the other elect ones who were with him in Babylon. The fact is established that when he wrote this Epistle Peter was in Babylon. But does this mean the literal Babylon on the banks of the Euphrates or the mystical Babylon, which is Rome? Roman Catholic writers claim that it means the city of Rome, and a large number of Protestant commentators side with this view. They claim that he was in Rome with Mark. They say that Babylon has the same meaning as the word has in the book of Revelation, that is, not the literal Babylon, but Rome.

There is no definite proof that Rome was universally called "Babylon" before John received it in his Patmos vision; it is claimed that the persecution under Nero led Christians to call Rome by the name of Babylon; but it is more likely that the name Babylon was widely used for Rome after John had written the Apocalypse. The Apocalypse was written some 25 or 30 years after Peter had written his Epistle, how, then could he have used this mystical name for Rome? Furthermore, a mystical name is out of keeping in an Epistle. It would be the only instance in the entire epistolar testimony where a place is camouflaged in this way. The use of a mystical name in an Epistle appears strained. It therefore must be the literal Babylon in Mesopotamia. And why should this not be? We read in the second chapter of Acts that among those who were in Jerusalem when the Holy Spirit came to earth were "Parthians, Medes, Elamites and dwellers in Mesopotamia." They heard Peter's testimony and some of them must have been converted. Many Jews dwelt there, and while in 41 A.D. Caligula instituted a persecution against the Jews in Babylon and many left, there was still a large company of them in the fast decaying city.

But the most conclusive evidence against Babylon, meaning Rome, is the complete silence of the Apostle Paul about Peter being in Rome. Paul sent his Epistle to the Roman Church in the year 58 A.D. In that Epistle he greets many believers who were in Rome. If Peter had been there, why did he not mention him also? He went to Rome as a prisoner in the year 61, but there is not a word about meeting Peter in Rome. Finally, when Paul penned his very last Epistle from Rome he makes the significant statement: "Only Luke is with me" (2 Tim. 4:11). This silence about Peter in the Pauline Epistle can only be explained by the fact that Peter was not in Rome at all.

Addressed to Believers in the Dispersion

The Epistle is addressed to the sojourners in the dispersion, that is, to Jewish believers who were scattered throughout Pontus, Galatia, Cappadocia, Asia and Bithynia, provinces in the northeastern part of Asia Minor. Many assemblies had been founded there and there were many believing Jews. They probably had their own gatherings, keeping aloof from the assemblies formed by believing Gentiles. They were the remnant and yet in having believed they were members of the body of Christ.

THE PURPOSE AND MESSAGE OF THE EPISTLE

When Peter wrote this Epistle he fulfilled the request of the Lord, when he told them "when thou art converted strengthen thy brethren." They needed strengthening and comfort for they were passing through all kinds of persecutions; their faith was being severely tested. As believers they were pilgrims and strangers on earth, their portion and calling was different from the unbelieving Jews about them, among whom they suffered. The Lord Jesus Christ who suffered in their behalf is repeatedly presented as a pattern for them in their persecutions, and blessed exhortations are linked with the Person and holy character of our Lord. The Epistle is not doctrinal, though the great doctrines of Christianity are in view throughout the Epistle. It is, like the Epistle of James, a practical Epistle, abounding in exhortations and references to Old Testament history suited to believing Jews in their trials. The keynote is *"Suffering and Glory."* The words suffering and suffer occur fifteen times and the word glory ten times.

The same error has been taught by some extremists in Biblical interpretation which we have pointed out already in the introduction to the Epistle of James, namely, that it has a Jewish character and does not belong to the Epistles in which the Church and the heavenly calling are revealed, and therefore the Church should not consider it. This is a most vital mistake. The first Epistle of Peter has an important message also for all believers at all times; to pass it over and not to heed its blessed message, its comfort and exhortations would mean a very serious loss. A one-sided Bible reading produces a one-sided Christian character and a one-sided Christian service. And there are only too many of such in the Church today.

The Division of First Peter

As stated in the introduction the keynote of the Epistle is "Suffering and Glory." The end of their pilgrimage, when all suffering ends, will be salvation and the possession of an inheritance incorruptible, undefiled and that fadeth not away. This salvation was the object of inquiry and searching by their own prophets. The Spirit of Christ who was in them testified beforehand the sufferings of Christ and the glory that should follow. So they as being His and identified with Him would also have suffering which in due time will be followed by glory. The glory comes with His revelation, His appearing, when He comes again.

We divide the Epistle into five sections, but somewhat different from the five chapters into which the Epistle is divided in our Bibles.

- I. **THE SUFFERING OF BELIEVERS AND EXHORTATION TO HOLY LIVING** (1:1-21)
- II. **THE BLESSINGS AND PRIVILEGES OF ALL BELIEVERS** (1:22—2:10)
- III. **CHRIST THE PATTERN FOR HIS SAINTS** (2:11—3:9)
- IV. **THE COMFORT IN THE MIDST OF TRIALS AND SUFFERING** (3:10—4)
- V. **EXHORTATIONS CONCERNING SERVICE AND CONFLICT** (5)

Analysis and Annotations

I. The Suffering of Believers and Exhortations to Holy Living

CHAPTER 1:1-21

1. The introduction and doxology (1:1-5)
2. Suffering and the coming glory (1:6-9)
3. As revealed in the prophets (1:10-12)
4. Exhortations to holy living (1:13-21)

Verses 1-5. As stated in the introduction, Peter writes to believing Jews in the dispersion throughout the provinces mentioned in the first verse. There is at once pointed out a contrast between them as true believers and their former condition. The nation to which they belonged was an elect nation, but they were "elect according to the foreknowledge of God the Father." It is something infinitely higher than a national election. Here is an individual election; they were foreknown of God the Father. In the Old Testament the Lord called Israel nationally "my first-born son," but no individual Israelite knew God as his Father, nor did an Israelite know himself individually as a son of God and a member of the family of God. They had received something better.

The nation had been set aside while those who believed were brought individually into the family of God, knowing God as their Father, while they became His children. Israel as a nation was set apart externally and by ordinances; but their setting apart, or sanctification, was through the Spirit. Their sanctification was unto the obedience and sprinkling of the blood of Jesus Christ. Their setting apart was vastly different from that separation which God had accorded to the nation as such. The Holy Spirit had set them apart unto the obedience of Christ, called them to obey as He obeyed, not to an obedience of the law. Connected with this obedience is the sprinkling of the blood of Jesus Christ, that precious blood typified by their former sacrifices which were unable to cleanse from sin, but the blood of Christ assures perfect forgiveness and justification, and that gives confidence and boldness before God, ànd liberty and power to practice the obedience of Christ, for which the believer is set apart.

"Blessed be the God and Father of our Lord Jesus Christ, who, according to His great mercy, hath begotten us again unto a living hope by the resurrection of Jesus Christ from among the dead." This is the doxology. It declares the new relationship into which they had been brought; for these Jewish believers it is no longer the God of Abraham, Isaac and Jacob, but "the God and Father of our Lord Jesus Christ." They were begotten again unto a living hope by the resurrection of Jesus Christ from among the dead. It is a joyful song of the better hope. We may think of what it meant to Peter, as well as to the other disciples. They had believed on Jesus as their promised, national Messiah. Their hope was in Him. As the two said on the way to Emmaus, "we trusted that it had been He which should have redeemed Israel." They hoped He would be King and take the throne of His father David. Then He who was their hope died on the shameful cross, and hope died. But the third day came and Christ arose from among the dead. Hope revived, yea, they werė begotten again unto a living hope. His resurrection was a begetting again to a living hope, no longer the hope of the earthly kingdom but a living hope "unto an inheritance incorruptible and undefiled that fadeth not away." And this living hope by the resurrection of Jesus Christ from among the dead, the hope which centers in Him as the living, risen and glorified One, is the hope of all His people.

Israel as a nation possessed an earthly inheritance, the promised land and with it corresponding earthly blessings. But now as the elect, according to the foreknowledge of the Father, they have a better inheritance. Earthly things are corruptible; the heavenly inheritance is incorruptible. Earthly things are defiled, pollution clings to the fairest and choicest; the coming inheritance is undefiled, nor can it ever be polluted by sin and its curse, it is eternally pure. Here on earth everything is fading, every beautiful flower has its roots in a grave, all is passing and fading away; but that inheritance which we shall receive is never-fading, it is always fresh and beautiful. And this inheritance is "preserved in heaven for you"; it is more than *reserved,* as we have it in our Bibles. It is with Him in the glory and He preserves it for His saints, so that the cruel hand of Satan cannot touch it nor take it away from man. And while that inheritance is preserved by the never-failing Lord in glory, saints are kept for the inheritance by the power of God through faith. Here is the real perseverance of the saints; the power to persevere and to keep is not in us but in God. That inheritance is ready to be revealed in the last times, that is when the Lord comes for His saints.

Verses 6-9. The way to the promised land for the literal Israel led through the desert sands with trials and testings. The way of the elect in Christ also leads through the desert with its wilderness experiences; faith too must be honored and glorified by testings. Faith is not only a precious thing for us, it is precious to God as well. It is His gold, that in which He rejoices. To bring out its value various trials are permitted by Him: "that the trial of your faith, being much more precious than of gold that perisheth, though it be tried with fire, might be found unto praise and honor and glory at the appearing of Jesus Christ." The goal of the hope, when the inheritance will be bestowed, is the appearing of Jesus Christ. This is His visible appearing. Peter writes as the apostle of circumcision and he does not write about the church as the body of Christ, the heavenly calling and destiny of the church, and therefore he does not say anything about the rapture preceding the revelation. Peter always speaks of His appearing or revelation; salvation as used in this chapter means the manifestation in glory, when He appears in visible glory and when we shall be manifested with Him in glory. Having mentioned His appearing, the Spirit of God directs the attention at once to the Person of

Christ. He must ever be the object of faith and occupation for the true believer. This brings into view the true character of Christianity.

"Whom having not seen ye love." It is a strange sound and fact at first, but in the end it is precious. Who ever loved a person that he never saw? We know that in human relations it is not so. In divine things it is precisely what shows the power and special character of a Christian's faith. "Whom having not seen, ye love, in whom, though now ye see Him not, yet believing, ye rejoice with joy unspeakable and full of glory: receiving the end of your faith, the salvation of your souls." This at once gives us a true and vivid picture of what Christianity is, of signal importance for the Jews to weigh, because they always looked forward for a visible Messiah as an object, the Son of David. But here it is altogether another order of ideas. It is a rejected Messiah who is the proper object of the Christian's love, though he never beheld Him; and who while unseen becomes so much the more simply and unmixedly the object of his faith, and the spring of "joy unspeakable and full of glory" (Wm. Kelly).

Verses 10-12. He directs their attention to the Prophets. The Spirit of Christ was in them and they testified before of the sufferings of Christ and the glories that should follow. This is the great message of these holy men of God who spoke as they were moved by the Holy Spirit. When our Lord said to the Jews "Search the Scriptures . . . they are they which testify of Me" He called attention to the same fact. They prophesied of the grace which was to come and though they did not understand their own prophecies, they sought diligently, they studied what they had written, searching and always searching, to find out what time, near or far, these things should come to pass. But they knew one thing, "To whom it was revealed, that not to themselves, but to us did they minister the things which are reported to you by those who have preached the gospel unto you by the Holy Spirit sent from heaven, into which things the angels desire to look." They knew that it was not for themselves, nor for their own times, that which the Spirit had announced, but for another time. The passage is illustrated by comparing Isaiah 64:4 with 1 Corinthians 2:9-10. The Spirit having come down from heaven after Christ had died and was raised from among the dead, has made known the fullness of redemption. And the angels desire to look into these things; they seek to explore and to fathom the wonders of that redemption and the coming glories which are connected with it.

Verses 13-21. The first exhortation is to gird up the loins of the mind. The man who girds the loins of the body is getting ready for service; the girding of the loins of the mind means to set the mind on these things, the things spiritual and unseen. To be sober means to be watchful and temperate, thus walking soberly, and "set your hope perfectly on the grace that is to be brought unto you at the revelation of Jesus Christ" (the correct translation). As they were now "obedient children" in the family of God, their responsibility and calling is to live and act as such. A holy God demands a holy people; this was God's call to His people Israel in the Old Testament, it is His call to the elect in the New Testament (Leviticus 11:44). This necessitates a walk in the Spirit as it is so fully revealed in the Epistles to the Romans and Galatians.

Next we find two great reasons for walking in holiness; the first reason is the relationship which believers have as children, God being their Father; the second, the redemption price which was paid.

"And if ye call on Him as Father, who without respect of persons judgeth according to each man's work, pass the time of your sojourn in fear, knowing that ye were redeemed not with corruptible things, with silver or gold, from your vain manner of life handed down from your fathers; but by precious blood, as of a lamb without blemish and without spot, the blood of Christ, foreknown indeed before the foundation of the world, but was manifested at the end of the times for your sake, who through Him believe in God, who raised Him from among the dead and gave Him glory, so that your faith and hope might be in God."

He has called us by His grace and we call Him Father. As Father, the head of His family, to which we belong, He must govern His house. As Father He exercises judgment in government regarding His children; He must chasten His children if they do not walk as it becometh those who are in possession of the divine nature. And though that government is one of love and grace, the Father's dealing with a beloved child, we must pass the time of our sojourn with fear. But this is not a slavish fear, nor a fear which has in it the elements of uncertainty as to salvation, a fear which trembles before a holy God, fearing His wrath. It is a godly, a holy fear, a fear that we might not please Him. This holy fear should be a passion to measure up to our calling as children and not to displease Him who is our Father, so that He does not need to exercise a Father's judgment upon us.

While the first reason to walk in holiness has to do with our conscience, the second concerns the affections. That blessed redemption by the blood of Christ, the Lamb without spot and blemish, foreknown before the foundation of the world, is the other great incentive to please God. It is not by silver or gold that He has redeemed us from all the vain things, whether vain religious traditions, or vain manner of life and all that goes with it, but by that which is the dearest, the most blessed and the most precious thing in the eyes of God and to the heart of God—the blood of Christ. No finite mind can understand the price God paid for our redemption. By Him we believe in God, who raised Him from among the dead and gave Him glory. And that acquired glory He received He has given to His own (John 17:22).

II. The Blessings and Privileges of All Believers

CHAPTER 1:22—2:10

1. The new birth (1:22-25)
2. Spiritual growth (2:1-3)
3. The privileges of believers as the holy and royal priesthood (2:4-10)

Verses 22-25. The relationship of those who are thus redeemed, whose faith and hope is in God, who raised Him from the dead and gave Him glory, whose souls are purified by obedience to the truth, unto unfeigned love of the brethren, is stated first: "Love one another with a pure heart fervently." All the elect through the foreknowledge of God the Father are covered by the same love, are redeemed by the same Lamb, washed in the same precious blood, have the same Father. They are one; they are brethren and as such love must characterize them. But this love, loving one another out of a pure heart fervently, is the fruit of the new nature which all possess who have believed and are redeemed by the precious blood of the Lamb. "Being born again, not of corruptible seed, but of incorruptible, by the Word of God, which liveth and abideth for ever." The Word of God, living and abiding, under the operation of the Spirit (the Word is "the water" of which our Lord spoke to Nicodemus) is the agent of the new birth. It is not corruptible seed, but incorruptible, hence the nature is an incorruptible, a holy nature. There are three incorruptible things mentioned in this chapter. An incorruptible inheritance, an incorruptible redemption price, and an incorruptible seed giving an incorruptible nature. And that new nature must love that which is of God, therefore the exhortation of loving one another, which is more fully developed in the great "family Epistle," the first Epistle of John.

But the new birth carries with it another blessing. "For all flesh is as grass and all the glory of it as the flower of the grass. The grass hath withered and the flower fallen, but the Word of the Lord endureth forever, and this is the Word which by the gospel is preached unto you."

The old creation is left behind, the world with all its glory and boastings, is judged. All is as grass and the glory of man as the flower of the grass. Those born again do no longer belong to this world, as He prayed: "They are not of the world, as I am not of the world." The words concerning the grass and the flower of the grass are a quotation from Isaiah (Isa. 40:6, 8). But the quotation is changed a little. In Isaiah we read: "The grass withereth, the flower fadeth," and here it is, "The grass hath withered and the flower fallen," that is how faith must look upon the world and all its glory, as withered and fallen, with no more attraction for the heart which knows God. But those who are born again are linked with that which abideth for ever, the Word of the Lord, preached in that ever blessed Gospel.

Verses 1-3. "Wherefore, laying aside all malice and all guile and hypocrisies and envyings and all evil-speakings as new born babes desire earnestly the pure milk of the Word that ye may grow by it unto salvation, if ye have tasted that the Lord is good."

Those who are born again of incorruptible seed, in possession of a new nature, are still in the world, though they are no longer of it. Evil is on all sides and there is still the old nature, the flesh, in every child of God though believers are reckoned as being no longer in the flesh (Rom. 8:9). The old things of the flesh must be put off, completely laid aside. This is the necessary thing for spiritual growth; if there is no putting off of these there can be no progress. Peter speaks of believers as "new-born babes."

The sense in which this expression is used here differs from the use of it in 1 Corinthians 3:1: "And I, brethren, could not speak unto you as unto spiritual, but as unto carnal, even as unto babes in Christ." The spiritual growth of the Corinthians had been arrested and dwarfed; they never developed, but remained babes, a spiritual monstrosity. But the meaning here is entirely different. Believers should be at all times like new-born babes hungering for that which the Lord has provided for spiritual growth, the milk in all its purity as found in His Word. The mother by which we are begotten again, that is the living and abiding Word of God, has also the nourishment for the life we have received. In this sense the child of God must always be like a healthy babe, always craving, hungering and thirsting for the pure milk as provided in His Word. All that we need, yea, every need is provided there, and as we go to that fountain which never runs dry, which never fails nor disappoints, we shall grow thereby.

One of the most subtle delusions is found among some pentecostal sects, who imagine that they are so filled with the Spirit that they can dispense with the reading of and feeding on the Word. In the authorized version two words are missing which belong in the text; they are the words *"unto salvation"* . . . "that ye may grow thereby unto salvation." They were omitted in some manuscripts, but belong here. Salvation here has the same meaning as in the first chapter, it looks forward to the end in glory.

And if we have felt that the Lord is gracious, have tasted of His loving kindness, we shall desire more and more of it, crave for still more. Peter surely had tasted that the Lord is gracious. We think of his denial, and when the Lord turned and looked upon him, Peter went out and wept bitterly. He had tasted that the Lord is gracious, and more so, when the Lord dealt so graciously with him at the meal His blessed hands had prepared for His disciples on the lakeshore (John 21), and His loving voice asked: "Simon, son of Jonas, lovest thou Me more than these?" The sentence, "If so be ye have tasted that the Lord is gracious," is a quotation from the Psalms (Psalm 34:8). David, like Peter, had shamefully failed and like Peter he had tasted that the Lord is gracious. All His saints have had the same experience of the graciousness of the Lord.

Verses 4-10. The testimony of Peter which follows is of great importance. The fisherman of Galilee knew nothing of what would happen centuries later. He did not know that ritualism would exalt him to a position of supremacy, claiming that he was and is the rock upon which the Church is built, that he was a bishop who communicated in Rome his apostolic authority to another, as it is claimed to one by name of Linus, and Linus handed over the same authority to Cletus and Cletus to Clemens, Clemens to Anacletus, Anacletus to Sixtus and so on from one generation to the other, each adding a little more till the harlot system of the mystical Babylon, the papacy became what it is today. But while Peter did not know the future, the Holy Spirit knew and He inspired his pen to write that which is the complete refutation of popery and a man-made priesthood.

Not Peter is the living stone upon which everything rests, but the Lord Jesus Christ is the rock foundation, the Stone upon whom all is built. Not Peter was rejected by men, then chosen of God and precious, but it is the Lord Jesus Christ. The Scriptures had announced this fact beforehand. Isaiah 28:16 is quoted in Verse 6. This is followed by a quotation from Psalm 118:22 and Isaiah 8:14. The Lord Jesus while on earth had made use of these prophecies given by His Spirit (Matthew 21:42). The Holy Spirit after Pentecost reminded the rulers, elders and scribes of the people once more of this great prophecy concerning the rejection of the Messiah by the nation (Acts 4:9-12). And when the Lord Jesus quoted this prophecy from Psalm 118 He added, what is cited here in verse 8, "whosoever shall fall on this stone shall be broken," that is what happened to the nation Israel.

The second half of this statement of our Lord in Matthew 21:44 is still unaccomplished—"but on whomsoever it shall fall, it will grind him to powder." This will happen at the close of the times of the Gentiles, when the stone strikes the feet of the prophetic image (Dan. 2). Israel had rejected the Stone and therefore was unfit as a nation to build the spiritual house, as the Lord had likewise announced: "the kingdom of God shall be taken from you, and given to a nation bringing forth the fruit thereof." They had as a nation a house called "The House of the Lord," where He delighted to dwell, but it was not a spiritual house, but a house made with hands, a shadow of the better things to come.

When Israel rejected the Messiah and the kingdom He had offered, when they had delivered Him up and He died, after His resurrection from among the dead and His exaltation to the right hand of God, the third person of the trinity, the Holy Spirit, came to earth for the purpose of building amongst men the habitation of God, a spiritual house, and that house is the church. Thus Peter bears witness to Christ as the Living Stone, the rock upon which the Church "the spiritual house" is being built. He with all other believers, including ourselves, are the living stones. As mentioned in the introduction, Christ is the *Petra, the Rock,* Peter and every other child of God is a *petros,* a little rock, a living stone with Himself (Matt. 16:17-18). And His Son whom man dishonored and rejected is precious to God; He is His delight; He is precious to those who have believed; He is our delight. While God says that His delight is in Him, we too confess that all our delight is in the Lord Jesus Christ.

Furthermore, all believers constitute a holy priesthood. Peter does not claim an exclusive priesthood vested in him, but his inspired testimony is that all members of the body of Christ, the living stones, are a priesthood. In the Old Testament the priesthood of Christ was foreshadowed in Aaron and the priesthood of believers by the sons of Aaron. (See annotations in Leviticus.) No longer are needed sacrifices of animals, for He has brought the one sacrifice, by which he has made the new and living way by His blood into the Holiest, so that every believer can draw nigh with a true heart and full assurance of faith, with hearts sprinkled from an evil conscience and bodies washed with pure water (Hebrews 10:19-22). This completely disposes of the ritualistic priesthood, vested in "ordained" men, that system which has been and still is and always will be, the corruption of Christianity. It also answers the blasphemous mass, which is an act of idolatry.

The function of the holy priesthood of believers consists in bringing spiritual sacrifices acceptable to God by Jesus Christ. "By Him therefore let us offer the sacrifice of praise to God continually, the fruit of our lips, giving thanks to His Name" (Hebrews 13:15). It is worship in the spirit and truth; it is praise and adoration as well as the ministry of intercession.

Once more Peter mentions the fact of the Christian priesthood. "But ye are a chosen generation, a royal priesthood, a holy nation, a peculiar people; that ye should shew forth the excellencies of Him who hath called you out of darkness into His marvellous light; which in time past were not a people, but are now the people of God; which had not obtained mercy, but now have obtained mercy" (Hosea 2:23). Israel was chosen, Israel was called to be a kingdom of priests and a holy nation, they were called "to show forth His praises." They never attained it, because they were not a holy nation, though constituted a separated nation by God's calling. But these believing Jews through grace in Christ had become a chosen generation, a royal priesthood, a holy nation, a peculiar people. As a remnant of the nation they possessed now what the nation never possessed. Of course that remnant was embodied in the church, and is a part of the body of Christ. Yet the application to them as a remnant must not be lost sight of.

Nor must we forget that there will be a future remnant of the nation, the nation which is now dispersed, which will become a holy nation, a royal priesthood in connection with the other nations. The promises, the gifts and callings of God, will all be accomplished, and those who had not obtained mercy will yet obtain mercy; that will be when He whom they pierced comes again and when they shall look upon Him in that day. Apart from this application to them as believing Jews, to whom the Epistle was addressed, all believers, whether Jews or Gentiles, have a royal priesthood. Christ is a holy Priest and a royal Priest; both aspects of His priesthood believers share in Him. We are holy priests to go in to God to represent man before God; we are royal priests to represent God before man, to show forth His excellencies. The royal priesthood of Christ, is the priesthood after the order of Melchisedec. He was the King-Priest who came to Abraham and made known God and His glory to Abraham. Thus in Christ we behold the glory of God and as identified with Christ, indwelt by Him, our royal priesthood is to make Him and His excellencies known among men.

III. Christ the Pattern for His Saints

CHAPTER 2:11—3:9

1. Abstinence and submission (2:11-17)
2. Christ the pattern for those who suffer (2:18-25)
3. Glorifying Christ in the marriage relation (3:1-7)
4. True Christian character (3:8-9)

Verses 11-17. The first exhortation is addressed to them as strangers and pilgrims. Such all true believers are. Because we belong to a heavenly home we cannot be at home in a world which lieth in the wicked one, which has cast out the Lord of glory, and which continues to reject Him. And it is only as a stranger here that we can do what we are exhorted to do, "to abstain from fleshly lusts which war against the soul." If our heart is where He is, if our affections are set upon the things on high, if we lose sight of the "vain things" which charm the natural man, and we realize in faith the heavenly calling and the heavenly home, then we shall not fight the lusts of the flesh, but willingly and joyfully abstain from them, fleeing them, as Paul exhorted Timothy.

A general exhortation follows. Their conversation is to be honest among the Gentiles who often spoke of them as evil-doers, accusing Christians of their own shameful conduct, as unsaved Gentiles, so that it might bring reproach upon "that worthy Name." By their godly lives the Gentiles should see their good works and when the day of visitation came, they would then glorify God. Does this mean a visitation in judgment, or the visitation in grace? It means the latter, though a visitation by the chastening hand of God is not excluded. When sorrows come, when earthly hopes are blasted, when sickness makes the enjoyment of the material things impossible, then the unbelievers often turn to the people of God for help and comfort, the grace of God will then be manifested in the day of visitation; this glorifies God.

Exhortation to submission is linked with this. "Submit yourselves therefore to every ordinance of man for the Lord's sake, whether unto the king as supreme; or to governors as sent by Him for the punishment of evil-doers, and for the praise of them that do well." We must remember that the kings and rulers mentioned here, under whom these believing Jews lived, were heathen and idolators. Yet they were to obey and to manifest patient submission. The exhortation has a special meaning for them as Jews, for naturally they were a rebellious people. The exhortation given to them before their captivity in Babylon, "to seek the peace of the city" where they would dwell has generally been disobeyed. These believing Jews probably were tempted to resist the powers which ruled. (It is a significant fact that many of the radicals, anarchists, or as they used to be called in Russia, nihilists, are apostate Jews. Many of the persecutions of the Jews, in which the innocent have to suffer with the guilty, are produced by Jews meddling with the politics of the nations among whom they are strangers and trying to overthrow these governments.) Therefore the exhortation to submit for the Lord's sake, though there are limitations to such submission. Such submission is "the will of God, that with well-doing ye may put to silence the ignorance of foolish men." Brief, but weighty, exhortations follow.

Verses 18-25. The exhortation after that is addressed to the servants, that is, to those Jewish believers who were slaves. To such the choicest words are addressed, God knowing that His own beloved Son had been on earth as a servant, that He was here not to be ministered to, but to minister and to give His life as a ransom for many. They were in the blessed position to "follow His steps." But the exhortation does not mean servants or slaves exclusively, it is written for all believers. "For this is acceptable, if a man for conscience toward God endure grief, suffering wrongfully. For what glory is it if, when ye sin, and are buffeted for it, ye take it patiently? but if, when ye do well and suffer, ye take it patiently, this is acceptable with God." To suffer wrongfully and take it patiently, without murmuring and without strife, is whereunto believers are called. It is then that they can show forth His excellencies and follow after Him. "Because Christ also suffered for you, leaving you an example that ye should follow His steps." And what an example has He left for us? He was the holy, spotless Son of God. Suffering for His own sins was an impossibility, for He was spotless. He knew no sin, neither could He sin. Yet He suffered. "Who did no sin, nor was guile found in His mouth; who when reviled, He reviled not again; when He suffered, threatened not; but committed Himself to Him who judgeth righteously."

Such is the pattern. But there is more than that. He knew no sin, did not sin and all His suffering, the shame and the suffering connected with the cross, was on account of our sins. "Who His own self bare our sins in His own body on the tree, that we, being dead to sins, should live unto righteousness; by whose stripes ye were healed. For ye were as sheep going astray; but are now returned unto the Shepherd and Bishop of your souls." The rendering, or, rather, paraphrase, some have adopted that Christ bore our sins "up to the tree" is erroneous and misleading. Our Lord did not bear our sins in His holy life before the cross, but He bore them on the cross, in His own body. And He bore them that "we, being dead to sins," not as revealed in Romans to *sin,* but to sins, that is, the practical giving up of our own wills, should live unto righteousness.

The fifty-third chapter of Isaiah is used by Peter in this paragraph. There it is written: "By His stripes we are healed," and the confession, "all we like sheep have gone astray." Of late the so-called "divine healers," men and women who claim gifts of healings, if not gifts to work miracles, speak of the sentence, "By His stripes we are healed," as meaning the healing of diseases. They claim that Christ died also for our bodily ills and that the stripes laid upon Him were specifically for the healing of our bodies, which Scripture so clearly states are "dead on account of sin." This is a most dangerous perversion of the truth. Christ died for our sins according to the Scriptures, but nowhere is it written that He died for our bodily diseases.

These believing Jews were in possession of the truth as revealed in Isaiah 53. They foreshadow that other Jewish remnant of the future which will some day use the fifty-third chapter of Isaiah as their great confession of Him whom they despised and rejected, and by whose stripes they also will be healed. Then Peter speaks of our Lord as Shepherd, the Shepherd who died for the sheep, the great Shepherd brought again from among the dead. He loves His sheep and shepherds them. Bishop means overseer. He is the only Bishop, who watches over all and guards all His blood-bought sheep.

Verses 1-7. The practical exhortations are now extended to the marriage relation, how wives and husbands should be royal priests, showing forth His excellencies in their divinely sanctioned union, as man and wife. The wife is mentioned first, for her place is the highest, the place of submission, which in God's eyes is the place of honor. The case of a wife is stated who has an unbelieving husband. Is she to submit to him, who is an unbeliever? Must she be obedient to such a one? How often wives placed in this position have listened to the evil councils of others, and, instead of submitting to the demands of an unbelieving husband, have resisted him, and as a result misery came upon them. Let it be noticed that the Holy Spirit insists on obedience; the fact of the disobedient husband is given as a reason for submission. Then there is a promise. The unbelieving husband is to be won without the Word, that is, without preaching in a public service, by the godly life of meekness and submission of the believing wife. This is the advice of the Holy Spirit, and many times the promise given to the believing wife has been made good.

Furthermore, there is a word concerning dress. The adorning is not to be outwardly in braiding of hair, wearing of gold, or putting on of apparel, but inwardly, "the hidden man of the heart, in that which is not corruptible, even the ornament of a meek and quiet spirit, which in the sight of God is of great price." The positive side is emphasized more than the negative. The greatest ornament a woman can wear is "a meek and quiet spirit," for it shows that in manifesting meekness and quietness, they learned and received from Him, who on earth was "meek and lowly of heart." This applies to every believer likewise. Wherever a meek and quiet spirit is manifested God is well pleased with it. What a contrast with the conditions in the world today. Women claim equality with men; in every walk of life they clamor to be heard; the female sex is breaking down the barriers set by the Creator and the Redeemer, demanding leadership in every sphere. The result will be disaster. But it must not be overlooked that here is also exhortation for the Christian woman to dress outwardly as becomes a follower of the Lord Jesus Christ. There should be a difference between the daughters of the world and those who are Christ's. On the other hand, shabbiness of dress, an unclean appearance, is no more an honor to the Gospel, than a dress which is after the latest fashion of the world.

And the husband is exhorted next. He is not told to claim submission, or to insist upon it as his peculiar right. He is exhorted to give the wife honor as the weaker vessel, hence he must show to her, as the weaker one, kindness, tenderness, consideration and loving sympathy, as we read in Ephesians: "Husbands, love your wives as Christ loved the church." The believing husband and the wife are "heirs together of the grace of life." Where this is practised there will be sweet companionship and fellowship in the Lord, nothing hindering them from bowing the knees together in His presence, expressing together their praise, their mutual needs and those of others.

Verses 8-9. General exhortations follow. What is found in these two verses constitutes a true Christian character.

IV. The Comfort in the Midst of Trials and Suffering

CHAPTER 3:10—4

1. The comfort in suffering (3:10-17)
2. Few saved as illustrated by Noah's preaching (3:18-22)
3. The new life in its transforming power (4:1-11)
4. Suffering and glory (4:12-19)

Verses 10-17. The words which stand in the beginning of this section are quoted from Psalm 34:12-16. It is interesting to note that the Spirit of God quotes from the three main divisions of the Hebrew Bible in the first three chapters of this Epistle. The Hebrew Bible is composed according to Jewish division of the law, the prophets and the writings. In the first chapter the law is quoted; in the second the prophets; and in the third we have a quotation from the Psalms. If we practice righteousness, the result of the new nature, produced by the new life, the promises of the Lord will not fail. To Israel in the Old Testament the Lord promised earthly blessings, and while to His heavenly people heavenly, spiritual blessings are vouchsafed, the earthly blessings are not excluded. It was true in olden times that "the eyes of the Lord are over the righteous, and His ears are open unto their prayers." It is so today, for He changes not. He looks for practical righteousness. Equally true is it that in His righteous government the face of the Lord is against them that do evil. And there is the comfort if we do right that none can harm us, for the Lord is on our side.

Suffering for righteousness' sake must be, but there is a "blessedness" connected with it. The Lord pronounced this in one of the beatitudes of the Sermon on the Mount (Matt. 5:10). How fitting it is that in this Epistle, in addressing these Jewish believers as a remnant of the nation, this should be mentioned. It is the comfort in persecution, "be not afraid of their terror, neither be troubled." The quotation in verse 15 is from Isaiah 8:12, 13. There it is a prophecy concerning the future remnant of Israel during their coming great tribulation, foreshadowed in Isaiah by the Assyrian invasion.

Verses 18-22. "For Christ also hath once suffered for sins, the just for the unjust, that He might bring us to God, being put to death in flesh but quickened by the Spirit: in which also He went and preached to the spirits in prison, who before time were disobedient when the long suffering of God waited in the days of Noah, while the ark was preparing; in which few, that is, eight souls, were saved through water; which figure does also now save you, even baptism (not the putting away of the filth of the flesh, but the request as before God of a good conscience), by the resurrection of Jesus Christ, who has gone into heaven and is at the right hand of God; angels and authorities and powers being subjected unto Him."

This difficult and much misunderstood passage demands a closer attention. It is the passage upon which Rome has built her obnoxious and unscriptural doctrine of a purgatory. Protestant expositors have also misinterpreted this passage; in some quarters of Protestantism a kind of a "Protestant purgatory" is now being taught. Many errors, like a second probation, another chance for the lost, the restitution of the wicked, are linked with the wrong exposition of the above words.

Even sound believers have adopted that which Peter does not mean at all, and which is unknown in the rest of the Word of God. Their teaching founded upon these statements by Peter is as follows: The Lord descended into Hades, the place of the departed spirits and preached there. The visit took place after His death and before His physical resurrection, that is, He made the visit in His unclothed state, while His body still rested in the tomb. As to the preaching, the opinions of these exegetes are divided. Some believe that He went to Hades to announce the certain doom of the lost. Others, and they are not a few, state that He preached, offering to the lost salvation, while still others claim that the spirits in prison are the righteous dead to whom Christ announced that their redemption had been wrought out for them, and that He announced His victory.

As to the result of the preaching, the teaching is that it was successful; this is by inference, as they say, otherwise it could not be mentioned among the blessed results of Christ's suffering. They also claim that inasmuch as early Christian literature has much to say about that fictitious "descent into Hades" (or, as generally stated, hell), it must be the true meaning of the passage. In giving these views on the meaning of the passage before us we give a very few; there are many others, like the late Bullinger's view, that the spirits were the fallen angels, and that He went to herald His triumph to them. Pages could be filled with the fanciful and unscriptural interpretations of this passage.

The chief question is: Did our Lord go to Hades in a disembodied state? In fact, all depends on the question of what is the true meaning of the sentence, "quickened by the Spirit." Now, according to the interpretations of the men who teach that the Lord visited Hades, the spirits in prison, during the interval between His death and the morning of the third day, He descended into these regions while His dead body was still in the grave. Therefore, these teachers claim that His human spirit was quickened, which necessitates that the spirit which the dying Christ commended into the Father's hands had also died. This is not only incorrect doctrine, but it is an unsound and evil doctrine. Was the holy humanity of our Lord, body, soul and spirit dead? A thousands times *No!* Only His body died; that is the only part of Him which could die. The text makes this clear: "He was put to death in flesh," that is, His body. There could be no quickening of His spirit, for His spirit was alive. Furthermore, the word quickening, as we learn from Ephesians 1:20 and 2:5-6, by comparing the two passages, applies to His physical resurrection, it is the quickening of His body. To teach that the Lord Jesus was made alive before His resurrection is unscriptural. The "quickened by the Spirit" means the raising up of His body. His human spirit needed no quickening; it was His body and *only* His body. And the Spirit who did the quickening is not His own spirit, that is, His human spirit, but the Holy Spirit. Romans 8:11 speaks of the Spirit as raising Jesus from among the dead.

We have shown that it was an impossibility that Christ was in any way quickened while His body was not yet raised, hence a visit to Hades is positively excluded between His death and resurrection. There is only another alternative. If it is true that He descended into these regions, then it must have been after His resurrection. But that is equally untenable. The so-called "Apostle's Creed" puts the descent between His death and resurrection and all the other theorists follow this view. We have shown what the passage *does not* mean. It cannot mean a visit of the disembodied Christ to Hades, for it speaks of the quickening by the Spirit, and that means His physical resurrection.

What, then, does the passage mean? It is very simple after all. He preached by the Spirit, or in the Spirit, that is, the same Spirit who raised Him from among the dead, the Holy Spirit of life and power, to the spirits who are *now* in prison. But when the preaching occurred they were not in prison. And who were they? All the wicked dead for 4,000 years? The text makes it clear that they are a special class of people. They were living in the days of Noah. It is incomprehensible how some of these teachers, misinterpreting this passage, can teach that it includes all the lost, or angels which fell, or the righteous dead. The Spirit of God preached to them, that is, the Spirit who quickened the body of Christ, the same Spirit preached to the generation of unbelievers in the days of Noah. The time of the preaching, then, did not occur between the death and resurrection of Christ, but it took place in Noah's day. Christ was not personally, or corporeally present, just as He is not present in person in this age when the gospel is preached; His Spirit is here.

So was He present by His Spirit in the days of Noah. It is written: "My Spirit shall not always strive with man, for that he also is flesh; yet his days shall be one hundred and twenty years" (Gen. 6:3). His Spirit was then on the earth. In long-suffering God was waiting for one hundred and twenty years while the ark was preparing. His Spirit preached then. But He needed an instrument. The instrument was Noah; in him was the Spirit of Christ and as the preacher of righteousness (2 Peter 2:5) he delivered the warning message of an impending judgment to those about him, who did not heed the message, passed on in disobedience, were swept away by the deluge and are now the spirits in prison. As the Spirit of Christ was in the prophets (chapter 1:11) testifying beforehand of the suffering of Christ and the glory that should follow, so the Spirit of Christ preached through Noah. This is the meaning of this passage, and any other is faulty and unscriptural.

This interpretation is in full keeping with Peter's testimony. It is to "strengthen his brethren," to encourage and comfort those who were suffering persecution and passed through many fiery trials. They thought it strange that they had to suffer, that they were few in number who were saved, while they lived in the midst of the vast multitudes which rejected the gospel and live on in sin and disobedience. For this reason the Spirit of God reminds them that such was also the case in the days of Noah, as it will be again at the close of the age, as the Lord Himself had announced. The multitudes in the days of Noah despised the warning; only eight souls were saved out of the judgment.

It must also be remembered that Peter's Epistle is not a doctrinal Epistle. He does not teach, but exhort. It is true many of the exhortations have for a foundation doctrines stated elsewhere in the Pauline Epistles. If it were Christian doctrine that Christ went to the prison of the wicked dead, such a doctrine should then be more fully stated somewhere else in the New Testament. But such is not the case. The passage in Ephesians 4, concerning Christ leading captivity captive has nothing to do with Peter's statement. (See annotations on Ephesians 4).

The concluding words, linked with this statement, are a typical comparison of the deluge and the ark with baptism. It has also been misunderstood, and some teach on account of it that baptism is a saving ordinance, which is another error. We quote a paragraph from the *Synopsis of the Bible* which clears this up in a way which cannot be improved upon.

"To this the apostle adds, the comparison of baptism to the ark of Noah in the deluge. Noah was saved through the water; we also; for the water of baptism typifies death, as the deluge, so to speak, was the death of the world. Now Christ has passed through death and is risen. We enter into death in baptism; but it is like the ark, because Christ suffered in death for us, and has come out of it in resurrection, as Noah came out of the deluge, to begin, as it were, a new life in a resurrection world. Now Christ, having passed through death, has atoned for sins; and we, by passing through it in spirit, leave all our sins in it, as Christ did in reality for us; for He was raised up without the sins which He expiated on the cross. And they were our sins; and thus, through the resurrection, we have a good conscience. We pass through death in spirit and in figure by baptism. The peace-giving force of the thing is the resurrection of Christ, after He had accomplished expiation; by which resurrection therefore we have a good conscience."

In other words our good conscience is not in having obeyed an ordinance, but it is by what Christ has done, who has gone into heaven and who is exalted at the right hand of God.

Verses 1-11. The opening sentence of the fourth chapter connects with chapter 3:18. The sufferings of Christ are thus brought to their attention once more. The reason is obvious. They were Jews and had been taught that earthly, temporal blessings, were the marks exclusively of divine favor; trials, sufferings and persecutions, on the other hand, according to Jewish conceptions, were evidences of disfavor. They were therefore disheartened and greatly perplexed when persecutions arose and they had to suffer. But these sufferings were the evidence that they followed Him who also suffered in the flesh. He suffered for us, that is, for our sins, and therefore believers must arm themselves with the same mind. They must expect suffering, not for sins, but from the side of an evil world. "For he that hath suffered in the flesh hath ceased from sin." The death of Christ for sin (not sins) demands from the believer that he also cease from sin, from living after the old nature.

If the Christian gratifies the old nature and yields to it, it will not entail any suffering, but if the believer lives as "dead unto sin," walks in separation from this evil age, the result will be that he has to suffer in some way. The life he lives is no longer "in the flesh to the lusts of men, but to the will of God." Such a walk brings with it the contradiction of sinners, the hatred of the world, such sufferings through which Christ also passed. Once they did as the heathen, the Gentiles, about them, walking in lasciviousness, lusts, excess of wine, revelings, banqueting, and abominable idolatries. But now their lives had been transformed; no longer did they run with them and do what the Gentiles did. Their former associates in sin and in the lusts of the flesh thought it strange that such should be the case, and they spoke evil of them. What evil they spoke about them is not stated. But for this they will have to give account to Him who is ready to judge the quick and the dead, even Christ.

The next verse has perplexed many, and has been misused by teachers of error and unsound doctrines, like the passage about the spirits in prison. "For to this end was the gospel preached also to the dead, that they might be judged as regards men after the flesh, but live according to God in the Spirit." It is strange that expositors should detach a verse like this from the context and then, without considering its connection, build upon one verse a new and vital doctrine. So it is claimed that the dead mentioned are those who died before the gospel was preached, or who never had a chance to hear the Gospel, but who hear it now in the abode of death, to obtain eternal life. But this is only one of a number of other interpretations.

The Apostle had spoken in the preceding verse of the judgment of the living and of the dead. He now mentions the dead to whom the gospel had been preached. It is a thing of the past and means that those who are dead now while they lived had heard the preaching of the gospel. He means only the righteous dead and the other dead are not in view at all. Those who are now dead passed through the same experience, as the living pass through it, judged according to men in the flesh, but living according to God in the Spirit. Thus the preaching to the dead as dead is not taught at all in this verse. If there were such a thing as preaching to the physical dead we should find it in the Epistle to the Romans, in that great document of the gospel, or somewhere else in the Pauline Epistles; but there is nothing mentioned about this anywhere.

The new life which is dead to sin and suffers with Christ must be manifested. Of this we read in the exhortations which follow (verses 7-11). The end of all things is at hand, the fact that this age will end must always be kept before the heart and mind. And if it was true then that the promised end is at hand how much more true is it now. As a result of waiting for His coming, expecting Him at any time, we are to be sober and watchful unto prayer, and manifest fervent love among and towards fellow-believers. There is to be hospitality without murmuring, ministering one to another, according as each has received. Public ministry in preaching or teaching is to be as the oracles of God, in dependence upon Him, as of the ability which God supplieth, that is, as enabled by His Spirit.

Verses 12-19. "Beloved, think it not strange concerning the fiery trial which cometh upon you, as though some strange thing happened unto you; but rejoice, inasmuch as ye are partakers of Christ's sufferings; that, when His glory shall be revealed, ye may be glad also with exceeding joy." With what love and tenderness, dear Peter, by the Spirit of God, touches again on their sufferings and trials! How perplexed they must have been when they read their own Scriptures and remembered the promises made to Israel as to earthly blessings; and here they were suffering want and privation, were persecuted and slandered by those about them. He writes to them not to think it strange, as if a strange thing happened unto them, when passing through fiery trials. It is the path the Shepherd went and the sheep must follow Him. He suffered, it is the believer's privilege to suffer with Him. When sufferings and trials come, then is the time for rejoicing and not for being disheartened. Sufferings become sweet and precious when we remember they constitute us partakers of Christ's sufferings. And there is coming a revelation of His glory. In anticipation of that we can rejoice, for that revelation will bring the end of all suffering, and glory as well.

"If ye are reproached for the name of Christ, blessed are ye, for the Spirit of glory and of God resteth upon you; on their part He is evil spoken of, but on your part He is glorified." Instead of trying to escape sufferings with Christ, a little reproach, a little contempt for Christ's sake, we should welcome all most gladly. There is a blessing in it, even when peopole call us narrow or by any other name of contempt, because we exalt Christ and are true to Him. The Spirit of glory and of God rests upon us whenever we are reproached for the name of Christ. And if we were but more faithful, more separated, more loyal and devoted, we also would have more reproach, and as a result know more of the blessed experience that we are the resting and dwelling place of the Spirit of glory.

But there are sufferings which are inconsistent with Christ's sufferings and with the character of a Christian. "But if any suffer as a Christian, let him not be ashamed; but let him glorify God on this behalf." It means to count reproach and suffering for Christ an honor and a glory. Peter had made this experience when with his fellow-apostles he had been beaten, "they departed from the presence of the council, rejoicing that they were counted worthy to suffer shame for His name" (Acts 5:41).

"For the time is come that judgment must begin at the house of God, and if it first begin at us, what shall the end be of them that obey not the gospel of God? And if the righteous scarcely be saved, where shall the ungodly and sinner appear?" The sufferings of believers are permitted by the Lord for their own good likewise; they are His loving chastenings. Thus He deals as a loving Father with His house, whose house are we (Hebrews 3:6), permitting and using afflictions, sorrows, losses, that we may be partakers of His holiness. But if such is the case with His house, with those who belong to Him and whom He loves, what shall be the end of those that disobey the gospel of God? If the righteous, the sinner saved by grace, in his walk through the wilderness can scarcely be saved, if it needs the very power of God to keep him, what shall be the fate of the ungodly and the sinner? Therefore, when the believer suffers he commits his soul to Him who is able to sustain and carry him through.

V. Exhortations Concerning Service and Conflict

CHAPTER 5

1. As to Christian service (5:1-7)
2. Conflict and victory (5:8-14)
3. The conclusion (5:12-14)

Verses 1-7. Peter now speaks in great tenderness exhorting to service. The exhortation is addressed to the elders and he speaks of himself as a "fellow-elder." Does he mean by this an official title or does he mean simply his age and experience? He is not writing in any official capacity, but the word elder has the meaning of old in years. He assumes no ecclesiastical authority to dictate, but speaks out of a ripe experience and a heart of love. How different from what ritualism has made him to be. He takes his place among the other elders and calls himself a fellow-elder, not claiming any authority or superiority whatever. He was a witness of the sufferings of Christ; he knew he would be a partaker of the glory which shall be revealed. The Lord had given him this assurance (Matt. 19:28,29).

He gives some important exhortations. We give it in a better rendering. "Tend the flock of God which is among you, exercising the oversight, not of constraint, but willingly; not for filthy lucre, but readily; neither as lording it over the charge allotted to you, but being ensamples to the flock." Believers here are called "the flock of God." In John 10:16 the Lord had given the announcement that there should be one flock (not one fold, as the Authorized Version). The flock of God is the Church, the body of Christ. The language so frequently heard in Christendom when preachers and pastors speak of those to whom they preach as "my flock" or "my people," is unscriptural and should be avoided. God's children do not belong to anybody but the Lord. As the Lord had commissioned Peter: "Feed My sheep," and "Feed My lambs," so Peter writes to the elders to tend the flock of God. It is the same Greek word used here which we find in John 21:16 and is really "shepherd"—shepherd the flock of God. It is not to be done for filthy lucre's sake, on account of gain, for money considerations.

All is prophetic, for exactly that which was not to be done is being done in Christendom today, hence many of those who claim to be shepherds of the flock are in reality nothing but hirelings; and often it happens that the hireling for the sake of better financial conditions will exchange "his flock" for another. Furthermore, there is to be no lording over the allotted charge (or over your allotments). The elder who has the oversight of the flock, called to shepherd the flock, minister to the flock as a servant, is not to take a place of superiority or spiritual dignity, claiming authority. This also is done in Christendom with its "Lord Bishops" and other titles of ecclesiastical authority. The word translated in the Authorized Version with "heritage" is in the Greek *"kleros,"* and means an allotment. From this word comes our English "clergy." There is no such thing in the body of Christ as a "clergy" and a "laity."

Instead of lording over their allotted charge, the elders are to be ensamples to the flock, in a godly life. Then comes the promise, "when the chief shepherd is manifested, ye shall receive a crown of glory that fadeth not away." The sheep of Christ for which He laid down His life are very precious to Him, and those who serve His sheep, who minister to their need, will be honored by Him and rewarded with the crown of glory in the day of His manifestation. There is to be submission by the younger to the elder, that is, the younger in years are to be subject to those older in years. The same rule of loving submission extends to all the flock of God, "be subject one to another."

Humility is to be the right clothing for the saints of God. "They are to gird themselves with humility in this way, humility being that which will keep everything rightly adjusted, as the girdle the robe, and which would thus enable for such activity as all are called to; for humility is a grand help against discouragement by the difficulties of the way, and necessarily against all that would search out any remnant of pride in us (F. W. Grant). Self-exaltation is the very essence of sin. God cannot tolerate it in His people. The example of Christ, who made of Himself no reputation, forbids it. God resisteth therefore always and in every way the proud, while He giveth grace to the humble. "Humble yourselves therefore under the mighty hand of God, that He may exalt you in due time." How little these great exhortations are considered in our times! Even among those who have the truth and believe in the revelation of God, while there is much increase in knowledge, there is little evidence of true humility. Humility will never leave us ashamed. We do not need to exalt ourselves; the Lord will do it for us.

Then there is the sweet comfort: "Casting all your care upon Him, for He careth for you." All means all—all cares, whatever they are; all burdens, all anxieties we can roll upon Him, with the perfect assurance that He does care. Alas! our anxieties, our heavy feelings, our worry and our hurry, all speak the same language of unbelief "Lord, dost Thou not care?" Well, it is if we look upon all burdens He permits to be laid upon us, as tokens of His love, by which we may learn His faithfulness afresh. Instead of murmuring then, we should sing and rejoice, being anxious for nothing, knowing He carries us and our burdens and cares as we can never do.

Verses 8-11. Once more we hear His exhortation: "Be sober, be watchful!" Why? Because there is an adversary and a conflict. In those days of persecution he was the roaring lion; in our days he sneaks about as an angel of light. No longer is it the persecution of the church; it is the corruption of the truth which is the work of the adversary today. But in Peter's day the enemy was engaged in active persecution, seeking to devour God's people. Once more he will assume this character during the coming great tribulation, the time of Jacob's trouble. Then the faithful Jewish remnant, like this remnant to whom Peter wrote, will have to face the roaring lion, as we read so frequently in the book of Revelation.

Then follows Peter's benediction, quite a different thing from the fraudulent benedictions, which come from the counterfeit successors of Peter: "But the God of all grace, who hath called you unto His eternal glory in Christ Jesus, when ye have suffered a little while, Himself shall perfect, stablish, strengthen and settle you. To Him be glory and dominion for ever and ever."

Verses 12-14. The Epistle was sent to them by Silvanus. It is the same Silvanus whose back had been lacerated in the prison of Philippi, whose feet had been in stocks, and who sang the praises of the Lord with beloved Paul in that night of pain and suffering. He knew what suffering with Christ meant and could equally sympathize with his brethren.

There is greeting from the other elect ones in Babylon, as we have shown in our introduction, in literal Babylon on the banks of the Euphrates. Salutation from Marcus is also given. This is John Mark, the cousin of Barnabas, whose failure in the book of Acts is recorded, and on account of whom the Apostle Paul had a falling out with Barnabas; it is the same Mark who wrote the Gospel which bears his name. The kiss of love is mentioned (Rom. 16:16; 1 Cor. 16:20; 2 Cor. 13:12; 1 Thess. 5:26). It was universally observed for centuries. "Peace be with you all in Christ Jesus. Amen."

THE SECOND EPISTLE OF

PETER

Introduction

The authenticity of this Second Epistle of Peter has occasioned a great deal of controversy and many are questioning it, as it has been done in the past. It is true the most ancient sources of post-apostolic writings do not mention this Epistle. What we have pointed out in the introductions of most of the other New Testament books, that their authenticity is confirmed by references in the fragments of the writings of the church fathers, such as Polycarp, Papias, Clement of Rome and others, cannot be done with this Epistle. Some scholars in their research claim that traces of this Epistle are discernable in the testimonies of Polycarp, Ignatius, in the letter of Barnabas and in the testimony of Clement of Rome, but they are so very faint and fanciful, that they are not reliable. But not finding a direct allusion in these sources does not mean anything at all. The greater portion of the writings of the men who were in touch with the Apostles and the direct disciples of the men who knew Peter and Paul, have been lost. If we had all they have written we would probably find in them references to this Epistle.

The Epistle is not found in the Peshito version. According to Bishop Westcott in his Canon of the New Testament there are in existence two classes of manuscripts of this version. Both omit the Second and Third Epistles of John, the Second Epistle of Peter, the Epistle of Jude and the Book of Revelation, but include all the other books. This Canon seems to have been generally maintained in the Syrian churches. It is reproduced in the Arabic version of Erpenius, which was taken from the Peshito. Cosmas, an Egyptian traveller of the sixth century, states that only three of the so-called "Catholic" Epistles were received by the Syrians. Later sources charge the Syrian churches with mutilating the New Testament by not having these books in their Bibles.

The Epistle is also omitted in the Latin version, that is, in the oldest editions. That the Vulgate is unreliable is well known. Westcott makes the following argument about the missing Second Epistle of Peter in the Latin version: "If we suppose that it was once received into the canon like the First Epistle, it would in all probability have been translated by the same person, as seems to have been the case with the Gospel of Luke and the Acts (both written by Luke), though their connection is less obvious; and while every allowance is made for the difference in style in the original Epistles, we must look for the same rendering of the same phrases. But when on the contrary, it appears that the Latin text of the Epistle not only exhibits constant and remarkable difference from the text of other parts of the Vulgate, but also differs from the First Epistle in the rendering of words common to both, when it further appears that it differs not less clearly from the Epistle of Jude in those parts which are almost identical in the Greek; then the supposition that it was admitted into the Canon at the same time with them becomes at once unnatural. It is indeed possible that the two Epistles may have been received at the same time and yet have found different translators." But this argument does not mean at all that this Epistle is spurious and should be excluded from the New Testament.

But while the Epistle is not mentioned in the Muratorian fragment, in the writings of Polycarp, Papias, Irenaeus and others, and while it is missing in the Peshito and the earlier editions of the Vulgate, Hippolytus (living in the first half of the third century) was evidently acquainted with the Epistle, for in writing on the Antichrist he makes use of 2 Peter 1:21. Eusebius, the church historian, gives incontrovertible testimony that the Epistle was positively known at the close of the second century as the second Epistle of Peter. He shows that Clement of Alexandria (about 190 A.D.) knew the Epistle as the work of Peter and used it. The successor of Clement, Origen, according to Eusebius wrote: "Peter has left one acknowledged Epistle, and possibly also a second, for it is disputed." It was through Jerome's (Eusebius Hieronymus, born 390 A.D.) efforts that the Epistle was added to the Vulgate. He wrote: "Peter wrote two Epistles, which are termed Catholic, the second of which is denied by most to be his, because of the disagreement of its style with that of the former Epistle." On account of these historical facts opinions among scholars have been very much divided. Many reject the Petrine authorship of this Epistle, but other scholars accept it without any question. Among those who defend the Epistle against those who deny it are scholars of the highest reputation like Alford, Olshausen, Keil and others.

The Sufficiency of Internal Evidence

The fact is that external evidences to confirm the authenticity of Second Peter are not needed, for the internal evidences are beyond controversy of such a nature as to establish the Petrine authorship. The Epistle starts with the name of Peter. In the Greek the name Simon is spelled "Symeon" or "Simeon." If we turn to Acts 15:14 we read that James called Peter "Symeon," the Aramaic form for Simon. Then the writer refers to the fact that he would have soon to put off this tabernacle "even as our Lord Jesus Christ hath showed me." He was now an old man, and the Lord had spoken to him at the lakeside. "When thou art old thou shalt stretch forth thy hands" (John 21). Still stronger is the reference of the writer to the transfiguration, where Peter was present, and he speaks of it as being an eyewitness of His coming and of His majesty. And, finally, the writer says: "This *second* Epistle, beloved, I now write unto you" (3:1).

Critical Claims and Evasions

This internal evidence destructive critics try to evade and offset. They claim that the writer was not Simon Peter, but that some unknown author, using Peter's name, wrote this document. It is the same foolish invention advanced by Old Testament critics as to the authorship of the book of Daniel.

To establish this theory they point to the fact that there was a tendency in the early church to use Peter's name in different pseudo documents, such spurious writings as "The Gospel of Peter; The Revelation of Peter; the Acts of Peter, and the travels of Peter." But the fact of these forgeries, some of which cover some of the text of the Second Epistle of Peter, is an evidence that a genuine writing exists. According to the opinions of the men who reject the authorship of Peter, the writer of this Epistle to give standing to his producton thought best to impersonate the Apostle Peter and so he started right in the beginning by saying he is Peter. And he is careful to select the Aramaic form of Peter's name, the name Symeon. Would a forger not rather have avoided that uncommon use of Peter's name? But, furthermore, he also tells us that the Lord had told him about His death; and yet this man was not Peter, nor had the Lord ever told him what He had spoken to Peter about the time and manner of His death. Then the writer of the Epistle claims to have been on the Mount of Transfiguration, that he beheld His glory there and heard the voice of the Father speaking. He is positive that he was present and was an eyewitness, the strongest possible claim.

Yet if it was not Peter who wrote this Epistle, then it must have been either John or James, because there were only three eyewitnesses of the transfiguration. But would John or James write thus, hiding his identity under the name of Peter? Then the writer, assuming the name of Peter, declares that he had written the first Epistle, which Peter beyond doubt wrote, yet he had *not* written that Epistle. Here are three (in plain English) *lies.* A man writes an Epistle claiming to be Peter, but he is not Peter at all; hence he is a fraud. The same man claims that he was at the lake of Tiberias, that the Lord told him about His death; yet he was not there, for he was not Peter; therefore this impersonator is a fraud. This is an especially strong point. The fact that the Lord had announced Peter's death was known to but a few at that time, when the Epistle was written, which we take was about the year 65 A.D.

The Gospel of John, where the Lord's prophecy as to Peter's future is recorded, had not yet been written. Furthermore, he says that he saw the transfiguration, which he did not see; hence he lied. The fourth lie is his claim that he wrote the first Epistle, which he did not write. It is astonishing what inventions the enemies of the Bible can bring forth simply to discredit the Word of God and to deny its authenticity. If Peter is not the writer of this Epistle the whole Epistle is a miserable fraud, a dishonest piece of work, a forgery of the worst kind, which every honest man must despise. The foolish babblings of critics: "it is a useful document and should be read by all Christians, though Peter did not write it himself," is ridiculous. Either Peter wrote it and then it must be be accepted; or Peter did not write it and in such a case the whole business is a forgery and a fraud. But would a fraud ever have written such a wonderful message as the one with which this second Epistle begins? Would a conscious fraud have warned against apostasy as found in the second chapter? Would he, could he, have exhorted fellow-believers in the way as it is done in this Epistle? It is a moral impossibility.

The Character of the Second Epistle

One of the critics makes the following statement in denying the Petrine authorship: "The fact that the only allusions to the incidents in the Lord's life found in the Epistle are such as would support the character as one writing as Peter does become, in view of the silence of the Epistle as to the passion, the resurrection, the ascension, and of the absence from it of allusions to the Lord's teaching as recorded in the gospel, are a serious ground for questioning the Petrine authorship of the Epistle" (Chase). Like most critics this one lacks in spiritual discernment. In fact, if critics had some spiritual insight in the majestic scope of God's holy Word, they would not be critics, but worshipers. All second Epistles, except Second Corinthians, have a peculiar character. Second Thessalonians, Second Timothy, Second and Third John, and the little Epistle of Jude are in reality prophetic. They all speak of the future, the coming evils in professing Christendom, the apostasy, and all warn against these things. The Second Epistle of Peter shares the same character with the other second Epistles and Jude's Epistle. There was no need for Peter to refer again to the passion being outside of the scope of this second letter, he had given his witness and testimony as to these facts so abundantly in his first Epistle. The two Epistles harmonize in many ways.

Another Supposed Difficulty

Another supposed difficulty is the similarity that exists between the second chapter of this Epistle and the Epistle of Jude. This difficulty will be taken up more fully, in connection with the annotations of the chapter and in the introduction to Jude's Epistle. The learned scholars have spent much time on the question whether Jude copied from Peter or Peter copied from Jude. Some claim that Peter had Jude's Epistle and used it; others claim that Jude imitated Peter. Even so good a scholar as the late Dean Alford says: "It is well known that, besides various scattered resemblances, a long passage occurs, included in the limits Jude 3-19; 2 Peter 2:1-19, describing in both cases the heretical enemies of the gospel, couched in terms so similar as to preclude all idea of entire independence. If considerations of human probability are here as everywhere else to be introduced into our estimate of sacred writings, then either one saw and used the text of the other, or both drew from a common document or a common source of oral apostolic teaching." This in reality affects the truth of inspiration, and leans towards criticism. If Peter sat down and copied Jude, what Peter wrote was not inspired, but copied. And if Jude sat down and wrote after the pattern of Peter, copied him, and worked over his testimony, then Jude is not inspired. But both, Peter and Jude were inspired, and therefore they wrote independent of each other, the Holy Spirit guiding their respective pens, in giving the same testimony of warning.

The Division of Second Peter

This Second Epistle of Peter may be looked upon as an appendix or complement of the First Epistle. It introduces a testimony as to the future, connected with the coming of the Lord, which the First Epistle so frequently mentions. While the First Epistle is silent as to the coming evils preceding the coming of the Lord, this Second Epistle sounds the warning and gives, as already stated in the preceding introduction, a prophetic picture of the conditions of Christendom when the age closes. Here, too, we find the exhortations of Peter, similar to those in the first letter. Peter himself states the purpose when he wrote: "This second Epistle, beloved, I now write unto you, in both of which I stir up your pure minds by way of remembrance." While the language may differ in some respects from the language of the First Epistle, the style and development of the Epistle is just like the first, which is even noticeable in our English version. He writes first of the gracious provisions, which are made for those of like precious faith through the righteousness of God and our Saviour Jesus Christ, which includes present provisions in precious promises, and the gift of all things that pertain unto life and godliness, as well as the gift of the Word of Prophecy.

The second chapter unfolds the coming dangers of the last days of this age. The false teachers and their pernicious doctrines are revealed with the corresponding warnings to beware of them. The concluding chapter is prophetic; it reveals the future, including the coming great transformation when the physical earth will pass through a judgment by fire, to come forth in an eternal resurrection glory as a new earth, surrounded by new heavens. We follow, therefore, in our annotations the division of the Epistle in three chapters as we have it in our Bibles.

I. THE GRACIOUS PROVISIONS OF GOD (1)

II. THE EVILS TO COME THROUGH FALSE TEACHERS (2)

III. THE FUTURE OF THE EARTH AND THE CONCLUSION (3)

Analysis and Annotations

I. The Gracious Provisions of God

CHAPTER 1

1. God's gracious provisions in Christ (1:1-4)
2. The development of the divine nature (1:5-11)
3. The promises of prophecy (1:12-21)

Verses 1-4. We are not left in doubt who the writer is, not a pseudo Peter, but Simon Peter, the fisherman of Galilee. With this second Epistle he finishes the task given him by the Lord "to strengthen his brethren." The opening verse of the third chapter shows that the Epistle is addressed to the same persons to whom he wrote the first Epistle. He gives his old name, Simon (or as in the Greek, Symeon), followed by the new name given him by the Lord, Peter. He calls himself a servant first before he mentions his apostleship. The word servant is the same as the word by which Paul designated himself, that is, a slave. Evidently Peter estimated his servantship higher than his apostleship.

He addresses his brethren no longer as he did in his first Epistle as strangers and elect by the foreknowledge of God. His purpose is a different one. No longer does he mention their trials, sufferings and persecutions; this was done abundantly in the preceding document. He addresses them instead as those "that have obtained like precious faith," that is, the faith in the Lord Jesus Christ, the Son of God, Saviour and Lord. This faith is obtained "through the righteousness of God and our Saviour Jesus Christ." In Romans the righteousness of God is the great theme as the ground of the believer's justification. (See annotations on Romans 3.) Here it has a somewhat different meaning. It is not the question of justification, but the question of God having been righteous, that is, faithful to His promises by Him who is Jehovah, their own promised Messiah. It was the faithfulness of the God of Israel which had bestowed upon them as a believing remnant this faith, which was now so precious to them, the faith in Jehovah-Jesus as Saviour.

Then follows the greeting: "Grace and peace be multiplied unto you through the knowledge of God, and of our Lord Jesus Christ." This form of greeting using the word "multiplied" is confined to the two Epistles of Peter and the Epistle of Jude. It is not without significance. When believers suffer, as seen in the First Epistle of Peter, they can count on God, to multiply grace and peace. But Second Peter and the Epistle of Jude look forward to the last days, the end of the age, with its predicted apostasy, and for those days God promises to multiply to His own grace, peace and mercy. But it must be noticed that this multiplication is "through the knowledge of God, and of our Lord Jesus Christ." It is not independent of a real heart knowledge of God and His Son, our Lord. There may be a head knowledge of God and of Christ, a barren knowledge which brings no fruit unto God. Of this we read in chapter 2:20-22 of our Epistle.

The knowledge of God is in Jesus Christ; through Him we know God in all His gracious fullness. (See 1 John 5:20.) The real heart knowledge of Him produces fruit because it carries with it divine power, which has given to the believer "all things that pertain to life and godliness, through the knowledge of Him that hath called us by glory and virtue." Life and glory are the gifts of grace; life is bestowed in the new birth which fits for glory, but godliness and virtue are the practical results of that grace in the life of the believer. The divine power for godliness and virtue which are to be manifested in the believer's life, that power which is able to act in us and give us the victory, must be laid hold on by faith. "How precious it is to know that faith can use this divine power, realized in the life of the soul, directing it toward glory in the end! What a safeguard from the efforts of the enemy, if we are really established in the consciousness of this divine power acting on our behalf in grace! The heart is led to make glory its object; and virtue, the strength of spiritual life, is developed on the way to it. Divine power has given all that is needed" *(Synopsis of the Bible.)*

Having called us by glory and virtue, He has in connection with it given us exceeding great and precious promises. These promises relate to both, glory and virtue. Through these promises we are made partakers of the divine nature, by the divine power acting in us, with the glory as the blessed goal. But by the same power promised unto us, we escape and are delivered from the corruption that is in the world through lust. Here is the real victorious life of a believer. It is not in some kind of a fixed "holiness experience" by which the old nature is eradicated, a teaching which is altogether against Scripture. The heart must be occupied with Christ and the glory by which we are called, as a result the divine power, the Holy Spirit in us, acts and victory over sin results.

Verses 5-11. While God promises to His people to add, that is, to multiply, daily grace and peace, they themselves in the faith which realizes the divine power and the glory to come, must add to that faith virtue, and that is to be done "by giving all diligence." The divine nature which the believer has received loves the will of God; it is a holy nature, and therefore abhors the corruption which is in the world by lust. But that divine nature is subject to growth and development in the life of the child of God, and that requires all care and diligence. If Christians say that they possess a new nature, are born again, saved by grace, and continue to live according to the old nature, enjoying the world and its sinful pleasures, without manifesting godliness and virtue, they are not only in a very unscriptural attitude, but on dangerous ground. It would prove that they belong to the class of professors described in chapter 2:20-22.

Seven things are to be added to faith. "Add to your faith virtue." This word means something different from its general meaning in English. It means moral courage, a courage which refuses the gratification of the old nature. It is the soldier's courage, who stands manfully against all opposition. It is an energy by which the heart is master of itself, and is able to choose the good, and to cast aside the evil, as a thing conquered and unworthy of one's self. Such courage to stand and withstand, this energy to deny one's self, makes full communion with God possible. If such virtue is added to faith it leads to knowledge, the next thing. The truth of God and the things of God are known and learned by obedience, by walking in them. Knowledge gained, without virtue practised, only puffs up and leads to hypocrisy.

A true knowledge of God is heart acquaintance with Him. This knowledge leads to temperance, which means self-restraint. And self-restraint, the government of the will, must be followed by patience, which means endurance. How easy it is to endure reproach, wrongs inflicted by others, sufferings—to endure it all in patience when faith looks to Him Who endured more than we are ever called upon to do. If such is the case, godliness will not be lacking. It is a walk with God, communion with Him, child-like trust and obedience and reverence. Out of such a heart of faith, which has moral courage, practises self-restraint, knowing God, endures and is godly—affections towards fellow-believers flow forth and brotherly love is added. This is what the knowledge of God teaches, "Ye yourselves are taught of God to love one another" (1 Thess. 4:9).

But there is something still higher than brotherly kindness and affection, and that is "love." It means divine love, which is the very nature of God Himself. "If divine love governs me, I love all my brethren; I love them because they belong to Christ; there is no partiality. I shall have greater *enjoyment* in a spiritual brother; but I shall occupy myself about my weaker brother with a love that rises above his weakness and has a tender consideration for it. I shall concern myself with my brother's sins, from love of God, in order to restore my brother, rebuking him, if needful; nor, if divine love be in exercise, can brotherly love be associated with disobedience. In a word, God will have His place in all my relationships" (John N. Darby).

Here, then, is food for self-examination and self-judgment. Does my faith in Christ, in whom all things are freely supplied pertaining to life and godliness, produce moral courage—does it produce heart knowledge of God, self-restraint, endurance in meekness, godliness and brotherly love and is all governed in me according to love, the very essence of God Himself? These things should be not only in us, but abound. It will not leave us barren or unfruitful. "But he that lacketh these things is blind, and cannot see afar off (short-sighted) and hath forgotten that he was cleansed from his former sins." There is not only the blindness of the natural man, but there may be a blindness and short-sightedness of a believer. It means that a believer whose new nature does not develop and manifest itself in these things, is short-sighted in respect to the heavenly things, the seen things which surround him are the objects which absorb his mind. Such a one forgets that he was cleansed from his former sins. The joy and peace in the Holy Spirit are no longer a present possession; his own heart condemns him and he lacks the reality of His salvation; the joy of it is gone, he has forgotten his cleansing from his former sins. When a believer remembers what God has done for Him in redemption, he will also long for a practical manifestation of that salvation in a godly life and walk.

He speaks next of making our calling and election sure. But is this not sure already? As far as God, who has called and elected us, is concerned, it is sure. To have a consciousness of our calling and election, the sureness of it, requires diligence to walk in the path which the Holy Spirit through the pen of Peter has so beautifully described. Those who walk thus will not stumble, and, finally, "an entrance shall be ministered unto you abundantly into the everlasting kingdom of our Lord and Saviour Jesus Christ."

Verses 12-21. Having mentioned the coming kingdom of Christ, the Holy Spirit now enlarges upon this. We pointed out in the first Epistle that salvation to be revealed, as repeatedly stated, means the visible and glorious appearing of our Lord to establish His kingdom on earth. Peter does not teach the coming of the Lord for His saints at all. He knew it, of course, for the Lord had revealed it through Paul. Inasmuch as Peter writes to this remnant of believing Jews, and that remnant is also representative of another remnant, which will, during the great tribulation, suffer and wait for the coming of the King, the second half of this chapter is therefore taken up with the kingdom in manifestation, as revealed in prophecy and foreshadowed by the transfiguration.

He speaks first of His coming departure; the Lord had told him about that long ago. But there was no doubt a special intimation from the Lord that this event would now soon be and he would have "to put off this tabernacle." So before his departure he was anxious to give them instructions by the Spirit of God, so that they might have these things always in remembrance. This makes it clear once more that Peter did not look for a chain of successors to become guardians and instructors of the faith.

He and the other apostles had not followed cunningly devised fables when they made known the power and coming of the Lord Jesus Christ. They had been eye witnesses of His majesty. But where and how? He speaks of the scene on the holy mount, when the Lord Jesus Christ was transfigured before them, when they heard the voice of the Father from the excellent glory. He stood upon that mount clothed with the glory of the Father; with Him Moses and Elijah, the one who had died, the other who went to heaven without dying. It was a foregleam of His coming glory and a fulfillment of the promise given in the last verse of Matthew 16. As He stood upon that mountain, so He will appear in His glory on earth again, bringing His saints with Him. It is His visible and glorious appearing to which Peter refers, and which was foreshadowed in the transfiguration, and not that coming promised to His own in John 14:1-3, to take them into the Father's house.

"We have also a more sure word of prophecy" should be rendered, "We have the word of prophecy made more sure." The Word of prophecy is, of course, in the Old Testament. But is not this sure enough? Why should it be made more sure? It must be understood in the sense of attesting, or confirming the word of prophecy. The transfiguration confirmed the prophecies in the Old Testament. The prophets describe such a scene like the transfiguration, when the Son of Man comes from heaven in power and glory; hence the word of prophecy has been confirmed, made more sure, by the scene on the holy mount. Let it be stated again that the Old Testament prophetic Word does not reveal that coming for His saints, which is for the Church "that blessed Hope." When Paul speaks of it in 1 Corinthians 15 he speaks of it as a mystery; it was hidden in former ages (1 Cor. 15:51). Yet in the verse before us Peter alludes to it when he speaks of the morning star.

There is a difficulty connected with this verse, and some have read it as if it meant that the morning star must arise in the heart of the individual, as it has been stated in the following comment: "The day star arising in our hearts will be the inner premonitions which announce the coming, as the day star heralds the dawn; such premonitions might be occasioned by observing the various signs of the coming." But it does not mean this at all, nor does it mean that prophecy is only to be used for encouragement till we possess the proper Christian hope. The suggested rendering in the *Numerical Bible* removes the difficulty. "We have also the prophetic Word confirmed, to which ye do well in taking heed (as to a lamp that shineth in an obscure place, until the day dawn and the morning star ariseth) in your hearts." It does not mean that the morning star is to arise in the heart of the believer; it means that we should take heed to prophecy in our hearts. And how the entire prophetic Word, that blessed lamp, is needed in these darkening days!

The day dawn is preceded by the rising of the morning star, or day star, and the morning star is the blessed emblem of the coming of the Lord for His saints. He is both the morning star and the sun of righteousness. He appears as the morning star for His saints and afterward in full glory as the sun of righteousness.

The closing statements of this chapter are also of much importance. "Knowing this first, that no prophecy of Scripture is of private interpretation. For no prophecy ever came by the will of man; but men spake from God, being moved by the Holy Spirit." Prophecy never could be produced by the will of man; only God knows the future and He has spoken concerning the future.

The fact of prophecy is one of the great evidences of the supernaturalness of the Bible. The men who were used to communicate prophecy spoke from God; they were moved by the Holy Spirit. For this reason the pernicious school of destructive criticism has always aimed at the prophetic Word, for if they concede that there is prophecy, they acknowledge their defeat. What denials and theories they have used in order to get rid of prophecy we cannot follow here. The next chapter shows what results have been brought about through the rejection of the truth stated by Peter, that God hath spoken. Of equal importance is the divine statement, "that no prophecy of Scripture is of private interpretation."

Rome has used the word "private" to uphold its awful lie, that Scripture should never be interpreted by a private individual. As a result Rome discourages in every way the reading of the Word of God. In the past that system burned the Bibles, often chaining the Bible to the martyr at the stake, burning the hated Book with the hated witness. Give Rome her old time power and she will do it again. The prophetic Word only is here in view. Prophecy shows a divine unity that is wonderful. Some have said that history must interpret prophecy, but that is not so. History is predicted in advance by prophecy. In interpreting prophecy, prophetic Scripture must be compared with prophetic Scripture. Prophecy must be taken as a whole. We have no business to say, as it is often done, "I think it means this or that." Prophecy starts in Genesis 3:15. The consummation of all prophecy is the kingdom of Christ, the victory of God in His Son, the complete defeat of Satan. Every prophecy is a part of prophecy, having one and the same object and can, therefore, not be interpreted by itself, independent of the rest of prophecy. All the confusion which is in the professing church today as to the prophetic forecasts of the Word of God is the result of having ignored this important injunction.

II. The Evil to Come Through False Teachers

CHAPTER 2

1. The source of the evil (2:1-3)
2. The lessons from the past. (2:4-10)
3. The description of the apostates (2:11-22)

Verses 1-3. The Apostle Peter is now being used by the Spirit of God to prophesy. He predicts the coming evil for the professing church, that apostate teachers would do their vicious work. As pointed out in the introduction every other writer of the Epistles bears the same witness and that witness is mostly found in the second Epistles and in the Epistle of Jude. (See 1 Tim. 4:1-2; 2 Tim. 3:1-5; 4:1-4; 2 Thess. 2; 1 John 2:18-23; 4:1-6; 2 John, verses 7-11; Jude.) He reminds them that among their own nation Israel there were false prophets. The false prophets appeared mostly, if not altogether, when judgment was impending for the nation, as we learn from the prophecies of Jeremiah and Ezekiel. These false prophets opposed the true prophets of God, who preached the God-given message, while the false prophets rejected the Word of the Lord and belittled it. They spoke out of their own hearts and spoke vanities and lies (Ezek. 13:2, 8). Their message was "peace" when there was no peace. As a result the people of Israel did not believe the Lord and His Word; they rejected Him.

The same, it is predicted, would be repeated in this Christian age, only with this difference, that not false prophets should appear, but "false teachers." And as this dispensation draws to its close apostasy would set in. (Consult annotations on 2 Thess. 2.) These false teachers, like the false prophets, reject first of all the Word of God; they, too, speak out of their own hearts, that is, vanities and lies. As a result they bring in "privily destructive heresies." All heresies have but one goal, and that is the denial of Christ and the gospel. Therefore Peter predicts "denying even the Master, who bought them."

This is the way of destructive criticism. One looks in vain among the many preachers and teachers who deny the virgin birth and with it the deity of Christ, for one who believes that the Bible is the inerrant Word of God. All those who deny the Master who bought them began with criticism of the Bible, rejecting first the writings of Moses, casting doubt upon other books, and finally abandoning any kind of faith in the Bible as the Word of God. Well is it called "the destructive criticism," for it is in the end destructive of everything. It is this which is poisoning everything in Christendom today and there is no denomination in which this leaven is not at work. Thus Peter's prediction is increasingly fulfilled in our days and will be much more as this age draws rapidly to its close.

We must also notice that it does not say that they deny "the Lord who redeemed them"; but "the Master who bought" or purchased "them." The difference between "purchase" and "redemption" is, that purchase is general, while redemption is limited to those who believe on Him and are thus redeemed by His precious blood. These false teachers never believed on Him as Lord, and, therefore, they are not redeemed by Him, though He paid the purchase price in their behalf. Be denying Him they disowned the purchase. And for such there is in store swift destruction. This pronounces the sentence of eternal doom upon all false teachers, upon destructive criticism as well as upon the cults which teach damnable heresies and, by doing it, deny the Master who bought them.

Here is also a prediction of the wide-spread success of these false teachers. "Many shall follow their pernicious (dissolute or lascivious) ways, through whom the way of truth shall be blasphemed." They speak of making the world better, they pose as teachers of morality and righteousness, but their ways are branded as pernicious. How can they be righteous when they deny that which alone can give righteousness to man? How often it has been brought to light that those who deny the truth and yet claim to be teachers of morality, were miserable hypocrites. Unbelief produces worldliness and immorality. Then the way of truth is being blasphemed and "that worthy Name" is being dishonored.

"And through covetousness shall they with feigned words make merchandise of you; whose judgment now from of old lingereth not, and their destruction slumbereth not." The people of God are their prey. They are covetous, seeking their own gratification in money, social standing, fame and everything else that the natural heart loves and desires. All is abundantly verified in the conditions about us. But retribution will surely come upon them.

Verses 4-10. Here we reach the section of second Peter, which is so much like the greater part of Jude's Epistle, that critics have claimed that one must have copied from the other. We have shown in the introduction that Peter and Jude wrote independently of each other as the direct instruments of the Holy Spirit. The correspondence of Peter's testimony with Jude's Epistle is more fully examined in the introduction to Jude.

The Spirit of God calls attention through Peter to that which happened in past history, showing that God deals with apostates who defy Him and are disobedient, while the godly He delivers. In Jude we shall find out, that while there is much similarity, the purpose of the testimony is quite different from that of Peter. First, mention is made of the angels who sinned and who are cast down to hell, the word being Tartarus (the very lowest pit), where they are kept in chains of darkness for the coming judgment. It is evident that this passage does not mean Satan and the angels who joined in his rebellion before ever man was created. Satan and the fallen angels are not now in the lowest pit awaiting there in a helpless condition the judgment; they are not in chains, but loose, and Satan, as the prince of this world, uses his angels in the pursuit of his work. Who, then, are these angels? They are the beings described in Genesis 6:1-4 as the "sons of God" (a term which in the Old Testament means angels) who came down and mingled with the daughters of men. These angels, as Jude tells us, did not keep their first estate, left their assigned place, and by their disobedience became the means of corrupting the race in such a manner that the judgment of God had to act in the deluge.

God has not been pleased to give a complete revelation of this sinister event. That it means this episode is learned that Peter at once speaks of the old world, which was not spared by God, "but saved Noah, the eighth person (with seven others), a preacher of righteousness, having brought in the flood upon the world of the ungodly." This testimony is closely linked with what Peter had written in the first Epistle (1 Peter 3:19-20). And here we are told that Noah was a preacher of righteousness. He and his house had found grace in the sight of the Lord, while the mass of the ungodly world who rejected His truth and His Spirit, who strove with them, were not spared but dealt with in judgment. It is so now. Another day is coming in which the Lord will judge the ungodly and unbelieving, while His people will be saved.

Sodom and Gomorrah are cited also as examples of God's holy judgment. These cities were turned into ashes, as an example of all those who live ungodly. The awful fruit of sin in the most terrible, unutterable corruption was manifested in these cities; the same corruption is found still in the world, and that mostly in the great centers of Christendom. (Romans 1:27 mentions the same corruption so often referred to by classic writers of Rome and Greece.) Lot, who was in Sodom, though not of Sodom, is called, nevertheless, righteous, was vexed from day to day with their lawless deeds. The Lord delivered him. It is another warning to the false teachers with their denials and heresies, for the rejection of God's Word brings in the flood of immorality, licentiousness, and lawlessness.

The God who turned Sodom and Gomorrah into ashes, by raining upon them fire and brimstone, will also deal with the apostasy at the close of this age, and with the teachers who deny the Master who bought them, in spite of their self-flattery that they are moral. That judgment comes "when the Lord Jesus shall be revealed from heaven with His mighty angels, in flaming fire taking vengeance on them that know not God and that obey not the gospel of our Lord Jesus Christ; who shall be punished with everlasting destruction from the presence of the Lord and from the glory of His power" (2 Thess. 1:7-9). These false teachers sneer at these words of Paul and call them quotations taken from the apocalyptic literature of the Jews, or something else; but the day will surely come when the Lord will vindicate His truth. In the meantime He knows the righteous, watches over them and knows how to deliver them.

Verses 11-22. This is one of the most solemn portions of the Word of God. It is prophetic, for here we have a description of the false teachers of the last days. Here is a startling picture of the baptized infidels of Christendom. It corresponds in a measure with 2 Timothy 3:1-5. They are bold (daring), self-willed, and tremble not to rail at dignities. They are unbridled in their talk and in their conduct. They are daring enough to assail every part of the truth of God, they call His revelation a myth, the virgin birth a legend, and despise the atoning work of the Son of God; they do what angels would never do, railing at dignities.

(Jude has more to say about this; it is a well-known fact that some of the liberal theology leaders have joined hands with socialism in its worst form, that is, the anarchistic side of it. They speak of helping the masses and they rail against existing law and order, and advocate their overthrow. The ringleader of an attempt in Western Canada against the government was an apostate preacher of an honored denomination. The so-called "parlor-bolshevists" belong to this class.)

As we read on let us remember that not Peter, but the Holy Spirit speaks. They are compared to beasts, just born to be caught and to be destroyed; they speak evil of the things of which they know nothing whatever. The meaning is that they were never born again, and therefore follow the flesh, though it may be under the guise of culture and learning. They shall perish in their own corruption. They count it pleasure to revel in the day-time, they delight in luxurious and sinful pleasures. More than that, they claim a Christian profession and fellowship, by attending the love feasts of believers, which they dishonor by their presence as spots and blemishes, while at the same time they glory in their deceivings, their false teachings and denials of the Master. The right (or straight) way which they professed to have taken, when they took the name of Christ upon themselves, they have now left, having gone astray. Therefore they have eyes full of adultery and cannot cease from sin; they entice unstable souls, leading them astray as they have gone astray themselves.

They are also following in the way of Balaam, who was rebuked for his iniquity by the speaking of the dumb ass. The love of money controls them, as it controlled the heathen prophet. Verses 17 and 18 give additional descriptions of the character of these false teachers. They are springs without water, men look to them for the refreshing water of life, because they profess to be teachers; "the hungry sheep look up and are not fed." They know nothing of the water of life. They are nothing but obscuring mists driven by the tempest of their natural hearts. The great swelling words are the divine estimate of empty, human rhetoric by which thousands are swayed, but they are words of vanity, instead of bringing souls to Christ and the knowledge of redemption, they allure them through the lusts of the flesh, while they promise liberty to others, they are themselves slaves of corruption. Such is the character of the false teachers, who deny the Master that bought them.

"For if, after having escaped the pollutions of the world through the knowledge of the Lord and Saviour Jesus Christ they are again entangled therein and overcome, the latter end is worse with them than the first. For it had been better for them not to have known the way of righteousness, than, having known it, to turn back from the holy commandment delivered unto them." Does this mean that these persons were at one time really begotten again, having received life and the Holy Spirit by trusting on Christ? These false teachers certainly were never born again; the description which we have of them is the proof of it. The last verse of this chapter gives the conclusive evidence. Believers, true Christians, are never compared to dogs or swine; they are the sheep of His flock. A sheep cannot be transformed into a dog or a swine, nor will a sheep do what a dog or a swine does. They were therefore never the true children of God. They had escaped the outward pollutions of the world, which is a different thing from the escape of the corruption which is in the world by lust; the latter stands for the inward deliverance by the new birth, the former for an outward reformation which had taken place when they professed the knowledge of the Lord and Saviour Jesus Christ, when for a time forsaking their evil ways so that they escaped the pollutions. But not having a new nature they became entangled therein and overcome, so that it was worse with them than in the beginning, before they had made a profession. They had known the way of righteousness as made known in the gospel of Christ, but the life which is offered in that way of righteousness, with the fruits of righteousness which follow, they had never accepted by a living faith. And this seems to be the case with the vast majority of the false teachers of today, the destructive critics, and those who deny the deity of our Lord. They were never born again; they never had a true experience of real salvation, hence they are but natural men, not having the Spirit.

III. The Future of the Earth and the Conclusion

CHAPTER 3

1. Mocking at the Lord's coming (3:1-7)
2. The future of the earth (3:8-10)
3. Exhortation and conclusion (3:11-18)

Verses 1-7. The opening statement shows conclusively that Peter is the author and that this second Epistle was sent to the same believers to whom the first Epistle was addressed. The critics claim that this chapter marks a separate Epistle in itself and that it was combined by mistake with the preceding two chapters. Like so much else the critics put forth this is a foolish speculation wholly unwarranted.

Peter states the reason for this second Epistle "to stir up their pure minds by way of remembrance." He had already used a similar statement in the first chapter (1:12), but now exhorts them to be mindful of the words which were spoken before by the holy prophets and the commandment of the Lord and Saviour through the apostles. The evil had been prophetically pictured by Peter and now he charges them to use the Word of God in the coming days of peril and apostasy, and remember especially its prophetic forecast. The apostle Paul did the same after he had given the warning of the coming of grievous wolves and false teachers (Acts 20:30).

Such is the resource of the true Church today, and in the degree, as we remember the words spoken by the prophets and by the apostles, give heed to them, we shall be kept in the perilous times. Both the prophets and the apostles warned of the evil to come as each age closes with apostasy and judgment; so did the Lord Himself when He predicted the future of the age and the conditions which precede His physical and glorious return. All have given the warning. Enoch was a prophet, as we learn from Jude; he prophesied about the coming of the Lord to execute judgment. There were apostates in his day who ridiculed his testimony and who spoke against him (Jude, verse 15).

Noah was a preacher of righteousness; he built the ark and sounded the warning, but no one paid any attention to him, and "as it was in the days of Noah so shall it be when the Son of Man cometh," said our Lord. The prophets warned of the judgment in store for Jerusalem; the warning was not heeded, and such a great one as Jeremiah was not believed, and cast into the dungeon. The prophet Amos speaks of those who "put far off the evil day." There were mockers and unbelievers each time an age ended. As already shown, the combined testimony of the apostles is on the same lines. Peter then writes: "Knowing this first, that in the last days mockers shall come with mockery, walking after their own lusts, and saying, Where is the promise of His coming? for, from the day the fathers fell asleep, all things continue as they were from the beginning of the creation."

While before Peter had shown the quality of the false teachers, he now points out by the revelation given unto him, that there would be unbelief and outright mockery touching the visible return of the Lord Jesus Christ. In both Epistles this great coming event, the coming of the Lord in the clouds of heaven, has a prominent place. The false teachers, whose doom will be sealed when Christ comes again, also ridicule and scoff at the idea that He will ever show Himself again. And why do they mock and sneer? It has its source in unbelief. These men are infidels. Every destructive critic is an infidel. The records of the past embodied in the Holy Scriptures are denied to be authentic and reliable. The prophets of God were Jewish patriots who dreamt of a great Jewish future. The magnificent prophecies as to the coming kingdom and the rule of the King of Kings are classed with the apocalyptic ramblings of the "Sibyline writings." The Lord Jesus Christ is even impeached as to His knowledge and is regarded as being under the ignorant prejudice of the times in which He lived. It all emanates from the rejection of the Bible as the inerrant revelation of God.

Never before has this prophecy been so literally fulfilled as now. The Holy Spirit has revived the study of prophecy. The midnight cry has gone forth. The blessed hope has been restored to the Church, and the forgotten prayer, "Even so, Come, Lord Jesus," is being prayed by the members of the body of Christ as never before. There is more preaching and teaching going on today on prophecy than ever before in the history of the church. It is one of the signs that the end of the age is very near. But the revival of prophecy has resulted in the activity of Satan. He both perverts and ridicules the coming of the Lord, and as that blessed event draws near, there will be increasing ridicule and mockery from the side of the apostates. (Of late certain presses of "evangelical denominations" have turned out tons of literature warning against the pre-millennial teachings. The Methodist church of Canada circulated a series of 5 pamphlets which attacked the blessed hope. They were the production of an infidel. The Chicago University and similar institutions also fight prophecy. Sneers and ridicule about His coming, the end of the age, the increase of evil and the coming are constantly multiplying. It is all a fulfillment of what Peter has written.)

The apostates dream of human progress, for they are "evolutionists." Their pet law, "the survival of the fittest," must work on till the last vestige of the beastly in man has worked itself out by a natural process, for they deny the need as well as the power of redemption. They call a belief in the coming of the Lord "pessimism," and have even attempted to brand those who believe in a catastrophic ending of this present evil age "enemies of civilization and human progress." What God hath spoken, what the mouth of all His holy prophets have declared, that the hope of the world is the coming and the enthronement of the Lord Jesus Christ, is extremely distasteful to them, for it conflicts with the program they have invented, a program which has no scriptural support whatever. They take the ground of an assumed unchangeableness of the world, that a sort of cycle governs nature, and thus they deny the positive statements of the Word of God and exclude God from His own creation. Science, meant to be a helpmeet to faith, is used by them to uphold their infidelity. They constantly speak of science contradicting revelation, which is not true.

The deluge which Peter mentions as an evidence of a past catastrophe, when the world was overflowed with water, they wilfully forget or, as it is now generally done, class it with myths of other nations, though science has abundantly proven that there happened such a judgment. But they do not want to believe that there can be a supernatural interference with the world. They believe in things continuing as they are and steadily improving. Up to the very time when the predicted sudden destruction shall come upon them, they say "Peace and safety" (1 Thess. 5). It was so, no doubt, when the deluge swept the unbelieving and secure generation of that time to eternal doom.

(Some apply the words relating to a past judgment to the judgment which passed over the original earth on account of Satan's fall. That there was such a judgment the second verse of the Bible teaches and geological facts confirm that the earth passed through a prehistoric destruction. But the reference is to the deluge. Almost every nation on earth has traditions of the deluge, though often in a perverted form. While the apostates and sneerers make everything of historical evidence and tradition, they ignore the universality of traditions concerning the flood.)

Verses 8-10. A great revelation follows. The heavens that are now, and the earth by the same word have been stored up, reserved for fire against a day of judgment and destruction of ungodly men. Then in verse 10, "But the day of the Lord will come as a thief; in which the heavens shall pass away with a great noise, and the elements shall be dissolved with fervent heat, and the earth and the works that are therein shall be burned up." As the earth was once judged by water so shall it be judged by fire in the future, and not the earth only but also the heavens, that is the heavens surrounding the earth. Years ago infidels used to ridicule the statement of Peter that the earth and the surrounding heavens would be consumed by fire. They spoke of it as an impossibility that the earth with its rivers, lakes and oceans could ever pass through such a conflagration, so that all is consumed. Well informed infidels no longer ridicule this statement, for astronomy with the help of the spectroscope has revealed the fact that other bodies in the heavens have passed through great conflagrations, that other globes have been burned up, and not a few astronomers have advanced the theory that this will be the fate of the earth on which we live. Peter had no telescope, nor did he know anything about astronomy. How did he find out that the earth would be destroyed by fire? It was the Spirit of God who revealed it to him.

The question arises what event is it of which Peter speaks here? He speaks of "the day of the Lord." What phrase of that coming day is it? It certainly is not the coming of the Lord for His saints as revealed in 1 Thess. 4. Nor is it the day of the Lord in its beginning, when the Lord appears in power and great glory. Now it is still "man's day," and when He appears the Day of the Lord begins. One day, Peter tells us, with the Lord is as a thousand years, and a thousand years as one day. From Revelation we learn that Christ will reign over the earth with His saints for a thousand years and that is "the Day of the Lord." The beginning of it will be as a thief, and it will bring fiery judgments, for He will be revealed "in flaming fire." But what Peter speaks of is not so much the beginning of that day of the Lord as it is the end, when the thousand years have expired.

When the thousand-year reign of Christ as King is over there follows a little season during which Satan is loosed from his prison; the revolt of which Revelation 20:8 speaks is followed by fire falling down from God out of heaven, and after that we see the great white throne, the judgment of the wicked dead. "And I saw a great white throne, and Him that sat on it, from whose face the earth and the heavens fled away, and there was found no place for them" (Rev. 20:11). It is this of which Peter writes, when the day of the Lord is ended, the earth and the surrounding heaven will pass away; it will be through a mighty conflagration from beneath and from above.[1] When Peter writes in verse 13 of new heavens and a new earth, he states what John beheld in his vision of chapter 21:1. "And I saw a new heaven and a new earth; for the first heaven and the first earth were passed away and there was no more sea."

Some of these Jewish believers were evidently thinking that the Lord was slack about the fulfillment of the promise concerning that day. The apostle tells them that the Lord's slackness is His long-suffering, "He is not willing that any should perish but all should come unto repentance."

Verses 11-18. In view of such a future the apostle exhorts once more to holy living and godliness, "waiting for and earnestly desiring the coming of the day of God." The thought which is often expressed in the words "hastening the coming of the day of God," that we might act and serve, sending the gospel to the heathen, and do other things, thus hastening the coming of the Lord, is not warranted by the text, nor is it true. God cannot be hastened by the creature, nor can He be delayed in the execution of His eternal purposes.

As stated in the preceding annotations, the fiery ending of the Day of the Lord, and with it the Day of God, the eternal Age, when God is all in all, is what Peter teaches. "But we, according to His promise, wait for new heavens and a new earth, wherein dwelleth righteousness." The promise is found in Isaiah 65:17, "For, behold, I create new heavens and a new earth; and the former shall not be remembered, nor come to mind." This is not the millennium, which in this chapter of Isaiah is described in verses 18-25, but that which comes into existence after the earth and the surrounding heavens have passed through the great conflagration. Once more Isaiah speaks of the earth and heavens which will remain forever.

---

[1]It will be observed, that the Spirit does not speak here of the coming of Christ, except to say that it will be scoffed at in the last days. He speaks of the day of God, in contrast with the trust of unbelievers in the stability of the material things of creation, which depends, as the apostle shows, on the word of God. And in that day everything on which unbelievers rested and will rest shall be dissolved and pass away. This will not be at the commencement of the day, but at its close; and here we are free to reckon this day, according to the apostle's word as a thousand years, or whatever length of period the Lord shall see fit. (*Synopsis of the Bible*).

(See Isaiah 66:22.) This new earth and the new heavens will be the glorious and eternal dwelling-place of the redeemed, for the new Jerusalem comes finally out of the highest heaven to find its eternal resting place there (Rev. 21). "Wherefore, beloved, seeing that ye wait for these things, be diligent to be found in Him in peace without spot and blameless."

In conclusion, Peter refers to Paul as "our beloved brother Paul." The Epistle to the Galatians was then in circulation and everybody could read there of Peter's failure in Antioch (Gal. 2:12-16). The loving remark by Peter shows that he had readily seen his mistake and that there was no clash between the two servants of the Lord Jesus Christ. The Epistle which Paul had written to the same Jewish Christians to whom Peter wrote is without question the Epistle to the Hebrews. (See Introduction to Hebrews.)

The Second Epistle of Peter ends with another warning, so well suited for our times, "Beware, lest, being carried away with the error of the wicked (destructive critics and deniers of Christ), ye fall from your own steadfastness." And the safeguard is "Grow in grace and in the knowledge of our Lord and Saviour Jesus Christ."

"To Him be Glory both now and forever, Amen."

THE FIRST EPISTLE OF JOHN

Introduction

This Epistle is not addressed to any one church nor does it mention, like the other New Testament Epistles, the author of the document; it is anonymous. We are not left in doubt who penned this Epistle in spite of its anonymous character. There can be no question that the author of the fourth Gospel is also the author of this Epistle. Its opening statement is linked with the opening of the Gospel and throughout it is written in the thought and language of the fourth Gospel. Inasmuch, then, as that Gospel is indisputably the work of John the Apostle, this Epistle is also the work of his inspired pen. "The internal testimony furnished by this Epistle to its author being the same with the author of the fourth Gospel is, it may well be thought, incontrovertible. To maintain a diversity of authorship would betray the very perverseness and exaggeration of that school of criticism which refuses to believe, be evidence never so strong" (Alford).

Historical Evidence

While the internal testimony confirms conclusively the Johannine authorship of the Epistle there is also a mass of historical evidence which attributes the Epistle to the beloved disciple. The oldest testimony is that of Polycarp, who was personally acquainted with the Apostle John. We refer to the introduction of the Gospel of John where we give fuller information on Polycarp and his testimony to the fourth Gospel. He makes, in one of his writings, a direct reference to 1 John 4:3, in fact, he quotes this verse almost verbatim. It is, therefore, a testimony to the genuineness and the authorship of this Epistle. Irenaeus, the disciple of Polycarp, frequently quotes the Epistle of John and states that it is John's. Notable is the reference in his work against heresies as quoted by Eusebius. He cites John 20:31 and connects it with 1 John 2:18 and 4:1-3 and 1 John 5:1. After these two witnesses, Polycarp, who knew John, and Irenaeus, the disciple of Polycarp, every authority among the church fathers mentions this Epistle as being the work of John the Apostle.

It is not necessary to quote all these references—by Clement of Alexandria, Tertullian, Cyprian, Origen, Dionysius of Alexandria, Eusebius, Jerome, and many others. We mention but one more of the ancient testimonies, that which is found in the Muratorian fragment. This old and very reliable source of the second century has in it the following paragraph: "What wonder is it, then, that John brings forward each detail with so much emphasis, even in this Epistle, saying of himself, "What we have seen with our eyes, and heard with our ears, and our hands have handled, these things have we written to you. For so he professes that he was not only an eye-witness, but a hearer, and, moreover, a historian of all the wonderful works of the Lord in order.

In harmony with this evidence is the testimony of the oldest fourth century Greek manuscripts, which give the title of the Epistle as *"Joannou-A"*—that is—"John 1." Its rejection by the gnostic Marcion is of no importance, for he excluded from the Scriptures all the writings of the Apostle because they deal a death-blow to his anti-Christian inventions. Lücke, one of the great scholars of bygone days, states that the Gospel of John and the Epistles of John are the genuine works of the apostle, and he adds, "Incontestably, then, our Epistle must be numbered among those canonical books which are most strongly upheld by ecclesiastical tradition."

It is, therefore, not necessary in face of such internal and external evidences to state the objections of destructive critics like Scaliger, S. G. Lange, Bretschneider and the Tübingen school. As it is with other portions of Scripture they have no case at all in attacking the authorship of this Epistle.

When and Where It Was Written

The Epistle itself gives no definite answer to these questions. Some have attempted to fix the date as being before the destruction of Jerusalem in the year 70 A.D. They base their assumption on chapter 2:18 and claim that "the last time" means the closing days for Jerusalem, which is incorrect. The term, "the last time," has in this Epistle the same meaning as in 1 Timothy 4:1 and 2 Timothy 3:1, and therefore does not mean the last days before the city of Jerusalem was destroyed. But it is clear that John wrote the fourth Gospel record first and his Epistle was written after the Gospel, so that the Epistle was written possibly about the year 90, preceding the Revelation, which was written about the year 96.

Irenaeus states that the Gospel was written by John in Ephesus; an ancient tradition states that the Epistle was written from the same place.

To Whom was it Written

The fact that this Epistle starts, unlike the other Epistles, without any address, introductory greeting or closing salutation, has led some to call it a treatise and not an Epistle. But the personal address and appeal, the style throughout fully sustains the epistolar character. Others, again, have termed the Epistle a second part of the Gospel (Michaelis), while others speak of it as an introduction to the Gospel. That the Epistle is closely related to the Gospel is very true, but that does not necessitate a closer external relationship.

Dr. Bullinger, in the *Companion Bible,* suggests that this Epistle also was originally addressed to believing Hebrews in the dispersion. This view was held by others before him (Benson and others); but there is nothing whatever in the Epistle to warrant such a conclusion. On account of a remark by Augustinus on 1 John 3:2 that John wrote "to the Parthians," many commentators have adopted this view, which is, however, without any foundation whatever. The Epistle was evidently not addressed to any one church but to believers in a number of assemblies. John was acquainted with these believers, who seemed to have been mostly Gentile converts. (See Chapter 5:21). If the tradition is true that the Epistle was written in Ephesus, it is not improbable that it was sent to the seven churches in the province of Asia, Ephesus, Smyrna, Pergamos, Thyatira, Sardis, Philadelphia and Laodicea, the churches to whom the Lord sent the messages a few years later when John was in Patmos.

The Purpose of the Epistle

The purpose of the Epistle is stated by the writer in two places; "These things write we unto you that your joy may be full" (1:4). "These things have I written unto you that believe on the name of the Son of God; that ye may know that ye have eternal life, and that ye may believe on the name of the Son of God" (5:13). According to the Gospel of John (chapter 20:31), this also is the purpose of the Gospel. He writes to those who believe on the Son of God and who have that eternal life which was manifested in the Lord Jesus, and which is imparted to all who believe on the Son of God and which establishes fellowship with the Father and the Son. The Epistle has been rightly called a family letter, that is, believers are viewed as the family of God, hence the repeated use of word *teknia,* children. The Gospel of John was written on account of the false teachings concerning the Person of Christ, which began in the second half of the first century. (See Introduction to John's Gospel.)

The Epistle of John is very outspoken against those errors touching the deity of the Lord Jesus Christ and His sacrificial work. They flourished later under the name of Gnosticism, Docetism, Montanism and others. Marcion, a Gnostic leader, when Polycarp, the disciple of John met him, was addressed by Polycarp with these words, "I know thee, thou firstborn of Satan." While these evil doctrines and denials were not yet fully developed in John's day, they existed and increased, hence the warnings in chapter 2:18-25 and 4:1-6. What antichristianity is will be learned from these passages. All the evil systems of today, which are sweeping with increasing force through Christendom towards their divinely appointed and revealed doom are exposed in this Epistle in their true character. Christian Science, falsely so called; the liberal theology, which denies that Christ is the virgin-born Son of God, the modern religion, the destructive criticism and other systems and cults are all branded by John as antichrists. These many antichrists are finally to be merged into a personal antichrist, the man of sin. Our annotations will enlarge upon all this.

The Message of the Epistle

The Epistle has a deep spiritual message for the children of God. As already stated, the Epistle, like the Gospel of John, witnesses to Christ as the Son of God and the eternal life which He is Himself and which He imparts to the believer. Thus the Epistle opens, "That which was from the beginning, which we have heard, which we have seen with our eyes, which we have looked upon and our hands have handled, of the Word of life. (And the life was manifested, and we have seen it, and bear witness, and shew unto you that eternal life, which was with the Father, and was manifested unto us.) That which we have seen and heard declare we unto you, that ye also may have fellowship with us; and truly our fellowship is with the Father and with his Son Jesus Christ."

The great truth which is developed by the Holy Spirit is not so much the life which the believer has in Christ, that is, the eternal life imparted unto him, but it is that life which is in the believer, and the manifestation of that life, a manifestation of the same characteristics as manifested by the Lord Jesus Christ in His blessed life. As born of God, believers have God as their Father, they are children of God. God is light and God is love and, therefore, those who are born of God, in whom there is eternal life, must also manifest light and love, walk in righteousness and in love. This is the message of the First Epistle of John. All the blessed things which cluster around it we shall discover in our analysis and annotations.

The Division of The First Epistle of John

The divisions of the First Epistle of John have always been considered a difficulty, so that leading expositors of the past have expressed the belief that there is no contextual connection at all in the Epistle. Calvin shares this belief as well as others. Bengel in his great work "The Gnomen" maintained that there is a logical and contextual arrangement. He divided the Epistle in three parts, naming them in Latin as follows: **I. Exordium**—Introduction 1:1-4. **II. Tractatio**—Treatment and discussion 1:5—5:12. **III.Conclusio**—Conclusion 5:13-21. The *Numerical Bible* gives also a three-fold division. I. God as Light and in the light and the light in us: 1—2:11. II. Growth by the truth, which is nothing else but the light manifested: 2:12-27. III. The manifestation of the children of God by the fruit found: 2:28—5. This is a helpful arrangement. *The Scofield Bible* gives two main divisions. I. The Family with the Father: 1—3:24. II. The Family and the world: 4—5.

We divide the Epistle into six sections as follows:

I. **THE LIFE MANIFESTED** (1:1-4)

II. **LIGHT AND DARKNESS AND THE TESTS** (1:5—2:17)

III. **ERROR AND TRUTH** (2:18-27)

IV. **RIGHTEOUSNESS AND LOVE AS MANIFESTED BY THE CHILDREN OF GOD** (2:28—3:18)

V. **HEREBY WE KNOW** (3:19—5:12)

VI. **THE CONCLUSION** (5:13-21)

Analysis and Annotations

I. The Life Manifested

CHAPTER 1:1-4

The opening verses of this Epistle are very precious and are the key to the whole Epistle. Three Scriptures speak of what was in the beginning. "In the beginning God created the heavens and the earth" (Gen. 1:1). This is the beginning of all things which God called into existence out of nothing. "In the beginning was the Word, and the Word was with God, and the Word was God" (John 1:1). This takes us beyond the first verse of the Bible. It reveals Him, by whom and for whom God created all things, in His eternal existence with God and as God.

The third Scripture is the first verse of John's Epistle. "That which was from the beginning, which we have heard, which we have seen with our eyes, which we have looked upon, and our hands have handled, the Word of life." This is a different beginning from the beginning in Genesis 1:1 and John 1:1; it means the manifestation of the Son of God in incarnation among men. He, who is the true God and the eternal life, the life and light, was manifested as man here below. This truth is stated by John in his Gospel in the fourteenth verse of the first chapter: "And the Word was made flesh and tabernacled among us (and we beheld His glory, the glory as of the Only Begotten of the Father), full of grace and truth." To this John refers in the first statement of his Epistle. John and his fellow-disciples had walked with Him and talked with Him.

It must be noted that the apostle speaks of Him as "the Word of Life"; he does not say therefore "who was from the beginning" but, which was from the begining. First he mentions what they had heard; but one may hear a person and not be near to that person. But they were closer to the Word of Life, he writes, "which we have seen with our eyes"; yet one may have seen a person without being close to that person; but they had more than a passing vision "which we have contemplated" which is more than a mere seeing, it denotes gazing with a purpose, with a desire and with admiration. A statement of still greater nearness follows, "our hands have handled"—John and the other disciples had known Him, the Word of Life, intimately.

"And the Life was manifested, and we have seen it, and bear witness, and shew unto you that eternal life which was with the Father, and hath been manifested unto us." He whom they heard, with whom they were in touch, whom they knew and gazed upon is the eternal Life which was with the Father. It is more than that He spoke of eternal Life and promised eternal Life; He Himself is eternal Life. He was with the Father and came into the world, to manifest what that life is. While He manifested the Father, as He witnessed "whosoever seeth Me seeth the Father," He also displayed as man what eternal life is in His blessed and perfect life He lived on earth. And this eternal life is communicated to all who believe on the Son of God. This life which was with the Father, manifested in the Lord Jesus on earth, is the life which is in us. ("The life has been manifested. Therefore we have no longer to seek for it, to grope after it in the darkness, to explore at random the indefinite, or the obscurity of our own hearts, in order to find it, to labor fruitlessly under the law, in order to obtain it. We behold it: it is revealed, it is here, in Jesus Christ. He who possesses Christ possesses that life.") To know then what life we possess as believers, we must not look in ourselves, or to other believers, but to Christ and the life He manifested on earth. As another has said, "When I turn my eyes to Jesus, when I contemplate all His obedience, His purity, His grace, His tenderness, His patience, His devotedness, His holiness, His love, His entire freedom from all self-seeking, I can say, that is *my* life. It may be that it is obscured in me; but it is none the less true, that it is my life."

"That which we have seen and heard declare we unto you, that ye also may have fellowship with us, and truly our fellowship is with the Father, and with His Son Jesus Christ. And these things write we unto you, that your joy may be full."

What they had seen and heard they have declared unto others, to those who also believe on Him, so that they too might share in the same fellowship, the fellowship of the Father and His Son Jesus Christ. The life which believers possess, the eternal life given through grace, the life He manifested on earth and which is in us, fits us for fellowship with both the Father and the Son. What such a fellowship demands and the tests of it are developed subsequently. To have such fellowship, bestowed through grace, is the blessed calling of all the saints of God. Such fellowship is eternal life and there is nothing beyond that in heaven itself, while we enjoy it here the fullness of it will be enjoyed in glory. But what is fellowship with the Father and with His Son Jesus Christ? It is but little understood in its real meaning. Fellowship means having things in common. The Father's delight is in Him who pleased Him so perfectly. For the Father, His blessed Son is the One altogether lovely.

Believers knowing the Son also find their delight in Him; He is for our hearts the One altogether lovely. As we then delight ourselves in Him, in His obedience, in what He is in love and devotion to the Father, we share the same feelings and thoughts with the Father, which is fellowship with the Father. Whenever the believer praises and thanks the Father for His Son, tells the Father of his deep appreciation of Him, how he loves Him, longs to be more like Him, walk even as He walked, then he is in fellowship with the Father. And the Son has given to us the knowledge of the Father. "No man knoweth the Son, but the Father; neither knoweth any man the Father, save the Son, and to whomsoever the Son will reveal Him" (Matt. 11:27). It is the Gospel of John where the blessed words of the Son concerning the Father are recorded. He manifested unto His own the name of the Father.

In the five chapters in the Gospel of John, beginning with the feet-washing and ending with the great intercessory prayer of our Lord (13—17) the word "Father" occurs fifty times. It is in this part of the Gospel the Son makes known the Father. Through the Son we have the knowledge of the Father and the knowledge of the Father's love. His delight was to glorify the Father in a life of devotion and obedience. And as the believer delights Himself in the Father, honors Him and yields obedience to Him, he has fellowship with the Son, has the same thing in common with the Son. Fellowship with the Father and with the Son is therefore not a feeling or some extraordinary experience.

"All this flows, whether in the one or the other point of view, from the Person of the Son. Herein our joy is full. What can we have more than the Father and the Son? What more perfect happiness than community of thoughts, feelings, joys and communion with the Father and the Son, deriving all our joy from themselves? And if it seem difficult to believe, let us remember that, in truth, it cannot be otherwise; for, in the life of Christ, the Holy Ghost is the source of my thoughts, feelings, communion, and He cannot give thoughts different from those of the Father and the Son. They must be in their nature the same. To say that they are adoring thoughts is in the very nature of things, and only makes them more precious. To say that they are feeble and often hindered, while the Father and the Son are divine and perfect, is, if true, to say the Father and the Son are God, are divine, and we feeble creatures. That surely none will deny. But if the blessed Spirit be the source, they must be the same as to nature and fact.

This is our Christian position then, here below in time, through the knowledge of the Son of God; as the apostle says, "These things write we unto you, that your joy may be full" (John N. Darby).

II. Light and Darkness and the Tests

CHAPTERS 1:5—2:17

1. God is light; walking in darkness and in light (1:5-7)
2. What the light manifests (1:8-10)
3. The advocacy of Christ to maintain the fellowship (2:1-2)
4. The tests of fellowship (2:4-17)

Chapter 1:5-7 The message they had heard of Him and which they declared to others is, that God is light and in Him is no darkness at all. Light, perfect, pure light is God's nature; He is absolutely holy, with no darkness in Him at all. That God is light was manifested in the life of the Lord Jesus, for He was and is holy. Fellowship with the Father and the Son means, therefore, to have fellowship with light, and that excludes a walk in darkness. "If we say that we have fellowship with Him and walk in darkness we lie and do not the truth." If one professes to have fellowship with God and walks in darkness, he lies, for darkness can have no fellowship with light. "But if we walk in the light as He is in the light, we have fellowship one with another and the blood of Jesus Christ His Son cleanseth us from all sin."

But what is this walk in the light? It is not the same thing as walking according to the light. It does not mean to live a perfect and sinless life. Walking in the light is not the question of *how* we walk, but *where* we walk, and the place where the believer walks is the light. It means to walk daily in His presence, with our will and conscience in the light and presence of God, judging everything that does not answer to that light. Whatever is not right is brought at once in His presence, exposed to the light, confessed, judged and put away. Such is the walk in the light which fellowship with God demands. The result of such a walk in the light is mutual fellowship among believers, because each has the same nature of God and the same Spirit, the same Christ as the object before the heart and the same Father. It cannot be otherwise. Then there is another thing stated, "The blood of Jesus Christ His Son cleanseth us from all sin." Walking in the light shows us what we are and we cannot say that we have no sin. But we have no consciousness of sin resting upon us before a holy God, though we know that sin is in us, but we have the assurance of being cleansed from it by His precious blood. Such is the blessed position of a true Christian. Fellowship with the Father and with His Son, walking in the light as He is in the light, fellowship one with another and the cleansing power of the blood.

Verses 8-10. The light makes known that sin is in us. If the believer, the child of God, says that he has no sin, the light contradicts him. If we say we have no sin, we deceive ourselves, and the truth is not in us. The denial of sin within is a delusion. This evil teaching that the old Adamic nature is eradicated in the believer is widespread in our day among Holiness, Pentecostal and other sects. True spirituality is to confess daily, walking in the light, that in our flesh there dwelleth no good thing. And if sin is committed it needs confession. He is faithful and just to forgive us our sins and to cleanse us from all unrighteousness.

The light also manifests another evil, the claim of a sinless perfection. If we say that we have not sinned, we make Him a liar and His Word is not in us. Some have applied this verse to the unsaved; it has nothing to do with the sinner, but relates to a true believer, who in presumption makes the claim that he lives without sinning. And the reason why children of God make such unscriptural claims is inattention to His

Word, for the Word makes manifest what sin is, and the Apostle says "If we say that we have not sinned . . . His word is not in us."

Chapter 2:1-2. For the first time John uses the endearing term "my little children," meaning the born ones of God, who are born into the family of God by having believed on the Son of God. One might conclude, inasmuch as belief in the eradication of the old nature and sinless perfection is a delusion, that the child of God must sin. But, while sin is within, and a sinless perfection is beyond our reach, it does not mean that the believer should continue in sin. He had written these things that they might not sin. But if any man sin a gracious provision has been made. Let it be noticed that the application, as it is often done, to the sinner who is outside, who knows not Christ at all, is totally wrong. It means the little children, the members of the family of God. If any true child of God sins we have an advocate with the Father (not God, it is the matter of the family), Jesus Christ the righteous. The advocacy of Christ restores the sinning believer to the communion with the Father and the Son which sin interrupted. He does not wait till we come repenting and confessing, but in the very moment we have sinned He exercises His blessed office as our Advocate with the Father and His intercession produces in us repentance, confession, and self-judgment. Thus we are maintained by Himself in the fellowship into which the grace of God has called and brought us.

When the believer sins it does not mean that he has lost his salvation. Many a child of God has been harassed through ignorance, and imagined that he committed the unpardonable sin. The sin of a believer does not make him unsaved or lost, but it makes fellowship with the Father and the Son impossible till the sin is judged and confessed. This is accomplished by His advocacy.

"The Lord Jesus as much lives to take up the failure of His own, as He died to put away their sins by His blood. This, too, is founded on propitiation; but there is besides the blessed fact that He is the righteousness of the believer in the presence of God. His one expiatory sacrifice avails in abiding value; His place is before God as our righteousness; and there for the failing He carries on His living active advocacy with the Father."

Verses 4-17. John now writes of the characteristics of the life which the believer has received, the eternal life and applies certain tests. The profession of a Christian is that He knows God. But how do we know that we know Him? The answer is, "If we keep His commandments." This is not legality in the least which puts the believer back under the law. John knows nothing of that. Obedience is the leading trait of the imparted life. It is set on doing the will of God. Christ walked on earth in obedience; His meat and drink was to do the will of Him that sent Him. Inasmuch as His life is in us as believers, it must manifest itself in obedience to the will of God. It is the same which we find in 1 Peter 1:2, sanctified, or set apart, unto the obedience of Jesus Christ. It is not a sinless obedience as it was in Him; while the believer has his heart set on obeying the Lord and doing His will, he often fails and stumbles, but he continues to aim at doing the will of God, for that is the nature of the new life. "He that saith, I know Him, and keepeth not His commandments, is a liar and the truth is not in him. But whoso keepeth His Word, in him verily is the love of God perfected; hereby know we that we are in Him."

One who professes to know God and does not manifest obedience is no Christian at all, but he is a liar, and the truth in the knowledge of the Lord is lacking in such a one. He is a mere professing Christian, one who has the outward form of godliness but does not know the power of it, because he has not the life in him, which is His life and in which he delights to obey. The first great test of the reality of the divine life in the believer is obedience.

Then follows a second test: "He that saith he abideth in Him ought himself also so to walk, even as He walked." In His prayer our Lord told the Father, "They are not of the world even as I am not of the world"; and again, "As Thou has sent me into the world so have I sent them into the world" (John 17:16, 18). Believers are not of the world as He is not of the world, because they are born again and have His life in them. They are in Him, abiding in Him, and therefore they must walk as He walked, which does not mean to be what He was, for He was without sin, but it is a walk after His own pattern, the reproduction of His character and life through the power of the Holy Spirit.

In the next two verses we read of the old commandment and of the new commandment (verses 7 and 8). The old commandment is explained, as the word which they had heard from the beginning, that is, the same beginning as mentioned in chapter 1:1, the manifestation of Christ on earth. But what is the commandment of which he speaks next? It is something new now, for the life which was in Him on earth is in believers now. Therefore, it is true in Him and in us because the darkness is passing away and the true light already shineth. Christ is life and light and as His life is in us we share it in Him; this is that which is new. It was true of Him first, and now it is true of us, too.

This is followed by another test. "He that saith he is in the light, and hateth his brother is in darkness even until now." The life must manifest itself in love. Light and love go together; both are manifested in Christ, He was light and love. If He is, therefore, in the believer, and he possesses that life, and professes to be in the light, and with such a profession hateth his brother, he shows thereby that he is in the darkness until now. Love cannot be separated from that life and light which was in Him and which is in us as believers. He that abideth in the light loveth his brother and because he does there is no occasion of stumbling in him. In him who loves there is neither darkness nor occasion of stumbling; in him who does not love there is both darkness and stumbling. He who hates his brother is a stumbling block to himself and stumbles against everything. Not loving the brethren and manifesting hatred against them is the sure sign of being in darkness and walking in darkness. Such are the tests of Christian profession; light and love, obedience and loving the brethren; where there is no life from God there is absence of love for the brethren and a walk in darkness and not in the light. It seems that many in John's day were in that deplorable condition, while today such is almost universally the case.

Verses 12-17 contain a message to those who are in the light, who possess that life and in whom it is manifested in obedience and in love. He addresses the fathers and the young men. Before he does this he mentions that which all believers, even the most feeble, possess. "I write unto you little children (the term of endearment which means the whole family of God) because your sins are forgiven you for His name's sake." This is blessedly true of every child of God. Each has "redemption through His blood, the forgiveness of sins." It is the thing which is settled for time and eternity for all those who are in Christ.

Then different grades are mentioned: fathers, young men and little children. The meaning is in the spiritual sense, fathers in Christ, young men in Christ and babes in Christ. The word "children" used in verses 13 and 18 is a different word from the one used in verse 12. In this chapter in verses 1, 12 and 28 the little children are all the family of God, but in verses 13 and 18 it means young converts.

The maturity of the fathers consists in knowing Him that was from the beginning, that is, the Lord Jesus Christ. Spiritual progress and maturity is a deep knowledge and appreciation of Christ. The Apostle Paul illustrates what real Christian maturity is. He had but one desire to know Him; not I but Christ; Christ is all. The Fathers have Christ for their fullest portion and walking in Him have learned the depths of His grace and the glory of His person. They are occupied not with their experience but with Himself. It has been well said, "All true experience ends with forgetting self and thinking of Christ." To know Him, to know Him still better, to be entirely dependent on Him, to have none other but Him, never losing sight of Him—that is the highest attainment of a Christian.

He speaks next of the young men, who have advanced in their Christian life. They had gone forward in undaunted faith and courage and overcame the difficulties; they overcame by faith the wicked one. The strength of the new life, that is, Christ, was manifested in them in conflict. The "babes," comes next, the young converts, who have not much experience in conflict. To them he writes, "Ye have known the Father." Every newborn babe in Christ cries, enabled by the Spirit of adoption, "Abba, Father." To know God as Father is the blessed birthright of every newborn soul.

Once more he writes the same to the fathers. He can add nothing to it for the highest attainment is to know Him, as the fathers know Him. But he has more to say to the young men. He tells them that they are strong, because the Word of God was abiding in them, which is the source of power and strength of every believer and because the Word of God abided in them they overcame the wicked one. Then follows the exhortation and warning not to love the world, the world of which John speaks later, "which lieth in the wicked one."

This world-system in every aspect, whether we call it the social world, the political world, the commerical word, the scientific world, the religious world—all is not of the Father. All its glory is not of the Father. The love of the world is, therefore, inconsistent with the love of the Father. The controlling principles in it are the lust of the flesh, the lust of the eyes and the pride of life. May we remember once more that our Lord speaks concerning His own, "They are not of the world, even as I am not of the world." Grace has taken us out of this old world, with its corruption which is there by lust and has put us into another world, so to speak, in which Christ is the center and the attraction. That new sphere is our place. The only way to escape this world with its beguiling influences is by separation from it. And that separation becomes real when we know Him, as the fathers know him, and find our joy and our satisfaction in Christ. "And the world passeth away, and the lust thereof; but he that doeth the will of God abideth forever." But if this exhortation was needed in John's day, how much more is it needed in our days, when, as never before, the god of this age blinds the eyes of them that believe not, when this world system, in its godless and seductive character, develops a power and attraction unknown before, and when on all sides professing Christians are "lovers of pleasure more than lovers of God."

III. Truth and Error

CHAPTER (2:18-27)

This section contains a warning which is addressed to the babes, the little children, young believers. Truth and error, are contrasted. Seducers were trying to lead them astray, for we read in verse 26: "These things have I written unto you concerning them that seduce you." He reminds them that it is "the last time," a striking expression, for since it was written centuries have come and gone, and what was true then is true now, that it is the last time; only the Lord is still patiently waiting, not willing that any should perish. Christ was manifested, the truth revealed in Him and the world rejected Him and His truth. Satan became the god of this age, with the mystery of iniquity working in it from the very beginning. Antichristianity is not a new thing of our times; it was here from the very beginning. John writes, "Even now there are many antichrists, whereby we know it is the last time." And the last time has its "last days" which are now upon us.

Antichristianity is increasing on all sides till *the* Antichrist, the man of sin, will be revealed (2 Thess. 2). An antichrist is not a vicious lawbreaker, an out and out immoral man. An antichrist is one who rejects Christ, who does not allow His claims; who denies that Jesus is the Son of God. It is of great significance that John speaks of the antichrists in his day as having gone out from among the professing body of Christians (verse 19). They were not true believers but only professed belief; they had left the flock and gone into apostasy, "that they might be made manifest that they were not all of us."

In verses 22 and 23 we have a picture of the antichrists of John's day and a prophecy of antichristianity down to the end of the age when the great opposer will appear in a person, the personal antichrist. "Who is a liar but he that denieth that Jesus is the Christ? He is antichrist that denieth the Father and the Son. Whosoever denieth the Son hath not the Father. He who confesseth the Son hath the Father also." Antichristianity is the denial that Jesus is the Christ. It includes every denial of the person of the Lord Jesus, the denial that He is the Son of God come into the flesh, His virgin birth and that He was sent by the Father. Such denials were prominent in John's lifetime. Gnosticism was troubling the Church. They denied the Messiahship and deity of the Lord Jesus Christ. Other systems were present in embryo, known later by the name of Arianism, etc. Denying the Son they denied the Father also.

These are important statements for our own days, the last days of the present age. What began in the days when the Holy Spirit penned this Epistle is now full-grown in the world. It is all about us in various forms throughout the professing church, only with this difference, the apostates in the beginning were more honest than the apostates in our times. They were in the professing church and when they began their denials they went out, separated themselves from the true Church.

The apostates of today remain in the professing church and maintain outwardly a Christian profession, so that it becomes the solemn duty of true believers to separate themselves from these enemies of the cross of Christ. They deny both the Jewish hope, which centers in the promises of the Messiah, and the Christian hope, which is the Father and the Son. They reject the truths of the Old and the New Testament. They speak of the God of Abraham, who promised the seed to come from Abraham, as a tribal god. They make common cause with the Jewish apostates in denying that there are predictions concerning the Messiah in the Old Testament.

We give but one illustration of this fact. Jews deny that the fifty-third chapter of Isaiah is a Messianic prophecy; the servant of Jehovah is explained to mean the nation Israel and not the

Christ of God. This infidel view is held today by many preachers and teachers in various evangelical denominations, in spite of the fact that the New Testament tells us that it is Christ of whom Isaiah spoke. Rejecting Isaiah 7:14, the prophecy concerning the virgin birth, they reject the virgin birth itself, and brazenly utter the greatest blasphemy which human lips can utter, that Christ was born like any other man. They speak of Him as a great leader and teacher, as having divinity in Himself, in a degree higher than found in the rest of the race. His absolute deity is not believed; that He is the propitiation for sins is sneered at, that He will ever appear again in His glorified humanity in a second visible and glorious manifestation is ridiculed.

Thus antichristianity is present with us in the camp of Christendom in such a marked and universal way as unknown before. With denying Christ they deny the Father. All that we have seen in this Epistle concerning Him, the true God and the eternal life, fellowship with the Father and with His Son, walking in the light, the advocacy of Christ and loving the brethren, is denied by them. They speak of "love"; they speak of toleration and the "Christ-spirit." But those who are the brethren, who contend for the faith once and for all delivered unto the saints, who believe on the Son of God, in His sacrificial work on the cross, are denounced by them, belittled and branded as fanatics. And the end is not yet. Let them continue in their evil ways under the guidance of the lying spirit of darkness and they may yet stoop to actual persecution of those who constitute the body of Christ. The conditions in Christendom today are the most solemn the true Church of Jesus Christ has faced. The heading up in "*the* Antichrist" cannot be far distant. As John writes these Christ-deniers, these blasphemers, who make the Holy Son of God the offspring of—we dare not finish the sentence! —may speak of "the Father," but they have not the Father, because only those who confess the Son of God, Christ come in the flesh, have the Father.

John writes all this to the babes, young believers, warning them against the lie. He useth the word "liar," for such the apostates are. In using this word repeatedly, he reveals his character as "Boanerges"—the son of thunder. Then he tells these babes how they may be guarded and kept. He reminds them that they have the anointing of the Holy One, that is, the Holy Spirit dwelling in their hearts and with Him they have the capacity to know and judge all these things. If they follow His guidance in and through the Word they would be kept in the truth and guarded from accepting the lie.

Let us again remember it is not the fathers, or the young men John addresses, but the babes. Here is a strong argument against the teaching so widespread among true believers, that the Holy Spirit is not given to a believer in regeneration, but that the gift of the Spirit must be sought in a definite experience after conversion. This is a serious error which opens the door to the most subtle delusions as found in certain Holiness sects and Pentecostalism. Verse 24 gives another instruction and exhortation. It is the truth concerning Christ, which they had heard from the beginning, which abiding in them will keep them. And besides "the anointing which ye have received of Him abideth in you, and ye need not that any man teach you, but as the same anointing teacheth you of all things, and is truth, and is no lie, and even as it hath taught you, ye shall abide in Him." The teachers in this instance who tried to seduce them (verse 26) were not gifts of Christ to His body, but false teachers, who came with a lying message. They did not need these teachers; the Holy Spirit was their teacher and infallible guide, but never apart from the written Word. All false teaching they were to repulse and fall back upon Him who guides in all truth. They were safe against all error as they abided in that.

IV. Righteousness and Love as Manifested by the Children of God

CHAPTERS 2:28—3:18

1. The children of God and their coming manifestation (2:28—3:3)
2. Sin and the new nature (3:4-9)
3. Righteousness and love (3:10-18)

Chapters 2:28—3:3. The address to the babes in Christ ended with the 27th verse, and now once more he speaks of the *teknia,* the little children, by which all believers are meant. The exhortation has been much misunderstood. It does not mean that by abiding in Him the believer may have confidence at His appearing. John speaks of himself and other servants of Christ, who minister the gospel and the truth of God. He urges the little children to abide in

Him, "that when He shall appear *we* may have confidence and not be ashamed before Him at His coming." He wants them to walk carefully, to be faithful in all things, so that John and the other servants may not be left ashamed in that coming day. It is the same truth which Paul mentions in 1 Thess. 2:19-20.

Verse 29 mentions the test of righteousness. It is an acid test. "If ye know that He is righteous, ye know that every one that doeth righteousness is born of Him." But the purpose of it is not to question the reality of their salvation as born again, to make them doubt, but the test is given so that they might be enabled to reject a spurious profession. Before he proceeds with the truth expressed in this verse, he mentions the fact that as born of God they are the children of God and what they shall be.

In verses 1 and 2 the word "sons of God" must be changed to *"children of God."* John never speaks of "sons of God" in his message. It is in the writings of Paul the Holy Spirit speaks of believers as "sons and heirs." But John unfolds the truth that believers are in the family of God by the new birth, hence the use of the word "children" to denote the community of nature as born of God. As children of God we are partakers of the divine nature. It is the love of the Father which has bestowed this upon all who believe. And most emphatically the Spirit of God assures us through the pen of John, "Now we are the children of God." There can be no doubt about it, it is our present and known position, because having believed on Him we are born again and are in possession of eternal life.

That which we shall be has not yet been manifested, but while it is not yet manifested we, nevertheless, know what we shall be. But how do we know? We know it because the Holy Spirit has revealed it in the Word of God. "But we know that when He shall appear, we shall be like Him; for we shall see Him as He is." This is our blessed assurance! To this God has called us; it is "the hope of His calling" (Ephesians 1:18). It is that to which we are predestined, to see Him as He is and then infinitely more than that "to be like Him." We see Him now by faith in His Word and are changed into the same image from glory to glory; when we shall see Him in that soon coming day, when He comes for His saints, we shall see Him bodily and then our bodies will be fashioned like unto His glorious body. Of all this the world knows nothing. It knew Him not, knew not His life, nor His glory; it does not know the life which is in the children of God and what glory awaits them. And this hope is a purifying hope. We see that John speaks of the blessed hope as Peter and James, addressing Jewish believers, do not.

Verses 4-9. He makes a contrast between sin and the new nature and shows the marks of one who abides in Christ and one who hath not seen Him neither knows Him. "Every one that practiseth sin, practiseth lawlessness; for sin is lawlessness," this is the correct rendering. The definition of sin as "transgression of the law" is misleading and incorrect. Before there ever was a law, sin was in the world (Romans 5:12, etc.); how then can sin be the transgression of the law? It is not *sins* of which John speaks, but *sin,* the evil nature of man. Here the apostle regards man as doing nothing else but his own, natural will; he lives as a natural man. He acts independently of God, and, as far as he is concerned, never does anything but his own will. John is, therefore, not speaking of positive overt acts, but of the natural man's habitual bent and character, his life and nature.

The sinner, then, sins, and in this merely shows in it his state and the moral root of his nature as a sinner, which is lawlessness. But the born one, the child of God, is in a different position. He knows that Christ was manifested to take away our sins and that in Him there was no sin. If one knows Him and abideth in Him, that one sinneth not. If the believer sins it is because he has lost sight of Christ and does not act in the new life imparted unto him. Another object usurps the place of Christ, and then acting in self-will he is readily exposed to the wiles of the devil using his old nature and the world to lead him astray. If a man lives habitually in sin, according to his old nature, he hath not seen Him nor known Him. A child of God may sin but he is no longer living in sin; if a professing believer lives constantly in sin it is the evidence that he has not known Him at all. There were such who tried to deceive them. Their teaching waas evidently a denial of holiness, that there was no need of righteousness. But the demand is for righteousness, while those who practise sin, live habitually in it, are of the devil. No true believer lives thus, for he knows the One whose life he possesses was manifested that He might destroy the works of the devil.

"Whosoever is begotton of God doth not practise sin, because his seed abideth in him, and he cannot sin, because he is begotten of God." This verse has puzzled many Christians, but it is quite simple. Every creature lives according to its nature. The fish has the nature of a fish and lives its nature in the water; a bird has its own nature and lives it in the air, and not under the water as the fish. Our Lord said to Nicodemus, "That which is born of the flesh is flesh." Man has a fallen nature, the nature of sin, and that nature can do nothing but sin. That is why He said, "Ye must be born again." In the new birth the divine nature is imparted. This nature is He Himself, Christ, the eternal life. Christ could not sin for He is God, and God cannot sin. The new nature believers possess cannot sin, for it is His nature. But why do new-born ones sin? Because the Christian has two natures, the old nature and the new nature. The old nature is not eradicated; a believer when he sins does so because he has given way to that old nature, has acted in the flesh. But the new nature followed will never lead to sin, for it is a holy nature, and for that nature it is impossible to sin. Some have suggested out of ignorance that the translation ought to be instead of cannot sin "ought not to sin," or "should not sin." The Greek text does not permit such a translation, anything different from "cannot sin" is an unscriptural paraphrase.

Verses 10-18. The test as to the children of God and the children of the devil follows in this section. Whosoever doeth not righteousness is not of God, neither he that loveth not his brother. The message from the beginning, that is the same beginning as in chapter 1:1—is that we should love one another. This was the commandment given by the Lord, "This is my commandment, That ye love one another, as I have loved you" (John 15:12). There is natural affection in the world, even in the animal creation. The natural man also can make himself amiable and speak of love and toleration. In fact an amiable character, a loving disposition through self-improvement is urged and practised among the antichristian cults, such as New Thought, Christian Science and the Liberalists, the advocates of the new theology.

But the love of which John speaks is exclusively of God and unknown to the natural heart of man. Yet all these antichrists go to the Epistle of John and quote him to confirm their evil doctrine of "the brotherhood of man and the universal fatherhood of God." John does not speak of loving man as such, but loving the brethren, the other born ones in the family of God, and that is a divine love. It is the great test of the divine nature, "We know that we have passed from death unto life, because we love the brethren." The world not only knows nothing of that divine love, but the world hates those who are born of God. "Marvel not, my brethren, if the world hate you." This fact is illustrated by Cain. He was of the devil. He slew his brother because Cain's works were evil, he was an unbeliever, and his brother's were righteous, Abel believed and that was counted to him for righteousness. And so the world hates the brethren, the children of God on the same ground and for the same reason. Then again he tests profession: "He who loveth not his brother abideth in death. . . . Whosoever hateth his brother is a murderer." Hating the brother is the evidence that the professing Christian is in the state of death and linked with the murderer from the beginning.

The better rendering of verse 16 is, "Hereby we know love, because He laid down His life for us." Such love must be manifested in practical ways towards the brethren.

"But 'we know that we have passed from death unto life, because we love the brethren.' Not because we love *certain* of the brethren, let us remember. We may love even the children of God for some other reason than *as* His children. We may love them, perhaps in gratitude to them for services that we may be receiving from them. Further than this, we may mistake for brotherly love that which is merely self-love in a subtler form. Men minister to our comfort, please us, and we think we love them; and in the true child of God there may be yet, after all, as to much that he counts love to the brethren, a similar mistake. A love to the children of God, as such, must find its objects wherever these children are, however little may be, so to speak, our gain from them; however, little they may fit to our tastes. The true love of the children of God must be far other than sociality, and cannot be sectarian. It is, as the Apostle says, 'without partiality, and without hypocrisy.' This does not, of course, deny that there may be differences that still obtain. He in whom God is most seen should naturally attract the heart of one who knows God according to the apostle's reasoning here. It is God seen in men whom we recognize in the love borne to them; but, then, God is in all His own, as the apostle is everywhere arguing; and, therefore, there is nothing self-contradictory in what has been just said."F. W. Grant.

V. HEREBY WE KNOW

CHAPTERS 3:19—5:13

1. Hereby we know that we are of the truth (3:19-24)
2. Hereby know ye the Spirit of God (4:1-4)
3. Hereby know we the Spirit of truth and of error (4:5-6)
4. The Love manifested toward us (4:7-19)
5. The final tests as to the possession of eternal life (4:20—5:13)

Verses 19-24. If the love of God dwells in the heart of the child of God it must be manifested in a practical way. Love must be expressed in deed and in truth, which is the fruit of true faith. If the believer does this he knows that he is of the truth. If it is lacking he is but an empty professing believer. But if we know that we are of the truth, by bearing such fruit of faith, we can assure our hearts before Him, and we can draw nigh with confidence. As our hearts do not condemn us, knowing that we are of the truth, we have confidence toward God and whatsoever we ask, we receive of Him, because we keep His commandments, and do those things that are pleasing in His sight. Where there is not a good conscience and the Holy Spirit is grieved real nearness to God and the effectual prayer which availeth much are impossible. It is the same blessed truth our Lord spoke in connection with the parable of the vine. "If ye abide in Me, and My words abide in you ye shall ask what ye will, and it shall be done unto you" (John 15:7).

But what is His commandment? Strange that some expositors have read into it the Ten Commandments. The context answers the question: "And this is His commandment, that we should believe on the name of His Son Jesus Christ, and love one another, as He gave us commandment. And He that keepeth His commandment dwelleth in Him, and He in him. And hereby we know that He abideth in us, by the Spirit He hath given to us."

Chapter 4:1-4. The last sentence of the preceding chapter gives the assurance that the believer has the Holy Spirit. There is no such thing as a true child of God without the Holy Spirit. The indwelling Spirit is the proof that He Himself dwells in us. But how do we know that it is the Spirit of God? How can a test be made? The sphere of the Spirit is the territory in which the spirit of error and darkness operates and where the liar from the beginning counterfeits. Many false prophets inspired by the spirit of darkness had gone out into the world and the apostle gives a warning not to believe every spirit but to try the spirits.[1] The true test is the person of the Lord Jesus Christ. Every spirit that confesseth that Jesus Christ is come in the flesh is of God.

But this means more than a mere confession with the lips, it means to own the person and lordship of Jesus Christ our Saviour. The demons know how to confess Him and yet they are demons (Matthew 8:29). The spirit of antichrist denies Him, does not confess that Jesus Christ is come in the flesh. This spirit which is not the Spirit of God manifests itself in the most subtle forms. It is called "true Christian charity" in our days to make common cause in what is called "social service" with those who do not confess Christ, who do not own Him as Saviour and Lord. These many antichrists speak of Him as man, they go so far as to call Christ a manifestation of God in human form, but they deny that He is very God come in the flesh.

As stated before the most prominent form of it is today the denial of His virgin birth. Anything which denies the full glory of the Lord Jesus Christ which in any way detracts from His glory, is the spirit of antichrist. About a hundred years ago a movement was in existence which claimed to be another Pentecost, just as there are movements today which claim the same unscriptural thing. The leader of that movement, Edward Irving, put great stress upon the incarnation, that Jesus came in the flesh. But after a while the demons which stood behind the movement brought forth the horrible doctrine of the peccability of Christ, that He had a corrupt nature like any other man. Such is the subtlety of Satan, the old serpent. He always strikes at Christ and His glory.

---

[1]"The false prophets are certainly no fewer in number at the present time than when the apostle spoke; yet, in general, we may say they assume less divine authority. We have sunk down so far into the wisdom of the world that man is credited with a place which God has lost. Inspiration is the inspiration of genius, rather than of God. We are more and more getting to lose the reality of the last, just as we are coming more and more to believe in the former. We believe in brilliancy, in eloquence, in intellect, in whatever you please in this way, but the assumption of speaking in any direct way by the Spirit of God no more exists, for the mass, except as one may say that the Spirit of God is as liberal as men are, and speaks in very diverse fashion—in poets, philosophers, and all the acknowledged leaders among men" (*Numerical Bible*).

Verses 5-6. The fifth verse has a good description of these antichrists and their following. These men, with their boasted learning and scholarship, their great swelling words, called eloquence, their natural amiability and cultured, courteous manners are of the world. They were never born again. If they had ever seen themselves lost and undone, and found in Christ their peace with God, they would yield complete obedience to Him and not deny His glory. When they speak they speak of the world. They speak of world conditions, and how they may be improved, of a better human society. Quite true they are even religious, but what they speak is not that which is of the Spirit, but what concerns the world system. The crowds want to hear that for it pleases the flesh, and thus the devil brings his audience to hear them. Such antichrists in cap and gown have multiplied by the thousands; they are found in the leading pulpits of all denominations.

The test as to the Spirit of truth and the spirit of error is stated in these words: "We are of God; He that knoweth God heareth us; he that is not of God heareth us not. Hereby know we the Spirit of truth and of error." The test is the apostle's doctrine. The Epistles are the full revelation of the doctrine of Christ, they contain the "many things" which the Lord spoke of when on earth, and which should be revealed when the Holy Spirit came. He has come and has made known the blessed things which eye hath not seen, nor ear heard, the things which God has prepared for them that love Him, but which are now revealed by His Spirit, the Spirit of truth (1 Corinthians 2:9-10). The spirit of error denies these doctrines. In our day the enemy has invested a most subtle slogan, "Back to Christ." It sounds well but behind it stands the father of lies. These men who speak of going back to Christ charge our beloved brother Paul with having a theological system of his own, which they claim Christ, on earth, never taught. They reject the great redemption truths made known by the Lord through the apostle to the Gentiles. Their cry "Back to Christ" is the spirit of antichrist.

Verses 7-19. These blessed words are addressed to the beloved, true believers. The great center of this passage is "God is Love." Love is of God. But how do we know that God is Love? Such an antichristian system as "Christian Science" babbles about the love of God, but that which alone expresses the love of God, and by which it is known that God is love, they reject completely. The question, how do we know that God is love? is answered in verses 9 and 10. "In this was manifested the love of God toward us, because that God sent His only begotten Son into the world, that we might live through Him. Herein is love, not that we loved God, but that He loved us, and sent His Son to be the propitiation for our sins." Apart from this there is no knowledge of the love of God. He who is born again knows that love, for in believing it (John 3:16) he receives eternal life, and that love was perfect in Him when we had no love for Him—not that we loved God, but that He loved us. In His great love He has met every need.

This love, the nature of God, is in those who are born again. Every one that loveth is born of God and knoweth God. He that loveth not knoweth not God. "Beloved, if God so loved us, we ought to love one another. If we love one another, God dwelleth in us, and His love is perfected in us." Love therefore is the very essence of the new nature and must be manifested towards all who are the objects of the love of God and are in the family of God by having believed that love.

"His presence, Himself, dwelling in us rises in the excellency of His nature above all the barriers of circumstances, and attaches us to those who are His. It is God in the power of His nature which is the source of thought and feeling and diffuses itself among them in whom it is. One can understand this. How is it that I love strangers from another land, persons of different habits, whom I have never known, more intimately than members of my own family after the flesh? How is it that I have thoughts in common, objects infinitely loved in common, affections powerfully engaged, a stronger bond with persons whom I have never seen, than with the otherwise dear companions of my childhood? It is because there is in them and in me a source of thoughts and affections which is not human. God is in it. God dwells in us. What happiness! What a bond! Does He not communicate Himself to the soul? Does He not render it conscious of His presence in love? Assuredly, yes. And if He is thus in us, the blessed source of our thoughts, can there be fear, or distance, or uncertainty, with regarding to what He is? None at all. His love is perfect in us" (John N. Darby).

His love is perfected in us by loving one another. Once more he uses the phrase "Hereby we know." "Hereby we know that we dwell in Him, and He in us, because He hath given us of His Spirit." "The Love of God is shed abroad in our hearts by the indwelling Spirit." He proceeds: "We have seen and testify that the Father sent the Son to be the Saviour of the world." Whosoever shall confess that Jesus is the son of God, God dwelleth in Him and he in God." What wonderful words these are! Can there be anything greater and more wonderful than dwelling in God and God dwelling in us! And this is true of every believer. If we confess that Jesus Christ is the Son of God, if we rest in His finished work as well, knowing the Father sent Him to be the Saviour, and our Saviour therefore, then the Holy Spirit dwells in us and as a result God dwelleth in us and we in God. There can be no question about it for God says so.

The enjoyment of it is a different matter. If it is not real to us and if we do not enjoy it there is something which hinders it in ourselves. If a great king should pay us a visit in our home and dwell there and we do not recognize the fact of the honor and privilege bestowed upon us, and if we do not trouble about it and show our appreciation of it, we would have no enjoyment in such a visit. To have the reality of it and enjoy the wonderful truth that God dwells in us and we in Him we must practise what our Lord said in John 14:23, "If a man love Me he will keep My words, and My Father will love him, and We will come unto him, and make Our abode in Him." We must dwell in love, the very nature of God, and that love is manifested towards Him and towards the brethren. Verses 12 and 16 make this clear. "And we have known and believed the love that God hath to us. God is love; and he that dwelleth in love dwelleth in God and God in him."

Another important fact is stated in the verses which follow: "Herein hath love been perfected with us, that we have boldness in the day of judgment, because as He is, even so are we in this world. There is no fear in love but perfect love casteth out fear, because fear has torment; and he that feareth is not perfected in love." It has nothing to do with *our* love, as some take it nor with seeking an experience of being "perfect in love." It is His love which casteth out fear, believing that love and dwelling in it. If we believe and know what God has made us in His infinite grace what Christ is, that as He is so are we, how can we fear anything! The coming day of judgment we await not only without any fear, but with boldness, for the day will only bring the full display of what Christ is and what we are in Him and with Him. The knowledge of His perfect love, the love which has reached down to us and lifted us so high, casteth out all fear.

("It is a blessed love that Christ came into the word for such sinners as we are. But then there is the day of judgment. When I think of the love, I am all happy; but when I think of the day of judgment, my conscience is not quite easy. Though the heart may have tasted the love, the conscience not being quite clear, when I think of judgment I am not quite happy. This is what is provided for here. 'As He is so are we in this world.' The love was shown in visiting us when we were sinners; it is enjoyed in communion: but it is completed in this, that I am in Christ, and that Christ must condemn Himself in the day of judgment, if He condemns me, because He is, so am I in the world, I am glorified before I get there. He changes this vile body and makes it like to His glorious body. When I am before the judgment seat, I am in this changed and glorified body; I am like my judge" *Synopsis of the Bible.*)

Verses 4:20—5:13. Once more brotherly love is applied as the test. "If a man say, I love God, and hateth his brother, he is a liar." God is in the believer, he is the object of God's love, if therefore the brother is not loved, but hated, it is an evidence that God does not dwell in such a heart and again the beloved disciple brands such an one as a liar.

"Whosoever believeth that Jesus is the Christ is born of God and every one that loveth Him that begat, loveth him also that is begotten of Him." This is very logical. Then he gives a counter test to show that it is genuine. "By this we know, that we love the children of God, when we love God and keep His commandments." If we love God and keep His commandments, we can rest assured that we love the children of God also. If the soul goes out to Him in love, and it is shown by unreserved fidelity to His will, then love for those begotten of Him, the other members of the family of God, will be the result. "For this is the love of God that we keep His commandments, and His commandments are not grievous." It is a different thing from the law which is called elsewhere a yoke which no one was able to bear (Acts 15:10). Keeping His commandments means to be obedient to His Word, being subject unto Him in all things, for love to God is the spirit of obedience. But the children of God are in the world, though no longer of it. There are hindrances all about in the world which knew Him not and which know not the children of God. All in this world is opposition to God and hinders true obedience. But that which is born of God overcometh the world. Our faith is the victory which overcometh the world. What faith is it? It is the faith which is occupied with the Son of God, which yields obedience to Him, does His will. Such a faith is the victory that overcomes the world and its attractions. This is stated in verse 5.

"And He, the Son of God, even Jesus Christ, came by water and blood—not by water only, but by water and blood." "And it is the Spirit that beareth witness, because the Spirit is truth" (verse 6). How beautiful is this passage and what divine perfection it reveals! Only John in his Gospel gives the account of the opened side of our adorable Saviour and that water and blood came forth out of the pierced side. "And he that saw it (John) bare record and his record is true and he knoweth that he saith true that ye might believe" (John 19:35). What the sinner needs is cleansing, a cleansing morally and a cleansing from guilt. The water is for cleansing, the blood telling of expiation cleanses from guilt. To make here of the water, baptism, and of the blood, the Lord's Supper, is as false as it is ridiculous. It is purification and propitiation as accomplished and provided for in the death of Christ for the believer. As a result the Holy Spirit is here on earth. Note the Apostle John does not put forward his own testimony here as given in the above passage, but the Holy Spirit Himself beareth witness to it. He is on earth for this purpose to bear witness to Christ and the work of Christ. How awful the rejection of that witness appears in the light of these words—that rejection which is so widespread and pronounced in antichristian modernism!

The seventh verse has no business in our Bibles. It must be stricken out. It is an interpolation and all the historical evidences are against it. The oldest manuscripts do not contain these words which we read in verse 7. Leaving out this inserted verse we notice the connection which exists between verse 6 and 8. "And there are three that bear witness on earth, the Spirit, and the water, and the blood; and these three are one." The Spirit is the abiding witness of accomplished redemption, and He dwells in the believer.

Verses 9-13 need no further detailed annotations. They are so plain and simple that only one wilfully blind can misunderstand them. God's witness is concerning His Son. The believer who believes on the Son of God hath the witness in himself, that is, by the indwelling Spirit, and by the salvation he possesses, the new nature, the eternal life. Any man who does not believe God's witness concerning His Son hath made Him a liar. Think of it, dear reader, the creature of the dust makes God, who cannot lie, a liar! This is the heinous sin of the great religious world. The record we have is, that God hath given to us eternal life, that this life is in His Son, that if we have the Son we have life, if we have not the Son we have not life. Verse 13 concludes the argument and teaching of the Epistle concerning eternal life.

VI. Conclusion

CHAPTER 5:14-21

The conclusion of this great Epistle mentions first the practical confidence which a believer may have, the outcome of that relationship and fellowship with the Father and His Son, which the doctrinal part so blessedly unfolds. We can come in prayer to Him with boldness and whatever we ask "according to His will He heareth us; and if we know that He heareth us, whatsoever we ask, we know that we have the petitions which we have asked of Him." As a loving Father He listens to the cry of His children and He answers if it is according to His will, and the child of God would not have it differently, and desire anything to be granted him which is contrary to the will of God. Our unanswered prayers we joyfully recognize as being not according to His will. It is not true faith when fanatics, like faith curists, say that God *must* do certain things. That is not faith but presumption.

But what is the sin unto death (verse 16)? God chastises the sinning believer often through sickness. And the chastisement may lead to the physical death of the child of God. Such was the case in Corinth (1 Corinth. 11:31). It is the same case as James 5:14, 15. If the sin is not unto physical death as a chastisement, we can pray for the brother and he will be restored. But there is a sin unto death. Ananias and Sapphira committed such a sin. No prayer in such a case does avail anything. God in His governmental dealings takes the offender away as to his life on earth. It does not affect the salvation of the soul, as those teach who think that one who has believed, has eternal life, and is a member of the family of God, can be lost again.

The conclusion of the Epistle consists in three statements that "we know": "We *know* that whosoever is born of God sinneth not; but He that is begotten of God keepeth himself and that wicked one toucheth him not." Sin is the touch of the wicked one. If the believer guards himself, by living in the fellowship with the Father and the Son, walking in the Light, the wicked one cannot reach him; he lives according to his new nature and sinneth not. *"We know* that we are of God and the whole world lieth in the wicked one." Hence God's children should be separated from the world. If a believer is not he moves on the very territory of the wicked one and the author of sin finds occasion to touch him and lead him to sin. *"We know* that the Son of God is come, and hath given us an understanding, that we may know Him that is true, and we are in Him that is true, even in His Son Jesus Christ. This is the true God and eternal life."

The final exhortation is "Little children (*teknia*—all God's children), keep yourselves from idols. Amen." What is an idol? Anything and everything that draws the affection and devotion of heart and soul from the Lord Jesus Christ. May He, through the power of His Spirit, keep us all from idols. And we shall be kept if we give in our hearts and lives the pre-eminence to our Lord and walk in the light as He is in the light.

THE SECOND AND THIRD EPISTLES OF
JOHN

Introduction

We treat these small documents together. No intelligent person can doubt that both Epistles were written by the same person. We do not need to investigate the objections and inventions of rationalists like Bretschneider, those of the so-called Tuebingen school and the modern critics, who deny the Johannine authorship and teach that the fictitious "John the Presbyter of Ephesus" wrote these two letters.

But all these modern conceptions are answered by the ancient authorities which ascribe both Epistles to the writer of the First Epistle, that is, the Apostle John. Irenaeus, who as a boy had listened to Polycarp, who knew John personally, bears witness to the genuineness of the Second Epistle, so does Clement of Alexandria, the Muratorian fragment, Dionysius of Alexandria, and others. Both Epistles seem to have been accepted from the very beginning as the inspired testimony of John.

The internal evidence is conclusive. Both Epistles are in tone, style and vocabulary like the Gospel of John and the First Epistle of John. The great characteristic words of the other writings of John (the Gospel and John I) "Love," "truth," "world," etc., are found in these two Epistles. They are, indeed, complementary to the First Epistle and give some of the truths contained in the First Epistle in a practical way. The warning contained in the Second Epistle concerning receiving one who does not bring the doctrine of Christ, that is, an antichrist, connects closely with the instructions of 1 John 4. There is no question but both Epistles are appendices to the First Epistle.

The Second Epistle

The Second Epistle is addressed by the elder unto the elect lady and her children. The word elder has the same meaning as it has in 1 Peter 5. Some take it that the elect lady means an assembly, and her children the members of the assembly. But this is a very strained application.

The word "Kyria" (lady) excludes this meaning, besides other reasons which we do not follow here. She was a Christian woman of note generally known and beloved, having children, whom the apostle had found walking in the truth. She had also a sister with children, who seems to have been in the same place where the apostle was, probably in Ephesus. This is indicated by the last verse of the Epistle, "The children of thy elect sister greet thee." The keynote of this message to the elect lady, unknown by name, is the word "truth." The apostle lets them know that he loves them, as well as all other believers in the truth. That is the ground of real love; every child of God—man, woman or child— is best beloved for the sake of the truth, the blessed truth so abundantly poured forth in the First Epistle, the truth which is Christ Himself. And that truth "dwelleth in us, and shall be with us forever." Thus the truth known binds together in closest fellowship all who know Him.

Then follows a blessed greeting, "Grace, mercy and peace shall be with you, from the Father, and from the Lord Jesus Christ, the Son of the Father, in truth and love." The statement, "the Son of the Father" is unique; it is not found elsewhere in the New Testament and is in full keeping with the object of this little Epistle, for the denial of Christ coming in the flesh, and the warning against these deceivers, is the chief message of the Epistle. The great joy of the Apostle was that he found them walking in the truth, that the children of the elect lady walked according to the commandment received from the Father (1 John 3:24). Having the truth necessitates walking in the truth. One who claims to have the truth and does not walk in it, shows that he does not know the truth in his heart. But walking in the truth is the result of having and knowing the truth.

What we have stated before, that these two Epistles are appendices of the First Epistle, is seen by the fifth verse (1 John 3:23-24). It is the old and new commandment. It was old because it was manifested in Christ Himself; new because it is just as true in us as in Him. Divine love flows from love, and reproduces itself in all who know the truth, that is, who know Christ. And this is love that we walk after His commandments. It means obedience to Him, and what else is obedience but love in exercise?

But why does he write all this? With the seventh verse he gives the reason and it is a very solemn one, indeed. Well may we look to these words in our own days for they have a great meaning for the children of God living in these closing days, as they had a meaning in the beginning of the dispensation. "For many deceivers are entered into the world, who confess not that Jesus Christ is come into the flesh. This is a deceiver and an antichrist." This was true in the beginning of the age, and all through the present age the old serpent has made its many attempts to attack Christ and foster the lies concerning His person and glory, but never before has this been so evident as in our own days. The reason is that the age is about to end. Denying that Jesus Christ is come in the flesh was mentioned by John in his First Epistle (chapter 4). It includes all phases of evil doctrines concerning Christ, the Son of the Father. It is a denial of His essential deity, His true humanity, His Virgin birth, His infallibility, His holy character, His physical resurrection, and His bodily presence in glory.

We need not mention again how many such antichrists are about in these days. And John brands them in plain words as deceivers. No matter what names they have, what scholarship and honors they claim, what beautiful characters they have assumed as natural men, if they deny anything about Christ, they are deceivers. He calls, therefore, to look diligently whether some of this awful leaven is not affecting them. If in any way they were contaminated with it they, John and the fellow teachers, might lose the full reward. (See 1 John 2:28). Then follow the instructions in verses 9-11.

"Whosoever transgresseth and abideth not in the doctrine of Christ hath not God. He that abideth in the doctrine of Christ, he hath both the Father and the Son." Even the smallest error about the person of Christ is a transgression of the doctrine of Christ and if followed will lead to a complete rejection of the truth, as it has been so often seen in cases of apostates. Such deniers have not God, while he who abideth in the doctrine of Christ hath both the Father and the Son. After this declaration comes a divine command which is just as binding as any other command in the Word of God. "If there come any unto you, and bring not this doctrine, receive him not in your house, neither bid him Godspeed; for he that biddeth him Godspeed is partaker of his evil deeds."

This is strong language and yet not too strong when we remember what is at stake. Any one who brings not the doctrine of Christ, the doctrine as unfolded in the previous Epistle, concerning Christ the Son of God come in the flesh, dying for sinners and all that clusters around it, is an antichrist. Furthermore he makes God a liar and in denying the doctrine of Christ robs God of His glory and man of his salvation. And every man who denies the virgin birth, or teaches the peccability of Christ, or denies His physical resurrection is such a one. He must be shunned. Fellowship with him is an impossibility. He is not to be welcomed to any Christian home, nor is he to be given the common greeting. If met anywhere there is to be no acknowledgement whatever, not even a "Good Morning" or "Good Night." This is the meaning of the expression "Godspeed."

But is not this intolerant? Yes, the intolerance of divine love. If such deceivers are welcomed and fellowship is had with them even in the slightest degree, the believer puts his sanction on a denier of Christ. God will hold all responsible who fellowship any man, any set of men, any institution or anything else, which deny His Son and His glory. This is unpalatable to many. Nowadays it is called "Christian charity and broadmindedness" to mingle with Unitarians, critics, and baptized infidels of various descriptions. His honor and glory is in the background. Happy are we if we stand firm and refuse such fellowship practising this divinely given injunction by the Apostle of love. God will be our rewarder.

"Having many things to write unto you, I would not write with paper and ink, but I trust to come unto you, and speak face to face, that our joy may be full. The children of the elect sister greet thee. Amen." Thus ends the Second Epistle.

The Third Epistle

The Third Epistle is addressed by the elder, the aged Apostle John, to a brother by name of Gaius. A Gaius is mentioned in Acts 19:29, 20:4, Romans 26:23 and 1 Corinthians 1:14. It is impossible to say whether this is the same. John calls him well-beloved, whom he loved in the truth. Thus he emphasizes the truth once more as he had done before. He wishes that he might prosper in his body, in health, as even his soul prospered. He had heard from the brethren who testified of the truth in him and that he walked in the truth. He rejoiced in this and declares "I have no greater joy than to hear that my children walk in truth." And this is not only the aged apostle's joy, but it is the joy of the Lord. How He must rejoice when His beloved children in whom He dwells walk in truth! Gaius had been very gracious and hospitable. Perhaps the brethren who gave such a good report to John were the recipients of Gaius's kindness. They had witnessed before the assembly how faithful he was in entertaining them, helping them on their journey in every way possible. He had done this not only with the brethren in his locality, but with brethren who were strangers, ministering servants of the Lord Jesus Christ, who went forth for His Name's sake, taking nothing of the Gentiles. In going forth in ministering the Word they depended on the Lord.

The evil of today, even among those who preach the truth, of demanding so much money for so much service was unknown in the Church. Nowhere do we read in the New Testament of a "salaried" ministry. The evils of going to the world for support of the Lord's work, or using the methods of the world are widespread and detrimental to true faith and a true testimony to the truth. The work of the Lord and the servants of Christ are to be supported only by the Lord's people and not by the unsaved. Such, then, who go forth for His Name's sake, taking nothing from the Gentiles (those who are outside) are to be received and those who receive them, help them on their journey as Gaius did, are fellow helpers to the truth. They are going to share in that coming day in the fruit of their labors. This is the true fellowship in the truth, as Paul expressed it in Galatians, "Let him that is taught in the Word communicate unto him that teaches in all good things" (Galatians 6:6). It is in contrast from what the Second Epistle demanded—withdrawal from those who bring not the doctrine of Christ, a complete separation from them; but here it is identification with those who know the truth and teach the truth.

This is a bright picture presented in Gaius. Alas! there is another side in this Third Epistle. There was one by name of Diotrephes. His name means "Nourished of God." Of him John writes as follows: "I wrote unto the church, but Diotrephes, who loveth to have the pre-eminence among them, received us not. Wherefore, if I come, I will remember his deeds which he doeth, prating against us with malicious words; and not content therewith, neither doth he himself receive the brethren, and casteth them out of the church." We let another speak on this. "We have another evil designated very clearly here. Diotrephes is the scriptural example of the clerical tribe, as contra-distinguished from the ministry of Christ. There is no service, because there is no love. He is the representative of the spirit which opposes the free action of the Holy Spirit, setting itself even against apostolic authority in order to gain or maintain his own individual pre-eminence.

Self-importance, jealousy of those over us, impatience of others equally called to serve, scorn of the assembly, yet sometimes humoring the least worthy for its own ends—such are the characteristics of clericalism. I do not mean in clergymen only; for there are men of God incomparably better than their position tends to make them; as on the other hand this evil thing is nowhere so offensive as where the truth that is owned, wholly condemns it" (William Kelly). Diotrephes wanted to be the leader of the assembly, a kind of a pope in embryo. He loved the pre-eminence and this self-love and seeking to maintain his position led him to act so outrageously that he excommunicated the brethren and dared to rise up against the apostle himself. What harm such jealousies, self-seeking, self-glorification and ecclesiastical bossism have worked and are working in the body of Christ! and nowhere so much as in circles where the full truth is known and confessed. But why did Diotrephes love to have the pre-eminence? Because, unlike the apostle and the beloved Gaius, he did not give the Lord Jesus Christ the pre-eminence in all things; he did not walk in the truth. When the Lord comes, before His judgment-seat, all these things will be brought to light and dealt with by Him.

John does not leave us with the sad picture of Diotrephes. "Beloved, follow not that which is evil, but that which is good. He that doeth good is of God; but he that doeth evil hath not seen God." It is another one of the tests as we found them in the First Epistle. Doing good is the active service of love. God does not do evil, but He does good, hence if we do good as believers in truth, we are of God. Then he mentions Demetrius. Perhaps he was one of the servants who went about doing good, preaching the truth, and whom Diotrephes would not receive. How blessed that the Holy Spirit through John's letter endorses and recommends him. "Demetrius hath good report of all, and of the truth itself; yea, and we also bear record, and ye know that our record is true." Such is the comfort of all true servants who walk in the truth, that the Lord knoweth. "I have many things to write, but I will not with ink and pen write unto thee. But I trust I shall shortly see thee, and we shall speak face to face. Peace be to thee. Our friends salute thee. Greet the friends by name." Both Epistles end, with a coming face to face meeting. Let us remember there is to be some blessed day a "face to face" meeting, when the saints of God will meet together for eternal fellowship, but above all when we shall be face to face with Him. How soon it may be! But while we wait for that meeting may we walk in the light and in the fullest enjoyment of our fellowship with the Father and with His Son, our blessed Lord. To Him be glory and dominion for ever. Amen.

THE EPISTLE OF
JUDE

Introduction

The Epistle of Jude is the last Epistle preceding the great final book with which the Holy Scriptures conclude, the book of Revelation. We believe the place given to this Epistle is the right one, for as we shall see, it reveals the conditions, religiously and morally, which prevail on earth before the great coming event takes place, of which Revelation has so much to say. Some have called it "the preface to the Revelation."

The Author

We are not left in doubt who the writer is, for he mentions himself in the beginning of it. It is Jude, the servant of Jesus Christ and brother of James. But who is this Jude or Judas? Among the disciples were two by the name of Judas. There was Judas Iscariot, who ended his miserable career, after he had become the instrument of the devil, by hanging. In John 14:22 we read, "Judas saith unto Him, not Iscariot, Lord, how is it that Thou wilt manifest Thyself unto us, and not unto the world?" The Spirit of God makes it plain that Judas Iscariot did not address Jesus by the name Lord, which expresses faith in His deity, but that there was another Judas in the apostolate who speaks here.

When we turn to the names of the twelve in Matthew 10:2-4, we find the name of Judas but once; it is the name of him who betrayed the Lord. The Judas whose words are recorded in the above passage in the Gospel of John, is called in Matthew 10:3 "'Lebbaeus whose surname was Thaddaeus." In Luke 6:16 and Acts 1:13, his name is given as Judas of James; it must be noticed that the words in the authorized version "the brother" are in italics, which means that they are supplied by the translators. It is not so in the first verse of this epistle; here the writer calls himself "brother of James."

But there is still another Judas found in the Gospels. His name is recorded in Matthew 13:55. "Is not this the carpenter's son? is not His mother called Mary? and His brethren, James, and Joses, and Simon, and Judas?" The James, the brother of the Lord mentioned in this passage, is the author of the Epistle of James. (See introduction to the Epistle of James). The question then arises, Is the writer of the Epistle before us, the Apostle Judas of James, also called Lebbaeus, surnamed Thaddaeus, or is it Judas, the one who is called one of the Lord's brethren, and therefore the natural brother of James, the writer of the Epistle of James? Some maintain that Jude is the Apostle Judas, while others see in Jude the brother of James, as given in Matthew 13:55. We endorse the latter view. We give the reasons why the writer of this Epistle cannot be the Apostle Judas.

1. He does not speak of himself as an apostle. He designates himself as a servant of Jesus Christ. Whenever an apostle calls himself a servant of Jesus Christ, he adds his apostleship, as we learn from Romans 1:1, Titus 1:1; 2 Peter 1:1. The only exception is the epistle to the Philippians, in which Paul associates with himself in the address Timothy, and then speaks of himself and Timothy as servants of Jesus Christ.

2. If he were the Apostle Judas, the brother of the Apostle James, the sons of Alphaeus, we have to face great difficulties, as Dean Alford states, involving the wholly unjustifiable hypothesis, that those who are called in Scripture the brethren of our Lord were not His brethren, but His cousins, sons of Alphaeus (Cleopas).

But why does the writer of this Epistle not speak of himself as "the brother of the Lord?" it has been asked. James does not do so in his Epistle either. He is silent about his relationship and so is his brother Jude. "The question, Why does not Jude mention his earthly relationship to the Lord? shows great ignorance of the true spirit of the writers of the New Testament. It would be the last thing I should expect, to find one of the brethren of the Lord asserting this relationship as a ground of reception for an Epistle. Almost all agree that the writer of the Epistle of James was the person known as the brother of the Lord. Yet there we have no designation. It would have been in fact altogether inconsistent with the true spirit of Christ (Luke 20:27, 28), and in harmony with those later superstitious feelings with which the next and following generations regarded His earthly relatives. Had such a designation as *"Adelphos tou Kyriou"* (brother of the Lord) been found in the address of an Epistle, it would have formed a strong à priori objection to its authenticity" (*Prolegomena*).

Jude is therefore the one mentioned in Matthew 13:55. Apart from this Epistle we know nothing more of him. The date of the Epistle is about the year 65.

Its Authenticity

It is authenticated by different ancient sources. The Muratorian fragment mentions it as Jude's Epistle. Clement of Alexandria cites it as Scripture, as well as Tertullian and others. The theories of some objecting critics need not to be considered.

To whom the Epistle was originally addressed is not stated. Some have surmised that like James and the Petrine Epistles Jude addressed originally Jewish believers. This may be true, for Jude mentions, prominently, like Peter, Old Testament facts, besides some Jewish traditional matters, which thereby are confirmed as facts. Concerning the apocryphal writings, which especially the book of Enoch, which Jude is charged with having used in the composition of his Epistle, we shall have more to say in the annotations.

Jude and 2 Peter 2

As stated in the introduction to the Second Epistle of Peter, Jude's testimony is very much like the testimony of the Apostle Peter in the second chapter of his second Epistle. Hence there has been a long controversy whether Jude copied from Peter or Peter copied from Jude. We have stated before that if Jude had copied from Peter, his epistle could not be an inspired Epistle, and so if Peter copied from Jude. Jude may have known Peter's Epistle, but that does not mean that he used Peter's Epistle, but the Holy Spirit gives a similar testimony through Jude, which is, after a closer examination, somewhat different from Peter's epistle. This is pointed out in the annotations.

The Message of Jude

It seems about the time when Jude wrote his letter a departure from the faith set in among believers. This is confirmed by the fact that other epistles written about the same time give warnings of the same nature as those given by Jude. The message of Jude may be called a prophetic history of the apostasy of Christendom from its beginning in apostolic days down to the end of the age, when the complete apostasy will be dealt with and completely destroyed by the coming of the Lord. It is the darkest forecast of the end of the age which the Spirit of God has given in the Epistles. While apostasy and antichristianity have held sway all through the history of Christendom, there is coming in the end of this age a consummation, the evils of which are pictured by the Holy Spirit through the pen of Jude. We know that we are living right in the midst of the fulfillment of Jude's message. The Epistle is, therefore, of great importance for our times.

Analysis and Annotations

I. The Introduction

Verses 1-2. Jude in his brief introduction speaks of the Christian believers, whom he addresses, as called ones, sanctified by God the Father, and preserved in Jesus Christ. The latter statement may also be translated "kept for Jesus Christ." What was true of the believers in Jude's day is true of all believers. Especially comforting is the fact, that, no matter how dark the days may be, however strong the current of evil, those who are "the beloved of God called saints" will be preserved in Jesus Christ and kept for Him as the members of His body, till He comes. He keeps His own. It is the blessed assurance that the believer's keeping rests in His own hands. In the Revelation we see in the glory vision that Christ holds seven stars in His right hand, which is the symbol of the hand of His power with which He keeps His own. Then there is the prayer that "mercy, and peace, and love may be multiplied."

II. The Purpose and Occasion of the Epistle

Verses 3-4. "Beloved, giving all diligence to write unto you of our common salvation, I was constrained to write unto you exhorting you to earnestly contend for the faith which was once delivered unto the saints."

It had evidently been upon the heart of Jude to write an epistle to the Christians whom he knew. He gave all diligence to carry out his intention. This must mean that he prayed and thought over this matter. He then decided to write about the common salvation. This is the gospel.

It is the nearest and the dearest object to every believer, for it is the matchless story of God's love. It reveals the Son of God, our Lord, who died for our sins, who was buried and rose again the third day. There are blessed depths and heights in this gospel, the salvation which believers have in common, which have never yet been measured. Jude thought to make this the theme of his epistle. Then something happened. The power which was to guide his pen constrained him to write about something else. The Holy Spirit constrained him to exhort Christians to contend earnestly for the faith once and for all delivered unto the saints. Here is a very fine illustration at the close of the New Testament of how the Word of God was given. Jude had a desire to write about the common salvation; but the Holy Spirit wanted him to write about something else and He constrained him to do so, not in his own words but in words given by God.

What faith is meant? Not a creed or confession of faith as formulated by a denomination, sect or party, but *the* faith, which has been delivered once for all unto the saints. It is the same faith concerning which our Lord asked the question, "Nevertheless when the Son of Man cometh, shall He find the faith on the earth?" (Luke 18:8) It is the faith revealed in the Word of God. The heart of that faith is the Son of God, our Lord Jesus Christ, and the apostles' doctrine made known by the Holy Spirit; it is therefore the whole body of revealed truth. This faith is given by revelation, a different thing from what is being taught today, as if this faith were the product of a process of evolution through the religious experiences of the race for thousands of years. The truths which man needs cannot be found by searching. This faith is "once for all delivered unto the saints." It is permanent, irrevocable and like Him who has revealed it, unchanging. Nor is this faith delivered to the world, but to the saints, that is to the body of Christ, the Church.

That faith was being corrupted when Jude received the commission to exhort Christians to contend earnestly for it. They were ungodly men, having taken on the Christian profession without possessing the reality of it. The evil they introduced was twofold. They turned the grace of God into lasciviousness and they denied the rights of Christ to be Lord and Master. They professed to believe in grace, but abused it so that they might indulge in their own lusts; they knew nothing of the power of godliness manifested in holy living and therefore they denied the authority of the Lord Jesus Christ.

III. Examples From the Past

Verses 5-10. The Spirit of God reminds them of certain apostasies in past history and how God in judgment dealt with it. If we compare this section of Jude's Epistle with 2 Peter 2:4-8 we shall see how both documents differ from each other. Peter speaks first of the angels that sinned; then of Noah and the flood and finally of Sodom and Gomorrha and the deliverance of Lot. Jude on the other hand does not mention Noah at all, nor Lot. He speaks first of the Israelites who had come out of Egypt and were destroyed in the wilderness because they believed not. This is followed by the angels who kept not their first estate; then comes Sodom and Gomorrha and the judgment which fell upon these cities, and finally Jude adds something which is not found elsewhere in the Word of God, the incident about Michael contending with the devil about the body of Moses. It is far fetched with this different testimony which Jude gives to charge him with having copied Peter, or Peter having used Jude.

When we examine these examples of the past, we discover that they are not chronologically arranged. If they were reported according to the time when they happened, Jude, like Peter, should have mentioned first the angels that sinned; after which Sodom and Gomorrha would be in order, followed by the Israelites who fell in the wilderness and after that Michael contending with the devil. Why this unchronological arrangement in this Epistle? There must be a purpose in it. We believe the arrangement is made in the manner as it is to teach us the starting point and the goal of apostasy. It starts with unbelief. The people had been saved out of Egypt, but they believed not and were destroyed in the wilderness, except those mentioned in the Word who believed.

Thus all apostasy starts with unbelief in what God has spoken. The angels which kept not their first estate, who left their own habitation, and who are now chained, are the same angels of whom Peter speaks, those who brought in the corruption described in the opening verses of Genesis 6. They gave up the place assigned to them. This is the next step in the progress of apostasy. Unbelief leads to rebellion against God. Sodom and Gomorrha come next. Here we find the grossest immoralities and going after strange flesh. These vicious things are still in the world, and why are they so prominent in our days? On account of unbelief. Then follows the statement, that these apostates are filthy dreamers who defile the flesh, despise dominion, and speak evil of dignities. This is lawlessness. This is the goal of all apostasy. The predicted lawlessness with which this age ends is the fruitage of infidelity. Such is the development of apostasy. Unbelief, rebellion against God and his revealed truth, immorality and anarchy. These steps may be traced in our own times.

To show that Michael, the archangel, would not rail against the fallen angel-prince, now the devil, as these apostates despise dominions, the incident concerning Michael contending against the devil about the body of Moses is introduced. He durst not bring a railing accusation against the former Lucifer, the son of the morning, for Michael still recognized in him the once great and glorious creature. It is stated by some of the early church fathers that this episode was recorded in a Jewish apocryphal book "Assumption of Moses." This book is no longer in existence. Another Jewish tradition has it that Michael had been given the custody of the grave of Moses.

Jude does not quote from tradition, nor does he quote from a source now no longer available, or, as others surmise, used one of Zechariah's visions (chapter 3), but the Holy Spirit revealed unto him what actually took place when Moses had died. It seems that Michael the archangel was commissioned by the Lord to conduct the funeral of Moses (Deut. 34:5-6). Then the devil appeared upon the scene claiming the body of the servant of the Lord, for what purpose is not revealed. (See annotations on Deuteronomy 25.) And Michael durst not bring against him a railing accusation but said, The Lord rebuke thee. But it is different with these apostates. They are compared with irrational animals, following their natural inclinations.

IV. A Further Description of the Apostates

Verses 11-13. The Spirit of God pronounces a woe upon them. The eleventh verse is of much importance. At the close of the New Testament we are reminded of Cain, the first murderer of the human race. Some expositors claim that his name is introduced here because he is a representative of all bad men; others think that he is mentioned because these apostates hated those who are of the truth, as Cain hated Abel. The way of Cain was the way of unbelief. He did not believe what God had spoken, while Abel believed. He had not faith like Abel, who offered unto God a more excellent sacrifice than Cain, by which he obtained witness that he was righteous. Cain was a religious man nevertheless, but his religion may be termed a "bloodless religion." He brought the labor of his hands, that which he had gathered from the land upon which the curse rested.

The apostates go in the same way of self-will and in that way they reject the record of God concerning His Son. They have no use for the blood of redemption; the salvation they preach is the salvation of "Do," by character. They rush also greedily after the error of Balaam. Money is the chief object with them. They teach error for reward, knowing all along that their teaching is contrary to the revelation of God. Money, honor and glory from men, self-exaltation and self-gratification are the leading motives of these men. The third characteristic is the sin of Core (Korah). The sin of Korah was open rebellion and opposition against the authority of God and the priesthood He had instituted. These apostates of the last days manifest the same spirit of rebellion and defiance. They have no use for the Lord Jesus Christ as the appointed mediator, priest and advocate. The perdition of Korah will overtake them likewise.

Not Jude, but the Holy Spirit, denounces them in the strongest language. (See annotations 2 Peter 2.) They are doubly dead, first in their own fallen nature, and in the second place by turning their ears from the truth and going into apostasy. They are like trees which give the promise of fruit in an imposing bloom, but which withers away; they do not yield any fruit whatever. They are plucked up by the roots without any hope of a revival. They are like the wild waves of the sea, foaming out their own shame (Isaiah 62:20-21); wandering stars to whom is reserved the blackness of darkness forever. The wandering stars in the universe belonged once to some great solar system. They detached themselves and began their wanderings. As they left their center they wandered further and further away, deeper and deeper into the immense space of cold and darkness. So these apostates left the center and became eccentric rushing, like these wandering stars of the heavens, into the outer darkness.

V. The Testimony of Enoch

Verses 14-16. The Holy Spirit introduces quite abruptly Enoch, the seventh from Adam. There is a deep spiritual significance in this. Enoch lived as an age was about to close. Before the evil days of Noah, with universal violence, corruption and wickedness, had come, Enoch walked with God and bore a prophetic testimony of what was to come in the future. He suffered on account of the testimony he bore to that generation. The ungodly spoke against him, but he kept on in his walk with God and in his testimony, till the day came when he was suddenly removed from the earth. "By faith Enoch was translated that he should not see death; and was not found, because God had translated him, for before his translation he had this testimony, that he pleased God" (Hebrews 11:5). Enoch represents prophetically the true Church living at the close of the age, bearing witness to the coming of the Lord, and waiting in faith for the promised translation. The Spirit of God mentions Enoch for this purpose and for our encouragement.

Much has been made by critics and rationalists about this reference to Enoch. What Jude writes about Enoch is found in a Jewish apocryphal book by the name of "The Book of Enoch." The book consists of supposed revelations which were given to Enoch and to Moses. Its object seems to be a vindication of the ways of providence and to set forth the coming and terrible retribution for sinners. The book was known to the early church fathers who refer to it often in their writings. For centuries it seems to have been lost. About the close of the 18th Century an Ethiopian translation was discovered in Abyssinia and translated into English and German. Critics claim that this book of Enoch was used by Jude, inasmuch as he inserted this reference to Enoch, which is almost verbatim found in that book. But according to these critics the book of Enoch was written in the second century and from this they reason that Jude did not write this Epistle in the year 65 A.D.

But there are other scholars who have ascertained that the book of Enoch was in existence before Christ. Even if the critics were correct that this book was written in the second century of our era, it is no evidence that Jude could not have written his Epistle in the year as stated above. The writers of the book of Enoch might have used Jude's statements about Enoch. The fact that Jude in giving by the Holy Spirit this paragraph concerning Enoch proves the record, whether it was handed down by tradition or written in the book of Enoch, to be true.

VI. The Exhortations

Verses 17-23. These exhortations are for the people of God, whose lot is cast in these predicted evil days. The first exhortation is to remember the words which were spoken before of the apostles of our Lord Jesus Christ. To hold fast these words and remember them is the great need in the days of apostasy. Peter bears the same witness (2 Peter 3:1-3). Building yourselves up on your most holy faith is the next exhortation. Nothing else is worth while building up for believers living in the last days. Prayer is needed. But it is not prayer *for* the Holy Spirit, for another Pentecost, which is nowhere promised, nor for another baptism with the Spirit, but it is prayer *in* the Spirit. The exhortation "Keep yourselves in the love of God" means to keep oneself in the consciousness in that fellowship with the Father and with the Son of which John speaks in his first epistle, that is enjoying the love of God in Christ Jesus our Lord. Looking for the mercy of our Lord Jesus Christ unto eternal life, which means, looking for Himself, for His coming. The final exhortations give instructions as to the believer's attitude towards those who have been led away.

VII. The Conclusion

Verses 24-25. "Now unto Him that is able to keep you from stumbling, and to present you faultless before the presence of His glory with exceeding joy, to the only wise God our Saviour, be glory and majesty, dominion and power, both now and ever. Amen."

Beautiful doxology with which this Epistle ends! His own are being kept in the evil days with which the age closes. They are the preserved in Jesus Christ kept for Him. And while we wait for Him, He is able to keep us not only from falling, but from stumbling. And then comes that day in which He will present His own, His beloved people, whom He bought by His own precious blood. He will present them faultless before the presence of His glory with exceeding joy. And what a day of joy and gladness, as well as of glory, it will be, when He shall see the travail of His soul and will be satisfied, the day in which He will present to Himself a glorious Church, not having spot or wrinkle, or any such thing; but that it should be holy and without blame! (Ephes. 5:27)

THE
REVELATION

Introduction

This great final Book of the Word of God may well be called the capstone of the entire Bible. A pyramid becomes a pyramid by the great capstone, and the Bibles becomes the full and complete revelation of God through this document "The Revelation of Jesus Christ." If this book were not in the Bible, the Bible would be an unfinished book; the issues raised in the preceding documents would be forever unsolved.

This disposes at once of the miserable attempts which have been made by critics and others to eliminate the book of Revelation from the canon of the New Testament. Revelation is a necessity. "A book which offers in some way or other to open up those secrets of God which yet lie hidden in the future, seems wholly in place in our sacred Scriptures. It is towards some such book that our thoughts have been moving as we travelled through the Gospels, the Acts and Epistles; for all alike point forward to a consummation of all things, to a time when the kingdom of God shall be finally and completely established, when all creation shall cease to groan and travail, when the inheritance of which we have received the first fruits shall be wholly ours. It is, moreover, towards some such book that our hearts seem to yearn as we travel through the earlier volumes of experience, discovering the contradictions between what should be and what is, accumulating impressions of the Protean forms and tremendous power of wickedness, and craving for the manifestation of triumphant righteousness. Thus both the Christian Bible and the Christian consciousness seem to demand a book of revelation for their completion or satisfaction" (C. Anderson Scott).

The Authorship

The title of the book as we find it in the King James Version is "The Revelation of St. John the Divine"; the better title would be to take the opening words of the book and call it "The Revelation of Jesus Christ." But the above title tells us that John is the author. This is confirmed by the book itself, for we read twice in the first chapter that the writer says "John to the seven churches," and again, "I, John, who also am your brother" (1:4, 9). Furthermore, at the close of the book he names himself again: "And I, John, saw these things" (22:8). The Church down to the middle of the third century has but one testimony as to the authorship of this book, and that is, the Johannine, that John, the beloved disciple, the son of Zebedee, wrote this book in the isle of Patmos when banished there. The only exceptions were the Alogians, a heretical sect which also rejected the Gospel of John, and a controversialist by name of Caius.

As it is of much interest to be acquainted with the testimony of the many early witnesses in refutation of the destructive critics, who attack this great book, we give a brief summary of these historical evidences.

The first witness is *Justin Martyr,* who wrote about the year 140 in the *Dialogue,* "that a certain man, whose name was John, one of the apostles of Christ, prophesied in an apocalypse (revelation) which came to him that believers should reign a thousand years in Jerusalem." *Melito,* Bishop of Sardis, according to the historian Eusebius, wrote treatises on "the devil and on the Apocalypse of John." This was about the year 170. Then follow the testimonies of *Theophilus,* Bishop of Antioch (180); and *Apollonius.*

A greater witness still is Irenaeus. We remind the reader of our introduction to the Gospel of John, and call to mind the fact that Irenaeus was in his youth acquainted with Polycarp, who was a disciple of the Apostle John. A number of times Irenaeus speaks of "Ioannes Domini disciplus" —John the disciple of the Lord—and that he had written the Apocalypse. *Tertullian* (about 200 A.D.) refers in his writings four times to the Revelation as being the work of the Apostle John. The so-called *Muratorian* fragments quote from the Revelation, and it can be shown by the context of the passage that the Apostle John was believed to be author.

Clement of Alexandria (about 200 A.D.) mentions also John, the beloved disciple as the writer of the book. A scholar of Clement was *Origen* (233 A.D.). He made careful research about the canonicity and genuineness of the books of the New Testament. While he reported carefully any doubts or disputes about different books, he has nothing to say about the Revelation and its author. He quotes from the book frequently, and it proves that in his time no question was raised about John being the author. *Hippolytus,* Bishop of Ostia (240 A.D.) quotes John's words many times and does not leave us in doubt that he means the son of Zebedee.

Then follow a host of witnesses. The first commentator, as far as we know, of the Revelation was Bishop *Victorinus.* He states positively that the Apostle John wrote the Revelation (about 303 A.D.). *Ephrem Syrus* (about 378), the greatest scholar in the Syrian church, repeatedly in his numerous writings, cites the Revelation as canonical and ascribes it to the Apostle John. The Syrian translation of the Bible, the Peshito, probably made in the second century, does not contain the book of Revelation, yet Ephrem Syrus possessed the Syrian translation. Scholars who have examined this question say that the Peshito in its original version had the book of Revelation, and that it was later detached, while others advanced the theory that the Peshito translation may have been made in the first century when the Apocalypse was not yet generally known.

After citing many more witnesses, including Athanasius, Gregory of Nyssa, Ambrose, Augustine and others, Dean Alford says: "The apostolic authorship rests on the firmest ground. We have it assured to us by one who had companied men who had known St. John himself; we have it held in continuous succession by Fathers in all parts of the Church. Nowhere, in primitive times, does there appear any counter-tradition on the subject."

The First Critic

This unquestionable historical evidence of the Johannine authorship of the Apocalypse was first attacked by Dionysius, the disciple of Origen and Bishop of Alexandria. In the second half of the third century this scholar raised his voice against the solid traditional view, declaring that not the same man could have written the fourth Gospel, the Epistles of John and Revelation. He also pointed out the contrast between the language, the grammar, and the diction of the Apocalypse and the other writings of the Apostle John. He suggested another man by name of John, a presbyter of Ephesus, as the author of the Revelation. He spoke of two tombs in Ephesus, one in which the body of the apostle was buried and in the other John the presbyter. But Dionysius spoke of this John the presbyter, yet he was entirely unknown to him. It was a new idea he invented to back up his contention, for such a person was wholly unknown to the ecclesiastical tradition in the church of Alexandria in the middle of the third century. Nor does it appear that his opinion on the authorship of the Revelation made any permanent impression on the Alexandrian church. That this "John the presbyter" is a fictitious person, who never existed, is fully demonstrated by the entire, the complete disappearance of John the presbyter from the memory of the Church of the second century.

But modern critics like Bleek, Duesterdieck, Ewald, and others have seized upon this man of straw and followed the invention of Dionysius about the two Johns. Other critics have gone a step further and reject wholly the tradition that the Apostle John lived and died in Ephesus, thus making the other John the sole outstanding bearer of the name in that community, ascribing to him not only the book of Revelation but also the fourth Gospel. Modern critics reject the Johannine authorship of the Revelation. They hold that a work of small compass, by somebody, nobody knows who wrote it, was worked over by somebody else, then expanded by somebody else, passing through three or four redactions till it took on the form of the book we call "The Revelation." They also claim that at best the Revelation is "a Christian redaction of a Jewish apocalypse."

The book also received a strange treatment from the different reformers. Luther for a time treated the Revelation with suspicion and questioned its inspiration; later he greatly modified this opinion. Zwingli followed the theory of Dionysius and attributed it to another John; he excluded it from the Bible. Calvin, however, believed in its canonicity and upheld the apostolic authorship. Melanchthon did the same.

All the criticism has not affected in the least the truth that John, the Apostle, the author of the Gospel of John and The Epistles, is the author also of the book of Revelation. The fact is, the Holy Spirit seems to have taken special care to preserve such historical evidences for the Revelation of Jesus Christ, which makes the true authorship and date unimpeachable.

"The apostolic authorship and canonicity of the Apocalypse were generally accepted, and went unchallenged, until toward the third century. Then contrary views began to make their appearance. But when the evidence, direct and indirect, on either side is weighed in respect of its date, its quantity, its quality, its freedom from bias, the external evidence in favor of the Johannine authorship, outweighs the other at every point."

The Date of the Book

It is interesting to find that the modern critics have done the opposite with the date of the book of Revelation from what they have done with the other Bible books. They generally fix the date of a book later than the traditional view holds; but they assign to the Apocalypse an earlier date than that which the Church has held in the past. Some have dated it during the reign of Nero. They do so on account of some particular interpretation of certain historical allusions. Of late some of the critics have adopted the later date, the year 96 A.D., that is, the traditional view held from the beginning. Irenaeus, the friend of Polycarp, who knew John, stated about the year 180 that "the Revelation was seen at Patmos at the end of Domitian's reign." Domitian reigned from 81 to 96 A.D. Then Clement of Alexandria left the testimony behind that John returned from his exile to the island of Patmos on the death of the emperor, which was Emperor Domitian, in the year 96. This is the correct date.

The Message and Interpretation

Revelation is marked out in the beginning as a book of prophecy (1:3). Of this we have more to say in the Preface and Key to Revelation, which follows this introduction. Furthermore, the book is in greater part written in symbolical language, which is a very important fact to be remembered in the interpretation. The message is prophetic, and this message is clothed in symbols, which are not difficult to interpret. Our analysis will show that the accusation brought against this book, as being disjointed, a veritable chaos, is wholly unfounded. Like all the other books of the Word of God it has a perfect arrangement.

There are three modes of interpreting this book, with its prophecies and symbols. The *historical* interpretation claims that the book covers the entire history of the Church and pictures the antagonism of the forces of evil in the world against the church. This method was in vogue during the Reformation period and for several centuries down to the nineteenth, especially during the Napoleonic upheavels, it was the acknowledged method of interpretation. It still has supporters. The Reformators saw in the Antichrist, the beast, the pope and the Romish church. Luther was very strong on that. On the other side, the Catholic exegetes, who also employed the same method, branded Protestantism as the Antichrist, and discovered that the mysterious 666 was contained in the name of Dr. Martin Luther. Then Napoleon was seen by believers living toward the end of the eighteenth and the beginning of the nineteenth centuries as fulfilling the thirteenth chapter in Revelation. Many predictions were made and the different numbers, the three years and a half, etc., applied to the stirring history of that time, just the same as men today are trying to figure out the duration of the "times of the Gentiles," and when certain events must occur.

The *Preterist* School of interpretation teaches that the greater part of the prophecies of this book have been fulfilled in the past in the struggles of the past, especially with the struggle of the Church with the Roman Empire, and that the victory of the Church as foretold in the book is accomplished. The third school is the so-called *Futurist.* This method of interpretation is the only satisfying one and in full harmony with the entire Prophetic Word. We follow this method in our annotations. Nothing beyond the third chapter of this book is fulfilled; all is still future, this is the claim of the Futurist school. The two chapters in which the word "Church" is exclusively found in Revelation (chapters 2 and 3) contain the prophecy concerning the Church on earth. This divinely given history of the Church is about finished and the predicted events from chapter 4 to the end of Revelation are yet to be accomplished. Chapters 5—19 contain the specific prophecy of the end of the age, the last seven years, the unfulfilled 70th week of Daniel's great prophecy. The scripturalness of this interpretation will be readily discovered by reading the "Preface and Key to Revelation."

There are other theories of interpretation. One of them is the Judaizing interpretation of the late Dr. Bullinger, who taught that nothing is fulfilled in the Apocalypse, that the seven churches in Asia are yet to come into existence. We request our readers and students of the Word to study carefully the article which follows this introduction and the analysis of the book.

PREFACE AND KEY TO THE REVELATION

"The Revelation of Jesus Christ, which God gave unto Him." This is the first sentence with which this last book in God's Word begins. The best title therefore is, "The Revelation of Jesus Christ." Our Lord received, according to this opening statement, a revelation from God. This must be understood in connection with Himself as the Son of Man. As the Only-Begotten He had no need of a revelation; in His deity He is acquainted with all the eternal purposes. One with God He knows the end from the beginning. But He, who is very God, took on in incarnation the form of a servant, and thus being in fashion as a man, He humbled Himself (Phil. 2:7-8). And as the Man who had passed through death, whom God raised from the dead, and exalted at His own right hand, God gave Him this revelation concerning the judgment of the earth and the glory of Himself. "God raised Him from the dead and gave Him glory" (1 Peter 1:21). What this glory is which He received from God is fully and blessedly revealed in this book. It is the revelation of His acquired glory and how this glory is to be manifested in connection with the earth. And this revelation He makes known to His servants, because His own are sharers with Him in all He received from God.

Pre-eminently His Revelation

The Revelation is pre-eminently His revelation; the revelation of His person and His glory. "In the volume of the book it is written of Me . . . " (Heb. 10:7) Martin Luther asked, "What Book and what person?" and answered, "There is only one Book—the Bible; and only one Person—Jesus Christ." The whole Book, the Word of God, bears witness of Him, Who is the living Word. He is the center, the sum total and the substance of the Holy Scriptures. The prayerful reader of the Bible will never read in vain if he approaches the blessed Book with the one desire to know Christ and His glory. His blessed face is seen on every page and the infallible Guide, the Holy Spirit, never fails to satisfy the longing of the believer's heart to know more of Christ. Inasmuch as this last Bible book is the Revelation of Jesus Christ, an "unveiling" of Himself, we find in it the completest revelation of His person and His glory.

It is here where many expositions of Revelation have missed the mark. Occupied chiefly with the symbols of the book, the mysteries, the judgments and the promised consummation, they have neglected to emphasize sufficiently Him, who throughout this book is pre-eminently the center of everything. The reader of Revelation does well to read first of all through the entire book with this object in mind, to see what is said of our Lord, of His person, His present and His future glory.

We shall find all the features of His person and His work mentioned. He is the Alpha and Omega, the first and the last (1:11); the Ancient of Days (1:14 compare with Daniel 7:9); the "I Am," that is, Jehovah, "I am He that liveth" (1:18); the Son of God (2:18). These terms speak of His deity. His earthly life in humiliation is touched upon in the statement, "the Faithful Witness" (1:5). His death on the cross is likewise mentioned—"He hath washed us from our sins in His blood" (1:5); "He was dead" (1:18); "the Lamb as it had been slain" (5:6); "worthy is the Lamb that was slain" (5:12). He is mentioned twenty-eight times as the Lamb in Revelation and each time it reminds us of the cross and the great work accomplished there. His resurrection is seen for He is called, "the First-begotten from the dead" (1:5), and He speaks of Himself as, "He that was dead, and, behold, I am alive forevermore" (1:18); and again, "these things saith the first and the last, who was dead and is alive" (2:8).

Then we behold Him "in the midst" in glory, seen face to face by all the redeemed and worshipped by them, as well as by the heavenly hosts and ultimately by every creature, the fulfillment of Phil. 2:10-11, "that at the name of Jesus every knee should bow, of things in heaven, and things on earth and things under the earth, and that every tongue should confess that Jesus Christ is Lord, to the glory of God the Father" (Rev. 5:13-14). After the fifth chapter we have His revelation as the executor of the decreed judgments. He opens the seals; He sends forth the seven angels with the judgment trumpets and the seven angels with the judgment vials, in which the wrath of God is completed. "The Father judgeth no man, but has committed all judgment unto the Son" (John 5:22). Then He is seen in the glorious union with the bride (19:7-10) and as the victorious Christ who passeth out of heaven followed by the armies of heaven (19:11-21), conquering the opposing forces of evil, executing the wrath of Almighty God, appearing as King of Kings and Lord of Lords. The twentieth chapter reveals Him as the reigning Christ. He and His saints with Him will reign over the earth for a thousand years. And all which follows reveals Him and His glory as well as the blessed and eternal results of His work.

A Book of Prophecy

Aside from the title of the book, which indicates that it deals with things future, there is a direct statement which determines its prophetic character. In the first beatitude of the seven which are found in the book, we read that it is a book of prophecy—"Blessed is he that readeth, and they that hear the words of this prophecy" (1:3). It is known to every intelligent student of the Bible that a good part of it is prophecy. The great prophecies concerning the people Israel and the nations of the world are found in the Old Testament Scriptures. In the New Testament there is but one book of Prophecy, the Revelation. As it is the capstone of the entire revelation of God, without which the Bible would be an unfinished book, we find in its pages the consummation of the great prophecies which were given by the prophets of God in Old Testament times.

For the study of this New Testament prophetic book, the knowledge of the chief content of the Old Testament Prophetic Word is therefore an absolute necessity. For instance, to a Christian who does not have a fair grasp of Daniel's great prophecies, or is ignorant of the place which the people Israel hold in the purposes of God, the book of Revelation is a sealed book, without any possible meaning. This is one of the chief reasons why this book has suffered so much both from the critics and from the hands of commentators. The Apostle Peter saith, "Knowing this first, that no prophecy of the Scripture is of any private interpretation. For the prophecy came not in old time by the will of man, but holy men of God spake as they were moved by the Holy Spirit" (2 Peter 1:20-21). The better translation for "private interpretation" is, "its own interpretation." It means that the interpretation of prophecy must be done by comparing Scripture with Scripture. The holy men of God, the prophets, were the instruments of the Holy Spirit and made known God's purposes in a progressive way. To understand any prophecy is only possible by taking the entire Prophetic Word into consideration. That there is a wonderful harmony in the great body of prophetic dispensational truths as found in the Bible we have demonstrated in another volume. (*Harmony of the Prophetic Word* has been used under God's blessing to open the minds of many to the meaning of prophecy.) This principle finds its strongest application in the interpretation of the Revelation.

The Three Classes

In 1 Corinthians 10:32 the Apostle Paul speaks of three classes into which the human race is divided: the Jews, the Gentiles, and the Church of God. In the Old Testament there was no Church of God, for the Church is a New Testament institution. As the Revelation is the book of consummation these three classes must be seen in the contents of this book. Many expositors have seen nothing but the struggles of the Church in her history in this book. This is true of the so-called Preterist school and also of the Historical school of interpretation. The Preterist school teaches a fulfillment of all the apocalyptic visions in the struggles of the Church in the past. The Historical school also teaches that the visions concern mostly the Church. These schools of interpretation leave out the Jews and what is written concerning them and their final history during the end of the age, preceding the glorious appearing of our Lord. Of late another school of interpreters has come into existence. They teach that the entire book of Revelation concerns the Jewish people and that there is nothing about the Church in this last book of the Bible. Any interpretation of Revelation which ignores the Jews, the people Israel and fulfillment of Old Testament predictions concerning them is wrong. And any interpretation which teaches that there is nothing about the Church in Revelation is equally wrong. The Church and her destiny on earth, the destiny of the true Church and the destiny of the apostate Church, or Christendom, is found in the book. The Jews and what concerns them in the end of the age, the Gentiles, the nations of the earth, and the judgments in store for them, as well as the future of the earth, a future of glory and blessing: all this is recorded in our New Testament book of prophecy.

The True Interpretation

There is a true interpretation of Revelation which is in harmony with all previous prophecies and which opens the book to our understanding. But how are we to find this true interpretation? We answer, the book itself furnishes it. This is an important fact, both convincing and conclusive. It is therefore of no profit to examine the different theories and schools of interpretation. We shall avoid the terms Preterist, Historical and Futurist, and not try, as it has been attempted, to reconcile these different modes of interpretation. There must be one true interpretation, and we claim that this is given to us by the Lord Himself in this book.

The Key Which Fits

It has often been truthfully said, every book in the Bible contains a key which unlocks the book. The Revelation is no exception. John the beloved disciple was in banishment in the isle of Patmos, as Daniel the man greatly beloved, was a captive in Babylon. The Lord called these two great servants to behold the panorama of the future. Both wrote down their visions. While in the book of Daniel we find no direct command to write, we find such a command in the first chapter of Revelation. John received divine instruction how to write the Revelation. We find this in the nineteenth verse, "Write therefore what thou hast seen, and the things that are, and the things that are about to be after these." (This is the correct translation of this important verse.) John, guided by the Holy Spirit then wrote the Revelation according to the divine direction. In examining this command to write we find that three things are mentioned. He is to write first the things he had seen, then the things which are, and finally the things that are about to be after these. When John received these instructions he had already seen something and the vision he had he was instructed to write down. Then present things, the things which are, and future things, to be after present things have passed away, must be located in this book. So we have the past, the present and the future in this key verse.

Three Divisions—Where are They

It is then clear that the book of Revelation must be divided into three main divisions. How are we to locate these divisions? They are marked, so that we are not left in doubt about it. In the beginning of the fourth chapter we find a significant statement which shows where the third division begins. After these things, that is after the contents of the opening three chapters were past, John heard the same voice speaking to him once more. He sees a door opened in heaven and is told, "Come up hither, and I will shew thee the things which must take place after these things" (4:1). There can be no doubt at all that with the fourth chapter the seer beheld the things which take place after the preceding things which are, have passed away. The third division of Revelation begins with the fourth chapter. John beholds future things from heaven into which he had been taken "in the Spirit." The things he had seen and the things which are, are therefore contained in the first three chapters of the book.

The first chapter contains the things he had seen. "What thou seest write in a book" was the first instruction John received (verse 11). In the nineteenth verse he is told, "Write therefore what thou has seen." Between verse 11 and verse 19 he saw a vision, which he was to write, and this vision constitutes the first section or division of the book. The second and third chapters form the second division, the things which are. The beginning of the fourth chapter to the end of the book is the final, the third division. There is no better and more logical key. And this key given in the book determines the true interpretation.

The Patmos Vision

"The thing thou has seen"—the first section of Revelation is the great Patmos vision, chapter 1:12-18. It is the vision of the glorified Son of Man in the midst of the seven golden candlesticks (or lampstands).

The Things Which Are

The things which are, the present things, begin the prophetic section of the Revelation. The second and third chapters of Revelation, the things which are, contain the messages of our Lord addressed to the seven churches of Asia Minor. These messages contain the first great prophecy of Revelation. The prophecy concerns the Church on earth. We shall show in our comment on these two chapters that we have in them a divine history of the Church on earth. It is one of the most remarkable sections of the Prophetic Word. What this present age is to be religiously and how it will end is made known in other parts of the New Testament. Our Lord in some of His kingdom parables (Matthew 13) reveals the characteristics of this age. The parables of the sower, the evil seed sown into the field, the mustard seed parable and the parable of the leaven are prophetic and teach, in part at least, what the Church messages reveal. The Holy Spirit in the Epistolar testimony also reveals the religious and moral characteristics of the age, and depicts its departure from the truth, and its end. The destiny of the true Church is heavenly. She has a "blessed hope," which is to be with the Lord in glory. She is the body of Christ, and He is the "Head of the body." The Church is also the bride of Christ and He is the Bridegroom. The body is united to the Head in Glory; the bride will be joined to the Bridegroom. 1 Thessalonians 4:13-18 is the Scripture which reveals this end for the true Church on earth.

The professing Church, Christendom, which rejects the doctrine of Christ and goes into apostasy has a far different destiny. The Lord will disown that which has denied His Name, and judgment and wrath is to be poured out upon apostate Christendom (2 Thess. 1:7-9). These predictions concerning the Church on earth are contained in the seven Church messages. When we come to the close of the third chapter we find a significant promise, and equally significant threat. "I also will keep thee from the hour of temptation (trial) which shall come upon all the world to try them that dwell upon the earth" (3:10). This is the promise. It tells of the removal of the true Church, composed of all true believers, from this earthly scene. "I will spew thee out of My mouth" (3:16). This is the threat to the apostate Church. Both the promise and the threat will be fulfilled. After the third chapter the word 'church' does not occur again in Revelation. The reason for this is obvious. The history of the Church on earth terminates with the close of the third chapter. Because the true Church is no longer here but has been taken up into glory, and that which professes to be the Church is disowned by the Lord, therefore no more mention of the Church is made in Revelation.

The Things Which Are After These

The future things, things after the removal of the true Church from the earth, occupy the greater part of this book. It is of the greatest importance to see that nothing whatever after the third chapter of Revelation has yet taken place. Some speak of a past and partial fulfillment of some of the visions found in this section. In view of the scope of the book that is impossible. The open door in heaven, the voice which calls the seer to pass through that open door into heaven, is symbolical of the great coming event, the realization of the blessed hope of the coming of the Lord for His saints. That this open door is mentioned immediately after the third chapter and John is suddenly in the spirit in the presence of the throne in heaven is very significant. It proves that the entire situation is now changed. And the first great vision is a vision of the saints in glory occupying thrones and worshipping God and the Lamb. With the sixth chapter the great judgment visions of this book begin. These great punitive dealings with the earth are executed from above. All transpires after the Lord has taken His saints into glory. No seal can be broken as long as this event has not been. But after the rapture, the seals of the book, which the Lamb received, are broken by Him, the trumpet and the vial judgments fall upon the earth. All this takes place after the home-going of the true Church and before the glorious appearing of our Lord Jesus Christ (19:11, etc.).

Now this portion of Revelation from chapter 6 to 19 contains the events which transpire during the end of the age. It is the unfulfilled seventieth week of the great prophecy in the book of Daniel (Dan. 9:24-27). This "end of the age" will last twice 1260 days, that is seven years. It is absolutely necessary to understand the scope of the seventy-week prophecy in Daniel in order to understand the greater part of these chapters in the Revelation. (*The Prophetic Daniel* by A. C. G. contains a very simple exegesis of Daniel's prophecies.) We are led back upon Jewish ground. Events in connection with the Jewish people and Jerusalem are before us. The times of the Gentiles have taken on their final form of ten kingdoms which Daniel saw on the fourth beast as ten horns, and Nebuchadnezzar on the image as ten toes. The empire in which these ten kingdoms come into existence is the Roman empire. It will have a revival and come into existence again. Then a wicked leader will take the headship of that resurrected Roman empire, and another beast, the false prophet, the Antichrist will domineer over the Jewish people and persecute their saints, the remnant of Israel, while the earth and the dwellers upon the earth experience the great judgments. The last half of these seven years is called the great tribulation. We must also remember that our Lord left behind a great prophecy concerning the end of the age. This prophecy is contained in the Olivet Discourse, the first part of which (Matt. 24:4-44) harmonizes in a striking manner with the events in Revelation 6—19. Our Lord calls special attention to Daniel and likewise speaks of the great tribulation. In our brief annotations we shall point out some of the interesting and convincing details.

The glorious climax is the visible manifestation of the Lord out of heaven, crowned with many crowns, the defeat and overthrow of the beast and the kings of the earth and their armies, the binding of Satan, and the reign of Christ with His saints for a thousand years. (Compare Revelation 19:11-21 with Daniel 7:11-

14 and Matthew 24:27-31.) After that follows the great white throne judgment, which is the judgment of the wicked dead, the glories of the new Jerusalem, the eternal destiny of the redeemed and the eternal destiny of the lost.

If this last great book of the Bible is studied in this divinely given order it will no longer be, as is so often said, a sealed book. All fanciful interpretations and applications of these great visions to past or present history can no longer be maintained as soon as we reckon with the fact that these visions are not yet fulfilled, and are going to be fulfilled after the true church is no longer on the earth.

The Promised Blessing

"Blessed is he that readeth, and they that hear the words of this prophecy, and keep those things which are written therein, for the time is at hand" (verse 3). A blessing is promised to him who readeth, and who hears and keeps. It does not say that a blessing is for him who understands and knows everything which is in this book. If such were the condition the writer and reader would have no claim on this promised blessing. The Bible teacher, or any other man, who says he knows and understands everything found in this great finale of God's Word is very much mistaken. We cannot be sure about everything in some of these visions and the full meaning of some may not be understood till the world sees the fulfillment. The blessing is promised to all His people who give attention to the Revelation of Jesus Christ. What is the blessing we may expect through the reading and prayerful study of the words of this prophecy?

First of all we receive through this book a wonderful vision of our Saviour and Lord. This is what we need as His people above everything else, and it is this which brings blessing into our lives. As stated before, this book is pre-eminently His revelation, a blessed unveiling of His person and glory. But we also get another blessing. In reading through this book we see what is in store for this age, what judgments will overtake the world, and how Satan's power will be manifested to the full upon those who rejected His grace. Judgment, tribulation and wrath are swiftly coming upon this age. Out of all this our gracious Lord has delivered us. There is no judgment, no wrath for us who know Him as our sinbearer and our hiding-place. Praise must fill our hearts when we read the words of this prophecy and remember the grace which has saved us from all which is coming upon this age. Another blessing is the assurance of ultimate victory and glory. Dark is the age, and becoming darker, but in Revelation we behold the glory which is coming for His saints first of all and after the judgment clouds are gone, for Jerusalem, the nations and the earth. Reading Revelation fills the heart with the assurance and certainty of the outcome of all. It is a solemn atmosphere which fills the whole book of Revelation. As we continue to read and continue to breathe this heavenly and solemn atmosphere it will result in a closer walk with God, a more spiritual worship and a greater and more unselfish service for Him "Who loveth us and hath washed us from our sins in His own blood, and hath made us priests and kings unto God His Father."

The Division of the Revelation

Title: The Revelation of Jesus Christ

I. THE PATMOS VISION OF THE GLORIFIED SON OF MAN (1)

II. THE THINGS WHICH ARE. THE SEVEN CHURCH MESSAGES REVEALING THE HISTORY OF THE CHURCH ON EARTH (2—3)

III. THE THINGS WHICH ARE AFTER THESE, THE END OF THE AGE, THE CONSUMMATION AND THE FINAL MESSAGES (4—22)

First Division: The Heavenly Scene and Before the Throne (4—5)

Second Division: The Opening of the Seven Seals (6—8:5)

Between the Sixth and Seventh Seal: A Parenthetical Vision (7)

Third Division: The Sounding of the Seven Trumpets (8:6—11:18)

Between the Sixth and Seventh Trumpets: Parenthetical Visions (10—11:14)

Fourth Division: Satan's Power and Satan's Masterpieces (11:19—13)

Fifth Division: The Power of God in Intervention: Grace and Judgment Manifested (14)

Sixth Division: The Seven Angels Having Seven Plagues and the Vials of Wrath (15—16)

Between the Sixth and Seventh Vial, Parenthetical Vision (16:13-16)
Seventh Division: The Great Harlot, Babylon, and her Judgment (17—18)
Eighth Division: The Manifestation of the King and the Millennium (19—20:6)
Ninth Division: After the Thousand Years and the Vision of the New Jerusalem (20:7—22:5)
Tenth Division: The Final Messages (22:6-21)

Analysis and Annotations

I. The Patmos Vision of the Glorified Son of Man

CHAPTER 1

1. The introduction (1:1-3)
2. Greeting and benediction (1:4-5)
3. The praise (1:6-7)
4. The testimony of the Almighty (1:8)
5. John in Patmos (1:9-11)
6. The vision of Christ in glory (1:12-16)
7. The commission (1:17-21)

Verses 1-3. The book does not contain "revelations" but it is one great revelation, "The Revelation of Jesus Christ." The third verse is of much importance. It pronounces a blessing upon all who read and hear the words of this prophecy and who keep the things that are written therein. Here, as already stated, we read that the Revelation is a great prophecy.

Verses 4-5. The churches addressed were in the Province of Asia. (See Acts 16:6; 19:10.) The words of greeting "Grace and peace unto you" tell of the two great possessions of the Church. Though the professing Church may fail in her testimony, grace and peace, even in the dark days of apostasy, will never fail. In the greeting here Jehovah-God, the great "I am"—Who is, Who was and Who is to come—stands first. Then follows the Holy Spirit in His own completeness and His diverse activities, spoken of as "the seven Spirits." And finally the name of our Lord. "He is the faithful witness," who lived as such in holiness and perfect obedience on earth. "The First-Begotten from the dead"; He died that shameful death on the cross and God raised Him from the dead. "The Prince of the kings of the earth." This is His future title and glory.

Verses 6-7. This is a true glory-song. It contains the blessed gospel of grace. What He has done for us; what He has made us; and what we shall be with Him. It is the first doxology in this book. See the swelling praise and worship two-fold, three-fold, four-fold and seven-fold in chapters 4:11; 5:13; 7:12. And then for the first time in this book His personal, visible and glorious coming is announced.

Verse 8. God, so to speak, puts His seal upon it. The words of the preceding verse, "Even so, Amen," must be read with this verse. The speaker is Jehovah, the Almighty.

Verses 9-11. John was in banishment in the Isle of Patmos. Patmos is a small rocky isle, and about ten miles long and six wide. According to ancient tradition this island was used as a place of exile for offenders who belonged to the better classes. John was exiled on account of his faithful witness to the Word of God and the testimony of Jesus. He came to be in the Spirit on the Lord's Day. Does this mean "the day of the Lord," that is, the day of His visible manifestation, or does it mean He was in the Spirit on the Lord's Day, the first day of the week? Dr. Bullinger teaches that the Lord's day means "the day of the Lord" (Isa. 2:12), and says: "John was not in a state of spiritual exaltation on any particular Sunday at Patmos, as the result of which he saw visions and dreamed dreams. But as we are told he found himself by the Spirit in the day of the Lord." But this view is not correct. It is not the prophetic day of the Lord, but the Lord's day, the day which the early Church from the beginning celebrated as the day of His resurrection. In Corinthians we read of "the Lord's Supper" in the same way as "the Lord's Day" is used here. Nor could John have been projected to the day of the Lord when his first message given to him by the glorified Christ concerned the church and her history on earth.

Verses 12-16. A voice had spoken, as of a trumpet telling him to write in a book what he was about to see and to send the message to the seven churches. And as he turned he beheld the greatest vision human eyes have ever seen. He saw seven golden candlesticks (lampstands); these represent the seven churches (verse 20) and are symbolical of the whole Church. "In the midst," John saw one "like unto a Son of Man." But He is more than Man, He is the Ancient of Days as well as Son of Man, the Alpha and the Omega, in His humiliation and in His exaltation. He was the Son of Man on earth; He is the Son of Man in glory. When He comes back to earth and receives the kingdom, He will receive it as Son of Man to judge the earth in righteousness.

Here we behold Him in His judicial character. The robe down to His feet expresses His dignity as the King-Priest, who is about to enter upon His future work. The golden girdle is symbolical of His divine righteousness. His white head and hair identify Him with the person whom Daniel saw sitting in judgment (Dan. 7:9-12). The flaming eyes, the fiery burning feet, the voice like the sound of many waters, the two-edged sword, all are symbolical of His glory and character.

There is one feature of the vision which needs an explanation. What do the seven stars mean, which are in the right hand of the Son of Man? Verse 20 gives the answer. They are the seven angels of the seven churches. Angels and stars are symbolical figures. The application of these terms to church-officers or bishops and pastors is incorrect. Stars are used in scripture to typify true believers. Stars are heavenly bodies which shine during the night; so are true believers in a heavenly position with the responsibility to shine in the night. The lampstands represent the visible, professing Church; the stars represent the true believing element in the Church. They are in the right hand of Himself, held securely there. Furthermore, only true believers have an ear to hear what the Spirit saith. The stars are called angels, because an angel is a messenger and true believers are likewise that.

Verses 17-20. John fell at His feet as dead. Compare with Daniel 10:4-11. The vision was overpowering. But graciously His hand rests upon His prostrated disciple, the same who once leaned upon His bosom, and he hears the blessed words His people know and love so well, "Fear not!" Once more He bears witness as to Himself. He is "He that liveth," the Jehovah, the Self-existing One; He was dead; He died the sinner's death and won the victory. He is alive forevermore; as the Risen One He has the key of Hades and of death. Then follows the commission which the reader finds fully explained in the Preface and Key to Revelation.

II. The Things Which Are, The Seven Church Messages, and Their Prophetic Meaning

CHAPTER 2

1. Ephesus: The post-apostolic period (2:1-7)
2. Smyrna: The period of persecution (2:8-11)
3. Pergamos: The corruption period (2:12-17)
4. Thyatira: The Romish corruption (2:18-29)

The two chapters which follow the introductory chapter contain seven messages to seven local churches which were in existence in the province of Asia in the days when the Apostle John was prisoner in the Isle of Patmos. The view held by the late Dr. Bullinger and a few of his followers that these churches are yet to come into existence in connection with believing Jews during the great tribulation with which the age closes, must be rejected as extremely fanciful. The omniscient Lord on the throne detected in each of these local assemblies certain traits which at different periods of His church on earth would become the leading features. We have therefore, in the seven messages the history of the entire Church in embryo. This assertion is fully confirmed by a closer study of these messages.

Verses 1-7. Ephesus was the church characterized by the greatest purity in doctrine and in walk. To the Ephesians, as "the faithful brethren in Christ," was addressed the most wonderful revelation God has given to man. It stands therefore for the model church in the apostolic age. But when Paul said farewell to the elders he predicted not smooth things, but the incoming failure (Acts 20). Ephesus means "desired" and that corresponds with her original holy character. He reveals Himself afresh as being in the midst and holding His own in His blessed pierced hands, so true of believers at all times. The descriptions of Ephesus suit the apostolic church, and immediately after the apostles had passed away, except John. But He finds fault with it. His omniscient eyes look to the heart and there He finds declension. "I have against thee that thou leavest thy first love." He, the one altogether lovely was no longer the all absorbing object before their hearts. Paul manifests the full meaning of first love. His constant cry was: "Not I but Christ"—"That I may know Him"; for him to live was Christ. Declension began in the church not with less service, less suffering or anything else, but with a decreasing heart-devotion to the Person of our Lord. That is where all backsliding begins. He calls to repentance, a return to Himself. The Nicolaitanes, whose works the church then hated, are mentioned again in the third message, where we shall define the word and the teaching of the Nicolaitanes. A promise to the overcomer follows.

Verses 8-11. Smyrna means "bitterness" and is a form of myrrh which was largely used for the embalming of the dead. When the wise men brought myrrh to the child, the new-born king of the Jews, the meaning of it was that the King would have to die. Smyrna was a suffering church, many of its members had to seal their faith by dying the martyr's death. Corresponding with this characteristic, the Lord speaks of Himself as "The First and the Last, who was dead and is alive." That is His comfort for the Church passing through the horrors of persecution and intense sufferings. In connection with this message to Smyrna the synagogue of Satan is mentioned. It means the Judaistic faction of the church, who, while they claimed to be Christians, also claimed to be Jews, observing the law, the Sabbath day and other parts of the legal system of Judaism. This synagogue of Satan helped in the afflictions of Smyrna. Nor is the same "synagogue of Satan" missing today in the professing sphere of Christendom.

He announces that the devil would cast some of them into prison, that they should have tribulation for ten days, and that it would require faithfulness unto death to gain the crown of life. The Apostolic age was followed by the martyr age, which lasted up to the beginning of the fourth century. Pagan emperors under the inspiration of Satan, the roaring lion, persecuted the Church. No one knows how many hundreds of thousands died the martyr's death, flayed and burned alive, cast before wild animals and cruelly tortured; thus they were faithful unto death and gained the crown of life. It is also significant that the address to Smyrna contains the number ten; Church history records ten great persecutions.

Verses 12-17. After the devil had played the roaring lion for several centuries, trying to exterminate the church of Jesus Christ, he discovered that "the blood of the martyrs is the seed of the church." He then stopped the persecutions suddenly and began to corrupt the Church. This is the meaning of the message to Pergamos, which means "twice married," a typical name for the professing Church which claims to be the bride of Christ, but is married to the world. Pergamos is dwelling where Satan has his throne. Milton described Satan being in hell.

> High on a throne of royal state,
> That far outshone the wealth
> of Ormuz or of Ind,
> Satan exalted sat.

But that is not Scripture. Satan will be in hell, in his final abode "the lake of fire," but he is not there now. He is the god of this world (age): his throne is right here on earth. And Pergamos had been married to the world. This is also indicated by the mention of Balaam, who cast a stumbling block before the children of Israel, by inducing them to take the daughters of the heathen and thus give up their God-demanded separation. The Church then gave up her pilgrim character, settled down in the world, became a world institution, as revealed by our Lord in the parable of the mustard seed. What happened in the beginning of the fourth century church-historians have proclaimed as the "triumph of Christianity." It was rather "the defeat of Christianity," for that happened which corrupted the Church of Christ.

The instrument of the devil used to bring about this was the emperor Constantine. He had a rival by the name of Maxentius, whom he faced in battle. Constantine claimed that the night before he had a vision of Christ bearing a cross with the words: *"In hoc signo vinces* (In this sign thou shalt conquer). He had the next morning a beautiful banner made, which was called *the Labarum,* and went forth to battle, in which Maxentius was defeated as well as another competitor by name of Licinus. Constantine then became emperor and nominally a Christian and head of the Church, while retaining his heathen title as *Pontifex Maximus,* the high-priest. Then the corruption of the Church resulted. The Church became a political world institution, like the mustard seed, rooting itself in the field (the world) became a great tree, opening its branches to the fowls of the air to defile (Matt. 13; see annotations there). Heathen priests became Christian priests. Heathen temples were changed into Christian churches; he demanded all children to be "christened," that is, made Christians by putting water upon their heads; heathen days of feasting and drinking were made into Christian days, like our "Christmas" and nearly all the other saints' days.

Here again the Nicolaitanes are mentioned, but, while the Ephesians hated the deeds of the Nicolaitanes, here in Pergamos we find the doctrine of the Nicolaitanes, and the Lord says: "which thing I hate." What is it, then? Some say that there was a certain Bishop Nicol who taught bad doctrines and his followers were called "the Nicolaitanes." But this Bishop Nicol is a fictitious person; he cannot be historically located.

Nicolaitanes is Greek; it is a compound. *Nikao* is a verb and means to have the upper hand, to domineer; *laos* means the people (our English "laity"). Nicolaitanes signifies "the domineerers of the people." A priestly class had sprung up in the Church, domineering over the rest of the people, the so-called laity. And this domineering class claimed a superior place in the body of Chirst. This evil was rejected in Ephesus, but is fully sanctioned and tolerated in Pergamos. Priestly assumption became then, and ever since has been, the corruption of Christianity. This is what our Lord hates and what He hates we must hate with Him.

Verses 18-29. The corruption which set in like a great flood with the fourth century increased till the depths of Satan (verse 24) were reached. Thyatira brings us into the period of the Papacy and its wickedness, ecclesiastical and otherwise. Here our Lord reveals Himself as "the Son of God." Rome speaks more of Him as the son of the virgin, the son of Mary, than as the Son of God. The Roman Catholic apostasy has put a woman in the place of the Son of God. Her corruption is fully revealed in verse 20. Jezebel, who called herself a prophetess, was permitted to teach and seduce God's servants to commit fornication and to eat things sacrificed unto idols. Jezebel the wicked woman represents the Papacy. Jezebel was a heathenish woman married to an Israelitish King. She was a queen and an idolatress and persecuted the true prophets of God (1 Kings 18—21).

Apply all this to the Romish church with her spiritual fornication and idolatry. The church, or, rather, the papacy, assumes the place of teacher and dictator and Christ is rejected. The name Jezebel has a twofold meaning. It means "a chaste one"; the other name is "dunghill." Rome claims to be the bride of Christ; in reality she is a harlot, and called so in chapter 27 and therefore a dunghill of all vileness and corruption. In verse 21 we find another important hint. It is said, "She repents not." Rome does not change. She is the same today in every respect as she was 500 years ago. She will continue in her perverted state of impenitence till her predicted doom will overtake her. (Compare verse 22 with chapter 17.) She is the woman of which our Lord spoke in the fourth kingdom parable in Matthew 13 (see annotations there) which took leaven (corruption) and put it into the three measures of meal (symbolical of the doctrine of Christ). It is noteworthy that beginning with the message to Thyatira the Lord announces His coming, that is, His second visible coming. Every following message speaks of it. This shows that the three preceding church periods and conditions are passed and the conditions pictured in Thyatira, Sardis, Philadelphia and Laodicea will continue till He comes. The apostolic age cannot be brought back; nor will there be again a persecution by Roman emperors nor will the church again become corrupted as in Pergamos. The Romish conditions continue to the end of the age.

CHAPTER 3

Sardis, Philadelphia, Laodicea

1. Sardis: The reformation period (3:1-6)
2. Philadelphia: The faithful remnant (3:7-13)
3. Laodicea: The indifferent and apostate Church (3:14-22)

Verses 1-6. We have traced briefly the decline during the 1450-1500 years of Church history. The climax is reached in Thyatira, prophetically the Roman abomination and apostasy. In Sardis we see the progress of evil stayed. Roman Catholicism, as already mentioned, is a fixed and unchanging religious system. Rome will yet have for a brief season a startling revival and get back her place as the mistress of the nations. But in Sardis we see a reaction. Sardis means "those escaping." It is the Reformation period, the movement which produced Protestantism. The Reformation itself was of God and the great men who were used were the most mighty instruments of the Holy Spirit. It was the greatest work, up to that time, since the days of the apostles. But out of it came the human systems which go by the name of Protestantism. The Reformation began well, but soon developed in the different Protestant systems into a dead, lifeless thing. They have a name to live but are dead. This is the verdict of our Lord upon the churches which sprung out of the reformation: "Thou hast a name that thou livest and art dead."

Verses 7-13. Philadelphia means "brotherly love." As Sardis came out of Thyatira, a protest against it, so Philadelphia comes out of Sardis and is a protest against the dead, lifeless, Spiritless condition prevailing in Protestantism. Out of the deadness of the state churches over and over again came forth companies of believers, energized by the Holy Spirit. Philadelphia has been variously applied to early Methodism, the evangelical movements, missionary efforts and to the revivals of the nineteenth century. But it is more than that. It is a complete return to the first principles. The message makes this clear.

It is the one message (besides Smyrna) in which the Lord does not say, "I have against thee," it is that which pleases Him and which He commends. It is a revival and turning back to the first love. The Lord Jesus Christ is once more as the all absorbing object before the heart; Philadelphia repudiates all that dishonors Him and owns alone that worthy, ineffable Name. It is a faithful remnant gathering around His Name as there was a faithful remnant in the closing days of the Old Testament (Mal. 3:16-17). All human pretensions are rejected. The truth of the unity of all believers is owned and manifested in brotherly love towards all the saints. They walk in the path of separation, in self-judgment, in lowliness of mind; they have a little strength, which means weakness; they are a feeble few. Twice the Lord speaks of obedience to His Word. "Thou hast kept My Word"—"Thou has kept the Word of My patience." And the Philadelphian does not deny His Name.

These are the two chief characteristics of this phase of Christianity during the closing days of the professing Church on earth: Obedience to His Word and faithfulness and devotion to His Name. The Word and the Name are denied in the last days. The apostasy of Christendom consists in the rejection of the written Word and the living Word. And turning their backs upon a dead profession, going on in confessed weakness are such paralyzed in their service? Far from it! The Lord promises to open the door for service which no man can shut. Every child of God may test this. True and continued service is the result of true and continued faithfulness to the Lord. Especially is this service to be blessed to those who hold to a perverted Judaism (verse 9). And there is the great promise, which they believe and hope for, the coming of Himself to keep them out of the great tribulation (verse 10). In Philadelphia there is a revival of prophetic truth, an earnest waiting for the coming of the Lord. Philadelphia is not a defined church-period, but rather a description of a loyal remnant called out by the Spirit of God and bearing the final testimony to the whole counsel of God by word and deed. If the reader desires to please the Lord, then study the details of the message to Philadelphia and walk accordingly.

Verses 14-22. Laodicea means "The judging or rights of the people." It is opposite of Nicolaitanism. The domineerers of the people still go on in Rome, but in Protestantism the people (the laity) arise and claim their rights and do the judging. This condition was also forseen by the Apostle Paul. "For the time will come when they (The laity) will not endure sound doctrine; but after their own lusts they shall heap to themselves teachers, having itching ears" (2 Tim. 4:3). We see in Laodicea the final religious and apostate conditions of protestant Christendom and the complete rejection of the professing body. "I will spew thee out of my mouth." He Himself is seen standing outside, which shows that He is rejected. But infinite grace! He knocks and is still willing to come in and bestow the riches of His grace.

The Philadelphian Christian, who is separated from the Laodicean state, whose heart is filled with the love of Christ can learn a lesson here. If our Lord stands outside and yet knocks and waits in patience, we too with Him outside of the camp where He is disowned, can try to gain admittance to the Laodicean hearts. Epaphras did this (Col. 4:12-13). Laodicea consists in a proudly boasting spirit with total indifference to the Lord Jesus Christ and to His Name. It is a religiousness without any truth nor the power of the Holy Spirit. Lukewarmness expresses it all. "Lukewarmness, a perfect jumble of sacred and worldly matters. The word does not point chiefly to half-heartedness. But as lukewarmness is produced by pouring of hot and cold water together in the same vessel, so in the Laodicean state, intense worldliness will be varnished over by plausible and humanitarian and religious pretences."

Great reformation movements for the advancement of religion and the betterment of the world, the rejection of the gospel as the power of God unto salvation, are characteristic features of this final phase of Christendom. It will continue and wax worse and worse till His patience is exhausted. Then the true Church will be caught up with the departed saints to meet Him in the air, and Laodicea will be spewed out of His mouth. It is important to notice that Thyatira (Rome), Sardis (Protestantism) and the two phases of Protestantism represented by Philadelphia and Laodicea co-exist. They go on together. This is seen by the fact that in each our Lord speaks of His second coming (2:25; 3:3; 10-11, 16). The Lord takes His own to Himself. Rome and an apostate Protestant Christendom continue on earth during the period of judgment, preceding the visible coming of the Lord.

III. The Things Which Are After These, The End of The Age, The Consummation, and Final Messages (4—22)

CHAPTERS 4—5

1. The open door and the vision of the throne (4:1-3)
2. The twenty-four elders and the throne (4:4-5)
3. The four living creatures and the worship (4:6-11)
4. Who is worthy to open the book? (5:1-3)
5. The answer (5:4-5)
6. The vision of the Lamb (5:6-7)
7. Worship and praise (5:8-14)

Verses 1-3. The scene changes suddenly. We are no longer on earth but are transported into heaven. The true Church is gone and the apostate Church, while still on earth to pass into the judgments of the great tribulation, is no longer owned by the Lord and, therefore, not mentioned. That is why the word "church" disappears entirely from the book after the third chapter. The open door and the voice which calls "come up hither" and John's presence in glory in the spirit, clearly indicate symbolically the fulfillment of 1 Thess. 4:15-17. That for which the faithful remnant waited, the blessed hope of the Church, has suddenly come to pass. The departure of the true Church from the earth will be as sudden as its beginning (Acts 2:1-2).

John's first vision in heaven is the established throne, the sign and symbol of the universal government of God. While thrones on earth begin to totter and to fall and man's day closes in the predicted upheavals, there is a throne which cannot be affected or disturbed. Yea, He who sitteth there and looks down upon earth and sees man's rebellion and madness laughs at them and holds them in derision (Psalm 2:4). The occupant of the throne was to look upon like a jasper (rather the diamond) and a sardine stone. Our Lord and the glory of His person are symbolically represented in these stones. His glory in the brilliant stone, His redemption work in the blood-red sardine. The rainbow in emerald-green tells us that in the judgment about to come upon the earth mercy will also be remembered. It is the covenant sign. Though judgments come, yet mercy is in store for Israel and the earth.

Verses 4-5. Who is represented by these twenty-four elders? They cannot be angels. Angels are never seated upon thrones (not seats, as in the Authorized Version), nor are they crowned, nor can they sing redemption's song as the elders do. There is only one possible meaning. They represent the redeemed, the saints in glory. They are priests (clothed in white) and they are kings (crowned); they are the royal priesthood in the presence of the throne. And why twenty-four? It points us back to the work David did for the temple. He appointed twenty-four courses of the priests (1 Chron. 24). Twice twelve would suggest the saints of the Old and New Testaments.

There were lightnings and voices and thunderings. This is repeatedly stated. See 8:5, 11:19, 16:18. It is the symbol of God's throne in its judicial aspect.

Verses 6-11. The sea of glass is a reminder of the great laver in Solomon's temple in which the priests had to wash. Now it is solidified because no more water is needed for the cleansing of the saints. The word "beast" should be changed to "living creatures" or "living ones." They are not symbolical of the Church, or a special class of saints, but they are the same supernatural beings seen in the Old Testament and always in connection with the throne and the presence of Jehovah. They are the cherubim of Ezekiel's great vision, chapters 1 and 10. Their constant cry, "Holy, Holy," reminds us of the seraphim also (Isa. 6). The worship here is the worship of Him who is the creator.

Chapter 5:1-3. Much has been written about the meaning of the book written within and and sealed with seven seals. What the book contains is no secret whatever. Beginning with the sixth chapter the seals are opened and after they are all broken the contents of the book are made known. The book contains the judgments for this earth preceding His coming in power and glory and the beginning of His reign. It is, therefore, the book of the righteous judgments of God, preceding the glorious manifestation of the King of Kings.

Verses 4-5. John receives the answer to the question the strong angel had proclaimed. One of the elders told him, "Behold the lion of the tribe of Judah, the root of David, has prevailed to open the book, and the seven seals thereof." No further comment is needed; the Lord Jesus Christ is the Lion of Judah and the Root of David. "The King's wrath is as a roaring lion" (Prov. 19:12). He is now to be revealed in mighty power and strength to execute judgment. (See Gen. 49:9.) And He is also the Root of David.

Verses 6-7. And now He is seen who alone is worthy to open the book. He does not appear as a lion in majesty, but He is seen by John as a Lamb standing, as having been slain. The Lamb slain is the lion. His victory was gained by dying, and, therefore, He must have as the lion the victory over all His enemies. Thrice the number seven is repeated revealing His perfection. Notice especially three descriptions. He is "in the midst." He is the center of God's government and of heaven itself, as He is for His people the center of all their thoughts and affections. He is seen "as a Lamb standing." Now He is seated at the right hand of God, but when the time comes when His enemies are about to be made His footstool, He will arise to act. He will arise and have mercy upon Zion (Psa. 102:13). And He is seen as "the Lamb slain." The Greek word here suggests "slain in sacrifice."

Verses 8-14. A great worship scene follows at once. The four living creatures join in with the elders, but the latter alone have harps and golden bowls full of incense, which are the prayers of the saints. The harps express their great joy and praise and the bowls full of incense denote the priestly ministry of the redeemed. Such is part of our glorious future, an endless praise of deepest joy, and perfect ministry. The prayers of the saints are not the prayers of the past, but the prayers of Jewish saints, so beautifully rewritten in the Psalms, when the time of Jacob's trouble is on the earth. And then the new song! This is redemption's song, the song of redeeming love; the old song was the praise of God as the Creator in His glory (Job 38:7). Redemption is now accomplished for the saints in glory; they look forward to the glorious manifestation with Himself and the great new song bursts forth. The praise of Him becomes universe-wide. The innumerable company of angels joins in it. "The number of them was myriads of myriads and thousands of thousands." (This is according to the Greek.) And the praise described here leads us on to the time when God will be all in all. It is the never-ending praise, the hallelujah-chorus of redeemed Creation! The four living creatures say "Amen"; the elders worship. Omit "Him that liveth forever and ever," as these words do not belong here.

CHAPTERS 6:1—8:5

The Opening of the Seven Seals

1. The first seal (6:1-2)
2. The second seal (6:3-4)
3. The third seal (6:5-6)
4. The fourth seal (6:7-8)
5. The fifth seal (6:9-11)
6. The sixth seal (6:12-17)
7. Parenthesis: The remnant of Israel (7:1-8)
8. The saved multitude (7:9-17)
9. The seventh seal (8:1-5)

Verses 1-2. The Lamb, invested with all the authority to execute judgment, having received His commission from God, begins now to open the seals of the book which is in His hands, the hands which were once nailed to the cross. It is evident that the breaking of the seals does not begin till His saints are gathered around the throne in glory. Until then it is still the day of grace. When the first seal is opened one of the living creatures said in voice of thunder, "Come." The words "and see" must be omitted here and in verses 3, 5 and 7. A rider upon a white horse appears; his is a bloodless conquest. He has a bow, but no arrow. He receives a crown and goes forth to conquer. Many expositors make this rider the Lord Jesus or some power which represents Him. It is positively incorrect. The rider here is a great counterfeit leader, not the personal Antichrist, but the little horn which Daniel saw coming out of the ten-horned beast (Dan. 7). This coming leader of the revived Roman empire will go forth to conquer and become its political head. He is Satan's man as we shall see later.

Verses 3-4. The second seal reveals a rider upon a red horse. He takes away the false peace, which the rider upon the white horse as a divine judgment act established. The universal peace of which the world dreams without the presence of the Prince of Peace, will be of short duration. Another awful war follows. It will not be war alone between nation and nation, but it will be a world-wide reign of terror and bloodshed, a carnage unknown before in the history of the world. See in Matthew 24 how our Lord mentions the great conflict of nation against nation and kingdom against kingdom.

Verses 5-6. The black horse rider brings famine, exactly what our Lord mentions next in Matthew 24: "There shall be famines." Famine follows war and inasmuch as the second seal brings the greatest war, the third seal will bring the greatest famine. The judgments of God fall then on the earth. Our Lord also mentions famines.

Verses 7-8. The next rider under the fourth seal is named death. And Hades, the region of the unseen (not hell), is populated. Sword, hunger, death, that is pestilences and the beasts of the earth, claim an awful harvest (Ezek. 14:21). And so our Lord spoke of "pestilences." These four seal judgments are hardening judgments.

Verses 9-11. The four living creatures have uttered their four-fold "Come." They are thus seen in connection with the providential government of the world. Under the fifth seal the scene changes completely. John saw under the altar the souls of them that had been slain. And they cry, "How long, O Lord!" Who are they? Not the martyrs of past ages. They are risen from the dead and are in glory with redeemed bodies. The words of the Lord in the Olivet discourse give us the key. Speaking to His Jewish disciples He said: "Then shall they deliver you up, and shall kill you and ye shall be hated of all nations for My Name's sake" (Matt. 24:9).

The Lord speaks of another company of Jewish disciples who will bear a witness during the end of the age, after the rapture of the Church. He will not leave Himself without a witness. He calls a remnant of His people Israel and they bear a witness to the coming of the Messiah, their coming Deliverer and King. Many of them suffer martyrdom. Their cry, "How long?" is the well-known prayer of Jewish saints; and their prayer to have their blood avenged is equally a Jewish prayer. Christians are not supplicating for vengeance on their foes. The prayer for vengeance refers us to the imprecatory psalms prewritten by the Holy Spirit in anticipation of the final persecution of Jewish believers. And the fellow-servants and their brethren, who are yet to be killed (verse 11), are the martyrs of that remnant during the final three and one-half years, which is the great tribulation.

Verses 12-17. Are the things mentioned under this seal to be taken in a literal sense or symbolically? Most of it is symbolical, yet at the same time great physical phenomena are also involved. The earthquake possibly means a literal earthquake. "Earthquakes in diverse places" our Lord predicted. And they increase as the age draws to its close. But the language is symbolical. Everything is being shaken in this poor world. The civil and governmental powers on earth all go to pieces; every class from kings to slaves is affected by it and terrorized. The political and ecclesiastical world is going to pieces. And when these shaking times have come, when thrones fall and anarchy reigns, when the great collapse of civilization and human society has come with signs on earth and in heaven, the earth-dwellers will see in anticipation the approaching day of wrath. Terror fills every breast and those who sneered at prayer, as the Christ-rejectors do now, will gather for a prayer-meeting to appeal to the rocks to cover them. Read the following Old Testament passages in connection with this seal: Isaiah 24, 34:2-4; Joel 2:30-31; Zephaniah 1; Haggai 2:6-7.

Chapter 7:1-8. This is the first parenthesis. It must not be taken chronologically. The six-seal judgments extend over the entire period of the ending age. The rider upon the white horse will be on the scene to the end, wars will continue to the end, and culminate in the battle of Armageddon, and so do the famines and pestilences. And the sixth seal brings the end in view. We shall see the correspondence with the seventh trumpet and seventh vial later. The trumpet and vial judgments are more intense and more terrible than the seal judgments. In a certain sense they are parallel; the effect of each is continuously felt. The parenthetical vision of the seventh chapter also covers the entire period of the last seven years and brings before us even the vision of what will be after the great tribulation.

How much confusion would have been avoided if expositors and Christians in searching for the meaning of this vision, had not lost sight of two great facts: 1. This chapter can have no application to the Church on earth, nor to the Church in glory, for the simple reason that the Church is already complete and translated to glory. 2. The vision states clearly that the sealed company is "of all the tribes of the children of Israel."

The sealed company is of Israel. After the Church is removed to glory, when the fulness of the Gentiles is come in (Rom. 11:26) the Lord will turn in mercy to Israel and call, before the judgments fall, a remnant which will also be sealed (See Ezek. 9). This remnant is frequently seen on the pages of Old Testament prophecy. This sealed company also bears a great testimony. They are the preachers of the gospel of the kingdom, as a witness to all nations before the end comes (Matt. 24:14). Therefore, during the time when the judgments are executed from above there will be a world-wide preaching of the gospel of the kingdom, proclaiming the coming of the King, calling to repentance and faith in His Name, and offering mercy still.

Verses 9-17. The application of this passage of Scripture to the redeemed Church in glory is wrong. This Scripture does not apply to the Church in glory, but to saved Gentiles on earth. It is a company which comes "out of the great tribulation." The Church enters the glory before that great tribulation begins. The great multitude represents those Gentiles who will hear the final testimony and believe. They will have turned in repentance to Him and will be washed in His precious blood. Our Lord speaks of them in the great judgment of the nations as sheep, who stand at His right hand and inherit the kingdom (Matt. 25:31, etc.). The brethren of our Lord mentioned in Matthew are the remnant of Israel. (For a complete exposition see *The Gospel of Matthew,* by the author of this volume.) This great company, therefore, does not stand before a heavenly throne, but before the millennial throne on earth. It is a millennial scene after the tribulation is passed.

Verses 8-15. The silence in heaven when the seventh seal is opened is indicative of the solemn things which are now to come. The scroll is now fully opened and there is an ominous hush as the seven angels prepare to sound their trumpets of judgment. John beholds these seven angels, but before they begin to sound "another angel" is seen standing at the altar. This angel is not a creature, but like *the* angel of Jehovah in the Old Testament, is our Lord Himself. He is seen as the Priest in behalf of the praying, suffering saints on earth. No angel can offer the prayers of the saints, but He, who is the one Intercessor, alone can do that. And for what do they pray on earth? For mercy for those who persecute the remnant of Israel? No! They pray for divine intervention, for the fire of judgment as Elijah did.

CHAPTERS 8:6—11:18

The Sounding of the Seven Trumpets

1. The first trumpet (8:6-7)
2. The second trumpet (8:8-9)
3. The third trumpet (8:10-11)
4. The fourth trumpet (8:12-13)
5. The fifth trumpet (9:1-12)
6. The sixth trumpet (9:13-21)
7. Parenthesis: The angel and the little book (10:1-11)
8. The temple (11:1-2)
9. The two witnesses (11:3-12)
10. The earthquake and the seventh trumpet (11:13-18)

Chapter 8:6-7. The judgments which follow can hardly be fully interpreted at this time. It would be folly to dogmatize about them. The historical application we reject, because the scope of the book makes it clear that these judgments have not yet taken place. What many of these things mean may perhaps never be fully understood till they are actually in fulfillment. The first four trumpet judgments evidently stand by themselves. The fire the Lord cast down is doing its work. The first trumpet manifests the same evidences of divine wrath as came upon Egypt, when Israel suffered there, under the seventh plague (Exodus 9:23). Hail (heat withdrawn), fire and blood are all symbols of divine wrath. The trees and the green grass were burned up. The green things are symbols of agricultural and commercial prosperity.

Verses 8-9. That this is not a literal mountain is obvious. A mountain in Scripture language represents a kingdom (Isaiah 2:2; Zech. 4:7; Psalm 46:2; and especially Jerem. 51:25). The sea is typical of nations. Some kingdom, internally on fire, signifying probably revolution, will be precipitated into the restless sea of nations, and the result will be a still greater destruction of life and commerce, which is represented by the ships.

Verses 10-11. In the preceding trumpet-judgments things were cast upon the earth, but here is a star which falls. It is some person who claimed authority and who becomes an apostate, whose fall produces the awful results given here. It may be the final Antichrist who first may have claimed to be for Israel a great teacher with divine authority and then takes the awful plunge. Wormwood is his name and the waters became wormwood and bitter.

Verses 12-13. The sun, the moon and the stars are now affected. The sun is the symbol of the highest authority; the moon, who has not her own light, is symbolical of derived authority; and the stars are symbolical of subordinate authority. The symbolical meaning of this trumpet judgment is that all authority within the revived Roman empire will be smitten by the hand of one above and as a result there will be the most awful moral darkness. These four-trumpet judgments tell of prosperity taken first from the earth; a great power burning with the fires of revolution affecting the nations; a great leader will fall and become wormwood; and authority disowned and smitten will fill the territory of the Roman empire (Europe) with the densest darkness.

Chapter 9:1-12. The remaining three trumpets have a "woe" attached to each. This is announced in the last verse of the preceding chapter, where the word angel should be "eagle." An eagle, the bird of prey, proclaims the threefold woe. He acts thus as a herald of great judgments (Matt. 24:28, Rev. 19:17-18). The fifth trumpet is a special judgment upon apostate Israel: because those who suffer are they "which have not the seal of God on their foreheads" (verse 4). The great tribulation in the second half of the week, comes now into prominence. If we turn to chapter 12:12 we read something similar to the eagle's message of woe. "Woe unto the inhabiters of the earth and of the sea! for the devil is come down unto you, having great wrath, because he knoweth that he hath but a short time."

Preceding the sounding of the fifth trumpet the eagle proclaimed the woe upon the inhabiters of the earth. The star which is seen fallen from heaven with the key of the pit of the abyss is Satan himself cast out of heaven. The details of this event we learn in the twelfth chapter. He has the key to the pit of the abyss, the same word "deep," used in Luke 8:31. "And they (the demons) besought Him that He would not command them to go out into the deep (abyss)." He unlocks the prison house of the fallen angels and the most awful satanic agencies come forth to begin their "dread" work of torment. The smoke first, symbolical of darkening; the locusts next, symbolical of these demon powers. Awful darkness prevails and the most diabolical delusions, producing fearful torments among apostate Israel and the inhabiters of the earth. It is the time of the strong delusion (2 Thess. 2:4-11) which has come. And over them is a king. His name is given in Greek and Hebrew, showing that it is both Jew and Gentile that come under His power. Both names mean distinction.

Verses 13-21. The sixth angel is commanded by a voice from the horns of the golden altar to loose the four angels who are found at Euphrates, and as a result an innumerable company of horsemen is released. (Greek: twice ten thousand times ten thousand, that is, 200 million. The number would indicate the immense, uncountable hordes.) They are prepared for a specific time to do their work. Euphrates is once more mentioned under the pouring out of the sixth vial. We believe the sixth vial judgment gives the key to these horsemen here. Euphrates does not mean the Turkish Empire, as we shall more fully show when we come to the sixth vial. This river was both the boundary line of the old Roman Empire and the land of Israel. Restraining influences held back the tide of nations on the other side of the river; this restraint is now removed and therefore a great invasion takes place. As the land of Israel is nearest it will suffer first, but the revived Roman empire will be the objective of these invading hordes. The "third part" stands for the Roman Empire, the coming European confederacy. This invasion is under the king of the north. It is seen in its beginning here and is consummated under the sixth vial. There the "kings of the sunrise" are included. And under the sixth vial they are more specifically gathered for the great day of God Almighty.

Chapter 10:1-11. The proclamation of the mighty angel is the first recorded event in this parenthesis. Who is this angel? It is Christ Himself. We saw our Lord in angel's form before the opening of the seventh seal and then He appeared in priestly dignity. Here before the sounding of the seventh trumpet He appears again in the same form, but He is called a mighty angel and we behold Him in royal dignity. The cloud, the rainbow, the face like the sun, His right foot upon the sea, the left on the earth, the voice like a lion and the seven thunders, all declare this to be correct. The hour is rapidly approaching when the kingdoms of this earth are to become His kingdom. This is seen under the seventh trumpet. And, therefore, He is seen now in this attitude of royal dignity. The words which He speaks (verses 6 and 7) bear out this interpretation. "There shall be no longer delay." Man's day is about to close. The mystery of God is now to be finished, "as He hath declared to His servants, the prophets"; or in better rendering "the mystery of God also shall be completed according to the good tidings which He declared by His own servants, the prophets." How great has been that mystery! Evil had apparently triumphed; the heavens for so long had been silent. Satan had been permitted to be the god of this age, deceiving the nations. And Israel, too, is included in this mystery. And now the time has come when the mystery of God will be completed, when the glorious messages, the good tidings of the prophets concerning Israel's blessing and the kingdom, will be fulfilled.

But what is the little book which the angel holds in His right hand? It is not a sealed book, but open. It stands for the prophecies in the Old Testament relating especially to Israel during the time of the great tribulation, which is yet to come upon the earth, culminating in the personal and glorious appearing of the Lord to begin His millennial reign.

Chapter 11:1-2. We see at once how Jewish things come now into view. To apply these verses to the Church and make the temple the Church is absolutely wrong. The temple and the altar are Jewish; the holy city is Jerusalem. After the Church has left the earth the Jewish people will be fully restored to their own land,

and their land restored to them. They will possess Jerusalem once more. When the Jews are once more masters in their own promised land they will erect another temple and then restore the Levitical worship as far as it is possible. Such a temple must be in Jerusalem. (See Isaiah 66:1-4.) In that temple the personal Antichrist, the beast out of the land of whom we shall read in chapter 13, will appear and claim divine worship. (See 2 Thess. 2:3-4.) Apostate Israel in corrupt alliance with equally apostate Gentiles is seen in the opening verses of this eleventh chapter, as the court without the temple. But in the midst of this corrupt mass, which will follow the delusion of the Antichrist and accept Satan's man as their Messiah, there will be the God-fearing remnant. This remnant is here divinely recognized as worshippers. Therefore that coming is called "the temple of God," because the Lord owns the true worshippers found in the midst of the unbelieving mass.

Verses 3-12. Much has been written on these two witnesses who will appear in Jerusalem. It is clear they are still future and their work will be in that city. Some make them Enoch and Elijah and others think they will be Moses and Elijah returned in person. Some have claimed to be a re-incarnation of Elijah. Such claims are fanatical. No second coming of Moses is anywhere promised in the Word. Something, however, is said about the work of Elijah in the future (Mal. 4:5-6). But the words of our Lord in Matt. 11:14, speaking of John the Baptist, and Matt. 17:12, seem to make to clear that no literal coming of the same Elijah, who went into glory, without dying, is meant. Yet the deeds of these two witnesses clearly link them with the work of Moses and Elijah. They each do both the things Moses and Elijah did separately. We take it then that these two witnesses represent the great testimony to be given in Jerusalem during the 1,260 days of the great tribulation. Perhaps the leaders will be two great instruments, manifesting the spirit of Moses and Elijah, endowed with supernatural power, but a large number of witnesses is unquestionably in view here. They maintain in the midst of the Satanic scenes a powerful testimony for God.

The period of the great tribulation was mentioned in verse 2. Here for the first time the beast is mentioned. This beast coming out of the pit of the abyss, the deep, is the revived Roman empire under the little horn, seen by Daniel on the four-horned beast (Dan. 7:8). While he dominates over the Gentiles, he will turn in fury against these Jewish saints, and the two witnesses will be slain. He makes war with the godly remnant (Dan. 7:21). A part of that remnant will be killed. The vileness of these coming days of Satan's rule on earth is seen in the treatment of the bodies of Jehovah's servants. The wicked are so elated over the silencing of the testimony that they refuse to permit their burial so that they may feast their eyes upon the sickening spectacle. They rejoice and make it a festive occasion, because torment had come to their consciences through the testimony of the slain.

Gentiles, who side with apostate Israel are mentioned, but especially a class which is called "they that dwell on the earth" rejoices over the end of the witnesses. The same class is mentioned several times. Study the passages where they are mentioned: Chapter 3:10, 6:9, 10; 8:13; 11:9, 10; 12:12; 14:6, 7; 17:8. They are the apostate, nominal Christians who are utterly blinded and hardened. Phil. 3:18-19 gives their character and destiny. They claim possession of the earth as belonging to them, but God is not only the God of heaven, He is also "the God of the earth" (Rev. 11:4). God's power is manifested in the physical resurrection and the visible translation of the two witnesses. Their enemies see a great miracle. The apostates who ridicule even now a physical resurrection, who sneer at the blessed hope of a coming translation of the saints, will witness these two great facts. No wonder that a great fear fell upon them. The raised witnesses belong to the first resurrection (20:4).

Verses 13-18. The terror becomes still greater when the whole city is shaken by a mighty earthquake. This is not a symbolical earthquake but a convulsion of nature by which the fourth part of the city falls and 7,000 men are killed. It marks the end of the second woe. Then those who escaped the visitation gave glory unto the God of heaven. It is only inspired by fear. They do not turn in repentance unto God. Here ends the parenthetical vision.

The seventh trumpet brings us to the very end of the tribulation and to the beginning of the millennial reign. It is Jerusalem's deliverance. He who alone is worthy receives the kingdom. How clear this ought to make the fact that our Lord has no earthly kingdom now, but He receives the promised kingdom on the earth at the end of these things. See Dan. 7:14. Heaven worships too; they celebrate the fact that He has taken His great power. It is a review of all that takes place and what follows when He appears out of heaven. The nations were full of wrath (Ps. 2; 46:6); His wrath is come; resurrection will follow; this points to the time after the kingdom (chapter 20:12). And His servants, the prophets and the saints, receive their rewards, to reign with Him.

CHAPTERS 11:19—13

Satan's Power and Masterpiece

1. The vision of the opened temple (11:19)
2. The woman with child (12:1-5)
3. The escape of the woman (12:6)
4. War in heaven (12:7-12)
5. The dragon persecuting the woman (12:13-17)
6. The beast out of the sea (13:1-10)
7. The beast out of the earth (13:11-18)

Chapter 11:19. What follows now brings the great tribulation, the 1,260 days, into prominence. As we have seen the seventh trumpet takes us right to the end. But now we are led back.

Verse 19 of chapter 11 belongs properly to the twelfth chapter. The ark contains the covenant made with Israel. This is now to be remembered and connected with it are the manifestations of coming wrath for those who oppress His people.

Chapter 12:1-5. Who is represented by the sun-clothed woman? Romanists have made out of her the Virgin Mary. Many expositors claim it is the Church which is represented by this woman. Some claim the woman is the professing Church and the manchild represents, according to their view, a class of overcomers who will escape the tribulation. This is a favored interpretation of some of the so-called "holiness people."

In the light of the scope of this book the woman cannot possibly have anything to do with the Church. Again, Christian Science has made the most absurd claim that this woman represents that instrument of Satan, the deluded woman, whom they worship as the founder of their cult. A hundred years ago another sect existed in England under the leadership of a woman, who also claimed to be the one of this vision. We do not need to seek long for the true meaning of the woman seen by John. She represents Israel. Everything in the symbolical statements bears this out, especially the crown with the twelve stars (Gen. 37:9).

"Thus she is seen clothed with the glory of the sun—that is, of Christ Himself as He will presently appear in supreme power as Sun of Righteousness (Mal. 4:2); for the sun is the ruler of the day. As a consequence, her glory of old, before the day-dawn, the reflected light of her typical system, is like the moon under her feet. Upon her head the crown of twelve stars speaks naturally of her twelve tribes, planets now around the central sun."

It is Israel, what she is in the purposes of God. And the child, the nation brought forth, is the Messiah, Christ. Even so Paul writes of Israel, "of whom as according to the flesh Christ came, who is over all, God blessed forever" (Rom. 9:5). The identity of the child is established beyond controversy by the fact that the child is caught up unto God and His throne, destined to rule all nations with a rod of iron (Psa. 2:9; Rev. 2:27). The great red dragon, the enemy of the woman and the child, is Satan. Seven crowns are symbolical of his authority as the god of this age and the ten horns symbolical of his power. These historical facts are seen first through this vision. But this is done for the one purpose of bringing into view what is yet in store of Israel during the end time. Christ ascended upon high, took His place at the right hand of God, is waiting till His enemies are made His footstool. Then the present Christian age began. It is not recorded in this vision at all. He who came from Israel and who was rejected by His own, is nevertheless Israel's Messiah, the hope of Israel. In Him and through Him alone the promises made to Israel can be fulfilled. The fulfillment of these promises is preceded by great sorrows and tribulation, the travail pains which come upon Israel during the great tribulation, before He, whom Israel once disowned, is revealed as Deliverer and King. And the red Dragon will do His most awful work during that period of tribulation, a work of hatred against the faithful seed of the woman.

Verse 6. The flight of the woman, Israel, has been taken by some to mean the dispersion of that nation during this age and Israel's miraculous preservation. But this is incorrect. It is true Israel has been miraculously preserved and Satan's hatred, too, has been against that nation. But here we have a special period mentioned, the 1,260 days, the last three and one-half years of Daniel's seventieth week. It means, therefore, that when the Dragon rises in all his furious power to exterminate the nation, God will preserve her. However, before we are told the details of that preservation and Satan's hatred, we read of the war in heaven. Satan is cast out of heaven, down upon the earth. Verses 15-17 and the entire chapter 13 will tell us what he will do on the earth.

Verses 7-12. This great scene takes place before the great tribulation begins. Satan's place is not in hell at this time. As we saw in the message to Pergamos his throne is on earth, he is the god of this age. His dominion is in the air, he is the prince of the power of the air (Eph. 2:2). Our present conflict as believers is "against principalities, against authorities, against the rulers of the darkness of this world, against the wicked spirits in the heavenlies" (Eph. 6:12). Satan as the accuser of the brethren has access even into the presence of God. His accusations are ended. All the redeemed are gathered before the throne. All the malice and power of Satan could not frustrate the purpose of God. His grace and power have been victorious. Thus when the saints come into the heavenly possession Satan's dominion there is at an end. The purchased possession, the region above, will be redeemed by the power of God (Eph. 1:13).

Michael and his angels will begin their short and decisive war against Satan and his angels. Michael is the one archangel mentioned in Scripture. It is not the first time he meets Satan face to face (Jude 9). And Daniel speaks of Michael, "And at that time shall Michael stand up, the great prince which standeth for the children of thy people; and there shall be a time of trouble, such as never was since there was a nation even to that same time; and at that time thy people shall be delivered, every one that shall be found written in the book" (Dan. 12:1). From this we learn that Michael will not only cause the expulsion of Satan out of heaven, but he will also stand up for the believing portion of Israel.

Satan is then cast out into the earth and his angels are cast out with him. It is identical with what we have seen already under the fifth trumpet, the star fallen out of heaven, opening the pit of the abyss with the darkening smoke and the locust swarms coming forth. Then there is joy in heaven because the accuser is cast down and his accusations are forever silenced. And the "woe" is pronounced upon those who dwell on the earth.

Verses 13-17. He turns in fury against the woman which brought forth the man-child. Satan realizes now that his time is short. His expulsion from heaven will soon be followed by his arrest and imprisonment in the pit for a thousand years, and after that there is prepared for him his eternal home of misery, the lake of fire. As he knows that Israel is mostly concerned in the final drama, and the believing portion of that nation will inherit the kingdom, he turns in wrath against them. Verse 6 should be connected with verse 14. It is symbolical language again we have here. The wilderness is a place of isolation, and the place prepared, speaks of God's care for them. But it is not the entire nation. The apostate part sides with Satan and with Satan's man, the Antichrist. But there is another part, which is preserved. This part is in the place of isolation among the nations. The water cast out by Satan is symbolical of the hatred which Satan stirs up against the people amongst the nations. But there will be other agencies in the earth by which this Satanic attempt to wipe from the face of the earth this faithful part of the nation will be frustrated.

Chapter 13:1-10. This chapter brings now fully into view the Satanic powers operating during the great tribulation—the forty-two months. Satan's masterpieces are on the earth; energized by him and endued with his powers they work together to stamp out all that is left of the truth on earth. Their combined efforts are directed against the godly remnant of Jews and against those Gentiles who accepted the message of the gospel of the kingdom.

And John sees this first beast having ten horns with crowns and seven heads and these heads have names of blasphemy. Daniel had seen Babylonia, Medo-Persia and Greco-Macedonia under the emblem of the lion, the bear and the leopard. John sees this beast here like a leopard, with bear's feet and lion's mouth. This revived Roman empire is an amalgamation of parts of the previous world empires. The preceding ones are absorbed by the last, the Roman empire. Therefore the revived Roman empire will contain the different elements in one great monster. This Roman empire will be revived in the first part of the final seven years. We saw this under the first seal. Here is the beginning of the period for which the dragon gives to him his power, and his throne and great authority. It becomes now fully possessed by Satan. The ten horns are the ten kingdoms which will exist in that empire. We are told later that these ten kings "have one mind and shall give their power and strength unto the beast" (17:13).

In the same chapter the beast is also seen coming out of the abyss (17:8) denoting its Satanic origin. The heads represent the seven forms of government which have characterized the empire in the past, the seventh becomes the eighth. One of the heads is especially mentioned; later we read "he is the eighth, and is of the seven, and goeth into perdition" (17:11). He was as it were wounded to death, and his deadly wound was healed, and all the world wondered after the beast. This head denotes the imperial form of government, which had died, and now is revived in the person of the leader, the prince of Daniel 9:27, the little horn, which Daniel saw in the midst of the ten horns. This will be Satan's man, one of his masterpieces. The whole earth will wonder after that beast and its Satan-possessed head.

Verses 11-18. The second beast is not an empire with a great leader, but a person. The first beast is out of the sea; the second out of the earth (land). The first has ten horns; the second has two. The beast out of the sea comes first; the other beast follows him. The first beast is a political power, the second is a religious leader. The first is a Gentile power and its head a Gentile; the second is a Jew. The first beast has Satanic power; so has the second beast. The second beast induced the worship of the first beast whose dominion is over the entire Roman world and after whom the whole earth wonders; the sphere of the second beast is Palestine. The first beast through its head makes in the beginning of the seven years a covenant with many of the Jews, but in the middle of the week he breaks that covenant (Dan. 9:27). That covenant will probably be the permission given to the Jews to build a temple and to resume their sacrificial worship.

The first and the second beast make a covenant, which marks the beginning of the seventieth week of Daniel. But when the little horn, the first beast, becomes energized by Satan, he breaks that covenant. Then the second beast demands the worship of the first beast as well as the worship of himself. This second beast is the final, personal Antichrist. He has two horns like a lamb, and speaks like a dragon. He is a counterfeit lamb and his two horns are an imitation of the priestly and kingly authority of Christ. He is the one of whose coming our Lord spoke (John 5:43). He is the man of sin, the son of perdition described by Paul in 2 Thess. 2. He must be a Jew or his claim of being Israel's true Messiah would not be accepted by the Jews.

Daniel also gives an interesting prophetic picture which bears out his Jewish character and his wicked, satanic ways. See Daniel 11:36-39. This second beast is also called the false prophet (16:13; 19:20; 20:10). He does lying wonders. He reigns as the false king in Jerusalem and sits as god in the temple. He will be the religious head of apostate Judaism and apostate Christendom. It is the strong delusion of the second chapter of Second Thessalonians. He also demands the worship of the first beast. He makes an image of the first beast and gives breath to it, so that it can speak. Whoever has not the mark of the beast on hand and forehead cannot buy nor sell, and whosoever does not worship the beast will be killed. And those who worship the beast and receive the mark are lost souls. Great will be the number of martyrs at that time. To find out what the mark is and some of the other details would only be guesswork. No one can imagine the horrors of that time when Satan rules for a short time on earth and produces the great tribulation, such as was not before on earth, nor ever can be again.

But what does the number 666 mean? If we were to state all the different views on this number and the different applications we would have to fill many pages and then we would not know what is right and wrong. Seven is the complete perfect number; six is incomplete and is man's number. Here we have three times six. It is humanity fallen, filled with pride, defying God. The number 666 signifies man's day and man's defiance of God under Satan's power in its culmination.

CHAPTER 14

Grace and Judgment

1. The Lamb and the 144,000 (14:1-5)
2. The everlasting gospel (14:6-7)
3. Fall of Babylon anticipated (14:8)
4. Wrath for the worshippers of the beast (14:9-11)
5. The blessed dead (14:12-13)
6. The harvest and the vintage (14:14-20)

Verses 1-5. A series of visions follow the dark scenes in chapter 13. The conditions under the domineering power of the two beasts are going to be changed. The Lord will answer the prayers of the persecuted Jewish people and deliver them by His personal coming out of the opened heaven. This glorious manifestation is fully revealed in the nineteenth chapter. Here it is anticipated. There is much said about this intervention in behalf of the suffering godly remnant in the Old Testament. As an illustration we call attention to Psalms 44 and 45. In the Forty-fourth Psalm we find a description of their suffering and the cry to heaven: "Arise for our help, and redeem us for Thy mercies' sake." In the Forty-fifth Psalm the answer to this prayer is recorded. The King riding in majesty, dealing with His enemies, surrounded by redeemed companies, is beheld in that Psalm. The entire book of Psalms should be studied from the viewpoint of prophecy; it will shed much light upon these events of this portion of Revelation.

But who are the 144,000 standing with the Lamb upon Mount Zion, having His Name and His Father's Name written on their foreheads? In the previous chapter we saw a company on earth who have the mark of the beast on their foreheads; but here is a company who have His Name and the Father's Name on the forehead. A good many have made of this company a portion of the Church, as first-fruits, who, according to this theory, have lived separated lives and are caught up into heaven, while the other believers, who did not live as near to God as they did, will have to suffer in the great tribulation.

The reader who has followed the unfolding of this book will see at once that such an interpretation is impossible. These 144,000 have nothing to do whatever with the Church. And the 144,000 learn to sing this new song. Who then are the harpers? They are the martyred company seen in connection with the fifth seal and they also include now their brethren which were slain during the great tribulation. The characteristics of the 144,000 are next given. Verse 4 must not be interpreted in a literal sense. Those who apply it to a first-fruits of the Church have done so, and it has led to much confusion and even worse things. Literal impurity is not in view. If it had a literal meaning this company would consist of men only. The woman, the great harlot Babylon and her daughters, the godless and christless religious world-systems (chapter 17) are then on earth. They did not defile themselves with the corruptions and idolatries prevalent on the earth. They kept themselves from spiritual fornication. They are the first-fruits and the earnest of the blessings soon in store for the earth. They were devoted to the Lamb and no lie (not guile) was in their mouth. The lie and delusion of the end-time were utterly repudiated by them.

Verses 6-7. This has nothing to do with the preaching of the gospel during this church-age. The angel must not be taken as a literal angel. The preaching of any gospel to those who dwell on earth is never committed to angels, but to men. This is true of the gospel of grace which redeemed sinners are privileged to proclaim during this age, and of the everlasting gospel during the end of the age. The gospel preached is the gospel of the kingdom and the preachers are this faithful remnant of God's earthly people. Nothing of this preaching was said in chapter 7, though the result, the gathered multitude coming out of the great tribulation is seen there. But here, where the moral and spiritual characteristics of the remnant of Israel are seen, their testimony also comes into view. What this everlasting gospel is we need not explain, for verse 7 gives us the information. It is everlasting because it concerns the Creator as the only object of worship. And it will sound the loudest and go forth in no uncertain sound at the time when pandemonium reigns on earth, and heaven is about to open to manifest the King of glory. How great is God's mercy! And the nations who hear and turn to God will enter the coming kingdom. Read in connection with verses 6 and 7 Psalm 96. It will give you a great deal of light on this portion of Revelation.

Verse 8. This is an anticipative announcement of what will also happen as the great tribulation nears its close. The particulars are not given here. These and what Babylon is and how Babylon the great (city must be omitted in this verse) falls, we shall find in chapters 17 and 18. God's intervention in judgment upon the great whore is simply mentioned here.

Verses 9-11. Here we have a third angelic announcement. It concerns the worshipers of the beast. They drink of the wrath of God. It is "without mixture," that is, no mercy is found in the cup of His indignation. It serves as a solemn warning. Babylon falls prior to the glorious appearing of the King, and the beast will afterward manifest his power as never before. Therefore, the warning concerning the inevitable fate of those who worship the beast and take its mark.

Verses 12-13. It is a voice which proclaims this. It refers especially to those who are martyrs at that time. Certainly all our loved ones who fall asleep in Jesus are blessed. They are absent from the body and consciously present with the Lord. But here is the comfort for those who faithfully resist the worship of the beast, who refuse to take the mark. They become martyrs. The book of Revelation will be read and studied during the great tribulation. Satan through the beasts, will try to annihilate it and the rest of the Bible. But it will be a failure as all former attempts to get the Bible out of the world have failed. Here then, is first the warning. If they worship the beast they will be lost forever. Then there is the alternative to resist the beast and be killed as to the body, but die in the Lord. "From henceforth" means during the tribulation when the great persecution goes on.

Verses 14-20. This brings now the coming of

the Son of Man with judgment power into view. The harvest and the vintage have come. The sickle is put in. The reapers used will be angels (Matt. 13:41). The day of vengeance has come. Read Isaiah 63:1-6; Joel 3; Zechariah 12—14. This will greatly help to a better understanding of the harvest and the vintage. The nations and their armies will be in the land; the Assyrian from the north, foreshadowed by the wicked work of Antiochus Epiphanes (Dan. 8) will do his awful work; the false prophet, the second beast is in Jerusalem. But then the judgment clouds break. The battle of Armageddon comes into view for the first time in verse 20. How we ought to praise Him for His infinite grace which has separated us from these awful judgments of vengeance and wrath. His people will be at home when these things come to pass.

CHAPTERS 15—16

The Seven Vials

1. The victors' song and worship (15:1-4)
2. The seven angels leave the temple (15:5-8)
3. The first vial (16:1-2)
4. The second vial (16:3)
5. The third vial (16:4-7)
6. The fourth vial (16:8-9)
7. The fifth vial (16:10-11)
8. The sixth vial (16:12)
9. Parenthesis: The seventh vial (16:13-21)

Chapter 15:1-4. And now the last seven angels appear; seven seal judgments first, followed by seven angels with trumpets and next the last seven angels. With these seven angels who have the seven last plagues for the world, the wrath of God is completed. Before these angels go forth we behold another worship scene. Who are they? Not the twenty-four elders, but they are the harpers which we saw harping and singing in chapter 14:2-3. They are the martyred company worshiping in glory. Here we are told of their victory and their song, the song of Moses and of the Lamb. The song of Moses (Exod. 15) is the song of an earthly deliverance and the song of the Lamb concerns a spiritual deliverance. They are redeemed by power and by blood.

Verses 5-8. A wonderful sight it is. There is again an ominous silence similar to the silence in connection with the opening of the seventh seal. The silence is not mentioned. But the text shows an impressive scene of silence. Quietly the procession of these ministers of judgment file out of the temple. They are clothed in pure, white linen; this is symbolical of the righteousness which demands the judgment wrath about to be poured out. And the golden girdles with which their breasts are girdled speak still more of divine righteousness. God in His righteousness must judge and now His wrath in completeness is about to be felt on the earth. The angels left the temple empty-handed, but the four living creatures give into their hands the bowls full of the wrath of God. And behind that smoke is the fire of judgment.

Chapter 16:1-2. The great voice commands the seven angels to go on their way and to empty the bowls upon the earth (Ps. 49:24). And these vials of judgments affect not only the Roman Empire, but the entire world, for the whole world is guilty before God. The first vial poured out produces a grievous sore upon the worshipers of the beast. While it is undoubtedly true that we have symbols also in these vial judgments, it is nevertheless possible that some of these plagues may have, besides the symbolical, also a literal meaning. The sixth plague which came upon Egypt, the first judgment upon the persons of the Egyptians, was also a sore (Exod. 9:10-11). The worshipers of the beast and of the image will be dreadfully afflicted.

Verse 3. This is poured out into the sea. The sea represents the Gentiles. These will now experience the wrath of God. See the plague in Egypt (Exod. 7:17-25). That was a literal thing; but not so here. Some apply it to the continued carnage which will be one of the leading features of the final history of the times of the Gentiles. That it presents a state of the most unspeakable corruption and spiritual death is obvious.

Verses 4-7. Another scene in which the blood is prominent. The apostates denied the blood, sneered at it as the Unitarians and Christian Scientists do in our own days, and now the angel of the waters saith, "Thou has given them blood to drink, for they are worthy." They have to feel the dreadful results of having rejected the Christ of God and accepted the man of sin. The children of Israel had to taste their own idolatry when Moses put the ashes of the burnt golden calf in the water and made them drink it (Exod. 32:20). They have to taste the vileness and bitterness of their apostasy. They reap what they sow. All the joys of life typified by rivers and fountains of water, are poisoned and corrupted. It is a retributive judgment of God falling upon the earth.

Verses 8-9. The fourth vial is poured into the sun and men are scorched with great heat. Some also apply this literally, but the symbolical meaning is to be preferred. There can be no doubt that the powers of nature will also bear witness to the wrath of God. Famines, droughts, great floods, volcanic disturbances, great and widespread earthquakes and other physical phenomena will occur throughout these days of tribulation. However, the sun here is not the physical sun, but means, as under the fourth trumpet, the supreme authority governing them (the Roman empire). Under the fourth trumpet great moral darkness came upon all; here it is fearful, fiery agony "scorched with great heat." The government, Satan-ruled as it is, becomes now the source of the most awful torment to those who are under its dominion. God, in judgment and in His wrath, permits those terrible things to come to pass. Everything under these vial judgments will become more aggravated than under the trumpet judgment.

Verses 10-11. Under the fifth trumpet we saw the star fallen from heaven. It synchronizes with chapter 12:7-12—Satan cast out of heaven. Then Satan fallen from heaven gave his power and authority to the beast, the head of the empire. Here the throne (not seat) of the beast is dealt with. His throne and his kingdom are deluged with wrath. All becomes darkness.

Verse 12. Once more the river Euphrates is mentioned. It dries up when the sixth bowl is poured out so that the way of the kings of the east (literal: from the rising of the sun) might be prepared. We have hinted before at the correspondence between the trumpet judgments and the pouring out of the vials. This now becomes very marked, for under the sixth trumpet the river Euphrates is also mentioned. There the forces which keep back hostile powers are removed and here the river is dried up.

As already stated the Euphrates was the boundary of the Roman empire and the land of Israel. It is a kind of barrier which separates the west from the east. This barrier symbolized by the river Euphrates is now completely removed, so that the kings from the sunrise can invade the land. This invasion is also seen in connection with the sixth trumpet. The nations must gather from all quarters in and about Palestine. We find much of this revealed in the Old Testament and it would be strange if the Revelation were silent on so important an event. Ezekiel describes a great invader, a confederacy of nations (Ezek. 38 and 39). Gog, Magog, the Prince of Rosh (Russia), Meshech, Tubel, Persia, Cush and Put are mentioned as forming this confederacy. The term "Kings of the sunrise" may even mean the far Eastern Asiatic nations, like China and Japan. The drying up of the Euphrates seems therefore to mean the removal of the barrier, so that the predicted gathering of the nations may take place (Joel 3:2). What began under the sixth trumpet is consummated when the sixth vial is poured out. It is an act of judgment-wrath, while at the same time these opposing nations are gathering for the great day of God Almighty.

Verses 13-21. Just as we had a parenthetical vision between the sixth and seventh seal, and between the sixth and seventh trumpet, so we find here a very brief one between the sixth and seventh vial judgments. Armageddon is not yet, but it now comes in view. Unclean spirits, like frogs, creatures of the slimy, evil-smelling swamps and of the night, now proceed out of the mouth of the trinity of evil. The dragon is Satan; the beast, the political head of the empire, and the false prophet, the Antichrist. Satanic influences, emanating from him and his two master-pieces are then at work; and they are of such a nature that we cannot fully understand them. They are the spirits of demons, working miracles.

The seventh angel pours his vial into the air. This is Satan's sphere. His power and dominion are now dealt with in wrath. While Satan was cast out of heaven, he may still maintain part of the atmosphere immediately above the earth, thus upholding his claim as the prince of the power of the air (Eph. 2:2). A great voice declares "It is done." All that follows shows that the climax is reached. The judgment shown is sweeping everything. A great earthquake as under the sixth seal and the seventh trumpet takes place. The great city Babylon is divided into three parts; the cities of the nations fall. It is the hour of collapse, when the stone from above does its smiting work (Dan. 2). "It is done!" The Lord has come. The nineteenth chapter will furnish us the particulars.

CHAPTERS 17—18

Babylon, the Harlot, and Her Judgment

1. The description of the woman (17:1-6)
2. The angel's interpretation (17:7-15)
3. The desolation of the whore (17:16-18)
4. The angelic announcement (18:1-3)
5. The call to separation (18:4-5)
6. Her pride and destruction (18:6-8)
7. Lamentation and jubilation (18:9-20)
8. Her utter and eternal destruction (18:21-24)

Chapter 17:1-6. Babylon was mentioned for the first time in this book in chapter 14:8; her fall was then anticipated. In two chapters we have a description of her and the details of her overthrow and complete destruction. Babylon is seen as a great, world-wide ecclesiastical, political and commercial system, and her dwelling-place, from where she exercises authority, is great city, which is the seven-hilled city Rome. There are many who believe that the literal Babylon is in view here in these two chapters. It is claimed that literal Babylon on the banks of the Euphrates is to become once more a large city and the seat of government during the end of this age. Literal Babylon never was a part of the Roman empire, and as the Babylon of Revelation 17 and 18 is seen in closest identification with the empire, and for a time at least is at its center and capital, the Babylon in Asia is ruled out at once. Rome was the great center of the Roman empire and Rome will once more become the seat where the woman pictured in this chapter will exercise her authority.

In the first part of this chapter we have a description of the great harlot Babylon. Who, then, is this woman, branded a harlot, whom one of the seven angels who poured out the vials showed to John? She represents the papal system in its final power and control in the world. We shall see how this assertion is fully confirmed by the words of this chapter.

We saw in the church-message to Thyatira, which stands for the papacy and its great corruption, that Rome is pictured as the woman Jezebel, corresponding to the woman in the parable of the leaven. And of Thyatira it is said "she repents not." This shows that Rome will continue in her corrupt ways to the end, till judgment overtakes her. She is to be cast into great tribulation (2:22).

When the true Church is caught up, the papal system, as we call it, the Roman Catholic "church" will see a great revival. For a time she has been stripped of the temporal power she once had, but it will be restored to her. Along with the revival of the Roman empire there will be a revival of papal Rome. But we must look very briefly at some of the descriptions of this woman, the harlot. "She sitteth upon many waters." We find the interpretation in verse 15. "The waters which thou sawest, where the whore sitteth are peoples, and multitudes, and nations and tongues." Rome even now can boast of her children among all nations. She gets her support from the whole world. And when she gets her revival she will have a still greater dominion. The kings of the earth will yield once more to her spiritual fornication. Then John saw the woman upon a scarlet colored beast, full of names of blasphemy, having seven heads and ten horns. Who is the Beast she rides? It is the first beast of chapter 13, the revived Roman empire. She becomes identified with that empire. Her attire is purple and scarlet and she is decked with gold, precious stones and pearls. The pope and his cardinals wear these colors. Purple and scarlet are the leading colors displayed in great Romish celebrations; gold, precious stones and pearls describe her enormous wealth and dazzling glory, so attractive to the natural man. And in her hand was a golden cup full of abominations and filthiness of her fornication.

How clearly this describes papal Rome. Her service, called worship, her rituals, her splendid edifices, etc., all are fair to behold and pleasing to the eye, like a golden cup. But inside we find her filthiness in doctrine and in practices. She encourages sin by her indulgences. With the celibacy there is also filth connected. And then the vileness and abomination of the confessional. Her shameless character is written upon her forehead. The true Church is to have His name upon the forehead and the great harlot-system bears an inscription.

Verses 7-15. The interpreting angel told John who the beast is, the beast, that was, and is not, and yet is (verse 8). It is the Roman empire as stated before. It was, in an imperial form in John's day. In the fifth century, A.D., it ceased existing as imperial Rome; it is not. But it is to be again, a revival which is here described as coming out of the pit of the abyss (chapter 13). Verse 9 shows Rome (seven mountains), where the woman sitteth. Therefore, Rome speaks of "the See of the Papacy," and "See" is derived from the Latin *Sedes,* which means seat or throne.

The seven kings or heads in verse 10, mean different forms of government of the Roman empire. Five are fallen; these were kings, consuls, dictators, decemvirs and military tribunes. These are past forms of government. But in John's day the empire had the imperial form of government. This is the meaning of "one is." The other and final form of the Roman empire "is not yet come." That is in John's day it had not yet come. It is the Satanic revival and control of the empire as we saw it in chapter 13. And the eighth head, which goeth into perdition, is the man who heads the empire, the little horn, which Daniel saw on the ten-horned beast.

The ten horns in verses 12-13 are kings. They correspond to the ten toes on Nebuchadnezzar's image and the ten horns on the fourth beast which Daniel saw coming out of the sea. And these ten kings yield their power and strength unto the beast. In verse 14, their awful future is seen. We shall see this more fully in chapter 19:11-21. They are going to make war with the Lamb, and the Lamb, who is Lord of Lords and King of Kings, will overcome them. With Him are the called, the chosen and the faithful, that is the redeemed, who come with Him and are manifested when He appears.

Verses 16-18. The woman rides the beast for a short time only. She will not be long successful in her regained power. The ten horns, the ten kingdoms, and the beast hate her and turn against the whore. ("And the Beast" is not in the Authorized Version; it is added in the Revised Version and belongs rightfully in the text.) First they were all for her and now they unite in making her desolate and naked and burn her with fire. But more than that "and shall eat her flesh," just as Jezebel was eaten by the dogs. It is God in His righteous judgment who decreed her desolation in this way.

Chapter 18:1-3. Babylon is now seen under another aspect. In the former chapter we have the religious center of Rome and her wicked idolatries, in the present chapter it includes also the whole system of apostate Christendom in its social and commercial aspect, the so-called "Christian civilization" in its final apostate condition and doom. Papal Rome in her short revival becomes the head of apostate Christendom and controls everything till her appointed doom comes upon her. While we saw in the preceding chapter the desolation of the whore by the ten kings and the beast, here we see how God views her and that He dethrones this system in His judgment. A strong angel comes down to announce her doom and to lay bare her inner and most awful corruption. A strong descending Angel whose glory lightened the earth, shows what the boasting thing, she, who bore the blessed name of Christ, has become. (This angel may represent the Lord Himself. If this is correct we have the third manifestation of our Lord in the garb of an angel: 8:3 in His priestly dignity; 10:1 in His royal dignity and here as the herald and executor of the vengeance of God upon Babylon.) She is seen to be the habitation of demons. Even now behind all the denials of the doctrine of Christ and the false doctrines which mark the onward march of the predicted apostatsy, demons are the leaders (1 Tim. 4:1).

And the nations drank eagerly her cup and the kings committed fornication with her. These kings are not the ten kings of the Empire for they are used in the judgment of the whore, while the kings mentioned here bewail her destruction (verse 9). And with the system there was connected great commerce; merchants through her became rich.

Verses 4-5. God always calls out His true children from that which is evil. His own must be a separate people. Saints in past centuries have heard this call and left behind the Romish abominations and thousands sealed their testimony with their blood. And in these days in which our lot is cast, days of increasing signs, heralding as never before the approaching end and the homecall of His people to meet Him in the air, in these days God demands the separation of His true children. Christendom is becoming daily more and more the religious camp of apostasy. And, therefore, He calls: "Let us go forth unto Him without the camp bearing His reproach" (Heb. 13:13). He who remains in that which denies His Name, is partaker of her sins (verse 4; compare with 2 John, verses 10-11). As all drifts back to Rome and the coming political and religious confederacy, this final Babylon looms up; God's people must hear that call. To whom is this call addressed? Undoubtedly to the remnant of God's ancient people, the believing remnant and also to that large number of Gentiles who hear the final message, the gospel of the kingdom.

Verses 6-8. Like ancient Babylon, the whole apostate system, Rome and all her offspring, was filled with pride. She was lifted up in all her earthly glory and now God breaks her completely. "She shall be utterly burned with fire." As her smoke is to arise forever and ever (19:3) it is possible that the proud city, Rome, the center of the system of apostasy and commerce, will be destroyed by volcanic action, and where the seven-hilled city once stood there may be instead an immense crater, testifying through the millennium of God's righteous retribution. In view of the volcanic conditions on the Italian peninsula this is more than possible.

Verses 9-20. And now follows the great and universal lamentation over the destruction of the great world-system. There is weeping and wailing when at last this anti-christian civilization, all Christendom united with Rome, and for a time controlling the commerce of the world, is wiped out by the hand of God. The kings, the merchants, the shipmasters, the company in ships and sailors, all are seen mourning, weeping and wailing. The destruction of the system and of its proud city affects them all. They bewail their great loss. Notice twenty-eight things are mentioned by them. The first is gold and the last is the souls of men. How this describes Rome! She is the trafficker in souls and the destroyer of souls as well. And in studying the articles of the commerce of apostate Christendom we notice that these are nearly all articles of luxury. The greatest panic has then come and there will be no recovery of the market. The rich men will weep and howl for their misery is come upon them (James 5:1). See also Zeph. 1:11, 18.

Heaven is called to rejoice over her, and three classes are mentioned (Revised Version), saints, apostles and prophets. "For God hath judged your judgment of her." This is the better rendering. The judgment which the saints pronounced on her is now executed. The next chapter shows us more fully the rejoicing heavens.

Verses 21-24. In Jeremiah 51:60-64 we read that Seraiah was commissioned by Jeremiah to attach a stone to the book containing the prophet's words and to cast it into the Euphrates. "And thou shalt say, thus shall Babylon sink and shall not rise from the evil that I will bring upon her and they shall be weary." Here an angel took up a millstone and cast it into the sea, showing by this action the complete and final destruction of the wicked system and the equally wicked city. And what revelation there is in the statement, "for by thy sorceries were all nations deceived." In chapter 20 we read that the old serpent deceives the nations. Sorceries, wicked spirits, demon-powers blinded the eyes of the nations to follow Rome's seductive lure. And thus it is with a lifeless, spiritless Protestantism and its bloodless gospel. The sorceries of Rome, the demons underneath it all, attract apostate Christendom so that all will be united in the great, final Babylon.

So that we may not question that both chapters refer to Rome, though the entire apostate Christendom is also in view, her blood-guiltiness is mentioned once more.

CHAPTERS 19—20:6

The Manifestation of the King and the Millennium

1. Heavenly hallelujahs and the marriage of the Lamb (19:1-6)
2. Heaven opened and His visible manifestation (19:11-16)
3. The battle of Armageddon (19:17-21)
4. The binding of Satan (20:1-3)
5. The thousand-year reign (20:4-6)

Verses 1-10. Once more we find the significant phrase "after these things" (chapter 4:1; 7:1; 18:1). "After these things"—the things which are described in chapters 17 and 18, the fall of Babylon and the complete destruction of the whore and the system over which she presided and domineered, after these things, voices in heaven are heard again. We were first introduced to the heavens in this book in the fourth chapter.

In chapter 18:20 we heard the words addressed to heaven, "Rejoice over her, thou heaven, and ye holy apostles and prophets, for God hath avenged you on her." And now we see heaven rejoicing. "I heard as it were a great voice of a great multitude in heaven saying, "Hallelujah." Hallelujah means "Praise ye Jehovah." This Hebrew word is not found elsewhere in the New Testament. Four times this word of praise is found in the beginning of this chapter; the Hallelujah times for heaven and earth are imminent. The book of Psalms closes with many hallelujahs; the blessed time which the Psalms so often anticipate, when the earth is judged in righteousness and the glory of the Lord is manifested, is now at hand. The praise here is on account of the righteousness of God exhibited in the judgment of the great whore "which did corrupt the earth with her fornication" and because the blood of God's servants shed by her is now avenged. The great multitude whose Hallelujah is heard first must be the company of martyrs who died during the tribulation. The souls under the altar and their brethren which were slain later utter this praise now. They are seen as a distinct company from the twenty-four elders. A second hallelujah is uttered by them, while the smoke of the destroyed city goes up forever and ever.

The whole redeemed company, Old and New Testament saints, add their amen and hallelujah to the outburst of praise on account of the execution of the righteous judgment. And they worship God, for it is of the righteousness which accomplished the destruction of the great whore. In the midst of this wonderful and impressive worship-scene the throne begins to be heard. A voice from the throne said: "Give Praise unto God all ye His servants and ye that fear Him both small and great." And the command is at once obeyed. John hears the fourth hallelujah and it is the greatest, the most magnificent. It is the great hallelujah-chorus of heaven. Like the voice of many roaring waters, like the voice of mighty thunderings, a great multitude saith, "Hallelujah for the Lord our God Omnipotent reigneth."

Who is this great multitude? In the first verse we heard the Hallelujah of the martyred companies. The twenty-four elders and four living creatures did not join in this first hallelujah. Their hallelujah followed. And now the great outburst of a great multitude. This multitude includes all the redeemed in glory. And they rejoice and give glory for an additional reason which is made known for the first time in this book. The marriage of the Lamb is about to be consummated. "Let us be glad and rejoice, and give honor to Him, for the marriage of the Lamb is come and His wife has made herself ready." The harlot, which claimed to be the bride, being judged, the true bride of Christ is seen in glory. And it is the marriage of the Lamb. His joy is now filled full for He receives her, who is bone of His bone and flesh of His flesh. The second Man, the last Adam, is joined to her who is to rule and reign with Him.

But who is the bride about to become the Lamb's wife? Some teach that it is Israel to be united with the Lord in the closest bonds. But these expositors forget that the scene is a heavenly one. This marriage does not take place on earth where the faithful remnant looks up expecting Him to appear for their deliverance, but this marriage is in glory. It is true such relationship is declared to be Israel's in the Old Testament. She was married to Jehovah in a legal covenant and on account of her faithless condition, because Jerusalem played the harlot (Ezek. 16:35), she was put away. For a time Israel was the wife of Jehovah (Is. 54:1) and then on account of her wickedness became divorced. She will be taken back in the day of her national repentance when the Lord comes. But as one who had been divorced she cannot be a bride again. The bride of Christ to become the Lamb's wife is the Church of the New Testament.

All who accepted Christ as Saviour and Lord since the day of Pentecost constitute the bride of Christ. The Church began on Pentecost and her completion will be the translation to glory (1 Thess. 4:17). She is both the body of Christ and the bride of Christ, as Eve was of the body of Adam and also his bride. The Church is the nearest and the most beloved object of His loving heart.

But how has she made herself ready? And what does it mean, "And to her was granted that she should be arrayed in fine linen, clean and white for the linen is the righteousness of the saints"? The grace of God has supplied the robe and the precious blood is her title to glory. In this respect she was ready. But the words here refer us to the judgment seat of Christ, that award seat before which we must appear. Then the hidden things are brought to light and the wood and the hay and stubble are burned (1 Cor. 3:12-15). Then "every man shall have praise of God" (1 Cor. 4:5) and what grace accomplished in each one and through each will be manifested. And the clean white linen "is the righteousness of the saints." The word "righteousness" is in the plural. It means more than the righteousness which we are in Christ or the faith in Him which is counted for righteousness (Rom. 4:3). It includes all the blessed results in life and service produced by the Holy Spirit, the practical righteousness of the saints. And yet even these need the washing in that precious blood without which all is unclean and unholy.

And so it is grace after all, as indicated by the word "given" (Revised Version); "it was given to her to be clothed in fine linen, bright and pure." He himself has made her ready and removed every spot, every wrinkle and every blemish. God grant that we His people may daily meditate on this coming glorious event, the marriage of the Lamb, and walk worthy of such a Lord and such a calling. Once more John is commissioned to write: "Write, Blessed are they which are bidden to the marriage supper of the Lamb." And who can estimate the blessedness of being in His ever blessed presence, at His table, at the marriage supper of the Lamb!

Verses 11-16. And now we reach the great even so often mentioned in the Old Testament, the event for which this world is waiting, the visible manifestation of Him, whom the heavens received, who returns to judge the earth, to receive the promised kingdom and rule over the earth for a thousand years. We have reached the great climax in the Revelation. His own words are now to be fulfilled. "Immediately after the tribulation of those days shall the sun be darkened, and the moon shall not give her light, and the stars shall fall from the heaven, and the powers of the heavens shall be shaken. And then shall appear the sign of the Son of Man in heaven, and then shall the tribes of the earth mourn, and they shall see the Son of Man coming in the clouds of heaven with power and great glory" (Matt. 24:29-30).

Impressive words—"And I saw heaven opened." Heaven was opened unto Him when He came out of Jordan at His baptism. While His baptism foreshadowed His death in the sinner's place, His resurrection and ascension are foreshadowed in coming out of the waters and the open heaven. In heaven at the right hand of God He has been ever since, unseen by human eyes. At last the time has come when God is to make His enemies as the footstool of His feet. Heaven is opened so that He might be revealed in His glorious majesty. And out of the opened heavens He comes forth. He comes as the mighty Victor to judge in righteousness and to make war. "And behold a white horse; and He that sat thereon was called Faithful and True and in righteousness He doth judge and make war." The white horse is symbolical of victorious warfare and glorious conquest. When, seven years before the first seal had been opened (6:1), a rider appeared upon a white horse achieving great conquest, it was the false king who was then seen in vision. He is as the beast on earth with the King and their armies to make war with the coming King who comes out of the opened heaven. Glorious sight! He is coming to conquer and to claim His inheritance. The appointed day has come in which God "will judge the world in righteousness by that man, whom He hath ordained; whereof He hath given assurance unto all men, in that He hath raised Him from the dead" (Acts 17:31). Upon His head are many diadems. The saints wear crowns, but He to whom belongs all power in heaven and on earth wears many diadems, encircling His head in dazzling splendor.

"And He had a name written, that no man knew but Himself." And again it is written, "His Name is called the Word of God." And on His vesture and on His thigh there is a name written, "King of Kings and Lord of Lords." The unknown Name is the name of His essential deity. No human name can express what He is in Himself. "No man knoweth the Son but the Father." His Name "the Word of God" refers us to the Gospel of John. As the Word He is the express image of God, that is, He makes God visible. He is the expression of God in His character, His thoughts and counsels. And the third name mentioned, "King of Kings and Lord of Lords," expresses what He is in relation to the earth.

"And he was clothed with a vesture dipped in blood"—"And out of His mouth goeth a sharp sword, that with it He should smite the nations, and He shall rule them with a rod of iron, and He treadeth the winepress of the fierceness and wrath of Almighty God." The blood-dipped vesture has nothing to do with His work on the cross. He is described in Isaiah 63:1-4 as the One who has the day of vengeance in His heart, and this passage in Isaiah is here being fulfilled. The two-edged sword refers us to Isaiah 11:4: "He shall smite the earth with the rod of His mouth and with the breath of His lips shall He slay the wicked."

But He is not alone. The armies of heaven follow the great King. They are, like Him, upon white horses and are clothed in fine linen, white and clean. These armies are not angels. It is true, angels will be with Him as He comes, for it is written, then He shall be revealed with His holy angels. Angels will be the reapers in the judgment (Matt. 13:41) when the age ends and they will be used in the regathering of Israel (Matt. 24:31). But the armies here are not angels. They are the glorified saints; the fine linen, white and clean, identifies them fully. In faith and blessed assurance, you, dear reader, and the writer can say, we shall be in that company with Himself as leader. The Son brings His many sons unto glory (Heb. 2:10). What a sight that will be for the earth-dwellers! Each in that company bears His own image; each reflects His own glory.

Verses 17-21. And what a sublime vision comes next! An angel is beheld by the Seer standing in the sun, and with a loud voice he summons the birds that fly in mid-heaven to gather themselves to the great supper of God to eat the flesh of the slain. The birds of prey are summoned in anticipation of the battle of Armageddon which is then imminent. And now the hour of judgment has come. An angel, standing in the sun, the place of supreme authority, gives the invitation to the birds of prey to be ready for the feast which a holy and righteous God will have for them. The day of wrath has come. The slain of the Lord shall be many (Isaiah 66:16).

And down on earth there is the greatest gathering of armies the world has ever seen. The beast, the head of the revived Roman Empire, is the commander-in-chief. The kings of the earth are with him. Vast armies camp on all sides. The great valley on the plains of Esdraelon is filled with soldiers. The hills and mountains swarm with armed men. Satan's power has gathered and blinded this vast multitude to the utmost. The unclean spirits, the demons working miracles, have brought them together to the battle of that day. And the hordes from the north, under the Prince of Rosh are coming later. These vast multitudes from the north and beyond Euphrates are described in Ezekiel 38—39. And in that Old Testament prophecy we find a statement which reminds us of the great supper of God in Revelation. "Speak unto every feathered fowl, and to every beast of the field, assemble yourselves and come; gather yourselves on every side to My sacrifice that I do sacrifice for you, even a great sacrifice upon the mountains of Israel, that ye may eat flesh, and drink blood" (Ezek. 39.17). "Thus shall ye be filled at My table with horses and chariots, with mighty men, and with all men of war, saith the Lord God" (verse 20).

Zechariah 14:2 is now being fulfilled. While the vast armies are covering valleys and hills, the objective will be Jerusalem. All nations are gathered against her. "For I will gather all nations against Jerusalem to battle; and the city shall be taken, and the houses rifled, and the women ravished; and half of the city shall go forth into captivity, and the residue of the people shall not be cut off from the city." And now as these armies are massed together the great battle of Armageddon takes place. They are ready to make war against Him, who comes through heaven's portals. "Then shall the Lord go forth, and fight against those nations" (Zech. 14:3). The battle does not consume much time. Sennacherib's army was suddenly smitten and they all perished, and here are armies in comparison with which Sennacherib's forces were insignificant. One mighty blow from above, one flash of glory and all their strength and power is gone. The stone has fallen (Dan. 2). With one blow the dominion and misrule of the Gentiles is at an end.

The kings of the present day might profitably listen to Nebuchadnezzar's letter in Daniel 4. He began at the times of the Gentiles, and has left this letter to be read by his successors. The words our Lord spoke while on earth "on whom this stone falls it shall grind him to powder" have been fulfilled (Matt. 21:44). Such is the awful fate which "Christian civilization" (?) and "Kultur" (!) and a Christless christendom is rapidly approaching. And while the armies perish as to the body and God's wrath sweeps the earth clean of the mass of apostates, taking vengeance on them that know not God and that obey not the gospel, the beast (the head of the empire) and the false prophet (the second beast of chapter 13), that is the false Messiah, the Antichrist, are cast alive into a lake of fire burning with brimstone. They were not annihilated, for a thousand years later we still find them there (20:10); and still they are in existence and will ever be as individuals in that place of eternal punishment. And those that were slain as to the body will be raised after the millennium and also share the place with the two, whom they followed and worshipped.

Chapter 20:1-3. And now Satan, who was cast out of heaven three and one-half years before the visible and glorious coming of the Lord, and who has been on earth in person, though not beheld by human eyes, is seized to be put into his prison for a thousand years. And the demons, who were liberated by Satan (chapter 9) are likewise shut up in the bottomless pit, though this is not mentioned because it is self-evident. The terms "key" and "great chain" are of course figurative. He is mentioned in all his infamous titles. He is called dragon on account of his horrible cruelty and vileness, the old serpent on account of his maliciousness, guile and deception; he is the devil, the arch-tempter of man, and Satan because he is the accuser of the brethren, the one who opposed Christ and His people. He is now dethroned as the god of this age, completely stripped of his power; and his dethronement means the complete enthronement of our Lord Jesus Christ. And here is the important statement that this being, the once glorious Lucifer, the Son of the morning and light-bearer, who fell through pride, has been the deceiver of the nations.

Verses 4-6. Thrones are seen next by the Seer. "And I saw thrones, and they sat upon them and judgment was given unto them." Daniel also saw thrones in connection with the judgment of the beast, but nothing is said of those occupying the thrones in Daniel's vision. Here we have the complete revelation, and several times the blessed statement is made that Christ and His saints shall reign with Him for a thousand years. The new age in which all things are put in subjection under His feet, the personal reign of Christ, in which all His redeemed people have a share, begins. It will last a thousand years. Six times we read of the thousand years in this chapter. Because this coming age will last a thousand years it has been called by the Latin word "millennium"' not a few have made the astonishing declaration that such a period of time during which Chirst and His saints reign over the earth has but little foundation in the Scripture.

It is quite true that the only place in which the duration of such an age is given is this great final book of Revelation. And that should be sufficient for any Christian to believe in such an age of a thousand years. However, this age of unspeakable blessing and glory for this earth is revealed throughout the entire Bible. The Old Testament contains hundreds of unfulfilled promises of blessing for Israel, the nations of the earth and even for all creation, which have never seen even a partial fulfillment. Isaiah is full of such promises. In the New Testament there are also passages which clearly teach and point to such an age of glory for this earth. Read Matt. 19:28; Acts 3:19-21; Romans 8:19-23; Eph. 1:10; Col. 1:20; Phil. 2:9-11. What awfully disheartening pessimism it would be if we had to believe that the terrible conditions prevailing on the earth now, conditions which have steadily become worse, were to continue and that man's work is to remedy them and produce something better. This earth has a bright and glorious future. Nations will some day no longer turn, as they do now, their plowshares into swords, but change their swords into plowshares. Righteousness and peace will surely kiss each other and creation's curse and travail pains will end. Mercy and truth meet together.

But when? Never as long as the great unfoldings of this book, which we have briefly followed, have not come to pass. There can be no better day for the earth as long as He is absent and not on the throne which belongs to Him. But when He comes, when He has appeared in glory and in majesty, then the earth will find her rest and groaning creation will be delivered. As we do not write on the great blessings and glories to come when He comes, we must refrain from following these things. Here in our book the revelation is given that Christ shall reign for a thousand years and His Saints shall reign with Him.

Let us notice briefly the different classes mentioned who are associated with Christ in His personal reign. The entire company of the redeemed, as we saw them under the symbolical figure of the twenty-four elders, occupying thrones and wearing crowns, are undoubtedly meant by the first statement, "they sat upon them and judgment was given unto them." They judge with Him. This is the raptured company whom we saw first in glory in chapters 4 and 5; and we, dear fellow-believer, belong to this company. Then follow the martyrs, whom we saw under the fifth seal (6:9-11): "And I saw the souls of them that had been beheaded on account of the testimony of Jesus and for the Word of God." Then we have a third company. "And I saw those who had not worshiped the beast, nor his image, and had not received his mark on their forehead, or in their hands." These are the other martyrs who were slain during the great tribulation, when the beast set up the image and demanded its worship (13). They lived and reigned with Christ a thousand years. The first resurrection is passed and all who have part in it reign with Christ, are priests of God and of Christ and shall reign with Him a thousand years.

Oh! wonderful grace which has saved us! Grace which has saved us in Christ and through His ever precious blood delivered us from eternal perdition! Grace which saved us from Satan's power, from sin and all its curse! Grace which has lifted into such heights of glory and has made us the sons of God and the joint-heirs of the Lord Jesus Christ! And how little after all we enter into all these things, which ought to be our daily joy and delight. How little we know of the power of the coming glory of being with Christ and reigning with Him!

CHAPTERS 20:7—22:5

After the Thousand Years and the New Jerusalem

1. Satan's last revolt (20:7-10)
2. The great white throne (20:11-15)
3. The eternal state (21:1-8)
4. The vision of the holy city (21:9-27)
5. The glories of the redeemed (22:1-5)

Verses 7-9. Satan who was put into the abyss a thousand years before, is now loosed out of his prison. God permits him to come forth once more. Who would have ever thought of such a thing! The archenemy who had done his vile and wicked work among the human race, for a thousand years put at least into the place of perfect restraint, and now loosed once more to continue, for a brief season, his work! And he finds nations ready for his deception, not a few, but a number "as the sand of the sea." God permits Satan to come out of his prison, so that the absolute corruption of man might be demonstrated. Man has been tried and tested under every possible condition. He has failed in every age. He failed under the law and he failed even more in the grace-dispensation; and now, under the most glorious conditions, during the millennium, when the Lord Himself is known in all the earth and reigns in righteousness, when want and nearly all the sorrows of a ruined creation are banished, when there is peace on earth, man also fails and does not fully respond to a gracious Lord.

But here is a difficulty which many have. Many a sincere post-Millennialist, who has studied the pre-millennial coming of our Lord, has asked this question, "If the whole word is converted during the millennium, how is it then that Satan finds nations ready to side with him after the thousand-year reign of Christ and then leads them on to destruction? The difficulty is far from being as great as it is generally made. In fact it is easily explained. As far as Israel is concerned, the "all Israel" living, when He comes, the trusting remnant of Israel, they will constitute the blessed nation in possession of all her promised blessings. They are not mentioned as siding with Satan. No more backsliding for that nation. Isaiah 59:20-21 vouches for this.

And the Gentile nations in the beginning of the millennium will also be converted. However, the human conditions of the earth will continue. The nations are not in a glorified state. Marriage will continue. Children will be born during the millennium. Indeed the earth will be populated as never before. Billions of human beings can be sustained upon our planet and they will come into existence by natural generation during the golden age of glory. Wars will be unknown. No longer will the flower of manhood be cruelly murdered by human passion in that legalized horrible thing called war. Earthquakes will no longer sweep thousands upon thousands into an untimely grave, nor can famines and pestilences claim their millions. Nor will there be the great infant mortality. Physical death will no longer be the univeral rule, but rather an exception (see Isaiah 65:20).

Now every child born during the millennium of the converted nations comes into the world the same as the children in the present age, it is still true, conceived and born in sin. And it is equally true, they must be born again.

As many children of pious, godly parents in this age are gospel-hardened and live on in sin, though they hear the gospel and see its power, so in the millennium, an enormous multitude will see the glory, live under the best and most glorious conditions the earth has seen since before the fall of man, and yet they will be glory-hardened and only submit to the righteousness of that age and yield obedience through fear, for disobedience to the governing laws of the kingdom on earth, will mean sudden and certain judgment. It is not the obedience produced by a believing, trusting heart, but only a feigned obedience. Three prophetic Psalms which speak of these millennial conditions make this clear, if we consider the marginal reading. "As soon as they hear of Me, they shall obey Me, the strangers shall yield feigned obedience unto Me" (Ps. 18:44). "Say unto God, How terrible art Thou in Thy works! Through the greatness of Thy power shall Thine enemies yield feigned obedience unto Thee" (Ps. 66:3). "The haters of the Lord yield feigned obedience unto Him, *but* their time might have endured forever" (Ps. 81:15). Study these Psalms in their millennial bearing. Thus many nations submit while sin is in their heart and in their blindness they long and hope for the day when they may cast off the restraint. And that day comes when Satan is loosed out of the prison to deceive these nations again.

It was the final attempt of the dethroned usurper to regain his lost dominion. For thousands of years, in the all-wise purposes of God, he was permitted to be the prince of the power of the air and the god of this age. We have followed his history in this book and seen how he was cast out of heaven upon the earth where he caused the great tribulation. Then we beheld him stripped of all his power. The kingdoms of the world became the kingdom of Christ and the old serpent was cast unto the abyss where he remained a thousand years. Loosed for a little season he tried once more to become earth's master. And fire out of heaven devoured the nations who had revolted.

The devil receives his final doom. He is cast into the lake of fire and brimstone. He goes to a fixed place, a locality where unspeakable and eternal torment is his portion. This place is prepared for the devil and his angels (Matt. 25:41). And all the wicked will share that place. And he finds others there. The first beings who were cast into this final abode were the beast (the emperor of the Roman empire, the little horn of Dan. 7), and the false prophet (the personal Antichrist, the second beast of chapter 13). They were put there a thousand years before, and as they are there as persons it shows they were not annihilated. And they shall be tormented day and night for ever and ever—for the ages of ages—never ending—for all eternity. What a solemn truth this is! Yet men meddle with it and deny future, conscious and eternal punishment. Besides these three persons, the nations who were judged and condemned in the beginning of the millennium, when the Son of Man sat upon the throne of His glory (Matt. 25:31), are also in the Lake of Fire.

Verses 11-15. And now we reach the last great judgment scene of God's holy Word. Much confusion prevails among Christians about this judgment. There is no such thing in the Word of God as a universal judgment, nor is there a universal resurrection. Every human being that has died will be raised at some time. Our Lord spoke (John 5:28) of two resurrections, a resurrection unto life and a resurrection unto judgment. The Revelation speaks of the first resurrection. "This is the first resurrection" (20:5). And previously the apostle wrote of a resurrection from among the dead (Phil. 3:11). The first resurrection was finished in the beginning of the millennium. "But the rest of the dead lived not again until the thousand years were finished." The rest of the dead come now into view and they are of necessity the wicked dead, who died in their sins, and whose is the resurrection unto judgment.

Some, like "Pastor" Russell, who echoes the evil teachings of others, have invented a third resurrection, a resurrection of the unsaved for a second chance. In the light of this final Bible book there is no room whatever for such a resurrection, which would give the lost another opportunity. Nor does the rest of the Bible mention such a third resurrection. And this great judgment is not a universal judgment. It is taught that the entire human race, the living and the dead, will appear before this great throne. But this is incorrect, for it saith, "I saw the dead, small and great, stand before God." No living people are there at all. Again the judgment-scene in Matthew 25:31, etc., is spoken of as being the universal judgment and identical with the judgment here in Revelation. But this is another error. In the judgment of Matthew 25 the dead are not there, but living nations are judged in the beginning of the millennium. And these nations are judged on account of the treatment of the Jewish preachers of the gospel of the kingdom heralded by them during the last seven years of the age. They did not accept the last offer of mercy and that is why they treated the messengers as they did.

Furthermore, the throne which the Son of Man occupies in Matthew 25 is upon the earth; the throne in Revelation 20:11 comes into view after earth and heaven fled away. The Church and the saints of God are not concerned at all in the judgment of Matthew 25, nor in the great white throne judgment. They are at that time in His own presence glorified. Every Christian should have these things clearly defined and know that for him, as in Christ, there is no more judgment or condemnation (John 5:24; Rom. 8:1). The judgment seat of Christ before which believers have to appear (2 Cor. 5:10) does not concern their eternal salvation, but their works and rewards.

Who is the occupant of this great white throne? Not God the Father, but God the Son. "The Father judgeth no man but hath committed all judgment unto the Son" (John 5:22). The earth and heaven fled from His face. Sin-stained and defiled as they were they flee away from the face of the Holy One. The great conflagration of 2 Peter 3:7-12 takes place. (See Annotations on 2 Peter 3.) Fire of judgment swept the earth before the millennium, the day of the Lord, began; but the all consuming fire comes after the millennium. Out of that great conflagration there arises a new heaven and a new earth (21:1).

But what about the millions of saved Israelites and Gentiles who are on the millennial earth? Where are they during this great conflagration? What becomes of them? That they share the eternal blessings and glories in the eternal state is certain. But their abode between the burning of the earth and the calling into existence of the new heaven and the new earth is unrevealed. Speculation on it would be wrong. We should accept the silences of Scripture as much in faith as we accept the promises of God.

And John sees the dead standing before the throne. Books were opened and another book was opened, the book of life. "And the dead were judged out of the things which were written in the books, according to their works." The books are symbolical; conscience and memory will speak loudly. Twice we read that they are judged according to their works. And in the "book of life" none of their names were written, or they would not have been in that company. "All this would seem to show that, though a millennium has passed since the first resurrection, yet no *righteous* dead can stand among this throng. The suggestion of the "book of life" has seemed to many to imply that there are such; but it is not said that there are, and the words "whosoever was not found written in the book of life was cast into the lake of fire" may be simply a solemn declaration (now affirmed by the result) that grace is man's only possible escape from the judgment" (*Numerical Bible*).

The second resurrection takes place. The sea gives up the dead and death and Hades give up the dead. Hades gives up the soul, and death, used here for the grave, gives up the bodies. Death and Hades were cast into the lake of fire. Both had come into existence because man had sinned, and, therefore, they are cast into the place where all belongs which is contrary to the holiness and righteousness of God. And then that solemn word! "And whosoever was not found written in the Book of Life was cast into the lake of fire." It corresponds to that other solemn statement in John 3:36. "He that believeth on the Son hath everlasting life; and he that believeth not the Son shall not see life, but the wrath of God abideth upon him." To be written in the "book of life" means to have life in Christ. Not our works, not our character, not our religiousness, not our tears, our prayers or our service can put our names in the "book of life." Grace alone can do it, and grace does it, as we believe on the Lord Jesus Christ. Reader! is *your* name written there?

The saints of God are in eternal glory; the wicked dead, the lost, are in an eternal lake of fire and suffer conscious, eternal punishment. And how man, blind, presumptuous man, yea, even such who know God, rise up against this solemn truth, the eternal punishment of the wicked. They accuse God of injustice, as if the judge of all the earth would not do right. That the suffering of the lost differs is obvious. It is eternal, because the evil condition remains unchanged. There is no repentence, no faith, no new birth in hell. As there are different rewards for the faithful service of the saints, so are there different degrees of punishment for the unsaved (Luke 12:47-48). This is the second death, not blotting out of existence, but endless in separation from God.

Chapter 21:1-8. And now the eternal state comes into view. "And I saw a new heaven and a new earth; for the first heaven and the first earth were passed away and the sea is no more." This is the revelation concerning the final and eternal state of the earth. "Thou hast established the earth and it abideth" (Ps. 119:90); "But the earth abideth forever" (Eccl. 1:4). These divine statements are now fulfilled. Many Christians have a very vague conception of the eternal state of the earth and the abode of the redeemed. They think of it as a spiritual state destitute of any locality. But it is not so. The earth and the heaven abide as definite places throughout all eternity. What a marvellous fact this is! In chapter 20:11 we read that the earth and the heaven fled away and there was found no place. We saw that at that time the great conflagration of which Peter speaks took place, when "the heavens shall pass away with a great noise, and the elements, shall be dissolved with fervent heat, the earth also, and the works that are therein shall be burned up" (2 Peter 3:10).

But we read in the same chapter "nevertheless we, according to His promise look for new heavens and a new earth, wherein dwelleth righteousness" (verse 13). During the millennium righteousness reigns upon the earth, but now a state comes for the earth when righteousness shall dwell there. The great burning up meant not an annihilation of the earth and the heavens; God does not annihilate anything, nor does Scripture teach an annihilation of material things and much less the annihilation of human beings, as false teachers claim. The conflagration of the earth and the heaven means their complete purification. The heaven mentioned cannot be the entire heavens; for there is a heaven which cannot be touched by these fires of purification. The heaven is that which surrounds the earth and which was once the peculiar sphere of the great usurper, the prince of the power in the air. And when Peter writes that all this is according to His promise, he has a well-known prophetic statement in Isaiah in mind. "For as the new heaven and the new earth, which I will make, shall remain before Me, saith the Lord, so shall your seed and your name remain" (Isaiah 66:22. See also 65:17).

From this statement we get definite information that the redeemed Israel established upon the new earth will throughout the eternal state be distinct from the saved nations. They will throughout all eternity bear witness of God's faithfulness as the covenant-keeping God. The new heaven and the new earth are therefore the abodes of the redeemed. The new earth, the eternal glory spot of redeemed Israel and the redeemed nations, and the new Jerusalem will come out of heaven to fill the new earth and the new heaven as well. "And I, John, saw the holy city, new Jerusalem, coming down from God out of heaven, prepared as a bride adorned for her husband."

The new Jerusalem, the holy city, comes into view. During the millennium the city of Jerusalem was known as the place of glory for the earth. Numerous Old Testament predictions were fulfilled. In chapter 20:9, she is called "the beloved city." But in Revelation 3:12 we have another Jerusalem mentioned, the same city which John sees coming down out of heaven, the place of the highest glory. It is the abode of the Church in all her glory; the statement "prepared as a bride adorned for her husband" establishes this beyond controversy. She is called "holy" for all is holy; and a "city" because the Saints are in blessed communion and fellowship there. In the highest glory she had her abode. But now she is being revealed in all her eternal glory and beauty.

During the millennial reign this wonderful city was above the earth and from there Christ reigned and His saints with Him. But here she comes down out of heaven. A thousand years before the marriage of the Lamb had taken place (19:7-8), and now after a thousand years of unspeakable glory, she is still seen "as a bride adorned for her husband." And yet all these things are given in figurative language. What will be the reality! The masterwork of God is at last fully manifested; what He accomplished through Him, who left the glory to die on the cross, is made known. The eternal, never ending riches, purchased by Him who was rich and became poor for our sakes, are beginning to be displayed in all their unfading splendor. Then the saints of God will learn to know the full meaning of Eph. 2:7, "that in the ages to come He might display the surpassing riches of His grace in kindness towards us through Christ Jesus." "And I heard a loud voice out of heaven, saying, Behold the tabernacle of God is with men, and He will dwell with them, and they shall be His people, and God Himself shall be with them, and be their God." This is the glorious consummation. It is the goal of a holy, loving God.

In Eden God visited man unfallen, walked and talked with Him. Then sin severed this fellowship. He dwelt in the midst of Israel in the holiest of the tabernacle. In this age the Church is His habitation by the Spirit, but the blessed consummation in the eternal state will result in God dwelling with His redeemed creatures. What holy, glorious, never-ending intimacy that will be! It is the time when God is all in all (1 Cor. 15:28). When that time has come all the former things are passed away. "And God shall wipe away every tear from their eyes, and there shall be no more death, nor sorrow, nor crying, neither shall there be any more pain; for the former things are passed away." Tears, death, sorrow, crying, pain and suffering, these came into existence through sin. And all these things, the effects of sin, are now gone. What relief and what joy!

And next comes the eternal state of those who have rejected the gospel, who lived in their sins and died in their sins, unsaved, unregenerated. "But the fearful, and unbelieving, and abominable, and murderers, and fornicators, and sorcerers, and idolaters, and all liars shall have their part in the lake which burneth with fire and brimstone, which is the second death." God still speaks. How many false teachers are meddling today with the solemn Scripture doctrine on the endless punishment of the wicked.

Verses 9-27. With the ninth verse we are brought back once more to the millennial state. What was briefly stated in chapter 20:4-6 is now more fully revealed and we have a description of the bride, the Lamb's wife, in her millennial glory, in relation to Israel and to the nations on the earth. One of the angels which had the seven vials appears on the scene to show something to the seer. We had a similar scene in chapter 17:1-3. There one of these angelic bearers of the vials showed to John the harlot woman and her judgment; but now he is to see the bride, the Lamb's wife. "And he carried me away in the Spirit, and set me on a great, high mountain and showed me the holy city, Jerusalem, coming down out of heaven from God." She is seen coming down out of heaven. This coming down precedes the one mentioned in verses 2-3 by a thousand years. Her coming down does not mean here that she actually comes down upon the earth, to dwell on the earth during the millennium. Her coming out of heaven in verses 2-3 is undoubtedly to the new earth. But here she comes down to be over the earth.

For a fuller exposition of the symbolical language we refer the reader to the larger exposition of Revelation by the author. We mention briefly that the foundations of the heavenly Jerusalem are twelve previous stones.

The jasper again stands first; the wall itself is of jasper, while the first foundation stone mentioned is also jasper. It stands for the glory of God. Then the stones follow in their order. The sapphire (blue); the chalcedony (a combination of grey, blue and yellow); the emerald (green); the sardonyx (a pale blue); the sardius (blood red); chrysolite (purple and green); the beryl (bluish green); the topaz (pale green or golden); the chrysoprasus (mixed blue, green and yellow); the jacinth (combination of red, violet and yellow), and the amethyst (purple). And what must be the deeper meaning of all these precious stones! What varied aspects of the glory of God they must represent! And the redeemed in their heavenly city shall know, understand and enjoy it all. What wonderful, unspeakable glory is ahead of us! May we look forward to it every day and willingly serve and suffer the little while down here.

The city itself was seen by John as of pure gold. Gold typifies the righteousness of God in His nature and such the holy city is, composed of the saints who were made through grace the partakers of the divine nature. "And the twelve gates were twelve pearls, each one of the several gates was of one pearl; and the street of the city was pure gold as it were transparent glass." How suitable the pearl to form each gate, the entrance to the city divine. The Pearl is a type of the Church. She is the one pearl of great price for which the Lord gave all He had (Matt. 13:45-46). And the golden street like unto pure glass shows that all the ways and walks in that city are according to righteousness and that defilement is eternally impossible.

And there was no temple in that city; the Lord God Almighty and the Lamb are the temple of it. There is no need any longer of a certain access into the presence of God, as it was on earth, but there is a free and unhindered fellowship with God and with His ever-blessed Son, the Lamb. Precious it is to hear Him again mentioned as the Lamb. His blessed work which He accomplished can never be forgotten by the saints in glory. And the light is not created light, but the light is the glory of God and the lamp thereof is the Lamb. The glory of God and Christ, the Lamb of God, will be the light and supersede all created light.

"And the nations shall walk by its light and the kings of the earth bring their glory and honor unto it (the better rendering); and the gates of it shall not be shut at all by day for there shall be no night there. And they shall bring the glory and honor of the nations unto it." From this we learn that the glory light which shines eternally and undiminished in the holy city is the light in which the saved millennial nations on the earth walk. And the kings of the earth bring their glory and honor unto it; not "into" it as it is rendered in the Authorized Version. The heavens then rule, for Christ and His co-heirs are in that holy city, and the government and rule over the earth proceeds from there. The kings bring their glory and honor unto it, they bow in homage in the presence of the holy city.

Heaven is acknowledged as the source of all light, glory and blessing. When the nations and the kings of the earth go up to Jerusalem to worship the Lord of Hosts during the millennial age (Psa. 72:8-11; Is. 60:1-3; Zech. 14:16) we doubt not, they will turn their faces upward. Mount Zion in Israel's land will have resting upon it the glory and above it the vision of the city in which the glory dwells and from which the glory emanates. And unto it they bring honor and glory. The open gates, never closed, denote security and suggest also communication and intercourse with the earth. "There shall be no night there"; the night of sin and sorrow is forever gone for the dwellers in the holy city. "And there shall in no wise enter into it anything that defileth, neither whatsoever worketh abomination, or maketh a lie, but they which are written in the Lamb's book of life."

Chapter 22:1-5. After the coming, Jerusalem and her blessings are once more revealed. In the opening verses of this chapter we find the glories of the redeemed.

Unspeakably beautiful and glorious are the concluding statements of this glory-section of the Revelation. Seven glories of the Redeemed are enumerated. 1. There will be no more curse. It means a perfect sinlessness; perfect holiness. 2. The throne of God and of the Lamb is there and the redeemed are forever linked with that throne. It is a perfect and blessed government which can never be disturbed by disorder. 3. His servant shall serve Him. Heaven will not consist in idleness. The holy city knows of service. And the service the saints will render to God in glory will be a perfect service. What will it be? We do not know what service it will be. God will have many surprises for His saints in glory. 4. There is also an eternal vision. "And they shall see His face." Oh! joy of all the joys in glory to see Him as He is and never lose sight of Him in all eternity. 5. His name shall be in their foreheads. It tells of eternal ownership and eternal possession. His name and the glory connected with it will be ours in eternal ages. 6. An eternal day. No more night; no need of any light. He is the light for all eternity. 7. An eternal reign. And they shall reign forever and ever. What glory and blessedness all this means. Such are the coming glories of the redeemed.

CHAPTER 22:6-21

The Final Messages

1. The angel's message (22:6-11)
2. The message of the Lord (22:12-13)
3. The two classes (22:14-15)
4. His final testimony (22:16)
5. The answer of the Spirit and the bride (22:17)
6. The final warning (22:18-19)
7. The final word—the final prayer (22:20-21)

Verses 6-11. Here it is an angel who speaks. "And the Lord God of the holy prophets (literal: of the spirits of the prophets) sent His angel to show unto His servants the things which must shortly be done." This reminds us of the beginning of the book, where we find a similar announcement. Suddenly some day these things will come to pass. The Lord will call His people to glory in a moment, in the twinkling of an eye, and then these things John had beheld will shortly come to pass. And then His own voice breaks in: "Behold I come quickly; Blessed is He that keepeth the sayings of the prophecy of this book." Three times we find this announcement in the last chapter (verses 7, 12 and 20). Here it is connected with the walk of the believer.

Just as in the beginning of the book a blessing is pronounced upon them that read the words of this prophecy (1:3), so we have at the close of Revelation a similar beatitude. And keeping these blessed words means more than believing in them; their power is to shape our conduct and walk. What godly lives God's people would live on earth, what unselfish and sacrificing lives, if they remembered constantly Him who thus testifies three times in the last chapter of the Bible, "Behold I come quickly." Note the awful results in Christendom today for not having kept the sayings of the Prophecy of this book.

Then the Seer is told not to seal the sayings of this prophecy. Daniel was told to do the opposite (Dan. 12:4). Old Testament prophecy reveals prophetic events in the far distance. They could then not be fully comprehended. But after Christ came and the full revelation of things to come is given, no sealing is needed; the events are at hand, yet grace has delayed and delays still the fulfillment. And the heavenly messenger announces also the fixed state of the two classes into which all humanity is divided. The unjust and filthy, the unsaved, continue to exist in the nature which they possess, and the fact that the desires of that corrupt nature can no longer be gratified must constitute in itself an unspeakable torment. The righteous and holy, those saved by grace, partakers of the divine nature, will always be righteous and holy.

Verses 12-13. And now the Lord speaks again. For the second time He announces His coming. Here it is in connection with rewards. "My reward is with Me." He Himself will receive His reward which is due Him as the sin-bearer. He will see the travail of His soul and be satisfied. And with His coming, His own people will receive their rewards. What a stimulating power His soon coming is to service! And the coming One is the Alpha and Omega, the first and the last, the beginning and the end.

Verses 14-15. Once more the two classes come into view. This is in fullest keeping with the end of the book and the end of the Bible. The Authorized Version here is faulty. Instead of "Blessed are they that do His commandments" the correct reading is "Blessed are they that wash their robes." The former is an interpolation; the latter is the divine statement. (All leading scholars like Alford, Darby, etc., make the change. Even the Vulgate has it "Beati, qui lavant stolas suas in sanguinem Agni.") Eternal life and eternal glory cannot be obtained by keeping commandments, by the works of the law. The blood of the Lamb alone is the title to glory. And then the other class. The one who rejects Christ, and thereby denies his lost condition and need of a Saviour, loveth and maketh a lie. He lives according to the old nature and the fruits of the flesh are there.

Verse 16. How He speaks in this last Bible book! In the beginning of Revelation we find His self-witness in the church-message and once more we hear His voice, bearing testimony to Himself. How majestic: I, Jesus! He reveals Himself once more by the name of humiliation. What comfort it must have been to John! What comfort it is to us! Then He speaks of Himself as the Root and Offspring of David. He is David's Lord and David's Son (Psalm 110:1). He is the hope of Israel and in Him the promises made to David will all be realized. This will be the case when He comes to reign in power and great glory. But He also speaks of Himself as "the bright and morning-star." His coming in power and glory is the sunrise for Israel and the Gentiles, the breaking of the millennial day. But for His Church He comes first as the morning-star, as the morning-star in the eastern sky precedes the rising of the sun in all its glory. The Lord will come as the morning-star some time in the interval between the 69th and 70th week of Daniel and as the Sun of Righteousness after that week has come to an end.

Verse 17. As soon as He mentions Himself as the morning-star, there is an answer from the earth. The Spirit now down here, for He came down from heaven on Pentecost, and the Bride, the Church, say, "Come." It is addressed to the Lord. They both long for His coming. And each individual believer who heareth is asked to join with this "Come." Surely in these days of darkness and world-confusion, the Spirit saith, "Come!" And never before were there so many individual believers on earth who say "Come," who wait for His coming. And the Come—from loving hearts—will increase and become a loud and pleading cry, till one blessed day He will answer and come to take His waiting people home. Here also is the final gospel message of the Bible. He that will, let him take the water of life freely. Once more a loving God makes it clear that the water of life is free to all who want it. It is the last "Whosoever" in the Bible.

Verses 18-19. And what a solemn warning is given! In a larger sense the warning applies to the entire Word of God. Higher criticism, which takes away, and false teachers, who add unto it, find written here their deserved judgment. But the Revelation is specially in view. Whosoever meddles with His Revelation must fall under the severest divine displeasure. Beware! oh ye critics! Beware! ye who call this book uninspired and warn against the study of it!

Verses 20-21. We reach the final statements of this great book. For the third time He announces His coming. "He that testifieth these things saith, surely I come quickly." It is the last time our Lord speaks from heaven. The next time His voice will be heard will be on that day when He descends out of heaven with a shout. While the two former announcements of His coming found in this chapter are preceded by the word, "Behold," this last one affirms the absolute certainty of the event. And there is the answer, the blessed response. "Amen. Even so, come, Lord Jesus." It is the Church which answers His positive and certain announcement. It is the last word recorded in the Bible coming from the lips of man.

The first word we hear man address to the Lord in the Bible is the solemn word "I heard Thy voice in the garden, and I was afraid" (Gen. 3:10). The last word addressed to the Lord by redeemed man is "even so, come, Lord Jesus." And between these two utterances in Genesis and Revelation is the story of redemption. Well might this final prayer of the Bible be termed the forgotten prayer. But it is equally true, with the revival of the study of prophecy, more hearts and lips are praying today for His coming, than ever before. And the prayer will be answered. May the reader and the writer pray for His coming daily and may our lives too bear witness to the fact that we expect Him to answer the petition of His people. The final benediction assures us once more of the grace of our Lord Jesus Christ. The better rendering is "The grace of our Lord Jesus Christ be with all the saints."

APPENDIX

Prominent Names and Their Symbolical Meaning in Revelation

Abaddon. (9:11) Destruction. The king over the locust army, denoting Satan and his agencies.

Abyss, The. (9:1; 20:1-3) The pit of the abyss or the deep. This expression occurs seven times in Revelation. Out of the deep, the lowest pit, there comes the demon and into the pit of the abyss Satan will be cast for 1,000 years. The lake of fire is a different place.

Accuser, The. Satan is the accuser of the brethren (12:10). His expulsion out of heaven occurs in the middle of the week, followed by the great tribulation on earth.

Alpha. The first letter in the Greek alphabet; Omega is the last letter. Therefore Alpha and Omega is equivalent to an A and Z. Symbolical of the first and last (1:8; 21:6; 22:13).

Amen, The. A name of our Lord. He is the "verily," the truth, and assurance and certainty are expressed by this word (1:18).

Angels. Angels are prominently mentioned throughout Revelation. The exposition shows that the angel mentioned in 8:1-5; 10:1 is the Lord Jesus Christ. Angels will be used in the end of the age to carry out the decreed judgments. On the angels of the different churches, the symbolical meaning, see the exposition, chapter 1:20.

The angels are the messengers who carried the Lord's message to the churches. They needed the power of the Spirit to do it. Hence the churches were to hear what the Spirit said to the churches (Rev. 2:7, etc.).

Antichrist, The. The final and personal Antichrist is mentioned for the first time in Revelation in chapter 13:11-18. He is also called the false prophet, because he heads up the ecclesiastical corruption and apostasy of the end of the age. He must not be confounded with the first beast out of the sea who is a political head, the emperor of the revived Roman empire, the little horn of Daniel 7, and the prince that shall come of Dan. 9:26.

Antipas. An unknown faithful martyr in Pergamos, known to Christ (2:13), meaning one against all.

Apollyon. (9:11) The Greek name of Abaddon, the King over the Locust army. The name means destruction or destroyer.

Ark, The. (11:19) It is seen by John in the temple. It means symbolically the assured presence of Jehovah with His people Israel, the faithful remnant, in the trying times of Jacob's trouble.

Armageddon. Mentioned for the first time in the parenthesis between the sixth and seventh vial. (16:12-16). It means "The hill of slaughter." The battle of Armageddon will be of brief duration. It is the stone of Nebuchadnezzar's dream smiting suddenly the ten toes, the ten kingdoms (Dan. 2). The battle of Armageddon is briefly described in chapter 19:19-20.

Alleluia. "Praise ye the Lord." The four hallelujahs are found in chapter 19:1-5.

Babylon. On the literal and mystical Babylon see exposition of chapter 17. The literal Babylon will undoubtedly be restored as a city of influence. But the city mentioned in chapter 17 is not the literal Babylon, but Rome. Not only will the Roman Empire be revived, *but* also papal Rome. Babylon the great, the mother of harlots, will see a great revival. The system in its corruption is described in chapter 18.

Balaam. The heathen prophet who could not curse Israel, but put a stumbling-block before the children of Israel. Used in Revelation to describe the corruption in the professing Church in giving up the divinely demanded separation from the world (chapter 2:14).

Beast, The. The expression "four beasts" in Rev. 4 and 5, etc., is faulty. The correct rendering is "the four living creatures" or the "four living ones." The term "beast" applies to the revived Roman empire and its head, the little horn of Daniel, also called beast in Daniel's vision. The Antichrist is likewise called a beast. The work of the two beasts is seen in chapter 13.

Birds, unclean and hateful. Symbolical of evil persons outwardly professing to be something but full of corruption. They describe the apostate masses of Christendom (Rev. 18:2. Also Matt. 13:31-32).

Black Horse. The black horse comes into view with the opening of the third seal. Black is the color of night, darkness and death.

Blood, with Hail and Fire. (8:7) Not literal things, but symbols of divine judgment for this earth.

Bow, The. (6:2) The bow without an arrow as in possession by the rider upon the white horse is the symbol of a bloodless conquest.

Bride, The. (21:2) the Bride of Christ, the Lamb's wife (19:7); it is not Israel but the church.

Brimstone and Fire. The symbols of divine wrath (Isa. 30:33).

Candlestick, Golden. Symbolical of that which gives light. Representing the seven assemblies. The Church is on earth to give light.

Crowns. The symbols of given glory and also rewards for service. The crowns seen upon the seven heads of the dragon (12:3) and upon the four horns of the Beast (13:1) denote despotic authority.

David, Key of. Symbolical of the right to open and to enter in. See Isa. 22:22. It is a prediction concerning Christ. The authority of the kingdom of heaven.

David, Root and Offspring. (22:16) Christ is the Root and offspring of David.

Demons. Fallen spirit beings; the wicked spirits over which Satan is the head. They will be worshipped by the apostates during the end of the age. Demon-worship is even now going on to some extent, for the Antichristian cults are produced by demons (1 Tim. 4:1). See Rev. 9:20-21. The word devils must be changed to demons. There is but one devil, but legions of demons.

Dwellers on the Earth. This class mentioned repeatedly in Revelation is the large number of professing Christians, who did not receive the love of the truth and rejecting the gospel follow the strong delusion and are utterly blinded, as well as hardened, during the tribulation.

Eagle. (8:13) The word angel must be changed to "eagle." Symbolical of the coming judgment, as an eagle is a bird of prey. Eagle's wings (12:13-17) are symbolical of swift motion, escape and deliverance.

Earth. The prophetic territory of the Roman Empire is mostly described by this form, though the entire earth is also indicated.

Earthquake. Symbolical of the shaking of all political and ecclesiastical institutions. But, as we show in our exposition, literal earthquakes will take place.

Elders, Twenty-four. The twenty-four elders typify all the redeemed in glory. Old and New Testament saints are included. After chapter 19 this term does not appear again, because the Church, the bride of Christ, is then seen separate from the entire company of the redeemed, and takes her exalted position as the Lamb's wife.

Eternal State, The. The eternal state is described in chapter 21:1-8.

Euphrates. This great river is mentioned twice in Revelation, 9:14 and 16:12. It is the boundary line of the Roman empire and the land of Israel. See exposition of these passages.

Everlasting Gospel. (14:6) The declaration of the gospel of the kingdom during the tribulation, and the proclamation of God as Creator to the heathen nations of the world, to prepare them for the gospel of the kingdom.

Fire. Often mentioned in this book and symbolical of the judgments which will be executed upon the earth as well as the everlasting wrath upon the unsaved.

Fornication. Spiritual wickedness in departing from the Truth of God, followed by the literal lusts of the flesh. The days of Lot will be on the earth before the Son of Man cometh.

Four. This number appears a number of times in Revelation. Four living creatures; four corners of the earth; four horns of the golden altar; four angels; four winds. Four is the number of universality.

Frogs. Mentioned between the sixth and seventh vial. Symbolical of demon influences, denoting filty and wicked things. Frogs come out of slimy and dark waters; evil doctrines.

Glass, Sea of. (4:6). Compare with Exod. 30:18-21 and 1 Kings 7:23, etc. Symbolical of fixed lasting holiness. No more water needed for cleansing from sin, for the saints in glory are delivered from the presence of sin itself.

God, Supper of. (19:17) Symbolical of God's judgment upon the wicked nations and the earth dwellers.

Gold. Symbolical of divine righteousness.

Grass. (8:7) Symbolical of human prosperity (Isa. 40:7 and 1 Peter 1:24).

Hades. The region of disembodied spirits; literally "the unknown." Christ has the keys. Hades with death, because they came into existence through sin, will be cast into the lake of fire.

Harvest of the Earth. The harvest is the end of the age. In chapter 14:14-15 we read of the Lord's judgment dealing with the earth.

Hidden Manna. (2:17) Symbolical of the reward those who overcome will receive from the Lord.

Horns. Horn is symbolical of power. Horns mean typically kings, and powers and kingdoms (Dan. 7:24).

Image of the Beast. (13:12-15) Compare with Dan. 3. It will be a literal image of the princely leader of the revived Roman empire, the first beast, which John saw rising out of the sea.

Islands. Mentioned under the sixth seal and the seventh vial. Mountains typify kingdoms and governments; islands are symbolical of smaller and isolated governments. All will be affected. No doubt when the great earthquakes will shake the very foundations of the earth, many islands will also disappear.

Jasper. A precious stone, most likely our diamond. See exposition of chapter 4.

Jerusalem. The earthly and the heavenly Jerusalem are mentioned in the book. During the tribulation the earthly Jerusalem will be the seat of the Antichrist, the false prophet. Jerusalem is for this reason called "Sodom and Egypt" (11:8). Then Jerusalem will pass through her worst history. A great siege will take place at the close of the tribulation period and the city will fall (Zech 14). After that Jerusalem will become the capital of the kingdom of Christ and a great temple will be erected, the universal place of worship during the millennium. The heavenly Jerusalem is above the earth. From there the glorious reign of Christ and the saints will be executed. This glorious city will come down out of heaven at the end of the millennium to find its eternal resting-place on the new earth (chapters 21—22).

Jezebel. Symbolical of the Papacy. The corruptress which claims to be the bride of Christ, but plays the harlot. See chapters 2 and 17.

Judgment. Judgment falls upon the earth during the seven years, which constitute the end of the age. When the Lord comes in His glory the great judgment of the nations takes place. Chapter 19:11, etc., compare with Matt. 25:31. After the millennium the second resurrection takes place and the great white throne judgment is the judgment of the wicked dead.

King of the Nations. (15:2-4) King of the saints should be changed to King of the nations. Our Lord is the King of the nations, the King of Kings.

Lake of Fire. The place which God has prepared for the devil and his angels. The beast and the false prophet will be cast there; also the Assyrian, the king of the north, the nations who followed the beast and all the wicked dead. Death and Hades will likewise be put into that place.

The Lamb. The Lamb (John 1:29), our Lord in His sacrificial character, is mentioned twenty-eight times in the Revelation. The Lamb is worshipped by all. Thus we find the song of the Lamb, the throne of the Lamb and the marriage of the Lamb, and the wife of the Lamb (the Church) in this book.

Lightning. Symbolical of the divine judgment, Wrath.

Locust Army. Symbolical of the host of demons, which come out of the abyss to torment mankind.

Lord's Day, The. Mentioned but once in 1:10. It is the first day of the week on which John saw the great Patmos vision.

Man-child. (Chapter 12) The Man-child is the Lord Jesus Christ.

Mark of the Beast. Some special mark which

declares ownership. As the Holy Spirit seals those who trust on Christ, so Antichrist will put his mark upon those who follow him.

Millennium, The. Millennium means "a thousand years." Six times this period of blessing and glory is mentioned in Rev. 20.

Moon as blood. The Moon is symbolical of derived authority. Blood is the symbol of death. Apostate Israel and the apostate Church passing through the most severe judgments are symbolized by this figure.

Morning Star, The. Christ in His coming for the Church (22:16; 2:28).

Mountain. A kingdom.

Mountains, Seven. Rome is the city built upon the seven hills. See exposition of chapter 17.

Nicolaitanes. Mentioned in the message of Ephesus and Pergamos. They signify the domineering, priestly class which assumed an unscriptural place of authority in the Church.

Palms. Emblems of victory.

Rainbow. The symbol of covenant and of mercy. Mentioned twice. Around the throne (chapter 4) and around His head (chapter 10).

Rest of the Dead. (20:5) Meaning those who had not part in the first resurrection, hence the wicked dead.

River of Life. (22:1) Symbolical of the fullness of life, glory and blessing.

Saints. The saints in Revelation include all the saints. The Old and New Testament saints are seen under the figure of the twenty-four elders. The suffering saints are the Jewish saints and the remnant of Israel, as well as the multitude of nations, who accept the final message and come out of the great tribulation (chapter 7).

Satan. The entire book reveals his person, his work and his destiny. His work may be traced in the church-messages. Then we have his work during the tribulation and his final work after the millennium.

Scorpions. Symbolical of the torment caused by the army of demons under the fifth trumpet judgment.

Sea. Symbol of the nations. Also the literal sea, which gives up the dead. Then there will be no more sea. All wickedness and restlessness will cease forever.

Seven. The divine number. No other book in the Bible contains so many "sevens" as this final Bible book, the Revelation. There are seven angels, churches, attributes of the Lord, heads, horns, eyes, spirits, lamps, seals, trumpets, vials, plagues, stars, thunders, times and a sevenfold doxology.

Song. The songs of the redeemed and the song of Moses and the Lamb are mentioned in the book.

Stars. See exposition on the meaning of the seven stars in His hand. Stars are also symbolical of lesser authorities, which will all fall during the tribulation period. Lights in the night.

Sun. The symbol of supreme authority.

Synagogue of Satan. Mentioned in the messages to Smyrna and Philadelphia. It means a Judaized Christianity as seen in ritualistic, professing Christendom.

Temple. The tribulation temple is in view in chapter 11:1-3. The millennial temple is seen in 7:15. Then there is the temple of heaven (16:17). In the heavenly Jerusalem there is no temple (21:22).

Third Part. Mentioned in connection with men, the sea, the stars of heaven, the sun and the moon. It probably refers exclusively to the Roman Empire, which in its different aspects and authorities, will be affected during these judgments.

Two horns. The beast out of the land has two horns like a lamb, but speaks like the dragon. He is the counterfeit Christ.

Waters, Many. Symbolical of peoples and nations over which the Romish whore has authority.

White. Color of righteousness and purity; also denoting victorious conquests. We have in Revelation, white robes, the white horses, white linen, a white cloud and a white throne.

Witnesses. See in Rev. 11 about the two witnesses.

Wrath. We read of the wrath of God and the wrath of the Lamb. The wrath of God is completed with the pouring out of the vials. The wrath of the Lamb will be executed when He comes in glory.

Zion. Mentioned only once in Rev., chapter 14:1. It means the literal Zion in Palestine. Upon that holy hill of Zion the glory will rest during the millennium. See Psalm 132:13-14.